Cathy Lambert

95

How to Use the Maps in *Western Civilization, 5th Edition*

Here are some basic map concepts that will help you to get the most out of the maps in this textbook.

- Always look at the scale, which allows you to determine the distance in miles or kilometers between locations on the map.
- Examine the legend carefully. It explains the colors and symbols used on the map.
- Note the locations of mountains, rivers, oceans, and other geographic features, and consider how these would affect such human activities as agriculture, commerce, travel, and warfare.
- Read the map caption thoroughly. It provides important information, sometimes not covered in the text itself, and poses a thought question to encourage you to think beyond the mere appearance of the map and make connections across chapters, regions, and concepts.
- Several "spot maps" appear in each chapter, to allow you to view in detail smaller areas that may not be apparent in larger maps. For example, a spot map in Chapter 3 lets you zoom in on the Piraeus, and one in Chapter 5 shows the city of Rome in detail.

Arctic Ocean
FINLAND
Helsinki
Tallinn
ESTONIA
Riga
LATVIA
LITHUANIA
Vilnius
Minsk
BELARUS
AND
Warsaw
RUSSIA
Moscow
Kiev
UKRAINE
Dnieper R.
Don R.
Volga R.
KAZAKHSTAN
BLIC
SLOVAKIA
Bratislava
Budapest
HUNGARY
MOLDOVA
Chisinau
ROMANIA
Bucharest
BOSNIA
YUGOSLAVIA
Sofia
BULGARIA
Skopje
Tirane
MACEDONIA
ALBANIA
GREECE
Athens
Crete
Black Sea
Caspian Sea
GEORGIA
Tbilisi
ARMENIA
Yerevan
Baku
AZERBAIJAN
Ankara
TURKEY
Tigris R.
Euphrates
Tehran
CYPRUS
SYRIA
LEBANON
Damascus
Beirut
Baghdad
IRAN
IRAQ
ISRAEL
Jerusalem
Amman
JORDAN
Cairo
Nile R.
Kuwait
KUWAIT
SAUDI ARABIA
LIBYA
EGYPT
erranean Sea

0 250 500 750 Kilometers
0 250 500 Miles
Norwegian Sea
ICELAND
Reykjavík
SWEDEN
NORWAY
Stockholm
Oslo
North Sea
Copenhagen
DENMARK
Dublin
UNITED KINGDOM
NETHERLANDS
Elbe R.
Berlin
IRELAND
Amsterdam
Rhine R.
London
BELGIUM
GERMANY
Brussels
Prague
LUXUMBOURG
Paris
Seine R.
Vienna
Atlantic Ocean
LIECHTENSTEIN.
AUSTRIA
Bern
FRANCE
Ljubljana
SWITZERLAND
SLOVENIA
Po R.
ITALY
Ebro R.
Rome
Corsica
PORTUGAL
Madrid
Sardinia
SPAIN
Balearic Isl.
Lisbon
Sicily
Tunis
Algiers
Rabat
TUNISIA
Tripoli
MOROCCO
ALGERIA

FIFTH EDITION

Western Civilization

Comprehensive Volume

Jackson J. Spielvogel
The Pennsylvania State University

THOMSON
WADSWORTH

Australia • Canada • Mexico • Singapore • Spain
United Kingdom • United States

HISTORY PUBLISHER: *Clark Baxter*
SENIOR DEVELOPMENT EDITOR: *Sue Gleason*
ASSISTANT EDITOR: *Julie Iannacchino*
EDITORIAL ASSISTANT: *Jonathan Katz*
EXECUTIVE MARKETING MANAGER: *Caroline Croley*
PRINT BUYER: *Vena Dyer*
PROJECT EDITOR: *Dianne Jensis Toop*
TECHNOLOGY PROJECT EDITOR: *Jennifer Ellis*
PERMISSIONS EDITOR: *Joohee Lee*
COPY EDITOR: *Bruce Emmer*
PHOTO RESEARCHER: *Image Quest*
PRODUCTION SERVICE: *Jon Peck, Dovetail Publishing Services*
MAPS: *Maps.com*
INTERIOR AND COVER DESIGNER: *Norman Baugher*
COMPOSITOR: *New England Typographic Service*
PRINTER/BINDER: *Von Hoffmann Press*
COVER PRINTER: *Phoenix Color Corp.*
COVER IMAGE: *Marriage at Cana, Paolo Veronese (1528–1588), Louvre, Paris, France, © Erich Lessing/Art Resource, NY*
PHOTO CREDITS: *begin on page 885*

Printed in the United States of America
2 3 4 5 6 7 06 05 04 03 02

For more information about our products, contact us at:
Thomson Learning Academic Resource Center
1-800-423-0563
For permission to use material from this text, contact us by:
Phone: 1-800-730-2214
Fax: 1-800-730-2215
Web: http://www.thomsonrights.com

Library of Congress Control Number: 2002107892

ISBN 0-534-60006-9

Wadsworth/Thomson Learning
10 Davis Drive
Belmont, CA 94002-3098
USA

Asia
Thomson Learning
5 Shenton Way, #01-01
UIC Building
Singapore 068808

Australia
Nelson Thomson Learning
102 Dodds Street
South Melbourne, Victoria 3205
Australia

Canada
Nelson Thomson Learning
1120 Birchmount Road
Toronto, Ontario M1K 5G4
Canada

Europe/Middle East/Africa
Thomson Learning
High Holborn House
50/51 Bedford Row
London WC1R 4LR
United Kingdom

Latin America
Thomson Learning
Seneca, 53
Colonia Polanco
11560 Mexico D.F.
Mexico

Spain
Paraninfo Thomson Learning
Calle/Magallanes, 25
28015 Madrid, Spain

About the Author

JACKSON J. SPIELVOGEL is associate professor emeritus of history at The Pennsylvania State University. He received his Ph.D. from The Ohio State University, where he specialized in Reformation history under Harold J. Grimm. His articles and reviews have appeared in such journals as Moreana, Journal of General Education, Catholic Historical Review, Archiv für Reformationsgeschichte, *and* American Historical Review. *He has also contributed chapters or articles to* The Social History of the Reformation, The Holy Roman Empire: A Dictionary Handbook, *the* Simon Wiesenthal Center Annual of Holocaust Studies, *and* Utopian Studies. *His work has been supported by fellowships from the Fulbright Foundation and the Foundation for Reformation Research. At Penn State, he helped inaugurate the Western civilization courses as well as a popular course on Nazi Germany. His book* Hitler and Nazi Germany *was published in 1987 (fourth edition, 2001). He is the coauthor (with William Duiker) of* World History, *first published in 1998 (third edition, 2001), and* The Essential World History *(first edition, 2002). Professor Spielvogel has won five major universitywide teaching awards. He held the Penn State Teaching Fellowship, the university's most prestigious teaching award, in 1988–89. In 1996, he won the Dean Arthur Ray Warnock Award for Outstanding Faculty Member, and in 2000, received the Schreyer Honors College Excellence in Teaching Award.*

To Diane,
whose love and support
made it all possible

Brief Contents

Detailed Contents

CHAPTER 24

An Age of Modernity, Anxiety, and Imperialism, 1894–1914 672

CHAPTER 25

The Beginning of the Twentieth-Century Crisis: War and Revolution 707

CHAPTER 26

The Futile Search for Stability: Europe Between the Wars, 1919–1939 739

Documents

This page constitutes an extension of the copyright page. We have made every effort to trace the ownership of all copyrighted material and to secure permission from copyright holders. In the event of any question arising as to the use of any material, we will be pleased to make the necessary corrections in future printings. Thanks are due to the following authors, publishers, and agents for permission to use the material indicated.

Continues on page 889

Maps

How to Use the Maps in *Western Civilization, 5th Edition*

Here are some basic map concepts that will help you to get the most out of the maps in this textbook.

- Always look at the scale, which allows you to determine the distance in miles or kilometers between locations on the map.
- Examine the legend carefully. It explains the colors and symbols used on the map.
- Note the locations of mountains, rivers, oceans, and other geographic features, and consider how these would affect such human activities as agriculture, commerce, travel, and warfare.
- Read the map caption thoroughly. It provides important information, sometimes not covered in the text itself, and poses a thought question to encourage you to think beyond the mere appearance of the map and make connections across chapters, regions, and concepts.
- Several "spot maps" appear in each chapter, to allow you to view in detail smaller areas that may not be apparent in larger maps. For example, a spot map in Chapter 3 lets you zoom in on the Piraeus, and one in Chapter 5 shows the city of Rome in detail.

Chronologies

Preface

WE ARE OFTEN REMINDED how important it is to understand today's world if we are to deal with our growing number of challenges. And yet that understanding will be incomplete if we in the Western world do not comprehend the meaning of Western civilization and the role Western civilization has played in history. Despite modern progress, we still greatly reflect our religious traditions, our political systems and theories, our economic and social structures, and our cultural heritage. I have written this history of Western civilization to assist a new generation of students in learning more about the past that has helped create them and the world in which they live.

At the same time, for the fifth edition, I have added considerable new material on world history to show the impact other parts of the world have made on the West. Certainly, the terrorist attacks on the World Trade Center Towers and the Pentagon on September 11, 2001, have made clear the intricate relationship between the West and the rest of the world. In this fifth edition, I have attempted to show not only how Western civilization has affected the rest of the world but also how it has been influenced since its beginnings by contacts with other peoples around the world.

Another of my goals was to write a well-balanced work in which the political, economic, social, religious, intellectual, cultural, and military aspects of Western civilization have been integrated into a chronologically ordered synthesis. I have been especially aware of the need to integrate the latest research on social history and women's history into each chapter of the book rather than isolating it either in lengthy topical chapters, which confuse the student by interrupting the chronological narrative, or in separate sections that appear at periodic intervals between chapters.

Another purpose in writing this history of Western civilization has been to put the story back in history. That story is an exciting one; yet many textbooks, often the product of several authors with different writing styles, fail to capture the imagination of their readers. Narrative history effectively transmits the knowledge of the past and is the form that best aids remembrance. At the same time, I have not overlooked the need for the kind of historical analysis that makes students aware that historians often disagree on their interpretations of the past.

To enliven the past and let readers see for themselves the materials that historians use to create their pictures of the past, I have included in each chapter primary sources (boxed documents) that are keyed to the discussion in the text. The documents include examples of the religious, artistic, intellectual, social, economic, and political aspects of Western life. Such varied sources as a Renaissance banquet menu, a student fight song in twentieth-century Britain, letters exchanged between a husband on the battle front and his wife in World War I, the Declaration of the Rights of Woman and the Female Citizen in the French Revolution, and a debate in the Reformation era all reveal in a vivid fashion what Western civilization meant to the individual men and women who shaped it by their activities.

Each chapter has a lengthy introduction and conclusion to help maintain the continuity of the narrative and to provide a synthesis of important themes. Anecdotes in the chapter introductions convey more dramatically the major theme or themes of each chapter. Detailed chronologies reinforce the events discussed in the text, while timelines at the end of each chapter enable students to review at a glance the major developments of an era. Many of the timelines have been revised to show parallel developments in different cultures or nations. An annotated bibliography at the end of each chapter reviews the most recent literature on each period and also gives references to some of the older, "classic" works in each field.

Extensive maps and illustrations serve to deepen the reader's understanding of the text. New to the fifth edition are map captions, designed to enrich students' awareness of the importance of geography to history, and a large number of spot maps, which enable students to see at a glance the region or subject being discussed in the text. The maps have also been revised where needed. To facilitate understanding of cultural movements, illustrations of artistic works discussed in the text are placed next to the discussions. Chapter outlines and focus questions, including analytical questions, at the beginning of each chapter help students with an overview and guide them to the main subjects of each chapter. A glossary of important terms and a pronunciation guide are included to enrich an understanding of the text.

As preparation for the revision of *Western Civilization,* I reexamined the entire book and analyzed the comments and reviews of many colleagues who have found the book to be a useful instrument for introducing their students to the history of Western civilization. In making revisions for the fifth edition, I sought to build on the strengths of the first four editions and, above all, to maintain the balance, synthesis, and narrative qualities that characterized those editions. To keep up with the ever-growing body of historical scholarship, new or revised material has been added throughout the book on many topics, including early civilizations around the world; early Egyptian civilization; Alexander and the Mauryan Empire in India; martyred Christian women; the Han Empire in China; the Mongol Empire; the Ottoman Empire; the Black Death; the development and use of cannons; the Maya, Aztecs, and Inca; the Mughal Empire; early Western encounters with Japan and China; the impact of Western expansion on indigenous peoples; the impact of expansion on European lifestyle and rivalries; the impact of travel literature on Western intellectuals; the impact of the discovery of the Pacific Islands in the eighteenth century; the defeat of Napoleon; slavery; the slave revolt in Haiti; how industrialized nations limited industrialization in their colonies; Latin America; Canada; the impact of renewed European imperialism; the Russian Revolution; the popular culture of the 1920s; the Nazis and women; the Asian theater of World War II; the end of European colonies after World War II; Postmodernism in literature and art; and international terrorism. Throughout the revising process, I also rewrote some sections and added new subheadings in order to facilitate the reader's comprehension of the content of the chapters.

To help put *Western Civilization* into a broader world context, I added a new chapter, "Europe and the World, 1500–1800." This new Chapter 14 brings together a wealth of material on the impact of Europe's first major outreach into the rest of the world and the results for Europe of this encounter with new peoples. Chapters 13 and 15 were also reorganized. Chapter 13 now deals with the Reformation and the religious wars of the sixteenth century; Chapter 15 focuses on seventeenth-century developments. Chapters 7, 9, and 10 were also reorganized to provide a more logical arrangement of the material. Moreover, the "Suggestions for Further Reading" at the end of each chapter were updated and condensed, and new illustrations were added to every chapter.

The enthusiastic response to the primary sources (boxed documents) led me to evaluate the content of each document carefully and add new documents throughout the text, including "The Politics of Aristotle," "Alexander Meets an Indian King," "A Woman's Defense of Learning," "An Imperial Edict to the King of England," "Columbus Lands in the New World," "The Portuguese Conquest of Malacca," "British Victory in India," "Marital Arrangements in the Eighteenth Century," "Justice in the Reign of Terror," and "Bloody Sunday."

Because courses in Western civilization at American and Canadian colleges and universities follow different chronological divisions, a one-volume edition, two two-volume editions, a three-volume edition, and a volume covering events since 1300 are being made available to fit the needs of instructors. Teaching and learning ancillaries include the following:

For the Instructor

Instructor's Manual with Test Bank Prepared by Eugene Larson, Los Angeles Pierce College. This new Instructor's Manual contains chapter outlines, chapter summaries, suggested lecture topics, and discussion questions for the maps and artwork as well as the primary source documents located in the text. Worldwide Web sites and resources, video collections, a Resource Integration Guide, and suggested student activities are also included. Exam questions include essays, identifications, and multiple-choice questions. Available in two volumes.

ExamView Instructors can create, deliver, and customize tests and study guides (both print and online) in minutes with this easy-to-use assessment and tutorial system. ExamView offers both a Quick Test Wizard and an Online Test Wizard that guide users step by step through the process of creating tests, while its unique WYSIWYG capability allows one to see the test on the screen exactly as it will print or display online. Instructors can build tests of up to 250 questions using up to a dozen question types. Using ExamView's complete word processing capabilities, they can enter an unlimited number of new questions or edit existing questions. Available for Windows and Macintosh.

Full-Color Map Acetate Package This package includes all 165 maps from the text. Map commentary is provided by James Harrison, Siena College.

Map Slides 100 full-color map slides.

Lecture Enrichment Slides Prepared by Dale Hoak and George Strong, College of William and Mary. These 100 slides contain images of famous paintings, statues, architectural achievements, and interesting photos. The authors supply commentary for each slide.

History Video Library A completely new selection of videos to go with the fifth edition. Over 50 titles to choose from, with coverage spanning from "Egypt: A Gift to Civilization" to "Children of the Holocaust."

CNN Today Videos For Western civilization, the perfect lecture launchers contain video clips ranging from one to five minutes long.

Sights and Sounds of History Uses focused video clips, photos, artwork, animations, music, and dramatic readings to bring history to life. The video segments average four minutes long and are available on VHS. These make excellent lecture launchers.

Multimedia Manager for Western Civilization, A Microsoft PowerPoint Link Tool An advanced PowerPoint presentation tool containing text-specific lecture outlines, figures, images, and CNN Video Clips that allows instructors to quickly deliver dynamic lectures. In addition, it provides the flexibility to customize each presentation by editing what we have provided or by adding one's own collection of slides, videos, and animations. All of the map acetates and selected photos have also been incorporated into each of the lectures. In addition, the extensive map commentaries for each map slide are available through the "Comments" feature of PowerPoint.

For the Student

Study Guide Prepared by James Baker, Western Kentucky University. Includes chapter outlines, chapter summaries, and seven different types of questions for each chapter. Available in two volumes.

Map Exercise Workbook This workbook, prepared by Cynthia Kosso, Northern Arizona University, has been thoroughly revised, including new easier to read maps. Over 20 maps and exercises ask students to identify important cities and countries and answer critical thinking questions. Available in two volumes.

MapTutor CD-ROM This interactive map tutorial helps students learn geography by having them locate geographical features, regions, cities, and sociopolitical movements. Each map exercise is accompanied by questions that test their knowledge and promote critical thinking. Animations vividly show movements such as the conquests of the Romans, the spread of Christianity, invasions, medieval trade routes, and the spread of the Black Death.

Document Exercise Workbook Prepared by Donna Van Raaphorst, Cuyahoga Community College. A collection of exercises based on primary sources. It contains a Web component that points students to museums and other useful sites. Available in two volumes.

Journey of Civilizations CD-ROM This CD-ROM takes the student on eighteen interactive journeys through history. Enhanced with QuickTime movies, animations, sound clips, maps, and more, the journeys allow students to engage in history as active participants rather than as readers of past events. Available for Windows.

History: Hits on the Web Recently revised for 2002, *Hits on the Web* (HOW) is an exciting, class-tested product specially designed to help history students utilize the Internet for studying, conducting research, and completing assignments. HOW is approximately 80 pages of valuable teaching tools that can be bundled with any Wadsworth textbook at a very affordable price. Available through Thomson Custom Publishing.

Exploring the European Past: Text and Images A new custom reader for Western civilization. Written by leading educators and historians, this fully customizable reader of primary and secondary sources is enhanced with an online module of visual sources, including maps, animations, and interactive exercises. Each reading also comes with an introduction and a series of questions. To learn more, visit http://etep.thomsonlearning.com or call Thomson Learning Custom Publishing at (800) 355-9983.

WebTutor This Internet-based teaching and learning tool is rich with study and mastery tools, communication tools, and course content. Instructors can use WebTutor to provide virtual office hours, post syllabi, set up threaded discussions, track student progress with the quizzing material, and more. For students, WebTutor offers real-time access to a full array of study tools, including flash cards (with audio), practice quizzes, tutorials, interactive maps and timelines, Internet activities, and Web links. Professors can customize the content by uploading images and other resources, adding Web links, or creating their own practice materials. WebTutor also provides rich communication tools, including a course calendar, asynchronous discussion, real-time chat, and an integrated e-mail system. Available in WebCT and Blackboard formats.

Magellan Atlas of Western Civilization Available to bundle with any Western civilization text; contains 44 four-color historical maps, including The Conflict in Afghanistan, 2001, and States of the World, 2001.

Internet Guide for History Prepared by John Soares. Provides up-to-date Internet exercises by topic. Available on the Web site.

Western Civilization, Canadian Supplement Prepared by Maryann Farkus, Dawson College. Discusses Canadian history and culture in the context of Western civilization.

Archer, Documents of Western Civilization Contains a broad selection of carefully chosen documents. Available in two volumes.

InfoTrac® College Edition Create your own collection of secondary readings from more than 900 popular and scholarly periodicals such as *Smithsonian, Historian,* and *Harper's* for four months. Students can browse, choose, and print any articles they want, twenty-four hours a day.

The Wadsworth History Web Site Both instructors and students will enjoy the Wadsworth History Web Site, with access to the chapter-by-chapter resources for Spielvogel's *Western Civilization.* Text-specific content for students includes interactive maps and timelines, tutorial quizzes, a glossary, hyperlinks, InfoTrac College Edition exercises, Internet activities, and Web links. Instructors also have access to the Instructor's Manual, lesson plans, and Microsoft® PowerPoint® slides (access code required). From the History homepage, instructors and students can access many selections, such as an Internet Guide for History, a career center, lessons on surfing the Web, the World History image bank and links to great history-related Web sites.

http://history.wadsworth.com

Acknowledgments

I began to teach at age five in my family's grape arbor. By the age of ten, I wanted to know and understand everything in the world, so I set out to memorize our entire set of encyclopedia volumes. At seventeen, as editor of the high school yearbook, I chose "patterns" as its theme. With that as my early history, followed by twenty rich years of teaching, writing, and family nurturing, it seemed quite natural to accept the challenge of writing a history of Western civilization as I approached that period in life often described as the age of wisdom. Although I see this writing adventure as part of the natural unfolding of my life, I gratefully acknowledge that without the generosity of many others, it would not have been possible.

David Redles gave generously of his time and ideas, especially for Chapters 28 and 29. Chris Colin provided research on the history of music, while Laurie Batitto, Alex Spencer, Stephen Maloney, Shaun Mason, Peter Angelos, and Fred Schooley offered valuable editorial assistance. I deeply appreciate the valuable technical assistance provided by Dayton Coles. I am deeply grateful to John Soares for his assistance in preparing the map captions, new to the fifth edition, and to Charmarie Blaisdell of Northeastern University for her detailed suggestions on women's history that were incorporated into the fourth edition. I am also thankful to the thousands of students whose questions and responses have caused me to see many aspects of Western civilization in new ways.

My ability to undertake a project of this magnitude was in part due to the outstanding European history teachers that I had as both an undergraduate and a graduate student. These included Kent Forster (modern Europe) and Robert W. Green (early modern Europe) at The Pennsylvania State University and Franklin Pegues (medieval), Andreas Dorpalen (modern Germany), William MacDonald (ancient), and Harold J. Grimm (Renaissance and Reformation) at The Ohio State University. These teachers provided me with profound insights into Western civilization and also taught me by their examples that learning only becomes true understanding when it is accompanied by compassion, humility, and open-mindedness.

I would like to thank the many teachers and students who have used the first four editions of my *Western Civilization.* Their enthusiastic response to a textbook that was intended to put the story back in history and capture the imagination of the reader has been very gratifying. I especially thank the many teachers and students who made the effort to contact me personally to share their enthusiasm. Thanks to Wadsworth's comprehensive review process, many historians were asked to evaluate my manuscript and review each edition. I am grateful to the following people for their innumerable suggestions, which have greatly improved my work:

Paul Allen
University of Utah
Gerald Anderson
North Dakota State University
Susan L. H. Anderson
Campbell University
Letizia Argenteri
University of San Diego
Roy A. Austensen
Illinois State University
James A. Baer
Northern Virginia Community College—Alexandria
James T. Baker
Western Kentucky University
Patrick Bass
Morningside College
John F. Battick
University of Maine
Frederic J. Baumgartner
Virginia Polytechnic Institute
Phillip N. Bebb
Ohio University
Anthony Bedford
Modesto Junior College
F. E. Beemon
Middle Tennessee State University
Leonard R. Berlanstein
University of Virginia
Douglas T. Bisson
Belmont University
Charmarie Blaisdell
Northeastern University
Stephen H. Blumm
Montgomery County Community College
Hugh S. Bonar
California State University
Werner Braatz
University of Wisconsin—Oshkosh
Alfred S. Bradford
University of Missouri
Maryann E. Brink
College of William & Mary
Blaine T. Browne
Broward Community College
J. Holden Camp, Jr.,
Hillyer College, University of Hartford
Jack Cargill
Rutgers University
Martha Carlin
University of Wisconsin—Milwaukee
Elizabeth Carney
Clemson University
Eric H. Cline
Xavier University
Robert Cole
Utah State University
William J. Connell
Rutgers University
Nancy Conradt
College of DuPage
Marc Cooper
Southwest Missouri State
Richard A. Cosgrove
University of Arizona
David A. Crain
South Dakota State University
Michael A. Crane, Jr. (student)
Everett Community College
Luanne Dagley
Pellissippi State Technical Community College
Michael F. Doyle
Ocean County College
James W. Ermatinger
University of Nebraska—Kearney
Porter Ewing
Los Angeles City College
Carla Falkner
Northeast Mississippi Community College
Steven Fanning
University of Illinois—Chicago
Ellsworth Faris
California State University—Chico
Gary B. Ferngren
Oregon State University
Mary Helen Finnerty
Westchester Community College
A. Z. Freeman
Robinson College
Marsha Frey
Kansas State University
Frank J. Frost
University of California—Santa Barbara
Frank Garosi
California State University — Sacramento
Richard M. Golden
University of North Texas
Manuel G. Gonzales
Diablo Valley College
Amy G. Gordon
Denison University
Richard J. Grace
Providence College
Hanns Gross
Loyola University
John F. Guilmartin
Ohio State University
Jeffrey S. Hamilton
Gustavus Adolphus College
J. Drew Harrington
Western Kentucky University
James Harrison
Siena College
A. J. Heisserer
University of Oklahoma
Betsey Hertzler
Mesa Community College
Robert Herzstein
University of South Carolina
Shirley Hickson
North Greenville College
Martha L. Hildreth
University of Nevada
Boyd H. Hill Jr.
University of Colorado—Boulder
Michael Hofstetter
Bethany College
Donald C. Holsinger
Seattle Pacific University
Frank L. Holt
University of Houston
W. Robert Houston
University of South Alabama

Paul Hughes
Sussex County Community College
Richard A. Jackson
University of Houston
Fred Jewell
Harding University
Jenny M. Jochens
Towson State University
William M. Johnston
University of Massachusetts
Jeffrey A. Kaufmann
Muscatine Community College
David O. Kieft
University of Minnesota
Patricia Killen
Pacific Lutheran University
William E. Kinsella, Jr.
Northern Virginia Community College—Annandale
James M. Kittelson
Ohio State University
Doug Klepper
Santa Fe Community College
Cynthia Kosso
Northern Arizona University
Clayton Miles Lehmann
University of South Dakota
Diana Chen Lin
Indiana University, Northwest
Ursula W. MacAffer
Hudson Valley Community College
Harold Marcuse
University of California—Santa Barbara
Mavis Mate
University of Oregon
T. Ronald Melton
Brewton Parker College
Jack Allen Meyer
University of South Carolina
Eugene W. Miller Jr.
The Pennsylvania State University—Hazleton
David Mock
Tallahassee Community College
John Patrick Montano
University of Delaware
Rex Morrow
Trident Technical College
Thomas M. Mulhern
University of North Dakota
Pierce Mullen
Montana State University
Frederick I. Murphy
Western Kentucky University
William M. Murray
University of South Florida
Otto M. Nelson
Texas Tech University
Sam Nelson
Willmar Community College
John A. Nichols
Slippery Rock University
Lisa Nofzinger
Albuquerque Technical Vocational Institute
Chris Oldstone-Moore
Augustana College
Donald Ostrowski
Harvard University
James O. Overfield
University of Vermont
Matthew L. Panczyk
Bergen Community College
Kathleen Parrow
Black Hills State University
Carla Rahn Phillips
University of Minnesota
Keith Pickus
Wichita State University
Linda J. Piper
University of Georgia
Janet Polasky
University of New Hampshire
Thomas W. Porter
Randolph-Macon College
Charles A. Povlovich
California State University—Fullerton
Nancy Rachels
Hillsborough Community College
Charles Rearick
University of Massachusetts—Amherst
Jerome V. Reel, Jr.
Clemson University
Joseph Robertson
Gadsden State Community College
Jonathan Roth
San Jose State University
Constance M. Rousseau
Providence College
Julius R. Ruff
Marquette University
Richard Saller
University of Chicago
Magdalena Sanchez
Texas Christian University
Jack Schanfield
Suffolk County Community College
Roger Schlesinger
Washington State University
Joanne Schneider
Rhode Island College
Thomas C. Schunk
University of Wisconsin—Oshkosh
Kyle C. Sessions
Illinois State University
Linda Simmons
Northern Virginia Community College—Manassas
Donald V. Sippel
Rhode Island College
Glen Spann
Asbury College
John W. Steinberg
Georgia Southern University
Paul W. Strait
Florida State University
James E. Straukamp
California State University—Sacramento
Brian E. Strayer
Andrews University
Fred Suppe
Ball State University
Roger Tate
Somerset Community College
Tom Taylor
Seattle University
Jack W. Thacker
Western Kentucky University
Thomas Turley
Santa Clara University
John G. Tuthill
University of Guam
Maarten Ultee
University of Alabama
Donna L. Van Raaphorst
Cuyahoga Community College
Allen M. Ward
University of Connecticut
Richard D. Weigel
Western Kentucky University
Michael Weiss
Linn-Benton Community College
Arthur H. Williamson
California State University—Sacramento
Katherine Workman
Wright State University
Judith T. Wozniak
Cleveland State University
Walter J. Wussow
University of Wisconsin—Eau Claire
Edwin M. Yamauchi
Miami University

The editors at Wadsworth Publishing Company have been both helpful and congenial at all times. I especially wish to thank Clark Baxter, whose clever wit, wisdom, gentle prodding, and good friendship have added much depth to our working relationship. Sue Gleason thoughtfully guided the overall development of the fifth edition, and Julie Iannacchino orchestrated the preparation of outstanding teaching and learning ancillaries. Jennifer Ellis managed construction of the Web site, including its new interactive maps and timelines. Dianne Jensis Toop, of Thomson Learning, and Jon Peck, of Dovetail Publishing Services, were extremely cooperative and competent in the production of the book.

Above all, I thank my family for their support. The gifts of love, laughter, and patience from my daughters, Jennifer and Kathryn; my sons, Eric and Christian; and my daughters-in-law, Liz and Laurie, were enormously appreciated. My wife and best friend, Diane, contributed editorial assistance, wise counsel, good humor, and the loving support that made it possible for me to accomplish a project of this magnitude. I could not have written the book without her.

Introduction to Students of Western Civilization

CIVILIZATION, as historians define it, first emerged between five thousand and six thousand years ago when people began to live in organized communities with distinct political, military, economic, and social structures. Religious, intellectual, and artistic activities also assumed important roles in these early societies. The focus of this book is on Western civilization, a civilization that for most of its history has been identified with the continent of Europe. Its origins, however, go back to the Mediterranean basin, including lands in North Africa, and the Near East as well as Europe itself. Moreover, the spread of Europeans abroad led to the development of offshoots of Western civilization in other parts of the world.

Because civilized life includes all the deeds and experiences of people organized in communities, the history of a civilization must encompass a series of studies. An examination of Western civilization requires that we study the political, economic, social, military, cultural, intellectual, and religious aspects that make up the life of that civilization and show how they are interrelated. In so doing, we need also at times to focus on some of the unique features of Western civilization. Certainly, science played a crucial role in the development of modern Western civilization. Although such societies as those of the Greeks, the Romans, and medieval Europeans were based largely on a belief in the existence of a spiritual order, Western civilization experienced a dramatic departure to a natural or material view of the universe in the seventeenth-century Scientific Revolution. Science and technology have been important in the growth of a modern and largely secular Western civilization, although antecedents to scientific development also existed in Greek, Islamic, and medieval thought and practice.

Many historians have also viewed the concept of political liberty, the fundamental value of every individual, and the creation of a rational outlook, based on a system of logical, analytical thought, as unique aspects of Western civilization. Of course, Western civilization has also witnessed the frightening negation of liberty, individualism, and reason. Racism, violence, world wars, totalitarianism—these, too, must form part of the story. Finally, regardless of our concentration on Western civilization and its characteristics, we need to take into account that other civilizations have influenced the West and it, in turn, has affected the development of other civilizations.

In our examination of Western civilization, we need also to be aware of the dating of time. In recording the past, historians try to determine the exact time when events occurred. World War II in Europe, for example, began on September 1, 1939, when Hitler sent German troops into Poland, and ended on May 7, 1945, when Germany surrendered. By using dates, historians can place events in order and try to determine the development of patterns over periods of time.

If someone asked you when you were born, you would reply with a number, such as 1983. In the United States, we would all accept that number without question because it is part of the dating system followed in the Western world (Europe and the Western Hemisphere). In this system, events are dated by counting backward or forward from the birth of Jesus Christ (assumed to be the year 1). An event that took place four hundred years before the birth of Christ would be dated 400 B.C. (before Christ). Dates after the birth of Christ are labeled A.D. These letters stand for the Latin words *anno Domini*, which mean "in the year of the Lord." Thus an event that took place two hundred years after the birth of Christ is written A.D. 200, or in the year of the Lord 200. It can also be written as 200, just as you would not give your birth year as A.D. 1983, but simply as 1983. Historians also make use of other terms to refer to time. A decade is ten years, a century is one hundred years, and a millennium is one thousand years. Thus "the fourth century B.C." refers to the fourth period of one hundred years counting backward from 1, the assumed date of the birth of Christ. Since the first century B.C. would be the years 100 B.C. to 1 B.C., the fourth century B.C. would be the years 400 B.C. to 301 B.C. We could say, then, that an event in 350 B.C. took place in the fourth century B.C.

"The fourth century A.D." refers to the fourth period of one hundred years after the birth of Christ. Since the first period of one hundred years would be the years 1 to 100, the fourth period or fourth century would be the years 301 to 400. We could say, then, that an event in 350 took place in the fourth century. Likewise, the first millennium B.C. refers to the years 1000 B.C. to 1 B.C.; the second millennium A.D. refers to the years 1001 to 2000. Some historians now prefer to use the abbreviations B.C.E. ("before the Common Era") and C.E. ("Common Era") instead of B.C. and A.D. This is especially true of world historians, who prefer to use symbols that are not so Western or Christian-oriented. The dates, of course, remain the same. Thus 1950 B.C.E. and 1950 B.C. would be the same year. In keeping with current usage by many historians of Western civilization, this book will use the terms B.C. and A.D.

The dating of events can also vary from people to people. Most people in the Western world use the Western calendar, also known as the Gregorian calendar after Pope Gregory XIII, who refined it in 1582. The Hebrew calendar uses a different system in which the year 1 is the equivalent of the Western year 3760 B.C., considered by Jews to be the date of the creation of the world. Thus the Western year 2002 is the year 5762 on the Hebrew calendar. The Islamic calendar begins year 1 on the day Muhammad fled Mecca, which is the year 622 on the Western calendar.

FIFTH EDITION

Western Civilization

C H A P T E R

1

The Ancient Near East: The First Civilizations

Erich Lessing/Art Resource, NY

CHAPTER OUTLINE

- The First Humans
- The Emergence of Civilization
- Civilization in Mesopotamia
- Egyptian Civilization: "The Gift of the Nile"
- On the Fringes of Civilization
- Conclusion

FOCUS QUESTIONS

- Where did the Neolithic agricultural revolution occur, and how did it affect the lives of men and women?
- What are the characteristics of civilization, and what are some explanations for why early civilizations emerged?
- How did geography contribute to the civilizations that arose in Mesopotamia and Egypt?
- What role did religion play in the civilizations of Mesopotamia and Egypt?
- What were the chief legacies of Mesopotamia and Egypt to later civilizations?
- In what ways were the civilizations of Mesopotamia and Egypt alike? In what ways were they different?

IN 1849, A DARING YOUNG Englishman made a hazardous journey into the deserts and swamps of southern Iraq. Moving south down the banks of the Euphrates River while braving high winds and temperatures that reached 120 degrees Fahrenheit, William Loftus led a small expedition in search of the roots of civilization. As he said, "From our childhood we have been led to regard this place as the cradle of the human race."

Guided by native Arabs into the southernmost reaches of Iraq, Loftus and his small group of explorers were soon overwhelmed by what they saw. He wrote, "I know of nothing more exciting or impressive than the first sight of one of these great piles, looming in solitary grandeur from the surrounding plains and marshes." One of these piles, known to the natives as the mound of Warka, contained the ruins of Uruk, one of the first cities in the world and part of the world's first civilization.

Southern Iraq, known to ancient peoples as Mesopotamia, was one area in the world where civilization began. Western civilization can be traced back to the ancient Near East, where people in Mesopotamia and Egypt developed organized societies and created the ideas and institutions that we associate with civilization. The later Greeks and Romans, who played such a crucial role in the development of Western civilization, were themselves nourished and influenced by these older societies in the Near East. It is appropriate, therefore, to begin our story of Western civilization in the ancient Near East with the early civilizations of Mesopotamia and Egypt. Before considering them, however, we must briefly examine humankind's prehistory and observe how human beings made the shift from hunting and gathering to agricultural communities and ultimately to cities and civilization.

C H R O N O L O G Y

The First Humans

Australopithecines	flourished c. 2–4 million years ago
Homo erectus	flourished c. 100,000–1.5 million years ago
Homo sapiens:	
Neanderthals	flourished c. 100,000–30,000 B.C.
Homo sapiens sapiens	emerged c. 200,000 B.C.

The First Humans

Historians rely primarily on documents to create their pictures of the past, but no written records exist for the prehistory of humankind. In their absence, the story of early humanity depends on archaeological and, more recently, biological information, which anthropologists and archaeologists use to formulate theories about our early past.

Although modern science has given us more precise methods for examining prehistory, much of our understanding of early humans still relies on conjecture. Given the rate of new discoveries, the following account of the current theory of early human life might well change in a few years. As the great British archaeologist Louis Leakey reminded us years ago: "Theories on prehistory and early man constantly change as new evidence comes to light."

The earliest humanlike creatures—known as hominids—existed in Africa as long as three to four million years ago. Known as Australopithecines, they flourished in East and South Africa and were the first hominids to make simple stone tools.

A second stage in early human development occurred around 1.5 million years ago when *Homo erectus* ("upright human being") emerged. *Homo erectus* made use of larger and more varied tools and was the first hominid to leave Africa and move into both Europe and Asia.

Around 250,000 years ago, a third—and crucial—stage in human development began with the emergence of *Homo sapiens* ("wise human being"). By 100,000 B.C., two groups of *Homo sapiens* had developed. One type was the Neanderthal, whose remains were first found in the Neander valley in Germany. Neanderthal remains have since been found in both Europe and the Middle East and have been dated to between 100,000 and 30,000 B.C. Neanderthals relied on a variety of stone tools and were the first early people to bury their dead.

The first anatomically modern humans, known as *Homo sapiens sapiens* ("wise, wise human being"), appeared in Africa between 200,000 and 150,000 years ago. Recent evidence indicates that they began to spread outside Africa around 100,000 years ago. Map 1.1 shows probable dates for different movements, although many of these are still controversial. By 30,000 B.C., *Homo sapiens sapiens* had replaced the Neanderthals, who had largely become extinct.

The movement of the first modern humans was rarely deliberate. Groups of people advanced beyond their old hunting grounds at a rate of only 2 or 3 miles per generation. This was enough, however, to populate the world in some tens of thousands of years. Based on recent evidence, some scholars have suggested that such advanced human creatures may have emerged independently in different parts of the world, rather than in Africa alone. In any case, by 10,000 B.C., members of the *Homo sapiens sapiens* species could be found throughout the world. By that time, it was the only human species left. All humans today, whether they are Europeans, Australian Aborigines, or Africans, belong to the same subspecies of human being.

The Hunter-Gatherers of the Old Stone Age

One of the basic distinguishing features of the human species is the ability to make tools. The earliest tools were made of stone, and the term *Paleolithic* (Greek for "old stone") Age is used to designate this early period of human history (c. 2,500,000–10,000 B.C.).

For hundreds of thousands of years, humans relied on hunting and gathering for their daily food. Paleolithic peoples had a close relationship with the world around them, and over a period of time, they came to know which

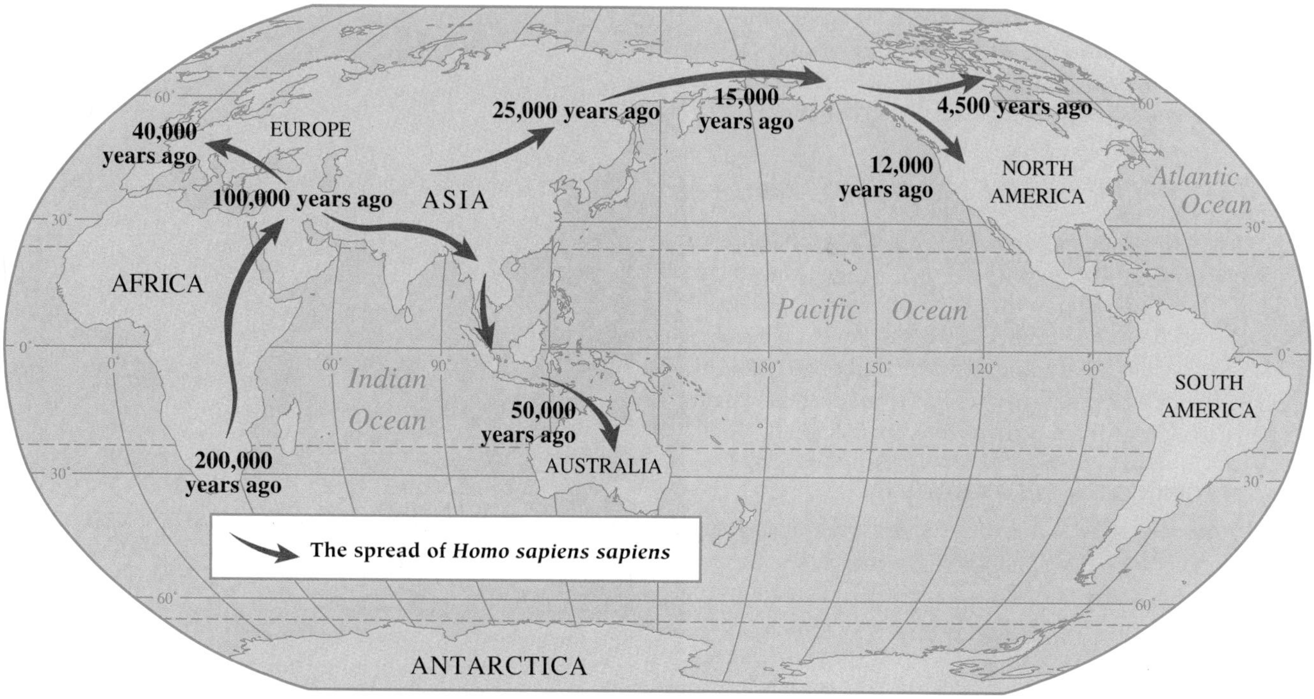

Map 1.1 The Spread of *Homo sapiens sapiens.* *Homo sapiens sapiens* spread from Africa beginning about 100,000 years ago. Living and traveling in small groups, these anatomically modern humans were hunter-gatherers. ■ Given that some diffusion of humans occurred during ice ages, how would such climate change affect humans and their movements, especially from Asia to Australia and Asia to North America?

animals to hunt and which plants to eat. They did not know how to grow crops or raise animals, however. They gathered wild nuts, berries, fruits, and a variety of wild grains and green plants. Around the world, they hunted and consumed various animals, including buffalo, horses, bison, wild goats, and reindeer. In coastal areas, fish were a rich source of nourishment.

The hunting of animals and the gathering of wild plants no doubt led to certain patterns of living. Archaeologists and anthropologists have speculated that Paleolithic people lived in small bands of twenty or thirty people. They were nomadic (they moved from place to place) since they had no choice but to follow animal migrations and vegetation cycles. Hunting depended on careful observation of animal behavior patterns and required a group effort to achieve any real degree of success. Over the years, tools became more refined and more useful. The invention of the spear, and later the bow and arrow, made hunting considerably easier. Harpoons and fishhooks made of bone increased the catch of fish.

Both men and women were responsible for finding food—the chief work of Paleolithic people. Since women bore and raised the children, they generally stayed close to the camps, but they played an important role in acquiring food by gathering berries, nuts, and grains. Men hunted the wild animals, an activity that took them far from camp. Because both men and women played important roles in providing for the band's survival, scientists have argued that a rough equality existed between men and women. Indeed, some speculate that both men and women made the decisions that affected the activities of the Paleolithic band.

These groups of Paleolithic people, especially those who lived in cold climates, found shelter in caves. Over time, they created new types of shelter as well. Perhaps the most common was a simple structure of wood poles or sticks covered with animal hides. Where wood was scarce, Paleolithic hunter-gatherers might use the bones of mammoths to build frames that were then covered with animal hides. The systematic use of fire, which archaeologists believe began around 500,000 years ago, made it possible for the caves and human-made structures to have a source of light and heat. Fire also enabled early humans to cook their food, making it taste better, last longer, and, in the case of some plants, such as wild grain, easier to chew and digest.

The making of tools and the use of fire—two important technological innovations of Paleolithic peoples—remind us how crucial the ability to adapt was to human survival. But Paleolithic peoples did more than just survive. The cave paintings of large animals found in southwestern France and northern Spain bear witness to the cultural activity of Paleolithic peoples. A cave discovered in southern France in 1994 contains more than three hundred paintings of lions, oxen, owls, panthers, and other animals. Most of these are animals that Paleolithic people did not hunt, which suggests that the paintings were made for religious or even decorative purposes.

The Neolithic Revolution (c. 10,000–4000 B.C.)

The end of the last ice age around 10,000 B.C. was followed by what is called the Neolithic Revolution, a significant change in living patterns that occurred in the New Stone Age (the word *neolithic* is Greek for "new stone"). The name New Stone Age is misleading, however. Although Neolithic peoples made a new type of polished stone ax, this was not the major change that occurred after 10,000 B.C.

Paleolithic Cave Painting. Cave paintings of large animals provide good examples of the cultural creativity of Paleolithic peoples. This scene is part of a large underground chamber found accidentally in 1940 at Lascaux, France, by some boys looking for their dog. This work is dated around 15,000 B.C.

AN AGRICULTURAL REVOLUTION

The biggest change was the shift from hunting animals and gathering plants for sustenance to producing food by systematic agriculture (see Map 1.2). The planting of grains and vegetables provided a regular supply of food, while the taming of animals, such as goats, cattle, pigs, and sheep, added a steady source of meat, milk, and fibers such as wool for clothing. Larger animals could also be used as beasts of burden. The growing of crops and the taming of food-producing animals created a new relationship between humans and nature. Historians like to speak of this as an agricultural revolution. Revolutionary change is dramatic and requires great effort, but the ability to acquire food on a regular basis gave humans greater control over their environment. It also enabled them to give up their nomadic way of life and begin to live in settled communities.

Systematic agriculture probably developed independently between 8000 and 7000 B.C. in four different areas

Map 1.2 The Development of Agriculture. Agriculture first began between 8000 and 7000 B.C. in four different areas. It allowed the establishment of permanent settlements where crops could be grown and domesticated animals that produced meat and milk could be easily tended. ■ What human and geographical factors might explain relationships between latitude and the beginning of agriculture?

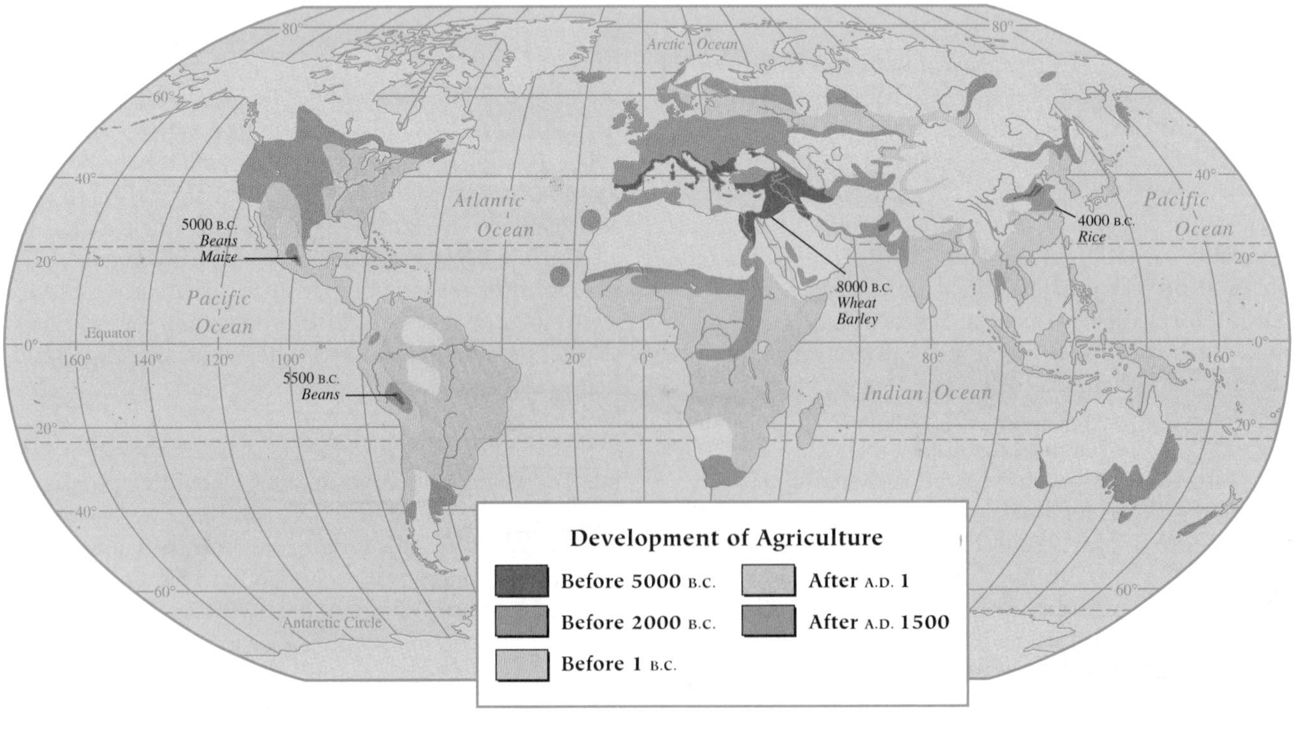

of the world. In each of these areas, different plants were cultivated: wheat, barley, and lentils in the Near East, rice and millet in southern Asia, millet and yams in western Africa, and beans, potatoes, and corn (maize) in the middle Americas. In the Near East as elsewhere, the Neolithic agricultural revolution needed a favorable environment. The upland areas above the Fertile Crescent (present-day northern Iraq and southern Turkey) were initially more conducive to systematic farming than the river valleys. This region received the necessary rainfall and was the home of two wild plant (barley, wheat) and four wild animal (pigs, cows, goats, sheep) species that humans eventually domesticated for their use.

CONSEQUENCES OF THE NEOLITHIC REVOLUTION

The growing of crops on a regular basis gave rise to more permanent settlements, which historians refer to as Neolithic farming villages or towns. One of the oldest and most extensive agricultural villages was Çatal Hüyük, located in modern-day Turkey. Its walls enclosed 32 acres, and its population probably reached six thousand inhabitants during its high point from 6700 to 5700 B.C. People lived in simple mudbrick houses that were built so close to one another that there were few streets. To get to their homes, people had to walk along the rooftops and then enter the house through a hole in the roof.

Archaeologists have discovered twelve cultivated products in Çatal Hüyük, including fruits, nuts, and three kinds of wheat. People grew their own food and stored it in storerooms in their homes. Domesticated animals, especially cattle, yielded meat, milk, and hides. Food surpluses also made it possible for people to do things other than farming. Some people became artisans and made weapons and jewelry that were traded with neighboring peoples.

Religious shrines housing figures of gods and goddesses have been found at Çatal Hüyük, as have a number of female statuettes. Molded with noticeably large breasts and buttocks, these "earth mothers" perhaps symbolically represented the fertility of both "our mother" earth and human mothers. Both the shrines and the statues point to the growing role of religion in the lives of these Neolithic people.

The Neolithic agricultural revolution had far-reaching consequences. Once people settled in villages or towns, they built houses for protection and other structures for the storage of goods. As organized communities stored food and accumulated material goods, they began to engage in trade. People also began to specialize in certain crafts, and a division of labor developed. Pottery was made from clay and baked in a fire to make it hard. The pots were used for cooking and to store grains. Woven baskets were also used for storage. Stone tools became refined as flint blades were developed to make sickles and hoes for use in the

Statues from Ain Ghazal. These life-size statues made of plaster and bitumen date from 6500 B.C. and were discovered in 1984 in Ain Ghazal, an archaeological site near Amman, Jordan. They are among the oldest statues ever found of the human figure. Archaeologists are studying the sculptures to try to understand their purpose and their meaning.

Courtesy of the Hashemite Kingdom of Jordan, Dept. of Antiquities

fields. In the course of the Neolithic Age, many of the food plants still in use today began to be cultivated. Moreover, vegetable fibers from such plants as flax and cotton were used to make thread that was woven into cloth.

The change to systematic agriculture in the Neolithic Age also had consequences for the relationship between men and women. Men assumed the primary responsibility for working in the fields and herding animals, jobs that kept them away from the home. Women remained behind, caring for the children and weaving clothes, making cheese from milk, and performing other tasks that required considerable labor in one place. In time, as work outside the home was increasingly perceived as more important than work done at home, men came to play the more dominant role in society, a basic pattern that would persist until our own times.

Other patterns set in the Neolithic Age also proved to be enduring elements of human history. Fixed dwellings, domesticated animals, regular farming, a division of labor, men holding power—all of these are part of the human story. For all our scientific and technological progress, human survival still depends on the growing and storing of food, an accomplishment of people in the Neolithic Age. The Neolithic Revolution was truly a turning point in human history.

Between 4000 and 3000 B.C., significant technical developments began to transform the Neolithic towns. The invention of writing enabled records to be kept, and the use of metals marked a new level of human control over the environment and its resources. Already before 4000 B.C., craftspeople had discovered that metal-bearing rocks could be heated to liquefy metals, which could then be cast in molds to produce tools and weapons that were more useful than stone instruments. Although copper was the first metal to be used in producing tools, after 4000 B.C., craftspeople in western Asia discovered that a combination of copper and tin produced bronze, a much harder and more durable metal than copper. Its widespread use has led historians to call the period from around 3000 to 1200 B.C. the Bronze Age; thereafter, bronze was increasingly replaced by iron.

At first, Neolithic settlements were hardly more than villages. But as their inhabitants mastered the art of farming, more complex human societies gradually emerged. As wealth increased, these societies began to develop armies and to build walled cities. By the beginning of the Bronze Age, the concentration of larger numbers of people in the river valleys of Mesopotamia and Egypt was leading to a whole new pattern for human life.

The Emergence of Civilization

As we have seen, early human beings formed small groups that developed a simple culture that enabled them to survive. As human societies grew and developed greater complexity, a new form of human existence—called civilization—came into being. A civilization is a complex culture in which large numbers of human beings share a variety of common elements. Historians have identified a number of basic characteristics of civilization. These include (1) an urban focus: cities became the centers of political, economic, social, cultural, and religious development; (2) a distinct religious structure: the gods were deemed crucial to the community's success, and professional priestly classes, as stewards of the gods' property, regulated relations with the gods; (3) new political and military structures: an organized government bureaucracy arose to meet the administrative demands of the growing population, and armies were organized to gain land and power; (4) a new social structure based on economic power: while kings and an upper class of priests, political leaders, and warriors dominated, there also existed a large group of free people (farmers, artisans, craftspeople) and at the very bottom, socially, a class of slaves; (5) the development of writing: kings, priests, merchants, and artisans used writing to keep records; and (6) new forms of significant artistic and intellectual activity: for example, monumental architectural structures, usually religious, occupied a prominent place in urban environments.

The civilizations that developed in Mesopotamia and Egypt, the forerunners of Western civilization, will be examined in detail in this chapter. But civilizations also developed independently in other parts of the world. Between 3000 and 1500 B.C., the valleys of the Indus River in India supported a flourishing civilization that extended hundreds of miles from the Himalayas to the coast of the Arabian Sea. Two major cities—Harappa and Mohenjo-Daro—were at the heart of this civilization in India. Many written records of this Indus valley civilization exist, but their language has not yet been deciphered. This Indus valley civilization carried on extensive trade with city-states in Mesopotamia.

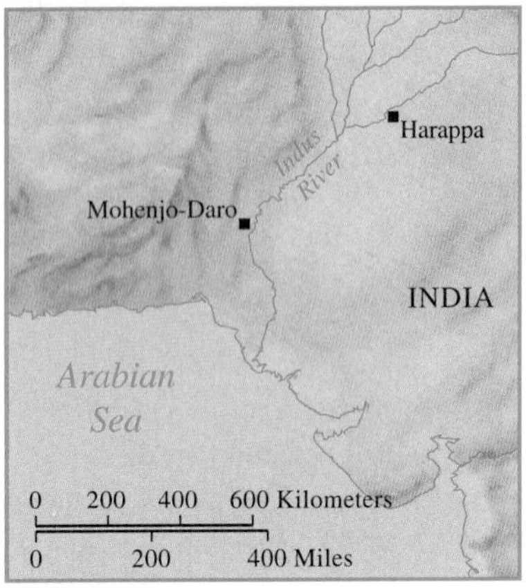

Harappa and Mohenjo-Daro

Another river valley civilization emerged along the Yellow River in northern China about 4,000 years ago. Under the Shang dynasty of kings, which ruled from 1750 to 1122 B.C., this civilization contained impressive cities with huge outer walls, royal palaces, and large royal tombs. A system of irrigation enabled early Chinese civilization to maintain a prosperous farming society ruled by an aristocratic class whose major concern was war.

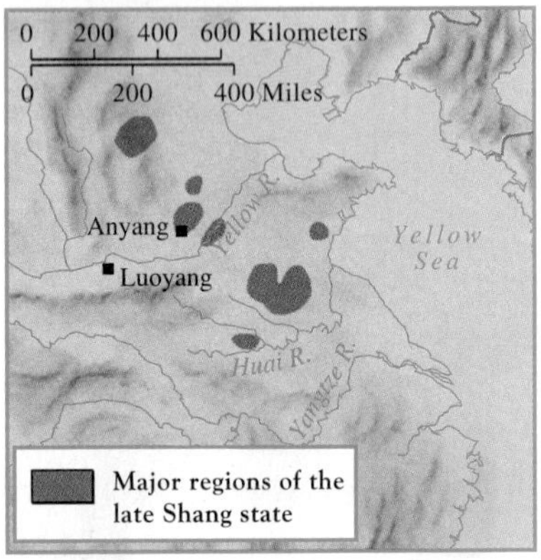

The Yellow River, China

Scholars have believed for a long time that civilization emerged only in four areas, in the fertile river valleys of the Tigris and Euphrates, the Nile, the Indus, and the Yellow River—that is, in Mesopotamia, Egypt, India, and China. Recently, however, archaeologists have discovered two

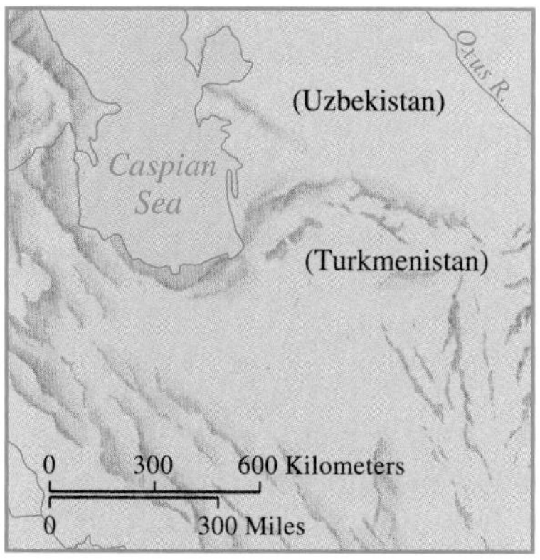

Central Asian Civilization

other early civilizations. One of these flourished in Central Asia (in what are now the republics of Turkmenistan and Uzbekistan) around 4,000 years ago. People in this civilization built mudbrick buildings, raised sheep and goats, had bronze tools, used a system of irrigation to grow wheat and barley, and had a writing system.

Another early civilization was discovered in the Supe River valley of Peru. At the center of this civilization was the city of Caral, which flourished around 2600 B.C. It contained buildings for officials, apartment houses, and grand residences, all built of stone. The inhabitants of Caral also developed a system of irrigation by diverting a river more than a mile upstream into their fields.

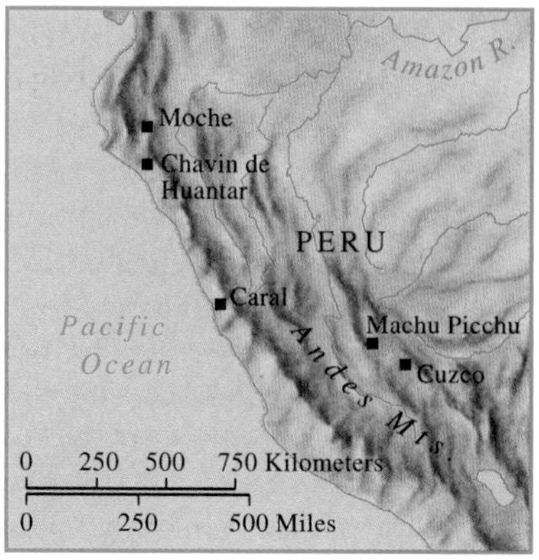

Caral, Peru

Why early civilizations developed remains difficult to explain. Since civilizations developed independently in different parts of the world, can general causes be identified that would explain why all of these civilizations emerged? A number of possible explanations of the beginning of civilization have been suggested. A theory of challenge and response maintains that challenges forced human beings to make efforts that resulted in the rise of civilization. Some scholars have adhered to a material explanation. Material forces, such

Map 1.3 The Ancient Near East. The Fertile Crescent encompassed land with access to water. Employing flood management and irrigation systems, the peoples of the region established civilizations based on agriculture. These civilizations developed writing, law codes, and economic specialization. ■ What geographical aspects of the Mesopotamian city-states made conflict between them likely?

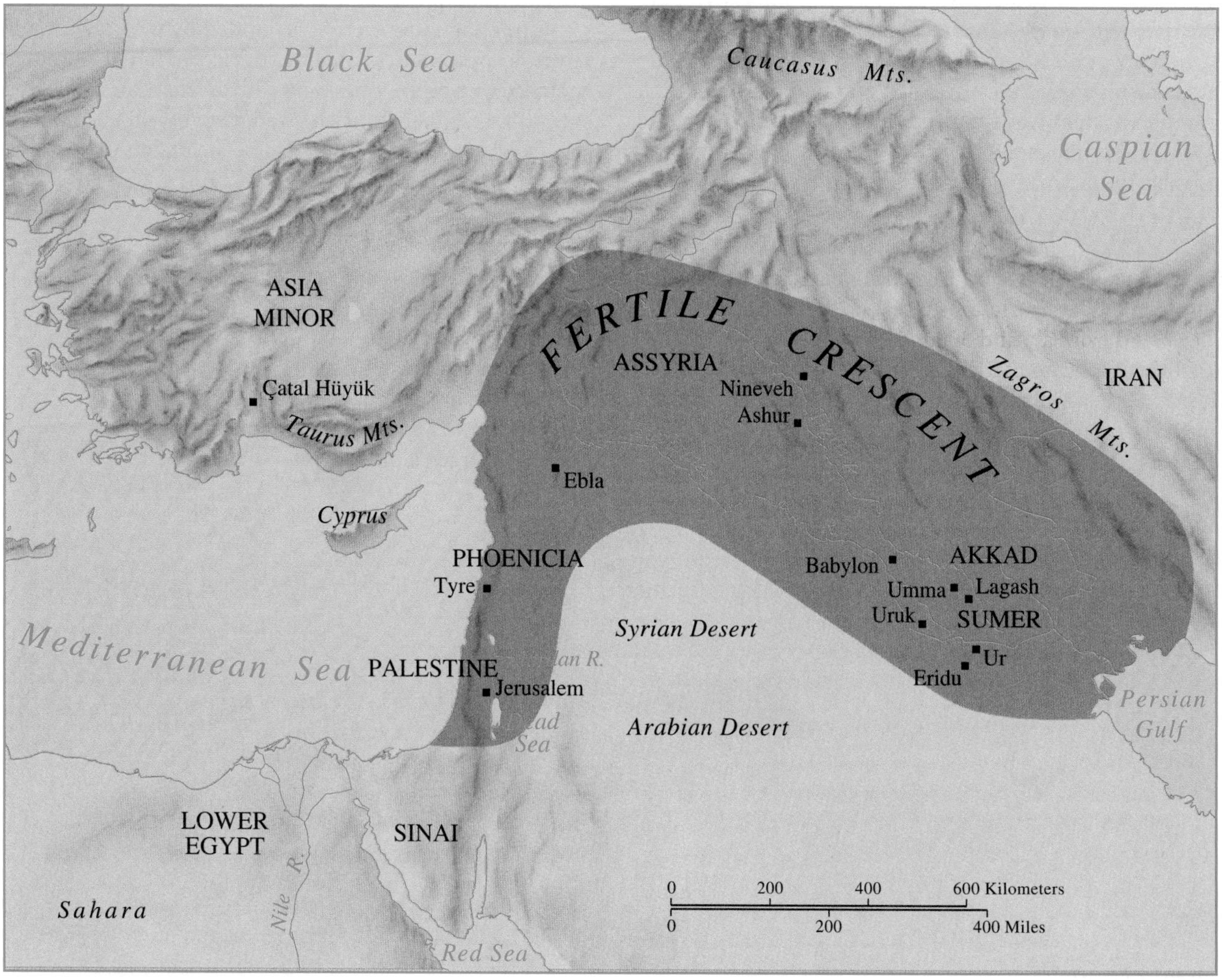

as the growth of food surpluses, made possible the specialization of labor and development of large communities with bureaucratic organization. But the area of the Fertile Crescent, in which Mesopotamian civilization emerged (see Map 1.3), was not naturally conducive to agriculture. Abundant food could only be produced with a massive human effort to carefully manage the water, an effort that created the need for organization and bureaucratic control and led to civilized cities. Some historians have argued that nonmaterial forces, primarily religious, provided the sense of unity and purpose that made such organized activities possible. Finally, some scholars doubt that we are capable of ever discovering the actual causes of early civilization.

CHRONOLOGY

The Birth of Early Civilizations

Egypt	c. 3100 B.C.
Mesopotamia	c. 3000 B.C.
India	c. 3000 B.C.
Peru	c. 2600 B.C.
China	c. 2000 B.C.
Central Asia	c. 2000 B.C.

Civilization in Mesopotamia

The Greeks spoke of the valley between the Tigris and Euphrates Rivers as Mesopotamia, the land "between the rivers." The region receives little rain, but the soil of the plain of southern Mesopotamia was enlarged and enriched over the years by layers of silt deposited by the two rivers. In late spring, the Tigris and Euphrates overflow their banks and deposit their fertile silt, but since this flooding depends on the melting of snows in the upland mountains where the rivers begin, it is unpredictable and sometimes catastrophic. In such circumstances, farming could be done only when people built irrigation and drainage ditches. A complex system was required to control the flow of the rivers and produce the crops. Large-scale irrigation made possible the expansion of agriculture in this region, and the abundant food provided the material base for the emergence of civilization in Mesopotamia.

The City-States of Ancient Mesopotamia

The creators of Mesopotamian civilization were the Sumerians, a people whose origins remain unclear. By 3000 B.C., they had established a number of independent cities in southern Mesopotamia, including Eridu, Ur, Uruk, Umma, and Lagash. As the cities grew larger, they came to exercise political and economic control over the surrounding countryside, forming city-states. These city-states were the basic units of Sumerian civilization.

Sumerian cities were surrounded by walls. Uruk, for example, occupied an area of approximately 1,000 acres encircled by a wall 6 miles long with defense towers located every 30 to 35 feet along the wall. City dwellings, built of sun-dried bricks, included both the small flats of peasants and the larger dwellings of the civic and priestly officials.

The "Royal Standard" of Ur. This detail is from the "Royal Standard" of Ur, a box dating from around 2700 B.C. that was discovered in a stone tomb from the royal cemetery of the Sumerian city-state of Ur. The scenes on the box depict the activities of the king and his military forces. Shown here in this scene is a Sumerian battle chariot. Each chariot held two men, one who held the reins and the other armed with a spear for combat. A special compartment in the chariot held a number of spears.

Although Mesopotamia had little stone or wood for building purposes, it did have plenty of mud. Mudbricks, easily shaped by hand, were left to bake in the hot sun until they were hard enough to use for building. People in Mesopotamia were remarkably inventive with mudbricks, inventing the arch and the dome and constructing some of the largest brick buildings in the world. Mudbricks are still used in rural areas of the Middle East today.

The most prominent building in a Sumerian city was the temple, which was dedicated to the chief god or goddess of the city and often built atop a massive stepped tower called a ziggurat. The Sumerians believed that the gods and goddesses owned the cities, and much wealth was used to build temples as well as elaborate houses for the priests and priestesses who served the gods. Priests and priestesses, who supervised the temples and their property, had great power. In fact, historians believe that in the early stages of the city-states, priests and priestesses played an important role in ruling. The Sumerians believed that the gods ruled the cities, making the state a theocracy (government by a divine authority). Eventually, however, ruling power was shared with worldly figures known as kings.

Sumerians viewed kingship as divine in origin—kings, they believed, derived their power from the gods and were the agents of the gods. As one person said in a petition to his king: "You in your judgment, you are the son of Anu [god of the sky]; your commands, like the word of a god, cannot be reversed; your words, like rain pouring down from heaven, are without number."[1] Regardless of their origins, kings had power—they led armies, initiated legislation, supervised the building of public works, provided courts, and organized workers for the irrigation projects on which Mesopotamian agriculture depended. The army, the government bureaucracy, and the priests and priestesses all aided the kings in their rule. Befitting their power, Sumerian kings lived in large palaces with their wives and children.

The economy of the Sumerian city-states was primarily agricultural, but commerce and industry became important as well. The people of Mesopotamia produced woolen textiles, pottery, and the metalwork for which they were especially well known. Foreign trade, which was primarily a royal monopoly, could be extensive. Royal officials imported luxury items, such as copper and tin, aromatic woods, and fruit trees, in exchange for dried fish, wool, barley, wheat, and the metal goods produced by Mesopotamian metalworkers. Traders traveled by land to the eastern Mediterranean in the west and by sea to India in the east. The invention of the wheel around 3000 B.C. led to carts with wheels that made the transport of goods easier.

Sumerian city-states contained three major social groups—nobles, commoners, and slaves. Nobles included royal and priestly officials and their families. Commoners included the nobles' clients who worked for the palace and temple estates and other free citizens who worked as farmers, merchants, fishers, scribes, and craftspeople. Probably 90 percent or more of the population were farmers. They could exchange their crops for the goods of the artisans in free town markets. Slaves belonged to palace officials, who used them mostly in building projects; temple officials, who used mostly female slaves to weave cloth and grind grain; and rich landowners, who used them for farming and domestic work.

Empires in Ancient Mesopotamia

As the number of Sumerian city-states grew and the states expanded, new conflicts arose as city-state fought city-state for control of land and water. During the Early Dynastic Age (3000–2340 B.C.), the fortunes of various cities rose and fell over the centuries. The constant wars, with their burning and sacking of cities, left many Sumerians in deep despair, as is evident in this Sumerian poem from the city of Ur: "Ur is destroyed, bitter is its lament. The country's blood now fills its holes like hot bronze in a mold. Bodies dissolve like fat in the sun. Our temple is destroyed, the gods have abandoned us, like migrating birds. Smoke lies on our city like a shroud."

Located on the flat, open land of Mesopotamia, the Sumerian city-states were also vulnerable to invasion. To the north of the Sumerian city-states were the Akkadians. We call them a Semitic people because of the type of language they spoke (see Table 1.1). Around 2340 B.C., Sargon, leader of the Akkadians, overran the Sumerian city-states and established a dynastic empire. Sargon's empire, including all of Mesopotamia as well as lands westward to the Mediterranean, inspired generations of Near Eastern leaders to emulate his accomplishment. Despite a period of economic growth, prosperity, and cultural flowering, Sargon's successors were ultimately unable to preserve his empire, however. Attacks from neighboring hill peoples caused the Akkadian empire to fall by 2100 B.C.

The end of the Akkadian empire brought a return to independent city-states in Mesopotamia until Ur-Nammu of Ur succeeded in reunifying much of Mesopotamia. The Third Dynasty of Ur (c. 2112–2000 B.C.) that he established witnessed a final flowering of Sumerian culture. The economy flourished, and new temples and canals were built. Invasion by nomadic tribes, a perennial problem in Mesopotamian history, proved disastrous for the Third Dynasty of Ur, however. After a lengthy period of fighting and confusion, the sixth king of the Amorite dynasty, Hammurabi, managed to establish power. Under Hammurabi,

Table 1.1 Some Semitic Languages

Akkadian
Arabic
Aramaic
Assyrian
Babylonian
Canaanitic
Hebrew
Phoenician
Syriac

Note: Languages in italic type are no longer spoken.

the Amorites or Old Babylonians, a large group of Semitic-speaking seminomads, created a new empire.

Hammurabi (1792–1750 B.C.) had a well-disciplined army of foot soldiers who carried axes, spears, and copper or bronze daggers. He learned to divide his opponents and subdue them one by one. Using such methods, he gained control of Sumer and Akkad and reunified Mesopotamia almost to the old borders established by Sargon. After his conquests, Hammurabi called himself "the sun of Babylon, the king who has made the four quarters of the world subservient," and established a new capital at Babylon.

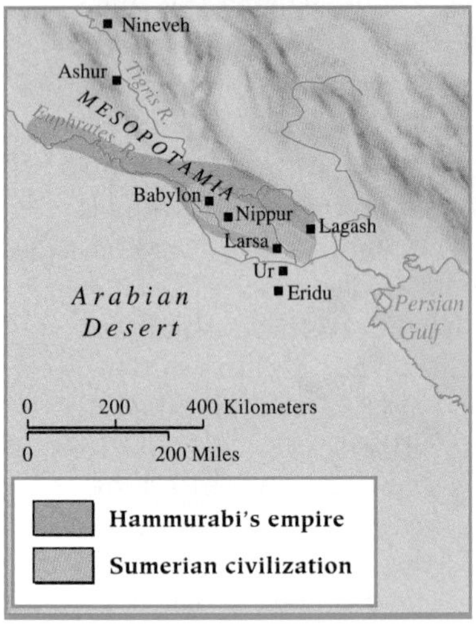

Hammurabi's Empire

Hammurabi, the man of war, was also a man of peace. He followed in the footsteps of previous conquerors by assimilating Mesopotamian culture with the result that Sumerian ways continued to exist despite the end of the Sumerians as a political entity. A collection of his letters, found by archaeologists, reveals that the king took a strong interest in state affairs. He built temples, defensive walls, and irrigation canals; encouraged trade; and brought about an economic revival. Hammurabi left his dynasty strong enough that it survived until the 1550s B.C. when the Kassites from the northeast took over.

CHRONOLOGY

Chief Events in Mesopotamian History

Sumerian city-states: Early Dynastic Age	c. 3000–2340 B.C.
Sargon's empire	c. 2340–2100 B.C.
Third Dynasty of Ur	c. 2112–2000 B.C.
Hammurabi's reign	1792–1750 B.C.
Invasion by Kassites	c. 1550 B.C.

The Code of Hammurabi

Hammurabi is best remembered for his law code, a collection of 282 laws. For centuries, laws had regulated people's relationships with one another in the lands of Mesopotamia, but only fragments of these earlier codes survive. Hammurabi's collection provides considerable insight into many aspects of everyday life and affords us a priceless glimpse of the values of this early society (see the box on p. 11).

The Code of Hammurabi reveals a society with a system of strict justice. Penalties for criminal offenses were severe and varied according to the social class of the victim. A crime against a member of the upper class (a noble) was punished more severely than the same offense against a member of the lower class. Moreover, the principle of retaliation ("an eye for an eye, a tooth for a tooth") was fundamental to this system of justice. It was applied in cases where members of the upper class committed crimes against their social equals. For crimes against members of the lower classes, a money payment was made instead.

Hammurabi's code took the responsibilities of public officials very seriously. The governor of an area and city officials were expected to catch burglars. If they failed to do so, officials in the district where the crime was committed had to replace the lost property. If murderers were not found, the officials had to pay a fine to the relatives of the murdered person. Soldiers were likewise expected to fulfill their duties and responsibilities for the order and maintenance of the state. If a soldier hired a substitute to fight for him, he was put to death, and the substitute was given control of his estate.

Stele of Hammurabi (Code of Hammurabi, King of Babylonia). Although the Sumerians compiled earlier law codes, Hammurabi's code was the most famous in early Mesopotamian history. The code recognized three social classes in Babylonia (nobles, freemen, and slaves) and included laws dealing with marriage and divorce, job performance, punishments for crime, and even sexual relations. The upper section of the stele depicts Hammurabi standing in front of the seated sun god Shamash, who orders the king to record the law. The lower section contains the actual code.

The Code of Hammurabi

Hammurabi's code is the most complete Mesopotamian law code, although not the earliest. It was inscribed on a stone stele topped by a bas-relief picturing Hammurabi receiving the inspiration for the law code from the sun god Shamash, who was also the god of justice. The law code emphasizes the principle of retribution ("an eye for an eye") and punishments that vary according to social status. The following examples illustrate these concerns.

The Code of Hammurabi

25. If fire broke out in a freeman's house and a freeman, who went to extinguish it, cast his eye on the goods of the owner of the house and has appropriated the goods of the owner of the house, that freeman shall be thrown into that fire.
129. If the wife of a freeman has been caught while lying with another man, they shall bind them and throw them into the water. If the husband of the woman wishes to spare his wife, then the king in turn may spare his subject.
131. If a freeman's wife was accused by her husband, but she was not caught while lying with another man, she shall make affirmation by god and return to her house.
196. If a freeman has destroyed the eye of a member of the aristocracy, they shall destroy his eye.
198. If he has destroyed the eye of a commoner or broken the bone of a commoner, he shall pay one mina of silver.
199. If he has destroyed the eye of a freeman's slave or broken the bone of a freeman's slave, he shall pay one-half his value.
209. If a freeman struck another freeman's daughter and has caused her to have a miscarriage, he shall pay ten shekels of silver for her fetus.
210. If that woman has died, they shall put his daughter to death.
211. If by a blow he has caused a commoner's daughter to have a miscarriage, he shall pay five shekels of silver.
212. If that woman has died, he shall pay one-half mina of silver.
213. If he struck a freeman's female slave and has caused her to have a miscarriage, he shall pay two shekels of silver.
214. If that female slave has died, he shall pay one-third mina of silver.

The law code also furthered the proper performance of work with what virtually amounted to consumer protection laws. Builders were held responsible for the buildings they constructed. If a house collapsed and caused the death of the owner, the builder was put to death. If the collapse caused the death of the son of the owner, the son of the builder was put to death. If goods were destroyed by the collapse, they had to be replaced and the house itself reconstructed at the builder's expense.

The number of laws in Hammurabi's code dedicated to land tenure and commerce reveal the importance of agriculture and trade in the Mesopotamian economy. Laws concerning land use and irrigation were especially strict, an indication of the danger of declining crop yields if the land was used incompetently. If landowners and tenants failed to keep dikes in good repair or to control water flow properly and thus caused damage to others' crops, they were required to pay for the grain that was destroyed. If they could not pay, they were sold into slavery and their goods sold and the proceeds divided among the injured parties.

Commercial activity was carefully regulated. Rates of interest on loans were watched closely. If the lender raised the interest rate after a loan was made, he lost the entire amount of the loan. The Code of Hammurabi even specified the precise wages of laborers and artisans, such as brickmakers and jewelers.

The largest number of laws in the Code of Hammurabi focused on marriage and the family. Parents arranged marriages for their children. After marriage, the parties involved signed a marriage contract; without it, no one was considered legally married. While the husband provided a bridal payment, the woman's parents were responsible for a dowry to the new husband.

As in many patriarchal societies, women possessed far fewer privileges and rights in the married relationship than men. A woman's place was in the home, and failure to fulfill her expected duties was grounds for divorce. If she was not able to bear children, her husband could divorce her, but he did have to return the dowry to the woman's family. If his wife tried to leave home to engage in business, thus neglecting her house, her husband could divorce her and did not have to repay the dowry. Furthermore, if his wife was a "gadabout, . . . neglecting her house [and] humiliating her husband," she could be drowned. We do know that in practice not all women remained at home. Some worked in business and were especially prominent in running taverns.

Women were guaranteed some rights, however. If a woman was divorced without good reason, she received the dowry back. A woman could seek divorce and get her dowry back if her husband was unable to show that she had done anything wrong. In theory, a wife was guaranteed the use of her husband's legal property in the event of his death. A mother could also decide which of her sons would receive an inheritance.

Sexual relations were strictly regulated as well. Husbands, but not wives, were permitted sexual activity outside marriage. A wife caught committing adultery was pitched into the river, although her husband could ask the king to pardon her. Incest was strictly forbidden. If a father committed incestuous relations with his daughter, he would be banished. Incest between a son and his mother resulted in both being burned.

Fathers ruled their children as well as their wives. Obedience was duly expected: "If a son has struck his father, they shall cut off his hand." If a son committed a serious enough offense, his father could disinherit him, although fathers were not permitted to disinherit their sons arbitrarily.

The Culture of Mesopotamia

A spiritual worldview was of fundamental importance to Mesopotamian culture. To the peoples of Mesopotamia, the gods were living realities who affected all aspects of life. It was crucial, therefore, that the correct hierarchies be observed. Leaders could prepare armies for war, but success really depended on a favorable relationship with the gods. This helps explain the importance of the priestly class and is the reason why even the kings took great care to dedicate offerings and monuments to the gods. The records of these dedications are among our earliest historical documents.

THE IMPORTANCE OF RELIGION

The Mesopotamians viewed their city-states as earthly copies of a divine model and order. Each city-state was sacred because it was linked to a god or goddess. Hence Nippur, the earliest center of Sumerian religion, was dedicated to Enlil, the god of wind. Moreover, located at the heart of each major city-state was a temple complex. Occupying several acres, this sacred area consisted of a ziggurat with a temple at the top dedicated to the god or goddess who owned the city. The temple complex was the true center of the community. The main god or goddess dwelt there symbolically in the form of a statue, and the ceremony of dedication included a ritual that linked the statue to the god or goddess and thus supposedly harnessed the power of the deity for the city's benefit. Considerable wealth was poured into the construction of temples and other buildings used for the residences of priests and priestesses who served the gods. Although the gods literally owned the city, the temple complex used only part of the land and rented out the remainder. The temples dominated individual and commercial life, an indication of the close relationship between Mesopotamian religion and culture.

The physical environment had an obvious impact on the Mesopotamian view of the universe. Ferocious floods, heavy downpours, scorching winds, and oppressive humidity were all part of the Mesopotamian climate. These conditions and resulting famines easily convinced Mesopotamians that this world was controlled by supernatural forces and that the days of human beings "are numbered; whatever he may do, he is but wind," as *The Epic of Gilgamesh* laments (see "Mesopotamian Literature" later in this chapter). In the presence of nature, Mesopotamians could easily feel helpless, as this poem relates:

The rampant flood which no man can oppose,
Which shakes the heavens and causes earth to tremble,
In an appalling blanket folds mother and child,
Beats down the canebrake's full luxuriant greenery,
And drowns the harvest in its time of ripeness.

Rising waters, grievous to eyes of man,
All-powerful flood, which forces the embankments
And mows down mighty trees,
Frenzied storm, tearing all things in massed confusion
With it in hurtling speed.[2]

The Mesopotamians discerned cosmic rhythms in the universe and accepted its order but perceived that it was not completely safe because of the presence of willful, powerful cosmic forces that they identified with gods and goddesses.

With its numerous gods and goddesses animating all aspects of the universe, Mesopotamian religion was polytheistic. The four most important deities were An, Enlil, Enki, and Ninhursaga. An was the god of the sky and hence the most important force in the universe. Since his basic essence was authority, he was also viewed as the source or active principle of all authority, including the earthly power of rulers and fathers alike. In one myth, the gods address him thus:

What you have ordered comes true!
The utterance of prince and lord is but what you have ordered, do agree with.
O An! your great command takes precedence, who could gainsay it?
O father of the gods, your command, the very foundations of heaven and earth, what god could spurn it?[3]

Robert Harding Picture Library

Ziggurat at Ur. This ziggurat, located at Ur, is rectangular, not square like later ones. Built around 2112 B.C., the ziggurat had a central staircase that led to the temple at the top. This temple was dedicated to the god believed to own the city.

A Creation Myth: "Let Man Carry the Labor-Basket of the Gods"

This selection is taken from *Atrahasis,* a Mesopotamian poem probably composed early in the second millennium B.C. It is a myth that relates the creation, destruction, and regeneration of the human race. In this excerpt, the gods create human beings to do the physical labor—digging canals—that they have grown to detest.

■ Atrahasis

When the gods, like man,
bore the work, carried the labor-basket—
the labor-basket of the great gods—
the work was heavy, much was the distress. . . .
Forty more years
they bore the labor night and day.
They wearied, complained,
grumbled in the workpits.
"Let us confront the throne-bearer
that he may remove from us our heavy labor.
Come on, let us confuse him in his dwelling,
Enlil, the counselor of the gods, the hero,
come on, let us confuse him in his dwelling. . . ."

[After the lesser gods who are digging the canals rebel against Enlil, who rules the surface of the earth, he agrees to create human beings to do the physical labor for the lesser gods.]

"While [Nintu the birth-goddess] is present,
let the birth-goddess create the offspring,
let man bear the labor-basket of the gods."
They called the goddess and asked her,
the midwife of the gods, wise Mami:
"You are the birth-goddess, creatress of man.
Create lullu-man, let him bear the yoke.
Let him bear the yoke, the work of Enlil;
let man carry the labor-basket of the gods. . . ."
At the new moon, the seventh day, and the full moon,
he set up a purifying bath.
We-ila, who had rationality,
they slaughtered in their assembly.
With his flesh and blood
Nintu mixed the clay.
Till the end of days they hear the drum [heartbeat].
From the flesh of the god there was spirit.
She proclaimed "alive" as its sign.
For the sake of not-forgetting there was a spirit.
After she had mixed the clay,
she called the Anunnaki, the great gods.
The Igigi, the great gods,
cast their spittle on the clay.
Mami opened her mouth
and said to the great gods,
"You commanded me a task—
I have completed it.
You slaughtered a god together with his rationality.
I have removed your heavy labor,
have placed your labor-basket on man.
You raised a cry for mankind;
I have loosened your yoke, have established freedom."

Enlil, god of wind, was considered the second greatest power of the visible universe. In charge of the wind and thus an expression of the legitimate use of force, Enlil became the symbol of the proper use of force on earth as well. Enki was the god of the earth. Since the earth was the source of life-giving waters, Enki was also the god of rivers, wells, and canals. More generally, he represented the waters of creativity and was responsible for inventions and crafts. Ninhursaga began as a goddess associated with soil, mountains, and vegetation. Eventually, however, she was worshiped as a mother goddess, a "mother of all children," who manifested her power by giving birth to kings and conferring the royal insignia on them.

Human beings' relationship with their gods was based on subservience since, according to Sumerian myth, human beings were created to do the manual labor the gods were unwilling to do for themselves (see the box above). Moreover, humans were insecure because they could never be sure what the gods would do. But humans did make attempts to circumvent or relieve their anxiety by discovering the intentions of the gods and by trying to influence them as well; these efforts gave rise to the development of the arts of divination.

Divination took a variety of forms. A common form, at least for kings and priests who could afford it, involved killing animals, such as sheep or goats, and examining their livers or other organs. Supposedly, features seen in the organs of the sacrificed animals foretold events to come. Thus one handbook states that if the animal organ has shape *x*, the outcome of the military campaign will be *y*. Private individuals relied on cheaper divinatory techniques. These included interpreting patterns of smoke from burning incense or the pattern formed when oil was poured into water.

The Mesopotamian arts of divination arose out of the desire to discover the purposes of the gods and goddesses. If people could decipher the signs that foretold events, the events would be predictable and humans could act wisely. But the Mesopotamians also developed cultic arts to influence good powers (gods and goddesses) whose decisions could determine human destiny and to ward off evil powers (demons). These cultic arts included ritualistic formulas, such as spells against evil spirits, and prayers or hymns to the gods to win their positive influence. Since only the priests knew the precise rituals, it is not hard to understand the important role they exercised in a society dominated by a belief in the reality of spiritual powers.

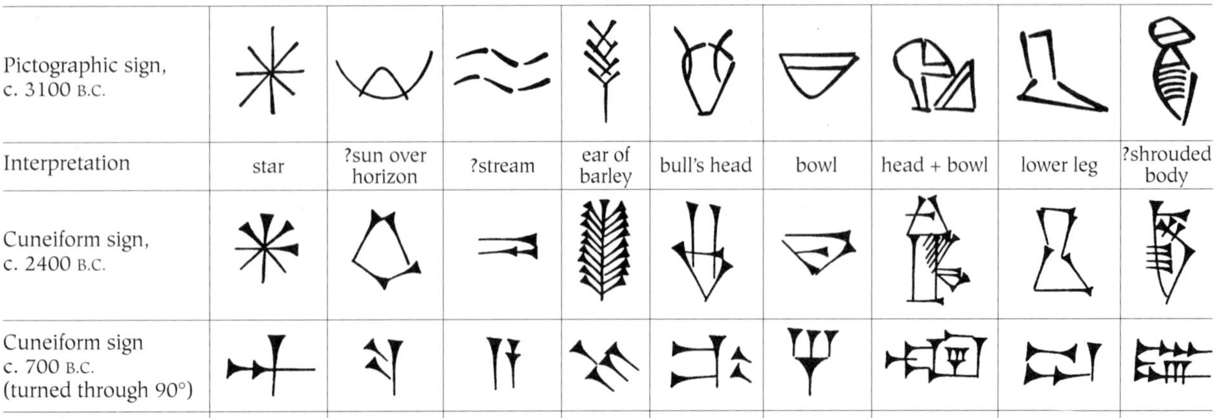

Pictographic sign, c. 3100 B.C.									
Interpretation	star	?sun over horizon	?stream	ear of barley	bull's head	bowl	head + bowl	lower leg	?shrouded body
Cuneiform sign, c. 2400 B.C.									
Cuneiform sign c. 700 B.C. (turned through 90°)									
Phonetic value*	dingir, an	u_4, ud	a	še	gu_4	nig_2, ninda	ku_2	du, gin, gub	lu_2
Meaning	god, sky	day, sun	water, seed, son	barley	ox	food, bread	to eat	to walk, to stand	man

*Some signs have more than one phonetic value and some sounds are represented by more than one sign; for example, u_4 means the fourth sign with the phonetic value *u*.

Michael Roaf/Andromeda, Oxford Limited, Oxford, England

The Development of Cuneiform. Pictured here is the cone of Uruinimgina, an example of cuneiform script from an early Sumerian dynasty. The inscription announces reductions in taxes. The table shows the evolution of writing from pictographic signs to cuneiform script.

WRITING

The realization of writing's great potential was another aspect of Mesopotamian culture. The oldest Mesopotamian texts date to around 3000 B.C. and were written by the Sumerians, who used a cuneiform ("wedge-shaped") system of writing. Using a reed stylus, they made wedge-shaped impressions on clay tablets, which were then baked or dried in the sun. Once dried, these tablets were virtually indestructible, and the several hundred thousand that have been found so far have provided a valuable source of information for modern scholars. Sumerian writing evolved from pictures of concrete objects to simplified and stylized signs, leading eventually to a phonetic system that made possible the written expression of abstract ideas.

Sumerian was the chief spoken and written language of Mesopotamia in the third millennium, but it was replaced in the second millennium by Akkadian. After 2500 B.C., Sumerian cuneiform was adapted by Semitic-speaking peoples (as seen in Old Akkadian) for their own written languages. Eventually, two dialects of Old Akkadian were used in Mesopotamia, Assyrian in the north and Babylonian in the south.

Mesopotamian peoples used writing primarily for record keeping. The most common cuneiform tablets record transactions of daily life: tallies of cattle kept by cowherds for their owners, production figures, lists of taxes and wage payments, accounts, contracts, and court decisions dealing with business matters. There are also monumental texts, documents that were intended to last forever, such as inscriptions etched in stone on statues and royal buildings.

Still another category of cuneiform inscriptions includes a large body of basic texts produced for teaching purposes (see the box on p. 15). Schools for scribes were in operation by 2500 B.C. They were necessary because considerable time was needed to master the cuneiform system of writing. The primary goal of scribal education was to produce professionally trained scribes for careers in the temples and palaces, the military, and government service. Pupils were male and primarily from wealthy families. Gradually, the schools became important centers for culture because Mesopotamian literature was used for instructional purposes. Moreover, new literary productions came out of the scribal schools.

A Sumerian Schoolboy

This document is a Sumerian essay narrating the daily activities of a schoolboy, written by a teacher as a copying exercise for pupils. The schoolboy experiences numerous trials and tribulations, including being beaten ("caned") for improper behavior. Scribal schools came into being in Sumer around 2500 B.C.

A Sumerian Essay for Schoolboys

"Schoolboy, where did you go from earliest day?"
"I went to school."
"What did you do in school?"
"I read my tablet, wrote it, finished it; then my prepared lines were prepared for me and in the afternoon, my hand copies were prepared for me."
Upon the school's dismissal, I went home, entered the house, there was my father sitting. I spoke to my father of my hand copies, then read the tablet to him, and my father was pleased; truly I found favor with my father.
"I am thirsty, give me drink, I am hungry, give me bread, wash my feet, set up the bed, I want to go to sleep; wake me early in the morning, I must not be late, or my teacher will cane me."
When I awoke early in the morning, I faced my mother, and said to her: "Give me my lunch, I want to go to school. . . ."
My mother gave me two "rolls," I went to school.
In the tablet-house, the monitor said to me: "Why are you late?" I was afraid, my heart beat fast. I entered before my teacher, took my place.
My "school-father" read my tablet to me, said "The . . . is cut off," caned me. . . .
Who was in charge of drawing said "Why when I was not here did you stand up?" caned me.
Who was in charge of the gate said "Why when I was not here did you go out?" caned me. . . .
My teacher said "Your hand is not good," caned me.

[At this point, the student decides he needs help and suggests to his father that he invite his teacher home for dinner. The father does so, thanks the teacher, and treats him to a feast and gifts. The teacher now responds to the student.]

Young man, because you did not neglect my work, did not forsake it,
May you reach the pinnacle of the scribal art, achieve it completely
Because you gave me that which you were by no means obliged to give,
You presented me with a gift over and above my earnings, have shown me great honor, may Nidaba, the queen of the guardian deities, be your guardian deity.
May she show favor to your fashioned reed,
May she take all evil from your hand copies.
Of your brothers, may you be their leader,
Of your companions, may you be their chief,
May you rank the highest of all the schoolboys.

MESOPOTAMIAN LITERATURE

Writing was important because it enabled a society to keep records and maintain knowledge of previous practices and events. Writing also made it possible for people to communicate ideas in new ways, which is especially evident in Mesopotamian literary works. The most famous piece of Mesopotamian literature was *The Epic of Gilgamesh.* This epic poem, Sumerian in origin but preserved in Akkadian, records the exploits of a legendary king of Uruk. Gilgamesh, wise, strong, and perfect in body, part man, part god, abused the citizens of Uruk:

> "Gilgamesh sounds the tocsin for his amusement," the people complained, "his arrogance has no bounds by day or night. No son is left with his father, for Gilgamesh takes them all, even the children. . . . His lust leaves no virgin to her lover, neither the warrior's daughter nor the wife of the noble. . . ."[4]

The citizens asked the gods to send a competitor to oppose Gilgamesh and keep him busy. The gods comply and send a hairy, barbaric beast named Enkidu whom Gilgamesh tries to weaken by sending a prostitute to seduce him. When Enkidu finally comes to Uruk, he and Gilgamesh engage in a fierce struggle that neither can win. The two become fast friends and set off in pursuit of heroic deeds. Ishtar (Sumerian Inanna), the goddess of love, attempts to seduce Gilgamesh, but he refuses her advances. In anger, she convinces her father Anu (Sumerian An) to send the Bull of Heaven to kill Gilgamesh and Enkidu. They manage to kill the bull instead, and the gods decide that in return one of them must die. Enlil, the god of wind, rules for Enkidu, and he falls ill and dies, much to the prolonged grief of Gilgamesh. Gilgamesh experiences the pain of mortality and enters upon a search for the secret of immortality. He finds the man who had been granted "everlasting life" by the gods, Utnapishtim. The latter tells him the story of how he survived the Great Flood sent by the gods to destroy humankind (see the box on p. 16). Regretting what they had done, the gods bestowed immortality on Utnapishtim, who now instructs Gilgamesh to dive to the bottom of a river and find a certain plant that gives the power to grow younger. Although Gilgamesh finds the plant, a snake snatches it away before he can eat it. Gilgamesh remains mortal. The desire for immortality, one of humankind's great searches, ends in complete

The Great Flood

The great epic poem of Mesopotamian literature, *The Epic of Gilgamesh*, includes an account by Utnapishtim (a Mesopotamian version of the later biblical Noah), who had built a ship and survived the flood unleashed by the gods to destroy humankind. This selection recounts how the god Ea advised Utnapishtim to build a boat and how he came to land his boat at the end of the flood. In this section, Utnapishtim is telling his story to Gilgamesh.

■ *The Epic of Gilgamesh*

"In those days the world teemed, the people multiplied, the world bellowed like a wild bull, and the great god was aroused by the clamor. Enlil heard the clamor and he said to the gods in council, 'The uproar of mankind is intolerable and sleep is no longer possible by reason of the babel.' So the gods agreed to exterminate mankind. Enlil did this, but Ea [Sumerian Enki, god of the waters] because of his oath warned me in a dream . . . 'tear down your house and build a boat, abandon possessions and look for life, despise worldly goods and save your soul alive. Tear down your house, I say, and build a boat. . . . Then take up into the boat the seed of all living creatures. . . .' [Utnapishtim did as he was told, and then the destruction came.]

"For six days and six nights the winds blew, torrent and tempest and flood overwhelmed the world, tempest and flood raged together like warring hosts. When the seventh day dawned the storm from the south subsided, the sea grew calm, the flood was stifled; I looked at the face of the world and there was silence, all mankind was turned to clay. The surface of the sea stretched as flat as a rooftop; I opened a hatch and the light fell on my face. Then I bowed low, I sat down and I wept, the tears streamed down my face, for on every side was the waste of water. I looked for land in vain, but fourteen leagues distant there appeared a mountain, and there the boat grounded; on the mountain of Nisir the boat held fast, she held fast and did not budge. . . . When the seventh day dawned I loosed a dove and let her go. She flew away, but finding no resting-place she returned. Then I loosed a swallow, and she flew away but finding no resting-place she returned. I loosed a raven, she saw that the waters had retreated, she ate, she flew around, she cawed, and she did not come back. Then I threw everything open to the four winds, I made a sacrifice and poured out a libation on the mountain top."

frustration. "Everlasting life," as this Mesopotamian epic makes clear, is only for the gods.

MATHEMATICS AND ASTRONOMY

People in Mesopotamia made outstanding achievements in mathematics and astronomy. In math, the Sumerians devised a number system based on 60, using combinations of 6 and 10 for practical solutions. They used the processes of multiplication and division and compiled tables for the computation of interest. Geometry was used for practical purposes, such as measuring fields and building projects. In astronomy, the Sumerians made use of units of 60 and charted the chief heavenly constellations. Their calendar was based on twelve lunar months and was brought into harmony with the solar year by adding an extra month from time to time.

Egyptian Civilization: "The Gift of the Nile"

Although contemporaneous with Mesopotamia, civilization in Egypt evolved along somewhat different lines. Of central importance to the development of Egyptian civilization was the Nile River. That the Egyptian people recognized its significance is apparent in this *Hymn to the Nile* (see the box on p. 18): "The bringer of food, rich in provisions, creator of all good, lord of majesty, sweet of fragrance. . . . He who . . . fills the magazines, makes the granaries wide, and gives things to the poor. He who makes every beloved tree to grow."[5] Egypt, like Mesopotamia, was a river valley civilization.

The Nile is a unique river, beginning in the heart of Africa and coursing northward for thousands of miles. It is the longest river in the world. Thanks to the Nile, an area several miles wide on both banks of the river was capable of producing abundant harvests. The "miracle" of the Nile was its annual flooding. The river rose in the summer from rains in Central Africa, crested in Egypt in September and October, and left a deposit of silt that enriched the soil. The Egyptians called this fertile land, dark from the silt and the lush crops that grew on it, the "Black Land." Beyond these narrow strips of fertile fields lay the deserts (the "Red Land").

Unlike the floods of Mesopotamia's rivers, the flooding of the Nile was gradual and usually predictable, and the river itself was seen as life enhancing, not life threatening. Although a system of organized irrigation was still necessary, the small villages along the Nile could make the effort without the massive state intervention that was required in Mesopotamia. Egyptian civilization consequently tended to remain more rural, with many small population centers congregated along a narrow band on both sides of the Nile. About 100 miles before it empties into the Mediterranean, the river splits into two major branches, forming the delta, a triangular-shaped territory called Lower Egypt to distinguish it from Upper Egypt, the land upstream to the south (see Map 1.4). Egypt's important cities developed at the tip of the delta. Even today, most of Egypt's 65 million people are crowded along the banks of the Nile River.

The surpluses of food that Egyptian farmers grew in the fertile Nile valley made Egypt prosperous. But the Nile also served as a unifying factor in Egyptian history. In ancient times, the Nile was the fastest way to travel through the land, making both transportation and communication easier. Winds from the north pushed sailboats south, and the current of the Nile carried them north. Often when they headed downstream (or north), people used long poles or paddles to propel their boats forward.

Unlike Mesopotamia, which was subject to constant invasion, Egypt was blessed by natural barriers that protected it from invasion and gave it a sense of security. These barriers included the deserts to the west and east; the cataracts (rapids) on the southern part of the Nile, which made defense relatively easy; and the Mediterranean Sea to the north. These barriers, however, did not prevent the development of trade. Indeed, there is evidence of very early trade between Egypt and Mesopotamia.

In essence, Egyptian geography and topography played important roles in the early history of the country. The regularity of the Nile floods and the relative isolation of the Egyptians created a sense of security that was accompanied by a feeling of changelessness. To the ancient Egyptians, when the Nile flooded each year, "the fields laugh and people's faces light up." Unlike people in Mesopotamia, Egyptians faced life with a spirit of confidence in the stability of things. Egyptian civilization was characterized by a remarkable degree of continuity over thousands of years. It was certainly no accident that Egyptians believed in cyclical rather than linear progress. Just as the sun passed through its daily cycle and the Nile its annual overflow, Egyptian kings reaffirmed the basic, unchanging principle of justice at the beginning of each new cycle of rule.

The Old and Middle Kingdoms

The basic framework for the study of Egyptian history was provided by Manetho, an Egyptian priest and historian who lived in the early third century B.C. He divided Egyptian history into thirty-one dynasties of kings. On the basis of Manetho's and other king lists, modern historians have divided Egyptian history into three major periods known as the Old Kingdom, the Middle Kingdom, and the New Kingdom. These were periods of long-term stability characterized by strong monarchical authority, competent bureaucracy, freedom from invasion, much construction of temples and pyramids, and considerable intellectual and cultural activity. But between the periods of stability were ages of political chaos known as the Intermediate Periods, which were characterized by weak political structures and rivalry for leadership, invasions, a decline in building activity, and a restructuring of society.

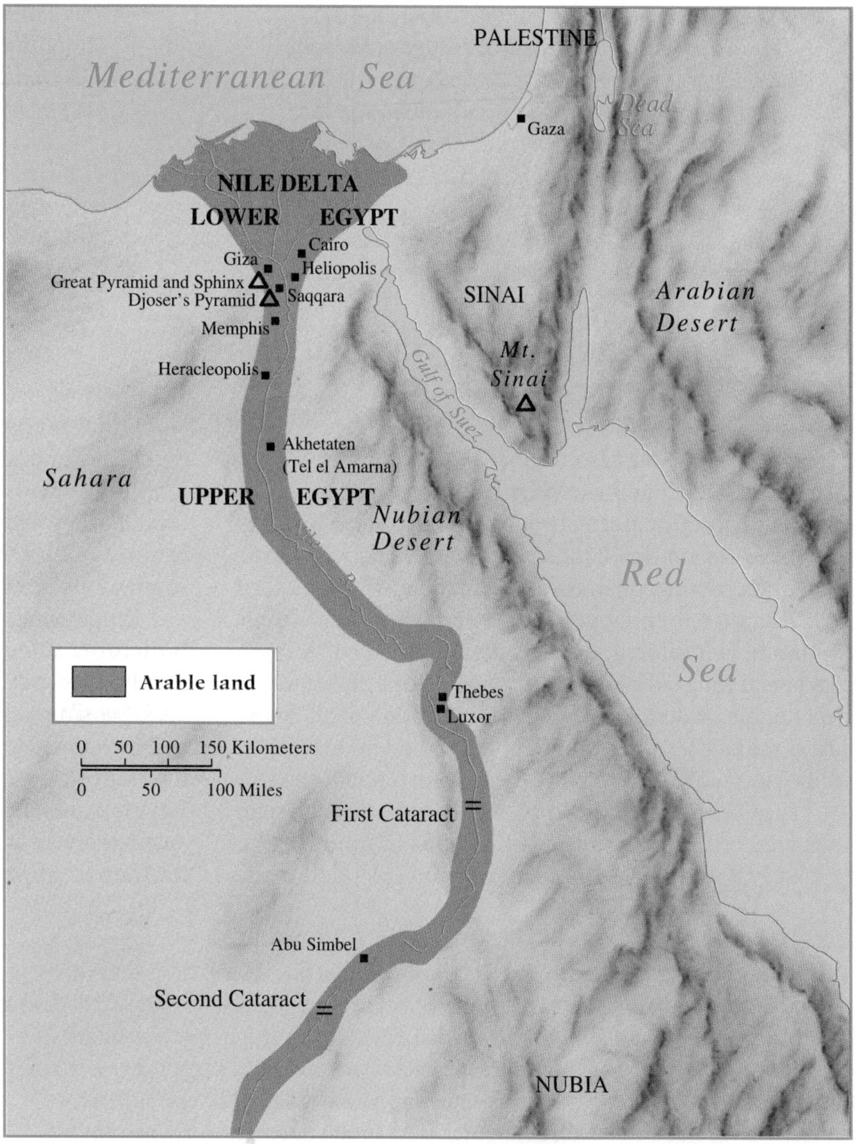

Map 1.4 Ancient Egypt. Egyptian civilization centered on the life-giving water and flood silts of the Nile River, with most of the population living in Lower Egypt, where the river splits to form the Nile delta. Most of the pyramids, built during the Old Kingdom, are clustered south and west of Cairo. How did the lands to the east and west of the river make invasions of Egypt difficult?

Significance of the Nile River and the Pharaoh

Two of the most important sources of life for the ancient Egyptians were the Nile River and the pharaoh. Egyptians perceived that the Nile River made possible the abundant food that was a major source of their well-being. This *Hymn to the Nile*, probably from the nineteenth and twentieth dynasties in the New Kingdom, expresses the gratitude Egyptians felt for the Nile.

Hymn to the Nile

Hail to you, O Nile, that issues from the earth and comes to keep Egypt alive! . . .
He that waters the meadows which Re created, in order to keep every kid alive.
He that makes to drink the desert and the place distant from water: that is his dew coming down from heaven. . . .
The lord of fishes, he who makes the marsh-birds to go upstream. . . .
He who makes barley and brings emmer [wheat] into being, that he may make the temples festive.
If he is sluggish, then nostrils are stopped up, and everybody is poor. . . .
When he rises, then the land is in jubilation, then every belly is in joy, every backbone takes on laughter, and every tooth is exposed.
The bringer of food, rich in provisions, creator of all good, lord of majesty, sweet of fragrance. . . .
He who makes every beloved tree to grow, without lack of them.

The Egyptian king, or pharaoh, was viewed as a god and the absolute ruler of Egypt. His significance and the gratitude of the Egyptian people for his existence are evident in this hymn from the reign of Sesotris III (c. 1880–1840 b.c.).

Hymn to the Pharaoh

He has come unto us that he may carry away Upper Egypt; the double diadem [crown of Upper and Lower Egypt] has rested on his head.
He has come unto us and has united the Two Lands; he has mingled the reed with the bee [symbols of Lower and Upper Egypt].
He has come unto us and has brought the Black Land under his sway; he has apportioned to himself the Red Land.
He has come unto us and has taken the Two Lands under his protection; he has given peace to the Two Riverbanks.
He has come unto us and has made Egypt to live; he has banished its suffering.
He has come unto us and has made the people to live; he has caused the throat of the subjects to breathe. . . .
He has come unto us and has done battle for his boundaries; he has delivered them that were robbed.

THE OLD KINGDOM

According to the Egyptians' own tradition, their land consisted initially of numerous populated areas ruled by tribal chieftains. Around 3100 B.C., during the Early Dynastic Period, the first Egyptian royal dynasty, under a king called Menes, united both Upper and Lower Egypt into a single kingdom. Henceforth, the king would be called "King of Upper and King of Lower Egypt," and the royal crown would be a double diadem, signifying the unification of all Egypt. Just as the Nile served to unite Upper and Lower Egypt physically, kingship served to unite the two areas politically.

The Old Kingdom encompassed the third through sixth dynasties of Egyptian kings, lasting from around 2686 to 2125 B.C. It was an age of prosperity and splendor, made visible in the construction of the greatest and largest pyramids in Egypt's history. The capital of the Old Kingdom was located at Memphis, south of the delta.

Kingship was a divine institution in ancient Egypt and formed part of a universal cosmic scheme (see the box above): "What is the king of Upper and Lower Egypt? He is a god by whose dealings one lives, the father and mother of all men, alone by

Harvard MFA Expedition. Courtesy Museum of Fine Arts, Boston.

Pair Statue of King Menkaure and His Queen. The period designated as the Old Kingdom began approximately four centuries after Egypt's unification (c. 3100 B.C.) and lasted until approximately 2125 B.C. During this period, Egypt's greatest and largest pyramids were constructed. The kings (eventually called "pharaohs") were regarded as gods, divine instruments who maintained the fundamental order and harmony of the universe and wielded absolute power. This statue depicts King Menkaure and his queen (fourth dynasty).

himself, without an equal."[6] In obeying their king, subjects helped maintain the cosmic order. A breakdown in royal power could only mean that citizens were offending divinity and weakening the universal structure. Among the various titles of Egyptian kings, that of pharaoh (originally meaning "great house" or "palace") eventually came to be the most common.

Although they possessed absolute power, Egyptian kings were supposed to rule not arbitrarily but according to set principles. The chief principle was called *Ma'at*, a spiritual precept that conveyed the idea of truth and justice, especially right order and harmony. To ancient Egyptians, this fundamental order and harmony had existed throughout the universe since the beginning of time. Pharaohs were the divine instruments who maintained it and were themselves subject to it.

Although theoretically absolute in their power, in practice Egyptian kings did not rule alone. Initially, members of the king's family performed administrative tasks, but by the fourth dynasty a bureaucracy with regular procedures had developed. Especially important was the office of vizier, "steward of the whole land." Directly responsible to the king, the vizier was in charge of the bureaucracy, with its numerous departments, including police, justice, river transport, and public works. Agriculture and the treasury were the most important departments. Agriculture was, of course, the backbone of Egyptian prosperity, and the treasury collected the taxes, which were paid in kind. A careful assessment of land and tenants was undertaken to establish the tax base.

For administrative purposes, Egypt was divided into provinces or nomes, as they were later called by the Greeks—twenty-two in Upper and twenty in Lower Egypt. A governor, called by the Greeks a nomarch, was head of each nome and was responsible to the king and vizier. Nomarchs, however, tended to build up large holdings of land and power within their nomes, creating a potential rivalry with the pharaohs.

THE MIDDLE KINGDOM

Despite the theory of divine order, the Old Kingdom eventually collapsed, ushering in an Intermediate Period of chaos (c. 2125–2055 B.C.). A so-called prophet named Nefer-Rohu (Neferti) described the scene:

> This land is so damaged that there is no one who is concerned with it, no one who speaks, no one who weeps. . . . The sun disc is covered over. It will not shine so that people may see. . . . The rivers of Egypt are empty, so that the water is crossed on foot. Men seek for water for the ships to sail on it. . . . This land is helter-skelter, and no one knows the result that will come about, which is hidden from speech, sight, or hearing.[7]

During this First Intermediate Period of chaos, new centers of power established rival dynasties, such as those at Heracleopolis near Lower Egypt and Thebes in Upper Egypt. Finally, the king of Thebes, Mentuhotep, defeated the ruler of Heracleopolis and achieved the reunification of all Egypt, thus beginning the Middle Kingdom, a new period of stability lasting from around 2055 to 1650 B.C.

CHRONOLOGY

The Egyptians

Early Dynastic Period (dynasties 1–2)	c. 3100–2686 B.C.
Old Kingdom (dynasties 3–6)	c. 2686–2125 B.C.
First Intermediate Period (dynasties 7–10)	c. 2125–2055 B.C.
Middle Kingdom (dynasties 11–12)	c. 2055–1650 B.C.
Second Intermediate Period (dynasties 13–17)	c. 1650–1550 B.C.
New Kingdom (dynasties 18–20)	c. 1550–1085 B.C.
Postempire Egypt (dynasties 21–31)	1085–30 B.C.

Much of the Middle Kingdom's history centered around the twelfth dynasty founded by Amenemhet I, a vizier who established himself and his successors as pharaohs. Egyptians later portrayed the Middle Kingdom as a golden age, a clear indication of its stability. Several factors contributed to its vitality. The nome structure was reorganized. The boundaries of each nome were now settled precisely, and the obligations of the nomes to the state were clearly delineated. Nomarchs were confirmed as hereditary officeholders but with the understanding that their duties must be performed faithfully. These included the collection of taxes for the state and the recruitment of labor forces for royal projects, such as stone quarrying.

The Middle Kingdom was characterized by a new concern on the part of the pharaohs for the people. In the Old Kingdom, the pharaoh had been viewed as an inaccessible god-king. Now he was portrayed as the shepherd of his people with the responsibility to build public works and provide for the public welfare. As one pharaoh expressed it: "He [a particular god] created me as one who should do that which he had done, and to carry out that which he commanded should be done. He appointed me herdsman of this land, for he knew who would keep it in order for him."[8]

As confirmation of its newfound strength, Egypt embarked on a period of expansion. Lower Nubia was conquered, and fortresses were built to protect the new southern frontier. The government also sent military expeditions into Palestine and Syria. Although they did not remain there, this campaign marks the beginning of Egyptian imperialism in those areas.

Society and Economy in Ancient Egypt

Egyptian society had a simple structure in the Old and Middle Kingdoms; basically, it was organized along hierarchical lines with the god-king at the top. The king was surrounded by an upper class of nobles and priests who participated in the elaborate rituals of life that surrounded the pharaoh. This ruling class ran the government and managed its own landed estates, which provided much of its wealth.

Below the upper classes were merchants and artisans. Merchants engaged in active trade up and down the Nile as well as in town and village markets. Some merchants also engaged in international trade; they were sent by the king to Crete and Syria, where they obtained wood and other products. Expeditions traveled into Nubia for ivory and down the Red Sea to Punt for incense and spices. Egyptian artisans displayed unusually high standards of craftsmanship and physical beauty and produced an incredible variety of goods: stone dishes; beautifully painted boxes made of clay; wooden furniture, especially of Lebanon cedar; gold, silver, and copper tools and containers; paper and rope made of papyrus; and linen clothes.

By far, the largest number of people in Egypt simply worked the land. In theory, the king owned all the land but granted out portions of it to his subjects. Large sections were in the possession of nobles and the temple complexes. Most of the lower classes were serfs, or common people who were bound to the land and cultivated the estates. They paid taxes in the form of crops to the king, nobles, and priests; lived in small villages or towns; and provided military service and labor for building projects.

The Culture of Egypt

Egypt produced a culture that dazzled and awed its later conquerors. The Egyptians' technical achievements alone, especially visible in the construction of the pyramids, demonstrated a measure of skill unique to the world of that time. To the Egyptians, all of these achievements were part of a cosmic order suffused with the presence of the divine.

SPIRITUAL LIFE IN EGYPTIAN SOCIETY

The Egyptians had no word for religion because it was an inseparable element of the world order to which Egyptian society belonged. Egypt was part of the universal cosmic scheme, and the pharaoh was the divine being whose function was to maintain its stability within that cosmic order.

The Egyptians possessed a remarkable number of gods associated with heavenly bodies and natural forces. Two groups, sun gods and land gods, came to have special prominence, hardly unusual in view of the importance of the sun, the river, and the fertile land along its banks to Egypt's well-being. The sun was the source of life and hence worthy of worship. A sun cult developed, especially at Heliopolis, now a suburb of modern Cairo. The sun god took on different forms and names, depending on his specific function. He was worshiped as Atum in human form and as Re, who had a human body but the head of a falcon. The pharaoh took the title "Son of Re" because he was regarded as the earthly embodiment of Re.

River and land deities included Osiris and Isis with their child Horus, who was related to the Nile and to the sun as well. Osiris became especially important as a symbol of resurrection. A famous Egyptian myth told of the struggle between Osiris, who brought civilization to Egypt,

Osiris as Judge of the Dead. According to the *Book of the Dead*, after making a denial of offenses (the "negative confession"), the deceased experienced the "weighing of the heart." Shown here is a judgment scene from the *Book of the Dead* of Hunefer, a royal scribe who died around 1285 B.C. Hunefer's heart is placed on one side of a balance scale; on the other side is the feather of Ma'at, the goddess of truth. For Hunefer, heart and feather are of equal weight, so the god Anubis ushers him into the presence of Osiris, seated on his throne at the right. A "Swallowing Monster," a hybrid creature of crocodile, lion, and hippopotamus, stood ready at the scale to devour the deceased if he failed the test.

and his evil brother Seth, who killed him, cut his body into fourteen parts, and tossed them into the Nile. Osiris's faithful wife Isis found the pieces and, with help from other gods, restored Osiris to life. As a symbol of resurrection and as judge of the dead, Osiris took on an important role for the Egyptians. By identifying with Osiris, one could hope to gain new life, just as Osiris had done. The dead, embalmed and mummified, were placed in tombs (in the case of kings, in pyramidal tombs), given the name of Osiris, and by a process of magical identification became Osiris. Like Osiris, they could then be reborn. The flood of the Nile and the new life it brought to Egypt were symbolized by Isis gathering all of Osiris's parts together and were celebrated each spring in the festival of the new land.

Later Egyptian spiritual practice began to emphasize morality by stressing Osiris's role as judge of the dead. The dead were asked to give an account of their earthly deeds to show whether they deserved a reward. Other means were also employed to gain immortality. As seen in the *Book of the Dead*, magical incantations were used to ensure a favorable journey to a happy afterlife. Specific instructions explained what to do when confronted by the judge of the dead. These instructions had two aspects. The negative confession gave a detailed list of what one had not done:

> What is said on reaching the Broad-Hall of the Two Justices [the place of the next-world judgment], absolving X [the name and title of the deceased] of every sin which he had committed, . . .
>
> I have not committed evil against men.
> I have not mistreated cattle. . . .
> I have not blasphemed a god. . . .
> I have not done violence to a poor man. . . .
> I have not defamed a slave to his superior.
> I have not made anyone sick.
> I have not made anyone weep.
> I have not killed. . . .
> I have not caused anyone suffering. . . .
> I have not had sexual relations with a boy.
> I have not defiled myself. . . .
> I have not driven cattle away from their pasturage.[9]

Later the supplicant made a speech listing his good actions: "I have done that which men said and that with which gods are content. . . . I have given bread to the hungry, water to the thirsty, clothing to the naked, and a ferry-boat to him who was marooned. I have provided divine offerings for the gods and mortuary offerings for the dead."[10]

At first the Osiris cult was reserved for the very wealthy, who could afford to take expensive measures to preserve the body after death. During the Middle Kingdom, however, the cult became "democratized"—extended to all Egyptians who aspired to an afterlife.

THE PYRAMIDS

One of the great achievements of Egyptian civilization, the building of pyramids, occurred in the time of the Old Kingdom. Pyramids were not built in isolation but as part of a larger complex dedicated to the dead—in effect, a city of the dead. The area included a large pyramid for the king's burial, smaller pyramids for his family, and mastabas, rectangular structures with flat roofs, as tombs for the pharaoh's noble officials. The tombs were well prepared for their residents. The rooms were furnished and stocked with numerous supplies, including chairs, boats, chests, weapons, games, dishes, and a variety of foods. The Egyptians believed that human beings had two bodies, a physical one and a spiritual one, which they called the *ka*. If the physical body was properly preserved (that is, mummified) and the tomb furnished with all the various objects of regular life, the *ka* could return and continue its life despite the death of the physical body.

To preserve the physical body after death, the Egyptians practiced mummification, a process of slowly drying a dead body to prevent it from rotting. Special workshops, run by priests, performed this procedure, primarily for the wealthy families who could afford it. Workers first removed the liver, lungs, stomach, and intestines and placed them in four special jars that were put in the tomb with the mummy. The priests also removed the brain by extracting it through the nose. They then covered the corpse with a natural salt that absorbed the body's water. Later, they filled the body with spices and wrapped it with layers of linen soaked in resin. At the end of the process, which took about seventy days, a lifelike mask was placed over the head and shoulders of the mummy, which was then sealed in a case and placed in its tomb.

Pyramids were tombs for the mummified bodies of pharaohs. The first pyramid was built in the third dynasty during the reign of King Djoser. The architect Imhotep, a priest of Heliopolis, the center dedicated to the sun cult, was responsible for the step pyramid at Saqqara. Beginning

The Pyramids at Giza. The three pyramids at Giza, across the Nile River from Cairo, are the most famous in Egypt. Pyramids served as tombs for both the king and his immediate family. At the rear is the largest of the three pyramids—the Great Pyramid of Khufu. Next to it is the pyramid of Khafre. In the foreground is the smaller pyramid of Menkaure standing behind the even smaller pyramids for the pharaohs' wives.

with Djoser, wives and immediate families of the kings were buried in pyramids, nobles and officials in mastabas.

The first real pyramid, with each side filled in to make an even surface, was constructed in the fourth dynasty around 2600 B.C. by King Snefru, who built three pyramids. But the largest and most magnificent of all was built under Snefru's son Khufu. Constructed at Giza around 2540 B.C., the famous Great Pyramid covers 13 acres, measures 756 feet at each side of its base, and stands 481 feet high. Its four sides are almost precisely oriented to the four points of the compass.

The building of the Great Pyramid was an enormous construction project that used limestone blocks as well as granite from Upper Egypt. The Greek historian Herodotus (see Chapter 3) reported the tradition that it took 100,000 Egyptians twenty years to build the Great Pyramid. But Herodotus wrote two thousand years after the event, and considerable controversy and speculation still surround the construction of the Great Pyramid, especially in view of the precision with which it was built. The stone slabs on the outside of the pyramid, for example, fit so closely side by side that a hair cannot be pushed into the joints between them. The Great Pyramid still stands as a symbol of the power of Egyptian kings of the Old Kingdom. No later pyramid ever matched its size or splendor. But an Egyptian pyramid was not just the king's tomb; it was also an important symbol of royal power. It could be seen for miles away as a visible reminder of the glory and might of the ruler, a living god on earth.

ART AND WRITING

Commissioned by kings or nobles for use in temples and tombs, Egyptian art was largely functional. Wall paintings and statues of gods and kings in temples served a strictly spiritual purpose. They were an integral part of the performance of ritual, which was thought necessary to preserve the cosmic order and hence the well-being of Egypt. Likewise, the mural scenes and sculptured figures found in the tombs had a specific function. They were supposed to aid the journey of the deceased into the afterworld.

Egyptian art was also formulaic. Artists and sculptors were expected to observe a strict canon of proportions that determined both form and presentation. This canon gave Egyptian art a distinctive appearance for thousands of years. Especially characteristic was the convention of combining the profile, semiprofile, and frontal views of the human body in relief work and painting in order to represent each part of the body accurately. This fashion created an art that was highly stylized yet still allowed distinctive features to be portrayed.

Map 1.5 The Egyptian and Hittite Empires. The Hittite empire was the dominant power north of Egypt for roughly two centuries. It assimilated important linguistic, political, and religious aspects of the peoples it conquered and thus helped transmit Mesopotamian culture to the eastern Mediterranean. ■ What made both the Hittite and Egyptian empires vulnerable to invasions by the Sea Peoples?

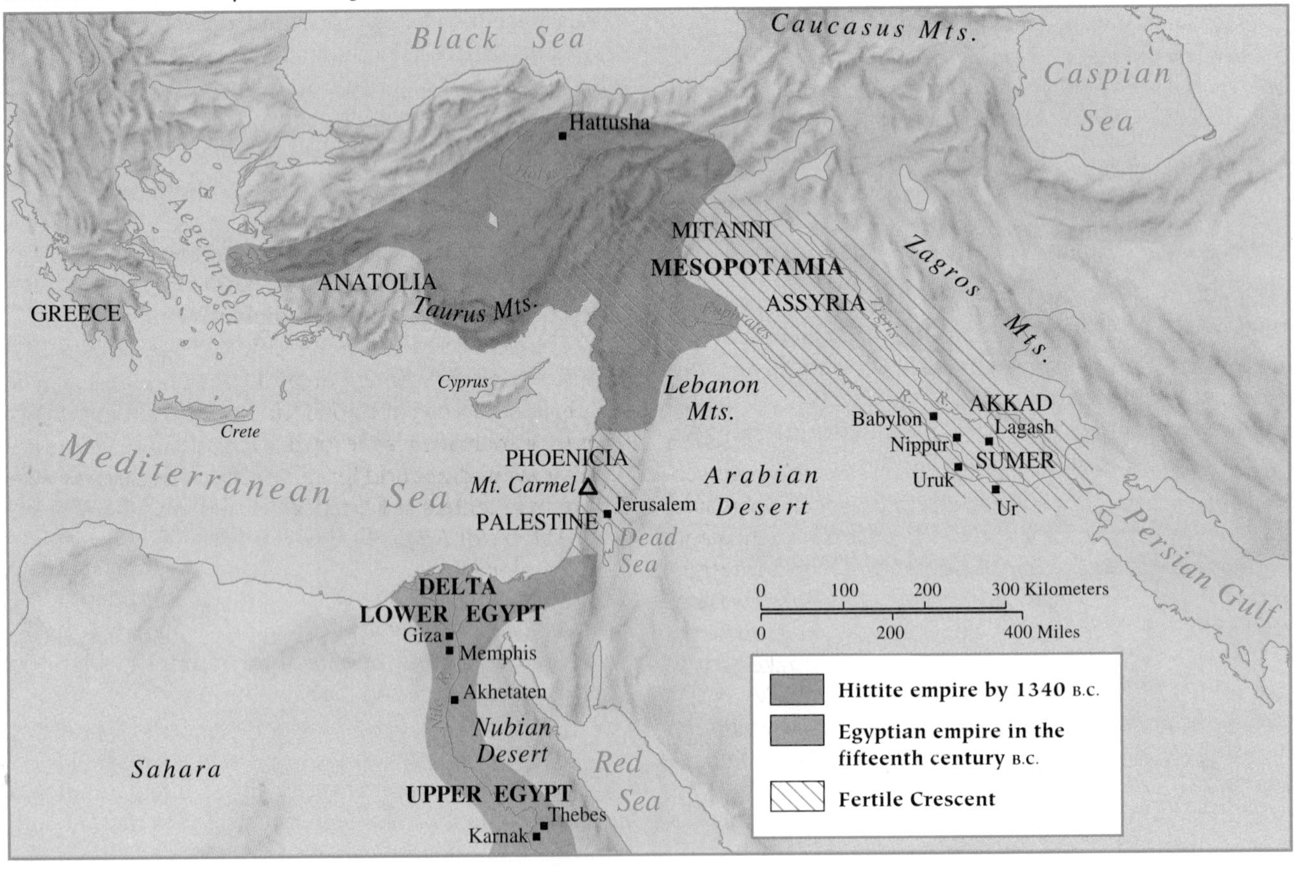

Akhenaten's Hymn to Aten

Amenhotep IV, more commonly known as Akhenaten, created a religious upheaval in Egypt by introducing the worship of Aten, god of the sun disk, as the chief god. Akhenaten's reverence for Aten is evident in this hymn. Some authorities have noted a similarity in spirit and wording to the 104th Psalm of the Old Testament.

■ *Hymn to Aten*

Your rays suckle every meadow.
When you rise, they live, they grow for you.
You make the seasons in order to rear all that you have made,
The winter to cool them,
And the heat that they may taste you.
You have made the distant sky in order to rise therein,
In order to see all that you do make.
While you were alone,
Rising in your form as the living Aten,
Appearing, shining, withdrawing or approaching,
You made millions of forms of yourself alone.
Cities, towns, fields, road, and river—
Every eye beholds you over against them,
For you are the Aten of the day over the earth. . . .
The world came into being by your hand,
According as you have made them.
When you have risen they live,
When you set they die.
You are lifetime your own self,
For one lives only through you.
Eyes are fixed on beauty until you set.
All work is laid aside when you set in the west.
But when you rise again,
Everything is made to flourish for the king . . .
Since you did found the earth
And raise them up for your son,
Who came forth from your body: the King of Upper and Lower Egypt, . . . Akh-en-Aten, . . . and the
Chief Wife of the King . . . Nefert-iti, living and youthful forever and ever.

Writing emerged in Egypt during the first two dynasties. It was the Greeks who later labeled Egyptian writing *hieroglyphics,* meaning "priest-carvings" or "sacred writings." Hieroglyphs were sacred characters used as picture signs that depicted objects and had a sacred value at the same time. Although hieroglyphs were later simplified for writing purposes into two scripts, they never developed into an alphabet. Egyptian hieroglyphs were initially carved in stone, but later the two simplified scripts were written on papyrus, a paper made from the papyrus reed that grew along the Nile. Most of the ancient Egyptian literature that has come down to us was written on papyrus rolls and wooden tablets.

■ *Chaos and a New Order: The New Kingdom*

The Middle Kingdom came to an end in the midst of another period of instability. An incursion into the delta region by a people known as the Hyksos initiated this second age of chaos. The Hyksos, a Semitic-speaking people, infiltrated Egypt in the seventeenth century B.C. and came to dominate much of Egypt during the Second Intermediate Period. However, the presence of the Hyksos was not entirely negative for Egypt. They introduced Bronze Age technology, teaching the Egyptians how to make bronze for use in new agricultural tools and weapons. More significantly, the Hyksos brought new aspects of warfare to Egypt, including the horse-drawn war chariot, a heavier sword, and the compound bow. Eventually, the Egyptians made use of their new weapons to throw off Hyksos domination.

It was the pharaoh Ahmose I who managed to defeat and expel the Hyksos from Egypt. He reunited Egypt, founded the eighteenth dynasty, established the New Kingdom (c. 1550–1085 B.C.), and launched the Egyptians along a new militaristic and imperialistic path. A more professional army was developed. Viziers, who were in charge of the state bureaucracy, were now chosen only from the ranks of military commanders.

During the period of the New Kingdom, Egypt became the most powerful state in the ancient Near East (see Map 1.5). Thutmosis III (c. 1480–c. 1450 B.C.) led seventeen military campaigns into Palestine and Phoenicia. The Egyptians occupied these lands but permitted local native princes to rule. Egypt, no longer content to remain in isolation, now pursued an active political and diplomatic policy.

The new Egyptian imperial state reached its height during the reign of Amenhotep III (c. 1412–1375 B.C.), the great-grandson of Thutmosis III. The achievements of the empire were made visible in the construction of magnificent new buildings and temples. Especially famous were the temple centers at Karnak and Luxor and the 70-foot-high statues of Amenhotep III in front of the mortuary temples along the Nile.

By the end of his reign, Amenhotep III faced a growing military challenge from a people known as the Hittites (see "The Impact of the Indo-Europeans" later in this chapter). His son, Amenhotep IV (c. 1364–1347 B.C.), proved even less able to deal with this threat, a failure that was due in large part to his preoccupation with a religious revolution that he had initiated in Egypt.

Amenhotep introduced the worship of Aten, god of the sun disk, as the chief god (see the box above) and pursued his worship with great enthusiasm. Changing his own name to Akhenaten ("It is well with Aten"), the pharaoh closed the temples of other gods and especially endeavored to lessen the power of the priesthood dedicated to the god Amon-Re at Thebes, which had become the chief landowner in Egypt. Akhenaten strove to reduce the priests' influence by replacing Thebes as the capital of Egypt with Akhetaten ("dedicated to Aten"), a new city located near modern Tel el Amarna, 200 miles north of Thebes.

Scala/Art Resource, NY

Akhenaten, Nefertiti, and Daughters. Shown here are Akhenaten, his wife Nefertiti, and their three daughters basking in the rays of Aten, god of the sun disk. During the reign of Akhenaten, artists broke with the formal type of portraiture and depicted figures in relaxed poses. After Akhenaten's death, artists returned to the traditional rigid style.

Akhenaten's attempt at religious change failed. It was too much to ask Egyptians to ignore their traditional ways and beliefs, especially since they saw the destruction of the old gods as subversive of the very cosmic order on which Egypt's survival and continuing prosperity depended. Moreover, the priests at Thebes were unalterably opposed to the changes, which diminished their influence and power. At the same time, Akhenaten's preoccupation with religion caused him to ignore foreign affairs and led to the loss of both Syria and Palestine. Akhenaten's changes were soon undone after his death by those who influenced his successor, the boy-pharaoh Tutankhamen (1347–1338 B.C.). Tutankhamen returned the government to Thebes and restored the old gods. The Aten experiment had failed to take hold, and the eighteenth dynasty itself came to an end with the rise to power of a military officer and vizier, Horemhab, who assumed the kingship in 1333 B.C.

The nineteenth dynasty managed to restore Egyptian power one more time. Under Rameses II (c. 1279–1213 B.C.), the Egyptians regained control of Palestine but were unable to reestablish the borders of their earlier empire. New invasions in the thirteenth century by the "Sea Peoples," as the Egyptians called them, destroyed Egyptian power in Palestine and drove the Egyptians back within their old frontiers. The days of Egyptian empire were ended, and the New Kingdom itself expired with the twentieth dynasty in 1085 B.C. For the next thousand years, despite periodic revivals of strength, Egypt was dominated by Libyans, Nubians, Assyrians, Persians, and finally Macedonians after the conquest of Alexander the Great (see Chapter 4). In the first century B.C., Egypt became a province in Rome's mighty empire.

Daily Life in Ancient Egypt

Ancient Egyptians had a very positive attitude toward daily life on earth and followed the advice of the wisdom literature, which suggested that people marry young and establish a home and family. Monogamy was the general rule, although a husband was allowed to keep additional wives if his first wife was childless. Pharaohs were entitled to harems; the queen was acknowledged, however, as the Great Wife, with a status higher than that of the other wives. The husband was master in the house, but wives were very much respected and in charge of the household and education of the children. From a book of wise sayings (which the Egyptians called "instructions") came this advice:

> If you are a man of standing, you should found your household and love your wife at home as is fitting. Fill her belly; clothe her back. Ointment is the prescription for her body. Make her heart glad as long as you live. She is a profitable field for her lord. You should not contend with her at law, and keep her far from gaining control. . . . Let her heart be soothed through what may accrue to you; it means keeping her long in your house.[11]

Women's property and inheritances remained in their hands, even in marriage. Although most careers and public offices were closed to women, some women did operate businesses. Peasant women worked long hours in the fields and at numerous domestic tasks. Upper-class women could function as priestesses, and a few queens even became pharaohs in their own right. Most famous was Hatshepsut in the New Kingdom. She initially served as regent for her stepson Thutmosis III but assumed the throne for herself and remained in power until her death.

Hatshepsut's reign was a prosperous one, as is especially evident in her building activity. She is most famous for the temple dedicated to herself at Deir el Bahri on the west bank of the Nile at Thebes. As pharaoh, Hatshepsut sent out military expeditions, encouraged mining, fostered agriculture, and sent a trading expedition up the Nile. Because pharaohs were almost always male, Hatshepsut's official statues show her clothed and bearded like a king. She was addressed as "His Majesty." That Hatshepsut was aware of her unusual position is evident from an inscription she had placed on one of her temples. It read: "Now my heart turns to and fro, in thinking what will the people say, they who shall see my monument in after years, and shall speak of what I have done."

Marriages were arranged by parents. The primary concerns were family and property, and the chief purpose of marriage was to produce children, especially sons (see the box on p. 26). From the New Kingdom came this piece of wisdom: "Take to yourself a wife while you are a youth, that she may produce a son for you."[12] Only sons could carry on the family name. Daughters were not slighted, however. Numerous tomb paintings show the close and affectionate relationship parents had with both sons and daughters. Although marriages were arranged, some of the surviving love poems from ancient Egypt would indicate an element of romance in some marriages. Here is the lament of a lovesick boy for his "sister" (lovers referred to each other as "brother" and "sister," although some scholars believe that the practice of brother-sister marriage in the Egyptian royal family probably reached down into the general population as well):

Seven days to yesterday I have not seen the sister,
and a sickness has invaded me;
My body has become heavy,
And I am forgetful of my own self.
If the chief physicians come to me,
My heart is not content with their remedies. . . .
What will revive me is to say to me: "Here she is!"
Her name is what will lift me up. . . .
My health is her coming in from outside:
When I see her, then I am well.[13]

Marriages could and did end in divorce, which was allowed, apparently with compensation for the wife. Adultery, however, was strictly prohibited, and punishments were severe, especially for women, who could have their noses cut off or be burned at the stake.

Under normal circumstances, Egypt was blessed by a material abundance that not only kept its entire population fed but also enabled its upper classes to lead a life of gracious leisure. These wealthy families had attractive homes located on walled estates. Much energy was devoted to the garden, which contained fruit trees and vegetables, as well as tree-lined paths and pools for the family's leisure time.

Tomb paintings indicate that the upper classes participated in numerous banquets where guests were lavishly fed and entertained. Although some people obviously got drunk, a collection of "instructions" advises more circumspect behavior:

> If you are one of those sitting at the table of one greater than yourself, take what he may give, when it is set before your nose. You should gaze at what is before you. . . . Let your face be cast down until he addresses you, and you should speak only when he addresses you. Laugh after he laughs, and it will be very pleasing to his heart and what you may do will be pleasing to the heart.[14]

Statue of Hatshepsut. Wife of Thutmosis II, Hatshepsut served as regent for her stepson Thutmosis III after her husband's death. In 1473 B.C., however, she proclaimed herself pharaoh. This red granite statue shows her as a woman, although most official statues portrayed her dressed and bearded like a king.

A Father's Advice

Upper-class Egyptians enjoyed compiling collections of wise sayings to provide guidance for leading an upright and successful life. This excerpt is taken from *The Instruction of the Vizier Ptah-hotep* and dates from around 2450 B.C. The vizier was the pharaoh's chief official. In this selection, Ptah-hotep advises his son on how to be a successful official.

The Instruction of the Vizier Ptah-hotep

Then he said to his son:

Let not your heart be puffed-up because of your knowledge; be not confident because you are a wise man. Take counsel with the ignorant as well as the wise. The full limits of skill cannot be attained, and there is no skilled man equipped to his full advantage. Good speech is more hidden than the emerald, but it may be found with maidservants at the grindstones. . . .

If you are a leader commanding the affairs of the multitude, seek out for yourself every beneficial deed, until it may be that your own affairs are without wrong. Justice is great, and its appropriateness is lasting; it has been disturbed since the time of him who made it, whereas there is punishment for him who passes over its laws. It is the right path before him who knows nothing. Wrongdoing has never brought its undertaking into port. It may be that it is fraud that gains riches, but the strength of justice is that it lasts. . . .

If you are a man of intimacy, whom one great man sends to another, be thoroughly reliable when he sends you. Carry out the errand for him as he has spoken. Do not be reserved about what is said to you, and beware of any act of forgetfulness. Grasp hold of truth, and do not exceed it. Mere gratification is by no means to be repeated. Struggle against making words worse, thus making one great man hostile to another through vulgar speech. . . .

If you are a man of standing and found a household and produce a son who is pleasing to god, if he is correct and inclines toward your ways and listens to your instruction, while his manners in your house are fitting, and if he takes care of your property as it should be, seek out for him every useful action. He is your son, . . . you should not cut your heart off from him.

But a man's seed often creates enmity. If he goes astray and transgresses your plans and does not carry out your instruction, so that his manners in your household are wretched, and he rebels against all that you say, while his mouth runs on in the most wretched talk, quite apart from his experience, while he possesses nothing, you should cast him off: he is not your son at all. He was not really born to you. Thus you enslave him entirely according to his own speech. He is one whom god has condemned in the very womb. . . .

The same collection of "instructions" warns that when one has been invited to a party, "beware of approaching the women. It does not go well with the place where that is done."[15]

Entertainment, especially music, was a regular feature of parties. The Egyptians used an astonishing variety of instruments: drums, tambourines, flutes, trumpets, and stringed instruments that were plucked rather than played with a bow. Singers, accompanying themselves on lute or harp, presented songs in praise of the host's generosity and of enjoying life.

Judging from the paintings in their tombs, the upper classes found a myriad of ways to entertain themselves as well. Fowling in the stands of papyrus reeds that grew along the riverbanks was a favorite pastime. Using a reed skiff, the huntsman used a boomerang to bring down his prey, much to the delight of his family, who accompanied him. Once the waterfowl was downed, Egyptian families used trained retriever cats to swim out into the water and bring back the birds. The hunting of animals was only for the men. The hunters rode in chariots and used dogs to pursue antelope, gazelles, and other creatures who were shot with bows and arrows. Indoor activities included board games among other things. The earliest known board games in the world have been found in Egyptian tombs.

A Hunting Scene. A favorite pastime of the Egyptian upper classes was hunting waterfowl in the stands of papyrus reeds that grew along the riverbanks. This tomb painting shows a wealthy Egyptian with members of his family hunting geese with throwsticks.

Erich Lessing/Art Resource, NY

© Adam Woolfit/Robert Harding Picture Library

Stonehenge. The Bronze Age in northwestern Europe is known for its megaliths, large standing stones. Between 3200 and 1500 B.C., standing stones that were placed in circles or lined up in rows were erected throughout the British Isles and northwestern France. By far the most famous of these megalithic constructions is Stonehenge in England.

Many are made of wood decorated with ivory or ebony. The games played on them involved moving pieces on the boards according to the roll of the dice.

On the Fringes of Civilization

Our story of the beginnings of Western civilization has been dominated so far by Mesopotamia and Egypt. But significant developments were also taking place on the fringes of these civilizations. Farming had spread into the Balkan peninsula of Europe by 6500 B.C., and by 4000 B.C. it was well established in southern France, central Europe, and the coastal regions of the Mediterranean. Although migrating farmers from the Near East may have brought some farming techniques into Europe, historians now believe that the Neolithic peoples of Europe domesticated animals and began to farm largely on their own.

One outstanding feature of late Neolithic Europe was the building of megalithic structures. *Megalith* is Greek for "large stone." Radiocarbon dating, a technique that allows scientists to determine the age of objects, shows that the first megalithic structures were built around 4000 B.C., more than a thousand years before the great pyramids were built in Egypt. Between 3200 and 1500 B.C., standing stones placed in circles or lined up in rows were erected throughout the British Isles and northwestern France. Other megalithic constructions have been found as far north as Scandinavia and as far south as the islands of Corsica, Sardinia, and Malta. Some archaeologists have demonstrated that the stone circles were used as observatories to detect not only such simple astronomical phenomena as the midwinter and midsummer sunrises but also such sophisticated observations as the major and minor standstills of the moon.

By far the most famous of these megalithic constructions is Stonehenge in England. Stonehenge consists of a series of concentric rings of standing stones. Its construction sometime between 2100 and 1900 B.C. was no small accomplishment. The eighty bluestones used at Stonehenge weigh 4 tons each and were transported to the site from their original source 135 miles away. Like other megalithic structures, Stonehenge indicates a remarkable awareness of astronomy on the part of its builders, as well as an impressive coordination of workers.

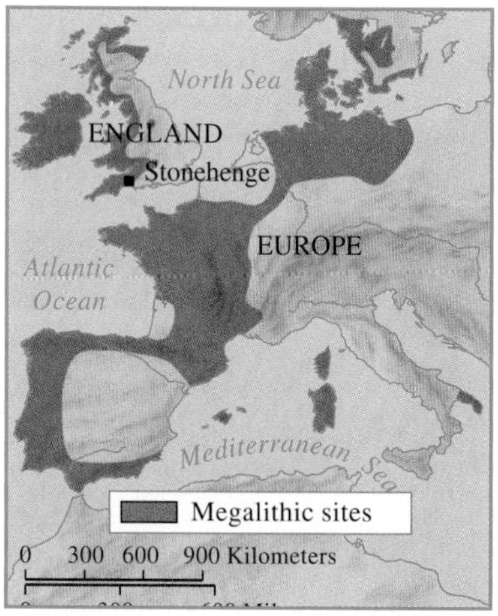

Stonehenge and Other Megalithic Sites in Europe

The Impact of the Indo-Europeans

For many historians, both the details of construction and the purpose of the megalithic structures of Europe remain a mystery. Also puzzling is the role of the Indo-European people. The term *Indo-European* refers to people who used a language derived from a single parent tongue. Indo-European languages include Greek, Latin, Persian, Sanskrit, and the Germanic languages (see Table 1.2). It has been

Table 1.2 Some Indo-European Languages

Subfamily	Languages
Indo-Iranian	*Sanskrit,* Persian
Balto-Slavic	Russian, Serbo-Croatian, Czech, Polish, Lithuanian
Hellenic	Greek
Italic	*Latin,* Romance languages (French, Italian, Spanish, Portuguese, Romanian)
Celtic	Irish, Gaelic
Germanic	Swedish, Danish, Norwegian, German, Dutch, English

Note: Languages in italic type are no longer spoken.

suggested that the original Indo-European–speaking peoples were based somewhere in the steppe region north of the Black Sea or in southwestern Asia, in modern Iran or Afghanistan. Although there had been earlier migrations, around 2000 B.C. they began major nomadic movements into Europe (including present-day Italy and Greece), India, and the Near East. The Indo-Europeans who moved into Asia Minor and Anatolia (modern Turkey) coalesced with the native peoples to form the Hittite kingdom around 1750 B.C. with its capital at Hattusha (Bogazköy in modern Turkey).

The Hittites began to spread outward around 1600 B.C., but it was not until the reign of Suppiluliumas (c. 1380–1340 B.C.) that the Hittites established a real empire. He destroyed the power of the Mitanni kingdom, which had been established in the sixteenth century B.C. by a people known as the Hurrians from the mountainous northern border of Mesopotamia. Suppiluliumas formed an alliance with the Egyptians and then conquered Syria. The Hittites were the first of the Indo-European peoples to make use of iron, enabling them to construct weapons that were stronger and cheaper to make because of the widespread availability of iron ore.

For the next hundred years, the Hittites were in conflict with Egypt until the Egyptian pharaoh Rameses II made a remarkable nonaggression treaty that stabilized relations between Egypt and the Hittites. The end of Hittite power came around 1200 B.C. when the Sea Peoples struck at both Egypt and the Hittite empire. Egypt managed to keep the invaders out but remained weakened thereafter. The Hittite empire was destroyed, however. By 1190 B.C., Hittite power was at an end.

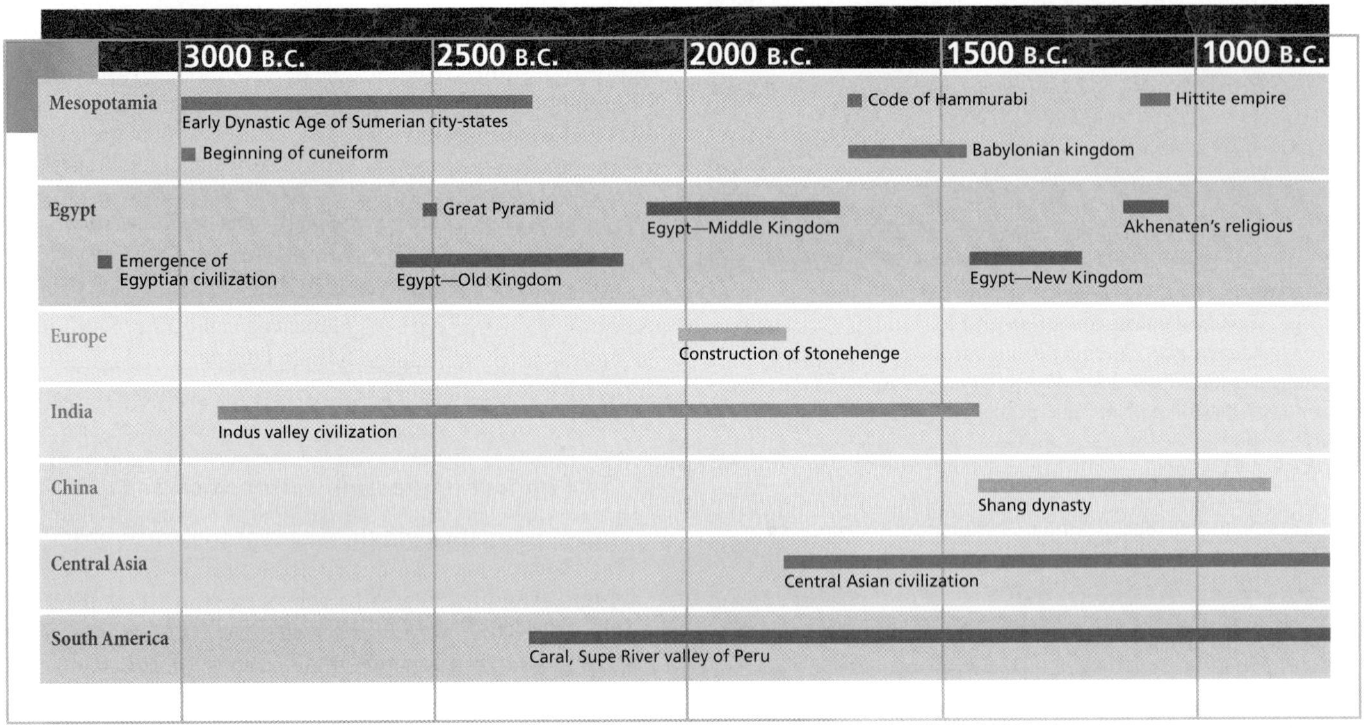

Conclusion

Although early civilizations emerged in different parts of the world, the foundations of Western civilization were laid by the Mesopotamians and the Egyptians. They developed cities and struggled with the problems of organized states. They developed writing to keep records and created literature. They constructed monumental architecture to please their gods, symbolize their power, and preserve their culture. They developed new political, military, social, and religious structures to deal with the basic problems of human existence and organization. These first literate civilizations left detailed records that allow us to view how they grappled with three of the fundamental problems that humans have pondered: the nature of human relationships, the nature of the universe, and the role of divine forces in that cosmos. Although later peoples in Western civilization would provide different answers from those of the Mesopotamians and Egyptians, it was they who first posed the questions, gave answers, and wrote them down. Human memory begins with these two civilizations.

By the middle of the second millennium B.C., much of the creative impulse of the Mesopotamian and Egyptian civilizations was beginning to wane. The invasion of the Sea Peoples around 1200 B.C. ushered in a whole new pattern of petty states and new kingdoms that would lead to the largest empires the ancient Near East had seen.

Notes

1. Quoted in Amélie Kuhrt, *The Ancient Near East, c. 3000–330 B.C.* (London, 1995), Vol. 1, p. 68.
2. Quoted in Thorkild Jacobsen, "Mesopotamia," in Henri Frankfort et al., *Before Philosophy* (Baltimore, 1949), p. 139.
3. Quoted in Thorkild Jacobsen, *The Treasures of Darkness: A History of Mesopotamian Religion* (New Haven, Conn., 1976), p. 97.
4. *The Epic of Gilgamesh*, trans. N. K. Sandars (London, 1972), p. 62.
5. James B. Pritchard, *Ancient Near Eastern Texts*, 3d ed. (Princeton, N.J., 1969), p. 372.
6. Quoted in Milton Covensky, *The Ancient Near Eastern Tradition* (New York, 1966), p. 51.
7. Pritchard, *Ancient Near Eastern Texts*, p. 445.
8. Quoted in B. G. Trigger, B. J. Kemp, D. O'Connor, and A. B. Lloyd, *Ancient Egypt: A Social History* (Cambridge, 1983), p. 74.
9. Pritchard, *Ancient Near Eastern Texts*, p. 34.
10. Ibid., p. 36.
11. Ibid., p. 413.
12. Ibid., p. 420.
13. Quoted in John A. Wilson, *The Culture of Ancient Egypt* (Chicago, 1956), p. 264.
14. Pritchard, *Ancient Near Eastern Texts*, p. 412.
15. Ibid., p. 413.

Suggestions for Further Reading

For a beautifully illustrated introduction to the ancient world, see *Past Worlds: The Times Atlas of Archaeology* (Maplewood, N.J., 1988), written by an international group of scholars. A detailed history of the ancient world with chapters written by different specialists is available in the twelve volumes of *The Cambridge Ancient History*, now in its third edition. A less detailed but sound survey can be found in L. De Blois and R. J. van der Spek, *An Introduction to the Ancient World*, trans. S. Mellor (London, 1997). The following works are of considerable value in examining the prehistory of humankind: M. N. Cohen, *The Food Crisis in Prehistory: Overpopulation and the Origins of Agriculture* (New Haven, Conn., 1977); R. Leakey, *The Making of Mankind* (London, 1981); R. J. Wenke, *Patterns in Prehistory: Humankind's First Three Million Years*, 4th ed. (New York, 1999); P. Mellars and C. Stringer, *The Human Revolution* (Edinburgh, 1989); D. O. Henry, *From Foraging to Agriculture* (Philadelphia, 1989); and C. Redman, *The Rise of Civilization* (San Francisco, 1978). For a study of the role of women in early human society, see E. Barber, *Women's Work: The First 20,000 Years* (New York, 1994).

An excellent reference tool on the ancient Near East can be found in P. Bienkowski and A. Milward, eds., *Dictionary of the Ancient Near East* (Philadelphia, 2000). General surveys of Mesopotamia and Egypt include A. B. Knapp, *The History and Culture of Ancient Western Asia and Egypt* (Chicago, 1987); W. von Soden, *The Ancient Orient: An Introduction to the Study of the Ancient Near East* (Grand Rapids, Mich., 1994); and H. J. Nissen, *The Early History of the Ancient Near East, 9000–2000 B.C.* (Chicago, 1988). For a detailed survey, see A. Kuhrt, *The Ancient Near East, c. 3000–330 B.C.*, 2 vols. (London, 1995). H. W. F. Saggs, *Babylonians* (Norman, Okla., 1995), provides an overview of the peoples of ancient Mesopotamia. On the economic and social history of the ancient Near East, see D. C. Snell, *Life in the Ancient Near East* (New Haven, Conn., 1997).

General works on ancient Mesopotamia include J. N. Postgate, *Early Mesopotamia: Society and Economy at the Dawn of History* (London, 1992), and A. L. Oppenheim, *Ancient Mesopotamia*, 2d ed. (Chicago, 1977). A beautifully illustrated survey can be found in M. Roaf, *Cultural Atlas of Mesopotamia and the Ancient Near East* (New York, 1996). The world of the Sumerians has been well described in S. N. Kramer, *The Sumerians* (Chicago, 1963) and *History Begins at Sumer* (New York, 1959). See also the summary of the historical and archaeological evidence by H. Crawford, *Sumer and the Sumerians* (Cambridge, 1991). The fundamental work on the spiritual perspective of ancient Mesopotamia is T. Jacobsen, *The Treasures of Darkness: A History of Mesopotamian Religion* (New Haven, Conn., 1976).

For a good introduction to ancient Egypt, see the beautifully illustrated works by M. Hayes, *The Egyptians* (New York, 1997), and D. P. Silverman, ed., *Ancient Egypt* (New York, 1997). Other general surveys include I. Shaw, ed., *The Oxford History of Ancient Egypt* (New York, 2000); N. Grant, *The Egyptians* (New York, 1996); and N. Grimal, *A History of Ancient Egypt*, trans. I. Shaw (Oxford, 1992). On Akhenaten and his religious changes, see D. Redford, *Akhenaten: The Heretic King* (Princeton, N.J., 1984). Egyptian religion is covered in H. Frankfort, *Ancient Egyptian Religion* (New York, 1948), a brief but superb study, and E. Hornung, *Conceptions of God in Ancient Egypt: The One and the Many* (Ithaca, N.Y., 1982). On Egyptian culture in general, see J. A. Wilson, *The Culture of Ancient Egypt* (Chicago, 1956). An important study on women is G. Robins, *Women in Ancient Egypt* (Cambridge, Mass., 1993). Daily life can be examined in E. Strouhal, *Life of the Ancient Egyptians* (Norman, Okla., 1992).

On the Sea Peoples, see the standard work by N. Sandars, *The Sea Peoples: Warriors of the Ancient Mediterranean* (London, 1978). A good introductory survey on the Hittites can be found in O. R. Gurney, *The Hittites*, 2d ed. (Harmondsworth, England, 1981).

For additional reading, go to InfoTrac College Edition, your online research library at http://web1.infotrac-college.com

Enter the search term *antiquities* using the Subject Guide.

Enter the search term *Mesopotamia* using Key Terms.

Enter the search term *archaeology research* using the Subject Guide.

Enter the search term *Egypt history* using the Subject Guide.

CHAPTER

2

The Ancient Near East: Peoples and Empires

© The British Museum

CHAPTER OUTLINE

- The Hebrews: "The Children of Israel"
- The Neighbors of the Israelites
- The Assyrian Empire
- The Neo-Babylonian Empire
- The Persian Empire
- Conclusion

FOCUS QUESTIONS

- In what ways was the Jewish faith unique in the ancient Near East, and how did it evolve over time?
- What effect did the other peoples of the ancient Near East have on the history of Israel and the development of the Jewish faith?
- What methods and institutions did the Assyrians and Persians use to amass and maintain their respective empires?
- What were the chief teachings of Zoroastrianism, and what role did it play in the Persian Empire?
- What is the relationship between the political history of the Israelites and the evolution of their religious beliefs?

AROUND 970 B.C., Solomon came to the throne of Israel, a small state in western Asia. He was lacking in military prowess but excelled in many other ways. Through trade and a series of foreign alliances, he created a strong, flourishing state. But he was especially famed for another of his qualities. When confronted with two women who each claimed that the child before them was her natural child, Solomon ordered his servant to cut the child in half and give half to each woman. The first woman objected: "Please, my lord, give her the living baby! Don't kill him!" The second woman replied, "Neither I nor you shall have him. Cut him in two!" Then Solomon rendered his judgment: "Give the living baby to the first woman. Do not kill him; she is his mother." According to the biblical account, "when all Israel heard the verdict the king had given, they held the king in awe, because they saw that he had wisdom from God to administer justice." After Solomon's death,

Israel's power began to crumble. But how had such a small nation been able to survive for as long as it did in a Near East dominated by mighty empires?

The destruction of the Hittite kingdom and the weakening of Egypt around 1200 B.C. temporarily left a power vacuum in the Near East, allowing a patchwork of petty kingdoms and city-states to emerge, especially in Syria and Palestine. One of these small states, the nation of Israel, has played a role in Western civilization completely disproportionate to its size. The Israelites were a minor factor in the politics of the ancient Near East, but their spiritual heritage—the Judeo-Christian values—is one of the basic pillars of Western civilization.

The small states did not last, however. Ever since the first city-states had arisen in the Near East around 3000 B.C., there had been a movement toward the creation of larger territorial states with more sophisticated systems of control. This process reached a high point in the first millennium B.C. with the appearance of empires that embraced the entire Near East. Between 1000 and 500 B.C., the Assyrians, Chaldeans, and Persians all created empires that encompassed most or all of the ancient Near East. Each had impressive and grandiose capital cities that emphasized the power and wealth of its rulers. Each brought peace and order for a period of time by employing new administrative techniques. Each eventually fell to other conquerors. In the long run, these large empires had less impact on Western civilization than did the Hebrew people of Israel. In human history, the power of ideas is often more significant than the power of empires.

The Hebrews: "The Children of Israel"

The Hebrews were a Semitic-speaking people who had a tradition concerning their origins and history that was eventually written down as part of the Hebrew Bible, known to Christians as the Old Testament. Describing them as nomads organized into clans, the Hebrews' tradition states that they were descendants of the patriarch Abraham who had migrated from Mesopotamia to the land of Palestine, where they became identified as the "Children of Israel." Again according to tradition, a drought in Palestine caused many Hebrews to migrate to Egypt, where they lived peacefully until they were enslaved by pharaohs who used them as laborers on building projects. They remained in bondage until Moses led his people out of Egypt in the well-known Exodus, which some historians have estimated would have occurred in the first half of the thirteenth century B.C. According to the biblical account, the Hebrews then wandered for many years in the desert until they entered Palestine. Organized into twelve tribes, they became embroiled in conflict with the Philistines, a people who had settled in the coastal area of Palestine but were beginning to move into the inland areas.

Many scholars today doubt that the early books of the Hebrew Bible reflect the true history of the early Israelites. They argue that the early books of the Bible, written centuries after the events described, preserve only what the Israelites came to believe about themselves and that recent archaeological evidence often contradicts the details of the biblical account. Some of these scholars have even argued that the Israelites were not nomadic invaders but indigenous peoples in the Palestinian hill country. What is generally agreed, however, is that between 1200 and 1000 B.C., the Israelites emerged as a distinct group of people, possibly organized into tribes or a league of tribes, who established a united kingdom known as Israel.

The United Kingdom

The first king of the Israelites was Saul (c. 1020–1000 B.C.), who initially achieved some success in the ongoing struggle with the Philistines. But after his death in a disastrous battle with this enemy, a brief period of anarchy ensued until one of Saul's lieutenants, David (c. 1000–970 B.C.), reunited the Israelites, defeated the Philistines, and established control over all of Palestine (see Map 2.1). According to the biblical account, some of his conquests led to harsh treatment for the conquered people: "David also defeated the Moabites. He made them lie down on the ground and measured them off with a length of cord. Every two lengths of them were put to death, and the third length was allowed to live. So the Moabites became subject to David and brought tribute."[1] Among David's conquests was the city of Jerusalem, which he made into the capital of a united kingdom. David centralized Israel's political organization and accelerated the integration of the Israelites into a settled community based on farming and urban life.

David's son Solomon (c. 970–930 B.C.) did even more to strengthen royal power. He expanded the political and military establishments and was especially active in extending the trading activities of the Israelites. Solomon is best known for his building projects, of which the most famous was the Temple in the city of Jerusalem. The Israelites viewed the Temple as the symbolic center of their religion, and hence of the kingdom of Israel itself. The Temple now housed the Ark of the Covenant, a holy chest containing the sacred relics of the Hebrew religion and, symbolically, the throne of the invisible God of Israel. Under Solomon, ancient Israel was at the height of its power, but his efforts to extend royal power throughout his kingdom led to dissatisfaction among some of his subjects.

The Divided Kingdom

After Solomon's death, tensions between the northern and southern tribes in Israel led to the establishment of two separate kingdoms—the kingdom of Israel, composed of the ten northern tribes, with its capital eventually at Samaria, and the southern kingdom of Judah, consisting of two tribes, with its capital at Jerusalem. The northern kingdom of Israel, especially under King Ahab (869–850 B.C.), joined with some small Syrian states to temporarily stop the onslaught of the Assyrians, who had consolidated their kingdom to the northeast (see "The Assyrian Empire" later in this chapter). But the power of Israel declined after Ahab, and by the end of the ninth century, the kingdom of Israel was forced to pay tribute to Assyria. In the next century, Israel itself was destroyed. The Assyrians overran the kingdom, destroyed the capital of Samaria in 722 B.C., and deported many Hebrews to other parts of the Assyrian Empire. These dispersed Hebrews (the "ten lost tribes") merged with neighboring peoples and gradually lost their identity.

The southern kingdom of Judah was also forced to pay tribute to Assyria but managed to survive as an independent state as Assyrian power declined. A new enemy, however, appeared on the horizon. The Chaldeans first demolished Assyria and then, under King Nebuchadnezzar II, conquered Judah and completely destroyed Jerusalem in 586 B.C. Many upper-class people from Judah were sent to Babylonia in exile, the memory of which is still evoked in the stirring words of Psalm 137:

By the rivers of Babylon, we sat and wept when we remembered Zion. . . .
How can we sing the songs of the Lord while in a foreign land?
If I forgot you, O Jerusalem, may my right hand forget its skill.
May my tongue cling to the roof of my mouth if I do not remember you, if I do not consider Jerusalem my highest joy.[2]

But the Babylonian captivity of the people of Judah did not last. Upon the destruction of the Chaldean kingdom by a new set of conquerors, the Persians, the people of Judah were allowed to return to Jerusalem and rebuild their city and the Temple, although Judah remained under Persian control until the conquests of Alexander the Great in the fourth century B.C. The people of Judah survived, eventually becoming known as the Jews and giving their name to Judaism, the religion of Yahweh, the Jewish God.

Map 2.1 Palestine in the First Millennium B.C. United under Saul, David, and Solomon, greater Israel split into two states—Israel and Judah—after the death of Solomon. With power divided, the Israelites could not resist invasions that dispersed many Jews from Palestine. Some, such as the "ten lost tribes," never returned. Others were sent to Babylon but were later allowed to return under the rule of the Persians. ■ Why was Israel more vulnerable to the Assyrian Empire than Judah was?

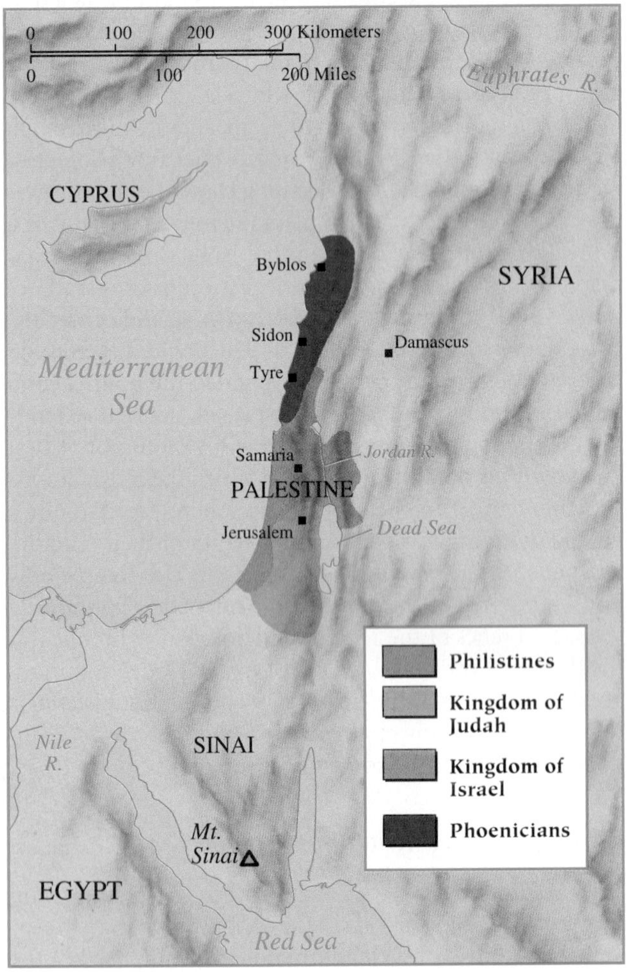

A Representation of the Ark of the Covenant. The most famous project carried out under King Solomon was the building of the Temple of Jerusalem, in which the Israelites placed the Ark of the Covenant, a holy chest containing the sacred relics of the Hebrew faith. The Ark was also considered the throne of the invisible God on earth. This representation of the Ark, believed to be one of the earliest, is from a second-century A.D. synagogue at Capernaum.

Ronald Sheridan/The Ancient Art & Architecture Collection

CHRONOLOGY

The Israelites

Saul—first king	c. 1020–1000 B.C.
King David	c. 1000–970 B.C.
King Solomon	c. 970–930 B.C.
Northern kingdom of Israel destroyed by Assyria	722 B.C.
Southern kingdom of Judah falls to Chaldeans; destruction of Jerusalem	586 B.C.
Return of exiles to Jerusalem	538 B.C.

The Spiritual Dimensions of Israel

The spiritual perspective of the Israelites evolved over time. Early Israelites probably worshiped many gods, including nature spirits dwelling in trees and rocks. For some Israelites, Yahweh was the chief god of Israel, but many, including kings of Israel and Judah, worshiped other gods as well. It was among the Babylonian exiles in the sixth century B.C. that Yahweh—the God of Israel—came to be seen as the only God. After the return of these exiles to Judah, their point of view eventually became dominant, and pure monotheism, or the belief that there is only one God for all peoples, came to be the major tenet of Judaism.

"I AM THE LORD YOUR GOD": RULER OF THE WORLD

According to the Jewish conception, there is but one God, whom the Jews called Yahweh. God is the creator of the world and everything in it. Indeed, Yahweh means "he causes to be." To the Jews, the gods of all other peoples were idols. The Jewish God ruled the world; he was subject to nothing. All peoples were his servants, whether they knew it or not. This God was also transcendent. He had created nature but was not in nature. The stars, moon, rivers, wind, and other natural phenomena were not divinities or suffused with divinity, as other peoples of the ancient Near East believed, but were God's handiwork. All of God's creations could be admired for their awesome beauty but not worshiped as gods.

This omnipotent creator of the universe was not removed from the life he had created, however, but was a just and good God who expected goodness from his people. If they did not obey his will, they would be punished. But he was also a God of mercy and love: "The Lord is gracious and compassionate, slow to anger and rich in love. The Lord is good to all; he has compassion on all he has made."[3] Despite the powerful dimensions of God as creator and sustainer of the universe, the Jewish message also emphasized that each person could have a personal relationship with this powerful being. As the psalmist sang: "My help comes from the Lord, the Maker of heaven and earth. He will not let your foot slip—he who watches over you will not slumber."[4]

The chief source of information about Israel's spiritual conceptions is the Hebrew Bible, which is the Old Testament of the Christian Bible. Its purpose was to teach the essential beliefs about the God of Israel after the Babylonian captivity of the Jews and their dispersal. During and after the Babylonian exile, the Jews recorded many of their traditions in order to preserve their identity. These writings became the core of the Hebrew Bible. The first five books (known as the Pentateuch), which cover the time from the beginning of the world until the Israelites' arrival in Palestine, constitute the Torah, or law code, governing the lives of worshipers and their relations to one another

The King of Israel Pays Tribute to the King of Assyria. By the end of the ninth century B.C., the kingdom of Israel had been forced to pay tribute to the Assyrian Empire. The Assyrians overran the kingdom in 722 B.C. and destroyed the capital city of Samaria. In this scene from a black obelisk, Jehu, king of Israel, is shown paying tribute to the king of Assyria.

The Covenant and the Law: The Book of Exodus

According to the biblical account, it was during the Exodus from Egypt that the Israelites supposedly made their covenant with Yahweh. They agreed to obey their God and follow his law. In return, Yahweh promised to take special care of his chosen people. This selection from the Book of Exodus describes the making of the covenant and God's commandments to the Israelites.

■ *Exodus 19:1–8*

In the third month after the Israelites left Egypt—on the very day—they came to the Desert of Sinai. After they set out from Rephidim, they entered the Desert of Sinai, and Israel camped there in the desert in front of the mountain. Then Moses went up to God, and the Lord, called to him from the mountain, and said, "This is what you are to say to the house of Jacob and what you are to tell the people of Israel: 'You yourselves have seen what I did to Egypt, and how I carried you on eagles' wings and brought you to myself. Now if you obey me fully and keep my covenant, then out of all nations you will be my treasured possession. Although the whole earth is mine, you will be for me a kingdom of priests and a holy nation.' These are the words you are to speak to the Israelites." So Moses went back and summoned the elders of the people and set before them all the words the Lord had commanded him to speak. The people all responded together, "We will do everything the Lord has said." So Moses brought their answer back to the Lord.

■ *Exodus 20:1–17*

And God spoke all these words, "I am the Lord your God, who brought you out of Egypt, out of the land of slavery. You shall have no other gods before me. You shall not make for yourself an idol in the form of anything in heaven above or on the earth beneath or in the waters below. You shall not bow down to them or worship them; for I, the Lord your God, am a jealous God, punishing the children for the sin of the fathers to the third and fourth generation of those who hate, but showing love to a thousand generations of those who love me and keep my commandments. You shall not misuse the name of the Lord your God, for the Lord will not hold anyone guiltless who misuses his name. Remember the Sabbath day by keeping it holy. Six days you shall labor and do all your work, but the seventh day is a Sabbath to the Lord your God. On it you shall not do any work, neither you, nor your son or daughter, nor your manservant or maidservant, nor your animals, nor the alien within your gates. For in six days the Lord made the heavens and the earth, the sea, and all that is in them, but he rested on the seventh day. Therefore the Lord blessed the Sabbath day and made it holy. Honor your father and your mother, so that you may live long in the land the Lord your God is giving you. You shall not murder. You shall not commit adultery. You shall not steal. You shall not give false testimony against your neighbor. You shall not covet your neighbor's house. You shall not covet your neighbor's wife, or his manservant or maidservant, his ox or donkey, or anything that belongs to your neighbor."

and to the non-Jewish population. The Hebrew Bible focuses on one basic theme: the necessity for the Jews to obey their God.

"YOU ONLY HAVE I CHOSEN": COVENANT, LAW, AND PROPHETS

Three aspects of the Jewish religious tradition had special significance: the covenant, the law, and the prophets. The Israelites believed that during the Exodus from Egypt, when Moses supposedly led his people out of bondage into a land of plenty promised to them by Yahweh, a special event occurred that determined the Jewish experience for all time. According to tradition, God entered into a covenant or contract with the tribes of Israel, who believed that Yahweh had spoken to them through Moses (see the box above). The Israelites promised to obey Yahweh and follow his law. In return, Yahweh promised to take special care of his people, "a peculiar treasure unto me above all people."

This covenant between Yahweh and his chosen people could be fulfilled, however, only by obedience to the law of God. Law became a crucial element of the Jewish world and had a number of different dimensions. In some instances, it set forth specific requirements, such as payments for offenses. Most important, since the major characteristic of God was his goodness, ethical concerns stood at the center of the law. Sometimes these took the form of specific standards of moral behavior: "You shall not murder. You shall not commit adultery. You shall not steal."[5] But these concerns were also expressed in decrees that regulated the economic, social, and political life of the community, for God's laws of morality applied to all areas of life. These laws made no class distinctions and emphasized the protection of the poor, widows, orphans, and slaves.

The Israelites believed that certain religious leaders or holy men, called prophets, were sent by God to serve as his voice to his people. In the ninth century B.C., the prophets were particularly vociferous about the tendency of the Israelites to accept other gods, chiefly the fertility and earth gods of other peoples in Palestine. They warned of the terrible retribution that God would exact from the Israelites if they did not keep the covenant to remain faithful to him alone and just in their dealings with one another (see the box on p. 35).

The golden age of prophecy began in the mid-eighth century and continued during the time when the people of Israel and Judah were threatened by Assyrian and Chaldean

The Hebrew Prophets: Micah, Isaiah, and Amos

The Hebrew prophets warned the Israelites that they must obey God's commandments or face punishment for breaking their covenant with God. These selections from the prophets Micah, Isaiah, and Amos make clear that God would punish the Israelites for their sins. Even the Assyrians, as Isaiah indicated, would be used as God's instrument to punish them.

■ *Micah 6:9–16*

Listen! The Lord is calling to the city—and to fear your name is wisdom—"Heed the rod and the One who appointed it. Am I still to forget, O wicked house, your ill-gotten treasures . . . ? Shall I acquit a man with dishonest scales, with a bag of false weights? Her rich men are violent; her people are liars and their tongues speak deceitfully. Therefore, I have begun to destroy you, to ruin you because of your sins. You will eat but not be satisfied; your stomach will still be empty. You will store up but save nothing, because what you save I will give to the sword. You will plant but not harvest; you will press olives but not use the oil on yourselves, you will crush grapes but not drink the wine. . . . Therefore I will give you over to ruin and your people to derision; you will bear the scorn of the nations."

■ *Isaiah 10:1–6*

Woe to those who make unjust laws, to those who issue oppressive decrees, to deprive the poor of their rights and withhold justice from the oppressed of my people, making their prey and robbing the fatherless. What will you do on the day of reckoning, when disaster comes from afar? To whom will you run for help? Where will you leave your riches? Nothing will remain but to cringe among the captives or fall among the slain. Yet for all this, his anger is not turned away, his hand is still upraised. "Woe to the Assyrian, the rod of my anger, in whose hand is the club of my wrath! I send him against a godless nation, I dispatch him against a people who anger me, to seize loot and snatch plunder, and to trample them down like mud in the streets."

■ *Amos 3:1–2*

Hear this word the Lord has spoken against you, O people of Israel—against the whole family I brought up out of Egypt: "You only have I chosen of all the families of the earth; therefore, I will punish you for all your sins."

Art Resource, NY

conquerors. These "men of God" went through the land warning the Israelites that they had failed to keep God's commandments and would be punished for breaking the covenant: "I will punish you for all your iniquities." Amos prophesied the fall of the northern kingdom of Israel to Assyria; twenty years later, Isaiah said the kingdom of Judah too would fall.

Out of the words of the prophets came new concepts that enriched the Jewish tradition and ultimately Western civilization, including a notion of universalism and a yearning for social justice. Although the Jews' religious practices gave them a sense of separateness from other peoples, the prophets transcended this by embracing a concern for all humanity. All nations would someday come to the God of Israel: "All the earth shall worship you." A universal community of all people under God would someday be established by Israel's effort. This vision encompassed the elimination of war and the establishment of peace for all the nations of the world. In the words of the prophet Isaiah: "He will judge between the nations and will settle disputes for many people. They will beat their swords into plowshares and their spears into pruning hooks. Nation

The Hebrew Bible. The Hebrew Bible was the main source of information about the spiritual conceptions of the Israelites. Shown here is a twelfth-century Hebrew manuscript of the Torah, the first five books of the Hebrew Bible.

will not take up sword against nation, nor will they train for war anymore."[6]

The prophets also cried out against social injustice. They condemned the rich for causing the poor to suffer, denounced luxuries as worthless, and threatened Israel with prophecies of dire punishments for these sins. God's command was to live justly, share with one's neighbors, care for the poor and the unfortunate, and act with compassion. When God's command was not followed, the social fabric of the community was threatened. These proclamations by Israel's prophets became a source for Western ideals of social justice, even if they have never been very perfectly realized.

Although the prophets ultimately developed a sense of universalism, the demands of the Jewish religion—the need to obey their God—encouraged a separation between the Jews and their non-Jewish neighbors. Unlike most other peoples of the Near East, Jews could not simply be amalgamated into a community by accepting the gods of their conquerors and their neighbors. To remain faithful to the demands of their God, they might even have to refuse loyalty to political leaders.

The Social Structure of the Hebrews

Originally, the Israelites had been organized along tribal lines, but a new social structure had evolved by the time of the monarchy as the Israelites settled in towns and villages. Although historians warn that the Israelites did not develop social classes in the modern sense of self-conscious groups opposed to one another, there were conspicuous "divisions of the population."

The "men of rank and influence" formed a special group of considerable importance in Hebrew society. This group included officials of the king, military officers, civil officials, and governors. Although simply servants to the kings, they held a privileged position in the society at large. The common people, sometimes called "people of the land," remained a body of free people having basic civil rights. Their livelihood came mostly from the land and from various crafts. These peasants and artisans sold their own produce and products directly to buyers in markets in their local town or village squares, thus eliminating intermediaries or traders. There was no real merchant class in ancient Israel. Commerce was carried on by foreigners, such as the Phoenicians. Not until the Diaspora, when Jews became scattered throughout the ancient world after their exile to Babylon, did they become merchants.

The family was the central social institution in Hebrew life and consisted of individuals connected by common blood and a common living place. A family living in one house could comprise husband and wife, married sons and their wives, and their children. The Hebrew family was patriarchal. The husband-father was master of his wife and possessed absolute authority over his children, including the power of life and death.

Marriage was an important aspect of Hebrew family life. In ancient Israel, under the monarchy, polygamy was an accepted form of marriage, especially for kings and wealthier citizens. Hebrew law limited kings to eighteen wives and citizens to four. In practice, only kings could afford a large harem. When others had more than one wife, it was usually because they desired more children; the first wife, for example, might be unable to have children or have produced only daughters.

Many Hebrews, however, believed that monogamy was the preferred form of marriage. Wives were honored for their faithfulness and dedication to their husbands. The Book of Proverbs in the Hebrew Bible provides a picture of what Hebrews considered a perfect wife:

> *A wife of noble character who can find? She is worth far more than rubies.*
> *Her husband has full confidence in her and lacks nothing of value.*
> *She brings him good, not harm, all the days of her life.*
> *She selects wool and flax and works with eager hands.*
> *She is like the merchant ships, bringing her food from afar.*
> *She gets up while it is still dark; she provides food for her family and portions for her servant girls.*
> *She considers a field and buys it; out of her earnings she plants a vineyard.*
> *She sets about her work vigorously; her arms are strong for her tasks.*
> *She sees that her trading is profitable, and her lamp does not go out at night.*
> *In her hand she holds the distaff and grasps the spindle with her fingers.*
> *She opens her arms to the poor and extends her hands to the needy. . . .*
> *She makes linen garments and sells them, and supplies the merchants with sashes.*
> *She is clothed with strength and dignity; she can laugh at the days to come.*
> *She speaks with wisdom, and faithful instruction is on her tongue.*
> *She watches over the affairs of her household, and does not eat the bread of idleness.*
> *Her children arise and call her blessed; her husband also, and he praises her.*[8]

Women were greatly valued, but their work was obviously never done.

Although the Hebrew Bible, a male-edited work, reveals a society dominated by men, it also includes stories of women who played heroic roles in the early history of Israel. Deborah, for example, played a prominent role in the defeat of the Canaanites at Mount Tabor. After the same battle, Jael killed Sisera, the leader of the Canaanites. According to the Song of Deborah, "Most blessed of women be Jael, . . . most blessed of tent-dwelling women. . . . Her hand reached for the tent peg, her right hand for the workman's hammer. She struck Sisera, she crushed his head, she shattered and pierced his temple. At her feet he sank, he fell; there he lay."[8]

But these accounts are not the norm. In the Hebrew Bible, women are mostly dependent on men. It should not

surprise us, then, to learn that a married woman was subject to her husband's authority. Unlike the Mesopotamians, the Hebrews did not develop the custom of a dowry from the bride's parents. They did, however, have a practice whereby the bridegroom's family paid a sum of money to the bride's family, not as a purchase price as such, but apparently as compensation to the family for the loss of their daughter. A married woman left her parents' home, lived with her husband's family, and became a member of their clan. Her children also belonged to the husband's clan.

Since boys and girls were married at a relatively young age, parents took the responsibility for matchmaking. Although marriages occurred between persons of different families and even with foreign women, it was customary to find marriage partners within one's own clan or extended family. Wives were expected to remain faithful to their husbands, an ideal that would later have an impact on Christian attitudes toward women.

The primary goal of marriage was to produce children. They were the "crown of man," and sons, in particular, were desired. Daughters would eventually leave the family house, but sons carried on the family line. Mothers were in charge of the early education of children, especially in regard to basic moral principles. As boys matured, their fathers took over responsibility for their education, which remained largely informal. This included religious instruction as well as general education for life. The rod was not spared as a matter of principle. Since trades were usually hereditary, fathers also provided their sons' occupational education. As one rabbi stated, "He who does not teach his son a useful trade is bringing him up to be a thief."[9] Additional education for boys came from priests, whose sacred mission was to instruct people in the Torah. An organized school system was not established until much later, possibly in the second century B.C. The only education girls received was from their mothers, who taught them the basic fundamentals of how to be good wives, mothers, and housekeepers.

The Neighbors of the Israelites

The Israelites were not the only people living in Palestine. The Philistines, who invaded from the sea, established five towns on the coastal plain of the region. They settled down as farmers and eventually came into conflict with the Israelites. The Phoenicians had resided in Palestine for some time but now found themselves with a new independence. A Semitic-speaking people, the Phoenicians resided along the Mediterranean coast on a narrow band of land 120 miles long. They had rebuilt their major cities, Byblos, Tyre, and Sidon, after destruction by the Sea Peoples. Their newfound political independence helped the Phoenicians expand the trade that was already the foundation of their prosperity. In fact, Byblos had been the principal distribution center for Egyptian papyrus outside Egypt (the Greek word for book, *biblos,* is derived from the name Byblos).

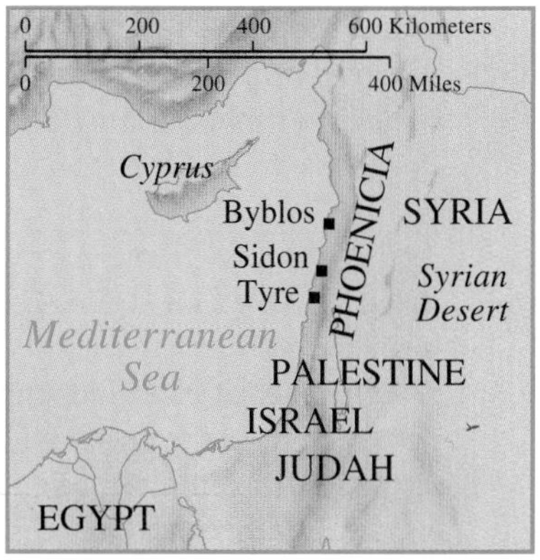

Phoenician Cities

All three chief cities of Phoenicia were seaports, but they also served as distribution centers for the lands to the east in Mesopotamia. The Phoenicians themselves produced a number of goods for foreign markets, including purple dye, glass, wine, and lumber from the famous cedars of Lebanon. In addition, the Phoenicians improved their ships and became great international sea traders. They charted new routes, not only in the Mediterranean but also in the Atlantic Ocean, where they reached Britain and sailed south along the west coast of Africa. The Phoenicians established a number of colonies in the western Mediterranean, including settlements in southern Spain, Sicily, and Sardinia. Most of the Phoenician colonies were trading stations, not permanent settlements. A major exception was Carthage, the Phoenicians' most famous colony, located on the North African coast.

Culturally, the Phoenicians are best known as transmitters. Instead of using pictographs or signs to represent whole words and syllables as the Mesopotamians and

Phoenician Plaque. The Phoenicians were a Semitic-speaking people dwelling in ancient Palestine who became the predominant sea traders of the ancient Near East. Ivory was one of the favorite materials of Phoenician artists of the ninth and eighth centuries B.C. This ivory plaque inlaid with glass stones shows a lioness attacking a slave boy.

Egyptians did, the Phoenicians simplified their writing by using twenty-two different signs to represent the sounds of their speech. These twenty-two characters or letters could be used to spell out all the words in the Phoenician language. Although the Phoenicians were not the only people to invent an alphabet, theirs would have special significance because it was eventually passed on to the Greeks. From the Greek alphabet was derived the Roman alphabet that we still use today (see Table 2.1). The Phoenicians achieved much while independent, but they ultimately fell subject to the Assyrians, Chaldeans, and Persians.

The Assyrian Empire

The existence of independent states in Palestine was only possible because of the power void that followed the destruction of the Hittite kingdom and the weakening of the Egyptian empire. But this state of affairs did not last; new empires soon arose and came to dominate vast stretches of the ancient Near East. The first of these empires emerged in Assyria, an area whose location on the upper Tigris River brought it into both cultural and political contact with southern Mesopotamia.

Although part of Mesopotamia, Assyria, with its hills and adequate, if not ample, rainfall, had a different terrain and climate. The Assyrians were a Semitic-speaking people who exploited the use of iron weapons to establish an empire by 700 B.C. that included Mesopotamia, sections of Asia Minor, Syria, Palestine, and Egypt down to Thebes (see Map 2.2). By 660 B.C., the Assyrian Empire had reached the height of its power.

Ashurbanipal (669–626 B.C.) was one of the strongest Assyrian rulers, but it was already becoming apparent during his reign that the Assyrian Empire was greatly overextended. Internal strife intensified as powerful Assyrian nobles gained control of vast territories and waged their own private military campaigns. Moreover, subject peoples greatly resented Assyrian rule. The hatred that the Babylonians felt after the brutal Assyrian sack of the city of Babylon in 689 B.C., for example, led them to rebel during the reign of Ashurbanipal. Soon after Ashurbanipal's death, the Assyrian Empire began to disintegrate. The capital city of Nineveh fell to a coalition of Chaldeans and Medes (see "The Neo-Babylonian Empire" later in this chapter) in 612 B.C., and in 605 B.C., the Neo-Babylonian Empire took over the rest of the empire.

At its height, the Assyrian Empire was ruled by kings whose power was considered absolute. Under their leadership, the empire became well organized. By eliminating governorships held by nobles on a hereditary basis and instituting a new hierarchy of local officials directly responsible to the king, the Assyrian kings gained greater control over the resources of the empire. The Assyrians also developed an efficient system of communication to administer their empire more effectively. A network of posting stages was established that used relays of horses (mules or donkeys in mountainous terrain) to carry messages

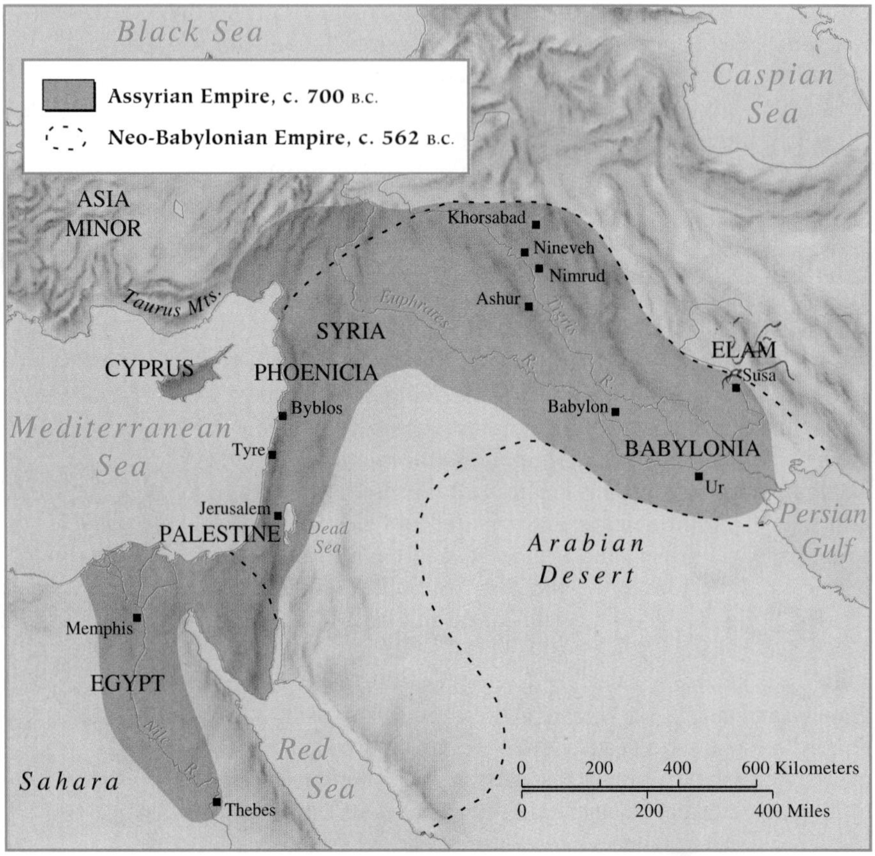

Map 2.2 The Assyrian and Neo-Babylonian Empires. The Assyrian Empire expanded in large part due to its brutal military methods. It maintained its rule through use of a common language and religion, along with extremely violent suppression of internal revolts. It was overthrown by Chaldeans in Babylonia, leading to the Neo-Babylonian Empire epitomized by Nebuchadnezzar. ■ Why was control of Babylonia crucial to both empires?

Table 2.1 The Phoenician, Greek, and Latin Alphabets

Phoenician			Greek			Latin	
Phoenician	*Phoenician Name*	*Modern Symbol*	*Early Greek*	*Classical Greek*	*Greek Name*	*Early Latin*	*Classical Latin*
𐤀	ʾaleph	ʾ	A	A	alpha	A	A
𐤁	beth	b	B	B	beta		B
𐤂	gimel	g	Γ	Γ	gamma		C
𐤃	daleth	d	Δ	Δ	delta	D	D
𐤄	he	h	Ǝ	E	epsilon	Ǝ	E
𐤅	waw	w	F		digamma	F	F
							G
𐤆	zayin	z	I	Z	zeta		
𐤇	ḥeth	h	H	H	eta	H	H
𐤈	teth	t	⊗	Θ	theta		
𐤉	yod	y	I	I	iota	I	I
							(J)
𐤊	kaph	k	K	K	kappa	K	K
𐤋	lamed	l	Λ	Λ	lambda		L
𐤌	mem	m	M	M	mu	M	M
𐤍	nun	n	N	N	nu	N	N
𐤎	samek	s			xi		
𐤏	ayin	ʿ	O	O	omnicron	O	O
𐤐	pe	p	Γ	Π	pi		P
𐤑	sade	s	M		saw		
𐤒	qoph	o	Ϙ		qoppa		Q
𐤓	reš	r	P	P	rho		R
𐤔	šin	sh/s	Σ	Σ	sigma	S	S
𐤕	taw	t	X		tau		T
				Y	upsilon	V	V
				X	chi		X
							Y
				Ω	omega		Z

SOURCE: Andrew Robinson, *The Story of Writing* (London: Thames & Hudson, 1995), p. 170.

Erich Lessing/Art Resource, NY

Ashurbanipal Destroys an Elamite City. Assyria was the first great empire to gain control over the ancient Near East in the first millennium B.C. The Assyrians had a highly efficient and well-organized military machine, capable of fighting under a variety of conditions. This relief depicts the army of King Ashurbanipal sacking an Elamite city in 647 B.C. Shown at the top are Assyrian soldiers destroying the city walls while below soldiers carry off the spoils of war.

throughout the empire. The system was so effective that a provincial governor anywhere in the empire (except Egypt) could send a question and receive an answer from the king in his palace within a week.

The Assyrian Military Machine

The ability of the Assyrians to conquer and maintain an empire derived from a combination of factors. Through years of practice, the Assyrians developed effective military leaders and fighters. They were able to enlist and deploy troops numbering in the hundreds of thousands, although most campaigns were not on such a large scale. In 845 B.C., Shalmaneser III led an army of 120,000 men across the Euphrates on a campaign. Size alone was not decisive, however. The Assyrian army was extremely well organized and disciplined. It included a standing army of infantry as its core, accompanied by cavalry and horse-drawn war chariots that were used as mobile platforms for shooting arrows. Moreover, the Assyrians had the advantage of having the first large armies equipped with iron weapons. The Hittites (see Chapter 1) had been the first to develop iron metallurgy, but iron came to be used extensively only after new methods for hardening it came into common use after 1000 B.C.

Another factor in the army's success was its ability to use different kinds of military tactics (see the box on p. 41). The Assyrian army was capable of waging guerrilla warfare in the mountains and set battles on open ground as well as laying siege to cities. The Assyrians were especially renowned for their siege warfare. They would hammer a city's walls with heavy, wheeled siege towers and armored battering rams while sappers dug tunnels to undermine the walls' foundations and cause them to collapse. The besieging Assyrian armies learned to cut off supplies so effectively that if a city did not fall to them, the inhabitants could be starved into submission.

A final factor in the effectiveness of the Assyrian military machine was its ability to create a climate of terror as an instrument of warfare. The Assyrians became famous for their terror tactics, although some historians believe their policies were no worse than those of other Near Eastern conquerors. As a matter of regular policy, the Assyrians laid waste the land in which they were fighting, smashing dams, looting and destroying towns, setting crops on fire, and cutting down trees, particularly fruit trees. The Assyrians were especially known for committing atrocities on their captives. King Ashurnasirpal recorded this account of his treatment of prisoners:

The Assyrian Military Machine

The Assyrians won a reputation for having a mighty military machine. They were able to use a variety of military tactics and were successful whether they were employing guerrilla warfare, fighting set battles, or laying siege to cities. In these three selections, Assyrian kings describe their military conquests.

King Sennacherib (704–681 B.C.) Describes a Battle with the Elamites in 691

At the command of the god Ashur, the great Lord, I rushed upon the enemy like the approach of a hurricane. . . . I put them to rout and turned them back. I transfixed the troops of the enemy with javelins and arrows. . . . I cut their throats like sheep. . . . My prancing steeds, trained to harness, plunged into their welling blood as into a river; the wheels of my battle chariot were bespattered with blood and filth. I filled the plain with the corpses of their warriors like herbage. . . . As to the lords of the Chaldeans, panic from my onslaught overwhelmed them like a demon. They abandoned their tents and fled for their lives, crushing the corpses of their troop as they went. . . . In their terror they passed scalding urine and voided their excrement into their chariots.

King Sennacherib Describes His Siege of Jerusalem (701 B.C.)

As to Hezekiah, the Jew, he did not submit to my yoke, I laid siege to 46 of his strong cities, walled forts and to the countless small villages in their vicinity, and conquered them by means of well-stamped earth-ramps, and battering-rams brought thus near to the walls combined with the attack by foot soldiers, using mines, breeches as well as sapper work. I drove out of them 200,150 people, young and old, male and female, horses, mules, donkeys, camels, big and small cattle beyond counting, and considered them booty. Himself I made a prisoner in Jerusalem, his royal residence, like a bird in a cage. I surrounded him with earthwork in order to molest those who were leaving his city's gate.

King Ashurbanipal (669–626 B.C.) Describes His Treatment of Conquered Babylon

I tore out the tongues of those whose slanderous mouths had uttered blasphemies against my god Ashur and had plotted against me, his god-fearing prince; I defeated them completely. The others, I smashed alive with the very same statues of protective deities with which they had smashed my own grandfather Sennacherib—now finally as a belated burial sacrifice for his soul. I fed their corpses, cut into small pieces, to dogs, pigs, . . . vultures, the birds of the sky and also to the fish of the ocean. After I had performed this and thus made quiet again the hearts of the great gods, my lords, I removed the corpses of those whom the pestilence had felled, whose leftovers after the dogs and pigs had fed on them were obstructing the streets, filling the places of Babylon, and of those who had lost their lives through the terrible famine.

> 3000 of their combat troops I felled with weapons. . . . Many of the captives taken from them I burned in a fire. Many I took alive; from some of these I cut off their hands to the wrist, from others I cut off their noses, ears, and fingers; I put out the eyes of many of the soldiers. . . . I burned their young men and women to death.

After conquering another city, the same king wrote: "I fixed up a pile of corpses in front of the city's gate. I flayed the nobles, as many as had rebelled, and spread their skins out on the piles. . . . I flayed many within my land and spread their skins out on the walls."[10] (Obviously, not a king to play games with!) Note that this policy of extreme cruelty to prisoners was not used against all enemies but was reserved primarily for those who were already part of the empire and then rebelled against Assyrian rule.

Assyrian Society and Culture

Unlike the Hebrews, the Assyrians were not fearful of mixing with other peoples. In fact, the Assyrian policy of deporting many prisoners of newly conquered territories to Assyria created a polyglot society in which ethnic differences were not very important. It has been estimated that over a period of three centuries, between four and five million people were deported to Assyria, resulting in a population that was racially and linguistically mixed. What gave identity to the Assyrians themselves was their language, although even that was akin to that of their southern neighbors in Babylonia. Religion was also a cohesive force. Assyria was literally, "the land of Ashur," a reference to its chief god. The king, as the human representative of the god Ashur, served as a final unifying focus.

Agriculture formed the principal basis of Assyrian life. Assyria was a land of farming villages with relatively few significant cities, especially in comparison to southern Mesopotamia. Unlike the river valleys, where farming required the minute organization of large numbers of people to control irrigation, Assyrian farms received sufficient moisture from regular rainfall.

Trade was second to agriculture in economic importance. For internal trade, metals, such as gold, silver, copper, and bronze, were used as a medium of exchange. Various agricultural products also served as a form of

King Ashurbanipal's Lion Hunt. This relief, sculptured on alabaster as a decoration for the northern palace in Nineveh, depicts King Ashurbanipal engaged in a lion hunt. Relief sculpture, one of the best-known forms of Assyrian art, reached its high point under Ashurbanipal at about the time that the Assyrian Empire began to disintegrate.

payment or exchange. Because of their geographical location, the Assyrians served as intermediaries and participated in an international trade in which they imported timber, wine, and precious metals and stones while exporting textiles produced in palaces, temples, and private villas.

The culture of the Assyrian Empire was a hybrid. The Assyrians assimilated much of Mesopotamian civilization and saw themselves as guardians of Sumerian and Babylonian culture. Ashurbanipal, for example, amassed a large library at Nineveh that included the available works of Mesopotamian history. Assyrian religion reflected this assimilation of other cultures as well. Although the Assyrians considered their own national god, Ashur, their chief deity, they recognized virtually all of the Mesopotamian gods and goddesses as well.

Among the best-known objects of Assyrian art are the relief sculptures found in the royal palaces in three of the Assyrian capital cities, Nimrud, Nineveh, and Khorsabad. These reliefs, which were begun in the ninth century and reached their high point in the reign of Ashurbanipal in the seventh century, depicted two different kinds of subject matter: ritual or ceremonial scenes revolving around the person of the king and scenes of hunting and war. The latter show realistic action scenes of the king and his warriors engaged in battle or hunting animals, especially lions. These reliefs depict a strongly masculine world where discipline, brute force, and toughness are the enduring values, indeed, the very values of the Assyrian military monarchy.

The Neo-Babylonian Empire

The Chaldeans, a Semitic-speaking people, had gained ascendancy in Babylonia by the seventh century and came to form the chief resistance to Assyrian control of Mesopotamia. The Chaldean king Nabopolassar (625–605 B.C.), who joined forces with the Medes to capture the Assyrian capital Nineveh in 612 B.C., was responsible for establishing a new Babylonian monarchy. But it was his son Nebuchadnezzar II (605–562 B.C.) who achieved the final defeat of the Assyrian Empire. Under his rule, the Chaldeans defeated Egypt to gain control of Syria and Palestine, destroyed Jerusalem, carried the people of Judah into exile in Babylon, and in the process regained for Babylonia a position as the leading power in the ancient Near East (see Map 2.2).

During Nebuchadnezzar's reign, Babylonia was renowned for a prosperity based on lush agricultural lands, lucrative trade routes, and industries, especially textiles and metals. Nebuchadnezzar rebuilt Babylon as the center of his empire, giving it a reputation as one of the great cities of the ancient world. Babylon was surrounded by towering walls, 8 miles in length, encircled by a moat filled by the Euphrates River. The Ishtar Gate opened onto the Triumphal Way, which led to the sacred precincts of Marduk, the chief Babylonian god. Babylon was adorned with temples and palaces; most famous of all were the Hanging Gardens, known as one of the Seven Wonders of the ancient world. These were supposedly built to satisfy Nebuchadnezzar's wife, a princess from the land of Media, who missed the mountains of her homeland. A series of terraces led to a plateau, an artificial mountain, at the top of which grew the lush gardens irrigated by water piped to the top. From a distance the gardens appeared to be suspended in air.

The splendor of the Neo-Babylonian Empire proved to be short-lived. Nabonidus (555–539 B.C.) was the last king of the Chaldean dynasty. He had a great interest in history and encouraged scholars to collect Sumerian texts and study the Sumerian language. But his policies aroused considerable internal dissent. Among other things, Nabonidus neglected the cult of Marduk, instead worshiping the moon god, Sin. When Babylon fell to the Persian conqueror Cyrus in 539 B.C., the Babylonians welcomed him as a liberator.

Ishtar Gate of Babylon. Under Nebuchadnezzar II, the Chaldeans finally succeeded in destroying the Assyrian Empire. Nebuchadnezzar rebuilt Babylon as the center of his empire and adorned it with such architectural wonders as the Ishtar Gate, which was built of blue glazed bricks and opened onto the Triumphal Way. This picture shows the Ishtar Gate as it was rebuilt in the Pergamum Museum in Berlin.

The Persian Empire

The Persians were an Indo-European-speaking people who lived in southwestern Iran. Primarily nomadic, the Persians were organized into tribes or clans led by petty kings assisted by a group of warriors who formed a class of nobles. At the beginning of the seventh century, the Persians became unified under the Achaemenid dynasty, based in Persis in southern Iran. One of the dynasty's members, Cyrus (559–530 B.C.), created a powerful Persian state that rearranged the political map of the ancient Near East (see Map 2.3).

Cyrus the Great

In 550 B.C., Cyrus established Persian control over Media, making it the first Persian satrapy or province. Three years later, Cyrus defeated the prosperous Lydian kingdom in western Asia Minor, and Lydia became another Persian satrapy. Cyrus' forces then went on to conquer the Greek city-states that had been established on the Ionian coast. Cyrus then turned eastward, subduing the eastern part of the Iranian plateau, Sogdiana, and even western India. His eastern frontiers secured, Cyrus entered Mesopotamia in 539 and captured Babylon (see the box on p. 44). His treatment of Babylonia showed remarkable restraint and wisdom. Babylonia was made into a Persian province under a Persian satrap, but many government officials were kept in their positions. Cyrus took the title "King of All, Great King, Mighty King, King of Babylon, King of the Land of Sumer and Akkad, King of the Four Rims (of the Earth), the Son of Cambyses the Great King, King of Anshan"[11] and insisted that he stood in the ancient, unbroken line of Babylonian kings. By appealing to the vanity of the Babylonians, he won their loyalty. Cyrus also issued an edict permitting the Jews, who had been brought to Babylon in the sixth century B.C., to return to Jerusalem with their sacred temple objects and to rebuild their Temple as well.

From 538 to 530 B.C., Cyrus consolidated his empire. Among other things, he constructed forts, especially in the northeast, to protect against nomadic incursions. It was there that he undertook his last campaign. In 530 B.C., he marched into the territory of the Massagetae, where he was killed in battle.

To his contemporaries, Cyrus the Great was deserving of his epithet. The Greek historian Herodotus recounted that the Persians viewed him as a "father," a ruler who was "gentle, and procured them all manner of goods."[12] Cyrus must have been an unusual ruler for his time, a man who demonstrated considerable wisdom and compassion in the conquest and organization of his empire. Cyrus obtained the favor of the priesthoods in his conquered lands by restoring temples and permitting religious toleration. He won approval by using not only Persians but also native peoples as government officials in their own states. He allowed Medes to be military commanders. Unlike the Assyrian rulers of an earlier empire, he had a reputation for mercy. Medes, Babylonians, and Jews all accepted him as their legitimate ruler. Some peoples portrayed him as a great leader and peacemaker. Indeed, a Hebrew prophet regarded him as the anointed one of God: "I am the Lord who says of Cyrus, 'He is my shepherd and will accomplish all that I please'; he will say of Jerusalem, 'Let it be rebuilt'; and of the temple, 'Let its foundations be laid.' This is what the Lord says to his anointed, to Cyrus, whose right hand I take hold of to subdue nations before him."[13]

The Fall of Babylon

Under the Chaldeans, Babylon became the center of an empire and gained a reputation as one of the great cities of the ancient world. But the Neo-Babylonian Empire did not last, and Babylon fell to the Persian forces under King Cyrus in 539 B.C. In his history of the Persian Wars, the ancient Greek historian Herodotus described how Cyrus supposedly captured Babylon.

Herodotus, The Persian Wars

Cyrus, with the first approach of the ensuing spring, marched forward against Babylon. The Babylonians, encamped without their walls, awaited his coming. A battle was fought at a short distance from the city, in which the Babylonians were defeated by the Persian king, whereupon they withdrew within their defenses. Here they shut themselves up, and made light of his siege, having laid in a store of provisions for many years in preparation against this attack; for when they saw Cyrus conquering nation after nation, they were convinced that he would never stop, and that their turn would come at last.

Cyrus was now reduced to great perplexity, as time went on and he made no progress against the place. In this distress, either some one made the suggestion to him, or he thought himself of a plan, which he proceeded to put in execution. He placed a portion of his army at the point where the river enters the city and another body at the back of the place where it issues forth, with orders to march into the town by the bed of the stream, as soon as the water became shallow enough: he then himself drew off with the unwarlike portion of his host, and made for the place where Nitocris [supposedly a queen of Babylon] dug the basin for the river, where he did exactly what she had done formerly: he turned the Euphrates by a canal into the basin, which was then a marsh, on which the river sank to such an extent that the natural bed of the stream became fordable. Hereupon the Persians who had been left for the purpose at Babylon by the river-side, entered the stream, which had now sunk so as to reach about midway up a man's thigh, and thus got into the town. Had the Babylonians been apprised of what Cyrus was about, or had they noticed their danger, they would not have allowed the entrance of the Persians within the city, which was what ruined them utterly, but would have made fast all the street-gates which gave upon the river, and mounting upon the walls along both sides of the stream, would so have caught the enemy as it were in a trap. But, as it was, the Persians came upon them by surprise and so took the city. Owing to the vast size of the place, the inhabitants of the central parts (as the residents at Babylon declare) long after the outer portions of the town were taken, knew nothing of what had chanced, but as they were engaged in a festival, continued dancing and reveling until they learned the capture but too certainly. Such, then, were the circumstances of the first taking of Babylon.

Cyrus had a genuine respect for ancient civilizations—in building his palaces, he made use of Assyrian, Babylonian, Egyptian, and Lydian practices. Indeed, Cyrus had a sense that he was creating a "world empire" that included peoples who had ancient and venerable traditions and institutions.

Expanding the Empire

Upon Cyrus' death in 530 B.C., his son Cambyses II assumed power as the Great King. Four years later, Cambyses undertook the invasion of Egypt, the only kingdom in the Near East not yet brought under Persian control. Aided by the Phoenician fleet, he defeated and captured the pharaoh and the Egyptian forces. Egypt was made into a satrapy with Memphis as its capital. In the summer of 525 B.C., Cambyses took the title of pharaoh.

After the death of Cambyses in 522, Darius emerged as Great King after a year of intense civil war. Once in charge, Darius (521–486 B.C.) turned to the task of strengthening the empire. He codified Egyptian law and built a canal to link the Red Sea and the Mediterranean. A campaign into western India led to the creation of a new Persian province that extended to the Indus River. Darius also moved into Europe proper, conquering Thrace and making the Macedonian king a vassal. A revolt of the Ionian Greek cities in 499 B.C. resulted in temporary freedom for these communities in western Asia Minor. Aid from the Greek mainland, most notably from Athens, led to a brief invasion of Lydia by the Ionians and the burning of Sardis, center of the Lydian satrapy. This event led to Darius' involvement with the mainland Greeks. After reestablishing control of the Ionian Greek cities, Darius undertook an invasion of the Greek mainland, which culminated in the famous Athenian victory in the Battle of Marathon in 490 B.C. (see Chapter 3).

Governing the Empire

By the reign of Darius, the Persians had created the largest empire the world had yet seen. It not only included all the old centers of power in the Near East, Egypt, Mesopotamia, and Assyria but also extended into Thrace and Asia Minor in the west and into India in the east.

For administrative purposes, the empire had been divided into approximately twenty provinces called satrapies. Each province was ruled by a governor or satrap, literally a "protector of the kingdom." Although Darius had not introduced the system of satrapies, he did see that it was organized more rationally. He created a sensible system for calculating the tribute that each satrapy owed

Darius, the Great King. Darius ruled the Persian Empire from 521 to 486 B.C. He is shown here on his throne in Persepolis, a new capital city that he built. In his right hand, Darius holds the royal staff. In his left hand, he grasps a lotus blossom with two buds, a symbol of royalty.

to the central government and gave satraps specific civil and military duties. They collected tributes, were responsible for justice and security, raised military levies, and normally commanded the military forces within their satrapies. In terms of real power, the satraps were miniature kings who established courts imitative of the Great King's.

From the time of Darius on, satraps were men of Persian descent. The major satrapies were given to princes of the king's family, and their position became essentially hereditary. The minor satrapies were placed in the hands of Persian nobles. Their offices, too, tended to pass from father to son. The hereditary nature of the governors' offices made it necessary to provide some checks on their power. Consequently, some historians think that there were officials at the satrapal courts, such as secretaries and generals in charge of the garrison, who reported directly to the Great King, keeping him informed of what was going on within the various satrapal governments. It is also possible that an official known as the "king's eye" or "king's messenger" made annual inspections of each satrapy.

CHRONOLOGY

The Empires

The Assyrians	
Height of power	660 B.C.
Ashurbanipal	669–626 B.C.
Capture of Nineveh	612 B.C.
Assyrian Empire destroyed	605 B.C.
The Chaldeans	
Ascendancy in Babylonia	600s B.C.
Nabopolassar establishes Neo-Babylonian monarchy	625–605 B.C.
Height of empire under King Nebuchadnezzar II	605–562 B.C.
Fall of Babylon	539 B.C.
The Persians	
Unification of Persians	600s B.C.
Conquests of Cyrus the Great	559–530 B.C.
Cambyses II and conquest of Egypt	530–522 B.C
Reign of Darius	521–486 B.C.

An efficient system of communication was considered crucial to sustaining the Persian Empire. Well-maintained roads facilitated the rapid transit of military and government personnel. One in particular, known as the Royal Road, stretched from Sardis, the center of Lydia in Asia Minor, to Susa, the chief capital of the Persian Empire. Like the Assyrians, the Persians established staging posts equipped with fresh horses for the king's messengers.

In this vast administrative system, the Persian king occupied an exalted position. Although not considered a god like the Egyptian pharaoh, he was nevertheless the elect one or regent of the Persian god Ahuramazda (see "Persian Religion" later in this chapter). All subjects were the king's servants, and he was the source of all justice, possessing the power of life and death over everyone. Persian kings were largely secluded and not easily available. They resided in a series of splendid palaces. Darius in particular was a palace builder on a grand scale. His description of the construction of a palace in the chief Persian capital of Susa demonstrated what a truly international empire Persia was:

> This is the . . . palace which at Susa I built. From afar its ornamentation was brought. . . . The cedar timber was brought from a mountain named Lebanon; the Assyrians brought it to Babylon, and from Babylon the Carians and Ionians brought it to Susa. Teakwood was brought from Gandara and from Carmania. The gold which was used here was brought from Sardis and from Bactria. The stone—lapis lazuli and carnelian—was

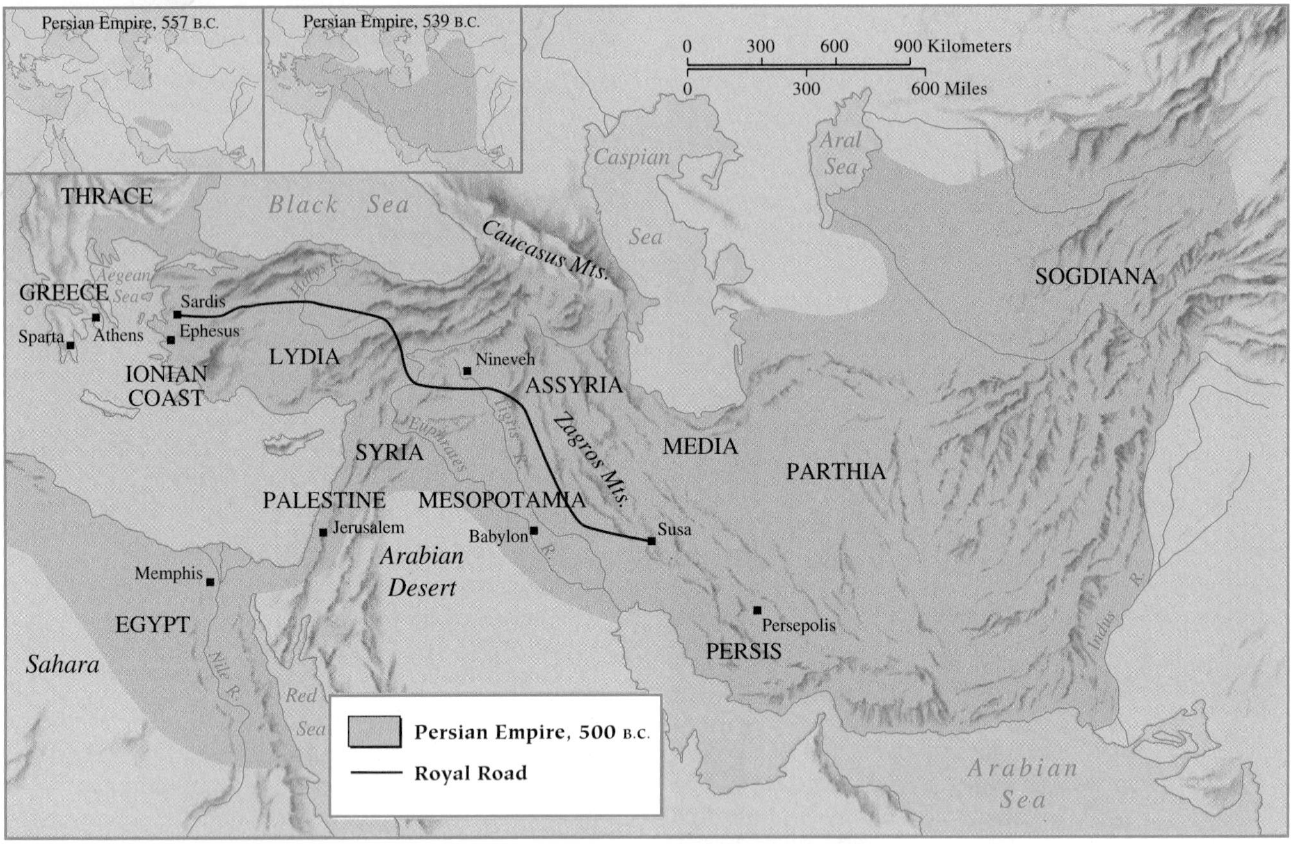

Map 2.3 The Persian Empire at the Time of Darius. Cyrus the Great united the Persians and led them in successful conquest of much of the Near East. By the time of Darius, the Persian Empire was the largest the world had yet seen. The Persians allowed a high degree of religious tolerance and gave some government positions to natives of conquered territories. ■ How did Persian policies attempt to overcome the difficulties of governing far-flung provinces?

> brought from Sogdiana. . . . The silver and copper were brought from Egypt. The ornamentation with which the wall was adorned was brought from Ionia. The ivory was brought from Ethiopia, from India, and from Arachosia. The stone pillars were brought from . . . Elam. The artisans who dressed the stone were Ionians and Sardians. The goldsmiths who wrought the gold were Medes and Egyptians. . . . Those who worked the baked brick [with figures] were Babylonians. The men who adorned the wall were Medes and Egyptians. At Susa here a splendid work was ordered; very splendid did it turn out.[14]

But Darius was unhappy with Susa. He did not really consider it his homeland, and it was oppressively hot in the summer months. He built another residence at Persepolis, a new capital located to the east of the old one and at a higher elevation.

The policies of Darius also tended to widen the gap between the king and his subjects. As the Great King himself said of all his subjects, "What was said to them by me, night and day it was done."[15] Over a period of time, the Great Kings in their greed came to hoard immense quantities of gold and silver in the various treasuries located in the capital cities. Both their hoarding of wealth and their later overtaxation of their subjects are seen as crucial factors in the ultimate weakening of the Persian Empire (see the box on p. 47).

In its heyday, however, the empire stood supreme, and much of its power depended on the military. By the time of Darius, the Persian monarchs had created a standing army of professional soldiers. This army was truly international, composed of contingents from the various peoples who made up the empire. At its core was a cavalry force of ten thousand and an elite infantry force of ten thousand Medes and Persians known as the Immortals because they were never allowed to fall below ten thousand in number. When one was killed, he was immediately replaced. The Persians made effective use of their cavalry, especially for operating behind enemy lines and breaking up lines of communication. The Persian navy consisted of ships from subject states, including the Phoenicians, Egyptians, Anatolians, and Ionian Greeks.

■ *Persian Religion*

Of all the Persians' cultural contributions, the most original was their religion. Before the advent of Zoroastrianism in the sixth century, the popular religion of the Iranians

A Dinner of the Persian King

The Persian kings lived in luxury as a result of their conquests and ability to levy taxes from their conquered subjects. In this selection, we read a description of how a Persian king dined with his numerous guests.

■ *Athenaeus,* The Deipnosophists, *4:145–146*

Heracleides of Cumae, author of the *Persian History,* writes in the second book of the work entitled *Equipment:* "All who attend upon the Persian kings when they dine first bathe themselves and then serve in white clothes, and spend nearly half the day on preparations for the dinner. Of those who are invited to eat with the king, some dine outdoors, in full sight of anyone who wishes to look on; others dine indoors in the king's company. Yet even these do not eat in his presence, for there are two rooms opposite each other, in one of which the king has his meal, in the other the invited guests. The king can see them through the curtain at the door, but they cannot see him. Sometimes, however, on the occasion of a public holiday, all dine in a single room with the king, in the great hall. And whenever the king commands a symposium [drinking-bout following the dinner] which he does often, he has about a dozen companions at the drinking. When they have finished dinner, that is the king by himself, the guests in the other room, these fellow-drinkers are summoned by one of the eunuchs; and entering they drink with him, though even they do not have the same wine; moreover, they sit on the floor, while he reclines on a couch supported by feet of gold, and they depart after having drunk to excess. In most cases the king breakfasts and dines alone, but sometimes his wife and some of his sons dine with him. And throughout the dinner his concubines sing and play the lyre; one of them is the soloist, the others sing in chorus. And so, Heracleides continues, the 'king's dinner,' as it is called, will appear prodigal to one who merely hears about it, but when one examines it carefully it will be found to have been got up with economy and even with parsimony; and the same is true of the dinners among other Persians of high station. For one thousand animals are slaughtered daily for the king; these comprise horses, camels, oxen, asses, deer, and most of the small animals; many birds are also consumed, including Arabian ostriches—and the creature is large—geese, and cocks. And of all these only moderate portions are served to each of the king's guests, and each of them may carry home whatever he leaves untouched at the meal. But the greater part of these meats and other foods are taken into the courtyard for the body-guard and light-armed troopers maintained by the king; there they divide all the half-eaten remnants of meat and bread and share them in equal portions. . . ."

Réunion des Musées Nationaux/Art Resource, NY

Archers of the Persian Guard. One of the main pillars supporting the Persian Empire was the military. This frieze, composed of enameled brick, depicts members of the famous infantry force known as the Immortals, so called because their number was never allowed to drop below ten thousand. Those killed would be replaced immediately. They carry the standard lance and bow and arrow of the infantry.

focused on the worship of the powers of nature, such as the sun, moon, fire, and winds. Mithra was an especially popular god of light and war who came to be viewed as a sun god. The people worshiped and sacrificed to these powers of nature with the aid of priests, known as Magi.

Zoroaster was a semilegendary figure who, according to Persian tradition, was born in 660 B.C. After a period of wandering and solitude, he experienced revelations that caused him to be revered as a prophet of the "true religion." It is difficult to know what Zoroaster's original teachings were, since the sacred book of Zoroastrianism, the *Zend Avesta,* was not written down until the third century A.D. Scholars believe, however, that the earliest section of the *Zend Avesta,* known as the *Yasna,* consisting of seventeen hymns or *gathas,* contains the actual writings of Zoroaster. This enables us to piece together his message.

Zoroaster did not introduce a new god but taught that Ahuramazda, who had long been one of the Iranians' deities, was the only God and that his religion was the only perfect one. Ahuramazda (the "Wise Lord") was the supreme deity who brought all things into being:

This I ask of You, O Ahuramazda; answer me well:
Who at the Creation was the first father of Justice?—
Who assigned their path to the sun and the stars?—
Who decreed the waxing and waning of the moon, if it
was not You?— . . .
Who has fixed the earth below, and the heaven above
with its clouds that it might not be moved?—
Who has appointed the waters and the green things upon
the earth?—
Who has harnessed to the wind and the clouds their
steeds?— . . .
Thus do I strive to recognize in You, O Wise One,
Together with the Holy Spirit, the Creator of all things.[16]

According to Zoroaster, Ahuramazda also possessed abstract qualities or states that all humans should aspire to, such as Good Thought, Right, and Piety. Although Ahuramazda was supreme, he was not unopposed. Right is opposed by the Lie, Truth by Falsehood, Life by Death. At the beginning of the world, the good spirit of Ahuramazda was opposed by the evil spirit (in later Zoroastrianism identified with Ahriman). Although it appears that Zoroaster saw it as simply natural that where there is good there will be evil, later followers had a tendency to make these abstractions concrete and overemphasize the reality of an evil spirit. Humans also played a role in this cosmic struggle between good and evil. Ahuramazda, the creator, gave all humans free will and the power to choose between right and wrong. The good person chooses the right way of Ahuramazda. Zoroaster taught that there would be an end to the struggle between good and evil. Ahuramazda would eventually triumph, and at the last judgment at the end of the world, the final separation of good and evil would occur. Zoroaster also provided for individual judgment as well. Each soul faced a final evaluation of its actions. A person who had performed good deeds would achieve paradise, the "House of Song" or the "Kingdom of Good Thought"; the soul of a person who had performed evil deeds would be thrown into an abyss, the "House of Worst Thought," where it would experience future ages of darkness, torment, and misery.

The spread of Zoroastrianism was due to its acceptance by the Great Kings of Persia. The inscriptions of Darius make clear that he believed Ahuramazda was the only God. Although Darius himself may have been a monotheist, dramatic changes occurred as the kings and Magi of Persia propagated Zoroaster's teachings on Ahuramazda. Zoroastrianism lost its monotheistic emphasis, and the old nature worship resurfaced. Soon Persian religion had returned to polytheism, with Ahuramazda the chief of a number of gods of light. Mithra, the sun god, became a helper of Ahuramazda and later, in Roman times, the source of another religion. Persian kings were also very tolerant of other religions, and gods and goddesses of those religions tended to make their way into the Persian pantheon. Moreover, Zoroaster's teachings, as frequently happens to the ideas of founders of religions, acquired concrete forms that he had never originally intended. The struggle between good and evil was taken beyond the abstractions of Zoroaster into a strong ethical dualism. The spirit of evil became an actual being who had to be warded off by the use of spells and incantations. Descriptions of the last judgment came to be filled with minute physical details. Some historians believe that Zoroastrianism, with its emphasis on good and evil, a final judgment, and individual judgment of souls, had an impact on Christianity, a religion that eventually surpassed it in significance.

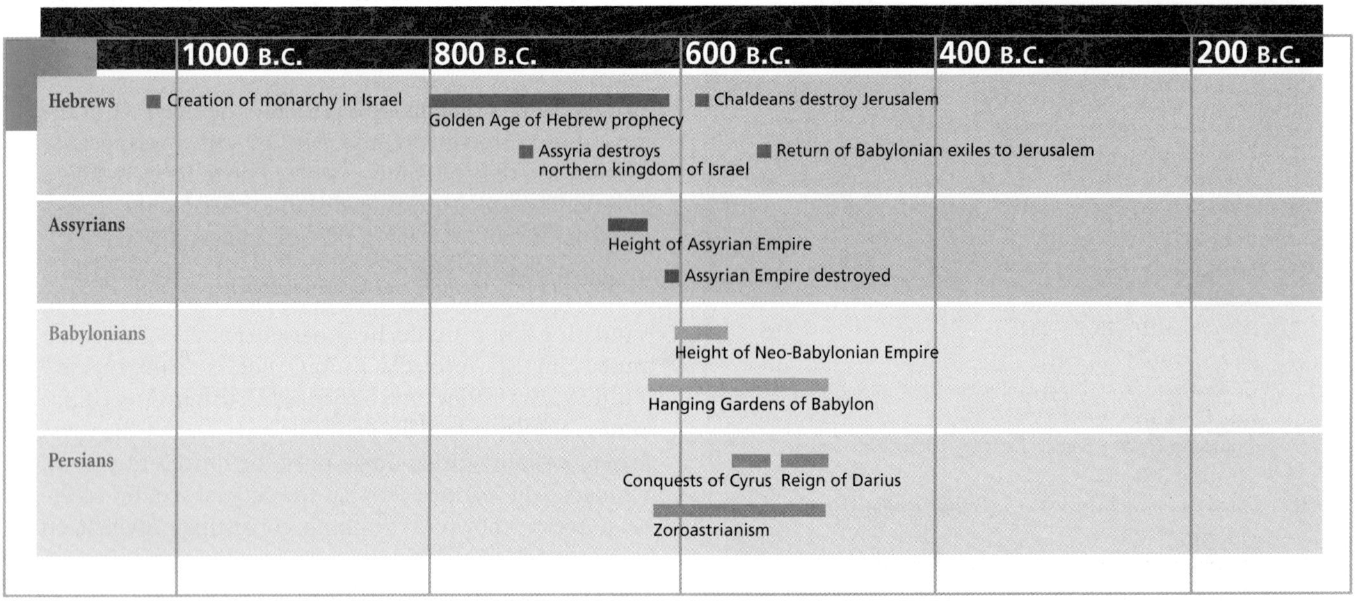

Conclusion

Around 1200 B.C., the decline of the Hittites and Egyptians had created a power vacuum that allowed a number of small states to emerge and flourish temporarily in the Near East. All of them were eventually overshadowed by the rise of the great empires of the Assyrians, Chaldeans, and Persians. The Assyrian Empire was the first to unite almost all of the ancient Near East. Far larger was the empire of the Great Kings of Persia. Although it owed much to the administrative organization created by the Assyrians, the Persian Empire had its own peculiar strengths. Persian rule was tolerant as well as efficient. Conquered peoples were allowed to keep their own religions, customs, and methods of doing business. The many years of peace that the Persian Empire brought to the region facilitated trade and the general well-being of its peoples. Many Near Eastern peoples expressed gratitude for being subjects of the Great Kings of Persia.

The Hebrews were one of these peoples. They created no empire and were dominated by the Assyrians, Chaldeans, and Persians. Nevertheless, they left a spiritual legacy that influenced much of the later development of Western civilization. The evolution of Hebrew monotheism created in Judaism one of the world's greatest religions; it influenced the development of both Christianity and Islam. When we speak of the Judeo-Christian heritage of Western civilization, we refer not only to the concept of monotheism but also to ideas of law, morality, and social justice that have become important parts of Western culture.

On the western fringes of the Persian Empire, another relatively small group of people, the Greeks, were creating cultural and political ideals that would also have an important impact on Western civilization. It is to the Greeks that we now turn.

Notes

1. 2 Samuel 8:2.
2. Psalms 137:1, 4–6.
3. Psalms 145:8–9.
4. Psalms 121:2–3.
5. Exodus 20:13–15.
6. Isaiah 2:4.
7. Proverbs 31:10–20, 24–28.
8. Judges 5:24–27.
9. Quoted in Roland de Vaux, *Ancient Israel: Its Life and Institutions* (New York, 1961), p. 49.
10. Quoted in H. W. F. Saggs, *The Might That Was Assyria* (London, 1984), pp. 261–262.
11. Quoted in John M. Cook, *The Persian Empire* (New York, 1983), p. 32.
12. Herodotus, *The Persian Wars,* trans. George Rawlinson (New York, 1942), p. 257.
13. Isaiah 44:28, 45:1.
14. Quoted in Albert T. Olmstead, *History of the Persian Empire* (Chicago, 1948), p. 168.
15. Quoted in Cook, *The Persian Empire,* p. 76.
16. Yasna 44:3–4, 7, as quoted in A. C. Bouquet, *Sacred Books of the World* (Harmondsworth, England, 1954), pp. 111–112.

Suggestions for Further Reading

For an excellent general survey of the material covered in this chapter, see A. Kuhrt, *The Ancient Near East, c. 3000–330 B.C.,* vol. 2 (London, 1995). There is an enormous literature on ancient Israel. Two good studies on the archaeological aspects are A. Mazar, *Archaeology of the Land of the Bible* (New York, 1992), and A. Ben-Tor, ed., *The Archaeology of Ancient Israel* (New Haven, Conn., 1992). For historical narratives, see especially J. Bright, *A History of Israel,* 3d ed. (Philadelphia, 1981), a fundamental study; J. M. Miller and J. H. Hayes, *A History of Ancient Israel and Judah* (Philadelphia, 1986); M. Grant, *The History of Ancient Israel* (New York, 1984); and H. Shanks, *Ancient Israel: A Short History from Abraham to the Roman Destruction of the Temple* (Englewood Cliffs, N.J., 1988). For a new perspective, see N. P. Lemche, *Ancient Israel: A New History of Israelite Society* (Sheffield, England, 1988). A brief summary of Hebrew history and thought can be found in J. H. Hexter, *The Judaeo-Christian Tradition* (New York, 1966). R. de Vaux, *Ancient Israel: Its Life and Institutions* (New York, 1961), is especially good on the social institutions of ancient Israel. On women in ancient Israel, see C. Meyers, *Discovering Eve: Ancient Israelite Women in Context* (New York, 1988).

For general studies on the religion of the Hebrews, see R. Albertz, *A History of Israelite Religion in the Old Testament Period* (Louisville, Ky., 1994), and W. J. Doorly, *The Religion of Israel* (New York, 1997). The role of the prophets is examined in J. Lindblom, *Prophecy in Ancient Israel* (Oxford, 1962), and R. B. Y. Scott, *The Relevance of the Prophets* (New York, 1968).

For a good account of Phoenician domestic and overseas expansion, see D. Harden, *The Phoenicians,* rev. ed. (Harmondsworth, England, 1980). See also M. E. Aubet, *The Phoenicians and the West: Politics, Colonies and Trade* (Cambridge, 1993).

A detailed account of Assyrian political, economic, social, military, and cultural history is H. W. F. Saggs, *The Might That Was Assyria* (London, 1984). A. T. Olmstead, *History of Assyria* (Chicago, 1975), is a basic survey of the Assyrian Empire. The Neo-Babylonian Empire can be examined in J. Oates, *Babylon* (London, 1979), and H. W. F. Saggs, *Babylonians* (Norman, Okla., 1995).

The classic work on the Persian Empire is A. T. Olmstead, *History of the Persian Empire* (Chicago, 1948), but J. M. Cook, *The Persian Empire* (New York, 1983), provides new material and fresh interpretations. Also of value is J. Curtis, *Ancient Persia* (Cambridge, Mass., 1990). On the history of Zoroastrianism, see R. C. Zaehner, *The Dawn and Twilight of Zoroastrianism* (London, 1961), and S. A. Nigosian, *The Zoroastrian Faith: Tradition and Modern Research* (New York, 1993).

For additional reading, go to InfoTrac College Edition, your online research library at http://web1.infotrac-college.com

Enter the search term *Assyrian* using Key Terms.

Enter the search term *Babylonian* using Key Terms.

Enter the search term *Phoenician* using Key Terms.

Enter the search term *Persian* using Key Terms.

C H A P T E R 3

The Civilization of the Greeks

Scala/Art Resource, NY

CHAPTER OUTLINE

- Early Greece
- The Greeks in a Dark Age (c. 1100–c. 750 B.C.)
- The World of the Greek City-States (c. 750–c. 500 B.C.)
- The High Point of Greek Civilization: Classical Greece
- Conclusion

FOCUS QUESTIONS

- How did the geography of Greece affect Greek history?
- What was the *polis,* or city-state, and how did the major city-states of Athens and Sparta differ?
- What effect did the two great conflicts of the fifth century—the Persian Wars and the Peloponnesian War—have on Greek civilization?
- Upon what ideals was classical Greek art based, and how were these ideals expressed?
- What questions did the Greek philosophers pose, and what answers did they suggest?
- Why are the Greeks considered the cornerstone of the Western intellectual tradition?

IN 431 B.C., WAR ERUPTED in Greece as two very different Greek city-states—Athens and Sparta—fought for domination of the Greek world. The people of Athens felt secure behind their walls and in the first winter of the war held a public funeral to honor those who had died in battle. On the day of the ceremony, the citizens of Athens joined in a procession, with the relatives of the dead wailing for their loved ones. As was the custom in Athens, one leading citizen was asked to address the crowd, and on this day it was Pericles who spoke to the people. He talked about the greatness of Athens and reminded the Athenians of the strength of their political system. "Our constitution," he said, "is called a democracy because power is in the hands not of a minority but of the whole people. When it is a question of settling private disputes, everyone is equal before the law. Just as our political life is free and open, so is our day-to-day life in our relations with each other. . . . Here each individual is interested not only in his own affairs but in the affairs of the state as well."

In this famous Funeral Oration, Pericles gave voice to the ideal of democracy and the importance of the individual. It was the Greeks who created the intellectual foundations of our Western heritage. They asked some basic questions about human life that still dominate our own intellectual pursuits: What is the nature of the universe? What is the purpose of human existence? What is our relationship to divine forces? What constitutes a community? What constitutes a state? What is true education? What are the true sources of law? What is truth itself, and how do we realize it? Not only did the Greeks provide answers to these questions, but they created a system of logical, analytical thought to examine them. This rational outlook has remained an important feature of Western civilization.

The story of ancient Greek civilization is a remarkable one that begins with the first arrival of the Greeks around 2000 B.C. By the eighth century B.C., the characteristic institution of ancient Greek life, the polis *or city-state, had emerged. Greek civilization flourished and reached its height in the classical era of the fifth century B.C., which has come to be closely identified with the achievements of Athenian democracy.*

Early Greece

Geography played an important role in the evolution of Greek history. Compared to the landmasses of Mesopotamia and Egypt, Greece occupied a small area, a mountainous peninsula that encompassed only 45,000 square miles of territory, about the size of the state of Louisiana. The mountains and the sea played especially significant roles in the development of Greek history. Much of Greece consists of small plains and river valleys surrounded by mountain ranges 8,000 to 10,000 feet high. The mountainous terrain had the effect of isolating Greeks from one another. Consequently, Greek communities tended to follow their own separate paths and develop their own way of life. Over a period of time, these communities became attached to their independence and were only too willing to fight one another to gain advantage. No doubt the small size of these independent Greek communities fostered participation in political affairs and unique cultural expressions, but the rivalry among these communities also led to the bitter warfare that ultimately devastated Greek society.

The sea also influenced the evolution of Greek society. Greece had a long seacoast, dotted by bays and inlets that provided numerous harbors. The Greeks also inhabited a number of islands to the west, the south, and particularly the east of the Greek mainland. It is no accident that the Greeks became seafarers who sailed out into the Aegean and Mediterranean Seas, first to make contact with the outside world and later to establish colonies that would spread Greek civilization throughout the Mediterranean world.

Greek topography helped determine the major territories into which Greece was ultimately divided. South of the Gulf of Corinth was the Peloponnesus, virtually an island connected to the mainland by a narrow land bridge (see Map 3.1). Consisting mostly of hills, mountains, and small valleys, the Peloponnesus was the location of Sparta, as well as the site of Olympia, where athletic games were held. Northeast of the Peloponnesus was the Attic peninsula (or Attica), the home of Athens, hemmed in by mountains to the north and west and surrounded by the sea to the south and east. Northwest of Attica was Boeotia in central Greece, with its chief city of Thebes. To the north of Boeotia was Thessaly, which contained the largest plains and became a great producer of grain and horses. To the north of Thessaly lay Macedonia, which was not of much importance in Greek history until 338 B.C., when the Macedonian king Philip II conquered the Greeks.

Minoan Crete

The earliest civilization in the Aegean region emerged on Crete. By 2800 B.C., a Bronze Age civilization that used metals, especially bronze, in making weapons had been established on the large island of Crete, southeast of the Greek mainland. The civilization of Minoan Crete was first discovered by the English archaeologist Arthur Evans, who named it "Minoan" after Minos, a legendary king of Crete. Evans's excavations on Crete at the beginning of the twentieth century led to the discovery of an enormous palace complex at Knossus, near modern Heracleion. The remains revealed a rich and prosperous culture with Knossus as the likely center of a far-ranging "sea empire," probably largely commercial. We know from archaeological remains that

The Minoan Sport of Bull Leaping. Minoan bull games were held in the great palaces on the island of Crete. As seen in this fresco from the east wing of the palace at Knossus, women and men acrobats (the man in red) somersaulted over the back of the bull. Another person waited behind the bull to catch the leapers.

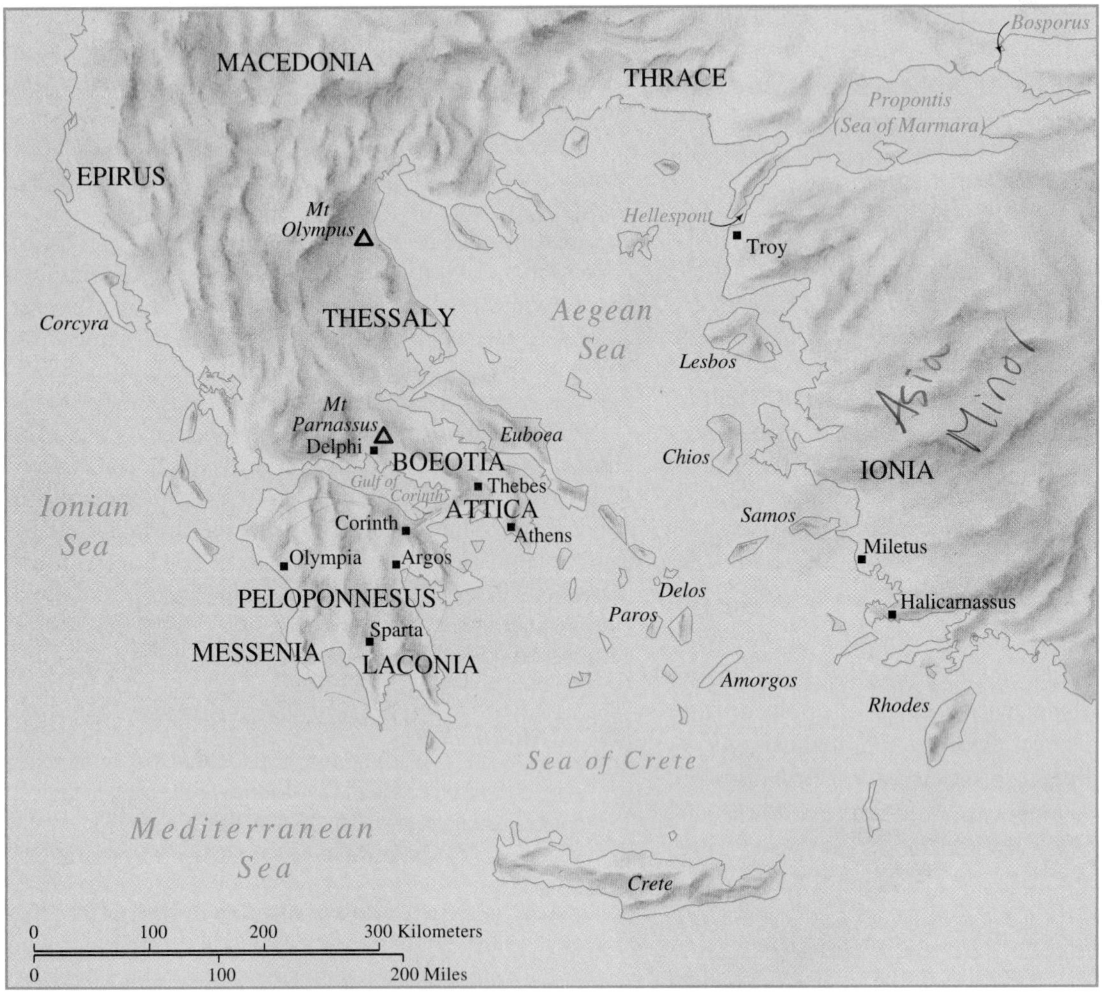

Map 3.1 Classical Greece. Classical Greece lasted from about 500 to 338 B.C. It encompassed the high points of Greek civilization in arts, science, philosophy, and politics, as well as the Persian Wars and the Peloponnesian War. ■ How does the geography of Greece help explain the rise and development of the Greek city-state?

the people of Minoan Crete were accustomed to sea travel and had made contact with the more advanced civilization of Egypt. Egyptian products have been found in Crete and Cretan products in Egypt. Minoan Cretans also made contact with and exerted influence on the Greek-speaking inhabitants of the Greek mainland.

The Minoan civilization reached its height between 2000 and 1450 B.C. The palace at Knossus, the royal seat of the kings, demonstrates the prosperity and power of this civilization. It was an elaborate structure built around a central courtyard and included numerous private living rooms for the royal family and workshops for making decorated vases, small sculptures, and jewelry. Even bathrooms, with elaborate drains, formed part of the complex. The rooms were decorated with frescoes in bright colors showing sporting events and naturalistic scenes that have led some observers to conclude that the Cretans had a great love of nature. Storerooms in the palace held enormous jars of oil, wine, and grain, presumably paid as taxes to the king.

The centers of Minoan civilization on Crete suffered a sudden and catastrophic collapse around 1450 B.C. The cause of this destruction has been vigorously debated. Some historians believe that a tsunami triggered by a powerful volcanic eruption on the island of Thera was responsible for the devastation. Most historians, however, maintain that the destruction was the result of invasion and pillage by mainland Greeks known as the Mycenaeans.

Mycenaean Greece

The term *Mycenaean* is derived from Mycenae, a remarkable fortified site first excavated by the amateur German archaeologist Heinrich Schliemann. Mycenae was one center in a Mycenaean Greek civilization that flourished between 1600 and 1100 B.C. The Mycenaean Greeks were part of the Indo-European family of peoples (see Chapter 2) who spread from their original Central Asian location into southern and western Europe, India, and Iran. One group entered the territory of Greece from the north around 1900 B.C. and managed to gain control of the Greek mainland and develop a civilization.

Mycenaean civilization reached its high point between 1400 and 1200 B.C. It is especially noted for its fortified palace-centers, which were built on hills surrounded by gigantic stone walls. The royal families lived within the walls of these complexes, while the civilian populations lived in scattered locations outside the walls.

Minoan Crete and Mycenaean Greece

Mycenaean civilization consisted of a number of powerful monarchies centered in the palace complexes, such as those found at Mycenae, Tiryns, Pylos, and Orchomenos. These various centers of power probably formed a loose confederacy of independent states, with Mycenae the strongest. According to tablets written in an early form of Greek script called Linear B, a Mycenaean king used the title of *wanax.* Next in importance to the king were commanders of the army, priests, and bureaucrats who kept careful records. The free citizenry included peasants, soldiers, and artisans, with the lowest rung of the social ladder consisting of serfs and slaves.

The Mycenaeans were above all a warrior people who prided themselves on their heroic deeds in battle. Archaeological evidence also indicates that the Mycenaean monarchies developed an extensive commercial network. Mycenaean pottery has been found throughout the Mediterranean basin, in Syria and Egypt to the east and Sicily and southern Italy to the west. But some scholars believe that the Mycenaeans, led by Mycenae itself, also spread outward militarily, conquering Crete and making it part of the Mycenaean world. Some of the Aegean islands also fell subject to Mycenaean control. The most famous of all the Mycenaeans' supposed military adventures has come down to us in the epic poetry of Homer (see the discussion of Homer in the next section). Did the Mycenaeans, led by Agamemnon, king of Mycenae, sack the city of Troy on the northwestern coast of Asia Minor around 1250 B.C.? Scholars have debated this question ever since Schliemann began his excavations in 1870. Many believe that Homer's account does have a basis in fact, even if the details have become shrouded in mystery.

By the late thirteenth century, Mycenaean Greece was showing signs of serious trouble. Mycenae itself was torched around 1190 B.C., and other Mycenaean centers show similar patterns of destruction as new waves of Greek-speaking invaders moved into Greece from the north. By 1100 B.C, the Mycenaean culture was coming to an end, and the Greek world was entering a new period of considerable insecurity.

Erich Lessing/Art Resource, NY

The Death Mask of Agamemnon. This death mask of thin gold was one of the first objects found by Heinrich Schliemann in his excavation of a series of graves at Mycenae. Schliemann claimed that he had found the mask of Agamemnon, king of Mycenae in Homer's *Iliad.*

The Greeks in a Dark Age (c. 1100–c. 750 B.C.)

After the collapse of the Mycenaean civilization, Greece entered a difficult period in which population declined and food production dropped. Because of the difficult conditions and our lack of knowledge about the period, historians refer to it as the Dark Age. Not until 850 B.C. did farming revive. At the same time, some new developments were forming the basis for a revived Greece.

During the Dark Age, large numbers of Greeks left the mainland and migrated across the Aegean Sea to various islands and especially to the southwestern shore of Asia Minor, a strip of territory that came to be called Ionia. Based on their dialect, the Greeks who resided there were called Ionians. Two other major groups of Greeks settled in established parts of Greece. The Aeolian Greeks, located in northern and central Greece, colonized the large island of Lesbos and the adjacent territory on the northwestern coast of Asia Minor. The Dorians established themselves in southwestern Greece, especially in the Peloponnesus, as well as on some of the southern Aegean islands, including Crete and Rhodes.

Other important activities occurred in this Dark Age as well. Greece saw a revival of some trade and some economic activity besides agriculture. Iron replaced bronze in the construction of weapons, making them affordable for more people. And farming tools made of iron helped reverse the decline in food production. At some point in the eighth century B.C., the Greeks adopted the Phoenician alphabet to give themselves a new system of writing. By reducing all words to a combination of twenty-four letters, the Greeks made learning to read and write simpler. Finally, near the end of this Dark Age appeared the work of Homer, who has come to be viewed as one of the great poets of all time.

Homer and Homeric Greece

The *Iliad* and the *Odyssey*, the first great epic poems of early Greece, were based on stories that had been passed on from generation to generation. It is generally assumed that early in the eighth century B.C., Homer made use of these oral traditions to compose the *Iliad*, his epic of the Trojan War. The war was caused by an act of Paris, a prince of Troy. By kidnapping Helen, wife of the king of the Greek state of Sparta, he outraged all the Greeks. Under the leadership of the Spartan king's brother, Agamemnon of Mycenae, the Greeks attacked Troy. Ten years later, the Greeks finally won and sacked the city.

But the *Iliad* is not so much the story of the war itself as it is the tale of the Greek hero Achilles and how the "wrath of Achilles" led to disaster. As is true of all great literature, the *Iliad* abounds in universal lessons. Underlying them all is the clear message, as one commentator has observed, that "men will still come and go like the generations of leaves in the forest; that he will still be weak, and the gods strong and incalculable; that the quality of a man matters more than his achievement; that violence and recklessness will still lead to disaster, and that this will fall on the innocent as well as on the guilty."[1]

The *Odyssey*, long considered Homer's other masterpiece, is an epic romance that recounts the journeys of one of the Greek heroes, Odysseus, after the fall of Troy and his ultimate return to his wife. But there is a larger vision here as well: the testing of the heroic stature of Odysseus until, by both cunning and patience, he prevails. In the course of this testing, the underlying moral message is "that virtue is a better policy than vice."[2]

Although the *Iliad* and the *Odyssey* supposedly deal with the heroes of the Mycenaean age of the thirteenth century B.C., many scholars believe that they really describe the social conditions of the Dark Age. According to the Homeric view, Greece was a society based on agriculture in which a landed warrior-aristocracy controlled much wealth and exercised considerable power. Homer's world reflects the values of aristocratic heroes.

This, of course, explains the importance of Homer to later generations of Greeks. Homer did not so much record history; he made it. The Greeks regarded the *Iliad* and the *Odyssey* as authentic history as recorded by one poet, Homer. These masterpieces gave the Greeks an ideal past with a cast of heroes and came to be used as standard texts for the education of generations of Greek males. As one Athenian stated, "My father was anxious to see me develop into a good man . . . and as a means to this end he compelled me to memorize all of Homer."[3] The values Homer taught were essentially the aristocratic values of courage and honor (see the box on p. 55). A hero strives

The Slaying of Hector. This scene from a late-fifth-century Athenian vase depicts the final battle between Achilles and the Trojan hero Hector. Achilles is shown lunging forward with his spear to deliver the fatal blow to the Trojan prince, a scene taken from Homer's *Iliad*. The *Iliad* is Homer's masterpiece and was important to later Greeks as a means of teaching the aristocratic values of courage and honor.

Homer's Ideal of Excellence

The *Iliad* and the *Odyssey*, epics that the Greeks believed were written by Homer, were used as basic texts for the education of Greeks for hundreds of years in antiquity. This passage from the *Iliad*, describing a conversation between Hector, prince of Troy, and his wife, Andromache, illustrates the Greek ideal of gaining honor through combat. At the end of the passage, Homer also reveals what became the Greek attitude toward women: women are supposed to spin and weave and take care of their households and their children.

Homer, Iliad

Hector looked at his son and smiled, but said nothing. Andromache, bursting into tears, went up to him and put her hand in his. "Hector," she said, "you are possessed. This bravery of yours will be your end. You do not think of your little boy or your unhappy wife, whom you will make a widow soon. Some day the Achaeans [Greeks] are bound to kill you in a massed attack. And when I lose you I might as well be dead. . . . I have no father, no mother, now. . . . I had seven brothers too at home. In one day all of them went down to Hades' House. The great Achilles of the swift feet killed them all. . . .

"So you, Hector, are father and mother and brother to me, as well as my beloved husband. Have pity on me now; stay here on the tower; and do not make your boy an orphan and your wife a widow. . . ."

"All that, my dear," said the great Hector of the glittering helmet, "is surely my concern. But if I hid myself like a coward and refused to fight, I could never face the Trojans and the Trojan ladies in their trailing gowns. Besides, it would go against the grain, for I have trained myself always, like a good soldier, to take my place in the front line and win glory for my father and myself. . . ."

As he finished, glorious Hector held out his arms to take his boy. But the child shrank back with a cry to the bosom of his girdled nurse, alarmed by his father's appearance. He was frightened by the bronze of the helmet and the horsehair plume that he saw nodding grimly down at him. His father and his lady mother had to laugh. But noble Hector quickly took his helmet off and put the dazzling thing on the ground. Then he kissed his son, dandled him in his arms, and prayed to Zeus and the other gods: "Zeus, and you other gods, grant that this boy of mine may be, like me, pre-eminent in Troy; as strong and brave as I; a mighty king of Ilium. May people say, when he comes back from battle, 'Here is a better man than his father.' Let him bring home the bloodstained armor of the enemy he has killed, and make his mother happy."

Hector handed the boy to his wife, who took him to her fragrant breast. She was smiling through her tears, and when her husband saw this he was moved. He stroked her with his hand and said: "My dear, I beg you not to be too much distressed. No one is going to send me down to Hades before my proper time. But Fate is a thing that no man born of woman, coward or hero, can escape. Go home now, and attend to your own work, the loom and the spindle, and see that the maidservants get on with theirs. War is men's business; and this war is the business of every man in Ilium, myself above all."

for excellence, which the Greeks called *arete*. In the warrior-aristocratic world of Homer, *arete* is won in a struggle or contest. Through his willingness to fight, the hero protects his family and friends, preserves his own honor and that of his family, and earns his reputation. In the Homeric world, aristocratic women, too, were expected to pursue excellence. Penelope, for example, the wife of Odysseus, the hero of the *Odyssey*, remains faithful to her husband and displays great courage and intelligence in preserving their household during her husband's long absence. Upon his return, Odysseus praises her for her excellence: "Madame, there is not a man in the wide world who could find fault with you. For your fame has reached heaven itself, like that of some perfect king, ruling a populous and mighty state with the fear of god in his heart, and upholding the right."[4] Homer gave the Greeks a model of heroism, honor, and nobility. But in time, as a new world of city-states emerged in Greece, new values of cooperation and community also transformed what Greeks learned from Homer.

The World of the Greek City-States (c. 750–c. 500 B.C.)

In the eighth century B.C., Greek civilization burst forth with new energies, beginning the period that historians have called the Archaic Age of Greece. Two major developments stand out in this era: the evolution of the *polis*, or city-state, as the central institution in Greek life and the Greeks' colonization of the Mediterranean and Black Seas.

The Polis

The Greek *polis* (plural, *poleis*) developed slowly during the Dark Age but by the eighth century B.C. had emerged as a unique and fundamental institution in Greek society. In a physical sense, the *polis* encompassed a town or city or even a village and its surrounding countryside. But the town or city or village served as the focus or central point where the citizens of the *polis* could assemble for political, social, and religious activities. In some *poleis*, this central meeting point was a hill, like the Acropolis at Athens, which could serve as a place of refuge during an attack and later in some locales came to be the religious center where temples and public monuments were erected. Below the acropolis would be an agora, an open space that served both as a place where citizens could assemble and as a market.

Poleis varied greatly in size, from a few square miles to a few hundred square miles. The larger ones were the product of consolidation. The territory of Attica, for example, had once had twelve *poleis* but eventually became a single *polis* (Athens) through a process of amalgamation. Athens grew to have a population of more than 300,000 by the fifth century B.C. Most *poleis* were much smaller, consisting of only a few hundred to several thousand people.

Although our word *politics* is derived from the Greek term *polis*, the *polis* itself was much more than just a political institution. It was, above all, a community of citizens in which all political, economic, social, cultural, and religious activities were focused. As a community, the *polis* consisted of citizens with political rights (adult males), citizens with no political rights (women and children), and noncitizens (slaves and resident aliens). All citizens of a *polis* possessed rights, but these rights were coupled with responsibilities. The Greek philosopher Aristotle argued that the citizen did not just belong to himself: "We must rather regard every citizen as belonging to the state." The unity of citizens was important and often meant that states would take an active role in directing the patterns of life. However, the loyalty that citizens had to their *poleis* also had a negative side. *Poleis* distrusted one another, and the division of Greece into fiercely patriotic sovereign units helped bring about its ruin.

A NEW MILITARY SYSTEM: THE HOPLITES

As the *polis* developed, so did a new military system. In earlier times, wars in Greece had been fought by aristocratic cavalry soldiers—nobles on horseback. These aristocrats, who were large landowners, also dominated the political life of their *poleis*. But at the end of the eighth century, a new military order came into being that was based on *hoplites*, heavily armed infantrymen who wore bronze or leather helmets, breastplates, and greaves (shin guards). Each carried a round shield, a short sword, and a thrusting spear about 9 feet long. Hoplites advanced into battle as a unit, shoulder to shoulder, forming a phalanx (a rectangular formation) in tight

The Hoplite Forces. The Greek hoplites were infantrymen equipped with large round shields and long thrusting spears. In battle they advanced in tight phalanx formation and were dangerous opponents as long as this formation remained unbroken. This vase painting from the seventh century B.C. shows two groups of hoplite warriors engaged in battle. The piper on the left is leading another line of soldiers preparing to enter the fray.

order, usually eight ranks deep. As long as the hoplites kept their order, were not outflanked, and did not break, they either secured victory or, at the very least, suffered no harm. The phalanx was easily routed, however, if it broke its order. The safety of the phalanx depended, above all, on the solidarity and discipline of its members. As one seventh-century B.C. poet noted, a good hoplite was "a short man firmly placed upon his legs, with a courageous heart, not to be uprooted from the spot where he plants his legs."[5]

The hoplite force, which apparently developed first in the Peloponnesus, had political as well as military repercussions. The aristocratic cavalry was now outdated. Since each hoplite provided his own armor, men of property, both aristocrats and small farmers, made up the new phalanx. Initially, this created a bond between the aristocrats and peasants, which minimized class conflict and enabled the aristocrats to dominate their societies. In the long run, however, those who could become hoplites and fight for the state could also challenge aristocratic control.

Colonization and the Growth of Trade

Greek expansion overseas was another major development of the Archaic Age. Between 750 and 550 B.C., large numbers of Greeks left their homeland to settle in distant lands. Poverty and land hunger created by the growing gulf between rich and poor, overpopulation, and the development of trade were all factors that led to the establishment of colonies. Some Greek colonies were simply trading posts or centers for the transshipment of goods to Greece. Most were larger settlements that included good agricultural land taken from the native populations found in those areas. Each colony was founded as a *polis* and was usually independent of the mother *polis* (*metropolis*) that had established it.

In the western Mediterranean, new Greek settlements were established along the coastline of southern Italy, including the cities of Tarentum (Taranto) and Neapolis (Naples) (see Map 3.2). So many Greek communities were established in southern Italy that the Romans later called it *Magna Graecia* ("Great Greece"). An important city was

Map 3.2 Greece and Its Colonies in the Archaic Age. Impelled by overpopulation and poverty, Greeks spread out from their homelands during the Archaic Age, establishing colonies in many parts of the Mediterranean. The colonies were independent city-states that traded with the older Greek city-states. ■ What aspects of the colonies' locations facilitated trade between them and city-states in Greece?

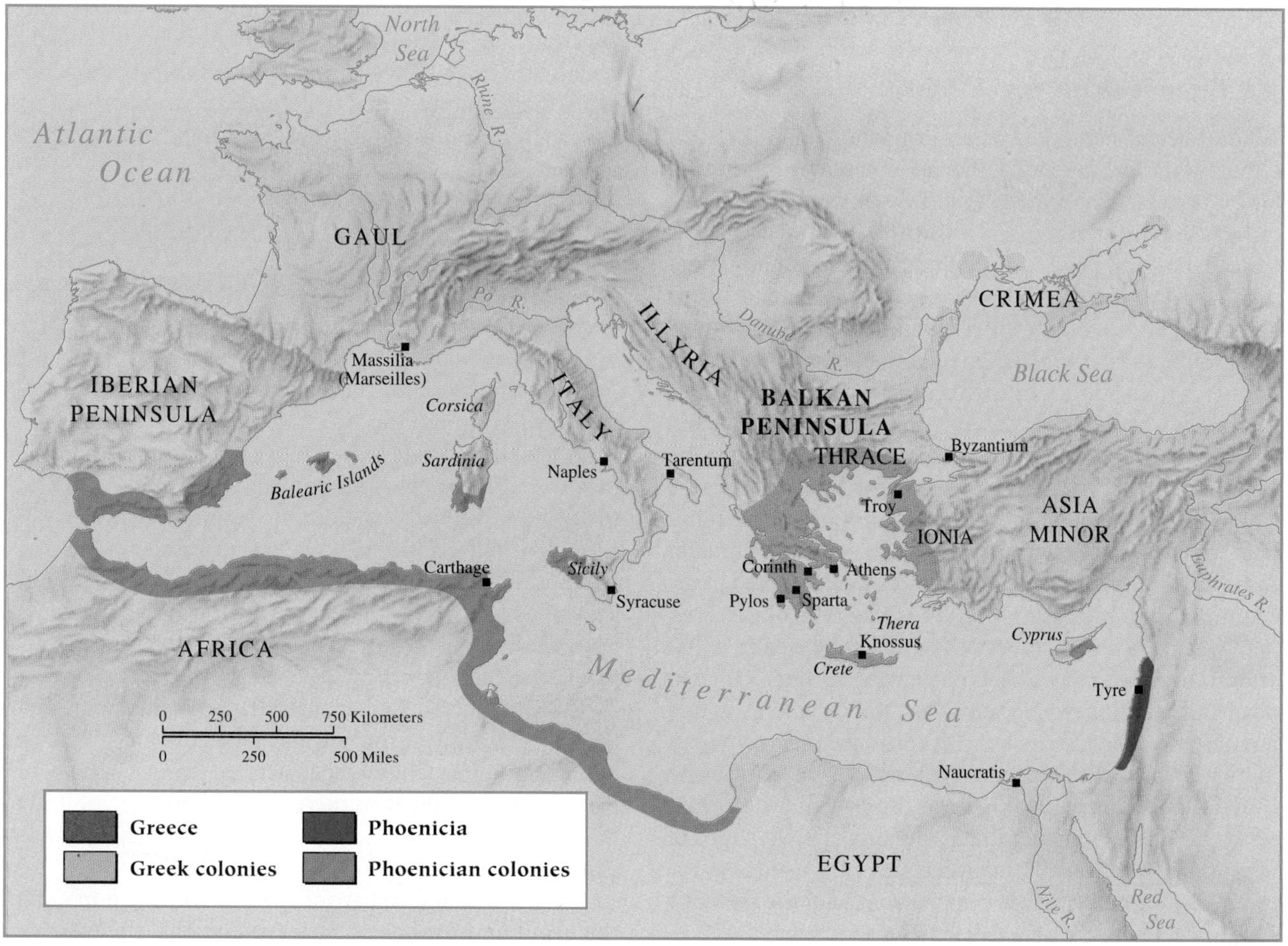

founded at Syracuse in eastern Sicily in 734 B.C. by the city-state of Corinth, one of the most active Greek states in establishing colonies. Greek settlements were also established in southern France (Massilia—modern Marseilles), eastern Spain, and northern Africa west of Egypt.

To the north, the Greeks set up colonies in Thrace, where they sought good agricultural lands to grow grains. Greeks also settled along the shores of the Black Sea and secured the approaches to it with cities on the Hellespont and Bosporus, most notably Byzantium, site of the later Constantinople (Istanbul). A trading post was established in Egypt, giving the Greeks access to both the products and the advanced culture of the East.

The establishment of these settlements over such a wide area had important effects. For one thing, they contributed to the diffusion of culture as the Greeks spread their culture throughout the Mediterranean basin. The later Romans, after all, made their first contact with the Greeks through the settlements in southern Italy. In addition, colonization led to increased trade and industry. The Greeks sent their pottery, wine, and olive oil to these areas; in return, they received grains and metals from the west and fish, timber, wheat, metals, and slaves from the Black Sea region. The expansion of trade and industry created a new group of rich men in many *poleis* who desired political privileges commensurate with their wealth but found them impossible to gain because of the power of the ruling aristocrats. The desire for change on the part of this group soon led to political crisis in many Greek states.

Tyranny in the Greek Polis

When the *polis* emerged as an important institution in Greece in the eighth century, monarchical power waned, and kings virtually disappeared in most Greek states or survived only as ceremonial figures with little or no real power. Instead, political power passed into the hands of local aristocracies. But increasing divisions between rich and poor and the aspirations of newly rising industrial and commercial groups in Greek *poleis* opened the door to the rise of tyrants in the seventh and sixth centuries B.C. They were not necessarily oppressive or wicked as our word *tyrant* connotes. Greek tyrants were rulers who seized power by force and who were not subject to the law. Support for the tyrants came from the new rich, who made their money in trade and industry, as well as from poor peasants, who were in debt to landholding aristocrats. Both groups were opposed to the domination of political power by aristocratic oligarchies.

Tyrants usually achieved power by a local coup d'état and maintained it by using mercenary soldiers. Once in power, they built new marketplaces, temples, and walls that not only glorified the city but also enhanced their own popularity. Tyrants also favored the interests of merchants and traders by encouraging the founding of new colonies, developing new coinage, and establishing new systems of weights and measures. In many instances, they added to the prosperity of their cities. By their patronage of the arts, they encouraged cultural development.

One of the most famous examples of tyranny can be found in Corinth. During the eighth and early seventh centuries B.C., Corinth had become one of the most prosperous states in Greece under the rule of an oligarchy led by the Bacchiad family. Their violent activities, however, made them unpopular and led Cypselus, a member of the family, to overthrow the oligarchy and assume sole control of Corinth.

Cypselus was so well liked that he could rule without a bodyguard. During his tyranny, Corinth prospered by exporting vast quantities of pottery and founding new colonies to expand its trade empire. Cypselus' son, Periander, took control of Corinth after his father's death but ruled with such cruelty that shortly after his death in 585 B.C., his own son, who succeeded him, was killed, and a new oligarchy soon ruled Corinth.

As in Corinth, tyranny elsewhere in Greece was largely extinguished by the end of the sixth century B.C. The children and grandchildren of tyrants, who tended to be corrupted by their inherited power and wealth, often became cruel and unjust rulers, making tyranny no longer seem such a desirable institution. Its very nature as a system outside the law seemed contradictory to the ideal of law in a Greek community. Tyranny did not last, but it played a significant role in the evolution of Greek history. The rule of narrow aristocratic oligarchies was destroyed. Once the tyrants were eliminated, the door was opened to the participation of more people in the affairs of the community. Although this trend culminated in the development of democracy in some communities, in other states expanded oligarchies of one kind or another managed to remain in power. Greek states exhibited considerable variety in their governmental structures; this can perhaps best be seen by examining the two most famous and most powerful Greek city-states, Sparta and Athens.

Sparta

The Greeks of Sparta and Athens spoke different dialects and developed different political systems. The Spartans sought stability and conformity and emphasized order. The Athenians allowed for individual differences and stressed freedom. Although the two states shared a common heritage, their differences grew so large in their own minds that they were ultimately willing to engage in a life-and-death struggle to support their separate realities. When they did so, the entire Greek world was the real loser.

Located in the southeastern Peloponnesus, in an area known as Laconia, the Spartans had originally occupied four small villages that eventually became unified into a single *polis*. This unification made Sparta a strong community in Laconia and enabled the Spartans to conquer their neighboring Laconians and subject them to serfdom. Known as helots (the name is derived from a Greek word for "capture"), these conquered Laconians were bound to the land and forced to work on farms and as household servants for the Spartans.

When the land in Laconia proved unable to maintain the growing number of Spartan citizens, the Spartans

The Lycurgan Reforms

To maintain their control over the helots, the Spartans instituted the reforms that created their military state. In this account of the lawgiver Lycurgus, the Greek historian Plutarch discusses the effect of these reforms on the treatment and education of boys.

Plutarch, Lycurgus

Lycurgus was of another mind; he would not have masters bought out of the market for his young Spartans, . . . nor was it lawful, indeed, for the father himself to breed up the children after his own fancy; but as soon as they were seven years old they were to be enrolled in certain companies and classes, where they all lived under the same order and discipline, doing their exercises and taking their play together. Of these, he who showed the most conduct and courage was made captain; they had their eyes always upon him, obeyed his orders, and underwent patiently whatsoever punishment he inflicted; so that the whole course of their education was one continued exercise of a ready and perfect obedience. The old men, too, were spectators of their performances, and often raised quarrels and disputes among them, to have a good opportunity of finding out their different characters, and of seeing which would be valiant, which a coward, when they should come to more dangerous encounters. Reading and writing they gave them just enough to serve their turn; their chief care was to make them good subjects, and to teach them to endure pain and conquer in battle. To this end, as they grew in years, their discipline was proportionately increased; their heads were close-clipped, they were accustomed to go barefoot, and for the most part to play naked.

After they were twelve years old, they were no longer allowed to wear any undergarments, they had one coat to serve them a year; their bodies were hard and dry, with but little acquaintance of baths and unguents; these human indulgences they were allowed only on some few particular days in the year. They lodged together in little bands upon beds made of the rushes which grew by the banks of the river Eurotas, which they were to break off with their hands with a knife; if it were winter, they mingled some thistledown with their rushes, which it was thought had the property of giving warmth. By the time they were come to this age there was not any of the more hopeful boys who had not a lover to bear him company. The old men, too, had an eye upon them, coming often to the grounds to hear and see them contend either in wit or strength with one another, and this as seriously . . . as if they were their fathers, their tutors, or their magistrates; so that there scarcely was any time or place without some one present to put them in mind of their duty, and punish them if they had neglected it.

[Spartan boys were also encouraged to steal their food.] They stole, too, all other meat they could lay their hands on, looking out and watching all opportunities, when people were asleep or more careless than usual. If they were caught, they were not only punished with whipping, but hunger, too, being reduced to their ordinary allowance, which was but very slender, and so contrived on purpose, that they might set about to help themselves, and be forced to exercise their energy and address. This was the principal design of their hard fare.

looked for land nearby and, beginning around 730 B.C., undertook the conquest of neighboring Messenia despite its larger size and population. Messenia possessed a spacious, fertile plain ideal for growing grain. After its conquest, which was not completed until the seventh century B.C., the Messenians were reduced to serfdom and forced to work for the Spartans. To ensure control over their conquered Laconian and Messenian helots, the Spartans made a conscious decision to create a military state.

Sometime between 800 and 600 B.C., the Spartans instituted a series of reforms that are associated with the name of the lawgiver Lycurgus (see the box above). Although historians are not sure that Lycurgus ever existed, there is no doubt about the result of the reforms that were made: Sparta was transformed into a perpetual military camp.

THE NEW SPARTA

The lives of Spartans were now rigidly organized. At birth, each child was examined by state officials who decided whether it was fit to live. Those judged unfit were exposed to the elements and left to die. Boys were taken from their mothers at the age of seven and put under control of the state. They lived in barracks, where they were subjected to harsh discipline to make them tough and given an education that stressed military training and obedience to authority. At twenty, Spartan males were enrolled in the army for regular military service. Although allowed to marry, they continued to live in the barracks and ate their meals in public dining halls with their fellow soldiers. Meals were simple; the famous Spartan black broth consisted of a piece of pork boiled in blood, salt, and vinegar, causing a visitor who ate in a public mess to remark that he now understood why Spartans were not afraid to die. At thirty, Spartan males were recognized as mature and allowed to vote in the assembly and live at home, but they remained in the army until the age of sixty.

While their husbands remained in military barracks until age thirty, Spartan women lived at home. Because of this separation, Spartan women had greater freedom of movement and greater power in the household than was common for women elsewhere in Greece. They were encouraged to exercise and remain fit to bear and raise healthy children. Like the men, Spartan women engaged in athletic exercises in the nude. At solemn feasts, the young women would march naked in processions, and in the presence of the young men, they would sing songs about those who had showed special gallantry or cowardice on the battlefield. Many Spartan women upheld the strict Spartan values, expecting their husbands and sons to be brave in war. The story is told that as a Spartan mother was burying her son, an old woman came up to her and said, "You poor woman, what a misfortune." "No," replied the other, "because I bore him so that he might die for Sparta and that is what has happened, as I wished."[6] Another Spartan woman saw her son off to war by telling him to come back carrying his shield or carried on it.

The Spartan social structure was rigidly organized. At the summit were the *Spartiates*—full Spartan citizens. Each Spartan citizen owned a piece of land, worked by the helots, to provide economic sustenance. With their material needs provided for them, Spartan citizens could dedicate themselves to their duties as a ruling class. Below the *Spartiates* were the *perioeci.* Though free, they did not possess the privileges of citizenship and served as small merchants and artisans. They were subject to military duty, however. At the bottom of the social scale were the helots, perpetually bound to the land. They were assigned to the lands of the Spartan citizens. The helots farmed the land and gave their masters one-half of the produce. According to one seventh-century Spartan poet, helots worked "like donkeys exhausted under heavy loads." A secret police force lived among them and was permitted to kill any helot considered dangerous. To legalize this murder, the state officially declared war on the helots at the beginning of each year.

THE SPARTAN STATE

The so-called Lycurgan reforms also reorganized the Spartan government, creating an oligarchy. Two kings from different families were primarily responsible for military affairs and served as the leaders of the Spartan army on its campaigns. Moreover, the kings served as the supreme priests within the state religion and had some role in foreign policy.

The two kings shared power with a body called the *gerousia*, a council of elders. It consisted of twenty-eight citizens over the age of sixty, who were elected for life, and the two kings. The primary task of the *gerousia* was to prepare proposals that would be presented to the *apella*, an assembly of all male citizens. The assembly did not debate but only voted on the proposals put before it by the *gerousia*; rarely did the assembly reject these proposals. The assembly also elected the *gerousia* and another body known as the *ephors.*

To balance the power of the kings and the *gerousia*, the Spartan state created a college of five *ephors.* Elected annually, their duties included convening the *gerousia* and supervising the education of youth and the conduct of all citizens. They also served as judges in all civil cases and could even bring charges against a king for wrongdoing.

To make their new military state secure, the Spartans deliberately turned their backs on the outside world. Foreigners, who might bring in new ideas, were discouraged from visiting Sparta. Nor were Spartans, except for military reasons, encouraged to travel abroad where they might pick up new ideas. Trade and commerce were likewise minimized. Spartan citizens were discouraged from pursuing philosophy, literature, the arts, or any subject that might foster novel thoughts dangerous to the stability of the state. The art of war and ruling was the Spartan ideal. All other arts were frowned on.

In the sixth century, Sparta used its military might and the fear it inspired to gain greater control of the Peloponnesus by organizing an alliance of almost all the Peloponnesian states. Sparta's strength enabled it to dominate this Peloponnesian League and determine its policies. By 500 B.C., the Spartans had organized a powerful military state that maintained order and stability in the Peloponnesus. Raised from early childhood to believe that total loyalty to the Spartan state was the basic reason for existence, the Spartans viewed their strength as justification for their militaristic ideals and regimented society.

Athens

By 700 B.C., Athens had established a unified *polis* on the peninsula of Attica. Although early Athens had been ruled by a monarchy, by the seventh century B.C., it had fallen under the control of its aristocrats. They possessed the best land and controlled political and religious life by means of a council of nobles called the Areopagus, assisted by a board of nine archons. Since the archons served only one year and entered the Areopagus afterward, the latter body held the real power. Although there was an *ecclesia* or assembly of full citizens, it possessed few powers.

Near the end of the seventh century B.C., Athens faced political turmoil because of serious economic problems. Many Athenian farmers found themselves sold into slavery when they were unable to repay the loans they had borrowed from their aristocratic neighbors, pledging themselves as collateral. Over and over, there were cries to cancel the debts and give land to the poor. Athens seemed on the verge of civil war.

Hoping to avoid tyranny, the ruling Athenian aristocrats responded to this crisis by choosing Solon, a reform-minded aristocrat, as sole archon in 594 B.C. and giving him full power to make reforms. Solon canceled all current land debts, outlawed new loans based on humans as collateral, and freed people who had fallen into slavery for debt. He refused, however, to carry out the redistribution of the land and hence failed to deal with the basic cause of the economic crisis.

Like his economic reforms, Solon's political measures were also a compromise. Though by no means eliminating the power of the aristocracy, they opened the door to the participation of new people, especially the nonaristocratic wealthy, in the government. Solon now divided all Athenian citizens into four classes on the basis of wealth. Only men in the first two classes (the wealthiest classes) could hold the archonship and be members of the Areopagus. Men in the third class could be elected to a new council of four hundred called the *boule*, whose function was to prepare the agenda for the assembly. The fourth (and poorest) class, though not allowed to hold any political offices, could now vote in the assembly. All four classes could also sit in the new popular court (the *heliaea*) instituted by Solon to hear appeals from cases tried before the archons.

THE MOVE TO TYRANNY

Solon's reforms, though popular, did not truly solve Athens's problems. Aristocratic factions continued to vie for power, and the poorer peasants resented Solon's failure to institute land redistribution. Internal strife finally led to the very institution Solon had hoped to avoid—tyranny. Pisistratus, an aristocrat and a distant relative of Solon, seized power in 560 B.C. and made himself a tyrant.

Pisistratus did not tamper very much with the constitution. The assembly, councils, and courts continued to function while he made sure that his supporters were elected as magistrates and council members. Pisistratus curried favor with an ambitious building program, aimed at beautifying the city. Pursuing a foreign policy that aided Athenian trade, Pisistratus maintained the support of the mercantile and industrial classes. Pisistratus' mild tyranny was popular with many Athenians, but the policies of his son Hippias (527–510 B.C.) eventually produced a reaction, and the Athenians sent Hippias into exile and ended the tyranny. Although the aristocrats attempted to reestablish an aristocratic oligarchy, Cleisthenes, an aristocratic reformer, opposed this plan and, with the backing of the Athenian people, gained the upper hand in 508 B.C. The reforms of Cleisthenes now established the basis for Athenian democracy.

THE REFORMS OF CLEISTHENES

A major aim of Cleisthenes' reforms was to weaken the power of traditional localities and regions, which had provided the foundation for aristocratic strength. He enrolled all citizens in ten new tribes, each of which contained inhabitants located in the country districts of Attica, the coastal areas, and Athens. The ten tribes thus contained a cross section of the population and reflected all of Attica, a move that diminished local interests and increased loyalty to the *polis*. Each of the ten tribes chose fifty members by lot each year for a new council of five hundred, which was responsible for the administration of both foreign and financial affairs and prepared the business that would be handled by the assembly. This assembly of all male citizens had final authority in the passing of laws after free and open debate; thus Cleisthenes' reforms strengthened the central role of the assembly of citizens in the Athenian political system.

The reforms of Cleisthenes laid the foundations for Athenian democracy. More changes would come in the fifth century when the Athenians themselves would begin to use the word *democracy* (from the Greek words *demas*, "people," and *kratia*, "power") to describe their system. By 500 B.C., Athens was more united than it had been and was about to assume a more important role in Greek affairs.

Greek Culture in the Archaic Age

The period after the Dark Age witnessed a revitalization of Greek life that is also evident in Greek art and literature. Some aspects of Archaic Greek culture, such as pottery and sculpture, were especially influenced by the East. Greek sculpture, particularly that of the Ionian Greek settlements in southwestern Asia Minor, demonstrates the impact of the considerably older Egyptian civilization. There we first see the life-size stone statues of young male nudes known as *kouros* figures. The *kouros* bears considerable

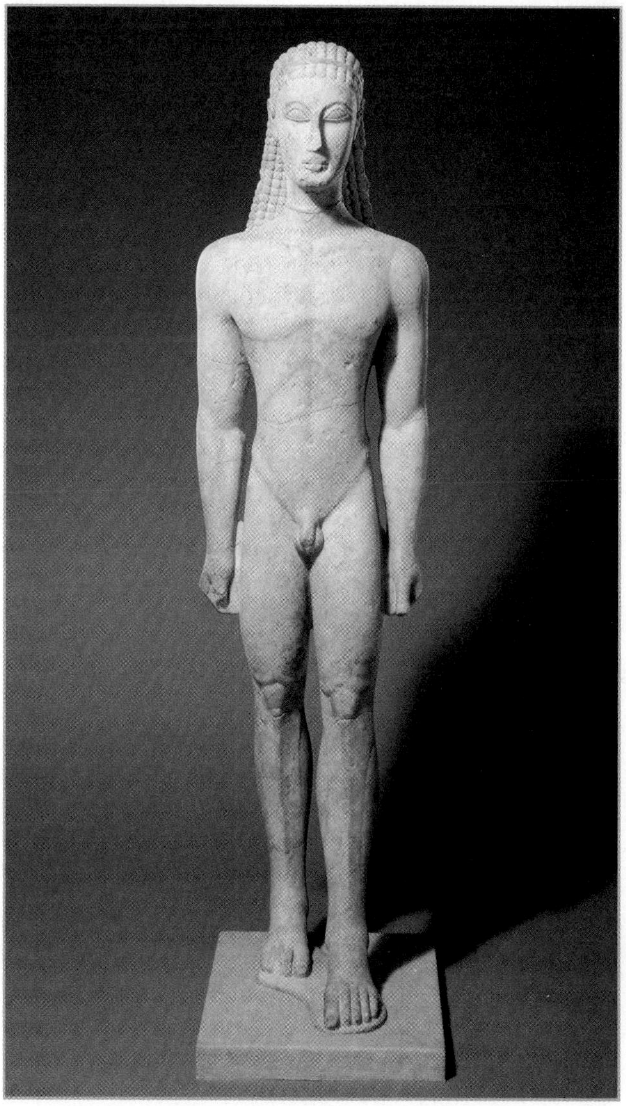

The Metropolitan Museum of Art, New York, Fletcher Fund, 1932 (32.11.1)

Kouros. This statue of a young male nude is from around 600 B.C., making it an early example of *kouros* sculpture. These statues, which were placed in temples (along with companion figures of young women, known as *korai*), were meant to be representations of the faithful dedicated to the gods.

CHRONOLOGY

Achaic Greece: Sparta and Athens

Sparta	
Conquest of Messenia	c. 730–710 B.C.
Beginning of Peloponnesian League	c. 560–550 B.C.
Athens	
Solon's reforms	594–593 B.C.
Tyranny of Pisistratus	c. 560–556 and 546–527 B.C.
Deposition of Hippias—end of tyranny	510 B.C.
Cleisthenes' reforms	c. 508–501 B.C.

resemblance to Egyptian statues of the New Kingdom. The figures are not realistic, but stiff, with a slight smile; one leg is advanced ahead of the other, and the arms are held rigidly at the sides of the body.

Greek literature of the seventh century is perhaps best known for its lyric poetry. The lyric is considerably shorter than epic poetry (such as Homer's) and focuses on personal emotions, usually the power of love and its impact on human lives. Later Greeks acknowledged Sappho as their greatest female lyric poet (see the box on p. 63). Born in the seventh century, Sappho lived on the island of Lesbos in the Aegean Sea, where she taught music and poetry to her young charges. Many of her poems are love songs to her female students. Our word *lesbian* is derived from Sappho's island of Lesbos. Sappho, like many upper-class Greeks, accepted that homosexual and heterosexual feelings could exist in the same individual. Sappho was a wife and a mother who also wrote poems about love between men and between women.

Archaic Greece is also known for poets who reflected the lifestyles of both aristocrats and peasants. A wide gulf, however, separated the wealthy aristocrat with his large landed estates from the poor peasants and small farmers who eked out their existence as best they could. Hesiod, a poet from Boeotia in central Greece who lived around 700 B.C., wrote a lengthy epic poem titled *Works and Days.* Himself a farmer, Hesiod distrusted aristocrats and looked down on what he considered the aristocratic emphasis on pride and war. One of his aims was to show that the gods punished injustice and that the way to success was to work: "Famine and blight do not beset the just, who till their well-worked fields and feast. The earth supports them lavishly." *Works and Days* is the first paean to work in Western literature.

Hesiod emphasized the importance of two things to the farmer's success. It depended, first of all, on proper respect for and treatment of divine forces: "Please the gods with incense and libations, when you go to bed, and when the holy light returns, that they may favor you, with gracious hearts and spirits, so that you may buy the lands of other men, and they may not buy yours." But success depended on more than prayer; therefore:

. . . you must learn to organize your work
So you may have full barns at harvest time.
From working, men grow rich in flocks and gold
And dearer to the deathless gods. In work
There is no shame; shame is in idleness.
And if you work, the lazy man will soon
Envy your wealth: a rich man can become
Famous and good. No matter what your luck,
To work is better; turn your foolish mind
From other men's possessions to your own,
And earn your living, as I tell you to.[7]

To Hesiod, hard work and honesty were the keys to success.

Theognis of Megara described a way of life considerably different from Hesiod's. Theognis was an aristocrat who lived and wrote primarily in the sixth century B.C. Because of revolutionary upheaval, he, like other aristocrats in sixth-century *poleis,* lost his position and probably his wealth. Sent into exile, he became a bitter man. In his poetry, he portrayed aristocrats as the only good people who are distinguished from others by their natural intelligence, virtue, honor, and moderation. The lower classes or common people were by nature bad and debased:

Only a fool does favors for the base;
You'd do as well to sow the gray salt sea.
No crop of corn would come up from the deep,
No gratitude, no favors from the base.
The scum are never sated. If you slip,
Just once, their former friendship melts away.
But put a gentleman once in your debt,
You have a friend for life; he won't forget.

Aristocrats, then, should associate only with other aristocrats: "Avoid low company, mix only with the better sort of men. . . . From them you will learn goodness. Men of little worth will spoil the natural beauty of your birth."[8] The poems of Theognis show clearly the political views and biases of a typical sixth-century aristocrat.

The High Point of Greek Civilization: Classical Greece

Classical Greece is the name given to the period of Greek history from around 500 B.C. to the conquest of Greece by the Macedonian king Philip II in 338 B.C. It was a period of brilliant achievement, much of it associated with the flowering of democracy in Athens under the leadership of Pericles. Many of the lasting contributions of the Greeks occurred during this period. The age began with a mighty confrontation between the Greek states and the mammoth Persian Empire.

The Lyric Poetry of Sappho

These love poems are examples of the work of Sappho of Lesbos, regarded as one of Greece's greatest lyric poets. She wrote directly about her personal world of emotions. Sappho is an unusual figure, an independent woman in a world dominated by males. Her attitude toward the Trojan War, as seen in the poem "To Anaktoria," is quite different from that found in Homer's *Iliad*.

Sappho, "To Anaktoria, Now a Soldier's Wife in Lydia"

Some say cavalry and some would claim
infantry or a fleet of long oars
is the supreme sight on the black earth.
I say it is

the girl you love. And easily proved.
Did not Helen, who was queen of mortal
beauty, choose as first among mankind
the very scourge

of Trojan honor? Haunted by Love
she forgot kinsmen, her own dear child
and wandered off to a remote country.
O weak and fitful

woman bending before any man:
so Anaktoria, although you are
far, do not forget your loving friends.
And I for one

would rather listen to your soft step
and see your radiant face—than watch
all the dazzling horsemen and armored
hoplites of Lydia.

"To Atthis"

So I shall never see Atthis again,
and really I long to be dead,
although she too cried bitterly

when she left and she said to me,
"Ah, what a nightmare we've suffered.
Sappho, I swear I go unwillingly."

And I answered, "Go, and be happy.
But remember me, for surely you
know how I worshiped you. If not,

then I want you to remember all
the exquisite days we too shared;
how when near me you would adorn

your hanging locks with violets and
tiny roses and your sapling throat
with necklets of a hundred blossoms;

how your young flesh was rich with kingly
myrrh as you leaned near my breasts on
the soft couch where delicate girls

served us all an Ionian could desire;
how we went to every hill, brook,
and holy place, and when early spring

filled the woods with noises of birds
and a choir of nightingales—we two
in solitude were wandering there."

The Challenge of Persia

As Greek civilization grew and expanded throughout the Mediterranean, it was inevitable that it would come into contact with the Persian Empire to the east. In his play *The Persians*, the Greek playwright Aeschylus reflected what some Greeks perceived to be the essential difference between themselves and the Persians. The Persian queen, curious to find out more about the Athenians, asks: "Who commands them? Who is shepherd of their host?" The chorus responds: "They are slaves to none, nor are they subject."[9] Thus at least some Greeks saw the struggle with the Persians as a contest between freedom and slavery.

The Ionian Greek cities in southwestern Asia Minor had already fallen subject to the Persian Empire by the mid-sixth century B.C. (see Chapter 2). But the Greek cities were restless under Persian control, and a revolt of the Ionian cities, led by Miletus, broke out against the Persians in 499 B.C. The Athenians sent twenty ships to aid the revolt and helped the Milesians capture and burn Sardis, the Persian capital of the Lydian satrapy. The success was temporary, however, and the Persians managed to sack Miletus and reestablish control. By 494 B.C., the rebellion had been suppressed. The Persian ruler Darius now decided to attack the mainland Greeks, in part, no doubt, to gain revenge for the Athenian action but also to expand his empire westward. In 490 B.C., a Persian expedition was sent to Greece.

The Persians sailed across the Aegean, captured Eretria on the island of Euboea across from Attica, and then transferred their army to the plain of Marathon, only 26 miles from Athens (see Map 3.3). The Athenians, aided by the Plataeans (from a neighboring town in Boeotia), confronted the Persians without additional assistance. The two armies were quite different. The Persians, with their light-armed troops, were more mobile and flexible and relied heavily on missiles; the Greek hoplites were armed with heavy shields and relied on spear thrusts at close range. The Athenians and Plataeans were clearly outnumbered, but led by Miltiades, one of the Athenian leaders who insisted

The Battle of Marathon

The Battle of Marathon (490 B.C.) was an important event in the struggle between the Greeks and the Persians. The defeat of the mighty Persians gave Athenian confidence a tremendous boost. In *The Persian Wars,* the Greek historian Herodotus gave an account of this momentous battle.

■ *Herodotus,* The Persian Wars

So when the battle was set in array, and the victims showed themselves favorable, instantly the Athenians, so soon as they were let go, charged the barbarians at a run. Now the distance between the two armies was little short of a mile. The Persians, therefore, when they saw the Greeks coming on at speed, made ready to receive them, although it seemed to them that the Athenians were bereft of their senses, and bent upon their own destruction; for they saw a mere handful of men coming on at a run without either horsemen or archers. Such was the opinion of the barbarians; but the Athenians in close array fell upon them, and fought in a manner worthy of being recorded. They were the first of the Greeks, so far as I know, who introduced the custom of charging the enemy at a run, and they were likewise the first who dared to look upon the Median garb, and to face men clad in that fashion. Until this time the very name of the Medes had been a terror to the Greeks to hear.

The two armies fought together on the plain of Marathon for a length of time; and in the mid battle, where the Persians themselves and the Sacae had their place, the barbarians were victorious, and broke and pursued the Greeks into the inner country; but on the two wings the Athenians and the Plataeans defeated the enemy. Having so done, they suffered the routed barbarians to fly at their ease, and joining the two wings in one, fell upon those who had broken their own center, and fought and conquered them. These likewise fled, and now the Athenians hung upon the runaways and cut them down, chasing them all the way to the shore, on reaching which they laid hold of the ships and called for fire. . . .

After the full of the moon 2,000 Lacedaemonians [Spartans] came to Athens. So eager had they been to arrive in time, that they took but three days to reach Attica from Sparta. They came, however, too late for the battle; yet, as they had a longing to behold the Medes, they continued their march to Marathon and there viewed the slain. Then, after giving the Athenians all praise for their achievement, they departed and returned home.

on attacking, the Greek hoplites charged across the plain of Marathon and crushed the Persian forces (see the box above). The Persians did not mount another attack against mainland Greece for ten years.

In the meantime, Athens had acquired a new leader, Themistocles, who persuaded his fellow citizens to pursue a new military policy, namely, the development of a navy. The Athenians used a new vein of silver from Laurium to finance the construction of ships and new port facilities. By 480 B.C., Athens had produced a navy of about two hundred vessels, primarily triremes (ships with three banks of oars).

A revolt in Egypt, compounded by the death of Darius in 486 B.C., kept the Persians from mounting another attack on Greece. Xerxes, the new Persian monarch, was bent on revenge and expansion, however. Some of the Greeks prepared by forming a defensive league under Spartan leadership, although many Greek states remained neutral; some even fought on the Persian side.

The Greek Trireme. The trireme became the standard warship of ancient Greece. Highly maneuverable, fast, and outfitted with metal prows, Greek triremes were especially effective at ramming enemy ships. The bas-relief shows a fifth-century B.C. Athenian trireme. The photo shows the *Olympias,* a trireme reconstructed by the Greek navy.

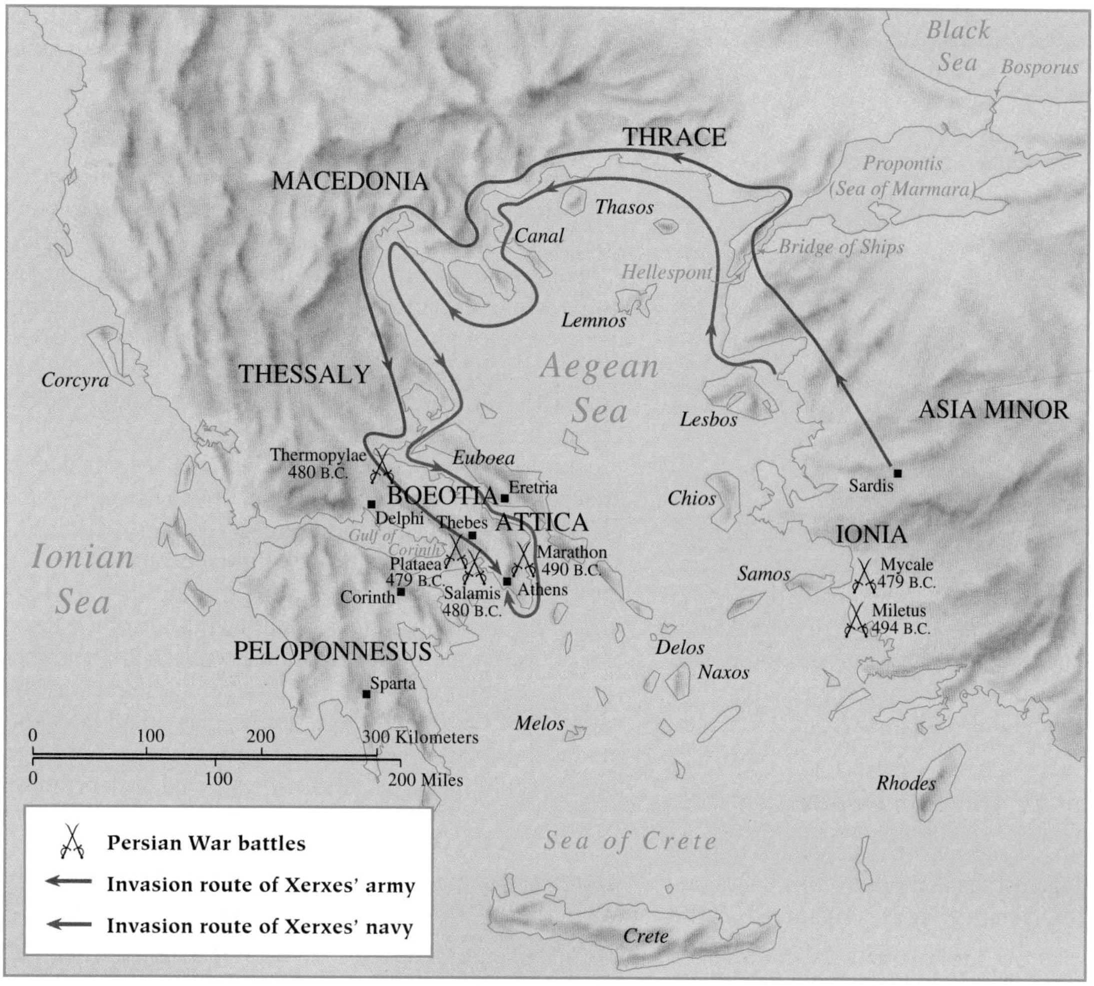

Map 3.3 The Persian Wars. The Athenians defeated Persia in 490 B.C. at Marathon. Athens later led a coalition of Greek city-states that decisively defeated Xerxes' navy at the Battle of Salamis in 480 B.C., leading Xerxes to withdraw most of his troops back to Asia. ■ How far did the Persian army have to walk to get to Athens, and through what types of terrain?

Xerxes and the Persians undertook their invasion in 480 B.C. Their military forces were massive: close to 150,000 troops, almost seven hundred naval ships, and hundreds of supply ships to feed their large army. The Persians crossed the Hellespont by a bridge of ships and then moved through Thrace and Macedonia on their way into Greece. The Greek plan, as it evolved, was to fight a delaying action at the pass of Thermopylae along the main road from Thessaly into Boeotia, probably to give the Greek fleet of three hundred ships at Artemisium, off northern Euboea, the chance to fight the Persian fleet. The Greeks knew that the Persian army depended on the fleet for supplies. A Greek force numbering close to nine thousand, under the leadership of the Spartan king Leonidas and his contingent of three hundred Spartans, held off the Persian army at Thermopylae for two days. The Spartan troops were especially brave. When told that Persian arrows would darken the sky in battle, one Spartan warrior supposedly responded, "That is good news. We will fight in the shade!" Unfortunately for the Greeks, a traitor told the Persians how to use a mountain path to outflank the Greek force. King Leonidas and the three hundred Spartans fought to the last man.

The Athenians, now threatened by the onslaught of the Persian forces, decided to abandon Athens and evacuated the population of Attica to the offshore island of Salamis. Meanwhile, the Greek fleet remained in the straits off Salamis while the Persians sacked Athens. The Peloponnesians wanted the Greeks to retreat to the Peloponnesus and the Greek ships to move to the isthmus as well. Themistocles' refusal and his threat to withdraw the Athenian ships altogether if a fight was not made forced the ships to remain and set up the naval Battle of Salamis. Although the Greeks were outnumbered, they managed to outmaneuver the Persian fleet (mostly Phoenicians and Ionians) and decisively defeated them. The Persians still had their army and much of their fleet intact, but Xerxes, frightened at the prospect of another Ionian revolt, decided to return to Asia. He left a Persian force in Thessaly under his general Mardonius.

Early in 479 B.C., the Greeks formed the largest Greek army seen up to that time. The Athenians forced the Spartans

CHRONOLOGY

The Persian Wars

Persian control of Greek cities in southwestern Asia Minor	By 540s B.C.
Rebellion of Greek cities in Asia Minor	499–494 B.C.
Battle of Marathon	490 B.C.
Xerxes invades Greece	480–479 B.C.
Battles of Thermopylae and Salamis	480 B.C.
Battles of Plataea and Mycale	479 B.C.

to move north of the Peloponnesus and take on the Persians at Plataea, northwest of Athens, where the Greek forces decisively defeated the Persian army. The remnants of the Persian forces returned to Asia. At the same time, the Greeks destroyed much of the Persian fleet in a naval battle at Mycale in Ionia. The Greeks were overjoyed at their victory but remained cautious. Would the Persians try again?

The Growth of an Athenian Empire

After the defeat of the Persians, Athens stepped in to provide new leadership against the Persians by forming a confederation called the Delian League. Organized in the winter of 478–477 B.C., the Delian League was dominated by the Athenians from the beginning. Its main headquarters was the island of Delos, sacred to the Ionian Greeks, but its chief officials, including the treasurers and commanders of the fleet, were Athenians. Athens also provided most of the league's three hundred ships. While the larger states in the league, such as Lesbos, Samos, and Chios, contributed ships, the smaller communities made payments in money.

Under the leadership of the Athenians, the Delian League pursued the attack against the Persian Empire. Virtually all of the Greek states in the Aegean were liberated from Persian control, and the Persian fleet and army were decisively defeated in 469 B.C. in southern Asia Minor. Arguing that the Persian threat was now over, some members of the Delian League wished to withdraw. Naxos did so in 470 and Thasos in 465 B.C. The Athenians responded vigorously. They attacked both states, destroyed their walls, took over their fleets, eliminated their liberty, and forced them to pay tribute. "No secession" became Athenian policy. The Delian League was rapidly becoming an instrument of Athenian imperialism and the nucleus of an Athenian empire.

THE AGE OF PERICLES

At home, Athenians favored the new imperial policy, especially after 461 B.C., when a political faction, led by a young aristocrat named Pericles, triumphed. Under Pericles, Athens embarked on a policy of expanding democracy at home while severing its ties with Sparta and expanding its new empire abroad. This period of Athenian and Greek history, which historians have subsequently labeled the Age of Pericles, witnessed the height of Athenian power and the culmination of its brilliance as a civilization.

In the age of Pericles, the Athenians became deeply attached to their democratic system. The sovereignty of the people was embodied in the assembly (*ecclesia*), which consisted of all male citizens over eighteen years of age. In the 440s, that was probably a group of about 43,000. Meetings of the assembly were held on the hillside of the Pnyx, east of the Acropolis. Not all could attend, and the number present seldom exceeded six thousand, which was the capacity of the Pnyx. The assembly passed all laws and made final decisions on war and foreign policy. Although anyone could speak, usually only respected leaders did so,

Pericles: Roman Copy of Fifth-Century Bronze Original. Pericles dominated Athenian politics from 461 to 429 B.C. In addition to increasing the Athenians' participation in their own democratic system, he pursued an imperialistic policy, expanding the Athenian empire both on the Greek mainland and abroad. Largely with funds taken from the treasury of the Delian League, Pericles also initiated a number of beautification projects for Athens.

Athenian Democracy: The Funeral Oration of Pericles

In his *History of the Peloponnesian War*, the Greek historian Thucydides presented his reconstruction of the eulogy given by Pericles in the winter of 431–430 B.C. to honor the Athenians killed in the first campaigns of the Great Peloponnesian War. It is a magnificent, idealized description of the Athenian democracy at its height.

Thucydides, History of the Peloponnesian War

Our constitution is called a democracy because power is in the hands not of a minority but of the whole people. When it is a question of settling private disputes, everyone is equal before the law; when it is a question of putting one person before another in positions of public responsibility, what counts is not membership of a particular class, but the actual ability which the man possesses. No one, so long as he has it in him to be of service to the state, is kept in political obscurity because of poverty. And, just as our political life is free and open, so is our day-to-day life in our relations with each other. We do not get into a state with our next-door neighbor if he enjoys himself in his own way, nor do we give him the kind of black looks which, though they do no real harm, still do hurt people's feeling. We are free and tolerant in our private lives; but in public affairs we keep to the law. This is because it commands our deep respect.

We give our obedience to those whom we put in positions of authority, and we obey the laws themselves, especially those which are for the protection of the oppressed, and those unwritten laws which it is an acknowledged shame to break. . . . Here each individual is interested not only in his own affairs but in the affairs of the state as well: even those who are mostly occupied with their own business are extremely well-informed on general politics—this is a peculiarity of ours: we do not say that a man who takes no interest in politics is a man who minds his own business; we say that he has no business here at all. We Athenians, in our own persons, take our decisions on polity or submit them to proper discussions: for we do not think that there is an incompatibility between words and deeds; the worst thing is to rush into action before the consequences have been properly debated. . . . Taking everything together then, I declare that our city is an education to Greece, and I declare that in my opinion each single one of our citizens, in all the manifold aspects of life, is able to show himself the rightful lord and owner of his own person and do this, moreover, with exceptional grace and exceptional versatility. And to show that this is no empty boasting for the present occasion, but real tangible fact, you have only to consider the power which our city possesses and which has been won by those very qualities which I have mentioned.

a feat that required considerable speaking ability in such a large crowd. Pericles expanded the Athenians' involvement in their democracy (see the box above). Lower-class citizens were now eligible for public offices formerly closed to them. Pericles also introduced state pay for officeholders, including the widely held jury duty. This meant that poor citizens could now afford to participate in public affairs.

The reforms of Cleisthenes had introduced the council of five hundred, elected by lot from the ten tribes. It prepared the agenda for the assembly and made recommendations for action. Thus the council served as a control on the assembly. The council was divided into ten smaller groups of fifty called prytanies. Each prytany held office for one-tenth of the year to supervise the execution of the laws passed by the assembly.

Routine administration of public affairs was handled by a large body of city magistrates, usually chosen by lot without regard to class. The general directors of policy, a board of ten officials known as generals (*strategoi*), were elected by public vote and were usually wealthy aristocrats, even though the people were free to select otherwise. The generals could be reelected, enabling individual leaders to play an important political role. Pericles, for example, was elected to the generalship thirty times between 461 and 429 B.C. But all public officials were subject to scrutiny and could be deposed from office if they lost the people's confidence. After 488 B.C., the Athenians began to make use of an instrument devised to protect the citizenry against overly ambitious politicians. Called ostracism, this practice enabled the members of the assembly to write on a broken pottery fragment (*ostrakon*) the name of the person they most disliked or considered most harmful to the *polis*. Frequently, this was a person whose policy, approved at first by the assembly, had failed. A person who received a majority (if at least six thousand votes were cast) was exiled for ten years, although the practical Athenians often recalled a man from exile if they needed him.

ATHENIAN IMPERIALISM

The Athenian pursuit of democracy at home was coupled with increasing imperialism abroad as Athens attempted to create both a land empire in Greece and a maritime empire in the Aegean. As we have seen, after 470 B.C., Athenian policies had the effect of converting the voluntary allies of the Delian League into the involuntary subjects of an Athenian naval empire. After 462 B.C., Athens attempted to expand its empire on the Greek mainland as well. The creation of a land empire, however, overextended

CHRONOLOGY

Events Between the Persian Wars and the Great Peloponnesian War

Delian League created	478–477 B.C.
Victory over Persians in southern Asia Minor	469 B.C.
Curtailment of Areopagus	461 B.C.
Beginning of First Peloponnesian War	c. 460 B.C.
Treasury of Delian League moved to Athens	454 B.C.
Thirty Years' Peace and end of First Peloponnesian War	445 B.C.

the Athenians and involved them in a series of skirmishes with Sparta and its allies known as the First Peloponnesian War (c. 460–445 B.C.). After a series of defeats in 445 B.C., the land empire of Athens disintegrated, and Athens agreed to a thirty years' peace with the Spartans in the following year. Athens consented to give up most of its land empire, and in return, Sparta recognized the existence of Athens' maritime empire.

While building its land empire, Athens continued its offensive against Persia and at the same time tightened its control over the Delian League. Citing the threat of the Persian fleet in the Aegean, the Athenians moved the treasury of the league from the island of Delos to Athens itself, possibly in 454 B.C. Members were, in effect, charged a fee (tribute) for the Athenian claim of protection. Pericles also used the treasury money of the league, without the approval of its members, to build new temples in Athens, a clear indication that the Delian League had become the Athenian empire. Henceforth, any protest by a league state against the tribute imposed by Athens could be heard only before an Athenian court. However, Athenian imperialism, pursued both in Greece and abroad, took its toll. Pericles recognized the dangers of Athenian exhaustion and sought a lull. After peace was made with Sparta in 445 B.C., the Athenians had a breathing space in which to beautify Athens and enjoy the fruits of empire, but it was not long before all of Greece was plunged into a new and prolonged struggle.

The Great Peloponnesian War (431–404 B.C.)

In the decades that followed the defeat of the Persians, the Greek world divided into two major camps: Sparta and its Peloponnesian League and the Athenian maritime empire.

In his classic *History of the Peloponnesian War*, the great Greek historian Thucydides pointed out that the fundamental, long-range cause of the war was the fear that Athens and its empire inspired in Sparta (see the box on p. 69). The Spartans were especially concerned that Athens would use its superior naval power to weaken Sparta's control of the Peloponnesian League. The immediate causes of the war involved conflicts between Corinth and Athens and between Athens and Megara. When these two allies of Sparta threatened to withdraw from the Peloponnesian League if Sparta did not back them, the Spartans sent an ultimatum to Athens: if the Athenians did not back down in their disputes with Corinth and Megara, it would mean war. The Athenians refused to compromise when Pericles convinced them that if they accepted Sparta's ultimatum, they would be admitting that Sparta was the dominant power in Greece.

At the beginning of the war in 431 B.C., both sides believed they had winning strategies. The Athenian plan was based on the navy. The citizens of Attica would be brought in behind the protective walls of Athens and the port of Piraeus, while the overseas empire and the navy would keep them supplied (see Map 3.4). Pericles knew perfectly well that the Spartans and their allies could beat the Athenians in pitched battles, which, of course, formed the focus of the Spartan strategy. The Spartans and their allies invaded Attica and ravaged the fields and orchards, hoping that the Athenians would send out their army to fight beyond the walls. But Pericles was convinced that Athens was secure behind its walls and retaliated by sending out naval excursions to ravage the seacoast of the Peloponnesus. In the second year of the war, however, a plague devastated the crowded city of Athens and wiped out possibly one-third of the Athenian population. Pericles himself died the following year (429 B.C.), a severe loss to Athens. Dominance now passed to Cleon, leader of the war party, who was opposed by Nicias, head of a conservative faction that favored peace. Despite the losses from the plague, the Athenians fought on in a struggle that witnessed numerous instances of futile destruction. Cleon achieved some successes for the Athenians; Brasidas came to be a dynamic general for the Spartans. At the Battle of Amphipolis in 422 B.C., both generals were killed and the new Athenian leader, Nicias, negotiated the Peace of Nicias (421 B.C.). Although both parties agreed to keep the peace for fifty years, the truce did not really solve the problems that had caused the war in the first place.

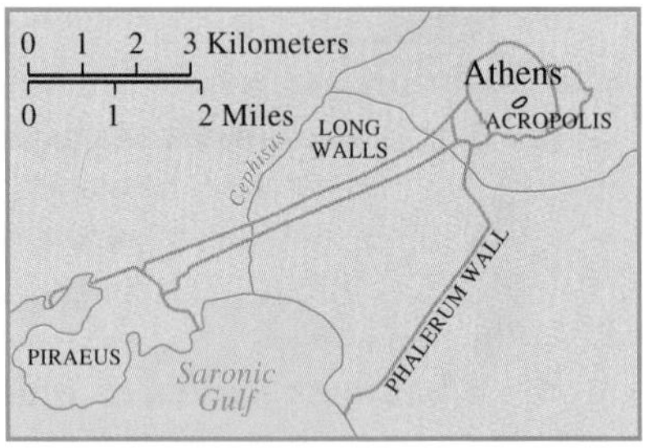

Piraeus and Athens

A second phase of the war began only six years after the fifty-year truce began. This phase was initiated by Alcibiades, a nephew of Pericles. Elected to the generalship in 420 B.C., he proved to be a poor choice because of his recklessness and self-seeking. In 415 B.C., he convinced the Athenians to invade the island of Sicily, arguing that its conquest would give the Athenians a strong source of support to carry on a lengthy war. But the expedition was ill-fated. Alcibiades himself was removed from leadership of the expedition on a charge of profaning the religious mysteries. Rather than stand trial, he fled to Sparta and advised the Spartans

The Significance of the Great Peloponnesian War

In his *History of the Peloponnesian War*, Thucydides gave a detailed account of the origins, course, and effects of the Great Peloponnesian War. Thucydides was an Athenian general who was banished from Athens for failing to win an important battle against the Spartans. Near the beginning of his history, he discussed the significance of this war to the Greeks and its underlying cause.

Thucydides, History of the Peloponnesian War

The greatest war in the past was the Persian War; yet in this war the decision was reached quickly as a result of two naval battles and two battles on land. The Peloponnesian War, on the other hand, not only lasted for a long time, but throughout its course brought with it unprecedented suffering for Greece. Never before had so many cities been captured and then devastated, whether by foreign armies or by the Greek Powers themselves; never had there been so many exiles; never such loss of life—both in the actual warfare and in internal revolutions. Old stories of past prodigies, which had not found much confirmation in recent experience, now became credible. Wide areas, for instance, were affected by violent earthquakes; there were more frequent eclipses of the sun than had ever been recorded before; in various parts of the country there were extensive droughts followed by famine; and there was the plague which did more harm and destroyed more life than almost any other single factor. All of these calamities fell together upon the Greeks after the outbreak of war.

War began when the Athenians and the Peloponnesians broke the Thirty Years' Truce which had been made after the capture of Euboea. As to the reasons why they broke the truce, I propose first to give an account of the causes of complaint which they had against each other and of the specific instances where their interests clashed: this is in order that there should be no doubt in anyone's mind about what led to this great war falling upon the Greeks. But the real reason for the war is, in my opinion, most likely to be disguised by such an argument. What made war inevitable was the growth of Athenian power and the fear which this caused in Sparta.

how to defeat Athens by getting help from Persia and assembling a navy with ships and money supplied by the Persians. The Spartans later followed his advice.

In the meantime, the Athenians pursued the Sicilian policy. A "great expedition" consisting of five thousand Athenian hoplites was sent out in 415 B.C. and reinforced two years later by an even larger army of Athenians and allies. All was in vain. The Athenians failed to take Syracuse and were captured during their retreat. All of the Athenians were killed or sold into slavery. These heavy losses at Syracuse had immediate domestic repercussions. The democracy was weakened, and an aristocratic oligarchy was temporarily established (411–410 B.C.).

Despite the disaster, the Athenians refused to give up; they raised new armies and sent out new fleets. The final crushing blow came, however, in 405 B.C., when the Athenian fleet was destroyed at Aegospotami on the Hellespont. Athens was besieged and surrendered the next year. Its walls were torn down, the navy was disbanded, and the Athenian empire was dissolved. The great war was finally over.

The Decline of the Greek States (404–338 B.C.)

The next seventy years of Greek history are a tale of continuing warfare among the Greeks, with the leading roles shifting among Sparta, Athens, and a new Greek power, the city-state of Thebes. After the defeat of Athens in 404 B.C., the Spartans established their own control over Greece. The Athenian empire was no more. Oligarchies, headed by local *decarchies* (ten-man boards) in cooperation with Spartan garrisons, were placed in control of the states "liberated" from Athenian imperialism. But oligarchical control proved ineffective, especially in Athens, where the ruling oligarchical faction of thirty, set up by the Spartans, earned their nickname of "Thirty Tyrants" by executing about fifteen hundred of their democratic opponents. This led to a reaction in which the Athenians were able to reestablish their democracy in 403 B.C. They also rebuilt their navy and again became an important force in the Greek world.

To maintain its newly organized leadership in Greek affairs, Sparta encouraged a Panhellenic crusade against the Persians as a common enemy. The Persians had taken advantage of the Greeks' internal struggle to reimpose their control over the Greek states in western Asia Minor. The Spartans, under King Agesilaus, led a Greek expedition into Asia Minor in 396 B.C. But the Persians had learned the lessons of Greek politics and offered financial support to Athens, Thebes, and other Greek states to oppose Spartan power within Greece itself, thus beginning a new war, the Corinthian War (395–386 B.C.). The war ended when the Greek states, weary of the struggles, accepted the King's Peace, dictated by the Great King of Persia.

The city-state of Thebes, in Boeotia north of Athens, now began to exert its influence. Under their leader Epaminondas, the Thebans dramatically defeated the Spartan army at the Battle of Leuctra in 371 B.C. Spartan power declined, to be replaced by the ascendancy of the Thebans. But Theban power was short-lived. After the death of Epaminondas in the Battle of Mantinea in 362 B.C., the

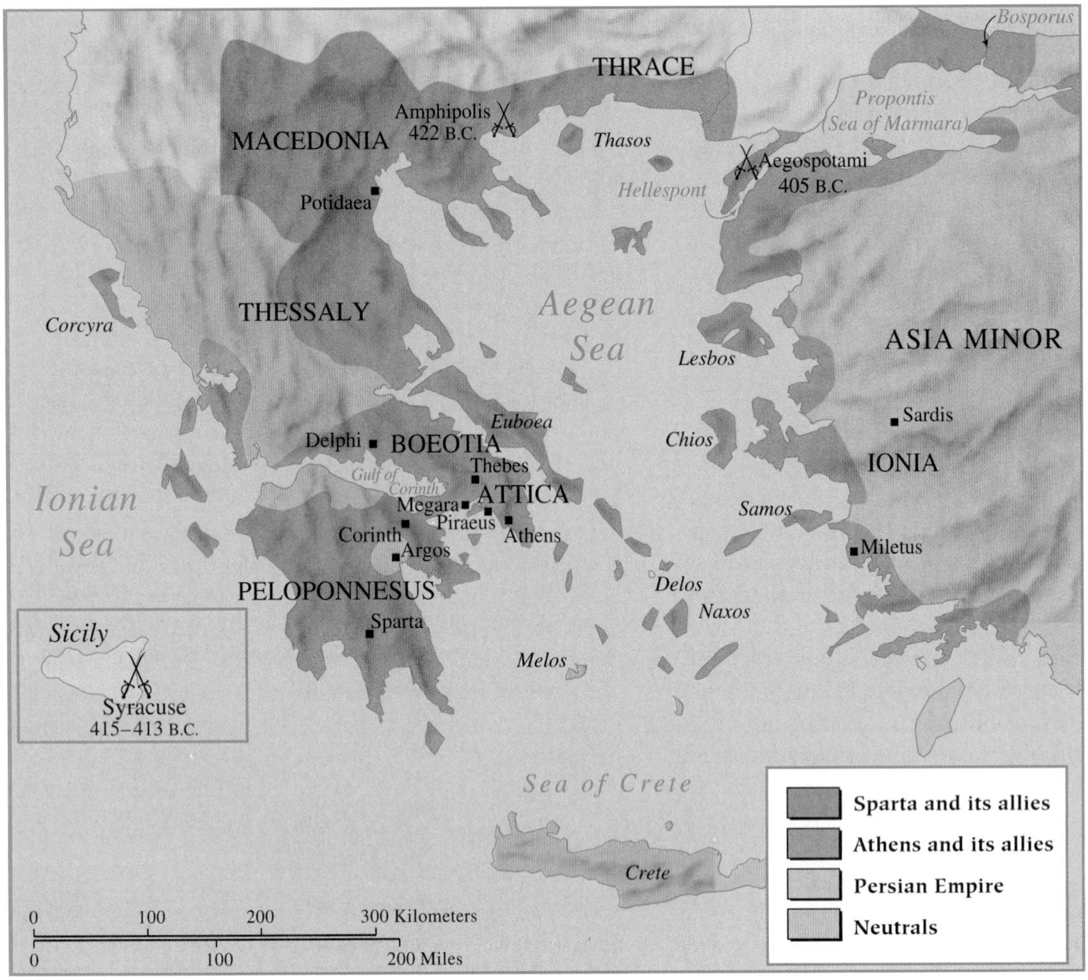

Map 3.4 The Great Peloponnesian War (431–404 B.C.). During much of the fifth century B.C., Athens sought to dominate Greece and the Aegean Sea. The Peloponnesian War ultimately saw Sparta and the Peloponnesian League defeat Athens and its allies, culminating in the destruction of Athens's navy and empire in 404 B.C. ■ How did Athens use its proximity to the ocean to forge and maintain its empire and to conduct the war?

Thebans could no longer dominate Greek politics. And yet the Greek states continued their petty wars, seemingly oblivious to the growing danger to the north, where King Philip II of Macedonia was developing a unified state that would finally end the destructive fratricide of the Greek states by imposing Macedonian authority.

The Culture of Classical Greece

Classical Greece saw a period of remarkable intellectual and cultural growth throughout the Greek world. Historians agree, however, that Periclean Athens was the most important center of Classical Greek culture. Indeed, the eighteenth-century French philosopher and writer Voltaire listed the Athens of Pericles as one of four happy ages "when the arts were brought to perfection and which, marking an era of the greatness of the human mind, are an example to posterity."[10]

THE WRITING OF HISTORY

History as we know it, the systematic analysis of past events, was a Greek creation. Herodotus (c. 484–c. 425 B.C.), a Dorian Greek from Asia Minor, was the author of *The Persian Wars*, a work commonly regarded as the first real history in Western civilization. The Greek word *historia* (from which we derive our word *history*) means "research" or "investigation," and it is in the opening line of Herodotus' work that we find the first recorded use of the word:

> Here are presented the researches (*historiae*) carried out by Herodotus of Halicarnassus. The purpose is to prevent the traces of human events from being erased by time, and to preserve the fame of the important and remarkable achievements produced by both Greeks and non-Greeks; among the matters covered is, in particular, the cause of the hostilities between Greeks and non-Greeks.[11]

CHRONOLOGY

The Great Peloponnesian War

Invasion of Attica	431 B.C.
Battle of Amphipolis	422 B.C.
Peace of Nicias	421 B.C.
Athenian invasion of Sicily	415–413 B.C.
Battle of Aegospotami	405 B.C.
Surrender of Athens	404 B.C.

The central theme of Herodotus' work is the conflict between the Greeks and the Persians, which he viewed as a struggle between Greek freedom and Persian despotism. Herodotus traveled widely for his information and was dependent for his sources on what we today would call oral history. Although he was a master storyteller and sometimes included considerable fanciful material, Herodotus was also capable of exhibiting a critical attitude toward the materials he used. Regardless of its weaknesses, Herodotus' history is an important source of information on the Persians and our chief source on the Persian Wars themselves.

Thucydides (c. 460–c. 400 B.C.) was by far the better historian; in fact, modern historians consider him the greatest of the ancient world. Thucydides was an Athenian and a participant in the Peloponnesian War. He had been elected a general, but a defeat in battle led the fickle Athenian assembly to send him into exile, which gave him the opportunity to write his *History of the Peloponnesian War*. In the book, he described his own activities in the war:

> I lived through the whole of it, being of an age to understand what was happening, and I put my mind to the subject so as to get an accurate view of it. It happened, too, that I was banished from my country for twenty years after my command at Amphipolis [422 B.C.]; I saw what was being done on both sides, particularly on the Peloponnesian side, because of my exile, and this leisure gave me rather exceptional facilities for looking into things.[12]

Unlike Herodotus, Thucydides was not concerned with underlying divine forces or gods as explanatory causal factors in history. He saw war and politics in purely rational terms, as the activities of human beings. He examined the long-range and immediate causes of the Peloponnesian War in a clear, methodical, objective fashion. Thucydides placed much emphasis on accuracy and the precision of his facts. As he stated:

> And with regard to my factual reporting of the events of the war I have made it a principle not to write down the first story that came my way, and not even to be guided by my own general impressions; either I was present myself at the events which I have described or else I heard of them from eyewitnesses whose reports I have checked with as much thoroughness as possible.

Thucydides also provided remarkable insight into the human condition. He believed that human nature was a constant: "It will be enough for me, however, if these words of mine are judged useful by those who want to understand clearly the events which happened in the past and which (human nature being what it is) will, at some time or other and in much the same ways, be repeated in the future."[13] He was not so naive as to believe in an exact repetition of events but felt that political situations recur in similar fashion and that the study of history is of great value in understanding the present.

GREEK DRAMA

Drama as we know it was created by the Greeks and was clearly intended to do more than entertain. It was used to educate citizens and was supported by the state for that reason. Plays were presented in outdoor theaters as part of religious festivals. The form of Greek plays remained rather stable. Three male actors who wore masks acted all the parts. A chorus, also male, spoke the important lines that explained what was going on. Action was very limited because the emphasis was on the story and its meaning. Content was generally based on myths or legends that the audience already knew.

The first Greek dramas were tragedies, plays based on the suffering of a hero and usually ending in disaster. Aeschylus (525–456 B.C.) is the first tragedian whose plays are known to us. Although he wrote ninety tragedies, only

Greek Tragedy: *The Eumenides*. The Greek artist Python depicted this detail on a fourth-century B.C. vase. Shown is a scene from *The Eumenides*, the third play of the *Oresteia* trilogy written by Aeschylus. In this play, Orestes is acquitted by Athena of the crime of killing his mother to avenge his father's death. The Furies, who had been pursuing Orestes for killing his mother, now become the Eumenides—the "Kindly Ones."

Athenian Comedy: Sex as an Antiwar Instrument

Aristophanes used his comedies to present political messages, especially to express his antiwar sentiments. The plot of *Lysistrata* centers on a sex strike by wives in order to get their husbands to end the Peloponnesian War. In this scene from the play, Lysistrata (whose name means "she who dissolves the armies") has the women swear a special oath.

Aristophanes, Lysistrata

LYSISTRATA: Lampito: all of you women: come, touch the bowl, and repeat after me: *I will have nothing to do with my husband or my lover*

KALONIKE: I will have nothing to do with my husband or my lover

LYSISTRATA: *Though he come to me in pitiful condition*

KALONIKE: Though he come to me in pitiful condition (Oh, Lysistrata! This is killing me!)

LYSISTRATA: *I will stay in my house untouchable*

KALONIKE: I will stay in my house untouchable

LYSISTRATA: *In my thinnest saffron silk*

KALONIKE: In my thinnest saffron silk

LYSISTRATA: *And make him long for me*

KALONIKE: And make him long for me

LYSISTRATA: *I will not give myself*

KALONIKE: I will not give myself

LYSISTRATA: *And if he constrains me*

KALONIKE: And if he constrains me

LYSISTRATA: *I will be as cold as ice and never move*

KALONIKE: I will be as cold as ice and never move

LYSISTRATA: *I will not lift my slippers toward the ceiling*

KALONIKE: I will not lift my slippers toward the ceiling

LYSISTRATA: *Or crouch on all fours like the lioness in the carving*

KALONIKE: Or crouch on all fours like the lioness in the carving

LYSISTRATA: *And if I keep this oath let me drink from this bowl*

KALONIKE: And if I keep this oath let me drink from this bowl

LYSISTRATA: *If not, let my own bowl be filled with water.*

KALONIKE: If not, let my own bowl be filled with water.

LYSISTRATA: You have all sworn?

MYRRHINE: We have.

seven have survived. As was customary in Greek tragedy, his plots are simple. The entire drama focuses on a single tragic event and its meaning. Greek tragedies were supposed to be presented in a trilogy (a set of three plays) built around a common theme. The only complete trilogy we possess, called the *Oresteia*, was composed by Aeschylus. The theme of this trilogy is derived from Homer. Agamemnon, the king of Mycenae, returns a hero from the defeat of Troy. His wife, Clytemnestra, avenges the sacrificial death of her daughter Iphigenia by murdering Agamemnon, who had been responsible for Iphigenia's death. In the second play of the trilogy, Agamemnon's son Orestes avenges his father by killing his mother. Orestes is now pursued by the avenging Furies, who torment him for killing his mother. Evil acts breed evil acts, and suffering is one's lot, suggests Aeschylus. But Orestes is put on trial and acquitted by Athena, the patron goddess of Athens. Personal vendetta has been eliminated, and law has prevailed.

Another great Athenian playwright was Sophocles (c. 496–406 B.C.), whose most famous play was *Oedipus the King*. The oracle of Apollo foretells that a man (Oedipus) will kill his own father and marry his mother. Despite all attempts at prevention, the tragic events occur. Although it appears that Oedipus suffered the fate determined by the gods, Oedipus also accepts that he himself as a free man must bear responsibility for his actions: "It was Apollo, friends, Apollo, that brought this bitter bitterness, my sorrows to completion. But the hand that struck me was none but my own."[14]

The third outstanding Athenian tragedian, Euripides (c. 485–406 B.C.), moved beyond his predecessors in creating more realistic characters. His plots also became more complex, reflecting a greater interest in real-life situations. Perhaps the greatest of all his plays was *The Bacchae*, which dealt with the introduction of the hysterical rites associated with Dionysus, god of wine. Euripides is often seen as a skeptic, who questioned traditional moral and religious values. Euripides was also critical of the traditional view that war was glorious. He portrayed war as brutal and barbaric and expressed deep compassion for the women and children who suffered from it.

Greek tragedies dealt with universal themes that are still relevant in our day. They probed such problems as the nature of good and evil, the conflict between spiritual values and the demands of the state or family, the rights of the individual, the nature of divine forces, and the nature of human beings. Over and over again, the tragic lesson was repeated: humans were free and yet could operate only within limitations imposed by the gods. The real task was to cultivate the balance and moderation that led to awareness of one's true position. But the pride in human accomplishment and independence is real. As the chorus chants in Sophocles' *Antigone:* "Is there anything more wonderful on earth, our marvellous planet, than the miracle of man?"[15]

Greek comedy developed later than tragedy. The plays of Aristophanes (c. 450–c. 385 B.C.), who used both grotesque masks and obscene jokes to entertain the Athenian audience, are examples of Old Comedy. But comedy in

Athens was also more clearly political than tragedy. It was used to attack or savagely satirize both politicians and intellectuals. In *The Clouds*, for example, Aristophanes characterized the philosopher Socrates as the operator of a thought factory where people could learn deceitful ways to handle other people. Later plays gave up the element of personal attack and featured contemporary issues. Of special importance to Aristophanes was his opposition to the Peloponnesian War. *Lysistrata,* performed in 411 B.C., at a time when Athens was in serious danger of losing the war, had a comic but effective message against the war (see the box on p. 72).

THE ARTS: THE CLASSICAL IDEAL

The artistic standards established by the Greeks of the Classical Period have largely dominated the arts of the Western world. Classical Greek art did not aim at experimentation for experiment's sake but was concerned with expressing eternally true ideals. Its subject matter was basically the human being, expressed harmoniously as an object of great beauty. The Classical Style, based on the ideals of reason, moderation, symmetry, balance, and harmony in all things, was meant to civilize the emotions.

In architecture, the most important form was the temple dedicated to a god or goddess. Since Greek religious ceremonies were held at altars in the open air, temples were not used to enclose the faithful, as modern churches are. At the center of Greek temples were walled rooms that housed the statues of deities and treasuries in which gifts to the gods and goddesses were safeguarded. These central rooms were surrounded by a screen of columns that make Greek temples open structures rather than closed ones. The columns were originally made of wood but changed to limestone in the seventh century and to marble in the fifth century B.C. The most significant formal element in Greek temples was the shape and size of the columns in combination with the features above and below the column (see the illustration below).

Some of the finest examples of Classical Greek architecture were built in fifth-century Athens. The development of Athenian architecture was aided tremendously by the massive rebuilding program funded from the treasury of the Delian League and instituted almost a half-century after the Persians destroyed Athens in the Persian Wars. New buildings were erected in the agora, but especially important was a series of constructions on the Acropolis begun in 448 B.C., which included a monumental entrance gate, a temple to Athena Nike (the Bringer of Victory), and the Erechtheum, a multilevel temple. These temples honored the gods and heroes who protected Athens.

The most famous building, regarded as the greatest example of the Classical Greek temple, was the Parthenon, built between 447 and 432 B.C. The master builders Ictinus and Callicrates directed the construction of this temple, which was consecrated to Athena, the patron goddess of Athens. The Parthenon typifies the principles of Classical architecture: the search for calm, clarity, and freedom from

Doric, Ionic, and Corinthian Orders. The size and shape of a column constituted one of the most important aspects of Greek temple architecture. The Doric order, with plain capitals and no base, developed first in the Dorian Peloponnesus and was rather simple in comparison to the slender Ionic column, which had an elaborate base and spiral-shaped capitals, and the Corinthian column, which featured leaf-shaped capitals.

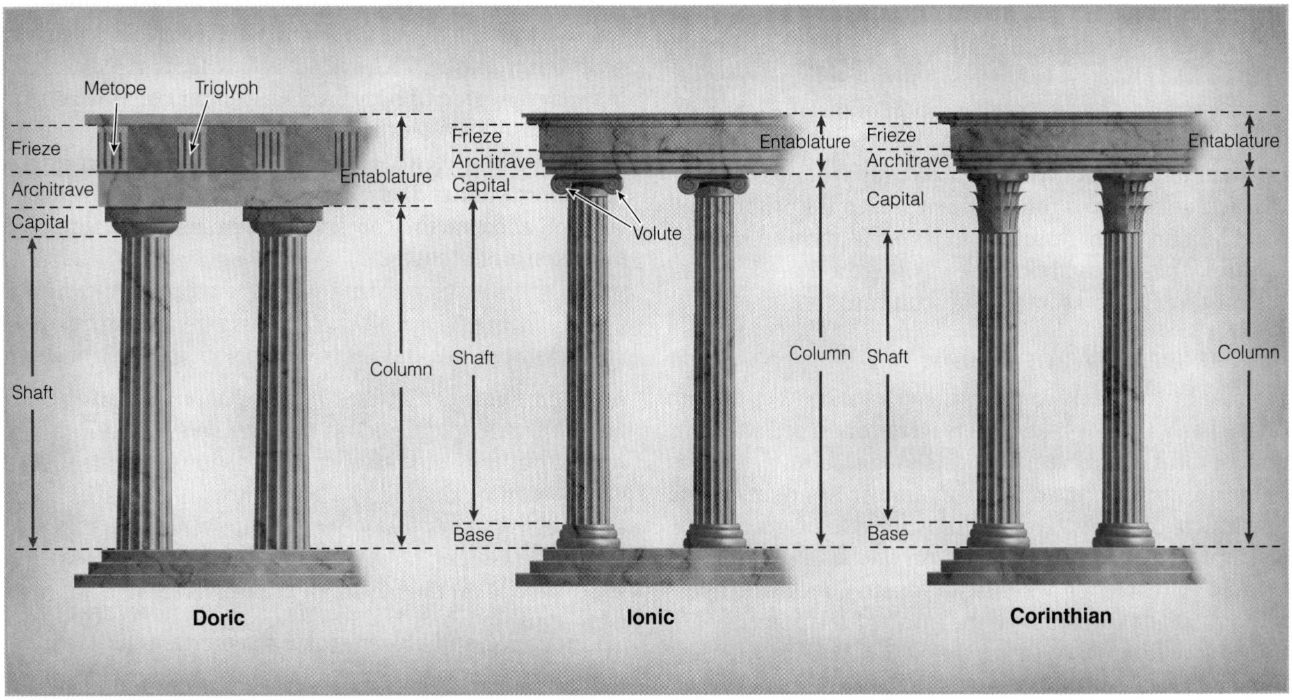

© Michael Holford, London

The Parthenon. The arts in Classical Greece were designed to express the eternal ideals of reason, moderation, symmetry, balance, and harmony. In architecture, the most important form was the temple, and the classic example of this kind of architecture is the Parthenon, built between 447 and 432 B.C. Located on the Acropolis, the Parthenon was dedicated to Athena, the patron goddess of the city, but it also served as a shining example of the power and wealth of the Athenian empire.

superfluous detail. The individual parts of the temple were constructed in accordance with certain mathematical ratios found in nature. The concern of the architects with these laws of proportion is paralleled by the attempt of Greek philosophers to understand the general laws of nature.

Greek sculpture also developed a Classical style that differed significantly from the artificial stiffness of the *kouros* figure of the Archaic Period. Statues of the male nude, the favorite subject of Greek sculptors, now exhibited more relaxed attitudes; their faces were self-assured, their bodies flexible and smooth-muscled. Although the figures possessed natural features that made them lifelike, Greek sculptors sought to achieve not realism but a standard of ideal beauty. Polyclitus, a fifth-century sculptor, wrote a treatise (now lost) on a canon of proportions that he illustrated in a work known as the *Doryphoros*. His theory maintained that the use of ideal proportions, based on mathematical ratios found in nature, could produce an ideal human form, beautiful in its perfected and refined features. This search for ideal beauty was the dominant feature of the Classical standard in sculpture.

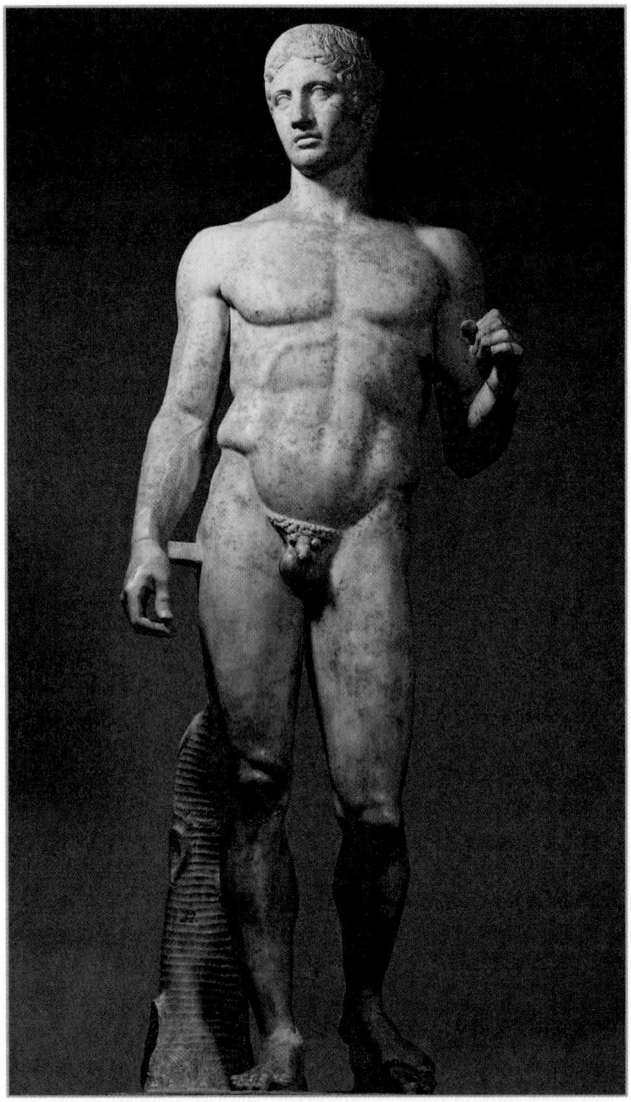

Scala/Art Resource, NY

Doryphoros. This statue, known as the *Doryphoros*, or spear-carrier, is a Roman copy of the original work by the fifth-century sculptor Polyclitus, who believed it illustrated the ideal proportions of the human figure. Classical Greek sculpture moved away from the stiffness of the *kouros* figure but retained the young male nude as the favorite subject matter. The statues became more lifelike, with relaxed poses and flexible, smooth-muscled bodies. The aim of sculpture, however, was not simply realism but rather the expression of ideal beauty.

THE GREEK LOVE OF WISDOM

Philosophy is a Greek word that literally means "love of wisdom." Early Greek philosophers were concerned with the development of critical or rational thought about the nature of the universe and the place of divine forces and souls in it.

Much of early Greek philosophy focused on the attempt to explain the universe on the basis of unifying principles. Thales of Miletus, an Ionian Greek who lived around 600 B.C., postulated the unity of the universe. All things were linked by water as the basic substance. Another Ionian Greek, Pythagoras (c. 580–c. 490 B.C.), taught that the essence of the universe could be found in music and number. These early Greek philosophers may have eliminated the role of the gods as they were portrayed in Greek myths, but they did not eliminate divinity itself from the world, tending instead to identify it with the underlying, unchanging forces that govern the universe.

Many Greeks, however, were simply not interested in speculations on the nature of the universe. The Sophists were a group of philosophical teachers in the fifth century who rejected such speculation as foolish; they argued that understanding the universe was beyond the reach of the human mind. It was more important for individuals to improve themselves, so the only worthwhile object of study was human behavior. The Sophists were wandering scholars who sold their services as professional teachers to the young men of Greece, especially those of Athens. The Sophists stressed the importance of rhetoric (the art of persuasive speaking) in winning debates and swaying an audience, a skill that was especially valuable in democratic Athens. To the Sophists, there was no absolute right or wrong—what was right for one individual might be wrong for another. True wisdom consisted of being able to perceive one's own good and to pursue its acquisition. Many people, however, viewed the Sophists as harmful to the traditional values of society and especially dangerous to the values of young people.

In Classical Greece, Athens became the foremost intellectual and artistic center. Its reputation is perhaps strongest of all in philosophy. After all, Socrates, Plato, and Aristotle raised basic questions that have been debated for more than two thousand years; these are still largely the same philosophical questions we wrestle with today.

Socrates (469–399 B.C.) left no writings, but we know about him from his pupils, especially his most famous one, Plato. By occupation, Socrates was a stonemason, but his true love was philosophy. He taught a number of pupils, but not for pay, because he believed that the goal of education was only to improve the individual. He made use of a teaching method that is still known by his name. The Socratic method employs a question-and-answer technique to lead pupils to see things for themselves using their own reason. Socrates believed that all real knowledge is within each person; only critical examination was needed to call it forth. This was the real task of philosophy, since "the unexamined life is not worth living."

Socrates' questioning of authority and public demonstrations of others' lack of knowledge led him into trouble. Athens had had a tradition of free thought and inquiry, but its defeat in the Peloponnesian War had created an environment intolerant of open debate and soul-searching. Socrates was accused and convicted of corrupting the youth of Athens by his teaching, and an Athenian jury sentenced him to death.

One of Socrates' disciples was Plato (c. 429–347 B.C.), considered by many scholars the greatest philosopher of Western civilization. Unlike his master Socrates, who wrote nothing, Plato wrote a great deal. In his dialogues, he used Socrates as his chief philosophical debater.

Plato's philosophical thought focused on the essence of reality and was centered in the concept of Ideas or ideal Forms. According to Plato, a higher world of eternal, unchanging Ideas or Forms has always existed. To know these Forms is to know truth. These ideal Forms constitute reality and can only be apprehended by a trained mind, which, of course, is the goal of philosophy. The objects that we perceive with our senses are simply reflections of the ideal Forms. Hence they are shadows, while reality is found in the Forms themselves.

Plato's ideas of government were set out in his dialogue titled *The Republic*. Based on his experience in Athens, Plato had come to distrust the workings of democracy. It was obvious to him that individuals could not attain an ethical life unless they lived in a just and rational state. This insight led him to construct an ideal state in which the population was divided into three basic groups. At the top was an upper class, a ruling elite, the famous philosopher-kings: "Unless either philosophers become kings in their countries or those who are now called kings and rulers come to be sufficiently inspired with a genuine desire for wisdom; unless, that is to say, political power and philosophy meet together . . . there can be no rest from troubles . . . . for states, nor yet, as I believe, for all mankind."[16] The second group consisted of the courageous; they would be the warriors who protected the society. All the rest made up the masses, essentially people driven not by wisdom or courage but by desire for material things. They would be the producers of society—the artisans, tradesmen, and farmers.

In Plato's ideal state, each group fulfilled its assigned role, creating a society that functioned harmoniously. The needs of the community, rather than the happiness of the individual, were Plato's concern, and he focused on the need for the guardians or rulers, above all, to be removed from any concerns for wealth or prestige so that they could strive for what was best for the community. To rid the guardians of these desires, Plato urged that they live together, forgoing both private property and family life. Plato believed that women, too, could be rulers; in this he departed radically from the actual practices of the Greek states.

Plato established a school at Athens known as the Academy. One of his pupils, who studied there for twenty years, was Aristotle (384–322 B.C.), who later became a tutor to Alexander the Great. Aristotle differed significantly from his teacher in that he did not accept Plato's theory of ideal Forms. He, like Plato, believed in universal principles or forms, but he believed that form and matter were inseparable. By examining individual objects, we can perceive their form and arrive at universal principles, but they do not exist as a separate higher world of reality beyond material things; rather they are a part of things themselves. Aristotle's interests, then, lay in analyzing and classifying things based on thorough research and investigation. His interests were wide-ranging, and he wrote treatises on an enormous number of subjects: ethics, logic, politics, poetry, astronomy, geology, biology, and physics.

Like Plato, Aristotle wished for an effective form of government that would rationally direct human affairs. Unlike Plato, he did not seek an ideal state based on embodiment of an ideal Form of justice; he tried to find the best form of government by a rational examination of existing governments. For his *Politics* (see the box on p. 76), Aristotle examined the constitutions of 158 states and arrived at general categories for organizing governments. He identified three good forms of government: monarchy, aristocracy, and constitutional government. But based on his examination, he warned that monarchy can easily turn into tyranny, aristocracy into oligarchy, and constitutional government into radical democracy or anarchy. He favored constitutional government as the best form for most people.

The Politics of Aristotle

Aristotle was one of the great philosophers of ancient Athens. His philosophical and political ideas would play an important role in the evolution of Western thought during the Middle Ages. In this selection from his *Politics,* Aristotle examines the nature of political community and of the *polis.*

Aristotle, Politics

From these considerations it is evident that the *polis* belongs to the class of things that exist by nature, and that man is by nature an animal intended to live in a *polis.* He who is without a *polis,* by reason of his own nature and not of some accident, is either a poor sport of being, or a being higher than man: he is the man of whom Homer wrote in denunciation: "Clanless and lawless and hearthless is he." The man who is such by nature [unable to join in the society of a *polis*] at once plunges into a passion for war; he is in the position of a solitary advanced piece in a game of [checkers].

The reason why man is a being meant for political association, in a higher degree than bees or other gregarious animals can ever associate, is evident. Nature, according to our theory, makes nothing in vain; and man alone of the animals is furnished with the faculty of language. The mere making of sounds serves to indicate pleasure and pain, is thus a faculty that belongs to animals in general: their nature enables them to attain the point at which they have perceptions of pleasure and pain, and can signify those perceptions to one another. But language serves to declare what is advantageous and what is the reverse, and it therefore serves to declare what is just and what is unjust. It is the peculiarity of man, in comparison with the rest of the animal world, that he alone possesses perception of good and evil, of the just and the unjust, and of other similar qualities; and it is association in [a common perception of] these things which makes a family and a *polis.*

We now proceed to add that [though the individual and the family are prior in the order of time] the *polis* is prior in the order of nature to the family and the individual.

Aristotle's philosophical and political ideas played an enormous role in the development of Western thought during the Middle Ages (see Chapter 10). So did his ideas on women. Aristotle believed that marriage was meant to provide mutual comfort between man and woman and contributed to the overall happiness of a community: "The community needs both male and female excellences or it can only be half-blessed." Nevertheless, Aristotle maintained that women were biologically inferior to men: "A woman is, as it were, an infertile male. She is female in fact on account of a kind of inadequacy." Therefore, according to Aristotle, women must be subordinated to men, not only in the community but also in marriage: "The association between husband and wife is clearly an aristocracy. The man rules by virtue of merit, and in the sphere that is his by right; but he hands over to his wife such matters as are suitable for her."[17]

Greek Religion

Greek religion was intricately connected to every aspect of daily life; it was both social and practical. Public festivals, which originated from religious practices, served specific functions: boys were prepared to be warriors, girls to be mothers. Since religion was related to every aspect of life, citizens had to have a proper attitude toward the gods. Religion was a civic cult necessary for the well-being of the state. Temples dedicated to a god or goddess were the major buildings of Greek society.

Homer gave an account of the gods that provided a definite structure to Greek religion. Over a period of time, most Greeks came to accept a common religion based on twelve chief gods who supposedly lived on Mount Olympus, the highest mountain in Greece. Among the twelve were Zeus, the chief deity and father of the gods; Athena, goddess of wisdom and crafts; Apollo, god of the sun and poetry; Aphrodite, goddess of love; and Poseidon, brother of Zeus and god of the seas and earthquakes.

The twelve Olympian gods were common to all Greeks, who thus shared a basic polytheistic religion. Each *polis* usually singled out one of the twelve Olympians as a guardian deity of its community. Athena was the patron goddess of Athens, for example. But each *polis* also had its own local deities who remained important to the community as a whole, and each family had patron gods as well. Because it was desirable to have the gods look favorably on one's activities, ritual assumed enormous proportions in Greek religion. Prayers were often combined with gifts to the gods based on the principle, "I give so that you [the gods] will give [in return]." Some prayers directly reflected this mutual benefit: "Protect our city. I believe that what I say is in our common interest. For a flourishing city honors the gods." Ritual meant sacrifices, whether of animals or agricultural products. Animal victims were burned on an altar in front of a temple or on a small altar in front of a home.

Festivals were also developed as a way to honor the gods and goddesses. Some of these (the Panhellenic celebrations) were important to all Greeks and were held at special locations, such as those dedicated to the worship of Zeus at Olympia, to Poseidon at the Isthmus of Corinth, and to Apollo at Delphi. The great festivals incorporated

An Animal Sacrifice. Animal sacrifice was a regular part of Greek religious ritual. This painted wooden tablet, which was found in a cave near Corinth and dates from the sixth century B.C., depicts the beginning stage of an animal sacrifice performed at a small altar.

numerous events in honor of the gods, including athletic competitions to which all Greeks were invited. According to tradition, the first such games were held at the Olympic festival in 776 B.C. and then held every four years thereafter to honor Zeus. Initially, the Olympic contests consisted of foot races and wrestling, but later, boxing, javelin throwing, and various other contests were added. Competitions were always between individuals, not groups.

As another practical side of Greek religion, Greeks wanted to know the will of the gods. There were seers who obtained omens from dreams, the flight of birds, or the entrails of sacrificial animals. But perhaps the most famous method of divining the will of the gods was the use of the oracle, a sacred shrine dedicated to a god or goddess who revealed the future. The most famous was the oracle of Apollo at Delphi, located on the side of Mount Parnassus, overlooking the Gulf of Corinth. At Delphi, a priestess listened to questions while in a state of ecstasy that was believed to be induced by Apollo. Her responses were interpreted by the priests and given in verse form to the person asking questions. Representatives of states and individuals traveled to Delphi to consult the oracle of Apollo. States might inquire whether they should undertake a military expedition; individuals might raise such questions as "Heracleidas asks the god whether he will have offspring from the wife he has now." Responses were often enigmatic and could be interpreted in more than one way. Croesus, the king of Lydia in Asia Minor who was known for his incredible wealth, sent messengers to the oracle at Delphi, asking whether he should go to war with the Persians. The oracle replied that if Croesus attacked the Persians, a mighty empire would be destroyed. Overjoyed to hear these words, Croesus made war on the Persians but was crushed by his enemy. A mighty empire—that of Croesus—was destroyed.

Greek religion, centered in ritual and a formal relationship with the gods, tended to lack a strong emotional component. It also offered no hope of life after death for most people. As a result, the Greeks sometimes turned to mystery religions, which included initiation into secret rites that promised a more emotional involvement with spiritual forces and a greater hope of immortality. The most important mysteries were those of the Eleusinian cult connected with the myth of Demeter. This was a fertility cult in which participants felt reborn and gained some hope for life after death. The Orphic cultists, who considered themselves followers of the legendary singer Orpheus, believed in cycles of reincarnation since the human soul had become trapped in the physical body. Their aim was to liberate the soul from its confinement.

Daily Life in Classical Athens

The Greek city-state was, above all, a male community: only adult male citizens took part in public life. In Athens, this meant the exclusion of women, slaves, and foreign residents, or roughly 85 percent of the total population of Attica. In the fifth century, Athens had the largest population of all the Greek city-states. There were probably 150,000 citizens, of whom about 43,000 were adult males who exercised political power. Resident foreigners, known as metics, numbered about 35,000 and received the protection of the laws, but they were also subject to some of the responsibilities of citizens, namely, military service and the funding of festivals. The remaining social group, the slaves, numbered around 100,000.

Metropolitan Museum of Art, New York, Fletcher Fund, 1931 (31.11.10)

Women in the Loom Room. In Athens, women were considered citizens and could participate in religious cults and festivals, but they were barred from any political activity. Women were thought to belong in the house, caring for the children and the needs of the household. A principal activity of Greek women was the making of clothes. This vase shows two women working on a warp-weighted loom.

SLAVERY AND THE ECONOMY

Slavery was a common institution in the ancient world. Economic necessity dictated the desirability of owning at least one slave, although the very poor in Athens did not own any. A soldier on campaign usually took along one slave to carry his armor. The really wealthy might own large numbers of slaves, but those who did usually employed them in industry. Most often slaves in Athens performed domestic tasks as cooks and maids or worked in the fields. Few peasants could afford more than one or two. Other slaves worked as unskilled and skilled laborers. Slaves who worked in public construction were paid the same as metics or citizens.

The Athenian economy was largely agricultural but highly diversified. Athenian farmers grew grains, vegetables, and fruit for local consumption; cultivated vines and olives for wine and olive oil, which were exportable products; and raised sheep and goats for wool and milk products. Given the size of the population in Attica and the lack of abundant fertile land, Athens had to import between 50 and 80 percent of its grain, a staple in the Athenian diet. Trade was thus very important to the Athenian economy. The building of the port at Piraeus and the Long Walls (a series of defensive walls 4 1/2 miles long connecting Athens and Piraeus) created the physical conditions that made Athens the leading trade center in the fifth-century Greek world.

Athens did not have large numbers of artisans, but those it had were important to the economy. Athens was the chief producer of high-quality painted pottery in the fifth century. Other crafts had moved beyond the small workshop into the factory through the use of slave labor.

FAMILY AND RELATIONSHIPS

The Athenian lifestyle was basically simple. Athenian houses were furnished with necessities bought from artisans, such as beds, couches, tables, chests, pottery, stools, baskets, and cooking utensils. Wives and slaves made clothes and blankets at home. The Athenian diet was rather plain. Basic foods consisted of barley, wheat, millet, lentils, grapes, figs, olives, almonds, bread made at home, vegetables, eggs, fish, cheese, and chicken. Olive oil was widely used, not only for eating but also for lighting lamps and for rubbing on the body after washing and exercise. Owners of country houses kept animals for reasons other than their flesh: oxen for plowing, sheep for wool, and goats for milk and cheese. Meat was consumed only on special occasions, such as festivals, when animals were sacrificed, cooked, and then eaten.

The family was an important institution in ancient Athens. It was composed of husband, wife, and children (a nuclear family), although other dependent relatives and slaves were regarded as part of the family because of its economic unity. The family's primary social function was to produce new citizens. Strict laws of the fifth century had stipulated that a citizen must be the offspring of a legally acknowledged marriage between two Athenian citizens. By law, property was divided by lot among all the surviving sons; as a result, marriages were usually sought within a close circle of relatives so as to preserve the family property. The family also served to protect and enclose women.

Women were citizens who could participate in most religious cults and festivals but were otherwise excluded from public life. They could not own property beyond personal items and always had a male guardian: if unmarried,

Household Management and the Role of the Athenian Wife

In Classical Athens, a woman's place was in the home. She had two major responsibilities: bearing and raising children and managing the household. In his dialogue on estate management, Xenophon relates the instructions of an Athenian to his new wife.

Xenophon, Oeconomicus

[Ischomachus addresses his new wife:] For it seems to me, dear, that the gods with great discernment have coupled together male and female, as they are called, chiefly in order that they may form a perfect partnership in mutual service. For, in the first place that the various species of living creatures may not fail, they are joined in wedlock for the production of children. Secondly, offspring to support them in old age is provided by this union, to human beings, at any rate. Thirdly, human beings live not in the open air, like beasts, but obviously need shelter. Nevertheless, those who mean to win stores to fill the covered place, have need of someone to work at the open-air occupations; since plowing, sowing, planting and grazing are all such open-air employments; and these supply the needful food. . . . For he made the man's body and mind more capable of enduring cold and heat, and journeys and campaigns; and therefore imposed on him the outdoor tasks. To the woman, since he had made her body less capable of such endurance, I take it that God has assigned the indoor tasks. And knowing that he had created in the woman and had imposed on her the nourishment of the infants, he meted out to her a larger portion of affection for newborn babes than to the man. . . .

Your duty will be to remain indoors and send out those servants whose work is outside, and superintend those who are to work indoors, and to receive the incomings, and distribute so much of them as must be spent, and watch over so much as is to be kept in store, and take care that the sum laid by for a year be not spent in a month. And when wool is brought to you, you must see that cloaks are made for those that want them. You must see too that the dry corn is in good condition for making food. One of the duties that fall to you, however, will perhaps seem rather thankless: you will have to see that any servant who is ill is cared for.

a father or male relative; if married, a husband; if widowed, a son or male relative.

The function of the Athenian woman as wife was very clear. Her foremost obligation was to bear children, especially male children who would preserve the family line. The marriage formula that Athenians used put it succinctly: "I give this woman for the procreation of legitimate children." A wife was also expected to take care of her family and her house, either doing the household work herself or supervising the slaves who did the actual work (see the box above).

Women were kept under strict control. Since they were married at fourteen or fifteen, they were taught about their responsibilities at an early age. Although many managed to learn to read and play musical instruments, they were often cut off from any formal education. And women were expected to remain at home out of sight unless they attended funerals or festivals, such as the women's festival of Thesmophoria. If they left the house, they were to be accompanied. A woman working alone in public was either poverty-stricken or not a citizen.

Women in Athens served males in other ways as well. Prostitution flourished in Classical Athens. Most female prostitutes were slaves in brothels run as a business or trade by an Athenian citizen. Another class of prostitutes in Athenian society occupied a more favorable position; these more refined courtesans were known as *hetairai*, literally "female companions." Usually ex-slaves or foreigners, these women were more sophisticated than ordinary prostitutes and were known for their intellectual and musical achievements as well as their physical ones. Athenian males continued the aristocratic practice of the symposium, the sophisticated drinking party, where *hetairai* were often present. Symposia were held in the men's dining rooms, and wives were not present. *Hetairai* danced, played musical instruments, and provided entertainment, including sex. Some *hetairai* achieved fortune and considerable renown. Aspasia was the most famous. A friend of Socrates and known for her learning, she was the mistress of Pericles and eventually became his wife.

Male homosexuality was also a prominent feature of Classical Athens. It was widely practiced and tolerated. Athenian law disfranchised a citizen who had prostituted his body to another male, but nothing was done to males who engaged in homosexual love with male prostitutes or other adult males for love or pleasure. The law did not eliminate male prostitution but assured that male prostitutes would be foreigners, not Athenian citizens.

The Greek homosexual ideal was a relationship between a mature man and a young male. It is likely that this was primarily an aristocratic ideal. While the relationship was frequently physical, the Greeks also viewed it as educational. The older male (the "lover") won the love of his "beloved" by his value as a teacher and by the devotion he demonstrated in training his charge. In a sense, this love relationship was seen as a way of initiating young males into the male world of political and military dominance. The Greeks did not feel that the coexistence of homosexual and heterosexual predilections created any special problems for individuals or their society.

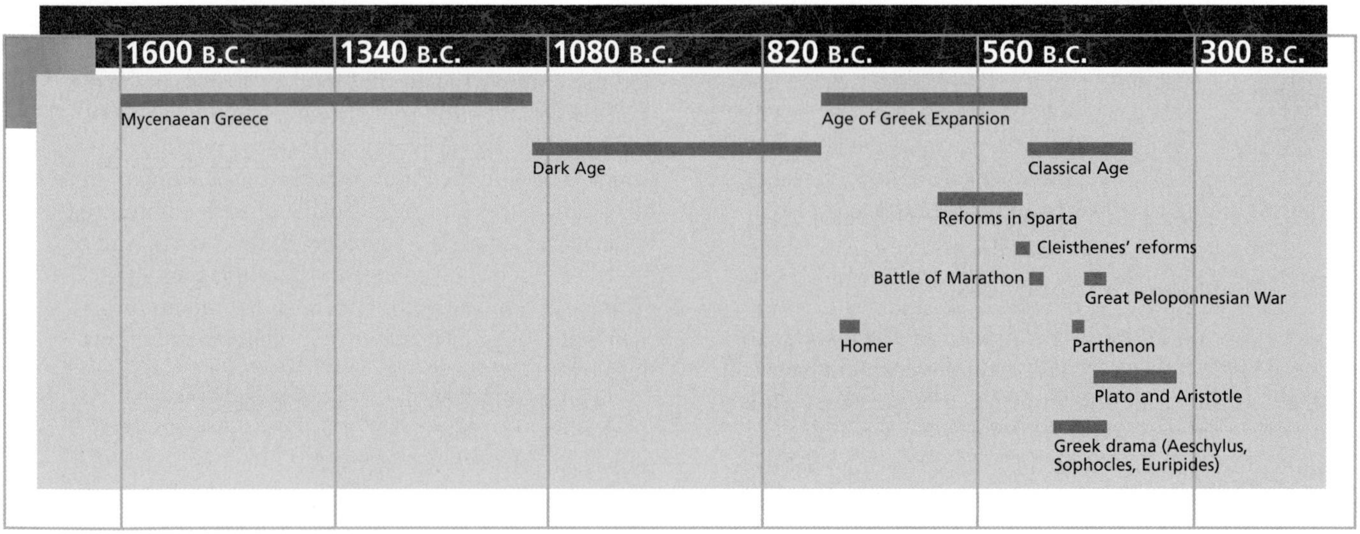

Conclusion

The civilization of the ancient Greeks was the fountainhead of Western culture. Socrates, Plato, and Aristotle established the foundations of Western philosophy. Herodotus and Thucydides created the discipline of history. Our literary forms are largely derived from Greek poetry and drama. Greek notions of harmony, proportion, and beauty have remained the touchstones for all subsequent Western art. A rational method of inquiry, so important to modern science, was conceived in ancient Greece. Many of our political terms are Greek in origin, and so are our concepts of the rights and duties of citizenship, especially as they were conceived in Athens, the first great democracy the world had seen. Especially during their Classical Period, the Greeks raised and debated the fundamental questions about the purpose of human existence, the structure of human society, and the nature of the universe that have concerned Western thinkers ever since.

All of these achievements came from a group of small city-states in ancient Greece. And yet Greek civilization also contains an element of tragedy. For all of their brilliant accomplishments, the Greeks were unable to rise above the divisions and rivalries that caused them to fight each other and undermine their own civilization.

Notes

1. H. D. F. Kitto, *The Greeks* (Harmondsworth, England, 1951), p. 64.
2. Homer, *Odyssey*, trans. E. V. Rieu (Harmondsworth, England, 1946), p. 337.
3. Xenophon, *Symposium*, trans. O. J. Todd (Cambridge, Mass., 1968), 3.5.
4. Homer, *Odyssey*, pp. 290–291.
5. Quoted in Thomas R. Martin, *Ancient Greece* (New Haven, Conn., 1996), p. 62.
6. These words from Plutarch are quoted in Elaine Fantham, Helene P. Foley, Natalie B. Kampen, Sarah B. Pomeroy, and H. Alan Shapiro, *Women in the Classical World* (New York, 1994), p. 64.
7. Hesiod, *Works and Days*, trans. Dorothea Wender (Harmondsworth, 1973), pp. 77, 69, 71, 68.
8. Theognis, *Elegies*, trans. Dorothea Wender (Harmondsworth, England, 1973), pp. 118, 100.
9. Aeschylus, *The Persians*, in *The Complete Greek Tragedies*, vol. 1, ed. David Grene and Richmond Lattimore (Chicago, 1959), p. 229.
10. Voltaire, *The Age of Louis XIV*, trans. Martyn Pollack (London, 1926), p. 1.
11. Herodotus, *The Persian Wars*, trans. Robin Waterfield (New York, 1998), p. 3.
12. Thucydides, *History of the Peloponnesian War*, trans. Rex Warner (Harmondsworth, England, 1954), p. 24.
13. Ibid.
14. Sophocles, *Oedipus the King*, trans. David Grene (Chicago, 1959), pp. 68–69.
15. Sophocles, *Antigone*, trans. Don Taylor (London, 1986), p. 146.
16. Plato, *The Republic*, trans. F. M. Cornford (New York, 1945), pp. 178–179.
17. Quotations from Aristotle are from Sue Blundell, *Women in Ancient Greece* (London, 1995), pp. 106, 186.

Suggestions for Further Reading

A standard one-volume reference work for Greek history is J. B. Bury and R. Meiggs, *A History of Greece to the Death of Alexander the Great*, 4th ed. (New York, 1975). For a beautifully illustrated introduction, see F. Durando, *Ancient Greece: The Dawn of the Western World* (New York, 1997). Other good general introductions to Greek history include *The Oxford History of the Classical World*, ed. J. Boardman, J. Griffin, and O. Murray (Oxford, 1986), pp. 19–314; T. R. Martin, *Ancient Greece* (New Haven, Conn., 1996); P. Cartledge, *The Cambridge Illustrated History of Ancient Greece* (Cambridge, 1998); and W. Donlan,

S. B. Pomeroy, J. T. Roberts, and S. M. Burstein, *Ancient Greece: A Political, Social, and Cultural History* (New York, 1998). Hoplite warfare is well covered in V. D. Hanson, *The Western Way of War: Infantry Battle in Classical Greece* (New York, 1989) and *Hoplites: The Classical Greek Battle Experience* (New York, 1991).

Early Greek history is examined in O. Murray, *Early Greece*, 2d ed. (Cambridge, Mass., 1993); M. I. Finley, *Early Greece: The Bronze and Archaic Ages*, 2d ed. (New York, 1982); and J. L. Fitton, *The Discovery of the Greek Bronze Age* (Cambridge, 1995). For an introduction to Homer, see J. Griffin, *Homer* (Oxford, 1980). On Homer and his world, see the modern classic by M. I. Finley, *The World of Odysseus*, 2d ed. (New York, 1979).

General works on Archaic Greece include A. M. Snodgrass, *Archaic Greece* (London, 1980), and M. Grant, *The Rise of the Greeks* (London, 1987). Economic and social history of the period is covered in C. Starr, *The Economic and Social Growth of Early Greece, 800–500* B.C. (Oxford, 1977). On colonization, see J. Boardman, *The Greeks Overseas*, rev. ed. (Baltimore, 1980). On tyranny, see J. F. McGlew, *Tyranny and Political Culture in Ancient Greece* (Ithaca, N.Y., 1993). On the culture of Archaic Greece, see W. Burkert, *The Orientalizing Revolution: Near Eastern Influence on Greek Culture in the Early Archaic Age* (Cambridge, Mass., 1992). The best histories of Sparta are W. Forrest, *A History of Sparta, 950–121 B.C.*, 2d ed. (London, 1980), and P. A. Cartledge, *Sparta and Laconia: A Regional History, 1300–362 B.C.* (London, 1979). See also P. Cartledge, *Spartan Reflections* (Berkeley, Calif., 2001). On early Athens, see the still valuable A. Jones, *Athenian Democracy* (London, 1957), and R. Osborne, *Demos* (New York, 1985). The Persian Wars are examined in P. Green, *The Greco-Persian Wars* (Berkeley, Calif., 1996).

A general history of Classical Greece can be found in S. Hornblower, *The Greek World, 479–323 B.C.* (London, 1983), and J. K. Davies, *Democracy and Classical Greece*, 2d ed. (Cambridge, Mass., 1993). Valuable works on Athens include D. Kagan, *Pericles of Athens and the Birth of Democracy* (New York, 1991); C. Farrar, *The Origins of Democratic Thinking: The Invention of Politics in Classical Athens* (Cambridge, 1988); C. W. Fornara and L. J. Samons II, *Athens from Cleisthenes to Pericles* (Berkeley, Calif., 1991); and D. Stockton, *The Classical Athenian Democracy* (Oxford, 1990). On the development of the Athenian empire, see R. Meiggs, *The Athenian Empire* (Oxford, 1975), and M. F. McGregor, *The Athenians and Their Empire* (Vancouver, 1987). The best way to examine the Great Peloponnesian War is to read the work of Thucydides, *History of the Peloponnesian War*, trans. Rex Warner (Harmondsworth, England, 1954). On fourth-century Athens, see M. H. Hansen, *The Athenian Democracy in the Age of Demosthenes* (Oxford, 1991).

For a comprehensive history of Greek art, see M. Robertson, *A History of Greek Art*, 2 vols. (Cambridge, 1975). On sculpture, see A. Stewart, *Greek Sculpture: An Exploration* (New Haven, Conn., 1990). A basic survey of architecture is H. W. Lawrence, *Greek Architecture*, rev. ed. (Harmondsworth, England, 1983). On Greek drama, see the general work by J. De Romilly, *A Short History of Greek Literature* (Chicago, 1985). For sound studies of Greek history writing, see J. A. S. Evans, *Herodotus* (Boston, 1982), and K. Dover, *Thucydides* (Oxford, 1973). On Greek philosophy, a detailed study is available in W. K. C. Guthrie, *A History of Greek Philosophy*, 6 vols. (Cambridge, 1962–81).

On Greek religion, see J. N. Bremmer, *Greek Religion* (Oxford, 1994); W. Burkert, *Greek Religion*, trans. J. Raffan (Cambridge, Mass., 1985); and R. Garland, *Religion and the Greeks* (New York, 1994).

On the family and women, see C. B. Patterson, *The Family in Greek History* (New York, 1998); M. Golden, *Children and Childhood in Classical Athens* (Baltimore, 1990); S. B. Pomeroy, *Goddesses, Whores, Wives, and Slaves* (New York, 1975); E. Fantham, H. P. Foley, N. B. Kampen, S. B. Pomeroy, and H. A. Shapiro, *Women in the Classical World* (New York, 1994); and S. Blundell, *Women in Ancient Greece* (London, 1995). On slavery, see Y. Garlan, *Slavery in Ancient Greece* (Ithaca, N.Y., 1988), and N. R. E. Fisher, *Slavery in Classical Greece* (New York, 1995). On homosexuality, see K. J. Dover, *Greek Homosexuality* (London, 1978), and E. Cantarella, *Bisexuality in the Ancient World* (New Haven, Conn., 1992).

For additional reading, go to InfoTrac College Edition, your online research library at http://web1.infotrac-college.com

Enter the search term *Greek history* using Key Terms.

Enter the search term *Greek mythology* using the Subject Guide.

Enter the search term *Peloponnesian War* using Key Terms.

C H A P T E R

4

The Hellenistic World

CHAPTER OUTLINE

FOCUS QUESTIONS

- How was Alexander able to amass his empire, and what might his rule have been like if he had lived longer?
- What role did cities play in the Hellenistic kingdoms?
- What were the chief political, economic, and social developments in the Hellenistic world?
- What achievements in science and medicine occurred during the Hellenistic period?
- Which schools of philosophy and which religions were prominent during the Hellenistic period, and what does their popularity suggest about Hellenistic society?
- How was the Hellenistic period different from the Greek Classical Age?

IN 334 B.C., ALEXANDER THE GREAT led an army of Greeks and Macedonians into western Asia to launch his attack on the Persian Empire. Years of campaigning resulted in the complete defeat of the Persians, and in 327 B.C. Alexander and his troops pushed eastward into India. But two more years of fighting in an exotic and difficult terrain exhausted his troops, who rebelled and refused to go on. Reluctantly, Alexander turned back, leading his men across the arid lands of southern Persia. Conditions in the desert were appalling; the blazing sun and lack of water led to thousands of deaths. At one point, when a group of his soldiers found a little water, they scooped it up in a helmet and gave it to Alexander. Then, according to Arrian, an ancient Greek historian, Alexander, "with a word of thanks for the gift, took the helmet and, in full view of his troops, poured the water on the ground. So extraordinary was the effect of this action that the water wasted by Alexander was as good as a drink for every man in the army." Ever the great military leader, Alexander had found yet another way to inspire his troops.

Alexander the Great was the son of King Philip II of Macedonia, who in 338 B.C. defeated the Greeks and established his control over the Greek peninsula. After Philip's death, Alexander became king and led the Macedonians and Greeks on a spectacular conquest of the Persian Empire and opened the door to the spread of Greek culture throughout the ancient Near East. Greek settlers poured into these lands as bureaucrats, traders, soldiers, and scholars. Alexander's triumph created a new series of kingdoms that blended together the achievements of the eastern world with the cultural outlook and attitudes of the Greeks. We use the term Hellenistic *to designate this new order. The Hellenistic world was the world of Greeks and non-Greek easterners, and it resulted, in its own way, in a remarkable series of accomplishments that are sometimes underestimated. They form the story of this chapter.*

The Rise of Macedonia

While the Greek city-states were continuing to fight each other, to their north a new and ultimately powerful kingdom was emerging in its own right. Its people, the Macedonians, were viewed as barbarians by their southern neighbors, the Greeks. The Macedonians were mostly rural folk and were organized into tribes rather than city-states. Not until the end of the fifth century B.C. did Macedonia emerge as an important kingdom. When King Philip II (359–336 B.C.) took control, he turned Macedonia into the chief power of the Greek world.

Philip had spent three years as a hostage in Thebes, where he had gained a great admiration for Greek culture and absorbed the latest Greek military developments. Philip understood the importance of having an efficient army if Macedonia was to be a strong state. Philip used Macedonian countrymen, sturdy peasants and shepherds, as the core of his phalanx of infantrymen. From the gold mines of Mount Pangaeus, he obtained the wealth to pay these soldiers and establish a standing professional army. The Macedonian phalanx was also armed with long thrusting spears and supported by strong cavalry contingents that served to break the opposing line of battle and create disorder in the enemy's ranks. Philip's new army defeated the Illyrians to the west and the Thracians to the north and east and was then drawn into the Greeks' interstate conflicts.

The Greeks had mixed reactions to Philip's growing strength. Many Athenians, especially the orator Demosthenes, came to have a strong distrust of the Macedonian leader's intentions. Demosthenes delivered a series of orations, known as the *Philippics*, in which he portrayed Philip as ruthless, deceitful, treacherous, and barbaric and called on the Athenians to undertake a struggle against him (see the box on p. 84). Other Athenians, such as Isocrates, a teacher of rhetoric, viewed Philip as a savior who would rescue the Greeks from themselves by uniting them and organizing the entire Greek world in a crusade against the common enemy, the Persians.

Demosthenes' repeated calls for action, combined with Philip's rapid expansion, finally spurred Athens into action. Allied with Thebes and some other smaller states, Athens fought the Macedonians at the Battle of Chaeronea, near Thebes, in 338 B.C. The Macedonian army crushed the Greek allies, and Philip was now free to consolidate his control over the Greek peninsula. While Thebes was punished severely, Athens was treated leniently out of respect for its past and expected cooperation in the future. The Greek states were joined together in an alliance that we call the Corinthian League because they met at Corinth. All members took an oath of loyalty: "I swear by Zeus, Earth, Sun, Poseidon, Athena, Ares, and all the gods and goddesses. I will abide by the peace, and I will not break the agreements with Philip the Macedonian, nor will I take up arms with hostile intent against any one of those who abide by the oaths either by land or by sea."[1]

Though based on the principle of self-governing, independent states, the league did have an army and a council.

Philip II. Having unified Macedonia, Philip built a powerful standing army from his Macedonian subjects and defeated the Greek city-states allied against him in 338 B.C. Philip did not hesitate to share his soldiers' dangers and was wounded a number of times, including the loss of an eye. This small ivory head of Philip II found at Vergina clearly shows the damage to his right eye.

Demosthenes Condemns Philip of Macedonia

Among the Greeks, Demosthenes, above all, reacted strongly to the growing strength and expansionary policies of the Macedonian king Philip II. Demosthenes delivered a series of orations to the Athenian assembly in which he portrayed Philip as a ruthless and barbaric man. This excerpt is from the *Third Philippic*, probably delivered in 341 B.C.

■ *Demosthenes,* The Third Philippic

I observe, however, that all men, and you first of all, have conceded to him something which has been the occasion of every war that the Greeks have ever waged. And what is that? The power of doing what he likes, of calmly plundering and stripping the Greeks one by one, and of attacking their cities and reducing them to slavery. Yet your hegemony in Greece lasted seventy-three years, that of Sparta twenty-nine, and in these later times Thebes too gained some sort of authority after the battle of Leuctra. But neither to you nor to the Thebans nor to the Spartans did the Greeks ever yet, men of Athens, concede the right of unrestricted action, or anything like it. On the contrary, when you, or rather the Athenians of that day, were thought to be showing a want of consideration in dealing with others, all felt it their duty, even those who had no grievance against them, to go to war in support of those who had been injured. . . . Yet all the faults committed by the Spartans in those thirty years, and by our ancestors in their seventy years of supremacy, are fewer, men of Athens, than the wrongs which Philip has done to the Greeks in the thirteen incomplete years in which he has been coming to the top—or rather, they are not a fraction of them. . . . Ay, and you know this also, that the wrongs which the Greeks suffered from the Spartans or from us, they suffered at all events at the hands of true-born sons of Greece, and they might have been regarded as the acts of a legitimate son, born to great possessions, who should be guilty of some fault or error in the management of his estate: so far he would deserve blame and reproach, yet it could not be said that it was not one of the blood, not the lawful heir who was acting thus. But if some slave or illegitimate bastard had wasted and squandered what he had no right to, heavens! how much more monstrous and exasperating all would have called it! Yet they have no such qualms about Philip and his present conduct, though he is not only no Greek, nor related to the Greeks, but not even a barbarian from any place that can be named with honor, but a pestilent knave from Macedonia, from where it was never yet possible to buy a decent slave.

Philip of Macedon was recognized as *hegemon* (leader) of the league and its army. Although Philip allowed the Greek city-states autonomy in domestic affairs, he retained the general direction of their foreign affairs. Many Greeks still objected to being subject to the less civilized master from the north, but Philip insisted that the Greek states end their bitter rivalries and cooperate with him in a war against Persia.

Before Philip could undertake his invasion of Asia, however, he was assassinated, leaving the task to his son Alexander. Although Alexander justly deserves credit for the destruction of the Persian Empire, it was Philip who really paved the way for the conquest. He had unified Macedonia, created a powerful military machine, and subdued the Greeks.

Alexander the Great

Alexander was only twenty when he became king of Macedonia. In only twelve years, he achieved so much that he has since been called Alexander the Great. The illustrious conqueror was in many ways groomed for kingship by his father, who had taken Alexander along on military campaigns and at the important Battle of Chaeronea had given him control of the cavalry. After his father's assassination, Alexander moved quickly to assert his authority, securing

Bust of Alexander the Great. This bust of Alexander the Great is a Roman copy of the head of a statue, possibly by Lysippus. Although he aspired to be another Achilles, the tragic hero of Homer's *Iliad*, Alexander also sought more divine honors. He claimed to be descended from Heracles, a Greek hero worshiped as a god, and as pharaoh of Egypt, he gained recognition as a living deity.

the Macedonian frontiers and smothering a rebellion in Greece. He then turned to his father's dream, the invasion of the Persian Empire.

Alexander's Conquests

There is no doubt that Alexander was taking a chance in attacking the Persian Empire. Although weakened in some respects, it was still a strong state. Alexander's fleet was inferior to the Persian navy, which drew its ships from the Phoenicians and other coastal peoples of western Asia, and his finances were shaky at best. His army would have to live off the countryside and win quick victories to gain the resources needed to continue the struggle. In the spring of 334 B.C., Alexander entered Asia Minor with an army of some 37,000 men. About half were Macedonians, the rest Greeks and other allies. The cavalry, which would play an important role as a striking force, numbered about five thousand. Architects, engineers, historians, and scientists accompanied the army, a clear indication of Alexander's grand vision and positive expectations at the beginning of his campaign.

His first confrontation with the Persians, at the Granicus River in 334 B.C. (see Map 4.1), nearly cost him his life but resulted in a major victory. By the spring of 333 B.C., the entire western half of Asia Minor was in Alexander's hands, and the Ionian Greek cities of southwestern Asia Minor had been "liberated" from the Persian oppressor. Not all of them wished to be liberated, and many regarded Alexander simply as their new master.

Meanwhile, the Persian king, Darius III, mobilized his forces to stop Alexander's army. Although the Persian troops outnumbered Alexander's, the Battle of Issus was fought on a narrow field that canceled the advantage of superior numbers and resulted in another Macedonian success. The Persian cause was certainly not helped when Darius made a spectacular exit from the battlefield before it was even clear who would be victorious. After his victory at Issus in 333 B.C., Alexander laid siege to the port cities of Tyre and Gaza to prevent Persian control of the sea. Egypt surrendered without a fight, and by the winter of 332 B.C., Syria, Palestine, and Egypt were under Alexander's domination. He took the traditional title of pharaoh of Egypt and was hailed as the "son of Amon," to the Greeks the equivalent of being called the son of Zeus. Alexander also built the first of a series of cities named after him (Alexandria) to be the Greek administrative capital of Egypt. It became (and remains today) one of the most important cities in the Mediterranean world.

In the meantime, Darius indicated his willingness to make a peace settlement, offering to cede all land west of the Euphrates River to Alexander. Alexander refused and renewed the offensive. He moved now into the territory of the ancient Mesopotamian kingdoms and fought a decisive battle with the Persians at Gaugamela in the summer of 331 B.C. At Gaugamela, Alexander's men were clearly outnumbered by the Persian forces, which had established the battle site on a broad, open plain where their war chariots could maneuver to best advantage. Alexander was able to break through the center of the Persian line with his heavy cavalry, followed by the infantry. The battle turned into a rout, although Darius managed to escape. After his victory, Alexander entered Babylon and then proceeded to the Persian capitals at Susa and Persepolis, where he acquired the Persian treasuries and took possession of vast quantities of gold and silver.

Alexander and Darius at the Battle of Issus. This late Hellenistic mosaic from Pompeii depicts the battle between Alexander and Darius III, king of Persia, at Issus in 333 B.C. Alexander landed his forces in western Asia Minor in 334 B.C. to begin his Persian campaign and first met Darius at Issus, where the narrow field made the greater numbers of the Persians useless.

Scala/Art Resource, NY

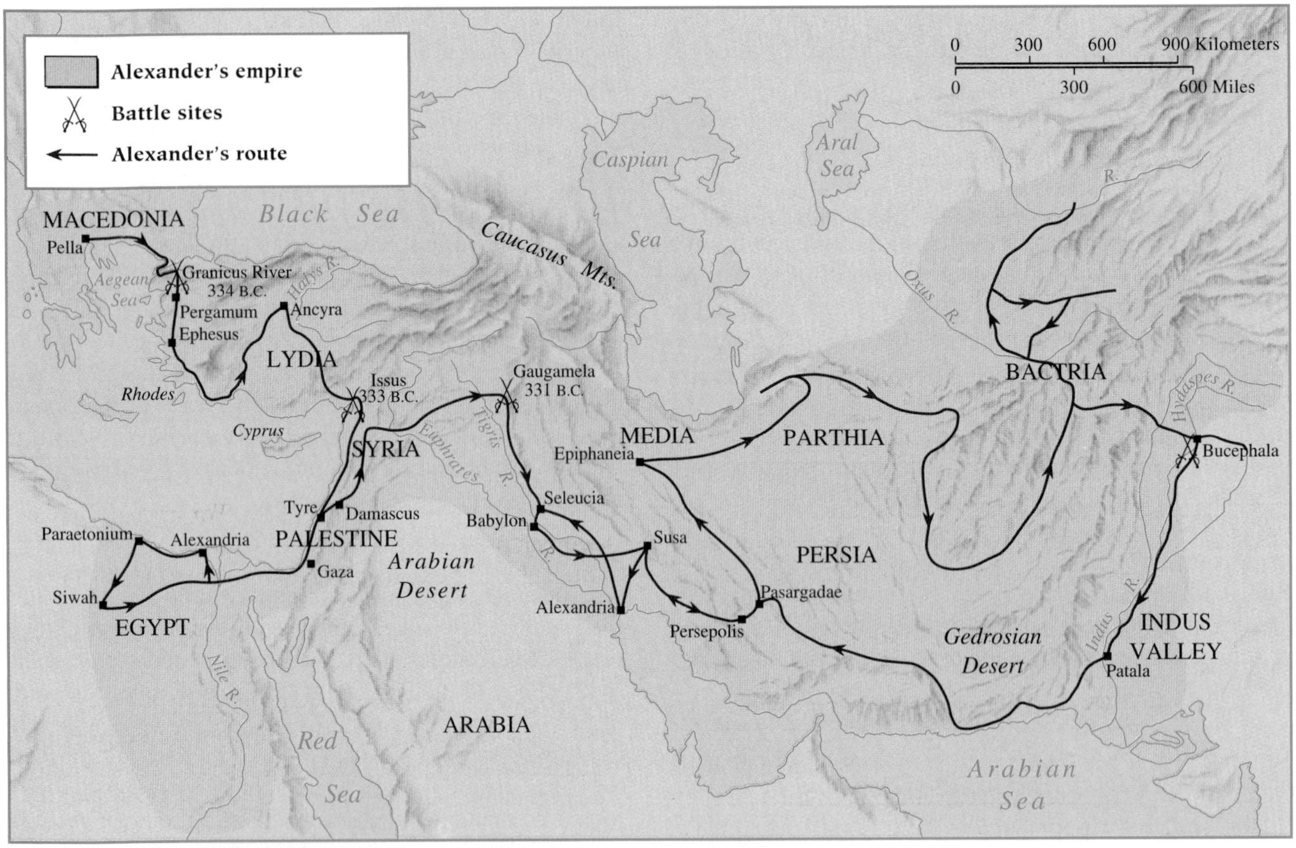

Map 4.1 The Conquests of Alexander the Great. In just twelve years, Alexander the Great conquered vast territories. Dominating lands from west of the Nile to east of the Indus, he brought the Persian Empire, Egypt, and much of the Middle East under his control and laid the foundations for the Hellenistic world. ■ Approximately how far did he and his troops travel during those twelve years?

By 330 B.C., Alexander was again on the march. After Darius was killed by one of his own men, Alexander took the title and office of the Great King of the Persians. But he was not content to rest with the spoils of the Persian Empire. Over the next three years, he moved east and northeast, as far as modern Pakistan. By the summer of 327 B.C., he had entered India, which at that time was divided into a number of warring states. In 326 B.C., Alexander and his armies arrived in the plains of northwestern India. At the Battle of the Hydaspes River, Alexander won a brutally fought battle (see the box on p. 87). When Alexander made clear his determination to march east to conquer more of India, his soldiers, weary of campaigning year after year, mutinied and refused to go further. Alexander surrendered to their demands and agreed to return, leading his troops through southern Persia across the Gedrosian Desert, where they suffered heavy losses from appalling desert conditions. Alexander and the remnant of his army went to Susa and then Babylon, where he planned more campaigns. But in June 323 B.C., weakened from wounds, fever, and probably excessive alcohol, he died at the young age of thirty-two.

Alexander's Ideals

Alexander is one of the most puzzling great figures in history. Historians relying on the same sources give vastly different pictures of him. Some portray him as an idealistic visionary and others as a ruthless Machiavellian. How did Alexander the Great view himself? We know that he sought to imitate Achilles, the warrior-hero of Homer's *Iliad*. Alexander kept a copy of the *Iliad*—and a dagger—under his pillow. He also claimed to be descended from Heracles, the Greek hero who came to be worshiped as a god. No doubt Alexander aspired to divine honors; as pharaoh of Egypt, he became a living god according to Egyptian tradition and at one point even sent instructions to the Greek cities to "vote him a god."

Some historians have argued that Alexander believed in an ideal of universal humanity. As evidence they cite the fact that he urged his soldiers to marry native women, and at Susa in 324 B.C. he celebrated the marriages of ten thousand of them en masse to local women. Alexander himself married easterners—Stateira, daughter of Darius, and Roxane, daughter of a Bactrian baron. Was Alexander pursuing a lofty ideal, or was he simply looking for a real-

Alexander Meets an Indian King

In his campaigns in India, Alexander fought a number of difficult battles. At the Battle of the Hydaspes River, he faced a strong opponent in the Indian king Porus. After defeating Porus, Alexander treated him with respect, according to Arrian, Alexander's ancient biographer.

Arrian, The Campaigns of Alexander

Throughout the action Porus had proved himself a man indeed, not only as a commander but as a soldier of the truest courage. When he saw his cavalry cut to pieces, most of his infantry dead, and his elephants killed or roaming riderless and bewildered about the field, his behavior was very different from that of the Persian King Darius: unlike Darius, he did not lead the scramble to save his own skin, but so long as a single unit of his men held together, he fought bravely on. It was only when he was himself wounded that he turned the elephant on which he rode and began to withdraw. . . . Alexander, anxious to save the life of this great and gallant soldier, sent . . . [to him] an Indian named Meroes, a man he had been told had long been Porus' friend. Porus listened to Meroes' message, stopped his elephant, and dismounted; he was much distressed by thirst, so when he had revived himself by drinking, he told Meroes to conduct him with all speed to Alexander.

Alexander, informed of his approach, rode out to meet him. . . . When they met, he reined in his horse and looked at his adversary with admiration: he was a magnificent figure of a man, over seven feet high and of great personal beauty; his bearing had lost none of its pride; his air was of one brave man meeting another, of a king in the presence of a king, with whom he had fought honorably for his kingdom.

Alexander was the first to speak. "What," he said, "do you wish that I should do with you?" "Treat me as a king ought," Porus is said to have replied. "For my part," said Alexander, pleased by his answer, "your request shall be granted. But is there not something you would wish for yourself? Ask it." "Everything," said Porus, "is contained in this one request."

The dignity of these words gave Alexander even more pleasure, and he restored to Porus his sovereignty over his subjects, adding to his realm other territory of even greater extent. Thus he did indeed use a brave man as a king ought, and from that time forward found him in every way a loyal friend.

istic way to unify his newly won domains? Early on in his conquests, he adopted features of Persian rule. He called himself the Great King and asked his subjects to bow before him in the Persian fashion. He wore Persian dress, used Persians as administrators, and trained native youths in Macedonian military methods. His fellow Macedonians objected to these trappings of eastern despotism and the equal treatment he accorded Persians. Some even went so far as to attempt his assassination. But Alexander must have felt a need to fuse the Macedonians, Greeks, and Persians into a ruling class that would enable him to control such an extensive empire. One is left with the impression that he aspired to autocratic monarchy rather than a lofty vision of the unity of humankind.

Alexander's Legacy

Regardless of his ideals, motives, or views about himself, one fact stands out: Alexander created a new age, the Hellenistic era. The word *Hellenistic* is derived from a Greek word meaning "to imitate Greeks." It is an appropriate way to describe an age that saw the extension of the Greek language and ideas to the non-Greek world of the ancient Near East. Alexander's destruction of the Persian monarchy had extended Greco-Macedonian rule over an enormous area. It created opportunities for Greek engineers, intellectuals, merchants, soldiers, and administrators. While the Greeks on the mainland might remain committed to the ideals of their city-states, those who followed Alexander and his successors participated in a new political unity based on the principle of monarchy. Alexander had transformed his army from a Macedonian force into an international one, owing loyalty only to himself. His successors used force to establish military monarchies that dominated the Hellenistic world after his death. Autocratic power, based on military strength and pretensions of divine rule, became a regular feature of those Hellenistic monarchies and was part of Alexander's political legacy to the Hellenistic world. His vision of empire no doubt inspired the Romans, who were, of course, the real heirs of Alexander's legacy.

But Alexander also left a cultural legacy. As a result of his conquests, Greek language, art, architecture, and literature spread throughout the Near East. The urban centers of the Hellenistic age, many founded by Alexander and his successors, became springboards for the diffusion of Greek culture. Alexander had established a number of cities and military colonies named Alexandria to guard strategic points and supervise wide areas. Most of the settlers were Greek mercenaries. It has been estimated that in the course of his campaigns, Alexander summoned some 60,000 to 65,000 additional mercenaries from Greece, at least 36,000 of whom took up residence in the garrisons and new cities. While the Greeks spread their culture in the east, they were also inevitably influenced by eastern ways. Thus Alexander's legacy became one of the hallmarks of the Hellenistic world: the clash and fusion of different cultures.

CHRONOLOGY

The Rise of Macedonia and the Conquests of Alexander

Reign of Philip II	359–336 B.C.
Battle of Chaeronea; Philip II conquers Greece	338 B.C.
Reign of Alexander the Great	336–323 B.C.
Alexander invades Asia; Battle of Granicus River	334 B.C.
Battle of Issus	333 B.C.
Battle of Gaugamela	331 B.C.
Fall of Persepolis, the Persian capital	330 B.C.
Alexander enters India	327 B.C.
Battle of Hydaspes River	326 B.C.
Death of Alexander	323 B.C.

The World of the Hellenistic Kingdoms

The united empire that Alexander created by his conquests disintegrated after his death. All too soon, Macedonian military leaders were engaged in a struggle for power. By 301 B.C., after the Battle of Ipsus, any hope of unity was dead, and eventually four Hellenistic kingdoms emerged as the successors to Alexander: Macedonia under the Antigonid dynasty, Syria and the east under the Seleucids, the Attalid kingdom of Pergamum, and Egypt under the Ptolemies (see Map 4.2).

In Macedonia, the struggles for power led to the extermination of Alexander the Great's dynasty. Not until 276 B.C. did Antigonus Gonatus, the grandson of one of Alexander's generals, succeed in establishing the Antigonid dynasty as rulers of Macedonia. The Antigonids viewed control of Greece as essential to their power but did not see outright conquest as necessary. Macedonia was, of course, also important to the Greeks. As one ancient commentator noted, "It is in the interest of the Greeks that the Macedonian dominion should be humbled for long, but by no means that it should be destroyed. For in that case . . . [the Macedonians] would very soon experience the lawless violence of the Thracians and Gauls, as they had on more than one occasion."[2] But the Greeks, like the Macedonians, eventually fell subject to Roman power.

Another Hellenistic monarchy was founded by the general Seleucus, who established the Seleucid dynasty of Syria. This was the largest of the Hellenistic kingdoms and controlled much of the old Persian Empire from Turkey in the west to India in the east, although the Seleucids found it increasingly difficult to maintain control of the eastern territories. In fact, an Indian ruler named Chandragupta Maurya (324–301 B.C.) created a new Indian state, the Mauryan Empire, and drove out the Seleucid forces. His grandson

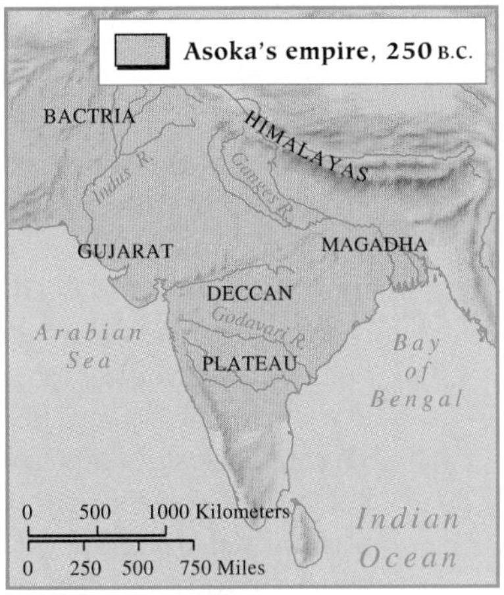

The Mauryan Empire Under Asoka

Giraudon/Art Resource, NY

A Gaul and His Wife: Monument to the Victory of a Hellenistic King. After the death of Alexander, the empire he had created collapsed, and four Hellenistic kingdoms arose in its place. Warfare continued to be of importance to these kingdoms, as it was through warfare that they were created, maintained, and expanded. They did not just fight among themselves, however; they also faced foreign enemies, such as the Gauls, who first entered the Hellenistic world in 279 B.C. This statue of a Gaulish chieftain and his wife was part of a larger monument erected to commemorate the victory of Attalus I of Pergamum over the Gauls, a victory that gave Pergamum control over much of Asia Minor.

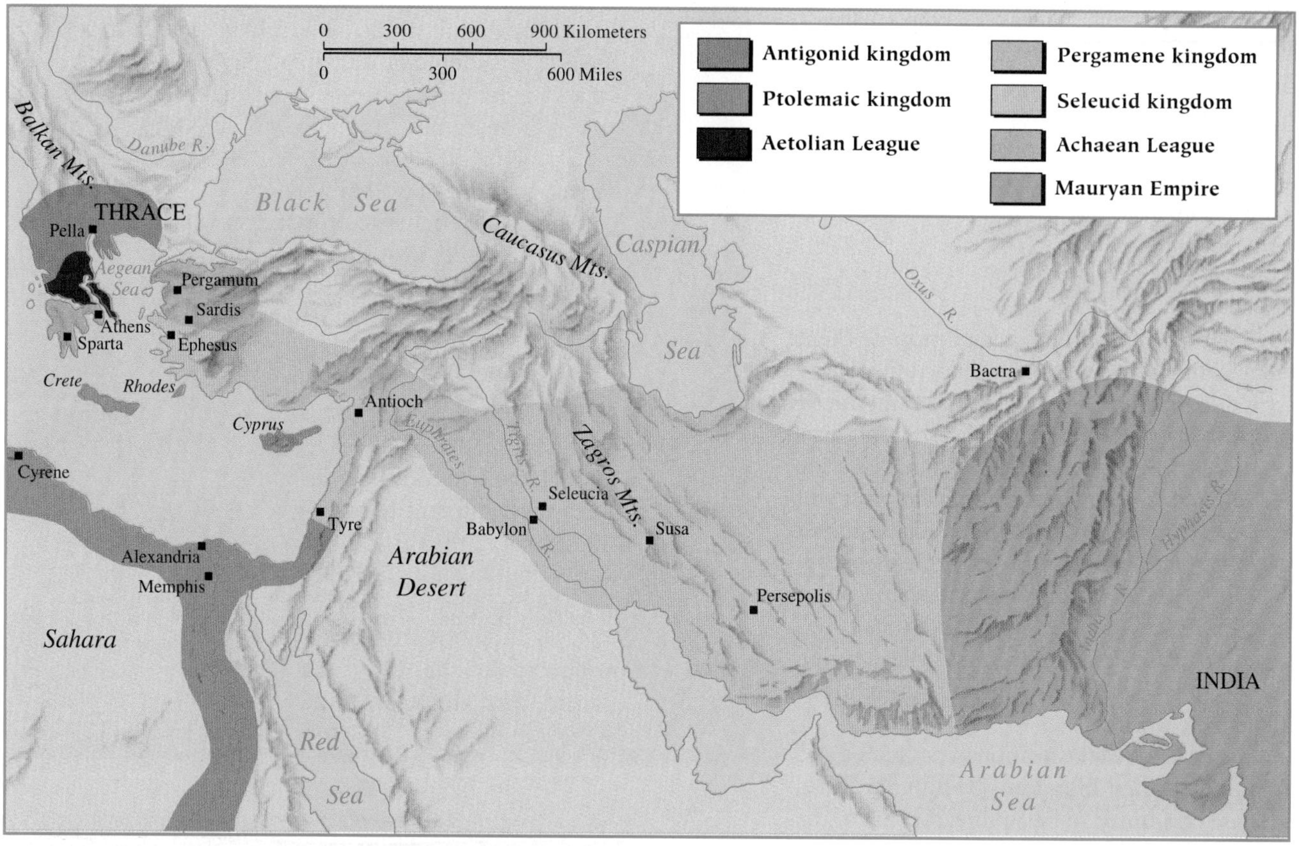

Map 4.2 The World of the Hellenistic Kingdoms. Alexander died unexpectedly at the age of thirty-two and did not designate a successor. Upon his death, his generals struggled for power, eventually creating four monarchies that spread Hellenistic culture and fostered trade and economic development. ■ Which kingdom encompassed most of the old Persian Empire?

Asoka (269–232 B.C.) extended the empire to include most of India and is considered the greatest ruler in India's history.

A third Hellenistic kingdom came into being by freeing itself from the Seleucids. This was the kingdom of Pergamum in western Asia Minor under the Attalid dynasty. It was Pergamum that brought the Romans into the area by seeking their aid first against the Antigonids and then against the Seleucids. This led to the Roman defeat of Antiochus III, probably the strongest of the Seleucid monarchs, in 191 B.C. The Seleucids declined thereafter until their small remaining territory was made a Roman province in 63 B.C. Seventy years before that, the last of the Attalid dynasty had bequeathed his kingdom to Rome in his will.

The fourth Hellenistic monarchy was Egypt, which had come under the control of Ptolemy, another Macedonian general. Named governor of Egypt after Alexander's death, Ptolemy had established himself as king by 305 B.C., creating the Ptolemaic dynasty of pharaohs. Hellenistic Egypt lasted longer than all the other Hellenistic monarchies; it was not until the reign of Cleopatra VII, who allied herself with the wrong side in the Roman civil wars (see Chapter 5), that Egypt fell to the Romans in 30 B.C.

The Hellenistic Monarchies

The Hellenistic monarchies created a semblance of stability for several centuries, even though Hellenistic kings refused to accept the new status quo and periodically engaged in wars to alter it. At the same time, an underlying strain always existed between the new Greco-Macedonian ruling class and the native populations. Together these factors created a certain degree of tension that was never truly ended until the vibrant Roman state to the west stepped in and imposed a new order.

The Hellenistic kingdoms shared a common political system that represented a break with their Greek past. To the Greeks, monarchy was an institution for barbarians, associated in their minds with people like the Persians. Although they retained democratic forms of government in their cities, the Greeks of the Hellenistic world were forced to accept monarchy as a new fact of political life.

Although Alexander the Great apparently had planned to fuse Greeks and easterners, Hellenistic monarchs relied primarily on Greeks and Macedonians to form the new ruling class. It has been estimated that in the Seleucid kingdom, for example, only 2.5 percent of the people in

Greek War Elephants. Some of the armies in the Hellenistic world made use of elephants obtained from North Africa and India. Pictured on this Italian plate is a Greek war elephant that was brought to the Mediterranean by one of Alexander's successors. The battle fortress on the back of the elephant was a Greek innovation.

Scala/Art Resource, NY

authority were non-Greek, and most of them were commanders of local military units. Those who did advance to important administrative posts had learned Greek (all government business was transacted in Greek) and had become Hellenized in a cultural sense. The policy of excluding non-Greeks from leadership positions, it should be added, was not due to the incompetence of the natives but to the determination of the Greek ruling class to maintain its privileged position. It was the Greco-Macedonian ruling class that provided the only unity in the Hellenistic world.

Since the Hellenistic monarchs created and maintained their kingdoms by military force, warfare continued to be an integral part of the Hellenistic world. The phalanx— heavily armed infantry with long spears (lengthened by this time to 18 feet)—and the cavalry still formed the core of the Hellenistic forces. Hellenistic warfare also saw some innovations. Most noticeable were the elephants, "the tanks of ancient warfare," which were especially prominent in the army of the Seleucids, who procured theirs from India, and the Ptolemies, who obtained them from North Africa. But even more important, since armies quickly learned tricks that neutralized the elephants, was the development of new siege machinery, especially the catapult and siege towers. In classical times, cities with good walls were virtually impregnable; Alexander and later Hellenistic rulers could capture cities by using their new equipment.

Hellenistic Cities

Cities played an especially important role in the Hellenistic kingdoms. Throughout his conquests, Alexander had founded a series of new cities and military settlements, and Hellenistic kings did likewise. The new population centers varied considerably in size and importance. Military settlements were meant to maintain order and might consist of only a few hundred men heavily dependent on the king. But there were also new independent cities with thousands of inhabitants. Alexandria in Egypt was the largest city in the Mediterranean region by the first century B.C.

Hellenistic rulers encouraged this massive spread of Greek colonists to the Near East because of their intrinsic value to the new monarchies. Greeks (and Macedonians) provided not only a recruiting ground for the army but also a pool of civilian administrators and workers who would contribute to economic development. Even architects, engineers, dramatists, and actors were in demand in the new Greek cities. Many Greeks and Macedonians were quick to see the advantages of moving to the new urban centers and gladly sought their fortunes in the Near East. Greeks of all backgrounds joined the exodus until around 250 B.C., when the outpouring began to slow significantly.

Within the Hellenistic cities, the culture was primarily Greek. The political institutions of the cities were modeled after those of the Greek *polis.* Greeks of the Classical Period would easily have recognized the councils, magistracies, assemblies, and codes of law. The physical layout of the new cities was likewise modeled after those of the Greek homeland. Using the traditional rectilinear grid, cities were laid out with temples, altars, and stone theaters.

Many of the new urban centers were completely dominated by Greeks, while the native populations remained cut off from all civic institutions. The Greeks commissioned purely Greek sculpture, read literature of the Classical Period, and had separate law courts for themselves. Complaints from resentful natives have been recorded. An Egyptian camel driver, for example, complained bitterly that he was not paid regularly because he did "not know how to behave like a Greek." Not only was it difficult for easterners to enter the ranks of the ruling class, but those who did so had to become thoroughly Hellenized. This often required alienation from one's own culture.

The Greeks' belief in their own cultural superiority provided an easy rationalization for their political dominance of the eastern cities. But Greek control of the new cities was also necessary because the kings frequently used the cities as instruments of government, enabling them to rule considerable territory without an extensive bureaucracy. At the same time, for security reasons, the Greeks needed the support of the kings. After all, the Hellenistic cities were islands of Greek culture in a sea of non-Greeks. The relationship between rulers and cities, therefore, was a symbiotic one that bore serious consequences for the cities.

In their political system, religious practices, and city architecture, the Greeks tried to re-create the *poleis* of their homeland in their new cities. But it was no longer possible to do so. The new cities were not autonomous entities and soon found themselves dependent on the power of the Hellenistic monarchies. Although the kings did not rule the cities directly, they restricted their freedom in other ways. Cities knew they could not conduct an independent foreign policy and did not try to do so. The kings also demanded tribute, which could be a heavy burden.

The Greek cities of the Hellenistic era were the chief agents for the spread of Hellenic culture in the Near East, as far, in fact, as modern Afghanistan and India. These Greek cities were also remarkably vibrant despite their subordination to the Hellenistic monarchies and persisted in being a focal point for the loyalty of their citizens. Their continuing vitality is perhaps most evident on the Greek mainland, where the Greek cities formed two important leagues, the Aetolian League in central Greece and the Achaean League in the Peloponnesus.

Economic Trends

Agriculture was still of primary importance to both the native populations and the new Greek cities of the Hellenistic world. The Greek cities continued their old agrarian patterns. A well-defined citizen body owned land and worked it with the assistance of slaves. But their farms were isolated units in a vast area of land ultimately owned by the king or assigned to large estate owners and worked by native peasants dwelling in villages. Overall, then, neither agricultural patterns nor methods of production underwent significant changes.

Few new products or manufacturing methods were introduced in the Hellenistic world, but the centers of manufacturing shifted significantly. Industry spread from Greece to the east—especially to Asia Minor, Rhodes, and Egypt. New textile centers were set up at Pergamum, and glass and silver crafts were developed in Syria. Leading all cities in manufacturing was Alexandria in Egypt, which became the center for the production of parchment, textiles, linens, oil, metalwork, and glass.

Commerce expanded considerably in the Hellenistic era. Indeed, trading contacts linked much of the Hellenistic world together. The decline in the number of political barriers encouraged more commercial traffic. Although Hellenistic monarchs still fought wars, the conquests of Alexander and the policies of his successors made possible greater trade between east and west. Two major trade routes connected the east with the Mediterranean world. The central route was the major one and led by sea from India to the Persian Gulf, up the Tigris River to Seleucia on the Tigris, which replaced Babylon as the center for waterborne traffic from the Persian Gulf and overland caravan routes as well. Overland routes from Seleucia then led to Antioch and Ephesus. A southern route wound its way from India by sea but went around Arabia and up the Red Sea to Petra or later Berenice. Caravan routes then led overland to Coptos on the Nile, thence to Alexandria and the Mediterranean.

An incredible variety of products was traded: gold and silver from Spain; iron from northern Armenia; salt from Asia Minor; timber from Macedonia; purple dye from Tyre; ebony, gems, ivory, and spices from India; frankincense (used on altars) from Arabia; slaves from Thrace, Syria, and Asia Minor; fine wines from Syria and western Asia Minor; olive oil from Athens; and numerous exquisite foodstuffs, such as the famous prunes of Damascus. The greatest trade, however, was in the basic staple of life—grain. The great exporting areas were Egypt, Sicily, and the Black Sea region, while Rhodes and Delos served as the major depots for the international grain trade.

Hellenistic Society

One of the noticeable features of social life in the Hellenistic world was the emergence of new opportunities for women—at least for upper-class women. No doubt this was related to the changes in Hellenistic society itself, since the subordination of the cities to the kings altered the way men related to their *polis* and to each other. Some historians maintain that the visible role of Hellenistic queens may also have contributed to a new model for upper-class women.

New Opportunities for Upper-Class Women

The creation of the Hellenistic monarchies, which represented a considerable departure from the world of the city-state, gave new scope to the role played by the monarchs' wives, the Hellenistic queens. In Macedonia, a pattern of alliances between mothers and sons provided openings for women to take an active role in politics, especially in political intrigue. In Egypt, opportunities for royal women were even greater after the Ptolemaic rulers adopted the Egyptian custom of kings marrying their own sisters. Of the first eight Ptolemaic rulers, four wed their sisters. Ptolemy II and his sister-wife Arsinoë II were both worshiped as gods in their lifetimes. Arsinoë played an energetic role in government and was involved in the expansion of the Egyptian navy. She was also the first Egyptian queen whose portrait appeared on coins with her husband.

Portrait of Queen Arsinoë II. Arsinoë II, sister and wife of King Ptolemy II, played an active role in Egyptian political affairs. This statue from around 270–240 B.C. depicts the queen in the traditional style of a pharaoh.

Hellenistic queens also showed an intense interest in culture. They wrote poems, collected art, and corresponded with intellectuals.

The most notable gains for upper-class women came in the economic area. Documents show increasing numbers of women involved in managing slaves, selling property, and making loans. Even then, legal contracts in which women were involved had to include their official male guardians, although in numerous instances these men no longer played an important function but were only listed to satisfy legal requirements. In Sparta, women were allowed to own land and manage their own economic affairs. As many of their husbands were absent or had died in war, many Spartan women became wealthy; females owned 40 percent of the privately held land in Sparta.

Spartan women, however, were an exception, especially on the Greek mainland. Women in Athens, for example, still remained highly restricted and supervised. Although a few philosophers welcomed female participation in men's affairs, many philosophers rejected equality between men and women and asserted that the traditional roles of wives and mothers were most satisfying for women. In her treatise "On Chastity," Phintys wrote that "serving as generals, public officials, and statesmen is appropriate for men," but "keeping house, remaining within, and taking care of husbands belongs to women."[3]

But the opinions of philosophers did not prevent upper-class women from making gains in areas other than the economic sphere (see the box on p. 93). New possibilities for females arose when women in some areas of the Hellenistic world were allowed to pursue education in the fields of literature, music, and even athletics. Education, then, provided new opportunities for women: female poets appeared again in the third century B.C., and there are instances of women involved in both scholarly and artistic pursuits.

Some wealthy aristocratic women even became politically active in the running of their cities. In the second century B.C., a number of cities passed decrees honoring women for their service to the community. Cyme, in Asia Minor, for example, paid homage to Archippe for her enormous financial contributions. In return, some women were given political rights and in a few instances were allowed to hold office as city magistrates. But often economic motives were attached to this generosity. When Phile of Priene was made a magistrate of her city, it was probably with the understanding that she would donate funds for public works. Once in office, she did build an aqueduct and a reservoir for the community.

Improvements in the position of females were largely restricted to upper-class women. A harsher reality existed for a large group of women condemned to the practice of prostitution. Inscriptional evidence indicates that small families were common in the Hellenistic world; boys were preferred, and rarely was more than one daughter raised. Unwanted girl babies were often exposed to the elements and left to die. Some of these infants were gathered up by eager entrepreneurs and raised to be slave prostitutes. Only the most beautiful and luckiest prostitutes came to be the companions (the *hetairai*) of upper-class men.

The Role of Slavery

The Hellenistic world witnessed the migration of large numbers of people from one area to another. Greeks and Macedonians went into the Hellenistic kingdoms of the east as administrators, mercenaries, engineers, scholars, artists, teachers, and merchants. Moreover, significantly large numbers of non-Greeks moved around for economic and military purposes. But the largest number of uprooted people were slaves. Slavery was viewed as a normal part of life in the Hellenistic world and in antiquity in general.

A New Autonomy for Women

There were noticeable gains for upper-class women in Hellenistic society. But even in the lives of ordinary women, a new assertiveness came to the fore despite the continuing domination of society by men. The first selection is taken from the letter of a wife to her husband, complaining about his failure to return home. In the second selection, a father complains that his daughter has abandoned him, contrary to Egyptian law providing that children who have been properly raised should support their parents.

Letter from Isias to Hephaistion, 168 B.C.

If you are well and other things are going right, it would accord with the prayer that I make continually to the gods. I myself and the child and all the household are in good health and think of you always. When I received your letter from Horos, in which you announce that you are in detention in the Serapeum at Memphis, for the news that you are well I straightway thanked the gods, but about your not coming home, when all the others who had been secluded there have come, I am ill-pleased, because after having piloted myself and your child through such bad times and been driven to every extremity owing to the price of wheat, I thought that now at least, with you at home, I should enjoy some respite, whereas you have not even thought of coming home nor given any regard to our circumstances, remembering how I was in want of everything while you were still here, not to mention this long lapse of time and these critical days, during which you have sent us nothing. As, moreover, Horos who delivered the letter has brought news of your having been released from detention, I am thoroughly ill-pleased. Notwithstanding, as your mother also is annoyed, for her sake as well as for mine please return to the city, if nothing more pressing holds you back. You will do me a favor by taking care of your bodily health. Farewell.

Letter from Ktesikles to King Ptolemy, 220 B.C.

I am wronged by Dionysios and by Nike my daughter. For though I raised her, my own daughter, and educated her and brought her to maturity, when I was stricken with bodily ill-health and was losing my eyesight, she was not minded to furnish me with any of the necessities of life. When I sought to obtain justice from her in Alexandria, she begged my pardon, and in the eighteenth year she swore me a written royal oath to give me each month twenty drachmas, which she was to earn by her own bodily labor. . . . But now corrupted by Dionysios, who is a comic actor, she does not do for me anything of what was in the written oath, despising my weakness and ill-health. I beg you, therefore, O King, not to allow me to be wronged by my daughter and by Dionysios the actor who corrupted her, but to order Diophanes the strategus [provincial administrator] to summon them and hear us out; and if I am speaking the truth, let Diophanes deal with her corrupter as seems good to him and compel my daughter Nike to do justice to me. If this is done I shall no longer be wronged but by fleeing to you, O King, I shall obtain justice.

Slaves were obtained from four chief sources: the children of slaves; children who were sold by their parents or abandoned to perish; persons kidnapped by pirates; and perhaps the largest source of all, prisoners of war. Delos, a major trading center, could handle ten thousand slaves a day in its markets. Although slaves came from everywhere, Thracians and Syrians were the most numerous. Slaves varied in price; Macedonians, Thracians, and Italians drew the highest prices.

Slaves were put to work in numerous ways in the Hellenistic world. States employed slaves as servants for government officials and in government-run industries such as weaving. Most slaves were used in domestic service, farming, and mines, but the situation could vary from state to state. Egypt had no slave class in the countryside, nor was there much domestic slavery outside Alexandria. But the Egyptians did use slave labor in state-run textile factories and made especially brutal use of them in mining operations (see the box on p. 94). Women were also sold as slaves to be concubines for Greek and Macedonian soldiers and civilians.

The effects of slavery could also be important. The employment of large numbers of slaves in the Hellenistic kingdoms contributed to the Hellenizing process. Slaves working in homes, farms, or factories had opportunities to absorb Greek ways. This is especially evident in the case of the slave-wives of Hellenistic soldiers.

The Transformation of Education

In the Hellenistic world, education underwent a significant transformation. In the classical period of Greek history, education had been left largely to private enterprise. Greek cities now began to supervise education in new ways. The Greek gymnasium, which had been primarily an athletic institution, evolved into a secondary school. The curriculum centered on music, physical exercise, and literature, especially the poetry of Homer. Wealthy individuals often provided the money for the schools and also specified how it should be spent. An inscription from the city of Teos in Asia Minor specified that Polythroos "gave 34,000 drachmas . . . for there to be appointed each year . . . three grammar-masters to teach the boys and the girls; . . . for two gymnastics-masters to be appointed, . . . for a lyre—or harp—player to be appointed . . . he will teach music and lyre—or harp—playing to the children."[4]

Treatment of Slaves in the Egyptian Gold Mines

Slavery was a common practice throughout antiquity. In both Classical Greece and the Hellenistic world, the worst-treated slaves were those who worked in the mines. The Egyptians were especially notorious for their treatment of slaves in the gold mines in Nubia, described in this account by Diodorus of Sicily, who lived in the first century B.C. His account was based on the now lost work of the second-century writer Agatharchides.

■ *Diodorus of Sicily,* Library of History

And those who have been condemned in this way—and they are a great multitude and are all bound in chains—work at their task unceasingly both by day and throughout the entire night, enjoying no respite and being carefully cut off from any means of escape; since guards of foreign soldiers who speak a language different from theirs stand watch over them, so that not a man, either by conversation or by some contact of a friendly nature, is able to corrupt one of his keepers. . . . And the entire operations are in charge of a skilled worker who distinguishes the stone and points it out to the laborers; and of those who are assigned to this unfortunate task the physically strongest break the quartz-rock with iron hammers, applying no skill to the task but only force, and cutting tunnels through the stone, not in a straight line but wherever the seam of gleaming rock may lead. Now these men, working in darkness as they do because of the bending and winding of the passages, carry lamps bound on their foreheads; and since much of the time they change the position of their bodies to follow the particular character of the stone they throw the blocks, as they cut them out, on the ground, and at this task they labor without ceasing beneath the sternness and blows of an overseer.

The boys there who have not yet come to maturity, entering through the tunnels into the galleries formed by the removal of the rock, laboriously gather up the rock as it is cast down piece by piece and carry it out into the open to the place outside the entrance. Then those who are above thirty years of age take this quarried stone from them and with iron pestles pound a specified amount of it in stone mortars, until they have worked it down to a smaller size. Thereupon the women and older men receive from them the rock of this size and cast it into mills of which a number stand there in a row, and taking their places in groups of two or three at the spoke or handle of each mill they grind it until they have worked down the amount given them to the consistency of the finest flour. And since no opportunity is afforded any of them to care for his body and they have no garment to cover their shame, no man can look upon the unfortunate wretches without feeling pity for them because of the exceeding hardships they suffer. For no leniency or respite of any kind is given to any man who is sick, or maimed or aged, or in the case of a woman for her weakness, but all without exception are compelled by blows to persevere in their labors, until through ill-treatment they die in the midst of their tortures. Consequently the poor unfortunates believe, because their punishment is so excessively severe, that the future will always be more terrible than the present and therefore look forward to death as more to be desired than life.

The school in Teos was unusual, however, in that education was ordinarily for upper-class male children. An official known as gymnasiarch served as the head of a gymnasium. This was a civic position of considerable prestige. He was not paid and was expected to provide money for sacrifices, competitions, entertainment, and even school repairs. Many cities passed decrees awarding praise and a "gold crown" to the gymnasiarch for his "munificence toward the people." The educational year culminated with various musical, academic, and athletic contests in which students competed for the honor of having their names inscribed on a victory column.

Hellenistic kings also served as patrons of gymnasia, recognizing their importance in training youths who might serve later as administrators of the state. The institution of the gymnasium played a significant role in the diffusion of Greek culture throughout the Hellenistic world. Whether an upper-class Greek youth lived on the Greek mainland, in Alexandria, or in another city in the east, he could imbibe Greek culture and maintain that sense of superiority that characterized the Greek overlords of the Hellenistic kingdoms.

Culture in the Hellenistic World

Although the Hellenistic kingdoms encompassed vast areas and many diverse peoples, the Greeks provided a sense of unity as a result of the diffusion of Greek culture throughout the Hellenistic world. The Hellenistic era was a period of considerable cultural accomplishment in many fields—literature, art, science, medicine, and philosophy. Although these achievements occurred throughout the Hellenistic world, certain centers, especially the great Hellenistic cities of Alexandria and Pergamum, stood out. In both cities, cultural developments were encouraged by the rulers themselves. Rich Hellenistic kings had considerable resources with which to patronize culture.

The Ptolemies in Egypt made Alexandria an especially important cultural center. The library became the largest in ancient times, with over half a million scrolls. The museum (literally, "temple of the Muses") created a favorable environment for scholarly research. Alexandria became home to poets, writers, philosophers, and scientists—schol-

The Pastoral Idyll of Theocritus

Little is known of the poet Theocritus (c. 315–250 B.C.). Born in Syracuse on the island of Sicily, he also lived in Miletus, Cos, and Alexandria. He is best known as the creator of pastoral idylls that portray his great love of nature. This selection is from the famous *Seventh Idyll* (called the "queen of pastorals"), which describes a delightful day on the island of Cos.

Theocritus, The Seventh Idyll

This I sang, and Lykidas laughed
again pleasantly, and gave me his stick
in fellowship of the Muses,
and turned left, taking the road
to Pyxa, but Eukritos
and handsome Amyntas and I
turned off at Phrasidamos's
and happily laid ourselves down
on beds of sweet grass and vine-leaves,
freshly picked. Overhead, many elms
and poplars rustled, and nearby
the sacred waters splashed down
from the Nymphs' cave. Brown cicadas
shrilled from the shady branches,
and far off the tree-frog whined
in the heavy underbrush.
Lark and finches sang, doves crooned,
and bees hummed about the spring.
Everything smelled of rich summer
and rich fruits. Pears lay at our feet,
apples in plenty rolled beside us,
and branches loaded down with plums
bent to the ground. And we broke
the four-year seals on the wine-jars.
Nymphs of Kastalia that live
on the slopes of Parnassos, tell me,
was it such a cup old Chiron
offered Herakles in Pholos'
rocky cave? Was it a drink like this
set Polyphemos dancing,
that mighty shepherd who grazed
his flocks beside the Anapos
and pelted ships with mountains—
such nectar as you mixed for us,
you Nymphs, that day by the altar
of Demeter of the Harvest?
May I plant the great winnowing-fan
another time in her grain-heaps,
while she stands and smiles at us
with wheat-sheaves and poppies in her hand.

ars of all kinds. The library encouraged the systematic study of language and literature. As a result of patronage from the Attalid dynasty, Pergamum, the greatest city in Asia Minor, also became a leading cultural center that attracted both scholars and artists. Its library was second only to that of Alexandria.

New Directions in Literature and Art

The Hellenistic Age produced an enormous quantity of literature, most of which has not survived. Hellenistic monarchs, who held literary talent in high esteem, subsidized writers on a grand scale. The Ptolemaic rulers of Egypt were particularly lavish. The combination of their largess and the famous library drew a host of scholars and authors to Alexandria, including a circle of poets. Theocritus (c. 315–250 B.C.), originally a native of the island of Sicily, wrote "little poems" or idylls dealing with erotic themes, lovers' complaints, and above all, pastoral themes expressing his love of nature and his appreciation of nature's beauty (see the box above).

In the Hellenistic era, Athens remained the theatrical center of the Greek world. While little remained of tragedy, a new kind of comedy developed that completely rejected political themes and sought only to entertain and amuse. The Athenian playwright Menander (c. 342–291 B.C.) was perhaps the best representative of New Comedy. Plots were simple: typically, a hero falls in love with a not-really-so-bad prostitute who turns out eventually to be the long-lost daughter of a rich neighbor. The hero marries her, and they live happily ever after.

The Hellenistic period saw a great outpouring of historical and biographical literature. The chief historian of the Hellenistic Age was Polybius (c. 203–c. 120 B.C.), a Greek who lived for some years in Rome. He is regarded by many historians as second only to Thucydides among Greek historians. His major work consisted of forty books narrating the history of the "inhabited Mediterranean world" from 221 to 146 B.C. Only the first five books are extant, although long extracts from the other books survive. His history focuses on the growth of Rome from a city-state to a vast empire. It is apparent that Polybius understood the significance of the Romans' achievement. He followed Thucydides in seeking rational motives for historical events. He also approached his sources critically and used firsthand accounts.

In addition to being patrons of literary talent, the Hellenistic monarchs were eager to spend their money to beautify and adorn the cities in their states. The founding of new cities and the rebuilding of old ones provided numerous opportunities for Greek architects and sculptors. The structures of the Greek homeland—gymnasia, baths, theaters, and of course, temples—lined the streets of these cities. Most noticeable in the construction of temples was the use

Scala/Art Resource, NY

Laocoön and His Sons. Three sculptors from Pergamum created this famous piece. This version is probably a Roman copy of the original. The scene illustrates an episode from the Trojan War when the gods sent serpents into Troy to kill the Trojan priest Laocoön and his sons. The intense struggles of the figures are reflected in the pained expressions on their faces.

Metropolitan Museum of Art, New York, Rogers Fund, 1909 (09.39)

Old Market Woman. Greek architects and sculptors were highly valued throughout the Hellenistic world, as kings undertook projects to beautify the cities of their kingdoms. The sculptors of this period no longer tried to capture ideal beauty in their sculpture, a quest that characterized Greek classicism, but moved toward a more emotional and realistic art. This statue of an old market woman is typical of this new trend in art.

of the more ornate Corinthian order (see Chapter 3), which became especially popular during the Hellenistic era.

Sculptors were patronized by Hellenistic kings and rich citizens. Thousands of statues, many paid for by their subjects, were erected in towns and cities all over the Hellenistic world. Hellenistic sculptors traveled widely, attracted by the material rewards offered by wealthy patrons. While maintaining the technical skill of the Classical Period, Hellenistic sculptors moved away from the idealism of fifth-century classicism to a more emotional and realistic art, seen in numerous statues of old women, drunks, and little children at play. They also placed a new emphasis on the female nude.

A Golden Age of Science and Medicine

The Hellenistic era witnessed a more conscious separation of science from philosophy. In Classical Greece, what we would call the physical and life sciences had been divisions of philosophical inquiry. Nevertheless, the Greeks, by the time of Aristotle, had already established an important principle of scientific investigation, empirical research, or systematic observation, as the basis for generalization. In the Hellenistic Age, the sciences tended to be studied in their own right.

One of the traditional areas of Greek science was astronomy, and two Alexandrian scholars continued this exploration. Aristarchus of Samos (c. 310–230 B.C.) developed a heliocentric view of the universe, contending that the sun and the fixed stars remain stationary while the earth rotates around the sun in a circular orbit. He also argued that the earth rotates around its own axis. This view was not widely accepted, and most scholars clung to the earlier geocentric view of the Greeks, which held that the earth was at the center of the universe. Another astronomer, Eratosthenes (c. 275–194 B.C.), determined that the earth was round and calculated the earth's circumference at 24,675 miles, an estimate that was within 200 miles of the actual figure.

A third Alexandrian scholar was Euclid, who lived around 300 B.C. He established a school in Alexandria but is primarily known for his work titled *Elements.* This was a systematic organization of the fundamental elements of geometry as they had already been worked out; it became the standard textbook of plane geometry and was used up to modern times.

Miraculous Cures

Although all gods and goddesses were believed to have healing powers, special curative powers were attributed to Asclepius, the god of healing. A cult of supernatural healing came to be associated with him. Dreams that people experienced when they slept in a sanctuary dedicated to Asclepius supposedly had curative powers, as these texts demonstrate.

Texts on the Miraculous Cures at Epidaurus

A man with the fingers of his hand paralyzed except for one came as a suppliant to the god, and when he saw the tablets in the sanctuary he would not believe the cures and was rather contemptuous of the inscriptions, but when he went to sleep he saw a vision: he thought that as he was playing dice below the sanctuary and was about to throw the dice, the god appeared, sprang on his hand and stretched out his fingers, and when the god moved away, the man thought he bent his hand and stretched out the fingers one by one. When he had straightened them all out, the god asked him whether he still did not believe the inscriptions on the tablets in the sanctuary, and the man said he did. The god said: "Since previously you would not believe them, although they are not incredible, in future let [your name] be 'Incredulous.'" When day came he went away cured.

Ambrosia from Athens, blind in one eye. She came as a suppliant to the god, and as she walked about the sanctuary she ridiculed some of the cures as being incredible and impossible, that persons who were lame and blind should be restored to health merely by seeing a dream. But when she went to sleep she saw a vision: she thought the god was standing next to her and saying that he would restore her to health, but she must dedicate in the sanctuary as a reward a silver pig, as a memorial of her stupidity. Having said this he split open the diseased eye and poured in a medicine. When day came she went away cured.

By far the most famous of the scientists of the Hellenistic period, Archimedes (287–212 B.C.), came from the western Mediterranean region. Archimedes was especially important for his work on the geometry of spheres and cylinders, for establishing the value of the mathematical constant pi, and for creating the science of hydrostatics. Archimedes was also a practical inventor. He may have devised the so-called Archimedean screw used to pump water out of mines and to lift irrigation water, as well as a compound pulley for transporting heavy weights. During the Roman siege of his native city of Syracuse, he constructed a number of devices to thwart the attackers. According to Plutarch's account, the Romans became so frightened "that if they did but see a little rope or a piece of wood from the wall, instantly crying out, that there it was again, Archimedes was about to let fly some engine at them, they turned their backs and fled."[5] Archimedes' accomplishments inspired a wealth of semilegendary stories. Supposedly, he discovered specific gravity by observing the water he displaced in his bath and became so excited by his realization that he jumped out of the water and ran home naked, shouting, "Eureka" ("I have found it"). He is said to have emphasized the importance of levers by proclaiming to the king of Syracuse: "Give me a lever and a place to stand on, and I will move the earth." The king was so impressed that he encouraged Archimedes to lower his sights and build defensive weapons instead.

The scientific foundations of medicine also made considerable strides in the Hellenistic period. This represents a continuation from the fifth century when Hippocrates, a contemporary of Socrates, is credited with having been the "first to separate medicine from philosophy" by stressing natural explanations and natural cures for disease. Herophilus and Erasistratus, both well-known physicians, were active in Alexandria in the first half of the third century B.C. Both were interested in anatomy and used dissection and vivisection (the dissection of living bodies) to expand their knowledge, or so the Roman author Celsus claimed:

> Moreover, as pains, and also various kinds of diseases, arise in the more internal parts, they hold that no one can apply remedies for these who is ignorant about the parts themselves; hence it becomes necessary to lay open the bodies of the dead and to scrutinize their viscera and intestines. They hold that Herophilus and Erasistratus did this in the best way by far, when they laid open men while alive—criminals received out of prison from the kings—and while these were still breathing, observed parts which beforehand nature had concealed, their position, color, shape, size, arrangement, hardness, softness, smoothness, relation, processes and depressions of each, and whether any part is inserted into or is received into another.[6]

Herophilus added significantly to the understanding of the brain, eye, liver, and the reproductive and nervous systems. Erasistratus made discoveries in the process of digestion.

It would be misleading to think of medicine in the Hellenistic world only in terms of scientific advances. Alongside these developments, a wide range of alternative methods of healing continued to exist. These included magical practices, such as the use of amulets to cast off evil spirits, herbal remedies, and the healing powers of deities, especially those of Asclepius, the god of healing (see the box above).

Philosophy: New Schools of Thought

While Alexandria and Pergamum became the renowned cultural centers of the Hellenistic world, Athens remained the prime center for philosophy. After Alexander the Great, the home of Socrates, Plato, and Aristotle continued to attract the most illustrious philosophers from the Greek world who chose to establish their schools there. New schools of philosophical thought (the Epicureans and Stoics) reinforced Athens's reputation as a philosophical center.

Epicurus (341–270 B.C.), the founder of Epicureanism, established a school in Athens near the end of the fourth century B.C. Epicurus' famous belief in a doctrine of "pleasure" began with his view of the world. Although he did not deny the existence of the gods, he did not believe they played any active role in the world. The universe ran on its own. This left human beings free to follow self-interest as a basic motivating force. Happiness was the goal of life, and the means to achieve it was the pursuit of pleasure, the only true good. But the pursuit of pleasure was not meant in a physical, hedonistic sense:

> When, therefore, we maintain that pleasure is the end, we do not mean the pleasures of profligates and those that consist in sensuality, as is supposed by some who are either ignorant or disagree with us or do not understand, but freedom from pain in the body and from trouble in the mind. For it is not continuous drinkings and revelings, nor the satisfaction of lusts, nor the enjoyment of fish and other luxuries of the wealthy table, which produce a pleasant life, but sober reasoning, searching out the motives for all choice and avoidance, and banishing mere opinions, to which are due the greatest disturbance of the spirit.

Pleasure was not satisfying one's desire in an active, gluttonous fashion but rather freedom from emotional turmoil, freedom from worry, the freedom that came from a mind at rest. To achieve this passive pleasure, one had to free oneself from public activity: "We must release ourselves from the prison of affairs and politics." They were too strenuous to give peace of mind. But this was not a renunciation of all social life, for to Epicurus, a life could be complete only when it was centered on the basic ideal of friendship: "Of all the things which wisdom acquires to produce the blessedness of the complete life, far the greatest is the possession of friendship."[7] Epicurus' own life in Athens was an embodiment of his teachings. He and his friends created their own private community where they could pursue their ideal of true happiness.

Epicureanism was eventually overshadowed by another school of thought known as Stoicism, which became the most popular philosophy of the Hellenistic world and persisted in the Roman Empire as well. It was the product of a teacher named Zeno (335–263 B.C.), who came to Athens and began to teach in a public colonnade known as the Painted Portico (the *Stoa Poikile*—hence Stoicism). Like Epicureanism, Stoicism was concerned with how individuals find happiness. But Stoics took a radically different approach. To them, happiness, the supreme good, could be found only in virtue, which meant essentially living in harmony with divine will: "And this very thing constitutes the virtue of the happy man and the smooth current of life, when all actions promote the harmony of the spirit dwelling in the individual man with the will of him who orders the universe."[8] One achieved happiness by choosing to follow divine will through the free exercise of one's own will. To the Stoics, divine will was the same as the will of nature since nature was simply a manifestation or expression of the gods. "Living according to nature," therefore, meant following divine will or the natural laws that the gods established to run the universe.

Virtuous living, then, was living in accordance with the laws of nature or submitting to divine will (see the box on p. 99). This led to the acceptance of whatever one received in life since divine will for us was by its very nature good. By accepting divine law, people mastered themselves and gained inner peace. Life's problems could not disturb such individuals, and they could bear whatever life offered (hence our word *stoic*).

Unlike Epicureans, Stoics did not believe in the need to separate oneself from the world and politics. Public service was regarded as noble. The real Stoic was a good

Metropolitan Museum of Art, New York, Rogers Fund, 1911 (11.90)

Portrait of Epicurus. Epicurus was the founder of the Epicurean school of philosophy, which became very popular during the Hellenistic period. He maintained an "atomic" theory of the universe—that the only things that exist are atoms moving through the void—and an ethical theory based on the pursuit of pleasure.

The Stoic Ideal of Harmony with God

The Stoic Cleanthes (331–232 B.C.) succeeded Zeno as head of this school of philosophy. One historian of Hellenistic civilization has called this work by Cleanthes the greatest religious hymn in Greek literature. Certainly it demonstrates that Stoicism, unlike Epicureanism, did have an underlying spiritual foundation. This poem has been compared to the great psalms of the Hebrews.

Cleanthes, Hymn to Zeus

Nothing occurs on the earth apart from you, O God,
nor in the heavenly regions nor on the sea,
except what bad men do in their folly;
but you know to make the odd even,
and to harmonize what is dissonant; to you the alien is akin.
And so you have wrought together into one all things that are good and bad,
So that there arises one eternal logos [rationale] of all things,
Which all bad mortals shun and ignore,
Unhappy wretches, ever seeking the possession of good things
They neither see nor hear the universal law of God,
By obeying which they might enjoy a happy life.

citizen and could even be a good government official. Because Stoics believed that a divine principle was present throughout the universe, each human being also contained a divine spark. This led to a belief in the oneness of humanity. The world constituted a single society of equal human beings. Although not equal in the outer world, the divine spark in each meant that all were free to follow divine will (what was best for each individual). All persons then, even slaves, though unfree in body, were equal at the level of the soul.

Epicureanism and especially Stoicism appealed to large numbers of people in the Hellenistic world. Both of these philosophies focused primarily on the problem of human happiness. Their popularity would suggest a fundamental change in the character of the Greek lifestyle. In the Classical Greek world, the happiness of individuals and the meaning of life were closely associated with the life of the *polis.* One found fulfillment within the community. In the Hellenistic kingdoms, although the *polis* continued to exist, the sense that one could find satisfaction and fulfillment through life in the *polis* had weakened. Not only did individuals seek new philosophies that offered personal happiness, but in the cosmopolitan world of the Hellenistic states, with their mixtures of peoples, a new openness to thoughts of universality could also emerge. For some people, Stoicism embodied this larger sense of community. The appeal of new philosophies in the Hellenistic era can also be explained by the apparent decline in certain aspects of traditional religion.

Religion in the Hellenistic World

When the Greeks spread throughout the Near East, they took their gods with them. Hellenistic cities increased the number of public festivals and celebrated them with great magnificence. But over a period of time, there was a noticeable decline in the vitality of the traditional Greek Olympian religion. Much of Greek religion had always revolved around ritual, but the civic cults based on the traditional gods no longer seemed sufficient to satisfy people's emotional needs.

The decline in traditional Greek religion left Greeks receptive to the numerous religious cults of the eastern world. The Greeks were always tolerant of other existing religious institutions. Hence in the Hellenistic cities of the Near East, the traditional civic cults of their own gods and foreign cults existed side by side. Alexandria had cults of the traditional Greek gods, Egyptian deities such as Isis and Horus, the Babylonian Astarte, and the Syrian Atargatis. The strongest appeal of eastern religions to the Greeks, however, came from the mystery religions. What was the source of their attraction?

The normal forms of religious worship in Hellenistic communities had lost some of their appeal. The practices of traditional, ritualized Greek religion in the civic cults seemed increasingly meaningless. For many people, the search for personal meaning remained unfulfilled, and they sought alternatives. Among educated Greeks, the philosophies of Epicureanism and especially Stoicism offered help. Another source of solace came in the form of mystery religions.

Mystery cults, with their secret initiations and promises of individual salvation, were not new to the Greek world. But the Greeks of the Hellenistic era were also strongly influenced by eastern mystery cults, such as those of Egypt, which offered a distinct advantage over the Greek mystery religions. The latter had usually been connected to specific locations (such as Eleusis), which meant that a would-be initiate had to undertake a pilgrimage in order to participate in the rites. In contrast, the eastern mystery religions were readily available since temples to their gods and goddesses were located throughout the Greek cities of the east.

All of the mystery religions were based on the same fundamental premises. Individuals could pursue a path to salvation and achieve eternal life by being initiated into a union with a savior god or goddess who had died and risen again. The ritual of initiation, by which the seeker identified with the god or goddess, was no doubt a highly emotional experience.

The Cult of Isis. The cult of Isis was one of the most popular mystery religions in the Hellenistic world. This fresco from Herculaneum in Italy depicts a religious ceremony in front of the temple of Isis. At the top a priest holds a golden vessel, while below him another priest leads the worshipers with a staff. A third priest fans the flames at the altar.

The Egyptian cult of Isis was one of the most popular of the mystery religions. The cult of Isis was very ancient but became truly universal in Hellenistic times. Isis was the goddess of women, marriage, and children, as one of her hymns states: "I am she whom women call goddess. I ordained that women should be loved by men: I brought wife and husband together, and invented the marriage contract. I ordained that women should bear children."[9] Isis was also portrayed as the giver of civilization who had brought laws and letters to all humankind. The cult of Isis offered a precious commodity to its initiates—the promise of eternal life. In many ways, the mystery religions of the Hellenistic era helped pave the way for Christianity.

The Jews in the Hellenistic World

In observing the similarities among their gods and goddesses, Greeks and easterners tended to assume they were the same beings with different names, giving rise to a process of syncretism. But a special position was occupied in the Hellenistic world by the Jews, whose monotheistic religion was exclusive and did not permit this kind of fusion of spiritual beings.

The Jewish province of Judaea was ruled by the Ptolemies until it fell under the control of the Seleucids by 200 B.C. In the reign of the Seleucid king Antiochus IV (175–163 B.C.), conflict erupted in Judaea. Hellenistic monarchs were generally tolerant of all religions, but problems with Rome prompted Antiochus to try to impose more cultural and religious unity in Judaea. When he sent troops to Jerusalem and seized the Temple, he sparked a Jewish uprising led by Judas Maccabaeus (164 B.C.). The rebels succeeded in recapturing the Temple, a joyous event that has been celebrated every year since in the Jewish holiday of Hanukkah (Hebrew for "rededication"). Although the conflict in Judaea continued, the Seleucids ultimately made concessions and allowed the Jews considerable freedom.

But since the Diaspora (see Chapter 2), large numbers of Jews no longer lived in Judaea. There was a large Jewish population in Egypt, particularly in Alexandria, as well as Jewish settlements throughout the cities of Asia Minor and Syria. In each city, Jews generally set up a synagogue and formed a private association for worship as other foreigners did. But some city authorities also allowed the Jews to form a political corporation that gave them greater rights than other resident aliens. Most important, they gained the privilege to live by their own laws and their own judicial system. The Jews were not really interested in citizenship in the cities in which they resided because full citizenship meant worship of the city's gods, anathema to Jews who believed only in Yahweh.

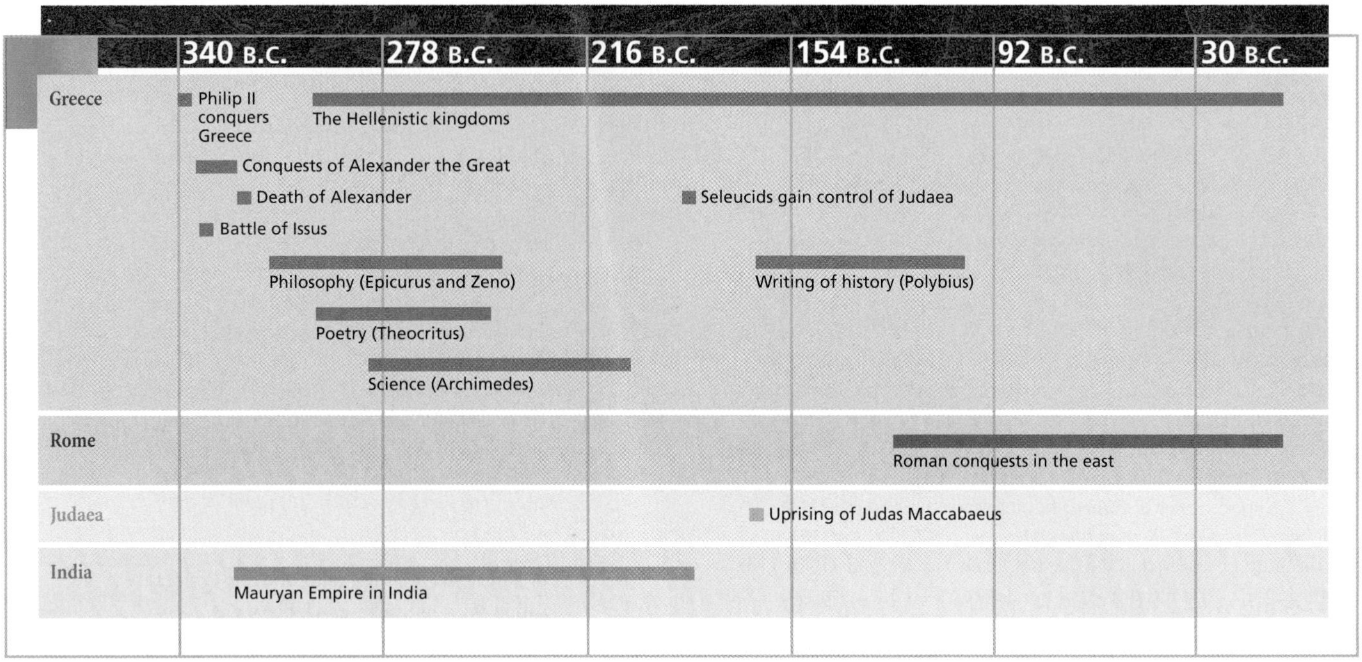

Conclusion

Although historians used to view the Hellenistic era as a period of stagnation after the brilliant Greek civilization of the fifth century B.C.*, our survey of the Hellenistic world has shown the weakness of that position. The Hellenistic period was, in its own way, a vibrant one. New cities arose and flourished. New philosophical ideas captured the minds of many people. Significant achievements occurred in art, literature, and science. Greek culture spread throughout the Near East and made an impact wherever it was carried. In some areas of the Hellenistic world, queens played an active role in political life, and many upper-class women found new avenues for expressing themselves.*

But serious problems remained. Hellenistic kings continued to engage in inconclusive wars. The gulf between rich and poor was indeed great. Much of the formal culture was the special preserve of the Greek conquerors, whose attitude of superiority kept them largely separated from the native masses of the Hellenistic kingdoms. Although the Hellenistic world achieved a degree of political stability, signs of decline were beginning to multiply by the late third century B.C. *Some of the more farsighted denizens of the Hellenistic world may have realized the danger represented by the growing power of Rome, which would ultimately inherit Alexander's empire. We must now try to understand what made the Romans such successful conquerors.*

Notes

1. Quoted in Sarah B. Pomeroy, Stanley M. Burstein, Walter Donlan, and Jennifer Tolbert Roberts, *Ancient Greece: A Political, Social, and Cultural History* (Oxford, 1999), p. 390.
2. Polybius, *The Histories*, trans. W. R. Paton (Cambridge, Mass., 1960), 18.37.8–10.
3. Maureen B. Fant and Mary R. Lefkowitz, *Women's Life in Greece and Rome: A Source Book in Translation* (Baltimore, 1992), no. 208.
4. Roger S. Bagnall and Peter Derow, *Greek Historical Documents: The Hellenistic Period* (Chico, Calif., 1981), p. 113.
5. Plutarch, *Life of Marcellus*, trans. John Dryden (New York, n.d.), p. 378.
6. Celsus, *De Medicina*, trans. W. G. Spencer (Cambridge, Mass., 1935), Prooemium 23–24.
7. *Epicurus: The Extant Remains*, trans. Cyril Bailey (Oxford, 1926), pp. 89–90, 115, 101.
8. Diogenes Laertius, *Life of Zeno*, vol. 2, trans. R. D. Hicks (London, 1925), p. 195.
9. Quoted in W. W. Tarn, *Hellenistic Civilization* (London, 1930), p. 324.

Suggestions for Further Reading

For a general introduction to the Hellenistic era, see J. Boardman, J. Griffin, and O. Murray, eds., *The Oxford History of the Classical World* (Oxford, 1986), pp. 315–385. The best general surveys are F. W. Walbank, *The Hellenistic World* (Cambridge, Mass., 1993), and G. Shipley, *The Greek World After Alexander, 323–300* B.C. (New York, 2000). Other studies include W. W. Tarn and G. T. Griffith, *Hellenistic Civilization*, 3d ed. (London, 1952); M. Grant, *From Alexander to Cleopatra: The Hellenistic World* (London, 1982); and P. Green,

Alexander to Actium: The Historic Evolution of the Hellenistic Age (Berkeley, Calif., 1990).

For a good introduction to the early history of Macedonia, see E. N. Borza, *In the Shadow of Olympus: The Emergence of Macedon* (Princeton, N.J., 1990), and R. M. Errington, *A History of Macedonia* (Berkeley, Calif., 1990). Philip II is covered well in G. L. Cawkwell, *Philip of Macedon* (London, 1978). There are considerable differences of opinion on Alexander the Great. Good biographies include R. L. Fox, *Alexander the Great* (London, 1973); J. R. Hamilton, *Alexander the Great* (London, 1973); N. G. L. Hammond, *Alexander the Great* (London, 1981); and P. Green, *Alexander of Macedon* (Berkeley, Calif., 1991).

Studies on the various Hellenistic monarchies include N. G. L. Hammond and F. W. Walbank, *A History of Macedonia*, vol. 3, *336–167 B.C.* (Oxford, 1988); S. Sherwin-White and A. Kuhrt, *From Samarkand to Sardis: A New Approach to the Seleucid Empire* (Berkeley, Calif., 1993); N. Lewis, *Greeks in Ptolemaic Egypt* (Oxford, 1986); and R. E. Allen, *The Attalid Kingdom* (Oxford, 1983).

A good survey of Hellenistic cities can be found in A. H. M. Jones, *The Greek City from Alexander to Justinian* (Oxford, 1940). Alexandria is covered in P. M. Fraser, *Ptolemaic Alexandria* (Oxford, 1972). On economic and social trends, see M. I. Finley, *The Ancient Economy*, 2d ed. (London, 1985), and the classic and still indispensable M. I. Rostovtzeff, *Social and Economic History of the Hellenistic World*, 3 vols., 2d ed. (Oxford, 1953).

Hellenistic women are examined in two works by S. B. Pomeroy, *Goddesses, Whores, Wives, and Slaves* (New York, 1975), pp. 120–148, and *Women in Hellenistic Egypt* (New York, 1984). Slavery is examined in W. L. Westermann, *The Slave-Systems of Greek and Roman Antiquity* (Philadelphia, 1955). The classic work on education is H. I. Marrou, *A History of Education in Antiquity* (London, 1956).

For a general introduction to Hellenistic culture, see J. Onians, *Art and Thought in the Hellenistic Age* (London, 1979). On art, see J. J. Pollitt, *Art in the Hellenistic Age* (New York, 1986). The best general survey of Hellenistic philosophy is A. A. Long, *Hellenistic Philosophy: Stoics, Epicureans, Skeptics*, 2d ed. (London, 1986). A superb work on Hellenistic science is G. E. R. Lloyd, *Greek Science After Aristotle* (London, 1973).

On various facets of Hellenistic religion, see L. Martin, *Hellenistic Religions: An Introduction* (New York, 1987), and R. E. Witt, *Isis in the Graeco-Roman World* (London, 1971).

On the entry of Rome into the Hellenistic world, see the basic work by E. S. Gruen, *The Hellenistic World and the Coming of Rome*, 2 vols. (Berkeley, Calif., 1984).

For additional reading, go to InfoTrac College Edition, your online research library at http://web1.infotrac-college.com

Enter the search term *Greek history* using Key Terms.

Enter the search term *Alexander the Great* using Key Terms.

Enter the search term *Archimedes* using Key Terms.

C H A P T E R

5

The Roman Republic

© Leonard von Matt/Photo Researchers, Inc.

CHAPTER OUTLINE

- The Emergence of Rome
- The Roman Republic (c. 509–264 B.C.)
- The Roman Conquest of the Mediterranean (264–133 B.C.)
- Society and Culture in the Roman Republic
- The Decline and Fall of the Roman Republic (133–31 B.C.)
- Conclusion

FOCUS QUESTIONS

- What influence did the Etruscans and Greeks have on early Roman history?
- What policies and institutions help explain the Romans' success in conquering first Italy and then the entire Mediterranean world?
- What were the characteristics of the Roman family, and how did the family change between the early and the late Republic?
- How did the acquisition of an empire affect Roman social and economic institutions, values and attitudes, and art and literature?
- What were the main problems Rome faced during the last century of the Republic, and how were they ultimately resolved?
- What did the Roman poet Horace mean when he wrote, "Captive Greece took captive her rude conqueror"?

EARLY ROMAN HISTORY is filled with legendary stories that tell of the heroes who made Rome great. One of the best known is the story of Horatius at the bridge. Threatened by attack from the neighboring Etruscans, Roman farmers abandoned their fields and moved into the city, where they would be protected by the walls. One weak point in the Roman defenses, however, was a wooden bridge over the Tiber River. Horatius was on guard at the bridge when a sudden assault by the Etruscans caused many Roman troops to throw down their weapons and flee. Horatius urged them to make a stand at the bridge to protect Rome; when they hesitated, as a last resort he told them to destroy the bridge behind him while he held the Etruscans back. Astonished at the sight of a single defender, the confused Etruscans threw their spears at Horatius, who caught them on his shield and barred the way. By the time the Etruscans had regrouped and were about to overwhelm the lone defender, the Roman soldiers brought down the bridge. When Horatius heard the bridge crash into the river behind him, he dived fully armed into the water and swam safely to the other side through a hail of arrows. Rome had been saved by the courageous act of a Roman who knew his duty and was determined to carry it out. Courage, duty, determination—these qualities would also serve the many Romans who believed that it was their mission to rule nations and peoples.

In the first millennium B.C.*, a group of Latin-speaking people established a small community on the plain of Latium on the Italian peninsula. This community, called Rome, was merely one of numerous Latin-speaking communities in Latium, and the Latin speakers, in turn, constituted only some of the many peoples in Italy. Roman history is basically the story of the Romans' conquest of the plain of Latium, then Italy, and finally the entire Mediterranean world. Why were the Romans able to do this? Scholars do not really know all the answers. The Romans made the right decisions at the right time; in other words, the Romans had political wisdom.*

The Romans were also practical. Unlike the Greeks, who reserved their citizenship for small, select groups, the Romans often offered citizenship to the peoples they conquered, thus laying the basis for a strong, integrated empire. The Romans also did not hesitate to borrow ideas and culture from the Greeks. Roman strength lay in government, law, and engineering. The Romans knew how to govern people, establish legal structures, and construct the roads that took them to the ends of the known world. Throughout their empire, they carried their law, their political institutions, their engineering skills, and their Latin language. And even after the Romans were gone, those same gifts continued to play an important role in the continuing saga of Western civilization.

The Emergence of Rome

Not much is known about the prehistoric peoples who lived in Italy. We do know that Indo-European peoples moved into Italy during the second half of the second millennium B.C. By the first millennium B.C., other peoples had also settled in Italy—the two most notable being the Greeks and the Etruscans. Before examining these peoples, however, we need to consider the influence geography had on the historical development of the peoples on the Italian peninsula.

Geography of the Italian Peninsula

Italy is a narrow peninsula extending about 750 miles from north to south but averaging only about 120 miles across (see Map 5.1). The Apennine Mountains traverse the peninsula from north to south, forming a ridge down the middle that divides west from east. Nevertheless, Italy has some fairly large fertile plains ideal for farming. Most important were the Po valley in the north, probably the most fertile agricultural area; the plain of Latium, on which Rome was located; and Campania to the south of Latium. East of the Italian peninsula is the Adriatic Sea and west the Tyrrhenian Sea and the large islands of Corsica and Sardinia. Sicily lies just west of the toe of the boot-shaped peninsula.

Geography had an impact on Roman history. Although the Apennines bisected Italy, they were less rugged than the mountain ranges of Greece and did not divide the peninsula into many small isolated communities. Italy also possessed considerably more productive farmland than Greece, enabling it to support a large population. Rome's location was favorable from a geographical point of view. Located 18 miles inland on the Tiber River, Rome had access to the sea but was far enough inland to be safe from pirates. Built on seven hills, it was easily defended, and because it was situated where the Tiber could be readily forded, Rome became a natural crossing point for north-south traffic in western Italy. All in all, Rome had a good central location in Italy from which to expand.

Moreover, the Italian peninsula juts into the Mediterranean Sea, making it an important crossroads between the western and eastern Mediterranean. Once Rome had

Map 5.1 Ancient Italy. Ancient Italy was home to several groups. Both the Etruscans in the north and the Greeks in the south had a major influence on the development of Rome. ■ Once Rome conquered the Etruscans, Sabines, Samnites, and other local groups, what aspects of the Italian peninsula helped make it defensible against outside enemies?

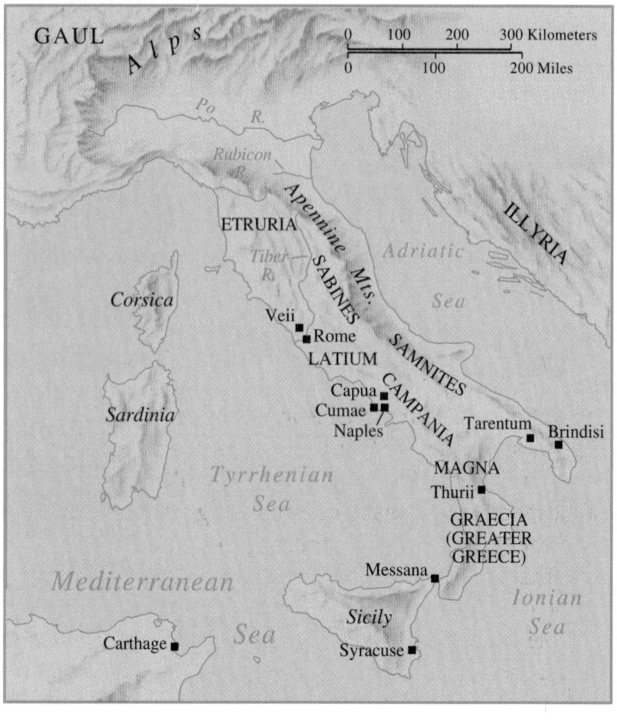

AKG, London

Etruscan Tomb Mural. Like the Egyptians, the Etruscans filled their tombs with furniture, bowls, and other objects of daily life, as well as murals showing diversions experienced in life and awaiting the dead in the afterlife. Shown in this mural found in an Etruscan tomb at Tarquinia are servants and musicians at a banquet. This mural was painted in the first half of the fifth century B.C.

unified Italy, involvement in Mediterranean affairs was natural. And after the Romans had conquered their Mediterranean empire, Italy's central location made their task of governing that empire considerably easier.

The Greeks

The Greeks arrived on the Italian peninsula in large numbers during the age of Greek colonization (750–550 B.C.—see Chapter 3). Initially, the Greeks settled in southern Italy. They founded Cumae in the Bay of Naples, Naples itself, and Tarentum and then crept around the coast and up the peninsula as far as Brindisi. They also occupied the eastern two-thirds of Sicily. In establishing their colonies, the Greeks planned permanent communities, secured the coastal plains for agriculture, and built walled cities with harbors to carry on trade. Ultimately, the Greeks had considerable influence on Rome. They cultivated the olive and the vine, passed on their alphabetic system of writing, and provided artistic and cultural models through their sculpture, architecture, and literature. Indeed, many historians view Roman culture as a continuation of Greek culture. While Greek influence initially touched Rome indirectly through the Etruscans, the Roman conquest of southern Italy and Sicily brought them into direct contact with the Greeks.

The Etruscans

The initial development of Rome was influenced most by a people known as the Etruscans, who had settled north of Rome in Etruria. They were a city-dwelling people who established their towns in commanding positions and fortified them with walls. Numerous inscriptions in tombs show that the Etruscans adopted alphabetic writing from the Greeks before 600 B.C.

The origins of the Etruscans are not clear, but after 650 B.C., they expanded in Italy and became the dominant cultural and economic force in a number of areas. To the north, they moved into north-central Italy. To the south, according to Roman tradition and archaeological evidence, they controlled Rome and possibly all of Latium. From Latium they moved south into Campania, founded a settlement at Capua, and came into direct contact with Greek colonists in southern Italy. In the sixth century B.C., the Etruscans were at the height of their power. But by 480 B.C., their power had begun to decline, and by 400 B.C., they were again limited to Etruria itself. Later they were invaded by the Gauls and then conquered by the Romans. But by then the Etruscans had already made an impact. By transforming villages into towns and cities, they brought urbanization to northern and central Italy (the Greeks brought urbanization to southern Italy). Rome was, of course, the Etruscans' most famous creation.

Early Rome

According to Roman legend, Rome was founded by the twin brothers Romulus and Remus in 753 B.C. Of course, the Romans invented this story to provide a noble ancestry for their city. Archaeologists have found, however, that by the eighth century there was a settlement consisting of huts on the tops of Rome's hills. The early Romans, basically a pastoral people, spoke Latin, which, like Greek, belongs to the Indo-European family of languages (see the table in Chapter 1). The Roman historical tradition also maintained that early Rome (753–509 B.C.) had been under the control of seven kings and that two of the last three had been Etruscans. Some historians believe that the king list may have some historical accuracy. What is certain is that Rome did fall under the influence of the Etruscans for about one hundred years during the period of the kings.

By the beginning of the sixth century, under Etruscan influence, Rome began to emerge as a city. The Etruscans were responsible for an outstanding building program. They constructed the first roadbed of the chief street through Rome—the Sacred Way—before 575 B.C. and oversaw the development of temples, markets, shops, streets, and houses.

By 509 B.C., supposedly when the monarchy was overthrown, a new Rome had emerged, essentially a product of the fusion of Etruscan and native Roman elements.

The Etruscans had an impact on Roman civilization in numerous ways, both large and small. Etruscan dress—the toga and short cloak—was adopted by the Romans. The insignia of the Etruscan kings became the insignia of Roman magistrates in the Republic. Most impressive was the *fasces,* an ax surrounded by a bundle of rods used as a symbol for the power to scourge and execute, hence to rule. In the Republic, the consuls as chief magistrates were preceded by twelve lictors bearing the *fasces.* The Romans were also indebted to the Etruscans for the alphabet. The Latin alphabet was a modification of the Etruscan one derived from the Greeks.

The City of Rome

The Romans traditionally associated the end of both monarchy and Etruscan domination with the rape of Lucretia, a Roman noblewoman of great virtue. Raped by a son of the king, Lucretia informed her father, husband, and their friends what had happened and then committed suicide "rather than be an example of unchastity to other wives," as an ancient Roman historian put it. Lucretia became the model Roman woman: a faithful wife and a pure and courageous woman who chose death rather than be seen as lacking in virtue. In revenge, the Roman nobles drove the king and his family from Rome and established a republican form of government, which ushered in the era of the Republic. According to the Romans of the late Republic, all this occurred in 509 B.C. Though interesting, the story has little historical foundation. It is more likely that the overthrow of the monarchy was accomplished by nobles who experienced a loss of power because of the shift from cavalry to heavy-armed infantry during the reign of Servius Tullius, the next-to-last king. The overthrow was not a patriotic uprising but an attempt by Roman nobles to maintain their position of power. Some scholars have even argued that the continuation of Etruscan influence at Rome into the fifth century necessitates dating the beginning of the Roman Republic to around 475 B.C., but most historians remain committed to a date close to the traditional 509 B.C.

The Roman Republic (c. 509–264 B.C.)

The transition from monarchy to republican government was not easy. Rome felt threatened by enemies from every direction and in meeting these threats embarked on a course of military expansion that led to the conquest of the entire Italian peninsula. During this period of expansion in Italy, the Roman Republic developed political institutions that were in many ways determined by the social divisions that existed within the community.

The Roman State

In politics and law, as in conquest, the Romans took a practical approach and fashioned political institutions in response to problems as they arose. Hence it is important

Alinari/Art Resource, NY

Lictors with *Fasces.* Pictured are lictors bearing the *fasces,* an ax surrounded by a bundle of rods tied with a red thong, an insignia borrowed from the Etruscan kings. The *fasces* was a symbol of the power to rule, and the consuls, the chief executives of the Roman Republic, were always preceded by twelve lictors bearing the *fasces.*

to remember that the political institutions we will discuss evolved over a period of centuries.

POLITICAL INSTITUTIONS

The Romans had a clear concept of executive authority, embodied in their word *imperium*, or "the right to command." Invested with *imperium*, the chief magistrates of the Roman state exercised a supreme power that was circumscribed only by extraneous means—officials held office for a limited term and could be tried for offenses committed in office once their term ended. While political institutions changed, the concept of *imperium* did not, and it is the one factor that gives Roman constitutional history continuity and unity.

The chief executive officers of the Roman Republic who possessed *imperium* were the consuls and praetors. Two consuls, chosen annually, administered the government and led the Roman army into battle. In 366 B.C., a new office, that of the praetor, was created. The praetor also possessed *imperium* and could govern Rome when the consuls were away from the city and could also lead armies. The praetor's primary function, however, was the execution of justice. He was in charge of the civil law as it applied to Roman citizens. In 242 B.C., reflecting Rome's growth, another praetor was added to judge cases in which one or both parties were noncitizens.

As Rome expanded into the Mediterranean, additional praetors were established to govern the newly conquered provinces (two in 227, two more in 197 B.C.). But as the number of provinces continued to grow, the Romans devised a new system in which ex-consuls and ex-praetors who had served their one-year terms were given the title of proconsul and propraetor, respectively, and sent out as provincial governors. This demonstrates once again the Romans' practical solution to an immediate problem. It was reasonable to assume that officials with governmental experience would make good provincial administrators, although this was not always true in practice due to the opportunities for financial corruption in the provinces.

Periodically, the Republic also created an extraordinary executive. In an emergency, the consuls would resign, and a dictator with unlimited power would be chosen to run the state. This office was supposed to last only for the duration of the emergency, the usual limit being six months. The Roman state also had administrative officials with specialized duties. Quaestors assisted consuls and praetors in the administration of financial affairs. Aediles supervised the public games and watched over the grain supply of the city, a major problem for a rapidly growing urban community that came to rely on imported grain to feed its population. Censors were chosen every five years with the chief responsibility of making an assessment of the population on the basis of age and property for purposes of taxes, military service, and officeholding.

The Roman senate came to hold an especially important position in the Republic. The senate or council of elders was a select group of about three hundred men who served for life. The senate was not a legislative body and could only advise the magistrates. This advice of the senate was not taken lightly, however, and by the third century B.C. had virtually the force of law. No doubt the prestige of the senate's members furthered this development. But it also helped that the senate met continuously, while the chief magistrates changed annually and the popular assemblies operated slowly and met only periodically.

The Roman Republic possessed a number of popular assemblies. By far the most important was the centuriate assembly, essentially the Roman army functioning in its political role. Organized by classes based on wealth, it was structured in such a way that the wealthiest citizens always had a majority. The centuriate assembly elected the chief magistrates and passed laws. It is important to remember, however, that the Romans passed few statutory laws and simply left much governance to magisterial authority. As a result of the struggle between the orders, another assembly, the council of the plebs, came into being in 471 B.C.

The government of the Roman Republic, then, consisted of three major elements. Two consuls and later other elected officials served as magistrates and ran the state. An assembly of adult males (the centuriate assembly), controlled by the wealthiest citizens, elected these officials, while the senate, a small group of large landowners, advised them. Thus the Roman state was an aristocratic republic controlled by a relatively small group of privileged people.

SOCIAL ORGANIZATION

The family was the basis of Roman society. At its head was the *paterfamilias*, who theoretically had unlimited power over his family. In the early Republic, for example, it is claimed that he had the right to put his children to death, although this actually occurred in very few instances. With the *paterfamilias* at the head, the family resembled a kind of miniature state within the state. When a father died, his sons became heads of their own families. Families were often grouped into social units known as *gentes* or clans, descended from the same ancestor and bearing the same family name.

Closely associated with clan and family was the practice of clientage. Clients constituted a dependent class, people who did not have the means to protect themselves or their families without the assistance of a patron. The patron, usually a wealthy member of the upper classes, gave protection and especially legal assistance to his clients. In return, clients provided their patrons with certain services, such as field labor, military assistance, and, especially important in the Republic, votes in the assemblies.

The most noticeable element in the social organization of early Rome was the division between two groups—the patricians and the plebeians. The word *patrician* is derived from *patres*—the fathers—as the members of the Roman senate were called. The patrician class in Rome consisted of those families who were descended from the original senators appointed during the period of the kings. Their initial prominence was probably due to their wealth as great landowners. Thus the patricians constituted an aristocratic governing class. Only they could be consuls, other magistrates, and senators. Through their patronage of large numbers of dependent clients, they could control the centuriate assembly and many other facets of Roman life.

The plebeians constituted the considerably larger group of "independent, unprivileged, poorer and vulnerable men" as well as nonpatrician large landowners, less wealthy landholders, artisans, merchants, and small farmers. Although they were citizens, they did not possess the same rights as the patricians and at the beginning of the fifth century B.C. began a struggle to rectify that situation. The plebeians who led the struggle for plebeian rights were large landowners who were equal in wealth to many patricians and therefore considered themselves equally qualified to enjoy the same privileges.

THE STRUGGLE OF THE ORDERS

Two major problems that existed in the fifth century probably fueled the struggle between the patricians and the plebeians. Both patricians and plebeians could vote, but only the patricians could be elected to governmental offices. Both had the right to make legal contracts and marriages, but intermarriage between patricians and plebeians was forbidden. The wealthy plebeians wanted political equality with the patricians, namely, the right to hold office, and social equality in the form of the right of intermarriage.

The first success for the plebeians came in 494 B.C., when they withdrew physically from the state. The patricians, who by themselves could not defend Rome, were forced to compromise. Two new officials known as tribunes of the plebs were instituted (later the number was raised to five and then ten). These tribunes were given the power to protect plebeians against arrest by patrician magistrates. Moreover, after a new popular assembly for plebeians only, called the council of the plebs, was created in 471 B.C., the tribunes became responsible for convoking and placing proposals before it. If adopted, these measures became *plebiscita* ("it is the opinion of the plebs"), but they were binding only on the plebeians, not on the patricians. Nevertheless, the plebeian council gave the plebeians considerable political leverage.

The next step for the plebeians involved the law. The plebeians came to realize that if they were to increase their power, they needed knowledge of the law and the legal and governmental procedures carefully guarded by the patricians. Due to plebeian pressure, a special commission of ten officials known as the *decemviri* ("ten men") was created with the task of regularizing and publishing the laws. This action resulted in the publication in 450 B.C. of the Twelve Tables of Law, which included the legal procedures for going to court; provisions on family, women, and divorce; regulations concerning private property; rules governing relationships and injuries to others; and a provision prohibiting intermarriage between patricians and plebeians (see the box on p. 109). This publication of the laws produced further agitation from the plebeians between 450 and 445 since they could now see how disadvantaged they were. In particular, they demanded the right of intermarriage and admission to the chief magistracies, especially the consulship. In 445 B.C., the Canuleian law allowed patricians and plebeians to intermarry. Once this was permitted, the division between the two groups became less important, and the solidarity of the patrician class against plebeian gains began to falter. But it was not until 367 B.C. that the consulship was opened to plebeians. The Licinian-Sextian laws stipulated that one consul could now be a plebeian. From 366 to 361 B.C., however, only two plebeians were elected to the consulship, and from 361 to 340, only three, a clear indication that only the most prominent plebeian families could obtain the office. In 342 B.C., another law stipulated that both consuls could be plebeians but at least one had to be plebeian.

CHRONOLOGY

The Struggle of the Orders

First secession of the plebeians; creation of tribunes of the plebs	494 B.C.
Creation of the council of the plebs	471 B.C.
Publication of the Twelve Tables of Law	450 B.C.
Canuleian law: Right of plebeians to marry patricians	445 B.C.
Licinian-Sextian laws: One consul may be a plebeian	367 B.C.
Both consuls may be plebeians; one must be	342 B.C.
Hortensian law: Laws passed by plebeian assembly are binding on all Romans	287 B.C.

The chief landmark in Roman constitutional history—and the climax of the struggle between the orders—came in 287 B.C. with the Hortensian law. Henceforth all *plebiscita* passed by the plebeian assembly had the force of law and were binding on the entire community, both plebeians and patricians. Moreover, unlike the laws passed by the centuriate assembly, these *plebiscita* did not need the approval of the senate.

The struggle between the orders, then, had a significant impact on the development of the Roman constitution. Plebeians could hold the highest offices of state, they could intermarry with the patricians, and they could help pass laws binding on the entire Roman community. Although the struggle had been long, the Romans had handled it by compromise, not violent revolution. Theoretically, by 287 B.C. all Roman citizens were equal under the law, and all could strive for political office. But in reality, as a result of the right of intermarriage, a select number of wealthy patrician and plebeian families formed a new senatorial aristocracy called the *nobiles,* which came to dominate the political offices. The Roman Republic had not become a democracy.

The Roman Conquest of Italy

At the beginning of the Republic, Rome was surrounded by enemies, including the Etruscans to the north and the Sabines, Volscians, and Aequi to the east and south. The Latin communities on the plain of Latium posed an even

The Twelve Tables

In 451 B.C., plebeian pressure led to the creation of a special commission of ten men who were responsible for codifying Rome's laws and making them public. In so doing, the plebeians hoped that they could restrict the arbitrary power of the patrician magistrates who alone had access to the laws. The Twelve Tables represents the first formal codification of Roman laws and customs. The laws dealt with litigation procedures, debt, family relations, property, and other matters of public and sacred law. The code was inscribed on bronze plaques, which were eventually destroyed. These selections are taken from reconstructions of the code preserved in the works of later writers.

Selections from the Twelve Tables

Table III: Execution; Law of Debt

When a debt has been acknowledged, or judgment about the matter has been pronounced in court, thirty days must be the legitimate time of grace. After that, the debtor may be arrested by laying on of hands. Bring him into court. If he does not satisfy the judgment, or no one in court offers himself as surety in his behalf, the creditor may take the defaulter with him. He may bind him either in stocks or in fetters. . . .

Unless they make a settlement, debtors shall be held in bond for sixty days. During that time they shall be brought before the praetor's court in the meeting place on three successive market days, and the amount for which they are judged liable shall be announced; on the third market day they shall suffer capital punishment or be delivered up for sale abroad, across the Tiber.

Table IV: Rights of Head of Family

Quickly kill . . . a dreadfully deformed child.

If a father three times surrenders a son for sale, the son shall be free from the father.

A child born ten months after the father's death will not be admitted into legal inheritance.

Table V: Guardianship; Succession

Females shall remain in guardianship even when they have attained their majority.

If a man is raving mad, rightful authority over his person and chattels shall belong to his agnates [nearest male relatives] or to his clansmen.

A spendthrift is forbidden to exercise administration over his own goods. . . . A person who, being insane or a spendthrift, is prohibited from administering his own goods shall be under trusteeship of agnates.

Table VII: Rights Concerning Land

Branches of a tree may be lopped off all round to a height of more than 15 feet. . . . Should a tree on a neighbor's farm be bent crooked by a wind and lean over your farm, action may be taken for removal of that tree.

It is permitted to gather up fruit falling down on another man's farm.

Table VIII: Torts or Delicts

If any person has sung or composed against another person a song such as was causing slander or insult to another, he shall be clubbed to death.

If a person has maimed another's limb, let there be retaliation in kind unless he makes agreement for settlement with him.

Any person who destroys by burning any building or heap of corn deposited alongside a house shall be bound, scourged, and put to death by burning at the stake, provided that he has committed the said misdeed with malice aforethought, but if he shall have committed it by accident, that is, by negligence, it is ordained that he repair the damage, or, if he be too poor to be competent for such punishment, he shall receive a lighter chastisement.

Table IX: Public Law

The penalty shall be capital punishment for a judge or arbiter legally appointed who has been found guilty of receiving a bribe for giving a decision.

Table XI: Supplementary Laws

Intermarriage shall not take place between plebeians and patricians.

more immediate threat. After the expulsion of the Etruscan kings, a league of Latin allies formed and challenged Roman leadership in Latium. But in 493 B.C., the Romans established an alliance with the Latin communities, which provided for a common defense of Latium.

Rome was under constant pressure from its neighbors for the next hundred years. If we are to believe Livy, one of the chief ancient sources for the history of the early Roman Republic, Rome was engaged in almost continuous warfare with its neighbors.

In his account of these years, Livy provided a detailed narrative of Roman efforts. Many of Livy's stories were legendary in character and indeed were modeled after events in Greek history. But Livy, writing in the first century B.C.,

Cincinnatus Saves Rome: A Roman Morality Tale

There is perhaps no better account of how the virtues of duty and simplicity enabled good Roman citizens to prevail during the travails of the fifth century B.C. than Livy's account of Cincinnatus. He was chosen dictator, supposedly in 457 B.C., to defend Rome against the attacks of the Aequi. The position of dictator was a temporary expedient used only in emergencies; the consuls would resign, and a leader with unlimited power would be appointed for a limited period (usually six months). In this account, Cincinnatus did his duty, defeated the Aequi, and returned to his simple farm in just fifteen days.

Livy, The Early History of Rome

The city was thrown into a state of turmoil, and the general alarm was as great as if Rome herself were surrounded. Nautius was sent for, but it was quickly decided that he was not the man to inspire full confidence; the situation evidently called for a dictator, and, with no dissenting voice, Lucius Quinctius Cincinnatus was named for the post.

Now I would solicit the particular attention of those numerous people who imagine that money is everything in this world, and that rank and ability are inseparable from wealth: let them observe that Cincinnatus, the one man in whom Rome reposed all her hope of survival, was at that moment working a little three-acre farm . . . west of the Tiber, just opposite the spot where the shipyards are today. A mission from the city found him at work on his land—digging a ditch, maybe, or plowing. Greetings were exchanged, and he was asked—with a prayer for divine blessing on himself and his country—to put on his toga and hear the Senate's instructions. This naturally surprised him, and, asking if all were well, he told his wife Racilia to run to their cottage and fetch his toga. The toga was brought, and wiping the grimy sweat from his hands and face he put it on; at once the envoys from the city saluted him, with congratulations, as Dictator, invited him to enter Rome, and informed him of the terrible danger of Municius' army. A state vessel was waiting for him on the river, and on the city bank he was welcomed by his three sons who had come to meet him, then by other kinsmen and friends, and finally by nearly the whole body of senators. Closely attended by all these people and preceded by his lictors he was then escorted to his residence through streets lined with great crowds of common folk who, be it said, were by no means so pleased to see the new Dictator, as they thought his power excessive and dreaded the way in which he was likely to use it.

[Cincinnatus proceeds to raise an army, march out, and defeat the Aequi.]

In Rome the Senate was convened by Quintus Fabius the City Prefect, and a decree was passed inviting Cincinnatus to enter in triumph with his troops. The chariot he rode in was preceded by the enemy commanders and the military standards, and followed by his army loaded with its spoils. . . . Cincinnatus finally resigned after holding office for fifteen days, having originally accepted it for a period of six months.

used these stories to teach Romans the moral values and virtues that had made Rome great. These included tenacity, duty, courage, and especially discipline (see the box above). Indeed, Livy recounted stories of military leaders who executed their own sons for leaving their place in battle, a serious offense since the success of the hoplite infantry depended on maintaining a precise order. These stories had little basis in fact, but like the story of George Washington and the cherry tree in American history, they provided mythical images to reinforce Roman patriotism.

In 340 B.C., Rome had to deal with a revolt of the Latin states in Latium, which had come to resent Rome's increasing domination of their alliance. The Romans crushed the revolt and established complete supremacy in Latium. Between 343 and 290 B.C., the Romans waged a fierce struggle with the Samnites, a hill people from the central Apennines, some of whom had settled in Campania, south of Rome. The conquest of the Samnites gave Rome considerable control over a large part of Italy and also brought it into direct contact with the Greek communities of southern Italy. Soon the Romans were involved in hostilities with some of these Greek cities. The Greek communities were primarily commercial cities and had no standing armies. They were accustomed to hiring mercenaries to fight their battles for them. Consequently, they bought the aid of King Pyrrhus of Epirus (approximately modern-day Epirus in Greece), who crossed the Adriatic with twenty thousand troops and defeated the Romans twice. In both battles, however, Pyrrhus experienced heavy losses, leading him to comment that one more victory would ruin him (hence our phrase "Pyrrhic victory"). After a diversion to Sicily, Pyrrhus came back for one more battle with the Romans and this time was decisively defeated by 267 B.C. The Romans completed their conquest of southern Italy. After crushing the remaining Etruscan states to the north, Rome had conquered all of Italy, except the extreme north, by 264 B.C.

To rule Italy, the Romans devised the Roman confederation. Under this system, Rome allowed some peoples—especially the Latins—to have full Roman citizenship. Most of the remaining communities were made allies. They remained free to run their own local affairs but were required to provide soldiers for Rome. Moreover, the Romans made it clear that loyal allies could improve their status and even aspire to becoming Roman citizens. Thus the Romans had found a way to give conquered states a stake in Rome's success.

CHRONOLOGY

The Roman Conquest of Italy

Alliance with Latin states	493 B.C.
Latin revolt	340–338 B.C.
Creation of the Roman confederation	338 B.C.
Samnite Wars	343–290 B.C.
Pyrrhic War	281–267 B.C.

SEF/Art Resource, NY

King Pyrrhus. By sinking a Roman fleet off its coast, the Greek city of Tarentum initiated the Pyrrhic War. The Tarentines bought the aid of King Pyrrhus of Epirus, who defeated the Romans in their first two encounters, but not without suffering heavy losses. In their third battle, in which the Romans stampeded Pyrrhus' war elephants into his own troops, Rome was victorious. Pictured is a marble bust of Pyrrhus found at Herculaneum.

In the course of their expansion throughout Italy, the Romans had pursued consistent policies that help explain their success. The Romans excelled in making the correct diplomatic decisions; they were superb diplomats. While firm and even cruel when necessary—rebellions were crushed without mercy—they were also shrewd in extending their citizenship and allowing autonomy in domestic affairs. Their conquest of Italy could hardly be said to be the result of a direct policy of expansion. Much of it was opportunistic. The Romans did not hesitate to act once they felt their security threatened. And surrounded by potential enemies, Rome in a sense never felt secure. The Romans were not only good soldiers but also persistent ones. The loss of an army or a fleet did not cause them to quit but spurred them on to build new armies and new fleets. Finally, the Romans had a practical sense of strategy. As

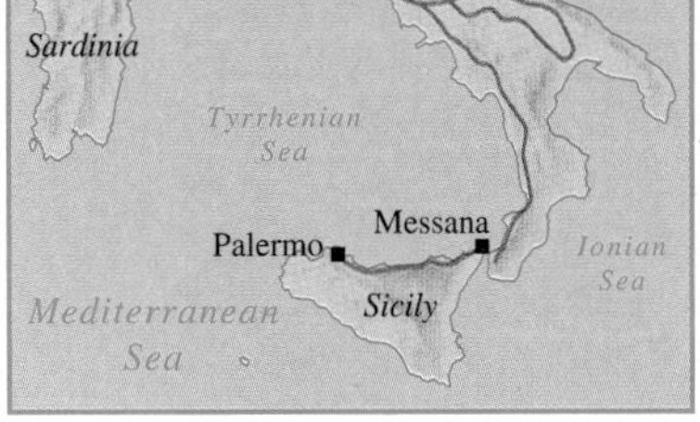

Roman Roads in Italy, c. 100 B.C.

The Art Archive, London/Museo di Villa Giulia/G. Dagli Orti (A)

A Roman Legionary. The Roman legionaries, famed for their courage and tenacity, made possible Roman domination of the Mediterranean Sea. This tablet, dating from the first half of the third century B.C. shows a Roman legionary during the period of the Republic.

they conquered, they settled Romans and Latins in new communities outside Latium. By 264 B.C., the Romans had established colonies—fortified towns—at all strategic locations. By building roads to these settlements and connecting them, the Romans assured themselves of an impressive military and communications network that enabled them to rule effectively and efficiently. By insisting on military service from the allies in the Roman confederation, Rome essentially mobilized the entire military manpower of all Italy for its wars.

The Roman Conquest of the Mediterranean (264–133 B.C.)

After their conquest of the Italian peninsula, the Romans found themselves face to face with a formidable Mediterranean power—Carthage. Founded around 800 B.C. by Phoenicians from Tyre, Carthage was located in a favorable position for commanding Mediterranean trade routes and had become an important commercial center (see Map 5.2). It had become politically and militarily strong as well. By the third century B.C., the Carthaginian empire included the coast of North Africa, southern Spain, Sardinia, Corsica, and western Sicily. With its monopoly of western Mediterranean trade, Carthage was the largest and richest state in the area. The presence of Carthaginians in Sicily made the Romans apprehensive about Carthaginian encroachment on the Italian coast. In 264 B.C., mutual suspicions drove the two powers into a lengthy struggle for control of the western Mediterranean.

The Struggle with Carthage

The First Punic War (264–241 B.C.)—the Latin word for Phoenician was *Punicus*—began when the Romans decided to intervene in a struggle between two Sicilian cities and sent an army to Sicily. The Carthaginians, who considered Sicily within their own sphere of influence, regarded this as just cause for war. In going to war, both sides determined on the conquest of Sicily. The Romans realized that the war would be long and drawn out if they could not supplement land operations with a navy and promptly developed a substantial fleet. The Carthaginians, however, had difficulty in finding mercenaries to continue the fight. After a long struggle in which both sides lost battles in North

Map 5.2 Roman Conquests in the Mediterranean, 264–133 B.C. Beginning with the Punic Wars, Rome expanded its holdings, first in the western Mediterranean at the expense of Carthage and later in Greece and western Asia Minor. ■ What aspects of Mediterranean geography, combined with the territorial holdings and aspirations of Rome and the Carthaginians, made the Punic Wars more likely?

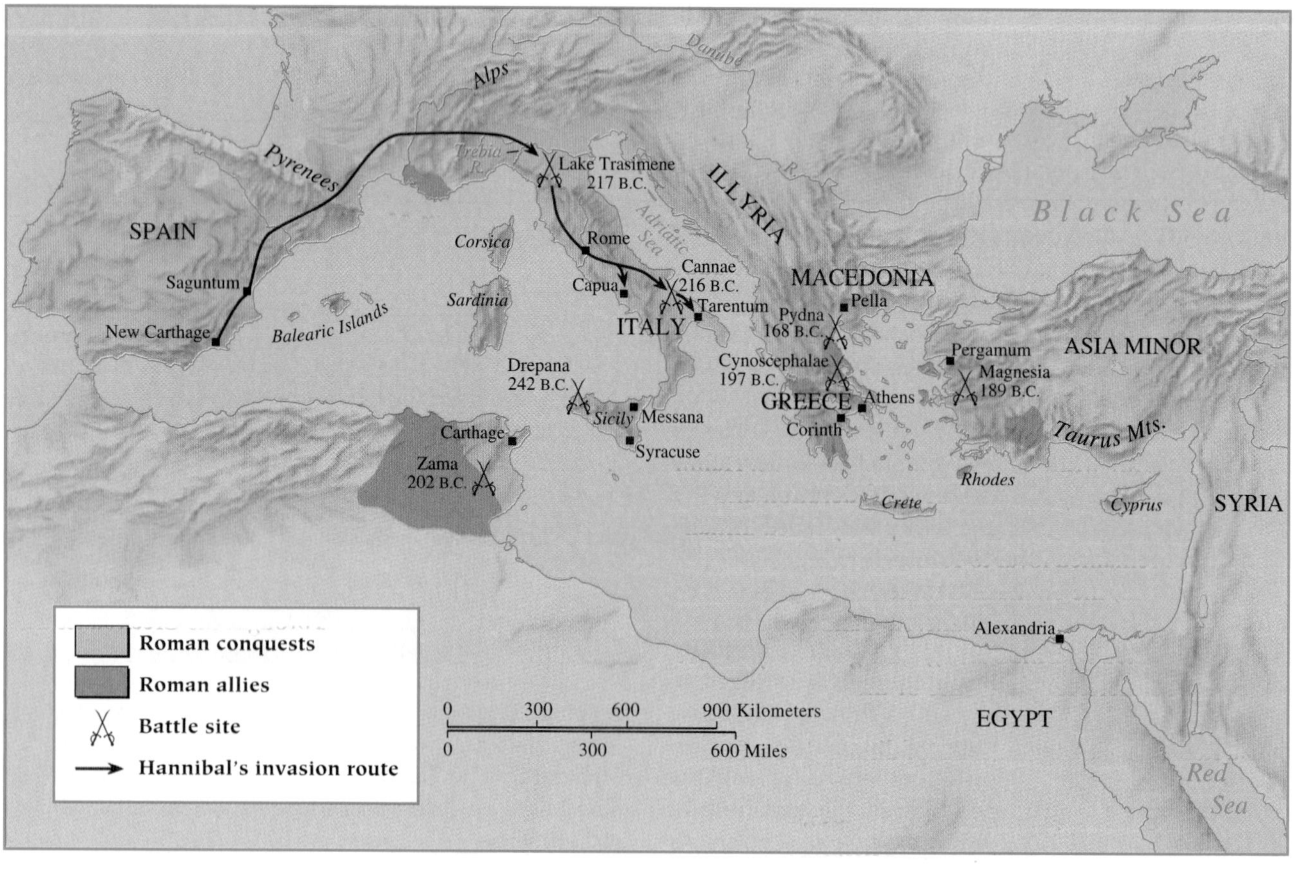

Africa and Sicily, a Roman fleet defeated the Carthaginian navy off Drepana near Sicily in 242 B.C. The cities of western Sicily that had been controlled by Carthage capitulated. Carthage sued for peace, and the war ended in 241 B.C. Carthage gave up all rights to Sicily and had to pay an indemnity. Three years later, Rome took advantage of Carthage's problems with its mercenaries to seize the islands of Sardinia and Corsica. This act so angered the Carthaginians that, according to one story, their leading general, Hamilcar Barca, made his nine-year-old son swear that he would hate Rome ever after. The son's name was Hannibal.

Between the wars, Carthage made an unexpected recovery under the leadership of the general who had been briefly successful in Sicily in the First Punic War, Hamilcar Barca. Hamilcar extended Carthage's domains in Spain to compensate for the territory lost to Rome. A major goal in creating the Spanish empire was to get manpower for Carthage. The Spanish natives made great soldiers, being physically strong and possessing excellent swords. Hamilcar and his successors proceeded to build up a formidable land army in the event of a second war with Rome because they realized that Carthage's success depended on defeating Rome on land. In 221 B.C., Hamilcar's son Hannibal, now twenty-five, took over direction of Carthaginian policy. Within three years, Rome and Carthage were again at war.

Carthage and Rome had agreed to divide Spain into respective spheres of influence. Although Saguntum was located in the Carthaginian sphere, Rome made an alliance with the city and encouraged its inhabitants in anti-Carthaginian activities. Thoroughly provoked by the Roman action, Hannibal attacked Saguntum, and the Romans declared war on Carthage in 218 B.C. This time the Carthaginian strategy aimed at bringing the war home to the Romans and defeating them in their own backyard. In an amazing march, Hannibal crossed the Alps with an army of thirty to forty thousand men and six thousand horses and elephants and advanced into northern Italy. After defeating the Romans at the Trebia River, he added thousands of Gauls to his army and proceeded into central Italy. At Lake Trasimene in Etruria, he again defeated the Romans. In desperation, the Romans elected as consul Quintus Fabius Maximus, who became known as the "Delayer" because of his tactics of following and delaying Hannibal's army without risking a pitched battle. Hannibal hoped to destroy the Roman confederation and win Italian cities away from Rome. The policy failed initially; virtually all remained loyal to Rome.

In 216 B.C., the Romans decided to meet Hannibal head on. It was a serious mistake. At Cannae, Hannibal's forces devastated a Roman army, killing as many as forty thousand soldiers. At last, some of the southern Italian cities rebelled against Roman rule and went over to Hannibal. Rome seemed on the brink of disaster but refused to give up and raised yet another army.

Rome gradually recovered. Although Hannibal remained free to roam in Italy, he had neither the men nor the equipment to lay siege to the major cities, including Rome itself. The Romans began to reconquer some of the rebellious Italian cities. More important, the Romans pursued a Spanish strategy that aimed at undermining the Carthaginian empire in Spain. Publius Cornelius Scipio, later known as Scipio Africanus the Elder, was given command of the Roman forces in Spain even though he was too young to hold the position legally. But he was a brilliant general who learned from Hannibal's tactics and by 206 B.C. had pushed the Carthaginians out of Spain.

The Romans then took the war directly to Carthage. Late in 204 B.C., Scipio led a Roman army from Sicily into North Africa and forced the Carthaginians to recall Hannibal from Italy. At the Battle of Zama in 202 B.C., Scipio decisively defeated Hannibal and the Carthaginian forces, and the war was over. By the peace treaty signed in 201, Carthage lost Spain, agreed to pay an indemnity, and promised not to go to war without Rome's permission. Spain, like Sicily, Corsica, and Sardinia earlier, was made into a Roman province. Rome had become the dominant power in the western Mediterranean.

But some Romans wanted even more. A number of prominent Romans, especially the conservative politician Cato, advocated the complete destruction of Carthage. Cato ended every speech he made to the senate with the words, "And I think Carthage must be destroyed." When the Carthaginians technically broke their peace treaty with Rome by going to war against one of Rome's North African allies who had been encroaching on Carthage's home territory, the Romans declared war. Led by Scipio Aemilianus Africanus the Younger, Roman forces undertook their third and last war with Carthage (149–146 B.C.). This time, Carthage was no match for the Romans, who seized this opportunity to carry out the final destruction of Carthage (see the box on p. 114). The territory of Carthage was made a province called Africa.

The Eastern Mediterranean

During the Punic Wars, Rome had become acutely aware of the Hellenistic states of the eastern Mediterranean when the king of Macedonia made an alliance with Hannibal after the Roman defeat at Cannae. But Rome was preoccupied with the Carthaginians, and it was not until after the defeat of Carthage that Rome became involved in the world of Hellenistic politics as an advocate for the freedom of the Greek states. This support of the Greeks brought the Romans into conflict with both Macedonia and the kingdom of the Seleucids. Roman military victories and diplomatic negotiations rearranged the territorial boundaries of the Hellenistic kingdoms and brought the Greek states their freedom in 196 B.C. For fifty years, the Romans tried to be a power broker in the affairs of the Greeks without direct control of their lands. When the effort failed, the Romans changed their policy.

Macedonia was made a Roman province in 148 B.C., and when some of the Greek states rose in revolt against Rome's restrictive policies, Rome acted decisively. The city

The Destruction of Carthage

The Romans used a technical breach of Carthage's peace treaty with Rome as a pretext to undertake a third and final war with Carthage (149–146 B.C.). Although Carthage posed no real threat to Rome's security, the Romans still remembered the traumatic experiences of the Second Punic War when Hannibal had ravaged much of their homeland. The hard-liners gained the upper hand in the senate and called for the complete destruction of Carthage. The city was razed, the survivors were sold into slavery, and the land was made a province of Rome. In this passage, the historian Appian of Alexandria describes the final destruction of Carthage by the Romans under the command of Scipio Aemilianus.

Appian, Roman History

Then came new scenes of horror. The fire spread and carried everything down, and the soldiers did not wait to destroy the buildings little by little, but pulled them all down together. So the crashing grew louder, and many fell with the stones into the midst dead. Others were seen still living, especially old men, women, and young children who had hidden in the inmost nooks of the houses, some of them wounded, some more or less burned, and uttering horrible cries. Still others, thrust out and falling from such a height with the stones, timbers, and fire, were torn asunder into all kinds of horrible shapes, crushed and mangled. Nor was this the end of their miseries, for the street cleaners, who were removing the rubbish with axes, mattocks, and boat-hooks, and making the roads passable, tossed with these instruments the dead and the living together into holes in the ground, sweeping them along like sticks and stones or turning them over with their iron tools, and man was used for filling up a ditch. Some were thrown in head foremost, while their legs, sticking out of the ground, writhed a long time. Others fell with their feet downward and their heads above the ground. Horses ran over them, crushing their faces and skulls, not purposely on the part of the riders, but in their headlong haste. Nor did the street cleaners either do these things on purpose; but the press of war, the glory of approaching victory, the rush of the soldiery, the confused noise of heralds and trumpeters all round, the tribunes and centurions changing guard and marching the cohorts here and there—all together made everybody frantic and heedless of the spectacle before their eyes.

Six days and nights were consumed in this kind of turmoil, the soldiers being changed so that they might not be worn out with toil, slaughter, lack of sleep, and these horrid sights. . . .

Scipio, beholding this city, which had flourished 700 years from its foundation and had ruled over so many lands, islands, and seas, as rich in arms and fleets, elephants, and money as the mightiest empires, but far surpassing them in hardihood and high spirit . . . now come to its end in total destruction—Scipio, beholding this spectacle, is said to have shed tears and publicly lamented the fortune of the enemy. After meditating by himself a long time and reflecting on the inevitable fall of cities, nations, and empires, as well as of individuals, upon the fate of Troy, that once proud city, upon the fate of the Assyrian, the Median, and afterwards of the great Persian empire, and, most recently of all, of the splendid empire of Macedon, either voluntarily or otherwise the words of the poet [Homer, *Iliad*] escaped his lips:

The day shall come in which our sacred Troy
And Priam, and the people over whom
Spear-bearing Priam rules, shall perish all.

Being asked by Polybius in familiar conversation (for Polybius had been his tutor) what he meant by using these words, Polybius says that he did not hesitate frankly to name his own country, for whose fate he feared when he considered the mutability of human affairs. And Polybius wrote this down just as he heard it.

of Corinth, leader of the revolt, was destroyed in 146 B.C. to teach the Greeks a lesson, and Greece was placed under the control of the Roman governor of Macedonia. Thirteen years later, in 133 B.C., the king of Pergamum deeded his kingdom to Rome, giving Rome its first province in Asia. Rome was now master of the Mediterranean Sea.

The Nature of Roman Imperialism

Rome's empire was built in three stages: the conquest of Italy, the conflict with Carthage and expansion into the western Mediterranean, and the involvement with and domination of the Hellenistic kingdoms in the eastern Mediterranean. The Romans did not have a master plan for the creation of an empire. Much of their expansion was opportunistic; once involved in a situation that threatened their security, the Romans did not hesitate to act. And the more they expanded, the more threats to their security appeared on the horizon, involving them in yet more conflicts. Indeed, the Romans liked to portray themselves as declaring war only for defensive reasons or to protect allies. That is only part of the story, however. It is likely, as some historians have recently suggested, that at some point a group of Roman aristocratic leaders emerged who favored expansion both for the glory it offered and for the economic benefits it provided. Certainly by the second century B.C., aristocratic senators perceived new opportunities for lucrative foreign commands, enormous spoils of war, and an abundant supply of slave labor for their growing landed estates. By that same time, as the destruction of

CHRONOLOGY

The Roman Conquest of the Mediterranean

First Punic War	264–241 B.C.
Rome seizes Corsica and Sardinia	238 B.C.
Second Punic War	218–201 B.C.
Battle of Cannae	216 B.C.
Scipio completes seizure of Spain	206 B.C.
Battle of Zama	202 B.C.
Third Punic War	149–146 B.C.
Incorporation of Macedonia as a Roman province	148 B.C.
Destruction of Carthage	146 B.C.
Roman acquisition of Pergamum	133 B.C.

Corinth and Carthage indicates, Roman imperialism had become more arrogant and brutal as well. Rome's foreign success also had enormous repercussions for the internal development of the Roman Republic.

Society and Culture in the Roman Republic

One of the most noticeable aspects of Roman society and culture is the impact of the Greeks. The Romans had experienced Greek influence early on through the Greek cities in southern Italy. By the end of the third century B.C., however, Greek civilization played an ever-increasing role in Roman culture. Greek ambassadors, merchants, and artists traveled to Rome and spread Greek thought and practices. After their conquest of the Hellenistic kingdoms, Roman military commanders shipped Greek manuscripts and art back to Rome. Multitudes of educated Greek slaves were used in Roman households. Greek models affected virtually every area of Roman life, from literature and philosophy to religion and education. Wealthy Romans hired Greek tutors and sent their sons to Athens to study. As the Roman poet Horace said, "Captive Greece took captive her rude conqueror." Greek thought captivated the less sophisticated Roman minds, and the Romans became willing transmitters of Greek culture—not, however, without some resistance from Romans who had nothing but contempt for Greek politics and feared the end of old Roman values. Even those who favored Greek culture, such as Scipio Aemilianus, blamed the Greeks for Rome's new vices, including luxury and homosexual practices.

Roman Religion

Every aspect of Roman society was permeated with religion. The official state religion focused on the worship of a pantheon of gods and goddesses, including Juno, the patron goddess of women; Minerva, the goddess of craftspeople; Mars, the god of war; and Jupiter Optimus Maximus (best and greatest), who became the patron deity of Rome and assumed a central place in the religious life of the city. As Rome developed and came into contact with other peoples and gods, the community simply adopted new deities. Hence the Greek Hermes became the Roman Mercury, and the Greek Demeter, Ceres. By the end of the third century B.C., a rather complete amalgamation of Greek and Roman religion had occurred. In general, the Romans were very tolerant of new religious cults and only occasionally outlawed them.

Roman religion focused on the worship of the gods for a very practical reason—human beings were thought to be totally dependent on them. The exact performance of ritual was crucial to establishing a right relationship with the gods. What was true for individuals was also valid for the

Scala/Art Resource, NY

Temple of Portunus. The Romans considered the proper worship of the gods an important element of their success. Typical of Roman religious architecture was the small urban temple located in the midst of a crowded commercial center. Pictured here is a rectangular temple built in Rome in the late second or early first century B.C. and dedicated to Portunus, the god of harbors. The temple was located in the cattle market close to the Tiber River.

state: it also had to observe correct ritual in order to receive its reward. Accurate performance of ritual was consequently important, and the Romans established a college of priests or pontiffs to carry out that responsibility. Initially three in number, by the first century B.C., they had increased to sixteen. The pontiffs were in charge of what the Romans called the divine law, maintaining the right relationship between the state and the gods. The pontiffs performed all public religious acts and supervised magistrates in the correct ritual for public political acts. If the rituals were performed correctly, the Romans would obtain the "peace of the gods." The Romans' success in creating an empire was no doubt taken as confirmation of divine favor. As Cicero, the first-century politician and writer, claimed, "We have overcome all the nations of the world, because we have realized that the world is directed and governed by the gods."[1]

In addition to the college of pontiffs, a college of augurs existed whose responsibility was to interpret the signs (auspices) or warnings that the gods gave to men. Before every important act of state, a magistrate with *imperium* took the auspices to make sure the gods approved. The Romans attributed great importance to this—if the omens were unfavorable, the act was invalid or the planned action was not auspicious. As Cicero later commented, the augurs had "the highest and most important authority in the State" because "no act of any magistrate at home or in the field can have any validity for any person without their authority."[2] Auspices were taken by observing the flights of birds, lightning and other natural phenomena, and the behavior of certain animals.

Just as the state had an official cult, so did families. Because the family was regarded as a small state within the state, it had its own household cults, which included Janus, the spirit of the doorway; Vesta, the goddess of the hearth; and the Penates, the spirits of the storehouse. Here, too, proper ritual was important, and it was the responsibility of the *paterfamilias* as head of the family to ensure the religious obligations were properly fulfilled.

One of the most important ceremonies involved purification. In his manual *On Agriculture*, Marcus Cato the Elder spelled out the proper ritual for purification of a landed estate. The ceremony included these words:

> Father Mars [god of vegetation as well as war], I beg and entreat you to be of good will and favorable to me and to our house and household, for which purpose I have ordered the swine-sheep-bull procession to be led around my land and fields and farm. And [I beg] that you will check, thrust back, and avert diseases seen and unseen, crop failure and crop destruction, sudden losses and storms, and that you will permit the annual crops, the grain crops, the vineyards, and tree and vine slips to grow and turn out well. And [that you] keep safe the shepherds and the flocks and give good health and strength to me and to our house and household: with these purposes in view . . . receive the honor of this suckling swine-sheep-bull sacrifice.[3]

Proper observance of the ritual was so crucial that any error necessitated a repetition of the entire ritual.

Religious festivals were an important part of Roman religious practice. There were two kinds: public festivals ordained and paid for by the state and private festivals celebrated by individuals and families. By the mid-second century B.C., six public festivals were celebrated annually, each lasting several days.

The practice of holding games also grew out of religious festivals. The games were inaugurated in honor of Jupiter Optimus Maximus but had become annual events by 366 B.C. In the late Republic, both the number of games and the number of days they lasted were increased. Consequently, state funds became inadequate for the magnificence expected, and the aediles, who were in charge of the games and hoped to use their office as a stepping-stone to higher political offices, paid additional expenses out of their own pocket. Originally, the games consisted of chariot racing in the Circus Maximus; later, animal hunts and theatrical performances were added. In the empire, gladiatorial contests would become the primary focus.

Education: The Importance of Rhetoric

The Romans did not possess a system of public education. In the early Republic, the family provided training in the various skills needed by a Roman citizen. Boys were expected to master the basic elements of farming, develop the physical skills needed to be good soldiers, learn the traditions of the state through the legends of heroic Roman ancestors, and become acquainted with public affairs. Girls were supposed to learn the skills needed to be good wives and mothers. Every upper-class Roman boy or girl was expected to learn to read.

Through contact with the Greek world, Roman education took on new ideals in the third and second centuries B.C. The wealthy classes wanted their children exposed to Greek studies and were especially attracted to the training in rhetoric and philosophy that would prepare their sons for a successful public career. For upper-class males, rhetoric—the art of persuasive speaking—was an especially important part of their education. To pursue a public career, they needed to learn good speaking skills that would enable them to win elections and lawsuits in the court. By winning lawsuits, a person could make a name for himself and build political support.

Since knowledge of Greek was a crucial ingredient in education, schools taught by professional teachers emerged to supply this need. Those who could afford to might provide Greek tutors for their children, but less well endowed families could turn to private schools where most of the instructors were educated slaves or freedmen, usually of Greek origin. After several years of primary instruction, whose aim was simply to teach the basics of reading, writing, and arithmetic, the pupil went to a secondary school run by a *grammaticus*, or grammarian. These schools had a standard curriculum based on the liberal arts: literature, dialectic (logic), arithmetic, geometry, astronomy, and music. The core of the liberal arts and the curriculum, how-

© Leslye and Roy Adkins Picture Library

Schoolmaster and Pupils. By the third and second centuries B.C., wealthy Romans sought to prepare their sons for successful public careers by a thorough education in rhetoric and philosophy. Pictured here is a Roman teacher with his two pupils, who are reading from papyrus scrolls.

ever, was Greek literature. As a result, by the second and first centuries B.C., educated Romans had become increasingly bilingual.

The Growth of Slavery

Slavery was a common institution throughout the ancient world, but no people possessed more slaves or relied so much on slave labor as the Romans eventually did. Before the third century B.C., a small Roman farmer might possess one or two slaves who would help farm his few acres and perform domestic chores. These slaves would most likely be from Italy and be regarded as part of the family household. Only the very rich would have large numbers of slaves.

The Roman conquest of the Mediterranean brought a drastic change in the use of slaves. Large numbers of foreign slaves were brought back to Italy. During the Republic, then, the chief source of slaves was from capture in war, followed by piracy. Of course, the children of slaves also became slaves. While some Roman generals brought back slaves to be sold to benefit the public treasury, ambitious generals of the first century, such as Pompey and Caesar, made personal fortunes by treating slaves captured by their armies as private property.

Slaves were used in many ways in Roman society. The rich, of course, owned the most and the best. In the late Republic, it became a badge of prestige to be attended by many slaves. Greeks were in much demand as tutors, musicians, doctors, and artists. Roman businesses would employ them as shop assistants or craftspeople. Slaves were also used as farm laborers; the large landed estates known as *latifundia* were worked by huge gangs of slaves living in pitiful conditions. Cato the Elder argued that it was cheaper to work slaves to death and then replace them than to treat them well. Many slaves of all nationalities were used as menial household workers, such as cooks, valets, waiters, cleaners, and gardeners. Contractors used slave labor to build roads, aqueducts, and other public facilities. The total number of slaves is difficult to judge—estimates range from one-fourth to one-half the number of free people.

It is also difficult to generalize about the treatment of Roman slaves. There are numerous instances of humane treatment by masters and situations where slaves even protected their owners from danger out of gratitude and esteem. But slaves were also subject to severe punishments, torture, abuse, and hard labor that drove some to run away or even revolt against their owners. The Republic had stringent laws against aiding a runaway slave. The murder of a master by a slave usually meant the execution of all the other household slaves. Near the end of the second century B.C., large-scale slave revolts occurred in Sicily, where enormous gangs of slaves were subjected to horrible

Household Slaves. It became a sign of status for upper-class Romans to have numerous specialist slaves at work in a household. This wall painting from central Italy depicts an elaborate dressing room where a female slave is arranging a girl's hair while the girl's mother and sister look on.

Erich Lessing/Art Resource, NY

A Roman Lady. Roman women, especially those of the upper class, developed comparatively more freedom than women in Classical Athens despite the persistent male belief that women required guardianship. This mural decoration was found in the remains of a villa destroyed by the eruption of Mount Vesuvius.

working conditions on large landed estates. Slaves were branded, beaten, fed inadequately, worked in chains, and housed at night in underground prisons. It took three years (from 135 to 132 B.C.) to crush a revolt of seventy thousand slaves, and the great revolt on Sicily (104–101 B.C.) involved most of the island and took a Roman army of seventeen thousand men to suppress. The most famous revolt on the Italian peninsula occurred in 73 B.C. Led by a Thracian gladiator named Spartacus, the revolt broke out in southern Italy and involved seventy thousand slaves. Spartacus managed to defeat several Roman armies before he was finally trapped and killed in southern Italy in 71 B.C. Six thousand of his followers were crucified, the traditional form of execution for slaves.

The Roman Family

At the heart of the Roman social structure stood the family, headed by the *paterfamilias*—the dominant male. The household also included the wife, sons with their wives and children, unmarried daughters, and slaves. As we have seen, a family was virtually a small state within the state, and the power of the *paterfamilias* paralleled that of the state magistrates over citizens. He held absolute authority over his children; he could sell them or have them put to death. Like the Greeks, Roman males believed that the weakness of the female sex necessitated male guardians (see the box on p. 119). The *paterfamilias* exercised that authority; on his death, sons or the nearest male relatives assumed the role of guardians. By the late Republic, however, although the rights of male guardians remained legally in effect, many upper-class women found numerous ways to circumvent the power of their guardians.

Fathers arranged the marriages of daughters, although there are instances of mothers and daughters influencing the choice. In the Republic, women married *cum manu,* "with legal control" passing from father to husband. By the mid-first century B.C., the dominant practice had changed to *sine manu,* "without legal control," which meant that married daughters officially remained within the father's legal power. Since the fathers of most married women were dead, not being in the "legal control" of a husband made possible independent property rights that forceful women could translate into considerable power within the household and outside it. Traditionally, Roman marriages were intended to be for life, but divorce was introduced in the third century and became relatively easy to obtain since either party could initiate it and no one needed to prove the breakdown of the marriage. Divorce became especially prevalent in the first century B.C.—a period of political turmoil—when marriages were used to cement political alliances.

Some parents in upper-class families provided education for their daughters. Some girls had private tutors, and others may have gone to primary schools. But at the age when boys were entering secondary schools, girls were pushed into marriage. The legal minimum age was twelve; fourteen was a more common age in practice. Although some Roman doctors warned that early pregnancies could be dangerous to young girls, early marriages persisted due to the desire to benefit from dowries as soon as possible and the reality of early mortality. A good example is Tullia, Cicero's beloved daughter. She was married at sixteen, widowed at twenty-two,

Cato the Elder on Women

During the Second Punic War, the Romans enacted the Oppian Law, which limited the amount of gold women could possess and restricted their dress. In 195 B.C., an attempt was made to repeal the law, and women demonstrated in the streets on behalf of the effort. According to the Roman historian Livy, the conservative Roman official Cato the Elder spoke against repeal and against the women favoring it. His words reflect a traditional male Roman attitude toward women.

Livy, The History of Rome

"If each of us, citizens, had determined to assert his rights and dignity as a husband with respect to his own spouse, we should have less trouble with the sex as a whole; as it is, our liberty, destroyed at home by female violence, even here in the Forum is crushed and trodden underfoot, and because we have not kept them individually under control, we dread them collectively. . . . But from no class is there not the greatest danger if you permit them meetings and gatherings and secret consultations. . . .

"Our ancestors permitted no woman to conduct even personal business without a guardian to intervene in her behalf; they wished them to be under the control of fathers, brothers, husbands; we (Heaven help us!) allow them now even to interfere in public affairs, yes, and to visit the Forum and our informal and formal sessions. What else are they doing now on the streets and at the corners except urging the bill of the tribunes and voting for the repeal of the law? Give loose rein to their uncontrollable nature and to this untamed creature and expect that they will themselves set no bounds to their license. Unless you act, this is the least of the things enjoined upon women by custom or law and to which they submit with a feeling of injustice. It is complete liberty or rather, if we wish to speak the truth, complete license that they desire.

"If they win in this, what will they not attempt? Review all the laws with which your forefathers restrained their license and made them subject to their husbands; even with all these bonds you can scarcely control them. What of this? If you suffer them to seize these bonds one by one and wrench themselves free and finally to be placed on a parity with their husbands, do you think you will be able to endure them? The moment they begin to be your equals, they will be your superiors. . . .

"Now they publicly address other women's husbands, and, what is more serious, they beg for a law and votes, and from various men they get what they ask. In matters affecting yourself, your property, your children, you, Sir, can be importuned; once the law has ceased to set a limit to your wife's expenditures you will never set it yourself. Do not think, citizens, that the situation which existed before the law was passed will ever return."

remarried one year later, divorced at twenty-eight, remarried at twenty-nine, and divorced at thirty-three. She died at thirty-four, not unusual for females in Roman society.

In contrast to upper-class Athenian women, Roman upper-class women were not segregated from males in the home. Wives were appreciated as enjoyable company and were at the center of household social life. Women talked to visitors and were free to shop, visit friends, and go to games, temples, and theaters. Nevertheless, they were not allowed to participate in public life, although there are examples of women exerting considerable political influence through their husbands. In fact, while upper-class men served the government abroad or in the military, they depended on their wives and mothers to manage their estates and protect their political interests.

The Evolution of Roman Law

One of Rome's chief gifts to the Mediterranean world of its day and to succeeding generations of Western civilization was its development of law. After the Twelve Tables of 450 B.C., there was no complete codification of Roman law until that of the Byzantine emperor Justinian in the sixth century A.D. (see Chapter 7). The Twelve Tables, though inappropriate for later times, were never officially abrogated and were still memorized by schoolboys in the first century B.C. Civil law (*ius civile*) derived from the Twelve Tables proved inadequate for later Roman needs, however, and gave way to corrections and additions by the praetors. On taking office, a praetor issued an edict listing his guidelines for dealing with different kinds of legal cases. The praetors were knowledgeable in law, but they also relied on Roman jurists—amateur law experts—for advice in preparing their edicts. The interpretations of the jurists, often embodied in the edicts of the praetors, created a body of legal principles.

In 242 B.C., the Romans appointed a second praetor who was responsible for examining suits between a Roman and a non-Roman as well as between two non-Romans. The Romans found that although some of their rules of law could be used in these cases, special rules were often needed. These rules gave rise to a body of law known as the *ius gentium*—the law of nations—defined by the Romans as "that part of the law which we apply both to ourselves and to foreigners." But the influence of Greek philosophy, primarily Stoicism, led Romans in the late Republic to develop the idea of *ius naturale*—natural law—or universal divine law derived from right reason. The Romans came to view their law of nations as derived from or identical to this natural law, thus giving Roman jurists a philosophical justification for systematizing Roman law according to basic principles.

The Development of Literature and Art

The Romans produced little literature before the third century B.C., and the Latin literature that emerged in that century was strongly influenced by Greek models. The demand for plays at public festivals eventually led to a growing number of native playwrights. The best known were Plautus and Terence.

Plautus (c. 254–184 B.C.) used plots from Greek New Comedy (see Chapter 4) for his own plays (see the box on p. 121). The actors wore Greek costumes and Greek masks and portrayed the same stock characters: dirty old men, clever slaves, prostitutes, and young men in love, whose pains are recounted in this brief excerpt:

Not the throes of all mankind
Equal my distracted mind.
I strain and I toss
On a passionate cross:
Love's goad makes me reel,
I whirl on Love's wheel,
In a swoon of despair
Hurried here, hurried there—
Torn asunder, I am blind
With a cloud upon my mind.[4]

While indebted to the Greeks, Plautus managed to infuse his plays with his own earthy Latin quality, incorporating elements that appealed to the Romans: drunkenness, gluttony, and womanizing. Plautus wrote for the masses and became a very popular playwright in Rome.

A second playwright of distinction was Terence (185–159 B.C.), who was born in Carthage and brought to Rome as a slave by a Roman senator who freed him. Terence died at an early age after he had written six plays. He also used plots from Greek New Comedy, but his plays contained less slapstick than those of Plautus. Terence was more concerned with the subtle portrayal of character and the artistry of his language. His refined Latin style appealed more to a cultivated audience than to the masses. In the prologue to *The Brothers,* he stated:

> The author . . . takes it as a high compliment if he can win the approval of men who themselves find favor with you all and with the general public, men whose services in war, in peace, and in your private affairs, are given at the right moment, without ostentation, to be available for each one of you.[5]

Terence wrote for Rome's aristocracy.

Latin prose developed later than poetry and playwriting and was often the product of Rome's ruling elite. These upper classes were interested in history as a means of

Roman Theater: Rehearsal of a Greek Play. This mosaic found at Pompeii shows Roman actors preparing to present a Greek play. The seated figure is the chorus master, who observes two actors dancing to the music of a pipe.

exalting their ideals and in oratory because it could be an important instrument for effective statecraft. Hence their emphasis in writing prose was on creating works of a practical value. This is a prominent feature of the oldest existing work of Latin prose, Cato the Elder's treatise *On Agriculture.* In effect, this was a technical manual reminiscent of the practical handbooks produced in the Hellenistic world.

Despite their attraction to the Greek world, Romans were generally repelled by much of Greek philosophy with the exception of Stoicism. The latter's emphasis on virtuous conduct and performance of duty (see Chapter 4) fit well with Roman ideals and the practical bent of the Roman character. Panaetius of Rhodes (c. 180–111 B.C.), whose works helped introduce Stoicism to the Romans, proved especially popular.

The Romans were also dependent on the Greeks for artistic inspiration. During the third and second centuries B.C., they adopted many features of the Hellenistic style of art (see Chapter 4). The Romans excelled in architecture, a highly practical art. In addition to their justly famous highways, they built sturdy bridges and aqueducts that made use of the arch. They also developed the technique of using concrete in construction projects, which enabled them to erect giant amphitheaters, public baths, and the high-rise tenement buildings that housed Rome's exploding population in the late second and first centuries B.C.

The Romans developed a taste for Greek statues, which they placed not only in public buildings but in their homes as well. When demand outstripped the supply of original works, reproductions of Greek statues became fashionable. The Romans' own portrait sculpture was characterized by an intense realism that included even unpleasant physical details.

Roman Comedy

This excerpt is a scene from one of the plays of Plautus. While Plautus made use of Greek New Comedy, his devious plots and earthiness were original. His farcical humor and buffoonery made his plays exceedingly popular, especially with the masses. This excerpt is from *Miles Gloriosus* ("The Swaggering Soldier"). This opening scene features a pompous general and a parasitical bootlicker. Plautus loved to create fantastic names for his characters. Pyrgopolynices means "Often victorious over fortresses," and Artotrogus means "Bread eater."

Plautus, The Swaggering Soldier

PYRGOPOLYNICES: My shield, there—have it burnished brighter than the bright splendor of the sun on any summer's day. Next time I have occasion to use it in the press of battle, it must flash defiance into the eyes of the opposing foe. My sword, too, I see, is pining for attention; poor chap, he's quite disheartened and cast down, hanging idly at my side so long; he's simply itching to get at an enemy and carve him into little pieces. . . . Where's Artotrogus?

ARTOTROGUS: Here, at his master's heels, close to his hero, his brave, his blessed, his royal, his doughty warrior—whose valor Mars himself could hardly challenge or outshine.

PYRGOPOLYNICES [*reminiscent*]: Ay—what of the man whose life I saved on the Curculionean field, where the enemy was led by Bumbomachides Clytomestoridysarchides, a grandson of Neptune?

ARTOTROGUS: I remember it well. I remember his golden armor, and how you scattered his legions with a puff of breath, like a wind sweeping up leaves or lifting the thatch from a roof.

PYRGOPOLYNICES [*modestly*]: It was nothing much, after all.

ARTOTROGUS: Oh, to be sure, nothing to the many more famous deeds you did—[aside] or never did. [*He comes down, leaving the captain attending to his men.*] If anyone ever saw a bigger liar or more conceited braggart than this one, he can have me for keeps. . . . The only thing to be said for him is, his cook makes a marvellous olive salad. . . .

PYRGOPOLYNICES [*missing him*]: Where have you got to, Artotrogus?

ARTOTROGUS [*obsequiously*]: Here I am, sir. I was thinking about that elephant in India, and how you broke his ulna with a single blow of your fist.

PYRGOPOLYNICES: His ulna, was it?

ARTOTROGUS: His femur, I should have said.

PYRGOPOLYNICES: It was only a light blow, too.

ARTOTROGUS: By Jove, yes, if you had really hit him, your arm would have smashed through the animal's hide, bones, and guts.

PYRGOPOLYNICES [*modestly*]: I'd rather not talk about it, really.

Values and Attitudes

The Romans were by nature a conservative people. They were very concerned about maintaining the *mos maiorum,* the customs or traditions of their ancestors. The Romans emphasized parental authority and, above all, their obligations to the state. The highest virtue was *pietas*—the dutiful execution of one's obligations to one's fellow citizens, to the gods, and to the state.

By the second century B.C., however, the creation of an empire had begun to weaken the old values. The Romans began to place greater stress on affluence, status, and material possessions. There was also more emphasis on individualism and less on collective well-being, on the old public spirit that had served Rome so well. Romans who worried about the decline of the old values blamed it on different causes. Some felt that after the destruction of Carthage, the Romans no longer had any strong enemies to challenge them. Others believed that the Romans had simply been overwhelmed by the affluence created by the new empire. And finally, there were those who blamed everything on the Greeks for importing ideas and practices baneful to the Romans.

Of course, Romans responded differently to the changes brought by the creation of an empire. Two examples from the second century demonstrate this well. Marcus Cato the Elder (234–149 B.C.) was a Roman praetor, consul, and member of the ruling class who became censor in 184. Cato scorned the "Greeklings"—people who followed Greek ways and read Greek philosophy and literature. He even introduced a decree to force all Greek philosophers to leave Rome. He wrote to his son:

> I shall speak about those Greek fellows in their proper place, son Marcus, and point out the results of my inquiries at Athens, and convince you what benefit comes from dipping into their literature, and not making a close study of it. They are a quite worthless people, and an intractable one, and you must consider my words prophetic. When that race gives us its literature it will corrupt all things.[6]

But Cato was not stupid. He not only learned Greek himself but also allowed his own son to study in Athens. He knew only too well that, like it or not, Greek was becoming a necessity for Roman political life.

Scipio Aemilianus (185–129 B.C.) was a member of a patrician family and a brilliant general who easily achieved the top offices of the Roman state. Scipio was also concerned about the traditional Roman values, but he was much more inclined to accept Rome's growing urbanization as it became the center of the Mediterranean world and was consequently more open to the Greeks as well. He was an admirer of Greek philosophy and literature. He created a group of intellectuals dedicated to Greek thought, which included Polybius, Terence, and Panaetius. While desirous of maintaining old Roman virtues, Scipio was well aware that the acquisition of an empire had created a new world with new demands and values.

The Decline and Fall of the Roman Republic (133–31 B.C.)

By the mid-second century B.C., Roman domination of the Mediterranean Sea was well established. Yet the process of building an empire had weakened and threatened the internal stability of Rome. This internal instability characterizes the period of Roman history from 133 until 31 B.C., when the armies of Octavian defeated Mark Antony and stood supreme over the Roman world. By that time, the constitution of the Roman Republic was in shambles (see the box on p. 123).

Background: Social, Economic, and Political Problems

By the second century B.C., the senate had become the effective governing body of the Roman state. It had achieved this position through its own initiative—not through law, but by custom. As always, it comprised some three hundred men drawn primarily from the landed aristocracy who remained senators for life and held the chief magistracies of the Republic. During the wars of the third and second centuries, the senate came to exercise enormous power. It directed the wars and took control of both foreign and domestic policy, including financial affairs. The advice of the senate to the consuls had come to have the force of law.

Moreover, the magistracies and senate were increasingly controlled by a relatively select circle of wealthy and powerful families—both patrician and plebeian—called the *nobiles* ("nobles"). The *nobiles* were essentially the men whose families were elected to the more important political offices of the Republic. In the hundred years from 233 to 133 B.C., 80 percent of the consuls came from twenty-six families; 50 percent came from only ten families. Hence the *nobiles* constituted a governing oligarchy that managed, through landed wealth, patronage, and intimidation, to maintain its hold over the magistracies and senate and thus guide the destiny of Rome while running the state in its own interests. When a new man—called a *novus homo*—did win a consulship, he and his descendants became members of this select oligarchy.

By the end of the second century B.C., two types of aristocratic leaders, called the *optimates* ("the best men") and the *populares* ("favoring the people"), became prominent. These were not political parties or even individual cliques but leaders who followed two different approaches to politics. *Optimates* and *populares* were terms of political rhetoric that were used by individuals within the aristocracy against fellow aristocratic rivals to distinguish one set of tactics from another. The *optimates* tended to be the *nobiles* who controlled the senate and wished to maintain their oligarchical privileges, while the *populares* were usually other ambitious aristocrats who used the people's assemblies, especially the council of the plebs, as instruments to break the domination of the *optimates*. The conflicts between these aristocratic leaders and their supporters engulfed the first century in political turmoil.

Another social group in Rome also became entangled in this political turmoil—the *equites* or equestrians, a name derived from the fact that they had once formed Rome's cavalry. Many equestrians had become extremely wealthy through a variety of means, often related to the creation of the empire. Some, for example, were private contractors who derived their wealth from government contracts for the collection of taxes, the outfitting of armies, and the construction of fleets and public works. In 218 B.C., the senate enacted a law that forbade senators to bid for state contracts or engage in commerce. The law effectively barred the equestrians from high office, since to serve in the senate they would have to give up their livelihoods. By the end of the second century B.C., the equestrians were seeking real political power commensurate with their financial stake in the empire. They would play an important role in the political turmoil that brought an end to the Republic.

Of course, equestrians and aristocrats together formed only a tiny minority of the Roman people. The backbone of the Roman state and army had traditionally been the small farmers who tilled their little plots of land and made up the chief source of recruits for the army. But economic changes that began in the period of the Punic Wars increasingly undermined the position of that group. This occurred for several reasons. Their lands had been severely damaged during the Second Punic War when Hannibal invaded Italy. Moreover, in order to win the wars, Rome had to increase the term of military service from two to six years. The Roman army was never meant to serve in distant wars but was called out for the "war season," after which the soldiers returned to their farms. Now when the soldiers returned home after many years of service abroad, they found their farms so deteriorated that they chose to sell out instead of remaining on the land. By this time, capitalistic agriculture was also increasing rapidly. Landed aristocrats had been able to develop large estates (called *latifundia*) by taking over state-owned land and by buying out small peasant owners. These large estates relied on slave and tenant labor and frequently concentrated on cash crops, such as grapes for wine, olives, and sheep for wool, which small farmers could not afford to do. Thus the rise of *latifundia* contributed to the decline in the number of small citizen farmers. Since the latter group traditionally formed the basis of the Roman army—Romans conscripted only people with a financial stake in the community—the number of men available for military service declined. Many of the newly

The Decline of the Roman Republic

Although Rome stood supreme over the Mediterranean world, by 133 B.C. the internal structure of the Republic had begun to disintegrate. Over the next hundred years, the Republic was afflicted with mob violence, assassinations, civil wars, and unscrupulous politicians who seized every opportunity to advance their own interests. The Roman historian Sallust (86–35 B.C.), who lived through many of these crises, reflected on the causes of Rome's problems. In this selection, he discusses the moral decline that set in after the destruction of Carthage in 146 B.C.

Sallust, The War with Catiline

Good morals were cultivated at home and in the field; [in the early Republic] there was the greatest harmony and little or no avarice; justice and honesty prevailed among them, thanks not so much to laws as to nature. Quarrels, discord, and strife were reserved for their enemies; citizen vied with citizen only for the prize of merit. They were lavish in their offerings to the gods, frugal in the home, loyal to their friends. By practicing these two qualities, boldness in warfare and justice when peace came, they watched over themselves and their country. In proof of these statements, I present this convincing evidence, firstly, in time of war punishment was more often inflicted for attacking the enemy contrary to orders, or for withdrawing too tardily when recalled from the field, than for venturing to abandon the standards or to give ground under stress; and secondly, in time of peace they ruled by kindness rather than by fear, and when wronged preferred forgiveness to vengeance.

But when our country had grown great through toil and the practice of justice, when great kings had been vanquished in war, savage tribes and mighty people subdued by force of arms, when Carthage, the rival of Rome's sway, had perished root and branch, and all seas and lands were open, then Fortune began to grow cruel and to bring confusion into all our affairs. Those who had found it easy to bear hardships and dangers, anxiety and adversity, found leisure and wealth, desirable under other circumstances, a burden and a curse. Hence the lust for power first, then for money, grew upon them; these were, I may say, the root of all evils. For avarice destroyed honor, integrity, and all other noble qualities; taught in their place insolence, cruelty, to neglect the gods, to set a price on everything. Ambition drove many men to become false; to have one thought locked in the breast, another ready on the tongue; to value friendships and enmities not on their merits but by the standard of self-interest, and to show a good front rather than a good heart. At first these vices grew slowly, from time to time they were punished; finally, when the disease had spread like a deadly plague, the state was changed and a government second to none in justice and excellence became cruel and intolerable.

landless families stayed in the countryside, finding agricultural work as best they could. Some of them, however, drifted to the cities, especially Rome, forming a large class of day laborers who possessed no property. This new class of urban proletariat formed a highly unstable mass with the potential for much trouble in depressed times. Thus Rome's economic, social, and political problems were serious and needed attention. In 133 B.C., a member of the aristocracy proposed a solution that infuriated his fellow aristocrats.

The Reforms of Tiberius and Gaius Gracchus

Tiberius Gracchus (163–133 B.C.) was a member of the *nobiles* who ruled Rome. Although concerned with the immediate problem of a shortage of military recruits, Tiberius believed that the underlying cause of Rome's problems was the decline of the small farmers. Tiberius was not a revolutionary, and his proposals for reform, drafted with the help of several prominent senators, were essentially conservative; he was looking backward to what had constituted the foundation of Rome's greatness.

Tiberius Gracchus was elected one of the tribunes of the plebs for 133 B.C. Without consulting the senate, where he knew his rivals would oppose his proposal, Tiberius took his legislation directly to the council of the plebs, which passed his land reform bill. It authorized the government to reclaim public land held by large landowners and to distribute it to landless Romans. Many senators, themselves large landowners whose estates included large tracts of public land, were furious, and a group of senators took the law into their own hands and assassinated Tiberius.

The efforts of Tiberius Gracchus were continued by his brother Gaius (153–121 B.C.), elected tribune for both 123 and 122 B.C. Gaius broadened his reform program to appeal to more people disenchanted with the current senatorial leadership. Gaius, too, pushed for the rapid distribution of land to displaced farmers. To win the support of the *equites,* he replaced the senators on the jury courts that tried provincial governors accused of extortion with members of the equestrian order and opened the new province of Asia to equestrian tax collectors. Thus Gaius gave the *equites* two instruments of public power: control over the jury courts that often tried provincial governors and control over provincial taxation. Fellow senators, hostile to Gaius' reforms and fearful of his growing popularity, made use of a constitutional innovation, a "final decree of the senate," which encouraged the consuls to "do everything possible to prevent any misfortune befalling the Republic." As a result, Gaius and many of his followers were killed in 121 B.C. The attempts of the Gracchus brothers to bring reforms by using the tribuneship and council of the plebs had opened the door to more instability and further violence and marked the beginning of the breakdown of the republican form of government.

Marius and the New Roman Army

In the closing years of the second century B.C., a series of military disasters gave rise to a fresh outburst of popular anger against the old leaders of the senate and resulted in the rise of Marius (157–86 B.C.).

Marius came to prominence during the war in North Africa against Jugurtha and the Numidians. The senate had badly bungled the war effort. Marius had served as legate to the senate-appointed commanding general Metellus but quarreled with his superior, returned to Rome, and ran for the consulship with "Win the war" as his campaign slogan. Despite being a *novus homo* from the equestrian order, Marius won and became a consul for 107 B.C. The council of the plebs then voted to give Marius command of the army in Africa, a definite encroachment on the senate's right to conduct wars. Generals no longer needed to be loyal to the senate.

Marius brought the Jugurthine War to a successful conclusion and was then called on to defeat the Celtic tribes (or Gauls, as the Romans called them), who had annihilated a Roman army and threatened an invasion of Italy. Marius was made consul for five years, from 104 to 100 B.C., raised a new army, and decisively defeated the Celts, leaving him in a position of personal ascendancy in Rome.

In raising a new army, Marius initiated military reforms that proved to have drastic consequences. The Roman army had traditionally been a conscript army of small landholders. Marius recruited volunteers from both the urban and the rural proletariat who possessed no property. These volunteers swore an oath of loyalty to the general, not the senate, and thus inaugurated a professional-type army that might no longer be subject to the state. Moreover, to recruit these men, a general would promise them land, so generals had to play politics to get legislation passed that would provide the land for their veterans. Marius left a powerful legacy. He had created a new system of military recruitment that placed much power in the hands of the individual generals. Roman republican politics was entering a new and potentially dangerous stage.

The Role of Sulla

After almost a decade of relative quiet, the Roman Republic was threatened with another crisis—the Italian or Social War (90–88 B.C.). This war resulted from Rome's unwillingness to deal constructively with the complaints of its Italian allies. These allies had fought loyally on Rome's side but felt they had not shared sufficiently in the lands and bonuses given to Roman veterans. In 90 B.C., the Italians rebelled and formed their own confederation. Two years of bitter fighting left Italy devastated and took an enormous number of lives. The Romans managed to end the rebellion but only by granting full rights of Roman citizenship to all free Italians. "Rome was now Italy, and Italy Rome,"[7] as one historian has written. This influx of new voters into the popular assemblies drastically altered the voting power structure in favor of the *populares,* who had earlier favored enfranchisement of the Italians.

During this war, a new figure came into prominence—Lucius Cornelius Sulla (138–78 B.C.), a member of the *nobiles.* Sulla had been made consul for 88 B.C. and been given command by the senate of the war against Mithridates, the king of Pontus in Asia Minor, who had rebelled against Roman power. However, Marius, who had retired from Roman politics, now returned to the scene. The council of the plebs, contradicting the senate's wishes, transferred command of the war against Mithridates to Marius. Considering this action illegal, Sulla marched on Rome with his army. Marius fled, and Sulla reestablished his command. After Sulla left again for the east, Marius joined forces with the consul Cinna, marched on Rome, seized control of the government, outlawed Sulla, and killed many of Sulla's supporters. Civil war had become a fact of life in Roman politics.

Marius soon died, but Cinna continued to use his forces to remain as consul. His control, however, really depended on the fortunes of Sulla and his army. After defeating Mithridates in the east, Sulla returned to Rome, crushed the armies opposing him in Italy, and seized Rome itself in 82 B.C. He forced the senate to grant him the title of dictator to "reconstitute the Republic." After conducting a reign of terror to wipe out all opposition, Sulla revised the constitution to restore power to the hands of the senate. He eliminated most of the powers of the popular assemblies and the tribunes of the plebs and restored the senators to the jury courts. He also enlarged the senate by adding men of the equestrian order. In 79 B.C., believing that he had restored the traditional Republic governed by a powerful senate, he resigned his office of dictator, retired, and soon died, leaving a power vacuum. But his real legacy was quite different from what he had intended. His example of how an army could be used to seize power would prove most attractive to ambitious men.

The Death of the Republic

For the next fifty years, Roman history would be characterized by two important features: the jostling for power by a number of powerful individuals and the civil wars generated by their conflicts.

THE RISE OF POMPEY

Not long after Sulla's attempts to revive senatorial power, the senate made two extraordinary military appointments that raised to prominence two very strong personalities—Crassus (c. 112–53 B.C.) and Pompey (106–48 B.C.). Crassus had fought for Sulla and had also become extremely rich—it was said that he owned most of Rome. In 73 B.C., the senate gave Crassus a military command against the slave rebellion led by Spartacus, which he successfully completed. Pompey had also fought for Sulla and was given an impor-

The Ny Carlsberg Glyptotek, Copenhagen

Pompey. A popular and powerful figure of the late Republic, Pompey was a successful general who joined with Caesar and Crassus in a coalition known as the First Triumvirate in order to secure his reorganization of the east and to obtain lands for his veterans. Later he opposed Caesar during the civil war of 49–45 B.C. Pictured is a marble copy of an earlier sculpted head of Pompey.

Scala/Art Resource, NY

Cicero. The great orator Marcus Tullius Cicero, whose writings provide much information about politics and upper-class life, rose to the highest offices in the Republic due to his oratorical skills. He was a supporter of the senate and wished to establish a "concord of the orders," cooperative rule by the equestrians and the senators.

tant military command in Spain in 77 B.C. When he returned six years later, he was hailed as a military hero.

Despite their jealousy of one another, Pompey and Crassus joined forces and were elected consuls for 70 B.C. Although both men had been supporters of Sulla, they undid his work. They restored the power of the tribunes and helped put *equites* back on the jury courts, thereby reviving the *populares* as a path to political power.

With their power reestablished by this action, friendly plebeian tribunes now proposed legislation that gave two important military commands to Pompey. In 67 B.C., he cleared the Mediterranean Sea of the pirates who were harassing Roman commerce. After this success, he was put in charge of the campaign against Mithridates, who thought he could take advantage of Rome's internal troubles to pursue his plans of conquest. Pompey defeated Mithridates and reorganized the east, winning immense success and prestige as well as enormous wealth. When he returned to Rome, he disbanded his army, expecting that the senate would automatically ratify his eastern settlement and give land to his veterans. But new forces and new personalities had risen to prominence during his absence, and his requests encountered complications.

Marcus Tullius Cicero (106–43 B.C.) was one of these new personalities. A *novus homo* from the equestrian order and the first of his family to achieve the consulship, Cicero made a name for himself as a lawyer, using his outstanding oratorical skills to defend people accused of crimes and to prosecute others, including a corrupt provincial governor (see the box on p. 126). He became consul in 63 B.C. and upheld the interests of the senate. While consul, he added to his reputation by acting forcefully to suppress a political conspiracy led by a desperate and bankrupt aristocrat named Catiline. Cicero was one of the few prominent politicians who attempted to analyze the problems of the Republic systematically. He believed in a "concord of the orders," meaning the cooperation of the equestrians and senators. In effect, Cicero harked back to the days of collective rule, a time when political leaders were motivated to work together for the good of the Roman state. But collective rule was no longer meaningful to ambitious men seeking personal power. Cicero himself had few military skills and could not command an army. He realized that the senate needed the support of a powerful general if the concord of the orders were to be made a reality. In 62 B.C., he saw Pompey as that man. But a large element in the senate felt that Pompey had become too powerful, and they now refused to grant his wishes after his return from the east. This same element in the senate treated Julius Caesar in a similar fashion when he returned from Spain. That turned out to be a big mistake.

THE STRUGGLE BETWEEN POMPEY AND CAESAR

Julius Caesar (100–44 B.C.) had been a spokesman for the *populares* from the beginning of his political career, an alliance that ran in the family—Marius was his uncle by marriage. Caesar pursued political power by appealing to many of the

Exploitation of the Provinces

As the Romans expanded their territory outside Italy, conquered lands were made provinces. These possessions were clearly distinguished from Italy in that their inhabitants were forced to pay tribute to the Roman state. Eventually, the senate came to control the appointment of the governors who administered the provinces. By the first century B.C., many provincial governors used their provinces to amass enormous fortunes through extortion, confiscation of property, and bribery. Although governors could be prosecuted after their term of office, the senators who served as judges often protected the accused, who were members of their own class. Cicero successfully prosecuted Verres, the corrupt governor of Sicily, and thereby gained prominence as a politician. This excerpt is taken from one of his speeches against Verres.

■ *Cicero,* Against Verres

But nowhere did he multiply and magnify the memorials and the proofs of all his evil qualities so thoroughly as in his governorship of Sicily; which island for the space of three years he devastated and ruined so effectually that nothing can restore it to its former condition, and it hardly seems possible that a long lapse of years and a succession of upright governors can in time bring it a partial revival of prosperity. So long as Verres was governing it, its people were protected neither by their own laws, nor by the decrees of the Roman Senate, nor by the rights that belong to all nations alike. . . .

For the space of three years, the law awarded nothing to anybody unless Verres chose to agree; and nothing was so undoubtedly inherited from a man's father or grandfather that the courts would not cancel his right to it, if Verres asked them to do so. Countless sums of money, under a new and unprincipled regulation, were wrung from the purses of the farmers; our most loyal allies were treated as if they were national enemies; Roman citizens were tortured and executed like slaves; the guiltiest criminals bought their legal acquittal, while the most honorable and honest men would be prosecuted in absence, and condemned and banished unheard; strongly fortified harbors, mighty and well-defended cities, were left open to the assaults of pirates and buccaneers; Sicilian soldiers and sailors, our allies and our friends, were starved to death; fine fleets, splendidly equipped, were to the great disgrace of our nation destroyed and lost to us. Famous and ancient works of art, some of them the gifts of wealthy kings, who intended them to adorn the cities where they stood, others the gifts of Roman generals, who gave or restored them to the communities of Sicily in the hour of victory—this same governor stripped and despoiled every one of them. Nor was it only the civic statues and works of art that he treated thus; he also pillaged the holiest and most venerated sanctuaries. . . . As to his adulteries and the like vile offenses, a sense of decency makes me afraid to repeat the tale of his acts of wanton wickedness: and besides, I would not wish, by repeating it, to add to the calamities of those who have not been suffered to save their children and their wives from outrage at the hands of this lecherous scoundrel. Is it alleged that he did these things so secretly that they were not known everywhere? I do not believe that one human being lives, who has heard the name of Verres spoken and cannot also repeat the tale of his evil doings.

same groups who had supported Marius. After serving as aedile and praetor, he sought a military command and was sent to Spain. He returned from Spain in 60 B.C. and requested a special dispensation so that he could both celebrate a triumph with his troops and run for the consulship, which would place him in the highest rank within the senate. Rival senators blocked his request. Consequently, Caesar joined with two fellow senators, Crassus and Pompey, who were also being stymied by the senate. Historians call their coalition the First Triumvirate. Though others had made political deals before, the combined wealth and power of these three men was enormous, enabling them to dominate the political scene. Caesar was elected consul for 59 B.C. and used the popular assemblies to achieve the basic aims of the triumvirs: Pompey received his eastern settlement and lands for his veterans; equestrian allies of Crassus were given a reduction on tax contracts for which they had overbid; and Caesar was granted a special military command in Gaul (modern France, Belgium, and parts of the Netherlands) for five years.

Caesar did so well in Gaul that Crassus and Pompey realized anew the value of military command. They became consuls again for 55 B.C. and garnered more benefits for the coalition: Caesar was given a five-year extension in Gaul; Crassus a command in Syria; and Pompey one in Spain. When Crassus was killed in battle in 53 B.C., his death left two powerful men with armies in direct competition. Caesar had used his time in Gaul to gain fame and military experience. He had waged numerous campaigns, costing the lives, it has been estimated, of almost two million men, women, and children. But his wars had also enabled him to amass enough booty and slaves to pay off all of the debts he had accumulated in gaining political offices. Moreover, he now had an army of seasoned veterans who were loyal to him. No doubt most senators would have preferred both Pompey

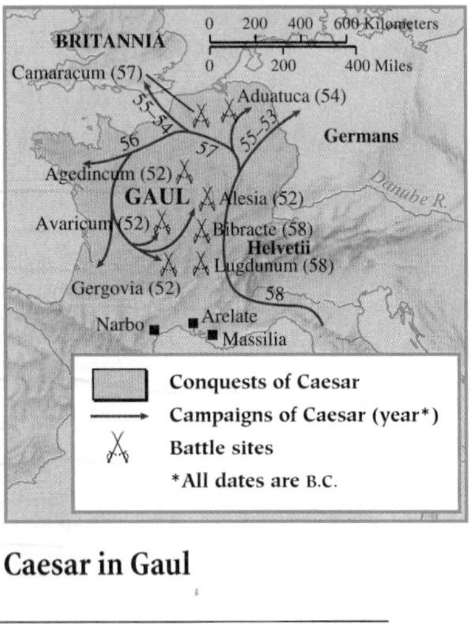

Caesar in Gaul

and Caesar to lay down their commands and give up their armies. Since both refused, the leading senators fastened on Pompey as the less harmful to their cause and voted for Caesar to lay down his command and return as a private citizen to Rome. Such a step was intolerable to Caesar, as it would leave him totally vulnerable to his enemies. He chose to keep his army and moved into Italy by crossing the Rubicon, the river that formed the southern boundary of his province, on January 10, 49 B.C. (The phrase "crossing the Rubicon" is still used today to mean being unable to turn back.)

Pompey and his followers fled to Greece, where they raised a new army. Meanwhile it took Caesar until the end of 49 to raise a fleet and ship his troops to Greece. In the spring of 48 B.C., at the Battle of Pharsalus, Caesar's veterans carried the day against Pompey's forces. The defeated Pompey fled to Egypt, where the king was one of his foreign clients, but one of the king's advisers had Pompey killed. The war continued, however, since some of the senators on his side, including Cato the Younger, had recruited new troops. After victories in North Africa and Spain, Caesar returned triumphant to Rome in 45 B.C.

No doubt Caesar realized that the old order of unfettered political competition could not be saved. He was unwilling to take the title of king, which was intensely disliked by the Roman upper classes, but he had no intention of giving up his control. Caesar had officially been made dictator in 47 B.C., and in 44 B.C. he was made dictator for life. He continued to hold elections for offices but saw to it that his supporters chose the people he recommended. As Rome's new ruler, he quickly instituted a number of ambitious reforms. He increased the senate to nine hundred members by filling it with many of his followers. He granted citizenship to a number of people in the provinces who had provided assistance to him. By establishing colonies of Roman citizens in North Africa, Gaul, and Spain, he initiated a process of Romanization in those areas. He tried to reorganize the administrative structures of cities in Italy in order to create some sense of rational order in their government.

Caesar was a generous victor and pardoned many of the republican leaders who had opposed him, allowing them to return to Rome. He also replaced the Roman calendar with the Egyptian solar year of 365 days (this so-called Julian calendar, with later changes made in 1582, became the basis of our modern calendar). He planned much more in the way of building projects and military adventures in the east but was not able to carry them out. In 44 B.C., a group of leading senators who resented his domination assassinated him, believing that the old republican system would now return (see the box on p. 128). In truth, however, they had set the stage for another civil war that delivered the final death blow to the Republic.

THE FINAL STRUGGLE: OCTAVIAN VERSUS ANTONY

A new struggle for power soon ensued. Caesar's heir and adopted son, his grandnephew Octavian, though only nineteen, took command of some of Caesar's legions. After forcing the senate to name him consul, he joined forces with Mark Antony, Caesar's ally and assistant, and Marcus Lepidus, who had been commander of Caesar's cavalry. Together, the three formed the Second Triumvirate, which was legally empowered to rule Rome. Their first act was to restore Sulla's policy of proscription, as described by the ancient historian Appian:

> As soon as they were on their own, the three drew up a list of those who were to die. They put on the list, both then and later, those of whom they were suspicious because of their ability, as well as their personal enemies, trading with each other for the lives of their own relations and friends. They decreed death and confiscation of property for about 300 senators and 2,000 equestrians, among them their own brothers and uncles, as well as senior officers serving under them who had had cause to offend them or their own colleagues.[8]

In addition to proscribing their enemies at home (Cicero was one of those killed), the three commanders pursued Caesar's assassins, who had in the meantime raised an army, and defeated them at Philippi in Macedonia. Lepidus was soon shunted aside, and Octavian and Antony then divided the Roman world between them—Octavian taking the west and Antony the east. But the empire of the Romans, large as it was, was still too small for two masters, and Octavian and Antony eventually came into conflict. Antony allied himself with the Egyptian queen

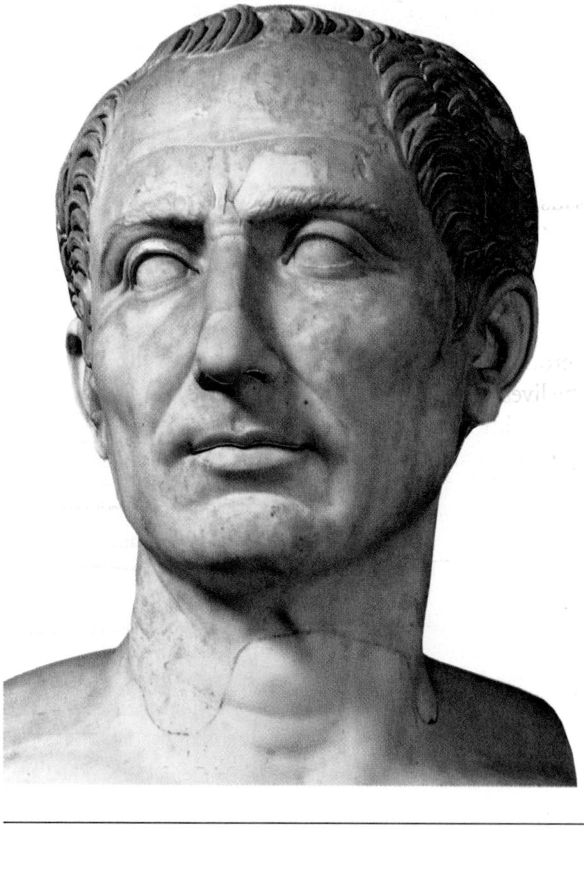

Scala/Art Resource, NY

Caesar. Conqueror of Gaul and member of the First Triumvirate, Julius Caesar is perhaps the best-known figure of the late Republic. Caesar became dictator of Rome in 47 B.C. and after his victories in the civil war was made dictator for life. Some members of the senate who resented his power assassinated him in 44 B.C. Pictured is a marble copy of a bust of Caesar.

The Assassination of Julius Caesar

When it became apparent that Julius Caesar had no intention of restoring the Republic as they conceived it, about sixty senators, many of them his friends or pardoned enemies, formed a conspiracy to assassinate the dictator. It was led by Gaius Cassius and Marcus Brutus, who naively imagined that this act would restore the traditional Republic. The conspirators set the Ides of March (March 15) of 44 B.C. as the date for the assassination. Caesar was in the midst of preparations for a campaign in the eastern part of the empire. Although warned about a plot against his life, he chose to disregard it. This account of Caesar's death is taken from his biography by the Greek writer Plutarch.

■ *Plutarch,* Life of Caesar

Fate, however, is to all appearance more unavoidable than unexpected. For many strange prodigies and apparitions are said to have been observed shortly before this event. . . . One finds it also related by many that a soothsayer bade him [Caesar] prepare for some great danger on the Ides of March. When this day was come, Caesar, as he went to the senate, met this soothsayer, and said to him mockingly, "The Ides of March are come," who answered him calmly, "Yes, they are come, but they are not past. . . ."

All these things might happen by chance. But the place which was destined for the scene of this murder, in which the senate met that day, was the same in which Pompey's statue stood, and was one of the edifices which Pompey had raised and dedicated with his theater to the use of the public, plainly showing that there was something of a supernatural influence which guided the action and ordered it to that particular place. Cassius, just before the act, is said to have looked toward Pompey's statue, and silently implored his assistance. . . . When Caesar entered, the senate stood up to show their respect to him, and of Brutus' confederates, some came about his chair and stood behind it, others met him, pretending to add their petitions to those of Tillius Cimber, in behalf of his brother, who was in exile; and they followed him with their joint applications till he came to his seat. When he sat down, he refused to comply with their requests, and upon their urging him further began to reproach them severely for their demand, when Tillius, laying hold of his robe with both his hands, pulled it down from his neck, which was the signal for the assault. Casca gave him the first cut in the neck, which was not mortal nor dangerous, as coming from one who at the beginning of such a bold action was probably very much disturbed; Caesar immediately turned about, and laid his hand upon the dagger and kept hold of it. And both of them at the same time cried out, he that received the blow, in Latin, "Vile Casca, what does this mean?" and he that gave it, in Greek to his brother, "Brother, help!" Upon this first onset, those who were not privy to the design were astonished, and their horror and amazement at what they saw were so great that they dared not fly nor assist Caesar, nor so much as speak a word. But those who came prepared for the business enclosed him on every side, with their naked daggers in their hands. Which way soever he turned he met with blows, and saw their swords leveled at his face and eyes, and was encompassed like a wild beast in the toils on every side. For it had been agreed they should each of them make a thrust at him, and flesh themselves with his blood: for which reason Brutus also gave him one stab in the groin. Some say that he fought and resisted all the rest, shifting his body to avoid the blows, and calling out for help, but that when he saw Brutus' sword drawn, he covered his face with his robe and submitted, letting himself fall, whether it were by chance or that he was pushed in that direction by his murderers, at the foot of the pedestal on which Pompey's statue stood, and which was thus wetted with his blood. So that Pompey himself seemed to have presided, as it were, over the revenge done upon his adversary, who lay here at his feet, and breathed out his soul through his multitude of wounds, for they say he received three-and-twenty. And the conspirators themselves were many of them wounded by each other while they all leveled their blows at the same person.

Cleopatra VII, with whom, like Caesar before him, he fell deeply in love. Octavian began a propaganda campaign, accusing Antony of catering to Cleopatra and giving away Roman territory to this "whore of the east." Finally, at the Battle of Actium in Greece in 31 B.C., Octavian's forces smashed the army and navy of Antony and Cleopatra. Both fled to Egypt, where, according to the Roman historian Florus, they committed suicide a year later:

> Antony was the first to commit suicide, by the sword. Cleopatra threw herself at Octavian's feet, and tried her best to attract his gaze: in vain, for his self-control was impervious to her beauty. It was not her life she was after, for that had already been granted, but a portion of her kingdom. When she realized this was hopeless and that she had been earmarked to feature in Octavian's triumph in Rome, she took advantage of her guard's carelessness to get herself into the mausoleum, as the royal tomb is called. Once there, she put on the royal robes which she was accustomed to wear, and lay down in a richly perfumed coffin beside her Antony. Then she applied poisonous snakes to her veins and passed into death as though into a sleep.[9]

Octavian, at the age of thirty-two, stood supreme over the Roman world (see Map 5.3). The civil wars had ended. And so had the Republic.

CHRONOLOGY

The Decline and Fall of the Roman Republic

Reforms of Tiberius Gracchus	133 B.C.
Reforms of Gaius Gracchus	123–122 B.C.
Jugurthine War	111–105 B.C.
Marius: First consulship	107 B.C.
Marius: Consecutive consulships	104–100 B.C.
Italian or Social War	90–88 B.C.
Sulla's march on Rome	88 B.C.
Sulla as dictator	82–79 B.C.
Pompey's command in Spain	77–71 B.C.
Campaign of Crassus against Spartacus	73–71 B.C.
Consulship of Crassus and Pompey	70 B.C.
First Triumvirate (Caesar, Pompey, Crassus)	60 B.C.
Caesar in Gaul	59–49 B.C.
Crassus and Pompey as consuls	55 B.C.
Crassus killed by Parthians	53 B.C.
Caesar crosses the Rubicon	49 B.C.
Battle of Pharsalus; Pompey killed in Egypt	48 B.C.
End of civil war	45 B.C.
Caesar as dictator	47–44 B.C.
Second Triumvirate (Octavian, Antony, Marcus Lepidus); Cicero killed	43 B.C.
Caesar's assassins defeated at Philippi	42 B.C.
Octavian defeats Antony at Actium	31 B.C.

Literature in the Late Republic

The last century of the Roman Republic had witnessed the completion of the union of Greek and Roman culture in a truly Greco-Roman civilization. After all, Greek was the language not only of Greece but of the entire Hellenistic world of the eastern Mediterranean, which Rome had conquered. Moreover, educated, upper-class Romans spoke Greek fluently. The influence of Greece would continue to be felt in the development of Latin literature.

In the last century of the Republic, the Romans began to produce a new poetry, less dependent on epic themes and more inclined to personal expression. Latin poets now took to using various Greek forms to express their own feelings about people, social and political life, and love. The finest example is the work of Catullus (c. 87–54 B.C.), the best lyric poet Rome produced and one of the greatest in world literature.

Like most of the great Roman writers of the first century B.C., Catullus was not from Rome. He grew up in northern Italy but came to Rome, where he joined a group of carefree, youthful aristocrats. He became a master at adapting and refining Greek forms of poetry to express emotions. He wrote a variety of poems on, among other things, political figures, social customs, the use of language, the death of his brother, and the travails of love. Catullus became infatuated with Clodia, the promiscuous sister of a tribune and wife of a provincial governor, and addressed a number of poems to her (he called her Lesbia), describing his passionate love and hatred for her (Clodia had many other lovers besides Catullus):

You used to say that you wished to know only Catullus, Lesbia,
and wouldn't take even Jove before me!
I didn't regard you just as my mistress then: I cherished you as
a father does his sons or his daughters' husbands.
Now that I know you, I burn for you even more fiercely,
though I regard you as almost utterly worthless.
How can that be, you ask? It's because such cruelty forces lust
to assume the shrunken place of affection.[10]

The ability of Catullus to express in simple fashion his intense feelings and curiosity about himself and his world had a noticeable impact on later Latin poets.

Another important poet of the late Republic was Lucretius (c. 94–55 B.C.), who followed an old Greek tradition of expounding philosophy in the form of poetry. Although Stoicism was the Greek school of philosophy that the Romans found most congenial, the philosophy of Epicurus also enjoyed a period of intense popularity between 60 and 40 B.C. Lucretius' lengthy poem *On the Nature of the Universe* played a role in furthering that philosophy. In this work, Lucretius attempted to set out poetically Epicurus' idea that the world and all its creatures had been created by an accidental combination of atoms and not by the operation of divine forces. Two themes are repeated: divine forces have no effect on us, and death is of no real consequence because the soul, like the body, is material and after death also dissolves into atoms. Lucretius was especially adept at using vivid imagery. Describing the movement of atoms in the void, he wrote:

Consider the rays of the sun that are always stealing
Into the shade of a house to pour their light.
There in the void you'll notice many and sundry
Dust flecks that mingle among the rays themselves,
Stirring up in a sort of ceaseless strife
Skirmishes, wars, realigning their squadrons, never
Stopping for breath, assailed by alliance, secession;
From this you can project how atoms are
Constantly tossed along the gulf of space.[11]

If the gods and death are of no significance, how then are we to lead our lives? Lucretius' Epicurean argument that a simple life free of political worries was the highest good ran counter to Roman ideals but had an obvious appeal to Romans sick of the civil discord of the first century B.C.

The development of Roman prose was greatly aided by the practice of oratory. Romans had great respect for oratory, for the ability to persuade people in public debate led to success in politics. Oratory was brought to perfection in a literary fashion by Cicero, the best exemplar of the literary and intellectual interests of the elite of the late Republic and, indeed, the greatest prose writer of that period. For

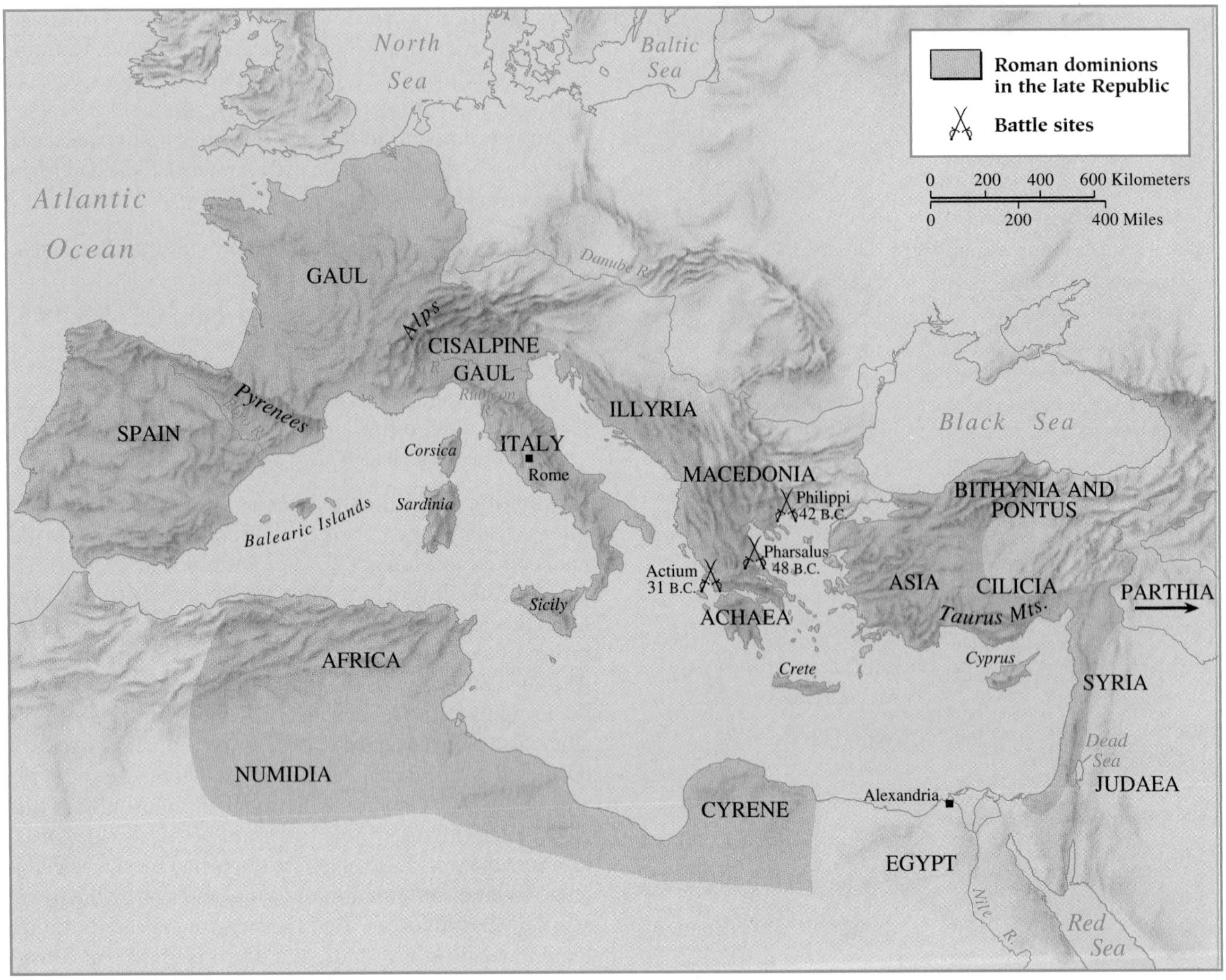

Map 5.3 Roman Dominions in the Late Republic, 31 B.C. Rome expanded its empire not only in response to military threats on its borders but also for increased access to economic resources and markets, in addition to the vanity of conquest itself. For comparison, look back at Map 5.2. ■ In what areas did the Romans gain the greatest amount of territory, and how?

Cicero, oratory was not simply skillful speaking. An orator was a statesman, a man who achieved his highest goal by pursuing an active life in public affairs.

Later, when the turmoil of the late Republic forced him into semiretirement politically, Cicero turned his attention to writing philosophical treatises. He performed a valuable service for Roman society by popularizing and making understandable the works of Greek philosophers. In his philosophical works, Cicero, more than anyone else, transmitted the classical intellectual heritage to the Western world. Cicero's original contributions to Western thought came in the field of politics. His works *On the Laws* and *On the Republic* provided fresh insights into political thought. His emphasis on the need to pursue an active life to benefit and improve humankind would greatly influence the later Italian Renaissance.

Rome's upper classes continued to have a strong interest in history. The best-known historian of the late Republic is Sallust (86–35 B.C.), who established an approach to historical studies that influenced later Roman historians. Sallust, who served as governor of the province of Africa, was on Caesar's side in the civil war and after Caesar's death went into retirement and turned to the writing of history. His two extant works are the *War with Jugurtha,* which discusses the Roman war with the African king from 111 to 105 B.C., and the *War with Catiline,* an account of the conspiracy of the disaffected aristocrat Catiline, whom Cicero had opposed during his consulship in 63 B.C.

Sallust modeled his style after that of the Greek historian Thucydides, whose historical work experienced a sudden wave of popularity in the 50s and 40s B.C. Sallust's works expressed his belief that the most important causative factor in Roman history was the moral degeneration of Roman society, which he attributed to the lack of a strong enemy after Carthage and the corrupting influence of the Greeks (see the box on p. 123).

Brief mention should also be made of the historical writing of Julius Caesar. Most famous is his *Commentaries on the Gallic War,* an account of his conquest of Gaul between 58 and 51 B.C. The work was published in 51 B.C., at a time when Caesar was afraid that his political enemies would take advantage of his absence from the Roman scene. Although the *Commentaries* served a partisan purpose by defending his actions in Gaul, Caesar presented his material in straightforward, concise prose. He referred to himself in the third person and, as the following passage indicates, was not averse to extolling his own bravery:

> Caesar saw that the situation was critical, and there was no reserve to throw in. He snatched a shield from a soldier in the rear—he had not brought one himself—and moved to the front line; he called upon the centurions by name, encouraged the men to advance, and directed them to open their lines out to give freer play to their swords. His coming inspired the men with hope and gave them new heart. Even in a desperate situation each man was anxious to do his utmost when his general was looking on, and the enemy's onset was somewhat slowed down.[12]

Caesar's work reminds us that some of the best prose of the late Republic was written by politicians who were concerned with enhancing their own position in a world of civil conflict.

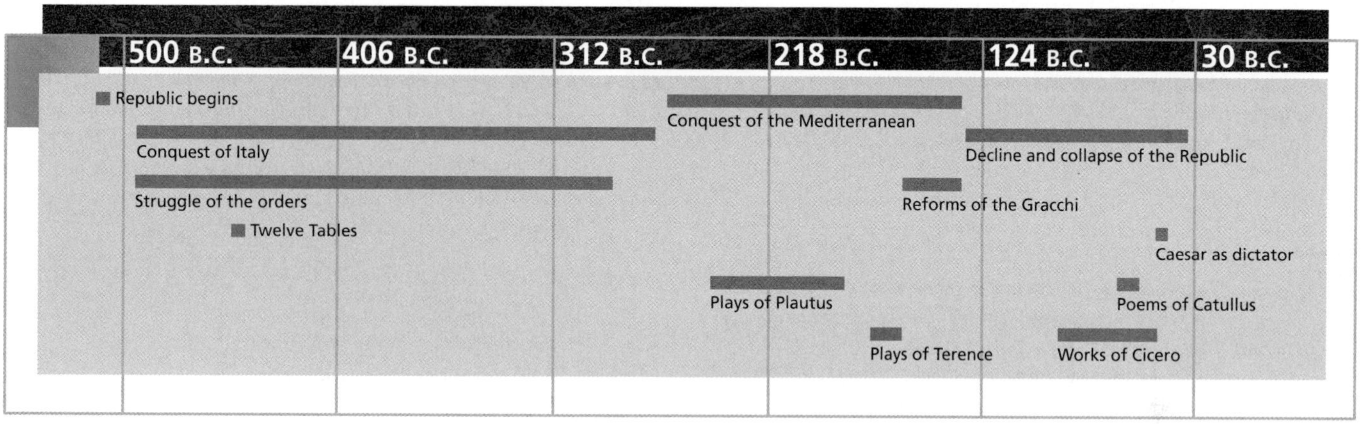

Conclusion

In the eighth and seventh centuries B.C., the pastoral community of Rome emerged as a true city. Between 509 and 264 B.C., the expansion of this city led to the union of almost all of Italy under Rome's control. Even more dramatically, between 264 and 133 B.C., Rome expanded to the west and east and became master of the Mediterranean Sea.

After 133 B.C., however, Rome's republican institutions proved inadequate for the task of ruling an empire. In the breakdown that ensued, ambitious individuals saw opportunities for power unparalleled in Roman history and succumbed to the temptations. After a series of bloody civil wars, peace was finally achieved when Octavian defeated Antony and Cleopatra. Octavian's real task was to create a new system of government that seemed to preserve the Republic while establishing the basis for a new order that would rule the empire in an orderly fashion. Octavian proved equal to the task of establishing a Roman imperial state.

Notes

1. Quoted in Chester Starr, *Past and Future in Ancient History* (Lanham, Md., 1987), pp. 38–39.
2. Cicero, *Laws,* trans. C. W. Keyes (Cambridge, Mass., 1966), 2.12.31.
3. Cato the Censor, *On Farming,* trans. Ernest Brehaut (New York, 1933), 141.
4. Quoted in J. Wright Duff, *A Literary History of Rome* (London, 1960), pp. 136–137.
5. Terence, *The Comedies,* trans. Betty Radice (Harmondsworth, England, 1976), p. 339.
6. Pliny, *Natural History,* trans. W. H. S. Jones (Cambridge, Mass., 1963), 29.7.
7. Mary Beard and Michael Crawford, *Rome in the Late Republic* (London, 1985), p. 3.
8. Appian, *Roman History: The Civil Wars,* trans. H. White (Cambridge, Mass., 1961), 4.2.149–151.
9. Florus, *Epitome of Roman History,* trans. E. S. Forster (Cambridge, Mass., 1960), 2.22.327.
10. *The Poems of Catullus,* trans. Charles Martin (Baltimore, 1990), p. 109.
11. Lucretius, *On the Nature of Things,* trans. Anthony M. Esolen (Baltimore, 1995), Bk. 2, ll. 115–123.
12. Julius Caesar, *The Gallic War and Other Writings,* trans. Moses Hadas (New York, 1957), 2.25.

Suggestions for Further Reading

For a general account of the Roman Republic, see J. Boardman, J. Griffin, and O. Murray, eds., *The Oxford History of the Roman World* (Oxford, 1991). A standard one-volume reference is M. Cary and H. H. Scullard, *A History of Rome down to the Reign of Constantine,* 3d ed. (New York, 1975). Good surveys of Roman history include M. H. Crawford, *The Roman Republic,* 2d ed. (Cambridge, Mass., 1993); H. H. Scullard, *History of the Roman World, 753–146 B.C.,* 4th ed.

(London, 1978), and *From the Gracchi to Nero,* 5th ed. (London, 1982); M. Le Glay, J.-L. Voisin, and Y. Le Bohec, *A History of Rome,* trans. A. Nevill (Oxford, 1996); and A. Kamm, *The Romans* (London, 1995). For a beautifully illustrated survey, see J. F. Drinkwater and A. Drummond, *The World of the Romans* (New York, 1993). The history of early Rome is well covered in T. J. Cornell, *The Beginnings of Rome: Italy and Rome from the Bronze Age to the Punic Wars (c. 1000–264 B.C.)* (London, 1995). A good work on the Etruscans is M. Pallottino, *The Etruscans,* rev. ed. (Bloomington, Ind., 1975).

Aspects of the Roman political structure can be studied in R. E. Mitchell, *Patricians and Plebeians: The Origin of the Roman State* (Ithaca, N.Y., 1990). Changes in Rome's economic life can be examined in A. H. M. Jones, *The Roman Economy* (Oxford, 1974). On the Roman social structure, see G. Alföldy, *The Social History of Rome* (London, 1985).

A general account of Rome's expansion in the Mediterranean is provided by R. M. Errington, *The Dawn of Empire: Rome's Rise to World Power* (Ithaca, N.Y., 1971). On the conquest of Italy, see J.-M. David, *The Roman Conquest of Italy,* trans. A. Nevill (Oxford, 1996). On Rome's struggle with Carthage, see N. Bagnall, *The Punic Wars* (London, 1990). Especially important works on Roman expansion and imperialism include W. V. Harris, *War and Imperialism in Republican Rome* (Oxford, 1979), and E. Badian, *Roman Imperialism in the Late Republic* (Oxford, 1968). On Roman expansion in the eastern Mediterranean, see A. N. Sherwin-White, *Roman Foreign Policy in the Greek East* (London, 1984).

Roman religion can be examined in J. Liebeschuetz, *Continuity and Change in Roman Religion* (Oxford, 1979), and H. H. Scullard, *Festivals and Ceremonies of the Roman Republic* (Ithaca, N.Y., 1981). A general study of daily life in Rome is available in F. Dupont, *Daily Life in Ancient Rome* (Oxford, 1994). On the Roman family, see S. Dixon, *The Roman Family* (Baltimore, 1992). Roman women are examined in J. Balsdon, *Roman Women,* rev. ed. (London, 1974); S. B. Pomeroy, *Goddesses, Whores, Wives, and Slaves: Women in Classical Antiquity* (New York, 1976), pp. 149–189; R. Baumann, *Women and Politics in Ancient Rome* (New York, 1995); and S. Dixon, *The Roman Mother* (Norman, Okla., 1988). On slavery and its consequences, see K. R. Bradley, *Slavery and Rebellion in the Roman World, 140–70 B.C.* (Bloomington, Ind., 1989). For a brief and readable survey of Latin literature, see R. M. Ogilvie, *Roman Literature and Society* (Harmondsworth, England, 1980). On Roman art and architecture, see R. Ling, *Roman Painting* (New York, 1991); D. E. Kleiner, *Roman Sculpture* (New Haven, Conn., 1992); and M. Wheeler, *Roman Art and Architecture* (London, 1964).

An excellent account of basic problems in the history of the late Republic can be found in M. Beard and M. H. Crawford, *Rome in the Late Republic* (London, 1985). Also valuable are D. Shotter, *The Fall of the Roman Republic* (London, 1994), and C. Nicolet, *The World of the Citizen in Republican Rome* (London, 1980). Numerous biographies provide many details on the politics of the period. Especially worthwhile are A. H. Bernstein, *Tiberius Sempronius Gracchus: Tradition and Apostasy* (Ithaca, N.Y., 1978); D. Stockton, *The Gracchi* (Oxford, 1979); C. Meier, *Caesar* (London, 1995); R. Seager, *Pompey: A Political Biography* (Berkeley, Calif., 1980); A. Ward, *Marcus Crassus and the Late Roman Republic* (Columbia, Mo., 1977); and D. Stockton, *Cicero: A Political Biography* (London, 1971).

For additional reading, go to InfoTrac College Edition, your online research library at http://web1.infotrac-college.com

Enter the search term *Rome history* using Key Terms.

Enter the search term *Roman Republic* using Key Terms.

Enter the search term *Roman mythology* using the Subject Guide.

Enter the search term *Roman law* using the Subject Guide.

CHAPTER

6

The Roman Empire

CHAPTER OUTLINE

- The Age of Augustus (31 B.C.–A.D. 14)
- The Early Empire (14–180)
- The Terrible Third Century
- The Restored Empire of the Fourth Century
- The Transformation of the Roman World: The Development of Christianity
- The Fall of the Western Roman Empire
- Conclusion

FOCUS QUESTIONS

- In his efforts to solve the problems Rome had faced during the late Republic, what changes did Augustus make in Rome's political, military, and social institutions?
- What were the chief features of the Roman Empire at its height during the second century?
- What problems did the Roman Empire face during the third century?
- What reforms did Diocletian and Constantine institute, and were they successful in solving the empire's problems?
- What characteristics of Christianity enabled it to grow and ultimately to triumph?
- What did one historian mean when he said that the Romans became Christians and the Christians became Romans?

WITH THE VICTORIES OF OCTAVIAN, peace finally settled on the Roman world. Although civil conflict still erupted occasionally, the new imperial state constructed by Octavian experienced a period of remarkable stability for the next two hundred years. The Romans imposed their peace on the largest empire established in antiquity. Indeed, Rome's writers proclaimed that "by heaven's will my Rome shall be capital of the world."[1] Rome's writers were not quite accurate, but few Romans were aware of the Han Empire, which flourished at the same time (202 B.C.–A.D. 221) and extended from Central Asia to the Pacific.

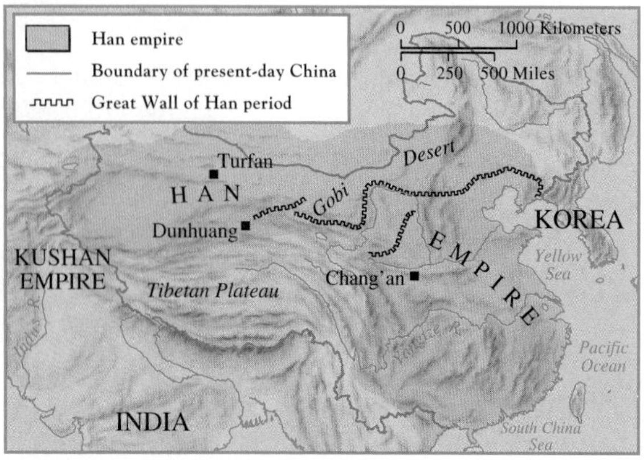

The Han Chinese Empire

Although there was little contact between them, the Han and Roman Empires had remarkable similarities: they lasted for centuries; they had remarkable success in establishing centralized control; and they maintained their law and political institutions, their technical skills, and their languages throughout the empire.

To the Romans, their divine mission was clearly to rule nations and peoples. Hadrian, one of the emperors of the second century A.D., was but one of many Roman rulers who believed in Rome's mission. He was a strong and intelligent ruler who took his responsibilities quite seriously. Between 121 and 132, he visited all of the provinces in the empire. According to his Roman biographer, Aelius Spartianus, "Hardly any emperor ever traveled with such speed over so much territory." When he arrived in a province, Hadrian dealt firsthand with any problems and bestowed many favors on the local population. He also worked to establish the boundaries of the provinces and provide for their defense. New fortifications, such as the 80-mile-long Hadrian's Wall across northern Britain, were built to defend the borders. Hadrian insisted on rigid discipline for frontier armies and demanded that the soldiers be kept in training "just as if war were imminent." He also tried to lead by personal example; according to his biographer, he spent time with the troops and "cheerfully ate out of doors such camp food as bacon, cheese, and vinegar." Moreover, he "would walk as much as twenty miles fully armed."

By the third century A.D., however, Rome's ability to rule nations and people began to weaken as the Roman Empire began to experience renewed civil war, economic chaos, and invasions. Although order was reestablished by the end of the third century and the beginning of the fourth, Rome's decline was halted only temporarily. In the meantime, the growth of Christianity, one of the remarkable success stories of Western civilization, led to the emergence of a vibrant and powerful institution that picked up the pieces left by Rome's collapse.

The Age of Augustus (31 B.C.–A.D. 14)

In 27 B.C., Octavian proclaimed the "restoration of the Republic." He understood that only traditional republican forms would satisfy the senatorial aristocracy. At the same time, Octavian was aware that the Republic could not be fully restored and managed to arrive at a compromise that worked, at least during his lifetime. In 27 B.C., the senate awarded him the title of Augustus—"the revered one." He preferred the title *princeps,* meaning chief citizen or first among equals. The system of rule that Augustus established is sometimes called the principate, conveying the idea of a constitutional monarch as coruler with the senate. But while Augustus worked to maintain this appearance, in reality, power was heavily weighted in favor of the *princeps.*

Augustus. Octavian, Caesar's adopted son, emerged victorious from the civil conflict that rocked the Republic after Caesar's assassination. Augustus operated through a number of legal formalities to ensure that control of the Roman state rested firmly in his hands. This marble statue from Prima Porta depicts the *princeps* Augustus.

Photo, Vatican Museums

The Achievements of Augustus

This excerpt is taken from a text written by Augustus and inscribed on a bronze tablet at Rome. Copies of the text in stone were displayed in many provincial capitals. Called "the most famous ancient inscription," the *Res Gestae* of Augustus summarizes his accomplishments in three major areas: his offices, his private expenditures on behalf of the state, and his exploits in war and peace. While factual in approach, it is a highly subjective account.

Augustus, Res Gestae

Below is a copy of the accomplishments of the deified Augustus by which he brought the whole world under the empire of the Roman people, and of the moneys expended by him on the state and the Roman people, as inscribed on two bronze pillars set up in Rome.

1. At the age of nineteen, on my own initiative and at my own expense, I raised an army by means of which I liberated the Republic, which was oppressed by the tyranny of a faction [Mark Antony and his supporters]....
2. Those who assassinated my father [Julius Caesar, his adoptive father] I drove into exile, avenging their crime by due process of law; and afterwards when they waged war against the state, I conquered them twice on the battlefield.
3. I waged many wars throughout the whole world by land and by sea, both civil and foreign, and when victorious I spared all citizens who sought pardon....
5. The dictatorship offered to me ... by the people and the senate, both in my absence and in my presence, I refused to accept....
17. Four times I came to the assistance of the treasury with my own money, transferring to those in charge of the treasury 150,000,000 sesterces. And in the consulship of Marcus Lepidus and Lucius Arruntius I transferred out of my own patrimony 170,000,000 sesterces to the soldiers' bonus fund, which was established on my advice for the purpose of providing bonuses for soldiers who had completed twenty or more years of service....
20. ... I repaired the conduits of the aqueducts which were falling into ruin in many places because of age....
22. I gave a gladiatorial show three times in my own name, and five times in the names of my sons or grandsons; at these shows about 10,000 fought....
25. I brought peace to the sea by suppressing the pirates. In that war I turned over to their masters for punishment nearly 30,000 slaves who had run away from their owners and taken up arms against the state....
26. I extended the frontiers of all the provinces of the Roman people on whose boundaries were peoples not subject to our empire....
27. I added Egypt to the empire of the Roman people....
28. I established colonies of soldiers in Africa, Sicily, Macedonia, in both Spanish provinces, in Achaea, Asia, Syria, Narbonese Gaul, and Pisidia. Italy, moreover, has twenty-eight colonies established by me, which in my lifetime have grown to be famous and populous....
35. When I held my thirteenth consulship, the senate, the equestrian order, and the entire Roman people gave me the title of "father of the country" and decreed that this title should be inscribed in the vestibule of my house, in the Julian senate house, and in the Augustan Forum on the pedestal of the chariot which was set up in my honor by decree of the senate. At the time I wrote this document I was in my seventy-sixth year.

The New Order

In the new constitutional order that Augustus created, the basic governmental structure consisted of the *princeps* (Augustus) and an aristocratic senate. Augustus retained the senate as the chief deliberative body of the Roman state. Its decrees, screened in advance by the *princeps*, now had the effect of law. The title of *princeps*—first citizen of the state—carried no power in itself, but each year until 23 B.C., Augustus held the office of consul, which gave him *imperium*, or the right to command (see Chapter 5). When Augustus gave up the consulship in 23 B.C., he was granted *maius imperium*—greater *imperium* than all others. The consulship was now unnecessary. Moreover, very probably in 23 B.C., Augustus was given the power of a tribune without actually holding the office itself; this power enabled him to propose laws and veto any item of public business. Although officials continued to be elected, Augustus' authority ensured that his candidates for office usually won. This situation caused participation in elections to decline. Consequently, the popular assemblies, shorn of any real role in elections and increasingly overshadowed by the senate's decrees, gradually declined in importance.

Augustus proved highly popular. As the Roman historian Tacitus commented, "Indeed, he attracted everybody's goodwill by the enjoyable gift of peace.... Opposition did not exist."[2] Certainly the ending of the civil wars had greatly bolstered Augustus' popularity (see the box above). At the same time, his continuing control of the army, while making possible the Roman peace, was a crucial source of his power.

The Army

The peace of the Roman Empire depended on the army, and so did the security of the *princeps*. Though primarily responsible for guarding the frontiers of the empire, the army was also used to maintain domestic order within the provinces. Moreover, the army played an important social role. It was an agent of upward mobility for both officers and recruits and provided impetus for Romanization wherever the legions were stationed. The colonies of veterans established by Augustus throughout the empire proved especially valuable in Romanizing the provinces.

Augustus maintained a standing army of twenty-eight legions. Since each legion at full strength numbered 5,400 soldiers, the Roman Empire had an army of about 150,000 men, certainly not large either by modern standards or in terms of the size of the empire itself (the population of the empire was probably close to fifty million). Roman legionaries served twenty years and were recruited only from the citizenry and, under Augustus, largely from Italy. Augustus also maintained a large contingent of auxiliary forces enlisted from the subject peoples. They served as both light-armed troops and cavalry and were commanded by Roman officers as well as tribal leaders. During the principate of Augustus, the auxiliaries numbered around 130,000. They were recruited only from noncitizens, served for twenty-four years, and along with their families received citizenship after their terms of service.

Augustus was responsible for establishing the praetorian guard. These "nine cohorts of elite troops," roughly nine thousand men, had the important task of guarding the person of the *princeps*. They were recruited from Roman citizens in Italy and served for sixteen years. Eventually, the praetorian guard would play an important role in making and deposing emperors.

The Praetorian Guard. Augustus was responsible for setting up the praetorian guard as an imperial bodyguard of elite troops. Pictured in this second-century relief are five members of the praetorian guard.

Réunion des Musées Nationaux/Art Resource, NY

The role of the *princeps* as military commander gave rise to a title by which this ruler eventually came to be known. When victorious, a military commander was acclaimed by his troops as *imperator*. Augustus was so acclaimed on a number of occasions. *Imperator* is our word *emperor*. Although such a title was applied to Augustus and his successors, Augustus still preferred to use the title *princeps*. Not until the reign of Vespasian (69–79) did *emperor* become the common title for the Roman ruler.

Roman Provinces and Frontiers

Augustus inaugurated a new system for governing the provinces. Under the Republic, the senate had appointed the provincial governors. Now certain provinces were allotted to the *princeps*, who assigned deputies known as legates to govern them. These legates were from the senatorial class and held office as long as the emperor chose. The remaining provinces were designated as senatorial provinces. They continued to be ruled by proconsuls and propraetors as governors who were appointed annually by lot for one year and reported directly to the senate. Although a dual system of provincial administration seemed to have been created, in reality the greater proconsular *imperium* that had been granted to Augustus gave him the power to overrule the senatorial governors and hence to establish a unified imperial policy. Because all provincial governors, whether of imperial or senatorial provinces, now received regular salaries, there was less need for the kind of extortion that had characterized provincial administration in the late Republic. In general, although there were still abuses, especially in the area of tax collection, provincial administration under Augustus was more efficient than under the Republic, and provincials were better protected against abuses of power.

Since a governor had relatively few administrative officials to assist him, effective government of the provinces necessitated considerable cooperation from local authorities. By supporting the power of local elites—the upper classes—in return for their cooperation, Roman policy encouraged a substantial degree of self-government and local autonomy in the cities. By fostering municipal life, Rome essentially made cities and city-states the basic units of imperial administration. City councils of leading citizens made for stable local government, and leading city officials were rewarded for their administrative services with Roman citizenship.

Augustus' frontier policy was not wholly defensive as it is sometimes portrayed. He was not immune to the glories of military conquest and in fact added more territory to the Roman Empire than any other single Roman. In the east, instead of creating new provinces, Augustus encouraged the establishment of client kingdoms, a policy that enabled him to minimize the Roman military presence in the east so that he could use his forces elsewhere. After the final pacification of Spain in 19 B.C., the *princeps* expended his greatest military efforts along the northern frontiers of the Roman Empire. He conquered the central and maritime Alps and then expanded Roman control of the Balkan peninsula up to the Danube River.

The extension of Roman power to the Danube now opened the door for Augustus' major military project—expansion into Germany. After 15 B.C., Roman forces advanced across the Rhine and by 9 B.C. had reached the Elbe River in eastern Germany. By A.D. 6, plans were coordinated for another advance between the Elbe and the Danube. This time, however, the Romans encountered a series of difficulties, including the great catastrophe of A.D. 9 when three Roman legions under Varus were massacred in the Teutoburg Forest by a coalition of German tribes led by Arminius, a German tribal leader who had served in the Roman auxiliary forces and had even received Roman citizenship. Roman historians blamed Varus for the disaster: "He [Varus] entertained the notion that the Germans were a people who were men only in voice and limbs. . . . With this purpose in mind, he entered the heart of Germany as though he were going among a people enjoying the blessings of peace."[3] The defeat severely dampened Augustus' enthusiasm for continued expansion in central Europe. Thereafter, the Romans were content to use the Rhine as the frontier between the Roman province of Gaul and the German tribes to the east. In fact, Augustus' difficulties had convinced him that "the empire should not be extended beyond its present frontiers."[4] His defeats in Germany taught Augustus that Rome's power was not unlimited. They also left him devastated; for months he would beat his head against a door and shout, "Varus, give me back my legions!"

Augustan Society

Roman society in the Early Empire was characterized by a system of social stratification, inherited from the Republic, in which Roman citizens were divided into three basic classes: the senatorial, equestrian, and lower classes.

Augustus had accepted the senatorial order as a ruling class for the empire. Senators filled the chief magistracies of the Roman government, held the most important military posts, and governed the provinces. One needed to possess property worth 1 million sesterces (an unskilled laborer in Rome received 3 sesterces a day; a Roman legionary, 900 sesterces a year in pay) to belong to the senatorial order. When Augustus took charge, the senate had over a thousand members. Augustus revised the senatorial list and reduced its size to six hundred but also added new men from wealthy families throughout Italy. Overall, Augustus was successful in winning the support of the senatorial class for his new order.

The equestrian order was expanded under Augustus and given a share of power in the new imperial state. The order was open to all Roman citizens of good standing who possessed property valued at 400,000 sesterces. They could now hold military and governmental offices, but the positions open to them were less important than those held by the senatorial order. At the end of his career, an equestrian might be rewarded by membership in the senatorial order.

Citizens not of the senatorial or equestrian orders belonged to the lower classes, who obviously constituted the overwhelming majority of the free citizens. The diminution of the power of the Roman assemblies ended whatever political power they may have possessed earlier in the Republic. Many of these people were provided with free grain and public spectacles to keep them from creating disturbances. Nevertheless, by gaining wealth and serving as lower officers in the Roman legions, it was sometimes possible for them to advance to the equestrian order.

Augustus was very concerned about certain aspects of Rome's social health. He believed that the civil strife of the first century B.C. had sapped the strength of public religion, which he considered the cornerstone of a strong state. Therefore, he restored traditional priesthoods that had fallen into disuse in the late Republic, rebuilt many ruined temples and shrines, and constructed new ones to honor the Roman gods.

Augustus also instituted a new religious cult that would serve to strengthen the empire. Since the Roman state was intimately tied to Roman religion, an imperial cult served as a unifying instrument for the Roman world. Augustus did not claim to be a god, but he did permit the construction of temples to his deified adoptive father, Julius Caesar. Augustus also permitted the building of temples to Augustus and Roma, the personification of the Roman state. The worship of Augustus and Roma became the foundation of the imperial cult. Its development was furthered when Augustus was acclaimed as a god upon his death.

Augustus' belief that Roman morals had been corrupted during the late Republic led him to initiate social legislation to arrest the decline. He thought that increased luxury had undermined traditional Roman frugality and simplicity and caused a decline in morals, evidenced by easy divorce, a falling birthrate among the upper classes, and lax behavior manifested in hedonistic parties and the love affairs of prominent Romans with fashionable women and elegant boys.

Through his new social legislation, Augustus hoped to restore respectability to the upper classes and reverse the declining birthrate as well. Expenditures for feasts were limited, and other laws made adultery a criminal offense. In fact, Augustus' own beloved daughter Julia was exiled for adultery. Augustus also revised the tax laws to penalize bachelors, widowers, and married persons who had fewer than three children.

A Golden Age of Latin Literature

The high point of Latin literature was reached in the time of Augustus. The literary accomplishments of the Augustan Age were such that the period has been called the golden age of Latin literature.

The most distinguished poet of the Augustan Age was Virgil (70–19 B.C.). The son of a small landholder in northern Italy, he welcomed the rule of Augustus and wrote his greatest work in the emperor's honor. Virgil's masterpiece was the *Aeneid,* an epic poem clearly meant to rival the work of Homer. The connection between Troy and Rome is made explicitly. Aeneas, the son of Anchises of Troy, survives the destruction of Troy and eventually settles in Latium; thus Roman civilization is linked to Greek history. The character of Aeneas is portrayed in terms that remind us of the ideal Roman—his virtues are duty, piety, and faithfulness. Virgil's overall purpose was to show that Aeneas had fulfilled his mission to establish the Romans in Italy and thereby start Rome on its divine mission to rule the world:

> *Let others fashion from bronze more lifelike, breathing images—*
> *For so they shall—and evoke living faces from marble;*
> *Others excel as orators, others track with their instruments*
> *The planets circling in heaven and predict when stars will appear.*
> *But, Romans, never forget that government is your medium!*
> *Be this your art:—to practice men in the habit of peace,*
> *Generosity to the conquered, and firmness against aggressors.*[5]

As Virgil expressed it, ruling was Rome's gift.

Another prominent Augustan poet was Horace (65–8 B.C.), a friend of Virgil. Horace was a very sophisticated writer whose overriding concern seems to have been to point out to his contemporaries the "follies and vices of his age." In the *Satires,* a medley of poems on a variety of subjects, Horace is revealed as a detached observer of human weaknesses. He directed his attacks against movements, not living people, and took on such subjects as sexual immorality, greed, and job dissatisfaction ("How does it happen, Maecenas, that no man alone is content with his lot?"[6]). Horace mostly laughs at the weaknesses of humankind and calls for forbearance: "Supposing my friend has got liquored and wetted my couch. . . . Is he for such a lapse to be deemed less dear as a friend, or because when hungry he snatched up before me a chicken from my side of the dish?"[7] In his final work, the *Epistles,* Horace used another Greek form—the imaginary letter in verse—to provide a portrait of his friends and society and the things he held most dear: a simple life, good friends, and his beloved countryside.

Ovid (43 B.C.–A.D. 18) was the last of the great poets of the golden age. He belonged to a privileged group of Roman youths who liked to ridicule old Roman values. In keeping with the spirit of this group, Ovid wrote a frivolous series of love poems known as the *Amores.* Intended to entertain and shock, they achieved their goal. Ovid's most popular work was the *Metamorphoses,* a series of fifteen complex mythological tales involving transformations of shapes, such as the change of chaos into order. A storehouse of mythological information, the *Metamorphoses* inspired many Western painters, sculptors, and writers, including Shakespeare.

Another of Ovid's works was *The Art of Love.* This was essentially a takeoff on didactic poems. Whereas authors of earlier didactic poems had written guides to farming, hunting, or some such subject, Ovid's work was a handbook on the seduction of women (see the box on p. 139). *The Art of Love* appeared to applaud the loose sexual morals of the Roman upper classes at a time when Augustus was trying to clean up the sexual scene in upper-class Rome. The *princeps* was not pleased. Ovid chose to ignore the wishes of Augustus and paid a price for it. In A.D. 8, Ovid was implicated in a sexual scandal, possibly involving the emperor's daughter Julia. He was banished to a small town on the coast of the Black Sea and died in exile.

The most famous Latin prose work of the golden age was written by the historian Livy (59 B.C.–A.D. 17). Livy's masterpiece was a history of Rome from the foundation of the city to 9 B.C., written in 142 books. Only 35 of the books have survived, although we do possess brief summaries of the whole work from other authors. Livy perceived history in terms of moral lessons. He stated in the preface:

> The study of history is the best medicine for a sick mind; for in history you have a record of the infinite variety of human experience plainly set out for all to see; and in that record you can find for yourself and your country both examples and warnings: fine things to take as models, base things, rotten through and through, to avoid.[8]

For Livy, human character was the determining factor in history.

Livy's history celebrated Rome's greatness. He built scene upon scene that not only revealed the character of the chief figures but also demonstrated the virtues that had made Rome great. Of course, he had serious weaknesses as a historian. He was not always concerned about the factual accuracy of his stories and was not overly critical of his sources. But he did tell a good tale, and his work remained the standard history of Rome for centuries.

The Augustan Age was a lengthy one. Augustus died in A.D. 14 after dominating the Roman world for forty-five years. He had created a new order while placating the old by restoring and maintaining traditional values, a fitting combination for a leader whose favorite maxim was "Make haste slowly." By the time of his death, his new order was so well established that few Romans agitated for an alternative. Indeed, as the Roman historian Tacitus pointed out, "Actium had been won before the younger men were born. Even most of the older generation had come into a world of civil wars. Practically no one had ever seen truly Republican government. . . . Political equality was a thing of the past; all eyes watched for imperial commands."[9] The Republic was now only a memory and, given its last century of warfare, an unpleasant one at that. The new order was here to stay.

The Early Empire (14–180)

There was no serious opposition to Augustus' choice of successor, his stepson Tiberius. By designating a family member as *princeps,* Augustus established the Julio-Claudian dynasty; the next four rulers were related either to his own family or to that of his wife, Livia.

Ovid and the Art of Love

Ovid has been called the last great poet of the Augustan golden age of literature. One of his most famous works was *The Art of Love*, a guidebook for the seduction of women. Unfortunately for Ovid, the work appeared at a time when Augustus was anxious to improve the morals of the Roman upper class. Augustus considered the poem offensive, and Ovid soon found himself in exile.

Ovid, The Art of Love

Now I'll teach you how to captivate and hold the woman of your choice. This is the most important part of all my lessons. Lovers of every land, lend an attentive ear to my discourse; let goodwill warm your hearts, for I am going to fulfill the promises I made you.

First of all, be quite sure that there isn't a woman who cannot be won, and make up your mind that you will win her. Only you must prepare the ground. Sooner would the birds cease their song in the springtime, or the grasshopper be silent in the summer, . . . than a woman resist the tender wooing of a youthful lover. . . .

Now the first thing you have to do is to get on good terms with the fair one's maid. She can make things easy for you. Find out whether she is fully in her mistress's confidence, and if she knows all about her secret dissipations. Leave no stone unturned to win her over. Once you have her on your side, the rest is easy. . . .

In the first place, it's best to send her a letter, just to pave the way. In it you should tell her how you dote on her; pay her pretty compliments and say all the nice things lovers always say. . . . And promise, promise, promise. Promises will cost you nothing. Everyone's a millionaire where promises are concerned. . . .

If she refuses your letter and sends it back unread, don't give up; hope for the best and try again. . . .

Don't let your hair stick up in tufts on your head; see that your hair and your beard are decently trimmed. See also that your nails are clean and nicely filed; don't have any hair growing out of your nostrils; take care that your breath is sweet, and don't go about reeking like a billy-goat. . . .

When you find yourself at a feast where the wine is flowing freely, and where a woman shares the same couch with you, pray to that god whose mysteries are celebrated during the night, that the wine may not overcloud your brain. 'Tis then you may easily hold converse with your mistress in hidden words whereof she will easily divine the meaning. . . .

By subtle flatteries you may be able to steal into her heart, even as the river insensibly overflows the banks which fringe it. Never cease to sing the praises of her face, her hair, her taper fingers and her dainty foot. . . .

Tears, too, are a mighty useful resource in the matter of love. They would melt a diamond. Make a point, therefore, of letting your mistress see your face all wet with tears. Howbeit, if you can't manage to squeeze out any tears—and they won't always flow just when you want them to—put your finger in your eyes.

The Julio-Claudians (14–68)

The Julio-Claudian rulers varied greatly in ability. Tiberius (14–37) was a competent general and able administrator who tried initially to involve the senate in government. Caligula (37–41) was a grandnephew of Tiberius and great-grandson of Augustus. He exhibited tyrannical behavior and was excessively erratic. Claudius (41–54) had been mistreated by his family because of a physical disability due to partial paralysis, but he was intelligent, well educated, and competent. He was followed by Nero (54–68), who was only sixteen when he came to power. Nero's interest in the arts caused him to neglect affairs of state, especially the military, and proved to be his undoing.

Several major tendencies emerged during the reigns of the four Julio-Claudians. In general, more and more of the responsibilities that Augustus had given to the senate tended to be taken over by the emperors. Moreover, an imperial bureaucracy was instituted under Claudius. He rationalized the central government by developing bureaucratic departments with talented freedmen as their chiefs. This practice further undermined the authority of the senators, who had previously shared in these responsibilities.

As the Julio-Claudian successors of Augustus began to behave openly like real rulers rather than "first citizens of the state," the opportunity for arbitrary and corrupt acts increased. Caligula, who became mentally unbalanced, wanted to be hailed as a god and neglected affairs of state while indulging his passions. Nero freely eliminated people he wanted out of the way, including his own mother, whom he had murdered. Without troops, the senators proved unable to oppose these excesses. Only the praetorian guard established by Augustus seemed capable of interfering with these rulers but did so in a manner that did not bode well for future stability. Caligula proved so capricious that the officers of the praetorian guard hatched a plot and assassinated him before he had ruled for four complete years. Afterward, they chose Claudius, uncle of Caligula, as the next emperor and forced the senate to confirm their act, thereby demonstrating the power of the military units stationed around Rome.

The downfall of the Julio-Claudian dynasty came during the reign of Nero. His early reign had been quite successful. The young emperor worked hard and with the assistance of his childhood tutor, the philosopher Seneca, gave the empire a sound government. But Nero soon tired of his duties and began to pursue other interests, including singing, acting, horse racing, and sexual activities. After Seneca resigned his position in disgust in 62, Nero's rule deteriorated. His obsession with singing and acting in public was greeted with contempt by the senatorial class. At the same time, he aroused animosity by executing a number of prominent figures, including a popular general, on a charge of treason. His actions finally led to a conspiracy, not by the praetorian guard, but by the Roman legions themselves. In 68, Galba, governor of one of the Spanish provinces, rose in revolt and secured the principate for himself. Nero, abandoned by his guards, chose to commit suicide by stabbing himself in the throat after uttering his final words, "What an artist the world is losing in me."

The Flavians (69–96)

Galba, however, was not readily accepted by the other provincial armies. The result was a civil war in 69, known as the year of the four emperors (see the box on p. 141). Finally, Vespasian, commander of the legions in the east, established himself as sole ruler and his family as a new dynasty known as the Flavians. The significance of the year 69 was summed up precisely by Tacitus when he stated that "a well-hidden secret of the principate had been revealed: it was possible, it seemed, for an emperor to be chosen outside Rome"[10]—chosen, of course, by members of the Roman army.

The accession of Vespasian to the imperial power demonstrated that it was no longer necessary to be descended from an ancient aristocratic family to be emperor. In fact, the family of Vespasian (69–79) was from the equestrian order. Once in control, he managed to reestablish the economy on a sound basis after the extravagances of Nero and the destruction wrought by the civil wars of 69. More important, Vespasian had no compunctions whatever about establishing the principle of dynastic succession for the principate. He was followed by his sons Titus (79–81) and Domitian (81–96). The Flavians, especially Domitian, dropped the pretense of the word *princeps* and began to use the title of *imperator*, emperor, freely. The emperor was rapidly becoming an absolute monarch.

The Five "Good Emperors" (96–180)

Many historians see the *Pax Romana* (the Roman peace) and the prosperity it engendered as the chief benefits of Roman rule during the first and second centuries A.D. These benefits were especially noticeable during the reigns of the five so-called good emperors. These rulers treated the ruling classes with respect, cooperated with the senate, ended arbitrary executions, maintained peace in the empire, and supported domestic policies generally beneficial to the empire. Though absolute monarchs, they were known for their tolerance and diplomacy.

The first of the five good emperors was Nerva (96–98), chosen by the senate after the assassination of Domitian. By chance, Nerva and his next three successors had no sons and had to resort to adoption to obtain heirs. As his successor, Nerva chose Trajan, a capable man who was also acceptable to the army, an increasingly important requirement. Trajan (98–117) had been born in Spain to an old Roman family and was the first emperor born outside Italy. He was succeeded by his second cousin Hadrian (117–138), who also came from a Roman family that had settled in Spain. Hadrian adopted as his successor Antoninus Pius (138–161), who achieved a reputation as the most beneficent of the five good emperors. Unlike Hadrian, who traveled extensively in the provinces, Antoninus Pius stayed in Rome and made even greater use of the senate. He in turn adopted Marcus Aurelius (161–180), who has been viewed as a philosopher-king of the sort Plato envisioned (see Chapter 3). Highly influenced by Stoicism, Marcus Aurelius wrote his *Meditations*, reflecting the ideal of Stoic duty as a religious concept.

Under the five good emperors, the powers of the emperor continued to expand at the expense of the senate. Increasingly, imperial officials appointed and directed by the emperor took over the running of the government. The five good emperors also extended the scope of imperial administration to areas previously untouched by the imperial government. Trajan established a program that provided state funds to assist poor parents in raising and educating their children. He was not motivated simply by benevolence, since he believed that such assistance would materially aid in creating a larger pool of young men in Italy eligible for military service.

The five good emperors were widely praised by their subjects for their extensive building programs. Trajan and Hadrian were especially active in constructing public works—aqueducts, bridges, roads, and harbor facilities—throughout the provinces and in Rome. Trajan built a new forum in Rome to provide a setting for his celebrated victory column. Hadrian's Pantheon, a temple of "all the gods," is one of the grandest ancient buildings surviving in Rome.

CHRONOLOGY

Rulers of the Early Empire

Julio-Claudian dynasty	
Augustus	31 B.C.–A.D. 14
Tiberius	14–37
Caligula	37–41
Claudius	41–54
Nero	54–68
Flavian dynasty	
Vespasian	69–79
Titus	79–81
Domitian	81–96
Five good emperors	
Nerva	96–98
Trajan	98–117
Hadrian	117–138
Antoninus Pius	138–161
Marcus Aurelius	161–180

The Fate of Cremona in the Year of the Four Emperors

After the death of Nero in A.D. 68, a power struggle ensued that resulted in a year of confusion with four different emperors, each the leader of a field army. Galba replaced Nero and was succeeded by Otho, who was then defeated by Vitellius. Finally, Vespasian established a new dynasty. Some of the Italian cities suffered greatly in these struggles between Roman legions loyal to their commanders. This excerpt is from Tacitus' account of the destruction of Cremona by the forces that had declared for Vespasian.

Tacitus, The Histories

Forty thousand armed men forced their way into the city. . . . Neither rank nor years saved the victims from an indiscriminate orgy in which rape alternated with murder and murder with rape. Graybeards and frail old women, who had no value as loot, were dragged off to raise a laugh. But any full-grown girl or good-looking lad who crossed their path was pulled this way and that in a violent tug-of-war between the would-be captors, and finally drove them to destroy each other. A single looter trailing a hoard of money or temple-offerings of massive gold was often cut to pieces by others who were stronger. Some few turned up their noses at the obvious finds and inflicted flogging and torture on the owners in order to rummage after hidden valuables and dig for buried treasure. In their hands they held firebrands, which, once they had got their spoil away, they wantonly flung into the empty houses and rifled temples. It is not surprising that, in an army of varied tongues and conventions, including Romans, allies and foreigners [auxiliaries], there was a diversity of wild desires, differing conceptions of what was lawful, and nothing barred. Cremona lasted them four days. While all its buildings, sacred and secular, collapsed in flames, only the temple of Melitis [goddess of pestilential vapors] outside the walls remained standing, defended by its position or the power of the divinity.

The Roman Empire at Its Height: Frontiers and Provinces

At its height in the second century, the Roman Empire (see Map 6.1) covered about 3.5 million square miles and had a population, like that of Han China, estimated at more than fifty million. While the emperors and the imperial administration provided a degree of unity, considerable leeway was given to local customs, and the privileges of Roman citizenship were extended to many people throughout the empire. In A.D. 212, the emperor Caracalla completed the process by giving Roman citizenship to every free inhabitant of the empire. Latin was the language of the western part of the empire, while Greek was used in the east. Although Roman culture spread to all parts of the empire, there were limits to Romanization since local languages persisted and many of the empire's residents spoke neither Latin nor Greek.

With the exception of Claudius' annexation of Britain, the first-century successors of Augustus had largely followed his advice to curb expansion and remain within the natural frontiers of the empire—the ocean to the west, the rivers in the north, and the desert in the east and south. Two areas prompted special concern. The Rhine-Danube frontier in the north became the most heavily fortified border area because of the threat from restless barbarian tribes. In the east, the Romans used a system of client states to serve as a buffer against the troublesome Parthians.

Although Trajan broke with Augustus' policy of defensive imperialism by extending Roman rule into Dacia (modern Romania), Mesopotamia, and the Sinai peninsula, his conquests represent the high-water mark of Roman expansion. His successors recognized that the empire was overextended and pursued a policy of retrenchment. Hadrian withdrew Roman forces from much of Mesopotamia. Although he retained Dacia and Arabia, he went on the defensive in his frontier policy, reinforcing the fortifications along a line connecting the Rhine and Danube Rivers and building a defensive wall 80 miles long across northern Britain. By the end of the second century, the vulnerability of the empire had become apparent. Frontiers were stabilized, and the Roman forces were established in permanent bases behind the frontiers. But when one frontier was attacked, troops had to be drawn from other frontiers, leaving them vulnerable. The empire lacked a real strategic reserve, and its weakness would become ever more apparent.

The Roman army was the primary instrument for the defense of the Roman frontiers. In A.D. 14, it numbered twenty-five legions but had increased to thirty by the time of Trajan. The auxiliaries were increased correspondingly, making a Roman army of about 400,000 by the end of the second century. Since legionaries had to be Roman citizens, most recruits in Augustus' time were from Italy. But in the course of the first century, the Italians' reluctance to serve in the military led to the recruitment of citizens from the provinces. By A.D. 100, only one in five of the legionaries was Italian.

In addition to defense and protection, the Roman army also served as an important instrument for Romanizing the provinces. Roman military camps became centers for the spread of the Latin language and Roman institutions and ways of thought and conduct. The presence of large numbers of troops and their dependent women and slaves encouraged the development of trade and local production to meet the army's need for supplies. Urban centers developed around army bases or nearby colonies. Many cities along the Rhine had their roots in legionary bases or

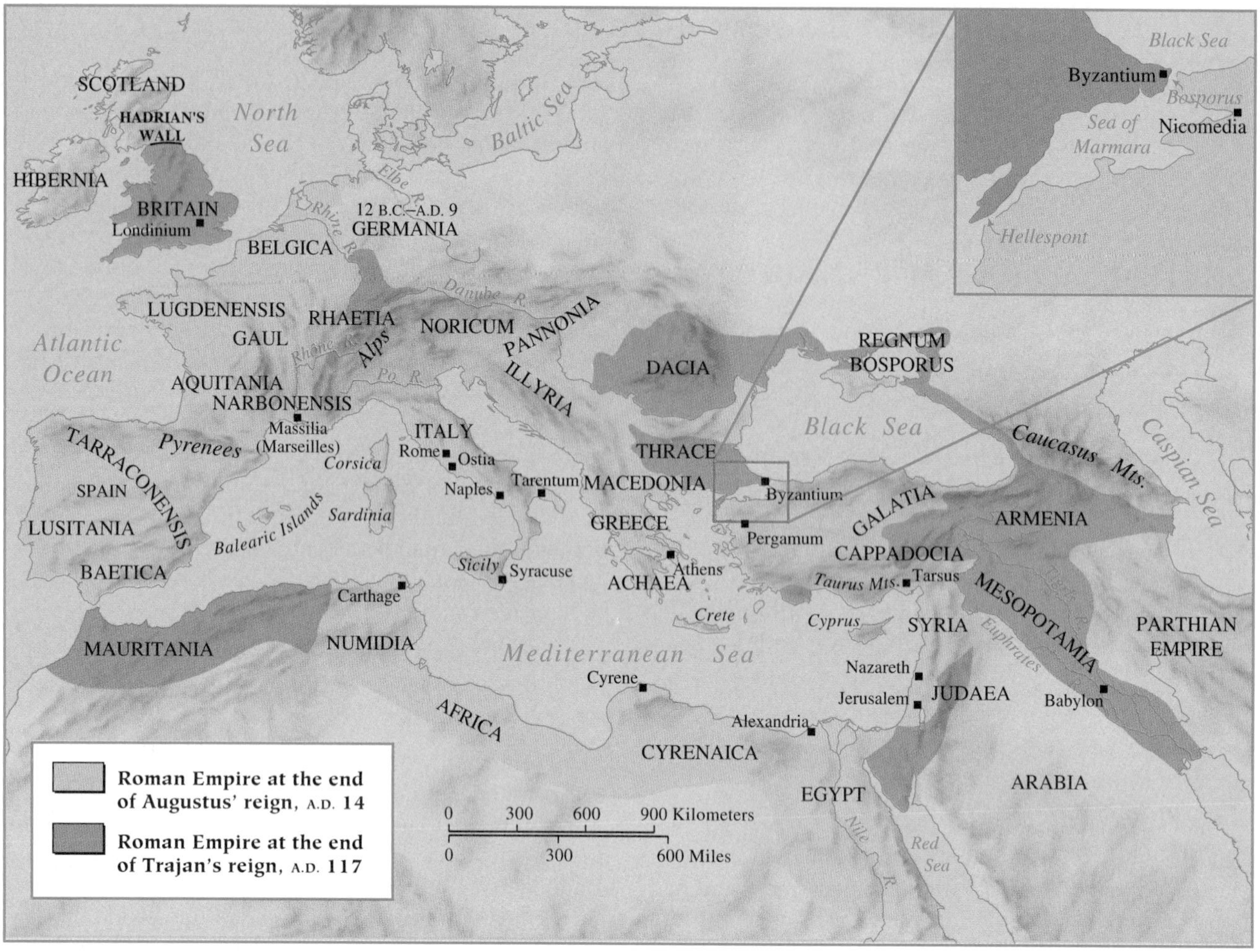

Map 6.1 The Roman Empire from Augustus to Trajan (14–117). Augustus and later emperors continued the expansion of the Roman Empire, adding more resources but also increasing the tasks of administration and keeping the peace. Compare this map with Map 5.3. ■ Which territories were conquered by Augustus, and which were added by the end of Trajan's reign?

auxiliary forts. The city of Cologne, for example, grew out of the military colony the Romans called Colonia Agrippinensis.

The administration and cultural life of the Roman Empire depended greatly on cities and towns. A provincial governor's staff was not large, so it was left to local city officials to act as Roman agents in carrying out many government functions, especially those related to taxes. Most towns and cities were not large by modern standards. The largest was Rome, but there were also some large cities in the east: Alexandria in Egypt numbered over 300,000 inhabitants, Ephesus in Asia Minor had 200,000, and Anti-

A Rome in Germany. The Roman army helped bring Roman culture and institutions to the provinces. Local production and trade grew up around the military camps to meet the soldiers' needs, and cities often developed from the bases themselves or from colonies located nearby. Pictured are the remains of the Porta Nigra, or gateway to the Roman city of Augusta Treverorum (modern Trier). In the early empire, Trier became the headquarters of the imperial procurator of Belgica and the two Germanies. Its close location to Roman military camps along the Rhine enabled it to flourish as one of the most significant cities in the Western Roman Empire.

och in Syria had around 150,000. In the west, cities were usually small, with only a few thousand inhabitants. Cities were important in the spread of things Roman. They were also uniform in physical appearance, with similar temples, markets, amphitheaters, and other public buildings.

Magistrates and town councillors chosen from the ranks of the wealthy upper classes directed municipal administration. These municipal offices were unsalaried but were nevertheless desired by wealthy citizens because the offices conferred prestige and power at the local level as well as Roman citizenship. Roman municipal policy effectively tied the upper classes to Roman rule and ensured that these classes would retain control over the rest of the population.

The process of Romanization in the provinces was reflected in significant changes in the governing classes of the empire. In the course of the first century, there was a noticeable decline in the number of senators from Italian families. By the end of the second century, Italian senators made up less than half the total. Increasingly, the Roman senate was being recruited from wealthy provincial equestrian families. The provinces also provided many of the legionaries for the Roman army and, beginning with Trajan, supplied many of the emperors.

The Shipping of Grain. Trade was an important ingredient in the prosperity of the Early Empire. This tomb painting from Ostia, the port of Rome at the mouth of the Tiber, shows workers loading grain onto the *Isis Giminiana,* a small merchant ship, for shipment upriver to Rome. The captain of the ship stands by the rudder. Next to him is Abascantus, the ship's owner.

Prosperity in the Early Empire

The Early Empire was a period of considerable prosperity. Internal peace resulted in unprecedented levels of trade (see Map 6.2). Merchants from all over the empire came to the chief Italian ports of Puteoli on the Bay of Naples and Ostia at the mouth of the Tiber. Trade extended beyond the Roman boundaries and included even goods from China. Chinese merchants traveled across Central Asia, forming part of the Silk Road, which became a regular overland route between west and east. By the first century A.D., Chinese goods, including silk and lacquerware, were being sent into the eastern part of the Roman Empire, in southwestern Asia, where they were traded for woolen textiles, glass, and precious stones. Moreover, the importation of large quantities of grain to feed the populace of Rome and an incredible quantity of luxury items for the wealthy upper classes in the west led to a steady drain of gold and silver coins from Italy and the west to the eastern part of the empire.

Increased trade helped stimulate manufacturing. The cities of the east still produced the items made in Hellenistic times (see Chapter 4). The first two centuries of the empire also witnessed the high point of industrial development in Italy. Some industries became concentrated in certain areas, such as bronze work in Capua and pottery in Arretium in Etruria. Other industries, such as brickmaking, were pursued in rural areas on large landed estates. Much industrial production remained small-scale and was done by individual artisans, usually freedmen or slaves. In the course of the first century, Italian centers of industry experienced increasing competition from the provinces. Pottery produced in Gaul, for example, began to outsell Italian pottery from Arretium.

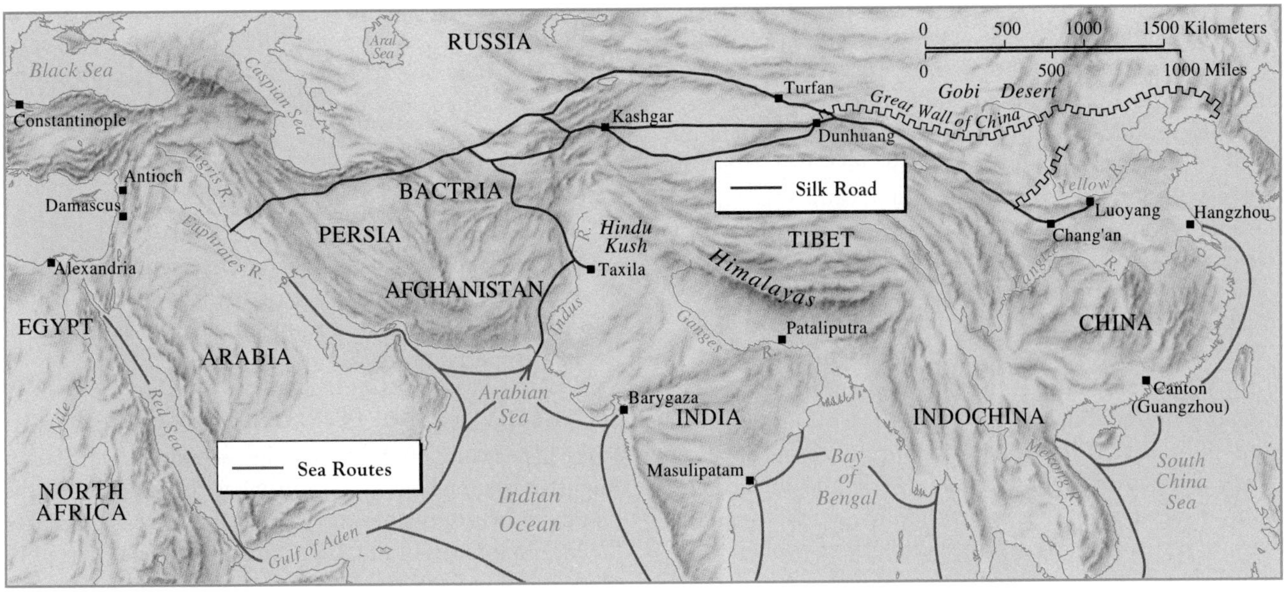

The Silk Road

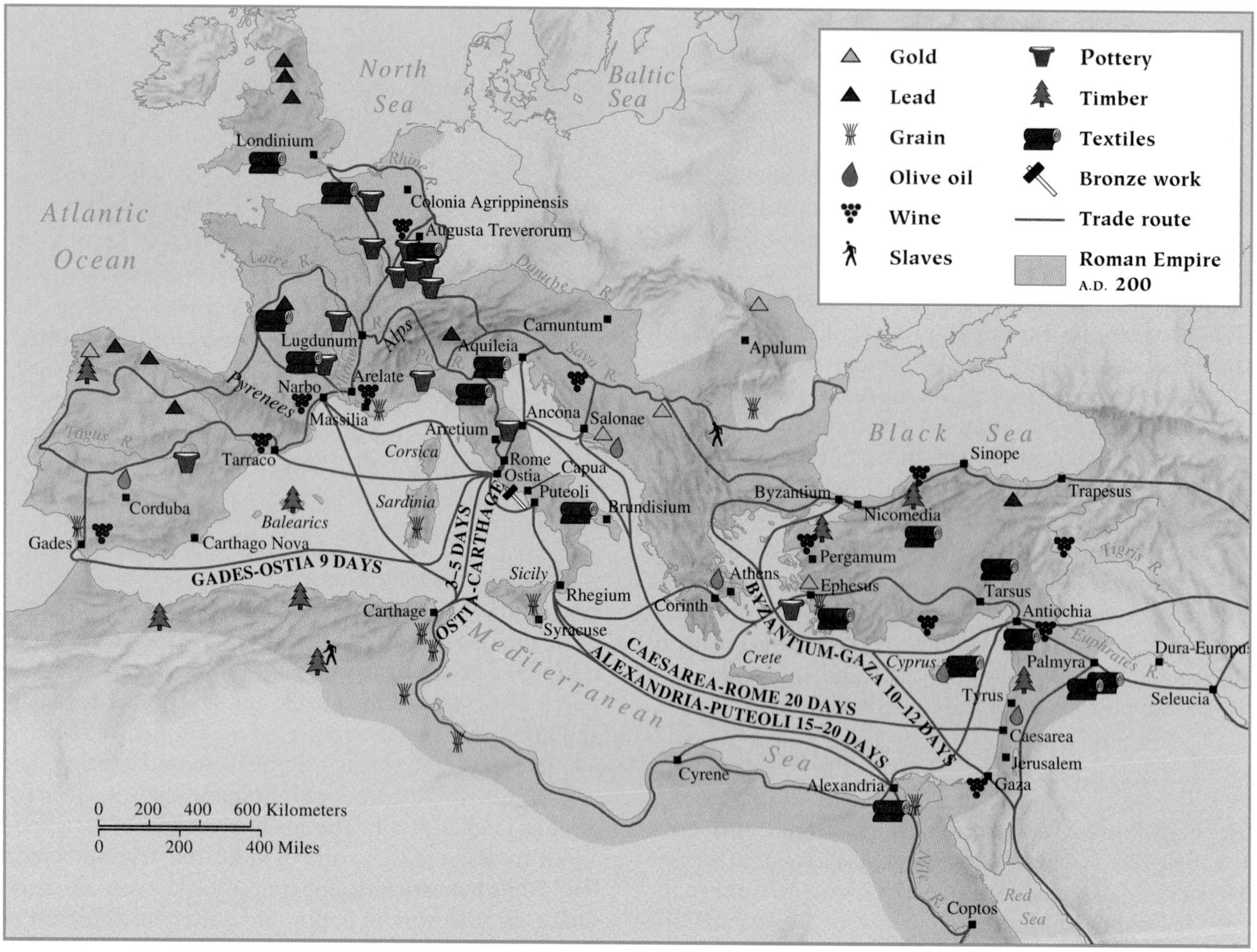

Map 6.2 Trade Routes and Products in the Roman Empire, c. 200. Although still primarily an agrarian economy, the Roman Empire provided the single currency and stable conditions necessary for an expansion of trade in various commodities and products. An extensive system of roads and shipping routes also facilitated trade. ■ What truth is there to the statement "All roads lead to Rome"?

Despite the prosperity from trade and commerce, agriculture remained the chief occupation of most people and the underlying basis of Roman prosperity. While the large landed estates, the *latifundia,* still dominated agriculture, especially in southern and central Italy, small peasant farms persisted, particularly in Etruria and the Po valley. Although large estates concentrating on sheep and cattle raising used slave labor, the lands of some *latifundia* were worked by free tenant farmers called *coloni.* The *colonus* was essentially a sharecropper who paid rent in labor, produce, or sometimes cash.

In considering the prosperity of the Roman world, it is important to remember the enormous gulf between rich and poor underlying it (see the box on p. 145). The development of towns and cities, so important to the creation of any civilization, is based to a large degree on the agricultural surpluses of the countryside. In ancient times, the margin of surplus produced by each farmer was relatively small. Therefore, the upper classes and urban populations had to be supported by the labor of a large number of agricultural producers who never found it easy to produce much more than enough for themselves. In lean years, when there were no surpluses, the townspeople often took what they wanted, leaving little for the peasants.

Roman Culture and Society in the Early Empire

Although the cultural and social developments of the Early Empire were similar to those of the last century of the Republic, there were also significant changes as a result of the new imperial order.

THE SILVER AGE OF LATIN LITERATURE

In the history of Latin literature, the century and a half after Augustus is often labeled the "silver age" to indicate that the literary efforts of the period, while good, were not equal to the high standards of the Augustan "golden age." The popularity of rhetorical training encouraged the use of clever literary expressions, often at the expense of original and

The Daily Life of an Upper-Class Roman

There was an enormous gulf between rich and poor in Roman society. The upper classes lived lives of great leisure and luxury in their villas and on their vast estates. Pliny the Younger (c. 62–c. 113) was an upper-class Roman who rose to the position of governor of Bithynia in Asia Minor. In this excerpt from one of his letters, Pliny describes a typical day vacationing at one of his Italian villas. Although Pliny owned four villas in Italy, we should note that he did not belong to the ranks of the really rich in Roman society.

Pliny, Letter to Fuscus Salinator

You want to know how I plan the summer days I spend in Tuscany. I wake when I like, usually about sunrise, often earlier but rarely later. My shutters stay closed, for in the stillness and darkness I feel myself surprisingly detached from any distractions and left to myself in freedom. . . . If I have anything on hand I work it out in my head, choosing and correcting the wording, and the amount I achieve depends on the ease or difficulty with which my thoughts can be marshaled and kept in my head. Then I call my secretary, the shutters are opened, and I dictate what I have put into shape; he goes out, is recalled, and again dismissed. Three or four hours after I first wake (but I don't keep to fixed times) I betake myself according to the weather either to the terrace or the covered arcade, work out the rest of my subject, and dictate it. I go for a drive, and spend the time in the same way as when walking or lying down; my powers of concentration do not flag and are in fact refreshed by the change. After a short sleep and another walk I read a Greek or Latin speech aloud and with emphasis, not so much for the sake of my voice as my digestion, though of course both are strengthened by this. Then I have another walk, am oiled, take exercise, and have a bath. If I am dining alone with my wife or with a few friends, a book is read aloud during the meal and afterward we listen to a comedy or some music; then I walk again with the members of my household, some of whom are educated. Thus the evening is prolonged with varied conversations, and even when the days are at their longest, comes to a satisfying end.

Sometimes I vary this routine, for, if I have spent a long time on my couch or taking a walk, after my siesta and reading I go out on horseback instead of a carriage so as to be quicker and take less time. Part of the day is given up to friends who visit me from neighboring towns and sometimes come to my aid with a welcome interruption when I am tired. Occasionally I go hunting, but not without my notebooks so that I shall have something to bring home even if I catch nothing. I also give some time to my tenants (they think it should be more) and the boorishness of their complaints gives fresh zest to our literary interests and the more civilized pursuits of town.

meaningful content. A good example of this trend can be found in the works of Seneca.

Educated in Rome, Seneca (c. 4 B.C.–A.D. 65) became strongly attached to the philosophy of Stoicism (see Chapter 4). After serving as tutor to Nero, he helped run the government during the first five years of Nero's reign. Seneca began to withdraw from politics after Nero took a more active role in government. In 65, he was charged with involvement in a conspiracy against Nero and committed suicide at Nero's command.

In letters written to a young friend, Seneca expressed the basic tenets of Stoicism: living according to nature, accepting events dispassionately as part of the divine plan, and a universal love for all humanity. Thus "the first thing philosophy promises us is the feeling of fellowship, of belonging to mankind and being members of a community. . . . Philosophy calls for simple living, not for doing penance, and the simple way of life need not be a crude one."[11] Viewed in retrospect, Seneca displays some glaring inconsistencies. While preaching the virtues of simplicity, he amassed a fortune and was ruthless at times in protecting it. His letters show humanity, benevolence, and fortitude, but his sentiments are often undermined by an attempt to be clever with words.

The silver age also produced a work called the *Satyricon,* described by some literary historians as the first picaresque novel in Western literature. It was written by Petronius (d. 66), probably a former governor of Bithynia who had joined Nero's inner circle. The *Satyricon* is a humorous satire on the excesses of the Roman social scene. Basically, it is the story of a young man and his two male companions who engage in a series of madcap escapades and homosexual antics. The longest surviving episode contains a description of an elaborate and vulgar dinner party given by Trimalchio, a freedman who had become a millionaire through an inheritance from his former master. In Trimalchio, Petronius gave a hilarious, satirical portrait of Rome's new rich.

The greatest historian of the silver age was Tacitus (c. 56–120). His main works included the *Annals* and the *Histories,* which presented a narrative account of Roman history from the reign of Tiberius through the assassination of Domitian in 96. Tacitus believed that history had a moral purpose: "It seems to me a historian's foremost duty to ensure that merit is recorded, and to confront evil deeds and words with the fear of posterity's denunciations."[12] As a member of the senatorial class, Tacitus was disgusted with the abuses of power perpetrated by the emperors and was determined that the "evil deeds" of wicked men would not be forgotten. Many historians believe he went too far in projecting the evils of his own day back into his account of the past. Tacitus' work *Germania* is especially important as a source of information about the early Germans. But it too is colored by his attempt to show the Germans as noble savages in contrast to the decadent Roman upper classes.

By the second century A.D., though still influenced by the familiar Greek models, Latin authors were increasingly imitating the great Latin writers of earlier ages. This was evident in the work of Juvenal, the best poet of the silver age. Juvenal (c. 55–c. 128) wrote five books of satires in which he pilloried the manners and vices of his generation. He attacked the affectations of Roman women, the abuse of slaves, the excesses of emperors, the eastern and Greek immigrants, his own poverty, and the inequities of Roman society. For example: "They demand that the teacher shall mold these tender minds. . . . 'See to it,' you're told, and when the school year's ended, you'll get as much as a jockey makes from a single race."[13] But Juvenal was not a reformer. Though he attacked many vices, he offered no basic critique of his society.

ART IN THE EARLY EMPIRE

The Romans contributed little that was original to painting and scupture. Much work was done by Greek artists and craftspeople who adhered to the Roman desire for realism and attention to details. Wall paintings and frescoes in the houses of the rich realistically depicted landscapes, portraits, and scenes from mythological stories.

SEF/Art Resource, NY

The Roman Aqueduct. As engineers and architects, the Romans not only followed Greek models but also made significant innovations, such as their extensive use of concrete and curvilinear forms. Their engineering skills enabled them to construct the massive Colosseum in Rome, the public baths built under Caracalla, approximately 50,000 miles of roads, and aqueducts such as this one in southern France, known as the Pont du Gard.

The Pantheon. Shown here is the Pantheon, one of Rome's greatest buildings. Constructed of brick, six kinds of concrete, and marble, it was a stunning example of the Romans' engineering skills. The outside porch of the Pantheon contained eighteen Corinthian granite columns, but it was the inside of the temple that amazed onlookers. The interior is a large circular space topped by a huge dome. A hole in the center of the roof was the only source of light. The dome, built up layer by layer, was made of concrete, weighing 5,000 tons. The walls holding the dome are almost 20 feet thick.

Magnum Photos

© COFBIS

In architecture, the Romans continued to imitate Greek styles and made use of colonnades, rectangular structures, and post-and-lintel construction. But the Romans were innovative in their own way. They made considerable use of curvilinear forms: the arch, vault, and dome. The Romans were the first people in antiquity to use concrete on a massive scale. By combining concrete and curvilinear forms, they were able to construct massive buildings—public baths, such as those of Caracalla, and amphitheaters, the most famous of which was the Colosseum in Rome. These large buildings were made possible by Roman engineering skills. These same skills were put to use in constructing roads (the Romans built a network of 50,000 miles of roads throughout their empire), aqueducts (in Rome, almost a dozen aqueducts kept a population of one million supplied with water), and bridges.

IMPERIAL ROME

At the center of the colossal Roman Empire was the ancient city of Rome (see Map 6.3). Truly a capital city, Rome had the largest population of any city in the empire. It is estimated that its population was close to one million by the time of Augustus. For anyone with ambitions, Rome was the place to be. A magnet to many people, Rome was extremely cosmopolitan. Nationalities from all over the empire resided there with entire sections inhabited by specific groups, such as Greeks and Syrians.

Rome was no doubt an overcrowded and noisy city. Because of the congestion, cart and wagon traffic was banned from the streets during the day. The noise from the resulting vehicular movement at night often made sleep difficult. Evening pedestrian travel was dangerous. Although Augustus had organized a police force, lone travelers might be assaulted, robbed, and soaked by filth thrown out of the upper-story windows of Rome's massive apartment buildings.

An enormous gulf existed between rich and poor in the city of Rome. While the rich had comfortable villas, the poor lived in apartment blocks called *insulae,* which might be six stories high. Constructed of concrete, they were often poorly built and prone to collapse. The use of wooden beams in the floors and movable stoves, torches, candles, and lamps for heat and light made the danger of fire a constant companion. Once started, fires were extremely difficult to put out. The famous conflagration of 64, which Nero was unjustly accused of starting, devastated a good part of the city. Besides the hazards of collapse and fire, living conditions were miserable. High rents forced entire families into one room. In the absence of plumbing and central heating, conditions were so uncomfortable that poorer Romans spent most of their time outdoors in the streets.

Fortunately for these people, Rome boasted public buildings unequaled anywhere in the empire. Its temples, forums, markets, baths, theaters, triumphal arches, governmental buildings, and amphitheaters gave parts of the city an appearance of grandeur and magnificence (see the box on p. 148).

Though the center of a great empire, Rome was also a great parasite. Beginning with Augustus, the emperors accepted responsibility for providing food for the urban populace, with about 200,000 people receiving free grain. Rome needed about six million sacks of grain a year and imported large quantities from its African and Egyptian provinces to meet these requirements. Even with the free grain, conditions were grim for the poor. Early in the second century A.D., a Roman doctor claimed that rickets was common among the city's children.

In addition to food, entertainment was also provided on a grand scale for the inhabitants of Rome. The poet Juvenal said of the Roman masses: "Nowadays, with no vote

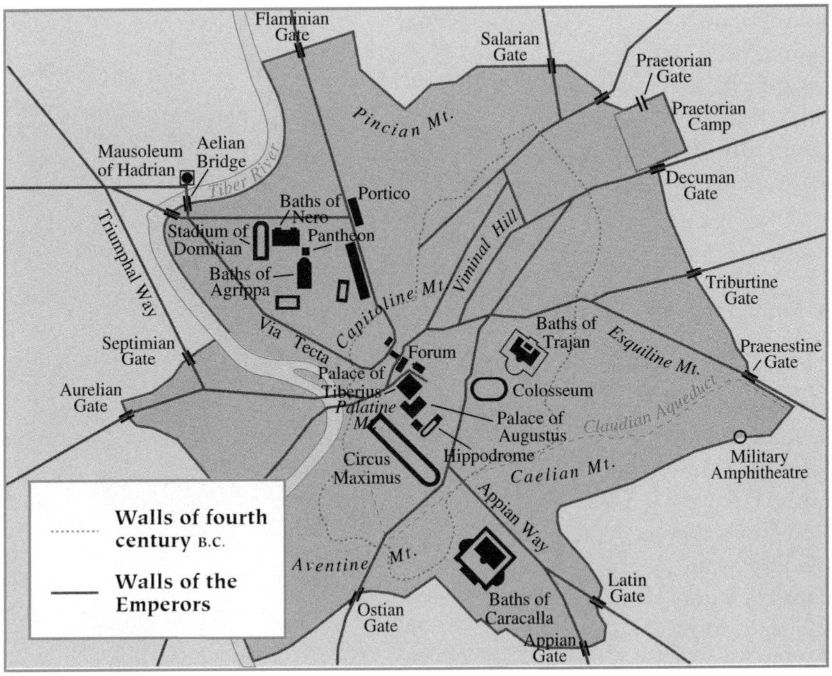

Map 6.3 Imperial Rome. A large, overcrowded, and dirty city, Rome was the political, economic, social, and cultural hub of the Roman Empire. Squalid and desperate living conditions for the poor contrasted dramatically with the city's magnificent architectural works. ■ How did roads from outside enter Rome, and what could possibly explain this?

The Public Baths of the Roman Empire

The public baths in Rome and other cities played an important role in urban life. Introduced to Rome in the second century B.C. as a result of Greek influence, the number of public baths grew at a rapid pace in the Early Empire as the emperors contributed funds for their construction. The public baths were especially noisy near the end of the afternoon when Romans stopped in after work to use the baths before dinner. The following description is by Lucian, a traveling lecturer who lived in the second century. This selection is taken from *Hippias, or the Bath*.

Lucian, Hippias, or the Bath

The building suits the magnitude of the site, accords well with the accepted idea of such an establishment, and shows regard for the principles of lighting. The entrance is high, with a flight of broad steps of which the tread is greater than the pitch, to make them easy to ascend. On entering, one is received into a public hall of good size, with ample accommodations for servants and attendants. On the left are the lounging rooms, also of just the right sort for a bath, attractive, brightly lighted retreats. Then, besides them, a hall larger than need be for the purposes of a bath, but necessary for the reception of richer persons. Next, capacious locker rooms to undress in, on each side, with a very high and brilliantly lighted hall between them, in which are three swimming pools of cold water. . . .

On leaving this hall, you come into another which is slightly warmed instead of meeting you at once with fierce heat; it is oblong, and has an apse on each side. Next to it, on the right, is a very bright hall, nicely fitted up for massage. . . . Then near this is another hall, the most beautiful in the world, in which one can stand or sit with comfort, linger without danger, and stroll about with profit. It also is radiant with Phrygian marble clear to the roof. Next comes the hot corridor, faced with Numidian marble. The hall beyond it is very beautiful, full of abundant light and aglow with color like that of purple hangings. It contains three hot tubs.

When you have bathed you need not go back through the same rooms, but can go directly to the cold room through a slightly warmed chamber. Everywhere there is copious illumination and full indoor daylight. . . . Why should I go on to tell you of the exercising floor and the cloak rooms? . . . Moreover, it is beautiful with all other marks of thoughtfulness—with two toilets, many exits, and two devices for telling time, a water clock that makes a bellowing sound and a sundial.

to sell, their motto is 'Couldn't care less.' Time was when their vote elected generals, heads of state, commanders of legions: but now they've pulled in their horns, there's only two things that concern them: Bread and Circuses."[14] The emperor and other state officials provided public spectacles as part of the great festivals—most of them religious in origin—celebrated by the state. More than one hundred days a year were given over to these public holidays. The festivals included three major types of entertainment. At the Circus Maximus, horse and chariot races attracted hundreds of thousands, while dramatic and other performances were held in theaters. But the most famous of all the public spectacles were the gladiatorial shows.

THE GLADIATORIAL SHOWS

The gladiatorial shows were an integral part of Roman society. They took place in amphitheaters; the first permanent one was constructed at Rome in 29 B.C. Perhaps the most famous was the Flavian amphitheater, called the Colosseum, constructed at Rome under Vespasian and his son Titus to seat fifty thousand spectators. Amphitheaters were constructed throughout the empire. They varied in size, with capacities ranging from a few thousand to tens of thousands. Considerable resources and ingenuity went into building them, especially in the arrangements for moving wild beasts efficiently into the arena. In most cities and towns, amphitheaters came to be the biggest

Interior of the Colosseum of Rome. The Colosseum was a large amphitheater constructed under the emperor Vespasian and his son Titus. Such amphitheaters, in which gladiatorial contests were held, were erected throughout the empire. They varied in size; this was the largest.

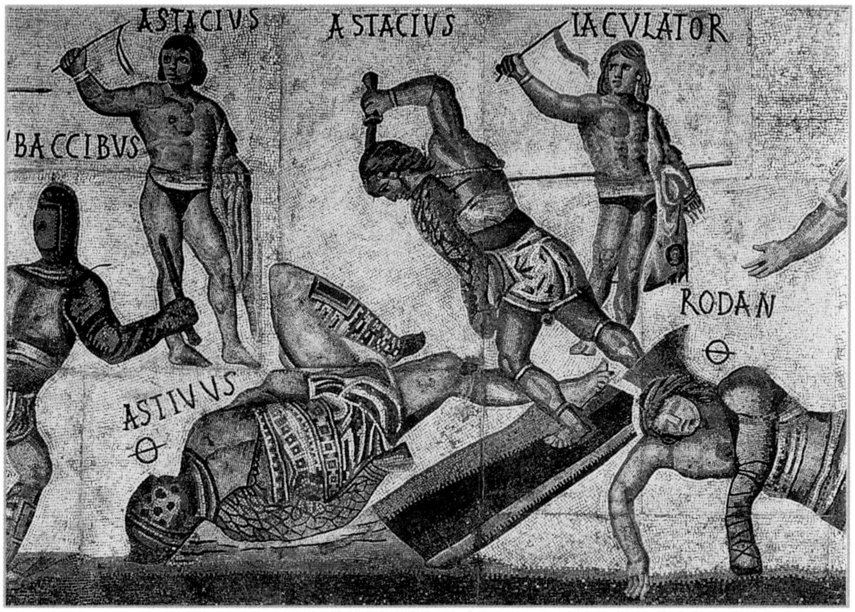

Scala/Art Resource, NY

The Gladiatorial Games. Although some gladiators were free men enticed by the possibility of rewards, most were condemned criminals, slaves, or prisoners of war who were trained in special schools. A great gladiator could win his freedom through the games. This mosaic from the fourth century A.D. depicts different aspects of gladiatorial fighting and clearly shows the bloody nature of the contests.

buildings, rivaled only by the circuses for races and the public baths. As we shall see repeatedly in the course of Western civilization, where a society invests its money gives an idea of its priorities. Since the amphitheater was the primary location for the gladiatorial games, it is fair to say that public slaughter was an important part of Roman culture.

Gladiatorial games were held from dawn to dusk. Their main features were contests to the death between trained fighters. Most gladiators were slaves or condemned criminals, although some free men lured by the hope of popularity and patronage by wealthy fans participated voluntarily. They were trained for combat in special gladiatorial schools.

Gladiatorial games included other forms of entertainment as well. Criminals of all ages and both sexes were sent into the arena without weapons to face certain death from wild animals who would tear them to pieces. Numerous kinds of animal contests were also held: wild beasts against each other, such as bears against buffalo; staged hunts with men shooting safely from behind iron bars; and gladiators in the arena with bulls, tigers, and lions. Reportedly, five thousand beasts were killed in one day of games when the emperor Titus inaugurated the Colosseum in A.D. 80. Enormous resources were invested in capturing and shipping wild animals for slaughter, and whole species were hunted to extinction in parts of the empire.

These bloodthirsty spectacles were extremely popular with the Roman people. Tacitus reported, "Few indeed are to be found who talk of any other subjects in their homes, and whenever we enter a classroom, what else is the conversation of the youths."[15] But the gladiatorial games served a purpose beyond mere entertainment. Like the other forms of public entertainment, the games fulfilled both a political and a social function. Certainly, the games served to divert the idle masses from political unrest. It was said of the emperor Trajan that he understood that although the distribution of grain and money satisfied the individual, spectacles were necessary for the "contentment of the masses."

THE ART OF MEDICINE

Although early Romans had no professional physicians, they did possess an art of medicine. Early Roman medicine was essentially herbal. The *paterfamilias* would prepare various remedies to heal wounds and cure illnesses. Knowledge of the healing properties of plants was passed down from generation to generation. This traditional herbal medicine continued to be used in the Early Empire. Of course, numerous recipes for nonillnesses, such as remedies to prevent baldness, were also passed on. One such formula consisted of wine, saffron, pepper, vinegar, *laserpicium* (the queen of Roman medicinal plants), and rat dung.

As in other areas of Roman life, Greek influence was also felt in medicine. At the end of the third century B.C., scientific medicine entered the Roman world through professional practitioners from the Hellenistic world. Doctors became fashionable in Rome, although prejudice against them was never completely abandoned. Many were Greek slaves who belonged to the households of large aristocratic families. The first public doctors in Rome were attached to the Roman army. Military practices were then extended to imperial officials and their families in the provinces and included the establishment of public hospitals. Gladiatorial schools had their own resident doctors as well. In fact, one of the most famous physicians, the Greek Galen (129–199), emerged from the ranks of gladiatorial doctors to become court physician to the emperor Marcus Aurelius. Roman scientific medicine also witnessed the development of numerous specialists. For example, Alcon, the famous surgeon of the Flavian age, specialized in bone diseases and hernia operations.

ROMAN LAW IN THE EARLY EMPIRE

The Early Empire experienced great progress in the study and codification of law. The second and early third centuries A.D. witnessed the "classical age of Roman law," a period in which a number of great jurists classified and compiled basic legal principles that have proved valuable to the Western world. Most jurists emphasized the emperor as the source of law: "What has pleased the emperor has the force of law."

In the "classical age of Roman law," the identification of the law of nations with natural law led to a concept of natural rights. According to the jurist Ulpian (d. 228), natural rights implied that all men are born equal and should therefore be equal before the law. In practice, however, such a principle was not applied, particularly in the third and later centuries.

The Romans, however, did establish standards of justice, applicable to all people, that included principles that we would immediately recognize. A person was regarded as innocent until proven otherwise. People accused of wrongdoing were allowed to defend themselves before a judge. A judge was expected to weigh evidence carefully before arriving at a decision. These principles lived on in Western civilization long after the fall of the Roman Empire.

SLAVES AND THEIR MASTERS

The number of slaves had increased dramatically in the Roman Republic as the empire was expanded through warfare. Consequently, slaves were highly visible in the Early Empire. The households of the rich were filled with slaves. Possessing a large number of slaves was a status symbol; a single residence might include dozens of slaves, serving as hairdressers, footmen, messengers, accountants, secretaries, carpenters, plumbers, librarians, goldsmiths, and doctors as well as ordinary domestic servants. The reliance on slaves, especially as skilled craftspeople, undoubtedly created unemployment among the free population. Some slaves worked at high-status jobs as architects and managers of businesses, while some imperial slaves held positions in the government bureaucracy. Slaves were also used on landed estates.

But the number of slaves probably peaked in the Early Empire. The defensive imperial policies pursued after Augustus led to a decline in the supply of slaves from foreign conquest. Manumission also contributed to the decline in the number of slaves. It had been customary in Rome for "good masters" to free their slaves, especially well-educated ones or good workers. Although freedmen became Roman citizens, they were not given full rights of citizenship. They could vote but not run for office.

Many authors have commented on the supposed advance in humanitarian attitudes toward slaves in the Early Empire, especially in the second century. They argue that the philosophy of Stoicism, with its emphasis on the universality of humanity, had an influence in this direction. Seneca stressed the need for kindness to slaves. Very likely, however, the practical Romans were as much, if not more, concerned about the usefulness of their slaves than about any humanitarian attitudes. New laws in the second century moralized more than they actually improved the condition of slaves. Hadrian, for example, forbade the sale of slaves for immoral or gladiatorial purposes. Such laws had little impact, however, on how masters actually treated their slaves. Despite the changes, there were still instances of slaves murdering their owners, and Romans continued to live in unspoken fear of their slaves (see the box on p. 151).

THE UPPER-CLASS ROMAN FAMILY

By the second century A.D., significant changes were occurring in the Roman family. The foundations of the authority of the *paterfamilias* over his family, which had already begun to weaken in the late Republic, were further undermined. The *paterfamilias* no longer had absolute authority over his children; he could no longer sell his children into slavery or have them put to death. Moreover, the husband's absolute authority over his wife also disappeared, a process that had begun in the late Republic. In the Early Empire, the idea of male guardianship continued to weaken significantly, and by the late second century, it had become a mere formality.

Upper-class Roman women in the Early Empire had considerable freedom and independence. They had acquired the right to own, inherit, and dispose of property. Upper-class women could attend races, the theater, and events in the amphitheater, although in the latter two places they were forced to sit in separate female sections. Moreover, ladies of rank were still accompanied by maids and companions when they went out. Some women operated businesses, such as shipping firms. Women still could not participate in politics, but the Early Empire saw a number of important women who influenced politics through their husbands, including Livia, the wife of Augustus; Agrippina, the mother of Nero; and Plotina, the wife of Trajan.

At the end of the first century and beginning of the second, there was a noticeable decline in the number of children among the upper classes, a trend that had already begun in the late Republic. Especially evident was an increase in childless marriages. Despite imperial laws aimed at increasing the number of children, the low birthrate persisted. Not only did infanticide continue to be practiced, but upper-class Romans also used contraception and abortion to limit their families. There were numerous techniques for contraception. Though highly touted, amulets, magical formulas, and potions to induce temporary sterility proved ineffective, as did the rhythm method, since Roman medical writers believed that a woman was most fertile just when menstruation was ending. A more dependable practice involved the use of oils, ointments, and soft wool to obstruct the opening of the uterus. Contraceptive techniques for males were also advocated. An early version of a condom involved using the bladder of a goat, but it was prohibitively expensive. Although the medical sources do not mention it, the Romans may also have used the ubiquitous coitus interruptus. Abortion was practiced, either

The Roman Fear of Slaves

The lowest stratum of the Roman population consisted of slaves. They were used extensively in households and the court, as craftspeople in industrial enterprises, as business managers, and in numerous other ways. Although some historians have argued that slaves were treated more humanely during the Early Empire, these selections by the Roman historian Tacitus and the Roman statesman Pliny indicate that slaves still rebelled against their masters because of mistreatment. Many masters continued to live in fear of their slaves, as witnessed by the saying, "As many enemies as you have slaves."

■ *Tacitus,* The Annals of Imperial Rome

The City Prefect, Lucius Pedanius Secundus, was murdered by one of his slaves [A.D. 61]. Either Pedanius had refused to free the murderer after agreeing to a price, or the slave, in a homosexual infatuation, found competition from his master intolerable. After the murder, ancient custom required that every slave residing under the same roof must be executed. But a crowd gathered, eager to save so many innocent lives; and rioting began. The senate-house was besieged. Inside, there was feeling against excessive severity, but the majority opposed any change. Among the latter was Gaius Cassius Longinus, who when his turn came spoke as follows. . . .

"An ex-consul has been deliberately murdered by a slave in his own home. None of his fellow-slaves prevented or betrayed the murderer, though the senatorial decree threatening the whole household with execution still stands. Exempt them from the penalty if you like. But then, if the City Prefect was not important enough to be immune, who will be? Who will have enough slaves to protect him if Pedanius' 400 were too few? Who can rely on his household's help if even fear for their own lives does not make them shield us?" [The sentence of death was carried out.]

■ *Pliny the Younger to Acilius*

This horrible affair demands more publicity than a letter—Larcius Macedo, a senator and ex-praetor, has fallen a victim to his own slaves. Admittedly he was a cruel and overbearing master, too ready to forget that his father had been a slave, or perhaps too keenly conscious of it. He was taking a bath in his house at Formiae when suddenly he found himself surrounded; one slave seized him by the throat while the others struck his face and hit him in the chest and stomach and—shocking to say—in his private parts. When they thought he was dead they threw him on to the hot pavement, to make sure he was not still alive. Whether unconscious or feigning to be so, he lay there motionless, thus making them believe that he was quite dead. Only then was he carried out, as if he had fainted with the heat, and received by his slaves who had remained faithful, while his concubines ran up, screaming fanatically. Roused by their cries and revived by the cooler air he opened his eyes and made some movement to show that he was alive, it being now safe to do so. The guilty slaves fled, but most of them have been arrested and a search is being made for the others. Macedo was brought back to life with difficulty, but only for a few days; at least he died with the satisfaction of having revenged himself, for he lived to see the same punishment meted out as for murder. There you see the dangers, outrages, and insults to which we are exposed. No master can feel safe because he is kind and considerate; for it is their brutality, not their reasoning capacity, which leads slaves to murder masters.

by the use of drugs or by surgical instruments. Ovid chastises Corinna: "Ah, women, why will you thrust and pierce with the instrument, and give dire poisons to your children yet unborn?"[16]

The Terrible Third Century

During the reign of Marcus Aurelius, the last of the five good emperors, a number of natural catastrophes struck Rome. Floods of the Tiber, famine, and plague brought back from the east by the army led to considerable loss of population and a shortage of military manpower. To many Romans, these natural disasters seemed to portend an ominous future for Rome. New problems arose soon after the death of Marcus Aurelius.

Unlike the first four good emperors, who chose capable successors by adopting competent men as their sons, Marcus Aurelius allowed his own son, Commodus (180–192), to become emperor. A cruel man, Commodus was a poor choice, and his assassination led to a brief renewal of civil war until Septimius Severus (193–211), who was born in North Africa and spoke Latin with an accent, used his legions to seize power. Septimius Severus' deathbed admonition to his sons "to pay the soldiers, and ignore everyone else" set the tone for the new dynasty he established. The Severan rulers (193–235) began to create a military monarchy. The army was expanded, soldiers' pay was increased, and military officers were appointed to important government positions.

Military monarchy was followed by military anarchy. For a period of almost fifty years, from 235 to 284, the Roman Empire was mired in the chaos of continual civil war as contenders for the imperial throne found that bribing soldiers was the primary way to become emperor. In these five decades, there were twenty-two emperors, only two of whom did not meet a violent death. At the same time, the empire was beset by a series of invasions, no doubt exacerbated by the civil wars. In the east, the Sassanid Persians made inroads into Roman territory. A fitting symbol of Rome's decline was the capture of the Roman emperor Valerian (253–260) by the Persians and his death in captivity, an event previously unheard of in Roman history. Germanic tribes also poured into the empire. The Goths overran the Balkans and moved into Greece and Asia Minor. The Franks advanced into Gaul and Spain. It was not until the reign of Aurelian (270–275) that most of the boundaries were restored.

Invasions, civil wars, and recurrence of the plague came close to causing an economic collapse of the Roman Empire in the third century. The population declined drastically, possibly by as much as one-third. There was a noticeable decline in trade and small industry. The manpower shortage created by the plague affected both military recruiting and the economy. Farm production deteriorated significantly. Fields were ravaged by barbarians and even more often by the defending Roman armies. Many farmers complained that Roman commanders and their soldiers were confiscating produce and livestock. Provincial governors seemed powerless to stop these depredations, and some even joined in the extortion.

The monetary system began to show signs of collapse as a result of debased coinage and the onset of serious inflation. Gold coins disappeared from circulation, and silver coins were diluted. The standard coin, the denarius, was now worth less than half of its first-century value. After further decline, it was replaced by new coins of even less value. Goods began to replace money as a medium of exchange.

Armies were needed more than ever, but financial strains made it difficult to enlist and pay the necessary soldiers. Whereas in the second century the Roman army had been recruited among the inhabitants of frontier provinces, by the mid-third century, the state had to rely on hiring barbarians to fight under Roman commanders. These soldiers had no understanding of Roman traditions and no real attachment to either the empire or the emperors.

The Restored Empire of the Fourth Century

At the end of the third century and beginning of the fourth, the Roman Empire gained a new lease on life through the efforts of two strong emperors, Diocletian and Constantine, who restored order and stability. The empire was virtually transformed into a new state, the so-called Late Empire, which included a new governmental structure, a rigid economic and social system, and a new state religion—Christianity.

Diocletian and Constantine: Political and Military Reforms

The emperor Diocletian (284–305) created a new administrative system for the restructured empire. The number of provinces was increased to almost one hundred by creating smaller districts superintended by more officials. In turn, the provinces were grouped into twelve dioceses, each headed by an official called a vicar. The twelve dioceses were grouped into four prefectures (see Map 6.4), and the entire Roman Empire was divided into two parts, east and west. Each part contained two prefectures and was ruled by an "Augustus." Diocletian ruled the east, and Maximian, a strong military commander, the west. Each Augustus was assisted by a chief lieutenant or "vice-emperor" called a "Caesar," who theoretically would eventually succeed to the position of Augustus. This new system was called the tetrarchy (rule by four). Diocletian had obviously come to believe that one man was incapable of ruling such an enormous empire, especially in view of the barbarian invasions of the third century. Each of the four tetrarchs—two Augusti and two Caesars—resided in a different administrative capital. Diocletian, for example, established his base at Nicomedia in Bithynia. Despite the appearance of four-man rule, however, it is important to note that Diocletian's military seniority enabled him to claim a higher status and hold the ultimate authority.

Soon after Diocletian's retirement in 305, a new struggle for power ensued. The victory of Constantine (306–337) in 312 led to his control of the entire west, although he continued to share imperial authority with Licinius, a fellow emperor. Twelve years later, in 324, Constantine's army routed Licinius' forces, and Constantine established himself as the sole ruler.

Constantine continued and even expanded the autocratic policies of Diocletian. Under these two rulers, the Roman Empire was transformed into a system where the emperor had far more personal power than Augustus, Trajan, or any of the other emperors had had during the *Pax Romana*. The emperor, now clothed in jewel-bedecked robes of gold and blue, was seen as a divinely sanctioned monarch whose will was law. Government officials were humble servants required to kneel before the emperor and kiss his robe. The Roman senate was stripped of any power and became merely the city council for Rome.

Diocletian and Constantine greatly strengthened and enlarged the administrative bureaucracies of the Roman Empire. Henceforth, civil and military bureaucracies were sharply separated. Each contained a hierarchy of officials who exercised control at the various levels. The emperor presided over both hierarchies and served as the only link between them. New titles of nobility—such as *illustres* ("illustrious ones") and *illustrissimi* ("most illustrious ones")—were instituted to dignify the holders of positions in the civil and military bureaucracies. Additional military reforms were also instituted. The army was enlarged to half a million men, including barbarian units. Mobile units were established that could be quickly moved to support frontier troops when the borders were threatened.

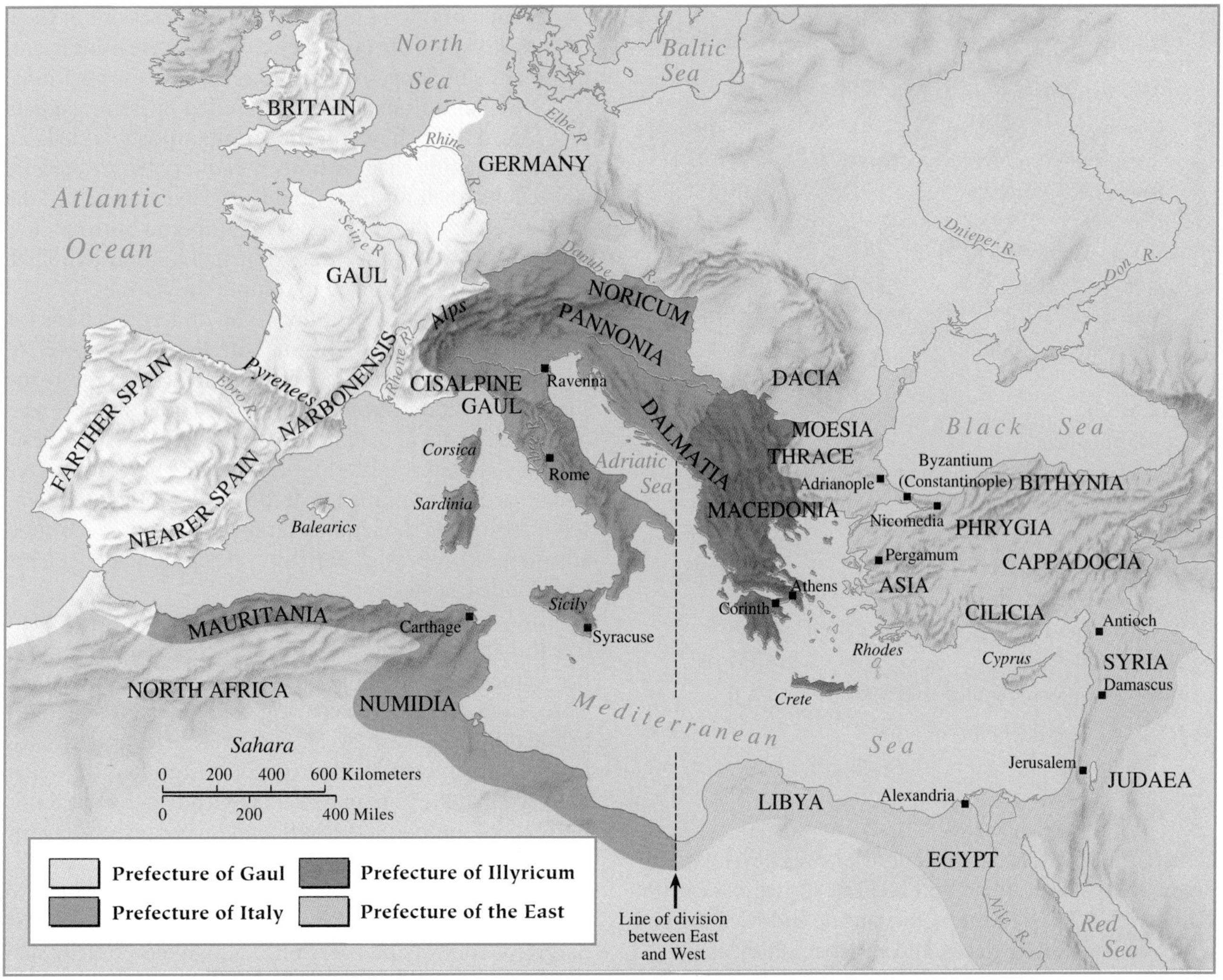

Map 6.4 Divisions of the Restored Roman Empire, c. 300. Diocletian imposed order and a new economic and administrative structure on the Late Empire. He divided the Roman Empire into four regions, each ruled by either an "Augustus" or a "Caesar," although Diocletian retained supreme power. Compare this map with Map 6.1. ■ How much territory was lost by the time of Diocletian?

Constantine was especially interested in building programs despite the strain they placed on the budget. Much of the construction took place in the provinces, since Rome had become merely a symbolic capital. It was no longer an imperial administrative center, as it was considered too far from the frontiers. Between 324 and 330, Constantine engaged in his biggest project, the construction of a new capital city in the east on the site of the Greek city of Byzantium on the shores of the Bosporus. Eventually renamed

The Emperor Constantine. Constantine played an important role in restoring order and stability to the Roman Empire at the beginning of the fourth century. This marble head of Constantine, which is 8 feet 6 inches high, was part of an enormous seated statue of the emperor in Rome. Constantine used these awe-inspiring statues throughout the empire to build support for imperial policies.

Scala/Art Resource, NY

CHRONOLOGY

Chief Events and Rulers of the Late Empire

Commodus	180–192
Military monarchy (Severan dynasty)	193–235
Septimius Severus	193–211
Caracalla	211–217
Military anarchy	235–284
Decius	249–251
Valerian	253–260
Aurelian	270–275
Diocletian	284–305
Constantine	306–337
Edict of Milan	313
Construction of Constantinople	324–330
Julian	360–363
Valens	364–378
Theodosius "the Great"	378–395
Division of the empire	395
Visigoths sack Rome	410
Vandals sack Rome	455
Odoacer deposes Romulus Augustulus	476

Constantinople (modern Istanbul), it was developed for defensive reasons; it had an excellent strategic location. Calling it his "New Rome," Constantine endowed the city with a forum, large palaces, and a vast amphitheater.

Diocletian and Constantine: Economic, Social, and Cultural Trends

The political and military reforms of Diocletian and Constantine greatly enlarged two institutions—the army and the civil service—that drained most of the public funds. Although more revenues were needed to pay for the military and the bureaucracy, the population was not growing, so the tax base could not be expanded. Diocletian and Constantine devised new economic and social policies to deal with these financial burdens. Like their political policies, these economic and social policies were all based on coercion and loss of individual freedom (see the box on p. 155).

To fight inflation, in 301 Diocletian resorted to issuing an edict that established maximum wages and prices for the entire empire. It was applied mostly in the east, but despite severe penalties, like most wage and price controls, it was largely unenforceable. The decline in circulation of coins led Diocletian to collect taxes and make government payments in produce. Constantine, however, managed to introduce a new gold coin—the solidus—and new silver coins that remained in circulation during his reign.

In the third century, the city councils, which had formed one of the most important administrative units of the empire, had begun to decline. Since the *curiales* (the city councillors) were forced to pay expenses out of their own pocket when the taxes they collected were insufficient, the wealthy no longer wanted to serve in these positions. Diocletian and Constantine responded by issuing edicts that forced the rich to continue in their posts as *curiales*, virtually making the positions hereditary. Some *curiales* realized that their fortunes would be wiped out and fled the cities to escape the clutches of the imperial bureaucracy. If caught, however, they were returned to their cities like runaway slaves and forced to resume their duties.

Coercion also came to form the underlying basis for numerous occupations in the Late Roman Empire. To ensure the tax base and keep the empire going despite the shortage of labor, the emperors issued edicts that forced people to remain in their designated vocations. Hence basic jobs, such as bakers and shippers, became hereditary. Free tenant farmers continued to decline and soon found themselves bound to the land by large landowners who took advantage of depressed agricultural conditions to enlarge their landed estates.

In addition to facing increased restrictions on their freedom, the lower classes were burdened with enormous taxes, since the wealthiest classes in the Late Roman Empire were either exempt from paying taxes or evaded them by bribing the tax collectors. These tax pressures undermined lower-class support for the regime. A fifth-century writer reported that the Roman peasants welcomed the Visigothic invaders of southern Gaul as liberators because the enemy was more lenient to them than the tax collectors.

In general, the economic and social policies of Diocletian and Constantine were based on an unprecedented degree of control and coercion. Though temporarily successful, in the long run such authoritarian policies stifled the very vitality the Late Empire needed to revive its sagging fortunes.

The Transformation of the Roman World: The Development of Christianity

The rise of Christianity marks a fundamental break with the dominant values of the Greco-Roman world. Christian views of God, human beings, and the world were quite different from those of the Greeks and Romans. Nevertheless, to understand the rise of Christianity, we must first examine both the religious environment of the Roman world and the Jewish background from which Christianity emerged.

The Religious World of the Roman Empire

Augustus had taken a number of steps to revive the Roman state religion, which had declined during the turmoil of the late Republic. The official state religion focused on the worship of a pantheon of Greco-Roman gods and goddesses, including

Compulsory Services in the Late Empire

The political, economic, and social policies of the restored empire under Diocletian and Constantine were based on coercion. This is especially evident in the edicts that forced people to remain in their occupations or in the city magistracies. These excerpts are taken from the Theodosian Code of 438, a compilation of imperial edicts going back to the reign of Constantine. These examples illustrate the plight of city councillors, shipmasters, bakers, and peasants.

Decrees from the Theodosian Code

Since we have learned that the municipal councils are being left deserted by persons who, though subject to them through origin, are requesting military service for themselves through supplications [to the emperor] and are running away to the legions and the various government offices, we order all municipal councils to be advised that if they catch any persons in government services less than twenty years who have either fled from [the duties of] their origin or, rejecting nomination [to municipal office], have enrolled themselves in the military service, they shall drag such person back to the municipal councils.

If any shipmaster by birth becomes captain of a lighter, he shall nonetheless continue right along to remain in the same group in which his parents appear to have been.

No breadmaker or any of his descendants shall be allowed to pass from his service by marriage with private persons or with persons of the stage or with persons held bound by the profession of charioteer, even if the assent of all the breadmakers should agree to such action.

Any person whatsoever in whose possession a *colonus* [tenant farmer] belonging to another is found not only shall restore the said *colonus* to his place of origin but shall also assume the capitation tax on him for the time [that he had him]. And as for *coloni* themselves, it will be proper for such as contemplate flight to be bound with chains to a servile status, so that by virtue of such condemnation to servitude they may be compelled to fulfill the duties that befit free men.

Jupiter, Juno, Minerva, and Mars. Observance of proper ritual by state priests theoretically brought the Romans into proper relationship with the gods and guaranteed security, peace, and prosperity. The polytheistic Romans were extremely tolerant of other religions. The Romans allowed the worship of native gods and goddesses throughout their provinces and even adopted some of the local gods. In addition, the imperial cult of Roma and Augustus was developed to bolster support for the emperors. After Augustus, dead emperors deified by the Roman senate were included in the official imperial cult.

The desire for a more emotional spiritual experience led many people to the mystery religions of the Hellenistic east, which flooded into the western Roman world during the Early Empire. The mystery religions offered secret teachings that supposedly brought special benefits. They promised their followers advantages unavailable through Roman religion: an entry into a higher world of reality and the promise of a future life superior to the present one. They also featured elaborate rituals with deep emotional appeal. By participating in their ceremonies and performing their rites, an adherent could achieve communion with spiritual beings and undergo purification that opened the door to life after death.

Although many mystery cults vied for attention in the Roman world, perhaps the most important was Mithraism. Mithra was the chief agent of Ahuramazda, the supreme god of light in Persian Zoroastrianism (see Chapter 2). In the Roman world, Mithra came to be identified with the sun god and was known by his Roman title of the Unconquered Sun. Mithraism had spread rapidly in Rome and the western provinces by the second century A.D. and was especially favored by soldiers who viewed Mithra as their patron deity. It was a religion for men only and featured an initiation ceremony in which devotees were baptized in the blood of a sacrificed bull. Mithraists paid homage to the sun on the first day of the week (Sunday), commemorated the sun's birthday around December 25, and celebrated ceremonial meals.

The Jewish Background

Jesus of Nazareth was a Palestinian Jew who was condemned to death by Pontius Pilate, the procurator of the Roman province of Judaea, which embraced the lands of the old Jewish kingdom of Judah (see Chapter 2). Christianity emerged out of Judaism, and it is to the Jewish political-religious world that we must turn to find the beginnings of Christianity.

In Hellenistic times, the Jewish people had enjoyed considerable independence under their Seleucid rulers (see Chapter 4). Roman involvement with the Jews began in 63 B.C., and by A.D. 6, Judaea had been made a province and placed under the direction of a Roman procurator. But unrest continued, augmented by divisions among the Jews themselves. The Sadducees favored a rigid adherence to Hebrew law, rejected the possibility of personal immortality, and favored cooperation with the Romans. The Pharisees adhered strictly to Jewish ritual and, although they wanted Judaea to be free from Roman control, did not advocate violent means to achieve this goal. The Essenes were a Jewish sect that lived in a religious community near the Dead Sea. As revealed in the Dead Sea Scrolls, a collection of documents first discovered in 1947, the Essenes, like many other Jews, awaited a Messiah who would save Israel from oppression,

Christian Ideals: The Sermon on the Mount

Christianity was simply one of many religions competing for attention in the Roman Empire during the first and second centuries. The rise of Christianity marked a fundamental break with the value system of the upper-class elites who dominated the world of classical antiquity. As these excerpts from the Sermon on the Mount in the Gospel of Matthew illustrate, Christians emphasized humility, charity, brotherly love, and a belief in the inner being and a spiritual kingdom superior to this material world. These values and principles were not those of classical Greco-Roman civilization as exemplified in the words and deeds of its leaders.

The Gospel According to Matthew

Now when he saw the crowds, he went up on a mountainside and sat down. His disciples came to him, and he began to teach them saying:

Blessed are the poor in spirit: for theirs is the kingdom of heaven.
Blessed are those who mourn: for they will be comforted.
Blessed are the meek: for they will inherit the earth.
Blessed are those who hunger and thirst for righteousness: for they will be filled.
Blessed are the merciful: for they will be shown mercy.
Blessed are the pure in heart: for they will see God.
Blessed are the peacemakers: for they will be called sons of God.
Blessed are those who are persecuted because of righteousness: for theirs is the kingdom of heaven. . . .

You have heard that it was said, "Eye for eye, and tooth for tooth." But I tell you, Do not resist an evil person. If someone strikes you on the right cheek, turn to him the other also. . . .

You have heard that it was said, "Love your neighbor, and hate your enemy." But I tell you, Love your enemies and pray for those who persecute you. . . .

Do not store up for yourselves treasures on earth, where moth and rust destroy, and where thieves break in and steal. But store up for yourselves treasures in heaven, where moth and rust do not destroy, and where thieves do not break in and steal. For where your treasure is, there your heart will be also. . . .

No one can serve two masters. Either he will hate the one and love the other, or he will be devoted to the one and despise the other. You cannot serve both God and Money.

Therefore I tell you, do not worry about your life, what you will eat or drink; or about your body, what you will wear. Is not life more important than food, and the body more important than clothes? Look at the birds of the air; they do not sow or reap to store away in barns, and yet your heavenly Father feeds them. Are you not much more valuable than they? . . . So do not worry, saying, What shall we eat? or What shall we drink? or What shall we wear? For the pagans run after all these things, and your heavenly Father knows that you need them. But seek first his kingdom and his righteousness, and all these things will be given to you as well.

usher in the kingdom of God, and establish a paradise on earth. A fourth group, the Zealots, were militant extremists who advocated the violent overthrow of Roman rule. A Jewish revolt in A.D. 66 was crushed by the Romans four years later. The Jewish Temple in Jerusalem was destroyed, and Roman power once more stood supreme in Judaea.

The Rise of Christianity

In the midst of the confusion and conflict in Judaea, Jesus of Nazareth (c. 6 B.C.–A.D. 30) began his public preaching. Jesus grew up in Galilee, an important center of the militant Zealots. Jesus' message was basically simple. He reassured his fellow Jews that he did not plan to undermine their traditional religion: "Do not think that I have come to abolish the Law or the Prophets; I have not come to abolish them but to fulfill them."[17] According to Jesus, what was important was not strict adherence to the letter of the law and attention to rules and prohibitions but the transformation of the inner person: "So in everything, do to others what you would have them do to you, for this sums up the Law and the Prophets."[18] God's command was a simple one—to love God and one another: "Love the Lord your God with all your heart and with all your soul and with all your mind and with all your strength. The second is this: Love your neighbor as yourself."[19] In the Sermon on the Mount (see the box above), Jesus presented the ethical concepts—humility, charity, and brotherly love—that would form the basis for the value system of medieval Western civilization. As we have seen, these were not the values of classical Greco-Roman civilization.

Although some people welcomed Jesus as the Messiah who would save Israel from oppression and establish God's kingdom on earth, Jesus spoke of a heavenly kingdom, not an earthly one: "My kingdom is not of this world."[20] Consequently, he disappointed the radicals. At the same time, conservative religious leaders believed Jesus was another false Messiah who was undermining respect for traditional Jewish religion. To the Roman authorities of Palestine and their local allies, the Nazarene was a potential revolutionary who might transform Jewish expectations of a messianic kingdom into a revolt against Rome. Therefore, Jesus found himself denounced on many sides and was given over to the Roman authorities. The procurator Pontius Pilate ordered his crucifixion. But that did not solve the problem. A few loyal followers of Jesus spread the story that he had overcome death, been resurrected, and then ascended into heaven. The belief in Jesus' resurrection became an important tenet of Christian doctrine. Jesus was now hailed as the "anointed one" (*Christ* in Greek), the Messiah who would return and usher in the kingdom of God on earth.

Christianity began, then, as a religious movement within Judaism and was viewed that way by Roman authorities for many decades. Although tradition holds that one of Jesus' disciples, Peter, founded the Christian church at Rome, the most important figure in early Christianity after Jesus was Paul of Tarsus (c. 5–c. 67). Paul reached out to non-Jews and transformed Christianity from a Jewish sect into a broader religious movement.

Called the "second founder of Christianity," Paul was a Jewish Roman citizen who had been strongly influenced by Hellenistic Greek culture. He believed that the message of Jesus should be preached not only to Jews but to Gentiles (non-Jews) as well. Paul was responsible for founding Christian communities throughout Asia Minor and along the shores of the Aegean.

It was Paul who provided a universal foundation for the spread of Jesus' ideas. He taught that Jesus was, in effect, a savior-God, the son of God, who had come to earth to save all humans, who were basically sinners as a result of Adam's original sin of disobedience against God. By his death, Jesus had atoned for the sins of all humans and made it possible for all men and women to experience a new beginning with the potential for individual salvation. By accepting Jesus as their savior, they, too, could be saved.

At first, Christianity spread slowly. Although the teachings of early Christianity were mostly disseminated by the preaching of convinced Christians, written materials also appeared. Paul had written a series of letters, or epistles, outlining Christian beliefs for different Christian communities. Some of Jesus' disciples may also have preserved some of the sayings of the master in writing and would have passed on personal memories that became the basis of the written gospels—the "good news" concerning Jesus—which attempted to give a record of Jesus' life and teachings and formed the core of the New Testament. Although Jerusalem was the first center of Christianity, its destruction by the Romans in A.D. 70 left individual Christian churches with considerable independence. By 100, Christian churches had been established in most of the major cities of the east and in some places in the western part of the empire. Many early Christians came from the ranks of Hellenized Jews and the Greek-speaking populations of the east. But in the second and third centuries, an increasing number of followers were Latin-speaking people. A Latin translation of the Greek New Testament that appeared soon after 200 aided this process.

Early Christian groups met in private homes in the evening to share a common meal called an *agape* or love feast and to celebrate what became known as the sacrament of the eucharist or Lord's Supper—the communal celebration of Jesus' Last Supper:

> While they were eating, Jesus took bread, gave thanks and broke it, and gave it to the disciples, saying, Take and eat; this is my body. Then he took the cup, gave thanks, and offered it to them, saying, Drink from it, all of you. This is my blood of the covenant, which is poured out for many for the forgiveness of sins.[21]

Early Christian communities were loosely organized, with both men and women playing significant roles. Some women held important positions, often as preachers. Local churches were under the leadership of boards of elders (presbyters), but by the beginning of the second century, officials known as bishops came to exercise considerable authority over the presbyters. These bishops based their

Jesus and His Apostles. Pictured is a fourth-century fresco from a Roman catacomb depicting Jesus and his apostles. Catacombs were underground cemeteries where early Christians buried their dead. Christian tradition holds that in times of imperial repression, Christians withdrew to the catacombs to pray and hide.

Scala/Art Resource, NY

superior position on apostolic succession—as the successors to Jesus' original twelve apostles, they were living representatives of Jesus' power. As Ignatius of Antioch wrote in 107, "It is clear that we must regard a bishop as the Lord Himself. . . . Your clergy . . . are attuned to their bishop like the strings of a harp, and the result is a hymn of praise to Jesus Christ from minds that are in unison."[22] Bishops were men, a clear indication that by the second century A.D., most Christian communities were following the views of Paul that Christian women should be subject to Christian men.

Although some of the fundamental values of Christianity differed markedly from those of the Greco-Roman world, the Romans initially did not pay much attention to the Christians, whom they regarded at first as simply another sect of Judaism. The structure of the Roman Empire itself aided the growth of Christianity. Christian missionaries, including some of Jesus' original twelve disciples or apostles, used Roman roads to travel throughout the empire spreading their "good news."

As time passed, however, the Roman attitude toward Christianity began to change. As we have seen, the Romans were tolerant of other religions except when they threatened public order or public morals. Many Romans came to view Christians as harmful to the order of the Roman state. These views were often based on misperceptions. The practice of the Lord's Supper, for example, led to rumors that Christians practiced horrible crimes, such as the ritualistic murder of children. While we know these rumors are untrue, some Romans believed them and used them to incite people against the Christians during times of crisis. Moreover, because Christians held their meetings in secret and seemed to be connected to Christian groups in other areas, the government could view them as potentially dangerous to the state.

Some Romans felt that Christians were overly exclusive and hence harmful to the community and public order. The Christians did not recognize other gods and therefore abstained from public festivals honoring these deities. Finally, Christians refused to participate in the worship of the state gods and imperial cult. Since the Romans regarded these as important to the state, the Christians' refusal undermined the security of the state and hence constituted an act of treason, punishable by death. It was also proof of atheism (disbelief in the gods) and subject to punishment on those grounds. But to the Christians, who believed there was only one real God, the worship of state gods and the emperors was idolatry and would endanger their own salvation.

Roman persecution of Christians in the first and second centuries was never systematic but sporadic and local. Persecution began during the reign of Nero. After the fire that destroyed much of Rome, the emperor used the Christians as scapegoats, accusing them of arson and hatred of the human race and subjecting them to cruel deaths in Rome. In the second century, Christians were often ignored as harmless. By the end of the reigns of the five good emperors, Christians still represented a small minority, but one of considerable strength. That strength lay in their conviction of the rightness of their path, a conviction that had been reinforced by the willingness of the first Christians to become martyrs for their faith.

The Growth of Christianity

The sporadic persecution of Christians by the Romans in the first and second centuries had done nothing to stop the growth of Christianity. It had, in fact, served to strengthen Christianity as an institution in the second and third centuries by causing it to shed the loose structure of the first century and move toward a more centralized organization of its various church communities. Crucial to this change was the emerging role of the bishops. Though still chosen by the community, bishops began to assume more control, with the bishop serving as leader and the presbyters emerging as clergy subject to the bishop's authority. By the third century, bishops were nominated by the clergy, simply approved by the congregation, and then officially ordained into office. The Christian church was creating a well-defined hierarchical structure in which the bishops and clergy were salaried officers separate from the laity or regular church members.

Christianity grew slowly in the first century, took root in the second, and had spread widely by the third. Why was Christianity able to attract so many followers? Historians are not really sure but have offered several answers. Certainly, the Christian message had much to offer the Roman world. The promise of salvation, made possible by Jesus' death and resurrection, had immense appeal in a world full of suffering and injustice. Christianity seemed to imbue life with a meaning and purpose beyond the simple material things of everyday reality. Second, Christianity was not entirely unfamiliar. It could be viewed as simply another eastern mystery religion, offering immortality as the result of the sacrificial death of a savior-god. At the same time, it offered advantages that the other mystery religions lacked. Jesus had been a human figure, not a mythological one, such as Isis or Mithra. Moreover, Christianity had universal appeal. Unlike Mithraism, it was not restricted to men. Furthermore, it did not require a difficult or expensive initiation rite as other mystery religions did. Initiation was accomplished simply by baptism—a purification by water—by which one entered into a personal relationship with Jesus. In addition, Christianity gave new meaning to life and offered what the Roman state religions could not—a personal relationship with God and a link to higher worlds.

Finally, Christianity fulfilled the human need to belong. Christians formed communities bound to one another in which people could express their love by helping each other and offering assistance to the poor, sick, widows, and orphans. Christianity satisfied the need to belong in a way that the huge, impersonal, and remote Roman Empire could never do.

Christianity proved attractive to all classes. The promise of eternal life was for all—rich, poor, aristocrats, slaves, men, and women. As Paul stated in his Epistle to the Colossians: "And [you] have put on the new self, which is being renewed in knowledge in the image of its Creator. Here there is no Greek nor Jew, circumcised or uncircumcised, barbarian, Scythian, slave or free, but Christ is all, and is in all."[23] Although it did not call for revolution or social upheaval, Christianity emphasized a sense of spiritual equality for all people.

Many women found that Christianity offered them new roles and new forms of companionship with other women. Christian women fostered the new religion in their own homes and preached their convictions to other people in their towns and villages. Many also died for their faith. Perpetua (d. 203) was an aristocratic woman who converted to Christianity. Her pagan family begged her to renounce her new faith, but she refused. Arrested by the Roman authorities, she chose instead to die for her faith and was one of a group of Christians who were slaughtered by wild beasts in the arena at Carthage on March 7, 203.

As the Christian church became more organized, two emperors in the third century responded with more systematic persecutions. The emperor Decius (249–251) blamed the Christians for the disasters befalling the Roman Empire in the terrible third century: it was they who had failed to acknowledge the state gods and consequently brought on the gods' retribution against the Romans. Moreover, as the administrative organization of the church grew, Christianity appeared to Decius even more like a state within a state that was undermining the empire. Accordingly, he initiated the first systematic persecution of Christians. All citizens were required to appear before their local magistrates and offer sacrifices to the Roman gods. Christians of course refused to do so. Decius' scheme, however, failed to work. Local officials did not cooperate, and Decius' reign was also not that long. The last great persecution was by Diocletian at the beginning of the fourth century, but by then it was too late. Christianity had become too strong to be eradicated by force. Most pagans had come to accept the existence of Christianity.

In the fourth century, Christianity prospered as never before. The emperor Constantine played an important role in Christianity's status. His support for Christianity supposedly began in 312, when his army was about to fight a crucial battle against the forces of Maxentius at the Milvian Bridge, which crossed the Tiber River just north of the city of Rome. According to the traditional story, before the battle, Constantine saw a vision of a Christian cross with the words, "In this sign you will conquer." Having won the battle, the story goes, Constantine was convinced of the power of the Christian God. Although he was not baptized until the end of his life, in 313 he issued the famous Edict of Milan, which officially tolerated the existence of Christianity. After Constantine, the emperors were Christian with the exception of Julian (360–363), who tried briefly to restore the traditional Greco-Roman polytheistic religion. But he died in battle, and his reign was too short to make a difference. Under Theodosius "the Great" (378–395), Christianity was made the official religion of the Roman Empire. Once in control, Christian leaders used their influence and power to outlaw pagan religious practices. Christianity had triumphed.

The Fall of the Western Roman Empire

The restored empire of Diocletian and Constantine limped along for more than a century. After Constantine, the empire continued to divide into western and eastern parts, a division that was made complete in 395, when the western and eastern parts of the empire became two independent states.

The west came under increasing pressure from invading barbarian forces. The major breakthrough into the Roman Empire came in the second half of the fourth century. Ferocious warriors from Asia, known as Huns, moved into eastern Europe and put pressure on the Germanic Visigoths, who in turn moved south and west, crossed the Danube into Roman territory, and settled down as Roman allies. But the Visigoths soon revolted, and the Roman attempt to stop them at Adrianople in 378 led to a crushing defeat and the death of the emperor Valens (364–378).

Increasing numbers of barbarians now crossed the frontiers. In 410, the Visigoths under Alaric sacked Rome. Vandals poured into southern Spain and Africa, Visigoths into Spain and Gaul. The Vandals crossed into Italy from North Africa and sacked Rome in 455. Twenty-one years later, the western emperor Romulus Augustulus (475–476) was deposed, and a series of Germanic kingdoms replaced the Roman Empire in the west while the Eastern Roman Empire continued with its center at Constantinople.

The end of the Roman Empire has given rise to numerous theories that attempt to provide a single, all-encompassing reason for the "decline and fall of the Roman Empire." These include the following: Christianity's emphasis on a spiritual kingdom undermined Roman military virtues and patriotism, traditional Roman values declined as non-Italians gained prominence in the empire, poisoning from lead water pipes and cups caused a mental decline, plague killed one-tenth of the population, Rome failed to advance technologically because of slavery, and Rome was unable to achieve a workable political system. There may be an element of truth in each of these theories, but each of them has also been challenged. History is an intricate web of relationships, causes, and effects. No single explanation will ever suffice to explain complex historical events. One thing is clear: the Roman army in the west was simply not able to fend off the hordes of people invading Italy and Gaul. In contrast, the Eastern Roman Empire, which would survive for another thousand years, remained largely free of invasion.

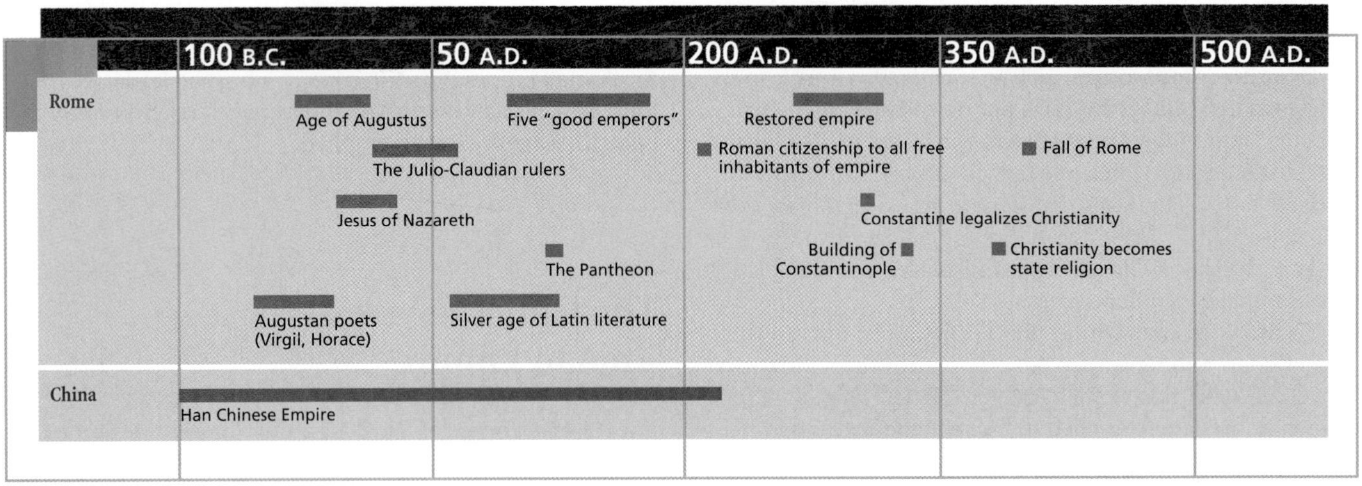

Conclusion

The Roman Republic had created one of the largest empires in antiquity, but its republican institutions had proved inadequate for the task of ruling an empire. After a series of bloody civil wars, Augustus created a new order that ruled the empire in an orderly fashion. His successors established a Roman imperial state.

Like its contemporary, the Han Empire in China, however, the Roman Empire eventually faced serious problems. Both empires suffered from overexpansion, and both fortified their long borders with walls, forts, and military garrisons to guard against invasions by nomadic peoples. Both empires were eventually overcome by these peoples: the Han dynasty was weakened by the incursions of the Xiongnu, and the Western Roman Empire eventually collapsed in the face of invasions by the Germanic peoples. Nevertheless, a significant difference between these two empires remained. Although the Han dynasty collapsed, the Chinese imperial tradition, along with the class structure and set of values that sustained it, continued, and the Chinese empire, under new dynasties, continued well into the twentieth century as a single political entity.

The Roman Empire, by contrast, collapsed and lived on only as an idea, although Roman achievements were bequeathed to the future. The Romance languages of today (French, Italian, Spanish, Portuguese, and Romanian) are based on Latin. Western practices of impartial justice and trial by jury owe much to Roman law. As great builders, the Romans left monuments to their skills throughout Europe, some of which, such as aqueducts and roads, are still in use today. Aspects of Roman administrative practices survived in the Western world for centuries. The Romans also preserved the intellectual heritage of the Greco-Roman world of antiquity. Nevertheless, while many aspects of the Roman world would continue, as we shall see in the next chapter, the heirs of Rome created new civilizations—European, Islamic, and Byzantine—that would dominate the Western world for centuries to come.

Notes

1. Livy, *The Early History of Rome,* trans. Aubrey de Sélincourt (Harmondsworth, England, 1960), p. 35.
2. Tacitus, *The Annals of Imperial Rome,* trans. Michael Grant (Harmondsworth, England, 1956), p. 30.
3. Velleius Paterculus, *Compendium of Roman History,* trans. Frederick Shipley (Cambridge, Mass., 1967), 2.117.
4. Tacitus, *Annals of Imperial Rome,* p. 37.
5. Virgil, *The Aeneid,* trans. C. Day Lewis (Garden City, N.Y., 1952), p. 154.
6. Horace, *Satires,* in *The Complete Works of Horace,* trans. Lord Dunsany and Michael Oakley (London, 1961), 1.1.
7. Ibid., 1.3.
8. Livy, *Early History of Rome,* p. 18.
9. Tacitus, *Annals of Imperial Rome,* p. 31.
10. Tacitus, *The Histories,* trans. Kenneth Wallesley (Harmondsworth, England, 1964), p. 23.
11. Seneca, *Letters from a Stoic,* trans. Robin Campbell (Harmondsworth, England, 1969), let. 5.
12. Tacitus, *Annals of Imperial Rome,* p. 147.
13. Juvenal, *The Sixteen Satires,* trans. Peter Green (Harmondsworth, England, 1967), satire 7, p. 171.
14. Ibid., satire 10, p. 207.
15. Tacitus, *A Dialogue on Oratory,* in *The Complete Works of Tacitus,* trans. Alfred Church and William Brodribb (New York, 1942), 29, p. 758.
16. Ovid, *The Amores,* trans. Grant Showerman (Cambridge, Mass., 1963), 2.14.26–27.
17. Matthew 5:17.
18. Matthew 7:12.

19. Mark 12:30–31.
20. John 18:36.
21. Matthew 26:26–28.
22. *Early Christian Writings* (Harmondsworth, England, 1968), pp. 76–77.
23. Colossians 3:10–11.

Suggestions for Further Reading

For a general account of the Roman Empire, see J. Boardman, J. Griffin, and O. Murray, eds., *The Oxford History of the Roman World* (Oxford, 1991). Good surveys of the Early Empire include P. Garnsey and R. P. Saller, *The Roman Empire: Economy, Society and Culture* (London, 1987); C. Wells, *The Roman Empire,* 2d ed. (London, 1992); J. Wacher, *The Roman Empire* (London, 1987); and F. Millar, *The Roman Empire and Its Neighbours,* 2d ed. (London, 1981).

Studies of Roman emperors of the first and second centuries include D. Shotter, *Augustus Caesar* (London, 1991); R. Seager, *Tiberius* (London, 1972); A. Barrett, *Caligula: The Corruption of Power* (New Haven, Conn., 1990); A. Momigliano, *Claudius: The Emperor and His Achievement,* trans. W. D. Hogarth (Cambridge, 1961); M. Griffin, *Nero: The End of a Dynasty* (London, 1984); and M. Hammond, *The Antonine Monarchy* (Rome, 1959). For brief biographies of all the Roman emperors, see M. Grant, *The Roman Emperors* (New York, 1985).

The Roman army is examined in J. B. Campbell, *The Emperor and the Roman Army* (Oxford, 1984). On the provinces and Roman foreign policy, see E. N. Luttwak, *The Grand Strategy of the Roman Empire from the First Century A.D. to the Third* (Baltimore, 1976); B. Isaac, *The Limits of Empire: The Roman Empire in the East* (Oxford, 1990); and S. L. Dyson, *The Creation of the Roman Frontier* (Princeton, N.J., 1985).

A good survey of Roman literature can be found in R. M. Ogilvie, *Roman Literature and Society* (Harmondsworth, England, 1980). More specialized studies include R. O. Lyne, *The Latin Love Poets from Catullus to Horace* (Oxford, 1980), and K. Galinsky, *Augustan Culture* (Princeton, N.J., 1996).

A survey of Roman art can be found in D. E. Strong, *Roman Art* (Harmondsworth, England, 1976). Architecture is covered in the standard work by J. B. Ward-Perkins, *Roman Imperial Architecture* (Harmondsworth, England, 1981).

Various aspects of Roman society are covered in L. Adkins and R. A. Adkins, *Handbook to Life in Ancient Rome* (New York, 1994). Also useful on urban life is J. E. Stambaugh, *The Ancient Roman City* (Baltimore, 1988). On public festivals, see P. Veyne, *Bread and Circuses* (London, 1992). On the gladiators, see T. Wiedemann, *Emperors and Gladiators* (New York, 1992). Studies on Roman women include J. P. V. D. Balsdon, *Roman Women: Their History and Habits* (London, 1969), and S. B. Pomeroy, *Goddesses, Whores, Wives, and Slaves: Women in Classical Antiquity* (New York, 1975), pp. 149–226. On slavery, see K. Bradley, *Slavery and Society at Rome* (New York, 1994).

For a general introduction to early Christianity, see J. Court and K. Court, *The New Testament World* (Cambridge, 1990). Useful works on early Christianity include W. A. Meeks, *The First Urban Christians* (New Haven, Conn., 1983); W. H. C. Frend, *The Rise of Christianity* (Philadelphia, 1984); and R. MacMullen, *Christianizing the Roman Empire* (New Haven, Conn., 1984). On Christian women, see D. M. Scholer, ed., *Women in Early Christianity* (New York, 1993), and R. Kraemer, *Her Share of the Blessings: Women's Religion Among the Pagans, Jews and Christians in the Graeco-Roman World* (Oxford, 1995).

The classic work on the "decline and fall" of the Roman Empire is E. Gibbon, *The Decline and Fall of the Roman Empire,* J. B. Bury ed. (London, 1909–1914). Also valuable is A. Cameron, *The Later Roman Empire* (Cambridge, Mass., 1993). On the fourth century, see M. Grant, *Constantine the Great: The Man and His Times* (New York, 1993), and T. D. Barnes, *The New Empire of Diocletian and Constantine* (Cambridge, Mass., 1982). Recent studies analyzing the aristocratic circles, the barbarian invasions, and the military problem include E. A. Thompson, *Romans and Barbarians* (Madison, Wis., 1982); A. Ferrill, *The Fall of the Roman Empire: The Military Explanation* (London, 1986); and J. M. O'Flynn, *Generalissimos of the Western Roman Empire* (Edmonton, Canada, 1983).

For additional reading, go to InfoTrac College Edition, your online research library at http://web1.infotrac-college.com

Enter the search term *Roman Empire* using Key Terms.

Enter the search term *Roman mythology* using the Subject Guide.

Enter the search term *Roman law* using the Subject Guide.

Enter the search term *Constantine* using the Subject Guide.

CHAPTER 7

The Passing of the Roman World and the Emergence of Medieval Civilization

CHAPTER OUTLINE

- Transformation of the Roman World: The Role of the Germanic Peoples
- The Role and Development of the Christian Church
- The Byzantine Empire
- The Rise of Islam
- Conclusion

FOCUS QUESTIONS

- What were the main features of Germanic law and society, and how did they differ from those of the Romans?
- How and why did the organization of the Christian church and its relations with the state change during the fourth and fifth centuries?
- What were the chief characteristics of Benedictine monasticism, and what role did monks play in both the conversion of Europe to Christianity and the intellectual life of the Germanic kingdoms?
- How did the Byzantine Empire that had emerged by the eighth century differ from the empire of Justinian and from the Germanic kingdoms in the west?
- What was the basic message of Islam, and why was it able to expand so successfully?
- In what ways were the Byzantine and Islamic civilizations different from the civilization developing in western Europe? In what ways were they similar?

THE PERIOD THAT SAW the disintegration of the western part of the Roman Empire also witnessed the emergence of medieval civilization. Scholars know that major historical transitions are never tidy; chaos is often the ground out of which new civilizations are born. The early medieval civilization that arose out of the dissolution of the Western Roman Empire was formed by the coalescence of three major elements: the Germanic peoples who moved into the western empire and established new kingdoms, the continuing attraction of the Greco-Roman cultural legacy, and the Christian church. Christianity was the most distinctive and most powerful component of the new medieval civilization. The church assimilated the classical tradition and through its clergy, especially the monks, brought Christianized civilization to the Germanic tribes.

The conversion to Christianity of the pagan leaders of German tribes was sometimes dramatic, at least as reported by the sixth-century historian Gregory of Tours. Clovis, leader of the Franks, married Clotilde, daughter of the king of the Burgundians. She was a Christian, but Clovis refused her pleas to become a Christian, telling her, "Your god can do nothing." But during a battle with the Alemanni, when Clovis's army was close to utter destruction, "he saw the danger; his heart was stirred; and he raised his eyes to heaven, saying, 'Jesus Christ, I beseech the glory of your aid. If you shall grant me victory over these enemies, I will believe in you and be baptized in your name.'" When he had uttered these words, the Alemanni began to flee. Clovis kept his vow and became a Christian.

While the Germanic kingdoms were putting down roots in the west, the eastern part of the old Roman Empire, increasingly Greek in culture, continued as the Byzantine Empire. Serving as a buffer between Europe and the peoples to the east, the Byzantine or Eastern Roman Empire also preserved the intellectual and legal accomplishments of Greek and Roman antiquity. At the same time, a new world of Islam emerged in the east; it occupied large parts of the old Roman Empire, preserved much of Greek culture, and created its own flourishing civilization. This chapter, then, largely concerns the heirs of Rome and the new world they created.

Transformation of the Roman World: The Role of the Germanic Peoples

The Germanic peoples were an important element of the new medieval civilization. Around 500 B.C., the Germans began to migrate from their northern Scandinavian homeland south into what are now the Baltic states and Germany and east into the fertile lands of Ukraine. Although the Romans had established a series of political frontiers in the western empire, Romans and Germans often came into contact across those boundaries. For some time, the Romans had hired Germanic tribes to fight other Germanic tribes that threatened Rome or enlisted groups of Germans to fight for Rome.

In the late fourth century, the Germanic tribes came under new pressure when the Huns, a fierce tribe of nomads from the steppes of Asia (see the box on p. 164), moved into the Black Sea region. They devastated the Germanic Gothic confederation that dominated the region and forced some tribes out. One of the largest displaced groups, the Visigoths, crossed the Danube, crushed a Roman army in 378, and settled along the Danube, within the Roman Empire. But they were soon on the move again. Under their king Alaric, they stormed into Italy and sacked Rome in 410. Then, at the urging of the emperor, they moved into Spain and southern Gaul as Roman allies (see Map 7.1).

The Roman experience with the Visigoths established a precedent. The emperors in the first half of the fifth century made alliances with whole groups of Germanic peoples, who settled peacefully in the western part of the empire. The Burgundians settled themselves in much of eastern Gaul, just south of another Germanic tribe called the Alemanni. Only the Vandals remained consistently hostile to the Romans. They sacked parts of Gaul, crossed the Pyrenees into Spain, and began to establish a Vandal kingdom there. Defeated by incoming Visigoths, the Vandals crossed the Strait of Gibraltar and conquered the province of Africa. In 455, the Vandals even attacked Rome and sacked it more ferociously than the Visigoths had in 410.

Increasingly, German military leaders dominated the imperial courts of the western empire. One such leader finally ended the charade of Roman imperial rule. In 476, Odoacer deposed the Roman emperor, Romulus Augustulus, and began to rule on his own. Meanwhile, another branch of the Goths, known as the Ostrogoths, under King Theodoric (493–526), marched into Italy, killed Odoacer, and established control of Italy in 493.

The New Kingdoms

By 500, the Western Roman Empire was being replaced politically by a series of kingdoms ruled by German kings (see Map 7.2). The pattern of settlement and the fusion of the Romans and Germans took different forms in the various Germanic kingdoms.

THE OSTROGOTHIC KINGDOM OF ITALY

More than any other Germanic state, the Ostrogothic kingdom of Italy managed to maintain the Roman tradition of government. The Ostrogothic king, Theodoric, had received a Roman education while a hostage in Constantinople. After taking control of Italy, he was eager to create a synthesis of Ostrogothic and Roman practices (see the box on p. 165). In addition to maintaining the entire structure of imperial Roman government, he established separate systems of rule for the Ostrogoths and Romans. The Italian population lived under Roman law administered by Roman officials. The Ostrogoths were governed by their own customs and their own officials.

After Theodoric's death in 526, it quickly became apparent that much of his success had been due to the force of his own personality. His successors soon found themselves face to face with opposition from the imperial forces of the Byzantine or Eastern Roman Empire. Under Emperor Justinian (527–565) (see "The Reign of Justinian" later in this chapter), Byzantine armies reconquered Italy between 535 and 552, devastating much of the peninsula and destroying Rome as one of the great urban centers of the Mediterranean world. The Byzantine reconquest proved ephemeral, however. Another German tribe, the Lombards, invaded Italy

The People of the Huns

The first selection is a description of the Huns by Ammianus Marcellinus (c. 330–c. 393), who has been called the "last great Roman historian." Ammianus wrote a history of Rome from A.D. 96 to his own day. Only the chapters that deal with the period from 354 to 378 have survived. Historians believe that his account of the Huns is largely based on stereotypes. The second selection is taken from an account by Priscus, an envoy from the Eastern Roman Empire to the court of Attila the Hun. His description of the Huns in 448 is quite different from that of Ammianus Marcellinus.

■ *Ammianus Marcellinus,* The Later Roman Empire

The people of the Huns . . . are quite abnormally savage. From the moment of their birth they make deep gashes in their children's cheeks, so that when in due course hair appears its growth is checked by the wrinkled scars; . . . They have squat bodies, strong limbs, and thick necks, and are so prodigiously ugly and bent that they might be two-legged animals, or the figures crudely carved from stumps which are seen on the parapets of bridges. Still, their shape, however disagreeable, is human; but their way of life is so rough that they have no use for fire or seasoned food, but live on the roots of wild plants and the half-raw flesh of any sort of animal, which they warm a little by placing it between their thighs and the backs of their horses. They have no buildings to shelter them, but avoid anything of the kind; . . . not so much as a hut thatched with reeds is to be found among them. . . . They wear garments of linen or of the skins of field-mice stitched together, and there is no difference between their clothing whether they are at home or abroad. Once they have put their necks in some dingy shirt they never take it off or change it till it rots and falls to pieces from incessant wear. They have round caps of fur on their heads, and protect their hairy legs with goatskins. Their shapeless shoes . . . make it hard to walk easily. In consequence they are ill-fitted to fight on foot, and remain glued to their horses, hardy but ugly beasts, on which they sometimes sit like women to perform their everyday business. Buying or selling, eating or drinking, are all done by day or night on horseback, and they even bow forward over their beasts' narrow necks to enjoy a deep and dreamy sleep. . . .

They sometimes fight by challenging their foes to single combat, but when they join battle they advance in packs, uttering their various warcries. Being lightly equipped and very sudden in their movements they can deliberately scatter and gallop about at random, inflicting tremendous slaughter; their extreme nimbleness enables them to force a rampart or pillage an enemy's camp before one catches sight of them. . . . None of them plows or ever touches a plow-handle. They have no fixed abode, no home or law or settled manner of life, but wander like refugees with the wagons in which they live. In these their wives weave their filthy clothing, mate with their husbands, and give birth to their children, and rear them to the age of puberty.

■ *Priscus,* An Account of the Court of Attila the Hun

[We were invited to a banquet with Attila.] When the hour arrived we went to Attila's palace, along with the embassy from the western Romans, and stood on the threshold of the hall in the presence of Attila. The cup-bearers gave us a cup, according to the national custom, that we might pray before we sat down. Having tasted the cup, we proceeded to take our seats, all the chairs being ranged along the walls of the room on either side. Attila sat in the middle on a couch; a second couch was set behind him, and from it steps led up to his bed, which was covered with linen sheets and coverlets. . . .

[First the king and his guests pledged one another with the wine.] When this ceremony was over the cup-bearers retired and tables, large enough for three or four, or even more, to sit at, were placed next the table of Attila, so that each could take of the food on the dishes without leaving his seat. The attendant of Attila first entered with a dish full of meat, and behind him came the other attendants with bread and other dishes, which they laid on the tables. A luxurious meal, served on silver plate, had been made ready for us and the other guests, but Attila ate nothing but meat on a wooden platter. In everything else, too, he showed himself temperate; his cup was of wood, while to the guests were given goblets of gold and silver. His dress, too, was quite simple, affecting only to be clean.

in 568 and conquered much of northern and central Italy. Unlike the Ostrogoths, the Lombards were harsh rulers and cared little for Roman structures and traditions.

THE VISIGOTHIC KINGDOM OF SPAIN

The Visigothic kingdom in Spain demonstrated a number of parallels to the Ostrogothic kingdom of Italy. Both favored coexistence between the Roman and German populations, both featured a warrior caste dominating a larger native population, and both continued to maintain much of the Roman structure of government while largely excluding Romans from power. There were also noticeable differences, however. Laws preventing intermarriage were dropped, and the Visigothic and Hispano-Roman peoples began to fuse together. A new body of law common to both peoples also developed.

The kingdom possessed one fatal weakness, however—the Visigoths fought constantly over the kingship. The Visi-

Theodoric and Ostrogothic Italy

The Ostrogothic king Theodoric (493–526), who had been educated in Constantinople, was determined to maintain Roman culture rather than destroy it. His attempt to preserve *civilitas,* the traditional Roman civic culture, was well expressed in the official letters written in his name by Cassiodorus, who became master of offices in 525. Theodoric's efforts were largely undone by opposition from the Roman nobility and especially by Justinian's reconquest of the Italian peninsula shortly after Theodoric's death.

Letters of Cassiodorus

King Theodoric to Colossaeus

We delight to entrust our mandates to persons of approved character. . . .

Show forth the justice of the Goths, a nation happily situated for praise, since it is theirs to unite the forethought of the Romans and the virtue of the Barbarians. Remove all ill-planted customs, and impress upon all your subordinates that we would rather that our Treasury lost a suit than that it gained one wrongfully, rather that we lost money than the taxpayer was driven to suicide.

King Theodoric to Unigis, the Sword-Bearer

We delight to live after the law of the Romans, whom we seek to defend with our arms; and we are as much interested in the maintenance of morality as we can possibly be in war. For what profit is there in having removed the turmoil of the Barbarians, unless we live according to law? . . . Let other kings desire the glory of battles won, of cities taken, of ruins made; our purpose is, God helping us, so to rule that our subjects shall grieve that they did not earlier acquire the blessing of our dominion.

King Theodoric to All the Jews of Genoa

The true mark of *civilitas* is the observance of law. It is this which makes life in communities possible, and which separates man from the brutes. We therefore gladly accede to your request that all the privileges which the foresight of antiquity conferred upon the Jewish customs shall be renewed to you, for in truth it is our great desire that the laws of the ancients shall be kept in force to secure the reverence due to us. Everything which has been found to conduce to *civilitas* should be held fast with enduring devotion.

King Theodoric to All the Goths Settled in Picenum and Samnium

The presence of the Sovereign doubles the sweetness of his gifts, and that man is like one dead whose face is not known to his lord. Come therefore by God's assistance, come all into our presence on the eighth day before the Ides of June [June 6], there solemnly to receive our royal largesse. But let there be no excesses by the way, no plundering the harvest of the cultivators nor trampling down their meadows, since for this cause do we gladly defray the expense of our armies that *civilitas* may be kept intact by armed men.

goths had no hereditary monarchy and no established procedure for choosing new rulers. Church officials tried to help develop a sense of order, as this canon from the Fourth Council of Toledo in 633 illustrates: "No one of us shall dare to seize the kingdom; no one shall arouse sedition among the citizenry; no one shall think of killing the king. . . ." Church decrees failed to stop the feuds, however, and assassinations remained a way of life in Visigothic Spain. In 711, Muslim invaders destroyed the Visigothic kingdom itself (see "The Rise of Islam" later in this chapter).

Kunsthistorisches Museum, Vienna

Amalsuntha, Theodoric's Successor. After Theodoric's death in 526, his daughter Amalsuntha, acting as regent for her son Athalaric, took control of Italy. But she was murdered by relatives in 535, and Italy soon fell subject to the forces of Justinian. This ivory panel of 530 shows Amalsuntha seated on a throne. The frame probably depicts part of Theodoric's palace at Ravenna.

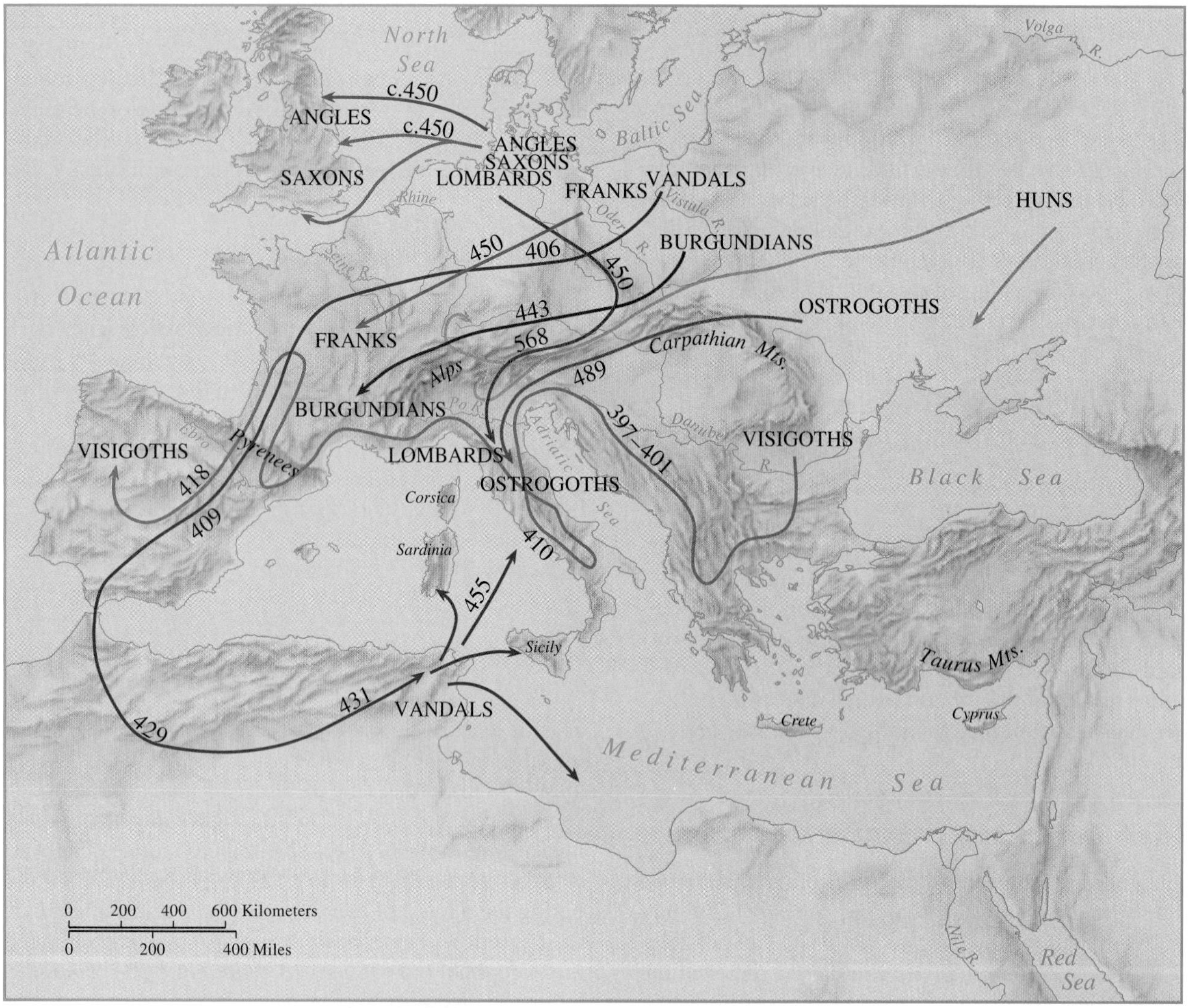

Map 7.1 Barbarian Migration and Invasion Routes. In the fifth century, extensive migrations of barbarians occurred in the Roman Empire. Pressure from Huns in the east forced some tribes west into the empire, and many tribes already in the empire experienced conflict. Some fought the empire, while others were induced to move to the empire's far regions. ■ How far did the Vandals travel in what period of time?

THE FRANKISH KINGDOM

Only one of the German states on the European continent proved long-lasting—the kingdom of the Franks. The establishment of a Frankish kingdom was the work of Clovis (c. 482–511), a member of the Merovingian dynasty who became a Catholic Christian around 500. He was not the first German king to convert to Christianity, but the others had joined the Arian sect of Christianity (see "Organization and Religious Disputes" later in this chapter). The Christian church in Rome, which had become known as the Roman Catholic church, regarded the Arians as heretics, people who believed in teachings that departed from the official church doctrine. Clovis found that his conversion to Catholic Christianity gained him the support of the Roman Catholic church, which was only too eager to obtain the friendship of a major Germanic ruler who was a Catholic Christian.

By 510, Clovis had established a powerful new Frankish kingdom stretching from the Pyrenees in the west to German lands in the east (modern-day France and western Germany). After the death of Clovis, however, his sons divided the newly created kingdom, as was the Frankish custom. During the sixth and seventh centuries, the once-united Frankish kingdom came to be partitioned into three major areas: Neustria in northern Gaul; Austrasia, consisting of the ancient Frankish lands on both sides of the Rhine; and the former kingdom of Burgundy. All three were ruled by members of the Merovingian dynasty.

At the beginning of the eighth century, the most important political development in the Frankish kingdom

Bibliotheque Nationale, Paris

Baptism of Clovis. The conversion of Clovis to Catholic Christianity was an important factor in gaining papal support for his Frankish kingdom. In this illustration from a medieval manuscript, bishops and nobles look on while Clovis is baptized. One of the nobles holds a crown while a dove, symbol of the Holy Spirit, descends from heaven bringing sacred oil for the ceremony.

CHRONOLOGY

The Germanic Kingdoms

Sack of Rome by Visigoths	410
Vandals in North Africa	429
Sack of Rome by Vandals	455
Odoacer deposes western emperor	476
Theodoric establishes an Ostrogothic kingdom in Italy	493
Frankish king Clovis converts to Christianity	c. 500
Reconquest of Italy by Byzantines	535–552
Lombards begin conquest of Italy	568
Muslims shatter Visigoths in Spain	711
Charles Martel defeats Muslims	732

was the rise of Charles Martel, who served as mayor of the palace (chief officer of the king's household) of Austrasia beginning in 714. Charles Martel led troops that defeated the Muslims near Poitiers in 732 and by the time of his death in 741 had become virtual ruler of the three Merovingian kingdoms. Though he was not king, Charles Martel's dynamic efforts put his family on the verge of creating a new dynasty that would establish an even more powerful Frankish state (see Chapter 8).

During the sixth and seventh centuries, the Frankish kingdom witnessed a process of fusion between Gallo-Roman and Frankish cultures and peoples, a process accompanied by a significant decline in Roman standards of civilization and commercial activity. The Franks were warriors and did little to encourage either urban life or trade. Commerce declined in the interior, though seacoast towns maintained some activity. By 750, Frankish Gaul was basically an agricultural society in which the old Roman *latifundia* system of the late empire had continued unimpeded. Institutionally, however, Germanic concepts of kingship and customary law had replaced the Roman governmental structure.

ANGLO-SAXON ENGLAND

The barbarian pressures on the Western Roman Empire had forced the emperors to withdraw the Roman armies and abandon Britain by the beginning of the fifth century. This opened the door to the Angles and Saxons, Germanic tribes from Denmark and northern Germany. Although these same peoples had made plundering raids for the past century, the withdrawal of the Roman armies enabled them to make settlements instead. They met with resistance from the Celtic Britons, however, who still controlled the western regions of Cornwall, Wales, and Cumberland at the beginning of the seventh century. The German invaders eventually succeeded in carving out small kingdoms throughout the island, Kent in southeast England being one of them. This wave of German invaders would eventually be converted to Christianity by new groups of Christian missionaries.

The Society of the Germanic Peoples in the New Kingdoms

As the Germans infiltrated the Roman Empire, they were influenced by the Roman society they encountered. Consequently, the Germanic peoples of the fifth, sixth, and seventh centuries were probably quite different from the Germans that the forces of Augustus encountered in the first century A.D. Moreover, there was a meaningful fusion of Roman and German upper classes in the new kingdoms. In Merovingian Frankish lands, upper-class Gallo-Romans intermarried with Frankish nobles to produce a new ruling class. Each influenced the other. Franks constructed Roman-style villas; Gallo-Romans adopted Frankish weapons.

The crucial social bond among the Germanic peoples was the family, especially the extended or patriarchal family of husbands, wives, children, brothers, sisters, cousins, and grandparents. In addition to working the land together and passing it down to succeeding generations, the extended family provided protection, which was sorely needed in the violent atmosphere of Merovingian times.

The German conception of family and kinship affected the way Germanic law treated the problem of crime and punishment. In the Roman system, as in our own, a crime such as murder was considered an offense against society or the state and was handled by a court that heard evidence

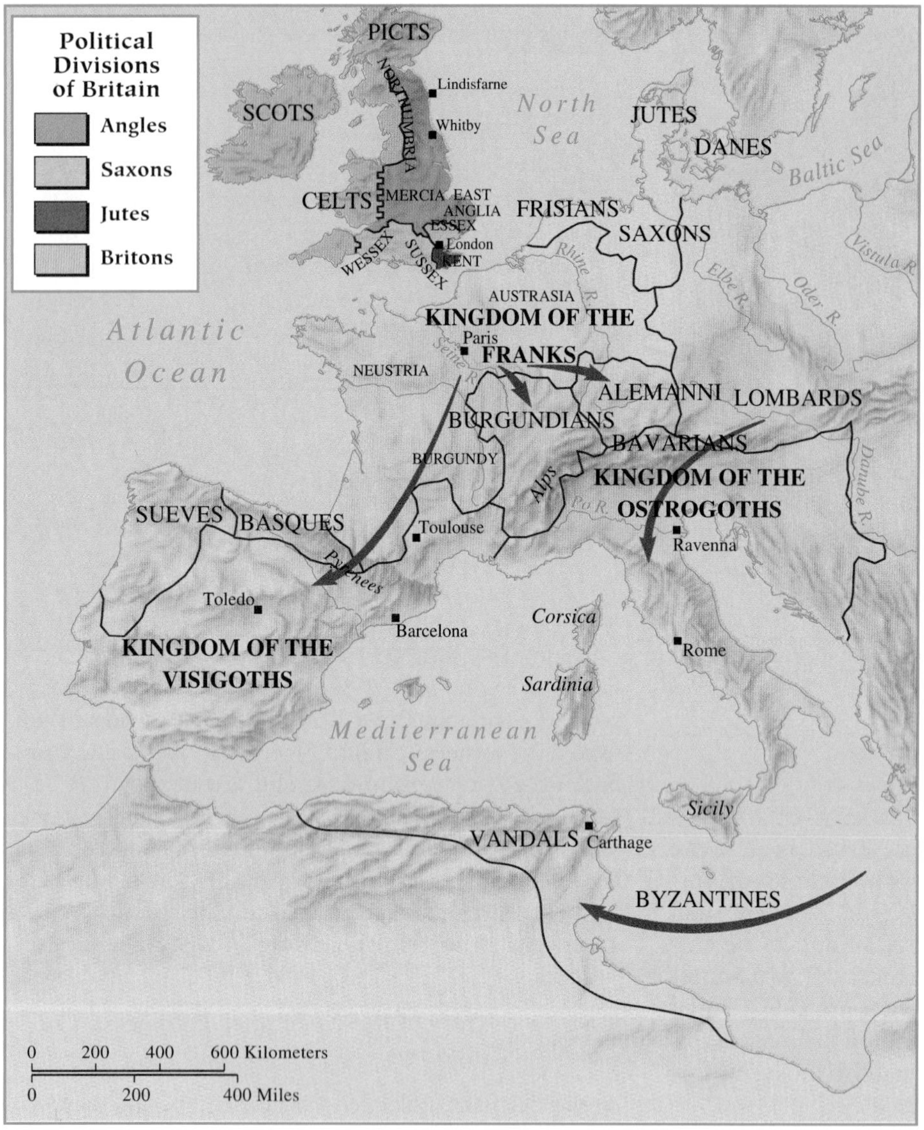

Map 7.2 The New Kingdoms of the Old Western Empire. The Germanic tribes filled the power vacuum caused by the demise of the Roman Empire, building states that blended elements of Germanic customs and laws with those of Roman culture, including large-scale conversions to Christianity. The Franks established the most durable of these Germanic states. ■ How did the movements of Franks during this period correspond to the borders of present-day France?

and arrived at a decision. Germanic law tended to be personal. An injury by one person against another could mean a blood feud in which the family of the injured party took revenge on the kin of the wrongdoer. Feuds could lead to savage acts of revenge, such as hacking off hands or feet, gouging out eyes, or slicing off ears and noses. Since this system had a tendency to get out of control and allow mayhem to multiply, an alternative system arose that made use of a fine called *wergeld.* This was the amount paid by a wrongdoer to the family of the person who had been injured or killed. *Wergeld,* which means "money for a man," was the value of a person in monetary terms. That value varied considerably according to social status. The law of the Salic Franks, which was first written down under Roman influence at the beginning of the sixth century, stated:

> If any one shall have killed a free Frank, or a barbarian living under the Salic law, and it have been proved on him, he shall be sentenced to 8,000 denars. . . .
> But if any one has slain a man who is in the service of the king, he shall be sentenced to 24,000 denars. . . .[1]

An offense against a noble obviously cost considerably more than one against a free person or a slave.

Under German customary law, compurgation and the ordeal were the two most commonly used procedures for determining whether an accused person was guilty and should have to pay *wergeld.* Compurgation was the swearing of an oath by the accused person, backed up by a group of "oathhelpers," numbering twelve or twenty-five, who would also swear that the accused person should be believed. The ordeal functioned in a variety of ways, all of which were based on the principle of divine intervention; divine forces (whether pagan or Christian) would not allow an innocent person to be harmed (see the box on p. 169).

THE FRANKISH FAMILY AND MARRIAGE

For the Franks, like other Germanic peoples of the Early Middle Ages, the extended family was at the center of social organization. The Frankish family structure was quite simple. Males were dominant and made all the important decisions. A woman obeyed her father until she married and then fell under the legal domination of her husband. A

Germanic Customary Law: The Ordeal

In Germanic customary law, the ordeal came to be a means by which accused persons might clear themselves. Although the ordeal took different forms, all involved a physical trial of some sort, such as holding a red-hot iron. It was believed God would protect the innocent and allow them to come through the ordeal unharmed. The sixth-century account by Gregory of Tours describes an ordeal by hot water.

Gregory of Tours, An Ordeal of Hot Water *(c. 580)*

An Arian priest disputing with a deacon of our religion made venomous assertions against the Son of God and the Holy Ghost, as is the habit of that sect [the Arians]. But when the deacon had discoursed a long time concerning the reasonableness of our faith and the heretic, blinded by the fog of unbelief, continued to reject the truth, . . . the former said: "Why weary ourselves with long discussions? Let acts approve the truth; let a kettle be heated over the fire and someone's ring be thrown into the boiling water. Let him who shall take it from the heated liquid be approved as a follower of the truth, and afterward let the other party be converted to the knowledge of the truth. And do you also understand, O heretic, that this our party will fulfill the conditions with the aid of the Holy Ghost; you shall confess that there is no discordance, no dissimilarity in the Holy Trinity [belief that God, Jesus (son of God), and Holy Spirit (Ghost) are three manifestations of the same unique Deity]." The heretic consented to the proposition and they separated after appointing the next morning for the trial. But the fervor of faith in which the deacon had first made this suggestion began to cool through the instigation of the enemy. Rising with the dawn he bathed his arm in oil and smeared it with ointment. But nevertheless he made the round of the sacred places and called in prayer on the Lord. . . . About the third hour they met in the market place. The people came together to see the show. A fire was lighted, the kettle was placed upon it, and when it grew very hot the ring was thrown into the boiling water. The deacon invited the heretic to take it out of the water first. But he promptly refused, saying, "You who did propose this trial are the one to take it out." The deacon all of a tremble bared his arm. And when the heretic saw it besmeared with ointment he cried out: "With magic arts you have thought to protect yourself, that you have made use of these salves, but what you have done will not avail." While they were thus quarreling there came up a deacon from Ravenna named Iacinthus and inquired what the trouble was about. When he learned the truth he drew his arm out from under his robe at once and plunged his right hand into the kettle. Now the ring that had been thrown in was a little thing and very light so that it was thrown about by the water as chaff would be blown about by the wind; and searching for it a long time he found it after about an hour. Meanwhile the flame beneath the kettle blazed up mightily so that the greater heat might make it difficult for the ring to be followed by the hand; but the deacon extracted it at length and suffered no harm, protesting rather that at the bottom the kettle was cold while at the top it was just pleasantly warm. When the heretic beheld this he was greatly confused and audaciously thrust his hand into the kettle saying, "My faith will aid me." As soon as his hand had been thrust in all the flesh was boiled off the bones clear up to the elbow. And so the dispute ended.

widow, however, could hold property without a male guardian. In Frankish law, the *wergeld* of a wife of childbearing age—of value because she could bear children—was considerably higher than that of a man. The Salic law stated: "If any one killed a free woman after she had begun bearing children, he shall be sentenced to 24,000 denars. . . . After she can have no more children, he who kills her shall be sentenced to 8,000 denars. . . ."[2]

Since marriage affected the extended family group, fathers or uncles could arrange marriages for the good of the family without considering their children's wishes. Most important was the engagement ceremony in which a prospective son-in-law made a payment symbolizing the purchase of paternal authority over the bride. The essential feature of the marriage itself involved placing the married couple in bed to achieve their physical union. In first marriages, it was considered important that the wife be a virgin so as to ensure that any children would be the husband's. A virgin symbolized the ability of the bloodline to continue. For this reason, adultery was viewed as pollution of the woman and her offspring, hence poisoning the future. Adulterous wives were severely punished (an adulterous woman could be strangled or even burned alive); adulterous husbands were not. Divorce was relatively simple and was initiated primarily by the husband. Divorced wives simply returned to their families.

For most women in the new Germanic kingdoms, their legal status reflected the material conditions of their lives. Archaeological evidence suggests that most women had life expectancies of only thirty or forty years and that about 10 to 15 percent of women died in their childbearing years, no doubt due to complications associated with childbirth. For most women, life consisted of domestic labor: providing food and clothing for the household, caring for the children, and assisting with numerous farming chores. Of all the duties of women, the most important was childbearing, because it was crucial to the maintenance of the family and its properties.

The Role and Development of the Christian Church

By the end of the fourth century, Christianity had become the predominant religion of the Roman Empire. As the official Roman state disintegrated, the Christian church played an increasingly important role in the new civilization built on the ruins of the old Roman Empire.

Organization and Religious Disputes

By the fourth century, the Christian church had developed a system of government based on a territorial plan borrowed from Roman administration. The Christian community in each city was headed by a bishop, whose area of jurisdiction was known as a bishopric or diocese. The bishoprics of each Roman province were clustered together under the direction of an archbishop. The bishops of four great cities, Rome, Jerusalem, Alexandria, and Antioch, held positions of special power in church affairs because the churches in these cities all asserted that they had been founded by the original apostles sent out by Jesus.

One reason the church needed a more formal organization was the problem of heresy. As Christianity developed and spread, contradictory interpretations of important doctrines emerged. Heresy came to be viewed as a teaching different from the official "catholic" or universal beliefs of the church. In a world where people were concerned about salvation, the question of whether Jesus' nature is divine or human took on great significance. These doctrinal differences also became political issues, creating political factions that actually warred with one another. It is highly unlikely, though, that ordinary people understood what these debates meant.

The two major heresies of the fourth century were Donatism and Arianism. Donatus was a priest in North Africa who taught that the sacraments of the church, the channels by which a Christian received God's grace, were not valid if administered by an immoral priest or one who had denied his faith under persecution. Donatus' deviation from traditional teaching on the subject created so much dissension that it came to the attention of the Emperor Constantine, who convened a council of western bishops to denounce it. It was not until a century later, in 411, however, that the church declared authoritatively that the efficacy of the sacraments was not dependent on the moral state of the priest administering them as long as the priest had been properly ordained.

Arianism was a product of the followers of Arius, a priest from Alexandria in Egypt. Arius postulated that Jesus had been human and thus not truly God. Arius was opposed by Athanasius, a bishop of Alexandria, who argued that Jesus was human but also truly God. Emperor Constantine, disturbed by the controversy, called the first ecumenical council of the church, a meeting composed of representatives from the entire Christian community. The Council of Nicaea, held in 325, condemned Arianism and stated that Jesus was of "the same substance" as God: "We believe in one God the Father All-sovereign, maker of all things visible and invisible; And in one Lord Jesus Christ, the Son of God, begotten of the Father, only-begotten, that is, of the substance of the Father, God of God, Light of Light, true God of true God, begotten not made, of one substance with the Father."[3] The Council of Nicaea did not end the controversy, however; not only did Arianism persist in some parts of the Roman Empire for many years, but even more important, many of the Germanic Goths who established states in the west converted to Arian Christianity. As a result of these fourth-century religious controversies, the Roman emperor came to play an increasingly important role in church affairs. At the same time, such divisions also created a need for leadership within the church.

The Power of the Pope

In the early centuries of Christianity, the churches in the larger cities had great influence in the administration of the church. It was only natural, then, that the bishops of those cities would also exercise considerable power. One of the far-reaching developments in the history of the Christian church was the emergence of one bishop—that of Rome—as the recognized leader of the western Christian church.

The doctrine of Petrine supremacy, based on the belief that the bishops of Rome occupied a preeminent position in the church, was grounded in Scripture. According to the Gospel of Matthew, when Jesus asked his disciples, "Who do you say I am?" Simon Peter answered:

> You are the Christ, the Son of the living God. Jesus replied, Blessed are you, Simon, son of Jonah, for this was not revealed by man, but by my Father in heaven. And I tell you that you are Peter, and on this rock I will build my church, and the gates of hell will not overcome it. I will give you the keys of the kingdom of heaven; whatever you bind on earth will be bound in heaven; and whatever you loose on earth will be loosed in heaven.[4]

According to church tradition, Jesus had given the keys to the kingdom of heaven to Peter, who was considered the chief apostle and the first bishop of Rome. Subsequent bishops of Rome were considered Peter's successors and later the "vicars of Christ" on earth. Though this exalted view of the bishops of Rome was by no means accepted by all early Christians, Rome's position as the traditional capital of the Roman Empire served to buttress this claim.

By the end of the fourth century, the bishops of Rome were using the title of *papa*, "father" (which became the English *pope*). Pope Leo I (440–461) was especially energetic in systematically expounding the doctrine of Petrine supremacy. He portrayed himself as the heir of Peter, whom Jesus had chosen to be head of the Christian church. But state authorities were also claiming some power over the church.

Church and State

Once the Roman emperors became Christians, they came to play a significant role in the affairs of the church. Christian emperors viewed themselves as God's representatives on earth. They not only built churches and influenced the structure of the church's organization but also became involved in church government and doctrinal controversies.

While emperors were busying themselves in church affairs, the spiritual and political vacuum left by the disintegration of the Roman state allowed bishops to play a more active role in imperial government. Increasingly, they served as advisers to Christian Roman emperors. Moreover, as imperial authority declined, bishops often played a noticeably independent political role. Ambrose (c. 339–397) of Milan was an early example of a strong and independent bishop. Through his activities and writings, Ambrose created an image of the ideal Christian bishop. Among other things, this ideal bishop would defend the independence of the church against the tendency of imperial officials to oversee church policy: "Exalt not yourself, but if you would reign the longer, be subject to God. It is written, God's to God and Caesar's to Caesar. The palace is the Emperor's, the Churches are the Bishop's."[5] When Emperor Theodosius I ordered the massacre of many citizens in Thessalonika for refusing to obey his commands, Ambrose denounced the massacre and refused to allow the emperor to take part in church ceremonies. Theodosius finally agreed to do public penance in the cathedral of Milan for his dastardly deed. Ambrose proved himself a formidable advocate of the position that spiritual authority should take precedence over temporal power, at least in spiritual matters.

The weakness of the political authorities on the Italian peninsula also contributed to the church's independence in that area. In the Germanic kingdoms, the kings controlled both churches and bishops. But in Italy a different tradition prevailed, fed by semilegendary accounts of papal deeds. Pope Leo I, for example, supposedly caused Attila the Hun to turn away from Rome in 452. Although plague rather than papal persuasion was probably more to account for Attila's withdrawal, the pope got the credit. Popes, then, played significant political roles in Italy, which only added to their claims of power vis-à-vis the secular authorities. Pope Gelasius I (492–496) could write to the emperor at Constantinople:

> There are two powers, august Emperor, by which this world is ruled from the beginning: the consecrated authority of the bishops, and the royal power. In these matters the priests bear the heavier burden because they will render account, even for rulers of men, at the divine judgment. Besides, most gracious son, you are aware that, although you in your office are the ruler of the human race, nevertheless you devoutly bow your head before those who are leaders in things divine and look to them for the means of your salvation.[6]

According to Gelasius, though there were two ruling powers, spiritual and temporal, with different functions, the church was ultimately the higher authority because all men, including emperors, must look to the church "for the means of . . . salvation."

Pope Gregory the Great

Although western Christians came to accept the bishop of Rome as head of the church, there was no unanimity on the extent of the powers the pope possessed as a result of his position. Nevertheless, the emergence in the sixth century of a strong pope, Gregory I, known as Gregory the Great, set the papacy and the Roman Catholic church on an energetic path that enabled the church in the seventh and eighth centuries to play an increasingly prominent role in civilizing the Germans and aiding the emergence of a distinctly new European civilization.

As pope, Gregory I (590–604) assumed direction of Rome and its surrounding territories, which had suffered enormously from the Ostrogothic-Byzantine struggle and the Lombard invasion of the sixth century. Gregory described the conditions in a sermon to the people of Rome:

> What Rome herself, once deemed the Mistress of the World, has now become, we see—wasted away with afflictions grievous and many, with the loss of citizens, the assaults of enemies, the frequent fall of ruined buildings. . . . Where is the Senate? Where is the people? The bones are all dissolved, the flesh is consumed, all the pomp of the dignities of this world is gone.[7]

Gregory took charge and made Rome and its surrounding area into an administrative unit that eventually came to be known as the Papal States. Although historians disagree about Gregory's motives in establishing papal temporal power, no doubt Gregory was probably only doing

Pope Gregory I. Pope Gregory the Great became one of the most important popes of the Early Middle Ages. This ninth-century manuscript illustration shows Gregory dictating a work to two monks. Over Gregory's right shoulder is a dove, symbol of the Holy Spirit, which is providing divine inspiration for what he is dictating.

Sonia Halliday Photographs

what he felt needed to be done: to provide for the defense of Rome against the Lombards, to establish a government for Rome, and to feed the people. Gregory remained loyal to the empire and continued to address the Byzantine emperor as the rightful ruler of Italy.

Gregory also pursued a policy of extending papal authority over the Christian church in the west. He intervened in ecclesiastical conflicts throughout Italy and corresponded with the Frankish rulers, urging them to reform the church in Gaul. He successfully initiated the efforts of missionaries to convert England to Christianity and was especially active in converting the pagan peoples of Germanic Europe. His primary instrument was the monastic movement.

The Monks and Their Missions

A monk (Latin *monachus,* meaning "someone who lives alone") was a man who sought to live a life divorced from the world, cut off from ordinary human society, in order to pursue an ideal of godliness or total dedication to the will of God. Christian monasticism, which developed first in Egypt, was initially based on the model of the solitary hermit who forsakes all civilized society to pursue spirituality. Saint Anthony (c. 250–350) was a prosperous Egyptian peasant who decided to follow Jesus' injunction in the Gospel of Mark: "Go your way, sell whatsoever you have, and give to the poor, and you shall have treasure in heaven: and come, take up the cross, and follow me."[8] Anthony gave his 300 acres of land to the poor and went into the desert to pursue his ideal of holiness (see the box on p. 173). Others did likewise, often to extremes. Saint Simeon the Stylite lived for three decades in a basket atop a pillar over 60 feet high. These spiritual gymnastics established a new ideal for Christianity. Whereas the early Christian model had been the martyr who died for the faith and achieved eternal life in the process, the new ideal was the monk who died to the world and achieved spiritual life through denial, asceticism, and mystical experience of God.

These early monks, however, soon found themselves unable to live in solitude. Their feats of holiness attracted followers on a wide scale, and as the monastic ideal spread throughout the east, a new form of monasticism, based on the practice of communal life, soon became the dominant form. Monastic communities soon came to be seen as the ideal Christian society that could provide a moral example to the wider society around them.

BENEDICTINE MONASTICISM

Saint Benedict of Nursia (c. 480–c. 543), who founded a monastic house for which he wrote a set of rules sometime between 520 and 530, established the fundamental form of monastic life in the western Christian church. Benedict's rules largely rejected the ascetic ideals of eastern monasticism, which had tended to emphasize such practices as fasting and self-inflicted torments (such as living atop pillars for thirty years), in favor of an ideal of moderation. In Chapter 40 of the rules, on the amount of drink a monk should imbibe, this sense of moderation becomes apparent:

> "Every man has his proper gift from God, one after this manner, another after that." And therefore it is with some misgiving that we determine the amount of food for someone else. Still, having regard for the weakness of some brothers, we believe that a hemina [a quarter liter] of wine per day will suffice for all. Let those, however, to whom God gives the gift of abstinence, know that they shall have their proper reward. But if either the circumstances of the place, the work, or the heat of summer necessitates more, let it lie in the discretion of the abbot to grant it. But let him take care in all things lest satiety or drunkenness supervene.

At the same time, moderation did not preclude a hard and disciplined existence based on the ideals of poverty, chastity, and obedience.

Life of Saint Benedict. This illustration with its six scenes is from an eleventh-century manuscript of Pope Gregory the Great's *Life of Saint Benedict,* written in 593 or 594. *Top left,* Benedict writes his rules; *top right,* the death of Benedict; *middle left,* his burial; *middle right* and *bottom left,* scenes of miracles attributed to Saint Benedict's intercession; *bottom right,* Gregory finishes his *Life of Saint Benedict.*

Foto Biblioteca Apostolica Vaticana

The Life of Saint Anthony

In the third and early fourth centuries, the lives of martyrs had provided important models for early Christianity. But in the course of the fourth century, monks who attempted to achieve spiritual perfection through asceticism, the denial of earthly life, and the struggle with demons became the new spiritual ideal for Christians. Consequently, spiritual biographies of early monks became a significant new form of Christian literature. Especially noteworthy was *The Life of Saint Anthony* by Saint Athanasius, the defender of Catholic orthodoxy against the Arians. His work had been translated into Latin before 386. This excerpt describes how Anthony fought off the temptations of Satan.

■ *Athanasius,* The Life of Saint Anthony

Now when the Enemy [Satan] saw that his craftiness in this matter was without profit, and that the more he brought temptation into Saint Anthony, the more strenuous the saint was in protecting himself against him with the armor of righteousness, he attacked him by means of the vigor of early manhood which is bound up in the nature of our humanity. With the goadings of passion he sued to trouble him by night, and in the daytime also he would vex him and pain him with the same to such an extent that even those who saw him knew from his appearance that he was waging war against the Adversary. But the more the Evil One brought unto him filthy and maddening thoughts, the more Saint Anthony took refuge in prayer and in abundant supplication, and amid them all he remained wholly chaste. And the Evil One was working upon him every shameful deed according to his wont, and at length he even appeared unto Saint Anthony in the form of a woman; and other things which resembled this he performed with ease, for such things are a subject for boasting to him.

But the blessed Anthony knelt down upon his knees on the ground, and prayed before Him who said, "Before you criest unto Me, I will answer you," and said, "O my Lord, this I entreat you. Let not Your love be blotted out from my mind, and behold, I am, by Your grace, innocent before You." And again the Enemy multiplied in him the thoughts of lust, until Saint Anthony became as one who was being burned up, not through the Evil One, but through his own lusts; but he girded himself about with the threat of the thought of the Judgment, and of the torture of Gehenna [Hell], and of the worm which does not die. And while meditating on the thoughts which could be directed against the Evil One, he prayed for thoughts which would be hostile to him. Thus, to the reproach and shame of the Enemy, these things could not be performed; for he who imagined that he could be God was made a mock of by a young man, and he who boasted over flesh and blood was vanquished by a man who was clothed with flesh. . . .

Benedict's rules divided each day into a series of activities with primary emphasis on prayer and manual labor. Physical work of some kind was required of all monks for several hours a day because "idleness is the enemy of the soul." At the very heart of community practice was prayer, the proper "work of God." While this included private meditation and reading, all monks gathered together seven times during the day for common prayer and chanting of psalms. A Benedictine life was a communal one; monks ate, worked, slept, and worshiped together.

Each Benedictine monastery was strictly ruled by an abbot, or "father" of the monastery, who had complete authority over the monks, who bent unquestioningly to the will of the abbot. Each Benedictine monastery owned lands that enabled it to be a self-sustaining community, isolated from and independent of the world surrounding it. Within the monastery, however, monks were to fulfill their vow of poverty: "Let all things be common to all, as it is written, lest anyone should say that anything is his own or arrogate it to himself."[9] By the eighth century, Benedictine monasticism had spread throughout the west.

Women, too, sought to withdraw from the world to dedicate themselves to God. Already in the third century, groups of women abandoned the cities to form communities in the deserts of Egypt and Syria. The first monastic rules for western women were produced by Caesarius of Arles for his sister in the fifth century. They strongly emphasized a rigid cloistering of female religious, known as nuns, to preserve them from dangers. Later in the west, in the seventh and eighth centuries, the growth of double monasteries allowed monks and nuns to reside close by and follow a common set of rules.

Not all women pursued the celibate life in the desert, however. In a number of cities in the fourth century, women organized religious communities in their own homes. A woman named Marcella, for example, led a group of aristocratic women in Rome in discussing the ideals of asceticism and practicing virginity as a spiritual discipline that would enable them to achieve salvation.

Monasticism played an indispensable role in early medieval civilization. Monks became the new heroes of Christian civilization. Their dedication to God became the highest ideal of Christian life. Moreover, as we shall see later, the monks played an increasingly significant role in spreading Christianity to the entire European world.

IRISH MONKS AS MISSIONARIES

Ireland had remained a Celtic world beyond the outposts of the Roman Empire and the Germanic invaders. The most famous of the Christian missionaries to Ireland in the fifth century was Saint Patrick (c. 390–461). Son of a Romano-British Christian, Patrick was kidnapped as a young man by

Irish raiders and kept as a slave in Ireland. After his escape to Gaul, he became a monk and chose to return to Ireland to convert the Irish to Christianity. Irish tradition ascribes to Patrick the title of "founder of Irish Christianity," a testament to his apparent success.

Since Ireland had not been part of the Roman world and was fairly isolated from the European continent even after its conversion, Irish Christianity tended to develop along lines somewhat different from Roman Christianity. Whereas Catholic ecclesiastical structure had followed Roman government models, the absence of these models in Ireland engendered a different pattern of church organization. Rather than bishoprics, monasteries became the fundamental units of church organization, and abbots, the heads of the monasteries, exercised far more control over the Irish church than bishops did.

By the sixth century, Irish monasticism was a flourishing institution with its own striking characteristics. It was strongly ascetic. Monks performed strenuous fasts, prayed and meditated frequently under extreme privations, and confessed their sins on a regular basis to their superiors. In fact, Irish monasticism gave rise to the use of penitentials or manuals that provided a guide for examining one's life to see what sins, or offenses against the will of God, one had committed (see the box on p. 175). A great love of learning also characterized Irish monasticism. The Irish eagerly absorbed both Latin and Greek culture and fostered education as a major part of their monastic life.

The Board of Trinity College, Dublin

The Book of Kells. The emphasis on education in Irish monasticism led to the production of elaborately illustrated manuscripts. Shown here is the figure of Jesus from the Book of Kells, a text believed to have been made by the monks of Iona.

The emphasis on asceticism led many Irish monks to go into voluntary exile. This "exile for the love of God" was not into isolation, however, but into missionary activity. Irish monks became fervid missionaries. Saint Columba (521–597) left Ireland in 565 as a "pilgrim for Christ" and founded a highly influential monastic community off the coast of Scotland on the island of Iona. From there Irish missionaries went to northern England to begin the process of converting the Angles and Saxons. Meanwhile, other Irish monks traveled to the European continent. New monasteries founded by the Irish became centers of learning wherever they were located.

THE CONVERSION OF ENGLAND

At the same time the Irish monks were busy bringing their version of Christianity to the Anglo-Saxons of Britain, Pope Gregory the Great had set in motion his own effort to convert England to Roman Christianity. His most important agent was Augustine, a monk from Saint Andrew's monastery in Rome, who arrived in England in 597. England at that time had a number of Germanic kingdoms. Augustine went first to Kent, where he converted King Ethelbert, whereupon most of the king's subjects followed suit. Pope Gregory's conversion techniques emphasized persuasion rather than force, and as seen in this excerpt from one of his letters, he was willing to assimilate old pagan practices in order to coax the pagans into the new faith:

> We wish you [Abbot Mellitus] to inform him [Augustine] that we have been giving careful thought to the affairs of the English, and have come to the conclusion that the temples of the idols among that people should on no account be destroyed. The idols are to be destroyed, but the temples themselves are to be sprinkled with holy water, altars set up in them, and relics deposited there. For if these temples are well-built, they must be purified from the worship of demons and dedicated to the service of the true God. In this way, we hope that the people, seeing that their temples are not destroyed, may abandon their error and, flocking more readily to their accustomed resorts, may come to know and adore the true God.[10]

Irish Monasticism and the Penitential

Irish monasticism became well known for its ascetic practices. Much emphasis was placed on careful examination of conscience to determine if one had committed a sin against God. To facilitate this examination, penitentials were developed that listed possible sins with appropriate penances. Penance usually meant fasting a number of days each week, taking only bread and water. Although these penitentials were eventually used throughout Christendom, they were especially important in Irish Christianity. This excerpt from the penitential of Cummean, an Irish abbot, was written about 650 and demonstrates a distinctive feature of the penitentials, an acute preoccupation with sexual sins.

The Penitential of Cummean

A bishop who commits fornication shall be degraded and shall do penance for twelve years.

A priest or a deacon who commits natural fornication, having previously taken the vow of a monk, shall do penance for seven years. He shall ask pardon every hour; he shall perform a special fast during every week except in the days between Easter and Pentecost.

He who defiles his mother shall do penance for three years, with perpetual pilgrimage.

So shall those who commit sodomy do penance every seven years.

He who merely desires in his mind to commit fornication, but is not able, shall do penance for one year, especially in the three forty-day periods.

He who is willingly polluted during sleep shall arise and sing nine psalms in order, kneeling. On the following day, he shall live on bread and water.

A cleric who commits fornication once shall do penance for one year on bread and water; if he begets a son he shall do penance for seven years as an exile; so also a virgin.

He who loves any woman, but is unaware of any evil beyond a few conversations, shall do penance for forty days.

He who is in a state of matrimony ought to be continent during the three forty-day periods and on Saturday and on Sunday, night and day, and in the two appointed week days [Wednesday and Friday], and after conception, and during the entire menstrual period.

After a birth he shall abstain, if it is a son, for thirty-three [days]; if a daughter, for sixty-six [days].

Boys talking alone and transgressing the regulations of the elders [in the monastery], shall be corrected by three special fasts.

Children who imitate acts of fornication, twenty days; if frequently, forty.

But boys of twenty years who practice masturbation together and confess [shall do penance] twenty or forty days before they take communion.

Freed of their pagan past, temples had become churches, as one Christian commentator noted with joy: "The dwelling place of demons has become a house of God. The saving light has come to shine, where shadows covered all. Where sacrifices once took place and idols stood, angelic choirs now dance. Where God was angered once, now God is made content."[11]

Likewise, old pagan feasts were to be given new names and incorporated into the Christian calendar. No doubt Gregory was aware that early Christians had done the same. The Christian feast of Christmas, for example, was held on December 25, the day of the pagan celebration of the winter solstice.

As Roman Christianity spread northward in Britain, it encountered Irish Christianity moving southward. Soon arguments arose over the differences between Celtic and Roman Christianity, especially over matters of discipline. At the Synod of Whitby, held in the kingdom of Northumbria in 664, the king of Northumbria accepted the arguments of the representatives of Roman Christianity and decided the issue in favor of Roman practices. A gradual fusion of Celtic and Roman Christianity now ensued. Despite its newfound unity and loyalty to Rome, the English church retained some Irish features. Most important was the concentration on monastic culture with special emphasis on learning and missionary work. By 700, the English clergy had become the best trained and most learned in western Europe.

Following the Irish example, English monks journeyed to the European continent to carry on the work of conversion (see Map 7.3). Most important was Boniface (c. 675–754), who undertook the conversion of pagan Germans in Frisia, Bavaria, and Saxony. By 740, Saint Boniface, the "Apostle of the Germans," had become the most famous churchman in Europe. Fourteen years later, he was killed while trying to convert the pagan Frisians. Boniface was a brilliant example of the numerous Irish and English monks whose tireless efforts made Europe the bastion of the Roman Catholic faith.

WOMEN AND MONASTICISM

Women, too, played an important role in the monastic missionary movement and the conversion of the Germanic kingdoms. Double monasteries, where both monks and nuns lived in separate houses but attended church services together, were found in both the English and Frankish kingdoms. The monks and nuns followed common rules under a common head—frequently an abbess rather than an abbot. Many of these abbesses belonged to royal houses, especially in Anglo-Saxon England. In the kingdom of

An Anglo-Saxon Abbess: Hilda of Whitby

Hilda, abbess of the monastery of Whitby, is a good example of the abbesses from royal families in Anglo-Saxon England who played important roles in English monastic institutions. Hilda was especially known for her exemplary life and high regard for learning. This account of her life is taken from Bede, considered by many the first major historian of the Middle Ages.

Bede, The Ecclesiastical History of the English People

In the following year, that is the year of our Lord 680, Hilda, abbess of the monastery of Whitby, a most religious servant of Christ, passed away to receive the reward of eternal life on the seventeenth of November at the age of sixty-six, after a life full of heavenly deeds. Her life fell into two equal parts, for she spent thirty-three years most nobly in secular occupations, and dedicated the remainder of her life even more nobly to our Lord in the monastic life. She was nobly born, the daughter of Hereric, nephew to King Edwin, with whom she received the Faith and sacraments of Christ through the preaching of Paulinus of blessed memory, first bishop of the Northumbrians, and she preserved this Faith inviolate until she was found worthy to see him in heaven....

When she had ruled this monastery (Heruteu) for some years, constantly occupied in establishing the regular life, she further undertook to found or organize a monastery at a place known as Streaneshalch, and carried out this appointed task with great energy. She established the same regular life as in her former monastery, and taught the observance of justice, devotion, purity, and other virtues, but especially in peace and charity. After the example of the primitive Church, no one there was rich or poor, for everything was held in common, and none possessed any personal property. So great was her prudence that not only ordinary folk, but kings and princes used to come and ask her advice in their difficulties. Those under her direction were required to make a thorough study of the Scriptures and occupy themselves in good works, in order that many might be found fitted for Holy Orders and the service of God's altar. Subsequently, five bishops were chosen from this monastery—Bosa, Hedda, Oftfor, John, and Wilfrid—all of them men of outstanding merit and holiness....

Christ's servant Abbess Hilda, whom all her acquaintances called Mother because of her wonderful devotion and grace, was not only an example of holy life to members of her own community, for she also brought about the amendment and salvation of many living far distant, who heard the inspiring story of her industry and goodness.... When Hilda ruled this monastery for many years, it pleased the Author of our salvation to try her holy soul by a long sickness, in order that, like the Apostle, her strength might be perfected in weakness. She was attacked by a burning fever that racked her continually for six years; but during all this time she never ceased to give thanks to her Maker, or to instruct the flock committed to her both privately and publicly. For her own example taught them all to serve God rightly when in health, and to render thanks to him faithfully when in trouble or bodily weakness. In the seventh year of her illness she suffered interior pains, and her last day came. About dawn she received holy Communion, and when she had summoned all the servants of Christ in the monastery, she urged them to maintain the gospel peace among themselves and with others. And while she was still speaking, she joyfully welcomed death, and in the words of our Lord, passed from death to life.

Northumbria, for example, Saint Hilda founded the monastery of Whitby in 657. As abbess, she was responsible for giving learning an important role in the life of the monastery; five future bishops were educated under her tutelage (see the box above). For female intellectuals, monasteries offered opportunities for learning not found elsewhere in the society of their day.

Nuns of the seventh and eighth centuries were not always as heavily cloistered as they once had been and were therefore able to play an important role in the spread of Christianity. The great English missionary Boniface relied on nuns in England for books and money. He also asked the abbess of Wimborne to send groups of nuns to establish convents in newly converted German lands. A nun named Leoba established the first convent in Germany at Bischofsheim.

It is difficult to assess what Christianity meant to the converted pagans, especially the peasants on whom the Irish and English monks expended their greatest efforts. As Pope Gregory had recommended, Christian beliefs and values were usually superimposed on older pagan customs. Though effective in producing quick conversions, it is an open question how much people actually understood of Christian theology. Popular belief tended to focus on God as a judge who needed to be appeased to avert disasters in daily life and gain salvation. Except for the promise of salvation, such an image of God was not all that different from Roman religious practices.

Christianity and Intellectual Life

Many early Christians expressed considerable hostility toward the pagan culture of the classical world. Tertullian (c. 160–c. 225), a Christian writer from Carthage, had proclaimed: "What has Jerusalem to do with Athens, the Church

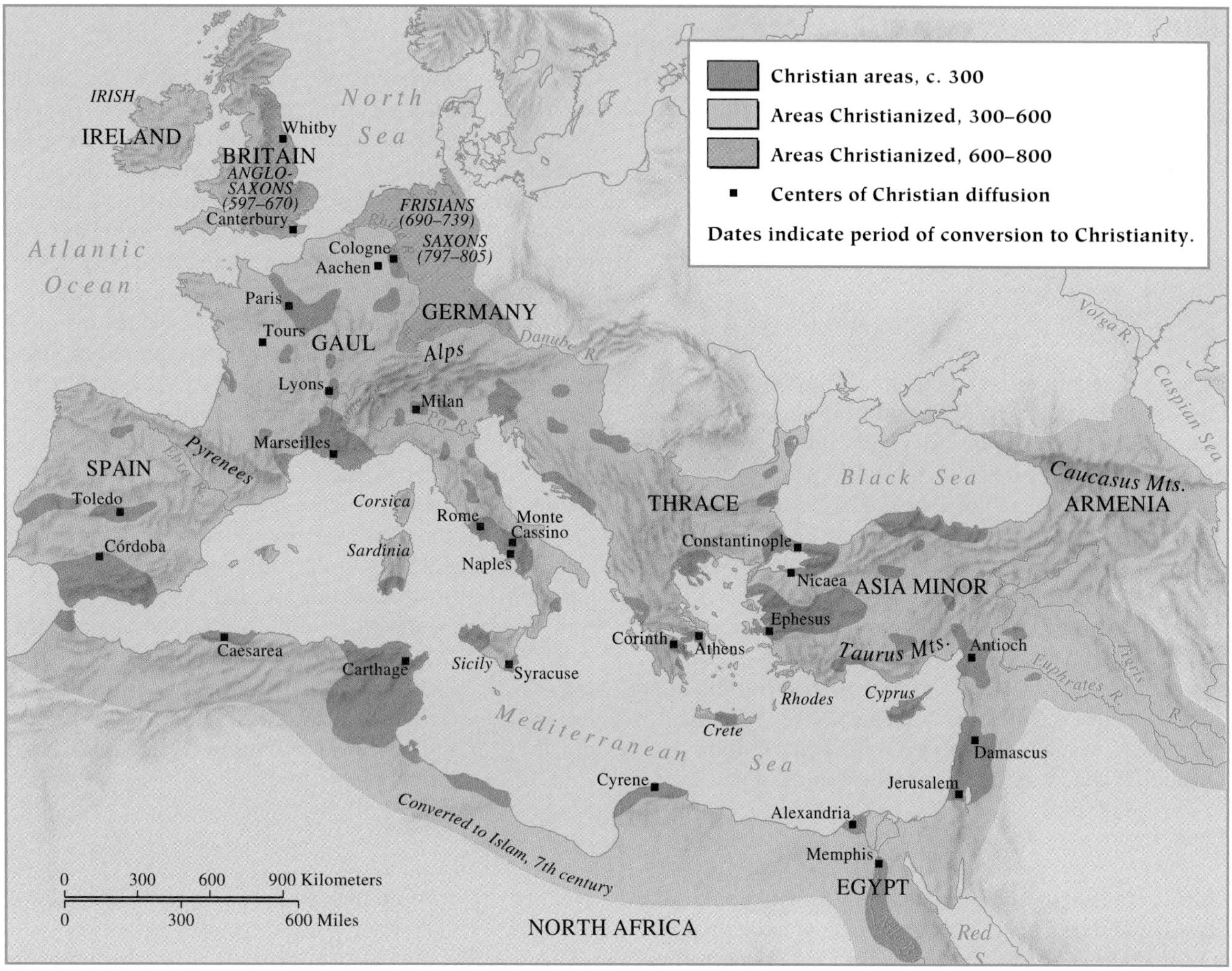

Map 7.3 The Spread of Christianity, A.D. 400–800. The Christian church had penetrated much of the Roman Empire by the end of the fifth century. It emerged as a major base of power after the fall of the empire, and it pushed its influence into new areas through the activities of missionaries. ■ What aspects of geography help explain the relatively late conversions of the Anglo-Saxons in Britain and the Frisians and Saxons east of the Rhine River?

with the Academy, the Christian with the heretic? . . . After Jesus Christ we have no need of speculation, after the Gospel no need of research."[12] To many early Christians, the Bible contained all the knowledge anyone needed.

Others, however, thought it was not possible to separate Christian theological thought from classical traditions and education and encouraged Christians to absorb the classical heritage. As it spread in the eastern Roman world, Christianity adopted Greek as its language. The New Testament was written in Greek. Christians also turned to Greek thought for help in expressing complicated theological concepts. An especially important influence was Neoplatonism, a revival of Platonic thought that reached its high point in the third century A.D. Neoplatonists believed that one could use reason to perceive the link between the invisible spiritual world and the visible material world. Christian theologians used Neoplatonic concepts to explain doctrines on Jesus, especially the distinction between his human and divine natures. In many ways, then, Christianity served to preserve Greco-Roman culture.

THE WORK OF AUGUSTINE

The work of Saint Augustine (354–430) provides one of the best examples of how Christian theologians used pagan culture in the service of Christianity. Born in North Africa, Augustine was reared by his mother, an ardent Christian. He eventually became a professor of rhetoric at Milan in 384. But two years later, after experiencing a profound and moving religious experience, Augustine gave up his teaching position and went back to North Africa, where he served as bishop of Hippo from 396 until his death in 430.

Augustine's two most famous works are the *Confessions* and *The City of God.* Written in 397, the *Confessions* was a

The Confessions of Augustine

Saint Augustine's spiritual and intellectual autobiography is a revealing self-portrait of the inner struggles of one of the intellectual giants of early Christianity. The first excerpt is taken from Book 8, in which Augustine describes how he heard a voice from heaven and was converted from his old habits. In the second excerpt, from Book 9, Augustine expresses joy and gratitude for his conversion.

Augustine, Confessions

So was I speaking and weeping in the most bitter contrition of my heart, when, lo! I heard from a neighboring house a voice as of boy or girl, I know not, chanting, and oft repeating, "Take up and read; Take up and read." Instantly, my countenance altered, I began to think most intently whether children were wont in any kind of play to sing such words: nor could I remember ever to have heard the like. So checking the torrent of my tears, I arose; interpreting it to be no other than a command from God to open the book, and read the first chapter I should find. For I had heard of Antony, that coming in during the reading of the Gospel, he received the admonition, as if what was being read was spoken to him: Go, sell all that you have, and give to the poor, and you shall have treasure in heaven, and come and follow me: and by such oracle he was forthwith converted unto You. Eagerly then I returned to the place where Alypius was sitting; for there I had laid the volume of the Apostle [Paul] when I arose thence. I seized, opened, and in silence read that section on which my eyes first fell: Not in rioting and drunkenness, not in chambering and wantonness, not in strife and envying; but put you on the Lord Jesus Christ, and make not provision for the flesh. . . . No further would I read; nor need I: for instantly at the end of this sentence, by a light as it were of serenity infused into my heart, all the darkness of doubt vanished away. . . .

O Lord I am your servant; I am your servant, and the son of your handmaid: You have broken my bonds in sunder. I will offer to You the sacrifice of praise. Let my heart and my tongue praise You; yea, let all my bones say, O Lord, who is like unto You? Let them say, and answer You me, and say unto my soul, I am your salvation. Who am I, and what am I? What evil have not been either my deeds, or if not my deeds, my words, or if not my words, my will? But You, O Lord, are good and merciful, and your right hand had respect unto the depth of my death, and from the bottom of my heart emptied that abyss of corruption.

self-portrait not of Augustine's worldly activities but of the "history of a heart," an account of his own personal and spiritual experiences, written to help others with their search. Augustine describes how he struggled throughout his early life to find God until in his thirty-second year he experienced a miraculous conversion (see the box above).

The City of God, Augustine's other major work, was a profound expression of a Christian philosophy of government and history. It was written in response to a line of argument that arose soon after the sack of Rome in 410. Some pagan philosophers maintained that Rome's problems stemmed from the Roman state's recognition of Christianity and abandonment of the old, traditional gods. Augustine argued that Rome's troubles began long before Christianity arose in the empire. In *The City of God,* Augustine theorized on the ideal relations between two kinds of societies existing throughout time—the City of God and the City of the World. Those who loved God would be loyal to the City of God, whose ultimate location was the kingdom of heaven. Earthly society would always be insecure because of human beings' fallen nature and inclination to sin. And yet the City of the World was still necessary, for it was the duty of rulers to curb the depraved instincts of sinful humans and maintain the peace necessary for Christians to live in the world. Hence Augustine posited that secular government and authority were necessary for the pursuit of the true Christian life on earth; in doing so, he provided a justification for secular political authority that would play an important role in medieval thought.

Augustine was also important in establishing the Christian church's views on sexual desire. Many early Christians had seen celibacy, or complete abstinence from sexual activity, as the surest way to holiness. Augustine, too, believed Christians should reject sex, but he maintained that many Christians were unable to do so. For them, marriage was a good alternative, but with the understanding that even in marriage, sex between a man and woman had to serve a purpose—the procreation of children. It was left to the clergy of the church to uphold the high ideal of celibacy.

JEROME AND THE BIBLE

Augustine came to be seen as one of the Latin Fathers of the Catholic church, intellectuals who wrote in Latin and profoundly influenced the development of Christian thought in the west. Another Latin Father was Jerome (345–420), who pursued literary studies in Rome and became a master of Latin prose. Jerome had mixed feelings about his love for liberal studies, however, and like Augustine experienced a spiritual conversion, after which he tried to dedicate himself more fully to Jesus. He had a dream in which Jesus appeared as his judge:

> Asked who and what I was, I replied: "I am a Christian." But He who presided said: "You lie, you are a follower of Cicero, not of Christ. For where your treasure is, there will your heart be also." Instantly, I became dumb. . . . Accordingly I made oath

> and called upon His name, saying: "Lord, if ever again I possess worldly books [the classics], or if ever again I read such, I have denied You."

After this dream, Jerome determined to "read the books of God with a zeal greater than I had previously given to the books of men."[13]

Ultimately, Jerome found a compromise by purifying the literature of the pagan world and then using it to further the Christian faith. Jerome was the greatest scholar among the Latin Fathers, and his extensive knowledge of both Hebrew and Greek enabled him to translate the Old and New Testaments into Latin. In the process, he created the so-called Latin Vulgate, or common text, of the Scriptures that became the standard edition for the Catholic church in the Middle Ages.

CASSIODORUS AND BEDE

Although the Christian church came to accept classical culture, it was not easy to do so in the new German kingdoms. Nevertheless, some Christian scholars managed to keep learning alive. Most prominent was Cassiodorus (c. 490–585), who came from an aristocratic Roman family and served as an official of the Ostrogothic king Theodoric. The conflicts that erupted after the death of Theodoric led Cassiodorus to withdraw from public life and retire to his landed estates in southern Italy, where he wrote his final work, *Divine and Human Readings,* a compendium of the literature of both Christian and pagan antiquity. Cassiodorus accepted the advice of earlier Christian intellectuals to make use of classical works while treasuring the Scriptures above all else.

Cassiodorus continued the tradition of late antiquity of classifying knowledge according to certain subjects. In assembling his compendium of authors, he followed the works of late ancient authors in placing all secular knowledge into the categories of the seven liberal arts, which were divided into two major groups: the *trivium,* consisting of grammar, rhetoric, and dialectic or logic, and the *quadrivium,* consisting of arithmetic, geometry, astronomy, and music. The seven liberal arts would be the cornerstone of Western education for nearly twelve hundred years.

The Venerable Bede (c. 672–735) was a scholar and product of Christian Anglo-Saxon England. He entered a monastery at Jarrow as a small boy and remained there most of the rest of his life. Many historians consider Bede the first major historian of the Middle Ages. His *Ecclesiastical History of the English People,* completed in 731, was a product of the remarkable flowering of English ecclesiastical and monastic culture in the eighth century. His history of England begins with the coming of Christianity to Britain. Although Bede shared the credulity of his age in regard to stories of miracles, he had a remarkable sense of history. He used his sources so judiciously that they remain our chief source of information about early Anglo-Saxon England (see the box on p. 176). His work was a remarkable accomplishment for a monk from a small corner of England and reflects the high degree of intellectual achievement of England in the eighth century.

The Byzantine Empire

In the fourth century, a noticeable separation between the western and eastern parts of the Roman Empire began to develop (see Chapter 6). In the course of the fifth century, while the Germans moved into the western part of the empire and established various kingdoms, the Roman Empire in the east, centered on Constantinople, continued to exist and even prosper.

The Reign of Justinian (527–565)

In the sixth century, the empire in the east came under the control of one of its most remarkable rulers, the emperor Justinian. As the nephew and heir of the previous emperor, Justinian had been well trained in imperial administration. He married Theodora, daughter of a lower-class circus trainer who was said to have been an actress and prostitute. She proved to be a remarkably strong-willed and intelligent woman who played a crucial role in giving Justinian the determination to crush a revolt against his rule in 532. Justinian was determined to reestablish the Roman Empire in the entire Mediterranean world and began his attempt to reconquer the west within a year after the revolt had failed.

Justinian's army under Belisarius, probably the best general of the late Roman world, presented a formidable force. Belisarius sailed to North Africa and quickly destroyed the Vandals in two major battles. From North Africa, he led his forces onto the Italian peninsula after occupying Sicily in 535. But it was not until 552 that the Ostrogoths were finally defeated. The struggle devastated Italy, which suffered more from Justinian's reconquest than from all of the previous barbarian invasions.

Justinian has been criticized for overextending his resources and bankrupting the empire. Historians now think, however, that a devastating plague in 542 and long-term economic factors were far more damaging to the Eastern Roman Empire than Justinian's conquests. Before he died, Justinian appeared to have achieved his goals. He had restored the imperial Mediterranean world; his empire included Italy, part of Spain, North Africa, Asia Minor, Palestine, and Syria (see Map 7.4). But the conquest of the western empire proved fleeting. Only three years after Justinian's death, the Lombards entered Italy. Although the eastern empire maintained the fiction of Italy as a province, its forces were limited to southern and central Italy, Sicily, and coastal areas, such as the territory around Ravenna.

THE CODIFICATION OF ROMAN LAW

Though his conquests proved short-lived, Justinian made a lasting contribution to Western civilization through his codification of Roman law. The eastern empire was heir to a vast quantity of materials connected to the development of Roman law. These included laws passed by the senate and assemblies, legal commentaries of jurists, decisions of praetors, and the edicts of emperors. Justinian had been well trained in imperial government and was well

The Emperor Justinian Surrounded by His Court. The Church of San Vitale at Ravenna contains some of the finest examples of sixth-century Byzantine mosaics. This mosaic depicts the Byzantine emperor Justinian and his court dressed in their elaborate court robes.

acquainted with Roman law. He wished to codify and simplify this mass of materials.

To accomplish his goal, Justinian authorized the jurist Trebonian to make a systematic compilation of imperial edicts. The result was the Code of Law, the first part of the *Corpus Iuris Civilis* (*The Body of Civil Law*), completed in 529. Four years later, two other parts of the *Corpus* appeared: the *Digest,* a compendium of writings of Roman jurists, and the *Institutes,* a brief summary of the chief principles of Roman law that could be used as a textbook on Roman law. The fourth part of the *Corpus* was the *Novels,* a compilation of the most important new edicts issued during Justinian's reign.

Justinian's codification of Roman law became the basis of imperial law in the Byzantine Empire until its end in 1453. More important, however, since it was written in Latin (it was, in fact, the last product of eastern Roman culture to be written in Latin, which was soon replaced by Greek), it was also eventually used in the west and in fact became the basis of the legal system of all of continental Europe.

INTELLECTUAL LIFE UNDER JUSTINIAN

The intellectual life of the Eastern Roman Empire was highly influenced by the traditions of classical civilization. Scholars actively strived to preserve the works of the ancient Greeks while basing a great deal of their own literature on classical models. Initially, however, the most outstanding literary achievements of the eastern empire were historical and religious works.

The best known of the early Byzantine historians was Procopius (c. 500–c. 562), court historian during the reign of Justinian. Procopius served as secretary to the great general Belisarius and accompanied him on his wars on behalf of Justinian. Procopius' best historical work, the *Wars,* is a firsthand account of Justinian's wars of reconquest in the western Mediterranean and his wars against the Persians in the east. Deliberately modeled after the work of his hero, the Greek historian Thucydides (see Chapter 3), Procopius' narrative features vivid descriptions of battle scenes, clear judgment, and noteworthy objectivity.

Procopius also wrote a work that many historians consider mostly scandalous gossip, his infamous *Secret History.* At the beginning of this work, Procopius informed his readers that "what I shall write now follows a different plan, supplementing the previous formal chronicle with a disclosure of what really happened throughout the Roman Empire."[14] What he revealed constituted a scathing attack upon Justinian and his wife Theodora for their alleged misdeeds.

LIFE IN CONSTANTINOPLE: THE EMPEROR'S BUILDING PROGRAM

After riots destroyed much of Constantinople in 532, Justinian rebuilt the city and gave it the appearance it would keep for almost a thousand years (see Map 7.5). With a population estimated in the hundreds of thousands, Constantinople was the largest city in Europe during the

Map 7.4 The Byzantine Empire in the Time of Justinian. The Byzantine emperor Justinian briefly restored much of the Mediterranean portion of the old Roman Empire. His general Belisarius quickly conquered the Vandals in North Africa but wrested Italy from the Ostrogoths only after a long and devastating struggle. Examine Map 6.1. ■ What former Roman territories lay outside Justinian's control?

Middle Ages. It viewed itself as the center of an empire and a special Christian city.

Until the twelfth century, Constantinople was Europe's greatest commercial center. The city was the chief entrepôt for the exchange of products between west and east. Highly desired in Europe were the products of the east: silk from China, spices from Southeast Asia and India, jewelry and ivory from India (the latter used by artisans for church items), wheat and furs from southern Russia, and flax and honey from the Balkans. Many of these eastern goods were then shipped to the Mediterranean area and northern Europe. Despite the Germanic incursions, European trade did not entirely end.

Moreover, imported raw materials were used in Constantinople for local industries. During Justinian's reign, two Christian monks smuggled silkworms from China to begin a silk industry. The state had a monopoly on the production of silk cloth, and the workshops themselves were housed in Constantinople's royal palace complex. European demand for silk cloth made it the city's most lucrative product. It is interesting to note that the upper classes, including emperors and empresses, were not discouraged from making money through trade and manufacturing. Indeed, one empress even manufactured perfumes in her bedroom.

Much of Constantinople's appearance in the Early Middle Ages was due to Justinian's program of rebuilding in the sixth century. Earlier, Emperor Theodosius II (408–450) had constructed an enormous defensive wall to protect the city on its land side. The city was dominated by an immense palace complex, a huge arena known as the Hippodrome, and hundreds of churches. No residential district was particularly fashionable; palaces, tenements, and slums ranged alongside one another. Justinian added many new buildings. His public works projects included roads, bridges, walls, public baths, law courts, and colossal underground reservoirs to hold the city's water supply. He also built hospitals, schools, monasteries, and churches. Churches were his special passion, and in Constantinople alone he built or rebuilt thirty-four of them. His greatest achievement was the famous Hagia Sophia—the Church of the Holy Wisdom.

Completed in 537, Hagia Sophia was designed by a Greek architect who did not use the simple, flat-roofed

Interior View of Hagia Sophia. Pictured here is the interior of the Church of the Holy Wisdom, constructed under Justinian by Anthemius of Tralles and Isidore of Milan. The pulpits and the great plaques bearing inscriptions from the Qur'an were introduced when the Turks converted this church to a mosque in the fifteenth century.

basilica of western architecture. The center of Hagia Sophia consisted of four enormous piers crowned by an enormous dome, which seemed to be floating in space. This effect was emphasized by Procopius, the court historian, who, at Justinian's request, wrote a treatise on the emperor's building projects: "From the lightness of the building, it does not appear to rest upon a solid foundation, but to cover the place beneath as though it were suspended from heaven by the fabled golden chain." In part, this impression was created by putting forty-two windows around the base of the dome, which allowed an incredible play of light within the cathedral. Light served to remind the worshipers of God; as Procopius commented:

> Whoever enters there to worship perceives at once that it is not by any human strength or skill, but by the favor of God that this work has been perfected; his mind rises sublime to commune with God, feeling that He cannot be far off, but must especially love to dwell in the place which He has chosen; and this takes place not only when a man sees it for the first time, but it always makes the same impression upon him, as though he had never beheld it before.[15]

As darkness is illumined by invisible light, so too it was believed the world is illumined by invisible spirit.

The royal palace complex, Hagia Sophia, and the Hippodrome were the three greatest buildings in Constantinople. This last was a huge amphitheater, constructed of brick covered by marble, holding between forty and sixty thousand spectators. Although gladiator fights were held there, the main events were the chariot races; twenty-four would usually be presented in one day. The citizens of Constantinople were passionate fans of chariot racing. Successful charioteers were acclaimed as heroes and honored with public statues. Crowds in the Hippodrome also took on political significance. Being a member of the two chief factions of charioteers—the Blues or Greens—was the only

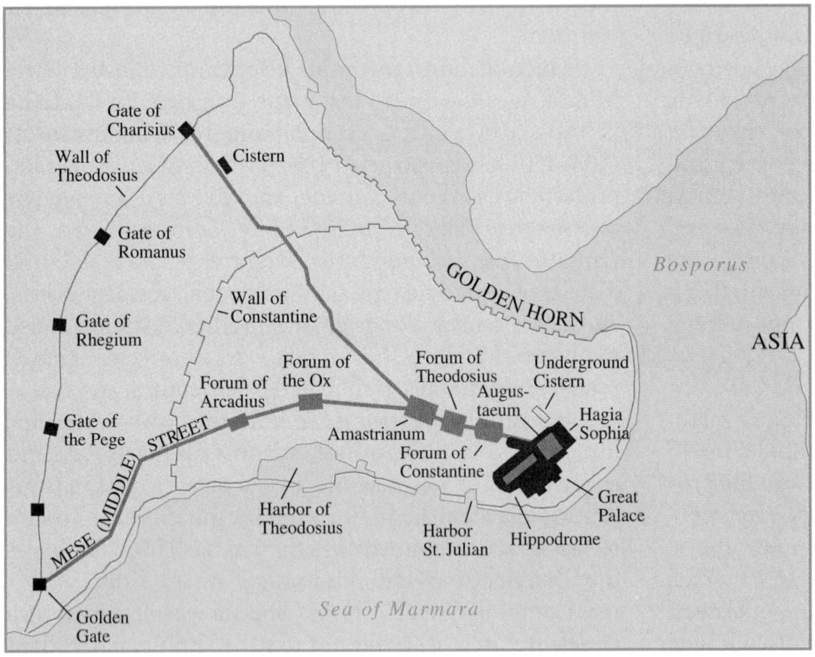

Map 7.5 Constantinople. Constantinople was the largest European city, and until the twelfth century, it was the nexus of trade between east and west. Emperor Justinian oversaw a massive building program that produced important architectural monuments such as the Hagia Sophia. ■ What natural and human-made aspects of the city helped protect it from invasion?

CHRONOLOGY

The Byzantine Empire

Protective walls of Theodosius II	408–450
Justinian codifies Roman law	529–533
Reconquest of Italy by the Byzantines	535–552
Completion of Hagia Sophia	537
Attacks on the empire in reign of Heraclius	610–641
Arab defeat of Byzantines at Yarmuk	636
Defeat by the Bulgars; losses in the Balkans	679

real outlet for political expression. Even emperors had to be aware of their demands and attitudes: the loss of a race in the Hippodrome frequenty resulted in bloody riots, and rioting could threaten the emperor's power.

From Eastern Roman to Byzantine Empire

Justinian's accomplishments had been spectacular, but when he died, he left the Eastern Roman Empire with serious problems: too much distant territory to protect, an empty treasury, a smaller population after the plague, and renewed threats to the frontiers. In the first half of the seventh century, during the reign of Heraclius (610–641), the empire faced attacks from the Persians to the east and the Slavs to the north.

The empire was left exhausted by these struggles. In the midst of them, it had developed a new system of defense by creating a new administrative unit, the *theme,* which combined civilian and military offices in the hands of the same person. Thus the civil governor was also the military leader of the area. Although this innovation helped the empire survive, it also fostered an increased militarization of the empire. By the mid-seventh century, it had become apparent that a restored Mediterranean empire was simply beyond the resources of the eastern empire, which now increasingly turned its back on the Latin west. A renewed series of external threats in the second half of the seventh century strengthened this development.

The most serious challenge to the eastern empire was presented by the rise of Islam, which unified the Arab tribes and created a powerful new force that swept through the east (see "The Rise of Islam" later in this chapter). The defeat of an eastern Roman army at Yarmuk in 636 meant the loss of the provinces of Syria and Palestine. The Arabs also moved into the old Persian Empire and conquered it. An Arab attempt to besiege Constantinople failed, in large part due to the use of Greek fire against the Arab fleets. Greek fire was a petroleum-based compound containing quicklime and sulfur. Because it would burn under water, the Byzantines created the equivalent of modern flamethrowers by using tubes to blow Greek fire onto wooden ships, with frightening effect. Arabs and eastern Roman forces now faced each other along a frontier in southern Asia Minor.

Problems also arose along the northern frontier, especially in the Balkans, where an Asiatic people known as the Bulgars had arrived earlier in the sixth century. In 679, the Bulgars defeated the eastern Roman forces and took possession of the lower Danube valley, setting up a strong Bulgarian kingdom.

By the beginning of the eighth century, the Eastern Roman Empire was greatly diminished in size, consisting only of the eastern Balkans and Asia Minor. It was now an eastern Mediterranean state. These external challenges had important internal repercussions as well. By the eighth century, the Eastern Roman Empire had been transformed into what historians call the Byzantine Empire, a civilization with its own unique character that would last until 1453 (Constantinople was built on the site of an older city named Byzantium—hence the term *Byzantine*).

The Byzantine Empire, c. 800

THE BYZANTINE EMPIRE IN THE EIGHTH CENTURY

The Byzantine Empire was a Greek state. Justinian's *Body of Civil Law* had been the last official work published in Latin. Increasingly, Latin fell into disuse as Greek became not only the common language of the Byzantine Empire but its official language as well.

The Byzantine Empire was also a Christian state, built on a faith in Jesus that was shared in a profound way by almost all its citizens. An enormous amount of artistic talent was poured into the construction of churches, church ceremonies, and church decoration. Spiritual principles deeply permeated Byzantine art. The importance of religion to the Byzantines explains why theological disputes took on an exaggerated form. The most famous of these disputes, the so-called iconoclastic controversy, threatened the stability of the empire in the first half of the eighth century.

Beginning in the sixth century, the use of religious images, especially in the form of icons or pictures of sacred figures, became so widespread that charges of idolatry, or the worship of images, began to be heard. The use of images or icons had been justified by the argument that icons were not worshiped but were simply used to help illiterate people understand their religion. This argument failed to stop the iconoclasts, as the opponents of icons were called.

A Byzantine Icon. The Byzantine Empire experienced considerable dissension over the use of icons, or pictures of sacred figures. Pictured here is an icon of the Virgin and Child, a fourteenth-century Byzantine miniature mosaic in which small pieces of colored glass were attached to a wooden panel.

Beginning in 730, the Byzantine emperor Leo III (717–741) outlawed the use of icons. Strong resistance ensued, especially from monks. Leo III also used the iconoclastic controversy to add to the prestige of the patriarch of Constantinople, the highest church official in the east and second in dignity only to the bishop of Rome. The Roman popes were opposed to the iconoclastic edicts, and their opposition created considerable dissension between the popes and the Byzantine emperors. Late in the eighth century, the Byzantine rulers reversed their stand on the use of images, but not before considerable damage had been done to the unity of the Christian church. Although the final separation between Roman Catholicism and Greek Orthodoxy (as the Christian church in the Byzantine Empire was called) did not occur until 1054, the iconoclastic controversy was important in moving both sides in that direction.

The emperor occupied a crucial position in the Byzantine state. Portrayed as chosen by God, the Byzantine emperor was crowned in sacred ceremonies, and his subjects were expected to prostrate themselves in his presence. His power was considered absolute and was limited in practice only by deposition or assassination. Because the emperor appointed the patriarch, he also exercised control over both church and state. The Byzantines believed that God had commanded their state to preserve the true faith—Orthodox Christianity. Emperor, clergy, and civic officials were all bound together in service to this ideal. It can be said that spiritual values truly held the Byzantine state together.

By 750, it was apparent that two of Rome's heirs, the Germanic kingdoms and the Byzantine Empire, were moving in different directions. Nevertheless, Byzantine influence on the medieval western world was significant. The images of a Roman imperial state that continued to haunt the west had a living reality in the Byzantine state. The legal system of the west came to owe much to Justinian's codification of Roman law. In addition, the Byzantine Empire served in part as a buffer state, protecting the west for a long time from incursions from the east. Although the Byzantine Empire would continue to influence the west until its demise in 1453, it went its own unique way. One of its bitterest enemies was the new power known as Islam.

The Rise of Islam

Like the Hebrews and the Assyrians, the Arabs were a Semitic-speaking people of the Near East with a long history. In Roman times, the Arabian peninsula came to be dominated by Bedouins, tribes of nomads who moved constantly to find water and food for their animals. Although some Arabs prospered from trading activities, especially in the north, the majority of the Arabs consisted of poor Bedouins, whose tribes were known for their independence, their warlike qualities, and their dislike of urban-dwelling Arabs.

Although these early Arabs were polytheistic, there was a supreme God named Allah (*Allah* is Arabic for God) who ruled over the other gods. There was no priesthood; all members of the tribe were involved in the practice of the faith. Allah was symbolized by a sacred stone, and each tribe had its own stone. All tribes, however, worshiped a massive black meteorite—the Black Stone, which had been placed in a central shrine called the *Ka'ba* in the city of Mecca.

In the fifth and sixth centuries A.D., the Arabian peninsula took on new importance. As a result of political disorder in Mesopotamia and Egypt, the usual trade routes in the region began to change. A new trade route—from the Mediterranean through Mecca to Yemen and then by ship across the Indian Ocean—became more popular, and communities in that part of the Arabian peninsula, such as Mecca, began to prosper from this caravan trade. As

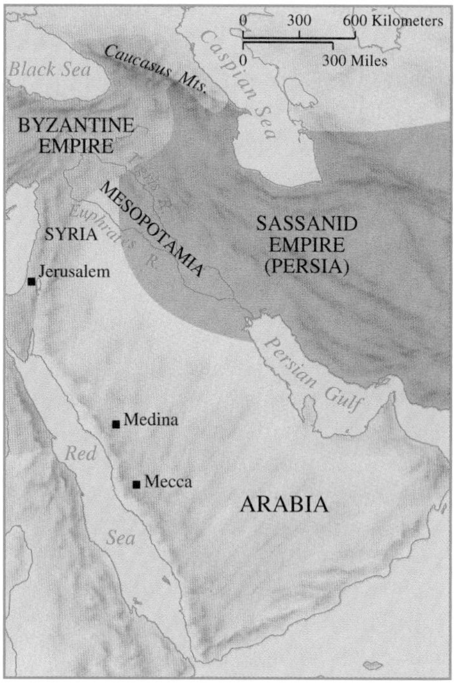

Arabia in the Time of Muhammad

a result, tensions arose between the Bedouins in the desert and the increasingly wealthy merchant classes in the towns. Into this intense world stepped Muhammad.

Born in Mecca to a merchant family, Muhammad (c. 570–632) was orphaned at the age of five. He grew up to become a caravan manager and eventually married a rich widow who was also his employer. In his middle years, he began to experience visions that he believed were inspired by Allah. Muhammad believed that while Allah had already revealed himself in part through Moses and Jesus—and thus through the Hebrew and Christian traditions—the final revelations were now being given to him. Out of these revelations, which were eventually written down, came the Qur'an or Koran, which contained the guidelines by which followers of Allah were to live. Muhammad's teachings formed the basis for the religion known as Islam, which means "submission to the will of Allah." Allah was the all-powerful being who had created the universe and everything in it. Humans must subject themselves to Allah if they wished to achieve everlasting life. His followers were called Muslims, meaning practitioners of Islam.

After receiving the revelations, Muhammad set out to convince the people of Mecca that the revelations were true. At first, many thought he was insane, and others feared that his attacks on the corrupt society around him would upset the established social and political order. Discouraged by the failure of the Meccans to accept his message, in 622 Muhammad and some of his closest supporters left the city and moved north to the rival city of Yathrib, later renamed Medina ("city of the Prophet"). The year of the journey to Medina, known in history as the *Hegira,* became year 1 in the official calendar of Islam.

Muhammad, who had been invited to the town by a number of prominent residents, soon began to win support from people in Medina as well as from members of Bedouin tribes in the surrounding countryside. From these groups, he formed the first Muslim community. Muslims saw no separation between political and religious authority; submission to the will of Allah meant submission to his Prophet, Muhammad. Muhammad soon became both a religious and a political leader. His political and military skills enabled him to put together a reliable military force, with which he returned to Mecca in 630, conquering the city and converting the townspeople to the new faith. From Mecca, Muhammad's ideas spread quickly across the Arabian peninsula and within a relatively short time had resulted in both the religious and the political union of Arab society.

At the heart of Islam was its sacred book, the Qur'an, with its basic message that there is no God but Allah and Muhammad is his prophet (see the box on p. 186). Essentially, the Qur'an contains Muhammad's revelations of a heavenly book written down by secretaries. Consisting of 114 chapters, the Qur'an recorded the beliefs of the Muslims and served as their code of ethics and law.

Islam was a direct and simple faith, emphasizing the need to obey the will of Allah. This meant following a basic ethical code consisting of the Five Pillars of Islam: belief in Allah and Muhammad as his Prophet; standard prayer five times a day and public prayer on Friday at midday to worship Allah; observance of the holy month of Ramadan (the ninth month in the Muslim calendar) by fasting from dawn to sunset; making a pilgrimage (known as the *hajj*) to

Muhammad on a Camel. This illustration is from a medieval manuscript of the *Universal History* by Rashid al-Din, a Persian historian. Here Jesus is shown riding on a donkey beside Muhammad, who rides on a camel. The purpose of the illustration is to show that while Jesus was accepted as a forerunner of the Prophet, his teachings were superseded by the message of Muhammad.

The Qur'an and the Spread of the Muslim Faith

The Qur'an is the sacred book of the Muslims, comparable to the Bible in Christianity. In this selection from Chapter 47, titled "Muhammad, Revealed at Medina," it is apparent that Islam encourages the spreading of the faith. Believers who died for Allah were promised a garden of paradise quite unlike the arid desert homeland of the Arab warriors.

■ *The Qur'an: Chapter 47, "Muhammad, Revealed at Medina"*

Allah will bring to nothing the deeds of those who disbelieve and debar others from His path. As for the faithful who do good works and believe in what is revealed to Muhammad—which is the truth from their Lord—He will forgive them their sins and ennoble their state.

This, because the unbelievers follow falsehood, while the faithful follow the truth from their Lord. Thus Allah coins their sayings for mankind.

When you meet the unbelievers in the battlefield strike off their heads and, when you have laid them low, bind your captives firmly. Then grant them their freedom or take ransom from them, until War shall lay down her armor.

Thus shall you do. Had Allah willed, He could Himself have punished them; but He has ordained it thus that He might test you, the one by the other.

As for those who are slain in the cause of Allah, he will not allow their works to perish. He will vouchsafe them guidance and ennoble their state; He will admit them to the Paradise He has made known to them.

Believers, if you help Allah, Allah will help you and make you strong. But the unbelievers shall be consigned to perdition. He will bring their deeds to nothing. Because they have opposed His revelations, He will frustrate their works.

Have they never journeyed through the land and seen what was the end of those who have gone before them? Allah destroyed them utterly. A similar fate awaits the unbelievers, because Allah is the protector of the faithful; because the unbelievers have no protector.

Allah will admit those who embrace the true faith and do good works to gardens watered by running streams. The unbelievers take their fill of pleasure and eat as the beasts eat: but Hell shall be their home. . . .

This is the Paradise which the righteous have been promised. There shall flow in it rivers of unpolluted water, and rivers of milk forever fresh; rivers of delectable wine and rivers of clearest honey. They shall eat therein of every fruit and receive forgiveness from their Lord. Is this like the lot of those who shall abide in Hell for ever and drink scalding water which will tear their bowels? . . .

Know that there is no god but Allah. Implore Him to forgive your sins and to forgive the true believers, men and women. Allah knows your busy haunts and resting-places.

Mecca in one's lifetime, if possible; and giving alms to the poor and unfortunate. The faithful who observed the law were guaranteed a place in an eternal paradise.

Islam was not just a set of religious beliefs but a way of life as well. After the death of Muhammad, Muslim scholars drew up a law code, called the *Shari'a,* to provide believers with a set of prescriptions to regulate their daily lives. Much of the *Shari'a* was drawn from the Qur'an. Believers' behavior was subject to strict guidelines. In addition to the Five Pillars, Muslims were forbidden to gamble, to eat pork, to drink alcoholic beverages, and to engage in dishonest behavior. Sexual practices were also strict. Marriages were to be arranged by parents, and contacts between unmarried men and women were discouraged. In accordance with Bedouin custom, males were permitted to have more than one wife, but Muhammad attempted to limit the practice by restricting the number of wives to four.

■ *The Expansion of Islam*

The death of Muhammad presented his followers with a dilemma. Although Muhammad had not claimed to be divine, Muslims saw no separation between religious and political authority. Submission to the will of Allah was the same thing as submission to his Prophet, Muhammad.

Bibliothèque Nationale, Paris

Muslims Celebrate the End of Ramadan. Ramadan is the holy month of Islam during which all Muslims must fast from dawn to sunset. Observance of this holy month is regarded as one of the Five Pillars of the faith. Muhammad instituted the fast during his stay at Medina. It was designed to replace the single Jewish Day of Atonement. This Persian miniature depicts Muslims on horseback celebrating the end of Ramadan.

According to the Qur'an: "Whoever obeys the messenger obeys Allah." But Muhammad had never named a successor, and although he had several daughters, he left no sons. In a male-oriented society, who would lead the community of the faithful? Shortly after Muhammad's death, a number of his closest followers selected Abu Bakr, a wealthy merchant who was Muhammad's father-in-law, as caliph, or temporal leader, of the Islamic community.

Muhammad and the early caliphs who succeeded him took up the Arab tribal custom of making raids against enemies. The Qur'an called this activity "striving in the way of the Lord," or *jihad.* Although misleadingly called a Holy War, the *jihad* grew out of the tradition of tribal raids, which were permitted as a way to channel the warlike energies of the Bedouin tribes. *Jihads* were not carried out to convert others because conversion to Islam was purely voluntary. Nonbelievers who did not convert were required only to submit to Muslim rule and pay taxes.

Once the Arabs had become unified under Abu Bakr, they began to direct the energy they had once expended against each other outward against neighboring peoples. The Byzantines and the Persians were the first to feel the strength of the newly united Arabs. At Yarmuk in 636, the Muslims defeated the Byzantine army, and by 640, they had taken possession of the province of Syria (see Map 7.6). To the east, the Arabs defeated Persian forces in 637 and then went on to conquer the entire Persian Empire by 650. In the meantime, Egypt and other areas of northern Africa had been added to the new Muslim empire. Led by a series of brilliant generals, the Arabs had put together a large and highly motivated army, whose valor was enhanced by the belief that Muslim warriors were guaranteed a place in paradise if they died in battle.

Early caliphs, ruling from Medina, organized their newly conquered territories into taxpaying provinces. By the mid-seventh century, problems arose again over the succession to the Prophet until Ali, Muhammad's son-in-law, was assassinated and the general Muawiya, the governor of Syria and one of Ali's chief rivals, became caliph in 661. Muawiya was known for one outstanding virtue: he used force only when necessary. As he said, "I never use my sword when my whip will do, nor my whip when my tongue will do."[16] Muawiya moved quickly to make the caliphate hereditary in his own family, thus establishing the Umayyad dynasty. As one of their first actions, the Umayyads moved the capital of the Muslim empire from Medina to Damascus in Syria. This

Map 7.6 The Expansion of Islam. Muhammad, the prophet of Islam, engaged in warfare against neighboring tribes, an activity sanctified in the new religion as *jihad*. Militaristic expansion continued with great zeal under the Prophet's successors. Islamic rule spread rapidly in the decades after Muhammad's death, stopped finally by the Byzantine Empire and the Franks. ■ Why was the continuance of the Byzantine Empire a key factor in stopping the spread of Islam into Europe?

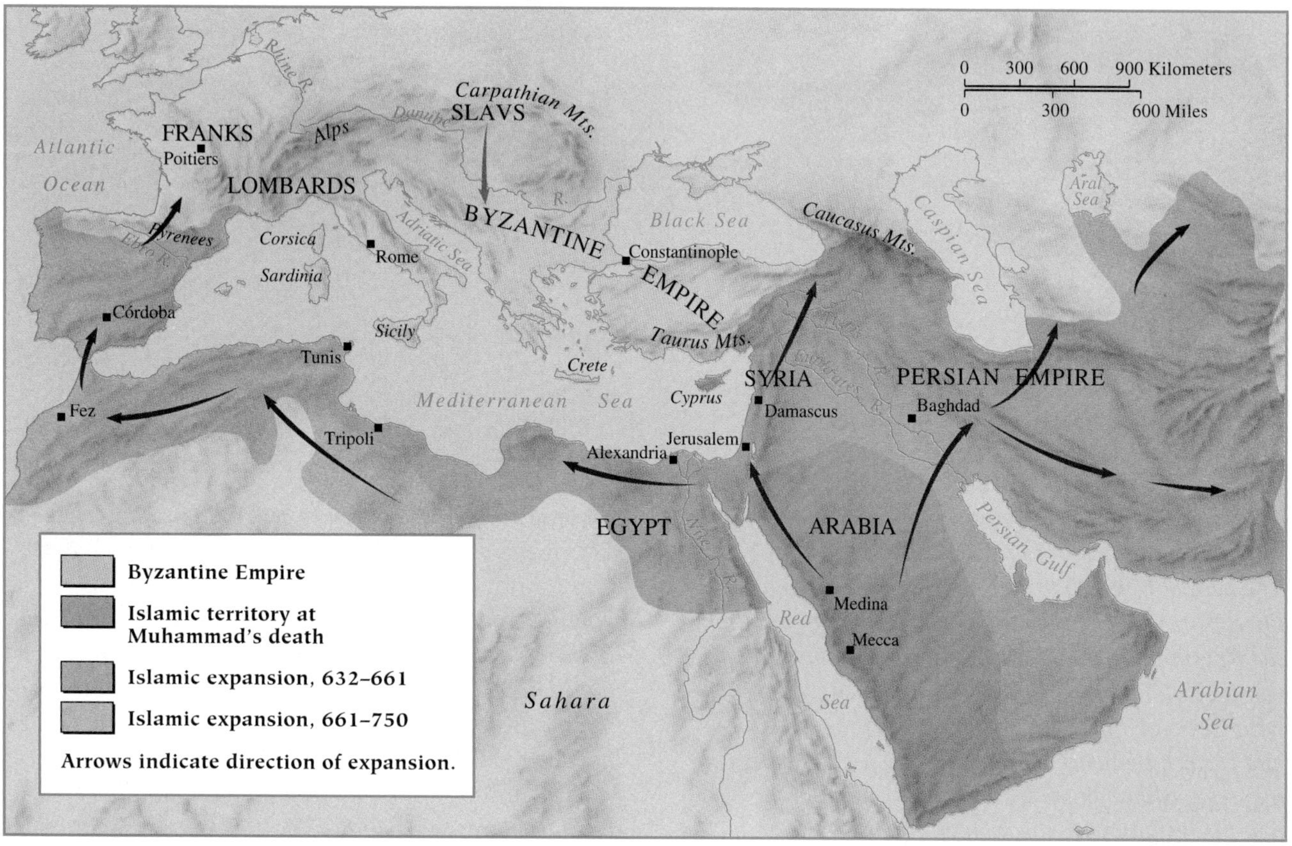

internal dissension over the caliphate created a split in Islam between the Shi'ites, or those who accepted only the descendants of Ali, Muhammad's son-in-law, as the true rulers, and the Sunnites, who claimed that the descendants of the Umayyads were the true caliphs. This seventh-century split in Islam has lasted until the present day.

The internal dissension did not stop the expansion of Islam, however. At the beginning of the eighth century, new attacks were made at both the western and eastern ends of the Mediterranean world. After sweeping across North Africa, the Muslims crossed the Strait of Gibraltar and moved into Spain around 710. The Visigothic kingdom collapsed, and by 725, most of Spain had become a Muslim state with its center at Córdoba. In 732, a Muslim army, making a foray into southern France, was defeated at the Battle of Tours near Poitiers. Muslim expansion in Europe came to a halt.

Meanwhile, in 717, another Muslim force had launched a naval attack on Constantinople with the hope of destroying the Byzantine Empire. In the spring of 718, the Byzantines destroyed the Muslim fleet and saved the Byzantine Empire and indirectly Christian Europe, since the fall of Constantinople would no doubt have opened the door to Muslim invasion of eastern Europe. The Byzantine Empire and Islam now established an uneasy frontier in southern Asia Minor.

The Arab advance had finally come to an end, but not before the southern and eastern Mediterranean parts of the old Roman Empire had been conquered. Islam had truly become heir to much of the old Roman Empire. The Umayyad dynasty at Damascus now ruled an enormous empire. While expansion had conveyed untold wealth and new ethnic groups into the fold of Islam, it also brought contact with Byzantine and Persian civilization. As a result, the new Arab empire would be influenced by Greek culture as well as the older civilizations of the ancient Near East. The children of the conquerors would be educated in new ways and produce a brilliant culture that would eventually influence western Europe intellectually.

CHRONOLOGY

The Rise of Islam

Birth of Muhammad	c. 570
Muhammad's flight from Mecca (*Hegira*)	622
Death of Muhammad	632
Defeat of Byzantines at Yarmuk	636
Seizure of Byzantine provinces of Syria and Egypt	640–642
Defeat of Persians	637–650
Invasion of Spain	c. 710
Arab failure to capture Constantinople	717–718
Defeat of Muslims near Poitiers	732

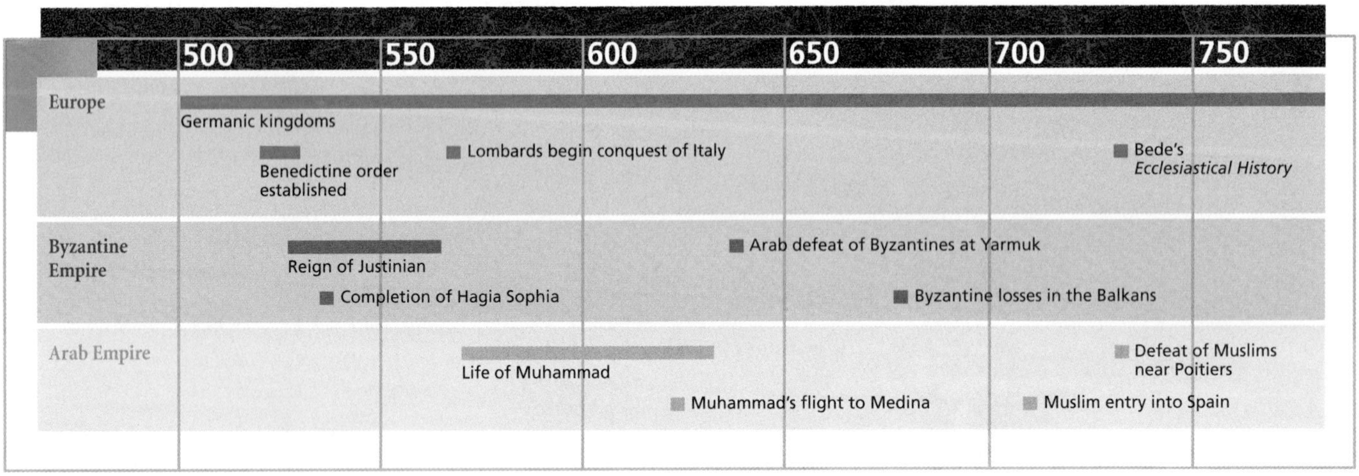

Conclusion

The period from 400 to 800 was both chaotic and creative. Three new entities fell heir to Roman civilization: the Germanic kingdoms, the Byzantine Empire, and the world of Islam. In the west, Roman elements combined with German and Celtic influences; in the east, Greek and eastern elements of late antiquity were of more consequence. Although the Germanic kingdoms of the west and the Byzantine civilization of the east came to share a common bond in Christianity, it proved incapable of keeping them in harmony politically as the two civilizations continued to move apart. Christianity, however, remained a dominant influence in both civilizations and in the west was especially important as a civilizing agent that brought pagan peoples into a new European civilization that was slowly being born. The rise of Islam, Rome's third heir, resulted in the loss of the southern and eastern Mediterranean worlds of the old Roman Empire to a religious power that was neither Roman nor Christian.

The new Islamic empire forced Europe proper back upon itself, and slowly, a new civilization emerged that became the heart of what we know as Western civilization.

Notes

1. Ernest F. Henderson, *Selected Historical Documents of the Middle Ages* (London, 1892), p. 182.
2. Ibid., p. 181.
3. "The Creed of Nicaea," in Henry Bettenson, ed., *Documents of the Christian Church* (London, 1963), p. 35.
4. Matthew, 16:15–19.
5. R. C. Petry, ed., *A History of Christianity: Readings in the History of Early and Medieval Christianity* (Englewood Cliffs, N.J., 1962), p. 70.
6. Brian Pullan, ed., *Sources for the History of Medieval Europe* (Oxford, 1966), p. 46.
7. Quoted in Sidney Painter and Brian Tierney, *Western Europe in the Middle Ages, 300–1475* (New York, 1983), p. 106.
8. Mark, 10:21.
9. Norman F. Cantor, ed., *The Medieval World, 300–1300* (New York, 1963), pp. 104, 101, 108, 103.
10. Bede, *A History of the English Church and People,* trans. Leo Sherley-Price (Harmondsworth, England, 1968), pp. 86–87.
11. Quoted in Peter Brown, *The Rise of Western Christendom: Triumph and Adversity, A.D. 200–1000* (Oxford, 1997), p. 98.
12. Tertullian, "The Prescriptions Against the Heretics," in *The Library of Christian Classics,* vol. 5, *Early Latin Theology,* ed. and trans. S. L. Greenslade (Philadelphia, 1956), p. 36.
13. Anne Fremantle, ed., *A Treasury of Early Christianity* (New York, 1953), p. 91.
14. Procopius, *Secret History,* trans. Richard Atwater (Ann Arbor, Mich., 1963), p. 3.
15. Procopius, *Buildings of Justinian* (Palestine Pilgrims' Text Society, 1897), pp. 9, 6–7, 11.
16. Quoted in Arthur Goldschmidt Jr., *A Concise History of the Middle East,* 4th ed. (Boulder, Colo., 1991), p. 56.

Suggestions for Further Reading

Good general histories of the entire medieval period can be found in S. Painter and B. Tierney, *Western Europe in the Middle Ages, 300–1475* (New York, 1983); E. Peters, *Europe and the Middle Ages,* 2d ed. (Englewood Cliffs, N.J., 1989); D. Nicholas, *The Evolution of the Medieval World: Society, Government, and Thought in Europe, 312–1500* (London, 1993); and G. Holmes, ed., *The Oxford Illustrated History of Medieval Europe* (Oxford, 1988). For a good general survey of the social history of the Middle Ages, see C. B. Bouchard, *Life and Society in the West: Antiquity and the Middle Ages* (San Diego, Calif., 1988). For excellent reference works on medieval history, see H. R. Loyn, *The Middle Ages: A Concise Encyclopedia* (New York, 1989), and J. R. Strayer, ed., *Dictionary of the Middle Ages,* 13 vols. (New York, 1982–1989). For a brief history of the period covered in this chapter, see R. Collins, *Early Medieval Europe, 300–1000* (New York, 1991).

For surveys of the German tribes and their migrations, see L. Musset, *The German Invasions* (University Park, Pa., 1975); T. S. Burns, *A History of the Ostrogoths* (Bloomington, Ind., 1984); F. P. Heather, *Goths and Romans* (Oxford, 1991); E. James, *The Franks* (Oxford, 1988); H. Wolfram, *The Goths,* trans. T. J. Dunlop (Berkeley, Calif., 1988); and I. N. Wood, *Merovingian Kingdoms* (London, 1994).

For a superb introduction to early Christianity, see P. Brown, *The Rise of Western Christendom: Triumph and Adversity, A.D. 200–1000* (Oxford, 1997). On Saints Augustine and Jerome, see H. Chadwick, *Augustine* (Oxford, 1986), and J. N. D. Kelly, *Saint Jerome* (London, 1975). For a good account of early monasticism, see C. H. Lawrence, *Medieval Monasticism,* 2d ed. (London, 1989). On Saint Benedict and the Benedictine ideal, see O. Chadwick, *The Making of the Benedictine Ideal* (London, 1981). For women in monastic life, see S. F. Wemple, *Women in Frankish Society: Marriage and the Cloister, 500–900* (Philadelphia, 1981). On women in general, see L. Bitel, "Women in Early Medieval Northern Europe," in R. Bridenthal, S. M. Stuard, and M. E. Wiesner, *Becoming Visible,* 3d ed. (New York, 1998), and D. Herlihy, *Opera Muliebria: Women and Work in Medieval Europe* (New York, 1990).

A brief survey of the development of the papacy can be found in G. Barraclough, *The Medieval Papacy* (New York, 1968). J. Richards, *The Popes and the Papacy in the Early Middle Ages, 476–752* (Boston, 1979), is a more detailed study of the early papacy. On Pope Gregory the Great, see C. Straw, *Gregory the Great: Perfection in Imperfection* (Berkeley, Calif., 1988). On Irish monasticism, see L. M. Bitel, *Isle of the Saints: Monastic Settlement and Christian Community in Early Ireland* (Ithaca, N.Y., 1990).

A brief but good introduction to Byzantine history can be found in J. Haldon, *Byzantium: A History* (Charleston, S.C., 2000). The best single political history is G. Ostrogorsky, *A History of the Byzantine State,* 2d ed. (New Brunswick, N.J., 1968). For a comprehensive survey of the Byzantine Empire, see W. Treadgold, *A History of the Byzantine State and Society* (Stanford, Calif., 1997). On Justinian, see J. Moorhead, *Justinian* (London, 1995), and J. A. S. Evans, *The Age of Justinian* (New York, 1996). On Constantinople, see D. T. Rice, *Constantinople: From Byzantium to Istanbul* (New York, 1965). The role of the Christian church is discussed in J. Hussey, *The Orthodox Church in the Byzantine Empire* (Oxford, 1986).

Good brief surveys of the Islamic Middle East include A. Goldschmidt Jr., *A Concise History of the Middle East,* 5th ed. (Boulder, Colo., 1995), and S. N. Fisher, *The Middle East: A History,* 5th ed. (New York, 1997). On the rise of Islam, see F. E. Peters, *Muhammad and the Origins of Islam* (Albany, N.Y., 1994); M. Lings, *Muhammad: His Life Based on the Earliest Sources* (New York, 1983); and F. Donner, *The Early Islamic Conquests* (Princeton, N.J., 1980).

For additional reading, go to InfoTrac College Edition, your online research library at http://web1.infotrac-college.com

Enter the search term *Byzantium* using the Subject Guide.

Enter the search term *early Christianity* using Key Terms.

Enter the search term *Augustine* using Key Terms.

Enter the search term *Middle Ages* using the Subject Guide.

CHAPTER

8

European Civilization in the Early Middle Ages, 750–1000

Bibliotheque Nationale, Paris

CHAPTER OUTLINE

FOCUS QUESTIONS

- What was the significance of Charlemagne's coronation as emperor?
- How did both the intellectual life and daily life in the Carolingian Empire represent a fusion of Gallo-Roman, Germanic, and Christian practices?
- What was fief-holding, and why did it develop?
- What was manorialism, and how was it related to fief-holding?
- What were the chief developments in the Byzantine Empire and the Islamic world between 750 and 1000?
- Why can it be said that Islamic civilization was superior to the civilization of western Europe in the ninth and tenth centuries?

IN 800, CHARLEMAGNE, the king of the Franks, journeyed to Rome to help Pope Leo III, who was barely clinging to power in the face of rebellious Romans. On Christmas Day, Charlemagne and his family, attended by Romans, Franks, and visitors from the Byzantine Empire, crowded into St. Peter's Basilica to hear Mass. Quite unexpectedly, according to a Frankish writer, "as the king rose from praying before the tomb of the blessed apostle Peter, Pope Leo placed a golden crown on his head." In keeping with ancient tradition, the people in the church shouted, "Long life and victory to Charles Augustus, crowned by God the great and pacific Emperor of the Romans." Seemingly, the Roman Empire in the west had been reborn, and Charles had become the first western emperor since 476. But this "Roman emperor" was actually a German king, and he had been crowned by the head of the western

Christian church. In truth, the coronation of Charlemagne was a sign not of the rebirth of the Roman Empire but of the emergence of a new European civilization.

By the year of Charlemagne's coronation, the contours of this new European civilization were beginning to emerge in western Europe. Increasingly, Europe would become the focus and center of Western civilization. Building on a fusion of Germanic, classical, and Christian elements, the medieval European world first became visible in the Carolingian Empire of Charlemagne. The agrarian foundations of the eighth and ninth centuries proved inadequate to maintain a large monarchical system, however, and a new political and military order based on the decentralization of political power subsequently evolved to become an integral part of the political world of the Middle Ages.

European civilization began on a shaky and uncertain foundation, however. In the ninth century, Vikings, Magyars, and Muslims posed threats that could easily have stifled the new society. But the Vikings and Magyars were assimilated, and recovery slowly began to set in. By 1000, European civilization was ready to embark on a period of dazzling vitality and expansion.

People and Environment

The number of people in early medieval Europe is a matter of considerable uncertainty. In all probability, the population of the eighth century had still not recovered from the losses caused by the plagues of the sixth and seventh centuries. Historians generally believe that in the Early Middle Ages, Europe was a sparsely populated landscape dotted with villages and clusters of villages of farmers and warriors. Although rivers, such as the Loire, Seine, Rhine, Elbe, and Oder, served as major arteries of communication, villages were still separated from one another by forests, swamps, and mountain ridges. Forests, which provided building and heating materials as well as game, covered the European landscape. In fact, it has been estimated that less than 10 percent of the land was cultivated, a figure so small that some economic historians believe that Europe had difficulty feeding even its modest population. Thus hunting and fishing were necessary to supplement the European diet.

The cultivation of new land proved especially difficult in the Early Middle Ages. Given the crude implements of the time, it was not easy to clear forests and cultivate new land. Moreover, German tribes had for centuries considered trees sacred and resisted cutting them down to clear land for farming. Even conversion to Christianity did not entirely change these attitudes. In addition, the heavy soils of northern Europe were not easily plowed. Agricultural methods also worked against significant crop yields. Land was allowed to lie fallow (idle) every other year to regain its fertility, but even so it produced low yields. Evidence indicates that Frankish estates yielded incredibly low ratios of two measures of grain to one measure of seed. Although climatic patterns show that European weather began to improve around 700 after a centuries-long period of wetter and colder conditions, natural disasters were still a threat, especially since the low yields meant that little surplus could be saved for bad times. Drought or too much rain could mean meager harvests, famine, and dietary deficiencies that made people particularly susceptible to a wide range of diseases. This was a period of low life expectancy. One study of Hungarian graves found that of every five skeletons, one was a child below the age of one, and two were children between one and fourteen; more than one in five was a woman below the age of twenty. Overall, then, the picture of early medieval Europe is of a relatively small population subsisting on the basis of a limited agricultural economy and leading, in most cases, a precarious existence.

The World of the Carolingians

By the eighth century, the Merovingian dynasty was losing its control of the Frankish lands. Charles Martel, the Carolingian mayor of the palace of Austrasia, became the virtual ruler of these territories. When Charles Martel died in 741, his son, Pepin, deposed the Merovingians and assumed the kingship of the Frankish state for himself and his family. Pepin's actions, which were approved by the pope, created a new form of Frankish kingship. Pepin (751–768) was crowned king and formally anointed by a representative of the pope with holy oil in imitation of an Old Testament practice. The anointing not only symbolized that the kings had been entrusted with a sacred office but also provides yet another example of how a Germanic institution fused with a Christian practice in the Early Middle Ages.

Charlemagne and the Carolingian Empire (768–814)

Pepin's death in 768 brought to the throne of the Frankish kingdom his son, a dynamic and powerful ruler known to history as Charles the Great or Charlemagne (*Carolus magnus* in Latin—hence our word *Carolingian*). Charlemagne was a determined and decisive man, highly intelligent and inquisitive. A fierce warrior, he was also a wise patron of learning and a resolute statesman (see the box on p. 192). He greatly expanded the territory of the Carolingian Empire during his lengthy rule.

EXPANSION OF THE CAROLINGIAN EMPIRE

In the tradition of the Germanic kings, Charlemagne was a determined warrior who undertook fifty-four military campaigns. Even though the Frankish army was relatively small—only eight thousand men gathered each spring for

The Achievements of Charlemagne

Einhard, the biographer of Charlemagne, was born in the valley of the Main River in Germany about 775. Raised and educated in the monastery of Fulda, an important center of learning, he arrived at the court of Charlemagne in 791 or 792. Although he did not achieve high office under Charlemagne, he served as private secretary to Louis the Pious, Charlemagne's son and successor. Einhard's *Life of Charlemagne,* written between 817 and 830, was modeled on Suetonius' *Lives of the Caesars,* especially his biography of Augustus. In this selection, Einhard discusses some of Charlemagne's accomplishments.

Einhard, Life of Charlemagne

Such are the wars, most skillfully planned and successfully fought, which this most powerful king waged during the forty-seven years of his reign. He so largely increased the Frank kingdom, which was already great and strong when he received it at his father's hands, that more than double its former territory was added to it.... He subdued all the wild and barbarous tribes dwelling in Germany between the Rhine and the Vistula, the Ocean and the Danube, all of which speak very much the same language, but differ widely from one another in customs and dress....

He added to the glory of his reign by gaining the good will of several kings and nations; so close, indeed, was the alliance that he contracted with Alfonso, King of Galicia and Asturias, that the latter, when sending letters or ambassadors to Charles, invariably styled himself his man.... The Emperors of Constantinople [the Byzantine emperors] sought friendship and alliance with Charles by several embassies; and even when the Greeks [the Byzantines] suspected him of designing to take the empire from them, because of his assumption of the title Emperor, they made a close alliance with him, that he might have no cause of offense. In fact, the power of the Franks was always viewed with a jealous eye, whence the Greek proverb, "Have the Frank for your friend, but not for your neighbor."

This King, who showed himself so great in extending his empire and subduing foreign nations, and was constantly occupied with plans to that end, undertook also very many works calculated to adorn and benefit his kingdom, and brought several of them to completion. Among these, the most deserving of mention are the basilica of the Holy Mother of God at Aix-la-Chapelle, built in the most admirable manner, and a bridge over the Rhine River at Mainz, half a mile long, the breadth of the river at this point.... Above all, sacred buildings were the object of his care throughout his whole kingdom; and whenever he found them falling to ruin from age, he commanded the priests and fathers who had charge of them to repair them, and made sure by commissioners that his instructions were obeyed.... Thus did Charles defend and increase as well as beautify his kingdom....

He cherished with the greatest fervor and devotion the principles of the Christian religion, which had been instilled into him from infancy. Hence it was that he built the beautiful church at Aix-la-Chapelle, which he adorned with gold and silver and lamps, and with rails and doors of solid brass. He had the columns and marbles for this structure brought from Rome and Ravenna, for he could not find such as were suitable elsewhere. He was a constant worshiper at this church as long as his health permitted, going morning and evening, even after nightfall, besides attending Mass....

He was very forward in caring for the poor, so much so that he not only made a point of giving in his own country and his own kingdom, but when he discovered that there were Christians living in poverty in Syria, Egypt, and Africa, at Jerusalem, Alexandria, and Carthage, he had compassion on their wants, and used to send money over the seas to them.... He sent great and countless gifts to the popes, and throughout his whole reign the wish that he had nearest at heart was to reestablish the ancient authority of the city of Rome under his care and by his influence, and to defend and protect the Church of St. Peter, and to beautify and enrich it out of his own store above all other churches.

campaigning—supplying it and transporting it to distant areas could still present serious problems. The Frankish army comprised mostly infantry, with some cavalry armed with swords and spears.

Charlemagne's campaigns took him to many areas of Europe. In 773, he led his army into Italy, crushed the Lombards, and took control of the Lombard state. Although his son was crowned king of Italy, Charlemagne was its real ruler. Four years after his invasion of Italy, Charlemagne and his forces advanced into northern Spain. This campaign proved disappointing; not only did the Basques harass his army as it crossed the Pyrenees on the way home, but they also ambushed and annihilated his rear guard.

Charlemagne was considerably more successful with his eastern campaigns into Germany, especially against the Saxons who had settled between the Elbe River and the North Sea. As Einhard, Charlemagne's biographer, recounted it:

> No war ever undertaken by the Frank nation was carried on with such persistence and bitterness, or cost so much labor, because the Saxons, like almost all the tribes of Germany, were a fierce people, given to the worship of devils, and hostile to our religion, and did not consider it dishonorable to transgress and violate all law, human and divine.[1]

Charlemagne's insistence that the Saxons convert to Christianity simply fueled their resistance. Not until 804, after

Bronze Equestrian Statue of Charlemagne. This small bronze statue is believed to represent the emperor Charles the Great. The figure dates from the ninth century, but the horse is a sixteenth-century restoration. The attire on the figure accords with Einhard's account of how Charlemagne dressed.

Réunion des Musées Nationaux/Art Resource, NY

eighteen campaigns, was Saxony finally pacified and added to the Carolingian domain.

In southeastern Germany, Charlemagne invaded the land of the Bavarians in 787 and brought them into his empire by the following year, an expansion that brought him into contact with the southern Slavs and the Avars. The latter disappeared from history after their utter devastation at the hands of Charlemagne's army. Now at its height, Charlemagne's empire covered much of western and central Europe (see Map 8.1); not until the time of Napoleon in the nineteenth century would an empire its size be seen again in Europe.

Map 8.1 The Carolingian Empire. Charlemagne inherited the Carolingian Empire from his father, Pepin. He expanded his territories in several directions, creating an empire that would not be rivaled in size until the conquests of Napoleon in the early nineteenth century. ■ How might Charlemagne's holdings in northern Italy have influenced his relationship with the pope?

GOVERNING THE EMPIRE

Charlemagne continued the efforts of his father in organizing the Carolingian kingdom. Because there was no system of public taxation, Charlemagne was highly dependent on the royal estates for the resources he needed to govern his empire. Food and goods derived from these lands provided support for the king, his household staff, and officials. To keep the nobles in his service, Charlemagne granted part of the royal lands as lifetime holdings to nobles who assisted him.

Besides the household staff, the administration of the empire depended on counts, who were the king's chief representatives in local areas, although in dangerous border districts officials known as margraves (literally, *mark graf*, count of the border district) were used. Counts were members of the nobility who had already existed under the Merovingians. They had come to control public services in their own lands and thus acted as judges, military leaders, and agents of the king. Gradually, as the rule of the Merovingian kings weakened, many counts had simply attached the royal lands and services performed on behalf of the king to their own family possessions.

In an effort to gain greater control over his kingdom, Charlemagne attempted to limit the power of the counts. They were required to serve outside their own family lands and were moved about periodically rather than being permitted to remain in a county for life. By making the offices appointive, Charlemagne tried to prevent the counts' children from automatically inheriting their offices. Moreover, as another check on the counts, Charlemagne instituted the *missi dominici* ("messengers of the lord king"), two men, one lay lord and one church official, who were sent out to local districts to ensure that the counts were executing the king's wishes. The counts also had assistants, but they were members of their households, not part of a bureaucratic office.

The last point is an important reminder that we should not think of Carolingian government in the modern sense of government offices run by officials committed to an impersonal ideal of state service. The Carolingian system was glaringly inefficient. Great distances had to be covered on horseback, making it impossible for Charlemagne and his household staff to exercise much supervision over local affairs. What held the system together was personal loyalty to a single ruler who was strong enough to ensure loyalty by force when necessary.

Charlemagne also realized that the Catholic church could provide invaluable assistance in governing his kingdom. By the late seventh century, the system of ecclesiastical government within the Christian church that had been created in the Late Roman Empire had largely disintegrated. Many church offices were not filled or were held by grossly unqualified relatives of the royal family. Both Pepin and his son Charlemagne took up the cause of church reform by creating new bishoprics and archbishoprics, restoring old ones, and seeing to it that the clergy accepted the orders of their superiors and executed their duties.

CHRONOLOGY

The Carolingian Empire

Pepin crowned king of the Franks	751
Reign of Charlemagne	768–814
Campaign in Italy	773–774
Campaign in Spain	778
Conquest of Bavarians	787–788
Charlemagne crowned emperor	800
Final conquest of Saxons	804
Reign of Louis the Pious	814–840
Treaty of Verdun divides Carolingian Empire	843

CHARLEMAGNE AS EMPEROR

As Charlemagne's power grew, so did his prestige as the most powerful Christian ruler; one monk even wrote of his empire as the "kingdom of Europe." Charlemagne acquired a new title—emperor of the Romans—in 800, but substantial controversy surrounds this event, and it can only be understood within the context of the relationship between the papacy and the Frankish monarchs.

Already during the reign of Pepin, a growing alliance had emerged between the kingdom of the Franks and the papacy. The popes welcomed this support, and in the course of the second half of the eighth century, they severed more and more of their ties with the Byzantine Empire and drew closer to the Frankish kingdom. Charlemagne encouraged this development. In 799, after a rebellion against his authority, Pope Leo III (795–816) managed to escape from Rome and flee to safety at Charlemagne's court. Charlemagne offered assistance, and when he went to Rome in November 800 to settle affairs, he was received by the pope like an emperor. On Christmas Day 800, after Mass, Pope Leo placed a crown on Charlemagne's head and proclaimed him emperor of the Romans.

The significance of this imperial coronation has been much debated by historians. We are not even sure whether the pope or Charlemagne initiated the idea or whether Charlemagne was pleased or displeased. His biographer Einhard claimed that "at first [he] had such an aversion that he declared that he would not have set foot in the Church the day that [it was] conferred, although it was a great feastday, if he could have foreseen the design of the Pope."[2] But Charlemagne also perceived the usefulness of the imperial title; after all, he was now on a level of equality with the Byzantine emperor, a status he did not reject. Moreover, the papacy now had a defender of great stature, although later popes in the Middle Ages would become involved in fierce struggles with emperors over who possessed the higher power.

In any case, Charlemagne's coronation as Roman emperor certainly demonstrated the strength, even after three hundred years, of the concept of an enduring Roman Empire. More important, it symbolized the fusion of the Roman,

The Granger Collection

The Coronation of Charlemagne. After a rebellion in 799 forced Pope Leo III to seek refuge at Charlemagne's court, Charlemagne went to Rome to settle the affair. There, on Christmas Day 800, he was crowned emperor of the Romans by the pope. This manuscript illustration shows Leo III placing a crown on Charlemagne's head.

Christian, and Germanic elements that constituted the foundation of European civilization. A Germanic king had been crowned emperor of the Romans by the spiritual leader of western Christendom. A new civilization had emerged.

The Carolingian Intellectual Renewal

Charlemagne had a strong desire to revive learning in his kingdom, an attitude that stemmed from his own intellectual curiosity as well as the need to provide educated clergy for the church and literate officials for the government. His efforts led to a revival of learning and culture that some historians have labeled a Carolingian Renaissance, or "rebirth" of learning.

For the most part, the revival of classical studies and the efforts to preserve Latin culture took place in the monasteries, many of which had been established by the Irish and English missionaries of the seventh and eighth centuries (see Chapter 7). By the ninth century, the work required of Benedictine monks was the copying of manuscripts. Monasteries established *scriptoria,* or writing rooms, where monks copied not only the works of early Christianity, such as the Bible and the treatises of the church fathers, but also the works of Latin classical authors.

Following the example of the Irish and English monks, their Carolingian counterparts developed new ways of

Monk as Copyist. Charlemagne's efforts to revive learning led to what has been called the Carolingian Renaissance. Through their copying of ancient manuscripts, Benedictine monks added an important element to this revival. Shown at work in this medieval miniature is a monk who is meant to represent Saint Luke, one of the four Gospel writers.

Bibliotheque Mazarine, Paris/Archives Charmet/Bridgeman Art Library

producing books. Their texts were written on pages made of parchment or sheepskin rather than papyrus and then bound in covers decorated with jewels and precious metals. The use of parchment made books very expensive; an entire herd of sheep could be required to make a Bible. (Papyrus was no longer available because Egypt was in Muslim hands, and the west could no longer afford to import it.) Carolingian monastic scribes also developed a new writing style called the Carolingian minuscule (see the illustration on p. 201). This was really hand printing rather than cursive writing and was far easier to read than the Merovingian script.

The production of manuscripts, some of which were illustrated, in Carolingian monastic *scriptoria* was a crucial factor in the preservation of the ancient legacy. About eight thousand manuscripts survive from Carolingian times. Virtually 90 percent of the ancient Roman works that we have today exist because they were copied by Carolingian monks.

Charlemagne personally promoted learning by establishing a palace school and encouraging scholars from all over Europe to come to the Carolingian court. These included men of letters from Italy, Spain, Germany, and Ireland. Best known was Alcuin, called by Einhard the "greatest scholar of that day." He was from the famous school at York that was a product of the great revival of learning in the Anglo-Saxon kingdom of Northumbria. From 782 to 796, while serving at Charlemagne's court as an adviser on ecclesiastical affairs, Alcuin also provided the leadership for the palace school. He concentrated on teaching classical Latin and adopted Cassiodorus' sevenfold division of knowledge known as the liberal arts (see Chapter 7), which became the basis for all later medieval education. All in all, the Carolingian Renaissance played a crucial role in keeping the classical heritage alive as well as maintaining the intellectual life of the Catholic church.

Life in the Carolingian World

In daily life as well as intellectual life, the newly emerging European world of the Carolingian era witnessed a fusion of Roman, Germanic, and Christian practices. The last in particular seem to have exercised an ever-increasing influence.

THE FAMILY AND MARRIAGE

By Carolingian times, the Catholic church had begun to make a significant impact on Frankish family life and marital and sexual attitudes. Marriages in Frankish society were arranged by fathers or uncles to meet the needs of the extended family. Although wives were expected to be faithful to their husbands, Frankish aristocrats often kept concubines, either slave girls or free women from their estates. Even the "most Christian king" Charlemagne had a number of concubines.

To limit such sexual license, the church increasingly emphasized its role in marriage and attempted to Christianize it. Although marriage was a civil arrangement, priests tried to add their blessings and strengthen the concept of a special marriage ceremony. Moreover, the church tried to serve as the caretaker of marriage by stipulating that a girl over fifteen must give her consent to her guardian's choice of a husband or her marriage would not be valid in the eyes of the church.

To stabilize marriages, the church also began to emphasize monogamy and permanence. A Frankish church council in 789 stipulated that marriage was an "indissoluble sacrament" and condemned the practice of concubinage and easy divorce; during the reign of Emperor Louis the Pious (814–840), the church finally established the right to prohibit divorce. Now a man who married was expected to remain with his wife "even though she were sterile, deformed, old, dirty, drunken, a frequenter of bad company, lascivious, vain, greedy, unfaithful, quarrelsome, abusive . . . for when that man was free, he freely engaged himself."[3] This was not easily accepted, since monogamy and indissoluble marriages were viewed as obstacles to the well-established practice of concubinage. Not until the thirteenth century was divorce largely stamped out among both the common people and the nobility.

The acceptance and spread of the Catholic church's views on the indissolubility of marriage encouraged the development of the nuclear family at the expense of the extended family. Although the kin was still an influential social and political force, the conjugal unit came to be seen as the basic unit of society. The new practice of young couples establishing their own households had a significant impact on women (see the box on p. 197). In the extended family, the eldest woman controlled all the other female members; in the nuclear family, the wife was still dominated by her husband, but at least she now had control of her own household and children.

CHRISTIANITY AND SEXUALITY

The early church fathers had stressed that celibacy and complete abstinence from sexual activity constituted an ideal state superior to marriage. Subsequently, the early church gradually developed a case for clerical celibacy, although it proved impossible to enforce in the Early Middle Ages.

The early fathers had also emphasized, however, that not all people had the self-discipline to remain celibate. It was thus permissible to marry, as Paul had indicated in his first epistle to the Corinthians: "It is good for a man not to touch a woman. Nevertheless, to avoid fornication, let every man have his own wife, and let every woman have her own husband. . . . I say therefore to the unmarried and widows, It is good for them if they abide even as I. But if they cannot contain, let them marry: for it is better to marry than to burn [with passion]."[4] The church thus viewed marriage as the lesser of two evils; it was a concession to human weakness and fulfilled the need for companionship, sex, and children. Although marriage was the subject of much debate in the early medieval church, it was generally agreed that marriage gave the right to indulge in sexual intercourse. Sex, then, was permissible within marriage, but only so long as it was used for the

Advice from a Carolingian Mother

The wife of a Carolingian aristocrat bore numerous responsibilities. She was entrusted with the management of the household and even the administration of extensive landed estates while her husband was absent in the royal service or on a military campaign. A wife was also expected to bear larger numbers of children and to supervise their upbringing. This selection by Dhouda, wife of Bernard, marquis of Septimania (in southern France), is taken from a manual she wrote to instruct her son on his duties to his new lord, King Charles the Bald (840–877).

Dhouda, Handbook for William

Direction on your comportment toward your lord.

You have Charles as your lord; you have him as lord because, as I believe, God and your father, Bernard, have chosen him for you to serve at the beginning of your career, in the flower of your youth. Remember that he comes from a great and noble lineage on both sides of his family. Serve him not only so that you please him in obvious ways, but also as one clearheaded in matters of both body and soul. Be steadfastly and completely loyal to him in all things. . . .

This is why, my son, I urge you to keep this loyalty as long as you live, in your body and in your mind. For the advancement that it brings you will be of great value both to you and to those who in turn serve you. May the madness of treachery never, not once, make you offer an angry insult. May it never give rise in your heart to the idea of being disloyal to your lord. There is harsh and shameful talk about men who act in this fashion. I do not think that such will befall you or those who fight alongside you because such an attitude has never shown itself among your ancestors. It has not been seen among them, it is not seen now, and it will not be seen in the future.

Be truthful to your lord, my son William, child of their lineage. Be vigilant, energetic, and offer him ready assistance as I have said here. In every matter of importance to royal power take care to show yourself a man of good judgment—in your own thoughts and in public—to the extent that God gives you strength. Read the sayings and the lives of the holy Fathers who have gone before us. You will there discover how you may serve your lord and be faithful to him in all things. When you understand this, devote yourself to the faithful execution of your lord's commands. Look around as well and observe those who fight for him loyally and constantly. Learn from them how you may serve him. Then, informed by their example, with the help and support of God, you will easily reach the celestial goal I have mentioned above. And may your heavenly Lord God be generous and benevolent toward you. May he keep you safe, be your kind leader and your protector. May he deign to assist you in all your actions and be your constant defender.

purpose of procreation, or the begetting of children, not for pleasure.

Because the church developed the tradition that sexual relations between man and wife were legitimate only if engaged in for procreation, it condemned all forms of contraception. The church also strongly condemned abortion, although its prohibition failed to stop the practice. Various herbal potions, whose formulas appear in writings from Roman and Byzantine doctors, were available to prevent conception or cause abortion. The Catholic church accepted only one way to limit children: abstinence from intercourse, either periodic or total.

The church's condemnation of sexual activity outside marriage also included homosexuality. Neither Roman religion nor Roman law had recognized any real difference between homosexual and heterosexual eroticism, and the Roman Empire had taken no legal measures against the practice of homosexuality between adults. Later, in the Byzantine Empire, Emperor Justinian in 538 condemned homosexuality, emphasizing that such practices brought down the wrath of God ("we have provoked Him to anger") and endangered the welfare of the state:

> For because of such crimes, there are famines, earthquakes, and pestilences; wherefore we admonish men to abstain from the aforesaid unlawful acts, that they may not lose their souls. . . . We order the most illustrious prefect of the capital to arrest those who persist in the aforesaid lawless and impious acts after they have been warned by us, and to inflict on them the extreme punishments, so that the city and the state may not come to harm by reason of such wicked deeds.[5]

Justinian recommended that the guilty parties be punished by castration. Although the church in the Early Middle Ages similarly condemned homosexuality, it also pursued a flexible policy in its treatment of homosexuals. In the Early Middle Ages, homosexuals were treated less harshly than married couples who practiced contraception.

NEW ATTITUDES TOWARD CHILDREN

The Catholic church also had an impact on another aspect of family life—children. The ancient Romans had limited their family size through infanticide, primarily the exposure of unwanted children, which was accepted in classical society. Romans then paid much attention to the children chosen to survive, as is especially evident in the education of upper-class children. In the emerging early medieval world, barbarian practices of child rearing became influential. As we saw in Chapter 7, the Germanic law codes listed *wergelds,* whose size represented a crude evaluation of a person's importance. According to a Visigothic code of the mid-seventh century, for example, male children were valued at 60 solidi. At the age of twenty, when they had become warriors, the *wergeld* increased fivefold to 300 solidi, where it remained until the adult male reached fifty, after which it again declined. The value of females was only half that of males, although it also jumped tremendously (to 250 solidi) for women between the ages of fifteen and forty because of their importance as bearers of children.

Although the Christian church condemned infanticide, it was not able to eliminate the practice, especially among the poor and among victims of seduction who did not want to keep their illegitimate offspring. Nevertheless, priests tried to discourage such practices by urging people to abandon unwanted children in churches. Often such children were taken in by monasteries and convents and raised to be monks and nuns. Following the example of Jesus' love for children, monks and nuns tended to respect and preserve the virtues of childhood. As children grew older, however, it was thought necessary to use strict discipline to control what was considered the natural inclination of children to sin, especially by disobeying their elders.

TRAVEL AND HOSPITALITY

Monasteries served another important function in the early medieval world as providers of hospitality. Both monasteries and aristocratic households were expected to provide a place to stay for weary travelers, who were ever at risk from thieves or violence of many kinds. Indeed, Burgundian law stipulated that "anyone who refused to offer a visitor shelter and warmth shall pay a fine of three solidi."[6] Hospitality, then, was a sacred duty, and monasteries were especially active in providing it. It was customary for monasteries to have two guest houses, one for the rich and another for the poor. The plan for the monastery of Saint Gall, for example, provided pilgrims and paupers with a house containing benches, two dormitories, and outbuildings. For travelers of high rank, there was a separate guest house with two heated rooms, servants' bedrooms, and stables for horses. One could not always be sure of hospitality in the Early Middle Ages, however. The famous English missionary to Germany, Saint Boniface, reported that female pilgrims to Rome had been forced to become prostitutes in every town along their route in order to obtain their sustenance and reach their goal. The church responded by forbidding females to go on such pilgrimages.

DIET

For both rich and poor, the main staple of the Carolingian diet was bread. The aristocratic classes, as well as the monks, consumed it in large quantities. Ovens at the monastery of Saint Gall were able to bake a thousand loaves of bread. Sometimes a gruel made of barley and oats was substituted for bread in the peasant diet.

The upper classes in Carolingian society enjoyed a much more varied diet than the peasants. Pork was the major meat. Domestic pigs, allowed to run wild in the forests to find their own food, were collected and slaughtered in the fall, then smoked and salted to be eaten during the winter months. Because Carolingian aristocrats were especially fond of roasted meat, hunting wild game became one of their favorite activities. They ate little beef or mutton, however, because cattle were kept as dairy cows and oxen to draw plows, and sheep were raised for wool.

Dairy products became prevalent in the Carolingian diet. Milk, which spoiled rapidly, was made into cheese and butter. Chickens were raised for their eggs. Vegetables also formed a crucial part of the diet of both rich and poor. These included legumes, such as beans, peas, and lentils, and roots, such as garlic, onions, and carrots.

The Carolingian diet, especially of the upper classes, was also heavily dependent on honey and spices. Honey was used as a sweetener, both for foods and for many drinks, including wine and ale. Spices included domestic varieties that were grown in home gardens, such as thyme, sage, and chives, and more exotic—and outrageously expensive—varieties imported from the East, such as pepper, cumin, cloves, and cinnamon. Aristocrats were especially fond of spicy dishes, not just for their taste but as a sign of prestige and wealth; spices were also believed to aid the digestion.

Both gluttony and drunkenness were vices shared by many people in Carolingian society. Monastic rations were greatly enlarged in the eighth century to include a daily allotment of 3.7 pounds of bread (nuns were permitted 3 pounds), $1\frac{1}{2}$ quarts of wine or ale, 2 or 3 ounces of cheese, and 8 ounces of vegetables (4 ounces for nuns). These

Travelers Arriving at an Inn. Inns provided refuge for the many pilgrims, merchants, and others who traveled Europe's dangerous roads in the Middle Ages. In this illustration, a group of merchants has stopped at an inn, which like most medieval inns provided basic necessities but not individual beds. Medieval people generally slept in the nude.

Medical Practices in the Early Middle Ages

A number of medical manuscripts written in Old English have survived from Anglo-Saxon England. Although most of the medical texts date from the tenth to twelfth centuries, scholars believe that they include copies of earlier works and contain older influences as well. As the following selections from three of these treatises illustrate, herbs were the basic materials of the Anglo-Saxon physicians (or leeches as they were called), and treatments consequently focused almost entirely on botanical remedies.

The Anglo-Saxon Herbal

Cress (Nasturtium)

1. In case a man's hair falls out, take juice of the plant which one names nasturtium and by another name cress, put it on the nose, the hair shall grow.
2. This plant is not sown but it is produced of itself in springs and in brooks; also it is written that in some lands it will grow against walls.
3. For a sore head, that is for scurf [dandruff] and for itch, take the seed of this same plant and goose grease, pound together, it draws from off the head the whiteness of the scurf.
4. For soreness of the body [indigestion], take this same plant nasturtium and pennyroyal, soak them in water and give to drink; the soreness and the evil departs.

The Leechbook of Bald

Here are wound salves for all wounds and drinks and cleansings of every sort, whether internally or externally. Waybroad beaten and mixed with old lard, the fresh is of no use. Again, a wound salve: take waybroad seed, crush it small, shed it on the wound and soon it will be better.

For a burn, if a man be burned with fire only, take woodruff and lily and brooklime; boil in butter and smear therewith. If a man be burned with a liquid, let him take elm rind and roots of the lily, boil them in milk, smear thereon three times a day. For sunburn, boil in butter tender ivy twigs and smear thereon.

The Peri-Didaxeon

For a Broken Head

For a broken or wounded head which is caused by the humors of the head. Take betony and pound it and lay it on the wound and it will relieve all the pain.

For Sleep

Thus must one do for the man who cannot sleep; take wormwood and rub it into wine or warm water and let the man drink it and soon it will be better with him.

For Sore Hands

This leechcraft is good for sore hands and for sore fingers which is called chilblains. Take white frankincense and silver cinders and brimstone and mingle together, then take oil and add it into this mixture, then warm the hands and smear them with the mixture thus made. Wrap up the hands in a linen cloth.

rations provided a total of 6,000 calories a day, and since only heavy and fatty foods—bread, milk, and cheese—were considered nourishing, we begin to understand why some Carolingians were known for their potbellies. Malnutrition, however, remained a widespread problem for common people in this period.

Everyone in Carolingian society, including abbots and monks, drank heavily and often to excess. Taverns became a regular feature of life and were found everywhere: in marketplaces, at pilgrimage centers, and on royal, episcopal, and monastic estates. Drinking contests were not unusual; one penitential stated: "Does drunken bravado encourage you to attempt to out-drink your friends? If so, thirty days' fast."

The aristocrats and monks favored wine above all other beverages, and much care was lavished on its production, especially by monasteries. Although ale was considered inferior in some quarters, it was especially popular in the northern and eastern parts of the Carolingian world. Water was also drunk as a beverage, but much care had to be taken to obtain pure sources from wells or clear streams. Monasteries were particularly active in going to the sources of water and building conduits to bring it to the cloister or kitchen fountains.

Water was also used for bathing. Although standards of personal hygiene were not high, medieval people did not ignore cleanliness. A royal palace, such as Charlemagne's, possessed both hot and cold baths. Carolingian aristocrats changed clothes and bathed at least once a week, on Saturdays. The Saturday bath was also a regular practice in many Carolingian monasteries. To monks, bathing more than once a week seemed an unnecessary luxury; to aristocrats, it often seemed desirable.

HEALTH

Medical practice in Carolingian times stressed the use of medicinal herbs (see the box above) and bleeding. Although the latter was practiced regularly, moderation was frequently recommended. Some advised carefulness as well: "Who dares to undertake a bleeding should see to it that his hand does not tremble."

Physicians were also available when people faced serious illnesses. Many were clerics, and monasteries trained their own. Monastic libraries kept medical manuscripts copied from ancient works and grew herbs to provide stocks of medicinal plants. Carolingian medical manuscripts contained scientific descriptions of illnesses, recipes for medical potions, and even gynecological advice, although monks in particular expended little effort on female medical needs. Some manuals even included instructions for operations, especially for soldiers injured in battle. Some sources clearly demonstrate that there were accurate techniques for amputating gangrenous limbs:

> If you must cut off an unhealthy limb from a healthy body, then do not cut to the limit of the healthy flesh, but cut further into the whole and quick flesh, so that a better and quicker cure may be obtained. When you set fire on the man [i.e., cauterize], take leaves of tender leek and grated salt, overlay the places so that the heat of the fire be more quickly drawn away.[7]

Although scholars are not sure whether anesthesia was used for such operations, medieval manuals recommended poppy, mandrake, and henbane for their narcotic properties.

Physicians of the Early Middle Ages supplemented their medicines and natural practices with appeals for otherworldly help. Magical rites and influences were carried over from pagan times; the Germanic tribes had used magical medicine for centuries. Physicians recommended that patients wear amulets and charms around their bodies to ward off diseases:

> Procure a little bit of the dung of a wolf, preferably some which contains small bits of bone, and pack it in a tube which the patient may easily wear as an amulet.
>
> For epilepsy take a nail of a wrecked ship, make it into a bracelet and set therein the bone of a stag's heart taken from its body whilst alive; put it on the left arm; you will be astonished at the result.[8]

But as pagans were converted to Christianity, miraculous healing through the intervention of God, Jesus, or the saints soon replaced pagan practices. Medieval chronicles abound with accounts of people healed by touching a saint's body. The use of Christian prayers, written down and used as amulets, however, reminds us that for centuries Christian and pagan medical practices survived side by side.

The Disintegration of the Carolingian Empire

The Carolingian Empire began to disintegrate soon after Charlemagne's death. Charlemagne was survived by his son Louis the Pious (814–840). Though a decent man, he was not a strong ruler and was unable to control either the Frankish aristocracy or his own four sons, who fought continually. In 843, after their father's death, the three surviving brothers signed the Treaty of Verdun. This agreement divided the Carolingian Empire among them into three major sections: Charles the Bald (843–877) obtained the western Frankish lands, which formed the core of the eventual kingdom of France; Louis the German (843–876) took the eastern lands, which became Germany; and Lothair (840–855) received the title of emperor and a "Middle Kingdom" extending from the North Sea to the Mediterranean, including the Netherlands, the Rhineland, and northern Italy. The territories of the Middle Kingdom became a source of incessant struggle between the other two Frankish rulers and their heirs. Indeed, France and Germany would fight over the territories of this Middle Kingdom for centuries.

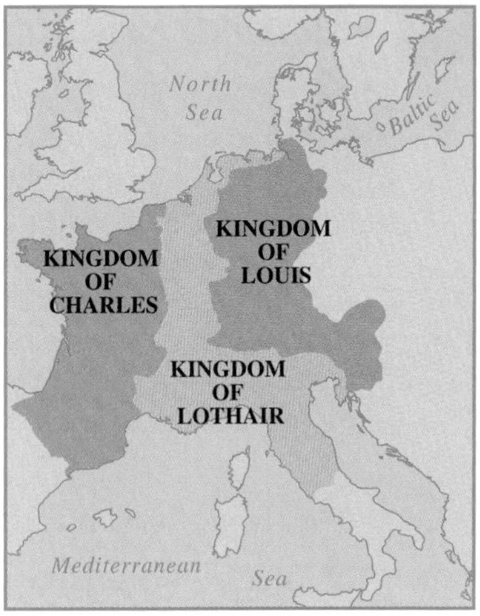

Division of the Carolingian Empire by the Treaty of Verdun, 843

Although this division of the Carolingian Empire was made for political and not nationalistic reasons (dividing a kingdom among the male heirs was a traditional Frankish custom), two different cultures began to emerge. By the ninth century, inhabitants of the western Frankish area were speaking a Romance language derived from Latin that became French. Eastern Franks spoke a Germanic dialect. The later kingdoms of France and Germany did not yet exist, however. In the ninth century, the frequent struggles among the numerous heirs of the sons of Louis the Pious led to further disintegration of the Carolingian Empire. In the meantime, while powerful aristocrats acquired even more power in their own local territories at the expense of the squabbling Carolingian rulers, the process of disintegration was abetted by external attacks on different parts of the old Carolingian world.

Invasions of the Ninth and Tenth Centuries

In the ninth and tenth centuries, western Europe was beset by a wave of invasions by several non-Christian peoples—one old enemy, the Muslims, and two new ones, the Magyars and Vikings (see Map 8.2). Although battered by these onslaughts, Christian Europe hung on and, with the exception of the Muslims, wound up assimilating the other two peoples into Christian European civilization.

MUSLIMS AND MAGYARS

The first great wave of Muslim expansion had ended at the beginning of the eighth century (see Chapter 7). Gradually, the Muslims built up a series of sea bases in their occupied territories in North Africa, Spain, and southern Gaul and began a new series of attacks in the Mediterranean in the ninth century. They raided the southern coasts of Europe, especially Italy, and even threatened Rome in 843. Their invasion of Sicily in 827 eventually led to a successful occu-

Bibliotheque Nationale, Paris

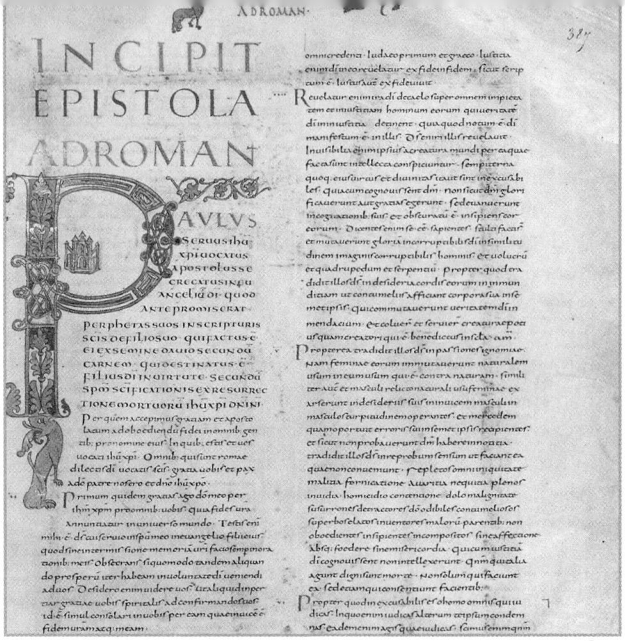

Bibliotheque Nationale, Paris

The First Bible of Charles the Bald. Charles the Bald, who took control of the western Frankish lands, is pictured here in an illustration from his first Bible, which dates from between 843 and 851. Illustrated Bibles were one of the finest achievements of Carolingian art. Also pictured is a page from the Bible, showing the use of the Carolingian minuscule style of writing.

pation of the entire island. Muslim forces also destroyed the Carolingian defenses in northern Spain and conducted forays into southern France.

The Magyars were a people from western Asia. When the Byzantine emperors encouraged them to attack the troublesome Bulgars, the latter in turn encouraged a people known as the Pechenegs to attack the Magyars instead. Consequently, the Magyars, under severe Pecheneg pressure, had moved west into eastern and central Europe by the end of the ninth century. They established themselves on the plains of Hungary and from there made raids into western Europe. The Magyars were finally crushed at the Battle of Lechfeld in Germany in 955. At the end of the tenth century, they were converted to Christianity and settled down to establish the kingdom of Hungary.

THE VIKINGS

By far the most devastating and far-reaching attacks of the time came from the Northmen or Norsemen of Scandinavia, also known to us as the Vikings. The Vikings were a Germanic people based in Scandinavia and constitute, in a sense, the final wave of Germanic migration. Why they moved is not very clear to historians. One common explanation focuses on overpopulation, although recent research indicates that this may have been true only in western Norway. Other reasons have included the Vikings' great love of adventure and their search for wealth and new avenues of trade.

Two features of Viking society help explain what the Vikings accomplished. First of all, they were warriors. Second, they were superb shipbuilders and sailors. Their ships were the best of the period. Long and narrow with beautifully carved arched prows, the Viking dragon ships carried about fifty men. They had banks of oars as well as a single great sail. Their shallow draft enabled them to sail up European rivers and attack places at some distance inland. Although Viking raids in the eighth century tended to be small-scale and sporadic, they became more regular and more devastating in the ninth. Vikings sacked villages and towns, destroyed churches, and easily defeated small local armies. Viking attacks frightened people and led many a clergyman to exhort his parishioners to change their behavior to appease God's anger, as in this sermon by an English archbishop in 1014:

> Things have not gone well now for a long time at home or abroad, but there has been devastation and persecution in every district again and again, and the English have been for a long time now completely defeated and too greatly disheartened through God's anger; and the pirates [Vikings] so strong with God's consent that often in battle one puts to flight ten, and sometimes less, sometimes more, all because of our sins. . . . We pay them continually and they humiliate us daily; they ravage and they burn, plunder, and rob and carry on board; and lo, what else is there in all these events except God's anger clear and visible over this people?[9]

Because there were different groups of Scandinavians, Viking expansion varied a great deal. Norwegian Vikings moved into Ireland and western England; Danes attacked eastern England, Frisia, and the Rhineland and navigated rivers to enter western Frankish lands. Swedish Vikings dominated the Baltic Sea and progressed into the Slavic areas to the east. Moving into northwestern Russia, they went down the rivers of Russia to Novgorod and Kiev and established fortified ports throughout these territories. There they made contact with the Byzantine Empire, either as traders or as invaders. They also made contact with Arab traders on the Volga River and the Sea of Azov.

Early Viking raids had been carried out largely in the summer; by the mid-ninth century, however, the Norsemen had begun to establish winter settlements in Europe from which they could make expeditions to conquer and settle new lands. By 850, groups of Norsemen had settled in Ireland, and the Danes occupied an area known as the Danelaw in northeastern England by 878. Agreeing to accept Christianity, the Danes were eventually assimilated into a larger Anglo-Saxon kingdom. Beginning in 911, the ruler of the western Frankish lands gave one band of Vikings land at the mouth of the Seine River, forming a section of France that ultimately came to be known as Normandy. This policy of settling the Vikings and converting them to Christianity was a deliberate one, since the new inhabitants served as protectors against additional Norsemen attacks.

The Vikings were also daring explorers. After 860, they sailed westward in their long ships across the north Atlantic, reaching Iceland in 874. Erik the Red, a Viking exiled from Iceland, traveled even farther west and discovered Greenland in 985. The only known Viking site in North America was found in Newfoundland.

By the tenth century, Viking expansion was drawing to a close. Greater control by the monarchs of Denmark, Norway, and Sweden over their inhabitants and the increasing Christianization of both the Scandinavian kings and peoples tended to inhibit Viking expansion, but not before Viking settlements had been established throughout many parts of Europe. Like the Magyars, the Vikings were also

The Vikings Attack England. An illustration from an eleventh-century English manuscript depicts a group of armed Vikings invading England. Two ships have already reached the shore, and a few Vikings are shown walking down a long gangplank onto English soil. Also shown is a replica of a well-preserved Viking ship found at Oseberg, Norway. The Oseberg ship was one of the largest Viking ships in its day.

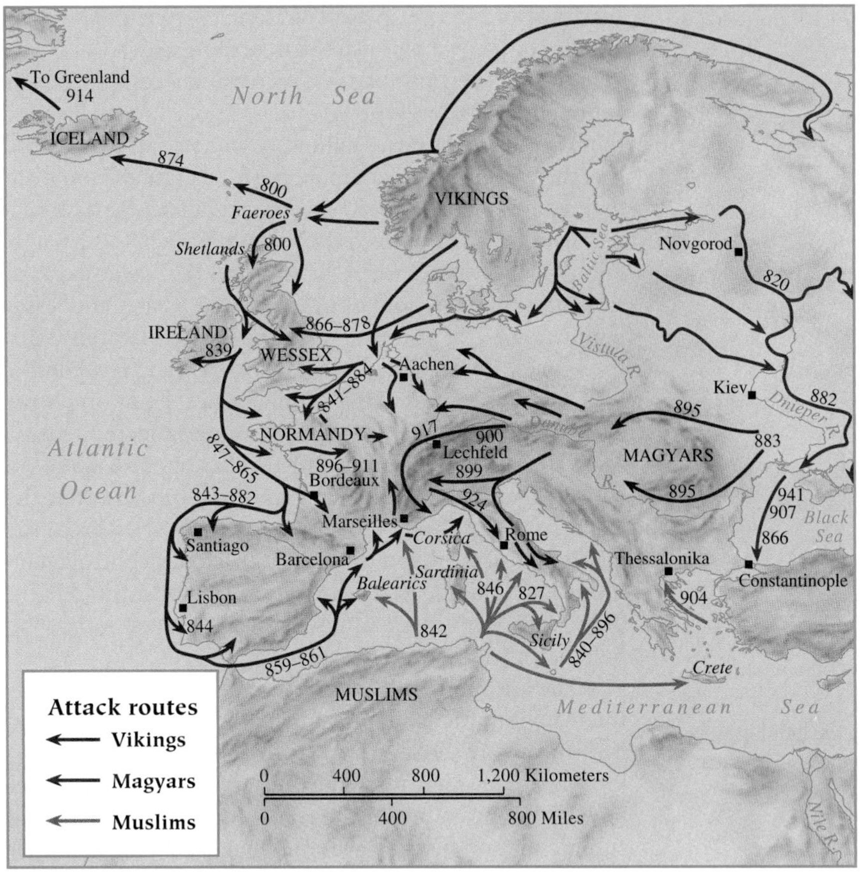

Map 8.2 Invasions of the Ninth and Tenth Centuries. Attacks by invading Vikings, Magyars, and Muslims terrorized much of Europe in the ninth and tenth centuries, disrupting economic development and spurring the development of fief-holding. The Vikings were the biggest problem, but they eventually formed settlements, converted to Christianity, and were assimilated. ■ Why was it important for the marauding Vikings to build sound boats and develop good seafaring skills?

assimilated into European civilization. Once again, Christianity proved a decisive civilizing force in Western civilization in its European form. Europe and Christianity were becoming virtually synonymous.

The Viking raids and settlements also had important political repercussions. The inability of royal authorities to protect their peoples against these incursions caused local populations to turn instead to the local aristocrats to provide security for them. In the process, the landed aristocrats not only increased their strength and prestige but also assumed even more of the functions of local government that had previously belonged to the kings; over time these developments led to a new political and military order.

The Emerging World of Lords and Vassals

The renewed invasions and the disintegration of the Carolingian world led to the emergence of a new type of relationship between free individuals. When governments ceased to be able to defend their subjects, it became important to find some powerful lord who could offer protection in exchange for service. The contract sworn between a lord and his subordinate is the basis of a form of social organization that later generations of historians called feudalism. But feudalism was never a system, and many historians today prefer to avoid using the term.

The practice of vassalage was derived from Germanic society, in which warriors swore an oath of loyalty to their leader. They fought for their chief, and he in turn took care of their needs. By the eighth century, an individual who served a lord in a military capacity was known as a vassal.

With the breakdown of governments, powerful nobles took control of large areas of land. They needed men to fight for them, so the practice arose of giving grants of land to vassals, who would in return fight for their lord. The Frankish army had originally consisted of foot soldiers, dressed in coats of mail and armed with swords. But in the eighth century, when larger horses and the stirrup were introduced, a military change began to occur. Earlier, horsemen had been throwers of spears. Now they wore armored coats of mail (the larger horse could carry the weight) and wielded long lances that enabled them to act as battering rams (the stirrups kept the riders on their horses). For almost five hundred years, warfare in Europe would be dominated by heavily armored cavalry, or knights as they came to be called. The knights came to have the greatest social prestige and formed the backbone of the European aristocracy.

Of course, a horse, armor, and weapons were expensive to purchase and maintain, and learning to wield these instruments skillfully from horseback took much time and practice. Consequently, lords who wanted men to fight for

A Knight's Equipment Showing Saddle and Stirrups. In return for his fighting skills, a knight received a piece of land from his lord that provided for his economic support. Pictured here is a charging knight with his equipment. The introduction of the high saddle, stirrup, and larger horses allowed horsemen to wear heavier armor and to wield long lances, vastly improving the fighting ability of the cavalry.

them had to grant each vassal a piece of land that provided for the support of the vassal and his family. In return for the land, the vassal provided his lord with one major service, his fighting skills. Each needed the other. In the society of the Early Middle Ages, where there was little trade and wealth was based primarily on land ownership, land became the most important gift a lord could give to a vassal in return for military service.

The relationship between lord and vassal was made official by a public ceremony. To become a vassal, a man performed an act of homage to his lord, as described in this passage from a medieval treatise of law:

> The man should put his hands together as a sign of humility, and place them between the two hands of his lord as a token that he vows everything to him and promises faith to him; and the lord should receive him and promise to keep faith with him. Then the man should say: "Sir, I enter your homage and faith and become your man by mouth and hands [i.e., by taking the oath and placing his hands between those of the lord], and I swear and promise to keep faith and loyalty to you against all others, and to guard your rights with all my strength.[10]

As in the earlier Germanic band, loyalty to one's lord was the chief virtue.

By the ninth century, the land granted to a vassal in return for military service had come to be known as a fief. In time, many vassals who held such grants of land came to exercise rights of jurisdiction or political and legal authority within their fiefs. As the Carolingian world disintegrated politically under the impact of internal dissension and invasions from without, an increasing number of powerful lords arose. Instead of a single government, many people were now responsible for keeping order.

Fief-holding also became increasingly complicated as subinfeudation developed. The vassals of a king, who were themselves great lords, might also have vassals who would owe them military service in return for a grant of land from their estates. Those vassals, in turn, might likewise have vassals, who at such a level would be simple knights with barely enough land to provide their equipment. The lord-vassal relationship, then, bound together both greater and lesser landowners. Historians used to speak of a hierarchy with the king at the top, greater lords on the next level, lesser lords on the next, and simple knights at the bottom; however, this was only a model and rarely reflected reality. Such a hierarchy implies a king at the top. The reality in the tenth-century west Frankish kingdom was that the Capetian kings (see "New Political Configurations in the Tenth Century" later in this chapter) actually controlled no more land than the Île-de-France, the region around Paris. They possessed little real power over the great lords who held fiefs throughout France.

The lord-vassal relationship at all levels always constituted an honorable relationship between free men and did not imply any sense of servitude. Since kings could no longer provide security in the midst of the breakdown created by the invasions of the ninth century, the system of subinfeudation became ever more widespread. With their rights of jurisdiction, fiefs gave lords virtual possession of the rights of government.

The new practice of lordship was basically a product of the Carolingian world, but it also spread to England, Germany, central Europe, and in some form to Italy. Fief-holding came to be characterized by a set of practices worked out in the course of the tenth century, although they became more prominent after 1000. These practices included a series of mutual obligations of lord toward vassal and vassal toward lord, but it is crucial to remember that such obligations varied considerably from place to place and even from fief to fief. As usual, practice almost always diverged from theory.

Since the basic objective of fief-holding was to provide military support, it is no surprise to learn that the major obligation of a vassal to his lord was to perform military service. In addition to his own personal service, a great lord was also responsible for providing a group of knights for the king's army. Moreover, vassals had to furnish suit at court; this meant that a vassal was obliged to appear at his lord's court when summoned, either to give advice to the lord or to sit in judgment in a legal case, since the important vassals of a lord were peers and only they could judge each other. Many vassals were also obliged to provide hospitality for their lord when he stayed at a vassal's castle. This obligation was especially important to medieval kings because they tended to be highly itinerant. Finally, vassals were responsible for aids, or financial payments, to the lord on a number of occasions, among them the knighting of the lord's eldest son, the marriage of his eldest daughter, and the ransom of the lord's person if the lord had been captured (see the box on p. 205).

Lords, Vassals, and Fiefs

The upheavals of the Early Middle Ages produced a number of new institutions—lordship, vassalage, fiefs. The first selection records the granting of a fief by a lord to a vassal. The second is the classic statement by Bishop Fulbert of Chartres in 1020 on the mutual obligations between lord and vassal.

Record of a Grant Made by Abbot Faritius to Robert, a Knight

Abbot Faritius also granted to Robert, son of William Mauduit, the land of four hides in Weston which his father had held from the former's predecessor, to be held as a fief. And he should do this service for it, to wit: that whenever the church of Abingdon should perform its knight's service he should do the service of half a knight for the same church; that is to say, in castle ward, in military service beyond and on this side of the sea, in giving money in proportion to the knights on the capture of the king, and in the rest of the services which the other knights of the church perform.

Bishop Fulbert of Chartres

Asked to write something concerning the form of fealty, I have noted briefly for you, on the authority of the books, the things which follow. He who swears fealty to his lord ought always to have these six things in memory: what is harmless, safe, honorable, useful, easy, practicable. *Harmless,* that is to say, that he should not injure his lord in his body; *safe,* that he should not injure him by betraying his secrets or the defenses upon which he relies for safety; *honorable,* that he should not injure him in his justice or in other matters that pertain to his honor; *useful,* that he should not injure him in his possessions; *easy* and *practicable,* that that good which his lord is able to do easily he make not difficult, nor that which is practicable he make not impossible to him.

That the faithful vassal should avoid these injuries is certainly proper, but not for this alone does he deserve his holding; for it is not sufficient to abstain from evil, unless what is good is done also. It remains, therefore, that in the same six things mentioned above he should faithfully counsel and aid his lord, if he wishes to be looked upon as worthy of his benefice and to be safe concerning the fealty which he has sworn.

The lord also ought to act toward his faithful vassal reciprocally in all these things. And if he does not do this, he will be justly considered guilty of bad faith, just as the former, if he should be detected in avoiding or consenting to the avoidance of his duties, would be perfidious and perjured.

In turn, a lord had responsibilities toward his vassals. His major obligation was to protect his vassal, either by defending him militarily or by taking his side in a court of law if necessary. The lord was also responsible for the maintenance of the vassal, usually by granting him a fief.

As this system of mutual obligations between lord and vassal evolved, certain practices became common. If a lord acted improperly toward his vassal, the bond between them could be dissolved. Likewise, if a vassal failed to fulfill his vow of loyalty, he was subject to forfeiture of his fief. Upon a vassal's death, his fief theoretically reverted to the lord, since it had been granted to the vassal for use, not as a possession. In practice, however, fiefs by the tenth century tended to be hereditary. Following the principle of primogeniture, the eldest son inherited the father's fief. If a man died without heirs, the lord could reclaim the fief.

New Political Configurations in the Tenth Century

In the tenth century, Europe began to recover from the great invasions of the century before. The disintegration of the Carolingian Empire and the emergence of great and powerful lords soon produced new political configurations.

In the east Frankish kingdom, the last Carolingian king died in 911, whereupon local rulers, especially the powerful dukes (the title of duke is derived from the Latin word *dux,* meaning "leader") of the Saxons, Swabians, Bavarians, Thuringians, and Franconians, who exercised much power in their large dukedoms, elected one of their own number, Conrad of Franconia, to serve as king of Germany (as we think of it) or of the eastern Franks (as contemporaries thought of it). But Conrad did not last long, and after his death, the German dukes chose Henry the Fowler, duke of Saxony, as the new king of Germany (919–936). The first of the Saxon dynasty of German kings, Henry was not particularly successful in creating a unified eastern Frankish kingdom, lacking the resources to impose effective rule over the entire area.

The best known of the Saxon kings of Germany was Otto I (936–973). He defeated the Magyars at the Battle of Lechfeld in 955 and encouraged an ongoing program of Christianization of both the Slavic and Scandinavian peoples. Even more than his father, he relied on bishops and abbots in governing his kingdom. This practice was in part a response to the tendency of the lay lords to build up their power at the expense of the king. Since the clergy were theoretically celibate, bishops and abbots could not make their offices hereditary, thus allowing the king to maintain more control over them.

Otto also intervened in Italian politics and for his efforts was crowned emperor of the Romans by the pope in 962, reviving a title that had fallen into disuse with the disintegration of Charlemagne's Carolingian Empire. Once again a pope had conferred the Roman imperial title on a king of the Franks, even though he was a Saxon king of the eastern Franks. Otto's creation of a new "Roman Empire" in the hands of the eastern Franks, or Germans as they came to be called, added a tremendous burden to the kingship of Germany. To the difficulties of governing Germany was appended the onerous task of ruling Italy as well. It proved a formidable and ultimately impossible task in the centuries to come.

In the ninth and tenth centuries, the Carolingian kings had little success in controlling the great lords of the western Frankish kingdom. The counts, who were supposed to serve as the chief administrative officials, often paid little attention to the wishes of the Carolingian kings. In 987, when the Carolingian king died, the western Frankish nobles and chief prelates of the church chose Hugh Capet, count of Orléans and Paris, as the new king (987–996).

The nobles who elected Hugh Capet did not intend to establish a new royal dynasty. After all, although Hugh was officially king of the western Franks and overlord of the great nobles of the kingdom, his own family controlled only the Île-de-France, the region around Paris. Other French nobles possessed lands equal to or greater than those of the Capetians and assumed that the king would be content to live off the revenues of his personal lands and not impose any burdensome demands on the nobility. Hugh Capet did succeed in making his position hereditary, however. He asked the nobles, and they agreed, to choose his eldest son Robert as his anointed associate in case Hugh died on a campaign to Spain in 987. And although Hugh Capet could not know it then, the Capetian dynasty would rule the western Frankish kingdom, or France as it came to be known, for centuries. In the late tenth century, however, the territory that would become France was not a unified kingdom but a loose alliance of powerful lords who treated the king of France as one of themselves. They assisted him only when it was in their own interests to do so.

England's development in the ninth and tenth centuries took a course somewhat different from that of the Frankish kingdoms. The long struggle of Anglo-Saxon England against the Danish invasions ultimately produced a unified kingdom. Alfred the Great, king of Wessex (871–899), played a crucial role. He defeated a Danish army in 879 and made peace with the Danes in 886. His successors reconquered the areas occupied by the Danes and established a unified Anglo-Saxon monarchy.

By the time of King Edgar (959–975), Anglo-Saxon England had a well-developed and strong monarchical government. Although the kingship was elective, only descendants of Alfred were chosen for the position. In the counties or shires, the administrative units into which England was divided, the king was assisted by an agent appointed and controlled by him, the shire-reeve or sheriff. An efficient chancery or writing office was responsible for issuing writs (or royal letters) conveying the king's orders to the sheriffs.

CHRONOLOGY

New Political Configurations of the Tenth Century

Eastern Franks	
Conrad of Franconia	911–918
Saxon dynasty: Henry I	919–936
Otto I	936–973
Defeat of Magyars	955
Coronation as emperor	962
Western Franks	
Election of Hugh Capet as king	987
Anglo-Saxon England	
Alfred the Great, king of Wessex	871–899
Peace with the Danes	886
Reign of King Edgar	959–975

The Manorial System

The landholding class of nobles and knights comprised a military elite whose ability to function as warriors depended on having the leisure time to pursue the arts of war. Landed estates, located on the fiefs given to a vassal by his lord and worked by a dependent peasant class, provided the economic sustenance that made this way of life possible. A manor or villa (see Map 8.3) was simply an agricultural estate operated by a lord and worked by peasants. Lords provided protection; peasants gave up their freedom, became tied to the lord's land, and provided labor services for him.

Manorialism grew out of the unsettled circumstances of the Early Middle Ages, when small farmers often needed protection or food in a time of bad harvests. Free peasants gave up their freedom to the lords of large landed estates in return for protection and use of the lord's land. Although a large class of free peasants continued to exist, increasing numbers of them became bound to the land as serfs. Unlike slaves, serfs could not be bought and sold, but they were subservient to their lords in a variety of ways. Serfs were required to provide labor services, pay rents, and be subject to the lord's jurisdiction. By the ninth century, probably 60 percent of the population of western Europe had become serfs.

A serf's labor services consisted of working the lord's demesne, the land retained by the lord, which might consist of one-third to one-half of the cultivated lands scattered throughout the manor (the rest would have been allotted to the serfs for their maintenance), as well as building barns and digging ditches. Although labor requirements varied from manor to manor and person to person, a common work obligation was three days a week.

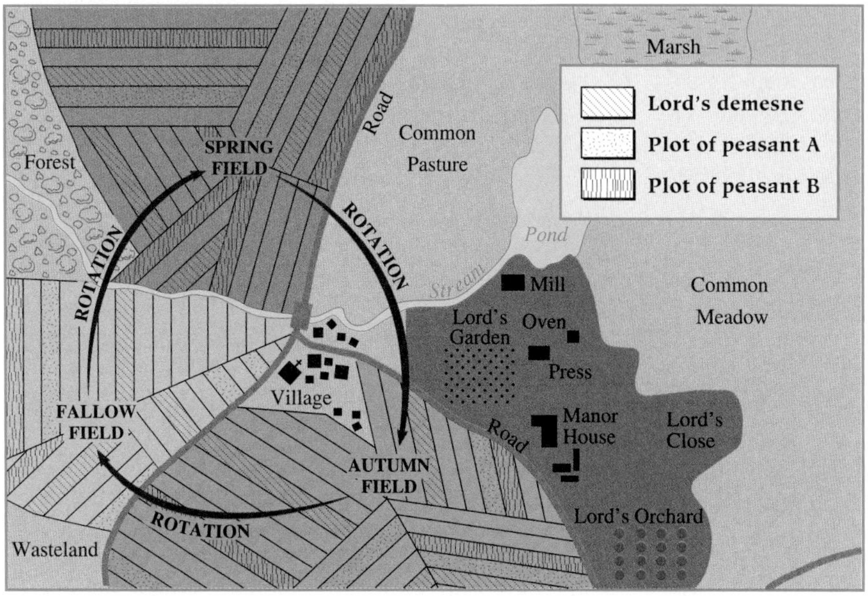

Map 8.3 A Typical Manor. The manorial system created small, tightly knit communities in which peasants were economically and physically bound to their lord. Crops were rotated, with roughly one-third of the fields lying fallow at any one time, which helped replenish soil nutrients. ■ How does the area of the lord's manor, other buildings, garden, and orchard compare to that of the peasant holdings in the village?

The serfs paid rents by giving the lords a share of every product they raised. Serfs also paid the lord for the use of the manor's common pasturelands, streams, ponds, and surrounding woodlands. For example, if tenants fished in the pond or stream on a manor, they turned over part of the catch to their lord. For grazing a cow in the common pasture, a serf paid a rent in cheese produced from the cow's milk. Serfs were also obliged to pay a tithe (a tenth of their produce) to their local village church.

Lords also possessed a variety of legal rights over their serfs. Serfs were legally bound to the lord's land; they could not leave without his permission. Although free to marry, serfs could not marry anyone outside their manor without the lord's approval. Moreover, lords sometimes exercised public rights or political authority on their lands. This gave the lord the right to try serfs in his own court, although only for lesser crimes (called "low justice"). In fact, the lord's manorial court provided the only law that most serfs

Peasants in the Manorial System. In the manorial system, peasants were required to provide labor services for their lord. This thirteenth-century illustration shows a group of English peasants harvesting grain. Overseeing their work is a bailiff, or manager, who supervised the work of the peasants.

The Manorial Court

The way of life of the medieval lord was made possible by the labors of the serfs on his manor. In addition to his right to collect rents, labor services, and fees from his serfs, the lord also possessed political authority over them, including the right to hold a manorial court to try tenants for crimes and infractions of the manor's rules. This selection, taken from the records of an English manorial court, lists the cases heard, the decisions of the jurors, and the subsequent penalties.

Select Pleas in Manorial Courts

John Sperling complains that Richard of Newmere on the Sunday next before S. Bartholomew's day [August 24] last past with his cattle, horses, and pigs wrongfully destroyed the corn on his (John's) land to his damage to the extent of one thrave of wheat, and to his dishonor to the extent of two shillings; and of this he produces suit. And Richard comes and defends all of it. Therefore let him go to the law six handed [with three companions who will swear to his innocence]. His pledges, Simon Combe and Hugh Frith [like bail bondsmen, pledges stood surety for a person ordered to show up in court or pay a fine].

Hugh Free in mercy [fined] for his beast caught in the lord's garden. Pledges, Walter Hill and William Slipper, Fine 6d. [sixpence].

(The) twelve jurors say that Hugh Cross has right in the bank and hedge about which there was a dispute between him and William White. Therefore let him hold in peace and let William be distrained [forced to comply by seizing his property] for his many trespasses. (Afterwards he made fine for 12d.)

From the whole township of Little Ogbourne, except seven, for not coming to wash the lord's sheep, 6s. 8d. [six shillings, eight pence].

Gilbert Richard's son gives 5s. for license to marry a wife. Pledge, Seaman. Term (for payments), the Purification [February 2].

William Jordan in mercy for bad plowing on the lord's land. Pledge, Arthur. Fine, 6d.

The parson of the Church is in mercy for his cow caught in the lord's meadow. Pledges, Thomas Ymer and William Coke.

From Martin Shepherd 6d. for the wound that he gave Pekin.

Ragenhilda of Bec. gives 2s. for having married without license. Pledge, William of Primer.

Walter Hull gives 13s. 4d. for license to dwell on the land of the Prior of Harmondsworth so long as he shall live and as a condition finds pledges, to wit, William Slipper, John Bisuthe, Gilbert Bisuthe, Hugh Tree, William Johnson, John Hulle, who undertake that the said Walter shall do to the lord all the services and customs which he would do if he dwelt on the lord's land. . . .

It was presented that Robert Carter's son by night invaded the house of Peter Burgess and in felony threw stones at his door so that the said Peter raised the hue [alarm]. Therefore let the said Robert be committed to prison. Afterwards he made fine with 2s.

All the plowmen of Great Ogbourne are convicted by the oath of twelve men . . . because by reason of their default (the land) of the lord is damaged to the amount of 9s. . . . And Walter Reaper is in mercy for concealing (i.e., not giving information as to) the said bad plowing. Afterwards he made fine with the lord with 1 mark [thirteen shillings, four pence].

knew (see the box above). Finally, the lord's political authority enabled him to establish monopolies on certain services that provided additional revenues. Serfs could be required to bring their grain to the lord's mill and pay a fee to have it ground into flour. Thus the rights a lord possessed on his manor gave him virtual control over both the lives and property of his serfs.

The administration of manors varied considerably. If the lord of a manor was a simple knight, he would probably live on the estate and supervise it in person. Great lords possessed many manors and relied on a steward or bailiff to run each estate. We should note that manors were controlled not only by lay lords but also by monasteries and cathedral churches. Monasteries tended to be far more conscientious about keeping accurate records of their manorial estates than lay lords, and their surveys provide some of the best sources of information on medieval village life. The relationship between manors and villages was highly variable. A single village might constitute a manor, or a large manor might encompass several villages.

In the Early Middle Ages, a vast majority of men and women, free or unfree—possibly as many as 90 percent—worked the land. This period had witnessed a precipitous decline in trade. Coins and jewelry were often hoarded, and at the local level, goods were frequently bartered because so few coins were in circulation. But trade never entirely disappeared. Even in an agrarian society, surplus products could be exchanged at local markets. More significant, however, was that both aristocrats and wealthy clerics desired merchandise not produced locally, such as spices, silk cloth, wine, gold, and silver jewelry, and it took trade to obtain these items.

Much trade in luxury goods, especially beginning in the ninth century, was with the Byzantine Empire, particularly the city of Constantinople, and the Islamic caliphs of Baghdad. Products from the west included iron, timber, furs, and slaves (many from eastern Europe, including captured Slavs, from whom the modern word *slave* is derived). Traders, often Jews, carried goods by boat on European rivers or on caravans with horses or mules. An Arab geographer of the ninth century left this account of Jewish traders from southern France:

> [They] speak Arabic, Persian, Greek, Frankish, Spanish, and Slavonic. They travel from west to east and from east to west, by land and by sea. From the west they bring eunuchs, slave-girls, boys, brocade, marten and other furs, and swords. They take ship from Frankland in the western Mediterranean sea and land at Farama, whence they take their merchandise on camel-back to Qulzum. . . . Then they sail on the eastern [Red] sea from Qulzum, and onward to India and China. From China they bring back musk, aloes, camphor, cinnamon, and other products of those parts, and return to Qulzum. Then they transport them to Farama and sail again on the western sea. Some sail with their goods to Constantinople and sell them to the Greeks, and some take them to the king of the Franks and sell them there.[11]

By 900, Italian merchants, especially the Venetians, were entering the trade picture. Overall, however, compared to the Byzantine Empire or Muslim caliphates, western Europe in the Early Middle Ages was an underdeveloped, predominantly agrarian society and could not begin to match the splendor of either of the other heirs of the Roman Empire.

The Zenith of Byzantine Civilization

In the seventh and eighth centuries, the Byzantine Empire had lost much of its territory to Slavs, Bulgars, and Muslims. By 750, the empire consisted only of Asia Minor, some lands in the Balkans, and the southern coast of Italy. Although Byzantium was beset with internal dissension and invasions in the ninth century, it was able to deal with them and not only endured but even expanded, reaching its high point in the tenth century, which some historians have called the golden age of Byzantine civilization.

During the reign of Michael III (842–867), the Byzantine Empire began to experience a revival. Iconoclasm was finally abolished in 843, and reforms were made in education, church life, the military, and the peasant economy. There was a noticeable intellectual renewal. But the Byzantine Empire under Michael was still plagued by persistent problems. The Bulgars mounted new attacks, and the Arabs continued to harass the empire. Moreover, a new church problem with political repercussions erupted over differences between the pope as leader of the western Christian church and the patriarch of Constantinople as leader of the eastern (or Orthodox) Christian church. Patriarch Photius condemned the pope as a heretic for accepting a revised form of the Nicene Creed stating that the Holy Spirit proceeded from the Father and the Son instead of "the Holy Spirit, who proceeds from the Father." A council of eastern bishops followed Photius' wishes and excommunicated the pope, creating the so-called Photian schism. Although the differences were later papered over, this controversy served to further the division between the eastern and western Christian churches.

The problems that arose during Michael's reign were effectively dealt with by a new dynasty of Byzantine emperors known as the Macedonians (867–1081), who managed to hold off the external enemies, go over to the offensive, and reestablish domestic order. Supported by the church, the emperors thought of the Byzantine Empire as a continuation of the Christian Roman Empire of late antiquity. Although for diplomatic reasons they occasionally recognized the imperial title of western emperors, such as Charlemagne and Otto I, they still regarded them as little more than barbarian parvenus.

The Macedonian emperors could boast of a remarkable number of achievements in the late ninth and tenth centuries. They worked to strengthen the position of the free farmers, who felt threatened by the attempts of landed aristocrats to expand their estates at the expense of the farmers. The emperors were well aware that the free farmers made up the rank and file of the Byzantine cavalry and provided the military strength of the empire. The Macedonian emperors also fostered a burst of economic prosperity by expanding trade relations with western Europe, especially by selling silks and metalwork. Thanks to this prosperity, the city of Constantinople flourished. Foreign visitors continued to be astounded by its size, wealth, and physical surroundings. To western Europeans, it was the stuff of legends and fables (see the box on p. 210).

In the midst of this prosperity, Byzantine cultural influence expanded during this period due to the active missionary efforts of eastern Byzantine Christians. Eastern Orthodox Christianity was spread to eastern European peoples, such as the Bulgars and Serbs. Perhaps the greatest missionary success occurred when the prince of Kiev in Russia converted to Christianity in 987.

Under the Macedonian rulers, Byzantium enjoyed a strong civil service, talented emperors, and military advances. The Byzantine civil service was staffed by well-educated, competent aristocrats from Constantinople who oversaw the collection of taxes, domestic administration, and foreign policy. At the same time, the Macedonian dynasty produced some truly outstanding emperors skilled in administration and law, including Leo VI (886–912) and Basil II (976–1025). In the tenth century, competent emperors combined with

A Western View of the Byzantine Empire

Bishop Liudprand of Cremona undertook diplomatic missions to Constantinople on behalf of two western kings, Berengar of Italy and Otto I of Germany. This selection is taken from the bishop's description of his mission to the Byzantine emperor Constantine VII as an envoy for Berengar, king of Italy from 950 until his overthrow by Otto I of Germany in 964. Liudprand had mixed feelings about Byzantium: admiration, yet also envy and hostility because of its superior wealth.

■ *Liudprand of Cremona,* Antapodosis

Next to the imperial residence at Constantinople there is a palace of remarkable size and beauty which the Greeks call Magnavra . . . the name being equivalent to "fresh breeze." In order to receive some Spanish envoys, who had recently arrived, as well as myself . . . , Constantine gave orders that his palace should be got ready. . . .

Before the emperor's seat stood a tree, made of bronze gilded over, whose branches were filled with birds, also made of gilded bronze, which uttered different cries, each according to its varying species. The throne itself was so marvelously fashioned that at one moment it seemed a low structure, and at another it rose high into the air. It was of immense size and was guarded by lions, made either of bronze or of wood covered over with gold, who beat the ground with their tails and gave a dreadful roar with open mouth and quivering tongue. Leaning upon the shoulders of two eunuchs I was brought into the emperor's presence. At my approach the lions began to roar and the birds to cry out, each according to its kind; but I was neither terrified nor surprised, for I had previously made enquiry about all these things from people who were well acquainted with them. So after I had three times made obeisance to the emperor with my face upon the ground, I lifted my head, and behold! The man whom just before I had seen sitting on a moderately elevated seat had now changed his raiment and was sitting on the level of the ceiling. How it was done I could not imagine, unless perhaps he was lifted up by some such sort of device as we use for raising the timbers of a wine press. On that occasion he did not address me personally . . . but by the intermediary of a secretary he enquired about Berengar's doings and asked after his health. I made a fitting reply and then, at a nod from the interpreter, left his presence and retired to my lodging.

It would give me some pleasure also to record here what I did then for Berengar. . . . The Spanish envoys . . . had brought handsome gifts from their masters to the emperor Constantine. I for my part had brought nothing from Berengar except a letter and that was full of lies. I was very greatly disturbed and shamed at this and I began to consider anxiously what I had better do. In my doubt and perplexity it finally occurred to me that I might offer the gifts, which on my account I had brought for the emperor, as coming from Berengar, and trick out my humble present with fine words. I therefore presented him with nine excellent curaisses, seven excellent shields with gilded bosses, two silver gilt cauldrons, some swords, spears and spits, and what was more precious to the emperor than anything, four carzimasia; that being the Greek name for young eunuchs who have had both their testicles and their penis removed. This operation is performed by traders at Verdun, who take the boys into Spain and make a huge profit.

Byzantine Visual Resources, Dumbarton Oaks, Washington, DC

Emperor Leo VI. Under the Macedonian dynasty, the Byzantine Empire achieved economic prosperity through expanded trade and gained new territories through military victories. This mosaic over the western door of the Hagia Sophia in Constantinople depicts the Macedonian emperor Leo VI prostrating himself before Jesus. This act of humility symbolized the emperor's function as an intermediary between God and the empire.

The Byzantine Empire in 1025

a number of talented generals to mobilize the empire's military resources and take the offensive. The Bulgars were defeated, and both the eastern and western parts of Bulgaria were annexed to the empire. The Byzantines went on to add the islands of Crete and Cyprus to the empire and defeat the Muslim forces in Syria, expanding the empire to the upper Euphrates. By the end of the reign of Basil II in 1025, the Byzantine Empire was the largest it had been since the beginning of the seventh century.

The Slavic Peoples of Central and Eastern Europe

North of Byzantium and east of the Carolingian Empire lay a spacious plain through which a number of Asiatic nomads, including the Huns, Bulgars, Avars, and Magyars, had pushed their way westward, terrorizing and plundering the settled peasant communities. Eastern Europe was ravaged by these successive waves of invaders, who found it relatively easy to create large empires that were in turn overthrown by the next invaders. Over a period of time, the invaders themselves were largely assimilated with the native Slavic peoples of the area.

The Slavic peoples were originally a single people in central Europe who through mass migrations and nomadic invasions were gradually divided into three major groups: the western, southern, and eastern Slavs (see Map 8.4). In the region east of the Germanic kingdom emerged the Polish and Bohemian kingdoms of the western Slavs. The Germans assumed responsibility for the conversion of these Slavic peoples because German emperors considered it their duty to spread Christianity to the barbarians. Of

Map 8.4 The Migrations of the Slavs. Originally from east-central Europe, the Slavic people broke into three groups. The western Slavs converted to Catholic Christianity, while the eastern Slavs and southern Slavs, under the influence of the Byzantine Empire, embraced the Eastern Orthodox faith. ■ What connections do these Slavic migrations have with what we today characterize as eastern Europe?

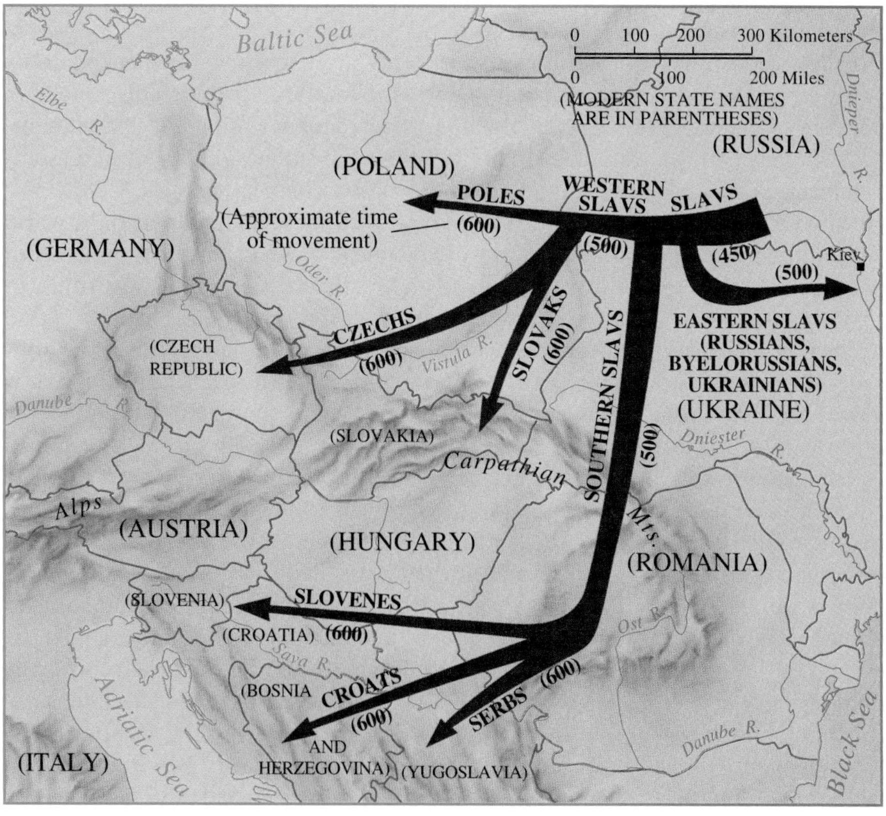

course, it also gave them the opportunity to extend their political authority as well. German missionaries had converted the Czechs in Bohemia by the end of the ninth century, and a bishopric eventually occupied by a Czech bishop was established at Prague in the tenth century. The Slavs in Poland were not converted until the reign of Prince Mieszko (c. 960–992). In 1000, an independent Polish archbishopric was set up at Gniezno by the pope. The non-Slavic kingdom of Hungary, which emerged after the Magyars settled down after their defeat at Lechfeld in 955, was also converted to Christianity by German missionaries. Saint Stephen, king of Hungary from 997 to 1038, facilitated the acceptance of Christianity by his people. The Poles, Czechs, and Hungarians all accepted Catholic or western Christianity and became closely tied to the Roman Catholic church and its Latin culture.

The southern and eastern Slavic populations took a different path because of their proximity to the Byzantine Empire. The southern Slavic peoples were converted to the Eastern Orthodox Christianity of the Byzantine Empire by two Byzantine missionary brothers, Cyril and Methodius, who began their activities in 863. They created a Slavonic (Cyrillic) alphabet, translated the Bible into Slavonic, and developed Slavonic church services. Although the southern Slavic peoples accepted Christianity, a split eventually developed between the Croats, who accepted the Roman church, and the Serbs, who remained loyal to eastern Christianity.

Although the Bulgars were originally an Asiatic people who conquered much of the Balkan peninsula, they were eventually absorbed by the larger native southern Slavic population. Together, by the ninth century, they formed a largely Slavic Bulgarian kingdom. Although the conversion to Christianity of this state was complicated by the rivalry between the Roman Catholic and Eastern Orthodox churches, the Bulgarians eventually accepted the latter. By the end of the ninth century, they embraced the Slavonic church services earlier developed by Cyril and Methodius. The acceptance of Eastern Orthodoxy by the southern Slavic peoples, the Serbs and Bulgarians, meant that their cultural life was also linked to the Byzantine state.

The eastern Slavic peoples, from whom the modern Russians, White Russians (Byelorussians), and Ukrainians are descended, had settled in the territory of present-day Ukraine and European Russia. There, beginning in the late eighth century, they began to encounter Viking invaders. Swedish Vikings, known to the eastern Slavs as Varangians, moved down the extensive network of rivers into the lands of the eastern Slavs in search of booty and new trade routes. After establishing trading links with the Byzantine state, the Varangians built trading settlements, became involved in the civil wars among the Slavic peoples, and eventually came to dominate the native peoples, just as their fellow Vikings were doing in parts of western Europe. According to the traditional version of the story, the semilegendary Rurik secured his ruling dynasty in the Slavic settlement of Novgorod in 862. Rurik and his fellow Vikings were called "the Rus," from which the name Russia is derived; eventually that name became attached to the state they founded (see the box on p. 213). Although much about Rurik is unclear, it is certain that his follower Oleg (c. 873–913) took up residence in Kiev and created the Rus state or union of eastern Slavic territories known as the principality of Kiev. Oleg's successors extended their control over the eastern Slavs and expanded the territory of Kiev until it encompassed the lands between the Baltic and Black Seas and the Danube and Volga Rivers. By marrying Slavic wives, the Viking ruling class was gradually assimilated into the Slavic population, a process confirmed by their assumption of Slavic names.

The growth of the principality of Kiev attracted religious missionaries, especially from the Byzantine Empire. One Rus ruler, Vladimir (c. 980–1015), married the Byzantine emperor's sister and officially accepted Christianity for himself and his people in 987. His primary motive was probably not spiritual. By all accounts, Vladimir was a cruel and vicious man who believed an established church would be helpful in developing an organized state. From the end of the tenth century on, Byzantine Christianity became the model for Russian religious life, just as Byzantine imperial ideals came to influence the outward forms of Russian political life.

The World of Islam

The Umayyad dynasty of caliphs had established Damascus as the center of an Islamic empire created by Arab expansion in the seventh and eighth centuries. But Umayyad rule created resentment, and the Umayyads also helped bring about their own end by their corrupt behavior. One caliph, for example, supposedly swam in a pool of wine and drank enough of it to lower the wine level considerably. Finally, in 750, Abu al-Abbas, a descendant of the uncle of Muhammad, brought an end to the Umayyad dynasty and established the Abbasid dynasty, which lasted until 1258.

The Abbasid rulers brought much change to the world of Islam. They tried to break down the distinctions between Arab and non-Arab Muslims. All Muslims, regardless of their ethnic background, could now hold both civil and military offices. This helped open Islamic life to the influences of the conquered civilizations. Many Arabs now began to intermarry with their conquered peoples.

In 762, the Abbasids built a new capital city, Baghdad, on the Tigris River far to the east of Damascus. The new capital was well placed. It took advantage of river traffic to the Persian Gulf and at the same time was located on the caravan route from the Mediterranean to Central Asia. The move eastward allowed Persian influence to come to the fore, encouraging a new cultural orientation. Under the Abbasids, judges, merchants, and government officials, rather than warriors, were viewed as the ideal citizens.

The new Abbasid dynasty experienced a period of splendid rule well into the ninth century. Best known of the caliphs of the time was Harun al-Rashid (786–809), whose

A Muslim's Description of the Rus

Despite the difficulties that travel presented, early medieval civilization did witness some contact among the various cultures. This might occur through trade, diplomacy, or the conquest and migration of peoples. This document is a description of the Swedish Rus who eventually merged with the native Slavic peoples to form the principality of Kiev, commonly regarded as the first Russian state. This account was written by Ibn Fadlan, a Muslim diplomat sent from Baghdad in 921 to a settlement on the Volga River. His comments on the filthiness of the Rus reflect the Muslim preoccupation with cleanliness.

Ibn Fadlan, Description of the Rus

I saw the Rus folk when they arrived on their trading-mission and settled at the river Atul (Volga). Never had I seen people of more perfect physique. They are tall as date-palms, and reddish in color. They wear neither coat nor kaftan, but each man carried a cape which covers one half of his body, leaving one hand free. No one is ever parted from his axe, sword, and knife. Their swords are Frankish in design, broad, flat, and fluted. Each man has a number of trees, figures, and the like from the fingernails to the neck. Each woman carried on her bosom a container made of iron, silver, copper or gold—its size and substance depending on her man's wealth. . . .

They [the Rus] are the filthiest of God's creatures. They do not wash after discharging their natural functions, neither do they wash their hands after meals. They are as lousy as donkeys. They arrive from their distant river, and there they build big houses on its shores. Ten or twenty of them may live together in one house, and each of them has a couch of his own where he sits and diverts himself with the pretty slave girls whom he had brought along for sale. He will make love with one of them while a comrade looks on; sometimes they indulge in a communal orgy, and, if a customer should turn up to buy a girl, the Rus man will not let her go till he has finished with her.

They wash their hands and faces every day in incredibly filthy water. Every morning the girl brings her master a large bowl of water in which he washes his hands and face and hair, then blows his nose into it and spits into it. When he has finished the girl takes the bowl to his neighbor—who repeats the performance. Thus the bowl goes the rounds of the entire household. . . .

If one of the Rus folk falls sick they put him in a tent by himself and leave bread and water for him. They do not visit him, however, or speak to him, especially if he is a serf. Should he recover he rejoins the others; if he dies they burn him. But if he happens to be a serf they leave him for the dogs and vultures to devour. If they catch a robber they hang him to a tree until he is torn to shreds by wind and weather. . . .

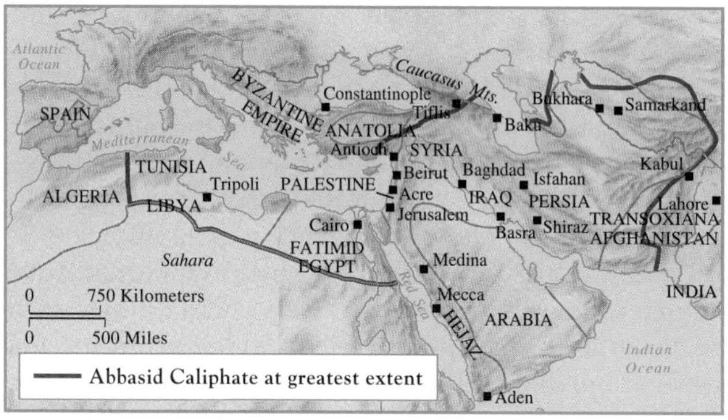

The Abbasid Caliphate at the Height of Its Power

reign is often described as the golden age of the Abbasid caliphate. His son al-Ma'mun (813–833) was a great patron of learning. He founded an astronomical observatory and created a foundation for translating classical Greek works. This was also a period of growing economic prosperity. After all, the Arabs had conquered many of the richest provinces of the old Roman Empire, and they now controlled the trade routes to the east. Baghdad became the center of an enormous trade empire that extended into Europe, Asia, and Africa, greatly adding to the wealth of the Islamic world.

Despite the prosperity, all was not quite well in the empire of the Abbasids. There was much fighting over the succession to the caliphate. When Harun al-Rashid died, his two sons fought to succeed him in a struggle that almost destroyed the city of Baghdad. As the tenth-century Muslim historian al-Mas'udi wrote: "Mansions were destroyed, most remarkable monuments obliterated; prices soared. . . . Brother turned his sword against brother, son against father, as some fought for Amin, others for Ma'mun. Houses and palaces fueled the flames; property was put to the sack."[12]

Vast wealth also gave rise to financial corruption. By awarding important positions to court favorites, the Abbasid caliphs began to undermine the foundations of their own power and soon became figureheads. Provincial rulers broke away from the control of the caliphs and established their own independent dynasties. Even earlier, in the eighth century, a separate caliphate had already been established in Spain when Abd al-Rahman of the Umayyad dynasty had fled there. In 756, he seized control of southern Spain and then expanded his power into the center of the peninsula. He took the title of emir, or commander, and set up the emirate of al-Andalus with its center at Córdoba. Under Abd al-Rahman's successors, a unique society developed in which all religions were

Scala/Art Resource, NY

Mosque at Córdoba. The first Great Mosque of Córdoba was built by Abd al-Rahman, founder of the Umayyad dynasty of Spain, in the eighth century. The mosque was later enlarged in the tenth century. Shown here is the interior of the sanctuary, with its two levels of arches. Although the Umayyad caliphs of Damascus were overthrown and replaced by the Abbasid dynasty in the eighth century, the independent Umayyad dynasty in Spain lasted until the eleventh century.

CHRONOLOGY

Byzantium, the Slavs, and the Islamic World

Byzantine Empire	
Michael III	842–867
Macedonian dynasty	867–1081
Leo VI	886–912
Basil II	976–1025
Slavic peoples of central and eastern Europe	
Establishment of Novgorod	c. 862
Cyril and Methodius begin to convert Moravian Slavs	863
Oleg creates principality of Kiev	c. 873–913
Reign of Prince Mieszko; Slavs in Poland converted to Christianity	c. 960–992
Vladimir's conversion to Christianity	987
Saint Stephen, king of Hungary	997–1038
World of Islam	
Overthrow of Umayyad dynasty by Abbasids	750
Creation of emirate of al-Andalus	756
Harun al-Rashid	786–809
al-Ma'mun	813–833
Establishment of Fatimid caliphate in Egypt	973

tolerated. The court also supported writers and artists, creating a brilliant and flourishing culture.

The breakup of the Islamic empire accelerated in the tenth century. The Fatimid family established a caliphate in Egypt in 973, and an independent dynasty also operated in North Africa. Despite the political disunity of the Islamic world, however, there was an underlying Islamic civilization based on two common bonds, the Qur'an and the Arabic language.

Islamic Civilization

From the beginning of their empire, Muslim Arabs had demonstrated a willingness to absorb the culture of their conquered territories. The Arabs were truly heirs to the remaining Greco-Roman culture of the Roman Empire. Just as readily, they assimilated Byzantine and Persian culture. In the eighth and ninth centuries, numerous Greek, Syrian, and Persian scientific and philosophical works were translated into Arabic. As the chief language in the southern Mediterranean and the Near East and the required language of Muslims, Arabic became a truly international tongue.

The Muslims created a brilliant urban culture at a time when western Europe was predominantly a rural world of farming villages. This can be seen in such new cities as Baghdad and Cairo, but also in Córdoba, the capital of the Umayyad caliphate in Spain. With a population of possibly 100,000, Córdoba was Europe's largest city after Constantinople. Its library was also the largest in Europe.

Islamic cities had a distinctive physical appearance due to their common use of certain architectural features, such as the pointed arch and traceried windows, and specific kinds of buildings. The latter included palaces and public buildings with fountains and secluded courtyards, mosques for worship, public baths, and bazaars or marketplaces. Muslims embellished their buildings with a unique decorative art that avoided representation of living things because of their religion's commandment that prohibited the making of graven images.

During the first few centuries of the Arab empire, it was the Islamic world that saved and spread the scientific and philosophical works of ancient civilizations. At a time when the ancient Greek philosophers were largely unknown in Europe, key works by Plato and Aristotle were translated into Arabic. They were put in a library called the House of Wisdom in Baghdad where they were read and studied by Muslim scholars. The library also contained texts on mathematics brought from India. The preservation of ancient texts was aided by the use of paper. The making of paper was introduced from China in the eighth century, and by the end of the century, paper factories had been established in Baghdad. Booksellers and libraries soon followed. European universities later benefited from this scholarship when these works were translated from Arabic into Latin.

Although Islamic scholars are rightly praised for preserving much of classical knowledge for the West, they also made considerable advances of their own. Nowhere is this more evident than in their contributions to mathematics and the natural sciences. The list of achievements in mathematics and astronomy alone is impressive. The Muslims adopted and passed on the numerical system of India, including the use of the zero. In Europe, it became known as the Arabic system. A ninth-century Persian mathematician created the discipline of algebra. Muslim astronomers studied the positions of the stars from the observatory established by al-Ma'mun at Baghdad. They were aware that the earth was round and named many stars. They also perfected the astrolabe, an instrument used by sailors to determine their location by observing the positions of heavenly bodies. It was the astrolabe that later made it possible for Europeans to sail to the Americas.

Muslim scholars also made many new discoveries in chemistry and developed medicine as a field of scientific study. Especially well known was Ibn Sina (known as Avicenna in the West, 980–1037), who wrote a medical encyclopedia that, among other things, stressed the contagious nature of certain diseases and showed how they could be spread by contaminated water supplies. After its translation into Latin, Avicenna's work became a basic medical textbook for medieval European university students. Avicenna was but one of many Muslim scholars whose work was translated into Latin and contributed to the development of intellectual life in Europe in the twelfth and thirteenth centuries.

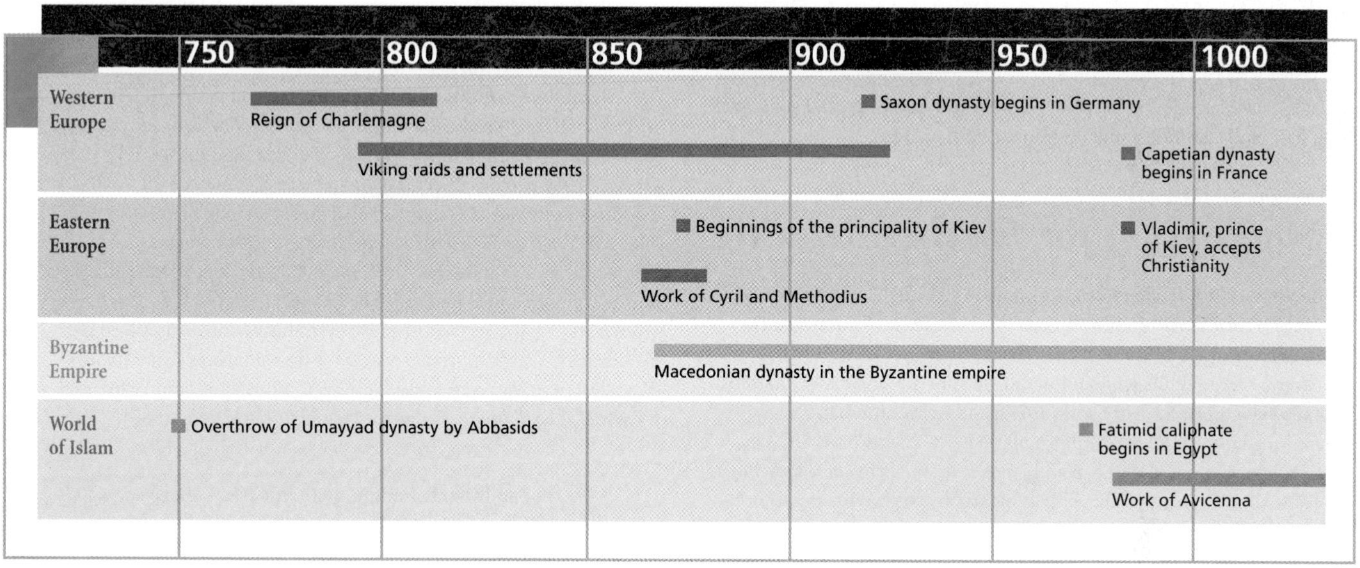

Conclusion

After the turmoil of the disintegration of the Roman Empire and the establishment of the Germanic states, a new European civilization began to emerge slowly in the Early Middle Ages. The coronation of Charlemagne, descendant of a Germanic tribe converted to Christianity, as Roman emperor in 800 symbolized the fusion of the three chief components of the new European civilization: the German tribes, the classical tradition, and Christianity. In the long run, the creation of a western empire fostered the idea of a distinct European identity and marked a shift of power from the south to the north. Italy and the Mediterranean had been the center of the Roman Empire. The lands north of the Alps now became the political center of Europe.

With the disintegration of the Carolingian Empire, new forms of political institutions in which lords exercised legal, administrative, and military power began to develop in Europe. The practice of fief-holding transferred public power into many private hands and seemed to provide the security sorely lacking in a time of weak central government and new invasions by Muslims, Magyars, and Vikings. While Europe struggled, the Byzantine and Islamic worlds continued to prosper and flourish, the brilliance of their urban cultures standing in marked contrast to the underdeveloped rural world of Europe. By 1000, however, that rural world had not only recovered but was beginning to expand in ways undreamed of by previous generations. Europe stood poised for a giant leap.

Notes

1. Einhard, *The Life of Charlemagne,* trans. Samuel Turner (Ann Arbor, Mich., 1960), p. 30.
2. Ibid., p. 57.
3. Quoted in Pierre Riché, *Daily Life in the World of Charlemagne,* trans. Jo Ann McNamara (Philadelphia, 1978), p. 56.
4. 1 Corinthians 7:1–2, 8–9.
5. Quoted in Derrick Bailey, *Homosexuality and the Western Christian Tradition* (London, 1955), p. 73.
6. Quoted in Paul Veyne, ed., *A History of Private Life,* vol. 1, *From Pagan Rome to Byzantium,* trans. Arthur Goldhammer (Cambridge, Mass., 1987), p. 440.
7. Stanley Rubin, *Medieval English Medicine* (New York, 1974), p. 136.
8. Quoted in Brian Inglis, *A History of Medicine* (New York, 1965), p. 51.
9. Quoted in Simon Keynes, "The Vikings in England, c. 790–1016," in Peter Sawyer, ed., *The Oxford Illustrated History of the Vikings* (Oxford, 1997), p. 81.
10. Quoted in Oliver Thatcher and Edgar McNeal, *A Source Book for Medieval History* (New York, 1905), p. 363.
11. Quoted in Bernard Lewis, *The Arabs in History* (London, 1958), p. 90.
12. al-Mas'udi, *The Meadows of Gold: The Abbasids,* ed. Paul Lunde and Caroline Stone (London, 1989), p. 151.

Suggestions for Further Reading

Surveys of Carolingian Europe include D. Bullough, *The Age of Charlemagne* (New York, 1966), and *Carolingian Renewal: Sources and Heritage* (New York, 1991); P. Riché, *The Carolingians: A Family Who Forged Europe* (Philadelphia, 1993); L. Halphen, *Charlemagne and the Carolingian Empire* (New York, 1977); and R. McKitterick, *The Frankish Kingdoms Under the Carolingians, 751–987* (London, 1983). On Charlemagne, see H. R. Loyn and J. Percival, *The Reign of Charlemagne* (New York, 1976), and the popular biography by R. Winston, *Charlemagne: From the Hammer to the Cross* (Indianapolis, 1954). On Carolingian culture, see R. McKitterick, *The Carolingians and the Written Word* (Cambridge, 1989), *Carolingian Culture: Emulation and Innovation* (New York, 1994), and the collection of essays titled *The Frankish Kings and Culture in the Early Middle Ages* (Brookfield, Vt., 1995).

Various aspects of social life in the Carolingian world are examined in P. Riché, *Daily Life in the World of Charlemagne,* trans. J. A. McNamara (Philadelphia, 1978); M. Rouche, "The Early Middle Ages in the West," in P. Veyne, ed., *A History of Private Life* (Cambridge, Mass., 1987), vol. 1, pp. 411–549; C. B. Bouchard, *Life and Society in the West: Antiquity and the Middle Ages* (San Diego, Calif., 1988), ch. 5; and S. F. Wemple, *Women in Frankish Society: Marriage and the Cloister* (Philadelphia, 1981). On children, see S. Shamar, *Childhood in the Middle Ages,* trans. C. Galai (London, 1992), and J. Boswell, *The Kindness of Strangers* (New York, 1988). On the attitudes toward sexuality in the early Christian church, see the important works by P. Brown, *The Body and Society* (New York, 1988), and E. Pagels, *Adam, Eve, and the Serpent* (New York, 1988).

The Vikings are examined in P. Sawyer, *Kings and Vikings* (London, 1982); F. D. Logan, *The Vikings in History,* 2d ed. (London, 1991); G. Jones, *A History of the Vikings,* rev. ed. (Oxford, 1984); and P. Sawyer, ed., *The Oxford Illustrated History of the Vikings* (New York, 1997).

Two introductory works on fief-holding are J. R. Strayer, *Feudalism* (Princeton, N.J., 1985), and the classic work by M. Bloch, *Feudal Society,* trans. L. A. Manyon (London, 1961). For an important revisionist view, see S. Reynolds, *Fiefs and Vassals* (Oxford, 1994). Works on the new political configurations that emerged in the tenth century are cited in Chapter 9.

For the economic history of the Early Middle Ages, see G. Duby, *The Early Growth of the European Economy: Warriors and Peasants from the Seventh to the Twelfth Century* (Ithaca, N.Y., 1974). On the manorial court, see Z. Razi and R. Smith, eds., *Medieval Society and the Manor Court* (New York, 1996).

Byzantine civilization in this period is examined in R. Jenkins, *Byzantium: The Imperial Centuries, 610–1071* (New York, 1969), and W. Treadgold, *The Byzantine Revival, 780–842* (Stanford, Calif., 1988). On the Slavic peoples of central and eastern Europe, see F. Dvornik, *The Slavs in European History and Civilization* (New Brunswick, N.J., 1962); A. P. Vlasto, *The Entry of the Slavs into Christendom* (Cambridge, 1970); Z. Vana, *The World of the Ancient Slavs* (London, 1983); and S. Franklin and J. Shepard, *The Emergence of Rus, 750–1200* (New York, 1996). The world of Islam in this period is discussed in H. Kennedy, *The Prophet and the Age of the Caliphates: The Islamic Near East from the Sixth to the Eleventh Century* (London, 1986), and J. Lassner, *The Shaping of Abbasid Rule* (Princeton, N.J., 1980).

For additional reading, go to InfoTrac College Edition, your online research library at http://web1.infotrac-college.com

Enter the search term *Carolingian* using Key Terms.

Enter the search term *Charlemagne* using Key Terms.

Enter the search term *Vikings not Minnesota* using Key Terms.

Enter the search term *feudalism* and also the search term *feudal* using the Subject Guide.

CHAPTER

9

The Recovery and Growth of European Society in the High Middle Ages

Staatliche Museen, Berlin, Photo © Bildarchiv Preussischer Kulturbesitz, Berlin

CHAPTER OUTLINE

- Land and People in the High Middle Ages
- The New World of Trade and Cities
- The Intellectual and Artistic World of the High Middle Ages
- Conclusion

FOCUS QUESTIONS

- What new agricultural practices arose in the High Middle Ages?
- What roles did peasants and aristocrats play in the civilization of the High Middle Ages?
- What developments contributed to the revival of trade during the High Middle Ages, and what areas were the primary beneficiaries of the revival?
- What were the major features of medieval cities?
- What were the major intellectual and cultural achievements of European civilization in the High Middle Ages?
- What is the relationship between economic and social changes and intellectual and artistic developments in the High Middle Ages?

THE NEW EUROPEAN CIVILIZATION that had emerged in the ninth and tenth centuries began to come into its own in the eleventh and twelfth centuries as Europeans established new patterns that reached their zenith in the thirteenth century. The High Middle Ages (1000–1300) was a period of recovery and growth for Western civilization, characterized by a greater sense of security and a burst of energy and enthusiasm. New agricultural practices that increased the food supply helped give rise to a commercial and urban revival that, accompanied by a rising population, created new dynamic elements in a formerly static society.

Townspeople themselves were often great enthusiasts for their new way of life. In the twelfth century, William Fitz-Stephen spoke of London as one of the noble cities of the world: "It is happy in the healthiness of its air, in the Christian religion, in the strength of its defences, the nature of its site, the honor of its citizens, the modesty of its women; pleasant in sports; fruitful of noble men." To Fitz-Stephen, London offered a myriad of opportunities and pleasures. Fairs and markets were held regularly, and "practically anything that man may need is brought daily not only into special places but even into the open squares." Any man, according to Fitz-Stephen, "if he is healthy and not a good-for-nothing, may earn his living expenses and esteem according to his station." Then, too, there are the happy inhabitants of the city: where else has one "ever met such a wonderful show of people this side or the other side of the sea?" Sporting events and leisure activities are available in every season of the year: "In Easter holidays they fight battles on water." In summer, "the youths are exercised in leaping, dancing, shooting, wrestling, casting the stone; the maidens dance as long as they can well see." In winter, "when the great fen, or moor, which waters the walls of the city on the north side, is frozen, many young men play upon the ice; some, striding as wide as they may, do slide swiftly." To Fitz-Stephen, "every convenience for human pleasure is known to be at hand" in London. One would hardly know from his cheerful description that medieval cities faced overcrowded conditions, terrible smells from rotting garbage and raw sewage, and the constant challenge of epidemics and fires.

By the twelfth and thirteenth centuries, both the urban centers and the urban population of Europe were experiencing a dramatic expansion. New forms of cultural and intellectual expression also arose in this new urban world. Although European society in the High Middle Ages remained overwhelmingly agricultural, the growth of trade and cities along with the development of a money economy and new commercial practices and institutions constituted a veritable commercial revolution that affected most of Europe.

Table 9.1 Population Estimates (in millions), 1000 and 1340

Area	1000	1340
Mediterranean		
Greece and Balkans	5	6
Italy	5	10
Iberia	7	9
Total	17	25
Western and Central Europe		
France and Low Countries	6	19
British Isles	2	5
Germany and Scandinavia	4	11.5
Total	12	35.5
Eastern Europe		
Russia	6	8
Poland	2	3
Hungary	1.5	2
Total	9.5	13
Grand Total	**38.5**	**73.5**

SOURCE: J. C. Russell, *The Control of Late Ancient and Medieval Population* (Philadelphia: American Philosophical Society, 1985), p. 36. Demographic specialists admit that these are merely estimates. Some figures, especially those for eastern Europe, could be radically revised by new research.

Land and People in the High Middle Ages

The period from 1000 to 1300 witnessed an improvement in climate as a small but nevertheless significant rise in temperature made for longer and better growing seasons. At the same time, the European population experienced a dramatic increase, virtually doubling between 1000 and 1300, from 38 million to 74 million people. As Table 9.1 indicates, the rate of growth tended to vary from region to region. This rise in population was physically evident in the growth of agricultural villages, towns, and cities and the increase in arable land.

Why this dramatic increase in population? Obviously, fertility rates increased sufficiently to gradually outstrip the relatively high mortality rates of medieval society, which were especially acute in infancy and the childhood years. Traditionally, historians have cited two factors to explain the population increase. For one, they attribute it to increased security stemming from more settled and peaceful conditions after the invasions of the Early Middle Ages had stopped. Moreover, agricultural production increased dramatically after 1000. Were it not for this increase in food supplies, the expansion in population could never have been sustained.

The New Agriculture

During the High Middle Ages, significant changes occurred in the way Europeans farmed. Although the warmer climate played an underlying role by improving growing conditions, another important factor in increasing the production of food was the expansion of cultivated or arable land. This was done primarily by clearing forested areas for cultivation. Millions of acres of forests were also cut down to provide timber for fuel, houses, mills, bridges, fortresses, ships, and charcoal for the iron industry (see the box on p. 219). Eager for land, peasants cut down trees, drained swamps, and in the area of the Netherlands even began to reclaim land from the sea. By the thirteenth century, the total acreage available for farming in Europe was greater than before or since.

Technological changes also furthered the expansion of agriculture. Many depended on the use of iron, which was mined in various areas of Europe and traded to places where it was not found. Iron was in demand to make swords and armor as well as scythes, axheads, new types of farming implements such as hoes, and saws, hammers, and nails for building purposes. It was crucial to the development of the heavy, wheeled plow, the *carruca,* which made an enormous impact on medieval agriculture north of the Alps.

The plow of the Mediterranean and Near Eastern worlds had been the *aratum,* a nonwheeled, light scratch plow made mostly of wood that was sufficient to break the top layer of the light soils of those areas. It could be pulled

The Elimination of Medieval Forests

One of the interesting environmental changes of the Middle Ages was the elimination of millions of acres of forest to create new areas of arable land and to meet the demand for timber. Timber was used as fuel and to build houses, mills of all kinds, bridges, fortresses, and ships. Incredible quantities of wood were burned to make charcoal for the iron forges. The clearing of the forests caused the price of wood to skyrocket by the thirteenth century. This document from 1140 illustrates the process. Suger, the abbot of Saint-Denis, needed 35-foot beams for the construction of a new church. His master carpenters told him that there were no longer any trees big enough in the area around Paris and that he would have to go far afield to find such tall trees. This selection recounts his efforts.

Suger's Search for Wooden Beams

On a certain night, when I had returned from celebrating Matins [a prayer service], I began to think in bed that I myself should go through all the forests of these parts. . . . Quickly disposing of all duties and hurrying up in the early morning, we hastened with our carpenters, and with the measurements of the beams, to the forest called Iveline. When we traversed our possession in the Valley of Chevreuse we summoned . . . the keepers of our own forests as well as men who know about the other woods, and questioned them under oath whether we would find there, no matter with how much trouble, any timbers of that measure. At this they smiled, or rather would have laughed at us if they had dared; they wondered whether we were quite ignorant of the fact that nothing of the kind could be found in the entire region, especially since Milon, the Castellan of Chevreuse, . . . had left nothing unimpaired or untouched that could be used for palisades and bulwarks while he was long subjected to wars both by our Lord the King and Amaury de Montfort. We however—scorning whatever they might say—began, with the courage of our faith as it were, to search through the woods; and toward the first hour we found one timber adequate to the measure. Why say more? By the ninth hour or sooner, we had, through the thickets, the depths of the forest and the dense, thorny tangles, marked down twelve timbers (for so many were necessary) to the astonishment of all.

by a single donkey, ox, or horse. But such a light plow was totally ineffective in the heavy clay soils north of the Alps. The *carruca,* a heavy, wheeled plow with an iron plowshare, came into widespread use by the tenth century. It could turn over heavy soils and allow them to drain. Because of its weight, a team of oxen was needed to pull it. Oxen were slow, however. Two new inventions for the horse made greater productivity possible. In the tenth century, a new horse collar was developed that distributed the weight around the shoulders and chest rather than the throat and could be used to hitch up a series of horses, enabling them to pull the new heavy plow faster and cultivate more land. The use of horseshoes, iron shoes nailed to a horse's hooves, produced greater traction and better protection against the rocky and heavy clay soils of northern Europe.

The use of the heavy, wheeled plow also led to cooperative agricultural villages. Because iron was expensive, a heavy, wheeled plow had to be purchased by the entire community. An individual family could not afford a team of animals, so villagers shared their beasts. Moreover, the plow's size and weight made it hard to maneuver, so land was cultivated in long strips to minimize the amount of turning that would have to be done.

Besides using horsepower, the High Middle Ages harnessed the power of water and wind to do jobs formerly

The Heavy, Wheeled Plow. The heavy, wheeled plow was an important invention that enabled peasants to turn over the heavy clay soil of northern Europe. This sixteenth-century illumination shows the heavy, wheeled plow pulled by draft horses with collars.

done by human or animal power. Although the watermill had been invented as early as the second century B.C., it did not come into widespread use until the High Middle Ages. Located along streams, watermills were used to grind grain into flour. Often dams were constructed to increase waterpower. The development of the cam enabled millwrights to mechanize entire industries; waterpower was used in certain phases of cloth production and to power trip-hammers for the working of metals.

Where rivers were unavailable or not easily dammed, Europeans developed windmills to yoke the power of the wind. By the end of the twelfth century, these were beginning to dot the European landscape. The watermill and windmill were the most important devices for the harnessing of power before the invention of the steam engine in the eighteenth century.

The shift from a two-field to a three-field system of crop rotation also contributed to the increase in agricultural production. In the Early Middle Ages, it was common to plant half of one's fields while allowing the other half to lie fallow to regain its fertility. Now estates were divided into three parts. One field was planted in the fall with grains such as rye and wheat, while spring-sown grains, such as oats and barley, and legumes, such as peas, beans, or lentils, were planted in the second field. The third was allowed to lie fallow. By rotating their use, only one-third, rather than one-half, of the land lay fallow at any time. The rotation of crops also prevented the soil from being exhausted so quickly, especially since legumes improve soil fertility because their roots fix nitrogen in the soil. Grain yields increased as well. The three-field system was not adopted everywhere, however. It was not used in Mediterranean lands, and even in northern Europe the two-field and three-field systems existed side by side for centuries.

By the thirteenth century, the growing demand for agricultural produce in the towns and cities led to higher food prices. This led lords to try to grow more food for profit. One way to do so was to lease their demesne land to their serfs. Labor services were then transformed into money payments or fixed rents, thereby converting many serfs into free peasants. Although many peasants still remained economically dependent on their lords, they were no longer legally tied to the land. Lords, in turn, became collectors of rents rather than operators of a manor with political and legal privileges. The political and legal powers formerly exercised by lords were increasingly reclaimed by the monarchical states.

The Life of the Peasantry

Peasant activities were largely determined by the seasons of the year. Each season brought a new round of tasks appropriate for the time, although some periods were considerably more hectic than others, especially summer and fall. The basic staple of the peasant diet was bread, so an adequate harvest of grains was crucial to survival in the winter months. A new cycle began in October when peasants prepared the ground for the planting of winter crops. In November came the slaughter of excess livestock because there was usually insuf-

Giraudon/Art Resource, NY

Peasant Activities. The seasons of the year largely determined the life of the European peasant. The kind of work that peasants did was dictated by the month and the season. This French calendar of 1460 shows a number of medieval farming activities, including sowing seeds, harvesting crops, pruning plants, shearing sheep, threshing, pressing grapes, and taking care of animals.

ficient fodder to keep animals all winter. The meat would be salted to preserve it for winter use. In February and March, the land was plowed for spring crops—oats, barley, peas, beans, and lentils. Early summer was a comparatively relaxed time, although there was still weeding and sheepshearing to be done. In every season, the serfs worked not only their own land but also the lord's demesne. They also tended the gardens adjacent to their dwellings where they grew the vegetables and fruits that made up part of their diet.

HOLIDAYS AND THE VILLAGE CHURCH

But peasants did not face a life of constant labor thanks to the feast days or holidays of the Catholic church, which commemorated the great events of the Christian faith or the lives of Christian saints or holy persons. The three great feasts of the Catholic church were Christmas (celebrating the birth of Jesus), Easter (celebrating the resurrection of Jesus), and Pentecost (celebrating the descent of the Holy Spirit on Jesus' disciples fifty days after his resurrection). Numerous other feasts dedicated to saints or the Virgin Mary, the mother of Jesus, were also celebrated, making a total of over fifty holidays.

Religious feast days, Sunday Mass, baptisms, marriages, and funerals all brought peasants into contact with the village church, a crucial part of manorial life. In the village church, the peasant was baptized as an infant, confirmed in the faith, sometimes married, and given the sacrament of Holy Communion as well as the last rites of the church before death. The village priest instructed the peasants in the basic elements of Christianity so that they might attain the Christian's ultimate goal—salvation. But village priests were often barely literate peasants themselves, and it is hard to know how much church doctrine the peasants actually understood. Very likely, they regarded God as an all-powerful force who needed to be appeased by prayer to bring good harvests.

THE PEASANT HOUSEHOLD AND FAMILY

Peasant dwellings were very simple. In timber-rich areas, peasant cottages had wood frames filled in with wattling (a lattice of laths) and plastered with a "daub" of clay, straw, animal hair, and dung. Roofs were often thatched with reeds or straw. In timber-poor areas, peasants built their houses out of stone. The houses of poorer peasants consisted of a single room, but others had at least two rooms—a main room for cooking, eating, and other activities and another room for sleeping. There was little privacy in a medieval household. A hearth in the main room was used for heating and cooking, but since there were few or no windows and no chimney, the smoke from fires in the hearth went out a hole in the roof or gable.

Surveys of monastic manors reveal that the typical peasant household consisted of a husband and wife with two or three children. Infant mortality rates were high. Peasant women occupied both an important and a difficult position in manorial society. They were expected to carry and bear children, do the spinning and weaving that provided the household's clothes, tend the family's vegetable garden, and provide the meals. A woman's ability to manage the household might determine whether her family would starve or survive in difficult times. At the same time, peasant women often worked with men in the fields, especially at harvest time.

Though simple, a peasant's daily diet was potentially nutritious when food was available. The basic staple of the peasant diet, and the medieval diet in general, was bread. While women made the dough for the bread, the loaves were usually baked in community ovens, which were a monopoly of the lord of the manor. Peasant bread was made of the cheaper grains (rye, barley, millet, and oats), rather than expensive wheat. It was dark and had a very heavy, hard texture. Bread was supplemented by legumes (peas and beans) from the household gardens, bacon from the family pig, cheese from cow's or goat's milk, and, where available, wild game and fish from hunting and fishing. Manorial lords tended to regulate fishing, however, and were especially reluctant to allow peasants to hunt so that game could be reserved for the nobility. Woodlands also provided nuts, berries, and a foraging area for pigs. Fruits, such as apples, pears, and cherries, were also available. Chickens provided eggs and occasionally meat. Peasants usually ate fresh meat only on the great feast days, such as Christmas, Easter, and Pentecost.

Grains were important not only for bread but also for making ale. In many northern European countries, ale was the most common drink of the poor. If records are accurate, enormous quantities of ale were consumed. A monastery in the twelfth century recorded a daily allotment of three gallons a day to each monk, far above the weekend consumption of many present-day college students. Peasants in the field undoubtedly consumed even more. This high consumption of alcohol might explain the large number of fights and accidents recorded in medieval court records.

The Aristocracy of the High Middle Ages

In the High Middle Ages, European society was dominated by a group of men whose primary preoccupation was warfare. King Alfred of England had said that a "well-peopled land" must have "men of prayer, men of war, and men of work," and medieval ideals held to a tripartite division of society into these three basic groups. The "men of war" were the aristocracy who came to form a distinct social group, albeit one with considerable variation in wealth among its members. Nevertheless, they, along with their wives and children, shared a common ethos and a distinctive lifestyle.

THE SIGNIFICANCE OF THE ARISTOCRACY

King Alfred's "men of war" were the lords and vassals of medieval society. The lords were the kings, dukes, counts, barons, and viscounts (and even bishops and archbishops) who held extensive lands and considerable political power. They formed an aristocracy or nobility that consisted of people who held real political, economic, and social power. Nobles relied for military help on knights, mounted warriors who fought for them in return for weapons and daily sustenance. Knights were by no means the social equals of nobles; many knights in fact possessed little more than peasants. But in the course of the twelfth and thirteenth centuries, knights improved their social status and joined the ranks of the nobility. In the process, *noble* and *knight* came to mean much the same thing, and warfare likewise tended to become a distinguishing characteristic of the nobleman. The great lords and knights came to form a common caste. Although social divisions based on extremes of wealth and landholdings persisted, they were all warriors united by the institution of knighthood.

Medieval theory maintained that the warlike qualities of the nobility were justified by their role as defenders of society. Knights, however, were also notorious for fighting each other. The Catholic church intervened, and though it could not stop the incessant bloodletting, it did at least try to limit it by instituting the "Peace of God." Beginning in the eleventh century, the church encouraged knights to take an oath to respect churches and pilgrimage centers and to refrain from attacking noncombatants, such as clergy, poor people, merchants, and women. It was, of course, permissible to continue killing each other. At the same time, the church initiated the "Truce of God," which forbade fighting on Sundays and the primary feast days.

In addition to trying to diminish fighting, the church also worked to redirect the nobility's warlike energy into different channels, such as the Crusades against the Muslims (see Chapter 10), and was quite willing to justify violence when used against peace-breakers and especially against non-Christians. Hence being a warrior on behalf of God easily vindicated the nobles' love of war and in fact justified their high social status as the defenders of Christian society. The church furthered this process by steeping knighthood in Christian symbols. A knight formally received his arms in a religious ceremony, and weapons were blessed by a priest for Christian service. Throughout the Middle Ages, a constant tension existed between the ideals of a religion founded on the ideal of peace and the ethos of a nobility based on the love of war.

The growth of the European nobility in the High Middle Ages was made visible by an increasing number of castles scattered across the landscape. Although castle architecture varied considerably, castles did possess two common features: they were permanent residences for the noble family, its retainers, and servants, and they were defensible fortifications. For defensive purposes, castles were surrounded by open areas and large stone walls. At the heart of the castle was the keep, a large, multistoried building that housed kitchens, stables, storerooms, a great hall for visitors, dining, and administrative business, and numerous rooms for sleeping and living. The growing wealth of the High Middle Ages made it possible for the European nobility to build more secure castles with thicker walls and more elaborately decorated interiors. As castles became more sturdily built, they proved to be more easily defended and harder to seize by force.

ARISTOCRATIC WOMEN

Although women could legally hold and inherit property, most women remained under the control of men—their fathers until they married and their husbands after they married. Nevertheless, aristocratic women had numerous opportunities to play important roles. Because the lord was often away at war, on Crusade, or at court, the lady of the castle had to manage the estate, a considerable responsibility in view of the fact that households, even of lesser aristocrats, could include large numbers of officials and servants. Supervising financial accounts, both for the household and for the landed estate, alone required considerable financial knowledge. The lady of the castle was also often responsible for overseeing the food supply and maintaining all other supplies for the smooth operation of the household.

Giraudon/Art Resource, NY

Castle and Aristocrats. This illustration from the *Trés Riches Heures* of Jean, duke of Berry, depicts the Chateau of Dourdan, France, and its surrounding lands. In the foreground, elaborately dressed aristocratic men and women are seen amusing themselves.

Women in Medieval Thought

Whether a nun or the wife of an aristocrat, townsman, or peasant, a woman in the Middle Ages was considered inferior to a man and subject to a man's authority. Although there are a number of examples of strong women who ignored such attitudes, church teachings also reinforced these notions. The first selection from Gratian, the twelfth-century jurist who wrote the first systematic work on canon law, supports this view. The second selection was written in the 1390s by a wealthy fifty-year-old Parisian who wanted to instruct his fifteen-year-old bride on how to be a good wife.

Gratian, Decretum

Women should be subject to their men. The natural order for mankind is that women should serve men and children their parents, for it is just that the lesser serve the greater.

The image of God is in man and it is one. Women were drawn from man, who has God's jurisdiction as if he were God's vicar, because he has the image of one God. Therefore woman is not made in God's image.

Woman's authority is nil; let her in all things be subject to the rule of man. . . . And neither can she teach, nor be a witness, nor give a guarantee, nor sit in judgment.

Adam was beguiled by Eve, not she by him. It is right that he whom woman led into wrongdoing should have her under his direction, so that he may not fail a second time through female levity.

A Merchant of Paris, On Marriage

I entreat you to keep his linen clean, for this is up to you. Because the care of outside affairs is men's work, a husband must look after these things, and go and come, run here and there in rain, wind, snow, and hail—sometimes wet, sometimes dry, sometimes sweating, other times shivering, badly fed, badly housed, badly shod, badly bedded—and nothing harms him because he is cheered by the anticipation of the care his wife will take of him on his return—of the pleasures, joys, and comforts she will provide, or have provided for him in her presence: to have his shoes off before a good fire, to have his feet washed, to have clean shoes and hose, to be well fed, provided with good drink, well served, well honored, well bedded in white sheets and white nightcaps, well covered with good furs, and comforted with other joys and amusements, intimacies, affections, and secrets about which I am silent. And on the next day fresh linen and garments . . .

Also keep peace with him. Remember the country proverb that says there are three things that drive a good man from his home: a house with a bad roof, a smoking chimney, and a quarrelsome woman. I beg you, in order to preserve your husband's love and good will, be loving, amiable, and sweet with him. . . . Thus protect and shield your husband from all troubles, give him all the comfort you can think of, wait on him, and have him waited on in your home. . . . If you do what is said here, he will always have his affection and his heart turned toward you and your service, and he will forsake all other homes, all other women, all other help, and all other households.

Childhood ended early for the daughters of aristocrats. Since aristocratic girls were married in their teens (usually at the age of fifteen or sixteen) and were expected by their husbands to assume their responsibilities immediately, the training of girls in a large body of practical knowledge could never start too early. Sent at a young age to the castles of other nobles to be brought up, girls were trained as ladies-in-waiting. The lady of the castle taught them how to sew and weave and instructed them in all the skills needed for running an estate. They also learned some reading and writing, dancing, singing, and how to play musical instruments.

Although women were expected to be subservient to their husbands (see the box above), there were many strong women who advised and sometimes even dominated their husbands. Perhaps the most famous was Eleanor of Aquitaine (c. 1122–1204), heiress to the duchy of Aquitaine in southwestern France. Married first to King Louis VII of France (1137–1180), Eleanor even accompanied her husband on a crusade, but her failure to bear sons led Louis to have their marriage annulled. Eleanor then married Henry, count of Anjou, who became King Henry II of England (1154–1189) and duke of Normandy. She bore him both sons and daughters and took an active role in politics, even assisting her sons in rebelling against Henry in 1173–1174. Imprisoned by her husband for her activities, after Henry's death she again assumed an active political life, providing both military and political support for her sons.

THE WAY OF THE WARRIOR

At the age of seven or eight, aristocratic boys were sent either to a clerical school to pursue a religious career or to another nobleman's castle, where they prepared for the life of a noble. Their chief lessons were military; they learned how to joust, hunt, ride, and handle weapons properly. Occasionally, aristocrats' sons might also learn the basic fundamentals of reading and writing. After his apprenticeship in knighthood, at about the age of twenty-one, a young man formally entered the adult world in the ceremony of "knighting." A sponsor girded a sword on the young candidate and struck him on the cheek or neck with an open hand (or later touched him three times on the shoulder with the blade of a sword), possibly signifying the passing of the sponsor's military valor to the new knight.

Visual Arts Library/Art Resource, NY

The Tournament. The tournament arose as a socially acceptable alternative to the private warfare that plagued the nobility in the Middle Ages. This fifteenth-century Flemish illustration shows a joust between two heavily armored knights. Shown watching are King Richard II in the middle and other onlookers at the right.

In the eleventh and twelfth centuries, under the influence of the church, an ideal of civilized behavior called chivalry gradually evolved among the nobility. Chivalry represented a code of ethics that knights were supposed to uphold. In addition to their oath to defend the church and the defenseless, knightly honor also demanded that unarmed knights should not be attacked. Chivalry also implied that knights should fight only for glory, but this account of a group of English knights by a medieval writer reveals another motive for battle: "The whole city was plundered to the last farthing, and then they proceeded to rob all the churches throughout the city, . . . and seizing gold and silver, cloth of all colors, women's ornaments, gold rings, goblets, and precious stones . . . They all returned to their own lords rich men."[1] Apparently, not all chivalric ideals were taken seriously.

After his formal initiation into the world of warriors, a young man returned home to find himself once again subject to his parents' authority. Young men were discouraged from marrying until their fathers died, at which time they could marry and become lords of the castle. Trained to be warriors but with no adult responsibilities, young knights naturally gravitated toward military activities and often furthered the private warfare endemic to the noble class.

In the twelfth century, tournaments began to appear as an alternative to the socially destructive fighting that the church was trying to curb. Initially, tournaments consisted of the "melee," in which warriors on horseback fought with blunted weapons in free-for-all combat. The goal was to take prisoners who would then be ransomed, making success in tournaments a path to considerable gain. Within an eight-month span, the English knight William Marshall made a tour of the tournament circuit, defeated 203 knights, and made so much money that he had to hire two clerks to take care of it.

By the late twelfth century, the melee was preceded by the joust, or individual combat between two knights. Gradually, jousts became the main part of the tournament. No matter how much the church condemned tournaments, knights themselves continued to see them as an excellent way to train for war. As one knight explained: "A knight cannot distinguish himself in that [war] if he has not trained for it in tourneys. He must have seen his blood flow, heard his teeth crack under fist blows, felt his opponent's weight bear down upon him as he lay on the ground and, after being twenty times unhorsed, have risen twenty times to fight."[2]

Marriage Patterns of the Aristocracy

Aristocratic marriages were expected to establish alliances with other families, bring new wealth, and provide heirs to carry on the family line. Parents therefore supervised the choice of spouses for their children. One of the most noticeable features of aristocratic marriages was the usu-

Bibliothèque Nationale, Paris

Marriage. Marriage festivities for members of the aristocracy were usually quite elaborate. As seen in this illustration of the marriage of Renaud de Montaubon and Clarisse, daughter of the ruler of Gascogne, after the festivities the wedding party would accompany the new couple to their bedroom to prepare them for the physical consummation of their marriage. Only after physical union was a medieval marriage considered valid.

ally wide discrepancy in the ages of the marital partners. Daughters of the nobles married at fifteen or sixteen, but their husbands might be in their thirties or even forties, since men did not marry until they came into their inheritances.

By the twelfth century, the efforts of the church since Carolingian times to end divorce (see Chapter 8) had borne much fruit. As a sacrament, marriage was intended to last for a lifetime and could not be dissolved. In certain cases, however, the church accepted the right of married persons to separate by granting them an annulment or official recognition that their marriage had not been valid in the first place. If it could be established that the couple had not consented to the marriage, that one or the other suffered from a sexual incapacity that prevented the consummation of the marriage, or that the couple were related by blood (more closely than sixth or, after 1215, third cousins), the church would approve an annulment of their marriage, and the partners would be free to marry again.

The New World of Trade and Cities

Medieval Europe was an overwhelmingly agrarian society with most people living in small villages. In the eleventh and twelfth centuries, however, new elements were introduced that began to transform the economic foundation of Western civilization: a revival of trade, considerable expansion in the circulation of money, a restoration of specialized craftspeople and artisans, and the growth and development of towns. These changes were made possible by the new agricultural practices and subsequent increase in food production, which freed some European families from the need to produce their own food. Merchants and craftspeople could now buy their necessities.

The Revival of Trade

The revival of commercial activity was a gradual process. During the chaotic conditions of the Early Middle Ages, large-scale trade had declined in western Europe except for Byzantine contacts with Italy and the Jewish traders who moved back and forth between the Muslim and Christian worlds. By the end of the tenth century, however, people with both the skills and the products for commercial activity were emerging in Europe.

Cities in Italy assumed a leading role in the revival of trade (see Map 9.1). By the end of the eighth century, Venice, on the northeastern coast, had emerged as a town with close trading ties to the Byzantine Empire. Venice developed a trading fleet and by the end of the tenth century had become the chief western trading center for Byzantine and Islamic commerce. Venice sent wine, grain, and timber to Constantinople in exchange for silk cloth, which was then peddled to other communities. Other coastal communities in western Italy, such as Genoa and Pisa, also opened new trade routes. By 1100, Italian merchants began to benefit from the Crusades and were able to establish new trading centers in eastern ports. There the merchants obtained silks, sugar, and spices, which they subsequently carried back to Italy and the West. At the same time, northern Italy began to experience rapid economic growth from the production of high-quality cloth, which was also in demand.

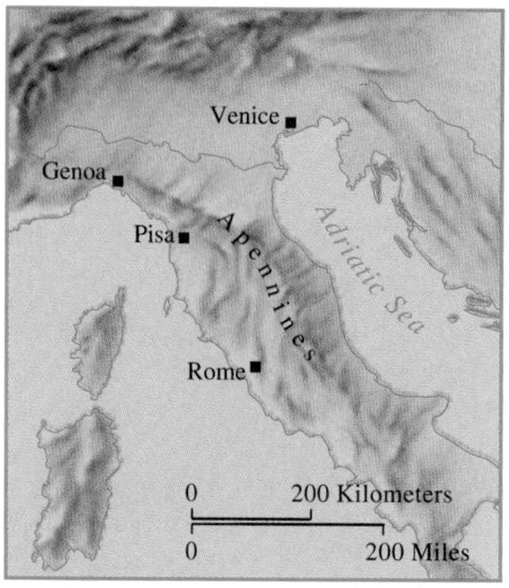

Commercial Cities in Italy: Venice, Genoa, and Pisa

While the northern Italian cities were busy trading in the Mediterranean, the towns of Flanders were doing likewise in northern Europe. Flanders, the area along the coast of present-day Belgium and northern France, was known for the production of a much desired high-quality woolen cloth. Flanders's location made it a logical entrepôt for the traders of northern Europe. Merchants from England, Scandinavia, France, and Germany converged there to trade their wares for woolen cloth. Flanders prospered in the eleventh and twelfth centuries, and such Flemish towns as Bruges and Ghent became centers for the trade and manufacture of woolen cloth.

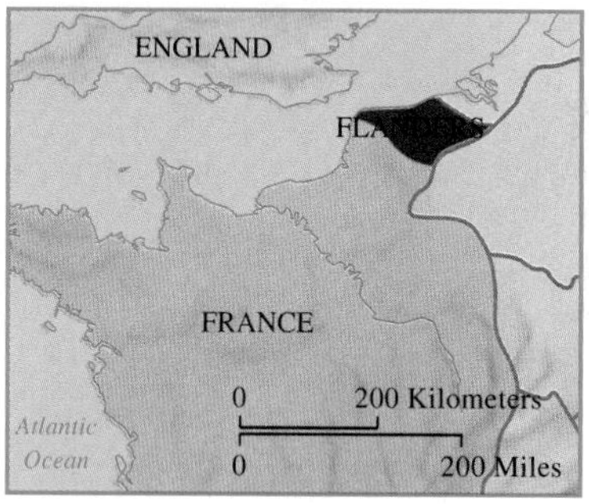

Flanders

By the twelfth century, it was almost inevitable that a regular exchange of goods would develop between Flanders and Italy. To encourage this trade, the counts of Champagne in northern France devised a series of six fairs held annually in the chief towns of their territory. They guaranteed the safety of visiting merchants, supervised the trading activities, and of course collected a sales tax on all goods exchanged at the fairs. The fairs of Champagne became the largest commercial marketplace in western Europe where the goods of northern Europe could be exchanged for the goods of southern Europe and the East. Northern merchants brought the furs, woolen cloth, tin, hemp, and honey of northern Europe and exchanged them for the cloth and swords of northern Italy and the silks, sugar, and spices of the East. The prosperity of the Champagne fairs caused lords everywhere to follow their example and establish trading fairs.

As trade increased, both gold and silver came to be in demand at fairs and trading markets of all kinds. Slowly, a money economy began to emerge. New trading companies as well as banking firms were set up to manage the exchange and sale of goods. All of these new practices were part of the rise of commercial capitalism, an economic

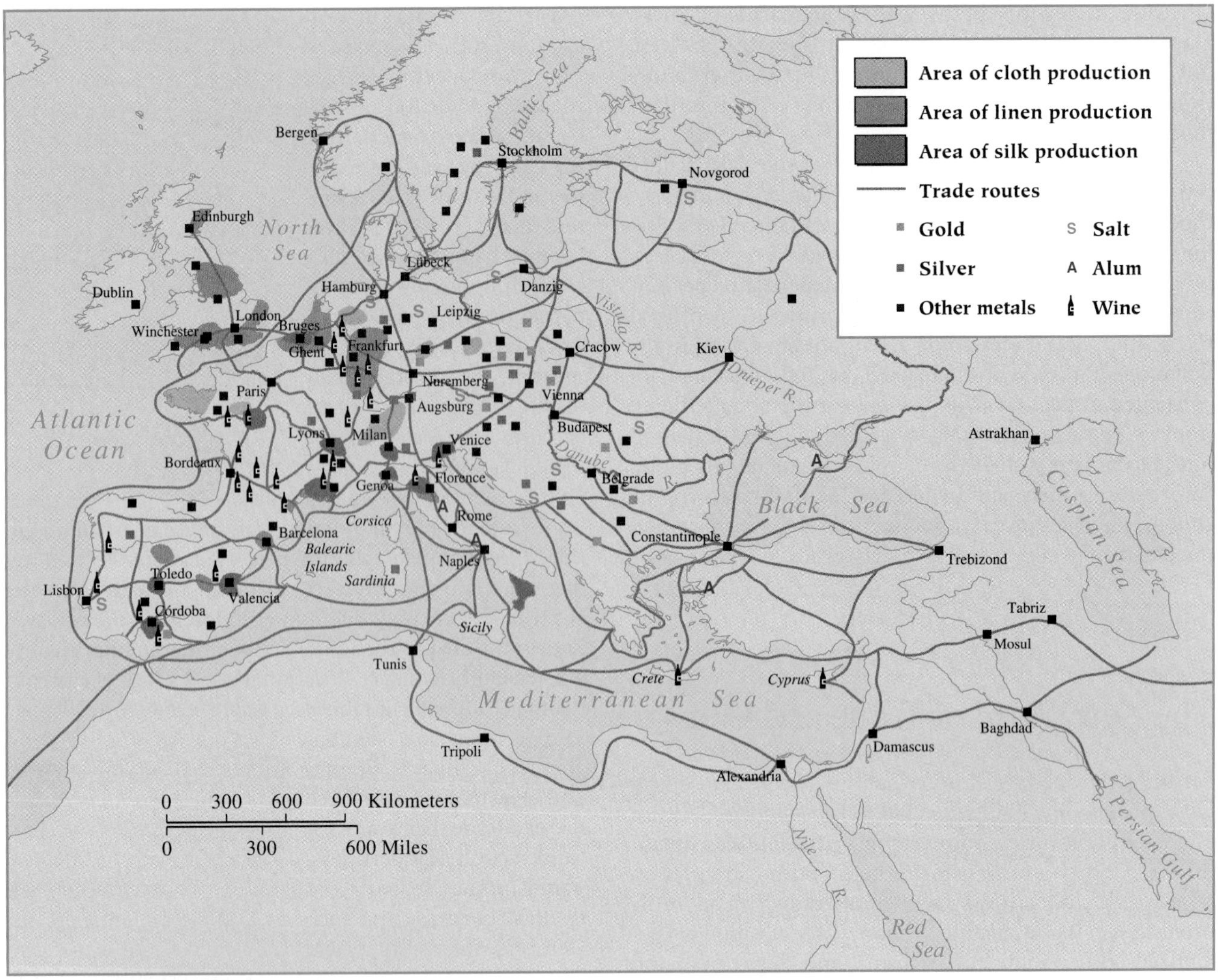

Map 9.1 Medieval Trade Routes. Italian cities and Flanders were the centers of gradually expanding trade in Europe. They fostered the exchange of goods from the Byzantine Empire and the Far East with those of various regions of Europe. The diminishing threats of violence over time greatly helped trade. ■ Look at Map 6.2. In what areas had trade expanded, and how can you account for this?

system in which people invested in trade and goods in order to make profits (see the box on p. 227).

The Growth of Cities

The revival of trade led to a revival of cities. Merchants needed places where they could live and build warehouses to store their goods. Towns had greatly declined in the Early Middle Ages, especially in Europe north of the Alps. Old Roman cities continued to exist but had dwindled in size and population. With the revival of trade, merchants began to settle in these old cities, followed by craftworkers or artisans, people who had developed skills on manors or elsewhere and now perceived the opportunity to ply their trade producing objects that could be sold by the merchants. In the course of the eleventh and twelfth centuries, the old Roman cities came alive with new populations and growth. By 1100, the old areas of these cities had been repopulated; soon the population outgrew the walls, necessitating the construction of new city walls outside the old.

In the Mediterranean world, cities had survived in a more visible fashion. Spain's Islamic cities had a flourishing urban life, and southern Italy still possessed such thriving cities as Bari, Salerno, Naples, and Amalfi. Although greatly reduced in size, Rome, the old capital of the Roman world, had survived as the center of papal administration. In northern Italy, Venice had already emerged as a town by the end of the eighth century because of its commercial connections to the Byzantine Empire.

Beginning in the late tenth century, many new cities or towns were founded, particularly in northern Europe. Usually, a group of artisans and merchants established a settlement near some fortified stronghold, such as a castle or monastery. Castles were particularly favored because they were usually located along major routes of transportation or at the intersection of two trade routes;

The Value of Money

With the emergence of a money economy came new attitudes toward money. Although the medieval church exalted poverty as a sure way to salvation, there were some medieval Christians who saw money differently. This is evident in the work of Juan Ruiz, a mid-fourteenth century Spanish writer, who was especially critical about the attitudes of the clergy.

Juan Ruiz, "The Power of Money"

Money can do much; it should be held in high esteem. It turns a tramp into a respected and honorable man; it makes the lame man run and the dumb man speak. Even a man without hands reaches out and grabs for money. A man may be an idiot or an ill-bred peasant, but money will make him a noble and a sage; the more money a man has, the more worthy he becomes, while the man who is penniless cannot call himself his own master. If you have money, you can have luxury, pleasure, and joy, and benefices from the Pope. You can buy Paradise and earn salvation. Piles of money bring forth piles of blessings.

Over in Rome, the seat of holiness, I myself observed them all curtseying and scraping before Money, and doing him solemn homage. They humble themselves as they do before the Crucifix. There, money created many priors, bishops and abbots, archbishops, doctors, patriarchs, and men of power. Money won dignities for many ignorant clerics; it turned truths into lies and lies into truths. Money created many clerics and priests, monks and nuns, certifying that they had sufficient knowledge, while the poor were informed that they lacked learning. Money bought judgments and verdicts galore, lived with crooked lawyers, and fostered unjust suits and settlements, so that finally, thanks to money, even absolution could be obtained. . . .

I have observed that Money always had the best, the largest, the most costly and elegant mansions; castles, estates, turreted palaces served Money and were bought by him. Money dined on exotic delicacies, decked himself in rich and gilded clothes, wore precious jewels, all this in leisure and pleasure, with rare ornaments and noble mounts. I have often heard monks in their sermons condemn money and its temptations—and immediately afterward grant pardons and offer prayers—for money. These monks may scorn money in the public square, but back in the cloister they hoard it in vases and chalices.

the lord of the castle also offered protection. If the settlement prospered and expanded, walls were built to protect it. The original meaning of the English *borough* or *burgh* and the German *Burg* as a fortress or walled enclosure is still evident in the names of many cities, such as Edinburgh and Hamburg. The merchants and artisans of these boroughs and burghs came to be called burghers or bourgeoisie.

Most towns were closely tied to their surrounding territories because they were dependent on the countryside for their food supplies. In addition, they were often part of the territory belonging to a lord and were subject to his jurisdiction. Although lords wanted to treat towns and townspeople as they would their vassals and serfs, cities had totally different needs and a different perspective. Townspeople needed mobility to trade. Consequently, the

Fortified Town of Carcassonne. The expansion of commerce and industry led to an ongoing growth of towns and cities in the High Middle Ages. As seen in this picture of the French town of Carcassonne, medieval towns were surrounded by walls strengthened by defensive towers and punctuated by gates. As is evident here, medieval urban skylines were dominated by towers of all kinds.

Wysocki/Explorer/Photo Researchers, Inc.

merchants and artisans of the towns constituted a revolutionary group who needed their own unique laws to meet their requirements. Since the townspeople were profiting from the growth of trade and sale of their products, they were willing to pay for the right to make their own laws and govern themselves. In many instances, lords and kings saw the potential for vast new sources of revenues and were willing to grant (or more accurately, sell) to the townspeople the liberties they were beginning to demand.

By 1100, townspeople were obtaining charters of liberties from their territorial lords that granted them the privileges they wanted, including the right to bequeath goods and sell property, freedom from military obligation to the lord, written urban law that guaranteed their freedom, and the right for serfs to become free after residing a year and a day in the town. The last provision made it possible for a runaway serf who could avoid capture to become a free person in a city. Almost all new urban communities gained these elementary liberties, but only some towns obtained the right to govern themselves by choosing their own officials and administering their own courts of law. Where townspeople experienced difficulty in obtaining privileges, they often swore an oath, forming an association called a commune, and resorted to force against their lay or ecclesiastical lords.

Communes made their first appearance in Italy, where even in the Early Middle Ages, urban communities continued to exist. In northern Italy, in the regions called Tuscany and Lombardy, towns were governed by their bishops, but the nobles whose lands surrounded the towns took an active interest in them. Bishops were usually supported by the emperors, who used them as their chief administrators. In the eleventh century, city residents rebelled against the rule of the bishops, swore communal associations with the bishops' noble vassals, and overthrew the authority of the bishops by force. The alliance between town residents and rural nobles was overwhelming, and in the course of the eleventh and twelfth centuries, bishops were shorn of their authority. Communes took over the rights of government and created new offices, such as consuls and city councils, for self-rule. Pisa, Milan, Arezzo, and Genoa all attained self-government by the end of the eleventh century.

Although communes were also sworn in northern Europe, especially in France and Flanders, townspeople did not have the support of rural nobles. Revolts against lay lords were usually brutally suppressed; those against bishops, as in Laon at the beginning of the twelfth century (see the box on p. 229), were more frequently successful. When they succeeded, communes received the right to choose their own officials, hold their own courts, and run their own cities. Unlike the towns in Italy, however, where the decline of the emperor's authority ensured that the northern Italian cities could function as self-governing republics, towns in France and England did not become independent city-states but remained ultimately subject to royal authority.

Medieval cities, then, possessed varying degrees of self-government, depending on the amount of control retained over them by the lord or king in whose territory they were located. Nevertheless, all towns, regardless of the degree of outside control, evolved institutions of government for running the affairs of the community.

Medieval cities defined citizenship narrowly and accorded it only to males who had been born in the city or who had lived there for some time. In many cities, citizens elected members of a city council that bore primary responsibility for running the affairs of the city. City councilors (known as consuls in Italy and southern France) not only enacted legislation but also served as judges and city magistrates. The electoral process was carefully engineered to ensure that only members of the wealthiest and most powerful families, who came to be called the patricians, were elected. They kept the reins of government in their hands despite periodic protests from lesser merchants and artisans. In the twelfth and thirteenth centuries, cities added some kind of sole executive leader, even if he was only a figurehead. Although the title varied from town to town, this executive officer was frequently called a mayor.

British Library, London

The Execution of Criminals. Violence was a common feature of medieval life. Criminals, if apprehended, were punished quickly and severely, and public executions were considered a deterrent to crime. As one can surmise from this illustration, executions were also a form of entertainment.

A Communal Revolt

When townspeople were unable to gain basic liberties for themselves from the lord in whose territory their town was located, they sometimes swore a "commune" to gain these privileges by force. This selection by a contemporary abbot describes the violence that accompanied the formation of a commune at Laon in France in 1116. The bishop of Laon, lord of the town, had granted privileges to the townspeople in return for a large payment. Later he rescinded his grant but kept the money, thereby angering the citizens.

The Autobiography of Guibert, Abbot of Nogent-sous-Coucy

All the efforts of the prelate and nobles in these days were reserved for fleecing their inferiors. But those inferiors were no longer moved by mere anger, but goaded into a murderous lust for the death of the bishop and his accomplices and bound themselves by oath to effect their purpose. Now they say that 400 took the oath. Such a mob could not be secret and when it came to the ears of Anselm [the bishop's assistant] toward evening of the holy Sabbath, he sent word to the bishop, as he was retiring to rest, not to go out to the early morning service, knowing that if he did he must certainly be killed. But he, infatuated with excessive pride said, "Fie, surely I shall not perish at the hands of such. . . ."

The next day, that is, the fifth in Easter week, after midday, as he [the bishop] was engaged in business with Archdeacon Walter about the getting of money, behold there arose a disorderly noise throughout the city, men shouting "Commune!" and . . . citizens now entered the bishop's court with swords, battle-axes, bows and hatchets, and carrying clubs and spears, a very great company. As soon as this sudden attack was discovered, the nobles rallied from all sides to the bishop, having sworn to give him aid against such an onset, if it should occur. . . . [Despite the assistance of the nobles, the commoners were victorious.]

Next the outrageous mob attacking the bishop and howling before the walls of his palace, he with some who were aiding him fought them off by hurling of stones and shooting of arrows. For he now, as at all times, showed great spirit as a fighter, but because he had wrongly and in vain taken up another sword, by the sword he perished. Therefore, being unable to stand against the reckless assaults of the people, he put on the clothes of one of his servants and flying to the vaults of the church hid himself in a cask, shut up in which with the head fastened on by a faithful follower he thought himself safely hidden. And as they ran hither and thither demanding where, not the bishop, but the hangdog, was, they seized one of his pages, but through his faithfulness could not get what they wanted. Laying hands on another, they learned from the traitor's nod where to look for him. Entering the vaults therefore, and searching everywhere, at last they found [him]. . . .

[The bishop] therefore, sinner though he was, yet the Lord's anointed, was dragged forth from the cask by the hair, beaten with many blows and brought out into the open air in the narrow lane of the clergy's cloister before the house of the chaplain Godfrey. And as he piteously implored them, ready to take oath that he would henceforth cease to be their bishop, that he would leave the country, and as they with hardened hearts jeered at him, one named Bernard . . . lifting his battle-axe brutally dashed out the brains of that sacred, though sinner's, head, and he slipping between the hands of those who held him, was dead before he reached the ground stricken by another thwart blow under the eye-sockets and across the middle of the nose. There brought to his end, his legs were cut off and many another wound inflicted. But Thibaut seeing the ring on the finger of the erstwhile prelate and not being able to draw it off, cut off the dead man's finger and took it. And so stripped to his skin he was thrown into a corner in front of his chaplain's house. My God, who shall recount the mocking words that were thrown at him by passersby, as he lay there, and with what clods and stones and dirt his corpse was covered?

City governments kept close watch over the activities of their community. To care for the welfare and safety of the community, a government might regulate air and water pollution; provide water barrels and delegate responsibility to people in every section of the town to fight fires, which were an ever-present danger; construct warehouses to stockpile grain in the event of food emergencies; and establish and supervise the standards of weights and measures used in the various local trades and industries.

Crime was not a major problem in the towns of the High Middle Ages because the relatively small size of communities made it difficult for criminals to operate openly. Nevertheless, medieval urban governments did organize town guards to patrol the streets by night and the city walls by day. People caught committing criminal acts were quickly tried for their offenses. Serious offenses, such as murder, were punished by execution, usually by hanging. Lesser crimes were punished by fines, flogging, branding, public exposure (as in the pillory), or expulsion.

Medieval cities remained relatively small in comparison to either ancient or modern cities. A large trading city would number about five thousand inhabitants. By 1300, London was the largest city in England, with eighty thousand people or more. Otherwise, north of the Alps, only a few great commercial urban centers, such as Bruges and Ghent, had a population close to forty thousand. Italian cities tended to be larger, with Venice, Florence, Genoa, Milan, and Naples numbering almost one hundred thousand. Even the largest European city, however, seemed insignificant alongside the Byzantine capital of Constantinople or the Arab cities of Damascus, Baghdad, and Cairo. For a long time to come, Europe remained predominantly rural, but in the long run, the rise of towns and the growth of trade laid the foundation for the eventual transformation of Europe from a rural agricultural society to an urban industrial one.

LIFE IN THE MEDIEVAL CITY

Medieval towns were surrounded by stone walls that were expensive to build, so the space within was precious and tightly filled. This gave medieval cities their characteristic appearance of narrow, winding streets with houses crowded against each other. Streets were generally left unpaved until the thirteenth century, and buildings fronted directly on them. To gain more space, inhabitants frequently added balconies or built the second and third stories of their dwellings out over the streets. Since dwellings were crowded so closely together and candles and wood fires were used for light and heat, the danger of fire was great.

A medieval urban skyline was dominated by the towers of castles and town halls, but especially of churches, whose number could be staggering. At the beginning of the thirteenth century, London had 120 monastic and parish churches. If a city was the center of a bishop's see, a large cathedral would dominate the other buildings and be visible for miles outside the city.

Most of the people who lived in the cities were merchants involved in trade and artisans engaged in manufacturing of some kind. Sometimes merchants and artisans had their own sections in a city. The merchant area included warehouses, inns, and taverns. Artisan sections were usually divided along craft lines, and each craft might have its own street where its activity was pursued.

The physical environment of medieval cities was not pleasant. They were often dirty and rife with smells from animal and human waste deposited in backyard privies or on the streets (see the box on p. 231). In some places, city governments required citizens to periodically collect garbage and waste and cart it outside the town. Atmospheric pollution was also a fact of life, not only from the ubiquitous wood fires but also from the use of coal, a cheap fuel that was used industrially by lime-burners, brewers, and dyers. Burning coal emitted ill-smelling, noxious fumes and was sometimes prohibited under pain of fine.

Cities were also unable to stop water pollution, especially from the animal-slaughtering and tanning industries. Butchers dumped blood and other waste products from their butchered animals into the river, while tanners unloaded tannic acids, dried blood, fat, hair, and the other waste products of their operations. Forcing both industries to locate downstream to avoid polluting the water used by the city upstream was only partially effective. Tanneries and slaughterhouses existed in every medieval town, so the river could rapidly become polluted from other towns' wastes.

Because of the pollution, cities were not inclined to use the rivers for drinking water but relied instead on wells. Occasionally, communities repaired the system of aqueducts or conduits left over from Roman times and sometimes even constructed new ones. Private and public baths also existed in medieval towns. Paris, for example, had thirty-two public baths for men and women. City laws did not allow lepers and people with "bad reputations" to use them, but such measures did not prevent the public baths from being known for permissiveness due to public nudity. One contemporary commented on what occurred in public bathhouses: "Shameful things. Men make a point of staying all night in the public baths and women at the break of day come in and through 'ignorance' find themselves in the men's rooms."[3] Authorities came under increasing pressure to close the baths down, and the great plague of the fourteenth century sealed their fate. The standards of medieval hygiene broke down, and late medieval and early modern European society would prove to be remarkably dirty.

Because of the limited space in medieval towns, houses were narrow, built next to one another, and usually multistoried. In many houses, the shops or workrooms of merchants and craftspeople occupied the ground floor. Inhabitants, who might include husband and wife, children, servants, and apprentices, would live upstairs.

For most ordinary merchants and artisans, home life and work life were thus closely intertwined. Merchants and

Shops in a Medieval Town. Most urban residents were merchants involved in trade and artisans who manufactured a wide variety of products. Master craftspeople had their workshops in the ground-level rooms of their houses. In this illustration, two well-dressed burghers are touring the shopping districts of a French town. Tailors, furriers, a barber, and a grocer (from left to right) are visible at work in their shops.

Bibliotheque Nationale, Paris

Pollution in a Medieval City

Environmental pollution is not new. Medieval cities and towns had their own problems with filthy living conditions. This excerpt is taken from an order sent by the king of England to the town of Boutham, a suburb of York, which was then being used by the king as headquarters in a war with the Scots. It demands rectification of the town's pitiful physical conditions.

The King's Command to Boutham

To the bailiffs of the abbot of St. Mary's, York, at Boutham. Whereas it is sufficiently evident that the pavement of the said town of Boutham is so very greatly broke up that all and singular passing and going through that town sustain immoderate damages and grievances, and in addition the air is so corrupted and infected by the pigsties situated in the king's highways and in the lanes of that town and by the swine feeding and frequently wandering about in the streets and lanes and by dung and dunghills and many other foul things placed in the streets and lanes, that great repugnance overtakes the king's ministers staying in that town and also others there dwelling and passing through, the advantage of more wholesome air is impeded; the state of men is grievously injured, and other unbearable inconveniences and many other injuries are known to proceed from such corruption, to the nuisance of the king's ministers aforesaid and of others there dwelling and passing through, and to the peril of their lives.... The king, being unwilling longer to tolerate such great and unbearable defects there, orders the bailiffs to cause the pavement to be suitably repaired within their liberty before All Saints next, and to cause the pigsties, aforesaid streets and lanes to be cleansed from all dung and dunghills, and to cause proclamation to be made throughout their bailiwick forbidding any one, under pain of grievous forfeiture, to cause or permit their swine to feed or wander outside his house in the king's streets or the lanes aforesaid.

artisans taught their trades to their children and their wives and apprentices, or their children might be apprenticed to another merchant or artisan. Women, in addition to supervising the household, purchasing food and preparing meals, washing clothes, and managing the family finances, were also often expected to help their husbands in their trades. While men produced goods at home, their wives often peddled them at markets or fairs.

Some women also developed their own trades to earn extra money. Margery Kempe, for example, although the daughter of a mayor and the wife of a wealthy merchant, pursued the trade of brewing ale. Other women worked at making hats and cloth. Widows often carried on their husband's trade. Some women in medieval towns were thus able to lead lives of considerable independence.

Industry in Medieval Cities

The revival of trade enabled cities and towns to become important centers for manufacturing a wide range of goods, such as cloth, metalwork, shoes, and leather goods. A host of crafts were carried on in houses along the narrow streets of the medieval cities. From the twelfth century on, merchants and artisans began to organize themselves into guilds, which came to play a leading role in the economic life of the cities.

By the thirteenth century, virtually every group of craftspeople, such as tanners, carpenters, and bakers, had their own guild, and specialized groups of merchants, such as dealers in silk, spices, wool, or banking, had their separate guilds as well. Florence alone, for example, had fifty different guilds. Some communities were so comprehensive in covering all trades that they even had guilds for prostitutes.

Craft guilds directed almost every aspect of the production process. They set standards for the articles produced, specified the actual methods of production to be used, and even fixed the price at which the finished goods could be sold. Guilds also determined the number of individuals who could enter a specific trade and the procedure they must follow to do so.

A person who wanted to learn a trade first became an apprentice to a master craftsman, usually at around the age of ten. Apprentices were not paid but did receive room and board from their masters. After five to seven years of service, during which they learned their craft, apprentices became journeymen (or journeywomen, although most were male) who then worked for wages for other masters. Journeymen aspired to become masters as well. To do so, a journeyman had to produce a "masterpiece," a finished piece in his craft that allowed the master craftsmen of the guild to judge whether the journeyman was qualified to become a master and join the guild.

Craft guilds continued to dominate manufacturing in industries where raw materials could be acquired locally and the products sold locally. But in industries that required raw materials from outside the local area to produce high-quality products for growing markets abroad, a new form of industry dependent on large concentrations of capital and unskilled labor began to emerge. It was particularly evident in the "putting-out" or domestic system used in the production of woolen cloth in both Flanders and northern Italy. An entrepreneur, whose initial capital outlay probably came from commercial activities, bought raw wool and distributed it to workers who carried out the various stages of carding, spinning, weaving, dyeing, and fulling to produce a finished piece of woolen cloth. These laborers worked in their own homes and were paid wages.

As wage earners, they were dependent on their employers and the fluctuations in prices that occurred periodically in the international market for the finished goods. The entrepreneur collected the final products and sold the finished cloth, earning a profit that could then be invested in more production. Woolen industries operated by capitalist entrepreneurs in seventeen principal centers in northern Europe, mostly in Flanders, produced most of the woolen cloth used in northern Europe. An Italian chronicler at the beginning of the fourteenth century estimated that the woolen industry in Florence produced eighty thousand pieces of cloth a year and employed thirty thousand men, women, and children, usually at pitiful wages.

The Intellectual and Artistic World of the High Middle Ages

The High Middle Ages was a time of tremendous intellectual and artistic vitality. The period witnessed the growth of educational institutions, a rebirth of interest in ancient culture, a quickening of theological thought, the revival of law, the development of a vernacular literature, and a burst of activity in art and architecture. Although monks continued to play an important role in intellectual activity, increasingly the secular clergy, cities, and courts, whether of kings, princes, or high church officials, began to exert a newfound influence. Especially significant were the new cultural expressions that emerged in towns and cities.

The Rise of Universities

The university as we know it with faculty, students, and degrees was a product of the High Middle Ages. The word *university* is derived from the Latin word *universitas,* meaning a corporation or guild, and referred to either a guild of teachers or a guild of students. Medieval universities were educational guilds or corporations that produced educated and trained individuals.

THE ORIGINS OF UNIVERSITIES

Education in the Early Middle Ages rested primarily with the clergy, especially the monks. Although monastic schools were the centers of learning from the ninth century, they were surpassed in the course of the eleventh century by the cathedral schools organized by the secular (nonmonastic) clergy. Cathedral schools, like the cities in which they were located, expanded rapidly in the eleventh century. There were twenty of them in 900, but by 1100 the number had grown to at least two hundred since every cathedral city felt compelled to establish one. The most famous were Chartres, Reims, Paris, Laon, and Soissons, all in France, which was the intellectual center of Europe by

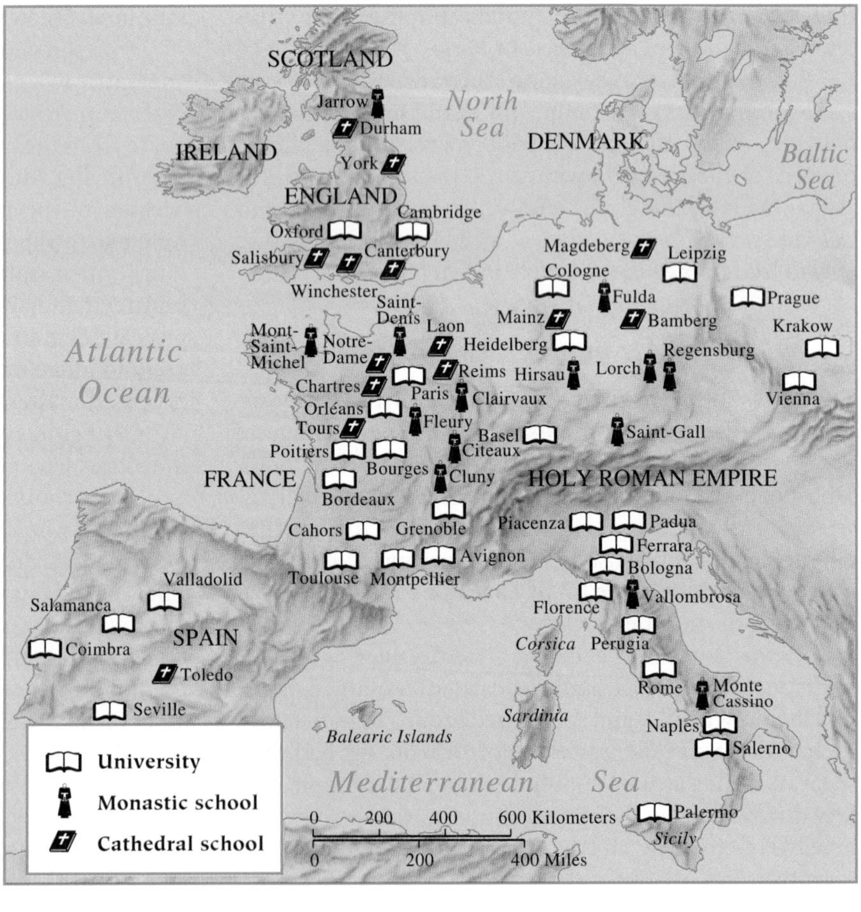

Map 9.2 Intellectual Centers of Medieval Europe. Products of the High Middle Ages, universities provided students with a basic liberal arts education and the opportunity to pursue further studies in law, medicine, or theology. Courses were taught in Latin, primarily by professors reading from books. There were no exams in individual courses, but students had to pass a comprehensive oral exam to gain a degree.
■ In what ways did France qualify as the intellectual capital of Europe?

the twelfth century (see Map 9.2). Although the primary purpose of cathedral schools was to educate priests to be more literate men of God, they also attracted other individuals who desired some education but did not want to become priests. Many university administrators today carry titles, such as chancellor, provost, and dean, that were originally used for the officials of cathedral chapters.

The first European university appeared in Bologna, Italy (unless one accords this distinction to the first medical school established earlier at Salerno, Italy). The emergence of the University of Bologna coincided with the revival of interest in Roman law, especially the rediscovery of Justinian's *Body of Civil Law* (see "The Revival of Roman Law" later in this chapter). In the twelfth century, a great teacher, such as Irnerius (1088–1125), attracted students from all over Europe. Most of them were laymen, usually older individuals who served as administrators to kings and princes and were eager to learn more about law so they could apply it in their jobs. To protect themselves, students at Bologna formed a guild or *universitas,* which was recognized by Emperor Frederick Barbarossa and given a charter in 1158. Although the faculty also organized itself as a group, the *universitas* of students at Bologna was far more influential. It obtained a promise of freedom for students from local authorities, regulated the price of books and lodging, and determined the curriculum, fees, and standards for their masters. Teachers were fined if they missed a class or began their lectures late. The University of Bologna remained the greatest law school in Europe throughout the Middle Ages.

In northern Europe, the University of Paris became the first recognized university. A number of teachers or masters who had received licenses to teach from the cathedral school of Notre-Dame in Paris began to take on extra students for a fee. By the end of the twelfth century, these masters teaching at Paris had formed a *universitas* or guild of masters. By 1200, the king of France, Philip Augustus, officially acknowledged the existence of the University of Paris. The University of Oxford in England, organized on the Paris model, first appeared in 1208. A migration of scholars from Oxford in 1209 led to the establishment of Cambridge University. In the Late Middle Ages, kings, popes, and princes vied to found new universities. By the end of the Middle Ages, there were eighty universities in Europe, most of them located in France, Italy, Germany, and England.

TEACHING IN THE MEDIEVAL UNIVERSITY

A student's initial studies at a medieval university centered around the traditional liberal arts curriculum. The trivium consisted of grammar, rhetoric, and logic, and the quadrivium was comprised of arithmetic, geometry, astronomy, and music. All classes were conducted in Latin, which provided a common means of communication for students, regardless of their country of origin. Basically, medieval university instruction used the lecture method. The word *lecture* is derived from Latin and means "to read." Before the development of the printing press in the fifteenth century, books were expensive, and few students could afford them, so masters read from a text (such as a collection of law if the subject were law) and then added commentaries, which came to be known as glosses. No exams were given after a series of lectures, but when a student applied for a degree, he (women did not attend universities in the Middle Ages) was given a comprehensive oral examination by a committee of teachers. These exams were taken after a four- or six-year period of study. The first degree a student could earn was an A.B., the *artium baccalaureus,* or bachelor of arts; later he might receive an A.M., *artium magister,* master of arts. All degrees were technically licenses to teach, although most students receiving them did not become teachers.

After completing the liberal arts curriculum, a student could go on to study law, medicine, or theology, which was the most highly regarded subject of the medieval curriculum. The study of law, medicine, or theology was a long process that could take a decade or more. A student who passed his final oral examinations was granted a doctor's degree, which officially enabled him to teach his subject. Most students who pursued advanced degrees received their master's degrees first and taught the arts curriculum while continuing to pursue their advanced degrees. Students who received degrees from medieval universities could pursue other careers besides teaching that proved to be much more lucrative. A law degree was deemed essential for those who wished to serve as advisers to kings and princes. The growing administrative bureaucracies of popes and kings also demanded a supply of clerks with a university education who could keep records and draw up official documents.

University Classroom. This illustration shows a university classroom in fourteenth-century Germany. As was customary in medieval classrooms, the master is reading from a text. The students vary considerably in age and in the amount of attention they are willing to give the lecturer.

STUDENTS IN THE MEDIEVAL UNIVERSITY

Students at medieval universities stemmed predominantly from the middle groups of medieval society, the families of lesser knights, merchants, and artisans. All were male; many were poor but ambitious and upwardly mobile. Many medieval students started when they were fourteen to eighteen years old and received their bachelor's or master's degrees by their early twenties. Study for a doctorate in one of the specialized schools of law, medicine, or theology entailed at least another ten years. It was not unusual for men to receive their doctorates in their late thirties or early forties.

There are obvious similarities between medieval and modern students. Then as now, many students took their studies seriously and worked hard. Then as now, alcohol, sex, and appeals for spending money were all too common. In medieval universities, handbooks provided form letters that students could use in requesting money from their fathers, guardians, or patrons. This is an example from Oxford:

> B. to his venerable master A., greeting. This is to inform you that I am studying at Oxford with the greatest of diligence, but the matter of money stands greatly in the way of my promotion, as it is now two months since I have spent the last of what you sent me. The city is expensive and makes many demands; I have to rent lodgings, buy necessaries, and provide for many other things which I cannot now specify. Wherefore I respectfully beg your paternity that by the promptings of divine pity you may assist me, so that I may be able to complete what I have well begun.[4]

Lack of studiousness is not just a modern phenomenon as this letter from a medieval father to his son illustrates:

> To his son G. residing at Orléans, P. of Besançon sends greetings with paternal zeal. It is written, 'He also that is slothful in his work is brother to him that is a great waster.' I have recently discovered that you live dissolutely and slothfully, preferring license to restraint and play to work and strumming a guitar while the others are at their studies, whence it happens that you have read but one volume of law while your more industrious companions have read several. Wherefore I have decided to exhort you herewith to repent utterly of your dissolute and careless ways, that you may no longer be called a waster and your shame may be turned to good repute.[5]

We have no idea whether the letter convinced the student to change his ways.

Medieval universities shared in the violent atmosphere of the age. Records from courts of law reveal numerous instances of disturbances at European universities. One German professor was finally dismissed for stabbing one too many of his colleagues in faculty meetings. A student in Bologna was attacked in the classroom by another student armed with a sword. Oxford regulations attempted to dampen the violence by forbidding students to bring weapons to class. Not uncommonly, town and gown struggles (gown refers to the academic robe worn by teachers and students) escalated into bloody riots between townspeople and students (see the box on p. 235).

Despite the violence, universities proved important to medieval civilization, not only for the growth of learning, which, after all, is the main task of the university, but also by providing a mechanism for training the personnel who served as teachers, administrators, lawyers, and doctors in an increasingly specialized society.

A Revival of Classical Antiquity

Another aspect of the intellectual revival of the High Middle Ages was a resurgence of interest in the works of classical antiquity—the works of the Greeks and Romans. In the twelfth century, western Europe was introduced to a large number of Greek scientific and philosophical works, including those of Galen and Hippocrates on medicine, Ptolemy on geography and astronomy, and Euclid on mathematics. Above all, the West now had available the complete works of Aristotle. During the second half of the twelfth century, all of Aristotle's scientific works were translated into Latin, which served as an international language for both speaking and writing in the West. This great influx of Aristotle's works had an overwhelming impact on the West. He came to be viewed as the "master of those who know," the man who seemed to have understood every field of knowledge.

The recovery of Greek scientific and philosophical works was not a simple process, however. Little knowledge of Greek had survived in Europe. Thus it was through the Muslim world that the West recovered Aristotle and other Greek works. The translation of Greek works into Arabic had formed but one aspect of a brilliant Muslim civilization. In the twelfth century, these writings were now translated from Arabic into Latin, making them available to the West. Wherever Muslim and Christian cultures met—in the Norman kingdom of Sicily, southern Italy, and above all Spain—the work of translation was carried on by both Arabic and Jewish scholars.

The Islamic world had more to contribute intellectually to the West than translations, however. Scientific work in the ninth and tenth centuries had enabled it to forge far ahead of the Western world, and in the twelfth and thirteenth centuries, Arabic works on physics, mathematics, medicine, and optics became available to the West in Latin translations. In addition, when Aristotle's works arrived in the West in the second half of the twelfth century, they were accompanied by commentaries written by outstanding Arabic and Jewish philosophers. One example was Ibn-Rushd or Averroës (1126–1198), who lived in Córdoba and composed a systematic commentary on virtually all of Aristotle's surviving works.

The Development of Scholasticism

Christianity's importance in medieval society probably made inevitable theology's central role in the European intellectual world. Whether in monastic or cathedral schools or the new universities, theology, the formal study of religion, reigned as "queen of the sciences."

University Students and Violence at Oxford

Medieval universities shared in the violent atmosphere of their age. Town and gown quarrels often resulted in bloody conflicts, especially during the universities' formative period. This selection is taken from an anonymous description of a student riot at Oxford at the end of the thirteenth century.

A Student Riot at Oxford

They [the townsmen] seized and imprisoned all scholars on whom they could lay hands, invaded their inns [halls of residence], made havoc of their goods and trampled their books under foot. In the face of such provocation the proctors [university officials] sent their assistants about the town, forbidding the students to leave their inns. But all commands and exhortations were in vain. By nine o'clock next morning, bands of scholars were parading the streets in martial array. If the proctors failed to restrain them, the mayor was equally powerless to restrain his townsmen. The great bell of St. Martin's rang out an alarm; oxhorns were sounded in the streets; messengers were sent into the country to collect rustic allies. The clerks [students and teachers], who numbered 3,000 in all, began their attack simultaneously in various quarters. They broke open warehouses in the Spicery, the Cutlery and elsewhere. Armed with bow and arrows, swords and bucklers, slings and stones, they fell upon their opponents. Three they slew, and wounded fifty or more. One band . . . took up a position in High Street between the Churches of St. Mary and All Saints', and attacked the house of a certain Edward Hales. This Hales was a longstanding enemy of the clerks. There were no half measures with him. He seized his crossbow, and from an upper chamber sent an unerring shaft into the eye of the pugnacious rector. The death of their valiant leader caused the clerks to lose heart. They fled, closely pursued by the townsmen and country-folk. Some were struck down in the streets, and others who had taken refuge in the churches were dragged out and driven mercilessly to prison, lashed with thongs and goaded with iron spikes.

Complaints of murder, violence and robbery were lodged straightway with the king by both parties. The townsmen claimed 3,000 pounds' damage. The commissioners, however, appointed to decide the matter, condemned them to pay 200 marks, removed the bailiffs, and banished twelve of the most turbulent citizens from Oxford.

Beginning in the eleventh century, the effort to apply reason or logical analysis to the church's basic theological doctrines had a significant impact on the study of theology. The word *scholasticism* is used to refer to the philosophical and theological system of the medieval schools. A primary preoccupation of scholasticism was the attempt to reconcile faith and reason, to demonstrate that what was accepted on faith was in harmony with what could be learned by reason. The scholastic method came to be the basic instructional mode of the universities. In essence, this method consisted of posing a question, presenting contradictory authorities on that question, and then arriving at conclusions. It was a system that demanded rigorous analytical thought. Although scholasticism reached its high point in the thirteenth century, it had its beginnings in the theological world of the eleventh and twelfth centuries, especially in the work of Peter Abelard.

Abelard (1079–1142) studied in northern France but scorned his teachers as insignificant and took up the teaching of theology in Paris. Possessed of a colorful personality, Abelard was a very popular teacher who attracted many students. A man with a strong ego, he became known for the zest with which he entered into arguments with fellow students as well as for his affair with his student Heloise. Heloise bore a child by Abelard and secretly married him. But her uncle, who had hired Abelard as a tutor for his niece, sought revenge, as Abelard related in an account of his life titled *History of My Misfortunes:* "One night they took from me a most cruel and shameful vengeance, as I was resting and sleeping in the inner room of my lodging. . . . For they cut off those parts of my body, by which I had committed the deed which sorrowed them."[6]

Above all others, Abelard was responsible for furthering the new scholastic approach to theology. In his most famous work, *Sic et Non* (*Yes and No*), he listed passages from Scripture and the church fathers that stood in direct contradiction to one another and stressed the need to use logic or dialectical reasoning to reconcile the apparent differences systematically. He summed up his method thus: "By doubting we come to inquiry, through inquiry to the truth."

Beginning in the twelfth century, a major controversy—the problem of universals—began to occupy many theologians. The basic issue involved the nature of reality itself: what constitutes what is real. Theologians were divided into two major schools of thought reflecting the earlier traditions of Greek thought, especially the divergent schools of Plato and Aristotle.

Following Plato, the scholastic realists took the position that the individual objects that we perceive with our senses, such as trees, are not real but merely manifestations of universal ideas ("treeness") that exist in the mind of God. All knowledge, then, is based on the ideas implanted in human reason by the creator. To the realists, truth can be discovered only by contemplating universals. The other school, the nominalists, were adherents of Aristotle's ideas and believed that only individual objects are real. In their view, universal ideas and concepts were simply names (Latin *nomina,* hence nominalism). Truth could be discovered only by examining individual objects.

By the thirteenth century, the scholastics were confronted by a new challenge—how to harmonize Christian revelation with the work of Aristotle. The great influx of Aristotle's works into the West in the High Middle Ages threw many theologians into consternation. Aristotle was so highly regarded that he was called "the philosopher," yet he had arrived at his conclusions by rational thought—not revelation—and some of his doctrines, such as the mortality of the individual soul, contradicted the teachings of the church. The most famous attempt to reconcile Aristotle and the doctrines of Christianity was that of Saint Thomas Aquinas.

Thomas Aquinas (1225–1274) studied theology at Cologne and Paris and taught at both Naples and Paris, and it was at the latter that he worked on his famous *Summa Theologica* (*A Summa of Theology*—a summa was a compendium of knowledge that attempted to bring together all the received learning of the preceding centuries on a given subject into a single whole). Aquinas' masterpiece was organized according to the dialectical method of the scholastics. Aquinas first posed a question, cited sources that offered opposing opinions on the question, and then resolved them by arriving at his own conclusions. In this fashion, Aquinas raised and discussed some six hundred articles or issues (see the box on p. 237).

Aquinas' reputation derives from his masterful attempt to reconcile faith and reason. He took it for granted that there were truths derived by reason and truths derived by faith. He was certain, however, that the two truths could not be in conflict with each other:

> The light of faith that is freely infused into us does not destroy the light of natural knowledge [reason] implanted in us naturally. For although the natural light of the human mind is insufficient to show us these things made manifest by faith, it is nevertheless impossible that these things which the divine principle gives us by faith are contrary to these implanted in us by nature [reason]. Indeed, were that the case, one or the other would have to be false, and since both are given to us by God, God would have to be the author of untruth, which is impossible. . . . It is impossible that those things which are of philosophy can be contrary to those thing which are of faith.[7]

The natural mind, unaided by faith, could arrive at truths concerning the physical universe. Without God's help, however, unaided reason alone could not grasp spiritual truths, such as the Trinity (the belief that God, Jesus, and the Holy Spirit are three manifestations of the same unique deity) or the Incarnation (the belief that Jesus in his lifetime was God in human form).

The Revival of Roman Law

A systematic approach to knowledge was also expressed in the area of law. Of special importance was the rediscovery of the great legal work of Justinian, the *Corpus Iuris Civilis* (*Body of Civil Law*), known to the medieval West before 1100 only at second hand. Initially, teachers of law, such as Irnerius of Bologna, were content merely to explain the meaning of Roman legal terms to their students. Gradually, they became more sophisticated so that by the mid-twelfth century, "doctors of law" had developed commentaries and systematic treatises on the legal texts. Italian cities, above all Pavia and Bologna, became prominent centers for the study of Roman law. By the thirteenth century, Italian jurists were systematizing the various professional commentaries on Roman law into a single commentary known as the ordinary gloss. Study of Roman law at the universities came to consist of learning the text of the law along with this gloss.

This revival of Roman law occurred in a world dominated by a body of law quite different from that of the Romans. European law comprised a hodgepodge of Germanic law codes, feudal customs, and urban regulations. The desire to know a more orderly world, already evident in the study of theology, perhaps made it inevitable that Europeans would enthusiastically welcome the more systematic approach of Roman law.

The training of students in Roman law at medieval universities led to further application of its principals as these students became judges, lawyers, scribes, and councilors for the towns and monarchies of western Europe. By the beginning of the thirteenth century, the old system of ordeal was being replaced by a rational, decision-making process based on the systematic collection and analysis of evidence, a clear indication of the impact of Roman law on the European legal system.

Literature in the High Middle Ages

Latin was the universal language of medieval civilization. Used in the church and schools, it enabled learned people to communicate anywhere in Europe. The intellectual revival of the High Middle Ages included an outpouring of Latin literature. While Latin continued to be used for literary purposes, by the twelfth century much of the creative literature was being written in the vernacular (the local languages, such as Spanish, French, English, or German). Throughout the Middle Ages, there had been a popular vernacular literature, especially manifest in the Germanic, Celtic, Old Icelandic, and Slavonic sagas. But a new market for vernacular literature appeared in the twelfth century when educated laypeople at courts and in the new urban society sought fresh avenues of entertainment.

Perhaps the most popular vernacular literature of the twelfth century was troubadour poetry, chiefly the product of nobles and knights. This poetry focused on themes of courtly love, the love of a knight for a lady, generally a married noble lady, who inspires him to become a braver knight and a better poet. A good example is found in the laments of a crusading noble Jaufré Rudel, who cherished a dream lady from afar whom he said he would always love but feared he would never meet:

Most sad, most joyous shall I go away,
Let me have seen her for a single day,
    My love afar,
I shall not see her, for her land and mine

The Dialectical Method of Thomas Aquinas

In his masterpiece of scholastic theology, the *Summa Theologica,* Thomas Aquinas attempted to resolve some six hundred theological issues by the dialectical method. This method consisted of posing a question, stating the objections to it, and then replying to the objections. This selection from the *Summa Theologica* focuses on Article 4 of Question 92, "The Production of the Woman."

Thomas Aquinas, Summa Theologica

Question 92: The Production of the Woman (in Four Articles)

We must next consider the production of the woman. Under this head there are four points of inquiry: (1) Whether the woman should have been made in that first production of things? (2) Whether the woman should have been made from man? (3) Whether of man's rib? (4) Whether the woman was made immediately by God? . . .

Fourth Article: Whether the Woman Was Formed Immediately by God?

We proceed thus to the Fourth Article:—

Objection 1. It would seem that the woman was not formed immediately by God. For no individual is produced immediately by God from another individual alike in species. But the woman was made from a man who is of the same species. Therefore she was not made immediately by God.

Objection 2. Further, Augustine says that corporeal things are governed by God through the angels. But the woman's body was formed from corporeal matter. Therefore it was made through the ministry of the angels, and not immediately by God.

Objection 3. Further, those things which preexist in creatures as to their causal virtues are produced by the power of some creature, and not immediately by God. But the woman's body was produced in its causal virtues among the first created works, as Augustine says. Therefore it was not produced immediately by God.

On the contrary, Augustine says, in the same work: *God alone, to Whom all nature owes its existence, could form or build up the woman from the man's rib.*

I answer that, As was said above, the natural generation of every species is from some determinate matter. Now the matter whence man is naturally begotten is the human semen of man or woman. Wherefore from any other matter an individual of the human species cannot naturally be generated. Now God alone, the Author of nature, can produce an effect into existence outside the ordinary course of nature. Therefore God alone could produce either a man from the slime of the earth, or a woman from the rib of a man.

Reply Objection 1. This argument is verified when an individual is begotten, by natural generation, from that which is like it in the same species.

Reply Objection 2. As Augustine says, we do not know whether the angels were employed by God in the formation of the woman; but it is certain that, as the body of man was not formed by the angels from the slime of the earth, so neither was the body of the woman formed by them from the man's rib.

Reply Objection 3. As Augustine says, The first creation of things did not demand that woman should be made thus; it made it possible for her to be thus made. Therefore the body of the woman did indeed preexist in these causal virtues, in the things first created; not as regards active potentiality, but as regards a potentiality passive in relation to the active potentiality of the Creator.

Are sundered, and the ways are hard to find,
So many ways, and I shall lose my way,
So wills it God.

Yet shall I know no other love but hers,
And if not hers, no other love at all.
She has surpassed all.
So fair she is, so noble, I would be
A captive with the hosts of paynimrie [the Muslims]
In a far land, if so be upon me
Her eyes might fall.[8]

Although it originated in southern France, troubadour poetry also spread to northern France, Italy, and Germany.

Another type of vernacular literature was the *chanson de geste,* or heroic epic. The earliest and finest example is the *Chanson de Roland* (*The Song of Roland*), which appeared around 1100 and was written in a dialect of French, a Romance language derived from Latin (see the box on p. 238). The *chansons de geste* were written for a male-dominated society. The chief events described in these poems, as in *The Song of Roland,* are battles and political contests. Their world is one of combat in which knights fight courageously for their kings and lords. Women play little or no role in this literary genre.

Although *chansons de geste* were still written in the twelfth century, a different kind of long poem, the courtly romance, also became popular. It was composed in rhymed

The Song of Roland

The Song of Roland is one of the best examples of the medieval *chanson de geste,* or heroic epic. Inspired by a historical event, it recounts the ambush of the rear guard of Charlemagne's Frankish army in the Pyrenees. It was written three hundred years after the event it supposedly describes, however, and reveals more about the eleventh century than about the age of Charlemagne. Christian Basques who ambushed Charlemagne's army have been transformed into Muslims, the Frankish soldiers into French knights. This selection describes the death of Roland, Charlemagne's nephew, who was the commander of the ill-fated rear guard.

The Song of Roland

Now Roland feels that he is at death's door;
Out of his ears the brain is running forth.
Now for his peers he prays God call them all,
And for himself St. Gabriel's aid implores;
Then in each hand he takes, lest shame befall,
His Olifant [horn] and Durendal his sword.
Far as a quarrel flies from a cross-bow drawn,
Toward land of Spain he goes, to a wide lawn,
And climbs a mound where grows a fair tree tall,
And marble stones beneath it stand by four.
Face downward there on the green grass he falls,
And swoons away, for he is at death's door. . . .
Now Roland feels death press upon him hard;
It's creeping down from his head to his heart.
Under a pine-tree he hastens him apart,
There stretches him face down on the green grass,
And lays beneath him his sword and Olifant.
He's turned his head to where the Paynims [Muslims] are,
And this he does for the French and for Charles,
Since fain is he that they should say, brave heart,
That he has died a conqueror at last.
He beats his breast full many a time and fast,
Gives, with his glove, his sins into God's charge.

Now Roland feels his time is at an end;
On the steep hill-side, toward Spain he's turned his head,
And with one hand he beats upon his breast;
Saying: "Mea culpa; Thy mercy, Lord, I beg
For all the sins, both the great and the less,
That e'er I did since first I drew my breath
Unto this day when I'm struck down by death."
His right-hand glove he unto God extends;
Angels from Heaven now to his side descend.

couplets and dwelt on a romantic subject matter: brave knights, virtuous ladies, evil magicians, bewitched palaces, fairies, talking animals, and strange forests. The story of King Arthur, the legendary king of the fifth-century Britons, became a popular subject for the courtly romance. The best versions of the Arthurian legends survive in the works of Chrétien de Troyes, a French writer in the second half of the twelfth century, whose courtly romances were viewed by contemporaries as the works of a master storyteller.

Romanesque Architecture: "A White Mantle of Churches"

The eleventh and twelfth centuries witnessed an explosion of building, both private and public. The construction of castles and churches absorbed most of the surplus resources of medieval society and at the same time reflected its basic preoccupations, warfare and God. The churches were by far the most conspicuous of the public buildings. As a chronicler of the eleventh century commented:

> As the year 1000 approached, people all over the world, but especially in Italy and France, began to rebuild their churches. Although most of them were well built and in little need of alterations, Christian nations were rivaling each other to have the most beautiful edifices. One might say the world was shaking herself, throwing off her old garments, and robing herself with a white mantle of churches. Then nearly all the cathedrals, the monasteries dedicated to different saints, and even the small village chapels were reconstructed more beautifully by the faithful.[9]

G. Dagli Orti

Barrel Vaulting. The eleventh and twelfth centuries witnessed an enormous amount of church construction. Utilizing the basilica shape, master builders replaced flat wooden roofs with long, round stone vaults known as barrel vaults. As this illustration of a Romanesque church in Vienne, France, indicates, the barrel vault limited the size of a church and left little room for windows.

Hundreds of new cathedrals and abbey and pilgrimage churches, as well as thousands of parish churches in rural villages, were built in the eleventh and twelfth centuries. This building spree reflected both the revived religious culture and the increased wealth of the period produced by agriculture, trade, and the growth of cities.

The cathedrals of the eleventh and twelfth centuries were built in a truly international style, the Romanesque. The construction of churches required the services of professional master builders, whose employment throughout Europe guaranteed an international unity in basic features. Prominent examples of Romanesque churches can be found in Germany, France, and Spain.

Romanesque churches were normally built in the rectangular basilica shape used in the construction of churches in the Late Roman Empire. Romanesque builders made a significant innovation by replacing the earlier flat wooden ceiling with a long, round stone vault called a barrel vault or a cross vault where two barrel vaults intersected (a vault is simply a curved roof made of masonry). The latter was used when a transept was added to create a church plan in the shape of a cross. Although barrel and cross vaults were technically difficult to construct, they were considered aesthetically pleasing and technically proficient and had fine acoustics.

Because stone vaults were extremely heavy, Romanesque churches required massive pillars and walls to hold them up. This left little space for windows, making Romanesque churches notoriously dark on the inside. Their massive walls and pillars gave the churches a sense of solidity and almost the impression of a fortress. Indeed, massive walls and slit windows were also characteristic of the castle architecture of the period.

The Gothic Cathedral. The Gothic cathedral was one of the greatest artistic triumphs of the High Middle Ages. Shown here is the cathedral of Notre-Dame in Paris. Begun in 1163, it was not completed until the beginning of the fourteenth century.

The Gothic Cathedral

Begun in the twelfth century and brought to perfection in the thirteenth, the Gothic cathedral remains one of the greatest artistic triumphs of the High Middle Ages. Soaring skyward, almost as if to reach heaven, it was a fitting symbol for medieval people's preoccupation with God.

Two fundamental innovations of the twelfth century made Gothic cathedrals possible. The combination of ribbed vaults and pointed arches replaced the barrel vault of Romanesque churches and enabled builders to make Gothic churches higher than their Romanesque counterparts. The use of pointed arches and ribbed vaults created an impression of upward movement, a sense of weightless upward thrust that implied the energy of God. Another technical innovation, the flying buttress, a heavy arched pier of stone built onto the outside of the walls, made it possible to distribute the weight of the church's vaulted ceilings

Interior of a Gothic Cathedral. The use of ribbed vaults and pointed arches gave the Gothic cathedral a feeling of upward movement. Moreover, due to the flying buttress, the cathedral could have thin walls with stained-glass windows that filled the interior with light. The flying buttress was a heavy pier of stone built onto the outside of the walls to bear the brunt of the weight of the church's vaulted ceiling.

outward and downward and thereby eliminate the heavy walls used in Romanesque churches to hold the weight of the massive barrel vaults. Thus Gothic cathedrals could be built with thin walls that were filled with magnificent stained-glass windows, which created a play of light inside that varied with the sun at different times of the day.

Medieval craftspeople of the twelfth and thirteenth centuries perfected the art of stained glass. Small pieces of glass were stained in glowing colors like jewels. The preoccupation with colored light in Gothic cathedrals was not accidental but was executed by people inspired by the belief that natural light was a symbol of the divine light of God. Light is invisible but enables people to see; so too is God invisible, but the existence of God allows the world of matter to be. Those impressed by the mystical significance of light were also impressed by the mystical significance of number. The proportions of Gothic cathedrals were based on mathematical ratios that their builders believed were derived from the ancient Greek school of Pythagoras and expressed the intrinsic harmony of the world as established by its creator.

The first fully Gothic church was the abbey church of Saint-Denis near Paris, inspired by Suger, the famous abbot of the monastery from 1122 to 1151, and built between 1140 and 1150. Although the Gothic style was the product of northern France, by the mid-thirteenth century French Gothic architecture had spread to England, Spain, Germany—indeed, to virtually all of Europe. This French Gothic style was seen most brilliantly in cathedrals in Paris (Notre-Dame), Reims, Amiens, and Chartres.

A Gothic cathedral was the work of an entire community. All classes contributed to its construction. Money was raised from wealthy townspeople who had profited from the new trade and industries as well as from kings and nobles. Master masons who were both architects and engineers designed the cathedrals. They drew up the plans and supervised the work of construction. Stonemasons and other craftspeople were paid a daily wage and provided the skilled labor to build the cathedrals. Indeed, these buildings were the first monumental structures of consequence built by free, salaried labor.

The building of cathedrals often became highly competitive as communities vied with one another to build the highest tower, a rivalry that sometimes ended in disaster. The cathedral of Beauvais in northern France collapsed in 1284 after reaching the height of 157 feet. Gothic cathedrals also depended on a community's faith. After all, it often took two or more generations to complete a cathedral, and the first generation of builders must have begun with the knowledge that they would not live to see the completed project. Most important, a Gothic cathedral symbolized the chief preoccupation of a medieval Christian community, its dedication to a spiritual ideal. As we have observed before, the largest buildings of an era reflect the values of its society. The Gothic cathedral, with its towers soaring toward heaven, gave witness to an age when a spiritual impulse still underlay most of existence.

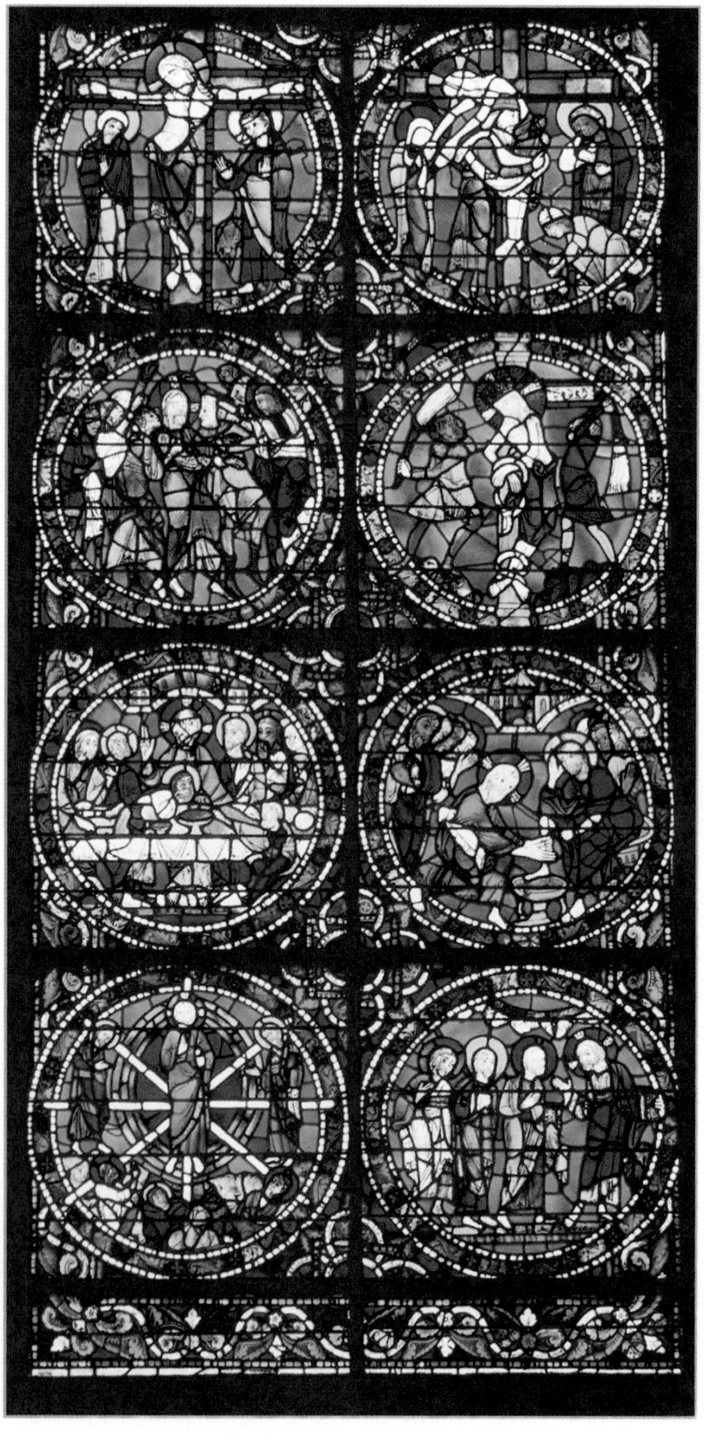

Sonia Halliday Photographs

Chartres Cathedral: Stained-Glass Window. The stained glass of Gothic cathedrals is remarkable for the beauty and variety of its colors. Stained-glass windows depicted a remarkable variety of scenes. The windows of Chartres cathedral, for example, present the saints, views of the everyday activities of ordinary men and women, and, as in this panel, scenes from the life of Jesus.

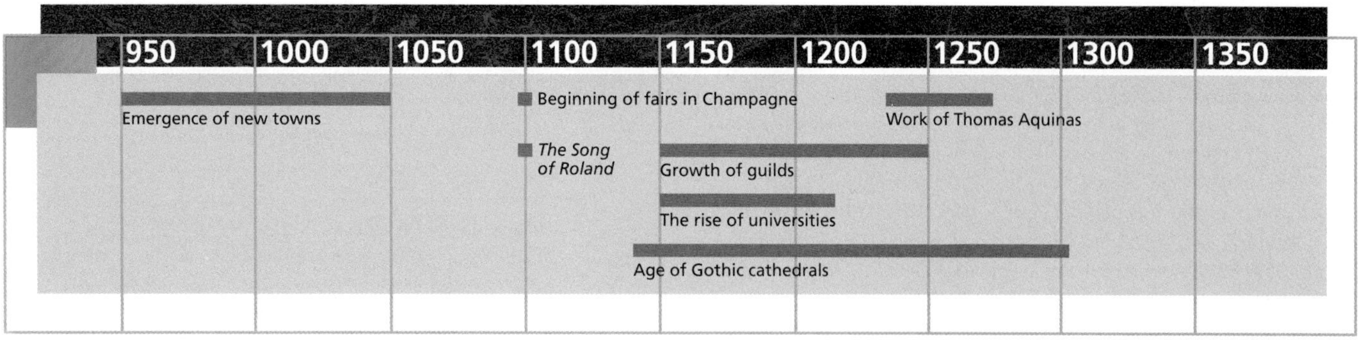

Conclusion

The new European civilization that had emerged in the Early Middle Ages began to flourish in the High Middle Ages. Better growing conditions, an expansion of cultivated land, and technological and agricultural changes combined to enable Europe's food supply to increase significantly after 1000. This increase helped sustain a dramatic rise in population that was physically apparent in the expansion of towns and cities.

The High Middle Ages witnessed economic and social changes that some historians believe set European civilization on a path that lasted until the eighteenth century. The revival of trade, the expansion of towns and cities, and the development of a money economy did not mean the end of a predominantly rural European society, but they did open the door to new ways to make a living and new opportunities for people to expand and enrich their lives. Eventually, they created the foundations for the development of a mostly urban industrial society.

The High Middle Ages also gave birth to a cultural revival. This cultural revival led to a rediscovery of important aspects of the classical heritage, to new centers of learning in the universities, to the use of reason to systematize the study of theology and law, to the development of a vernacular literature that appealed both to knights and to townspeople, and to a dramatic increase in the number and size of churches.

Notes

1. Quoted in Joseph and Frances Gies, *Life in a Medieval Castle* (New York, 1974), p. 175.
2. Quoted in Robert Delort, *Life in the Middle Ages,* trans. Robert Allen (New York, 1972), p. 218.
3. Quoted in Jean Gimpel, *The Medieval Machine* (Harmondsworth, England, 1977), p. 92.
4. Quoted in Charles H. Haskins, *The Rise of Universities* (Ithaca, N.Y., 1957), pp. 77–78.
5. Ibid., pp. 79–80.
6. Quoted in David Herlihy, *Medieval Culture and Society* (New York, 1968), p. 204.
7. Quoted in John Mundy, *Europe in the High Middle Ages, 1150–1309* (New York, 1973), pp. 474–475.
8. Helen Waddell, *The Wandering Scholars* (New York, 1961), p. 222.
9. Quoted in John W. Baldwin, *The Scholastic Culture of the Middle Ages, 1000–1300* (Lexington, Mass., 1971), p. 15.

Suggestions for Further Reading

For a good introduction to this period, see C. N. L. Brooke, *Europe in the Central Middle Ages, 962–1154,* rev. ed. (New York, 1988); M. Barber, *The Two Cities: Medieval Europe, 1050–1320* (London, 1992); and R. Bartlett, *The Making of Europe: Conquest, Colonization, and Cultural Change, 950–1350* (Princeton, N.J., 1993). On peasant life, see R. Fossier, *Peasant Life in the Medieval West* (New York, 1988). Technological changes are discussed in J. Gimpel, *The Medieval Machine* (Harmondsworth, England, 1976), and J. Langdon, *Horses, Oxen, and Technological Innovation* (New York, 1986).

Works on the function and activities of the nobility in the High Middle Ages include S. Reynolds, *Kingdoms and Communities in Western Europe, 900–1300* (Oxford, 1984); R. W. Barber, *The Knight and Chivalry* (Rochester, N.Y., 1995); and the classic work by M. Bloch, *Feudal Society* (London, 1961). Various aspects of the social history of the nobility can be found in G. Duby, *The Knight, the Lady, and the Priest* (London, 1984), on noble marriages; R. Barber and J. Barker, *Tournaments: Jousts, Chivalry, and Pageants in the Middle Ages* (New York, 1989), on tournaments; N. J. G. Pounds, *The Medieval Castle in England and Wales: A Social and Political History* (New York, 1990); and C. B. Bouchard, *Life and Society in the West: Antiquity and the Middle Ages* (San Diego, Calif., 1988), ch. 6. On women, see R. T. Morewedge, ed., *The Role of Women in the Middle Ages* (Albany, N.Y., 1975), and S. M. Stuard, ed., *Women in Medieval Society* (Philadelphia, 1976).

On the revival of trade, see R. S. Lopez, *The Commercial Revolution of the Middle Ages, 950–1350* (Englewood Cliffs, N.J., 1971). Urban history is covered in D. Nicholas, *The Growth of the Medieval City: From Late Antiquity to the Early Fourteenth Century* (New York, 1997), and the classic work of H. Pirenne, *Medieval Cities* (Princeton, N.J., 1969). For a good collection of essays on urban culture, see B. Hanawalt and K. I. Reyerson, eds., *City and Spectacle in Medieval Europe* (Minneapolis, Minn., 1994). On women in the cities, see B. Hanawalt, ed., *Women and Work in Preindustrial Europe* (Bloomington, Ind., 1986).

A general work on medieval intellectual life is M. L. Colish, *Medieval Foundations of the Western Intellectual Tradition, 400–1400*

(New Haven, Conn., 1997). The development of universities is covered in S. Ferruolo, *The Origin of the University* (Stanford, Calif., 1985); A. B. Cobban, *The Medieval Universities* (London, 1975); and the brief older work by C. H. Haskins, *The Rise of Universities* (Ithaca, N.Y., 1957). Various aspects of the intellectual and literary developments of the High Middle Ages are examined in J. W. Baldwin, *The Scholastic Culture of the Middle Ages, 1000–1300* (Lexington, Mass., 1971); J. Marenbon, *The Philosophy of Peter Abelard* (New York, 1997); and H. Waddell, *The Wandering Scholars* (London, 1934). A good biography of Thomas Aquinas is J. Weisheipl, *Friar Thomas d'Aquino: His Life, His Thought and Work* (New York, 1974).

For a good introduction to the art and architecture of the Middle Ages, see A. Shaver-Crandell, *The Middle Ages,* in the Cambridge Introduction to Art Series (Cambridge, 1982). A good introduction to Romanesque style is A. Petzold, *Romanesque Art* (New York, 1995). On the Gothic movement, see M. Camille, *Gothic Art: Glorious Visions* (New York, 1996). Good books on the construction of Gothic cathedrals are J. Gimpel, *The Cathedral Builders* (New York, 1961), and A. Erlande-Brandenburg, *Cathedrals and Castles: Building in the Middle Ages* (New York, 1995).

For additional reading, go to InfoTrac College Edition, your online research library at http://web1.infotrac-college.com

Enter the search term *peasantry* using the Subject Guide.

Enter the search term *cities and towns, medieval* using the Subject Guide.

Enter the search term *Middle Ages* using the Subject Guide.

CHAPTER

10

The Rise of Kingdoms and the Growth of Church Power

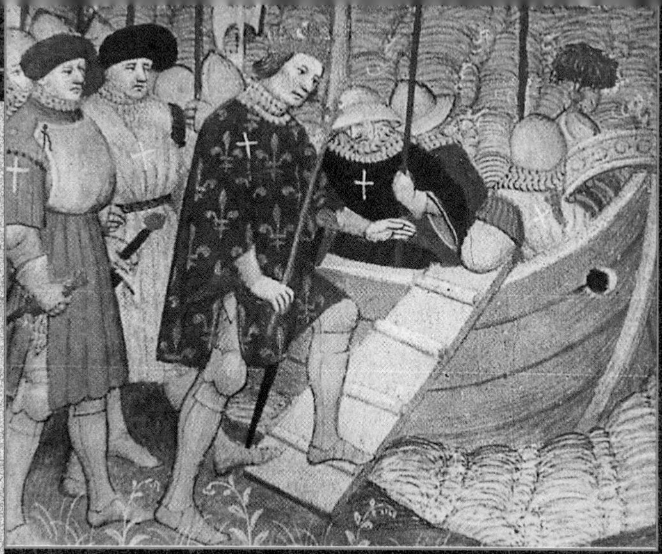

The Granger Collection

CHAPTER OUTLINE

- The Emergence and Growth of European Kingdoms, 1000–1300
- The Recovery and Reform of the Catholic Church
- Christianity and Medieval Civilization
- The Crusades
- Conclusion

FOCUS QUESTIONS

- What steps did the rulers of England and France take during the High Middle Ages to reverse the decentralizing tendencies of fief-holding?
- What was at issue in the Investiture Controversy, and what effect did the controversy have on the church and on Germany?
- What were the characteristics of the papal monarchy and the new religious orders of the High Middle Ages, and what role did women play in the religious life of the period?
- What was the church's attitude toward heretics and Jews during the High Middle Ages?
- Why did centralized kingdoms develop in some parts of Europe and not in others?

THE RECOVERY AND GROWTH of European civilization in the High Middle Ages also affected the state and the church. Both lords and vassals and the Catholic church recovered from the invasions and internal dissension of the Early Middle Ages. Although lords and vassals seemed forever mired in endless petty conflicts, some medieval kings began to exert a centralizing authority and inaugurated the process of developing new kinds of monarchical states. By the thirteenth century, European monarchs were solidifying their governmental institutions in pursuit of greater power.

The recovery of the Catholic church produced a reform movement that led to exalted claims of papal authority and subsequent conflict with state authorities. At the same time, vigorous papal leadership combined with new dimensions of religious life to make the Catholic church a forceful presence in every area of life. The role of the church in the new European civilization was quite evident in the career of a man named Samson, who became abbot, or head, of the great English abbey of Bury St. Edmonds in 1182. According to

Jocelyn of Brakeland, a monk who assisted him, Abbot Samson was a devout man who wore "undergarments of horsehair and a horsehair shirt." He loved virtue and "abhorred liars, drunkards and talkative folk." His primary concern was the spiritual well-being of his monastery, but he spent much of his time working on problems in the world beyond the abbey walls. Since the monastery had fallen into debt under his predecessors, Abbot Samson toiled tirelessly to recoup the abbey's fortunes by carefully supervising its manors. He also rounded up murderers to stand trial in St. Edmunds and provided knights for the king's army. But his actions were not always tolerant or beneficial. He was instrumental in driving the Jews from the town and was not above improving the abbey's possessions at the expense of his neighbors: "He built up the bank of the fish-pond at Babwell so high, for the service of a new mill, that by keeping back the water there is not a man, rich or poor, but has lost his garden and his orchards." The abbot's worldly cares weighed heavily on him, but he had little choice if his abbey were to flourish and fulfill its spiritual and secular functions. But he did have regrets, as he confided to Jocelyn: "If he could have returned to the circumstances he had enjoyed before he became a monk, he would never have become a monk or an abbot."

The Emergence and Growth of European Kingdoms, 1000–1300

The domination of society by the nobility reached its apex in the High Middle Ages. During this time, however, kings began the process of extending their power in more effective ways. Out of this growth in the monarchies would eventually come the European states that dominated much of later European history.

In theory, kings were regarded as the heads of their kingdoms and were expected to lead their vassals and subjects into battle. The king's power, however, was strictly limited. He had to honor the rights and privileges of his vassals, and if he failed to observe his vassals' rights, they could and did rebel. Weak kings were overthrown or, like the later Carolingians, replaced by another ruling dynasty.

However, kings did possess some sources of power that other lords did not. Kings were anointed by holy oil in ceremonies reminiscent of Old Testament precedents; thus their positions seemed sanctioned by divine favor. War and marriage alliances enabled them to increase their power, and their conquests enabled them to reward their followers with grants of land and bind powerful nobles to them. In the High Middle Ages, kings found ways to strengthen governmental institutions and consequently to extend their powers. The revival of commerce, the growth of cities, and the emergence of a money economy eventually enabled monarchs to hire soldiers and officials and to rely less on their vassals.

England in the High Middle Ages

At the beginning of the eleventh century, Anglo-Saxon England had fallen subject to Scandinavian control after a successful invasion by the Danes in 1016. King Canute (1016–1035), however, continued English institutions and laws and even supported the Catholic church. His dynastic line proved unable to maintain itself, and in 1042, the Anglo-Saxon line of kings was restored in the person of Edward the Confessor (1042–1066). After his death, the kingship was taken by Harold Godwinson, who belonged to one of England's greatest noble families.

A cousin of Edward the Confessor, William of Normandy, laid claim to the throne of England, however, and invaded England in the fall of 1066. The forces of Harold Godwinson and Duke William met at Hastings on October 14, 1066. The Saxon infantry was soundly defeated by the heavily armed Norman knights, and William was crowned king of England at Christmas in London.

Michael Holford

Norman Conquest of England. The Bayeux tapestry, which consists of woolen embroidery on a linen backing, was made by English needlewomen before 1082 for Bayeux Cathedral. It depicts scenes from the Norman invasion of England. This segment shows the Norman cavalry charging the shield wall of the Saxon infantry during the Battle of Hastings.

After his conquest, William (1066–1087) treated all of England as a royal possession. Based on the Domesday Book, which William commissioned in 1086 by sending out royal officials to ascertain who owned or held land in tenancy, modern historians have estimated that the Norman royal family took possession of about one-fifth of the land in England as the royal demesne (or domain). The remaining English land was held by nobles or the church as fiefs of the king; each of these vassals in turn was responsible for supplying a quota of knights for the royal army. The great landed nobles were allowed to divide their lands among their subvassals as they wished. In 1086, however, by the Oath of Salisbury Plain, William required all subvassals to swear loyalty to him as their king and liege lord. Henceforth, all subvassals owed their primary loyalty to the king rather than to their immediate lords.

Thus the Norman conquest of England had brought a dramatic change. In Anglo-Saxon England, the king had held limited lands while great families controlled large stretches of land and acted rather independently of the king. In contrast, the Normans established a hierarchy of nobles holding land as fiefs from the king. William of Normandy had created a strong, centralized monarchy. Gradually, a process of fusion between the victorious Normans and the defeated Anglo-Saxons created a new England. Although the Norman ruling class spoke French, the intermarriage of the Norman-French with the Anglo-Saxon nobility gradually merged Anglo-Saxon and French into a new English language.

William maintained the Anglo-Saxon administrative system in which counties (shires) were divided into hundreds (groups of villages). Within each shire, the sheriff was the chief royal officer responsible for leading the military forces of the county, collecting royal tolls, and presiding over the county court. William retained the office but replaced the Anglo-Saxon sheriffs with Normans. William also more fully developed the system of taxation and royal courts begun by the Anglo-Saxon and Danish kings of the tenth and eleventh centuries.

The Norman conquest of England had repercussions in France as well. Because the new king of England was still the duke of Normandy (see Map 10.1), he was both a king (of England) and at the same time a vassal to a king (of France), but a vassal who was now far more powerful than his lord. This connection with France kept England heavily involved in Continental affairs throughout the High Middle Ages.

In the twelfth century, the power of the English monarchy was greatly enlarged during the reign of Henry II (1154–1189), the founder of the Plantagenet dynasty. The new king was particularly successful in developing administrative and legal institutions that strengthened the royal government. First of all, Henry continued the development of the exchequer, or permanent royal treasury. Royal officials, known as "barons of the exchequer," received taxes collected by the sheriffs while seated around a table covered by a checkered cloth that served as a counting device. (*Exchequer* is derived from the French word for chessboard.) The barons gave receipts to the sheriffs, while clerks recorded the accounts on sheets of parchment that were then rolled up. These so-called pipe rolls have served as an important source of economic and social information for historians.

Perhaps even more significant than Henry's financial reforms were his efforts to strengthen the royal courts. Henry expanded the number of criminal cases tried in the king's court and also devised ways of taking property cases from local courts to the royal courts. Henry's goals were clear: expanding the jurisdiction of royal courts extended the king's power and, of course, brought revenues into his coffers. Moreover, because the royal courts were now found throughout England, a body of common law (law that was common to the whole kingdom) began to replace the local law codes, which often varied from place to place.

Henry was less successful at imposing royal control over the church. The king claimed the right to punish clergymen in the royal courts, but Thomas à Becket, archbishop of Canterbury and therefore the highest-ranking English cleric, claimed that only church courts could try clerics. Attempts at compromise failed, and the angry king publicly expressed the desire to be rid of Becket: "Who will free me of this priest?" he screamed. Four knights took the challenge, went to Canterbury, and murdered the archbishop in the cathedral (see the box on p. 246). Faced with public outrage, Henry was forced to allow the right of appeal from English church courts to the papal court.

Many English nobles came to resent the ongoing growth of the king's power and rose in rebellion during the reign of Henry's son, King John (1199–1216). At Runnymede in 1215, John was forced to assent to Magna Carta, the Great Charter of feudal liberties. Much of Magna Carta was aimed at limiting government practices that affected the relations between the king and his vassals on the one hand and between the king and the church on the other (see the box on p. 247).

Magna Carta remains, above all, a feudal document. Feudal custom had always recognized that the relationship between king and vassals was based on mutual rights and obligations. Magna Carta gave written recognition to that fact and was used in subsequent years to underscore the concept that the monarch should be limited rather than absolute.

In the late thirteenth century, a very talented and powerful monarch ascended the throne in the person of Edward I (1272–1307). He began the process of uniting all of the British Isles into a single kingdom. Although Wales was finally conquered and pacified, his attempt to subdue Scotland failed. Edward managed merely to begin a lengthy conflict between England and Scotland that lasted for centuries.

Edward was successful in reestablishing monarchical rights after a period of baronial control. During his reign, the role of the English Parliament, an institution of great importance in the development of representative government, began to be defined.

Murder in the Cathedral

The conflict between King Henry II and Thomas à Becket, archbishop of Canterbury, was the most dramatic confrontation between church and state in English medieval history. Although Henry did not order the archbishop's murder, he certainly caused it by his reckless public words expressing his desire to be free of Becket. This excerpt is from a letter by John of Salisbury, who served as secretary to Theobald, archbishop of Canterbury, and his successor, Thomas à Becket. John was present at the murder of the archbishop in 1170.

John of Salisbury to John of Canterbury, Bishop of Poitiers

The martyr [Becket] stood in the cathedral, before Christ's altar, as we have said, ready to suffer; the hour of slaughter was at hand. When he heard that he was sought—heard the knights who had come for him shouting in the throng of clerks and monks "Where is the archbishop?"—he turned to meet them on the steps which he had almost climbed, and said with steady countenance: "Here am I! What do you want?" One of the knight-assassins flung at him in fury: "That you die now! That you should live longer is impossible." No martyr seems ever to have been more steadfast in his agony than he, . . . and thus, steadfast in speech as in spirit, he replied: "And I am prepared to die for my God, to preserve justice and my church's liberty. If you seek my head, I forbid you on behalf of God almighty and on pain of anathema to do any hurt to any other man, monk, clerk or layman, of high or low degree. Do not involve them in the punishment, for they have not been involved in the cause: on my head not on theirs be it if any of them have supported the church in its troubles. I embrace death readily, so long as peace and liberty for the Church follow from the shedding of my blood. . . ." He spoke, and saw that the assassins had drawn their swords; and bowed his head like one in prayer. His last words were "To God and St. Mary and the saints who protect and defend this church, and to the blessed Denis, I commend myself and the church's cause." No one could dwell on what followed without deep sorrow and choking tears. A son's affection forbids me to describe each blow the savage assassins struck, spurning all fear of God, forgetful of all fealty and any human feeling. They defiled the cathedral and the holy season [Christmas] with a bishop's blood and with slaughter; but that was not enough. They sliced off the crown of his head, which had been specially dedicated to God by anointing with holy oil—a fearful thing even to describe; then they used their evil swords, when he was dead, to spill his brain and cruelly scattered it, mixed with blood and bones, over the pavement. . . . Through all the agony the martyr's spirit was unconquered, his steadfastness marvelous to observe; he spoke not a word, uttered no cry, let slip no groan, raised no arm nor garment to protect himself from an assailant, but bent his head, which he had laid bare to their swords with wonderful courage, till all might be fulfilled. Motionless he held it, and when at last he fell his body lay straight; and he moved neither hand nor foot.

Originally, the word *parliament* was applied to meetings of the king's Great Council in which the greater barons and chief prelates of the church met with the king's judges and principal advisers to deal with judicial affairs. But in his need for money, in 1295 Edward I invited two knights from every county and two residents from each city and town (called burgesses) to meet with the Great Council to consent to new taxes. This was the first Parliament.

The English Parliament, then, came to be composed of two knights from every county and two burgesses from every town or city, as well as the barons and ecclesiastical lords. Eventually, the barons and church lords formed the House of Lords; the knights and burgesses, the House of Commons. The Parliaments of Edward I granted taxes, discussed politics, passed laws, and handled judicial business. Although not yet the important body it would eventually become, the English Parliament had clearly emerged as an institution by the end of the thirteenth century. The law of the realm was beginning to be determined not by the king alone but by the king in consultation with representatives of various groups that constituted the community. By the beginning of the fourteenth century, England had begun to develop a unique system of national monarchy.

The Growth of the French Kingdom

The Capetian dynasty of French kings had emerged at the end of the tenth century. Although they bore the title of king, the Capetians had little real power. They controlled as the royal domain (the lands of the king) only the lands around Paris known as the Île-de-France. As kings of France, the Capetians were formally the overlords of the great lords of France, such as the dukes of Normandy, Brittany, Burgundy, and Aquitaine. In reality, however, many of the dukes were considerably more powerful than the Capetian kings. It would take the Capetian dynasty hundreds of years to create a truly centralized monarchical authority in France.

The reign of King Philip II Augustus (1180–1223) was an important turning point. He perceived that the power of the French monarch would never be extended until the Plantagenets' power was defeated. After all, Henry II and his sons were not only kings of England but also rulers of the French territories of Normandy, Maine, Anjou, and Aquitaine. Accordingly, Philip II waged war against the Plantagenet rulers of England and was successful in wresting control of Normandy, Maine, Anjou, and Touraine from the

Magna Carta

After the dismal failure of King John to reconquer Normandy from the French king, some of the English barons rebelled against their king. At Runnymede in 1215, King John agreed to seal Magna Carta, the Great Charter of liberties regulating the relationship between the king and his vassals. What made Magna Carta an important historical document was its more general clauses defining rights and liberties. These were later interpreted in broader terms to make them applicable to all the English people.

Magna Carta

John, by the Grace of God, king of England, lord of Ireland, duke of Normandy and Aquitaine, count of Anjou, to the archbishops, bishops, abbots, earls, barons, justiciars, foresters, sheriffs, reeves, servants, and all bailiffs and his faithful people greeting.

1. In the first place we have granted to God, and by this our present charter confirmed, for us and our heirs forever, that the English church shall be free, and shall hold its rights entire and its liberties uninjured. . . . We have granted moreover to all free men of our kingdom for us and our heirs forever all the liberties written below, to be had and holden by themselves and their heirs from us and our heirs.
2. If any of our earls or barons, or others holding from us in chief by military service shall have died, and when he had died his heir shall be of full age and owe relief, he shall have his inheritance by the ancient relief; that is to say, the heir or heirs of an earl for the whole barony of an earl a hundred pounds; the heir or heirs of a baron for a whole barony a hundred pounds; the heir or heirs of a knight, for a whole knight's fee, a hundred shillings at most; and who owes less let him give less according to the ancient custom of fiefs.
3. If moreover the heir of any one of such shall be under age, and shall be in wardship, when he comes of age he shall have his inheritance without relief and without a fine. . . .

12. No scutage or aid shall be imposed in our kingdom except by the common council of our kingdom, except for the ransoming of our body, for the making of our oldest son a knight, and for once marrying our oldest daughter, and for these purposes it shall be only a reasonable aid. . . .
13. And the city of London shall have all its ancient liberties and free customs, as well by land as by water. Moreover, we will and grant that all other cities and boroughs and villages and ports shall have all their liberties and free customs.
14. And for holding a common council of the kingdom concerning the assessment of an aid otherwise than in the three cases mentioned above, or concerning the assessment of a scutage we shall cause to be summoned the archbishops, bishops, abbots, earls, and greater barons by our letters under seal; and besides we shall cause to be summoned generally, by our sheriffs and bailiffs all those who hold from us in chief, for a certain day, that is at the end of forty days at least, and for a certain place; and in all the letters of that summons, we will express the cause of the summons, and when the summons has thus been given the business shall proceed on the appointed day, on the advice of those who shall be present, even if not all of those who were summoned have come. . . .

39. No free man shall be taken or imprisoned or dispossessed, or outlawed, or banished, or in any way destroyed, nor will we go upon him, nor send upon him, except by the legal judgment of his peers or by the law of the land. . . .

60. Moreover, all those customs and franchises mentioned above in which we have conceded in our kingdom, and which are to be fulfilled, as far as pertains to us, in respect to our men; all men of our kingdom, as well as clergy as laymen, shall observe as far as pertains to them, in respect to their men.

English kings. Through these conquests, Philip II quadrupled the income of the French monarchy and greatly enlarged its power. To administer justice and collect royal revenues in his new territories, Philip appointed new royal officials, thus inaugurating a French royal bureaucracy.

Capetian rulers after Philip II continued to add lands to the royal domain. Although Philip had used military force, other kings used both purchase and marriage to achieve the same end. Much of the thirteenth century was dominated by Louis IX (1226–1270), one of the most celebrated of the medieval French kings. A deeply religious man, he was later canonized as a saint by the church, an unusual action regardless of the century. Louis was known for his attempts to bring justice to his people and ensure their rights. He sent out royal agents to check on the activities of royal officials after hearing complaints that they were abusing their power. Sharing in the religious sentiments of his age, Louis played a major role in two of the later Crusades (see "The Crusades" later in this chapter). Both were failures, and he met his death during an invasion of North Africa.

One of Louis's successors, Philip IV the Fair (1285–1314), was particularly effective in strengthening the French monarchy. The machinery of government became even more specialized. French kings going back to the early Capetians had possessed a household staff for running their

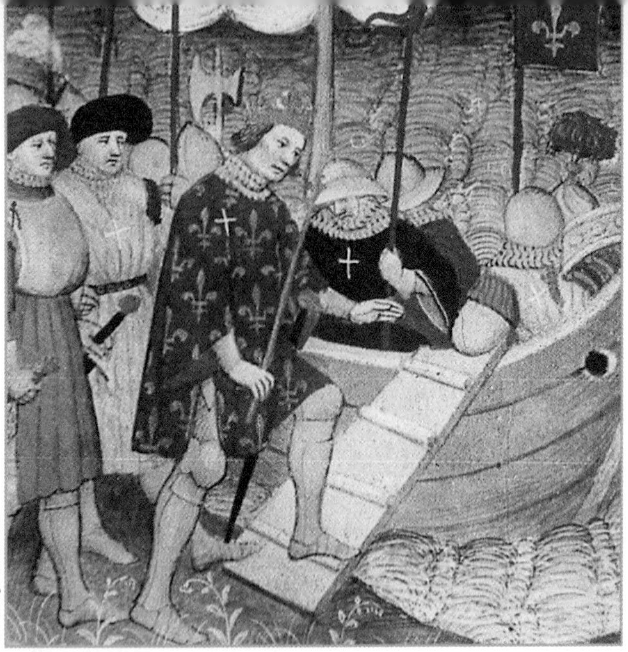
The Granger Collection

Louis IX Departs for Tunis. The pious French king Louis IX organized the last two major Crusades of the thirteenth century. Both failed miserably. This illustration shows a robust Louis IX setting out for Tunis in 1270. In truth, the king was so weak that he had to be carried to the ship.

affairs. In effect, the division and enlargement of this household staff produced the three major branches of royal administration: a council for advice; a chamber of accounts, for finances; and the *Parlement,* or royal court. By the beginning of the fourteenth century, the Capetians had established an efficient royal bureaucracy.

Philip IV also brought a French parliament into being. After he became involved in a struggle with the pope, Philip summoned representatives of the church, nobility, and towns to meet with him in 1302, thereby inaugurating the

Map 10.1 England and France in the High Middle Ages: (*left*) England and Its French Holdings; (*right*) Growth of the French State. King Philip II Augustus of France greatly expanded the power of the Capetian royal family through his victories over the Plantagenet monarchy of England, which gained Philip control over much of north-central France. ■ How could the presence of the English Channel have made it more difficult for England to rule its French possessions?

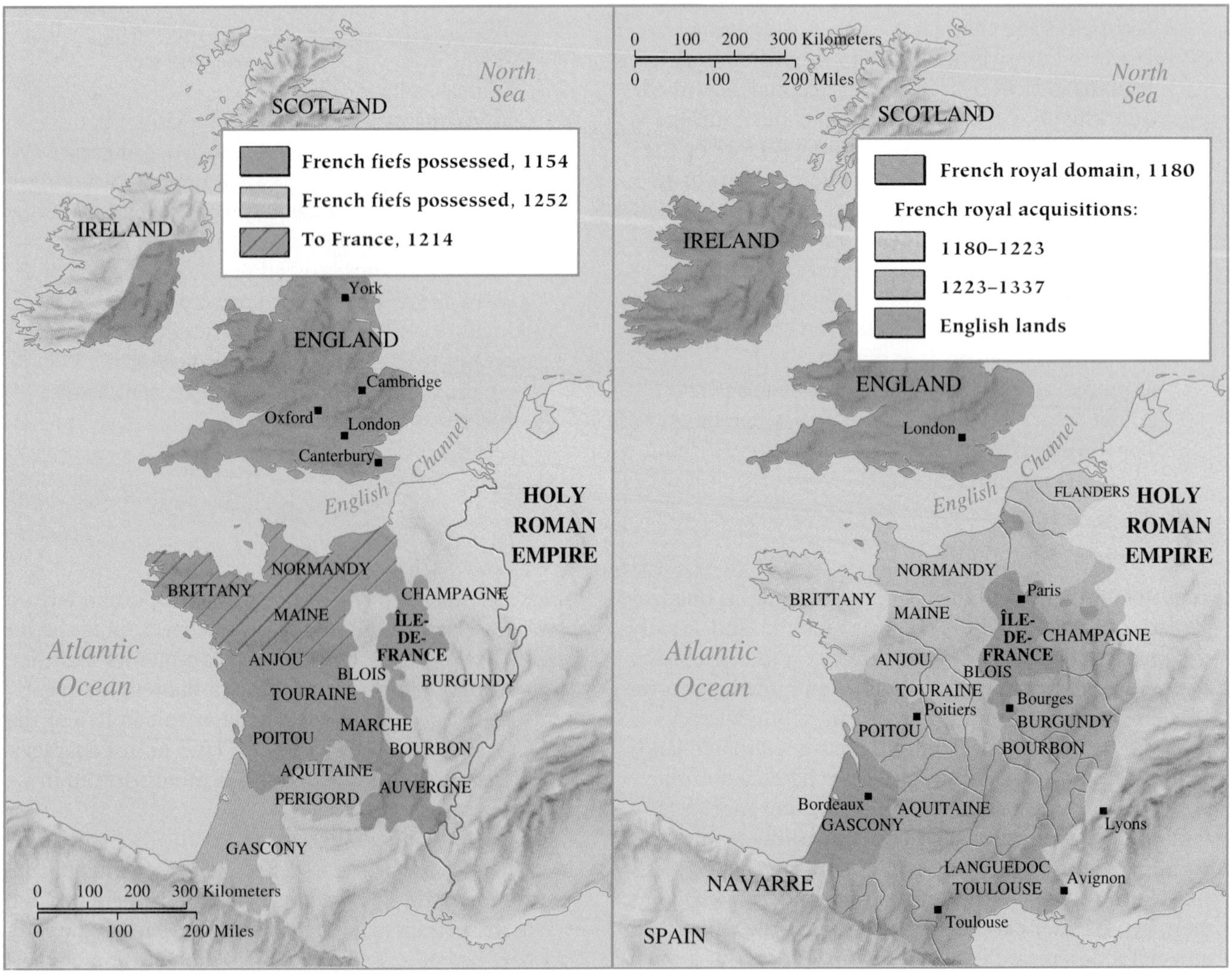

Estates-General, the first French parliament. The Estates-General came to function as an instrument to bolster the king's power because he could ask representatives of the major French social classes to change the laws or grant new taxes. By the end of the thirteenth century, France was the largest, wealthiest, and best-governed monarchical state in Europe.

Christian Reconquest: The Spanish Kingdoms

Much of Spain had been part of the Islamic world since the eighth century. Muslim Spain had flourished in the Early Middle Ages. Córdoba became a major urban center with a population exceeding 300,000 people. Agriculture prospered, and Spain became known for excellent leather, wool, silk, and paper. Beginning in the tenth century, however, the most noticeable feature of Spanish history was the weakening of Muslim power and the beginning of a Christian reconquest that lasted until the final expulsion of the Muslims at the end of the fifteenth century.

By the beginning of the eleventh century, five small Christian kingdoms in northern Spain—Leon, Castile, Navarre, Aragon, and Barcelona—took the offensive against the Muslims. By the end of the twelfth century, the northern half of Spain had been consolidated into the Christian kingdoms of Castile, Navarre, Aragon, and Portugal, which had first emerged as a separate kingdom in 1139 (see Map 10.2). The southern half of Spain remained under the control of the Muslims. But in the thirteenth century, Aragon, Castile, and Portugal made significant conquests of Muslim territory. Castile subdued most of Andalusia in the south, down to the Atlantic and Mediterranean; at the same time, Aragon conquered Valencia. The Muslims remained ensconced only in the kingdom of Granada in the southeast of the Iberian peninsula, which remained an independent Muslim state.

To encourage other settlers to move into the newly conquered regions, Spanish kings issued written privileges that guaranteed rule in accordance with the law for most of the communities in their kingdoms. These privileges, or *fueros,* stipulated the punishments for crimes committed within community boundaries and the means for resolving civil disputes. They also established regulations for acquiring citizenship in the community, rules for service in the community militia, and laws protecting the rights of women and children living in the towns. Kings of the different regions of Spain freely borrowed from the *fueros* of other regions in an effort to develop attractive customs for their towns so that immigrants would be lured into establishing residency there. By the thirteenth century, kings were increasingly required to swear that they would respect these community customs before they were confirmed in office by assemblies of their leading citizens.

The Spanish kingdoms followed no consistent policy in the treatment of the conquered Muslim population. Muslim farmers continued to work the land but were forced to pay very high rents in Aragon. In Castile, King Alfonso X (1252–1284), who called himself the "King of Three Religions," encouraged the continued development of a cosmopolitan culture shared by Christians, Jews, and Muslims.

The Lands of the Holy Roman Empire: Germany and Italy

The Saxon kings of the tenth century had strengthened their hold over the German kingdom and revived the empire of Charlemagne. A new dynasty, known as the Salian kings, began in 1024 with the election of Conrad II (1024–1039) of Franconia (see Map 10.3). Both Conrad and his successors, Henry III (1039–1056) and Henry IV (1056–1106), managed to create a strong German monarchy and a powerful empire by leading armies into Italy.

Map 10.2 Christian Reconquests in the Western Mediterranean. Muslims seized most of Spain in the eighth century, near the end of the period of rapid Islamic expansion. In the eleventh century, small Christian kingdoms in the north began the *Reconquista,* finally conquering the last Moors near the end of the fifteenth century. ■ How can you explain the roughly north-to-south conquest of the Muslim lands in Spain?

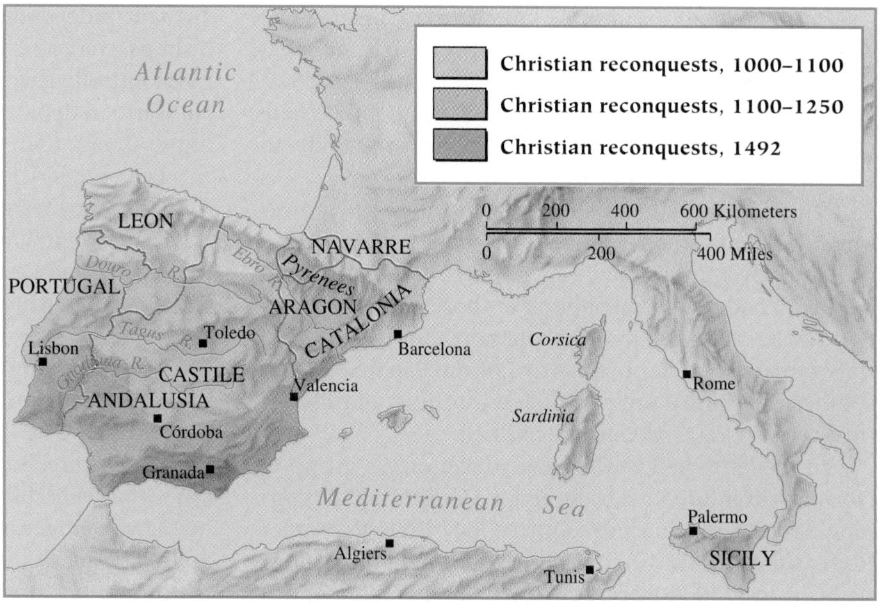

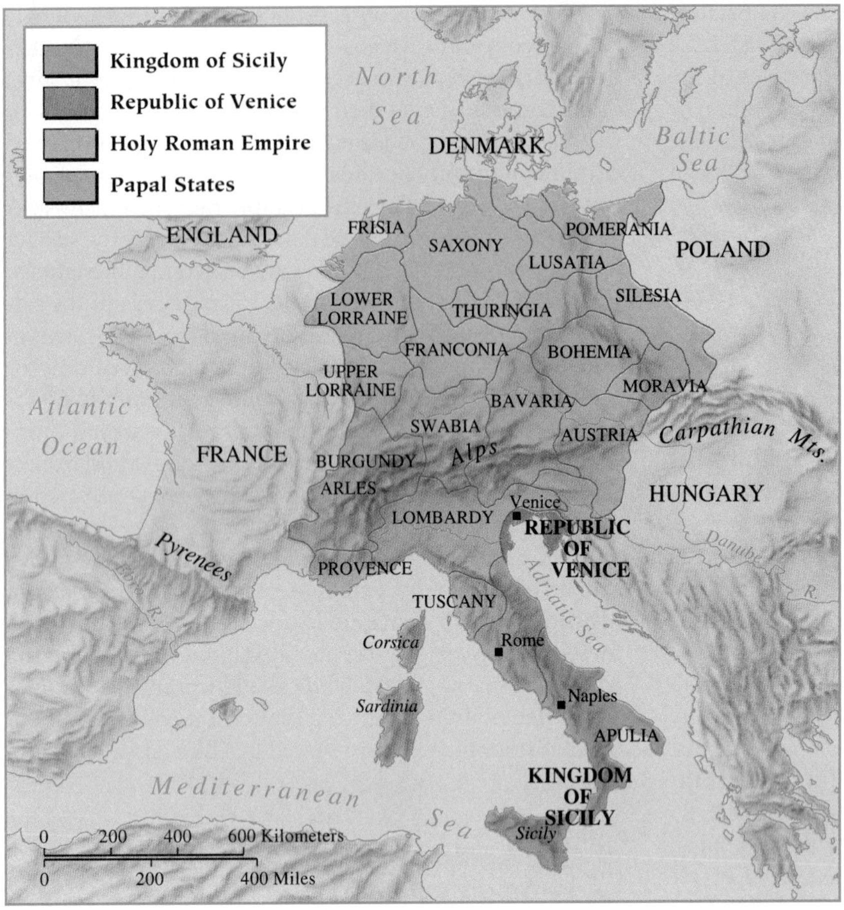

Map 10.3 The Holy Roman Empire in the Twelfth Century. The Hohenstaufen rulers Frederick I and Frederick II sought to expand the Holy Roman Empire to include all of Italy. Frederick II had only fleeting success: after his death, several independent city-states arose in northern Italy, while at home, German nobles had virtually free reign within their domains. ■ Why did the territorial conquests of the Holy Roman Empire cause alarm in the papacy?

The great lords of Germany took advantage of the early death of Henry III and the minority of Henry IV to extend their own power at the expense of the latter. The elective nature of the German monarchy posed a problem for the German kings. Although some dynasties were strong enough for their members to be elected regularly, the great lords who were the electors did at times deliberately choose otherwise. It was to their advantage to select a weak king.

To compensate for their weaknesses, German kings had come to rely on their ability to control the church and select bishops and abbots whom they could then use as royal administrators. But the struggle between church and state during the reign of Henry IV weakened the king's ability to use church officials in this way.

The German kings also tried to bolster their power by using their position as emperors to exploit the resources of Italy. Italy appeared to be a likely area for intervention because it had no central political authority. While important nobles struggled to dominate northern Italy, central Italy remained under the control of the Papal States. In southern Italy, the Lombard dukes, Muslims, and Byzantines seemed to be in constant conflict.

In the latter half of the eleventh century, a group of Norman adventurers led by Robert the Guiscard ("the cunning") conquered much of southern Italy. Robert's brother Roger subdued Muslim Sicily in 1091 after a thirty-year struggle. In 1130, Roger II, the son of Roger of Sicily, was crowned king of Sicily. By the end of the twelfth century, the Norman kingdom was one of the most powerful in Europe as well as one of the most fascinating. A melting pot of Christian, Jewish, and Muslim culture, the state issued its official documents in Latin, Greek, and Arabic.

The Norman kingdom in southern Italy was beyond any claims of the German kings, but the wealthy cities of northern Italy, which by the twelfth century had become virtually independent after overthrowing the rule of their bishops, were a tempting prize to the German kings who never entirely gave up their dreams of a restored empire. No German dynasty proved more susceptible to the allure of this dream than the Hohenstaufens.

Both Frederick I (1152–1190) and Frederick II (1212–1250) tried to create a foundation for a new kind of empire. Frederick I, known as Barbarossa or Redbeard to the Italians, was a powerful lord from the Swabian house of Hohenstaufen when he was elected king. Previous German kings had focused on building a strong German kingdom, to which Italy might be added as an appendage. Frederick I, however planned to get his chief revenues from Italy as the center of a "holy empire," as he called it—the Holy Roman Empire. But his attempt to conquer northern Italy ran into severe difficulties. The pope opposed him, fearful that the emperor wanted to include Rome and the Papal States as part of his empire. The cities of northern Italy, which had become used to their freedom, were also not

The Deeds of Emperor Frederick II

Frederick II, king of Germany and Sicily and would-be ruler of all Italy, was viewed even by contemporaries as one of the most unusual rulers of his time. This account of his "idiosyncrasies" is by Salimbene de Adam, a Franciscan friar whose *Chronicle* is one of the richest sources of information about medieval life in thirteenth-century Italy. He was, however, also known to be notoriously biased against Frederick II.

Salimbene de Adam, Chronicle

Note that Frederick almost always enjoyed having discord with the Church and fighting her on all sides, although she had nourished him, defended him, and raised him up. He held the true faith to be worthless. He was a cunning, crafty man, avaricious, lecherous, and malicious, easily given to wrath.

At times, however, Frederick was a worthy man, and when he wished to show his good, courtly side, he could be witty, charming, urbane, and industrious. He was adept at writing and singing, and was well-versed in the art of writing lyrics and songs. He was a handsome, well-formed man of medium height. I myself saw him and, at one time, loved him. For he once wrote Brother Elias, Minister General of the Friars Minor, on my behalf asking him to return me to my father. He also could speak many and various languages. In short, if he had been a good Catholic and had loved God, the Church, and his own soul, he would scarcely have had an equal as an emperor in the world. . . .

Now, it is necessary to speak of Frederick's idiosyncrasies.

His first idiosyncrasy is that he had the thumb of a certain notary cut off because he had written his name in a way different from the way the Emperor desired. . . .

His second idiosyncrasy was that he wanted to discover what language a child would use when he grew up if he had never heard anyone speak. Therefore, he placed some infants in the care of wet-nurses, commanding them to bathe and suckle the children, but by no means ever to speak to or fondle them. For he wanted to discover whether they would speak Hebrew, the first language, or Greek, Latin, Arabic, or the language of their parents. But he labored in vain, because all of the infants died. . . .

Furthermore, Frederick had many other idiosyncrasies: idle curiosity, lack of faith, perversity, tyranny, and accursedness, some of which I have written about in another chronicle. Once, for example, he sealed up a live man in a cask and kept him there until he died in order to prove that the soul totally perished with the body. . . . For Frederick was an Epicurean, and so he and the learned men of his court searched out whatever Biblical passage they could find to prove that there is no life after death. . . .

This sixth example of Frederick's idiosyncrasy and idle curiosity . . . was that he fed two men a fine meal, and he sent one to bed to sleep, the other out hunting. And that evening he had both men disemboweled in his presence, in order to determine which one had digested his food the best. The decisions by his doctors went to the man who had slept after the meal. . . .

I have heard and known many other idiosyncrasies of Frederick, but I keep quiet for the sake of brevity, and because reporting so many of the Emperor's foolish notions is tedious to me.

willing to be Frederick's subjects. An alliance of these northern Italian cities, with the support of the papacy, defeated the forces of the Emperor Frederick at Legnano in 1176.

Later Frederick returned to Italy and arranged a settlement with the northern Italian cities by which they retained their independence in return for an annual payment to the emperor. Frederick now had the financial base he had sought. Moreover, by marrying his son (who became Henry VI, 1190–1197) to the heiress of the Norman kingdom of southern Italy, Frederick seemed to be creating the foundation for making the Holy Roman Empire a reality and for realizing the pope's nightmare: the encirclement of Rome and the Papal States. After Frederick's death, Henry VI's control of Germany and both northern and southern Italy made him the strongest European ruler since Charlemagne. Henry's empire soon collapsed however, for he died prematurely, leaving as his heir a son only two years old.

The son, Frederick II, grew up to become the most brilliant of the Hohenstaufen rulers. King of Sicily in 1198, king of Germany in 1212, and crowned emperor in 1220, Frederick II was a truly remarkable man who awed his contemporaries (see the box above). Frederick was raised in Sicily, with its diverse peoples, languages, and religions. His court there brought together a brilliant array of lawyers, poets, artists, and scientists, and he himself took a deep interest in their work.

Until 1220, Frederick spent much time in Germany; once he left in 1220, he rarely returned. He gave the German princes full control of their territories, voluntarily surrendering any real power over Germany in exchange for revenues while he pursued his main goal, the establishment of a strong centralized state in Italy dominated by his kingdom in Sicily. Frederick's major task was to gain control of northern Italy. In reaching to extend his power in Italy, he became involved in a deadly struggle with the popes, who realized that a single ruler of northern and southern Italy meant the end of papal secular power in central Italy. The northern Italian cities were also unwilling to give up their freedom. Frederick waged a bitter struggle in northern Italy, winning many battles but ultimately losing the war.

The Coronation of Frederick II. Shown here is the coronation of Frederick II of Germany as Holy Roman Emperor by Pope Honorius II in Rome on November 22, 1220. The pope agreed to do so after Frederick promised to lead a Crusade to the Holy Land, a promise that he took years to fulfill. This scene is taken from a fifteenth-century French manuscript on the monarchs of Europe.

Frederick's preoccupation with the creation of an empire in Italy left Germany in confusion and chaos until 1273, when the major German princes, serving as electors, chose an insignificant German noble, Rudolf of Habsburg, as the new German king. In choosing a weak king, the princes were ensuring that the German monarchy would remain impotent and incapable of reestablishing a centralized monarchical state. The failure of the Hohenstaufens had led to a situation where his exalted majesty, the German king and Holy Roman Emperor, had no real power over either Germany or Italy. Unlike France and England, neither Germany nor Italy created a unified national monarchy in the Middle Ages. Both became geographical designations for loose confederations of hundreds of petty independent states under the vague direction of king or emperor. In fact, neither Germany nor Italy would become united until the nineteenth century.

Following the death of Frederick II, Italy fell into considerable political confusion. While the papacy remained in control of much of central Italy, the defeat of imperial power left the cities and towns of northern Italy independent of any other authority. Gradually, the larger ones began to emerge as strong city-states. Florence assumed the leadership of Tuscany, while Milan, under the guidance of the Visconti family, took control of the Lombard region. With its great commercial wealth, the republic of Venice dominated the northeastern part of the peninsula.

New Kingdoms in Northern and Eastern Europe

The Scandinavian countries of northern Europe had little political organization before 1000, and it was not until the second half of the tenth century and the first half of the eleventh that the three Scandinavian kingdoms—Denmark, Norway, and Sweden (see Map 10.4)—emerged with a noticeable political structure. At the same time, the three kingdoms were converted to Christianity by kings who believed that an organized church was a necessary accompaniment to an organized state. The adoption of Christianity, however, did not eliminate the warlike tendencies of the Scandinavians. Not only did the three kingdoms fight each other in the eleventh and twelfth centuries, but rival families were in regular conflict over the throne in each state. This period also witnessed the growth of a powerful noble landowning class.

To the south, in eastern Europe, Hungary, which had been a Christian state since 1000, remained relatively stable throughout the High Middle Ages, but the history of Poland and Russia was far more turbulent. In the thirteenth century, eastern Europe was beset by two groups of invaders, the Teutonic Knights from the west and the Mongols from the east.

In the eleventh century, a Polish kingdom existed as a separate state but with no natural frontiers. Consequently, German settlers encroached on its territory on a regular basis, leading to considerable intermarriage between Slavs and Germans. During the thirteenth century, relations between the Germans and the Slavs of eastern Europe worsened due to the aggression of the Teutonic Knights. The Teutonic Knights had been founded near the end of the twelfth century to protect the Christian Holy Land. In the early thirteenth century, however, these Christian knights found greater opportunity to the east of Germany, where they attacked the pagan Slavs. East Prussia was given to the military order in 1226, and five years later, the knights moved beyond the Vistula River, where they waged war against the Slavs for another thirty years. By the end of the thirteenth century, Prussia had become German and Christian as the pagan Slavs were forced to convert.

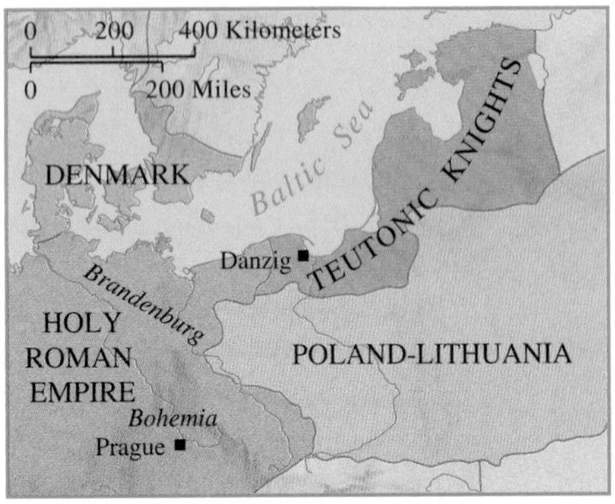

Settlements of the Teutonic Knights

Central and eastern Europe had periodically been subject to invasions from fierce Asiatic nomads, such as the

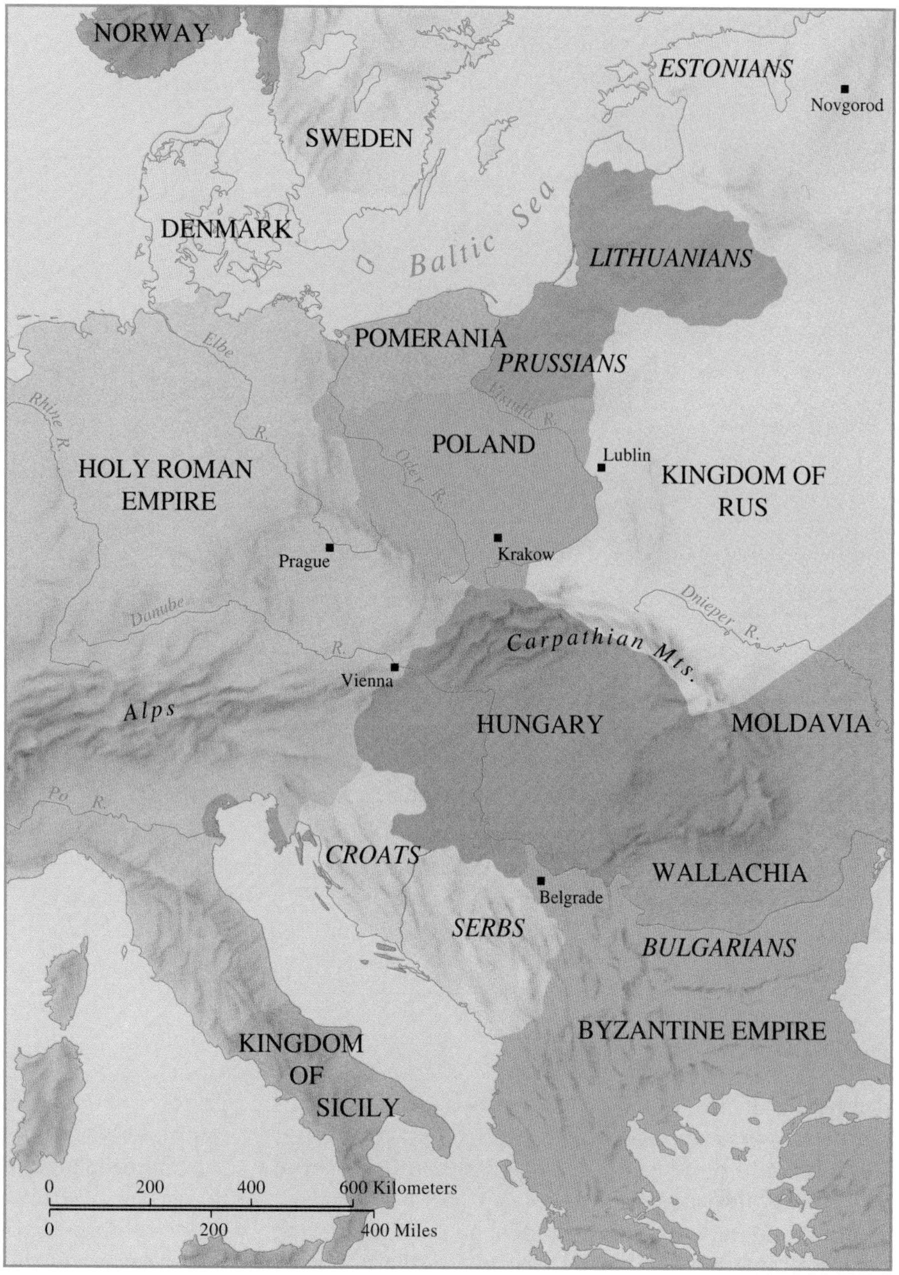

Map 10.4 Northern and Eastern Europe. Acceptance of Christianity gave many northern and eastern European kingdoms greater control over their subjects. Warfare was common in the region: dynastic struggles occurred in Scandinavia, and the Teutonic Knights, based in East Prussia, attacked pagan Slavs. ■ Which areas of northern and eastern Europe had large Slavic populations? (Look back at Map 8.4 for help.)

Huns, Avars, Bulgars, and Magyars. In the thirteenth century, the Mongols exploded upon the scene, causing far more disruption than earlier invaders.

The Mongol Empire

The Mongols rose to power in Asia with stunning speed. They were a pastoral people in the region of modern-day Outer Mongolia organized loosely into clans and tribes, often warring with each other. This changed when one leader, Temuchin, unified the Mongol tribes and gained the title of Genghis Khan (c. 1162–1227), which means "universal ruler." From that time on, Genghis Khan created a powerful military force and devoted himself to fighting. "Man's highest joy," Genghis Khan remarked, "is in victory: to conquer one's enemies, to pursue them, to deprive them of their possessions, to make their beloved weep, to ride on their horses, and to embrace their wives and daughters."[1] Genghis Khan was succeeded by equally competent sons and grandsons.

The Mongols burst upon the scene in the thirteenth century. They advanced eastward, eventually conquering China and Korea. One of Genghis Khan's grandsons, Khubilai Khan, completed the conquest of China and established a new Chinese dynasty of rulers known as the Yuan. In 1279, Khubilai Khan moved the capital of China northward to Khanbaliq (the city of the khan), which later would be known by the Chinese name Beijing.

The Mongols also moved westward against the Islamic empire. Persia fell by 1233, and by 1258, they had conquered Baghdad and destroyed the Abbasid caliphate.

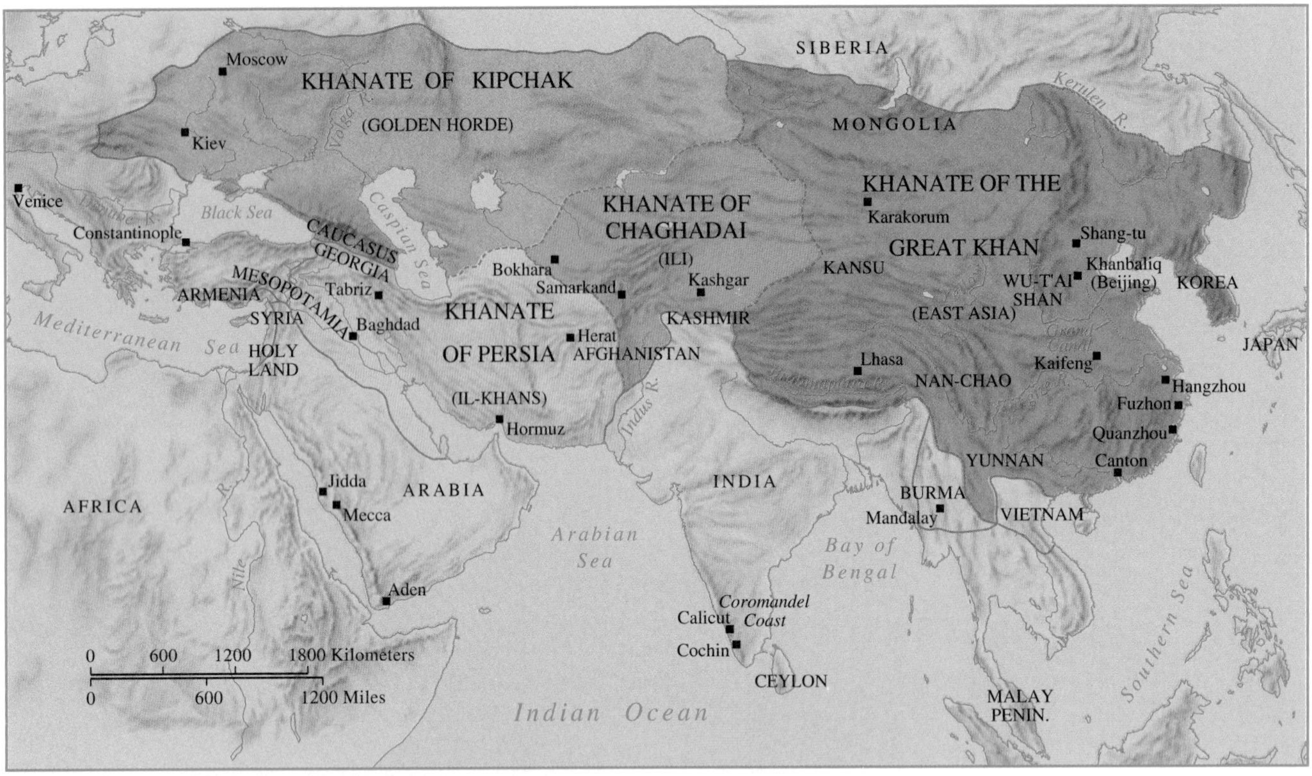

Map 10.5 The Mongol Empire. Beginning with the exploits of Genghis Khan, the Mongols used unorthodox but effective military tactics to establish an empire that stretched from Russia to China and included India and South Asia. The empire was divided into khanates. The Golden Horde, the khanate in Russia, was eventually overwhelmed by Moscow princes who went on to establish the Russian state. ■ Why would it be difficult for one khan to effectively rule the entire Mongol Empire?

Beginning in the 1230s, the Mongols had moved into Europe. They conquered Russia, advanced into Poland and Hungary, and destroyed a force of Poles and Teutonic Knights in Silesia in 1241 (see Map 10.5). Europe then seemingly got lucky when the Mongol hordes turned back because of internal fighting; western and southern Europe escaped the wrath of the Mongols. Over the long run, the Mongols left little of any real importance in Europe, although their occupation of Russia had some residual effects on that land.

The Development of Russia

The Kievan Rus state, which had become formally Christian in 987, prospered considerably afterward, reaching its high point in the first half of the eleventh century. Kievan society was dominated by a noble class of landowners known as the boyars. Kievan merchants maintained regular trade with Scandinavia to the northwest and the Islamic and Byzantine worlds to the south. But destructive civil wars and new invasions by Asiatic nomads caused the principality of Kiev to disintegrate into a number of constituent parts. The sack of Kiev by North Russian princes in 1169 brought an inglorious end to the first Russian state.

The fundamental civilizing and unifying force of early Russia was the Christian church. The Russian church imitated the liturgy and organization of the Byzantine Empire, whose Eastern Orthodox priests had converted the Kievan Rus to Christianity at the end of the tenth century. The Russian church became known for its rigid religious orthodoxy. Although Christianity provided a common bond between Russian and European civilization, Russia's religious development guaranteed an even closer affinity between Russian and Byzantine civilization.

In the thirteenth century, the Mongols conquered Russia and cut it off even more from western Europe. The Mongols were not numerous enough to settle the vast Russian lands but were content to rule directly an area along the lower Volga and north of the Caspian and Black Seas to Kiev and rule indirectly elsewhere. In the latter territories, Russian princes were required to pay tribute to the Mongol overlords.

One Russian prince soon emerged as more visible and powerful than the others. Alexander Nevsky (c. 1220–1263), prince of Novgorod, defeated a German invading army

CHRONOLOGY

The Growth of the European Kingdoms

England	
King Canute	1016–1035
Battle of Hastings	1066
William the Conqueror	1066–1087
Henry II, first of the Plantagenet dynasty	1154–1189
Murder of Thomas à Becket	1170
John	1199–1216
Magna Carta	1215
Edward I	1272–1307
The "greater Parliaments"	1295, 1297
France	
Philip II Augustus	1180–1223
Louis IX	1226–1270
Philip IV	1285–1314
First Estates-General	1302
Spain	
Establishment of Portugal	1139
Alfonso X of Castile	1252–1284
Germany, the Empire, and Italy	
Conrad II, first of the Salian dynasty	1024–1039
Henry III	1039–1056
Henry IV	1056–1106
Frederick I Barbarossa	1152–1190
Lombard League defeats Frederick at Legnano	1176
Henry VI	1190–1197
Frederick II	1212–1250
Election of Rudolf of Habsburg as king of Germany	1273
Eastern Europe	
East Prussia given to the Teutonic Knights	1226
Genghis Khan and the rise of the Mongols	c. 1162–1227
Mongol conquest of Russia	1230s
Alexander Nevsky, prince of Novgorod	c. 1220–1263
Defeat of the Germans	1242

at Lake Peipus in northwestern Russia in 1242. His cooperation with the Mongols, which included denouncing his own brother and crushing native tax revolts, won him their favor. The khan, the acknowledged leader of the western part of the Mongol Empire, rewarded Alexander Nevsky with the title of grand-prince, enabling his descendants to become the princes of Moscow and eventually leaders of all Russia.

The Recovery and Reform of the Catholic Church

In the Early Middle Ages, the Catholic church had played a leading role in converting and civilizing first the Germanic invaders and later the Vikings and Magyars. Although highly successful, this had not been accomplished without challenges that undermined the spiritual life of the church itself.

The Problems of Decline

Since the fifth century, the popes of the Catholic church had reigned supreme over the affairs of the church. They had also come to exercise control over the territories in central Italy that came to be known as the Papal States; this kept popes involved in political matters, often at the expense of their spiritual obligations. At the same time, the church became increasingly entangled in the evolving lord-vassal relationships. High officials of the church, such as bishops and abbots, came to hold their offices as fiefs from nobles. As vassals, they were obliged to carry out the usual duties, including military service. Of course, lords assumed the right to choose their vassals, even when those vassals included bishops and abbots. Because lords often selected their vassals from other noble families for political reasons, these bishops and abbots were often worldly figures who cared little about their spiritual responsibilities.

The monastic ideal had also suffered during the Early Middle Ages. Benedictine monasteries had sometimes been exemplary centers of Christian living and learning, but the invasions of Vikings, Magyars, and Muslims wreaked havoc with many monastic establishments. Discipline declined, and with it the monastic reputation for learning and holiness. At the same time, a growing number of monasteries fell under the control of local lords, as did much of the church. A number of people believed that the time for reform had come.

The Cluniac Reform Movement

Reform of the Catholic church began in Burgundy in eastern France in 910 when Duke William of Aquitaine founded the abbey of Cluny. The monastery began with a renewed dedication to the highest spiritual ideals of the Benedictine rules and was fortunate in having a series of abbots in the tenth century who maintained these ideals. Cluny was deliberately kept independent from any local control. As Duke William stipulated in his original charter: "It has pleased us also to insert in this document that, from this day, those same monks there congregated shall be subject neither to our yoke, nor to that of our relatives, nor to the sway of the royal might, nor to that of any earthly power."[2] The new monastery at Cluny tried to eliminate some of the abuses that had crept into religious communities by stressing the need for work, replacing manual labor with the copying of manuscripts, and demanding more community worship and less private prayer.

The Cluniac reform movement sparked an enthusiastic response, first in France and eventually in all of western and central Europe. Hundreds of new monasteries were founded based on Cluniac ideals, and previously existing monasteries rededicated themselves by adopting the Cluniac program. The movement also began to reach beyond monasticism and into the papacy itself, which was in dire need of help.

The Reform of the Papacy

By the eleventh century, a movement for change, led by a series of reforming popes, was sweeping through the Catholic church. One of the reformers' primary goals was to free the church from the interference of lords in the election of church officials. This issue was dramatically taken up by the greatest of the reform popes of the eleventh century, Gregory VII (1073–1085).

Elected pope in 1073, Gregory was absolutely certain that he had been chosen by God to reform the church. In pursuit of those aims, Gregory claimed that he—the pope—was truly God's "vicar on Earth," and that the pope's authority extended over all of Christendom and included the right to depose emperors if they disobeyed his wishes. Gregory sought nothing less than the elimination of lay investiture (both lay interference in elections and lay participation in the installation of prelates). Only in this way could the church regain its freedom, by which Gregory meant the right of the church to elect prelates and to run its own affairs. If rulers did not accept these "divine" commands, then they could be deposed by the pope acting in his capacity as the vicar of Christ (see the box on p. 257). Gregory VII soon found himself in conflict with the king of Germany over these claims. (The king of Germany was also the emperor-designate since it had been accepted by this time that only kings of Germany could be emperors, but they did not officially use the title "emperor" until they were crowned by the pope.)

King Henry IV (1056–1106) of Germany was just as determined as the pope. For many years, German kings had appointed high-ranking clerics, especially bishops, as their vassals in order to use them as administrators. Without them, the king could not hope to maintain his own power vis-à-vis the powerful German nobles. In 1075, Pope Gregory issued a decree forbidding important clerics from receiving investiture from lay leaders: "We decree that no one of the clergy shall receive the investiture with a bishopric or abbey or church from the hand of an emperor or king or of any lay person."[3] Henry had no intention of obeying a decree that challenged the very heart of his administration.

The immediate cause of the so-called Investiture Controversy was a disputed election to the bishopric of Milan in northern Italy, an important position because the bishop was also the ruler of the city. Control of the bishopric was crucial if the king wished to reestablish German power in northern Italy. Since Milan was considered second only to Rome in importance as a bishopric, papal interest in the office was also keen. Pope Gregory VII and King Henry IV backed competing candidates for the position.

To gain acceptance of his candidate, the pope threatened the king with excommunication. Excommunication is a censure by which a person is deprived of receiving the sacraments of the church. To counter this threat, the king called a synod or assembly of German bishops, all of whom he had appointed, and had them depose the pope.

Pope Gregory VII responded by excommunicating the king and freeing his subjects from their allegiance to him. The latter was a clever move. The German nobles were only too eager to diminish the power of a centralized monarchy because of the threat it posed to their own power, and they welcomed this opportunity to rebel against the king. Both the nobles and the bishops of Germany agreed to hold a meeting in Germany with the pope to solve the problem, possibly by choosing a new king. Gregory set out for Germany. Henry, realizing the threat to his power, forestalled the pope by traveling to northern Italy, where he met the pope at Canossa, a castle belonging to Countess Matilda of Tuscany, an avid supporter of the papal reform program. There, in January 1077, the king admitted his transgressions and begged for forgiveness and absolution. Although he made the king wait three days, the pope was constrained by his priestly responsibility to grant absolution to a penitent sinner and lifted the ban of excommunication. This did not end the problem, however. Within three years, pope and king were again locked in combat.

The struggle continued until 1122, when a new German king and a new pope achieved a compromise called the Concordat of Worms. Under this agreement, a bishop in Germany was first elected by church officials. After election, the nominee paid homage to the king as his secular lord, who in turn invested him with the symbols of temporal office. A representative of the pope, however, then invested the new bishop with the symbols of his spiritual office.

This struggle between church and state was an important element in the history of Europe in the High Middle Ages. In the Early Middle Ages, popes had been dependent on emperors and had allowed them to exercise considerable authority over church affairs. But a set of new ideals championed by activist reformers in the eleventh century now supported the "freedom of the church," which meant not only the freedom of the church to control its own affairs but also extreme claims of papal authority. Not only was the pope superior to all other bishops, but popes now claimed the right to depose kings under certain circumstances. Such papal claims ensured further church-state confrontations.

The "Gregorian Revolution": Papal Claims

In the eleventh century, a dynamic group of reformers pushed for the "freedom of the church." This came to mean not only papal control over the affairs of the church but also the elimination of lay investiture. The reformers saw the latter as the chief issue at the heart of lay control of the church. In trying to eliminate it, the reforming popes, especially Gregory VII, extended papal claims to include the right to oversee the secular authorities and, in particular, to depose rulers under certain circumstances. The following selection is from a document that was entered in the papal register in 1075. It consisted of twenty-seven assertions that probably served as headings, or a table of contents, for a collection of ecclesiastical writings that supported the pope's claims.

The Dictates of the Pope

1. That the Roman church was founded by God alone.
2. That the Roman pontiff alone can with right be called universal.
3. That he alone can depose or reinstate bishops.
4. That, in a council, his legate, even if a lower grade, is above all bishops, and can pass sentence of deposition against them.
5. That the pope may depose the absent.
6. That, among other things, we ought not to remain in the same house with those excommunicated by him. . . .
8. That he alone may use the imperial insignia.
9. That of the pope alone all princes shall kiss the feet.
10. That his name alone shall be spoken in the churches.
11. That this is the only name in the world.
12. That it may be permitted to him to depose emperors.
13. That he may be permitted to transfer bishops if need be. . . .
17. That no chapter and no book shall be considered canonical without his authority.
18. That a sentence passed by him may be retracted by no one; and that he himself, alone of all, may retract it.
19. That he himself may be judged by no one.
20. That no one shall dare to condemn one who appeals to the apostolic chair.
21. That to the latter should be referred the more important cases of every church.
22. That the Roman church has never erred; nor will it err to all eternity, the Scripture bearing witness.
23. That the Roman pontiff, if he have been canonically ordained, is undoubtedly made a saint by the merits of St. Peter. . . .
25. That he may depose and reinstate bishops without assembling a synod.
26. That he who is not at peace with the Roman church shall not be considered catholic.
27. That he may absolve subjects from their fealty to wicked men.

Christianity and Medieval Civilization

Christianity was an integral part of the fabric of medieval European society and the consciousness of Europe. Papal directives affected the actions of kings and princes alike, while Christian teaching and practices touched the economic, social, intellectual, cultural, and daily lives of all Europeans.

Growth of the Papal Monarchy

The popes of the twelfth century did not abandon the reform ideals of Gregory VII, but they were less dogmatic and more inclined to consolidate their power and build a strong administrative system. By the twelfth century, the Catholic church possessed a clearly organized, hierarchical structure. The pope and papal curia were at the apex of the administrative structure. The curia was staffed by high church officials known as cardinals, who served as major advisers and administrators to the popes; at the pope's death, the college of cardinals, as they were collectively called, elected the new pope. Below the pope and cardinals were the archbishops, each of whom controlled a large region called an archdiocese. Each archdiocese was divided into smaller units called dioceses, each headed by a bishop. Each diocese was divided into parishes, each headed by a priest. Theoretically, the bishop chose all priests in his diocese, administered his diocese, and was responsible only to the pope.

In the thirteenth century, the Catholic church reached the height of its political, intellectual, and secular power. The papal monarchy extended its sway over both ecclesiastical and temporal affairs, as was especially evident during the papacy of Pope Innocent III (1198–1216). At the beginning of his pontificate, in a letter to a priest, Innocent made a clear statement of his views on papal supremacy:

> As God, the creator of the universe, set two great lights in the firmament of heaven, the greater light to rule the day, and the lesser light to rule the night, so He set two great dignities in the

firmament of the universal church, . . . the greater to rule the day, that is, souls, and the lesser to rule the night, that is, bodies. These dignities are the papal authority and the royal power. And just as the moon gets her light from the sun, and is inferior to the sun . . . so the royal power gets the splendor of its dignity from the papal authority.[4]

Innocent's actions were those of a man who believed that he, the pope, was the supreme judge of European affairs. He forced King Philip II Augustus of France to take back his wife and queen after Philip had coerced a group of French prelates into annulling his marriage. The pope intervened in German affairs and established his candidate as emperor. He compelled King John of England to accept the papal choice for the position of archbishop of Canterbury. To achieve his political ends, Innocent did not hesitate to use the spiritual weapons at his command, especially the interdict. An interdict was imposed on a region or country rather than a person; it forbade priests there to dispense the sacraments of the church in the hope that the people, deprived of the comforts of religion, would exert pressure against their ruler. Pope Innocent's interdict was so effective that it caused King Philip Augustus to restore his wife to her rightful place as queen of France.

Pope Innocent III. Innocent III was an active and powerful pope during the High Middle Ages. He approved the creation of the Franciscan and Dominican religious orders and inaugurated the Fourth Crusade. He is shown here with the papal bull he issued to establish the monastery of Sacro Speco in Subiaco, Italy.

New Religious Orders and Spiritual Ideals

In the second half of the eleventh century and the first half of the twelfth, a wave of religious enthusiasm seized Europe, leading to a spectacular growth in the number of monasteries and the emergence of new monastic orders. Most important was the Cistercian order, founded in 1098 by a group of monks dissatisfied with the lack of strict discipline at their Benedictine monastery. Cistercian monasticism spread rapidly from southern France into the rest of Europe.

The Cistercians were strict. They ate a simple diet and possessed only a single robe apiece. All decorations were eliminated from their churches and monastic buildings. More time for prayer and manual labor was provided by shortening the number of hours spent at religious services. The Cistercians played a major role in developing a new activist spiritual model for twelfth-century Europe. A Benedictine monk often spent hours in prayer to honor God. The Cistercian ideal had a different emphasis: "Arise, soldier of Christ, arise! Get up off the ground and return to the battle from which you have fled! Fight more boldly after your flight, and triumph in glory!"[5] These were the words of Saint Bernard of Clairvaux (1090–1153), who more than any other person embodied the new spiritual ideal of Cistercian monasticism (see the box on p. 260).

Women were also active participants in the spiritual movements of the age. The number of women joining religious houses increased perceptibly with the spread of the new orders of the twelfth century. In the High Middle Ages, most nuns were from the ranks of the landed aristocracy. Convents were convenient for families unable or unwilling to find husbands for their daughters and for aristocratic women who did not wish to marry. Female intellectuals found them a haven for their activities. Most of the learned women of the Middle Ages, especially in Germany, were nuns. One of the most distinguished was Hildegard of Bingen (1098–1179), who became abbess of a convent at Disibodenberg in western Germany.

Hildegard shared in the religious enthusiasm of the twelfth century. Soon after becoming abbess, she began to write an account of the mystical visions she had experienced for years. "A great flash of light from heaven pierced my brain and . . . in that instant my mind was imbued with the meaning of the sacred books," she wrote in a description typical of the world's mystical literature. Eventually she produced three books based on her visions. Hildegard gained considerable renown as a mystic and prophet, and popes, emperors, kings, dukes, and bishops eagerly sought her advice.

LIVING THE GOSPEL LIFE

In the early thirteenth century, two religious leaders, Saint Francis and Saint Dominic, founded two new religious orders whose members did not remain in the cloister like the monks of the contemplative orders, such as the Benedictines and Cistercians, but rather went out into the secular arena of the towns to preach the word of God. By their example, the new orders, known as mendicant ("begging") orders for their deliberate poverty, strove to provide a more personal religious experience for ordinary people.

Saint Bernard. One of the most important religious figures of the twelfth century was Saint Bernard of Clairvaux, who advocated a militant expression of Christian ideas while favoring a more personalized understanding of the relationship between humans and God. Here Saint Bernard is shown preaching a sermon to his fellow Cistercians.

Giraudon/Art Resource, NY

A Group of Nuns. Although still viewed by the medieval church as inferior to men, women were as susceptible to the spiritual fervor of the twelfth century as men, and female monasticism grew accordingly. This miniature shows a group of Flemish nuns listening to the preaching of an abbot, Gilles li Muisis. The nun at the far left wearing a white robe is a novice.

A Miracle of Saint Bernard

Saint Bernard of Clairvaux has been called the most widely respected holy man of the twelfth century. He was an outstanding preacher, wholly dedicated to the service of God. His reputation reportedly influenced many young men to join the Cistercian order. He also inspired a myriad of stories dealing with his miracles.

A Miracle of Saint Bernard

A certain monk, departing from his monastery. . . . threw off his habit, and returned to the world at the persuasion of the Devil. And he took a certain parish living; for he was a priest. Because sin is punished with sin, the deserter from his Order lapsed into the vice of lechery. He took a concubine to live with him, as in fact is done by many, and by her he had children.

But as God is merciful and does not wish anyone to perish, it happened that many years after, the blessed abbot [Saint Bernard] was passing through the village in which the same monk was living, and went to stay at his house. The renegade monk recognized him, and received him very reverently, and waited on him devoutly . . . but as yet the abbot did not recognize him.

On the morrow, the holy man said Matins and prepared to be off. But as he could not speak to the priest, since he had got up and gone to the church for Matins, he said to the priest's son "Go, give this message to your master." Now the boy had been born dumb. He obeyed the command and feeling in himself the power of him who had given it, he ran to his father and uttered the words of the Holy Father clearly and exactly. His father, on hearing his son's voice for the first time, wept for joy, and made him repeat the same words . . . and he asked what the abbot had done to him. "He did nothing to me," said the boy, "except to say 'Go and say this to your father.' "

At so evident a miracle the priest repented, and hastened after the holy man and fell at his feet saying "My Lord and Father, I was your monk so-and-so, and at such-and-such a time I ran away from your monastery. I ask your Paternity to allow me to return with you to the monastery, for in your coming God has visited my heart." The saint replied unto him, "Wait for me here, and I will come back quickly when I have done my business, and I will take you with me." But the priest, fearing death (which he had not done before), answered, "Lord, I am afraid of dying before then." But the saint replied, "Know this for certain, that if you die in this condition, and in this resolve, you will find yourself a monk before God."

The saint [eventually] returned and heard that the priest had recently died and been buried. He ordered the tomb to be opened. And when they asked him what he wanted to do, he said, "I want to see if he is lying as a monk or a clerk in his tomb." "As a clerk," they said; "we buried him in his secular habit." But when they had dug up the earth, they found that he was not in the clothes in which they had buried him; but he appeared in all points, tonsure and habit, as a monk. And they all praised God.

Saint Francis of Assisi (1182–1226) was born to a wealthy Italian merchant family, but as a young man he abandoned all worldly goods and began to live and preach in poverty after a series of dramatic spiritual experiences. His simplicity, joyful nature, and love for others soon attracted a band of followers, all of whom took vows of absolute poverty, agreeing to reject all property and live by working and begging for their food. Francis drew up a simple rule for his followers that consisted merely of biblical precepts focusing on the need to preach and the importance of poverty. He sought approval for his new rule from Pope Innocent III, who confirmed the new order as the Order of Friars Minor, more commonly known as the Franciscans. The Franciscans struck a responsive chord among many Europeans and became very popular. The Franciscans lived among the people, preaching repentance and aiding the poor. Their calls for a return to the simplicity and poverty of the early church, reinforced by their own example, were especially effective. The Franciscans had a female branch as well, known as the Poor Clares, which was founded by Saint Clare, an aristocratic lady of Assisi who was a great admirer of Francis.

The second new religious order of the early thirteenth century arose out of the desire to defend orthodox church teachings from heresy (see "Voices of Protest and Intolerance" later in this chapter). The Order of Preachers, popularly known as the Dominicans, was created through the efforts of a Spanish priest, Dominic de Guzmán (1170–1221). Unlike Francis, Dominic was an intellectual who was particularly appalled by the recent growth of heretical movements. He came to believe that a new religious order of men who lived lives of poverty but were learned and capable of preaching effectively would best be able to attack heresy. With the approval of Pope Innocent III, the Dominicans became an order of mendicant friars in 1215.

In addition to the friars, the thirteenth century witnessed the development of yet another kind of religious order. Known as Beguines, these were communities of women dwelling together in poverty. Devout and dedicated to prayer, they begged for their daily support or worked as laundresses in hospitals or at other menial tasks. They did not take religious vows and were free to leave the community at will. Although the Beguines originated in the

Low Countries, they eventually became quite strong in the Rhineland area of Germany as well.

Popular Religion in the High Middle Ages

We have witnessed the actions of popes, bishops, and monks. But what of ordinary clergy and laypeople? What were their religious hopes and fears? What were their spiritual aspirations?

The sacraments of the Catholic church ensured that the church was an integral part of people's lives, from birth to death. There were (and still are) seven sacraments, administered only by the clergy. Sacraments, such as baptism and the Eucharist (the Lord's Supper), were viewed as outward symbols of an inward grace (grace was God's freely given gift that enabled humans to be saved) and were considered imperative for a Christian's salvation. Therefore, the clergy were seen to have a key role in the attainment of salvation.

Other church practices were also important to ordinary people. Saints, it was believed, were men and women who, through their holiness, had achieved a special position in heaven, enabling them to act as intercessors before God. The saints' ability to protect poor souls enabled them to take on great importance at the popular level. Jesus' apostles were, of course, recognized throughout Europe as saints, but there were also numerous local saints that were of special significance to the area. New cults rapidly developed, particularly in the intense religious atmosphere of the eleventh and twelfth centuries. The English introduced Saint Nicholas, the patron saint of children, who remains instantly recognizable today through his identification with Santa Claus.

Of all the saints, the Virgin Mary, the mother of Jesus, occupied the foremost position in the High Middle Ages. Mary was viewed as the most important mediator with her son Jesus, the judge of all sinners. Moreover, from the eleventh century on, a fascination with Mary as Jesus' human mother became more evident. A sign of Mary's importance was the growing number of churches all over Europe that were dedicated to her in the twelfth and thirteenth centuries, including the cathedral of Notre-Dame in Paris.

Emphasis on the role of the saints was closely tied to the use of relics, which also increased noticeably in the High Middle Ages. Relics were usually the bones of saints or objects intimately connected to saints that were considered worthy of veneration by the faithful. A twelfth-century English monk began his description of the abbey's relics by saying, "There is kept there a thing more precious than gold, . . . the right arm of St. Oswald. . . . This we have seen with our own eyes and have kissed, and have handled with our own hands. . . . There are kept here also part of his ribs and of the soil on which he fell."[6] The monk went on to list additional purported relics possessed by the abbey, which included two pieces of Jesus' swaddling clothes, pieces of Jesus' manger, and part of the five loaves of bread with which Jesus miraculously fed five thousand people. Because the holiness of the saint was considered to be inherent in his relics, these objects were believed to be capable of healing people or producing other miracles.

In the High Middle Ages, it became a regular practice of the church to attach indulgences to these relics. Indulgences brought a remission of time spent in purgatory. Purgatory was believed to be a place of punishment in which the soul of the departed could be purified before ascending to heaven. The living could ease that suffering by Masses and prayers offered on behalf of the deceased or by indulgences. Indulgences were granted for good works such as charitable contributions and viewing the relics of saints. The church

Bibliothèque Nationale, Paris

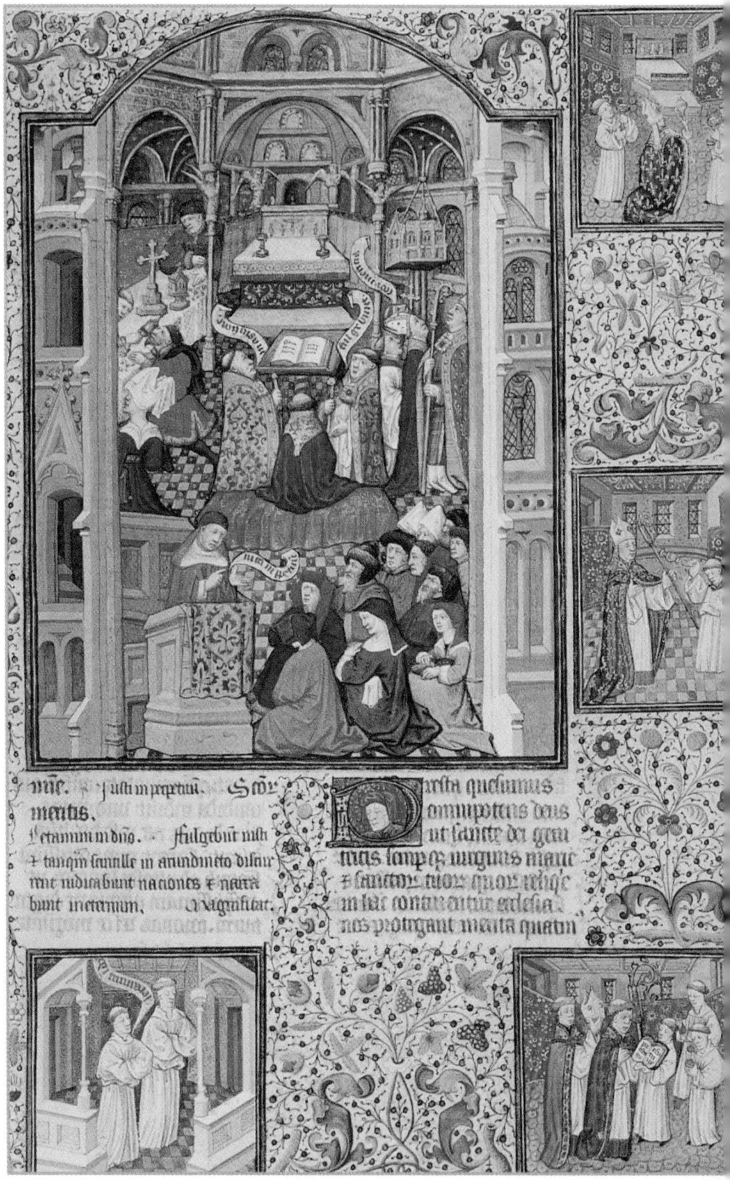

Mass of the Holy Relics. It was customary for churches that possessed relics to hold a special Mass honoring those saints. At that time, the reliquaries would be brought out for the faithful to venerate. The large picture shows the celebration of this special Mass of the holy relics. The reliquary is shown on a table to the left. The small pictures illustrate various stages of the Mass.

specified the number of years and days of each indulgence, enabling the soul to spend less time in purgatory.

Medieval Christians believed a pilgrimage to a holy shrine was of particular spiritual benefit. The greatest shrine but the most difficult to reach was the Holy City of Jerusalem (see Map 10.6). On the Continent, two pilgrim centers were especially popular in the High Middle Ages: Rome, which contained the relics of Saints Peter and Paul, and the town of Santiago de Compostela, supposedly the site of the tomb of the Apostle James. Local attractions, such as shrines dedicated to the Virgin Mary, also became pilgrimage centers.

Voices of Protest and Intolerance

The desire for more personal and deeper religious experience, which characterized the spiritual revival of the High Middle Ages, also led people into directions hostile to the institutional church. From the twelfth century on, heresy, the holding of religious doctrines different from the orthodox teachings of the church, became a serious problem for the Catholic church.

The best-known heresy of the twelfth and thirteenth centuries was Catharism. The Cathars (the word *Cathar* means "pure") were often called Albigensians after the city of Albi, one of their strongholds in southern France. They believed in a dualist system in which good and evil were separate and distinct. The things of the spirit were good because they were created by the God of light; the things of the world were evil because they were created by Satan, the prince of darkness. Humans, too, were enmeshed in dualism. Their souls, which were good, were trapped in material bodies, which were evil. According to the Cathars, the Catholic church, itself a materialistic institution, had nothing to do with God and was essentially evil. There was no need to follow its teachings or recognize its authority. The Cathar movement gained valuable support from important nobles in southern France and northern Italy.

The spread of heresy in southern France alarmed the church authorities. Pope Innocent III appealed to the nobles of northern France for a Crusade (a military campaign in defense of Christendom) against the heretics. The Crusade against the Albigensians, which began in the summer of 1209 and lasted for almost two decades, was a bloody one. Thousands of heretics (and the innocent) were slaughtered, including entire populations of some towns. In Béziers, for example, seven thousand men, women, and children were massacred when they took refuge in the local church.

Southern France was devastated, but Catharism remained, which caused the Catholic church to devise a regular method for discovering and dealing with heretics. This led to the emergence of the Holy Office, as the papal Inquisition was called, a formal court whose job it was to ferret

Map 10.6 Pilgrimage Routes in the Middle Ages. Some Christians sought spiritual solace by traveling to pilgrimage sites. Many went to local shrines honoring the Virgin Mary, but Jerusalem, Rome, and Santiago de Compostela were the most desired locations. ■ Roughly how far would a pilgrim from Lübeck have to travel to reach Jerusalem, and how long would the journey take if he walked 20 miles per day?

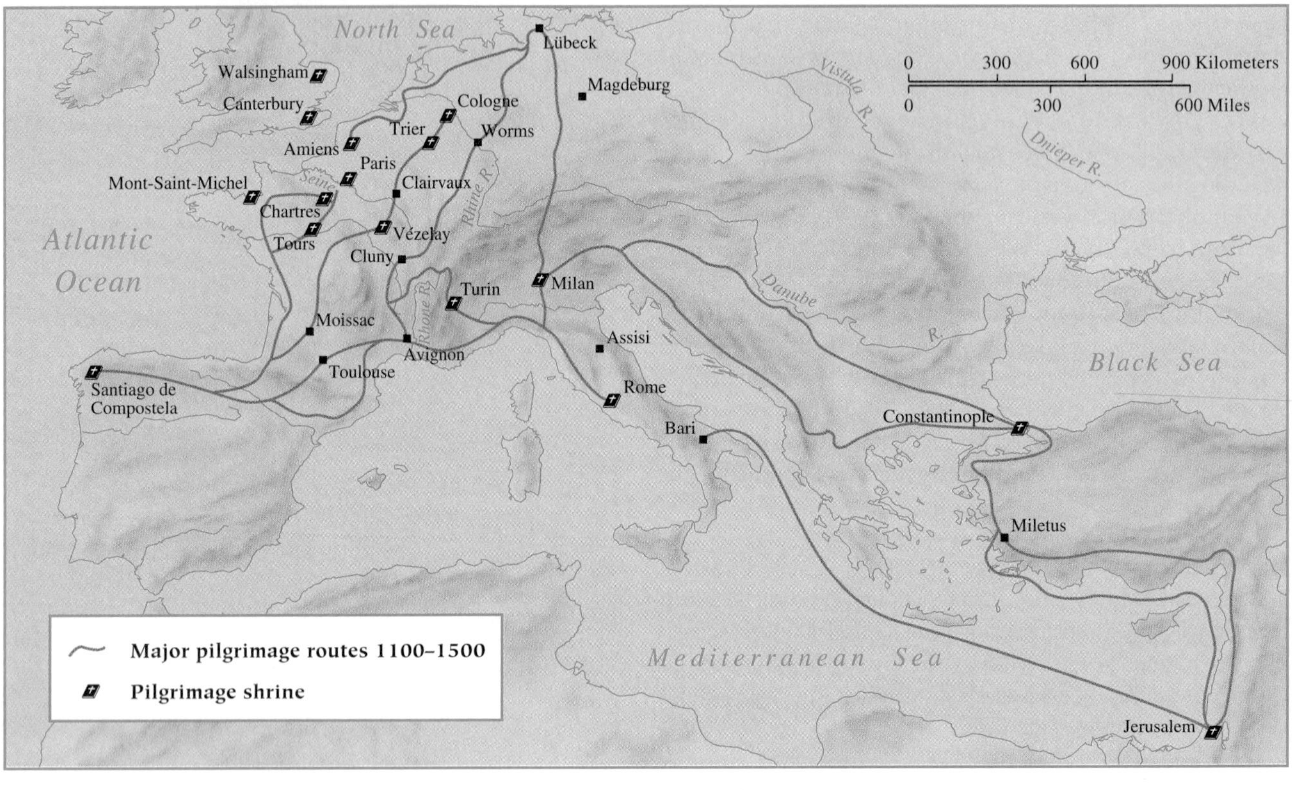

British Library, London/Bridgeman Art Library

Expulsion of Albigensian Heretics. In 1209, Pope Innocent III authorized a Crusade against the heretical Albigensians. In this medieval illustration, French knights are shown expelling Albigensian heretics from the town of Caracassonne near Albi, an Albigensian stronghold in southern France.

out and try heretics. Anyone accused of heresy who refused to confess and was still considered guilty was turned over to the secular authorities for execution. To the Christians of the thirteenth century, who believed that there was only one path to salvation, heresy was a crime against God and against humanity, and force was justified to save souls from damnation. The fanaticism and fear unleashed in the struggle against heretics were also used against others, especially the best-known outgroup of Western society, the Jews.

PERSECUTION OF THE JEWS

The Jews constituted the only religious minority in Christian Europe that was allowed to practice a non-Christian religion. In the Early Middle Ages, Jews were actively involved in trade and crafts. Later, after being excluded from practicing most trades by the guild system, some Jews turned to moneylending as a way to survive.

There is little certainty about the number of Jews in Europe. England had relatively few Jews, probably 2,500 to 3,000, or one of every thousand inhabitants. Larger numbers lived in southern Italy, Spain, France, and Germany. In southern Europe, Jews served an important function as cultural and intellectual intermediaries between the Muslim and Christian worlds.

The religious enthusiasm of the High Middle Ages produced an outburst of intolerance against the supposed enemies of Christianity. Although this was evident in the crusades against the Muslims (see "The Crusades" later in this chapter), Christians also took up the search for enemies at home, persecuting Jews in France and the Rhineland at the time of the first Crusades. Jews in Speyer, Worms, Mainz, and Cologne were all set upon by bands of Christian crusaders. A contemporary chronicler described how a band of English crusaders who stopped at Lisbon, Portugal, en route to the Holy Land "drove away the pagans and Jews, servants of the king, who dwelt in the city and plundered their property and possessions, and burned their houses; and they then stripped their vineyards, not leaving them so much as a grape or a cluster."[7] Even people who tried to protect the Jews were in danger. When the archbishop of Mainz provided shelter for the Jews, a mob stormed his palace and forced him to flee. Popes also came to the Jews' defense by issuing decrees ordering that Jews were not to be persecuted.

In the thirteenth century, in the supercharged religious atmosphere created by the struggle with heretics, Jews were more and more persecuted (see the box on p. 264). Friars urged action against these "murderers of Christ," referring to the traditional Christian view of the Jews as being responsible for the death of Jesus, and organized public burnings of Jewish books. The Fourth Lateran Council in 1215 decreed that Jews must wear distinguishing clothing to separate themselves from Christians. The same council encouraged the development of Jewish ghettos, or walled enclosures, not to protect the Jews but to isolate them from Christians. The persecutions and the new image of the hated Jew stimulated a tradition of anti-Semitism that proved to be one of Christian Europe's most insidious contributions to the Western heritage.

By the end of the thirteenth century, European kings, who had earlier portrayed themselves as protectors of the Jews, had fleeced the Jewish communities of their money and then renounced their protection. Edward I expelled all Jews from England in 1290. The French king followed suit in 1306, readmitted the Jews in 1315, and expelled them again in 1322. As this policy spread into central Europe, most northern European Jews were forced to move into Poland as a last refuge.

INTOLERANCE OF HOMOSEXUALITY

The climate of intolerance that characterized thirteenth-century attitudes toward Muslims, heretics, and Jews was also evident toward another minority group, homosexuals. Although the church had condemned homosexuality in the Early Middle Ages, it had not been overly concerned with homosexual behavior, an attitude also prevalent in the secular world. By the thirteenth century, however, these tolerant attitudes had altered drastically. Some historians see this change as part of the century's climate of fear and intolerance toward any minority group that deviated from the standards of the majority. A favorite approach of the critics was to identify homosexuals with other detested groups. Homosexuality was portrayed as a regular practice of Muslims and such notorious heretics as the Albigensians. Between 1250 and 1300, what had been tolerated in most of Europe became a criminal act deserving of death.

The legislation against homosexuality commonly referred to it as a "sin against nature." This is precisely the

Treatment of the Jews

The new religious sensibilities that emerged in the High Middle Ages also had a negative side, the turning of Christians against their supposed enemies. Although the Crusades provide the most obvious example, Christians also turned on their supposed enemies, the "murderers of Christ," the Jews. As a result, Jews suffered increased persecution. These three documents show different sides of the picture. The first is Canon 68 of the decrees of the Fourth Lateran Council called by Pope Innocent III in 1215. The decree specifies the need for special dress, one of the ways Christians tried to separate Jews from their community. The second excerpt is a chronicler's account of the most deadly charge levied against the Jews—that they were guilty of the ritual murder of Christian children to obtain Christian blood for the Passover service. This charge led to the murder of many Jews. The third document, taken from a list of regulations issued by the city of Avignon, France, illustrates the contempt Christian society held for the Jews.

Canon 68

In some provinces a difference in dress distinguishes the Jews or Saracens [Muslims] from the Christians, but in certain others such a confusion has grown up that they cannot be distinguished by any difference. Thus it happens at times that through error Christians have relations with the women of Jews or Saracens, and Jews or Saracens with Christian women. Therefore, that they may not, under pretext of error of this sort, excuse themselves in the future for the excesses of such prohibited intercourse, we decree that such Jews and Saracens of both sexes in every Christian province and at all times shall be marked off in the eyes of the public from other peoples through the character of their dress. . . .

Moreover, during the last three days before Easter and especially on Good Friday, they shall not go forth in public at all, for the reason that some of them on these very days, as we hear, do not blush to go forth better dressed and are not afraid to mock the Christians who maintain the memory of the most holy Passion by wearing signs of mourning.

An Accusation of the Ritual Murder of a Christian Child by Jews

. . . [The eight-year-old boy] Harold, who is buried in the Church of St. Peter the Apostle, at Gloucester . . . is said to have been carried away secretly by Jews, in the opinion of many, on Feb. 21, and by them hidden till March 16. On that night, on the sixth of the preceding feast, the Jews of all England coming together as if to circumcise a certain boy, pretend deceitfully that they are about to celebrate the feast [Passover] appointed by law in such case, and deceiving the citizens of Gloucester with the fraud, they tortured the lad placed before them with immense tortures. It is true no Christian was present, or saw or heard the deed, nor have we found that anything was betrayed by any Jew. But a little while after when the whole convent of monks of Gloucester and almost all the citizens of that city, and innumerable persons coming to the spectacle, saw the wounds of the dead body, scars of fire, the thorns fixed on his head, and liquid wax poured into the eyes and face, and touched it with the diligent examination of their hands, those tortures were believed or guessed to have been inflicted on him in that manner. It was clear that they had made him a glorious martyr to Christ, being slain without sin, and having bound his feet with his own girdle, threw him into the river Severn.

The Regulations of Avignon, 1243

Likewise, we declare that Jews or whores shall not dare to touch with their hands either bread or fruit put out for sale, and that if they should do this they must buy what they have touched.

argument developed by Thomas Aquinas, who formed Catholic opinion on the subject for centuries to come. In his *Summa Theologica*, Aquinas argued that because the purpose of sex was procreation, it could only legitimately take place in ways that did not exclude this possibility. Hence homosexuality was "contrary to nature" and a deviation from the natural order established by God. This argument and laws prohibiting homosexual activity on pain of severe punishment remained the norm in Europe and elsewhere in the Christian world until the twentieth century.

The Crusades

Another manifestation of the wave of religious enthusiasm that seized Europe in the High Middle Ages was a series of Crusades mounted against the Muslims. The Crusades gave the revived papacy of the High Middle Ages yet another opportunity to demonstrate its influence over European society. The Crusades were a curious mix of God and warfare, two of the chief concerns of the Middle Ages.

Background to the Crusades

Although European civilization developed in relative isolation, it had never entirely lost contact with the lands and empires of the East. At the end of the eleventh century, that contact increased, in part because developments in the Islamic and Byzantine worlds prompted the first major attempt of the new European civilization to expand beyond Europe proper.

ISLAM AND THE SELJUK TURKS

By the mid-tenth century, the Islamic empire led by the Abbasid caliphate in Baghdad was disintegrating. An attempt was made in the tenth century to unify the Islamic world under the direction of a Shi'ite dynasty known as the Fatimids. Their origins lay in North Africa, but they managed to conquer Egypt and establish the new city of Cairo as their capital. In establishing a Shi'ite caliphate, they became rivals to the Sunni caliphate of Baghdad and divided the Islamic world.

Nevertheless, the Fatimid dynasty prospered and surpassed the Abbasid caliphate as the dynamic center of Islam. Benefiting from their position in the heart of the Nile delta, the Fatimids played a major role in the regional trade passing from the Mediterranean to the Red Sea and beyond. They were tolerant in matters of religion and created a strong army by using nonnative peoples as mercenaries. One of these peoples, the Seljuk Turks, soon posed a threat to the Fatimids themselves.

The Seljuk Turks were a nomadic people from Central Asia who had been converted to Islam and flourished as military mercenaries for the Abbasid caliphate. Moving gradually into Persia and Armenia, their numbers grew until by the eleventh century they were able to take over the eastern provinces of the Abbasid empire. In 1055, a Turkish leader captured Baghdad and assumed command of the Abbasid empire with the title of sultan ("holder of power"). By the last quarter of the eleventh century, the Seljuk Turks were exerting military pressure on Egypt and the Byzantine Empire. When the Byzantine emperor foolishly challenged the Turks, the latter routed the Byzantine army at Manzikert in 1071. In dire straits, the Byzantines looked west for help, setting in motion the papal pleas that led to the Crusades. To understand the complexities of the situation, however, we need to look first at the Byzantine Empire.

THE BYZANTINE EMPIRE

The Macedonian dynasty of the tenth and eleventh centuries had restored much of the power of the Byzantine Empire; its incompetent successors, however, reversed most of the gains. After the Macedonian dynasty was extinguished in 1056, the empire was beset by internal struggles for power between ambitious military leaders and aristocratic families who attempted to buy the support of the great landowners of Anatolia by allowing them greater control over their peasants. This policy was self-destructive, however, because the peasant-warrior was the traditional backbone of the Byzantine state.

The growing division between the Catholic church of the West and the Eastern Orthodox church of the Byzantine Empire also weakened the Byzantine state. The Eastern Orthodox church was unwilling to accept the pope's claim that he was the sole head of the church. This dispute reached a climax in 1054 when Pope Leo IX and Patriarch Michael Cerularius, head of the Byzantine church, formally excommunicated each other, initiating a schism between the two great branches of Christianity that has not been completely healed to this day.

The Byzantine Empire faced external threats to its security as well. The greatest challenge came from the Seljuk Turks who had moved into Asia Minor—the heartland of the empire and its main source of food and manpower. After the Byzantine forces were disastrously defeated at Manzikert by a Turkish army in 1071, the Turks advanced into Anatolia, where many peasants, already disgusted by their exploitation at the hands of Byzantine landowners, readily accepted Turkish control.

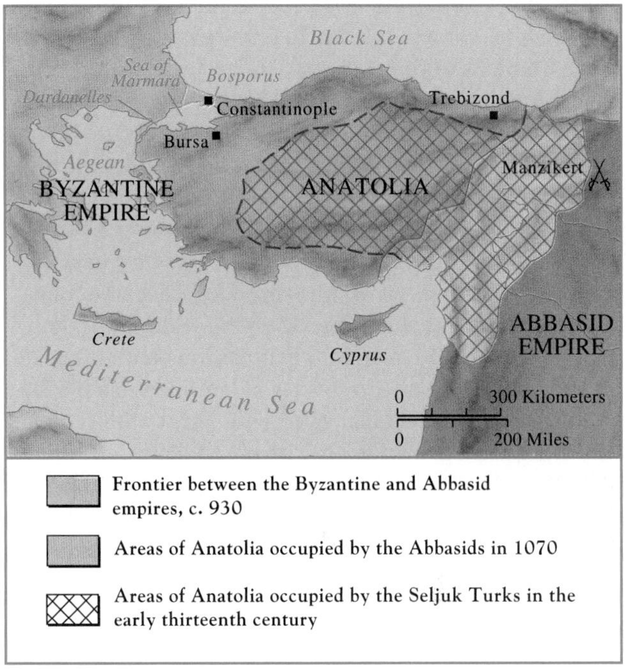

The Seljuk Turks and the Byzantines

A new dynasty, however, soon breathed new life into the Byzantine Empire. The Comneni, under Alexius I Comnenus (1081–1118), were victorious on the Greek Adriatic coast against the Normans, defeated the Pechenegs in the Balkans, and stopped the Turks in Anatolia. Lacking the resources to undertake additional campaigns against the Turks, Emperor Alexius I turned to the West for military assistance. The positive response to the emperor's request led to the Crusades. The Byzantine Empire lived to regret it.

Pope Urban II Proclaims a Crusade

Toward the end of the eleventh century, the Byzantine emperor Alexius I sent Pope Urban II a request for aid against the Seljuk Turks. At the Council of Clermont, Urban II appealed to a large crowd to take up weapons and recover Palestine from the Muslims. This description of Urban's appeal is taken from an account by Fulcher of Chartres.

Pope Urban II

Pope Urban II . . . addressed them [the French] in a very persuasive speech, as follows: "O race of the Franks, O people who live beyond the mountain [that is, north of the Alps], O people loved and chosen of God, as is clear from your many deeds, distinguished over all nations by the situation of your land, your catholic faith, and your regard for the holy church, we have a special message and exhortation for you. For we wish you to know what a grave matter has brought us to your country. The sad news has come from Jerusalem and Constantinople that the people of Persia, an accursed and foreign race [the Seljuk Turks], enemies of God, . . . have invaded the lands of those Christians and devastated them with the sword, rapine, and fire. Some of the Christians they have carried away as slaves, others they have put to death. The churches they have either destroyed or turned into mosques. They desecrate and overthrow the altars. They circumcise the Christians and pour the blood from the circumcision on the altars or in the baptismal fonts. Some they kill in a horrible way by cutting open the abdomen, taking out a part of the entrails and tying them to a stake; they then beat them and compel them to walk until all their entrails are drawn out and they fall to the ground. Some they use as targets for their arrows. They compel some to stretch out their necks and then they try to see whether they can cut off their heads with one strike of the sword. It is better to say nothing of their horrible treatment of the women. They have taken from the Greek empire a tract of land so large that it takes more than two months to walk through it. Whose duty is to avenge this and recover that land, if not yours? For to you more than to any other nations the Lord has given the military spirit, courage, agile bodies, and the bravery to strike down those who resist you. Let your minds be stirred to bravery by the deeds of your forefathers, and by the efficiency and greatness of Karl the Great [Charlemagne], . . . and of the other kings who have destroyed Turkish kingdoms, and established Christianity in their lands. You should be moved especially by the holy grave of our Lord and Savior which is now held by unclean peoples, and by the holy places which are treated with dishonor and irreverently befouled with their uncleanness. . . ."

"O bravest of knights, descendants of unconquered ancestors, do not be weaker than they, but remember their courage. . . . Set out on the road to the holy sepulchre, take the land from that wicked people, and make it your own. . . . Jerusalem is the best of all lands, more fruitful than all others. . . . This land our Savior made illustrious by his birth, beautiful with his life, and sacred with his suffering. . . . This royal city is now held captive by her enemies, and made pagan by those who know not God. She asks and longs to be liberated and does not cease to beg you to come to her aid. . . . Set out on this journey and you will obtain the remission of your sins and be sure of the incorruptible glory of the kingdom of heaven."

When Pope Urban had said this and much more of the same sort, all who were present were moved to cry out with one accord, "It is the will of God, it is the will of God." When the pope heard this he raised his eyes to heaven and gave thanks to God, and commanding silence with a gesture of his hand, he said: "My dear brethren, today there is fulfilled in you that which the Lord says in the Gospel, 'Where two or three are gathered together in my name, there am I in the midst.' For unless the Lord God had been in your minds you would not all have said the same thing. . . . So I say unto you, God, who put those words into your hearts, has caused you to utter them. Therefore let these words be your battle cry, because God caused you to speak them. Whenever you meet the enemy in battle, you shall all cry out, 'It is the will of God, it is the will of God. . . .' Whoever therefore shall determine to make this journey and shall make a vow to God and shall offer himself as a living sacrifice, holy, acceptable to God, shall wear a cross on his brow or on his breast. And when he returns after having fulfilled his vow he shall wear the cross on his back."

The Early Crusades

The Crusades were based on the idea of a holy war against the infidel or unbeliever. The wrath of Christians was directed against the Muslims, and at the end of the eleventh century, Christian Europe found itself with a glorious opportunity to attack them. The immediate impetus for the Crusades came when the Byzantine emperor, Alexius I, asked Pope Urban II (1088–1099) for help against the Seljuk Turks. The pope saw a golden opportunity to provide papal leadership for a great cause: to rally the warriors of Europe for the liberation of Jerusalem and the Holy Land from the infidel. At the Council of Clermont in southern France near the end of 1095, Urban challenged Christians to take up their weapons against the infidel and join in a holy war to recover the Holy Land (see the box above). The pope promised remission of sins: "All who die by the way, whether by land or by sea, or in battle against the pagans, shall have immediate remission of sins. This I grant them through the power of God with which I am invested."[8]

The Siege of Jerusalem: Christian and Muslim Perspectives

During the First Crusade, Christian knights laid siege to Jerusalem in June 1099. The first excerpt is taken from an account by Fulcher of Chartres, who accompanied the crusaders to the Holy Land. The second selection is by a Muslim writer, Ibn al-Athir, whose account of the First Crusade can be found in his history of the Muslim world.

Fulcher of Chartres, Chronicle of the First Crusade

Then the Franks entered the city magnificently at the noonday hour on Friday, the day of the week when Christ redeemed the whole world on the cross. With trumpets sounding and with everything in an uproar, exclaiming: "Help, God!" they vigorously pushed into the city, and straightway raised the banner on the top of the wall. All the heathen, completely terrified, changed their boldness to swift flight through the narrow streets of the quarters. The more quickly they fled, the more quickly they put to flight.

Count Raymond and his men, who were bravely assailing the city in another section, did not perceive this until they saw the Saracens [Muslims] jumping from the top of the wall. Seeing this, they joyfully ran to the city as quickly as they could, and helped the others pursue and kill the wicked enemy.

Then some, both Arabs and Ethiopians, fled into the Tower of David; others shut themselves in the Temple of the Lord and of Solomon, where in the halls a very great attack was made on them. Nowhere was there a place where the Saracens could escape swordsmen.

On the top of Solomon's Temple, to which they had climbed in fleeing, many were shot to death with arrows and cast down headlong from the roof. Within this Temple, about ten thousand were beheaded. If you had been there, your feet would have been stained up to the ankles with the blood of the slain. What more shall I tell? Not one of them was allowed to live. They did not spare the women and children.

Account of Ibn al-Athir

In fact Jerusalem was taken from the north on the morning of Friday 22 Sha'ban 492 / 15 July 1099. The population was put to the sword by the Franks, who pillaged the area for a week. A band of Muslims barricaded themselves into the Oratory of David and fought on for several days. They were granted their lives in return for surrendering. The Franks honored their word, and the group left by night for Ascalon. In the Masjid al-Aqsa the Franks slaughtered more than 70,000 people, among them a large number of Imams and Muslim scholars, devout and ascetic men who had left their homelands to live lives of pious seclusion in the Holy Place. The Franks stripped the Dome of the Rock of more than forty silver candelabra, each of them weighing 3,600 drams, and a great silver lamp weighing forty-four Syrian pounds, as well as a hundred and fifty smaller candelabra and more than twenty gold ones, and a great deal more booty. Refugees from Syria reached Baghdad in Ramadan, among them the qadi Abu sa'd al-Harawi. They told the Caliph's ministers a story that wrung their hearts and brought tears to their eyes. On Friday they went to the Cathedral Mosque and begged for help, weeping so that their hearers wept with them as they described the sufferings of the Muslims in that Holy City: the men killed, the women and children taken prisoner, the homes pillaged. Because of the terrible hardships they had suffered, they were allowed to break the fast.

The warriors of western Europe, particularly France, formed the first crusading armies. The knights who made up this first serious crusading host were motivated by religious fervor, but there were other attractions as well. Some sought adventure and welcomed a legitimate opportunity to pursue their favorite pastime—fighting. Others saw an opportunity to gain territory, riches, status, possibly a title, and even salvation—had the pope not offered a full remission of sins for those who participated in these "armed pilgrimages"? From the perspective of the pope and European monarchs, the Crusades offered a way to rid Europe of contentious young nobles who disturbed the peace and wasted lives and energy fighting each other. Then, too, merchants in many Italian cities sought new trading opportunities in Muslim lands.

Three organized crusading bands of noble warriors, most of them French, made their way to the east (see Map 10.7). The crusading army probably numbered several thousand cavalry and as many as ten thousand foot soldiers. After the capture of Antioch in 1098, much of the crusading host proceeded down the coast of Palestine, evading the garrisoned coastal cities, and reached Jerusalem in June 1099. After a five-week siege, the Holy City was taken amid a horrible massacre of the inhabitants, men, women, and children (see the box above).

After further conquest of Palestinian lands, the crusaders ignored the wishes of the Byzantine emperor (who foolishly believed the crusaders were working on his behalf) and organized four crusader states (Edessa, Antioch, Tripoli, and Jerusalem). Because the crusader states were surrounded by Muslim enemies, they grew increasingly dependent on the Italian commercial cities for supplies from Europe. Some Italian cities, such as Genoa, Pisa, and above all Venice, became rich and powerful in the process.

But it was not easy for the crusader states to maintain themselves in the east. Already by the 1120s, the Muslims had begun to strike back. In 1144, Edessa became the first of the four Latin states to be recaptured. Its fall led to renewed calls for another Crusade, especially from the monastic firebrand Saint Bernard of Clairvaux, who exclaimed: "Now, on account of our sins, the sacrilegious enemies of the cross have begun to show their faces. . . . What are you doing, you servants of the cross? Will you throw to the dogs that which is most holy? Will you cast pearls before swine?"[9] Bernard aimed his message at knights and even managed to enlist two powerful rulers, King Louis VII of France and Emperor Conrad III of Germany. Their Second Crusade, however, proved to be a total failure.

The Third Crusade was a reaction to the fall of the Holy City of Jerusalem in 1187 to the Muslim forces under Saladin. Now all of Christendom was ablaze with calls for a new Crusade in the Middle East. Three major monarchs agreed to lead new crusading forces in person: Emperor Frederick Barbarossa of Germany (1152–1190), King Richard I the Lionhearted of England (1189–1199), and Philip II Augustus, king of France (1180–1223). Some of the crusaders finally arrived in the Middle East by 1189 only to encounter problems. Frederick Barbarossa drowned while swimming in a local river, and his army quickly fell apart. The English and French arrived by sea and met with success against the coastal cities, where they had the support of their fleets, but when they moved inland, they failed

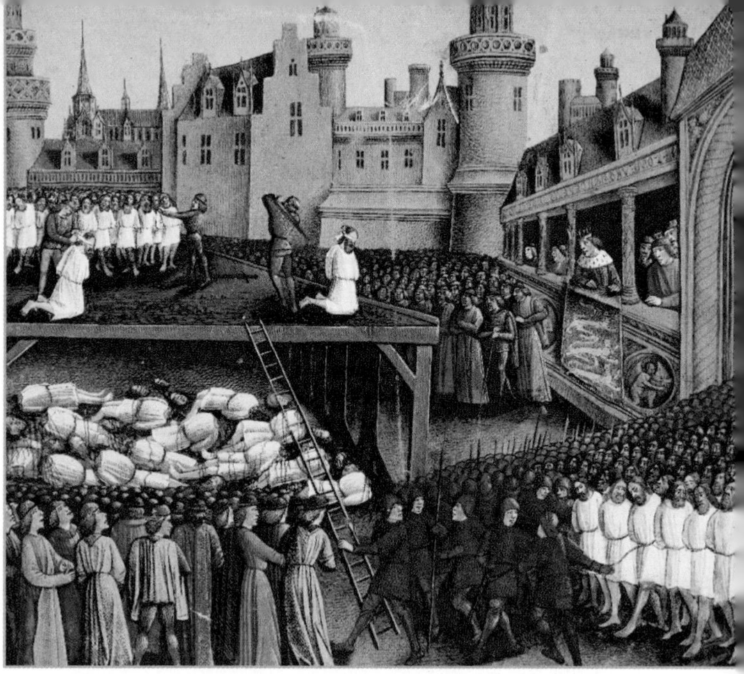

Bibliotheque Nationale, Paris

Richard the Lionhearted Executes Muslims at Acre. The Third Crusade was organized in response to the capture of the kingdom of Jerusalem by the Sunni Muslims under the leadership of Saladin. Though Saladin forbade the massacre of Christians, his Christian foes were more harsh. Here Richard the Lionhearted (at right with crown) watches the execution of 2,700 Muslims at Acre.

Map 10.7 The Early Crusades. Pope Urban II launched the Crusades to recapture the Holy Land from the "enemies of God," a call met with great enthusiasm in Europe. The fighters of the First Crusade massacred the inhabitants of Jerusalem and established the Crusader States. ■ In the Third Crusade, which countries sent crusaders by land and which by sea, and why would they choose these methods of travel?

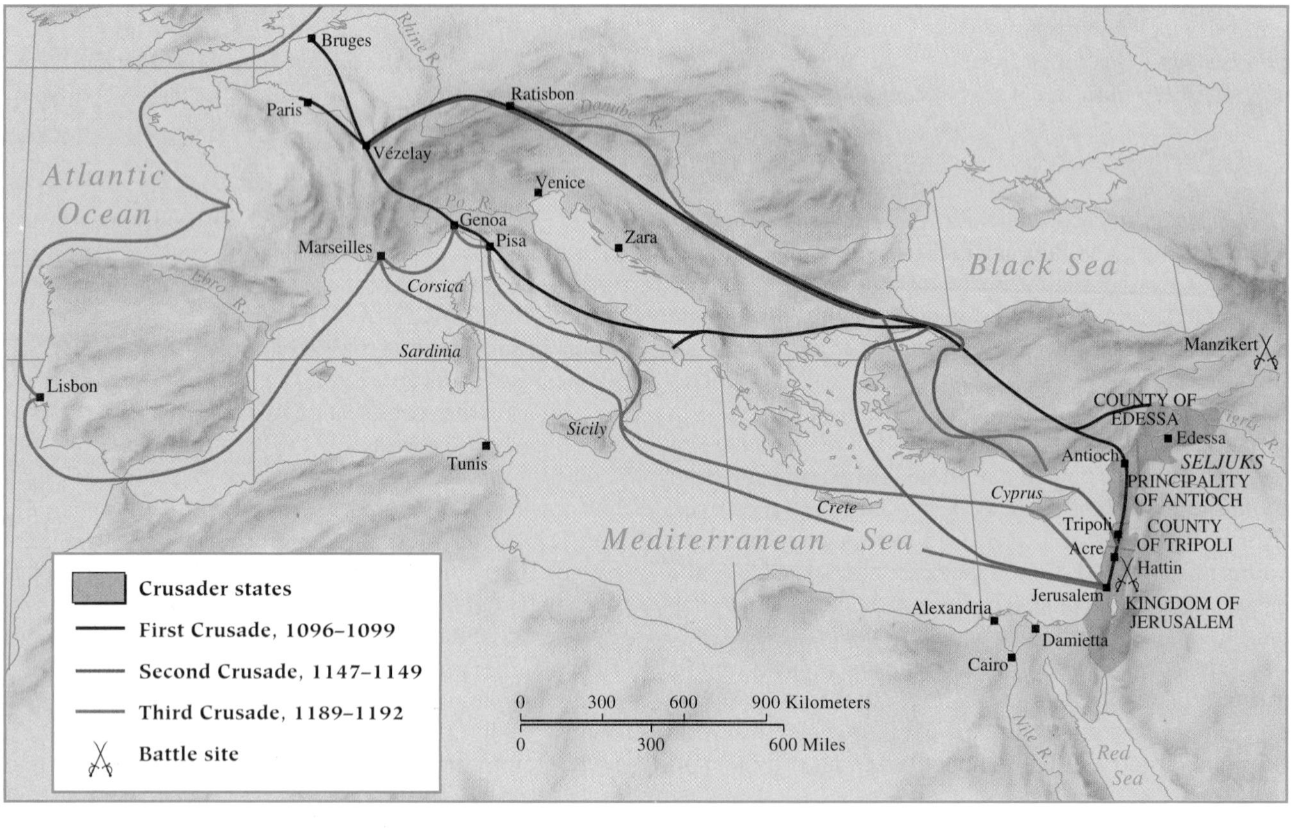

miserably. Eventually, after Philip went home, Richard negotiated a settlement whereby Saladin agreed to allow Christian pilgrims free access to Jerusalem.

The Crusades of the Thirteenth Century

After the death of Saladin in 1193, Pope Innocent III initiated the Fourth Crusade (see Map 10.8). On its way to the Holy Land, the crusading army became involved in a dispute over the succession to the Byzantine throne. The Venetian leaders of the Fourth Crusade saw an opportunity to neutralize their greatest commercial competitor, the Byzantine Empire. Diverted to Constantinople, the crusaders sacked the great capital city in 1204 and created a new Latin Empire of Constantinople. Not until 1261 did a Byzantine army recapture Constantinople. The Byzantine Empire had been saved, but it was no longer a great Mediterranean power. The restored empire now comprised only the city of Constantinople and its surrounding territory as well as some lands in Asia Minor. Though reduced in size, the empire limped along for another 190 years until its weakened condition finally enabled the Ottoman Turks to conquer it in 1453.

Despite the failures, the crusading ideal was not yet completely lost. In Germany in 1212, a youth known as Nicholas of Cologne announced that God had inspired him to lead a Children's Crusade to the Holy Land. Thousands of young people joined Nicholas and made their way down the Rhine and across the Alps to Italy, where the pope told them to go home. Most tried to do so. The next Crusade of adult warriors was hardly more successful. The Fifth Crusade (1219–1221) attempted to recover the Holy Land by way of the powerful Muslim state of Egypt. The Crusade achieved some early successes, but its ultimate failure marked an end to papal leadership of the western crusaders.

The Sixth Crusade, which was led by the German emperor Frederick II, took place without papal support because the emperor had been excommunicated by the

CHRONOLOGY

The Crusades

Pope Urban II's call for a Crusade at Clermont	1095
First Crusade	1096–1099
Fall of Edessa	1144
Second Crusade	1147–1149
Saladin's conquest of Jerusalem	1187
Third Crusade	1189–1192
Fourth Crusade—sack of Constantinople	1204
Latin Empire of Constantinople	1204–1261
Children's Crusade	1212
Fifth Crusade	1219–1221
Frederick II occupies Jerusalem (Sixth Crusade)	1228
First Crusade of Louis IX (Seventh Crusade)	1248–1254
Second Crusade of Louis IX (Eighth Crusade)	1270
Surrender of Acre and end of Christian presence in the Holy Land	1291

Bibliotheque Nationale, Paris

Siege and Capture of Constantinople. This thirteenth-century miniature is a depiction of the siege and capture of Constantinople during the Fourth Crusade in 1204. At the right, soldiers use a catapult to shower the city with stones while knights use a tower to attack the walls. In the stained-glass windows above the battle are scenes from the Passion of Christ, a deliberate and ironic reminder that the purpose of the Crusades was to capture the Holy City of Jerusalem.

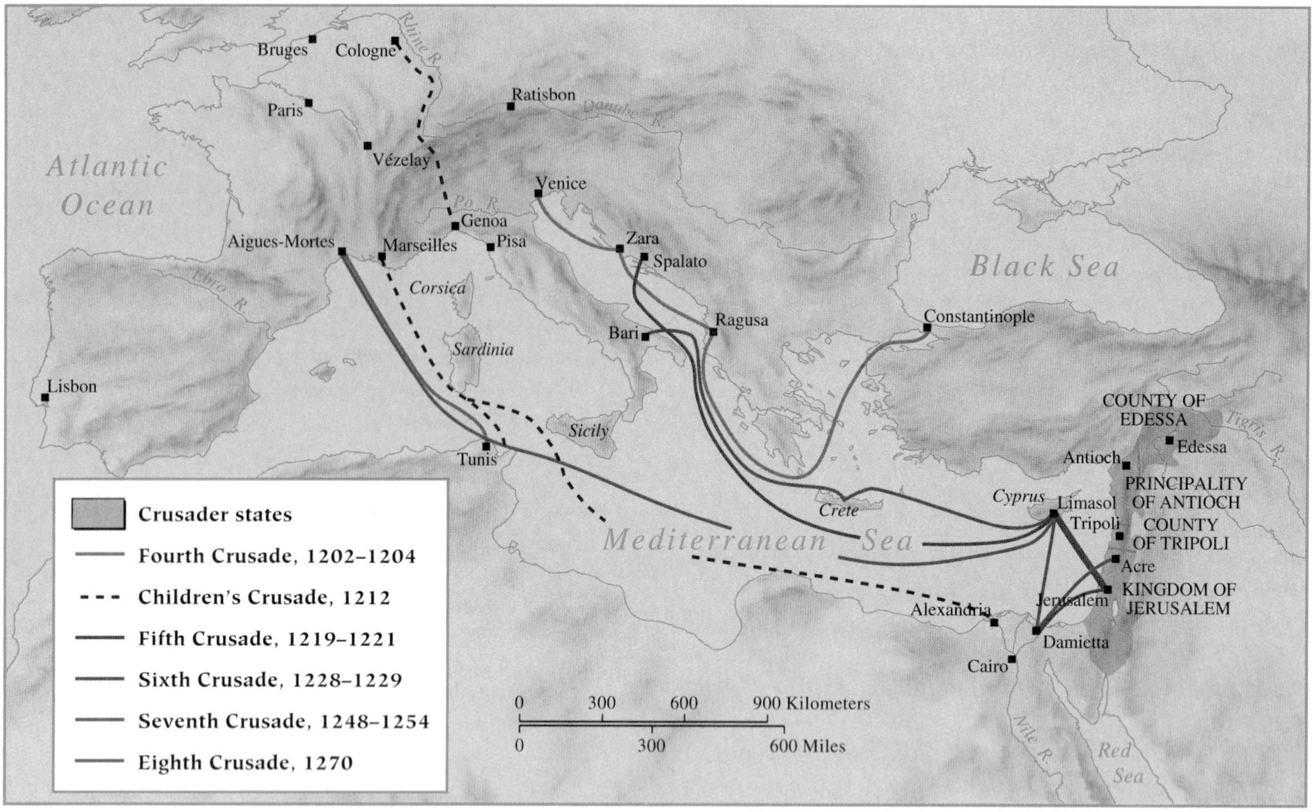

Map 10.8 The Crusades of the Thirteenth Century. The Fourth Crusade saw the crusaders sack Constantinople, a major blow that severely weakened the Byzantine Empire. Later Crusades achieved only temporary successes or were dismal failures. By the end of the thirteenth century, Christians had lost all territory in the Holy Land. ■ How would the great distances between the crusaders and their homelands affect the holy warriors' ability to fight successfully?

pope for starting late. In 1228, Frederick marched into Jerusalem and accepted the crown as king of Jerusalem after he had made an agreement with the sultan of Egypt. The Holy City had been taken without a fight and without papal support. Once Frederick left, however, the city fell once again, this time to a group of Turks allied with the sultan of Egypt. The last two major Crusades, poorly organized by the pious king of France, Louis IX, were complete failures. Soon the remaining Christian possessions in the Middle East were retaken. Acre, the last foothold of the crusaders, surrendered in 1291. All in all, the Crusades had failed to accomplish their primary goal of holding the Holy Land for the Christian West.

Effects of the Crusades

Whether the Crusades had much effect on European civilization is debatable. The crusaders made little long-term impact on the Middle East, where the only visible remnants of their conquests were their castles. There may have been some of the broadening of perspective that comes from the exchange between two cultures, but the interaction of Christian Europe with the Muslim world was actually both more intense and more meaningful in Spain and Sicily than in the Holy Land.

Did the Crusades help stabilize European society by removing large numbers of young warriors who would have fought each other in Europe? Some historians think so and believe that western monarchs established their control more easily as a result. There is no doubt that the Crusades did contribute to the economic growth of the Italian port cities, especially Genoa, Pisa, and Venice. But it is important to remember that the growing wealth and population of twelfth-century Europe had made the Crusades possible in the first place. The Crusades may have enhanced the revival of trade, but they certainly did not cause it. Even without the Crusades, Italian merchants would have pursued new trade contacts with the Eastern world.

The Crusades prompted evil side effects that would haunt European society for generations. The first widespread attacks on the Jews began with the Crusades. As some Christians argued, to undertake holy wars against infidel Muslims while the "murderers of Christ" ran free at home was unthinkable. The massacre of Jews became a regular feature of medieval European life.

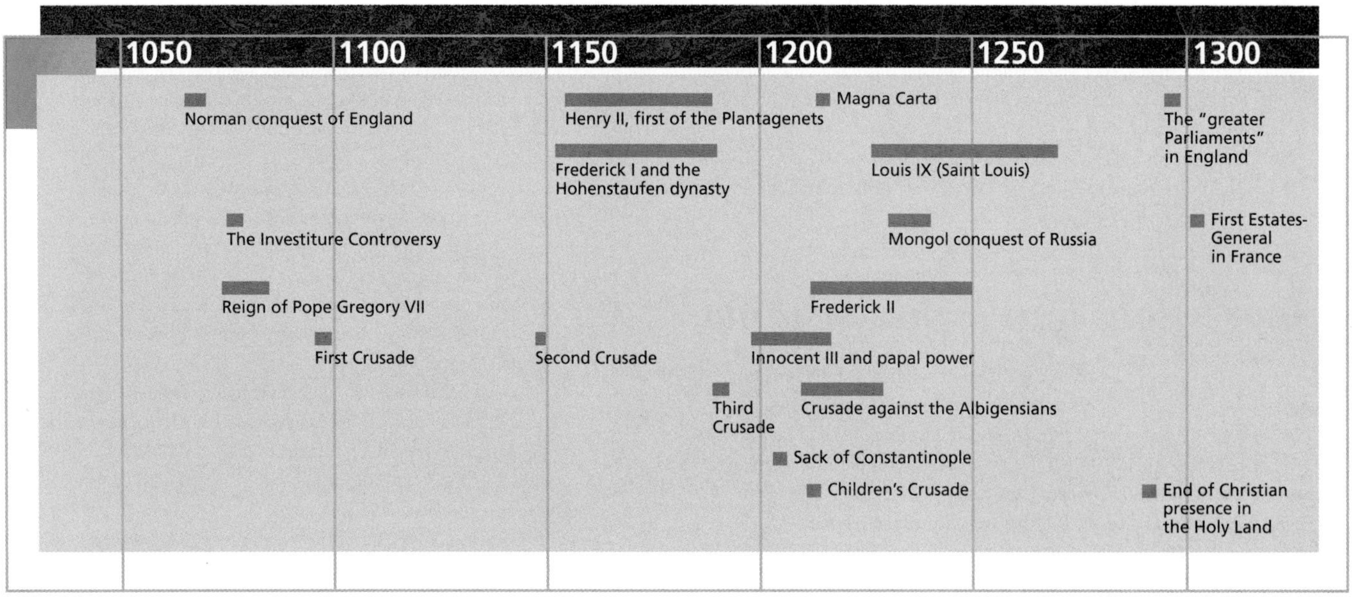

Conclusion

The period from 1000 to 1300 was a dynamic one in the development of Western civilization. The nobles, whose warlike attitudes were rationalized by labeling them as the defenders of Christian society, continued to dominate the medieval world politically, economically, and socially. But quietly and surely, within this world of castles and private power, kings gradually began to extend their public powers. Although the popes sometimes treated rulers as if they were the popes' servants, by the thirteenth century, monarchs themselves were developing the machinery of government that would enable them to challenge these exalted claims of papal power and become the centers of political authority in Europe. Although they could not know it then, the actions of these medieval monarchs laid the foundation for the European kingdoms that in one form or another have dominated the European political scene ever since.

The Catholic church shared in the challenge of new growth by reforming itself and striking out on a path toward greater papal power, both within the church and over European society. The High Middle Ages witnessed a spiritual renewal that led to numerous and even divergent paths: revived papal leadership, the development of centralized administrative machinery that buttressed papal authority, and new dimensions to the religious life of the clergy and laity. At the same time, this spiritual renewal also gave rise to the crusading "holy warrior" who killed for God.

The religious enthusiasm of the twelfth century continued well into the thirteenth as new orders of friars gave witness to spiritual growth and passion, but underneath the calm exterior lay seeds of discontent and change. Dissent from church teaching and practices grew, leading to a climate of fear and intolerance as the church responded with inquisitorial procedures to enforce conformity to its teachings. At the same time, papal claims of supremacy over secular authorities were increasingly challenged by the rising power of a new breed of monarchical authorities, who, thanks to the growth of cities, the revival of trade, and the emergence of a money economy, were now able to hire soldiers and officials to carry out their wishes.

The High Middle Ages of the eleventh, twelfth, and thirteenth centuries had been a period of great innovation, evident in significant economic, social, political, religious, intellectual, and cultural changes. And yet by the end of the thirteenth century, certain tensions had begun to creep into European society. As we shall see in the next chapter, these tensions soon became a torrent of troubles.

Notes

1. Quoted in John K. Fairbank, Edwin O. Reischauer, and Albert M. Craig, *East Asia: Tradition and Transformation* (Boston, 1973), p. 164.
2. Ernest F. Henderson, ed., *Selected Historical Documents of the Middle Ages* (London, 1892), p. 332.
3. Ibid., p. 365.
4. Oliver J. Thatcher and Edgar H. McNeal, eds., *A Source Book for Medieval History* (New York, 1905), p. 208.
5. Quoted in R. H. C. Davis, *A History of Medieval Europe from Constantine to Saint Louis,* 2d ed. (New York, 1988), p. 252.

6. Quoted in Rosalind Brooke and Christopher N. L. Brooke, *Popular Religion in the Middle Ages* (London, 1984), p. 19.
7. Henry T. Riley, ed., *Memorials of London and London Life in the Thirteenth, Fourteenth, and Fifteenth Centuries* (London, 1868), vol. 2, pp. 148–149.
8. Thatcher and McNeal, *Source Book for Medieval History,* p. 517.
9. Quoted in Hans E. Mayer, *The Crusades,* trans. John Gillingham (New York, 1972), pp. 99–100.

Suggestions for Further Reading

There are numerous works on the different medieval states. On England, see R. Frame, *The Political Development of the British Isles, 1100–1400* (Oxford, 1990), and M. T. Clanchy, *England and Its Rulers, 1066–1272* (New York, 1983). On France, see J. Dunbabin, *France in the Making, 843–1180* (Oxford, 1985), and E. M. Hallam, *Capetian France, 987–1328* (London, 1980), a well-done general account. On Spain, see B. F. Reilly, *The Medieval Spains* (Cambridge, 1993). On Germany, see A. Haverkamp, *Medieval Germany* (Oxford, 1988); H. Fuhrmann, *Germany in the High Middle Ages, c. 1050–1250* (Cambridge, 1986), an excellent account; and B. Arnold, *Princes and Territories in Medieval Germany* (Cambridge, 1991). On Italy, see D. J. Herlihy, *Cities and Society in Medieval Italy* (London, 1980). On eastern Europe and Scandinavia, see N. Davies, *God's Playground: A History of Poland* (Oxford, 1981); T. K. Derry, *A History of Scandinavia* (London, 1979); J. Fennell, *The Crisis of Medieval Russia, 1200–1304* (New York, 1983); and the books listed for Chapter 8.

For specialized studies in the political history of the thirteenth century, see D. Abulafia, *Frederick II: A Medieval Emperor* (London, 1987); M. W. Labarge, *St. Louis: The Life of Louis IX of France* (London, 1968); and C. J. Halperin, *Russia and the Golden Horde: The Mongol Impact on Medieval Russian History* (Bloomington, Ind., 1987).

For a good survey of religion in medieval Europe, see B. Hamilton, *Religion in the Medieval West* (London, 1986). On Europe during the time of the Investiture Controversy, see U.-R. Blumenthal, *The Investiture Controversy* (Philadelphia, 1988). For a general survey of church life, see R. W. Southern, *Western Society and the Church in the Middle Ages,* rev. ed. (New York, 1990).

On the papacy in the High Middle Ages, see the general surveys by C. Morris, *The Papal Monarchy* (Oxford, 1989), and I. S. Robinson, *The Papacy* (Cambridge, 1990). The papacy of Innocent III is covered in J. E. Sayers, *Innocent III, Leader of Europe, 1198–1216* (New York, 1994).

Good works on monasticism include B. Bolton, *The Medieval Reformation* (London, 1983), and C. H. Lawrence, *Medieval Monasticism* (London, 1984), a good general account. On the Cistercians, see L. J. Lekai, *The Cistercians* (Kent, Ohio, 1977). S. Flanagan, *Hildegard of Bingen,* 2d ed. (London, 1998), is a good account of the twelfth-century mystic. For a good introduction to popular religion in the eleventh and twelfth centuries, see R. Brooke and C. N. L. Brooke, *Popular Religion in the Middle Ages* (London, 1984). The image of women in the secular and religious realms is discussed in P. S. Gold, *The Lady and the Virgin: Image, Attitude and Experience in Twelfth-Century France* (Chicago, 1985).

On dissent and heresy, see M. Lambert, *Medieval Heresy* (New York, 1977), and J. Strayer, *The Albigensian Crusades,* 2d ed. (New York, 1992). On the Inquisition, see B. Hamilton, *The Medieval Inquisition* (New York, 1981). The persecution of Jews in the thirteenth century can be examined in J. Cohen, *The Friars and the Jews* (Oxford, 1985). The basic study on intolerance and homosexuality is J. Boswell, *Christianity, Social Tolerance, and Homosexuality* (Chicago, 1980).

Two good general surveys of the Crusades are H. E. Mayer, *The Crusades,* 2d ed. (New York, 1988), and J. Riley-Smith, *The Crusades: A Short History* (New Haven, Conn., 1987). Also see J. Riley-Smith, ed., *The Oxford Illustrated History of the Crusades* (New York, 1995). For works on the Byzantine and Islamic empires, see the reading suggestions at the end of Chapter 8 and M. Angold, *The Byzantine Empire, 1025–1204* (London, 1984). The disastrous Fourth Crusade is examined in J. Godfrey, *1204: The Unholy Crusade* (Oxford, 1980). On the later Crusades, see N. Housley, *The Later Crusades, 1274–1580* (New York, 1992).

For additional reading, go to InfoTrac College Edition, your online research library at http://web1.infotrac-college.com

Enter the search term *medieval Germany* using Key Terms.

Enter the search term *medieval England* using Key Terms.

Enter the search term *Saint Francis* using Key Terms.

Enter the search term *Crusades* using the Subject Guide.

C H A P T E R

11

The Later Middle Ages: Crisis and Disintegration in the Fourteenth Century

Bibliotheque Nationale, Paris

CHAPTER OUTLINE

- A Time of Troubles: Black Death and Social Crisis
- War and Political Instability
- The Decline of the Church
- The Cultural World of the Fourteenth Century
- Society in an Age of Adversity
- Conclusion

FOCUS QUESTIONS

- What was the Black Death, and what was its impact on European society?
- What major problems did European states face in the fourteenth century?
- How and why did the authority and prestige of the papacy decline in the fourteenth century?
- What were the major developments in art and literature in the fourteenth century?
- How did the adversities of the fourteenth century affect urban life and medical practices?
- To what extent were climate and disease the key factors in producing economic, social, and political changes in the fourteenth century?

AS A RESULT OF THEIR CONQUESTS in the thirteenth and fourteenth centuries, the Mongols created a vast empire stretching from Russia in the west to China in the east. Mongol rule brought stability to the Eurasian trade routes; increased trade brought prosperity but also avenues for the spread of flea-infested rats that carried bubonic plague to both East Asia and Europe. The mid-fourteenth century witnessed one of the most destructive natural disasters in history—the Black Death. One contemporary observer named Henry Knighton, a canon of Saint Mary of the Meadow Abbey in Leicester, England, was simply overwhelmed by the magnitude of the catastrophe. Knighton began his account of the great plague with these words: "In this year [1348] and in the following one there was a general mortality of people throughout the whole world." Few were left untouched; the plague struck even isolated monasteries: "At Montpellier, there remained out of a hundred and forty friars only seven." Animals, too, were devastated: "During this same year, there was a great mortality of sheep everywhere in the kingdom; in one place and in one pasture, more than five thousand sheep died and became so putrefied that neither beast nor bird wanted to touch them." Knighton was also stunned by the economic and social consequences of the Black Death. Prices dropped: "And the price of everything was cheap, because of the fear of death; there were very few who took any care for their wealth, or for anything else." Meanwhile laborers were scarce, so their wages increased: "In the following autumn, one could not hire a reaper at a lower wage than eight pence with food, or a mower at less than twelve pence with food. Because of this, much grain rotted in the fields for lack of harvesting." So many people died that some towns were deserted and some villages disappeared altogether: "Many small villages and hamlets were completely deserted; there was not one house left in them, but all those who had lived in them were dead." Some people thought the end of the world was at hand.

Plague was not the only disaster in the fourteenth century. Signs of disintegration were everywhere: famine, economic depression, war, social upheaval, a rise in crime and violence, and a decline in the power of the universal Catholic church. Periods of disintegration, however, are often fertile ground for change and new developments. Out of the dissolution of medieval civilization came a rebirth of culture that many historians have labeled the Renaissance.

A Time of Troubles: Black Death and Social Crisis

Well into the thirteenth century, Europe had experienced good harvests and an expanding population. By the end of the thirteenth century, however, a period of disastrous changes had begun.

Famine and Population

By the end of the thirteenth century, noticeable changes in weather patterns were occurring as Europe entered a period that has been called a "little ice age." A small drop in overall temperatures resulted in shortened growing seasons and disastrous weather conditions, including heavy storms and constant rain. Between 1315 and 1317, heavy rains in northern Europe destroyed harvests and caused serious food shortages, resulting in extreme hunger and starvation. The great famine expanded to other parts of Europe in an all-too-familiar pattern, as is evident in this scene described by a contemporary chronicler:

> We saw a large number of both sexes, not only from nearby places but from as much as five leagues away, barefooted and maybe even, except for women, in a completely nude state, together with their priests coming in procession at the Church of the Holy Martyrs, their bones bulging out, devoutly carrying bodies of saints and other relics to be adorned hoping to get relief.[1]

Some historians estimate that famine killed 10 percent of the European population in the first half of the fourteenth century.

Europe had experienced a great increase in population in the High Middle Ages. By 1300, however, indications are that Europe had reached the upper limit of its population, not in an absolute sense, but in the number of people who could be supported by existing agricultural production and technology. Virtually all productive land was being farmed, including many marginal lands that needed intensive cultivation and proved easily susceptible to changing weather patterns.

We know that there was also a movement from overpopulated rural areas to urban locations. Eighteen percent of the people in the village of Broughton in England, for example, migrated between 1288 and 1340. There is no certainty that these migrants found better economic opportunities in urban areas. We might in fact conclude the opposite, based on the reports of increasing numbers of poor people in the cities. In 1330, for example, one chronicler estimated that of the 100,000 inhabitants of Florence, 17,000 were paupers. Moreover, evidence suggests that because of the increase in population, individual peasant holdings by 1300 were shrinking in size to an acreage that could no longer support a peasant family. Europe seemed to have reached an upper limit to population growth, and the number of poor appeared to have increased noticeably.

Some historians have pointed out that famine may have led to chronic malnutrition, which in turn contributed to increased infant mortality, lower birthrates, and higher susceptibility to disease because malnourished people are less able to resist infection. This, they argue, helps explain the high mortality of the great plague known as the Black Death.

The Black Death

The Black Death of the mid-fourteenth century was the most devastating natural disaster in European history, ravaging Europe and causing economic, social, political, and cultural upheaval. Contemporary chroniclers lamented that parents abandoned their children; one related the words: "Oh father, why have you abandoned me? . . . Mother, where have you gone?"[2] People were horrified by an evil force they could not understand and by the subsequent breakdown of all normal human relations.

Bubonic plague, which was the most common and most important form of plague in the diffusion of the Black

Death, was spread by black rats infested with fleas who were host to the deadly bacterium *Yersinia pestis.* Symptoms of bubonic plague included high fever, aching joints, swelling of the lymph nodes, and dark blotches caused by bleeding beneath the skin. Bubonic plague was actually the least toxic form of plague but nevertheless killed 50 to 60 percent of its victims. In pneumonic plague, the bacterial infection spread to the lungs, resulting in severe coughing, bloody sputum, and the relatively easy spread of the bacillus from human to human by coughing.

The Black Death was all the more horrible because it was the first major epidemic disease to strike Europe since the seventh century, an absence that helps explain medieval Europe's remarkable population growth. This great plague originated in Asia. After disappearing from Europe and the Middle East in the Middle Ages, bubonic plague continued to haunt areas of southwestern China, especially isolated rural territories. The arrival of Mongol troops in this area in the mid-thirteenth century became the means for the spread of the plague as flea-infested rats carrying the bacteria accompanied the Mongols into central and northwestern China and Central Asia. From there, trading caravans brought the plague to Caffa on the Black Sea in 1346.

The plague reached Europe in October 1347, when Genoese merchants brought it from Caffa to the island of Sicily off the coast of southern Italy. It spread quickly, reaching southern Italy and southern France and Spain by the end of 1347 (see Map 11.1). Usually, the diffusion of the Black Death followed commercial trade routes. In 1348, the plague spread through France and the Low Countries and into Germany. By the end of that year, it had moved to England, ravaging it in 1349. By the end of 1349, it had expanded to northern Europe and Scandinavia. Eastern Europe and Russia were affected by 1351, although

Map 11.1 Spread of the Black Death. The plague started in Sicily in 1347 and within three years had killed between one-quarter and one-half of Europe's population. Outbreaks continued into the early eighteenth century, and it took Europe two hundred years to return to the population level it had before the Black Death. ■ Is there a general pattern between distance from Sicily and the elapsed time before a region was infected with the plague?

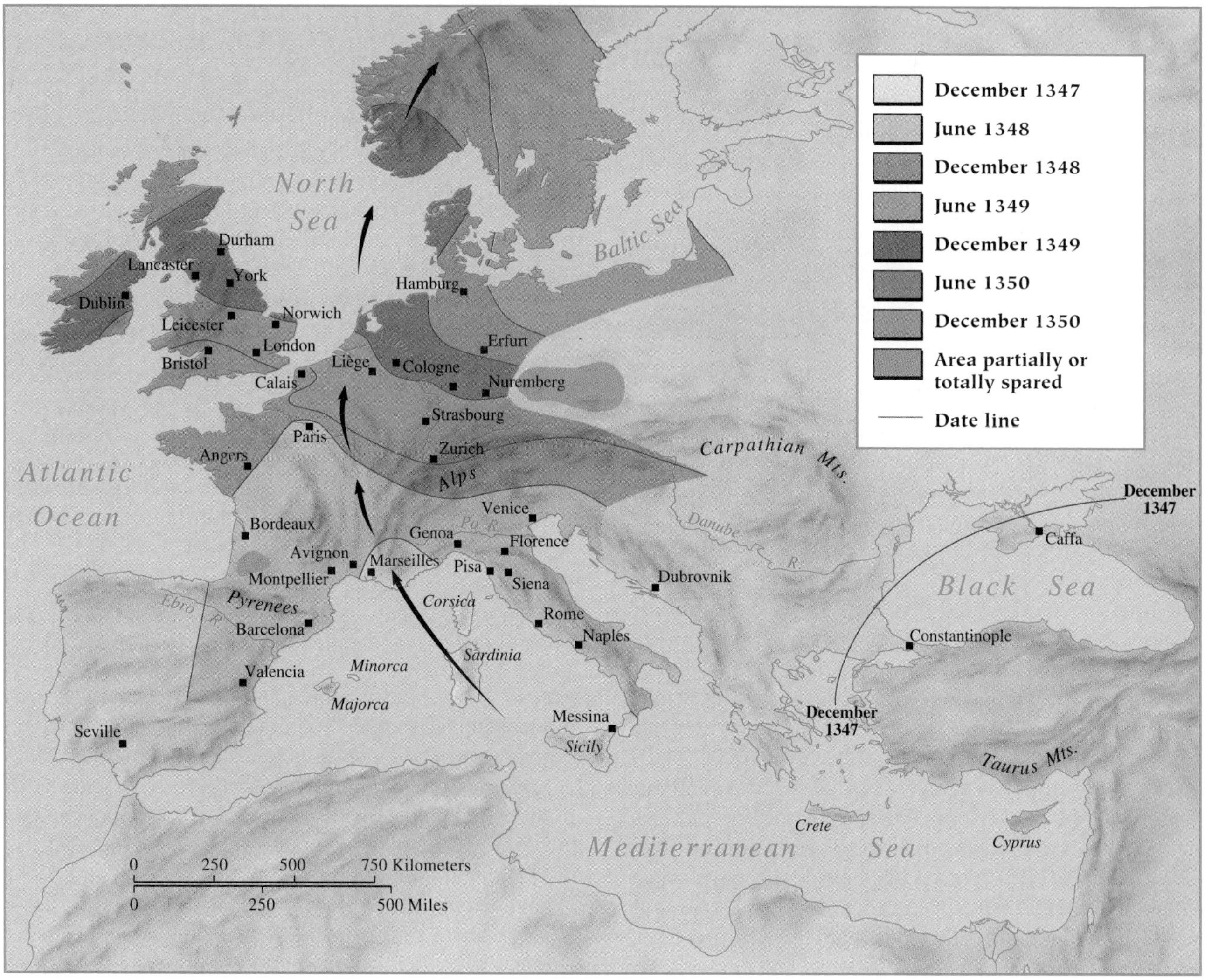

Mass Burial of Plague Victims. The Black Death spread to northern Europe by the end of 1348. Shown here is a mass burial of victims of the plague in Tournai, located in modern Belgium. As is evident in the illustration, at this stage of the plague, there was still time to make coffins for the victims' burial. Later, as the plague intensified, the dead were thrown into open pits.

mortality rates were never as high in eastern Europe as they were in western and central Europe.

Mortality figures for the Black Death were incredibly high. Italy was especially hard hit. As the commercial center of the Mediterranean, Italy possessed scores of ports where the plague could be introduced. Italy's crowded cities, whether large, such as Florence, Genoa, and Venice with populations near 100,000, or small, such as Orvieto and Pistoia, suffered losses of 50 to 60 percent (see the box on p. 277). France and England were also particularly devastated. In northern France, farming villages suffered mortality rates of 30 percent, while cities such as Rouen were more severely affected and experienced losses as high as 40 percent. In England and Germany, entire villages simply disappeared. In Germany, of approximately 170,000 inhabited locations, only 130,000 were left by the end of the fourteenth century.

It has been estimated that the European population declined by 25 to 50 percent between 1347 and 1351. If we accept the recent scholarly assessment of a European population of 75 million in the early fourteenth century, this means a death toll of 19 to 38 million people in four years. And the plague did not end in 1351. There were major outbreaks again in 1361–1362 and 1369 and then recurrences every five or six to ten or twelve years, depending on climatic and ecological conditions, until the end of the fifteenth century. The European population thus did not begin to recover until around 1500 and took several generations after that to reattain thirteenth-century levels.

LIFE AND DEATH: REACTIONS TO THE PLAGUE

Natural disasters of the magnitude of the great plague produce extreme psychological reactions. Knowing they could be dead in a matter of days, people began living for the moment; some threw themselves with abandon into sexual and alcoholic orgies. The fourteenth-century Italian writer Giovanni Boccaccio gave a classic description of this kind of reaction to the plague in Florence in the preface to his famous *Decameron:*

> [Some people] held that plenty of drinking and enjoyment, singing and free living and the gratification of the appetite in every possible way, letting the devil take the hindmost, was the best preventative . . . ; and as far as they could, they suited the action to the word. Day and night they went from one tavern to another drinking and carousing unrestrainedly. At the least inkling of something that suited them, they ran wild in other people's houses, and there was no one to prevent them, for everyone had abandoned all responsibility for his belongings as well as for himself, considering his days numbered.[3]

Wealthy and powerful people fled to their country estates, as Boccaccio recounted: "Still others . . . maintained that no remedy against plagues was better than to leave them miles behind. Men and women without number . . . , caring for nobody but themselves, abandoned the city, their houses and estates, their own flesh and blood even, and their effects, in search of a country place."[4]

The attempt to explain the Black Death and mitigate its harshness led to extreme sorts of behavior. To many people, the plague had either been sent by God as a pun-

The Black Death

The Black Death was the most terrifying natural calamity of the Middle Ages. This contemporary description of the great plague in Florence is taken from the preface to *The Decameron* by the fourteenth-century Italian writer Giovanni Boccaccio.

Giovanni Boccaccio, The Decameron

In the year of Our Lord 1348 the deadly plague broke out in the great city of Florence, most beautiful of Italian cities. Whether through the operation of the heavenly bodies or because of our own iniquities which the just wrath of God sought to correct, the plague had arisen in the East some years before, causing the death of countless human beings. It spread without stop from one place to another, until, unfortunately, it swept over the West. Neither knowledge nor human foresight availed against it, though the city was cleansed of much filth by chosen officers in charge and sick persons were forbidden to enter it, while advice was broadcast for the preservation of health. Nor did humble supplications serve. Not once but many times they were ordained in the form of processions and other ways for the propitiation of God by the faithful, but, in spite of everything, toward the spring of the year the plague began to show its ravages. . . .

It did not manifest itself as in the East, where if a man bled at the nose he had certain warning of inevitable death. At the onset of the disease both men and women were afflicted by a sort of swelling in the groin or under the armpits which sometimes attained the size of a common apple or egg. Some of these swellings were larger and some smaller, and were commonly called boils. From these two starting points the boils began in a little while to spread and appear generally all over the body. Afterwards, the manifestation of the disease changed into black or livid spots on the arms, thighs, and the whole person. In many these blotches were large and far apart, in others small and closely clustered. Like the boils, which had been and continued to be a certain indication of coming death, these blotches had the same meaning for everyone on whom they appeared.

Neither the advice of physicians nor the virtue of any medicine seemed to help or avail in the cure of these diseases. Indeed, . . . not only did few recover, but on the contrary almost everyone died within three days of the appearance of the signs—some sooner, some later. . . . The virulence of the plague was all the greater in that it was communicated by the sick to the well by contact, not unlike fire when dry or fatty things are brought near it. But the evil was still worse. Not only did conversation and familiarity with the diseased spread the malady and even cause death, but the mere touch of the clothes or any other object the sick had touched or used, seemed to spread the pestilence. . . .

More wretched still were the circumstances of the common people and, for a great part, of the middle class, for, confined to their homes either by hope of safety or by poverty, and restricted to their own sections, they fell sick daily by thousands. There, devoid of help or care, they died almost without redemption. A great many breathed their last in the public streets, day and night; a large number perished in their homes, and it was only by the stench of their decaying bodies that they proclaimed their death to their neighbors. Everywhere the city was teeming with corpses. . . .

So many bodies were brought to the churches every day that the consecrated ground did not suffice to hold them, particularly according to the ancient custom of giving each corpse its individual place. Huge trenches were dug in the crowded churchyards and the new dead were piled in them, layer upon layer, like merchandise in the hold of a ship. A little earth covered the corpses of each row, and the procedure continued until the trench was filled to the top.

ishment for humans' sins or been caused by the devil. Some resorted to extreme asceticism to cleanse themselves of sin and gain God's forgiveness. Such were the flagellants, whose movement became popular in 1348, especially in Germany. Groups of flagellants, both men and women, wandered from town to town, flogging themselves with whips to win the forgiveness of God, whom they believed had sent the plague to punish humans for their sinful ways. One contemporary chronicler described a flagellant procession:

> The penitents went about, coming first out of Germany. They were men who did public penance and scourged themselves with whips of hard knotted leather with little iron spikes. Some made themselves bleed very badly between the shoulder blades and some foolish women had cloths ready to catch the blood and smear it on their eyes, saying it was miraculous blood. While they were doing penance, they sang very mournful songs about the nativity and the passion of Our Lord. The object of this penance was to put a stop to the mortality, for in that time . . . at least a third of all the people in the world died.[5]

The flagellants attracted attention and created mass hysteria wherever they went. The Catholic church, however, became alarmed when flagellant groups began to kill Jews and attack clergy who opposed them. Some groups also developed a millenarian aspect, placing their emphasis

Metropolitan Museum of Art, New York, The Cloisters Collection

The Flagellants. Reactions to the plague were extreme at times. Believing that asceticism could atone for humanity's sins and win God's forgiveness, flagellants wandered from town to town flogging themselves and each other with whips, as in this illustration.

on the coming end of the world, the return of Jesus, and the establishment of a thousand-year kingdom under his governance. Pope Clement VI condemned the flagellants in October 1349 and urged the public authorities to crush them. By the end of 1350, most of the flagellant movement had been destroyed.

An outbreak of virulent anti-Semitism also accompanied the Black Death. Jews were accused of causing the plague by poisoning town wells. Although Jews were persecuted in Spain, the worst organized massacres, or pogroms, against this helpless minority were carried out in Germany; more than sixty major Jewish communities in Germany had been exterminated by 1351 (see the box on p. 279). Many Jews fled eastward to Russia and especially to Poland, where the king offered them protection. Eastern Europe became home to large Jewish communities.

The prevalence of death because of the plague and its recurrences affected people in profound ways. Some survivors apparently came to treat life as something cheap and passing. Violence and violent death appeared to be more common after the plague than before. Postplague Europe also demonstrated a morbid preoccupation with death. In their sermons, priests reminded parishioners that each night's sleep might be their last. Tombstones were decorated with macabre scenes of naked corpses in various stages of decomposition with snakes entwined in their bones and their innards filled with worms.

Economic Dislocation and Social Upheaval

The population collapse of the fourteenth century had dire economic and social consequences. Economic dislocation was accompanied by social upheaval. Between 1000 and 1300, Europe had been relatively stable. The division of society into the three estates of clergy (those who pray), nobility (those who fight), and laborers (those who work) had already begun to disintegrate in the thirteenth century, however. In the fourteenth century, a series of urban and rural revolts rocked European society.

NOBLE LANDLORDS AND PEASANTS

Both peasants and noble landlords were affected by the demographic crisis of the fourteenth century. Most noticeably, Europe experienced a serious labor shortage that caused a dramatic rise in the price of labor. At Cuxham manor in England, for example, a farm laborer who had received two shillings a week in 1347 was paid seven in 1349 and almost eleven by 1350. At the same time, the decline in population depressed or held stable the demand for agricultural produce, resulting in stable or falling prices for output (although in England prices remained high until the 1380s). The chronicler Henry Knighton observed: "And the price of everything was cheap. . . . A man could buy a horse for half a mark [six shillings], which before was worth forty shillings."[6] Because landlords were having to pay more for labor at the same time that their rents or incomes were declining, they began to experience considerable adversity and lower standards of living. In England, aristocratic incomes dropped more than 20 percent between 1347 and 1353.

Aristocrats responded to adversity by seeking to lower the wage rate. The English Parliament passed the Statute of Laborers (1351), which attempted to limit wages to preplague levels and forbid the mobility of peasants as well. Although such laws proved largely unworkable, they did keep wages from rising as high as they might have in a free market. Overall, the position of landlords continued to deteriorate during the late fourteenth and early fifteenth centuries. At the same time, the position of peasants improved, though not uniformly throughout Europe.

The decline in the number of peasants after the Black Death accelerated the process of converting labor services to rents, freeing peasants from the obligations of servile tenure and weakening the system of manorialism. But there were limits to how much the peasants could advance. They faced the same economic hurdles as the lords, while the latter attempted to impose wage restrictions, reinstate old forms of labor service, and create new obligations. New governmental taxes also hurt. Peasant complaints became widespread and soon gave rise to rural revolts.

PEASANT REVOLTS

In 1358, a peasant revolt, known as the *Jacquerie,* broke out in northern France. The destruction of normal order by the Black Death and the subsequent economic dislo-

A Medieval Holocaust: The Cremation of the Strasbourg Jews

In their attempt to explain the widespread horrors of the Black Death, medieval Christian communities looked for scapegoats. As at the time of the Crusades, the Jews were blamed for poisoning wells and hence spreading the plague. This selection by a contemporary chronicler, written in 1349, gives an account of how Christians in the town of Strasbourg in the Holy Roman Empire dealt with their Jewish community. It is apparent that financial gain was also an important motive in killing the Jews.

■ *Jacob von Königshofen, "The Cremation of the Strasbourg Jews"*

In the year 1349 there occurred the greatest epidemic that ever happened. Death went from one end of the earth to the other. . . . And from what this epidemic came, all wise teachers and physicians could only say that it was God's will. . . . This epidemic also came to Strasbourg in the summer of the above-mentioned year, and it is estimated that about sixteen thousand people died.

In the matter of this plague the Jews throughout the world were reviled and accused in all lands of having caused it through the poison which they are said to have put into the water and the wells—that is what they were accused of—and for this reason the Jews were burnt all the way from the Mediterranean into Germany. . . .

[The account then goes on to discuss the situation of the Jews in the city of Strasbourg.]

On Saturday . . . they burnt the Jews on a wooden platform in their cemetery. There were about two thousand people of them. Those who wanted to baptise themselves were spared. [About one thousand accepted baptism.] Many small children were taken out of the fire and baptized against the will of their fathers and mothers. And everything that was owed to the Jews was canceled, and the Jews had to surrender all pledges and notes that they had taken for debts. The council, however, took the cash that the Jews possessed and divided it among the working-men proportionately. The money was indeed the thing that killed the Jews. If they had been poor and if the lords had not been in debt to them, they would not have been burnt. . . .

Thus were the Jews burnt at Strasbourg, and in the same year in all the cities of the Rhine, whether Free Cities or Imperial Cities or cities belonging to the lords. In some towns they burnt the Jews after a trial, in others, without a trial. In some cities the Jews themselves set fire to their houses and cremated themselves.

It was decided in Strasbourg that no Jew should enter the city for 100 years, but before 20 years had passed, the council and magistrates agreed that they ought to admit the Jews again into the city for 20 years. And so the Jews came back again to Strasbourg in the year 1368 after the birth of our Lord.

cation were important factors in causing the revolt, but the ravages created by the Hundred Years' War also affected the French peasantry (see "War and Political Instability" later in this chapter). Both the French and English forces followed a deliberate policy of laying waste to peasants' lands while bands of mercenaries lived off the land by taking peasants' produce as well.

Peasant anger was also exacerbated by growing class tensions. Landed nobles were eager to hold on to their politically privileged position and felt increasingly threatened in the new postplague world of higher wages and lower prices. Many aristocrats looked upon peasants with utter contempt. A French tale

Bibliothèque Nationale, Paris

Peasant Rebellion. The fourteenth century witnessed a number of revolts of the peasantry against noble landowners. Although the revolts often met with initial success, they were soon crushed. This fifteenth-century illustration shows nobles massacring the rebels in the French *Jacquerie* of 1358.

told to upper-class audiences contained this remarkable passage:

> Tell me, Lord, if you please, by what right or title does a villein [peasant] eat beef? . . . Should they eat fish? Rather let them eat thistles and briars, thorns and straw and hay on Sunday and peapods on weekdays. They should keep watch without sleep and have trouble always; that is how villeins should live. Yet each day they are full and drunk on the best wines, and in fine clothes. The great expenditures of villeins come as a high cost, for it is this that destroys and ruins the world. It is they who spoil the common welfare. From the villein comes all unhappiness. Should they eat meat? Rather should they chew grass on the heath with the horned cattle and go naked on all fours.[7]

The peasants reciprocated this contempt for their so-called social superiors.

The outburst of peasant anger led to savage confrontations. Castles were burned and nobles murdered (see the box on p. 281). Such atrocities did not go unanswered, however. The *Jacquerie* soon failed as the privileged classes closed ranks, savagely massacred the rebels, and ended the revolt.

The English Peasants' Revolt of 1381 was the most prominent of all. It was a product not of desperation but of rising expectations. After the Black Death, the condition of the English peasants had improved as they enjoyed greater freedom and higher wages or lower rents. Aristocratic landlords had fought back with legislation to depress wages and attempted to reimpose old feudal dues. The most immediate cause of the revolt, however, was the monarchy's attempt to raise revenues by imposing a poll tax or a flat charge on each adult member of the population. Peasants in eastern England, the wealthiest part of the country, refused to pay the tax and expelled the collectors forcibly from their villages.

This action sparked a widespread rebellion of both peasants and townspeople led by a well-to-do peasant called Wat Tyler and a preacher named John Ball. The latter preached an effective message against the noble class, as recounted by the French chronicler Jean Froissart:

> Good people, things cannot go right in England and never will, until goods are held in common and there are no more villeins and gentlefolk, but we are all one and the same. In what way are those whom we call lords greater masters than ourselves? How have they deserved it? Why do they hold us in bondage? If we all spring from a single father and mother, Adam and Eve, how can they claim or prove that they are lords more than us, except by making us produce and grow the wealth which they spend?[8]

The movement developed a famous jingle based on Ball's preaching: "When Adam delved and Eve span, who was then a gentleman?"

The revolt was initially successful as the rebels burned down the manor houses of aristocrats, lawyers, and government officials and murdered several important officials, including the archbishop of Canterbury. After the peasants marched on London, the young king Richard II, age fifteen, promised to accept the rebels' demands if they returned to their homes. They accepted the king's word and dispersed, but the king reneged and with the assistance of the aristocrats arrested hundreds of the rebels. The poll tax was eliminated, however, and in the end most of the rebels were pardoned.

REVOLTS IN THE CITIES

Revolts also erupted in the cities. Commercial and industrial activity suffered almost immediately from the Black Death. An oversupply of goods and an immediate drop in demand led to a decline in trade after 1350. Some industries suffered greatly. Florence's woolen industry, one of the giants, produced 70,000 to 80,000 pieces of cloth in 1338; in 1378, it was yielding only 24,000 pieces. Bourgeois merchants and manufacturers responded to the decline in trade and production by attempting to restrict competition and resist the demands of the lower classes.

In urban areas, where capitalist industrialists paid low wages and managed to prevent workers from forming organizations to help themselves, industrial revolts broke out throughout Europe. Ghent experienced one in 1381, Rouen in 1382. Most famous, however, was the revolt of the *ciompi* in Florence in 1378. The *ciompi* were wool workers in Florence's most prominent industry. In the 1370s, not only was the woolen industry depressed, but the wool workers saw their real wages decline when the coinage in which they were paid was debased. Their revolt won them some concessions from the municipal government, including the right to form guilds and be represented in the government. But their newly won rights were short-lived; authorities ended *ciompi* participation in the government by 1382.

Although the peasant and urban revolts sometimes resulted in short-term gains for the participants, it is also true that the uprisings were quickly crushed and their gains lost. Accustomed to ruling, the established classes easily combined and quashed dissent. Nevertheless, the rural and urban revolts of the fourteenth century ushered in an age of social conflict that characterized much of later European history.

War and Political Instability

Famine, plague, economic turmoil, social upheaval, and violence were not the only problems of the fourteenth century. War and political instability must also be added to the list. Of all the struggles that ensued in the fourteenth century, the Hundred Years' War was the most famous and the most violent.

Causes of the Hundred Years' War

In 1259, the English king, Henry III, had relinquished his claims to all the French territories previously held by the English monarchy except for one relatively small possession known as the duchy of Gascony. As duke of Gascony, the English king pledged loyalty as a vassal to the French

A Revolt of French Peasants

In 1358, French peasants rose up in a revolt known as the *Jacquerie.* The relationship between aristocrats and peasants had degenerated as a result of the social upheavals and privations caused by the Black Death and the Hundred Years' War. This excerpt from the chronicle of an aristocrat paints a horrifying picture of the barbarities that occurred during the revolt.

Jean Froissart, Chronicles

There were very strange and terrible happenings in several parts of the kingdom of France. . . . They began when some of the men from the country towns came together in the Beauvais region. They had no leaders and at first they numbered scarcely 100. One of them got up and said that the nobility of France, knights and squires, were disgracing and betraying the realm, and that it would be a good thing if they were all destroyed. At this they all shouted: "He's right! He's right! Shame on any man who saves the nobility from being wiped out!"

They banded together and went off, without further deliberation and unarmed except for pikes and knives, to the house of a knight who lived nearby. They broke in and killed the knight, with his lady and his children, big and small, and set fire to the house. Next they went to another castle and did much worse; for, having seized the knight and bound him securely to a post, several of them violated his wife and daughter before his eyes. Then they killed the wife, who was pregnant, and the daughter and all the other children, and finally put the knight to death with great cruelty and burned and razed the castle.

They did similar things in a number of castles and big houses, and their ranks swelled until there were a good 6,000 of them. Wherever they went their numbers grew, for all the men of the same sort joined them. The knights and squires fled before them with their families. They took their wives and daughters many miles away to put them in safety, leaving their houses open with their possessions inside. And those evil men, who had come together without leaders or arms, pillaged and burned everything and violated and killed all the ladies and girls without mercy, like mad dogs. Their barbarous acts were worse than anything that ever took place between Christians and Saracens [Muslims]. Never did men commit such vile deeds. They were such that no living creature ought to see, or even imagine or think of, and the men who committed the most were admired and had the highest places among them. I could never bring myself to write down the horrible and shameful things which they did to the ladies. But, among other brutal excesses, they killed a knight, put him on a spit, and turned him at the fire and roasted him before the lady and her children. After about a dozen of them had violated the lady, they tried to force her and the children to eat the knight's flesh before putting them cruelly to death.

king. But this territory gave rise to numerous disputes between the kings of England and France. By the thirteenth century, the Capetian monarchs had greatly increased their power over their more important vassals, the great lords of France. Royal officials interfered regularly in the affairs of the vassals' fiefs, especially in matters of justice. Although this policy irritated all the vassals, it especially annoyed the king of England, who considered himself the peer of the French king.

A dispute over the right of succession to the French throne also complicated the struggle between the French and the English. In the fourteenth century, the Capetian dynasty failed to produce a male heir for the first time in almost four hundred years. In 1328, the senior branch of the Capetian dynasty became extinct in the male line with the death of Charles IV. As the son of the daughter of King Philip IV, King Edward III of England (1327–1377) had a claim to the French throne as a close male relative. French practice, however, emphasized descent through the male line, and a cousin of the Capetians, Philip, duke of Valois, became king as Philip VI (1328–1350).

The immediate cause of the war between France and England was yet another quarrel over Gascony. In 1337, when Edward III, the king of England and duke of Gascony, refused to do homage to Philip VI for Gascony, the French king seized the duchy. Edward responded by declaring war on Philip, the "so-called King of France." There is no doubt that the personalities of the two monarchs also had much to do with the outbreak of the Hundred Years' War. Both Edward and Philip loved luxury and shared a desire for the glory and prestige that came from military engagements. Both were only too willing to use their respective nation's resources to satisfy their own desires. Moreover, for many nobles, the promise of plunder and territorial gain was an incentive to follow the disruptive path of their rulers.

Conduct and Course of the War

The Hundred Years' War began in a burst of knightly enthusiasm. Trained to be warriors, knights viewed the clash of battle as the ultimate opportunity to demonstrate their fighting abilities. But this struggle would change the nature of warfare, for as it dragged on, the outcomes of battles were increasingly determined not by knights but by peasant foot soldiers. The French army of 1337, with its heavily armed noble cavalry, resembled its twelfth- and thirteenth-century forebears. The noble cavalrymen considered themselves the fighting elite and looked with contempt on the foot soldiers and crossbowmen, their social inferiors.

The English army, however, had evolved differently and had included peasants as paid foot soldiers since at least Anglo-Saxon times. Armed with pikes, many of these foot soldiers had also adopted the longbow, invented by the Welsh. The longbow had a more rapid speed of fire than the more powerful crossbow. Although the English made use of heavily armed cavalry, they relied even more on large numbers of foot soldiers.

Edward III's early campaigns in France achieved little. When Edward renewed his efforts in 1346 with an invasion of Normandy, Philip responded by raising a large force to crush the English army and met Edward's forces at Crécy, just south of Flanders. The larger French army followed no battle plan but simply attacked the English lines in a disorderly fashion. The arrows of the English archers devastated the French cavalry. As Jean Froissart described it, "The English continued to shoot [their longbows] into the thickest part of the crowd, wasting none of their arrows. They impaled or wounded horses and riders, who fell to the ground in great distress, unable to get up again [because of their heavy armor] without the help of several men."[9] It was a stunning victory for the English. Edward followed up by capturing the French port of Calais to serve as a staging ground for future invasions.

The Battle of Crécy was not decisive, however. The English simply did not possess the resources to subjugate all of France. Truces, small-scale hostilities, and some major operations were combined in an orgy of seemingly incessant struggle. The English campaigns were waged by Edward III and his son Edward, the prince of Wales, known as the Black Prince. The Black Prince's campaigns in France were devastating (see the box on p. 283). Avoiding pitched battles, his forces deliberately ravaged the land, burning crops and entire unfortified villages and towns and stealing anything of value. For the English, such campaigns were profitable; for the French people, they meant hunger, deprivation, and death. When the army of the Black Prince was finally forced to do battle, the French, under their king,

CHRONOLOGY

The Hundred Years' War

Outbreak of hostilities	1337
Battle of Crécy	1346
Battle of Poitiers	1356
Peace of Brétigny	1359
Death of Edward III	1377
Twenty-year truce declared	1396
Henry V (1413–1422) renews the war	1415
Battle of Agincourt	1415
French recovery under Joan of Arc	1429–1431
End of the war	1453

Battle of Crécy. This fifteenth-century manuscript illustration depicts the Battle of Crécy, the first of several military disasters suffered by the French in the Hundred Years' War, and shows why the English preferred the longbow to the crossbow. At the left, the French crossbowmen stop shooting and prime their weapons by cranking the handle, while English archers continue to shoot their longbows (a skilled archer could launch ten arrows a minute).

Bibliotheque Nationale, Paris/Bridgeman Art Library

The Hundred Years' War

In his account of the Hundred Years' War, the fourteenth-century French chronicler Jean Froissart described the sack of the fortified French town of Limoges by the Black Prince, Edward, the prince of Wales. It provides a vivid example of how noncombatants fared during the war.

Jean Froissart, Chronicles

For about a month, certainly not longer, the Prince of Wales remained before Limoges. During that time he allowed no assaults or skirmishes, but pushed on steadily with the mining. The knights inside and the townspeople, who knew what was going on, started a countermine in the hope of killing the English miners, but it was a failure. When the Prince's miners who, as they dug, were continually shoring up their tunnel, had completed their work, they said to the Prince: "My lord, whenever you like now we can bring a big piece of wall down into the moat, so that you can get into the city quite easily and safely."

The Prince was very pleased to hear this. "Excellent," he said. "At six o'clock tomorrow morning, show me what you can do."

When they knew it was the right time for it, the miners started a fire in their mine. In the morning, just as the Prince had specified, a great section of the wall collapsed, filling the moat at the place where it fell. For the English, who were armed and ready waiting, it was a welcome sight. Those on foot could enter as they liked, and did so. They rushed to the gate, cut through the bars holding it and knocked it down. They did the same with the barriers outside, meeting with no resistance. It was all done so quickly that the people in the town were taken unawares. Then the Prince, the Duke of Lancaster, the Earl of Cambridge, Sir Guichard d'Angle, with all the others and their men burst into the city, followed by pillagers on foot, all in a mood to wreak havoc and do murder, killing indiscriminately, for those were their orders. There were pitiful scenes. Men, women, and children flung themselves on their knees before the Prince, crying: "Have mercy on us, gentle sir!" But he was so inflamed with anger that he would not listen. Neither man nor woman was heeded, but all who could be found were put to the sword, including many who were in no way to blame. I do not understand how they could have failed to take pity on people who were too unimportant to have committed treason. Yet they paid for it, and paid more dearly than the leaders who had committed it.

There is no man so hard-hearted that, if he had been in Limoges on that day, and had remembered God, he would not have wept bitterly at the fearful slaughter which took place. More than 3,000 persons, men, women, and children, were dragged out to have their throats cut. May God receive their souls, for they were true martyrs.

John II (1350–1364), were once again defeated. This time even the king was captured. This Battle of Poitiers (1356) ended the first phase of the Hundred Years' War. Under the Peace of Brétigny (1359), the French agreed to pay a large ransom for King John, the English territories in Gascony were enlarged, and Edward renounced his claims to the throne of France in return for John's promise to give up control over English lands in France. This first phase of the war made it clear that despite their victories, the English were not really strong enough to subdue all of France and make Edward III's claim to the French monarchy a reality.

Monarchs, however, could be slow learners. The Treaty of Brétigny was never really enforced. In the next phase of the war, in the capable hands of John's son Charles V (1364–1380), the French recovered what they had previously lost. The English returned to plundering the French countryside and avoiding pitched battles. That pleased Charles, who did not want to engage in set battles, preferring to use armed bands to reduce the English fortresses systematically. By 1374, the French had recovered their lost lands, although France itself continued to be plagued by "free companies" of mercenaries who, no longer paid by the English, simply lived off the land by plunder and ransom. Nevertheless, for the time being, the war seemed over, especially when a twenty-year truce was negotiated in 1396.

In 1415, however, the English king, Henry V (1413–1422), renewed the war. At the Battle of Agincourt (1415), the French suffered a disastrous defeat, and fifteen hundred French nobles died when the heavy, armor-plated French knights attempted to attack across a field turned to mud by heavy rain. Henry went on to reconquer Normandy and forge an alliance with the duke of Burgundy, making the English masters of northern France (see Map 11.2).

The seemingly hopeless French cause fell into the hands of Charles the dauphin (heir to the throne), who governed the southern two-thirds of French lands from Bourges. Charles was weak and timid and was unable to rally the French against the English, who in 1428 had turned south and were besieging the city of Orléans to gain access to the valley of the Loire. The French monarch was saved, quite unexpectedly, by a French peasant woman.

Joan of Arc was born in 1412 to well-to-do peasants from the village of Domrémy in Champagne. Deeply religious, Joan experienced visions and came to believe that her favorite saints had commanded her to free France and have the dauphin crowned as king. In February 1429, Joan made her way to the dauphin's court, where her sincerity

Giraudon/Art Resource, NY

Joan of Arc. Pictured here in a suit of armor, Joan of Arc is holding aloft a banner that shows Jesus and two angels. This portrait dates from the late fifteenth century; there are no known portraits of Joan made from life.

and simplicity persuaded Charles to allow her to accompany a French army to Orléans. Apparently inspired by the faith of the peasant girl, the French armies found new confidence in themselves and liberated Orléans, changing the course of the war. Within a few weeks, the entire Loire valley had been freed of the English. In July 1429, fulfilling Joan's other task, the dauphin was crowned king of France and became Charles VII (1422–1461). In accomplishing the two commands of her angelic voices, Joan had brought the war to a decisive turning point.

Joan, however, did not live to see the war concluded. She was captured by the Burgundian allies of the English in 1430. Wishing to eliminate the "Maid of Orléans" for obvious political reasons, the English turned Joan over to the Inquisition on charges of witchcraft (see the box on p. 285). In the fifteenth century, spiritual visions were thought to be inspired by either God or the devil. Because Joan dressed in men's clothing, it was easy for her enemies to believe that she was in league with the "prince of darkness." She was condemned to death as a heretic and burned at the stake in 1431, at the age of nineteen. To the end, as the flames rose up around her, she declared that her voices came from God and had not deceived her. Twenty-five years later, a church court exonerated her of these charges. In 1920, she was made a saint of the Roman Catholic church.

Joan of Arc's accomplishments proved decisive. Although the war dragged on for another two decades, defeats of English armies in Normandy and Aquitaine led to French victory. Important to the French success was the use of the cannon, a new weapon made possible by the invention of gunpowder. The Chinese had invented gunpowder in the eleventh century and devised a simple cannon by the thirteenth century. The Mongols greatly improved this technology, developing more accurate cannons and cannonballs; both spread to the Middle East by the thirteenth century and to Europe by the fourteenth.

The death of England's best commanders and the instability of the English government under King Henry VI (1421–1471) also contributed to England's defeat. By 1453, the only part of France that was left in England's hands was the coastal town of Calais, which remained English for another century.

Political Instability

The fourteenth century was a period of adversity for the internal political stability of European governments. Although government bureaucracies grew ever larger, at the same time the question of who should control the bureaucracies led to internal conflict and instability. Like the lord-serf relationship, the lord-vassal relationship based on land and military service was being replaced by a contract based on money. Especially after the Black Death, money payments called scutage were increasingly substituted for military service. Monarchs welcomed this development because they could now hire professional soldiers, who tended to be more reliable anyway. As lord-vassal relationships became less personal and less important, new relationships based on political advantage began to be formed, creating new avenues for political influence—and for corruption as well. Especially noticeable as the landed aristocrats suffered declining rents and social uncertainties with the new relationships was the formation of factions of nobles who looked for opportunities to advance their power and wealth at the expense of other noble factions and of their monarchs. Other nobles went to the royal courts, offering to serve the kings.

The kings had their own problems, however. By the mid-fifteenth century, reigning monarchs in many European countries were not the direct descendents of the rulers of 1300. The founders of these new dynasties had to struggle for position as factions of nobles vied to gain material advantages for themselves. As the fifteenth century began, there were two claimants to the throne of France, two aristocratic factions fighting for control of England, and three German princes struggling to be recognized as Holy Roman Emperor.

Fourteenth-century monarchs of old dynasties and new faced financial problems as well. The shift to using mercenary soldiers left monarchs perennially short of cash. Traditional revenues, especially rents from property, increasingly proved insufficient to meet their needs.

The Trial of Joan of Arc

Feared by the English and Burgundians, Joan of Arc was put on trial on charges of witchcraft and heresy after her capture. She was condemned for heresy and burned at the stake on May 30, 1431. This excerpt is taken from the records of Joan's trial, which presented a dramatic confrontation between the judges, trained in the complexities of legal questioning, and a nineteen-year-old woman who relied only on the "voices" of saints who gave her advice. In this selection, Joan describes what these voices told her to do.

The Trial of Joan of Arc

She declared that at the age of thirteen she had a voice from God to help her and guide her. And the first time she was much afraid. And this voice came toward noon, in summer, in her father's garden. . . . She heard the voice on her right, in the direction of the church; and she seldom heard it without a light. This light came from the same side as the voice, and generally there was a great light. . . .

Asked what instruction this voice gave her for the salvation of her soul: she said it taught her to be good and to go to church often. . . . She said that the voice told her to come, and she could no longer stay where she was; and the voice told her again that she should raise the siege of the city of Orléans. She said moreover that the voice told her that she, Joan, should go to Robert de Baudricourt, in the town of Vaucouleurs of which he was captain, and he would provide an escort for her. And the said Joan answered that she was a poor maid, knowing nothing of riding or fighting. She said she went to an uncle of hers, and told him she wanted to stay with him for some time; and she stayed there about eight days. And she told her uncle she must go to the said town of Vaucouleurs, and so her uncle took her.

Then she said that when she reached Vaucouleurs she easily recognized Robert de Baudricourt, although she had never seen him before; and she knew him through her voice, for the voice had told her it was he. . . . The said Robert twice refused to hear her and repulsed her; the third time he listened to her and gave her an escort. And the voice had told her that it would be so.

Monarchs attempted to generate new sources of revenues, especially through taxes, which often meant going through parliaments. This opened the door for parliamentary bodies to gain more power by asking for favors first. Although unsuccessful in most cases, the parliaments simply added another element of uncertainty and confusion to fourteenth-century politics. Turning now to a survey of western and central European states (eastern Europe will be examined in Chapter 12), we can see how these disruptive factors worked.

The Growth of England's Political Institutions

The fifty-year reign of Edward III (1327–1377) was important for the evolution of English political institutions in the fourteenth century. Parliament increased in prominence and developed its basic structure and functions during Edward's reign. Due to his constant need for money to fight the Hundred Years' War, Edward came to rely on Parliament to levy new taxes. In return for regular grants, Edward made several concessions, including a commitment to levy no direct tax without Parliament's consent and to allow Parliament to examine the government accounts to ensure that the money was being spent properly. By the end of Edward's reign, Parliament had become an important component of the English governmental system.

During this same period, Parliament began to assume the organizational structure it has retained to this day. The Great Council of barons became the House of Lords and evolved into a body composed of the chief bishops and abbots of the realm and aristocratic peers whose position in Parliament was hereditary. The representatives of the shires and boroughs, who were considered less important than the lay and ecclesiastical lords, held collective meetings and soon came to be regarded as the House of Commons. Together, the House of Lords and House of Commons constituted Parliament. Although the House of Commons did little beyond approving measures proposed by the Lords, during Edward's reign the Commons did begin the practice of drawing up petitions, which, if accepted by the king, became law.

After Edward III's death, England began to experience the internal instability of aristocratic factionalism that was racking other European countries. The early years of the reign of Edward's grandson, Richard II (1377–1399), began inauspiciously with the Peasants' Revolt that ended only when the king made concessions. Richard's reign was troubled by competing groups of nobles who sought to pursue their own interests. One faction, led by Henry of Lancaster, defeated the king's forces and then deposed and killed him. Henry of Lancaster became King Henry IV (1399–1413). In the fifteenth century, factional conflict would lead to a devastating series of civil wars known as the War of the Roses.

The Problems of the French Kings

At the beginning of the fourteenth century, France was the most prosperous monarchy in Europe. By the end of the century, much of its wealth had been dissipated, and rival factions of aristocrats had made effective monarchical rule a virtual impossibility.

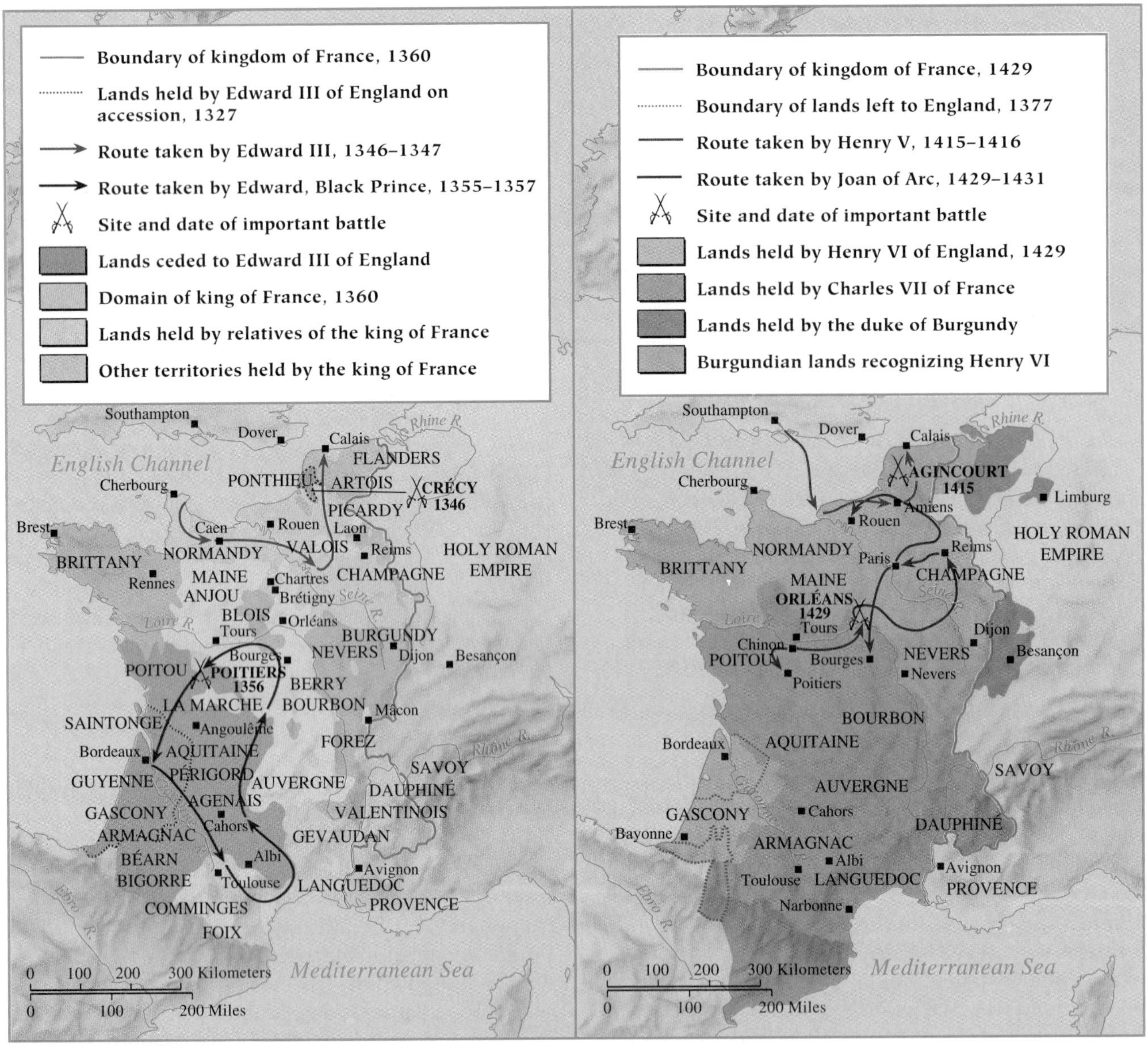

Map 11.2 The Hundred Years' War. This long, exhausting struggle began in 1337 and dragged on until 1453. The English initially gained substantial French territory, but in the later phases of the war, France turned the tide, eventually expelling the English from all Continental lands except the port of Calais. ■ What gains had the English made by 1429, and how do they correlate to proximity to England and the ocean?

The French monarchical state had always had an underlying inherent weakness that proved its undoing in difficult times. Although Capetian monarchs had found ways to enlarge their royal domain and extend their control by developing a large and effective bureaucracy, the various territories that made up France still maintained their own princes, customs, and laws. The parliamentary institutions of France provide a good example of France's basic lack of unity. The French parliament, known as the Estates-General and composed of representatives of the clergy, the nobility, and the Third Estate (everyone else), usually represented only the north of France, not the entire kingdom. The southern provinces had their own estates, and local estates existed in other parts of France. Unlike the English Parliament, which was evolving into a crucial part of the English government, the French Estates-General was simply one of many such institutions.

When Philip VI (1328–1350) became involved in the Hundred Years' War with England, he found it necessary to devise new sources of revenue, including a tax on salt known as the *gabelle* and a hearth tax eventually called the *taille.* These taxes weighed heavily on the French peasantry and middle class. Consequently, when additional taxes were needed to pay for the ransom of King John II after his capture at the Battle of Poitiers, the middle-class inhabitants of the towns tried to use the Estates-General to reform the French government and tax structure.

At the meeting of the Estates-General in 1357, under the leadership of the Parisian provost Étienne Marcel, representatives of the Third Estate granted taxes in exchange for a promise from King John's son, the dauphin Charles, not to tax without the Estates-General's permission and to allow the Estates-General to meet on a regular basis and participate in important political decisions. After Marcel's movement was crushed in 1358, this attempt to make the Estates-General a functioning part of the French government collapsed. The dauphin became King Charles V (1364–1380) and went on to recover much of the land lost to the English. His military successes underscored his efforts to reestablish strong monarchical powers. He undermined the role of the Estates-General by getting it to grant him taxes with no fixed time limit. Charles's death in 1380 soon led to a new time of troubles for the French monarchy, however.

The insanity of Charles VI (1380–1422), which first became apparent in 1392, opened the door to rival factions of French nobles aspiring to power and wealth. The dukes of Burgundy and Orléans competed to control Charles and the French monarchy. Their struggles created chaos for the French government and the French people. Many nobles supported the Orléanist faction while Paris and other towns favored the Burgundians. By the beginning of thc fifteenth century, France seemed hopelessly mired in a civil war. When the English renewed the Hundred Years' War in 1415, the Burgundians supported the English cause and the English monarch's claim to the throne of France.

The German Monarchy

England and France had developed strong national monarchies in the High Middle Ages. By the end of the fourteenth century, they seemed in danger of disintegrating due to dynastic problems and the pressures generated by the Hundred Years' War. In contrast, the Holy Roman Empire, whose core consisted of the lands of Germany, had already begun to fall apart in the High Middle Ages. Northern Italy, which the German emperors had tried to include in their medieval empire, had been free from any real imperial control since the end of the Hohenstaufen dynasty in the thirteenth century. In Germany itself, the failure of the Hohenstaufens ended any chance of centralized monarchical authority, and Germany became a land of hundreds of virtually independent states. These varied in size and power and included princely states, such as the duchies of Bavaria and Saxony; free imperial city-states (self-governing cities directly under the control of the Holy Roman Emperor rather than a German territorial prince), such as Nuremberg; modest territories of petty imperial knights; and ecclesiastical states, such as the archbishopric of Cologne, in which an ecclesiastical official, such as a bishop, archbishop, or abbot, served in a dual capacity as an administrative official of the Catholic church and as secular lord over the territories of the state. Although all of the rulers of these different states had some obligations to the German king and Holy Roman Emperor, more and more they acted independently.

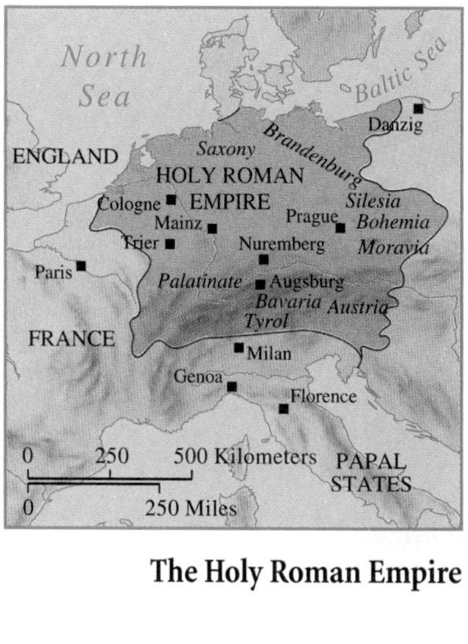

The Holy Roman Empire

Because of its unique pattern of development in the High Middle Ages, the German monarchy had become established on an elective rather than hereditary basis. This principle of election was standardized in 1356 by the Golden Bull issued by Emperor Charles IV (1346–1378). This document stated that four lay princes (the count palatine of the Rhine, the duke of Saxony, the margrave of Brandenburg, and the king of Bohemia) and three ecclesiastical rulers (the archbishops of Mainz, Trier, and Cologne) would serve as electors with the legal power to elect the "king of the Romans and future emperor, to be ruler of the world and of the Christian people."[10] "King of the Romans" was the official title of the German king; after his imperial coronation, he would also have the title of emperor.

In the fourteenth century, the electoral principle further ensured that kings of Germany were generally weak. Their ability to exercise effective power depended on the extent of their own family possessions. At the beginning of the fifteenth century, three emperors claimed the throne. Although the dispute was quickly settled, Germany entered the fifteenth century in a condition that verged on anarchy. Princes fought princes and leagues of cities. The emperors were virtually powerless to control any of them.

The States of Italy

By the fourteenth century, Italy, too, had failed to develop a centralized monarchical state. Papal opposition to the rule of the Hohenstaufen emperors in northern Italy had virtually guaranteed that. Moreover, southern Italy was divided into the kingdom of Naples, ruled by the French house of Anjou, and Sicily, whose kings came from the Spanish house of Aragon. The center of the peninsula remained under the rather shaky control of the papacy. Lack of centralized authority had enabled numerous city-states in northern Italy to remain independent of any political authority.

In fourteenth-century Italy, two general tendencies can be discerned: the replacement of republican governments by tyrants and the expansion of the larger city-states at the expense of the less powerful ones. Nearly all the cities of northern Italy began their existence as free communes with republican governments. But in the fourteenth century, intense internal strife led city-states to resort to temporary expedients, allowing rule by one man with dictatorial powers. Limited rule, however, soon became long-term despotism, as tyrants proved willing to use force to maintain themselves in power. Eventually, such tyrants tried to legitimize their power by purchasing titles from the emperor (still nominally ruler of northern Italy as Holy Roman Emperor). In this fashion, the Visconti became the dukes of Milan and the d'Este, the dukes of Ferrara.

The other change of great significance was the development of larger, regional states as the larger states expanded at the expense of the smaller ones. To fight their battles, city-states came to rely on mercenary soldiers, whose leaders, called *condottieri,* sold the services of their bands to the highest bidder. These mercenaries wreaked havoc on the countryside, living by blackmail and looting when they were not actively engaged in battles. Many were foreigners who flocked to Italy during the periods of truce of the Hundred Years' War. By the end of the fourteenth century, three major states came to dominate northern Italy, the despotic state of Milan and the republican states of Florence and Venice.

In the fertile Po valley, where the chief trade routes from Italian coastal cities to the Alpine passes crossed, Milan was one of the richest city-states in Italy. Politically, it was also one of the most agitated until the Visconti family established itself as the hereditary despots of Milan in 1322. Giangaleazzo Visconti, who ruled from 1385 to 1402, transformed this despotism into a hereditary duchy by purchasing the title of duke from the emperor in 1395. Under Giangaleazzo's direction, the duchy of Milan extended its power over all of Lombardy and even threatened to conquer much of northern Italy until the duke's untimely death before the gates of Florence in 1402.

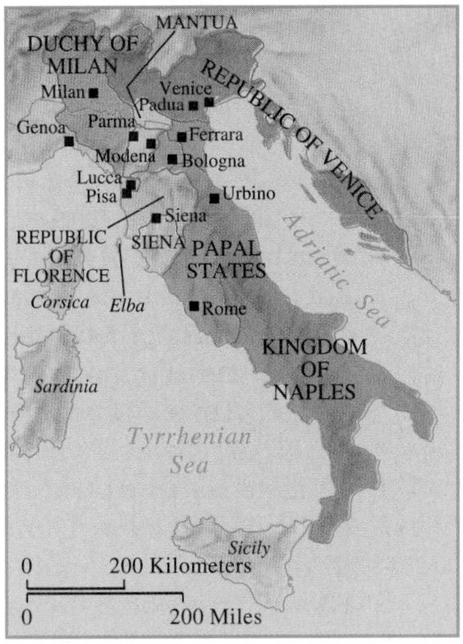

The States of Italy

Florence, like the other Italian towns, was initially a free commune dominated by a patrician class of nobles known as the *grandi.* But the rapid expansion of Florence's economy made possible the development of a wealthy merchant-industrialist class known as the *popolo grasso*—literally the "fat people." In 1293, the *popolo grasso* assumed a dominant role in government by establishing a new constitution known as the Ordinances of Justice. It provided for a republican government controlled by the seven major guilds of the city, which represented the interests of the wealthier classes. Executive power was vested in the hands of a council of elected priors (the *signoria*) and a standard-bearer of justice called the *gonfaloniere,* assisted by a number of councils with advisory and overlapping powers. Near the mid-fourteenth century, revolutionary activity by the *popolo minuto,* the small shopkeepers and artisans, won them a share in the government. Even greater expansion occurred briefly when the *ciompi,* or industrial wool workers, were allowed to be represented in the government after their revolt in 1378. Only four years later, however, a coun-

Mercenaries as Looters. Mercenary soldiers, like medieval armies in general, were notorious for causing havoc by looting when they were not engaged in battle. This mid-fourteenth-century manuscript illustration shows soldiers ransacking a house in Paris.

British Library

CHRONOLOGY

The States of Western and Central Europe

England	
Edward III	1327–1377
Richard II	1377–1399
Henry IV	1399–1413
France	
Philip VI	1328–1350
John II	1350–1364
Capture at Poitiers	1356
Crushing of the *Jacquerie* and Étienne Marcel	1358
Charles V	1364–1380
Charles VI	1380–1422
The German Monarchy	
Golden Bull	1356
Italy	
Florence	
Ordinances of Justice	1293
Venice	
Closing of Great Council	1297
Milan	
Visconti established themselves as rulers of Milan	1322
Giangaleazzo Visconti purchases title of duke	1395

terrevolution brought the "fat people" back into virtual control of the government. After 1382, the Florentine government was controlled by a small merchant oligarchy that manipulated the supposedly republican government. By that time, Florence had also been successful in a series of wars against its neighbors. It had conquered most of Tuscany and established itself as a major territorial state in northern Italy.

The other major northern Italian state was the republic of Venice, which had grown rich from commercial activity throughout the eastern Mediterranean and into northern Europe. A large number of merchant families became extremely wealthy. In the constitution of 1297, these patricians took control of the republic. In this year, the Great Council, the source of all political power, was closed to all but the members of about two hundred families. Since all other magistrates of the city were either chosen from or by this council, these families now formed a hereditary patriciate that completely dominated the city. Although the doge (or duke) had been the executive head of the republic since the Early Middle Ages, by 1300 he had become largely a figurehead. Actual power was vested in the hands of the Great Council and the legislative body known as the Senate, while an extraordinary body known as the Council of Ten, first formed in 1310, came to be the real executive power of the state. Venetian government was respected by contemporaries for its stability. A sixteenth-century Italian historian noted that Venice had "the best government of any city not only in our own times but also in the classical world."[11]

In the fourteenth century, Venice also embarked on a policy of expansion. By the end of the century, it had created a commercial empire by establishing colonies and trading posts in the eastern Mediterranean and Black Sea as well as continuing its commercial monopolies in the Byzantine Empire. At the same time, Venice began to conquer the territory adjoining it in northern Italy.

The Decline of the Church

The papacy of the Roman Catholic church reached the height of its power in the thirteenth century. Theories of papal supremacy included a doctrine of "fullness of power" as the spiritual head of Christendom and claims to universal temporal authority over all secular rulers. But papal claims of temporal supremacy were increasingly out of step with the growing secular monarchies of Europe and ultimately brought the papacy into a conflict with the territorial states that it was unable to win.

Boniface VIII and the Conflict with the State

The struggle between the papacy and the secular monarchies began during the pontificate of Pope Boniface VIII (1294–1303). One major issue appeared to be at stake between the pope and King Philip IV (1285–1314) of France. In his desire to acquire new revenues, Philip claimed the right to tax the French clergy. Boniface VIII responded that the clergy of any state could not pay taxes to their secular ruler without the pope's consent. Underlying this issue, however, was a basic conflict between the claims of the papacy to universal authority over both church and state, which necessitated complete control over the clergy, and the claims of the king that all subjects, including the clergy, were under the jurisdiction of the crown and subject to the king's authority on matters of taxation and justice. In short, the fundamental issue was the universal sovereignty of the papacy versus the royal sovereignty of the monarch.

Boniface VIII asserted his position in a series of papal bulls or letters, the most important of which was *Unam Sanctam,* issued in 1302. It was the strongest statement ever made by a pope on the supremacy of the spiritual authority over the temporal authority (see the box on p. 290). When it became apparent that the pope had decided to act on his principles by excommunicating Philip IV, the latter sent a small contingent of French forces to capture Boniface and bring him back to France for trial. The pope was captured in Anagni, although Italian nobles from the surrounding countryside soon rescued him. The shock of this experience, however, soon led to the pope's death.

Boniface VIII's Defense of Papal Supremacy

One of the most remarkable documents of the fourteenth century was the exaggerated statement of papal supremacy issued by Pope Boniface VIII in 1302 in the heat of his conflict with the French king Philip IV. Ironically, this strongest statement ever made of papal supremacy was issued at a time when the rising power of the secular monarchies made it increasingly difficult for the premises to be accepted.

■ *Pope Boniface VIII,* Unam Sanctam

We are compelled, our faith urging us, to believe and to hold—and we do firmly believe and simply confess—that there is one holy catholic and apostolic church, outside of which there is neither salvation nor remission of sins. . . . In this church there is one Lord, one faith and one baptism. . . . Therefore, of this one and only church there is one body and one head . . . Christ, namely, and the vicar of Christ, St. Peter, and the successor of Peter. For the Lord himself said to Peter, feed my sheep. . . .

We are told by the word of the gospel that in this His fold there are two swords—a spiritual, namely, and a temporal. . . . Both swords, the spiritual and the material, therefore, are in the power of the church; the one, indeed, to be wielded for the church, the other by the church; the one by the hand of the priest, the other by the hand of kings and knights, but at the will and sufferance of the priest. One sword, moreover, ought to be under the other, and the temporal authority to be subjected to the spiritual. . . .

Therefore if the earthly power err it shall be judged by the spiritual power; but if the lesser spiritual power err, by the greater. But if the greatest, it can be judged by God alone, not by man, the apostle bearing witness. A spiritual man judges all things, but he himself is judged by no one. This authority, moreover, even though it is given to man and exercised through man, is not human but rather divine, being given by divine lips to Peter and founded on a rock for him and his successors through Christ himself whom he has confessed; the Lord himself saying to Peter: "Whatsoever you shall bind, etc." Whoever, therefore, resists this power thus ordained by God, resists the ordination of God. . . .

Indeed, we declare, announce and define, that it is altogether necessary to salvation for every human creature to be subject to the Roman pontiff.

Philip's strong-arm tactics had produced a clear victory for the national monarchy over the papacy, and no later pope has dared renew the extravagant claims of Boniface VIII.

To ensure his position and avoid any future papal threat, Philip IV brought enough pressure to bear on the college of cardinals to achieve the election of a Frenchman as pope in 1305, Clement V (1305–1314). Using the excuse of turbulence in the city of Rome, the new pope took up residence in Avignon on the east bank of the Rhône River. Although Avignon was located in the Holy Roman Empire and was not a French possession, it lay just across the river from the territory of King Philip IV. Clement may have intended to return to Rome, but he and his successors remained in Avignon for the next seventy-two years, thereby creating yet another crisis for the church.

British Library, London

Pope Boniface VIII. The conflict between church and state in the Middle Ages reached its height in the struggle between Pope Boniface VIII and Philip IV of France. This fourteenth-century miniature depicts Boniface VIII presiding over a gathering of cardinals.

The Papacy at Avignon (1305–1377)

The residency of the popes in Avignon for most of the fourteenth century led to a decline in papal prestige and growing antipapal sentiment. The city of Rome was the traditional capital of the universal church. The pope was the bishop of Rome, and his position was based on being the successor to the apostle Peter, traditionally considered the first bishop of Rome. It was unseemly that the head of the Catholic church should reside elsewhere. In the 1330s, the popes began to construct a stately palace in Avignon, a clear indication that they intended to stay for some time.

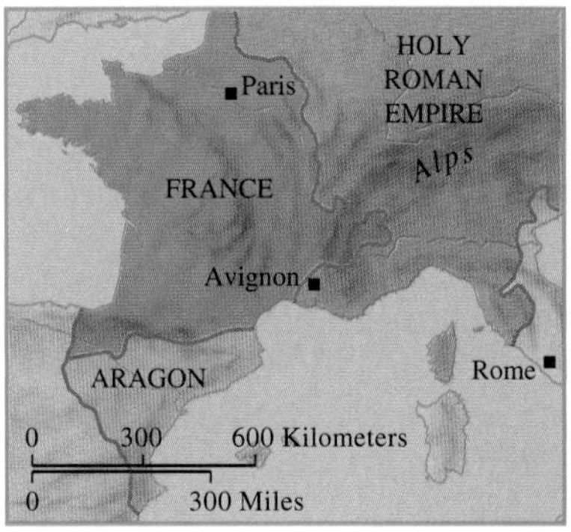

Avignon

Other factors also led to a decline in papal prestige during the Avignonese residency. It was widely believed that the popes at Avignon were captives of the French monarchy. Although questionable, since Avignon did not belong to the French monarchy, it was easy to believe in view of Avignon's proximity to French lands. Moreover, during the seventy-two years of the Avignonese papacy, of the 134 new cardinals created by the popes, 113 of them were French.

The papal residency at Avignon was also an important turning point in the church's attempt to adapt itself to the changing economic and political conditions of Europe. Like the growing monarchical states, the popes centralized their administration by developing a specialized bureaucracy. In fact, the papal bureaucracy in the fourteenth century under the leadership of the pope and college of cardinals became the most sophisticated administrative system in the medieval world.

At the same time, the popes attempted to find new sources of revenue to compensate for their loss of income from the Papal States and began to impose new taxes on the clergy. Furthermore, the splendor in which the pope and cardinals were living in Avignon led to a highly vocal criticism of both clergy and papacy in the fourteenth century. Avignon had become a powerful symbol of abuses within the church, and many people began to call for the pope's return to Rome.

One of the most prominent calls came from Catherine of Siena (c. 1347–1380), whose saintly demeanor and claims of visions from God led the city of Florence to send her on a mission to Pope Gregory XI (1370–1378) in Avignon. She told the pope: "Because God has given you authority and because you have accepted it, you ought to use your virtue and power; if you do not wish to use it, it might be better for you to resign what you have accepted; it would give more honor to God and health to your soul."[12]

The Great Schism

Catherine of Siena's admonition seemed to be heeded in 1377, when at long last Pope Gregory XI, perceiving the disastrous decline in papal prestige, returned to Rome. He died soon afterward, however, in the spring of 1378. When the college of cardinals met in conclave to elect a new pope, the citizens of Rome, fearful that the French majority would choose another Frenchman who would return the papacy to Avignon, threatened that the cardinals would not leave Rome alive unless a Roman or at least an Italian were elected pope. Indeed, the guards of the conclave warned the cardinals that they "ran the risk of being torn in pieces" if they did not choose an Italian. Wisely, the terrified cardinals duly elected the Italian archbishop of Bari, who was subsequently crowned as Pope Urban VI (1378–1389) on Easter Sunday. Five months later, a group of dissenting cardinals—the French ones—declared Urban's election null and void and chose one of their number, a Frenchman, who took the title of Clement VII and promptly returned to Avignon. Because Urban remained in Rome, there were now two popes, initiating what has been called the Great Schism of the church. Europe's loyalties became divided: France, Spain, Scotland, and southern Italy supported Clement, while England, Germany, Scandinavia, and most of Italy supported Urban. These divisions generally followed political lines and reflected the bitter division between the English and the French in the Hundred Years' War. Because the French supported the Avignonese pope, so did their allies; their enemies, particularly England and its allies, supported the Roman pope. The need for political support caused both popes to subordinate their policies to the policies of these states.

The Great Schism lasted for nearly forty years and had a baleful effect on the Catholic church and Christendom in general. The schism greatly aggravated the financial abuses that had developed within the church during the Avignonese papacy. Two papal administrative systems (with only one-half the accustomed revenues) worked to increase taxation. At the same time, the schism badly damaged the faith of Christian believers. The pope was widely believed to be the leader of Christendom and, as Boniface VIII had pointed out, held the keys to the kingdom of heaven. Since both lines of popes denounced the other as the Antichrist, such a spectacle could not help but undermine the institution that had become the very foundation of the church.

New Thoughts on Church and State and the Rise of Conciliarism

As dissatisfaction with the papacy grew, so did the calls for a revolutionary approach to solving the church's institutional problems. One of the most systematic was provided by Marsiglio of Padua (c.1270–1342), rector of the University of Paris and author of a remarkable book, *Defender of the Peace.*

Marsiglio denied that the temporal authority was subject to the spiritual authority, as popes from Innocent III to Boniface VIII had maintained. Instead, he argued that the church was only one element of society and must confine itself solely to spiritual functions. Furthermore, Marsiglio argued, the church was a community of the faithful in which all authority is ultimately derived from the entire community. The clergy hold no special authority from God but serve only to administer the affairs of the church on behalf of all Christians. Final authority in spiritual matters must reside not with the pope but with a general church council representing all members.

The Great Schism led large numbers of churchmen to take up this theory, known as conciliarism, in the belief that only a general council of the church could end the schism and bring reform to the church in its "head and members." The only serious issue left to be decided was who should call the council. Church law held that only a pope could convene a council. Professors of theology argued, however, that since the competing popes would not do so, either members of the church hierarchy or even secular princes, especially the Holy Roman Emperor, could convene a council to settle all relevant issues.

In desperation, a group of cardinals from both camps finally convened a general council on their own. This Council of Pisa, which met in 1409, deposed the two popes and elected a new one, Alexander V. The council's action proved disastrous when the two deposed popes refused to step down. There were now three popes, and the church seemed more hopelessly divided than ever.

Leadership in convening a new council now passed to the Holy Roman Emperor, Sigismund. As a result of his efforts, a new ecumenical church council met at Constance from 1414 to 1418. Ending the schism proved a surprisingly easy task: after the three competing popes either resigned or were deposed, a new conclave elected Cardinal Oddone Colonna, a member of a prominent Roman family, as Pope Martin V (1417–1431). The Great Schism had finally been ended.

CHRONOLOGY

The Decline of the Church

Pope Boniface VIII	1294–1303
Unam Sanctam	1302
The papacy at Avignon	1305–1377
Pope Gregory XI returns to Rome	1377
The Great Schism begins	1378
Pope Urban VI	1378–1389
Failure of Council of Pisa to end schism; election of Alexander V	1409
Council of Constance	1414–1418
End of schism; election of Martin V	1417

Popular Religion in an Age of Adversity

The concern of popes and leading clerics with finances and power during the struggles of Boniface VIII, the Avignonese papacy, and the Great Schism could not help but lead to a decline in prestige and respect for the institutional church, especially the papacy. At the same time, in the fourteenth century, the Black Death and its recurrences made an important impact on the religious life of ordinary Christians by heightening their preoccupation with death and salvation. The church often failed to provide sufficient spiritual comfort as many parish priests fled from the plague.

Christians responded in different ways to the adversities of the fourteenth century. First of all, there was a tendency to stress the performance of good works, including acts of charity, as a means of ensuring salvation. Bequests to hospitals and other charitable foundations increased. Family chapels were established, served by priests whose primary responsibility was to say Mass for the good of the souls of deceased family members. These chapels became even more significant as the importance of purgatory rose. Purgatory was defined by the church as the place where souls went after death to be purged of punishment for sins committed in life. In effect, the soul was purified in purgatory before it ascended into heaven. It was believed that like indulgences, prayers and private Masses for the dead could shorten the amount of time souls spent in purgatory.

All of these developments were part of a larger trend—a new emphasis in late medieval Christianity on a mechanical path to salvation. Chalking up good deeds to ensure salvation was done in numerous ways but was nowhere more evident than in the growing emphasis on indulgences. We should also note that pilgrimages, which became increasingly popular, and charitable contributions were good works that could be accomplished without the involvement of clerics, a reflection of the loss of faith in the institutional church and its clergy and another noticeable feature of popular religious life. At the same time, interest in Christianity itself did not decline. Indeed, people sought to play a more active role in their own salvation. This is particularly evident in the popularity of mysticism and lay piety in the fourteenth century.

MYSTICISM AND LAY PIETY

The mysticism of the fourteenth century was certainly not new, for Christians throughout the Middle Ages had claimed to have had mystical experiences. Simply defined, mysticism is the immediate experience of oneness with God. It is this experience that characterized the teaching of Meister Eckhart (1260–1327), who sparked a mystical movement in western Germany. Eckhart was a well-educated Dominican theologian who wrote learned Latin works on theology, but he was also a popular preacher whose message on the union of the soul with God was typical of mysticism. According to Eckhart, such a union was attainable for those who pursued it wholeheartedly.

Eckhart's movement spread from Germany into the Low Countries, where it took on a new form, called the Modern Devotion, founded by Gerard Groote (1340–1384). After a religious conversion, Groote entered a monastery for several years of contemplation before reentering the world. His messages were typical of a practical mysticism. To achieve true spiritual communion with God, people must imitate Jesus and lead lives dedicated to serving the needs of their fellow human beings. Groote emphasized a simple inner piety and morality based on Scripture and an avoidance of the complexities of theology.

Eventually, Groote attracted a group of followers who came to be known as the Brothers of the Common Life. From this small beginning, a movement developed that spread through the Netherlands and back into Germany. Houses of the Brothers, as well as separate houses for women (Sisters of the Common Life), were founded in one city after another. The Sisters and Brothers of the Common Life did not constitute regular religious orders. They were laypeople who took no formal monastic vows but were nevertheless regulated by quasi-monastic rules that they imposed on their own communities. They also established schools throughout Germany and the Netherlands in which they stressed their message of imitating the life of Jesus by serving others. The Brothers and Sisters of the Common Life attest to the vitality of spiritual life among lay Christians in the fourteenth century.

A number of female mystics had their own unique spiritual experiences. For them, fasting and receiving the Eucharist (the communion wafer that supposedly contains the body of Jesus) became the mainstay of their religious practices. Catherine of Siena, for example, gave up eating any solid food at the age of twenty-three and thereafter lived only on cold water and herbs that she sucked and then spat out. Her primary nourishment, however, came from the Eucharist. She wrote: "The immaculate lamb [Christ] is food, table, and servant. . . . And we who eat at that table become like the food [that is, Christ], acting not for our own utility but for the honor of God and the salvation of neighbor."[13] For Catherine and a number of other female mystics, reception of the Eucharist was their primary instrument in achieving a mystical union with God.

Changes in Theology

The fourteenth century presented challenges not only to the institutional church but also to its theological framework, especially evidenced in the questioning of the grand synthesis attempted by Thomas Aquinas. In the thirteenth century, Thomas Aquinas's grand synthesis of faith and reason was not widely accepted outside his own Dominican order. At the same time, differences with Aquinas were kept within a framework of commonly accepted scholastic thought. In the fourteenth century, however, the philosopher William of Occam (1285–1329) posed a severe challenge to the scholastic achievements of the High Middle Ages.

Occam posited a radical interpretation of nominalism. He asserted that all universals or general concepts were simply names and that only individual objects perceived by the senses were real. Although the mind was capable of analyzing individual objects, it could not establish any truths about the nature of external, higher reality. Reason could not be used to substantiate spiritual truths. It could not, for example, prove the statement "God exists." For William of Occam as a Christian believer, this did not mean that God did not exist, however. It simply indicated that the truths of religion were not demonstrable by reason but could only be known by an act of faith. The acceptance of Occam's nominalist philosophy at the University of Paris brought an element of uncertainty to late medieval theology by seriously weakening the synthesis of faith and reason that had characterized the theological thought of the High Middle Ages. Nevertheless, Occam's emphasis on using reason to analyze the observable phenomena of the world had an important impact on the development of physical science by creating support for rational and scientific analysis. Some late medieval theologians came to accept the compatibility of rational analysis of the material world with mystical acceptance of spiritual truths.

The Cultural World of the Fourteenth Century

The cultural life of the fourteenth century was also characterized by ferment. In literature, several writers used their vernacular languages to produce notable works. In art, the Black Death and other problems of the century left their mark as many artists turned to morbid themes, but the period also produced Giotto, whose paintings expressed a new realism that would be developed further by the artists of the next century.

The Development of Vernacular Literature

Although Latin remained the language of the church liturgy and the official documents of both church and state, the fourteenth century witnessed the rapid growth of vernacular literature, especially in Italy. The development of an Italian vernacular literature was mostly the result of the efforts of three writers in the fourteenth century: Dante, Petrarch, and Boccaccio. Their use of the Tuscan dialect common in Florence and its surrounding countryside ensured that it would become the basis of the modern Italian language.

Dante (1265–1321) came from an old Florentine noble family that had fallen on hard times. Although he had held high political office in republican Florence, factional conflict led to his exile from the city in 1302. Until the end of his life, Dante hoped to return to his beloved Florence, but his wish remained unfulfilled.

Dante's masterpiece in the Italian vernacular was the *Divine Comedy*, written between 1313 and 1321. Cast in a typical medieval framework, the *Divine Comedy* is basically the story of the soul's progression to salvation, a fundamental medieval preoccupation. The lengthy poem was divided into three major sections corresponding to the realms of the afterworld: hell, purgatory, and heaven or

Dante's Vision of Hell

The *Divine Comedy* of Dante Alighieri is regarded as one of the greatest literary works of all time. Many consider it the supreme summary of medieval thought. It combines allegory with a remarkable amount of contemporary history. Indeed, forty-three of the seventy-nine people consigned to hell in the "Inferno" were Florentines. This excerpt is taken from Canto 18 of the "Inferno," in which Dante and Virgil visit the eighth circle of hell, which is divided into ten trenches containing the souls of people who had committed malicious frauds upon their fellow human beings.

■ *Dante, "Inferno,"* Divine Comedy

We had already come to where the walk
crosses the second bank, from which it lifts
another arch, spanning from rock to rock.

Here we heard people whine in the next chasm,
and knock and thump themselves with open palms,
and blubber through their snouts as if in a spasm.

Steaming from that pit, a vapor rose
over the banks, crusting them with a slime
that sickened my eyes and hammered at my nose.

That chasm sinks so deep we could not sight
its bottom anywhere until we climbed
along the rock arch to its greatest height.

Once there, I peered down; and I saw long lines
of people in a river of excrement
that seemed the overflow of the world's latrines.

I saw among the felons of that pit
one wraith who might or might not have been
tonsured—
one could not tell, he was so smeared with shit.

He bellowed: "You there, why do you stare at me
more than at all the others in this stew?"
And I to him: "Because if memory

serves me, I knew you when your hair was dry.
You are Alessio Interminelli da Lucca.
That's why I pick you from this filthy fry."

And he then, beating himself on his clown's head:
"Down to this have the flatteries I sold
the living sunk me here among the dead."

And my Guide prompted then: "Lean forward a bit
and look beyond him, there—do you see that one
scratching herself with dungy nails, the strumpet

who fidgets to her feet, then to a crouch?
It is the whore Thäis who told her lover
when he sent to ask her, 'Do you thank me much?'

'Much? Nay, past all believing!' And with this
Let us turn from the sight of this abyss."

paradise. In the "Inferno" (see the box above), Dante is led by his guide, the classical author Virgil, who is a symbol of human reason. But Virgil (or reason) can only lead the poet so far on his journey. At the end of "Purgatory," Beatrice (the true love of Dante's life), who represents revelation—which alone can explain the mysteries of heaven—becomes his guide into "Paradise." Here Beatrice presents Dante to Saint Bernard, a symbol of mystical contemplation. The saint turns Dante over to the Virgin Mary, since grace is necessary to achieve the final step of entering the presence of God, where one beholds "the love that moves the sun and the other stars."[14]

Like Dante, Petrarch (1304–1374) was a Florentine who spent much of his life outside his native city. Petrarch's role in the revival of the classics made him a seminal figure in the literary Italian Renaissance (see Chapter 12). His primary contribution to the development of the Italian vernacular was made in his sonnets. He is considered one of the greatest European lyric poets. His sonnets were inspired by his love for a married lady named Laura, whom he had met in 1327. While honoring an idealized female figure was a long-standing medieval tradition, Laura was very human and not just an ideal. She was a real woman with whom Petrarch was involved for a long time. He poured forth his lamentations in sonnet after sonnet:

I am as tired of thinking as my thought
Is never tired to find itself in you,
And of not yet leaving this life that brought
Me the too heavy weight of signs and rue;

And because to describe your hair and face
And the fair eyes of which I always speak,
Language and sound have not become too weak
And day and night your name they still embrace.

And tired because my feet do not yet fail
After following you in every part,
Wasting so many steps without avail,

From whence derive the paper and the ink
That I have filled with you; if I should sink,
It is the fault of Love, not of my art.[15]

In analyzing every aspect of the unrequited lover's feelings, Petrarch appeared less concerned to sing his lady's praise than to immortalize his own thoughts. This interest in his own personality reveals a sense of individuality stronger than in any previous medieval literature.

Although he too wrote poetry, Boccaccio (1313–1375) is known primarily for his prose. Another Florentine, he also used the Tuscan dialect. While working for the Bardi banking house in Naples, he fell in love with a noble lady whom he called his Fiammetta, his Little Flame. Under her inspiration, Boccaccio began to write prose romances. His best-known work, *The Decameron,* however, was not written until after he had returned to Florence. *The Decameron* is set at the time of the Black Death. Ten young people flee to a villa outside Florence to escape the plague and decide to while away the time by telling stories. Although the stories are not new and still reflect the acceptance of basic Christian values, Boccaccio does present the society of his time from a secular point of view. It is the seducer of women, not the knight or philosopher or pious monk, who is the real hero. Perhaps, as some historians have argued, *The Decameron* reflects the immediate easygoing, cynical postplague values. Boccaccio's later work certainly became gloomier and more pessimistic; as he grew older, he even rejected his earlier work as irrelevant. He commented in a 1373 letter, "I am certainly not pleased that you have allowed the illustrious women in your house to read my trifles. . . . You know how much in them is less than decent and opposed to modesty, how much stimulation to wanton lust, how many things that drive to lust even those most fortified against it."[16]

Another leading vernacular author was Geoffrey Chaucer (c. 1340–1400), who brought a new level of sophistication to the English vernacular language in his famous *Canterbury Tales.* His beauty of expression and clear, forceful language were important in transforming his East Midland dialect into the chief ancestor of the modern English language. *The Canterbury Tales* is a collection of stories told by a group of twenty-nine pilgrims journeying from the London suburb of Southwark to the tomb of Saint Thomas à Becket at Canterbury. This format gave Chaucer the chance to portray an entire range of English society, both high- and low-born. Among others, he presented the Knight, the Yeoman, the Prioress, the Monk, the Merchant, the Student, the Lawyer, the Carpenter, the Cook, the Doctor, the Plowman, and, of course, "A Good Wife was there from beside the city of Bath—a little deaf, which was a pity." The stories these pilgrims told to while away the time on the journey were just as varied as the storytellers themselves: knightly romances, fairy tales, saints' lives, sophisticated satires, and crude anecdotes.

Chaucer also used some of his characters to criticize the corruption of the church in the late medieval period. His portrayal of the Friar leaves no doubt of Chaucer's disdain for the corrupt practices of clerics. Of the Friar, he says:

He knew the taverns well in every town.
The barmaids and innkeepers pleased his mind
Better than beggars and lepers and their kind.[17]

And yet Chaucer was still a pious Christian, never doubting basic Christian doctrines and remaining optimistic that the church could be reformed.

One of the extraordinary vernacular writers of the age was Christine de Pizan (c. 1364–1430). Because of her father's position at the court of Charles V of France, she received a good education. Her husband died when she was only twenty-five (they had been married for ten years), leaving her with little income and three small children and her mother to support. Christine took the unusual step of becoming a writer in order to earn her living. Her poems were soon in demand, and by 1400 she had achieved financial security.

Christine de Pizan is best known, however, for her French prose works written in defense of women. In *The Book of the City of Ladies,* written in 1404, she denounced the many male writers who had argued that women needed to be controlled by men because women by their very nature were prone to evil, unable to learn, and easily swayed. With the help of Reason, Righteousness, and Justice, who appear to her in a vision, Christine refutes these antifeminist attacks. Women, she argues, are not evil by nature, and they could learn as well as men if they were permitted to attend the same schools: "Should I also tell you whether a woman's nature is clever and quick enough to learn speculative sciences as well as to discover them, and likewise the manual arts. I assure you that women are equally well-suited and skilled

The Vision of Christine de Pizan. Christine de Pizan is one of the extraordinary vernacular writers of the late fourteenth and early fifteenth centuries. She is pictured here in a cover illustration from her *Book of the City of Ladies,* which depicts Reason, Righteousness, and Justice appearing to Christine in a dream.

British Library, London

to carry them out and to put them to sophisticated use once they have learned them."[18] Much of the book includes a detailed discussion of women from the past and present who have distinguished themselves as leaders, warriors, wives, mothers, and martyrs for their religious faith. She ends by encouraging women to defend themselves against the attacks of men, who are incapable of understanding them.

Art and the Black Death

The fourteenth century produced an artistic outburst in new directions as well as a large body of morbid work influenced by the Black Death and the recurrences of the plague. The city of Florence witnessed the first dramatic break with medieval tradition in the work of Giotto (1266–1337), often considered a forerunner of Italian Renaissance painting. Born into a peasant family, Giotto acquired his painting skills in a workshop in Florence. Although he worked throughout Italy, his most famous works were done in Padua and Florence. Coming out of the formal Byzantine school, Giotto transcended it with a new kind of realism, a desire to imitate nature that Renaissance artists later identified as the basic component of classical art. Giotto's figures were solid and rounded; placed realistically in relationship to each other and their background, they conveyed three-dimensional depth. The expressive faces and physically realistic bodies gave his sacred figures human qualities with which spectators could identify. Although Giotto had no direct successors, Florentine painting in the early fifteenth century pursued even more dramatically the new direction his work represents.

The Black Death made a visible impact on art. For one thing, it wiped out entire guilds of artists. At the same time, survivors, including the newly rich who patronized artists, were no longer so optimistic. Some were more guilty about enjoying life and more concerned about gaining salvation. Postplague art began to concentrate on pain and death. A fairly large number of artistic works came to exhibit a morbid concern with death, depicting coffins, decomposing bodies, and grim figures of Death, sometimes in the form of a witch flying through the air swinging a large scythe.

Society in an Age of Adversity

In the midst of disaster, the fourteenth century proved creative in its own way. New inventions made an impact on daily life at the same time that the effects of plague were felt in many areas of medieval urban life.

Changes in Urban Life

One immediate by-product of the Black Death was greater regulation of urban activities. Authorities tried to keep cities cleaner by enacting new ordinances against waste products in the streets. Viewed as unhealthy places, bath-

Scala/Art Resource, NY

Giotto, *Pietà*. The work of Giotto marked the first clear innovation in fourteenth-century painting, making him a forerunner of the early Renaissance. In this fresco, which was part of an elaborate series in the Arena chapel in Padua begun in 1305, the solidity of Giotto's human figures gives them a three-dimensional sense.

The Legal Rights of Women

During the High and Later Middle Ages, as women were increasingly viewed as weak beings who were unable to play independent roles, legal systems also began to limit the rights of women. These excerpts are taken from a variety of legal opinions in France, England, and a number of Italian cities.

Excerpts from Legal Opinions

France, 1270: No married woman can go to court . . . unless someone has abused or beaten her, in which case she may go to court without her husband. If she is a tradeswoman, she can sue and defend herself in matters connected with her business, but not otherwise.

England [probably fifteenth century]: Every Feme Covert [married woman] is a sort of infant. . . . It is seldom, almost never that a married woman can have any action to use her wit only in her own name: her husband is her stern, her prime mover, without whom she cannot do much at home, and less abroad. . . . It is a miracle that a wife should commit any suit without her husband.

England [probably fifteenth century]: The very goods which a man gives to his wife, are still his own, her chain, her bracelets, her apparel, are all the goodman's goods. . . . A wife however gallant she be, glitters but in the riches of her husband, as the moon has no light but it is the sun's. . . . For thus it is, if before marriage the woman was possessed of horses . . . , sheep, corn, wool, money, plate and jewels, all manner of movable substance is presently . . . the husband's to sell, keep or bequeath if she die.

Pesaro, Italy [exact date unknown]: No wife can make a contract without the consent of her husband.

Florence, Italy, 1415: A married woman with children cannot draw up a last will in her own right, nor dispose of her dowry among the living to the detriment of husband and children.

Lucca, Italy [exact date unknown]: No married woman . . . can seal or give away [anything] unless she has the agreement of her husband and nearest [male] relative.

houses were closed down, leading to a noticeable decline in cleanliness. Efforts at regulation also affected the practice of female prostitution.

Medieval society had tolerated prostitution as a lesser evil; it was better for males to frequent prostitutes than to seduce virgins or married women. Since many males in medieval towns married late, the demand for prostitutes was high and was met by a regular supply, derived no doubt from the need of many poor girls and women to survive. The recession of the fourteenth century probably increased the supply of prostitutes, while the new hedonism prevalent after the Black Death also increased demand. As a result, cities intensified their regulation of prostitution.

By organizing brothels, city authorities could supervise as well as tax prostitutes. Officials granted charters to citizens who were allowed to set up brothels, provided they were located only in certain areas of town. Prostitutes were also expected to wear special items of clothing—such as red hats—to distinguish them from other women.

FAMILY LIFE AND SEX ROLES IN LATE MEDIEVAL CITIES

The basic unit of the late medieval town was the nuclear family of husband, wife, and children. Especially in wealthier families, there might also be servants, apprentices, and other relatives, including widowed mothers and the husband's illegitimate children.

Before the Black Death, late marriages were common for urban couples. It was not unusual for husbands to be in their late thirties or forties and wives in their early twenties. The expense of setting up a household probably necessitated the delay in marriage. But the situation changed dramatically after the plague, reflecting new economic opportunities for the survivors and a new reluctance to postpone living in the presence of so much death.

The economic difficulties of the fourteenth century also had a tendency to strengthen the development of sex roles and to set new limits on employment opportunities for women. Based on the authority of Aristotle, Thomas Aquinas and other scholastic theologians had advanced the belief that according to the natural order, men were active and domineering while women were passive and submissive. As more and more lawyers, doctors, and priests, who had been trained in universities where these notions were taught, entered society, these ideas about the different natures of men and women became widely accepted. This was evident in legal systems, many of which limited the legal capacity of women (see the box above). Increasingly, women were expected to give up any active functions in society and remain subject to direction from males. A fourteenth-century Parisian provost commented that among glass cutters, "no master's widow who keeps working at his craft after her husband's death may take on apprentices, for the men of the craft do not believe that a woman can master it well enough to teach a child to master it, for the craft is a very delicate one."[19] Although this statement suggests that some women were, in fact, running businesses, it also reveals that they were viewed as incapable of undertaking all of men's activities. Europeans in the fourteenth century imposed a division of labor roles between men and women that persisted until the Industrial Revolution.

MEDIEVAL CHILDREN

Parents in the High and Later Middle Ages invested considerable resources and affection in rearing their children. The dramatic increase in specialized roles that accompanied the spread of commerce and the growth of cities demanded a commitment to educating children in the marketable skills needed for the new occupations. Philip of Navarre noted in the twelfth century that boys ought to be taught a trade "as soon as possible. Those who early become and long remain apprentices ought to be the best masters."[20] Some cities provided schools to educate the young. A Florentine chronicler related that between eight and ten thousand boys and girls between the ages of six and twelve attended the city's grammar schools, a figure that probably represented half of all school-aged children. Although grammar school completed education for girls, around eleven hundred boys went on to six secondary schools that prepared them for business careers, while another six hundred studied Latin and logic in four other schools that readied them for university training and a career in medicine, law, or the church. In the High Middle Ages, then, urban communities demonstrated a commitment to the training of the young.

As a result of the devastating effects of the plague and its recurrences, these same communities became concerned about investing in the survival and health of children. Although a number of hospitals existed in both Florence and Rome in the fourteenth century, it was not until the 1420s and 1430s that hospitals were established that catered only to the needs of foundlings, supporting them until boys could be taught a trade and girls could marry.

New Directions in Medicine

The medical community comprised a number of functionaries. At the top of the medical hierarchy were the physicians, usually clergymen, who received their education in the universities, where they studied ancient authorities, such as Hippocrates and Galen. As a result, physicians were highly trained in theory but had little or no clinical practice. By the fourteenth century, they were educated in six chief medical schools—Salerno, Montpellier, Bologna, Oxford, Padua, and Paris. Paris was regarded as the most prestigious.

The preplague medicine of university-trained physicians was theoretically grounded in the classical Greek theory of the "four humors," each connected to a particular organ: blood (from the heart), phlegm (from the brain), yellow bile (from the liver), and black bile (from the spleen). The four humors corresponded in turn to the four elemental qualities of the universe, earth (black bile), air (blood), fire (yellow bile), and water (phlegm), making a human being a microcosm of the cosmos. Good health resulted from a perfect balance of the four humors; sickness meant that the humors were out of balance. The task of the medieval physician was to restore proper order by a number of cures, such as rest, diet, herbal medicines, or bloodletting.

Beneath the physicians in the hierarchy of the medical profession stood the surgeons, whose activities included performing operations, setting broken bones, and bleeding patients. Their knowledge was largely based on practical experience. Below surgeons were midwives and the barber-surgeons, who were less trained and performed menial tasks such as bloodletting and setting simple bone fractures. Barber-surgeons supplemented their income

Birth of a Child. This scene from *Birth of the Virgin* by an unknown German artist is actually a painting of a wealthy fourteenth-century mother who has just given birth to a child. Female attendants prepare the water for the child's first bath while the mother holds her newborn in her canopied bed.

Meister des Marienlebens, "Geburt Mariae," Alte Pinakothek, Munich. Photo © Artothek by shaving and cutting hair and pulling teeth. Apothecaries also constituted part of the medical establishment. They filled herbal prescriptions recommended by physicians and also prescribed drugs on their own authority.

All of these medical practitioners proved unable to deal with the plague. When King Philip VI of France requested the opinion of the medical faculty of the University of Paris on the plague, their advice proved worthless. This failure to understand the Black Death, however, produced a crisis in medieval medicine that resulted in some new approaches to health care.

One result was the rise of surgeons to greater prominence because of their practical knowledge. Surgeons were now recruited by universities, which placed them on an equal level with physicians and introduced a greater emphasis on practical anatomy into the university curriculum. Connected to this was a burgeoning of medical textbooks, often written in the vernacular and stressing practical, how-to approaches to medical and surgical problems.

Finally, as a result of the plague, cities, especially in Italy, gave increased attention to public health and sanitation. Public health laws were instituted, and municipal boards of health came into being. The primary concern of the latter was to prevent plague, but gradually they came to control almost every aspect of health and sanitation. Boards of public health, consisting of medical practitioners and public officials, were empowered to enforce sanitary conditions, report on and attempt to isolate epidemics by quarantine (rarely successful), and regulate the activities of doctors.

A Medical Textbook. This illustration is taken from a fourteenth-century surgical textbook that stressed a how-to approach to surgical problems. *Top left,* a surgeon shows how to remove an arrow from a patient; *top right,* how to open a patient's chest; *bottom left,* how to deal with an injury to the intestines; *bottom right,* how to diagnose an abscess.

British Library, London

Inventions and New Patterns

Despite its problems, the fourteenth century witnessed a continuation of the technological innovations that had characterized the High Middle Ages. The most extraordinary of these inventions, and one that made a visible impact on European cities, was the clock. The mechanical clock was invented at the end of the thirteenth century but not perfected until the fourteenth. The time-telling clock was actually a by-product of a larger astronomical clock. The best-designed one was constructed by Giovanni di Dondi in the mid-fourteenth century. Dondi's clock contained the signs of the zodiac but also struck on the hour. Since clocks were expensive, they were usually installed only in the towers of churches or municipal buildings. The first clock striking equal hours was in a church in Milan; in 1335, a chronicler described it as "a wonderful clock, with a very large clapper which strikes a bell twenty-four times according to the twenty-four hours of the day and night and thus at the first hour of the night gives one sound, at the second two strikes . . . and so distinguishes one hour from another, which is of greatest use to men of every degree."[21]

Clocks introduced a wholly new conception of time into the lives of Europeans; they revolutionized how people thought about and used time. Throughout most of the Middle Ages, time was determined by natural rhythms (daybreak and nightfall) or church bells that were rung at more or less regular three-hour intervals, corresponding to the ecclesiastical offices of the church. Clocks made it possible to plan one's day and organize one's activities around the regular striking of bells. This brought a new regularity into the life of workers and merchants, defining urban existence and enabling merchants and bankers to see the value of time in a new way.

Like clocks, eyeglasses were introduced in the thirteenth century but not refined until the fourteenth. Even then they were not particularly effective by modern standards and were still extremely expensive. The high cost of parchment forced people to write in extremely small script; eyeglasses made it more readable. At the same time, a significant change in writing materials occurred in the fourteenth century when parchment was supplemented by much cheaper paper made from cotton rags. Although it was more subject to insect and water damage than parchment, medieval paper was actually superior to modern papers made of high-acid wood pulp.

Invented earlier by the Chinese, gunpowder also made its appearance in the West in the fourteenth century. The use of gunpowder eventually brought drastic changes to European warfare. Its primary use was in cannons, although early cannons were prone to blow up, making them as dangerous to the people firing them as to the enemy. Even as late as 1460, an attack on a castle using the "Lion," an enormous Flemish cannon, proved disastrous for the Scottish king James II when the "Lion" blew up, killing the king and a number of his retainers. Continued improvement in the construction of cannons, however, soon made them extremely valuable in reducing both castles and city walls. Gunpowder made castles, city walls, and armored knights obsolete.

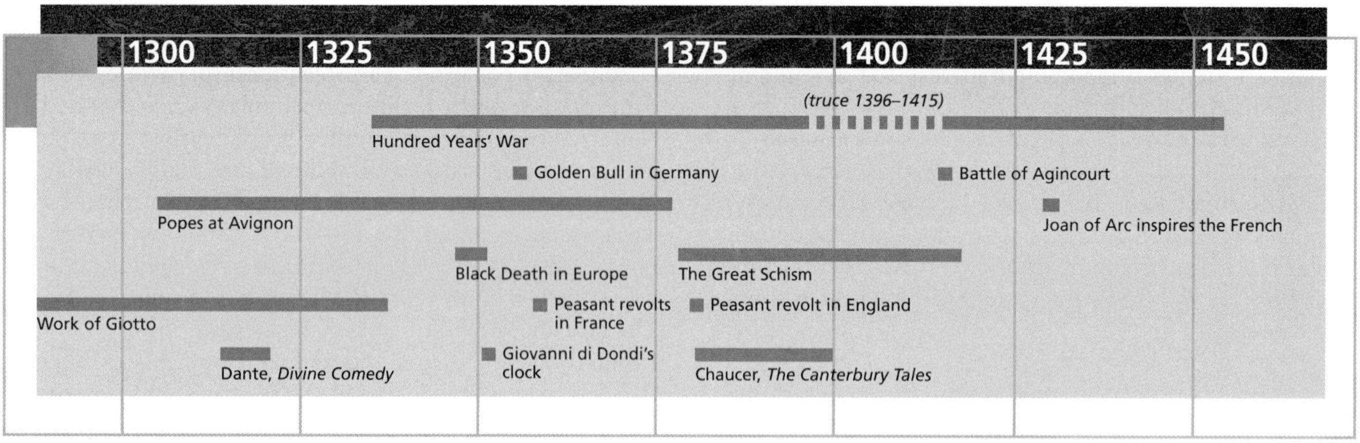

Conclusion

In the eleventh, twelfth, and thirteenth centuries, European civilization developed many of its fundamental features. Territorial states, parliaments, capitalist trade and industry, banks, cities, and vernacular literatures were all products of that fertile period. During the same time, the Catholic church under the direction of the papacy reached its apogee. Fourteenth-century European society, however, was challenged by an overwhelming number of crises. Devastating plague, declining trade and industry, bank failures, peasant revolts pitting lower classes against the upper classes, seemingly constant warfare, aristocratic factional conflict that undermined political stability, the absence of the popes from Rome, and even the spectacle of two popes condemning each other as the Antichrist all seemed to overpower Europeans in this "calamitous century." Not surprisingly, much of the art of the period depicted the Four Horsemen of the Apocalypse described in the New Testament book of Revelation: Death, Famine, Pestilence, and War. No doubt, to some people, the last days of the world appeared to be at hand.

The new European society, however, proved remarkably resilient. Periods of crisis are usually paralleled by the emergence of new ideas and new practices. Intellectuals of the period saw themselves as standing on the threshold of a new age or a rebirth of the best features of classical civilization. It is their perspective that led historians to speak of a Renaissance in the fifteenth century.

Notes

1. Quoted in H. S. Lucas, "The Great European Famine of 1315, 1316, and 1317," *Speculum* 5 (1930): 359.
2. Quoted in David Herlihy, *The Black Death and the Transformation of the West,* ed. Samuel K. Cohn Jr. (Cambridge, Mass., 1997), p. 9.
3. Giovanni Boccaccio, *The Decameron,* trans. Frances Winwar (New York, 1955), p. xxv.
4. Ibid., p. xxvi.
5. Jean Froissart, *Chronicles,* ed. and trans. Geoffrey Brereton (Harmondsworth, England, 1968), p. 111.
6. Quoted in James B. Ross and Mary M. McLaughlin, *The Portable Medieval Reader* (New York, 1949), pp. 218–219.
7. Quoted in Barbara W. Tuchman, *A Distant Mirror* (New York, 1978), p. 175.
8. Froissart, *Chronicles,* p. 212.
9. Ibid., p. 89.
10. Oliver J. Thatcher and Edgar H. McNeal, eds., *A Source Book for Medieval History* (New York, 1905), p. 288.
11. Quoted in D. S. Chambers, *The Imperial Age of Venice, 1380–1580* (London, 1970), p. 30.
12. Quoted in Robert Coogan, *Babylon on the Rhône: A Translation of Letters by Dante, Petrarch, and Catherine of Siena* (Washington, D.C., 1983), p. 115.
13. Quoted in Caroline Walker Bynum, *Holy Feast and Holy Fast: The Religious Significance of Food to Medieval Women* (Berkeley, Calif., 1987), p. 180.
14. Dante Alighieri, *Divine Comedy,* trans. Dorothy Sayers (New York, 1962), "Paradise," canto 33, line 145.
15. Petrarch, *Sonnets and Songs,* trans. Anna Maria Armi (New York, 1968), no. 74, p. 127.
16. Quoted in Millard Meiss, *Painting in Florence and Siena After the Black Death* (Princeton, N.J., 1951), p. 161.
17. Geoffrey Chaucer, *The Canterbury Tales,* in *The Portable Chaucer,* ed. Theodore Morrisoon (New York, 1949), p. 67.

18. Christine de Pizan, *The Book of the City of Ladies,* trans. E. Jeffrey Richards (New York, 1982), pp. 83–84.
19. Quoted in Susan Mosher Stuard, "The Dominion of Gender, or How Women Fared in the High Middle Ages," in Renate Bridenthal, Claudia Koonz, and Susan Stuard, eds., *Becoming Visible: Women in European History,* 3d ed. (Boston, 1998), p. 147.
20. Quoted in David Herlihy, "Medieval Children," in Bede K. Lackner and Kenneth R. Philp, eds., *Essays on Medieval Civilization* (Austin, Texas, 1978), p. 121.
21. Quoted in Jean Gimpel, *The Medieval Machine* (New York, 1976), p. 168.

Suggestions for Further Reading

For a general introduction to the fourteenth century, see D. P. Waley, *Later Medieval Europe,* 2d ed. (London, 1985); G. Holmes, *Europe: Hierarchy and Revolt, 1320–1450* (New York, 1975); and the well-written popular history by B. Tuchman, *A Distant Mirror* (New York, 1978).

On famine in the early fourteenth century, see W. C. Jordan, *The Great Famine: Northern Europe in the Early Fourteenth Century* (Princeton, N.J., 1996). On the Black Death, see P. Ziegler, *The Black Death* (New York, 1969), and D. Herlihy, *The Black Death and the Transformation of the West,* ed. S. K. Cohn Jr. (Cambridge, Mass., 1997).

Recent accounts of the Hundred Years' War include A. Curry, *The Hundred Years' War* (New York, 1993), and R. H. Neillands, *The Hundred Years' War* (New York, 1990). On Joan of Arc, see M. Warner, *Joan of Arc: The Image of Female Heroism* (New York, 1981). On the political history of the period, see B. Guenée, *States and Rulers in Later Medieval Europe,* trans. J. Vale (Oxford, 1985). Works on individual countries include P. S. Lewis, *Later Medieval France: The Polity* (London, 1968); A. R. Myers, *England in the Late Middle Ages* (Harmondsworth, England, 1952); and F. R. H. Du Boulay, *Germany in the Later Middle Ages* (London, 1983). On the Italian political scene, see J. Larner, *Italy in the Age of Dante and Petrarch, 1216–1380* (London, 1980).

A good general study of the church in the fourteenth century can be found in F. P. Oakley, *The Western Church in the Later Middle Ages* (Ithaca, N.Y., 1980). On the Avignonese papacy, see Y. Renouard, *The Avignon Papacy, 1305–1403* (London, 1970). On the role of food in the spiritual practices of medieval women, see C. W. Bynum, *Holy Feast and Holy Fast: The Religious Significance of Food to Medieval Women* (Berkeley, Calif., 1987).

A classic work on the life and thought of the Later Middle Ages is J. Huizinga, *The Autumn of the Middle Ages,* trans. R. J. Payton and U. Mammitzsch (Chicago, 1996). On the impact of the plague on culture, see the brilliant study by M. Meiss, *Painting in Florence and Siena After the Black Death* (New York, 1964). On Dante, see J. Freccero, *Dante and the Poetics of Conversion* (Cambridge, Mass., 1986). On Chaucer, see G. Kane, *Chaucer* (New York, 1984). The best work on Christine de Pizan is by C. C. Willard, *Christine de Pizan: Her Life and Works* (New York, 1984).

A wealth of material on everyday life is provided in the second volume of *A History of Private Life,* edited by G. Duby, *Revelations of the Medieval World* (Cambridge, Mass., 1988). On women in the Later Middle Ages, see S. Shahar, *The Fourth Estate: A History of Women in the Middle Ages,* trans. C. Galai (London, 1983), and D. Herlihy, *Women, Family, and Society: Historical Essays, 1978–1991* (Providence, R.I., 1995). On childhood, see B. Hanawalt, *Growing Up in Medieval London* (New York, 1993). The subject of medieval prostitution is examined in L. L. Otis, *Prostitution in Medieval Society* (Chicago, 1984). Poor people are discussed in M. Mollat, *The Poor in the Middle Ages* (New Haven, Conn., 1986). For a general introduction to the changes in medicine, see T. McKeown, *The Role of Medicine* (Princeton, N.J., 1979). The importance of inventions is discussed in J. Gimpel, *The Medieval Machine* (New York, 1976). Another valuable discussion of medieval technology can be found in J. Le Goff, *Time, Work, and Culture in the Middle Ages* (Chicago, 1980).

For additional reading, go to InfoTrac College Edition, your online research library at http://web1.infotrac-college.com

Enter the search term *Middle Ages* using the Subject Guide.

Enter the search term *Black Death* using Key Terms.

Enter the search term *Edward III* using Key Terms.

Enter the search term *Hundred Years' War* using Key Terms.

CHAPTER

12

Recovery and Rebirth: The Age of the Renaissance

Staatliche Landesbildstelle Hamburg

CHAPTER OUTLINE

- Meaning and Characteristics of the Italian Renaissance
- The Making of Renaissance Society
- The Italian States in the Renaissance
- The Intellectual Renaissance in Italy
- The Artistic Renaissance
- The European State in the Renaissance
- The Church in the Renaissance
- Conclusion

FOCUS QUESTIONS

- What characteristics distinguish the Renaissance from the Middle Ages?
- How did Machiavelli's works reflect the political realities of Renaissance Italy?
- What was humanism, and what effect did it have on philosophy, education, attitudes toward politics, and the writing of history?
- What were the chief characteristics of Renaissance art, and how did it differ in Italy and northern Europe?
- Why do historians sometimes refer to the monarchies of the late fifteenth century as "new monarchies" or "Renaissance states"?
- How did Renaissance art and the humanist movement reflect the political, economic, and social developments of the period?

WERE THE FOURTEENTH and fifteenth centuries a continuation of the Middle Ages or the beginning of a new era? Both positions can be defended. Although the disintegrative patterns of the fourteenth century continued into the fifteenth, at the same time there were elements of recovery that made the fifteenth century a period of significant political, economic, artistic, and intellectual change. The humanists or intellectuals of the age called their period (from the mid-fourteenth to the mid-sixteenth century) an age of rebirth, believing that they had restored arts and letters to new glory after they had been "neglected" or "dead" for centuries. The humanists also saw their age as one of great individuals who dominated the landscape of their time. Michelangelo, the great Italian artist of the early sixteenth century, and Pope Julius II, the "warrior pope," were two such titans. The artist's temperament and the pope's temper led to many lengthy and often loud quarrels between the two. The pope had hired Michelangelo to paint the ceiling of the Sistine Chapel in Rome, a difficult task for a man long accustomed to being a sculptor. Michelangelo undertook the project but refused for a long time to allow anyone, including the pope, to see his work. Julius grew anxious, pestering Michelangelo on a regular basis about when the ceiling would be finished. Exasperated by the pope's requests, Michelangelo once replied, according to Giorgio Vasari, his contemporary biographer, that the ceiling would be completed "when it satisfies me as an artist." The pope responded, "And we want you to satisfy us and finish it soon," and then threatened that if Michelangelo did not "finish the ceiling quickly," the pope would "have him thrown down from the scaffolding." Fearing the pope's anger, Michelangelo "lost no time in doing all that was wanted" and quickly completed the ceiling, one of the great masterpieces in the history of Western art.

The humanists' view of their age as a rebirth of the classical civilization of the Greeks and Romans ultimately led historians to use the word Renaissance *to identify this age. Although recent historians have emphasized the many elements of continuity between the Middle Ages and the Renaissance, the latter age was also distinguished by its own unique characteristics.*

Meaning and Characteristics of the Italian Renaissance

The word *Renaissance* means "rebirth." A number of people who lived in Italy between 1350 and 1550 believed that they had witnessed a rebirth of antiquity or Greco-Roman civilization, marking a new age. To them, the thousand or so years between the end of the Roman Empire and their own era was a middle period (hence the "Middle Ages"), characterized by darkness because of its lack of classical culture. Historians of the nineteenth century later used similar terminology to describe this period in Italy. The Swiss historian and art critic Jacob Burckhardt created the modern concept of the Renaissance in his celebrated *Civilization of the Renaissance in Italy,* published in 1860. He portrayed Italy in the fourteenth and fifteenth centuries as the birthplace of the modern world (the Italians were "the firstborn among the sons of modern Europe") and saw the revival of antiquity, the "perfecting of the individual," and secularism ("worldliness of the Italians") as its distinguishing features. Burckhardt exaggerated the individuality and secularism of the Renaissance and failed to recognize the depths of its religious sentiment; nevertheless, he established the framework for all modern interpretations of the Renaissance. Although contemporary scholars do not believe that the Renaissance represents a sudden or dramatic cultural break with the Middle Ages, as Burckhardt argued—there was, after all, much continuity in economic, political, and social life between the two periods—the Renaissance can still be viewed as a distinct period of European history that manifested itself first in Italy and then spread to the rest of Europe.

Renaissance Italy was largely an urban society. As a result of its commercial preeminence and political evolution, northern Italy by the mid-fourteenth century was mostly a land of independent cities that dominated the country districts around them. These city-states became the centers of Italian political, economic, and social life. Within this new urban society, a secular spirit emerged as increasing wealth created new possibilities for the enjoyment of worldly things (see the box on p. 304).

Above all, the Renaissance was an age of recovery from the "calamitous fourteenth century." Italy and Europe began a slow process of recuperation from the effects of the Black Death, political disorder, and economic recession. This recovery was accompanied by a rebirth of the culture of classical antiquity. Increasingly aware of their own historical past, Italian intellectuals became intensely interested in the Greco-Roman culture of the ancient Mediterranean world. This new revival of classical antiquity (the Middle Ages had in fact preserved much of ancient Latin culture) affected activities as diverse as politics and art and led to new attempts to reconcile the pagan philosophy of the Greco-Roman world with Christian thought, as well as new ways of viewing human beings.

A revived emphasis on individual ability became characteristic of the Italian Renaissance. As the fifteenth-century Florentine architect Leon Battista Alberti expressed it: "Men can do all things if they will."[1] A high regard for human dignity and worth and a realization of individual potentiality created a new social ideal of the well-rounded personality or universal person (*l'uomo universale*) who was capable of achievements in many areas of life.

These general features of the Italian Renaissance were not characteristic of all Italians but were primarily the preserve of the wealthy upper classes, who constituted a small percentage of the total population. The achievements of the Italian Renaissance were the product of an elite, rather than a mass, movement. Nevertheless, indirectly it did have some impact on ordinary people, especially in the cities, where so many of the intellectual and artistic accomplishments of the period were most visible.

The Making of Renaissance Society

After the severe economic reversals and social upheavals of the fourteenth century, the European economy gradually recovered as the volume of manufacturing and trade increased.

A Renaissance Banquet

As in Greek and Roman society, the Renaissance banquet was an occasion for good food, interesting conversation, music, and dancing. In Renaissance society, it was also a symbol of status and an opportunity to impress people with the power and wealth of one's family. Banquets were held to celebrate public and religious festivals, official visits, anniversaries, and weddings. The following menu lists the foods served at a grand banquet given by Pope Pius V in the sixteenth century.

A Sixteenth-Century Banquet

First Course:
Cold Delicacies from the Sideboard

Pieces of marzipan and marzipan balls
Neapolitan spice cakes
Malaga wine and Pisan biscuits
Fresh grapes
Prosciutto cooked in wine, served with capers and grape pulp
Salted pork tongues cooked in wine, sliced
Spit-roasted songbirds, cold, with their tongues sliced over them
Sweet mustard

Second Course:
Hot Foods from the Kitchen, Roasts

Fried veal sweetbreads and liver
Spit-roasted skylarks with lemon sauce
Spit-roasted quails with sliced eggplants
Stuffed spit-roasted pigeons with capers sprinkled over them
Spit-roasted rabbits, with sauce and crushed pine nuts
Partridges larded and spit-roasted, served with lemon
Heavily seasoned poultry with lemon slices
Slices of veal, spit-roasted, with a sauce made from the juices
Leg of goat, spit-roasted, with a sauce made from the juices
Soup of almond paste, with the flesh of three pigeons to each serving

Third Course:
Hot Foods from the Kitchen, Boiled Meats and Stews

Stuffed fat geese, boiled Lombard style and covered with sliced almonds
Stuffed breast of veal, boiled, garnished with flowers
Very young calf, boiled, garnished with parsley
Almonds in garlic sauce
Turkish-style rice with milk, sprinkled with cinnamon
Stewed pigeons with mortadella sausage and whole onions
Cabbage soup with sausages
Poultry pie, two chickens to each pie
Fricasseed breast of goat dressed with fried onions
Pies filled with custard cream
Boiled calves' feet with cheese and egg

Fourth Course:
Delicacies from the Sideboard

Bean tarts
Quince pastries
Pear tarts, the pears wrapped in marzipan
Parmesan cheese and Riviera cheese
Fresh almonds on vine leaves
Chestnuts roasted over the coals and served with salt and pepper
Milk curds
Ring-shaped cakes
Wafers made from ground grain

Economic Recovery

By the fourteenth century, Italian merchants were carrying on a flourishing commerce throughout the Mediterranean and had also expanded their lines of trade north along the Atlantic seaboard. The great galleys of the Venetian Flanders Fleet maintained a direct sea route from Venice to England and the Netherlands, where Italian merchants came into contact with the increasingly powerful Hanseatic League of merchants. Hard hit by the plague, the Italians lost their commercial preeminence while the Hanseatic League continued to prosper.

As early as the thirteenth century, a number of North German coastal towns had formed a commercial and military association known as the Hansa, or Hanseatic League. By 1500, more than eighty cities belonged to the League, which had established settlements and commercial bases in many cities in England and northern Europe, including the chief towns of Denmark, Norway, and Sweden. For almost two hundred years, the Hansa had a monopoly on northern European trade in timber, fish, grain, metals, honey, and wines. Its southern outlet in Flanders, the port city of Bruges, became the economic crossroads of Europe in the fourteenth century, serving as the meeting place between Hanseatic merchants and the Flanders Fleet of Venice. In the fifteenth century, however, silting of the port caused Bruges to enter a slow decline. So did the Hanseatic League as it proved increasingly

Harbor Scene at Hamburg. Hamburg was a founding member of the Hanseatic League. This illustration from a fifteenth-century treatise on the laws of Hamburg shows a busy port with ships of all sizes. At the left, a crane is used to unload barrels. In the building at the right, customs officials collect their dues. Merchants and townspeople are shown talking at dockside.

unable to compete with the developing larger territorial states.

Overall, trade recovered dramatically from the economic contraction of the fourteenth century. The Italians and especially the Venetians, despite new restrictive pressures on their eastern Mediterranean trade from the Ottoman Turks (see "The Ottoman Turks and the End of the Byzantine Empire" later in this chapter), continued to maintain a wealthy commercial empire. Not until the sixteenth century, when transatlantic discoveries gave new importance to the states along the ocean, did the petty Italian city-states begin to suffer from the competitive advantages of the ever-growing and more powerful national territorial states.

The economic depression of the fourteenth century also affected patterns of manufacturing. The woolen industries of Flanders and the northern Italian cities had been particularly devastated. By the beginning of the fifteenth century, however, the Florentine woolen industry had begun to recover. At the same time, the Italian cities began to develop and expand luxury industries, especially silk, glassware, and handworked items in metal and precious stones.

Other new industries, especially printing, mining, and metallurgy, began to rival the textile industry in importance in the fifteenth century. New machinery and techniques for digging deeper mines and for separating metals from ore and purifying them were developed. When rulers began to transfer their titles to underground minerals to financiers as collateral for loans, these entrepreneurs quickly developed large mining operations to produce copper, iron, and silver. Especially valuable were the rich mineral deposits in central Europe, Hungary, the Tyrol, Bohemia, and Saxony. Expanding iron production and new skills in metalworking in turn contributed to the development of firearms that were more effective than the crude weapons of the fourteenth century.

The city of Florence regained its preeminence in banking in the fifteenth century, due primarily to the Medici family. The Medici had expanded from cloth production into commerce, real estate, and banking. In its best days (in the fifteenth century), the House of Medici was the greatest bank in Europe, with branches in Venice, Milan, Rome, Avignon, Bruges, London, and Lyons. Moreover, the family had controlling interests in industrial enterprises for wool, silk, and the mining of alum, used in the dyeing of textiles. Except for a brief interruption, the Medici were also the principal bankers for the papacy, a position that produced big profits and influence at the papal court. Despite its great success in the early and middle part of the fifteenth century, the Medici bank suffered a rather sudden decline at the end of the century due to poor leadership and a series of bad loans, especially uncollectible loans to rulers. In 1494, when the French expelled the Medici from Florence and confiscated their property, the Medici financial edifice collapsed.

Social Changes in the Renaissance

The Renaissance inherited its social structure from the Middle Ages. Society remained fundamentally divided into three estates: the First Estate, the clergy, whose preeminence was grounded in the belief that people should be guided to spiritual ends; the Second Estate, the nobility, whose privileges were based on the principle that the nobles provided security and justice for society; and the Third Estate, which consisted of the peasants and inhabitants of the towns and cities. This social order experienced certain adaptations in the Renaissance, which we can see by examining the Second and Third Estates (the clergy will be examined in Chapter 13).

THE NOBILITY

Throughout much of Europe, the landholding nobles faced declining real incomes during the greater part of the fourteenth and fifteenth centuries, while the expense of maintaining noble status was rising. Nevertheless, members of the old nobility survived, and new blood infused its ranks. A reconstruction of the aristocracy was well under way by 1500.

As a result, the nobles, old and new, who constituted between 2 and 3 percent of the population in most countries, managed to dominate society as they had done in the Middle Ages, serving as military officers and holding important political posts as well as advising the king. Increasingly in the sixteenth century, members of the aristocracy pursued education as the means to maintain their role in government.

By 1500, certain ideals came to be expected of the aristocrat. These were best expressed in *The Book of the Courtier* by the Italian Baldassare Castiglione (1478–1529). First published in 1528, Castiglione's work soon became popular throughout Europe and remained a fundamental handbook for European aristocrats for centuries. In it, Castiglione described the three basic attributes of the perfect courtier. First, nobles should possess fundamental native endowments, such as impeccable character, grace, talents, and noble birth. The perfect courtier must also cultivate certain achievements. Primarily, he should participate in military and bodily exercises, because the principal profession of a courtier was bearing arms. But unlike the medieval knight, who had been required only to have military skill, the Renaissance courtier was also expected to have a classical education and to adorn his life with the arts by playing a musical instrument, drawing, and painting. In Castiglione's hands, the Renaissance ideal of the well-developed personality became a social ideal of the aristocracy. Finally, the aristocrat was expected to follow a certain standard of conduct. Nobles were expected to make good impressions; while being modest, they should not hide their accomplishments but show them with grace.

What was the purpose of these courtly standards? Castiglione wrote:

> I think that the aim of the perfect Courtier, which we have not spoken of up to now, is so to win for himself, by means of the accomplishments ascribed to him by these gentlemen, the favor and mind of the prince whom he serves that he may be able to tell him, and always will tell him, the truth about everything he needs to know, without fear or risk of displeasing him; and that when he sees the mind of his prince inclined to a wrong action, he may dare to oppose him . . . so as to dissuade him of every evil intent and bring him to the path of virtue.[2]

The aim of the perfect noble, then, was to serve his prince in an effective and honest way. Nobles would adhere to these principles for hundreds of years while they continued to dominate European life socially and politically.

PEASANTS AND TOWNSPEOPLE

Peasants made up the overwhelming mass of the Third Estate and continued to constitute 85 to 90 percent of the European population, except in the highly urbanized areas of northern Italy and Flanders. The most noticeable trend produced by the economic crisis of the fourteenth century was the decline of the manorial system and the continuing elimination of serfdom. This process had already begun in the twelfth century when the introduction of a money economy made possible the conversion of servile labor dues into rents paid in money, although they also continued to be paid in kind or labor. The contraction of the peasantry after the Black Death simply accelerated this process, since lords found it convenient to deal with the peasants by granting freedom and accepting rents. The lords' lands were then tilled by hired workers or rented out. By the end of the fifteenth century, serfdom was declining in western Europe, and more and more peasants were becoming legally free.

The remainder of the Third Estate centered around the inhabitants of towns and cities, originally the merchants and artisans who formed the burghers. The Renaissance town or city of the fifteenth century actually possessed a multitude of townspeople widely separated socially and economically.

At the top of urban society were the patricians, whose wealth from capitalistic enterprises in trade, industry, and banking enabled them to dominate their urban communities economically, socially, and politically. Below them were the petty burghers—the shopkeepers, artisans, guildmasters, and guild members, who were largely concerned with providing goods and services for local consumption.

Below these two groups were the propertyless workers earning pitiful wages and the unemployed, living squalid and miserable lives; these people constituted 30 to 40 percent of the population living in cities. In many places in Europe in the late fourteenth and fifteenth centuries, urban poverty increased dramatically. One rich merchant of Florence wrote:

> Those that are lazy and indolent in a way that does harm to the city, and who can offer no just reason for their condition, should either be forced to work or expelled from the Commune. The city would thus rid itself of that most harmful part of the poorest class. . . . If the lowest order of society earn enough food to keep them going from day to day, then they have enough.[3]

But even this large group was not at the bottom of the social scale; beneath them were the slaves, especially in the Italian cities.

SLAVERY IN THE RENAISSANCE

Agricultural slavery existed in the Early Middle Ages but had declined for economic reasons and been replaced by serfdom by the ninth century. Although some domestic slaves remained, slavery in European society had largely disappeared by the eleventh century. It reappeared first in Spain, where both Christians and Muslims used captured prisoners as slaves during the lengthy *Reconquista.* In the second half of the fourteenth century, the shortage of workers after the Black Death led Italians to introduce slavery on a fairly large scale. In 1363, for example, the government of Florence authorized the unlimited importation of foreign slaves.

In the Italian cities, slaves were used as skilled workers, making handcrafted goods for their masters, or as household workers. Girls served as nursemaids and boys as playmates. Fiammetta Adimari wrote to her husband in 1469: "I must remind you that when Alfonso is weaned we ought to get a little slave-girl to look after him, or else one of the black boys to keep him company."[4] In Florence, wealthy merchants might possess two or three slaves. Often men of the household took slaves as concubines, which sometimes led to the birth of illegitimate children. In 1392, the wealthy merchant Francesco Datini fathered an illegitimate daughter by Lucia, his twenty-year-old slave. His wife, Margherita, who was unable to bear any children, reluctantly agreed to raise the girl as their own daughter. Many illegitimate children were not as fortunate.

Slaves for the Italian market were obtained primarily from the eastern Mediterranean and the Black Sea region and included Tartars, Russians, Albanians, and Dalmatians. There were also slaves from Africa, either Moors or Ethiopians, and Muslims from Spain. Because of the lucrative nature of the slave trade, Italian merchants became involved in the transportation of slaves. Between 1414 and 1423, ten thousand slaves were sold on the Venetian market. Most slaves were females, many of them young girls.

By the end of the fifteenth century, slavery had declined dramatically in the Italian cities. Many slaves had been freed by their owners for humanitarian reasons, and the major source of slaves dried up as the Black Sea slave markets were closed to Italian traders after the Turks conquered the Byzantine Empire. Although some other sources remained, prices rose dramatically, further cutting demand. Moreover, a general feeling had arisen that slaves—the "domestic enemy," as they were called—were dangerous and not worth the effort. By the sixteenth century, slaves were in evidence only at princely courts, where they were kept as curiosities; this was especially true of black slaves.

In the fifteenth century, the Portuguese had imported increasing numbers of African slaves for southern European markets. It has been estimated that between 1444 and 1505, some 140,000 slaves were shipped from Africa. The presence of blacks in European society was not entirely new. Saint Maurice, a Christian martyr of the fourth century, was portrayed by medieval artists as a black knight and became the center of a popular cult in the twelfth and thirteenth centuries. The number of blacks in Europe was small, however, until their importation as slaves.

THE FAMILY IN RENAISSANCE ITALY

The family played an important role in Renaissance Italy. Family meant, first of all, the extended household of parents, children, and servants (if the family was wealthy) and could also include grandparents, widowed mothers, and even unmarried sisters. Families that were related and bore the same surname often lived near each other and might dominate an entire urban district. Old family names—Strozzi, Rucellai, Medici—conferred great status and prestige. The family bond was a source of great security in a dangerous and violent world, and its importance helps explain the vendetta in the Italian Renaissance. A crime committed by one family member fell on the entire family, ensuring that retaliation by the offended family would be a bloody affair involving large numbers of people.

To maintain the family, careful attention was given to marriages arranged by parents, often to strengthen business or family ties. Details were worked out well in advance, sometimes when children were only two or three, and reinforced by a legally binding marriage contract (see the box on p. 309). The important aspect of the contract was the size of the dowry, money presented by the wife's family to the husband upon marriage. The dowry could involve large sums and was expected of all families. The size of the dowry was an indication of whether the bride was moving upward or downward in society. With a large dowry, a daughter could marry a man of higher social status, thereby enabling her family to move up in society; if the daughter married a man of lower social status, however, her dowry would be smaller because the reputation of her family would raise the status of the husband's family.

The father-husband was the center of the Italian family. He gave it his name, was responsible for it in all legal matters, managed all finances (his wife had no share in his wealth), and made the crucial decisions that determined his children's lives. A father's authority over his children

Private Collection/Bridgeman Art Library

Wedding Banquet. Parents arranged marriages in Renaissance Italy to strengthen business or family ties. A legally binding marriage contract was considered a necessary part of the marital arrangements. So was a wedding feast. This painting by Botticelli shows the wedding banquet in Florence that celebrated the marriage of Nastagio degli Onesti and the daughter of Paulo Traversaro.

was absolute until he died or formally freed his children. In Renaissance Italy, children did not become adults on reaching a certain age; adulthood came only when the father went before a judge and formally emancipated them. The age of emancipation varied from early teens to late twenties.

The wife managed the household, a position that gave women a certain degree of autonomy in their daily lives. Most wives, however, also knew that their primary function was to bear children. Upper-class wives were frequently pregnant; Alessandra Strozzi of Florence, for example, who had been married at the age of sixteen, bore eight children in ten years. Poor women did not conceive at the same rate because they nursed their own babies. Wealthy women gave their infants out to wet nurses, which enabled them to become pregnant more quickly after the birth of a child.

For women in the Renaissance, childbirth was a fearful occasion. Not only was it painful, but it could be deadly; as many as 10 percent of mothers died in childbirth. In his memoirs, the Florentine merchant Gregorio Dati recalled that three of his four wives had died in childbirth. His third wife, after bearing eleven children in fifteen years, "died in childbirth after lengthy suffering, which she bore with remarkable strength and patience."[5] Nor did the tragedies end with childbirth. Surviving mothers often faced the death of their children. In Florence in the fifteenth century, for example, almost 50 percent of the children born to merchant families died before the age of twenty. Given these mortality rates, many upper-class families sought to have as many children as possible to ensure that there would be a surviving male heir to the family fortune. This concern is evident in the Florentine humanist Leon Battista Alberti's treatise *On the Family*, where one of the characters remarks, "How many families do we see today in decadence and ruin! . . . Of all these families not only the magnificence and greatness but the very men, not only the men but the very names are shrunk away and gone. Their memory . . . is wiped out and obliterated."[6]

Considering that marriages were arranged, marital relationships ran the gamut from deep emotional attachments to purely formal ties. The lack of emotional attachment from arranged marriages did encourage extramarital relationships, especially among groups whose lifestyle offered special temptations. Although sexual license for males was the norm for princes and their courts, women were supposed to follow different guidelines. The first wife of Duke Filippo Maria Visconti of Milan had an affair with the court musician and was executed for it.

The great age difference between husbands and wives in Italian Renaissance marriage patterns also heightened the need for sexual outlets outside marriage. In Florence in 1427–1428, the average difference was thirteen years. Though females married between the ages of sixteen and eighteen, factors of environment, wealth, and demographic

Marriage Negotiations

Marriages were so important in maintaining families in Renaissance Italy that much energy was put into arranging them. Parents made the choices for their children, most often for considerations that had little to do with the modern notion of love. This selection is taken from the letters of a Florentine matron of the illustrious Strozzi family to her son Filippo in Naples. The family's considerations were complicated by the fact that the son was in exile.

Alessandra Strozzi to Her Son Filippo in Naples

[April 20, 1464] . . . Concerning the matter of a wife [for you], it appears to me that if Francesco di Messer Tanagli wishes to give his daughter, that it would be a fine marriage. . . . Now I will speak with Marco [Parenti, Alessandra's son-in-law], to see if there are other prospects that would be better, and if there are none, then we will learn if he wishes to give her [in marriage]. . . . Francesco Tanagli has a good reputation, and he has held office, not the highest, but still he has been in office. You may ask: "Why should he give her to someone in exile?" There are three reasons. First, there aren't many young men of good family who have both virtue and property. Second, she has only a small dowry, 1,000 florins, which is the dowry of an artisan [although not a small sum, either—senior officials in the government bureaucracy earned 300 florins a year]. . . . Third, I believe that he will give her away, because he has a large family and he will need help to settle them. . . .

[July 26, 1465] . . . Francesco is a good friend of Marco and he trusts him. On S. Jacopo's day, he spoke to him discreetly and persuasively, saying that for several months he had heard that we were interested in the girl and . . . that when we had made up our minds, she will come to us willingly. [He said that] you were a worthy man, and that his family had always made good marriages, but that he had only a small dowry to give her, and so he would prefer to send her out of Florence to someone of worth, rather than to give her to someone here, from among those who were available, with little money. . . . We have information that she is affable and competent. She is responsible for a large family (there are twelve children, six boys and six girls), and the mother is always pregnant and isn't very competent. . . .

[August 31, 1465] . . . I have recently received some very favorable information [about the Tanagli girl] from two individuals. . . . They are in agreement that whoever gets her will be content. . . . Concerning her beauty, they told me what I had already seen, that she is attractive and well-proportioned. Her face is long, but I couldn't look directly into her face, since she appeared to be aware that I was examining her . . . and so she turned away from me like the wind. . . . She reads quite well . . . and she can dance and sing. . . .

So yesterday I sent for Marco and told him what I had learned. And we talked about the matter for a while, and decided that he should say something to the father and give him a little hope, but not so much that we couldn't withdraw, and find out from him the amount of the dowry. . . . May God help us to choose what will contribute to our tranquility and to the consolation of us all.

[September 13, 1465] . . . Marco came to me and said that he had met with Francesco Tanagli, who had spoken very coldly, so that I understand that he had changed his mind. . . .

[Filippo Strozzi eventually married Fiametta di Donato Adimari in 1466.]

trends favored relatively late ages for the first marriages of males, who were usually in their thirties or even early forties. The existence of large numbers of young, unmarried males encouraged extramarital sex as well as prostitution. Prostitution was viewed as a necessary vice; since it could not be eliminated, it should be regulated. In Florence in 1415, the city fathers established communal brothels:

> Desiring to eliminate a worse evil by means of a lesser one, the lord priors . . . have decreed that the priors . . . may authorize the establishment of two public brothels in the city of Florence, in addition to the one which already exists. . . . [They are to be located] in suitable places or in places where the exercise of such scandalous activity can best be concealed, for the honor of the city and of those who live in the neighborhood in which these prostitutes must stay to hire their bodies for lucre.[7]

A prostitute in Florence was required to wear a traditional garb of "gloves on her hands and a bell on her head."

The Italian States in the Renaissance

By the fifteenth century, five major powers dominated the Italian peninsula: Milan, Venice, Florence, the Papal States, and Naples (see Map 12.1).

The Five Major States

Northern Italy was divided between the duchy of Milan and the republic of Venice. After the death of the last Visconti ruler of Milan in 1447, Francesco Sforza, one of the leading *condottieri* (see Chapter 11) of the time, turned on his Milanese employers, conquered the city, and became its new duke. Both the Visconti and the Sforza rulers worked to create a highly centralized territorial state. They were especially successful in devising systems of taxation that

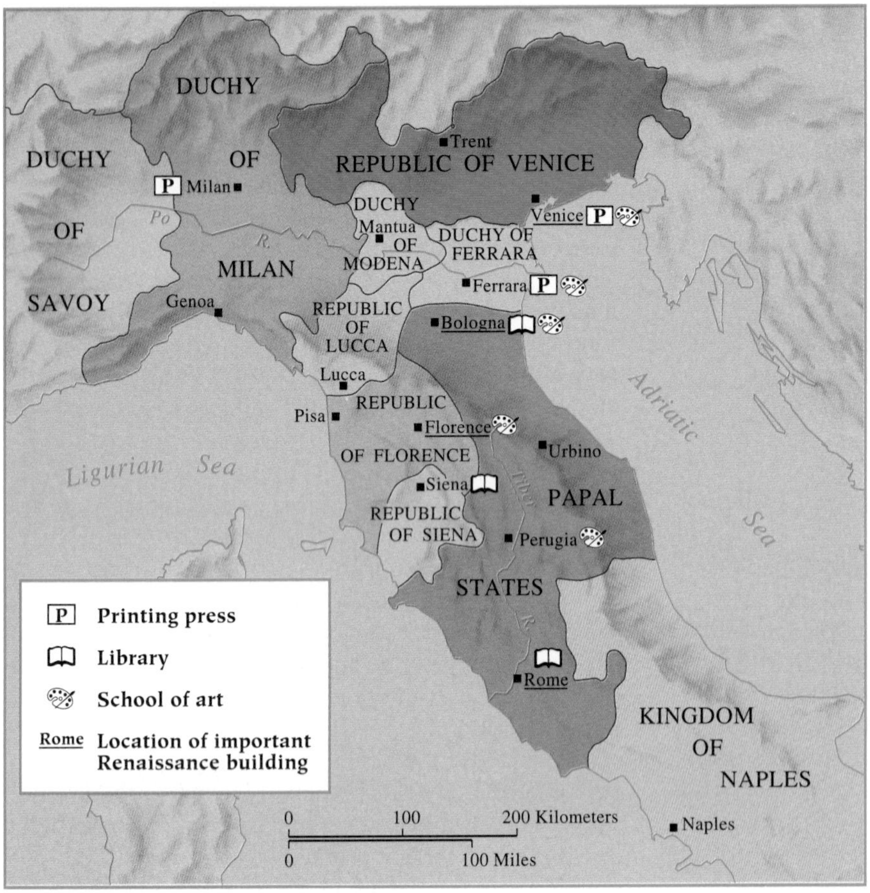

Map 12.1 Renaissance Italy. Italy in the late fourteenth century was a land of five major states and numerous independent city-states. Increased prosperity and a supportive intellectual climate helped create the atmosphere for the middle and upper classes to "rediscover" Greco-Roman culture. Modern diplomacy was also a product of Renaissance Italy. ■ Could the presence of several other powers within easy marching distance make a ruler recognize the importance of diplomacy?

generated enormous revenues for the government. The maritime republic of Venice remained an extremely stable political entity governed by a small oligarchy of merchant-aristocrats. Its commercial empire brought in enormous revenues and gave it the status of an international power. At the end of the fourteenth century, Venice embarked on the conquest of a territorial state in northern Italy to protect its food supply and its overland trade routes. Although expansion on the mainland made sense to the Venetians, it frightened Milan and Florence, which worked to curb what they perceived as the expansionary designs of the Venetians.

The republic of Florence dominated the region of Tuscany. By the beginning of the fifteenth century, Florence was governed by a small merchant oligarchy that manipulated the apparently republican government. In 1434, Cosimo de' Medici took control of this oligarchy. Although the wealthy Medici family maintained republican forms of government for appearance' sake, it ran the government from behind the scenes. Through their lavish patronage and careful courting of political allies, Cosimo (1434–1464), and later his grandson Lorenzo the Magnificent (1469–1492), were successful in dominating the city at a time when Florence was the center of the cultural Renaissance.

The Papal States lay in central Italy. Nominally under the political control of the popes, papal residence in Avignon and the Great Schism had enabled individual cities and territories, such as Urbino, Bologna, and Ferrara, to become independent of papal authority. The Renaissance popes of the fifteenth century directed much of their energy toward reestablishing their control over the Papal States (see "The Renaissance Papacy" later in this chapter).

The kingdom of Naples, which encompassed most of southern Italy and usually the island of Sicily, was fought over by the French and the Aragonese until the latter established their domination in the mid-fifteenth century. Throughout the Renaissance, the kingdom of Naples remained a backward monarchy with a population consisting largely of poverty-stricken peasants dominated by unruly nobles. It shared little in the cultural glories of the Renaissance.

■ *Independent City-States*

Besides the five major states, there were a number of independent city-states under the control of powerful ruling families that became brilliant centers of Renaissance culture in the fifteenth century. These included Mantua under the enlightened rule of the Gonzaga lords, Ferrara governed by the flamboyant d'Este family, and perhaps the most famous, Urbino, ruled by the Montefeltro dynasty.

Federigo da Montefeltro, who ruled Urbino from 1444 to 1482, received a classical education typical of the famous humanist school in Mantua run by Vittorino da Feltre. He had also learned the skills of fighting, since the Mon-

Scala/Art Resource, NY

Scala/Art Resource, NY

Piero della Francesca, *Duke and Duchess of Urbino.* Federigo da Montefeltro and his wife, Battista Sforza, ruled the small central Italian principality of Urbino. These profile portraits by Piero della Francesca gave a realistic rendering of the two figures. Visible in the background are the hills and valleys of Urbino.

tefeltro family compensated for the poverty of Urbino by hiring themselves out as *condottiere.* Federigo was not only a good ruler, but also a rather unusual *condottiere* by fifteenth-century standards. Although not a brilliant general, he was reliable and honest. He did not break his promises, even when urged to do so by a papal legate. At the same time, Duke Federigo was one of the greatest patrons of Renaissance culture. Under his direction, Urbino became a well-known cultural and intellectual center. Though a despot, Federigo was also benevolent. It was said of him that he could walk safely through the streets of Urbino unaccompanied by a bodyguard, a feat few Renaissance rulers dared to emulate.

A noticeable feature of these smaller Renaissance courts was the important role played by women. Battista Sforza, niece of the ruler of Milan, was the wife of Federigo da Montefeltro. The duke called his wife "the delight of both my public and my private hours." An intelligent woman, she was well versed in both Greek and Latin and did much to foster art and letters in Urbino. As a prominent *condottiere,* Federigo was frequently absent, and like the wives of medieval lords, Battista Sforza was respected for governing the state "with firmness and good sense."

Perhaps the most famous of the Renaissance ruling women was Isabella d'Este (1474–1539), daughter of the duke of Ferrara, who married Francesco Gonzaga, marquis of Mantua. Their court was another important center of art and learning in the Renaissance. Educated at the brilliant court of Ferrara, Isabella was known for her intelligence and political wisdom. Called the "first lady of the world," she attracted artists and intellectuals to the Mantuan court and was responsible for amassing one of the finest libraries in all of Italy. Her numerous letters to friends, family, princes, and artists all over Europe disclose her political acumen as well as a good sense of humor (see the box on p. 312). Both before and after the death of her husband, she effectively ruled Mantua and won a reputation as a clever negotiator.

Warfare in Italy

The fragmented world of the Italian territorial states gave rise to a political practice that was later used on a larger scale by competing European states. This was the concept of a balance of power, designed to prevent the aggrandizement of any one state at the expense of the others. This

The Letters of Isabella d'Este

Many Italian and European rulers at the beginning of the sixteenth century regarded Isabella d'Este as an important political figure. These excerpts from her letters reveal Isabella's political skills and her fierce determination. After her husband was taken prisoner by the Venetians in 1509, she refused to accept the condition for his release—namely, that her son Federico be kept as a hostage by the Venetians or the Holy Roman Emperor. She wrote to both the emperor and her husband, refusing to do as they asked.

Letter of Isabella d'Este to the Imperial Envoy

As to the demand for our dearest first-born son Federico, besides being a cruel and almost inhuman thing for any one who knows the meaning of a mother's love, there are many reasons which render it difficult and impossible. Although we are quite sure that his person would be well cared for and protected by His Majesty [the Holy Roman Emperor], how could we wish him to run the risk of this long and difficult journey, considering the child's tender and delicate age? And you must know what comfort and solace, in his father's present unhappy condition, we find in the presence of this dear son, the hope and joy of all our people and subjects. To deprive us of him, would be to deprive us of life itself, and of all we count good and precious. If you take Federico away you might as well take away our life and state. . . . Once for all, we will suffer any loss rather than part from our son, and this you may take to be our deliberate and unchanging resolution.

Letter of Isabella d'Este to Her Husband, Who Had Ordered Her to Send the Boy to Venice

If in this matter Your Excellency were to despise me and deprive me of your love and grace, I would rather endure such harsh treatment, I would rather lose our State, than deprive us of our children. I am hoping that in time your own prudence and kindness will make you understand that I have acted more lovingly toward you than you have to yourself.

Have patience! You can be sure that I think continuously of your liberation and when the time comes I will not fail you, as I have not relaxed my efforts. As witness I cite the Pope, the Emperor, the King of France, and all the other reigning heads and potentates of Christendom. Yes, and the infidels as well [she had written to the Turkish sultan for help]. If it were *really* the only means of setting you free, I would not only send Federico but all the other children as well. I will do everything imaginable. Some day I hope I can make you understand. . . .

Pardon me if this letter is badly written and worse composed, but I do not know if I am dead or alive.

Isabella, who desires the best for Your Excellency, written with her own hand

[Isabella's husband was not pleased with her response and exclaimed angrily: "That whore of my wife is the cause of it all. Send me into battle alone, do what you like with me. I have lost in one blow my state, my honor and my freedom. If she does not obey, I'll cut her vocal cords."]

system was especially evident after 1454 when the Italian states signed the Peace of Lodi, which ended almost a half-century of war and inaugurated a relatively peaceful era in Italy until 1494. An alliance system (Milan, Florence, and Naples versus Venice and the papacy) was then created that led to a workable balance of power within Italy. It failed, however, to establish lasting cooperation among the major powers or a common foreign policy.

The growth of powerful monarchical states (see "The European State in the Renaissance" later in this chapter) led to trouble for the Italians. Italy soon became a battlefield for the great power struggle between the French and Spanish monarchies. Italian wealth and splendor would probably have been inviting to its northern neighbors under any circumstances, but it was actually the breakdown of the Italian balance of power that encouraged the invasions and began the Italian wars. Feeling isolated, Ludovico Sforza, the duke of Milan, foolishly invited the French to intervene in Italian politics. The French king Charles VIII (1483–1498) was eager to do so, and in 1494, with an army of thirty thousand men, he advanced through Italy and occupied the kingdom of Naples. Other Italian states turned to the Spanish for help, and Ferdinand of Aragon indicated his willingness to intervene. For the next fifteen years, the French and Spanish competed to dominate Italy. After 1510, the war was continued by a new generation of rulers, Francis I of France and Charles I of Spain (see Chapter 13). This war was part of a long struggle for power throughout Europe between the Valois and Habsburg dynasties. Italy was only a pawn for the two great powers, a convenient arena for fighting battles. The terrible sack of Rome in 1527 by the armies of the Spanish king Charles I brought a temporary end to the Italian wars. Thereafter, the Spaniards dominated Italy.

Although some Italians had developed a sense of national consciousness and differentiated between Italians and "barbarians" (all foreigners), few Italians conceived of creating an alliance or confederation of states that could repel foreign invaders. Italians remained fiercely loyal to their own petty states, making invasion a fact of life in Italian history for all too long. Italy would not achieve unification and nationhood until 1870.

CHRONOLOGY

The Italian States in the Renaissance

Duchy of Milan	
The Viscontis	1311–1447
The Sforzas	1450–1494
Florence	
Cosimo de' Medici	1434–1464
Lorenzo de' Medici	1469–1492
Peace of Lodi	1454
Beginning of Italian wars—French invasion of Italy	1494
Sack of Rome	1527

The Birth of Modern Diplomacy

The modern diplomatic system was a product of the Italian Renaissance. There were ambassadors in the Middle Ages, but they were used only on a temporary basis. Moreover, an ambassador, regardless of whose subject he was, regarded himself as the servant of all Christendom, not just of his particular employer. As a treatise on diplomacy stated: "An ambassador is sacred because he acts for the general welfare." Since he was the servant of all Christendom, "the business of an ambassador is peace."[8]

This concept of an ambassador changed during the Italian Renaissance because of the political situation in Italy. A large number of states existed, many so small that their security was easily threatened by their neighbors. To survive, the Italian states began to send resident diplomatic agents to each other to ferret out useful information. During the Italian wars, the practice of resident diplomats spread to the rest of Europe, and in the course of the sixteenth and seventeenth centuries, Europeans developed the diplomatic machinery still in use today, such as the rights of ambassadors in host countries and the proper procedures for conducting diplomatic business.

With the use of permanent resident agents or ambassadors, the conception of the purpose of the ambassador also changed. A Venetian diplomat attempted to define the function of an ambassador in a treatise written at the end of the fifteenth century. He wrote: "The first duty of an ambassador is exactly the same as that of any other servant of a government, that is, to do, say, advise, and think whatever may best serve the preservation and aggrandizement of his own state."[9] An ambassador was now simply an agent of the territorial state that sent him, not the larger body of Christendom. He could use any methods that were beneficial to the political interests of his own state. We are at the beginning of modern politics when the interests of the state supersede all other considerations.

Machiavelli and the New Statecraft

No one gave better expression to the Renaissance preoccupation with political power than Niccolò Machiavelli (1469–1527). He entered the service of the Florentine republic in 1498, four years after the Medici family had been expelled from the city. As a secretary to the Florentine Council of Ten, he made numerous diplomatic missions, including trips to France and Germany, and saw the workings of statecraft firsthand. Since Italy had been invaded in 1494, Machiavelli was active during a period of Italian tribulation and devastation. In 1512, French defeat and Spanish victory led to the reestablishment of Medici power in Florence. Staunch republicans, including Machiavelli, were sent into exile. Forced to give up politics, the great love of his life, Machiavelli now reflected on political power and wrote books, including *The Prince* (1513), one of the most famous treatises on political power in the Western world.

Machiavelli's ideas on politics stemmed from two major sources, his preoccupation with Italy's political problems and his knowledge of ancient Rome. His major concerns in *The Prince* were the acquisition and expansion of political power as the means to restore and maintain order

© ARCHIV/Photo Researchers, Inc.

Niccolò Machiavelli. In *The Prince,* Machiavelli gave concrete expression to the Renaissance preoccupation with political power. This slender volume remains one of the most famous and most widely read Western treatises on politics. Machiavelli is seen here in a portrait by Santi di Tito.

Machiavelli: "Is It Better to Be Loved Than Feared?"

In 1513, Niccolò Machiavelli wrote a short treatise on political power that, justly or unjustly, has given him a reputation as a political opportunist. In this passage from Chapter 17 of *The Prince,* Machiavelli analyzes whether it is better for a ruler to be loved than to be feared.

Machiavelli, The Prince

This leads us to a question that is in dispute: Is it better to be loved than feared, or vice versa? My reply is one ought to be both loved and feared; but, since it is difficult to accomplish both at the same time, I maintain it is much safer to be feared than loved, if you have to do without one of the two. For of men one can, in general, say this: They are ungrateful, fickle, deceptive and deceiving, avoiders of danger, eager to gain. As long as you serve their interests, they are devoted to you. They promise you their blood, their possessions, their lives, and their children, as I said before, so long as you seem to have no need of them. But as soon as you need help, they turn against you. Any ruler who relies simply on their promises and makes no other preparations, will be destroyed. For you will find that those whose support you buy, who do not rally to you because they admire your strength of character and nobility of soul, these are people you pay for, but they are never yours, and in the end you cannot get the benefit of your investment. Men are less nervous of offending someone who makes himself lovable, than someone who makes himself frightening. For love attaches men by ties of obligation, which, since men are wicked, they break whenever their interests are at stake. But fear restrains men because they are afraid of punishment, and this fear never leaves them. Still, a ruler should make himself feared in such a way that, if he does not inspire love, at least he does not provoke hatred. For it is perfectly possible to be feared and not hated. You will only be hated if you seize the property or the women of your subjects and citizens. Whenever you have to kill someone, make sure that you have a suitable excuse and an obvious reason; but, above all else, keep your hands off other people's property; for men are quicker to forget the death of their father than the loss of their inheritance. Moreover, there are always reasons why you might want to seize people's property; and he who begins to live by plundering others will always find an excuse for seizing other people's possessions; but there are fewer reasons for killing people, and one killing need not lead to another.

When a ruler is at the head of his army and has a vast number of soldiers under his command, then it is absolutely essential to be prepared to be thought cruel; for it is impossible to keep an army united and ready for action without acquiring a reputation for cruelty.

in his time. Late medieval political theorists believed that a ruler was justified in exercising political power only if it contributed to the common good of the people he served. The ethical side of a prince's activity—how a ruler ought to behave based on Christian moral principles—was the focus of many late medieval treatises on politics. Machiavelli bluntly contradicted this approach:

> My hope is to write a book that will be useful, at least to those who read it intelligently, and so I thought it sensible to go straight to a discussion of how things are in real life and not waste time with a discussion of an imaginary world. . . . For the gap between how people actually behave and how they ought to behave is so great that anyone who ignores everyday reality in order to live up to an ideal will soon discover he had been taught how to destroy himself, not how to preserve himself.[10]

Machiavelli considered his approach far more realistic than that of his medieval forebears.

From Machiavelli's point of view, a prince's attitude toward power must be based on an understanding of human nature, which he perceived as basically self-centered: "For of men one can, in general, say this: They are ungrateful, fickle, deceptive and deceiving, avoiders of danger, eager to gain." Political activity, therefore, could not be restricted by moral considerations. The prince acts on behalf of the state and for the sake of the state must be willing to let his conscience sleep. As Machiavelli put it:

> You need to understand this: A ruler, and particularly a ruler who is new to power, cannot conform to all those rules that men who are thought good are expected to respect, for he is often obliged, in order to hold on to power, to break his word, to be uncharitable, inhumane, and irreligious. So he must be mentally prepared to act as circumstances and changes in fortune require. As I have said, he should do what is right if he can; but he must be prepared to do wrong if necessary.[11]

Machiavelli found a good example of the new Italian ruler in Cesare Borgia, the son of Pope Alexander VI, who used ruthless measures to achieve his goal of carving out a new state in central Italy. As Machiavelli said: "So anyone who decides that the policy to follow when one has newly acquired power is to destroy one's enemies, to secure some allies, to win wars, whether by force or by fraud, to make oneself both loved and feared by one's subjects, . . . cannot hope to find, in the recent past, a better model to imitate than Cesare Borgia."[12] Machiavelli was among the first to abandon morality as the basis for the analysis of political activity (see the box above).

The Intellectual Renaissance in Italy

Individualism and secularism—two characteristics of the Italian Renaissance—were most noticeable in the intellectual and artistic realms. Italian culture had matured by the fourteenth century. For the next two centuries, Italy was the cultural leader of Europe. This new Italian culture was primarily the product of a relatively wealthy, urban lay society. The most important literary movement associated with the Renaissance is humanism.

Italian Renaissance Humanism

Renaissance humanism was an intellectual movement based on the study of the classical literary works of Greece and Rome. Humanists studied the liberal arts—grammar, rhetoric, poetry, moral philosophy or ethics, and history—all based on the writings of ancient Greek and Roman authors. These are the subjects we call the humanities.

The central importance of literary preoccupations in Renaissance humanism is evident in the professional status or occupations of the humanists. Some of them were teachers of the humanities in secondary schools and universities, where they either gave occasional lectures or held permanent positions, often as professors of rhetoric. Others served as secretaries in the chancelleries of Italian city-states or at the courts of princes or popes. All of these occupations were largely secular, and most humanists were laymen rather than members of the clergy.

THE EMERGENCE OF HUMANISM

Petrarch (1304–1374) has often been called the father of Italian Renaissance humanism (see Chapter 11 on Petrarch's use of the Italian vernacular). Petrarch had rejected his father's desire that he become a lawyer and took up a literary career instead. Although he lived in Avignon for a time, most of his last decades were spent in Italy as the guest of various princes and city governments. With his usual lack of modesty, Petrarch once exclaimed, "Some of the greatest kings of our time have loved me and cultivated my friendship. . . . When I was their guest it was more as if they were mine."[13]

Petrarch did more than any other individual in the fourteenth century to foster the development of Renaissance humanism. He was the first intellectual to characterize the Middle Ages as a period of darkness, promoting the mistaken belief that medieval culture was ignorant of classical antiquity. Petrarch's interest in the classics led him on a quest for forgotten Latin manuscripts and set in motion a ransacking of monastic libraries throughout Europe. In his preoccupation with the classics and their secular content, Petrarch worried at times whether he was sufficiently attentive to spiritual ideals (see the box on p. 316). His qualms, however, did not prevent him from inaugurating the humanist emphasis on the use of pure classical Latin, making it fashionable for humanists to use Cicero as a model for prose and Virgil for poetry. As Petrarch said, "Christ is my God; Cicero is the prince of the language."

HUMANISM IN FIFTEENTH-CENTURY ITALY

In Florence, the humanist movement took a new direction at the beginning of the fifteenth century when it became closely tied to Florentine civic spirit and pride, giving rise to what one modern scholar has labeled "civic humanism." Fourteenth-century humanists such as Petrarch had described the intellectual life as one of solitude. They rejected family and a life of action in the community. In the busy civic world of Florence, however, intellectuals began to take a new view of their role as intellectuals. The classical Roman Cicero, who was both a statesman and an intellectual, became their model. Leonardo Bruni (1370–1444), a humanist, Florentine patriot, and chancellor of the city, wrote a biography of Cicero titled the *New Cicero,* in which he waxed enthusiastic about the fusion of political action and literary creation in Cicero's life. From Bruni's time on, Cicero served as the inspiration for the Renaissance ideal that it was the duty of an intellectual to live an active life for one's state. An individual only "grows to maturity—both intellectually and morally—through participation" in the life of the state. Civic humanism reflected the values of the urban society of the Italian Renaissance. Humanists came to believe that their study of the humanities should be put to the service of the state. It is no accident that humanists served the state as chancellors, councillors, and advisers.

Also evident in the humanism of the first half of the fifteenth century was a growing interest in classical Greek civilization. One of the first Italian humanists to gain a thorough knowledge of Greek was Leonardo Bruni, who became an enthusiastic pupil of the Byzantine scholar Manuel Chrysoloras, who taught in Florence from 1396 to 1400. Humanists eagerly perused the works of Plato as well as Greek poets, dramatists, historians, and orators, such as Thucydides, Euripides, and Sophocles, all of whom had been ignored by the scholastics of the High Middle Ages as irrelevant to the theological questions they were examining.

By the fifteenth century, a consciousness of being humanists had emerged. This was especially evident in the career of Lorenzo Valla (1407–1457). Valla was brought up in Rome and educated in both Latin and Greek. Eventually, he achieved his chief ambition of becoming a papal secretary. Valla's major work, *The Elegances of the Latin Language,* was an effort to purify medieval Latin and restore Latin to its proper position over the vernacular. The treatise examined the proper use of classical Latin and created a new literary standard. Early humanists had tended to take as classical models any author (including Christians) who had written before the seventh century A.D. Valla identified different stages in the growth of the Latin language and accepted only the Latin of the last century of the Roman Republic and the first century of the empire.

Petrarch: Mountain Climbing and the Search for Spiritual Contentment

Petrarch has long been regarded as the father of Italian Renaissance humanism. One of his literary masterpieces was *The Ascent of Mount Ventoux,* a colorful description of an attempt to climb a mountain in Provence in southern France and survey the world from its top. Petrarch's primary interest is in presenting an allegory of his own soul's struggle to achieve a higher spiritual state. The work is addressed to a professor of theology in Paris who had initially led Petrarch to read Augustine. The latter had experienced a vivid conversion to Christianity almost a thousand years earlier.

■ *Petrarch,* The Ascent of Mount Ventoux

Today I ascended the highest mountain in this region, which, not without cause, they call the Windy Peak. Nothing but the desire to see its conspicuous height was the reason for this undertaking. For many years I have been intending to make this expedition. You know that since my early childhood, as fate tossed around human affairs, I have been tossed around in these parts, and this mountain, visible far and wide from everywhere, is always in your view. So I was at last seized by the impulse to accomplish what I had always wanted to do. . . .

[After some false starts, Petrarch finally achieves his goal and arrives at the top of Mount Ventoux.]

I was glad of the progress I had made, but I wept over my imperfection and was grieved by the fickleness of all that men do. In this manner I seemed to have somehow forgotten the place I had come to and why, until I was warned to throw off such sorrows, for which another place would be more appropriate. I had better look around and see what I had intended to see in coming here. The time to leave was approaching, they said. . . . Like a man aroused from sleep, I turned back and looked toward the west. . . . One could see most distinctly the mountains of the province of Lyons to the right and, to the left, the sea near Marseilles as well as the waves that break against Aigues-Mortes. . . . The Rhône River was directly under our eyes.

I admired every detail, now relishing earthly enjoyment, now lifting up my mind to higher spheres after the example of my body, and I thought it fit to look in the volume of Augustine's *Confessions* which I owe to your loving kindness and preserve carefully, keeping it always in my hands, in remembrance of the author as well as the donor. . . . I opened it with the intention of reading whatever might occur to me first: . . . I happened to hit upon the tenth book of the work. . . . Where I fixed my eyes first, it was written: "And men go to admire the high mountains, the vast floods of the sea, the huge streams of the rivers, the circumference of the ocean, and the revolutions of the stars—and desert themselves." I was stunned, I confess. I bade my brother [who had accompanied him], who wanted to hear more, not to molest me, and closed the book, angry with myself that I still admired earthly things. Long since I ought to have learned, even from pagan philosophers, that "nothing is admirable besides the soul; compared to its greatness nothing is great."

I was completely satisfied with what I had seen of the mountain and turned my inner eye toward myself. From this hour nobody heard me say a word until we arrived at the bottom. These words occupied me sufficiently. I could not imagine that this had happened to me by chance: I was convinced that whatever I had read there was said to me and to nobody else. I remembered that Augustine once suspected the same regarding himself, when, while he was reading the Apostolic Epistles, the first passage that occurred to him was, as he himself relates: "Not in banqueting and drunkenness, not in chambering and wantonness, not in strife and envying; but put you on the Lord Jesus Christ, and make no provision for the flesh to fulfill your lusts."

HUMANISM AND PHILOSOPHY

In the second half of the fifteenth century, a dramatic upsurge of interest in the works of Plato occurred, especially evident among the members of the Florentine Platonic Academy. This academy was not a formal school but rather an informal discussion group. Cosimo de' Medici, the de facto ruler of Florence, became its patron and commissioned a translation of Plato's dialogues by Marsilio Ficino (1433–1499), one of the academy's leaders. Ficino dedicated his life to the translation of Plato and the exposition of the Platonic philosophy known as Neoplatonism.

In two major works, Ficino undertook the synthesis of Christianity and Platonism into a single system. His Neoplatonism was based on two primary ideas, the Neoplatonic hierarchy of substances and a theory of spiritual love. The former postulated the idea of a hierarchy of substances, or great chain of being, from the lowest form of physical matter (plants) to the purest spirit (God), in which humans occupied a central or middle position. They were the link between the material world (through the body) and the spiritual world (through the soul), and their highest duty was to ascend toward that union with God that was the true end of human existence. Ficino's theory of spiritual or Platonic love maintained that just as all people are bound together in their common humanity by love, so too are all parts of the universe held together by bonds of sympathetic love.

Renaissance Hermeticism was another product of the Florentine intellectual environment of the late fifteenth century. At the request of Cosimo de' Medici, Ficino translated into Latin a Greek work titled the *Corpus Hermeticum.*

Pico della Mirandola and the Dignity of Man

Giovanni Pico della Mirandola was one of the foremost intellects of the Italian Renaissance. Pico boasted that he had studied all schools of philosophy, which he tried to demonstrate by drawing up nine hundred theses for public disputation at the age of twenty-four. As a preface to his theses, he wrote his famous *Oration on the Dignity of Man,* in which he proclaimed the unlimited potentiality of human beings.

Pico della Mirandola, Oration on the Dignity of Man

At last the best of artisans [God] ordained that that creature to whom He had been able to give nothing proper to himself should have joint possession of whatever had been peculiar to each of the different kinds of being. He therefore took man as a creature of indeterminate nature, and assigning him a place in the middle of the world, addressed him thus: "Neither a fixed abode nor a form that is yours alone nor any function peculiar to yourself have we given you, Adam, to the end that according to your longing and according to your judgment you may have and possess what abode, what form, and what functions you yourself desire. The nature of all other beings is limited and constrained within the bounds of laws prescribed by Us. You, constrained by no limits, in accordance with your own free will, in whose hand We have placed you, shall ordain for yourself the limits of your nature. We have set you at the world's center that you may from there more easily observe whatever is in the world. We have made you neither of heaven nor of earth, neither mortal nor immortal, so that with freedom of choice and with honor, as though the maker and molder of yourself, you may fashion yourself in whatever shape you shall prefer. You shall have the power to degenerate into the lower forms of life, which are brutish. You shall have the power, out of your soul's judgment, to be reborn into the higher forms, which are divine."

O supreme generosity of God the Father, O highest and most marvelous felicity of man! To him it is granted to have whatever he chooses, to be whatever he wills. Beasts as soon as they are born bring with them from their mother's womb all they will ever possess. Spiritual beings, either from the beginning or soon thereafter, become what they are to be for ever and ever. On man when he came into life the Father conferred the seeds of all kinds and the germs of every way of life. Whatever seeds each man cultivates will grow to maturity and bear in him their own fruit. If they be vegetative, he will be like a plant. If sensitive, he will become brutish. If rational, he will grow into a heavenly being. If intellectual, he will be an angel and the son of God.

The Hermetic manuscripts contained two kinds of writings. One type stressed the occult sciences, with an emphasis on astrology, alchemy, and magic. The other focused on theological and philosophical beliefs and speculations. Some parts of the Hermetic writings were distinctly pantheistic, seeing divinity embodied in all aspects of nature and in the heavenly bodies as well as in earthly objects. As Giordano Bruno, one of the most prominent of the sixteenth-century Hermeticists stated: "God as a whole is in all things."[14]

For Renaissance intellectuals, the Hermetic revival offered a new view of humankind. They believed that human beings had been created as divine beings endowed with divine creative power but had freely chosen to enter the material world (nature). Humans could recover their divinity, however, through a regenerative experience or purification of the soul. Thus regenerated, they became true sages or magi, as the Renaissance called them, who had knowledge of God and of truth. In regaining their original divinity, they reacquired an intimate knowledge of nature and the ability to employ the powers of nature for beneficial purposes.

In Italy, the most prominent magi in the late fifteenth century were Ficino and his friend and pupil, Giovanni Pico della Mirandola (1463–1494). Pico produced one of the most famous pieces of writing of the Renaissance, the *Oration on the Dignity of Man.* Pico combed diligently through the works of many philosophers of different backgrounds for the common "nuggets of universal truth" that he believed were all part of God's revelation to humanity. In the *Oration* (see the box above), Pico offered a ringing statement of unlimited human potential: "To him it is granted to have whatever he chooses, to be whatever he wills."[15] Like Ficino, Pico took an avid interest in Hermetic philosophy, accepting it as the "science of the Divine," which "embraces the deepest contemplation of the most secret things, and at last the knowledge of all nature."[16]

Education in the Renaissance

The humanist movement had a profound effect on education. Renaissance humanists believed that human beings could be dramatically changed by education. They wrote books on education and developed secondary schools based on their ideas. Most famous was the one founded in 1423 by Vittorino da Feltre (1378–1446) at Mantua, where the ruler of that small Italian state, Gian Francesco I Gonzaga, wished to provide a humanist school for his children. Vittorino based much of his educational system on the ideas of classical authors, particularly Cicero and Quintilian.

At the core of the academic training Vittorino offered were the "liberal studies." The Renaissance view of the value of the liberal arts was most strongly influenced by a treatise on education called *Concerning Character* by Pietro

Paolo Vergerio (1370–1444). This work stressed the importance of the liberal arts as the key to true freedom, enabling individuals to reach their full potential. According to Vergerio, "We call those studies liberal which are worthy of a free man; those studies by which we attain and practice virtue and wisdom; that education which calls forth, trains, and develops those highest gifts of body and mind which ennoble men."[17] The liberal studies included history, moral philosophy, eloquence (rhetoric), letters (grammar and logic), poetry, mathematics, astronomy, and music. The purpose of a liberal education was thus to produce individuals who followed a path of virtue and wisdom and possessed the rhetorical skills with which to persuade others to do the same. Following the Greek precept of a sound mind in a sound body, Vittorino's school at Mantua also stressed physical education. Pupils were taught the skills of javelin throwing, archery, and dancing and encouraged frequently to run, wrestle, hunt, and swim.

Although a small number of children from the lower classes were provided free educations, humanist schools such as Vittorino's were primarily geared for the education of an elite, the ruling classes of their communities. Also largely absent from such schools were females. Vittorino's only female pupils were the two daughters of the Gonzaga ruler of Mantua. Though these few female students studied the classics and were encouraged to know some history and to ride, dance, sing, play the lute, and appreciate poetry, they were discouraged from learning mathematics and rhetoric. In the educational treatises of the time, religion and morals were thought to "hold the first place in the education of a Christian lady."

Nevertheless, some women in Italy who were educated in the humanist fashion went on to establish their own literary careers. Isotta Nogarola, born to a noble family in Verona, mastered Latin and wrote numerous letters and treatises that brought her praise from male Italian intellectuals. Cassandra Fedele of Venice, who learned both Latin and Greek from humanist tutors hired by her family, became prominent in Venice for her public recitations of orations. Laura Cereta was educated in Latin by her father, a physician from Brescia. Laura defended the ability of women to pursue scholarly pursuits (see the box on p. 319).

Humanist education was thought to be a practical preparation for life. Its aim was not to create great scholars but rather to produce complete citizens who could participate in the civic life of their communities. As Vittorino said: "Not everyone is obliged to excel in philosophy, medicine, or the law, nor are all equally favored by nature; but all are destined to live in society and to practice virtue."[18] Humanist schools, combining the classics and Christianity, provided the model for the basic education of the European ruling classes until the twentieth century.

Humanism and History

Humanism had a strong impact on the writing of history. Influenced by Roman and Greek historians, the humanists approached the writing of history differently from the chroniclers of the Middle Ages. The humanists' belief that classical civilization had been followed by an age of barbarism (the Middle Ages), which had in turn been succeeded by their own age, with its rebirth of the study of the classics, enabled them to think in terms of the passage of time, of the past as past. Their division of the past into ancient world, dark ages, and their own age provided a new sense of chronology or periodization in history.

The humanists were also responsible for secularizing the writing of history. Humanist historians reduced or eliminated the role of miracles in historical interpretation, not because they were anti-Christian but because they took a new approach to sources. They wanted to use documents and exercised their newly developed critical skills in examining them. Greater attention was paid to the political events and forces that affected their city-states or larger territorial units. Thus Leonardo Bruni wrote the *History of the Florentine People.* The new emphasis on secularization was also evident in the humanists' conception of causation in history. In much medieval historical literature, historical events were often portrayed as being caused by God's active involvement in human affairs. Humanists deemphasized divine intervention in favor of human motives, stressing political forces or the role of individuals in history.

The high point of Renaissance historiography was achieved at the beginning of the sixteenth century in the works of Francesco Guicciardini (1483–1540). He has been called by some Renaissance scholars the greatest historian between Tacitus in the first century (see Chapter 6) and Voltaire and Gibbon in the eighteenth century (see Chapter 17). His *History of Italy* and *History of Florence* represent the beginning of "modern analytical historiography." To Guicciardini, the purpose of writing history was to teach lessons, but he was so impressed by the complexity of historical events that he felt those lessons were not always obvious. From his extensive background in government and diplomatic affairs, he developed the political skills that enabled him to analyze political situations precisely and critically. Emphasizing political and military history, his works relied heavily on personal examples and documentary sources.

The Impact of Printing

The Renaissance witnessed the invention of printing, one of the most important technological innovations of Western civilization. The art of printing made an immediate impact on European intellectual life and thought.

Printing from hand-carved wooden blocks had been done in the West since the twelfth century and in China even before that. What was new to Europe in the fifteenth century was multiple printing with movable metal type. The development of printing from movable type was a gradual process that culminated between 1445 and 1450; Johannes Gutenberg of Mainz played an important role in bringing the process to completion. Gutenberg's Bible, completed in 1455 or 1456, was the first true book in the West produced from movable type.

A Woman's Defense of Learning

As a young woman, Laura Cereta was proud of her learning but condemned by a male world that found it unseemly for women to be scholars. One monk said to her father, "She gives herself to things unworthy of her—namely, the classics." Before being silenced, Laura Cereta wrote a series of letters, including one to a male critic who had argued that her work was so good it could not have been written by a woman.

Laura Cereta, Defense of the Liberal Instruction of Women

My ears are wearied by your carping. You brashly and publicly not merely wonder but indeed lament that I am said to possess as fine a mind as nature ever bestowed upon the most learned man. You seem to think that so learned a woman has scarcely before been seen in the world. You are wrong on both counts. . . .

I would have been silent. . . . But I cannot tolerate your having attacked my entire sex. For this reason my thirsty soul seeks revenge, my sleeping pen is aroused to literary struggle, raging anger stirs mental passions long chained by silence. With just cause I am moved to demonstrate how great a reputation for learning and virtue women have won by their inborn excellence, manifested in every age as knowledge. . . .

Only the question of the rarity of outstanding women remains to be addressed. The explanation is clear: women have been able by nature to be exceptional, but have chosen lesser goals. For some women are concerned with parting their hair correctly, adorning themselves with lovely dresses, or decorating their fingers with pearls and other gems. Others delight in mouthing carefully composed phrases, indulging in dancing, or managing spoiled puppies. Still others wish to gaze at lavish banquet tables, to rest in sleep, or, standing at mirrors, to smear their lovely faces. But those in whom a deeper integrity yearns for virtue, restrain from the start their youthful souls, reflect on higher things, harden the body with sobriety and trials, and curb their tongues, open their ears, compose their thoughts in wakeful hours, their minds in contemplation, to letters bonded to righteousness. For knowledge is not given as a gift, but [is gained] with diligence. The free mind, not shirking effort, always soars zealously toward the good, and the desire to know grows ever more wide and deep. It is because of no special holiness, therefore, that we [women] are rewarded by God the Giver with the gift of exceptional talent. Nature has generously lavished its gifts upon all people, opening to all the doors of choice through which reason sends envoys to the will, from which they learn and convey its desires. The will must choose to exercise the gift of reason. . . .

I have been praised too much; showing your contempt for women, you pretend that I alone am admirable because of the good fortune of my intellect. . . . Do you suppose, O most contemptible man on earth, that I think myself sprung [like Athena] from the head of Jove? I am a school girl, possessed of the sleeping embers of an ordinary mind. Indeed I am too hurt, and my mind, offended, too swayed by passions, sighs, tormenting itself, conscious of the obligation to defend my sex. For absolutely everything—that which is within us and that which is without—is made weak by association with my sex.

The new printing spread rapidly throughout Europe in the second half of the fifteenth century. Printing presses were established throughout the Holy Roman Empire in the 1460s and within ten years had spread to Italy, England, France, the Low Countries, Spain, and eastern Europe. Especially well known as a printing center was Venice, home by 1500 to almost one hundred printers who had produced almost two million volumes.

By 1500, there were more than one thousand printers in Europe who had published almost forty thousand titles (between eight and ten million copies). Probably 50 percent of these books were religious—Bibles and biblical commentaries, books of devotion, and sermons. Next in importance were the Latin and Greek classics, medieval grammars, legal handbooks, works on philosophy, and an ever-growing number of popular romances.

Printing became one of the largest industries in Europe, and its effects were soon felt in many areas of European life. The printing of books encouraged the development of scholarly research and the desire to attain knowledge. Moreover, printing facilitated cooperation among scholars and helped produce standardized and definitive texts. Printing also stimulated the development of an ever-expanding lay reading public, a development that had an enormous impact on European society. Indeed, without the printing press, the new religious ideas of the Reformation would never have spread as rapidly as they did in the sixteenth century.

The Artistic Renaissance

Leonardo da Vinci, one of the great Italian Renaissance artists, once explained: "Hence the painter will produce pictures of small merit if he takes for his standard the pictures of others, but if he will study from natural objects he will bear good fruit . . . those who take for their standard any one but nature . . . weary themselves in vain."[19] Renaissance artists considered the imitation of nature their primary goal. Their search for naturalism became an end in itself: to persuade onlookers of the reality of the object or event they were portraying. At the same time, the new artistic standards reflected a new attitude of mind as well, one in which human beings became the focus of attention, the "center and measure of all things," as one artist proclaimed.

Leonardo and other Italians maintained that it was Giotto in the fourteenth century (see Chapter 11) who began the imitation of nature. But what Giotto had begun was not taken up again until the work of Masaccio (1401–1428) in Florence. Masaccio's cycle of frescoes in the Brancacci Chapel has long been regarded as the first masterpiece of Early Renaissance art. With his use of monumental figures, demonstration of a more realistic relationship between figures and landscape, and visual representation of the laws of perspective, a new realistic style of painting was born. Onlookers become aware of a world of reality that appears to be a continuation of their own world. Masaccio's massive, three-dimensional human figures provided a model for later generations of Florentine artists.

This new Renaissance style was absorbed and modified by other Florentine painters in the fifteenth century. Especially important was the development of an experimental trend that took two directions. One emphasized the mathematical side of painting, the working out of the laws of perspective and the organization of outdoor space and light by geometry and perspective. In the work of Paolo Uccello (1397–1475), figures became mere stage props to show off his mastery of the laws of perspective. The other aspect of the experimental trend involved the investigation of movement and anatomical structure. *The Martyrdom of Saint Sebastian* by Antonio Pollaiuolo (c. 1432–1498) revels in classical motifs and attempts to portray the human body under stress. Indeed, the realistic portrayal of the human nude became one of the foremost preoccupations of Italian Renaissance art. The fifteenth century, then, was a period of experimentation and technical mastery.

During the last decades of the fifteenth century, a new sense of invention emerged in Florence, especially in the circle of artists and scholars who formed part of the court of the city's leading citizen, Lorenzo the Magnificent. One of this group's prominent members was Sandro Botticelli (1445–1510), whose interest in Greek and Roman mythology was well reflected in one of his most famous works, *Primavera* (Spring). The painting is set in the garden of Venus, a garden of eternal spring. Though Botticelli's figures are well defined, they also possess an otherworldly quality that is far removed from the realism that characterized the painting of the Early Renaissance.

The revolutionary achievements of Florentine painters in the fifteenth century were matched by equally stunning advances in sculpture and architecture. Donato di Donatello (1386–1466) spent time in Rome studying and copying the statues of antiquity. His subsequent work in Florence reveals how well he had mastered the essence of what he saw. Among his numerous works was a statue of David, which is the first known "lifesize freestanding bronze nude in European art since antiquity." With the severed head of the giant Goliath beneath David's feet, Donatello's

Masaccio, *Tribute Money.* With the frescoes of Masaccio, regarded by many as the first great works of Early Renaissance art, a new realistic style of painting was born. *Tribute Money* was one of a series of frescoes that Masaccio painted in the Brancacci Chapel of the Church of Santa Maria del Carmine in Florence. In illustrating a story from the Bible, Masaccio used a rational system of perspective to create a realistic relationship between the figures and their background.

Botticelli, *Primavera.* This work reflects Botticelli's strong interest in classical antiquity. At the center of the painting is Venus, the goddess of love. At the right stands Flora, a Roman goddess of flowers and fertility, while the Three Graces dance playfully at the left. Cupid, the son of Venus, aims his arrow at the Three Graces. At the far left of the picture is Mercury, the messenger of the gods. Later in his life, Botticelli experienced a profound religious crisis, leading him to reject his earlier preoccupation with pagan gods and goddesses. He burned many of his early paintings and then produced only religious works.

statue celebrated Florentine heroism in the triumph of the Florentines over the Milanese in 1428. Like Donatello's other statues, *David* also radiated a simplicity and strength that reflected the dignity of humanity.

Filippo Brunelleschi (1377–1446) was a friend of Donatello and accompanied him to Rome. Brunelleschi drew much inspiration from the architectural monuments of Roman antiquity, and when he returned to Florence, he poured his new insights into the creation of a new architecture. When the Medici commissioned him to design the Church of San Lorenzo, Brunelleschi, inspired by Roman models, created a church interior very different from that of the great medieval cathedrals. San Lorenzo's classical columns, rounded arches, and coffered ceiling created an environment that did not overwhelm the worshiper

Donatello, *David.* Donatello's *David* first stood in the courtyard of the Medici Palace. On its base was an inscription praising Florentine heroism and virtue, leading art historians to assume that the statue was meant to commemorate the victory of Florence over Milan in 1428.

Scala/Art Resource, NY

Brunelleschi, Interior of San Lorenzo. Cosimo de' Medici contributed massive amounts of money to the rebuilding of the Church of San Lorenzo. As seen in this view of the nave and choir of the church, Brunelleschi's architectural designs were based on the basilica plan borrowed by early Christians from pagan Rome. San Lorenzo's simplicity, evident in its rows of slender Corinthian columns, created a human-centered space.

materially and psychologically, as Gothic cathedrals did, but comforted as a space created to fit human, not divine, measurements. Like painters and sculptors, Renaissance architects sought to reflect a human-centered world.

The new assertion of human individuality, evident in Early Renaissance art, was also reflected in the new emphasis on portraiture. Patrons appeared in the corners of sacred pictures, and monumental tombs and portrait statues honored many of Florence's prominent citizens. By the mid-fifteenth century, artists were giving an accurate rendering of their subjects' facial features while revealing the inner qualities of their personalities. The portraits of the duke and duchess of Urbino by Piero della Francesca (c. 1410–1492) provide accurate representations as well as a sense of both the power and the wealth of the rulers of Urbino (see p. 311).

By the end of the fifteenth century, Italian painters, sculptors, and architects had created a new artistic environment. Many artists had mastered the new techniques for a scientific observation of the world around them and were now ready to move into individualistic forms of creative expression. This final stage of Renaissance art, which flourished between 1480 and 1520, is called the High Renaissance. The shift to the High Renaissance was marked by the increasing importance of Rome as a new cultural center of the Italian Renaissance.

The High Renaissance was dominated by the work of three artistic giants: Leonardo da Vinci (1452–1519),

Leonardo da Vinci, *The Last Supper.* Leonardo da Vinci was the impetus behind the High Renaissance concern for the idealization of nature, moving from a realistic portrayal of the human figure to an idealized form. Evident in Leonardo's *Last Supper* is his effort to depict a person's character and inner nature by the use of gesture and movement. Unfortunately, Leonardo used an experimental technique in this fresco, which soon led to its physical deterioration.

Scala/Art Resource, NY

Raphael (1483–1520), and Michelangelo (1475–1564). Leonardo represents a transitional figure in the shift to High Renaissance principles. He carried on the fifteenth-century experimental tradition by studying everything and even dissecting human bodies to more clearly see how nature worked. But Leonardo stressed the need to advance beyond such realism and initiated the High Renaissance's preoccupation with the idealization of nature, or the attempt to generalize from realistic portrayal to an ideal form. Leonardo's *Last Supper,* painted in Milan, is a brilliant summary of fifteenth-century trends in its organization of space and use of perspective to depict subjects three-dimensionally in a two-dimensional medium. But it is also more. The figure of Philip is idealized, and there are profound psychological dimensions to the work. The words of Jesus that "one of you shall betray me" are experienced directly as each of the apostles reveals his personality and his relationship to Jesus. Through gestures and movement, Leonardo hoped to reveal a person's inner life.

Raphael blossomed as a painter at an early age; at twenty-five, he was already regarded as one of Italy's best painters. Raphael was acclaimed for his numerous madonnas, in which he attempted to achieve an ideal of beauty far surpassing human standards. He is well known for his frescoes in the Vatican Palace; his *School of Athens* reveals a world of balance, harmony, and order—the underlying principles of the art of the classical world of Greece and Rome.

Michelangelo, an accomplished painter, sculptor, and architect, was another giant of the High Renaissance. Fiercely driven by his desire to create, he worked with great passion and energy on a remarkable number of projects. Michelangelo was influenced by Neoplatonism, especially evident in his figures on the ceiling of the Sistine Chapel in Rome. These muscular figures reveal an ideal type of human being with

Raphael, *School of Athens.* Raphael arrived in Rome in 1508 and began to paint a series of frescoes commissioned by Pope Julius II for the papal apartments at the Vatican. In the *School of Athens,* painted in 1510 or 1511, Raphael created an imaginary gathering of ancient philosophers. In the center stand Plato and Aristotle. At the left is Pythagoras, showing his system of proportions on a slate. At the right is Ptolemy, holding a celestial globe.

Erich Lessing/Art Resource, NY

Photo, Vatican Museums

Michelangelo, *Creation of Adam.* In 1508, Pope Julius II called Michelangelo to Rome and commissioned him to decorate the ceiling of the Sistine Chapel. This colossal project was not completed until 1512. Michelangelo attempted to tell the story of the Fall of Man by depicting nine scenes from the biblical Book of Genesis. In this scene, the well-proportioned figure of Adam, meant by Michelangelo to be a reflection of divine beauty, awaits the divine spark.

perfect proportions. In good Neoplatonic fashion, their beauty is meant to be a reflection of divine beauty; the more beautiful the body, the more God-like the figure.

Another manifestation of Michelangelo's search for ideal beauty was his *David,* a colossal marble statue commissioned by the Florentine government in 1501 and completed in 1504. Michelangelo maintained that the form of a statue already resided in the uncarved piece of stone: "I only take away the surplus, the statue is already there."[20] Out of a piece of marble that had remained unused for fifty years, Michelangelo created a 14-foot-high figure, the largest piece of sculpture in Italy since the time of Rome. An awe-inspiring hero, Michelangelo's *David* proudly proclaims the beauty of the human body and the glory of human beings.

A High Renaissance in architecture was also evident, especially in the work of Donato Bramante (1444–1514). He came from Urbino but took up residence in Rome, where he designed a small temple on the supposed site of Saint Peter's martyrdom. The Tempietto, or little temple, with its Doric columns surrounding a sanctuary enclosed by a dome, summarized the architectural ideals of the High Renaissance. Columns, dome, and sanctuary form a monumental and harmonious whole. Inspired by antiquity, Bramante had recaptured the grandeur of ancient Rome. His achievement led Pope Julius II to commission him to design a new basilica for Rome, which eventually became the great Saint Peter's.

Scala/Art Resource, NY

Michelangelo, *David.* This statue of David, cut from an 18-foot-high piece of marble, exalts the beauty of the human body and is a fitting symbol of the Italian Renaissance's affirmation of human power. Completed in 1504, *David* was moved by Florentine authorities to a special location in front of the Palazzo Vecchio, the seat of the Florentine government.

The Genius of Leonardo da Vinci

During the Renaissance, artists came to be viewed as creative geniuses with almost divine qualities. One individual who helped create this image was himself a painter. Giorgio Vasari was an avid admirer of Italy's great artists and wrote a series of brief biographies of them. This excerpt is taken from his account of Leonardo da Vinci.

Giorgio Vasari, Lives of the Artists

In the normal course of events many men and women are born with various remarkable qualities and talents; but occasionally, in a way that transcends nature, a single person is marvelously endowed by heaven with beauty, grace, and talent in such abundance that he leaves other men far behind, all his actions seem inspired, and indeed everything he does clearly comes from God rather than from human art.

Everyone acknowledged that this was true of Leonardo da Vinci, an artist of outstanding physical beauty who displayed infinite grace in everything he did and who cultivated his genius so brilliantly that all problems he studied he solved with ease. He possessed great strength and dexterity; he was a man of regal spirit and tremendous breadth of mind; and his name became so famous that not only was he esteemed during his lifetime but his reputation endured and became even greater after his death. . . .

He was marvelously gifted, and he proved himself to be a first-class geometrician in his work as a sculptor and architect. In his youth Leonardo made in clay several heads of women, with smiling faces, of which plaster casts are still being made, as well as some children's heads executed as if by a mature artist. He also did many architectural drawings both of ground plans and of other elevations, and, while still young, he was the first to propose reducing the Arno River to a navigable canal between Pisa and Florence. He made designs for mills, fulling machines, and engines that could be driven by waterpower; and as he intended to be a painter by profession he carefully studied drawing from life. . . . Altogether, his genius was so wonderfully inspired by the grace of God, his powers of expression were so powerfully fed by a willing memory and intellect, and his writing conveyed his ideas so precisely, that his arguments and reasonings confounded the most formidable critics. In addition, he used to make models and plans showing how to excavate and tunnel through mountains without difficulty, so as to pass from one level to another; and he demonstrated how to lift and draw great weights by means of levers and hoists and ways of cleaning harbors and using pumps to suck up water from great depths.

The Artist and Social Status

Early Renaissance artists began their careers as apprentices to masters in craft guilds. Apprentices with unusual talent might eventually become masters and run their own workshops. As in the Middle Ages, artists were still largely viewed as artisans. Since guilds depended on commissions for their projects, patrons played an important role in the art of the Early Renaissance. The wealthy upper classes determined both the content and purpose of the paintings and pieces of sculpture they commissioned.

By the end of the fifteenth century, a transformation in the position of the artist had occurred. Especially talented individuals, such as Leonardo, Raphael, and Michelangelo, were no longer seen as artisans but as artistic geniuses with creative energies akin to the divine (see the box above). Artists were heroes, individuals who were praised more for their creativity than for their competence as craftspeople. Michelangelo, for example, was frequently addressed as "Il Divino"—the Divine One. As society excused their eccentricities and valued their creative

Bramante, Tempietto. Ferdinand and Isabella of Spain commissioned Donato Bramante to design a small building in Rome that would commemorate the place where Saint Peter supposedly was crucified. Completed in 1502, the temple reflected Bramante's increasing understanding of ancient Roman remains.

genius, the artists of the High Renaissance became the first to embody the modern concept of the artist.

As respect for artists grew, so did their ability to profit economically from their work and to rise on the social scale. Now welcomed as equals into the circles of the upper classes, they mingled with the political and intellectual elite of their society and became more aware of new intellectual theories, which they then embodied in their art. The Platonic Academy and Renaissance Neoplatonism had an especially important impact on Florentine painters.

The Northern Artistic Renaissance

In trying to provide an exact portrayal of their world, the artists of the north (especially the Low Countries) and Italy took different approaches. In Italy, the human form became the primary vehicle of expression as Italian artists sought to master the technical skills that allowed them to portray humans in realistic settings. The large wall spaces of Italian churches had given rise to the art of fresco painting, but in the north, the prevalence of Gothic cathedrals with their stained-glass windows resulted in more emphasis on illuminated manuscripts and wooden panel painting for altarpieces. The space available in these works was limited, and great care was required to depict each object, leading northern painters to become masters at rendering details.

The most influential northern school of art in the fifteenth century was centered in Flanders. Jan van Eyck (c. 1390–1441) was among the first to use oil paint, a medium that enabled the artist to use a varied range of colors and make changes to create fine details. In the famous *Giovanni Arnolfini and His Bride,* van Eyck's attention to detail is staggering: precise portraits, a glittering chandelier, and a mirror reflecting the objects in the room. Although each detail was rendered as observed, it is evident that van Eyck's comprehension of perspective was still uncertain. His work is truly indicative of northern Renaissance painters, who, in their effort to imitate nature, did so not by mastery of the laws of perspective and proportion but by empirical observation of visual reality and the accurate portrayal of details. Moreover, northern painters placed great emphasis on the emotional intensity of religious feeling and created great works of devotional art, especially in their altarpieces. Michelangelo summarized the difference between northern and Italian Renaissance painting in these words:

> In Flanders, they paint, before all things, to render exactly and deceptively the outward appearance of things. The painters choose, by preference, subjects provoking transports of piety, like the figures of saints or of prophets. But most of the time they paint what are called landscapes with plenty of figures. Though the eye is agreeably impressed, these pictures have neither choice of values nor grandeur. In short, this art is without power and without distinction; it aims at rendering minutely many things at the same time, of which a single one would have sufficed to call forth a man's whole application.[21]

By the end of the fifteenth century, however, artists from the north began to study in Italy and were visually influenced by what artists were doing there.

Van Eyck, *Giovanni Arnolfini and His Bride.* Northern painters took great care in depicting each object and became masters at rendering details. This emphasis on a realistic portrayal is clearly evident in this oil painting, supposedly a portrait of Giovanni Arnolfini, an Italian merchant who had settled in Bruges, and his wife, Giovanna Cenami.

One northern artist of this later period who was greatly affected by the Italians was Albrecht Dürer (1471–1528) from Nuremberg. Dürer made two trips to Italy and absorbed most of what the Italians could teach, as is evident in his mastery of the laws of perspective and Renaissance theories of proportion. He wrote detailed treatises on both subjects. At the same time, as in his famous *Adoration of the Magi,* Dürer did not reject the use of minute details characteristic of northern artists. He did try, however, to integrate those details more harmoniously into his works and, like the Italian artists of the High Renaissance, to achieve a standard of ideal beauty by a careful examination of the human form.

Music in the Renaissance

For much of the fifteenth century, an extraordinary cultural environment was fostered in the domains of the dukes of Burgundy in northern Europe. The court of the dukes attracted some of the best artists and musicians of the time. Among them was Guillaume Dufay (c. 1400–1474), perhaps the most important composer of his time. Born in northern France, Dufay lived for a few years in Italy and was thus well suited to combine the late medieval style of France with

Alinari/Art Resource, NY

Dürer, *Adoration of the Magi.* By the end of the fifteenth century, northern artists had begun to study in Italy and to adopt many of the techniques used by Italian painters. As is evident in this painting, which was the central panel for an altarpiece done for Frederick the Wise in 1504, Albrecht Dürer masterfully incorporated the laws of perspective and the ideals of proportion into his works. At the same time, he did not abandon the preoccupation with detail typical of northern artists.

the early Renaissance style of Italy. One of Dufay's greatest contributions was a change in the composition of the Mass. He was the first to use secular tunes to replace Gregorian chants as the fixed melody that served as the basis for the Mass. Dufay also composed a number of secular songs, an important reminder that during the Renaissance, music ceased to be used chiefly in the service of God and moved into the secular world of courts and cities. In Italy and France, the chief form of secular music was the madrigal.

The Renaissance madrigal was a poem set to music, and its origins were in the fourteenth-century Italian courts. The texts were usually twelve-line poems written in the vernacular, and their theme was emotional or erotic love. By the mid-sixteenth century, most madrigals were written for five or six voices and employed a technique called text painting, in which the music tried to portray the literal meaning of the text. Thus the melody would rise for the word *heaven* or use a wavelike motion to represent the word *water.* By the mid-sixteenth century, the madrigal had also spread to England, where the most popular form was characterized by the *fa-la-la* refrain like that found in the English carol "Deck the Halls."

The European State in the Renaissance

In the first half of the fifteenth century, European states continued the disintegrative patterns of the previous century. In the second half of the fifteenth century, however, recovery set in, and attempts were made to reestablish the centralized power of monarchical governments. To characterize the results, some historians have used the label "Renaissance states"; others have spoken of the "new monarchies," especially those of France, England, and Spain at the end of the fifteenth century (see Map 12.2). Whereas monarchs succeeded to varying degrees at extending their political authority in western Europe, rulers in central and eastern Europe were often weak and unable to impose their authority.

The Growth of the French Monarchy

The Hundred Years' War had left France prostrate. Depopulation, desolate farmlands, ruined commerce, and independent and unruly nobles had made it difficult for the kings to assert their authority. But the war had also developed a strong degree of French national feeling toward a common enemy that the kings could use to reestablish monarchical power. The need to prosecute the war provided an excuse to strengthen the authority of the king, already evident in the policies of Charles VII (1422–1461) after he was crowned king at Reims. With the consent of the Estates-General, Charles established a royal army composed of cavalry and archers. He received from the Estates-General the right to levy the *taille,* an annual direct tax usually on land or property, without any need for further approval from the Estates-General. Losing control of the purse meant less power for this parliamentary body.

The process of developing a French territorial state was greatly advanced by King Louis XI (1461–1483), known as the Spider because of his wily and devious ways. By retaining the *taille* as a permanent tax imposed by royal authority, Louis secured a sound, regular source of income. Louis was not, however, completely successful in repressing the French nobility, whose independence posed a threat to his own state building. A major problem was his supposed vassal, Charles the Bold, duke of Burgundy (1467–1477). Charles attempted to create a middle kingdom between

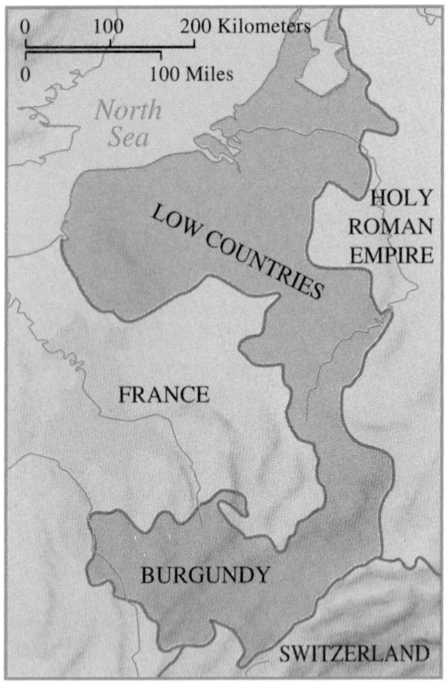

Lands of Charles the Bold

France and Germany, stretching from the Low Countries to Switzerland. Louis opposed his action, and when Charles was killed in 1477 fighting the Swiss, Louis added part of Charles's possessions, the duchy of Burgundy, to his own lands. Three years later, the provinces of Anjou, Maine, Bar, and Provence were brought under royal control. Many historians believe that Louis created a base for the later development of a strong French monarchy.

England: Civil War and a New Monarchy

The Hundred Years' War had also strongly affected the other protagonist in that conflict. The cost of the war in its final years and the losses in manpower strained the English economy. Moreover, even greater domestic turmoil came to England when the War of the Roses broke out in the 1450s. This civil war pitted the ducal house of Lancaster, whose symbol was a red rose, against the ducal house of York, whose symbol was a white rose. Many aristocratic families of England were drawn into the conflict. Finally, in 1485, Henry Tudor, duke of Richmond, defeated the last Yorkist king, Richard III (1483–1485), at Bosworth Field and established the new Tudor dynasty.

As the first Tudor king, Henry VII (1485–1509) worked to reduce internal dissension and establish a strong monarchical government. Henry ended the private wars of the nobility by abolishing "livery and maintenance," the practice by which wealthy aristocrats maintained private armies of followers dedicated to the service of their lord. Since England, unlike France and Spain, did not possess a standing army, the king relied on special commissions to trusted nobles to raise troops for a specific campaign, after which the troops were disbanded. Henry also controlled the irresponsible activity of the nobles by establishing the Court of Star Chamber, which did not use juries and allowed torture to be used to extract confessions.

Henry VII was particularly successful in extracting income from the traditional financial resources of the English monarch, such as the crown lands, judicial fees and fines, and customs duties. By using diplomacy to avoid wars, which are always expensive, the king avoided having to call Parliament on any regular basis to grant him funds. By not overburdening the landed gentry and middle class with taxes, Henry won their favor, and they provided much support for his monarchy. Henry's policies enabled him to leave England with a stable and prosperous government and an enhanced status for the monarchy itself.

The Unification of Spain

During the Middle Ages, several independent Christian kingdoms had emerged in the course of the long reconquest of the Iberian peninsula from the Muslims. Aragon and Castile were the strongest Spanish kingdoms; in the west was the independent monarchy of Portugal; in the north, the small kingdom of Navarre, oriented toward France; and in the south, the Muslim kingdom of Granada (see Map 12.3). Few people at the beginning of the fifteenth century could have predicted the unification of the Iberian kingdoms.

A major step in that direction was taken with the marriage of Isabella of Castile (1474–1504) and Ferdinand of Aragon (1479–1516) in 1469. This marriage was a dynastic union of two rulers, not a political union. Both kingdoms maintained their own parliaments (Cortes), courts, laws, coinage, speech, customs, and political organs. Nevertheless, the two rulers worked to strengthen royal control of government, especially in Castile. The royal council, which was supposed to supervise local administration and oversee the implementation of government policies, was stripped of aristocrats and filled primarily with middle-class lawyers. Trained in the principles of Roman law, these officials operated on the belief that the monarchy embodied the power of the state.

Seeking to replace the undisciplined feudal levies they had inherited with a more professional royal army, Ferdinand and Isabella reorganized the military forces of Spain. The development of a strong infantry force as the heart of the new Spanish army made it the best in Europe by the sixteenth century.

Ferdinand and Isabella recognized the importance of controlling the Catholic church, with its vast power and wealth. They secured from the pope the right to select the most important church officials in Spain, virtually making the clergy an instrument of royal power. Ferdinand and Isabella also pursued a policy of strict religious uniformity. Spain possessed two large religious minorities, Jews and Muslims, both of whom had been largely tolerated in medieval Spain. Increased persecution in the fourteenth century, however, led the majority of Spanish Jews to convert to Christianity. But complaints about the sincerity of these Jewish converts prompted Ferdinand and Isabella to ask the pope to introduce the Inquisition into Spain in 1478. Under royal control, the Inquisition worked with cruel efficiency to guarantee the orthodoxy of the converts, but had no authority over practicing Jews. Consequently, in 1492, flush with the success of their conquest of Muslim Granada, Ferdinand and Isabella took the drastic step of expelling all professed Jews from Spain. It is estimated that 150,000 out of possibly 200,000 Jews fled.

Muslims, too, were "encouraged" to convert to Christianity after the conquest of Granada. In 1502, Isabella issued a decree expelling all professed Muslims from her kingdom. To a very large degree, the "Most Catholic" monarchs had achieved their goal of absolute religious orthodoxy as a basic ingredient of the Spanish state. To be Spanish was to be Catholic, a policy of uniformity enforced by the Inquisition.

Map 12.2 Europe in the Renaissance. By the second half of the fifteenth century, states in western Europe, particularly France, Spain, and England, had begun the process of modern state building. With varying success, they reined in the power of the church and nobles, increased the ability to levy taxes, and established effective government bureaucracies. ■ What aspects of Europe's political boundaries help explain why France and the Holy Roman Empire were often at war with each other?

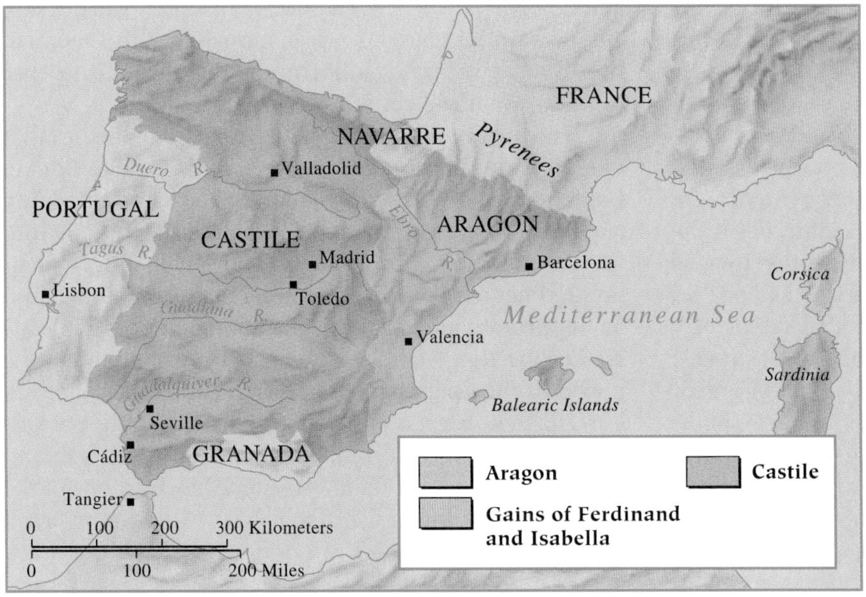

Map 12.3 The Iberian Peninsula. The marriage of Isabella of Castile to Ferdinand of Aragon laid the foundation for the unification of Spain and its rise as a major European power. The two monarchs instituted military and bureaucratic reforms and forced Jews and Muslims to flee the country. ■ What aspects of Portugal's geography help explain why it became a major seafaring nation, with little overland trade with Europe?

The Holy Roman Empire: The Success of the Habsburgs

Unlike France, England, and Spain, the Holy Roman Empire failed to develop a strong monarchical authority. After 1438, the position of Holy Roman Emperor remained in the hands of the Habsburg dynasty. Having gradually acquired a number of possessions along the Danube, known collectively as Austria, the house of Habsburg had become one of the wealthiest landholders in the empire and by the mid-fifteenth century began to play an important role in European affairs.

Much of the Habsburg success in the fifteenth century was due not to military success but to a well-executed policy of dynastic marriages. As the old Habsburg motto said: "Leave the waging of wars to others! But you, happy Austria, marry; for the realms which Mars [god of war] awards to others, Venus [goddess of love] transfers to you." By marrying his son Maximilian to Mary, the daughter of Duke Charles the Bold of Burgundy, Emperor Frederick III (1440–1493) gained Franche-Comté in east-central France, Luxembourg, and a large part of the Low Countries. The addition of these territories made the Habsburg dynasty an international power and brought it the undying opposition of the French monarchy because the rulers of France feared they would be surrounded by the Habsburgs.

Much was expected of the flamboyant Maximilian I (1493–1519) when he became emperor. Through the Reichstag, the imperial diet or parliament, Maximilian attempted to centralize the administration by creating new institutions common to the entire empire. Opposition from the German princes doomed these efforts, however. Maximilian's only real success lay in his marriage alliances. Philip of Burgundy, the son of Maximilian's marriage to Mary, was married to Joanna, the daughter of Ferdinand and Isabella. Philip and Joanna produced a son, Charles, who, through a series of unexpected deaths, became heir to all three lines, the Habsburg, Burgundian, and Spanish, making him the leading monarch of his age (see Chapter 13).

The Struggle for Strong Monarchy in Eastern Europe

In eastern Europe, rulers struggled to achieve the centralization of their territorial states but faced serious obstacles. Although the population was mostly Slavic, there were islands of other ethnic groups that caused untold difficulties. Religious differences also troubled the area, as Roman Catholics, Greek Orthodox Christians, and pagans confronted each other.

Much of Polish history revolved around a bitter struggle between the crown and the landed nobility until the end of the fifteenth century, when the preoccupation of Poland's rulers with problems in Bohemia and Hungary as well as war with the Russians and Turks enabled the aristocrats to reestablish their power. Through their control of the *Sejm* or national diet, the magnates reduced the peasantry to serfdom by 1511 and established the right to elect their kings. The Polish kings proved unable to establish a strong royal authority.

Bohemia, Poland's neighbor, was part of the Holy Roman Empire, but distrust of the Germans and close ethnic ties to the Poles and Slovaks encouraged the Czechs of Bohemia to associate with their northeastern Slavic neighbors. The Hussite wars (see "The Problems of Heresy and Reform" later in this chapter) led to further dissension and civil war. Because of a weak monarchy, the Bohemian nobles increased their authority and wealth at the expense of both crown and church.

The history of Hungary had been closely tied to that of central and western Europe by its conversion to Roman Catholicism by German missionaries. The church became a large and prosperous institution. Wealthy bishops, along with the great territorial lords, became powerful, independent political figures. For a brief while, Hungary developed into an important European state, the dominant power in eastern Europe. King Matthias Corvinus (1458–1490) broke the power of the wealthy lords and created a well-organized bureaucracy. Like a typical Renaissance prince, he patronized the new humanist culture, brought Italian scholars and artists to his capital at Buda, and made his court one of the most brilliant outside Italy. After his death, Hungary returned to weak rule, and the work of Corvinus was largely undone.

CHRONOLOGY

The European State in the Renaissance

France	
Charles VII	1422–1461
Louis XI the Spider	1461–1483
England	
War of the Roses	1450s–1485
Richard III	1483–1485
Henry VII	1485–1509
Spain	
Isabella of Castile	1474–1504
Ferdinand of Aragon	1479–1516
Marriage of Ferdinand and Isabella	1469
Introduction of Inquisition	1478
Expulsion of the Jews	1492
Expulsion of the Muslims	1502
Holy Roman Empire	
Frederick III	1440–1493
Maximilian I	1493–1519
Eastern Europe	
Hungary: Matthias Corvinus	1458–1490
Russia: Ivan III	1462–1505
Fall of Constantinople and Byzantine Empire	1453

Since the thirteenth century, Russia had been under the domination of the Mongols. Gradually, the princes of Moscow rose to prominence by using their close relationship to the Mongol khans to increase their wealth and expand their possessions. In the reign of the great prince Ivan III (1462–1505), a new Russian state—the principality of Moscow—was born. Ivan III annexed other Russian principalities and took advantage of dissension among the Mongols to throw off their yoke by 1480.

The Ottoman Turks and the End of the Byzantine Empire

Eastern Europe was increasingly threatened by the steadily advancing Ottoman Turks (see Map 12.4). The Byzantine Empire had, of course, served as a buffer between the Muslim Middle East and the Latin West for centuries. It was severely weakened by the sack of Constantinople in 1204 and its occupation by the West. Although the Palaeologus dynasty (1260–1453) had tried to reestablish Byzantine power in the Balkans after the overthrow of the Latin empire, the threat from the Turks finally doomed the long-lasting empire.

Beginning in northeastern Asia Minor in the thirteenth century, the Ottoman Turks spread rapidly, seizing the lands of the Seljuk Turks and the Byzantine Empire. In 1345, they bypassed Constantinople and moved into the Balkans, which they conquered by the end of the century. Finally, in 1453, the great city of Constantinople fell to the Turks after a siege of several months. After consolidating their power, the Turks prepared to exert renewed pressure on the West, both in the Mediterranean and up the Danube valley toward Vienna. By the end of the fifteenth century, they were threatening Hungary, Austria, Bohemia, and Poland. The Holy Roman Emperor, Charles V, became their bitter enemy in the sixteenth century.

The Church in the Renaissance

As a result of the efforts of the Council of Constance, the Great Schism had finally been brought to an end in 1417 (see Chapter 11). The ending of the schism proved to be the council's easiest task; it was much less successful in dealing with the problems of heresy and reform.

The Problems of Heresy and Reform

Heresy was not a new problem, and in the thirteenth century, the church had developed inquisitorial machinery to deal with it. But two widespread movements in the fourteenth and early fifteenth centuries—Lollardy and Hussitism—posed new threats to the church.

English Lollardy was a product of the Oxford theologian John Wyclif (c. 1328–1384), whose disgust with clerical corruption led him to a far-ranging attack on papal authority and medieval Christian beliefs and practices. Wyclif alleged that there was no basis in Scripture for papal claims of temporal authority and advocated that the popes be stripped of their authority and their property. Believing that the Bible should be a Christian's sole authority, Wyclif urged that it be made available in the vernacular languages so that every Christian could read it. Rejecting all practices not mentioned in Scripture, Wyclif condemned pilgrimages, the veneration of saints, and a whole series of rituals and rites that had developed in the medieval church. Wyclif attracted a number of followers who came to be known as Lollards.

A marriage between the royal families of England and Bohemia enabled Lollard ideas to spread to Bohemia, where they reinforced the ideas of a group of Czech reformers led by the chancellor of the university at Prague, John Hus (1374–1415). In his call for reform, Hus urged the elimination of the worldliness and corruption of the clergy and attacked the excessive power of the papacy within the Catholic church. Hus's objections fell on receptive ears, since the Catholic church, as one of the largest landowners in Bohemia, was already widely criticized. Moreover, many clergymen were German, and the native Czechs' strong resentment of the Germans who dominated Bohemia also contributed to Hus's movement.

The Council of Constance attempted to deal with the growing problem of heresy by summoning John Hus to the council. Granted safe conduct by Emperor Sigismund, Hus went in the hope of a free hearing of his ideas. Instead he was arrested, condemned as a heretic (by a narrow vote), and burned at the stake in 1415. This action turned the unrest in Bohemia into revolutionary upheaval, and the resulting Hussite wars racked the Holy Roman Empire until a truce was arranged in 1436.

The reform of the church was even less successful than the attempt to eradicate heresy. Two reform decrees were passed by the Council of Constance. *Sacrosancta* stated that a general council of the church received its authority from God; hence every Christian, including the pope, was subject to its authority. The decree *Frequens* provided for the regular holding of general councils to ensure that church reform would continue. Taken together, *Sacrosancta* and *Frequens* provided for a legislative system within the church superior to the popes.

Decrees alone, however, proved insufficient to reform the church. Councils could issue decrees, but popes had to execute them, and popes would not cooperate with councils that diminished their authority. Beginning as early as Martin V in 1417, successive popes worked steadfastly for thirty years to defeat the conciliar movement. The final blow came in 1460, when Pope Pius II issued the papal bull *Execrabilis,* condemning appeals to a council over the head of a pope as heretical.

By the mid-fifteenth century, the popes had reasserted their supremacy over the Catholic church. No longer, however, did they have any possibility of asserting supremacy over temporal governments as the medieval papacy had. Although the papal monarchy had been maintained, it had lost much moral prestige. In the fifteenth century, the Renaissance papacy contributed to an even further decline in the moral leadership of the popes.

The Renaissance Papacy

The Renaissance papacy refers to the line of popes from the end of the Great Schism (1417) to the beginnings of the Reformation in the early sixteenth century. The primary concern of the papacy is governing the Catholic church as its spiritual leader. But as heads of the church, popes had temporal preoccupations as well, and the story of the Renaissance papacy is really an account of how the latter came to overshadow the popes' spiritual functions.

The manner in which Renaissance popes pursued their interests in the Papal States and Italian politics, especially their use of intrigue and even bloodshed, seemed shocking. Of all the Renaissance popes, Julius II (1503–1513) was most involved in war and politics. The fiery "warrior-pope" personally led armies against his enemies, much to the disgust of pious Christians, who viewed the pope as a spiritual leader. As one intellectual wrote: "How, O bishop

CHRONOLOGY

The Church in the Renaissance

Council of Constance	1414–1418
Burning of John Hus	1415
End of the Great Schism	1417
Pius II issues the papal bull *Execrabilis*	1460
The Renaissance papacy	
Sixtus IV	1471–1484
Alexander VI	1492–1503
Julius II	1503–1513
Leo X	1513–1521

Map 12.4 The Ottoman Empire and Southeastern Europe. Long a buffer between Christian Europe and the Muslim Middle East, the Byzantine Empire quickly waned in power and territory after Constantinople was sacked by Crusaders in 1204. The Ottoman Turks slowly gained Byzantine territory and ended the thousand-year reign with the fall of Constantinople in 1453 ■ Why would the Byzantine Empire have found it difficult to make alliances by 1403?

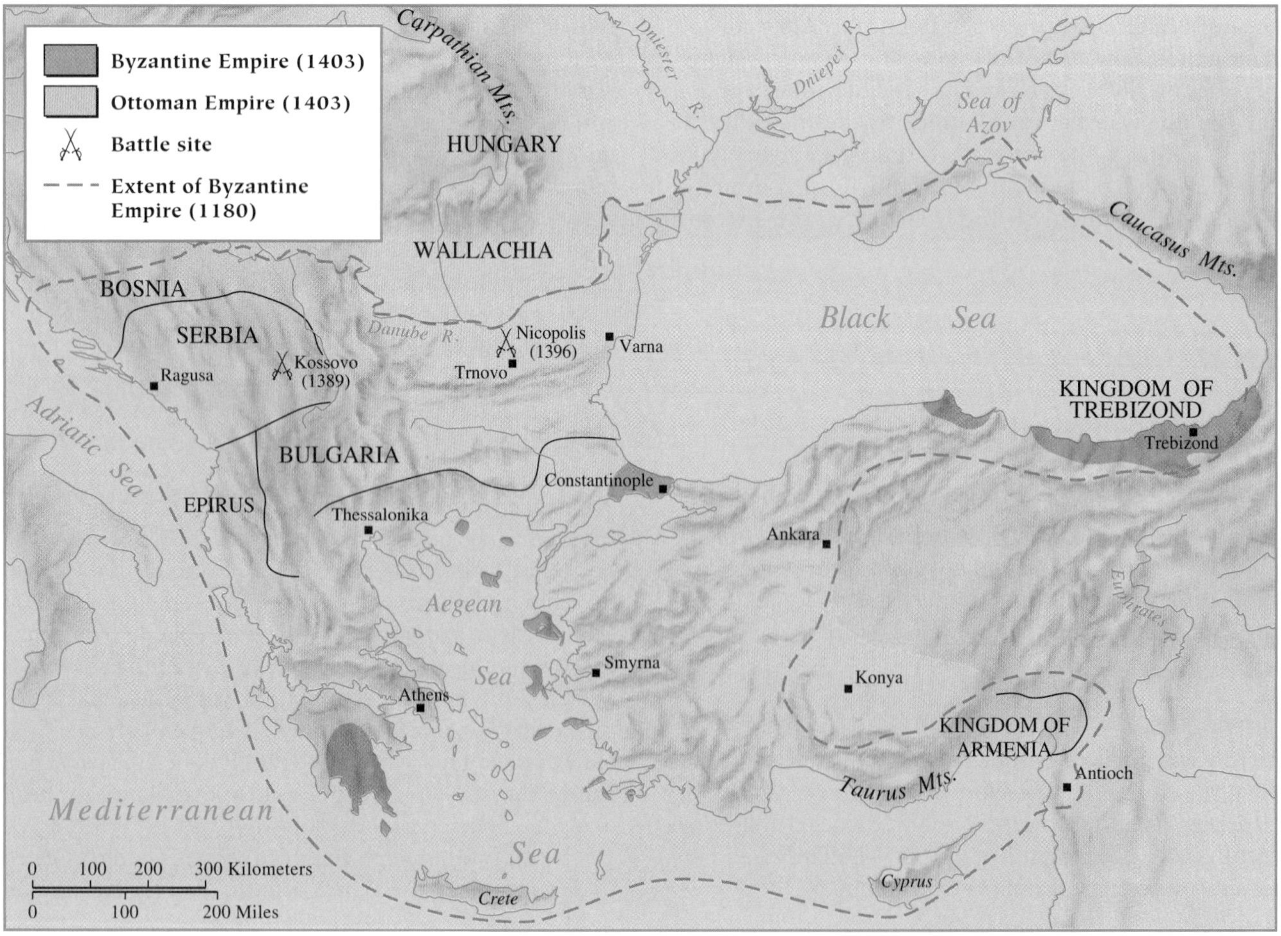

A Renaissance Pope: Leo X. The Renaissance popes allowed secular concerns to overshadow their spiritual duties. Shown here is the Medici pope Leo X. Raphael portrays the pope as a collector of books, looking up after examining an illuminated manuscript with a magnifying glass. At the left is the pope's cousin Guilio, a cardinal. Standing behind the pope is Luigi de' Rossi, another relative who had also been made a cardinal.

Scala/Art Resource, NY

standing in the room of the Apostles, dare you teach the people the things that pertain to war?"

To further their territorial aims in the Papal States, the popes needed loyal servants. Because they were not hereditary monarchs, popes could not build dynasties over several generations and came to rely on the practice of nepotism to promote their families' interests. Pope Sixtus IV (1471–1484), for example, made five of his nephews cardinals and gave them an abundance of church offices to build up their finances (the word *nepotism* is in fact derived from the Greek *nepos,* meaning "nephew"). Alexander VI (1492–1503), a member of the Borgia family who was known for his debauchery and sensuality, raised one son, one nephew, and the brother of one mistress to the cardinalate. A Venetian envoy stated that Alexander, "joyous by nature, thought of nothing but the aggrandizement of his children." Alexander scandalized the church by encouraging his son Cesare to carve a state for himself in central Italy out of the territories of the Papal States.

The Renaissance popes were great patrons of Renaissance culture, and their efforts made Rome a cultural leader at the beginning of the sixteenth century. For the warrior-pope Julius II, the patronage of Renaissance culture was mostly a matter of policy as he endeavored to add to the splendor of his pontificate by tearing down the Basilica of Saint Peter, which had been built by the emperor Constantine, and beginning construction of the greatest building in Christendom, the present Saint Peter's Basilica. Julius's successor, Leo X (1513–1521), was also a patron of Renaissance culture, not as a matter of policy, but as a deeply involved participant. Such might be expected of the son of Lorenzo de' Medici. Made an archbishop at the age of eight and a cardinal at thirteen, he acquired a refined taste in art, manners, and social life among the Florentine Renaissance elite. He became pope at the age of thirty-seven, supposedly remarking to the Venetian ambassador, "Let us enjoy the papacy, since God has given it to us." Raphael was commissioned to do paintings, and the construction of Saint Peter's was accelerated as Rome became the literary and artistic center of the Renaissance.

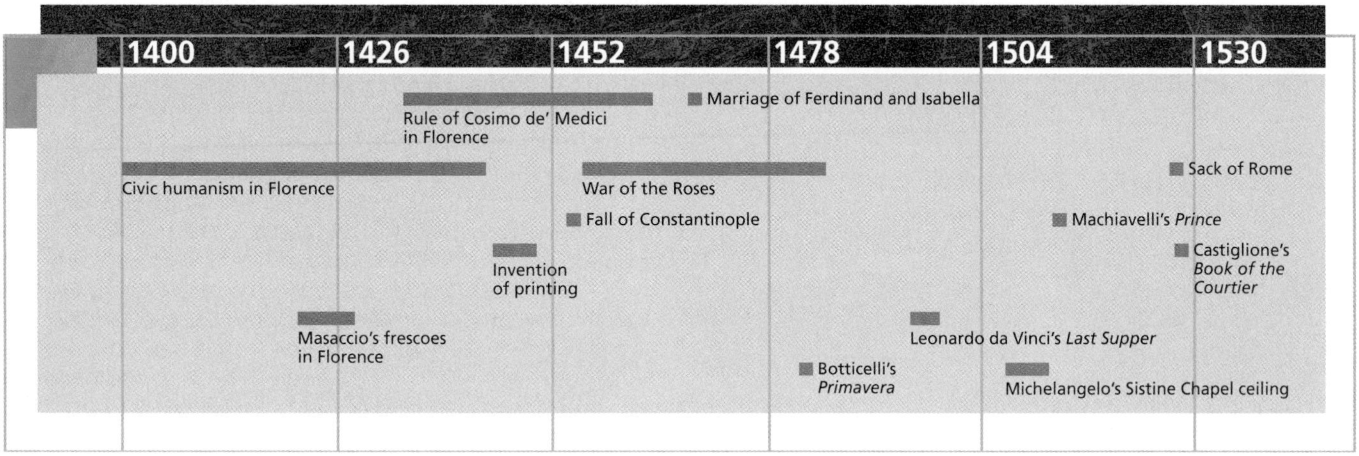

Conclusion

The Renaissance was a period of transition that witnessed a continuation of the economic, political, and social trends that had begun in the High Middle Ages. It was also a movement in which intellectuals and artists proclaimed a new vision of humankind and raised fundamental questions about the value and importance of the individual. Of course, intellectuals and artists wrote and painted for the upper classes, and the brilliant intellectual, cultural, and artistic accomplishments of the Renaissance were products of and for the elite. The ideas of the Renaissance did not have a broad base among the masses of the people. As Lorenzo the Magnificent, ruler of Florence, once commented: "Only men of noble birth can obtain perfection. The poor, who work with their hands and have no time to cultivate their minds, are incapable of it."

The Renaissance did, however, raise new questions about medieval traditions. In advocating a return to the early sources of Christianity and criticizing current religious practices, the humanists raised fundamental issues about the Catholic church, which was still an important institution. In the sixteenth century, the intellectual revolution of the fifteenth century gave way to a religious renaissance that touched the lives of people, including the masses, in new and profound ways. After the Reformation, Europe would never again be the unified Christian commonwealth it once believed it was.

Notes

1. Quoted in Jacob Burckhardt, *The Civilization of the Renaissance in Italy,* trans. S. G. C. Middlemore (London, 1960), p. 81.
2. Baldassare Castiglione, *The Book of the Courtier,* trans. Charles S. Singleton (Garden City, N.Y., 1959), pp. 288–289.
3. Quoted in De Lamar Jensen, *Renaissance Europe* (Lexington, Mass., 1981), p. 94.
4. Quoted in Iris Origo, "The Domestic Enemy: The Eastern Slaves in Tuscany in the Fourteenth and Fifteenth Centuries," *Speculum* 30 (1955): 333.
5. Gene Brucker, ed., *Two Memoirs of Renaissance Florence* (New York, 1967), p. 132.
6. Quoted in Margaret L. King, *Women of the Renaissance* (Chicago, 1991), p. 3.
7. Gene Brucker, ed., *The Society of Renaissance Florence* (New York, 1971), p. 190.
8. Quoted in Garrett Mattingly, *Renaissance Diplomacy* (Baltimore, 1964), p. 42.
9. Ibid., p. 95.
10. Niccolò Machiavelli, *The Prince,* trans. David Wootton (Indianapolis, 1995), p. 48.
11. Ibid., p. 55.
12. Ibid., p. 27.
13. Petrarch, "Epistle to Posterity," *Letters from Petrarch,* trans. Morris Bishop (Bloomington, Ind., 1966), pp. 6–7.
14. Quoted in Frances Yates, *Giordano Bruno and the Hermetic Tradition* (Chicago, 1964), p. 211.
15. Giovanni Pico della Mirandola, *Oration on the Dignity of Man,* in E. Cassirer, P. O. Kristeller, and J. H. Randall Jr., eds., *The Renaissance Philosophy of Man* (Chicago, 1948), p. 225.
16. Ibid., pp. 247–249.
17. W. H. Woodward, *Vittorino da Feltre and Other Humanist Educators* (Cambridge, 1897), p. 102.
18. Quoted in Iris Origo, "The Education of Renaissance Man," *The Light of the Past* (New York, 1959), p. 136.
19. Quoted in Elizabeth G. Holt, ed., *A Documentary History of Art* (Garden City, N.Y., 1957), vol.1, p. 286.
20. Quoted in Rosa M. Letts, *The Cambridge Introduction to Art: The Renaissance* (Cambridge, 1981), p. 86.
21. Quoted in Johan Huizinga, *The Waning of the Middle Ages* (Garden City, N.Y., 1956), p. 265.

Suggestions for Further Reading

The classic study of the Italian Renaissance is J. Burckhardt, *The Civilization of the Renaissance in Italy,* trans. S. G. C. Middlemore (London, 1960), first published in 1860. General works on the Renaissance in Europe include D. L. Jensen, *Renaissance Europe* (Lexington, Mass., 1981); P. Burke, *The European Renaissance: Centres and Peripheries* (Oxford, 1998); E. Breisach, *Renaissance Europe, 1300–1517* (New York, 1973); J. Hale, *The Civilization of Europe in the Renaissance* (New York, 1994); and the classic work by M. P. Gilmore, *The World of Humanism, 1453–1517* (New York, 1962). Although many of its interpretations are outdated, W. Ferguson's *Europe in Transition, 1300–1520* (Boston, 1962), contains a wealth of information. The brief study by P. Burke, *The Renaissance,* 2d ed. (New York, 1997), is a good summary of recent literature on the Renaissance. For beautifully illustrated introductions to the Renaissance, see G. Holmes, *Renaissance* (New York, 1996), and M. Aston, ed., *The Panorama of the Renaissance* (New York, 1996).

Brief but basic works on Renaissance economic matters are H. A. Miskimin, *The Economy of Early Renaissance Europe, 1300–1460* (New York, 1975) and *The Economy of Later Renaissance Europe, 1460–1600* (New York, 1978). For a reinterpretation of economic matters, see L. Jardine, *Worldly Goods* (New York, 1996). On family and marriage, see D. Herlihy, *The Family in Renaissance Italy* (St. Louis, Mo., 1974); C. Klapisch-Zuber, *Women, Family, and Ritual in Renaissance Italy* (Chicago, 1985); and the well-told story by G. Brucker, *Giovanni and Lusanna: Love and Marriage in Renaissance Florence* (Berkeley, Calif., 1986). On women, see M. L. King, *Women of the Renaissance* (Chicago, 1991), and N. Z. Davis and A. Farge, eds., *A History of Women: Renaissance and Enlightenment Paradoxes* (Cambridge, Mass., 1993).

The best overall study of the Italian city-states is L. Martines, *Power and Imagination: City-States in Renaissance Italy* (New York, 1979); D. Hay and J. Law, *Italy in the Age of the Renaissance* (London, 1989), is also a good survey. There is an enormous literature on Renaissance Florence. The best introduction is G. A. Brucker, *Renaissance Florence,* rev. ed. (Berkeley, Calif., 1983). On the *condottieri,* see M. Mallett, *Mercenaries and Their Masters: Warfare in Renaissance Italy* (Totowa, N.J., 1974). The work by G. Mattingly, *Renaissance Diplomacy* (Boston, 1955), remains the basic one on the subject. Machiavelli's life can be examined in Q. Skinner, *Machiavelli* (Oxford, 1981).

Brief introductions to Renaissance humanism can be found in D. R. Kelley, *Renaissance Humanism* (Boston, 1991); C. G. Nauert Jr., *Humanism and the Culture of Renaissance Europe* (Cambridge, 1995); and F. B. Artz, *Renaissance Humanism, 1300–1550* (Oberlin, Ohio, 1966). The fundamental work on fifteenth-century civic humanism is H. Baron, *The Crisis of the Early Italian Renaissance,* 2d ed. (Princeton, N.J., 1966). The impact of printing is exhaustively examined in E. Eisenstein, *The Printing Press as an Agent of Change,* 2 vols. (New York, 1978).

For brief introductions to Renaissance art, see R. M. Letts, *The Cambridge Introduction to Art: The Renaissance* (Cambridge, 1981), and B. Cole and A. Gealt, *Art of the Western World* (New York, 1989), ch. 6–8. Good surveys of Renaissance art include F. Hartt, *History of Italian Renaissance Art,* 4th ed. (Englewood Cliffs, N.J., 1994); S. Elliott, *Italian Renaissance Painting,* 2d ed. (London, 1993); R. Turner, *Renaissance Florence: The Invention of a New Art* (New York, 1997); and L. Murray, *The High Renaissance* (New York, 1967). For studies of individual artists, see J. H. Beck, *Raphael* (New York, 1994); M. Kemp, *Leonardo da Vinci: The Marvellous Works of Nature and of Man* (London, 1981); and A. Hughes, *Michelangelo* (London, 1997).

For a general work on the political development of Europe in the Renaissance, see J. H. Shennan, *The Origins of the Modern European State, 1450–1725* (London, 1974). On France, see D. Potter, *A History of France, 1460–1560* (London, 1995). Early Renaissance England is examined in J. R. Lander, *Crown and Nobility, 1450–1509* (London, 1976). Good coverage of Renaissance Spain can be found in J. N. Hillgarth, *The Spanish Kingdoms, 1250–1516,* vol. 2, *Castilian Hegemony, 1410–1516* (New York, 1978). Two good works on eastern Europe include P. W. Knoll, *The Rise of the Polish Monarchy* (Chicago, 1972), and C. A. Macartney, *Hungary: A Short History* (Edinburgh, 1962). On the Ottomans and their expansion, see H. Inalcik, *The Ottoman Empire: The Classical Age, 1300–1600* (London, 1973), and the classic work by S. Runciman, *The Fall of Constantinople, 1453* (Cambridge, 1965).

On problems of heresy and reform, see C. Crowder, *Unity, Heresy and Reform, 1378–1460* (London, 1977). Aspects of the Renaissance papacy can be examined in E. Lee, *Sixtus IV and Men of Letters* (Rome, 1978), and M. Mallett, *The Borgias* (New York, 1969). On Rome, see especially P. Partner, *Renaissance Rome, 1500–1559: A Portrait of a Society* (Berkeley, Calif., 1976).

For additional reading, go to InfoTrac College Edition, your online research library at http://web1.infotrac-college.com

Enter the search term *Renaissance* using the Subject Guide.

Enter the search term *Machiavelli* using Key Terms.

Enter the search term *humanism* using the Subject Guide.

Enter the search term *Leonardo da Vinci* using Key Terms.

C H A P T E R

13

Reformation and Religious Warfare in the Sixteenth Century

The Royal Collection © Her Majesty Queen Elizabeth II

CHAPTER OUTLINE

- Prelude to Reformation
- Martin Luther and the Reformation in Germany
- Germany and the Reformation: Religion and Politics
- The Spread of the Protestant Reformation
- The Social Impact of the Protestant Reformation
- The Catholic Reformation
- Politics and the Wars of Religion in the Sixteenth Century

FOCUS QUESTIONS

- Who were the Christian humanists, and how did they differ from the Protestant reformers?
- What were Martin Luther's main disagreements with the Roman Catholic church, and why did the movement he began spread so quickly across Europe?
- What impact did the Protestant Reformation have on the society of the sixteenth century?
- What measures did the Roman Catholic church take to reform itself and to combat Protestantism in the sixteenth century?
- What role did religion play in the European wars of the sixteenth century?
- What were the main tenets of the major Protestant groups, and how did they differ from each other and from Catholicism? What were the results of these differences?

ON APRIL 18, 1520, a lowly monk stood before the emperor and princes of Germany in the city of Worms. He had been called before this august gathering to answer charges of heresy, charges that could threaten his very life. The monk was confronted with a pile of his books and asked if he wished to defend them all or reject a part. Courageously, Martin Luther defended them all and asked to be shown where any part was in error on the basis of "Scripture and plain reason." The emperor was outraged by Luther's response and made his own position clear the next day: "Not only I, but you of this noble German nation, would be forever disgraced if by our negligence not only heresy but the very suspicion of heresy were to survive. After having heard yesterday the obstinate defense of Luther, I regret that I have so long delayed in proceeding against him and his false teaching. I will have no more to do with him." Luther's appearance at Worms set the stage for a serious challenge to the authority of the Catholic church. This was by no means the first crisis in the church's fifteen-hundred-year history, but its consequences were more far-reaching than anyone at Worms in 1520 could have imagined.

Throughout the Middle Ages, the Catholic church continued to assert its primacy of position. It had overcome defiance of its temporal authority by emperors, and challenges to its doctrines had been crushed by the Inquisition and combated by new religious orders that carried its message of salvation to all the towns and villages of medieval Europe. The growth of the papacy had paralleled the growth of the church, but by the end of the Middle Ages, challenges to papal authority from the rising power of monarchical states had resulted in a loss of papal temporal authority. An even greater threat to papal authority and church unity arose in the sixteenth century when the unity of Christendom was shattered by the Reformation.

The movement begun by Martin Luther when he made his dramatic stand quickly spread across Europe, a clear indication of dissatisfaction with Catholic practices. Within a short time, new forms of religious practices, doctrines, and organizations, including Zwinglianism, Calvinism, Anabaptism, and Anglicanism, were attracting adherents all over Europe. Although seemingly helpless to stop the new Protestant churches, the Catholic church also underwent a religious renaissance and managed by the mid-sixteenth century to revive its fortunes. All too soon, the doctrinal divisions between Protestants and Catholics led to a series of religious wars that dominated the history of western Europe in the second half of the sixteenth century.

Prelude to Reformation

Martin Luther's reform movement was by no means the first. During the second half of the fifteenth century, the new classical learning that was part of Italian Renaissance humanism spread to northern Europe and spawned a movement called Christian or northern Renaissance humanism whose major goal was the reform of Christianity.

Christian or Northern Renaissance Humanism

Like their Italian counterparts, northern humanists cultivated a knowledge of the classics, the one common bond that united all humanists into a kind of international fellowship. In returning to the writings of antiquity, northern humanists (also called Christian humanists because of their profound preoccupation with religion) focused on the sources of early Christianity, the Holy Scriptures and the writings of such church fathers as Augustine, Ambrose, and Jerome. In these early Christian writings, they discovered a simple religion that they came to feel had been distorted by the complicated theological arguments of the Middle Ages.

The most important characteristic of northern humanism was its reform program. With their belief in the ability of human beings to reason and improve themselves, the northern humanists felt that through education in the sources of classical, and especially Christian, antiquity, they could instill a true inner piety or an inward religious feeling that would bring about a reform of the church and society. For this reason, Christian humanists supported schools, brought out new editions of the classics, and prepared new editions of the Bible and writings of the church fathers. In the preface to his edition of the Greek New Testament, the famous humanist Erasmus wrote:

> Indeed, I disagree very much with those who are unwilling that Holy Scripture, translated into the vulgar tongue, be read by the uneducated, as if Christ taught such intricate doctrines that they could scarcely be understood by very few theologians, or as if the strength of the Christian religion consisted in men's ignorance of it. . . . I would that even the lowliest women read the Gospels and the Pauline Epistles. And I would that they were translated into all languages so that they could be read and understood not only by Scots and Irish but also by Turks and Saracens. . . . Would that, as a result, the farmer sing some portion of them at the plow, the weaver hum some parts of them to the movement of his shuttle, the traveler lighten the weariness of the journey with stories of this kind![1]

This belief in the power of education would remain an important characteristic of European civilization. Like later intellectuals, Christian humanists believed that to change society, they must first change the human beings who compose it. Although some have viewed the Christian humanists as naive, they themselves were very optimistic. The turmoil of the Reformation, however, shattered much of this intellectual optimism, as the lives and careers of two of the most prominent Christian humanists, Desiderius Erasmus and Thomas More, illustrate.

ERASMUS

The most influential of all the Christian humanists was Desiderius Erasmus (1466–1536), who formulated and popularized the reform program of Christian humanism. Born in Holland, Erasmus was educated at one of the schools of the Brothers of the Common Life. He wandered to France, England, Italy, Germany, and Switzerland, conversing everywhere in the classical Latin that might be called his mother tongue. The *Handbook of the Christian Knight,* printed in 1503, reflected his preoccupation with religion. He called his conception of religion "the philosophy of Christ," by which he meant that Christianity should be a guiding philosophy for the direction of daily life rather than the system of dogmatic beliefs and practices that the medieval church seemed to stress. In other words, he emphasized inner piety and deemphasized the external forms of religion (such as the sacraments, pilgrimages, fasts, veneration of saints, and relics). To return to the simplicity of the early church, people needed to understand the original meaning of the Scriptures and early church fathers. Because Erasmus thought that the standard Latin edition of the Bible, known as the Vulgate, contained errors, he edited the Greek text of the New Testament from the earliest available manuscripts and published it, along with a new Latin translation, in 1516.

To Erasmus, the reform of the church meant spreading an understanding of the philosophy of Jesus, providing enlightened education in the sources of early Christianity, and making commonsense criticism of the abuses in the church. This last is especially evident in *The Praise of Folly,* written in 1511, in which Erasmus was able to engage in a humorous yet effective criticism of the most corrupt practices of his own society. He was especially harsh on the abuses within the ranks of the clergy (see the box on p. 339).

Erasmus' program did not achieve the reform of the church that he so desired. His moderation and his emphasis on education were quickly overwhelmed by the passions of the Reformation. Undoubtedly, though, his work helped prepare the way for the Reformation; as contemporaries proclaimed, "Erasmus laid the egg that Luther hatched." Yet Erasmus eventually disapproved of Luther and the Protestant reformers. He had no intention of destroying the unity of the medieval Christian church; rather, his whole program was based on reform within the church.

Oeffentliche Kunstsammlung Basel, Kunstmuseum: Colorphoto Hans Hinz

Erasmus. Desiderius Erasmus was the most influential of the northern Renaissance humanists. He sought to restore Christianity to the early simplicity found in the teachings of Jesus. This portrait of Erasmus was painted in 1523 by Hans Holbein the Younger, who had formed a friendship with the great humanist while they were both in Basel.

THOMAS MORE

The son of a London lawyer, Thomas More (1478–1535) received the benefits of a good education. Although trained in the law, he took an avid interest in the new classical learning and became proficient in both Latin and Greek. Like the Italian humanists who believed in putting their learning at the service of the state, More embarked on a public career that ultimately took him to the highest reaches of power as lord chancellor of England.

His career in government service, however, did not keep More from the intellectual and spiritual interests that were so dear to him. He was well acquainted with other English humanists and became an intimate friend of Erasmus. He made translations from Greek authors and wrote both prose and poetry in Latin. A deeply devout man, he spent many hours in prayer and private devotions. Many praised his household as a shining model of Christian family life.

More's most famous work, and one of the most controversial of his age, was *Utopia,* written in 1516. This literary masterpiece is an account of the idealistic life and institutions of the community of Utopia (Greek for "nowhere"), an imaginary island in the vicinity of the New World. It reflects More's own concerns with the economic, social, and political problems of his day. He presented a new social system in which cooperation and reason replaced power and fame as the proper motivating agents for human society. Utopian society, therefore, is based on communal ownership rather than private property. All persons work nine hours a day, regardless of occupation, and are rewarded according to their needs. Possessing abundant leisure time and relieved of competition and greed, Utopians were free to do wholesome and enriching things. More envisioned Utopia as an orderly world where social relations, recreation, and even travel were carefully controlled for the moral welfare of society and its members.

Erasmus: In Praise of Folly

The Praise of Folly is one of the most famous pieces of literature of the sixteenth century. Erasmus, who wrote it in a short period of time during a visit to the home of Thomas More, considered it a "little diversion" from his "serious work." Yet both contemporaries and later generations have appreciated "this laughing parody of every form and rank of human life." In this selection, Erasmus belittles one of his favorite objects of scorn, the monks.

Erasmus, The Praise of Folly

Those who are the closest to these [the theologians] in happiness are generally called "the religious" or "monks," both of which are deceiving names, since for the most part they stay as far away from religion as possible and frequent every sort of place. I cannot, however, see how any life could be more gloomy than the life of these monks if I [Folly] did not assist them in many ways. Though most people detest these men so much that accidentally meeting one is considered to be bad luck, the monks themselves believe that they are magnificent creatures. One of their chief beliefs is that to be illiterate is to be of a high state of sanctity, and so they make sure that they are not able to read. Another is that when braying out their gospels in church they are making themselves very pleasing and satisfying to God, when in fact they are uttering these psalms as a matter of repetition rather than from their hearts. . . .

Moreover, it is amusing to find that they insist that everything be done in fastidious detail, as if employing the orderliness of mathematics, a small mistake in which would be a great crime. Just so many knots must be on each shoe and the shoelace may be of only one specified color; just so much lace is allowed on each habit; the girdle must be of just the right material and width; the hood of a certain shape and capacity; their hair of just so many fingers' length; and finally they can sleep only the specified number of hours per day. Can they not understand that, because of a variety of bodies and temperaments, all this equality of restrictions is in fact very unequal? Nevertheless, because of all this detail that they employ they think that they are superior to all other people. And what is more, amid all their pretense of Apostolic charity, the members of one order will denounce the members of another order clamorously because of the way in which the habit has been belted or the slightly darker color of it. . . .

Many of them work so hard at protocol and at traditional fastidiousness that they think one heaven hardly a suitable reward for their labors; never recalling, however, that the time will come when Christ will demand a reckoning of that which he had prescribed, namely charity, and that he will hold their deeds of little account. One monk will then exhibit his belly filled with every kind of fish; another will profess a knowledge of over a hundred hymns. Still another will reveal a countless number of fasts that he has made, and will account for his large belly by explaining that his fasts have always been broken by a single large meal. Another will show a list of church ceremonies over which he has officiated so large that it would fill seven ships.

In serving King Henry VIII, More came face to face with the abuses and corruption he had criticized in *Utopia.* But he did not allow idealism to outweigh his own ultimate realism, and in *Utopia* itself he justified his service to the king:

> If you can't completely eradicate wrong ideas, or deal with inveterate vices as effectively as you could wish, that's no reason for turning your back on public life altogether. You wouldn't abandon ship in a storm just because you couldn't control the winds. On the other hand, it's no use attempting to put across entirely new ideas, which will obviously carry no weight with people who are prejudiced against them. You must go to work indirectly. You must handle everything as tactfully as you can, and what you can't put right you must try to make as little wrong as possible. For things will never be perfect, until human beings are perfect—which I don't expect them to be for quite a number of years.[2]

More's religious devotion and belief in the universal Catholic church proved even more important than his service to the king, however. Always the man of conscience, More willingly gave up his life opposing England's break with the Roman Catholic church over the divorce of King Henry VIII.

Church and Religion on the Eve of the Reformation

Corruption in the Catholic church was another factor that encouraged people to want reform. No doubt the failure of the Renaissance popes to provide spiritual leadership had affected the spiritual life of all Christendom. The papal court's preoccupation with finances had an especially strong impact on the clergy. So did the economic changes of the fourteenth and fifteenth centuries. The highest positions among the clergy were increasingly held by either nobles or the wealthy members of the bourgeoisie. Moreover, to increase their revenues, high church officials (bishops, archbishops, and cardinals) took over more than one church office. This so-called pluralism led in turn to absenteeism: church officeholders ignored their duties and hired underlings who often had even less interest in the job. Complaints about the ignorance and ineptness of parish priests became widespread in the fifteenth century.

While the leaders of the church were failing to meet their responsibilities, ordinary people were clamoring for meaningful religious expression and certainty of salvation.

As a result, for some the salvation process became almost mechanical. As more and more people sought certainty of salvation through veneration of relics, collections of such objects grew. Frederick the Wise, elector of Saxony and Martin Luther's prince, had amassed over five thousand relics to which were attached indulgences that could reduce one's time in purgatory by 1,443 years. (An indulgence, you will recall, is a remission, after death, of all or part of the punishment for sin.) Other people sought certainty of salvation in the popular mystical movement known as the Modern Devotion, which downplayed religious dogma and stressed the need to follow the teachings of Jesus. Thomas à Kempis, author of *The Imitation of Christ*, wrote that "truly, at the day of judgment we shall not be examined by what we have read, but what we have done; not how well we have spoken, but how religiously we have lived."

What is striking about the revival of religious piety in the fifteenth century—whether expressed through such external forces as the veneration of relics and the buying of indulgences or the mystical path—was its adherence to the orthodox beliefs and practices of the Catholic church. The agitation for certainty of salvation and spiritual peace occurred within the framework of the "holy mother Church." But disillusionment grew as the devout experienced the clergy's inability to live up to their expectations. The deepening of religious life, especially in the second half of the fifteenth century, found little echo among the worldly-wise clergy, and this environment helps explain the tremendous and immediate impact of Luther's ideas.

Martin Luther and the Reformation in Germany

The Protestant Reformation began with a typical medieval question: What must I do to be saved? Martin Luther, a deeply religious man, found an answer that did not fit within the traditional teachings of the late medieval church. Ultimately, he split with that church, destroying the religious unity of western Christendom. That other people were concerned with the same question is evident in the rapid spread of the Reformation. But religion was so entangled in the social, economic, and political forces of the period that the Protestant reformers' hope of transforming the church quickly proved illusory.

The Early Luther

Martin Luther was born in Germany on November 10, 1483. His father wanted him to become a lawyer, so Luther enrolled at the University of Erfurt, where he received his bachelor's degree in 1502. In 1505, after becoming a master in the liberal arts, the young Martin began to study law. But Luther was not content, not in small part due to his longstanding religious inclinations. That summer, while returning to Erfurt after a brief visit home, he was caught in a ferocious thunderstorm and vowed that if he survived unscathed, he would become a monk. He then entered the monastic order of the Augustinian Hermits in Erfurt, much to his father's disgust. In the monastery, Luther focused on his major concern, the assurance of salvation. The traditional beliefs and practices of the church seemed unable to relieve his obsession with this question, especially evident in his struggle with the sacrament of penance or confession. The sacraments were a Catholic's chief means of receiving God's grace; confession offered the opportunity to have one's sins forgiven. Luther spent hours confessing his sins, but he was always doubtful. Had he remembered all of his sins? Even more, how could a hopeless sinner be acceptable to a totally just and all-powerful God? Luther threw himself into his monastic routine with a vengeance:

> I was indeed a good monk and kept my order so strictly that I could say that if ever a monk could get to heaven through monastic discipline, I was that monk. . . . And yet my conscience would not give me certainty, but I always doubted and said, "You didn't do that right. You weren't contrite enough. You left that out of your confession." The more I tried to remedy an uncertain, weak and troubled conscience with human traditions, the more I daily found it more uncertain, weaker and more troubled.[3]

Despite his herculean efforts, Luther achieved no certainty.

Martin Luther. This painting by Lucas Cranach the Elder in 1533 shows Luther at the age of fifty. By this time, Luther's reforms had taken hold in many parts of Germany, and Luther himself was a happily married man with five children.

Luther and the Ninety-Five Theses

To most historians, the publication of Luther's Ninety-Five Theses marks the beginning of the Reformation. To Luther, they were simply a response to what he considered Johann Tetzel's blatant abuses in selling indulgences. Although written in Latin, Luther's statements were soon translated into German and disseminated widely across Germany. They made an immense impression on Germans already dissatisfied with the ecclesiastical and financial policies of the papacy.

Martin Luther, Selections from the Ninety-Five Theses

5. The Pope has neither the will nor the power to remit any penalties beyond those he has imposed either at his own discretion or by canon law.
20. Therefore the Pope, by his plenary remission of all penalties, does not mean "all" in the absolute sense, but only those imposed by himself.
21. Hence those preachers of Indulgences are wrong when they say that a man is absolved and saved from every penalty by the Pope's Indulgences.
27. It is mere human talk to preach that the soul flies out [of purgatory] immediately the money clinks in the collection-box.
28. It is certainly possible that when the money clinks in the collection-box greed and avarice can increase; but the intercession of the Church depends on the will of God alone.
50. Christians should be taught that, if the Pope knew the exactions of the preachers of Indulgences, he would rather have the basilica of St. Peter reduced to ashes than built with the skin, flesh and bones of his sheep.
81. This wanton preaching of pardons makes it difficult even for learned men to redeem respect due to the Pope from the slanders or at least the shrewd questionings of the laity.
82. For example: "Why does not the Pope empty purgatory for the sake of most holy love and the supreme need of souls? This would be the most righteous of reasons, if he can redeem innumerable souls for sordid money with which to build a basilica, the most trivial of reasons."
86. Again: "Since the Pope's wealth is larger than that of the crassest Crassi of our time, why does he not build this one basilica of St. Peter with his own money, rather than with that of the faithful poor?"
90. To suppress these most conscientious questionings of the laity by authority only, instead of refuting them by reason, is to expose the Church and the Pope to the ridicule of their enemies, and to make Christian people unhappy.
94. Christians should be exhorted to seek earnestly to follow Christ, their Head, through penalties, deaths, and hells.
95. And let them thus be more confident of entering heaven through many tribulations rather than through a false assurance of peace.

To help overcome his difficulties, his superiors recommended that the intelligent yet disturbed monk study theology. He received his doctorate in 1512 and then became a professor in the theological faculty at the University of Wittenberg, lecturing on the Bible. Probably sometime between 1513 and 1516, through his study of the Bible, he arrived at an answer to his problem.

Catholic doctrine had emphasized that both faith and good works were required of a Christian to achieve personal salvation. In Luther's eyes, human beings, weak and powerless in the sight of an almighty God, could never do enough good works to merit salvation. Through his study of the Bible, especially his work on Paul's Epistle to the Romans, Luther rediscovered another way of viewing this problem. To Luther, humans are saved not through their good works but through faith in the promises of God, made possible by the sacrifice of Jesus on the cross. The doctrine of salvation or justification by grace through faith alone became the primary doctrine of the Protestant Reformation (justification is the act by which a person is made deserving of salvation). Because Luther had arrived at this doctrine from his study of the Bible, the Bible became for Luther, as for all other Protestants, the chief guide to religious truth. Justification by faith and the Bible as the sole authority in religious affairs were the twin pillars of the Protestant Reformation.

Luther did not see himself as either an innovator or a heretic, but his involvement in the indulgence controversy propelled him into an open confrontation with church officials and forced him to see the theological implications of justification by faith alone. In 1517, Pope Leo X had issued a special jubilee indulgence to finance the ongoing construction of Saint Peter's Basilica in Rome. Johann Tetzel, a rambunctious Dominican, hawked the indulgences in Germany with the slogan "As soon as the coin in the coffer rings, the soul from purgatory springs."

Luther was greatly distressed by the sale of indulgences, certain that people were simply guaranteeing their eternal damnation by relying on these pieces of paper to assure themselves of salvation. Greatly angered, he issued his Ninety-Five Theses, although scholars are unsure whether he nailed them to a church door in Wittenberg, as is traditionally alleged, or mailed them to his ecclesiastical superior. In either case, his theses were a stunning indictment of the abuses in the sale of indulgences (see the box above). It is doubtful that Luther intended any break with the church over the issue of indulgences. If the pope had clarified

Staatliche Museen Preussischer Kulturbesitz, Kupferstichkabinett, Berlin, Photo: Jorg P. Anders

Woodcut: Luther Versus the Pope. In the 1520s, after Luther's return to Wittenberg, his teachings began to spread rapidly, ending ultimately in a reform movement supported by state authorities. Pamphlets containing picturesque woodcuts were important in the spread of Luther's ideas. In the woodcut shown here, the crucified Jesus attends Luther's service on the left, while on the right the pope is at a table selling indulgences.

the use of indulgences, as Luther wished, he would probably have been satisfied and the controversy would have ended. But Pope Leo X did not take the issue seriously and is even reported to have said that Luther was simply "some drunken German who will amend his ways when he sobers up." A German translation of the Ninety-Five Theses was quickly printed in thousands of copies and received sympathetically in a Germany that had a long tradition of dissatisfaction with papal policies and power.

The controversy reached an important turning point with the Leipzig Debate in July 1519. In Leipzig, Luther's opponent, the capable Catholic theologian Johann Eck, forced Luther to move beyond indulgences and deny the authority of popes and councils. In effect, Luther was compelled to see the consequences of his new theology. At the beginning of 1520, he proclaimed: "Farewell, unhappy, hopeless, blasphemous Rome! The Wrath of God has come upon you, as you deserve. We have cared for Babylon, and she is not healed: let us then, leave her, that she may be the habitation of dragons, spectres, and witches."[4] At the same time, Luther was convinced that he was doing God's work and had to proceed regardless of the consequences.

In three pamphlets published in 1520, Luther moved toward a more definite break with the Catholic church. The *Address to the Nobility of the German Nation* was a political tract written in German in which Luther called on the German princes to overthrow the papacy in Germany and establish a reformed German church. *The Babylonian Captivity of the Church,* written in Latin for theologians, attacked the sacramental system as the means by which the pope and church had held the real meaning of the Gospel in captivity for a thousand years. He called for the reform of monasticism and for the clergy to marry. Though virginity is good, Luther argued, marriage is better, and freedom of choice is best. *On the Freedom of a Christian Man* was a short treatise on the doctrine of salvation. It is faith alone, not good works, that justifies, frees, and brings salvation through Jesus. Being saved and freed by his faith in Jesus, however, does not free the Christian from doing good works. Rather, he performs good works out of gratitude to God. "Good works do not make a good man, but a good man does good works."[5]

Unable to accept Luther's forcefully worded dissent from traditional Catholic teachings, the church excommunicated him in January 1521. He was also summoned to appear before the Reichstag, the imperial diet of the Holy Roman Empire, in Worms, convened by the newly elected Emperor Charles V (1519–1556). Expected to recant the heretical doctrines he had espoused, Luther refused and made the famous reply that became the battle cry of the Reformation:

> Since then Your Majesty and your lordships desire a simple reply, I will answer without horns and without teeth. Unless I am convicted by Scripture and plain reason—I do not accept the authority of popes and councils, for they have contradicted each other—my conscience is captive to the Word of God. I cannot and I will not recant anything, for to go against conscience is neither right nor safe. Here I stand, I cannot do otherwise. God help me. Amen.[6]

Emperor Charles was outraged at Luther's audacity and gave his opinion that "a single friar who goes counter to all Christianity for a thousand years must be wrong." By the Edict of Worms, Martin Luther was made an outlaw within the empire. His works were to be burned, and Luther himself was to be captured and delivered to the emperor.

The Rise of Lutheranism

After a brief period of hiding, Luther returned to Wittenberg in Electoral Saxony at the beginning of 1522 and began to organize a reformed church. Lutheranism had wide appeal and spread rapidly. The preaching of evangelical sermons, based on a return to the original message of the Bible, found favor throughout Germany. In city after city, the arrival of preachers presenting Luther's teachings was soon followed by a public debate in which the new preachers proved victorious. A reform of the church was then instituted by state authorities. Also useful to the spread of the Reformation were pamphlets illustrated with vivid woodcuts portraying the pope as a hideous Antichrist and titled with catchy phrases such as "I Wonder Why There Is No Money in the Land" (which, of course, was an attack on papal greed). Luther also insisted on the use of music as a means to teach the Gospel, and his own composition, "A Mighty Fortress Is Our God," became the battle hymn of the Reformation:

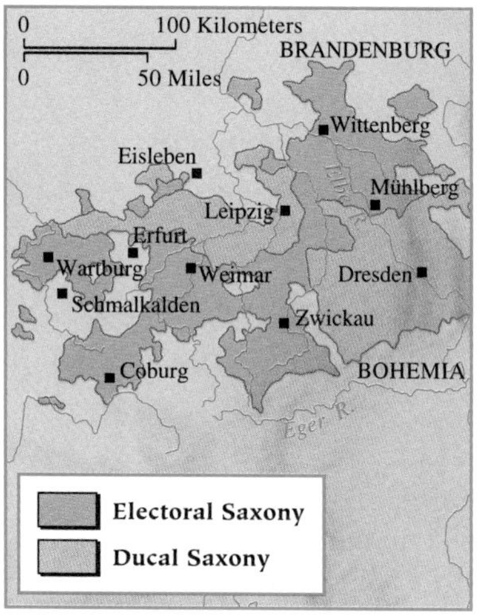

Luther's Saxony

> *Standing alone are we undone, the Fiend would soon enslave us;*
> *but for us fights a mighty One whom God has sent to save us.*
> *Ask you who is this? Jesus Christ is He, Lord God of Hosts*
> *There is no other God; He can and will uphold us.*

Lutheranism spread to both princely and ecclesiastical states in northern and central Germany as well as to two-thirds of the free imperial cities, especially those of southern Germany, where prosperous burghers, for both religious and secular reasons, became committed to Luther's cause. Nuremberg, where an active city council led by the dynamic city secretary Lazarus Spengler brought a conversion as early as 1525, was the first imperial city to convert to Lutheranism. At its outset, the Reformation in Germany was largely an urban phenomenon.

A series of crises in the mid-1520s made it apparent, however, that spreading the word of God was not as easy as Luther had originally envisioned, the usual plight of most reformers. Luther experienced dissent within his own ranks in Wittenberg from people such as Andreas Carlstadt, who wished to initiate a more radical reform by abolishing all relics, images, and the Mass. Luther had no sooner dealt with them when he faced defection from the Christian humanists. Many had initially supported Luther, believing that he shared their goal of reforming the abuses within the church. But when it became apparent that Luther's movement threatened the unity of Christendom, the older generation of Christian humanists, including Erasmus, broke with the reformer. A younger generation of Christian humanists, however, played a significant role in Lutheranism. Philip Melanchthon (1497–1560) arrived in Wittenberg in 1518 at the age of twenty-one to teach Greek and Hebrew, was immediately attracted to Luther's ideas, and became his staunch supporter.

Luther's greatest challenge in the mid-1520s, however, came from the Peasants' War. Peasant dissatisfaction in Germany stemmed from several sources. Many peasants had not been touched by the gradual economic improvement of the early sixteenth century. In some areas, especially southwestern Germany, influential local lords continued to abuse their peasants, and new demands for taxes and other services caused them to wish for a return to "the good old days." Social discontent soon became entangled with religious revolt as peasants looked to Martin Luther for support. It was not Luther, however, but one of his ex-followers, the radical Thomas Müntzer, who inflamed the peasants against their rulers with his fiery language: "Strike while the iron is hot!" Revolt first erupted in southwestern Germany in June 1524 and spread northward and eastward.

Luther reacted quickly and vehemently against the peasants. In his pamphlet *Against the Robbing and Murdering Hordes of Peasants,* he called on the German princes to "smite, slay and stab" the stupid and stubborn peasantry (see the box on p. 344). Luther, who knew how much his reformation of the church depended on the full support of the German princes and magistrates, supported the rulers. To Luther, the state and its rulers were ordained by God and given the authority to maintain the peace and order necessary for the spread of the Gospel. It was the duty of princes to suppress all revolt. By May 1525, the German princes had ruthlessly suppressed the peasant hordes. By this time, Luther

Luther and the "Robbing and Murdering Hordes of Peasants"

The Peasants' War of 1524–1525 encompassed a series of uprisings by German peasants who were suffering from economic changes they did not comprehend. Led by radical religious leaders, the revolts quickly became entangled with the religious revolt set in motion by Luther's defiance of the church. But it was soon clear that Luther himself did not believe in any way in social revolution. This excerpt is taken from Luther's pamphlet written in May 1525 at the height of the peasants' power but not published until after their defeat.

Martin Luther, Against the Robbing and Murdering Hordes of Peasants

The peasants have taken on themselves the burden of three terrible sins against God and man, by which they have abundantly merited death in body and soul. In the first place they have sworn to be true and faithful, submissive and obedient, to their rulers, as Christ commands, when he says, "Render unto Caesar the things that are Caesar's," and in Romans XIII, "Let everyone be subject unto the higher powers." Because they are breaking this obedience, and are setting themselves against the higher powers, willfully and with violence, they have forfeited body and soul, as faithless, perjured, lying, disobedient knaves and scoundrels are wont to do. . . .

In the second place, they are starting a rebellion, and violently robbing and plundering monasteries and castles which are not theirs, by which they have a second time deserved death in body and soul, if only as highwaymen and murderers. . . . For rebellion is not simple murder, but is like a great fire, which attacks and lays waste a whole land. . . . Therefore, let everyone who can, smite, slay and stab, secretly or openly, remembering that nothing can be more poisonous, hurtful or devilish than a rebel. . . .

In the third place, they cloak this terrible and horrible sin with the Gospel, call themselves "Christian brothers," receive oaths and homage, and compel people to hold with them to these abominations. Thus they become the greatest of all blasphemers of God and slanderers of his holy Name, serving the devil, under the outward appearance of the Gospel, thus earning death in body and soul ten times over. . . . It does not help the peasants, when they pretend that, according to Genesis I and II, all things were created free and common, and that all of us alike have been baptized. . . . For baptism does not make men free in body and property, but in soul; and the Gospel does not make goods common. . . . Since the peasants, then, have brought both God and man down upon them and are already so many times guilty of death in body and soul, . . . I must instruct the worldly governors how they are to act in the matter with a clear conscience.

First, I will not oppose a ruler who, even though he does not tolerate the Gospel, will smite and punish these peasants without offering to submit the case to judgment. For he is within his rights, since the peasants are not contending any longer for the Gospel, but have become faithless, perjured, disobedient, rebellious murderers, robbers and blasphemers, whom even heathen rulers have the right and power to punish; nay, it is their duty to punish them, for it is just for this purpose that they bear the sword, and are "the ministers of God upon him that doeth evil."

found himself ever more dependent on state authorities for the growth and maintenance of his reformed church.

Church and State

Justification by faith alone was the starting point for most of Protestantism's major doctrines. Since Luther downplayed the role of good works in salvation, the sacraments also had to be redefined. No longer were they merit-earning works; they were now divinely established signs signifying the promise of salvation. Based on his interpretation of scriptural authority, Luther kept only two of the Catholic church's seven sacraments, baptism and the Lord's Supper. Baptism signified rebirth through grace. Regarding the Lord's Supper, Luther denied the Catholic doctrine of transubstantiation, which taught that the substance of the bread and wine consumed in the rite is miraculously transformed into the body and blood of Jesus. Yet he continued to insist on the real presence of Jesus' body and blood in the bread and wine given as a testament to God's forgiveness of sin.

Luther's emphasis on the importance of Scripture led him to reject the Catholic belief that the authority of Scripture must be supplemented by the traditions and decrees of the church. The word of God as revealed in the Bible was sufficient authority in religious affairs. A hierarchical priesthood was thus unnecessary since all Christians who followed the word of God were their own priests ("priesthood of all believers"). Though Luther thus considered the true church to be an invisible one, the difficulties of actually creating a reformed church led him to believe that a visible, organized church was needed. Since the Catholic ecclesiastical hierarchy had been scrapped, Luther came to rely increasingly on the princes or state authorities to organize and guide the new Lutheran reformed churches. He had little choice. By the sixteenth century, secular authorities in Germany as elsewhere were already playing an important role in church affairs. By 1530, in the German states that had converted to Lutheranism, both princes and city councils appointed officials who visited churches in their territories and regulated matters of worship. The

Lutheran churches in Germany (and later in Scandinavia) quickly became territorial or state churches in which the state supervised and disciplined church members.

As part of the development of these state-dominated churches, Luther also instituted new religious services to replace the Mass. These featured a worship service consisting of a German liturgy that focused on Bible reading, preaching the word of God, and song. Following his own denunciation of clerical celibacy, Luther married a former nun, Katherina von Bora, in 1525. His union provided a model of married and family life for the new Protestant minister.

Germany and the Reformation: Religion and Politics

From its very beginning, the fate of Luther's movement was closely tied to political affairs. In 1519, Charles I, king of Spain and grandson of Emperor Maximilian, was elected Holy Roman Emperor as Charles V (1519–1556). Charles V ruled over an immense empire, consisting of Spain and its overseas possessions, the traditional Austrian Habsburg lands, Bohemia, Hungary, the Low Countries, and the kingdom of Naples in southern Italy (see Map 13.1). The extent of his possessions was reflected in the languages he used: "I speak Spanish to God, Italian to women, French to men, and German to my horse." Politically, Charles wanted to maintain his dynasty's control over his enormous empire; religiously, he hoped to preserve the unity of the Catholic faith throughout his empire. Despite his strengths, Charles spent a lifetime in futile pursuit of his goals. Four major problems—the French, the papacy, the Turks, and Germany's internal situation—cost him both his dream and his health. At the same time, the emperor's problems gave Luther's movement time to grow and organize before facing the concerted onslaught of the Catholic forces.

The French, the Papacy, and the Turks

Charles V's chief political concern was his rivalry with the Valois king of France, Francis I (1515–1547). Encircled by the possessions of the Habsburg empire, Francis became embroiled in conflict with Charles over disputed territories in southern France, the Netherlands, the Rhineland, northern Spain, and Italy. These conflicts, known as the Habsburg-Valois Wars, were fought intermittently for twenty four years (1521–1544), preventing Charles from concentrating on the Lutheran problem in Germany.

Meanwhile, Charles faced two other enemies. The Habsburg emperor expected papal cooperation in dealing with the Lutheran heresy. Papal policy, however, was guided by political considerations, not religious ones. Fearful of Charles's power in Italy, Pope Clement VII (1523–1534) joined the side of Francis I in the second Habsburg-Valois War (1527–1529), but with catastrophic results. In April 1527, the Spanish-imperial army of Charles V went berserk while attacking Rome and gave the capital of Catholicism a fearful and bloody sacking. Sobered by the experience, Clement came to terms with the emperor, and by 1530, Charles V stood supreme over much of Italy.

In the meantime, a new threat to the emperor's power had erupted in the eastern part of his empire. The Ottoman Turks, under Suleiman the Magnificent (1520–1566), had defeated and killed King Louis of Hungary, Charles's brother-in-law, at the Battle of Mohács in 1526. Subsequently, the Turks overran most of Hungary, moved into Austria, and advanced as far as Vienna, where they were finally repulsed in 1529.

Charles V. Charles V sought to create religious unity throughout his vast empire by keeping all his subjects within the bounds of the Catholic church. Due to his conflict with Francis I in addition to his difficulties with the Turks, the papacy, and the German princes, Charles was never able to check the spread of Lutheranism. This portrait of Charles V is by the Venetian painter Titian.

Alte Pinakothek, Munich

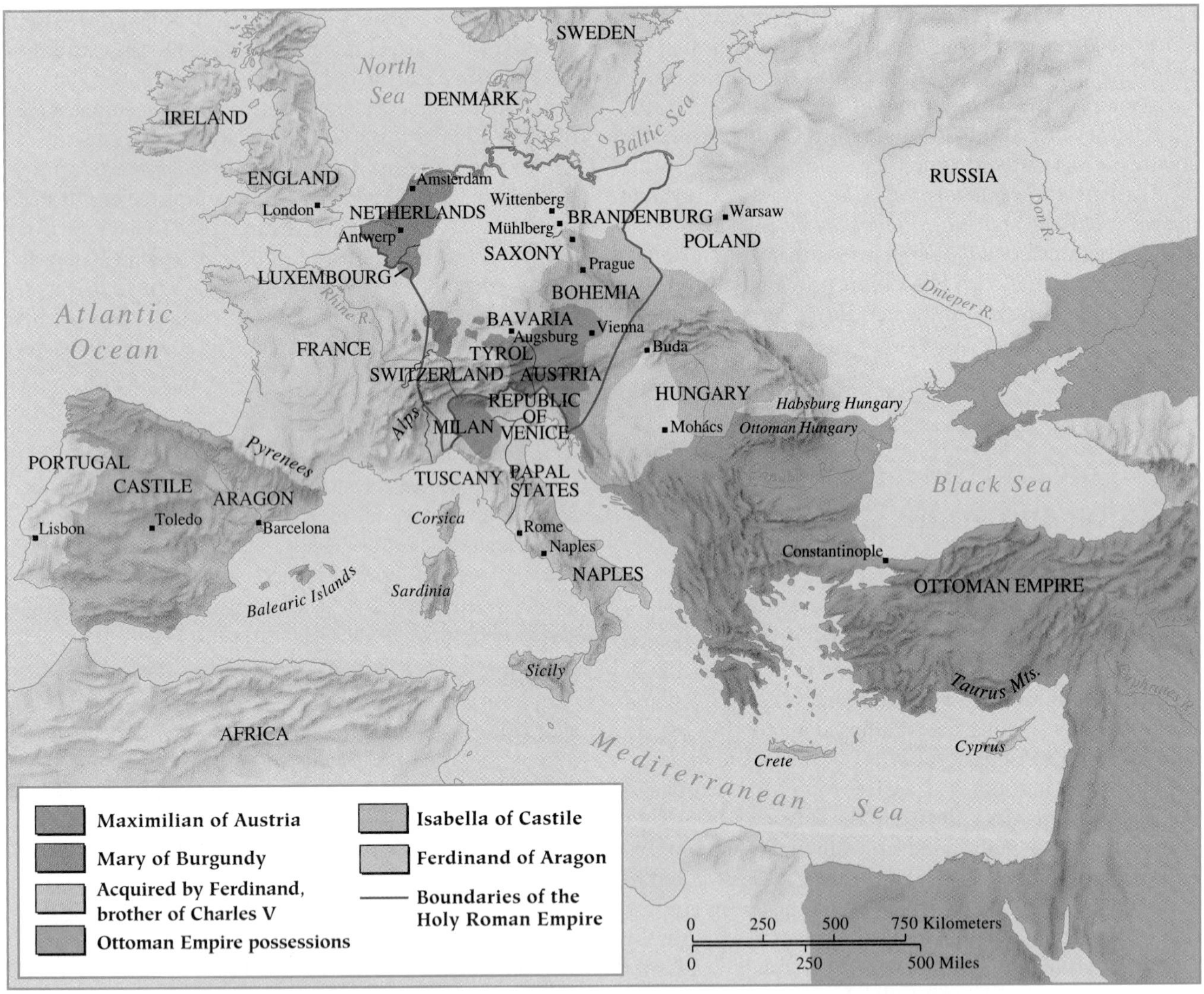

Map 13.1 The Empire of Charles V. Charles V spent much of his reign fighting wars in Italy, against France and the Ottoman Empire, and within the borders of the Holy Roman Empire. He failed in his main goal to secure Europe for Catholicism: the 1555 Peace of Augsburg recognized the equality of Catholicism and Protestantism and let each German prince choose his realm's religion. ■ Why would France feel threatened by the empire of Charles V?

Politics in Germany

By the end of 1529, Charles was ready to deal with Germany. The second Habsburg-Valois War had ended, the Turks had been defeated temporarily, and the pope had been subdued. The internal political situation in the Holy Roman Empire was not in his favor, however. Germany was a land of several hundred territorial states: princely states, ecclesiastical principalities, and free imperial cities. Though all owed loyalty to the emperor, Germany's medieval development had enabled these states to become quite independent of imperial authority. They had no desire to have a strong emperor.

Charles's attempt to settle the Lutheran problem at the Diet of Augsburg in 1530 proved completely inadequate, and the emperor wound up demanding that the Lutherans return to the Catholic church by April 15, 1531. In February 1531, fearful of Charles's intentions, eight princes and eleven imperial cities—all Lutheran—formed a defensive alliance known as the Schmalkaldic League. These Protestant German states vowed to assist each other "whenever any one of us is attacked on account of the Word of God and the doctrine of the Gospel." Religion was dividing the empire into two armed camps.

The renewed threat of the Turks against Vienna forced Charles once again to seek compromise instead of war with the Protestant authorities. From 1532 to 1535, Charles was forced to fight off a Turkish, Arab, and Barbary attack on the Mediterranean coasts of Italy and Spain. Two additional Habsburg-Valois Wars (1535–1538 and 1542–1544) soon followed and kept Charles preoccupied with military campaigns in southern France and the Low Countries. Finally, Charles made peace with Francis in 1544 and the Turks in 1545. Fifteen years after the Diet of Augsburg, Charles was finally free to resolve his problem in Germany.

CHRONOLOGY

Politics and the German Reformation

First Habsburg-Valois War	1521–1525
Battle of Mohács	1526
Second Habsburg-Valois War	1527–1529
Defeat of the Turks at Vienna	1529
Diet of Augsburg	1530
Formation of Schmalkaldic League	1531
Third Habsburg-Valois War	1535–1538
Fourth Habsburg-Valois War	1542–1544
Schmalkaldic Wars	1546–1555
Peace of Augsburg	1555

By the time of Luther's death in February 1546, all hopes of a peaceful compromise had faded. Charles brought a sizable imperial army of German, Dutch, Italian, and Spanish troops to do battle with the Protestants. In the first phase of the Schmalkaldic Wars (1546–1547), the emperor's forces decisively defeated the Lutherans at the Battle of Mühlberg. Charles V was at the zenith of his power, and the Protestant cause seemed doomed.

Appearances proved misleading, however. The Schmalkaldic League was soon reestablished, and the German Protestant princes allied themselves with the new French king, Henry II (1547–1559)—a Catholic—to revive the war in 1552. This time Charles was less fortunate and was forced to negotiate a truce. Exhausted by his efforts to maintain religious orthodoxy and the unity of his empire, Charles abandoned German affairs to his brother Ferdinand, abdicated all of his titles in 1556, and retired to his country estate in Spain to spend the remaining two years of his life in solitude.

An end to religious warfare in Germany came in 1555 with the Peace of Augsburg, which marked an important turning point in the history of the Reformation. The division of Christianity was formally acknowledged, with Lutheranism granted equal legal standing with Catholicism. Moreover, the peace settlement accepted the right of each German ruler to determine the religion of his subjects (but not the right of the subjects to choose their religion). Charles's hope for a united empire had been completely dashed, and the ideal of medieval Christian unity was irretrievably lost. The rapid proliferation of new Protestant groups served to underscore that new reality.

The Spread of the Protestant Reformation

For both Catholics and Protestant reformers, Luther's heresy raised the question of what constituted the correct interpretation of the Bible. The inability to agree on this issue led not only to theological confrontations but also to bloody warfare as each Christian group was unwilling to admit that it could be wrong.

Lutheranism in Scandinavia

In 1397, the Union of Kalmar had brought about the unification of Denmark, Norway, and Sweden under the rule of one monarch, the king of Denmark. This union, however, failed to achieve any real social or political unification of the three states, particularly since the independent-minded landed nobles worked to frustrate any increase in monarchical centralization. By the beginning of the sixteenth century, the union was on the brink of disintegration. In 1520, Christian II (1513–1523) of Denmark, ruler of the three Scandinavian kingdoms, was overthrown by Swedish barons led by Gustavus Vasa. Three years later, Vasa became king of an independent Sweden (1523–1560) and took the lead in establishing a Lutheran Reformation in his country. By the 1530s, the Swedish Lutheran National Church had been created.

Meanwhile, Christian II had also been deposed as the king of Denmark by the Danish nobility; he was succeeded by his uncle, who became Frederick I (1523–1533). Frederick encouraged Lutheran preachers to spread their evangelical doctrines and to introduce a Lutheran liturgy into the Danish church service. In the 1530s, under Frederick's successor, Christian III (1534–1559), a Lutheran state church was installed with the king as the supreme authority in all ecclesiastical affairs. Christian was also instrumental in spreading Lutheranism to Norway. By the 1540s, Scandinavia had become a Lutheran stronghold. Like the German princes, the Scandinavian monarchs had been the dominant force in establishing state-run churches.

The Zwinglian Reformation

In the sixteenth century, the Swiss Confederation was a loose association of thirteen self-governing states called cantons. Theoretically part of the Holy Roman Empire, they had become virtually independent in 1499. The six forest cantons were democratic republics; the seven urban cantons, which included Zürich, Bern, and Basel, were mostly governed by city councils controlled by narrow oligarchies of wealthy citizens.

Zwingli's Zürich

Ulrich Zwingli (1484–1531) was ordained a priest in 1506 and accepted an appointment as a cathedral priest in the Great Minster of Zürich in

National Gallery of Scotland, Edinburgh/Bridgeman Art Library

Zwingli. Ulrich Zwingli began the Reformation in Switzerland through his preaching in Zürich. Zwingli's theology was accepted in Zürich and soon spread to other Swiss cities. This portrait of Zwingli was done by Hans Asper, probably in 1531.

1518. Through his preaching there, Zwingli began the Reformation in Switzerland. Zwingli's preaching of the Gospel caused such unrest that in 1523 the city council held a public disputation or debate in the town hall. The disputation became a standard method of spreading the Reformation to many cities. It gave an advantage to reformers, since they had the power of new ideas and Catholics were not used to defending their teachings. Zwingli's party was accorded the victory, and the council declared that "Mayor, Council and Great Council of Zürich, in order to do away with disturbance and discord, have upon due deliberation and consultation decided and resolved that Master Zwingli should continue as heretofore to proclaim the Gospel and the pure sacred Scripture."[7]

Over the next two years, evangelical reforms were promulgated in Zürich by a city council strongly influenced by Zwingli. Zwingli looked to the state to supervise the church. "A church without the magistrate is mutilated and incomplete," he declared. Relics and images were abolished; all paintings and decorations were removed from the churches and replaced by whitewashed walls. The Mass was replaced by a new liturgy consisting of Scripture reading, prayer, and sermons. Music was eliminated from the service as a distraction from the pure word of God. Monasticism, pilgrimages, the veneration of saints, clerical celibacy, and the pope's authority were all abolished as remnants of papal Christianity. Zwingli's movement soon spread to other cities in Switzerland, including Bern in 1528 and Basel in 1529.

By 1528, Zwingli's reform movement faced a serious political problem as the forest cantons remained staunchly Catholic. Zürich feared an alliance between them and the Habsburgs. To counteract this danger, Zwingli attempted to build a league of evangelical cities by seeking an agreement with Luther and the German reformers. An alliance between them seemed possible, since the Reformation had spread to the southern German cities, especially Strasbourg, where a moderate reform movement containing characteristics of both Luther's and Zwingli's movements had been instituted by Martin Bucer (1491–1551). Both the German and the Swiss reformers realized the need for unity to defend against imperial and conservative opposition. Protestant political leaders, especially Landgrave Philip of Hesse, fearful of Charles V's ability to take advantage of the division between the reformers, attempted to promote an alliance of the Swiss and German reformed churches by persuading the leaders of both groups to attend a colloquy (or conference) at Marburg to resolve their differences. Able to agree on virtually everything else, the gathering splintered over the interpretation of the Lord's Supper (see the box on p. 349). Zwingli believed that the scriptural words "This is my body, This is my blood" should be taken figuratively, not literally, and refused to accept Luther's insistence on the real presence of the body and blood of Jesus "in, with, and under the bread and wine." The Marburg Colloquy of 1529 produced no agreement and no evangelical alliance.

In October 1531, war erupted between the Swiss Protestant and Catholic cantons. Zürich's army was routed, and Zwingli was found wounded on the battlefield. His enemies killed him, cut up his body, and burned the pieces, scattering the ashes. This Swiss civil war of 1531 provided an early indication of what religious passions would lead to in the sixteenth century. Unable to find peaceful ways to agree on the meaning of the Gospel, the disciples of Christianity resorted to violence and decision by force. When he heard of Zwingli's death, Martin Luther, who had not forgotten the confrontation at Marburg, is supposed to have remarked that Zwingli got what he deserved.

The Radical Reformation: The Anabaptists

Although many reformers were ready to allow the state to play an important, if not dominant, role in church affairs, some people rejected this kind of magisterial reformation and favored a far more radical reform movement. Collectively called the Anabaptists, these radicals actually formed a large variety of groups who nevertheless shared some common characteristics. Anabaptism was especially attractive to the peasants, weavers, miners, and artisans who had been adversely affected by the economic changes of the age.

A Reformation Debate: The Marburg Colloquy

Debates played a crucial role in the Reformation period. They were a primary instrument in introducing the Reformation into innumerable cities as well as a means of resolving differences among like-minded Protestant groups. This selection contains an excerpt from the vivacious and often brutal debate between Luther and Zwingli over the sacrament of the Lord's Supper at Marburg in 1529. The two protagonists failed to reach agreement.

The Marburg Colloquy, 1529

THE HESSIAN CHANCELLOR FEIGE: My gracious prince and lord [Landgrave Philip of Hesse] has summoned you for the express and urgent purpose of settling the dispute over the sacrament of the Lord's Supper.... And let everyone on both sides present his arguments in a spirit of moderation, as becomes such matters.... Now then, Doctor Luther, you may proceed.

LUTHER: Noble prince, gracious lord! Undoubtedly the colloquy is well intentioned.... Although I have no intention of changing my mind, which is firmly made up, I will nevertheless present the grounds of my belief and show where the others are in error.... Your basic contentions are these: In the last analysis you wish to prove that a body cannot be in two places at once, and you produce arguments about the unlimited body which are based on natural reason. I do not question how Christ can be God and man and how the two natures can be joined. For God is more powerful than all our ideas, and we must submit to his word.

Prove that Christ's body is not there where the Scripture says, "This is my body!" Rational proofs I will not listen to.... God is beyond all mathematics and the words of God are to be revered and carried out in awe. It is God who commands, "Take, eat, this is my body." I request, therefore, valid scriptural proof to the contrary.

Luther writes on the table in chalk, "This is my body," and covers the words with a velvet cloth.

OECOLAMPADIUS [leader of the reform movement in Basel and a Zwinglian partisan]: The sixth chapter of John clarifies the other scriptural passages. Christ is not speaking there about a local presence. "The flesh is of no avail," he says. It is not my intention to employ rational, or geometrical, arguments—neither am I denying the power of God—but as long as I have the complete faith I will speak from that. For Christ is risen; he sits at the right hand of God; and so he cannot be present in the bread. Our view is neither new nor sacrilegious, but is based on faith and Scripture....

ZWINGLI: I insist that the words of the Lord's Supper must be figurative. This is ever apparent, and even required by the article of faith: "taken up into heaven, seated at the right hand of the Father." Otherwise, it would be absurd to look for him in the Lord's Supper at the same time that Christ is telling us that he is in heaven. One and the same body cannot possibly be in different places....

LUTHER: I call upon you as before: your basic contentions are shaky. Give way, and give glory to God!

ZWINGLI: And we call upon you to give glory to God and to quit begging the question! The issue at stake is this: Where is the proof of your position? I am willing to consider your words carefully—no harm meant! You're trying to outwit me. I stand by this passage in the sixth chapter of John, verse 63, and shall not be shaken from it. You'll have to sing another tune.

LUTHER: You're being obnoxious.

ZWINGLI: (*excitedly*) Don't you believe that Christ was attempting in John 6 to help those who did not understand?

LUTHER: You're trying to dominate things! You insist on passing judgment! Leave that to someone else!... It is your point that must be proved, not mine. But let us stop this sort of thing. It serves no purpose.

ZWINGLI: It certainly does! It is for you to prove that the passage in John 6 speaks of a physical repast.

LUTHER: You express yourself poorly and make about as much progress as a cane standing in a corner. You're going nowhere.

ZWINGLI: No, no, no! This is the passage that will break your neck!

LUTHER: Don't be so sure of yourself. Necks don't break this way. You're in Hesse, not Switzerland.

Anabaptists everywhere held certain ideas in common. All felt that the true Christian church was a voluntary association of believers who had undergone spiritual rebirth and had then been baptized into the church. Anabaptists advocated adult rather than infant baptism. They also tried to return literally to the practices and spirit of early Christianity. Adhering to the accounts of early Christian communities in the New Testament, they followed a strict sort of democracy in which all believers were considered equal. Each church chose its own minister, who might be any member of the community, since all Christians were considered priests (though women were often excluded). Those chosen as ministers had the duty to lead services, which were very simple and contained nothing not found in the early church. Anabaptists rejected theological speculation in favor of simple Christian living according to what they believed was the pure word of God. The Lord's Supper was interpreted as a remembrance, a meal of fellowship celebrated in the evening in private houses according to Jesus' example. Finally, unlike the Catholics and other Protestants, most Anabaptists believed in the complete separation of church and state. Not only was government to be excluded from the realm of religion, but it was not even supposed to exercise political jurisdiction over real Christians. Anabaptists refused to hold political office or bear arms because many took literally the commandment "Thou shall not kill," although some Anabaptist groups did become quite violent. Their political beliefs as much as their religious beliefs caused the Anabaptists to be regarded as dangerous radicals who threatened the very fabric of sixteenth-century society. Indeed, the chief thing Protestants and Catholics could agree on was the need to persecute Anabaptists.

One early group of Anabaptists known as the Swiss Brethren arose in Zürich. Their ideas frightened Zwingli, and they were soon expelled from the city. As their teachings spread through southern Germany, the Austrian Habsburg lands, and Switzerland, Anabaptists suffered ruthless persecution, especially after the Peasants' War of 1524–1525, when the upper classes resorted to repression. Virtually stamped out in Germany, Anabaptist survivors emerged in Moravia and Poland, and in the Netherlands, Anabaptism took on a strange form.

In the 1530s, the city of Münster in Westphalia in northwestern Germany near the Dutch border was the site of an Anabaptist uprising that determined the fate of Dutch Anabaptism. Seat of a powerful Catholic prince-bishop, Münster had experienced severe economic disasters, including crop failure and plague. Although converted to Lutheranism in 1532, Münster experienced a more radical mass religious hysteria that led to legal recognition for the Anabaptists. Soon Münster became a haven for Anabaptists from the surrounding neighborhood, especially the more wild-eyed variety known as Melchiorites who adhered to a vivid millenarianism. They believed that the end of the world was at hand and that they would usher in the kingdom of God with Münster as the New Jerusalem. By the end of February 1534, these millenarian Anabaptists had taken control of the city, driven out those they considered godless or unbelievers, burned all books except the Bible, and proclaimed communal ownership of all property. Eventually, the leadership of this New Jerusalem fell into the hands of one man, John of Leiden, who proclaimed himself king of the New Jerusalem. As king, he would lead out the elect from Münster to cover the entire world and purify it of evil by the sword in preparation for Jesus' Second Coming and the creation of a New Age. In this new kingdom, John of Leiden believed, all goods would be held in common and the saints would live without suffering.

But it was not to be. As the Catholic prince-bishop of Münster gathered a large force and laid siege to the city, the new king repeatedly had to postpone the ushering forth from Münster. Finally, after many inhabitants had starved, a joint army of Catholics and Lutherans recaptured the city in June 1535 and executed the radical Anabaptist leaders in a gruesome fashion. The New Jerusalem had ceased to exist.

Purged of its fantasies and its more extreme elements, Dutch Anabaptism reverted to its pacifist tendencies, especially evident in the work of Menno Simons (1496–1561), the man most responsible for rejuvenating Dutch Anabaptism. A popular leader, Menno dedicated his life to the spread of a peaceful, evangelical Anabaptism that stressed separation from the world in order to truly emulate the life of Jesus. Simons imposed strict discipline on his followers and banned those who refused to conform to the rules. The Mennonites, as his followers were called, spread from the Netherlands into northwestern Germany and eventually into Poland and Lithuania as well as the New World. Both the Mennonites and the Amish, who are also descended from the Anabaptists, maintain communities in the United States today.

The Reformation in England

The English Reformation was initiated by an act of state. King Henry VIII (1509–1547) wanted to divorce his first wife, Catherine of Aragon, who had failed to produce a male heir. Furthermore, Henry had fallen in love with Anne Boleyn, a lady-in-waiting to Queen Catherine. Anne's unwillingness to be only the king's mistress and the king's desire to have a legitimate male heir made their marriage imperative, but the king's first marriage stood in the way.

Henry relied on Cardinal Wolsey, the highest-ranking English church official and lord chancellor to the king, to obtain from Pope Clement VII an annulment of the king's marriage. Normally, the pope might have been willing to oblige, but the sack of Rome in 1527 had made the pope dependent on the Holy Roman Emperor Charles V, who happened to be the nephew of Queen Catherine. Discretion dictated delay in granting the English king's request. Impatient with the process, Henry dismissed Wolsey in 1529.

Two new advisers now became the king's agents in fulfilling his wishes. These were Thomas Cranmer (1489–1556), who became archbishop of Canterbury in 1532, and Thomas Cromwell (1485–1540), the king's principal secretary after the fall of Wolsey. They advised the king to obtain an annulment of his marriage in England's own ecclesiastical courts. The most important step toward this goal was the promulgation by Parliament of an act cutting off all appeals from English church courts to Rome, a piece of legislation that essentially abolished papal authority in England. Henry no longer needed the pope to obtain his annulment. He was now in a hurry because Anne Boleyn had become pregnant and he had secretly married her in January 1533 to legitimize the expected heir. In May, as archbishop of Canterbury and head of the highest ecclesiastical court in England, Thomas Cranmer ruled that the king's marriage to Catherine was "null and absolutely void" and then validated Henry's marriage to Anne. At the beginning of June, Anne was crowned queen. Three months later, a child was born. Much to the king's disappointment, the baby was a girl, whom they named Elizabeth.

In 1534, Parliament completed the break of the Church of England with Rome by passing the Act of Supremacy, which declared that the king was "taken, accepted, and reputed the only supreme head on earth of the Church of England." This meant that the English monarch now controlled the church in all matters of doctrine, clerical appointments, and discipline. In addition, Parliament passed the Treason Act, making it punishable by death to deny that the king was the supreme head of the church.

Few challenged the new order. One who did was Thomas More, the humanist and former lord chancellor, who saw clearly to the heart of the issue: loyalty to the pope in Rome was now treason in England. More refused to support the new laws and was duly tried for treason. At his trial, he asked, rhetorically, what the effect of the actions of the king and Parliament would be: "Therefore am I not bound . . . to conform my conscience to the Council of one realm [England] against the general Council of Christendom?"[8] Because his conscience could not accept the victory of the national state over the church, nor would he, as a Christian, bow his head to a secular ruler in matters of faith, More was beheaded in London on July 6, 1535.

Thomas Cromwell worked out the details of the Tudor government's new role in church affairs based on the centralized power exercised by the king and Parliament. Cromwell also came to his extravagant king's financial rescue with a daring plan for the dissolution of the monasteries. About four hundred religious houses were closed in 1536, and their land and possessions were confiscated by the king. Many were sold to nobles, gentry, and some merchants. The king added enormously to his treasury and also to his ranks of supporters, who now had a stake in the new Tudor order.

Although Henry VIII had broken with the papacy, little change occurred in matters of doctrine, theology, and ceremony. Some of his supporters, such as Archbishop Thomas Cranmer, wished to have a religious reformation as well as an administrative one, but Henry was unyielding. The last decade of Henry's reign was preoccupied with foreign affairs, factional intrigue, and a continued effort to find the perfect wife. Henry soon tired of Anne Boleyn and had her beheaded in 1536 on a charge of adultery. His third wife, Jane Seymour, produced the long-awaited male heir but died during childbirth. His fourth marriage to Anne of Cleves, a German princess, was arranged for political reasons and on the basis of a painted portrait. Henry was shocked at her physical appearance when he first saw her in person and soon divorced her. His fifth wife, Catherine Howard, was more attractive but less moral. When she committed adultery, Henry had her beheaded. His last wife was Catherine Parr, who married the king in 1543 and outlived him. Henry was succeeded by the underage and sickly Edward VI (1547–1553), the son of his third wife.

Since the new king was only nine years old at the time of his accession to the throne, real control of England passed to a council of regency. During Edward's reign, Archbishop Cranmer and others inclined toward Protestant doctrines were able to move the Church of England in a more Protestant direction. New acts of Parliament instituted the right of the clergy to marry, the elimination of images, and the creation of a revised Protestant liturgy that was elaborated in a new prayer book and liturgical guide known as the Book of Common Prayer. These rapid changes in doctrine and liturgy aroused much opposition and prepared the way for the reaction that occurred when Mary, Henry's first daughter by Catherine of Aragon, came to the throne.

There was no doubt that Mary (1553–1558) was a Catholic who intended to restore England to Roman

Henry VIII, His Wife, and His Children. The desire of Henry VIII for a male heir played a significant role in his break with the Catholic church. Pictured here in the central panel of this 1545 portrait by an unknown artist are Henry VIII, Jane Seymour, his third wife, and Prince Edward, who became King Edward VI in 1547. On the far left is Princess Mary and on the far right is Princess Elizabeth.

Catholicism. But her restoration of Catholicism, achieved by joint action of the monarch and Parliament, aroused opposition. There was widespread antipathy to Mary's unfortunate marriage to Philip II, the son of Charles V and the future king of Spain. Philip was strongly disliked in England, and Mary's foreign policy of alliance with Spain aroused further hostility, especially when her forces lost Calais, the last English possession from the Hundred Years' War. The burning of more than three hundred Protestant heretics aroused further ire against "bloody Mary." As a result of her policies, Mary managed to achieve the opposite of what she had intended: England was more Protestant by the end of her reign than it had been at the beginning. When she came to power, Protestantism had become identified with church destruction and religious anarchy. Now people identified it with English resistance to Spanish interference. The death of Mary in 1558 ended the restoration of Catholicism in England.

John Calvin and Calvinism

Of the second generation of Protestant reformers, one stands out as the systematic theologian and organizer of the Protestant movement—John Calvin (1509–1564). Calvin received a remarkably diverse education in humanistic studies and law in his native France. He was also influenced by Luther's writings, which were being circulated and read by French intellectuals as early as 1523. In 1533, Calvin experienced a religious crisis that determined the rest of his life's work. He described it in these words:

> God, by a sudden conversion, subdued and brought my mind to a teachable frame, which was more hardened in such matters than might have been expected from one at my early period of life. Having thus received some taste and knowledge of true godliness, I was immediately inflamed with so intense a desire to make progress therein, although I did not leave off other studies, I yet pursued them with less ardor.[9]

Calvin's conversion was solemn and straightforward. He was so convinced of the inner guidance of God that he became the most determined of all the Protestant reformers.

After his conversion and newfound conviction, Calvin was no longer safe in Paris, since King Francis I periodically persecuted Protestants. Eventually, Calvin made his way to Basel, where in 1536 he published the first edition of the *Institutes of the Christian Religion,* a masterful synthesis of Protestant thought that immediately secured his reputation as one of the new leaders of Protestantism.

On most important doctrines, Calvin stood very close to Luther. He adhered to the doctrine of justification by faith alone to explain how humans achieved salvation. But Calvin also placed much emphasis on the absolute sovereignty of God or the "power, grace, and glory of God." Thus "God asserts his possession of omnipotence, and claims our acknowledgment of this attribute; not such as is imagined by sophists, vain, idle, and almost asleep, but vigilant, efficacious, operative and engaged in continual action."[10]

One of the ideas derived from his emphasis on the absolute sovereignty of God—predestination—gave a unique cast

John Calvin. After a conversion experience, John Calvin abandoned his life as a humanist and became a reformer. In 1536, Calvin began working to reform the city of Geneva, where he remained until his death in 1564. This sixteenth-century portrait of Calvin pictures him near the end of his life.

to Calvin's teachings. This "eternal decree," as Calvin called it, meant that God had predestined some people to be saved (the elect) and others to be damned (the reprobate). According to Calvin, "He has once for all determined, both whom he would admit to salvation, and whom he would condemn to destruction."[11] Calvin identified three tests that might indicate possible salvation: an open profession of faith, a "decent and godly life," and participation in the sacraments of baptism and communion. In no instance did Calvin ever suggest that worldly success or material wealth was a sign of election. Most important, although Calvin stressed that there could be no absolute certainty of salvation, some of his followers did not always make this distinction. The practical psychological effect of predestination was to give some later Calvinists an unshakable conviction that they were doing God's work on earth. Thus Calvinism became a dynamic and activist faith. It is no accident that Calvinism became the militant international form of Protestantism.

To Calvin, the church was a divine institution responsible for preaching the word of God and administering the sacraments. Calvin kept only two sacraments, baptism and the Lord's Supper. Baptism was a sign of the remission of sins. Calvin believed in the real presence of Jesus in the

The Role of Discipline in the "Most Perfect School of Christ on Earth"

John Calvin had emphasized in his reform movement that the church should have the ability to enforce proper behavior. Consequently, the Ecclesiastical Ordinances of 1541, the constitution of the church in Geneva, provided for an order of elders whose function was to cooperate with the pastors in maintaining discipline, "to have oversight of the life of everyone," as Calvin expressed it. These selections form the official records of the Consistory show the nature of its work.

Reports of the Genevan Consistory

Donna Jane Peterman is questioned concerning her faith and why she does not receive communion and attend worship. She confesses her faith and believes in one God and wants to come to God and the holy Church and has no other faith. She recited the Lord's Prayer in the vernacular. She said that she believes what the Church believes. Is questioned why she never participates in communion when it is celebrated in this town, but goes to other places. She answers that she goes where it seems good to her. Is placed outside the faith.

The sister of Sr. Curtet, Lucresse, to whom remonstrances have been made on account of her going with certain monies to have Masses said at Nessy by the monks of St. Claire. Questioned whether she has no scruples as to what she says. Replied that her father and mother have brought her up to obey a different law from the one now in force here. However, she does not desire the present law. Asked as to when was the festival of St. Felix, she replied that it was yesterday. Asked if she had not fasted, she replied that she fasted when it pleased her. Asked if she did not desire to pray to a single God; said that she did. Asked if she did not pray to St. Felix; said that she prayed to St. Felix and other saints who interceded for her. She is very obstinate. Decision that she be sent to some minister of her choice every sermon day and that the Lord's Supper be withheld from her.

At about this time, by resolution of the Consistory . . . the marriage contracted between the widow of Jean Archard, aged more than 70, and a servant of hers, aged about 27 or 28, was dissolved because of the too great inequality of age. The Consistory resolved further that Messieurs should be requested to make a ruling on this matter for the future.

sacrament of the Lord's Supper, but only in a spiritual sense. Jesus' body is at the right hand of God and thus cannot be in the sacrament, but to the believer, Jesus is spiritually present in the Lord's Supper.

Up to 1536, John Calvin had essentially been a scholar. But in that year, he took up a ministry in Geneva that lasted until his death in 1564. Calvin achieved a major success in 1541 when the city council accepted his new church constitution, known as the Ecclesiastical Ordinances. This document created a church government that used both clergy and laymen in the service of the church. The Consistory, a special body for enforcing moral discipline, was set up as a court to oversee the moral life and doctrinal purity of Genevans (see the box above). As its power increased, the Consistory went from "fraternal corrections" to the use of public penance and excommunication. More serious cases could be turned over to the city council for punishments greater than excommunication. During Calvin's last years, stricter laws against blasphemy were enacted and enforced with banishment and public whippings.

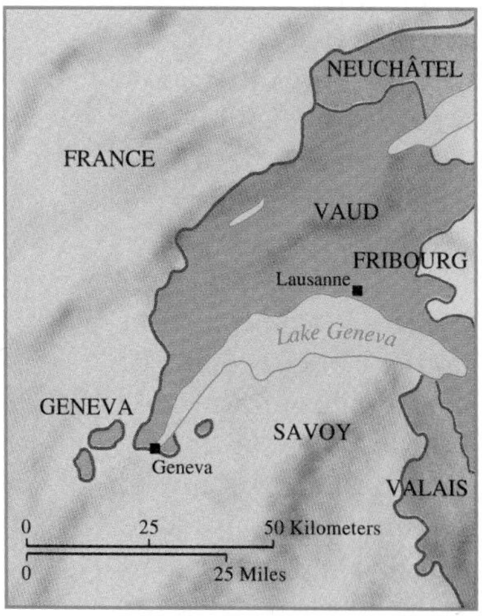

Calvin's Geneva

Calvin's success in Geneva enabled the city to become a vibrant center of Protestantism. John Knox, the Calvinist reformer of Scotland, called it "the most perfect school of Christ on earth." Following Calvin's lead, missionaries trained in Geneva were sent to all parts of Europe. Calvinism became established in France, the Netherlands, Scotland, and central and eastern Europe. By the mid-sixteenth century, Calvinism had replaced Lutheranism as the international form of Protestantism, and Calvin's Geneva stood as the fortress of the Reformation.

The Social Impact of the Protestant Reformation

Because Christianity was such an integral part of European life, it was inevitable that the Reformation would have an impact on the family, education, and popular religious practices.

The Family

For centuries, Catholicism had praised the family and sanctified its existence by making marriage a sacrament. But the Catholic church's high regard for abstinence from sex as the surest way to holiness made the celibate state of the clergy preferable to marriage. Nevertheless, because not all men

A Protestant Woman

In the initial zeal of the Protestant Reformation, women were frequently allowed to play unusual roles. Katherine Zell of Germany (c. 1497–1562) first preached beside her husband in 1527. After the death of her two children, she devoted the rest of her life to helping her husband and their Anabaptist faith. This selection is taken from one of her letters to a young Lutheran minister who had criticized her activities.

Katherine Zell to Ludwig Rabus of Memmingen

I, Katherine Zell, wife of the late lamented Mathew Zell, who served in Strasbourg, where I was born and reared and still live, wish you peace and enhancement in God's grace. . . .

From my earliest years I turned to the Lord, who taught and guided me, and I have at all times, in accordance with my understanding and His grace, embraced the interests of His church and earnestly sought Jesus. Even in youth this brought me the regard and affection of clergymen and others much concerned with the church, which is why the pious Mathew Zell wanted me as a companion in marriage; and I, in turn, to serve the glory of Christ, gave devotion and help to my husband, both in his ministry and in keeping his house. . . . Ever since I was ten years old I have been a student and a sort of church mother, much given to attending sermons. I have loved and frequented the company of learned men, and I conversed much with them, not about dancing, masquerades, and worldly pleasures but about the kingdom of God. . . .

Consider the poor Anabaptists, who are so furiously and ferociously persecuted. Must the authorities everywhere be incited against them, as the hunter drives his dog against wild animals? Against those who acknowledge Christ the Lord in very much the same way we do and over which we broke with the papacy? Just because they cannot agree with us on lesser things, is this any reason to persecute them and in them Christ, in whom they fervently believe and have often professed in misery, in prison, and under the torments of fire and water?

Governments may punish criminals, but they should not force and govern belief, which is a matter for the heart and conscience not for temporal authorities. . . . When the authorities pursue one, they soon bring forth tears, and towns and villages are emptied.

could remain chaste, marriage offered the best means to control sexual intercourse and give it a purpose, the procreation of children. To some extent, this attitude persisted among the Protestant reformers; Luther, for example, argued that sex in marriage allowed one to "make use of this sex in order to avoid sin," and Calvin advised that every man should "abstain from marriage only so long as he is fit to observe celibacy." If "his power to tame lust fails him," then he must marry.

But the Reformation did bring some change to the conception of the family. Both Catholic and Protestant clergy preached sermons advocating a more positive side to family relationships. The Protestants were especially important in developing this new view of the family. Because Protestantism had eliminated any idea of special holiness for celibacy, abolishing both monasticism and a celibate clergy, the family could be placed at the center of human life, and a new stress on "mutual love between man and wife" could be extolled. But were doctrine and reality the same? For more radical religious groups, at times they were (see the box above). One Anabaptist wrote to his wife before his execution: "My faithful helper, my loyal friend. I praise God that he gave you to me, you who have sustained me in all my trial."[12] But more often reality reflected the traditional roles of husband as the ruler and wife as the obedient servant whose chief duty was to please her husband. Luther stated it clearly:

> The rule remains with the husband, and the wife is compelled to obey him by God's command. He rules the home and the state, wages war, defends his possessions, tills the soil, builds, plants, etc. The woman on the other hand is like a nail driven into the wall . . . so the wife should stay at home and look after the affairs of the household, as one who has been deprived of the ability of administering those affairs that are outside and that concern the state. She does not go beyond her most personal duties.[13]

But obedience to her husband was not a wife's only role; her other important duty was to bear children. To Calvin and Luther, this function of women was part of the divine plan. God punishes women for the sins of Eve by the burdens of procreation and feeding and nurturing their children, but, said Luther, "it is a gladsome punishment if you consider the hope of eternal life and the honor of motherhood which had been left to her."[14] Although the Protestant reformers sanctified this role of woman as mother and wife, viewing it as a holy vocation, Protestantism also left few alternatives for women. Because monasticism had been destroyed, that career avenue was no longer available; for most Protestant women, family life was their only destiny. At the same time, by emphasizing the father as "ruler" and hence the center of household religion, Protestantism even removed the woman from her traditional role as controller of religion in the home.

Protestant reformers called on men and women to read the Bible and participate in religious services together. In this way, the reformers provided a stimulus for the education of girls so they could read the Bible and other religious literature. The city council of Zwickau, for example, established a girls' school in 1525. But these schools were designed to encourage proper moral values rather than intellectual development and really did little to improve the position of women in society. Likewise, when women attempted to take more active roles in religious life, reformers—Lutheran and Calvinist alike—shrank back in horror. To them, the equality of the Gospel did not mean overthrowing the inequality of social classes or the sexes. Overall, the Protestant Reformation did not noticeably transform women's subordinate place in society.

Education in the Reformation

The Reformation had an important effect on the development of education in Europe. Renaissance humanism had significantly altered the content of education, and Protestant educators were very successful in implementing and using humanist methods in Protestant secondary schools and universities. Unlike the humanist schools, however, which had been mostly for an elite, the sons and a few daughters of the nobility and wealthier bourgeoisie, Protestant schools were aimed at a much wider audience. Protestantism created an increased need for at least a semiliterate body of believers who could read the Bible for themselves.

While adopting the classical emphasis of humanist schools, Protestant reformers broadened the base of the people being educated. Convinced of the need to provide the church with good Christians and good pastors as well as the state with good administrators and citizens, Martin Luther advocated that all children should have the opportunity of an education provided by the state. To that end, he urged the cities and villages of Saxony to establish schools paid for by the public. Luther's ideas were shared by his Wittenberg coworker, Philip Melanchthon, whose educational efforts earned him the title of *Praecepter Germaniae,* the Teacher of Germany. In his scheme for education in Saxony, Melanchthon divided students into three classes or divisions based on their age or capabilities.

Following Melanchthon's example, the Protestants in Germany were responsible for introducing the gymnasium, or secondary school, where the humanist emphasis on the liberal arts based on instruction in Greek and Latin was combined with religious instruction. Most famous was the school in Strasbourg founded by Johannes Sturm in 1538, which served as a model for other Protestant schools. John Calvin's Genevan Academy, founded in 1559, was organized in two distinct parts. The "private school" or gymnasium was divided into seven classes for young people who were taught Latin and Greek grammar and literature as well as logic. In the "public school," students were taught philosophy, Hebrew, Greek, and theology. The Genevan Academy, which eventually became a university, came to concentrate on preparing ministers to spread the Calvinist view of the Gospel.

Religious Practices and Popular Culture

The attacks of Protestant reformers on the Catholic church led to radical changes in religious practices. The Protestant Reformation abolished or severely curtailed such customary practices as indulgences, the veneration of relics and saints, pilgrimages, monasticism, and clerical celibacy. The elimination of saints put an end to the numerous celebrations of religious holy days and changed a community's sense of time. Thus in Protestant communities, religious ceremonies and imagery, such as processions and statues, tended to be replaced with individual private prayer, family worship, and collective prayer and worship at the same time each week on Sunday.

In addition to abolishing saints' days and religious carnivals, some Protestant reformers even tried to eliminate customary forms of entertainment. The Puritans (as English Calvinists were called), for example, attempted to ban drinking in taverns, dramatic performances, and dancing. Dutch Calvinists denounced the tradition of giving small presents to children on the feast of Saint Nicholas, in

A Sixteenth-Century Classroom. Protestants in Germany developed secondary schools that combined instruction in the liberal arts with religious education. This scene from a painting by Ambrosius Holbein shows a schoolmaster instructing a pupil in the alphabet while his wife helps a little girl.

early December. Many of these Protestant attacks on popular culture were unsuccessful, however. The importance of taverns in English social life made it impossible to eradicate them, and celebrating at Christmas time persisted in the Dutch Netherlands.

The Catholic Reformation

By the mid-sixteenth century, Lutheranism had become established in parts of Germany and Scandinavia, and Calvinism in parts of Switzerland, France, the Netherlands, and eastern Europe (see Map 13.2). In England, the split from Rome had resulted in the creation of a national church. The situation in Europe did not look particularly favorable for the Roman Catholic church. But even at the beginning of the sixteenth century, constructive, positive forces were at work for reform within the Catholic church, and by the mid-sixteenth century, they came to be directed by a revived and reformed papacy, giving the Catholic church new strength. We call the story of the revival of Roman Catholicism the Catholic Reformation, although some historians prefer to use the term Counter-Reformation, especially for those elements of the Catholic Reformation that were directly aimed at stopping the spread of Protestantism.

The Catholic Reformation was a mixture of old and new elements. The best features of medieval Catholicism were revived and then adjusted to meet new conditions, a situation most apparent in the revival of mysticism and monasticism. The emergence of a new mysticism, closely tied to the traditions of Catholic piety, was especially evident in the life of the Spanish mystic Saint Teresa of Avila (1515–1582). A nun of the Carmelite order, Teresa experienced a variety of mystical visions that she claimed resulted in the ecstatic union of her soul with God. But Teresa also believed that mystical experience should lead to an active life of service on behalf of her Catholic faith. Consequently, she founded a new order of barefoot Carmelite nuns and worked to foster their mystical experiences.

The regeneration of religious orders also proved valuable to the reform of Catholicism. Old orders, such as the Benedictines and Dominicans, were reformed and renewed. The Capuchins emerged when a group of Franciscans decided to return to the simplicity and poverty of Saint Francis of Assisi, the medieval founder of the Franciscan order. In addition to caring for the sick and the poor, the Capuchins focused on preaching the Gospel directly to the people and emerged as an effective force against Protestantism.

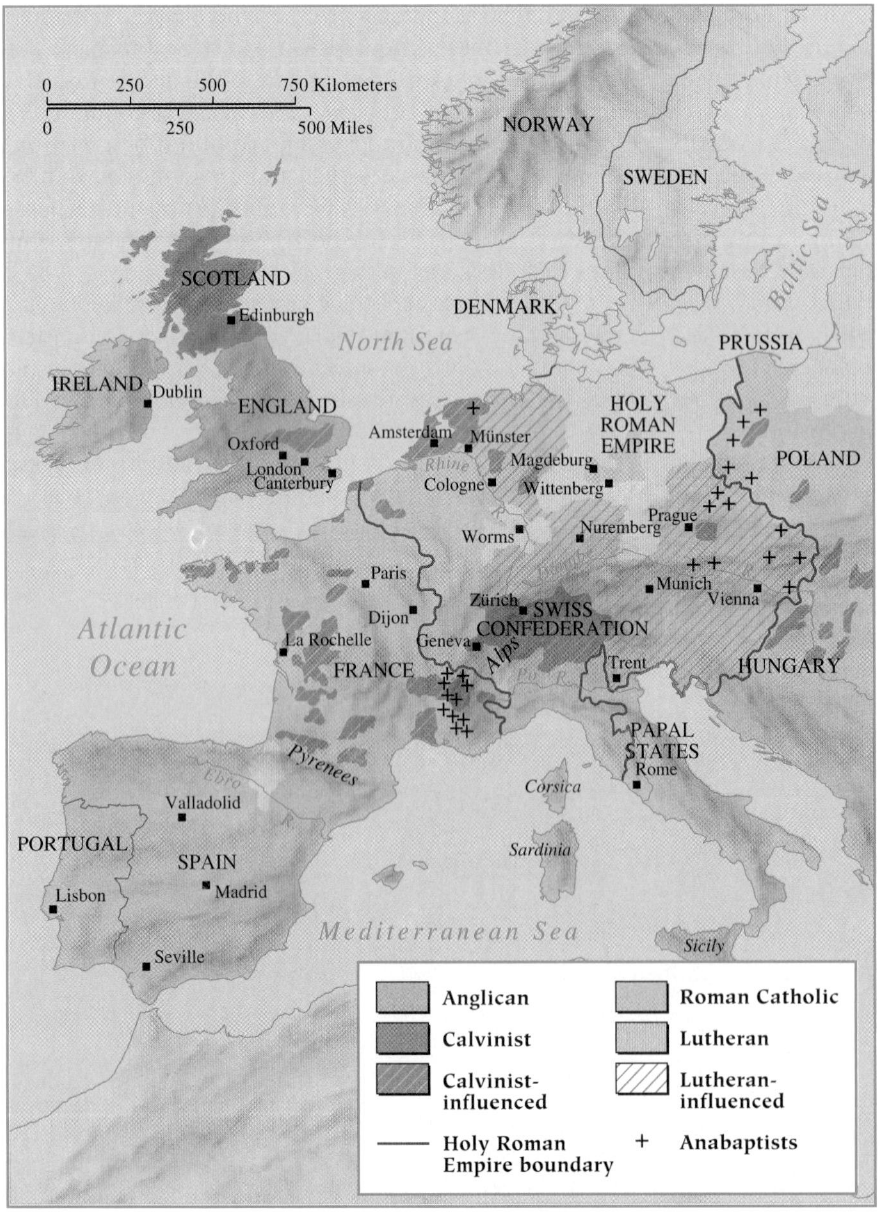

Map 13.2 Catholics and Protestants in Europe by 1560. The Reformation continued to evolve beyond the basic split of the Lutherans from the Catholics. Several Protestant sects broke away from the teachings of Martin Luther, each with a separate creed and different ways of worship. In England, Henry VIII broke with the Catholic church for political and dynastic reasons. ■ Which areas of Europe were solidly Catholic, which were solidly Lutheran, and which were neither?

New religious orders and brotherhoods were also created. The Theatines, founded in 1524, placed their emphasis on reforming the secular clergy and encouraging those clerics to fulfill their duties among the laity. The Theatines also founded orphanages and hospitals to care for the victims of war and plague. The Ursulines, a new order of nuns founded in Italy in 1535, focused their attention on establishing schools for the education of girls.

The Oratory of Divine Love, first organized in Italy in 1497, was not a new religious order but an informal group of clergy and laymen who worked to foster reform by emphasizing personal spiritual development and outward acts of charity. The "philosophy of Christ," advocated by the Christian humanist Erasmus, was especially appealing to many of them. The Oratory's members included a number of cardinals who favored the reform of the Catholic church.

The Society of Jesus

Of all the new religious orders, the most important was the Society of Jesus, known as the Jesuits, who became the chief instrument of the Catholic Reformation. The Society of Jesus was founded by a Spanish nobleman, Ignatius of Loyola (1491–1556), whose injuries in battle cut short his military career. Loyola experienced a spiritual torment similar to Luther's but, unlike Luther, resolved his problems not by a new doctrine but by a decision to submit his will to the will of the church. Unable to be a real soldier, he vowed to be a soldier of God. Over a period of twelve years, Loyola prepared for his lifework by prayer, pilgrimages, going to school, and working out a spiritual program in his brief but powerful book, *The Spiritual Exercises.* This was a training manual for spiritual development emphasizing exercises by which the human will could be strengthened and made to follow the will of God as manifested through his instrument, the Catholic church (see the box on p. 358).

Loyola gathered together a small group of individuals who were eventually recognized as a religious order, the Society of Jesus, by a papal bull in 1540. The new order was grounded on the principles of absolute obedience to the papacy, a strict hierarchical order for the society, the use of education to achieve its goals, and a dedication to engage in "conflict for God." Jesuit organization came to resemble the structure of a military command. A two-year novitiate weeded out all but the most dedicated. Executive leadership was put in the hands of a general, who nominated all-important positions in the order and was to be revered as the absolute head of the order. Loyola served as the first general of the order until his death in 1556. A special vow of absolute obedience to the pope made the Jesuits an important instrument for papal policy.

The Jesuits pursued three major activities. They established highly disciplined schools, borrowing freely from humanist schools for their educational methods. To the Jesuits, the thorough education of young people was crucial to combating the advance of Protestantism. In the course of the sixteenth century, the Jesuits took over the premier academic posts in Catholic universities, and by 1600, they were the most famous educators in Europe. Another prominent Jesuit activity was the propagation of the Catholic faith among non-Christians. Francis Xavier (1506–1552), one of the original members of the Society of Jesus, carried the message of Catholic Christianity to the East, ministering to India and Japan before dying of fever. Although conversion efforts in Japan proved short-lived,

Ignatius of Loyola. The Jesuits became the most important new religious order of the Catholic Reformation. Shown here in a sixteenth-century painting by an unknown artist is Ignatius of Loyola, founder of the Society of Jesus. Loyola is seen kneeling before Pope Paul III, who officially recognized the Jesuits in 1540.

Loyola and Obedience to "Our Holy Mother, the Hierarchical Church"

In his *Spiritual Exercises,* Ignatius of Loyola developed a systematic program for "the conquest of self and the regulation of one's life" for service to the hierarchical Catholic church. Ignatius' supreme goal was the commitment of the Christian to active service under Jesus' banner in the Church of Christ (the Catholic church). In the final section of the *Spiritual Exercises,* Loyola explained the nature of that commitment in a series of "Rules for Thinking with the Church."

Ignatius of Loyola, "Rules for Thinking with the Church"

The following rules should be observed to foster the true attitude of mind we ought to have in the Church militant.

1. We must put aside all judgment of our own, and keep the mind ever ready and prompt to obey in all things the true Spouse of Jesus Christ, our holy Mother, the hierarchical Church.
2. We should praise sacramental confession, the yearly reception of the Most Blessed Sacrament [the Lord's Supper], and praise more highly monthly reception, and still more weekly Communion. . . .
3. We ought to praise the frequent hearing of Mass, the singing of hymns, psalmody, and long prayers whether in the church or outside. . . .
4. We must praise highly religious life, virginity, and contingency; and matrimony ought not be praised as much as any of these.
5. We should praise vows of religion, obedience, poverty, chastity, and vows to perform other works of supererogation conducive to perfection. . . .
6. We should show our esteem for the relics of the saints by venerating them and praying to the saints. We should praise visits to the Station Churches, pilgrimages, indulgences, jubilees, the lighting of candles in churches.
7. We must praise the regulations of the Church, with regard to fast and abstinence, for example, in Lent, on Ember Days, Vigils, Fridays, and Saturdays.
8. We ought to praise not only the building and adornment of churches, but also images and veneration of them according to the subject they represent.
9. Finally, we must praise all the commandments of the Church, and be on the alert to find reasons to defend them, and by no means in order to criticize them.
10. We should be more ready to approve and praise the orders, recommendations, and way of acting of our superiors than to find fault with them. Though some of the orders, etc., may not have been praiseworthy, yet to speak against them, either when preaching in public or in speaking before the people, would rather be the cause of murmuring and scandal than of profit. As a consequence, the people would become angry with their superiors, whether secular or spiritual. But while it does harm in the absence of our superiors to speak evil of them before the people, it may be profitable to discuss their bad conduct with those who can apply a remedy. . . .
13. If we wish to proceed securely in all things, we must hold fast to the following principle: What seems to me white, I will believe black if the hierarchical Church so defines. For I must be convinced that in Christ our Lord, the bridegroom, and in His spouse the Church, only one Spirit holds sway, which governs and rules for the salvation of souls.

Jesuit activity in China, especially that of the Italian Matteo Ricci, was more long-lasting. Finally, the Jesuits were determined to carry the Catholic banner and fight Protestantism. Jesuit missionaries proved singularly successful in restoring Catholicism to parts of Germany and eastern Europe. Poland was largely won back for the Catholic church through Jesuit efforts.

A Revived Papacy

The involvement of the Renaissance papacy in dubious finances and Italian political and military affairs had given rise to numerous sources of corruption. The meager steps taken to control corruption left the papacy still in need of serious reform, and it took the jolt of the Protestant Reformation to bring it about.

The pontificate of Pope Paul III (1534–1549) proved to be a turning point in the reform of the papacy. Raised in the lap of Renaissance luxury, Paul III continued Renaissance papal practices by appointing his nephews as cardinals, involving himself in politics, and patronizing arts and letters on a lavish scale. Nevertheless, he perceived the need for change and expressed it decisively. Advocates of reform, such as Gasparo Contarini and Gian Pietro Caraffa, were made cardinals. In 1535, Paul took the audacious step of appointing a reform commission to study the church's condition. The commission's report in 1537 blamed the church's problems on the corrupt policies of popes and cardinals. Paul III also formally recognized the Jesuits and summoned the Council of Trent (see next section).

A decisive turning point in the direction of the Catholic Reformation and the nature of papal reform came in the 1540s. In 1541, a colloquy had been held at Regensburg in a final attempt to settle the religious division peacefully. Here Catholic moderates, such as Cardinal Contarini, who favored concessions to Protestants in the hope of restoring Christian unity, reached a compromise with Protestant moderates on a number of doctrinal issues.

When Contarini returned to Rome with these proposals, Cardinal Caraffa and other hard-liners, who regarded all compromise with Protestant innovations as heresy, accused him of selling out to the heretics. It soon became apparent that the conservative reformers were in the ascendancy when Caraffa was able to persuade Paul III to establish the Roman Inquisition or Holy Office in 1542 to ferret out doctrinal errors. There was to be no compromise with Protestantism.

When Cardinal Caraffa was chosen pope as Paul IV (1555–1559), he so increased the power of the Inquisition that even liberal cardinals were silenced. This "first true pope of the Catholic Counter-Reformation," as he has been called, also created the Index of Forbidden Books, a list of books that Catholics were not allowed to read. It included all the works of Protestant theologians as well as authors considered "unwholesome," a category general enough to include the works of Erasmus. Rome, the capital of Catholic Christianity, was rapidly becoming Fortress Rome; any hope of restoring Christian unity by compromise was fast fading. The activities of the Council of Trent made compromise virtually impossible.

The Council of Trent

In 1542, Pope Paul III took the decisive step of calling for a general council of Christendom to resolve the religious differences created by the Protestant revolt. It was not until March 1545, however, that a group of cardinals, archbishops, bishops, abbots, and theologians met in the city of Trent on the border between Germany and Italy and initiated the Council of Trent, which met intermittently from 1545 to 1563 in three major sessions. Moderate Catholic reformers hoped compromises would be made in formulating doctrinal definitions that would encourage Protestants to return to the church. Conservatives, however, favored an uncompromising restatement of Catholic doctrines in strict opposition to Protestant positions. The latter group won, although not without a struggle.

The final doctrinal decrees of the Council of Trent reaffirmed traditional Catholic teachings in opposition to Protestant beliefs. Scripture and tradition were affirmed as equal authorities in religious matters; only the church could interpret Scripture. Both faith and good works were declared necessary for salvation. The seven sacraments, the Catholic doctrine of transubstantiation, and clerical celibacy were all upheld. Belief in purgatory and in the efficacy of indulgences was affirmed, although the hawking of indulgences was prohibited. Of the reforming decrees that were passed, the most important established theological seminaries in every diocese for the training of priests.

After the Council of Trent, the Roman Catholic church possessed a clear body of doctrine and a unified church under the acknowledged supremacy of the popes, who had triumphed over bishops and councils. The Roman Catholic church had become one Christian denomination among many with an organizational framework and doctrinal pattern that would not be significantly altered for four hundred years. With a new spirit of confidence, the Catholic church entered a militant phase, as well prepared as the Calvinists to do battle for the Lord. An era of religious warfare was about to unfold.

Politics and the Wars of Religion in the Sixteenth Century

By the middle of the sixteenth century, Calvinism and Catholicism had become militant religions dedicated to spreading the word of God as they interpreted it. Although this struggle for the minds and hearts of Europeans is at the heart of the religious wars of the sixteenth century, economic, social, and political forces also played an important role in these conflicts. Of the sixteenth-century religious wars, none were more momentous or shattering than the French civil wars known as the French Wars of Religion.

The French Wars of Religion (1562–1598)

Religion was at the heart of the French civil wars of the sixteenth century. Concerned by the growth of Calvinism, the French kings tried to stop its spread by persecuting Calvinists but had little success. Huguenots (as the French Calvinists were called) came from all levels of society: artisans and shopkeepers hurt by rising prices and a rigid guild system; merchants and lawyers in provincial towns whose local privileges were tenuous; and members of the nobility. Possibly 40 to 50 percent of the French nobility became Huguenots, including the house of Bourbon, which stood next to the Valois in the royal line of succession and ruled the southern French kingdom of Navarre. The conversion of so many nobles made the Huguenots a potentially dangerous political threat to monarchical power. Though the Calvinists constituted only about 7 percent of the population, they were a strong-willed and well-organized minority.

The Catholic majority greatly outnumbered the Calvinist minority. The Valois monarchy was staunchly Catholic, and its control of the Catholic church gave it little incentive to look favorably upon Protestantism. When King Henry II (1547–1559) was killed accidentally in a tournament, he was succeeded by a series of weak and neurotic sons, two of whom were dominated by their mother, Catherine de' Medici (1519–1589). As regent for her sons, the moderate Catholic Catherine looked to religious compromise as a way to defuse the political tensions but found to her consternation that both sides possessed their share of religious fanatics unwilling to make concessions. The extreme Catholic party—known as the ultra-Catholics—favored strict opposition to the Huguenots and was led by the Guise family. Possessing the loyalty of Paris and large sections of northern and northwestern France through their client-patronage system, they could recruit and pay for large armies and received support abroad from the papacy and Jesuits who favored the Guises' uncompromising Catholic position.

The religious issue was not the only factor that contributed to the French civil wars. Towns and provinces, which had long resisted the growing power of monarchical centralization, were only too willing to join a revolt against the monarchy. This was also true of the nobility, and because so many of them were Calvinists, they formed an important base of opposition to the crown. The French Wars of Religion, then, presented a major constitutional crisis for France and temporarily halted the development of the French centralized territorial state. The claim of the state's ruling dynasty to a person's loyalties was temporarily superseded by loyalty to one's religious belief. For some people, the unity of France was less important than religious truth. But there also emerged in France a group of public figures who placed politics before religion and believed that no religious truth was worth the ravages of civil war. These *politiques* ultimately prevailed, but not until both sides were exhausted by bloodshed.

The wars erupted in 1562 when the powerful duke of Guise massacred a peaceful congregation of Huguenots at Vassy. In the decade of the 1560s, the Huguenots held their own. Too small a group to conquer France, their armies were so good at defensive campaigns that they could not be defeated either, despite the infamous Saint Bartholomew's Day massacre.

This massacre of Huguenots in August 1572 occurred at a time when the Catholic and Calvinist parties had apparently been reconciled through the marriage of the sister of the reigning Valois king, Charles IX (1560–1574), and Henry of Navarre, the Bourbon ruler of Navarre. Henry was the son of Jeanne d'Albret, queen of Navarre, who had been responsible for introducing Calvinist ideas into her kingdom. Henry was also the acknowledged political leader of the Huguenots, and many Huguenots traveled to Paris for the wedding.

But the Guise family persuaded the king and his mother, Catherine de' Medici, that this gathering of Huguenots posed a threat to them. Charles and his advisers decided to eliminate the Huguenot leaders with one swift blow. According to one French military leader, Charles and his advisers believed that civil war would soon break out anyway and that "it was better to win a battle in Paris, where all the leaders were, than to risk it in the field and fall into a dangerous and uncertain war."[15]

The massacre began early in the day on August 24 when the king's guards sought out and killed some prominent Huguenot leaders. These murders soon unleashed a

The Saint Bartholomew's Day Massacre. Although the outbreak of religious war seemed unlikely in France, the collapse of the strong monarchy with the death of Henry II unleashed forces that led to a series of civil wars. Pictured here is the Saint Bartholomew's Day massacre of 1572. This contemporary painting by the Huguenot artist François Dubois depicts a number of the incidents of that day when approximately three thousand Huguenots were murdered in Paris.

Musée cantonal des Beaux-Arts de Lausanne

CHRONOLOGY

The French Wars of Religion (1562–1598)

Henry II	1547–1559
Charles IX	1560–1574
Duke of Guise massacres Huguenot congregation at Vassy	1562
Saint Bartholomew's Day massacre	1572
Henry III	1574–1589
Formation of the Holy League	1576
War of the Three Henries	1588–1589
Assassination of Henry III	1589
Coronation of Henry IV	1594
Edict of Nantes	1598

wave of violence that gripped the city of Paris. For three days, frenzied Catholic mobs roamed the streets of Paris, killing Huguenots in an often cruel and bloodthirsty manner. According to one eyewitness account: "Then they took her [Françoise Lussault] and dragged her by the hair a long way through the streets, and spying the gold bracelets on her arms, without having the patience to unfasten them, cut off her wrists."[16] Three days of killing left three thousand Huguenots dead, although not Henry of Navarre, who saved his life by promising to turn Catholic. Thousands more were killed in provincial towns. The massacre boomeranged, however, because it discredited the Valois dynasty without ending the conflict.

The fighting continued. The Huguenots rebuilt their strength, and in 1576, the ultra-Catholics formed a "holy league," vowing to exterminate heresy and seat a true Catholic champion—Henry, duke of Guise—on the French throne in place of the ruling king, Henry III (1574–1589), who had succeeded his brother Charles IX. The turning point in the conflict came in the War of the Three Henries in 1588–1589. Henry, duke of Guise, in the pay of Philip II of Spain, seized Paris and forced King Henry III to make him chief minister. To rid himself of Guise influence, Henry III assassinated the duke of Guise and then joined with Henry of Navarre (who meanwhile had returned to Calvinism), who was next in line to the throne, to crush the Catholic Holy League and retake the city of Paris. Although successful, Henry III in turn was assassinated in 1589 by a monk who was repelled by the spectacle of a Catholic king cooperating with a Protestant. Henry of Navarre now claimed the throne. Realizing, however, that he would never be accepted by Catholic France, Henry took the logical way out and converted once again to Catholicism. With his coronation in 1594, the French Wars of Religion finally came to an end.

Nevertheless, the religious problem persisted until the Edict of Nantes was issued in 1598. The edict acknowledged Catholicism as the official religion of France but guaranteed the Huguenots the right to worship in selected places in every district and allowed them to retain a number of fortified towns for their protection. In addition, Huguenots were allowed to enjoy all political privileges, including the holding of public offices. Although the Edict of Nantes recognized the rights of the Protestant minority and ostensibly the principle of religious toleration, it did so only out of political necessity, not out of conviction.

Philip II and the Cause of Militant Catholicism

The greatest advocate of militant Catholicism in the second half of the sixteenth century was King Philip II of Spain (1556–1598), the son and heir of Charles V. Philip's reign ushered in an age of Spanish greatness, both politically and culturally.

Scala/Art Resource, NY

Philip of Spain. This portrait by Titian depicts Philip II of Spain. The king's attempts to make Spain a great power led to large debts and crushing taxes, and his military actions in defense of Catholicism ended in failure and misfortune in both France and the Netherlands.

The first major goal of Philip II was to consolidate and secure the lands he had inherited from his father, Charles V. These included Spain, the Netherlands, and possessions in Italy and the New World (see Map 13.3). For Philip, this meant strict conformity to Catholicism, enforced by aggressive use of the Spanish Inquisition, and the establishment of strong, monarchical authority. The latter was not an easy task because Philip had inherited a governmental structure in which each of the various states and territories of his empire stood in an individual relationship to the king. Philip did manage, however, to expand royal power in Spain by making the monarchy less dependent on the traditional landed aristocracy. Philip tried to be the center of the whole government and supervised the work of all departments, even down to the smallest details. Unwilling to delegate authority, he failed to distinguish between important and trivial matters and fell weeks behind on state correspondence, where he was inclined to make marginal notes and even correct spelling. One Spanish official said, "If God used the Escorial [the royal palace where Philip worked] to deliver my death sentence, I would be immortal."

One of Philip's aims was to make Spain a dominant power in Europe. To a great extent, Spain's preeminence depended on a prosperous economy fueled by its importation of gold and silver from its New World possessions, its agriculture, its commerce, and its industry, especially in textiles, silk, and leather goods. The importation of silver had detrimental effects as well, however, as it helped set off a spiraling inflation that disrupted the Spanish economy, eventually hurting both textile production and agriculture. Moreover, the expenses of war, especially after 1580, proved devastating to the Spanish economy. American gold and silver never constituted more than 20 percent of the royal revenue, leading the government to impose a crushing burden of direct and indirect taxes. Even then the government was forced to borrow. Philip repudiated his debts seven times; still, two-thirds of state income went to pay interest on the debt by the end of his reign. The attempt to make Spain a great power led to its decline after Philip's reign.

Crucial to an understanding of Philip II is the importance of Catholicism to the Spanish people and their ruler. Driven by a heritage of crusading fervor, the Spanish had little difficulty seeing themselves as a nation of people divinely chosen to save Catholic Christianity from the Protestant heretics. Philip II, the "Most Catholic King," became the champion of Catholicism throughout Europe, a role that led to spectacular victories and equally spectacular defeats for the Spanish king. Spain's leadership of a holy league against Turkish encroachments in the Mediterranean, especially the Muslim attack on the island of

Map 13.3 The Height of Spanish Power Under Philip II. Like his father, Charles V, Philip II, the "Most Catholic King," was a champion of the Catholic cause against Protestantism. He sought to maintain Habsburg control in the Netherlands by combating a Protestant revolt, a rebellion eventually supported by Queen Elizabeth of England. Spain's 1588 attempt to invade England ended in disaster. ■ Why would England feel threatened by Spanish territory in the Netherlands?

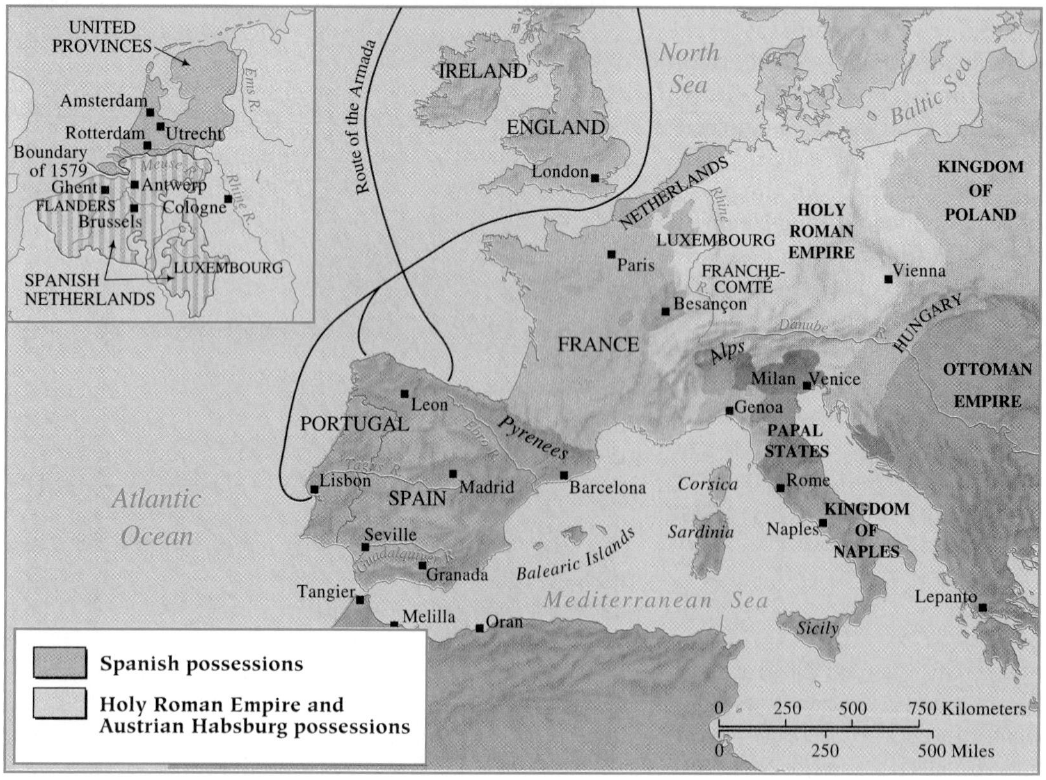

Cyprus, resulted in a stunning victory over the Turkish fleet in the Battle of Lepanto in 1571. Philip's greatest misfortunes came from his attempt to crush the revolt in the Netherlands and his tortured relations with Queen Elizabeth of England.

The Revolt of the Netherlands

As one of the richest parts of Philip's empire, the Spanish Netherlands was of great importance to the Most Catholic King. The Netherlands consisted of seventeen provinces (modern Netherlands, Belgium, and Luxembourg). The seven northern provinces were largely Germanic in culture and Dutch-speaking, while the French- and Flemish-speaking southern provinces were closely tied to France. Situated at the commercial crossroads of northwestern Europe, the Netherlands had become prosperous through commerce and a flourishing textile industry. Because of its location, the Netherlands was open to the religious influences of the age. Though some inhabitants had adopted Lutheranism or Anabaptism, by the time of Philip II, Calvinism was also making inroads. These provinces had no real political bond holding them together except their common ruler, and that ruler was Philip II, a foreigner who was out of touch with the situation in the Netherlands.

Philip II hoped to strengthen his control in the Netherlands, regardless of the traditional privileges of the separate provinces. This was strongly opposed by the nobles, towns, and provincial states, which stood to lose politically if their jealously guarded privileges and freedoms were weakened. Resentment against Philip was also aroused when the residents of the Netherlands realized that the taxes they paid were being used for Spanish interests. Finally, religion became a major catalyst for rebellion when Philip attempted to crush Calvinism. Violence erupted in 1566 when Calvinists—especially nobles—began to destroy statues and stained-glass windows in Catholic churches. Philip responded by sending the duke of Alva with ten thousand veteran Spanish and Italian troops to crush the rebellion.

The repressive policies of the duke proved counterproductive. The levying of a permanent sales tax alienated many merchants and commoners who now joined the nobles and Calvinists in the struggle against Spanish rule. A special tribunal, known as the Council of Troubles (nicknamed by the Dutch the Council of Blood), inaugurated a reign of terror in which even powerful aristocrats were executed. As a result, the revolt now became organized, especially in the northern provinces where William of Nassau, the prince of Orange, also known as William the Silent, and Dutch pirates known as the "Sea Beggars" mounted growing resistance. In 1573, Philip removed the duke of Alva and shifted to a more conciliatory policy to bring an end to the costly revolt.

William of Orange wished to unify all seventeen provinces, a goal seemingly realized in 1576 with the Pacification of Ghent. This agreement stipulated that all the provinces would stand together under William's leadership, respect religious differences, and demand that Spanish troops be withdrawn. But religious differences proved too strong for any lasting union. When the duke of Parma, the next Spanish leader, arrived in the Netherlands, he astutely played on the religious differences of the provinces and split their united front. The southern provinces formed a Catholic union—the Union of Arras—in 1579 and accepted Spanish control. To counter this, William of Orange organized the northern, Dutch-speaking states into a Protestant union—the Union of Utrecht—determined to oppose Spanish rule. The Netherlands was now divided along religious, geographical, and political lines into two hostile camps. The struggle dragged on until 1609, when a twelve-year truce ended the war, virtually recognizing the independence of the northern provinces. These "United Provinces" soon emerged as the Dutch Republic, although the Spanish did not formally recognize them as independent until 1648. The ten southern provinces remained a Spanish possession (see Map 13.3).

CHRONOLOGY

Philip II and Militant Catholicism

Philip II	1556–1598
Outbreak of revolt in the Netherlands	1566
Battle of Lepanto	1571
Pacification of Ghent	1576
Union of Arras	1579
The Spanish Armada	1588
Twelve-year truce (Spain and Netherlands)	1609
Independence of the United Provinces	1648

The England of Elizabeth

After the death of Queen Mary in 1558, her half-sister Elizabeth ascended the throne of England. During Elizabeth's reign, England rose to prominence as the relatively small island kingdom became the leader of the Protestant nations of Europe, laid the foundations for a world empire, and experienced a cultural renaissance.

The daughter of King Henry VIII and Anne Boleyn, Elizabeth had had a difficult early life. During Mary's reign, she had even been imprisoned for a while and had learned early to hide her true feelings from both private and public sight. Intelligent, cautious, and self-confident, she moved quickly to solve the difficult religious problem she had inherited from Mary, who had become extremely unpopular when she tried to return England to the Catholic fold.

Elizabeth's religious policy was based on moderation and compromise. As a ruler, she wished to prevent England from being torn apart over matters of religion. Parliament cooperated with the queen in initiating the Elizabethan

Procession of Queen Elizabeth I. Intelligent and learned, Elizabeth Tudor was familiar with Latin and Greek and spoke several European languages. Served by able administrators, Elizabeth ruled for nearly forty-five years and generally avoided open military action against any major power. This picture, painted near the end of her reign, shows the queen in a ceremonial procession.

religious settlement in 1559. The Catholic legislation of Mary's reign was repealed, and the new Act of Supremacy designated Elizabeth as "the only supreme governor of this realm, as well in all spiritual or ecclesiastical things or causes, as temporal." The Act of Uniformity restored the church service of the Book of Common Prayer from the reign of Edward VI with some revisions to make it more acceptable to Catholics. Elizabeth's religious settlement was basically Protestant, but it was a moderate Protestantism that avoided overly subtle distinctions and extremes.

The new religious settlement worked, at least to the extent that it smothered religious differences in England in the second half of the sixteenth century. Two groups, however, the Catholics and the Puritans, continued to oppose it. One of Elizabeth's greatest challenges came from her Catholic cousin, Mary, queen of Scots, who was next in line to the English throne. Mary was ousted from Scotland by rebellious Calvinist nobles in 1568 and fled for her life to England. There Elizabeth placed her under house arrest and for fourteen years tolerated her involvement in a number of ill-planned Catholic plots designed to kill Elizabeth and replace her on the throne with the Catholic Mary. Finally, in 1587, after Mary became embroiled in a far more serious plot, Elizabeth had her cousin beheaded to end the threats to her regime.

Potentially more dangerous to Anglicanism in the long run were the Puritans. The word *Puritan* first appeared in 1564 when it was used to refer to Protestants within the Anglican church who, inspired by Calvinist theology, wanted to remove any trace of Catholicism from the Church of England. Elizabeth managed to keep the Puritans in check during her reign.

Elizabeth proved as adept in government and foreign policy as in religious affairs. She was well served administratively by the principal secretary of state. The talents of Sir William Cecil and Sir Francis Walsingham, who together held the office for thirty-two years, ensured much of Elizabeth's success in foreign and domestic affairs. Elizabeth also handled Parliament with much skill; it met only thirteen times during her entire reign (see the box on p. 365).

Caution, moderation, and expediency also dictated Elizabeth's foreign policy. Fearful of other countries' motives, Elizabeth realized that war could be disastrous for her island kingdom and her own rule. Unofficially, however, she encouraged English seamen to raid Spanish ships and colonies. Francis Drake was especially adept at plundering Spanish fleets loaded with gold and silver from Spain's New World empire. While encouraging English piracy and providing clandestine aid to French Huguenots and Dutch Calvinists to weaken France and Spain, Elizabeth pretended complete aloofness and avoided alliances that would force her into war with any major power.

Queen Elizabeth Addresses Parliament (1601)

Queen Elizabeth I ruled England from 1558 to 1603 with a consummate skill that contemporaries considered unusual in a woman. Though shrewd and paternalistic, Elizabeth, like other sixteenth-century monarchs, depended for her power on the favor of her people. This selection is taken from her speech to Parliament in 1601, when she had been forced to retreat on the issue of monopolies after vehement protest by members of Parliament. Although the speech was designed to make peace with Parliament, some historians also feel that it was a sincere expression of the rapport that existed between the queen and her subjects.

Queen Elizabeth I, "The Golden Speech"

I do assure you there is no prince that loves his subjects better, or whose love can countervail our love. There is no jewel, be it of never so rich a price, which I set before this jewel: I mean your love. For I do esteem it more than any treasure of riches. . . . And, though God has raised me high, yet this I count the glory of my crown, that I have reigned with your loves. This makes me that I do not so much rejoice that God has made me to be a Queen, as to be a Queen over so thankful a people. . . .

Of myself I must say this: I never was any greedy, scraping grasper, nor a strait, fast-holding Prince, nor yet a waster. My heart was never set on any worldly goods, but only for my subjects' good. What you bestow on me, I will not hoard it up, but receive it to bestow on you again. Yea, mine own properties I account yours, to be expended for your good. . . .

I have ever used to set the Last-Judgement Day before mine eyes, and so to rule as I shall be judged to answer before a higher judge, to whose judgement seat I do appeal, that never thought was cherished in my heart that tended not unto my people's good. And now, if my kingly bounties have been abused, and my grants turned to the hurt of my people, contrary to my will and meaning, and if any in authority under me neglected or perverted what I have committed to them, I hope God will not lay their culps [crimes] and offenses to my charge; who, though there were danger in repealing our grants, yet what danger would I not rather incur for your good, than I would suffer them still to continue?

There will never Queen sit in my seat with more zeal to my country, care for my subjects, and that will sooner with willingness venture her life for your good and safety, than myself. For it is my desire to live nor reign no longer than my life and reign shall be for your good. And though you have had and may have many princes more mighty and wise sitting in this seat, yet you never had nor shall have any that will be more careful and loving.

Gradually, however, Elizabeth was drawn into more active involvement in the Netherlands. This move accelerated the already mounting friction between Spain and England. After years of resisting the idea of invading England as too impractical, Philip II of Spain was finally persuaded to do so by advisers who assured him that the people of England would rise against their queen when the Spaniards arrived. Moreover, Philip was easily convinced that the revolt in the Netherlands would never be crushed as long as England provided support for it. In any case, a successful invasion of England would mean the overthrow of heresy and the return of England to Catholicism, surely an act in accordance with the will of God. Accordingly, Philip ordered preparations for a fleet of warships that would rendezvous with the army of the duke of Parma in Flanders and escort his troops across the English Channel for the invasion.

The armada proved to be a disaster. The Spanish fleet that finally set sail had neither the ships nor the troops that Philip had planned to send. A conversation between a papal emissary and an officer of the Spanish fleet before the armada departed reveals the fundamental flaw:

> "And if you meet the English armada in the Channel, do you expect to win the battle?" "Of course," replied the Spaniard.
>
> "How can you be sure?" [asked the emissary].
>
> "It's very simple. It is well known that we fight in God's cause. So, when we meet the English, God will surely arrange matters so that we can grapple and board them, either by sending some strange freak of weather or, more likely, just by depriving the English of their wits. If we can come to close quarters, Spanish valor and Spanish steel (and the great masses of soldiers we shall have on board) will make our victory certain. But unless God helps us by a miracle the English, who have faster and handier ships than ours, and many more long-range guns, and who know their advantage just as well as we do, will never close with us at all, but stand aloof and knock us to pieces with their culverins [cannons], without our being able to do them any serious hurt. So," concluded the captain, and one fancies a grim smile, "we are sailing against England in the confident hope of a miracle."[17]

The hoped-for miracle never materialized. The Spanish fleet, battered by a number of encounters with the English, sailed back to Spain by a northward route around Scotland and Ireland, where it was further battered by storms. Although the English and Spanish would continue their war for another sixteen years, the defeat of the Spanish Armada guaranteed for the time being that England would remain a Protestant country. Although Spain made up for its losses within a year and a half, the defeat was a psychological blow to the Spaniards.

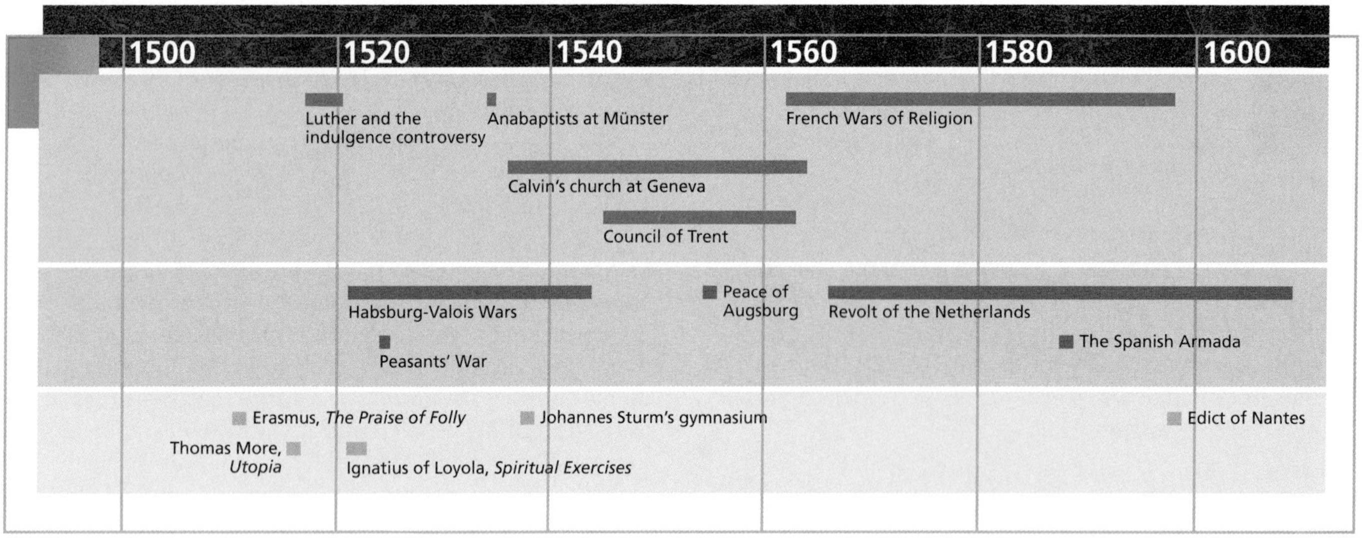

Conclusion

When the Augustinian monk Martin Luther burst onto the scene with a series of theses on indulgences, few people suspected that his observations would eventually split all of Europe along religious lines. But the yearning for reform of the church and meaningful religious experience caused a seemingly simple dispute to escalate into a powerful movement.

Although Luther felt that his revival of Christianity based on his interpretation of the Bible should be acceptable to all, others soon appeared who also read the Bible but interpreted it in different ways. Protestantism fragmented into different sects, which, though united in their dislike of Catholicism, were themselves divided over the interpretation of the sacraments and religious practices. As reform ideas spread, religion and politics became ever more intertwined.

By 1555, Lutheranism had lost much of its momentum; its energy was largely replaced by the new Protestant form of Calvinism, which had a clarity of doctrine and a fervor that made it attractive to a whole new generation of Europeans. Although Calvinism's militancy enabled it to expand across Europe, Catholicism was also experiencing its own revival and emerged as a militant faith, prepared to do combat for the souls of the faithful. An age of religious passion was followed by an age of religious warfare.

That people who were disciples of the Apostle of Peace would kill each other—often in brutal and painful fashion—aroused skepticism about Christianity itself. As one German writer put it, "Lutheran, popish, and Calvinistic, we've got all these beliefs here; but there is some doubt about where Christianity has got."[18] *It is surely no accident that the search for a stable, secular order of politics and for order in the universe through natural laws soon came to play important roles. Before we look at this search for order in the seventeenth century, however, we need first to look at the adventures that plunged Europe into its new role in the world.*

Notes

1. Erasmus, *The Paraclesis,* in John Olin, ed., *Christian Humanism and the Reformation: Selected Writings of Erasmus,* 3d ed. (New York, 1987), p. 101.
2. Thomas More, *Utopia,* trans. Paul Turner (Harmondsworth, England, 1965), p. 76.
3. Quoted in Alister E. McGrath, *Reformation Thought: An Introduction* (Oxford, 1988), p. 72.
4. Quoted in Gordon Rupp, *Luther's Progress to the Diet of Worms* (New York, 1964), p. 82.
5. *On the Freedom of a Christian Man,* quoted in E. G. Rupp and Benjamin Drewery, eds., *Martin Luther* (New York, 1970), p. 50.
6. Quoted in Roland Bainton, *Here I Stand: A Life of Martin Luther* (New York, 1950), p. 144.
7. Quoted in De Lamar Jensen, *Reformation Europe* (Lexington, Mass., 1981), p. 83.
8. Quoted in A. G. Dickens and Dorothy Carr, eds., *The Reformation in England to the Accession of Elizabeth I* (New York, 1968), p. 72.
9. Quoted in Lewis W. Spitz, *The Renaissance and Reformation Movements* (Chicago, 1971), p. 414.
10. John Calvin, *Institutes of the Christian Religion,* trans. John Allen (Philadelphia, 1936), vol. 1, p. 220.
11. Ibid., vol. 1, p. 228; vol. 2, p. 181.
12. Quoted in Roland Bainton, *Women of the Reformation in Germany and Italy* (Minneapolis, 1971), p. 154.
13. Quoted in Bonnie S. Anderson and Judith P. Zinsser, *A History of Their Own: Women in Europe from Prehistory to the Present* (New York, 1988), vol. 1, p. 259.
14. Quoted in John A. Phillips, *Eve: The History of an Idea* (New York, 1984), p. 105.

15. Quoted in R. J. Knecht, *The French Wars of Religion, 1559–1598,* 2d ed. (New York, 1996), p. 47.
16. Quoted in Mack P. Holt, *The French Wars of Religion, 1562–1629* (Cambridge, 1995), p. 86.
17. Quoted in Garrett Mattingly, *The Armada* (Boston, 1959), pp. 216–217.
18. Quoted in Theodore Schieder, *Handbuch der Europäischen Geschichte* (Stuttgart, 1979), vol. 3, p. 579.

Suggestions for Further Reading

Basic surveys of the Reformation period include H. J. Grimm, *The Reformation Era, 1500–1650,* 2d ed. (New York, 1973); C. Lindberg, *The European Reformations* (Cambridge, Mass., 1996); D. L. Jensen, *Reformation Europe* (Lexington, Mass., 1981); G. R. Elton, *Reformation Europe, 1517–1559* (Cleveland, Ohio, 1963); and E. Cameron, *The European Reformation* (New York, 1991). The significance of the Protestant Reformation is examined in S. Ozment, *Protestants: The Birth of a Revolution* (New York, 1992). A brief but very useful introduction to the theology of the Reformation can be found in A. McGrath, *Reformation Thought: An Introduction,* 2d ed. (Oxford, 1993).

The development of humanism outside Italy is examined in C. G. Nauert Jr., *Humanism and the Culture of Renaissance Europe* (Cambridge, 1995). On Thomas More, see R. Marius, *Thomas More: A Biography* (New York, 1984). On Erasmus, see J. McConica, *Erasmus* (Oxford, 1991).

The classic account of Martin Luther's life is R. Bainton, *Here I Stand: A Life of Martin Luther* (New York, 1950). More recent works include H. A. Oberman, *Luther* (New York, 1992), and J. M. Kittelson, *Luther the Reformer: The Story of the Man and His Career* (Minneapolis, 1986). On the Peasants' War, see especially P. Blickle, *The Revolution of 1525: The German Peasants' War from a New Perspective* (Baltimore, 1981). The spread of Luther's ideas in Germany can be examined in M. Hannemann, *The Diffusion of the Reformation in Southwestern Germany, 1518–1534* (Chicago, 1975), and B. Moeller, *Imperial Cities and the Reformation* (Durham, N.C., 1982).

The best account of Ulrich Zwingli is G. R. Potter, *Zwingli* (Cambridge, 1976), although W. P. Stephens' *Zwingli* (Oxford, 1994) is an important study of the man's ideas. The most comprehensive account of the various groups and individuals who are called Anabaptists is G. H. Williams, *The Radical Reformation,* 2d ed. (Kirksville, Mo., 1992).

Two worthwhile surveys of the English Reformation are A. G. Dickens, *The English Reformation,* 2d ed. (New York, 1989), and G. R. Elton, *Reform and Reformation: England, 1509–1558* (Cambridge, Mass., 1977). On John Calvin, see A. McGrath, *A Life of John Calvin: A Study in the Shaping of Western Culture* (Cambridge, Mass., 1990), and W. J. Bouwsma, *John Calvin* (New York, 1988).

On the impact of the Reformation on the family, see J. F. Harrington, *Reordering Marriage and Society in Reformation Germany* (New York, 1995). M. E. Wiesner's *Working Women in Renaissance Germany* (New Brunswick, N.J., 1986) covers primarily the sixteenth century. There is also a good collection of essays in S. Marshall, ed., *Women in Reformation and Counter-Reformation Europe: Public and Private Worlds* (Bloomington, Ind., 1989). On education, see G. Strauss, *Luther's House of Learning* (Baltimore, 1978).

A good introduction to the Catholic Reformation can be found in the beautifully illustrated brief study by A. G. Dickens, *The Counter-Reformation* (New York, 1969). Also valuable are M. R. O'Connell, *The Counter-Reformation, 1559–1610* (New York, 1974), and R. Po-chia Hsia, *The World of Catholic Renewal, 1540–1770* (Cambridge, 1998). On Loyola, see P. Caravan, *Ignatius Loyola: A Biography of the Founder of the Jesuits* (San Francisco, 1990). J. O'Malley, *The First Jesuits* (Cambridge, Mass., 1995), offers a clear discussion of the founding of the Jesuits.

For good introductions to the French Wars of Religion, see M. P. Holt, *The French Wars of Religion, 1562–1629* (Cambridge, 1995), and R. J. Knecht, *The French Wars of Religion, 1559–1598,* 2d ed. (New York, 1996). A good history of Spain in the sixteenth century is J. Lynch, *Spain, 1516–1598: From Nation-State to World Empire* (Cambridge, Mass., 1994). On Philip II, see G. Parker, *Philip II,* 3d ed. (Chicago, 1995). On the revolt of the Netherlands, see the classic work by P. Geyl, *The Revolt of the Netherlands, 1555–1609* (London, 1962), and the more recent work of G. Parker, *The Dutch Revolt* (London, 1977). Elizabeth's reign can be examined in two good biographies: C. Haigh, *Elizabeth I,* 2d ed. (New York, 1998), and W. T. MacCaffrey, *Elizabeth I* (London, 1993). The classic work on the Spanish Armada is the beautifully written book *The Armada* by G. Mattingly (Boston, 1959).

For additional reading, go to InfoTrac College Edition, your online research library at http://web1.infotrac-college.com

Enter the search term *Reformation* using the Subject Guide.

Enter the search term *Counter-Reformation* using the Subject Guide.

Enter the search term *Martin and Luther not King* using Subject Guide.

Enter the search term *John Calvin* using the Subject Guide.

Enter the search term *Elizabeth I* using Key Terms.

CHAPTER

14

Europe and the World: New Encounters, 1500–1800

CHAPTER OUTLINE

- On the Brink of a New World
- New Horizons: The Portuguese and Spanish Empires
- New Rivals on the World Stage
- Toward a World Economy
- The Impact of European Expansion
- Conclusion

FOCUS QUESTIONS

- Why did Europeans begin to embark on voyages of discovery and expansion at the end of the fifteenth century?
- How did Portugal and Spain acquire their overseas empires, and how did their empires differ?
- How did the arrival of the Dutch, British, and French on the world scene in the seventeenth and eighteenth centuries affect Africa, India, Southeast Asia, China, and Japan?
- What were the main features of the African slave trade, and what effects did it have on Africa?
- What was mercantilism, and what was its relationship to colonial empires?
- How was European expansion into the rest of the world both a positive and a negative experience for Europeans and non-Europeans?

WHILE MANY EUROPEANS were occupied with the problems of dynastic expansion and religious reform, others were taking voyages that propelled Europeans far beyond the medieval walls in which they had been enclosed for almost a thousand years. One of these adventurers was the Portuguese explorer Ferdinand Magellan. Convinced that he could find a sea passage to Asia through America, Magellan persuaded the king of Spain to finance an exploratory voyage. On August 10, 1519, Magellan set sail on the Atlantic with five ships and a Spanish crew of 277 men. After a stormy and difficult crossing of the Atlantic, Magellan's fleet moved down the coast of South America, searching for the elusive strait that would take him through. His Spanish ship captains thought he was crazy: "The fool is obsessed with his search for a strait," one remarked. "On the flame of his ambition he will crucify us all." At last, in October 1520, he found it, passing through a narrow waterway (later named the Strait of Magellan) and emerging into an unknown ocean that he called the Pacific Sea. Magellan reckoned that it would then be a short distance to the Spice Islands of the East, but he was badly mistaken. Week after week, he and his crew sailed on across the Pacific as their food supplies dwindled. According to one account, "When their last biscuit had gone, they scraped the maggots out of the casks, mashed them and served them as gruel. They made cakes out of sawdust soaked with the urine of rats—the rats themselves, as delicacies, had long since been hunted to extinction." At last they reached the Philippines (named after King Philip II of Spain), where Magellan met his death at the hands of the natives. Although only one of his original fleet of five ships survived and returned to Spain, Magellan is still remembered as the first person to circumnavigate the world.

At the beginning of the sixteenth century, European adventurers like Magellan had begun launching small fleets into the vast reaches of the Atlantic Ocean. They were hardly aware that they were beginning a new era, not only for Europe, but for the peoples of Asia, Africa, and the Americas as well. Nevertheless, the voyages of these Europeans marked the beginning of a process that led to radical changes in the political, economic, and cultural life of the entire world.

Between 1500 and 1800, European power engulfed the world. In the Americas, Europeans established colonies that spread their laws, religions, and cultures. In the island regions of Southeast Asia, Europeans firmly established their rule. In Africa and other parts of Asia, their trading activities dramatically affected the local peoples.

On the Brink of a New World

Nowhere has the dynamic and even ruthless energy of Western civilization been more apparent than in its expansion into the rest of the world. By the sixteenth century, the Atlantic seaboard had become the center of a commercial activity that raised Portugal and Spain and later the Dutch Republic, England, and France to prominence. The age of expansion was a crucial factor in the European transition from the agrarian economy of the Middle Ages to a commercial and industrial capitalistic system. Expansion also led Europeans into new and lasting contacts with non-European peoples that inaugurated a new age of world history in the sixteenth century.

The Motives

For almost a millennium, Catholic Europe had been confined to one geographical area. Its one major attempt to expand beyond those frontiers, the Crusades, had largely failed. Of course, Europe had never completely lost touch with the outside world: the goods of Asia and Africa made their way into medieval castles, the works of Muslim philosophers were read in medieval universities, and in the ninth and tenth centuries, the Vikings had even made their way to the eastern fringes of North America. But in all cases, contacts with non-European civilizations remained limited until the end of the fifteenth century, when Europeans embarked on a remarkable series of overseas journeys. What caused Europeans to undertake such dangerous voyages to the ends of the earth?

Europeans had long been attracted to lands outside Europe. Indeed, a large body of fantasy literature about "other worlds" blossomed in the Middle Ages. In the fourteenth century, the author of *The Travels of John Mandeville* spoke of realms (which he had never seen) filled with precious stones and gold. Other lands were more frightening. In one country, "the folk be great giants of twenty-eight foot long, or thirty foot long. . . . And they eat more gladly man's flesh than any other flesh." Farther north was a land inhabited by "full cruel and evil women. And they have precious stones in their eyes. And they be of that kind that if they behold any man with wrath they slay him at once with the beholding."[1] Other writers spoke of mysterious Christian kingdoms: the magical kingdom of Prester John in Africa and a Christian community in southern India that was supposedly founded by Thomas, the apostle of Jesus.

Although Muslim control of Central Asia cut Europe off from the countries farther east, the Mongol conquests in the thirteenth century had reopened the doors. The most famous medieval travelers to the East were the Polos of Venice. Niccolò and Maffeo, merchants from Venice, accompanied by Niccolò's son Marco, undertook the lengthy journey to the court of the great Mongol ruler Khubilai Khan (1259–1294) in 1271. An account of Marco's experiences, the *Travels*, was the most informative of all the descriptions of Asia by medieval European travelers. Others followed the Polos, but in the fourteenth century, the conquests of the Ottoman Turks and then the breakup of the Mongol Empire reduced Western traffic to the East. With the closing of the overland routes, a number of people in Europe became interested in the possibility of reaching Asia by sea to gain access to the spices and other precious items of the region. Christopher Columbus had a copy of Marco Polo's *Travels* in his possession when he began to envision his epoch-making voyage across the Atlantic Ocean.

An economic motive thus looms large in Renaissance European expansion. Merchants, adventurers, and government officials had high hopes of finding precious metals and new areas of trade, especially more direct access to the spices of the East. These continued to come to Europe via Arab intermediaries but were outrageously expensive. Many European explorers and conquerors did not hesitate to express their desire for material gain. One Spanish conquistador explained that he and his kind went to the New World to "serve God and His Majesty, to give light to those who were in darkness, and to grow rich, as all men desire to do."[2]

This statement expresses another major reason for the overseas voyages—religious zeal. A crusading mentality was particularly strong in Portugal and Spain, where the Muslims had largely been driven out in the Middle Ages. Contemporaries of Prince Henry the Navigator of Portugal (see opposite page) said that he was motivated by "his great desire to make increase in the faith of our Lord Jesus Christ and to bring him all the souls that should be saved." Although most scholars believe that the religious motive was secondary to economic considerations, it would be foolish to overlook the genuine desire on the part of both explorers and conquistadors, let alone missionaries, to convert the heathen to Christianity. Hernán Cortés, the conqueror of Mexico, asked his Spanish rulers if it was not their duty to ensure that the native Mexicans "are introduced into and instructed in the holy Catholic faith" and predicted that if "the devotion, trust and hope which they now have in their idols turned so as to repose with the divine power of the true God . . . they would work many miracles."[3] Spiritual and secular affairs were closely intertwined in the sixteenth century. No doubt, grandeur and glory as well as plain intellectual curiosity and spirit of adventure also played some role in European expansion.

The Means

If "God, glory, and gold" were the primary motives, what made the voyages possible? First of all, the expansion of Europe was connected to the growth of centralized monarchies during the Renaissance. Although historians still debate the degree of that centralization, the reality is that Renaissance expansion was a state enterprise. By the second half of the fifteenth century, European monarchies had increased both their authority and their resources and were in a position to turn their energies beyond their borders. For France, that meant the invasion of Italy, but for Portugal, a state not strong enough to pursue power in Europe, it meant going abroad. The Spanish monarchy was strong enough by the sixteenth century to pursue power both in Europe and beyond.

At the same time, Europeans had achieved a level of wealth and technology that enabled them to make a regular series of voyages beyond Europe. Although the highly schematic and symbolic medieval maps were of little help to sailors, the *portolani*, or detailed charts made by medieval navigators and mathematicians in the thirteenth and fourteenth centuries, were more useful. With details on coastal contours, distances between ports, and compass readings, these charts proved of great value for voyages in European waters. But because the *portolani* were drawn on a flat scale and took no account of the curvature of the earth, they were of little use for longer overseas voyages. Only when seafarers began to venture beyond the coast of Europe did they begin to accumulate information about the actual shape of the earth. By the end of the fifteenth century, cartography had developed to the point that Europeans possessed fairly accurate maps of the known world.

One of the most important world maps available to Europeans at the end of the fifteenth century was that of Ptolemy, an astronomer of the second century A.D. Ptolemy's work, the *Geography*, had been known to Arab geographers as early as the eighth century, but it was not until the fifteenth century that a Latin translation was made of the work. Printed editions of Ptolemy's *Geography*, which contained his world map, became available from 1477 on. Ptolemy's map (as seen in the illustration below) showed the world as spherical with three major landmasses—Europe, Asia, and Africa—and only two oceans. In addi-

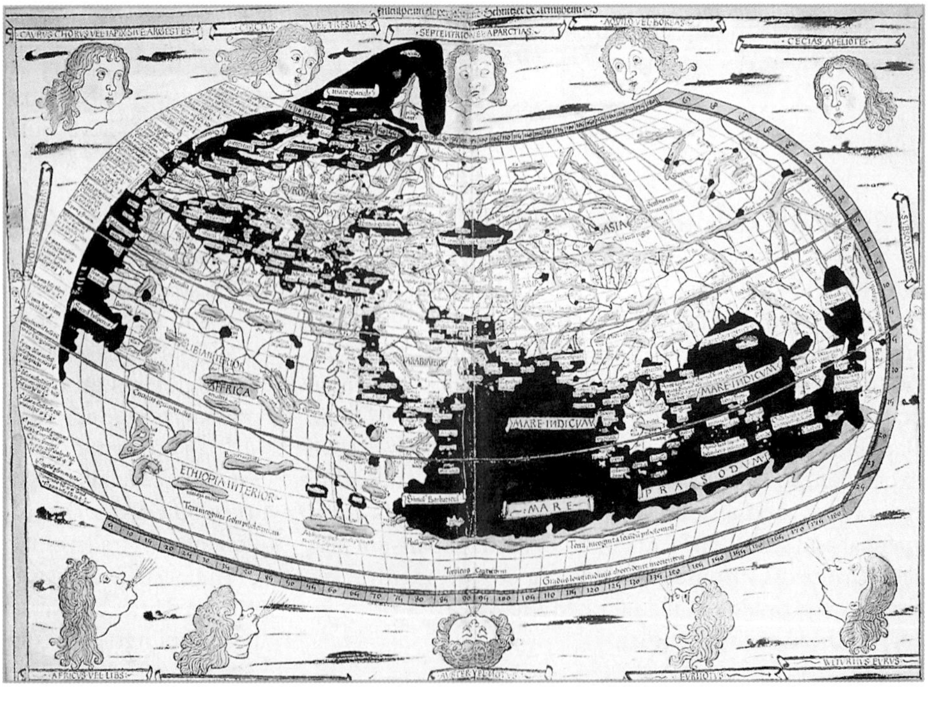

Ptolemy's World Map. Contained in the Latin translation of Ptolemy's *Geography* was this world map, which did not become available to Europeans until the late fifteenth century. Scholars quickly accepted it as the most accurate map of its time. The twelve wind-faces, meant to show wind currents around the earth, were a fifteenth-century addition to the ancient map.

The Huntington Library, San Marino, CA: Claudius Ptolemy, Cosmographia, Ulm, 1482 tion to showing the oceans as considerably smaller than the landmasses, Ptolemy had also dramatically underestimated the circumference of the earth, which led Columbus and other adventurers to believe that it would be feasible to sail west from Europe to reach Asia.

Europeans had developed remarkably seaworthy ships as well as new navigational techniques. European shipmakers had mastered the use of the axial rudder (an import from China) and had learned to combine the use of lateen sails with a square rig. With these innovations, they could construct ships mobile enough to sail against the wind and engage in naval warfare and also large enough to mount heavy cannons and carry a substantial amount of goods over long distances. Previously, sailors had used a quadrant and their knowledge of the position of the Pole Star to ascertain their latitude. Below the equator, however, this technique was useless. Only with the assistance of new navigational aids such as the compass and the astrolabe were they able to explore the high seas with confidence.

A final spur to exploration was the growing knowledge of the wind patterns in the Atlantic Ocean. The first European fleets sailing southward along the coast of West Africa had found their efforts to return hindered by the strong winds that blew steadily from the north along the coast. By the late fifteenth century, however, sailors had learned to tack out into the ocean, where they were able to catch westerly winds in the vicinity of the Azores that brought them back to the coast of western Europe. Christopher Columbus used this technique in his voyages to the Americas, and others relied on their new knowledge of the winds to round the continent of Africa in search of the Spice Islands.

New Horizons: The Portuguese and Spanish Empires

Portugal took the lead in the European age of expansion when it began to explore the coast of Africa under the sponsorship of Prince Henry the Navigator (1394–1460). His motives were a blend of seeking a Christian kingdom as an ally against the Muslims, acquiring trade opportunities for Portugal, and extending Christianity.

The Development of a Portuguese Maritime Empire

In 1419, Prince Henry founded a school for navigators on the southwestern coast of Portugal. Shortly thereafter, Portuguese fleets began probing southward along the western coast of Africa in search of gold, which had been carried northward from south of the Atlas Mountains in central Morocco for centuries. In 1441, Portuguese ships reached the Senegal River, just north of Cape Verde, and brought home a cargo of black Africans, most of whom were then sold as slaves to wealthy buyers elsewhere in Europe. Within a few years, an estimated one thousand slaves were shipped annually from the area back to Lisbon.

Through regular expeditions, the Portuguese gradually crept down the African coast, and in 1471, they discovered a new source of gold along the southern coast of the hump of West Africa (an area that would henceforth be known to Europeans as the Gold Coast). A few years

Hulton/Archive/Getty Images

The Port of Lisbon. This sixteenth-century engraving by Theodore de Bry shows the port of Lisbon with several caravels in the harbor. The caravel was the workhorse of the Age of Exploration. Prior to the fifteenth century, most European ships were either small craft with lateen sails used in the Mediterranean or slow, unwieldy square-rigged vessels operating in the North Atlantic. By the sixteenth century, European naval architects began to build ships that combined the maneuverability and speed offered by lateen sails with the carrying capacity and seaworthiness of the square-riggers.

later, they established contact with the state of Bakongo, near the mouth of the Zaire (Congo) River in Central Africa. To facilitate trade in gold, ivory, and slaves (some of the latter were brought back to Lisbon, while others were bartered to local merchants for gold), the Portuguese leased land from local rulers and built stone forts along the coast.

Hearing reports of a route to India around the southern tip of Africa, Portuguese sea captains continued their probing. In 1488, Bartholomeu Dias (c. 1450–1500) took advantage of westerly winds in the South Atlantic to round the Cape of Good Hope, but he feared a mutiny from his crew and returned (see Map 14.1). Ten years later, a fleet under the command of Vasco da Gama (c. 1460–1524) rounded the cape and stopped at several ports controlled by Muslim merchants along the coast of East Africa. Then da Gama's fleet crossed the Arabian Sea and reached the port of Calicut, on the southwestern coast of India, on May 18, 1498. On arriving in Calicut, da Gama announced to his surprised hosts that he had arrived in search of "Christians and spices." He found no Christians, but he did find the spices he sought. Although he lost two ships en route, da Gama's remaining vessels returned to Europe with their holds filled with ginger and cinnamon, a cargo that earned the investors a profit of several thousand percent.

For the next several years, Portuguese fleets returned annually to the area, seeking to destroy Arabic shipping and establish a monopoly in the spice trade. In 1509, a Portuguese armada defeated a combined fleet of Turkish and Indian ships off the coast of India and began to impose a

Map 14.1 Discoveries and Possessions in the Fifteenth and Sixteenth Centuries. Desire for wealth was the main motivation of the early explorers, though spreading Christianity was also an important factor. Portugal under Prince Henry the Navigator initiated the first voyages in the early fifteenth century; Spain's explorations began at the century's end. ■ Which regions of the globe were primarily explored by Portugal, and which were the main focus of Spain's voyages?

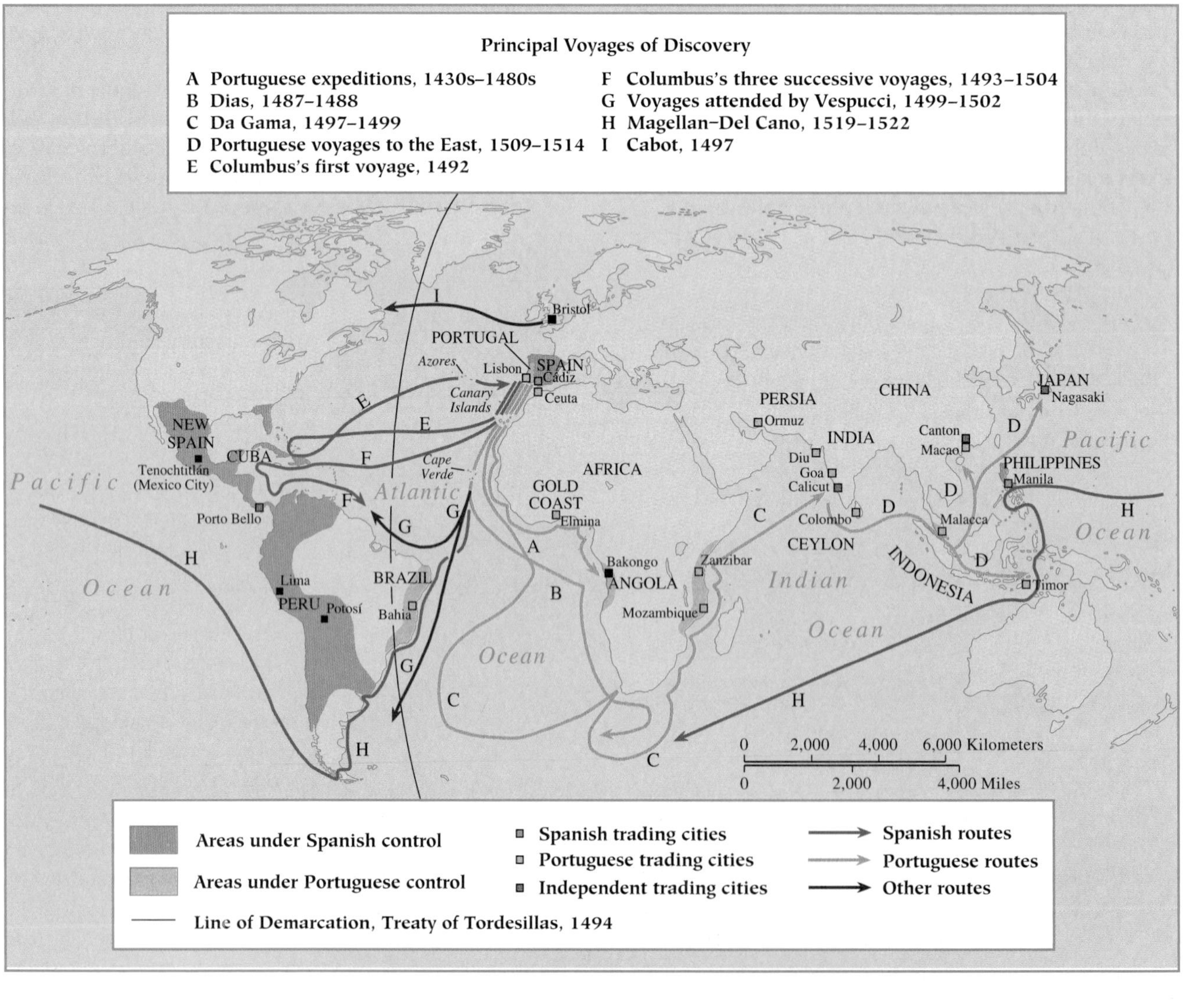

The Portuguese Conquest of Malacca

In 1511, a Portuguese fleet led by Afonso de Albuquerque attacked the Muslim sultanate at Malacca, on the west coast of the Malay peninsula. Occupation of the port gave the Portuguese control over the strategic Strait of Malacca and the route to the Spice Islands. In this passage, Albuquerque tells his men the reasons for the attack. Note that he sees control of Malacca as a way to reduce the power of the Muslim world.

The Commentaries of the Great Afonso de Albuquerque

Although there be many reasons which I could allege in favor of our taking this city and building a fortress therein to maintain possession of it, two only will I mention to you, on this occasion. . . .

The first is the great service which we shall perform to Our Lord in casting the Muslims out of this country. . . . If we can only achieve the task before us, it will result in the Muslims resigning India altogether to our rule, for the greater part of them—or perhaps all of them—live upon the trade of this country and are become great and rich, and lords of extensive treasures. . . . For when we were committing ourselves to the business of cruising in the Straits [of the Red Sea], where the King of Portugal had often ordered me to go (for it was there that His Highness considered we could cut down the commerce which the Muslims of Cairo, of Mecca, and of Judah carry on with these parts), Our Lord for his service thought right to lead us here, for when Malacca is taken the places on the Straits must be shut up, and the Muslims will never more be able to introduce their spices into those places.

And the other reason is the additional service which we shall render to King Manuel in taking this city, because it is the headquarters of all the spices and drugs which the Muslims carry every year hence to the Straits without our being able to prevent them from so doing; but if we deprive them of this their ancient market there, there does not remain for them a single port, nor a single situation, so commodious in the whole of these parts, where they can carry on their trade in these things. . . . I hold it as very certain that if we take this trade of Malacca away out of their hands, Cairo and Mecca are entirely ruined, and to Venice will no spices be conveyed except that which her merchants go and buy in Portugal.

blockade on the entrance to the Red Sea to cut off the flow of spices to Muslim rulers in Egypt and the Ottoman Empire. The following year, seeing the need for a land base in the area, Admiral Alfonso de Albuquerque (c. 1462–1515) set up port facilities at Goa, on the western coast of India south of present-day Bombay. Goa henceforth became the headquarters for Portuguese operations throughout the entire region. Although Indian merchants were permitted to continue their trading activities, the Portuguese conducted raids against Arab shippers, provoking the following brief report from an Arab source: "In this year the vessels of the Portuguese appeared at sea en route for India and those parts. They took about seven vessels, killing those on board and making some prisoner. This was their first action, may God curse them."[4]

The Portuguese now began to range more widely in search of the source of the spice trade. In 1511, Albuquerque sailed into the harbor of Malacca on the Malay peninsula. Malacca had been transformed by its Muslim rulers into a thriving port and a major stopping point for the spice trade. For Albuquerque, control of Malacca would serve two purposes. It could help destroy the Arab spice trade and also provide the Portuguese with a way station on the route to the Moluccas, then known as the Spice Islands (see the box above). After a short but bloody battle, the Portuguese seized the city and massacred the local Arab population. This slaughter initiated a fierce and brutal struggle between the Portuguese and the Arabs. According to one account, "to enhance the terror of his name he [Albuquerque] always separated Arabs from the other inhabitants of a captured city, and cut off the right hand of the men, and the noses and ears of the women."[5]

From Malacca, the Portuguese launched expeditions farther east, to China and the Spice Islands. There they signed a treaty with a local ruler for the purchase and export of cloves to the European market. The new trading empire was now complete. Within a few years, the Portuguese had managed to seize control of the spice trade from Muslim traders and had garnered substantial profits for the Portuguese monarchy. Nevertheless, the Portuguese Empire remained limited, consisting only of trading posts on the coasts of India and China. The Portuguese lacked the power, the population, and the desire to colonize the Asian regions.

Why were the Portuguese so successful? Basically, their success was a matter of guns and seamanship. The first Portuguese fleet to arrive in Indian waters was relatively modest in size, consisting of three ships and twenty guns, a force sufficient for self-defense and intimidation but not for serious military operations. Later Portuguese fleets, which began to arrive with regularity early in the sixteenth century, were more heavily armed and were able not only to intimidate but also to inflict severe defeats if necessary on local naval and land forces. The Portuguese by no means possessed a monopoly on the use of firearms and explosives, but their effective use of naval technology, their heavy guns that could be mounted in the hulls of their sturdy vessels, and their tactics gave them military superiority over lightly armed rivals that they were able to exploit until the arrival of other European forces several decades later.

Voyages to the New World

While the Portuguese were seeking access to the spice trade of the Indies by sailing eastward through the Indian Ocean, the Spanish were attempting to reach the same destination by sailing westward across the Atlantic. Although the Spanish came to overseas discovery and exploration after the initial efforts of Henry the Navigator, their greater resources enabled them to establish a far grander overseas empire quite different from that of the Portuguese.

An important figure in the history of Spanish exploration was an Italian known as Christopher Columbus (1451–1506). Knowledgeable Europeans were aware that the world was round but had little understanding of its circumference or the extent of the continent of Asia. Convinced that the circumference of the earth was less than contemporaries believed and that Asia was larger than people thought, Columbus felt that Asia could be reached by sailing west instead of around Africa. After being rejected by the Portuguese, he persuaded Queen Isabella of Spain to finance his exploratory expedition.

With three ships, the *Santa María*, the *Niña*, and the *Pinta*, manned by ninety men, Columbus set sail on August 3, 1492. On October 12, he reached the Bahamas and then went on to explore the coastline of Cuba and the northern shores of Hispaniola (present-day Haiti and the Dominican Republic). Columbus believed that he had reached Asia, and in his reports to Queen Isabella and King Ferdinand, he assured them not only that he would eventually find gold but also that they had a golden opportunity to convert the natives—whom Columbus persisted in calling "Indians"—to Christianity (see the box on p. 375). In three subsequent voyages (1493, 1498, 1502), Columbus sought in vain to find a route through the outer lands to the Asian mainland. In his four voyages, Columbus reached all the major islands of the Caribbean and the mainland of Central America.

Although Columbus clung to his belief until his death, other explorers soon realized that he had discovered a new frontier altogether. State-sponsored explorers joined the race to the New World. A Venetian seaman, John Cabot, explored the New England coastline of the Americas under a license from King Henry VII of England. The continent of South America was discovered accidentally by the Portuguese sea captain Pedro Cabral in 1500. Amerigo Vespucci, a Florentine, accompanied several voyages and wrote a series of letters describing the geography of the New World. The publication of these letters led to the use of the name "America" (after Amerigo) for the new lands.

The first two decades of the sixteenth century witnessed numerous overseas voyages that explored the eastern coasts of both North and South America. Vasco Nuñez de Balboa, a Spanish explorer, led an expedition across the Isthmus of Panama and reached the Pacific Ocean in 1513. Perhaps the most dramatic of all these expeditions was the journey of Ferdinand Magellan (1480–1521) in 1519. After passing through the straits named after him at the southern tip of South America, he sailed across the Pacific Ocean and reached the Philippines, where he met his death at the hands of the natives. Although only one of his original fleet of five ships survived and returned to Spain, Magellan's name is still associated with the first known circumnavigation of the earth.

The Europeans referred to the newly discovered territories as the New World, even though they possessed flourishing civilizations populated by millions of people. But the Americas were indeed new to the Europeans, who quickly saw opportunities for conquest and exploitation. The Spanish, in particular, were interested because the 1494 Treaty of Tordesillas had divided up the newly discovered world into separate Portuguese and Spanish spheres of influence, and it turned out that most of South America fell within the Spanish sphere. Hereafter the route east around the Cape of Good Hope was to be reserved for the Portuguese while the route across the Atlantic

Christopher Columbus. Columbus was an Italian explorer who worked for the queen of Spain. He has become a symbol for two entirely different perspectives. To some, he was a great and heroic explorer who discovered the New World; to others, especially in Latin America, he was responsible for beginning a process of invasion that led to the destruction of an entire way of life. This painting by the Italian Sebastiano del Piombo in 1519 is the earliest known portrait of Columbus, but it was done thirteen years after his death and reveals as much about the painter's conception of Columbus as it does about the explorer himself.

Columbus Lands in the New World

On returning from America, which he believed was the coast of Asia, Christopher Columbus wrote about his experience. In this passage from a letter describing his first voyage, he tells of his arrival on the island of Hispaniola (Haiti). Historians believe that Columbus wrote this letter for public consumption.

Letter to Raphael Sanchez, Treasurer to the King and Queen of Spain

Thirty-three days after my departure from Cadiz I reached the Indian sea, where I discovered many islands, thickly peopled, of which I took possession without resistance in the name of our most illustrious Monarch, by public proclamation and with unfurled banners. To the first of these islands, I gave the name of the blessed Saviour (San Salvador), relying upon whose protection I had reached this as well as the other islands; to each of these I also gave a name. . . .

The inhabitants of both sexes in this island, and in all the others which I have seen, or of which I have received information, go always naked as they were born, with the exception of some of the women, who use the covering of a leaf, or small bough, or an apron of cotton which they prepare for that purpose. None of them are possessed of any iron, neither have they weapons, being unacquainted with, and indeed incompetent to use them, not from any deformity of body (for they are well-formed), but because they are timid and full of fear. . . . As soon however as they see that they are safe, and have laid aside all fear, they are very simple and honest, and exceedingly liberal with all they have; none of them refusing any thing he may possess when he is asked for it. . . . They also give objects of great value for trifles, and content themselves with very little or nothing in return.

I however forbade that these trifles and articles of no value (such as pieces of dishes, plates, and glass, keys, and leather straps) should be given to them, although if they could obtain them, they imagined themselves to be possessed of the most beautiful trinkets in the world. . . . Thus they bartered, like idiots, cotton and gold for fragments of bows, glasses, bottles, and jars. . . .

In all these islands there is no difference of physiognomy, of manners, or of language, but they all clearly understand each other, a circumstance very propitious for the realization of what I conceive to be the principal wish of our most serene King, namely, the conversion of these people to the holy faith of Christ, to which indeed, as far as I can judge, they are very favourable and well-disposed. . . .

Finally, to compress into a few words the entire summary of my voyage and speedy return, and of the advantages derivable therefrom, I promise, that with a little assistance afforded me by our most invincible sovereigns, I will procure them as much gold as they need, and as great a quantity of spices and cotton. . . . Let Christ rejoice on earth, as he rejoices in heaven in the prospect of the salvation of the souls of so many nations hitherto lost. Let us also rejoice as well on account of the exaltation of our faith as on account of the increase of our temporal prosperity, of which not only Spain but all Christendom will be partakers.

(except for the eastern hump of South America) was assigned to Spain.

The Spanish Empire in the New World

The Spanish conquistadors were hardy individuals motivated by a typical sixteenth-century blend of glory, greed, and religious crusading zeal. Although authorized by the Castilian crown, these groups were financed and outfitted privately, not by the government. Their superior weapons, organizational skills, and determination brought the conquistadors incredible success. They also benefited from rivalries among the native peoples.

EARLY CIVILIZATIONS IN MESOAMERICA

Before the Spaniards arrived in the New World, Mesoamerica (modern Mexico and Central America) had already hosted a number of flourishing civilizations. Beginning around A.D. 300, a people known as the Maya had built on the Yucatán peninsula one of the most sophisticated civilizations in the Americas. The Maya built splendid temples and pyramids, were accomplished artists, and developed a sophisticated calendar, as accurate as any in existence in the world at that time. The Maya were an agrarian people who cleared the dense rain forests, developed farming, and built a patchwork of city-states. Mayan civilization came to include much of Central America and southern Mexico. For unknown reasons, Mayan civilization began to decline around 800 and had collapsed less than a hundred years later.

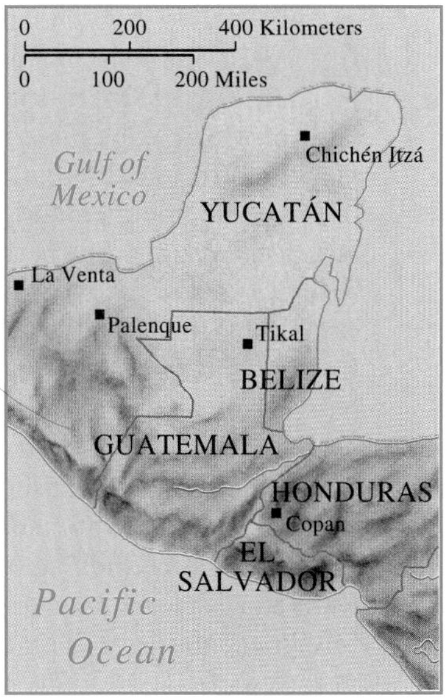

The Maya

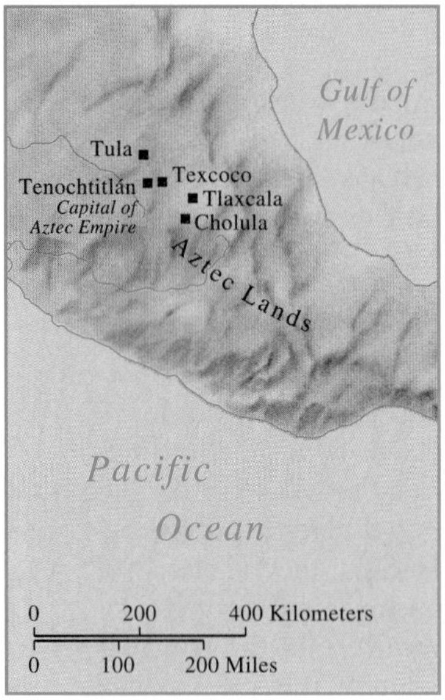

The Aztecs

Sometime during the early twelfth century A.D., a people known as the Aztecs began a long migration that brought them to the Valley of Mexico. They established their capital at Tenochtitlán, on an island in the middle of Lake Texcoco (now the location of Mexico City). For the next hundred years, the Aztecs built their city, constructing temples, other public buildings, houses, and causeways of stone across Lake Texcoco to the north, south, and west, linking the many islands to the mainland. At the beginning of the fifteenth century, they constructed an aqueduct to bring fresh water from a spring 4 miles away.

The Aztecs were outstanding warriors, and while they were building their capital city, they also set out to bring the entire area around the city under their control. By the early fifteenth century, they had become the leading city-state in the lake region. For the remainder of the fifteenth century, the Aztecs consolidated their rule over much of what is modern Mexico, from the Atlantic to the Pacific Oceans and as far south as the Guatemalan border. The new kingdom was not a centralized state but a collection of semi-independent territories governed by local lords. These rulers were confirmed in their authority by the Aztec ruler in return for the payment of tribute. Their loose political organization would later be a cause of the downfall of the Aztec Empire.

SPANISH CONQUEST OF THE AZTEC EMPIRE

In 1519, a Spanish expedition under the command of Hernán Cortés (1485–1547) landed at Veracruz, on the Gulf of Mexico. He marched to the city of Tenochtitlán (see the box on p. 378) at the head of a small contingent of troops (550 soldiers and 16 horses); as he went, he made alliances with city-states that had tired of the oppressive rule of the Aztecs. Especially important was Tlaxcala, a state that the Aztecs had not been able to conquer. In November, Cortés arrived at Tenochtitlán, where he received a friendly welcome from the Aztec monarch Moctezuma (often called Montezuma). At first, Moctezuma believed that his visitor was a representative of Quetzalcoatl, the god who had departed from his homeland centuries before and had promised that he would return. Riddled with fears, Moctezuma offered gifts of gold to the foreigners and gave them a palace to use while they were in the city.

But trouble eventually erupted between the Spaniards and the Aztecs. The Spaniards took Moctezuma hostage and began to pillage the city. In the fall of 1520, one year after Cortés had arrived, the local population revolted and drove the invaders from the city. Many of the Spaniards were killed, but the Aztecs soon experienced new disasters. As one Aztec related: "At about the time that the Spaniards had fled from Mexico, there came a great sickness, a pestilence, the smallpox." With no natural immunity to the diseases of Europeans, many Aztecs fell sick and died. Meanwhile, Cortés received fresh soldiers from his new allies; the state of Tlaxcala alone provided fifty thousand warriors. After four months, the city capitulated. And then the destruction began. The pyramids, temples, and palaces were leveled, and the stones were used to build Spanish government buildings and churches. The rivers and canals were filled in. The mighty Aztec Empire on mainland Mexico was no more. Between 1531 and 1550, the Spanish gained control of northern Mexico.

THE INCA AND THE SPANISH

In the late fourteenth century, the Inca were a small community in the area of Cuzco, a city located at an altitude of 10,000 feet in the mountains of southern Peru. In the 1440s, however, under the leadership of their powerful ruler Pachakuti, the Inca launched a campaign of conquest that eventually brought the entire region under their control.

Pachakuti created a highly centralized state. The capital of Cuzco was transformed from a city of mud and

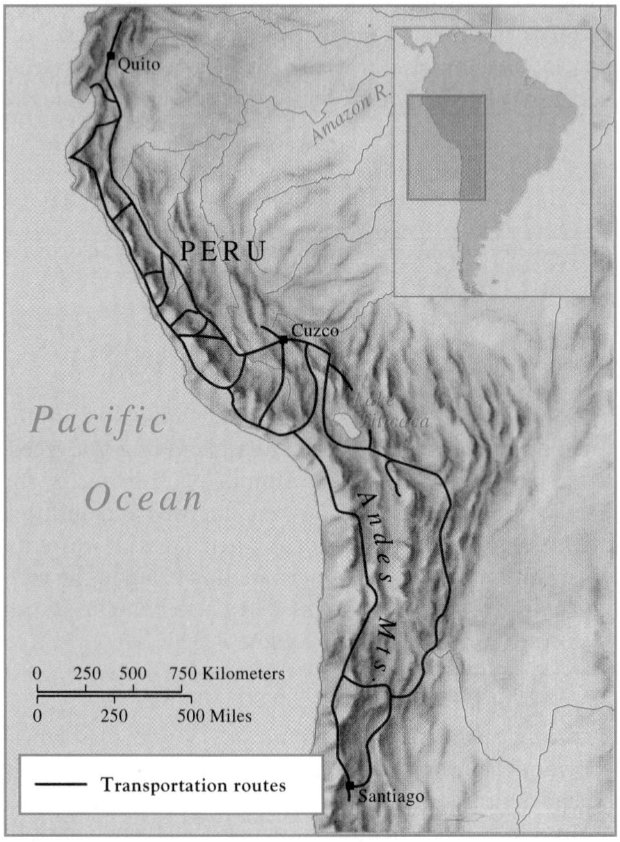

The Inca

Slaughter of the Natives. Fearful of growing Aztec resistance, the Spaniards responded by slaughtering many natives. This sixteenth-century watercolor shows the massacre of the Cholula people, carried out on the orders of Cortés. The Cholula had refused to provide supplies to the forces of a Spanish expedition.

thatch into an imposing city of stone. Under Pachakuti and his immediate successors, Topa Inca and Huayna Inca (the word *Inca* means "ruler"), the boundaries of the Inca Empire were extended as far as Ecuador, central Chile, and the edge of the Amazon basin. The empire included perhaps twelve million people.

To create a well-organized empire, Pachakuti divided his realm into four quarters, each ruled by a governor. The quarters were in turn divided into provinces, each also ruled by a governor. The individuals chosen to be governors were usually related to the royal family. Each province was supposed to contain about ten thousand residents. At the top of the entire system was the emperor, who was believed to be descended from the sun god.

The Inca were great builders. One major project was a system of 24,800 miles of roads that extended from the border of modern-day Colombia to a point south of modern-day Santiago, Chile. Two major roadways extended in a north-south direction, one through the Andes Mountains and the other along the coast, with connecting routes between them. Rest houses, located a day's walk apart, and storage depots were placed along the roads. Various types of bridges, including some of the finest examples of suspension bridges in premodern times, were built over ravines and waterways.

The Inca Empire was still flourishing when the first Spanish expeditions arrived in the area. In December 1530, Francisco Pizarro (c. 1475–1541) landed on the Pacific coast of South America with a band of about 180 men, but like Cortés, he had steel weapons, gunpowder, and horses, none of which were familiar to his hosts. Pizarro was also lucky because the Inca Empire had already succumbed to an epidemic of smallpox. Like the Aztecs, the Inca had no immunities to European diseases, and all too soon, smallpox was devastating entire villages. In another stroke of good fortune for Pizarro, even the Inca emperor was a victim. Upon

The Spanish Conquistador: Cortés and the Conquest of Mexico

Hernán Cortés was a minor Spanish nobleman who came to the New World in 1504 to seek his fortune. Contrary to his superior's orders, Cortés waged an independent campaign of conquest and overthrew the Aztec Empire in Mexico (1519–1521). Cortés wrote a series of five reports to Emperor Charles V to justify his action. The second report includes a description of Tenochtitlán, the capital of the Aztec Empire. The Spanish conquistador and his men were obviously impressed by this city, awesome in its architecture yet built by people who lacked European technology, such as wheeled vehicles and tools of hard metal.

Cortés's Description of Tenochtitlán

The great city Tenochtitlán is built in the midst of this salt lake, and it is two leagues from the heart of the city to any point on the mainland. Four causeways lead to it, all made by hand and some twelve feet wide. The city itself is as large as Seville or Córdoba. The principal streets are very broad and straight, the majority of them being of beaten earth, but a few and at least half of the smaller thoroughfares are waterways along which they pass in their canoes. Moreover, even the principal streets have openings at regular distances so that the water can freely pass from one to another, and these openings which are very broad are spanned by great bridges of huge beams, very stoutly put together, so firm indeed that over many of them ten horsemen can ride at once. Seeing that if the natives intended any treachery against us they would have every opportunity from the way in which the city is built, for by removing the bridges from the entrances and exits they could leave us to die of hunger with no possibility of getting to the mainland, I immediately set to work as soon as we entered the city on the building of four brigs, and in a short space of time had them finished so that we could ship 300 men and the horses to the mainland whenever we so desired.

The city has many open squares in which markets are continuously held and the general business of buying and selling proceeds. One square in particular is twice as big as that of Salamanca and completely surrounded by arcades where there are daily more than 60,000 folk buying and selling. Every kind of merchandise such as may be met with in every land is for sale there, whether of food and victuals, or ornaments of gold and silver, or lead, brass, copper, tin, precious stones, bones, shells, snails and feathers; limestone for building is likewise sold there, stone both rough and polished, bricks burnt and unburnt, wood of all kinds and in all stages of preparation. . . . There is a street of herb-sellers where there are all manner of roots and medicinal plants that are found in the land. There are houses as it were of apothecaries where they sell medicines made from these herbs, both for drinking and for use as ointments and salves. There are barbers' shops where you may have your hair washed and cut. There are other shops where you may obtain food and drink. . . .

Finally, to avoid being wordy in telling all the wonders of this city, I will simply say that the manner of living among the people is very similar to that in Spain, and considering that this is a barbarous nation shut off from a knowledge of the true God or communication with enlightened nations, one may well marvel at the orderliness and good government which is everywhere maintained.

The actual service of Montezuma and those things which call for admiration by their greatness and state would take so long to describe that I assure your Majesty I do not know where to begin with any hope of ending. For as I have already said, what could there be more astonishing than that a barbarous monarch such as he should have reproductions made in gold, silver, precious stones, and feathers of all things to be found in his land, and so perfectly reproduced that there is no goldsmith or silversmith in the world who could better them, nor can one understand what instrument could have been used for fashioning the jewels; as for the featherwork its like is not to be seen in either wax or embroidery; it is so marvelously delicate.

the emperor's death, two sons claimed the throne, leading to a civil war. Pizarro took advantage of the situation by seizing Atahualpa, whose forces had just defeated his brother's. Armed only with stones, arrows, and light spears, Incan soldiers provided little challenge to the charging horses of the Spanish, let alone their guns and cannons. After executing Atahualpa, Pizarro and his soldiers, aided by their Incan allies, marched on Cuzco and captured the Incan capital. By 1535, Pizarro had established a capital at Lima for a new colony of the Spanish Empire.

ADMINISTRATION OF THE SPANISH EMPIRE

Spanish policy toward the Indians of the New World was a combination of confusion, misguided paternalism, and cruel exploitation. Whereas the conquistadors made decisions based on expediency and their own interests, Queen Isabella declared the natives to be subjects of Castile and instituted the Spanish *encomienda*, a system that permitted the conquering Spaniards to collect tribute from the natives and use them as laborers. In return, the holders of an *encomienda* were supposed to protect the Indi-

Las Casas and the Spanish Treatment of the American Natives

Bartolomé de Las Casas (1474–1566) participated in the conquest of Cuba and received land and Indians in return for his efforts. But in 1514 he underwent a radical transformation and came to believe that the Indians had been cruelly mistreated by his fellow Spaniards. He became a Dominican friar and spent the remaining years of his life (he lived to the age of ninety-two) fighting for the Indians. This selection is taken from his most influential work, which is known to English readers as *The Tears of the Indians.* This work was largely responsible for the "black legend" of the Spanish as inherently "cruel and murderous fanatics." Most scholars feel that Las Casas may have exaggerated his account in order to shock his contemporaries into action.

Bartolomé de Las Casas, The Tears of the Indians

There is nothing more detestable or more cruel, than the tyranny which the Spaniards use toward the Indians for the getting of pearl. Surely the infernal torments cannot much exceed the anguish that they endure, by reason of that way of cruelty; for they put them under water some four or five ells [15 to 18 feet] deep, where they are forced without any liberty of respiration, to gather up the shells wherein the pearls are; sometimes they come up again with nets full of shells to take breath, but if they stay any while to rest themselves, immediately comes a hangman row'd in a little boat, who as soon as he has well beaten them, drags them again to their labor. Their food is nothing but filth, and the very same that contains the pearl, with a small portion of that bread which that country affords; in the first whereof there is little nourishment; and as for the latter, it is made with great difficulty, besides that they have not enough of that neither for sustenance; they lie upon the ground in fetters, lest they should run away; and many times they are drown'd in this labor, and are never seen again till they swim upon the top of the waves: oftentimes they also are devoured by certain sea monsters, that are frequent in those seas. Consider whether this hard usage of the poor creatures be consistent with the precepts which God commands concerning charity to our neighbor, by those that cast them so undeservedly into the dangers of a cruel death, causing them to perish without any remorse or pity, or allowing them the benefit of the sacraments, or the knowledge of religion; it being impossible for them to live any time under the water; and this death is so much the more painful, by reason that by the constricting of the breast, while the lungs strive to do their office, the vital parts are so afflicted that they die vomiting the blood out of their mouths. Their hair also, which is by nature black, is hereby changed and made of the same color with that of the sea wolves; their bodies are also so besprinkled with the froth of the sea, that they appear rather like monsters than men.

ans, pay them wages, and supervise their spiritual needs. In practice, this meant that the settlers were free to implement the paternalistic system of the government as they pleased. Three thousand miles from Spain, Spanish settlers largely ignored their government and brutally used the Indians to pursue their own economic interests. Indians were put to work on plantations and in the lucrative gold and silver mines. Forced labor, starvation, and especially disease took a fearful toll of Indian lives. With little or no natural resistance to European diseases, the Indians of America were ravaged by the smallpox, measles, and typhus that came with the explorers and the conquistadors. Although scholarly estimates of native populations vary drastically, a reasonable guess is that 30 to 40 percent of the natives died. On Hispaniola alone, out of an initial population of 100,000 natives when Columbus arrived in 1493, only 300 Indians survived by 1570. In 1542, largely in response to the publications of Bartolomé de Las Casas, a Dominican friar who championed the Indians (see the box above), the government abolished the *encomienda* system and provided more protection for the natives.

In the New World, the Spanish developed an administrative system based on viceroys. Spanish possessions were initially divided into two major administrative units: New Spain (Mexico, Central America, and the Caribbean islands), with its center in Mexico City, and Peru (western South America), governed by a viceroy in Lima. Each viceroy served as the king's chief civil and military officer and was aided by advisory groups called *audiencias*, which also functioned as supreme judicial bodies.

By papal agreement, the Catholic monarchs of Spain were given extensive rights over ecclesiastical affairs in the New World. They could appoint all bishops and clergy, build churches, collect fees, and supervise the affairs of the various religious orders that sought to Christianize the heathen. Catholic missionaries—especially the Dominicans, Franciscans, and Jesuits—fanned out across the Spanish Empire, where they converted and baptized hundreds of thousands of Indians in the early years of the conquest.

The mass conversion of the Indians brought the organizational and institutional structures of Catholicism to the New World. Dioceses, parishes, cathedrals, schools, and hospitals—all the trappings of civilized European society—soon appeared in the Spanish Empire. So, too, did the Spanish Inquisition, established first in Peru in 1570 and then in Mexico in 1571.

CHRONOLOGY

The Portuguese and Spanish Empires in the Sixteenth Century

Bartholomeu Dias sails around the tip of Africa	1488
The voyages of Columbus	1492–1502
Treaty of Tordesillas	1494
Vasco da Gama lands at Calicut in India	1498
Portuguese seize Malacca	1511
Landing of Portuguese ships in southern China	1514
First boatload of African slaves to America	1518
Magellan's voyage around the world	1519–1522
Spanish conquest of Mexico	1519–1522
Pizarro's conquest of the Incas	1530–1535

New Rivals on the World Stage

Portugal and Spain had been the first Atlantic nations to take advantage of the Age of Exploration, starting in the late fifteenth century, and both had become great colonial powers. In the seventeenth century, however, their European neighbors to the north—first the Dutch and then the French and British—moved to replace the Portuguese and Spanish and create their own colonial empires. The new rivals and their rivalry soon had an impact on much of the rest of the world—in Africa, Asia, and the Americas.

Africa: The Slave Trade

Although the primary objective of the Portuguese in sailing around Africa was to find a sea route to the Spice Islands, they soon discovered that profits could be made in Africa itself. So did other Europeans.

The Portuguese built forts on both the western and eastern coasts of Africa and tried, above all, to dominate the trade in gold. During the mid-seventeenth century, however, the Dutch seized a number of Portuguese forts along the West African coast and at the same time took control of much of the Portuguese trade across the Indian Ocean.

The Dutch East India Company, a trading company established under government sponsorship, also set up a settlement in southern Africa, at the Cape of Good Hope, which was meant to serve as a base to provide food and other provisions to Dutch ships en route to the Spice Islands. Eventually, however, it developed into a permanent colony. Dutch farmers, known as Boers, began to settle in areas outside the city of Cape Town. The area's moderate climate and freedom from tropical diseases made it desirable for Europeans to settle there.

The European exploration of the African coastline did not affect most Africans living in the interior of the continent, but for peoples living on or near the coast, the impact was great indeed. As the trade in slaves increased during the sixteenth through the eighteenth centuries, thousands and then millions of Africans were removed from their homes and forcibly shipped to plantations in the New World.

Of course, traffic in slaves was not new. As in other areas of the world, slavery had been practiced in Africa since ancient times. In the fifteenth century, it continued at a fairly steady level. The primary market for African slaves was the Middle East, where most were used as domestic servants. Slavery also existed in many European countries, where some slaves from Africa or war captives from the regions north of the Black Sea were used for domestic purposes or as agricultural workers.

At first, the Portuguese simply replaced European slaves with African ones. During the second half of the fifteenth century, about a thousand slaves were taken to Portugal each year. Most wound up serving as domestic servants for affluent families in Europe. But the discovery of the Americas in the 1490s and the planting of sugarcane in South America and the islands of the Caribbean changed the situation drastically.

Cane sugar had first been introduced to Europeans from the Middle East during the Crusades. At the end of the fifteenth century, the Portuguese set up sugar plantations worked by African laborers on an island off the central coast of Africa. During the sixteenth century, sugarcane plantations were set up along the eastern coast of Brazil and on several islands in the Caribbean. Because the growing of cane sugar demands both skill and large quantities of labor, the new plantations required more workers than could be provided by the small American Indian population in the New World, decimated by diseases imported from the Old World. Since the climate and soil of much of West Africa were not conducive to the cultivation of sugar, African slaves began to be shipped to Brazil and the Caribbean to work on the plantations. The first were sent from Portugal, but in 1518, a Spanish ship carried the first boatload of African slaves directly from Africa to the New World.

GROWTH IN THE SLAVE TRADE

During the next two centuries, the trade in slaves grew dramatically. An estimated 275,000 enslaved Africans were exported to other countries during the sixteenth century, with 2,000 going annually to the Americas alone (see Map 14.2). In the seventeenth century, the total climbed to over a million and jumped to 6 million in the eighteenth century, when the trade spread from West and Central Africa to East Africa. Even during the nineteenth century, when Great Britain and other European countries tried to end

The Atlantic Slave Trade

One of the most odious practices of early modern Western society was the Atlantic slave trade, which reached its height in the eighteenth century. Blacks were transported in densely packed cargo ships from the western coast of Africa to the Americas to work as slaves in the plantation economy. Not until late in the eighteenth century did a rising chorus of voices raise serious objections to this trade in human beings. This excerpt presents a criticism of the slave trade from an anonymous French writer.

Diary of a Citizen

As soon as the ships have lowered their anchors off the coast of Guinea, the price at which the captains have decided to buy the captives is announced to the Negroes who buy prisoners from various princes and sell them to Europeans. Presents are sent to the sovereign who rules over that particular part of the coast, and permission to trade is given. Immediately the slaves are brought by inhuman brokers like so many victims dragged to a sacrifice. White men who cover that portion of the human race receive them in a little house they have erected on the shore, where they have entrenched themselves with two pieces of cannon and twenty guards. As soon as the bargain is concluded, the Negro is put in chains and led aboard the vessel, where he meets his fellow sufferers. Here sinister reflections come to his mind; everything shocks and frightens him and his uncertain destiny gives rise to the greatest anxiety. . . .

The vessel sets sail for the Antilles, and the Negroes are chained in a hold of the ship, a kind of lugubrious prison where the light of day does not penetrate, but into which the air is introduced by means of a pump. Twice a day some disgusting food is distributed to them. Their consuming sorrow and the sad state to which they are reduced would make them commit suicide if they were not deprived of all the means for an attempt upon their lives. Without any kind of clothing it would be difficult to conceal from the watchful eyes of the sailors in charge any instrument apt to alleviate their despair. The fear of a revolt, such as sometimes happens on the voyage from Guinea, is the basis of a common concern and produces as many guards as there are men in the crew. The slightest noise or a secret conversation among two Negroes is punished with utmost severity. All in all, the voyage is made in a continuous state of alarm on the part of the white men, who fear a revolt, and in a cruel state of uncertainty on the part of the Negroes, who do not know the fate awaiting them.

When the vessel arrives at a port in the Antilles, they are taken to a warehouse where they are displayed, like any merchandise, to the eyes of buyers. The plantation owner pays according to the age, strength, and health of the Negro he is buying. He has him taken to his plantation, and there he is delivered to an overseer who then and there becomes his tormentor. In order to domesticate him, the Negro is granted a few days of rest in his new place, but soon he is given a hoe and a sickle and made to join a work gang. Then he ceases to wonder about his fate; he understands that only labor is demanded of him. But he does not know yet how excessive this labor will be. As a matter of fact, his work begins at dawn and does not end before nightfall; it is interrupted for only two hours at dinnertime. The food a full-grown Negro is given each week consists of two pounds of salt beef or cod and two pots of tapioca meal. . . . A Negro of twelve or thirteen years or under is given only one pot of meal and one pound of beef or cod. In place of food some planters give their Negroes the liberty of working for themselves every Saturday; others are even less generous and grant them this liberty only on Sundays and holidays.

the slave trade, nearly 2 million were exported. Altogether as many as 10 million African slaves were transported to the Americas between the early sixteenth and nineteenth centuries. It is estimated that 50 percent of African slaves were transported in British ships, with the rest divided among French, Dutch, Portuguese, Danish, and later, American ships.

One reason for the astonishing numbers of slaves, of course, was the high death rate. African slaves were closely packed into cargo ships, 300 to 450 per ship, and chained in holds without sanitary facilities or enough space to stand up; there they remained during the voyage to America, which took at least 100 days (see the box above). Mortality rates averaged 10 percent; longer journeys due to storms or adverse winds resulted in even higher death rates. The Africans who survived the journey were subject to high death rates from diseases to which they had little or no immunity. Death rates were lower for slaves born and raised in the New World: the new generation developed immunity to many of the more fatal diseases. Owners, however, rarely encouraged their slaves to have children. Many slave owners, especially in the West Indies, believed that buying a new slave was less expensive than raising a child from birth to working age at adolescence.

Before the coming of Europeans in the fifteenth century, most slaves in Africa were prisoners of war. Many served as domestic servants or as wageless workers for the local ruler. When Europeans first began to take part in the

Bibliotheque des Arts Decoratifs, Paris/Archives Charmet/Bridgeman Art Library

The Sale of Slaves. In the eighteenth century, the slave trade was a highly profitable commercial enterprise. This painting shows a Western slave merchant negotiating with a local African leader over slaves at Gorée, Senegal, West Africa, in the late eighteenth century.

slave trade, they bought slaves from local African merchants at slave markets in return for gold, guns, or other European goods such as textiles or copper or iron utensils.

At first, local slave traders obtained their supply from regions nearby, but as demand increased, they had to move farther inland to find their victims. In a few cases, local rulers became concerned about the impact of the slave trade on the well-being of their societies. In a letter to the king of Portugal in 1526, King Affonso of Congo (Bakongo) complained, "So great, Sire, is the corruption and licentiousness that our country is being completely depopulated."[6] Protests from Africans were generally ignored by Europeans as well as by other Africans. As a general rule, local rulers viewed the slave trade as a source of income, and many sent raiders into defenseless villages in search of unsuspecting victims.

Historians once thought that Europeans controlled the terms of the slave trade and were able to obtain victims at bargain prices. However, it is now clear that African middlemen—merchants, local elites, or rulers—were very active in the process and were often able to dictate the price and number of slaves to European purchasers. Payment to the slave merchant was often made in goods, such as textiles, furniture, and guns.

EFFECTS OF THE SLAVE TRADE

The effects of the slave trade varied from area to area. Of course, it had tragic effects on the lives of individual victims and their families. There was also an economic price as the importation of cheap manufactured goods from Europe undermined local cottage industries and forced countless families into poverty. The slave trade also led to the depopulation of some areas and deprived many African communities of their youngest and strongest men and women.

The political effects of the slave trade were also devastating. The need to maintain a constant supply of slaves led to increased warfare and violence as African chiefs and their followers, armed with guns acquired from the trade in slaves, increased their raids and wars on neighboring peoples. A few Europeans lamented what they were doing to traditional African societies. One Dutch slave trader remarked: "From us they have learned strife, quarrelling, drunkenness, trickery, theft, unbridled desire for what is not one's own, misdeeds unknown to them before, and the accursed lust for gold."[7] But the slave trade continued with devastating effects for some African states. The case of

Benin in West Africa is a good example. A brilliant and creative society in the sixteenth century, Benin was pulled into the slave trade. As the population declined and warfare increased, the people of Benin lost faith in their gods, their art deteriorated, and human sacrifice became more common. When the British arrived there at the end of the nineteenth century, they found a corrupt and savage place. It took years to discover the brilliance of the earlier culture destroyed by slavery.

Despite a rising chorus of humanitarian sentiments from European intellectuals, the use of black slaves remained largely acceptable to Western society. Europeans continued to view blacks as inferior beings fit primarily for slave labor. Not until the Society of Friends, known as the Quakers, began to criticize slavery in the 1770s and exclude from their church any member adhering to slave trafficking, did European sentiment against slavery begin to build. Even then, it was not until the radical stage of the French Revolution in the 1790s that the French abolished slavery. The British followed suit in 1807. Despite the elimination of the African source, slavery continued in the newly formed United States until the Civil War of the 1860s.

The West in Southeast Asia

Portugal's efforts to dominate the trade of Southeast Asia were never totally successful. The Portuguese lacked both the numbers and the wealth to overcome local resistance and colonize the Asian regions. Portugal's empire was simply too large and Portugal too small to maintain it. One Portuguese chronicler lamented: "My country, oh my country. Too heavy is the task that has been laid on your shoulders. Day after day I watch the ships leaving your shores filled always with your best and bravest men. And too many do not return. . . . Who then is left to till the fields, to harvest the grapes, to keep the enemy on our frontiers at bay?"[8] By the end of the sixteenth century, new European rivals had entered the fray.

One of them was Spain. The Spanish had established themselves in the region when Magellan had landed in the Philippines. Although he was killed there, the Spanish were able to gain control over the Philippines, which eventually became a major Spanish base in the trade across the Pacific. Spanish ships carried silk and other luxury goods to Mexico in return for silver from the mines of Mexico.

Map 14.2 The Slave Trade. Although slavery had long existed in Europe itself, the traffic in African slaves flourished from the early sixteenth century to the late eighteenth century. Most African slaves went to the Americas, where they primarily worked on sugar plantations in the Caribbean and eastern Brazil and later on large holdings in the southern United States.
■ What were the important source regions for slaves, and where were most of them taken?

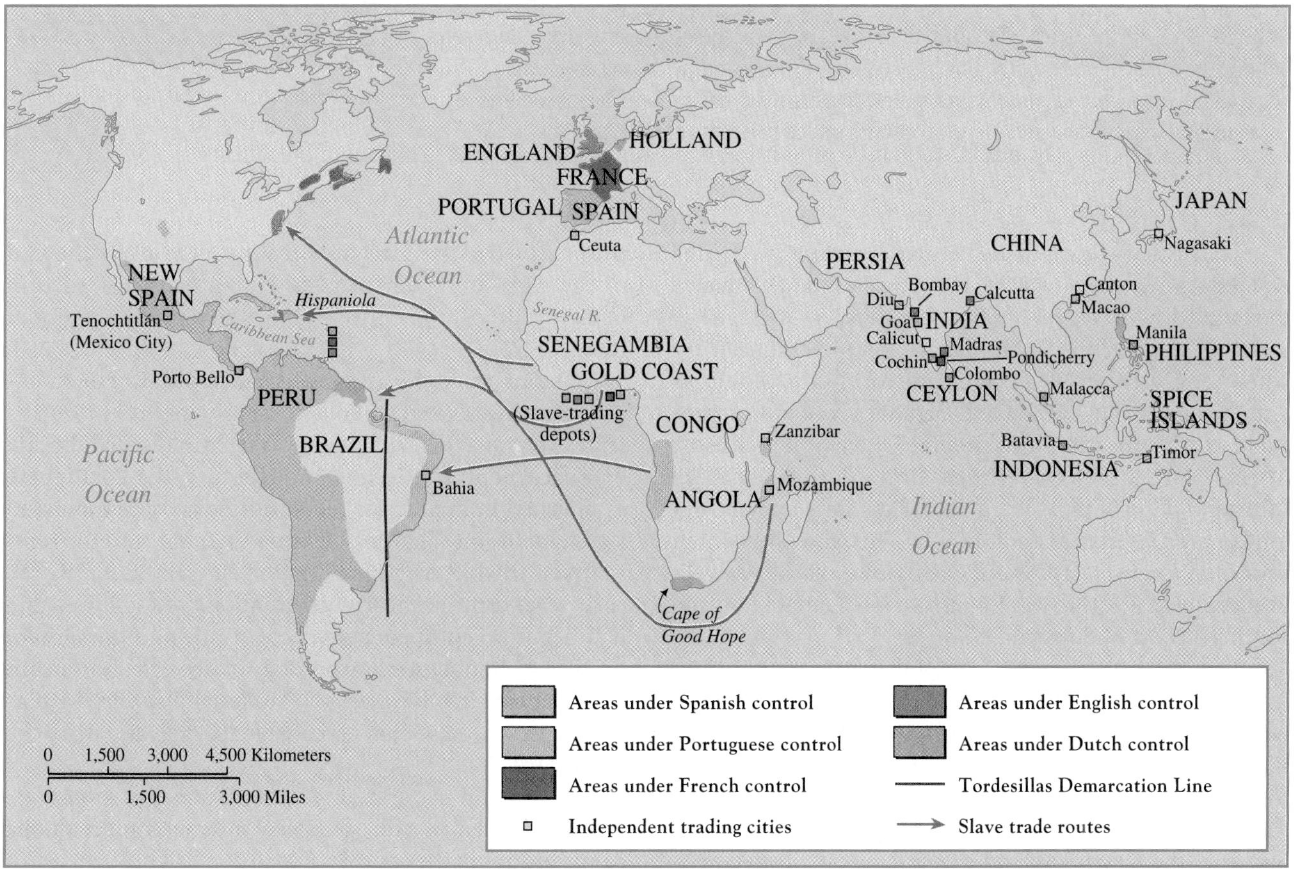

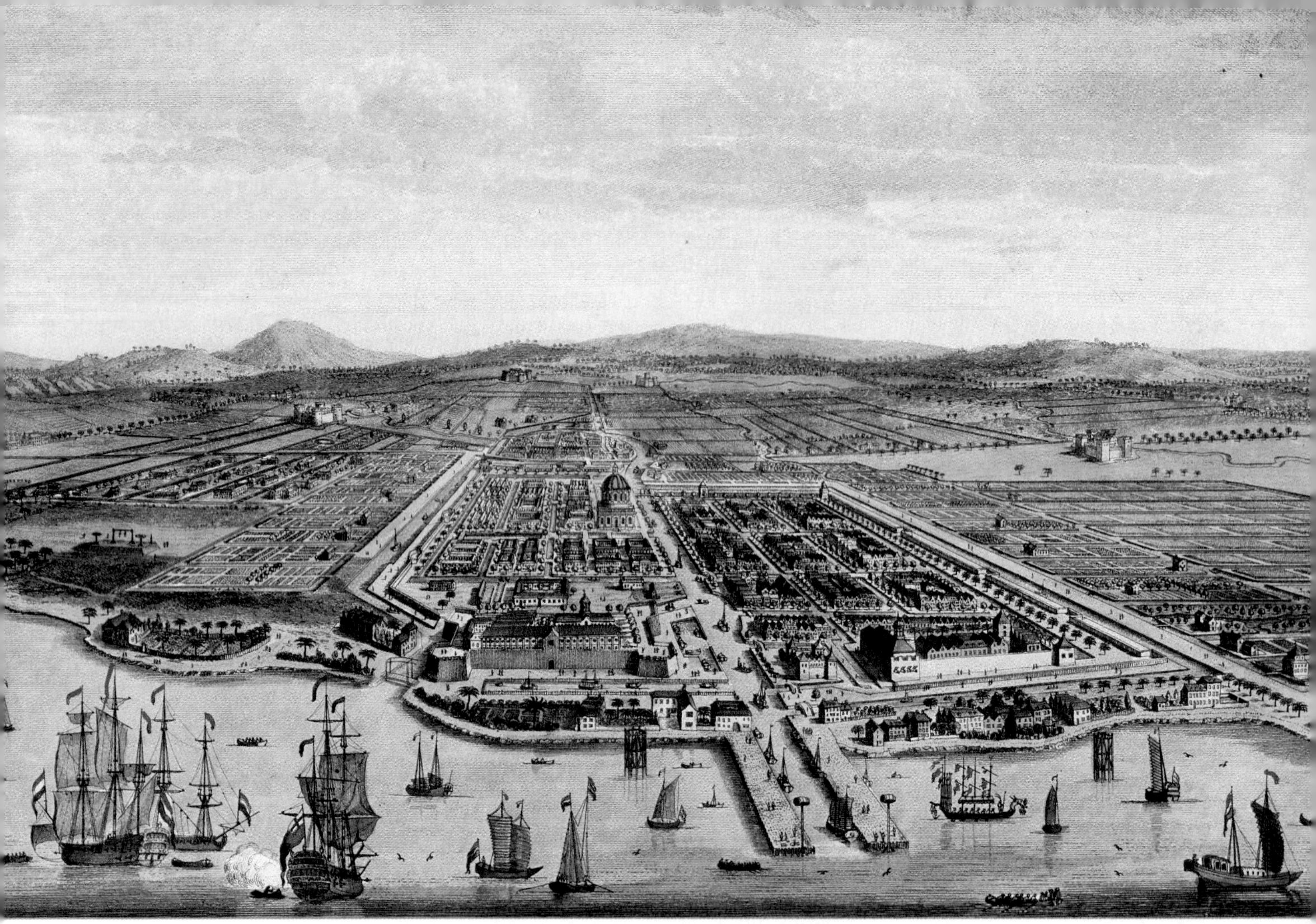

The Art Archive/London

Batavia. In 1619, the Dutch established themselves on the island of Java at Batavia, which soon became the center of power of the Dutch East Indies. The city's numerous canals (seen in this illustration), swamps, and ponds served as breeding areas for malaria-bearing mosquitoes; consequently, the mortality rate of the Dutch who settled here was enormously high.

The primary threat to the Portuguese Empire in Southeast Asia, however, came with the arrival of the Dutch and the English, who were better financed than the Portuguese. The shift in power began in the early seventeenth century when the Dutch seized a Portuguese fort in the Moluccas and then gradually pushed the Portuguese out of the spice trade. During the next fifty years, the Dutch occupied most of the Portuguese coastal forts along the trade routes throughout the Indian Ocean, including the island of Ceylon (today's Sri Lanka) and Malacca. The aggressive Dutch drove the English traders out of the spice market as well, eventually restricting the English to a single port on the southern coast of Sumatra.

The Dutch also began to consolidate their political and military control over the entire area. On the island of Java, where they had established a fort at Batavia (modern Jakarta) in 1619, the Dutch found that it was necessary to bring the inland regions under their control to protect their position. On Java and the neighboring island of Sumatra, the Dutch East India Company established pepper plantations, which soon became the source of massive profits for Dutch merchants in Amsterdam. By the end of the eighteenth century, the Dutch had succeeded in bringing almost the entire Indonesian archipelago under their control.

The arrival of the Europeans had less impact on mainland Southeast Asia, where strong monarchies in Burma (now Myanmar), Thailand, and Vietnam resisted foreign encroachment. In the sixteenth century, the Portuguese established limited trade relations with several mainland states, including Thailand, Burma Vietnam, and the remnants of the old Angkor kingdom in Cambodia. By the early seventeenth century, other nations had followed and had begun to compete actively for trade and missionary privileges. To obtain economic advantages, the Europeans soon became involved in local factional disputes. In general, however, these states were able to unite and drive the Europeans out.

In Vietnam, the arrival of Western merchants and missionaries coincided with a period of internal conflict among ruling groups in the country. Expansion had brought a civil war that temporarily divided the country into two separate states, one in the south and one in the north. After their arrival in the mid-seventeenth century, the European powers began to take sides in local politics, with the Portuguese and the Dutch supporting rival factions. The Europeans also set up trading posts for their merchants, but by the end of the seventeenth century, when it became clear that economic opportunities were limited, most of them were abandoned. French missionaries attempted to remain, but their efforts were blocked by the authorities, who viewed converts to Catholicism as a threat to the prestige of the Vietnamese emperor (see the box on p. 386).

Why were the mainland states better able to resist the European challenge than the states in the Malay world? One factor, no doubt, was the cohesive nature of these states. The mainland states in Burma, Thailand, and Vietnam had begun to define themselves as distinct political entities. The Malay states had less cohesion. Moreover, the Malay states were victims of their own resources. The spice trade was enormously profitable. European merchants and rulers were determined to gain control of the sources of the spices, and that determination led them to take direct control of the Indonesian archipelago.

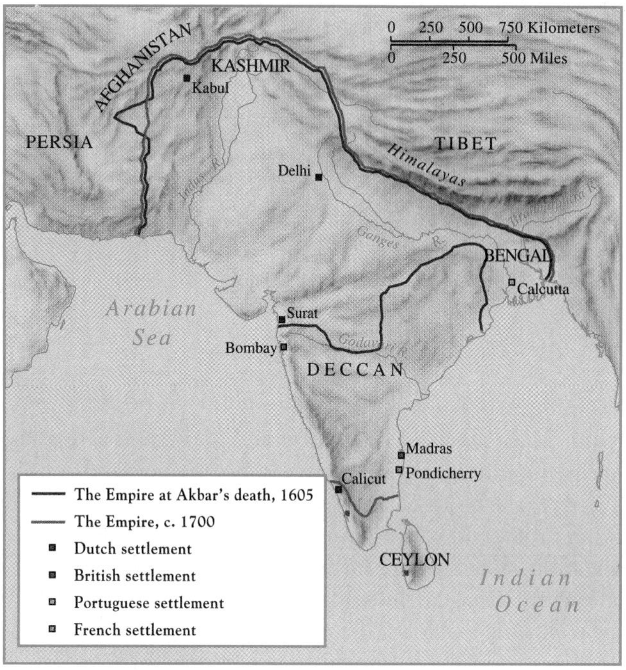

The Mughal Empire

The French and British in India

When a Portuguese fleet arrived at the port of Calicut in the spring of 1498, the Indian subcontinent was divided into a number of Hindu and Muslim kingdoms. But it was on the verge of a new era of unity that would be brought about by a foreign dynasty called the Mughals. The founders of the Mughal Empire were not natives of India but came from the mountainous region north of the Ganges River valley. The founder of the dynasty, Babur, had an illustrious background. His father was descended from the great Asian conqueror Tamerlane; his mother, from the Mongol conqueror Genghis Khan. It was Babur's grandson, however, who brought Mughal rule to most of India, creating the greatest Indian empire since the Mauryan dynasty nearly two thousand years earlier.

THE IMPACT OF THE WESTERN POWERS

As we have seen, the first Europeans to arrive in India were the Portuguese. At first, Portugal dominated regional trade in the Indian Ocean, but at the end of the sixteenth century, the British and the Dutch arrived on the scene. Soon both powers were competing with Portugal, and with each other, for trading privileges in the region.

During the first half of the seventeenth century, the British presence in India steadily increased. By 1650, British trading posts had been established at Surat (a thriving port along the northwestern coast of India), Fort William (now the great city of Calcutta) near the Bay of Bengal, and Madras on the southeastern coast. From Madras, British ships carried Indian-made cotton goods to the East Indies, where they were bartered for spices, which were shipped back to Britain.

British success in India attracted rivals, including the Dutch and the French. The Dutch abandoned their interests to concentrate on the spice trade in the middle of the seventeenth century, but the French were more persistent and established their own forts on the east coast. For a brief period, the French competed successfully with the British, even capturing the British fort at Madras.

But the British were saved by the military genius of Sir Robert Clive, an aggressive British empire-builder who eventually became the chief representative of the East India Company in India. The British were aided as well by the refusal of the French government to provide financial support for French efforts in far-off India. Eventually the French were restricted to the fort at Pondicherry and a handful of small territories on the southeastern coast (see Map 14.3).

In the meantime, Clive began to consolidate British control in Bengal, where the local ruler had attacked Fort William and imprisoned the local British population in the "Black Hole of Calcutta" (an underground prison for holding the prisoners, many of whom died in captivity). In 1757, a small British force numbering about three thousand defeated a Mughal-led army more than ten times its size in the Battle of Plassey. As part of the spoils of victory, the British East India Company received from the now-decrepit Mughal court the authority to collect taxes from lands in the area surrounding Calcutta. During the Seven Years' War (1756–1763), the British forced the French to withdraw completely from India (see Chapter 18).

To officials of the East India Company, the expansion of their authority into the interior of the subcontinent probably seemed like a simple economic decision. It made sense to seek regular revenues that would pay for increasingly expensive military operations in India. To historians, it marks a major step in the gradual transfer of all of the Indian subcontinent to the British East India Company and later, in 1858, to the British crown as a colony (see Chapter 24).

West Meets East: An Exchange of Royal Letters

Economic gain was not the only motivation of Western rulers who wished to establish a European presence in the East. In 1681, King Louis XIV of France wrote a letter to the king of Tonkin (the Trinh family head, then acting as viceroy to the Vietnamese emperor) asking permission for Christian missionaries to proselytize in Vietnam. The king of Tonkin politely declined the request.

A Letter to the King of Tonkin

Most high, most excellent, most mighty and most magnanimous Prince, our very dear and good friend, may it please God to increase your greatness with a happy end!

We hear from our subjects who were in your Realm what protection you accorded them. We appreciate this all the more since we have for you all the esteem that one can have for a prince as illustrious through his military valor as he is commendable for the justice which he exercises in his Realm. . . . Since the war which we have had for several years, in which all of Europe had banded together against us, prevented our vessels from going to the Indies, at the present time, when we are at peace after having gained many victories and expanded our Realm through the conquest of several important places, we have immediately given orders to the Royal Company to establish itself in your kingdom as soon as possible. . . . We have given orders to have brought to you some presents which we believe might be agreeable to you. But the one thing in the world which we desire most, both for you and for your Realm, would be to obtain for your subjects who have already embraced the law of the only true god of heaven and earth, the freedom to profess it, since this law is the highest, the noblest, the most sacred and especially the most suitable to have kings reign absolutely over the people.

We are even quite convinced that, if you knew the truths and the maxims which it teaches, you would give first of all to your subjects the glorious example of embracing it. We wish you this incomparable blessing together with a long and happy reign, and we pray God that it may please Him to augment your greatness with the happiest of endings.

Your very dear and good friend,
Louis

Answers from the King of Tonkin

The King of Tonkin sends to the King of France a letter to express to him his best sentiments. . . . Your communication, which comes from a country which is a thousand leagues away, and which proceeds from the heart as a testimony of your sincerity, merits repeated consideration and infinite praise. Politeness toward strangers is nothing unusual in our country. There is not a stranger who is not well received by us. How then could we refuse a man from France, which is the most celebrated among the kingdoms of the world and which for love of us wishes to frequent us and bring us merchandise? These feelings of fidelity and justice are truly worthy to be applauded. As regards your wish that we should cooperate in propagating your religion, we do not dare to permit it, for there is an ancient custom, introduced by edicts, which formally forbids it. Now, edicts are promulgated only to be carried out faithfully; without fidelity nothing is stable. How could we disdain a well-established custom to satisfy a private friendship? . . . This then is my letter. We send you herewith a modest gift which we offer you with a glad heart.

This letter was written at the beginning of winter and on a beautiful day.

China

In 1514, a Portuguese fleet dropped anchor off the coast of China. It was the first direct contact between the Chinese Empire and Europe since the journeys of Marco Polo two hundred years earlier. At the time, the Chinese thought little of the event. China appeared to be at the height of its power as the most magnificent civilization on the face of the earth. Its empire stretched from the steppes of Central Asia to the China Sea, from the Gobi Desert to the tropical rain forests of Southeast Asia. From the lofty perspective of the imperial throne in Beijing, the Europeans could only be seen as an unusual form of barbarian. To the Chinese ruler, the rulers of all other countries were simply "younger brothers" of the Chinese emperor, who was viewed as the Son of Heaven.

By the time the Portuguese fleet arrived off the coast of China, the Ming dynasty, which ruled from 1369 to 1644, had already begun a new era of greatness in Chinese history. Under a series of strong rulers, China extended its rule into Mongolia and Central Asia. The Ming even briefly reconquered Vietnam. Along the northern frontier, they strengthened the Great Wall and made peace with the nomadic tribesmen who had troubled China for centuries.

But the days of the Ming dynasty were numbered. After a period of prosperity and growth, the Ming gradually began to decline. During the late sixteenth century, a series of weak rulers led to a period of government

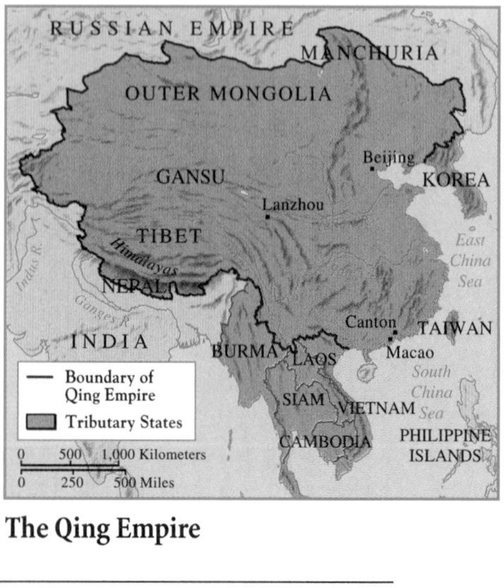

The Qing Empire

An Imperial Edict to the King of England

In 1793, the British emissary Lord Macartney visited the Qing Empire to request the opening of trading relations between his country and China. Emperor Qianlong's reply, addressed to King George III of England, illustrates how the imperial court in Beijing viewed the world. King George cannot have been pleased.

An Imperial Edict to the King of England

You, O King, are so inclined toward our civilization that you have sent a special envoy across the seas to bring to our Court your memorial of congratulations on the occasion of my birthday and to present your native products as an expression of your thoughtfulness. On perusing your memorial, so simply worded and sincerely conceived, I am impressed by your genuine respectfulness and friendliness and greatly pleased.

As to the request made in your memorial, O King, to send one of your nationals to stay at the Celestial Court to take care of your country's trade with China, this is not in harmony with the state system of our dynasty and will definitely not be permitted. Traditionally people of the European nations who wished to tender some service under the Celestial Court have been permitted to come to the capital. But after their arrival they are obliged to wear Chinese court costumes, are placed in a certain residence and are never allowed to return to their own countries. This is the established rule of the Celestial Dynasty with which presumably you, O King, are familiar. Now you, O King, wish to send one of your nationals to live in the capital, but he is not like the Europeans, who come to Beijing as Chinese employees, live there and never return home again, nor can he be allowed to go and come and maintain any correspondence. This is indeed a useless undertaking. . . .

The Celestial Court has pacified and possessed the territory within the four seas. Its sole aim is to do its utmost to achieve good government and to manage political affairs, attaching no value to strange jewels and precious objects. The various articles presented by you, O King, this time are accepted by my special order to the office in charge of such functions in consideration of the offerings having come from a long distance with sincere good wishes. As a matter of fact, the virtue and prestige of the Celestial Dynasty having spread far and wide, the kings of the myriad nations come by land and sea with all sorts of precious things. Consequently there is nothing we lack, as your principal envoy and others have themselves observed. We have never set much store on strange objects, nor do we need any more of your country's manufactures.

corruption. As always, internal problems went hand in hand with unrest along the northern frontier. The Ming had tried to come to terms with the frontier tribes by making alliances with them. One of the alliances was with the Manchus, who lived northeast of the Great Wall in the area known today as Manchuria. In 1644, the Manchus overthrew the last Ming emperor and declared the creation of a new dynasty with the reign title of the Qing (Ch'ing, "Pure"). The Qing were blessed with a series of strong early rulers who pacified the country, corrected the most serious social and economic ills, and restored peace and prosperity. Two Qing monarchs, Kangxi and Qianlong, ruled China for well over a century, from the middle of the seventeenth century to the end of the eighteenth. They were responsible for much of the greatness of Manchu China.

WESTERN INROADS

Although China was at the height of its power and glory in the mid-eighteenth century, the first signs of the internal decay of the Manchu dynasty were beginning to appear. Qing military campaigns along the frontier cost much money and placed heavy demands on the treasury. At the same time, growing pressure on the land because of population growth led to economic hardship for many peasants and even rebellion.

Unfortunately for China, the decline of the Qing dynasty occurred just as Europe was increasing pressure for more trade. The first conflict had come from the north, where Russian traders sought skins and furs. Formal diplomatic relations between China and Russia were established in 1689 and provided for regular trade between the two countries.

Dealing with the foreigners who arrived by sea was more difficult. By the end of the seventeenth century, the English had replaced the Portuguese as the dominant force in European trade. Operating through the East India Company, which served as both a trading unit and the administrator of English territories in Asia, the English established their first trading post at Canton in 1699. Over the next decades, trade with China, notably the export of tea and silk to England, increased rapidly. To limit contacts between Europeans and Chinese, the Qing government confined all European traders to a small island just outside the city walls of Canton and permitted them to reside there only from October through March.

For a while, the British accepted this system, which brought considerable profit to the East India Company. But by the end of the eighteenth century, some British traders had begun to demand access to other cities along the Chinese coast and insist that the country be opened to British manufactured goods. In 1793, a British mission under Lord Macartney visited Beijing to press for liberalization of trade restrictions. But Emperor Qianlong expressed no interest in British products (see the box above). An exasperated Macartney compared the Chinese Empire to "an old, crazy, first-rate man-of-war" that had once awed its neighbors "merely by her bulk and appearance" but was now destined under incompetent leadership to be "dashed to pieces on the shore." The Chinese would later pay for their rejection of the British request (see Chapter 24).

Japan

At the end of the fifteenth century, Japan was at a point of near anarchy, but in the course of the sixteenth century, a number of powerful individuals achieved the unification of Japan. One of them, Tokugawa Ieyasu (1543–1616), took the title of shogun ("general") in 1603, an act that initiated the most powerful and long-lasting of all the Japanese shogunates. The Tokugawa rulers completed the restoration of central authority and remained in power until 1868.

OPENING TO THE WEST

Portuguese traders had landed on the islands of Japan in 1543, and in a few years, Portuguese ships began stopping at Japanese ports on a regular basis to take part in the regional trade between Japan, China, and Southeast Asia. The first Jesuit missionary, Francis Xavier, arrived in 1549 and had some success in converting the local population to Christianity.

Initially, the visitors were welcomed. The curious Japanese were fascinated by tobacco, clocks, eyeglasses, and other European goods, and local nobles were interested in purchasing all types of European weapons and armaments. Japanese rulers found the new firearms especially helpful in defeating their enemies and unifying the islands. The effect on Japanese military architecture was especially striking, as local lords began to erect castles in stone on the European model.

The success of Catholic missionaries, however, created a strong reaction against the presence of Westerners. When the missionaries interfered in local politics, Tokugawa Ieyasu, newly come to power, expelled all missionaries. Japanese Christians were now persecuted. When a group of Christian peasants on the island of Kyushu revolted in 1637, they were bloodily suppressed.

The European merchants were the next to go. The government closed the two major foreign trading posts on the island of Hirado and at Nagasaki. Only a small Dutch community in Nagasaki was allowed to remain in Japan. The Dutch, unlike the Spanish and Portuguese, had not allowed missionary activities to interfere with their trade interests. But the conditions for staying were strict. Dutch ships were allowed to dock at Nagasaki harbor once a year and could remain for only two or three months.

The Americas

In the sixteenth century, Spain and Portugal had established large colonial empires in the Americas. Portugal continued to profit from its empire in Brazil. The Spanish also maintained an enormous South American empire, but Spain's importance as a commercial power declined rapidly in the seventeenth century because of a drop in the output of the silver mines and the poverty of the Spanish monarchy. By the beginning of the seventeenth century, both Portugal and Spain found themselves with new challenges to their

The Portuguese Arrive at Nagasaki. Portuguese traders landed accidentally in Japan in 1543. In a few years, they arrived regularly, taking part in a regional trade network between Japan, China, and Southeast Asia. In these panels, done in black lacquer and gold leaf, we see a late-sixteenth-century Japanese interpretation of the first Portuguese landing at Nagasaki.

American empires from the Dutch, British, and French, who increasingly sought to create their own colonial empires in the New World.

THE WEST INDIES

Both the French and British colonial empires in the New World included large parts of the West Indies. The British held Barbados, Jamaica, and Bermuda, and the French possessed Saint Domingue, Martinique, and Guadeloupe. On these tropical islands, both the British and the French had developed plantation economies, worked by African slaves, which produced tobacco, cotton, coffee, and sugar, all products increasingly in demand in Europe.

The "sugar factories," as the sugar plantations in the Caribbean were called, played an especially prominent role. By the last two decades of the eighteenth century, the British colony of Jamaica, one of Britain's most important, was producing 50,000 tons of sugar annually with the slave labor of 200,000 blacks. The French colony of Saint Domingue (later Haiti) had 500,000 slaves working on three thousand plantations at the same time. This colony produced 100,000 tons of sugar a year, but at the expense of a high death rate from the brutal treatment of the slaves. It is not surprising that Saint Domingue was the site of the first successful slave uprising in 1793.

NORTH AMERICA

Although Spain claimed all of North America as part of its American overseas empire, other nations largely ignored its claim. The British argued that "prescription without possession availeth nothing." The Dutch were among the first to establish settlements on the North American continent after Henry Hudson, an English explorer hired by the Dutch, discovered in 1609 the river that bears his name. Within a few years, the Dutch had established the mainland colony of New Netherlands, which stretched from the mouth of the Hudson River as far north as Albany, New York. Present-day names such as Staten Island and Harlem remind us that it was the Dutch who initially settled the Hudson River valley. In the second half of the seventeenth century, competition from the English and French and years of warfare with those rivals led to the decline of the Dutch commercial empire. In 1664, the English seized the colony of New Netherlands and renamed it New York; soon afterward, the Dutch West India Company went bankrupt.

In the meantime, the English had begun to establish their own colonies in North America. The first permanent English settlement in America was Jamestown, founded in 1607 in modern Virginia. It barely survived, which made it evident that the colonizing of American

A Sugar Mill in the West Indies. Cane sugar was one of the most valuable products produced in the West Indies. By 1700, sugar was replacing honey as a sweetener for increasing numbers of Europeans. This seventeenth-century French illustration shows the operation of a sugar mill in the French West Indies.

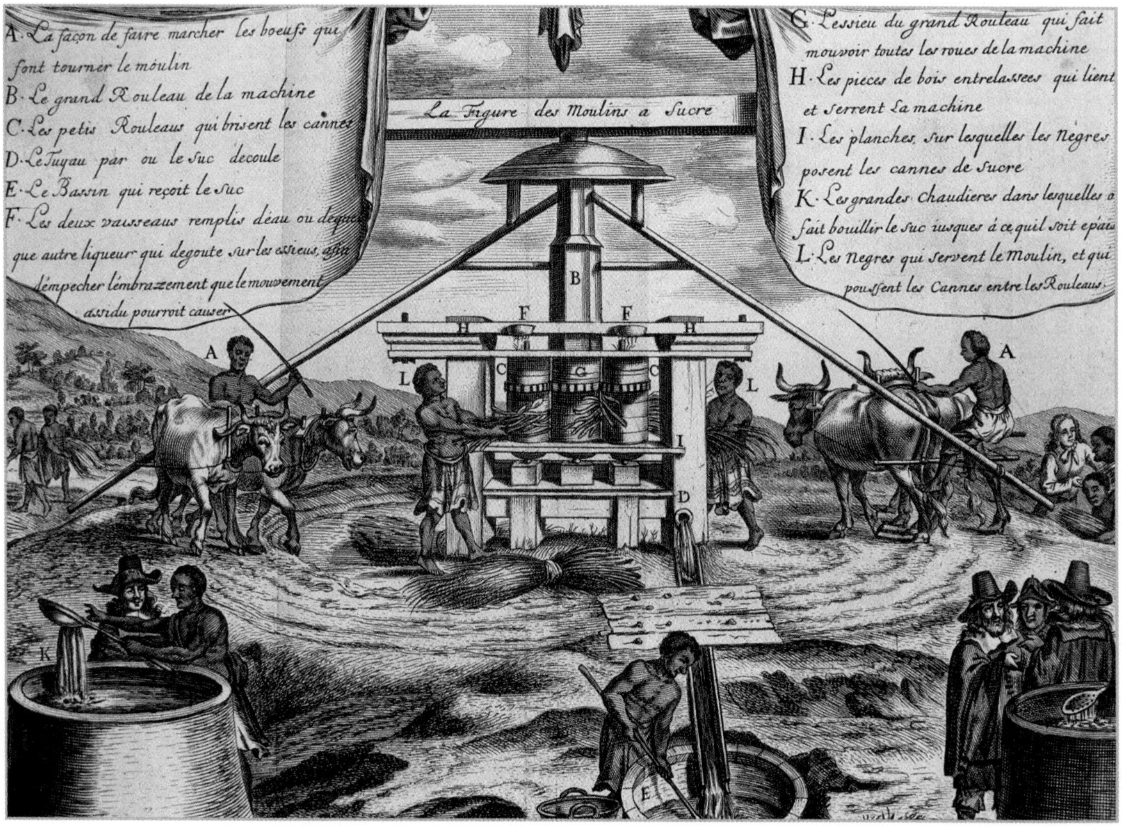

The Art Archive/London

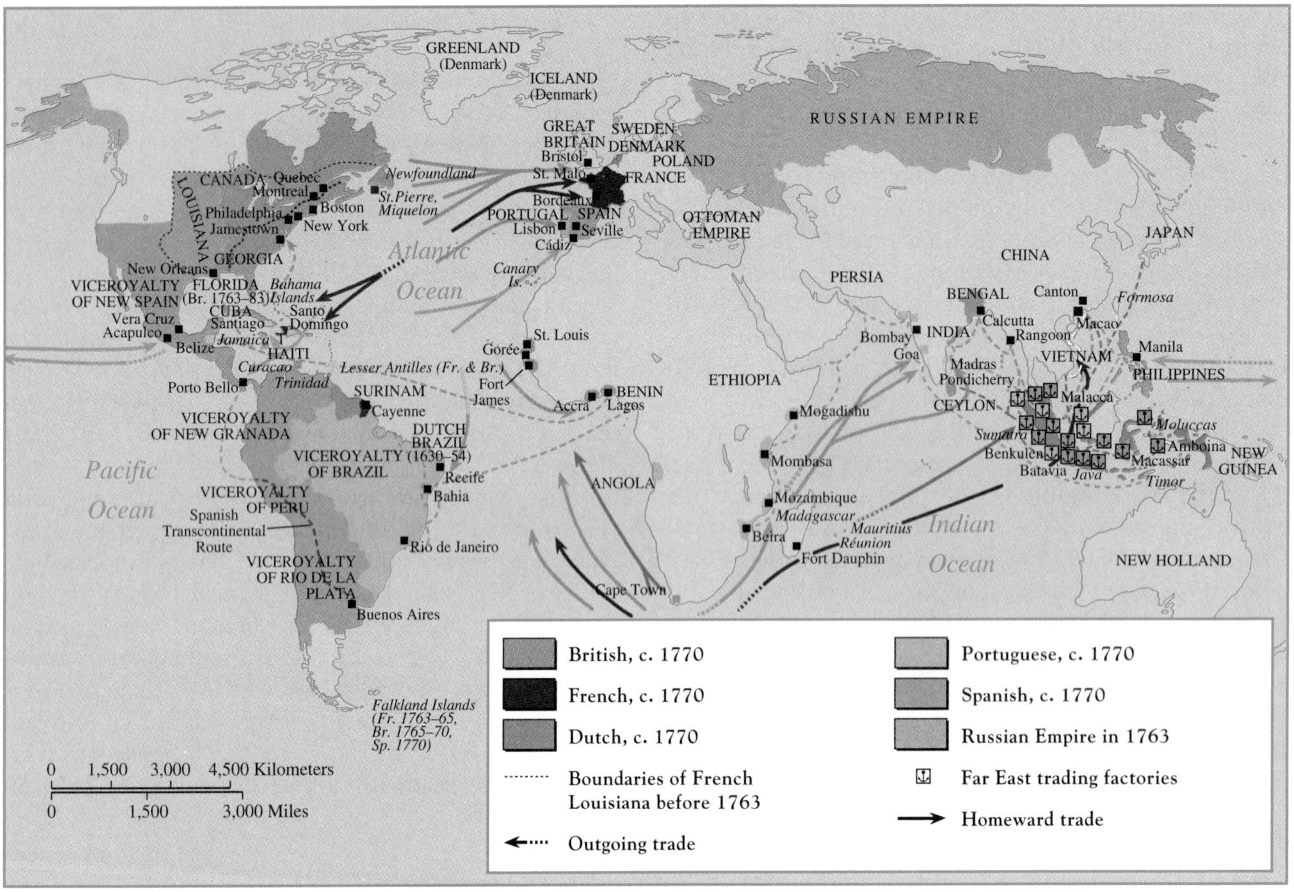

Map 14.3 Global Trade Patterns of the European States in the Eighteenth Century. In the eighteenth century, most European trade was still conducted within Europe, but the earlier advent of colonialism led to a large increase in trade across the oceans. This emerging global economy was dominated by Britain, the largest naval power, after it won much of France's overseas empire in the Seven Years' War. ■ With what regions did Britain conduct most of its trade?

lands was not necessarily conducive to quick profits. But the desire to practice one's own religion, combined with economic interests, could lead to successful colonization, as the Massachusetts Bay Company demonstrated. The Massachusetts colony had four thousand settlers in its early years but by 1660 had swelled to forty thousand. By the end of the seventeenth century, the English had established control over most of the eastern seaboard of the present United States.

British North America came to consist of thirteen colonies. They were thickly populated, containing about 1.5 million people by 1750, and were also prosperous. Supposedly run by the British Board of Trade, the Royal Council, and Parliament, these thirteen colonies had legislatures that tended to act independently. Merchants in such port cities as Boston, Philadelphia, New York, and Charleston resented and resisted regulation from the British government.

Both the North American and West Indian colonies of Britain were assigned roles in keeping with mercantilist theory (see "Mercantilism" later in this chapter). They provided raw materials for the mother country while buying the latter's manufactured goods. Navigation acts regulated what could be taken from and sold to the colonies. Theoretically, the system was supposed to provide a balance of trade favorable to the mother country.

The French also established a colonial empire in North America. Already in 1534, the French explorer Jacques Cartier had discovered the Saint Lawrence River and laid claim to Canada as a French possession. It was not, however, until Samuel de Champlain established a settlement at Quebec in 1608 that the French began to take a more serious interest in Canada as a colony. In 1663, Canada was made the property of the French crown and administered by a French governor like a French province.

French North America was run autocratically as a vast trading area, where valuable furs, leather, fish, and timber were acquired. However, the inability of the French state to get its people to emigrate to their Canadian possessions left them thinly populated. By the mid-eighteenth century, there were about fifteen thousand French Canadians, most of whom were hunters, trappers, missionaries, and explorers. The French failed to provide adequate men or money, allowing their Continental wars to take precedence over the conquest of the North American continent. Already in 1713, by the Treaty of Utrecht, the French began to cede some of their American possessions to their English rival. As a result of the Seven Years' War, they would surrender the rest of their Canadian lands in 1763 (see Chapter 18).

British and French rivalry was also evident in the Spanish and Portuguese colonial empires in Latin America. The decline of Spain and Portugal had led these two states to depend even more on resources from their colonies, and they imposed strict mercantilist rules to keep others out. Spain, for example, tried to limit all trade with its colonies to Spanish ships. But the British and French were too powerful to be excluded. The British cajoled the Portuguese into allowing them into the lucrative Brazilian trade. The French, however, were the first to break into the Spanish Latin American market when the French Bourbons became kings of Spain. Britain's entry into Spanish American markets first came in 1713, when the British were granted the privilege, known as the *asiento,* of transporting 4,500 slaves a year into Spanish Latin America.

CHRONOLOGY

New Rivals on the World Stage

Portuguese traders land in Japan	1543
British East India Company formed	1600
Dutch East India Company formed	1602
English settlement at Jamestown	1607
Champlain establishes settlement at Quebec	1608
Dutch fort established at Batavia	1619
Dutch seize Malacca from the Portuguese	1641
English seize New Netherlands	1664
English establish trading post at Canton	1699
Battle of Plassey	1757
French cede Canada to British	1763
British mission to China	1793

Toward a World Economy

During the High Middle Ages, Europeans had engaged in a commercial revolution that created new opportunities for townspeople in a basically agrarian economy. Although this commercial thrust was slowed by the devastating crises of the fourteenth century, the beginning of Europe's discovery of the world outside in the fifteenth century led to an even greater burst of commercial activity and the inception of a world market.

Economic Conditions in the Sixteenth Century

Inflation was a major economic problem in the sixteenth and early seventeenth centuries. This so-called price revolution was a Europe-wide phenomenon, although different areas were affected at different times. Though the inflation rate was probably a relatively low 2 to 3 percent a year, it was noticeable in a Europe accustomed to stable prices. Foodstuffs were most subject to price increases, especially evident in the price of wheat. An upward surge in wheat prices was first noticed in the Mediterranean area—in Spain, southern France, and Italy—and reached its peak there in the 1590s.

Although precise data are lacking, economic historians believe that as a result of the price revolution, wages failed to keep up with price increases. Wage earners, especially agricultural laborers and salaried workers in urban areas, saw their standard of living drop. At the same time, landed aristocrats, who could raise rents, managed to prosper. Commercial and industrial entrepreneurs also benefited from the price revolution because of rising prices, expanding markets, and relatively cheaper labor costs. Some historians regard this profit inflation as a valuable stimulus to investment and the growth of capitalism, helping to explain the economic expansion and prosperity of the sixteenth century. Governments were likewise affected by inflation. They borrowed heavily from bankers and imposed new tax burdens on their subjects, often stirring additional discontent.

The causes of the price revolution are a subject of much historical debate. Already in the 1560s, European intellectuals had associated the rise in prices with the great influx of precious metals from the New World. Although this view was accepted for a long time, many economic historians now believe that the increase in population in the sixteenth century played an important role in creating inflationary pressures. A growing population increased the demand for land and food and drove up prices for both.

The Growth of Commercial Capitalism

The flourishing European trade of the sixteenth century revolved around three major areas: the Mediterranean in the south, the Low Countries and the Baltic region in the north, and central Europe, whose inland trade depended on the Rhine and Danube Rivers. As overseas trade expanded, however, the Atlantic seaboard began to play a more important role, linking the Mediterranean, Baltic, and central European trading areas together and making the whole of Europe into a more integrated market that was all the more vulnerable to price shifts. With their cheaper and faster ships, the Dutch came to monopolize both European and world trade, although they were increasingly challenged by the English and French in the seventeenth century.

The commercial expansion of the sixteenth and seventeenth centuries was made easier by new forms of commercial organization, especially the joint-stock trading company. Individuals bought shares in a company and received dividends on their investment while a board of directors ran the company and made the important business decisions. The return on investments could be spectacular. During its first ten years, investors received 30 percent on their money from the Dutch East India Company, which opened the Spice Islands and Southeast Asia to Dutch activity. The joint-stock company made it easier to raise large amounts of capital for world trading ventures.

Enormous profits were also being made in shipbuilding and in mining and metallurgy, where technological innovations, such as the use of pumps and new methods of extracting metals from ores, proved highly successful. The mining industry was closely tied to sixteenth-century family banking firms. In exchange for arranging large loans to Charles V, Jacob Fugger was given a monopoly over silver, copper, and mercury mines in the Habsburg possessions of central Europe that produced profits in excess of 50 percent per year. Though these close relationships between governments and entrepreneurs could lead to stunning successes, they could also be precarious. The House of Fugger went bankrupt at the end of the sixteenth century when the Habsburgs defaulted on their loans.

By the seventeenth century, the traditional family banking firms were no longer able to supply the numerous services needed for the commercial capitalism of the seventeenth century. New institutions arose to take their place. The city of Amsterdam created the Bank of Amsterdam in 1609 as both a deposit and a transfer institution and the Amsterdam Bourse, or Exchange, where the trading of stocks replaced the exchange of goods. By the first half of the seventeenth century, the Amsterdam Exchange had emerged as the hub of the European business world, just as Amsterdam itself had replaced Antwerp as the greatest commercial and banking center of Europe.

Jacob Fugger the Rich. Jacob Fugger, head of one of the wealthiest banking firms of the sixteenth century, is pictured here with his faithful secretary, Matthaus Schwartz, who painted this scene in 1516. The cabinet in the background lists the names of the cities where Fugger's firm had branch offices, including Milan, Innsbruck, Nuremberg, and Lisbon.

Herzog Anton Ulrich Museum, Braunschweig

Despite the growth of commercial capitalism, most of the European economy still depended on an agricultural system that had experienced few changes since the thirteenth century. At least 80 percent of Europeans still worked on the land. Almost all of the peasants of western Europe were free of serfdom, although many still owed a variety of feudal dues to the nobility. Despite the expanding markets and rising prices, European peasants saw little or no improvement in their lot as they faced increased rents and fees and higher taxes imposed by the state. In eastern Europe, the peasants' position even worsened as they were increasingly tied to the land in a new serfdom enforced by powerful landowners (see Chapter 15).

Mercantilism

Mercantilism is the name historians use to identify a set of economic tendencies that came to dominate economic practices in the seventeenth century. Fundamental to mercantilism was the belief that the total volume of trade was unchangeable. Colbert, a French financier, observed that "trade causes perpetual conflict, both in war and in peace, among the nations of Europe, as to who should carry off the greatest part. The Dutch, the English and the French are the actors in this conflict."[9] Since one nation could expand its trade and hence its prosperity only at the expense of others, to mercantilists, economic activity was war carried on by peaceful means.

According to the mercantilists, the prosperity of a nation depended on a plentiful supply of bullion, or gold and silver. For this reason, it was desirable to achieve a favorable balance of trade in which goods exported were of greater value than those imported, promoting an influx of gold and silver payments that would increase the quantity of bullion. Furthermore, to encourage exports, governments should stimulate and protect export industries and trade by granting trade monopolies, encouraging investment in new industries through subsidies, importing foreign artisans, and improving transportation systems by building roads, bridges, and canals. By placing high tariffs on foreign goods, they could be kept out of the country and prevented from competing with domestic industries. Colonies were also deemed valuable as sources of raw materials and markets for finished goods.

Mercantilism focused on the role of the state, believing that state intervention in some aspects of the economy was desirable for the sake of the national good. Government regulations to ensure the superiority of export goods, the construction of roads and canals, and the granting of subsidies to create trade companies were all predicated on government involvement in economic affairs.

Overseas Trade and Colonies: Movement Toward Globalization

Mercantilist theory on the role of colonies was matched in practice by Europe's overseas expansion. With the development of colonies and trading posts in the Americas and the East, Europeans embarked on an adventure in international commerce in the seventeenth century. Although some historians speak of a nascent world economy, we should remember that local, regional, and intra-European trade still predominated. At the end of the seventeenth century, for example, English imports totaled 360,000 tons, but only 5,000 tons came from the East Indies. About one-tenth of English and Dutch exports were shipped across the Atlantic; slightly more went to the East. What made the transoceanic trade rewarding, however, was not the volume but the value of its goods. Dutch, English, and French merchants were bringing back products that were still consumed largely by the wealthy but were beginning to make their way into the lives of artisans and merchants. Pepper and spices from the Indies, West Indian and Brazilian sugar, and Asian coffee and tea were becoming more readily available to European consumers.

Trade within Europe remained strong throughout the eighteenth century as wheat, timber, and naval stores from the Baltic, wines from France, wool and fruit from Spain, and silk from Italy were exchanged along with a host of other products. But this trade increased only slightly while overseas trade boomed. From 1716 to 1789, total French exports quadrupled; intra-European trade, which constituted 75 percent of these exports in 1716, accounted for only 50 percent of the total in 1789. This increase in overseas trade has led some historians to proclaim the emergence of a truly global economy in the eighteenth century. Trade patterns now interlocked Europe, Africa, the East, and the Americas. For example, British merchant ships carried British manufactured goods to Africa, where they were traded for a cargo of slaves, which were then shipped to the West Indies or Virginia, where the slaves would be auctioned. The British ships would then carry sugar, tobacco, and other valuable products from the Americas back to Europe to be sold.

The Impact of European Expansion

Between 1500 and 1800, the Atlantic nations of Europe moved into all parts of the world. The first had been Spain and Portugal, the two great colonial powers of the sixteenth century, followed by the Dutch, who built their colonial empire in the seventeenth century as Portugal and Spain declined. The Dutch were soon challenged by the British and French, who outstripped the others in the eighteenth century while becoming involved in a bitter rivalry. By the end of the eighteenth century, it appeared that Great Britain would become the great European imperial power. European expansion made a great impact on both the conquerors and the conquered.

The Conquered

The native American civilizations, which had their own unique qualities and a degree of sophistication not much appreciated by Europeans, were virtually destroyed. In addition to devastating losses of population from European diseases, ancient social and political structures were ripped up and replaced by European institutions, religion, language, and culture. In Africa, European involvement in the slave trade led to devastating effects, especially in coastal areas. Before 1800, however, European influence generally did not penetrate into the interior of Africa. The Portuguese trading posts in the East had little direct impact on native Asian civilizations, although Dutch control of the Indonesian archipelago was more pervasive. China and Japan were still little affected by Westerners, although India was subject to ever-growing British encroachment.

In Central and South America, a new civilization arose that we have come to call Latin America. It was a multiracial society. Spanish and Portuguese settlers who arrived in the Western Hemisphere were few in number compared to the native Indians; many of the newcomers were males who not only used female natives for their sexual pleasure but married them as well. Already by 1501, Spanish rulers had authorized intermarriage between Europeans and native American Indians, whose offspring became known as mestizos. Another group of people brought to Latin America were the Africans. Over a period of three centuries, possibly as many as eight million slaves were brought to Spanish and Portuguese America to work the

The Mission

In 1609, two Jesuit priests embarked on a missionary calling with the Guaraní Indians in eastern Paraguay. Eventually, the Jesuits established more than thirty missions in the region. Well organized and zealous, the Jesuits transformed their missions into profitable businesses. This description of a Jesuit mission in Paraguay was written by Félix de Azara, a Spanish soldier and scientist.

Félix de Azara, Description and History of Paraguay and Rio de la Plata

Having spoken of the towns founded by the Jesuit fathers, and of the manner in which they were founded, I shall discuss the government which they established in them. . . . In each town resided two priests, a curate and a subcurate, who had certain assigned functions. The subcurate was charged with all the spiritual tasks, and the curate with every kind of temporal responsibility. . . .

The curate allowed no one to work for personal gain; he compelled everyone, without distinction of age or sex, to work for the community, and he himself saw to it that all were equally fed and dressed. For this purpose the curates placed in storehouses all the fruits of agriculture and the products of industry, selling in the Spanish towns their surplus of cotton, cloth, tobacco, vegetables, skins, and wood, transporting them in their own boats down the nearest rivers, and returning with implements and whatever else was required.

From the foregoing one may infer that the curate disposed of the surplus funds of the Indian towns, and that no Indian could aspire to own private property. This deprived them of any incentive to use reason or talent, since the most industrious, able, and worthy person had the same food, clothing, and pleasures as the most wicked, dull, and indolent. It also follows that although this form of government was well designed to enrich the communities it also caused the Indian to work at a languid pace, since the wealth of his community was of no concern to him.

It must be said that although the Jesuit fathers were supreme in all respects, they employed their authority with a mildness and a restraint that command admiration. They supplied everyone with abundant food and clothing. They compelled the men to work only half a day, and did not drive them to produce more. Even their labor was given a festive air, for they went in procession to the fields, to the sound of music . . . and the music did not cease until they had returned in the same way they had set out. They gave them many holidays, dances, and tournaments, dressing the actors and the members of the municipal councils in gold or silver tissue and the most costly European garments, but they permitted the women to act only as spectators.

They likewise forbade the women to sew; this occupation was restricted to the musicians, sacristans, and acolytes. But they made them spin cotton; and the cloth that the Indians wove, after satisfying their own needs, they sold together with the surplus cotton in the Spanish towns, as they did with the tobacco, vegetables, wood, and skins. The curate and his companion, or subcurate, had their own plain dwellings, and they never left them except to take the air in the great enclosed yard of their college. They never walked through the streets of the town or entered the house of any Indian or let themselves be seen by any woman—or indeed, by any man, except for those indispensable few through whom they issued their orders.

plantations. Africans also contributed to Latin America's multiracial character. Mulattoes—the offspring of Africans and whites—joined mestizos and descendants of whites, Africans, and native Indians to produce a unique society in Latin America. Unlike Europe, and unlike British North America, which remained a largely white offshoot of Europe, Latin America developed a multiracial society with less rigid attitudes about race.

The ecology of conquered areas was also affected by the European presence. Europeans brought horses and cattle to the Americas. Horses revolutionized the life of the Plains Indians; South America would later become a great exporter of beef. Europeans brought new crops, such as wheat and cane sugar, to be cultivated on large plantations by native or imported slave labor. In their trips to other parts of the world, Europeans also carried New World plants with them. Thus Europeans introduced sweet potatoes and maize (Indian corn) to Africa in the sixteenth century.

CATHOLIC MISSIONARIES

Although there were some Protestant missionaries in the world outside Europe, Catholic missionaries were far more active in spreading Christianity. From the beginning of their conquest of the New World, Spanish and Portuguese rulers were determined to Christianize the native peoples. This policy gave the Catholic church an important role to play in the New World, and one that added considerably to church power. Catholic missionaries—especially the Dominicans, Franciscans, and Jesuits—fanned out to different parts of the Spanish Empire.

To facilitate their efforts, missionaries brought Indians together into villages, where the natives could be converted, taught trades, and encouraged to grow crops. These missions enabled the missionaries to control the lives of the Indians and helped ensure that they would remain docile members of the empire (see the box on p. 394). In such frontier districts as California and Texas, missions also served as military barriers to foreign encroachment.

The Catholic church constructed hospitals, orphanages, and schools. Monastic schools instructed Indian students in the rudiments of reading, writing, and arithmetic. The Catholic church also provided outlets for women other than marriage. Nunneries were places of prayer and quiet contemplation, but women in religious orders, many of them of aristocratic background, often lived well and worked outside their establishments by running schools and hospitals. Indeed, one of these nuns, Sor Juana Inés de la Cruz (1651–1695), was one of seventeenth-century Latin America's best-known literary figures. She wrote poetry and prose and urged that women be educated.

Christian missionaries had also made the long voyage to China on European merchant ships. The Jesuits were among the most active and the most effective. Many of the early Jesuit missionaries to China were highly educated men who were familiar with European philosophical and scientific developments. They brought along clocks and various other instruments that impressed Chinese officials and made them more open to Western ideas.

The Jesuits used this openness to promote Christianity. To make it easier for the Chinese to accept Christianity, the Jesuits pointed to similarities between Christian morality and Confucian ethics. The Italian priest Matteo Ricci described the Jesuit approach:

> In order that the appearance of a new religion might not arouse suspicion among the Chinese people, the Jesuit Fathers did not speak openly about religious matters when they began to appear in public. . . . They did, however, try to teach this pagan people in a more direct way, namely, by virtue of their example and by the sanctity of their lives. In this way they attempted to win the good will of the people and little by little to dispose their minds to receive what they could not be persuaded to accept by word of mouth. . . . From the time of their entrance they wore the ordinary Chinese outer garment, which was somewhat similar to their own religious habits; a long robe reaching down to the heels and with very ample sleeves, which are much in favor with the Chinese.[10]

The efforts of the Christian missionaries, Dominicans and Franciscans as well as Jesuits, reached their height in the early eighteenth century. Several hundred Chinese officials became Catholics, as did an estimated 300,000 ordinary Chinese. But ultimately the Christian effort was undermined by squabbling among the religious orders themselves. To make it easier for the Chinese to convert, the Jesuits had allowed the new Catholics to continue the practice of ancestor worship. Jealous Dominicans and Franciscans complained to the pope, who condemned the practice. Soon Chinese authorities began to suppress Christian activities throughout China.

The Jesuits also had some success in Japan, where they converted a number of local nobles. By the end of the sixteenth century, thousands of Japanese on the southernmost islands of Kyushu and Shikoku had become Christians. But the Jesuit practice of destroying local idols and shrines and turning some temples into Christian schools or churches caused a severe reaction. When a new group of Spanish Franciscans continued the same policies, the government ordered the execution of nine missionaries and a number of their Japanese converts. When missionaries continued to interfere in local politics, Tokugawa Ieyasu expelled all missionaries. Japanese Christians were now persecuted.

The Conquerors

For some Europeans, expansion abroad brought hopes for land, riches, and social advancement. One Spaniard commented in 1572 that many "poor young men" left Spain for Mexico, where they might hope to acquire landed estates and call themselves "gentlemen." Although some wives accompanied their husbands abroad, many ordinary European women found new opportunities for marriage in the New World because of the lack of white women. Indeed, as one commentator bluntly put it, even "a whore, if handsome, [can] make a wife for some rich planter."[11] In the violence-prone world of early Spanish America, a number of women also found themselves rich after their husbands were killed unexpectedly. In one area of Central America, women owned about 25 percent of the landed estates by 1700.

European expansion also had other economic effects on the conquerors. Wherever they went in the New World, Europeans sought to find sources of gold and silver. One Aztec commented that the Spanish conquerors "longed and lusted for gold. Their bodies swelled with greed, and their hunger was ravenous; they hungered like pigs for that gold."[12] Rich silver deposits were found and exploited in Mexico and southern Peru (modern Bolivia). When the mines at Potosí in Peru were opened in 1545, the value of precious metals imported into Europe quadrupled. Between 1503 and 1650, an estimated 16 million kilograms (over 35 million pounds) of silver and 185,000 kilograms (407,000 pounds) of gold entered the port of Seville and set off a price revolution that affected the Spanish economy.

But gold and silver were only two of the products that became part of the exchange between the New World and the Old. Historians refer to the reciprocal importation and exportation of plants and animals between Europe and the Americas as the Columbian exchange (see Map 14.4). While Europeans were bringing horses, cattle, and wheat to the New World, they were taking new agricultural products such as potatoes, chocolate, corn, tomatoes, and tobacco back to Europe.

The European lifestyle was greatly affected by new products from abroad. In addition to new foods, new drinks also appeared in Europe. Chocolate, which had been brought to Spain from Aztec Mexico, became a common drink by 1700. The first coffee and tea houses opened in

London in the 1650s and spread rapidly to other parts of Europe. In the eighteenth century, a craze for Chinese furniture and porcelain spread among the upper classes. Chinese ideas would also make an impact on intellectual attitudes (see Chapter 17).

European expansion, which was in part a product of European rivalries, also deepened those rivalries and increased the tensions among European states. Bitter conflicts arose over the cargoes coming from the New World and Asia. The Anglo-Dutch trade wars and the British-French rivalry over India and North America became part of a new pattern of worldwide warfare in the eighteenth century (see Chapter 18). Bitter rivalries also led to state-sponsored piracy in which governments authorized private captains to attack enemy shipping and keep part of the proceeds for themselves.

In the course of their expansion, Europeans also came to have a new view of the world. When the travels began in the fifteenth century, Europeans were dependent on maps that were often fanciful and inaccurate. Their explorations led them to create new maps that gave a more realistic portrayal of the world, as well as new techniques called map projections in order to represent the round surface of a sphere on a flat piece of paper. The most famous map projection in history is the Mercator projection, the work of a Flemish cartographer, Gerardus Mercator (1512–1594). The Mercator projection is what mapmakers call a conformal projection. This tries to show the true shape of landmasses, but only of a limited area. On the Mercator projection, the shapes of lands near the equator are quite accurate, but it greatly enlarges areas in the polar regions, far away from the equator. For example, the island of Greenland on a Mercator projection appears to be larger than the continent of South America. In fact, Greenland is about one-ninth the size of South America. The Mercator projection, however, was valuable to ship captains. Every straight line on a Mercator projection is a line of true direction, whether north, south, east, or west. For four centuries, ship captains were very grateful to Mercator.

Map 14.4 The Columbian Exchange. In addition to their diseases, which killed vast numbers of indigenous inhabitants of the Americas, Europeans transplanted many of their crops and domestic animals to the New World. Europeans also imported plants from the New World that increased food production and nutrition in Europe. ■ Where were the main source regions for native plants imported into Europe?

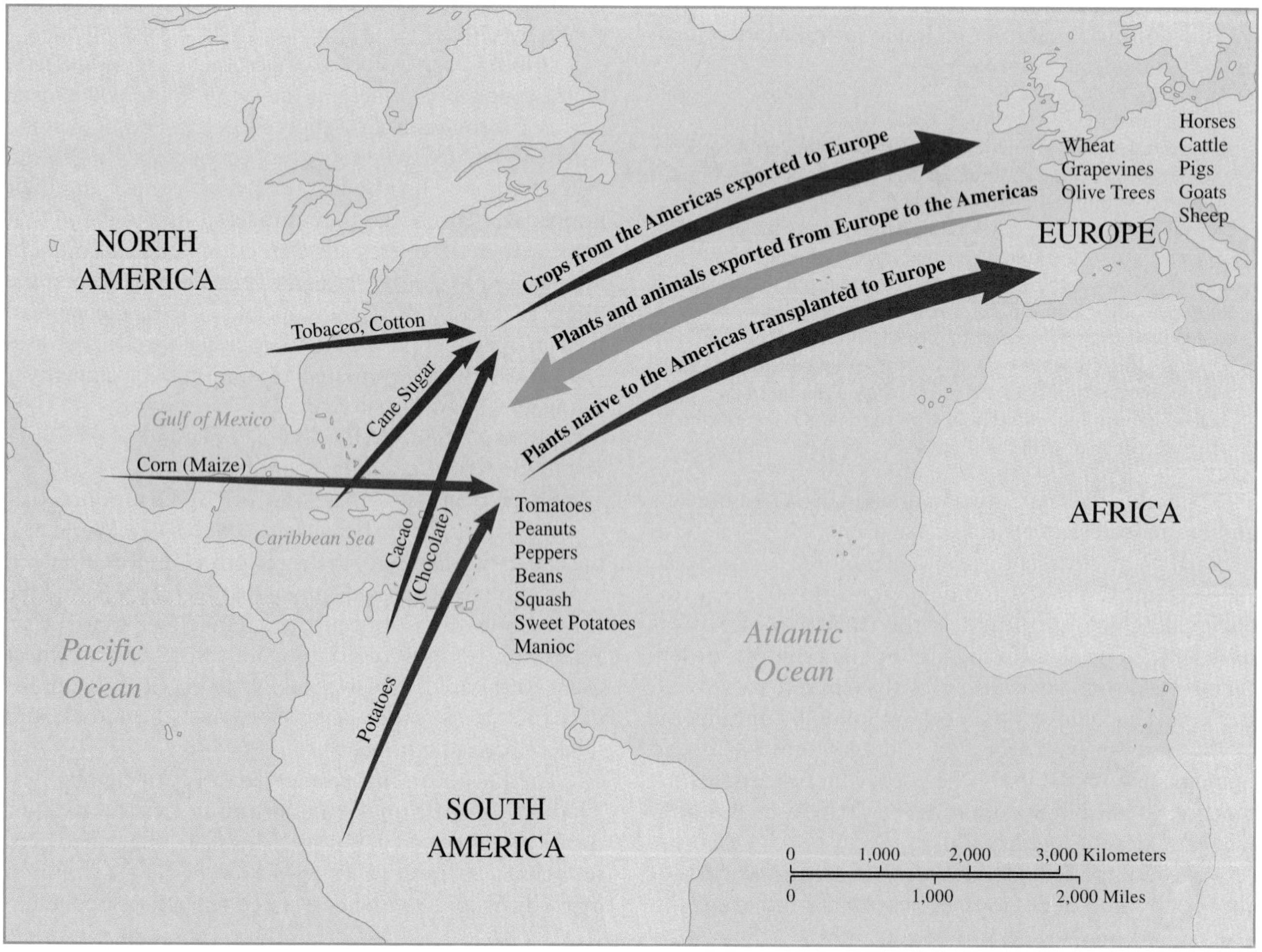

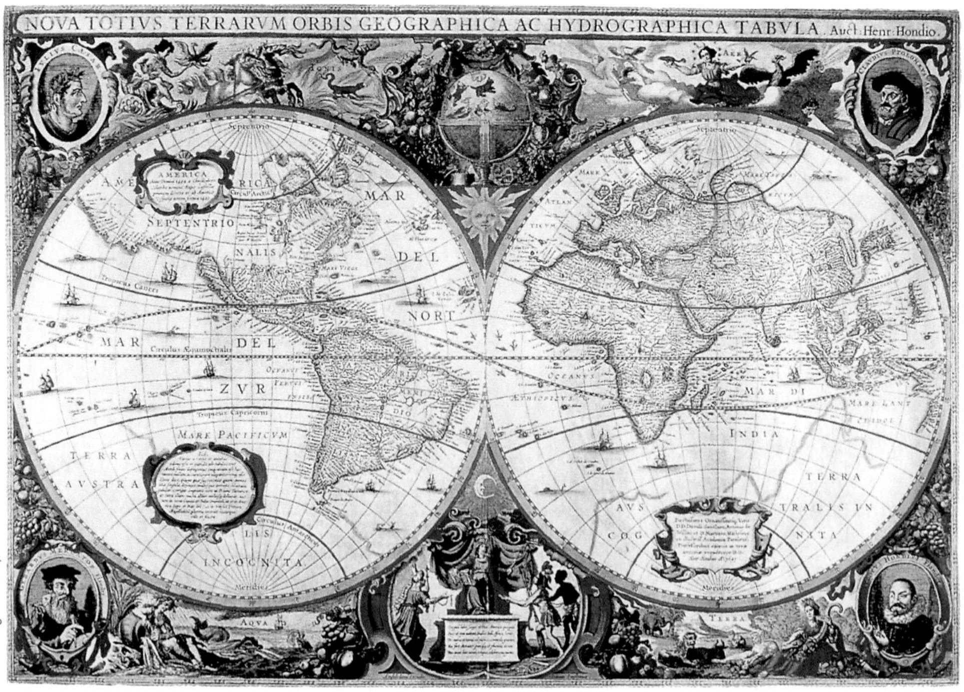

The Huntington Library, San Marino, CA

A Seventeenth-Century World Map. This beautiful world map was prepared in 1630 by Henricus Hondius. The four portraits are of Caesar, the Roman statesman; Ptolemy, the second-century astronomer; Mercator, the Flemish cartographer whose map projection Hondius followed; and Hondius himself. By comparing this map to the one of Ptolemy on page 370, one can see how much Europeans had learned about the shape of the world by the seventeenth century.

The psychological impact of colonization on the colonizers is awkward to evaluate but hard to deny. The relatively easy European success in dominating native peoples reinforced Christian Europe's belief in the inherent superiority of European civilization and religion. The Scientific Revolution of the seventeenth century (see Chapter 16), the Enlightenment of the eighteenth (see Chapter 17), and the imperialism of the nineteenth (see Chapter 24) would all bolster this Eurocentric perspective, which has pervaded Western civilization's relationship with the rest of the world.

	1450	1500	1550	1600	1650	1700	1750	1800
Portugal	Dias sails around tip of Africa	Portuguese seize Malacca						
Spain	Voyages of Columbus; Spanish conquest of Mexico	First boatload of African slaves to America; Pizarro's conquest of Incas						
France				Champlain establishes settlement at Quebec				
Netherlands			Dutch fort established at Batavia		Dutch seize Malacca from Portuguese			
England					English seize New Netherlands	English establish trading post at Canton	Battle of Plassey; French cede Canada to British	British mission to China

Conclusion

At the end of the fifteenth century, Europeans sailed out into the world in all directions. Beginning with the handful of Portuguese ships that ventured southward along the West African coast in the mid-fifteenth century, the process accelerated with the epochal voyages of Christopher Columbus to the Americas and Vasco da Gama to the Indian Ocean in the 1490s. Soon a number of other European states had joined in the adventure, and by the end of the eighteenth century, they had created a global trade network dominated by Western ships and Western power.

In less than three hundred years, the European Age of Exploration changed the shape of the world. In some areas, such as the Americas and the Spice Islands, it led to the destruction of indigenous civilizations and the establishment of European colonies. In others, as in Africa, India, and mainland Southeast Asia, it left native regimes intact but had a strong impact on local societies and regional trade patterns.

At the time, many European observers viewed the process in a favorable light. It not only expanded wealth through world trade and exchanged crops and discoveries between the Old and the New Worlds, they believed, but it also introduced "heathen peoples" to the message of Jesus Christ. No doubt the conquest of the Americas and expansion into the rest of the world brought out the worst and some of the best of European civilization. The greedy plundering of resources and the brutal repression and enslavement were hardly balanced by attempts to create new institutions, convert the natives to Christianity, and foster the rights of the indigenous peoples. In any case, Europeans had begun to change the face of the world and would continue on the new path they had started.

Notes

1. Quoted in J. R. Hale, *Renaissance Exploration* (New York, 1968), p. 32.
2. Quoted in J. H. Parry, *The Age of Reconnaissance: Discovery, Exploration, and Settlement, 1450 to 1650* (New York, 1963), p. 33.
3. Quoted in Richard B. Reed, "The Expansion of Europe," in Richard DeMolen, ed., *The Meaning of the Renaissance and Reformation* (Boston, 1974), p. 308.
4. Quoted in K. N. Chaudhuri, *Trade and Civilization in the Indian Ocean: An Economic History from the Rise of Islam to 1750* (Cambridge, 1985), p. 65.
5. Quoted in Ian Cameron, *Explorers and Exploration* (New York, 1991), p. 42.
6. Quoted in Basil Davidson, *Africa in History: Themes and Outlines*, rev. ed. (New York, 1991), p. 213.
7. Quoted in ibid., p. 198.
8. Quoted in Cameron, *Explorers and Exploration*, p. 42.
9. Quoted in H. G. Koenigsberger, *Early Modern Europe, 1500–1798* (London, 1987), p. 172.
10. Quoted in Louis J. Gallagher, ed. and trans., *China in the Sixteenth Century: The Journals of Matthew Ricci* (New York, 1953), p. 154.
11. Quoted in G. V. Scammell, *The First Imperial Age: European Overseas Expansion, c. 1400–1715* (London, 1989), p. 62.
12. Miguel Leon-Portilla, ed., *The Broken Spears: The Aztec Account of the Conquest of Mexico* (Boston, 1969), p. 51.

Suggestions for Further Reading

The best general accounts of European discovery and expansion are G. V. Scammell, *the First Imperial Age: European Overseas Expansion, c. 1400–1715* (London, 1989); J. H. Parry, *The Age of Reconnaissance: Discovery, Exploration, and Settlement, 1450 to 1650* (New York, 1963); and B. Penrose, *Travel and Discovery in the Renaissance, 1420–1620* (New York, 1962). On the medieval background to European expansion, see J. R. S. Phillips, *The Medieval Expansion of Europe* (New York, 1988). On European perceptions of the world outside Europe, see M. Campbell, *The Witness and the Other World: Exotic European Travel Writing, 400–1600* (Ithaca, N.Y., 1991), and J. B. Friedman, *The Monstrous Races in Medieval Art and Thought* (Cambridge, Mass., 1981). On the technological aspects, see R. C. Smith, *Vanguard of Empire: Ships of Exploration in the Age of Columbus* (Oxford, 1993).

On Portuguese expansion, see the fundamental work by C. R. Boxer, *The Portuguese Seaborne Empire, 1415–1825* (New York, 1969); W. B. Diffie and G. D. Winius, *Foundations of the Portuguese Empire, 1415–1580* (Minneapolis, 1979); and S. Subrahmanyam, *The Portuguese Empire in Asia, 1500–1700: A Political and Economic History* (New York, 1993). On Columbus, see F. Fernandez-Armesto, *Columbus* (New York, 1991), and W. D. Phillips and C. R. Phillips, *The Worlds of Christopher Columbus* (Cambridge, 1992). On the Spanish Empire in the New World, see J. H. Parry, *The Spanish Seaborne Empire* (New York, 1966). For a theoretical discussion of violence and gender in America, see R. Trexler, *Sex and Conquest: Gendered Violence, Political Order, and the European Conquest of the Americas* (Ithaca, N.Y., 1995). On the conquistadors, see the beautifully illustrated work by M. Wood, *Conquistadors* (Berkeley, 2000). On the destructive nature of the Spanish conquest of the Americas, see D. E. Standard, *American Holocaust: Columbus and the Conquest of the New World* (New York, 1993).

The subject of mercantile empires and worldwide trade is covered in J. H. Parry, *Trade and Dominion: Overseas Empires in the Eighteenth Century* (London, 1971); D. K. Fieldhouse, *The Colonial Empires* (New York, 1971); J. D. Tracy, *The Rise of Merchant Empires: Long-Distance Trade in the Early Modern World, 1350–1750* (Cambridge, 1990); and T. Benjamin, T. Hall, and D. Rutherford, eds., *The Atlantic World in the Age of Empire* (New York, 2001). See also A. Pagden, *Lords of All the Worlds: Ideologies of Empire in Spain, Britain and France, c. 1500–c. 1850* (New Haven, Conn., 1995). On the African slave trade, see H. Thomas, *The Slave Trade: The Story of the Atlantic Slave Trade, 1440–1870* (New York, 1997); the collection of articles in D. Northrup, ed., *The Atlantic Slave Trade* (Lexington, Mass., 1994); I. Berlin, *Thousands Gone* (Cambridge, Mass., 1998); and C. Palmer, *The First Passage: Blacks in the Americas, 1501–1617* (New York, 1995). On the Dutch colonial empire, see J. I. Israel, *Dutch Primacy in World Trade, 1585–1740* (Oxford, 1989). The effects of European trade in Southeast Asia are discussed in A. Reid, *Southeast Asia in the Age of*

Commerce, 1450–1680 (New Haven, Conn., 1989). On Asia, see H. Furber, *Rival Empires of Trade in the Orient, 1600–1800* (Minneapolis, 1976).

On the economic dimensions of expansion, there are the three volumes by F. Braudel, *Civilization and Capitalism in the 15th to 18th Century: The Structures of Everyday Life* (London, 1981), *The Wheels of Commerce* (London, 1982), and *The Perspective of the World* (London, 1984). On mercantilism, see L. Magnusson, *Mercantilism: The Shaping of an Economic Language* (New York, 1994). On the concept of a world economy, see A. K. Smith, *Creating a World Economy: Merchant Capital, Colonialism, and World Trade, 1400–1825* (Boulder, Colo., 1991).

The impact of expansion on European consciousness is explored in A. Pagden, *European Encounters with the New World: From Renaissance to Romanticism* (New Haven, Conn., 1993). The human and ecological effects of the interaction of New World and Old World cultures are examined thoughtfully in A. W. Crosby, *The Columbian Exchange: Biological and Cultural Consequences of 1492* (Westport, Conn., 1972), and *Ecological Imperialism: The Biological Expansion of Europe* (New York, 1986). For a general view of the interaction of cultures, see J. Diamond, *Guns, Germs, and Steel* (New York, 1997). The native American female experience with the European encounter is presented in R. Gutierrez, *When Jesus Came the Corn Mother Went Away: Marriage, Sexuality, and Power in New Mexico, 1500–1846* (Stanford, Calif., 1991).

For additional reading, go to InfoTrac College Edition, your online research library at http://web1.infotrac-college.com

Enter the search terms *Vasco da Gama* using Key Terms.

Enter the search terms *Ferdinand Magellan* using Key Terms.

Enter the search terms *Christopher Columbus* using Subject Guide.

Enter the search term *mercantilism* using Subject Guide.

C H A P T E R

15

State Building and the Search for Order in the Seventeenth Century

CHAPTER OUTLINE

- Social Crises, War, and Rebellions
- The Practice of Absolutism: Western Europe
- Absolutism in Central, Eastern, and Northern Europe
- Limited Monarchy and Republics
- The Flourishing of European Culture
- Conclusion

FOCUS QUESTIONS

- What economic, social, and political crises did Europe experience in the first half of the seventeenth century?
- What theories of government were proposed by Jacques Bossuet, Thomas Hobbes, and John Locke, and how did their respective theories reflect concerns and problems of the seventeenth century?
- What was absolutism in theory, and how did its actual practice in France reflect or differ from the theory?
- What developments enabled Brandenburg-Prussia, Austria, and Russia to emerge as major powers in the seventeenth century?
- What were the main issues in the struggle between king and Parliament in seventeenth-century England, and how were they resolved?
- How did the artistic and literary achievements of this era reflect the political and economic developments of the period?

BY THE END of the sixteenth century, Europe was beginning to experience a decline in religious passions and a growing secularization that affected both the political and intellectual worlds (on the intellectual effect, see Chapter 16). Some historians like to speak of the seventeenth century as a turning point in the evolution of a modern state system in Europe. The ideal of a united Christian Europe gave way to the practical realities of a system of secular states in which matters of state took precedence over the salvation of subjects' souls. By the seventeenth century, the credibility of Christianity had been so weakened through religious wars that more and more Europeans came to think of politics in secular terms.

One of the responses to the religious wars and other crises of the time was a yearning for order. As the internal social and political rebellions and revolts died down, it became apparent that the privileged classes of society—the aristocrats—remained in control, although the various states exhibited important differences in political forms. The most general trend saw an extension of monarchical power as a stabilizing force. This development, which historians have called absolute monarchy or absolutism, was most evident in France during the flamboyant reign of Louis XIV, regarded by some as the perfect embodiment of an absolute monarch. In his memoirs, the duc de Saint-Simon, who had firsthand experience of French court life, said that Louis was "the very figure of a hero, so imbued with a natural but most imposing majesty that it appeared even in his most insignificant gestures and movements." The king's natural grace gave him a special charm as well: "He was as dignified and majestic in his dressing gown as when dressed in robes of state, or on horseback at the head of his troops." He spoke well and learned quickly. He was naturally kind and "loved truth, justice, order, and reason." His life was orderly: "Nothing could be regulated with greater exactitude than were his days and hours." His self-control was impeccable: "He did not lose control of himself ten times in his whole life, and then only with inferior persons." But even absolute monarchs had imperfections, and Saint-Simon had the courage to point them out: "Louis XIV's vanity was without limit or restraint," which led to his "distaste for all merit, intelligence, education, and, most of all, for all independence of character and sentiment in others," as well as "to mistakes of judgment in matters of importance."

But absolutism was not the only response to the search for order in the seventeenth century. Other states, such as England, reacted differently to domestic crisis, and another very different system emerged where monarchs were limited by the power of their representative assemblies. Absolute and limited monarchy were the two poles of seventeenth-century state building.

Social Crises, War, and Rebellions

The inflation-fueled prosperity of the sixteenth century showed signs of slackening by the beginning of the seventeenth. Economic contraction was evident in some parts of Europe in the 1620s. In the 1630s and 1640s, as imports of silver from the Americas declined, economic recession intensified, especially in the Mediterranean area. Once the industrial and financial center of Europe in the Renaissance, Italy was now becoming an economic backwater. Spain's economy was also seriously failing by the 1640s.

Population trends of the sixteenth and seventeenth centuries also reveal Europe's worsening conditions. The sixteenth century was a period of expanding population, possibly related to a warmer climate and increased food supplies. It has been estimated that the population of Europe increased from 60 million in 1500 to 85 million by 1600, the first major recovery of European population since the devastation of the Black Death in the mid-fourteenth century. However, records also indicate a leveling off of the population by 1620 and even a decline by 1650, especially in central and southern Europe. Only the Dutch, English, and to a lesser degree, the French grew in number in the first half of the seventeenth century. Europe's longtime adversaries—war, famine, and plague—continued to affect population levels. Another "little ice age" after the middle of the sixteenth century, when average temperatures fell, affected harvests and caused famines. These problems created social tensions that were also evident in the witchcraft craze.

The Witchcraft Craze

Hysteria over witchcraft affected the lives of many Europeans in the sixteenth and seventeenth centuries. Witchcraft trials were prevalent in England, Scotland, Switzerland, Germany, some parts of France and the Low Countries, and even New England in America.

Witchcraft was not a new phenomenon. Its practice had been part of traditional village culture for centuries, but it came to be viewed as both sinister and dangerous when the medieval church began to connect witches to the activities of the devil, thereby transforming witchcraft into a heresy that had to be wiped out. After the establishment of the Inquisition in the thirteenth century, some people were accused of a variety of witchcraft practices and, following the biblical injunction "Thou shalt not suffer a witch to live," were turned over to secular authorities for burning at the stake or, in England, hanging.

What distinguished witchcraft in the sixteenth and seventeenth centuries from these previous developments was the increased number of trials and executions of presumed witches. Perhaps more than 100,000 people were prosecuted throughout Europe on charges of witchcraft. As more and more people were brought to trial, the fear of witches as well as the fear of being accused of witchcraft escalated to frightening proportions. Although larger cities were affected first, the trials also spread to smaller towns and rural areas as the hysteria persisted well into the seventeenth century (see the box on p. 402).

The accused witches usually confessed to a number of practices, most often after intense torture. But even when people confessed voluntarily, certain practices stand out. Many said that they had sworn allegiance to the devil and attended sabbats or nocturnal gatherings where they feasted, danced, and even copulated with the devil in sexual orgies.

A Witchcraft Trial in France

Persecutions for witchcraft reached their high point in the sixteenth and seventeenth centuries when tens of thousands of people were brought to trial. In this excerpt from the minutes of a trial in France in 1652, we can see why the accused witch stood little chance of exonerating herself.

The Trial of Suzanne Gaudry

28 May, 1652. . . . Interrogation of Suzanne Gaudry, prisoner at the court of Rieux. . . . [During interrogations on May 28 and May 29, the prisoner confessed to a number of activities involving the devil.]

Deliberation of the Court—June 3, 1652

The undersigned advocates of the Court have seen these interrogations and answers. They say that the aforementioned Suzanne Gaudry confesses that she is a witch, that she had given herself to the devil, that she had renounced God, Lent, and baptism, that she has been marked on the shoulder, that she has cohabited with the devil and that she has been to the dances, confessing only to have cast a spell upon and caused to die a beast of Philippe Cornié. . . .

Third Interrogation—June 27

This prisoner being led into the chamber, she was examined to know if things were not as she had said and confessed at the beginning of her imprisonment.

—Answers no, and that what she has said was done so by force.

Pressed to say the truth, that otherwise she would be subjected to torture, having pointed out to her that her aunt was burned for this same subject.

—Answers that she is not a witch. . . .

She was placed in the hands of the officer in charge of torture, throwing herself on her knees, struggling to cry, uttering several exclamations, without being able, nevertheless to shed a tear. Saying at every moment that she is not a witch.

The Torture

On this same day, being at the place of torture.

This prisoner, before being strapped down, was admonished to maintain herself in her first confessions and to renounce her lover.

—Says that she denies everything she has said, and that she has no lover. Feeling herself being strapped down, says that she is not a witch, while struggling to cry . . . and upon being asked why she confessed to being one, said that she was forced to say it.

Told that she was not forced, that on the contrary she declared herself to be a witch without any threat.

—Says that she confessed it and that she is not a witch, and being a little stretched [on the rack] screams ceaselessly that she is not a witch. . . .

Asked if she did not confess that she had been a witch for twenty-six years.

—Says that she said it, that she retracts it, crying that she is not a witch.

Asked if she did not make Philippe Cornié's horse die, as she confessed.

—Answers no, crying Jesus-Maria, that she is not a witch.

The mark having been probed by the officer, in the presence of Doctor Bouchain, it was adjudged by the aforesaid doctor and officer truly to be the mark of the devil.

Being more tightly stretched upon the torture-rack, urged to maintain her confessions.

—Said that it was true that she is a witch and that she would maintain what she had said.

Asked how long she has been in subjugation to the devil.

—Answers that it was twenty years ago that the devil appeared to her, being in her lodgings in the form of a man dressed in a little cow-hide and black breeches. . . .

Verdict

July 9, 1652. In the light of the interrogations, answers and investigations made into the charge against Suzanne Gaudry, . . . seeing by her own confessions that she is said to have made a pact with the devil, received the mark from him, . . . and that following this, she had renounced God, Lent, and baptism and had let herself be known carnally by him, in which she received satisfaction. Also, seeing that she is said to have been a part of nocturnal carols and dances.

For expiation of which the advice of the undersigned is that the office of Rieux can legitimately condemn the aforesaid Suzanne Gaudry to death, tying her to a gallows, and strangling her to death, then burning her body and burying it here in the environs of the woods.

More common, however, were admissions of using evil incantations and special ointments and powders to wreak havoc on neighbors by killing their livestock, injuring their children, or raising storms to destroy their crops.

A number of contributing factors have been suggested to explain why the witchcraft craze became so widespread in the sixteenth and seventeenth centuries. Religious uncertainties clearly played some part. Many witchcraft trials occurred in areas where Protestantism had been recently victorious or in regions, such as southwestern Germany, where Protestant-Catholic controversies still raged. As religious passions became inflamed, accusations of being in league with the devil became common on both sides.

Recently, however, historians have emphasized the importance of social conditions, especially the problems of a society in turmoil, in explaining the witchcraft hysteria. At a time when the old communal values that stressed working together for the good of the community were disintegrating before the onslaught of a new economic ethic that emphasized that one should look out for oneself, property owners became more fearful of the growing numbers of poor in their midst and transformed them psychologically into agents of the devil. Old women were particularly susceptible to suspicion. Many of them, no longer the recipients of the local charity available in traditional society, may even have tried to survive by selling herbs, potions, or secret remedies for healing. When problems arose—and there were many in this crisis-laden period—these women were handy scapegoats.

That women should be the chief victims of witchcraft trials was hardly accidental. Nicholas Rémy, a witchcraft judge in France in the 1590s, found it "not unreasonable that this scum of humanity [witches] should be drawn chiefly from the feminine sex." To another judge, it came as no surprise that witches would confess to sexual experiences with Satan: "The Devil uses them so, because he knows that women love carnal pleasures, and he means to bind them to his allegiance by such agreeable provocations."[1] Of course, not only witch hunters held women in such low esteem. Most theologians, lawyers, and philosophers in early modern Europe believed in the natural inferiority of women and thus would have found it plausible that women would be more susceptible to witchcraft.

By the mid-seventeenth century, the witchcraft hysteria began to subside. The destruction caused by the religious wars had at least forced people to accept a grudging toleration, causing religious passions to subside. Moreover, as governments began to stabilize after the period of crisis, fewer magistrates were willing to accept the unsettling and divisive conditions generated by the trials of witches. Finally, by the end of the seventeenth and beginning of the eighteenth centuries, more and more educated people were questioning altogether their old attitudes toward religion and finding it especially contrary to reason to believe in the old view of a world haunted by evil spirits.

The Thirty Years' War

Although many Europeans responded to the upheavals of the second half of the sixteenth century with a desire for peace and order, the first fifty years of the seventeenth century continued to be plagued by crises. A devastating war that affected much of Europe and rebellions seemingly everywhere protracted the atmosphere of disorder and violence.

Religion, especially the struggle between a militant Catholicism and a militant Calvinism, certainly played an important role in the outbreak of the Thirty Years' War, often called the "last of the religious wars." As the war progressed, however, it became increasingly clear that secular, dynastic-nationalist considerations were far more important.

Although much of the fighting in the Thirty Years' War (1618–1648) took place in the Germanic lands of the Holy Roman Empire, the war became a Europe-wide struggle (see Map 15.1). In fact, some historians view it as part of a larger conflict between the Bourbon dynasty of France and the Habsburg dynasties of Spain and the Holy Roman Empire for European leadership and date it from 1609 to 1659.

The Peace of Augsburg in 1555 had brought an end to the religious warfare between German Catholics and Lutherans. Religion, however, continued to play a divisive role in German life as Lutherans and Catholics persisted in vying for control of various principalities. In addition, although the treaty had not recognized the rights of Calvinists, a number of German states had adopted Calvinism as their state church. At the beginning of the seventeenth century, the Calvinist ruler of the Palatinate, the Elector Palatine Frederick IV, assumed the leadership in forming a league of German Protestant states called the Protestant Union. To counteract it, a Catholic League of German states was organized by Duke Maximilian of the south German state of Bavaria. By 1609, then, Germany was dividing into two armed camps in anticipation of religious war.

The religious division was exacerbated by a constitutional issue. The desire of the Habsburg emperors to consolidate their authority in the Holy Roman Empire was resisted by the princes who fought for their "German liberties," their constitutional rights and prerogatives as individual rulers. To pursue their policies, the Habsburg emperors looked to Spain (ruled by another branch of the Habsburgs) for assistance while the princes turned to the enemies of Spain, especially France, for help against the emperors. The divisions in the Holy Roman Empire and Europe made it almost inevitable that if war did erupt, it would be widespread and difficult to stop.

THE BOHEMIAN PHASE

Historians have traditionally divided the Thirty Years' War into four major phases. The Bohemian phase (1618–1625) began in one of the Habsburgs' own territories. In 1617, the Bohemian Estates (primarily the nobles) accepted the Habsburg Archduke Ferdinand as their king but soon found themselves unhappy with their choice. Though many of the nobles were Calvinists, Ferdinand was a devout Catholic who began a process of re-Catholicizing Bohemia and strengthening royal power. The Protestant nobles rebelled against Ferdinand in May 1618 and proclaimed their resistance by throwing two of the Habsburg governors and a secretary out of the window of the royal castle in Prague, the seat of Bohemian government. The Catholic side claimed that their seemingly miraculous escape from death in the 70-foot fall from the castle was due to the intercession of the Virgin Mary, while Protestants pointed out that they fell into a manure pile. The Bohemian rebels now seized control of Bohemia, deposed Ferdinand, and elected as his replacement the Protestant ruler of the Palatinate, Elector Frederick V, who was also head of the Protestant Union.

Ferdinand, who in the meantime had been elected Holy Roman Emperor, refused to accept his deposition. Aided by the imposing forces of Maximilian of Bavaria and the Catholic League, the imperial forces defeated Frederick and the Bohemian nobles at the Battle of White Mountain outside Prague on November 8, 1620. Spanish troops took advantage of Frederick's predicament by invading the Palatinate and conquering it by the end of 1622. The unfortunate Frederick, who had lost two crowns—Bohemia and the Palatinate—fled into exile in Holland. The Spanish took control of the western part of the Palatinate (to gain the access route from Italy to the Netherlands that they had wanted), and Duke Maximilian of Bavaria took the rest of the territory. Reestablished as king of Bohemia, Emperor Ferdinand declared Bohemia a hereditary Habsburg possession, confiscated the land of the Protestant nobles, and established Catholicism as the sole religion. The Spanish renewed their attack on the Dutch, and the forces of Catholicism seemed on the road to victory. But the war was far from over.

THE DANISH PHASE

The second phase of the war, the Danish phase (1625–1629), began when King Christian IV of Denmark (1588–

Map 15.1 The Thirty Years' War. The conflict began in the German states as Europe's major powers backed either the northern Protestant Union or the southern Catholic League. As the war progressed, religion receded in importance, replaced by a dynastic struggle between the French Bourbons and the Spanish and Austrian Habsburgs. ■ Compare this map with Map 13.2. Which countries engaged in the war were predominantly Protestant, which were predominantly Catholic, and which were mixed?

1648), a Lutheran, intervened on behalf of the Protestant cause by leading an army into northern Germany. The imperial forces were now led by a brilliant and enigmatic commander, Albrecht von Wallenstein, a Bohemian nobleman who had taken advantage of Ferdinand's victory to become the country's wealthiest landowner. Wallenstein marched the imperial army north, utterly defeated the Danes, and occupied parts of northern Germany, including the Baltic ports of Hamburg, Lübeck, and Bremen. Christian IV's total defeat meant the end of Danish supremacy in the Baltic.

After the success of the imperial armies, Emperor Ferdinand II was at the height of his power and took this opportunity to issue the Edict of Restitution in March 1629. His proclamation prohibited Calvinist worship and restored to the Catholic church all property taken by Protestant princes or cities during the past seventy-five years. But this sudden growth in the power of the Habsburg emperor frightened many German princes, who feared for their independent status and reacted by forcing the emperor to dismiss Wallenstein.

THE SWEDISH PHASE

The Swedish phase (1630–1635) marked the entry of Gustavus Adolphus, king of Sweden (1611–1635), into the war. Gustavus Adolphus was responsible for reviving Sweden and making it into a great Baltic power. A military genius, he brought a disciplined and well-equipped Swedish army to northern Germany. He was also a devout Lutheran who felt compelled to aid his coreligionists in Germany.

Gustavus's army swept the imperial forces out of the north and moved into the heart of Germany. In desperation, the imperial side recalled Wallenstein, who was given command of the imperial army that met Gustavus's troops near Leipzig. At the Battle of Lützen (1632), the Swedish forces prevailed but paid a high price for the victory when the Swedish king was killed in the battle. Although the Swedish forces remained in Germany, they proved much less effective. Despite the loss of Wallenstein, who was assassinated in 1634 by one of his own captains, the imperial army decisively defeated the Swedes at the Battle of Nördlingen at the end of 1634 and drove them out of southern Germany. This imperial victory guaranteed that southern Germany would remain Catholic. The emperor used this opportunity to make peace with the German princes by agreeing to annul the Edict of Restitution of 1629. But peace failed to come to war-weary Germany. The Swedes wished to continue, while the French, under the direction of Cardinal Richelieu, the chief minister of King Louis XIII, entered the war directly, beginning the fourth and final phase of the war, the Franco-Swedish phase (1635–1648).

THE FRANCO-SWEDISH PHASE

By this time, religious issues were losing their significance. The Catholic French were now supporting the Protestant Swedes against the Catholic Habsburgs of Germany and Spain. The Battle of Rocroi in 1643 proved decisive as the French beat the Spanish and brought an end to Spanish military greatness. The French then moved on to victories over the imperialist-Bavarian armies in southern Germany. By this time, all parties were ready for peace, and after five years of protracted negotiations, the war in Germany was officially ended by the Peace of Westphalia in 1648. The war between France and Spain, however, continued until the Peace of the Pyrenees in 1659. By that time, Spain had become a second-class power, and France had emerged as the dominant nation in Europe.

OUTCOMES OF THE WAR

What were the results of this "basically meaningless conflict," as one historian has called it? The Peace of Westphalia ensured that all German states, including the Calvinist ones, were free to determine their own religion. Territorially, France gained parts of western Germany, part of Alsace, and the three cities of Metz, Toul, and Verdun, giving the French control of the Franco-German border area. While Sweden and the German states of Brandenburg and Bavaria gained some territory in Germany, the Austrian Habsburgs did not really lose any but did see their authority as rulers of Germany further diminished. The more than three hundred states that made up the Holy Roman Empire were recognized as virtually independent states, since each received the power to conduct its own foreign policy; this brought an end to the Holy Roman Empire as a political entity and ensured German disunity for another two hundred years. The Peace of Westphalia also made it clear that religion and politics were now separate worlds. The pope was completely ignored in all decisions at Westphalia, and political motives became the guiding forces in public affairs as

CHRONOLOGY

The Thirty Years' War

The Protestant Union	1608
The Catholic League	1609
Election of Habsburg Archduke Ferdinand as king of Bohemia	1617
Bohemian revolt against Ferdinand	1618
Bohemian Phase	1618–1625
Battle of White Mountain	1620
Spanish conquest of Palatinate	1622
Danish Phase	1625–1629
Edict of Restitution	1629
Swedish Phase	1630–1635
Battle of Lützen	1632
Battle of Nördlingen	1634
Franco-Swedish Phase	1635–1648
Battle of Rocroi	1643
Peace of Westphalia	1648
Peace of the Pyrenees	1659

Giraudon/Art Resource, NY

Soldiers Pillaging a Farm. This painting shows a group of soldiers running amok on a French peasant's farm. This scene was typical of many that occurred during the Thirty Years' War, especially in Germany, where the war caused enormous destruction.

religion moved closer to becoming primarily a matter of personal conviction and individual choice.

The economic and social effects of the Thirty Years' War on Germany are still debated. The most recent work pictures a ruined German economy and a decline in German population from 21 to 16 million between 1618 and 1650. Some areas of Germany were completely devastated, but others remained relatively untouched and even experienced economic growth. In any case, the Thirty Years' War was undoubtedly the most destructive conflict Europeans had yet experienced (see the box on p. 407).

A Military Revolution?

By the seventeenth century, war played an increasingly important role in European affairs. Military power was considered essential to a ruler's reputation and power; thus the pressure to build an effective military machine was intense. Some historians believe that the changes that occurred in the science of warfare between 1560 and 1650 warrant the title of military revolution.

Medieval warfare, with its mounted knights and supplementary archers, had been transformed in the Renaissance by the employment of infantry armed with pikes and halberds and arranged in massed rectangles, known as squadrons or battalions. The use of firearms required adjustments to the size and shape of the massed infantry and made the cavalry less effective.

It was Gustavus Adolphus, the king of Sweden, who developed the first standing army of conscripts, notable for the flexibility of its tactics. The infantry brigades of Gustavus's army were composed of equal numbers of musketeers and pikemen, standing six men deep. They employed the salvo, in which all rows of the infantry fired at once instead of row by row. These salvos of fire, which cut up the massed ranks of the opposing infantry squadrons, were followed by a pike charge, giving the infantry a primarily offensive deployment. Gustavus also used the cavalry in a more mobile fashion. After shooting a pistol volley, they charged the enemy with their swords. Additional flexibility was obtained by using lighter artillery pieces that were more easily moved during battle. All of these changes required coordination, careful training, and better discipline, forcing rulers to move away from undisciplined mercenary forces. Naturally, the success of Gustavus Adolphus led to imitation.

The military changes between 1560 and 1650 included increased use of firearms and cannons, greater flexibility and mobility in tactics, and better-disciplined and better-trained armies. These innovations necessitated standing armies, based partly on conscription, which grew ever larger and more expensive as the seventeenth century progressed. Such armies could be maintained only by levying

The Face of War in the Seventeenth Century

We have a firsthand account of the face of war in Germany from a picaresque novel called *Simplicius Simplicissimus,* written by Jakob von Grimmelshausen. The author's experiences as a soldier in the Thirty Years' War give his descriptions of the effect of the war on ordinary people a certain vividness and reality. This selection describes the fate of a peasant farm, an experience all too familiar to thousands of German peasants between 1618 and 1648.

Jakob von Grimmelshausen, Simplicius Simplicissimus

The first thing these horsemen did in the nice back rooms of the house was to put in their horses. Then everyone took up a special job, one having to do with death and destruction. Although some began butchering, heating water, and rendering lard, as if to prepare for a banquet, others raced through the house, ransacking upstairs and down; not even the privy chamber was safe, as if the golden fleece of Jason might be hidden there. Still others bundled up big packs of cloth, household goods, and clothes, as if they wanted to hold a rummage sale somewhere. What they did not intend to take along they broke and spoiled. Some ran their swords into the hay and straw, as if there hadn't been hogs enough to stick. Some shook the feathers out of beds and put bacon slabs, hams, and other stuff in the ticking, as if they might sleep better on these. Others knocked down the hearth and broke the windows, as if announcing an everlasting summer. They flattened out copper and pewter dishes and baled the ruined goods. They burned up bedsteads, tables, chairs, and benches, though there were yards and yards of dry firewood outside the kitchen. Jars and crocks, pots and casseroles all were broken, either because they preferred their meat broiled or because they thought they'd eat only one meal with us. In the barn, the hired girl was handled so roughly that she was unable to walk away, I am ashamed to report. They stretched the hired man out flat on the ground, stuck a wooden wedge in his mouth to keep it open, and emptied a milk bucket full of stinking manure drippings down his throat; they called it a Swedish cocktail. He didn't relish it and made a very wry face. By this means they forced him to take a raiding party to some other place where they carried off men and cattle and brought them to our farm. Among those were my father, mother, and Ursula [sister].

Then they used thumbscrews, which they cleverly made out of their pistols, to torture the peasants, as if they wanted to burn witches. Though he had confessed to nothing as yet, they put one of the captured hayseeds in the bake-oven and lighted a fire in it. They put a rope around someone else's head and tightened it like a tourniquet until blood came out of his mouth, nose, and ears. In short, every soldier had his favorite method of making life miserable for peasants, and every peasant had his own misery. My father was, as I thought, particularly lucky because he confessed with a laugh what others were forced to say in pain and martyrdom. No doubt because he was the head of the household, he was shown special consideration; they put him close to a fire, tied him by his hands and legs, and rubbed damp salt on the bottoms of his feet. Our old nanny goat had to lick it off and this so tickled my father that he could have burst laughing. This seemed so clever and entertaining to me—I had never seen or heard my father laugh so long—that I joined him in laughter, to keep him company or perhaps to cover up my ignorance. In the midst of such glee he told them the whereabouts of hidden treasure much richer in gold, pearls, and jewelry than might have been expected on a farm.

I can't say much about the captured wives, hired girls, and daughters because the soldiers didn't let me watch their doings. But I do remember hearing pitiful screams from various dark corners and I guess that my mother and our Ursula had it no better than the rest.

heavier taxes, making war an economic burden and an ever more important part of the early modern European state. The creation of large bureaucracies to supervise the military resources of the state led to a growth in the power of state governments.

Rebellions

Before, during, and after the Thirty Years' War, a series of rebellions and civil wars stemming from the discontent of both nobles and commoners rocked the domestic stability of many European governments. To strengthen their power, monarchs attempted to extend their authority at the expense of traditional powerful elements who resisted the rulers' efforts. At the same time, to fight their battles, governments increased taxes and created such hardships that common people also rose in opposition.

Between 1590 and 1640, peasant and lower-class revolts erupted in central and southern France, Austria, and Hungary. In the decades of the 1640s and 1650s, even greater unrest occurred. Portugal and Catalonia rebelled against the Spanish government in 1640. The common people in Naples and Sicily revolted against both the government and the landed nobility in 1647. Russia, too, was rocked by urban uprisings in 1641, 1645, and 1648. Nobles rebelled in France from 1648 to 1652 to halt the growth of royal power. The northern states of Sweden, Denmark, and Holland were also not immune from upheavals involving clergy, nobles, and mercantile groups. By far the most famous and wide-ranging struggle, however, was the civil war and rebellion in England, commonly known as the English Revolution (discussed later in this chapter).

The Practice of Absolutism: Western Europe

Absolute monarchy or absolutism meant that the sovereign power or ultimate authority in the state rested in the hands of a king who claimed to rule by divine right. But what did sovereignty mean? The late-sixteenth-century political theorist Jean Bodin believed that sovereign power consisted of the authority to make laws, tax, administer justice, control the state's administrative system, and determine foreign policy. These powers made a ruler sovereign.

One of the chief theorists of divine-right monarchy in the seventeenth century was the French theologian and court preacher Bishop Jacques Bossuet (1627–1704), who expressed his ideas in a book titled *Politics Drawn from the Very Words of Holy Scripture.* Bossuet argued first that government was divinely ordained so that humans could live in an organized society. God established kings and through them reigned over all the peoples of the world. Since kings received their power from God, their authority was absolute. They were responsible to no one (including parliaments) except God. There was, however, a large gulf between the theory of absolutism as expressed by Bossuet and the practice of absolutism. A monarch's absolute power was often limited greatly by practical realities.

France and Absolute Monarchy

France during the reign of Louis XIV (1643–1715) has traditionally been regarded as the best example of the practice of absolute monarchy in the seventeenth century. French culture, language, and manners reached into all levels of European society. French diplomacy and wars shaped the political affairs of western and central Europe. The court of Louis XIV seemed to be imitated everywhere in Europe. Of course, the stability of Louis's reign was magnified by the instability that had preceded it.

FOUNDATIONS OF FRENCH ABSOLUTISM

The fifty years of French history before Louis XIV came to power were a time in which royal and ministerial governments struggled to avoid the breakdown of the state. The line between order and anarchy was often a narrow one. The situation was especially complicated by the fact that both Louis XIII (1610–1643) and Louis XIV were only boys when they succeeded to the throne in 1610 and 1643, respectively, leaving the government dependent on royal ministers. Two especially competent ministers played crucial roles in maintaining monarchical authority.

Cardinal Richelieu, Louis XIII's chief minister from 1624 to 1642, initiated policies that eventually strengthened the power of the monarchy. By eliminating the political and military rights of the Huguenots while preserving their religious ones, Richelieu transformed the Huguenots into more reliable subjects. Richelieu acted more cautiously in "humbling the pride of the great men," the important French nobility. He understood the influential role played by the nobles in the French state. The dangerous ones were those who asserted their territorial independence when they were excluded from participating in the central government. Proceeding slowly but determinedly, Richelieu developed an efficient network of spies to uncover noble

Cardinal Richelieu. A key figure in the emergence of a strong monarchy in France was Cardinal Richelieu, pictured here in a portrait by Philippe de Champagne. Chief minister to Louis XIII, Richelieu strengthened royal authority by eliminating the private armies and fortified cities of the Huguenots and by crushing aristocratic conspiracies.

plots and then crushed the conspiracies and executed the conspirators, thereby eliminating a major threat to royal authority.

To reform and strengthen the central administration, initially for financial reasons, Richelieu sent out royal officials called *intendants* to the provinces to execute the orders of the central government. As the functions of the intendants grew, they came into conflict with provincial governors. Since the intendants were victorious in most of these disputes, they further strengthened the power of the crown. Richelieu proved less capable in financial matters, however. Not only was the basic system of state finances corrupt, but so many people benefited from the system's inefficiency and injustice that the government faced strong resistance when it tried to reform it. The *taille* (an annual direct tax usually levied on land or property) was increased—in 1643 it was two and a half times what it had been in 1610—and crown lands were mortgaged again. Expenditures, especially the cost of war preparations, soon outstripped the additional revenues, however, and French debt continued its upward spiral under Richelieu.

Richelieu died in 1642, followed five months later by King Louis XIII, who was succeeded by his son Louis XIV, then but four years old. This necessitated a regency under Anne of Austria, wife of the dead king. But she allowed Cardinal Mazarin, Richelieu's trained successor, to dominate the government. An Italian who had come to France as a papal legate and then become naturalized, Mazarin attempted to carry on Richelieu's policies until his death in 1661.

The most important event during Mazarin's rule was a revolt known as the Fronde. As a foreigner, Mazarin was greatly disliked by all elements of the French population. The nobles, who particularly resented the centralized administrative power being built up at the expense of the provincial nobility, temporarily allied with the members of the Parlement of Paris, who opposed the new taxes levied by the government to pay the costs of the Thirty Years' War, and with the masses of Paris, who were also angry at the additional taxes. The Parlement of Paris was the most important court in France, with jurisdiction over half of the kingdom, and its members formed the nobles of the robe, the service nobility of lawyers and administrators. These nobles of the robe led the first Fronde (1648–1649), which broke out in Paris and was ended by compromise. The second Fronde, begun in 1650, was led by the nobles of the sword, whose ancestors were medieval nobles. They were interested in overthrowing Mazarin for their own purposes: to secure their positions and increase their own power. The second Fronde was crushed by 1652, a task made easier when the nobles began fighting each other instead of Mazarin. With the end of the Fronde, the vast majority of the French concluded that the best hope for stability in France lay in the crown. When Mazarin died in 1661, the greatest of the seventeenth-century monarchs, Louis XIV, took over supreme power.

THE REIGN OF LOUIS XIV (1643–1715)

The day after Cardinal Mazarin's death, Louis XIV, at the age of twenty-three, expressed his determination to be a real king and the sole ruler of France:

> Up to this moment I have been pleased to entrust the government of my affairs to the late Cardinal. It is now time that I govern them myself. You [secretaries and ministers of state] will assist me with your counsels when I ask for them. I request and order you to seal no orders except by my command, . . . I order you not to sign anything, not even a passport . . . without my command; to render account to me personally each day and to favor no one.[2]

His mother, who was well aware of Louis's proclivity for fun and games and getting into the beds of the maids in the royal palace, laughed aloud at these words. But Louis was quite serious.

Louis proved willing to pay the price of being a strong ruler (see the box on p. 410). He established a conscientious routine from which he seldom deviated, but he did not look upon his duties as drudgery since he considered his royal profession "grand, noble, and delightful." Eager for glory (in the French sense of achieving what was expected of one in an important position), Louis created a grand and majestic spectacle at the court of Versailles. Consequently, Louis and his court came to set the standard for monarchies and aristocracies all over Europe. Less than fifty years after the king's death, the great French writer Voltaire dubbed the period from 1661 to 1715 the "Age of Louis XIV," and historians have tended to call it that ever since.

Although Louis may have believed in the theory of absolute monarchy and consciously fostered the myth of himself as the Sun King, the source of light for all of his people, historians are quick to point out that the realities fell far short of the aspirations. Despite the centralizing efforts of Cardinals Richelieu and Mazarin, seventeenth-century France still possessed a bewildering system of overlapping authorities. Provinces had their own regional courts, their own local Estates, their own sets of laws. Members of the high nobility, with their huge estates and clients among the lesser nobility, still exercised much authority. Both towns and provinces possessed privileges and powers seemingly from time immemorial that they would not easily relinquish.

One of the keys to Louis's power was that he was able to restructure the central policy-making machinery of government because it was part of his own court and household. The royal court located at Versailles was an elaborate structure that served different purposes: it was the personal household of the king, the location of central governmental machinery, and the place where powerful subjects came to find favors and offices for themselves and their clients as well as the main arena where rival aristocratic factions jostled for power. The greatest danger to Louis's personal rule came from the very high nobles and princes of the blood (the royal princes), who considered it their natural function to assert the policy-making role of royal ministers.

Louis XIV: Kingly Advice

Throughout his reign, Louis XIV was always on stage, acting the role of the wise "grand monarch." In 1661, after he became a father, Louis began his *Memoirs for the Dauphin,* a frank collection of precepts for the education of his oldest son and heir to the throne. He continued to add to the *Memoirs* over the next twenty years.

■ *Louis XIV,* Memoirs for the Dauphin

Kings are often obliged to do things which go against their inclinations and offend their natural goodness. They should love to give pleasure and yet they must often punish and destroy persons on whom by nature they wish to confer benefits. The interest of the state must come first. One must constrain one's inclinations and not put oneself in the position of berating oneself because one could have done better in some important affair but did not because of some private interest, because one was distracted from the attention one should have for the greatness, the good and the power of the state. Often there are troublesome places where it is difficult to make out what one should do. One's ideas are confused. As long as this lasts, one can refrain from making a decision. But as soon as one has fixed one's mind upon something which seems best to do, it must be acted upon. This is what enabled me to succeed so often in what I have done. The mistakes which I made, and which gave me infinite trouble, were the result of the desire to please or of allowing myself to accept too carelessly the opinions of others. Nothing is more dangerous than weakness of any kind whatsoever. In order to command others, one must raise oneself above them and once one has heard the reports from every side one must come to a decision upon the basis of one's own judgment, without anxiety but always with the concern not to command anything which is of itself unworthy either of one's place in the world or of the greatness of the state. Princes with good intentions and some knowledge of their affairs, either from experience or from study and great diligence in making themselves capable, find numerous cases which instruct them that they must give special care and total application to everything. One must be on guard against oneself, resist one's own tendencies, and always be on guard against one's own natural bent. The craft of a king is great, noble and delightful when one feels worthy of doing well whatever one promises to do. But it is not exempt from troubles, weariness and worries. Sometimes uncertainty causes despair, and when one has spent a reasonable time in examining an affair, one must make a decision and take the step which one believes to be best. When one has the state in view, one works for one's self. The good of the one constitutes the glory of the other. When the former is fortunate, eminent and powerful, he who is the cause thereof becomes glorious and consequently should find more enjoyment than his subjects in all the pleasant things of life for himself and for them. When one has made a mistake, it must be corrected as soon as possible, and no other consideration must stand in the way, not even kindness.

Louis eliminated this threat by removing them from the royal council, the chief administrative body of the king and overseer of the central machinery of government, and enticing them to his court, where he could keep them preoccupied with court life and out of politics. Instead of the high nobility and royal princes, Louis relied for his ministers on nobles who came from relatively new aristocratic families. His ministers were expected to be subservient; said Louis, "I had no intention of sharing my authority with them."

Louis's domination of his ministers and secretaries gave him control of the central policy-making machinery of government and thus authority over the traditional areas of monarchical power: the formulation of foreign policy, the making of war and peace, the assertion of the secular power of crown against any religious authority, and the ability to levy taxes to fulfill these functions. However, Louis had considerably less success with the internal administration of the kingdom. The traditional groups and institutions of French society—the nobles, officials, town councils, guilds, and representative Estates in some provinces—were simply too powerful for the king to have direct control over the lives of his subjects. Consequently, control of the provinces and the people was achieved largely by bribing the individuals responsible for executing the king's policies. Nevertheless, local officials could still obstruct execution of policies they disliked, indicating clearly that a so-called absolute monarch was not always that absolute.

The maintenance of religious harmony had long been considered an area of monarchical power. The desire to keep it led Louis into conflict with the French Huguenots. Louis XIV did not want to allow Protestants to practice their faith in largely Catholic France. Perhaps he was motivated by religion, but it is more likely that Louis, who believed in the motto, "one king, one law, one faith," felt that the existence of this minority undermined his own political authority. In October 1685, Louis issued the Edict of Fontainebleau. In addition to revoking the Edict of Nantes, the new edict provided for the destruction of Huguenot churches and the closing of Protestant schools. It is estimated that 200,000 Huguenots defied the prohibition on their leaving France and sought asylum in England, the United Provinces, and the German states.

The cost of building Versailles and other palaces, maintaining his court, and pursuing his wars made finances a crucial issue for Louis XIV. He was most fortunate in having the services of Jean-Baptiste Colbert (1619–1683) as controller general of finances. Colbert sought to increase

Réunion des Musées Nationaux/Art Resource, NY

Louis XIV. Louis XIV was determined to be the sole ruler of France. He eliminated the threat of the nobles by removing them from the royal council and replacing them with relatively new aristocrats whom he could dominate. This portrait by Hyacinth Rigaud captures the king's sense of royal dignity and grandeur.

the wealth and power of France through general adherence to mercantilism, which stressed government regulation of economic activities to benefit the state. To decrease the need for imports and increase exports, Colbert attempted to expand the quantity and improve the quality of French manufactured goods. He founded new luxury industries, such as the royal tapestry works at Beauvais; invited Venetian glassmakers and Flemish clothmakers to France; drew up instructions regulating the quality of goods produced; oversaw the training of workers; and granted special privileges, including tax exemptions, loans, and subsidies, to those who established new industries. To improve communications and the transportation of goods internally, he built roads and canals. To decrease imports directly, he raised tariffs on foreign manufactured goods, especially English and Dutch cloth, and created a merchant marine to facilitate the conveyance of French goods.

Although Colbert's policies are given much credit for fostering the development of manufacturing, some historians are dubious about the usefulness of many of his mercantilistic policies. Regulations were often evaded, and the imposition of high tariffs brought foreign retaliation. French trading companies entered the scene too late to be really competitive with the English and the Dutch. And above all, Colbert's economic policies, which were geared to making his king more powerful, were ultimately self-defeating. The more revenue Colbert collected to enable the king to make war, the faster Louis depleted the treasury. At the same time, the burden of taxes fell increasingly on the peasants, who still constituted the overwhelming majority of the French population.

DAILY LIFE AT THE COURT OF VERSAILLES

The court of Louis XIV at Versailles set a standard that was soon followed by other European rulers. In 1660, Louis, who disliked Paris as a result of his humiliating experiences at the hands of Parisian mobs during the Fronde, decided to convert a hunting lodge at Versailles, not far from the city, into a chateau. Not until 1688, after untold sums of money had been spent and tens of thousands of workers had labored incessantly, was most of the construction completed on the enormous palace that housed thousands of people.

Versailles served many purposes. It was the residence of the king, a reception hall for state affairs, an office building for the members of the king's government, and the home of thousands of royal officials and aristocratic courtiers. Versailles became a symbol for the French absolutist state and the power of the Sun King, Louis XIV. As

The Palace of Versailles As Seen in an Eighteenth-Century Engraving. Louis XIV spent untold sums of money on the construction of a new royal residence at Versailles. The enormous palace also housed the members of the king's government and served as home for thousands of French nobles. As the largest royal residence in Europe, Versailles impressed foreigners and became a source of envy for other rulers.

a visible manifestation of France's superiority and wealth, this lavish court was intended to overawe subjects and impress foreign powers.

Versailles also served a practical political purpose. It became home to the high nobility and princes of the blood (the royal princes), those powerful figures who had aspired to hold the policy-making role of royal ministers. By keeping them involved in the myriad activities that made up daily life at the court of Versailles, Louis excluded them from real power while allowing them to share in the mystique of power as companions of the king.

Life at Versailles became a court ceremony with Louis XIV at the center of it all. The king had little privacy; only when he visited his wife or mother or mistress or met with ministers was he free of the noble courtiers who swarmed about the palace. Most daily ceremonies were carefully staged, such as those attending Louis's rising from bed, dining, praying, attending Mass, and going to bed. A mob of nobles aspired to assist the king in carrying out these solemn activities. It was considered a great honor for a noble to be chosen to hand the king his shirt while dressing. But why did nobles participate in so many ceremonies, some of which were so obviously demeaning? Active involvement in the activities at Versailles was the king's prerequisite for obtaining the offices, titles, and pensions that only he could grant. This policy reduced great nobles and ecclesiastics, the "people of quality," to a plane of equality, allowing Louis to exercise control over them and prevent them from interfering in the real lines of power. To maintain their social prestige, the "people of quality" were

Giraudon/Art Resource, NY

Interior of Versailles: The Hall of Mirrors. Pictured here is the exquisite Hall of Mirrors at Versailles. A number of daily and occasional ceremonies dominated the lives of the residents of Versailles. Rules of etiquette became so complex that they guided virtually every aspect of behavior.

expected to adhere to rigid standards of court etiquette appropriate to their rank.

Indeed, court etiquette became a complex matter. Nobles and royal princes were arranged in an elaborate order of seniority and expected to follow certain rules of precedence. Who could sit down and on what kind of chair was a subject of much debate. When Philip of Orleans, the king's brother, and his wife Charlotte sought to visit their daughter, the duchess of Lorraine, they encountered problems with Louis. Charlotte told why in one of her letters:

> The difficulty is that the Duke of Lorraine claims that he is entitled to sit in an armchair in the presence of Philip and myself because the Emperor gives him an armchair. To this the King [Louis] replied that the Emperor's ceremonial is one thing and the King's another, and that, for example, the Emperor gives the cardinals armchairs, whereas here they may never sit at all in the King's presence.[3]

Louis refused to compromise; the duke of Lorraine was only entitled to a stool. The duke balked, and Philip and Charlotte canceled their visit.

Who could sit where at meals with the king was also carefully regulated. On one occasion, when the wife of a minister sat closer to the king than a duchess at dinner, Louis XIV became so angry that he did not eat for the rest of the evening. Another time, Louis reproached his talkative brother for the sin of helping himself to a dish before Louis had touched it with the biting words: "I perceive that you are no better able to control your hands than your tongue."[4]

Daily life at Versailles also included numerous forms of entertainment. Walks through the gardens, boating trips, performances of tragedies and comedies, ballets, and concerts all provided sources of pleasure (see the box on p. 414). Three evenings a week, from seven to ten, Louis also held an *appartement* where he was at "home" to his court. The *appartement* was characterized by a formal informality. Relaxed rules of etiquette even allowed people to sit down in the presence of their superiors. The evening's entertainment began with a concert, followed by games of billiards or cards, and ended with a sumptuous buffet.

One form of entertainment—gambling—became an obsession at Versailles. Although a few of the courtiers made a living by their gambling skill, many others were simply amateurs. This did not stop them from playing regularly and losing enormous sums of money. One princess described the scene: "Here in France as soon as people get together they do nothing but play [cards]; they play for frightful sums, and the players seem bereft of their senses. . . . One shouts at the top of his voice, another strikes the table with his fist, a third blasphemes. . . . it is horrible to watch them."[5] Louis did not share the princess's sensibilities; he was not horrified by an activity that kept the Versailles nobles busy and out of mischief.

Travels with the King

The duc de Saint-Simon was one of many noble courtiers who lived at Versailles and had firsthand experience of court life there. In his *Memoirs,* he left a controversial and critical account of Louis XIV and his court. In this selection, Saint-Simon describes the price court ladies paid for the "privilege" of riding with the great king.

■ *Duc de Saint-Simon,* Memoirs

The King always traveled with his carriage full of women: His mistresses, his bastard daughters, his daughters-in-law, sometimes Madame [the wife of the king's brother], and the other ladies of the court when there was room. This was the case for hunts, and trips to Fontainebleau, Chantilly, Compiègne, and the like. . . . In his carriage during these trips there was always an abundance and variety of things to eat: meats, pastries, and fruit. Before the carriage had gone a quarter league the King would ask who was hungry. He never ate between meals, not even a fruit, but he enjoyed watching others stuff themselves. It was mandatory to eat, with appetite and good grace, and to be gay; otherwise; he showed his displeasure by telling the guilty party she was putting on airs and trying to be coy. The same ladies or princesses who had eaten that day at the King's table were obliged to eat again as though they were weak from hunger. What is more, the women were forbidden to mention their personal needs, which in any case they could not have relieved without embarrassment, since there were guards and members of the King's household in front and in back of the carriage, and officers and equerries riding alongside the doors. The dust they kicked up choked everyone in the carriage, but the King, who loved fresh air, insisted that all the windows remain open. He would have been extremely displeased if one of the ladies had pulled a curtain to protect herself from the sun, the wind, or the cold.

He pretended not to notice his passengers' discomfort, and always traveled very fast, with the usual number of relays. Sickness in the carriage was a demerit which ruled out further invitations. . . . When the king had to relieve himself he did not hesitate to stop the carriage and get out; but the ladies were not allowed to budge.

THE WARS OF LOUIS XIV

Both the increase in royal power that Louis pursued and his desire for military glory led the king to wage war. Under the secretary of war, François-Michel Le Tellier, the marquis of Louvois, France developed a professional army numbering 100,000 men in peacetime and 400,000 in time of war. Louis made war an almost incessant activity of his reign. To achieve the prestige and military glory befitting the Sun King as well as to ensure the domination of his Bourbon dynasty over European affairs, Louis waged four wars between 1667 and 1713 (see Map 15.2).

In 1667, Louis began his first war by invading the Spanish Netherlands to his north and Franche-Comté to the east. But a Triple Alliance of the Dutch, English, and Swedes forced Louis to sue for peace in 1668 and accept a few towns in the Spanish Netherlands for his efforts. He never forgave the Dutch for arranging the Triple Alliance, and in 1672, after isolating the Dutch, France invaded the United Provinces with some initial success. But the French victories led Brandenburg, Spain, and the Holy Roman Emperor to form a new coalition that forced Louis to end the Dutch War by making peace at Nimwegen in 1678. While Dutch territory remained intact, France received Franche-Comté from Spain, which served merely to stimulate Louis's appetite for even more land.

This time, Louis moved eastward against the Holy Roman Empire, which he perceived from his previous war as feeble and unable to resist. The gradual annexation of the provinces of Alsace and Lorraine was followed by the occupation of the city of Strasbourg, a move that led to widespread protest and the formation of a new coalition. The creation of this League of Augsburg, consisting of Spain, the Holy Roman Emperor, the United Provinces, Sweden, and England, led to Louis's third war, the War of the League of Augsburg (1689–1697). This bitterly contested eight-year struggle brought economic depression and famine to France. The Treaty of Ryswick ending the war forced Louis to give up most of his conquests in the empire, although he was allowed to keep Strasbourg and part of Alsace. The gains were hardly worth the bloodshed and the misery he had caused the French people.

Louis's fourth war, the War of the Spanish Succession (1702–1713), was over bigger stakes, the succession to the Spanish throne. Charles II, the sickly and childless Habsburg ruler, left the throne of Spain in his will to a grandson of Louis XIV. When the latter became King Philip V of Spain after Charles's death, the suspicion that Spain and France would eventually be united in the same dynastic family caused the formation of a new coalition, determined to prevent a Bourbon hegemony that would mean the certain destruction of the European balance of power. This coalition of England, Holland, Habsburg Austria, and German states opposed France and Spain in a war that dragged on in Europe and the colonial empires in North America from 1702 to 1713. In a number of battles, including the memorable defeat of the French forces at Blenheim in 1704 by allied troops led by the English commander, John Churchill, duke of Marlborough, the coalition wore down Louis's forces. An end to the war finally came with the Peaces of Utrecht in 1713 and Rastatt in 1714. Although these peace treaties confirmed Philip V as the Spanish ruler, initiating a Spanish Bourbon dynasty that would last into the twentieth century, they also affirmed that the thrones of Spain and France were to remain separated. The Spanish Netherlands, Milan, and Naples were given to Austria, and the emerging state of Brandenburg-Prussia gained additional territories. The real winner at Utrecht, however, was England, which received Gibraltar as well as the French possessions in America of Newfoundland, Hudson's Bay Territory, and Nova Scotia. Though France, by its sheer size and position, remained a great power, England had emerged as a formidable naval force.

Only two years after the treaty, the Sun King was dead, leaving France impoverished and surrounded by enemies. On his deathbed, the seventy-six-year-old monarch seemed remorseful when he told his successor:

> Soon you will be King of a great kingdom. I urge you not to forget your duty to God; remember that you owe everything to Him. Try to remain at peace with your neighbors. I loved war too much. Do not follow me in that or in overspending. Take advice in everything; try to find the best course and follow it. Lighten your people's burden as soon as possible, and do what I have had the misfortune not to do myself.[6]

Did Louis mean it? Did Louis ever realize how tarnished the glory he had sought had become? One of his subjects wrote ten years before the end of his reign: "Even the people . . . who have so much loved you, and have placed such trust in you, begin to lose their love, their trust, and even their respect. . . . They believe you have no pity for their sorrows, that you are devoted only to your power and your glory."[7] In any event, the advice to his successor was probably not remembered; his great-grandson was only five years old.

The Decline of Spain

At the beginning of the seventeenth century, Spain possessed the most populous empire in the world, controlling almost all of South America and a number of settlements in Asia and Africa. To most Europeans, Spain still seemed the greatest power of the age, but the reality was quite different. The treasury was empty; Philip II went bankrupt in 1596 from excessive expenditures on war, and his successor, Philip III, did the same in 1607 by spending a fortune on his court. The armed forces were out-of-date, the government was inefficient, and the commercial class was weak in the midst of a suppressed peasantry, a luxury-loving class of nobles, and an oversupply of priests and monks. Spain continued to play the role of a great power, but appearances were deceiving.

During the reign of Philip III (1598–1621), many of Spain's weaknesses became apparent. Interested only in court luxury or miracle-working relics, Philip III allowed

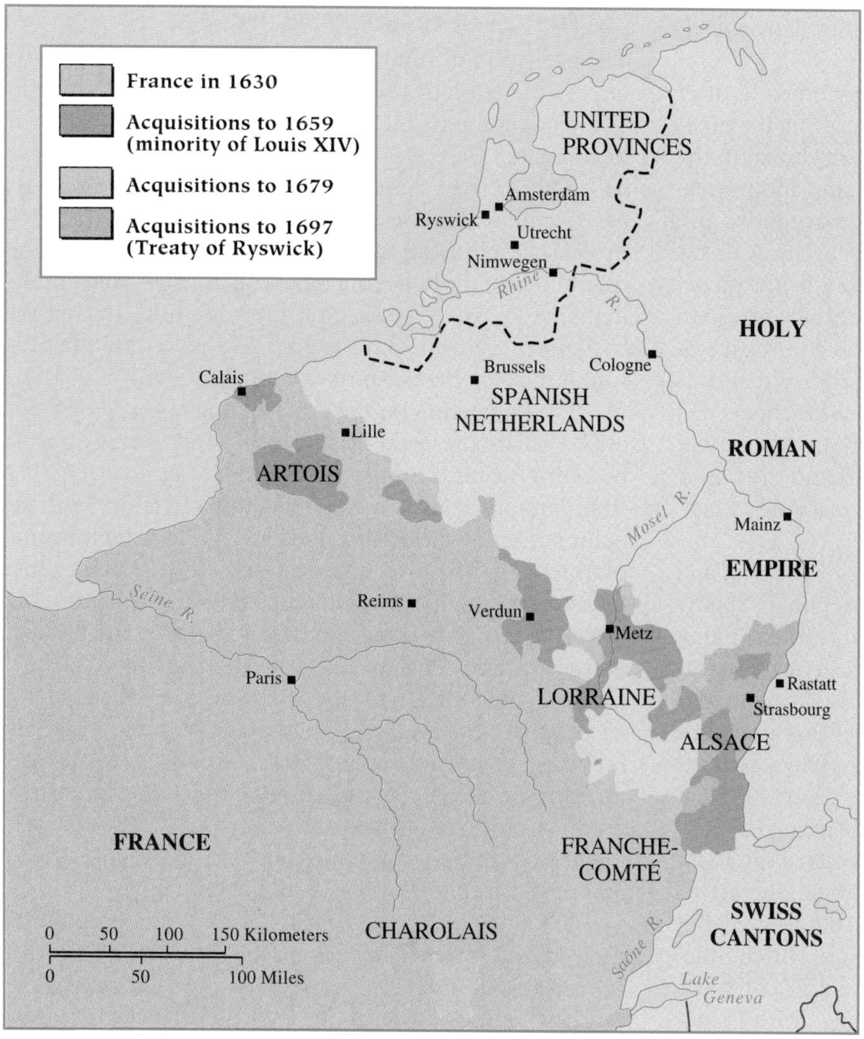

Map 15.2 The Wars of Louis XIV. The Sun King instigated several wars in his efforts to expand the power of France and the Bourbon dynasty. Each military thrust was met by a coalition of European states that kept French gains minimal compared to the amount of blood spilled and capital spent. ■ Louis XIV made his territorial acquisitions primarily at the expense of what countries?

CHRONOLOGY

Absolutism in Western Europe

France	
Louis XIII	1610–1643
Cardinal Richelieu as chief minister	1624–1642
Ministry of Cardinal Mazarin	1642–1661
First Fronde	1648–1649
Second Fronde	1650–1652
Louis XIV	1643–1715
First war (vs. Triple Alliance)	1667–1668
Dutch War	1672–1678
Edict of Fontainebleau	1685
War of the League of Augsburg	1689–1697
War of the Spanish Succession	1702–1713
Spain	
Philip III	1598–1621
Philip IV	1621–1665

his first minister, the greedy duke of Lerma, to run the country. The aristocratic Lerma's primary interest was accumulating power and wealth for himself and his family. As important offices were filled with his relatives, crucial problems went unsolved.

The reign of Philip IV (1621–1665) seemed to offer hope for a revival of Spain's energies, especially in the capable hands of his chief minister, Gaspar de Guzman, the count of Olivares. This clever, hardworking, and power-hungry statesman dominated the king's every move and worked to revive the interests of the monarchy. A flurry of domestic reform decrees, aimed at curtailing the power of the Catholic church and the landed aristocracy, was soon followed by a political reform program whose purpose was to further centralize the government of all Spain and its possessions in monarchical hands. All of these efforts met with little real success, however, because both the number (estimated at one-fifth of the population) and the power of the Spanish aristocrats made them too strong to curtail in any significant fashion.

At the same time, most of the efforts of Olivares and Philip were undermined by their desire to pursue Spain's imperial glory and by a series of internal revolts. Spain's involvement in the Thirty Years' War led to a series of frightfully expensive military campaigns that incited internal revolts and years of civil war. Unfortunately for Spain, the campaigns also failed to produce victory. As Olivares wrote to King Philip IV, "God wants us to make peace; for He is depriving us visibly and absolutely of all the means of war."[8] The defeats in Europe and the internal revolts of the 1640s ended any illusions about Spain's greatness. The actual extent of Spain's economic difficulties is still debated, but there is no question about its foreign losses. Dutch independence was formally recognized by the Peace of Westphalia in 1648, and the Peace of the Pyrenees with France in 1659 meant the surrender of Artois and the outlying defenses of the Spanish Netherlands as well as certain border regions that went to France.

Absolutism in Central, Eastern, and Northern Europe

During the seventeenth century, a development of great importance for the modern Western world took place in central and eastern Europe, the appearance of three new powers: Prussia, Austria, and Russia.

The German States

The Peace of Westphalia, which officially ended the Thirty Years' War in 1648, left each of the states in the Holy Roman Empire virtually autonomous and sovereign. Properly speaking, there was no longer a German state but rather more than three hundred little Germanies. Of these, two emerged as great European powers in the seventeenth and eighteenth centuries.

THE RISE OF BRANDENBURG-PRUSSIA

The evolution of Brandenburg into a powerful state was largely the work of the Hohenzollern dynasty, which in 1415 had come to rule the insignificant principality in northeastern Germany (see Map 15.3). In 1609, the Hohenzollerns inherited some lands in the Rhine valley in western Germany; nine years later, they received the duchy of Prussia (East Prussia). By the seventeenth century, then, the dominions of the house of Hohenzollern, now called Brandenburg-Prussia, consisted of three disconnected masses in western, central, and eastern Germany; only the person of the Hohenzollern ruler connected them.

The foundation for the Prussian state was laid by Frederick William the Great Elector (1640–1688), who came to power in the midst of the Thirty Years' War. Realizing that Brandenburg-Prussia was a small, open territory with no natural frontiers for defense, Frederick William built a competent and efficient standing army. By 1678, he possessed a force of forty thousand men that absorbed more than 50 percent of the state's revenues. To sustain the army and his own power, Frederick William established the General War Commissariat to levy taxes for the army and oversee its growth and training. The Commissariat soon evolved into an agency for civil government as well. Directly responsible to the elector, the new bureaucratic machine became his chief instrument for governing the state. Many of its officials were members of the Prussian landed aristocracy, the Junkers, who also served as officers in the all-important army.

The nobles' support for Frederick William's policies derived from the tacit agreement that he made with them. In order to eliminate the power that the members of the nobility could exercise in their provincial Estates-

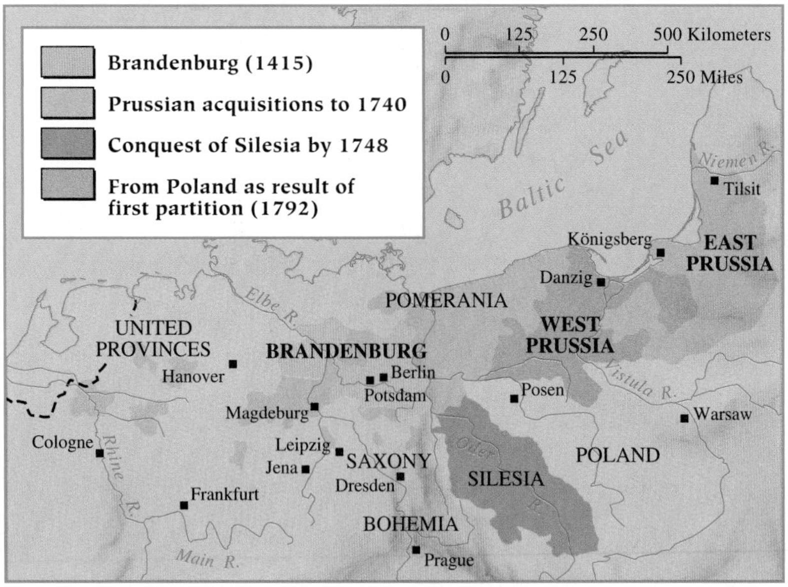

Map 15.3 The Growth of Brandenburg-Prussia. Frederick William the Great Elector laid the foundation for a powerful state when he increased the size and efficiency of the army, raised taxes and created an efficient bureaucracy to collect them, and gained the support of the landed aristocracy. Later rulers added more territory. ■ Why was the acquisition of Pomerania and West Prussia important for the continued rise in power of Brandenburg-Prussia?

General, Frederick William made a deal with the nobles. In return for a free hand in running the government (in other words, for depriving the provincial Estates of their power), he gave the nobles almost unlimited power over their peasants, exempted the nobles from taxation, and awarded them the highest ranks in the army and the Commissariat with the understanding that they would not challenge his political control. As for the peasants, the nobles were allowed to appropriate their land and bind them to the soil as serfs.

To build Brandenburg-Prussia's economy, Frederick William followed the fashionable mercantilist policies, using high tariffs, subsidies, and monopolies for manufacturers to stimulate domestic industry and the construction of roads and canals. At the same time, however, Frederick William continued to favor the interests of the nobility at the expense of the commercial and industrial middle classes in the towns.

Frederick William laid the groundwork for the Prussian state; his son Frederick III (1688–1713) made one further significant contribution: in return for aiding the Holy Roman Emperor in the War of the Spanish Succession, he was officially granted the title of king of Prussia. Thus was Elector Frederick III transformed into King Frederick I of an important new player on the European stage.

THE EMERGENCE OF AUSTRIA

The Austrian Habsburgs had long played a significant role in European politics as Holy Roman Emperors, but by the end of the Thirty Years' War, the Habsburg hopes of creating an empire in Germany had been dashed. In the seventeenth century, the house of Austria made an important transition; the German empire was lost, but a new empire was created in eastern and southeastern Europe.

The nucleus of the new Austrian Empire remained the traditional Austrian hereditary possessions: Lower and Upper Austria, Carinthia, Carniola, Styria, and Tyrol (see Map 15.4). To these had been added the kingdom of Bohemia and parts of northwestern Hungary in the sixteenth century.

In the seventeenth century, Leopold I (1658–1705) encouraged the eastward movement of the Austrian Empire, but he was sorely challenged by the revival of Turkish power in the seventeenth century. Having moved into Transylvania, the Turks eventually pushed westward and laid siege to Vienna in 1683. A European army, led by the Austrians, counterattacked and decisively defeated the Turks in 1687. By the Treaty of Karlowitz in 1699, Austria took control of Hungary, Transylvania, Croatia, and Slovenia, thus establishing an Austrian Empire in southeastern Europe. At the end of the War of the Spanish Succession, Austria gained possession of the Spanish Netherlands and received formal recognition of its occupation of the Spanish possessions in Italy, namely, Milan, Mantua, Sardinia, and Naples. By the beginning of the eighteenth century, the house of Austria had acquired a new empire of considerable size.

The Austrian monarchy, however, never became a highly centralized, absolutist state, primarily because it included so many different national groups. The Austrian Empire remained a collection of territories held together by a personal union. The Habsburg emperor was archduke of Austria, king of Bohemia, and king of Hungary. Each of these areas had its own laws, Estates-General, and political life. The landed aristocrats throughout the empire were connected by a common bond of service to the house of Habsburg, as military officers or government bureaucrats, but no other common sentiment tied the regions together. Nevertheless, by the beginning of the eighteenth century, Austria was a populous empire in central Europe of great potential military strength.

■ *Italy: From Spanish to Austrian Rule*

By 1530, Emperor Charles V had managed to defeat the French armies in Italy and become the arbiter of Italy (see Chapter 13). Initially, he was content to establish close ties with many native Italian rulers and allow them to rule, provided that they recognize his dominant role. But in 1540, he gave the duchy of Milan to his son Philip II and transferred all imperial rights over Italy to the Spanish monarchy.

From the beginning of Philip II's reign in 1559 until 1713, the Spanish presence was felt everywhere in Italy.

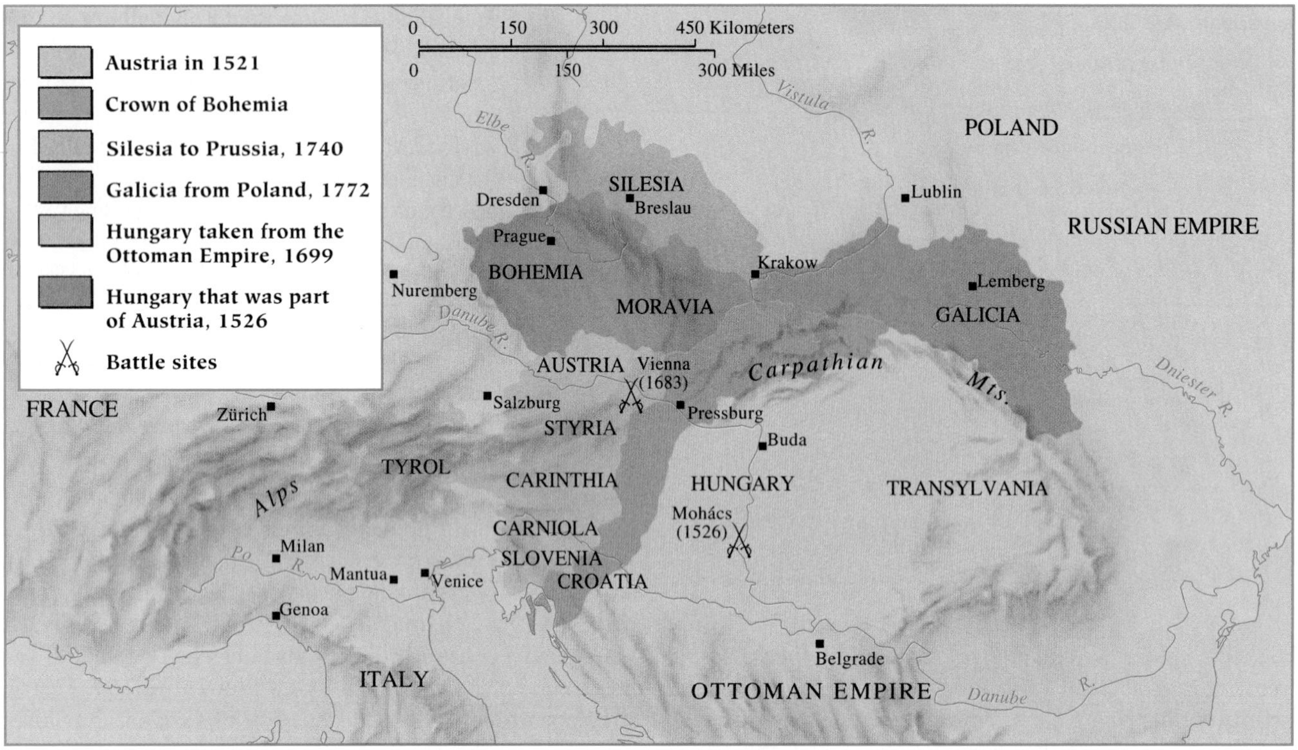

Map 15.4 The Growth of the Austrian Empire. The Habsburgs had hoped to establish an empire of Germans, but the results of the Thirty Years' War crushed the dream. So Austria expanded to the east and the south, primarily at the expense of the Ottoman Empire, and also gained the Spanish Netherlands and former Spanish territories in Italy. ■ In which areas did the Austrian Empire have access to the Mediterranean Sea, and why would that potentially be important?

Only Florence, the Papal States, and Venice managed to maintain relatively independent policies. At the same time, the influence of the papacy became oppressive in Italy as the machinery of the Catholic Counter-Reformation—the Inquisition, Index, and the Jesuits—was used to stifle all resistance to the Catholic orthodoxy created by the Council of Trent (see Chapter 13).

At the beginning of the eighteenth century, Italy suffered further from the struggles between France and Spain. But it was Austria, not France, that benefited the most from the War of the Spanish Succession. By gaining Milan, Mantua, Sardinia, and Naples, Austria supplanted Spain as the dominant power in Italy.

Russia: From Fledgling Principality to Major Power

A new Russian state had emerged in the fifteenth century under the leadership of the principality of Moscow and its grand dukes (see Chapter 12). In the sixteenth century, Ivan IV the Terrible (1533–1584), who was the first ruler to take the title of tsar, expanded the territories of Russia eastward after finding westward expansion blocked by the powerful Swedish and Polish states. Ivan also extended the autocracy of the tsar by crushing the power of the Russian nobility, known as the boyars. Ivan's dynasty came to an end in 1598 and was followed by a resurgence of aristocratic power in a period of anarchy known as the Time of Troubles. It did not end until the Zemsky Sobor, or national assembly, chose Michael Romanov (1613–1645) as the new tsar, beginning a dynasty that lasted until 1917.

In the seventeenth century, Muscovite society was highly stratified. At the top was the tsar, who claimed to be a divinely ordained autocratic ruler. Russian society was dominated by an upper class of landed aristocrats who, in the course of the seventeenth century, managed to bind their peasants to the land. An abundance of land and a shortage of peasants made serfdom desirable to the landowners. Townspeople were also controlled. Many merchants were not allowed to move from their cities without government permission or to sell their businesses to anyone outside their class. In the seventeenth century, merchant and peasant revolts as well as a schism in the Russian Orthodox church created very unsettled conditions. In the midst of these political and religious upheavals, seventeenth-century Moscow was experiencing more frequent contacts with the West, and Western ideas were beginning to penetrate a few Russian circles. At the end of the seventeenth century, Peter the Great noticeably accelerated this westernizing process.

THE REIGN OF PETER THE GREAT (1689–1725)

Peter the Great was an unusual character. A strong man, towering 6 feet, 9 inches tall, Peter was coarse in his tastes and rude in his behavior. He enjoyed a low kind of humor—belching contests, crude jokes, comical funerals—and vicious punishments including floggings, impalings, roastings, and beard burnings (see the box on p. 420). Peter gained a firsthand view of the West when he made a trip there in 1697–1698 and returned to Russia with a firm determination to westernize or Europeanize his realm. Perhaps too much has been made of Peter's desire to westernize a "backward country." Peter's policy of Europeanization was largely technical. He admired European technology and gadgets and desired to transplant these to Russia. Only this kind of modernization could give him the army and navy he needed to make Russia a great power.

As could be expected, one of his first priorities was the reorganization of the army and the creation of a navy. Employing both Russians and Europeans as officers, he conscripted peasants for twenty-five-year stints of service to build a standing army of 210,000 men. Peter has also been given credit for forming the first Russian navy.

Peter reorganized the central government, partly along Western lines. In 1711, Peter created the Senate to supervise the administrative machinery of the state while he was away on military campaigns. In time, the Senate became something like a ruling council, but its ineffectiveness caused Peter to borrow the Western institution of "colleges," or boards of administrators entrusted with specific functions, such as foreign affairs, war, and justice. To impose the rule of the central government more effectively throughout the land, Peter divided Russia into eight provinces and later, in 1719, into fifty. Although he hoped to create a "police state," by which he meant a well-ordered community governed in accordance with law, few of his bureaucrats shared his concept of honest service and duty to the state. Peter hoped for a sense of civic duty, but his own forceful personality created an atmosphere of fear that prevented it. He wrote to one administrator, "According to these orders act, act, act. I won't write more, but you will pay with your head if you interpret orders again."[9]

To further his administrative aims, Peter demanded that all members of the landholding class serve in either military or civil offices. Moreover, in 1722, Peter instituted the Table of Ranks to create opportunities for nonnobles to serve the

Peter the Great. Peter the Great wished to westernize Russia, especially in the realm of technical skills. His foremost goal was the creation of a strong army and navy in order to make Russia a great power. A Dutch painter created this portrait of the armored tsar during his visit to the West in 1697.

Russian School, *Czar Peter the Great*, Rijksmuseum, Amsterdam

Peter the Great Deals with a Rebellion

During his first visit to the West in 1697–1698, Peter received word that the Streltsy, an elite military unit stationed in Moscow, had revolted against his authority. Peter hurried home and crushed the revolt in a very savage fashion. This selection is taken from an Austrian account of how Peter dealt with the rebels.

■ *Peter and the Streltsy*

How sharp was the pain, how great the indignation, to which the tsar's Majesty was mightily moved, when he knew of the rebellion of the Streltsy, betraying openly a mind panting for vengeance! He was still tarrying at Vienna, quite full of the desire of setting out for Italy; but, fervid as was his curiosity of rambling abroad, it was, nevertheless, speedily extinguished on the announcement of the troubles that had broken out in the bowels of his realm. Going immediately to Lefort . . . , he thus indignantly broke out: "Tell me, Francis, how I can reach Moscow by the shortest way, in a brief space, so that I may wreak vengeance on this great perfidy of my people, with punishments worthy of their abominable crime. Not one of them shall escape with impunity. Around my royal city, which, with their impious efforts, they planned to destroy, I will have gibbets and gallows set upon the walls and ramparts, and each and every one of them will I put to a direful death." Nor did he long delay the plan for his justly excited wrath; he took the quick post, as his ambassador suggested, and in four weeks' time he had got over about 300 miles without accident, and arrived the 4th of September, 1698—a monarch for the well deposed, but an avenger for the wicked.

His first anxiety after his arrival was about the rebellion—in what it consisted, what the insurgents meant, who dared to instigate such a crime. And as nobody could answer accurately upon all points, and some pleaded their own ignorance, others the obstinacy of the Streltsy, he began to have suspicions of everybody's loyalty. . . . No day, holy or profane, were the inquisitors idle; every day was deemed fit and lawful for torturing. There was as many scourges as there were accused, and every inquisitor was a butcher. . . . The whole month of October was spent in lacerating the backs of culprits with the knout and with flames; no day were those that were left alive exempt from scourging or scorching; or else they were broken upon the wheel, or driven to the gibbet, or slain with the ax. . . .

To prove to all people how holy and inviolable are those walls of the city which the Streltsy rashly meditated scaling in a sudden assault, beams were run out from all the embrasures in the walls near the gates, in each of which two rebels were hanged. This day beheld about two hundred and fifty die that death. There are few cities fortified with as many palisades as Moscow has given gibbets to her guardian Streltsy.

state and join the nobility. All civil offices were ranked according to fourteen levels; a parallel list of fourteen grades was also created for all military offices. Every official was then required to begin at level one and work his way up the ranks. When a nonnoble reached the eighth rank, he acquired noble status. This attempt by Peter to create a new nobility based on merit was not carried on by his successors.

To obtain the enormous amount of money needed for an army and navy that absorbed as much as four-fifths of the state revenue, Peter adopted Western mercantilistic policies to stimulate economic growth. He tried to increase exports and develop new industries while exploiting domestic resources like the iron mines in the Urals. But his military needs were endless, and he came to rely on the old expedient of simply raising taxes, imposing additional burdens on the hapless peasants, who were becoming ever more oppressed in Peter's Russia.

Peter also sought to gain state control of the Russian Orthodox church. In 1721, he abolished the position of patriarch and created a body called the Holy Synod to make decisions for the church. At its head stood a procurator, a layman who represented the interests of the tsar and assured Peter of effective domination of the church.

Shortly after his return from the West in 1698, Peter had begun to introduce Western customs, practices, and manners into Russia. He ordered the preparation of the first Russian book of etiquette to teach Western manners. Among other things, it pointed out that it was not polite to spit on the floor or to scratch oneself at dinner. Because Europeans at that time did not wear beards or traditional long-skirted coats, Russian beards had to be shaved and coats shortened, a reform Peter personally enforced at court by shaving off his nobles' beards and cutting their coats at the knees with his own hands. Outside the court, barbers and tailors planted at town gates enforced the edicts by cutting the beards and cloaks of those who entered or left. Anyone who failed to conform was to be "beaten without mercy."

One group of Russians benefited greatly from Peter's cultural reforms—women. Having watched women mixing freely with men in Western courts, Peter shattered the seclusion of upper-class Russian women and demanded that they remove the traditional veils that covered their faces. Peter also decreed that social gatherings bc held three times a week in the large houses of Saint Petersburg where men and women could mix for conversation, card games, and dancing, which Peter had learned in the West. The tsar also now insisted that women could marry of their own free will.

The object of Peter's domestic reforms was to make Russia into a great state and a military power. His primary goal was to "open a window to the West," meaning an ice-free port easily accessible to Europe. This could only be achieved on the Baltic, but at that time the Baltic coast was controlled by Sweden, the most important power in northern Europe. Desirous of these lands, Peter, with the support of Poland and Denmark, attacked Sweden in the summer of 1700 believing that the young king of Sweden, Charles XII, could easily be defeated. Charles, however, proved to be a brilliant general. He smashed the Danes, flattened the Poles, and with a well-disciplined force of only eight thousand men, routed the Russian army of forty thousand at the Battle of Narva (1700). The Great Northern War (1701–1721) soon ensued.

But Peter fought back. He reorganized his army along Western lines and at the Battle of Poltava in 1709 defeated Charles's army decisively. Although the war dragged on for another twelve years, the Peace of Nystadt in 1721 gave formal recognition to what Peter had already achieved: the acquisition of Estonia, Livonia, and Karelia (see Map 15.5). Sweden had become a second-rate power, while Russia was now the great European state Peter had wanted. And he was building it a fine capital. Early in the war, in the northern marshlands along the Baltic, Peter had begun to construct a new city, Saint Petersburg, his window on the West and a symbol that Russia was looking westward to Europe. Though its construction cost the lives of thousands of peasants, the city was completed during Peter's lifetime. It remained the Russian capital until 1917.

Peter modernized and westernized Russia to the extent that it became a great military power and, by his death in 1725, an important member of the European state system. But his policies were also detrimental to Russia. Westernization was a bit of a sham, because Western culture reached only the upper classes, and the real object of the reforms, the creation of a strong military, only added more burdens to the masses of the Russian people. The forceful way in which Peter the Great imposed westernization led his people not to embrace Europe and Western civilization but to distrust it.

■ *The Growth of Monarchy in Sweden*

As the economic thoroughfare between the products of eastern Europe and the West, the Baltic Sea bestowed special importance on the lands surrounding it. In the sixteenth century, Sweden had broken its ties with Denmark and emerged as an independent state (see Chapter 13). Despite their common Lutheran religion, Denmark's and Sweden's territorial ambitions in northern Europe kept them in rather constant rivalry in the seventeenth century.

Compared to Denmark, Sweden seemed a relatively poor country, and historians have had difficulty explaining why it played such a large role in European affairs in the seventeenth century. Sweden's economy was weak, and the monarchy was still locked in conflict with the powerful Swedish nobility. During the reign of Gustavus Adolphus (1611–1632), his wise and dedicated chief minister, Axel Oxenstierna, persuaded the king to adopt a new policy in which the nobility formed a "first estate" occupying

Map 15.5 Russia: From Principality to Nation-State. Russia had swelled in size since its emergence in the fifteenth century. However, Peter the Great modernized the country, instituting bureaucratic and taxation reforms and building up the military. He won territory on the Baltic from Sweden, giving Russia an ice-free port. ■ Why would the later westward expansion of Russia during Catherine the Great's reign affect the international balance of power in Europe?

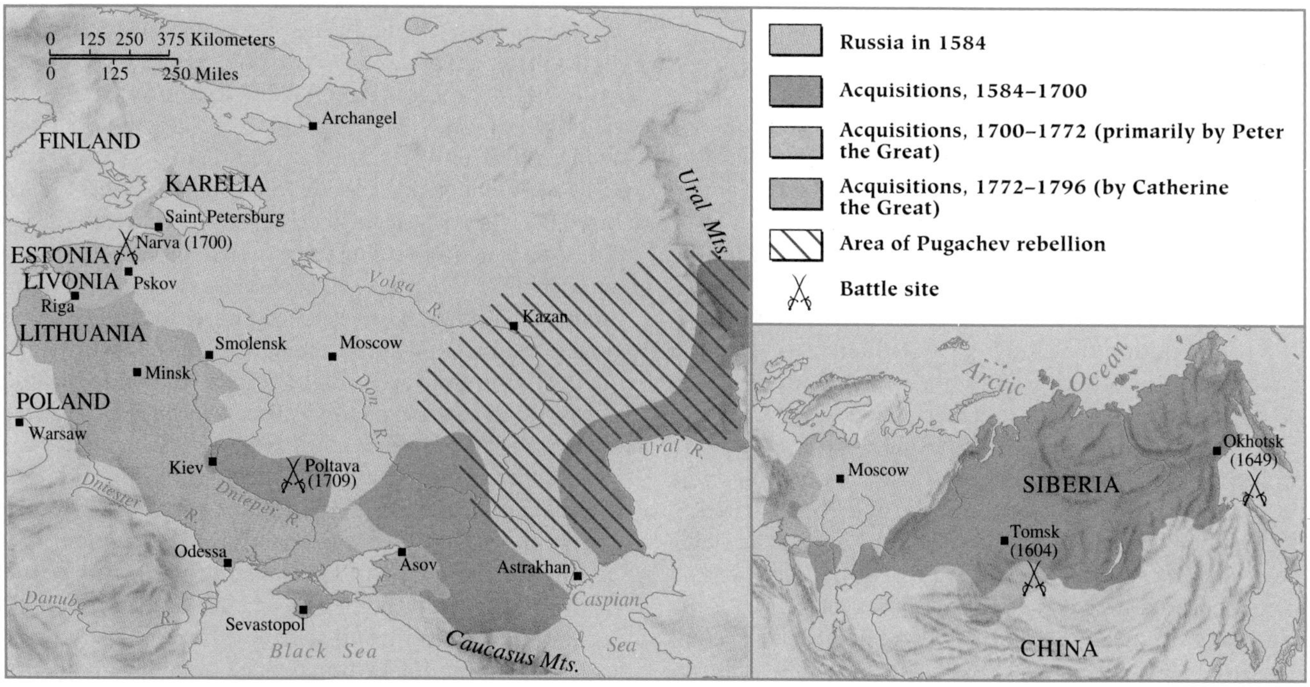

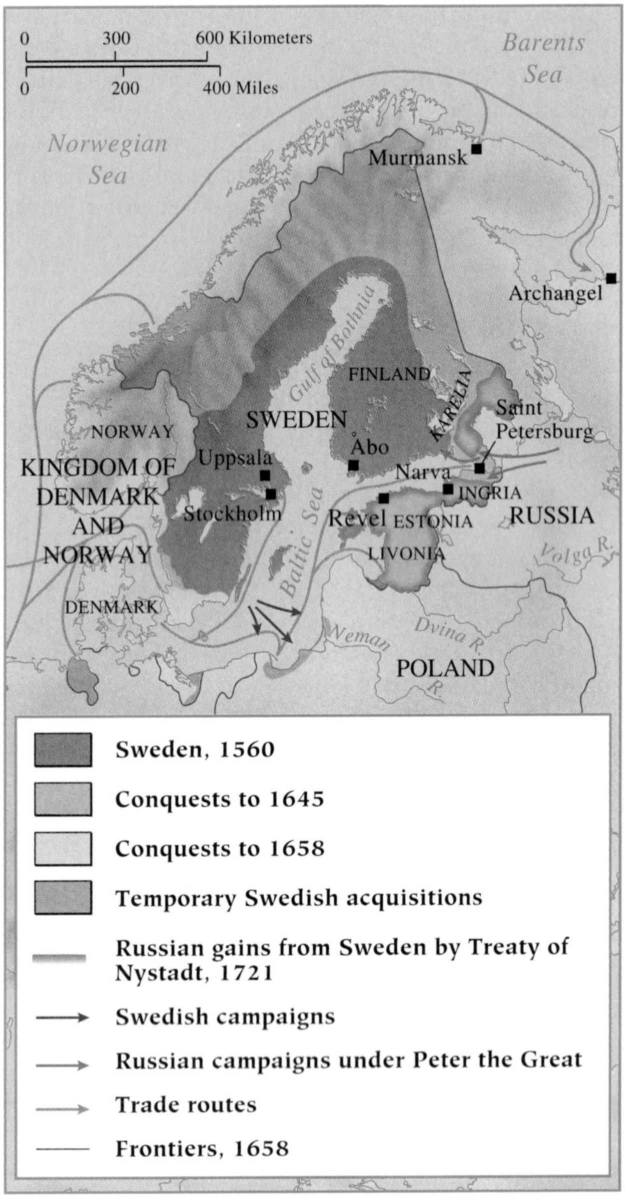

Sweden in the Seventeenth Century

the bureaucratic positions of an expanded central government. This created a stable monarchy and freed the king to raise a formidable army and participate in the Thirty Years' War, only to be killed in battle in 1632.

Sweden experienced a severe political crisis after the death of Gustavus Adolphus. His daughter Christina (1633–1654) proved to be far more interested in philosophy and religion than ruling. Her tendency to favor the interests of the nobility led the other estates of the Riksdag, Sweden's parliament—the burghers, clergy, and peasants—to protest. In 1654, tired of ruling and wishing to become a Catholic, which was forbidden in Sweden, Christina abdicated in favor of her cousin, who became King Charles X (1654–1660). His accession to the throne defused a potentially explosive peasant revolt against the nobility.

Charles X reestablished domestic order, but it was his successor, Charles XI (1660–1697), who did the painstaking work of building the Swedish monarchy along the lines of an absolute monarchy. He built up a bureaucracy, subdued both the Riksdag and the church, improved the army and navy, and left to his son, Charles XII (1697–1718), a well-organized Swedish state that dominated northern Europe.

Charles XII was primarily interested in military affairs. Energetic and regarded as a brilliant general, his grandiose plans and strategies, which involved Sweden in conflicts with Poland, Denmark, and Russia, proved to be Sweden's undoing. By the time he died in 1718, Charles XII had lost much of Sweden's northern empire to Russia, and Sweden's status as a first-class northern power had proved to be short-lived.

The Ottoman Empire

After their conquest of Constantinople in 1453, the Ottoman Turks tried to complete their conquest of the Balkans, where they had been established since the fourteenth century (see Map 15.6). Although they were successful in taking the Romanian territory of Wallachia in 1476, the resistance of the Hungarians kept them from advancing up the Danube valley. From 1480 to 1520, internal problems and the need to consolidate their eastern frontiers kept the Turks from any further attacks on Europe.

The reign of Sultan Suleiman I the Magnificent (1520–1566), however, brought the Turks back to Europe's attention. Advancing up the Danube, the Turks seized Belgrade in 1521 and Hungary by 1526, although their attempts to conquer Vienna in 1529 were repulsed. At the same time, the Turks extended their power into the western Mediterranean, threatening to turn it into a Turkish lake until a large Turkish fleet was destroyed by the Spanish at Lepanto in 1571. Despite the defeat, the Turks continued to hold nominal control over the southern shores along the Mediterranean.

Although Europeans frequently spoke of new Christian crusades against the infidel Turks, by the beginning of the seventeenth century the Ottoman Empire was being treated like another European power by European rulers seeking alliances and trade concessions. The Ottoman Empire possessed a highly effective governmental system, especially when it was led by strong sultans or powerful grand viziers (prime ministers). The splendid capital, Constantinople, possessed a population far larger than that of any European city. Nevertheless, Ottoman politics periodically degenerated into bloody intrigues as factions fought each other for influence and the throne. In one particularly gruesome practice, a ruling sultan would murder his brothers to avoid challenges to his rule. Despite the periodic bouts of civil chaos, a well-trained bureaucracy of civil servants continued to administer state affairs efficiently.

A well-organized military system also added to the strength of the Ottoman Empire. Especially outstanding were the Janissaries, composed of Christian boys who had been taken from their parents, converted to the Muslim faith, and subjected to rigid military discipline to form an elite core of eight thousand troops personally loyal to the sultan.

In the first half of the seventeenth century, the Ottoman Empire was a "sleeping giant." Occupied by domestic bloodletting and severely threatened by a challenge from Persia, the Ottomans were content with the sta-

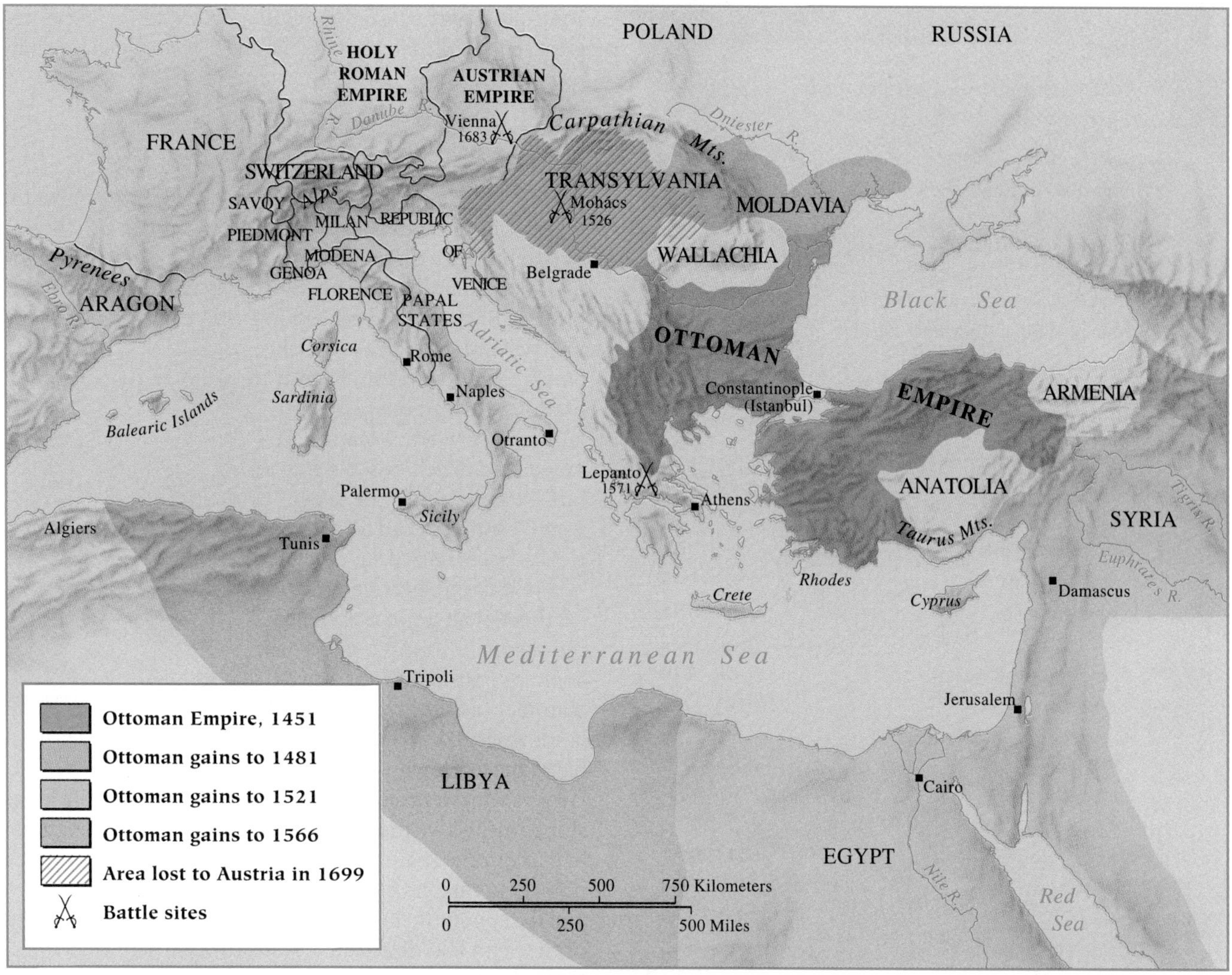

Map 15.6 The Ottoman Empire. In the sixteenth and seventeenth centuries, the Ottoman Empire possessed an effective bureaucracy and military. During this period, it conquered much of the Balkans and made inroads into eastern Europe; however, by 1699 it had lost the farthest reaches of its European territory and would never again pose a serious threat to Europe. ■ In what region did the Ottomans make the greatest territorial gains in the sixteenth century?

tus quo in eastern Europe. But under a new line of grand viziers in the second half of the seventeenth century, the Ottoman Empire again took the offensive. By 1683, the Ottomans had marched through the Hungarian plain and laid siege to Vienna. Repulsed by a mixed army of Austrians, Poles, Bavarians, and Saxons, the Turks retreated and were pushed out of Hungary by a new European coalition. Although they retained the core of their empire, the Ottoman Turks would never again be a threat to Europe.

The Limits of Absolutism

In recent decades, historical studies of local institutions have challenged the traditional picture of absolute monarchs. We now recognize that their power was far from absolute, and it is misleading to think that they actually controlled the lives of their subjects. In 1700, government for most people still meant the local institutions that affected their lives: local courts, local tax collectors, and local organizers of armed forces. Kings and ministers might determine policies and issue guidelines, but they still had to function through local agents and had no guarantee whatever that their wishes would be carried out. A mass of urban and provincial privileges, liberties, and exemptions (including from taxation) and a whole host of corporate bodies and interest groups—provincial and national Estates, clerical officials, officeholders who had bought or inherited their positions, and provincial nobles—limited what monarchs could achieve. The most successful rulers were not those who tried to destroy the old system but rather those like Louis XIV, who knew how to use the old system to their advantage. Above all other considerations stood the landholding nobility. Everywhere in the seventeenth century, the landed aristocracy played an important

CHRONOLOGY

Absolutism in Central, Eastern, and Northern Europe

Brandenburg-Prussia	
Hohenzollerns established in Brandenburg	1415
Hohenzollerns acquire lands along the Rhine	1609
Hohenzollerns acquire East Prussia	1618
Frederick William the Great Elector	1640–1688
Elector Frederick III (King Frederick I)	1688–1713
Austrian Empire	
Leopold I	1658–1705
Turkish siege of Vienna	1683
Treaty of Karlowitz	1699
Russia	
Ivan IV the Terrible	1533–1584
Time of Troubles	1598–1613
Michael Romanov	1613–1645
Peter the Great	1689–1725
First trip to the West	1697–1698
Great Northern War	1701–1721
Construction of Saint Petersburg begins	1703
Battle of Poltava	1709
Sweden	
Gustavus Adolphus	1611–1632
Christina	1633–1654
Charles X	1654–1660
Charles XI	1660–1697
Charles XII	1697–1718
Ottoman Empire	
Suleiman I the Magnificent	1520–1566
Battle of Lepanto	1571
Turkish defeat at Vienna	1683

role in the European monarchical system. As military officers, judges, officeholders, and landowners in control of vast, untaxed estates, their power remained immense. In some places, their strength put severe limits on how effectively even absolute monarchs could rule.

Limited Monarchy and Republics

Almost everywhere in Europe in the seventeenth century, kings and their ministers were in control of central governments that sought to impose order by strengthening their powers. But not all European states followed the pattern of absolute monarchy. In eastern Europe, the Polish aristocracy controlled a virtually powerless king. In western Europe, two great states—the Dutch Republic and England—successfully resisted the power of hereditary monarchs.

The Weakness of the Polish Monarchy

Poland had played a major role in eastern Europe in the fifteenth century and ruled Lithuania and much of Ukraine by the end of the sixteenth. After the elective throne of Poland had been won by the Swede Sigismund III (1587–1631), Poland had a king who even thought seriously of creating a vast Polish empire that would include at least Russia and possibly Finland and Sweden. Poland not only failed to achieve this goal, but by the end of the seventeenth century, it had become a weak, decentralized state.

Poland in the Seventeenth Century

It was the elective nature of the Polish monarchy that reduced it to impotence. The Sejm, or Polish diet, was a two-chamber assembly in which landowners completely dominated the few townspeople and lawyers who were also members. To be elected to the kingship, prospective monarchs (who were mostly foreigners) had to agree to share power with the Sejm (in effect with the nobles) in matters of taxation, foreign and military policy, and the appointment of state officials and judges. The power of the Sejm had disastrous results for central monarchical authority, for the real aim of most of its members was to ensure that central authority would not affect their local interests. The acceptance of the liberum veto in 1652, whereby the meetings of the Sejm could be stopped by a single dissenting member, reduced government to virtual chaos.

Poland, then, was basically a confederation of semi-independent estates of landed nobles. By the late seventeenth century, it also became a battleground for foreign powers, who found the nation easy to invade but difficult to rule.

The Golden Age of the Dutch Republic

The seventeenth century has often been called the golden age of the Dutch Republic as the United Provinces held center stage as one of Europe's great powers. Like France and England, the United Provinces was an Atlantic power, underlining the importance of the shift of political and economic power from the Mediterranean basin to the countries on the Atlantic seaboard. As a result of the sixteenth-century revolt of the Netherlands, the seven northern provinces, which began to call themselves the United Provinces of the Netherlands in 1581, became the core of the modern Dutch state. The new state was officially recognized by the Peace of Westphalia in 1648.

With independence came internal dissension. There were two chief centers of political power in the new state.

Each province had an official known as a stadholder who was responsible for leading the army and maintaining order. Beginning with William of Orange and his heirs, the house of Orange occupied the stadholderate in most of the seven provinces and favored the development of a centralized government with themselves as hereditary monarchs. The States General, an assembly of representatives from every province, opposed the Orangist ambitions and advocated a decentralized or republican form of government. For much of the seventeenth century, the republican forces were in control. But in 1672, burdened with war against both France and England, the United Provinces turned to William III (1672–1702) of the house of Orange to establish a monarchical regime. But his death in 1702 without a direct heir enabled the republican forces to gain control once more. The Dutch Republic would not be seriously threatened again by monarchical forces.

Underlying Dutch prominence in the seventeenth century was its economic prosperity, fueled by the role of the Dutch as carriers of European trade. But warfare proved disastrous to the Dutch Republic. Wars with France and England placed heavy burdens on Dutch finances and manpower. English shipping began to challenge what had been Dutch commercial supremacy, and by 1715, the Dutch were experiencing a serious economic decline.

LIFE IN SEVENTEENTH-CENTURY AMSTERDAM

By the beginning of the seventeenth century, Amsterdam had replaced Antwerp as the financial and commercial capital of Europe. In 1570, Amsterdam had thirty thousand inhabitants; by 1610, that number had doubled as refugees poured in, especially from the Spanish Netherlands. In 1613, this rapid growth caused the city government to approve an "urban expansion plan" that increased the city's territory from 500 to 1,800 acres through the construction of three large concentric canals. Builders prepared plots for the tall, narrow-fronted houses that were characteristic of the city by hammering wooden columns through the mud to the firm sand underneath. The canals in turn made it possible for merchants and artisans to use the upper stories of their houses as storerooms for their goods. Wares carried by small boats were hoisted to the top windows of these dwellings by block and tackle beams fastened to the gables of the roofs. Amsterdam's physical expansion was soon matched by its population as the city grew to 200,000 by 1660.

The exuberant expansion of Amsterdam in the seventeenth century owed much to the city's role as the commercial and financial center of Europe. But what had made this possible? For one thing, Amsterdam merchants possessed vast fleets of ships, many of which were used for the lucrative North Sea herring catch. Amsterdam-based ships were also important carriers for the products of other countries. The Dutch invention of the *fluyt,* a shallow-draft ship of large capacity, enabled the transport of enormous quantities of cereals, timber, and iron.

Amsterdam merchants unloaded their cargoes at Dam Square, where all goods weighing more than 50 pounds were recorded and tested for quality. The quantity of goods brought to Amsterdam soon made the city a crossroads for many of Europe's chief products. Amsterdam was also, of course, the chief port for the Dutch West and East Indian

Dam Square. This work by Jacob van der Ulft, done in 1659, shows Dam Square in Amsterdam. Merchants unloaded their cargoes here, making Dam Square one of the busiest centers of the city.

Giraudon/Art Resource, NY

trading companies. Moreover, city industries turned imported raw materials into finished goods, making Amsterdam an important producer of woolen cloth, refined sugar and tobacco products, glass, beer, paper, books, jewelry, and leather goods. Some of the city's great wealth came from war profits: by 1700, Amsterdam was the principal supplier of military goods in Europe; its gun foundries had customers throughout the Continent.

A third factor in Amsterdam's prosperity was its importance as a financial center. Trading profits provided large quantities of capital for investment. Its financial role was greatly facilitated by the foundation in 1609 of the Exchange Bank of Amsterdam, long the greatest public bank in northern Europe. The city also founded the Amsterdam Stock Exchange for speculating in commodities.

At the very top of Amsterdam's society stood a select number of very prosperous manufacturers, shipyard owners, and merchants, whose wealth enabled them to control the city government of Amsterdam as well as the Dutch Republic's States General. In the first half of the seventeenth century, the Calvinist background of the wealthy Amsterdam burghers led them to adopt a simple lifestyle. They wore dark clothes and lived in substantial but simply furnished houses known for their steep, narrow stairways. The oft-quoted phrase that "cleanliness is next to godliness" was literally true for these self-confident Dutch burghers. Their houses were clean and orderly; foreigners often commented that Dutch housewives always seemed to be scrubbing. But in the second half of the seventeenth century, the wealthy burghers began to reject their Calvinist heritage, a transformation that is especially evident in their more elaborate and colorful clothes.

England and the Emergence of Constitutional Monarchy

One of the most prominent examples of resistance to absolute monarchy came in seventeenth-century England, where king and Parliament struggled to determine the role each should play in governing the nation. But the struggle over this political issue was complicated by a deep and profound religious controversy. With the victory of Parliament came the foundation for constitutional monarchy by the end of the seventeenth century.

KING JAMES I AND PARLIAMENT

With the death of Queen Elizabeth in 1603, the Tudor dynasty became extinct, and the Stuart line of rulers was inaugurated with the accession to the throne of Elizabeth's cousin, King James VI of Scotland (son of Mary, queen of Scots), who became James I (1603–1625) of England. Although used to royal power as king of Scotland, James understood little about the laws, institutions, and customs of the English. He espoused the divine right of kings, the belief that kings receive their power directly from God and are responsible to no one except God. This viewpoint alienated Parliament, which had grown accustomed under the Tudors to act on the premise that monarch and Parliament together ruled England as a "balanced polity." Parliament expressed its displeasure with James's claims by refusing his requests for additional monies needed by the king to meet the increased cost of government. Parliament's power of the purse proved to be its trump card in its relationship with the king.

Some members of Parliament were also alienated by James's religious policy. The Puritans—Protestants in the Anglican church inspired by Calvinist theology—wanted James to eliminate the episcopal system of church organization used in the Church of England (in which the bishop or *episcopos* played the major administrative role) in favor of a Presbyterian model (used in Scotland and patterned after Calvin's church organization in Geneva, where ministers and elders—also called presbyters—played an important governing role). James refused because he realized that the Anglican church, with its bishops appointed by the crown, was a major support of monarchical authority. But the Puritans were not easily cowed and added to the rising chorus of opposition to the king. Many of England's gentry, mostly well-to-do landowners below the level of the nobility, had become Puritans, and these Puritan gentry not only formed an important and substantial part of the House of Commons, the lower house of Parliament, but also held important positions locally as justices of the peace and sheriffs. It was not wise to alienate them.

CHARLES I AND THE MOVE TOWARD REVOLUTION

The conflict that had begun during the reign of James came to a head during the reign of his son, Charles I (1625–1649). In 1628, Parliament passed the Petition of Right, which the king was supposed to accept before being granted any tax revenues. This petition prohibited taxation without Parliament's consent, arbitrary imprisonment, the quartering of soldiers in private houses, and the declaration of martial law in peacetime. Although he initially accepted it, Charles later reneged on the agreement because of its limitations on royal power. In 1629, Charles decided that since he could not work with Parliament, he would not summon it to meet. From 1629 to 1640, Charles pursued a course of personal rule, which forced him to find ways to collect taxes without the cooperation of Parliament. One expedient was a tax called ship money, a levy on seacoast towns to pay for coastal defense, which was now collected annually by the king's officials throughout England and used to finance other government operations besides defense. This use of ship money aroused opposition from middle-class merchants and landed gentry, who objected to the king's attempts to tax without Parliament's consent.

The king's religious policy also proved disastrous. His marriage to Henrietta Maria, the Catholic sister of King Louis XIII of France, aroused suspicions about the king's own religious inclinations. Even more important, however, the efforts of Charles and William Laud, the archbishop of Canterbury, to introduce more ritual into the Anglican church struck the Puritans as a return to Catholic popery. Grievances mounted. Charles might have survived unscathed if he could have avoided calling Parliament, which alone could provide a focus for the many cries of discontent throughout the land. But when the king and Archbishop Laud attempted to impose the Anglican Book of Common Prayer on the Scottish Presbyterian church, the Scots rose up in rebellion against the king. Financially strapped and unable to raise troops to defend against the Scots, the king was forced to call Parliament into session. Eleven years of frustration welled up to create a Parliament determined to deal the king his due.

In its first session, from November 1640 to September 1641, the so-called Long Parliament (because it lasted in one form or another from 1640 to 1660) took a series of steps that placed severe limitations on royal authority. These included the abolition of arbitrary courts, the abolition of taxes that the king had collected without Parliament's consent, such as ship money, and the passage of the revolutionary Triennial Act, which specified that Parliament must meet at least once every three years, with or without the king's consent. By the end of 1641, one group in Parliament was prepared to go no further, but a group of more radical parliamentarians pushed for more change, including the elimination of bishops in the Anglican church. When the king tried to take advantage of the split by arresting some members of the more radical faction in Parliament, a large group in Parliament led by John Pym and his fellow Puritans decided that the king had gone too far. England slipped into civil war.

CIVIL WAR IN ENGLAND

Parliament proved victorious in the first phase of the English Civil War (1642–1646). Most important to Parliament's success was the creation of the New Model Army by Oliver Cromwell. The New Model Army was composed primarily of more extreme Puritans known as the Independents, who believed they were doing battle for the Lord. It is striking to read in Cromwell's military reports such statements as "Sir, this is none other but the hand of God; and to Him alone belongs the glory." We might also attribute some of the credit to Cromwell himself, since his crusaders were well disciplined and trained in the latest military tactics. Supported by the New Model Army, Parliament ended the first phase of the civil war with the capture of King Charles I in 1646.

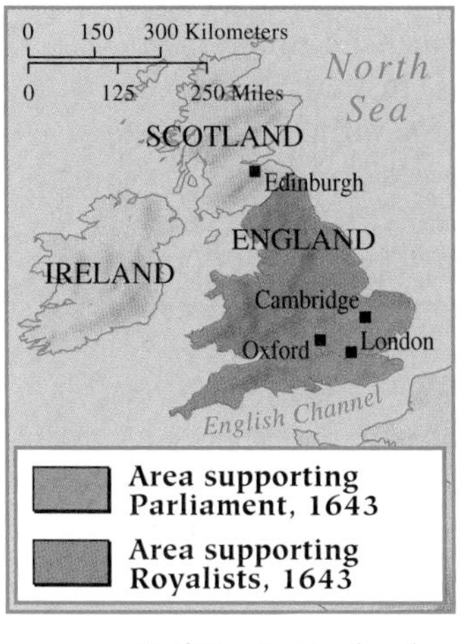

Civil War in England

A split now occurred in the parliamentary forces. A Presbyterian majority wanted to disband the army and restore Charles I with a Presbyterian state church. The army, composed mostly of the more radical Independents, who opposed an established Presbyterian church, marched on London in 1647 and began negotiations with the king. Charles took advantage of this division to flee and seek help from the Scots. Enraged by the king's treachery, Cromwell and the army engaged in a second civil war (1648) that ended with Cromwell's victory and the capture of the king. This time, Cromwell was determined to achieve a victory for the army's point of view. The Presbyterian members of Parliament were purged, leaving a Rump Parliament of fifty-three members of the House of Commons who then tried and condemned the king on a charge of treason and adjudged that "he, the said Charles Stuart, as a tyrant, traitor, murderer, and public enemy to the good people of this nation, shall be put to death by the severing of his head from his body." On January 30, 1649, Charles was beheaded, a most uncommon act in the seventeenth century. The revolution had triumphed, and the monarchy in England had been destroyed, at least for the moment.

CROMWELL AND NEW GOVERNMENTS

After the death of the king, the Rump Parliament abolished the monarchy and the House of Lords and proclaimed England a republic or commonwealth (1649–1653). This was not an easy period for Cromwell. As commander in chief of the army, he had to crush a Catholic uprising in Ireland, which he accomplished with a brutality that earned him the eternal enmity of the Irish people, as well as an uprising in Scotland on behalf of the son of Charles I.

Cromwell also faced opposition at home, especially from more radically minded groups who took advantage

Oliver Cromwell. Oliver Cromwell was a dedicated Puritan who formed the New Model Army and defeated the forces supporting King Charles I. Unable to work with Parliament, he came to rely on military force to rule England. Cromwell is pictured here in 1649, on the eve of his military campaign in Ireland.

Courtesy of the National Portrait Gallery

of the upheaval in England to push their agendas. The Levellers, for example, advocated such advanced ideas as freedom of speech, religious toleration, and a democratic republic, arguing for the right to vote for all male householders over the age of twenty-one. The Levellers also called for annual Parliaments, women's equality with men, and government programs to care for the poor. As one Leveller said, "The poorest he that is in England has a life to live as the greatest he." To Cromwell, a country gentleman, only people of property had the right to participate in the affairs of state, and he warned in a fit of rage: "I tell you . . . you have no other way to deal with these men but to break them or they will break you; . . . and make void all that work that, with so many years' industry, toil, and pains, you have done. . . . I tell you again, you are necessitated to break them."[10] And break them he did; Cromwell smashed the radicals by force. Only two centuries later would their ideas of democracy and equality become fashionable.

At the same time that Cromwell was dealing with the Levellers, he also found it difficult to work with the Rump Parliament and finally dispersed it by force. As the members of Parliament departed (April 1653), he shouted after them: "It's you that have forced me to do this, for I have sought the Lord night and day that He would slay me rather than put upon me the doing of this work." With the certainty of one who is convinced he is right, Cromwell had destroyed both king and Parliament.

The army provided a new government when it drew up the Instrument of Government, England's first and last written constitution. Executive power was vested in the Lord Protector (a position held by Cromwell) and legislative power in a reconstituted Parliament. But the new system failed to work. Cromwell found it difficult to work with the Parliament, especially when its members debated his authority and advocated once again the creation of a Presbyterian state church. In 1655, Cromwell dissolved Parliament and divided the country into eleven regions, each ruled by a major general who served virtually as a military governor. To meet the cost of military government, Cromwell levied a 10 percent land tax on all former Royalists. Unable to establish a constitutional basis for a working government, Cromwell had resorted to military force to maintain the rule of the Independents, ironically using even more arbitrary policies than those of Charles I.

Oliver Cromwell died in 1658. After floundering for eighteen months, the military establishment decided that arbitrary rule by the army was no longer feasible and reestablished the monarchy in the person of Charles II, the son of Charles I. The restoration of the Stuart monarchy ended England's time of troubles, but it was not long before yet another constitutional crisis arose.

RESTORATION OF THE MONARCHY

After eleven years of exile, Charles II (1660–1685) returned to England. As he entered London amid the acclaim of the people, he remarked sardonically, "I never knew that I was so popular in England." The restoration of the monarchy and the House of Lords did not mean, however, that the work of the English Revolution was undone. Parliament kept much of the power it had won: its role in government was acknowledged, the necessity for its consent to taxation was accepted, and arbitrary courts were still abolished. Yet Charles continued to push his own ideas, some of which were clearly out of step with many of the English people.

A serious religious problem disturbed the tranquility of Charles II's reign. After the restoration of the monarchy, a new Parliament (the Cavalier Parliament) met in 1661 and restored the Anglican church as the official church of England. In addition, laws were passed to force everyone, particularly Catholics and Puritan Dissenters, to conform to the Anglican church. Charles, however, was sympathetic to and perhaps even inclined toward Catholicism. Moreover, Charles's brother James, heir to the throne, did not hide the fact that he was a Catholic. Parliament's suspicions were therefore aroused in 1672 when Charles took the audacious step of issuing the Declaration of Indulgence, which suspended the laws that Parliament had passed against Catholics and Puritans. Parliament would have none of it and induced the king to suspend the declaration. Propelled by a strong anti-Catholic sentiment, Parliament then passed the Test Act of 1673, specifying that only Anglicans could hold military and civil offices.

A purported Catholic plot to assassinate King Charles and place his brother James on the throne, though soon exposed as imaginary, inflamed Parliament to attempt to pass a bill that would have barred James from the throne as a professed Catholic. Although these attempts failed, the debate over the bill created two political groupings: the Whigs, who wanted to exclude James and establish a Protestant king with toleration of Dissenters, and the Tories, who supported the king, despite their dislike of James as a Catholic, because they did not believe Parliament should tamper with the lawful succession to the throne. To foil these efforts, Charles dismissed Parliament in 1681, relying on French subsidies to rule alone. When he died in 1685, his Catholic brother came to the throne.

The accession of James II (1685–1688) virtually guaranteed a new constitutional crisis for England. An open and devout Catholic, his attempt to further Catholic interests made religion once more a primary cause of conflict between king and Parliament. Contrary to the Test Act, James named Catholics to high positions in the government, army, navy, and universities. In 1687, he issued a new Declaration of Indulgence, which suspended all laws barring Catholics and Dissenters from office. Parliamentary outcries against James's policies stopped short of rebellion because members knew that he was an old man and his successors were his Protestant daughters Mary and Anne, born to his first wife. But on June 10, 1688, a son was born to James II's second wife, also a Catholic. Suddenly the specter of a Catholic hereditary monarchy loomed large.

The Bill of Rights

In 1688, the English experienced yet another revolution, a rather bloodless one in which the Stuart king James II was replaced by Mary, James's daughter, and her husband, William of Orange. After William and Mary had assumed power, Parliament passed the Bill of Rights, which specified the rights of Parliament and laid the foundation for a constitutional monarchy.

■ The Bill of Rights

Whereas the said late King James II having abdicated the government, and the throne being thereby vacant, his Highness the prince of Orange (whom it has pleased Almighty God to make the glorious instrument of delivering this kingdom from popery and arbitrary power) did (by the device of the lords spiritual and temporal, and diverse principal persons of the Commons) cause letters to be written to the lords spiritual and temporal, being Protestants, and other letters to the several counties, cities, universities, boroughs, and Cinque Ports, for the choosing of such persons to represent them, as were of right to be sent to parliament, to meet and sit at Westminster upon the two and twentieth day of January, in this year 1689, in order to such an establishment as that their religion, laws, and liberties might not again be in danger of being subverted; upon which letters elections have been accordingly made.

And thereupon the said lords spiritual and temporal and Commons, pursuant to their respective letters and elections, being now assembled in a full and free representation of this nation, taking into their most serious consideration the best means for attaining the ends aforesaid, do in the first place (as their ancestors in like case have usually done), for the vindication and assertion of their ancient rights and liberties, declare:

1. That the pretended power of suspending laws, or the execution of laws, by regal authority, without consent of parliament is illegal.
2. That the pretended power of dispensing with the laws, or the execution of law by regal authority, as it has been assumed and exercised of late, is illegal.
3. That the commission for erecting the late court of commissioners for ecclesiastical causes, and all other commissions and courts of like nature, are illegal and pernicious.
4. That levying money for or to the use of the crown by pretense of prerogative, without grant of parliament, for longer time or in other manner than the same is or shall be granted, is illegal.
5. That it is the right of the subjects to petition the king, and all commitments and prosecutions for such petitioning are illegal.
6. That the raising or keeping a standing army within the kingdom in time of peace, unless it be with consent of parliament, is against law.
7. That the subjects which are Protestants may have arms for their defense suitable to their conditions, and as allowed by law.
8. That election of members of parliament ought to be free.
9. That the freedom of speech, and debates or proceedings in parliament, ought not to be impeached or questioned in any court or place out of parliament.
10. That excessive bail ought not to be required, nor excessive fines imposed, nor cruel and unusual punishments inflicted.
11. That jurors ought to be duly impaneled and returned, and jurors which pass upon men in trials for high treason ought to be freeholders.
12. That all grants and promises of fines and forfeitures of particular persons before conviction are illegal and void.
13. And that for redress of all grievances, and for the amending, strengthening, and preserving of the laws, parliament ought to be held frequently.

A GLORIOUS REVOLUTION

A group of seven prominent English noblemen invited William of Orange, husband of James's daughter Mary, to invade England. An inveterate foe of Louis XIV, William welcomed this opportunity to fight France with England's resources. William and Mary raised an army and invaded England while James, his wife, and their infant son fled to France. With almost no bloodshed, England had embarked on a "Glorious Revolution," not over the issue of whether there would be a monarchy but rather over who would be monarch.

The events of late 1688 set the Glorious Revolution in motion. The far more important part was the Revolution Settlement, which confirmed William and Mary as monarchs. In January 1689, the Convention Parliament asserted that James had tried to subvert the constitution "by breaking the original contract between king and people" and declared the throne of England vacant. It then offered the throne to William and Mary, who accepted it along with the provisions of a declaration of rights, later enacted into law as the Bill of Rights in 1689 (see the box above). The Bill of Rights affirmed Parliament's right to make laws and levy taxes and made it impossible for kings to oppose or do

CHRONOLOGY

Limited Monarchy and Republics

Poland	
Sigismund III	1587–1631
Beginning of liberum veto	1652
United Provinces	
Official recognition of United Provinces	1648
House of Orange	
William III	1672–1702
England	
James I	1603–1625
Charles I	1625–1649
Petition of Right	1628
First Civil War	1642–1646
Second Civil War	1648
Execution of Charles I	1649
Commonwealth	1649–1653
Death of Cromwell	1658
Restoration of monarchy	1660
Charles II	1660–1685
Cavalier Parliament	1661
Declaration of Indulgence	1672
Test Act	1673
James II	1685–1688
Declaration of Indulgence	1687
Glorious Revolution	1688
Bill of Rights	1689

without Parliament by stipulating that standing armies could be raised only with the consent of Parliament. Both elections and debates of Parliament had to be free, meaning that the king could not interfere. The rights of citizens to petition the sovereign, keep arms, have a jury trial, and not be subject to excessive bail were also confirmed. The Bill of Rights helped fashion a system of government based on the rule of law and a freely elected Parliament, thus laying the foundation for a constitutional monarchy.

The Bill of Rights did not settle the religious questions that had played such a large role in England's troubles in the seventeenth century. The Toleration Act of 1689 granted Puritan Dissenters the right of free public worship (Catholics were still excluded), although they did not yet have full civil and political equality since the Test Act was not repealed. Although the Toleration Act did not mean complete religious freedom and equality, it marked a departure in English history: few people would ever again be persecuted for religious reasons.

Many historians have viewed the Glorious Revolution as the end of the seventeenth-century struggle between king and Parliament. By deposing one king and establishing another, Parliament had demolished the divine-right theory of kingship (William was, after all, king by grace of Parliament, not God) and confirmed its right to participate in the government. Parliament did not have complete control of the government, but it now had an unquestioned role in affairs of state. Over the next century, it would gradually prove to be the real authority in the English system of constitutional monarchy.

RESPONSES TO REVOLUTION

The English revolutions of the seventeenth century prompted very different responses from two English political thinkers—Thomas Hobbes and John Locke. Thomas Hobbes (1588–1679), who lived during the English Civil War, was alarmed by the revolutionary upheavals in his contemporary England. Hobbes's name has since been associated with the state's claim to absolute authority over its subjects, a topic that he elaborated in his major treatise on political thought known as the *Leviathan,* published in 1651.

Hobbes claimed that in the state of nature, before society was organized, human life was "solitary, poor, nasty, brutish, and short." Humans were guided not by reason and moral ideals but by animalistic instincts and a ruthless struggle for self-preservation. To save themselves from destroying each other (the "war of every man against every man"), people contracted to form a commonwealth, which Hobbes called "that great Leviathan (or rather, to speak more reverently, that mortal god) to which we owe our peace and defense." This commonwealth placed its collective power into the hands of a sovereign authority, preferably a single ruler, who served as executor, legislator, and judge. This absolute ruler possessed unlimited power. In Hobbes's view, subjects may not rebel; if they do, they must be suppressed.

John Locke (1632–1704) viewed the exercise of political power quite differently from Hobbes and argued against the absolute rule of one man. Locke's experience of English politics during the Glorious Revolution was incorporated into a political work called *Two Treatises of Government.* Like Hobbes, Locke began with the state of nature before human existence became organized socially. But unlike Hobbes, Locke believed that humans lived then in a state of equality and freedom rather than a state of war. In this state of nature, humans had certain inalienable natural rights—to life, liberty, and property. Like Hobbes, Locke did not believe all was well in the state of nature. Since there was no impartial judge in the state of nature, people found it difficult to protect these natural rights. So they mutually agreed to establish a government to ensure the protection of their rights. This agreement established mutual obligations: government would protect the rights of the people while the people would act reasonably toward government. But if a government broke this agreement—for example, if a monarch failed to live up to his obligation to protect the natural rights or claimed absolute authority and made laws without the consent of the community—the people might form a new government. For Locke, however, the community of people was primarily the landholding aristocracy who were represented in Parliament, not the landless masses. Locke was hardly an advocate of political democracy, but his ideas proved important to both the Americans and the French in the eighteenth century and were used to support demands for constitutional government, the rule of law, and the protection of rights.

The Flourishing of European Culture

In the midst of religious wars and the growth of absolutism, European culture continued to flourish. The era was blessed with a number of prominent artists and writers.

The Changing Faces of Art

After the Renaissance, European art passed through a number of stylistic stages. The artistic Renaissance came to an end when a new movement called Mannerism emerged in Italy in the 1520s and 1530s.

MANNERISM

The Reformation's revival of religious values brought much political turmoil. Especially in Italy, the worldly enthusiasm of the Renaissance gave way to anxiety, uncertainty, suffering, and a yearning for spiritual experience. Mannerism reflected this environment in its deliberate attempt to break down the High Renaissance principles of balance, harmony, and moderation (the term *Mannerism* derives from critics who considered their contemporary artists to be second-rate imitators, painting "in the manner of" Michelangelo's late style). Italian Mannerist painters deliberately distorted the rules of proportion by portraying elongated figures that conveyed a sense of suffering and a strong emotional atmosphere filled with anxiety and confusion.

Mannerism spread from Italy to other parts of Europe and perhaps reached its apogee in the work of El Greco (1541–1614). Doménikos Theotocópoulos (called "the Greek"—El Greco) was from Crete, but after studying in Venice and Rome, he moved in the 1570s to Spain, where he became a church painter in Toledo. El Greco's elongated and contorted figures, portrayed in unusual shades of

El Greco, *Laocoön.* Mannerism reached its height of expression in the work of El Greco. Born in Crete, trained in Venice and Rome, and settling finally in Spain, El Greco worked as a church painter in Toledo. Pictured here is his version of the *Laocoön,* a Hellenistic sculpture discovered in Rome in 1506. The elongated, contorted bodies project a world of suffering while the somber background scene of the city of Toledo and threatening sky add a sense of terror and doom.

National Gallery of Art, Washington: Samuel H. Kress Collection

Scala/Art Resource, NY

Gian Lorenzo Bernini, *Ecstasy of Saint Theresa.* One of the greatest figures of the Baroque period was the Italian sculptor and architect Gian Lorenzo Bernini. *The Ecstasy of Saint Theresa,* created for the Cornaro Chapel in the Church of Santa Maria della Vittoria in Rome, was one of Bernini's most famous pieces of sculpture. Bernini sought to convey visually Theresa's own description of her mystical experience when an angel supposedly pierced her heart repeatedly with a golden arrow.

Giraudon/Art Resource, NY

Artemisia Gentileschi, *Judith Beheading Holofernes.* Artemisia Gentileschi painted a series of pictures portraying scenes from the lives of courageous Old Testament women. In this painting, a determined Judith, armed with her victim's sword, struggles to saw off the head of Holofernes. Gentileschi realistically and dramatically shows the gruesome nature of Judith's act.

yellow and green against an eerie background of turbulent grays, reflect well the artist's desire to create a world of intense emotion.

THE BAROQUE PERIOD

Mannerism was eventually replaced by a new movement—the Baroque—that began in Italy in the last quarter of the sixteenth century and spread to the rest of Europe. The style was most wholeheartedly embraced by the Catholic reform movement, as is evident at the Catholic courts, especially those of the Habsburgs in Madrid, Prague, Vienna, and Brussels. Although it was resisted in France, England, and Holland, eventually the Baroque style spread to all of Europe and to Latin America.

Baroque artists sought to bring together the classical ideals of Renaissance art with the spiritual feelings of the sixteenth-century religious revival. The Baroque painting style was known for its use of dramatic effects to arouse the emotions. In large part, though, Baroque art and architecture reflected the search for power that was such a large part of the seventeenth-century ethos. Baroque churches and palaces were magnificent and richly detailed. Kings and princes wanted other kings and princes as well as their subjects to be in awe of their power.

Perhaps the greatest figure of the Baroque was the Italian architect and sculptor Gian Lorenzo Bernini (1598–1680), who completed Saint Peter's Basilica at the Vatican and designed the vast colonnade enclosing the piazza in front of it. Action, exuberance, profusion, and dramatic effects mark the work of Bernini in the interior of Saint Peter's, where his *Throne of Saint Peter* hovers in mid-air, held by the hands of the four great doctors of the Catholic church. Above the chair, rays of golden light drive a mass of clouds and angels toward the spectator. In his most striking sculptural work, the *Ecstasy of Saint Theresa,* Bernini depicts a moment of mystical experience in the life of the sixteenth-century Spanish saint. The elegant draperies and the expression on her face create a sensuously real portrayal of physical ecstasy.

Less well known than the male artists who dominated the art world of seventeenth-century Italy but prominent in her own right was Artemisia Gentileschi (1593–1653). Born in Rome, she studied painting under her father's direction. In 1616, she moved to Florence and began a successful career as a painter. At the age of twenty-three, she became the first woman to be elected to the Florentine Academy of Design. Although she was known internationally in her day as a portrait painter, her fame now rests

Nicholas Poussin, *Landscape with the Burial of Phocian.* France became the new cultural leader of Europe in the second half of the seventeenth century. French Classicism upheld the values of High Renaissance style, but in a more static version. In Nicholas Poussin's work, we see the emphasis of French Classicism on the use of scenes from classical sources and the creation of a sense of grandeur and noble strength in both human figures and landscape.

on a series of pictures of heroines from the Old Testament. Most famous is *Judith Beheading Holofernes,* a dramatic rendering of the biblical scene in which Judith slays the Assyrian general Holofernes to save her besieged town from the Assyrian army.

FRENCH CLASSICISM

In the second half of the seventeenth century, France replaced Italy as the cultural leader of Europe. Rejecting the Baroque style as overly showy and impassioned, the French remained committed to the classical values of the High Renaissance. French late Classicism, with its emphasis on clarity, simplicity, balance, and harmony of design, was, however, a rather austere version of the High Renaissance style. Its triumph reflected the shift in seventeenth-century French society from chaos to order. Though it rejected the emotionalism and high drama of the Baroque, French Classicism continued the Baroque's conception of grandeur in the portrayal of noble subjects, especially those from classical antiquity. Nicholas Poussin (1594–1665) exemplified these principles in his paintings. His choice of scenes from classical mythology, the orderliness of his landscapes, the postures of his figures copied from the sculptures of antiquity, and his use of brown tones all reflect French Classicism of the late seventeenth century.

DUTCH REALISM

The supremacy of Dutch commerce in the seventeenth century was paralleled by a brilliant flowering of Dutch painting. Wealthy patricians and burghers of Dutch urban society commissioned works of art for their guild halls, town halls, and private dwellings. The interests of this burgher society were reflected in the subject matter of many Dutch paintings: portraits of themselves, group portraits of their military companies and guilds, landscapes, seascapes, genre scenes, still lifes, and the interiors of their residences. Neither classical nor Baroque, Dutch painters were primarily interested in the realistic portrayal of secular everyday life.

The finest product of the golden age of Dutch painting was Rembrandt van Rijn (1606–1669). During his early career, Rembrandt painted opulent portraits and grandiose scenes that were often quite colorful. He was prolific and successful, but he turned away from materialistic success to follow his own artistic path; in the process, he lost public support and died bankrupt.

Rembrandt van Rijn, *Syndics of the Cloth Guild.* The Dutch experienced a golden age of painting during the seventeenth century. The burghers and patricians of Dutch urban society commissioned works of art, and these quite naturally reflected the burghers' interests, as this painting by Rembrandt illustrates.

Although Rembrandt shared the Dutch predilection for realistic portraits, he became more introspective as he grew older. He refused to follow his contemporaries, whose pictures were largely secular; half of his own paintings depicted scenes from biblical tales. Since the Protestant tradition of hostility to religious pictures had discouraged artistic expression, Rembrandt stands out as the one great Protestant painter of the seventeenth century.

A Wondrous Age of Theater

In England and Spain, writing reached new heights between 1580 and 1640. All of these impressive new works were written in the vernacular. Except for academic fields, such as theology, philosophy, jurisprudence, and the sciences, Latin was no longer a universal literary language.

The greatest age of English literature is often called the Elizabethan era because much of the English cultural flowering of the late sixteenth and early seventeenth centuries occurred during the reign of Queen Elizabeth I. Elizabethan literature exhibits the exuberance and pride associated with England's international exploits at the time. Of all the forms of Elizabethan literature, none expressed the energy and intellectual versatility of the era better than drama. And of all the dramatists, none is more famous than William Shakespeare (1564–1616).

Shakespeare was the son of a prosperous glovemaker from Stratford-upon-Avon. When he appeared in London in 1592, Elizabethans were already addicted to the stage. In Greater London, as many as six theaters were open six afternoons a week. London theaters ranged from the Globe, which was a circular unroofed structure holding three thousand spectators, to the Blackfriars, which was roofed and held only five hundred. In the former, an admission charge of one or two pennies enabled even the lower classes to attend; the higher prices in the latter ensured an audience of the well-to-do. Elizabethan audiences varied greatly, putting pressure on playwrights to write works that pleased nobles, lawyers, merchants, and even vagabonds.

William Shakespeare: In Praise of England

William Shakespeare is one of the most famous playwrights of the Western world. He was a universal genius, outclassing all others in his psychological insights, depth of characterization, imaginative skills, and versatility. His historical plays reflected the patriotic enthusiasm of the English in the Elizabethan era, as this excerpt from *Richard II* illustrates.

William Shakespeare, Richard II

This royal throne of kings, this sceptered isle,
This earth of majesty, this seat of Mars,
This other Eden, demi-Paradise,
This fortress built by Nature for herself
Against infection and the hand of war,
This happy breed of men, this little world,
This precious stone set in the silver sea,
Which serves it in the office of a wall
Or as a moat defensive to a house
Against the envy of less happier lands—
This blessed plot, this earth, this realm, this England,
This nurse, this teeming womb of royal kings,
Feared by their breed and famous by their birth,
Renowned for their deeds as far from home,
For Christian service and true chivalry,
As is the sepulcher in stubborn Jewry [the Holy
Sepulcher in Jerusalem]
Of the world's ransom, blessed Mary's Son—
This land of such dear souls, this dear dear land,
Dear for her reputation through the world,
Is now leased out, I die pronouncing it,
Like a tenement or pelting farm.
England, bound in with the triumphant sea,
Whose rocky shore beats back the envious siege
Of watery Neptune, is now bound in with shame,
With inky blots and rotten parchment bonds.
That England, what was wont to conquer others,
Hath made a shamful conquest of itself.
Ah, would the scandal vanish with my life,
How happy then were my ensuing death!

William Shakespeare was a "complete man of the theater." Although best known for writing plays, he was also an actor and shareholder in the chief company of the time, the Lord Chamberlain's Company, which played in theaters as diverse as the Globe and the Blackfriars. Shakespeare has long been recognized as a universal genius. A master of the English language, he was instrumental in codifying a language that was still in a period of transition. His technical proficiency, however, was matched by an incredible insight into human psychology. In tragedies as well as comedies, Shakespeare exhibited a remarkable understanding of the human condition (see the box above).

The theater was also one of the most creative forms of expression during Spain's golden century. The first professional theaters established in Seville and Madrid in the 1570s were run by actors' companies, as in England. Soon a public playhouse could be found in every large town, including Mexico City in the New World. Touring companies brought the latest Spanish plays to all parts of the Spanish Empire.

Beginning in the 1580s, the agenda for playwrights was set by Lope de Vega (1562–1635). Like Shakespeare, he was from a middle-class background. He was an incredibly prolific writer; almost one-third of his 1,500 plays survive. They have been characterized as witty, charming, action-packed, and realistic. Lope de Vega made no apologies for the fact that he wrote his plays to please his audiences. In a treatise on drama written in 1609, he stated that the foremost duty of the playwright was to satisfy public demand. Shakespeare undoubtedly believed the same thing, since his livelihood depended on public approval, but Lope de Vega was considerably more cynical about it: he remarked that if anyone thought he had written his plays for fame, "undeceive him and tell him that I wrote them for money."

As the great age of theater in England and Spain was drawing to a close around 1630, a new dramatic era began to dawn in France that lasted into the 1680s. Unlike Shakespeare in England and Lope de Vega in Spain, French playwrights wrote more for an elite audience and were forced to depend on royal patronage. Louis XIV used theater as he did art and architecture—to attract attention to his monarchy.

French dramatists cultivated a classical style that emphasized the clever, polished, and correct over the emotional and imaginative. Many of the French works of the period derived both their themes and their plots from Greek and Roman sources, especially evident in the works of Jean-Baptiste Racine (1639–1699). In *Phédre,* which has been called his best play, Racine followed closely the plot of the Greek tragedian Euripides' *Hippolytus.* Like the ancient tragedians, Racine, who perfected the French neoclassical tragic style, focused on conflicts, such as between love and honor or inclination and duty, that characterized and revealed the tragic dimensions of life.

Jean-Baptiste Molière (1622–1673) enjoyed the favor of the French court and benefited from the patronage of King Louis XIV. Molière wrote, produced, and acted in a series of comedies that often satirized the religious and social world of his time. In *Tartuffe,* he ridiculed religious hypocrisy. His satires, however, sometimes got him into trouble. The Paris clergy did not find *Tartuffe* funny and had it banned for five years. Only the protection of the king saved Molière from more severe harassment.

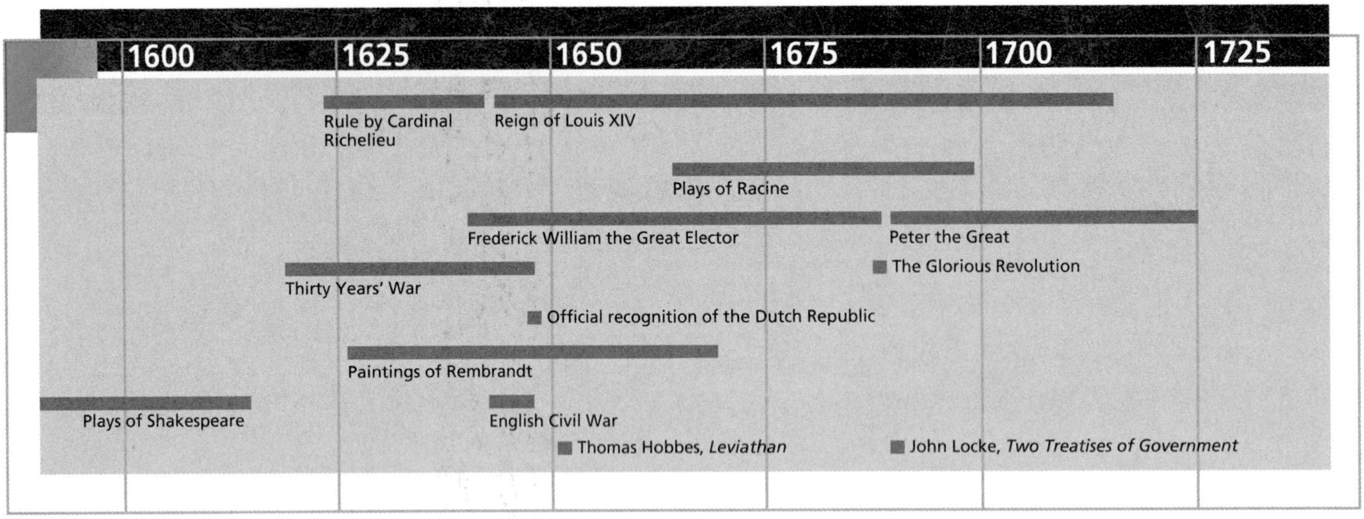

Conclusion

To many historians, the seventeenth century has assumed extraordinary proportions. The divisive effects of the Reformation had been assimilated and the concept of a united Christendom, held as an ideal since the Middle Ages, had been irrevocably destroyed by the religious wars, making possible the emergence of a system of nation-states in which power politics took on an increasing significance. The growth of political thought focusing on the secular origins of state power reflected the changes that were going on in seventeenth-century society.

Within those states, there slowly emerged some of the machinery that made possible a growing centralization of power. In those states called absolutist, strong monarchs with the assistance of their aristocracies took the lead in providing the leadership for greater centralization. But in England, where the landed aristocracy gained power at the expense of the monarchs, the foundations were laid for a constitutional government in which Parliament provided the focus for the institutions of centralized power. In all the major European states, a growing concern for power and dynastic expansion led to larger armies and greater conflict. War remained an endemic feature of Western civilization.

But the search for order and harmony continued, evident in art and literature. At the same time, religious preoccupations and values were losing ground to secular considerations. The seventeenth century was a period of transition toward the more secular spirit that has characterized modern Western civilization to the present. No stronger foundation for this spirit could be found than in the new view of the universe that was ushered in by the Scientific Revolution of the seventeenth century, and it is to that story that we now turn.

Notes

1. Quoted in Joseph Klaits, *Servants of Satan: The Age of the Witch Hunts* (Bloomington, Ind., 1985), p. 68.
2. Quoted in John B. Wolf, *Louis XIV* (New York, 1968), p. 134.
3. Quoted in James B. Collins, *The State in Early Modern France* (Cambridge, 1995), p. 130.
4. Quoted in W. H. Lewis, *The Splendid Century* (Garden City, N.Y., 1953), pp. 39–40.
5. Quoted in Wolf, *Louis XIV,* p. 284.
6. Quoted in ibid., p. 618.
7. Quoted in D. H. Pennington, *Europe in the Seventeenth Century,* 2d ed. (New York, 1989), p. 494.
8. Quoted in J. H. Elliot, *Imperial Spain, 1469–1716* (New York, 1963), p. 306.
9. Quoted in B. H. Sumner, *Peter the Great and the Emergence of Russia* (New York, 1962), p. 122.
10. Quoted in Simon Schama, *A History of Britain,* Vol. 2: *The Wars of the British, 1603–1776* (New York, 2001), pp. 182, 185.

Suggestions for Further Reading

For general works on the seventeenth century, see D. H. Pennington, *Europe in the Seventeenth Century,* 2d ed. (New York, 1989); T. Munck, *Seventeenth-Century Europe, 1598–1700* (London, 1990); and R. S. Dunn, *The Age of Religious Wars, 1559–1715,* 2d ed. (New York, 1979).

The story of the witchcraft craze can be examined in three recent works: J. Klaits, *Servants of Satan: The Age of the Witch Hunts* (Bloomington, Ind., 1985); J. B. Russell, *A History of Witchcraft* (London, 1980); and B. P. Levack, *The Witch-Hunt in Early Modern Europe* (London, 1987).

The classic study on the Thirty Years' War is C. V. Wedgwood, *The Thirty Years' War* (Garden City, N.Y., 1961), but it needs to be supplemented by the more recent works by G. Parker, ed., *The Thirty Years' War,* 2d ed. (London, 1997); R. G. Asch, *The Thirty Years' War: The Holy Roman Empire and Europe, 1618–1648* (New York, 1997); and the brief study by S. J. Lee, *The Thirty Years' War* (London, 1991).

For succinct accounts of seventeenth-century French history, see R. Briggs, *Early Modern France, 1560–1715* (Oxford, 1977), and

J. B. Collins, *The State in Early Modern France* (Cambridge, 1995). A solid and very readable biography of Louis XIV is J. B. Wolf, *Louis XIV* (New York, 1968). For a shorter study, see P. R. Campbell, *Louis XIV, 1661–1715* (London, 1993). A now classic work on life in Louis XIV's France is W. H. Lewis, *The Splendid Century* (Garden City, N.Y., 1953). Well-presented summaries of revisionist views on Louis's monarchical power are R. Mettam, *Power and Faction in Louis XIV's France* (Oxford, 1988), and W. Beik, *Absolutism and Society in Seventeenth-Century France* (Cambridge, 1985).

Good general works on seventeenth-century Spanish history include J. Lynch, *Spain Under the Habsburgs,* 2d ed. (New York, 1981), and the relevant sections of J. H. Elliott, *Imperial Spain, 1469–1716* (New York, 1963, 1977).

An important work on the German states is M. Hughes, *Early Modern Germany, 1477–1806* (Philadelphia, 1992). On the creation of Austria, see R. J. W. Evans, *The Making of the Habsburg Monarchy, 1550–1700* (Oxford, 1979), and C. Ingrao, *The Habsburg Monarchy, 1618–1815* (Cambridge, 1994). F. L. Carsten, *The Origins of Prussia* (Oxford, 1954), remains an outstanding study of early Prussian history. For an introduction to Polish history, see N. Davies, *God's Playground: A History of Poland,* Vol. 1, *The Origins to 1795* (Oxford, 1981).

On Russian history before Peter the Great, see the classic work by V. O. Klyuchevsky, *A Course in Russian History: The Seventeenth Century* (Chicago, 1968). Works on Peter the Great include L. Hughes, *Russia in the Age of Peter the Great* (New Haven, Conn., 1998), and M. S. Anderson, *Peter the Great,* 2d ed. (New York, 1995).

Good general works on the period of the English Revolution include M. A. Kishlansky, *A Monarchy Transformed* (London, 1996); G. E. Aylmer, *Rebellion or Revolution? England, 1640–1660* (New York, 1986); and A. Hughes, *The Causes of the English Civil War* (New York, 1991). On Oliver Cromwell, see R. Howell Jr., *Cromwell* (Boston, 1977), and P. Gaunt, *Oliver Cromwell* (Cambridge, Mass., 1996). For a general survey of the post-Cromwellian era, see J. R. Jones, *Country and Court: England, 1658–1714* (London, 1978). On Charles II, see the scholarly biography by R. Hutton, *Charles II* (Oxford, 1989). Locke's political ideas are examined in J. H. Franklin, *John Locke and the Theory of Sovereignty* (London, 1978). On Thomas Hobbes, see D. D. Raphael, *Hobbes* (London, 1977).

On the United Provinces, J. Israel, *The Dutch Republic: Its Rise, Greatness, and Fall* (New York, 1995), is a valuable but very lengthy study. Of much value is S. Schama, *The Embarrassment of Riches: An Interpretation of Dutch Culture in the Golden Age* (New York, 1987).

A brief, readable guide to Mannerism is L. Murray, *The Late Renaissance and Mannerism* (New York, 1967). For a general survey of Baroque culture, see M. Mainstone and L. Mainstone, *The Cambridge Introduction to Art: The Seventeenth Century* (Cambridge, 1981), and J. S. Held, *Seventeenth and Eighteenth Century Art: Baroque Painting, Sculpture, Architecture* (New York, 1971). The literature on Shakespeare is enormous. For a biography, see A. L. Rowse, *The Life of Shakespeare* (New York, 1963). French theater and literature are examined in A. Adam, *Grandeur and Illusion: French Literature and Society, 1600–1715,* trans. J. Tint (New York, 1972). For an examination of French and Dutch art, see A. Merot, *French Painting in the Seventeenth Century* (New Haven, Conn., 1995), and S. Slive, *Dutch Painting, 1600–1800* (New Haven, Conn., 1993).

For additional reading, go to InfoTrac College Edition, your online research library at http://web1.infotrac-college.com

Enter the search term *Thirty Years' War* using Key Terms.

Enter the search term *Peter the Great* using Key Terms.

Enter the search term *Oliver Cromwell* using Key Terms.

Enter the search term *Louis XIV* using Key Terms.

CHAPTER

16

Toward a New Heaven and a New Earth: The Scientific Revolution and the Emergence of Modern Science

Giraudon/Art Resource, NY

CHAPTER OUTLINE

- Background to the Scientific Revolution
- Toward a New Heaven: A Revolution in Astronomy
- Advances in Medicine
- Women in the Origins of Modern Science
- Toward a New Earth: Descartes, Rationalism, and a New View of Humankind
- The Scientific Method
- Science and Religion in the Seventeenth Century
- The Spread of Scientific Knowledge
- Conclusion

FOCUS QUESTIONS

- What developments during the Middle Ages and the Renaissance contributed to the Scientific Revolution of the seventeenth century?
- What did Copernicus, Kepler, Galileo, and Newton contribute to a new vision of the universe, and how did it differ from the Ptolemaic conception of the universe?
- What role did women play in the Scientific Revolution?
- What problems did the Scientific Revolution present for organized religion, and how did both the church and the emerging scientists attempt to solve these problems?
- How were the ideas of the Scientific Revolution disseminated, and what impact did they have on society?
- In what ways were the intellectual, political, social, and religious developments of the seventeenth century related?

IN ADDITION TO THE political, economic, social, and international crises of the seventeenth century, we need to add an intellectual one. The Scientific Revolution questioned and ultimately challenged conceptions and beliefs about the nature of the external world and reality that had crystallized into a rather strict orthodoxy by the Late Middle Ages. Derived from the works of ancient Greeks and Romans and grounded in Christian thought, the medieval worldview had become formidable. But the breakdown of Christian unity during the Reformation and the subsequent religious wars had created an environment in which Europeans became more comfortable with challenging both the ecclesiastical and political realms. Should it surprise us that a challenge to intellectual authority soon followed?

The Scientific Revolution taught Europeans to view the universe and their place in it in a new way. The shift from an earth-centered to a sun-centered cosmos had an emotional as well as an intellectual effect on the people who understood it. Thus the Scientific Revolution, popularized in the eighteenth-century Enlightenment, stands as the major force in the transition to the largely secular, rational, and materialistic perspective that has defined the modern Western mentality since its full acceptance in the nineteenth and twentieth centuries.

The transition to a new worldview, however, was far from easy. In the seventeenth century, the Italian scientist Galileo Galilei, an outspoken advocate of the new worldview, found that his ideas were strongly opposed by the authorities of the Catholic church. Galileo's position was clear: "I hold the sun to be situated motionless in the center of the revolution of the celestial bodies, while the earth rotates on its axis and revolves about the sun." Moreover, "nothing physical that sense-experience sets before our eyes . . . ought to be called in question (much less condemned) upon the testimony of Biblical passages." But the church had a different view, and in 1633, Galileo, now sixty-eight and in ill health, was called before the dreaded Inquisition in Rome. He was kept waiting for two months before he was tried and found guilty of heresy and disobedience. Completely shattered by the experience, he denounced his errors: "With a sincere heart and unfeigned faith I curse and detest the said errors and heresies contrary to the Holy Church. Legend holds that when he left the trial room, Galileo muttered to himself: "And yet it does move!" Galileo had been silenced, but his writings remained, and they spread through Europe. The Inquisition had failed to stop the new ideas of the Scientific Revolution.

In one sense, the Scientific Revolution was not a revolution. It was not characterized by the explosive change and rapid overthrow of traditional authority that we normally associate with the word revolution. *The Scientific Revolution did overturn centuries of authority, but only in a gradual and piecemeal fashion. Nevertheless, its results were truly revolutionary. The Scientific Revolution was a key factor in setting Western civilization along its modern secular and material path.*

Background to the Scientific Revolution

To say that the Scientific Revolution brought about a dissolution of the medieval worldview is not to say that the Middle Ages was a period of scientific ignorance. Many educated Europeans took an intense interest in the world around them since it was, after all, "God's handiwork" and therefore an appropriate subject for study. Late medieval scholastic philosophers had advanced mathematical and physical thinking in many ways, but the subjection of these thinkers to a strict theological framework and their unquestioning reliance on a few ancient authorities, especially Aristotle and Galen, limited where they could go. Many "natural philosophers," as medieval scientists were called, preferred refined logical analysis to systematic observations of the natural world. A number of changes and advances in the fifteenth and sixteenth centuries may have played a major role in helping "natural philosophers" abandon their old views and develop new ones.

Whereas medieval scholars had made use of Aristotle, Galen, and Ptolemy in Latin translations to develop many of their positions in the fields of physics, medicine, and astronomy, the Renaissance humanists had mastered Greek as well as Latin and made available new works of Galen, Ptolemy, and Archimedes as well as Plato and the pre-Socratics. These writings made it apparent that even the unquestioned authorities of the Middle Ages, Aristotle and Galen, had been contradicted by other thinkers. The desire to discover which school of thought was correct stimulated new scientific work that sometimes led to a complete rejection of the classical authorities.

Renaissance artists have also been credited with making an impact on scientific study. Their desire to imitate nature led them to rely on a close observation of nature. Their accurate renderings of rocks, plants, animals, and human anatomy established new standards for the study of natural phenomena. At the same time, the "scientific" study of the problems of perspective and correct anatomical proportions led to new insights. "No painter," one Renaissance artist declared, "can paint well without a thorough knowledge of geometry."[1] Renaissance artists were frequently called on to be practicing mathematicians as well. Leonardo da Vinci devised "war machines," and Albrecht Dürer made designs for the fortifications of cities.

Technical problems such as calculating the tonnage of ships accurately also served to stimulate scientific activity because they required careful observation and accurate measurements. The fifteenth and sixteenth centuries witnessed a proliferation of books dedicated to machines and technology, all of which espoused the belief that innovation in techniques was necessary. The relationship between technology and the Scientific Revolution is not a simple one, however, for many technological experts did not believe in abstract or academic learning. Indeed, many of the technical innovations of

Magic and Science: The Case of Girolamo Cardano

Girolamo Cardano, or Jerome Cardan (1501–1576), was a very important figure in the history of mathematics. He also became a physician and professor of medicine at Pavia in 1547. Like many other intellectuals in the sixteenth century, Cardano was a student of magic and astrology. In this selection taken from his autobiography, *The Book of My Life,* Cardano discusses the presence in his life of what we would call paranormal powers, including prescient dreams, extrasensory perception, and intuitive flashes of direct understanding.

■ *Girolamo Cardano,* The Book of My Life

I am conscious that some influence from without seems to bring a murmuring sound to my ear from precisely that direction or region where some one is discussing me. If this discussion be fair, the sound seems to come to rest on the right side; or, if perchance it approaches from the left, it penetrates to the right and becomes a steady hum. If, however, the talk be contentious, strangely conflicting sounds are heard; when evil is spoken, the noise rests in the left ear, and comes from the quarter exactly whence the voices of my detractors are making disturbance, and, accordingly, may approach from any side of my head. . . . Very often when the discussion about me has taken place in the same city, it has happened that the vibration has scarcely ceased before a messenger has appeared who addresses me in the name of my detractors. But if the conversation has taken place in another state and the messenger should appear, one has but to compute the space of time which had elapsed between the discussion and the beginning of the messenger's journey, and the moment I heard the voices and the time of the discussion itself will fall out the same. . . .

A few years later, eight perhaps, that is, about 1534, I began to see in my dreams the events shortly to come to pass. If these events were due to happen on the day following the dream, I used to have clear and defined visions of them just after sunrise, so that even on occasion I saw the motion for my admission to the College of Physicians straightway brought to vote, to a decision, and the motion lost. I dreamed, as well, that I was about to obtain my appointment to the professorship at Bologna. This manifestation by dreams ceased in the year just preceding the cessation of the former manifestation, that is, about 1567. . . . And so it had lasted about thirty-three years.

A third peculiarity is an intuitive flash of direct knowledge. This I employed with gradually increasing advantage. It originated about the year 1529; its effectiveness was increased but it could never be rendered infallible, except toward the close of 1573. For a period between the end of August of that year and the beginning of September 1574, and particularly, as it seems to me, now in this year 1575, I have considered it infallible. It is, moreover, a gift which has not deserted me, and it replaces the power of those two latter faculties which did; it prepares me to meet my adversaries, and for any pressing necessity. Its component parts are an ingeniously exercised employment of the intuitive faculty, and an accompanying lucidity of understanding.

the Middle Ages and the Renaissance were accomplished outside the universities by people who emphasized practical rather than theoretical knowledge. In any case, the invention of new instruments and machines, such as the telescope and the microscope, often made new scientific discoveries possible. The printing press had an indirect but crucial role in spreading innovative ideas quickly and easily.

Mathematics, so fundamental to the scientific achievements of the sixteenth and seventeenth centuries, was promoted in the Renaissance by the rediscovery of the works of ancient mathematicians and the influence of Plato, who had emphasized the importance of mathematics in explaining the universe. While mathematics was applauded as the key to navigation, military science, and geography, the Renaissance also held the widespread belief that mathematics was the key to understanding the nature of things. According to Leonardo da Vinci, since God eternally geometrizes, nature is inherently mathematical: "Proportion is not only found in numbers and measurements but also in sounds, weights, times, positions, and in whatsoever power there may."[2] Moreover, mathematical reasoning was seen as promoting a degree of certainty that was otherwise impossible. In the words of Leonardo da Vinci: "There is no certainty where one can neither apply any of the mathematical sciences nor any of those which are based upon the mathematical sciences."[3] Copernicus, Kepler, Galileo, and Newton were all great mathematicians who believed that the secrets of nature were written in the language of mathematics.

Another factor in the origins of the Scientific Revolution may have been magic. Renaissance magic was the preserve of an intellectual elite from all of Europe (see the box above). By the end of the sixteenth century, Hermetic magic had become fused with alchemical thought into a single intellectual framework. This tradition believed that the world was a living embodiment of divinity. Humans, who it was believed also had that spark of divinity within, could use magic, especially mathematical magic, to understand and dominate the world of nature or employ the powers of nature for beneficial purposes. Was it Hermeticism, then, that inaugurated the shift in consciousness that made the Scientific Revolution possible, since the desire to control and dominate the natural world was a crucial motivating force in the Scientific Revolution? One scholar has argued:

> It is a movement of the will which really originates an intellectual movement. A new center of interest arises, surrounded by emotional excitement; the mind turns where the will has directed it and new attitudes, new discoveries follow. Behind the emergence of modern science there was a new direction of the will toward the world, its marvels, and mysterious workings, a new longing and determination to understand those workings and to operate with them.[4]

"This time," the author continues, "the return to the occult [Hermetic tradition] stimulates the genuine science."[5] Scholars debate the issue, but histories of the Scientific Revolution frequently overlook the fact that the great names we associate with the revolution in cosmology—Copernicus, Kepler, Galileo, and Newton—all had a serious interest in Hermetic ideas and the fields of astrology and alchemy. The mention of these names also reminds us of one final consideration in the origins of the Scientific Revolution: it largely resulted from the work of a handful of great intellectuals.

Toward a New Heaven: A Revolution in Astronomy

The greatest achievements in the Scientific Revolution of the sixteenth and seventeenth centuries came in the fields most dominated by the ideas of the Greeks—astronomy, mechanics, and medicine. The cosmological views of the Late Middle Ages had been built on a synthesis of the ideas of Aristotle, Claudius Ptolemy (the greatest astronomer of antiquity, who lived in the second century A.D.), and Christian theology. In the resulting Ptolemaic or geocentric conception, the universe was seen as a series of concentric spheres with a fixed or motionless earth at its center. Composed of the material substances of earth, air, fire, and water, the earth was imperfect and constantly changing. The spheres that surrounded the earth were made of a crystalline, transparent substance and moved in circular orbits around the earth. Circular movement, according to Aristotle, was the most "perfect" kind of motion and hence appropriate for the "perfect" heavenly bodies thought to consist of a nonmaterial, incorruptible "quintessence." These heavenly bodies, pure orbs of light, were embedded in the moving, concentric spheres and in 1500 numbered ten. Working outward from the earth, eight spheres contained the moon, Mercury, Venus, the sun, Mars, Jupiter, Saturn, and the fixed stars. The ninth sphere imparted to the eighth sphere of the fixed stars its motion, and the tenth sphere was frequently described as the prime mover that moved itself and imparted motion to the other spheres. Beyond the tenth sphere was the Empyrean Heaven—the location of God and all the saved souls. This Christianized Ptolemaic universe, then, was a finite one. It had a fixed outer boundary in harmony with Christian thought and expectations. God and the saved souls were at one end of the universe while humans were at the center. They had been given power over the earth, but their real purpose was to achieve salvation.

This conception of the universe, however, did not satisfy professional astronomers, who wished to ascertain the precise paths of the heavenly bodies across the sky. Finding that their observations did not always correspond to the accepted scheme, astronomers tried to "save appearances" by developing an elaborate system of devices. They proposed, for example, that the planetary bodies traveled on epicycles, concentric spheres within spheres, that would enable the paths of the planets to correspond more precisely to observations while adhering to Aristotle's ideas of circular planetary movement.

Copernicus

Nicolaus Copernicus (1473–1543) had studied both mathematics and astronomy first at Krakow in his native Poland and later at the Italian universities of Bologna and Padua. Before he left Italy in 1506, he had become aware of ancient views that contradicted the Ptolemaic, earth-centered conception of the universe. Between 1506 and 1530, he completed the manuscript of his famous book, *On the Revolutions of the Heavenly Spheres*, but his own timidity and fear of ridicule from fellow astronomers kept him from publishing it until May 1543, shortly before his death.

Copernicus was not an accomplished observational astronomer and relied for his data on the records of his predecessors. But he was a mathematician who felt that Ptolemy's geocentric system was too complicated and failed to accord with the observed motions of the heavenly bodies (see the box on p. 444). Copernicus hoped that his heliocentric or sun-centered conception would offer a simpler and more accurate explanation.

Copernicus argued that the universe consisted of eight spheres with the sun motionless at the center and the sphere of the fixed stars at rest in the eighth sphere. The planets revolved around the sun in the order of Mercury, Venus, the earth, Mars, Jupiter, and Saturn. The moon, however, revolved around the earth. Moreover, according to Copernicus, what appeared to be the movement of the sun and the fixed stars around the earth was really explained by the daily rotation of the earth on its axis and the journey of the earth around the sun each year.

Copernicus, however, was basically conservative. He did not reject Aristotle's principle of the existence of heavenly spheres moving in circular orbits. As a result, when he put forth the calculations to prove his new theory, he retained Ptolemy's epicycles and wound up with a system almost as complicated as that of the Alexandrian astronomer.

Nevertheless, the shift from an earth-centered to a sun-centered system was significant and raised serious questions about Aristotle's astronomy and physics despite Copernicus' own adherence to Aristotle. It also seemed to create uncertainty about the human role in the universe as well as God's location. Protestant reformers, adhering to a literal interpretation of Scripture, were the first to attack

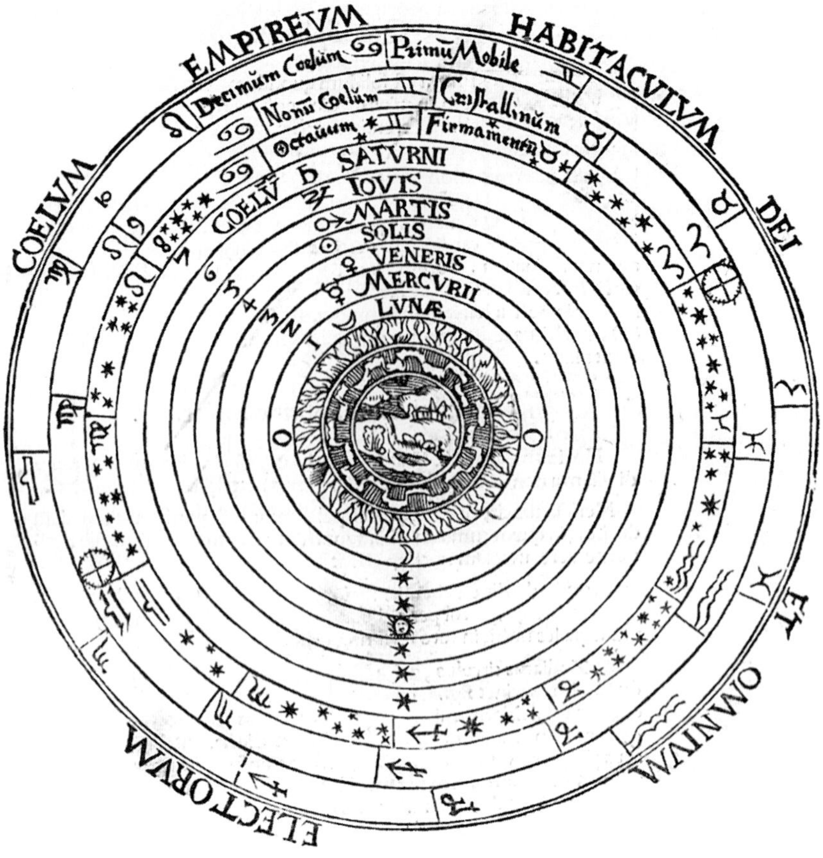

Medieval Conception of the Universe. As this sixteenth-century illustration shows, the medieval cosmological view placed the earth at the center of the universe, surrounded by a series of concentric spheres. The earth was imperfect and constantly changing, whereas the heavenly bodies that surrounded it were perfect and incorruptible. Beyond the tenth and final sphere was heaven, where God and all the saved souls were located.

Courtesy of the Lilly Library, Indiana University, Bloomington, Indiana

the new ideas. Martin Luther thundered against "the new astrologer who wants to prove that the earth moves and goes round. . . . The fool wants to turn the whole art of astronomy upside down. As Holy Scripture tells us, so did Joshua bid the sun stand still and not the earth." Luther's cohort at Wittenberg, Philip Melanchthon, condemned Copernicus as well:

> The eyes are witness that the heavens revolve in the space of twenty-four hours. But certain men, either from the love of novelty, or to make a display of ingenuity, have concluded that the earth moves, and they maintain that neither the eighth sphere [of the fixed stars] nor the sun revolves. . . . Now it is a want of honesty and decency to assert such notions publicly, and the example is pernicious. It is the part of a good mind to accept the truth as revealed by God and to acquiesce in it.[6]

The Catholic church remained silent for the time being; it did not denounce Copernicus until the work of Galileo appeared. The denunciation came at a time when an increasing number of astronomers were being attracted to Copernicus' ideas.

Brahe and Kepler

Copernicus did not have a great impact immediately, but doubts about the Ptolemaic system were growing. The next step in destroying the geocentric conception and supporting the Copernican system was taken by Johannes Kepler. It has been argued, however, that Kepler's work would not have occurred without the material provided by Tycho Brahe.

A Danish nobleman, Tycho Brahe (1546–1601) was granted possession of an island near Copenhagen by King Frederick II. On it, Brahe built the elaborate Uraniborg castle, which he outfitted with a library, observatories, and instruments he had designed for more precise astronomical observations. For twenty years, Brahe patiently concentrated on compiling a detailed record of his observations of the positions and movements of the stars and planets, a series of observations described as the most accurate up to that time. This body of data led him to reject the Aristotelian-Ptolemaic system, but at the same time he was unable to accept Copernicus' suggestion that the earth actually moved. Brahe's last years were spent in Prague as imperial mathematician to Emperor Rudolf II, who took a keen interest in astronomy, astrology, and the Hermetic tradition. While he was in Prague, Brahe took on an assistant by the name of Johannes Kepler.

Johannes Kepler (1571–1630) had been destined by his parents for a career as a Lutheran minister. While studying theology at the university at Tübingen, however, he fell under the influence of Michael Mästlin, Germany's best-known astronomer, and spent much time pursuing his real interests, mathematics and astronomy. He abandoned theology and became a teacher of mathematics and astronomy at Graz in Austria.

Kepler's work illustrates well the narrow line that often separated magic and science in the early Scientific Revolution. An avid astrologer, Kepler possessed a keen interest in Hermetic mathematical magic. In a book written in 1596,

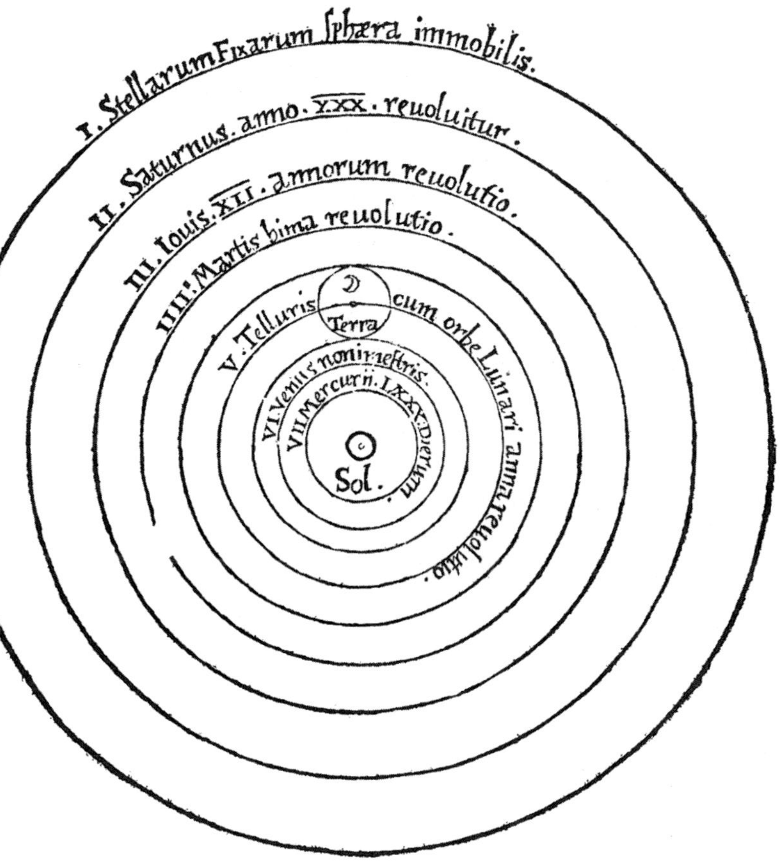

The Copernican System. The Copernican system was presented in *On the Revolutions of the Heavenly Spheres,* published shortly before Copernicus' death. As shown in this illustration from the first edition of the book, Copernicus maintained that the sun was the center of the universe and that the planets, including the earth, revolved around it. Moreover, the earth rotated daily on its axis.

he elaborated on his theory that the universe was constructed on the basis of geometric figures, such as the pyramid and the cube (see the box on p. 445). Believing that the harmony of the human soul (a divine attribute) was mirrored in the numerical relationships existing between the planets, he focused much of his attention on discovering the "music of the spheres." Kepler was also a brilliant mathematician and astronomer and, after Brahe's death, succeeded him as imperial mathematician to Rudolf II. There he gained possession of Brahe's detailed astronomical data and, using them, arrived at his three laws of planetary motion. These laws may have confirmed Kepler's interest in the "music of the spheres," but more important, they confirmed Copernicus' heliocentric theory while modifying it in some ways. Above all, they drove another nail into the coffin of the Aristotelian-Ptolemaic system.

Kepler published his first two laws of planetary motion in 1609. Although at Tübingen he had accepted Copernicus' heliocentric ideas, in his first law he rejected Copernicus by showing that the orbits of the planets around the

Johannes Kepler. Abandoning theology in favor of mathematics and astrology, Kepler was a key figure in the rise of the new astronomy. Building on Tycho Brahe's vast astronomical data, Kepler discovered the three laws of planetary motion that both confirmed and modified the Copernican theory. They also eliminated the Ptolemaic-Aristotelian ideas of uniform circular motion and crystalline spheres moving in circular orbits.

On the Revolutions of the Heavenly Spheres

Nicolaus Copernicus began a revolution in astronomy when he argued that the sun and not the earth was at the center of the universe. Expecting controversy and scorn, Copernicus hesitated to publish the work in which he put forth his heliocentric theory. He finally relented, however, and managed to see a copy of it just before he died.

Nicolaus Copernicus, On the Revolutions of the Heavenly Spheres

For a long time, then, I reflected on this confusion in the astronomical traditions concerning the derivation of the motions of the universe's spheres. I began to be annoyed that the movements of the world machine, created for our sake by the best and most systematic Artisan of all [God], were not understood with greater certainty by the philosophers, who otherwise examined so precisely the most insignificant trifles of this world. For this reason I undertook the task of rereading the works of all the philosophers which I could obtain to learn whether anyone had ever proposed other motions of the universe's spheres than those expounded by the teachers of astronomy in the schools. And in fact first I found in Cicero that Hicetas supposed the earth to move. Later I also discovered in Plutarch that certain others were of this opinion. I have decided to set his words down here, so that they may be available to everybody:

> Some think that the earth remains at rest. But Philolaus the Pythagorean believes that, like the sun and moon, it revolves around the fire in an oblique circle. Heraclides of Pontus and Ecphantus the Pythagorean make the earth move, not in a progressive motion, but like a wheel in a rotation from the west to east about its own center.

Therefore, having obtained the opportunity from these sources, I too began to consider the mobility of the earth. And even though the idea seemed absurd, nevertheless I knew that others before me had been granted the freedom to imagine any circles whatever for the purpose of explaining the heavenly phenomena. Hence I thought that I too would be readily permitted to ascertain whether explanations sounder than those of my predecessors could be found for the revolution of the celestial spheres on the assumption of some motion of the earth.

Having thus assumed the motions which I ascribe to the earth later on in the volume, by long and intense study I finally found that if the motions of the other planets are correlated with the orbiting of the earth, and are computed for the revolution of each planet, not only do their phenomena follow therefrom but also the order and size of all the planets and spheres, and heaven itself is so linked together that in no portion of it can anything be shifted without disrupting the remaining parts and the universe as a whole. . . .

Hence I feel no shame in asserting that this whole region engirdled by the moon, and the center of the earth, traverse this grand circle amid the rest of the planets in an annual revolution around the sun. Near the sun is the center of the universe. Moreover, since the sun remains stationary, whatever appears as a motion of the sun is really due rather to the motion of the earth.

sun were not circular but elliptical, with the sun at one focus of the ellipse rather than at the center. In his second law, he demonstrated that the speed of a planet is greater when it is closer to the sun and decreases as its distance from the sun increases. This proposition destroyed a fundamental Aristotelian tenet that Copernicus had shared—that the motion of the planets was steady and unchanging. Published ten years later, Kepler's third law established that the square of a planet's period of revolution is proportional to the cube of its average distance from the sun. In other words, planets with larger orbits revolve at a slower average velocity than those with smaller orbits.

Kepler's three laws effectively eliminated the idea of uniform circular motion as well as the idea of crystalline spheres revolving in circular orbits. The basic structure of the traditional Ptolemaic system had been disproved, and people had been freed to think in new ways of the actual paths of planets revolving around the sun in elliptical orbits. By the end of Kepler's life, the Ptolemaic system was rapidly losing ground to the new ideas. Important questions remained unanswered, however: What were the planets made of? And how does one explain motion in the universe? It was an Italian scientist who achieved the next important breakthrough to a new cosmology by answering the first question and making important strides toward answering the second.

Galileo

Galileo Galilei (1564–1642) taught mathematics, first at Pisa and later at Padua, one of the most prestigious universities in Europe. Galileo was the first European to make systematic observations of the heavens by means of a telescope, thereby inaugurating a new age in astronomy. He had heard of a Flemish lens grinder who had created a "spyglass" that magnified objects seen at a distance and soon constructed his own after reading about it. Instead of peering at terrestrial objects, Galileo turned his telescope to the skies and made a remarkable series of discoveries: mountains and craters on the moon, four moons revolving around Jupiter, the phases of Venus, and sunspots. Galileo's observations seemed to destroy yet another aspect of the

Kepler and the Emerging Scientific Community

The exchange of letters between intellectuals was an important avenue for scientific communication. After receiving a copy of Johannes Kepler's first major work, the Italian Galileo Galilei wrote to Kepler, inaugurating a correspondence between them. This selection contains samples of their letters to each other.

Galileo to Kepler, Padua, August 4, 1597

Your book, highly learned gentleman, which you sent me through Paulus Amberger, reached me not days ago but only a few hours ago, and as this Paulus just informed me of his return to Germany, I should think myself indeed ungrateful if I should not express to you my thanks by this letter. I thank you especially for having deemed me worthy of such a proof of your friendship. . . . So far I have read only the introduction, but have learned from it in some measure your intentions and congratulate myself on the good fortune of having found such a man as a companion in the exploration of truth. For it is deplorable that there are so few who seek the truth and do not pursue a wrong method of philosophizing. But this is not the place to mourn about the misery of our century but to rejoice with you about such beautiful ideas proving the truth. . . . I would certainly dare to approach the public with my ways of thinking if there were more people of your mind. As this is not the case, I shall refrain from doing so. . . . I shall always be at your service. Farewell, and do not neglect to give me further good news of yourself.

Yours in sincere friendship,
Galilaeus Galilaeus
Mathematician at the Academy of Padua

Kepler to Galileo, Graz, October 13, 1597

I received your letter of August 4 on September 1. It was a double pleasure to me. First because I became friends with you, the Italian, and second because of the agreement in which we find ourselves concerning Copernican cosmography. As you invite me kindly at the end of your letter to enter into correspondence with you, and I myself feel greatly tempted to do so, I will not let pass the occasion of sending you a letter with the present young nobleman. For I am sure, if your time has allowed it, you have meanwhile obtained a closer knowledge of my book. And so a great desire has taken hold of me, to learn your judgment. For this is my way, to urge all those to whom I have written to express their candid opinion. Believe me, the sharpest criticism of one single understanding man means much more to me than the thoughtless applause of the great masses.

I would, however, have wished that you who have such a keen insight into everything would choose another way to reach your practical aims. By the strength of your personal example you advise us, in a cleverly veiled manner, to go out of the way of general ignorance and warn us against exposing ourselves to the furious attacks of the scholarly crowd. . . . But after the beginning of a tremendous enterprise has been made in our time, and furthered by so many learned mathematicians, and after the statement that the earth moves can no longer be regarded as something new, would it not be better to pull the rolling wagon to its destination with united effort. . . . For it is not only you Italians who do not believe that they move unless they feel it, but we in Germany, too, in no way make ourselves popular with this idea. Yet there are ways in which we protect ourselves against these difficulties. . . . Be of good cheer, Galileo, and appear in public. If I am not mistaken there are only a few among the distinguished mathematicians of Europe who would dissociate themselves from us. So great is the power of truth. If Italy seems less suitable for your publication and if you have to expect difficulties there, perhaps Germany will offer us more freedom. But enough of this. Please let me know, at least privately if you do not want to do so publicly, what you have discovered in favor of Copernicus.

traditional cosmology in that the universe seemed to be composed of material substance similar to that of the earth rather than ethereal or perfect and unchanging substance.

Galileo's revelations, published in *The Starry Messenger* in 1610 (see the box on p. 446), stunned his contemporaries and probably did more to make Europeans aware of the new picture of the universe than the mathematical theories of Copernicus and Kepler did. The English ambassador in Venice wrote to the chief minister of King James I in 1610:

> I send herewith unto His Majesty the strangest piece of news . . . that he has ever yet received from any part of the world; which is the annexed book of the Mathematical Professor at Padua [Galileo], who by the help of an optical instrument . . . has discovered four new planets rolling about the sphere of Jupiter. . . . So upon the whole subject he has first overthrown all former astronomy. . . . By the next ship your Lordship shall receive from me one of the above instruments [a telescope], as it is bettered by this man.[7]

During a trip to Rome, Galileo was received by scholars as a conquering hero. Grand Duke Cosimo II of Florence offered him a new position as his court mathematician, which Galileo readily accepted. But even in the midst of his newfound acclaim, Galileo found himself increasingly suspect by the authorities of the Catholic church.

In *The Starry Messenger,* Galileo had revealed himself as a firm proponent of Copernicus' heliocentric system. The Roman Inquisition (or Holy Office) of the Catholic

The Starry Messenger

The Italian Galileo Galilei was the first European to use a telescope to make systematic observations of the heavens. His observations, as reported in *The Starry Messenger* in 1610, stunned European intellectuals by revealing that the celestial bodies were not perfect and immutable but composed of material substance similar to that of the earth. In this selection, Galileo describes how he devised a telescope and what he saw with it.

Galileo Galilei, The Starry Messenger

About ten months ago a report reached my ears that a certain Fleming had constructed a spyglass by means of which visible objects, though very distant from the eye of the observer, were distinctly seen as if nearby. Of this truly remarkable effect several experiences were related, to which some persons gave credence while others denied them. A few days later the report was confirmed to me in a letter from a noble Frenchman at Paris, Jacques Badovere, which caused me to apply myself wholeheartedly to inquire into the means by which I might arrive at the invention of a similar instrument. This I did shortly afterwards, my basis being the theory of refraction. First I prepared a tube of lead, at the ends of which I fitted two glass lenses, both plane on one side while on the other side one was spherically convex and the other concave. Then placing my eye near the concave lens I perceived objects satisfactorily large and near, for they appeared three times closer and nine times larger than when seen with the naked eye alone. Next I constructed another one, more accurate, which represented objects as enlarged more than sixty times. Finally, sparing neither labor nor expense, I succeeded in constructing for myself so excellent an instrument that objects seen by means of it appeared nearly one thousand times larger and over thirty times closer than when regarded without natural vision.

It would be superfluous to enumerate the number and importance of the advantages of such an instrument at sea as well as on land. But forsaking terrestrial observations, I turned to celestial ones, and first I saw the moon from as near at hand as if it were scarcely two terrestrial radii. After that I observed often with wondering delight both the planets and the fixed stars, and since I saw these latter to be very crowded, I began to seek (and eventually found) a method by which I might measure their distances apart. . . .

Now let us review the observations made during the past two months, once more inviting the attention of all who are eager for true philosophy to the first steps of such important contemplations. Let us speak first of that surface of the moon which faces us. For greater clarity I distinguish two parts of this surface, a lighter and a darker; the lighter part seems to surround and to pervade the whole hemisphere, while the darker part discolors the moon's surface like a kind of cloud, and makes it appear covered with spots. . . . From observation of these spots repeated many times I have been led to the opinion and conviction that the surface of the moon is not smooth, uniform, and precisely spherical as a great number of philosophers believe it (and the other heavenly bodies) to be, but is uneven, rough, and full of cavities and prominences, being not unlike the face of the earth, relieved by chains of mountains and deep valleys.

church condemned Copernicanism and ordered Galileo to reject the Copernican thesis. As one cardinal commented, "The intention of the Holy Spirit is to teach us not how the heavens go, but how to go to heaven." The report of the Inquisition ran: "That the doctrine that the sun was the center of the world and immovable was false and absurd, formally heretical and contrary to Scripture, whereas the doctrine that the earth was not the center of the world but moved, and has further a daily motion, was philosophically false and absurd and theologically at least erroneous."[8] Galileo was told, however, that he could continue to discuss Copernicanism as long as he maintained that it was not a fact but a mathematical supposition. It is apparent from the Inquisition's response that the church attacked the Copernican system because it threatened not only Scripture but also an entire conception of the universe. The heavens were no longer a spiritual world but a world of matter. Humans were no longer at the center, and God was no longer in a specific place. The new system raised such uncertainties that it seemed prudent simply to condemn it.

Galileo, however, never really accepted his condemnation. In 1632, he published his most famous work, *Dialogue on the Two Chief World Systems: Ptolemaic and Copernican.* Unlike most scholarly treatises, it was written in Italian rather than Latin, making it more widely available to the public, which no doubt alarmed the church authorities. The work took the form of a dialogue among Simplicio, a congenial but somewhat stupid supporter of Aristotle and Ptolemy; Sagredo, an open-minded layman; and Salviati, a proponent of Copernicus' ideas. There is no question who wins the argument, and the *Dialogue* was quickly perceived as a defense of the Copernican system. Galileo was dragged once more before the Inquisition in 1633, found guilty of teaching the condemned Copernican system, and forced to recant his errors. Placed under house arrest on his estate near Florence, he spent the remaining eight years of his life studying mechanics, a field in which he made significant contributions.

One of the problems that fell under the heading of mechanics was the principle of motion. The Aristotelian

Galileo's Trial. Galileo's work seemed to support the Copernican system, a position that the Catholic church found heretical. This painting shows Galileo at his trial in 1633, seated in the center opposite the group of church leaders who had accused him of defending the Copernican heresy. Galileo was found guilty and forced to retract his views.

conception, which dominated the late medieval world, held that an object remained at rest unless a force was applied against it. If a force was constantly exerted, then the object moved at a constant rate, but if it was removed, then the object stopped. This conception encountered some difficulties, especially with a projectile thrown out of a cannon. Late medieval theorists had solved this problem by arguing that the rush of air behind the projectile kept it in motion. The Aristotelian principle of motion also raised problems in the new Copernican system. In the Ptolemaic system, the concentric spheres surrounding the earth were weightless, but in the Copernican system, if a constant force had to be applied to objects to cause movement, then what power or force kept the heavy earth and other planets in motion?

Galileo made two contributions to the problem of motion. First, he demonstrated by experiments that if a uniform force was applied to an object, it would move at an accelerated speed rather than a constant speed. Moreover, Galileo discovered the principle of inertia when he argued that a body in motion continues in motion forever unless deflected by an external force. Thus a state of uniform motion is just as natural as a state of rest. Before Galileo, natural philosophers had tried to explain motion; now their task was to explain changes in motion.

The condemnation of Galileo by the Inquisition seriously hampered further scientific work in Italy, which had been at the forefront of scientific innovation. Leadership in science now passed to the northern countries, especially England, France, and the Dutch Netherlands. By the 1630s and 1640s, no reasonable astronomer could overlook that Galileo's discoveries, combined with Kepler's mathematical laws, had made nonsense of the Ptolemaic-Aristotelian world system and clearly established the reasonableness of the Copernican model. Nevertheless, the problem of explaining motion in the universe and tying together the ideas of Copernicus, Galileo, and Kepler had not yet been solved. This would be the work of an Englishman who has long been considered the greatest genius of the Scientific Revolution.

Newton

Born in the little English village of Woolsthorpe in 1642, the young Isaac Newton showed little brilliance until he attended Cambridge University. Newton experienced his first great burst of creative energy in 1666 when the fear of plague closed Cambridge and forced him to return to Woolsthorpe for eighteen months. There Newton discovered his creative talents: "In those days I was in the prime of my life for invention and minded mathematics and philosophy more than at any time since."[9] During this period, he invented the calculus, a mathematical means of calculating rates of change, began his investigations into the composition of light, and inaugurated his work on the law of universal gravitation. Two years after his return to Cambridge, in 1669, he accepted a chair in mathematics at the university. During a second intense period of creativity from 1684 to 1686, he wrote his famous *Principia* (see the box on p. 448). After a nervous breakdown in 1693, he sought and received an administrative post as warden of the royal mint and was advanced to master of the mint by 1699, a post he held until his death in 1727. Made president of the Royal Society (see "The Scientific Societies" later in

Newton's Rules of Reasoning

In 1687, Isaac Newton published his masterpiece, the *Mathematical Principles of Natural Philosophy*. In this work, Newton demonstrated the mathematical proofs for his universal law of gravitation and completed the new cosmology begun by Copernicus, Kepler, and Galileo. He also described the rules of reasoning by which he arrived at his universal law.

Isaac Newton, *Rules of Reasoning in Philosophy*

■ *Rule 1*

We are to admit no more causes of natural things than such as are both true and sufficient to explain their appearances.

To this purpose the philosophers say that Nature does nothing in vain, and more is in vain when less will serve; for Nature is pleased with simplicity, and affects not the pomp of superfluous causes.

■ *Rule 2*

Therefore to the same natural effects we must, as far as possible, assign the same causes.

As to respiration in a man and in a beast; the descent of stones in Europe and in America; the light of our culinary fire and of the sun; the reflection of light in the earth and in the planets.

■ *Rule 3*

The qualities of bodies, which admit neither intensification nor remission of degrees, and which are found to belong to all bodies within the reach of our experiments, are to be esteemed the universal qualities of all bodies whatsoever.

For since qualities of bodies are only known to us by experiments, we are to hold for universal all such as universally agree with experiments; and such as are not liable to diminution can never be quite taken away.

■ *Rule 4*

In experimental philosophy we are to look upon propositions inferred by general induction from phenomena as accurately or very nearly true, notwithstanding any contrary hypotheses that may be imagined, till such time as other phenomena occur, by which they may either be made more accurate, or liable to exceptions.

This rule we must follow, that the argument of induction may not be evaded by hypotheses.

this chapter) in 1703 and knighted in 1705 for his great achievements, Sir Isaac Newton wound up the only English scientist to be buried in Westminster Abbey.

Although Newton occupies a very special place in the history of modern science, we need to remember that he, too, remained extremely interested in aspects of the occult world. He left behind hundreds of manuscript pages of his studies of alchemy, and in fact, his alchemical experiments were a major feature of his life until he moved to London in 1696 to become warden of the royal mint. The British economist John Maynard Keynes said of Newton after examining his manuscripts in 1936:

> Newton was not the first of the age of reason. He was the last of the magicians. . . . He looked on the whole universe and all that is in it as a riddle, as a secret which could be read by applying pure thought to certain evidence, certain mystic clues which God had laid about the world to allow a sort of philosopher's treasure hunt to the esoteric brotherhood. He believed that these clues were to be found partly in the evidence of the heavens and in the constitution of elements, . . . but also partly in certain papers and traditions handed down by the brethren in an unknown chain back to the original cryptic revelation in Babylonia.[10]

Although Newton may have considered himself a representative of the Hermetic tradition, he chose, it has been recently argued, for both political and psychological reasons to repress that part of his being, and it is as the "symbol of Western science" that Newton came to be viewed.

Newton's major work, the "hinge point of modern scientific thought," was his *Mathematical Principles of Natural Philosophy,* known simply as the *Principia,* by the first word of its Latin title. In this work, the last highly influential book in Europe to be written in Latin, Newton spelled out the mathematical proofs demonstrating his universal law of gravitation. Newton's work was the culmination of the theories of Copernicus, Kepler, and Galileo. Though each had undermined some part of the Ptolemaic-Aristotelian cosmology, until Newton no one had pieced together a coherent synthesis for a new cosmology.

In the first book of the *Principia,* Newton defined the basic concepts of mechanics by elaborating the three laws of motion: every object continues in a state of rest or uniform motion in a straight line unless deflected by a force, the rate of change of motion of an object is proportional to the force acting on it, and to every action there is always an equal and opposite reaction. In Book Three, Newton applied his theories of mechanics to the problems of astronomy by demonstrating that these three laws of motion govern the planetary bodies as well as terrestrial objects. Integral to his whole argument was the universal law of gravitation, which explained why the planetary bodies did not go off in straight lines but continued in elliptical orbits about

National Portrait Gallery, London

Isaac Newton. With a single law, that of universal gravitation, Isaac Newton was able to explain all motion in the universe. His great synthesis of the work of his predecessors created a new picture of the universe, one in which the universe was viewed as a great machine operating according to natural laws. This portrait of Newton was painted by Sir Godfrey Kneller.

the sun. In mathematical terms, Newton explained that every object in the universe was attracted to every other object with a force (that is, gravity) that is directly proportional to the product of their masses and inversely proportional to the square of the distances between them.

The implications of Newton's universal law of gravitation were enormous, even though it took another century before they were widely recognized. Newton had demonstrated that one universal law, mathematically proved, could explain all motion in the universe, from the movements of the planets in the celestial world to an apple falling from a tree in the terrestrial world. The secrets of the natural world could be known by human investigations. At the same time, the Newtonian synthesis created a new cosmology in which the world was seen largely in mechanistic terms. The universe was one huge, regulated, and uniform machine that operated according to natural laws in absolute time, space, and motion. Although Newton believed that God was "everywhere present" and acted as the force that moved all bodies on the basis of the laws he had discovered, later generations dropped his spiritual assumptions. Newton's world-machine, conceived as operating absolutely in time, space, and motion, dominated the Western worldview until the twentieth century, when the Einsteinian revolution based on a concept of relativity superseded the Newtonian mechanistic concept.

Newton's ideas were soon accepted in England, possibly out of national pride and conviction and, as has been argued recently, for political reasons (see "Science and Society" later in this chapter). Natural philosophers on the Continent resisted Newton's ideas, and it took much of the eighteenth century before they were generally accepted everywhere in Europe. They were also reinforced by developments in other fields, especially medicine.

Advances in Medicine

Although the Scientific Revolution of the sixteenth and seventeenth centuries is associated primarily with the dramatic changes in astronomy and mechanics that precipitated a new perception of the universe, a third field that had been dominated by Greek thought in the Late Middle Ages, that of medicine, also experienced a transformation. Late, medieval medicine was dominated not by the teachings of Aristotle but by those of the Greek physician Galen, who had lived in the second century A.D.

Galen's influence on the medieval medical world was pervasive in anatomy, physiology, and disease. Galen had relied on animal, rather than human, dissection to arrive at a picture of human anatomy that was quite inaccurate in many instances. Even when Europeans began to practice human dissection in the Later Middle Ages, instruction in anatomy still relied on Galen. While a professor read a text of Galen, an assistant dissected a cadaver for illustrative purposes. Physiology, or the functioning of the body, was also dominated by Galenic hypotheses, including the belief that there were two separate blood systems. One controlled muscular activities and contained bright red blood moving upward and downward through the arteries; the other governed the digestive functions and contained dark red blood that ebbed and flowed in the veins.

Treatment of disease was highly influenced by Galen's doctrine of four bodily humors: blood, considered warm and moist; yellow bile, warm and dry; phlegm, cold and moist; and black bile, cold and dry. Since disease was supposedly the result of an imbalance of humors that could be discerned from the quantity and color of urine, the examination of a patient's urine became the chief diagnostic tool. Although purging and bleeding to remedy the imbalance were often harmful to patients, treatment with traditional herbal medicines sometimes proved beneficial.

Three figures are associated with the changes in medicine in the sixteenth and seventeenth centuries: Paracelsus, Andreas Vesalius, and William Harvey. Philippus Aureolus von Hohenheim (1493–1541), who renamed himself Paracelsus ("greater than Celsus," the ancient physician), was born in a small town near Zürich. After leaving home at the age of fourteen, Paracelsus traveled widely and may have been awarded a medical degree from the University of Ferrara. He achieved a moment of glory when he was appointed city physician and professor of medicine at Basel in 1527. But this, like so many other appointments, proved short-lived due to his vanity and quick temper. He could never disguise his contempt for universities and physicians who did not agree with his new ideas:

> I am *monarcha medicorum,* monarch of physicians, and I can prove to you what you cannot prove. . . . It was not the constellations that made me a physician: God made me. . . . I need not don a coat of mail or a buckler against you, for you are not learned or experienced enough to refute even one word of mine. . . . Let me tell you this: every little hair on my neck knows more than you and all your scribes, and my shoebuckles are more learned than your Galen and Avicenna, and my beard has more experience than all your high colleges.[11]

Paracelsus was not easy to get along with, and he was forced to wander from one town to another until his death in 1541.

Paracelsus rejected the work of both Aristotle and Galen and attacked the universities as centers of their moribund philosophy. He and his followers hoped to replace the traditional system with a new chemical philosophy that was based on a new understanding of nature derived from fresh observation and experiment. This chemical philosophy was in turn closely connected to a view of the universe based on the macrocosm-microcosm analogy. According to this view, a human being was a small replica (microcosm) of the larger world (macrocosm). All parts of the universe were represented within each person. As Paracelsus said: "For the sun and the moon and all planets, as well as the stars and the whole chaos, are in man. . . . For what is outside is also inside; and what is not outside man is not inside. The outer and the inner are one thing."[12] In accordance with the macrocosmic-microcosmic principle, Paracelsus believed that the chemical reactions of the universe as a whole were reproduced in human beings on a smaller scale. Disease, then, was not caused by an imbalance of the four humors, as Galen had argued, but was due to chemical imbalances that were localized in specific organs and could be treated by chemical remedies.

Although others had used chemical remedies, Paracelsus and his followers differed from them in giving careful attention to the proper dosage of their chemically prepared metals and minerals. Paracelsus had turned against the Galenic principle that "contraries cure" in favor of the ancient Germanic folk principle that "like cures like." The poison that caused a disease would be its cure if used in proper form and quantity. This use of toxic substances to cure patients was, despite its apparent effectiveness (Paracelsus did have a strong reputation for actually curing his patients), viewed by Paracelsus' opponents as the practice of a "homicide physician." Later generations came to view Paracelsus more favorably, and historians who have stressed Paracelsus' concept of disease and recognition of "new drugs" for medicine have viewed him as a father of modern medicine. Others have argued that his macrocosmic-microcosmic philosophy and use of "like cures like" drugs make him the forerunner of both homeopathy and the holistic medicine of the postmodern era.

Historians usually associate the name of Paracelsus with the diagnosis and treatment of disease. The new anatomy of the sixteenth century, however, was the work of Andreas Vesalius (1514–1564). His study of medicine at Paris involved him in the works of Galen. Especially important to him was a recently discovered text of Galen, *On Anatomical Procedures,* that led Vesalius to emphasize practical research as the principal avenue for understanding human anatomy. After receiving a doctorate in medicine at the University of Padua in 1536, he accepted a position there as professor of surgery. In 1543, he published his masterpiece, *On the Fabric of the Human Body.*

This book was based on his Paduan lectures, in which he deviated from traditional practice by personally dissecting a body to illustrate what he was discussing. Vesalius' anatomical treatise presented a careful examination of the individual organs and general structure of the human body. The book would not have been feasible without both the artistic advances of the Renaissance and technical developments in the art of printing. Together, they made possible the creation of illustrations superior to any hitherto produced.

Vesalius' "hands-on" approach to teaching anatomy enabled him to rectify some of Galen's most glaring errors. He did not hesitate, for example, to correct Galen's assertion that the great blood vessels originated from the liver since his own observations made it apparent that they came from the heart. Nevertheless, Vesalius still clung to a number of Galen's erroneous assertions, including the Greek physician's ideas on the ebb and flow of two kinds of blood in the veins and arteries. It was not until William Har-

CHRONOLOGY

Important Works of the Scientific Revolution

Copernicus, *On the Revolutions of the Heavenly Spheres*	1543
Vesalius, *On the Fabric of the Human Body*	1543
Galileo, *The Starry Messenger*	1610
Harvey, *On the Motion of the Heart and Blood*	1628
Galileo, *Dialogue on the Two Chief World Systems*	1632
Cavendish, *Grounds of Natural Philosophy*	1668
Newton, *Principia*	1687

vey's work on the circulation of the blood that this Galenic misperception was corrected.

William Harvey (1578–1657) attended Cambridge University and later Padua, where he received a doctorate of medicine in 1602. His reputation rests on his book *On the Motion of the Heart and Blood,* published in 1628. Although questions had been raised in the sixteenth century about Galen's physiological principles, no major break from his system had occurred. Harvey's work, which was based on meticulous observations and experiments, led him to demolish the ancient Greek's erroneous contentions. Harvey demonstrated that the heart and not the liver was the beginning point of the circulation of blood in the body, that the same blood flows in both veins and arteries, and most important, that the blood makes a complete circuit as it passes through the body. Although Harvey's work dealt a severe blow to Galen's theories, his ideas did not begin to achieve general recognition until the 1660s, when capillaries, which explained how the blood passed from the arteries to the veins, were discovered. Harvey's theory of the circulation of the blood laid the foundation for modern physiology.

Women in the Origins of Modern Science

During the Middle Ages, except for members of religious orders, women who sought a life of learning were severely hampered by the traditional attitude that a woman's proper role was as a daughter, wife, and mother. But in the late fourteenth and early fifteenth centuries, new opportunities for elite women emerged as enthusiasm for the new secular learning called humanism encouraged Europe's privileged and learned men to encourage women to read and study classical and Christian texts. The ideal of a humanist education for some of the daughters of Europe's elite persisted into the seventeenth century, but only for some privileged women.

Much as they were drawn to humanism, women were also attracted to the Scientific Revolution. Unlike females educated formally in humanist schools, women attracted to science had to obtain a largely informal education. European nobles had the leisure and resources that gave them easy access to the world of learning. This door was also open to noblewomen who could participate in the informal scientific networks of their fathers and brothers. One of the most prominent female scientists of the seventeenth century, Margaret Cavendish (1623–1673), came from an aristocratic background. Cavendish was not a popularizer of science for women but a participant in the crucial scientific debates of her time. Despite her achievements, however, she was excluded from membership in the Royal Society (see "The Scientific Societies" later in this chapter), although she was once allowed to attend a meeting. She

Margaret Cavendish. Shown in this portrait is Margaret Cavendish, the duchess of Newcastle. Her husband, who was thirty years older, encouraged her to pursue her literary interests. In addition to scientific works, she wrote plays, an autobiography, and a biography of her husband titled *The Life of the Thrice Noble, High and Puissant Prince William Cavendish, Duke, Marquess and Earl of Newcastle.* The autobiography and biography led one male literary critic to call her "a mad, conceited and ridiculous woman."

CORBIS

wrote a number of works on scientific matters, including *Observations upon Experimental Philosophy* and *Grounds of Natural Philosophy*. In these works, she did not hesitate to attack what she considered the defects of the rationalist and empiricist approaches to scientific knowledge and was especially critical of the growing belief that through science, humans would be masters of nature: "We have no power at all over natural causes and effects . . . for man is but a small part . . . his powers are but particular actions of Nature, and he cannot have a supreme and absolute power."[13]

As an aristocrat, Cavendish was a good example of the women in France and England who worked in science. In Germany, women interested in science came from a different background. There the tradition of female participation in craft production enabled some women to become involved in observational science, especially entomology and astronomy. Between 1650 and 1710, one of every seven German astronomers was a woman.

A good example of female involvement in the Scientific Revolution stemming from the craft tradition was Maria Sibylla Merian (1647–1717), who had established a reputation as an important entomologist by the beginning of the eighteenth century. Merian's training came from working in her father's workshop, where she learned the art of illustration, a training of great importance since her exact observation of insects and plants was demonstrated through the superb illustrations she made. In 1699, she undertook an expedition into the wilds of the Dutch colony of Surinam to collect and draw samples of plants and insect life. This led to her major scientific work, the *Metamorphosis of the Insects of Surinam*, in which she used sixty illustrations to show the reproductive and developmental cycles of Surinam's insect life.

The craft organization of astronomy also gave women opportunities to become involved in science. Those who did worked in family observatories; hence daughters and wives received training as apprentices to fathers or husbands. The most famous of the female astronomers in Germany was Maria Winkelmann (1670–1720). She was educated by her father and uncle and received advanced training in astronomy from a nearby self-taught astronomer. Her opportunity to be a practicing astronomer came when she married Gottfried Kirch, Germany's foremost astronomer. She became his assistant at the astronomical observatory operated in Berlin by the Academy of Science. She made some original contributions, including a hitherto undiscovered comet, as her husband related:

> Early in the morning (about 2:00 A.M.) the sky was clear and starry. Some nights before, I had observed a variable star, and my wife (as I slept) wanted to find and see it for herself. In so doing, she found a comet in the sky. At which time she woke me, and I found that it was indeed a comet. . . . I was surprised that I had not seen it the night before.[14]

Moreover, Winkelmann corresponded with the famous scientist Gottfried Leibniz (who invented the calculus independently of Newton), who praised her effusively as "a most learned woman who could pass as a rarity." When her husband died in 1710, she applied for a position as assistant astronomer for which she was highly qualified. As a woman—with no university degree—she was denied the post by the Berlin Academy, which feared that it would establish a precedent by hiring a woman ("mouths would gape").

Winkelmann's difficulties with the Berlin Academy reflect the obstacles women faced in being accepted in scientific work, which was considered a male preserve. Although no formal statutes excluded women from membership in the new scientific societies, no woman was invited to join either the Royal Society of England or the French Academy of Sciences until the twentieth century. All of these women scientists were exceptional, since a life devoted to any kind of scholarship was still viewed as being at odds with the domestic duties women were expected to perform.

The nature and value of women had been the subject of an ongoing, centuries-long debate known as the *querelles des femmes*—arguments about women. Male opinions in the debate were largely a carryover from medieval times and were not favorable. Women were portrayed as inherently base, prone to vice, easily swayed, and "sexually insatiable." Hence men needed to control them. Learned women were viewed as having overcome female liabilities to become like men. One man in praise of a woman scholar remarked that her writings were so good that you "would hardly believe they were done by a woman at all."

In the early modern era, women joined this debate by arguing against these male images of women. They argued that women also had rational minds and could grow from education. Further, since most women were pious, chaste, and temperate, there was no need for male authority over them. These female defenders of women emphasized education as the key to women's ability to move into the world. How, then, did the era of the Scientific Revolution affect this debate over the nature of women? As an era of intellectual revolution in which traditional authorities were being overthrown, we might expect significant change in men's views of women. But by and large, instead of becoming an instrument for liberation, science was used to find new support for the old, stereotypical views about a woman's place in the scheme of things.

An important project in the new anatomy of the sixteenth and seventeenth centuries was the attempt to illustrate the human body and skeleton. For Vesalius, the portrayal of physical differences between males and females was limited to external bodily form (the outlines of the body) and the sexual organs. Vesalius saw no difference in skeletons and portrayed them as the same for men and women. It was not until the eighteenth century, in fact, that a new anatomy finally prevailed. Drawings of female skeletons between 1730 and 1790 varied, but females tended to have a larger pelvic area, and, in some instances, female skulls were portrayed as smaller than those of males. Eighteenth-century studies on the anatomy and physiology of sexual differences provided "scientific evidence" to reaffirm the

The "Natural" Inferiority of Women

Despite the shattering of old views and the emergence of a new worldview in the Scientific Revolution of the seventeenth century, attitudes toward women remained tied to traditional perspectives. In this selection, the philosopher Benedict de Spinoza argues for the "natural" inferiority of women to men.

■ *Benedict de Spinoza,* A Political Treatise

But, perhaps, someone will ask, whether women are under men's authority by nature or institution? For if it has been by mere institution, then we had no reason compelling us to exclude women from government. But if we consult experience itself, we shall find that the origin of it is in their weakness. For there has never been a case of men and women reigning together, but wherever on the earth men are found, there we see that men rule, and women are ruled, and that on this plan, both sexes live in harmony. But on the other hand, the Amazons, who are reported to have held rule of old, did not suffer men to stop in their country, but reared only their female children, killing males to whom they gave birth. But if by nature women were equal to men, and were equally distinguished by force of character and ability, in which human power and therefore human right chiefly consist; surely among nations so many and different some would be found, where both sexes rule alike, and others, where men are ruled by women, and so brought up, that they can make less use of their abilities. And since this is nowhere the case, one may assert with perfect propriety, that women have not by nature equal right with men: but that they necessarily give way to men, and that thus it cannot happen, that both sexes should rule alike, much less that men should be ruled by women. But if we further reflect upon human passions, how men, in fact, generally love women merely from the passion of lust, and esteem their cleverness and wisdom in proportion to the excellence of their beauty, and also how very ill-disposed men are to suffer the women they love to show any sort of favor to others, and other facts of this kind, we shall easily see that men and women cannot rule alike without great hurt to peace.

traditional inferiority of women. The larger pelvic area "proved" that women were meant to be childbearers, and the larger skull "demonstrated" the superiority of the male mind. Male-dominated science had been used to "prove" male social dominance.

At the same time, during the seventeenth and eighteenth centuries, women even lost the traditional spheres of influence they had possessed, especially in the science-related art of midwifery. Women serving as midwives had traditionally been responsible for birthing. Similar to barber-surgeons or apothecaries (see Chapter 17), midwives had acquired their skills through apprenticeship. But the impact of the Scientific Revolution caused traditional crafts to be upgraded and then even professionalized as males took over. When medical men entered this arena, they also began to use devices and techniques derived from the study of anatomy. These were increasingly used to justify the male takeover of the traditional role of midwives. By the end of the eighteenth century, midwives were simply accessories to the art they had once controlled, except among the poor. Since little money was to be made in serving the lower classes, midwives were allowed to continue to practice their traditional art among them.

Overall, the Scientific Revolution reaffirmed traditional ideas about women. Male scientists used the new science to spread the view that women were inferior by nature, subordinate to men, and suited by nature to play a domestic role as nurturing mothers (see the box above). The widespread distribution of books ensured the continuation of these ideas. Jean de La Bruyère, the seventeenth-century French moralist, was typical when he remarked that an educated woman was like a gun that was a collector's item, "which one shows to the curious, but which has no use at all, any more than a carousel horse."[15]

Toward a New Earth: Descartes, Rationalism, and a New View of Humankind

The fundamentally new conception of the universe contained in the cosmological revolution of the sixteenth and seventeenth centuries inevitably had an impact on the Western view of humankind. Nowhere is this more evident than in the work of René Descartes (1596–1650), an extremely important figure in Western history. Descartes began by reflecting the doubt and uncertainty that seemed pervasive in the confusion of the seventeenth century and ended with a philosophy that dominated Western thought until the twentieth century.

Descartes was born into a family of the French lower nobility. After a Jesuit education, he studied law at Poitiers but traveled to Paris to study by himself. In 1618, at the beginning of the Thirty Years' War, Descartes volunteered for service in the army of Maurice of Nassau, but his motives seem to have been guided less by the desire for military action than for travel and leisure time to think. On the night of November 10, 1619, Descartes underwent what one historian has called an experience comparable to the "ecstatic illumination of the mystic." Having perceived in one night the outlines of a new rational-mathematical system, with a sense of divine approval he made a new commitment to mind, mathematics, and a mechanical universe. For the rest of his life, Descartes worked out the details of his vision.

The starting point for Descartes's new system was doubt, as he explained at the beginning of his most famous work, *Discourse on Method,* written in 1637:

> From my childhood I have been familiar with letters; and as I was given to believe that by their means a clear and assured knowledge can be acquired of all that is useful in life, I was extremely eager for instruction in them. As soon, however, as I had completed the course of study, at the close of which it is customary to be admitted into the order of the learned, I entirely changed my opinion. For I found myself entangled in so many doubts and errors that, as it seemed to me, the endeavor to instruct myself had served only to disclose to me more and more of my ignorance.[16]

Descartes decided to set aside all that he had learned and begin again. One fact seemed beyond doubt—his own existence:

> But I immediately became aware that while I was thus disposed to think that all was false, it was absolutely necessary that I who thus thought should be something; and noting that this truth, *I think, therefore I am,* was so steadfast and so assured that the suppositions of the skeptics, to whatever extreme they might all be carried, could not avail to shake it, I concluded that I might without scruple accept it as being the first principle of the philosophy I was seeking.[17]

With this emphasis on the mind, Descartes asserted that he would accept only those things that his reason said were true.

From his first postulate, Descartes deduced an additional principle, the separation of mind and matter. Descartes argued that since "the mind cannot be doubted but the body and material world can, the two must be radically different." From this came an absolute duality between mind and body, what has been called Cartesian dualism. Using mind or human reason, the path to certain knowledge, and its best instrument, mathematics, humans can understand the material world because it is pure mechanism, a machine that is governed by its own physical laws because it was created by God, the great geometrician.

Descartes's conclusions about the nature of the universe and human beings had important implications. His separation of mind and matter allowed scientists to view matter as dead or inert, as something that was totally separate from themselves and could be investigated independently by reason. The split between mind and body led Westerners to equate their identity with mind and reason rather than with the whole organism. Descartes has rightly been called the father of modern rationalism (see the box on p. 455). His books were placed on the papal Index of Forbidden Books and condemned by many Protestant theologians. The radical Cartesian split between mind and matter, and between mind and body, had devastating implications not only for traditional religious views of the universe but also for how Westerners viewed themselves.

The Scientific Method

In the course of the Scientific Revolution, attention was also paid to the problem of establishing the proper means to examine and understand the physical realm. This development of a scientific method was crucial to the evolution of science in the modern world.

Curiously enough, it was an Englishman with few scientific credentials who attempted to put forth a new method of acquiring knowledge that made an impact on the Royal Society in England in the seventeenth century and other European scientists in the eighteenth century. Francis Bacon (1561–1626), a lawyer and lord chancellor, rejected Copernicus and Kepler and misunderstood Galileo. And yet in his unfinished work, *The Great Instauration,* he called for his contemporaries "to commence a total reconstruction of sciences, arts, and all human knowledge, raised upon the proper foundations." Bacon did not doubt humans' ability to know the natural world, but he believed that they had proceeded incorrectly: "The entire

Descartes with Queen Christina of Sweden. René Descartes was one of the primary figures in the Scientific Revolution. Claiming to use reason as his sole guide to truth, Descartes posited a sharp distinction between mind and matter. He is shown here standing to the right of Queen Christina of Sweden. The queen had a deep interest in philosophy and invited Descartes to her court.

The Father of Modern Rationalism

René Descartes has long been viewed as the founder of modern rationalism and modern philosophy because he believed that human beings could understand the world—itself a mechanical system—by the same rational principles inherent in mathematical thinking. In his *Discourse on Method,* he elaborated on his approach to discovering truth.

René Descartes, Discourse on Method

In place of the numerous precepts which have gone to constitute logic, I came to believe that the four following rules would be found sufficient, always provided I took the firm and unswerving resolve never in a single instance to fail in observing them.

The first was to accept nothing as true which I did not evidently know to be such, that is to say, scrupulously to avoid precipitance and prejudice, and in the judgments I passed to include nothing additional to what had presented itself to my mind so clearly and so distinctly that I could have no occasion for doubting it.

The second, to divide each of the difficulties I examined into as many parts as may be required for its adequate solution.

The third, to arrange my thoughts in order, beginning with things the simplest and easiest to know, so that I may then ascend little by little, as it were step by step, to the knowledge of the more complex, and in doing so, to assign an order of thought even to those objects which are not of themselves in any such order of precedence.

And the last, in all cases to make enumerations so complete, and reviews so general, that I should be assured of omitting nothing.

Those long chains of reasonings, each step simple and easy, which geometers are wont to employ in arriving even at the most difficult of their demonstrations, have led me to surmise that all the things we human beings are competent to know are interconnected in the same manner, and that none are so remote as to be beyond our reach or so hidden that we cannot discover them—that is, provided we abstain from accepting as true what is not thus related, i.e., keep always to the order required for their deduction one from another. And I had no great difficulty in determining what the objects are with which I should begin, for that I already knew, namely, that it was with the simplest and easiest. Bearing in mind, too, that of all those who in time past have sought for truth in the sciences, the mathematicians alone have been able to find any demonstrations, that is to say, any reasons which are certain and evident, I had no doubt that it must have been by a procedure of this kind that they had obtained them.

fabric of human reason which we employ in the inquisition of nature is badly put together and built up, and like some magnificent structure without foundation."

Bacon's new foundation—a correct scientific method—was to be built on inductive principles. Rather than beginning with assumed first principles from which logical conclusions could be deduced, he urged scientists to proceed from the particular to the general. From carefully organized experiments and thorough, systematic observations, correct generalizations could be developed.

Bacon was clear about what he believed his method could accomplish. His concern was more for practical than for pure science. He stated that "the true and lawful goal of the sciences is none other than this: that human life be endowed with new discoveries and power." He wanted science to contribute to the "mechanical arts" by creating devices that would benefit industry, agriculture, and trade. Bacon was prophetic when he said that "I am laboring to lay the foundation, not of any sect or doctrine, but of human utility and power." And how would this "human power" be used? To "conquer nature in action."[18] The control and domination of nature became a central proposition of modern science and the technology that accompanied it. Only in the twentieth century did some scientists begin to ask whether this assumption might not be at the heart of the earth's ecological crisis.

Descartes proposed a different approach to scientific methodology by emphasizing deduction and mathematical logic. As Descartes explained in *Discourse on Method,* each step in an argument should be as sharp and well founded as a mathematical proof:

> These long chains of reasonings which geometers are accustomed to using to reach their most difficult demonstrations, had given me cause to imagine that everything which can be encompassed by man's knowledge is linked in the same way, and that provided only that one abstains from accepting any for true which is not true, and that one always keeps the right order for one thing to be deduced from that which precedes it, there can be nothing so distant that one does not reach it eventually, or so hidden that one cannot discover it.[19]

Descartes believed then that one could start with self-evident truths, comparable to geometrical axioms, and deduce more complex conclusions. His emphasis on deduction and mathematical order complemented Bacon's stress on experiment and induction. It was Sir Isaac Newton who synthesized them into a single scientific methodology by uniting Bacon's empiricism with Descartes's rationalism. This scientific method began with systematic observations and experiments, which were used to arrive at general concepts. New deductions derived from these general concepts could then be tested and verified by precise experiments.

The scientific method, of course, was valuable in answering the question as to *how* something works, and its success in doing this gave others much confidence in the method. It did not attempt to deal with the question of *why* something happens or the purpose and meaning behind the world of nature. This allowed religion to retain its central importance in the seventeenth century.

Science and Religion in the Seventeenth Century

In Galileo's struggle with the inquisitorial Holy Office of the Catholic church, we see the beginning of the conflict between science and religion that has marked the history of modern Western civilization. Since time immemorial, theology had seemed to be the queen of the sciences. It was natural that the churches would continue to believe that religion was the final measure of all things. To the emerging scientists, however, it often seemed that theologians knew not of what they spoke. These "natural philosophers" then tried to draw lines between the knowledge of religion and the knowledge of "natural philosophy" or nature. Galileo had clearly felt that it was unnecessary to pit science against religion when he wrote:

> In discussions of physical problems we ought to begin not from the authority of scriptural passages, but from sense-experiences and necessary demonstrations; for the holy Bible and the phenomena of nature proceed alike from the divine word, the former as the dictate of the Holy Ghost and the latter as the observant executrix of God's commands. It is necessary for the Bible, in order to be accommodated to the understanding of every man, to speak many things which appear to differ from the absolute truth so far as the bare meaning of the words is concerned. But Nature, on the other hand, is inexorable and immutable; she never transgresses the laws imposed upon her, or cares a whit whether her abstruse reasons and methods of operation are understandable to men.[20]

To Galileo, it made little sense for the church to determine the nature of physical reality on the basis of biblical texts that were subject to radically divergent interpretations. The church, however, decided otherwise in Galileo's case and lent its great authority to one scientific theory, the Ptolemaic-Aristotelian cosmology, no doubt because it fit so well with its own philosophical views of reality. But the church's decision had tremendous consequences, just as the rejection of Darwin's ideas did in the nineteenth century. For educated individuals, it established a dichotomy between scientific investigations and religious beliefs. As the scientific beliefs triumphed, it became almost in-evitable that religious beliefs would suffer, leading to a growing secularization in European intellectual life—precisely what the church had hoped to combat by opposing Copernicanism. Many seventeenth-century intellectuals were both religious and scientific and believed that the implications of this split would be tragic. Some believed that the split was largely unnecessary, while others felt the need to combine God, humans, and a mechanistic universe into a new philosophical synthesis. Two individuals—Spinoza and Pascal—illustrate the wide diversity in the response of European intellectuals to the implications of the cosmological revolution of the seventeenth century.

Spinoza

Benedict de Spinoza (1632–1677) was a philosopher who grew up in the relatively tolerant atmosphere of Amsterdam. He was excommunicated from the Amsterdam synagogue at the age of twenty-four for rejecting the tenets of Judaism. Ostracized by the local Jewish community and major Christian churches alike, Spinoza lived a quiet, independent life, earning a living by grinding optical lenses and refusing to accept an academic position in philosophy at the University of Heidelberg for fear of compromising his freedom of thought. Spinoza read a great deal of the new scientific literature and was influenced by Descartes.

Spinoza was unwilling to accept the implications of Descartes's ideas, especially the separation of mind and matter and the apparent separation of an infinite God from the finite world of matter. God was not simply the creator of the universe; he was the universe. All that is is in God, and nothing can be apart from God. This philosophy of pantheism (or monism) was set out in Spinoza's book *Ethics Demonstrated in the Geometrical Manner,* which was not published until after his death.

To Spinoza, human beings are not "situated in nature as a kingdom within a kingdom" but are as much a part of God or nature or the universal order as other natural objects. The failure to understand God had led to many misconceptions—for one, that nature exists only for one's use:

> As they find in themselves and outside themselves many means which assist them not a little in their search for what is useful, for instance, eyes for seeing, teeth for chewing, herbs and animals for yielding food, the sun for giving light, the sea for breeding fish, they come to look on the whole of nature as a means for obtaining such conveniences.[21]

Furthermore, unable to find any other cause for the existence of these things, they attributed them to a creator-God who must be worshiped to gain their ends: "Hence also it follows, that everyone thought out for himself, according to his abilities, a different way of worshiping God, so that God might love him more than his fellows, and direct the whole course of nature for the satisfaction of his blind cupidity and insatiable avarice." Then, when nature appeared unfriendly in the form of storms, earthquakes, and diseases, "they declared that such things happen, because the gods are angry at some wrong done them by men, or at some fault committed in their worship," rather than realizing "that good and evil fortunes fall to the lot of pious and impious alike."[22] Likewise, human beings made moral condemnations of others because they failed to understand that human emotions, "passions of hatred, anger, envy and so, considered in themselves, follow from the same necessity and efficacy of nature" and "nothing comes to pass in nature in contravention to her universal laws." To explain human emotions, like everything else, we need to analyze them as we would the movements of planets: "I shall, therefore, treat of the nature and strength of my emotions according to the same method as I employed heretofore in my investigations concerning God and the mind. I shall consider human actions and desires in exactly the same manner as though I were concerned with lines, planes, and solids."[23] Everything has a rational explanation, and humans are capable of finding it. In using reason, people can find true happiness. Their real freedom comes when they understand the order and necessity of nature and achieve detachment from passing interests.

Pascal

Blaise Pascal (1623–1662) was a French scientist who sought to keep science and religion united. He had a brief but checkered career. An accomplished scientist and a brilliant mathematician, he excelled at both the practical, by inventing a calculating machine, and the abstract, by devising a theory of chance or probability and doing work on conic sections. After a profound mystical vision on the night of November 23, 1654, which assured him that God cared for the human soul, he devoted the rest of his life to religious matters. He planned to write an "apology for the Christian religion" but died before he could do so. He did leave a set of notes for the larger work, however, which in published form became known as *Pensées* (*Thoughts*).

In *Pensées*, Pascal tried to convert rationalists to Christianity by appealing to both their reason and their emotions. Humans were, he argued, frail creatures, often deceived by their senses, misled by reason, and battered by their emotions. And yet they were beings whose very nature involved thinking: "Man is but a reed, the weakest in nature; but he is a thinking reed."[24]

Pascal was determined to show that the Christian religion was not contrary to reason: "If we violate the principles of reason, our religion will be absurd, and it will be laughed at." Christianity, he felt, was the only religion that recognized people's true state of being as both vulnerable and great. To a Christian, a human being was both fallen and at the same time God's special creation. But it was not necessary to emphasize one at the expense of the other—to view humans as only rational or only hopeless. Pascal even had an answer for skeptics in his famous wager. God is a reasonable bet; it is worthwhile to assume that God exists. If he does, then we win all; if he does not, we lose nothing.

Despite his own background as a scientist and mathematician, Pascal refused to rely on the scientist's world of order and rationality to attract people to God: "If we

Réunion des Musées Nationaux/Art Resource, NY

Blaise Pascal. Blaise Pascal was a brilliant scientist and mathematician who hoped to keep science and Christianity united. In his *Pensées,* he made a passionate argument on behalf of the Christian religion. He is pictured here in a posthumous portrait by Quesnel.

Pascal: "What Is a Man in the Infinite?"

Perhaps no intellectual in the seventeenth century gave greater expression to the uncertainties generated by the cosmological revolution than Blaise Pascal. Himself a scientist, Pascal's work, *Pensées,* consisted of notes for a large unfinished work justifying the Christian religion. In this selection, Pascal presents his musings on the human place in an infinite world.

Blaise Pascal, Pensées

Let man then contemplate the whole of nature in her full and exalted majesty. Let him turn his eyes from the lowly objects which surround him. Let him gaze on that brilliant light set like an eternal lamp to illumine the Universe; let the earth seem to him a dot compared with the vast orbit described by the sun, and let him wonder at the fact that this vast orbit itself is no more than a very small dot compared with that described by the stars in their revolutions around the firmament. But if our vision stops here, let the imagination pass on; it will exhaust its powers of thinking long before nature ceases to supply it with material for thought. All this visible world is no more than an imperceptible speck in nature's ample bosom. No idea approaches it. We may extend our conceptions beyond all imaginable space; yet produce only atoms in comparison with the reality of things. It is an infinite sphere, the center of which is everywhere, the circumference nowhere. In short, it is the greatest perceptible mark of God's almighty power that our imagination should lose itself in that thought.

Returning to himself, let man consider what he is compared with all existence; let him think of himself as lost in his remote corner of nature; and from this little dungeon in which he finds himself lodged—I mean the Universe—let him learn to set a true value on the earth, its kingdoms, and cities, and upon himself. What is a man in the infinite?...

For, after all, what is a man in nature? A nothing in comparison with the infinite, an absolute in comparison with nothing, a central point between nothing and all. Infinitely far from understanding these extremes, the end of things and their beginning are hopelessly hidden from him in an impenetrable secret. He is equally incapable of seeing the nothingness from which he came, and the infinite in which he is engulfed. What else then will he perceive but some appearance of the middle of things, in an eternal despair of knowing either their principle or their purpose? All things emerge from nothing and are borne onward to infinity. Who can follow this marvelous process? The Author of these wonders understands them. None but He can.

submit everything to reason, there will be no mystery and no supernatural element in our religion." In the new cosmology of the seventeenth century, "finite man," Pascal believed, was lost in the new infinite world, a realization that frightened him: "The eternal silence of those infinite spaces strikes me with terror" (see the box above). The world of nature, then, could never reveal God: "Because they have failed to contemplate these infinites, men have rashly plunged into the examination of nature, as though they bore some proportion to her. . . . Their assumption is as infinite as their object." A Christian could only rely on a God who through Jesus cared for human beings. In the final analysis, after providing reasonable arguments for Christianity, Pascal came to rest on faith. Reason, he believed, could take people only so far: "The heart has its reasons of which the reason knows nothing." As a Christian, faith was the final step: "The heart feels God, not the reason. This is what constitutes faith: God experienced by the heart, not by the reason."[25]

In retrospect, it is obvious that Pascal failed to achieve his goal of uniting Christianity and science. Increasingly, the gap between science and traditional religion grew wider as Europe continued along its path of secularization. Of course, traditional religions were not eliminated, nor is there any evidence that churches had yet lost their followers. That would happen later. Nevertheless, more and more of the intellectual, social, and political elites began to act on the basis of secular rather than religious assumptions.

The Spread of Scientific Knowledge

During the seventeenth century, scientific learning and investigation began to increase dramatically. Major universities in Europe established new chairs of science, especially in medicine. Royal and princely patronage of individual scientists became an international phenomenon. The king of Denmark constructed an astronomical observatory for Tycho Brahe, Emperor Rudolf II hired Brahe and Kepler as imperial mathematicians, and the grand duke of Tuscany appointed Galileo to a similar post. Of greater importance to the work of science, however, was the emergence of new learned societies and journals that enabled the new scientists to communicate their ideas to each other and to disseminate them to a wider, literate public.

The Scientific Societies

The first of these scientific societies appeared in Italy, but those of England and France were ultimately of more significance. The English Royal Society evolved out of informal gatherings of scientists at London and Oxford in the 1640s, although it did not receive a formal charter from King Charles II until 1662. The French Royal Academy of Sciences also arose out of informal scientific meetings in Paris during the 1650s. In 1666, Louis XIV formally recognized the

Louis XIV and Colbert Visit the Academy of Sciences. In the seventeenth century, individual scientists received royal and princely patronage, and a number of learned societies were established. In France, Louis XIV, urged on by his minister Colbert, gave formal recognition to the French Academy in 1666. In this painting by Henri Testelin, Louis XIV is shown seated, surrounded by Colbert and members of the French Royal Academy of Sciences.

group. The French Academy received abundant state support and remained under government control; its members were appointed and paid salaries by the state. In contrast, the Royal Society of England received little government encouragement, and its fellows simply co-opted new members.

Early on, both the English and the French scientific societies formally emphasized the practical value of scientific research. The Royal Society created a committee to investigate technological improvements for industry; the French Academy collected tools and machines. This concern with the practical benefits of science proved short-lived, however, as both societies came to focus their primary interest on theoretical work in mechanics and astronomy. The construction of observatories at Paris in 1667 and at Greenwich, England, in 1675 greatly facilitated research in astronomy by both groups. The French Academy, however, since it was controlled by the state, was forced by the war minister of France, the marquis de Louvois, to continue its practical work to benefit both "the king and the state." The French example was especially important as a model for the scientific societies established in neighboring Germany. German princes and city governments encouraged the foundation of small-scale scientific societies of their own. Most of them were sponsored by governments and were mainly devoted to the betterment of the state. Although both the English and the French societies made useful contributions to scientific knowledge in the second half of the seventeenth century, their true significance arose from their example that science should proceed as a cooperative venture.

Scientific journals furthered this concept of cooperation. The French *Journal des Savants,* published weekly beginning in 1665, printed results of experiments as well as general scientific knowledge. Its format appealed to both scientists and the educated public interested in the new

The Royal Observatory at Greenwich. To facilitate their astronomical investigations, both the English and the French constructed observatories such as the one pictured here, which was built at Greenwich, England, in 1675. Here the royal astronomer works at the table while his two assistants make observations.

CHRONOLOGY

The Impact of the Scientific Revolution: Important Works

Bacon, *The Great Instauration*	1620
Descartes, *Discourse on Method*	1637
Pascal, *Pensées*	1669
Spinoza, *Ethics Demonstrated in the Geometrical Manner*	1677

science. The *Philosophical Transactions* of the Royal Society, however, also initiated in 1665, published papers of its members and learned correspondence and was aimed at practicing scientists. It became a prototype for the scholarly journals of later learned and academic societies and a crucial instrument for circulating news of scientific and academic activities.

Science and Society

The importance of science in the history of modern Western civilization is usually taken for granted. No doubt the Industrial Revolution of the nineteenth century provided tangible proof of the effectiveness of science and ensured its victory over Western minds. But how did science become such an integral part of Western culture in the seventeenth and eighteenth centuries? Recent research has stressed that one cannot simply assert that people perceived that science was a rationally superior system. Two important social factors, however, might explain the relatively rapid acceptance of the new science.

It has been argued that the literate mercantile and propertied elites of Europe were attracted to the new science because it offered new ways to exploit resources for profit. Some of the early scientists made it easier for these groups to accept the new ideas by showing how they could be applied directly to specific industrial and technological needs. Galileo, for example, consciously sought an alliance between science and the material interests of the educated elite when he assured his listeners that the science of mechanics would be quite useful "when it becomes necessary to build bridges or other structures over water, something occurring mainly in affairs of great importance." At the same time, Galileo stressed that science was fit for the "minds of the wise" and not for "the shallow minds of the common people." This made science part of the high culture of Europe's wealthy elites at a time when that culture was being increasingly separated from the popular culture of the lower classes (see Chapter 17).

It has also been argued that political interests used the new scientific conception of the natural world to bolster social stability. One scholar has recently argued that "no single event in the history of early modern Europe more profoundly shaped the integration of the new science into Western culture than did the English Revolution (1640–1660)."[26] Fed by their millenarian expectations that the end of the world would come and usher in a thousand-year reign of the saints, Puritan reformers felt it was important to reform and renew their society. They seized on the new science as a socially useful instrument to accomplish this goal. The Puritan Revolution's role in the acceptance of science, however, stemmed even more from the reaction to the radicalism spawned by the revolutionary ferment. The upheavals of the Puritan Revolution gave rise to groups, such as the Levellers, Diggers, and Ranters, who advocated not only radical political ideas but also a new radical science based on Paracelsus and the natural magic associated with the Hermetic tradition. The chaplain of the New Model Army said that the radicals wanted "the philosophy of Hermes, revived by the Paracelsian schools." The propertied and educated elites responded vigorously to these challenges to the established order by supporting the new mechanistic science and appealing to the material benefits of science. Hence the founders of the Royal Society were men who wanted to pursue an experimental science that would remain detached from radical reforms of church and state. Although willing to make changes, they now viewed those changes in terms of an increase in food production and commerce. By the eighteenth century, the Newtonian world-machine had been readily accepted, and Newtonian science would soon be applied to trade and industry by a mercantile and landed elite that believed that they "could retain a social order that primarily rewarded and enriched themselves while still improving the human condition."

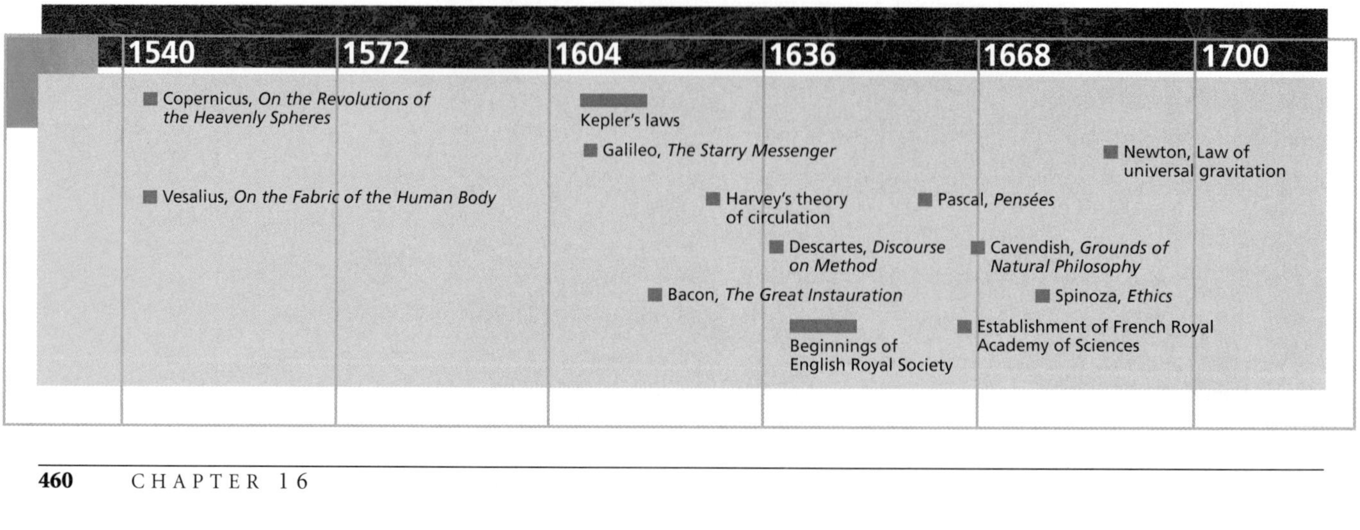

Conclusion

The Scientific Revolution represents a major turning point in modern Western civilization. In the Scientific Revolution, the Western world overthrew the medieval, Ptolemaic-Aristotelian worldview and arrived at a new conception of the universe: the sun at the center, the planets as material bodies revolving around the sun in elliptical orbits, and an infinite rather than finite world. With the changes in the conception of "heaven" came changes in the conception of "earth." The work of Bacon and Descartes left Europeans with the separation of mind and matter and the belief that by using only reason they could in fact understand and dominate the world of nature. The development of a scientific method furthered the work of scientists, while the creation of scientific societies and learned journals spread its results. Although traditional churches stubbornly resisted the new ideas and a few intellectuals pointed to some inherent flaws, nothing was able to halt the replacement of the traditional ways of thinking by new ways of thinking that created a more fundamental break with the past than that represented by the breakup of Christian unity in the Reformation.

The Scientific Revolution forced Europeans to change their conception of themselves. At first, some were appalled and even frightened by its implications. Formerly, humans on earth had been at the center of the universe. Now the earth was only a tiny planet revolving around a sun that was itself only a speck in a boundless universe. Most people remained optimistic despite the apparent blow to human dignity. After all, had Newton not demonstrated that the universe was a great machine governed by natural laws? Newton had found one—the universal law of gravitation. Could others not find other laws? Were there not natural laws governing every aspect of human endeavor that could be found by the new scientific method? Thus the Scientific Revolution leads us logically to the Enlightenment in the eighteenth century.

Notes

1. Quoted in Alan G. R. Smith, *Science and Society in the Sixteenth and Seventeenth Centuries* (London, 1972), p. 59.
2. Edward MacCurdy, *The Notebooks of Leonardo da Vinci* (London, 1948), vol. 1, p. 634.
3. Ibid., p. 636.
4. Frances Yates, *Giordano Bruno and the Hermetic Tradition* (New York, 1964), p. 448.
5. Ibid., p. 450.
6. Quoted in Smith, *Science and Society,* p. 97.
7. Logan P. Smith, *Life and Letters of Sir Henry Wotton* (Oxford, 1907), vol. 1, pp. 486–487.
8. Quoted in John H. Randall, *The Making of the Modern Mind* (Boston, 1926), p. 234.
9. Quoted in Smith, *Science and Society,* p. 124.
10. Quoted in Betty J. Dobbs, *The Foundations of Newton's Alchemy* (Cambridge, 1975), pp. 13–14.
11. Jolande Jacobi, ed., *Paracelsus: Selected Writings* (New York, 1965), pp. 5–6.
12. Ibid., p. 21.
13. Quoted in Londa Schiebinger, *The Mind Has No Sex? Women in the Origins of Modern Science* (Cambridge, Mass., 1989), pp. 52–53.
14. Ibid., p. 85.
15. Quoted in Phyllis Stock, *Better than Rubies: A History of Women's Education* (New York, 1978), p. 16.
16. René Descartes, *Philosophical Writings,* ed. and trans. Norman K. Smith (New York, 1958), p. 95.
17. Ibid., pp. 118–119.
18. Francis Bacon, *The Great Instauration,* trans. Jerry Weinberger (Arlington Heights, Ill., 1989), pp. 2, 8, 16, 21.
19. Descartes, *Discourse on Method,* in *Philosophical Writings,* p. 75.
20. Stillman Drake, ed. and trans., *Discoveries and Opinions of Galileo* (New York, 1957), p. 182.
21. Benedict de Spinoza, *Ethics,* trans. R. H. M. Elwes (New York, 1955), pp. 75–76.
22. Ibid., p. 76.
23. Spinoza, *Letters,* quoted in Randall, *The Making of the Modern Mind,* p. 247.
24. Blaise Pascal, *Pensées,* trans. J. M. Cohen (Harmondsworth, England, 1961), p. 100.
25. Ibid., pp. 31, 52–53, 164, 165.
26. Margaret C. Jacob, *The Cultural Meaning of the Scientific Revolution* (New York, 1988), p. 73.

Suggestions for Further Reading

Four general surveys of the entire Scientific Revolution are A. G. R. Smith, *Science and Society in the Sixteenth and Seventeenth Centuries* (London, 1972); J. R. Jacob, *The Scientific Revolution: Aspirations and Achievements, 1500–1700* (Atlantic Highlands, N.J., 1998); S. Shapin, *The Scientific Revolution* (Chicago, 1996); and J. Henry, *The Scientific Revolution and the Origins of Modern Science* (New York, 1997). Also of much value is A. G. Debus, *Man and Nature in the Renaissance* (Cambridge, 1978), which covers the mid-fifteenth through mid-seventeenth centuries. On the relationship of magic to the beginnings of the Scientific Revolution, see the pioneering works by F. Yates, *Giordano Bruno and the Hermetic Tradition* (New York, 1964) and *The Rosicrucian Enlightenment* (London, 1975).

A good introduction to the transformation from the late medieval to the early modern worldview is A. Koyré, *From the Closed World to the Infinite Universe* (New York, 1958). On the important figures of the revolution in astronomy, see E. Rosen, *Copernicus and the Scientific Revolution* (New York, 1984); M. Sharratt, *Galileo: Decisive Innovator* (Oxford, 1994); S. Drake, *Galileo, Pioneer Scientist* (Toronto, 1990); M. Casper, *Johannes Kepler,* trans. C. D. Hellman (London, 1959), the standard biography; and R. S. Westfall, *The Life of Isaac Newton* (New York, 1993). On Newton's relationship to alchemy, see the valuable study by B. J. Dobbs, *The Foundations of Newton's Alchemy* (Cambridge, 1975), and M. White, *Isaac Newton: The Last Sorcerer* (Reading, Mass., 1997).

The worldview of Paracelsus and his followers can be examined in A. G. Debus, *The Chemical Philosophy: Paracelsian Science and Medicine in the Sixteenth and Seventeenth Centuries,* 2 vols. (New York, 1977). The standard biography of Vesalius is C. D. O'Malley, *Andreas Vesalius of Brussels, 1514–1564* (Berkeley, Calif., 1964). The work of Harvey is discussed in G. Whitteridge, *William Harvey and the Circulation of the Blood* (London, 1971).

The importance of Francis Bacon in the early development of science is underscored in P. Zagorin, *Francis Bacon* (Princeton, N.J., 1998). A good introduction to the work of Descartes can be found in G. Radis-Lewis, *Descartes: A Biography* (Ithaca, N.Y., 1998). The standard biography of Spinoza in English is S. Hampshire, *Spinoza* (New York, 1961).

For histories of the scientific academies, see R. Hahn, *The Anatomy of a Scientific Institution: The Paris Academy of Sciences, 1666–1803* (Berkeley, Calif., 1971), and M. Purver, *The Royal Society, Concept and Creation* (London, 1967).

On the subject of women and early modern science, see the comprehensive and highly informative work by L. Schiebinger, *The Mind Has No Sex? Women in the Origins of Modern Science* (Cambridge, Mass., 1989). See also C. Merchant, *The Death of Nature: Women, Ecology, and the Scientific Revolution* (San Francisco, 1980). There is a chapter on Maria Sibylla Merian in N. Davis, *Women on the Margins* (Cambridge, Mass., 1995). The social and political context for the triumph of science in the seventeenth and eighteenth centuries is examined in M. Jacobs, *The Cultural Meaning of the Scientific Revolution* (New York, 1988) and *The Newtonians and the English Revolution, 1689–1720* (Ithaca, N.Y., 1976).

For additional reading, go to InfoTrac College Edition, your online research library at http://web1.infotrac-college.com

Enter the search term *Copernicus* using Key Terms.

Enter the search term *Galileo not Jupiter* using Key Terms.

Enter the search term *Isaac Newton* using Key Terms.

Enter the search term *René Descartes* using Key Terms.

CHAPTER

17

The Eighteenth Century: An Age of Enlightenment

Réunion des Musées Nationaux/Art Resource, NY

CHAPTER OUTLINE

- The Enlightenment
- Culture and Society in the Enlightenment
- Religion and the Churches
- Conclusion

FOCUS QUESTIONS

- What intellectual developments led to the emergence of the Enlightenment?
- Who were the leading figures of the Enlightenment, and what were their main contributions?
- In what type of social environment did the philosophes thrive, and what role did women play in that environment?
- What innovations in art, music, and literature occurred in the eighteenth century?
- How did popular culture and popular religion differ from high culture and institutional religion in the eighteenth century?
- What is the relationship between the Scientific Revolution and the Enlightenment?

THE EARTH-SHATTERING WORK of the "natural philosophers" in the Scientific Revolution had affected only a relatively small number of Europe's educated elite. In the eighteenth century, this changed dramatically as a group of intellectuals known as the philosophes popularized the ideas of the Scientific Revolution and used them to undertake a dramatic reexamination of all aspects of life. In Paris, the cultural capital of Europe, women took the lead in bringing together groups of men and women to discuss the new ideas of the philosophes. At her fashionable home in the Rue Saint-Honoré, Marie-Thérèse de Geoffrin, the wife of a wealthy merchant, held sway over gatherings that became the talk of France and even Europe. Distinguished foreigners, including a future king of Sweden and a future king of Poland, competed to receive invitations. When Madame Geoffrin made a visit to Vienna, she was so well received that she exclaimed, "I am better known here than a couple of yards from my own house." Madame Geoffrin was an amiable but firm hostess who allowed wide-ranging discussions as long as they remained in good taste. When she found that artists and philosophers did not mix particularly well (the artists were high-strung and the philosophers talked too much), she set up separate meetings. Artists were invited only on Mondays; philosophers, on Wednesdays. These gatherings were among the many avenues for the spread of the ideas of the philosophes. And those ideas had such a widespread impact on their society that historians ever since have called the eighteenth century the Age of Enlightenment.

For most of the philosophes, "enlightenment" included the rejection of traditional Christianity. The religious wars and intolerance of the sixteenth and seventeenth centuries had so alienated intellectuals that they were open and even eager to embrace the new ideas of the Scientific Revolution. Whereas the great scientists of the seventeenth century believed that their work exalted God, the intellectuals of the eighteenth century read those scientific conclusions a different way and increasingly turned their backs on Christian orthodoxy. Consequently, European intellectual life in the eighteenth century was marked by the emergence of the secularization that has characterized the modern Western mentality ever since. Ironically, at the same time that reason and materialism were beginning to replace faith and worship, a great outburst of religious sensibility manifested itself in music and art. Clearly, the growing secularization of the eighteenth century had not yet captured the hearts and minds of all European intellectuals and artists.

The Enlightenment

In 1784, the German philosopher Immanuel Kant defined the Enlightenment as "man's leaving his self-caused immaturity." Whereas earlier periods had been handicapped by the inability to "use one's intelligence without the guidance of another," Kant proclaimed as the motto of the Enlightenment: "Dare to know! Have the courage to use your own intelligence!" The eighteenth-century Enlightenment was a movement of intellectuals who dared to know. They were greatly impressed with the accomplishments of the Scientific Revolution, and when they used the word *reason*—one of their favorite words—they were advocating the application of the scientific method to the understanding of all life. All institutions and all systems of thought were subject to the rational, scientific way of thinking if only people would free themselves from the shackles of old, worthless traditions, especially religious ones. If Isaac Newton could discover the natural laws regulating the world of nature, they too by using reason could find the laws that governed human society. This belief in turn led them to hope that they could make progress toward a better society than the one they had inherited. *Reason, natural law, hope, progress*—these were common words in the heady atmosphere of the eighteenth century.

The Paths to Enlightenment

The intellectuals of the eighteenth century were especially influenced by the revolutionary thinkers of the seventeenth century. What were the major intellectual changes that culminated in the intellectual movement of the Enlightenment?

THE POPULARIZATION OF SCIENCE

Although the philosophes of the eighteenth century were much influenced by the scientific ideas of the seventeenth, they did not always acquire this knowledge directly from the original sources. Newton's *Principia* was not an easy book to read or comprehend. Scientific ideas were spread to ever-widening circles of educated Europeans not so much by scientists themselves as by popularizers. Especially important as the direct link between the Scientific Revolution of the seventeenth century and the philosophes of the eighteenth was Bernard de Fontenelle (1657–1757), secretary of the French Royal Academy of Science from 1691 to 1741.

Although Fontenelle neither performed any scientific experiments nor made any scientific discoveries, he possessed a deep knowledge of all the scientific work of earlier centuries and his own time. Moreover, he was able to communicate that body of scientific knowledge in a clear and even witty fashion that appealed to his upper-class audiences in a meaningful way. One of his most successful books, *Plurality of Worlds*, was actually presented in the form of an intimate conversation between a lady aristocrat and her lover who are engaged in conversation under the stars. What are they discussing? "Tell me," she exclaims, "about these stars of yours." Her lover proceeds to tell her of the tremendous advances in cosmology after the foolish errors of their forebears:

> There came on the scene a certain German, one Copernicus, who made short work of all those various circles, all those solid skies, which the ancients had pictured to themselves. The former he abolished; the latter, he broke in pieces. Fired with the noble zeal of a true astronomer, he took the earth and spun it very far away from the center of the universe, where it had been installed, and in that center he put the sun, which had a far better title to the honor.[1]

In the course of two evenings under the stars, the lady learned the basic fundamentals of the new mechanistic universe. So too did scores of the educated elite of Europe. What bliss it was to learn the "truth" in such lighthearted fashion.

Thanks to Fontenelle, science was no longer the monopoly of experts but part of literature. He was especially fond of downplaying the religious backgrounds of the seventeenth-century scientists. Himself a skeptic, Fontenelle contributed to the growing skepticism toward

The Popularization of Science: Fontenelle and the *Plurality of Worlds*. The most important popularizer of the ideas of the Scientific Revolution was Bernard de Fontenelle, who, though not a scientist himself, had much knowledge of scientific matters. In this frontispiece illustration to his *Plurality of Worlds,* an aristocratic lady listens while her astronomer-friend explains the details of the new cosmology.

religion at the end of the seventeenth century by portraying the churches as enemies of scientific progress.

A NEW SKEPTICISM

The great scientists of the seventeenth century, including Kepler, Galileo, and Newton, had pursued their work in a spirit of exalting God, not undermining Christianity. But as scientific knowledge spread, more and more educated men and women began to question religious truths and values. Skepticism about religion and a growing secularization of thought were especially evident in the work of Pierre Bayle (1647–1706), who remained a Protestant while becoming a leading critic of traditional religious attitudes. Bayle attacked superstition, religious intolerance, and dogmatism. In his view, compelling people to believe a particular set of religious ideas (as Louis XIV was doing at the time in Bayle's France) was wrong. It simply created hypocrites and in itself was contrary to what religion should be about. Individual conscience should determine one's actions. Bayle argued for complete religious toleration, maintaining that the existence of many religions would benefit rather than harm the state.

Bayle was one of a number of intellectuals who believed that the new rational principles of textual criticism should be applied to the Bible as well as secular documents. In his most famous work, the *Historical and Critical Dictionary,* Bayle demonstrated the results of his own efforts with a famous article on the Israelite King David. Undermining the traditional picture of the heroic David, he portrayed the king as a sensual, treacherous, cruel, and basically evil man. Bayle's *Dictionary,* which attacked traditional religious practices and heroes, was well known to eighteenth-century philosophes. One critic regarded it as the "Bible of the eighteenth century."

THE IMPACT OF TRAVEL LITERATURE

Skepticism about both Christianity and European culture itself was nourished by travel reports. In the course of the seventeenth century, traders, missionaries, medical practitioners, and explorers began to publish an increasing number of travel books that gave accounts of many different cultures. Then, too, the new geographical adventures of the eighteenth century, especially the discovery of the Pacific island of Tahiti and of New Zealand and Australia by James

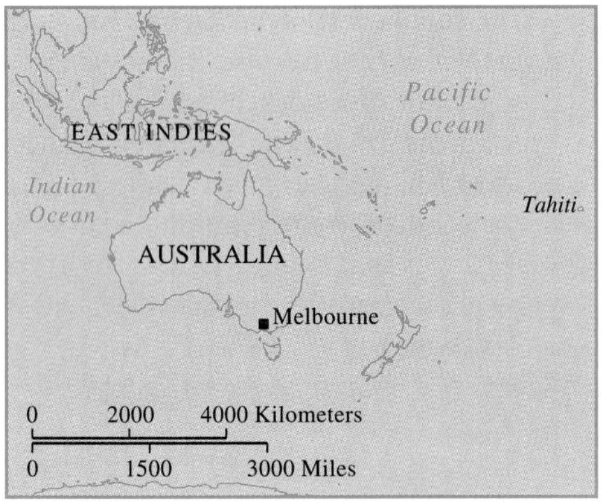

Pacific Discoveries

Cook, aroused much enthusiasm. Cook's *Travels,* an account of his journey, became a best-seller. Educated Europeans responded to these accounts of lands abroad in different ways.

For some intellectuals, the existence of exotic peoples, such as the natives of Tahiti, presented an image of a "natural man" who was far happier than many Europeans. One intellectual wrote:

> The life of savages is so simple, and our societies are such complicated machines! The Tahitian is close to the origin of the world, while the European is closer to its old age.... [The Tahitians] understand nothing about our manners or our laws, and they are bound to see in them nothing but shackles disguised in a hundred different ways. Those shackles could only provoke the indignation and scorn of creatures in whom the most profound feeling is a love of liberty.[2]

The idea of the "noble savage" would play an important role in the political work of some philosophes.

The travel literature of the seventeenth and eighteenth centuries also led to the realization that there were highly developed civilizations with different customs in other parts of the world. China was especially singled out. One German university professor praised Confucian morality as superior to the intolerant attitudes of Christianity. Some European intellectuals began to evaluate their own civilization relative to others. What had seemed to be practices grounded in reason now appeared to be matters of custom. Certainties about European practices gave way to cultural relativism.

Cultural relativism was accompanied by religious skepticism. As these travel accounts made clear, the Christian perception of God was merely one of many. Some people were devastated by this revelation: "Some complete their demoralization by extensive travel, and lose whatever shreds of religion remained to them. Every day they see a new religion, new customs, new rites."[3]

THE LEGACY OF LOCKE AND NEWTON

The intellectual inspiration for the Enlightenment came primarily from two Englishmen, Isaac Newton and John Locke, acknowledged by the philosophes as great minds. Newton was frequently singled out for praise as the "greatest and rarest genius that ever rose for the ornament and instruction of the species." One English poet declared: "Nature and Nature's Laws lay hid in Night; God said, 'Let Newton be,' and all was Light." Enchanted by the grand design of the Newtonian world-machine, the intellectuals of the Enlightenment were convinced that by following Newton's rules of reasoning, they could discover the natural laws that governed politics, economics, justice, religion, and the arts. The world and everything in it were like a giant machine.

John Locke's theory of knowledge especially influenced the philosophes. In his *Essay Concerning Human Understanding,* written in 1690, Locke denied Descartes's belief in innate ideas. Instead, argued Locke, every person was born with a *tabula rasa,* a blank mind:

> Let us then suppose the mind to be, as we say, white paper, void of all characters, without any ideas. How comes it to be furnished? Whence comes it by that vast store which the busy and boundless fancy of man has painted on it with an almost endless variety? Whence has it all the materials of reason and knowledge? To this I answer, in one word, from experience.... Our observation, employed either about external sensible objects or about the internal operations of our minds perceived and reflected on by ourselves, is that which supplies our understanding with all the materials of thinking.[4]

Our knowledge, then, is derived from our environment, not from heredity; from reason, not from faith. Locke's philosophy implied that people were molded by their environment, by the experiences that they received through their senses from their surrounding world. By changing the environment and subjecting people to proper influences, they could be changed and a new society created. And how should the environment be changed? Newton had already paved the way by showing how reason enabled enlightened people to discover the natural laws to which all institutions should conform. No wonder the philosophes were enamored of Newton and Locke. Taken together, their ideas seemed to offer the hope of a "brave new world" built on reason.

The Philosophes and Their Ideas

The intellectuals of the Enlightenment were known by the French term *philosophes,* although not all of them were French and few were philosophers in the strict sense of the word. They were literary people, professors, journalists, statesmen, economists, political scientists, and above all, social reformers. They came from both the nobility and the middle class, and a few even stemmed from lower origins. Although it was a truly international and cosmopolitan movement, the Enlightenment also enhanced the dominant role being played by French culture. Paris was its recognized capital, and most of the leaders of the Enlightenment were French. The French philosophes in turn affected intellectuals elsewhere and created a movement that engulfed the entire Western world, including the British and Spanish colonies in America (see Map 17.1).

Although the philosophes faced different political circumstances depending on the country in which they lived, they shared common bonds as part of a truly international movement. Although they were called philosophers, what did philosophy mean to them? The role of philosophy was to change the world, not just discuss it. As one writer said, the philosophe is one who "applies himself to the study of society with the purpose of making his kind better and happier." To the philosophes, rationalism did not mean the creation of a grandiose system of thought to explain all things. Reason was scientific method, and it meant an appeal to facts and experience. A spirit of rational criticism was to be applied to everything, including religion and politics.

The philosophes' call for freedom of expression is a reminder that their work was done in an atmosphere of censorship. The philosophes were not free to write whatever they chose. State censors decided what could be published, and protests from any number of government bodies could result in the seizure of books and the imprisonment of their authors, publishers, and sellers.

The philosophes found ways to get around state censorship. Some published under pseudonyms or anonymously or abroad, especially in Holland. The use of double meanings, such as talking about the Persians when they meant the French, became standard procedure for many. Books were also published and circulated secretly or in manuscript form to avoid the censors. As frequently happens with attempted censorship, the government's announcement that a book had been burned often made the book more desirable and more popular.

Map 17.1 The Enlightenment in Europe. "Have the courage to use your own intelligence!" Kant's words epitomize the role of the individual in using reason to understand all aspects of life—the natural world and the sphere of human nature, behavior, and institutions. ■ Which countries or regions were at the center of the Enlightenment, and what reasons could account for peripheral regions being less involved?

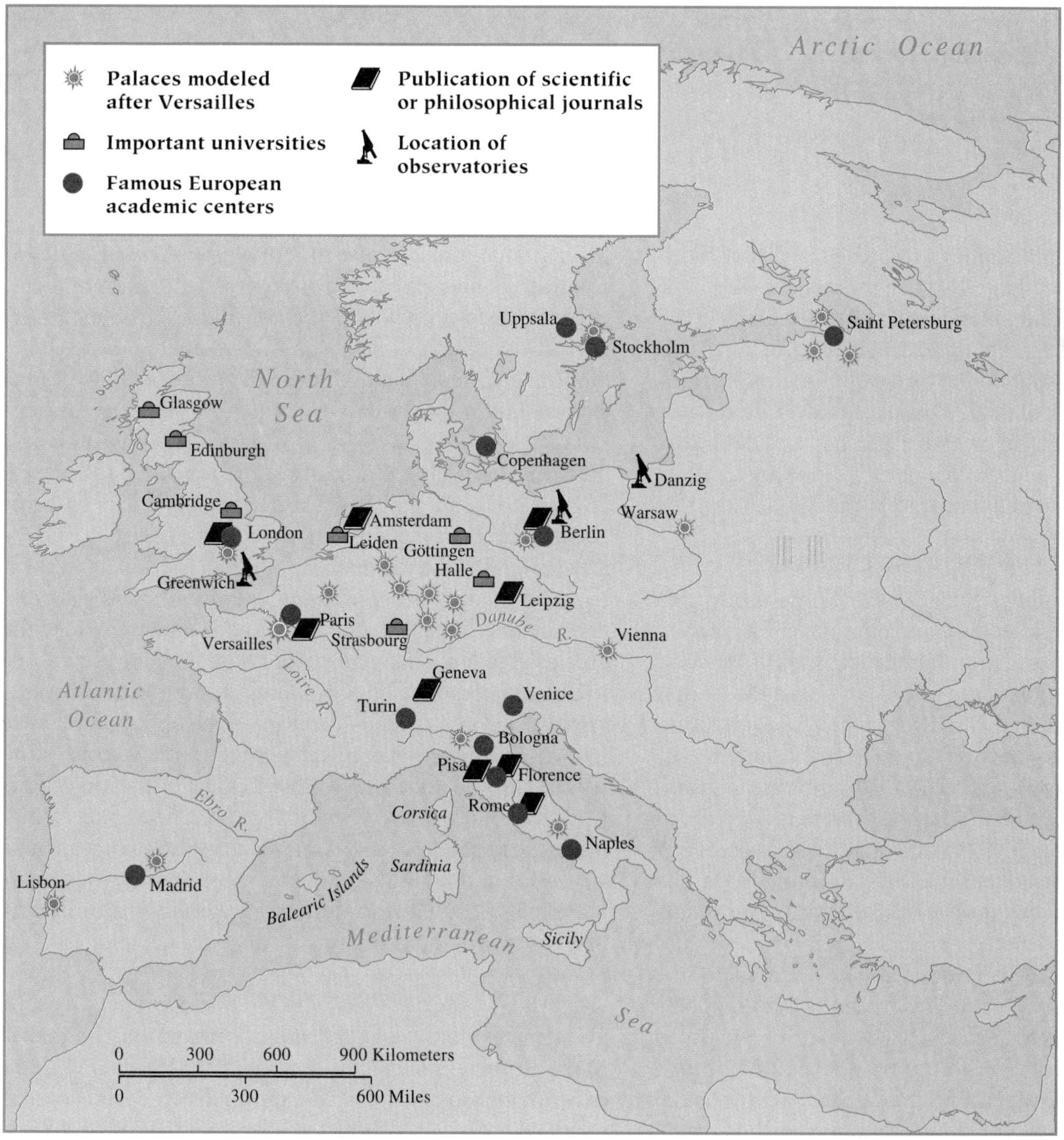

The Separation of Powers

The Enlightenment affected the new world of America as much as it did the old world of Europe. American philosophes were well aware of the ideas of European Enlightenment thinkers. This selection from Montesquieu's *Spirit of the Laws* enunciates the "separation of powers" doctrine.

Montesquieu, *The Spirit of the Laws*

Of the Constitution of England

In every government there are three sorts of power: the legislative; the executive in respect to things dependent on the law of nations; and the executive in regard to matters that depend on the civil law.

By virtue of the first, the prince or magistrate enacts temporary or perpetual laws, and amends or abrogates those that have been already enacted. By the second, he makes peace or war, sends or receives embassies, establishes the public security, and provides against invasions. By the third, he punishes criminals, or determines the disputes that arise between individuals. The latter we shall call the judiciary power, and the other simply the executive power of the state.

The political liberty of the subject is a tranquillity of mind arising from the opinion each person has of his safety. In order to have this liberty, it is requisite the government be so constituted as one man need not be afraid of another.

When the legislative and executive powers are united in the same person, or in the same body of magistrates, there can be no liberty; because apprehensions may arise, lest the same monarch or senate should enact tyrannical laws, to execute them in a tyrannical manner.

Again, there is no liberty, if the judiciary power be not separated from the legislative and executive. Were it joined with the legislative, the life and liberty of the subject would be exposed to arbitrary control; for the judge would be then the legislator. Were it joined to the executive power, the judge might behave with violence and oppression.

There would be an end of everything, were the same man or the same body, whether of the nobles or of the people, to exercise those three powers, that of enacting laws, that of executing the public resolutions, and of trying the causes of individuals.

Although the philosophes constituted a kind of "family circle" bound together by common intellectual bonds, they often disagreed. Spanning almost an entire century, the Enlightenment evolved over time, with each succeeding generation becoming more radical as it built on the contributions of the previous one. A few people, however, dominated the landscape completely, and we might best begin our survey of the ideas of the philosophes by looking at three French giants—Montesquieu, Voltaire, and Diderot.

MONTESQUIEU AND POLITICAL THOUGHT

Charles de Secondat, the baron de Montesquieu (1689–1755), came from the French nobility. He received a classical education and then studied law. In his first work, the *Persian Letters,* published in 1721, he used the format of two Persians supposedly traveling in western Europe and sending their impressions back home to enable him to criticize French institutions, especially the Catholic church and the French monarchy. Much of the program of the French Enlightenment is contained in this work: the attack on traditional religion, the advocacy of religious toleration, the denunciation of slavery, and the use of reason to liberate human beings from their prejudices.

Montesquieu's most famous work, *The Spirit of the Laws,* was published in 1748. This treatise was a comparative study of governments in which Montesquieu attempted to apply the scientific method to the social and political arena to ascertain the "natural laws" governing the social relationships of human beings. Montesquieu distinguished three basic kinds of governments: republics, suitable for small states and based on citizen involvement; monarchy, appropriate for middle-sized states and grounded in the ruling class's adherence to law; and despotism, apt for large empires and dependent on fear to inspire obedience. Montesquieu used England as an example of the second category, and it was his praise and analysis of England's constitution that led to his most far-reaching and lasting contribution to political thought—the importance of checks and balances created by means of a separation of powers (see the box above). He believed that England's system, with its separate executive, legislative, and judicial powers that served to limit and control each other, provided the greatest freedom and security for a state. In large part, Montesquieu misread the English situation and insisted on a separation of powers because he wanted the nobility of France (of which he was a member) to play an active role in the running of the French government. The translation of his work into English two years after publication ensured that it would be read by American philosophes, such as Benjamin Franklin, James Madison, John Adams, Alexander Hamilton, and Thomas Jefferson, who incorporated its principles into the U.S. Constitution (see Chapter 19).

VOLTAIRE AND THE ENLIGHTENMENT

The greatest figure of the Enlightenment was François-Marie Arouet, known simply as Voltaire (1694–1778). Son of a prosperous middle-class family from Paris, Voltaire received a classical education typical of Jesuit schools.

The Attack on Religious Intolerance

Voltaire's lucid prose, biting satire, and clever wit caused his works to be widely read and all the more influential. These two selections present different sides of Voltaire's attack on religious intolerance. The first is from a straightforward treatise, *The Ignorant Philosopher,* and the second is from his only real literary masterpiece, the novel *Candide,* where he uses humor to make the same fundamental point about religious intolerance.

Voltaire, The Ignorant Philosopher

The contagion of fanaticism then still subsists. . . . The author of the Treatise upon Toleration has not mentioned the shocking executions wherein so many unhappy victims perished in the valleys of Piedmont. He has passed over in silence the massacre of six hundred inhabitants of Valtelina, men, women, and children, who were murdered by the Catholics in the month of September, 1620. I will not say it was with the consent and assistance of the archbishop of Milan, Charles Borome, who was made a saint. Some passionate writers have averred this fact, which I am very far from believing; but I say, there is scarce any city or borough in Europe, where blood has not been spilt for religious quarrels; I say, that the human species has been perceptibly diminished, because women and girls were massacred as well as men; I say, that Europe would have had a third larger population, if there had been no theological disputes. In fine, I say, that so far from forgetting these abominable times, we should frequently take a view of them, to inspire an eternal horror for them; and that it is for our age to make reparation by toleration, for this long collection of crimes, which has taken place through the want of toleration, during sixteen barbarous centuries.

Let it not then be said, that there are no traces left of that shocking fanaticism, of the want of toleration; they are still everywhere to be met with, even in those countries that are esteemed the most humane. The Lutheran and Calvinist preachers, were they masters, would, perhaps, be as little inclined to pity, as obdurate, as insolent as they upbraid their antagonists with being.

Voltaire, Candide

At last he [Candide] approached a man who had just been addressing a big audience for a whole hour on the subject of charity. The orator peered at him and said:

"What is your business here? Do you support the Good Old Cause?"

"There is not effect without a cause," replied Candide modestly. "All things are necessarily connected and arranged for the best. It was my fate to be driven from Lady Cunégonde's presence and made to run the gauntlet, and now I have to beg my bread until I can earn it. Things should not have happened otherwise."

"Do you believe that the Pope is Antichrist, my friend?" said the minister.

"I have never heard anyone say so," replied Candide; "but whether he is or he isn't, I want some food."

"You don't deserve to eat," said the other. "Be off with you, you villain, you wretch! Don't come near me again or you'll suffer for it."

The minister's wife looked out of the window at that moment, and seeing a man who was not sure that the Pope was Antichrist, emptied over his head a chamber pot, which shows to what lengths ladies are driven by religious zeal.

Although he studied law, he wished to be a writer and achieved his first success as a playwright. By his mid-twenties, Voltaire had been hailed as the successor to Racine (see Chapter 15) for his tragedy *Œdipe* and his epic *Henriade* on his favorite king, Henry IV. His wit made him a darling of the Parisian intellectuals but also involved him in a quarrel with a dissolute nobleman that forced him to flee France and live in England for almost two years.

Well received in English literary and social circles, the young playwright was much impressed by England. His *Philosophic Letters on the English,* written in 1733, expressed a deep admiration of English life, especially its freedom of the press, its political freedom, and its religious toleration. In judging the English religious situation, he made the famous remark that "if there were just one religion in England, despotism would threaten, if there were two religions, they would cut each other's throats, but there are thirty religions, and they live together peacefully and happily." Although he clearly exaggerated the freedoms England possessed, in a roundabout way Voltaire had managed to criticize many of the ills oppressing France, especially royal absolutism and the lack of religious toleration and freedom of thought.

Upon his return to France, Voltaire's reputation as the author of the *Philosophic Letters* made it necessary for him to retire to Cirey, near France's eastern border, where he lived in semiseclusion on the estate of his mistress, Madame de Châtelet. He eventually settled on a magnificent estate at Ferney. Located in France near the Swiss border, Ferney gave Voltaire the freedom to write what he wished. By this time, through his writings, inheritance, and clever investments, Voltaire had become wealthy and now had the leisure to write an almost endless stream of pamphlets, novels, plays, letters, and histories.

Although he touched on all of the themes of importance to the philosophes, Voltaire was especially well known for his criticism of traditional religion and his strong attachment to the ideal of religious toleration (see the box above). He lent his prestige and skills as a polemicist to fight cases of

Mary Evans Picture Library

Voltaire. François-Marie Arouet, better known as Voltaire, achieved his first success as a playwright. A philosophe, Voltaire was well known for his criticism of traditional religion and his support of religious toleration.

intolerance in France. The most famous incident was the Calas affair. Jean Calas was a Protestant from Toulouse who was accused of murdering his own son to stop him from becoming a Catholic. Tortured to confess his guilt, Calas died shortly thereafter. An angry and indignant Voltaire published devastating broadsides that aroused public opinion and forced a retrial in which Calas was exonerated when it was proved that his son had actually committed suicide. The family was paid an indemnity, and Voltaire's appeals for toleration appeared all the more reasonable. In 1763, he penned his *Treatise on Toleration,* in which he argued that religious toleration had created no problems for England and Holland and reminded governments that "all men are brothers under God." As he grew older, Voltaire became ever more strident in his denunciations. "Crush the infamous thing," he thundered repeatedly—the infamous thing being religious fanaticism, intolerance, and superstition.

Throughout his life, Voltaire championed not only religious tolerance but also deism, a religious outlook shared by most other philosophes. Deism was built on the Newtonian world-machine, which implied the existence of a mechanic (God) who had created the universe. Voltaire said: "In the opinion that there is a God, there are difficulties, but in the contrary opinion there are absurdities." To Voltaire and most other philosophes, God had no direct involvement in the world he had created and allowed it to run according to its own natural laws. God did not extend grace or answer prayers as Christians liked to believe. Jesus might be a "good fellow," as Voltaire called him, but he was not divine, as Christianity claimed.

DIDEROT AND THE *ENCYCLOPEDIA*

Denis Diderot (1713–1784), the son of a skilled craftsman from eastern France, became a freelance writer so that he could study many subjects and read in many languages. One of his favorite topics was Christianity, which he condemned as fanatical and unreasonable. As he grew older, his literary attacks on Christianity grew more vicious. Of all religions, he maintained, Christianity was the worst, "the most absurd and the most atrocious in its dogma" (see the box on p. 471). Near the end of his life, he argued for an essentially materialistic conception of life: "This world is only a mass of molecules."

Diderot's most famous contribution to the Enlightenment was the twenty-eight-volume *Encyclopedia, or Classified Dictionary of the Sciences, Arts, and Trades,* that he edited and called the "great work of his life." Its purpose, according to Diderot, was to "change the general way of thinking." It did precisely that in becoming a major weapon of the philosophes' crusade against the old French society. The contributors included many philosophes who expressed their major concerns. They attacked religious superstition and advocated toleration as well as a program for social,

Réunion des Musées Nationaux/Art Resource, NY

Denis Diderot. Editor of the *Encyclopedia,* Diderot was a major figure in propagating the ideas of the French philosophes. He had diverse interests and penned an incredible variety of literary works. He is shown here in a portrait by Jean-Honoré Fragonard.

Diderot Questions Christian Sexual Standards

Denis Diderot was one of the boldest thinkers of the Enlightenment. In his *Supplement to the Voyage of Bougainville,* he constructed a dialogue between Orou, a Tahitian who symbolizes the wisdom of a philosophe, and a chaplain who defends Christian sexual mores. The dialogue gave Diderot the opportunity to criticize the practice of sexual chastity and monogamy.

■ *Denis Diderot,* Supplement to the Voyage of Bougainville

[Orou:] "You are young and healthy [speaking to the chaplain] and you have just had a good supper. He who sleeps alone sleeps badly; at night a man needs a woman at his side. Here is my wife and here are my daughters. Choose whichever one pleases you most, but if you would like to do me a favor, you will give your preference to my youngest girl, who has not yet had any children. . . ."

The chaplain replied that his religion, his holy orders, his moral standards and his sense of decency all prevented him from accepting Orou's invitation.

Orou answered: "I don't know what this thing is that you call religion, but I can only have a low opinion of it because it forbids you to partake of an innocent pleasure to which Nature, the sovereign mistress of us all, invites everybody. It seems to prevent you from bringing one of your fellow creatures into the world, from doing a favor asked of by a father, a mother and their children, from repaying the kindness of a host, and from enriching a nation by giving it an additional citizen. . . . Look at the distress you have caused to appear on the faces of these four women—they are afraid you have noticed some defect in them that arouses your distaste. . . ."

The Chaplain: "You don't understand—it's not that. They are all four of them equally beautiful. But there is my religion! My holy orders! . . . [God] spoke to our ancestors and gave them laws; he prescribed to them the way in which he wishes to be honored; he ordained that certain actions are good and others he forbade them to do as being evil."

Orou: "I see. And one of these evil actions which he has forbidden is that of a man who goes to bed with a woman or girl. But in that case, why did he make two sexes?"

The Chaplain: "In order that they might come together—but only when certain conditions are satisfied and only after certain initial ceremonies one man belongs to one woman and only to her; one woman belongs to one man and only to him."

Orou: "For their whole lives?"

The Chaplain: "For their whole lives. . . ."

Orou: "I find these strange precepts contrary to nature, and contrary to reason. . . . Furthermore, your laws seem to me to be contrary to the general order of things. For in truth is there anything so senseless as a precept that forbids us to heed the changing impulses that are inherent in our being, or commands that require a degree of constancy which is not possible, that violate the liberty of both male and female by chaining them perpetually to one another? . . . I don't know what your great workman [God] is, but I am very happy that he never spoke to our forefathers, and I hope that he never speaks to our children, for if he does, he may tell them the same foolishness, and they may be foolish enough to believe it."

legal, and political improvements that would lead to a society that was more cosmopolitan, more tolerant, more humane, and more reasonable. In later editions, the price of the *Encyclopedia* was drastically reduced, dramatically increasing its sales and making it available to doctors, clergy, teachers, lawyers, and even military officers. The ideas of the Enlightenment were spread even further as a result.

THE NEW "SCIENCE OF MAN"

The Enlightenment belief that Newton's scientific methods could be used to discover the natural laws underlying all areas of human life led to the emergence in the eighteenth century of what the philosophes called the "science of man," or what we would call the social sciences. In a number of areas, philosophes arrived at natural laws that they believed governed human actions. If these "natural laws" seem less than universal to us, it reminds us how much the philosophes were people of their times reacting to the conditions they faced. Nevertheless, their efforts did at least lay the foundations for the modern social sciences.

That a science of man was possible was a strong belief of the Scottish philosopher David Hume (1711–1776). An important figure in the history of philosophy, Hume has also been called "a pioneering social scientist." In his *Treatise on Human Nature,* which he subtitled "An Attempt to Introduce the Experimental Method of Reasoning into Moral Subjects," Hume argued that observation and reflection, grounded in "systematized common sense," made conceivable a "science of man." Careful examination of the experiences that constituted human life would lead to the knowledge of human nature that would make this science possible.

The Physiocrats and Adam Smith have been viewed as founders of the modern discipline of economics. The leader of the Physiocrats was François Quesnay (1694–1774), a highly successful French court physician. Quesnay and the Physiocrats claimed they would discover the natural economic laws that governed human society. Their first principle was that land constituted the only source of wealth and that wealth itself could be increased only by agriculture because all other economic activities were unproductive and sterile. Even the state's revenues should come from a single tax on the land rather than the hodgepodge of inequitable taxes and privileges currently in place. In stressing the economic primacy of agricultural production, the Physiocrats were rejecting the mercantilist emphasis on the significance of money—that is, gold and silver—as the primary determinants of wealth (see Chapter 14).

Their second major "natural law" of economics also represented a repudiation of mercantilism, specifically, its emphasis on a controlled economy for the benefit of the state. Instead the Physiocrats stressed that the existence of the natural economic forces of supply and demand made it imperative that individuals should be left free to pursue their own economic self-interest. In doing so, all of society would ultimately benefit. Consequently, they argued that the state should in no way interrupt the free play of natural economic forces by government regulation of the economy but rather should just leave it alone, a doctrine that subsequently became known by its French name, *laissez-faire* (noninterference; literally, to let people do as they choose).

The best statement of laissez-faire was made in 1776 by a Scottish philosopher, Adam Smith (1723–1790), when he published his famous *Inquiry into the Nature and Causes of the Wealth of Nations,* known simply as *The Wealth of Nations.* In the process of enunciating three of his basic principles of economics, Smith presented a strong attack on mercantilism. First, he condemned the mercantilist use of protective tariffs to protect home industries. If one country can supply another country with a product cheaper than the latter can make it, it is better to purchase than to produce it. To Smith, free trade was a fundamental economic principle. Smith's second principle was his labor theory of value. Like the Physiocrats, he claimed that gold and silver were not the source of a nation's true wealth, but unlike the Physiocrats, he did not believe that soil was either. Rather labor—the labor of individual farmers, artisans, and merchants—constituted the true wealth of a nation. Finally, like the Physiocrats, Smith believed that the state should not interfere in economic matters; indeed, he assigned to government only three basic functions: it should protect society from invasion (army), defend individuals from injustice and oppression (police), and keep up certain public works, such as roads and canals, that private individuals could not afford. Thus in Smith's view, the state should stay out of the lives of individuals. In emphasizing the economic liberty of the individual, the Physiocrats and Adam Smith laid the foundation for what became known in the nineteenth century as economic liberalism.

THE LATER ENLIGHTENMENT

By the late 1760s, a new generation of philosophes who had grown up with the worldview of the Enlightenment began to move beyond their predecessors' beliefs. Baron Paul d'Holbach (1723–1789), a wealthy German aristocrat who settled in Paris, preached a doctrine of strict atheism and materialism. In his *System of Nature,* written in 1770, he argued that everything in the universe consisted of matter in motion. Human beings were simply machines; God was a product of the human mind and was unnecessary for leading a moral life. People needed only reason to live in this world: "Let us persuade men to be just, beneficent, moderate, sociable; not because the gods demand it, but because they must please men. Let us advise them to abstain from vice and crimes; not because they will be punished in the other world, but because they will suffer for it in this."[5] Holbach shocked almost all of his fellow philosophes with his uncompromising atheism. Most intellectuals remained more comfortable with deism and feared the effect of atheism on society.

Marie-Jean de Condorcet (1743–1794), another French philosophe, made an exaggerated claim for progress. Condorcet was a victim of the turmoil of the French Revolution and wrote his chief work, *The Progress of the Human Mind,* while in hiding during the Reign of Terror (see Chapter 19). His survey of human history convinced him that humans had progressed through nine stages of history. Now, with the spread of science and reason, humans were about to enter the tenth stage, one of perfection, in which they will see that "there is no limit to the perfecting of the powers of man; that human perfectibility is in reality indefinite, that the progress of this perfectibility . . . has no other limit than the duration of the globe upon which nature has placed us." Shortly after composing this work, the prophet of humankind's perfection died in a French revolutionary prison.

ROUSSEAU AND THE SOCIAL CONTRACT

No one was more critical of the work of his predecessors than Jean-Jacques Rousseau (1712–1778). Born in Geneva, he spent his youth wandering about France and Italy holding various jobs. He went back to school for a while to study music and the classics (he could afford to do so after becoming the paid lover of an older woman). Eventually, he made his way to Paris, where he was introduced into the circles of the philosophes. He never really liked the social life of the cities, however, and frequently withdrew into long periods of solitude.

Rousseau's political beliefs were presented in two major works. In his *Discourse on the Origins of the Inequality of Mankind,* Rousseau began with humans in their primitive condition (or state of nature—see Chapter 15) where they were happy. There were no laws, no judges; all people were equal. But what had gone wrong?

> The first man who, having enclosed a piece of ground, thought of saying, This is mine, and found people simple enough to believe him, was the true founder of civil society. How many crimes, wars, murders; how much misery and horror the human race would have been spared if someone had pulled up the stakes and filled in the ditch, and cried to his fellow men: "Beware of listening to this impostor. You are lost if you forget that the fruits of the earth belong to everyone and that the earth itself belongs to no one!"[6]

In order to preserve their private property, people adopted laws and governors. In so doing, they rushed headlong not to liberty but into chains. "What then is to be done? Must societies be totally abolished? . . . Must we return again to the forest to live among bears?" No, civilized humans could

A Social Contract

Although Jean-Jacques Rousseau was one of the French philosophes, he has also been called "the father of Romanticism." His political ideas have proved extremely controversial. Though some people have hailed him as the prophet of democracy, others have labeled him an apologist for totalitarianism. This selection is taken from one of his most famous books, *The Social Contract.*

Jean-Jacques Rousseau, *The Social Contract*

■ *Book 1, Chapter 6: "The Social Pact"*

"How to find a form of association which will defend the person and goods of each member with the collective force of all, and under which each individual, while uniting himself with the others, obeys no one but himself, and remains as free as before." This is the fundamental problem to which the social contract holds the solution. . . .

■ *Chapter 7: "The Sovereign"*

Despite their common interest, subjects will not be bound by their commitment unless means are found to guarantee their fidelity.

For every individual as a man may have a private will contrary to, or different from, the general will that he has as a citizen. His private interest may he speak with a very different voice from that of the public interest; his absolute and naturally independent existence may make him regard what he owes to the common cause as a gratuitous contribution, the loss of which would be less painful for others than the payment is onerous for him; and fancying that the artificial person which constitutes the state is a mere rational entity, he might seek to enjoy the rights of a citizen without doing the duties of a subject. The growth of this kind of injustice would bring about the ruin of the body politic.

Hence, in order that the social pact shall not be an empty formula, it is tacitly implied in that commitment—which alone can give force to all others—that whoever refused to obey the general will shall be constrained to do so by the whole body, which means nothing other than that he shall be forced to be free; for this is the condition which, by giving each citizen to the nation, secures him against all personal dependence, it is the condition which shapes both the design and the working of the political machine, and which alone bestows justice on civil contracts—without it, such contracts would be absurd, tyrannical and liable to the grossest abuse.

Allan Ramsay, *Jean-Jacques Rousseau,* National Gallery of Scotland

Jean-Jacques Rousseau. By the late 1760s, a new generation of philosophes arose who began to move beyond and even to question the beliefs of their predecessors. Of the philosophes of the late Enlightenment, Rousseau was perhaps the most critical of his predecessors.

"no longer subsist on plants or acorns or live without laws and magistrates." Government was an evil, but a necessary one.

In his celebrated treatise *The Social Contract,* published in 1762, Rousseau tried to harmonize individual liberty with governmental authority (see the box above). The social contract was basically an agreement on the part of an entire society to be governed by its general will. If any individual wished to follow his own self-interest, he should be compelled to abide by the general will. "This means nothing less than that he will be forced to be free," said Rousseau, because the general will represented a community's highest aspirations, whatever was best for the entire community. Thus liberty was achieved through being forced to follow what was best for all people because, he believed, what was best for all was best for each individual. True freedom is adherence to laws that one has imposed on oneself. To Rousseau, because everybody was responsible for framing the general will, the creation of laws could never be delegated to a parliamentary institution:

> Thus the people's deputies are not and could not be its representatives; they are merely its agents; and they cannot decide anything finally. Any law which the people has not ratified in person is void; it is not law at all. The English people believes itself to be free; it is gravely mistaken; it is free only during the election of Members of Parliament; as soon as the Members are elected, the people is enslaved; it is nothing.[7]

This is an extreme and idealistic statement, but it is the ultimate statement of participatory democracy.

Another influential treatise by Rousseau also appeared in 1762. Titled *Émile,* it is one of the Enlightenment's most important works on education. Written in the form of a novel, the work is really a general treatise "on the education of the natural man." Rousseau's fundamental concern was that education should foster rather than restrict children's natural instincts. Life's experiences had shown Rousseau the importance of the promptings of the heart, and what he sought was a balance between heart and mind, between sentiment and reason. This emphasis on heart and sentiment made him a precursor of the intellectual movement called Romanticism that dominated Europe at the beginning of the nineteenth century.

But Rousseau did not necessarily practice what he preached. His own children were sent to foundling homes, where many children died young. Rousseau also viewed women as "naturally" different from men: "To fulfill [a woman's] functions, an appropriate physical constitution is necessary to her.... She needs a soft sedentary life to suckle her babies. How much care and tenderness does she need to hold her family together." In Rousseau's *Émile,* Sophie, who was Émile's intended wife, was educated for her role as wife and mother by learning obedience and the nurturing skills that would enable her to provide loving care for her husband and children. Not everyone in the eighteenth century agreed with Rousseau, however, making ideas of gender an important issue in the Enlightenment.

THE "WOMAN'S QUESTION" IN THE ENLIGHTENMENT

For centuries, men had dominated the debate about the nature and value of women. In general, many male intellectuals had argued that the base nature of women made them inferior to men and made male domination of women necessary (see Chapter 16). In the seventeenth and eighteenth centuries, many male thinkers reinforced this view by arguing that it was based on "natural" biological differences between men and women. Like Rousseau, they argued that the female constitution made women mothers. Male writers, in particular, were critical of the attempts of some women in the Enlightenment to write on intellectual issues, arguing that women were by nature intellectually inferior to men. Nevertheless, some Enlightenment thinkers offered more positive views of women. Diderot, for example, maintained that men and women were not all that different, and Voltaire asserted that "women are capable of all that men are" in intellectual affairs.

It was women thinkers, however, who added new perspectives to the "woman's question" by making specific suggestions for improving the condition of women. Mary Astell (1666–1731), daughter of a wealthy English coal merchant, argued in 1697 in *A Serious Proposal to the Ladies* that women needed to become better educated. Men, she believed, would resent her proposal, "but they must excuse me, if I be as partial to my own sex as they are to theirs, and think women as capable of learning as men are, and that it becomes them as well."[8] In a later work titled *Some Reflections upon Marriage,* Astell argued for the equality of the sexes in marriage: "If absolute sovereignty be not necessary in a state, how comes it to be so in a family...? For if arbitrary power is evil in itself, and an improper method of governing rational and free agents, it ought not be practiced anywhere.... If all men are born free, how is it that all women are born slaves?"[9]

The strongest statement for the rights of women in the eighteenth century was advanced by the English writer Mary Wollstonecraft (1759–1797), viewed by many as the founder of modern European feminism. In *Vindication of the Rights of Woman,* written in 1792, Wollstonecraft pointed out two contradictions in the views of women held by such Enlightenment thinkers as Rousseau. To argue that women must obey men, she said, was contrary to the beliefs of the same individuals that a system based on the arbitrary power of monarchs over their subjects or slave owners over their slaves was wrong. The subjection of women to men was equally wrong. In addition, she argued that the Enlightenment was based on an ideal of reason innate in all human beings. If women have reason, then they too are entitled to the same rights that men have. Women, Wollstonecraft declared, should have equal rights with men in education and in economic and political life as well (see the box on p. 475).

The Social Environment of the Philosophes

The social background of the philosophes varied considerably, from the aristocratic Montesquieu to the lower-middle-class Diderot and Rousseau. The Enlightenment was not the preserve of any one class, although obviously its greatest appeal was to the aristocracy and upper middle classes of the major cities. The common people, especially the peasants, were little affected by the Enlightenment.

Of great importance to the Enlightenment was the spread of its ideas to the literate elite of European society. Although the publication and sale of books and treatises were crucial to this process, the salon was also a factor. Salons came into being in the seventeenth century but rose to new heights in the eighteenth. The salons were the elegant drawing rooms in the urban houses of the wealthy where invited philosophes and guests gathered together and engaged in witty, sparkling conversations often centered on the new ideas of the philosophes. In France's rigid hierarchical society, the salons were important in bringing together writers and artists with aristocrats, government officials, and wealthy bourgeoisie.

As hostesses of the salons, women found themselves in a position to affect the decisions of kings, sway political opinion, and influence literary and artistic taste. Salons provided havens for people and views unwelcome in the royal court. When the *Encyclopedia* was suppressed by the French authorities, Marie-Thérèse de Geoffrin (1699–1777), a wealthy bourgeois widow whose father had been a valet, welcomed the encyclopedists to her salon and offered financial assistance to complete the work in secret. Madame Geoffrin was not without rivals, however. The marquise du Deffand (1697–1780) had abandoned her husband in the provinces and established herself in Paris, where her ornate drawing room attracted many of the Enlightenment's great figures, including Montesquieu, Hume, and Voltaire.

The Rights of Women

Mary Wollstonecraft responded to an unhappy childhood in a large family by seeking to lead an independent life. Few occupations were available for middle-class women in her day, but she survived by working as a teacher, chaperone, and governess to aristocratic children. All the while, she wrote and developed her ideas on the rights of women. This excerpt is taken from her *Vindication of the Rights of Woman,* written in 1792. This work led to her reputation as the foremost British feminist thinker of the eighteenth century.

■ *Mary Wollstonecraft,* Vindication of the Rights of Woman

It is a melancholy truth—yet such is the blessed effect of civilization—the most respectable women are the most oppressed; and, unless they have understandings far superior to the common run of understandings, taking in both sexes, they must, from being treated like contemptible beings, become contemptible. How many women thus waste life away the prey of discontent, who might have practiced as physicians, regulated a farm, managed a shop, and stood erect, supported by their own industry, instead of hanging their heads surcharged with the dew of sensibility, that consumes the beauty to which it at first gave luster. . . .

Proud of their weakness, however, [women] must always be protected, guarded from care, and all the rough toils that dignify the mind. If this be the fiat of fate, if they will make themselves insignificant and contemptible, sweetly to waste "life away," let them not expect to be valued when their beauty fades, for it is the fate of the fairest flowers to be admired and pulled to pieces by the careless hand that plucked them. In how many ways do I wish, from the purest benevolence, to impress this truth on my sex; yet I fear that they will not listen to a truth that dear-bought experience has brought home to many an agitated bosom, nor willingly resign the privileges of rank and sex for the privileges of humanity, to which those have no claim who do not discharge its duties. . . .

Would men but generously snap our chains, and be content with the rational fellowship instead of slavish obedience, they would find us more observant daughters, more affectionate sisters, more faithful wives, and more reasonable mothers—in a word, better citizens. We should then love them with true affection, because we should learn to respect ourselves; and the peace of mind of a worthy man would not be interrupted by the idle vanity of his wife.

Although the salons were run by women, the reputation of a salon depended on the stature of the males a hostess was able to attract. Despite this male domination, however, both French and foreign observers complained that females exerted undue influence in French political affairs. Though exaggerated, this perception led to the decline of salons during the French Revolution.

The salon served an important role in promoting conversation and sociability between upper-class men and women as well as spreading the ideas of the Enlightenment. But other means of spreading Enlightenment ideas were also available. Coffeehouses, cafés, reading clubs, and public lending libraries established by the state were gathering places to exchange ideas. Learned societies were formed in cities

Giraudon/Art Resource, NY

The Salon of Madame Geoffrin. An important factor in the development of the Enlightenment was the spread of new ideas to the literate elites of European society. Salons were an important part of this process. Madame Geoffrin, who presided over one of the best-known Parisian salons, is shown here, the third figure from the right in the front row.

CHRONOLOGY

Works of the Philosophes

Montesquieu, *Persian Letters*	1721
Voltaire, *Philosophic Letters on the English*	1733
Hume, *Treatise on Human Nature*	1739–1740
Montesquieu, *The Spirit of the Laws*	1748
Voltaire, *The Age of Louis XIV*	1751
Diderot, *Encyclopedia*	1751–1765
Rousseau, *The Social Contract, Émile*	1762
Voltaire, *Treatise on Toleration*	1763
Beccaria, *On Crimes and Punishments*	1764
Holbach, *System of Nature*	1770
Smith, *The Wealth of Nations*	1776
Gibbon, *The Decline and Fall of the Roman Empire*	1776–1788
Wollstonecraft, *Vindication of the Rights of Woman*	1792
Condorcet, *The Progress of the Human Mind*	1794

throughout Europe and America. At such gatherings as the Select Society of Edinburgh, Scotland, and the American Philosophical Society in Philadelphia, lawyers, doctors, and local officials gathered to discuss Enlightened ideas. Secret societies also developed. The most famous was the Freemasons, established in London in 1717, France and Italy in 1726, and Prussia in 1744. It was no secret that the Freemasons were sympathetic to the ideas of the philosophes.

Culture and Society in the Enlightenment

The intellectual adventure fostered by the philosophes was accompanied by both traditional practices and important changes in the eighteenth-century world of culture and society.

Innovations in Art, Music, and Literature

Although the Baroque and Neoclassical styles that had dominated the seventeenth century continued into the eighteenth century, by the 1730s a new style known as Rococo had begun to affect decoration and architecture all over Europe. Unlike the Baroque, which stressed majesty, power, and movement, Rococo emphasized grace and gentle action. Rococo rejected strict geometrical patterns and had a fondness for curves; it liked to follow the wandering lines of natural objects, such as seashells and flowers. It made much use of interlaced designs colored in gold with delicate contours and graceful curves. Highly secular, its lightness and charm spoke of the pursuit of pleasure, happiness, and love.

Antoine Watteau, *The Pilgrimage to Cythera.* Antoine Watteau was one of the most gifted painters in eighteenth-century France. His portrayal of aristocratic life reveals a world of elegance, wealth, and pleasure. In this painting, Watteau depicts a group of aristocratic pilgrims about to depart the island of Cythera, where they have paid homage to Venus, the goddess of love.

Réunion des Musées Nationaux/Art Resource, NY

Courtesy of James R. Spencer

Vierzehnheiligen, Interior View. Pictured here is the interior of the Vierzehnheiligen, the pilgrimage church designed by Balthasar Neumann. Elaborate detail, blazing light, rich colors, and opulent decoration were blended together to create a work of stunning beauty. The pilgrim in search of holiness is struck by an incredible richness of detail. Persuaded by joy rather than fear, the believer is lifted toward heaven on a cloud of rapture.

Some of Rococo's appeal is evident already in the work of Antoine Watteau (1684–1721), whose lyrical views of aristocratic life—refined, sensual, civilized, with gentlemen and ladies in elegant dress—revealed a world of upper-class pleasure and joy. Underneath that exterior, however, was an element of sadness as the artist revealed the fragility and transitory nature of pleasure, love, and life.

Another aspect of Rococo was that its decorative work could easily be used with Baroque architecture. The palace of Versailles had made an enormous impact on Europe. "Keeping up with the Bourbons" became important as the Austrian emperor, the Swedish king, German princes and prince-bishops, Italian princes, and even a Russian tsar built grandiose palaces. While emulating Versailles's size, they were modeled less after the French classical style of Versailles than after the seventeenth-century Italian Baroque, as modified by a series of brilliant German and Austrian sculptor-architects. This Baroque-Rococo architectural style of the eighteenth century was used in both palaces and churches, and often the same architects designed both. This

Scala/Art Resource, NY

Vierzehnheiligen, Exterior View. Balthasar Neumann, one of the most prominent architects of the eighteenth century, used the Baroque-Rococo style of architecture to design some of the most beautiful buildings of the century. Pictured here is the exterior of his pilgrimage church of the Vierzehnheiligen (The Fourteen Saints), located in southern Germany.

Jacques-Louis David, *Oath of the Horatii.* The Frenchman David was one of the most famous Neoclassical artists of the late eighteenth century. In order to immerse himself in the world of classical antiquity, he painted the *Oath of the Horatii* in Rome. With its emphasis on patriotic duty, the work became an instant success in both Paris and Rome.

is evident in the work of one of the greatest architects of the eighteenth century, Balthasar Neumann (1687–1753).

Neumann's two masterpieces are the pilgrimage church of the Vierzehnheiligen (The Fourteen Saints) in southern Germany and the Bishop's Palace, known as the Residenz, the residential palace of the Schönborn prince-bishop of Würzburg. Secular and spiritual become easily interchangeable as lavish and fanciful ornament, light, bright colors, and elaborate and rich detail greet the visitor in both buildings.

Despite the popularity of the Rococo style, Neoclassicism continued to maintain a strong appeal and in the late eighteenth century emerged in France as an established movement. Neoclassical artists wanted to recapture the dignity and simplicity of the classical style of ancient Greece and Rome. Some were especially influenced by the recent excavations of the ancient Roman cities of Herculaneum and Pompeii. Classical elements are evident in the work of Jacques-Louis David (1748–1825). In the *Oath of the Horatii*, he re-created a scene from Roman history in which the three Horatius brothers swore an oath before their father, proclaiming their willingness to sacrifice their lives for their country. David's Neoclassical style, with its moral seriousness and its emphasis on honor and patriotism, made him extremely popular during the French Revolution.

THE DEVELOPMENT OF MUSIC

The seventeenth and eighteenth centuries were the formative years of classical music and saw the rise of the opera and oratorio, the sonata, the concerto, and the symphony. The Italians were the first to develop these genres but were soon followed by the Germans, Austrians, and English. As in previous centuries, most musicians depended on a patron—a prince, a well-endowed ecclesiastic, or an aristocrat. The many individual princes, archbishops, and bishops, each with his own court, provided the patronage that made Italy and Germany the musical leaders of Europe.

Many of the techniques of the Baroque musical style, which dominated Europe between 1600 and 1750, were perfected by two composers—Bach and Handel—who stand out as musical geniuses. Johann Sebastian Bach (1685–1750) came from a family of musicians. Bach held the post of organist and music director at a number of small German courts before becoming director of church music at the Church of Saint Thomas in Leipzig in 1723. There Bach composed his Mass in B Minor, his Saint Matthew's Passion, and the cantatas and motets that have established his reputation as one of the greatest composers of all time. For Bach, music was above all a means to worship God; in his own words, his task in life was to make "well-ordered music in the honor of God."

The other great musical giant of the early eighteenth century, George Frederick Handel (1685–1759) was, like Bach, born in Saxony in Germany and in the same year. In contrast to Bach's quiet provincial life, however, Handel experienced a stormy international career and was profoundly secular in temperament. After studying in Italy, where he began his career by writing operas in the Italian manner, in 1712 he moved to England where he spent most of his adult life attempting to run an opera company. Although patronized by the English royal court, Handel wrote music for large public audiences and was not averse to writing huge, unusual-sounding pieces. The band for his Fireworks Music, for example, was supposed to be accompanied by 101 cannons. Although he wrote more than forty operas and much other secular music, the worldly Handel is, ironically, probably best known for his religious music. His *Messiah* has been called "one of those rare works that appeal immediately to everyone, and yet is indisputably a masterpiece of the highest order."[10]

Although Bach and Handel composed many instrumental suites and concerti, orchestral music did not come to the fore until the second half of the eighteenth century, when new instruments such as the piano appeared. A new musical period, the classical era (1750–1830), also emerged,

Musée Conde, Chantilly; Photo, Giraudon/Art Resource, NY

Mozart as Child Prodigy. This painting, done in Paris between 1763 and 1764, shows the seven-year-old Mozart playing at the harpsichord while his composer-father Leopold plays the violin and his sister Nannerl sings. Crowds greeted the young Mozart enthusiastically throughout the family's three-year tour of northern Europe.

represented by two great innovators—Haydn and Mozart. Their renown caused the musical center of Europe to shift from Italy and Germany to the Austrian Empire.

Franz Joseph Haydn (1732–1809) spent most of his adult life as musical director for the wealthy Hungarian princes, the Esterhazy brothers. Haydn was incredibly prolific, composing 104 symphonies in addition to string quartets, concerti, songs, oratorios, and Masses. His visits to England in 1790 and 1794 introduced him to another world, where musicians wrote for public concerts rather than princely patrons. This "liberty," as he called it, induced him to write his two great oratorios, *The Creation* and *The Seasons,* both of which were dedicated to the common people.

The concerto, symphony, and opera all reached their zenith in the works of Wolfgang Amadeus Mozart (1756–1791), a child prodigy who gave his first harpsichord concert at six and wrote his first opera at twelve. He, too, sought a patron, but his discontent with the overly demanding archbishop of Salzburg forced him to move to Vienna, where his failure to find a permanent patron made his life miserable. Nevertheless, he wrote music prolifically and passionately until he died a debt-ridden pauper at thirty-five. Mozart carried the tradition of Italian comic opera to new heights with *The Marriage of Figaro,* based on a Parisian play of the 1780s in which a valet outwits and outsings his noble employers, and *Don Giovanni,* a "black comedy" about the havoc Don Giovanni wrought on earth before he descended into hell. *The Marriage of Figaro, The Magic Flute,* and *Don Giovanni* are three of the world's greatest operas. Mozart composed with an ease of melody and a blend of grace, precision, and emotion that arguably no one has ever excelled. Haydn remarked to Mozart's father that "your son is the greatest composer known to me either in person or by reputation."

THE DEVELOPMENT OF THE NOVEL

The eighteenth century was also decisive in the development of the novel. The novel was not a completely new literary genre but grew out of the medieval romances and the picaresque stories of the sixteenth century. The English are credited with establishing the modern novel as the chief vehicle for fiction writing. With no established rules, the novel was open to much experimentation. It also proved especially attractive to women readers and women writers.

Samuel Richardson (1689–1761) was a printer by trade who did not turn to writing until his fifties. His first novel, *Pamela: or, Virtue Rewarded,* focused on a servant girl's resistance to numerous seduction attempts by her master. Finally, by reading the girl's letters describing her feelings about his efforts, the master realizes that she has a good mind as well as body and marries her. Virtue is rewarded. *Pamela* won Richardson a large audience as he appealed to the growing cult of sensibility in the eighteenth century—the taste for the sentimental and emotional. Samuel Johnson, another great English writer of the century and an even greater wit, remarked, "If you were to read Richardson for the story . . . you would hang yourself. But you must read him for the sentiment."

Reacting against the moral seriousness of Richardson, Henry Fielding (1707–1754) wrote novels about people without scruples who survived by their wits. His best work was *The History of Tom Jones, a Foundling,* a lengthy novel about the numerous adventures of a young scoundrel. Fielding presented scenes of English life from the hovels of London to the country houses of the aristocracy. In a number of hilarious episodes, he described characters akin to real types in English society. Although he emphasized

Gibbon and the Idea of Progress

Edward Gibbon's *Decline and Fall of the Roman Empire* was one of the great historical masterpieces of the eighteenth century. Like some of the philosophes, Gibbon believed in the idea of progress and, in reflecting on the decline and fall of Rome, expressed his optimism about the future of European civilization and the ability of Europeans to avoid the fate of the Romans.

Edward Gibbon, The Decline and Fall of the Roman Empire

It is the duty of a patriot to prefer and promote the exclusive interest and glory of his native county; but a philosopher may be permitted to enlarge his views, and to consider Europe as one great republic, whose various inhabitants have attained almost the same level of politeness and cultivation. The balance of power will continue to fluctuate, and the prosperity of our own, or the neighboring kingdoms, may be alternately exalted or depressed; but these partial events cannot essentially injure our general state of happiness, the system of arts, and laws, and manners, which so advantageously distinguish, above the rest of mankind, the Europeans and their colonies. The savage nations of the globe are the common enemies of civilized society; and we may inquire, with anxious curiosity, whether Europe is still threatened with a repetition of those calamities, which formerly oppressed the arms and institutions of Rome. Perhaps the same reflections will illustrate the fall of the mighty empire, and explain the probable causes of our actual security. . . .

Should these speculations be found doubtful or fallacious, there still remains a more humble source of comfort and hope. The discoveries of ancient and modern navigators, and the domestic history, or tradition, of the most enlightened nations, represent the *human* savage, naked both in mind and body, and destitute of laws, of arts, of ideas, and almost of language. From this abject condition, perhaps the primitive and universal state of man, he has gradually arisen to command the animals, to fertilize the earth, to traverse the oceans, and to measure the heavens. His progress in the improvement and exercise of his mental and corporeal faculties has been irregular and various; infinitely slow in the beginning, and increasing by degree with redoubled velocity: ages of laborious ascent have been followed by a moment of rapid downfall; and the several climates of the globe have felt the vicissitudes of light and darkness. Yet the experience of four thousand years should enlarge our hopes, and diminish our apprehensions: we cannot determine to what height the human species may aspire in their advances toward perfection; but it may safely be presumed, that no people, unless the face of nature is changed, will relapse into their original barbarism. . . . Fortunately for mankind, the more useful, or, at least, more necessary arts, can be performed without superior talents, or national subordination. . . . Each village, each family, each individual must always possess both ability and inclination, to perpetuate the use of fire and of metals; the propagation and service of domestic animals; the methods of hunting and fishing; the rudiments of navigation; the imperfect cultivation of corn, or other nutritive grain; and the simple practice of the mechanic trades. Private genius and public industry may be extirpated; but these hardy plants survive the tempest, and strike an everlasting root into the most unfavorable soil. The splendid days of Augustus and Trajan were eclipsed by a cloud of ignorance: and the Barbarians subverted the laws and palaces of Rome. But the scythe . . . still continued annually to mow the harvests of Italy. . . .

Since the first discovery of the arts, war, commerce, and religious zeal have diffused, among the savages of the Old and New World, these inestimable gifts: they have been successively propagated; they can never be lost. We may therefore acquiesce in the pleasing conclusion, that every age of the world has increased, and still increases, the real wealth, the happiness, the knowledge, and perhaps the virtue of the human race.

action rather than inner feeling, Fielding did his own moralizing by attacking the hypocrisy of his age.

THE WRITING OF HISTORY

The philosophes were responsible for creating a revolution in the writing of history. Their secular orientation caused them to eliminate the role of God in history and freed them to concentrate on events themselves and search for causal relationships in the natural world. Earlier, the humanist historians of the Renaissance had also placed their histories in purely secular settings, but not with the same intensity and complete removal of God.

The philosophe-historians also broadened the scope of history from the humanists' preoccupation with politics. Politics still predominated in the work of Enlightenment historians, but they also paid attention to economic, social, intellectual, and cultural developments. As Voltaire explained in his masterpiece, *The Age of Louis XIV:* "It is not merely the life of Louis XIV that we propose to write; we have a wider aim in view. We shall endeavor to depict for posterity, not the actions of a single man, but the spirit of men in the most enlightened age the world has ever seen."[11] In seeking to describe the "totality of past human experience," Voltaire initiated the modern ideal of social history.

The weaknesses of these philosophe-historians stemmed from their preoccupations as philosophes. Following the ideals of the classics that dominated their minds, the philosophes sought to instruct as well as entertain.

Their goal was to help civilize their age, and history could play a role by revealing its lessons according to their vision. Their emphasis on science and reason and their dislike of Christianity made them less than sympathetic to the period we call the Middle Ages. This is particularly noticeable in the other great masterpiece of eighteenth-century historiography, the six-volume *Decline and Fall of the Roman Empire* by Edward Gibbon (see the box on p. 480). Although Gibbon thought that the decline of Rome had many causes, he portrayed the growth of Christianity as a major reason for Rome's eventual collapse.

The High Culture of the Eighteenth Century

Historians and cultural anthropologists have grown accustomed to distinguishing between a civilization's high culture and its popular culture. High culture usually means the literary and artistic world of the educated and wealthy ruling classes; popular culture refers to the written and unwritten lore of the masses, most of which is passed down orally. By the eighteenth century, European high culture consisted of a learned world of theologians, scientists, philosophers, intellectuals, poets, and dramatists, for whom Latin remained a truly international language. Their work was supported by a wealthy and literate lay group, the most important of whom were the landed aristocracy and the wealthier upper classes in the cities.

Especially noticeable in the eighteenth century was an expansion of both the reading public and publishing. One study of French publishing, for example, reveals that French publishers were issuing about 1,600 titles yearly in the 1780s, up from 300 titles in 1750. Though many of these titles were still aimed at small groups of the educated elite, many were also directed to the new reading public of the middle classes, which included women and even urban artisans. The growth of publishing houses made it possible for authors to make money from their works and be less dependent on wealthy patrons.

An important aspect of the growth of publishing and reading in the eighteenth century was the development of magazines for the general public. Great Britain, an important center for the new magazines, saw 25 periodicals published in 1700, 103 in 1760, and 158 in 1780. Although short-lived, the best known was Joseph Addison's and Richard Steele's *Spectator,* begun in 1711. Its goal was "to enliven Morality with wit, and to temper Wit with Morality. . . . To bring Philosophy out of the closets and libraries, schools and colleges, to dwell in clubs and assemblies, at tea-tables and coffeehouses." In keeping with one of the chief intellectual goals of the philosophes, the *Spectator* wished to instruct and entertain at the same time. With its praise of family, marriage, and courtesy, the *Spectator* also had a strong appeal to women. Some of the new magazines were aimed specifically at women, such as *The Female Spectator* in England, which was also edited by a woman, Eliza Haywood, and featured articles by female writers.

Along with magazines came daily newspapers. The first was printed in London in 1702, but by 1780, thirty-seven other English towns had their own newspapers. Filled with news and special features, they were relatively cheap and were provided free in coffeehouses. Books, too, received wider circulation through the development of public libraries in the cities as well as private circulating libraries, which offered books for rental.

A London Coffeehouse. Coffeehouses first appeared in Venice and Constantinople but quickly spread throughout Europe by the beginning of the eighteenth century. In addition to drinking coffee, patrons of coffeehouses could read magazines and newspapers, exchange ideas, play chess, smoke, and even engage in business transactions. In this scene from a London coffeehouse of 1705, well-attired gentlemen make bids on commodities. Bidding went on until pins, which had been placed in lit candles, fell to the table. When patrons "heard a pin drop," bidding stopped.

EDUCATION AND UNIVERSITIES

By the eighteenth century, Europe was home to a large number of privately endowed secondary schools, such as the grammar and public school in England, the gymnasium in German-speaking lands, and the *collège* in France and Spain. These schools tended to be elitist, designed to meet the needs of the children of the upper classes of society. Basically, European secondary schools perpetuated the class hierarchy of Europe rather than creating avenues for social mobility. In fact, most of the philosophes reinforced the belief that education should function to keep people in their own social class. Baron d'Holbach said, "Education should teach princes to reign, the ruling classes to distinguish themselves by their merit and virtue, the rich to use their riches well, the poor to live by honest industry."

The curriculum of these secondary schools still largely concentrated on the Greek and Latin classics with little attention paid to mathematics, the sciences, and modern languages. Complaints from philosophe-reformers, as well as from merchants and other middle-class people who wanted their sons to have a more practical education, led to the development of new schools designed to provide a broader education. In Germany, the first *Realschule* was opened in Berlin in 1747 and offered modern languages, geography, and bookkeeping to prepare boys for careers in business. New schools of this kind were also created for upper-class girls, although they focused primarily on religion and domestic skills.

The most common complaint about universities, especially from the philosophes, was the old-fashioned curriculum that emphasized the classics and Aristotelian philosophy and provided no training in the sciences or modern languages. Before the end of the century, this criticism led to reforms that introduced new ideas in the areas of physics, astronomy, and even mathematics into the universities. It is significant, however, that very few of the important scientific discoveries of the eighteenth century occurred in the universities.

Crime and Punishment

By the eighteenth century, most European states had developed a hierarchy of courts to deal with crimes. Except in England, judicial torture remained an important means of obtaining evidence before a trial. Courts used the rack, thumbscrews, and other instruments to obtain confessions in criminal cases. Punishments for crimes were often cruel and even spectacular. Public executions were a basic part of traditional punishment and were regarded as a necessary means of deterring potential offenders in an age when a state's police forces were too weak to assure the capture of criminals. Although nobles were executed by simple beheading, lower-class criminals condemned to death were tortured, broken on the wheel, or drawn and quartered (see the box on p. 483). The death penalty was still commonly used in property as well as criminal cases. By 1800, more than two hundred crimes were subject to the death penalty in England. In addition to executions, European states resorted to forced labor in mines, forts, and navies. England also sent criminals as indentured servants to colonies in the New World and, after the American Revolution, to Australia.

Appalled by the unjust laws and brutal punishments of their times, some philosophes sought to create a new approach to justice. The most notable effort was made by an Italian philosophe, Cesare Beccaria (1738–1794). In his essay *On Crimes and Punishments,* written in 1764, Beccaria argued that punishments should serve only as deterrents, not as exercises in brutality: "Such punishments . . . ought to be chosen as will make the strongest and most lasting impressions on the minds of others, with the least torment to the body of the criminal."[12] Beccaria was also opposed to the use of capital punishment. It was spectacular, but it failed to stop others from committing crimes. Imprisonment—the deprivation of freedom—made a far more lasting impression. Moreover, capital punishment was harmful to society because it set an example of barbarism: "Is it not absurd that the laws, which detest and punish homicide, should, in order to prevent murder, publicly commit murder themselves?"

By the end of the eighteenth century, a growing sentiment against executions and torture led to a decline in both corporal and capital punishment. A new type of prison, in which criminals were placed in cells and subjected to discipline and regular work to rehabilitate them, began to replace the public spectacle of barbarous punishments.

The World of Medicine

In the eighteenth century, medicine was practiced by a hierarchy of practitioners. At the top stood the physicians, who were university graduates and enjoyed a high social status. Despite the scientific advances of the seventeenth and eighteenth centuries, however, university medical education was still largely conducted in Latin and was based primarily on Galen's work. New methods emphasizing clinical experience did begin to be introduced at the University of Leiden, which replaced Padua as the foremost medical school of Europe in the first half of the seventeenth century, only to be surpassed in the second half of that century by Vienna. A graduate with a doctorate in medicine from a university needed to receive a license before he could be a practicing member of the physicians' elitist corporate body. In England, the Royal College of Physicians licensed only one hundred physicians in the early eighteenth century. Only officially licensed physicians could hold regular medical consultations with patients and receive payments, already regarded in the eighteenth century as outrageously high.

Below the physicians were the surgeons, who were still known as barber-surgeons well into the eighteenth century from their original dual occupation. Their primary functions were to bleed patients and perform surgery; the latter was often done crudely, without painkillers and in filthy conditions, because there was no understanding of anesthesia or infection. Bleeding was widely believed to be beneficial in reducing fevers and combating a variety of illnesses.

The Punishment of Crime

Torture and capital punishment remained common features of European judicial systems well into the eighteenth century. Public spectacles were especially gruesome as this excerpt from the *Nocturnal Spectator* of Restif de la Bretonne demonstrates.

Restif de la Bretonne, *Nocturnal Spectator*

"The Broken Man"

I went home by way of rue Saint-Antoine and the Place de Gréve. Three murderers had been broken on the wheel there, the day before. I had not expected to see any such spectacle, one that I had never dared to witness. But as I crossed the square I caught sight of a poor wretch, pale, half dead, wracked by the pains of the interrogation inflicted on him twenty hours earlier; he was stumbling down from the Hôtel de Ville supported by the executioner and the confessor. These two men, so completely different, inspired an inexpressible emotion in me! I watched the latter embrace a miserable man consumed by fever, filthy as the dungeons he came from, swarming with vermin! And I said to myself, "O Religion, here is your greatest glory! . . ."

I saw a horrible sight, even though the torture had been mitigated. . . . The wretch had revealed his accomplices. He was garroted before he was put to the wheel. A winch set under the scaffold tightened a noose around the victim's neck and he was strangled; for a long while the confessor and the hangman felt his heart to see whether the artery still pulsed, and the hideous blows were dealt only after it beat no longer. . . . I left, with my hair standing on end in horror.

The surgeons underwent significant changes in the course of the eighteenth century. In the 1740s, they began to separate themselves from the barbers and organize their own guilds. At the same time, they started to undergo additional training by dissecting corpses and studying anatomy more systematically. As they became more effective, the distinction between physicians and surgeons began to break down, and surgeons were examining patients in a fashion similar to physicians by the end of the century. Moreover, surgeons also began to be licensed. In England, the Royal College of Surgeons required clinical experience before granting the license.

Other medical practitioners, such as apothecaries, midwives, and faith healers, primarily served the common people in the eighteenth century. Although their main function was to provide herbs and potions as recommended by physicians, apothecaries or pharmacists also acted independently in diagnosing illnesses and selling remedies. In the course of the eighteenth century, male doctors increasingly supplanted midwives in delivering babies. However, the tradition of faith healing, so prominent in medieval medicine, continued to be practiced, especially in the rural areas of Europe.

Hospitals in the eighteenth century seemed more a problem than an aid in dealing with disease and illness. That conditions were bad is evident in this description by the philosophe Denis Diderot, who characterized the Hôtel-Dieu in Paris, France's "biggest, roomiest, and richest" hospital, in these words:

> Imagine a long series of communicating wards filled with sufferers of every kind of disease who are sometimes packed three, four, five or even six into a bed, the living alongside the dead and dying, the air polluted by this mass of unhealthy bodies, passing pestilential germs of their afflictions from one to the other, and the spectacle of suffering and agony on every hand. That is the Hôtel-Dieu.
>
> The result is that many of these poor wretches come out with diseases they did not have when they went in, and often pass them on to the people they go back to live with.[13]

Despite appeals, efforts at hospital reform in the eighteenth century remained ineffectual.

Popular Culture

Popular culture refers to the written and unwritten literature and the social activities and pursuits that are fundamental to the lives of most people. The distinguishing characteristic of popular culture is its collective and public nature. Group activity was especially evident in the festival, a broad name used to cover a variety of celebrations: community festivals in Catholic Europe that celebrated the feast day of the local patron saint; annual festivals, such as Christmas and Easter that go back to medieval Christianity; and Carnival, the most spectacular form of festival, which was celebrated in the Mediterranean world of Spain, Italy, and France as well as in Germany and Austria. All of these festivals were special occasions on which people ate, drank, and celebrated to excess. In traditional societies, festival was a time for relaxation and enjoyment because much of the rest of the year was a time of unrelieved work. As the poet Thomas Gray said of Carnival in Turin in 1739: "This Carnival lasts only from Christmas to Lent; one half of the remaining part of the year is passed in remembering the last, the other in expecting the future Carnival."[14]

Carnival was celebrated for weeks leading up to the beginning of Lent, the forty-day period of fasting and purification preceding Easter. Carnival was, understandably, a time of great indulgence, just the reverse of Lent, when people were expected to abstain from meat, sex, and most recreations. Hearty consumption of food, especially meat and other delicacies, and heavy drinking were the norm during Carnival; so was intense sexual activity. Songs with double meanings that would be considered offensive at other times could be sung publicly at this time of year. A float of Florentine "key-makers," for example, sang this ditty to the ladies: "Our tools are fine, new and useful; We always carry them with us; They are good for anything; If you want to touch them, you can."[15] Finally, Carnival was a time of aggression, a time to release pent-up feelings. Most often this took the form of verbal aggression, since people were allowed to openly insult other people and even criticize their social superiors and authorities. Certain acts of physical violence were also permitted. People pelted each other with apples, eggs, flour, and pig's bladders filled with water.

The same sense of community evident in festival was also present in the chief gathering places of the common people, the local taverns or cabarets. Taverns functioned as regular gathering places for neighborhood men to talk, play games, conduct small business matters, and drink. In some countries, the favorite drinks of poor people, such as gin in England and vodka in Russia, proved devastating as poor people regularly drank themselves into oblivion. Gin was cheap; the classic sign in English taverns, "Drunk for a penny, dead drunk for two pence," was literally true. In England, the consumption of gin rose from 2 to 5 million gallons between 1714 and 1733 and declined only when complaints finally led to strict laws to restrict sales in the 1750s. Of course, the rich drank too. Samuel Johnson once remarked: "All the decent people in Lichfield got drunk every night and were not the worse thought of." But unlike the poor, the rich drank port and brandy, usually in large quantities.

This difference in drinking habits between rich and poor reminds us of the ever-widening separation between the elite and poor in the eighteenth century. In 1500, popular culture was for everyone; a second culture for the elite, it was the only culture for the rest of society. But between 1500 and 1800, the nobility, clergy, and bourgeoisie had abandoned popular culture to the lower classes. This was, of course, a gradual process, and in abandoning the popular festivals, the upper classes were also abandoning the popular worldview as well. The new scientific outlook had brought a new mental world for the upper classes, and they now viewed such things as witchcraft, faith healing, fortune telling, and prophecy as the beliefs of "such as are of the weakest judgment and reason, as women, children, and ignorant and superstitious persons."

Popular culture had always included a vast array of traditional songs and stories that were passed down from generation to generation. But popular culture was not entirely based on an oral tradition; a popular literature existed as well. So-called chapbooks, printed on cheap paper, were short brochures sold by itinerant peddlers to the lower classes. They contained both spiritual and secular material: lives of saints and inspirational stories competed with crude satires and adventure stories.

It is apparent from the chapbooks that popular culture did not have to remain primarily oral. Its ability to change was dependent on the growth of literacy. Studies in France indicate that literacy rates for men increased from 29 percent in the late seventeenth century to 47 percent in the late eighteenth century; for women, the increase was from 14 to 27 percent during the same period. Of course, certain groups were more likely to be literate than others. Upper-class elites and the upper middle classes in the cities were mostly all literate. However, the figures also indicate dramatic increases for lower-middle-class artisans in urban areas. Recent research in the city of Marseilles, for example, indicates that literacy of male artisans and workers increased from 28 percent in 1710 to 85 percent in 1789, though the rate for women remained at 15 percent. Peasants, who constituted as much as 75 percent of the French population, remained largely illiterate.

The spread of literacy was closely connected to primary education. In Catholic Europe, primary education was largely a matter of local community effort, leading to little real growth. Only in the Habsburg Austrian Empire was a system of state-supported primary schools (*Volkschulen*) established, although only one in four school-age children actually attended.

The emphasis of the Protestant reformers on reading the Bible had led Protestant states to take a greater interest in primary education. Some places, especially the Swiss cantons, Scotland, and the German states of Saxony and Prussia, witnessed the emergence of universal primary schools that provided a modicum of education for the masses. But effective systems of primary education were hindered by the attitudes of the ruling classes, who feared the consequences of teaching the lower classes anything beyond the virtues of hard work and deference to their superiors. Hannah More, an English writer who set up a network of Sunday schools, made clear the philosophy of her charity school for poor children: "My plan of instruction is extremely simple and limited. They learn on weekdays such coarse work as may fit them for servants. I allow of no writing for the poor. My object is to train up the lower classes in habits of industry and piety."

Religion and the Churches

The music of Bach and the pilgrimage and monastic churches of southern Germany and Austria make us aware of a curious fact. Though much of the great art and music of the time was religious, the thought of the time was antireligious as life became increasingly secularized and men of reason attacked the established churches. And yet most Europeans were still Christians. Even many of those most critical of the churches accepted that society could not function without religious faith.

The Institutional Church

In the eighteenth century, the established Catholic and Protestant churches were basically conservative institutions that upheld society's hierarchical structure, privileged classes, and traditions. Although churches experienced change because of new state policies, they did not sustain any dramatic internal changes. In both Catholic and Protestant countries, the parish church run by priest or pastor remained the center of religious practice. In addition to providing religious services, the parish church kept records of births, deaths, and marriages; provided charity for the poor; supervised whatever primary education there was; and cared for orphans.

CHURCH-STATE RELATIONS

Early on, the Protestant Reformation had solved the problem of the relationship between church and state by establishing the principle of state control over the churches. In the eighteenth century, Protestant state churches flourished throughout Europe: Lutheranism in Scandinavia and the north German states, Anglicanism in England, and Calvinism (or Reformed churches) in Scotland, the United Provinces, and some of the Swiss cantons and German states (see Map 17.2). There were also Protestant minorities in other European countries.

In 1700, the Catholic church still exercised much power in Catholic European states: Spain, Portugal, France, Italy, the Habsburg Empire, Poland, and most of southern Germany. The church also continued to possess enormous wealth. In Spain, 3,000 monastic institutions housing 100,000 men and women controlled enormous landed estates.

Map 17.2 Religious Populations of Eighteenth-Century Europe. Christianity was still a dominant force in eighteenth-century Europe—even many of the philosophes remained Christians while attacking the authority and power of the established Catholic and Protestant churches. However, by the end of the century, most monarchs had increased royal power at the expense of religious institutions. ■ To what extent are religious majorities geographically concentrated in certain areas, and what accounts for this?

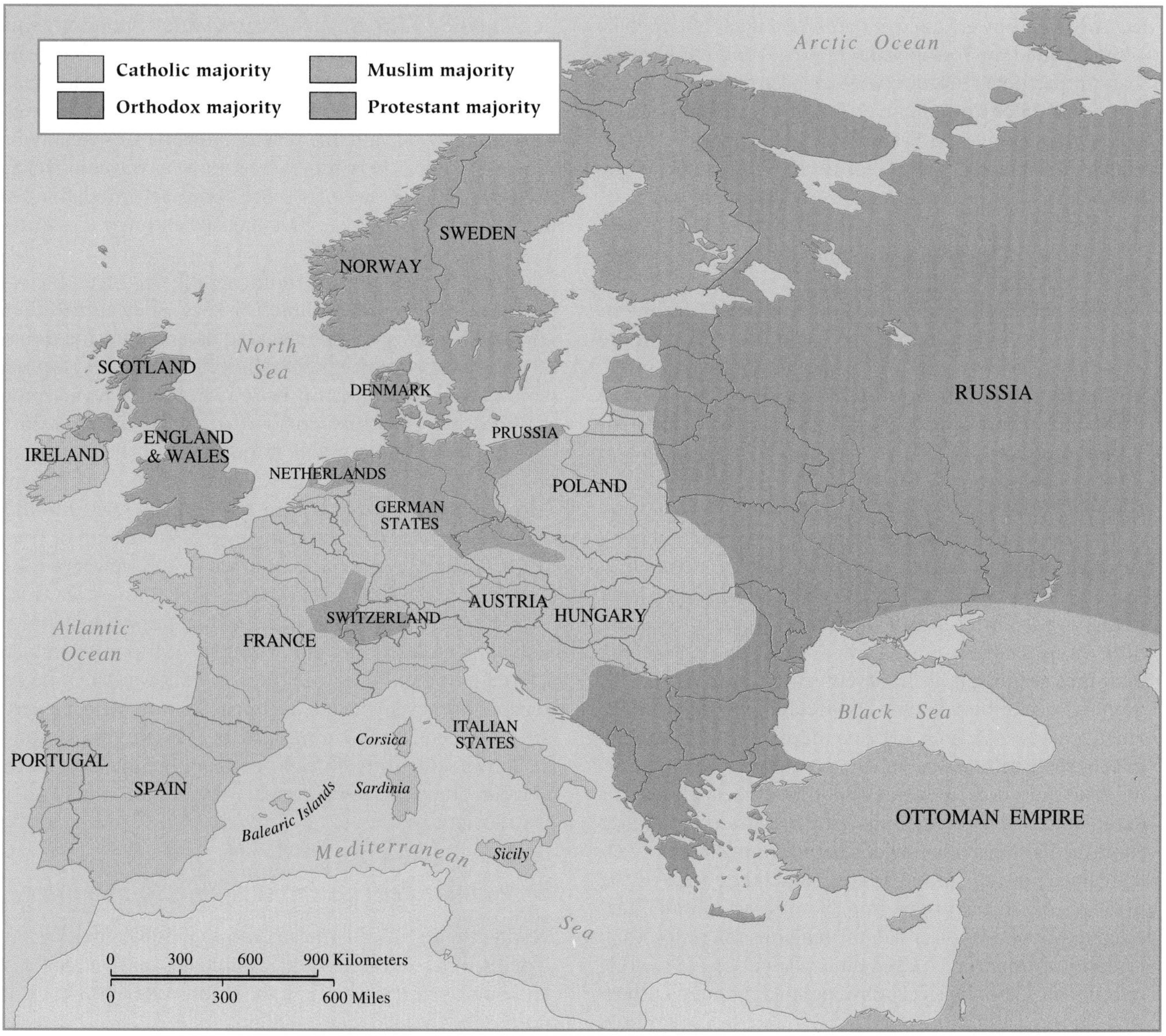

The Catholic church remained hierarchically structured. In most Catholic countries, the highest clerics, such as bishops, archbishops, abbots, and abbesses, were members of the upper class, especially the landed nobility, and received enormous revenues from their landed estates and tithes from the faithful. A wide gulf existed between the upper and lower clergy. While the French bishop of Strasbourg, for example, received 100,000 livres a year, parish priests were paid only 500.

In the eighteenth century, the governments of many Catholic states began to seek greater authority over the churches in their countries. This "nationalization" of the Catholic church meant controlling the papacy and in turn the chief papal agents, the Society of Jesus. The Jesuits had proved extremely successful, perhaps too successful for their own good. They had created special enclaves, virtually states within states, in the French, Spanish, and Portuguese colonies in the New World. As advisers to Catholic rulers, the Jesuits exercised considerable political influence. But the high profile they achieved through their successes led to a wide range of enemies, and a series of actions soon undermined Jesuit power. The Portuguese monarch destroyed the powerful Jesuit state in Paraguay and then in 1759 expelled the Jesuits from Portugal and confiscated their property. In 1764, they were expelled from France and three years later from Spain and the Spanish colonies. In 1773, when Spain and France demanded that the entire society be dissolved, Pope Clement XIV reluctantly complied. The dissolution of the Jesuit order, the pillar of Catholic fanaticism and strength, was yet another victory for Catholic governments determined to win control over their churches.

The end of the Jesuits was paralleled by a decline in papal power. Already by the mid-eighteenth century, the papacy played only a minor role in diplomacy and international affairs. The nationalization of the churches by the states meant the loss of the papacy's power to appoint high clerical officials.

TOLERATION AND RELIGIOUS MINORITIES

One of the chief battle cries of the philosophes had been a call for religious toleration. Out of political necessity, a certain level of tolerance of different creeds had occurred in the seventeenth century, but many rulers still found it difficult to accept. Louis XIV had turned back the clock in France at the end of the seventeenth century, insisting on religious uniformity and suppressing the rights of the Huguenots (see Chapter 15). Even devout rulers continued to believe that there was only one path to salvation; it was the true duty of a ruler not to allow subjects to be condemned to hell by being heretics. Persecution of heretics continued; the last burning of a heretic took place in 1781.

Nevertheless, some progress was made toward the principle of religious toleration. No ruler was more interested in the philosophes' call for religious toleration than Joseph II of Austria. His Toleration Patent of 1781, while recognizing Catholicism's public practice, granted Lutherans, Calvinists, and Greek Orthodox the right to worship privately. In all other ways, all subjects were now equal: "Non-Catholics are in future admitted under dispensation to buy houses and real property, to practice as master craftsmen, to take up academic appointments and posts in public service, and are not to be required to take the oath in any form contrary to their religious tenets."[16]

TOLERATION AND THE JEWS

The Jews remained the despised religious minority of Europe. The largest number of Jews (known as the Ashkenazic Jews) lived in eastern Europe. Except in relatively tolerant Poland, Jews were restricted in their movements, forbidden to own land or hold many jobs, forced to pay burdensome special taxes, and also subject to periodic outbursts of popular wrath. The resulting pogroms, in which Jewish communities were looted and massacred, made Jewish existence precarious and dependent on the favor of their territorial rulers.

Another major group was the Sephardic Jews, who had been expelled from Spain in the fifteenth century. Although many had migrated to Turkish lands, some of them had settled in cities, such as Amsterdam, Venice, London, and Frankfurt, where they were relatively free to participate in the banking and commercial activities that Jews had practiced since the Middle Ages. The highly successful ones came to provide valuable services to rulers, especially in central Europe, where they were known as the court Jews. But even these Jews were insecure because their religion set them apart from the Christian majority and served as a catalyst to social resentment.

Some Enlightenment thinkers in the eighteenth century favored a new acceptance of Jews. They argued that Jews and Muslims were human and deserved the full rights of citizenship despite their religion. Many philosophes denounced persecution of the Jews but made no attempt to hide their hostility and ridiculed Jewish customs. Diderot, for example, said that the Jews had "all the defects peculiar to an ignorant and superstitious nation." Many Europeans favored the assimilation of the Jews into the mainstream of society, but only by the conversion of Jews to Christianity as the basic solution to the "Jewish problem." This, of course, was not acceptable to most Jews.

The Austrian emperor Joseph II attempted to adopt a new policy toward the Jews, although it too was limited. It freed Jews from nuisance taxes and allowed them more freedom of movement and job opportunities, but they were still restricted from owning land and worshiping in public. At the same time, Joseph II encouraged Jews to learn German and work toward greater assimilation into Austrian society.

Popular Religion in the Eighteenth Century

Despite the rise of skepticism and the intellectuals' belief in deism and natural religion, it would appear that religious devotion remained strong in the eighteenth century.

CATHOLIC PIETY

It is difficult to assess precisely the religiosity of Europe's Catholics. The Catholic parish church remained an important center of life for the entire community. How many people went to church regularly cannot be known exactly, but it has been established that 90 to 95 percent of Catholic populations did go to Mass on Easter Sunday, one of the church's most special celebrations.

Catholic religiosity proved highly selective, however. Despite the Reformation, much popular devotion was still directed to an externalized form of worship focusing on prayers to saints, pilgrimages, and devotion to relics and images. This bothered many clergymen, who felt that their parishioners were "more superstitious than devout," as one Catholic priest put it. Many common people continued to fear witches and relied on the intervention of the saints and the Virgin Mary to save them from personal disasters caused by the devil.

PROTESTANT REVIVALISM

After the initial century of religious fervor that created Protestantism in the sixteenth century, Protestant churches in the seventeenth century had settled down into well-established patterns controlled by state authorities and served by a well-educated clergy. Protestant churches became bureaucratized and bereft of religious enthusiasm. In Germany and England, where rationalism and deism had become influential and moved some theologians to a more "rational" Christianity, the desire of ordinary Protestant churchgoers for greater depths of religious experience led to new and dynamic religious movements.

Pietism in Germany was a response to this desire for a deeper personal devotion to God. Begun in the seventeenth century by a group of German clerics who wished their religion to be more personal, Pietism was spread by the teachings of Count Nikolaus von Zinzendorf (1700–1760). To Zinzendorf and his Moravian Brethren, as his sect was called, it was the mystical dimensions—the personal experience of God—in one's life that constituted true religious experience. He was utterly opposed to what he perceived as the rationalistic approach of orthodox Lutheran clergy, who were being educated in new "rational" ideas. As Zinzendorf commented: "He who wishes to comprehend God with his mind becomes an atheist."

After the civil wars of the seventeenth century, England too had arrived at a respectable, uniform, and complacent state church. A pillar of the establishment, the Anglican church seemed to offer little spiritual excitement, especially to the masses of people. The dissenting Protestant groups—Puritans, Quakers, Baptists—were relatively subdued, while the growth of deism seemed to challenge Christianity itself. The desire for deep spiritual experience seemed unmet until the advent of John Wesley (1703–1791).

An ordained Anglican minister, John Wesley experienced a deep spiritual crisis and underwent a mystical experience: "I felt I did trust in Christ alone for salvation; and an assurance was given me, that He had taken away my sins, even mine, and saved me from the law of sin and death. I felt my heart strangely warmed." To Wesley, "the gift of God's grace" assured him of salvation and led him to become a missionary to the English people, bringing the "glad tidings" of salvation to all people, despite opposition from the Anglican church, which criticized this emotional mysticism or religious enthusiasm as superstitious nonsense. To Wesley, all could be saved by experiencing God and opening the doors to his grace.

By courtesy of the National Portrait Gallery, London

John Wesley. In leading a deep spiritual revival in Britain, John Wesley founded a religious movement that came to be known as Methodism. He loved to preach to the masses, and this 1766 portrait by Nathaniel Hope shows him as he might have appeared before a crowd of people.

In taking the Gospel to the people, Wesley preached to the masses in open fields, appealing especially to the lower classes neglected by the socially elitist Anglican church. He tried, he said, "to lower religion to the level of the lowest people's capacities." Wesley's charismatic preaching often provoked highly charged and even violent conversion experiences (see the box on p. 488). Afterward, converts were organized into so-called Methodist societies or chapels in

The Conversion Experience in Wesley's Methodism

After his own conversion experience, John Wesley traveled extensively to bring the "glad tidings" of Jesus to other people. It has been estimated that he preached over forty thousand sermons, some of them to audiences numbering twenty thousand listeners. Wesley gave his message wherever people gathered—in the streets, hospitals, private houses, and even pubs. In this selection from his journal, Wesley describes how emotional and even violent conversion experiences could be.

■ The Works of the Reverend John Wesley

Sunday, May 20 [1759], being with Mr. B—11 at Everton, I was much fatigued, and did not rise: but Mr. B. did, and observed several fainting and crying out, while Mr. Berridge was preaching: afterwards at Church, I heard many cry out, especially children, whose agonies were amazing: one of the eldest, a girl of ten or twelve years old, was full in my view, in violent contortions of body, and weeping aloud, I think incessantly, during the whole service. . . . The Church was equally crowded in the afternoon, the windows being filled within and without, and even the outside of the pulpit to the very top; so that Mr. B. seemed almost stifled by their breath; yet feeble and sickly as he is, he was continually strengthened, and his voice, for the most part, distinguishable; in the midst of all the outcries. I believe there were present three times more men than women, a great part of whom came from far; thirty of them having set out at two in the morning, from a place thirteen miles off. The text was, *Having a form of godliness, but denying the power thereof.* When the power of religion began to be spoken of, the presence of God really filled the place: and while poor sinners felt the sentence of death in their souls, what sounds of distress did I hear! The greatest number of them who cried or fell, were men: but some women, and several children, felt the power of the same almighty Spirit, and seemed just sinking into hell. This occasioned a mixture of several sounds; some shrieking, some roaring aloud. The most general was a loud breathing, like that of people half strangled and gasping for life: and indeed almost all the cries were like those of human creatures, dying in bitter anguish. Great numbers wept without any noise: others fell down as death: some sinking in silence; some with extreme noise and violent agitation. I stood on the pew-seat, as did a young man in the opposite pew, an able-bodied, fresh, healthy countryman: but in a moment, while he seemed to think of nothing less, down he dropped with a violence inconceivable. The adjoining pews seemed to shake with his fall: I heard afterwards the stamping of his feet; ready to break the boards, as he lay in strong convulsions, at the bottom of the pew. Among several that were struck down in the next pew, was a girl, who was as violently seized as he. . . . Among the children who felt the arrows of the Almighty, I saw a sturdy boy, about eight years old, who roared above his fellows, and seemed in his agony to struggle with the strength of a grown man. His face was as red as scarlet: and almost all on whom God laid his hand, turned either very red or almost black. . . .

The violent struggling of many in the above-mentioned churches, has broken several pews and benches. Yet it is common for people to remain unaffected there, and afterwards to drop down on their way home. Some have been found lying as dead on the road: others, in Mr. B.'s garden; not being able to walk from the Church to his house, though it is not two hundred yards.

which they could aid each other in doing the good works that Wesley considered a component of salvation. Although Wesley sought to keep Methodism within the Anglican church, after his death it became a separate and independent sect. Methodism was an important revival of Christianity and proved that the need for spiritual experience had not been expunged by the eighteenth-century search for reason.

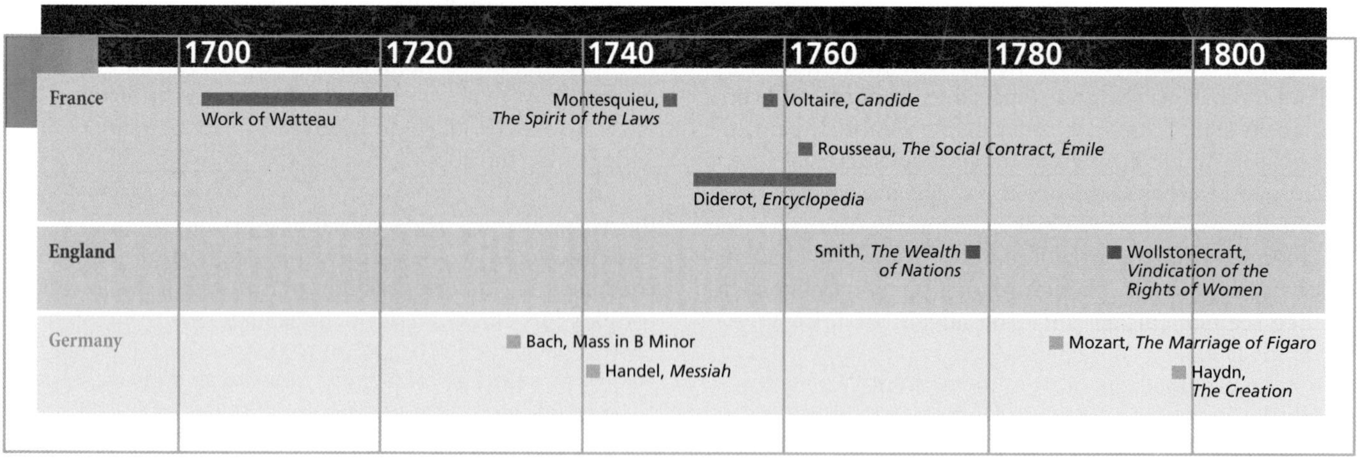

Conclusion

One prominent historian of the eighteenth century has appropriately characterized it as a century of change and tradition. Highly influenced by the new worldview created by the Scientific Revolution and especially the ideas of Locke and Newton, the philosophes hoped that they could create a new society by using reason to discover the natural laws that governed it. Like the Christian humanists of the fifteenth and sixteenth centuries, they believed that education could create better human beings and a better human society. By attacking traditional religion as the enemy and creating a new "science of man" in economics, politics, justice, and education, the philosophes laid the foundation for a modern worldview based on rationalism and secularism.

But it was also an age of tradition. Although secular thought and rational ideas began to pervade the mental world of the ruling elites, most people in eighteenth-century Europe still lived by seemingly eternal verities and practices—God, religious worship, and farming. The most brilliant architecture and music of the age were religious. And yet the forces of secularization were too strong to stop. In the midst of intellectual change, economic, political, and social transformations of great purport were taking shape and by the end of the eighteenth century were to lead to both political and social upheavals.

Notes

1. Quoted in Paul Hazard, *The European Mind, 1680–1715* (New York, 1963), pp. 304–305.
2. Quoted in Dorinda Outram, *The Enlightenment* (Cambridge, 1995), p. 67.
3. Quoted in Hazard, *The European Mind,* p. 12.
4. John Locke, *An Essay Concerning Human Understanding* (New York, 1964), pp. 89–90.
5. Baron d'Holbach, *Common Sense,* as quoted in Frank E. Manuel, ed., *The Enlightenment* (Englewood Cliffs, N.J., 1965), p. 62.
6. Jean-Jacques Rousseau, *A Discourse on Inequality,* trans. Maurice Cranston (Harmondsworth, England, 1984), p. 109.
7. Jean-Jacques Rousseau, *The Social Contract,* trans. Maurice Cranston (Harmondsworth, England, 1968), p. 141.
8. Mary Astell, *A Serious Proposal to the Ladies,* in Moira Ferguson, ed., *First Feminists: British Women Writers, 1578–1799* (Bloomington, Ind., 1985). p. 190.
9. Ibid., p. 193.
10. Kenneth Clark, *Civilization* (New York, 1969), p. 231.
11. Voltaire, *The Age of Louis XIV,* trans. Martyn P. Pollack (New York, 1961), p. 1.
12. Cesare Beccaria, *An Essay on Crimes and Punishments,* trans. E. D. Ingraham (Philadelphia, 1819), pp. 59–60.
13. Quoted in René Sand, *The Advance to Social Medicine* (London, 1952), pp. 86–87.
14. Quoted in Peter Burke, *Popular Culture in Early Modern Europe* (New York, 1978), p. 179.
15. Quoted in ibid., p. 186.
16. Quoted in C. A. Macartney, *The Habsburg and Hohenzollern Dynasties in the Seventeenth and Eighteenth Centuries* (New York, 1970), p. 157.

Suggestions for Further Reading

Two sound, comprehensive surveys of eighteenth-century Europe are I. Woloch, *Eighteenth-Century Europe* (New York, 1982), and M. S. Anderson, *Europe in the Eighteenth Century* (London, 1987). See also R. Birn, *Crisis, Absolutism, Revolution: Europe, 1648–1789,* 2d ed. (Fort Worth, Tex., 1992).

Good introductions to the Enlightenment can be found in N. Hampson, *A Cultural History of the Enlightenment* (New York, 1968); U. Im Hof, *The Enlightenment* (Oxford, 1994); D. Goodman, *The Republic of Letters: A Cultural History of the French Enlightenment* (Ithaca, N.Y., 1994); and D. Outram, *The Enlightenment* (Cambridge, 1995). A more detailed synthesis can be found in P. Gay, *The Enlightenment: An Interpretation,* 2 vols. (New York, 1966–69). For a short, popular survey on the French philosophes, see F. Artz, *The Enlightenment in France* (Kent, Ohio, 1968). Also of value are E. J. Wilson and P. H. Reill, *Encyclopedia of the Enlightenment* (New York, 1996), and J. W. Yolton, ed., *The Blackwell Companion to the Enlightenment* (Cambridge, Mass., 1995). Studies of the major Enlightenment intellectuals include J. Sklar, *Montesquieu* (Oxford, 1987); H. T. Mason, *Voltaire: A Biography* (Baltimore, 1981); P. N. Furbank, *Diderot: A Critical Biography* (New York, 1992); and M. Cranston, *The Noble Savage: Jean-Jacques Rousseau* (New York, 1991). On women in the eighteenth century, see N. Z. Davis and A. Farge, eds., *A History of Women: Renaissance and Enlightenment Paradoxes* (Cambridge, Mass., 1993); C. Lougee, *Le Paradis des Femmes: Women, Salons, and Social Stratification* (Princeton, N.J., 1976); O. Hufton, *The Prospect Before Her: A History of Women in Western Europe, 1500–1800* (New York, 1998); and B. S. Anderson and J. P. Zinsser, *A History of Their Own,* vol. 2 (New York, 1988).

Two readable general surveys on the arts and literature are M. Levy, *Rococo to Revolution* (London, 1966), and H. Honour, *Neo-Classicism* (Harmondsworth, England, 1968). On the eighteenth-century novel, see G. J. Barker-Benfield, *The Culture of Sensibility: Sex and Society in the Eighteenth-Century English Novel* (Chicago, 1992). On Gibbon, see W. B. Carnuchan, *Gibbon's Solitude: The Inward World of the Historian* (London, 1987). On the growth of literacy, see R. A. Houston, *Literacy in Early Modern Europe: Culture and Education, 1500–1800* (New York, 1988). Different facets of crime and punishment are examined in the important works by M. Foucault, *Discipline and Punish: The Birth of the Prison* (New York, 1977), and J. Langbein, *Torture and the Law of Proof* (Chicago, 1977). On the medical profession, see A. Cunningham and R. French, eds., *The Medical Enlightenment of the Eighteenth Century* (New York, 1990).

Important studies on popular culture include P. Burke, *Popular Culture in Early Modern Europe* (New York, 1978), and R. Darnton, *The Great Cat Massacre and Other Episodes in French Cultural History* (New York, 1984).

A good introduction to the religious history of the eighteenth century can be found in G. R. Cragg, *The Church and the Age of Reason, 1648–1789* (London, 1966). The problem of religious toleration is examined in J. I. Israel, *European Jewry in the Age of Mercantilism, 1550–1750,* 2d ed. (New York, 1989). On Pietism, see R. Gawthorp, *Pietism and the Making of Eighteenth-Century Prussia* (New York, 1993). On John Wesley, see H. Rack, *Reasonable Enthusiast: John Wesley and the Rise of Methodism* (New York, 1989).

For additional reading, go to InfoTrac College Edition, your online research library at http://web1.infotrac-college.com

Enter the search term *Enlightenment* using the Subject Guide.

Enter the search term *Voltaire* using Key Terms.

Enter the search term *Diderot* using Key Terms.

Enter the search term *Rousseau* using Key Terms.

CHAPTER

18

The Eighteenth Century: European States, International Wars, and Social Change

CHAPTER OUTLINE

- The European States
- Wars and Diplomacy
- Economic Expansion and Social Change
- The Social Order of the Eighteenth Century
- Conclusion

FOCUS QUESTIONS

- What do historians mean by the term *enlightened absolutism,* and to what degree did eighteenth-century Prussia, Austria, and Russia exhibit its characteristics?
- How did the concepts of "balance of power" and "reason of state" influence international relations in the eighteenth century?
- What were the causes and results of the Seven Years' War?
- What changes occurred in agriculture, finance, industry, and trade during the eighteenth century?
- Who were the main groups making up the European social order in the eighteenth century, and how did the conditions in which they lived differ both between groups and between different parts of Europe?
- What was the relationship between political, economic, and social changes in the eighteenth century?

HISTORIANS HAVE OFTEN defined the eighteenth century chronologically as spanning the years from 1715 to 1789. Politically, this makes sense since 1715 marks the end of the age of Louis XIV and 1789 was the year in which the French Revolution erupted. This period has often been portrayed as the final phase of Europe's old order, before the violent upheaval and reordering of society associated with the French Revolution. Europe's old order, still largely agrarian, dominated by kings and landed aristocrats, and grounded in privileges for nobles, clergy, towns, and provinces, seemed to continue a basic pattern that had prevailed in Europe since medieval times. But new ideas and new practices were also beginning to emerge. Just as a new intellectual order based on rationalism and secularism was emerging from the intellectual revolution of the Scientific Revolution and the Enlightenment, demographic, economic, and social patterns were beginning to change in ways that reflected a modern new order.

The ideas of the Enlightenment seemed to proclaim a new political age as well. Catherine the Great, who ruled Russia from 1762 to 1796, wrote to Voltaire: "Since 1746 I have been under the greatest obligations to you. Before that period I read nothing but romances, but by chance your works fell into my hands, and ever since then I have never ceased to read them, and have no desire for books less well written than yours, or less instructive." The empress of Russia also invited Diderot to Russia and, when he arrived, urged him to speak frankly "as man to man." Diderot did, offering her advice for a far-ranging program of political and financial reform. But Catherine's apparent eagerness to make enlightened reforms was tempered by skepticism. She said of Diderot: "If I had believed him everything would have been turned upside down in my kingdom; legislation, administration, finance—all would have been turned topsy-turvy to make room for impractical theories." For Catherine, enlightened reform remained more a dream than a reality, and in the end, the waging of wars to gain more power was more important.

In the eighteenth century, the process of centralization that had characterized the growth of states since the Middle Ages continued as most European states enlarged their bureaucratic machinery and consolidated their governments in order to collect the revenues and build the armies they needed to compete militarily with the other European states. International competition continued to be the favorite pastime of eighteenth-century rulers. Within the European state system, the nations that would dominate Europe until World War I—Britain, France, Austria, Prussia, and Russia—emerged as the five great powers of Europe. Their rivalries led to major wars, which some have called the first world wars because they were fought outside as well as inside Europe. In the midst of this state building and warmaking, dramatic demographic, economic, and social changes heralded the emergence of a radical transformation in the way Europeans would raise food and produce goods.

The European States

Most European states in the eighteenth century were ruled by monarchs. Although the justifications of the previous century for strong monarchy continued to hold sway, divine-right assumptions were gradually superseded by influential utilitarian arguments as Europe became increasingly secularized. The Prussian king Frederick II expressed this new thinking well when explaining the services a monarch must provide for his people:

> These services consisted in the maintenance of the laws; a strict execution of justice; an employment of his whole powers to prevent any corruption of manners; and defending the state against its enemies. It is the duty of this magistrate to pay attention to agriculture; it should be his care that provisions for the nation should be in abundance, and that commerce and industry should be encouraged. He is a perpetual sentinel, who must watch the acts and the conduct of the enemies of the state. . . . If he be the first general, the first minister of the realm, it is not that he should remain the shadow of authority, but that he should fulfill the duties of such titles. He is only the first servant of the state.[1]

This utilitarian argument was reinforced by the praises of the philosophes.

Enlightened Absolutism?

There is no doubt that Enlightenment thought had some impact on the political development of European states in the eighteenth century. Closely related to the Enlightenment idea of natural laws was the belief in natural rights, which were thought to be inalterable privileges that ought not to be withheld from any person. These natural rights included equality before the law, freedom of religious worship, freedom of speech and press, and the right to assemble, hold property, and seek happiness. The American Declaration of Independence summarized the Enlightenment concept of natural rights in its opening paragraph: "We hold these truths to be self-evident, that all men are created equal; that they are endowed by their creator with certain unalienable rights; that among these are life, liberty and the pursuit of happiness."

But how were these natural rights to be established and preserved? In the opinion of most philosophes, most people needed the direction provided by an enlightened ruler. What made rulers enlightened? They must allow religious toleration, freedom of speech and press, and the right to hold private property. They must foster the arts, sciences, and education. Above all, they must not be arbitrary in their rule; they must obey the laws and enforce them fairly for all subjects. Only strong monarchs seemed capable of overcoming vested interests and effecting the reforms society needed. Reforms then should come from above—from the rulers rather than from the people. Distrustful of the masses, the philosophes believed that absolute rulers, swayed by enlightened principles, were the best hope of reforming their societies.

The extent to which rulers actually did so is frequently discussed in the political analyses of Europe in the eighteenth century. Many historians once asserted that a new type of monarchy emerged in the late eighteenth century, which they called "enlightened despotism" or "enlightened absolutism." Monarchs such as Frederick II of Prussia, Catherine the Great of Russia, and Joseph II of Austria supposedly followed the advice of the philosophes and ruled by enlightened principles, establishing a path to modern nationhood. Recent scholarship, however, has questioned the usefulness of the concept of "enlightened absolutism." We can best determine the extent to which it can be applied by surveying the development of the European states in the eighteenth century and then making a judgment about the "enlightened absolutism" of the century's later years.

The Atlantic Seaboard States

As a result of overseas voyages in the sixteenth century, the European economic axis began to shift from the Mediterranean to the Atlantic seaboard. In the seventeenth century, the English and Dutch expanded as Spain and Portugal declined. By the eighteenth century, Dutch power had waned, and it was left to the English and French to build the commercial empires that created a true global economy.

FRANCE: THE LONG RULE OF LOUIS XV

In the eighteenth century, France experienced an economic revival as the Enlightenment gained strength. The French monarchy, however, was not overly influenced by the philosophes and resisted reforms while the French aristocracy grew stronger.

Louis XIV had left France with enlarged territories, an enormous debt, an unhappy populace, and a five-year-old great-grandson as his successor. The governing of France fell into the hands first of the regent, the duke of Orléans, whose good intentions were thwarted by his drunken and immoral behavior, and later of Cardinal Fleury, the king's minister. France pulled back from foreign adventures while commerce and trade expanded and the government promoted the growth of industry, especially in coal and textiles. The budget was even balanced for a while. When Fleury died in 1743, Louis XV (1715–1774) decided to rule alone. But Louis was both lazy and weak, and ministers and mistresses soon began to influence the king, control the affairs of state, and undermine the prestige of the monarchy. One mistress—probably the most famous of eighteenth-century Europe—was Madame de Pompadour. An intelligent and beautiful woman, she charmed Louis XV and gained both wealth and power, often making important government decisions and giving advice on appointments and foreign policy. The loss of an empire in the Seven Years' War, accompanied by burdensome taxes, an ever-mounting public debt, more hungry people, and a court life at Versailles that remained frivolous and carefree, forced even Louis to realize the growing disgust with his monarchy.

Perhaps all might not have been in vain if Louis had been succeeded by a competent king. But the new king, Louis's twenty-year-old grandson who became Louis XVI (1774–1792), knew little about the operations of the French government and lacked the energy to deal decisively with state affairs (see the box on p. 494). His wife, Marie Antoinette, was a spoiled Austrian princess who devoted much of her time to court intrigues. As France's financial crises worsened, neither Louis nor his queen seemed able to fathom the depths of despair and discontent that soon led to violent revolution (see Chapter 19).

GREAT BRITAIN: KING AND PARLIAMENT

The success of the Glorious Revolution in England had prevented absolutism without clearly inaugurating constitutional monarchy. The eighteenth-century British political system was characterized by a sharing of power between king and Parliament, with Parliament gradually gaining the upper hand. (The United Kingdom of Great Britain came into existence in 1707 when the governments of England and Scotland were united; the term *British* came to refer to both English and Scots.) The king chose ministers responsible to himself who set policy and guided Parliament; Parliament had the power to make laws, levy taxes, pass the budget, and indirectly influence the king's ministers. The eighteenth-century British Parliament was dominated by a landed aristocracy that historians usually divide into two groups: the peers, who sat for life in the House of Lords, and the landed gentry, who sat in the House of Commons and served as justices of the peace in the counties. There is much historical debate over whether it makes sense to distinguish between the aristocracies because the two groups had much in common. Both were landowners with similar economic interests, and they frequently intermarried.

Although the British monarchy faced a powerful aristocracy that monopolized Parliament and held most of the important governing posts locally and nationally, it still exercised considerable power. Because the aristocracy was divided by factional struggles based on family rivalries, the kings could take advantage of the divisions to win aristocratic supporters through patronage, awarding them titles, government posts, and positions in the church and household staff.

What enabled the British system of political patronage to work was the structure of parliamentary elections. The deputies to the House of Commons were chosen from the boroughs and counties, but not by popular vote and hardly in any equitable fashion. Of the almost five hundred deputies in the House of Commons, about four hundred were chosen from the boroughs. Past history rather than population determined the number of delegates from each borough, however, so in one borough six people might choose two representatives whereas new cities like Manchester had no delegates at all despite their growing populations. Who could vote also varied wildly, enabling wealthy landed aristocrats to gain support through patronage and bribery; the result was a number of "pocket boroughs" controlled by a single person ("in his pocket"). The duke of Newcastle, for example, controlled the representatives from seven boroughs. It has been estimated that out of 405 borough deputies, 293 were chosen by fewer than 500 voters. This aristocratic control also extended to the county

The French King's Bedtime

Louis XIV had used court etiquette to magnify the dignity of kingship. During the reign of Louis XVI (1774–1792), however, court etiquette degenerated to ludicrous depths. This excerpt from the *Memoirs of the Comtesse de Boigne* describes the king's *coucher,* the formal ceremony in which the king retired for the night.

■ *Comtesse de Boigne,* Memoirs

The king [Louis XVI] went to his *coucher.* The so-called *coucher* took place every evening at half past nine. The gentlemen of the court assembled in the bedroom of Louis XVI (but Louis XVI did not sleep there). I believe that all those who had been presented at court were permitted to attend.

The king came in from an adjoining room, followed by his domestic staff. His hair was in curlers, and he was not wearing his decorations. Without paying attention to anybody, he stepped behind the handrail surrounding the bed, and the chaplain on duty was given the prayer book and a tall taperstand with two candles by one of the valets. He then joined the king behind the handrail, handed him the book, and held the taperstand during the king's prayer, which was short. The king then went to the part of the room where the courtiers were, and the chaplain gave the taperstand back to the first valet who, in turn, took it over to a person indicated by the king. This person held it as long as the *coucher* lasted. This distinction was very much sought after. . . .

The king had his coat, vest and finally shirt removed. He was naked to the waist, scratching and rubbing himself as if alone, though he was in the presence of the whole court and often a number of distinguished foreigners.

The first valet handed the nightshirt to the most qualified person. . . . If it was a person with whom the king was on familiar terms, he often played little tricks before donning it, missed it, passed it, and ran away, accompanying this charming nonsense with hearty laughter, making those who were sincerely attached to him suffer. Having donned the nightshirt, he put on his robe and three valets unfastened the belt and the knee buckles of his trousers, which fell down to his feet. Thus attired, hardly able to walk so absurdly encumbered, he began to make the round of the circle.

The duration of this reception was by no means fixed; sometimes it lasted only a few minutes, sometimes almost an hour; it depended on who was there. . . . When the king had enough, he dragged himself backward to an easy chair which had been pushed to the middle of the room and fell heavily into it, raising both legs. Two pages on their knees seized his shoes, took them off, and dropped them on the floor with a thump, which was part of the etiquette. When he heard it, the doorman opened the door and said, "This way, gentlemen." Everybody left, and the ceremony was over. However, the person who held the taperstand was permitted to stay if he had anything special to say to the king. This explains the high price attached to this strange favor.

delegates, two from each of England's forty counties. Although all holders of property worth at least 40 shillings a year could vote, members of the leading landed gentry families were elected over and over again.

Since the ministers were responsible for exercising the king's patronage, who became his chief ministers took on great political significance. In 1714, a new dynasty—the Hanoverians—was established when the last Stuart ruler, Queen Anne (1702–1714), died without an heir. The crown was offered to the Protestant rulers of the German state of Hanover. Both George I (1714–1727) and George II (1727–1760) relied on Robert Walpole as their chief or prime minister and the duke of Newcastle as their main dispenser of patronage, putting the latter at the center of British politics. Since the first Hanoverian king did not speak English and neither George had much familiarity with the British system, the chief ministers were allowed to handle Parliament and dispense patronage. Many historians feel that this exercise of ministerial power was an important step in the development of the modern cabinet system in British government.

Walpole served as prime minister from 1721 to 1742 and pursued a peaceful foreign policy to avoid new land taxes. But burgeoning trade and industry in eighteenth-century Britain led the ever-increasing middle class to favor expansion of trade and world empire. The exponents of empire found a spokesman in William Pitt the Elder, who became prime minister in 1757 and furthered imperial ambitions by acquiring Canada and India in the Seven Years' War (see "The Seven Years' War" later in this chapter).

Despite his successes, however, Pitt was dismissed by the new king, George III (1760–1820), in 1761 and replaced by the king's favorite, Lord Bute. George III was determined to strengthen monarchical authority and to wield the power of patronage personally. However, as a growing number of newspapers spread Enlightenment ideas to an expanding reading public, the clamor for the reform of both patronage and the electoral system began to increase. The saga of John Wilkes soon intensified the public outcry.

An ambitious middle-class member of the House of Commons, John Wilkes was an outspoken journalist who publicly criticized the king's ministers. Arrested and soon released, Wilkes was expelled from his seat in Parliament. When he persevered and won another parliamentary seat from the county of Middlesex, near London, he was again denied the right to take his place in Parliament. Wilkes's cause quickly became identified with liberty, and the slogan "Wilkes and Liberty" was frequently used by his sup-

National Portrait Gallery

The British House of Commons. A sharing of power between king and Parliament characterized the British political system in the eighteenth century. Parliament was divided into the House of Lords and the House of Commons. This painting shows the House of Commons in session in 1793 during a debate over the possibility of war with France. William Pitt is addressing the House.

porters, who came from two major social groups: the common people of London, who had no voting rights, and a middle element of voting freeholders, such as guild masters and small merchants in London and the surrounding counties. The cry for liberty soon spilled over into calls for the reform of Parliament and an end to parliamentary privileges. In 1780, the House of Commons affirmed that "the influence of the crown has increased, is increasing, and ought to be diminished." At the same time, criticism at home was exacerbated by criticism abroad, especially by the American colonists, whose discontent with the British system had led to rebellion and separation (see Chapter 19). Although minor reforms of the patronage system were made in 1782, King George III managed to avoid more drastic change by appointing William Pitt the Younger (1759–1806), son of William Pitt the Elder, as prime minister in 1783. Supported by the merchants, industrial classes, and the king, who used patronage to gain support for Pitt in the House of Commons, the latter managed to stay in power through the French revolutionary and Napoleonic eras. George III, however, remained an uncertain supporter because of periodic bouts of insanity (he once thought a tree in Windsor Park was the king of Prussia). With Pitt's successes, serious reform of the corrupt parliamentary system was avoided for another generation.

THE DECLINE OF THE DUTCH REPUBLIC

After its century in the sun, the Dutch Republic or United Netherlands suffered a decline in economic prosperity. Both local and national political affairs were dominated by the oligarchies that governed the Dutch Republic's towns. In the eighteenth century, the struggle continued between these oligarchs (or regents, as they were called, from their governing positions) and the house of Orange, who as stadholders headed the executive branch of government. The regents sought to reduce the power of the Orangists but soon became divided when Dutch burghers who called themselves the Patriots (artisans, merchants, and shopkeepers) began to agitate for democratic reforms that would open up the municipal councils to greater participation than that of the oligarchs. The success of the Patriots, however, led to foreign interference when the Prussian king sent troops to protect his sister, wife of the Orangist stadholder. The Patriots were crushed, and both Orangists and regents reestablished the old system. The intervention by Prussia serves to remind us of the growing power of the central European states.

Absolutism in Central and Eastern Europe

Of the five major European states, three were located in central and eastern Europe and came to play an increasingly important role in European international politics (see Map 18.1).

PRUSSIA: THE ARMY AND THE BUREAUCRACY

Two able Prussian kings in the eighteenth century, Frederick William I and Frederick II, further developed the two major institutions—the army and the bureaucracy—that were the backbone of Prussia. Frederick William I (1713–1740) promoted the evolution of Prussia's highly efficient civil bureaucracy by establishing the General Directory. It served as the chief administrative agent of the central government, supervising military, police, economic, and financial affairs. Because Prussia's disjointed territories could hardly have been preserved without a centralized administrative machine, Frederick William strove to maintain a highly efficient bureaucracy of civil service workers. It had its own code, in which the supreme values were obedience, honor, and service to the king as the highest duty. As Frederick William asserted: "One must serve the king with life and limb, with goods and chattels, with honor

CHRONOLOGY

The European States: The Atlantic Seaboard States

France	
Louis XV	1715–1774
Louis XVI	1774–1792
Great Britain	
The Stuarts	
Queen Anne	1702–1714
The Hanoverians	
George I	1714–1727
George II	1727–1760
Robert Walpole	1721–1742
William Pitt the Elder	1757–1761
George III	1760–1820
William Pitt the Younger	1783–1801

and conscience, and surrender everything except salvation. The latter is reserved for God. But everything else must be mine."[2] For his part, Frederick William personally kept a close watch over his officials to ensure that they performed their duties. As the Saxon minister at Berlin related:

> Every day His Majesty gives new proofs of his justice. Walking recently at Potsdam at six in the morning, he saw a post-coach arrive with several passengers who knocked for a long time at the post-house which was still closed. The King, seeing that no one opened the door, joined them in knocking and even knocked in some window-panes. The master of the post then opened the door and scolded the travelers, for no one recognized the King. But His Majesty let himself be known by giving the official some good blows of his cane and drove him from his house and his job after apologizing to the travelers for his laziness. Examples of this sort, of which I could relate several others, make everybody alert and exact.[3]

Close personal supervision of the bureaucracy became a hallmark of the eighteenth-century Prussian rulers.

Under Frederick William I, the rigid class stratification that had emerged in seventeenth-century Brandenburg-

Map 18.1 Europe in 1763. By the middle of the eighteenth century, five major powers dominated Europe—Prussia, Austria, Russia, Britain, and France. Each sought to enhance its power both domestically, through a bureaucracy that collected taxes and ran the military, and internationally, by capturing territory or preventing other powers from capturing territory.
■ Given the distribution of Prussian and Habsburg holdings, in what areas of Europe were they most likely to compete for land and power?

Prussia persisted. The nobility or landed aristocracy known as Junkers, who owned large estates with many serfs, still played a dominating role in the Prussian state. The Junkers held a complete monopoly over the officer corps of the Prussian army, which Frederick William passionately continued to expand. By the end of his reign, the army had grown from 45,000 to 83,000 men. Though tenth in physical size and thirteenth in population among the European states, Prussia had the fourth largest army, after France, Russia, and Austria.

By using nobles as officers, Frederick William ensured a close bond between the nobility and the army and, in turn, the loyalty of the nobility to the absolute monarch. As officers, the Junker nobility became imbued with a sense of service to the king or state. All the virtues of the Prussian nobility were, in effect, military virtues: duty, obedience, sacrifice. At the same time, because of its size and reputation as one of the best armies in Europe, the Prussian army was the most important institution in the state. "Prussian militarism" became synonymous with the extreme exaltation of military virtues. Indeed, one Prussian minister remarked around 1800 that "Prussia was not a country with an army, but an army with a country which served as headquarters and food magazine."[4]

The remaining classes in Prussia were considerably less important than the nobility. The peasants were born on their lords' estates and spent most of the rest of their lives there or in the army. They had few real rights and even needed their Junker's permission to marry. For the middle class, the only opportunity for any social prestige was in the Prussian civil service, where the ideal of loyal service to the state became a hallmark of the middle-class official. Frederick William allowed and even encouraged men of non-noble birth to serve in important administrative posts. When he died in 1740, only three of his eighteen privy councillors were of noble birth.

Frederick II, known as the Great (1740–1786), was one of the best educated and most cultured monarchs in the eighteenth century. He was well versed in Enlightenment thought and even invited Voltaire to live at his court for several years. His intellectual interests were despised by his father, who forced his intelligent son to prepare for a career in ruling (see the box on p. 498). A believer in the king as the "first servant of the state," Frederick the Great became a conscientious ruler who made few innovations in the administration of the state. His diligence in overseeing its operation, however, made the Prussian bureaucracy well known for both its efficiency and its honesty.

For a time, Frederick seemed quite willing to follow the philosophes' recommendations for reform. He established a single code of laws for his territories that eliminated the use of torture except in treason and murder cases. He also granted a limited freedom of speech and press as well as complete religious toleration—no difficult task since he had no strong religious convictions. Although Frederick was well aware of the philosophes' condemnation of serfdom, he was too dependent on the Prussian nobility to interfere with it or with the hierarchical

Frederick II at Sans-Souci. Frederick II was one of the most cultured and best educated European monarchs. In this painting, he is shown (holding walking stick) visiting the building site of his residential retreat, Sans-Souci, at Potsdam, accompanied by the marquis of Argens.

Frederick the Great and His Father

As a young man, the future Frederick the Great was quite different from his strict and austere father, Frederick William I. Possessing a high regard for French culture, poetry, and flute playing, Frederick resisted his father's wishes that he immerse himself in governmental and military affairs. Eventually, Frederick capitulated to his father's will and accepted the need to master affairs of state. These letters, written when Frederick was sixteen, illustrate the difficulties in their relationship.

Frederick to His Father, Frederick William I (September 11, 1728)

I have not ventured for a long time to present myself before my dear papa, partly because I was advised against it, but chiefly because I anticipated an even worse reception than usual and feared to vex my dear papa still further by the favor I have now to ask; so I have preferred to put it in writing.

I beg my dear papa that he will be kindly disposed toward me. I do assure him that after long examination of my conscience I do not find the slightest thing with which to reproach myself; but if, against my wish and will, I have vexed my dear papa, I hereby beg most humbly for forgiveness, and hope that my dear papa will give over the fearful hate which has appeared so plainly in his whole behavior and to which I cannot accustom myself. I have always thought hitherto that I had a kind father, but now I see the contrary. However, I will take courage and hope that my dear papa will think this all over and take me again into his favor. Meantime I assure him that I will never, my life long, willingly fail him, and in spite of his disfavor I am still, with most dutiful and childlike respect, my dear papa's

Most obedient and faithful servant and son,

Frederick

Frederick William to His Son Frederick

A bad, obstinate boy, who does not love his father; for when one does one's best, and especially when one loves one's father, one does what he wishes not only when he is standing by but when he is not there to see. Moreover you know very well that I cannot stand an effeminate fellow who has no manly tastes, who cannot ride or shoot (to his shame be it said!), is untidy about his person, and wears his hair curled like a fool instead of cutting it; and that I have condemned all these things a thousand times, and yet there is no sign of improvement. For the rest, haughty, offish as a country lout, conversing with none but a favored few instead of being affable and popular, grimacing like a fool, and never following my wishes out of love for me but only when forced into it, caring for nothing but to have his own way, and thinking nothing else is of any importance. This is my answer.

Frederick William

structure of Prussian society. In fact, Frederick was a social conservative who made Prussian society even more aristocratic than it had been before. Frederick reversed his father's policy of allowing commoners to rise to power in the civil service and reserved the higher positions in the bureaucracy for members of the nobility. The upper ranks of the bureaucracy came close to constituting a hereditary caste over time.

Like his predecessors, Frederick the Great took a great interest in military affairs and enlarged the Prussian army (to 200,000 men). Unlike his predecessors, he had no objection to using it. Frederick did not hesitate to take advantage of a succession crisis in the Habsburg monarchy to seize the Austrian province of Silesia for Prussia. This act aroused Austria's bitter hostility and embroiled Frederick in two major wars, the War of the Austrian Succession and the Seven Years' War (see "Wars and Diplomacy" later in this chapter). Although the latter war left his country exhausted, Frederick succeeded in keeping Silesia. After the wars, the first partition of Poland with Austria and Russia in 1772 gave him the Polish territory between Prussia and Brandenburg and created greater unity for the scattered lands of Prussia. By the end of his reign, Prussia was recognized as a great European power.

THE AUSTRIAN EMPIRE OF THE HABSBURGS

The Austrian Empire had become one of the great European states by the beginning of the eighteenth century. The city of Vienna, center of the Habsburg monarchy, was filled with magnificent palaces and churches built in the Baroque style and became the music capital of Europe. And yet Austria, a sprawling empire composed of many different nationalities, languages, religions, and cultures, found it difficult to provide common laws and a centralized administration for its people.

Empress Maria Theresa (1740–1780), however, stunned by the loss of Austrian Silesia to Prussia in the War of the Austrian Succession, resolved to reform her empire in preparation for the seemingly inevitable next conflict with rival Prussia. Although Maria Theresa was forced to accept the privileges of the Hungarian nobility and the right of her Hungarian subjects to have their own laws, she did abolish the Austrian and Bohemian chancelleries and replaced them with departments of foreign affairs, justice, war, commerce, and internal affairs that functioned for both territories. Maria Theresa also curtailed the role of the diets or provincial assemblies in taxation and local administration. Now clergy and nobles were forced to pay

Kunsthistorisches Museum, Vienna

Maria Theresa and Her Family. Maria Theresa governed the vast possessions of the Austrian Empire from 1740 to 1780. Of her ten surviving children, Joseph II (shown here in red standing to the left of his mother) succeeded her; Leopold became grand-duke of Tuscany and the ruler of Austria after Joseph's death; Ferdinand was made duke of Modena; and Marie Antoinette became the bride of King Louis XVI of France.

property and income taxes to royal officials rather than the diets. The Austrian and Bohemian lands were divided into ten provinces and subdivided into districts, all administered by royal officials rather than representatives of the diets, making part of the Austrian Empire more centralized and more bureaucratic. But these administrative reforms were done for practical reasons—to strengthen the power of the Habsburg state—and were accompanied by an enlargement and modernization of the armed forces. Maria Theresa remained staunchly Catholic and conservative and was not open to the wider reform calls of the philosophes. But her successor was.

Joseph II (1780–1790) was determined to make changes; at the same time, he carried on his mother's chief goal of enhancing Habsburg power within the monarchy and Europe. Joseph was an earnest man who believed in the need to sweep away anything standing in the path of reason. As he expressed it: "I have made philosophy the lawmaker of my empire; her logical applications are going to transform Austria."

Joseph's reform program was far-reaching. He abolished serfdom and tried to give the peasants hereditary rights to their holdings. He abandoned economic restraints by eliminating internal trade barriers, ending monopolies, and removing guild restrictions. A new penal code was instituted that abrogated the death penalty and established the principle of equality of all before the law. Joseph introduced drastic religious reforms as well, including complete religious toleration and restrictions on the Catholic church. Altogether, Joseph II issued six thousand decrees and eleven thousand laws in his effort to transform Austria.

Joseph's reform program proved overwhelming for Austria, however. He alienated the nobility by freeing the serfs and alienated the church by his attacks on the monastic establishment. Even the serfs were unhappy, unable to comprehend the drastic changes inherent in Joseph's policies. His attempt to rationalize the administration of the empire by imposing German as the official bureaucratic language alienated the non-German nationalities. As Joseph complained, there were not enough people for the kind of bureaucracy he needed. His deep sense of failure is revealed in the epitaph he wrote for his gravestone: "Here lies Joseph II, who was unfortunate in everything that he undertook." His successors undid many of his reform efforts.

RUSSIA UNDER CATHERINE THE GREAT

Peter the Great's six successors fell under the thumb of the palace guard. The last of these six was Peter III, whose German wife, Catherine, learned Russian and won the favor of the guard. Peter was murdered by a faction of nobles, and Catherine II the Great (1762–1796) emerged as autocrat of all of Russia.

Catherine was an intelligent woman who was familiar with the works of the philosophes. She claimed that she wished to reform Russia along the lines of Enlightenment ideas, but she was always shrewd enough to realize that her success depended on the support of the palace guard and the gentry class from which it stemmed. She could not afford to alienate the Russian nobility.

Initially, Catherine seemed eager to pursue reform. She called for the election of an assembly in 1767 to debate the details of a new law code. In her *Instruction,* written as a guide to the deliberations, Catherine questioned the institutions of serfdom, torture, and capital punishment and even advocated the principle of the equality of all people in the eyes of the law (see the box on p. 500). But a year and a half of negotiation produced little real change.

In fact, Catherine's subsequent policies had the effect of strengthening the landholding class at the expense of all others, especially the Russian serfs. In order to reorganize local government, Catherine divided Russia into fifty provinces, each of which was in turn subdivided into

The Proposals of Catherine II for a New Law Code

Catherine the Great of Russia appeared for a while to be an enlightened ruler. In 1767, she convened a legislative commission to prepare a new code of laws for Russia. In her famous *Instruction*, she gave the delegates a detailed guide to the principles they should follow. Although the guidelines were obviously culled from the liberal ideas of the philosophes, the commission itself accomplished nothing, and Catherine's *Instruction* was soon forgotten.

Catherine II, Proposals for a New Law Code

13. What is the true End of Monarchy? Not to deprive People of their natural Liberty; but to correct their Actions, in order to attain the supreme good.
33. The Laws ought to be so framed, as to secure the Safety of every Citizen as much as possible.
34. The Equality of the Citizens consists in this; that they should all be subject to the same Laws.
38. A Man ought to form in his own Mind an exact and clear Idea of what Liberty is. Liberty is the Right of doing whatsoever the Laws allow: And if any one Citizen could do what the Laws forbid, there would be no more Liberty; because others would have an equal Power of doing the same.
123. The Usage of Torture is contrary to all the Dictates of Nature and Reason; even Mankind itself cries out against it, and demands loudly the total Abolition of it.
180. That Law, therefore, is highly beneficial to the Community where it is established, which ordains that every Man shall be judged by his Peers and Equals. For when the Fate of a Citizen is in Question, all Prejudices arising from the Difference of Rank or Fortune should be stifled; because they ought to have no Influence between the Judges and the Parties accused.
194. No Man ought to be looked upon as guilty, before he has received his judicial Sentence; nor can the Laws deprive him of their Protection, before it is proved that he has forfeited all Right to it. What Right therefore can Power give to any to inflict Punishment upon a Citizen at a Time, when it is yet dubious, whether he is Innocent or guilty?
270. It is highly necessary that the Law should prescribe a Rule to the Lords, for a more judicious Method of raising their Revenues; and oblige them to levy such a Tax, as tends least to separate the Peasant from His House and Family; this would be the Means by which Agriculture would become more extensive, and Population be more increased in the Empire.

Scala/Art Resource, NY

Catherine the Great. Autocrat of Russia, Catherine was an intelligent ruler who favored reform. She found it expedient, however, to retain much of the old system in order to keep the support of the landed nobility. In this portrait by Dmitry Levitsky, she is shown in legislative regalia in the Temple of Justice in 1783.

districts whose ruling officials were chosen by the nobles. In this way, the local nobility became responsible for the day-to-day governing of Russia. Moreover, the gentry were now formed into corporate groups with special legal privileges, including the right to trial by peers and exemption from personal taxation and corporal punishment. The Charter of the Nobility formalized these rights in 1785.

Catherine's policy of favoring the landed nobility led to even worse conditions for the Russian peasantry. The attempt of the Russian government to impose restrictions on free peasants in the border districts of the Russian Empire soon led to a full-scale revolt that spread to the Volga valley. It was intensified by the support of the Cossacks, independent tribes of fierce warriors who had at times fought for the Russians against the Turks but now resisted the government's attempt to absorb them into the empire.

An illiterate Cossack, Emelyan Pugachev, succeeded in welding the disparate elements of discontent into a mass revolt. Beginning in 1773, Pugachev's rebellion spread

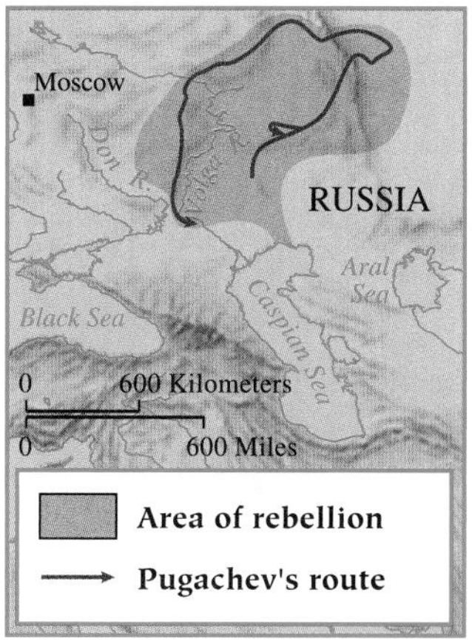

Pugachev's Rebellion

across southern Russia from the Urals to the Volga River. Initially successful, Pugachev won the support of many peasants when he issued a manifesto in July 1774 freeing all peasants from oppressive taxes and military service. Encouraged by Pugachev to seize their landlords' estates, the peasants responded by killing more than fifteen hundred estate owners and their families. The rebellion soon faltered, however, as government forces rallied and became more effective. Betrayed by his own subordinates, Pugachev was captured, tortured, and executed. The rebellion collapsed completely, and Catherine responded with even greater repression of the peasantry. All rural reform was halted, and serfdom was expanded into newer parts of the empire.

Catherine proved a worthy successor to Peter the Great by expanding Russia's territory westward into Poland and southward to the Black Sea. Russia spread southward by defeating the Turks. In the Treaty of Kuchuk-Kainarji in 1774, the Russians gained some land, the privilege of protecting Greek Orthodox Christians in the Ottoman Empire, and the right to sail in Turkish waters. Russian expansion westward occurred at the expense of neighboring Poland. In the three partitions of Poland, Russia gained about 50 percent of Polish territory.

THE DESTRUCTION OF POLAND

Poland was an excellent example of why a strong monarchy was needed in early modern Europe. The Polish king was elected by the Polish nobles and forced to accept drastic restrictions on his power, including limited revenues, a small bureaucracy, and a standing army of no more than twenty thousand soldiers. For Polish nobles, these limitations eliminated an absolute king; for Poland's powerful neighbors, they were an invitation to meddle in its affairs.

The total destruction of the Polish state in the eighteenth century resulted from the rivalries of its three great neighbors, Austria, Russia, and Prussia. To avoid war, the leaders of these powers decided to compensate themselves by dividing Poland. To maintain the balance of power in central and eastern Europe, the three great powers cynically agreed to the acquisition of roughly equal territories at Poland's expense.

In 1772, Poland lost about 30 percent of its land and 50 percent of its population (see Map 18.2). Austria gained the agriculturally rich district of Galicia, Russia took the largest slice of land in eastern Poland, and Prussia acquired West Prussia, the smallest but most valuable territory because it united two of the chief sections of Prussia.

The remaining Polish state was supposedly independent; in truth, it was dominated by the Russians, who even kept troops on Polish territory. After the Poles attempted to establish a stronger state under a hereditary monarchy in 1791, the Russians gained the support of Austria and Prussia and intervened militarily in May 1792. In the following year, Russia and Prussia undertook a second partition of Polish territory. Finally, after a heroic but hopeless rebellion in 1794–1795 under General Thaddeus Kosciuszko, the remaining Polish state was obliterated by Austria, Prussia, and Russia in the third partition of Poland (1795). Many historians have pointed to Poland's demise as a cogent example of why building a strong, absolutist state was essential to survival in the seventeenth and eighteenth centuries.

CHRONOLOGY

The European States: Absolutism in Central and Eastern Europe

Prussia	
Frederick William I	1713–1740
Frederick II the Great	1740–1786
Austrian Empire	
Maria Theresa	1740–1780
Joseph II	1780–1790
Russia	
Peter III	1762
Catherine II the Great	1762–1796
Pugachev's rebellion	1773–1775
Charter of the Nobility	1785
Poland	
First partition	1772
Second partition	1793
Third partition	1795

The Mediterranean World

At the beginning of the eighteenth century, Spain experienced a change of dynasties from the Habsburgs to the Bourbons. Bourbon rule temporarily rejuvenated Spain and at least provided an opportunity to centralize the institutions of the state. Under Philip V (1700–1746), the laws, administrative institutions, and language of Castile were established in the other Spanish kingdoms, making the king of Castile truly the king of Spain. Moreover, French-style ministries replaced the old conciliar system of government, and officials similar to French *intendants* were introduced into the various Spanish provinces.

Since the Treaty of Utrecht in 1713 had taken the Italian territories and Netherlands away from Spain, the latter now had fewer administrative problems and less drain on its already overtaxed economic resources. In the second half of the eighteenth century, especially during the reign of Charles III (1759–1788), the Catholic church was also brought under control when the king banished the Jesuits and circumscribed the activities of the Inquisition. The

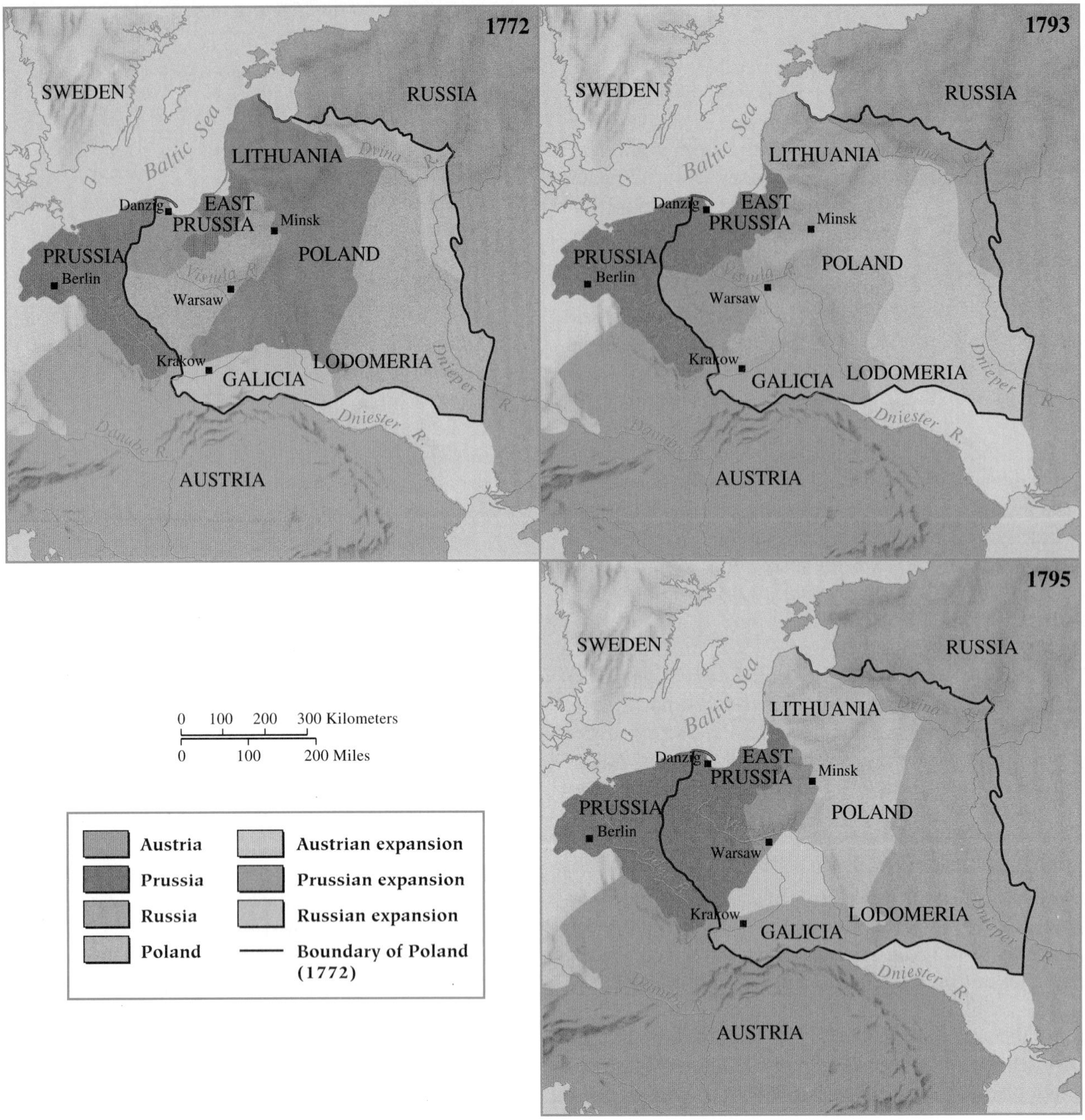

Map 18.2 The Partitions of Poland. Crowded by three great powers, Poland lay primarily on a plain with few easily defensible borders. This fact, combined with a weak and ineffectual monarchy, laid the seeds for Poland's destruction. By 1795, Austria, Prussia (Germany in 1870), and Russia had long borders with each other, a situation that would contribute to the outbreak of World War I in 1914. ■ Which country gained the most territory at the expense of Poland?

landed aristocracy continued to exercise substantial power throughout the eighteenth century, however.

Portugal had experienced decline since the glorious days of empire in the sixteenth century. Nevertheless, during the long ministry of the marquis of Pombal (1699–1782), who served as chief minister to a series of Portuguese kings, the nobility and Catholic church were curtailed and the Portuguese empire temporarily revived. After Pombal was removed from office, the nobility and church regained much of their power.

After the Treaty of Utrecht, Austria had replaced Spain as the dominant force in Italy in the eighteenth century. The duchy of Milan, Sardinia, and the kingdom of Naples were all surrendered to the Habsburg emperors, and Sicily was given to the northern Italian state of Savoy, which was slowly emerging as a state with an appetite for territorial expansion. In 1734, the Bourbons of Spain reestablished control over Naples and Sicily. Though some Italian states, such as Venice and Genoa, remained independent, they grew increasingly impotent in international affairs.

CHRONOLOGY

The European States: The Mediterranean World and Scandinavia

Spain	
Philip V, the first Bourbon king	1700–1746
Charles III	1759–1788
Portugal	
Marquis of Pombal	1699–1782
Sweden	
Charles XII	1697–1718
Gustavus III	1771–1792
Denmark	
Christian VII	1766–1808

The Scandinavian States

In the seventeenth century, Sweden had become the dominant power in northern Europe, but after the Battle of Poltava in 1709, Swedish power declined rapidly. Following the death of the powerful Charles XII in 1718, the Swedish nobility, using the Swedish diet as its instrument, gained control of public life and reduced the monarchy to puppet status. But the division of the nobility into pro-French and pro-Russian factions eventually enabled King Gustavus III (1771–1792) to reassert the power of the monarchy. Gustavus proved to be one of the most enlightened monarchs of his age. By decree, he established freedom of religion, speech, and press and instituted a new code of justice that eliminated the use of torture. Moreover, his economic reforms smacked of laissez-faire: he reduced tariffs, abolished tolls, and encouraged trade and agriculture. In 1792, however, a group of nobles, incensed at these reforms and their loss of power, assassinated the king, but they proved unable to fully restore the rule of the aristocracy.

Denmark also saw an attempt at enlightened reforms by King Christian VII (1766–1808) and his chief minister, John Frederick Struensee. Aristocratic opposition stymied their efforts, however, and led to Struensee's death in 1772.

Enlightened Absolutism Revisited

Of the three major rulers traditionally associated most closely with enlightened absolutism—Joseph II, Frederick II, and Catherine the Great—only Joseph II sought truly radical changes based on Enlightenment ideas. Both Frederick and Catherine liked to be cast as disciples of the Enlightenment, expressed interest in enlightened reforms, and even attempted some, but the policies of neither seemed seriously affected by Enlightenment thought. Necessities of state and maintenance of the existing system took precedence over reform. Indeed, many historians feel that Joseph, Frederick, and Catherine were all guided primarily by a concern for the power and well-being of their states and that their policies were not all that different from those of their predecessors. In the final analysis, heightened state power was used to amass armies and wage wars to gain more power. Nevertheless, in their desire to build stronger state systems, these rulers did pursue such enlightened practices as legal reform, religious toleration, and the extension of education because these served to create more satisfied subjects and strengthened the state in significant ways.

It would be foolish, however, to overlook the fact that political and social realities limited the ability of enlightened rulers to make reforms. Everywhere in Europe, the hereditary aristocracy still held the most power in society. Enlightened reforms were often limited to changes in the administrative and judicial systems that did not seriously undermine the powerful interests of the European nobility. Although aristocrats might join the populace in opposing monarchical extension of centralizing power, as the chief beneficiaries of a system based on traditional rights and privileges for their class, they were certainly not willing to support a political ideology that trumpeted the principle of equal rights for all.

Wars and Diplomacy

The philosophes condemned war as a foolish waste of life and resources in stupid quarrels of no value to humankind. Rulers, however, paid little attention to these comments and continued their costly struggles. By the eighteenth century, the European system of self-governing, individual states was grounded largely in the principle of self-interest. Because international relations were based on considerations of power, the eighteenth-century concept of a "balance of power" was predicated on how to counterbalance the power of one state by another to prevent any one power from dominating the others. This balance of power, however, did not imply a desire for peace. Large armies created to defend a state's security were often used for offensive purposes as well. As Frederick the Great of Prussia remarked, "The fundamental rule of governments is the principle of extending their territories." Nevertheless, the regular use of diplomacy served at times to lead to compromise.

The diplomacy of the eighteenth century still focused primarily on dynastic interests or the desire of ruling families to provide for their dependents and extend their dynastic holdings. But the eighteenth century also saw the emergence of the concept of "reason of state," on the basis of which a ruler such as Frederick II and a minister such as William Pitt the Elder looked beyond dynastic interests to the long-term future of their states.

International rivalry and the continuing centralization of the European states were closely related. The need for taxes to support large armies and navies created its own imperative for more efficient and effective control of power in the hands of bureaucrats who could collect taxes and organize states for the task of winning wars. At the same time, the development of large standing armies ensured that political disputes would periodically be resolved by armed conflict rather than diplomacy. Between 1715 and 1740, it had seemed that Europe preferred peace. But in 1740, a major conflict erupted over the succession to the Austrian throne.

The War of the Austrian Succession (1740–1748)

Unable to produce a male heir to the Austrian throne, the Habsburg emperor Charles VI (1711–1740) so feared the consequences of the succession of his daughter Maria Theresa that he spent much of his reign negotiating the Pragmatic Sanction, by which different European powers agreed to recognize his daughter as his legal heir.

After Charles's death, however, the Pragmatic Sanction was conveniently pushed aside, especially by Frederick II, who had just succeeded to the throne of Prussia. The new Prussian ruler took advantage of the new empress to invade Austrian Silesia. The vulnerability of Maria Theresa encouraged France to enter the war against its traditional enemy Austria; in turn, Maria Theresa made an alliance with Great Britain, who feared French hegemony over Continental affairs. All too quickly, the Austrian succession had set off a worldwide conflagration. The war was fought not only in Europe, where Prussia seized Silesia and France occupied the Austrian Netherlands, but in the East, where France took Madras in India from the British, and in North America, where the British captured the French fortress of Louisbourg at the entrance to the Saint Lawrence River. By 1748, all parties were exhausted and agreed to stop. The peace treaty of Aix-la-Chapelle promised the return of all occupied territories except Silesia to their original owners. Prussia's refusal to return Silesia guaranteed another war, at least between the two hostile central European powers of Prussia and Austria.

The Seven Years' War (1756–1763)

Maria Theresa refused to accept the loss of Silesia and prepared for its return by rebuilding her army while working diplomatically through her able foreign minister, Count Wenzel von Kaunitz, to separate Prussia from its chief ally, France. In 1756, Austria achieved what was soon labeled a diplomatic revolution. Bourbon-Habsburg rivalry had been a fact of European diplomacy since the late sixteenth century. But two new rivalries made this old one seem superfluous: Britain and France over colonial empires, and Austria and Prussia over Silesia. France now abandoned Prussia and allied with Austria. Russia, which saw Prussia as a major hindrance to Russian goals in central Europe, joined the new alliance. In turn, Great Britain allied with Prussia. This diplomatic revolution of 1756 now led to another worldwide war.

There were three major areas of conflict: Europe, India, and North America (see Map 18.3). Europe witnessed the clash of the two major alliances: the British and Prussians against the Austrians, Russians, and French. With his superb army and military prowess, Frederick the Great was able for some time to defeat the Austrian, French, and Russian armies. He won a spectacular victory at the Battle of Rossbach in Saxony (1757) over combined French-Austrian forces that far outnumbered his own troops. Under attack from three different directions, however, the forces of Frederick II were gradually worn down and faced utter defeat when they were saved by the death of Tsarina Elizabeth of Russia, which brought her nephew Peter III to power. A great admirer of Frederick the Great, Peter withdrew the Russian troops from the conflict and from the Prussian lands that they had occupied. His withdrawal guaranteed a stalemate and led to a desire for peace. The European conflict was ended by the Peace of Hubertusburg in 1763. All occupied territories were returned, and Austria officially recognized Prussia's permanent control of Silesia.

The Anglo-French struggle in the rest of the world had more decisive results. Known as the Great War for Empire, it was fought in India and North America. The French had returned Madras to Britain after the War of the Austrian Succession, but jockeying for power continued as the French and British supported opposing native Indian princes. The British under Robert Clive (1725–1774) ultimately won out, not because they had better forces but because they were more persistent (see the box on p. 506). By the Treaty of Paris in 1763, the French withdrew and left India to the British.

By far the greatest conflicts of the Seven Years' War took place in North America (where it was known as the French and Indian War). There were two primary areas of contention. One consisted of the waterways of the Gulf of Saint Lawrence, guarded by the fortress of Louisbourg and by forts near the Great Lakes and Lake Champlain that protected French Quebec and French traders. The other was the unsettled Ohio River valley. As the French moved south from the Great Lakes and north from their garrisons along the Mississippi, they began to establish forts from

CHRONOLOGY

The Mid-Century Wars

War of the Austrian Succession	1740–1748
Peace of Aix-la-Chapelle	1748
The Seven Years' War	1756–1763
Diplomatic revolution	1756
Battle of Rossbach	1757
British capture of Forts Duquesne and Louisbourg	1758
Battle of Quebec	1759
Peace of Hubertusburg	1763
Treaty of Paris	1763

Robert Clive in India. Robert Clive was the leader of the army of the British East India Company. He had been commanded to fight the ruler of Bengal in order to gain trading privileges. To make his job easier, Clive arranged a meeting with Mir Jaffier, the commander of Bengal's army, in order to win him over to the British side. Although not present at the meeting, British artist Francis Hayman imaginatively recreated the scene in this 1760 painting.

the Appalachians to the Mississippi River. To British settlers in the thirteen colonies to the east, this French activity threatened to cut off a vast area from British expansion. The French found allies among the Indians, who considered the French traders less threatening than the British settlers.

Despite initial French successes, British fortunes were revived by the efforts of William Pitt the Elder, who was convinced that the destruction of the French colonial empire was a necessary prerequisite for the creation of Britain's own colonial empire. Accordingly, Pitt decided to make a minimal effort in Europe while concentrating resources, especially the British navy, on the colonial war. Although French troops were greater in number, the ability of the French to use them in the New World was contingent on naval support. The defeat of French fleets in major naval battles in 1759 gave the British an advantage since the French could no longer easily reinforce their garrisons. A series of British victories soon followed. In 1758, Forts Louisbourg and Duquesne were captured. On the night of September 13, 1759, British forces led by General James Wolfe scaled the heights outside Quebec and defeated the French under General Louis-Joseph Montcalm on the Plains of Abraham. Both generals died in the battle. The British went on to seize Montreal, the Great Lakes area, and the Ohio valley. The French were forced to make peace. By the Treaty of Paris, they ceded Canada and the lands east of the Mississippi to Britain. Their ally Spain transferred Spanish Florida to British control; in return, the French gave their Louisiana territory to the Spanish. By 1763, Great Britain had become the world's greatest colonial power.

European Armies and Warfare

The professional standing army, initiated in the seventeenth century, became a standard feature of eighteenth-century Europe. Especially noticeable was the increase in the size of armies, which paralleled the development of absolutist states. Between 1740 and 1780, the French army grew from 190,000 to 300,000 men; the Prussian from 83,000 to 200,000; the Austrian from 108,000 to 282,000; and the Russian from 130,000 to 290,000.

The composition of these armies reflected the hierarchical structure of European society and the great chasm that separated the upper and lower classes. Officers were primarily from the landed aristocracy, which had for centuries regarded military activity as one of its major functions.

British Victory in India

The success of the British in defeating the French in India was due to Robert Clive, who, in this excerpt from one of his letters, describes his famous victory at Plassey, north of Calcutta (June 23, 1757). This battle demonstrated the inability of native Indian soldiers to compete with Europeans and signified the beginning of British control in Bengal. Clive claimed to have a thousand Europeans, two thousand sepoys (local soldiers), and eight cannons available for this battle.

Robert Clive's Account of His Victory at Plassey

At daybreak we discovered the [governor's army] moving toward us, consisting, as we since found, of about fifteen thousand horse and thirty-five thousand foot, with upwards of forty pieces of cannon. They approached apace, and by six began to attack with a number of heavy cannon, supported by the whole army, and continued to play on us very briskly for several hours, during which our situation was of the utmost service to us, being lodged in a large grove with good mud banks. To succeed in an attempt on their cannon was next to impossible, as they were planted in a manner round us and at considerable distances from each other. We therefore remained quiet in our post, in expectation of a successful attack upon their camp at night. About noon the enemy drew off their artillery and retired to their camp....

On finding them make no great effort to dislodge us, we proceeded to take possession of one or two more eminences lying very near an angle of their camp, from whence, and an adjacent eminence in their possession, they kept a smart fire of musketry upon us. They made several attempts to bring out their cannon, but our advanced fieldpieces played so warmly and so well upon them that they were always driven back. Their horse exposing themselves a good deal on this occasion, many of them were killed, and among the rest four or five officers of the first distinction; by which the whole army being visibly dispirited and thrown into some confusion, we were encouraged to storm both the eminence and the angle of their camp, which were carried at the same instant, with little or no loss; though the latter was defended (exclusively of blacks) by forty French and two pieces of cannon; and the former by a large body of blacks, both horse and foot. On this a general rout ensued, and we pursued the enemy six miles, passing upwards of forty pieces of cannon they had abandoned, with an infinite number of carts and carriages filled with baggage of all kinds.... It is computed there are killed of the enemy about five hundred. Our loss amounted to only twenty-two killed and fifty wounded, and those chiefly blacks.

Middle-class individuals were largely kept out of the higher ranks of the officer corps while being admitted to the middle ranks.

Rank-and-file soldiers came mostly from the lower classes of society. Some states, such as Prussia and Russia, conscripted able-bodied peasants. But many states realized that this was counterproductive since they could not afford to waste their farmers. For that reason, eighteenth-century armies were partly composed of foreign troops, many from Switzerland or the petty German states. Of the great powers, Britain alone had no regular standing army and relied on mercenaries, evident in its use of German troops in America. Most troops in European armies, especially the French and Austrian, were natives who enlisted voluntarily for six-year terms. Some were not exactly volunteers; often vagabonds and the unemployed were pressed into service. Most, however, came from the lower classes—peasants and also artisans from the cities—who saw the military as an opportunity to escape from hard times or personal problems.

The maritime powers, such as Britain and the Dutch Republic, regarded navies as more important than armies. In the second half of the eighteenth century, the British possessed 174 warships manned by eighty thousand sailors. Conditions on these ships were often poor. Diseases such as scurvy and yellow fever were rampant, and crews were frequently press-ganged into duty.

The dramatic increase in the size of armies and navies did not necessarily result in more destructive warfare in eighteenth-century Europe. For one thing, war was no longer driven by ideology as the religious conflicts of the sixteenth and seventeenth centuries had been. By their very nature, ideological wars are often violent and destructive. Moreover, since the larger armies depended on increased tax revenues, rulers regarded the wanton destruction of civilian taxpayers as foolish. Finally, the costliness of eighteenth-century armies as well as the technology and tactical traditions of the age created a system of warfare based on limited objectives.

Since generals were extremely reluctant to risk the destruction of their armies in pitched battles, clever and elaborate maneuvers, rather than direct confrontation, became fashionable. A system of formalities accepted by all sides allowed defeated opponents to withdraw without being captured or destroyed. This mentality also encouraged the construction of vast fortresses to secure major roads and the enormous quantities of supplies needed by eighteenth-century armies. With its own set patterns of tactics, siege warfare often became, as one French critic said disgustedly, "the art of surrendering strongholds honorably after certain conventional formalities." Nevertheless, despite the maneuvering and the sieges, European warfare in the eighteenth century also involved many battles and considerable risk.

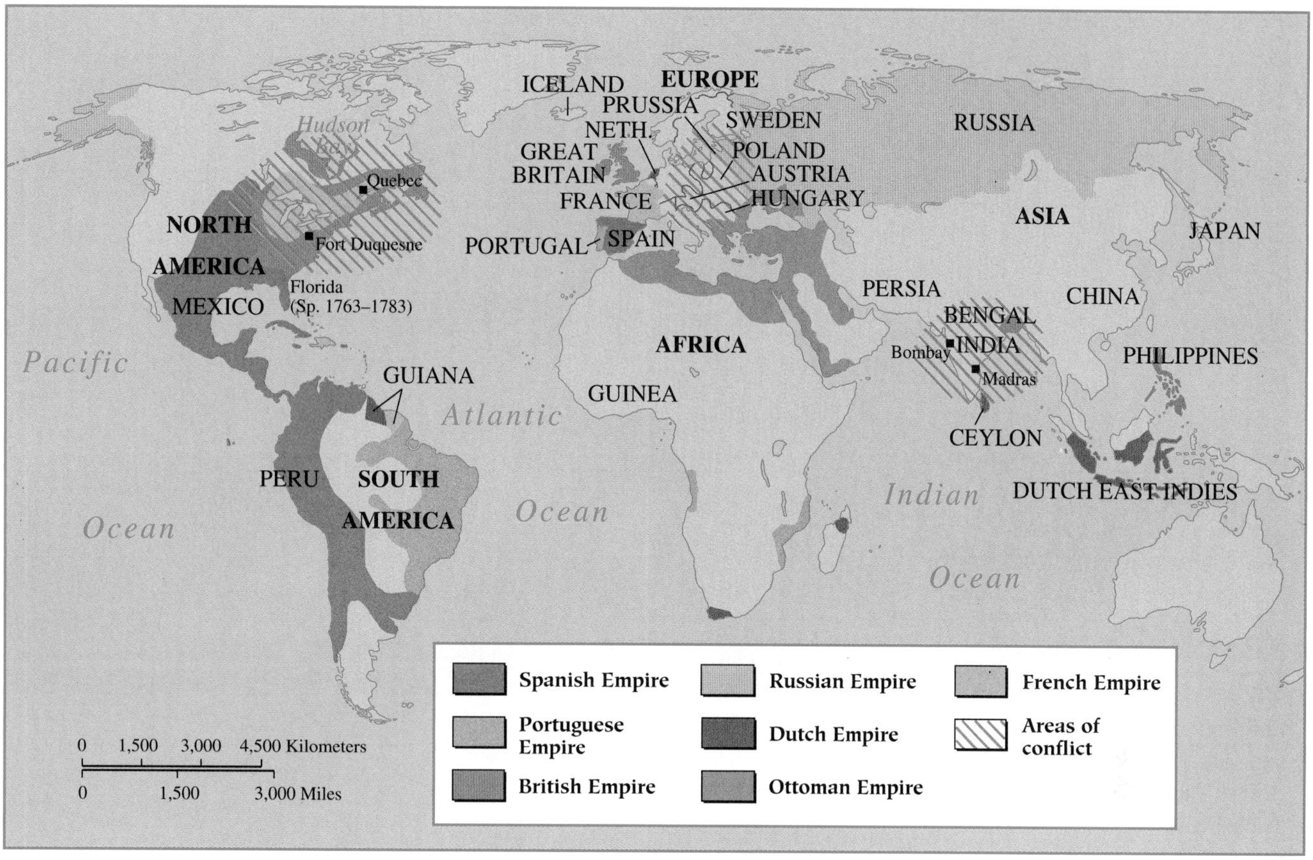

Map 18.3 The Battlefields of the Seven Years' War. A major struggle between the five great powers, the Seven Years' War was truly a worldwide conflict. In central Europe, Prussia survived against the combined forces of France, Austria, and Russia, while Britain emerged victorious against France in the struggle for empire, gaining control of French North America and India. ■ Why were naval strength and ability important in the conflict between Britain and France?

Economic Expansion and Social Change

The depressed economic conditions of the seventeenth century began to improve in the early eighteenth century. Rapid population growth, expansion in banking and trade, an agricultural revolution (at least in Britain), the stirrings of industrialization, and an increase in worldwide trade characterized the economic patterns of the eighteenth century.

Growth of the European Population

Europe's population began to grow around 1750 and experienced a slow but steady upward movement, with some regional variations. It has been estimated that the total European population was around 120 million in 1700, expanded to 140 million by 1750, and then grew to 190 million by 1790; thus the growth rate in the second half of the century was double that of the first half. Individual states also experienced rapid growth between 1700 and 1790: Russia's population went from 14 million to 28 million (much of it due to territorial expansion); France from 20 to 26 or 27 million; Spain from 6 to 10 million; Brandenburg-Prussia from 1.5 to 5.5 million (over half of this came from territorial acquisition); and Britain from 5 or 6 to 9 million. These increases occurred during the same time that several million Europeans were going abroad as colonists.

Perhaps the most important cause of population growth was a decline in the death rate, thanks, no doubt, to more plentiful food and better transportation of food supplies, which led to improved diets and some relief from devastating famines. Also of great significance was the end of the bubonic plague, the last great outbreak of which in western Europe occurred in 1720 in southern France. Nevertheless, death was still a ubiquitous feature of everyday life. Diseases such as typhus, smallpox, influenza, and dysentery were rampant, especially since hygienic conditions remained poor—little bathing, dirty clothes, and no systematic elimination of human wastes. Despite the improved transportation, famine and hunger could still be devastating.

Children of the Upper Classes. This painting of John Bacon and his family illustrates an important feature of upper-class family life in Great Britain in the first half of the eighteenth century. The children appear as miniature adults, dressed in clothes modeled after the styles of their parents.

Family, Marriage, and Birthrate Patterns

The family, rather than the individual, was still at the heart of Europe's social organization. For the most part, people still thought of the family in traditional terms, as a patriarchal institution with the husband dominating his wife and children. The upper classes in particular were still concerned for the family as a "house," an association whose collective interests were more important than those of its individual members. Parents (especially the fathers) still generally selected marriage partners for their children, based on the interests of the family (see the box on p. 510). One French noble responded to his son's inquiry about his upcoming marriage: "Mind your own business."

CHILD CARE

At the beginning of the eighteenth century, traditional attitudes also prevailed in the care of children. Generally, lower-class women breast-fed their own children because it provided the best nourishment. Moreover, since there were strong taboos in various parts of Europe against sexual intercourse while one was breast-feeding, mothers might also avoid another immediate pregnancy; if the infant died, they could then have another child. Lower-class women, however, also served as wet nurses for children of the aristocratic and upper middle classes. Mothers from these higher social strata considered breast-feeding undignified and hired wet nurses instead. Even urban mothers, the wives of artisans, for economic reasons sent their babies to wet nurses in the countryside if they could, making the practice widespread in the eighteenth century.

In the second half of the eighteenth century, traditional attitudes began to alter, especially in western Europe. The impact of Enlightenment thought, such as Rousseau's *Émile,* and the increasing survival of more infants led to new attitudes toward children. Childhood was more and more viewed as a phase in human development. One result was a shift to dressing children in more comfortable clothes appropriate to their age rather than dressing them in clothes modeled after adult styles. Shops for children's clothes appeared for the first time. Primogeniture, the practice of treating the first son as the favorite, also came under attack. All children, it was argued, deserve their parents' attention. Appeals for women to breast-feed their own children rather than use wet nurses soon followed. In England, games and toys specifically for children now appeared. The jigsaw puzzle was invented in the 1760s, and books, such as *Little Pretty Pocket-Book* (1744), aimed to please as well as teach children. These changes, however, were limited mostly to the upper classes of western European society and did not extend to the peasants. For most Europeans, children were still a source of considerable anxiety. They represented a health risk to the mothers who bore them and more mouths to feed if they survived. In times of economic crisis, children proved such a burden to some families that they resorted to infanticide or abandonment to foundling homes.

Despite being punishable by death, infanticide remained a solution to the problem of too many children. So many

Germanisches Nationalmuseum

The Practice of Infanticide. Infanticide remained one of the solutions to the problem of too many children in the eighteenth century. This engraving recounts the story of one infanticide in Germany. *Top left:* The infant is discovered, smothered under a mattress. *Bottom left:* The mother is taken from prison to be executed. *Right:* A large crowd observes the execution of the mother for her crime.

children were being "accidentally" suffocated while in their parents' bed that in Austria in 1784 a law was enacted that forbade parents to place children under five years old in bed with them. More common than infanticide was the placement of unwanted children in foundling homes or hospitals, which became a favorite charity of the rich in eighteenth-century Europe. The largest of its kind, located in Saint Petersburg, Russia, was founded by members of the nobility. By the end of the century, it was taking in 5,000 new babies a year and caring for 25,000 children at one time.

But severe problems arose as the system became overburdened. One historian has estimated that in the 1770s, one-third of all babies born in Paris were taken to foundling institutions by parents or desperate unmarried mothers, creating serious overcrowding. Foundling institutions often proved fatal for infants. Mortality rates ranged from 50 percent to as high as 90 percent (in a sense making foundling homes a legalized form of infanticide). Children who survived were usually sent to miserable jobs. The suffering of poor children was one of the blackest pages of eighteenth-century European history.

MARRIAGE AND BIRTHRATES

In most of Europe, newly married couples established their own households independent of their parents. This nuclear family, which had its beginning in the Middle Ages, had become a common pattern, especially in northwestern Europe. In order to save what they needed to establish their own households, both men and women (outside the aristocracy) married quite late; the average age for men in northwestern Europe was between twenty-seven and twenty-eight; for women, between twenty-five and twenty-seven.

Late marriages imposed limits on the birthrate; in fact, they might be viewed as a natural form of birth control. But was this limitation offset by the number of babies born illegitimately? From the low illegitimacy rate of 1 percent in some places in France and 5 percent in some English parishes, it would appear that it was not, at least in the first half of the eighteenth century. After 1750, however, illegitimacy appears to have increased. Studies in Germany, for example, show that rates of illegitimacy increased from 2 percent in 1700 to 5 percent in 1760 and to 10 percent in 1800, followed by an even more dramatic increase in the early nineteenth century.

For married couples, the first child usually appeared within one year of marriage, and additional children came at intervals of two or three years, producing an average number of five births per family. It would appear then that the birthrate had the potential of creating a significant increase in population. This possibility was restricted, however, because 40 to 60 percent of European women of child-bearing age (between fifteen and forty-four) were not married at any given time. Moreover, by the end of the eighteenth century, especially among the upper classes in France and Britain, birth control techniques were being used to limit the number of children. Figures for the French aristocracy indicate that the average number of children

Marital Arrangements

In the eighteenth century, upper-class parents continued to choose marriage partners for their children. This practice and the turmoil it could cause are evident in this selection from *The Rivals*, a play written in 1775 by Richard Sheridan. Sheridan was an Irish playwright who quit writing plays in order to pursue a political career. In this scene from *The Rivals*, a father, Sir Anthony Absolute, informs his son, Captain Jack Absolute, of the arrangements he has made for his son's marriage. Jack, in love with another woman, is dumbfounded by his father's proposal.

Richard Sheridan, The Rivals

ABSOLUTE: Now, Jack, I am sensible that the income of your commission, and what I have hitherto allowed you, is but a small pittance for a lad of your spirit.

CAPTAIN JACK: Sir, you are very good.

ABSOLUTE: And it is my wish, while yet I live, to have my boy make some figure in the world. I have resolved, therefore, to fix you at once in a noble independence.

CAPTAIN JACK: Sir, your kindness overpowers me—such generosity makes the gratitude of reason more lively than the sensations even of filial affection.

ABSOLUTE: I am so glad you are so sensible of my attention—and you shall be master of a large estate in a few weeks.

CAPTAIN JACK: Let my future life, sir, speak my gratitude; I cannot express the sense I have of your munificence. —Yet, sir, I presume you would not wish me to quit the army?

ABSOLUTE: Oh, that shall be as your wife chooses.

CAPTAIN JACK: My wife, sir!

ABSOLUTE: Ay, ay, settle that between you—settle that between you.

CAPTAIN JACK: A wife, sir, did you say?

ABSOLUTE: Ay, a wife—why, did I not mention her before?

CAPTAIN JACK: Not a word of her, sir.

ABSOLUTE: Odd, so! I mus'n't forget her though. —Yes, Jack, the independence I was talking of is by marriage—the fortune is saddled with a wife—but I suppose that makes no difference.

CAPTAIN JACK: Sir! Sir! You amaze me!

ABSOLUTE: Why, what the devil's the matter with you, fool? Just now you were all gratitude and duty.

CAPTAIN JACK: I was, sir—you talked of independence and a fortune, but not a word of a wife!

ABSOLUTE: Why—what difference does that make? Odds life, sir! If you had an estate, you must take it with the live stock on it, as it stands!

CAPTAIN JACK: If my happiness is to be the price, I must beg leave to decline the purchase. Pray, sir, who is the lady?

ABSOLUTE: What's that to you, sir? Come, give me your promise to love, and to marry her directly.

CAPTAIN JACK: Sure, sir, this is not very reasonable. . . . You must excuse me, sir, if I tell you, once for all, that in this point I cannot obey you. . . .

ABSOLUTE: Sir, I won't hear a word—not one word! . . .

CAPTAIN JACK: What, sir, promise to link myself to some mass of ugliness!

ABSOLUTE: Zounds! Sirrah! The lady shall be as ugly as I choose: she shall have a hump on each shoulder; she shall be as crooked as the crescent; her one eye shall roll like the bull's in Cox's Museum; she shall have a skin like a mummy, and the beard of a Jew—she shall be all this, sirrah! Yet I will make you ogle her all day, and sit up all night to write sonnets on her beauty.

declined from six in the period between 1650 and 1700 to three between 1700 and 1750 and to two between 1750 and 1780. These figures are even more significant when one considers that aristocrats married at younger ages than the rest of the population. Coitus interruptus remained the most commonly used form of birth control.

Among the working classes, whether peasants or urban workers, the contributions of women and children to the "family economy" were often crucial. In urban areas, both male and female children either helped in the handicraft manufacturing done in the home or were sent out to work as household servants. In rural areas, children worked on the land or helped in the activities of cottage industry. Married women grew vegetables in small plots, tended livestock, and sold eggs, vegetables, and milk. Wives of propertyless agricultural workers labored in the fields or as textile workers, spinning or knitting. In the cities, wives of artisans helped their husbands at their crafts or worked as seamstresses. The wives of unskilled workers labored as laundresses and cleaners for the rich or as peddlers of food or used clothing to the lower classes. But the family economy was often precarious. Bad harvests in the countryside or a downturn in employment in the cities often reduced people to utter poverty and a life of begging.

An Agricultural Revolution?

Did improvements in agricultural practices and methods in the eighteenth century lead to an agricultural revolution? The topic is much debated. Some historians have noted the beginning of agrarian changes already in the seventeenth century, especially in the Low Countries. Others, however, have questioned the use of the term, arguing that significant changes occurred only in England and noting that even there the upward trend in agricultural production was not maintained after 1750.

Eighteenth-century agriculture was characterized by increases in food production that can be attributed to four

Propaganda for the New Agriculture

Enthusiastic supporters of the new English agricultural practices went to the Continent to examine less efficient kinds of farming. One of these Englishmen, Arthur Young, wrote an account of his travels in which he blamed the low yields of French farmers on the old system of allowing part of the land to lie fallow and the small size of the farms. The latter factor was especially important to English aristocratic landholders, who wished to justify the enclosure movement. This selection is taken from Young's account.

■ *Arthur Young,* Travels During the Years 1787, 1788, and 1789 . . . in the Kingdom of France

The Englishman, in eleven years, gets three bushels more of wheat than the Frenchman. He gets three crops of barley, tares, or beans, which produce nearly twice as many bushels per acre, as what the three French crops of spring corn produce. And he farther gets, at the same time, three crops of turnips, and two of clover, the turnips worth 40s. the acre, and the clover 60s. That is 121 for both. What an enormous superiority. More wheat; almost double of the spring corn; and above 20s. per acre per annum in turnips and clover. But farther; the Englishman's land, by means of the manure arising from the consumption of the turnips and clover is in a constant state of improvement, while the Frenchman's farm is stationary.

The great populousness of France, I attribute very much to the division of the lands into small properties, which takes place in that country to a degree of which we have in England but little conception. . . . It has been said to me in France, "Would you leave uncultivated lands wastes, rather than let them be cultivated in small portions, through a fear of population?" I certainly would not: I would, on the contrary, encourage their culture; but I would prohibit the division of small farms, which is as mischievous to cultivation, as it is sure to be distressing to the people. . . . Go to districts where the properties are minutely divided, and you will find (at least I have done it) universally, great distress, and even misery, and probably very bad agriculture. Go to others, where such sub-division has not taken place, and you will find a better cultivation, and infinitely less misery. When you are engaged in this political tour, finish it by seeing England, and I will show you a set of peasants well clothed, well nourished, and tolerably drunken from superfluity, well-lodged, and at their ease.

interrelated factors: more farmland, increased yields per acre, healthier and more abundant livestock, and an improved climate. Climatologists believe that the "little ice age" of the seventeenth century declined in the eighteenth, especially evident in moderate summers that provided more ideal growing conditions.

The amount of land under cultivation was increased by abandoning the old open-field system, in which part of the land was allowed to lie fallow to renew it. The formerly empty fields were now planted with new crops, such as alfalfa, turnips, and clover, which stored nitrogen in their roots and thereby restored the soil's fertility. They also provided winter fodder for livestock, enabling landlords to maintain an ever-larger number of animals.

The more numerous livestock increased the amount of meat in the European diet and enhanced food production by making available more animal manure, which was used to fertilize fields and produce better yields per acre. Increased yields were also encouraged by landed aristocrats, who shared in the scientific experimentation of the age. In England, Jethro Tull (1674–1741) discovered that using a hoe to keep the soil loose allowed air and moisture to reach plants and enabled them to grow better. He also used a drill to plant seeds in rows instead of scattering them by hand, a method that had lost much seed to the birds.

The eighteenth century witnessed greater yields of vegetables, including two important American crops, the potato and maize (Indian corn). Although they were not grown in quantity until after 1700, both had been brought to Europe from America in the sixteenth century. The potato became a staple in Germany, the Low Countries, and especially Ireland, where repression by English landlords forced large numbers of poor peasants to survive on small pieces of marginal land. The potato took relatively little effort to produce in large quantities. High in carbohydrates and calories, rich in vitamins A and C, it could be easily stored for winter use.

The new agricultural techniques were considered best suited to large-scale farms. Consequently, a change in landholding accompanied the increase in food production. Large landowners or yeomen farmers enclosed the old open fields, combining the many small holdings that made up the fields into larger units. The end of the open-field system led to the demise of the cooperative farming of the village community. In England, where small landholders resisted this process, Parliament, dominated by the landed aristocracy, enacted legislation allowing agricultural lands to be legally enclosed. As a result of these enclosure acts, England gradually became a land of large estates, and many small farmers were forced to become wage laborers or tenant farmers working farms of 100 to 500 acres. The enclosure movement and new agricultural practices largely destroyed the traditional patterns of English village life.

In the eighteenth century, the English were the leaders in adopting the new techniques that have been characterized as an agricultural revolution (see the box above).

This early modernization of English agriculture, with its noticeable increase in productivity, made possible the feeding of an expanding population about to enter a new world of industrialization and urbanization.

New Methods of Finance

A decline in the supply of gold and silver in the seventeenth century had created a chronic shortage of money that undermined the efforts of governments to meet their needs. The establishment of new public and private banks and the acceptance of paper notes made possible an expansion of credit in the eighteenth century.

Perhaps the best example of this process can be observed in England, where the Bank of England was founded in 1694. Unlike other banks accustomed to receiving deposits and exchanging foreign currencies, the Bank of England also made loans. In return for lending money to the government, the bank was allowed to issue paper "banknotes" backed by its credit. These soon became negotiable and provided a paper substitute for gold and silver currency. In addition, the issuance of government bonds paying regular interest, backed by the Bank of England and the London financial community, created the notion of a public or "national debt" distinct from the monarch's personal debts. This process meant that capital for financing larger armies and other government undertakings could be raised in ever-greater quantities.

These new financial institutions and methods were not risk-free, however. In both Britain and France in the early eighteenth century, speculators provided opportunities for people to invest in colonial trading companies. The French company under John Law was also tied to his attempt to create a national bank and paper currency for France. When people went overboard and drove the price of the stock to incredibly high levels, the bubble burst. Law's company and bank went bankrupt, leading to a loss of confidence in paper money that prevented the formation of a French national bank. Consequently, French public finance developed slowly in the eighteenth century.

This was not the case in Britain, however. Despite crises, public confidence in the new financial institutions enabled the British government to borrow large sums of money at relatively low rates of interest, giving it a distinct advantage in the struggle with France. According to a contemporary observer, Britain's public credit was "the permanent miracle of her policy, which has inspired both astonishment and fear in the States of Europe."[5] Despite Britain's growing importance in finance, however, the Dutch Republic remained the leader in Europe's financial life, and Amsterdam continued to be the center of international finance until London replaced it in the nineteenth century. One observer noted in 1769:

> If ten or twelve businessmen of Amsterdam of the first rank meet for a banking operation, they can in a moment send circulating throughout Europe over two hundred million florins in paper money, which is preferred to cash. There is no Sovereign who could do as much. . . . This credit is a power which the ten or twelve businessmen will be able to exert over all the States of Europe, in complete independence of any authority.[6]

The decline of Dutch trade, industry, and power meant that Dutch capitalists were inclined to lend money abroad because they had fewer opportunities at home.

European Industry

The most important product of European industry in the eighteenth century was textiles. Woolen cloth made up 75 percent of Britain's exports in the early part of the century. France, too, was a leader in the production of woolen cloth, and other major states emulated both France and Britain by encouraging the development of their own textile industries.

Most textiles were still produced by traditional methods. In cities that were textile centers, master artisans used timeworn methods to turn out finished goods in their guild workshops. But by the eighteenth century, textile production was beginning to shift to the countryside in parts of Europe. In the countryside, textiles were produced by the "putting-out" or "domestic" system, in which a merchant-capitalist entrepreneur bought the raw materials, mostly wool and flax, and "put them out" to rural workers, who spun the raw material into yarn and then wove it into cloth on simple looms. Capitalist-entrepreneurs sold the finished product, made a profit, and used it to manufacture more. This system became known as the cottage industry because spinners and weavers did their work on spinning wheels and looms in their own cottages. The cottage industry was truly a family enterprise since women and children could spin while men wove on the looms, enabling rural people to earn incomes that supplemented their pitiful wages as agricultural laborers.

The cottage system employed traditional methods of manufacturing and spread to many areas of rural Europe in the eighteenth century. But significant changes in industrial production also began to occur in the second half of the century, pushed along by the introduction of cotton, originally imported from India. The importation of raw cotton from slave plantations encouraged the production of cotton cloth in Europe, where a profitable market developed because of the growing demand for lightweight cotton clothes that were less expensive than linens and woolens. But the traditional methods of the cottage industry proved incapable of keeping up with the growing demand, leading English cloth entrepreneurs to develop new methods and new machines. The flying shuttle sped up the process of weaving on a loom, thereby increasing the need for large quantities of yarn. In response, Richard Arkwright (1732–1792) invented a "water frame," powered by horse or water, which turned out yarn much faster than cottage spinning wheels. This abundance of yarn, in turn, led to the development of mechanized looms, invented in the 1780s but not widely adopted until the early nineteenth century. By that time, Britain was in the throes

Hulton/Archive by Getty Images

Cottage Industry. One important source of textile production in the eighteenth century was the cottage industry, truly a family enterprise. Shown here is a family at work producing knitwear. It was customary in the cottage industry for women to spin and wind the yarn and for men to weave the yarn into cloth on looms.

of an industrial revolution, but already at the end of the eighteenth century, rural workers, perceiving that the new machines threatened their traditional livelihood, had begun to call for the machines' destruction (see the box on p. 514).

The Social Order of the Eighteenth Century

The pattern of Europe's social organization, first established in the Middle Ages, continued well into the eighteenth century. Social status was still largely determined not by wealth and economic standing but by the division into the traditional "orders" or "estates" determined by heredity. This divinely sanctioned division of society into traditional orders was supported by Christian teaching, which emphasized the need to fulfill the responsibilities of one's estate. Although Enlightenment intellectuals attacked these traditional distinctions, they did not die easily. In the Prussian law code of 1794, marriage between noble males and middle-class females was forbidden without a government dispensation. Even without government regulation, however, different social groups remained easily distinguished everywhere in Europe by the distinctive, traditional clothes they wore.

Nevertheless, some forces of change were at work in this traditional society. The ideas of the Enlightenment made headway as reformers argued that the idea of an unchanging social order based on privilege was hostile to the progress of society. However, not until the revolutionary upheavals at the end of the eighteenth century did the old order finally begin to crumble.

The Peasants

Because society was still mostly rural in the eighteenth century, the peasantry constituted the largest social group, making up as much as 85 percent of Europe's population. There were rather large differences, however, between peasants from area to area. The most important distinction, at least legally, was between the free peasant and the serf. Peasants in Britain, northern Italy, the Low Countries, Spain, most of France, and some areas of western Germany were legally free, though not exempt from burdens. Some free peasants in Andalusia in Spain, southern Italy, Sicily, and Portugal lived in a poverty more desperate than that of many serfs in Russia and eastern Germany. In France, 40 percent of free peasants owned little or no land whatever by 1789.

Small peasant proprietors or tenant farmers in western Europe were also not free from compulsory services. Most owed tithes, often one-third of their crops. Although tithes were intended for parish priests, in France only 10 percent of the priests received them. Instead the tithes wound up in the hands of towns and aristocratic landowners. Moreover, peasants could still owe a variety of dues and fees. Local aristocrats claimed hunting rights on peasant land and had monopolies over the flour mills, community ovens, and wine and oil presses needed by the peasants. Hunting rights, dues, fees, and tithes were all deeply resented.

Eastern Europe continued to be dominated by large landed estates owned by powerful lords and worked by serfs. Serfdom had come late to the east, having largely been imposed in the sixteenth and seventeenth centuries. Peasants in eastern Germany were bound to the lord's estate, had to perform labor services on the lord's land, and could not marry or move without permission and payment of a tax. By the eighteenth century, landlords also possessed

The Beginnings of Mechanized Industry: The Attack on New Machines

Already by the end of the eighteenth century, mechanization was bringing changes to the traditional cottage industry of textile manufacturing. Rural workers who depended on the extra wages earned in their own homes often reacted by attacking the machinery that threatened their livelihoods. This selection is a petition that English wool workers published in their local newspapers asking that machines no longer be used to prepare wool for spinning.

■ *The Leeds Woolen Workers' Petition (1786)*

To the Merchants, Clothiers and all such as wish well to the Staple Manufactory of this Nation.

The Humble ADDRESS and PETITION of Thousands, who labor in the Cloth Manufactory.

The Scribbling-Machines have thrown thousands of your petitioners out of employ, whereby they are brought into great distress, and are not able to procure a maintenance for their families, and deprived them of the opportunity of bringing up their children to labor: We have therefore to request, that prejudice and self-interest may be laid aside, and that you may pay that attention to the following facts, which the nature of the case requires.

The number of Scribbling-Machines extending about seventeen miles southwest of LEEDS, exceed all belief, being no less than *one hundred and seventy!* and as each machine will do as much work in twelve hours, as ten men can in that time do by hand (speaking within bounds) and they working night and day, one machine will do as much work in one day as would otherwise employ twenty men.

As we do not mean to assert any thing but what we can prove to be true, we allow four men to be employed at each machine twelve hours, working night and day, will take eight men in twenty-four hours; so that, upon a moderate computation twelve men are thrown out of employ for every single machine used in scribbling; and as it may be supposed the number of machines in all the other quarters together, nearly equal those in the South-West, full four thousand men are left to shift for a living how they can, and must of course fall to the Parish, if not time relieved. Allowing one boy to be bound apprentice from each family out of work, eight thousand hands are deprived of the opportunity of getting a livelihood.

We therefore hope, that the feelings of humanity will lead those who have it in their power to prevent the use of those machines, to give every discouragement they can to what has a tendency so prejudicial to their fellow-creatures. . . .

We wish to propose a few queries to those who would plead for the further continuance of these machines:

How are those men, thus thrown out of employ to provide for their families; and what are they to put their children apprentice to, that the rising generation may have something to keep them at work, in order that they may not be like vagabonds strolling about in idleness? Some say, Begin and learn some other business. —Suppose we do, who will maintain our families, whilst we undertake the arduous task; and when we have learned it, how do we know we shall be any better for all our pains; for by the time we have served our second apprenticeship, another machine may arise, which may take away that business also. . . .

But what are our children to do; are they to be brought up in idleness? Indeed as things are, it is no wonder to hear of so many executions; for our parts, though we may be thought illiterate men, our conceptions are, that bringing children up to industry, and keeping them employed, is the way to keep them from falling into those crimes, which an idle habit naturally leads to.

legal jurisdiction, giving them control over the administration of justice. Only in the Habsburg empire had a ruler attempted to improve the lot of the peasants through a series of reforms. With the exception of the clergy and a small merchant class, eighteenth-century Russia, unlike the rest of Europe, was still largely a society of landlords and serfs. Russian peasants were not attached to the land but to the landlord and thus existed in a condition approaching slavery.

The local villages in which they dwelt remained the centers of peasants' social lives. The village, especially in western Europe, maintained public order; provided poor relief, a village church, and sometimes a schoolmaster; collected taxes for the central government; maintained roads and bridges; and established common procedures for sowing, plowing, and harvesting crops. But villages were often dominated by the wealthiest peasants and proved highly resistant to innovations, such as new agricultural practices.

The diet of the peasants in the eighteenth century did not vary much from that of the Middle Ages. Dark bread, made of roughly ground wheat and rye flour, remained the basic staple. It was quite nourishing and high in vitamins, minerals, and even proteins, since the bran and germ were not ground out. Peasants drank water, wine, and beer and ate soups and gruel made of grains and vegetables. The new foods of the eighteenth century, potatoes and American corn, added important elements to the peasant diet. Of course, when harvests were bad, hunger and famine became the peasants' lot in life, making them even more susceptible to the ravages of disease.

The Nobility

The nobles, who constituted about 2 or 3 percent of the European population, played a dominating role in society. Being born a noble automatically guaranteed a place at the top of the social order, with all the attendant special privileges and rights. The legal privileges of the nobility included judgment by their peers, immunity from severe punishment, and exemption from many forms of taxation. Especially in central and eastern Europe, the rights of landlords over their serfs were overwhelming. In Poland until 1768, the nobility even possessed the right of life or death over their serfs.

In many countries, nobles were self-conscious about their unique lifestyle, which set them apart from the rest of society. This did not mean, however, that they were unwilling to bend the conventions of that lifestyle if there were profits to be made. For example, by convention, nobles were expected to live off the yields of their estates. But although nobles almost everywhere talked about trade being beneath their dignity, many were not averse to mercantile endeavors. Many were also all too eager to profit from industries based on the exploitation of raw materials found on their estates; as a result, many nobles were involved in mining, metallurgy, and glassmaking. Their diet also set them off from the rest of society. Aristocrats consumed enormous quantities of meat and fish dishes accompanied by cheeses, nuts, and a variety of sweets.

Nobles also played important roles in military and government affairs. Since medieval times, landed aristocrats had served as military officers. Although monarchs found it impossible to exclude commoners from the ranks of officers, tradition maintained that nobles made the most natural and hence the best officers. Moreover, the eighteenth-century nobility played a significant role in the administrative machinery of state. In some countries, such as Prussia, the entire bureaucracy reflected aristocratic values. Moreover, in most of Europe, landholding nobles controlled much of the local government in their districts.

The nobility or landowning class was not a homogeneous social group. Landlords in England leased their land to tenant farmers, while those in eastern Europe used the labor services of serfs. Nobles in Russia and Prussia served the state, but those in Spain and Italy had few official functions. Differences in wealth, education, and political power also led to differences within countries as well. The gap between rich and poor nobles could be enormous. As the century progressed, poor nobles sometimes sank into the ranks of the unprivileged masses of the population. It has been estimated that the number of European nobles declined by one-third between 1750 and 1815.

Although the nobles clung to their privileged status and struggled to keep others out, almost everywhere a person with money found it possible to enter the ranks of the nobility. Rights of nobility were frequently attached to certain lands, so purchasing the lands made one a noble; the acquisition of government offices also often conferred noble status.

THE ARISTOCRATIC WAY OF LIFE: THE COUNTRY HOUSE

One aristocrat who survived the French Revolution once commented that "no one who did not live before the Revolution" could know the real sweetness of living. Of course, he spoke not for the peasants whose labor maintained the system but for the landed aristocrats. For them, the eighteenth century was a final century of "sweetness" before the Industrial Revolution and bourgeois society diminished their privileged way of life.

In so many ways, the court of Louis XIV had provided a model for other European monarchs, who built palaces and encouraged the development of a court society as a center of culture. As at Versailles, these courts were peopled by members of the aristocracy whose income from rents or officeholding enabled them to participate in this lifestyle. This court society, whether in France, Spain, or Germany, manifested common characteristics: participation in intrigues for the king's or prince's favor, serene walks in formal gardens, and duels to maintain one's honor.

The majority of aristocratic landowners, however, remained on their country estates and did not participate in court society; their large houses continued to give witness to their domination of the surrounding countryside. This was especially true in England, where the court of the Hanoverian kings (Georges I–III, from 1714 to 1820) made little impact on the behavior of upper-class society. English landed aristocrats invested much time, energy, and money in their rural estates, giving the English country house an important role in English social life. One American observer remarked, "Scarcely any persons who hold a leading place in the circles of their society live in London. They have houses in London, in which they stay while Parliament sits, and occasionally visit at other seasons; but their homes are in the country."[7]

Although there was much variety in country houses, many in the eighteenth century were built in the Georgian style (named after the Hanoverian kings). This style was greatly influenced by the classical serenity and sedateness of the sixteenth-century Venetian architect Andrea Palladio, who had specialized in the design of country villas. The Georgian country house combined elegance with domesticity, and its interior was often characterized as possessing a comfort of home that combined visual delight and usefulness.

The country house also fulfilled a new desire for greater privacy that was reflected in the growing separation between the lower and upper floors. The lower floors were devoted to public activities—dining, entertaining, and leisure. A central entrance hall provided the setting for the ceremonial arrival and departure of guests on formal occasions. From the hall, guests could proceed to a series of downstairs common rooms. The largest was the drawing room (larger houses possessed two), which contained

Collection of the Earl of Pembroke, Wilton House, Wilts., UK/Bridgeman Art Library

The Aristocratic Way of Life. The eighteenth-century country house in Britain fulfilled the desire of aristocrats for both elegance and greater privacy. The painting above by Richard Wilson shows a typical English country house of the eighteenth century surrounded by a simple and serene landscape. Thomas Gainsborough's *Conversation in the Park,* shown at right, captures the relaxed life of two aristocrats in the park of their country estate.

Erich Lessing/Art Resource, NY

musical instruments and was used for dances or card games, a favorite pastime. Other common rooms included a formal dining room, informal breakfast room, library, study, gallery, billiard room, and conservatory. The entrance hall also featured a large staircase that led to the upstairs rooms, which consisted of bedrooms for husbands and wives, sons, and daughters. These rooms were used not only for sleeping but also for private activities, such as playing for the children and sewing, writing, and reading for wives. "Going upstairs" literally meant leaving the company of others in the downstairs common rooms to be alone in the privacy of one's bedroom. This eighteenth-century desire for privacy also meant keeping servants at a distance. They were now housed in their own wing of rooms and alerted to their employers' desire for assistance by a new invention—long-distance cords connected to bells in the servants' quarters.

Although the arrangement of the eighteenth-century Georgian house originally reflected male interests, the influence of women was increasingly evident by the second half of the century. Already in the seventeenth century, it had become customary for the sexes to separate after dinner; while the men preoccupied themselves with brandy and cigars in the dining room, women would exit to a "withdrawing room" for their own conversation. In the course of the eighteenth century, the drawing room became a larger, more feminine room with comfortable pieces of furniture grouped casually in front of fireplaces to create a cozy atmosphere.

Aristocratic landowners, especially in Britain, also sought to expand the open space around their country houses to separate themselves from the lower classes in the villages and to remove farmland from their view. Often these open spaces were then enclosed by walls to create parks (as they were called in England) to provide even more privacy. Sometimes entire villages were destroyed to create a park, causing one English poet to lament the social cost:

> *The man of wealth and pride*
> *Takes up the space that many poor supplied;*
> *Space for his lake, his park's extended bounds,*
> *Space for his horses, equipage and hounds.*[8]

Along with a sense of privacy, parks gave landed aristocrats the ability to reshape their property to meet their leisure needs.

THE ARISTOCRATIC WAY OF LIFE: THE GRAND TOUR

One characteristic of the high culture of the Enlightenment was its cosmopolitanism, reinforced by education in the Latin classics and the use of French as an international language. Travel was another manifestation of the Enlightenment's cosmopolitanism and interest in new vistas. One important aspect of eighteenth-century travel was the grand tour, in which the sons of aristocrats completed their education by making a tour of Europe's major cities. The

English aristocracy in particular regarded the grand tour as crucial to their education. The great-aunt of Thomas Coke wrote to him upon his completion of school: "Sir, I understand you have left Eton and probably intend to go to one of those Schools of Vice, the Universities. If, however, you choose to travel I will give you 500 pounds [about $12,500] per annum."[9] Coke was no fool and went on the grand tour, along with many others. In one peak year alone, forty thousand Englishmen were traveling in Europe.

Travel was not easy in the eighteenth century. Crossing the English Channel could be difficult in rough seas and might take anywhere from three to twelve hours. The trip from France to Italy could be made by sea, where the traveler faced the danger of pirates, or overland by sedan chair over the Alps, where narrow passes made travel an adventure in terror. Inns, especially in Germany, were populated by thieves and the ubiquitous bedbugs. The English in particular were known for spending vast sums of money during their travels; as one observer recounted: "The French usually travel to save money, so that they sometimes leave the places where they sojourn worse off than they found them. The English, on the other hand, come over with plenty of cash, plenty of gear, and servants to wait on them. They throw their money about like lords."[10]

Since the trip's purpose was educational, young Englishmen in particular were usually accompanied by a tutor who ensured that his charges spent time looking at museum collections of natural history and antiquities. But tutors were not able to stop young men from also pursuing wine, women, and song. After crossing the Channel, English visitors went to Paris for a cram course on how to act sophisticated. They then went on to Italy, where their favorite destinations were Florence, Venice, and Rome. In Florence, the studious and ambitious studied art in the Uffizi Gallery. The less ambitious followed a less vigorous routine; according to the poet Thomas Gray, they "get up at twelve o'clock, breakfast till three, dine till five, sleep till six, drink cooling liquors till eight, go to the bridge till ten, sup till two, and so sleep till twelve again." In Venice, where sophisticated prostitutes had flourished since Renaissance times, the chief attraction for young English males was women. As Samuel Johnson remarked, "If a young man is wild, and must run after women and bad company, it is better this should be done abroad." Rome was another "great object of our pilgrimage," where travelers visited the "modern" sights, such as Saint Peter's and, above all, the ancient ruins. To a generation raised on a classical education, souvenirs of ruins and Piranesi's etchings of classical ruins were required purchases. The accidental rediscovery of the ancient Roman towns of Herculaneum and Pompeii made them a popular eighteenth-century tourist attraction.

The Inhabitants of Towns and Cities

Townspeople were still a distinct minority of the total population, except in the Dutch Republic, Britain, and parts of Italy. At the end of the eighteenth century, about one-sixth of the French population lived in towns of 2,000 people or more. The biggest city in Europe was London, with 1 million inhabitants, while Paris numbered between 550,000 and 600,000. Altogether, Europe had at least twenty cities in twelve countries with populations over 100,000, including Naples, Lisbon, Moscow, Saint Petersburg, Vienna, Amsterdam, Berlin, Rome, and Madrid.

Although urban dwellers were vastly outnumbered by rural inhabitants, towns played an important role in Western culture. The contrasts between a large city, with its education, culture, and material consumption, and the surrounding, often poverty-stricken countryside were striking, evident in this British traveler's account of Russia's Saint Petersburg in 1741:

> The country about Petersburg has full as wild and desert a look as any in the Indies; you need not go above 200 paces out of the town to find yourself in a wild wood of firs, and such a low, marshy, boggy country that you would think God when he created the rest of the world for the use of mankind had created this for an inaccessible retreat for all sorts of wild beasts.[11]

Peasants often resented the prosperity of towns and their exploitation of the countryside to serve urban interests. Palermo in Sicily used one-third of the island's food production while paying only one-tenth of the taxes. Towns lived off the countryside not by buying peasant produce but by acquiring it through tithes, rents, and dues.

Many cities in western and even central Europe had a long tradition of patrician oligarchies that continued to control their communities by dominating town and city councils. Despite their domination, patricians constituted only a small minority of the urban population. Just below the patricians stood an upper crust of the middle classes: nonnoble officeholders, financiers and bankers, merchants, wealthy rentiers who lived off their investments, and important professionals, including lawyers. Another large urban group was the petty bourgeoisie or lower middle class, made up of master artisans, shopkeepers, and small traders. Below them were the laborers or working classes. Much urban industry was still carried on in small guild workshops by masters, journeymen, and apprentices. Apprentices who acquired the proper skills became journeymen before entering the ranks of the masters, but increasingly in the eighteenth century, guilds became closed oligarchies as membership was restricted to the relatives of masters. Many skilled artisans were then often forced to become low-paid workers. Urban communities also had a large group of unskilled workers who served as servants, maids, and cooks at pitifully low wages.

Despite an end to the ravages of plague, eighteenth-century cities still experienced high death rates, especially among children, because of unsanitary living conditions, polluted water, and a lack of sewerage facilities. One observer compared the stench of Hamburg to an open sewer that could be smelled for miles around. Overcrowding also exacerbated urban problems as cities continued to grow from an influx of rural immigrants. But cities proved no paradise for them as unskilled workers found few

Poverty in France

Unlike the British, who had a system of public-supported poor relief, the French responded to poverty with ad hoc policies when conditions became acute. This selection is taken from an *intendant's* report to the controller general at Paris describing his suggestions for a program to relieve the grain shortages expected for the winter months.

M. de la Bourdonnaye, Intendant of Bordeaux, to the Controller General, September 30, 1708

Having searched for the means of helping the people of Agen in this cruel situation and having conferred with His Eminence, the Bishop, it seems to us that three things are absolutely necessary if the people are not to starve during the winter.

Most of the inhabitants do not have seed to plant their fields. However, we decided that we would be going too far if we furnished it, because those who have seed would also apply [for more]. Moreover, we are persuaded that all the inhabitants will make strenuous efforts to find some seed, since they have every reason to expect prices to remain high next year. . . .

But this project will come to nothing if the collectors of the taille continue to be as strict in the exercise of their functions as they have been of late and continue to employ troops [to force collection]. Those inhabitants who have seed grain would sell it to be freed from an oppressive garrison, while those who must buy seed, since they have none left from their harvest and have scraped together a little money for this purchase, would prefer to give up that money [for taxes] when put under police constraint. To avoid this, I feel it is absolutely necessary that you order the receivers-general to reduce their operations during this winter, at least with respect to the poor. . . .

We are planning to import wheat for this region from Languedoc and Quercy, and we are confident that there will be enough. But there are two things to be feared: one is the greed of the merchants. When they see that general misery has put them in control of prices, they will raise them to the point where the calamity is almost as great as if there were no provisions at all. The other fear is that the artisans and the lowest classes, when they find themselves at the mercy of the merchants, will cause disorders and riots. As a protective measure, it would seem wise to establish two small storehouses. Ten thousand ecus [30,000 livres] would be sufficient for each. . . .

A third point demanding our attention is the support of beggars among the poor, as well as of those who have no other resources than their wages. Since there will be very little work, these people will soon be reduced to starvation. We should establish public workshops to provide work as was done in 1693 and 1694. I should choose the most useful kind of work, located where there are the greatest number of poor. In this manner, we should rid ourselves of those who do not want to work and assure the others a moderate subsistence. For these workshops, we would need about 40,000 livres, or altogether 100,000 livres. The receiver-general of the taille of Agen could advance this sum. The 60,000 livres for the storehouses he would get back very soon. I shall await your orders on all of the above.

Marginal Comments by the Controller General

Operations for the collection of the taille are to be suspended. The two storehouses are to be established; great care must be taken to put them to good use. The interest on the advances will be paid by the king. His Majesty has agreed to the establishment of the public workshops for the able-bodied poor and is willing to spend up to 40,000 livres on them this winter.

employment opportunities. The result was a serious problem of poverty in the eighteenth century.

THE PROBLEM OF POVERTY

Poverty was a highly visible problem in the eighteenth century both in cities and in the countryside (see the box above). In Venice, licensed beggars made up 3 to 5 percent of the population, and unlicensed beggars may have constituted as much as 13 to 15 percent. Beggars in Bologna were estimated at 25 percent of the population; in Mainz, figures indicate that 30 percent of the people were beggars or prostitutes. Prostitution was often an alternative to begging. In France and Britain by the end of the century, an estimated 10 percent of the people depended on charity or begging for their food.

Earlier in Europe, the poor had been viewed as blessed children of God; assisting them was a Christian duty. A change of attitude that had begun in the latter part of the sixteenth century became even more apparent in the eighteenth century. Charity to poor beggars, it was argued, simply encouraged their idleness and led them to vice and crime. A French official stated, "Beggary is the apprenticeship of crime; it begins by creating a love of idleness which will always be the greatest political and moral evil. In this state the beggar does not long resist the temptation to steal."[12] Although private charitable institutions such as the religious Order of Saint Vincent de Paul and the Sisters of Charity had been founded to help such people, they were soon overwhelmed by the increased numbers of indigent in the eighteenth century.

Museo Civico di Torino

A Market in Turin. Below the wealthy patrician elites who dominated the towns and cities were a number of social groups with a wide range of incomes and occupations. This remarkable diversity is evident in this view of a market square in the Italian city of Turin.

Although some "enlightened" officials argued that the state should become involved in the problem, mixed feelings prevented concerted action. Since the sixteenth century, vagrancy and begging had been considered crimes. In the eighteenth century, French authorities attempted to round up vagrants and beggars and incarcerate them for eighteen months to act as a deterrent. This effort accomplished little, however, since the basic problem was socioeconomic. These people had no work. In the 1770s, the French tried to use public works projects, such as road building, to give people jobs, but not enough funds were available to accomplish much. The problem of poverty remained as another serious blemish on the quality of eighteenth-century life.

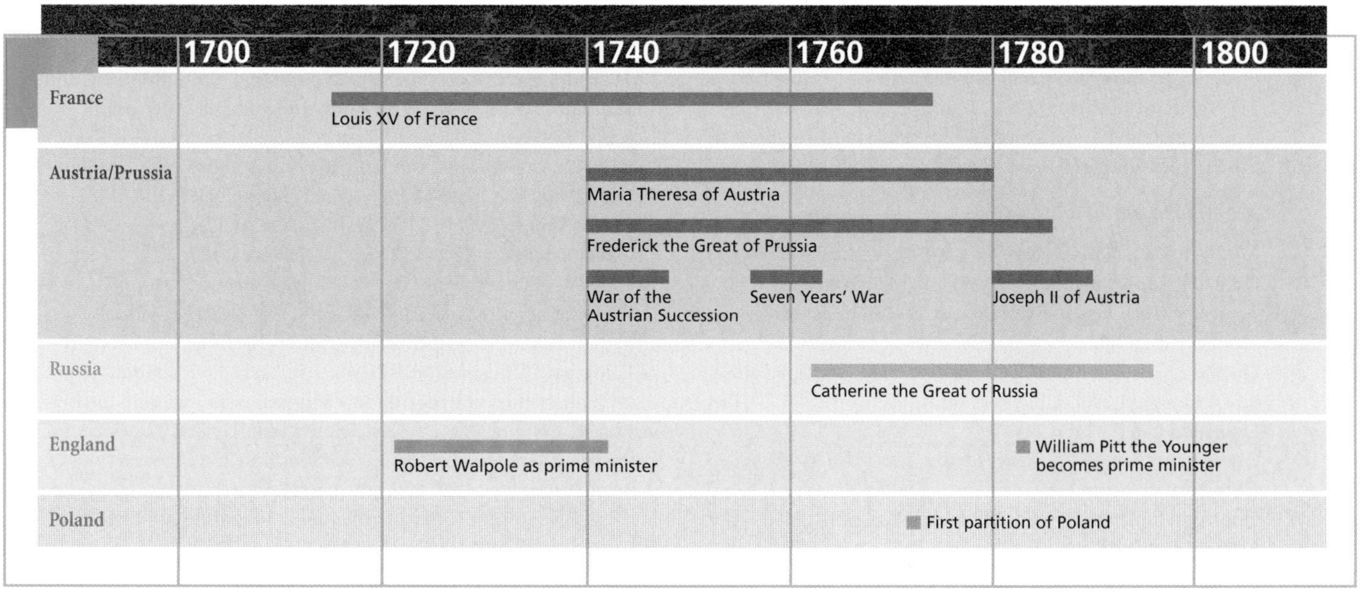

Conclusion

Everywhere in Europe at the beginning of the eighteenth century, the old order remained strong. Nobles, clerics, towns, and provinces all had privileges, some medieval in origin, others the result of the attempt of monarchies in the sixteenth and seventeenth centuries to gain financial support from their subjects. Everywhere in the eighteenth century, monarchs sought to enlarge their bureaucracies to raise taxes to support the new large standing armies that had originated in the seventeenth century. The existence of these armies made wars more likely. The existence of five great powers, two of them (France and Britain) in conflict in the East and the New World, initiated a new scale of confrontation: the Seven Years' War can legitimately be viewed as the first world war. The wars altered some boundaries on the European continent but were perhaps most significant for the British victories that marked the emergence of Great Britain as the world's greatest naval and colonial power. Everywhere in Europe, increased demands for taxes to support these conflicts led to attacks on the privileged orders and a desire for change not met by the ruling monarchs.

At the same time, sustained population growth, dramatic changes in finance, trade, and industry, and increased poverty created tensions that undermined the traditional foundations of European society. The inability of the old order to deal meaningfully with these changes led to a revolutionary outburst at the end of the eighteenth century that brought the beginning of the end for that old order.

Notes

1. Frederick II, *Forms of Government,* in Eugen Weber, *The Western Tradition* (Lexington, Mass., 1972), pp. 538, 544.
2. Quoted in Reinhold A. Dorwart, *The Administrative Reforms of Frederick William I of Prussia* (Cambridge, Mass., 1953), p. 36.
3. Quoted in Sidney B. Fay, *The Rise of Brandenburg-Prussia to 1786,* rev. Klaus Epstein (New York, 1964), p. 92.
4. Quoted in Hans Rosenberg, *Bureaucracy, Aristocracy, and Autocracy: The Prussian Experience, 1660–1815* (Cambridge, Mass., 1958), p. 40.
5. Quoted in Fernand Braudel, *Civilization and Capitalism* (London, 1981–1984), vol. 3, p. 378.
6. Quoted in ibid., p. 245.
7. Quoted in Witold Rybczynski, *Home: A Short History of an Idea* (New York, 1986), p. 105.
8. Quoted in Jonathan Dewald, *The European Nobility, 1400–1800* (Cambridge, 1996), pp. 91–92.
9. Quoted in Peter Gay, *Age of Enlightenment* (New York, 1966), p. 87.
10. Quoted in Paul Hazard, *The European Mind, 1680–1715* (Cleveland, Ohio, 1963), pp. 6–7.
11. Igor Vinogradoff, "Russian Missions to London, 1711–1789: Further Extracts from the Cottrell Papers," *Oxford Slavonic Papers,* New Series (1982), 15:76.
12. Quoted in Jeffrey Kaplow, *The Names of Kings: The Parisian Laboring Poor in the Eighteenth Century* (New York, 1972), p. 134.

Suggestions for Further Reading

For a good introduction to the political history of the eighteenth century, see the relevant chapters in the general works by Woloch, Anderson, and Birn listed in Chapter 17. See also G. Treasure, *The Making of Modern Europe, 1648–1780* (London, 1985), and O. Hufton, *Europe: Privilege and Protest, 1730–1789* (London, 1980). On enlightened absolutism, see H. M. Scott, ed., *Enlightened Absolutism: Reform and Reformers in Later Eighteenth-Century Europe* (Ann Arbor, Mich., 1990). Good studies of individual states include J. B. Owen, *The Eighteenth Century, 1714–1815* (London, 1975), on England; S. Schama, *Patriots and Liberators: Revolution in the Netherlands, 1780–1813* (New York, 1977); P. R. Campbell, *The Ancien Régime in France* (Oxford, 1988); E. Wangermann, *The Austrian Achievement, 1700–1800* (London, 1973); R. Vierhaus, *Germany in the Age of Absolutism* (Cambridge, 1988); J. Gagliardo, *Germany Under the Old Regime* (London, 1991); J. Lynch, *Bourbon Spain, 1700–1808* (Oxford, 1989); H. W. Koch, *A History of Prussia* (London, 1978); P. Dukes, *The Making of Russian Absolutism, 1613–1801,* 2d ed. (London, 1990); and D. Kirby, *Northern Europe in the Early Modern Period* (London, 1991). Good biographies of some of Europe's monarchs include R. Asprey, *Frederick the Great, The Magnificent Enigma* (New York, 1986); I. De Madariaga, *Catherine the Great: A Short History* (New Haven, Conn., 1990); volume 1 of D. Deales, *Joseph II* (Cambridge, 1987); T. C. W. Blanning, *Joseph II* (New York, 1994); and J. Brooke, *King George III* (London, 1972).

The warfare of this period is examined in M. S. Anderson, *War and Society in Europe of the Old Regime, 1615–1789* (New York, 1988). R. S. Browning, *The War of Austrian Succession* (London, 1995), is illuminating.

A good introduction to European population can be found in M. W. Flinn, *The European Demographic System, 1500–1820* (Brighton, 1981). One of the best works on family and marriage patterns is L. Stone, *The Family, Sex, and Marriage in England, 1500–1800* (New York, 1977). On wet nurses and infanticide, see G. Sussman, *Selling Mother's Milk: The Wet-Nursing Business* (Bloomington, Ind., 1982), and M. Jackson, *Newborn Child Murder: Women, Illegitimacy, and the Courts in Eighteenth-Century England* (New York, 1996).

A different perspective on economic history can be found in F. Braudel, *Capitalism and Material Life, 1400–1800* (New York, 1973). On England's agricultural revolution, see J. D. Chambers and G. E. Mingay, *The Agricultural Revolution, 1750–1880* (London, 1966). Eighteenth-century cottage industry and the beginnings of industrialization are examined in the early chapters of D. Landes, *The Unbound Prometheus: Technological Change and Industrial Development in Western Europe from 1750 to the Present* (New York, 1969), and in M. Berg, *The Age of Manufactures: Industry, Innovation, and Work in Britain, 1700–1820* (Oxford, 1985).

On the European nobility, see J. Dewald, *The European Nobility, 1400–1800* (Cambridge, 1996), and H. M. Scott, *The European Nobility in the Seventeenth and Eighteenth Centuries* (London, 1995). On the peasantry, see J. Blum, *The End of the Old Order in Rural Europe* (Princeton, N.J., 1978), and R. Evans, ed., *The German Peasantry* (New York, 1986). On European cities, see J. de Vries, *European Urbanization, 1500–1800* (Cambridge, Mass., 1984). On the lower urban classes, see J. Kaplow, *The Names of Kings: The Parisian Laboring Poor in the Eighteenth Century* (New York, 1972); R. M. Schwartz, *Policing the Poor in Eighteenth-Century France* (Chapel Hill, N.C., 1988); and B. Hill, *Servants: English Domestics in the Eighteenth Century* (New York, 1996). There is no better work on the problem of poverty than O. Hufton, *The Poor of Eighteenth-Century France* (Oxford, 1974).

For additional reading, go to InfoTrac College Edition, your online research library at http://web1.infotrac-college.com

Enter the search term *William Pitt* using Key Terms.

Enter the search term *Frederick II* or *Frederick the Great* using Key Terms.

Enter the search term *Joseph II* using Key Terms.

Enter the search term *Catherine the Great* using Key Terms.

C H A P T E R

19

A Revolution in Politics: The Era of the French Revolution and Napoleon

Giraudon/Art Resource, NY

CHAPTER OUTLINE

- The Beginnings of the Revolutionary Era: The American Revolution
- Background to the French Revolution
- The French Revolution
- The Age of Napoleon
- Conclusion

FOCUS QUESTIONS

- What were the causes and results of the American Revolution, and what impact did it have on Europe?
- What were the long-range and immediate causes of the French Revolution?
- What were the main events of the French Revolution between 1789 and 1799?
- What role did each of the following play in the French Revolution: lawyers, peasants, women, the clergy, the Jacobins, the sans-culottes, the French Revolutionary Army, and the Committee of Public Safety?
- What aspects of the French Revolution did Napoleon preserve, and which did he destroy?
- In what ways were the French Revolution and the seventeenth-century English revolutions alike? In what ways were they different?

ON THE MORNING of July 14, 1789, a Parisian mob of eight thousand people in search of weapons streamed toward the Bastille, a royal armory filled with arms and ammunition. The Bastille was also a state prison, and although it now contained only seven prisoners, in the eyes of these angry Parisians, it was a glaring symbol of the government's despotic policies. The armory was defended by the marquis de Launay and a small garrison of 114 men. The attack began in earnest in the early afternoon, and after three hours of fighting, de Launay and the garrison surrendered. Angered by the loss of ninety-eight of their members, the victorious mob beat de Launay to death, cut off his head, and carried it aloft in triumph through the streets of Paris. When King Louis XVI was told the news of the fall of the Bastille by the duc de La

Rochefoucauld-Liancourt, he exclaimed, "Why, this is a revolt." "No, Sire," replied the duc, "it is a revolution."

Historians have long assumed that the modern history of Europe began with two major transformations—the French Revolution (discussed in this chapter) and the Industrial Revolution (see Chapter 20). Accordingly, the French Revolution has been portrayed as the major turning point in European political and social history, when the institutions of the "old regime" were destroyed and a new order was created based on individual rights, representative institutions, and a concept of loyalty to the nation rather than the monarch. This perspective does have certain limitations, however.

France was only one of a number of areas in the Western world where the assumptions of the old order were challenged. Although some historians have called the upheavals of the eighteenth and early nineteenth centuries a "democratic revolution," it is probably more appropriate to speak of a liberal movement to extend political rights and power to the bourgeoisie in possession of capital—citizens besides the aristocracy who were literate and had become wealthy through capitalist enterprises in trade, industry, and finance. The years preceding and accompanying the French Revolution included attempts at reform and revolt in the North American colonies, Britain, the Dutch Republic, some Swiss cities, and the Austrian Netherlands. The success of the American and French Revolutions makes them the center of attention for this chapter.

Not all of the decadent privileges that characterized the old European regime were destroyed in 1789, however. The revolutionary upheaval of the era, especially in France, did create new liberal and national political ideals, summarized in the French revolutionary slogan, "Liberty, Equality, Fraternity," that transformed France and were then spread to other European countries through the conquests of Napoleon. After Napoleon's defeat, however, the forces of reaction did their best to restore the old order and resist pressures for reform.

The Beginnings of the Revolutionary Era: The American Revolution

At the end of the Seven Years' War in 1763, Great Britain had become the world's greatest colonial power. In North America, Britain controlled Canada and the lands east of the Mississippi (see Map 19.1). After the Seven Years' War, British policy makers sought to obtain new revenues from the thirteen American colonies to pay for British army expenses in defending the colonists. An attempt to levy new taxes by a stamp act in 1765 led to riots and the law's quick repeal.

The Americans and the British had different conceptions of empire. The British envisioned a single empire with Parliament as the supreme authority throughout. Only Parliament could make laws for all the people in the empire, including the American colonists. The Americans, in contrast, had their own representative assemblies. They believed that neither the king nor Parliament had any right to interfere in their internal affairs and that no tax could be levied without the consent of an assembly whose members actually represented the people.

Crisis followed crisis in the 1770s until 1776, when the colonists decided to declare their independence from the British Empire. On July 4, 1776, the Second Continental Congress approved a declaration of independence written by Thomas Jefferson (see the box on p. 524). A stirring political document, the declaration affirmed the Enlightenment's natural rights of "life, liberty, and the pursuit of happiness" and declared the colonies to be "free and independent states absolved from all allegiance to the British crown." The war for American independence had formally begun.

Of great importance to the colonies' cause was the assistance provided by foreign countries that were eager to gain revenge for earlier defeats at the hands of the British. The French supplied arms and money to the rebels from the beginning of the war, and French officers and soldiers also served in the American Continental Army under George Washington as commander in chief. When the British army of General Cornwallis was forced to surrender to a combined American and French army and French fleet under Washington at Yorktown in 1781, the British government decided to call it quits. The Treaty of Paris, signed in 1783, recognized the independence of the American colonies and granted the Americans control of the western territory from the Appalachians to the Mississippi River.

Forming a New Nation

The thirteen American colonies had gained their independence as the United States of America, but a fear of concentrated power and concern for their own interests caused them to have little enthusiasm for establishing a united nation with a strong central government. The Articles of Confederation, ratified in 1781, did little to provide for a strong central government. A movement for a different form of national government soon arose. In the summer of 1787, fifty-five delegates attended a convention in Philadelphia to revise the Articles of Confederation. The convention's delegates—wealthy, politically experienced, well educated—rejected revision and decided to devise a new constitution.

The proposed constitution created a central government distinct from and superior to the governments of the individual states. The national government was given the

The Argument for Independence

On July 2, 1776, the Second Continental Congress adopted a resolution declaring the independence of the American colonies. Two days later, the delegates approved the Declaration of Independence, which gave the reasons for their action. Its principal author was Thomas Jefferson, who basically restated John Locke's theory of revolution (see Chapter 15).

The Declaration of Independence

When in the course of human events it becomes necessary for one people to dissolve the political bands which have connected them with another, and to assume among the Powers of the earth, the separate and equal station to which the Laws of Nature and of Nature's God entitle them, a decent respect to the opinions of mankind requires that they should declare the causes which impel them to the separation.

We hold these truths to be self-evident, that all men are created equal, that they are endowed by their Creator with certain unalienable Rights, that among these are Life, Liberty and the pursuit of Happiness. That to secure these rights, Governments are instituted among Men, deriving their just powers from the consent of the governed, That whenever any Form of Government becomes destructive of these ends, it is the Right of the People to alter or to abolish it and to institute new Government, laying its foundation on such principles and organizing its powers in such form, as to them shall seem most likely to effect their Safety and Happiness. Prudence, indeed, will dictate that Governments long established should not be changed for light and transient causes; and accordingly all experience has shown, that mankind are more disposed to suffer, while evils are sufferable, than to right themselves by abolishing the forms to which they are accustomed. But when a long train of abuses and usurpations, pursuing invariably the same Object evinces a design to reduce them under absolute Despotism, it is their right, it is their duty, to throw off such Government, and to provide new Guards for their future security. —Such has been the patient sufferance of these Colonies; and such is now the necessity which constrains them to alter their former Systems of government. The history of the present King of Great Britain is a history of repeated injuries and usurpations, all having in direct object the establishment of an absolute Tyranny over these States.

power to levy taxes, raise a national army, regulate domestic and foreign trade, and create a national currency. The central or federal government was divided into three branches, each with some power to check the functioning of the others. A president would serve as the chief executive with the power to execute laws, veto the legislature's acts, supervise foreign affairs, and direct military forces. Legislative power was vested in the second branch of government, a bicameral legislature composed of the Senate, elected by the state legislatures, and the House of Representatives, elected directly by the people. The Supreme Court and other courts "as deemed necessary" by Congress served as the third branch of government. They would enforce the Constitution as the "supreme law of the land."

The United States Constitution was approved by the states—by a slim margin—in 1788. Important to its success was a promise to add a bill of rights to it as the new government's first piece of business. Accordingly, in March 1789, the new Congress proposed twelve amendments to the Constitution; the ten that were ratified by the states have been known ever since as the Bill of Rights. These guaranteed freedom of religion, speech, press, petition, and assembly, as well as the right to bear arms, protection against unreasonable searches and arrests, trial by jury, due process of law, and protection of property rights. Many of these rights were derived from the natural rights philosophy of the eighteenth-century philosophes, which was popular among the American colonists. Is it any wonder that many European intellectuals saw the American Revolution as the embodiment of the Enlightenment's political dreams?

The Impact of the American Revolution on Europe

The year 1789 witnessed two far-reaching events, the beginning of a new United States of America and the eruption of the French Revolution. Was there a connection between the two great revolutions of the late eighteenth century?

There is no doubt that the American Revolution had an important impact on Europeans. Books, newspapers, and magazines provided a newly developing reading public with numerous accounts of American events. To many in Europe, it seemed to portend an era of significant changes, including new arrangements in international politics. The Venetian ambassador to Paris astutely observed in 1783 that "if only the union of the [American] provinces is preserved, it is reasonable to expect that, with the favorable effects of time, and of European arts and sciences, it will become the most formidable power in the world."[1] But the American Revolution also meant far more than that. It proved to many Europeans that the liberal political ideas of the Enlightenment were not merely the vapid utterances of intellectuals. The rights of man, ideas of liberty and equality, popular sovereignty, freedom of religion, thought, and press, and the separation of powers were not merely utopian ideals. The Americans had created a new social contract, embodied it in a written constitution, and made concepts of liberty and representative government a reality. The premises of the Enlightenment seemed confirmed; a new age and a better world could be achieved. As a Swiss philosophe expressed it: "I am tempted to believe that

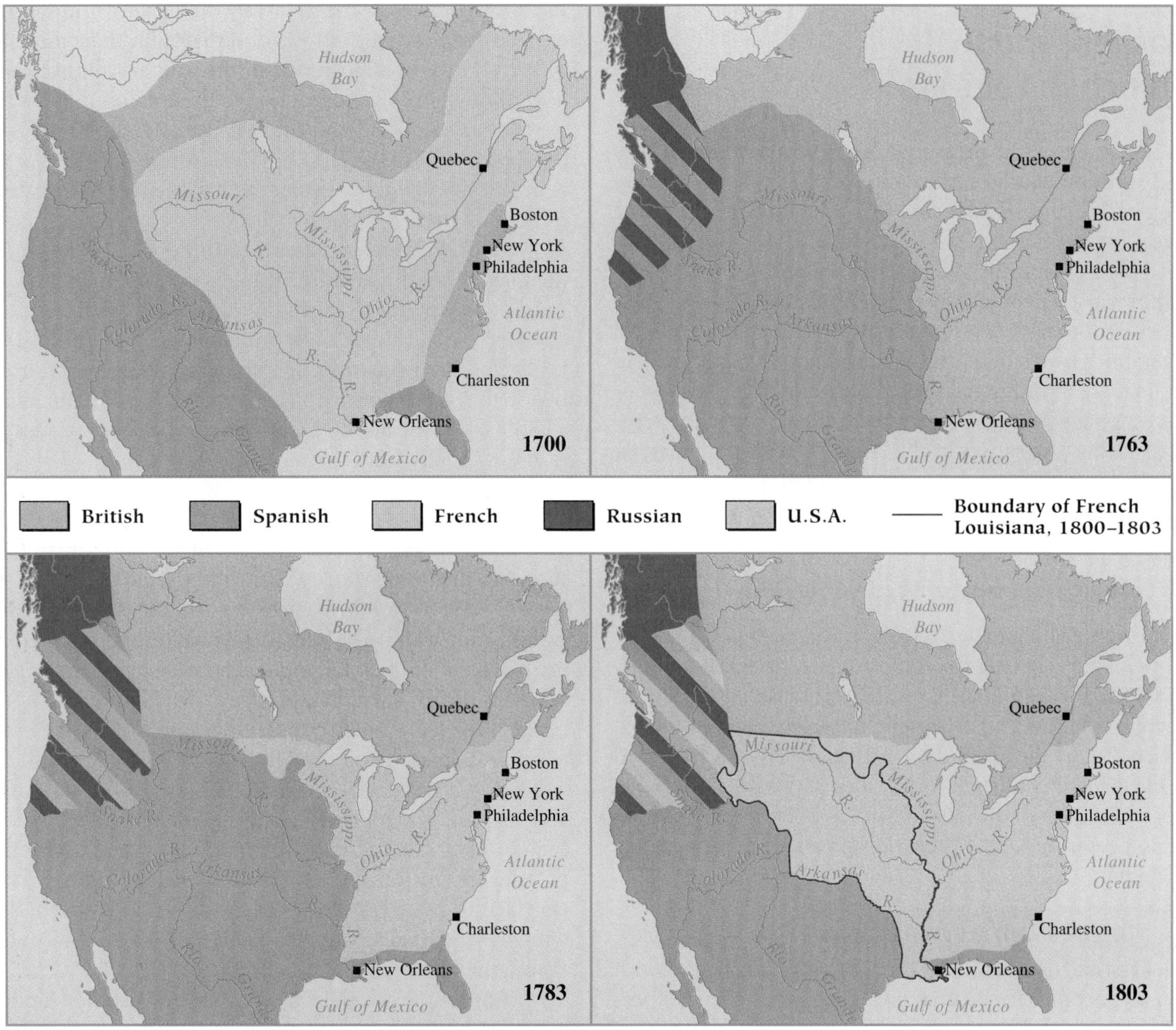

Map 19.1 North America, 1700–1803. The Seven Years' War gained Britain much territory in eastern North America, but asking the American colonies to help pay for the war sparked the American Revolution. The 1803 Louisiana Purchase nearly doubled the size of the United States and spurred westward expansion to the Pacific Ocean. ■ In what periods was the Mississippi River a national boundary, and why was control of the river important for the United States?

North America is the country where reason and humanity will develop more rapidly than anywhere else."[2]

Europeans obtained much of their information about America from returning soldiers, especially the hundreds of French officers who had served in the American war. One of them, the aristocratic marquis de Lafayette, had volunteered for service in America in order to "strike a blow against England," France's old enemy. Closely associated with George Washington, Lafayette returned to France with ideas of individual liberties and notions of republicanism and popular sovereignty. He became a member of the Society of Thirty, a club composed of people from the Paris salons. These "lovers of liberty" were influential in the early stages of the French Revolution. The Declaration of the Rights of Man and the Citizen (see "The Destruction of the Old Regime" later in this chapter) showed unmistakable signs of the influence of the American Declaration of Independence as well as the American state constitutions. Yet for all of its obvious impact, the American Revolution proved in the long run to be far less important to Europe than the French Revolution. The French Revolution was more complex, more violent, and far more radical in its attempt to construct both a new political order and a new social order. The French Revolution provided a model of revolution for Europe and much of the rest of the world; to many analysts, it remains the political movement that truly inaugurated the modern political world.

Background to the French Revolution

Although we associate events like the French Revolution with sudden changes, the causes of such events involve long-range problems as well as immediate, precipitating forces. Revolutions, as has been repeatedly shown, are not necessarily the result of economic collapse and masses of impoverished people hungering for change. In fact, in the fifty years before 1789, France had experienced a period of economic growth due to an expansion of foreign trade and an increase in industrial production, although many people, especially peasants, no doubt failed to share in the prosperity. Thus the causes of the French Revolution must be found in a multifaceted examination of French society and its problems in the late eighteenth century.

Social Structure of the Old Regime

Although France experienced an increase in economic growth in the eighteenth century, the wealth was not evenly distributed. The long-range or indirect causes of the French Revolution must first be sought in the condition of French society. Before the Revolution, French society was grounded in the inequality of rights or the idea of privilege. The population of 27 million was divided, as it had been since the Middle Ages, into legal categories known as the three orders or estates.

THE FIRST AND SECOND ESTATES

The First Estate consisted of the clergy and numbered about 130,000 people. The church owned approximately 10 percent of the land. Clergy were exempt from the *taille,* France's chief tax, although the church had agreed to pay a "voluntary" contribution every five years to the state. Clergy were also radically divided, since the higher clergy, stemming from aristocratic families, shared the interests of the nobility while the parish priests were often poor commoners.

The Second Estate was the nobility, composed of no more than 350,000 people who nevertheless owned about 25 to 30 percent of the land. Under Louis XV and Louis XVI, the nobility had continued to play an important and even crucial role in French society, holding many of the leading positions in the government, the military, the law courts, and the higher church offices. Much heavy industry in France was controlled by nobles, either through investment or by ownership of mining and metallurgical enterprises. The French nobility was also divided. The nobility of the robe derived their status from officeholding, a pathway that had often enabled commoners to attain noble rank. These nobles now dominated the royal law courts and important administrative offices. The nobility of the sword claimed to be descendants of the original medieval nobility. As a group, the nobles sought to expand their privileges at the expense of the monarchy—to defend liberty by resisting the arbitrary actions of monarchy, as some nobles asserted—and to maintain their monopolistic control over positions in the military, church, and government. In 1781, in reaction to the ambitions of aristocrats newly arrived from the bourgeoisie, the Ségur Law attempted to limit the sale of military officerships to fourth-generation nobles, thus excluding newly enrolled members of the nobility.

Although there were many poor nobles, on the whole the fortunes of the wealthy aristocrats outstripped those of most others in French society. Generally, the nobles tended to marry within their own ranks, making the nobility a fairly closed group. Although their privileges varied from region to region, the very possession of privileges remained a hallmark of the nobility. Common to all were tax exemptions, especially from the *taille.*

THE THIRD ESTATE

The Third Estate, the commoners of society, constituted the overwhelming majority of the French population. They were divided by vast differences in occupation, level of education, and wealth. The peasants who alone constituted 75 to 80 percent of the total population were by far the largest segment of the Third Estate. They owned about 35 to 40 percent of the land, although their landholdings varied from area to area and over half had no or little land on which to survive. Serfdom no longer existed on any large scale in France, but French peasants still had obligations to their local landlords that they deeply resented. These relics of feudalism included the payment of fees for the use of village facilities, such as the flour mill, community oven, and winepress, as well as tithes to the clergy. The nobility also maintained the right to hunt on peasants' land.

Another part of the Third Estate consisted of skilled artisans, shopkeepers, and other wage earners in the cities. Although the eighteenth century had been a period of rapid urban growth, 90 percent of French towns had fewer than ten thousand inhabitants; only nine cities had more than fifty thousand. In the eighteenth century, consumer prices rose faster than wages, with the result that these urban groups experienced a decline in purchasing power. In Paris, for example, income lagged behind food prices and especially behind a 140 percent rise in rents for working people in skilled and unskilled trades. The economic discontent of this segment of the Third Estate—and often simply their struggle for survival—led them to play an important role in the Revolution, especially in the city of Paris. Insubordination, one observer noted, "has been visible among the people for some years now and above all among craftsmen." One historian has charted the ups and downs of revolutionary riots in Paris by showing their correlation to changes in bread prices. Sudden increases in the price of bread, which constituted three-fourths of an ordinary person's diet and cost one-third to one-half of his or her income, immediately affected public order. People expected bread prices to be controlled. They grew desperate when prices rose, and their only recourse was mob action to try

© Bettmann/CORBIS

The Three Estates. This French political cartoon from 1789 reveals a critical view of France's privileged orders. Shown in the cartoon is a naked common man held in chains and being ridden by an aristocrat, a clergyman, and a judge. The message is clear: most ordinary French people (the Third Estate) are suffering horribly as a result of the privileges of the First and Second Estates.

to change the situation. The towns and cities were also home to large groups of unskilled workers. One magistrate complained that "misery . . . has thrown into the towns people who overburden them with their uselessness, and who find nothing to do, because there is not enough for the people who live there."[3]

About 8 percent, or 2.3 million people, constituted the bourgeoisie or middle class, who owned about 20 to 25 percent of the land. This group included the merchants, industrialists, and bankers who controlled the resources of trade, manufacturing, and finance and benefited from the economic prosperity after 1730. The bourgeoisie also included professional people—lawyers, holders of public offices, doctors, and writers. Many members of the bourgeoisie sought security and status through the purchase of land. They had their own set of grievances because they were often excluded from the social and political privileges monopolized by the nobles. These resentments of the middle class were for a long time assumed to be a major cause of the French Revolution. But although these tensions existed, the situation was not a simple case of a unified bourgeoisie against a unified noble class. As is evident, neither group was monolithic. Nobles were separated by vast differences in wealth and importance. A similar gulf separated wealthy financiers from local lawyers in French provincial towns.

Remarkable similarities existed at the upper levels of society between the wealthier bourgeoisie and the nobility. It was still possible for wealthy middle-class individuals to enter the ranks of the nobility by obtaining public offices and entering the nobility of the robe. In fact, between 1774 and 1789, the not insignificant number of 2,500 wealthy bourgeoisie entered the ranks of the nobility. Over the century as a whole, 6,500 new noble families were created. In addition, as we saw in Chapter 18, the aristocrats were also engaging in capitalist activities on their landed estates, such as mining, metallurgy, and glassmaking, and were even investing in foreign trade. Viewed in terms of economic function, many members of the bourgeoisie and nobility formed a single class. Finally, the new and critical ideas of the Enlightenment proved attractive to both aristocrats and bourgeoisie. Members of both groups shared a common world of liberal political thought. The old view that the French Revolution was the result of the conflict between two rigid orders, the bourgeoisie and the nobility, has been enlarged and revised. Both aristocratic and bourgeois elites, long accustomed to a new socioeconomic reality based on wealth and economic achievement, were increasingly frustrated by a monarchical system resting on privileges and on an old and rigid social order based on the concept of estates. The opposition of these elites to the old order ultimately led them to take drastic action against the monarchical regime, although they soon split over the question of how far to proceed in eliminating traditional privileges. In a real sense, the revolution had its origins in political grievances.

Other Problems Facing the French Monarchy

Although the long-range causes of the French Revolution can thus be found in part in the growing frustration at the monarchy's inability to deal with new social realities and problems, other factors were also present. The failure of the French monarchy was exacerbated by specific problems in the 1780s. Although the country had enjoyed fifty years of growth overall, periodic economic crises still occurred. Bad harvests in 1787 and 1788 and the beginnings of a manufacturing depression resulted in food shortages, rising prices for food and other necessities, and unemployment in the cities. The number of poor, estimated by some at almost one-third of the population, reached crisis proportions on the eve of the Revolution. An English traveler noted the misery of the poor in the countryside: "All the country girls and women are without shoes or stockings; and the plowmen at their work have neither sabots nor stockings to their feet. This is a poverty that strikes at the root of national prosperity."[4]

Increased criticism of existing privileges as well as social and political institutions also characterized the eighteenth century. Although the philosophes did not advocate revolution, their ideas were widely circulated among the literate bourgeois and noble elites of France. The actual influence of the ideas of the philosophes is difficult to prove, but once the Revolution began, the revolutionary leaders frequently quoted Enlightenment writers, especially Rousseau.

The French Parlements often frustrated efforts at reform. Responsible for registering royal decrees, these thirteen law courts could block royal edicts by not registering them. Although Louis XIV had forced them into submission, the Parlements had gained new strength in the eighteenth century as they and their noble judges assumed the role of defenders of "liberty" against the arbitrary power of the monarchy. As noble defenders, however, they often pushed their own interests as well, especially by blocking new taxes. This last point reminds us that one of the fundamental problems facing the monarchy was financial.

The immediate cause of the French Revolution was the near collapse of government finances. French governmental expenditures continued to grow due to costly wars and royal extravagance. Since the government responded by borrowing, by 1788 the interest on the debt alone constituted half of the government's spending. The king's finance ministry wrestled with the problem but met with resistance. In 1786, Charles de Calonne, the controller general of finance, proposed a complete revamping of the fiscal and administrative system of the state. To gain support, Calonne convened an "assembly of notables" early in 1787. This gathering of nobles, prelates, and magistrates refused to cooperate, and the government's attempt to go it alone brought further disaster. On the verge of a complete financial collapse, the government was finally forced to call a meeting of the Estates-General, the French parliamentary body that had not met since 1614. By calling the Estates-General, the government was virtually admitting that the consent of the nation was required to raise taxes.

The French Revolution

In summoning the Estates-General, the government was merely looking for a way to solve the immediate financial crisis. The monarchy had no wish for a major reform of the government, nor did the delegates who arrived at Versailles come with plans for the revolutionary changes that ultimately emerged. Yet over the next years, through the interplay of the deputies meeting in various legislative assemblies, the common people in the streets of Paris and other cities, and the peasants in the countryside, much of the old regime would be destroyed, and Europe would have a new model for political and social change.

From Estates-General to a National Assembly

The Estates-General consisted of representatives from the three orders of French society. In the elections for the Estates-General, the government had ruled that the Third Estate should get double representation (it did, after all, constitute 97 percent of the population). Consequently, while both the First Estate (the clergy) and the Second (the nobility) had about 300 delegates each, the commoners had almost 600 representatives. Two-thirds of the latter were people with legal training, and three-fourths were from towns with over two thousand inhabitants, giving the Third Estate a particularly strong legal and urban representation. Of the 282 representatives of the nobility, about 90 were liberal-minded, urban-oriented, and interested in the enlightened ideas of the century; half of them were under forty years of age. The activists of the Third Estate and reform-minded individuals among the First and Second Estates had common ties in their youth, urban background, and hostility to privilege. The *cahiers de doléances,* or statements of local grievances, which were drafted throughout France during the elections to the Estates-General, advocated a regular constitutional government that would abolish the fiscal privileges of the church and nobility as the major way to regenerate the country.

The Estates-General opened at Versailles on May 5, 1789. It was divided from the start over the question of whether voting should be by order or by head (each delegate having one vote). The Parlement of Paris, consisting of nobles of the robe, had advocated voting by order according to the form used in 1614. Each order would vote separately; each would have veto power over the other two, thus guaranteeing aristocratic control over reforms. But opposition to the Parlement's proposal had arisen from a group of reformers calling themselves patriots or "lovers of liberty." Although they claimed to represent the nation, they consisted primarily of bourgeoisie and nobles. One group of patriots known as the Society of Thirty drew most of its members from the salons of Paris. Some of this largely noble group had been directly influenced by the American Revolution, but all had been affected by the ideas of the Enlightenment and favored reforms made in the light of reason and utility.

THE NATIONAL ASSEMBLY

The failure of the government to assume the leadership at the opening of the Estates-General created an opportunity for the Third Estate to push its demands for voting by head. Since it had double representation, with the assistance of liberal nobles and clerics, it could turn the three estates into a single-chamber legislature that would reform France in its own way. One representative, the Abbé Sieyès, issued a pamphlet in which he asked, "What is the Third Estate? Everything. What has it been thus far in the political order? Nothing. What does it demand? To become something." Sieyès's sentiment, however, was not representative of the general feeling in 1789. Most delegates still wanted to make changes within a framework of respect for the authority of the king; revival or reform did not mean the overthrow of traditional institutions. When the First Estate declared in favor of voting by order, the Third Estate felt compelled to respond in a significant fashion. On June 17, 1789, the Third Estate voted to constitute itself a "National Assembly" and decided to draw up a constitution. Three days later, on June 20, the deputies of the Third Estate arrived at their meeting place only to find the doors locked; thereupon they moved to a nearby indoor tennis court and swore (in what has come to be known as the Tennis Court Oath) that they would continue to meet until they had produced a French constitution. These actions of June 17 and June 20 constituted the first step in the French Revolution, since the Third Estate had no legal right to act as the National Assembly. This revolution, largely the work of the lawyers of the Third Estate, was soon in jeopardy, however, as the king sided with the First Estate and threatened to dissolve the Estates-General. Louis XVI now prepared to use force. The revolution of the lawyers appeared doomed.

INTERVENTION OF THE COMMON PEOPLE

The common people, however, in a series of urban and rural uprisings in July and August 1789, saved the Third Estate from the king's attempt to stop the revolution. From now on, the common people would be mobilized by both revolutionary and counterrevolutionary politicians and used to support their interests. The common people had their own interests as well and would use the name of the Third Estate to wage a war on the rich, claiming that the aristocrats were plotting to destroy the Estates-General and retain its privileges. This war was not what the deputies of the Third Estate had planned.

The most famous of the urban risings was the fall of the Bastille (see the box on p. 531). The king's attempt to take defensive measures by increasing the number of troops at the arsenals in Paris and along the roads to Versailles served not to intimidate but rather to inflame public opinion. Increased mob activity in Paris led Parisian leaders to form the so-called Permanent Committee to keep order. Needing arms, they organized a popular force to capture the Invalides, a royal armory, and on July 14 attacked the Bastille, another royal armory. But the Bastille had also been

Giraudon/Art Resource, NY

The Tennis Court Oath. Finding themselves locked out of their regular meeting place on June 20, 1789, the deputies of the Third Estate met instead in the nearby tennis courts of the Jeu de Paume and committed themselves to continue to meet until they established a new constitution for France. In this painting, the Neoclassical Jacques-Louis David presents a dramatic rendering of the Tennis Court Oath.

Storming of the Bastille. Louis XVI planned to use force to dissolve the Estates-General, but a number of rural and urban uprisings by the common people prevented this action. The fall of the Bastille, pictured here in an anonymous painting, is perhaps the most famous of the urban risings.

a state prison, and though it now contained only seven prisoners (five forgers and two insane people), its fall quickly became a popular symbol of triumph over despotism. Paris was abandoned to the insurgents, and Louis XVI was soon informed that the royal troops were unreliable. Louis's acceptance of that reality signaled the collapse of royal authority; the king could no longer enforce his will. Louis then confirmed the appointment of the marquis de Lafayette as commander of a newly created citizens' militia known as the National Guard. The fall of the Bastille had saved the National Assembly.

At the same time, independently of what was going on in Paris, popular revolutions broke out in numerous cities. In Nantes, permanent committees and national guards were created to maintain order after crowds had seized the chief citadels. This collapse of royal authority in the cities was paralleled by peasant revolutions in the countryside.

A growing resentment of the entire seigneurial system, with its fees and obligations, greatly exacerbated by the economic and fiscal activities of the great estate holders—whether noble or bourgeois—in the difficult decade of the 1780s, created the conditions for a popular uprising. The fall of the Bastille and the king's apparent capitulation to the demands of the Third Estate now encouraged peasants to take matters into their own hands. From July 19 to August 3, peasant rebellions occurred in five major areas of France. Patterns varied. In some places, peasants simply forced their lay and ecclesiastical lords to renounce dues and tithes; elsewhere they burned charters listing their obligations. The peasants were not acting in blind fury; they knew what they were doing. Many also believed that the king supported their actions. As a contemporary chronicler wrote: "For several weeks, news went from village to village. They announced that the Estates-

The Fall of the Bastille

On July 14, 1789, Parisian crowds in search of weapons attacked and captured the royal armory known as the Bastille. It had also been a state prison, and its fall marked the triumph of "liberty" over despotism. This intervention of the Parisian populace saved the Third Estate from Louis XVI's attempted counterrevolution.

A Parisian Newspaper Account of the Fall of the Bastille

First, the people tried to enter this fortress by the Rue St.-Antoine, this fortress, which no one has even penetrated against the wishes of this frightful despotism and where the monster still resided. The treacherous governor had put out a flag of peace. So a confident advance was made; a detachment of French Guards, with perhaps five to six thousand armed bourgeois, penetrated the Bastille's outer courtyards, but as soon as some six hundred persons had passed over the first drawbridge, the bridge was raised and artillery fire mowed down several French Guards and some soldiers; the cannon fired on the town, and the people took fright; a large number of individuals were killed or wounded; but then they rallied and took shelter from the fire. . . . Meanwhile, they tried to locate some cannon; they attacked from the water's edge through the gardens of the arsenal, and from there made an orderly siege; they advanced from various directions, beneath a ceaseless round of fire. It was a terrible scene. . . . The fighting grew steadily more intense; the citizens had become hardened to the fire; from all directions they clambered onto the roofs or broke into the rooms; as soon as an enemy appeared among the turrets on the tower, he was fixed in the sights of a hundred guns and mown down in an instant; meanwhile cannon fire was hurriedly directed against the second drawbridge, which it pierced, breaking the chains; in vain did the cannon on the tower reply, for most people were sheltered from it; the fury was at its height; people bravely faced death and every danger; women, in their eagerness, helped us to the utmost; even the children, after the discharge of fire from the fortress, ran here and there picking up the bullets and shot; [and so the Bastille fell and the governor, de Launay, was captured]. . . . Serene and blessed liberty, for the first time, has at last been introduced into this abode of horrors, this frightful refuge of monstrous despotism and its crimes.

Meanwhile, they get ready to march; they leave amidst an enormous crowd; the applause, the outbursts of joy, the insults, the oaths hurled at the treacherous prisoners of war; everything is confused; cries of vengeance and of pleasure issue from every heart; the conquerors, glorious and covered in honor, carry their arms and the spoils of the conquered, the flags of victory, the militia mingling with the soldiers of the fatherland, the victory laurels offered them from every side, all this created a frightening and splendid spectacle. On arriving at the square, the people, anxious to avenge themselves, allowed neither de Launay nor the other officers to reach the place of trial; they seized them from the hands of their conquerors, and trampled them underfoot one after the other. De Launay was struck by a thousand blows, his head was cut off and hoisted on the end of a pike with blood streaming down all sides. . . . This glorious day must amaze our enemies, and finally usher in for us the triumph of justice and liberty. In the evening, there were celebrations.

General was going to abolish tithes, quitrents and dues, that the King agreed but that the peasants had to support the public authorities by going themselves to demand the destruction of titles."[5]

The agrarian revolts served as a backdrop to the Great Fear, a vast panic that spread like wildfire through France between July 20 and August 6. Fear of invasion by foreign troops, aided by a supposed aristocratic plot, encouraged the formation of more citizens' militias and permanent committees. The greatest impact of the agrarian revolts and the Great Fear was on the National Assembly meeting in Versailles. We will now examine its attempt to reform France.

Destruction of the Old Regime

One of the first acts of the National Assembly (also called the Constituent Assembly because from 1789 to 1791 it was writing a new constitution) was to destroy the relics of feudalism or aristocratic privileges. To some deputies, this measure was necessary to calm the peasants and restore order in the countryside, although many urban bourgeois were willing to abolish feudalism as a matter of principle. On the night of August 4, 1789, the National Assembly in an astonishing session voted to abolish seigneurial rights as well as the fiscal privileges of nobles, clergy, towns, and provinces.

THE DECLARATION OF THE RIGHTS OF MAN AND THE CITIZEN

On August 26, the assembly provided the ideological foundation for its actions and an educational device for the nation by adopting the Declaration of the Rights of Man and the Citizen (see the box on p. 532). This charter of basic liberties reflected the ideas of the major philosophes of the French Enlightenment and also owed much to the American Declaration of Independence and American state constitutions. The declaration began with a ringing affirmation of "the natural and imprescriptible rights of man"

Declaration of the Rights of Man and the Citizen

One of the important documents of the French Revolution, the Declaration of the Rights of Man and the Citizen, was adopted in August 1789 by the National Assembly. The declaration affirmed that "men are born and remain free and equal in rights," that governments must protect these natural rights, and that political power is derived from the people.

Declaration of the Rights of Man and the Citizen

The representatives of the French people, organized as a national assembly, considering that ignorance, neglect, and scorn of the rights of man are the sole causes of public misfortunes and of corruption of governments, have resolved to display in a solemn declaration the natural, inalienable, and sacred rights of man, so that this declaration, constantly in the presence of all members of society, will continually remind them of their rights and their duties. . . . Consequently, the National Assembly recognizes and declares, in the presence and under the auspices of the Supreme Being, the following rights of man and citizen:

1. Men are born and remain free and equal in rights; social distinctions can be established only for the common benefit.
2. The aim of every political association is the conservation of the natural and imprescriptible rights of man; these rights are liberty, property, security, and resistance to oppression.
3. The source of all sovereignty is located in essence in the nation; no body, no individual can exercise authority which does not emanate from it expressly.
4. Liberty consists in being able to do anything that does not harm another person. . . .
6. The law is the expression of the general will; all citizens have the right to concur personally or through their representatives in its formation; it must be the same for all, whether it protects or punishes. All citizens being equal in its eyes are equally admissible to all honors, positions, and public employments, according to their capabilities and without other distinctions than those of their virtues and talents.
7. No man can be accused, arrested, or detained except in cases determined by the law, and according to the forms which it has prescribed. . . .
10. No one may be disturbed because of his opinions, even religious, provided that their public demonstration does not disturb the public order established by law.
11. The free communication of thoughts and opinions is one of the most precious rights of man: every citizen can therefore freely speak, write, and print. . . .
12. The guaranteeing of the rights of man and citizen necessitates a public force; this force is therefore instituted for the advantage of all, and not for the private use of those to whom it is entrusted. . . .
14. Citizens have the right to determine for themselves or through their representatives the need for taxation of the public, to consent to it freely, to investigate its use, and to determine its rate, basis, collection, and duration.
15. Society has the right to demand an accounting of his administration from every public agent.
16. Any society in which guarantees of rights are not assured nor the separation of powers determined has no constitution.
17. Property being an inviolable and sacred right, no one may be deprived of it unless public necessity, legally determined, clearly requires such action, and then only on condition of a just and prior indemnity.

to "liberty, property, security, and resistance to oppression." It went on to affirm the destruction of aristocratic privileges by proclaiming an end to exemptions from taxation, freedom and equal rights for all men, and access to public office based on talent. The monarchy was restricted, and all citizens were to have the right to take part in the legislative process. Freedom of speech and press were coupled with the outlawing of arbitrary arrests.

The Declaration also raised another important issue. Did the proclamation's ideal of equal rights for "all men" also include women? Many deputies insisted that it did, at least in terms of civil liberties, provided that, as one said, "women do not aspire to exercise political rights and functions." Olympe de Gouges, a playwright and pamphleteer, refused to accept this exclusion of women from political rights. Echoing the words of the official declaration, she penned a Declaration of the Rights of Woman and the Female Citizen, in which she insisted that women should have all the same rights as men (see the box on p. 533). The National Assembly ignored her demands.

THE WOMEN'S MARCH TO VERSAILLES

In the meantime, Louis XVI had remained inactive at Versailles. He did refuse, however, to promulgate the decrees on the abolition of feudalism and the declaration of rights, but an unexpected turn of events soon forced the king to change his mind. On October 5, after marching to the Hôtel de Ville, the city hall, to demand bread, crowds of Parisian women numbering in the thousands set off for Versailles, 12 miles away, to confront the king and the National Assembly. One eyewitness was amazed at the sight of "detachments of women coming up from every

Declaration of the Rights of Woman and the Female Citizen

Olympe de Gouges (a pen name for Marie Gouze) was a butcher's daughter who wrote plays and pamphlets. She argued that the Declaration of the Rights of Man and the Citizen did not apply to women and composed her own Declaration of the Rights of Woman in 1791.

Declaration of the Rights of Woman and the Female Citizen

... Mothers, daughters, sisters and representatives of the nation demand to be constituted into a national assembly. Believing that ignorance, omission, or scorn for the rights of woman are the only causes of public misfortunes and of the corruption of governments, the women have resolved to set forth in a solemn declaration the natural, inalienable, and sacred rights of woman in order that this declaration, constantly exposed before all the members of the society, will ceaselessly remind them of their rights and duties....

Consequently, the sex that is as superior in beauty as it is in courage during the sufferings of maternity recognizes and declares in the presence and under the auspices of the Supreme Being, the following Rights of Woman and of Female Citizens.

1. Woman is born free and lives equal to man in her rights. Social distinctions can be based only on the common utility.
2. The purpose of any political association is the conservation of the natural and imprescriptible rights of woman and man; these rights are liberty, property, security, and especially resistance to oppression.
3. The principle of all sovereignty rests essentially with the nation, which is nothing but the union of woman and man; no body and no individual can exercise any authority which does not come expressly from it [the nation].
4. Liberty and justice consist of restoring all that belongs to others; thus, the only limits on the exercise of the natural rights of woman are perpetual male tyranny; these limits are to be reformed by the laws of nature and reason....
6. The law must be the expression of the general will; all female and male citizens must contribute either personally or through their representatives to its formation; it must be the same for all: male and female citizens, being equal in the eyes of the law, must be equally admitted to all honors, positions, and public employment according to their capacity and without other distinctions besides those of their virtues and talents.
7. No woman is an exception; she is accused, arrested, and detained in cases determined by law. Women, like men, obey this rigorous law....
10. No one is to be disquieted for his very basic opinions; woman has the right to mount the scaffold; she must equally have the right to mount the rostrum, provided that her demonstrations do not disturb the legally established public order.
11. The free communication of thought and opinions is one of the most precious rights of woman, since that liberty assured the recognition of children by their fathers....
12. The guarantee of the rights of woman and the female citizen implies a major benefit; this guarantee must be instituted for the advantage of all, and not for the particular benefit of those to whom it is entrusted....
14. Female and male citizens have the right to verify, either by themselves or through their representatives, the necessity of the public contribution. This can only apply to women if they are granted an equal share, not only of wealth, but also of public administration, and in the determination of the proportion, the base, the collection, and the duration of the tax.
15. The collectivity of women, joined for tax purposes to the aggregate of men, has the right to demand an accounting of his administration from any public agent.
16. No society has a constitution without the guarantee of rights and the separation of powers; the constitution is null if the majority of individuals comprising the nation have not cooperated in drafting it.
17. Property belongs to both sexes whether united or separate; for each it is an inviolable and sacred right; no one can be deprived of it, since it is the true patrimony of nature, unless the legally determined public need obviously dictates it, and then only with a just and prior indemnity.

direction, armed with broomsticks, lances, pitchforks, swords, pistols and muskets." After meeting with a delegation of these women, who tearfully described how their children were starving for lack of bread, Louis XVI promised them grain supplies for Paris, thinking that this would end the protest. But the women's action had forced the Paris National Guard under Lafayette to follow their lead and march to Versailles. The crowd now insisted that the royal family return to Paris. On October 6, the king complied. As a goodwill gesture, he brought along wagonloads of flour from the palace stores. All were escorted by women armed with pikes (some of which held the severed heads of the king's guards) singing, "We are bringing back the baker, the baker's wife, and the baker's boy"

The Women's March to Versailles. On October 5, 1789, thousands of Parisian women marched to Versailles to confront King Louis XVI and to demand bread for their starving children. This contemporary print shows a group of dedicated marchers armed with pikes and other weapons and pulling an artillery piece.

(the king, queen, and their son). The king now accepted the National Assembly's decrees; it was neither the first nor the last occasion when Parisian crowds would affect national politics. The king was virtually a prisoner in Paris, and the National Assembly, now meeting in Paris, would also feel the influence of Parisian insurrectionary politics.

THE CATHOLIC CHURCH

The Catholic church was viewed as an important pillar of the old order, and it soon also felt the impact of reform. Because of the need for money, most of the lands of the church were confiscated, and *assignats,* a form of paper money, were issued based on the collateral of the newly nationalized church property. The church was also secularized. In July 1790, the new Civil Constitution of the Clergy was put into effect. Both bishops and priests of the Catholic church were to be elected by the people and paid by the state. All clergy were also required to swear an oath of allegiance to the Civil Constitution. Since the pope forbade it, only 54 percent of the French parish clergy took the oath, and the majority of bishops refused. This was a critical development because the Catholic church, still an important institution in the life of the French people, now became an enemy of the revolution. The Civil Constitution has often been viewed as a serious tactical blunder on the part of the National Assembly, for by arousing the opposition of the church, it gave counterrevolution a popular base from which to operate.

A NEW CONSTITUTION

By 1791, the National Assembly had completed a new constitution that established a limited constitutional monarchy. There was still a monarch (now called "king of the French"), but he enjoyed few powers not subject to review by the new Legislative Assembly. The assembly, in which sovereign power was vested, was to sit for two years and consist of 745 representatives chosen by an indirect system of election that preserved power in the hands of the more affluent members of society. A distinction was drawn between active and passive citizens. Although all had the same civil rights, only active citizens (men over the age of twenty-five paying taxes equivalent in value to three days' unskilled labor) could vote. The active citizens probably numbered 4.3 million in 1790. These citizens did not elect the members of the Legislative Assembly directly but voted for electors (men paying taxes equal in value to ten days' labor). This relatively small group of fifty thousand electors chose the deputies. To qualify as a deputy, one had to pay at least a "silver mark" in taxes, an amount equivalent to fifty-four days' labor.

The National Assembly also undertook an administrative restructuring of France. In 1789, it abolished all the old local and provincial divisions and divided France into eighty-three departments, roughly equal in size and population. Departments were in turn divided into districts and communes, all supervised by elected councils and officials who oversaw financial, administrative, judicial, and ecclesiastical institutions within their domains. Although both bourgeois and aristocrats were eligible for offices based on property qualifications, few nobles were elected, leaving local and departmental governments in the hands of the bourgeoisie, especially lawyers of various types.

By 1791, France had moved into a revolutionary reordering of the old regime that had been achieved by a revolutionary consensus that was largely the work of the wealthier members of the bourgeoisie. By mid-1791, however, this consensus faced growing opposition from clerics angered by the Civil Constitution of the Clergy, lower classes hurt by the rise in the cost of living resulting from the inflation of the *assignats,* peasants who remained opposed to dues that had still not been abandoned, and political clubs offering more radical solutions to the nation's problems. The most famous were the Jacobins, who first emerged as a gathering of more radical deputies at the beginning of the revolution, especially during the events of the night of August 4, 1789. After October 1789, they occupied the former Jacobin convent in Paris. Jacobin clubs also formed in the provinces, where they served primarily as discussion groups. Eventually, they joined together in an extensive correspondence network and by spring 1790 were seeking affiliation with the Parisian club. One year later, there were nine hundred Jacobin clubs in France associated with the Parisian center. Members were usually the elite of their local societies, but they also included artisans and tradespeople.

In addition, by mid-1791, the government was still facing severe financial difficulties due to massive tax evasion. Despite all of their problems, however, the bourgeois politicians in charge remained relatively unified on the basis of their trust in the king. But Louis XVI disastrously undercut them. Quite upset with the whole turn of revolutionary events, he sought to flee France in June 1791 and almost succeeded before being recognized, captured at Varennes, and brought back to Paris. Though radicals called for the king to be deposed, the members of the National Assembly, fearful of the popular forces in Paris calling for a republic, chose to ignore the king's flight and pretended that he had been kidnapped. In this unsettled situation, with a discredited and seemingly disloyal monarch, the new Legislative Assembly held its first session in October 1791.

Because the National Assembly had passed a "self-denying ordinance" that prohibited the reelection of its members, the composition of the Legislative Assembly tended to be quite different from that of the National Assembly. The clerics and nobles were largely gone. Most of the representatives were men of property; many were lawyers. Although lacking national reputations, most had gained experience in the new revolutionary politics and prominence in their local areas through the National Guard, the Jacobin clubs, and the many elective offices spawned by the administrative reordering of France. The king made what seemed to be a genuine effort to work with the new Legislative Assembly, but France's relations with the rest of Europe soon led to Louis's downfall.

OPPOSITION FROM ABROAD

Over a period of time, some European countries had become concerned about the French example and feared that revolution would spread to their countries. On August 27, 1791, Emperor Leopold II of Austria and King Frederick William II of Prussia issued the Declaration of Pillnitz, which invited other European monarchs to take "the most effectual means . . . to put the king of France in a state to strengthen, in the most perfect liberty, the bases of a monarchical government equally becoming to the rights of sovereigns and to the wellbeing of the French Nation."[6] But European monarchs were too suspicious of each other to undertake such a plan, and in any case, French enthusiasm for war led the Legislative Assembly to declare war on Austria on April 20, 1792. But why take such a step in view of its obvious dangers? Many people in France wanted war. Reactionaries hoped that a preoccupation with war would cool off the revolution; French defeat, which seemed likely in view of the army's disintegration, might even lead to the restoration of the old regime. Leftists hoped that war would consolidate the revolution at home and spread it to all of Europe.

The French fared badly in the initial fighting, and loud recriminations were soon heard in Paris. A frantic search for scapegoats began; as one observer noted: "Everywhere you hear the cry that the king is betraying us, the generals are betraying us, that nobody is to be trusted; . . . that Paris will be taken in six weeks by the Austrians. . . . We are on a volcano ready to spout flames."[7] Defeats in war coupled with economic shortages in the spring reinvigorated popular groups that had been dormant since the previous summer and led to renewed political demonstrations, especially against the king. Radical Parisian political groups, declaring themselves an insurrectionary commune, organized a mob attack on the royal palace and Legislative Assembly in August 1792, took the king captive, and forced the Legislative Assembly to suspend the monarchy and call for a national convention, chosen on the basis of universal male suffrage, to decide on the future form of government. The French Revolution was about to enter a more radical stage as power passed from the assembly to the new Paris Commune, composed of many who proudly called themselves the *sans-culottes,* ordinary patriots without fine clothes. Although it has become customary to equate the more radical sans-culottes with working people or the poor, many were merchants and better-off artisans who were often the elite of their neighborhoods and trades.

The Radical Revolution

Before the National Convention met, the Paris Commune dominated the political scene. Led by the newly appointed minister of justice, Georges Danton (1759–1794), the sans-culottes sought revenge on those who had aided the king and resisted the popular will. Thousands of presumed traitors were arrested and then massacred as ordinary Parisian tradespeople and artisans solved the problem of overcrowded prisons by mass executions of their inmates. In September 1792, the newly elected National Convention began its sessions. Although it was called to draft a new constitution, it also acted as the sovereign ruling body of France.

Socially, the composition of the National Convention was similar to its predecessors. Dominated by lawyers, professionals, and property owners, it also included for the first time a handful of artisans. Two-thirds of the deputies were under age forty-five, and almost all had had political experience as a result of the revolution. Almost all were also intensely distrustful of the king and his activities. It was therefore no surprise that the convention's first major step on September 21 was to abolish the monarchy and establish a republic. But that was about as far as members of the convention could agree, and the National Convention soon split into factions over the fate of the king. The two most important were the Girondins and the Mountain. Both were members of the Jacobin club.

DOMESTIC CRISES

Representing primarily the provinces, the Girondins came to fear the radical mobs in Paris and were disposed to keep the king alive as a hedge against future eventualities. The Mountain represented the interests of the city of Paris and owed much of its strength to the radical and popular elements in the city, although the members of the Mountain themselves were middle-class. The Mountain won out at the beginning of 1793 when it passed a decree condemning Louis XVI to death, by a very narrow margin. On January 21, 1793, the king was executed, and the destruction of the old regime was complete. Now there could be no turning back. But the execution of the king produced further challenges by creating new enemies for the revolution both at home and abroad while strengthening those who were already its enemies.

Factional disputes between the Girondins and the Mountain were only one aspect of France's domestic crisis in 1792 and 1793. In Paris, the local government was controlled by the Commune, which drew a number of its leaders from the city's artisans and shopkeepers. The Commune favored radical change and put constant pressure on the National Convention, pushing it to ever more radical positions. As one man warned his fellow deputies: "Never forget that you were sent here by the sans-culottes."[8] At the end of May and the beginning of June 1793, the Commune organized a demonstration, invaded the National Convention, and forced the arrest and execution of the leading Girondins, thus leaving the Mountain in control of the convention. The National Convention itself still did not rule all of France. The authority of the convention was repudiated in western France, particularly in the department of the Vendée, by peasants who revolted against the new military draft (see "A Nation in Arms" later in this chapter). The Vendéan rebellion soon escalated into a full-blown counterrevolutionary appeal: "Long live the king and our good priests. We want our king, our priests and the old regime." Some of France's major provincial cities, including Lyons and Marseilles, also began to break away from the central authority. Arguing as Marseilles did that "it is time for the anarchy of a few men of blood to stop,"[9] these cities favored a decentralized republic to free themselves from the ascendancy of Paris. In no way did they favor breaking up the "indivisible republic."

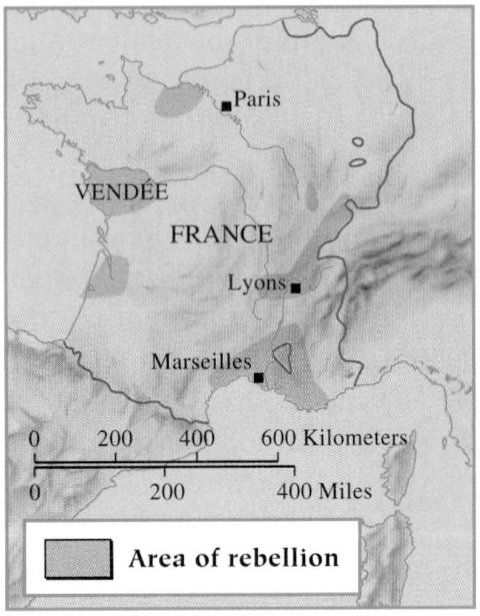

Rebellion in France

FOREIGN CRISIS

Domestic turmoil was paralleled by a foreign crisis. Early in 1793, after Louis XVI had been executed, much of Europe—an informal coalition of Austria, Prussia, Spain, Portugal, Britain, and the Dutch Republic—was pitted

The Art Archive

Execution of the King. At the beginning of 1793, the National Convention decreed the death of the king, and on January 21 of that year, Louis XVI was executed. As seen in this engraving by Carnavalet, the execution of the king was accomplished by a new revolutionary device: the guillotine.

against France. Carried away by initial successes and their own rhetoric, the French welcomed the struggle. Danton exclaimed to the convention: "They threaten you with kings! You have thrown down your gauntlet to them, and this gauntlet is a king's head, the signal of their coming death."[10] Grossly overextended, the French armies began to experience reverses, and by late spring some members of the anti-French coalition were poised for an invasion of France. If successful, both the revolution and the revolutionaries would be destroyed and the old regime reestablished. The revolution had reached a decisive moment.

To meet these crises, the program of the National Convention became one of curbing anarchy and counterrevolution at home while attempting to win the war by a great national mobilization. To administer the government, the convention gave broad powers to an executive committee known as the Committee of Public Safety, which was dominated initially by Danton. Maximilien Robespierre (1758–1794) eventually became one of its most important members. For the next twelve months, virtually the same twelve members were reelected and gave the country the leadership it needed to weather the domestic and foreign crises of 1793.

A NATION IN ARMS

To meet the foreign crisis and save the Republic from its foreign enemies, the Committee of Public Safety decreed a universal mobilization of the nation on August 23, 1793:

> Young men will fight, young men are called to conquer. Married men will forge arms, transport military baggage and guns and will prepare food supplies. Women, who at long last are to take their rightful place in the revolution and follow their true destiny, will forget their futile tasks: their delicate hands will work at making clothes for soldiers; they will make tents and they will extend their tender care to shelters where the defenders of the Patrie [nation] will receive the help that their wounds require. Children will make lint of old cloth. It is for them that we are fighting: children, those beings destined to gather all the fruits of the revolution, will raise their pure hands toward the skies. And old men, performing their missions again, as of yore, will be guided to the public squares of the cities where they will kindle the courage of young warriors and preach the doctrines of hate for kings and the unity of the Republic.[11]

In less than a year, the French revolutionary government had raised an army of 650,000; by September 1794, it numbered 1,169,000. The Republic's army was the largest ever seen in European history. It now pushed the allies back across the Rhine and even conquered the Austrian Netherlands (see Map 19.2). By May 1795, the anti-French coalition of 1793 was breaking up.

Historians have focused on the importance of the French revolutionary army in the creation of modern nationalism. Previously, wars had been fought between governments or ruling dynasties by relatively small armies of professional soldiers. The new French army, however, was the creation of a "people's" government; its wars were now "people's" wars. The entire nation was to be involved in the war. But when dynastic wars became people's wars, warfare increased in ferocity and lack of restraint. Although innocent civilians had suffered in the earlier struggles, now the carnage became appalling at times. The wars of the French revolutionary era opened the door to the total war of the modern world.

Giraudon/Art Resource, NY

Citizens Enlisting in the New French Army. To save the Republic from its foreign enemies, the National Convention created a revolutionary army of unprecedented size. In this painting, citizens joyfully hasten to sign up at the recruitment tables set up in the streets. On this occasion, officials are distributing coins to those who have enrolled.

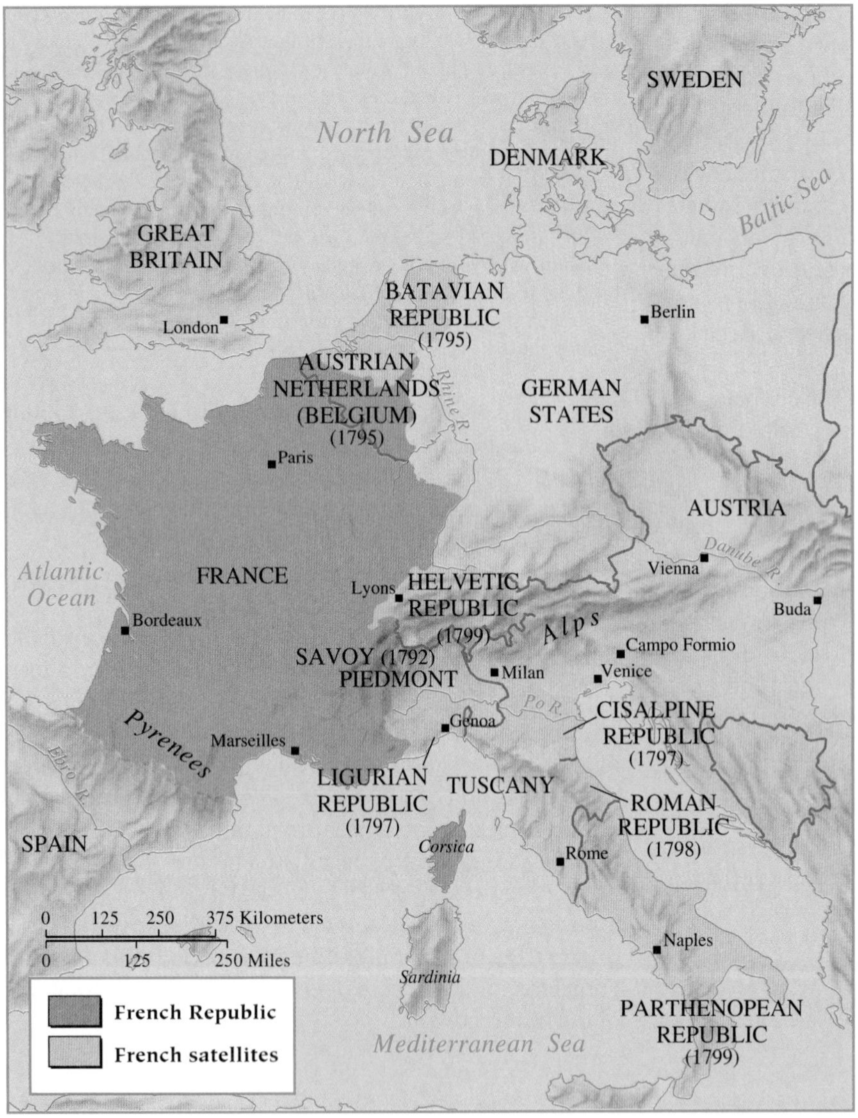

Map 19.2 French Conquests During the Revolutionary Wars, 1792–1799. The conservative rulers of Europe, appalled at the republican character of the French Revolution, took up arms to restore the power of the Bourbon monarchy. The French responded with a people's army, the largest ever seen, which pushed the invaders out of France and seized the Austrian Netherlands, Switzerland, and much territory in Italy. ■ Why would Austria desire cooperation from the German states if it wanted to wage war on France?

THE COMMITTEE OF PUBLIC SAFETY AND THE REIGN OF TERROR

To meet the domestic crisis, the National Convention and the Committee of Public Safety established the "Reign of Terror." Revolutionary courts were organized to protect the revolutionary Republic from its internal enemies, those "who either by their conduct, their contacts, their words or their writings, showed themselves to be supporters of tyranny or enemies of liberty" or those "who have not constantly manifested their attachment to the revolution."[12] Victims of the Terror ranged from royalists, such as Queen Marie Antoinette, to former revolutionary Girondins, including Olympe de Gouges, the chief advocate for political rights for women, and even included thousands of peasants. Many victims were persons who had opposed the radical activities of the sans-culottes. In the course of nine months, sixteen thousand people were officially killed under the blade of the guillotine, a revolutionary device for the quick and efficient separation of heads from bodies. But the true number of the Terror's victims was probably closer to fifty thousand (see the box on p. 539). The bulk of the Terror's executions took place in the Vendée and in cities such as Lyons and Marseilles, places that had been in open rebellion against the authority of the National Convention.

Military force in the form of revolutionary armies was used to bring recalcitrant cities and districts back under the control of the National Convention. Marseilles fell to a revolutionary army in August. Starving Lyons surrendered early in October after two months of bombardment and resistance. Since Lyons was France's second city after Paris and had defied the National Convention during a time when the Republic was in peril, the Committee of Public Safety decided to make an example of it. By April 1794, some 1,880 citizens of Lyons had been executed. When guillotining proved too slow, cannon fire and grapeshot were used to blow condemned men into open graves. A German observed:

> . . . whole ranges of houses, always the most handsome, burnt. The churches, convents, and all the dwellings of the former patricians were in ruins. When I came to the guillotine, the blood of those who had been executed a few hours beforehand

Justice in the Reign of Terror

The Reign of Terror created a repressive environment in which revolutionary courts often acted quickly to condemn traitors to the revolutionary cause. In this account, an English visitor describes the court, the procession to the scene of execution, and the final execution procedure.

J. G. Milligen, The Revolutionary Tribunal *(Paris, October 1793)*

In the center of the hall, under a statue of Justice, holding scales in one hand, and a sword in the other, sat Dumas, the President, with the other judges. Under them were seated the public accuser, Fourquier-Tinville, and his scribes. . . . To the right were benches on which the accused were placed in several rows, and *gendarmes* with carbines and fixed bayonets by their sides. To the left was the jury.

Never can I forget the mournful appearance of these funereal processions to the place of execution. The march was opened by a detachment of mounted *gendarmes*—the carts followed; they were the same carts as those that are used in Paris for carrying wood; four boards were placed across them for seats, and on each board sat two, and sometimes three victims; their hands were tied behind their backs, and the constant jolting of the cart made them nod their heads up and down, to the great amusement of the spectators. On the front of the cart stood Samson, the executioner, or one of his sons or assistants; *gendarmes* on foot marched by the side; then followed a hackney, in which was the reporting clerk, whose duty it was to witness the execution, and then return to the public accuser's office to report the execution of what they called the law.

The process of execution was also a sad and heart-rending spectacle. In the middle of the Place de la Revolution was erected a guillotine, in front of a colossal statue of Liberty, represented seated on a rock, a cap on her head, a spear in her hand, the other reposing on a shield. On one side of the scaffold were drawn out a sufficient number of carts, with large baskets painted red, to receive the heads and bodies of the victims. Those bearing the condemned moved on slowly to the foot of the guillotine; the culprits were led out in turn, and if necessary, supported by two of the executioner's assistants, but their assistance was rarely required. Most of these unfortunates ascended the scaffold with a determined step—many of them looked up firmly on the menacing instrument of death, beholding for the last time the rays of the glorious sun, beaming on the polished axe: and I have seen some young men actually dance a few steps before they went up to be strapped to the perpendicular plane, which was then tilted to a horizontal plane in a moment, and ran on the grooves until the neck was secured and closed in by a moving board, when the head passed through what was called, in derision, "the republican toilet seat"; the weighty knife was then dropped with a heavy fall; and, with incredible dexterity and rapidity, two executioners tossed the body into the basket, while another threw the head after it.

> was still running in the street. . . . I said to a group of sans-culottes that it would be decent to clear away all this human blood. Why should it be cleared? one of them said to me. It's the blood of aristocrats and rebels. The dogs should lick it up.[13]

In the Vendée, revolutionary armies were also brutal in defeating the rebel armies. After destroying one army on December 12, the commander of the revolutionary army ordered that no quarter be given: "The road to Laval is strewn with corpses. Women, priests, monks, children, all have been put to death. I have spared nobody." The Terror was at its most destructive in the Vendée. Forty-two percent of the death sentences during the Terror were passed in territories affected by the Vendée rebellion. Perhaps the most notorious act of violence occurred in Nantes, where victims were executed by sinking them in barges in the Loire River.

Contrary to popular opinion, the Terror demonstrated no class prejudice. Estimates are that the nobles constituted 8 percent of its victims; the middle classes, 25 percent; the clergy, 6; and the peasant and laboring classes, 60. To the Committee of Public Safety, this bloodletting was only a temporary expedient. Once the war and domestic emergency were over, "the republic of virtue" would ensue, and the Declaration of the Rights of Man and the Citizen would be fully established. Although theoretically a republic, the French government during the Terror was led by a group of twelve men who ordered the execution of people as enemies of the Republic. But how did they justify this? Louis Saint-Just, one of the younger members of the Committee of Public Safety, explained their rationalization in a speech to the convention: "Since the French people has manifested its will, everything opposed to it is outside the sovereign. Whatever is outside the sovereign is an enemy."[14] Clearly, Saint-Just was referring to Rousseau's concept of the general will, but it is equally apparent that these twelve men, in the name of the Republic, had taken upon themselves the right to ascertain the sovereign will of the French people (see the box on p. 540) and to kill their enemies as "outside the sovereign."

THE "REPUBLIC OF VIRTUE"

Along with the Terror, the Committee of Public Safety took other steps both to control France and to create a new republican order and new republican citizens. By spring 1793, they were sending "representatives on mission" as agents of the central government to all departments to explain the war emergency measures and to implement the laws dealing with the wartime emergency.

Robespierre and Revolutionary Government

In its time of troubles, the National Convention, under the direction of the Committee of Public Safety, instituted the Reign of Terror to preserve the revolution from its internal enemies. In this selection, Maximilien Robespierre, one of the committee's leading members, tries to justify the violence to which these believers in republican liberty resorted.

■ *Robespierre,* Speech on Revolutionary Government

The theory of revolutionary government is as new as the Revolution that created it. It is as pointless to seek its origins in the books of the political theorists, who failed to foresee this revolution, as in the laws of the tyrants, who are happy enough to abuse their exercise of authority without seeking out its legal justification. And so this phrase is for the aristocracy a mere subject of terror or a term of slander, for tyrants an outrage and for many an enigma. It behooves us to explain it to all in order that we may rally good citizens, at least, in support of the principles governing the public interest.

It is the function of government to guide the moral and physical energies of the nation toward the purposes for which it was established.

The object of constitutional government is to preserve the Republic; the object of the revolutionary government is to establish it.

Revolution is the war waged by liberty against its enemies; a constitution is that which crowns the edifice of freedom once victory has been won and the nation is at peace.

The revolutionary government has to summon extraordinary activity to its aid precisely because it is at war. It is subjected to less binding and less uniform regulations, because the circumstances in which it finds itself are tempestuous and shifting above all because it is compelled to deploy, swiftly and incessantly, new resources to meet new and pressing dangers.

The principal concern of constitutional government is civil liberty; that of revolutionary government, public liberty. Under a constitutional government little more is required than to protect the individual against abuses by the state, whereas revolutionary government is obliged to defend the state itself against the factions that assail it from every quarter.

To good citizens revolutionary government owes the full protection of the state; to the enemies of the people it owes only death.

The committee also attempted to provide some economic controls, especially since members of the more radical working class were advocating them. They established a system of requisitioning food supplies for the cities enforced by the forays of revolutionary armies into the countryside. The Law of the General Maximum established price controls on goods declared of first necessity, ranging from food and drink to fuel and clothing. The controls failed to work very well because the government lacked the machinery to enforce them.

Women continued to play an active role in this radical phase of the French Revolution. As spectators at sessions of revolutionary clubs and the National Convention, women made the members and deputies aware of their demands. When on Sunday, February 25, 1793, a group of women appealed formally to the National Convention for lower bread prices, the convention reacted by adjourning until Tuesday. The women responded bitterly by accosting the deputies: "We are adjourned until Tuesday; but as for us, we adjourn ourselves until Monday. When our children ask us for milk, we don't adjourn them until the day after tomorrow."[15] In 1793, two women—an actress and a chocolate manufacturer—founded the Society for Revolutionary Republican Women. Composed largely of working-class women, this Parisian group viewed itself as a "family of sisters" and vowed "to rush to the defense of the Fatherland."

Despite the importance of women to the revolutionary cause, male revolutionaries reacted disdainfully to female participation in political activity. In the radical phase of the revolution, the Paris Commune outlawed women's clubs and forbade women to be present at its meetings. One of its members explained why:

> It is horrible, it is contrary to all laws of nature for a woman to want to make herself a man. The Council must recall that some time ago these denatured women, these viragos, wandered through the markets with the red cap to sully that badge of liberty and wanted to force all women to take off the modest headdress that is appropriate for them [the bonnet]. . . . Is it the place of women to propose motions? Is it the place of women to place themselves at the head of our armies?[16]

Most men—radical or conservative—agreed that a woman's place was in the home and not in military or political affairs. As one man asked, "Since when is it considered normal for a woman to abandon the pious care of her home, the cradle of her children, to listen to speeches in the public forum?"[17]

DECHRISTIANIZATION AND A NEW CALENDAR

In its attempt to create a new order, the National Convention also pursued a policy of dechristianization. The word *saint* was removed from street names, churches were pillaged and closed by revolutionary armies, and priests were encouraged to marry. In Paris, the cathedral of Notre-Dame

Giraudon/Art Resource, NY

Women Patriots. Women played a variety of roles in the events of the French Revolution. This picture shows a women's patriotic club discussing the decrees of the National Convention, an indication that some women had become highly politicized by the upheavals of the revolution.

was designated the Temple of Reason. In November 1793, a public ceremony dedicated to the worship of reason was held in the former cathedral; patriotic maidens adorned in white dresses paraded before a temple of reason where the high altar once stood. At the end of the ceremony, a female figure personifying Liberty rose out of the temple. As Robespierre came to realize, dechristianization backfired because France was still overwhelmingly Catholic. In fact, dechristianization created more enemies than friends.

Yet another manifestation of dechristianization was the adoption of a new republican calendar on October 5, 1793. Years would no longer be numbered from the birth of Jesus but from September 22, 1792, the day the French Republic was proclaimed. Thus at the time the calendar was adopted, the French were already living in year II. The calendar contained twelve months; each month consisted of three ten-day weeks (*décades*) with the tenth day of each week a rest day (*décadi*). This eliminated Sundays and Sunday worship services and put an end to the ordering of French lives by a Christian calendar that emphasized Sundays, saints' days, and church holidays and festivals. The latter were to be replaced by revolutionary festivals. Especially important were the five days (six in leap years) left over in the calendar at the end of the year. These days were to form a half-week of festivals to celebrate the revolutionary virtues—Virtue, Intelligence, Labor, Opinion, and Rewards. The sixth extra day in a leap year would be a special festival day when French citizens would "come from all parts of the Republic to celebrate liberty and equality, to cement by their embraces the national fraternity." Of course, ending church holidays also reduced the number of nonworking holidays from fifty-six to thirty-two, a goal long recommended by eighteenth-century economic theorists.

The anti-Christian purpose of the calendar was reinforced in the naming of the months of the year. The months were given names that were supposed to evoke the seasons, the temperature, or the state of the vegetation: Vendémiaire (harvest—the first month of thirty days beginning September 22), Brumaire (mist), Frimaire (frost), Nivôse (snow), Pluviôse (rain), Ventôse (wind), Germinal (seeding), Floréal (flowering), Prairial (meadows), Messidor (wheat harvest), Thermidor (heat), and Fructidor (ripening).

The new calendar faced intense popular opposition, and the revolutionary government relied primarily on coercion to win its acceptance. Journalists, for example, were commanded to use republican dates in their newspaper articles. But many people refused to give up the old calendar, as one official reported:

> Sundays and Catholic holidays, even if there are ten in a row, have for some time been celebrated with as much pomp and splendor as before. The same cannot be said of *décadi,* which is observed by only a small handful of citizens. The first to disobey the law are the wives of public officials, who dress up on the holidays of the old calendar and abstain from work more religiously than anyone else.[18]

The government could hardly expect peasants to follow the new calendar when government officials were ignoring it. Napoleon later perceived that the revolutionary calendar was politically unpopular, and he simply abandoned it on January 1, 1806 (11 Nivôse XIV).

In addition to its anti-Christian function, the revolutionary calendar had also served to mark the revolution as a new historical beginning, a radical break in time. Revolutionary upheavals often project millenarian expectations, the hope that a new age is dawning. The revolutionary dream of a new order presupposed the creation of a new human being freed from the old order and its symbols, a new citizen surrounded by a framework of new habits. Restructuring time itself offered the opportunity to forge new habits and create a lasting new order.

EQUALITY AND SLAVERY

Early in the French Revolution, the desire for equality led to a discussion of what to do about slavery. A club called Friends of the Blacks advocated the abolition of slavery, which was achieved in France in September 1791. However, French planters in the West Indies, who profited greatly from the use of slaves on their sugar plantations, opposed the abolition of slavery in the French colonies. When the National Convention came into power, the issue was revisited, and on February 4, 1794, guided by ideals of equality, the government abolished slavery in the colonies.

In one French colony, slaves had already rebelled for their freedom. In 1791, black slaves in the French sugar colony of Saint Domingue (the western third of the island of Hispaniola), inspired by the ideals of the revolution occurring in France, revolted against French plantation owners. Led by Toussaint L'Ouverture (1746–1803), a son of African slaves, over 100,000 black slaves rose in revolt and seized control of all of Hispaniola. Later, an army sent by Napoleon captured L'Ouverture, who died in captivity in France. But the French soldiers, weakened by disease, soon succumbed to the slave forces. On January 1, 1804, the western part of Hispaniola, now called Haiti, announced its freedom and became the first independent state in Latin America. One of the French revolutionary ideals had triumphed abroad.

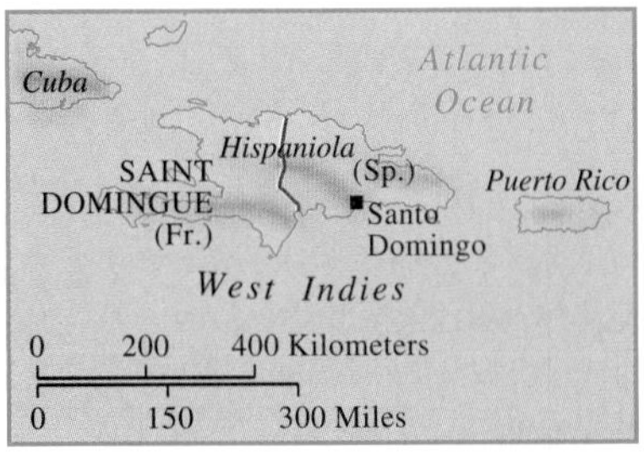

Revolt in Saint Domingue

THE DECLINE OF THE COMMITTEE OF PUBLIC SAFETY

Maintaining the revolutionary ideals in France proved not to be easy. By the Law of 14 Frimaire (passed on December 4, 1793), the Committee of Public Safety sought to centralize the administration of France more effectively and to exercise greater control in order to check the excesses of the Reign of Terror. The activities of both the representatives on mission and the revolutionary armies were scrutinized more carefully, and the campaign against Christianity was also dampened. Finally, in 1794, the Committee of Public Safety turned against its radical Parisian supporters, executed the leaders of the revolutionary Paris Commune, and turned it into a docile tool. This might have been a good idea for the sake of order, but in suppressing the people who had been its chief supporters, the National Convention alienated an important group. At the same time, the French had been successful against their foreign foes. The military successes meant that the Terror no longer served much purpose. But the Terror continued because Robespierre, now its dominant figure, had become obsessed with purifying the body politic of all the corrupt. Only then could the Republic of Virtue follow. Many deputies in the National Convention feared, however, that they were not safe while Robespierre was free to act. An anti-Robespierre coalition in the National Convention, eager now to destroy Robespierre before he destroyed them, gathered enough votes to condemn him. Robespierre was guillotined on July

Robespierre. Maximilien Robespierre eventually came to exercise much control over the Committee of Public Safety. Robespierre and the committee worked to centralize the administration of France and curb the excesses of the Reign of Terror. However, fear of Robespierre led many in the National Convention to condemn him, and on July 28, 1794, he was executed.

Giraudon/Art Resource, NY

28, 1794, beginning a reaction that brought an end to this radical stage of the French Revolution.

The National Convention and its Committee of Public Safety had accomplished a great deal. By creating a nation in arms, they preserved the French Revolution and prevented it from being destroyed by its foreign enemies, who, if they had succeeded, would have reestablished the old monarchical order. Domestically, the revolution had also been saved from the forces of counterrevolution. The committee's tactics, however, provided an example for the use of violence in domestic politics that has continued to bedevil the Western world to this day.

Reaction and the Directory

After the death of Robespierre on July 28, 1794, revolutionary fervor began to give way to the Thermidorean Reaction, named after the month of Thermidor. The Terror began to abate. The National Convention curtailed the power of the Committee of Public Safety, shut down the Jacobin club, and attempted to provide better protection for its deputies against the Parisian mobs. Churches were allowed to reopen for public worship, and a decree of February 21, 1795, gave freedom of worship to all cults. Economic regulation was dropped in favor of laissez-faire policies, another clear indication that moderate forces were regaining control of the Revolution. In addition, a new constitution was written in August 1795 that reflected this more conservative republicanism or a desire for a stability that did not sacrifice the ideals of 1789.

To avoid the dangers of another single legislative assembly, the Constitution of 1795 established a national legislative assembly consisting of two chambers: a lower house, known as the Council of 500, whose function was to initiate legislation, and an upper house of 250 members, the Council of Elders, composed of married or widowed members over age forty, which accepted or rejected the proposed laws. The 750 members of the two legislative bodies were chosen by electors who had to be owners or renters of property worth between one hundred and two hundred days' labor, a requirement that limited their number to thirty thousand, an even smaller base than the Constitution of 1791 had provided. The electors were chosen by the active citizens, now defined as all male taxpayers over the age of twenty-one. The Council of Elders elected five directors from a list presented by the Council of 500 to act as the executive authority or Directory. To ensure some continuity from the old order to the new, the members of the National Convention ruled that two-thirds of the new members of the National Assembly must be chosen from their ranks. This decision produced disturbances in Paris and an insurrection at the beginning of October that was dispersed after fierce combat by an army contingent under the artillery general Napoleon Bonaparte. This would be the last time in the great French Revolution that the city of Paris would attempt to impose its wishes on the central government. Even more significant and ominous was this use of the army, which made it clear that the Directory from the beginning had to rely on the military for survival.

CHRONOLOGY

The French Revolution

National Assembly (Constituent Assembly)	*1789–1791*
Meeting of Estates-General	May 5, 1789
Formation of National Assembly	June 17, 1789
Tennis Court Oath	June 20, 1789
Fall of the Bastille	July 14, 1789
Great Fear	Summer 1789
Abolition of feudalism	August 4, 1789
Declaration of the Rights of Man and the Citizen	August 26, 1789
Women's march to Versailles; king's return to Paris	October 5–6, 1789
Civil Constitution of the Clergy	July 12, 1790
Flight of the king	June 20–21, 1791
Declaration of Pillnitz	August 27, 1791
Legislative Assembly	*1791–1792*
France declares war on Austria	April 20, 1792
Attack on the royal palace	August 10, 1792
National Convention	*1792–1795*
Abolition of the monarchy	September 21, 1792
Execution of the king	January 21, 1793
Universal mobilization of the nation	August 23, 1793
Execution of Robespierre	July 28, 1794
Directory	*1795–1799*
Constitution of 1795 is adopted	August 22, 1795

The period of the Directory was an era of stagnation, corruption, and graft, a materialistic reaction to the suffering and sacrifices that had been demanded in the Reign of Terror and the Republic of Virtue. Speculators made fortunes in property by taking advantage of the government's severe monetary problems. Elaborate fashions, which had gone out of style because of their identification with the nobility, were worn again. Gambling and roulette became popular once more.

The government of the Directory had to contend with political enemies from both ends of the political spectrum. On the right, royalists who dreamed of restoring the monarchy continued their agitation; some still toyed with violent means. On the left, Jacobin hopes of power were revived by continuing economic problems, especially the total collapse in the value of the *assignats.* Some radicals even went beyond earlier goals, especially Gracchus Babeuf, who raised the question "What is the French Revolution? An open war between patricians and plebeians, between rich and poor." Babeuf, who was appalled at the misery of the common people, wanted to abolish private property and eliminate private enterprise. His Conspiracy of Equals was crushed in 1796, and he was executed in 1797.

New elections in 1797 created even more uncertainty and instability. Battered by the left and right, unable to find a definitive solution to the country's economic problems, and still carrying on the wars left from the Committee of Public Safety, the Directory increasingly relied on the military to maintain its power. This led to a coup d'état in 1799 in which the successful and popular general Napoleon Bonaparte was able to seize power.

The Age of Napoleon

Napoleon dominated both French and European history from 1799 to 1815. The coup that brought him to power occurred exactly ten years after the outbreak of the French Revolution. In a sense, Napoleon brought the revolution to an end in 1799, but he was also a child of the revolution; he called himself the Son of the Revolution. The French Revolution had made possible his rise first in the military and then to supreme power in France. Even beyond this, Napoleon had once said, "I am the revolution," and he never ceased to remind the French that they owed to him the preservation of all that was beneficial in the revolutionary program.

The Rise of Napoleon

Napoleon was born in Corsica in 1769, only a few months after France had annexed the island. The son of a lawyer whose family stemmed from the Florentine nobility, the young Napoleon obtained a royal scholarship to study at a military school in France. His military education led to his commission in 1785 as a lieutenant, although he was not well liked by his fellow officers because he was short, spoke with an Italian accent, and had little money. For the next seven years, Napoleon spent much of his time reading the works of the philosophes and educating himself in military matters by studying the campaigns of great military leaders from the past. The French Revolution and the European war that followed broadened his sights and presented him with new opportunities.

Napoleon rose quickly through the ranks. In 1792, he became a captain and in the following year performed so well as an artillery commander that he was promoted to the rank of brigadier general in 1794, when he was only twenty-five. In October 1795, he saved the National Convention from the Parisian mob and in 1796 was made commander of the French army in Italy (see the box on p. 545). There he turned a group of ill-disciplined soldiers into an effective fighting force and in a series of stunning victories

Napoleon as a Young Officer. Napoleon had risen quickly through the military ranks, being promoted to the rank of brigadier general at the age of twenty-five. This painting of Napoleon by the Romantic painter Baron Gros presents an idealized, heroic image of the young leader.

Réunion des Musées Nationaux/Art Resource, NY

Napoleon and Psychological Warfare

In 1796, at the age of twenty-seven, Napoleon Bonaparte was given command of the French army in Italy, where he won a series of stunning victories. His use of speed, deception, and surprise to overwhelm his opponents is well known. In this selection from a proclamation to his troops in Italy, Napoleon also appears to be a master of psychological warfare.

■ *Napoleon Bonaparte,* Proclamation to the French Troops in Italy *(April 26, 1796)*

Soldiers:

In a fortnight you have won six victories, taken twenty-one standards, fifty-five pieces of artillery, several strong positions, and conquered the richest part of Piedmont [in northern Italy]; you have captured 15,000 prisoners and killed or wounded more than 10,000 men.... You have won battles without cannon, crossed rivers without bridges, made forced marches without shoes, camped without brandy and often without bread. Soldiers of liberty, only republican troops could have endured what you have endured. Soldiers, you have our thanks! The grateful Patrie [nation] will owe its prosperity to you....

The two armies which but recently attacked you with audacity are fleeing before you in terror; the wicked men who laughed at your misery and rejoiced at the thought of the triumphs of your enemies are confounded and trembling.

But, soldiers, as yet you have done nothing compared with what remains to be done.... Undoubtedly the greatest obstacles have been overcome; but you still have battles to fight, cities to capture, rivers to cross. Is there one among you whose courage is abating? No.... All of you are consumed with a desire to extend the glory of the French people; all of you long to humiliate those arrogant kings who dare to contemplate placing us in fetters; all of you desire to dictate a glorious peace, one which will indemnify the Patrie for the immense sacrifices it has made; all of you wish to be able to say with pride as you return to your villages, "I was with the victorious army of Italy!"

defeated the Austrians and dictated peace to them in 1797. Throughout his Italian campaigns, Napoleon won the confidence of his men by his energy, charm, and ability to comprehend complex issues quickly and make decisions rapidly. These qualities, combined with his keen intelligence, ease with words, and supreme confidence in himself, enabled him throughout the rest of his life to influence people and win their firm support (see the box on p. 546).

In 1797, Napoleon returned to France as a conquering hero and was given command of an army training to invade England. Believing that the French were unready for such an invasion, he proposed instead to strike indirectly at Britain by taking Egypt and threatening India, a major source of British wealth. But the British controlled the seas and by 1799 had cut off supplies from Napoleon's army in Egypt. Seeing no future in certain defeat, Napoleon did not hesitate to abandon his army and return to Paris, where he participated in the coup d'état that ultimately led to his virtual dictatorship of France. He was only thirty years old at the time.

With the coup of 1799, a new form of the Republic was proclaimed with a constitution that established a bicameral legislative assembly elected indirectly to reduce the role of elections. Executive power in the new government was vested in the hands of three consuls, although, as Article 42 of the constitution said, "the decision of the First Consul shall suffice." As first

Réunion des Musées Nationaux/Art Resource, NY

The Coronation of Napoleon. In 1804, Napoleon restored monarchy to France when he crowned himself emperor. In the coronation scene painted by Jacques-Louis David, Napoleon is shown crowning the empress Josephine while the pope looks on. Shown seated in the box in the background is Napoleon's mother, even though she was not at the ceremony.

The Man of Destiny

Napoleon possessed an overwhelming sense of his own importance. Among the images he fostered, especially as his successes multiplied and his megalomaniacal tendencies intensified, were those of the man of destiny and the great man who masters luck.

Selections from Napoleon

When a deplorable weakness and ceaseless vacillations become manifest in supreme councils; when, yielding in turn to the influences of opposing parties, making shift from day to day, and marching with uncertain pace, a government has proved the full measure of its impotence; when even the most moderate citizens are forced to admit that the State is no longer governed; when, in fine, the administration adds to its nullity at home the gravest guilt it can acquire in the eyes of a proud nation—I mean its humiliation abroad—then a vague unrest spreads through the social body, the instinct of self-preservation is stirred, and the nation casts a sweeping eye over itself, as if to seek a man who can save it.

This guardian angel a great nation harbors in its bosom at all times; yet sometimes he is late in making his appearance. Indeed, it is not enough for him to exist: he also must be known. He must know himself. Until then, all endeavors are in vain, all schemes collapse. The inertia of the masses protects the nominal government, and despite its ineptitude and weakness the efforts of its enemies fail. But let that impatiently awaited savior give a sudden sign of his existence, and the people's instinct will divine him and call upon him. The obstacles are smoothed before his steps, and a whole great nation, flying to see him pass, will seem to be saying: "Here is the man!"

. . . A consecutive series of great actions never is the result of chance and luck; it always is the product of planning and genius. Great men are rarely known to fail in their most perilous enterprises. . . . Is it because they are lucky that they become great? No, but being great, they have been able to master luck.

consul, Napoleon directly controlled the entire executive authority of government. He had overwhelming influence over the legislature, appointed members of the bureaucracy, controlled the army, and conducted foreign affairs. In 1802, Napoleon was made consul for life and in 1804 returned France to monarchy when he crowned himself Emperor Napoleon I. This step undoubtedly satisfied his enormous ego but also stabilized the regime and provided a permanence not possible in the consulate. The revolutionary era that had begun with an attempt to limit arbitrary government had ended with a government far more autocratic than the monarchy of the old regime. As his reign progressed and the demands of war increased, Napoleon's regime became ever more dictatorial.

The Domestic Policies of Emperor Napoleon

Napoleon often claimed that he had preserved the gains of the revolution for the French people. The ideal of republican liberty had, of course, been destroyed by Napoleon's thinly disguised autocracy. But were revolutionary ideals maintained in other ways? An examination of his domestic policies will enable us to judge the truth or falsehood of Napoleon's assertion.

NAPOLEON AND THE CATHOLIC CHURCH

In 1801, Napoleon made peace with the oldest and most implacable enemy of the revolution, the Catholic church. Napoleon himself was devoid of any personal faith; he was an eighteenth-century rationalist who regarded religion at most as a convenience. In Egypt, he called himself a Muslim; in France, a Catholic. But Napoleon saw the necessity to come to terms with the Catholic church in order to stabilize his regime. In 1800, he had declared to the clergy of Milan: "It is my firm intention that the Christian, Catholic, and Roman religion shall be preserved in its entirety. . . . No society can exist without morality; there is no good morality without religion. It is religion alone, therefore, that gives to the State a firm and durable support."[19] Soon after making this statement, Napoleon opened negotiations with Pope Pius VII to reestablish the Catholic church in France.

Both sides gained from the Concordat that Napoleon arranged with the pope in 1801. Although the pope gained the right to depose French bishops, this gave him little real control over the French Catholic church, since the state retained the right to nominate bishops. The Catholic church was also permitted to hold processions again and reopen the seminaries. But Napoleon gained more than the pope. Just by signing the Concordat, the pope acknowledged the accomplishments of the revolution. Moreover, the pope agreed not to raise the question of the church lands confiscated during the revolution. Contrary to the pope's wishes, Catholicism was not reestablished as the state religion; Napoleon was only willing to recognize Catholicism as the religion of a majority of the French people. The clergy would be paid by the state, but to avoid the appearance of a state church, Protestant ministers were also put on the state payroll. As a result of the Concordat, the Catholic church was no longer an enemy of the French government. At the same time, the agreement reassured those who had acquired church lands during the revolution that they would not be stripped of them, an assurance that obviously made them supporters of the Napoleonic regime.

A NEW CODE OF LAWS

Before the Revolution, France did not have a single set of laws but rather some three hundred different legal systems. Efforts were made during the revolution to codify laws for the entire nation, but it remained for Napoleon to bring the work to completion in seven codes, the most important of which was the Civil Code (also known as the Code Napoléon). This preserved most of the revolutionary gains by recognizing the principle of the equality of all citizens before the law, the right of individuals to choose their professions, religious toleration, and the abolition of serfdom and feudalism. Property rights continued to be carefully protected, while the interests of employers were safeguarded by outlawing trade unions and strikes. The Civil Code clearly reflected the revolutionary aspirations for a uniform legal system, legal equality, and protection of property and individuals.

But the rights of some people were strictly curtailed by the Civil Code. During the radical phase of the French Revolution, new laws had made divorce an easy process for both husbands and wives, restricted the rights of fathers over their children (they could no longer have their children put in prison arbitrarily), and allowed all children (including daughters) to inherit property equally. Napoleon's Civil Code undid most of this legislation. The control of fathers over their families was restored. Divorce was still allowed but was made more difficult for women to obtain. A wife caught in adultery, for example, could be divorced by her husband and even imprisoned. A husband, however, could only be accused of adultery if he moved his mistress into his home. Women were now "less equal than men" in other ways as well. When they married, their property was brought under the control of their husbands. In lawsuits, they were treated as minors, and their testimony was regarded as less reliable than that of men.

THE FRENCH BUREAUCRACY

Napoleon also worked on rationalizing the bureaucratic structure of France by developing a powerful centralized administrative machine. During the revolution, the National Assembly had divided France into eighty-three departments and replaced the provincial estates, nobles, and *intendants* with self-governing assemblies. Napoleon kept the departments but eliminated the locally elected assemblies and instituted new officials, the most important of which were the prefects. As the central government's agents, appointed by the first consul (Napoleon), the prefects were responsible for supervising all aspects of local government. Yet they were not local men, and their careers depended on the central government.

As part of Napoleon's overhaul of the administrative system, tax collection became systematic and efficient (which it had never been under the old regime). Taxes were now collected by professional collectors employed by the state who dealt directly with each individual taxpayer. No tax exemptions due to birth, status, or special arrangement were granted. In principle, these changes had been introduced in 1789, but not until Napoleon did they actually work. In 1802, the first consul proclaimed a balanced budget.

Administrative centralization required a bureaucracy of capable officials, and Napoleon worked hard to develop one. Early on, the regime showed its preference for experts and cared little whether that expertise had been acquired in royal or revolutionary bureaucracies. Promotion, whether in civil or military offices, was to be based not on rank or birth but only on demonstrated abilities. This was, of course, what many bourgeois had wanted before the revolution. Napoleon, however, also created a new aristocracy based on merit in the state service. Napoleon created 3,263 nobles between 1808 and 1814; nearly 60 percent were military officers, and the remainder came from the upper ranks of the civil service or were other state and local officials. Socially, only 22 percent of Napoleon's aristocracy came from the nobility of the old regime; almost 60 percent were bourgeois in origin.

In his domestic policies, then, Napoleon both destroyed and preserved aspects of the revolution. Although equality was preserved in the law code and the opening of careers to talent, the creation of a new aristocracy, the strong protection accorded to property rights, and the use of conscription for the military make it clear that much equality had been lost. Liberty had been replaced by an initially benevolent despotism that grew increasingly arbitrary. Napoleon shut down sixty of France's seventy-three newspapers and insisted that all manuscripts be subjected to government scrutiny before they were published. Even the mail was opened by government police. One prominent writer, Germaine de Staël, refused to accept Napoleon's growing despotism. Educated in Enlightenment ideas, Madame de Staël wrote novels and political works that denounced Napoleon's rule as tyrannical. Napoleon banned her books in France and exiled her to the German states, where she continued to write.

Napoleon's Empire and the European Response

When Napoleon became consul in 1799, France was at war with a second European coalition of Russia, Great Britain, and Austria. Napoleon realized the need for a pause. He remarked to a Prussian diplomat "that the French Revolution is not finished so long as the scourge of war lasts. . . . I want peace, as much to settle the present French government as to save the world from chaos."[20] The peace he sought was achieved at Amiens in March 1802 and left France with new frontiers and a number of client territories from the North Sea to the Adriatic. But the peace did not last because the British and French both regarded it as temporary and had little intention of adhering to its terms. In 1803, war was renewed with Britain, which was soon joined by Austria, Russia, and Prussia in the Third Coalition. In a series of battles at Ulm, Austerlitz, Jena, and Eylau from 1805 to 1807, Napoleon's Grand Army defeated the Continental members of the coalition, giving him the opportunity to create a new European order.

NAPOLEON'S GRAND EMPIRE

The Grand Empire was composed of three major parts: the French empire, a series of dependent states, and allied states (see Map 19.3). The French empire, the inner core of the Grand Empire, consisted of an enlarged France extending to the Rhine in the east and including the western half of Italy north of Rome. Dependent states included Spain, the Netherlands, the kingdom of Italy, the Swiss Republic, the Grand Duchy of Warsaw, and the Confederation of the Rhine (a union of all German states except Austria and Prussia). Allied states were those defeated by Napoleon and forced to join his struggle against Britain; they included Prussia, Austria, and Russia). Although the internal structure of the Grand Empire varied outside its inner core, Napoleon considered himself the leader of the whole: "Europe cannot be at rest except under a single head who will have kings for his officers, who will distribute his kingdom to his lieutenants."

Within his empire, Napoleon demanded obedience, in part because he needed a common front against the British and in part because his growing egotism required obedience to his will. But as a child of the Enlightenment and the revolution, Napoleon also sought acceptance everywhere of certain revolutionary principles, including legal equality, religious toleration, and economic freedom. As he explained to his brother Jerome, shortly after making him king of the new German state of Westphalia:

> What the peoples of Germany desire most impatiently is that talented commoners should have the same right to your esteem and to public employments as the nobles, that any trace of serfdom and of an intermediate hierarchy between the sovereign and the lowest class of the people should be

Map 19.3 Napoleon's Grand Empire. Napoleon's Grand Army won a series of victories against Britain, Austria, Prussia, and Russia that gave the French emperor full or partial control over much of Europe by 1807. ■ On the Continent, what is the overall relationship between distance from France and degree of French control, and how can you account for this?

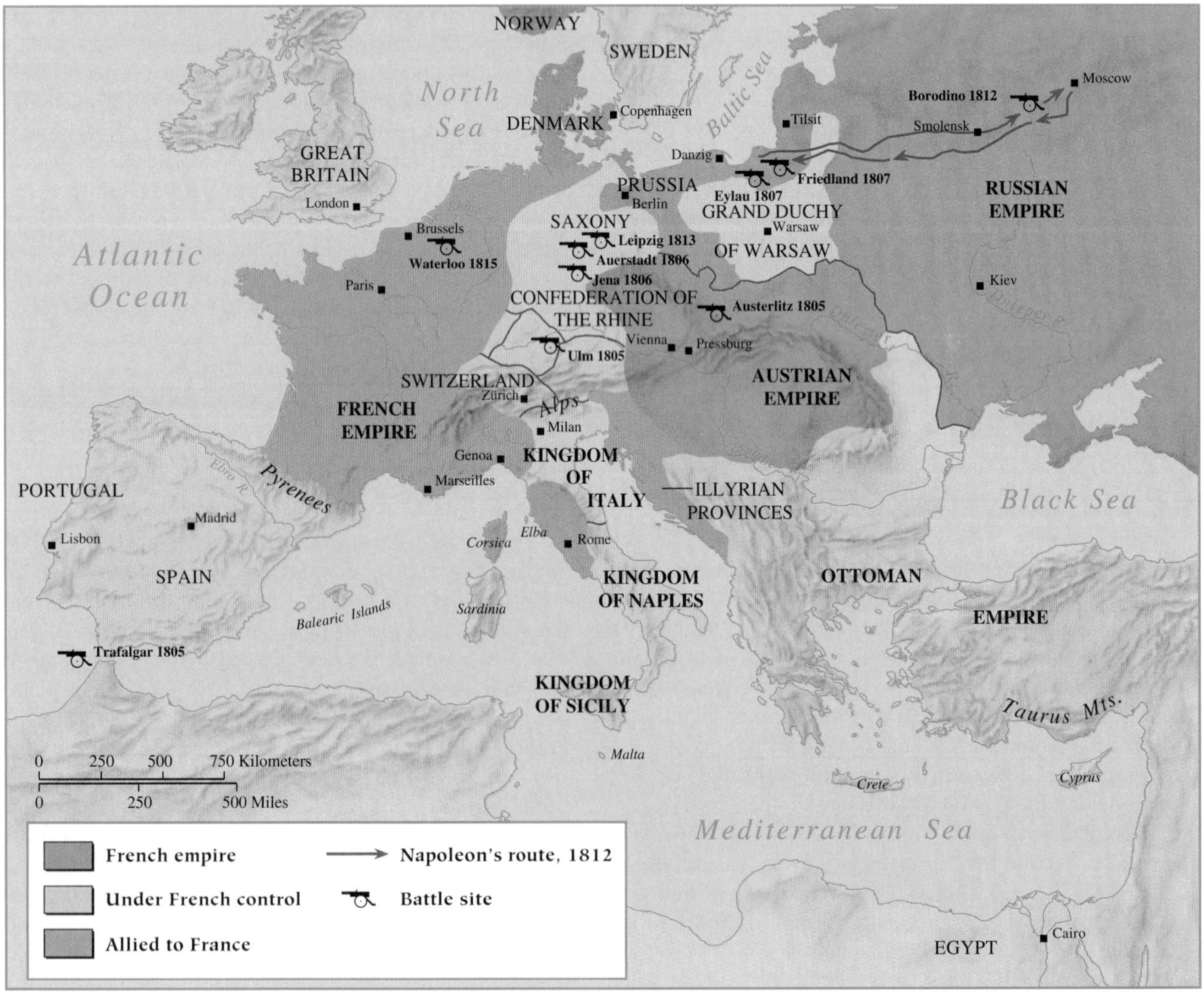

> completely abolished. The benefits of the Code Napoléon, the publicity of judicial procedure, the creation of juries must be so many distinguishing marks of your monarchy. . . . What nation would wish to return under the arbitrary Prussian government once it had tasted the benefits of a wise and liberal administration? The peoples of Germany, the peoples of France, of Italy, of Spain all desire equality and liberal ideas. I have guided the affairs of Europe for many years now, and I have had occasion to convince myself that the buzzing of the privileged classes is contrary to the general opinion. Be a constitutional king.[21]

In the inner core and dependent states of his Grand Empire, Napoleon tried to destroy the old order. Nobility and clergy everywhere in these states lost their special privileges. He decreed equality of opportunity with offices open to talent, equality before the law, and religious toleration. This spread of French revolutionary principles was an important factor in the development of liberal traditions in these countries. These reforms have led some historians to view Napoleon as the last of the enlightened absolutists.

CHRONOLOGY

The Napoleonic Era, 1799–1815

Napoleon as first consul	1799–1804
Concordat with Catholic church	1801
Peace of Amiens	1802
Emperor Napoleon I	1804–1815
Battles of Austerlitz, Trafalgar, Ulm	1805
Battle of Jena	1806
Continental System established	1806
Battle of Eylau	1807
Invasion of Russia	1812
War of liberation	1813–1814
Exile to Elba	1814
Battle of Waterloo; exile to Saint Helena	1815
Death of Napoleon	1821

PROBLEMS: GREAT BRITAIN AND NATIONALISM

Like Hitler 130 years later, Napoleon hoped that his Grand Empire would last for centuries; like Hitler's empire, it collapsed almost as rapidly as it had been formed. Two major reasons help explain this, the survival of Great Britain and the force of nationalism. Britain's survival was due primarily to its seapower. As long as Britain ruled the waves, it was almost invulnerable to military attack. Although Napoleon contemplated an invasion of England and even collected ships for it, he could not overcome the British navy's decisive defeat of a combined French-Spanish fleet at Trafalgar in 1805. Napoleon then turned to his Continental System to defeat Britain. Put into effect between 1806 and 1807, it attempted to prevent British goods from reaching the European continent in order to weaken Britain economically and destroy its capacity to wage war. But the Continental System failed. Allied states resented the ever-tightening French economic hegemony; some began to cheat and others to resist, thereby opening the door to British collaboration. New markets in the eastern Mediterranean and in Latin America also provided compensation for the British. Indeed, by 1810, British overseas exports were approaching record highs.

A second important factor in the defeat of Napoleon was nationalism. This political creed had arisen during the French Revolution in the French people's emphasis on brotherhood (*fraternité*) and solidarity against other peoples. Nationalism involved the unique cultural identity of a people based on common language, religion, and national symbols. The spirit of French nationalism had made possible the mass armies of the revolutionary and Napoleonic eras. But Napoleon's spread of the principles of the French Revolution beyond France inadvertently brought a spread of nationalism as well. The French aroused nationalism in two ways: by making themselves hated oppressors and thus arousing the patriotism of others in opposition to French nationalism and by showing the people of Europe what nationalism was and what a nation in arms could do. The lesson was not lost on other peoples and rulers. A Spanish uprising against Napoleon's rule, aided by British support, kept a French force of 200,000 pinned down for years.

THE FALL OF NAPOLEON

The beginning of Napoleon's downfall came in 1812 with his invasion of Russia. The latter's defection from the Continental System left Napoleon with little choice. Although aware of the risks in invading such a large country, he also knew that if the Russians were allowed to challenge the Continental System unopposed, others would soon follow suit. In June 1812, Napoleon's Grand Army of more than 600,000 men entered Russia. Napoleon's hopes for victory depended on quickly meeting and defeating the Russian armies, but the Russian forces refused to give battle and retreated hundreds of miles while torching their own villages and countryside to prevent Napoleon's army from finding food and forage. When the Russians did stop to fight at Borodino, Napoleon's forces won an indecisive and costly victory. When the remaining troops of the Grand Army arrived in Moscow, they found the city ablaze. Lacking food and supplies, Napoleon abandoned Moscow late in October and made the "Great Retreat" across Russia in terrible winter conditions. Only 40,000 troops managed to straggle back to Poland in January 1813. This military disaster then led to a war of liberation all over Europe, culminating in Napoleon's defeat in April 1814.

The defeated emperor of the French was allowed to play ruler on the island of Elba, off the cost of Tuscany, while the Bourbon monarchy was restored to France in the person of Louis XVIII, brother of the executed king. But the new king had little support, and Napoleon, bored on Elba, slipped back into France. When troops were sent to capture him, Napoleon opened his coat and addressed them: "Soldiers of the fifth regiment, I am your Emperor. . . . If there is a man among you would kill his Emperor, here I am!" No one fired a shot. Shouting "Vive l'Empéreur! Vive l'Empéreur," the troops went over to his side, and Napoleon entered Paris in triumph on March 20, 1815.

The powers that had defeated him pledged once more to fight this person they called the "Enemy and Disturber of the Tranquility of the World." Having decided to strike first at his enemies, Napoleon raised yet another army and moved to attack the nearest allied forces stationed in Belgium. At Waterloo on June 18, Napoleon met a combined British and Prussian army under the duke of Wellington and suffered a bloody defeat. This time, the victorious allies exiled him to Saint Helena, a small and forsaken island in the South Atlantic. Only Napoleon's memory would continue to haunt French political life.

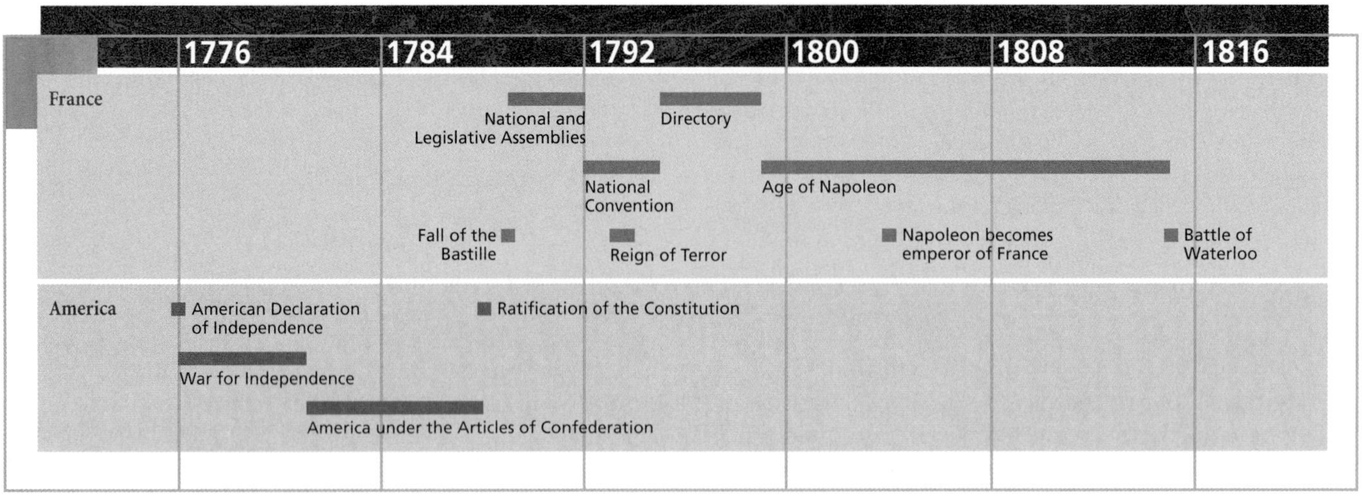

Conclusion

The revolutionary era of the late eighteenth century witnessed a dramatic political transformation. Revolutionary upheavals, beginning in North America and continuing in France, produced movements for political liberty and equality. The documents created by these revolutions, the Declaration of Independence and the Declaration of the Rights of Man and the Citizen, embodied the fundamental ideas of the Enlightenment and set forth a liberal political agenda based on a belief in popular sovereignty—the people as the source of political power—and the principles of liberty and equality. Liberty, frequently limited in practice, meant, in theory, freedom from arbitrary power as well as the freedom to think, write, and worship as one chose. Equality meant equality in rights and equality of opportunity based on talent rather than birth. In practice, equality remained limited; those who owned property had greater opportunities for voting and officeholding, and there was certainly no equality between men and women.

The leaders of France's liberal revolution, achieved between 1789 and 1791, were men of property, both bourgeois and noble, but they were assisted by commoners, both sans-culottes and peasants. Yet the liberal revolution, despite the hopes of the men of property, was not the end of the revolution. The decision of the revolutionaries to go to war "revolutionized the revolution," opening the door to a more radical, democratic, and violent stage. The excesses of the Reign of Terror, however, led to a reaction, first under the Directory and then under Napoleon, when men of property were willing to give up liberty in exchange for order, security, and economic opportunity. Napoleon, while diminishing freedom by establishing order and centralizing the government, shrewdly preserved equality of rights and the opening of careers to talent and integrated the bourgeoisie and old nobility into a new elite of property owners. For despite the antiaristocratic revolutionary rhetoric and the loss of their privileges, nobles remained important landowners. Though the nobles lost some of their lands during the revolution, they were still the largest proprietors in the early 1800s. The great gainers from the redistribution of clerical and noble property, however, had been the bourgeoisie, who also gained dramatically when important government and military positions were opened to men of talent. After 1800, an elite group of property owners, both noble and middle class, dominated French society.

The French Revolution defined the modern revolutionary concept. No one had foreseen or consciously planned the upheaval that began in 1789, but after 1789, "revolutionaries" knew that mass uprisings could succeed in overthrowing unwanted governments. The French revolution became the classical political and social model for revolution. At the same time, the liberal and national political ideals created by the revolution and spread through Europe by Napoleon's conquests dominated the political landscape of the nineteenth and early twentieth centuries.

Notes

1. Quoted in R. R. Palmer, *The Age of the Democratic Revolutions* (Princeton, N.J., 1959), vol. 1, p. 239.
2. Quoted in ibid., p. 242.
3. Quoted in O. J. Hufton, "Toward an Understanding of the Poor of Eighteenth-Century France," in J. F. Bosher, ed., *French Government and Society, 1500–1850* (London, 1973), p. 152.
4. Arthur Young, *Travels in France During the Years 1787, 1788, and 1789* (Cambridge, 1929), p. 23.
5. Quoted in D. M. G. Sutherland, *France, 1789–1815: Revolution and Counter-Revolution* (New York, 1986), p. 74.
6. Quoted in William Doyle, *The Oxford History of the French Revolution* (Oxford, 1989), p. 156.
7. Quoted in ibid., p. 184.
8. Quoted in J. Hardman, ed., *French Revolution Documents* (Oxford, 1973), vol. 2, p. 23.
9. Quoted in W. Scott, *Terror and Repression in Revolutionary Marseilles* (London, 1973), p. 84.
10. Quoted in H. Morse Stephens, *The Principal Speeches of the Statesmen and Orators of the French Revolution* (Oxford, 1892), vol. 2, p. 189.
11. Quoted in Leo Gershoy, *The Era of the French Revolution* (Princeton, N.J., 1957), p. 157.
12. Quoted in J. M. Thompson, ed., *French Revolution Documents* (Oxford, 1933), pp. 258–259.
13. Quoted in Doyle, *Oxford History of the French Revolution,* p. 254.
14. Quoted in R. R. Palmer, *Twelve Who Ruled* (New York, 1965), p. 75.
15. Quoted in Darline Gay Levy, Harriet Branson Applewhite, and Mary Durham Johnson, eds., *Women in Revolutionary Paris, 1789–1795* (Urbana, Ill., 1979), p. 132.
16. Ibid., pp. 219–220.
17. Quoted in Elizabeth G. Sledziewski, "The French Revolution as the Turning Point," in Geneviève Fraisse and Michelle Perrot, eds., *A History of Women in the West* (Cambridge, 1993), vol. 4, p. 39.
18. Quoted in François Furet and Mona Ozouf, *A Critical Dictionary of the French Revolution,* trans. Arthur Goldhammer (Cambridge, Mass., 1989), p. 545.
19. Quoted in Felix Markham, *Napoleon* (New York, 1963), pp. 92–93.
20. Quoted in Doyle, *Oxford History of the French Revolution,* p. 381.
21. Quoted in J. Christopher Herold, ed., *The Mind of Napoleon* (New York, 1955), pp. 74–75.

Suggestions for Further Reading

A well-written, up-to-date introduction to the French Revolution can be found in W. Doyle, *The Oxford History of the French Revolution* (Oxford, 1989). For the entire revolutionary and Napoleonic eras, see O. Connelly, *The French Revolution and Napoleonic Era,* 3d ed. (Fort Worth, Tex., 2000), and D. M. G. Sutherland, *France, 1789–1815: Revolution and Counter-Revolution* (New York, 1986). Two brief works are A. Forrest, *The French Revolution* (Oxford, 1995), and J. M. Roberts, *The French Revolution,* 2d ed. (New York, 1997). Three comprehensive reference works are S. F. Scott and B. Rothaus, eds., *Historical Dictionary of the French Revolution,* 2 vols. (Westport, Conn., 1985); F. Furet and M. Ozouf, *A Critical Dictionary of the French Revolution,* trans. A. Goldhammer (Cambridge, Mass., 1989); and O. Connelly et al., *Historical Dictionary of Napoleonic France, 1799–1815* (Westport, Conn., 1985).

The origins of the French Revolution are examined in W. Doyle, *Origins of the French Revolution* (Oxford, 1988). See also R. Chartier, *The Cultural Origins of the French Revolution* (Durham, N.C., 1991). On the early years of the revolution, see M. Kennedy, *The Jacobin Clubs in the French Revolution: The First Years* (Princeton, N.J., 1982); N. Hampson, *Prelude to Terror* (Oxford, 1988); T. Tackett, *Becoming a Revolutionary* (Princeton, N.J., 1996), on the deputies to the National Assembly; and J. Markoff, *The Abolition of Feudalism: Peasants, Lords, and Legislators in the French Revolution* (University Park, Pa., 1996). Important works on the radical stage of the French Revolution include N. Hampson, *The Terror in the French Revolution* (London, 1981); A. Soboul, *The Sans-Culottes* (New York, 1972); R. R. Palmer, *Twelve Who Ruled* (New York, 1965); and R. Cobb, *The People's Armies* (London, 1987). For a biography of Robespierre, one of the leading figures of this period, see N. Hampson, *The Life and Opinions of Maximilien Robespierre* (London, 1974). The importance of the revolutionary wars in the radical stage of the revolution is underscored in T. C. W. Blanning, *The French Revolutionary Wars, 1787–1802* (New York, 1996). On the Directory, see M. Lyons, *France Under the Directory* (Cambridge, 1975), and R. B. Rose, *Gracchus Babeuf* (Stanford, Calif., 1978).

The religious history of the French Revolution is covered in J. McManners, *The French Revolution and the Church* (London, 1969). On the Great Fear, see the classic work by G. Lefebvre, *The Great Fear of 1789: Rural Panic in Revolutionary France* (London, 1973). On the role of women in revolutionary France, see O. J. Hufton, *Women and the Limits of Citizenship in the French Revolution* (Toronto, 1992); J. Landes, *Women and the Public Sphere in the Age of the French Revolution* (Ithaca, N.Y., 1988); and the essays in G. Fraisse and M. Perrot, eds., *A History of Women in the West,* vol. 4 (Cambridge, Mass., 1993).

The best brief biography of Napoleon is F. Markham, *Napoleon* (New York, 1963). Also valuable are G. J. Ellis, *Napoleon* (New York, 1997); M. Lyons, *Napoleon Bonaparte and the Legacy of the French Revolution* (New York, 1994); and the massive biographies by F. J. McLynn, *Napoleon: A Biography* (London, 1997), and A. Schom, *Napoleon Bonaparte* (New York, 1997). On Napoleon's wars, see S. J. Woolf, *Napoleon's Integration of Europe* (New York, 1991).

A history of the revolutionary era in America can be found in R. Middlekauff, *The Glorious Cause: The American Revolution, 1763–1789* (New York, 1982), and C. Bonwick, *The American Revolution* (Charlottesville, Va., 1991). The importance of ideology is treated in G. Wood, *The Radicalism of the American Revolution* (New York, 1992). A comparative study that puts the American Revolution into a larger context is R. R. Palmer, *The Age of the Democratic Revolutions: A Political History of Europe and America, 1760–1800,* 2 vols. (Princeton, N.J., 1959–1964).

For additional reading, go to InfoTrac College Edition, your online research library at http://web1.infotrac-college.com

Enter the search term *French Revolution* using Key Terms.

Enter the search term *American Revolution* using Key Terms.

Enter the search term *Napoleon* using Key Terms.

Enter the search term *Napoleonic Wars* using Key Terms.

CHAPTER

20

The Industrial Revolution and Its Impact on European Society

CHAPTER OUTLINE

- The Industrial Revolution in Great Britain
- The Spread of Industrialization
- The Social Impact of the Industrial Revolution
- Conclusion

FOCUS QUESTIONS

- What conditions and developments coalesced in Great Britain to bring about the first Industrial Revolution?
- What were the basic features of the new industrial system created by the Industrial Revolution?
- How did the Industrial Revolution spread from Great Britain to the Continent and the United States, and how did industrialization in those areas differ from British industrialization?
- What effects did the Industrial Revolution have on urban life, social classes, family life, and standards of living?
- What were working conditions like in the early decades of the Industrial Revolution, and what efforts were made to improve them?
- What was the role of government in the industrial development of the Western world?

THE FRENCH REVOLUTION dramatically and quickly altered the political structure of France, and the Napoleonic conquests spread many of the revolutionary principles in an equally rapid and stunning fashion to other parts of Europe. During the late eighteenth and early nineteenth centuries, another revolution—an industrial one—was transforming the economic and social structure of Europe, although more slowly and less dramatically.

The Industrial Revolution caused a quantum leap in industrial production. New sources of energy and power, especially coal and steam, replaced wind and water to build and run machines that dramatically decreased the use of human and animal labor and at the same time increased productivity. This in turn called for new ways of organizing human labor to maximize the benefits and profits from the new machines;

factories replaced workshops and home workrooms. Many early factories were dreadful places with difficult working conditions. Reformers, appalled at these conditions, were especially critical of the treatment of married women. One reported: "We have repeatedly seen married females, in the last stage of pregnancy, slaving from morning to night beside these never-tiring machines, and when . . . they were obliged to sit down to take a moment's ease, and being seen by the manager, were fined for the offense." But there were also examples of well-run factories. William Cobbett described one in Manchester in 1830: "In this room, which is lighted in the most convenient and beautiful manner, there were five hundred pairs of looms at work, and five hundred persons attending those looms; and, owing to the goodness of the masters, the whole looking healthy and well-dressed."

During the Industrial Revolution, Europe experienced a shift from a traditional, labor-intensive economy based on farming and handicrafts to a more capital-intensive economy based on manufacturing by machines, specialized labor, and industrial factories. Although the Industrial Revolution took decades to spread, it was truly revolutionary in the way it fundamentally changed Europeans, their society, and their relationship to the rest of the world. The development of large factories encouraged mass movements of people from the countryside to urban areas, where impersonal coexistence replaced the traditional intimacy of rural life. Higher levels of productivity led to a search for new sources of raw materials, new consumption patterns, and a revolution in transportation that allowed raw materials and finished products to be moved quickly around the world. The creation of a wealthy industrial middle class and a huge industrial working class (or proletariat) substantially transformed traditional social relationships.

The Industrial Revolution in Great Britain

Although the Industrial Revolution evolved over a long period of time, historians generally agree that it began in Britain sometime after 1750. By 1850, the Industrial Revolution had made Great Britain the wealthiest country in the world; it had also spread to the European continent and the New World. In another fifty years, both Germany and the United States would surpass Britain in industrial production.

Origins

A number of factors or conditions coalesced in Britain to produce the first Industrial Revolution. One of these was the agricultural revolution of the eighteenth century. The changes in the methods of farming and stock breeding that characterized this agricultural transformation led to a significant increase in food production. British agriculture could now feed more people at lower prices with less labor. Unlike the rest of Europe, even ordinary British families did not have to use most of their income to buy food, giving them the potential to purchase manufactured goods. At the same time, a rapid growth of population in the second half of the eighteenth century provided a pool of surplus labor for the new factories of the emerging British industry. Rural workers in cottage industries also provided a potential labor force for industrial enterprises.

Britain had a ready supply of capital for investment in the new industrial machines and the factories that were needed to house them. In addition to profits from trade and the cottage industry, Britain possessed an effective central bank and well-developed, flexible credit facilities. Nowhere in Europe were people so accustomed to using paper instruments to facilitate capital transactions. Many early factory owners were merchants and entrepreneurs who had profited from the eighteenth-century cottage industry. Of 110 cotton-spinning mills in operation in the area known as the Midlands between 1769 and 1800, fully 62 were established by hosiers, drapers, mercers, and others involved in some fashion in the cottage textile industry.

But capital is only part of the story. Britain had a fair number of individuals who were interested in making profits if the opportunity presented itself (see the box on p. 554). The British were a people, as one historian has said, "fascinated by wealth and commerce, collectively and individually." No doubt the English revolutions of the seventeenth century had helped create an environment in Britain, unlike that of the absolutist states on the Continent, where political power rested in the hands of a progressive group of people who favored innovation in economic matters.

Nevertheless, these early industrial entrepreneurs faced considerable financial hazards. Fortunes were made quickly and lost just as quickly. The structure of early firms was fluid. An individual or family proprietorship was the usual mode of operation, but entrepreneurs also brought in friends to help—and just as easily jettisoned them. John Marshall, who made money in flax spinning, threw his partners out: "As they could neither of them be of any further use, I released them from the firm and took the whole upon myself."[1]

Britain had ample supplies of important mineral resources, such as coal and iron ore, needed in the manufacturing process. Britain was also small, and the relatively short distances made transportation nonproblematic. In addition to nature's provision of abundant rivers, from the mid-seventeenth century onward, both private and public investment poured into the construction of new roads, bridges, and, beginning in the 1750s and 1760s, canals. By 1780, roads, rivers, and canals linked the major industrial centers of the North, the Midlands, London, and the Atlantic. Unlike the Continental countries, Britain had no internal customs barriers to hinder domestic trade.

Britain's government also played a significant role in the process of industrialization. Parliament contributed to

The Traits of the British Industrial Entrepreneur

Richard Arkwright (1732–1792), inventor of a spinning frame and founder of cotton factories, was a good example of the successful entrepreneur in the early Industrial Revolution in Britain. In this selection, Edward Baines, who wrote *The History of the Cotton Manufacture in Great Britain* in 1835, discusses the traits that explain the success of Arkwright and presumably other British entrepreneurs.

Edward Baines, The History of the Cotton Manufacture in Great Britain

Richard Arkwright rose by the force of his natural talents from a very humble condition in society. He was born at Preston on the 23rd of December, 1732, of poor parents: being the youngest of thirteen children, his parents could only afford to give him an education of the humblest kind, and he was scarcely able to write. He was brought up to the trade of a barber at Kirkham and Preston, and established himself in that business at Bolton in the year 1760. Having become possessed of a chemical process for dyeing human hair, which in that day (when wigs were universal) was of considerable value, he traveled about collecting hair, and again disposing of it when dyed. In 1761, he married a wife from Leigh, and the connections he thus formed in that town are supposed to have afterwards brought him acquainted with Highs's experiments in making spinning machines. He himself manifested a strong bent for experiments in mathematics, which he is stated to have followed with so much devotedness as to have neglected his business and injured his circumstances. His natural disposition was ardent, enterprising, and stubbornly persevering: his mind was as coarse as it was bold and active, and his manners were rough and unpleasing. . . .

The most marked traits in the character of Arkwright were his wonderful ardor, energy, and perseverance. He commonly laboured in his multifarious concerns from five o'clock in the morning till nine at night; and when considerably more than fifty years of age,—feeling that the defects of his education placed him under great difficulty and inconvenience in conducting his correspondence, and in the general management of his business,—he encroached upon his sleep, in order to gain an hour each day to learn English grammar, and another hour to improve his writing and orthography [spelling]! He was impatient of whatever interfered with his favorite pursuits; and the fact is too strikingly characteristic not to be mentioned, that he separated from his wife not many years after their marriage, because she, convinced that he would starve his family [because of the impractical nature of his schemes], broke some of his experimental models of machinery. Arkwright was a severe economist of time; and, that he might not waste a moment, he generally traveled with four horses, and at a very rapid speed. His concerns in Derbyshire, Lancashire, and Scotland were so extensive and numerous, as to [show] at once his astonishing power of transacting business and his all grasping spirit. In many of these he had partners, but he generally managed in such a way, that, whoever lost, he himself was a gainer.

the favorable business climate by providing a stable government and passing laws that protected private property. Moreover, Britain was remarkable for the freedom it provided for private enterprise. It placed fewer restrictions on private entrepreneurs than any other European state.

Finally, a supply of markets gave British industrialists a ready outlet for their manufactured goods. British exports quadrupled from 1660 to 1760. In the course of its eighteenth-century wars and conquests, Great Britain had developed a vast colonial empire at the expense of its leading Continental rivals, the Dutch Republic and France. Britain also possessed a well-developed merchant marine that was able to transport goods to any place in the world. A crucial factor in Britain's successful industrialization was the ability to produce cheaply the articles most in demand abroad. And the best markets abroad were not in Europe, where countries protected their own incipient industries, but in the Americas, Africa, and the East, where people wanted sturdy, inexpensive clothes rather than costly, highly finished luxury items. Britain's machine-produced textiles fulfilled that demand. Nor should we overlook the British domestic market. Britain had the highest standard of living in Europe and a rapidly growing population. As Daniel Defoe noted already in 1728:

> For the rest, we see their Houses and Lodgings tolerably furnished, at least stuff'd well with useful and necessary household Goods: Even those we call poor People, Journey-men, working and Pains-taking People do thus; they lye warm, live in Plenty, work hard, and [need] know no Want. These are the People that carry off the Gross of your Consumption; 'tis for these your Markets are kept open late on Saturday nights; because they usually receive their Week's Wages late. . . . In a Word, these are the Life of our whole Commerce, and all by their Multitude: Their Numbers are not Hundreds or Thousands, or Hundreds of Thousands, but Millions; . . . by their Wages they are able to live plentifully, and it is by their expensive, generous, free way of living, that the Home Consumption is rais'd to such a Bulk, as well of our own, as of foreign Production.[2]

This demand from both domestic and foreign markets and the inability of the old system to fulfill it led entrepreneurs to seek and adopt the new methods of manufacturing that a series of inventions provided. In so doing, these individuals initiated the Industrial Revolution.

Technological Changes and New Forms of Industrial Organization

In the 1770s and 1780s, the cotton textile industry took the first major step toward the Industrial Revolution with the creation of the modern factory.

THE COTTON INDUSTRY

Already in the eighteenth century, Great Britain had surged ahead in the production of cheap cotton goods using the traditional methods of the cottage industry. The development of the flying shuttle had sped the process of weaving on a loom and enabled weavers to double their output. This caused shortages of yarn, however, until James Hargreaves's spinning jenny, perfected by 1768, enabled spinners to produce yarn in greater quantities. Richard Arkwright's water frame spinning machine, powered by water or horse, and Samuel Crompton's so-called mule, which combined aspects of the water frame and the spinning jenny, increased yarn production even more. Edmund Cartwright's power loom, invented in 1787, allowed the weaving of cloth to catch up with the spinning of yarn. Even then, early power looms were grossly inefficient, enabling cottage, hand-loom weavers to continue to prosper, at least until the mid-1820s. After that, they were gradually replaced by the new machines. In 1813, there were 2,400 power looms in operation in Great Britain; they numbered 14,150 in 1820, 100,000 in 1833 and 250,000 by 1850. In the 1820s, there were still 250,000 hand-loom weavers in Britain; by 1860, only 3,000 were left.

The water frame, Crompton's mule, and power looms presented new opportunities to entrepreneurs. It was much more efficient to bring workers to the machines and organize their labor collectively in factories located next to rivers and streams, the sources of power for many of these early machines, than to leave the workers dispersed in their cottages. The concentration of labor in the new factories also brought the laborers and their families to live in the new towns that rapidly grew up around the factories.

The early devices used to speed up the processes of spinning and weaving were the products of weavers and spinners—in effect, of artisan tinkerers. But the subsequent expansion of the cotton industry and the ongoing demand for even more cotton goods created additional pressure for new and more complicated technology. The invention that pushed the cotton industry to even greater heights of productivity was the steam engine.

THE STEAM ENGINE

The invention of the steam engine played a major role in the Industrial Revolution. It revolutionized the production of cotton goods and caused the factory system to spread to other areas of production, thereby creating whole new industries. The steam engine secured the triumph of the Industrial Revolution.

As in much of the Industrial Revolution, one kind of change forced other changes. In many ways, the steam engine was the result of the need for more efficient pumps to eliminate water seepage from deep mines. Deep coal mines were in turn the result of Britain's need and desire to find new sources of energy to replace wood. By the early eighteenth century, the British were acutely aware of a growing shortage of timber, which was used in heating, to build homes and ships, and in enormous quantities to produce the charcoal used in smelting iron ore to make pig iron. At the beginning of the eighteenth century, the discovery of new processes for smelting iron ore with coal and coke led to deeper and deeper mines for more intensive mining of coal. But as mines were dug below the water table, they filled with water. An early solution to the problem was the use of mechanical pumps powered by horses walking in a circle. In one coal mine in Warwickshire, for example, five hundred horses were used to lift the water from the mine, bucket by bucket. The need for more efficient pumps led Thomas Newcomen to develop a steam pump or, as it was called, an "atmospheric engine" that was first used in 1712. Though better than horses, it was still inefficient.

In the 1760s, a Scottish engineer, James Watt (1736–1819), was asked to repair a Newcomen engine. Instead he added a separate condenser and steam pump and transformed Newcomen's machine into a genuine steam engine. Power was derived not from air pressure, as in Newcomen's atmospheric engine, but from steam itself. Much more efficient than a Newcomen engine, Watt's engine could pump water three times as quickly. Initially, it possessed one major liability, however; as a contemporary noted in 1778: "The vast consumption of fuel in these engines is an immense drawback on the profit of our mines, for every fire-engine of magnitude consumes £3000 worth of coals per annum. This heavy tax amounts almost to a prohibition."[3] As steam engines were made more efficient, however, they also became cheaper to use.

In 1782, James Watt enlarged the possibilities of the steam engine when he developed a rotary engine that could turn a shaft and thus drive machinery. Steam power could now be applied to spinning and weaving cotton, and before long, cotton mills using steam engines were multiplying across Britain. By 1850, seven-eighths of the power available to the entire British cotton industry came from steam. Since steam engines were fired by coal, they did not need to be located near rivers; entrepreneurs now had greater flexibility in their choice of location.

The new boost given to cotton textile production by technological changes became readily apparent. In 1760, Britain had imported 2.5 million pounds of raw cotton, which was farmed out to cottage industries. All work was done by hand either in workers' homes or in the small shops of master weavers. In 1787, the British imported 22 million pounds of cotton; most of it was spun on machines, some powered by water in large mills. By 1840, 366 million pounds of cotton were imported annually, much of it from the American South, where it was grown by plantation owners using slave labor. By this time, cotton cloth was Britain's most important product by value and was produced mainly in factories, although some hand-loom weavers still worked

A Boulton and Watt Steam Engine. Encouraged by his business partner, Matthew Boulton, James Watt developed the first genuine steam engine. Pictured here is a typical Boulton and Watt engine. Steam pressure in the cylinder on the left drives the beam upward and sets the flywheel in motion.

in their cottages. The price of yarn was now one-twentieth what it had been. The cheapest labor in India could not compete in quality or quantity with Britain. British cotton goods sold everywhere in the world. And in Britain itself, cheap cotton cloth made it possible for millions of poor people to wear undergarments, long a preserve of the rich who could afford underwear made with expensive linen cloth. New work clothing that was tough, comfortable against the skin, and yet cheap and easily washable became common. Even the rich liked the colorful patterns of cotton prints and their light weight for summer wear.

The steam engine was indispensable in Britain's Industrial Revolution. In 1800, engines were generating 10,000 horsepower; fifty years later, 500,000 horsepower was being generated by stationary engines and 790,000 by mobile engines, largely in locomotives. Unlike horses, the steam engine was a tireless source of power and depended for fuel on a substance—coal—that seemed then to be in unlimited supply. The popular saying that "steam is an Englishman" had real significance by 1850. The steam engine also replaced waterpower in such places as flour and sugar mills. Just as the need for more coal had helped lead to the steam engine, so the success of the steam engine increased the demand for coal and led to an expansion in coal production; between 1815 and 1850, the output of coal quadrupled. In turn, new processes using coal furthered the development of the iron industry.

THE IRON INDUSTRY

The British iron industry was radically transformed during the Industrial Revolution. Britain had large resources of iron ore, but at the beginning of the eighteenth century, the basic process of producing iron had altered little since the Middle Ages and still depended heavily on charcoal. In the early eighteenth century, new methods of smelting iron ore to produce cast iron were devised, based on the use of coke derived from coal. Still, a better quality of iron was not possible until the 1780s, when Henry Cort developed a system called puddling in which coke was used to burn away impurities in pig iron to produce an iron of high quality. A boom then ensued in the British iron industry. In 1740, Britain produced 17,000 tons of iron; in the 1780s, almost 70,000 tons; by the 1840s, over 2 million tons; and by 1852, almost 3 million tons, more than the rest of the world combined.

The development of the iron industry was in many ways a response to the demand for the new machines. The high-quality wrought iron produced by the Cort process made it the most widely used metal until the production of cheaper steel in the 1860s. The growing supply of less costly metal encouraged the use of machinery in other industries, most noticeably in new means of transportation.

A REVOLUTION IN TRANSPORTATION

The eighteenth century had witnessed an expansion of transportation facilities in Britain as entrepreneurs realized the need for more efficient means of moving resources and goods. Turnpike trusts constructed new roads, and between 1760 and 1830, a network of canals was built. But both roads and canals were soon overtaken by a new form of transportation that dazzled people with its promise. To many economic historians, railroads were the "most important single factor in promoting European economic progress in the 1830s and 1840s." Again, Britain was the leader in the revolution.

The railways got their start in mining operations in Germany as early as 1500 and in British coal mines after 1600, where small handcarts filled with coal were pushed along parallel wooden rails. The rails reduced friction, enabling horses to haul more substantial loads. By 1700, some entrepreneurs began to replace wooden rails with cast-iron rails, and by the early nineteenth century, railways—still dependent on horsepower—were common in British mining and industrial districts. The development of the steam engine led to a radical transformation of the railways.

In 1804, Richard Trevithick pioneered the first steam-powered locomotive on an industrial rail line in south

Mansell/TimePix

Railroad Line from Liverpool to Manchester. The railroad line from Liverpool to Manchester, first opened in 1830, relied on steam locomotives. As is evident in this illustration, carrying passengers was the railroad's main business. First-class passengers rode in covered cars; second- and third-class passengers, in open cars.

Wales. It pulled 10 tons of ore and seventy people at 5 miles per hour. Better locomotives soon followed. The engines built by George Stephenson and his son proved superior, and it was in their workshops in Newcastle-upon-Tyne that the locomotives for the first modern railways in Britain were built. George Stephenson's *Rocket* was used on the first public railway line, which opened in 1830, extending 32 miles from Liverpool to Manchester. *Rocket* sped along at 16 miles per hour. Within twenty years, locomotives had reached 50 miles per hour, an incredible speed to contemporary passengers. During the same period, new companies were formed to build additional railroads as the infant industry proved to be not only technically but financially successful. In 1840, Britain had almost 2,000 miles of railroads; by 1850, 6,000 miles of railroad track crisscrossed much of the country (see Map 20.1 on p. 561).

The railroad contributed significantly to the success and maturing of the Industrial Revolution. The railroad's demands for coal and iron furthered the growth of those industries. British supremacy in civil and mechanical engineering, so evident after 1840, was in large part based on the skills acquired in railway building. The huge capital demands necessary for railway construction encouraged a whole new group of middle-class investors to invest their money in joint-stock companies (see "Limitations to Industrialization" later in this chapter). Railway construction created new job opportunities, especially for farm laborers and peasants, who had long been accustomed to finding work outside their local villages. Perhaps most important, a cheaper and faster means of transportation had a rippling effect on the growth of an industrial economy. By reducing the price of goods, larger markets were created; increased sales necessitated more factories and more machinery, thereby reinforcing the self-sustaining nature of the Industrial Revolution, which marked a fundamental break with the traditional European economy. The great productivity of the Industrial Revolution enabled entrepreneurs to reinvest their profits in new capital equipment, further expanding the productive capacity of the economy. Continuous, even rapid, self-sustaining economic growth came to be seen as a fundamental characteristic of the new industrial economy.

The railroad was the perfect symbol of this aspect of the Industrial Revolution. The ability to transport goods and people at dramatic speeds also provided visible confirmation of a new sense of power. When railway engineers penetrated mountains with tunnels and spanned chasms

Opening of the Royal Albert Bridge. This painting by Thomas Robins shows the ceremonies attending the official opening of the Royal Albert Bridge. I. K. Brunel, one of Britain's great engineers, designed this bridge, which carried a railroad line across the Tamar River into Cornwall. As is evident in the picture, the bridge was high enough to allow ships to pass underneath.

Elton Collection/Ironbridge Gorge

with breathtaking bridges, contemporaries experienced a sense of power over nature not felt before in Western civilization.

THE INDUSTRIAL FACTORY

Initially the product of the new cotton industry, the factory became the chief means of organizing labor for the new machines. As the workplace shifted from the artisan's shop and the peasant's cottage to the factory, the latter was not viewed as just a larger work unit. Employers hired workers who no longer owned the means of production but were simply paid wages to run the machines.

From its beginning, the factory system demanded a new type of discipline from its employees. Factory owners could not afford to let their expensive machinery stand idle. Workers were forced to work regular hours and in shifts to keep the machines producing at a steady pace for maximum output. This represented a massive adjustment for early factory laborers.

Preindustrial workers were not accustomed to a timed format. Agricultural laborers had always kept irregular hours; hectic work at harvest time might be followed by periods of inactivity. Even in the burgeoning cottage industry of the eighteenth century, weavers and spinners who worked at home might fulfill their weekly quotas by working around the clock for two or three days, followed by a leisurely pace until the next week's demands forced another work spurt.

Factory owners therefore faced a formidable task. They had to create a system of time-work discipline that would accustom employees to working regular, unvarying hours during which they performed a set number of tasks over and over again as efficiently as possible. One early industrialist said that his aim was "to make such machines of the men as cannot err." Such work, of course, tended to be repetitive and boring, and factory owners resorted to tough methods to accomplish their goals. Factory regulations were minute and detailed (see the box on p. 559). Adult workers were fined for a wide variety of minor infractions, such as being a few minutes late for work, and dismissed for more serious misdoings, especially drunkenness. Drunkenness was viewed as particularly offensive because it set a bad example for younger workers and also courted disaster amid dangerous machinery. Employers found that dismissals and fines worked well for adult employees; in a time when great population growth had produced large numbers of unskilled workers, dismissal could be disastrous. Children were less likely to understand the impli-

A British Textile Factory. The development of the factory changed the relationship between workers and employers as workers were encouraged to adjust to a new system of discipline that forced them to work regular hours under close supervision. This 1851 illustration shows women working in a British textile factory.

Discipline in the New Factories

Workers in the new factories of the Industrial Revolution had been accustomed to a lifestyle free of overseers. Unlike the cottages, where workers spun thread and wove cloth in their own rhythm and time, the factories demanded a new, rigorous discipline geared to the requirements of the machines. This selection is taken from a set of rules for a factory in Berlin in 1844. They were typical of company rules everywhere the factory system had been established.

Factory Rules, Foundry and Engineering Works of the Royal Overseas Trading Company, Berlin

In every large works, and in the co-ordination of any large number of workmen, good order and harmony must be looked upon as the fundamentals of success, and therefore the following rules shall be strictly observed.

1. The normal working day begins at all seasons at 6 A.M. precisely and ends, after the usual break of half an hour for breakfast, an hour for dinner and half an hour for tea, at 7 P.M., and it shall be strictly observed. . . .

   Workers arriving 2 minutes late shall lose half an hour's wages; whoever is more than 2 minutes late may not start work until after the next break; or at least shall lose his wages until then. Any disputes about the correct time shall be settled by the clock mounted above the gatekeeper's lodge. . . .

3. No workman, whether employed by time or piece, may leave before the end of the working day, without having first received permission from the overseer and having given his name to the gatekeeper. Omission of these two actions shall lead to a fine of ten silver groschen [pennies] payable to the sick fund.
4. Repeated irregular arrival at work shall lead to dismissal. This shall also apply to those who are found idling by an official or overseer, and refused to obey their order to resume work. . . .
6. No worker may leave his place of work otherwise than for reasons connected with his work.
7. All conversation with fellow-workers is prohibited; if any worker requires information about his work, he must turn to the overseer, or to the particular fellow-worker designated for the purpose.
8. Smoking in the workshops or in the yard is prohibited during working hours; anyone caught smoking shall be fined five silver groschen for the sick fund for every such offense. . . .
10. Natural functions must be performed at the appropriate places, and whoever is found soiling walls, fences, squares, etc., and similarly, whoever is found washing his face and hands in the workshop and not in the places assigned for the purpose, shall be fined five silver groschen for the sick fund. . . .
12. It goes without saying that all overseers and officials of the firm shall be obeyed without question, and shall be treated with due deference. Disobedience will be punished by dismissal.
13. Immediate dismissal shall also be the fate of anyone found drunk in any of the workshops. . . .
14. Every workman is obliged to report to his superiors any acts of dishonesty or embezzlement on the part of his fellow workmen. If he omits to do so, and it is shown after subsequent discovery of a misdemeanor that he knew about it at the time, he shall be liable to be taken to court as an accessory after the fact and the wage due to him shall be retained as punishment.

cations of dismissal, so they were sometimes disciplined more directly—by beating.

The efforts of factory owners in the early Industrial Revolution to impose a new set of values were frequently reinforced by the new evangelical churches. Methodism, in particular, emphasized that people "reborn in Jesus" must forgo immoderation and follow a disciplined path. Laziness and wasteful habits were sinful. The acceptance of hardship in this life paved the way for the joys of the next. Evangelical values paralleled the efforts of the new factory owners to instill laborers with their own middle-class values of hard work, discipline, and thrift. In one crucial sense, the early industrialists proved successful. As the nineteenth century progressed, the second and third generations of workers came to view a regular working week as a natural way of life. It was, of course, an attitude that made possible Britain's incredible economic growth in that century.

Britain's Great Exhibition of 1851

In 1851, the British organized the world's first industrial fair. It was housed at Kensington in London in the Crystal Palace, an enormous structure made entirely of glass and iron, a tribute to British engineering skills. Covering 19 acres, the Crystal Palace contained 100,000 exhibits that showed the wide variety of products created by the Industrial Revolution. Six million people visited the fair in six months. Though most of them were Britons who had traveled to London by train, foreign visitors were also prominent. The Great Exhibition displayed Britain's wealth to the world; it was a gigantic symbol of British success. Even trees were brought inside the Crystal Palace as a visible symbol of how the Industrial Revolution had achieved human domination over nature. Prince Albert, Queen Victoria's husband, expressed the sentiments of the age when he described the exhibition as a sign that "man is approaching

Guildhall Library, Corporation of London, UK/Bridgeman Art Library

The Crystal Palace. The Great Exhibition of 1851 was a symbol of the success of Great Britain, which had become the world's first and richest industrial nation. Over 100,000 exhibits were housed in the Crystal Palace, a giant structure of cast iron and glass. This illustration shows the front of the palace and some of its numerous visitors.

a more complete fulfillment of that great and sacred mission which he has to perform in this world . . . to conquer nature to his use." Not content with that, he also linked British success to divine will: "In promoting [the progress of the human race], we are accomplishing the will of the great and blessed God."[4]

By the year of the Great Exhibition, Great Britain had become the world's first and richest industrial nation. Britain was the "workshop, banker, and trader of the world." It produced one-half of the world's coal and manufactured goods; its cotton industry alone in 1851 was equal in size to the industries of all other European countries combined. The quantity of goods produced was growing at three times the growth rate in 1780. No doubt, Britain's certainty about its mission in the world in the nineteenth century was grounded in its incredible material success story.

The Spread of Industrialization

Beginning first in Great Britain, industrialization spread to the Continental countries of Europe and the United States at different times and speeds during the nineteenth century. First to be industrialized on the Continent were Belgium, France, and the German states; the first in North America was the new nation of the United States. Not until after 1850 did the Industrial Revolution spread to the rest of Europe and other parts of the world.

Limitations to Industrialization

In 1815, the Low Countries, France, and the German states were still largely agrarian. During the eighteenth century, some of the Continental countries had experienced developments similar to those of Britain. They, too, had achieved population growth, made agricultural improvements, expanded their cottage industries, and witnessed growth in foreign trade. But whereas Britain's economy began to move in new industrial directions in the 1770s and 1780s, Continental countries lagged behind because they did not share some of the advantages that had made Britain's Industrial Revolution possible. Lack of good roads and problems with river transit made transportation difficult. Toll stations on important rivers and customs barriers along state boundaries increased the costs and prices of goods. Guild restrictions were also more prevalent, creating impediments that pioneer industrialists in Britain did not have to face. Finally, Continental entrepreneurs were generally less enterprising than their British counterparts and tended to adhere to traditional business attitudes, such as a dislike of competition, a high regard for family security coupled with an unwillingness to take risks in investment, and an excessive worship of thriftiness.

One additional factor also affected most of the Continent between 1790 and 1812: the upheavals associated with the wars of the French revolutionary and Napoleonic eras. Disruption of regular communications between Britain and the Continent made it difficult for Continental countries to keep up with the new British technology. Moreover, the wars wreaked havoc with trade, caused much physical destruction and loss of manpower, weakened currencies, and led to political and social instability. Napoleon's Continental System helped ruin a number of hitherto prosperous ports. The elimination of European markets for British textiles did temporarily revive the woolen industry in France and Belgium and stimulated textile manufacturing along the Rhine and in Silesia. After 1815, however, when cheap British goods again flooded European markets, the European textile industry suffered.

In the long run, the revolutionary and Napoleonic wars created an additional obstacle to rapid industrialization by widening the gap between British and Continental industrial machinery. By 1815, after Napoleon had finally been defeated and normal communication between Britain and the Continent had been restored, British industrial equip-

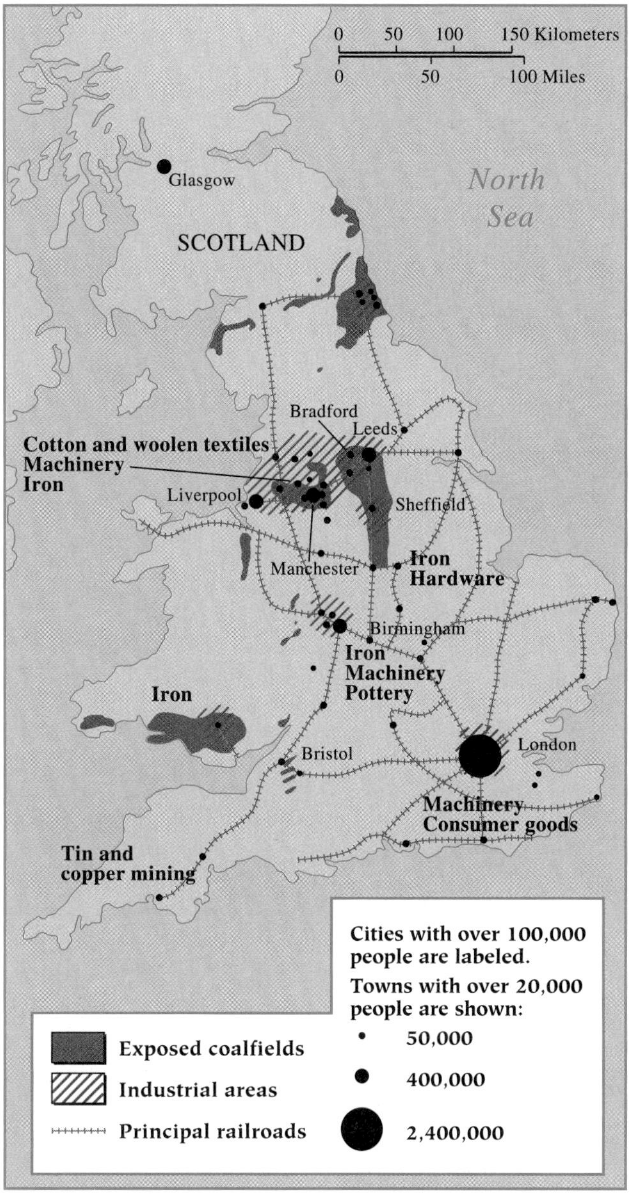

Map 20.1 The Industrial Revolution in Britain. The Industrial Revolution began in the mid-1700s. Increased food production, rapid population growth, higher incomes, plentiful capital, solid banking and financial institutions, an abundance of mineral resources, and easy transport all furthered the process, making the country the world's wealthiest by 1850. ■ How well does the railroad system connect important British industrial areas?

ment had grown larger and become more expensive. As a result, self-financed family enterprises were either unable or unwilling to raise the amount of capital necessary to modernize by investing in the latest equipment. Instead, most entrepreneurs in France, Belgium, and Germany initially chose to invest in used machines and less productive mills. Consequently, industrialization on the Continent faced numerous hurdles, and as it proceeded in earnest after 1815, it did so along lines that were somewhat different from Britain's.

Lack of technical knowledge was initially a major obstacle to industrialization. But the Continental countries possessed an advantage here; they could simply borrow British techniques and practices. Of course, the British tried to prevent that. Until 1825, British artisans were prohibited from leaving the country; until 1842, the export of important machinery and machine parts, especially for textile production, was forbidden. Nevertheless, the British were not able to control this situation by legislation. Already by 1825, there were at least two-thousand skilled British mechanics on the Continent, and British equipment was also being sold abroad, legally or illegally.

Although many Britons who went abroad to sell their skills were simply skilled mechanics, a number of them were accomplished entrepreneurs who had managerial as well as technical skills. John Cockerill, for example, was an aggressive businessman who established a highly profitable industrial plant at Seraing near Liège in southern Belgium in 1817. Cockerill thought nothing of pirating the innovations of other British industrialists to further his own factories. Aware of their importance, British technicians abroad were often contentious and arrogant, arousing the anger of Continental industrialists. Fritz Harkort, who initiated the engineering industry in Germany, once exclaimed that he could scarcely wait for Germans to be trained "so that the Englishmen could all be whipped out: we must even now tread softly with them, for they're only too quick to speak of quitting if one does so little as not look at them in a friendly fashion."[5]

Gradually, the Continent achieved technological independence as local people learned all the skills their British teachers had to offer. By the 1840s, a new generation of skilled mechanics from Belgium and France was spreading their knowledge east and south, playing the same role that the British had earlier. Even more important, however, Continental countries, especially France and the German states, began to establish a wide range of technical schools to train engineers and mechanics.

That government played an important role in this regard brings us to a second difference between British and Continental industrialization. Governments in most of the Continental countries were accustomed to playing a significant role in economic affairs. Furthering the development of industrialization was a logical extension of that attitude. Hence governments provided for the costs of technical education, awarded grants to inventors and foreign entrepreneurs, exempted foreign industrial equipment from import duties, and in some places even financed factories. Of equal if not greater importance in the long run, governments actively bore much of the cost of building roads and canals, deepening and widening river channels, and constructing railroads. By 1850, a network of iron rails had spread across Europe, although only Germany and Belgium had completed major parts of their systems by that time (see Map 20.2). Even though European markets did not feel the real impact of the railroad until after 1850, railroad construction itself in the 1830s and 1840s gave great impetus to the metalworking and engineering industries.

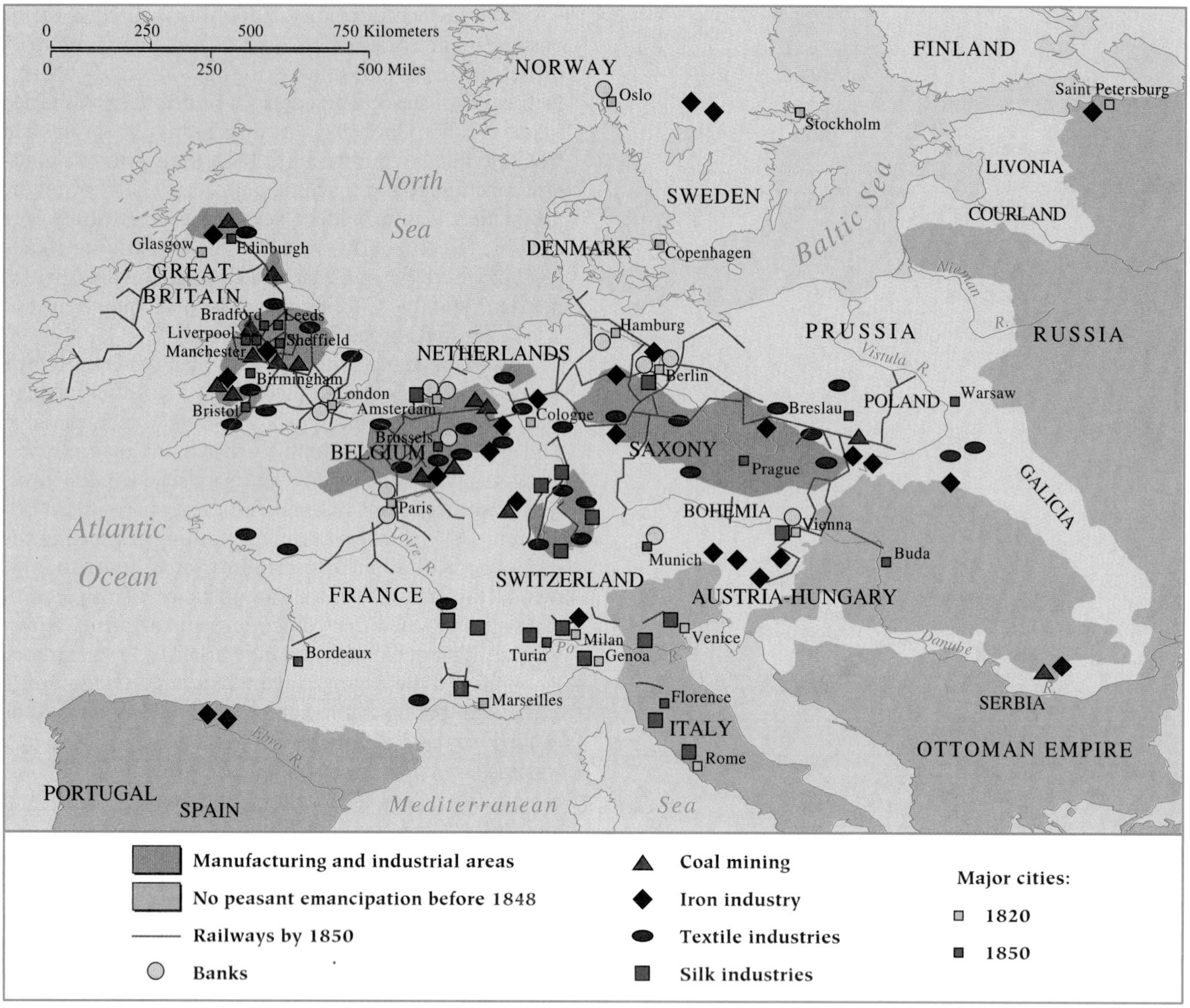

Map 20.2 The Industrialization of Europe by 1850. Great Britain was Europe's first industrialized country; however, by the middle of the nineteenth century, several regions on the Continent had made significant advances in industrialization, especially in Belgium, France, and the German states. ■ What reasons could explain why coal mining and iron industries are densely clustered in manufacturing and industrial areas?

Governments on the Continent also used tariffs to further industrialization. After 1815, cheap British goods flooded Continental markets. The French responded with high tariffs to protect their fledgling industries. The most systematic exposition for the use of tariffs, however, was made by a German writer, Friedrich List (1789–1846), who emigrated to America and returned to Germany as a United States consul. In his *National System of Political Economy,* written in 1844, List advocated a rapid and large-scale program of industrialization as the surest path to develop a nation's strength. To assure that path to industrialization, he felt that a nation must use protective tariffs. If countries followed the British policy of free trade, then cheaper British goods would inundate national markets and destroy infant industries before they had a chance to grow. Germany, he insisted, could not compete with Britain without protective tariffs.

A third significant difference between British and Continental industrialization was the role of the joint-stock investment bank on the Continent. Such banks mobilized the savings of thousands of small and large investors, creating a supply of capital that could then be plowed back into industry. Previously, Continental banks had been mostly merchant or private banks, but in the 1830s two Belgian banks, the Société Générale and the Banque de Belgique, took a new approach. By accepting savings from many depositors, they developed large capital resources that they invested on a large scale in railroads, mining, and heavy industry. Shareholders in these joint-stock corporations had limited liability; they could be held responsible only for the amount of their investment.

Similar institutions emerged in France and German-speaking lands as well in the 1850s with the establishment of the Crédit Mobilier in France, the Darmstadt Bank in Germany, and the Kreditanstalt in Austria. They, too, took in savings of small investors and bought shares in the new industries. The French consul in Leipzig noted their significance: "Every town and state [in Germany]," he pointed out, "however small it may be, wants its bank and its Crédit Mobilier." These investments were essential to Continental industrialization. By starting with less expensive machines, the British had been able to industrialize largely through the private capital of successful individuals who reinvested their profits. On the Continent, advanced industrial machines necessitated large amounts of capital; joint-stock industrial banks provided it.

Centers of Continental Industrialization

The Industrial Revolution on the Continent occurred in three major centers between 1815 and 1850—Belgium, France, and the German states. Here, too, cotton played an important role, although it was not as significant as heavy industry. France was the Continental leader in the manufacture of cotton goods but still lagged far behind Great Britain. In 1849, France used 64,000 tons of raw cotton, Belgium, 11,000, and Germany, 20,000, whereas Britain used 286,000 tons. Continental cotton factories were older, used less efficient machines, and had less productive labor. In general, Continental technology in the cotton industry was a generation behind Great Britain. But that is not the whole story. With its cheap coal and scarce water, Belgium gravitated toward the use of the steam engine as the major source of power and invested in the new machines. By the mid-1840s, Belgium had the most modern cotton-manufacturing system on the Continent.

The development of cotton manufacturing on the Continent and in Britain differed in two significant ways. Unlike Britain, where cotton manufacturing was mostly centered in Lancashire (in northwestern England) and the Glasgow area of Scotland, cotton mills in France, Germany, and, to a lesser degree, Belgium were dispersed through many regions. Noticeable, too, was the mixture of old and new. The old techniques of the cottage system, such as the use of hand looms, held on much longer. In the French district of Normandy, for example, in 1849, eighty-three mills were still driven by hand or animal power.

As traditional methods persisted alongside the new methods in cotton manufacturing, the new steam engine came to be used primarily in mining and metallurgy on the Continent rather than in textile manufacturing. At first, almost all of the steam engines on the Continent came from Britain; not until the 1820s was a domestic machine industry developed.

In Britain, the Industrial Revolution had been built on the cotton industry; on the Continent, the iron and coal of heavy industry led the way. As in textiles, however, heavy industry on the Continent before 1850 was a mixture of old and new. The adoption of new techniques, such as coke-smelted iron and puddling furnaces, coincided with the expansion of old-type charcoal blast furnaces. Before 1850, Germany lagged significantly behind both Belgium and France in heavy industry, and most German iron manufacturing remained based on old techniques. Not until the 1840s was coke-blast iron produced in the Rhineland. At that time, no one had yet realized the treasure of coal buried in the Ruhr valley. A German official wrote in 1852 that "it is clearly not to be expected that Germany will ever be able to reach the level of production of coal and iron currently attained in England. This is implicit in our far more limited resource endowment." Little did he realize that although the industrial development of Continental Europe was about a generation behind Britain at midcentury, after 1850 an incredibly rapid growth in Continental industry would demonstrate that Britain was not, after all, destined to remain the world's greatest industrial nation.

The Industrial Revolution in the United States

In 1800, the United States was an agrarian society. There were no cities over 100,000, and six out of every seven American workers were farmers. By 1860, however, the population had grown from 5 to 30 million people, larger than Great Britain. Almost half of them lived west of the Appalachian Mountains. The number of states had more than doubled, from sixteen to thirty-four, and nine American cities had over 100,000 in population. Only 50 percent of American workers were farmers. Between 1800 and the eve of the Civil War, the United States had experienced its own Industrial Revolution and the urbanization that accompanied it.

The initial application of machinery to production was accomplished, as in Continental Europe, by borrowing from Great Britain. A British immigrant, Samuel Slater, established the first textile factory using water-powered spinning machines in Rhode Island in 1790. By 1813, factories with power looms copied from British versions were being established. Soon thereafter, however, Americans began to equal or surpass British technical inventions. The Harpers Ferry arsenal, for example, built muskets with interchangeable parts. Because all the individual parts of a musket were identical (for example, all triggers were the same), the final product could be put together quickly and easily; this enabled Americans to avoid the more costly system in which skilled workers fitted together individual parts made separately. The so-called American system reduced costs and revolutionized production by saving labor, important to a society that had few skilled artisans.

Unlike Britain, the United States was a large country. The lack of a good system of internal transportation seemed to limit American economic development by making the transport of goods prohibitively expensive. This deficiency was gradually remedied, however. Thousands of

North Wind Picture Archives

The Steamboat. The steamboat was an important means of transportation for American products and markets. Steamboats like the one shown in this illustration regularly plied the Mississippi, moving the farm products of the Midwest and the southern plantations to markets in New Orleans. After the American Civil War, railroads began to replace steamboats on many routes.

miles of roads and canals were built linking east and west. The steamboat facilitated transportation on the Great Lakes, Atlantic coastal waters, and rivers. It was especially important to the Mississippi valley; by 1860, one thousand steamboats plied that river (see the box on p. 565). Most important of all in the development of the American transportation system was the railroad. Beginning with 100 miles in 1830, by 1860 more than 27,000 miles of railroad track covered the United States. This transportation revolution turned the United States into a single massive market for the manufactured goods of the Northeast, the early center of American industrialization.

Labor for the growing number of factories in this area came primarily from rural New England. The United States did not possess a large number of craftspeople, but it did have a rapidly expanding farm population; its size in the Northeast soon outstripped the available farmland. While some of this excess population, especially men, went west, others, mostly women, found work in the new textile and shoe factories of New England. Indeed, women made up more than 80 percent of the laboring force in the large textile factories. In Massachusetts mill towns, company boarding houses provided rooms for large numbers of young women who worked for several years before marriage. Outside Massachusetts, factory owners sought entire families including children to work in their mills; one mill owner ran this advertisement in a newspaper in Utica, New York: "Wanted: A few sober and industrious families of at least five children each, over the age of eight years, are wanted at the Cotton Factory in Whitestown. Widows with large families would do well to attend this notice." When a decline in rural births threatened to dry up this labor pool in the 1830s and 1840s, European immigrants, especially poor and unskilled Irish, English, Scottish, and Welsh, appeared in large numbers to replace American women and children in the factories.

Women, children, and these immigrants had one thing in common as employees; they were largely unskilled laborers. Unskilled labor pushed American industrialization into a capital-intensive pattern. Factory owners invested heavily in machines that could produce in quantity at the hands of untrained workers. In Britain, the pace of mechanization was never as rapid because Britain's supply of skilled artisans made it more profitable to pursue a labor-intensive economy.

By 1860, the United States was well on its way to being an industrial nation. In the Northeast, the most industrialized section of the country, per capita income was 40 percent higher than the national average. Diets, it has been argued, were better and more varied; machine-made clothing was more abundant. Industrialization did not necessarily lessen economic disparities, however. Despite a growing belief in a myth of social mobility based on equality of economic opportunity, the reality was that the richest 10 percent of the population in the cities held 70 to 80 percent of the wealth, compared to 50 percent in 1800. Nevertheless, American historians generally argue that while

"S-t-e-a-m-boat a-coming!"

Steamboats and railroads were crucial elements in a transportation revolution that enabled industrialists to expand markets by shipping goods cheaply and efficiently. At the same time, these marvels of technology aroused a sense of power and excitement that was an important aspect of the triumph of industrialization. The American novelist Mark Twain captured this sense of excitement in this selection from *Life on the Mississippi*.

Mark Twain, Life on the Mississippi

After all these years I can picture that old time to myself now, just as it was then: the white town drowsing in the sunshine of a summer's morning; the streets empty, or pretty nearly so; one or two clerks sitting in front of the Water street stores, with their splint-bottomed chairs tilted back against the walls, chins on breasts, hats slouched over their faces, asleep; . . . two or three lonely little freight piles scattered about the "levee"; a pile of "skids" on the slope of the stone-paved wharf, and the fragrant town drunkard asleep in the shadow of them; . . . the great Mississippi, the majestic, the magnificent Mississippi, rolling its mile-wide along, shining in the sun; the dense forest away on the other side; the "point" above the town, and the "point" below, bounding the river glimpse and turning it into a sort of sea, and withal a very still and brilliant and lonely one. Presently a film of dark smoke appears above on those remote "points"; instantly a negro drayman, famous for his quick eye and prodigious voice, lifts up to cry, "S-t-e-a-m-boat a-coming!" and the scene changes! The town drunkard stirs, the clerks wake up, a furious clatter of drays follows, every house and store pours out a human contribution, and all in a twinkling the dead town [Hannibal, Missouri] is alive and moving. Drays, carts, men, boys, all go hurrying from many quarters to a common center, the wharf. Assembled there, the people fasten their eyes upon the coming boat as upon a wonder they are seeing for the first time. And the boat is rather a handsome sight, too. She is long and sharp and trim and pretty; she has two tall, fancy-topped chimneys, with a gilded device of some kind swung between them; a fanciful pilot-house, all glass and "ginger bread," perched on top of the "texas" deck behind them; the paddle-boxes are gorgeous with a picture or with gilded rays above the boat's name; the boiler deck, the hurricane deck, and the texas deck are fenced and ornamented with clean white railings; there is a flag gallantly flying from the jack-staff; the furnace doors are open and the fires glaring bravely; the upper decks are black with passengers; the captain stands by the big bell, calm, imposing, the envy of all; great volumes of the blackest smoke are rolling and tumbling out of the chimneys—a husbanded grandeur created with a bit of pitch pine just before arriving at a town; the crew are grouped on the forecastle; the broad stage is run far out over the port bow, and an envied deck-hand stands picturesquely on the end of it with a coil of rope in his hand; the pent steam is screaming through the gaugecocks; the captain lifts his hand, a bell rings, the wheels stop; then they turn back, churning the water to foam, and the steam is at rest. Then such a scramble as there is to get aboard, and to get ashore, and to take in freight and discharge freight, all at one and the same time; and such a yelling and cursing as the mates facilitate it all with! Ten minutes later the steamer is under way again, with no flag on the jack-staff and no black smoke issuing from the chimneys. After ten more minutes the town is dead again, and the town drunkard asleep by the skids once more.

the rich got richer, the poor, thanks to an increase in their purchasing power, did not get poorer.

Limiting the Spread of Industrialization in the Nonindustrialized World

Before 1870, the industrialization that had developed in western and central Europe and the United States did not extend in any significant way to the rest of the world. Even in eastern Europe, industrialization lagged far behind. Russia, for example, remained largely rural and agricultural, and its autocratic rulers kept the peasants in serfdom. There was not much of a middle class, and the tsarist regime, fearful of change, preferred to import industrial goods in return for the export of raw materials, such as grain and timber. Russia would not have its Industrial Revolution until the end of the nineteenth century.

In other parts of the world where they had established control, newly industrialized European states pursued a deliberate policy of preventing the growth of mechanized industry. A good example is India. In the eighteenth century, India had become one of the world's greatest exporters of cotton cloth produced by hand labor. In the first half of the nineteenth century, much of India fell under the control of the British East India Company (see Chapter 24). With British control came inexpensive British factory-produced textiles, and soon thousands of Indian spinners and hand-loom weavers were unemployed. British policy encouraged Indians to export their raw materials while buying British-made goods. Although some limited forms of industrial factories for making textiles and jute (used in making rope) were opened in India in the 1850s, a lack of local capital and the advantages given to British imports limited the growth of new manufacturing operations. India, then, provides an excellent example of how some of the rapidly industrializing nations of Europe worked to deliberately thwart the spread of the Industrial Revolution to their colonial dominions.

The Social Impact of the Industrial Revolution

Eventually, the Industrial Revolution radically altered the social life of Europe and the world. Although much of Europe remained bound by its traditional ways, already in the first half of the nineteenth century, the social impact of the Industrial Revolution was being felt, and future avenues of growth were becoming apparent. Vast changes in the number of people and where they lived were already dramatically evident.

Population Growth

Population increases had already begun in the eighteenth century, but they became dramatic in the nineteenth. They were also easier to discern because record keeping became more accurate. In the nineteenth century, governments began to take periodic censuses and systematically collect precise data on births, deaths, and marriages. In Britain, for example, the first census was taken in 1801, and a systematic registration of births, deaths, and marriages was begun in 1836. In 1750, the total European population stood at an estimated 140 million; by 1800, it had increased to 187 million and by 1850 to 266 million, almost twice its 1750 level.

This population explosion cannot be explained by a higher birthrate, for birthrates were declining after 1790. Between 1790 and 1850, Germany's birthrate dropped from 40 per 1,000 to 36.1; Great Britain's, from 35.4 to 32.6; and France's, from 32.5 to 26.7. The key to the expansion of population was the decline in death rates evident throughout Europe. Historians now believe that two major causes explain this decline. There was a drop in the number of deaths from famines, epidemics, and war. Major epidemic diseases, such as plague and smallpox, declined noticeably, although small-scale epidemics broke out now and then. The ordinary death rate also declined as a general increase in the food supply, already evident in the agricultural revolution of Britain in the late eighteenth century, spread to more areas. More food enabled a greater number of people to be better fed and therefore more resistant to disease. Famine largely disappeared from western Europe, although there were dramatic exceptions in isolated areas, Ireland being the most significant.

Although industrialization itself did not cause population growth, industrialized areas did experience a change in the composition of the population. By 1850, the proportion of the active population involved in manufacturing, mining, or building had risen to 48 percent in Britain, 37 percent in Belgium, and 27 percent in France. But the actual areas of industrialization in 1850 were minimal, being concentrated in northern and central England, northern France, Belgium, and sections of western and eastern Germany. One author characterized them as "islands in an agricultural sea."

This minimal industrialization in light of the growing population meant severe congestion in the countryside, where ever-larger numbers of people divided the same amount of land into ever-smaller plots and also gave rise to an ever-increasing mass of landless peasants. Overpopulation, especially noticeable in parts of France, northern Spain, southern Germany, Sweden, and Ireland, magnified the already existing problem of rural poverty. In Ireland, it produced the century's greatest catastrophe.

THE GREAT HUNGER

Ireland was one of the most oppressed areas in western Europe. The predominantly Catholic peasant population rented land from mostly absentee British Protestant landlords whose primary concern was collecting their rents. Irish peasants lived in mud hovels in desperate poverty. The cultivation of the potato, a nutritious and relatively easy food to grow that produced three times as much food per acre as grain, gave Irish peasants a basic staple that enabled them to survive and even expand in numbers. As only an acre or two of potatoes was sufficient to feed a family, Irish men and women married earlier than elsewhere and started having children earlier as well. This led to significant growth in the population. Between 1781 and 1845, the Irish population doubled from four to eight million. Probably half of this population depended on the potato for survival. In the summer of 1845, the potato crop in Ireland was struck by blight due to a fungus that turned the potatoes black. Between 1845 and 1851, the Great Famine decimated the Irish population (see the box on p. 567). Over one million died of starvation and disease, and almost two million emigrated to the United States and Britain. Of all the European nations, only Ireland had a declining population in the nineteenth century. But other countries, too, faced problems of dire poverty and declining standards of living as their populations exploded.

The flight of so many Irish to America reminds us that the traditional safety valve for overpopulation has always been emigration. Between 1821 and 1850, the number of emigrants from Europe averaged about 110,000 a year. Most of these emigrants came from places like Ireland and southern Germany, where peasant life had been reduced to marginal existence. Times of agrarian crisis resulted in great waves of emigration. Bad harvests in Europe in 1846–1847 (such as the catastrophe in Ireland) produced massive numbers of emigrants. In addition to the estimated 1.6 million from Ireland, for example, 935,000 people left Germany between 1847 and 1854. More often than emigrating, however, the rural masses sought a solution to their poverty by moving to towns and cities within their own countries to find work. It should not astonish us, then, that the first half of the nineteenth century was a period of rapid urbanization.

The Growth of Cities

Although the Western world would not become a predominantly urban society until the twentieth century, cities and towns had already grown dramatically in the first half of the nineteenth century, a phenomenon related to industrialization. Cities had traditionally been centers for

The Great Irish Famine

The Great Irish Famine was one of the nineteenth century's worst natural catastrophes. Overly dependent on a single crop, the Irish were decimated by the potato blight. In this selection, an Irish nationalist reported what he had witnessed in Galway in 1847.

John Mitchel, The Last Conquest of Ireland

In the depth of winter we traveled to Galway, through the very center of that fertile island, and saw sights that will never wholly leave the eyes that beheld them—cowering wretches, almost naked in the savage weather, prowling in turnip-fields, and endeavoring to grub up roots which had been left, but running to hide as the mail-coach rolled by;—very large fields where small farms had been "consolidated," showing dark bars of fresh mold running through them where the ditches had been leveled;—groups and families, sitting or wandering on the high-road, with failing steps and dim patient eyes, gazing hopelessly into infinite darkness; before them, around them, above them, nothing but darkness and despair—parties of tall brawny men, once the flower of Meath and Galway, stalking by with a fierce but vacant scowl; as if they knew that all this ought not to be, but knew not whom to blame, saw none whom they could rend in their wrath. . . . Around those farmhouses which were still inhabited were to be seen hardly any stacks of grain; the poor-rate collector, the rent agent, the county-cess collector had carried it off; and sometimes I could see in front of the cottages little children leaning against a fence when the sun shone out—for they could not stand—their limbs fleshless, their bodies half naked, their faces bloated yet wrinkled, and of a pale greenish hue,—children who would never, it was too plain, grow up to be men and women.

princely courts, government and military offices, churches, and commerce. By 1850, especially in Great Britain and Belgium, cities were rapidly becoming places for manufacturing and industry. With the steam engine, entrepreneurs could locate their manufacturing plants in urban centers where they had ready access to transportation facilities and unemployed people from the country looking for work.

In 1800, Great Britain had one major city, London, with a population of one million, and six cities between 50,000 and 100,000. Fifty years later, London's population had swelled to 2,363,000, and there were nine cities over 100,000 and eighteen cities with populations between 50,000 and 100,000. All together, these twenty-eight cities accounted for 5.7 million, or one-fifth, of the total British

A New Industrial Town. Cities and towns grew dramatically in Britain in the first half of the nineteenth century, largely as a result of industrialization. Pictured here is Saltaire, a model textile factory and town founded near Bradford by Titus Salt in 1851. To facilitate the transportation of goods, the town was built on the Leeds and Liverpool canals.

population. When the populations of cities under 50,000 are added to this total, we realize that more than 50 percent of the British population lived in towns and cities by 1850. Britain was forced to become a food importer rather than an exporter as the number of people involved in agriculture declined to 20 percent of the population.

Urban populations also grew on the Continent, but less dramatically. Paris had 547,000 inhabitants in 1800, but only two other French cities had populations of 100,000: Lyons and Marseilles. In 1851, Paris had grown to a million while Lyons and Marseilles were still under 200,000. German and Austrian lands had only three cities with over 100,000 inhabitants (Vienna had 247,000) in 1800; fifty years later, there were only five, but Vienna had grown to 440,000. As these figures show, urbanization did not proceed as rapidly here as in Britain; of course, neither had industrialization. Even in Belgium, the most heavily industrialized country on the Continent, almost 50 percent of the male workforce was still engaged in agriculture by mid-century.

URBAN LIVING CONDITIONS IN THE EARLY INDUSTRIAL REVOLUTION

The dramatic growth of cities in the first half of the nineteenth century produced miserable living conditions for many of the inhabitants. Of course, the quality of life had been poor for centuries for many people in European cities, but the rapid urbanization associated with the Industrial Revolution intensified the problems in the first half of the nineteenth century and made these wretched conditions all the more apparent. City authorities of whatever kind either felt little responsibility for these conditions or more frequently did not have the skills to cope with the complex new problems associated with such rapidly growing populations. City authorities might also often be factory owners who possessed little or no tradition of public service or public responsibility.

Wealthy, middle-class inhabitants, as usual, insulated themselves as best they could, often living in suburbs or the outer ring of the city, where they could have individual houses and gardens. In the inner ring of the city stood the small row houses, some with gardens, of the artisans and the lower middle class. Finally, located in the center of most industrial towns were the row houses of the industrial workers. This report on working-class housing in the British city of Birmingham in 1843 gives an idea of the general conditions they faced:

> The courts [of working-class row houses] are extremely numerous; . . . a very large portion of the poorer classes of the inhabitants reside in them. . . . The courts vary in the number of the houses which they contain, from four to twenty, and

Slums of Industrial London. Industrialization and rapid urban growth produced dreadful living conditions in many nineteenth-century cities. Filled with garbage and human waste, cities often smelled terrible and were extremely unhealthy. This drawing by Gustave Doré shows a London slum district overshadowed by rail viaducts.

Billy Rose Theatre Collection, the New York Public Library, Astor Lenox and Tilden Foundations

> most of these houses are three stories high, and built, as it is termed, back to back. There is a wash-house, an ash-pit, and a privy at the end, or on one side of the court, and not unfrequently one or more pigsties and heaps of manure. Generally speaking, the privies in the old courts are in a most filthy condition. Many which we have inspected were in a state which renders it impossible for us to conceive how they could be used; they were without doors and overflowing with filth.

The people who lived in such houses were actually the fortunate; the truly unfortunate were those forced to live in cellars. One reformer asked, "How can a hole underground of from 12 to 15 feet square admit of ventilation so as to fit it for a human habitation?" Rooms were not large and were frequently overcrowded, as this government report of 1838 revealed: "I entered several of the tenements. In one of them, on the ground floor, I found six persons occupying a very small room, two in bed, ill with fever. In the room above this were two more persons in one bed ill with fever." Another report said: "There were 63 families where there were at least five persons to one bed; and there were some in which even six were packed in one bed, lying at the top and bottom—children and adults."[6]

Sanitary conditions in these towns were appalling. Due to the lack of municipal direction, city streets were often used as sewers and open drains: "In the center of this street is a gutter, into which potato parings, the refuse of animal and vegetable matters of all kinds, the dirty water from the washing of clothes and of the houses, are all poured, and there they stagnate and putrefy."[7] Unable to deal with human excrement, cities in the new industrial era smelled horrible and were extraordinarily unhealthy. Towns and cities were fundamentally death traps. As deaths outnumbered births in most large cities in the first half of the nineteenth century, only a constant influx of people from the country kept them alive and growing.

Adding to the deterioration of urban life was the adulteration of food. Consumers were defrauded in a variety of ways: alum was added to make bread look white and hence more expensive; beer and milk were watered down; and red lead, despite its poisonous qualities, was substituted for pepper. The government refused to intervene; a parliamentary committee stated that "more benefit is likely to result from the effects of a free competition . . . than can be expected to result from any regulations." It was not until 1875 that an effective food and drugs act was passed in Britain.

Our knowledge of the pathetic conditions in the early industrial cities is largely derived from an abundance of social investigations. Such investigations began in France in the 1820s. In Britain, the Poor Law Commissioners produced detailed reports. The investigators were often struck by the physically and morally debilitating effects of urban industrial life on the poor. They observed, for example, that young working-class men were considerably shorter and scrawnier than the sons of middle-class families and much more subject to disease. They were especially alarmed by what they considered the moral consequences of such living conditions: prostitution, crime, and sexual immoralities, all of which they saw as the effect of such squalid lives.

URBAN REFORMERS

To many of the well-to-do middle classes, this situation presented a clear danger to society. Were not these masses of workers, sunk in crime, disease, and immorality, a potential threat to their own well-being? Might not the masses be organized and used by unscrupulous demagogues to overthrow the established order? One of the most eloquent British reformers of the 1830s and 1840s, James Kay-Shuttleworth, described them as "volcanic elements, by whose explosive violence the structure of society may be destroyed." Another observer spoke more contemptuously in 1850:

> They live precisely like brutes, to gratify . . . the appetites of their uncultivated bodies, and then die, to go they have never thought, cared, or wondered whither. . . . Brought up in the darkness of barbarism, they have no idea that it is possible for them to attain any higher condition; they are not even sentient enough to desire to change their situation. . . . They eat, drink, breed, work and die; and . . . the richer and more intelligent classes are obliged to guard them with police.[8]

Some observers were less arrogant, however, and wondered if the workers should be held responsible for their fate.

One of the best of a new breed of urban reformers was Edwin Chadwick (1800–1890). With a background in law, Chadwick became obsessed with eliminating the poverty and squalor of the metropolitan areas. He became a civil servant and was soon appointed to a number of government investigatory commissions. As secretary of the Poor Law Commission, he initiated a passionate search for detailed facts about the living conditions of the working classes. After three years of investigation, Chadwick summarized the results in his *Report on the Condition of the Labouring Population of Great Britain,* published in 1842. In it, he concluded that "the various forms of epidemic, endemic, and other disease" were directly caused by the "atmospheric impurities produced by decomposing animal and vegetable substances, by damp and filth, and close overcrowded dwellings [prevailing] amongst the population in every part of the kingdom." Such conditions, he argued, could be eliminated. As to the means: "The primary and most important measures, and at the same time the most practicable, and within the recognized province of public administration, are drainage, the removal of all refuse of habitations, streets, and roads, and the improvement of the supplies of water."[9] In other words, Chadwick was advocating a system of modern sanitary reforms consisting of efficient sewers and a supply of piped water. Six years after his report and largely due to his efforts, Britain's first Public Health Act created the National Board of Health, empowered to form local boards that would establish modern sanitary systems.

Many middle-class citizens were quite willing to support the public health reforms of men like Chadwick because of their fear of cholera. Outbreaks of this deadly disease had ravaged Europe in the early 1830s and late 1840s and were especially rampant in the overcrowded cities. As city authorities and wealthier residents became convinced that filthy conditions helped spread the disease, they began to support the call for new public health measures.

New Social Classes: The Industrial Middle Class

The rise of industrial capitalism produced a new middle-class group. The bourgeoisie or middle class was not new; it had existed since the emergence of cities in the Middle Ages. Originally, the bourgeois was the burgher or town dweller, active as a merchant, official, artisan, lawyer, or scholar, who enjoyed a special set of rights from the charter of the town. As wealthy townspeople bought land, the original meaning of the word *bourgeois* became lost, and the term came to include people involved in commerce, industry, and banking as well as professionals, such as lawyers, teachers, physicians, and government officials at various levels. At the lower end of the economic scale were master craftspeople and shopkeepers.

Lest we make the industrial middle class too much of an abstraction, we need to look at who the new industrial entrepreneurs actually were. These were the people who constructed the factories, purchased the machines, and figured out where the markets were. Their qualities included resourcefulness, single-mindedness, resolution, initiative, vision, ambition, and often, of course, greed. As Jedediah Strutt, the cotton manufacturer said, the "getting of money . . . is the main business of the life of men."

But this was not an easy task. The early industrial entrepreneurs were called on to superintend an enormous array of functions that are handled today by teams of managers; they raised capital, determined markets, set company objectives, organized the factory and its labor, and trained supervisors who could act for them. The opportunities for making money were great, but the risks were also tremendous. The cotton trade, for example, which was so important to the early Industrial Revolution, was intensely competitive. Only through constant expansion could one feel secure, so early entrepreneurs reinvested most of their initial profits. Fear of bankruptcy was constant, especially among small firms. Furthermore, most early industrial enterprises were small. Even by the 1840s, only 10 percent of British industrial firms employed more than five thousand workers; 43 percent had fewer than one hundred. As entrepreneurs went bankrupt, new people could enter the race for profits, especially since the initial outlay required was not gigantic. In 1816, only one mill in five in the important industrial city of Manchester was in the hands of its original owner.

The social origins of industrial entrepreneurs were incredibly diverse. Many of the most successful came from a mercantile background. Three London merchants, for example, founded a successful ironworks in Wales that owned eight steam engines and employed five thousand men. In Britain, land and domestic industry were often interdependent. Joshua Fielden, for example, acquired sufficient capital to establish a factory by running a family sheep farm while working looms in the farmhouse. Intelligent, clever, and ambitious apprentices who had learned their trades well could also strike it rich. William Radcliffe's family engaged in agriculture and spinning and weaving at home; he learned quickly how to succeed:

> Availing myself of the improvements that came out while I was in my teens . . . with my little savings and a practical knowledge of every process from the cotton bag to the piece of cloth . . . I was ready to commence business for myself and by the year 1789 I was well established and employed many hands both in spinning and weaving as a master manufacturer.[10]

By 1801, Radcliffe was operating a factory employing a thousand workers.

Members of dissenting religious minorities were often prominent among the early industrial leaders of Britain. The Darbys and Lloyds, who were iron manufacturers; the Barclays and Lloyds, who were bankers; and the Trumans and Perkins, who were brewers, were all Quakers. These were expensive trades and depended on the financial support that coreligionists in religious minorities provided for each other. Most historians believe that a major reason members of these religious minorities were so prominent in business was that they lacked other opportunities. Legally excluded from many public offices, they directed their ambitions into the new industrial capitalism.

It is interesting to note that in Britain in particular, aristocrats also became entrepreneurs. The Lambtons in Northumberland, the Curwens in Cumberland, the Norfolks in Yorkshire, and the Dudleys in Staffordshire all invested in mining enterprises. This close relationship between land and industry helped Britain assume the leadership role in the early Industrial Revolution.

By 1850, in Britain at least, the kind of traditional entrepreneurship that had created the Industrial Revolution was declining and was being replaced by a new business aristocracy. This new generation of entrepreneurs stemmed from the professional and industrial middle classes, especially as sons inherited the successful businesses established by their fathers. It must not be forgotten, however, that even after 1850, a large number of small businesses existed in Britain, and some were still being founded by people from humble backgrounds. Indeed, the age of large-scale corporate capitalism did not begin until the 1890s (see Chapter 23).

Increasingly, the new industrial entrepreneurs—the bankers and owners of factories and mines—came to amass much wealth and play an important role alongside the traditional landed elites of their societies. The Industrial Revolution began at a time when the preindustrial agrarian world was still largely dominated by landed elites. As the new bourgeoisie bought great estates and acquired social respectability, they also sought political power, and in the course of the nineteenth century, their wealthiest members would merge with those old elites.

New Social Classes: Workers in the Industrial Age

At the same time that the members of the industrial middle class were seeking to reduce the barriers between themselves and the landed elite, they also were trying to separate themselves from the laboring classes below them. The working class was actually a mixture of groups in the first half of the nineteenth century. In the course of the century, factory workers would form an industrial proletariat, but in the first half of that century, they did not constitute a majority of the working class in any major city, even in Britain. According to the 1851 census in Britain, there were 1.8 million agricultural laborers and 1 million domestic servants but only 811,000 workers in the cotton and woolen industries. Even one-third of these were still working in small workshops or in their own homes.

In the cities, artisans or craftspeople remained the largest group of urban workers during the first half of the nineteenth century. They worked in numerous small industries, such as shoemaking, glovemaking, bookbinding, printing, and bricklaying. Some craftspeople formed a kind of aristocracy of labor, especially those employed in such luxury trades as coachbuilding and clockmaking, who earned higher wages than others. Artisans were not factory workers; they were traditionally organized in guilds, where they passed on their skills to apprentices. But guilds were increasingly losing their power, especially in industrialized countries. Fearful of losing out to the new factories that could produce goods more cheaply, artisans tended to support movements against industrialization. Industrialists welcomed the decline of skilled craftspeople, as one perceptive old tailor realized in telling his life story:

> It is upwards of 30 years since I first went to work at the tailoring trade in London. . . . I continued working for the honorable trade and belonging to the Society [for tailors] for about 15 years. My weekly earnings then averaged £1 16s. a week while I was at work, and for several years I was seldom out of work. . . . No one could have been happier than I was. . . . But then, with my sight defective . . . I could get no employment at the honorable trade, and that was the ruin of me entirely; for working there, of course, I got "scratched" from the trade society, and so lost all hope of being provided for by them in my helplessness. The workshop . . . was about seven feet square, and so low, that as you [sat] on the floor you could touch the ceiling with the tip of your finger. In this place seven of us worked. [The master] paid little more than half the regular wages, and employed such men as myself—only those who couldn't get anything better to do. . . . I don't think my wages there averaged above 12s. a week. . . . I am convinced I lost my eyesight by working in that cheap shop. . . . It is by the ruin of such men as me that these masters are enabled to undersell the better shops. . . . That's the way, sir, the cheap clothes is produced, by making blind beggars of the workmen, like myself, and throwing us on the parish in our old age.[11]

Servants also formed another large group of urban workers, especially in major cities like London and Paris. Many were women from the countryside who became utterly dependent on their upper- and middle-class employers.

WORKING CONDITIONS FOR THE INDUSTRIAL WORKING CLASS

Workers in the new industrial factories also faced wretched working conditions. We have already observed the psychological traumas workers experienced from their employers' efforts to break old preindustrial work patterns and create a well-disciplined labor force. But what were the physical conditions of the factories?

Unquestionably, in the early decades of the Industrial Revolution, "places of work," as early factories were called, were dreadful. Work hours ranged from twelve to sixteen hours a day, six days a week, with a half hour for lunch and dinner. There was no security of employment and no minimum wage. The worst conditions were in the cotton mills, where temperatures were especially debilitating. One report noted that "in the cotton-spinning work, these creatures are kept, fourteen hours in each day, locked up, summer and winter, in a heat of from eighty to eighty-four degrees." Mills were also dirty, dusty, and unhealthy:

> Not only is there not a breath of sweet air in these truly infernal scenes, but . . . there is the abominable and pernicious stink of the gas to assist in the murderous effects of the heat. In addition to the noxious effluvia of the gas, mixed with the steam, there are the dust, and what is called cotton-flyings or fuz, which the unfortunate creatures have to inhale; and . . . the notorious fact is that well constitutioned men are rendered old and past labor at forty years of age, and that children are rendered decrepit and deformed, and thousands upon thousands of them slaughtered by consumptions [lung diseases], before they arrive at the age of sixteen.[12]

Thus ran a report on working conditions in the cotton industry in 1824.

Conditions in the coal mines were also harsh. The introduction of steam power meant only that steam-powered engines mechanically lifted coal to the top. Inside the mines, men still bore the burden of digging the coal out while horses, mules, women, and children hauled coal carts on rails to the lift. Dangers abounded in coal mines; cave-ins, explosions, and gas fumes (called "bad air") were a way of life. The cramped conditions—tunnels often did not exceed 3 or 4 feet in height—and constant dampness in the mines resulted in deformed bodies and ruined lungs.

Both children and women were employed in large numbers in early factories and mines. Children had been an important part of the family economy in preindustrial times, working in the fields or carding and spinning wool at home with the growth of the cottage industry. In the Industrial Revolution, however, child labor was exploited more than ever and in a considerably more systematic fashion (see the boxes on pp. 572–573). The owners of cotton factories appreciated certain features of child labor. Children had an especially delicate touch as spinners of cotton. Their smaller size made it easier for them to crawl under machines to gather loose cotton. Moreover, children were more easily broken to factory work. Above all, children

Child Labor: Discipline in the Textile Mills

Child labor was not new, but in the early Industrial Revolution, it was exploited more systematically. These selections are taken from the Report of Sadler's Committee, which was commissioned in 1832 to inquire into the condition of child factory workers.

How They Kept the Children Awake

It is a very frequent thing at Mr. Marshall's [at Shrewsbury] where the least children were employed (for there were plenty working at six years of age), for Mr. Horseman to start the mill earlier in the morning than he formerly did; and provided a child should be drowsy, the overlooker walks round the room with a stick in his hand, and he touches that child on the shoulder, and says, "Come here." In a corner of the room there is an iron cistern; it is filled with water; he takes this boy, and takes him up by the legs, and dips him over head in the cistern, and sends him to work for the remainder of the day. . . .

What means were taken to keep the children to their work?—Sometimes they would tap them over the head, or nip them over the nose, or give them a pinch of snuff, or throw water in their faces, or pull them off where they were, and job them about to keep them waking.

The Sadistic Overlooker

Samuel Downe, age 29, factory worker living near Leeds; at the age of about ten began work at Mr. Marshall's mills at Shrewsbury, where the customary hours when work was brisk were generally 5 A.M. to 8 P.M., sometimes from 5:30 A.M. to 8 or 9:

What means were taken to keep the children awake and vigilant, especially at the termination of such a day's labor as you have described?—There was generally a blow or a box, or a tap with a strap, or sometimes the hand.

Have you yourself been strapped?—Yes, most severely, till I could not bear to sit upon a chair without having pillows, and through that I left. I was strapped both on my own legs, and then I was put upon a man's back, and then strapped and buckled with two straps to an iron pillar, and flogged, and all by one overlooker; after that he took a piece of tow, and twisted it in the shape of a cord, and put it in my mouth, and tied it behind my head.

He gagged you?—Yes; and then he orders me to run round a part of the machinery where he was overlooker, and he stood at one end, and every time I came there he struck me with a stick, which I believe was an ash plant, and which he generally carried in his hand, and sometimes he hit me, and sometimes he did not; and one of the men in the room came and begged me off, and that he let me go, and not beat me any more, and consequently he did.

You have been beaten with extraordinary severity?—Yes, I was beaten so that I had not power to cry at all, or hardly speak at one time. What age were you at that time?—Between 10 and 11.

represented a cheap supply of labor. In 1821, just about half of the British population was under twenty years of age. Hence children made up a particularly abundant supply of labor, and they were paid only about one-sixth to one-third of what a man was paid. In the cotton factories in 1838, children under eighteen made up 29 percent of the total workforce; children as young as seven worked twelve to fifteen hours per day, six days a week, in cotton mills.

Especially terrible in the early Industrial Revolution was the use of so-called pauper apprentices. These were orphans or children abandoned by their parents who had wound up in the care of local parishes. To save on their upkeep, parish officials found it convenient to apprentice them to factory owners looking for a cheap source of labor. These children worked long hours under strict discipline and received inadequate food and recreation; many became

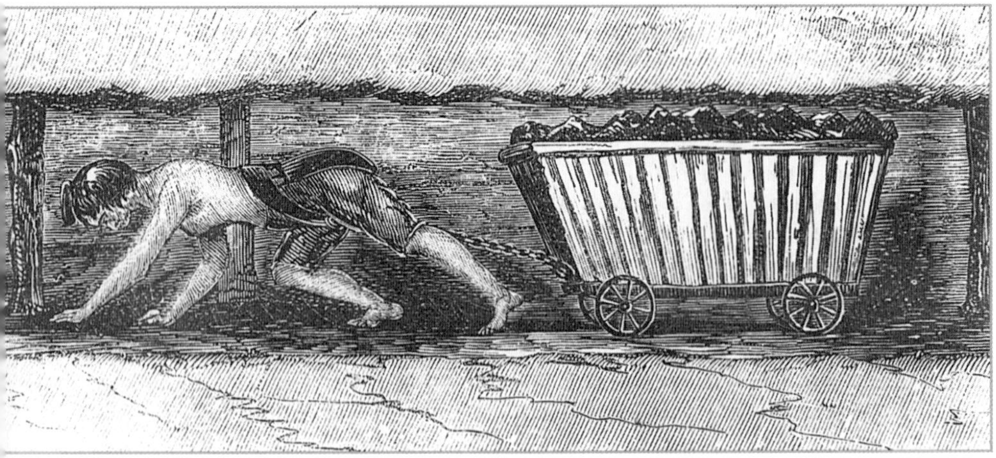

CORBIS

Women in the Mines. Both women and children were often employed in the early factories and mines of the nineteenth century. As is evident in this illustration of a woman dragging a cart loaded with coal behind her, they often worked under very trying conditions.

Child Labor: The Mines

After examining conditions in British coal mines, a government official commented that "the hardest labour in the worst room in the worst-conducted factory is less hard, less cruel and less demoralizing than the labour in the best of coal-mines." Yet it was not until 1842 that legislation was passed eliminating the labor of boys under ten from the mines. This selection is taken from a government report on the mines in Lancashire.

The Black Holes of Worsley

Examination of Thomas Gibson and George Bryan, witnesses from the coal mines at Worsley:

Have you worked from a boy in a coal mine?—(Both) Yes.

What had you to do then?—Thrutching the basket and drawing. It is done by little boys; one draws the basket and the other pushes it behind. Is that hard labor?—Yes, very hard labor.

For how many hours a day did you work?—Nearly nine hours regularly; sometimes twelve; I have worked about thirteen. We used to go in at six in the morning, and took a bit of bread and cheese in our pocket, and stopped two or three minutes; and some days nothing at all to eat.

How was it that sometimes you had nothing to eat?—We were over-burdened. I had only a mother, and she had nothing to give me. I was sometimes half starved. . . .

Do they work in the same way now exactly?—Yes, they do; they have nothing more than a bit of bread and cheese in their pocket, and sometimes can't eat it all, owing to the dust and damp and badness of air; and sometimes it is as hot as an oven; sometimes I have seen it so hot as to melt a candle.

What are the usual wages of a boy of eight?—They used to get 3d or 4d a day. Now a man's wages is divided into eight eighths; and when a boy is eight years old he gets one of those eighths; at eleven, two eighths; at thirteen, three eighths; at fifteen, four eighths; at twenty, man's wages.

What are the wages of a man?—About 15s if he is in full employment, but often not more than 10s, and out of that he has to get his tools and candles. He consumes about four candles in nine hours' work, in some places six; 6d per pound, and twenty-four candles to the pound.

Were you ever beaten as a child?—Yes, many a score of times; both kicks and thumps.

Are many girls employed in the pits?—Yes, a vast of those. They do the same kind of work as the boys till they get about 14 years of age, when they get the wages of half a man, and never get more, and continue at the same work for many years.

Did they ever fight together?—Yes, many days together. Both boys and girls; sometimes they are very loving with one another.

deformed from being kept too long in unusual positions. Although economic liberals and some industrialists were against all state intervention in economic matters, Parliament eventually remedied some of the worst ills of child abuse in factories and mines (see "Efforts at Change: Reformers and Government" later in this chapter). The legislation of the 1830s and 1840s, however, primarily affected child labor in textile factories and mines. It did not touch the use of children in small workshops or the nonfactory trades that were not protected. As these trades were in competition with the new factories, conditions there were often even worse. Pottery works, for example, were not investigated until the 1860s, when it was found that 17 percent of the workers were under eleven years of age. One investigator reported what he found:

> The boys were kept in constant motion throughout the day, each carrying from thirty to fifty dozen of molds into the stoves, and remaining . . . long enough to take the dried earthenware away. The distance thus run by a boy in the course of a day . . . was estimated at seven miles. From the very nature of this exhausting occupation children were rendered pale, weak and unhealthy. In the depth of winter, with the thermometer in the open air sometimes below zero, boys, with little clothing but rags, might be seen running to and fro on errands or to their dinners with the perspiration on their foreheads, "after laboring for hours like little slaves." The inevitable result of such transitions of temperature were consumption, asthma and acute inflammation.[13]

Little wonder that child labor legislation enacted in 1864 included pottery works.

By 1830, women and children made up two-thirds of the cotton industry's labor. However, as the number of children employed declined under the Factory Act of 1833, their places were taken by women, who came to dominate the labor forces of the early factories. Women made up 50 percent of the labor force in textile (cotton and woolen) factories before 1870. They were mostly unskilled labor and were paid half or less of what men received. Excessive working hours for women were outlawed in 1844, but only in textile factories and mines; not until 1867 were they outlawed in craft workshops.

The employment of children and women in large part represents a continuation of a preindustrial kinship pattern. The cottage industry had always involved the efforts of the entire family, and it seemed perfectly natural to continue this pattern. Men migrating from the countryside to industrial towns and cities took their wives and children with them into the factory or into the mines. Of 136 employees in Robert Peel's factory at Bury in 1801, 95 were members of the same twenty-six families. The impetus for this family work often came from the family itself. The factory owner Jedediah Strutt was opposed to child labor under age ten but was forced by parents to take children as young as seven.

The employment of large numbers of women in factories did not produce a significant transformation in female working patterns, as was once assumed. Studies of urban households in France and Britain, for example, have revealed that throughout the nineteenth century, traditional types of female labor still predominated in the women's work world. In 1851, fully 40 percent of the female workforce in Britain consisted of domestic servants. In France, the largest group of female workers, 40 percent, worked in agriculture. In addition, only 20 percent of female workers in Britain labored in factories, and only 10 percent did so in France. Regional and local studies have also found that most of the workers were single women. Few married women worked outside the home.

The factory acts that limited the work hours of children and women also began to break up the traditional kinship pattern of work and led to a new pattern based on a separation of work and home. Men came to be regarded as responsible for the primary work obligations as women assumed daily control of the family and performed low-paying jobs such as laundry work that could be done in the home. Domestic industry made it possible for women to continue their contributions to family survival.

Historians have also reminded us that if the treatment of children in the mines and factories seems particularly cruel and harsh, contemporary treatment of children in general was often brutal. Beatings, for example, had long been regarded, even by dedicated churchmen and churchwomen, as the best way to discipline children.

Standards of Living

One of the most heated debates on the Industrial Revolution concerns the standard of living. Most historians assume that in the long run, the Industrial Revolution increased living standards dramatically in the form of higher per capita incomes and greater consumer choices. But did the first generation of industrial workers experience a decline in their living standards and suffer unnecessarily? Some historians have argued that early industrialization required huge profits to be reinvested in new and ever more expensive equipment; thus to make the requisite profits, industrialists had to keep wages low. Others have questioned that argument, pointing out that initial investments in early machinery were not necessarily large, nor did they need to be. What certainly did occur in the first half of the nineteenth century was a widening gap between rich and poor. One estimate, based on income tax returns in Britain, is that the wealthiest 1 percent of the population increased its share of the national product from 25 percent in 1801 to 35 percent in 1848.

Wages, prices, and consumption patterns are some of the criteria used for measuring the standard of living. Between 1780 and 1850, as far as we can determine from the available evidence, both wages and prices fluctuated widely. Most historians believe that during the Napoleonic wars, the increase in prices outstripped wages. Between 1815 and 1830, a drop in prices was accompanied by a slight increase in wages. But from 1830 to the late 1840s, real wages seem to have improved, although regional variations make generalizations dangerous.

When we look at consumption patterns, we find, on the one hand, that in Britain in 1850, tea, sugar, and coffee were still semiluxuries consumed primarily by the upper and middle classes and better-off artisans. Meat consumption per capita was less in 1840 than in 1780. On the other hand, a mass market had developed in the cheap cotton goods so important to the Industrial Revolution. As a final note on the question of the standard of living, some historians who take a positive view of the early Industrial Revolution have questioned what would have happened to Britain's growing population without the Industrial Revolution. Would it have gone the way of Ireland's in the Great Hunger of the mid-nineteenth century? No one really knows.

No doubt the periodic crises of overproduction that haunted industrialization from its beginnings caused even further economic hardship. Short-term economic depressions brought high unemployment and increased social tensions. Unemployment figures could be astronomical. During one of these economic depressions in 1842, for example, 60 percent of the factory employees in Bolton were laid off. Cyclical depressions were particularly devastating in towns whose prosperity rested on one industry.

Overall we can say that some evidence exists for an increase in real wages for the working classes between 1790 and 1850, especially in the 1840s. But can standards of living be assessed only in terms of prices, wages, and consumption patterns? No doubt those meant little to people who faced dreadful housing, adulterated food, public health hazards, and the psychological traumas associated with a complete change in work habits and way of life. The real gainers in the early Industrial Revolution were members of the middle class—and some skilled workers whose jobs were not eliminated by the new machines. But industrial workers themselves would have to wait until the second half of the nineteenth century to reap the benefits of industrialization.

Efforts at Change: The Workers

Before long, workers looked to the formation of labor organizations to gain decent wages and working conditions. The British government, reacting against the radicalism of the French revolutionary working classes, had passed the Combination Acts in 1799 and 1800 outlawing associations of workers. The legislation failed to prevent the formation of trade unions, however. Similar to the craft societies of earlier times, these new associations were formed by skilled workers in a number of new industries, including the cotton spinners, ironworkers, coal miners, and shipwrights.

These unions served two purposes. One was to preserve their own workers' position by limiting entry into their trade; another was to gain benefits from the employers. These early trade unions had limited goals. They favored a working-class struggle against employers, but only to win improvements for the members of their own trades.

Some trade unions were even willing to strike to gain their goals. Bitter strikes were carried out by hand-loom weavers in Glasgow in 1813, cotton spinners in Manchester in 1818, and miners in Northumberland and Durham in 1810. Such blatant illegal activity caused Parliament to repeal the Combination Acts in 1824, accepting the argument of some members that the acts themselves had so alienated workers that they had formed unions. Unions were now tolerated, but other legislation enabled authorities to keep close watch over their activities.

In the 1820s and 1830s, the union movement began to focus on the creation of national unions. One of the leaders in this effort was a well-known cotton magnate and social reformer, Robert Owen (1771–1858). Owen came to believe in the creation of voluntary associations that would demonstrate to others the benefits of cooperative rather than competitive living (see Chapter 21 on the utopian socialists). Although Owen's program was not directed specifically to trade unionists, his ideas had great appeal to some of their leaders. Under Owen's direction, plans emerged for the Grand National Consolidated Trades Union, which was formed in February 1834. As a national federation of trade unions, its primary purpose was to coordinate a general strike for the eight-hour working day. Rhetoric, however, soon outpaced reality, and by the summer of that year, the lack of real working-class support led to the federation's total collapse, and the union movement reverted to trade unions for individual crafts. The largest and most successful of these unions was the Amalgamated Society of Engineers, formed in 1850. Its provision of generous unemployment benefits in return for a small weekly payment was precisely the kind of practical gains these trade unions sought. Larger goals would have to wait.

Trade unionism was not the only type of collective action by workers in the early decades of the Industrial Revolution. The Luddites were skilled craftspeople in the Midlands and northern England who in 1812 attacked the machines that they believed threatened their livelihoods. These attacks failed to stop the industrial mechanization of Britain and have been viewed as utterly naive. Some historians, however, have also seen them as an intense eruption of feeling against unrestrained industrial capitalism. The inability of twelve thousand troops to find the culprits provides stunning evidence of the local support they received in their areas.

A much more meaningful expression of the attempts of British workers to improve their condition developed in the movement known as Chartism. It was the "first important political movement of working men organized during the nineteenth century." Its aim was to achieve political democracy. A "people's charter," drawn up in 1838, demanded universal male suffrage, payment for members of Parliament, and annual sessions of Parliament (see the box on p. 576). Two national petitions incorporating these points, affixed with millions of signatures, were presented to Parliament in 1839 and 1842. Both were rejected by the members of Parliament, who were not at all ready for political democracy. As one member said, universal suffrage would be "fatal to all the purposes for which government exists" and was "utterly incompatible with the very existence of civilization." After 1848, Chartism as a movement had largely played itself out. It had never really posed a serious threat to the British establishment, but it had not been a total failure either. Its true significance stemmed from its ability to arouse and organize millions of working-class men and women, to give them a sense of working-class consciousness that they had not really possessed before. This political education of working people was important to the ultimate acceptance of all the points of the people's charter in the future.

A Trade Union Membership Card. Skilled workers in a number of new industries formed trade unions in an attempt to gain higher wages, better working conditions, and special benefits. The scenes at the bottom of this membership card for the Associated Shipwright's Society illustrate some of the medical and social benefits it provided for its members.

Trades Union Congress, London/Bridgeman Art Library

The Political Demands of the Chartist Movement

In the late 1830s and early 1840s, working-class protest centered on achieving a clear set of political goals, particularly universal male suffrage, as the means to achieve economic and social improvements. This selection is taken from one of the national petitions presented to Parliament by the Chartist movement. Although the petition failed, Chartism helped arouse and organize millions of workers.

National Petition (1839)

To the Honorable the Commons of the United Kingdom of Great Britain and Ireland, in Parliament assembled, the Petition of the undersigned, their suffering countrymen, HUMBLY SHOWS,—

The energies of a mighty kingdom have been wasted in building up the power of selfish and ignorant men, and its resources squandered for their aggrandizement. The good of a part has been advanced at the sacrifice of the good of the nation. The few have governed for the interest of the few, while the interests of the many have been sottishly neglected, or insolently . . . trampled upon. . . . We come before your honorable house to tell you, with all humility, that this state of things must not be permitted to continue. That it cannot long continue, without very seriously endangering the stability of the throne, and the peace of the kingdom, and that if, by God's help, and all lawful and constitutional appliances, an end can be put to it, we are fully resolved that it shall speedily come to an end. . . . Required, as we are universally, to support and obey the laws, nature and reason entitle us to demand that in the making of the laws the universal voice shall be implicitly listened to. We perform the duties of freemen; we must have the privileges of freemen. Therefore, we demand universal suffrage.

The suffrage, to be exempt from the corruption of the wealthy and the violence of the powerful, must be secret. . . . To public safety, as well as public confidence, frequent elections are essential. Therefore, we demand annual parliaments. With power to choose, and freedom in choosing, the range of our choice must be unrestricted. We are compelled, by existing laws, to take for our representatives men who are incapable of appreciating our difficulties, or have little sympathy with them; merchants who have retired from trade and no longer feel its harassings; proprietors of land who are alike ignorant of its evils and its cure; lawyers by whom the notoriety of the senate is courted only as a means of obtaining notice in the courts. . . . We demand that in the future election of members of your . . . house, the approbation of the constituency shall be the sole qualification, and that to every representative so chosen, shall be assigned out of the public taxes, a fair and adequate remuneration for the time which he is called upon to devote to the public service. . . . Universal suffrage will, and it alone can, bring true and lasting peace to the nation; we firmly believe that it will also bring prosperity. May it therefore please your honorable house, to take this our petition into your most serious consideration, and to use your utmost endeavours, by all constitutional means, to have a law passed, granting to every male of lawful age, sane mind, and unconvicted of crime, the right of voting for members of parliament, and directing all future elections of members of parliament to be in the way of secret ballot, and ordaining that the duration of parliament, so chosen, shall in no case exceed one year, and abolishing all property qualifications in the members, and providing for their due remuneration while in attendance on their parliamentary duties.

Efforts at Change: Reformers and Government

Efforts to improve the worst conditions of the industrial factory system also came from outside the ranks of the working classes. From its beginning, the Industrial Revolution had drawn much criticism. Romantic poets like William Wordsworth (see Chapter 21) decried the destruction of the natural world:

I grieve, when on the darker side
Of this great change I look; and there behold
Such outrage done to nature as compels
The indignant power to justify herself.

Reform-minded individuals, be they factory owners who felt twinges of conscience or social reformers in Parliament, campaigned against the evils of the industrial factory, especially condemning the abuse of children. One hoped for the day "that these little ones should once more see the rising and setting of the sun."

As it became apparent that the increase in wealth generated by the Industrial Revolution was accompanied by ever-increasing numbers of poor people, more and more efforts were made to document and deal with the problems. As reports from civic-minded citizens and parliamentary commissions intensified and demonstrated the extent of poverty, degradation, and suffering, the reform efforts began to succeed.

Their first success was a series of factory acts passed between 1802 and 1819 that limited labor for children between the ages of nine and sixteen to twelve hours a day; the employment of children under nine years old was forbidden. Moreover, the laws stipulated that children were to receive instruction in reading and arithmetic during working hours. But these acts applied only to cotton mills, not to factories or mines where some of the worst abuses were taking place. Just as important, no provision was made for enforcing the acts through a system of inspection.

In the reform-minded decades of the 1830s and 1840s, new legislation was passed. The Factory Act of 1833 strengthened earlier labor legislation. All textile factories were now included. Children between nine and thirteen could work only eight hours a day; those between thirteen and eighteen, twelve hours. Factory inspectors were appointed with the power to fine those who broke the law. Another piece of legislation in 1833 required that children between nine and thirteen have at least two hours of elementary education during the working day. In 1847, the Ten Hours Act reduced the workday for children between thirteen and eighteen to ten hours. Women were also now included in the ten-hour limitation. In 1842, the Coal Mines Act eliminated the employment of boys under ten and women in mines. Eventually, men too would benefit from the move to restrict factory hours.

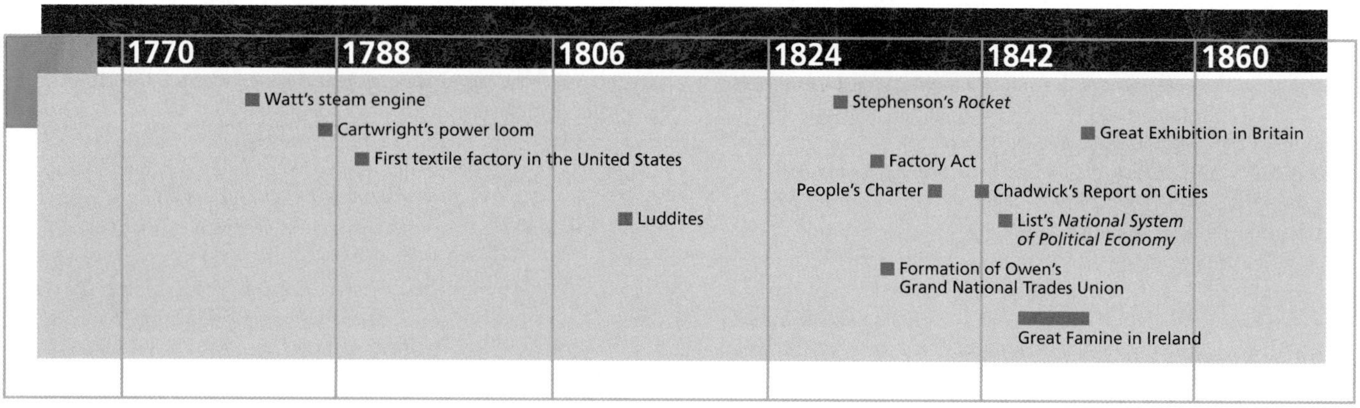

Conclusion

The Industrial Revolution was one of the major forces of change in the nineteenth century as it led Western civilization into the industrial era that has characterized the modern world. Beginning in Britain, its spread to the Continent and the new American nation ensured its growth and domination of the Western world.

The Industrial Revolution seemed to prove to Europeans the underlying assumption of the Scientific Revolution of the seventeenth century—that human beings were capable of dominating nature. By rationally manipulating the material environment for human benefit, people could attain new levels of material prosperity and produce machines not dreamed of in their wildest imaginings. Lost in the excitement of the Industrial Revolution were the voices that pointed to the dehumanization of the workforce and the alienation from one's work, one's associates, oneself, and the natural world.

The Industrial Revolution also transformed the social world of Europe. The creation of an industrial proletariat produced a whole new force for change. The development of a wealthy industrial middle class presented a challenge to the long-term hegemony of landed wealth. Though that wealth had been threatened by the fortunes of commerce, it had never been overturned. But the new bourgeoisie was more demanding. How, in some places, this new industrial bourgeoisie came to play a larger role in the affairs of state will become evident in the next chapter.

Notes

1. Quoted in W. Gordon Rimmer, *Marshall's of Leeds, Flax-Spinners, 1788–1886* (Cambridge, 1960), p. 40.
2. Daniel Defoe, *A Plan of the English Commerce* (Oxford, 1928), pp. 76–77.
3. Quoted in David Landes, *The Unbound Prometheus: Technological Change and Industrial Development in Western Europe from 1750 to the Present* (Cambridge, 1969), pp. 99–100.
4. Quoted in Albert Tucker, *A History of English Civilization* (New York, 1972), p. 583.
5. Quoted in Landes, *The Unbound Prometheus,* pp. 149–150.
6. Quotations can be found in E. Royston Pike, *Human Documents of the Industrial Revolution in Britain* (London, 1966), pp. 320, 313, 314, 343.
7. Ibid., p. 315.
8. Quoted in A. J. Donajgrodzi, ed., *Social Control in Nineteenth-Century Britain* (London, 1977), p. 141.
9. Quoted in Pike, *Human Documents of the Industrial Revolution in Britain,* pp. 343–344.
10. Quoted in Eric J. Evans, *The Forging of the Modern State: Early Industrial Britain, 1783–1870* (London, 1983), p. 113.
11. Henry Mayhew, *London Labour and the London Poor* (London, 1851), vol.1, pp. 342–343.
12. Quoted in Pike, *Human Documents,* pp. 60–61.
13. Quoted in Evans, *Forging of the Modern State,* p. 124.

Suggestions for Further Reading

The well-written work by D. Landes, *The Unbound Prometheus: Technological Change and Industrial Development in Western Europe from 1750 to the Present* (Cambridge, 1969), is a good introduction to the

Industrial Revolution. Although more technical, also of value are C. Trebilcock, *The Industrialization of the Continental Powers, 1780–1914* (London, 1981), and S. Pollard, *Peaceful Conquest: The Industrialization of Europe, 1760–1970* (Oxford, 1981). There are good collections of essays in P. Mathias and J. A. Davis, eds., *The First Industrial Revolutions* (Oxford, 1989), and M. Teich and R. Porter, eds., *The Industrial Revolution in National Context: Europe and the USA* (Cambridge, 1996). See also D. Fisher, *The Industrial Revolution* (New York, 1992). For a broader perspective, see P. Stearns, *The Industrial Revolution in World History* (Boulder, Colo., 1993). On the Industrial Revolution in Britain, see P. Mathias, *The First Industrial Nation: An Economic History of Britain, 1700–1914*, 2d ed. (New York, 1983), and R. Brown, *Society and Economy in Modern Britain, 1700–1850* (London, 1991). On the spread of industrialization to the Continent, see T. Kemp, *Industrialization in Nineteenth-Century Europe*, 2d ed. (London, 1985).

Given the importance of Great Britain in the Industrial Revolution, a number of books are available that place it in a broader context. See E. J. Evans, *The Forging of the Modern State: Early Industrial Britain, 1783–1870* (London, 1983), and P. K. O'Brien and R. Quinault, eds., *The Industrial Revolution and British Society* (New York, 1993).

The early industrialization of the United States is examined in B. Hindle and S. Lubar, *Engines of Change: The American Industrial Revolution, 1790–1860* (Washington, D.C., 1986). On the economic ties between Great Britain and the United States, see D. Jeremy, *Transatlantic Industrial Revolution: The Diffusion of Textile Technology Between Britain and America, 1790–1830* (Cambridge, Mass., 1981).

A general discussion of population growth in Europe can be found in T. McKeown, *The Modern Rise of Population* (London, 1976). For an examination of urban growth, see the classic work of A. F. Weber, *The Growth of Cities in the Nineteenth Century: A Study in Statistics* (Ithaca, N.Y., 1963); A. R. Sutcliffe, *Towards the Planned City: Germany, Britain, the United States and France, 1780–1914* (Oxford, 1981); and L. D. Schwarz, *London in the Age of Industrialization* (New York, 1992). C. Kinealy, *A Death-Dealing Famine: The Great Hunger in Ireland* (Chicago, 1997), is a good account of the great Irish tragedy. Many of the works cited here have much information on the social impact of the Industrial Revolution, but additional material is available in F. Crouzet, *The First Industrialists: The Problems of Origins* (Cambridge, 1985), on British entrepreneurs; J. Merriman, *The Margins of City Life* (New York, 1991), on French cities; P. Pilbeam, *The Middle Classes in Europe, 1789–1914* (Basingstoke, England, 1990); and T. Koditschek, *Class Formation and Urban Industrial Society* (New York, 1990). G. Himmelfarb, *The Idea of Poverty: England in the Early Industrial Age* (New York, 1984), traces the concepts of poverty and poor from the mid-eighteenth century to the mid-nineteenth century. See M. J. Maynes, *Taking the Hard Road* (Chapel Hill, N.C., 1995), on the lives of workers. A classic work on female labor patterns is L. A. Tilly and J. W. Scott, *Women, Work, and Family* (New York, 1978). See also J. Lown, *Women and Industrialization: Gender at Work in Nineteenth-Century England* (Minneapolis, Minn., 1990), and L. L. Frader, "Doing Capitalism's Work: Women in the Western European Industrial Economy," in R. Bridenthal, S. M. Stuard, and M. E. Wiesner, eds., *Becoming Visible*, 3d ed. (Boston, 1998).

For additional reading, go to InfoTrac College Edition, your online research library at http://web1.infotrac-college.com

Enter the search term *Industrial Revolution* using Key Terms.

Enter the search term *industrial development* using the Subject Guide.

Enter the search term *Chartism* using the Subject Guide.

C H A P T E R

21

Reaction, Revolution, and Romanticism, 1815–1850

Giraudon/Art Resource, NY

CHAPTER OUTLINE

- The Conservative Order (1815–1830)
- The Ideologies of Change
- Revolution and Reform (1830–1850)
- The Emergence of an Ordered Society
- Culture in an Age of Reaction and Revolution: The Mood of Romanticism
- Conclusion

FOCUS QUESTIONS

- What were the goals of the Congress of Vienna and the Concert of Europe, and how successful were they in achieving those goals?
- What were the main tenets of conservatism, liberalism, nationalism, and utopian socialism, and what role did each ideology play in Europe in the first half of the nineteenth century?
- What forces for change were present in France and Great Britain between 1830 and 1848, and how did each nation respond?
- What were the causes of the revolutions of 1848, and why did the revolutions fail?
- What were the characteristics of Romanticism, and how were they reflected in literature, art, and music?
- In what ways were intellectual and artistic developments related to the political and social forces of the age?

IN SEPTEMBER 1814, hundreds of foreigners began to converge on Vienna, the capital city of the Austrian Empire. Many were members of European royalty—kings, archdukes, princes, and their wives—accompanied by their diplomatic advisers and scores of servants. Their congenial host was the Austrian emperor, Francis I, who never tired of regaling Vienna's guests with concerts, glittering balls, sumptuous feasts, and innumerable hunting parties. One participant remembered, "Eating, fireworks, public illuminations. For eight or ten days, I haven't been able to work at all. What a life!" Of course, not every waking hour was spent in pleasure during this gathering of notables, known to history as the Congress of Vienna. These people were also representatives of all the states that had fought Napoleon, and their real business was to arrange a final peace settlement after almost a decade of war. On June 8, 1815, they finally completed their task.

The forces of upheaval unleashed during the French revolutionary and Napoleonic wars were temporarily quieted in 1815 as rulers sought to restore stability by reestablishing much of the old order to a Europe ravaged by war. Kings, landed aristocrats, and bureaucratic elites regained their control over domestic governments, and internationally the forces of conservatism tried to maintain the new status quo; some states even used military force to intervene in the internal affairs of other countries in their desire to crush revolutions.

But the Western world had been changed, and it would not readily go back to the old system. New ideologies, especially liberalism and nationalism, both products of the revolutionary upheaval initiated in France, had become too powerful to be contained. Not content with the status quo, the forces of change gave rise first to the revolts and revolutions that periodically shook Europe in the 1820s and 1830s and then to the widespread revolutions of 1848. Some of the revolutions and revolutionaries were successful; most were not. Although the old order usually appeared to have prevailed, by 1850 it was apparent that its days were numbered. This perception was reinforced by the changes wrought by the Industrial Revolution. Together the forces unleashed by the dual revolutions—the French Revolution and the Industrial Revolution—made it impossible to return to prerevolutionary Europe. Nevertheless, although these events ushered in what historians like to call the modern European world, remnants of the old remained amid the new.

The Conservative Order (1815–1830)

The immediate response to the defeat of Napoleon was the desire to contain revolution and the revolutionary forces by restoring much of the old order.

The Peace Settlement

In March 1814, even before Napoleon had been defeated, his four major enemies—Great Britain, Austria, Prussia, and Russia—had agreed to remain united, not only to defeat France but also to ensure peace after the war. After Napoleon's defeat, this Quadruple Alliance restored the Bourbon monarchy to France in the person of Louis XVIII and agreed to meet at a congress in Vienna in September 1814 to arrange a final peace settlement.

The leader of the Congress of Vienna was the Austrian foreign minister, Prince Klemens von Metternich (1773–1859). An experienced diplomat who was also conceited and self-assured, Metternich described himself in his memoirs in 1819: "There is a wide sweep about my mind. I am always above and beyond the preoccupation of most public men; I cover a ground much vaster than they can see. I cannot keep myself from saying about twenty times a day: 'How right I am, and how wrong they are.'"[1]

Metternich claimed that he was guided at Vienna by the principle of legitimacy. To reestablish peace and stability in Europe, he considered it necessary to restore the legitimate monarchs who would preserve traditional institutions. This had already been done in the restoration of the Bourbons in France and Spain, as well as in the return of a number of rulers to their thrones in the Italian states. Elsewhere, however, the principle of legitimacy was largely ignored and completely overshadowed by more practical considerations of power. The congress's treatment of Poland, to which Russia, Austria, and Prussia all had claims, illustrates this approach. Prussia and Austria were allowed to keep some Polish territory. A new, nominally independent Polish kingdom, about three-quarters of the size of the duchy of Warsaw, was established, with the Romanov dynasty of Russia as its hereditary monarchs. Although Poland was guaranteed its independence, the kingdom's foreign policy (and

Metternich. Prince Klemens von Metternich, the foreign minister of Austria, played a major role at the Congress of Vienna as the chief exponent of the principle of legitimacy. To maintain the new conservative order after 1815, Metternich espoused the principle of intervention, by which he meant that the great powers had the right to intervene militarily in other countries to crush revolutionary movements against legitimate rulers.

Austrian Information Service

the kingdom itself) remained under Russian control. Prussia was compensated for its loss of Polish lands by receiving two-fifths of Saxony, the Napoleonic German kingdom of Westphalia, and the left bank of the Rhine. Austria was compensated for its loss of the Austrian Netherlands by being given control of two northern Italian provinces, Lombardy and Venetia (see Map 21.1).

In making these territorial rearrangements, the powers at Vienna believed they were forming a new balance of power that would keep any one country from dominating Europe. For example, to balance Russian gains, Prussia and Austria had been strengthened. According to Metternich, this arrangement had clearly avoided a great danger: "Prussia and Austria are completing their systems of defense; united, the two monarchies form an unconquerable barrier against the enterprises of any conquering prince who might perhaps once again occupy the throne of France or that of Russia."[2]

Considerations of the balance of power also dictated the allied treatment of France. France had not been significantly weakened; it remained a great power. The fear that France might again upset the European peace remained so strong that the great powers attempted to establish major defensive barriers against possible French expansion. To the north of France, they created a new enlarged kingdom of the Netherlands composed of the former Dutch Republic and the Austrian Netherlands (Belgium) under a new ruler, King William I of the House of Orange. To the southeast, Piedmont (officially part of the kingdom of Sardinia) was enlarged. On France's eastern frontier, Prussia was strengthened by giving it control of the territory along the east bank of the Rhine. The British at least expected Prussia to be the major bulwark against French expansion in central Europe, but the Congress of Vienna also created a new league of German states, the Germanic Confederation, to replace the Napoleonic Confederation of the Rhine.

Napoleon's escape from Elba and his One Hundred Days in the midst of the Congress of Vienna delayed the negotiations but did not significantly alter the overall agreement. It was decided, however, to punish the French people for their enthusiastic response to Napoleon's return. France's borders were returned to those of 1790, and it was forced to pay an indemnity and accept an army of occupation for five years. The Congress of Vienna established a European order that managed to avoid a general European conflict for almost a century.

The Ideology of Conservatism

The peace arrangements of 1815 were but the beginning of a conservative reaction determined to contain the liberal and nationalist forces unleashed by the French Revolution. Metternich and his kind were representatives of the ideology known as conservatism (see the box on p. 582). As a

Map 21.1 Europe After the Congress of Vienna. The Congress of Vienna imposed order on Europe based on the principles of monarchical government and a balance of power. Monarchs were restored in France, Spain, and other states recently under Napoleon's control, and much territory changed hands, often at the expense of small and weak states.
■ How did Europe's major powers manipulate territory to decrease the probability that France could again threaten the Continent's stability?

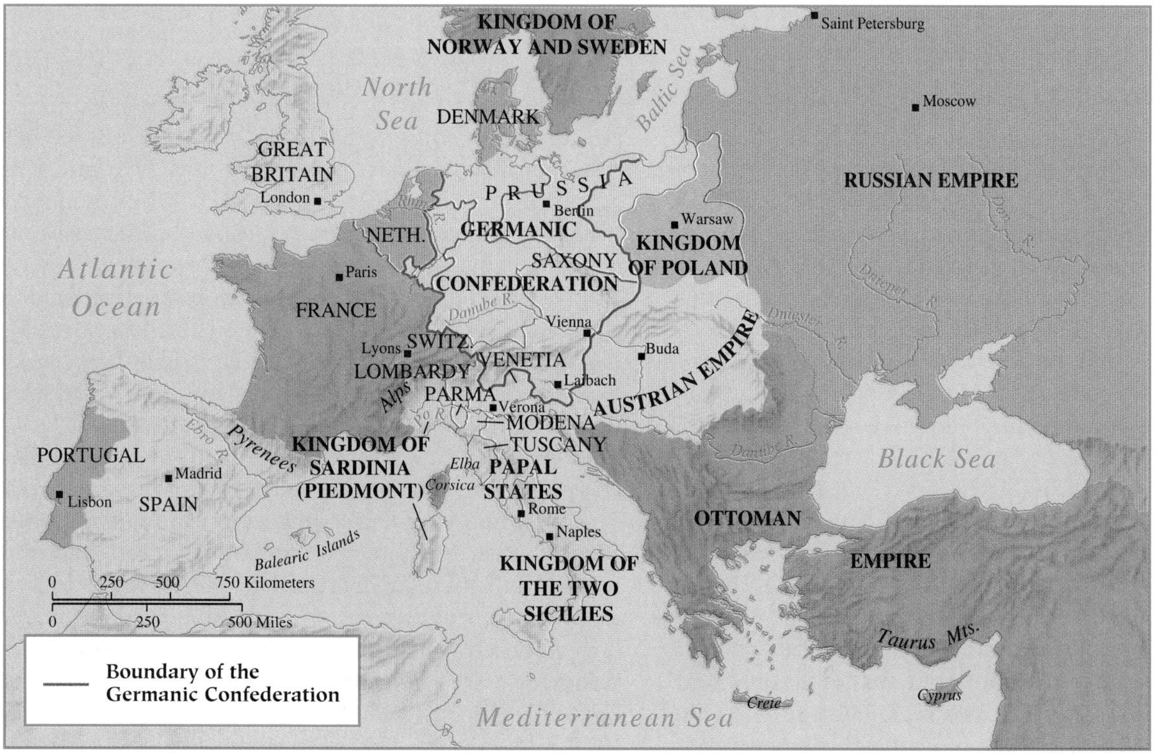

The Voice of Conservatism: Metternich of Austria

There was no greater symbol of conservatism in the first half of the nineteenth century than Prince Klemens von Metternich of Austria. Metternich played a crucial role at the Congress of Vienna and worked tirelessly for thirty years to repress the "revolutionary seed," as he called it, that had been spread to Europe by the "military despotism of Bonaparte."

Klemens von Metternich, Memoirs

We are convinced that society can no longer be saved without strong and vigorous resolutions on the part of the Governments still free in their opinions and actions.

We are also convinced that this may be, if the Governments face the truth, if they free themselves from all illusion, if they join their ranks and take their stand on a line of correct, unambiguous, and frankly announced principles.

By this course the monarchs will fulfill the duties imposed upon them by Him who, by entrusting them with power, has charged them to watch over the maintenance of justice, and the rights of all, to avoid the paths of error, and tread firmly in the way of truth. . . .

If the same elements of destruction which are now throwing society into convulsions have existed in all ages—for every age has seen immoral and ambitious men, hypocrites, men of heated imaginations, wrong motives, and wild projects—yet ours, by the single fact of the liberty of the press, possesses more than any preceding age the means of contact, seduction, and attraction whereby to act on these different classes of men.

We are certainly not alone in questioning if society can exist with the liberty of the press, a scourge unknown to the world before the latter half of the seventeenth century, and restrained until the end of the eighteenth, with scarcely any expectations but England—a part of Europe separated from the continent by the sea, as well as by her language and by her peculiar manners.

The first principle to be followed by the monarchs, united as they are by the coincidence of their desires and opinions, should be that of maintaining the stability of political institutions against the disorganized excitement which has taken possession of men's minds; the immutability of principles against the madness of their interpretation; and respect for laws actually in force against a desire for their destruction. . . .

The first and greatest concern for the immense majority of every nation is the stability of the laws, and their uninterrupted action—never their change. Therefore, let the Governments govern, let them maintain the groundwork of their institutions, both ancient and modern; for if it is at all times dangerous to touch them, it certainly would not now, in the general confusion, be wise to do so. . . .

Let them maintain religious principles in all their purity, and not allow the faith to be attacked and morality interpreted according to the social contract or the visions of foolish sectarians.

Let them suppress Secret Societies, that gangrene of society. . . .

To every great State determined to survive the storm there still remain many chances of salvation, and a strong union between the States on the principles we have announced will overcome the storm itself.

modern political philosophy, conservatism dates from 1790 when Edmund Burke (1729–1797) wrote his *Reflections on the Revolution in France* in reaction to the French Revolution, especially its radical republican and democratic ideas. Burke maintained that society was a contract, but "the state ought not to be considered as nothing better than a partnership agreement in a trade of pepper and coffee, to be taken up for a temporary interest and to be dissolved by the fancy of the parties." The state was a partnership but one "not only between those who are living, but between those who are living, those who are dead and those who are to be born."[3] No one generation has the right to destroy this partnership; each generation has the duty to preserve and transmit it to the next. Burke advised against the violent overthrow of a government by revolution, but he did not reject the possibility of change. Sudden change was unacceptable, but that did not eliminate gradual or evolutionary improvements.

Burke's conservatism, however, was not the only kind. The Frenchman Joseph de Maistre (1753–1821) was the most influential spokesman for a counterrevolutionary and authoritarian conservatism. De Maistre espoused the restoration of hereditary monarchy, which he regarded as a divinely sanctioned institution. Only absolute monarchy could guarantee "order in society" and avoid the chaos generated by movements like the French Revolution.

Despite their differences, most conservatives held to a general body of beliefs. They favored obedience to political authority, believed that organized religion was crucial to social order, hated revolutionary upheavals, and were unwilling to accept either the liberal demands for civil liberties and representative governments or the nationalistic aspirations generated by the French revolutionary era. The community took precedence over individual rights; society must be organized and ordered, and tradition remained the best guide for order. After 1815, the political philosophy of conservatism was supported by hereditary monarchs, government bureaucracies, landowning aristocracies, and revived churches, be they Protestant or Catholic. The conservative forces appeared dominant after 1815, both internationally and domestically.

Conservative Domination: The Concert of Europe

The great powers' fear of revolution and war led them to develop the Concert of Europe as a means to maintain the new status quo they had constructed. This Concert of Europe grew out of the reaffirmation of the Quadruple Alliance in November 1815. Great Britain, Russia, Prussia, and Austria renewed their commitment against any attempted restoration of Bonapartist power and agreed to meet periodically in conferences to discuss their common interests and examine measures that "will be judged most salutary for the repose and prosperity of peoples, and for the maintenance of peace in Europe."

In accordance with the agreement for periodic meetings, four congresses were held between 1818 and 1822. The first, held in 1818 at Aix-la-Chapelle, was by far the most congenial. "Never have I known a prettier little congress," said Metternich. The four great powers agreed to withdraw their army of occupation from France and to add France to the Concert of Europe. The Quadruple Alliance became a quintuple alliance.

The next congress proved far less pleasant. This session at Troppau was called in the autumn of 1820 to deal with the outbreak of revolution in Spain and Italy. The revolt in Spain was directed against Ferdinand VII, the Bourbon king who had been restored to the throne in 1814. In southern Italy, the restoration of another Bourbon, Ferdinand I, as king of Naples and Sicily sparked a rebellion that soon spread to the Piedmont in northern Italy.

Metternich was especially disturbed by the revolts in Italy because he saw them as a threat to Austria's domination of the peninsula. At Troppau, he proposed a protocol that established the principle of intervention. It read:

> States which have undergone a change of Government due to revolution, the results of which threaten other states, *ipso facto* cease to be members of the European Alliance, and remain excluded from it until their situation gives guarantees for legal order and stability. If, owing to such situations, immediate danger threatens other states, the Powers bind themselves, by peaceful means, or if need be by arms, to bring back the guilty state into the bosom of the Great Alliance.[4]

The principle of intervention meant the great powers had the right to send armies into countries where there were revolutions to restore legitimate monarchs to their thrones. Britain refused to agree to the principle, arguing that it had never been the intention of the Quadruple Alliance to interfere in the internal affairs of other states, except in France. Ignoring the British response, Austria, Prussia, and Russia met in a third congress at Laibach in January 1821 and authorized the sending of Austrian troops to Naples. These forces crushed the revolt, restored Ferdinand I to the throne, and then moved north to suppress the rebels in the Piedmont. At the fourth postwar conference, held at Verona in October 1822, the same three powers authorized France to invade Spain to crush the revolt against Ferdinand VII. In the spring of 1823, French forces restored the Bourbon monarch.

This success for the policy of intervention came at a price, however. The Concert of Europe had broken down when the British rejected Metternich's principle of intervention. And although the British had failed to thwart allied intervention in Spain and Italy, they were successful in keeping the Continental powers from interfering with the revolutions in Latin America.

THE REVOLT OF LATIN AMERICA

Although much of North America had been freed of European domination in the eighteenth century by the American Revolution, Latin America remained in the hands of the Spanish and Portuguese. Napoleon's Continental wars at the beginning of the nineteenth century, however, soon had repercussions in Latin America. When the Bourbon monarchy of Spain was toppled by Napoleon, Spanish authority in its colonial empire was weakened. By 1810, the disintegration of royal power in Argentina had led to that nation's independence. In Venezuela, a bitter struggle for independence was led by Simón Bolívar (1783–1830), hailed as the Liberator. His forces freed Colombia in 1819 and Venezuela in 1821. A second liberator was José de San Martín (1778–1850), who freed Chile in 1817 and then in

José de San Martín. José de San Martín of Argentina was one of the famous leaders of the Latin American independence movement. His forces liberated Argentina, Chile, and Peru from Spanish authority. In this painting by Theodore Gericault, San Martín is shown leading his troops at the Battle of Chacabuco in Chile in 1817.

1821 moved on to Lima, Peru, the center of Spanish authority. He was soon joined by Bolívar, who assumed the task of crushing the last significant Spanish army in 1824. Mexico and the Central American provinces also achieved their freedom, and by 1825, after Portugal had recognized the independence of Brazil, almost all of Latin America had been freed of colonial domination (see Map 21.2).

However, flushed by their success in crushing rebellions in Spain and Italy, the victorious Continental powers favored the use of troops to restore Spanish control in Latin America. This time, British opposition to intervention prevailed. Eager to gain access to an entire continent for investment and trade, the British proposed joint action with the United States against European interference in Latin America. Distrustful of British motives, President James Monroe acted alone in 1823, guaranteeing the independence of the new Latin American nations and warning against any further European intervention in the New World in the famous Monroe Doctrine. Actually, British ships were more important to Latin American independence than American words. Britain's navy stood between Latin America and any European invasion force, and the Continental powers were extremely reluctant to challenge British naval power.

Map 21.2 Latin America in the First Half of the Nineteenth Century. Latin American colonies took advantage of Spain's weakness during the Napoleonic wars to fight for independence, beginning with Argentina in 1810 and spreading throughout the region over the next decade with the help of leaders like Simón Bolívar and José de San Martín. ■ How many South American countries are sources of rivers that feed the Amazon, and roughly what percentage of the continent is contained within the Amazon's watershed?

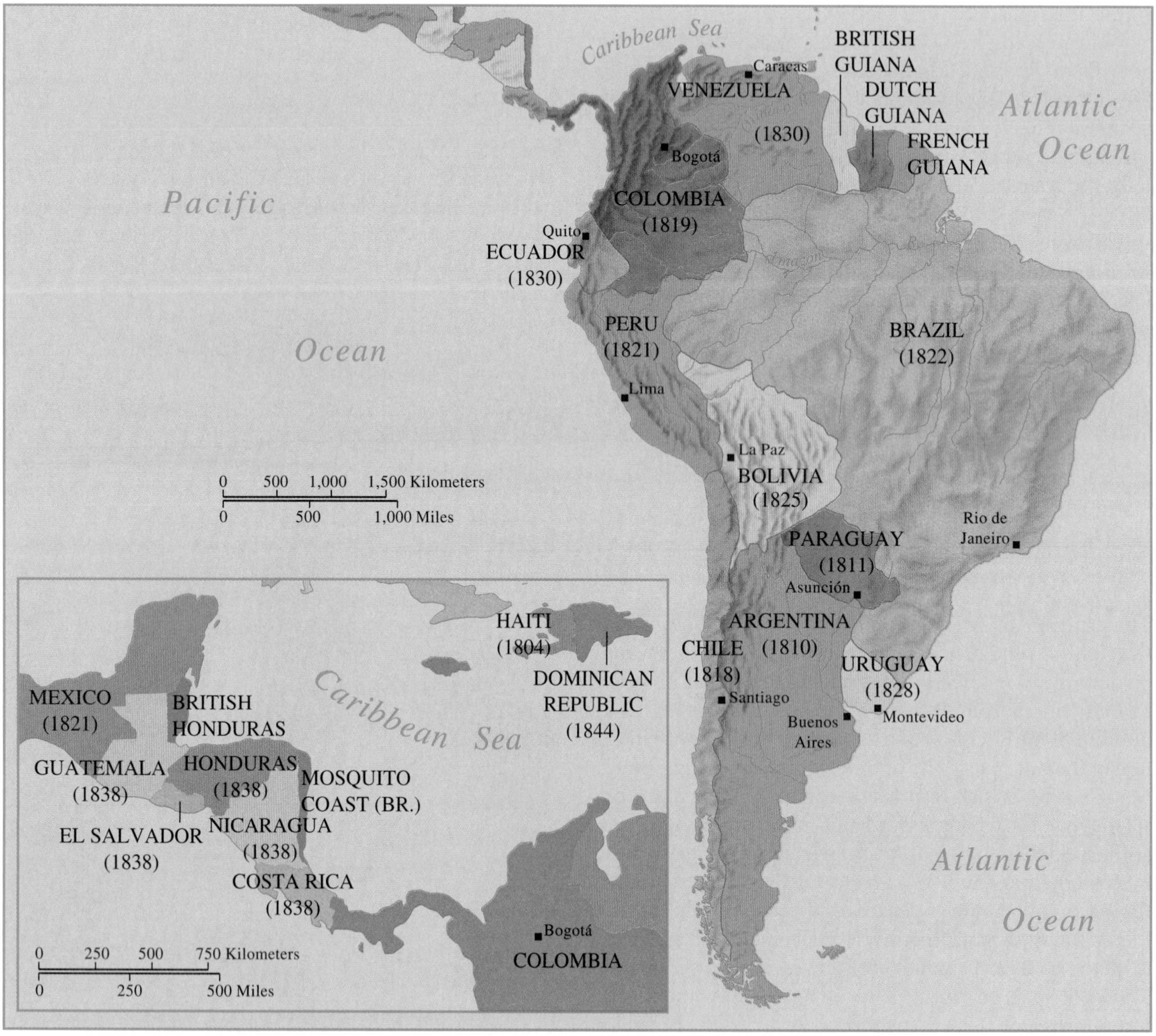

Although political independence brought economic independence to Latin America, old patterns were quickly reestablished. Instead of Spain and Portugal, Great Britain now dominated the Latin American economy. British merchants moved in in large numbers, while British investors poured in funds, especially in the mining industry. Old trade patterns soon reemerged. Because Latin America served as a source of raw materials and foodstuffs for the industrializing nations of Europe and the United States, exports—especially of wheat, tobacco, wool, sugar, coffee, and hides—to the North Atlantic countries increased noticeably. At the same time, finished consumer goods, especially textiles, were imported in increasing quantities, causing a decline in industrial production in Latin America. The emphasis on exporting raw materials and importing finished products ensured the ongoing domination of the Latin American economy by foreigners.

THE GREEK REVOLT

The principle of intervention proved to be a double-edged sword. Designed to prevent revolution, it could also be used to support revolution if the great powers found it in their interest to do so. In 1821, the Greeks revolted against their Ottoman Turkish masters. Although subject to Muslim control for four hundred years, the Greeks had been allowed to maintain their language and their Greek Orthodox faith. A revival of Greek national sentiment at the beginning of the nineteenth century added to the growing desire for liberation "from the terrible yoke of Turkish oppression." The Greek revolt was soon transformed into a noble cause by an outpouring of European sentiment for the Greeks' struggle.

In 1827, a combined British and French fleet went to Greece and defeated a large Ottoman armada. A year later, Russia declared war on the Ottoman Empire and invaded its European provinces of Moldavia and Wallachia. By the Treaty of Adrianople in 1829, which ended the Russian-Turkish war, the Russians received a protectorate over the two provinces. By the same treaty, the Ottoman Empire agreed to allow Russia, France, and Britain to decide the fate of Greece. In 1830, the three powers declared Greece an independent kingdom, and two years later, a new royal dynasty was established. The revolution had been successful only because the great powers themselves supported it. Until 1830, the Greek revolt was the only successful one in Europe; the conservative domination was still largely intact.

The Balkans by 1830

CHRONOLOGY

Conservative Domination: The Concert of Europe

Congress of Vienna	1814–1815
Reaffirmation of the Quadruple Alliance	1815
Congress of Aix-la-Chapelle	1818
Revolutions in Latin America	1819–1824
Congress of Troppau	1820
Congress of Laibach	1821
Crushing of revolt in southern Italy	1821
Greek revolt against the Ottoman Empire	1821
Congress of Verona	1822
Crushing of revolt in Spain	1823
Monroe Doctrine	1823
Treaty of Adrianople	1829
Greek independence	1830

Conservative Domination: The European States

Between 1815 and 1830, the conservative domination of Europe evident in the Concert of Europe was also apparent in domestic affairs as conservative governments throughout Europe worked to maintain the old order.

GREAT BRITAIN: RULE OF THE TORIES

In 1815, Great Britain was governed by the aristocratic landowning classes that dominated both houses of Parliament. Suffrage for elections to the House of Commons, controlled by the landed gentry, was restricted and unequal, especially in light of the changing distribution of the British population due to the Industrial Revolution. Large new industrial cities such as Birmingham and Manchester had no representatives, while landowners used pocket and rotten boroughs (see Chapter 18) to control seats in the House of Commons. Although the monarchy was not yet powerless, in practice the power of the crown was largely in the hands of the ruling party in Parliament.

There were two political factions in Parliament, the Tories and Whigs. Both were still dominated by members of the landed classes, although the Whigs were beginning to receive support from the new industrial middle class. Tory ministers largely dominated the government until 1830 and had little desire to change the existing political and electoral system.

Popular discontent grew apace after 1815 because of severe economic difficulties. The Tory government's response to falling agricultural prices was the Corn Law of 1815, a measure that placed extraordinarily high tariffs on foreign grain. Though beneficial to the landowners, subsequent high prices for bread made conditions for the working classes more difficult. Mass protest meetings took a nasty turn when a squadron of cavalry attacked a crowd of sixty thousand demonstrators at Saint Peter's Fields in Manchester in 1819. The death of eleven people, called the Peterloo Massacre by government detractors, led Parliament to take even more repressive measures. The government restricted large public meetings and the dissemination of pamphlets among the poor. At the same time, by making minor reforms in the 1820s, the Tories managed to avoid meeting the demands for electoral reforms—at least until 1830 (see "Reform in Great Britain" later in this chapter).

RESTORATION IN FRANCE

In 1814, the Bourbon family was restored to the throne of France in the person of Louis XVIII (1814–1824). Louis understood the need to accept some of the changes brought to France by the revolutionary and Napoleonic eras. He accepted Napoleon's Civil Code with its recognition of the principle of equality before the law (see Chapter 19). The property rights of those who had purchased confiscated lands during the revolution were preserved. A bicameral (two-house) legislature was established, consisting of the Chamber of Peers, chosen by the king, and the Chamber of Deputies, chosen by an electorate restricted to slightly fewer than 100,000 wealthy people.

Louis's grudging moderation, however, was opposed by liberals eager to extend the revolutionary reforms and by a group of ultraroyalists who criticized the king's willingness to compromise and retain so many features of the Napoleonic era. The ultras hoped to return to a monarchical system dominated by a privileged landed aristocracy and to restore the Catholic church to its former position of influence.

The initiative passed to the ultraroyalists in 1824 when Louis XVIII died and was succeeded by his brother, the count of Artois, who became Charles X (1824–1830). In 1825, Charles granted an indemnity to aristocrats whose lands had been confiscated during the revolution. Moreover, the king pursued a religious policy that encouraged the Catholic church to reestablish control over the French educational system. Public outrage, fed by liberal newspapers, forced the king to compromise in 1827 and even to accept the principle of ministerial responsibility—that the ministers of the king were responsible to the legislature. But in 1829, he violated his commitment. A protest by the deputies led the king to dissolve the legislature in 1830 and call for new elections. France was on the brink of another revolution.

INTERVENTION IN THE ITALIAN STATES AND SPAIN

The Congress of Vienna had established nine states in Italy, including Piedmont (part of the kingdom of Sardinia) in the north, ruled by the house of Savoy; the kingdom of the Two Sicilies (Naples and Sicily); the Papal States; a handful of small duchies ruled by relatives of the Austrian emperor; and the important northern provinces of Lombardy and Venetia, which were now part of the Austrian Empire. Much of Italy was under Austrian domination, and all the states had extremely reactionary governments eager to smother any liberal or nationalist sentiment. Nevertheless, secret societies motivated by nationalistic dreams and known as the Carbonari ("charcoal burners") continued to conspire and plan for revolution.

Italy, 1815

In Spain, another Bourbon dynasty had been restored in the person of Ferdinand VII in 1814. Ferdinand (1814–1833) had agreed to observe the liberal constitution of 1812, which allowed for the functioning of an elected parliamentary assembly known as the Cortes. But the king soon reneged on his promises, tore up the constitution, dissolved the Cortes, and persecuted its members, which led a combined group of army officers, upper-middle-class merchants, and liberal intellectuals to revolt. The king capitulated in March 1820 and promised once again to restore the constitution and the Cortes. But Metternich's policy of intervention came to Ferdinand's rescue. In April 1823, a French army moved into Spain and forced the revolutionary government to flee Madrid. By August of that year, the king had been restored to his throne.

REPRESSION IN CENTRAL EUROPE

After 1815, the forces of reaction were particularly successful in central Europe. The Habsburg empire and its chief agent, Prince Klemens von Metternich, played an important role. Metternich boasted: "You see in me the chief Minister of Police in Europe. I keep an eye on everything. My contacts are such that nothing escapes me."[5] Metternich's spies were everywhere, searching for evidence of liberal or nationalist plots. Although both liberalism and nationalism emerged in the German states and the Austrian Empire, they were initially weak as central Europe tended to remain under the domination of aristocratic landowning classes and autocratic, centralized monarchies.

The Vienna settlement in 1815 had recognized the existence of thirty-eight sovereign states in what had once been the Holy Roman Empire. Austria and Prussia were the two great powers; the other states varied considerably in size. Together these states formed the Germanic Confederation, but the confederation had little power. It had no real executive, and its only central organ was the federal diet, which needed the consent of all member states to take action, making it virtually powerless. However, it also came to serve as Metternich's instrument to repress revolutionary movements within the German states.

Initially, Germans who favored liberal principles and German unity looked to Prussia for leadership. During the

University Students and German Unity

In the early nineteenth century, university students and professors were the chief supporters of German nationalism. Especially important were the *Burschenschaften,* student societies that espoused the cause of German unity. In this selection, the liberal Heinrich von Gagern explains the purpose of the *Burschenschaften* to his father.

Heinrich von Gagern, Letter to His Father

It is very hard to explain the spirit of the student movement to you, but I shall try, even though I can only give you a few characteristics.... It speaks to the better youth, the man of heart and spirit and love for all this good, and gives him nourishment and being. For the average student of the past, the university years were a time to enjoy life, and to make a sharp break with his own background in defiance of the philistine world, which seemed to him somehow to foreshadow the tomb. Their pleasures, their organizations, and their talk were determined by their *status* as students, and their university obligation was only to avoid failing the examination and scraping by adequately—bread-and-butter learning. They were satisfied with themselves if they thought they could pass the examination. There are still many of those nowadays, indeed the majority over-all. But at several universities, and especially here, another group—in my eyes a better one—has managed to get the upper hand in the sense that it sets the mood. I prefer really not to call it a mood; rather, it is something that presses hard and tried to spread its ideas....

Those who share in this spirit have then quite another tendency in their student life, Love of Fatherland is their guiding principle. Their purpose is to make a better future for the Fatherland, each as best he can, to spread national consciousness, or to use the much ridiculed and maligned Germanic expression, more folkishness, and to work for better constitutions....

We want more sense of community among the several states of Germany, greater unity in their policies and in their principles of government; no separate policy for each state, but the nearest possible relations with one another; above all, we want Germany to be considered *one* land and the German people *one* people. In the forms of our student comradeship we show how we want to approach this as nearly as possible in the real world. Regional fraternities are forbidden, and we live in a German comradeship, one people in spirit, as we want it for all Germany in reality. We give our selves the freest of constitutions, just as we should like Germany to have the freest possible one, insofar as that is suitable for the German people. We want a constitution for the people that fits in with the spirit of the times and with the people's own level of enlightenment, rather than what each prince gives his people according to what he likes and what serves his private interest. Above all, we want the princes to understand and to follow the principle that they exist for the country and not the country for them. In fact, the prevailing view is that the constitution should not come from the individual states at all. The main principles of the German constitution should apply to all states in common, and should be expressed by the German federal assembly. This constitution should deal not only with the absolute necessities, like fiscal administration and justice, general administration and church and military affairs and so on; this constitution ought to be extended to the education of the young, at least at the upper age levels, and to many other such things.

Napoleonic era, King Frederick William III (1797–1840), following the advice of his two chief ministers, Baron Heinrich von Stein and Baron Karl von Hardenberg, instituted political and institutional reforms in response to Prussia's defeat at the hands of Napoleon. The reforms included the abolition of serfdom, municipal self-government through town councils, the expansion of primary and secondary schools, and universal military conscription to form a national army. The reforms, however, did not include the creation of a legislative assembly or representative government as Stein and Hardenberg wished. After 1815, Frederick William grew more reactionary and was content to follow Metternich's lead. Though reforms had made Prussia strong, it remained largely an absolutist state with little interest in German unity.

Liberal and national movements in the German states seemed largely limited to university professors and students. The latter began to organize *Burschenschaften,* student societies dedicated to fostering the goal of a free, united Germany (see the box above). Their ideas and their motto, "Honor, Liberty, Fatherland," were in part inspired by Friedrich Ludwig Jahn, who had organized gymnastic societies during the Napoleonic wars to promote the regeneration of German youth. Jahn encouraged Germans to pursue their Germanic heritage and urged his followers to disrupt the lectures of professors whose views were not nationalistic.

From 1817 to 1819, the *Burschenschaften* pursued a variety of activities that alarmed German governments. At an assembly held at the Wartburg Castle in 1817, marking the three-hundredth anniversary of Luther's Ninety-Five Theses, the crowd burned books written by conservative authors. When a deranged student assassinated a reactionary playwright, Metternich had the diet of the Germanic Confederation draw up the Karlsbad Decrees of 1819. These closed the *Burschenschaften,* provided for censorship of the press, and placed the universities under close supervision and control. Thereafter, except for a minor flurry of activity from 1830 to 1832, Metternich and the cooperative German rulers maintained the conservative status quo.

The Austrian Empire was a multinational state, a collection of different peoples under the Habsburg emperor, who provided a common bond. The empire contained eleven peoples of different national origin, including Germans, Czechs, Magyars (Hungarians), Slovaks, Romanians, Slovenes, Poles, Serbians, and Italians. The Germans, though only a quarter of the population, were economically the most advanced and played a leading role in governing Austria. Essentially, the Austrian Empire was held together by the dynasty, the imperial civil service, the imperial army, and the Catholic church. But its national groups, especially the Hungarians, with their increasing desire for autonomy, acted as forces to break the empire apart.

Still Metternich managed to hold it all together. His antipathy to liberalism and nationalism was understandably grounded in the realization that these forces threatened to tear the empire apart. The growing liberal belief that each national group had the right to its own system of government could only mean disaster for the multinational Austrian Empire. While the forces of liberalism and nationalism grew, the Austrian Empire largely stagnated.

RUSSIA: AUTOCRACY OF THE TSARS

At the beginning of the nineteenth century, Russia was overwhelmingly rural, agricultural, and autocratic. The Russian tsar was still regarded as a divine-right monarch. Alexander I (1801–1825) had been raised in the ideas of the Enlightenment and initially seemed willing to make reforms. With the aid of his liberal adviser, Michael Speransky, he relaxed censorship, freed political prisoners, and reformed the educational system. He refused, however, to grant a constitution or free the serfs in the face of opposition from the nobility. After the defeat of Napoleon, Alexander became a reactionary, and his government reverted to strict and arbitrary censorship. Soon opposition to Alexander arose from a group of secret societies.

One of these societies, known as the Northern Union, was composed of young aristocrats who had served in the Napoleonic wars and had become aware of the world outside Russia as well as intellectuals alienated by the censorship and lack of academic freedom in Russian universities. The Northern Union favored the establishment of a constitutional monarchy and the abolition of serfdom. The sudden death of Alexander in 1825 offered them their opportunity.

Although Alexander's brother Constantine was the legal heir to the throne, he had renounced his claims in favor of his brother Nicholas. Constantine's abdication had not been made public, however, and during the ensuing confusion in December 1825, the military leaders of the Northern Union rebelled against the accession of Nicholas. This so-called Decembrist Revolt was soon crushed by troops loyal to Nicholas, and its leaders were executed.

Portrait of Nicholas I. Tsar Nicholas I was a reactionary ruler who sought to prevent rebellion in Russia by strengthening the government bureaucracy, increasing censorship, and suppressing individual freedom by the use of political police. One of his enemies remarked about his facial characteristics: "The sharply retreating forehead and the lower jaw were expressive of iron will and feeble intelligence."

The revolt transformed Nicholas I (1825–1855) from a conservative into a reactionary determined to avoid another rebellion. He strengthened both the bureaucracy and the secret police. The political police, known as the Third Section of the tsar's chancellery, were given sweeping powers over much of Russian life. They deported suspicious or dangerous persons, maintained close surveillance of foreigners in Russia, and reported regularly to the tsar on public opinion.

Matching Nicholas's fear of revolution at home was his fear of revolution abroad. There would be no revolution in Russia during the rest of his reign; if he could help it, there would be none in Europe either. Contemporaries called him the Policeman of Europe because of his willingness to use Russian troops to crush revolutions.

The Ideologies of Change

Although the conservative forces were in the ascendancy from 1815 to 1830, powerful movements for change were also at work. These depended on ideas embodied in a series of political philosophies or ideologies that came into their own in the first half of the nineteenth century.

Liberalism

One of these ideologies was liberalism, which owed much to the Enlightenment of the eighteenth century and to the American and French Revolutions at the end of that century. In addition, liberalism became even more significant as the Industrial Revolution made rapid strides because the developing industrial middle class largely adopted the doctrine as its own. There were divergences of opinion among people classified as liberals, but all began with the belief that people should be as free from restraint as possible. This opinion is evident in both economic and political liberalism.

Also called classical economics, economic liberalism had as its primary tenet the concept of laissez-faire, the belief that the state should not interrupt the free play of natural economic forces, especially supply and demand. Government should not restrain the economic liberty of the individual and should restrict itself to only three primary functions: defense of the country, police protection of individuals, and the construction and maintenance of public works too expensive for individuals to undertake. If individuals were allowed economic liberty, ultimately they would bring about the maximum good for the maximum number and benefit the general welfare of society.

The case against government interference in economic matters was greatly enhanced by Thomas Malthus (1766–1834). In his major work, *Essay on the Principles of Population,* Malthus argued that population, when unchecked, increases at a geometric rate while the food supply correspondingly increases at a much slower arithmetic rate. The result will be severe overpopulation and ultimately starvation for the human race if this growth is not held in check. According to Malthus, nature imposes a major restraint: "Unwholesome occupations, severe labor and exposure to the seasons, extreme poverty, bad nursing of children, great towns, excesses of all kinds, the whole train of common disease, and epidemics, wars, plague and famine." Misery and poverty were simply the inevitable result of the law of nature; no government or individual should interfere with its operation.

The ideas of Thomas Malthus were further developed by David Ricardo (1772–1823). In his *Principles of Political Economy,* written in 1817, Ricardo developed his famous "iron law of wages." Following Malthus, Ricardo argued that an increase in population means more workers; more workers in turn cause wages to fall below the subsistence level. The result is misery and starvation, which then reduce the population. Consequently, the number of workers declines, and wages rise above the subsistence level again, which in turn encourages workers to have larger families as the cycle is repeated. According to Ricardo, raising wages arbitrarily would be pointless since it would accomplish little but perpetuate this vicious circle.

Politically, liberals came to hold a common set of beliefs. Chief among them was the protection of civil liberties or the basic rights of all people, which included equality before the law; freedom of assembly, speech, and press; and freedom from arbitrary arrest. All of these freedoms should be guaranteed by a written document, such as the American Bill of Rights or the French Declaration of the Rights of Man and the Citizen. In addition to religious toleration for all, most liberals advocated separation of church and state. The right of peaceful opposition to the government in and out of parliament and the making of laws by a representative assembly (legislature) elected by qualified voters constituted two other liberal demands. Many liberals believed, then, in a constitutional monarchy or constitutional state with limits on the powers of government in order to prevent despotism and in written constitutions that would help guarantee these rights.

Many liberals also advocated ministerial responsibility, a system in which the king's ministers were responsible to the legislature rather than to the king, giving the legislative branch a check on the power of the executive. Liberals in the first half of the nineteenth century also believed in a limited suffrage. Although all people were entitled to equal civil rights, they should not have equal political rights. The right to vote and hold office would be open only to men who met certain property qualifications. As a political philosophy, liberalism was tied to middle-class men, especially industrial middle-class men who favored the extension of voting rights so that they could share power with the landowning classes. They had little desire to let the lower classes share that power. Liberals were not democrats.

One of the most prominent advocates of liberalism in the nineteenth century was the English philosopher John Stuart Mill (1806–1873). *On Liberty,* his most famous work, published in 1859, has long been regarded as a classic statement on the liberty of the individual (see the box on p. 590). Mill argued for an "absolute freedom of opinion and sentiment on all subjects" that needed to be protected from both government censorship and the tyranny of the majority.

Mill was also instrumental in expanding the meaning of liberalism by becoming an enthusiastic supporter of women's rights. When his attempt to include women in the voting reform bill of 1867 failed, Mill published an essay titled *On the Subjection of Women,* which he had written earlier with his wife, Harriet Taylor. He argued that "the legal subordination of one sex to the other" was wrong. Differences between women and men, he claimed, were due not to different natures but simply to social practices. With equal education, women could achieve as much as men. *On the Subjection of Women* would become an important work in the nineteenth-century movement for women's rights.

Nationalism

Nationalism was an even more powerful ideology for change in the nineteenth century. Nationalism arose out of an awareness of being part of a community that has common institutions, traditions, language, and customs. This community constitutes a "nation," and it, rather than a dynasty, city-state, or other political unit, becomes the focus of the individual's primary political loyalty. Nationalism

The Voice of Liberalism: John Stuart Mill on Liberty

John Stuart Mill was one of Britain's most famous philosophers of liberalism. Mill's *On Liberty* is viewed as a classic statement of the liberal belief in the unfettered freedom of the individual. In this excerpt, Mill defends freedom of opinion from both government and the coercion of the majority.

■ *John Stuart Mill,* On Liberty

The object of this Essay is to assert one very simple principle, as entitled to govern absolutely the dealings of society with the individual in the way of compulsion and control, whether the means used by physical force in the form of legal penalties, or the moral coercion of public opinion. That principle is, that the sole end for which mankind are warranted, individually or collectively, interfering with the liberty of action of any of their number, is self-protection. That the only purpose for which power can be rightfully exercised over any member of a civilized community, against his will, is to prevent harm to others. His own good, either physical or moral, is not a sufficient warrant.... These are good reasons for remonstrating with him, or reasoning with him, or persuading him, or entreating him, but not for compelling him, or visiting him with any evil in case he do otherwise. To justify that, the conduct from which it is desired to deter him, must be calculated to produce evil to some one else. The only part of the conduct of any one, for which he is amenable to society, is that which concerns others. In the part which merely concerns himself, his independence is, of right, absolute. Over himself, over his own body and mind, the individual is sovereign....

Society can and does execute its own mandates: and if it issues wrong mandates instead of right, or any mandates at all in things with which it ought not to meddle, it practices a social tyranny more formidable than many kinds of political oppression, since, though not usually upheld by such extreme penalties, it leaves fewer means of escape, penetrating more deeply into the details of life, and enslaving the soul itself. Protection, therefore, against the tyranny of the magistrate is not enough: there needs protection also against the tyranny of prevailing opinion and feeling, against the tendency of society to impose, by other means than civil penalties, its own ideas and practices as rules of conduct on those who dissent from them....

But there is a sphere of action in which society, as distinguished from the individual has, if any, only an indirect interest; comprehending all that portion of a person's life and conduct which affects only himself, or if it also affects others, only with their free, voluntary and undeceived consent and participation.... This then is the appropriate region of human liberty. It comprises, first, the inward domain of consciousness; demanding liberty of conscience in the most comprehensive sense; liberty of thought and feeling; absolute freedom of opinion and sentiment on all subjects, practical or speculative, scientific, moral, or theological....

Let us suppose, therefore, that the government is entirely at one with the people, and never thinks of exerting any power of coercion unless in agreement with what it conceives to be their voice. But I deny the right of the people to exercise such coercion, either by themselves or by their government. The power itself is illegitimate. The best government has no more title to it than the worst. It is as noxious, or more noxious, when exerted in accordance with public opinion, than when in opposition to it. If all mankind minus one were of one opinion, and only one person were of the contrary opinion, mankind would be no more justified in silencing that one person, than he, if he had the power, would be justified in silencing mankind.... The peculiar evil of silencing the expression of an opinion is, that it is robbing the human race; posterity as well as the existing generation; those who dissent from the opinion, still more than those who hold it. If the opinion is right, they are deprived of the opportunity of exchanging error for truth: if wrong, they lose, what is almost as great a benefit, the clearer perception and livelier impression of truth, produced by its collision with error.

did not become a popular force for change until the French Revolution. From then on, nationalists came to believe that each nationality should have its own government. Thus a divided people such as the Germans wanted national unity in a German nation-state with one central government. Subject peoples, such as the Hungarians, wanted national self-determination, or the right to establish their own autonomy rather than be subject to a German minority in a multinational empire.

Nationalism threatened to upset the existing political order, both internationally and nationally (see Map 21.3). A united Germany or united Italy would upset the balance of power established in 1815. By the same token, an independent Hungarian state would mean the breakup of the Austrian Empire. Because many European states were multinational, it is evident why conservatives tried so hard to repress the radical threat of nationalism.

At the same time, in the first half of the nineteenth century, nationalism and liberalism became strong allies. Most liberals believed that liberty could only be realized by peoples who ruled themselves. One British liberal said, "It is in general a necessary condition of free institutions that the boundaries of governments should coincide in the main with those of nationalities." Many nationalists believed that once each people obtained its own state, all nations could be linked together into a broader community of all humanity.

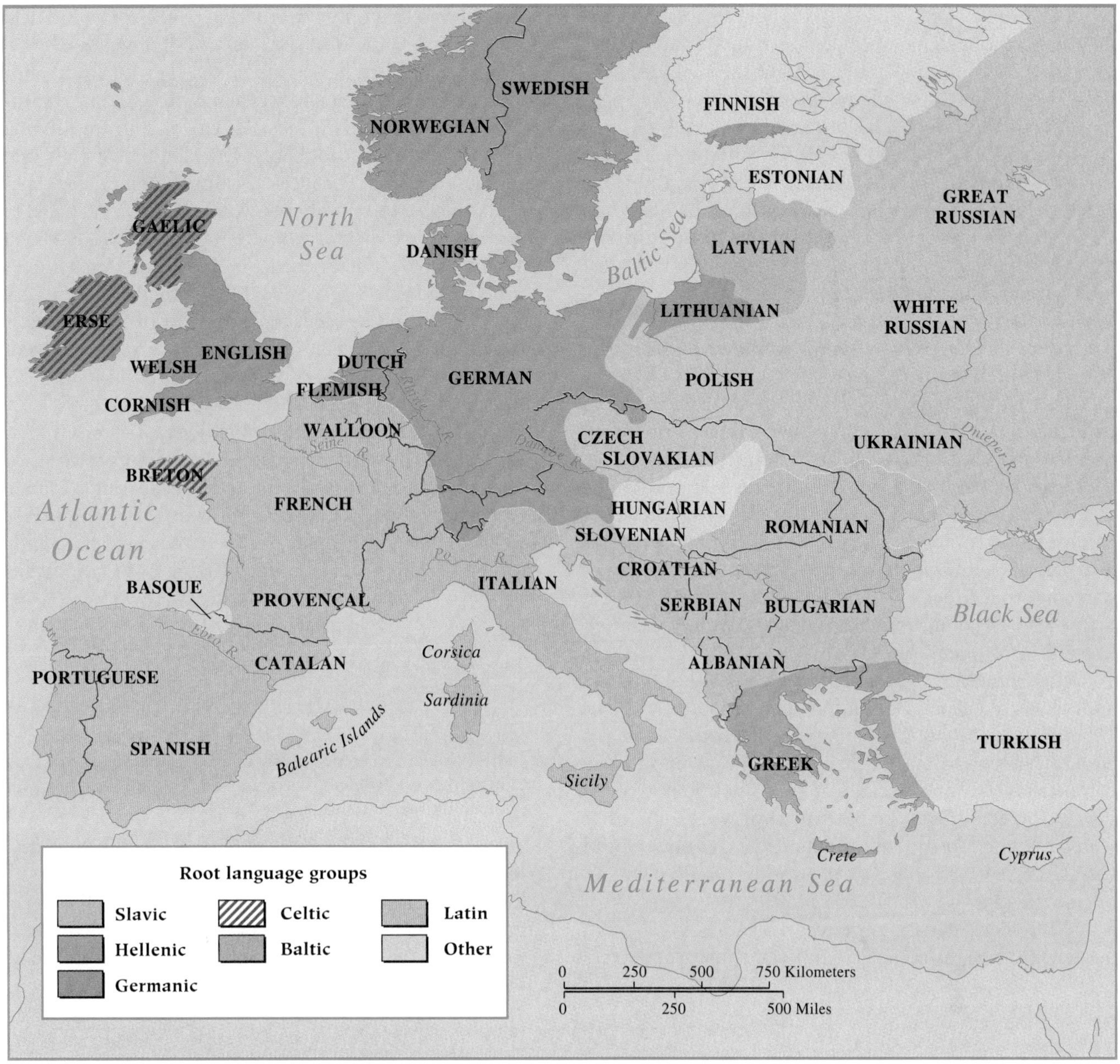

Map 21.3 The Distribution of Languages in Nineteenth-Century Europe. Numerous languages were spoken in Europe. People who used the same language often had a shared history and culture, which laid the seeds for growing nationalism in the nineteenth century. Such nationalism eventually led to unification for Germany and Italy but spelled trouble for the polyglot Habsburg empire. ■ Look at the distribution of Germanic, Latin, and Slavic languages. What patterns emerge, and how can you explain them?

Early Socialism

In the first half of the nineteenth century, the pitiful conditions found in the slums, mines, and factories of the Industrial Revolution gave rise to another ideology for change known as socialism. The term eventually became associated with a Marxist analysis of human society (see Chapter 22), but early socialism was largely the product of political theorists or intellectuals who wanted to introduce equality into social conditions and believed that human cooperation was superior to the competition that characterized early industrial capitalism. To later Marxists, such ideas were impractical dreams, and they contemptuously labeled the theorists utopian socialists. The term has endured to this day.

The utopian socialists were against private property and the competitive spirit of early industrial capitalism. By eliminating these things and creating new systems of social organization, they thought that a better environment for humanity could be achieved. Early socialists proposed a variety of ways to accomplish that task.

One group of early socialists sought to create voluntary associations that would demonstrate the advantages of cooperative living. Charles Fourier (1772–1838) proposed the creation of small model communities called phalansteries. These were self-contained cooperatives, each consisting ideally of 1,620 people. Communally housed, the inhabitants of the phalanstery would live and work together for their mutual benefit. Work assignments would be rotated frequently to relieve workers of undesirable tasks. Unable to gain financial backing for his phalansteries, Fourier's plan remained untested.

Robert Owen (1771–1858), the British cotton manufacturer, also believed that humans would reveal their true natural goodness if they lived in a cooperative environment. At New Lanark in Scotland, he was successful in transforming a squalid factory town into a flourishing, healthy community. But when he attempted to create a self-contained cooperative community at New Harmony, Indiana, in the United States in the 1820s, bickering within the community eventually destroyed his dream. One of Owen's disciples, a wealthy woman named Frances Wright, bought slaves in order to set up a model community at Nashoba, Tennessee. The community failed, but Wright continued to work for women's rights.

The Frenchman Louis Blanc (1813–1882) offered yet another early socialist approach to a better society. In *The Organization of Work,* he maintained that social problems could be solved by government assistance. Denouncing competition as the main cause of the economic evils of his day, he called for the establishment of workshops that would manufacture goods for public sale. The state would finance these workshops, but the workers would own and operate them.

With their plans for the reconstruction of society, utopian socialists attracted a number of female supporters who believed that only a reordering of society would help women. Zoé Gatti de Gamond, a Belgian follower of Fourier, established her own phalanstery, which was supposed to provide men and women with the same educational and job opportunities. As part of collective living, men and women were to share responsibilities for child care and housecleaning. The ideas of Saint-Simon proved especially attractive to a number of women who participated in the growing activism of women in politics that had been set in motion during the French Revolution. Saint-Simon's cooperative society recognized the principle of equality between men and women, and a number of working-class women, including Suzanne Voilquin, Claire Démar, and Reine Guindorf, published a newspaper dedicated to the emancipation of women.

One female utopian socialist, Flora Tristan (1803–1844), even attempted to foster a "utopian synthesis of socialism and feminism." She traveled through France preaching the need for the liberation of women. Her *Worker's Union,* published in 1843, advocated the application of Fourier's ideas to reconstruct both family and work:

> Workers, be sure of it. If you have enough equity and justice to inscribe into your Charter the few points I have just outlined, this declaration of the rights of women will soon pass into custom, from custom into law, and before twenty-five years pass you will then see inscribed in front of the book of laws which will govern French society: THE ABSOLUTE EQUALITY of man and woman. Then, my brothers, and only then, will human unity be constituted.[6]

She envisioned this absolute equality as the only hope to free the working class and transform civilization.

Flora Tristan, like the other utopian socialists, was largely ignored by her contemporaries. Although criticized for their impracticality, the utopian socialists at least laid

Children at New Lanark. Robert Owen created an early experiment in utopian socialism by establishing a model industrial community at New Lanark, Scotland. In this illustration, the children of factory workers are shown dancing the quadrille.

The Art Archive, London

the groundwork for later attacks on capitalism that would have a far-reaching result. In the first half of the nineteenth century, however, socialism remained merely a fringe movement compared to liberalism and nationalism.

Revolution and Reform (1830–1850)

Beginning in 1830, the forces of change began to break through the conservative domination of Europe, more successfully in some places than in others. Finally, in 1848, a wave of revolutionary fervor moved through Europe, causing liberals and nationalists everywhere to think that they were on the verge of creating a new order.

Another French Revolution

The new elections Charles X had called in 1830 produced another victory for the French liberals; at this point, the king decided to seize the initiative. On July 26, 1830, Charles issued a set of edicts (the July Ordinances) that imposed rigid censorship on the press, dissolved the legislative assembly, and reduced the electorate in preparation for new elections. Charles's actions produced an immediate rebellion—the July Revolution. Barricades went up in Paris as a provisional government led by a group of moderate, propertied liberals was hastily formed and appealed to Louis-Philippe, the duke of Orléans, a cousin of Charles X, to become the constitutional king of France. Charles X fled to Britain; a new monarchy had been born.

Louis-Philippe (1830–1848) was soon called the bourgeois monarch because political support for his rule came from the upper middle class. Louis-Philippe even dressed like a member of the middle class in business suits and hats. Constitutional changes that favored the interests of the upper bourgeoisie were instituted. Financial qualifications for voting were reduced yet remained sufficiently high that the number of voters only increased from 100,000 to barely 200,000, guaranteeing that only the wealthiest people would vote.

To the upper middle class, the bourgeois monarchy represented the stopping place for political progress. To the lesser bourgeoisie and the Parisian working class, who had helped overthrow Charles X in 1830, it was a severe disappointment because they had been completely excluded from political power. The rapid expansion of French industry in the 1830s and 1840s gave rise to an industrial working class concentrated in certain urban areas. Terrible working and living conditions and the periodic economic crises that created high levels of unemployment led to worker unrest and sporadic outbursts of violence.

Even in the legislature—the Chamber of Deputies—there were differences of opinion about the bourgeois monarchy and the direction in which it should grow. Two groups rapidly emerged, although both were composed of upper-middle-class representatives. The Party of Movement, which was led by Adolphe Thiers, favored ministerial

The July Revolution in Paris. In 1830, the forces of change began to undo the conservative domination of Europe. In France, the reactionary Charles X was overthrown. In this painting, students, former soldiers of the empire, and middle-class citizens are seen joining the rebels who are marching on city hall to demand a republic. The forces of Charles X, seen firing from a building above, failed to halt the rebels.

Giraudon/Art Resource, NY

responsibility, the pursuit of an active foreign policy, and limited expansion of the franchise. The Party of Resistance was led by François Guizot, who believed that France had finally reached the "perfect form" of government and needed no further institutional changes. After 1840, the Party of Resistance dominated the Chamber of Deputies. Guizot cooperated with Louis-Philippe in suppressing ministerial responsibility and pursuing a policy favoring the interests of the wealthier manufacturers and tradespeople.

Revolutionary Outbursts in Belgium, Poland, and Italy

Supporters of liberalism played a primary role in the July Revolution in France, but nationalism was the crucial force in three other revolutionary outbursts in 1830. In an effort to create a stronger, larger state on France's northern border, the Congress of Vienna had added the area once known as the Austrian Netherlands to the Dutch Republic. The combination of two states with different languages, traditions, and religions was never really acceptable to the Belgians, and in 1830, they rose up against the Dutch and succeeded in convincing the major European powers to accept an independent, neutral Belgium. Leopold of Saxe-Coburg, a minor German prince, was designated to be the new king, and a Belgian national congress established a constitutional monarchy for the new state.

The revolutionary scenarios in Italy and Poland were much less successful. Metternich sent Austrian troops to crush revolts in three Italian states. Poland, too, had a nationalist uprising in 1830 when revolutionaries tried to end Russian control of their country. But the Polish insurgents failed to get hoped-for support from France and Britain, and by September 1831, the Russians had crushed the revolt and established an oppressive military dictatorship over Poland.

Reform in Great Britain

In 1830, new parliamentary elections brought the Whigs to power in Britain. At the same time, the successful July Revolution in France served to catalyze change in Britain. The Industrial Revolution had led to an expanding group of industrial leaders who objected to the corrupt British electoral system, which excluded them from political power. The Whigs, though also members of the landed classes, realized that concessions to reform were superior to revolution; the demands of the wealthy industrial middle class could no longer be ignored. In 1830, the Whigs introduced an election reform bill that was enacted in 1832 after an intense struggle (see the box on p. 595).

The Reform Act gave explicit recognition to the changes wrought in British life by the Industrial Revolution. It disfranchised fifty-six rotten boroughs and enfranchised forty-two new towns and cities and reapportioned others. This gave the new industrial urban communities some voice in government. A property qualification (of £10 annual rent) for voting was retained, however, so the number of voters increased from 478,000 to only 814,000, a figure that still meant that only one in every thirty people was represented in Parliament. Thus the Reform Act of 1832 primarily benefited the upper middle class; the lower middle class, artisans, and industrial workers still had no vote. Moreover, the change did not significantly alter the composition of the House of Commons. One political leader noted that the Commons chosen in the first election after the Reform Act seemed "to be very much like every other parliament." Nevertheless, a significant step had been taken. The industrial middle class had been joined to the landed interests in ruling Britain.

The 1830s and 1840s witnessed considerable reform legislation. The aristocratic landowning class was usually (but not always) the driving force for legislation that halted some of the worst abuses in the industrial system by instituting government regulation of working conditions in the factories and mines. The industrialists and manufacturers now in Parliament opposed such legislation and were usually (but not always) the driving forces behind legislation that favored the principles of economic liberalism. The Poor Law of 1834 was based on the theory that giving aid to the poor and unemployed only encouraged laziness and increased the number of paupers. The Poor Law tried to remedy this by making paupers so wretched they would choose to work. Those unable to support themselves were crowded together in workhouses where living and working conditions were intentionally miserable so that people would be encouraged to find profitable employment.

Another piece of liberal legislation involved the repeal of the Corn Laws. This was primarily the work of the manufacturers Richard Cobden and John Bright, who formed the Anti–Corn Law League in 1838 to help workers by lowering bread prices. But abolishing the Corn Laws would also aid the industrial middle classes, who, as economic liberals, favored the principles of free trade. Repeal came in 1846 when Robert Peel (1788–1850), leader of the Tories, persuaded some of his associates to support free trade principles and abandon the Corn Laws.

The year 1848, which witnessed revolutions in most of Europe, ended without a major crisis in Britain. On the Continent, middle-class liberals and nationalists were at the forefront of the revolutionary forces. In Britain, however, the middle class had been largely satisfied by the Reform Act of 1832 and the repeal of the Corn Laws in 1846.

The Revolutions of 1848

Despite the successes of revolutions in France, Belgium, and Greece, the conservative order remained in control of much of Europe. But liberalism and nationalism continued to grow. In 1848, these forces of change erupted once more. Yet again, revolution in France provided the spark for other countries, and soon most of central and southern Europe was ablaze with revolutionary fires (see Map 21.4). Tsar Nicholas I of Russia lamented to Queen Victoria in April 1848, "What remains standing in Europe? Great Britain and Russia."

The Voice of Reform: Macaulay on the Reform Act of 1832

Thomas Babington Macaulay (1800–1859) was a historian and a Whig member of Parliament. This selection is an excerpt from his speech given in Parliament in support of the Reform Act of 1832, which extended the right to vote to the industrial middle classes of Britain. His argument was very simple: it is better to reform than to have a political revolution.

■ *Thomas Babington Macaulay, Speech of March 2, 1831*

My hon. friend the member of the University of Oxford tells us that, if we pass this law, England will soon be a Republic. The reformed House of Commons will, according to him, before it has sat ten years, depose the King, and expel the Lords from their House. Sir, if my hon. friend could prove this, he would have succeeded in bringing an argument for democracy infinitely stronger than any that is to be found in the works of Paine. His proposition is, in fact, this—that our monarchical and aristocratical institutions have no hold on the public mind of England; that these institutions are regarded with aversion by a decided majority of the middle class. . . . Now, sir, if I were convinced that the great body of the middle class in England look with aversion on monarchy and aristocracy, I should be forced, much against my will, to come to this conclusion, that monarchical and aristocratical institutions are unsuited to this country. Monarchy and aristocracy, valuable and useful as I think them, are still valuable and useful as means, and not as ends. The end of government is the happiness of the people; and I do not conceive that, in a country like this, the happiness of the people can be promoted by a form of government in which the middle classes place no confidence, and which exists only because the middle classes have no organ by which to make their sentiments known. But, sir, I am fully convinced that the middle classes sincerely wish to uphold the royal prerogatives, and the constitutional rights of the Peers. . . .

But let us know our interest and our duty better. Turn where we may—within, around—the voice of great events is proclaiming to us, "Reform, that you may preserve." Now, therefore, while everything at home and abroad forebodes ruin to those who persist in a hopeless struggle against the spirit of the age; now, while the crash of the proudest throne of the Continent is still resounding in our ears; . . . now, while the heart of England is still sound; now, while the old feelings and the old associations retain a power and a charm which may too soon pass away; now, in this your accepted time; now, in this your day of salvation, take counsel, not of prejudice, not of party spirit, not of the ignominious pride of a fatal consistency, but of history, of reason, of the ages which are past, of the signs of this most portentous time. Pronounce in a manner worthy of the expectation with which this great debate has been anticipated, and of the long remembrance which it will leave behind. Renew the youth of the State. Save property divided against itself. Save the multitude, endangered by their own ungovernable passions. Save the aristocracy, endangered by its own unpopular power. Save the greatest, and fairest, and most highly civilized community that ever existed, from calamities which may in a few days sweep away all the rich heritage of so many ages of wisdom and glory. The danger is terrible. The time is short. If this Bill should be rejected, I pray to God that none of those who concur in rejecting it may ever remember their votes with unavailing regret, amidst the wreck of laws, the confusion of ranks, the spoliation of property, and the dissolution of social order.

YET ANOTHER FRENCH REVOLUTION

A severe industrial and agricultural depression beginning in 1846 brought great hardship to the French lower middle class, workers, and peasants. One-third of the workers in Paris were unemployed by the end of 1847. Scandals, graft, and corruption were rife, and the government's persistent refusal to extend the suffrage angered the disfranchised members of the middle class.

As Louis-Philippe's government continued to refuse to make changes, opposition grew. Radical republicans and socialists, joined by the upper middle class under the leadership of Adolphe Thiers, agitated for the dismissal of Guizot. Since they were forbidden by law to stage political rallies, they used the political banquet to call for reforms. Almost seventy such banquets were held in France during the winter of 1847–1848; a grand culminating banquet was planned for Paris on February 22. When the government forbade it, people came anyway; students and workers threw up barricades in Paris. Although Louis-Philippe now proposed reform, he was unable to form another ministry and abdicated on February 24 and fled to Britain. A provisional government was established by a group of moderate and radical republicans; the latter even included the socialist Louis Blanc. The provisional government ordered that representatives for a constituent assembly convened to draw up a new constitution be elected by universal manhood suffrage.

The provisional government also established national workshops under the influence of Louis Blanc. As Blanc envisioned them, the workshops were to be cooperative factories run by the workers. In fact, the workshops came to provide jobs, consisting primarily of leaf raking and ditch digging, for unemployed workers. The cost of the program became increasingly burdensome to the government.

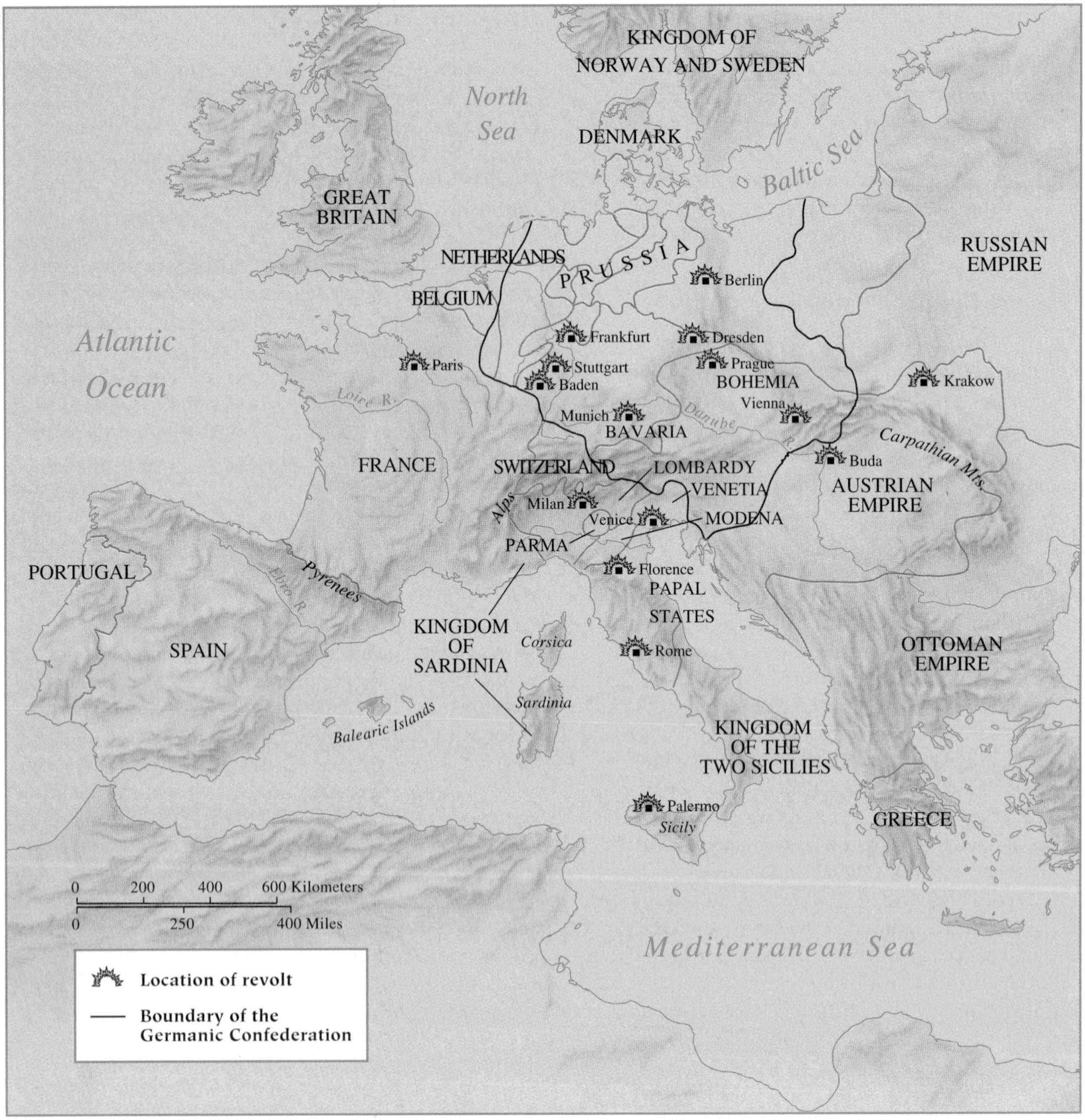

Map 21.4 The Revolutions of 1848–1849. Beginning in Paris, revolutionary fervor fueled by liberalism and nationalism spread to the east and the south. After initial successes, the revolutionaries failed to maintain unity: propertied classes feared the working masses, and nationalists such as the Hungarians could not agree that all national groups deserved self-determination. The old order rallied its troops and prevailed. ■ Which regions saw a great deal of revolutionary activity in 1848–1849, and which did not?

The result was a growing split between the moderate republicans, who had the support of most of France, and the radical republicans, whose main support came from the Parisian working class. In the elections for the National Assembly, five hundred seats went to moderate republicans and three hundred to avowed monarchists, while the radicals gained only one hundred. From March to June, the number of unemployed enrolled in the national workshops rose from 10,000 to almost 120,000, emptying the treasury and frightening the moderates, who responded by closing the workshops on June 23. The workers refused to accept this decision and poured into the streets. Four days of bitter and bloody fighting by government forces crushed the working-class revolt. Thousands were killed, and four thousand prisoners were deported to the French colony of Algeria in North Africa.

The new constitution, ratified on November 4, 1848, established a republic (the Second Republic) with a uni-

Revolutionary Excitement: The 1848 Revolution in Germany

The excitement with which German liberals and nationalists received the news of the February Revolution in France and their own expectations for Germany are well captured in this selection from the *Reminiscences* of Carl Schurz (1829–1906). Schurz made his way to the United States after the failure of the German revolution and eventually became a U.S. senator.

Carl Schurz, Reminiscences

One morning, toward the end of February, 1848, I sat quietly in my attic-chamber, working hard at my tragedy of "Ulrich von Hutten" [a sixteenth-century German knight] when suddenly a friend rushed breathlessly into the room, exclaiming: "What, you sitting here! Do you not know what has happened?"

"No; what?"

"The French have driven away Louis Philippe and proclaimed the republic."

I threw down my pen—and that was the end of "Ulrich von Hutten." I never touched the manuscript again. We tore down the stairs, into the street, to the market-square, the accustomed meeting-place for all the student societies after their midday dinner. Although it was still forenoon, the market was already crowded with young men talking excitedly. There was no shouting, no noise, only agitated conversation. What did we want there? This probably no one knew. But since the French had driven away Louis Philippe and proclaimed the republic, something of course must happen here, too. . . . We were dominated by a vague feeling as if a great outbreak of elemental forces had begun, as if an earthquake was impending of which we had felt the first shock, and we instinctively crowded together. . . .

The next morning there were the usual lectures to be attended. But how profitless! The voice of the professor sounded like a monotonous drone coming from far away. What he had to say did not seem to concern us. The pen that should have taken notes remained idle. At last we closed with a sigh the notebook and went away, impelled by a feeling that now we had something more important to do—to devote ourselves to the affairs of the fatherland. And this we did by seeking as quickly as possible again the company of our friends, in order to discuss what had happened and what was to come. In these conversations, excited as they were, certain ideas and catchwords worked themselves to the surface, which expressed more or less the feelings of the people. Now had arrived in Germany the day for the establishment of "German Unity," and the founding of a great, powerful national German Empire. In the first line the convocation of a national parliament. Then the demands for civil rights and liberties, free speech, free press, the right of free assembly, equality before the law, a freely elected representation of the people with legislative power, responsibility of ministers, self-government of the communes, the right of the people to carry arms, the formation of a civic guard with elective officers, and so on—in short, that which was called a "constitutional form of government on a broad democratic basis." Republican ideas were at first only sparingly expressed. But the word democracy was soon on all tongues, and many, too, thought it a matter of course that if the princes should try to withhold from the people the rights and liberties demanded, force would take the place of mere petition. Of course the regeneration of the fatherland must, if possible, be accomplished by peaceable means. . . . Like many of my friends, I was dominated by the feeling that at last the great opportunity had arrived for giving to the German people the liberty which was their birthright and to the German fatherland its unity and greatness, and that it was now the first duty of every German to do and to sacrifice everything for this sacred object.

cameral (one-house) legislature of 750 elected by universal male suffrage for three years and a president, also elected by universal male suffrage, for four years. In the elections for the presidency held in December 1848, four republicans who had been associated with the early months of the Second Republic were resoundingly defeated by Charles Louis Napoleon Bonaparte, the nephew of Napoleon Bonaparte. Within four years, President Napoleon would become Emperor Napoleon (see Chapter 22).

REVOLUTION IN CENTRAL EUROPE

News of the revolution in Paris in February 1848 triggered upheavals in central Europe as well (see the box above). Revolutionary cries for change caused many German rulers to promise constitutions, a free press, jury trials, and other liberal reforms. In Prussia, concessions were also made to appease the revolutionaries. King Frederick William IV (1840–1861) agreed to abolish censorship, establish a new constitution, and work for a united Germany. This last promise had its counterpart throughout all the German states as governments allowed elections by universal male suffrage for deputies to an all-German parliament to meet in Frankfurt, the seat of the German Confederation. Its purpose was to fulfill a liberal and nationalist dream—the preparation of a constitution for a new united Germany.

This Frankfurt Assembly was dominated by well-educated, articulate, middle-class delegates, many of them professors, lawyers, and bureaucrats. When it came to nationalism, many were ahead of the times and certainly ahead of the governments of their respective states. From the beginning, the assembly aroused controversy by claiming to be the government for all of Germany. Then it became embroiled in a sticky debate over the composition of the new German state. Supporters of a *Grossdeutsch* ("Big German") solution wanted to include the German province of Austria, whereas proponents of a *Kleindeutsch* ("Small German") solution favored excluding Austria and making the Prussian king the emperor of the new German state. The problem was solved when the Austrians withdrew, leaving the field to the supporters of the *Kleindeutsch* solution. Their victory was short-lived, however, as Frederick William IV gruffly refused the assembly's offer of the title of "emperor of the Germans" in March 1849 and ordered the Prussian delegates home.

The Frankfurt Assembly soon disbanded. Although some members spoke of using force, they had no real means of compelling the German rulers to accept the constitution they had drawn up. The attempt of the German liberals at Frankfurt to create a German state had failed.

The Austrian Empire also had its social, political, and nationalist grievances and needed only the news of the revolution in Paris to encourage it to erupt in flames in March 1848. The Hungarian liberals under Louis Kossuth agitated for "commonwealth" status; they were willing to keep the Habsburg monarch but wanted their own legislature. In March, demonstrations in Buda, Prague, and Vienna led to Metternich's dismissal, and the archsymbol of the conservative order fled abroad. In Vienna, revolutionary forces, carefully guided by the educated and propertied classes, took control of the capital and insisted that a constituent assembly be summoned to draw up a liberal constitution. Hungary was granted its wish for its own legislature, a separate national army, and control over its foreign policy and budget. Allegiance to the Habsburg dynasty was now Hungary's only tie to the Austrian Empire. In Bohemia, the Czechs began to demand their own government as well.

Although Emperor Ferdinand I (1835–1848) and Austrian officials had made concessions to appease the revolutionaries, they awaited an opportunity to reestablish their firm control. As in the German states, the conservatives were increasingly encouraged by the divisions between radical and moderate revolutionaries and played on the middle-class fear of a working-class social revolution. Their first success came in June 1848 when a military force under General Alfred Windischgrätz ruthlessly suppressed the Czech rebels in Prague. In October, the death of the minister for war at the hands of a Viennese mob gave Windischgrätz the pretext for an attack on Vienna. By the end of the month, radical rebels there had been crushed. In December, the feebleminded Ferdinand I agreed to abdicate in favor of his nephew, Francis Joseph I (1848–1916), who worked vigorously to restore the imperial government in Hungary. The Austrian armies, however, were unable to defeat Kossuth's forces, and it was only through the intervention of Nicholas I, who sent a Russian army of 140,000 men to aid the Austrians, that the Hungarian revolution was finally crushed in 1849. The revolutions in Austria had also failed.

Austrian Students in the Revolutionary Civil Guard. In 1848, revolutionary fervor swept the European continent and toppled governments in France, central Europe, and Italy. In the Austrian Empire, students joined the revolutionary civil guard in taking control of Vienna and forcing the Austrian emperor to call a constituent assembly to draft a liberal constitution.

The Voice of Italian Nationalism: Giuseppe Mazzini and Young Italy

After the failure of the uprisings in Italy in 1830–1831, Giuseppe Mazzini emerged as the leader of the Italian *risorgimento*—the movement for Italian nationhood. In 1831, he founded an organization known as Young Italy whose goal was the creation of a united Italian republic. This selection is excerpted from the oath that the members of young Italy were required to take.

■ *Giuseppe Mazzini,* The Young Italy Oath

Young Italy is a brotherhood of Italians who believe in a law of Progress and Duty, and are convinced that Italy is destined to become one nation,—convinced also that she possesses sufficient strength within herself to become one, and that the ill success of her former efforts is to be attributed not to the weakness, but to the misdirection of the revolutionary elements within her,—that the secret of force lies in constancy and unity of effort. They join this association in the firm intent of consecrating both thought and action to the great aim of reconstituting Italy as one independent sovereign nation of free men and equals. . . .

Each member will, upon his initiation into the association of Young Italy, pronounce the following form of oath, in the presence of the initiator:

In the name of God and of Italy;

In the name of all the martyrs of the holy Italian cause who have fallen beneath foreign and domestic tyranny;

By the duties which bind me to the land wherein God has placed me, and to the brothers whom God has given me;

By the love—innate in all men—I bear to the country that gave my mother birth, and will be the home of my children. . . .

By the sufferings of the millions,—

I, . . . believing in the mission intrusted by God to Italy, and the duty of every Italian to strive to attempt its fulfillment; convinced that where God has ordained that a nation shall be, He has given the requisite power to create it; that the people are the depositaries of that power, and that in its right direction for the people, and by the people, lies the secret of victory; convinced that virtue consists in action and sacrifice, and strength in union and constancy of purpose: I give my name to Young Italy, an association of men holding the same faith, and swear:

To dedicate myself wholly and forever to the endeavor with them to constitute Italy one free, independent, republican nation; to promote by every means in my power—whether by written or spoken word, or by action—the education of my Italian brothers toward the aim of Young Italy; toward association, the sole means of its accomplishment, and to virtue, which alone can render the conquest lasting; to abstain from enrolling myself in any other association from this time forth; to obey all the instructions, in conformity with the spirit of Young Italy, given me by those who represent with me the union of my Italian brothers; and to keep the secret of these instructions, even at the cost of my life; to assist my brothers of the association both by action and counsel—NOW AND FOREVER.

Autocratic government was restored; emperor and propertied classes remained in control, and the numerous nationalities were still subject to the Austrian government.

REVOLTS IN THE ITALIAN STATES

The failure of revolutionary uprisings in Italy in 1830–1831 had encouraged the Italian movement for unification to take a new direction. The leadership of Italy's *risorgimento* ("resurgence") passed into the hands of Giuseppe Mazzini (1805–1872), a dedicated Italian nationalist who founded an organization known as Young Italy in 1831 (see the box above). This group set as its goal the creation of a united Italian republic. In his work *The Duties of Man,* Mazzini urged Italians to dedicate their lives to the Italian nation: "O my Brother! Love your Country. Our Country is our home." A number of Italian women also took up Mazzini's call. Especially notable was Cristina Belgioioso, a wealthy aristocrat who worked to bring about Italian unification. Pursued by the Austrian authorities, she fled to Paris and started a newspaper espousing the Italian cause.

The dreams of Mazzini and Belgioioso seemed on the verge of fulfillment when a number of Italian states rose in revolt in 1848. Beginning in Sicily, rebellions spread northward as ruler after ruler granted a constitution to his people. Citizens in Lombardy and Venetia also rebelled against their Austrian overlords. The Venetians declared a republic in Venice. The king of the northern Italian state of Piedmont, Charles Albert (1831–1849), took up the call and assumed the leadership for a war of liberation from Austrian domination. His invasion of Lombardy proved unsuccessful, however, and by 1849, the Austrians had reestablished complete control over Lombardy and Venetia. Counterrevolutionary forces also prevailed throughout Italy. French forces helped Pope Pius IX regain control of Rome. Elsewhere Italian rulers managed to recover power on their own. Only Piedmont was able to keep its liberal constitution.

THE FAILURES OF 1848

Throughout Europe in 1848, popular revolts had initiated revolutionary upheavals that had led to the formation of liberal constitutions and liberal governments. But how could so many immediate successes in 1848 be followed by so many disasters only months later? Two reasons stand out. The unity of the revolutionaries had made the revolutions possible, but divisions soon shattered their ranks.

CHRONOLOGY

Reform, Reaction, and Revolution: The European States, 1815–1850

Great Britain	
Peterloo Massacre	1819
Reform Act	1832
Poor Law	1834
Repeal of Corn Laws	1846
France	
Louis XVIII	1814–1824
Charles X	1824–1830
July Revolution	1830
Louis-Philippe	1830–1848
Abdication of Louis-Philippe; formation of provisional government	1848 (February 22–24)
June Days: workers' revolt in Paris	1848 (June)
Establishment of Second Republic	1848 (November)
Election of Louis Napoleon as French president	1848 (December)
Low Countries	
Union of Netherlands and Belgium	1815
Belgian revolt	1830
German States	
Frederick William III of Prussia	1797–1840
Germanic Confederation established	1815
Karlsbad Decrees	1819
Frederick William IV of Prussia	1840–1861
Revolution in Germany	1848
Frankfurt Assembly	1848–1849
Austrian Empire	
Emperor Ferdinand I	1835–1848
Revolt in Austrian Empire; Metternich dismissed	1848 (March)
Austrian forces under General Windischgrätz crush Czech rebels	1848 (June)
Viennese rebels crushed	1848 (October)
Francis Joseph I	1848–1916
Defeat of Hungarians with help of Russian troops	1849
Italian States	
Revolts in southern Italy and Sardinia crushed	1821
King Charles Albert of Piedmont	1831–1849
Revolutions in Italy	1848
Charles Albert attacks Austrians	1848
Austrians reestablish control in Lombardy and Venetia	1849
Russia	
Tsar Alexander I	1801–1825
Decembrist Revolt	1825
Tsar Nicholas I	1825–1855
Polish uprising	1830
Suppression of Polish revolt	1831

Except in France, moderate liberals from the propertied classes failed to extend suffrage to the working classes who had helped to achieve the revolutions. But as radicals pushed for universal male suffrage, liberals everywhere pulled back. Concerned about their property and security, they rallied to the old ruling classes for the sake of order and out of fear of social revolution by the working classes. All too soon, established governments were back in power.

In 1848, nationalities everywhere had also revolted in pursuit of self-government. But here too, frightfully little was achieved as divisions among nationalities proved utterly disastrous. Though the Hungarians demanded autonomy from the Austrians, at the same time they refused the same to their minorities—the Slovenes, Croats, and Serbs. Instead of joining together against the old empire, minorities fought each other. No wonder that one Czech could remark in April 1848: "If the Austrian state had not already existed for so long, it would have been in the interests of Europe, indeed of humanity itself, to endeavor to create it as soon as possible."[7] The Austrians' efforts to recover the Hungarian provinces met with little success until they began to play off Hungary's rebellious minority nationalities against the Hungarians.

The Growth of the United States

The U.S. Constitution, ratified in 1789, committed the United States to two of the major forces of the first half of the nineteenth century, liberalism and nationalism. Initially, this constitutional commitment to national unity was challenged by divisions over the power of the federal government vis-à-vis the individual states. Bitter conflict erupted between the Federalists and the Republicans. Led by Alexander Hamilton (1757–1804), the Federalists favored a financial program that would establish a strong central government. The Republicans, guided by Thomas Jefferson (1743–1826) and James Madison (1751–1836), feared centralization and its consequences for popular liberties. These divisions were intensified by European rivalries because the Federalists were pro-British and the Republicans pro-French. The successful conclusion of the

War of 1812 brought an end to the Federalists, who had opposed the war, while the surge of national feeling generated by the war served to heal the nation's divisions.

Another strong force for national unity came from the Supreme Court while John Marshall (1755–1835) was chief justice from 1801 to 1835. Marshall made the Supreme Court into an important national institution by asserting the right of the Court to overrule an act of Congress if the Court found it to be in violation of the Constitution. Under Marshall, the Supreme Court contributed further to establishing the supremacy of the national government by curbing the actions of state courts and legislatures.

The election of Andrew Jackson (1767–1845) as president in 1828 opened a new era in American politics. Jacksonian democracy introduced mass democratic politics. The electorate was expanded by dropping traditional property qualifications; by the 1830s, suffrage had been extended to almost all adult white males. During the period from 1815 to 1850, the traditional liberal belief in the improvement of human beings was also given concrete expression. Americans developed detention schools for juvenile delinquents and new penal institutions, both motivated by the liberal belief that the right kind of environment would rehabilitate those in need of it.

The Emergence of an Ordered Society

Everywhere in Europe, the revolutionary upheavals of the late eighteenth and early nineteenth centuries made the ruling elite nervous about social disorder and the potential dangers to their lives and property. At the same time, the influx of large numbers of people from the countryside into rapidly growing cities had led to horrible living conditions, poverty, unemployment, and great social dissatisfaction. The first half of the nineteenth century witnessed a significant increase in crime rates, especially against property, in Britain, France, and Germany. The rise in property crimes caused a severe reaction among middle-class urban inhabitants, who feared that the urban poor posed a threat to their security and possessions. New police forces soon appeared to defend the propertied classes from criminals and social misfits.

New Police Forces

The first major contribution of the nineteenth century to the development of a disciplined or ordered society in Europe was a regular system of police. A number of European states established civilian police forces—groups of well-trained law enforcement officers who were to preserve property and lives, maintain domestic order, investigate crime, and arrest offenders. It was hoped that their very presence would prevent crime. That the new police existed to protect citizens eventually made them acceptable, and by the end of the nineteenth century, many Europeans viewed them approvingly.

This new approach to policing made its first appearance in France in 1828 when Louis-Maurice Debelleyme, the prefect of Paris, proclaimed his goal: "The essential object of our municipal police is the safety of the inhabitants of Paris. Safety by day and night, free traffic movement, clean streets, the supervision of and precaution against accidents, the maintenance of order in public places, the seeking out of offenses and their perpetrators."[8] In March 1829, the new police, known as *serjents,* became visible on Paris streets. They were dressed in blue uniforms to make them easily recognizable by all citizens. They were also lightly armed with a white cane during the day and a saber at night, underscoring the fact that they made up a civilian, not a military, body. Initially, there were not many of the new police officers. Paris had eighty-five by August 1829 and only five hundred in 1850. Before the end of the century, their number had increased to four thousand.

The British, fearful of the powers exercised by military or secret police in authoritarian Continental states, had long resisted the creation of a professional police force. Instead, Britain depended on a system of unpaid constables recruited by local authorities. Often these local constables were incapable of keeping order, preventing crimes,

The London Police. One response to the revolutionary upheavals of the late eighteenth and early nineteenth centuries was the development of civilian police forces that would be responsible for preserving property, arresting criminals, and maintaining domestic order. This early photograph shows a group of London policemen, who came to be known as bobbies after Sir Robert Peel, the man responsible for introducing the legislation that initiated the London police force.

Mansell/TimePix

The New British Police: "We Are Not Treated as Men"

The new British police forces, organized first in London in 1829, were generally well established throughout a good part of Britain by the 1840s. As professionalism rose in the ranks of the forces, so too did demands for better pay and treatment. In these two selections, police constables make clear their demands and complaints.

Petition for Higher Pay by a Group of Third-Class Constables (1848)

Men joining the Police service as 3rd Class Constables and having a wife and 3 children to support on joining, are not able properly to do so on the pay of 16/8d. Most of the married men on joining are somewhat in debt, and are unable to extricate themselves on account of rent to pay and articles to buy which are necessary for support of wife and children. We beg leave to state that a married man having a wife and 2 children to support on joining, that it is as much as he can do upon 16/8d per week, and having to remain upon that sum for the first 12 to 18 months.

Complaints from Constables of D Division of the London Metropolitan Police

We are not treated as men but as slaves we englishmen do not like to be terrorized by a set of Irish Sergeants who are only lenient to their own countrymen we the D division of Paddington are nearly all ruled by these Irish Sergeants after we have done our night-Duty may we not have the privilege of going to Church or staying at home to Suit our own inclination when we are ordered by the Superintendent to go to church in our uniform on wednesday we do not object to the going to church we like to go but we do not like to be ordered there and when we go on Sunday nights we are asked like so many schoolboys have we been to church should we say no let reason be what it may it does not matter we are forthwith ordered from Paddington to Marylebone lane the next night—about 2 hours before we go to Duty that is 2 miles from many of our homes being tired with our walk there and back we must either loiter about the streets or in some public house and there we do not want to go for we cannot spare our trifling wages to spend them there but there is no other choice left—for us to make our time out to go on Duty at proper time on Day we are ordered there for that offense another Man may faultlessly commit—the crime of sitting 4 minutes during the night—then we must be ordered there another to Shew his old clothes before they are given in even we must go to the expense of having them put in repair we have indeed for all these frightful crimes to walk 3 or 4 miles and then be wasting our time that makes our night 3 hours longer than they ought to be another thing we want to know who has the money that is deducted out of our wages for fines and many of us will be obliged to give up the duty unless we can have fair play as to the stationing of us on our beats why cannot we follow round that may all and each of us go over every beat and not for the Sergeants to put their favorites on the good beats and the others kept back their favorites are not the best policemen but those that will spend the most with them at the public house there are a great many of these things to try our temper.

or apprehending criminals. Such jobs could also be dangerous and involve incidents like the one reported by a man passing by a local pub in 1827:

> I saw Thomas Franklin [constable of the village of Leighton Buzzard] coming out backwards. John Brandon . . . was opposite and close to the constable. I saw the said John Brandon strike the said constable twice "bang full in the face" the blows knocked the constable down on his back. John Brandon fell down with him. Sarah Adams . . . got on top of the constable and jostled his head against the ground. . . . The constable appeared very much hurt and his face was all over blood.[9]

The failure of the local constables led to a new approach. Between September 1829 and May 1830, three thousand uniformed police officers appeared on the streets of London. They came to be known as bobbies after Sir Robert Peel, who had introduced the legislation that created the force.

As is evident from the first instruction book for the new British police, their primary goal was to prevent crime: "Officers and police constables should endeavour to distinguish themselves by such vigilance and activity as may render it impossible for any one to commit a crime within that portion of the town under their charge."[10] The municipal authorities soon found, however, that the police were also useful for imposing order on working-class urban inhabitants. On Sundays, they were called on to clean up after Saturday night's drinking bouts. As demands for better pay and treatment led to improved working conditions, British police began to develop a sense of professionalism (see the box above).

Police systems were reorganized throughout the Western world during the nineteenth century. After the revolutions of 1848 in Germany, a state-financed police force called the *Schutzmannschaft,* modeled after the London police, was established for the city of Berlin. The *Schutzmannschaft* began as a civilian body, but already by 1851, the force had become organized more along military lines and was used for political purposes. Its military nature was reinforced by the force's weaponry, which included swords, pistols, and brass knuckles. One observer noted that "a German policeman on patrol is armed as if for war."[11]

Although the new police alleviated some of the fears about the increase in crime, contemporary reformers approached the problem in other ways. Some of them believed that the increase in crime was related to the dramatic increase in poverty. As one commented in 1816: "Poverty, misery are the parents of crime." Strongly influenced by the middle-class belief that unemployment was the result of sheer laziness, European states passed poor laws that attempted to force paupers to find work on their own or enter workhouses designed to make people so utterly uncomfortable they would choose to reenter the labor market.

Meanwhile, another group of reformers was arguing that poor laws failed to address the real problem, which was that poverty was a result of the moral degeneracy of the lower classes, increasingly labeled the "dangerous classes" because of the perceived threat they posed to middle-class society. This belief led one group of secular reformers to form institutes to instruct the working classes in the applied sciences in order to make them more productive members of society. The London Mechanics' Institute, established in Britain, and the Society for the Diffusion of Useful Knowledge in the Field of Natural Sciences, Technical Science, and Political Economy, founded in Germany, are but two examples of this approach to the "dangerous classes."

Organized religion took a different approach. British evangelicals set up Sunday schools to improve the morals of working children, and in Germany, evangelical Protestants established nurseries for orphans and homeless children, women's societies to care for the sick and poor, and prison societies that prepared women to work in prisons. The Catholic church attempted the same kind of work through a revival of its religious orders; dedicated priests and nuns used spiritual instruction and recreation to turn young male workers away from the moral vices of gambling and drinking and female workers from lives of prostitution.

Prison Reform

The increase in crime led to a rise in arrests. By the 1820s in most countries, the indiscriminate use of capital punishment, even for crimes against property, was increasingly being viewed as ineffective and was replaced by imprisonment. Although the British had shipped people convicted of serious offenses to their colonial territory of Australia, that practice began to slow down in the late 1830s when the colonists loudly objected. Incarceration, then, was the only alternative. Prisons served to isolate criminals from society, but a growing number of reformers questioned their purpose and effectiveness, especially when prisoners were subjected to harsh and even humiliating work as punishment. By the 1830s, European governments were seeking ways to reform their penal systems. Motivated by the desire not just to punish but to rehabilitate and transform criminals into new persons, the British and French sent missions to the United States in the early 1830s to examine how the two different systems then used in American prisons accomplished this goal. At the Auburn Prison in New York, for example, prisoners were separated at night but worked together in the same workshop during the day. At Walnut Street Prison in Philadelphia, prisoners were separated into individual cells.

After examining the American prisons, both the French and the British constructed prisons on the Walnut Street model with separate cells that isolated prisoners from one another. At Petite Roquette in France and Pentonville in Britain, prisoners wore leather masks while they exercised and sat in separate stalls when in chapel. Solitary confinement, it was believed, forced prisoners back on their own consciences, led to greater remorse, and increased the possibility that they would change their evil ways. One supporter of the separate-cell system noted:

> A few months in the solitary cell renders a prisoner strangely impressible. The chaplain can then make the brawny navvy cry like a child; he can work on his feelings in almost any way he pleases; he can, so to speak, photograph his thoughts, wishes and opinions on his patient's mind, and fill his mouth with his own phrases and language.[12]

As prison populations increased, however, solitary confinement proved expensive and less feasible. The French even returned to their custom of sending prisoners to French Guiana to handle the overload.

Prison reform and police forces were geared toward one primary end, the creation of a more disciplined society. Disturbed by the upheavals associated with revolutions and the social discontent wrought by industrialization and urbanization, the ruling elites sought to impose some order on society.

Culture in an Age of Reaction and Revolution: The Mood of Romanticism

At the end of the eighteenth century, a new intellectual movement known as Romanticism emerged to challenge the Enlightenment's preoccupation with reason in discovering truth. The Romantics tried to balance the use of reason by stressing the importance of intuition, feeling, emotion, and imagination as sources of knowing. As one German Romantic put it, "It was my heart that counseled me to do it, and my heart cannot err."

The Characteristics of Romanticism

Romantic writers emphasized emotion, sentiment, and inner feelings in their works. An important model for Romantics was the tragic figure in *The Sorrows of the Young Werther,* a novel by the great German writer Johann Wolfgang von Goethe (1749–1832), who later rejected Romanticism in favor of Classicism. Werther was a Romantic figure who sought freedom in order to fulfill himself. Misunderstood and rejected by society, he continued to believe in his own worth through his inner feelings, but his deep love for a girl who did not love him finally led him to commit suicide. After Goethe's *Sorrows of the Young Werther,* numerous novels and plays appeared whose plots revolved around young maidens tragically carried off at an early age (twenty-three was most common) by disease (usually tuberculosis, at that time a protracted disease that was usually fatal) to the sorrow and sadness of their male lovers.

Another important characteristic of Romanticism was individualism, an interest in the unique traits of each person. The Romantics' desire to follow their inner drives led them to rebel against middle-class conventions. Long hair, beards, and outrageous clothes served to reinforce the individualism that young Romantics were trying to express.

Sentiment and individualism came together in the Romantics' stress on the heroic. The Romantic hero was a solitary genius who was ready to defy the world and sacrifice his life for a great cause. In the hands of the British writer Thomas Carlyle (1795–1881), however, the Romantic hero did not destroy himself in ineffective protests against society but transformed society instead. In his historical works, Carlyle stressed that historical events were largely determined by the deeds of such heroes.

Many Romantics possessed a passionate interest in the past. This historical focus was manifested in many ways. In Germany, the Grimm brothers collected and published local fairy tales, as did Hans Christian Andersen in Denmark. The revival of medieval Gothic architecture left European countrysides adorned with pseudo-medieval castles and cities bedecked with grandiose neo-Gothic cathedrals, city halls, parliamentary buildings, and even railway stations. Literature, too, reflected this historical consciousness. The novels of Walter Scott (1771–1832) became European best-sellers in the first half of the nineteenth century. *Ivanhoe,* in which Scott tried to evoke the clash between Saxon and Norman knights in medieval England, became one of his most popular works.

To the history-mindedness of the Romantics could be added an attraction to the bizarre and unusual. In an exaggerated form, this preoccupation gave rise to so-called Gothic literature (see the box on p. 605), chillingly evident in the short stories of horror by the American Edgar Allan Poe (1808–1849) and in *Frankenstein* by Mary Shelley (1797–1851). Shelley's novel was the story of a mad scientist who brings into being a humanlike monster who goes berserk. Some Romantics even sought the unusual in their own lives by pursuing extraordinary states of experience in dreams, nightmares, frenzies, and suicidal depression or by experimenting with cocaine, opium, and hashish to produce altered states of consciousness.

Romantic Poets and the Love of Nature

To the Romantics, poetry ranked above all other literary forms because they believed it was the direct expression of one's soul. The Romantic poets were viewed as seers who could reveal the invisible world to others. Their incredible sense of drama made some of them the most colorful figures of their era, living intense but short lives. Percy Bysshe Shelley (1792–1822), expelled from school for advocating atheism, set out to reform the world. His *Prometheus Unbound,* completed in 1820, is a portrait of the revolt of human beings against the laws and customs that oppress them. He drowned in a storm in the Mediterranean. Lord Byron (1788–1824) dramatized himself as the melancholy Romantic hero that he had described in his work, *Childe Harold's Pilgrimage.* He participated in the movement for Greek independence and died in Greece fighting the Ottomans.

Romantic poetry gave full expression to one of the most important characteristics of Romanticism: love of nature,

Neo-Gothic Revival: British Houses of Parliament. The Romantic movement of the first half of the nineteenth century led, among other things, to a revival of medieval Gothic architecture that left European cities bedecked with neo-Gothic buildings. After the Houses of Parliament in London burned down in 1834, they were replaced with new buildings of neo-Gothic design, as seen in this photograph.

Gothic Literature: Edgar Allan Poe

American writers and poets made significant contributions to the movement of Romanticism. Although Edgar Allan Poe (1809–1849) was influenced by the German Romantic school of mystery and horror, many literary historians give him the credit for pioneering the modern short story. This selection from the conclusion of "The Fall of the House of Usher" gives a sense of the nature of so-called Gothic literature.

Edgar Allan Poe, "The Fall of the House of Usher"

No sooner had these syllables passed my lips, than—as if a shield of brass had indeed, at the moment, fallen heavily upon a floor of silver—I became aware of a distinct, hollow, metallic, and clangorous, yet apparently muffled, reverberation. Completely unnerved, I leaped to my feet; but the measured rocking movement of Usher was undisturbed. I rushed to the chair in which he sat. His eyes were bent fixedly before him, and throughout his whole countenance there reigned a stony rigidity. But, as I placed my hand upon his shoulder, there came a strong shudder over his whole person; a sickly smile quivered about his lips and I saw that he spoke in a low, hurried, and gibbering murmur, as if unconscious of my presence. Bending closely over him, I at length drank in the hideous import of his words.

"Not hear it?—yes, I hear it, and *have* heard it. Long-long-long-many minutes, many hours, many days, have I heard it—yet I dared not—oh, pity me, miserable wretch that I am!—I dared not—I *dared* not speak! *We have put her living in the tomb!* Said I not that my senses were acute? I now tell you that I heard her first feeble movements in the hollow coffin. I heard them—many, many days ago—yet I dared not—I *dared not speak!* And now—to-night . . . the rending of her coffin, and the grating of the iron hinges of her prison, and her struggles within the coppered archway of the vault! Oh whither shall I fly? Will she not be here anon? Is she not hurrying to upbraid me for my haste? Have I not heard her footstep on the stair? Do I not distinguish that heavy and horrible beating of her heart? MADMAN!"—here he sprang furiously to his feet, and shrieked out his syllables, as if in the effort he were giving up his soul—"MADMAN! I TELL YOU THAT SHE NOW STANDS WITHOUT THE DOOR!"

As if in the superhuman energy of his utterance there had been found the potency of a spell, the huge antique panels to which the speaker pointed threw slowly back, upon the instant, their ponderous and ebony jaws. It was the work of the rushing gust—but then without those doors there DID stand the lofty and enshrouded figure of the lady Madeline of Usher. There was blood upon her white robes, and the evidence of some bitter struggle upon every portion of her emaciated frame. For a moment she remained trembling and reeling to and fro upon the threshold, then, with a low moaning cry, fell heavily inward upon the person of her brother, and in her violent and now final death-agonies, bore him to the floor a corpse, and a victim to the terrors he had anticipated.

especially evident in the works of William Wordsworth (1770–1850). His experience of nature was almost mystical as he claimed to receive "authentic tidings of invisible things":

One impulse from a vernal wood
May teach you more of man,
Of Moral Evil and of good,
Than all the sages can.[13]

To Wordsworth, nature contained a mysterious force that the poet could perceive and learn from. Nature served as a mirror into which humans could look to learn about themselves. Nature was, in fact, alive and sacred:

To every natural form, rock, fruit or flower,
Even the loose stones that cover the high-way,
I gave a moral life, I saw them feel,
Or link'd them to some feeling: the great mass
Lay bedded in a quickening soul, and all
That I beheld, respired with inward meaning.[14]

Other Romantics carried this worship of nature further into pantheism by identifying the great force in nature with God. The Romantics would have nothing to do with the deist God of the Enlightenment, the remote creator of the world-machine. As the German Romantic poet Friedrich Novalis said, "Anyone seeking God will find him anywhere."

The worship of nature also led Wordsworth and other Romantic poets to critique the mechanistic materialism of eighteenth-century science, which, they believed, had reduced nature to a cold object of study. Against that view of the natural world, Wordsworth offered his own vivid and concrete experience. To him, the scientists' dry, mathematical approach left no room for the imagination or for the human soul. The poet who left to the world "one single moral precept, one single affecting sentiment," Wordsworth said, did more for the world than scientists who were soon forgotten. The monster created by Frankenstein in Mary Shelley's Gothic novel symbolized well the danger of science when it tries to conquer nature. Many Romantics were convinced that the emerging industrialization would cause people to become alienated from their inner selves and the natural world around them.

Romanticism in Art and Music

Like the literary arts, the visual arts were also deeply affected by Romanticism. Although their works varied widely, Romantic artists shared at least two fundamental

Caspar David Friedrich, *Man and Woman Gazing at the Moon.* The German artist Caspar David Friedrich sought to express in painting his own mystical view of nature. "The divine is everywhere," he once wrote, "even in a grain of sand." In this painting, two solitary wanderers are shown from the back gazing at the moon. Overwhelmed by the all-pervasive presence of nature, the two figures express the human longing for infinity.

characteristics. All artistic expression to them was a reflection of the artist's inner feelings; a painting should mirror the artist's vision of the world and be the instrument of his own imagination. Moreover, Romantic artists deliberately rejected the principles of Classicism. Beauty was not a timeless thing; its expression depended on one's culture and one's age. The Romantics abandoned classical restraint for warmth, emotion, and movement. Through an examination of three painters, we can see how Romanticism influenced the visual arts.

The early life experiences of Caspar David Friedrich (1774–1840) left him with a lifelong preoccupation with God and nature. Friedrich painted landscapes with an interest that transcended the mere presentation of natural details. His portrayal of mountains shrouded in mist, gnarled trees bathed in moonlight, and the stark ruins of monasteries surrounded by withered trees all conveyed a feeling of mystery and mysticism. For Friedrich, nature was a manifestation of divine life, as is evident in *Man and Woman Gazing at the Moon.* To Friedrich, the artistic process depended on one's inner vision. He advised artists: "Shut your physical eye and look first at your picture with your spiritual eye; then bring to the light of day what you have seen in the darkness."

Another artist who dwelled on nature and made landscape his major subject was the Englishman Joseph Malford William Turner (1775–1851). Turner was an incredibly prolific artist who produced over twenty

J. M. W. Turner, *Rain, Steam, and Speed—The Great Western Railway.* Although Turner began his artistic career by painting accurate representations of the natural world, he increasingly sought to create an atmosphere through the skillful use of light and color. In this painting, Turner eliminates specific details and uses general fields of color to convey the impression of a locomotive rushing toward the spectator.

thousand paintings, drawings, and watercolors. Turner's concern with nature manifested itself in innumerable landscapes and seascapes, sunrises and sunsets. He did not idealize nature or reproduce it with realistic accuracy, however. He sought instead to convey its moods by using a skilled interplay of light and color to suggest natural effects. In allowing his objects to melt into their surroundings, he anticipated the Impressionist painters of the second half of the nineteenth century (see Chapter 24). John Constable, a contemporary English Romantic painter, described Turner's paintings as "airy visions, painted with tinted steam."

Eugène Delacroix (1798–1863) was the most famous French Romantic artist. Largely self-taught, he was fascinated by the exotic and had a passion for color. Both characteristics are visible in *The Death of Sardanapalus.* Significant for its use of light and its patches of interrelated color, this portrayal of the world of the last Assyrian king was criticized at the time for its garishness. Delacroix rejoiced in combining theatricality and movement with a daring use of color. Many of his works reflect his own belief that "a painting should be a feast to the eye."

To many Romantics, music was the most Romantic of the arts because it enabled the composer to probe deeply into human emotions. One Romantic writer noted, "It has been rightly said that the object of music is the awakening of emotion. No other art can so sublimely arouse human sentiments in the innermost heart of man."[15] Although music historians have called the eighteenth century the age of Classicism and the nineteenth the era of Romanticism, there was much carryover of classical forms from one century to the next. One of the greatest composers of all time, Ludwig van Beethoven, served as a bridge between Classicism and Romanticism.

Beethoven (1770–1827) is one of the few composers who was able singlehandedly to transform the art of music. Set ablaze by the events in France, a revolutionary mood burned brightly across Europe, and Beethoven, like other creative personalities, yearned to communicate his cherished beliefs. He said, "I *must* write, for what weighs on my heart, I *must* express." For Beethoven, music had to reflect his deepest inner feelings.

Born in Bonn, Beethoven came from a family of musicians who worked for the electors of Cologne. He became an assistant organist at the court by the age of thirteen and soon made his way to Vienna, the musical capital of Europe, where he studied briefly under Haydn. Beginning in 1792, this city became his permanent residence.

Eugène Delacroix, *The Death of Sardanapalus.* Delacroix's *Death of Sardanapalus* was based on Lord Byron's verse account of the last dramatic moments of the decadent Assyrian king. Besieged by enemy troops and with little hope of survival, Sardanapalus orders that his harem women and prize horses go to their death with him. At the right, a guard stabs one of the women as the king looks on.

During his first major period of composing, which extended from 1792 to 1800, his work was still largely within the classical framework of the eighteenth century, and the influences of Haydn and Mozart are paramount. But with the composition of the Third Symphony (1804), also called the *Eroica,* which was originally intended for Napoleon, Beethoven broke through to the elements of Romanticism in his use of uncontrolled rhythms to create dramatic struggle and uplifted resolutions. E. T. A. Hoffman, a contemporary composer and writer, said, "Beethoven's music opens the flood gates of fear, of terror, of horror, of pain, and arouses that longing for the eternal which is the essence of Romanticism. He is thus a pure Romantic composer."[16] Beethoven went on to write a vast quantity of works, but in the midst of this productivity and growing fame, he was more and more burdened by his growing deafness. One of the most moving pieces of music of all time, the chorale finale of his Ninth Symphony, was composed when Beethoven was totally deaf.

Beethoven served as a bridge from the classical era to Romanticism; after him came a number of musical geniuses who composed in the Romantic style. The Frenchman Hector Berlioz (1803–1869) was one of the most outstanding. His father, a doctor in Grenoble, intended that his son should also study medicine. The young Berlioz eventually rebelled, however, maintaining to his father's disgust that he would be "no doctor or apothecary but a great composer." Berlioz managed to fulfill his own expectations, achieving fame in Germany, Russia, and Britain, although the originality of his work kept him from receiving any real recognition in his native France.

Berlioz was one of the founders of program music, which was an attempt to use the moods and sound effects of instrumental music to depict the actions and emotions inherent in a story, event, or even a personal experience. This development of program music was evident in his most famous piece, the first complete program symphony, known as the *Symphonie Fantastique.* In this work, Berlioz used music to evoke the passionate emotions of a tortured love affair, including a fifth movement in which he musically creates an opium-induced nightmare of a witches' gathering.

The Revival of Religion in the Age of Romanticism

After 1815, Christianity experienced a revival. In the eighteenth century, Catholicism had lost its attraction for many of the educated elite as even the European nobility flirted with the ideas of the Enlightenment. The restoration of the nobility brought a new appreciation for the Catholic faith as a force for order in society. This appreciation was greatly reinforced by the Romantic movement. The attraction of Romantics to the Middle Ages and their emphasis on emotion led them to their own widespread revival of Christianity.

Catholicism, in particular, benefited from this Romantic enthusiasm for religion. Especially among German Romantics, there were many conversions to the Catholic faith. One of the most popular expressions of this Romantic revival of Catholicism was found in the work of the Frenchman François-René de Chateaubriand (1768–1848). His book *Genius of Christianity,* published in 1802, was soon labeled the "Bible of Romanticism." His defense of Catholicism was based not on historical, theological, or even rational grounds but largely on Romantic sentiment. As a faith, Catholicism echoed the harmony of all things. Its cathedrals brought one into the very presence of God; according to Chateaubriand: "You could not enter a Gothic church without feeling a kind of awe and a vague sentiment of the Divinity. . . . Every thing in a Gothic church reminds you of the labyrinths of a wood; every thing excites a feeling of religious awe, of mystery, and of the Divinity."[17]

Protestantism also experienced a revival. That revival, or awakening, as it was called, had already begun in the eighteenth century with the enthusiastic emotional experiences of Methodism in Britain and Pietism in Germany (see Chapter 17). Methodist missionaries from England and Scotland carried their messages of sin and redemption to liberal Protestant churches in France and Switzerland, winning converts to their strongly evangelical message. Germany, too, witnessed a Protestant awakening as enthusiastic evangelical preachers found that their messages of hellfire and their methods of emotional conversion evoked a ready response among people alienated by the highly educated establishment clergy of the state churches.

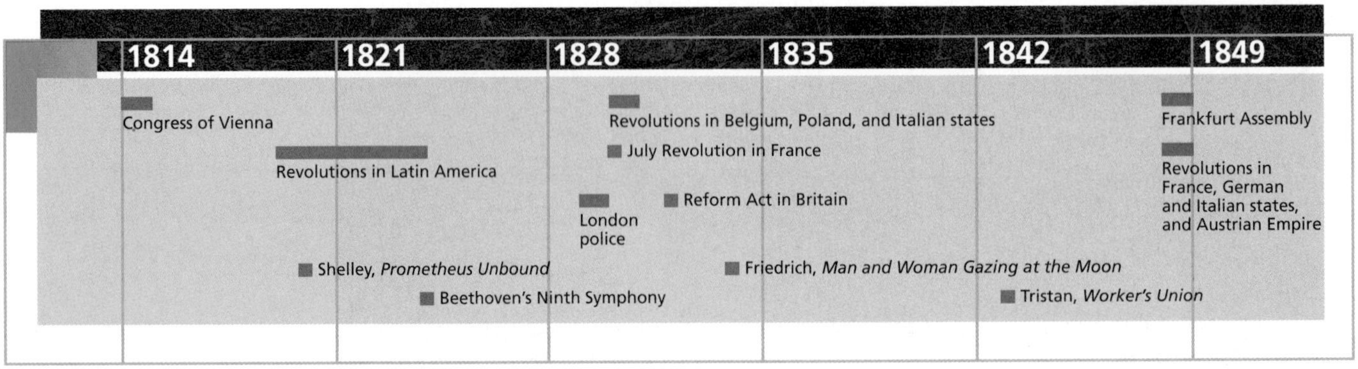

Conclusion

In 1815, a conservative order was reestablished throughout Europe, and the cooperation of the great powers, embodied in the Concert of Europe, tried to ensure its durability. But the revolutionary waves of the 1820s and 1830s made it clear that the ideologies of liberalism and nationalism, unleashed by the French Revolution and now reinforced by the spread of the Industrial Revolution, were still alive and active. They faced enormous difficulties, however, as failed revolutions in Poland, Russia, Italy, and Germany all testify. At the same time, reform legislation in Britain and successful revolutions in Greece, France, and Belgium demonstrated the continuing strength of these forces of change. In 1848, they erupted once more all across Europe. And once more they failed. But not all was lost. Both liberalism and nationalism would succeed in the second half of the nineteenth century, but in ways not foreseen by the idealistic liberals and nationalists, who were utterly convinced that their time had come when they manned the barricades in 1848.

Notes

1. Quoted in Charles Breunig, *The Age of Revolution and Reaction, 1789–1850* (New York, 1970), p. 119.
2. Quoted in M. S. Anderson, *The Ascendancy of Europe, 1815–1914,* 2d ed. (London, 1985), p. 1.
3. Quotations from Burke can be found in Peter Viereck, *Conservatism* (Princeton, N.J., 1956), pp. 27, 114.
4. Quoted in René Albrecht-Carrié, *The Concert of Europe* (New York, 1968), p. 48.
5. Quoted in G. de Berthier de Sauvigny, *Metternich and His Times* (London, 1962), p. 105.
6. Quoted in S. Joan Moon, "Feminism and Socialism: The Utopian Synthesis of Flora Tristan," in Marilyn J. Boxer and Jean H. Quataert, eds., *Socialist Women* (New York, 1978), p. 38.
7. Quoted in Stanley Z. Pech, *The Czech Revolution of 1848* (Chapel Hill, N.C., 1969), p. 82.
8. Quoted in Clive Emsley, *Policing and Its Context, 1750–1870* (New York, 1984), p. 58.
9. Quoted in Clive Emsley, *Crime and Society in England, 1750–1900* (London, 1987), p. 173.
10. Quoted in Emsley, *Policing and Its Context,* p. 66.
11. Quoted in ibid., p. 102.
12. Quoted in Emsley, *Crime and Society in England,* p. 226.
13. William Wordsworth, "The Tables Turned," *Poems of Wordsworth,* ed. Matthew Arnold (London, 1963), p. 138.
14. William Wordsworth, *The Prelude* (Harmondsworth, England, 1971), p. 109.
15. Quoted in H. G. Schenk, *The Mind of the European Romantics* (Garden City, N.Y., 1969), p. 205.
16. Quoted in Siegbert Prawer, ed., *The Romantic Period in Germany* (London, 1970), p. 285.
17. Quoted in John B. Halsted, ed., *Romanticism* (New York, 1969), p. 156.

Suggestions for Further Reading

For a good survey of the entire nineteenth century, see R. Gildea, *Barricades and Borders: Europe, 1800–1914,* 2d ed. (Oxford, 1996), in the Short Oxford History of the Modern World series. Also valuable is M. S. Anderson, *The Ascendancy of Europe, 1815–1914,* 2d ed. (London, 1985). For surveys of the period covered in this chapter, see M. Broers, *Europe After Napoleon: Revolution, Reaction, and Romanticism, 1814–1848* (New York, 1996), and C. Breunig, *The Age of Revolution and Reaction, 1789–1850,* 2d ed. (New York, 1979). There are also some useful books on individual countries that cover more than the subject of this chapter. These include R. Magraw, *France, 1815–1914: The Bourgeois Century* (London, 1983); D. Saunders, *Russia in the Age of Reaction and Reform, 1801–1881* (London, 1992); J. J. Sheehan, *German History, 1770–1866* (New York, 1989); A. Sked, *The Decline and Fall of the Habsburg Empire, 1815–1918* (London, 1989); S. J. Woolf, *A History of Italy, 1700–1860* (London, 1979); R. Carr, *Spain, 1808–1939* (Oxford, 1991); and N. McCord, *British History, 1815–1906* (New York, 1991).

On the peace settlement of 1814–1815, see T. Chapman, *The Congress of Vienna* (London, 1998). A concise summary of the international events of the entire nineteenth century can be found in R. Bullen and F. R. Bridge, *The Great Powers and the European States System, 1815–1914* (London, 1980). See also N. Rich, *Great Power Diplomacy, 1814–1914* (New York, 1992). On the man whose conservative policies dominated this era, see the brief but good biography by A. Palmer, *Metternich* (New York, 1972). On the revolutions in Europe in 1830, see C. Church, *Europe in 1830: Revolution and Political Change* (Chapel Hill, N.C., 1983). On Great Britain's reform legislation, see M. Brock, *Great Reform Act* (London, 1973), and D. C. Moore, *The Politics of Deference: A Study of the Mid-Nineteenth-Century English Political System* (New York, 1976). The Greek revolt is examined in detail in D. Dakin, *The Greek Struggle for Independence, 1821–33* (Berkeley, Calif., 1973).

The best introduction to the revolutions of 1848 is J. Sperber, *The European Revolutions, 1848–1851* (New York, 1994). Good accounts of the revolutions in individual countries include G. Duveau, *1848: The Making of a Revolution* (New York, 1967); R. J. Rath, *The Viennese Revolution of 1848* (Austin, Tex., 1957); I. Déak, *The Lawful Revolution: Louis Kossuth and the Hungarians, 1848–49* (New York, 1979); R. Stadelmann, *Social and Political History of the German 1848 Revolution* (Athens, Ohio, 1975); and P. Ginsborg, *Daniele Manin and the Venetian Revolution of 1848–49* (New York, 1979). On Mazzini, see D. M. Smith, *Mazzini* (New Haven, Conn., 1994).

Good introductions to the major ideologies of the first half of the nineteenth century, including both analysis and readings from the major figures, can be found in H. Kohn, *Nationalism* (Princeton, N.J., 1955); J. S. Schapiro, *Liberalism: Its Meaning and History* (Princeton, N.J., 1958); and P. Viereck, *Conservatism* (Princeton, N.J., 1956). For a more detailed examination of liberalism, see J. Gray, *Liberalism* (Minneapolis, Minn., 1995).

On changes in the treatment of crime and punishment, see M. Foucault, *Discipline and Punish: The Birth of the Prison* (New York,

1977). The new police forces are examined in C. Emsley, *Policing and Its Context, 1750–1870* (New York, 1984).

On the ideas of the Romantics, see H. G. Schenk, *The Mind of the European Romantics* (Garden City, N.Y., 1969), and M. Cranston, *The Romantic Movement* (Oxford, 1994). An excellent collection of writings by Romantics is J. B. Halsted, ed., *Romanticism* (New York, 1969). On Wordsworth and English Romanticism, see J. Wordsworth, *William Wordsworth and the Age of English Romanticism* (New Brunswick, N.J., 1987). For an introduction to the arts, see W. Vaughan, *Romanticism and Art* (New York, 1994). A briefer survey (with illustrations) can be found in D. M. Reynolds, *Cambridge Introduction to the History of Art: The Nineteenth Century* (Cambridge, 1985).

For additional reading, go to InfoTrac College Edition, your online research library at http://web1.infotrac-college.com

Enter the search term *Romanticism* using the Subject Guide.

Enter the search term *Habsburg* and also the term *Hapsburg* using Key Terms.

Enter the search term *John Stuart Mill* using Key Terms.

Enter the search term *Goethe* using Key Terms.

C H A P T E R 22

An Age of Nationalism and Realism, 1850–1871

CHAPTER OUTLINE

- The France of Napoleon III
- National Unification: Italy and Germany
- Nation Building and Reform: The National State in Mid-Century
- Industrialization and the Marxist Response
- Science and Culture in an Age of Realism
- Conclusion

FOCUS QUESTIONS

- What were the characteristics of Napoleon III's government, and how did his foreign policy contribute to the unification of Italy and Germany?
- What actions did Cavour and Bismarck take to bring about unification in Italy and Germany, respectively, and what role did war play in their efforts?
- What efforts for reform occurred in the Austrian Empire and in Russia between 1850 and 1870, and how successful were they in alleviating each nation's problems?
- What were the main ideas of Karl Marx?
- How did the belief that the world should be viewed realistically manifest itself in science, art, and literature in the second half of the nineteenth century?
- What was the relationship between nationalism and reform between 1850 and 1871?

ACROSS THE EUROPEAN CONTINENT, the revolutions of 1848 had failed. The forces of liberalism and nationalism appeared to have been decisively defeated as authoritarian governments reestablished their control almost everywhere in Europe by 1850. And yet within twenty-five years, many of the goals sought by the liberals and nationalists during the first half of the nineteenth century seemed to have been achieved. National unity became a reality in Italy and Germany, and many European states were governed by constitutional monarchies, even though the constitutional-parliamentary features were frequently facades.

All the same, these goals were not achieved by liberal and nationalist leaders but by a new generation of conservative leaders who were proud of being practitioners of Realpolitik, *the "politics of reality." One reaction to the failure of the revolutions of 1848 had been a new toughness of mind in which people prided themselves on being realistic in their handling of power. The new conservative leaders used armies and power politics to achieve their foreign policy goals. And they did not hesitate to manipulate liberal means to achieve conservative ends at home. Nationalism had failed as a revolutionary movement in 1848–1849, but between 1850 and 1871, these new leaders found a variety of ways to pursue nation building. One of the most successful was the Prussian Otto von Bismarck, who used both astute diplomacy and war to achieve the unification of Germany. On January 18, 1871, Bismarck and six hundred German princes, nobles, and generals filled the Hall of Mirrors in the palace of Versailles, outside Paris. The Prussian army had defeated the French, and the assembled notables were gathered for the proclamation of the Prussian king as the new emperor of a united German state. When the words "Long live His Imperial Majesty, the Emperor William!" rang out, the assembled guests took up the cry. One participant wrote, "A thundering cheer, repeated at least six times, thrilled through the room while the flags and standards waved over the head of the new emperor of Germany." European rulers who feared the power of the new German state were not so cheerful. "The balance of power has been entirely destroyed," declared the British prime minister.*

The France of Napoleon III

After 1850, a new generation of conservative leaders came to power in Europe. Foremost among them was Napoleon III (1852–1870) of France, who taught his contemporaries how authoritarian governments could use liberal and nationalistic forces to bolster their own power. It was a lesson others quickly learned.

Louis Napoleon: Toward the Second Empire

Even after his election as the president of the French Republic, many of his contemporaries dismissed Napoleon "the Small" as a nonentity whose success was due only to his name. But Louis Napoleon was a clever politician who was especially astute at understanding the popular forces of his day. After his election, he was clear about his desire to have personal power. He wrote: "I shall never submit to any attempt to influence me. . . . I follow only the promptings of my mind and heart. . . . Nothing, nothing shall trouble the clear vision of my judgment or the strength of my resolution."[1]

Louis Napoleon was a patient man. For three years, he persevered in winning the support of the French people, and when the National Assembly rejected his wish to revise the constitution and be allowed to stand for reelection, Louis used troops to seize control of the government on December 1, 1851. After restoring universal male suffrage, Louis Napoleon asked the French people to restructure the government by electing him president for ten years (see the box on p. 613). By an overwhelming majority, 7.5 million yes votes to 640,000 no votes, they agreed. A year later, on November 21, 1852, Louis Napoleon returned to the people to ask for the restoration of the empire. This time, 97 percent responded affirmatively, and on December 2, 1852, Louis Napoleon assumed the title of Napoleon III (the first Napoleon had abdicated in favor of his son, Napoleon II, on April 6, 1814). The Second Empire had begun.

Emperor Napoleon III. On December 2, 1852, Louis Napoleon took the title of Napoleon III and then proceeded to create an authoritarian monarchy. As opposition to his policies intensified in the 1860s, Napoleon III began to liberalize his government. However, a disastrous military defeat at the hands of Prussia in 1870–1871 brought the collapse of his regime.

Réunion des Musées Nationaux/Art Resource, NY

Louis Napoleon Appeals to the People

After his coup d'état on December 1, 1851, Louis Napoleon asked the French people to approve his actions. By making this appeal, the clever politician was demonstrating how universal male suffrage, considered a democratic and hence revolutionary device, could be used to bolster a basically authoritarian regime. This selection is from Louis Napoleon's proclamation to the French people in 1851.

Louis Napoleon, Proclamation to the People *(1851)*

Frenchmen! The present situation cannot last much longer. Each passing day increases the danger to the country. The [National] Assembly, which ought to be the firmest supporter of order, has become a center of conspiracies. . . . It attacks the authority that I hold directly from the people; it encourages all evil passions; it jeopardizes the peace of France: I have dissolved it and I make the whole people judge between it and me. . . .

I therefore make a loyal appeal to the whole nation, and I say to you: If you wish to continue this state of uneasiness which degrades us and makes our future uncertain, choose another in my place, for I no longer wish an authority which is powerless to do good, makes me responsible for acts I cannot prevent, and chains me to the helm when I see the vessel speeding toward the abyss.

If, on the contrary, you still have confidence in me, give me the means to accomplish the great mission that I hold from you. This mission consists in bringing to a close the era of revolutions by satisfying the legitimate wants of the people and by protecting them against subversive passions. It consists, especially, in creating institutions that may survive men and that may be at length foundations on which something durable can be established.

Persuaded that the instability of authority and the preponderance of a single Assembly are permanent causes of trouble and discord, I submit to you the following fundamental bases of a constitution which the Assemblies will develop later.

1. A responsible chief elected for ten years.
2. Ministers dependent upon the executive power alone.
3. A Council of State composed of the most distinguished men to prepare the laws and discuss them before the legislative body.
4. A legislative body to discuss and vote the laws, elected by universal [male] suffrage. . . .

This system, created by the First Consul [Napoleon I] at the beginning of the century, has already given France calm and prosperity; it will guarantee them to her again.

Such is my profound conviction. If you share it, declare that fact by your votes. If, on the contrary, you prefer a government without force, monarchical or republican, borrowed from I know not what past or from which chimerical future, reply in the negative. . . .

If I do not obtain a majority of your votes, I shall then convoke a new assembly, and I shall resign to it the mandate that I received from you. But if you believe that the cause of which my name is the symbol, that is, France regenerated by the revolution of 1789 and organized by the Emperor, is forever yours, proclaim it by sanctioning the powers that I ask from you. Then France and Europe will be saved from anarchy, obstacles will be removed, rivalries will disappear, for all will respect the decree of Providence in the decision of the people.

The Second Napoleonic Empire

The government of Napoleon III was clearly authoritarian in a Bonapartist sense. Louis Napoleon had asked, "Since France has carried on for fifty years only by virtue of the administrative, military, judicial, religious and financial organization of the Consulate and Empire, why should she not also adopt the political institutions of that period?"[2] As chief of state, Napoleon III controlled the armed forces, police, and civil service. Only he could introduce legislation and declare war. The Legislative Corps gave an appearance of representative government since its members were elected by universal male suffrage for six-year terms. But they could neither initiate legislation nor affect the budget.

The first five years of Napoleon III's reign were a spectacular success as he reaped the benefits of worldwide economic prosperity as well as of some of his own economic policies. Napoleon believed in using the resources of government to stimulate the national economy and took many steps to encourage industrial growth. Government subsidies were used to foster the rapid construction of railroads as well as harbors, roads, and canals. The major French railway lines were completed during Napoleon's reign, and industrial expansion was evident in the tripling of iron production. In his concern to reduce tensions and improve the social welfare of the nation, Napoleon provided hospitals and free medicine for the workers and advocated better housing for the working class.

In the midst of this economic expansion, Napoleon III undertook a vast reconstruction of the city of Paris. Under the direction of Baron Haussmann, the medieval Paris of narrow streets and old city walls was destroyed and replaced by a modern Paris of broad boulevards, spacious buildings, circular plazas, public squares, an underground sewage system, a new public water supply, and gaslights. The new Paris served a military as well as an aesthetic purpose.

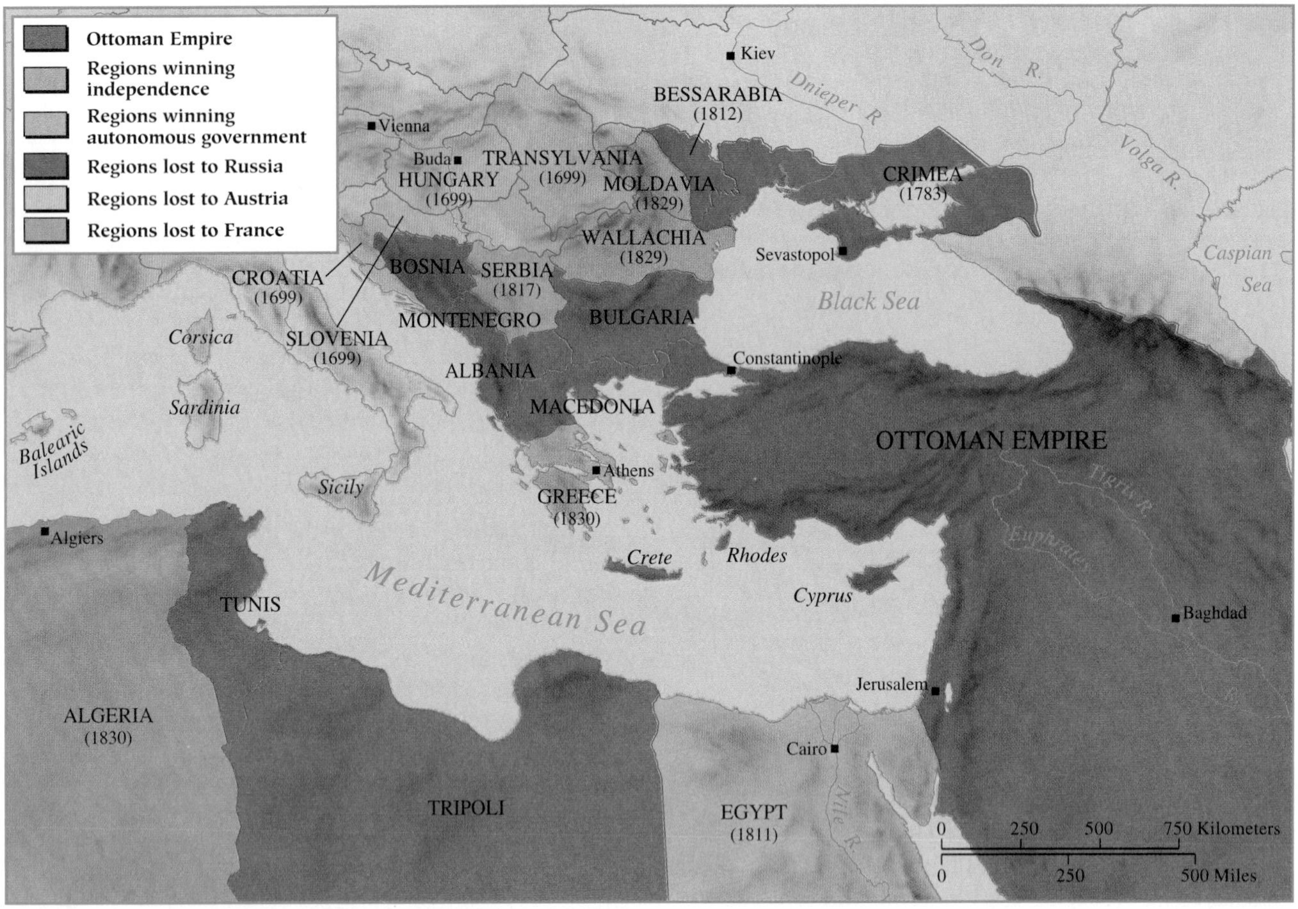

Map 22.1 Decline of the Ottoman Empire. The decline in Ottoman fortunes began in 1699 with major losses to the Austrian Empire. The slide accelerated in the nineteenth century with nationalist revolts in the European provinces and defeat in the Crimean War. Being on the losing side of World War I would complete its destruction. ■ What is the relationship between distance from Constantinople and independence date, and how can you explain it?

Broad streets made it more difficult for would-be insurrectionists to throw up barricades and easier for troops to move rapidly through the city in the event of revolts.

In the 1860s, as opposition to some of the emperor's policies began to mount, Napoleon III liberalized his regime. He reached out to the working class by legalizing trade unions and granting them the right to strike. He also began to liberalize the political process. The Legislative Corps had been closely controlled during the 1850s. In the 1860s, opposition candidates were allowed greater freedom to campaign, and the Legislative Corps was permitted more say in affairs of state, including debate over the budget. Napoleon's liberalization policies did serve initially to strengthen the hand of the government. In a plebiscite in May 1870 on whether to accept a new constitution that might have inaugurated a parliamentary regime, the French people gave Napoleon another resounding victory. This triumph was short-lived, however. Foreign policy failures led to growing criticism, and war with Prussia in 1870 turned out to be the death blow for Napoleon III's regime (see "The Franco-Prussian War, 1870–1871" later in this chapter).

Foreign Policy: The Crimean War

As heir to the Napoleonic Empire, Napoleon III was motivated by the desire to free France from the restrictions of the peace settlements of 1814–1815 and to make France the chief arbiter of Europe. Although his foreign policy ultimately led to disaster and his own undoing, Napoleon had an initial success in the Crimean War (1854–1856).

THE OTTOMAN EMPIRE

The Crimean War was yet another chapter in the story of the Eastern Question: Who would be the chief beneficiaries of the disintegration of the Ottoman Empire? In the seventeenth century, the Ottoman Empire had control of southeastern Europe but in 1699 had lost Hungary, Transylvania, Croatia, and Slovenia to the expanding Austrian Empire. The Russian Empire to its north also encroached on the Ottoman Empire by seizing the Crimea in 1783 and Bessarabia in 1812 (see Map 22.1).

By the beginning of the nineteenth century, the Ottoman Empire had begun a fresh period of decline. Nationalist revolts led to the creation of an independent

Serbia in 1817 and to the freedom of Greece in 1830. The Russians had gained a protectorate over the Danubian provinces of Moldavia and Wallachia in 1829.

As Ottoman authority over the outlying territories in southeastern Europe waned, European governments began to take an active interest in the empire's apparent demise. Russia's proximity to the Ottoman Empire and the religious bonds between the Russians and the Greek Orthodox Christians in Ottoman-dominated southeastern Europe naturally gave it special opportunities to enlarge its sphere of influence. Other European powers not only feared Russian ambitions but also had ambitions of their own in the area. Austria craved more land in the Balkans, a desire that inevitably meant conflict with Russia, and France and Britain were interested in commercial opportunities and naval bases in the eastern Mediterranean.

THE WAR

War erupted between Russia and the Ottoman Empire in 1853 when the Russians demanded the right to protect Christian shrines in Palestine, a privilege that had already been extended to the French. When the Ottomans refused, the Russians invaded Moldavia and Wallachia. Failure to resolve the dispute by negotiations led the Ottoman Empire to declare war on Russia on October 4, 1853. The following year, on March 28, Great Britain and France declared war on Russia.

Why did Britain and France take such a step? Concern over the prospect of an upset in the balance of power was clearly one reason. The British in particular feared that an aggressive Russia would try to profit from the obvious weakness of the Ottoman government by seizing Ottoman territory or the long-coveted Dardanelles. Such a move would make Russia the major power in eastern Europe and would enable the Russians to challenge British naval control of the eastern Mediterranean. Napoleon III felt that the Russians had insulted France, first at the Congress of Vienna and now by their insistence on replacing the French as the protectors of Christians living in the Ottoman Empire. The Russians assumed that they could count on support from the Austrians (since Russian troops had saved the Austrian government in 1849). However, the Austrian prime minister blithely explained, "We will astonish the world by our ingratitude," and Austria remained neutral. Since the Austrians had perceived that it was not in their best interest to intervene, Russia had to fight alone.

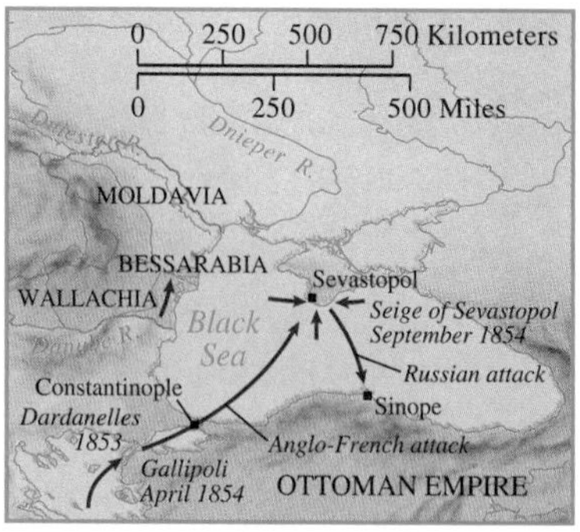

The Crimean War

The Crimean War was poorly planned and poorly fought. Britain and France decided to attack Russia's Crimean peninsula in the Black Sea. After a long siege and at a terrible cost in manpower for both sides, the main Russian fortress of Sevastopol fell in September 1855, six months after the death of Tsar Nicholas I. His successor, Alexander II, soon sued for peace. By the Treaty of Paris, signed in March 1856, Russia was forced to give up Bessarabia at the mouth of the Danube and accept the neutrality of the Black Sea. In addition, the Danubian principalities of Moldavia and Wallachia were placed under the protection of all five great powers.

The Crimean War proved costly to both sides. More than 250,000 soldiers died in the war, 60 percent of the deaths coming from disease (especially cholera). Even more would have died on the British side if it had not been for the efforts of Florence Nightingale (1820–1910). Her insistence on strict sanitary conditions saved many lives and helped make nursing a profession of trained, middle-class women.

Wellcome Institute Library, London

Florence Nightingale. By her efforts in the Crimean War, the British nurse Florence Nightingale helped make nursing a modern profession for middle-class women. She is shown here supervising her hospital at Scutari. Her attention to strict hygiene greatly reduced the death rate for wounded British soldiers.

The Crimean War broke up long-standing European power relationships and effectively destroyed the Concert of Europe. Austria and Russia, the two chief powers maintaining the status quo in the first half of the nineteenth century, were now enemies because of Austria's unwillingness to support Russia in the war. Russia, defeated, humiliated, and weakened by the obvious failure of its serf-armies, withdrew from European affairs for the next two decades to set its house in order. Great Britain, disillusioned by its role in the war, also pulled back from Continental affairs. Austria, paying the price for its neutrality, was now without friends among the great powers. Not until the 1870s were new combinations formed to replace those that had disappeared, and in the meantime, the European international situation remained fluid. Leaders who were willing to pursue the "politics of reality" found themselves in a situation rife with opportunity. It was this new international situation that made possible the unification of Italy and Germany.

National Unification: Italy and Germany

The breakdown of the Concert of Europe opened the way for the Italians and the Germans to establish national states. Their successful unifications transformed the power structure of the European continent. Well into the twentieth century, Europe would still be dealing with the consequences.

The Unification of Italy

In 1850, Austria was still the dominant power on the Italian peninsula. After the failure of the revolution of 1848–1849, a growing number of advocates for Italian unification focused on the northern Italian state of Piedmont as their best hope to achieve their goal. The royal house of Savoy ruled the kingdom of Piedmont, which also included the island of Sardinia (see Map 22.2). Although soundly defeated by the Austrians in 1848–1849, Piedmont under King Charles Albert had made a valiant effort; it seemed reasonable that Piedmont would now assume the leading role in the cause of national unity. The little state seemed unlikely to supply the needed leadership, however, until the new king, Victor Emmanuel II (1849–1878), named Count Camillo di Cavour (1810–1861) as his prime minister in 1852.

Cavour was a liberal-minded nobleman who had made a fortune in agriculture and went on to make even more money in banking, railroads, and shipping. Cavour was a moderate who favored constitutional government. He was a consummate politician with the ability to persuade others of the rightness of his own convictions. After becoming prime minister in 1852, he pursued a policy of economic expansion, encouraging the building of roads, canals, and railroads and fostering business enterprise by expanding credit and stimulating investment in new industries. The growth in the Piedmontese economy and the subsequent increase in government revenues enabled Cavour to pour money into equipping a large army.

Cavour had no illusions about Piedmont's military strength and was only too well aware that he could not challenge Austria directly. He would need the French. In 1858, Cavour came to an agreement with Napoleon III. The emperor agreed to ally with Piedmont in driving the Austrians out of Italy. Once the Austrians were driven out, Italy would be reorganized. Piedmont would be extended into the kingdom of Upper Italy by adding Lombardy, Venetia, Parma, Modena, and part of the Papal States to its territory. In compensation for its efforts, France would receive the Piedmontese provinces of Nice and Savoy. A kingdom of Central Italy would be created for Napoleon III's cousin, Prince Napoleon, who would be married to the younger daughter of King Victor Emmanuel. This agreement between Napoleon and Cavour seemed to assure the French ruler of the opportunity to control Italy. Confident that the plan would work, Cavour provoked the Austrians into invading Piedmont in April 1859.

In the initial stages of fighting, it was the French who were largely responsible for defeating the Austrians in two major battles at Magenta and Solferino. It was also the French who made peace with Austria on July 11, 1859, without informing their Italian ally. Why did Napoleon withdraw so hastily? For one thing, he realized that despite two losses, the Austrian army had not yet been defeated; the struggle might be longer and more costly than he had anticipated. Moreover, the Prussians were mobilizing in support of Austria, and Napoleon III had no desire to take on two enemies at once. As a result of Napoleon's peace with Austria, Piedmont received only Lombardy; Venetia remained under Austrian control. Cavour was furious at the French perfidy, but events in northern Italy now turned in his favor. Soon after the war with Austria had begun, some northern Italian states, namely, Parma, Modena, Tuscany, and part of the Papal States, had been taken over by nationalists. In plebiscites held in 1860, these states agreed to join Piedmont. Napoleon, in return for Nice and Savoy, agreed to the annexations.

Meanwhile, in southern Italy, a new leader of Italian unification had come to the fore. Giuseppe Garibaldi (1807–1882), a dedicated Italian patriot who had supported Mazzini and the republican cause of Young Italy, raised an army of a thousand Red Shirts, as his volunteers were called because of their distinctive dress, and on May 11, 1860, landed in Sicily, where a revolt had broken out against the Bourbon king of the Two Sicilies.

Although his forces were greatly outnumbered, Garibaldi's daring tactics won the day (see the box on p. 618). By the end of July 1860, most of Sicily had been pacified under Garibaldi's control. In August, Garibaldi and his forces crossed over to the mainland and began a victorious march up the Italian peninsula. Naples and the kingdom of the Two Sicilies fell in early September. At this point, Cavour reentered the scene. Aware that Garibaldi

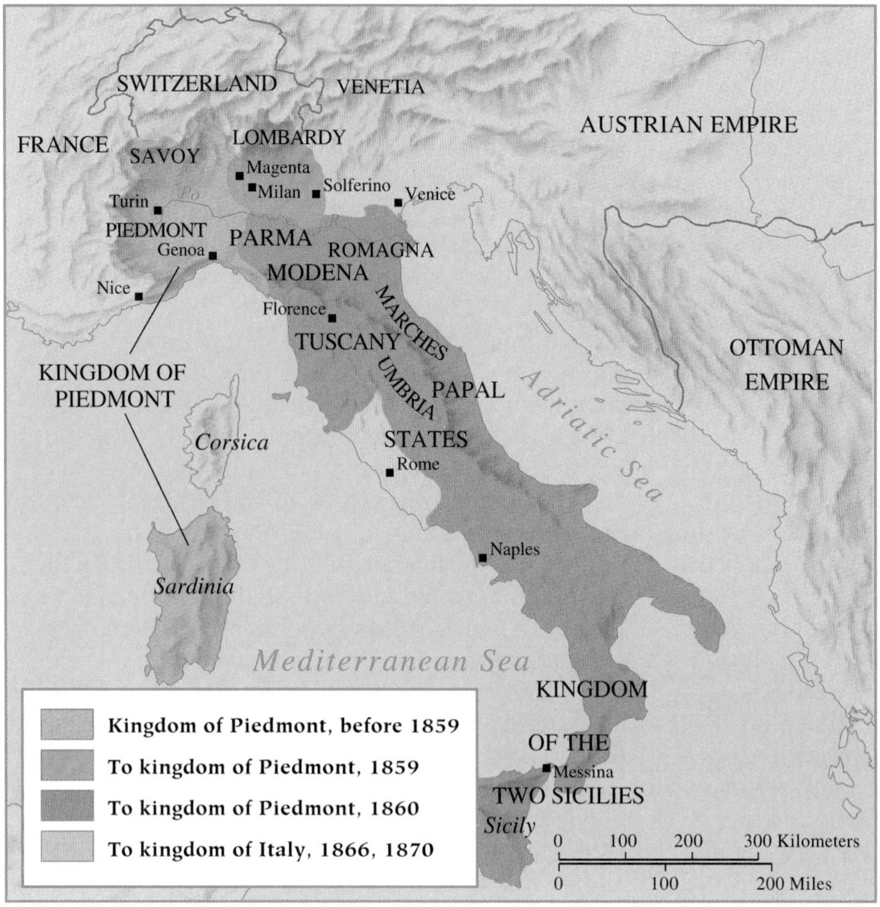

Map 22.2 The Unification of Italy. Piedmont under the able guidance of Count Camillo di Cavour provided the nucleus for Italian unification. Alliances with France and Prussia, combined with the military actions of republican nationalists like Giuseppe Garibaldi, led to complete unification in 1870. ■ Of the countries displayed on this map, which would likely, taking geographic and population-size factors into account, pose the greatest military threat to the new Italian state?

planned to march on Rome, Cavour feared that such a move would bring war with France as the defender of papal interests. Moreover, Garibaldi and his men favored a democratic republicanism; Cavour did not and acted quickly to preempt Garibaldi. The Piedmontese army invaded the Papal States and, bypassing Rome, moved into the kingdom of Naples. Ever the patriot, Garibaldi chose to yield to Cavour's fait accompli rather than provoke a civil war and retired to his farm. Plebiscites in the Papal States and the kingdom of the Two Sicilies resulted in overwhelming support for union with Piedmont. On March 17, 1861, the new kingdom of Italy was proclaimed under a centralized government subordinated to the control of Piedmont and King Victor Emmanuel II (1861–1878) of the house of Savoy. Worn out by his efforts, Cavour died three months later.

Despite the proclamation of the new kingdom, the task of unification was not yet complete since Venetia in the north was still held by Austria and Rome was under papal control, supported by French troops. To attack either one meant war with a major European state, which the Italian army was not prepared to handle. It was the Prussian army that indirectly

Garibaldi Arrives in Sicily. The dream of Italian nationalists for a united Italian state finally became a reality by 1870. An important figure in the cause of unification was Giuseppe Garibaldi, a determined Italian patriot. Garibaldi is shown here arriving in Sicily on May 11, 1860, with his band of Red Shirts.

Stock Montage

Garibaldi and Romantic Nationalism

Giuseppe Garibaldi was one of the most colorful figures involved in the unification of Italy. Accompanied by only one thousand of his famous Red Shirts, the Italian soldier of fortune left Genoa on the night of May 5, 1860, for an invasion of the kingdom of the Two Sicilies. The ragged band entered Palermo, the chief city on the island of Sicily, on May 31. This selection is taken from an account by a correspondent for *Times* of London, the Hungarian-born Nandor Eber.

London Times, *June 13, 1860*

PALERMO, May 31—Anyone in search of violent emotions cannot do better than set off at once for Palermo. However blasé he may be, or however milk-and-water his blood, I promise it will be stirred up. He will be carried away by the tide of popular feeling....

In the afternoon Garibaldi made a tour of inspection round the town. I was there, but find it really impossible to give you a faint idea of the manner in which he was received everywhere. It was one of those triumphs which seem to be almost too much for a man.... The popular idol, Garibaldi, in his red flannel shirt, with a loose colored handkerchief around his neck, and his worn "wide-awake" [a soft-brimmed felt hat], was walking on foot among those cheering, laughing, crying, mad thousands; and all his few followers could do was to prevent him from being bodily carried off the ground. The people threw themselves forward to kiss his hands, or, at least, to touch the hem of his garment, as if it contained the panacea for all their past and perhaps coming suffering. Children were brought up, and mothers asked on their knees for his blessing; and all this while the object of this idolatry was calm and smiling as when in the deadliest fire, taking up the children and kissing them, trying to quiet the crowd, stopping at every moment to hear a long complaint of houses burned and property sacked by the retreating soldiers, giving good advice, comforting, and promising that all damages should be paid for....

One might write volumes of horrors on the vandalism already committed, for every one of the hundred ruins has its story of brutality and inhumanity.... In these small houses a dense population is crowded together even in ordinary times. A shell falling on one, and crushing and burying the inmates, was sufficient to make people abandon the neighboring one and take refuge a little further on, shutting themselves up in the cellars. When the Royalists retired they set fire to those of the houses which had escaped the shells, and numbers were thus burned alive in their hiding places....

If you can stand the exhalation, try and go inside the ruins, for it is only there that you will see what the thing means and you will not have to search long before you stumble over the remains of a human body, a leg sticking out here, an arm there, a black face staring at you a little further on. You are startled by a rustle. You look round and see half a dozen gorged rats scampering off in all directions, or you see a dog trying to make his escape over the ruins.... I only wonder that the sight of these scenes does not convert every man in the town into a tiger and every woman into a fury. But these people have been so long ground down and demoralized that their nature seems to have lost the power of reaction.

completed the task of Italian unification. In the Austro-Prussian War of 1866, the new Italian state became an ally of Prussia. Although the Italian army was defeated by the Austrians, Prussia's victory left the Italians with Venetia. In 1870, the Franco-Prussian War resulted in the withdrawal of French troops from Rome. The Italian army then annexed the city on September 20, 1870, and Rome became the new capital of the united Italian state.

The Unification of Germany

After the failure of the Frankfurt Assembly to achieve German unification in 1848–1849, German nationalists focused on Austria and Prussia as the only two states powerful enough to dominate German affairs. Austria had long controlled the existing Germanic Confederation, but Prussian power had grown, strongly reinforced by economic expansion in the 1850s. Prussia had formed the *Zollverein,* a German customs union, in 1834. By eliminating tolls on rivers and roads among member states, the *Zollverein* had stimulated trade and added to the prosperity of its member states. By 1853, all the German states except Austria had joined the Prussian-dominated customs union. A number of middle-class liberals now began to see Prussia in a new light; some even looked openly to Prussia to bring about the unification of Germany.

In 1848, Prussia had framed a constitution that at least had the appearance of constitutional monarchy in that it had established a bicameral legislature with the lower house elected by universal male suffrage. However, the voting population was divided into three classes determined by the amount of taxes they paid, a system that allowed the biggest taxpayers to gain the most seats. Unintentionally, by 1859, this system had allowed control of the lower house to fall largely into the hands of the rising middle classes, whose numbers were growing as a result of continuing industrialization. Their desire was to have a real parliamentary system, but the king's executive power remained too strong; royal ministers answered for their actions only to the king, not the parliament. Nevertheless, the parliament had been granted important legislative and taxation powers on which it could build.

CHRONOLOGY

The Unification of Italy

Victor Emmanuel II	1849–1878
Count Cavour becomes prime minister of Piedmont	1852
Agreement with Napoleon III	1858
Austrian War	1859
Plebiscites in the northern Italian states	1860
Garibaldi's invasion of the kingdom of the Two Sicilies	1860
Kingdom of Italy is proclaimed	1861
Italy's annexation of Venetia	1866
Italy's annexation of Rome	1870

In 1861, King Frederick William IV died and was succeeded by his brother. King William I (1861–1888) had definite ideas about the Prussian army because of his own military training. He and his advisers believed that the army was in dire need of change if Prussia was to remain a great power. The king planned to double the size of the army and institute three years of compulsory military service for all young men.

Middle-class liberals in the parliament, while willing to have reform, feared compulsory military service because they believed the government would use it to inculcate obedience to the monarchy and strengthen the influence of the conservative-military clique in Prussia. When the Prussian legislature rejected the new military budget submitted to parliament in March 1862, William I appointed a new prime minister, Count Otto von Bismarck (1815–1898). Bismarck, regarded even by the king as too conservative, came to determine the course of modern German history. Until 1890, he dominated both German and European politics.

Otto von Bismarck was born into the Junker class, the traditional, landowning aristocracy of Prussia, and remained loyal to it throughout his life. "I was born and raised as an aristocrat," he once said. As a university student, Bismarck indulged heartily in wine, women, and song yet managed to read widely in German history. After earning a law degree, he embarked on a career in the Prussian civil service but soon tired of bureaucratic, administrative routine and retired to manage his country estates. Comparing the civil servant to a musician in an orchestra, he responded, "I want to play the tune the way it sounds good to me or not at all. . . . My pride bids me command rather than obey."[3] In 1847, desirous of more excitement and power than he could find in the country, he reentered public life. Four years later, he began to build a base of diplomatic experience as the Prussian delegate to the diet (parliament) of the Germanic Confederation. This, combined with his experience as Prussian ambassador to Russia and later to France, gave him opportunities to acquire a wide knowledge of European affairs and to learn how to assess the character of rulers.

Because Bismarck succeeded in guiding Prussia's unification of Germany, it is often assumed that he had determined on a course of action that led precisely to that goal. That is hardly the case. Bismarck was a consummate politician and opportunist. He was not a political gambler but a moderate who waged war only when all other diplomatic alternatives had been exhausted and when he was reasonably sure that all the military and diplomatic advantages were on his side. Bismarck has often been portrayed as the ultimate realist, the foremost nineteenth-century practitioner of *Realpolitik*. He was also quite open about his strong dislike of anyone who opposed him. He said one morning to his wife, "I could not sleep the whole night; I hated throughout the whole night."

In 1862, Bismarck resubmitted the army appropriations bill to parliament along with a passionate appeal to his liberal opponents: "Germany does not look to Prussia's liberalism but to her power. . . . Not by speeches and majorities will the great questions of the day be decided—that was the mistake of 1848–1849—but by iron and blood."[4] His opponents were not impressed and rejected the bill once again. Bismarck went ahead, collected the taxes, and reorganized the army anyway, blaming the liberals for causing the breakdown of constitutional government. From 1862 to 1866, Bismarck governed Prussia by largely ignoring parliament. Unwilling to revolt, parliament did nothing. In the meantime, opposition to his domestic policy determined Bismarck on an active foreign policy, which in 1864 led to his first war.

THE DANISH WAR (1864)

In the three wars that he waged, Bismarck's victories were as much diplomatic and political as they were military. Before war was declared, Bismarck always saw to it that Prussia would be fighting only one power and that that opponent was isolated diplomatically.

The Danish War arose over the duchies of Schleswig and Holstein. In 1863, contrary to international treaty, the Danish government moved to incorporate the two duchies into Denmark. German nationalists were outraged since both duchies had large German populations and were regarded as German states. The diet of the Germanic Confederation urged its member states to send troops against Denmark, but Bismarck did not care to subject Prussian policy to the Austrian-dominated German diet. Instead, he persuaded the Austrians to join Prussia in declaring war on Denmark on February 1, 1864. The Danes were quickly defeated and surrendered Schleswig and Holstein to the victors (see Map 22.3). Austria and Prussia then agreed to divide the administration of the two duchies; Prussia took Schleswig while Austria administered Holstein. The plan was Bismarck's. By this time, Bismarck had come to the realization that for Prussia to expand its power by dominating the northern, largely Protestant part of the Germanic Confederation, Austria would have to be excluded from German affairs or, less likely, be willing to accept Prussian domination of Germany.

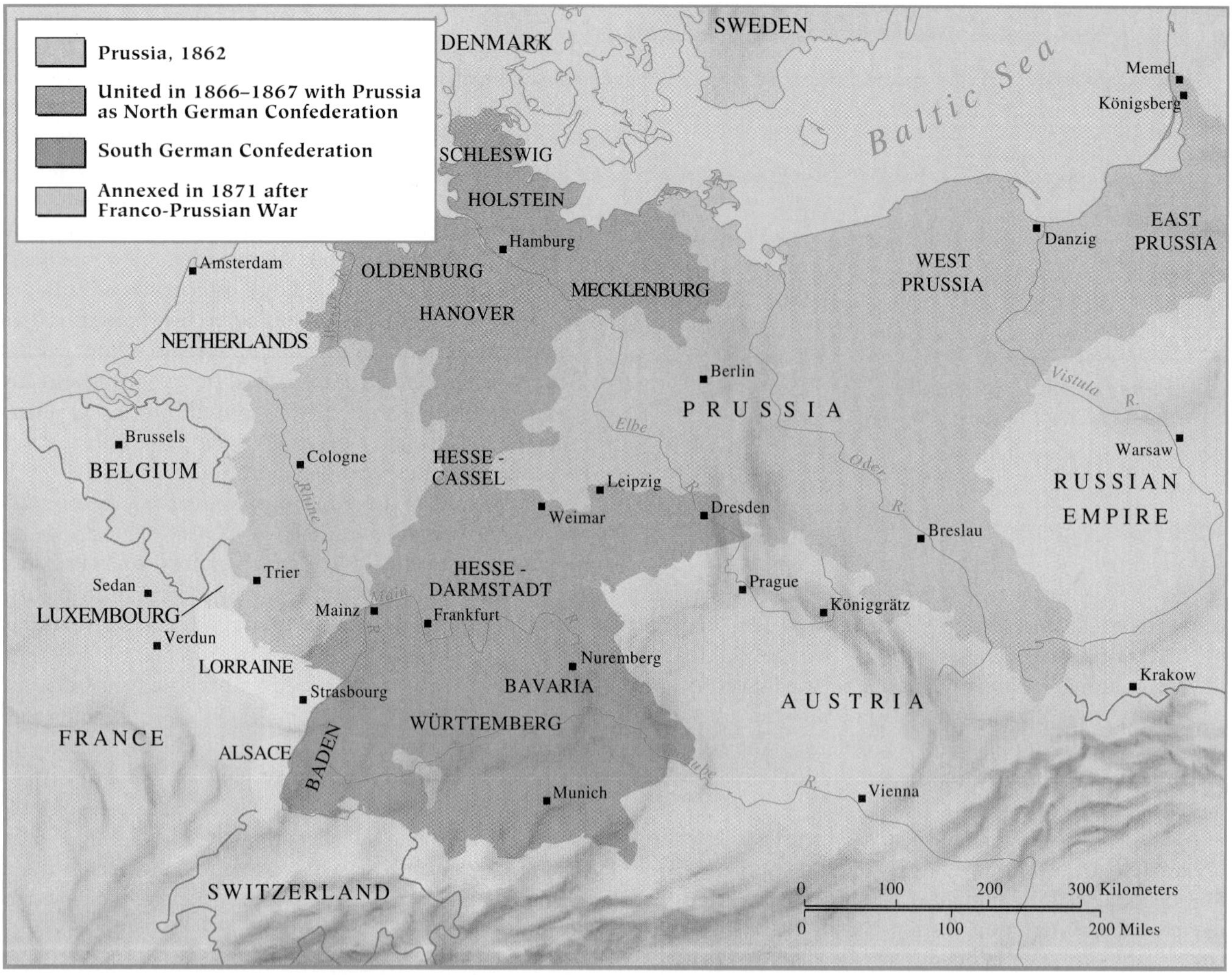

Map 22.3 The Unification of Germany. Count Otto von Bismarck, the Prussian prime minister, skillfully combined domestic policies with wars with Denmark, Austria, and France to achieve the creation of the German Empire in 1871. ■ From the Prussian perspective of increasing its military power and ability to rule all parts of its lands, which was more important: formation of the North German Confederation or absorption of the South German Confederation?

The joint administration of the two duchies offered plenty of opportunities to create friction with Austria and provide a reason for war if it came to that. While he pursued negotiations with Austria, he also laid the foundations for the isolation of Austria.

THE AUSTRO-PRUSSIAN WAR (1866)

Bismarck had no problem gaining Russia's agreement to remain neutral in the event of an Austro-Prussian war because Prussia had been the only great power to support Russia's repression of a Polish revolt in 1863. Napoleon III was a thornier problem, but Bismarck was able to buy his neutrality with vague promises of territory in the Rhineland. Finally, Bismarck made an alliance with the new Italian state and promised it Venetia in the event of Austrian defeat.

With the Austrians isolated, Bismarck used the joint occupation of Schleswig-Holstein to goad the Austrians into a war on June 14, 1866. Many Europeans, including Napoleon III, expected a quick Austrian victory, but they overlooked the effectiveness of the Prussian military reforms of the 1860s. The Prussian breech-loading needle gun had a much faster rate of fire than the Austrian muzzle-loader, and a superior network of railroads enabled the Prussians to mass troops quickly. At Königgrätz (Sadowa) on July 3, the Austrian army was decisively defeated. Looking ahead, Bismarck refused to create a hostile enemy by burdening Austria with a harsh peace as the Prussian king wanted. Austria lost no territory except Venetia to Italy but was excluded from German affairs. The German states north of the Main River were organized into the North German Confederation, controlled by Prussia. The southern German states, largely Catholic, remained independent but were coerced into signing military agreements with Prussia. In addition to Schleswig and Holstein, Prussia annexed Hanover and Hesse-Cassel because they had openly sided with Austria.

The Austrian war was a rather decisive turning point in Prussian domestic affairs. After the war, Bismarck asked the Prussian parliament to pass a bill of indemnity, retroactively legalizing the taxes he had collected illegally since 1862. Even most of the liberals voted in favor of the bill because they had been won over by Bismarck's successful use of military power. With his victory over Austria and the creation of the North German Confederation, Bismarck had proved Napoleon III's dictum that nationalism and authoritarian government could be combined. In using nationalism to win support from liberals and prevent governmental reform, Bismarck showed that liberalism and nationalism, the two major forces of change in the early nineteenth century, could be separated.

He showed the same flexibility in the creation of a new constitution for the North German Confederation. Each German state kept its own local government, but the king of Prussia was head of the confederation, and the chancellor (Bismarck) was responsible directly to the king. Both the army and foreign policy remained in the hands of the king and his chancellor. Parliament consisted of two bodies: the Bundesrat, or federal council, composed of delegates nominated by the states, and a lower house, the Reichstag, elected by universal male suffrage. Like Napoleon, Bismarck believed that the peasants and artisans who made up most of the population were conservative at heart and could be used to overcome the advantages of the liberals.

THE FRANCO-PRUSSIAN WAR (1870–1871)

Bismarck and William I had achieved a major goal by 1866. Prussia now dominated all of northern Germany, and Austria had been excluded from any significant role in German affairs. Nevertheless, unsettled business led to new international complications and further change. Bismarck realized that France would never be content with a strong German state to its east because of the potential threat to French security. At the same time, after a series of setbacks, Napoleon III needed a diplomatic triumph to offset his serious domestic problems. The French were not happy with the turn of events in Germany and looked for opportunities to humiliate the Prussians.

After a successful revolution had deposed Queen Isabella II, the throne of Spain was offered to Prince Leopold of Hohenzollern-Sigmaringen, a distant relative of the Hohenzollern king of Prussia. Bismarck welcomed this possibility for the same reason that the French objected to it. If Leopold were placed on the throne of Spain, France would be virtually encircled by members of the Hohenzollern dynasty. French objections caused King William I to force his relative to withdraw his candidacy. Bismarck was disappointed with the king's actions, but at this point, the French overreached themselves. Not content with their diplomatic victory, they pushed William I to make a formal apology to France and promise never to allow Leopold to be a candidate again. When Bismarck received a telegram from the king informing him of the French request, Bismarck edited it to make it appear even more insulting to the French, knowing that the French would be angry and declare war (see the box on p. 622). The French reacted as Bismarck expected they would and declared war on Prussia on July 15, 1870. The French prime minister remarked, "We go to war with a light heart."

Unfortunately for the French, a "light heart" was not enough. They proved no match for the better-led and better-organized Prussian forces. The southern German states honored their military alliances with Prussia and joined the war effort against the French. The Prussian armies advanced into France, and at Sedan on September 2, 1870, an entire French army and Napoleon III himself were captured. The Second French Empire collapsed, but the war was not yet over. After four months of bitter resistance, Paris finally capitulated on January 28, 1871, and an official peace treaty was signed in May. France had to pay an indemnity of 5 billion francs (about $1 billion) and give up the provinces of Alsace and Lorraine to the new German state, a loss that angered the French and left them burning for revenge.

Even before the war had ended, the southern German states had agreed to enter the North German Confederation.

The Unification of Germany. Under Prussian leadership, a new German Empire was proclaimed on January 18, 1871, in the Hall of Mirrors in the palace at Versailles. King William of Prussia became Emperor William I of the Second German Empire. In this painting by Anton von Werner, Otto von Bismarck, the man who had been so instrumental in creating the new German state, is shown, resplendently attired in his white uniform, standing at the foot of the throne.

Bismarck "Goads" France into War

After his meeting with the French ambassador at Ems, King William I of Prussia sent a telegram to Bismarck with a report of their discussions. By editing the telegram from King William I before releasing it to the press, Bismarck made it sound as if the Prussian king had treated the ambassador in a demeaning fashion. Six days later, France declared war on Prussia.

The Abeken [Privy Councillor] Text, Ems, July 13, 1870

To the Federal Chancellor, Count Bismarck. His Majesty the King writes to me:

"M. Benedetti intercepted me on the Promenade in order to demand of me most insistently that I should authorize him to telegraph immediately to Paris that I shall obligate myself for all future time never again to give my approval to the candidacy of the Hohenzollerns should it be renewed. I refused to agree to this, the last time somewhat severely, informing him that one dare not and cannot assume such obligations *à tout jamais* [forever]. Naturally, I informed him that I had received no news as yet, and since he had been informed earlier than I by way of Paris and Madrid, he could easily understand why my government was once again out of the matter."

Since then His Majesty has received a dispatch from the Prince [father of the Hohenzollern candidate for the Spanish throne]. As His Majesty has informed Count Benedetti that he was expecting news from the Prince, His Majesty himself, in view of the above-mentioned demand and in consonance with the advice of Count Eulenburg and myself, decided not to receive the French envoy again but to inform him through an adjutant that His Majesty had now received from the Prince confirmation of the news which Benedetti had already received from Paris, and that he had nothing further to say to the Ambassador. His Majesty leaves it to the judgment of Your Excellency whether or not to communicate at once the new demand by Benedetti and its rejection to our ambassadors and to the press.

Bismarck's Edited Version

After the reports of the renunciation by the hereditary Prince of Hohenzollern had been officially transmitted by the Royal Government of Spain to the Imperial Government of France, the French Ambassador presented to His Majesty the King at Ems the demand to authorize him to telegraph to Paris that His Majesty the King would obligate himself for all future time never again to give his approval to the candidacy of the Hohenzollerns should it be renewed.

His Majesty the King thereupon refused to receive the French envoy again and informed him through an adjutant that His Majesty had nothing further to say to the Ambassador.

On January 18, 1871, in the Hall of Mirrors in Louis XIV's palace at Versailles, William I was proclaimed kaiser or emperor of the Second German Empire (the first was the medieval Holy Roman Empire). German unity had been achieved by the Prussian monarchy and the Prussian army. In a real sense, Germany had been merged into Prussia, not Prussia into Germany. German liberals also rejoiced. They had dreamed of unity and freedom, but the achievement of unity now seemed much more important. One old liberal proclaimed:

> I cannot shake off the impression of this hour. I am no devotee of Mars; I feel more attached to the goddess of beauty and the mother of graces than to the powerful god of war, but the trophies of war exercise a magic charm even upon the child of peace. One's view is involuntarily chained and one's spirit goes along with the boundless row of men who acclaim the god of the moment—success.[5]

The Prussian leadership of German unification meant the triumph of authoritarian, militaristic values over liberal, constitutional sentiments in the development of the new German state. With its industrial resources and military might, the new state had become the strongest power on the Continent. A new European balance of power was at hand.

Nation Building and Reform: The National State in Mid-Century

While European affairs were dominated by the unification of Italy and Germany, other states were also undergoing transformations (see Map 22.4). War, civil war, and changing political alignments served as catalysts for domestic reforms.

The Austrian Empire: Toward a Dual Monarchy

After the Habsburgs had crushed the revolutions of 1848–1849, they restored centralized, autocratic government to the empire. What seemed to be the only lasting result of the revolution of 1848 was the act of emancipation of September 7, 1848, that freed the serfs and eliminated all compulsory labor services. Nevertheless, the development of industrialization after 1850, especially in Vienna and the provinces of Bohemia and Galicia, served to bring some economic and social change to the empire in the form of an urban proletariat, labor unrest, and a new industrial middle class.

In 1851, the revolutionary constitutions were abolished and a system of centralized autocracy was imposed on the empire. Under the leadership of Alexander von Bach (1813–1893), local privileges were subordinated to a unified system of administration, law, and taxation implemented by German-speaking officials. Hungary was subjected to the rule of military officers, and the Catholic church was declared the state church and given control of education. Economic troubles and war, however, soon brought change. After Austria's defeat in the Italian war in 1859, the Emperor Francis Joseph (1848–1916) attempted to establish an imperial parliament (*Reichsrat*) with a nominated upper house and an elected lower house of representatives. Although the system was supposed to provide representation for the nationalities of the empire, the

CHRONOLOGY

The Unification of Germany

King William I of Prussia	1861–1888
Bismarck becomes minister-president of Prussia	1862
Danish War	1864
Austro-Prussian War	1866
Battle of Königgrätz	1866 (July 3)
Franco-Prussian War	1870–1871
Battle of Sedan	1870 (September 2)
Fall of Paris	1871 (January 28)
German Empire is proclaimed	1871 (January 18)

Map 22.4 Europe in 1871. By 1871, most of the small states of Europe had been absorbed into larger ones, leaving the major powers uncomfortably rubbing shoulders with one another. Meanwhile, the power equation was shifting: the German Empire increased in power while Austria-Hungary and the Ottoman Empire declined. ■ Of the great powers, which had the greatest overall exposure to the others in terms of shared borders and sea access?

complicated formula used for elections ensured the election of a German-speaking majority, serving once again to alienate the ethnic minorities, particularly the Hungarians.

Only when military disaster struck again in the Austro-Prussian War did the Austrians deal with the fiercely nationalistic Hungarians. The result was the negotiated *Ausgleich*, or Compromise, of 1867, which created the dual monarchy of Austria-Hungary. Each part of the empire now had a constitution, its own bicameral legislature, its own governmental machinery for domestic affairs, and its own capital (Vienna for Austria and Buda—soon to be united with Pest, across the river—for Hungary). Holding the two states together were a single monarch (Francis Joseph was emperor of Austria and king of Hungary) and a common army, foreign policy, and system of finances. In domestic affairs, the Hungarians had become an independent nation. The *Ausgleich* did not, however, satisfy the other nationalities that made up the multinational Austro-Hungarian Empire (see Map 22.5). The dual monarchy simply enabled the German-speaking Austrians and Hungarian Magyars to dominate the minorities, especially the Slavic peoples (Poles, Croats, Czechs, Serbs, Slovaks, Slovenes, Little Russians), in their respective states. As the Hungarian nationalist Louis Kossuth remarked: "Dualism is the alliance of the conservative, reactionary and any apparently liberal elements in Hungary with those of the Austrian Germans who despise liberty, for the oppression of the other nationalities and races."[6] The nationalities problem persisted until the demise of the empire at the end of World War I.

Imperial Russia

Russia's defeat in the Crimean War at the hands of the British and French revealed the blatant deficiencies behind the facade of absolute power and made it clear even to staunch conservatives that Russia was falling hopelessly

Map 22.5 Ethnic Groups in the Dual Monarchy, 1867. Nationalism continued to be a problem in the Austrian Empire after suppression of the 1848–1849 revolutions. Military defeats led Emperor Francis Joseph to create the Dual Monarchy, giving Hungary power over its domestic affairs. However, the demands of other ethnic minorities went largely unmet.
■ Which ethnic group was most widely dispersed throughout the Dual Monarchy?

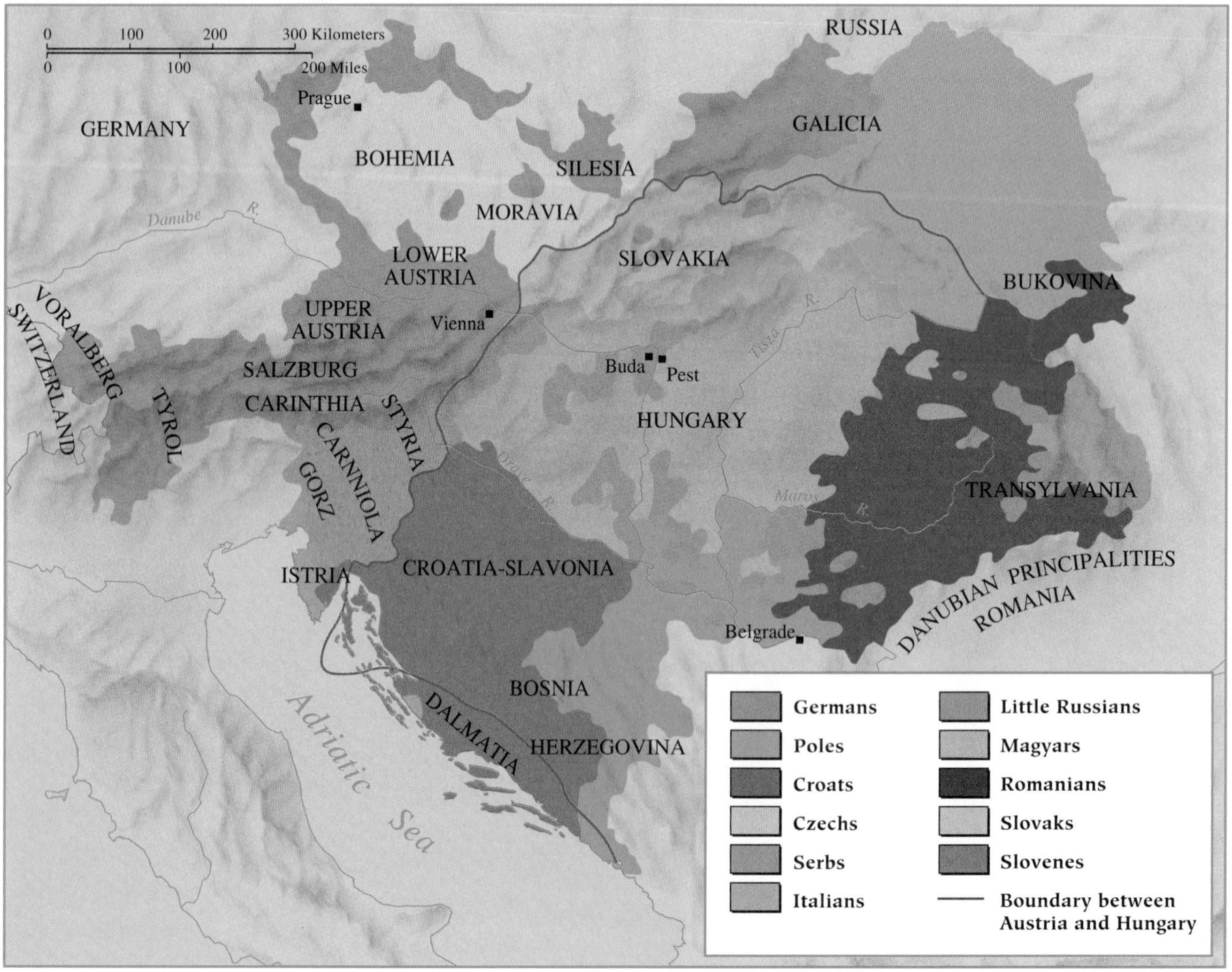

Emancipation: Serfs and Slaves

Although overall their histories have been quite different, Russia and the United States shared a common feature in the 1860s. They were the only states in the Western world that still had large enslaved populations (the Russian serfs were virtually slaves). The leaders of both countries issued emancipation proclamations within two years of each other. The first excerpt is taken from the Imperial Decree of March 3, 1861, which freed the Russian serfs. The second excerpt is from Abraham Lincoln's Emancipation Proclamation, issued on January 1, 1863.

Tsar Alexander II, Imperial Decree, March 3, 1861

By the grace of God, we, Alexander II, Emperor and Autocrat of all the Russias, King of Poland, Grand Duke of Finland, etc., to all our faithful subjects, make known:

Called by Divine Providence and by the sacred right of inheritance to the throne of our ancestors, we took a vow in our innermost heart to respond to the mission which is intrusted to us as to surround with our affection and our Imperial solicitude all our faithful subjects of every rank and of every condition, from the warrior, who nobly bears arms for the defense of the country to the humble artisan devoted to the works of industry; from the official in the career of the high offices of the State to the laborer whose plow furrows the soil. . . .

We thus came to the conviction that the work of a serious improvement of the condition of the peasants was a sacred inheritance bequeathed to us by our ancestors, a mission which, in the course of events, Divine providence called upon us to fulfill. . . .

In virtue of the new dispositions above mentioned, the peasants attached to the soil will be invested within a term fixed by the law with all the rights of free cultivators. . . .

At the same time, they are granted the right of purchasing their close, and, with the consent of the proprietors, they may acquire in full property the arable lands and other appurtenances which are allotted to them as a permanent holding. By the acquisition in full property of the quantity of land fixed, the peasants are free from their obligations toward the proprietors for land thus purchased, and they enter definitely into the condition of free peasants—landholders.

President Abraham Lincoln, Emancipation Proclamation, January 1, 1863

Now therefore, I, Abraham Lincoln, President of the United States, by virtue of the power in me vested as Commander-in-Chief of the Army and Navy of the United States in time of actual armed rebellion against the authority and government of the United States, and as a fit and necessary war measure for suppressing such rebellion, do, on this 1st day of January, A.D. 1863, and in accordance with my purpose to do so, . . . order and designate as the States and parts of States wherein the people thereof, respectively, are this day in rebellion against the United States the following, to wit:

Arkansas, Texas, Louisiana, . . . Mississippi, Alabama, Florida, Georgia, South Carolina, North Carolina, and Virginia. . . .

And by virtue of the power for the purpose aforesaid, I do order and declare that all persons held as slaves within said designated States and parts of States are, and henceforward shall be free; and that the Executive Government of the United States, including the military and naval authorities thereof, will recognize and maintain the freedom of said persons.

behind the western European powers. Tsar Alexander II (1855–1881), who came to power in the midst of the Crimean War, turned his energies to a serious overhaul of the Russian system.

Serfdom was the most burdensome problem in tsarist Russia. The continuing subjugation of millions of peasants to the land and their landlords was an obviously corrupt and failing system. Reduced to antiquated methods of production based on serf labor, Russian landowners were economically pressed and unable to compete with foreign agriculture. The serfs, who formed the backbone of the Russian infantry, were uneducated and consequently increasingly unable to deal with the more complex machines and weapons of war. Then, too, peasant dissatisfaction still led to local peasant revolts that disrupted the countryside. Alexander II seemed to recognize the inevitable: "The existing order of serfdom," he told a group of Moscow nobles, "cannot remain unchanged. It is better to abolish serfdom from above than to wait until it is abolished from below."

On March 3, 1861, Alexander issued his emancipation edict (see the box above). Peasants could now own property, marry as they chose, and bring suits in the law courts. Nevertheless, the benefits of emancipation were limited. The government provided land for the peasants by purchasing it from the landowners, but the landowners often chose to keep the best lands. The Russian peasants soon found that they had inadequate amounts of good arable land to support themselves, a situation that worsened as the peasant population increased rapidly in the second half of the nineteenth century.

Nor were the peasants completely free. The state compensated the landowners for the land given to the peasants, but the peasants were expected to repay the state in long-term installments. To ensure that the payments were made, peasants were subjected to the authority of their *mir*, or

Emancipation of the Serfs. On March 3, 1861, Tsar Alexander II issued his emancipation edict for the Russian serfs. This photograph shows a Russian noble on the steps of his country house reading the edict to a gathering of his serfs.

Novosti Agency

village commune, which was collectively responsible for the land payments to the government. In a very real sense, then, the village commune, not the individual peasants, owned the land the peasants were purchasing. And since the village communes were responsible for the payments, they were reluctant to allow peasants to leave their land. Emancipation, then, led not to a free, landowning peasantry along the Western model but to an unhappy, land-starved peasantry that largely followed the old ways of farming.

Alexander II also attempted other reforms. In 1864, he instituted a system of *zemstvos,* or local assemblies, that provided a moderate degree of self-government. Representatives to the zemstvos were to be elected from the noble landowners, townspeople, and peasants, but the property-based system of voting gave a distinct advantage to the nobles. Zemstvos were given a limited power to provide public services, such as education, famine relief, and road and bridge maintenance. They could levy taxes to pay for these services, but their efforts were frequently disrupted by bureaucrats, who feared any hint of self-government. The hope of liberal nobles and other social reformers that the zemstvos would be expanded into a national parliament remained unfulfilled. The legal reforms of 1864, which created a regular system of local and provincial courts and a judicial code that accepted the principle of equality before the law, proved successful, however.

Even the autocratic tsar was unable to control the forces he unleashed by his reform program. Reformers wanted more and rapid change; conservatives opposed what they perceived as the tsar's attempts to undermine the basic institutions of Russian society. By 1870, Russia was witnessing an increasing number of reform movements. One of the most popular stemmed from the radical writings of Alexander Herzen (1812–1870), a Russian exile living in London, whose slogan, "Land and Freedom," epitomized his belief that the Russian peasant must be the chief instrument for social reform. Herzen believed that the peasant village commune could serve as an independent, self-governing body that would form the basis of a new Russia. Russian students and intellectuals who followed Herzen's ideas formed a movement called populism whose aim was to create a new society through the revolutionary acts of the peasants. The peasants' lack of interest in these revolutionary ideas, however, led some of the populists to resort to violent means to overthrow tsarist autocracy. One such group of radicals, known as the People's Will, succeeded in assassinating Alexander II in 1881. His son and successor, Alexander III (1881–1894), turned against reform and returned to the traditional methods of repression.

Great Britain: The Victorian Age

Like Russia, Britain was not troubled by revolutionary disturbances during 1848, although for quite different reasons. The Reform Act of 1832 had opened the door to political representation for the industrial middle class, and in the 1860s, Britain's liberal parliamentary system demonstrated once more its ability to make both social and political reforms that enabled the country to remain stable and prosperous.

One of the reasons for Britain's stability was its continuing economic growth. After 1850, middle-class prosperity was at last coupled with some improvements for the working classes. Real wages for laborers increased more than 25 percent between 1850 and 1870. The British feeling of national pride was well reflected in Queen Victoria, whose reign from 1837 to 1901 was the longest in English history. Her sense of duty and moral respectability reflected the attitudes of her age, which has ever since been known as the Victorian Age.

Queen Victoria and Her Family. Queen Victoria, who ruled Britain from 1837 to 1901, married her German first cousin, Prince Albert of Saxe-Coburg-Gotha, in 1840 and subsequently gave birth to four sons and five daughters, who married into a number of European royal families. When she died at age eighty-one, she had thirty-seven great-grandchildren. Victoria is seated at the center of this 1881 photograph, surrounded by members of her family.

Politically, this was an era of uneasy stability as the aristocratic and upper-middle-class representatives who dominated Parliament blurred party lines by their internal strife and shifting positions. One political figure who stood out was Henry John Temple, Lord Palmerston (1784–1865), who was prime minister for most of the period from 1855 to 1865. Although a Whig, Palmerston was without strong party loyalty and found it easy to make political compromises. He was not a reformer, however, and opposed expanding the franchise. He said, "We should by such an arrangement increase the number of Bribeable Electors and overpower Intelligence and Property by Ignorance and Poverty."

After Palmerston's death in 1865, the movement for the extension of the franchise only intensified. Although the Whigs (now called the Liberals), who had been responsible for the Reform Act of 1832, talked about passing additional reform legislation, it was actually the Tories (now called the Conservatives) who carried it through. The Tory leader in Parliament, Benjamin Disraeli (1804–1881), was apparently motivated by the desire to win over the newly enfranchised groups to the Conservative Party. The Reform Act of 1867 was an important step toward the democratization of Britain. By lowering the monetary requirements for voting (taxes paid or income earned), it by and large enfranchised many male urban workers. The number of voters increased from about one million to slightly over two million. Although Disraeli believed that this would benefit the Conservatives, industrial workers helped produce a huge Liberal victory in 1868.

The extension of the right to vote had an important by-product as it forced the Liberal and Conservative Parties to organize carefully in order to manipulate the electorate. Party discipline intensified, and the rivalry between the two well-established political parties, the Liberals and Conservatives, became a regular feature of parliamentary life. In large part this was due to the personal and political opposition of the two leaders of these parties, William Gladstone (1809–1898) and Disraeli.

The first Liberal administration of William Gladstone, from 1868 to 1874, was responsible for a series of impressive reforms. Legislation and government orders opened civil service positions to competitive exams rather than patronage, introduced the secret ballot for voting, and abolished the practice of purchasing military commissions. The Education Act of 1870 attempted to make elementary schools available for all children (see Chapter 24). These reforms were typically liberal. By eliminating abuses and enabling people with talent to compete fairly, they sought to strengthen the nation and its institutions.

The United States: Civil War and Reunion

By the mid-nineteenth century, American national unity was increasingly threatened by the issue of slavery. Both North and South had grown dramatically in population during the first half of the nineteenth century. But their development was quite different. The cotton economy and social structure of the South were based on the exploitation of enslaved black Africans and their descendants. The importance of cotton is evident from production figures. In 1810, the South produced a raw cotton crop of 178,000 bales worth $10 million. By 1860, it was generating 4.5 million bales of cotton with a value of $249 million. Ninety-three percent of southern cotton in 1850 was produced by a slave population that had grown dramatically in fifty years. Although new slave imports had been barred in 1808, there were four million Afro-American slaves in the South by 1860—four times the number sixty years earlier. The cotton economy and plantation-based slavery were intimately related, and the attempt to maintain them in the course of the first half of the nineteenth century led the South to become increasingly defensive, monolithic, and isolated. At the same time, the rise of an abolitionist movement in the North challenged the southern order and created an "emotional chain reaction" that led to civil war.

By the 1850s, the slavery question had caused the Whig Party to become defunct and the Democrats to split along North-South lines. The Kansas-Nebraska Act of 1854, which allowed slavery in the Kansas and Nebraska territories to be determined by popular sovereignty, created a firestorm in the North and led to the creation of a new sectional party. The Republicans were united by antislavery principles and were especially driven by the fear that the "slave power" of the South would attempt to spread the slave system throughout the country.

As polarization over the issue of slavery intensified, compromise became less feasible. When Abraham Lincoln, the man who had said in a speech in Illinois in 1858 that "this government cannot endure permanently half slave and half free," was elected president in November 1860, the die was cast. Lincoln carried only 2 of the 1,109 counties in the South; the Republicans were not even on the ballot in ten southern states. On December 20, 1860, a South Carolina convention voted to repeal the state's ratification of the U.S. Constitution. In February 1861, six more southern states did the same, and a rival nation—the Confederate States of America—was formed (see Map 22.6). In April fighting erupted between North and South.

The American Civil War (1861–1865) was an extraordinarily bloody struggle, a foretaste of the total war to come in the twentieth century. More than 600,000 soldiers died, either in battle or from deadly infectious diseases spawned by filthy camp conditions. Over a period of four years, the Union states mobilized their superior assets and gradually wore down the South. As the war dragged on, it had the effect of radicalizing public opinion in the North. What began as a war to save the Union became a war against slavery. On January 1, 1863, Lincoln's Emancipation Proclamation made most of the nation's slaves "forever free" (see the box on p. 625). The increasingly effective Union blockade of the

Map 22.6 The United States: The West and the Civil War. By 1860, the North had developed an economy based on industry and commerce, whereas the South had remained a primarily agrarian economy based on black slave labor. The question of the continuance of slavery itself and the expansion of slavery into western territories led to the Civil War, in which the South sought to create an independent country. ■ Why would its inhabitants want to create a separate state of West Virginia?

CHRONOLOGY

National States

France	
Louis Napoleon is elected president	1848
Coup d'état by Louis Napoleon	1851
Creation of the Second Empire	1852
Emperor Napoleon III	1852–1870
"Authoritarian empire"	1852–1860
Crimean War	1854–1856
Treaty of Paris	1856
"Liberal empire"	1860–1870
Austrian Empire	
Establishment of imperial parliament	1859
Ausgleich: the Dual Monarchy	1867
Russia	
Tsar Alexander II	1855–1881
Emancipation edict	1861 (March 3)
Creation of zemstvos and legal reforms	1864
Great Britain	
Queen Victoria	1837–1901
Ministry of Palmerston	1855–1865
Reform Act	1867
First Liberal ministry of William Gladstone	1868–1874
United States	
Kansas-Nebraska Act	1854
Election of Lincoln and secession of South Carolina	1860
Outbreak of Civil War	1861
Surrender of Lee	1865 (April 9)
Canada	
Formation of the Dominion of Canada	1867

South, combined with a shortage of fighting men, made the Confederate cause desperate by the end of 1864. The final push of Union troops under General Ulysses S. Grant forced General Robert E. Lee's army to surrender on April 9, 1865. Although problems lay ahead, the Union victory confirmed that the United States would be "one nation, indivisible."

The Emergence of a Canadian Nation

To the north of the United States, the process of nation building was also making progress. By the Treaty of Paris in 1763, Canada—or New France, as it was called—passed into the hands of the British. By 1800, most Canadians favored more autonomy, although the colonists disagreed on the form this autonomy should take. Upper Canada (now Ontario) was predominantly English-speaking, whereas Lower Canada (now Quebec) was dominated by French Canadians. A dramatic increase in immigration to Canada from Great Britain (almost one million immigrants between 1815 and 1850) also fueled the desire for self-government.

In 1837, a number of Canadian groups rose in rebellion against British authority. Rebels in Lower Canada demanded separation from Britain, creation of a republic, universal male suffrage, and freedom of the press. Although the rebellions were crushed by the following year, the British government now began to seek ways to satisfy some of the Canadian demands. The American Civil War proved to be a turning point. Fearful of American designs on Canada during the war and eager to reduce the costs of maintaining the colonies, the British government finally capitulated to Canadian demands. In 1867, Parliament established the Canadian nation—the Dominion of Canada—with its own constitution. Canada now possessed a parliamentary system and ruled itself, although foreign affairs still remained under the control of the British government.

Industrialization and the Marxist Response

Between 1850 and 1871, Continental industrialization came of age. The innovations of the British Industrial Revolution—mechanized factory production, the use of coal, the steam engine, and the transportation revolution—all became regular features of economic expansion. Although marred periodically by economic depression (1857–1858) or recession (1866–1867), this was an age of considerable economic prosperity, particularly evident in the growth of domestic and foreign markets.

Industrialization on the Continent

The transformation of textile production from hand looms to power looms had largely been completed in Britain by the 1850s (for cotton) and 1860s (for wool). On the Continent, the period from 1850 to 1870 witnessed increased mechanization of the cotton and textile industries, although Continental countries still remained behind Britain. By 1870, hand looms had virtually disappeared in Britain, whereas in France there were still 200,000 of them, along with 80,000 power looms. However, this period of industrial expansion on the Continent was fueled not so much by textiles as by the growth of railroads. Between 1850 and 1870, European railroad track mileage increased from 14,500 to almost 70,000. The railroads, in turn, stimulated growth in both the iron and coal industries.

Between 1850 and 1870, Continental iron industries made the transition from charcoal iron smelting to coke-blast smelting. Despite the dramatic increases in the production of pig iron, the Continental countries had not yet come close to surpassing British iron production. In 1870, the British iron industry produced one-half of the world's pig iron, four times as much as Germany and five times as much as France. In the middle decades of the nineteenth century, the textile, mining, and metallurgical industries on the Continent also rapidly converted to the use of the steam engine.

An important factor in the expansion of markets was the elimination of barriers to international trade. Essential international waterways were opened up by the elimination of restrictive tolls. The Danube River in 1857 and the Rhine in 1861, for example, were declared freeways for all ships. The negotiation of trade treaties in the 1860s reduced or eliminated protective tariffs throughout much of western Europe.

Governments also played a role in first allowing and then encouraging the formation of joint-stock investment banks (see Chapter 20). These banks were crucial to Continental industrial development because they mobilized enormous capital resources for investment. In the 1850s and 1860s, they were very important in the promotion of railway construction, although they were not always a safe investment. During a trip to Spain to examine possibilities for railroad construction, the locomotive manufacturer George Stephenson reported: "I have been a month in the country, but have not seen during the whole of that time enough people of the right sort to fill a single train."[7] His misgivings proved to be well founded. In 1864, the Spanish banking system, which depended largely on investments in railway shares, collapsed.

Before 1870, capitalist factory owners remained largely free to hire labor on their own terms based on market forces. Although workers formed trade unions as organizations that would fight for improved working conditions and reasonable wages, the unions tended to represent only a small part of the industrial working class and proved largely ineffective. Real change for the industrial proletariat would come only with the development of socialist parties and socialist trade unions. These emerged after 1870, but the theory that made them possible had already been developed by mid-century in the work of Karl Marx.

Marx and Marxism

The beginnings of Marxism can be traced to the 1848 publication of a short treatise titled *The Communist Manifesto,* written by two Germans, Karl Marx (1818–1883) and Friedrich Engels (1820–1895). Marx was born into a relatively prosperous middle-class family in Trier in western Germany. He descended from a long line of rabbis, although his father, a lawyer, had become a Protestant to keep his job. Marx enrolled at the University of Bonn in 1835, but his carefree student ways soon led his father to send him to the more serious-minded University of Berlin, where he encountered the ideas of the German philosopher Georg Wilhelm Friedrich Hegel. After receiving a Ph.D. in philosophy, Marx planned to teach at a university. Unable to obtain a position because of his professed atheism, Marx decided on a career in journalism and eventually became the editor of a liberal bourgeois newspaper in Cologne in 1842. After the newspaper was suppressed because of his radical views, Marx moved to Paris. There he met Friedrich Engels, who became his lifelong friend and financial patron.

Engels, the son of a wealthy German cotton manufacturer, had worked in Britain at one of his father's factories in Manchester. There he had acquired a firsthand knowledge of what he came to call the "wage slavery" of the British working classes, which he detailed in a damning indictment of industrial life titled *The Conditions of the Working Class in England,* written in 1844. Engels would contribute his knowledge of actual working conditions as

Opening of the Suez Canal. Between 1850 and 1871, Continental Europeans built railways, bridges, and canals as part of the ever-spreading process of industrialization. A French diplomat, Ferdinand de Lesseps, was the guiding force behind the construction of the Suez Canal, which provided a link between the Mediterranean and Red Seas. Work on the canal began in 1859 and was completed ten years later. As seen here, an elaborate ceremony marked the opening of the canal. A French vessel led the first convoy of ships through the canal.

The Granger Collection, New York

Karl Marx. Karl Marx was a radical journalist who joined with Friedrich Engels to write *The Communist Manifesto,* which proclaimed the ideas of a revolutionary socialism. After the failure of the 1848 revolution in Germany, Marx fled to Britain, where he continued to write and became involved in the work of the first International Working Men's Association.

well as monetary assistance to the financially strapped Marx.

In 1847, Marx and Engels joined a tiny group of primarily German socialist revolutionaries known as the Communist League. By this time, both Marx and Engels were enthusiastic advocates of the radical working-class movement and agreed to draft a statement of their ideas for the league. The resulting *Communist Manifesto,* published in German in January 1848, appeared on the eve of the revolutions of 1848. One would think from its opening lines that the pamphlet alone had caused this revolutionary upheaval: "A spectre is haunting Europe—the spectre of Communism. All the Powers of Old Europe have entered into a holy alliance to exorcise this spectre: Pope and Czar, Metternich and Guizot, French Radicals and German police spies."[8] In fact, *The Communist Manifesto* was known to only a few of Marx's friends. Although its closing words—"The proletarians have nothing to lose but their chains. They have a world to win. WORKING MEN OF ALL COUNTRIES, UNITE!"—were clearly intended to rouse the working classes to action, they passed unnoticed in 1848. The work, however, became one of the most influential political treatises in modern European history.

According to Engels, Marx's ideas were partly a synthesis of French and German thought. The French provided Marx with ample documentation for his assertion that a revolution could totally restructure society. They also provided him with several examples of socialism. From the German idealistic philosophers such as Hegel, Marx took the idea of dialectic: everything evolves, and all change in history is the result of clashes between antagonistic elements. Marx was particularly impressed by Hegel, but he disagreed with Hegel's belief that history is determined by ideas manifesting themselves in historical forces. Instead, said Marx, the course of history is determined by material forces.

Marx and Engels began the *Manifesto* with the statement that "the history of all hitherto existing society

The Classless Society

In *The Communist Manifesto,* Karl Marx and Friedrich Engels projected the creation of a classless society as the end product of the struggle between the bourgeoisie and the proletariat. In this selection, they discuss the steps by which that classless society would be reached.

Karl Marx and Friedrich Engels, The Communist Manifesto

We have seen . . . that the first step in the revolution by the working class is to raise the proletariat to the position of ruling class . . . The proletariat will use its political supremacy to wrest, by degrees, all capital from the bourgeoisie, to centralize all instruments of production in the hands of the State, i.e., of the proletariat organized as the ruling class; and to increase the total of productive forces as rapidly as possible.

Of course, in the beginning, this cannot be effected except by means of despotic inroads on the rights of property, and on the conditions of bourgeois production; by means of measures, therefore, which appear economically insufficient and untenable, but which, in the course of the movement, outstrip themselves, necessitate further inroads upon the old social order, and are unavoidable as a means of entirely revolutionizing the mode of production.

These measures will of course be different in different countries.

Nevertheless, in the most advanced countries, the following will be pretty generally applicable:

1. Abolition of property in land and application of all rents of land to public purposes.
2. A heavy progressive or graduated income tax.
3. Abolition of all right of inheritance. . . .
5. Centralization of credit in the hands of the State, by means of a national bank with State capital and an exclusive monopoly.
6. Centralization of the means of communication and transport in the hands of the State.
7. Extension of factories and instruments of production owned by the State. . . .
8. Equal liability of all to labor. Establishment of industrial armies, especially for agriculture.
9. Combination of agriculture with manufacturing industries; gradual abolition of the distinction between town and country, by a more equable distribution of the population over the country.
10. Free education for all children in public schools. Abolition of children's factory labor in its present form. . . .

When, in the course of development, class distinctions have disappeared, and all production has been concentrated in the whole nation, the public power will lose its political character. Political power, properly so called, is merely the organized power of one class for oppressing another. If the proletariat during its contest with the bourgeoisie is compelled, by the force of circumstances, to organize itself as a class, if, by means of a revolution, it makes itself the ruling class, and, as such, sweeps away by force the old conditions of production, then it will, along with these conditions, have swept away the conditions for the existence of class antagonisms and of classes generally, and will thereby have abolished its own supremacy as a class.

In place of the old bourgeois society, with its classes and class antagonisms, we shall have an association, in which the free development of each is the condition for the free development of all.

is the history of class struggles." Throughout history, oppressed and oppressor have "stood in constant opposition to one another." In an earlier struggle, the feudal classes of the Middle Ages were forced to accede to the emerging middle class or bourgeoisie. As the bourgeoisie took control in turn, its ideas became the dominant views of the era, and government became its instrument. Marx and Engels declared: "The executive of the modern State is but a committee for managing the common affairs of the whole bourgeoisie."[9] In other words, the government of the state reflected and defended the interests of the industrial middle class and its allies.

Although bourgeois society had emerged victorious out of the ruins of feudalism, Marx and Engels insisted that it had not triumphed completely. Now once again the members of the bourgeoisie were antagonists in an emerging class struggle, but this time they faced the proletariat, or the industrial working class. The struggle would be fierce; in fact, Marx and Engels predicted that the workers would eventually overthrow their bourgeois masters. After this victory, the proletariat would form a dictatorship to reorganize the means of production. Then a classless society would emerge, and the state—itself an instrument of the bourgeoisie—would wither away since it no longer represented the interests of a particular class. Class struggles would then be over (see the box above). Marx believed that the emergence of a classless society would lead to progress in science, technology, and industry and to greater wealth for all.

After the failure of the revolutions of 1848, Marx went to London, where he spent the rest of his life. He continued his writing on political economy, especially his famous work, *Das Kapital (Capital),* only one volume of which he completed. After his death, the remaining volumes were edited by his friend Engels.

One of the reasons *Capital* was not finished was Marx's own preoccupation with organizing the working-class movement. In *The Communist Manifesto,* Marx had defined the communists as "the most advanced and resolute section of the working-class parties of every country." Their advantage was their ability to understand "the line of march, the conditions, and the ultimate general results of the proletarian movement." Marx saw his role in this light and participated enthusiastically in the activities of the International Working Men's Association. Formed in 1864 by British and French trade unionists, this "First International" served as an umbrella organization for working-class interests. Marx was the dominant personality on the organization's General Council and devoted much time to its activities. Internal dissension within the ranks soon damaged the organization, and it failed in 1872. Although it would be revived in 1889, the fate of socialism by that time was in the hands of national socialist parties.

Science and Culture in an Age of Realism

Between 1850 and 1870, two major intellectual developments are evident: the growth of scientific knowledge, with its rapidly increasing impact on the Western worldview, and the shift from Romanticism and its focus on the inner world of reality to Realism and its turning toward the outer, material world.

A New Age of Science

By the mid-nineteenth century, science was having a greater and greater impact on European life. The Scientific Revolution of the sixteenth and seventeenth centuries had fundamentally transformed the Western worldview and created a modern, rational approach to the study of the natural world. Even in the eighteenth century, however, these intellectual developments had remained the preserve of an educated elite and resulted in few practical benefits. Moreover, the technical advances of the early Industrial Revolution had depended little on pure science and much more on the practical experiments of technologically oriented amateur inventors. Advances in industrial technology, however, fed an interest in basic scientific research, which in turn, in the 1830s and afterward, resulted in a rash of basic scientific discoveries that were soon converted into technological improvements that affected everybody.

The development of the steam engine was important in encouraging scientists to work out its theoretical foundations, a preoccupation that led to thermodynamics, the science of the relationship between heat and mechanical energy. The laws of thermodynamics were at the core of nineteenth-century physics. In biology, the Frenchman Louis Pasteur formulated the germ theory of disease, which had enormous practical applications in the development of modern scientific medical practices (see "A Revolution in Health Care" later in this chapter). In chemistry, in the 1860s, the Russian Dmitri Mendeleyev classified all the material elements then known on the basis of their atomic weights and provided the systematic foundation for the periodic law. The Englishman Michael Faraday discovered the phenomenon of electromagnetic induction and put together a primitive generator that laid the foundation for the use of electricity, although economically efficient generators were not built until the 1870s.

The steadily increasing and often dramatic material gains generated by science and technology led to a growing faith in the benefits of science. The popularity of scientific and technological achievement produced a widespread acceptance of the scientific method, based on observation, experiment, and logical analysis, as the only path to objective truth and objective reality. This in turn undermined the faith of many people in religious revelation and truth. It is no accident that the nineteenth century was an age of increasing secularization, particularly evident in the growth of materialism or the belief that everything mental, spiritual, or ideal was simply an outgrowth of physical forces. Truth was to be found in the concrete material existence of human beings and not, as Romanticists imagined, in revelations gained by feeling or intuitive flashes. The importance of materialism was strikingly evident in the most important scientific event of the nineteenth century, the development of the theory of organic evolution according to natural selection. On the theories of Charles Darwin could be built a picture of humans as material beings that were simply part of the natural world.

Charles Darwin and the Theory of Organic Evolution

Charles Darwin (1809–1882), like many of the great scientists of the nineteenth century, was a scientific amateur. Born into an upper-middle-class family, he studied theology at Cambridge University while pursuing an intense side interest in geology and biology. In 1831, at the age of twenty-two, his hobby became his vocation when he accepted an appointment as a naturalist to study animals and plants on an official Royal Navy scientific expedition aboard the H.M.S. *Beagle.* Its purpose was to survey and study the landmasses of South America and the South Pacific. Darwin's specific job was to study the structure of various forms of plant and animal life. He was able to observe animals on islands virtually untouched by external influence and compare them to animals on the mainland. As a result, Darwin came to discard the notion of a special creation and to believe that animals evolved over time and in response to their environment. When he returned to Britain, he eventually formulated an explanation for evolution in the principle of natural selection, a theory that he presented in 1859 in his celebrated book, *On the Origin of Species by Means of Natural Selection.*

The basic idea of this book was that all plants and animals had evolved over a long period of time from earlier and simpler forms of life, a principle known as organic

Darwin and the Descent of Man

Darwin published his theory of organic evolution in 1859, followed twelve years later by *The Descent of Man,* in which he argued that human beings, like other animals, evolved from lower forms of life. The theory provoked a firestorm of criticism, especially from the clergy. One critic described Darwin's theory as a "brutal philosophy—to wit, there is no God, and the ape is our Adam."

■ *Charles Darwin,* The Descent of Man

The main conclusion here arrived at, and now held by many naturalists, who are well competent to form a sound judgment, is that man is descended from some less highly organized form. The grounds upon which this conclusion rests will never be shaken, for the close similarity between man and the lower animals in embryonic development, as well as in innumerable points of structure and constitution, both of high and of the most trifling importance,—the rudiments which he retains, and the abnormal reversions to which he is occasionally liable,—are facts which cannot be disputed. They have long been known, but until recently they told us nothing with respect to the origin of man. Now when viewed by the light of our knowledge of the whole organic world, their meaning is unmistakable. The great principle of evolution stands up clear and firm, when these groups of facts are considered in connection with others, such as the mutual affinities of the members of the same group, their geographical distribution in past and present times, and their geological succession. It is incredible that all these facts should speak falsely. He who is not content to look, like a savage, at the phenomena of nature as disconnected, cannot any longer believe that man is the work of a separate act of creation. He will be forced to admit that the close resemblance of the embryo of man to that, for instance, of a dog—the construction of his skull, limbs and whole frame on the same plan with that of other mammals, independently of the uses to which the parts may be put—the occasional reappearance of various structures, for instance of several muscles, which man does not normally possess . . . —and a crowd of analogous facts—all point in the plainest manner to the conclusion that man is the co-descendant with other mammals of a common progenitor. . . .

Man may be excused for feeling some pride at having risen, though not through his own exertions, to the very summit of the organic scale; and the fact of his having thus risen, instead of having been aboriginally placed there, may give him hope for a still higher destiny in the distant future. But we are not here concerned with hopes or fears, only with the truth as far as our reason permits us to discover it; and I have given the evidence to the best of my ability. We must, however, acknowledge, as it seems to me, that man with all his noble qualities, with sympathy which feels for the most debased, with benevolence which extends not only to other men but to the humblest living creature, with his god-like intellect which has penetrated into the movements and constitution of the solar system—with all these exalted powers—Man still bears in his bodily frame the indelible stamp of his lowly origin.

evolution. Darwin was important in explaining how this natural process worked. He took the first step from Thomas Malthus's theory of population: in every species, "many more individuals of each species are born than can possibly survive." This results in a "struggle for existence." Darwin believed that "as more individuals are produced than can possibly survive, there must in every case be a struggle for existence, either one individual with another of the same species, or with the individuals of distinct species, or with the physical conditions of life." Those who succeeded in this struggle for existence had adapted better to their environment, a process made possible by the appearance of "variants." Chance variations that occurred in the process of inheritance enabled some organisms to be more adaptable to the environment than others, a process that Darwin called natural selection: "Owing to this struggle [for existence], variations, however slight . . . , if they be in any degree profitable to the individuals of a species, in their infinitely complex relations to other organic beings and to their physical conditions of life, will tend to the preservation of such individuals, and will generally be inherited by the offspring."[10] Those that were naturally selected for survival ("survival of the fit") survived. The unfit did not and became extinct. The fit who survived propagated and passed on the variations that enabled them to survive until, from Darwin's point of view, a new separate species emerged.

In *On the Origin of Species,* Darwin discussed plant and animal species only. He was not concerned with humans themselves and only later applied his theory of natural selection to humans. In *The Descent of Man,* published in 1871, he argued for the animal origins of human beings: "man is the co-descendant with other mammals of a common progenitor." Humans were not an exception to the rule governing other species (see the box above).

Darwin's ideas were highly controversial at first. Some people fretted that Darwin's theory made human beings ordinary products of nature rather than unique beings. Others were disturbed by the implications of life as a struggle for survival, of "nature red in tooth and claw." Was there a place in the Darwinian world for moral values? For those who believed in a rational order in the world, Darwin's theory seemed to eliminate purpose and design from the universe. Gradually, however, Darwin's theory was accepted by scientists and other intellectuals. In the process of accepting Darwin's ideas, some people even tried to apply them to society, yet another example of science's increasing prestige.

A Revolution in Health Care

The application of natural science to the field of medicine in the nineteenth century led to revolutionary breakthroughs in health care. The first steps toward a more scientific basis for medicine were taken in Paris hospitals during the first half of the nineteenth century. Clinical observation, consisting of an active physical examination of patients, was combined with the knowledge gained from detailed autopsies to create a new clinical medicine. Nevertheless, the major breakthrough toward a scientific medicine occurred with the discovery of microorganisms, or germs, as the agents causing disease. The germ theory of disease was largely the work of Louis Pasteur (1822–1895). Pasteur was not a doctor but a chemist who approached medical problems in a scientific fashion. In 1857, Pasteur went to Paris as director of scientific studies at the École Normale, where experiments he conducted proved that microorganisms of various kinds were responsible for the process of fermentation, thus launching the science of bacteriology.

Government and private industry soon perceived the inherent practical value of Pasteur's work. His examination of a disease threatening the wine industry led to the development in 1863 of a process—subsequently known as pasteurization—for heating a product to destroy the organisms causing spoilage. In 1877, Pasteur turned his attention to human diseases. His desire to do more than simply identify disease-producing organisms led him in 1885 to a preventive vaccination against rabies. In the 1890s, the principle of vaccination was extended to diphtheria, typhoid fever, cholera, and plague, creating a modern immunological science.

The work of Pasteur and the many others who followed him in isolating the specific bacteriological causes of numerous diseases had a far-reaching impact. By providing a rational means of treating and preventing infectious diseases, they transformed the medical world. Both the practice of surgery and public health experienced a renaissance.

Surgeons had already experienced a new professionalism by the end of the eighteenth century (see Chapter 17), but the discovery of germs and the introduction of anesthesia created a new environment for surgical operations. Surgeons had traditionally set broken bones, treated wounds, and amputated limbs, usually shattered in war. One major obstacle to more successful surgery was the inevitable postoperative infection, which was especially rampant in hospitals.

Joseph Lister (1827–1912), who developed the antiseptic principle, was one of the first people to deal with this problem. Following the work of Pasteur, Lister perceived that bacteria might enter a wound and cause infection. His use of carbolic acid, a newly discovered disinfectant, proved remarkably effective in eliminating infections during surgery. Lister's discoveries dramatically transformed surgery wards as patients no longer succumbed regularly to what was called "hospital gangrene."

The second great barrier to large-scale surgery stemmed from the inability to lessen the pain of the patient.

Jefferson Medical College of Thomas Jefferson University, Philadelphia, PA

Thomas Eakins, *The Gross Clinic.* This painting, completed in 1875, shows Dr. Samuel Gross, one of the foremost surgeons in the United States, scalpel in hand, pausing midway in surgery on a young man's leg to discuss the operation with his students in the amphitheater of the Jefferson Medical College. Various tasks are performed by assistant doctors, including the anesthetist, who holds his cloth over the youth's face. Eakins's painting is a realistic portrayal of the new medical science at work.

Alcohol and opiates had been used for centuries during surgical operations, but even their use did not allow unhurried operative maneuvers. After experiments with numerous agents, sulfuric ether was first used successfully in an operation at the Massachusetts General Hospital in 1846 (see the box on p. 636). Within a year, chloroform began to rival ether as an anesthetic agent.

Although the great discoveries of bacteriology came after the emergence of the first public health movement, they significantly furthered its development. Based on the principle of preventive rather than curative medicine, the urban public health movement of the 1840s and 1850s was largely a response to the cholera epidemic (see Chapter 23). One medical man, in fact, called cholera "our best ally" in furthering public hygiene. The prebacteriological hygiene movement focused on providing clean water, adequate sewage disposal, and less crowded housing conditions. Bacterial discoveries led to greater emphasis on preventive measures, such as the pasteurization of milk, improved purification of water supplies, immunization against disease, and control of waterborne diseases. The public health movement also resulted in the government's hiring

Anesthesia and Modern Surgery

Modern scientific medicine became established in the nineteenth century. Important to the emergence of modern surgery was the development of anesthetic agents that would block the patient's pain and enable surgeons to complete their surgery without the haste that had characterized earlier operations. This document is an eyewitness account of the first successful use of ether anesthesia, which took place at the Massachusetts General Hospital in 1846.

The First Public Demonstration of Ether Anesthesia, October 16, 1846

The day arrived; the time appointed was noted on the dial, when the patient was led into the operating-room, and Dr. Warren and a board of the most eminent surgeons in the State were gathered around the sufferer. "All is ready—the stillness oppressive." It had been announced "that a test of some preparation was to be made for which the astonishing claim had been made that it would render the person operated upon free from pain." These are the words of Dr. Warren that broke the stillness.

Those present were incredulous, and, as Dr. Morton had not arrived at the time appointed and fifteen minutes had passed, Dr. Warren said, with significant meaning, "I presume he is otherwise engaged." This was followed with a "derisive laugh," and Dr. Warren grasped his knife and was about to proceed with the operation. At that moment Dr. Morton entered a side door, when Dr. Warren turned to him and in a strong voice said, "Well, sir, your patient is ready." In a few minutes he was ready for the surgeon's knife, when Dr. Morton said, "Your patient is ready, sir."

Here the most sublime scene ever witnessed in the operating-room was presented, when the patient placed himself voluntarily upon the table, which was to become the altar of future fame. Not that he did so for the purpose of advancing the science of medicine, nor for the good of his fellow-men, for the act itself was purely a personal and selfish one. He was about to assist in solving a new and important problem of therapeutics, whose benefits were to be given to the whole civilized world, yet wholly unconscious of the sublimity of the occasion or the art he was taking.

That was a supreme moment for a most wonderful discovery, and, had the patient died upon the operation, science would have waited long to discover the hypnotic effects of some other remedy of equal potency and safety, and it may be properly questioned whether chloroform would have come into use as it has at the present time.

The heroic bravery of the man who voluntarily placed himself upon the table, a subject for the surgeon's knife, should be recorded and his name enrolled upon parchment, which should be hung upon the walls of the surgical amphitheater in which the operation was performed. His name was Gilbert Abbott.

The operation was for a congenital tumor on the left side of the neck, extending along the jaw to the maxillary gland and into the mouth, embracing a margin of the tongue. The operation was successful; and when the patient recovered he declared he had suffered no pain. Dr. Warren turned to those present and said, "Gentlemen, this is no humbug."

medical doctors not just to treat people but to deal with issues of public health as well.

The new scientific developments also had an important impact on the training of doctors for professional careers in health care. Although there were a few medical schools at the beginning of the nineteenth century, most medical instruction was still done by a system of apprenticeship. In the course of the nineteenth century, virtually every Western country founded new medical schools, but attempts to impose uniform standards on them through certifying bodies met considerable resistance. Entrance requirements were virtually nonexistent, and degrees were granted after several months of lectures. Professional organizations founded around the mid-century, such as the British Medical Association in 1832, the American Medical Association in 1847, and the German Doctors' Society in 1872, attempted to elevate professional standards but achieved little until the end of the century. The establishment of the Johns Hopkins University School of Medicine in 1893, with its four-year graded curriculum, clinical training for advanced students, and use of laboratories for teaching purposes, provided a new model for medical training that finally became standard practice in the twentieth century.

During most of the nineteenth century, medical schools in Europe and the United States were closed to female students. When Harriet Hunt applied to Harvard Medical School, the male students drew up resolutions that prevented her admission:

> Resolved, that no woman of true delicacy would be willing in the presence of men to listen to the discussion of subjects that necessarily come under consideration of the students of medicine.
>
> Resolved, that we object to having the company of any female forced upon us, who is disposed to unsex herself, and to sacrifice her modesty by appearing with men in the lecture room.[11]

Elizabeth Blackwell (1821–1910) achieved the first major breakthrough for women in medicine. Although she had been admitted to the Geneva College of Medicine in New York by mistake, Blackwell's perseverance and intelligence won her the respect of her fellow male students. She received her M.D. degree in 1849 and eventually established a clinic in New York City.

European women experienced difficulties similar to Blackwell's. In Britain, Elizabeth Garret and Sophia Jex-Blake had to struggle for years before they were finally admitted to the practice of medicine. The unwillingness of medical schools to open their doors to women led to the formation of separate medical schools for women. The Female Medical College of Pennsylvania, established in 1850, was the first in the United States, and the London School of Medicine for women was founded in 1874. But even after graduation from such institutions, women faced obstacles when they tried to practice as doctors. Many were denied licenses, and hospitals often closed their doors to them. In Britain, Parliament finally capitulated to pressure and passed a bill in 1876 allowing women the right to take qualifying examinations. Soon women were entering medical schools in ever-larger numbers. By the 1890s, universities in Great Britain, Sweden, Denmark, Norway, Finland, Russia, and Belgium were admitting women to medical training and practice. Germany and Austria did not do so until after 1900. Even then, medical associations refused to accept women as equals in the medical profession. Women were not given full membership in the American Medical Association until 1915.

Science and the Study of Society

The importance of science in the nineteenth century perhaps made it inevitable that a scientific approach would be applied to the realm of human activity. The attempt to apply the methods of science systematically to the study of society was perhaps most evident in the work of the Frenchman Auguste Comte (1798–1857). His major work, titled *System of Positive Philosophy,* was published between 1837 and 1842 but had its real impact after 1850.

Comte created a system of "positive knowledge" based on a hierarchy of all the sciences. Mathematics was the foundation on which the physical sciences, earth sciences, and biological sciences were built. At the top was sociology, the science of human society, which for Comte incorporated economics, anthropology, history, and social psychology. Comte saw sociology's task as a difficult one. The discovery of the general laws of society would have to be based on the collection and analysis of data on humans and their social environment. Although his schemes were often complex and dense, Comte played an important role in the growing popularity of science and materialism in the mid-nineteenth century.

Realism in Literature and Art

The belief that the world should be viewed realistically, frequently expressed after 1850, was closely related to the materialistic outlook. The term *Realism* was first employed in 1850 to describe a new style of painting and soon spread to literature.

THE REALISTIC NOVEL

The literary Realists of the mid-nineteenth century were distinguished by their deliberate rejection of Romanticism. The literary Realists wanted to deal with ordinary characters from real life rather than Romantic heroes in unusual settings. They also sought to avoid flowery and sentimental language by using careful observation and accurate description, an approach that led them to eschew poetry in favor of prose and the novel. Realists often combined their interest in everyday life with a searching examination of social questions.

The leading novelist of the 1850s and 1860s, the Frenchman Gustave Flaubert (1821–1880), perfected the Realist novel. His *Madame Bovary* (1857) was a straightforward description of barren and sordid small-town life in France. Emma Bovary, a woman of some vitality, is trapped in a marriage to a drab provincial doctor. Impelled by the images of romantic love she has read about in novels, she seeks the same thing for herself in adulterous affairs. Unfulfilled, she is ultimately driven to suicide, unrepentant to the end for her lifestyle. Flaubert's contempt for bourgeois society was evident in his portrayal of middle-class hypocrisy and smugness.

William Thackeray (1811–1863) wrote Britain's prototypical Realist novel, *Vanity Fair: A Novel Without a Hero,* in 1848. Thackeray deliberately flouted the Romantic conventions. A novel, Thackeray said, should "convey as strongly as possible the sentiment of reality as opposed to a tragedy or poem, which may be heroical." Perhaps the greatest of the Victorian novelists was Charles Dickens (1812–1870), whose realistic novels focusing on the lower and middle classes in Britain's early industrial age became extraordinarily successful. His descriptions of the urban poor and the brutalization of human life were vividly realistic (see the box on p. 639).

REALISM IN ART

In the first half of the nineteenth century, Romanticism in art had been paralleled by the classical school of painting, but both were superseded by the new mood of the mid-nineteenth century. In art, too, Realism became dominant after 1850, although Romanticism was by no means dead. Among the most important characteristics of Realism are a desire to depict the everyday life of ordinary people, whether peasants, workers, or prostitutes; an attempt at photographic realism; and an interest in the natural environment. The French became leaders in Realist painting.

Gustave Courbet (1819–1877) was the most famous artist of the Realist school. In fact, the word *Realism* was first coined in 1850 to describe one of his paintings. Courbet reveled in a realistic portrayal of everyday life. His subjects were factory workers, peasants, and the wives of saloon keepers. "I have never seen either angels or goddesses, so I am not interested in painting them," he exclaimed. One of his famous works, *The Stonebreakers,* painted in 1849, shows two road workers engaged in the

Gemaldegalerie Neue Meister, Staatliche Kunstsammlungen Dresden, Photo by Reinhold, Leipzig-Molkau

Gustave Courbet, *The Stonebreakers.* Realism, largely developed by French painters, aimed at a lifelike portrayal of the daily activities of ordinary people. Gustave Courbet was the most famous of the Realist artists. As is evident in *The Stonebreakers,* he sought to portray things as they really appear. He shows an old road builder and his young assistant in their tattered clothes, engrossed in their dreary work of breaking stones to construct a road.

Jean-François Millet, *The Gleaners.* Jean-François Millet, another prominent French Realist painter, took a special interest in the daily activities of French peasants, although he tended to transform his peasants into heroic figures who dominated their environment. In *The Gleaners,* for example, the three peasant women who are engaged in the backbreaking work of gathering grain left after the harvest still appear as powerful figures, symbolizing the union of humans with the earth.

Erich Lessing/Art Resource, NY

Realism: Charles Dickens and an Image of Hell on Earth

Charles Dickens was one of Britain's greatest novelists. Though he realistically portrayed the material, social, and psychological milieu of his time, an element of Romanticism still pervaded his novels. This is evident in this selection from *The Old Curiosity Shop* in which his description of the English mill town of Birmingham takes on the imagery of Dante's Hell.

Charles Dickens, The Old Curiosity Shop

A long suburb of red brick houses,—some with patches of garden ground, where coal-dust and factory smoke darkened the shrinking leaves, and coarse rank flowers; and where the struggling vegetation sickened and sank under the hot breath of kiln and furnace, making them by its presence seem yet more blighting and unwholesome than in the town itself,—a long, flat, straggling suburb passed, they came by slow degrees upon a cheerless region, where not a blade of grass was seen to grow; where not a bud put forth its promise in the spring; where nothing green could live but on the surface of the stagnant pools, which here and there lay idly sweltering by the black roadside.

Advancing more and more into the shadow of this mournful place, its dark depressing influence stole upon their spirits, and filled them with a dismal gloom. On every side, and as far as the eye could see into the heavy distance, tall chimneys, crowding on each other, and presenting that endless repetition of the same dull, ugly form, which is the horror of oppressive dreams, poured out their plague of smoke, obscured the light, and made foul the melancholy air. On mounds of ashes by the wayside, sheltered only by a few rough boards, or rotten pent-house roofs, strange engines spun and writhed like tortured creatures; clanking their iron chains, shrieking in their rapid whirl from time to time as though in torment unendurable, and making the ground tremble with their agonies. Dismantled houses here and there appeared, tottering to the earth, propped up by fragments of others that had fallen down, unroofed, windowless, blackened, desolate, but yet inhabited. Men, women, children, wan in their looks and ragged in attire, tended the engines, fed their tributary fires, begged upon the road, or scowled half-naked from the doorless houses. Then came more of the wrathful monsters, whose like they almost seemed to be in their wildness and their untamed air, screeching and turning to the right and left, with the same interminable perspective of brick towers, never ceasing in their black vomit, blasting all things living or inanimate, shutting out the face of day, and closing in on all these horrors with a dense dark cloud.

But night-time in this dreadful spot!—night, when the smoke was changed to fire; when every chimney spurted up its flame; and places, that had been dark vaults all day, now shone red-hot, with figures moving to and fro within their blazing jaws, and calling to one another with hoarse cries—night, when the noise of every strange machine was aggravated by the darkness; when the people near them looked wilder and more savage; when bands of unemployed laborers paraded in the roads, or clustered by torchlight round their leaders, who told them in stern language of their wrongs, and urged them on by frightful cries and threats; when maddened men, armed with sword and firebrand, spurning the tears and prayers of women who would restrain them, rushed forth on errands of terror and destruction, to work no ruin half so surely as their own—night, when carts came rumbling by, filled with rude coffins (for contagious disease and death had been busy with the living crops); or when orphans cried, and distracted women shrieked and followed in their wake—night, when some called for bread, and some for drink to drown their cares; and some with tears, and some with staggering feet, and so with bloodshot eyes, went brooding home—night, which, unlike the night that Heaven sends on earth, brought with it no peace, nor quiet, nor signs of blessed sleep—who shall tell the terrors of the night to that young wandering child!

deadening work of breaking stones to build a road. This representation of human misery was a scandal to those who objected to his "cult of ugliness." To Courbet, no subject was too ordinary, too harsh, or too ugly to interest him.

Jean-François Millet (1814–1875) was preoccupied with scenes from rural life, especially peasants laboring in the fields, although his Realism still contained an element of Romantic sentimentality. In *The Gleaners,* his most famous work, three peasant women gather grain in a field, a centuries-old practice that for Millet showed the symbiotic relationship between humans and nature. Millet made landscape and country life an important subject matter for French artists, but he, too, was criticized by his contemporaries for crude subject matter and unorthodox technique.

Music: The Twilight of Romanticism

The mid-nineteenth century witnessed the development of a new group of musicians known as the New German School. It emphasized emotional content rather than abstract form and championed new methods of using music to express literary or pictorial ideas.

Hungarian-born composer Franz Liszt (1811–1886) best exemplifies the achievements of the New German School. A child prodigy, he established himself as an outstanding concert artist by the age of twelve. Liszt's performances and his dazzling personality made him the most highly esteemed virtuoso of his age. He has been called the greatest pianist of all time and has been credited with introducing the concept of the modern piano recital.

Liszt's compositions consist mainly of piano pieces, although he composed in other genres as well, including sacred music. He invented the term *symphonic poem* to refer to his orchestral works, which did not strictly obey traditional forms and were generally based on a literary or pictorial idea. Under the guidance of Liszt and the New German School, Romantic music reached its peak.

Although Liszt was an influential mentor to a number of young composers, he was most closely associated with his eventual son-in-law Richard Wagner (1813–1883). Building on the advances made by Liszt and the New German School, Wagner ultimately realized the German desire for a truly national opera. Wagner was not only a composer but also a propagandist and writer in support of his unique conception of dramatic music. Called both the culmination of the Romantic era and the beginning of the avant-garde, Wagner's music may be described as a monumental development in classical music.

Believing that opera is the best form of artistic expression, Wagner transformed opera into "music drama" through his *Gesamtkunstwerk* ("total art work"), a musical composition for the theater in which music, acting, dance, poetry, and scenic design are synthesized into a harmonious whole. He abandoned the traditional divisions of opera, which interrupted the dramatic line of the work, and instead used a device called a leitmotiv, a recurring musical theme in which the human voice combined with the line of the orchestra instead of rising above it. His operas incorporate literally hundreds of leitmotivs in order to convey the story. For his themes, Wagner looked to myth and epic tales from the past. His most ambitious work was *The Ring of the Nibelung,* a series of four music dramas dealing with the mythical gods of the ancient German epic.

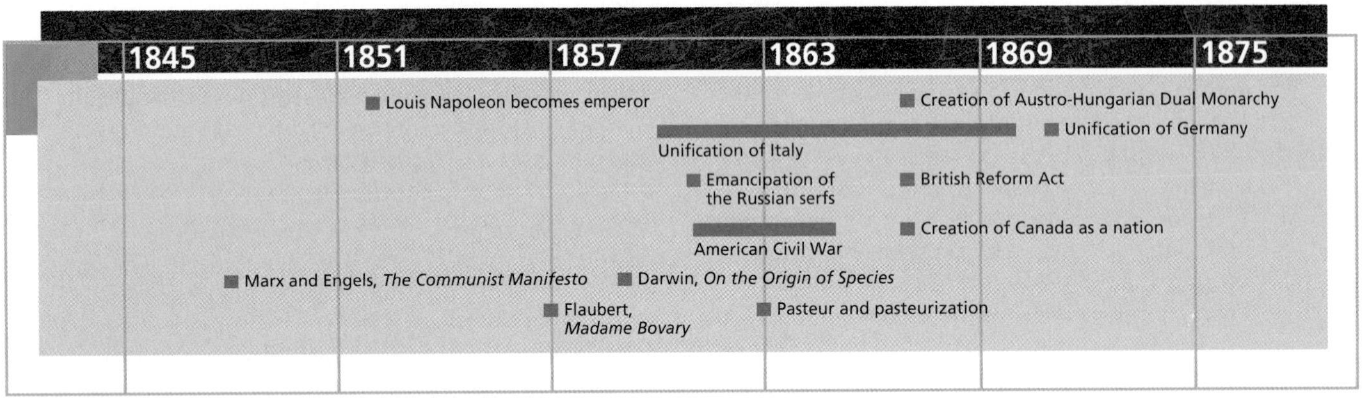

Conclusion

Between 1850 and 1871, the national state became the focus of people's loyalty. Wars, both foreign and civil, were fought to create unified nation-states. Political nationalism had emerged during the French revolutionary era and had become a powerful force of change during the first half of the nineteenth century, but its triumph came only after 1850. Associated initially with middle-class liberals, by the end of the nineteenth century, it would have great appeal to the broad masses as well. In 1871, however, the political transformations stimulated by the force of nationalism were by no means complete. Significantly large minorities, especially in the polyglot empires controlled by the Austrians, Turks, and Russians, had not achieved the goal of their own national states. Moreover, the nationalism that had triumphed by 1871 was no longer the nationalism that had been closely identified with liberalism. Liberal nationalists had believed that unified nation-states would preserve individual rights and lead to a greater community of European peoples. Rather than unifying people, however, the new, loud, and chauvinistic nationalism of the late nineteenth century divided them as the new national states became embroiled in bitter competition after 1871.

Europeans, however, were hardly aware of nationalism's dangers in 1871. The spread of industrialization and the wealth of scientific and technological achievements were sources of optimism. After the revolutionary and military upheavals of the mid-century decades, many Europeans undoubtedly believed that they stood on the verge of a new age of progress.

Notes

1. Quoted in James F. McMillan, *Napoleon III* (New York, 1991), p. 37.
2. Quoted in Robert Gildea, *Barricades and Borders: Europe, 1800–1914,* 2d ed. (Oxford, 1996), p. 170.
3. Quoted in Otto Pflanze, *Bismarck and the Development of Germany: The Period of Unification, 1815–1871* (Princeton, N.J., 1963), p. 60.

4. Louis L. Snyder, ed., *Documents of German History* (New Brunswick, N.J., 1958), p. 202.
5. Quoted in Pflanze, *Bismarck and the Development of Germany*, p. 327.
6. Quoted in György Szabad, *Hungarian Political Trends Between the Revolution and the Compromise, 1849–1867* (Budapest, 1977), p. 163.
7. Quoted in Rondo Cameron, "Crédit Mobilier and the Economic Development of Europe," *Journal of Political Economy* 61 (1953): 470.
8. Karl Marx and Friedrich Engels, *The Communist Manifesto* (Harmondsworth, England, 1967), p. 79.
9. Ibid., pp. 79, 81, 82.
10. Charles Darwin, *On the Origin of Species* (New York, 1872), vol. 1, pp. 77, 79.
11. Quoted in Albert Lyons and R. Joseph Petrucelli, *Medicine: An Illustrated History* (New York, 1978), p. 569.

Suggestions for Further Reading

Three general surveys of the mid-century decades are N. Rich, *The Age of Nationalism and Reform, 1850–1890,* 2d ed. (New York, 1979); E. Hobsbawm, *The Age of Capital, 1845–1875* (London, 1975); and J. A. S. Grenville, *Europe Reshaped, 1848–1878* (London, 1976). In addition to the books listed for individual countries in Chapter 21 that also cover the material of this chapter, see G. Craig, *Germany, 1866–1945* (Oxford, 1981); the two detailed volumes of T. Zeldin, *France, 1848–1945* (Oxford, 1973–1977); A. J. May, *The Habsburg Monarchy, 1867–1914* (Cambridge, Mass., 1951); and D. Read, *England, 1868–1914* (London, 1979).

For a good introduction to the French Second Empire, see A. Plessis, *The Rise and Fall of the Second Empire, 1852–1871,* trans. J. Mandelbaum (New York, 1985). Napoleon's role can be examined in J. F. McMillan, *Napoleon III* (New York, 1991). The Crimean War and its impact are examined in P. W. Schroeder, *Austria, Great Britain, and the Crimean War: The Destruction of the European Concert* (Ithaca, N.Y., 1972), and N. Rich, *Why the Crimean War?* (Hanover, N.H., 1985).

The unification of Italy can be examined in F. Coppa, *The Origins of the Italian Wars of Independence* (New York, 1992); the works of D. M. Smith, *Victor Emmanuel, Cavour and the Risorgimento* (London, 1971) and *Cavour* (London, 1985); and H. Hearder, *Cavour* (New York, 1994). The unification of Germany can be pursued first in W. Carr, *The Origins of the Wars of German Unification* (New York, 1991); and two good biographies of Bismarck, E. Crankshaw, *Bismarck* (New York, 1981), and G. O. Kent, *Bismarck and His Times* (Carbondale, Ill., 1978). See also the brief study by B. Waller, *Bismarck,* 2d ed. (Oxford, 1997). Also valuable is O. Pflanze, *Bismarck and the Development of Germany: The Period of Unification, 1815–1871* (Princeton, N.J., 1963). On the position of liberals in the unification of Germany, see J. J. Sheehan, *German Liberalism in the Nineteenth Century* (Chicago, 1978).

On the emancipation of the Russian serfs, see D. Field, *The End of Serfdom: Nobility and Bureaucracy in Russia, 1855–1861* (Cambridge, 1976). On Disraeli, see I. Machlin, *Disraeli* (London, 1995). On the background to the American Civil War, see D. Potter, *The Impending Crisis, 1845–1861* (New York, 1976), and M. Holt, *The Political Crisis of the 1850's* (New York, 1978). A good one-volume survey of the Civil War can be found in P. J. Parish, *The American Civil War* (New York, 1975).

In addition to the general works on economic development listed in Chapters 20 and 21, some specialized works on this period are worthwhile. These include W. O. Henderson, *The Rise of German Industrial Power, 1834–1914* (Berkeley, Calif., 1975), and F. Crouzet, *The Victorian Economy* (London, 1982). On Marx, the standard work is D. McLellan, *Karl Marx: His Life and Thought* (New York, 1975), but it can be supplemented by the interesting and comprehensive work by L. Kolakowski, *Main Currents of Marxism,* 3 vols. (Oxford, 1978).

For an introduction to the intellectual changes of the nineteenth century, see O. Chadwick, *The Secularization of the European Mind in the Nineteenth Century* (Cambridge, 1975). A detailed biography of Darwin can be found in J. Bowlby, *Charles Darwin: A Biography* (London, 1990). For an introduction to the transformation of medical practices in the nineteenth century, see the appropriate chapters in L. N. Magner, *A History of Medicine* (New York, 1992), and A. S. Lyons and R. J. Petrucelli, *Medicine: An Illustrated History* (New York, 1978). On Realism, J. Malpas, *Realism* (Cambridge, 1997), is a good introduction.

For additional reading, go to InfoTrac College Edition, your online research library at http://web1.infotrac-college.com

Enter the search term *Crimean War* using Key Terms.

Enter the search term *Victorian* using Key Terms.

Enter the search term *Karl Marx* using Key Terms.

Enter the search term *Charles Darwin* using Key Terms.

CHAPTER

23

The Mass Society in an "Age of Progress," 1871–1894

Verein fur Geschichte der Arbeiterbewegung, Vienna

CHAPTER OUTLINE

- The Growth of Industrial Prosperity
- The Emergence of a Mass Society
- The National State
- Conclusion

FOCUS QUESTIONS

- What was the Second Industrial Revolution, and what effects did it have on European economic and social life?
- What roles did socialist parties and trade unions play in improving conditions for the working classes?
- What is a *mass society,* and what were its main characteristics?
- What role were women expected to play in society and family life in the latter half of the nineteenth century, and how closely did patterns of family life correspond to this ideal?
- What general political trends were evident in the nations of western Europe in the last decades of the nineteenth century, and how did these trends differ from the policies pursued in Germany, Austria-Hungary, and Russia?
- What was the relationship between economic, social, and political developments between 1871 and 1894?

IN THE LATE 1800S, Europe entered a dynamic period of material prosperity. Bringing with it new industries, new sources of energy, and new goods, a second Industrial Revolution transformed the human environment, dazzled Europeans, and led them to believe that their material progress meant human progress. Scientific and technological achievements, many naively believed, would improve humanity's condition and solve all human problems. The doctrine of progress became an article of great faith.

The new urban and industrial world created by the rapid economic changes of the nineteenth century led to the emergence of a mass society by the late nineteenth century. Mass society meant improvements for the lower classes, who benefited from the extension of voting rights, a better standard of living, and education. It also brought mass leisure. New work patterns established the "weekend" as a distinct time of recreation and fun, and new forms of mass transportation—railroads and streetcars—enabled even ordinary workers to make excursions to amusement parks. Coney Island was only 8 miles from central New York City; Blackpool in England was a short train ride from nearby industrial towns. With their Ferris wheels and other daring rides that threw young men and women together, amusement parks offered a whole new world of entertainment. Thanks to the railroad, seaside resorts, once the preserve of the wealthy, also became accessible to more people for weekend visits, much to the disgust of one upper-class regular, who complained about the new "day-trippers": "They swarm upon the beach, wandering listlessly about with apparently no other aim than to get a mouthful of fresh air." Enterprising entrepreneurs in resorts like Blackpool welcomed the masses of new visitors, however, and built piers laden with food, drink, and entertainment to serve them.

The coming of mass society also created new roles for the governments of Europe's nation-states, which now fostered national loyalty, created national armies by conscription, and took more responsibility for public health and housing measures in their cities. By 1871, the national state had become the focus of Europeans' lives. Within many of these nation-states, the growth of the middle class had led to the triumph of liberal practices: constitutional governments, parliaments, and principles of equality. The period after 1871 also witnessed the growth of political democracy as the right to vote was extended to all adult males; women, though, would still have to fight for the same political rights. With political democracy came a new mass politics and a new mass press. Both would become regular features of the twentieth century.

The Growth of Industrial Prosperity

At the heart of Europeans' belief in progress after 1871 was the stunning material growth produced by what historians have called the Second Industrial Revolution. The First Industrial Revolution had given rise to textiles, railroads, iron, and coal. In the second revolution, steel, chemicals, electricity, and petroleum led the way to new industrial frontiers.

New Products

The first major change in industrial development after 1870 was the substitution of steel for iron. New methods of rolling and shaping steel made it useful in the construction of lighter, smaller, and faster machines and engines, as well as railways, ships, and armaments. In 1860, Great Britain, France, Germany, and Belgium together produced 125,000 tons of steel; by 1913, the total was 32 million tons. Whereas in the early 1870s, Britain had produced twice as much steel as Germany, by 1910, German production was double that of Great Britain. Both had been surpassed by the United States in 1890.

Great Britain also fell behind in the new chemical industry. A change in the method of making soda enabled France and Germany to take the lead in producing the alkalies used in the textile, soap, and paper industries. German laboratories soon overtook the British in the development of new organic chemical compounds, such as artificial dyes. By 1900, German firms had cornered 90 percent of the market for dyestuffs and also led in the development of photographic plates and film.

Electricity was a major new form of energy that proved to be of great value since it could be easily converted into other forms of energy, such as heat, light, and motion, and moved relatively effortlessly through space over wires. In the 1870s, the first commercially practical generators of electrical current were developed. By 1881, Britain had its first public power station. By 1910, hydroelectric power stations and coal-fired steam-generating plants enabled entire districts to be tied in to a single power distribution system that provided a common source of power for homes, shops, and industrial enterprises.

Electricity spawned a whole series of inventions. The invention of the lightbulb by the American Thomas Edison (1847–1931) and the Briton Joseph Swan opened homes and cities to illumination by electric lights. A revolution in communications was fostered when Alexander Graham Bell (1847–1922) invented the telephone in 1876 and Guglielmo Marconi (1874–1937) sent the first radio waves across the Atlantic in 1901. Although most electricity was initially used for lighting, it was eventually put to use in transportation. The first electric railway was installed in Berlin in 1879. By the 1880s, streetcars and subways had appeared in major European cities and had begun to replace horse-drawn buses. Electricity also transformed the factory. Conveyor belts, cranes, machines, and machine tools could all be powered by electricity and located anywhere. In the First Industrial Revolution, coal had been the major source of energy. Countries without adequate coal supplies lagged behind in industrialization. Thanks to electricity, they could now enter the industrial age.

The development of the internal combustion engine had a similar effect. The first internal combustion engine, fired by gas and air, was produced in 1878. It proved unsuitable for widespread use as a source of power in transportation until the development of liquid fuels—petroleum and its distilled derivatives. An oil-fired engine was made in 1897, and by 1902, the Hamburg-Amerika Line had switched from coal to oil on its new ocean liners. By the end of the nineteenth century, some naval fleets had been converted to oil burners as well.

The development of the internal combustion engine gave rise to the automobile and the airplane. Gottlieb

The Fotomas Index

An Age of Progress. In the decades after 1871, the Second Industrial Revolution led many Europeans to believe that they were living in an age of progress when most human problems would be solved by scientific achievements. This illustration is taken from a special issue of the *Illustrated London News* celebrating the Diamond Jubilee of Queen Victoria in 1897. On the left are scenes from 1837, when Victoria came to the British throne; on the right are scenes from 1897. The vivid contrast underscored the magazine's conclusion: "The most striking… evidence of progress during the reign is the ever increasing speed which the discoveries of physical science have forced into everyday life. Steam and electricity have conquered time and space to a greater extent during the last sixty years than all the preceding six hundred years witnessed."

Daimler's invention of a light engine in 1886 was the key to the development of the automobile. In 1900, world production stood at nine thousand cars; by 1906, Americans had overtaken the initial lead of the French. It was an American, Henry Ford (1863–1947), who revolutionized the car industry with the mass production of the Model T. By 1916, Ford's factories were producing 735,000 cars a year. Air transportation began with the Zeppelin airship in 1900. In 1903, at Kitty Hawk, North Carolina, the Wright brothers made the first flight in a fixed-wing plane powered by a gasoline engine. It took World War I to stimulate the aircraft industry, however, and the first regular passenger air service was not established until 1919.

New Markets

The growth of industrial production depended on the development of markets for the sale of manufactured goods. After 1870, the best foreign markets were already heavily saturated, forcing Europeans to take a renewed look at their domestic markets. As Europeans were the richest consumers in the world, those markets offered abundant possibilities. The dramatic population increases after 1870 (see "Population Growth and Emigration" later in this chapter) were accompanied by a steady rise in national incomes. The leading industrialized nations, Britain and Germany, doubled or tripled their national incomes. Between 1850 and 1900, real wages increased by two-thirds in Britain and by one-third in Germany. As the prices of both food and manufactured goods declined due to lower transportation costs, Europeans could spend more on consumer products. Businesses soon perceived the value of using new techniques of mass marketing to sell the consumer goods made possible by the development of the steel and electrical industries. By bringing together a vast array of new products in one place, they created the department store (see the box on p. 645). The desire to own sewing machines, clocks, bicycles, electric lights, and typewriters rapidly created a new consumer ethic that became a crucial part of the modern economy.

Meanwhile, increased competition for foreign markets and the growing importance of domestic demand led to a

The Department Store and the Beginnings of Mass Consumerism

Domestic markets were especially important for the sale of the goods being turned out by Europe's increasing number of industrial plants. New techniques of mass marketing were developed to encourage people to purchase the new consumer goods. The Parisians pioneered the department store, and this selection is taken from a contemporary's account of the growth of these stores in the French capital city.

E. Lavasseur, On Parisian Department Stores

It was in the reign of Louis-Philippe that department stores for fashion goods and dresses, extending to material and other clothing began to be distinguished. The type was already one of the notable developments of the Second Empire; it became one of the most important ones of the Third Republic. These stores have increased in number and several of them have become extremely large. Combining in their different departments all articles of clothing, toilet articles, furniture and many other ranges of goods, it is their special object so to combine all commodities as to attract and satisfy customers who will find conveniently together an assortment of a mass of articles corresponding to all their various needs. They attract customers by permanent display, by free entry into the shops, by periodic exhibitions, by special sales, by fixed prices, and by their ability to deliver the goods purchased to customers' homes, in Paris and to the provinces. Turning themselves into direct intermediaries between the producer and the consumer, even producing sometimes some of their articles in their own workshops, buying at lowest prices because of their large orders and because they are in a position to profit from bargains, working with large sums, and selling to most of their customers for cash only, they can transmit these benefits in lowered selling prices. They can even decide to sell at a loss, as an advertisement or to get rid of out-of-date fashions. Taking 5–6 percent on 100 million brings them in more than 20 percent would bring to a firm doing a turnover of 50,000 francs.

The success of these department stores is only possible thanks to the volume of their business and this volume needs considerable capital and a very large turnover. Now capital, having become abundant, is freely combined nowadays in large enterprises, although French capital has the reputation of being more wary of the risks of industry than of State or railway securities. On the other hand, the large urban agglomerations, the ease with which goods can be transported by the railways, the diffusion of some comforts to strata below the middle classes, have all favored these developments.

As example we may cite some figures relating to these stores, since they were brought to the notice of the public in the *Revue des Deux-Mondes*. . . .

Le Louvre, dating to the time of the extension of the rue de Rivoli under the Second Empire, did in 1893 a business of 120 million at a profit of 6.4 percent. *Le Bon-Marché,* which was a small shop when Mr. Boucicaut entered it in 1852, already did a business of 20 million at the end of the Empire. During the republic its new buildings were erected; Mme. Boucicaut turned it by her will into a kind of cooperative society, with shares and an ingenious organization; turnover reached 150 million in 1893, leaving a profit of 5 percent. . . .

According to the tax records of 1891, these stores in Paris, numbering 12, employed 1,708 persons and were rated on their site values at 2,159,000 francs; the largest had then 542 employees. These same stores had, in 1901, 9,784 employees; one of them over 2,000 and another over 1,600; their site value has doubled (4,089,000 francs).

reaction against free trade. To many industrial and political leaders, protective tariffs guaranteed domestic markets for the products of their own industries. That is why, after a decade of experimentation with free trade in the 1860s, Europeans returned to tariff protection.

During this same period, cartels were being formed to decrease competition internally. In a cartel, independent enterprises worked together to control prices and fix production quotas, thereby restraining the kind of competition that led to reduced prices. Cartels were especially strong in Germany, where banks moved to protect their investments by eliminating the "anarchy of competition." German businesses established cartels in potash, coal, steel, and chemicals.

The formation of cartels was paralleled by a move toward ever-larger manufacturing plants, especially in the iron and steel, machinery, heavy electrical equipment, and chemical industries. Although evident in Britain, France, and Belgium, the trend was most pronounced in Germany. Between 1882 and 1907, the number of people working in German factories with over one thousand employees rose from 205,000 to 879,000. This growth in the size of industrial plants led to pressure for greater efficiency in factory production at the same time that competition led to demands for greater economy. The result was a desire to streamline or rationalize production as much as possible. One way to accomplish this was by cutting labor costs through the mechanization of transport within plants, such as using electric cranes to move materials. Even more important, the development of precision tools enabled manufacturers to produce interchangeable parts, which in turn led to the creation of the assembly line for production. First used in the United States for small arms and clocks, the assembly line had moved to Europe by 1850. In the second half of the nineteenth century, it was used primarily in manufacturing nonmilitary goods, such as sewing machines, typewriters, bicycles, and finally the automobile. Principles of scientific management were also introduced by 1900 to maximize workers' efficiency.

The emergence of protective tariffs and cartels was clearly a response to the growth of the multinational industrial system. Economic competition intensified the political rivalries of the age. The growth of the national state, which had seemed to be the answer to old problems in the mid-nineteenth century, now seemed to be creating new ones.

New Patterns in an Industrial Economy

The Second Industrial Revolution played a role in the emergence of basic economic patterns that have characterized much of modern European economic life. Although we have described the period after 1871 as an age of material prosperity, recessions and crises were still very much a part of economic life. Although some historians question the appropriateness of characterizing the period from 1873 to 1895 as a great depression, Europeans did experience a series of economic crises during those years. Prices, especially those of agricultural products, fell dramatically. Slumps in the business cycle reduced profits, although recession occurred at different times in different countries. France and Britain, for example, sank into depression in the 1880s while Germany and the United States were recovering from their depression of the 1870s. However, from 1895 until World War I, Europe overall experienced an economic boom and achieved a level of prosperity that encouraged people later to look back to that era as *la belle époque*—a golden age in European civilization.

GERMAN INDUSTRIAL LEADERSHIP

After 1870, Germany replaced Great Britain as the industrial leader of Europe. Within two decades, Germany's superiority was evident in new areas of manufacturing, such as organic chemicals and electrical equipment, and increasingly apparent in its ever-greater share of worldwide trade. Why had industrial leadership passed from Britain to Germany?

Britain's early lead in industrialization gave it an established industrial plant and made it more difficult to shift to the new techniques of the Second Industrial Revolution. As later entrants to the industrial age, the Germans could build the latest and most efficient industrial plants. British entrepreneurs made the situation worse by their tendency to be suspicious of innovations and their reluctance to invest in new plants and industries. As one manufacturer remarked, "One wants to be thoroughly convinced of the superiority of a new method before condemning as useless a large plant that has hitherto done good service."[1] German managers, by contrast, were accustomed to change, and the formation of large cartels encouraged German banks to provide enormous sums for investment. Then, too, unlike the Germans, the British were not willing to encourage formal scientific and technical education.

After 1870, the relationship of science and technology grew closer. Newer fields of industrial activity, such as organic chemistry and electrical engineering, required more scientific knowledge than the commonsense tinkering once employed by amateur inventors. Companies began to invest capital in laboratory equipment for their own research or hired scientific consultants for advice. Nowhere was the relationship between science and technology more apparent than in Germany. In 1899, German technical schools were allowed to award doctorate degrees, and by 1900, they were turning out three to four thousand graduates a year. Many of these graduates made their way into industrial firms.

EUROPEAN ECONOMIC ZONES

The struggle for economic (and political) supremacy between Great Britain and Germany should not cause us to overlook the other great polarization of the age. By 1900, Europe was divided into two economic zones. Great Britain, Belgium, France, the Netherlands, Germany, the western part of the Austro-Hungarian Empire, and northern Italy constituted an advanced industrialized core that had a high standard of living, decent systems of transportation, and relatively healthy and educated peoples (see Map 23.1). Another part of Europe, the backward and little industrialized area to the south and east, consisting of southern Italy, most of Austria-Hungary, Spain, Portugal, the Balkan kingdoms, and Russia, was still largely agricultural and relegated by the industrial countries to the function of providing food and raw materials. The presence of Romanian oil, Greek olive oil, and Serbian pigs and prunes in western Europe served as reminders of an economic division of Europe that continued well into the twentieth century.

The growth of an industrial economy also led to new patterns for European agriculture. An abundance of grain and lower transportation costs caused the prices of farm commodities to plummet. Some countries responded with tariff barriers against lower-priced foodstuffs. Where agricultural labor was scarce and hence expensive, as in Britain and Germany, landowners introduced machines for threshing and harvesting. The slump in grain prices also led some countries to specialize in other food products. Denmark, for example, exported eggs, butter, and cheese; sugar beets predominated in Bohemia and northern France; fruit in Mediterranean countries; and wine in Spain and Italy. This age also witnessed the introduction of chemical fertilizers. Large estates could make these adjustments easily, but individual small farmers could not afford them and formed farm cooperatives that provided capital for making improvements and purchasing equipment and fertilizer.

A WORLD ECONOMY

The economic developments of the late nineteenth century, combined with the transportation revolution that saw the growth of marine transport and railroads, also fostered a true world economy. By 1900, Europeans were importing beef

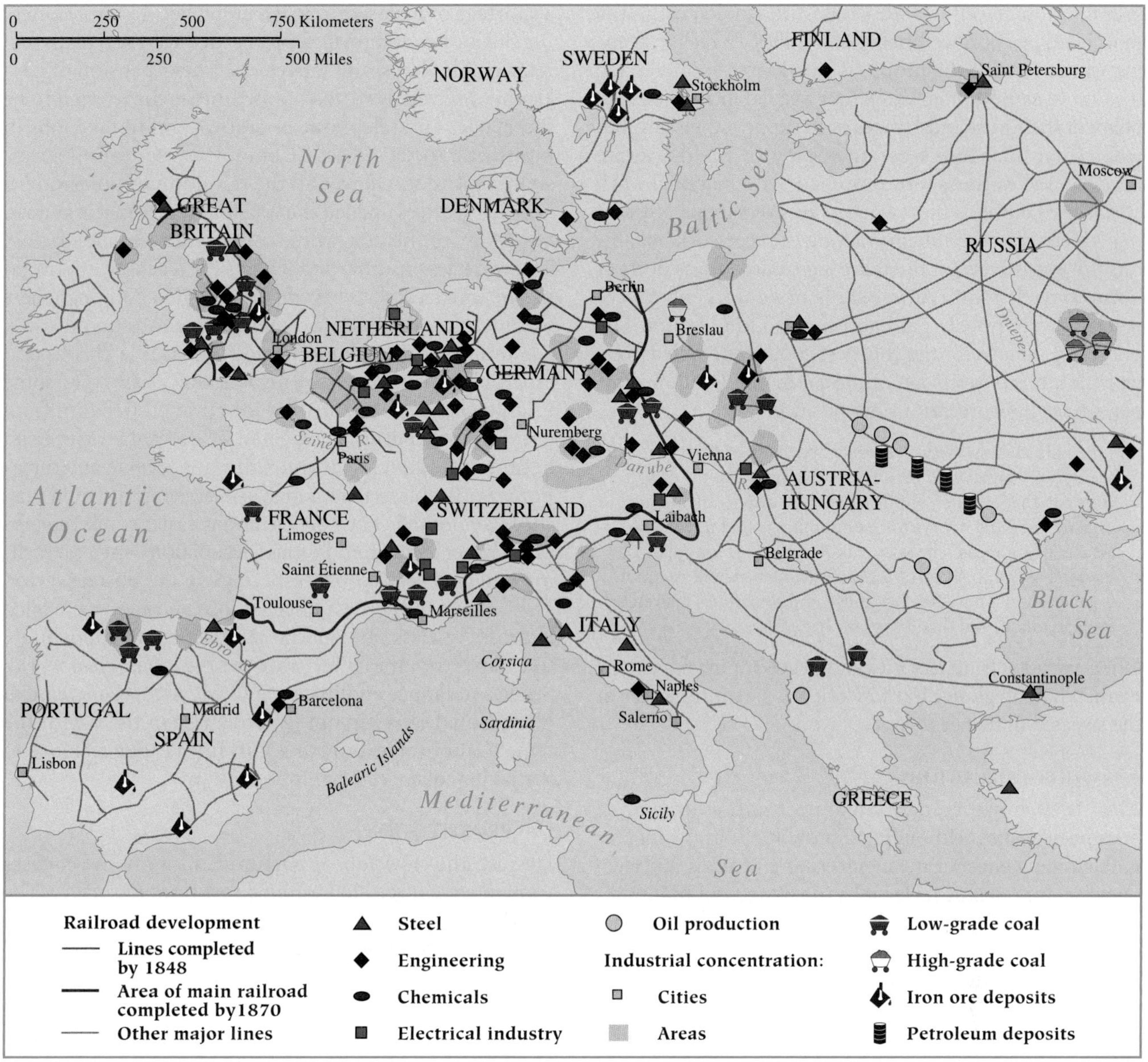

Map 23.1 The Industrial Regions of Europe at the End of the Nineteenth Century. By the end of the nineteenth century, the Second Industrial Revolution—in steelmaking, electricity, petroleum, and chemicals—had spurred substantial economic growth and prosperity in western and central Europe; it also sparked economic and political competition between Great Britain and Germany. ■ Look back at Map 20.2: What parts of Europe not industrialized in 1850 had become industrialized in the ensuing decades?

and wool from Argentina and Australia, coffee from Brazil, nitrates from Chile, iron ore from Algeria, and sugar from Java. European capital was also invested abroad to develop railways, mines, electrical power plants, and banks. High rates of return, such as 11.3 percent on Latin American banking shares that were floated in London, provided plenty of incentive. Of course, foreign countries also provided markets for the surplus manufactured goods of Europe. With its capital, industries, and military might, Europe dominated the world economy by the end of the nineteenth century.

Women and Work: New Job Opportunities

The Second Industrial Revolution had an enormous impact on the position of women in the labor market. During the course of the nineteenth century, considerable controversy erupted over a woman's "right to work." Working-class organizations tended to reinforce the underlying ideology of domesticity: women should remain at home to bear and nurture children and should not be allowed in the industrial workforce. Working-class men argued that keeping women out of industrial work would ensure the moral and physical well-being of families. In reality, keeping women out of the industrial workforce simply made it easier to exploit them when they needed income to supplement their husbands' wages or to support their families when their husbands were unemployed. The desperate need to work at times forced women to do marginal work at home or labor as pieceworkers in sweatshops. "Sweating" referred to the subcontracting of piecework usually, but not exclusively, in the tailoring trades; it was done at home since it required few skills or equipment. Pieceworkers were poorly paid and worked long hours. The poorest-paid jobs for the cheapest goods were called "slop work." In this description of the room of a London slopper, we see how precarious her position was:

> I then directed my steps to the neighborhood of Drury-lane, to see a poor woman who lived in an attic on one of the closest courts in that quarter. On the table was a quarter of an ounce of tea. Observing my eye to rest upon it, she told me it was all she took. "Sugar," she said, "I broke myself of long ago; I couldn't afford it. A cup of tea, a piece of bread, and an onion is generally all I have for my dinner, and sometimes I haven't even an onion, and then I sops my bread."[2]

Often excluded from factories and in need of income, many women had no choice but to work for the pitiful wages of the sweated industries.

WHITE-COLLAR JOBS

After 1870, however, new job opportunities for women became available. Although the growth of heavy industry in the mining, metallurgy, engineering, chemicals, and electrical sectors meant fewer jobs for women in manufacturing, the development of larger industrial plants and the expansion of government services created a large number of service or white-collar jobs. The increased demand for white-collar workers at relatively low wages, coupled with a shortage of male workers, led employers to hire women. Big businesses and retail shops needed clerks, typists, secretaries, file clerks, and salesclerks. The expansion of government services created opportunities for women to be secretaries and telephone operators and to take jobs in health and social services. Compulsory education necessitated more teachers, and the development of modern hospital services opened the way for an increase in nurses.

Many of the new white-collar jobs were unexciting. The work was routine and, except for teaching and nursing, required few skills beyond basic literacy. Although there was little hope for advancement, these jobs had distinct advantages for the daughters of the middle classes and especially the upward-aspiring working classes. For some middle-class women, the new jobs offered freedom from the domestic patterns expected of them. Nevertheless, because middle-class women did not receive an education comparable to that of men, the careers they could pursue were limited. Thus they found it easier to fill the jobs at the lower end of middle-class occupations, such as teaching and civil service jobs, especially in the postal service.

Most of the new white-collar jobs, however, were filled by working-class women who saw them as an opportunity to escape from the "dirty" work of the lower-class world. Studies in France and Britain indicate that the increase in white-collar jobs did not lead to a rise in the size of the female labor force, only to a shift from industrial jobs to the white-collar sector of the economy.

PROSTITUTION

Despite the new job opportunities, many lower-class women were forced to become prostitutes to survive. The rural, working-class girls who flocked into the cities in search of new opportunities were often naive and vulnerable. Employment was unstable, and wages were low. No longer protected by family or village community and church, some girls faced only one grim alternative—prostitution. In Paris, London, and many other large cities with transient populations, thousands of prostitutes plied their trade. One journalist estimated that there were sixty thousand prostitutes in London in 1885. Most prostitutes were active for a short time, usually from their late teens through their early twenties. Many eventually rejoined the regular workforce or married when they could.

In most European countries, prostitution was licensed and regulated by government and municipal authorities. Although the British government provided minimal regulation of prostitution, it did attempt to enforce the Contagious Diseases Acts in the 1870s and 1880s by giving authorities the right to examine prostitutes for venereal disease. Prostitutes found to be infected were confined for some time to special institutions called lock hospitals, where they were given moral instruction. But opposition to the Contagious Diseases Acts soon arose from middle-class female reformers. Their leader was Josephine Butler (1828–1906), who objected to laws that punished women but not men who suffered from venereal disease. Known as the "shrieking sisters" because they discussed sexual mat-

New Jobs for Women: The Telephone Exchange. The invention of the telephone in 1876 soon led to its widespread use. As is evident from this illustration of a telephone exchange in Paris in 1904, most of the telephone operators were women. This was but one of a number of new job opportunities for women created by the Second Industrial Revolution.

ters in public, Butler and her fellow reformers were successful in gaining the repeal of the acts in 1886.

Organizing the Working Classes

The desire to improve their working and living conditions led many industrial workers to form political parties and labor unions. One of the most important of the working-class or socialist parties was formed in Germany in 1875.

SOCIALIST PARTIES

Under the direction of its two Marxist leaders, Wilhelm Liebknecht and August Bebel, the German Social Democratic Party (SPD) espoused revolutionary Marxist rhetoric while organizing itself as a mass political party competing in elections for the Reichstag (the German parliament). Once in the Reichstag, SPD delegates worked to enact legislation to improve the condition of the working class. As August Bebel explained: "Pure negation would not be accepted by the voters. The masses demand that something should be done for today irrespective of what will happen on the morrow."[3] Despite government efforts to destroy it (see "Central and Eastern Europe: Persistence of the Old Order" later in this chapter), the German Social Democratic Party continued to grow. In 1890, it received 1.5 million votes and thirty-five seats in the Reichstag. When it received four million votes in the 1912 elections, it became the largest single party in Germany.

"Proletarians of the World, Unite." To improve their working and living conditions, many industrial workers, inspired by the ideas of Karl Marx, joined working-class or socialist parties. Pictured here is a socialist-sponsored poster that proclaims in German the closing words of *The Communist Manifesto:* "Proletarians of the World, Unite!"

Verein fur Geschichte der Arbeiterbewegung, Vienna

Socialist parties also emerged in other European states, although none proved as successful as the German Social Democrats. France had a variety of socialist parties, including a Marxist one. The leader of French socialism, Jean Jaurès (1859–1914), was an independent socialist who looked to the French revolutionary tradition rather than Marxism to justify revolutionary socialism. In 1905, the French socialist parties succeeded in unifying themselves into a single mostly Marxist-oriented socialist party. Social democratic parties on the German model were founded in Belgium, Austria, Hungary, Bulgaria, Poland, Romania, and the Netherlands before 1900. The Marxist Social Democratic Labor Party had been organized in Russia by 1898.

As the socialist parties grew, agitation for an international organization that would strengthen their position against international capitalism also grew. In 1889, leaders of the various socialist parties formed the Second International, which was organized as a loose association of national groups. Although the Second International took some coordinated actions—May Day (May 1), for example, was made an international labor day to be marked by strikes and mass labor demonstrations—differences often wreaked havoc at the organization's congresses. Two issues proved particularly divisive: revisionism and nationalism.

REVISIONISM AND NATIONALISM

Some Marxists believed in a pure Marxism that accepted the imminent collapse of capitalism and the need for socialist ownership of the means of production. The guiding light of the German Social Democrats, August Bebel, confided to another socialist that "every night I go to sleep with the thought that the last hour of bourgeois society strikes soon." Earlier, Bebel had said, "I am convinced that the fulfillment of our aims is so close, that there are few in this hall who will not live to see the day."[4] But a severe challenge to this orthodox Marxist position arose in the form of revisionism.

Most prominent among the revisionists was Eduard Bernstein (1850–1932), a member of the German Social Democratic Party who had spent years in exile in Britain, where he had been influenced by moderate English socialism and the British parliamentary system. In 1899, Bernstein challenged Marxist orthodoxy with a book titled *Evolutionary Socialism* in which he argued that some of Marx's ideas had turned out to be quite wrong (see the box on p. 650). The capitalist system had not broken down, said Bernstein. Contrary to Marx's assertion, the middle class was actually expanding, not declining. At the same time, the proletariat was not sinking further down; instead, its position was improving as workers experienced a higher standard of living. In the face of this reality, Bernstein

The Voice of Evolutionary Socialism: Eduard Bernstein

The German Marxist Eduard Bernstein was regarded as the foremost late-nineteenth-century theorist of Marxist revisionism. In his book *Evolutionary Socialism,* Bernstein argued that Marx had made some fundamental mistakes and that socialists needed to stress cooperation and evolution rather than class conflict and revolution.

■ *Eduard Bernstein,* Evolutionary Socialism

It has been maintained in a certain quarter that the practical deductions from my treatises would be the abandonment of the conquest of political power by the proletariat organized politically and economically. That is quite an arbitrary deduction, the accuracy of which I altogether deny.

I set myself against the notion that we have to expect shortly a collapse of the bourgeois economy, and that social democracy should be induced by the prospect of such an imminent, great, social catastrophe to adapt its tactics to that assumption. That I maintain most emphatically.

The adherents of this theory of a catastrophe base it especially on the conclusions of the *Communist Manifesto.* This is a mistake in every respect.

The theory which the *Communist Manifesto* sets forth of the evolution of modern society was correct as far as it characterized the general tendencies of that evolution. But it was mistaken in several special deductions, above all in the estimate of the time the evolution would take.... But it is evident that if social evolution takes a much greater period of time than was assumed, it must also take upon itself forms and lead to forms that were not foreseen and could not be foreseen then.

Social conditions have not developed to such an acute opposition of things and classes as is depicted in the *Manifesto.* It is not only useless, it is the greatest folly to attempt to conceal this from ourselves. The number of members of the possessing classes is today not smaller but larger. The enormous increase of social wealth is not accompanied by a decreasing number of large capitalists but by an increasing number of capitalists of all degrees. The middle classes change their character but they do not disappear from the social scale....

In all advanced countries we see the privileges of the capitalist bourgeoisie yielding step by step to democratic organizations. Under the influence of this, and driven by the movement of the working classes which is daily becoming stronger, a social reaction has set in against the exploiting tendencies of capital, a counteraction which, although it still proceeds timidly and feebly, yet does exist, and is always drawing more departments of economic life under its influence. Factory legislation, the democratizing of local government, and the extension of its area of work, the freeing of trade unions and systems of cooperative trading from legal restrictions, the consideration of standard conditions of labor in the work undertaken by public authorities—all these characterize this phase of the evolution.

But the more the political organizations of modern nations are democratized the more the needs and opportunities of great political catastrophes are diminished.... But is the conquest of political power by the proletariat simply to be by a political catastrophe? Is it to be the appropriation and utilization of the power of the State by the proletariat exclusively against the whole non-proletarian world?...

No one has questioned the necessity for the working classes to gain the control of government. The point at issue is between the theory of a social cataclysm and the question whether, with the given social development in Germany and the present advanced state of its working classes in the towns and the country, a sudden catastrophe would be desirable in the interest of the social democracy. I have denied it and deny it again, because in my judgment a greater security for lasting success lies in a steady advance than in the possibilities offered by a catastrophic crash.

discarded Marx's emphasis on class struggle and revolution. The workers, he asserted, must continue to organize in mass political parties and even work together with the other advanced elements in a nation to bring about change. With the extension of the right to vote, workers were in a better position than ever to achieve their aims through democratic channels. Evolution by democratic means, not revolution, would achieve the desired goal of socialism. German and French socialist leaders, as well as the Second International, condemned revisionism as heresy and opportunism. But many socialist parties, including the German Social Democrats, while spouting revolutionary slogans, followed Bernstein's revisionist, gradualist approach.

A second divisive issue for international socialism was nationalism. Marx and Engels had said that "the working men have no country" and that "national differences and antagonisms between peoples are daily more and more vanishing, owing to the development of the bourgeoisie."[5] They proved drastically wrong. Congresses of the Second International passed resolutions in 1907 and 1910 advocating joint action by workers of different countries to avert war but provided no real machinery to implement the resolutions. In truth, socialist parties varied from country to country and remained tied to national concerns and issues. Socialist leaders always worried that in the end, national loyalties might outweigh class loyalties among the masses. When World War I came in 1914, not only the working-class masses but even many of their socialist party leaders supported the war efforts of their national governments. Nationalism had proved a much more powerful force than socialism.

THE ROLE OF TRADE UNIONS

Workers also formed trade unions to improve their working conditions. Attempts to organize the workers did not come until after unions had won the right to strike in the 1870s. Strikes proved necessary to achieve the workers' goals. A walkout by female workers in the match industry in 1888 and by dockworkers in London the following year led to the establishment of trade union organizations for both groups. By 1900, two million workers were enrolled in British trade unions, and by the outbreak of World War I, this number had risen to between three and four million, although this was still less than one-fifth of the total workforce.

Trade unions failed to develop as quickly on the Continent as they had in Britain. In France, the trade union movement was from the beginning closely tied to socialist ideology. As there were a number of French socialist parties, the socialist trade unions remained badly splintered. Not until 1895 did French unions create a national organization called the General Confederation of Labor. Its decentralization and failure to include some of the more important individual unions, however, kept it weak and ineffective.

German trade unions, also closely attached to political parties, were first formed in the 1860s. Although there were liberal trade unions comprised of skilled artisans and Catholic or Christian trade unions, the largest German trade unions were those of the socialists. By 1899, even the latter had accepted the practice of collective bargaining with employers. As strikes and collective bargaining achieved successes, German workers were increasingly inclined to forgo revolution for gradual improvements. By 1914, its three million members made the German trade union movement the second largest in Europe, after Great Britain's. Almost 85 percent of these three million belonged to socialist unions. Trade unions in the rest of Europe had varying degrees of success, but by the beginning of World War I, they had made considerable progress in bettering both the living and the working conditions of the laboring classes.

THE ANARCHIST ALTERNATIVE

Despite the revolutionary rhetoric, socialist parties and trade unions gradually became less radical in pursuing their goals. Indeed, this lack of revolutionary fervor drove some people from Marxist socialism into anarchism, a movement that was especially prominent in less industrialized and less democratic countries.

Initially, anarchism was not a violent movement. Early anarchists believed that people were inherently good but had been corrupted by the state and society. True freedom could be achieved only by abolishing the state and all existing social institutions. In the second half of the nineteenth century, however, anarchists in Spain, Portugal, Italy, and Russia began to advocate using radical means to accomplish this goal. The Russian Michael Bakunin, for example, believed that small groups of well-trained, fanatical revolutionaries could perpetrate so much violence that the state and all its institutions would disintegrate. To revolutionary anarchists, that would usher in the anarchist golden age. The Russian anarchist Lev Aleshker wrote shortly before his execution:

> Slavery, poverty, weakness, and ignorance—the external fetters of man—will be broken. Man will be at the center of nature. The earth and its products will serve everyone dutifully. Weapons will cease to be a measure of strength and gold a measure of wealth; the strong will be those who are bold and daring in the conquest of nature, and riches will be the things that are useful. Such a world is called "Anarchy." It will have no castles, no place for masters and slaves. Life will be open to all. Everyone will take what he needs—this is the anarchist ideal. And when it comes about, men will live wisely and well. The masses must take part in the construction of this paradise on earth.[6]

After Bakunin's death in 1876, anarchist revolutionaries used assassination as their primary instrument of terror. The list of victims of anarchist assassins at the turn of the century included a Russian tsar (1881), a president of the French Republic (1894), the king of Italy (1900), and a president of the United States (1901). Despite anarchist hopes, these states did not collapse.

The Emergence of a Mass Society

The new patterns of industrial production, mass consumption, and working-class organization that we identify with the Second Industrial Revolution were only one aspect of the new mass society that emerged in Europe after 1870. A larger and vastly improved urban environment, new patterns of social structure, gender issues, mass education, and mass leisure were also important features of European society.

Population Growth and Emigration

The European population increased dramatically between 1850 and 1910, rising from 270 million to over 460 million by 1910 (see Table 23.1). Between 1850 and 1880, the main cause of the population increase was a rising birthrate, at least in western Europe, but after 1880, a noticeable decline in death rates largely explains the increase in population. Although the causes of this decline have been debated, two major factors—medical discoveries and environmental conditions—stand out. Some historians have stressed the importance of developments in medical science. Smallpox vaccinations, for example, were compulsory in many European countries by the mid-1850s. More important were improvements in the urban environment in the second half of the nineteenth century that greatly reduced fatalities from such diseases as diarrhea, dysentery, typhoid fever, and cholera, which had been spread through contaminated water supplies and improper elimination of sewage. Improved nutrition also made a significant difference in the health of the population. The increase in agricultural productivity combined with improvements in transportation facilitated the shipment of food supplies from areas of

Table 23.1 European Populations, 1851–1911 (in thousands)

	1851	1881	1911
England and Wales	17,928	25,974	36,070
Scotland	2,889	3,736	4,761
Ireland	6,552	5,175	4,390
France	35,783	37,406	39,192
Germany	33,413	45,234	64,926
Belgium	4,530	5,520	7,424
Netherlands	3,309	4,013	5,858
Denmark	1,415	1,969	2,757
Norway	1,490	1,819	2,392
Sweden	3,471	4,169	5,522
Spain	15,455	16,622	19,927
Portugal	3,844	4,551	5,958
Italy	24,351	28,460	34,671
Switzerland	2,393	2,846	3,753
Austria	17,535	22,144	28,572
Hungary	18,192	15,739	20,886
Russia	68,500	97,700	160,700
Romania	—	4,600	7,000
Bulgaria	—	2,800	4,338
Greece	—	1,679	2,632
Serbia	—	1,700	2,912

Source: Data from B. R. Mitchell, *European Historical Statistics, 1750–1970* (1975).

surplus to regions with poor harvests. Better nutrition and food hygiene were especially instrumental in the decline in infant mortality by 1900. The pasteurization of milk reduced intestinal disorders that had been a major cause of infant deaths.

Although growing agricultural and industrial prosperity supported an increase in the European population, it could not do so indefinitely, especially in areas that had little industrialization and severe rural overpopulation. Some of the excess labor from underdeveloped areas migrated to the industrial regions of Europe (see Map 23.2). By 1913, more than 400,000 Poles were working in the heavily industrialized Ruhr region of western Germany, and thousands of Italian laborers had migrated to France. The industrialized regions of Europe, however, were not able to absorb the entire surplus population of heavily agricultural regions like southern Italy, Spain, Hungary, and Romania, where the land could not support the growing numbers of people. The booming economies of North America after 1898 and cheap shipping fares after 1900 led to mass emigration from southern and eastern Europe to North America at the beginning of the twentieth century. In 1880, about 500,000 people left Europe each year on average; between 1906 and 1910, annual departures increased to 1.3 million, many of them from southern and eastern Europe. Altogether, between 1846 and 1932, probably 60 million Europeans left Europe, half of them bound for the United States and most of the rest for Canada or Latin America (see Table 23.2).

It was not only economic motives that caused people to leave eastern Europe. Migrants from Austria and Hungary, for example, were not the dominant nationalities, the Germans and Magyars, but mostly their oppressed minorities, such as Poles, Slovaks, Serbs, Croats, Romanians, and Jews. Between 1880 and 1914, 3.5 million Poles from Russia, Austria, and Germany went to the United States. Jews, who were severely persecuted, constituted 40 percent of the Russian emigrants to the United States between 1900 and 1913 and almost 12 percent of all emigrants to the United States during the first five years of the twentieth century.

Transformation of the Urban Environment

One of the most important consequences of industrialization and the population explosion of the nineteenth century was urbanization. In the course of the nineteenth century, urban dwellers came to make up an ever-increasing percentage of the European population. In 1800, they consti-

The Emigrants. In this painting done in 1880, C. J. Staniland presented a sentimental image of the scene faced by the tens of millions of Europeans who migrated to other parts of the world, especially the United States, Canada, and Latin America. Shown in the painting are people boarding a ship, saying farewell to family members and loved ones they might never see again. Ships were often crowded, making conditions uncomfortable during the journey.

Bradford Art Galleries & Museums, *West Yorkshire*, UK/Bridgeman Art Library

Table 23.2 European Emigration, 1876–1910 (Average Annual Emigration to Non-European Countries per 100,000 Population)

	1876–1880	1881–1885	1886–1890	1891–1895	1896–1900	1901–1905	1906–1910
Europe	94	196	213	185	147	271	322
Ireland	650	1,422	1,322	988	759	743	662
Great Britain	102	174	162	119	88	127	172
Denmark	157	380	401	338	117	292	275
Norway	432	1,105	819	597	312	903	746
Sweden	301	705	759	587	249	496	347
Germany	108	379	207	163	47	50	44
Belgium	—	—	86	50	23	57	69
Netherlands	32	136	111	76	25	45	58
France	8	14	49	14	13	12	12
Spain	—	280	437	434	446	391	758
Portugal	258	356	423	609	417	464	694
Italy	396	542	754	842	974	1,706	1,938
Austria	48	90	114	182	182	355	469
Hungary	—	92	156	134	205	437	616
Russia	6	13	42	47	32	63	67

SOURCE: Robert Gildea, *Barricades and Borders: Europe, 1800–1914* (Oxford, 1987), p. 283.

tuted 40 percent of the population in Britain, 25 percent in France and Germany, and only 10 percent in eastern Europe. By 1914, urban inhabitants had increased to 80 percent of the population in Britain, 45 percent in France, 60 percent in Germany, and 30 percent in eastern Europe. The size of cities also expanded dramatically, especially in industrialized countries. In 1800, there were 21 European cities with populations over 100,000; by 1900, there were 147. Between 1800 and 1900, London's population grew from 960,000 to 6.5 million and Berlin's from 172,000 to 2.7 million.

Urban populations grew faster than the general population primarily because of the vast migration from rural areas to cities. People were driven from the countryside to the cities by sheer economic necessity—unemployment, land hunger, and physical want. Urban centers offered something positive as well, usually mass employment in factories and later in service trades and professions. But cities also grew faster in the second half of the nineteenth century because health and living conditions in them were improving.

IMPROVING LIVING CONDITIONS

In the 1840s, a number of urban reformers, such as Edwin Chadwick in Britain (see Chapter 20) and Rudolf Virchow and Solomon Neumann in Germany, had pointed to filthy living conditions as the primary cause of epidemic disease and urged sanitary reforms to correct the problem. Soon legislative acts created boards of health that brought governmental action to bear on public heath issues. Urban medical officers and building inspectors were authorized to inspect dwellings for public health hazards. New building regulations made it more difficult for private contractors to build shoddy housing. The Public Health Act of 1875 in Britain, for example, prohibited the construction of new buildings without running water and an internal drainage system. For the first time in Western history, the role of municipal governments had been expanded to include detailed regulations for the improvement of the living conditions of urban dwellers.

Essential to the public health of the modern European city was the ability to bring clean water into the city and to expel sewage from it. The accomplishment of those two tasks was a major engineering feat in the second half of the nineteenth century. The problem of fresh water was solved by a system of dams and reservoirs that stored the water and aqueducts and tunnels that carried it from the countryside to the city and into individual dwellings. Regular private baths became accessible to more people as gas heaters in the 1860s and later electric heaters made hot baths possible. The shower had appeared by the 1880s.

The treatment of wastewater was improved by building mammoth underground pipes that carried raw sewage far from the city for disposal. In the late 1860s, a number of German cities began to construct sewer systems. Frankfurt began its program after a lengthy public campaign enlivened by the slogan "From the toilet to the river in half an hour." London devised a system of five enormous sewers that discharged their loads 12 miles from the city, where the waste was chemically treated. Unfortunately, in many places, new underground sewers simply discharged their raw sewage into what soon became highly polluted lakes and rivers. Nevertheless, the development of pure water and sewerage systems dramatically improved the public health of European cities.

HOUSING NEEDS

Middle-class reformers who denounced the unsanitary living conditions of the working classes also focused on their housing needs. Overcrowded, disease-ridden slums were viewed as dangerous not only to physical health but also to

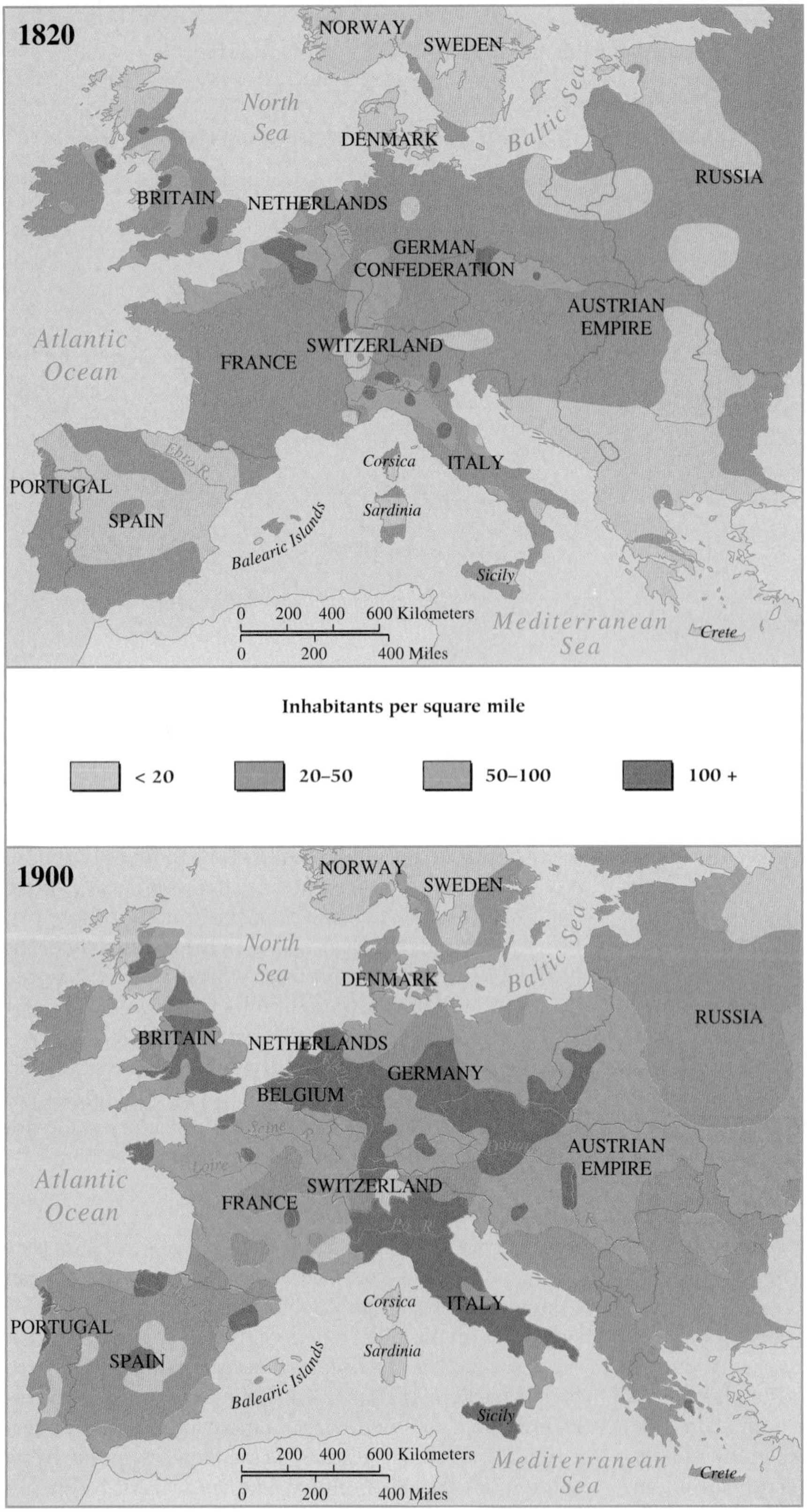

Map 23.2 Population Growth in Europe, 1820–1900. European population increased steadily throughout the nineteenth century. Advances in medical science, hygiene, nutrition, living conditions, and standards of living help account for the population increase, even though emigration to the United States, South America, and other regions reduced the total growth numbers. ■ Which regions experienced the greatest population growth between 1820 and 1900, and how can you account for this?

the political and moral health of the entire nation. V. A. Huber, the foremost early German housing reformer, wrote in 1861: "Certainly it would not be too much to say that the home is the communal embodiment of family life. Thus the purity of the dwelling is almost as important for the family as is the cleanliness of the body for the individual."[7] To Huber, good housing was a prerequisite for a stable family life and hence a stable society.

Early efforts to attack the housing problem emphasized the middle-class, liberal belief in the efficacy of private

The Housing Venture of Octavia Hill

Octavia Hill was a practical-minded British housing reformer who believed that workers and their families were entitled to happy homes. At the same time, she was convinced that the poor needed guidance and encouragement, not charity. In this selection, she describes her housing venture.

Octavia Hill, Homes of the London Poor

About four years ago I was put in possession of three houses in one of the worst courts of Marylebone. Six other houses were bought subsequently. All were crowded with inmates.

The first thing to be done was to put them in decent tenantable order. The set last purchased was a row of cottages facing a bit of desolate ground, occupied with wretched, dilapidated cow-sheds, manure heaps, old timber, and rubbish of every description. The houses were in a most deplorable condition—the plaster was dropping from the walls; on one staircase a pail was placed to catch the rain that fell through the roof. All the staircases were perfectly dark; the banisters were gone, having been burnt as firewood by tenants. The grates, with large holes in them, were falling forward into the rooms. The wash-house, full of lumber belonging to the landlord, was locked up; thus the inhabitants had to wash clothes, as well as to cook, eat and sleep in their small rooms. The dustbin, standing in the front part of the houses, was accessible to the whole neighborhood, and boys often dragged from it quantities of unseemly objects and spread them over the court. The state of the drainage was in keeping with everything else. The pavement of the back-yard was all broken up, and great puddles stood in it, so that the damp crept up the outer walls. . . .

As soon as I entered into possession, each family had an opportunity of doing better: those who would not pay, or who led clearly immoral lives, were ejected. The rooms they vacated were cleansed; the tenants who showed signs of improvement moved into them, and thus, in turn, an opportunity was obtained for having each room distempered and papered. The drains were put in order, a large slate cistern was fixed, the wash-house was cleared of its lumber, and thrown open on stated days to each tenant in turn. The roof, the plaster, the woodwork were repaired; the staircase walls were distempered; new grates were fixed; the layers of paper and rag (black with age) were torn from the windows, and glass put in; out of 192 panes only eight were found unbroken. The yard and footpath were paved.

The rooms, as a rule, were re-let at the same prices at which they had been let before; but tenants with large families were counseled to take two rooms, and for these much less was charged than if let singly: this plan I continue to pursue. In-coming tenants are not allowed to take a decidedly insufficient quantity of room, and no sub-letting is permitted. . . .

The pecuniary result has been very satisfactory. Five percent has been paid on all the capital invested. A fund for the repayment of capital is accumulating. A liberal allowance has been made for repairs. . . .

My tenants are mostly of a class far below that of mechanics. They are, indeed, of the very poor. And yet, although the gifts they have received have been next to nothing, none of the families who have passed under my care during the whole four years have continued in what is called "distress," except such as have been unwilling to exert themselves. Those who will not exert the necessary self-control cannot avail themselves of the means of livelihood held out to them. But, for those who are willing, some small assistance in the form of work has, from time to time, been provided—not much, but sufficient to keep them from want or despair.

enterprise. Reformers such as Huber believed that the construction of model dwellings renting at a reasonable price would force other private landlords to elevate their housing standards. A fine example of this approach was the work of Octavia Hill, granddaughter of a celebrated social reformer (see the box above). With the financial assistance of a friend, she rehabilitated some old dwellings and constructed new ones to create housing for 3,500 tenants.

Other wealthy reformer-philanthropists took a different approach to the housing problem. In 1887, Lord Leverhulme began construction of a model village called Port Sunlight outside Liverpool for the workers at his soap factory. Port Sunlight offered pleasant living conditions in the belief that good housing would ensure a healthy and happy workforce. Yet another approach was the garden city. At the end of the nineteenth century, Ebenezer Howard founded the British garden city movement, which advocated the construction of new towns separated from each other by open country that would provide the recreational areas, fresh air, and sense of community that would encourage healthy family life. Letchward Garden City, started in 1903, was the first concrete result of Howard's theory.

As the number and size of cities continued to mushroom, governments by the 1880s came to the conclusion—reluctantly—that private enterprise could not solve the housing crisis. In 1890, a British law empowered local town councils to collect new taxes and construct cheap housing for the working classes. London and Liverpool were the first communities to take advantage of their new powers. Similar activity had been set in motion in Germany by 1900. In 1894, the French government took a lesser step by providing easy credit for private contractors to build working-class housing. Everywhere, however, these lukewarm measures failed to do much to meet the real housing

Hulton Archive/Getty Images

Working-Class Housing in London. Although urban workers experienced some improvements in the material conditions of their lives after 1871, working-class housing remained drab and depressing. This 1912 photograph of working-class housing in the East End of London shows rows of similar-looking buildings on treeless streets. Most often, these buildings had no gardens or green areas.

needs of the working classes. In Britain, for example, only 5 percent of all dwellings erected between 1890 and 1914 were constructed by municipalities under the Housing Act of 1890. Nevertheless, by the start of World War I, the need for planning had been recognized, and after the war municipal governments moved into housing construction on a large scale. In housing, as in so many other areas of life in the late nineteenth century, the liberal principle that the government that governs least governs best had simply proved untrue. More and more, governments were stepping into areas of activity that they would never have touched earlier.

REDESIGNING THE CITIES

Housing was but one area of urban reconstruction after 1870. As urban populations expanded in the nineteenth century, the older layout, confining the city to a compact area enclosed by defensive walls, seemed restrictive and utterly useless. In the second half of the nineteenth century, many of the old defensive walls—worthless anyway from a military standpoint—were pulled down, and the areas were converted into parks and boulevards. In Vienna, for example, the great boulevards of the Ringstrasse replaced the old medieval walls. While the broad streets served a military purpose—the rapid deployment of troops to crush civil disturbances—they also offered magnificent views of the city hall, the university, and the parliament building, all powerful symbols of middle-class social values.

Like Vienna, many European urban centers were redesigned during the second half of the nineteenth century. The reconstruction of Paris after 1850 by Emperor Napoleon III was perhaps the most famous project and provided a model for other urban centers. The old residential districts in the central city, many of them working-class slums, were demolished and replaced with town halls, government office buildings, retail stores, including the new department stores, museums, cafés, and theaters, all of which provided for the shopping and recreational pleasures of the middle classes.

As cities expanded and entire groups of people were displaced from urban centers by reconstruction, city populations spilled over into the neighboring villages and countrysides, which were soon incorporated into the cities. The construction of streetcar and commuter train lines by the turn of the century enabled both working-class and middle-class populations to live in their own suburban neighborhoods far removed from their places of work. Cheap, modern transportation essentially separated home and work for many Europeans.

Social Structure of the Mass Society

Historians generally agree that after 1871, the average person enjoyed an improving standard of living. The real wages of British workers, for example, probably doubled between 1871 and 1910. We should not allow this increase in the standard of living to mislead us, however. Great poverty did remain in Western society, and the gap between rich and poor was enormous. There were many different groups of varying wealth between the small group of the elite at the top and the large number of very poor at the bottom.

THE ELITE

At the top of European society stood a wealthy elite, constituting only 5 percent of the population but controlling between 30 and 40 percent of its wealth. In the course of the nineteenth century, aristocrats coalesced with the most successful industrialists, bankers, and merchants to form this new elite. Big business had produced this group of wealthy plutocrats, while aristocrats, whose income from landed estates declined, invested in railway shares, public utilities, government bonds, and businesses, sometimes on their own estates. Gradually, the greatest fortunes shifted into the hands of the upper middle class. In Great Britain, for example, landed aristocrats constituted 73 percent of the country's millionaires at mid-century, while commercial and financial magnates made up 14 percent. By the period 1900–1914, landowners had declined to 27 percent. The wealthiest person in Germany was not an aristocrat but Bertha Krupp, granddaughter of Alfred Krupp and heiress to the business dynasty left by her father Friedrich, who committed suicide in 1902.

Increasingly, aristocrats and plutocrats fused as the wealthy upper middle class purchased landed estates to join the aristocrats in the pleasures of country living and the aristocrats bought lavish town houses for part-time urban life. Common bonds were also forged when the sons of wealthy middle-class families were admitted to the elite schools dominated by the children of the aristocracy. At Oxford, the landed upper class made up 40 percent of the student body in 1870, but only 15 percent in 1910, while undergraduates from business families went from 7 to 21 percent during the same period. This educated elite, whether aristocratic or middle-class in background, assumed leadership roles in government bureaucracies and military hierarchies. Marriage also served to unite the two groups. Daughters of tycoons acquired titles, while aristocratic heirs gained new sources of cash. Wealthy American heiresses were in special demand. When Consuelo Vanderbilt married the duke of Marlborough, the new duchess brought £2 million (approximately $10 million) to her husband.

It would be misleading, however, to assume that the alliance of the wealthy business elite and traditional aristocrats was always harmonious. In Germany, class lines were sometimes well drawn, especially if they were complicated by anti-Semitism. Albert Ballin, the wealthy director of the Hamburg-Amerika luxury liners, may have been close to Emperor William II, who entertained him on a regular basis, but the Prussian aristocracy snubbed Ballin because of his Jewish origins. Although the upper middle class was allowed into the bureaucracy of the German Empire, the diplomatic corps remained an aristocratic preserve.

THE MIDDLE CLASSES

The middle classes consisted of a variety of groups. Below the upper middle class was a level that included such traditional groups as professionals in law, medicine, and the civil service as well as moderately well-to-do industrialists and merchants. The industrial expansion of the nineteenth century also added new groups to this segment of the middle class. These included business managers and new professionals, such as the engineers, architects, accountants, and chemists who formed professional associations as the symbols of their newfound importance. A lower middle class of small shopkeepers, traders, manufacturers, and prosperous peasants provided goods and services for the classes above them.

Standing between the lower middle class and the lower classes were new groups of white-collar workers who were the product of the Second Industrial Revolution. They were the traveling sales representatives, bookkeepers, bank tellers, telephone operators, department store salesclerks, and secretaries. Although largely propertyless and often paid little more than skilled laborers, these white-collar workers were often committed to middle-class ideals and optimistic about improving their status.

The moderately prosperous and successful middle classes shared a common lifestyle and values that dominated nineteenth-century society. The members of the middle class were especially active in preaching their worldview to their children and to the upper and lower classes of their society. This was particularly evident in Victorian Britain, often considered a model of middle-class society. It was the European middle classes who accepted and promulgated the importance of progress and science. They believed in hard work, which they viewed as the primary human good, open to everyone and guaranteed to have positive results. They were also regular churchgoers who believed in the good conduct associated with traditional Christian morality. The middle class was concerned with propriety, the right way of doing things, which gave rise to an incessant number of books aimed at the middle-class market with such titles as *The Habits of Good Society* or *Don't: A Manual of Mistakes and Improprieties More or Less Prevalent in Conduct and Speech.*

THE LOWER CLASSES

The lower classes of European society constituted almost 80 percent of the European population. Many of them were landholding peasants, agricultural laborers, and sharecroppers, especially in eastern Europe. This was less true, however, in western and central Europe. About 10 percent of the British population worked in agriculture; in Germany, the figure was 25 percent. Many prosperous, landowning peasants shared the values of the middle class. Military conscription brought peasants into contact with the other groups of society, and state-run elementary schools forced the children of peasants to speak the national dialect and accept national loyalties.

The urban working class consisted of many different groups, including skilled artisans in such trades as cabinetmaking, printing, and jewelry making. Semiskilled laborers, who included such people as carpenters, bricklayers, and many factory workers, earned wages that were about two-thirds of those of highly skilled workers. At the bottom of the working-class hierarchy stood the largest group of workers, the unskilled laborers. They included day laborers, who worked irregularly for very low wages, and large numbers of domestic servants. One out of every seven employed persons in Great Britain in 1900 was a domestic servant. Most were women.

Urban workers did experience a real betterment in the material conditions of their lives after 1871. For one thing, urban improvements meant better living conditions. A rise in real wages, accompanied by a decline in many consumer costs, especially in the 1880s and 1890s, made it possible for workers to buy more than just food and housing. French workers in 1900, for example, spent 60 percent of their income on food, down from 75 percent in 1870. Workers' budgets now provided money for more clothes and even leisure at the same time that strikes and labor agitation were providing shorter (ten-hour) workdays and Saturday afternoons off.

"The Woman Question": The Role of Women

"The woman question" was the catchphrase used to refer to the debate over the role of women in society. In the nineteenth century, women remained legally inferior, economically dependent, and largely defined by family and household roles. Many women still aspired to the ideal of femininity popularized by writers and poets. Alfred, Lord Tennyson's poem *The Princess* expressed it well:

> *Man for the field and woman for the hearth:*
> *Man for the sword and for the needle she:*
> *Man with the head and woman with the heart:*
> *Man to command and woman to obey;*
> *All else confusion.*

Historians have pointed out that this traditional characterization of the sexes, based on gender-defined social roles, was elevated to the status of universal male and female attributes in the nineteenth century, largely due to the impact of the Industrial Revolution on the family. As the chief family wage earners, men worked outside the home, while women were left with the care of the family, for which they were paid nothing. Of course, the ideal did not always match reality, especially for the lower classes, where the need for supplemental income drove women to do sweatwork.

Throughout most of the nineteenth century, marriage was viewed as the only honorable and available career for most women. Though the middle class glorified the ideal of domesticity (see the box on p. 659), for most women, marriage was a matter of economic necessity. The lack of meaningful work and the lower wages paid to women made it difficult for single women to earn a living. Retiring to convents as in the past was no longer an option; many spinsters who could not find sufficiently remunerative work therefore elected to enter domestic service as live-in servants. Most women chose instead to marry, which was reflected in an increase in marriage rates and a decline in illegitimacy rates in the course of the nineteenth century.

Birthrates also dropped significantly at this time. A very important factor in the evolution of the modern family was the decline in the number of offspring born to the average woman. The change was not necessarily due to new technological products. Although the invention of vulcanized rubber in the 1840s made possible the production of condoms and diaphragms, they were not widely used as effective contraceptive devices until World War I. Some historians maintain that the change in attitude that led parents to deliberately limit the number of offspring was more important than the method used. Although some historians attribute increased birth control to more widespread use of coitus interruptus, or male withdrawal before ejaculation, others have emphasized the ability of women to restrict family size through abortion and even infanticide or abandonment. That a change in attitude occurred was apparent in the emergence of a movement to increase awareness of birth control methods. Authorities prosecuted those who spread information about contraception for "depraving public morals" but were unable to stop them. In 1882 in Amsterdam, Dr. Aletta Jacob founded Europe's first birth control clinic. Initially, "family planning" was the suggestion of reformers who thought that the problem of poverty could be solved by reducing the number of children among the lower classes. In fact, the practice spread quickly among the propertied classes, rather than among the impoverished, a good reminder that considerable differences still remained between middle-class and working-class families.

THE MIDDLE-CLASS FAMILY

The family was the central institution of middle-class life. Men provided the family income, while women focused on household and child care. The use of domestic servants in many middle-class homes, made possible by an abundant supply of cheap labor, reduced the amount of time middle-class women had to spend on household work. At the same time, by reducing the number of children in the family, mothers could devote more time to child care and domestic leisure. The idea that leisure should be used for constructive purposes supported and encouraged the cult of middle-class domesticity.

Advice to Women: Be Dependent

Industrialization had a strong impact on middle-class women as gender-based social roles became the norm. Men worked outside the home to support the family, while women provided for the needs of their children and husband at home. In this selection, one woman gives advice to middle-class women on their proper role and behavior.

Elizabeth Poole Sanford, Woman in Her Social and Domestic Character

The changes wrought by Time are many. It influences the opinions of men as familiarity does their feelings; it has a tendency to do away with superstition, and to reduce every thing to its real worth.

It is thus that the sentiment for woman has undergone a change. The romantic passion which once almost deified her is on the decline; and it is by intrinsic qualities that she must now inspire respect. She is no longer the queen of song and the star of chivalry. But if there is less of enthusiasm entertained for her, the sentiment is more rational, and, perhaps, equally sincere; for it is in relation to happiness that she is chiefly appreciated.

And in this respect it is, we must confess, that she is most useful and most important. Domestic life is the chief source of her influence; and the greatest debt society can owe to her is domestic comfort; for happiness is almost an element of virtue; and nothing conduces more to improve the character of men than domestic peace. A woman may make a man's home delightful, and may thus increase his motives for virtuous exertion. She may refine and tranquilize his mind,—may turn away his anger or allay his grief. Her smile may be the happy influence to gladden his heart, and to disperse the cloud that gathers on his brow. And in proportion to her endeavors to make those around her happy, she will be esteemed and loved. She will secure by her excellence that interest and that regard which she might formerly claim as the privilege of her sex, and will really merit the deference which was then conceded to her as a matter of course. . . .

Perhaps one of the first secrets of her influence is adaptation to the tastes, and sympathy in the feelings, of those around her. This holds true in lesser as well as in graver points. It is in the former, indeed, that the absence of interest in a companion is frequently most disappointing. Where want of congeniality impairs domestic comfort, the fault is generally chargeable on the female side. It is for woman, not for man, to make the sacrifice, especially in indifferent matters. She must, in a certain degree, be plastic herself if she would mold others. . . .

Nothing is so likely to conciliate the affections of the other sex as a feeling that woman looks to them for support and guidance. In proportion as men are themselves superior, they are accessible to this appeal. On the contrary, they never feel interested in one who seems disposed rather to offer than to ask assistance. There is, indeed, something unfeminine in independence. It is contrary to nature, and therefore it offends. We do not like to see a woman affecting tremors, but still less do we like to see her acting the amazon. A really sensible woman feels her dependence. She does what she can; but she is conscious of inferiority, and therefore grateful for support. She knows that she is the weaker vessel, and that as such she should receive honor. In this view, her weakness is an attraction, not a blemish.

In every thing, therefore, that women attempt, they should show their consciousness of dependence. If they are learners, let them evince a teachable spirit; if they give an opinion, let them do it in an unassuming manner. There is something so unpleasant in female self-sufficiency that it not unfrequently deters instead of persuading, and prevents the adoption of advice which the judgment even approves.

The middle-class family fostered an ideal of togetherness. The Victorians created the family Christmas with its yule log, Christmas tree, songs, and exchange of gifts. In the United States, Fourth of July celebrations changed from drunken revels to family picnics by the 1850s. The education of middle-class females in domestic crafts, singing, and piano playing prepared them for their function of providing a proper environment for home recreation.

The new domestic ideal had an impact on child raising and children's play. Late-eighteenth-century thought, beginning with Rousseau, had encouraged a new view of children as unique beings, not small adults, which had carried over into the nineteenth century. They were entitled to a long childhood involved in activities with other children their own age. The early environment in which they were raised, it was thought, would determine how they turned out. And mothers were seen as the most important force in protecting children from the harmful influences of the adult world. New children's games and toys, including mass-produced dolls for girls, appeared in middle-class homes. The middle-class emphasis on the functional value of knowledge was also evident in these games. One advice manual maintained that young children should learn checkers because it "calls forth the resources of the mind in the most gentle as well as the most successful manner."

Since the sons of the middle-class family were expected to follow careers like their father's, they were sent to schools where they were kept separate from the rest of society until the age of sixteen or seventeen. Sport was used in the schools to "toughen boys up," and their leisure activities centered around both national military concerns and

A Middle-Class Family. Nineteenth-century middle-class moralists considered the family the fundamental pillar of a healthy society. The family was a crucial institution in middle-class life, and togetherness constituted one of the important ideals of the middle-class family. This painting by William P. Frith, titled *Many Happy Returns of the Day,* shows a family birthday celebration for a little girl in which grandparents, parents, and children take part. The servant at the left holds the presents for the little girl.

character building. This combination was especially evident in the establishment of the Boy Scouts in Britain in 1908. Boy Scouts provided organized recreation for boys between the ages of twelve and eighteen; adventure was combined with the discipline of earning merit badges and ranks in such a way as to instill ideals of patriotism and self-sacrifice. Many men viewed such activities as a corrective to the possible dangers that female domination of the home posed for male development. As one scout leader wrote: "The REAL Boy Scout is not a sissy. [He] adores his mother [but] is not hitched to [her] apron strings." There was little organized recreational activity of this type for girls, although Robert Baden-Powell, the founder of the Boy Scouts, did encourage his sister to establish a girls' division as an afterthought. Its goal is evident from Agnes Baden-Powell's comment that "you do not want to make tomboys of refined girls, yet you want to attract, and thus raise, the slum girl from the gutter. The main object is to give them all the ability to be better mothers and Guides to the next generation."[8] Despite her comment, most organizations of this kind were for middle-class children, although some reformers tried to establish boys' clubs for working-class youths to reform them.

The new ideal of the middle-class woman as nurturing mother and wife who "determined the atmosphere of the household" through her character, not her work, frequently did not correspond to reality. Recent research indicates that in France, Germany, and even mid-Victorian Britain, relatively few families could actually afford to hire a host of servants. More often, middle-class families had one servant, usually a young working-class or country girl not used to middle-class lifestyles. Women, then, were often forced to work quite hard to maintain the expected appearance of the well-ordered household. A German housekeeping manual makes this evident:

> It often happens that even high-ranking ladies help at home with housework, and particularly with kitchen chores, scrubbing, etc., so that, above all the hands have good cause to become very rough, hard, and calloused. When these ladies appear in society, they are extremely upset at having such rough-looking hands. In order to perform the hardest and most ordinary chores . . . and, at the same time, to keep a soft hand like those fine ladies who have no heavier work to do than embroidering and sewing, always keep a piece of fresh bacon, rub your hands with it just before bedtime, and you will fully achieve your goal. You will, as a result, have the inconvenience of having to sleep with gloves on, in order not to soil the bed.[9]

Many middle-class wives, then, were caught in a no-win situation. Often for the sake of the advancement of her husband's career, she was expected to maintain in public the image of the "idle" wife, freed from demeaning physical labor and able to pass her days in ornamental pursuits. In truth, it was frequently the middle-class woman who paid the price for this facade in a life of unpaid work, carefully managing the family budget and participating in housework that could never be done by only one servant girl. As one historian has argued, the reality of many middle-class women's lives was that "what appears at first glance to be idleness is revealed, on closer examination, to be difficult and tiresome work."

THE WORKING-CLASS FAMILY

Hard work was, of course, standard fare for women in working-class families. Daughters in working-class families were expected to work until they married; even after marriage, they often did piecework at home to help support the family. For the children of the working classes, childhood was over by the age of nine or ten, when they became apprentices or were employed in odd jobs.

Between 1890 and 1914, however, family patterns among the working class began to change. High-paying jobs in heavy industry and improvements in the standard of living made it possible for working-class families to depend on the income of husbands and the wages of grown children. By the early twentieth century, some working-class mothers could afford to stay at home, following the pattern of middle-class women. At the same time, new consumer products, such as sewing machines, clocks, bicycles, and cast-iron stoves, spurred consumerism, focusing society on ever-higher levels of consumption.

Working-class families also followed the middle classes in limiting the size of their families. Children began to be viewed as dependents rather than as potential wage earners as child labor laws and compulsory education moved children out of the workforce and into schools. Improvements in public health as well as advances in medicine and a better diet resulted in a decline in infant mortality rates for the lower classes, especially noticeable in the cities after 1890, and made it easier for working-class families to choose to have fewer children. At the same time, strikes and labor agitation led to laws that reduced work hours to ten per day by 1900 and eliminated work on Saturday afternoons, which enabled working-class parents to devote more attention to their children and develop deeper emotional ties with them. Even working-class fathers became involved in their children's lives. One observer in the French town of Belleville in the 1890s noted that "the workingman's love for his children borders on being an obsession."[10] Interest in educating children as a way to improve their future also grew.

Education and Leisure in the Mass Society

Mass education was a product of the mass society of the late nineteenth century. Being "educated" in the early nineteenth century meant attending a secondary school or possibly even a university. Secondary schools emphasized a classical education based on the study of Greek and Latin. Secondary and university education was primarily for the elite, the sons of government officials, nobles, or wealthier middle-class families. After 1850, secondary education was expanded as more middle-class families sought employment in public service and the professions or entry into elite scientific and technical schools.

At the beginning of the nineteenth century, European states showed little interest in primary education. Only in the German states was there a state-run system for it. In 1833, the French government created a system of state-run, secular schools by instructing local government to establish an elementary school for both boys and girls. None of these primary schools required attendance, however, which tended to be irregular at best. In rural society, children were still expected to work in the fields. In industrializing countries like Britain and France, both employers and parents were eager to maintain the practice of child labor.

In the decades after 1870, the functions of the state were extended to include the development of mass education in state-run systems. Most Western governments began to offer at least primary education to both boys and girls between the ages of six and twelve. In most countries, it was not optional. Austria had established free, compulsory elementary education in 1869. In France, an 1882 law made primary education compulsory for all children between six and thirteen. Elementary education was made compulsory in Britain in 1880, but it was not until 1902 that an act of Parliament brought all elementary schools under county and town control. States also assumed responsibility for the quality of teachers by establishing teacher-training schools. By 1900, many European states, especially in northern and western Europe, were providing state-financed primary schools, salaried and trained teachers, and free, compulsory elementary education for the masses.

Why did European states make this commitment to mass education? Liberals believed that education was important to personal and social improvement and also sought, as in France, to supplant Catholic education with moral and civic training based on secular values. Even conservatives were attracted to mass education as a means of improving the quality of military recruits and training people in social discipline. In 1875, a German military journal stated: "We in Germany consider education to be one of the principal ways of promoting the strength of the nation and above all military strength."[11]

Another incentive for mass education came from industrialization. In the early Industrial Revolution, unskilled labor was sufficient to meet factory needs, but the new firms of the Second Industrial Revolution demanded skilled labor. Both boys and girls with an elementary education had new possibilities of jobs beyond their villages or small towns, including white-collar jobs in railways, subway stations, post offices, banking and shipping firms, teaching, and nursing. To industrialists, then, mass education furnished the trained workers they needed.

Nevertheless, the chief motive for mass education was political. For one thing, the expansion of voting rights necessitated a more educated electorate. Even more important, however, mass compulsory education instilled patriotism and nationalized the masses, providing an opportunity for even greater national integration. As people lost their ties to local regions and even to religion, nationalism supplied a new faith. The use of a single national language created greater national unity than loyalty to a ruler did.

A nation's motives for universal elementary education largely determined what was taught in its elementary schools. Indoctrination in national values took on great importance. At the core of the academic curriculum were reading, writing, arithmetic, national history (especially geared to a patriotic view), geography, literature, and some singing and drawing. The education of boys and girls varied, however. Where possible, the sexes were separated. Girls did less math and no science but concentrated on such domestic skills as sewing, washing, ironing, and cooking, all prerequisites for providing a good home for husband and children. Boys were taught some practical skills, such as carpentry, and even some military drill. Most of the elementary schools also inculcated the middle-class virtues of hard work, thrift, sobriety, cleanliness, and respect for the family. For most students, elementary education led to apprenticeship and a job.

The development of compulsory elementary education created a demand for teachers, and most of them were female. In the United States, for example, women constituted two-thirds of all teachers by the 1880s. Many men viewed the teaching of children as an extension of women's "natural role" as nurturers of children. Moreover, females were paid lower salaries, in itself a considerable incentive for governments to encourage the establishment of teacher-training institutes for women. The first colleges for women were really teacher-training schools. In Britain, the women's colleges of Queen's and Bedford were established in the 1840s to provide teacher training for middle-class spinsters who needed to work. A pioneer in the development of female education was Barbara Bodichon (1827–1891), who established her own school where girls were trained for economic independence as well as domesticity. Not until the beginning of the twentieth century were women permitted to enter the male-dominated universities. In France, 3 percent of university students in 1902 were women; by 1914, their number had increased to 10 percent of the total.

The most immediate result of mass education was an increase in literacy. Compulsory elementary education and the growth of literacy were directly related. In Germany, Great Britain, France, and the Scandinavian countries, adult illiteracy was virtually eliminated by 1900. Where there was less schooling, the story is very different. Adult illiteracy rates were 79 percent in Serbia, 78 percent in Romania, 72 percent in Bulgaria, and 79 percent in Russia. All of these countries had made only a minimal investment in compulsory mass education.

With the dramatic increase in literacy after 1871 came the rise of mass-circulation newspapers, such as the *Evening News* (1881) and *Daily Mail* (1896) in London, which sold millions of copies a day. Known as the "yellow press" in the United States, these newspapers shared some common characteristics. They were written in an easily understood style and tended toward the sensational. Unlike eighteenth-century newspapers, which were full of serious editorials and lengthy political analyses, these tabloids provided lurid details of crimes, jingoistic diatribes, gossip, and sports news. There were other forms of cheap literature as well. Specialty magazines, such as the *Family Herald* for the entire family, and women's magazines began in the 1860s. Pulp fiction for adults included the extremely popular westerns with their innumerable variations on conflicts between cowboys and Indians. Literature for the masses was but one feature of the new mass culture; another was the emergence of new forms of leisure.

MASS LEISURE

In the preindustrial centuries, play or leisure activities had been closely connected to work patterns based on the seasonal or daily cycles typical of the life of peasants and arti-

Courtesy of Vassar College Library

A Women's College. Women were largely excluded from male-dominated universities before 1900. Consequently, the demand of women for higher education led to the foundation of women's colleges, most of which were primarily teacher-training schools. This photograph shows a group of women in an astronomy class at Vassar College in the United States in 1878. Maria Mitchell, a famous female astronomer, was head of the department.

The Fight Song: Sports in the English Public School

In the second half of the nineteenth century, organized sports were often placed at the center of the curriculum in English public schools. These sports were not just for leisure but were intended to instill character, strength, and teamwork. This "fight song" was written by H. B. Tristam for the soccer team at Loretto School.

H. B. Tristam, "Going Strong"

Sing Football the grandest of sports in the world,
And you know it yourself if your pluck's never curled,
If you've gritted your teeth and gone hard to the last,
And sworn that you'll never let anyone past.

Chorus
Keeping close upon the ball—we drive it through them all,
And again we go rushing along, along, along;
O the tackle and the run, and the matches we have won,
From the start to the finish going strong, strong, strong, going strong!

If you live to be a hundred you'll never forget
How they hacked in the scrum, how you payed back the debt;
The joy of the swing when you tackled your man,
The lust of the fray when the battle began.

Long hence when you look with a quivering eye
On the little white tassel you value so high;
You'll think of the matches you've played in and won,
And you'll long for the days that are over and done.

sans. The process of industrialization in the nineteenth century had an enormous impact on those traditional patterns. The factory imposed new work patterns that were determined by the rhythms of machines and clocks and removed work time completely from the family environment of farms and workshops. Work and leisure became opposites as leisure came to be viewed as what people did for fun when not on the job. In fact, the new leisure hours created by the industrial system—evening hours after work, weekends, and later a week or two in the summer—largely determined the contours of the new mass leisure.

New technology and business practices also determined the forms of leisure pursuits. New technology created novelties such as the Ferris wheel at amusement parks. The mechanized urban transportation systems of the 1880s meant that even the working classes were no longer dependent on neighborhood taverns but could make their way to athletic events, amusement parks, and dance halls. Likewise, railroads could take people to the beaches on weekends.

Music and dance halls appeared in the second half of the nineteenth century. The first music hall in London was constructed in 1849 for a lower-class audience. As is evident from one Londoner's observation, music halls were primarily for males:

> [They were a] popular place of Saturday night resort with working men, as at them they can combine the drinking of the Saturday night glass and smoking of the Saturday night pipe, with the seeing and hearing of a variety of entertainments, ranging from magnificent ballets and marvelous scenic illusions to inferior tumbling, and from well-given operatic selections to the most idiotic of the so-called comic songs of the Jolly Dogs Class.[12]

By the 1880s, there were five hundred music halls in London. Promoters gradually made them more respectable and broadened their fare to entice both women and children to attend the programs. The new dance halls, which were all the rage by 1900, were more strictly oriented toward adults. Contemporaries were often shocked by the sight of young people engaged in sexually suggestive dancing.

The upper and middle classes had created the first market for tourism, but as wages increased and workers were given paid vacations, tourism became another form of mass leisure. Thomas Cook (1808–1892) was a British pioneer of mass tourism. Secretary to a British temperance group, Cook had been responsible for organizing a railroad trip to temperance gatherings in 1841. This experience led him to offer trips on a regular basis after he found that he could make substantial profits by renting special trains, lowering prices, and increasing the number of passengers. In 1867, he offered tours to Paris and by the 1880s to Switzerland. Of course, overseas tours were for the industrial and commercial middle classes, but soon, thanks to savings clubs, even British factory workers were able to take weekend excursions.

Team sports had also developed into yet another form of mass leisure by the late nineteenth century. Sports were by no means a new activity. Unlike the old rural games, however, they were no longer chaotic and spontaneous activities but became strictly organized, with written rules and officials to enforce them. The rules were the products of organized athletic groups, such as the English Football Association (1863) and the American Bowling Congress (1895).

The new sports were not just for fun; like other forms of middle-class recreation, they were intended to provide training for people, especially adolescents. Not only could the participants develop individual skills, but they could also acquire a sense of teamwork useful for military service. These characteristics were already evident in the British public schools (which were really private boarding schools) in the 1850s and 1860s when such schools as Harrow, Uppingham, and Loretto placed organized sports at the center of the curriculum (see the box above). At Loretto, for example, education was supposed to instill "First—Character.

Hulton Archive/Getty Images

Soccer Moments. Until 1863, soccer in Britain was an aggressive sport with no set rules. One of the first things the new English Football Association did after it was established on October 26, 1863, was to set up fourteen rules of play. Shown here in sketches from a magazine called *The Graphic* are some scenes from a soccer game between England and Scotland in 1872. Both teams followed the new rules.

Second—Physique. Third—Intelligence. Fourth—Manners. Fifth—Information."

The new team sports rapidly became professionalized. In Britain, soccer had its Football Association in 1863 and rugby its Rugby Football Union in 1871. In the United States, the first national association to recognize professional baseball players was formed in 1863. By 1900, the National League and American League had a complete monopoly over professional baseball. The development of urban transportation systems made possible the construction of stadiums where thousands could attend, making mass spectator sports a big business. In 1872, some 2,000 people watched the British Soccer Cup finals. By 1885, the crowd had increased to 10,000 and by 1901 to 100,000. Professional teams became objects of mass adulation by crowds of urbanites who compensated for their lost sense of identity in mass urban areas by developing these new loyalties. Spectator sports even reflected class differences. Upper-class soccer teams in Britain viewed working-class teams as vicious and prone to "money-grubbing, tricks, sensational displays, and utter rottenness."

The sports cult of the late nineteenth century was mostly male-oriented. Many men believed that females were not particularly suited for "vigorous physical activity," although it was permissible for middle-class women to indulge in less active sports such as croquet and lawn tennis. Eventually, some athletics crept into women's colleges and girls' public schools in England.

Standardized forms of amusement drew mass audiences. Although some authorities argued that the new amusements were important for improving people, in truth, they served primarily to provide entertainment and distract people from the realities of their work lives. The new mass leisure also represented a significant change from earlier forms of popular culture. Festivals and fairs had been based on active and spontaneous community participation, whereas the new forms of mass leisure were businesses, standardized for largely passive mass audiences and organized to make profits.

The National State

Within the major European states, considerable progress was made in achieving liberal practices (constitutions, parliaments, and individual liberties) and reforms that encouraged the expansion of political democracy through voting rights for men and the creation of mass political parties. At the same time, however, these developments were strongly resisted in parts of Europe where the old political forces remained strong.

Western Europe: The Growth of Political Democracy

In general, parliamentary government was most firmly rooted in the western European states. Both Britain and France saw an expansion of the franchise, but liberal reforms proved less successful in Spain and Italy.

REFORM IN BRITAIN

The growth of political democracy was one of the preoccupations of British politics after 1871, and its cause was pushed along by the expansion of suffrage. Much advanced by the Reform Act of 1867 (see Chapter 22), the right to vote was further extended during the second ministry of William Gladstone (1880–1885) with the passage of the Reform Act of 1884. It gave the vote to all men who paid regular rents or taxes, thus largely enfranchising agricultural workers, a group previously excluded. The following year, the Redistribution Act eliminated historic boroughs and counties and established constituencies with approximately equal populations and one representative each. The payment of salaries to members of the House of Commons beginning in 1911 further democratized that institution by at least opening the door to people other than the wealthy. The British system of gradual reform through parliamentary institutions had become the way of British political life.

Gradual reform failed to solve the problem of Ireland, however. The Irish had long been subject to British rule, and the Act of Union of 1801 had united the English and Irish parliaments. Like other unfree ethnic groups in Europe, the Irish developed a sense of national self-consciousness. They detested the absentee British landlords and their burdensome rents.

In 1870, William Gladstone attempted to alleviate Irish discontent by enacting limited land reform, but as Irish tenants continued to be evicted in the 1870s, the Irish peasants responded with terrorist acts. When the government reacted in turn with more force, Irish Catholics began to demand independence. Although the Liberals introduced home rule bills that would have given Ireland self-government in 1886 and 1893, the bills failed to win a majority vote. When the Liberals finally enacted a Home Rule Act in 1914, an explosive situation in Ireland itself created more problems. Irish Protestants in northern Ireland, especially in the province of Ulster, wanted no part of an Irish Catholic state. The outbreak of World War I enabled the British government to sidestep the potentially explosive issue and to suspend Irish home rule for the duration of the war.

THE THIRD REPUBLIC IN FRANCE

The defeat of France by the Prussian army in 1870 brought the downfall of Louis Napoleon's Second Empire. French republicans initially set up a provisional government, but the victorious Otto von Bismarck intervened and forced the French to choose a government by universal male suffrage. The French people rejected the republicans and overwhelmingly favored the monarchists, who won 400 of the 630 seats in the new National Assembly. In response, on March 26, 1871, radical republicans formed an independent republican government in Paris known as the Commune.

But the National Assembly refused to give up its power and decided to crush the revolutionary Commune. Vicious fighting broke out in April. Many working-class men and women stepped forth to defend the Commune. At first, women's activities were the traditional ones: caring for the

Mansell/TimePix

William Gladstone in His Later Years. The first Liberal ministry of William Gladstone had been responsible for a series of significant liberal reforms. During his second ministry, Gladstone and the Liberals expanded the right to vote by enfranchising agricultural workers.

A Leader of the Paris Commune

Louise Michel was a schoolteacher in Paris who took an interest in radical ideas. She became active among revolutionary groups in Paris in 1870 and then emerged as a leader of the Paris Commune in 1871. Exiled to New Caledonia after the crushing of the Commune, she was allowed in 1880 to return to France, where she became a heroic figure among radical groups. Later, she spent three years in prison and then lived much of the time in England in self-imposed exile. In her memoirs, Michel discusses what happened on March 18,1871, when the National Assembly sent troops to seize cannons that had been moved earlier to the hills of Montmartre. She also reflected on her activities in the Commune.

Louise Michel, Memoirs

Learning that the Versailles soldiers [troops of the National Assembly] were trying to seize the cannon, men and women of Montmartre swarmed up the Butte in a surprise maneuver. Those people who were climbing believed they would die, but they were prepared to pay the price.

The Butte of Montmartre was bathed in the first light of day, through which things were glimpsed as if they were hidden behind a thin veil of water. Gradually the crowd increased. The other districts of Paris, hearing of the events taking place on the Butte of Montmartre, came to our assistance.

The women of Paris covered the cannon with their bodies. When their officers ordered the soldiers to fire, the men refused. The same army that would be used to crush Paris two months later decided now that it did not want to be an accomplice of the reaction. They gave up their attempt to seize the cannon from the National Guard. They understood that the people were defending the Republic by defending the arms that the royalists and imperialists would have turned on Paris in agreement with the Prussians. When we had won our victory, I looked around and noticed my poor mother, who had followed me to the Butte of Montmartre, believing that I was going to die.

On this day, the eighteenth of March, the people awakened. If they had not, it would have been the triumph of some king; instead it was a triumph of the people. The eighteenth of March could have belonged to the allies of kings, or to foreigners, or to the people. It was the people's. . . .

During the entire time of the Commune, I only spent one night at my poor mother's. I never really went to bed during that time. I just napped a little whenever there was nothing better to do, and many other people lived the same way. Everybody who wanted deliverance gave himself totally to the cause. . . . During the Commune I went unhurt except for a bullet that grazed my wrist, although my hat was literally riddled with bullet holes.

wounded soldiers and feeding the troops. Gradually, however, women expanded their activities to include taking care of weapons, working as scouts, and even setting up their own fighting brigades. Louise Michel (1830–1905), a schoolteacher, emerged as one of the leaders of the Paris Commune (see the box above). She proved tireless in forming committees for the defense of the revolutionary Commune.

All of these efforts were in vain, however. In the last week of May, government troops massacred thousands of the Commune's defenders. Estimates are that twenty thousand were shot; another ten thousand (including Louise Michel) were shipped to the French penal colony of New Caledonia in the South Pacific. The brutal repression of the Commune bequeathed a legacy of hatred that continued to plague French politics for decades. The split between the middle and working classes, begun in the revolutionary hostilities of 1848–1849, had widened immensely. The harsh punishment of women who participated in the revolutionary activity also served to discourage any future efforts by working-class women to improve their conditions.

Although a majority of the members of the monarchist-dominated National Assembly wished to restore a monarchy to France, inability to agree on who should be king caused the monarchists to miss their opportunity and led in 1875 to an improvised constitution that established a republican form of government as the least divisive compromise. This constitution established a bicameral legislature with an upper house, the Senate, elected indirectly and a lower house, the Chamber of Deputies, chosen by universal male suffrage; a president, selected by the legislature for a term of seven years, served as executive of the government. The Constitution of 1875, intended only as a stopgap measure, solidified the republic—the Third Republic—which lasted sixty-five years. New elections in 1876 and 1877 strengthened the hands of the republicans who managed by 1879 to institute ministerial responsibility and establish the power of the Chamber of Deputies. The prime minister or premier and his ministers were now responsible not to the president but to the Chamber of Deputies.

Although the government's moderation gradually encouraged more and more middle-class and peasant support, the position of the Third Republic remained precarious because monarchists, Catholic clergy, and professional army officers were still its enemies.

A major crisis in the 1880s, however, actually served to strengthen the republican government. General Georges

Boulanger (1837–1891) was a popular military officer who attracted the public attention of all those discontented with the Third Republic: the monarchists, Bonapartists, aristocrats, and nationalists who favored a war of revenge against Germany. Boulanger appeared as the strong man on horseback, the savior of France. By 1889, just when his strength had grown to the point where many expected a coup d'état, he lost his nerve and fled France, a completely discredited man. In the long run, the Boulanger crisis served to rally support for the resilient republic.

SPAIN AND ITALY

In Spain, a new constitution, drafted in 1875 under King Alfonso XII (1874–1885), established a parliamentary government dominated by two political groups, the Conservatives and the Liberals, whose members stemmed from the same small social group of great landowners allied with a few wealthy industrialists. Because suffrage was limited to the propertied classes, Liberals and Conservatives alternated in power but followed basically the same conservative policies. Spain's defeat in the Spanish-American War in 1898 and the loss of Cuba and the Philippines to the United States increased the discontent with the status quo. When a group of young intellectuals known as the Generation of 1898 called for political and social reforms, both Liberals and Conservatives attempted to enlarge the electorate and win the masses' support for their policies. The attempted reforms did little to allay the unrest, however, and the growth of industrialization in some areas resulted in more workers being attracted to the radical solutions of socialism and anarchism. When violence erupted in Barcelona in July 1909, the military forces brutally suppressed the rebels. The revolt and its repression made clear that reform would not be easily accomplished because the Catholic church, large landowners, and the army remained tied to a conservative social order.

By 1870, Italy had emerged as a geographically united state with pretensions to great power status. Its internal weaknesses, however, gave that claim a particularly hollow ring. Sectional differences—a poverty-stricken south and an industrializing north—weakened any sense of community. Chronic turmoil between workers and industrialists undermined the social fabric. The Italian government was unable to deal effectively with these problems because of the extensive corruption among government officials and the lack of stability created by ever-changing government coalitions. The granting of universal male suffrage in 1912 did little to correct the extensive corruption and weak government. Even Italy's pretensions to great power status proved hollow when Italy became the first European power to lose to an African state—Ethiopia.

Central and Eastern Europe: Persistence of the Old Order

Germany, Austria-Hungary, and Russia pursued political policies that were quite different from those of the western European nations. The central European states (Germany and Austria-Hungary) had the trappings of parliamentary government, including legislative bodies and elections by universal male suffrage, but authoritarian forces, especially powerful monarchies and conservative social groups, remained strong. In eastern Europe, especially Russia, the old system of autocracy was barely touched by the winds of change.

GERMANY

Despite unification, important divisions remained in German society that could not simply be papered over by the force of nationalism. These divisions were already evident in the new German constitution that provided for a federal system with a bicameral legislature. The Bundesrat, or upper house, represented the twenty-five states that made up Germany. Individual states, such as Bavaria and Prussia, kept their own kings, their own post offices, and even their own armies in peacetime. The lower house of the German parliament, the Reichstag, was elected on the basis of universal male suffrage, but it did not have ministerial responsibility. Ministers of government, the most important of which was the chancellor, were responsible not to the parliament but to the emperor. The emperor also commanded the armed forces and controlled foreign policy and internal administration. Though the creation of a parliament elected by universal male suffrage presented opportunities for the growth of a real political democracy, it failed to develop in Germany before World War I. The army and Bismarck were two major reasons why it did not.

The German (largely Prussian) army viewed itself as the defender of monarchy and aristocracy and sought to escape any control by the Reichstag by operating under a general staff responsible only to the emperor. Prussian military tradition was strong, and military officers took steps to ensure the loyalty of their subordinates to the emperor, which was easy as long as Junker landowners were officers. As the growth of the army made it necessary to turn to the middle class for officers, extreme care was taken to choose only sons "of honorable bourgeois families in whom the love for King and Fatherland, a warm heart for the soldier's calling, and Christian morality are planted and nurtured."

The policies of Bismarck, who served as chancellor of the new German state until 1890, often served to prevent the growth of more democratic institutions. At first, Bismarck worked with the liberals to achieve greater centralization of Germany through common codes of criminal and commercial law. The liberals also joined Bismarck in his attack on the Catholic church, the so-called *Kulturkampf*, or "struggle for civilization." Like Bismarck, middle-class liberals distrusted Catholic loyalty to the new Germany. Bismarck's strong-arm tactics against Catholic clergy and Catholic institutions proved counterproductive, however, and Bismarck welcomed an opportunity in 1878 to abandon the attack on Catholicism by making an abrupt shift in policy.

In 1878, Bismarck abandoned the liberals and began to persecute the socialists. When the Social Democratic Party elected twelve deputies to the Reichstag in 1877, Bismarck grew alarmed. He genuinely believed that the socialists' antinationalistic, anticapitalistic, and antimonarchical stance represented a danger to the empire. In 1878, Bismarck got parliament to pass a stringent antisocialist law that outlawed the Social Democratic Party and limited socialist meetings and publications, although socialist candidates were still permitted to run for the Reichstag. In addition to repressive measures, Bismarck also attempted to woo workers away from socialism by enacting social welfare legislation (see the box on p. 669). Between 1883 and 1889, the Reichstag passed laws that established sickness, accident, and disability benefits as well as old-age pensions financed by compulsory contributions from workers, employers, and the state. Bismarck's social security system was the most progressive the world had yet seen, although even his system left much to be desired, as the Social Democrats pointed out. A full pension, for example, was payable only at age seventy after forty-eight years of contributions. In the event of a male worker's death, no benefits were paid to his widow or children.

Both the repressive and the social welfare measures failed to stop the growth of socialism, however. The Social Democratic Party continued to grow. In his frustration, Bismarck planned still more repressive measures in 1890, but before he could carry them out, the new emperor, William II (1888–1918), eager to pursue his own policies, cashiered the aged chancellor.

CHRONOLOGY

The National States, 1871–1894

Great Britain	
Second ministry of William Gladstone	1880–1885
Reform Act	1884
France	
Surrender of French provisional government to Germany	1871 (January 28)
Paris Commune	1871 (March–May)
Republican constitution (Third Republic)	1875
Boulanger is discredited	1889
Spain	
King Alfonso XII	1874–1885
New constitution	1875
Defeat in Spanish-American War	1898
Germany	
Bismarck as chancellor	1871–1890
Antisocialist law	1878
Social welfare legislation	1883–1889
Austria-Hungary	
Emperor Francis Joseph	1848–1916
Count Edward von Taaffe as prime minister	1879–1893
Russia	
Tsar Alexander III	1881–1894

CORBIS

Bismarck and William II. In 1890, Bismarck sought to undertake new repressive measures against the Social Democrats. Disagreeing with this policy, Emperor William II forced him to resign. This political cartoon shows William II reclining on a throne made of artillery and cannonballs and holding a doll labeled "socialism." Bismarck bids farewell as Germany, personified as a woman, looks on with grave concern.

Bismarck and the Welfare of the Workers

In his attempt to win workers away from socialism, Bismarck favored an extensive program of social welfare benefits, including old-age pensions and compensation for absence from work due to sickness, accident, and disability. This selection is taken from Bismarck's address to the Reichstag on March 10, 1884, in which he explained his motives for social welfare legislation.

■ *Bismarck,* Address to the Reichstag

The positive efforts began really only in the year . . . 1881 . . . with the imperial message . . . in which His Majesty William I said: "Already in February of this year, we have expressed our conviction that the healing of social ills is not to be sought exclusively by means of repression of Social Democratic excesses, but equally in the positive promotion of the welfare of the workers."

In consequence of this, first of all the insurance law against accidents was submitted. . . . And it reads . . . "But those who have, through age or disability, become incapable of working have a confirmed claim on all for a higher degree of state care than could have been their share heretofore. . . ."

The workers' real sore point is the insecurity of his existence. He is not always sure he will always have work. He is not sure he will always be healthy, and he foresees some day he will be old and incapable of work. But also if he falls into poverty as a result of long illness, he is completely helpless with his own powers, and society hitherto does not recognize relief, even when he has worked ever so faithfully and diligently before. But ordinary poor relief leaves much to be desired, especially in the great cities where it is extraordinarily much worse than in the country. . . . We read in Berlin newspapers of suicide because of difficulty in making both ends meet, of people who died from direct hunger and have hanged themselves because they have nothing to eat, of people who announce in the paper they were tossed out homeless and have no income. . . . For the worker it is always a fact that falling into poverty and onto poor relief in a great city is synonymous with misery, and this insecurity makes him hostile and mistrustful of society. That is humanly not unnatural, and as long as the state does not meet him halfway, just as long will this trust in the state's honesty be taken from him by accusations against the government, which he will find where he wills; always running back again to the socialist quacks . . . and, without great reflection, letting himself be promised things, which will not be fulfilled. On this account, I believe that accident insurance, with which we show the way, . . . will still work on the anxieties and ill-feeling of the working class.

AUSTRIA-HUNGARY

After the creation of the Dual Monarchy of Austria-Hungary in 1867, the Austrian part received a constitution that established a parliamentary system with the principle of ministerial responsibility. But Emperor Francis Joseph largely ignored ministerial responsibility and proceeded to personally appoint and dismiss his ministers and rule by decree when parliament was not in session.

The problem of the minorities continued to trouble the empire. The ethnic Germans, who made up only one-third of Austria's population, governed Austria but felt increasingly threatened by the Czechs, Poles, and other Slavic groups within the empire. The difficulties in dealing with this problem were especially evident from 1879 to 1893 when Count Edward von Taaffe served as prime minister. Taaffe attempted to "muddle through" by relying on a coalition of German conservatives, Czechs, and Poles to maintain a majority in parliament. But his concessions to national minorities, such as allowing the Slavic languages as well as German to be used in education and administration, served to antagonize the German-speaking Austrian bureaucracy and aristocracy, two of the basic pillars of the empire. Opposition to Taaffe's policies brought his downfall in 1893 but did not solve the nationalities problem. While the dissatisfied non-German groups demanded concessions, the ruling Austrian Germans resisted change. The granting of universal male suffrage in 1907 served only to make the problem worse as nationalities that had played no role in the government now agitated in the parliament for autonomy. This led prime ministers after 1900 to ignore the parliament and rely increasingly on imperial emergency decrees to govern.

Unlike Austria, Hungary had a working parliamentary system, but it was controlled by the great Magyar landowners who dominated both the Hungarian peasantry and the other ethnic groups in Hungary. The Hungarians attempted to solve their nationalities problem by systematic Magyarization. The Magyar language was imposed on all schools and was the only language that could be used by government and military officials.

RUSSIA

In Russia, the government made no concession whatever to liberal and democratic reforms. The assassination of Alexander II in 1881 convinced his son and successor, Alexander III (1881–1894), that reform had been a mistake, and he quickly instituted what he said were "exceptional measures." The powers of the secret police were expanded. Advocates of constitutional monarchy and social reform, along with revolutionary groups, were persecuted. Entire districts of Russia were placed under martial law if the government suspected the inhabitants of treason. The powers of the zemstvos, created by the reforms of Alexander II, were sharply curtailed. When Alexander III died, his weak son and successor, Nicholas II (1894–1917), adopted his father's conviction that the absolute power of the tsars should be preserved: "I shall maintain the principle of autocracy just as firmly and unflinchingly as did my unforgettable father."[13] But conditions were changing, especially with the growth of industrialization, and the tsar's approach was not realistic in view of the new circumstances he faced.

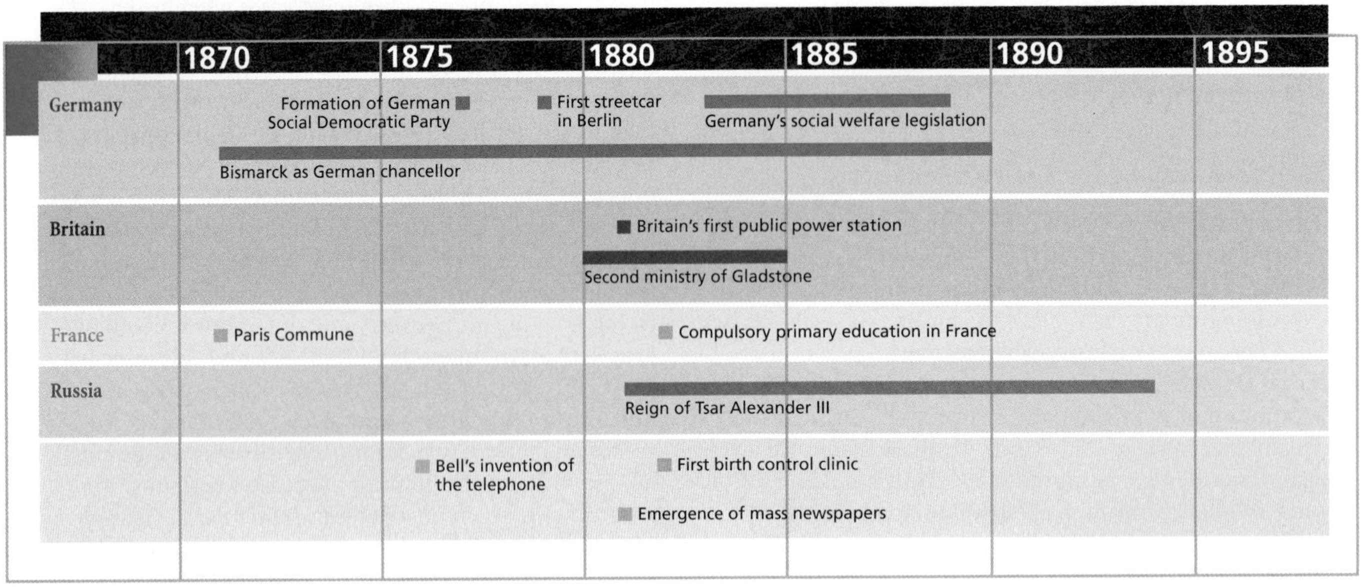

Conclusion

The Second Industrial Revolution helped create a new material prosperity that led Europeans to believe they had ushered in a new age of progress. A major feature of this age was the emergence of a mass society. The lower classes in particular benefited from the right to vote, a higher standard of living, and new schools that provided them with a modicum of education. New forms of mass transportation, combined with new work patterns, enabled large numbers of people to enjoy weekend excursions to amusement parks and seaside resorts and to participate in new leisure activities.

By 1871, the national state had become the focus of people's lives. Liberal and democratic reforms brought new possibilities for greater participation in the political process, although women were still largely excluded from political rights. After 1871, the national state also began to expand its functions beyond all previous limits. Fearful of the growth of socialism and trade unions, governments attempted to appease the working masses by adopting such social insurance measures as protection against accidents, illness, and old age. These social welfare measures were narrow in scope and limited in benefits, but they signaled a new direction for state action to benefit the mass of its citizens. The enactment of public health and housing measures, designed to curb the worst ills of urban living, were yet another indication of how state power could be used to benefit the people.

This extension of state functions took place in an atmosphere of increased national loyalty. After 1871, nation-states increasingly sought to solidify the social order and win the active loyalty and support of their citizens by deliberately cultivating national feelings. Yet this policy contained potentially great dangers. As we shall see in the next chapter, nations had discovered once again that imperialistic adventures and military successes could arouse nationalistic passions and smother domestic political unrest. But they also found that nationalistic feelings could lead to intense international rivalries that made war almost inevitable.

Notes

1. Quoted in David Landes, *The Unbound Prometheus: Technological Change and Industrial Development in Western Europe from 1750 to the Present* (Cambridge, 1969), p. 353.
2. Quoted in Barbara Franzoi, ". . . With the Wolf Always at the Door: Women's Work in Domestic Industry in Britain and Germany," in Marilyn J. Boxer and Jean H. Quataert, eds., *Connecting Spheres: Women in the Western World, 1500 to the Present* (New York, 1987), p. 151.
3. Quoted in W. L. Guttsman, *The German Social Democratic Party, 1875–1933* (London, 1981), p. 63.
4. Quoted in Leslie Derfler, *Socialism Since Marx: A Century of the European Left* (New York, 1973), p. 58.
5. Karl Marx and Friedrich Engels, *The Communist Manifesto* (Harmondsworth, England, 1967), p. 102.

6. Quoted in Paul Avrich, *The Russian Anarchists* (Princeton, N.J., 1971), p. 67.
7. Quoted in Nicholas Bullock and James Read, *The Movement for Housing Reform in Germany and France, 1840–1914* (Cambridge, 1985), p. 42.
8. Quoted in Gary Cross, *A Social History of Leisure Since 1600* (State College, Pa., 1990), pp. 116, 119.
9. Quoted in Sibylle Meyer, "The Tiresome Work of Conspicuous Leisure: On the Domestic Duties of the Wives of Civil Servants in the German Empire (1871–1918)," in Boxer and Quataert, *Connecting Spheres,* p. 161.
10. Quoted in Lenard R. Berlanstein, *The Working People of Paris, 1871–1914* (Baltimore, 1984), p. 141.
11. Quoted in Robert Gildea, *Barricades and Borders: Europe, 1800–1914,* 2d ed. (Oxford, 1996), pp. 240–241.
12. Quoted in Cross, *Social History of Leisure,* p. 130.
13. Quoted in Shmuel Galai, *The Liberation Movement in Russia, 1900–1905* (Cambridge, 1973), p. 26.

Suggestions for Further Reading

In addition to the general works on the nineteenth century and individual European countries cited in Chapters 21 and 22, two more specialized works on the subject matter of this chapter are available in N. Stone, *Europe Transformed, 1878–1919* (London, 1983), and F. Gilbert, *The End of the European Era, 1890 to the Present,* 4th ed. (New York, 1991).

The subject of the Second Industrial Revolution is well covered in D. Landes, *The Unbound Prometheus,* cited in Chapter 20. For a fundamental survey of European industrialization, see A. S. Milward and S. B. Saul, *The Development of the Economies of Continental Europe, 1850–1914* (Cambridge, Mass., 1977). For an introduction to the development of mass consumerism in Britain, see W. H. Fraser, *The Coming of the Mass Market, 1850–1914* (Hamden, Conn., 1981). The impact of the new technology on European thought is imaginatively discussed in S. Kern, *The Culture of Time and Space, 1880–1918* (Cambridge, Mass., 1983).

For an introduction to international socialism, see A. Lindemann, *A History of European Socialism* (New Haven, Conn., 1983), and L. Derfler, *Socialism Since Marx: A Century of the European Left* (New York, 1973). On the emergence of German social democracy, see W. L. Guttsman, *The German Social Democratic Party, 1875–1933* (London, 1981). A good introduction to anarchism is R. D. Sonn, *Anarchism* (New York, 1992).

Demographic problems are examined in T. McKeown, *The Modern Rise of Population* (New York, 1976). On European emigration, see L. P. Moch, *Moving Europeans: Migration in Western Europe Since 1650* (Bloomington, Ind., 1993).

For a good introduction to housing reform on the Continent, see N. Bullock and J. Read, *The Movement for Housing Reform in Germany and France, 1840–1914* (Cambridge, 1985). Working-class housing in Paris during its reconstruction is the subject of A. L. Shapiro, *Housing the Poor of Paris, 1850–1902* (Madison, Wis., 1985).

An interesting work on aristocratic life is D. Cannadine, *The Decline and Fall of the British Aristocracy* (New Haven, Conn., 1990). On the middle classes, see P. Pilbeam, *The Middle Classes in Europe, 1789–1914* (Basingstoke, England, 1990). On the working classes, see L. Berlanstein, *The Working People of Paris, 1871–1914* (Baltimore, 1984), and R. Magraw, *A History of the French Working Class* (Cambridge, Mass., 1992).

There are good overviews of women's experiences in the nineteenth century in B. G. Smith, *Changing Lives: Women in European History Since 1700* (Lexington, Mass., 1989), and M. J. Boxer and J. H. Quataert, eds., *Connecting Spheres: Women in the Western World, 1500 to the Present* (New York, 1987). The world of women's work is examined in L. A. Tilly and J. W. Scott, *Women, Work, and Family* (New York, 1978). Important studies of women include M. J. Peterson, *Family, Love and Work in the Lives of Victorian Gentlewomen* (Bloomington, Ind., 1989); B. G. Smith, *Ladies of the Leisure Class: The Bourgeoises of Northern France in the Nineteenth Century* (Princeton, N.J., 1981); P. Robertson, *An Experience of Women: Pattern and Change in Nineteenth-Century Europe* (Philadelphia, 1982); and B. Franzoi, *At the Very Least She Pays the Rent: Women and German Industrialization, 1871–1914* (Westport, Conn., 1985). Prostitution is discussed in J. R. Walkowitz, *Prostitution and Victorian Society: Women, Class and the State* (Cambridge, 1980).

On various aspects of education, see M. J. Maynes, *Schooling in Western Europe: A Social History* (Albany, N.Y., 1985), and J. S. Hurt, *Elementary Schooling and the Working Classes, 1860–1918* (London, 1979). A concise and well-presented survey of leisure patterns is G. Cross, *A Social History of Leisure Since 1600* (State College, Pa., 1990).

The domestic politics of the period can be examined in the general works on individual countries listed in the bibliographies for Chapters 21 and 22. There are also specialized works on aspects of each country's history. On Britain, see D. Read, *The Age of Urban Democracy: England, 1868–1914* (New York, 1994). The Irish problem is covered in O. MacDonagh, *States of Mind: A Study of Anglo-Irish Conflict, 1780–1980* (London, 1983). For a detailed examination of French history during the Third Republic, see J. M. Mayeur and M. Reberioux, *The Third Republic from Its Origins to the Great War, 1871–1914* (Cambridge, 1984). On the Paris Commune, see R. Tombs, *The War Against Paris, 1871* (Cambridge, 1981). On Italy, see C. Seton-Watson, *Italy from Liberalism to Fascism* (London, 1967). On Germany, see W. J. Mommsen, *Imperial Germany, 1867–1918* (New York, 1995), and V. R. Berghahn, *Imperial Germany, 1871–1914* (Providence, R.I., 1995). On the nationalities problem in the Austro-Hungarian Empire, see R. Kann, *The Multinational Empire: Nationalism and National Reform in the Habsburg Monarchy, 1848–1918,* 2 vols. (New York, 1950). On aspects of Russian history, see H. Rogger, *Russia in the Age of Modernization and Revolution, 1881–1917* (London, 1983).

For additional reading, go to InfoTrac College Edition, your online research library at http://web1.infotrac-college.com

Enter the search term *Marxism* using Key Terms.

Enter the search term *anarchism* using Key Terms.

Enter the search term *family nineteenth century* using Key Terms.

Enter the search term *socialism history* using Key Terms.

CHAPTER

24

An Age of Modernity, Anxiety, and Imperialism, 1894–1914

CHAPTER OUTLINE

- Toward the Modern Consciousness: Intellectual and Cultural Developments
- Politics: New Directions and New Uncertainties
- The New Imperialism
- International Rivalry and the Coming of War
- Conclusion

FOCUS QUESTIONS

- What developments in science, intellectual affairs, and the arts in the late nineteenth and early twentieth centuries "opened the way to a modern consciousness," and how did this consciousness differ from earlier worldviews?
- What difficulties did women, Jews, and the working classes face in the late nineteenth and early twentieth centuries, and how successful were they in achieving their goals?
- What were the causes of the new imperialism that took place after 1880, and what effects did the European quest for colonies have on Africa and Asia?
- What was the Bismarckian system of alliances, and how successful was it at keeping the peace?
- What issues lay behind the international crises that Europe faced in the late nineteenth and early twentieth centuries?
- What is the connection between the "new imperialism" of the late nineteenth century and the underlying causes for World War I?

MANY EUROPEANS after 1894 continued to believe they lived in an era of material and human progress. For some, however, progress entailed much struggle. Emmeline Pankhurst, who became the leader of the women's suffrage movement in Britain, said that her determination to fight for women's rights stemmed from a childhood memory: "My father bent over me, shielding the candle flame with his big hand and I heard him say, somewhat sadly, 'What a pity she wasn't born a lad.'" Eventually, Emmeline Pankhurst and her daughters marched and fought for women's right to vote. The struggle was often violent: "They came in bruised, hatless, faces scratched, eyes swollen, noses bleeding," one of the Pankhurst daughters recalled. Arrested and jailed in 1908, Pankhurst informed her judges: "If you had the power to send us to prison, not for six months, but for six years, or for our lives, the Government must not think they could stop this agitation. It would go on!" It did go on, and women in Britain did eventually receive the right to vote; to some, this was yet another confirmation of Europe's progress.

But the period after 1894 was not just a time of progress; it was also a time of great tension as imperialist adventures, international rivalries, and cultural uncertainties disturbed the apparent calm. After 1880, Europeans engaged in a great race for colonies around the world. This competition for lands abroad greatly intensified existing antagonisms among European states.

Ultimately, Europeans proved incapable of finding constructive ways to cope with their international rivalries. The development of two large alliance systems—the Triple Alliance and the Triple Entente—may have helped preserve peace for a time, but eventually the alliances made it easier for the European nations to be drawn into World War I. The alliances helped maintain a balance of power but also led to the creation of large armies, enormous military establishments, and immense arsenals. The alliances also generated tensions that were unleashed when Europeans rushed into the catastrophic carnage of World War I.

The cultural life of Europe in the decades before 1914 reflected similar dynamic tensions. The advent of mass education produced better-informed citizens, but also made it easier for governments to stir up the masses by nationalistic appeals through the new mass journalism. At the same time, despite the appearance of progress, European philosophers, writers, and artists were creating modern cultural expressions that questioned traditional ideas and values and incited a crisis of confidence. Before 1914, many intellectuals had a sense of unease about the direction society was heading, accompanied by a feeling of imminent catastrophe. They proved remarkably prophetic.

Toward the Modern Consciousness: Intellectual and Cultural Developments

Before 1914, most Europeans continued to believe in the values and ideals that had been generated by the Scientific Revolution and the Enlightenment. *Reason, science,* and *progress* were still important words in the European vocabulary. The ability of human beings to improve themselves and achieve a better society seemed to be well demonstrated by a rising standard of living, urban improvements, and mass education. Such products of modern technology as electric lights, phonographs, and automobiles reinforced the popular prestige of science and the belief in the ability of the human mind to comprehend the universe through the use of reason. Near the end of the nineteenth century, however, a dramatic transformation in the realm of ideas and culture challenged many of these assumptions. A new view of the physical universe, an appeal to the irrational, alternative views of human nature, and radically innovative forms of literary and artistic expression shattered old beliefs and opened the way to a modern consciousness. These new ideas called forth a sense of confusion and anxiety that would become even more pronounced after World War I.

Developments in the Sciences: The Emergence of a New Physics

Science was one of the chief pillars supporting the optimistic and rationalistic view of the world that many Westerners shared in the nineteenth century. Supposedly based on hard facts and cold reason, science offered a certainty of belief in the orderliness of nature that was comforting to many people for whom traditional religious beliefs no longer had much meaning. Many naively believed that the application of already known scientific laws would give humanity a complete understanding of the physical world and an accurate picture of reality. The new physics dramatically altered that perspective.

Throughout much of the nineteenth century, Westerners adhered to the mechanical conception of the universe postulated by the classical physics of Isaac Newton. In this perspective, the universe was viewed as a giant machine in which time, space, and matter were objective realities that existed independently of the people observing them. Matter was thought to be composed of indivisible solid material bodies called atoms.

These views were first seriously questioned at the end of the nineteenth century. The French scientist Marie Curie (1867–1934) and her husband Pierre (1859–1906) discovered that the element radium gave off rays of radiation that apparently came from within the atom itself. Atoms were not simply hard, material bodies but small worlds containing such subatomic particles as electrons and protons that behaved in seemingly random and inexplicable fashion. Inquiry into the disintegrative process within atoms became a central theme of the new physics.

Building on this work, in 1900, a Berlin physicist, Max Planck (1858–1947), rejected the belief that a heated body radiates energy in a steady stream but maintained instead that energy is radiated discontinuously, in irregular packets that he called "quanta." The quantum theory raised fundamental questions about the subatomic realm of the atom. By 1900, the old view of atoms as the basic building blocks of the material world was being seriously questioned, and the world of Newtonian physics was in trouble.

AP/Wide World Photos

Marie Curie. Marie Curie was born in Warsaw, Poland, but studied at the University of Paris, where she received degrees in both physics and mathematics. She was the first woman to win two Nobel Prizes, one in 1903 in physics and another in chemistry in 1911. She is shown here in her Paris laboratory in 1921.

Albert Einstein (1879–1955), a German-born patent officer working in Switzerland, pushed these new theories of thermodynamics into new terrain. In 1905, Einstein published a paper titled "The Electro-dynamics of Moving Bodies" that contained his special theory of relativity. According to relativity theory, space and time are not absolute but relative to the observer, and both are interwoven into what Einstein called a four-dimensional space-time continuum. Neither space nor time had an existence independent of human experience. As Einstein later explained simply to a journalist: "It was formerly believed that if all material things disappeared out of the universe, time and space would be left. According to the relativity theory, however, time and space disappear together with the things."[1] Moreover, matter and energy reflected the relativity of time and space. Einstein concluded that matter was nothing but another form of energy. His epochal formula $E = mc^2$—each particle of matter is equivalent to its mass times the square of the velocity of light—was the key theory explaining the vast energies contained within the atom. It led to the atomic age.

Many scientists were unable to comprehend Einstein's ideas, but during a total eclipse of the sun in May 1919, scientists were able to demonstrate that light was deflected in the gravitational field of the sun, just as Einstein had predicted. This confirmed Einstein's general theory of relativity and opened the scientific and intellectual world to his ideas. The 1920s would become the "heroic age" of physics.

Toward a New Understanding of the Irrational

Intellectually, the decades before 1914 witnessed a combination of contradictory developments. Thanks to the influence of science, confidence in human reason and progress still remained a dominant thread. At the same time, however, a small group of intellectuals attacked the idea of optimistic progress, dethroned reason, and glorified the irrational.

Friedrich Nietzsche (1844–1900) was one of the intellectuals who glorified the irrational. According to Nietzsche, Western bourgeois society was decadent and incapable of any real cultural creativity, primarily because of its excessive emphasis on the rational faculty at the expense of emotions, passions, and instincts. Reason, Nietzsche claimed, actually played little role in human life because humans were at the mercy of irrational life forces.

Nietzsche believed that Christianity should shoulder much of the blame for Western civilization's enfeeblement. The "slave morality" of Christianity, he believed, had obliterated the human impulse for life and had crushed the human will:

> I call Christianity the one great curse, the one enormous and innermost perversion. . . . I call it the one immortal blemish of mankind. . . . Christianity has taken the side of everything weak, base, ill-constituted, it has made an ideal out of opposition to the preservative instincts of strong life. . . . Christianity is called the religion of pity.—Pity stands in antithesis to the basic emotions which enhance the energy of the feeling of life: it has a depressive effect. One loses force when one pities.[2]

How, then, could Western society be renewed? First, said Nietzsche, one must recognize that "God is dead." Europeans had killed God, he said, and it was no longer possible to believe in some kind of cosmic order. Eliminating God and hence Christian morality had liberated human beings and made it possible to create a higher kind of being Nietzsche called the superman: "I teach you the Superman. Man is something that is to be surpassed."[3] Superior intellectuals must free themselves from the ordinary thinking of the masses, create their own values, and lead the masses. Nietzsche rejected and condemned political democracy, social reform, and universal suffrage.

Another popular revolutionary against reason in the 1890s was Henri Bergson (1859–1941), a French philosopher whose lectures at the University of Paris made him one of the most important influences in French thought in the early twentieth century. Bergson accepted rational, sci-

Freud and the Concept of Repression

Freud's psychoanalytical theories resulted from his attempt to understand the world of the unconscious. This excerpt is taken from a lecture given in 1909 in which Freud describes how he arrived at his theory of the role of repression. Although Freud valued science and reason, his theories of the unconscious produced a new image of the human being as governed less by reason than by irrational forces.

Sigmund Freud, Five Lectures on Psychoanalysis

I did not abandon it [his technique of encouraging patients to reveal forgotten experiences], however, before the observations I made during my use of it afforded me decisive evidence. I found confirmation of the fact that the forgotten memories were not lost. They were in the patient's possession and were ready to emerge in association to what was still known by him; but there was some force that prevented them from becoming conscious and compelled them to remain unconscious. The existence of this force could be assumed with certainty, since one became aware of an effort corresponding to it if, in opposition to it, one tried to introduce the unconscious memories into the patient's consciousness. The force which was maintaining the pathological condition became apparent in the form of resistance on the part of the patient.

It was on this idea of resistance, then, that I based my view of the course of physical events in hysteria. In order to effect a recovery, it had proved necessary to remove these resistances. Starting out from the mechanism of cure, it now became possible to construct quite definite ideas of the origin of the illness. The same forces which, in the form of resistance, were now offering opposition to the forgotten material's being made conscious, must formerly have brought about the forgetting and must have pushed the pathogenic experiences in question out of consciousness. I gave the name of "repression" to this hypothetical process, and I considered that it was proved by the undeniable existence of resistance.

The further question could then be raised as to what these forces were and what the determinants were of the repression in which we now recognized the pathogenic mechanism of hysteria. A comparative study of the pathogenic situations which we had come to know through the cathartic procedure made it possible to answer this question. All these experiences had involved the emergence of a wishful impulse which was in sharp contrast to the subject's other wishes and which proved incompatible with the ethical and aesthetic standards of his personality. There had been a short conflict, and the end of this internal struggle was that the idea which had appeared before consciousness as the vehicle of this irreconcilable wish fell a victim to repression, was pushed out of consciousness with all its attached memories, and was forgotten. Thus the incompatibility of the wish in question with the patient's ego was the motive for the repression; the subject's ethical and other standards were the repressing forces. An acceptance of the incompatible wishful impulse or a prolongation of the conflict would have produced a high degree of unpleasure; this unpleasure was avoided by means of repression, which was thus revealed as one of the devices serving to protect the mental personality.

entific thought as a practical instrument for providing useful knowledge but maintained that it was incapable of arriving at truth or ultimate reality. To him, reality was the "life force" that suffused all things; it could not be divided into analyzable parts. Reality was a whole that could only be grasped intuitively and experienced directly. When we analyze it, we have merely a description, no longer the reality we have experienced.

Georges Sorel (1847–1922), a French political theorist, combined Bergson's and Nietzsche's ideas on the limits of rational thinking with his own passionate interest in revolutionary socialism. Sorel understood the political potential of the nonrational and advocated violent action as the only sure way to achieve the aims of socialism. To destroy capitalist society, he recommended the use of the general strike, envisioning it as a mythic image that had the power to inspire workers to take violent, heroic action against the capitalist order. Sorel also came to believe that the new socialist society would have to be governed by a small elite ruling body because the masses were incapable of ruling themselves.

Sigmund Freud and Psychoanalysis

Around the turn of the twentieth century, a Viennese doctor, Sigmund Freud (1856–1939), put forth a series of theories that undermined optimism about the rational nature of the human mind. Freud's thought, like the new physics and the irrationalism of Nietzsche, added to the uncertainties of the age. His major ideas were published in 1900 in *The Interpretation of Dreams,* which contained the basic foundation of what came to be known as psychoanalysis.

According to Freud, human behavior was strongly determined by the unconscious, by earlier experiences and inner forces of which people were largely oblivious. To explore the content of the unconscious, Freud relied not only on hypnosis but also on dreams, but the latter were dressed in an elaborate code that had to be deciphered if the content were to be properly understood.

But why did some experiences whose influence persisted in controlling an individual's life remain unconscious? According to Freud, the answer was repression (see the box above), a process by which unsettling experiences were

Sigmund Freud. Freud was one of the intellectual giants of the nineteenth century. His belief that unconscious forces strongly determine human behavior formed the foundation for twentieth-century psychoanalysis.

blotted from conscious awareness but still continued to influence behavior because they had become part of the unconscious. To explain how repression worked, Freud elaborated an intricate theory of the inner life of human beings.

According to Freud, a human being's inner life was a battleground of three contending forces: the id, ego, and superego. The id was the center of unconscious drives and was ruled by what Freud termed the pleasure principle. As creatures of desire, human beings directed their energy toward pleasure and away from pain. The id contained all kinds of lustful drives and desires and crude appetites and impulses. The ego was the seat of reason and hence the coordinator of the inner life. It was governed by the reality principle. Although humans were dominated by the pleasure principle, a true pursuit of pleasure was not feasible. The reality principle meant that people rejected pleasure so that they might live together in society. The superego was the locus of conscience and represented the inhibitions and moral values that society in general and parents in particular imposed on people. The superego served to force the ego to curb the unsatisfactory drives of the id.

The human being was thus a battleground among id, ego, and superego. Ego and superego exerted restraining influences on the unconscious id and repressed or kept out of consciousness what they wanted to. The most important repressions, according to Freud, were sexual, and he went on to develop a theory of infantile sexual drives embodied in the Oedipus complex (Electra complex for females), or the infant's craving for exclusive possession of the parent of the opposite sex. Repression began in childhood, and psychoanalysis was accomplished through a dialogue between psychotherapist and patient in which the therapist probed deeply into memory in order to retrace the chain of repression all the way back to its childhood origins. By making the conscious mind aware of the unconscious and its repressed contents, the patient's psychic conflict was resolved.

Although many of Freud's ideas have been shown to be wrong in many details, he is still regarded as an important figure because of the impact his theories have had.

The Impact of Darwin: Social Darwinism and Racism

In the second half of the nineteenth century, scientific theories were sometimes wrongly applied to achieve other ends. The application of Darwin's principle of organic evolution to the social order came to be known as social Darwinism. The most popular exponent of social Darwinism was the British philosopher Herbert Spencer (1820–1903). Using Darwin's terminology, Spencer argued that societies were organisms that evolved through time from a struggle with their environment. Progress came from "the struggle for survival," as the "fit"—the strong—advanced while the weak declined. As Spencer expressed it in 1896 in his book *Social Statics:*

> Pervading all Nature we may see at work a stern discipline which is a little cruel that it may be very kind. . . . Meanwhile, the well-being of existing humanity and the unfolding of it into this ultimate perfection, are both secured by the same beneficial though severe discipline to which the animate creation at large is subject. It seems hard that an unskillfulness, which with all his efforts he cannot overcome, should entail hunger upon the artisan. It seems hard that a laborer, incapacitated by sickness from competing with his stronger fellows, should have to bear the resulting privations. It seems hard that widows and orphans should be left to struggle for life or death. Nevertheless, when regarded not separately but in connection with the interests of universal humanity, these harsh fatalities are seen to be full of beneficence—the same beneficence which brings to early graves the children of diseased parents, and singles out the intemperate and the debilitated as the victims of an epidemic.[4]

The state should not intervene in this natural process.

Darwin's ideas were also applied to human society in an even more radical way by rabid nationalists and racists. In their pursuit of national greatness, extreme nationalists argued that nations, too, were engaged in a "struggle for existence" in which only the fittest survived. The German general Friedrich von Bernhardi argued in 1907:

> War is a biological necessity of the first importance, a regulative element in the life of mankind which cannot be dispensed with, since without it an unhealthy development will follow, which excludes every advancement of the race, and therefore all real civilization. "War is the father of all things." The sages of antiquity long before Darwin recognized this.[5]

Numerous nationalist organizations preached the same doctrine as Bernhardi. The Nationalist Association of Italy, for example, founded in 1910, declared that "we must teach Italy the value of international struggle. But international struggle is war? Well, then, let there be war! And nationalism will arouse the will for a victorious war, . . . the only way to national redemption."[6]

Racism, too, was dramatically revived and strengthened by new biological arguments. Perhaps nowhere was the combination of extreme nationalism and racism more evident and more dangerous than in Germany. The concept of the *Volk* (nation, people, or race) had been an underlying idea in German history since the beginning of the nineteenth century. One of the chief propagandists for German volkish ideology at the turn of the twentieth century was Houston Stewart Chamberlain (1855–1927), an Englishman who became a German citizen. His book *The Foundations of the Nineteenth Century,* published in 1899, made a special impact on Germany. Modern-day Germans, according to Chamberlain, were the only pure successors of the "Aryans," who were portrayed as the true and original creators of Western culture. The Aryan race, under German leadership, must be prepared to fight for Western civilization and save it from the destructive assaults of such lower races as Jews, Negroes, and Orientals. Increasingly, Jews were singled out by German volkish nationalists as the racial enemy in biological terms and as parasites who wanted to destroy the Aryan race.

The Attack on Christianity and the Response of the Churches

The growth of scientific thinking as well as the forces of modernization presented new challenges to the Christian churches. Industrialization and urbanization had an especially adverse effect on religious institutions. The mass migration of people from the countryside to the city meant a change from the close-knit, traditional ties of the village in which the church had been a key force to new urban patterns of social life from which the churches were often excluded. The established Christian churches had a weak hold on workers.

The political movements of the late nineteenth century were also hostile to the established Christian churches. Beginning during the eighteenth-century Enlightenment and continuing well into the nineteenth century, European governments, especially in predominantly Catholic countries, had imposed controls over church courts, religious orders, and appointments of the clergy. But after the failure of the revolutions of 1848, governments were eager to use the churches' aid in reestablishing order and therefore relaxed these controls.

Eventually, however, the close union of state authorities with established churches produced a backlash in the form of anticlericalism, especially in the liberal nation-states of the late nineteenth century. As one example, in the 1880s, the French republican government substituted civic training for religious instruction in order to undermine the Catholic church's control of education. In 1901, Catholic teaching orders were outlawed, and four years later, in 1905, church and state were completely separated.

Science became one of the chief threats to all the Christian churches and even to religion itself in the nineteenth century. Darwin's theory of evolution, accepted by ever-larger numbers of educated Europeans, seemed to contradict the doctrine of divine creation. By seeking to suppress Darwin's books and to forbid the teaching of the evolutionary hypothesis, the churches often caused even more educated people to reject established religions.

The scientific spirit also encouraged a number of biblical scholars to apply critical principles to the Bible, leading to the so-called higher criticism. One of its leading exponents was Ernst Renan (1823–1892), a French Catholic scholar. In his *Life of Jesus,* Renan questioned the historical accuracy of the Bible and presented a radically different picture of Jesus. He saw Jesus not as the son of God but as a human being whose value lay in the example he provided by his life and teaching.

One response of the Christian churches to these attacks was the outright rejection of modern ideas and forces. Protestant fundamentalist sects were especially important in maintaining a literal interpretation of the Bible. The Catholic church under Pope Pius IX (1846–1878) also took a rigid stand against modern ideas. In 1864, Pope Pius issued a papal encyclical called the *Syllabus of Errors* in which he stated that it is "an error to believe that the Roman Pontiff can and ought to reconcile himself to, and agree with, progress, liberalism, and modern civilization." He condemned nationalism, socialism, religious toleration, and freedom of speech and press.

Rejection of the new was not the churches' only response, however. A religious movement called Modernism included an attempt by the churches to reinterpret Christianity in the light of new developments. The modernists viewed the Bible as a book of useful moral ideas, encouraged Christians to become involved in social reforms, and insisted that the churches must provide a greater sense of community. The Catholic church condemned Modernism in 1907 and had driven it underground by the beginning of World War I.

Yet another response of the Christian churches to modern ideas was compromise, an approach especially evident in the Catholic church during the pontificate of Leo XIII (1878–1903). Pope Leo permitted the teaching of evolution as a hypothesis in Catholic schools and also responded to the challenges of modernization in the economic and social spheres. In his encyclical *De Rerum Novarum,* issued in 1891, he upheld the individual's right to private property but at the same time criticized "naked" capitalism for the poverty and degradation in which it had left the working classes. Much in socialism, he declared, was Christian in principle, but he condemned Marxist socialism for its materialistic and antireligious foundations. The pope recommended that Catholics form socialist parties and labor unions of their own to help the workers.

Other religious groups also made efforts to win support for Christianity among the working-class poor and to restore religious practice among the urban working classes. Sects of evangelical missionaries were especially successful; a prime example is the Salvation Army, founded in London in 1865 by William Booth, the army's first "general." The Salvation Army established food centers, shelters where the homeless could sleep, and "rescue homes" for women, but all these had a larger purpose, as Booth admitted: "It is primarily and mainly for the sake of saving the soul that I seek the salvation of the body."[7]

The Culture of Modernity

The revolution in physics and psychology was paralleled by a revolution in literature and the arts. Before 1914, writers and artists were rebelling against the traditional literary and artistic styles that had dominated European cultural life since the Renaissance. The changes that they produced have since been called Modernism.

NATURALISM AND SYMBOLISM IN LITERATURE

Throughout much of the late nineteenth century, literature was dominated by Naturalism. Naturalists accepted the material world as real and felt that literature should be realistic. By addressing social problems, writers could contribute to an objective understanding of the world. Although Naturalism was a continuation of Realism, it lacked the underlying note of liberal optimism about people and society that had been prevalent in the 1850s. The Naturalists were pessimistic about Europe's future and often portrayed characters caught in the grip of forces beyond their control.

The novels of the French writer Émile Zola (1840–1902) provide a good example of Naturalism. Against a backdrop of the urban slums and coalfields of northern France, Zola showed how alcoholism and different environments affected people's lives. He had read Darwin's *Origin of Species* and had been impressed by its emphasis on the struggle for survival and the importance of environment and heredity. These themes were central to his *Rougon-Macquart,* a twenty-volume series of novels on the "natural and social history of a family." Zola maintained that the artist must analyze and dissect life as a biologist would a living organism. He said, "I have simply done on living bodies the work of analysis which surgeons perform on corpses."

The second half of the nineteenth century was a golden age for Russian literature. The nineteenth-century realistic novel reached its high point in the works of Leo Tolstoy (1828–1910) and Fyodor Dostoevsky (1821–1881). Tolstoy's greatest work was *War and Peace,* a lengthy novel played out against the historical background of Napoleon's invasion of Russia in 1812. It is realistic in its vivid descriptions of military life and character portrayal. Each person is delineated clearly and analyzed psychologically. Upon a great landscape, Tolstoy imposed a fatalistic view of history that ultimately proved irrelevant in the face of life's enduring values of human love and trust.

Dostoevsky combined narrative skill and acute psychological and moral observation with profound insights into human nature. He maintained that the major problem of his age was a loss of spiritual belief. Western people were attempting to gain salvation through the construction of a materialistic paradise built only by human reason and human will. Dostoevsky feared that the failure to incorporate spirit would result in total tyranny. His own life experiences led him to believe that only through suffering and faith could the human soul be purified, views that are evident in his best-known works, *Crime and Punishment* and *The Brothers Karamazov.*

At the turn of the century, a new group of writers, known as the Symbolists, reacted against Realism. Primarily interested in writing poetry, the Symbolists believed that an objective knowledge of the world was impossible. The external world was not real but only a collection of symbols that reflected the true reality of the individual human mind. Art, they believed, should function for its own sake instead of serving, criticizing, or seeking to understand society. In the works of such Symbolist poets as W. B. Yeats and Rainer Maria Rilke, poetry ceased to be part of popular culture because only through a knowledge of the poet's personal language could one hope to understand what the poem was saying (see the box on p. 683).

MODERNISM IN THE ARTS

Since the Renaissance, artists had tried to represent reality as accurately as possible. By the late nineteenth century, however, artists were seeking new forms of expression. The preamble to modern painting can be found in Impressionism, a movement that originated in France in the 1870s when a group of artists rejected the studios and museums and went out into the countryside to paint nature directly. Camille Pissarro (1830–1903), one of Impressionism's founders, expressed what they sought:

> Precise drawing is dry and hampers the impression of the whole, it destroys all sensations. Do not define too closely the outlines of things; it is the brush stroke of the right value and color which should produce the drawing. . . . Work at the same time upon sky, water, branches, ground, keeping everything going on an equal basis and unceasingly rework until you have got it. . . . Don't proceed according to rules and principles, but paint what you observe and feel. Paint generously and unhesitatingly, for it is best not to lose the first impression.[8]

Impressionists like Pissarro sought to put into painting their impressions of the changing effects of light on objects in nature.

Pissarro's suggestions are visibly portrayed in the work of Claude Monet (1840–1926). He was especially enchanted with water and painted many pictures in which he sought to capture the interplay of light, water, and atmosphere, espe-

Scala/Art Resource, NY

Claude Monet, *Impression, Sunrise.* Impressionists rejected "rules and principles" and sought to paint what they observed and felt in order "not to lose the first impression." As is evident in *Impression, Sunrise,* Monet sought to capture his impression of the fleeting moments of sunrise through the simple interplay of light, water, and atmosphere.

cially evident in *Impression, Sunrise.* But the Impressionists did not just paint scenes from nature. Streets and cabarets, rivers, and busy boulevards—wherever people congregated for work and leisure—formed their subject matter.

Another important Impressionist painter was Berthe Morisot (1841–1895), who broke with the practice of women being only amateur artists and became a professional painter. Her dedication to the new style of painting won her the disfavor of the traditional French academic artists. Morisot believed that women had a special vision, which was, as she said, "more delicate than that of men." Her special touch is evident in the lighter colors and flowing brush strokes of *Young Girl by the Window.* Near the end of her life, Morisot lamented the refusal of men to take her work seriously: "I don't think there has ever been a man who treated a woman as an equal, and that's all I would have asked, for I know I'm worth as much as they."[9]

By the 1880s, a new movement known as Post-Impressionism arose in France but soon

Erich Lessing/Art Resource, NY

Berthe Morisot, *Young Girl by the Window.* Berthe Morisot came from a wealthy French family that settled in Paris when she was seven. The first female painter to join the Impressionists, she developed her own unique Impressionist style. Her gentle colors and strong use of pastels are especially evident in *Young Girl by the Window,* painted in 1878. Many of her paintings focus on women and domestic scenes.

Paul Cézanne, *Woman with Coffee Pot.* Post-Impressionists sought above all to express their inner feelings and capture on canvas their own vision of reality. In *Woman with Coffee Pot,* Paul Cézanne tried to relate the geometric shapes of his central female figure to the geometric shapes of the coffeepot and the rectangles of the door panels.

Réunion des Musées Nationaux/Art Resource, NY

spread to other European countries. Post-Impressionism retained the Impressionist emphasis on light and color but revolutionized it even further by paying more attention to structure and form. Post-Impressionists sought to use both color and line to express inner feelings and produce a personal statement of reality rather than an imitation of objects. Impressionist paintings had retained a sense of realism, but the Post-Impressionists shifted from objective reality to subjective reality and in so doing began to withdraw from the artist's traditional task of depicting the external world. Post-Impressionism was the real beginning of modern art.

Paul Cézanne (1839–1906) was one of the most important Post-Impressionists. Initially, he was influenced by the Impressionists but soon rejected their work. In his paintings, such as *Woman with Coffee Pot,* Cézanne sought to express visually the underlying geometric structure and form of everything he painted. As Cézanne explained to one young painter: "You must see in nature the cylinder, the sphere, and the cone."

Another famous Post-Impressionist was a tortured and tragic figure, Vincent van Gogh (1853–1890). For van Gogh, art was a spiritual experience. He was especially interested in color and believed that it could act as its own form of language. Van Gogh maintained that artists should paint what they feel, which is evident in his *Starry Night.*

By the beginning of the twentieth century, the belief that the task of art was to represent "reality" had lost much of its meaning. By that time, psychology and the new physics had made it evident that many people were not sure what constituted reality anyway. Then, too, the development of photography gave artists another reason to reject visual realism. First invented in the 1830s, photography became popular and widespread after George Eastman produced the first Kodak camera for the mass market in 1888. What was the point of an artist doing what the camera did better? Unlike the camera, which could only mirror reality, artists could create reality. As in literature, so also in modern art, individual consciousness became the source of meaning. Between 1905 and 1914, this search for individual expression produced a wide variety of schools of painting, all of which had their greatest impact after World War I.

In 1905, one of the most important figures in modern art was just beginning his career. Pablo Picasso (1881–1973) was from Spain but settled in Paris in 1904. Picasso was extremely flexible and painted in a remarkable variety of styles. He was instrumental in the development of a new style called Cubism that used geometric designs as visual stimuli to re-create reality in the viewer's mind. Picasso's 1907 work *Les Demoiselles d'Avignon* has been called the first Cubist painting.

The modern artist's flight from "visual reality" reached a high point in 1910 with the beginning of abstract painting. A Russian who worked in Germany, Wassily Kandinsky (1866–1944), was one of the founders of abstract painting. As is evident in his *Painting with White Border,* Kandinsky sought to avoid representation altogether. He believed that art should speak directly to the soul. To do so, it must avoid any reference to visual reality and concentrate on color.

MODERNISM IN MUSIC

In the first half of the nineteenth century, the Romantics' attraction to exotic and primitive cultures had sparked a fascination with folk music, which became increasingly important as musicians began to look for ways to express their national identities. In the second half of the century, new flames of nationalistic spirit were fanned in both literary and musical circles.

One example of this new nationalistic spirit may be found in the Scandinavian composer Edvard Grieg (1843–1907), who remained a dedicated supporter of Norwegian nationalism throughout his life. Grieg's nationalism expressed itself in the lyric melodies found in the folk music of his homeland. Among his best-known works is the *Peer Gynt Suite* (1876), incidental music to a play by

The Museum of Modern Art, New York

Vincent van Gogh, *The Starry Night.* The Dutch painter Vincent van Gogh was a major figure among the Post-Impressionists. His originality and power of expression made a strong impact on his artistic successors. In *The Starry Night,* painted in 1889, van Gogh's subjective vision was given full play as the dynamic swirling forms of the heavens above overwhelmed the village below. The heavens seem alive with a mysterious spiritual force.

Henrik Ibsen. Grieg's music paved the way for the creation of a national music style in Norway.

The Impressionist movement in music followed its artistic counterpart by some thirty years. Impressionist music stressed elusive moods and haunting sensations and is distinct in its delicate beauty and elegance of sound. The composer most tangibly linked to the Impressionist movement was Claude Debussy (1862–1918), whose musical compositions were often inspired by the visual arts. One of Debussy's most famous works, *Prelude to the Afternoon of a Faun* (1894), was actually inspired by a poem, "Afternoon of a Faun," composed by his friend, the Symbolist poet Stéphane Mallarmé. But Debussy did not tell a story in music; rather, *Prelude to the Afternoon of a Faun* re-created in sound the overall feeling of the poem. Said Mallarmé upon hearing Debussy's piece, "I was not expecting anything like this. This music prolongs the emotion of my poem, and evokes the scene more vividly than color."[10]

Other composers adopted stylistic idioms that imitated presumably primitive forms in an attempt to express less refined and therefore more genuine feelings. A chief exponent of musical primitivism was Igor Stravinsky (1882–1971), one of the twentieth century's most important composers, both for his compositions and for his impact on other composers. He gained international fame as a ballet composer and together with the Ballet Russe, under the direction of Sergei Diaghilev (1872–1929), revolutionized the world of music with a series of ballets. The three most significant ballets Stravinsky composed for Diaghilev's company were *The Firebird* (1910), *Petrushka* (1911), and *The Rite of Spring* (1913). All three were based

Pablo Picasso, *Les Demoiselles d'Avignon.* Pablo Picasso, a major pioneer and activist of modern art, experimented with a remarkable variety of modern styles. *Les Demoiselles d'Avignon* (1907) was the first great example of Cubism, which one art historian has called "the first style of this century to break radically with the past." Geometric shapes replace traditional forms, forcing the viewer to re-create reality in his or her own mind.

on Russian folk tales. *The Rite of Spring* proved to be a revolutionary piece in the development of music. At the premiere on May 29, 1913, the pulsating rhythms, sharp dissonances, and unusual dancing overwhelmed the Paris audience and caused a riot at the theater. Like the intellectuals of his time, Stravinsky sought a new understanding of irrational forces in his music, which became an important force in inaugurating a modern musical movement.

Politics: New Directions and New Uncertainties

The uncertainties in European intellectual and cultural life were paralleled by growing anxieties in European political life. The seemingly steady progress in the growth of liberal principles and political democracy after 1871 was soon slowed or even halted altogether after 1894. The new mass politics had opened the door to changes that many nineteenth-century liberals found unacceptable, and liberals themselves were forced to move in new directions. The appearance of a new right-wing politics based on racism added an ugly note to the already existing anxieties. With their newfound voting rights, workers elected socialists who demanded new reforms when they took their places in legislative bodies. Women, too, made new demands, insisting on the right to vote and using new tactics to gain it. In central and eastern Europe, tensions grew as authoritarian governments refused to meet the demands of reformers. And outside Europe, a new giant appeared in the Western world as the United States emerged as a great industrial power with immense potential.

The Movement for Women's Rights

In the 1830s, a number of women in the United States and Europe, who worked together in several reform movements, became frustrated by the apparent prejudices against females. They sought improvements for women by focusing on specific goals. Family and marriage laws were especially singled out because it was difficult for women to secure divorces and property laws gave husbands almost complete control over the property of their wives. These early efforts were not particularly successful, however. For

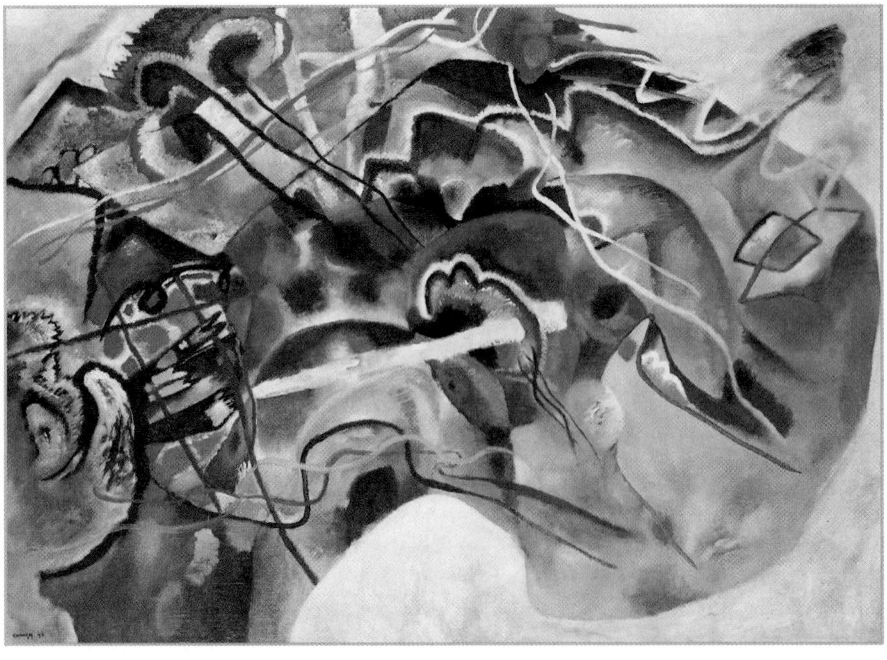

Wassily Kandinsky, *Composition VIII, No. 2 (Painting with White Border).* One of the founders of abstract painting was the Russian Wassily Kandinsky, who sought to eliminate representation altogether by focusing on color and avoiding any resemblance to visual reality. In *Painting with White Border* (1913), Kandinsky used color "to send light into the darkness of men's hearts." He believed that color, like music, could fulfill a spiritual goal of appealing directly to the human being.

Symbolist Poetry: Art for Art's Sake

Arthur Rimbaud was one of Symbolism's leading practitioners in France. Although his verses seem to have little real meaning, they were not meant to describe the external world precisely but to enchant the mind. Art was not meant for the masses but only for "art's sake." Rimbaud wrote, "By the alchemy of the words, I noted the inexpressible. I fixed giddiness."

Arthur Rimbaud, The Drunken Boat

As I floated down impassable rivers,
I felt the boatmen no longer guiding me.
After them came redskins who with war cries
Nailed them naked to the painted poles.

I was oblivious to the crew,
I who bore Flemish wheat and English cotton.
When the racket was finished with my boatmen,
The waters let me drift my own free way.

In the tide's furious pounding,
I, the other winter, emptier than children's minds,
I sailed! And the unmoored peninsulas
Have not suffered more triumphant turmoils.

The tempest blessed my maritime watches.
Lighter than a cork I danced on the waves,
Those eternal rollers of victims,
Ten nights, without regretting the lantern-foolish eye!

Sweeter than the bite of sour apples to a child,
The green water seeped through my wooden hull,
Rinsed me of blue wine stains and vomit,
Broke apart grappling iron and rudder.

And then I bathed myself in the poetry
Of the star-sprayed milk-white sea,
Devouring the azure greens; where, pale
And ravished, a pensive drowned one sometimes floats;

Where, suddenly staining the blueness, frenzies
And slow rhythms in the blazing of day,
Stronger than alcohol, vaster than our lyres,
The russet bitterness of love ferments. . . .

I have dreamed of the green night bedazzled with snow,
A kiss climbing slowly to the eyes of the sea,
The flow of unforgettable sap,
And the yellow-blue waking of singing phosphorous!

Long months I have followed, like maddened cattle,
The surge assaulting the rocks
Without dreaming that the Virgin's luminous feet
Could force a muzzle on the panting ocean!

I have struck against the shares of incredible Floridas
Mixing panther-eyed flowers like human skins!
Rainbows stretched like bridle reins
Under the ocean's horizon, toward sea-green troops!

I have seen the fermenting of monstrous marshes,
Nets where a whole Leviathan rots in the reeds!
The waters collapsing in the middle of the calm,
And horizons plunging toward the abyss!

Glaciers, silver suns, waves of pearl, charcoal skies,
Hideous beaches at the bottom of brown gulfs
Where giant serpents devoured by vermin
Tumble from twisted trees with black perfumes!

I would have liked to show the children those dolphins
On the blue waves, those golden singing fish.
—The froth of flowers lulled my voyagings,
Ineffable winds gave me wings by the moment. . . .

example, women did not gain the right to their own property until 1870 in Britain, 1900 in Germany, and 1907 in France. Although the British legalized divorce in 1857, the French state permitted only a limited degree of divorce in 1884. In Catholic countries such as Spain and Italy, women had no success at all in achieving the right to divorce their husbands.

Custody and property rights were only a beginning for the women's movement, however. Some middle- and upper-middle-class women gained access to higher education, and others sought entry into occupations dominated by men. The first to fall was teaching. Because medical training was largely closed to women, they sought alternatives in the development of nursing. One nursing pioneer was Amalie Sieveking (1794–1859), who founded the Female Association for the Care of the Poor and Sick in Hamburg, Germany. As she explained: "To me, at least as important were the benefits which [work with the poor] seemed to promise for those of my sisters who would join me in such a work of charity. The higher interests of my sex were close to my heart."[11] Sieveking's work was followed by the more famous British nurse, Florence Nightingale (1820–1910), whose efforts during the Crimean War, along with those of Clara Barton (1821–1912) in the American Civil War, transformed nursing into a profession of trained, middle-class "women in white."

By the 1840s and 1850s, the movement for women's rights had entered the political arena with the call for equal political rights. Many feminists believed that the right to vote was the key to all other reforms to improve the position of women. The British women's movement was the most vocal and active in Europe, but it divided over tactics. The liberal Millicent Fawcett (1847–1929) organized a moderate group who believed that women must demonstrate that they

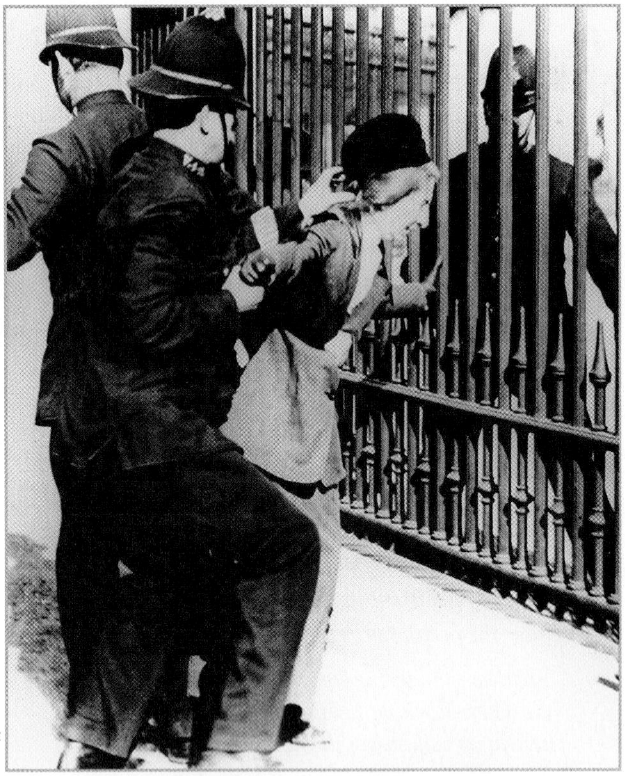

© Popperfoto

The Arrest of a Suffragist. For many feminists, the right to vote came to represent the key to other reforms that would benefit women. In Britain, suffragists attracted attention to their cause by unusual publicity stunts. This photograph shows the arrest of a suffragist who had chained herself to the railings of Buckingham Palace in London.

would use political power responsibly if they wanted Parliament to grant them the right to vote. Another group, however, favored a more radical approach. Emmeline Pankhurst (1858–1928) and her daughters, Christabel and Sylvia, founded the Women's Social and Political Union in 1903, which enrolled mostly middle- and upper-class women. Pankhurst's organization realized the value of the media and used unusual publicity stunts to call attention to its demands. Derisively labeled "suffragettes" by male politicians, they pelted government officials with eggs, chained themselves to lampposts, smashed the windows of department stores on fashionable shopping streets, burned railroad cars, and went on hunger strikes in jail. In 1913, Emily Davison accepted martyrdom for the cause when she threw herself in front of the king's horse at the Epsom Derby horse race. Suffragists had one fundamental aim: the right of women to full citizenship in the nation-state.

Although few women elsewhere in Europe used the Pankhursts' confrontational methods, demands for women's rights were heard throughout Europe and the United States before World War I. Nevertheless, only in Finland, Norway, and some American states did women actually receive the right to vote before 1914. It would take the dramatic upheaval of World War I before male-dominated governments capitulated on this basic issue (see Chapter 25).

Women reformers took on other issues besides suffrage. In many countries, women supported peace movements. Bertha von Suttner (1843–1914) became the head of the Austrian Peace Society and protested against the growing arms race of the1890s. Her novel *Lay Down Your Arms* became a best-seller and brought her the Nobel Peace Prize in 1905. Lower-class women also took up the cause of peace. In 1911, a group of female workers marched in Vienna and demanded: "We want an end to armaments, to the means of murder and we want these millions to be spent on the needs of the people."[12]

THE NEW WOMAN

Bertha von Suttner was but one example of the "new women" who were becoming more prominent at the turn of the century. These women renounced traditional feminine roles (see the box on p. 685). Although some of them supported political ideologies such as socialism that flew in the face of the ruling classes, others simply sought new freedom outside the household and new roles other than those of wives and mothers.

Maria Montessori (1870–1952) was a good example of the "new woman." Breaking with tradition, she attended medical school at the University of Rome. Although often isolated by the male students, she persisted and in 1896 became the first Italian woman to receive a medical degree. Three years later, she undertook a lecture tour in Italy on the subject of the "new woman," whom she characterized as a woman who followed a rational, scientific perspective. In keeping with this ideal, Montessori put her medical background to work in a school for mentally retarded children. She devised new teaching materials that enabled these children to read and write and became convinced, as she later wrote, "that similar methods applied to normal students would develop or set free their personality in a marvelous and surprising way." Subsequently, she established a system of childhood education based on natural and spontaneous activities in which students learned at their own pace. By the 1930s, hundreds of Montessori schools had been established in Europe and the United States. As a professional woman and an unwed mother, Montessori also embodied some of the freedoms of the "new woman."

Jews Within the European Nation-State

Near the end of the nineteenth century, a revival of racism combined with extreme nationalism to produce a new right-wing politics aimed primarily at the Jews. Of course, anti-Semitism was not new to European civilization. Since the Middle Ages, Jews had been portrayed as the murderers of Jesus and subjected to mob violence; their rights had been restricted, and they had been physically separated from Christians in quarters known as ghettos.

In the nineteenth century, as a result of the ideals of the Enlightenment and the French Revolution, Jews were

Advice to Women: Be Independent

Although a majority of women probably followed the nineteenth-century middle-class ideal of women as keepers of the household and nurturers of husband and children, an increasing number of women fought for the rights of women. This selection is taken from Act III of Henrik Ibsen's 1879 play *A Doll's House,* in which the character Nora Helmer declares her independence from her husband's control.

■ *Henrik Ibsen,* A Doll's House

NORA (*Pause*): Does anything strike you as we sit here?

HELMER: What should strike me?

NORA: We've been married eight years; does it not strike you that this is the first time we two, you and I, man and wife, have talked together seriously?

HELMER: Seriously? What do you mean, *seriously*?

NORA: For eight whole years, and more—ever since the day we first met—we have never exchanged one serious word about serious things. . . .

HELMER: Why, my dearest Nora, what have you to do with serious things?

NORA: There we have it! You have never understood me. I've had great injustice done to me, Torvald; first by father, then by you.

HELMER: What! Your father *and* me? We, who have loved you more than all the world!

NORA (*Shaking her head*): You have never loved me. You just found it amusing to think you were in love with me.

HELMER: Nora! What a thing to say!

NORA: Yes, it's true, Torvald. When I was living at home with father, he told me his opinions and mine were the same. If I had different opinions, I said nothing about them, because he would not have liked it. He used to call me his doll-child and played with me as I played with my dolls. Then I came to live in your house.

HELMER: What a way to speak of our marriage!

NORA (*Undisturbed*): I mean that I passed from father's hands into yours. You arranged everything to your taste and I got the same tastes as you; or pretended to—I don't know which—both, perhaps; sometimes one, sometimes the other. When I look back on it now, I seem to have been living here like a beggar, on handouts. I lived by performing tricks for you, Torvald. But that was how you wanted it. You and father have done me a great wrong. It is your fault that my life has come to naught.

HELMER: Why, Nora, how unreasonable and ungrateful! Haven't you been happy here?

NORA: No, never. I thought I was, but I never was.

HELMER: Not—not happy! . . .

NORA: I must stand quite alone if I am ever to know myself and my surroundings; so I cannot stay with you.

HELMER: Nora! Nora!

NORA: I am going at once. I daresay [my friend] Christina will take me in for tonight.

HELMER: You are mad! I shall not allow it! I forbid it!

NORA: It's no use your forbidding me anything now. I shall take with me only what belongs to me; from you I will accept nothing, either now or later.

HELMER: This is madness!

NORA: Tomorrow I shall go home—I mean to what was my home. It will be easier for me to find a job there.

HELMER: On, in your blind inexperience—

NORA: I must try to gain experience, Torvald.

HELMER: Forsake your home, your husband, your children! And you don't consider what the world will say.

NORA: I can't pay attention to that. I only know that I must do it.

HELMER: This is monstrous! Can you forsake your holiest duties?

NORA: What do you consider my holiest duties?

HELMER: Need I tell you that? Your duties to your husband and children.

NORA: I have other duties equally sacred.

HELMER: Impossible! What do you mean?

NORA: My duties toward myself.

HELMER: Before all else you are a wife and a mother.

NORA: That I no longer believe. Before all else I believe I am a human being just as much as you are—or at least that I should try to become one. I know that most people agree with you, Torvald, and that they say so in books. But I can no longer be satisfied with what most people say and what is in books. I must think things out for myself and try to get clear about them.

increasingly granted legal equality in many European countries. The French revolutionary decrees of 1790 and 1791 emancipated the Jews and admitted them to full citizenship. After the revolutions of 1848, emancipation became a fact of life for Jews throughout western and central Europe. For many Jews, emancipation enabled them to leave the ghetto and become assimilated as hundreds of thousands of Jews entered what had been the closed worlds of parliaments and universities. In 1880, for example, Jews made up 10 percent of the population of the city of Vienna, Austria, but 39 percent of its medical students and 23 percent of its law students. "A Jew could leave his Jewishness" behind, as the career of Benjamin Disraeli, who became prime minister of Great Britain, demonstrated. Many other Jews became eminently successful as bankers, lawyers, scientists, scholars, journalists, and stage performers.

These achievements represent only one side of the picture, however, as is evident from the Dreyfus affair in

France. Alfred Dreyfus, a Jew, was a captain in the French general staff. Early in 1895, a secret military court found him guilty of selling army secrets and condemned him to life imprisonment on Devil's Island. During his trial, right-wing mobs yelled "Death to the Jews." Soon after the trial, however, evidence emerged that pointed to Dreyfus's innocence. The government pardoned Dreyfus in 1899, and in 1906, he was fully exonerated.

In Austrian politics, the Christian Socialists combined agitation for workers with a virulent anti-Semitism. They were most powerful in Vienna, where they were led by Karl Lueger, mayor of Vienna from 1897 to 1910. Imperial Vienna at the turn of the century was a brilliant center of European culture, but it was also the home of an insidious German nationalism that blamed Jews for the corruption of German culture. It was in Vienna between 1907 and 1913 that Adolf Hitler later claimed to have found his worldview, one that was largely based on violent German nationalism and rabid anti-Semitism.

Germany, too, had its right-wing anti-Semitic parties, such as Adolf Stocker's Christian Social Workers. These parties used anti-Semitism to win the votes of traditional lower-middle-class groups who felt threatened by the new economic forces of the times. These German anti-Semitic parties were based on race. In medieval times, Jews could convert to Christianity and escape from their religion. To modern racial anti-Semites, Jews were racially stained; this could not be altered by conversion. One could not be both a German and a Jew. Hermann Ahlwardt, an anti-Semitic member of the German Reichstag, made this clear in a speech to that body:

> The Jew is no German. . . . A Jew who was born in Germany does not thereby become a German; he is still a Jew. Therefore it is imperative that we realize that Jewish racial characteristics differ so greatly from ours that a common life of Jews and Germans under the same laws is quite impossible because the Germans will perish.[13]

After 1898, the political strength of the German anti-Semitic parties began to decline.

The worst treatment of Jews in the last two decades of the nineteenth century and the first decade of the twentieth occurred in eastern Europe, where 72 percent of the entire world Jewish population lived. Russian Jews were admitted to secondary schools and universities only under a quota system and were forced to live in certain regions of the country. Persecutions and pogroms (organized massacres) were widespread. Between 1903 and 1906, pogroms took place in almost seven hundred Russian towns and villages, mostly in the Ukraine. Hundreds of thousands of Jews decided to emigrate to escape the persecution. Between 1881 and 1899, an average of 23,000 Jews left Russia each year. Many of them went to the United States and Canada, although some (probably about 25,000) moved to Palestine, which soon became the focus for a Jewish nationalist movement called Zionism.

The emancipation of the nineteenth century had presented vast opportunities for some Jews but dilemmas for others. Did emancipation mean full assimilation, and did assimilation mean the disruption of traditional Jewish life? Many Jews paid the price willingly, but others questioned its value and advocated a different answer, a return to Palestine. For many Jews, Palestine, the land of ancient Israel, had long been the land of their dreams. During the nineteenth century, as nationalist ideas spread and Italians, Poles, Irish, Greeks, and others sought national emancipation, so did the idea of national independence capture the imagination of some Jews. A key figure in the growth of political Zionism was Theodor Herzl (1860–1904). In 1896, he published a book called *The Jewish State* (see the box on p. 687) in which he advocated that "the Jews who wish it will have their state." Financial support for the development of *yishuvs,* or settlements in Palestine, came from wealthy Jewish banking families who wanted a refuge in Palestine for persecuted Jews. Even settlements were difficult because Palestine was then part of the Ottoman Empire and Ottoman authorities were opposed to Jewish immigration. In 1891, one Jewish essayist pointed to the problems this would create:

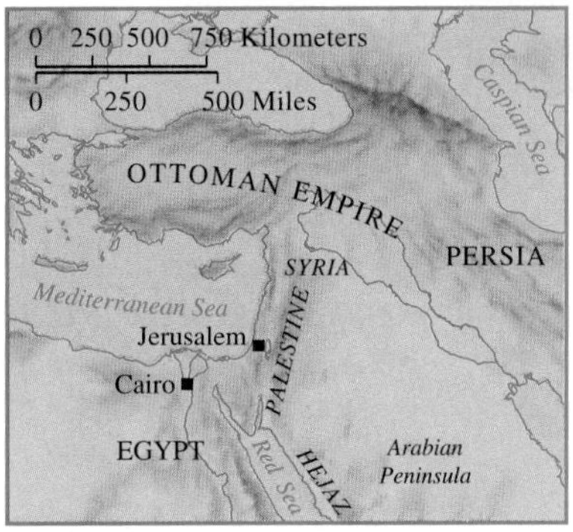

Palestine

> We abroad are accustomed to believe that Erez Israel [the land of Israel] is almost totally desolate at present . . . but in reality it is not so. . . . Arabs, especially those in towns, see and understand our activities and aims in the country but keep quiet and pretend as if they did not know, . . . and they try to exploit us, too, and profit from the new guests while laughing at us in their hearts. But if the time comes and our people make such progress as to displace the people of the country . . . they will not lightly surrender the place.[14]

Despite the warnings, however, the First Zionist Congress, which met in Switzerland in 1897, proclaimed as its aim the creation of a "home in Palestine secured by public law" for the Jewish people. One thousand Jews migrated to Palestine in 1901, and the number rose to three thousand annually between 1904 and 1914; but on the eve of World War I, the Zionist dream remained just that.

The Transformation of Liberalism: Great Britain and Italy

In dealing with the problems created by the new mass politics, liberal governments often followed policies that undermined the basic tenets of liberalism. This was certainly true in Great Britain, where the demands of the working-class movement caused Liberals to move away from their ideals. Liberals were forced to adopt significant social reforms due to the pressure of two new working-class organizations: trade unions and the Labour Party.

Trade unions began to advocate more radical change of the economic system, calling for "collective ownership

The Voice of Zionism: Theodor Herzl and the Jewish State

The Austrian Jewish journalist Theodor Herzl wrote *The Jewish State* in the summer of 1895 in Paris while he was covering the Dreyfus case for his Vienna newspaper. During several weeks of feverish composition, he set out to analyze the fundamental causes of anti-Semitism and devise a solution to the "Jewish problem." In this selection, he discusses two of his major conclusions.

Theodor Herzl, The Jewish State

I do not intend to arouse sympathetic emotions on our behalf. That would be a foolish, futile, and undignified proceeding. I shall content myself with putting the following questions to the Jews: Is it true that, in countries where we live in perceptible numbers, the position of Jewish lawyers, doctors, technicians, teachers, and employees of all descriptions becomes daily more intolerable? True, that the Jewish middle classes are seriously threatened? True, that the passions of the mob are incited against our wealthy people? True, that our poor endure greater sufferings than any other proletariat?

I think that this external pressure makes itself felt everywhere. In our economically upper classes it causes discomfort, in our middle classes continual and grave anxieties, in our lower classes absolute despair.

Everything tends, in fact, to one and the same conclusion, which is clearly enunciated in that classic Berlin phrase: "Juden 'raus!" (Out with the Jews!)

I shall now put the Jewish Question in the curtest possible form: Are we to "get out" now? And if so, to what place?

Or, may we yet remain? And if so, how long?

Let us first settle the point of staying where we are. Can we hope for better days, can we possess our souls in patience, can we wait in pious resignation till the princes and peoples of this earth are more mercifully disposed toward us? I say that we cannot hope for a change in the current of feeling. And why not? Were we as near to the hearts of princes as are their other subjects, even so they could not protect us. They would only feed popular hatred of Jews by showing us too much favor. By "too much," I really mean less than is claimed as a right by every ordinary citizen, or by every race. The nations in whose midst Jews live are all, either covertly or openly, Anti-Semitic. . . .

The whole plan is in its essence perfectly simple, as it must necessarily be if it is to come within the comprehension of all.

Let the sovereignty be granted us over a portion of the globe large enough to satisfy the rightful requirements of a nation; the rest we shall manage for ourselves.

The creation of a new State is neither ridiculous nor impossible. We have in our day witnessed the process in connection with nations which were not in the bulk of the middle class, but poorer, less educated, and consequently weaker than ourselves. The Governments of all countries scourged by Anti-Semitism will be keenly interested in assisting us to obtain the sovereignty we want. . . .

Palestine is our ever-memorable historic home. The very name of Palestine would attract our people with a force of marvelous potency. Supposing his Majesty the Sultan were to give us Palestine, we could in return undertake to regulate the whole finances of Turkey. We should there form a portion of the rampart of Europe against Asia, an outpost of civilization as opposed to barbarism. We should as a neutral State remain in contact with all Europe, which would have to guarantee our existence. The sanctuaries of Christendom would be safeguarded by assigning to them an extra-territorial status such as is well known to the law of nations. We should form a guard of honor about these sanctuaries, answering for the fulfillment of this duty with our existence. This guard of honor would be the great symbol of the solution of the Jewish Question after eighteen centuries of Jewish suffering.

and control over production, distribution, and exchange." At the same time, a movement for laborers emerged among a group of intellectuals known as the Fabian Socialists who stressed the need for the workers to use their right to vote to capture the House of Commons and pass legislation that would benefit the laboring class. Neither the Fabian Socialists nor the British trade unions were Marxist. They did not advocate class struggle and revolution but evolution toward a socialist state by democratic means. In 1900, representatives of the trade unions and Fabian Socialists coalesced to form the Labour Party. By 1906, they had managed to elect twenty-nine members to the House of Commons.

The Liberals, who gained control of the House of Commons in that year and held the government from 1906 to 1914, perceived that they would have to enact a program of social welfare or lose the support of the workers. The policy of reform was especially advanced by David Lloyd George (1863–1945), a brilliant orator from Wales who had been deeply moved by the misery of Welsh coal miners. The Liberals abandoned the classical principles of laissez-faire and voted for a series of social reforms. The National Insurance Act of 1911 provided benefits for workers in case of sickness and unemployment, to be paid for by compulsory contributions from workers, employers, and the state. Additional legislation provided a small pension for retirees over seventy and compensation for workers injured on the job. To pay for the new program, Lloyd George increased the tax burden on the wealthy classes. Though both the benefits of the program and the tax increases were modest, they were the first hesitant steps toward the future British welfare state. Liberalism, which had been based on the principle that the government that governs least governs best, had been transformed.

Liberals had even greater problems in Italy. A certain amount of stability was achieved from 1903 to 1914 when the liberal leader Giovanni Giolitti served intermittently as prime minister. Giolitti was a master of using *trasformismo* or transformism, a system in which old political groups were transformed into new government coalitions by political and economic bribery. In the long run, however, Giolitti's devious methods made Italian politics even more corrupt and unmanageable. When urban workers turned to violence to protest their living and working conditions, Giolitti tried to appease them with social welfare legislation and universal male suffrage in 1912. To strengthen his popularity, he also aroused nationalistic passions by conquering Libya. Despite his efforts, however, worker unrest continued, and in 1914 government troops had to be used to crush rioting workers.

Growing Tensions in Germany

The new imperial Germany begun by Bismarck in 1871 continued as an "authoritarian, conservative, military-bureaucratic power state" during the reign of Emperor William II (1888–1918). Unstable and aggressive, the emperor was inclined to tactless remarks, as when he told the soldiers of a Berlin regiment that they must be prepared to shoot their fathers and mothers if he ordered them to do so. A small group of about twenty powerful men joined William in setting government policy.

By 1914, Germany had become the strongest military and industrial power on the Continent. New social configurations had emerged as over 50 percent of German workers had jobs in industry while only 30 percent of the workforce was still in agriculture. Urban centers had mushroomed in number and size. The rapid changes in William's Germany helped produce a society torn between modernization and traditionalism.

The growth of industrialization led to even greater expansion for the Social Democratic Party. Despite the enactment of new welfare legislation to favor the working classes, William II was no more successful than Bismarck at slowing the growth of the Social Democrats. By 1912, it had become the largest single party in the Reichstag. At the same time, the party increasingly became less revolutionary and more revisionist in its outlook. Nevertheless, its growth frightened the middle and upper classes, who blamed labor for their own problems.

With the expansion of industry and cities came demands for more political participation and growing sentiment for reforms that would produce greater democratization. Conservative forces, especially the landowning nobility and representatives of heavy industry, two of the powerful ruling groups in Germany, tried to block it by supporting William II's activist foreign policy (see "New Directions and New Crises" later in this chapter). Expansionism, they believed, would divert people from further democratization.

The tensions in German society created by the conflict between modernization and traditionalism were also manifested in a new, radicalized, right-wing politics. A number of pressure groups arose to support nationalistic goals. Such groups as the Pan-German League stressed strong German nationalism and advocated imperialism as a tool to overcome social divisions and unite all classes. They were also anti-Semitic and denounced Jews as the destroyers of the national community.

Industrialization and Revolution in Imperial Russia

Starting in the 1890s, Russia experienced a massive surge of state-sponsored industrialism under the guiding hand of Sergei Witte (1849–1915), the minister for finance from 1892 to 1903. Count Witte saw industrial growth as crucial to Russia's national strength. Believing that railroads were a powerful weapon in economic development, Witte pushed the government toward a program of massive railroad construction. By 1900, 35,000 miles of railroads, including large parts of the 5,000-mile trans-Siberian line between Moscow and Vladivostok, on the Pacific Ocean, had been built. Witte also encouraged a system of protective tariffs to help Russian industry and persuaded Tsar Nicholas II (1894–1917) that foreign capital was essential for rapid industrial development. Witte's program made possible the rapid growth of a modern steel and coal industry in the Ukraine, making Russia by 1900 the fourth largest producer of steel behind the United States, Germany, and Great Britain.

With industrialization came factories, an industrial working class, industrial suburbs around Saint Petersburg and Moscow, and the pitiful working and living conditions that accompanied the beginnings of industrialization everywhere. Socialist thought and socialist parties developed, although repression in Russia soon forced them to go underground and become revolutionary. The Marxist Social Democratic Party, for example, held its first congress in Minsk in 1898, but the arrest of its leaders caused the next one to be held in Brussels in 1903, attended by Russian émigrés. The Social Revolutionaries worked to overthrow the tsarist autocracy and establish peasant socialism. Having no other outlet for their opposition to the regime, they advocated political terrorism and attempted to assassinate government officials and members of the ruling dynasty. The growing opposition to the tsarist regime finally exploded into revolution in 1905.

THE REVOLUTION OF 1905

As had happened elsewhere in Europe in the nineteenth century, defeat in war led to political upheaval at home. Russia's territorial expansion to the south and east, especially its designs on northern Korea, led to a confrontation with Japan. Japan made a surprise attack on the Russian

Bloody Sunday

On January 9, 1905, a massive procession of workers led by a Russian Orthodox priest loyal to the tsar, Father Gregory Gapon, carried pictures of the tsar and a petition to present to him at his imperial palace in Saint Petersburg. Although the tsar was not even there, government officials ordered troops to fire on the crowd. This account is by the leader of the procession, Father Gapon.

An Account of Bloody Sunday

We were not more than thirty yards from the soldiers, being separated from them only by the bridge over the Tarakanovskii Canal, which here marks the border of the city, when suddenly, without any warning and without a moment's delay, was heard the dry crack of many rifle-shots. I was informed later on that a bugle was blown, but we could not hear it above the singing, and even if we had heard it we should not have known what it meant.

Vasiliev, with whom I was walking hand in hand, suddenly left hold of my arm and sank upon the snow. One of the workmen who carried the banners fell also. Immediately one of the two police officers to whom I had referred shouted out, "What are you doing? How dare you fire upon the portrait of the Tsar?" This, of course, had no effect, and both he and the other officer were shot down—as I learned afterwards, one was killed and the other dangerously wounded.

I turned rapidly to the crowd and shouted to them to lie down, and I also stretched myself out upon the ground. As we lay thus another volley was fired, and another, and yet another, till it seemed as though the shooting was continuous. The crowd first kneeled and then lay flat down, hiding their heads from the rain of bullets, while the rear rows of the procession began to run away. The smoke of the fire lay before us like a thin cloud, and I felt it stiflingly in my throat. An old man named Lavrentiev, who was carrying the Tsar's portrait, had been one of the first victims. Another old man caught the portrait as it fell from his hands and carried it till he too was killed by the next volley. With his last gasp the old man said, "I may die, but I will see the Tsar." One of the banner-carriers had his arm broken by a bullet. A little boy of ten years, who was carrying a church lantern, fell pierced by a bullet, but still held the lantern tightly and tried to rise again, when another shot struck him down. Both the smiths who had guarded me were killed, as well as all those who were carrying the icons and banners; and all these emblems now lay scattered on the snow....

Horror crept into my heart. The thought flashed through my mind, "And this is the work of our Little Father, the Tsar." Perhaps this anger saved me, for now I knew in very truth that a new chapter was opened in the book of the history of our people. I stood up, and a little group of workmen gathered round me again. Looking backward, I saw that our line, though still stretching away into the distance, was broken and that many of the people were fleeing. It was in vain that I called to them, and in a moment I stood there, the center of a few scores of men, trembling with indignation amid the broken ruins of our movement.

eastern fleet at Port Arthur on February 8, 1904. In turn, Russia sent its Baltic fleet halfway around the world to the East, only to be defeated by the new Japanese navy at Tsushima Strait off the coast of Japan. Much to the astonishment of many Europeans, who could not believe that an Asian state was militarily superior to a great European power, the Russians admitted defeat and sued for peace in 1905.

In the midst of the war, the growing discontent of increased numbers of Russians rapidly led to upheaval. A middle class of business and professional people longed for liberal institutions and a liberal political system. Nationalities were dissatisfied with their domination by an ethnic Russian population that constituted only 45 percent of the empire's total population. Peasants were still suffering from lack of land, and laborers felt oppressed by their working and living conditions in Russia's large cities. The breakdown of the transport system caused by the Russo-Japanese War led to food shortages in the major cities of Russia. As a result, on January 9, 1905, a massive procession of workers went to the Winter Palace in Saint Petersburg to present a petition of grievances to the tsar. Troops foolishly opened fire on the peaceful demonstration, killing hundreds and launching a revolution (see the box above). This "Bloody Sunday" incited workers to call strikes and form unions; meanwhile, zemstvos demanded parliamentary government, ethnic groups revolted, and peasants burned the houses of landowners. After a general strike in October 1905, the government capitulated. Nicholas II issued the October Manifesto, in which he granted civil liberties and agreed to create a legislative assembly known as the Duma, elected directly by a broad franchise. This satisfied the middle-class moderates, who now supported the government's repression of a workers' uprising in Moscow at the end of 1905.

But real constitutional monarchy proved short-lived. Under Peter Stolypin, who served as the tsar's chief adviser from late 1906 until his assassination in 1911, important agrarian reforms dissolved the village ownership of land and opened the door to private ownership by enterprising peasants. Nicholas II, however, was no friend of reform. Already by 1907, the tsar had curtailed the power of the Duma, and after Stolypin's murder, he fell back on the army and bureaucracy to rule Russia.

Nicholas II. The last tsar of Russia hoped to preserve the traditional autocratic ways of his predecessors. In this photograph, Nicholas II and his wife, Alexandra, are shown returning from a church at Tsarskoe-Selo.

The Rise of the United States

Between 1860 and 1914, the United States made the shift from an agrarian to a mighty industrial nation. American heavy industry stood unchallenged in 1900. In that year, the Carnegie Steel Company alone produced more steel than Great Britain's entire steel industry. Industrialization also led to urbanization. While established cities, such as New York, Philadelphia, and Boston, grew even larger, other moderate-size cities, such as Pittsburgh, grew by leaps and bounds because of industrialization. Whereas 20 percent of Americans lived in cities in 1860, over 40 percent did in 1900. Four-fifths of the population growth in cities came from migration. Eight to ten million Americans moved from rural areas into the cities, and fourteen million foreigners came from abroad.

The United States had become the world's richest nation and greatest industrial power. Yet serious questions remained about the quality of American life. In 1890, the richest 9 percent of Americans owned an incredible 71 percent of all the wealth. Labor unrest over unsafe working conditions, strict work discipline, and periodic cycles of devastating unemployment led workers to organize. By the turn of the century, one national organization, the American Federation of Labor, emerged as labor's dominant voice. Its lack of real power, however, is reflected in its membership figures. In 1900, it included only 8.4 percent of the American industrial labor force.

During the so-called Progressive Era after 1900, an age of reform swept across the United States. State governments enacted economic and social legislation, such as laws that governed hours, wages, and working conditions, especially for women and children. The realization that state laws were ineffective in dealing with nationwide problems, however, led to a Progressive movement at the national level. The Meat Inspection Act and Pure Food and Drug Act provided for a limited degree of federal regulation of corrupt industrial practices. The presidency of Woodrow Wilson (1913–1921) witnessed the creation of a graduated federal income tax and the establishment of the Federal Reserve System, which permitted the federal government to play a role in important economic decisions formerly made by bankers. Like European nations, the United States was slowly adopting policies that extended the functions of the state.

The Growth of Canada

Canada faced problems of national unity at the end of the nineteenth century. In 1870, the Dominion of Canada had four provinces: Quebec, Ontario, Nova Scotia, and New Brunswick. With the addition of two more—Manitoba and British Columbia—the following year, Canada extended from the Atlantic to the Pacific.

Real unity was difficult to achieve, however, because of the distrust between the English-speaking and French-speaking Canadians. Wilfred Laurier, who became the first French Canadian prime minister in 1896, was able to reconcile Canada's two major groups. During his administration, industrialization boomed, especially the production of textiles, furniture, and railway equipment. Hundreds of thousands of immigrants, primarily from Europe, also flowed into Canada. Many settled on lands in the west, thus helping populate Canada's vast territories.

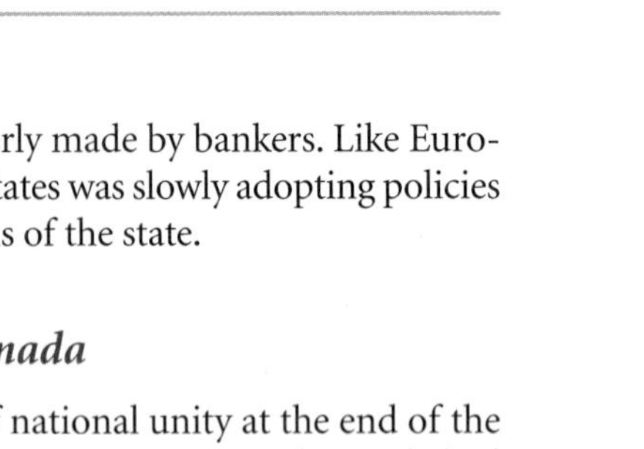

Canada, 1871

The New Imperialism

In the 1880s, European states embarked on an intense scramble for overseas territory. This revival of imperialism, or the "new imperialism," as some have called it, led Europeans to carve up Asia and Africa. What explains this mad scramble for colonies after 1880?

CHRONOLOGY

Politics, 1894–1914

Reign of Emperor William II	1888–1918
Reign of Tsar Nicholas II	1894–1917
Dreyfus affair in France	1895–1899
Theodor Herzl, *The Jewish State*	1896
Austrian Christian Socialists under Karl Lueger	1897–1910
First congress of Social Democratic Party in Russia	1898
Beginning of the Progressive Era in the United States	1900
Formation of Labour Party in Britain	1900
Pankhursts establish Women's Social and Political Union	1903
Ministries of Giovanni Giolitti in Italy	1903–1914
Russo-Japanese War	1904–1905
Revolution in Russia	1905
National Insurance Act in Britain	1911
Universal male suffrage in Italy	1912
Social Democratic Party becomes largest party in Germany	1912

Causes of the New Imperialism

The existence of competitive nation-states after 1870 was undoubtedly a major determinant in the growth of the new imperialism. As European affairs grew tense, heightened competition led European states to acquire colonies abroad that provided ports and coaling stations for their navies. Colonies were also a source of international prestige. Once the scramble for colonies began, failure to enter the race was perceived as a sign of weakness, totally unacceptable to an aspiring great power. Late-nineteenth-century imperialism was thus closely tied to nationalism.

Imperialism was tied to social Darwinism and racism, too. Social Darwinists believed that in the struggle between nations, the fit are victorious and survive. Superior races must dominate inferior races by military force to show how strong and virile they are. As British professor of mathematics Karl Pearson argued in 1900: "The path of progress is strewn with the wrecks of nations; traces are everywhere to be seen of the [slaughtered remains] of inferior races.... Yet these dead people are, in very truth, the stepping stones on which mankind has arisen to the higher intellectual and deeper emotional life of today."[15] Others were equally blunt. One Englishman wrote: "To the development of the White Man, the Black Man and the Yellow must ever remain inferior, and as the former raised itself higher and yet higher, so did these latter seem to shrink out of humanity and appear nearer and nearer to the brutes."[16]

Some Europeans took a more religious or humanitarian approach to imperialism when they argued that Europeans had a moral responsibility to civilize ignorant peoples. This notion of the "white man's burden" (see the box on p. 694) helped at least the more idealistic individuals rationalize imperialism in their own minds. Nevertheless, the belief that the superiority of their civilization obligated them to impose modern industries and new medicines on supposedly primitive nonwhites was yet another form of racism.

Some historians have emphasized an economic motivation for imperialism. There was a great demand for natural resources and products not found in Western countries, such as rubber, oil, and tin. Instead of just trading for these products, European investors advocated direct control of the areas where the raw materials were found. The large surpluses of capital that bankers and industrialists were accumulating often encouraged them to seek higher rates of profit in underdeveloped areas. All of these factors combined to create an economic imperialism whereby European finance dominated the economic activity of a large part of the world. This economic imperialism, however, was not

Soap and the White Man's Burden. The concept of the "white man's burden" included the belief that the superiority of their civilization obligated Europeans to impose their practices on supposedly primitive nonwhites. This advertisement for Pears' Soap clearly communicates the Europeans' view of their responsibility toward other peoples.

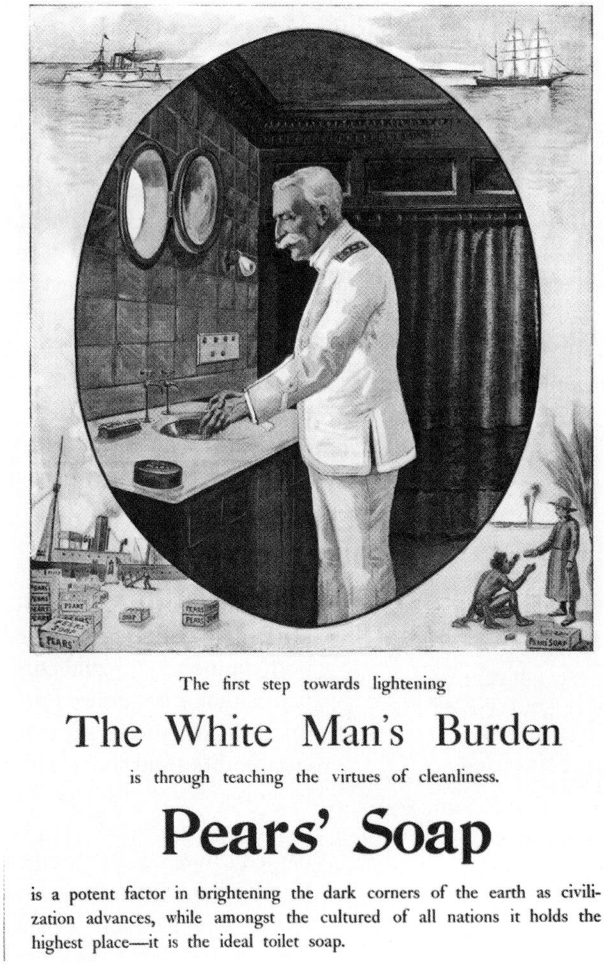

North Wind Picture Archives

necessarily the same thing as colonial expansion. Businesses invested where it was most profitable, not necessarily where their own countries had colonial empires.

Followers of Karl Marx were especially eager to argue that imperialism was economically motivated because they associated imperialism with the ultimate demise of the capitalist system. Marx had hinted at this argument, but it was one of his followers, the Russian V. I. Lenin (see Chapter 25), who in *Imperialism, the Highest Stage of World Capitalism* developed the idea that capitalism leads to imperialism. According to Lenin, as the capitalist system concentrates more wealth in ever-fewer hands, the possibility for investment at home is exhausted, and capitalists are forced to invest abroad, establish colonies, and exploit small, weak nations. In his view, then, the only cure for imperialism was the destruction of capitalism.

CHRONOLOGY

The New Imperialism: Africa

Great Trek of the Boers	1835
Opening of the Suez Canal	1869
Leopold of Belgium establishes settlements in the Congo	1876
British seizure of Transvaal	1877
French conquest of Algeria	1879
British expeditionary force in Egypt	1882
Ethiopians defeat the Italians	1896
Battle of Omdurman in the Sudan	1898
Boer War	1899–1902
Union of South Africa	1910
Italians seize Tripoli	1911
French protectorate over Morocco	1912

The Creation of Empires

Whatever the reasons for the new imperialism, it had a dramatic effect on Africa and Asia as European powers competed for control of these two continents.

THE SCRAMBLE FOR AFRICA

Europeans controlled relatively little of the African continent before 1880. During the Napoleonic wars, the British had established themselves in South Africa by taking control of Cape Town, originally founded by the Dutch. After the wars, the British encouraged settlers to come to what they called the Cape Colony. British policies disgusted the Boers or Afrikaners, as the descendants of the Dutch colonists were called, and led them in 1835 to migrate north on the Great Trek to the region between the Orange and Vaal Rivers (later known as the Orange Free State) and north of the Vaal River (the Transvaal). Hostilities between the British and the Boers continued, however. In 1877, the British governor of the Cape Colony seized the Transvaal, but a Boer revolt led the British government to recognize Transvaal as the independent South African Republic. These struggles between the British and the Boers did not prevent either white group from massacring and subjugating the Zulu and Xhosa peoples of South Africa.

In the 1880s, British policy in South Africa was largely determined by Cecil Rhodes (1853–1902). Rhodes founded both diamond and gold companies that monopolized production of these precious commodities and enabled him to gain control of a territory north of Transvaal that he named Rhodesia after himself. Rhodes was a great champion of British expansion. He said once, "If there be a God, I think what he would like me to do is to paint as much of Africa British red as possible." One of his goals was to create a series of British colonies "from the Cape to Cairo," all linked by a railroad. His imperialist ambitions led to his downfall in 1896, however, when the British government forced him to resign as prime minister of the Cape Colony after he conspired to overthrow the Boer government of the South African Republic without British approval. Although the British government had hoped to avoid war with the Boers, it could not stop extremists on both sides from precipitating a conflict. The Boer War dragged on from 1899 to 1902, when the Boers were overwhelmed by the larger British army. British policy toward the defeated Boers was remarkably conciliatory. Transvaal and the Orange Free State had representative governments by 1907, and in 1910, the Union of South Africa was created. Like Canada, Australia, and New Zealand, it became a fully self-governing dominion within the British Empire.

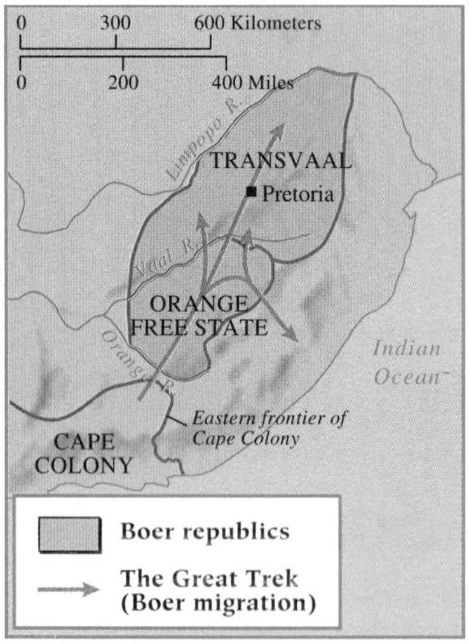

The Struggle for South Africa

Before 1880, the only other European settlements in Africa had been made by the French and the Portuguese. The Portuguese had held on to their settlements in Angola on the west coast and Mozambique on the east coast. The French had started the conquest of Algeria in Muslim North Africa in 1830, although it was not until 1879 that French civilian rule was established there. The next year, 1880, the European scramble for possession of Africa began in earnest. By 1900, the French had added the huge area of French West Africa and Tunisia to their African empire. In 1912, they established a protectorate over much of Morocco; the rest was left to Spain.

The British took an active interest in Egypt after the Suez Canal was opened by the French in 1869. Believing that the canal was their lifeline to India, the British sought to control the canal area. Egypt was a well-established state with an autonomous Muslim government, but that did not stop the British from landing an expeditionary force there in 1882. Although they asserted that their occupation was only temporary, they soon established a protectorate over

Egypt. From Egypt, the British moved south into Sudan and seized it after narrowly averting a war with France. Not to be outdone, Italy joined in the imperialist scramble. Their humiliating defeat by the Ethiopians in 1896 only led the Italians to try again in 1911, when they invaded and seized Ottoman Tripoli, which they renamed Libya.

Central Africa was also added to the list of European colonies. Popular interest in the forbiddingly dense tropical jungles of central Africa was first aroused in the 1860s and 1870s by explorers, such as the Scottish missionary David Livingstone and the British-American journalist Henry M. Stanley. But the real driving force for the colonization of central Africa was King Leopold II (1865–1909) of Belgium, who had rushed enthusiastically into the pursuit of empire in Africa: "To open to civilization," he said, "the only part of our globe where it has not yet penetrated, to pierce the darkness which envelops whole populations, is a crusade, if I may say so, a crusade worthy of this century of progress." Profit, however, was far more important to Leopold than progress; his treatment of the Africans was so brutal that even other Europeans condemned his actions. In 1876, Leopold created the International Association for the Exploration and Civilization of Central Africa and engaged Henry Stanley to establish Belgian settlements in the Congo. Alarmed by Leopold's actions, the French also moved into the territory north of the Congo River.

Between 1884 and 1900, most of the rest of Africa was carved up by the European powers. Germany also entered the ranks of the imperialist powers at this time. Initially, Bismarck had downplayed the significance of colonies, but as domestic political pressures for a German empire intensified, Bismarck became a political convert to colonialism. As he expressed it: "All this colonial business is a sham, but we need it for the elections." The Germans established colonies in South-West Africa, the Cameroons, Togoland, and Tanganyika in East Africa.

By 1914, Britain, France, Germany, Belgium, Spain, and Portugal had carved up the entire African continent (see Map 24.1). Only Liberia, founded by emancipated

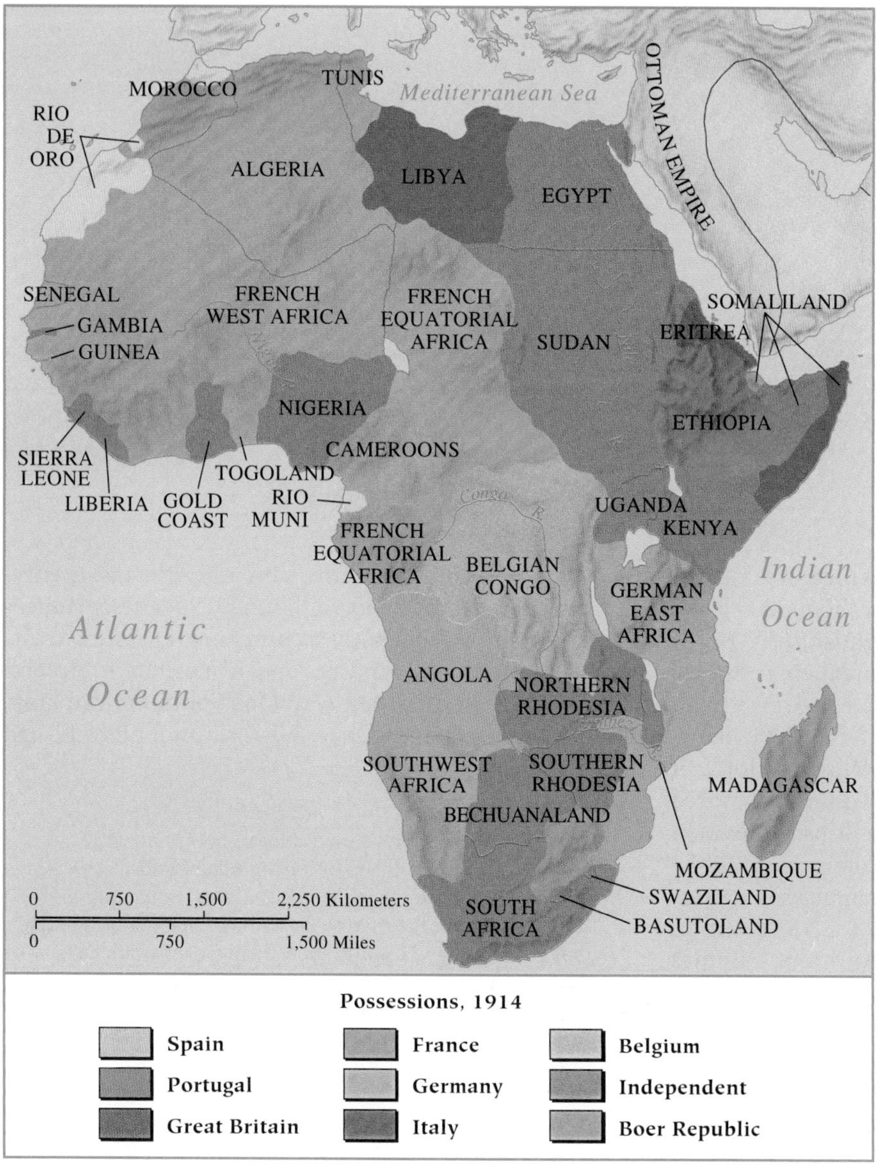

Map 24.1 Africa in 1914. The rush to acquire colonies by Europe's major powers was motivated by a combination of factors: ports and fueling stations for navies, enhancement of international prestige, outlets for nationalist feelings, expression of social Darwinism, and a desire to "civilize" non-Europeans. ■ Of the two countries with the largest amount of territory in Africa, which one had colonies that were the most geographically concentrated, and what could be the benefits of this?

The White Man's Burden

One of the justifications for European imperialism was the notion that superior white peoples had the moral responsibility to raise ignorant native peoples to a higher level of civilization. The British poet Rudyard Kipling (1865–1936) captured this notion in his poem "The White Man's Burden."

■ Rudyard Kipling, "The White Man's Burden"

Take up the White Man's burden—
Send forth the best ye breed—
Go bind your sons to exile
to serve your captives' needs;
To wait in heavy harness,
On fluttered folk and wild—
Your new-caught sullen peoples,
Half-devil and half-child.

Take up the White Man's burden—
In patience to abide,
To veil the threat of terror
And check the show of pride;
By open speech and simple,
An hundred times made plain
To seek another's profit,
And work another's gain.

Take up the White Man's burden—
The savage wars of peace—
Fill full the mouth of Famine
And bid the sickness cease;
And when your goal is nearest
The end for others sought,
Watch sloth and heathen Folly
Bring all your hopes to nought.

Take up the White Man's burden—
No tawdry rule of kings,
But toil of serf and sweeper—
The tale of common things.
The ports ye shall not enter,
The roads ye shall not tread,
Go mark them with your living,
And mark them with your dead.

Take up the White Man's burden—
And reap his old reward:
The blame of those ye better,
The hate of those ye guard—
The cry of hosts ye humour
(Ah, slowly;) toward the light—
'Why brought he us from bondage,
Our loved Egyptian night?'

Take up the White Man's burden—
Ye dare not stoop to less—
Nor call too loud on Freedom
To cloke your weariness;
By all ye cry or whisper,
By all you leave or do,
The silent, sullen peoples
Shall weigh your gods and you.

Take up the White Man's burden—
Have done with childish days—
The lightly proferred laurel,
The easy, ungrudged praise.
Comes now, to search your manhood
Through all the thankless years,
Cold, edged with dear-bought wisdom,
The judgment of your peers!

American slaves, and Ethiopia remained free states. Despite the humanitarian rationalizations about the "white man's burden," Africa had been conquered by European states determined to create colonial empires (see the box on p. 695). Any peoples who dared to resist (with the exception of the Ethiopians, who defeated the Italians) were simply devastated by the superior military force of the Europeans. In 1898, Sudanese tribesmen attempted to defend their independence and stop a British expedition armed with the recently developed machine gun. In the ensuing Battle of Omdurman, the Sudanese were massacred. One observer noted: "It was not a battle but an execution. . . . The bodies were not in heaps—bodies hardly ever are; but they spread evenly over acres and acres. Some lay very composedly with their slippers placed under their heads for a last pillow; some knelt, cut short in the middle of a last prayer. Others were torn to pieces."[17] The battle casualties at Omdurman tell the story of the one-sided conflicts between Europeans and Africans: twenty-eight British deaths to eleven thousand Sudanese. Military superiority was frequently accompanied by brutal treatment of blacks. Nor did Europeans hesitate to deceive the Africans to gain their way. One South African king, Lo Bengula, informed Queen Victoria about how he had been cheated:

> Some time ago a party of men came to my country, the principal one appearing to be a man called Rudd. They asked me for a place to dig for gold, and said they would give me certain things for the right to do so. I told them to bring what they could give and I would show them what I would give. A document was written and presented to me for signature. I asked what it contained, and was told that in it were my words and the words of those men. I put my hand to it. About three months afterwards I heard from other sources that I had given by that document the right to all the minerals of my country.[18]

The Black Man's Burden

The Western justification of imperialism that was based on a sense of moral responsibility, evident in Rudyard Kipling's poem, was often hypocritical. Edward Morel, a British journalist who spent time in the Congo, pointed out the destructive effects of Western imperialism on Africans in his book *The Black Man's Burden.*

■ *Edward Morel,* The Black Man's Burden

It is [the Africans] who carry the "Black man's burden." They have not withered away before the white man's occupation. Indeed . . . Africa has ultimately absorbed within itself every Caucasian and, for that matter, every Semitic invader, too. In hewing out for himself a fixed abode in Africa, the white man has massacred the African in heaps. The African has survived, and it is well for the white settlers that he has. . . .

What the partial occupation of his soil by the white man has failed to do; what the mapping out of European political "spheres of influence" has failed to do; what the Maxim [machine gun] and the rifle, the slave gang, labor in the bowels of the earth and the lash, have failed to do; what imported measles, smallpox and syphilis have failed to do; whatever the overseas slave trade failed to do; the power of modern capitalistic exploitation, assisted by modern engines of destruction, may yet succeed in accomplishing.

For from the evils of the latter, scientifically applied and enforced, there is no escape for the African. Its destructive effects are not spasmodic: they are permanent. In its permanence resides its fatal consequences. It kills not the body merely, but the soul. It breaks the spirit. It attacks the African at every turn, from every point of vantage. It wrecks his polity, uproots him from the land, invades his family life, destroys his natural pursuits and occupations, claims his whole time, enslaves him in his own home. . . .

In Africa, especially in tropical Africa, which a capitalistic imperialism threatens and has, in part, already devastated, man is incapable of reacting against unnatural conditions. In those regions man is engaged in a perpetual struggle against disease and an exhausting climate, which tells heavily upon childbearing; and there is no scientific machinery for saving the weaker members of the community. The African of the tropics is capable of tremendous physical labors. But he cannot accommodate himself to the European system of monotonous, uninterrupted labor, with its long and regular hours, involving, moreover, as it frequently does, severance from natural surroundings and nostalgia, the condition of melancholy resulting from separation from home, a malady to which the African is specially prone. Climatic conditions forbid it. When the system is forced upon him, the tropical African droops and dies.

Nor is violent physical opposition to abuse and injustice henceforth possible for the African in any part of Africa. His chances of effective resistance have been steadily dwindling with the increasing perfectibility in the killing power of modern armament. . . .

Thus the African is really helpless against the material gods of the white man, as embodied in the trinity of imperialism, capitalistic exploitation, and militarism. . . .

To reduce all the varied and picturesque and stimulating episodes in savage life to a dull routine of endless toil for uncomprehended ends, to dislocate social ties and disrupt social institutions; to stifle nascent desires and crush mental development; to graft upon primitive passions the annihilating evils of scientific slavery, and the bestial imaginings of civilized man, unrestrained by convention or law; in fine, to kill the soul in a people—this is a crime which transcends physical murder.

ASIA IN AN AGE OF IMPERIALISM

Although Asia had been open to Western influence since the sixteenth century, not much of its immense territory had fallen under direct European control. The Dutch were established in the East Indies, the Spanish were in the Philippines, and the French and Portuguese had trading posts on the Indian coast. China, Japan, Korea, and Southeast Asia had largely managed to exclude Westerners. The British and the Russians, however, had acquired the most Asian territory.

It was not until the explorations of Australia by Captain James Cook between 1768 and 1771 that Britain took an active interest in the East. The availability of land for grazing sheep and the discovery of gold in Australia led to an influx of free settlers who slaughtered many of the indigenous inhabitants. In 1850, the British government granted the various Australian colonies virtually complete self-government, and fifty years later, on January 1, 1901, all the colonies were unified into the Commonwealth of Australia. Nearby New Zealand, which the British had declared a colony in 1840, was granted dominion status in 1907.

A private trading company known as the British East India Company had been responsible for subjugating much of India. In 1858, however, after a revolt of the sepoys, or Indian troops of the East India Company's army, had been crushed, the British Parliament transferred the company's powers directly to the government in London. In 1876, the title Empress of India was bestowed on Queen Victoria; Indians were now her colonial subjects.

Russian expansion in Asia was a logical outgrowth of its traditional territorial aggrandizement. Russian explorers had penetrated the wilderness of Siberia in the seventeenth century and reached the Pacific coast in 1637. In the eighteenth century, Russians established a claim on Alaska, which they sold to the United States in 1867. Gradually, Russian settlers moved into cold and forbidding Siberia. Altogether seven million Russians settled in Siberia between 1800 and 1914, by which time 90 percent of the Siberian population was Slavic, not Asiatic.

The Russians also moved south, attracted by warmer climes and the crumbling Ottoman Empire. By 1830, the Russians had established control over the entire northern coast of the Black Sea and then pressed on into Central Asia, securing the trans-Caspian area by 1881 and Turkestan in 1885. These advances brought the Russians to the borders of Persia and Afghanistan, where the British also had interests because of their desire to protect their holdings in India. In 1907, the Russians and British agreed to make Afghanistan a buffer state between Russian Turkestan and British India and to divide Persia into two spheres of influence. Halted by the British in their expansion to the south, the Russians moved east in Asia. The Russian occupation of Manchuria and an attempt to move into Korea brought war with the new imperialist power, Japan. After losing the Russo-Japanese War in 1905, the Russians agreed to a Japanese protectorate in Korea, and their Asian expansion was brought to a temporary halt (see Map 24.2).

The thrust of imperialism after 1880 led Westerners to move into new areas of Asia hitherto largely free of Western influence. By the nineteenth century, the ruling Manchu dynasty of the Chinese Empire was showing signs of decline. In 1842, the British had obtained (through war) the island of Hong Kong and trading rights in a number of Chinese cities. Other Western nations soon rushed in to gain similar trading privileges. Chinese attempts to resist this encroachment of foreigners led to military defeats and new demands. Only rivalry among the great powers themselves prevented the complete dismemberment of the Chinese Empire. Instead, Britain, France, Germany, Russia, the United States, and Japan established spheres of influence and long-term leases of Chinese territory. In 1899, urged along by the American secretary of state, John Hay, they agreed to an "open-door" policy in which one country would not restrict the commerce of the other countries in its sphere of influence.

Japan avoided Western intrusion until 1853–1854, when American naval forces under Commodore Matthew Perry forced the Japanese to grant the United States trading and diplomatic privileges. Japan, however, managed to avoid China's fate. Korea had also largely excluded Westerners. The fate of Korea was determined by the struggle first between China and Japan in 1894–1895 and later between Japan and Russia in 1904–1905. Japan's victories gave it clear superiority, and in 1910, Japan formally annexed Korea.

In Southeast Asia, Britain established control over Burma and the Malay States, and France played an active role in subjugating Indochina. The city of Saigon was occupied in 1858, and four years later, Cochin China was taken. In the 1880s, the French extended "protection" over Cambodia, Annam, Tonkin, and Laos and organized them into the Union of French Indochina. Only Siam (Thailand) remained free as a buffer state because of British-French rivalry.

The Pacific islands were also the scene of great power competition and witnessed the entry of the United States onto the imperialist stage. The Samoan Islands became the first important American colony; the Hawaiian Islands were the next to fall. Soon after Americans had made Pearl Harbor into a naval station in 1887, American settlers gained control of the sugar industry on the islands. When Hawaiian natives tried to reassert their authority, the U.S. Marines were brought in to "protect" American lives. Hawaii was annexed by the United States in 1898 during the era of American nationalistic fervor generated by the Spanish-American War. The American defeat of Spain encouraged Americans to extend their empire by acquiring Puerto Rico, Guam, and the Philippine Islands. Although the Filipinos hoped for independence, the Americans refused to grant it. As President William McKinley said, the United States had the duty "to educate the Filipinos and uplift and Christianize them," a remarkable statement in view of the fact that most of them had been Roman Catholics for centuries. It took three years and sixty thousand troops to pacify the Philippines and establish American control.

CHRONOLOGY

The New Imperialism: Asia

Britain obtains Hong Kong and trading rights from Chinese government	1842
Australian colonies receive self-government	1850
Mission of Commodore Perry to Japan	1853–1854
Rebellion of sepoys in India	1857–1858
French occupy Saigon	1858
Overthrow of the shogun in Japan	1867
Emperor Mutsuhito and the Meiji Restoration	1867–1912
Queen Victoria is made empress of India	1876
Russians in Central Asia (trans-Caspian area)	1881
Formation of Indian National Congress	1883
Japanese defeat of China	1894–1895
Spanish-American War; United States annexes Philippines	1898
"Open-door" policy in China	1899
Boxer Rebellion in China	1900–1901
Commonwealth of Australia	1901
Commonwealth of New Zealand	1907
Russian-British agreement over Afghanistan and Persia	1907
Japan annexes Korea	1910
Overthrow of Manchu dynasty in China	1912

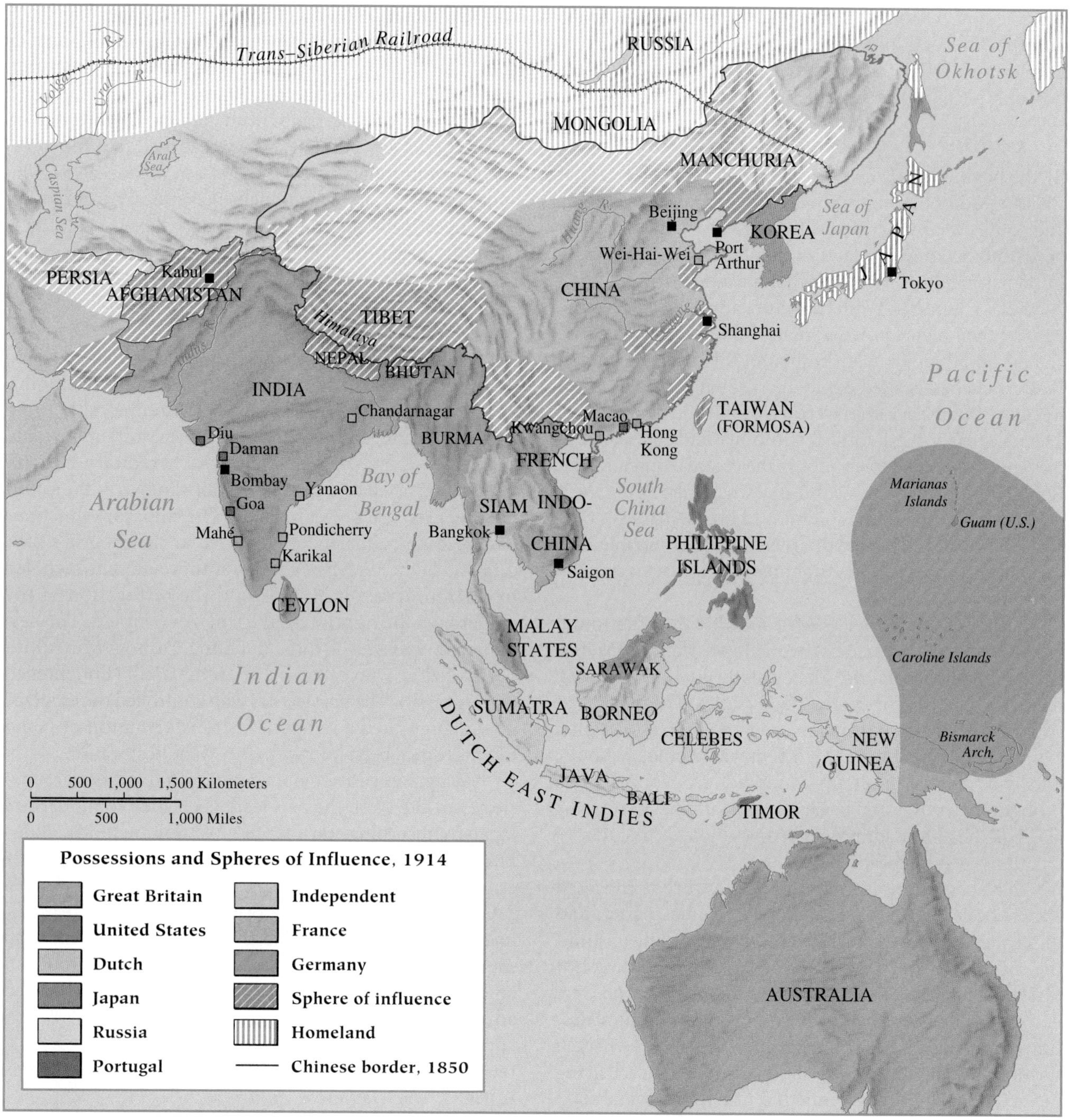

Map 24.2 Asia in 1914. Asia became an important arena of international competition in the nineteenth and early twentieth centuries. Beset by economic stagnation and an inability to modernize, a weak China was unable to withstand the demands of the United States, European powers, and a westernizing Japan. Britain, France, Russia, Japan, and the United States had direct or indirect control of nearly all of Asia by 1914. ■ Why would both Russia and Japan covet Manchuria?

Responses to Imperialism

When Europeans imposed their culture on peoples they considered inferior, how did the conquered peoples respond? Initial attempts to expel the foreigners only led to devastating defeats at the hands of Westerners, whose industrial technology gave them modern weapons of war with which to crush the indigenous peoples. Accustomed to rule by small elites, most people simply accepted their new governors, making Western rule relatively easy. The conquered peoples subsequently adjusted to foreign rule in different ways. Traditionalists sought to maintain their cultural traditions, but modernizers believed that adoption of Western ways would enable them to reform their societies and eventually challenge Western rule. Most people probably stood somewhere between these two extremes. Four examples illustrate different approaches to the question of how indigenous peoples responded to foreign rule.

AFRICA

By the beginning of the twentieth century, a new class of African leaders had emerged. Educated in colonial schools and some even in the West, they were the first generation of Africans to know a great deal about the West and to write in the language of their colonial masters. Although this "new class" admired Western culture and even disliked the ways of their own countries, many came to resent the foreigners and their arrogant contempt for colonial peoples. Westerners had exalted democracy, equality, and political freedom, but these values were not applied in the colonies. There were few democratic institutions, and colonial peoples could only hold lowly jobs in the colonial bureaucracy. Equally important, the economic prosperity of the West was never brought to the colonies. To many Africans, colonialism meant the loss of their farmlands or terrible jobs on plantations or in sweatshops and factories run by foreigners.

Although middle-class Africans did not suffer to the extent that poor peasants or workers on plantations did, they too had complaints. They usually qualified only for menial jobs in the government or business. The purported superiority of the Europeans over the natives was also expressed in a variety of ways. Segregated clubs, schools, and churches were set up as more European officials brought their wives and began to raise families. Europeans also had a habit of addressing natives by their first names or calling an adult male "boy."

Such conditions led many of the new urban educated class to be very confused toward their colonial masters and the civilization they represented. They were willing to admit the superiority of many aspects of Western culture, but these new intellectuals fiercely hated colonial rule and were determined to assert their own nationality and cultural destiny. Out of this mixture of hopes and resentments emerged the first stirrings of modern nationalism in Africa. During the first quarter of the twentieth century, in colonial societies across Africa, educated native peoples began to organize political parties and movements seeking the end of foreign rule.

CHINA

The humiliation of China by the Western powers led to much antiforeign violence, but the Westerners used this lawlessness as an excuse to extort further concessions from the Chinese. A major outburst of violence against foreigners occurred in the Boxer Rebellion in 1900–1901. Boxers was the popular name given to Chinese who belonged to a secret organization called the Society of Harmonious Fists, whose aim was to push the foreigners out of China. The Boxers murdered foreign missionaries, Chinese who had converted to Christianity, railroad workers, foreign businessmen, and even the German envoy to Beijing. Response to the killings was immediate and overwhelming. An allied army consisting of British, French, German, Russian, American, and Japanese troops attacked Beijing, restored order, and demanded more concessions from the Chinese government. The imperial government was so weakened that the forces of the revolutionary leader Sun Yat-sen (1866–1925), who adopted a program of "nationalism, democracy, and socialism," overthrew the Manchu dynasty in 1912. The new Republic of China remained weak and ineffective, and China's travails were far from over.

JAPAN

In the late 1850s and early 1860s, it looked as if Japan would follow China's fate and be carved up into spheres of influence by aggressive Western powers. A remarkably rapid transformation, however, produced a very different result. Before 1868, the shogun, a powerful hereditary military governor assisted by a warrior nobility known as the samurai, exercised real power in Japan. The emperor's functions had become primarily religious. After the shogun's concessions to the Western nations, antiforeign sentiment led to a samurai revolt in 1867 and the restoration of the emperor as the rightful head of the government. The new emperor was the astute, dynamic, young Mutsuhito (1867–1912), who called his reign the Meiji (Enlightened Government). The new leaders who controlled the emperor now inaugurated a remarkable transformation of Japan that has since been known as the Meiji Restoration.

Recognizing the obvious military and industrial superiority of the West, the new leaders decided to modernize Japan by absorbing and adopting Western methods. Thousands of young Japanese were sent abroad to receive Western educations, especially in the social and natural sciences. A German-style army and a British-style navy were established. The Japanese copied the industrial and financial methods of the United States and developed a modern commercial and industrial system. A highly centralized administrative system copied from the French replaced the old system. Initially, the Japanese adopted the French principles of social and legal equality, but by 1890, they had created a political system that was democratic in form but authoritarian in practice.

In imitating the West, Japan also developed a powerful military state. Universal military conscription was introduced in 1872, and a modern peacetime army of 240,000 was eventu-

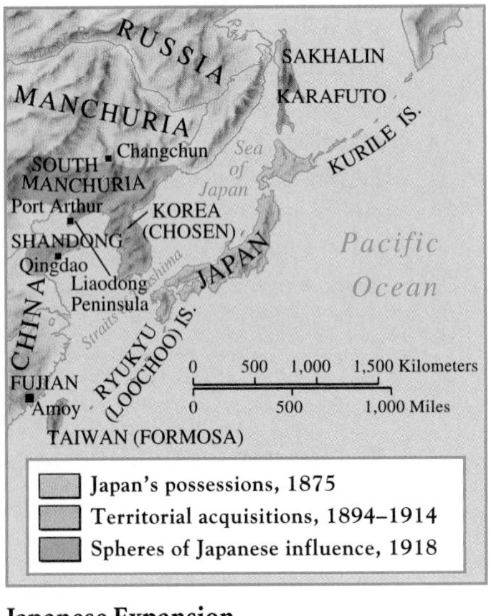

Japanese Expansion

The West and Japan. In their attempt to modernize, the Japanese absorbed and adopted Western methods. They were also influenced by Western culture as Western fashions became the rage in elite circles. Baseball was even imported from the United States. This 1889 Japanese painting shows a music recital at a music school in Tokyo. The musicians and singers wore Western clothing and performed Western music.

ally established. The Japanese avidly pursued the Western imperialistic model. They defeated China in 1894–1895, annexed some Chinese territory, and established their own sphere of influence in China. After they had defeated the Russians in 1905, the Japanese made Korea a colony under harsh rule. The Japanese had proved that an Asian power could play the "white man's" imperialistic game and provided a potent example to peoples in other regions of Asia and Africa.

INDIA

The British government had been in control of India since the mid-nineteenth century. After crushing a major revolt in 1858, the British ruled India directly. Under Parliament's supervision, a small group of British civil servants directed the affairs of India's almost 300 million people.

The British brought order to a society that had been divided by civil wars for some time and created a relatively honest and efficient government. They also brought Western technology—railroads, banks, mines, industry, medical knowledge, and hospitals. The British introduced Western-style secondary schools and colleges where the Indian upper and middle classes and professional classes were educated so that they could serve as trained subordinates in the government and army.

But the Indian people paid a high price for the peace and stability brought by British rule. Due to population growth in the nineteenth century, extreme poverty was a way of life for most Indians; almost two-thirds of the population was malnourished in 1901. British industrialization brought little improvement for the masses. British manufactured goods destroyed local industries, and Indian wealth was used to pay British officials and a large army. The system of education served only the elite, upper-class Indians, and it was conducted only in the rulers' English language while 90 percent of the population remained illiterate. Even for the Indians who benefited the most from their Western educations, British rule was degrading. The best jobs and the best housing were reserved for Britons. Despite their education, the Indians were never considered equals of the British, whose racial attitudes were made quite clear by Lord Kitchener, one of Britain's foremost military commanders in India, when he said: "It is this consciousness of the inherent superiority of the European which has won for us India. However well educated and clever a native may be, and however brave he may prove himself, I believe that no rank we can bestow on him would cause him to be considered an equal of the British officer."[19] Such smug racial attitudes made it difficult for British rule, no matter how beneficent, ever to be ultimately accepted and led to the rise of an Indian nationalist movement. By 1883, when the Indian National Congress was formed, moderate, educated Indians were beginning to seek self-government. By 1919, in response to British violence and British insensitivity, Indians were demanding complete independence.

International Rivalry and the Coming of War

Before 1914, Europeans had experienced almost fifty years of peace. There had been wars (including wars of conquest in the non-Western world), but none had involved the great powers. A series of crises had occurred, however, that might easily have led to general war. One reason they did not is that until 1890, Bismarck of Germany exercised a restraining influence on the Europeans.

The Bismarckian System

Bismarck knew that the emergence of a unified Germany in 1871 had upset the balance of power established at Vienna in 1815. Fearing the French desire for revenge over their loss of Alsace-Lorraine in the Franco-Prussian War, Bismarck made an alliance in 1873 with the traditionally conservative powers Austria-Hungary and Russia. The Three Emperors' League, as it was called, failed to work very well, however, primarily because of Russian-Austrian rivalry in the Balkans.

THE BALKANS: DECLINE OF OTTOMAN POWER

The problem in the Balkans was yet another chapter in the story of the disintegration of the Ottoman Empire. Subject peoples in the Balkans clamored for independence, while corruption and inefficiency weakened the Ottoman government. Only the interference of the great European powers, who were fearful of each other's designs on its territories, kept the Ottoman Empire alive. Complicating the situation was the rivalry between Russia and Austria, which both had designs on the Balkans. For Russia, the Balkans provided the shortest overland route to Constantinople and the Straits. Austria viewed the Balkans as fertile ground for Austrian expansion. Although Germany had no real interests in the Balkans, Bismarck was fearful of the consequences of a war between Russia and Austria over the Balkans and served as a restraining influence on both powers. Events in the Balkans, however, precipitated a new crisis.

In 1876, the Balkan states of Serbia and Montenegro declared war on the Ottoman Empire. Both were defeated, but Russia, with Austrian approval, attacked and defeated the Ottomans. By the Treaty of San Stefano in 1878, a large Bulgarian state, extending from the Danube in the north to the Aegean Sea in the south, was created (see Map 24.3). As Bulgaria was viewed as a Russian satellite, this Russian success caused the other great powers to call for a congress of European powers to discuss a revision of the treaty.

The Congress of Berlin, which met in the summer of 1878, was dominated by Bismarck. The congress effectively demolished the Treaty of San Stefano, much to Russia's humiliation. The new Bulgarian state was considerably reduced, and the rest of the territory was returned to Ottoman control. The three Balkan states of Serbia, Montenegro, and Romania, until then nominally under Ottoman control, were recognized as independent. The other Balkan territories of Bosnia and Herzegovina were placed under Austrian protection; Austria could occupy but not annex them. Although the Germans received no territory, they believed they had at least preserved the peace among the great powers.

NEW ALLIANCES

After the Congress of Berlin, the European powers sought new alliances to safeguard their security. Angered by the Germans' actions at the congress, the Russians had terminated the Three Emperors' League. Bismarck then made an alliance with Austria in 1879 that was joined by Italy in 1882. The Triple Alliance of 1882 committed Germany, Austria, and Italy to support the existing political order while providing a defensive alliance against France or "two or more great powers not members of the alliance." At the same time, Bismarck sought to remain on friendly terms with the Russians and signed the Reinsurance Treaty with Russia in 1887, hoping to prevent a French-Russian alliance that would threaten Germany with the possibility of a two-front war. The Bismarckian system of alliances, geared to preserving peace and the status quo, had worked, but in 1890, Emperor William II dismissed Bismarck and began to chart a new direction for Germany's foreign policy.

New Directions and New Crises

After Bismarck's dismissal, Emperor William II embarked on an activist foreign policy dedicated to enhancing German power by finding, as he put it, Germany's rightful "place in the sun." One of his changes in Bismarck's foreign policy was to drop the Reinsurance Treaty with Russia, which he viewed as being at odds with Germany's alliance with Austria. Although William II tried to remain friendly with Russia, the ending of the alliance achieved what Bismarck had feared: it brought France and Russia together. Long isolated by Bismarck's policies, republican France leaped at the chance to draw closer to tsarist Russia, and in 1894, the two powers concluded a military alliance.

The attitude of the British now became crucial. Secure in their vast empire, the British had long pursued a policy of "splendid isolation" toward the Continent. The British were startled, however, when many Europeans condemned their activity in the Boer War in South Africa. Fearful of an anti-British Continental alliance, they recognized the weakness of isolation and sought an alliance with a Continental power. Initially, neither France nor Russia seemed a logical choice. Britain's traditional enmity with France had only intensified because of their imperialistic rivalries in Africa and Asia. Likewise, British and Russian imperialistic interests had frequently collided.

The Emperor's Big Mouth

Emperor William II had the unfortunate tendency to stir up trouble by his often tactless public remarks. In this 1908 interview, for example, William intended to strengthen Germany's ties with Britain. His words had just the opposite effect and raised a storm of protest in both Britain and Germany.

Daily Telegraph *Interview, October 28, 1908*

His Majesty [William II] honored me with a long conversation, and spoke with impulsive and unusual frankness. "You English," he said, "are mad, mad, mad as March hares. What has come over you that you are so completely given over to suspicions quite unworthy of a great nation? What more can I do than I have done? I declared with all the emphasis at my command, in my speech at Guildhall, that my heart is set upon peace, and that it is one of my dearest wishes to live on the best of terms with England. Have I ever been false to my word? Falsehoods and prevarication are alien to my nature. My actions ought to speak for themselves, but you listen not to them but to those who misinterpret and distort them. That is a personal insult which I feel and resent. To be forever misjudged, to have my repeated offers of friendship weighed and scrutinized with jealous, mistrustful eyes, taxes my patience severely. I have said time after time that I am a friend of England, and your Press—or, at least, a considerable section of it—bids the people of England to refuse my proffered hand, and insinuates that the other holds a dagger. How can I convince a nation against its will?

"I repeat," continued his Majesty, "that I am a friend of England, but you make things difficult for me. My task is not of the easiest. The prevailing sentiment among large sections of the middle and lower classes of my own people is not friendly to England. I am, therefore, so to speak, in a minority in my own land, but it is a minority of the best elements as it is in England with respect to Germany. That is another reason why I resent your refusal to accept my pledged word that I am the friend of England. I strive without ceasing to improve relations, and you retort that I am your arch-enemy. You make it hard for me. Why is it? . . .

"But, you will say, what of the German Navy? Surely, that is a menace to England! Against whom but England are my squadrons being prepared? If England is not in the minds of those Germans who are bent on creating a powerful fleet, why is Germany asked to consent to such new and heavy burdens of taxation? My answer is clear. Germany is a young and growing Empire. She has a world-wide commerce, which is rapidly expanding, and to which the legitimate ambition of patriotic Germans refuses to assign any bounds. Germany must have a powerful fleet to protect that commerce, and her manifold interests in even the most distant seas. She expects those interests to go on growing, and she must be able to champion them manfully in any quarter of the globe. Germany looks ahead. Her horizons stretch far away. She must be prepared for any eventualities in the Far East. Who can foresee what may take place in the Pacific in the days to come, days not so distant as some believe, but days, at any rate, for which all European Powers with Far Eastern interests ought steadily to prepare? Look at the accomplished rise of Japan; think of the possible national awakening of China; and then judge of the vast problems of the Pacific. Only those Powers which have great navies will be listened to with respect, when the future of the Pacific comes to be solved; and, if for that reason only, Germany must have a powerful fleet. It may even be that England herself will be glad that Germany has a fleet when they speak together on the same side in the great debates of the future."

Germany, therefore, seemed the most likely potential ally. Certainly, some people in both Britain and Germany believed that their common German heritage (Anglo-Saxons from Germany had settled in Britain in the Early Middle Ages) made them "natural allies." But Britain was not particularly popular in Germany, nor did the British especially like the Germans. Industrial and commercial rivalry had created much ill feeling, and William II's imperial posturing and grabbing for colonies made the British suspicious of Germany's ultimate aims (see the box above). Especially worrisome to the British was the Germans' construction of a large navy, including a number of battleships advocated by the persistent Admiral von Tirpitz, secretary of the German navy. The British now turned to their traditional enemy, France, and in 1904 concluded the Entente Cordiale by which the two settled all of their outstanding colonial disputes.

German response to the Entente was swift, creating what has been called the First Moroccan Crisis in 1905. The Germans chose to oppose French designs on Morocco in order to humiliate them and drive a wedge between the two new allies, Britain and France. Germany's foolish saber rattling had the opposite effect of what had been intended and succeeded only in uniting Russia, France, Great Britain, and even the United States against Germany. A conference at Algeciras, Spain, in January 1906 awarded control of Morocco to France.

The First Moroccan Crisis of 1905–1906 had important repercussions. France and Britain drew closer together as both began to view Germany as a threat to European

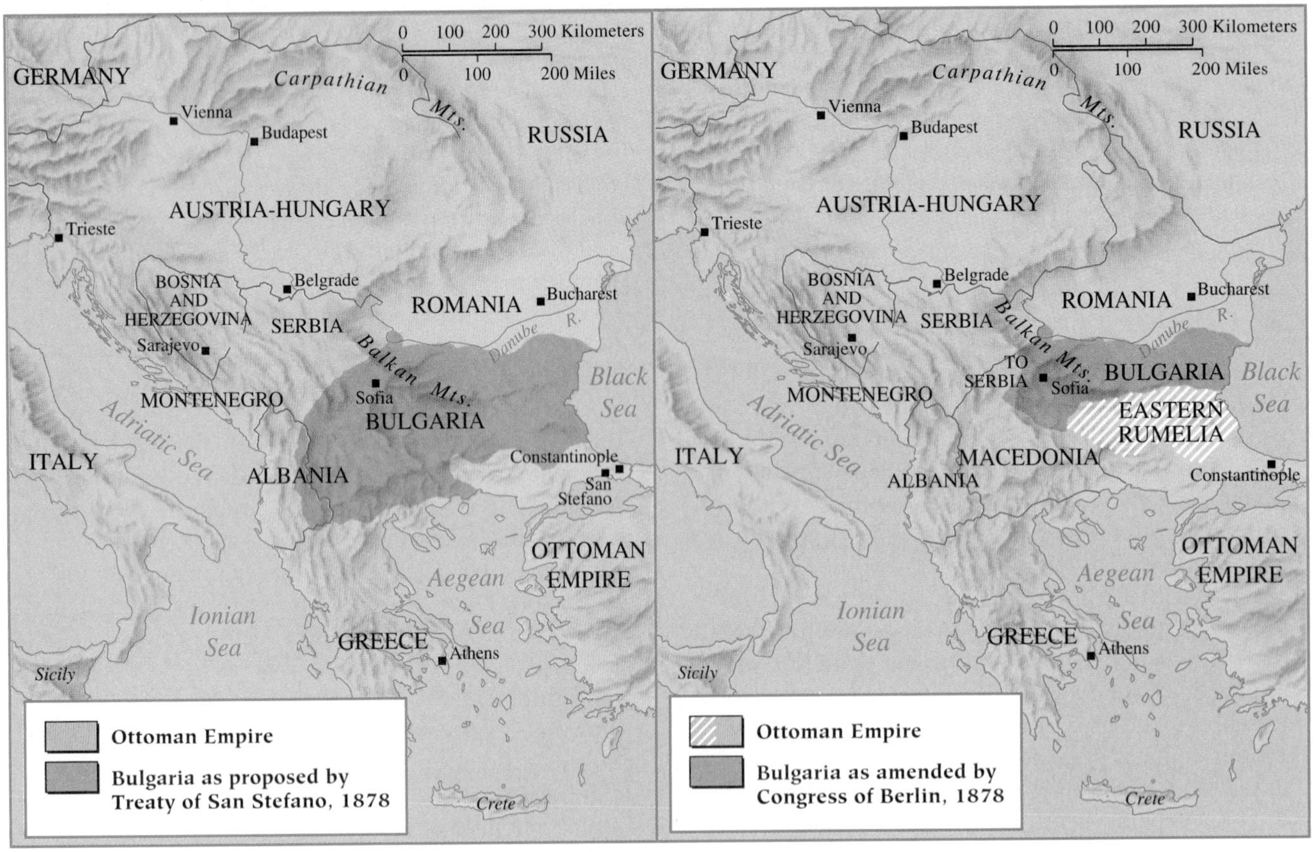

Map 24.3 The Balkans in 1878. As the Ottoman Empire weakened, nationalist groups in the Balkans clamored for independence. After Russia intervened against the Ottomans in the mid-1870s, Germany's Bismarck stepped in, brokering a deal that recognized the independence of Serbia, Romania, and Montenegro and reduced Russian influence in the Balkans. ■ What territories were gained and lost by the Ottoman Empire at the 1878 Congress of Berlin relative to the Treaty of San Stefano?

peace. German leaders, for their part, began to speak of sinister plots to encircle Germany and hinder its emergence as a world power. Russia, too, grew more and more suspicious of the Germans and signed an agreement in 1907 with Great Britain. By that year, Europe's division into two major blocs—the Triple Alliance of Germany, Austria-Hungary, and Italy and the Triple Entente, as the loose association of Russia, France, and Great Britain was called—grew increasingly rigid at the same time that the problems in the Balkans were heating up, setting the stage for all-out war.

CRISES IN THE BALKANS, 1908–1913

The Bosnian Crisis of 1908–1909 initiated a chain of events that eventually went out of control. Since 1878, Bosnia and Herzegovina had been under the protection of Austria, but in 1908, Austria took the drastic step of annexing these two Slavic-speaking territories. Serbia became outraged at this action because it dashed the Serbs' hopes of creating a large Serbian kingdom that would include most of the southern Slavs. This was why the Austrians had annexed Bosnia and Herzegovina. To the Austrians, a large Serbia would be a threat to the unity of the Austro-Hungarian Empire, with its large Slavic population. The Russians, as protectors of their fellow Slavs and with their own desire to increase their authority in the Balkans, supported the Serbs and opposed the Austrian action. Backed by the Russians, the Serbs prepared for war against Austria. At this point, William II intervened and demanded that the Russians accept Austria's annexation of Bosnia and Herzegovina or face war with Germany. Weakened from their defeat in the Russo-Japanese War in 1904–1905, the Russians were afraid to risk war and backed down. Humiliated, the Russians vowed revenge.

European attention returned to the Balkans in 1912 when Serbia, Bulgaria, Montenegro, and Greece organized the Balkan League and defeated the Ottomans in the First Balkan War. When the victorious allies were unable to agree on how to divide the conquered Ottoman provinces of Macedonia and Albania, the Second Balkan War erupted in 1913. Greece, Serbia, Romania, and the Ottoman Empire attacked and defeated Bulgaria. As a result, Bulgaria obtained only a small part of Macedonia, and most of the rest was divided between Serbia and Greece (see Map 24.4). Yet Serbia's aspirations remained unfulfilled. The two Balkan wars left the inhabitants embittered and created more tensions among the great powers.

One of Serbia's major ambitions had been to acquire Albanian territory that would give it a port on the Adriatic. At the London Conference arranged by Austria at the end of the two Balkan wars, the Austrians had blocked Serbia's wishes by creating an independent Albania. The Germans, as Austrian allies, had supported this move. In their frustration, Serbian nationalists increasingly portrayed the Austrians as evil monsters who were keeping the Serbs from becoming a great nation. As Serbia's chief supporters, the Russians were also upset by the turn of events in the Balkans. A feeling had grown among Russian leaders that they could not back down again in the event of a confrontation with Austria or Germany in the Balkans. One Russian military journal even stated early in 1914: "We are preparing for a war in the west. The whole nation must accustom itself to the idea that we arm ourselves for a war of annihilation against the Germans."

Austria-Hungary had achieved another of its aims, but it was still convinced that Serbia was a mortal threat to its empire and must at some point be crushed. Meanwhile, the French and Russian governments renewed their alliance

CHRONOLOGY

European Diplomacy

Three Emperors' League	1873
Serbia and Montenegro attack the Ottoman Empire	1876
Treaty of San Stefano	1878
Congress of Berlin	1878
Defensive alliance: Germany and Austria	1879
Triple Alliance: Germany, Austria, and Italy	1882
Reinsurance Treaty: Germany and Russia	1887
Military alliance: Russia and France	1894
Entente Cordiale: France and Britain	1904
First Moroccan Crisis	1905–1906
Triple Entente: France, Britain, and Russia	1907
First Balkan War	1912
Second Balkan War	1913

The Art Archive, London

Ottoman Army in Retreat. In 1912, a coalition of Serbia, Bulgaria, Montenegro, and Greece defeated the Ottomans and took possession of the Ottoman provinces of Macedonia and Albania. This picture shows the Ottoman army in retreat, pursued by Bulgarian forces.

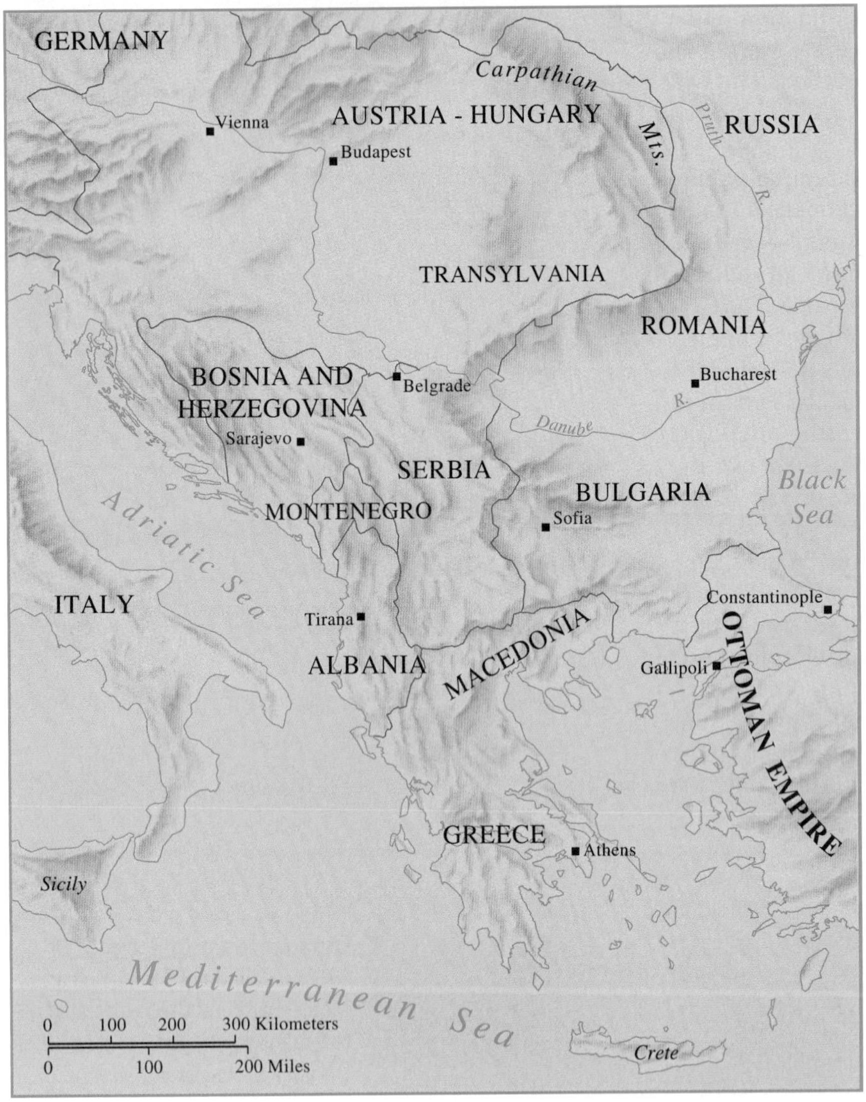

Map 24.4 The Balkans in 1913. The First Balkan War (1912) liberated most of the region from Ottoman control; the Second Balkan War (1913) increased the size of Greece and Serbia at Bulgaria's expense. Russia supported the ambitions of fellow Slavs in Serbia, who sought to rule a large Slavic kingdom in the Balkans. Austria and its ally Germany opposed Serbia's ambitions. ■ Look at Map 24.3: What territories had the Ottomans lost by the end of 1913?

and promised each other that they would not back down at the next crisis. Britain drew closer to France. By the beginning of 1914, the two armed camps viewed each other with suspicion. An American in Europe observed, "The whole of Germany is charged with electricity. Everybody's nerves are tense. It only needs a spark to set the whole thing off." The German ambassador to France noted at the same time that "peace remains at the mercy of an accident." The European "age of progress" was about to come to an inglorious and bloody end.

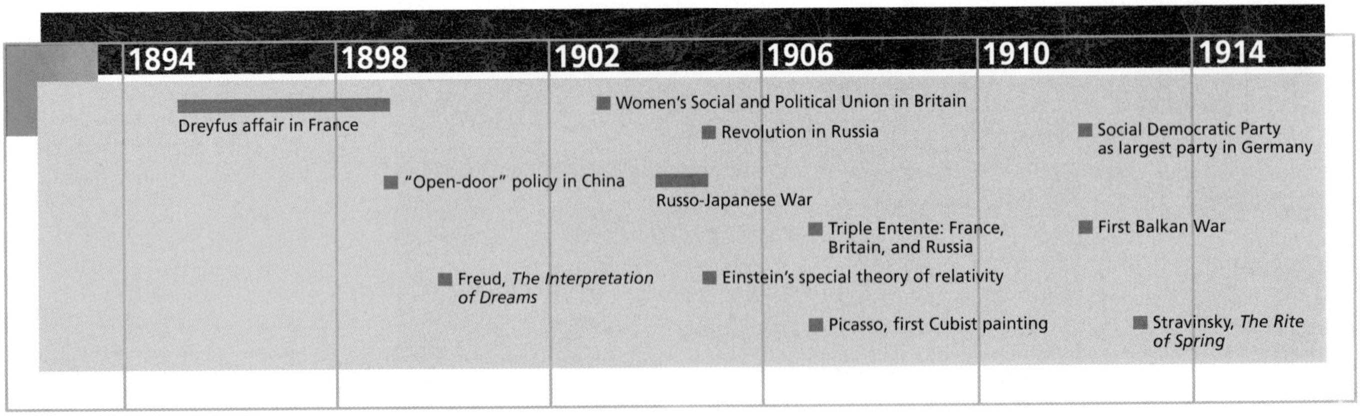

Conclusion

What many Europeans liked to call their "age of progress" in the decades before 1914 was also an era of anxiety. Frenzied imperialist expansion had created vast European empires and spheres of influence around the globe. This feverish competition for colonies, however, had markedly increased the existing antagonisms among the European states. At the same time, the Western treatment of non-Western peoples as racial inferiors caused educated, non-Western elites in these colonies to initiate movements for national independence. Before these movements could be successful, however, the power that Europeans had achieved through their mass armies and technological superiority had to be weakened. The Europeans soon inadvertently accomplished this task for their colonial subjects by demolishing their own civilization on the battlegrounds of Europe.

The cultural revolutions before 1914 had also produced anxiety and a crisis of confidence in European civilization. A brilliant minority of intellectuals had created a modern consciousness that questioned most Europeans' optimistic faith in reason, the rational structure of nature, and the certainty of progress. The devastating experiences of World War I turned this culture of uncertainty into a way of life after 1918.

Notes

1. Quoted in Arthur E. E. McKenzie, *The Major Achievements of Science* (New York, 1960), vol. 1, p. 310.
2. Friedrich Nietzsche, *Twilight of the Idols and the Anti-Christ,* trans. R. J. Hollingdale (New York, 1972), pp. 117–118.
3. Friedrich Nietzsche, *Thus Spake Zarathustra,* in *The Philosophy of Nietzsche* (New York, 1954), p. 6.
4. Herbert Spencer, *Social Statics* (New York, 1896), pp. 146–150.
5. Friedrich von Bernhardi, *Germany and the Next War,* trans. Allen H. Powles (New York, 1914), pp. 18–19.
6. Quoted in Edward R. Tannenbaum, *1900: The Generation Before the Great War* (Garden City, N.Y., 1976), p. 337.
7. William Booth, *In Darkest England and the Way Out* (London, 1890), p. 45.
8. Quoted in John Rewald, *The History of Impressionism* (New York, 1961), pp. 456–458.
9. Quoted in Anne Higonnet, *Berthe Morisot's Images of Women* (Cambridge, Mass., 1992), p. 19.
10. Quoted in Craig Wright, *Listening to Music* (Saint Paul, Minn., 1992), p. 327.
11. Quoted in Catherine M. Prelinger, "Prelude to Consciousness: Amalie Sieveking and the Female Association for the Care of the Poor and the Sick," in John C. Fout, ed., *German Women in the Nineteenth Century: A Social History* (New York, 1984), p. 119.
12. Quoted in Bonnie G. Smith, *Changing Lives: Women in European History Since 1700* (Lexington, Mass., 1989), p. 379.
13. Quoted in Paul Massing, *Rehearsal for Destruction: A Study of Political Anti-Semitism in Imperial Germany* (New York, 1949), p. 147.
14. Quoted in Abba Eban, *Heritage: Civilization and the Jews* (New York, 1984), p. 249.
15. Karl Pearson, *National Life from the Standpoint of Science* (London, 1905), p. 184.
16. Quoted in John Ellis, *The Social History of the Machine Gun* (New York, 1975), p. 80.
17. Quoted in ibid., p. 86.
18. Quoted in Louis L. Snyder, ed., *The Imperialism Reader* (Princeton, N.J., 1962), p. 220.
19. Quoted in K. M. Panikkar, *Asia and Western Dominance* (London, 1959), p. 116.

Suggestions for Further Reading

A well-regarded study of Freud is P. Gay, *Freud: A Life for Our Time* (New York, 1988). Also see J. Neu, ed., *The Cambridge Companion to Freud* (New York, 1991). Nietzsche is examined in R. C. Holub, *Friedrich Nietzsche* (New York, 1995). On Bergson, see A. E. Pilkington, *Henri Bergson and His Influence* (Cambridge, 1976). The basic study on Sorel is J. J. Roth, *The Cult of Violence: Sorel and the Sorelians* (Berkeley, Calif., 1980). A useful study on the impact of Darwinian thought on religion is J. Moore, *The Post-Darwinian Controversies: A Study of the Protestant Struggle to Come to Terms with Darwin in Great Britain and America, 1870–1900* (Cambridge, 1979). Studies of the popular religion of the period include T. A. Kselman, *Miracles and Prophesies in Nineteenth-Century France* (New Brunswick, N.J., 1983), and J. Sperber, *Popular Catholicism in Nineteenth-Century Germany* (Princeton, N.J., 1984). Very valuable on modern art are M. Powell-Jones, *Impressionism* (London, 1994); B. Denvir, *Post-Impressionism* (New York, 1992); and T. Parsons, *Post-Impressionism: The Rise of Modern Art* (London, 1992). On literature, see R. Pascal, *From Naturalism to Expressionism: German Literature and Society, 1880–1918* (New York, 1973).

The rise of feminism is examined in J. Rendall, *The Origins of Modern Feminism: Women in Britain, France and the United States* (London, 1985). The subject of modern anti-Semitism is covered in J. Katz, *From Prejudice to Destruction* (Cambridge, Mass., 1980), and A. S. Lindemann, *Esau's Tears: Modern Anti-Semitism and the Rise of the Jews* (New York, 1997). European racism is analyzed in G. L. Mosse, *Toward the Final Solution* (New York, 1980); German anti-Semitism as a political force is examined in P. J. Pulzer, *The Rise of Political Anti-Semitism in Germany and Austria* (New York, 1964). Anti-Semitism in France is the subject of E. Cahm, *The Dreyfus Affair in French Society and Politics* (New York, 1996). The problems of Jews in Russia are examined in J. Frankel, *Prophecy and Politics: Socialism, Nationalism and the Russian Jews, 1862–1917* (Cambridge, 1981). For a recent biography of Theodor Herzl, see J. Kornberg, *Theodor Herzl: From Assimilation to Zionism* (Bloomington, Ind., 1993). The beginnings of the Labour Party are examined in H. Pelling, *The Origins of the Labour Party,* 2d ed. (Oxford, 1965). There are good introductions to the political world of William II's Germany in T. A. Kohut, *Wilhelm II and the Germans: A Study in Leadership* (New York, 1991), and J. C. G. Röhl, *The Kaiser and His Court: Wilhelm II and the Government of Germany* (New York, 1994). On Russia, see A. Ascher, *The Revolution of 1905: Russia in Disarray,* 2 vols. (Stanford, Calif., 1988–1992).

For broad perspectives on imperialism, see T. Smith, *The Pattern of Imperialism* (Cambridge, 1981); M. W. Doyle, *Empires* (Ithaca, N.Y., 1986); and P. Darby, *Three Faces of Imperialism: British and American Approaches to Asia and Africa, 1870–1970* (New Haven, Conn., 1987). Different aspects of imperialism are covered in R. Robinson and J. Gallagher, *Africa and the Victorians,* 2d ed. (New York, 1981); A. Burton, *Burdens of History: British Feminists, Indian Women, and Imperial Culture, 1865–1915* (Chapel Hill, N.C., 1994); M. Strobel, *European Women and the Second British Empire* (Bloomington, Ind., 1991); P. J. Marshall, ed., *The Cambridge Illustrated History of the British Empire* (Cambridge, 1996); and T. Pakhenham, *The Scramble for Africa* (New York, 1991).

Two fundamental works on the diplomatic history of the period are W. L. Langer, *European Alliances and Alignments,* 2d ed. (New York, 1966), and *The Diplomacy of Imperialism,* 2d ed. (New York, 1965). Also valuable are G. Kennan, *The Decline of Bismarck's European Order: Franco-Prussian Relations, 1875–1890* (Princeton, N.J., 1979), and the masterful study by P. Kennedy, *The Rise of Anglo-German Antagonism, 1860–1914* (London, 1982).

For additional reading, go to InfoTrac College Edition, your online research library at http://web1.infotrac-college.com

Enter the search term *Nietzsche* using Key Terms.

Enter the search term *Sigmund Freud* using Key Terms.

Enter the search term *social Darwinism* using Key Terms.

Enter the search term *imperialism* using the Subject Guide.

CHAPTER

25

The Beginning of the Twentieth-Century Crisis: War and Revolution

Libraire Larousse, Paris

CHAPTER OUTLINE

- The Road to World War I
- The War
- War and Revolution
- The Peace Settlement
- Conclusion

FOCUS QUESTIONS

- What were the long-range and immediate causes of World War I?
- What did the belligerents expect at the beginning of World War I, and why did the course of the war turn out to be so different from their expectations?
- How did World War I affect the belligerents' governmental and political institutions, economic affairs, and social life?
- What were the causes of the Russian Revolution of 1917, and why did the Bolsheviks prevail in the civil war and gain control of Russia?
- What were the objectives of the chief participants at the Paris Peace Conference of 1919, and how closely did the final settlement reflect these objectives?
- What was the relationship between World War I and the Russian Revolution?

ON JULY 1, 1916, British and French infantry forces attacked German defensive lines along a 25-mile front near the Somme River in France. Each soldier carried almost 70 pounds of equipment, making it "impossible to move much quicker than a slow walk." German machine guns soon opened fire: "We were able to see our comrades move forward in an attempt to cross No-Man's Land, only to be mown down like meadow grass," recalled one British soldier. "I felt sick at the sight of this carnage and remember weeping." In one day more than 21,000 British soldiers died. After six months of fighting, the British had advanced 5 miles; one million British, French, and German soldiers had been killed or wounded.

World War I (1914–1918) was the defining event of the twentieth century. It devastated the prewar economic, social, and political order of Europe, and its uncertain outcome served to prepare the way for an even more destructive war. Overwhelmed by the size of its battles, the number of its casualties, and the extent of its impact on all facets of European life, contemporaries referred to it simply as the Great War.

The Great War was all the more disturbing to Europeans because it came after a period that many believed to have been an age of progress. There had been international crises before 1914, but somehow Europeans had managed to avoid serious and prolonged military confrontations. When smaller European states had gone to war, as in the Balkans in 1912 and 1913, the great European powers had shown the ability to keep the conflict localized. Material prosperity and a fervid belief in scientific and technological progress had convinced many people that Europe stood on the verge of creating the utopia that humans had dreamed of for centuries. The historian Arnold Toynbee expressed what the pre–World War I era had meant to his generation:

> *[It was expected] that life throughout the World would become more rational, more humane, and more democratic and that, slowly, but surely, political democracy would produce greater social justice. We had also expected that the progress of science and technology would make mankind richer, and that this increasing wealth would gradually spread from a minority to a majority. We had expected that all this would happen peacefully. In fact we thought that mankind's course was set for an earthly paradise.*[1]

After 1918, it was no longer possible to maintain naive illusions about the progress of Western civilization. As World War I was followed by the destructiveness of World War II and the mass murder machines of totalitarian regimes, it became all too apparent that instead of a utopia, European civilization had become a nightmare. The Great War resulted not only in great loss of life and property but also in the annihilation of one of the basic intellectual precepts on which Western civilization had been thought to have been founded—the belief in progress. A sense of hopelessness and despair soon replaced blind faith in progress. World War I and the revolutions it spawned can properly be seen as the first stage in the crisis of the twentieth century.

The Road to World War I

On June 28, 1914, the heir to the Austrian throne, the Archduke Francis Ferdinand, was assassinated in the Bosnian city of Sarajevo. Although this event precipitated the confrontation between Austria and Serbia that led to World War I, war was not inevitable. Previous assassinations of European leaders had not led to war, and European statesmen had managed to localize such conflicts. Although the decisions that European statesmen made during this crisis were crucial in leading to war, there were also long-range underlying forces that were propelling Europeans toward armed conflict.

Nationalism and Internal Dissent

In the first half of the nineteenth century, liberals had maintained that the organization of European states along national lines would lead to a peaceful Europe based on a sense of international fraternity. They had been very wrong. The system of nation-states that had emerged in Europe in the second half of the nineteenth century led not to cooperation but to competition. Rivalries over colonial and commercial interests intensified during an era of frenzied imperialist expansion, and the division of Europe's great powers into two loose alliances (Germany, Austria, and Italy and France, Great Britain, and Russia) only added to the tensions (see Map 25.1). The series of crises that tested these alliances in the early years of the new century had taught European states a dangerous lesson. Governments that had exercised restraint in order to avoid war wound up being publicly humiliated, whereas those that went to the brink of war to maintain their national interests had often been praised for having preserved national honor. In either case, by 1914, the major European states had come to believe that their allies were important and that their security depended on supporting those allies, even when they took foolish risks.

Diplomacy based on brinkmanship was especially frightening in view of the nature of the European state system. Each nation-state regarded itself as sovereign, subject to no higher interest or authority. Each state was motivated by its own self-interest and success. As Emperor William II of Germany remarked: "In questions of honor and vital interests, you don't consult others." Such attitudes made war an ever-present possibility, particularly since most statesmen considered war an acceptable way to preserve the power of their national states.

The growth of nationalism in the nineteenth century had yet another serious consequence. Not all ethnic groups had achieved the goal of nationhood. Slavic minorities in the Balkans and the Austrian Empire, for example, still dreamed of creating their own national states. So did the Irish in the British Empire and the Poles in the Russian Empire.

National aspirations, however, were not the only source of internal strife at the beginning of the twentieth century. Socialist labor movements had grown more powerful and were increasingly inclined to use strikes, even violent ones, to achieve their goals. Some conservative leaders, alarmed at the increase in labor strife and class division, even feared that European nations were on the verge of revolution. Did these statesmen opt for war in 1914 because they believed that "prosecuting an active foreign policy," as one leader expressed it, would smother "internal troubles"? Some historians have argued that the desire to suppress internal disorder may have encouraged some leaders to take the plunge into war in 1914.

Militarism

The growth of large mass armies after 1900 not only heightened the existing tensions in Europe but made it inevitable that if war did come, it would be highly destructive. Conscription had been established as a regular prac-

Map 25.1 Europe in 1914. By 1914, two alliances dominated Europe: the Triple Entente of Britain, France, and Russia and the Triple Alliance of Germany, Austria-Hungary, and Italy. Russia sought to bolster fellow Slavs in Serbia, whereas Austria-Hungary was intent on increasing its power in the Balkans and thwarting Serbia's ambitions. Thus the Balkans became the flash point for World War I. ■ Which nonaligned nations were positioned between the two alliances?

tice in most Western countries before 1914 (the United States and Britain were major exceptions). European military machines had doubled in size between 1890 and 1914. With its 1.3 million men, the Russian army had grown to be the largest, but the French and Germans were not far behind with 900,000 each. The British, Italian, and Austrian armies numbered between 250,000 and 500,000 soldiers. Most European land armies were filled with peasants, since many young, urban working-class males were unable to pass the physical examinations required for military service.

Militarism, however, involved more than just large armies. As armies grew, so did the influence of military leaders, who drew up vast and complex plans for quickly mobilizing millions of men and enormous quantities of supplies in the event of war. Fearful that changes in these plans would cause chaos in the armed forces, military leaders insisted that their plans could not be altered. In the crises during the summer of 1914, the generals' lack of flexibility forced European political leaders to make decisions for military instead of political reasons.

The Outbreak of War: The Summer of 1914

Militarism, nationalism, and the desire to stifle internal dissent may all have played a role in the coming of World War I, but the decisions made by European leaders in the summer of 1914 directly precipitated the conflict. It was another crisis in the Balkans that forced this predicament on European statesmen.

As we have seen, states in southeastern Europe had struggled to free themselves from Ottoman rule in the course of the nineteenth and early twentieth centuries. But the rivalry between Austria-Hungary and Russia for domination of these new states created serious tensions in the region. The crises between 1908 and 1913 had only intensified the antagonisms. By 1914, Serbia, supported by Russia, was determined to create a large, independent Slavic state in the Balkans, but Austria, which had its own Slavic minorities to contend with, was equally set on preventing that possibility. Many Europeans perceived the inherent dangers in this combination of Serbian ambition bolstered by Russian hatred of Austria and Austrian conviction that Serbia's success would mean the end of its empire. The British ambassador to Vienna wrote in 1913:

> Serbia will some day set Europe by the ears, and bring about a universal war on the Continent. . . . I cannot tell you how exasperated people are getting here at the continual worry which that little country causes to Austria under encouragement from Russia. . . . It will be lucky if Europe succeeds in avoiding war as a result of the present crisis. The next time a Serbian crisis arises . . . , I feel sure that Austria-Hungary will refuse to admit of any Russian interference in the dispute and that she will proceed to settle her differences with her little neighbor by herself.[2]

It was against this backdrop of mutual distrust and hatred between Austria-Hungary and Russia, on the one hand, and Austria-Hungary and Serbia, on the other, that the events of the summer of 1914 were played out.

The assassination of the Austrian Archduke Francis Ferdinand and his wife, Sophia, on June 28, 1914, was carried out by a Bosnian activist who worked for the Black Hand, a Serbian terrorist organization dedicated to the creation of a pan-Slavic kingdom. Although the Austrian government did not know whether the Serbian government had been directly involved in the archduke's assassination, it saw an opportunity to "render Serbia impotent once and for all by a display of force," as the Austrian foreign minister put it. Fearful of Russian intervention on Serbia's behalf, Austrian leaders sought the backing of their German allies. Emperor William II and his chancellor, Theobald von Bethmann-Hollweg, responded with the infamous "blank check," their assurance that Austria-Hungary could rely on Germany's "full support," even if "matters went to the length of a war between Austria-Hungary and Russia." Much historical debate has focused on this "blank check" extended to the Austrians. Did the Germans realize that an Austrian-Serbian war could lead to a wider war? If so, did they actually want one? Historians are still seriously divided on the answers to these questions.

Strengthened by German support, Austrian leaders issued an ultimatum to Serbia on July 23. Austrian leaders made their demands so extreme that Serbia had little choice but to reject some of them in order to preserve its sovereignty. Austria then declared war on Serbia on July 28. Although both Germany and Austria had hoped to keep the war limited to Serbia and Austria in order to ensure Austria's success in the Balkans, these hopes soon vanished.

Still smarting from its humiliation in the Bosnian crisis of 1908, Russia was determined to support Serbia's cause. On July 28, Tsar Nicholas II ordered partial mobilization of the Russian army against Austria. At this point, the rigidity of the military war plans played havoc with diplomatic and political decisions. The Russian General Staff informed the tsar that their mobilization plans were based on a war against both Germany and Austria simultaneously. They could not execute partial mobilization without creating chaos in the army. Consequently, the Russian government ordered full mobilization of the Russian army on July 29, knowing that the Germans would consider this an act of war against them (see the box on p. 711). Germany responded to Russian mobilization with its own ultimatum that the Russians must halt their mobilization within twelve hours. When the Russians ignored it, Germany declared war on Russia on August 1.

At this stage of the conflict, German war plans determined whether France would become involved in the war.

C H R O N O L O G Y

The Road to World War I

	1914
Assassination of Archduke Francis Ferdinand	June 28
Austria's ultimatum to Serbia	July 23
Austria declares war on Serbia	July 28
Russia mobilizes	July 29
German ultimatum to Russia	July 31
Germany declares war on Russia	August 1
Germany declares war on France	August 3
German troops invade Belgium	August 4
Great Britain declares war on Germany	August 4

CORBIS

Apprehension of an Assassin. World War I was precipitated by the assassination of the Archduke Francis Ferdinand, heir to the Austrian throne, on June 28, 1914. His assassin was Gavrillo Princip, an eighteen-year-old Bosnian activist and student who favored the creation of a pan-Slavic kingdom at Austria's expense. As shown here, he was arrested soon after killing the archduke and his wife.

"You Have to Bear the Responsibility for War or Peace"

After Austria declared war on Serbia on July 28, 1914, Russian support of Serbia and German support of Austria threatened to escalate the conflict in the Balkans into a wider war. As we can see in these last-minute telegrams between the Russians and Germans, neither side was able to accept the other's line of reasoning.

Communications Between Berlin and Saint Petersburg on the Eve of World War I

Emperor William II to Tsar Nicholas II, July 28, 10:45 P.M.

I have heard with the greatest anxiety of the impression which is caused by the action of Austria-Hungary against Servia [Serbia]. The inscrupulous agitation which has been going on for years in Servia, has led to the revolting crime of which Archduke Franz Ferdinand has become a victim. The spirit which made the Servians murder their own King and his consort still dominates that country. Doubtless You will agree with me that both of us, You as well as I, and all other sovereigns, have a common interest to insist that all those who are responsible for this horrible murder shall suffer their deserved punishment. . . .

Your most sincere and devoted friend and cousin

(Signed)
Wilhelm

Tsar Nicholas II to Emperor William II, July 29, 1:00 P.M.

I am glad that you are back in Germany. In this serious moment I ask You earnestly to help me. An ignominious war has been declared against a weak country and in Russia the indignation which I full share is tremendous. I fear that very soon I shall be unable to resist the pressure exercised upon me and that I shall be forced to take measures which will lead to war. To prevent a calamity as a European war would be, I urge You in the name of our old friendship to do all in Your power to restrain Your ally from going too far.

(Signed)
Nicolas

Emperor William II to Tsar Nicholas II, July 29, 6:30 P.M.

I have received Your telegram and I share Your desire for the conservation of peace. However: I cannot—as I told You in my first telegram—consider the action of Austria-Hungary as an "ignominious war." Austria-Hungary knows from experience that the promises of Servia as long as they are merely on paper are entirely unreliable. . . . I believe that a direct understanding is possible and desirable between Your Government and Vienna, an understanding which I—as I have already telegraphed You—my Government endeavors to aid with all possible effort. Naturally military measures by Russia, which might be construed as a menace by Austria-Hungary, would accelerate a calamity which both of us desire to avoid and would undermine my position as mediator which—upon Your appeal to my friendship and aid—I willingly accepted.

(Signed)
Wilhelm

Emperor William II to Tsar Nicholas II, July 30, 1:00 A.M.

My Ambassador has instructions to direct the attention of Your Government to the dangers and serious consequences of a mobilization. I have told You the same in my last telegram. Austria-Hungary has mobilized only against Servia, and only a part of her army. If Russia, as seems to be the case, according to Your advice and that of Your Government, mobilizes against Austria-Hungary, the part of the mediator with which You have entrusted me in such friendly manner and which I have accepted upon Your express desire, is threatened if not made impossible. The entire weight of decision now rests upon Your shoulders, You have to bear the responsibility for war or peace.

(Signed)
Wilhelm

German Chancellor to German Ambassador at Saint Petersburg, July 31, URGENT

In spite of negotiations still pending and although we have up to this hour made no preparations for mobilization, Russia has mobilized her entire army and navy, hence also against us. On account of these Russian measures, we have been forced, for the safety of the country, to proclaim the threatening state of war, which does not yet imply mobilization. Mobilization, however, is bound to follow if Russia does not stop every measure of war against us and against Austria-Hungary within 12 hours, and notifies us definitely to this effect. Please to communicate this at once to M. Sasonof and wire hour of communication.

Under the guidance of General Alfred von Schlieffen, chief of staff from 1891 to 1905, the German General Staff had devised a military plan based on the assumption of a two-front war with France and Russia, since the two powers had formed a military alliance in 1894. The Schlieffen Plan called for a minimal troop deployment against Russia while most of the German army would make a rapid invasion of western France by way of neutral Belgium. After the planned quick defeat of the French, the German army expected to redeploy to the east against Russia. Under the Schlieffen Plan, Germany could not mobilize its troops solely against Russia and therefore declared war on France on August 3 after issuing an ultimatum to Belgium on August 2 demanding the right of German troops to pass through Belgian territory. On August 4, Great Britain declared war on Germany, officially over this violation of Belgian neutrality but in fact over the British desire to maintain world power. As one British diplomat argued, if Germany and Austria were to win the war, "what would be the position of a friendless England?" By August 4, all the great powers of Europe were at war. Through all the maneuvering of the last few days before the war, one fact stands out—all the great powers seemed willing to risk the Great War. They were not disappointed.

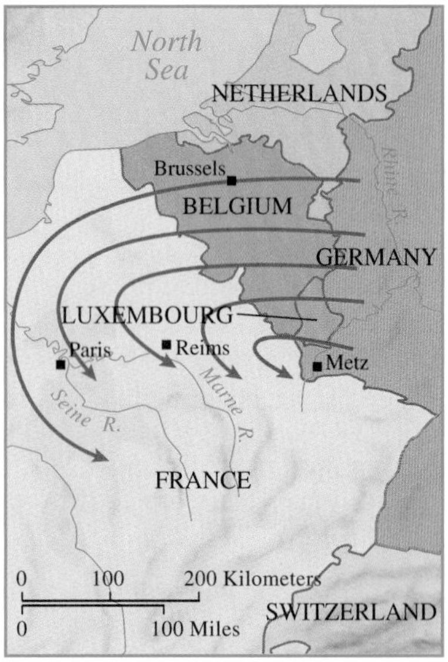

The Schlieffen Plan

The War

Before 1914, many political leaders had become convinced that war involved so many political and economic risks that it was not worth fighting. Others had believed that "rational" diplomats could control any situation and prevent the outbreak of war. At the beginning of August 1914, both of these prewar illusions were shattered, but the new illusions that replaced them soon proved to be equally foolish.

1914–1915: Illusions and Stalemate

Europeans went to war in 1914 with remarkable enthusiasm (see the box on p. 713). Government propaganda had been successful in stirring up national antagonisms before the war. Now, in August 1914, the urgent pleas of governments for defense against aggressors fell on receptive ears in every belligerent nation. Most people seemed genuinely convinced that their nation's cause was just. Even domestic differences were temporarily shelved in the midst of war fever. Socialists had long derided "imperialist war" as a blow against the common interests that united the working classes of all countries. Nationalism, however, proved more powerful than working-class solidarity in the summer of 1914 as socialist parties everywhere dropped plans for strikes and workers expressed their readiness to fight for their country. The German Social Democrats, for example, decided that it was imperative to "safeguard the culture and independence of our own country."

A new set of illusions fed the enthusiasm for war. Almost everyone in August 1914 believed that the war would be over in a few weeks. People were reminded that all European wars since 1815 had in fact ended in a matter of weeks, conveniently overlooking the American Civil War (1861–1865), which was the true prototype for World War I. The illusion of a short war was also bolstered by another illusion, the belief that in an age of modern industry, war could not be conducted for more than a few months without destroying a nation's economy. Both the soldiers who exuberantly boarded the trains for the war front in August 1914 and the jubilant citizens who bombarded them with flowers when they departed believed that the warriors would be home by Christmas.

The Excitement of War. World War I was greeted with incredible enthusiasm. Each of the major belligerents was convinced of the rightness of its cause. Everywhere in Europe, jubilant civilians sent their troops off to war with joyous fervor. Their belief that the soldiers would be home by Christmas proved to be a pathetic illusion.

Librairie Larousse, Paris

The Excitement of War

The incredible outpouring of patriotic enthusiasm that greeted the declaration of war at the beginning of August 1914 demonstrated the power that nationalistic feeling had attained at the beginning of the twentieth century. Many Europeans seemingly believed that the war had given them a higher purpose, a renewed dedication to the greatness of their nation. This selection is taken from the autobiography of Stefan Zweig, an Austrian writer who captured well the orgiastic celebration of war in Vienna in 1914.

Stefan Zweig, The World of Yesterday

The next morning I was in Austria. In every station placards had been put up announcing general mobilization. The trains were filled with fresh recruits, banners were flying, music sounded, and in Vienna I found the entire city in a tumult. . . . There were parades in the street, flags, ribbons, and music burst forth everywhere, young recruits were marching triumphantly, their faces lighting up at the cheering. . . .

And to be truthful, I must acknowledge that there was a majestic, rapturous, and even seductive something in this first outbreak of the people from which one could escape only with difficulty. And in spite of all my hatred and aversion for war, I should not like to have missed the memory of those days. As never before, thousands and hundreds of thousands felt what they should have felt in peace time, that they belonged together. A city of two million, a country of nearly fifty million, in that hour felt that they were participating in world history, in a moment which would never recur, and that each one was called upon to cast his infinitesimal self into the glowing mass, there to be purified of all selfishness. All differences of class, rank, and language were flooded over at that moment by the rushing feeling of fraternity. Strangers spoke to one another in the streets, people who had avoided each other for years shook hands, everywhere one saw excited faces. Each individual experienced an exaltation of his ego, he was no longer the isolated person of former times, he had been incorporated into the mass, he was part of the people, and his person, his hitherto unnoticed person, had been given meaning. . . .

What did the great mass know of war in 1914, after nearly half a century of peace? They did not know war, they had hardly given it a thought. It had become legendary, and distance had made it seem romantic and heroic. They still saw it in the perspective of their school readers and of paintings in museums; brilliant cavalry attacks in glittering uniforms, the fatal shot always straight through the heart, the entire campaign a resounding march of victory—"We'll be home at Christmas," the recruits shouted laughingly to their mothers in August of 1914. . . . A rapid excursion into the romantic, a wild, manly adventure—that is how the war of 1914 was painted in the imagination of the simple man, and the younger people were honestly afraid that they might miss this most wonderful and exciting experience of their lives; that is why they hurried and thronged to the colors, and that is why they shouted and sang in the trains that carried them to the slaughter; wildly and feverishly the red wave of blood coursed through the veins of the entire nation.

Then, too, war held a fatal attraction for many people. To some, war was an exhilarating release from humdrum bourgeois existence, from a "world grown old and cold and weary," as one poet wrote. To some, war meant a glorious adventure, as a young German student wrote to his parents: "My dear ones, be proud that you live in such a time and in such a nation and that you . . . have the privilege of sending those you love into so glorious a battle."[3] And finally, some believed that the war would have a redemptive effect, that millions would abandon their petty preoccupations with material life, ridding the nation of selfishness and sparking a national rebirth based on self-sacrifice, heroism, and nobility. All of these illusions about war died painful deaths on the battlefields of World War I.

German hopes for a quick end to the war rested on a military gamble. The Schlieffen Plan had called for the German army to make a vast encircling movement through Belgium into northern France that would sweep around Paris and encircle most of the French army. German troops crossed into Belgium on August 4 and by the first week of September had reached the Marne River, only 20 miles from Paris. The Germans seemed on the verge of success but had underestimated the speed with which the British would be able to mobilize and put troops into battle in France. An unexpected counterattack by British and French forces under the French commander General Joseph Joffre stopped the Germans at the First Battle of the Marne (September 6–10; see Map 25.2). The German troops fell back, but the exhausted French army was unable to pursue its advantage. The war quickly turned into a stalemate as neither the Germans nor the French could dislodge the other from the trenches they had begun to dig for shelter. Two lines of trenches soon extended from the English Channel to the frontiers of Switzerland. The Western Front had become bogged down in trench warfare, which kept both sides immobilized in virtually the same positions for four years.

In contrast to the west, the war in the east was marked by much more mobility, although the cost in lives was equally enormous. At the beginning of the war, the Russian army moved into eastern Germany but was decisively defeated at the Battles of Tannenberg on August 30 and the Masurian Lakes on September 15 (see Map 25.3 on p. 721). These battles established the military reputations of the commanding general, Paul von Hindenburg, and his chief of staff, General Erich Ludendorff. The Russians were no longer a threat to German territory.

Roger-Viollet/Getty Images

The Horrors of War. The slaughter of millions of men in the trenches of World War I created unimaginable horrors for the participants. For the sake of survival, many soldiers learned to harden themselves against the stench of decomposing bodies and the sight of bodies horribly dismembered by artillery barrages.

The Austrians, Germany's allies, fared less well initially. They had been defeated by the Russians in Galicia and thrown out of Serbia as well. To make matters worse, the Italians betrayed the Germans and Austrians and entered the war on the Allied side by attacking Austria in May 1915. By this time, the Germans had come to the aid of the Austrians. A German-Austrian army defeated and routed the Russian army in Galicia and pushed the Russians back 300 miles into their own territory. Russian casualties stood at 2.5 million killed, captured, or wounded; the Russians had almost been knocked out of the war. Buoyed by their success, the Germans and Austrians, joined by the Bulgarians in September 1915, attacked and eliminated Serbia from the war.

1916–1917: The Great Slaughter

The successes in the east enabled the Germans to move back to the offensive in the west. The early trenches dug in 1914 had by now become elaborate systems of defense. Both lines of trenches were protected by barbed wire entanglements 3 to 5 feet high and 30 yards wide, concrete machine-gun nests, and mortar batteries, supported further back by heavy artillery. Troops lived in holes in the ground, separated from each other by a "no-man's land."

The unexpected development of trench warfare baffled military leaders, who had been trained to fight wars of

The Destruction of Verdun. In 1916, the German High Command decided to take the offensive against the French fortifications at Verdun, 125 miles east of Paris. The ferocious Battle of Verdun cost 700,000 lives and resulted in an exchange of only a few square miles of land. The city of Verdun was subjected to massive artillery shelling, and its population dropped from fifteen thousand to three thousand during the course of the ten-month battle.

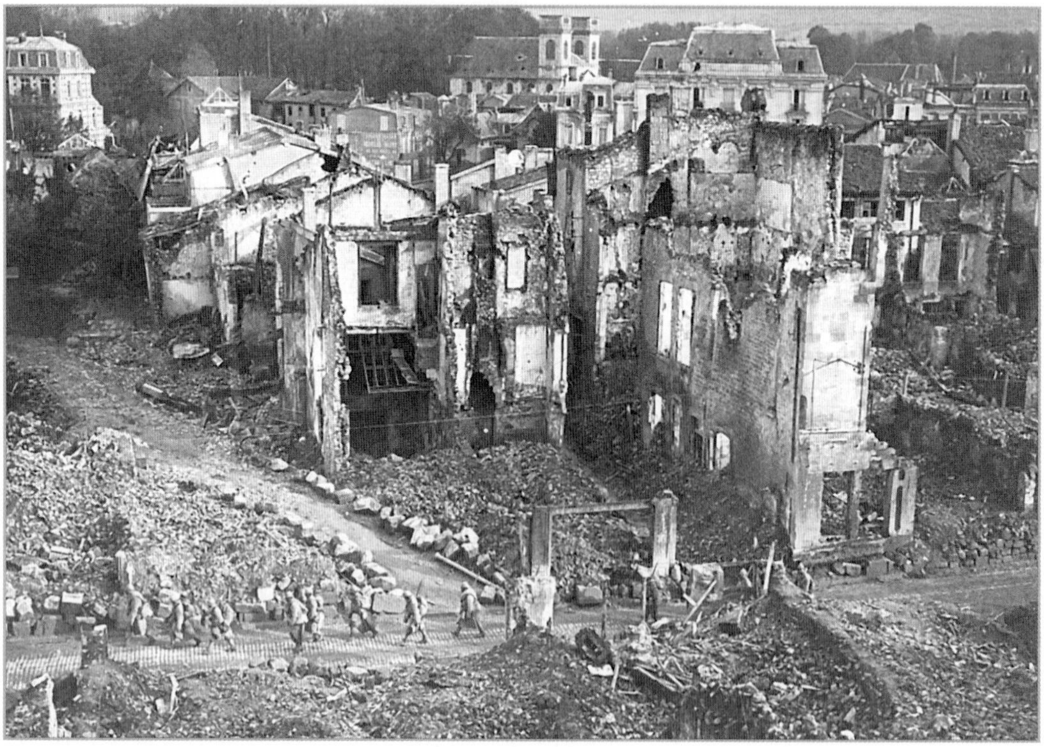

Libraire Larousse, Paris

Map 25.2 The Western Front, 1914–1918. The Western Front was the site of massive carnage: millions of soldiers died in offensives and counteroffensives as they moved battle lines a few miles at a time in France and Belgium. Soldiers in the trenches were often surrounded by the rotting bodies of dead comrades. ■ What is the approximate distance between the armistice line near Sedan and the closest approach of the Germans to Paris?

movement and maneuver. But public outcries for action put them under heavy pressure. The only plan generals could devise was to attempt a breakthrough by throwing masses of men against enemy lines that had first been battered by artillery barrages. Once the decisive breakthrough had been achieved, they thought, they could then return to the war of movement that they knew best. Periodically, the high command on either side would order an offensive that would begin with an artillery barrage to flatten the enemy's barbed wire and leave the enemy in a state of shock. After "softening up" the enemy in this fashion, a mass of soldiers would climb out of their trenches with fixed bayonets and try to work their way toward the enemy trenches. The attacks rarely worked; the machine gun put hordes of men advancing unprotected across open fields at a severe disadvantage. In 1916 and 1917, millions of young men were sacrificed in the search for the elusive breakthrough. In the German offensive at Verdun in 1916, the British campaign on the Somme in 1916, and the French attack in the Champagne in 1917, the senselessness of trench warfare became all too obvious. In ten months at Verdun, 700,000 men lost their lives over a few square miles of terrain.

DAILY LIFE IN THE TRENCHES

Warfare in the trenches of the Western Front produced unimaginable horrors (see the box on p. 718). Many participants commented on the cloud of confusion that covered the battlefields. When attacking soldiers entered "no-man's land," the noise, machine-gun fire, and exploding artillery shells often caused them to panic and lose their sense of direction; they went forward only because they were carried on by the momentum of the soldiers beside them. Rarely were battles as orderly as they were portrayed on military maps and in civilian newspapers.

Battlefields were hellish landscapes of barbed wire, shell holes, mud, and injured and dying men. The introduction of poison gas in 1915 produced new forms of injuries, as one British writer described:

> I wish those people who write so glibly about this being a holy war could see a case of mustard gas . . . could see the poor things burnt and blistered all over with great mustard-colored suppurating blisters with blind eyes all sticky . . . and stuck together, and always fighting for breath, with voices a mere whisper, saying that their throats are closing and they know they will choke.[4]

Archive/Getty Images

Impact of the Machine Gun. Trench warfare on the Western Front stymied military leaders, who had expected to fight a war based on movement and maneuver. Their efforts to effect a breakthrough by sending masses of men against enemy lines were the height of folly in view of the brutal efficiency of the machine gun. This photograph shows a group of German soldiers in their machine-gun nest.

Soldiers in the trenches also lived with the persistent presence of death. Since combat went on for months, they had to carry on in the midst of countless bodies of dead men or the remains of men dismembered by artillery barrages. Many soldiers remembered the stench of decomposing bodies and the swarms of rats that grew fat in the trenches.

Soldiers on the Western Front did not spend all of their time on the front line or in combat when they were on the front line. An infantryman spent one week out of every month in the front-line trenches, one week in the reserve lines, and the remaining two weeks somewhere behind the lines. Daily life in the trenches was predictable. Thirty minutes before sunrise, troops had to "stand to" or be ready to repel any attack. If no attack were forthcoming that day, the day's routine consisted of breakfast followed by inspection, sentry duty, restoration of the trenches, care of personal items, or whiling away the time as best they could. Soldiers often recalled the boredom of life in the dreary, lice-ridden, muddy or dusty trenches.

At many places along the opposing lines of trenches, a "live and let live" system evolved based on the realization that neither side was going to drive out the other anyway. The "live and let live" system resulted in such arrangements as not shelling the latrines or attacking during breakfast. Some parties even worked out agreements to make noise before lesser raids so that the opposing soldiers could retreat to their bunkers.

On both sides, troops produced their own humorous magazines to help pass the time and fulfill the need to laugh in the midst of their daily madness. The British trench magazine, the *B.E.F. Times,* devoted one of its issues to defining military terms. A typical definition "DUDS—These are of two kinds. A shell on impact failing to explode is called a dud. They are unhappily not as plentiful as the other kind, which often draws a big salary and explodes for no reason. These are plentiful away from the fighting areas."[5] Soldiers' songs also captured a mixture of the sentimental and the frivolous (see the box on p. 719).

The Widening of the War

As another response to the stalemate on the Western Front, both sides sought to gain new allies who might provide a winning advantage. The Ottoman Empire had already come into the war on Germany's side in August 1914. Russia, Great Britain, and France declared war on the Ottoman Empire in November. Although the forces of the British Empire attempted to open a Balkan front by landing forces at Gallipoli, southwest of Constantinople, in April 1915, the entry of Bulgaria into the war on the side of the Central Powers (as Germany, Austria-Hungary, and the Ottoman Empire were called) and a disastrous campaign at Gallipoli caused them to withdraw. The Italians, as we have seen, entered the war on the Allied side after France and Britain promised to further their acquisition of Austrian territory. In the long run, however, Italian military incompetence forced the Allies to come to the assistance of Italy.

By 1917, the war that had begun in Europe was having an increasing impact on other parts of the world. In the Middle East, a British officer who came to be known as Lawrence of Arabia incited Arab princes to revolt against their Ottoman overlords. In 1918, British forces from Egypt destroyed the rest of the Ottoman Empire in the Middle East. For their Middle East campaigns, the British mobilized forces from India, Australia, and New Zealand. The Allies also took advantage of Germany's preoccupations in Europe and lack of naval strength to seize German colonies in the rest of the world.

ENTRY OF THE UNITED STATES

The United States tried to remain neutral in the Great War but found it more difficult to do so as the war dragged on. Although there was considerable sentiment for the

Bilderdienst Suddeutscher Verlag, Munich

Victims of the Machine Gun. Masses of men weighed down with equipment and advancing slowly across open land made magnificent targets for opponents armed with machine guns. This photograph shows French soldiers moving across a rocky terrain, all open targets for their enemies manning the new weapons.

British side in the conflict, the immediate cause of American involvement grew out of the naval conflict between Germany and Great Britain. Only once did the German and British naval forces engage in direct combat—at the Battle of Jutland on May 31, 1916, when the Germans won an inconclusive victory.

Britain used its superior naval power to maximum effect, however, by imposing a naval blockade on Germany. Germany retaliated with a counterblockade enforced by the use of unrestricted submarine warfare. At the beginning of 1915, the German government declared the area around the British Isles a war zone and threatened to torpedo any ship caught in it. Strong American protests over the German sinking of passenger liners, especially the British ship *Lusitania* on May 7, 1915, on which more than one hundred Americans lost their lives, forced the German government to modify its policy of unrestricted submarine warfare starting in September 1915 and to briefly suspend unrestricted submarine warfare a year later.

In January 1917, however, eager to break the deadlock in the war, the Germans decided on another military gamble by returning to unrestricted submarine warfare. German naval officers convinced Emperor William II that the use of unrestricted submarine warfare could starve the British into submission within five months. When the emperor expressed concern about the Americans, he was told not to worry. The Americans, the chief of the German Naval Staff said, were "disorganized and undisciplined." The British would starve before the Americans could act. And even if the Americans did intervene, Admiral Holtzendorff assured the emperor, "I give your Majesty my word as an officer, that not one American will land on the Continent."

The return to unrestricted submarine warfare brought the United States into the war on April 6, 1917. Although American troops did not arrive in large numbers in Europe until the following year, the entry of the United States into the war in 1917 gave the Allied Powers a psychological boost when they needed it. The year 1917 was not a good one for them. Allied offensives on the Western Front were disastrously defeated. The Italian armies were smashed in October, and in November, the Bolshevik Revolution in Russia led to Russia's withdrawal from the war (see "The Russian Revolution" later in this chapter). The cause of the Central Powers looked favorable, although war weariness in the Ottoman Empire, Bulgaria, Austria-Hungary, and Germany was beginning to take its toll. The home front was rapidly becoming a cause for as much concern as the war front.

The Home Front: The Impact of Total War

The prolongation of World War I made it a total war that affected the lives of all citizens, however remote they might be from the battlefields. World War I transformed the governments, economies, and societies of the European belligerents in fundamental ways. The need to organize masses of men and matériel for years of combat (Germany alone had 5.5 million men in active units in 1916) led to increased centralization of government powers, economic regimentation, and manipulation of public opinion to keep the war effort going.

TOTAL WAR: POLITICAL CENTRALIZATION AND ECONOMIC REGIMENTATION

As we have seen, the outbreak of World War I was greeted with a rush of patriotism; even socialists joined enthusiastically into the fray. As the war dragged on, governments realized, however, that more than patriotism would be needed. Since the war was expected to be short, little thought had been given to economic problems and

The Reality of War: Trench Warfare

The romantic illusions about the excitement and adventure of war that filled the minds of so many young men who marched off to battle (see the box on p. 713) quickly disintegrated after a short time in the trenches on the Western Front. This description of trench warfare is taken from the most famous novel that emerged from World War I, Erich Maria Remarque's *All Quiet on the Western Front,* written in 1929. Remarque had fought in the trenches in France.

■ *Erich Maria Remarque,* All Quiet on the Western Front

We wake up in the middle of the night. The earth booms. Heavy fire is falling on us. We crouch into corners. We distinguish shells of every caliber.

Each man lays hold of his things and looks again every minute to reassure himself that they are still there. The dug-out heaves, the night roars and flashes. We look at each other in the momentary flashes of light, and with pale faces and pressed lips shake our heads.

Every man is aware of the heavy shells tearing down the parapet, rooting up the embankment and demolishing the upper layers of concrete. . . . Already by morning a few of the recruits are green and vomiting. They are too inexperienced. . . .

The bombardment does not diminish. It is falling in the rear too. As far as one can see it spouts fountains of mud and iron. A wide belt is being raked.

The attack does not come, but the bombardment continues. Slowly we become mute. Hardly a man speaks. We cannot make ourselves understood.

Our trench is almost gone. At many places it is only eighteen inches high, it is broken by holes, and craters, and mountains of earth. A shell lands square in front of our post. At once it is dark. We are buried and must dig ourselves out. . . .

Towards morning, while it is still dark, there is some excitement. Through the entrance rushes in a swarm of fleeing rats that try to storm the walls. Torches light up the confusion. Everyone yells and curses and slaughters. The madness and despair of many hours unloads itself in this outburst. Faces are distorted, arms strike out, the beasts scream; we just stop in time to avoid attacking one another. . . .

Suddenly it howls and flashes terrifically, the dug-out cracks in all its joints under a direct hit, fortunately only a light one that the concrete blocks are able to withstand. It rings metallically, the walls reel, rifles, helmets, earth, mud, and dust fly everywhere. Sulphur fumes pour in. . . . The recruit starts to rave again and two others follow suit. One jumps up and rushes out, we have trouble with the other two. I start after the one who escapes and wonder whether to shoot him in the leg—then it shrieks again, I fling myself down and when I stand up the wall of the trench is plastered with smoking splinters, lumps of flesh, and bits of uniform. I scramble back.

The first recruit seems actually to have gone insane. He butts his head against the wall like a goat. We must try tonight to take him to the rear. Meanwhile we bind him, but so that in case of attack he can be released.

Suddenly the nearer explosions cease. The shelling continues but it has lifted and falls behind us, our trench is free. We seize the hand-grenades, pitch them out in front of the dug-out and jump after them. The bombardment has stopped and a heavy barrage now falls behind us. The attack has come.

No one would believe that in this howling waste there could still be men; but steel helmets now appear on all sides out of the trench, and fifty yards from us a machine-gun is already in position and barking.

The wire-entanglements are torn to pieces. Yet they offer some obstacle. We see the storm-troops coming. Our artillery opens fire. Machine-guns rattle, rifles crack. The charge works its way across. Haie and Kropp begin with the hand-grenades. They throw as fast as they can, others pass them, the handles with the strings already pulled. Haie throws seventy-five yards, Kropp sixty, it has been measured, the distance is important. The enemy as they run cannot do much before they are within forty yards.

We recognize the distorted faces, the smooth helmets: they are French. They have already suffered heavily when they reach the remnants of the barbed-wire entanglements. A whole line has gone down before our machine-guns; then we have a lot of stoppages and they come nearer.

I see one of them, his face upturned, fall into a wire cradle. His body collapses, his hands remain suspended as though he were praying. Then his body drops clean away and only his hands with the stumps of his arms, shot off, now hang in the wire.

long-term wartime needs. Governments had to respond quickly, however, when the war machines failed to achieve their knockout blows and made ever-greater demands for men and matériel.

The extension of government power was a logical outgrowth of these needs. Most European countries had already devised some system of mass conscription or military draft. It was now carried to unprecedented heights as countries mobilized tens of millions of young men for that elusive breakthrough to victory. Even countries that traditionally relied on volunteers (Great Britain had the largest volunteer army in modern history—one million men—in 1914 and 1915) were forced to resort to conscription, especially to ensure that skilled workers did not enlist but remained in factories that were crucial to the production of munitions. In 1916, despite widespread resis-

The Songs of World War I

On the march, in bars, in trains, and even in the trenches, the soldiers of World War I spent time singing. The songs sung by soldiers of different nationalities varied considerably. A German favorite, "The Watch on the Rhine," focused on heroism and patriotism. British war songs often partook of black humor, as in "The Old Barbed Wire." An American favorite was the rousing "Over There," written by the professional songwriter George M. Cohan.

From "The Watch on the Rhine"

There sounds a call like thunder's roar,
Like the crash of swords, like the surge of waves.
To the Rhine, the Rhine, the German Rhine!
Who will the stream's defender be?
Dear Fatherland, rest quietly
Sure stands and true the Watch,
The Watch on the Rhine.

To heaven he gazes.
Spirits of heroes look down.
He vows with proud battle-desire:
O Rhine! You will stay as German as my breast!
Dear Fatherland, [etc.]
Even if my heart breaks in death,
You will never be French.
As you are rich in water
Germany is rich in hero's blood.
Dear Fatherland, [etc.]

So long as a drop of blood still glows,
So long a hand the dagger can draw,
So long an arm the rifle can hold—
Never will an enemy touch your shore.
Dear Fatherland, [etc.]

From "The Old Barbed Wire"

If you want to find the old battalion,
I know where they are,
I know where they are.
If you want to find a battalion,
I know where they are,
They're hanging on the old barbed wire.
I've seen 'em, I've seen 'em,
Hanging on the old barbed wire,
I've seen 'em,
Hanging on the old barbed wire.

George M. Cohan, "Over There"

Over There
Over There
Send the word
Send the word
Over There
That the boys are coming
The drums rum-tuming everywhere.
Over There
Say a prayer
Send the word
Send the word
To beware.
It will be over.
We're coming over
And we won't come back
Till it's over
Over There.

Johnnie get your gun
get your gun
get your gun
Back in town to run
Home to run
Home to run
Hear them calling you and me
Every son of liberty
Hurry right away
Don't delay go today
Make your Daddy glad
To have had such a lad
Tell your sweetheart not to pine
To be proud their boy's in line.

tance to this extension of government power, compulsory military service was introduced in Great Britain.

Throughout Europe, wartime governments expanded their powers over their economies. Free market capitalistic systems were temporarily shelved as governments experimented with price, wage, and rent controls, the rationing of food supplies and materials, the regulation of imports and exports, and the nationalization of transportation systems and industries. Some governments even moved toward compulsory employment. In effect, to mobilize the entire resources of their nations for the war effort, European nations had moved toward planned economies directed by government agencies. Under total war mobilization, the distinction between soldiers at war and civilians at home was narrowed. In the view of political leaders, all citizens constituted a national army dedicated to victory. As the American president, Woodrow Wilson, expressed it, the men and women "who remain to till the soil and man the factories are no less a part of the army than the men beneath the battle flags."

Not all European nations made the shift to total war equally well. Germany had the most success in developing a planned economy. At the beginning of the war, the government asked Walter Rathenau, head of the German General Electric Company, to use his business methods to organize the War Raw Materials Board, which would allocate strategic raw materials to produce the goods that were most needed. Rathenau made it possible for the German war machine to be effectively supplied. The Germans were much less successful with the rationing of food, however. Even before the war, Germany had had to import about 20 percent of its food supply. The British blockade of Germany and a decline in farm labor made food shortages inevitable. Daily food rations in Germany were cut from 1,350 calories in 1916 to 1,000 by 1917, barely adequate for survival. As a result of a poor potato harvest in the winter of 1916–1917, turnips became the basic staple for the poor. An estimated 750,000 German civilians died of hunger during World War I.

The German war government was eventually consolidated under military authority. The two popular military heroes of the war, General Paul von Hindenburg, chief of the General Staff, and Erich Ludendorff, deputy chief of staff, came to control the government by 1916 and virtually became the military dictators of Germany. In 1916, Hindenburg and Ludendorff decreed a system of complete mobilization for total war. In the Auxiliary Service Law of December 2, 1916, they required all male noncombatants between the ages of seventeen and sixty to work only in jobs deemed crucial for the war effort.

Germany, of course, had already possessed a rather authoritarian political system before the war began. France and Britain did not, but even in those countries, the power of the central government was dramatically increased. At first, Great Britain tried to fight the war by continuing its liberal tradition of limited government interference in the economy. The pressure of circumstances, however, forced the British government to take a more active role in economic matters. The need to ensure an adequate production of munitions led to the creation in July 1915 of the Ministry of Munitions under a dynamic leader, David Lloyd George. The Ministry of Munitions took numerous steps to ensure that private industry would produce war matériel at limited profits. It developed a vast bureaucracy of 65,000 clerks to oversee munitions plants. Beginning in 1915, it was given the power to take over plants manufacturing war goods that did not cooperate with the government. The British government also rationed food supplies and imposed rent controls.

The French were less successful than the British and Germans in establishing a strong war government during much of the war. For one thing, the French faced a difficult obstacle in organizing a total war economy. German occupation of northeastern France cost the nation 75 percent of its coal production and almost 80 percent of its steelmaking capacity. Then, too, the relationship between civil and military authorities in France was extraordinarily strained. For the first three years of the war, military and civil authorities

The Leaders of Germany. Over the course of the war, the power of central governments was greatly enlarged in order to meet the demands of total war. In Germany, the two military heroes of the war, Paul von Hindenburg (left) and Erich Ludendorff (right), became virtual military dictators by 1916. The two are shown here with Emperor William II (center), whose power declined as the war dragged on.

CORBIS

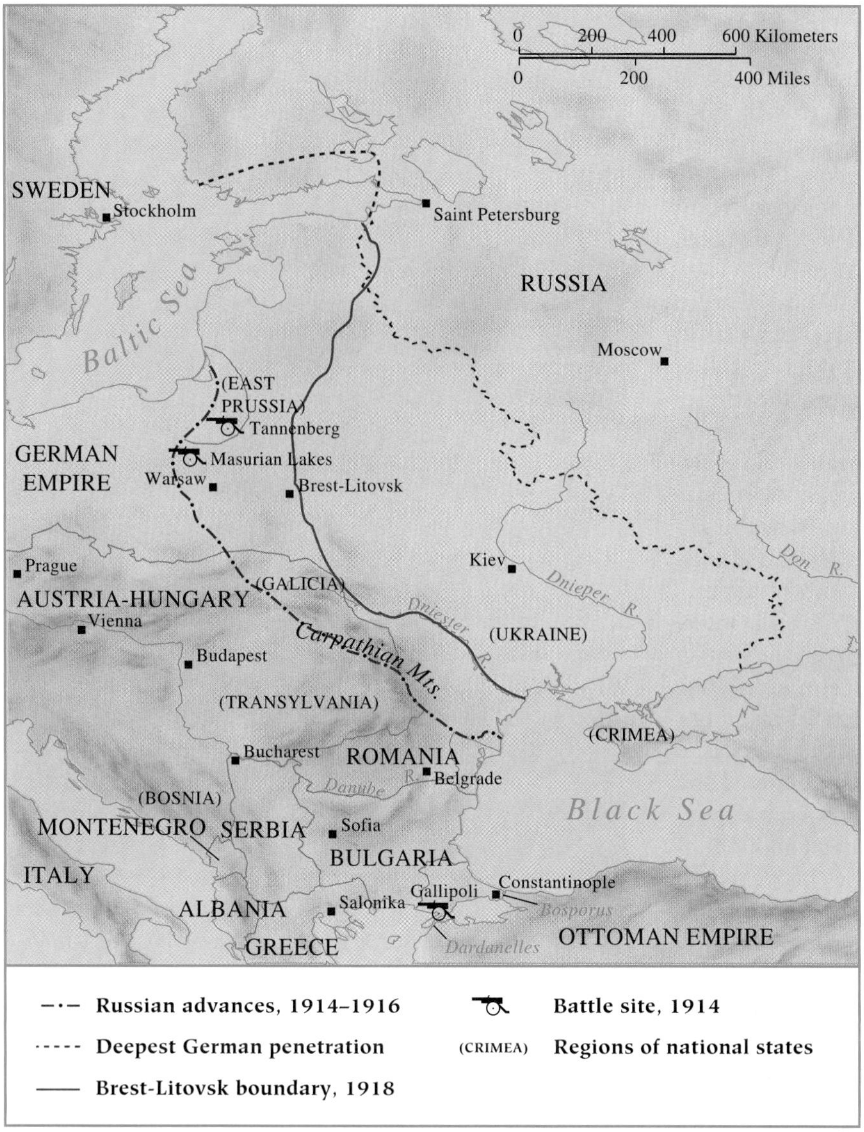

Map 25.3 The Eastern Front, 1914–1918. Russia made early gains but then was pushed far back into its own territory by the German army. After the Bolsheviks seized power, they negotiated the Treaty of Brest-Litovsk, which extracted Russia from the war at the cost of substantial Russian territory (see Map 25.4). ■ What is the approximate average distance between the farthest advances of Russia into Germany and the farthest advances of Germany into Russia?

struggled over who would oversee the conduct of the war. Not until the end of 1917 did the French war government find a strong leader in Georges Clemenceau. Declaring that "war is too important to be left to generals," Clemenceau established clear civilian control of a total war government.

The three other major belligerents—Russia, Austria-Hungary, and Italy—had much less success than Great Britain, Germany, and France in mobilizing for total war. The autocratic empires of Russia and Austria-Hungary had backward economies that proved incapable of turning out the quantity of war matériel needed to fight a modern war. The Russians, for example, conscripted millions of men but could arm only one-fourth of them. Unarmed Russian soldiers were sent into battle anyway and advised to pick up rifles from their dead colleagues. With their numerous minorities, both the Russian and Austro-Hungarian Empires found it difficult to achieve the kind of internal cohesion needed to fight a prolonged total war. Italy, too, lacked both the public enthusiasm and the industrial resources needed to wage a successful total war.

PUBLIC ORDER AND PUBLIC OPINION

As the Great War dragged on and both casualties and privations worsened, internal dissatisfaction replaced the patriotic enthusiasm that had marked the early stages of the war. By 1916, there were numerous signs that civilian morale was beginning to crack under the pressure of total war.

The first two years of the war witnessed only a few scattered strikes, but thereafter strike activity had increased dramatically. In 1916, fifty thousand German workers carried out a three-day work stoppage in Berlin to protest the arrest of a radical socialist leader. In France and Britain, the number of strikes increased significantly. Even worse was the violence that erupted in Ireland when members of the Irish Republican Brotherhood and Citizens Army occupied government buildings in Dublin on Easter Sunday (April 24) in 1916. British forces crushed the Easter Rebellion and then condemned its leaders to death.

Internal opposition to the war came from two major sources in 1916 and 1917, liberals and socialists. Liberals in both Germany and Britain sponsored peace resolutions calling for a negotiated peace without any territorial acquisitions. They were largely ignored. Socialists in Germany and Austria also called for negotiated settlements. By 1917, war morale had so deteriorated that more dramatic protests took place. Mutinies in the Italian and French armies were put down with difficulty. Czech leaders in the Austrian Empire openly called for an independent democratic Czech state. In April 1917, some 200,000 workers in Berlin went out on strike for a week to protest the reduction of bread rations. Only the threat of military force and prison brought them back to their jobs. Despite the strains, all of the belligerent countries except Russia survived the stresses of 1917 and fought on.

War governments also fought back against the growing opposition to the war. Authoritarian regimes, such as those of Germany, Russia, and Austria-Hungary, had always relied on force to subdue their populations. Under the pressures of the war, however, even parliamentary regimes resorted to an expansion of police powers to stifle internal dissent. At the very beginning of the war, the British Parliament passed the Defence of the Realm Act, which allowed the public authorities to arrest dissenters as traitors. The act was later extended to authorize public officials to censor newspapers by deleting objectionable material and even to suspend newspaper publication. In France, government authorities had initially been lenient about public opposition to the war. But by 1917, they began to fear that open opposition to the war might weaken the French will to fight. When Georges Clemenceau became premier near the end of 1917, the lenient French policies came to an end, and basic civil liberties were suppressed for the duration of the war. The editor of an antiwar newspaper was even executed on a charge of treason.

Wartime governments made active use of propaganda to arouse enthusiasm for the war. At the beginning, public officials needed to do little to achieve this goal. The British and French, for example, exaggerated German atrocities in Belgium and found that their citizens were only too willing to believe these accounts. But as the war progressed and morale sagged, governments were forced to devise new techniques to stimulate declining enthusiasm. In one British recruiting poster, for example, a small daughter asked her father, "Daddy, what did *you* do in the Great War?" while her younger brother played with toy soldiers and cannons.

The Art Archive, London

British Recruiting Poster. As the conflict persisted month after month, governments resorted to active propaganda campaigns to generate enthusiasm for the war. In this British recruiting poster, the government tried to pressure men into volunteering for military service. By 1916, the British were forced to adopt compulsory military service.

THE SOCIAL IMPACT OF TOTAL WAR

Total war made a significant impact on European society, most visibly by bringing an end to unemployment. The withdrawal of millions of men from the labor market to fight, combined with the heightened demand for wartime products, led to jobs for everyone able to work.

The cause of labor also benefited from the war. The enthusiastic patriotism of workers was soon rewarded with a greater acceptance of trade unions. To ensure that labor problems would not disrupt production, war governments in Britain, France, and Germany not only sought union cooperation but also for the first time allowed trade unions to participate in making important government decisions on labor matters. In return, unions cooperated on wage limits and production schedules. Labor gained two benefits from this cooperation: it opened the way to the collective bargaining practices that became more widespread after World War I and increased the prestige of trade unions, enabling them to attract more members.

World War I also created new roles for women. With so many men off fighting at the front, women were called on to take over jobs and responsibilities that had not been open to them before. These included certain clerical jobs that only small numbers of women had held earlier. In Britain, for example, the number of women who worked in banking rose from 9,500 to almost 64,000 in the course of the war, while the number of women in commerce rose from a half million to almost one million. Overall, 1,345,000 women in Britain obtained new jobs or replaced men during the war. Women were also now employed in jobs that had been considered "beyond the capacity of women." These included such occupations as chimney

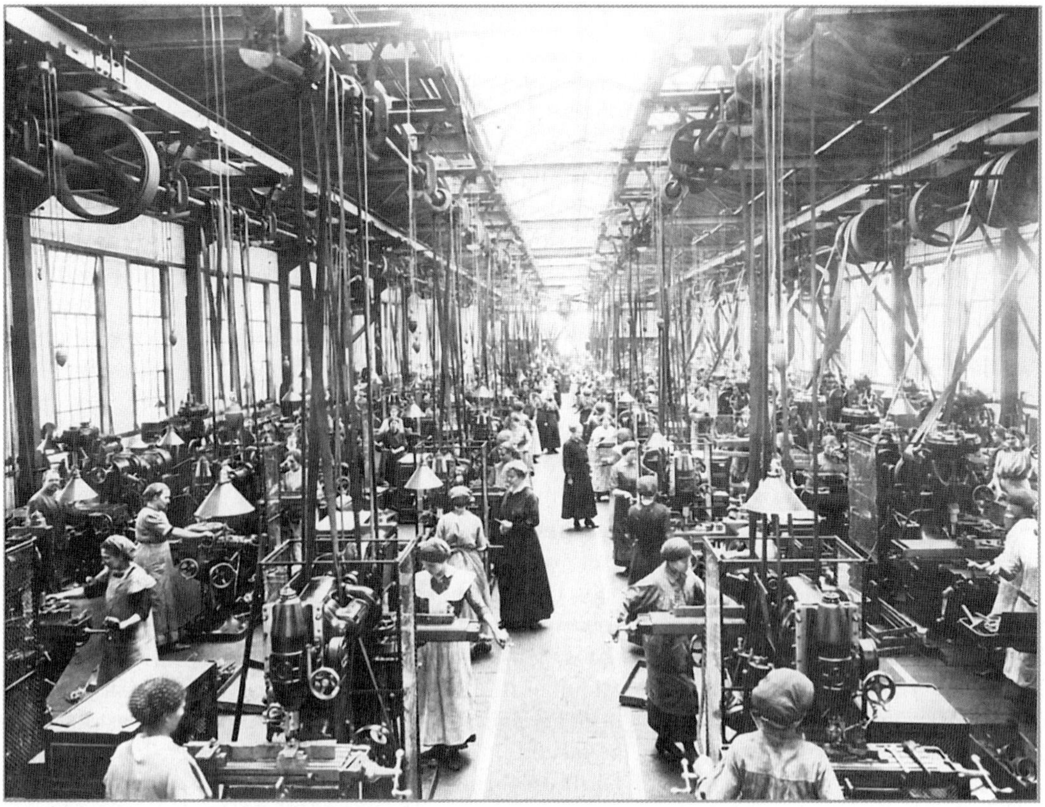

Women Workers in a German Munitions Factory. World War I created new job opportunities for women. They were now employed in jobs that had earlier been considered beyond their capacity. As seen in this picture, this included factory work in heavy industry. These German women are performing a variety of tasks in a shell factory. Between 1913 and 1917, female metalworkers increased from 5 to 28 percent of the total labor force.

sweeps, truck drivers, farm laborers, and, above all, factory workers in heavy industry (see the box on p. 724). In France, 684,000 women worked in armaments plants for the first time; in Britain, the figure was 920,000. Thirty-eight percent of the workers in the Krupp armaments works in Germany in 1918 were women.

Male resistance, however, often made it difficult for women to enter these new jobs, especially in heavy industry. One Englishwoman who worked in a munitions factory recalled her experience: "I could quite see it was hard on the men to have women coming into all their pet jobs and in some cases doing them a good deal better. I sympathized with the way they were torn between not wanting the women to undercut them, and yet hating them to earn as much."[6] While male workers expressed concern that the employment of females at lower wages would depress their own wages, women began to demand equal-pay legislation. The French government passed a law in July 1915 that established a minimum wage for women homeworkers in textiles, an industry that had grown dramatically because of the need for military uniforms. In 1917, the government decreed that men and women should receive equal rates for piecework. Despite the noticeable increase in women's wages that resulted from government regulations, women's industrial wages still were not equal to men's wages by the end of the war.

Even worse, women had achieved little real security about their place in the workforce. Both men and women seemed to think that many of the new jobs for women were only temporary, an expectation quite evident in the British poem "War Girls," written in 1916:

> *There's the girl who clips your ticket for the train,*
> *And the girl who speeds the lift from floor to floor,*
> *There's the girl who does a milk-round in the rain,*
> *And the girl who calls for orders at your door.*
> *Strong, sensible, and fit,*
> *They're out to show their grit,*
> *And tackle jobs with energy and knack.*
> *No longer caged and penned up,*
> *They're going to keep their end up*
> *Till the khaki soldier boys come marching back.*[7]

At the end of the war, governments moved quickly to remove women from the jobs they had encouraged them to take earlier. By 1919, there were 650,000 unemployed women in Britain, and wages for women who were still employed were also lowered. The work benefits for women from World War I seemed to be short-lived.

Women in the Factories

During World War I, women were called on to assume new job responsibilities, including factory work. In this selection, Naomi Loughnan, a young, upper-middle-class woman, describes the experiences in a munitions plant that considerably broadened her perspective on life.

Naomi Loughnan, "Munition Work"

We little thought when we first put on our overalls and caps and enlisted in the Munition Army how much more inspiring our life was to be than we had dared to hope. Though we munition workers sacrifice our ease we gain a life worth living. Our long days are filled with interest, and with the zest of doing work for our country in the grand cause of Freedom. As we handle the weapons of war we are learning great lessons of life. In the busy, noisy workshops we come face to face with every kind of class, and each one of these classes has something to learn from the others. . . .

Engineering mankind is possessed of the unshakable opinion that no woman can have the mechanical sense. If one of us asks humbly why such and such an alteration is not made to prevent this or that drawback to a machine, she is told, with a superior smile, that a man has worked her machine before her for years, and that therefore if there were any improvement possible it would have been made. As long as we do exactly what we are told and do not attempt to use our brains, we give entire satisfaction, and are treated as nice, good children. Any swerving from the easy path prepared for us by our males arouses the most scathing contempt in their manly bosoms. . . . Women have, however, proved that their entry into the munition world has increased the output. Employers who forget things personal in their patriotic desire for large results are enthusiastic over the success of women in the shops. But their workmen have to be handled with the utmost tenderness and caution lest they should actually imagine it was being suggested that women could do their work equally well, given equal conditions of training—at least where muscle is not the driving force. . . .

The coming of the mixed classes of women into the factory is slowly but surely having an educative effect upon the men. "Language" is almost unconsciously becoming subdued. There are fiery exceptions who make our hair stand up on end under our close-fitting caps, but a sharp rebuke or a look of horror will often straighten out the most savage. . . . It is grievous to hear the girls also swearing and using disgusting language. Shoulder to shoulder with the children of the slums, the upper classes are having their eyes opened at last to the awful conditions among which their sisters have dwelt. Foul language, immorality, and many other evils are but the natural outcome of overcrowding and bitter poverty. . . . Sometimes disgust will overcome us, but we are learning with painful clarity that the fault is not theirs whose actions disgust us, but must be placed to the discredit of those other classes who have allowed the continued existence of conditions which generate the things from which we shrink appalled.

Nevertheless, in some countries, the role played by women in the wartime economies did have a positive impact on the women's movement for social and political emancipation. The most obvious gain was the right to vote that was given to women in Germany and Austria immediately after the war (in Britain already in January 1918). The Nineteenth Amendment to the U.S. Constitution gave women in the United States the right to vote in 1920. Contemporary media, however, tended to focus on the more noticeable yet in some ways more superficial social emancipation of upper- and middle-class women. In ever-larger numbers, these young women took jobs, had their own apartments, and showed their new independence by smoking in public and wearing shorter dresses, cosmetics, and boyish hairstyles.

In one sense, World War I had been a great social leveler. Death in battle did not distinguish between classes. Although all social classes suffered casualties in battle, two groups were especially hard-hit. Junior officers who led the charges across the "no-man's land" that separated the lines of trenches experienced death rates that were three times higher than regular casualty rates. Many of these junior officers were members of the aristocracy (see the box on p. 725). The unskilled workers and peasants who made up the masses of soldiers mowed down by machine guns also suffered heavy casualties. The fortunate ones were the skilled laborers who gained exemptions from military service because they were needed at home to train workers in the war industries.

The burst of patriotic enthusiasm that marked the beginning of the war deceived many into believing that the war was creating a new sense of community that meant the end of the class conflict that had marked European society at the end of the nineteenth and beginning of the twentieth centuries. David Lloyd George, who became the British prime minister in 1916, wrote in September 1914 that "all classes, high and low, are shedding themselves of selfishness. . . . It is bringing a new outlook to all classes. . . . We can see for the first time the fundamental things that matter in life, and that have been obscured from our vision by the . . . growth of prosperity."[8] Lloyd George's optimistic opinion proved to be quite misguided, however. The Great War did not eliminate the class conflict that had characterized pre-1914 Europe, and this became increasingly apparent as the war progressed.

The economic impact of the war was felt unevenly. One group of people who especially benefited were the

The Reality of War: War and the Family

John Mott was a captain in the British army. He came from an aristocratic family with a strong military tradition. He married Muriel Backhouse in 1907, and they had three sons before he was called up for service in World War I. These excerpts are taken from four of Mott's letters to his wife and a letter informing her of her husband's death during the Gallipoli campaign. The human experience of World War I was made up of millions of stories like that of John Mott and his family.

■ *One Family's War*

1 July [1915]

My darling Childie,

I hope you got home safely. I have been promised that I shall know the ship we go on tomorrow. But it will be no good writing to Gibraltar as we should get there before the letter. Try Malta as that goes over land. If you get overdrawn go and see Cox. Goodbye Darling. Don't worry I shall come back alright. Your devoted husband John F. Mott

13 July

Mediterranean field force, Mudros

My darling Childie,

This island is very hot indeed but beastly windy. We have absolutely no news from the Front. Troops are pouring out now and I expect we shall be in it next week.

We have all gone through our little bout of diarrhea. I was not too bad and only had pains in my stomach otherwise I am very well indeed.

Everyone is standing the heat very well. The Brigadier has a tent but everybody else is out in the blazing sun.

31 July

My darling Childie,

I got more letters from you today dated 5th, 6th, 7th. I had no idea till I read the letter that they could do all that about writs. I would never have left things in such a muddle, I only hope you can get straight.

Yesterday I left here at 5:30 am to go to the trenches with the Brigadier. We had an awful day, and I am not at all keen to go into that lot at all events. We sailed over in a trawler and had a long walk in the open under shrapnel fire. It was not very pleasant. Then we got to the communications trenches and had a mile and a half of them to go up. When we got to the fire trenches the stink was awful. Arms and legs of Turks sticking out of the trench parapets and lying dead all round. In one place the bottom of the trench was made up by dead Turks, but this has been abandoned as the place was too poisonous.

Our battle ships have been shelling very heavily so there may be an attack on. I must write to my mother tonight. All my love and kisses for ever Your loving husband John F. Mott

6 August

My darling Childie,

We are off today just as we stand up, with four days rations. I can't say where we are going but we shall see spots. I shall not get a chance to write again for a bit as we shall be on the move. I expect you have got a map of the place by now and perhaps you will hear where we have gone.

Very good to get away. All my love and kisses for ever
Your loving husband John F. Mott
Best love to all kids and baby

Pte A Thompson
6 Batt Y and L Red Cross Hospital

We landed on the 6th of Aug and took 2 hills and at daybreak on the 7th advanced across an open plain to the left of Salt Lake and got an awful shelling. We came to a small hill which was flat on top and it was about 2 hundred yards further on where the Capt was hit. They gave us it worse than ever when we got on there and I might have been happen 50 yds away when I saw the Capt and about 5 men fall badly hit. I could not say whether it was shrapnel or common shell but I think it was most probably shrapnel as they use that mostly. It was that thick that no one could get to the Capt at the time and I don't think he lived very long, well he could not the way they were hit and was afterwards buried when things had quietened down in the evening and a cross was put on his grave with an inscription and he got as good a burial as could be given out there. Well I think I have told you all I know about Capt Mott. I only wishe I could have given you better news, so I will close with Kind Regards
Yours Obediently,
Pte Thompson

owners of the large industries manufacturing the weapons of war. Despite public outrage, governments rarely limited the enormous profits made by the industrial barons. In fact, in the name of efficiency, wartime governments tended to favor large industries when scarce raw materials were allocated. Small firms considered less essential to the war effort even had to shut down because of a lack of resources.

Growing inflation also caused inequities. The combination of full employment and high demand for scarce consumer goods caused prices to climb. Many skilled workers were able to earn wages that enabled them to keep up with inflation, but this was not true for unskilled workers or those in nonessential industries. Only in Great Britain did the wages of workers outstrip prices. Everywhere else in Europe, people experienced a loss of purchasing power.

Many middle-class people were hit especially hard by inflation. They included both those who lived on fixed incomes, such as retired people on pensions, and professional people, such as clerks, lesser civil servants, teachers, small shopkeepers, and members of the clergy, whose incomes remained stable at a time when prices were rising. By the end of the war, many of these people were actually doing less well economically than skilled workers. Their discontent would find expression after the war.

War and Revolution

By 1917, total war was creating serious domestic turmoil in all of the European belligerent states. Most countries were able to prop up their regimes and convince their peoples to continue the war for another year, but others were coming close to collapse. In Austria, for example, a government minister warned that "if the monarchs of the Central Powers cannot make peace in the coming months, it will be made for them by their peoples." Russia, however, was the only belligerent that actually experienced the kind of complete collapse in 1917 that others were predicting might happen throughout Europe. Out of Russia's collapse came the Russian Revolution, whose impact would be widely felt in Europe for decades to come.

The Russian Revolution

After the Revolution of 1905 had failed to bring any substantial changes to Russia, Tsar Nicholas II relied on the army and bureaucracy to uphold his regime. But World War I magnified Russia's problems and severely challenged the tsarist government.

Russia was unprepared both militarily and technologically for the total war of World War I. Competent military leadership was lacking. The tsar, alone of all European monarchs, insisted on taking personal charge of the armed forces despite his lack of training for such an awesome burden. Russian industry was unable to produce the weapons needed for the army. Ill-led and ill-armed, Russian armies suffered incredible losses. Between 1914 and 1916, two million soldiers were killed while another four to six million were wounded or captured. By 1917, the Russian will to fight had vanished.

The tsarist government was unprepared for the tasks that it faced in 1914. The surge of patriotic enthusiasm that greeted the outbreak of war was soon dissipated by a government that distrusted its own people. When leading industrialists formed committees to improve factory production, a government suspicious of their motives undermined their efforts. Although the middle classes and liberal aristocrats still hoped for a constitutional monarchy, they were sullen over the tsar's revocation of the political concessions made during the Revolution of 1905. Peasant discontent flourished as conditions worsened. The concentration of Russian industry in a few large cities made workers' frustrations all the more evident and dangerous. In the meantime, Tsar Nicholas II was increasingly insulated from events by his wife, Alexandra.

This German-born princess was a well-educated woman who had fallen under the influence of Rasputin, a Siberian peasant whom the tsarina regarded as a holy man because he alone seemed able to stop the bleeding of her hemophiliac son, Alexis. Rasputin's influence made him a power behind the throne, and he did not hesitate to interfere in government affairs. As the leadership at the top experienced a series of military and economic disasters, the middle class, aristocrats, peasants, soldiers, and workers grew more and more disenchanted with the tsarist regime. Even conservative aristocrats who supported the monarchy felt the need to do something to reverse the deteriorating situation. For a start, they assassinated Rasputin in December 1916. By then it was too late to save the monarchy, and its fall came quickly at the beginning of March 1917.

THE MARCH REVOLUTION

At the beginning of March, a series of strikes broke out in the capital city of Petrograd (formerly Saint Petersburg). Here the actions of working-class women helped to change the course of Russian history. In February 1917, the government had introduced bread rationing in the capital city after the price of bread had skyrocketed. Many of the women who stood in the lines waiting for bread were also factory workers who had put in twelve-hour days. The number of women working in Petrograd factories had doubled since 1914. The Russian government had become aware of the volatile situation in the capital from a police report:

> Mothers of families, exhausted by endless standing in line at stores, distraught over their half-starving and sick children, are today perhaps closer to revolution than [the liberal opposition leaders] and of course they are a great deal more dangerous because they are the combustible material for which only a single spark is needed to burst into flame.[9]

On March 8, a day celebrated since 1910 as International Women's Day, about ten thousand Petrograd women marched through the city shouting "Peace and Bread" and "Down with Autocracy." Soon the women were joined by other workers, and together they called for a general strike that succeeded in shutting down all the factories in the city on March 10. The tsarina wrote to Nicholas II at the battlefront that "this is a hooligan movement. If the weather were very cold they would all probably stay at home." Nicholas ordered the troops to disperse the crowds by shooting them if necessary. Initially, the troops did so, but soon significant numbers of the soldiers joined the demonstrators. The situation was out of the tsar's control. The Duma, or legislature, which the tsar had tried to dissolve, met anyway and on March 12 declared that it was assuming governmental responsibility. It established a provisional government on March 15; the tsar abdicated the same day.

In just one week, the tsarist regime had fallen apart. It was not really overthrown, since there had been no delib-

Sovfoto

The Women's March in Petrograd. After the imposition of bread rationing in Petrograd, ten thousand women engaged in mass demonstrations and demanded "Peace and Bread" for the families of soldiers. This photograph shows the women marching through the streets of Petrograd on March 8, 1917.

erate revolution. Even conscious revolutionaries were caught by surprise at the rapidity of the monarchy's disintegration. Although no particular group had been responsible for the outburst, the moderate Constitutional Democrats were responsible for establishing the provisional government. They represented primarily a middle-class and liberal aristocratic minority. Their program consisted of a nineteenth-century liberal agenda: freedom of speech, religion, and assembly and various civil liberties. Their determination to carry on the war to preserve Russia's honor was a major blunder since it satisfied neither the workers nor the peasants, who fervently wanted an end to the war.

The provisional government also faced another authority, the soviets, or councils of workers' and soldiers' deputies. The soviet of Petrograd had been formed in March 1917; around the same time, soviets sprang up spontaneously in army units, factory towns, and rural areas. The soviets represented the more radical interests of the lower classes and were largely composed of socialists of various kinds. Most numerous were the Socialist Revolutionaries, who wished to establish peasant socialism by seizing the great landed estates and creating a rural democracy. Since the beginning of the twentieth century, the Socialist Revolutionaries had come to rely on the use of political terrorism to accomplish their goals. Since 1893, Russia had also had a Marxist Social Democratic Party, which had divided in 1903 into two factions known as the Mensheviks and the Bolsheviks. The Mensheviks wanted the Social Democrats to be a mass electoral socialist party based on a Western model. Like the Social Democrats of Germany, they were willing to cooperate temporarily in a parliamentary democracy while working toward the ultimate achievement of the socialist state.

The Bolsheviks were a small faction of Russian Social Democrats who had come under the leadership of Vladimir Ulianov, known to the world as V. I. Lenin (1870–1924). Born in 1870 to a middle-class family, Lenin received a legal education and became a lawyer. In 1887, he turned into a dedicated enemy of tsarist Russia when his older brother was executed for planning to assassinate the tsar. Lenin's search for a revolutionary faith led him to Marxism, and in 1894 he moved to Saint Petersburg, where he organized an illegal group known as the Union for the Liberation of the Working Class. Arrested for this activity, Lenin was shipped to Siberia. After his release, he chose to go into exile in Switzerland and eventually assumed the leadership of the Bolshevik wing of the Russian Social Democratic Party.

Under Lenin's direction, the Bolsheviks became a party dedicated to a violent revolution that would destroy the capitalist system. He believed that a "vanguard" of activists must form a small party of well-disciplined professional revolutionaries to accomplish the task. Between 1900 and 1917, Lenin spent most of his time in Switzerland. When the provisional government was formed in March 1917, he believed that an opportunity for the Bolsheviks to seize power had come. In April 1917, with the connivance of the German High Command, who hoped to create disorder in Russia, Lenin, his wife, and a small group of his followers were shipped to Russia in a "sealed train" by way of Finland.

Lenin's arrival in Russia in April opened a new stage in the Russian Revolution. In his "April Theses," issued on April 20, Lenin presented a blueprint for revolutionary action based on his own version of Marxist theory. According to Lenin, it was not necessary for Russia to experience a bourgeois revolution before it could move toward socialism, as orthodox Marxists had argued. Instead, Russia could move directly into socialism. In the "April Theses," Lenin maintained that the soviets of soldiers, workers, and peasants were ready-made instruments of power. The Bolsheviks must work toward gaining control of these groups and then use them to overthrow the provisional government. At the same time, the Bolsheviks articulated the discontent and aspirations of the people, promising an end to the war, the redistribution of all land to the peasants, the transfer of factories and industries from capitalists to committees of workers, and relegation of government power from the provisional government to the soviets. Three simple slogans summed up the Bolshevik program: "Peace, Land, Bread," "Worker Control of Production," and "All Power to the Soviets."

In late spring and early summer, while the Bolsheviks set about winning over the masses to their program and gaining a majority in the Petrograd and Moscow soviets, the provisional government struggled to gain control of Russia against almost overwhelming obstacles. Although the provisional government promised that a constitutional convention called for the fall of 1917 would confiscate and redistribute royal and monastic lands, the offer was meaningless since many peasants had already started seizing lands on their own in March. The military situation was also deteriorating. The Petrograd soviet had issued its Army Order No. 1 in March to all Russian military forces, encouraging them to remove their officers and replace them with committees composed of "the elected representatives of the lower ranks" of the army. Army Order No. 1 led to the collapse of all discipline and created military chaos. When the provisional government attempted to initiate a new military offensive in July, the army simply dissolved as masses of peasant soldiers turned their backs on their officers and returned home to join their families in seizing lands.

THE BOLSHEVIK REVOLUTION

In July 1917, Lenin and the Bolsheviks were falsely accused of inciting an attempt to overthrow the provisional government, and Lenin was forced to flee to Finland. But the days of the provisional government were numbered. In July 1917, Alexander Kerensky, a Socialist Revolutionary, had become prime minister in the provisional government. In September, when General Lavr Kornilov attempted to march on Petrograd and seize power, Kerensky released Bolsheviks from prison and turned to the Petrograd soviet for help. Although General Kornilov's forces never reached Petrograd, Kerensky's action had strengthened the hands of the Petrograd soviet and had shown Lenin how weak the provisional government really was.

By the end of October, the Bolsheviks had achieved a slight majority in the Petrograd and Moscow soviets. The number of party members had also grown from 50,000 to 240,000. Reports of unrest abroad had convinced Lenin that "we are on the threshold of a world proletarian revolution," and he tried to persuade his fellow Bolsheviks that the time was ripe for the overthrow of the provisional government. Although he faced formidable opposition within the Bolshevik ranks, he managed to gain support for his policy. With Leon Trotsky (1877–1940), a fervid revolutionary, as chairman of the Petrograd soviet, the Bolsheviks were in a position to seize power in the name of the soviets. During the night of November 6, pro-soviet and pro-Bolshevik forces took control of Petrograd under the immensely popular slogan "All Power to the Soviets." The provisional government quickly collapsed with little bloodshed. The following night, the all-Russian Congress of Soviets, representing local soviets from all over the country, affirmed the transfer of power. At the second session, the night of November 8, Lenin announced the new Soviet government, the Council of People's Commissars, with himself as its head (see the box on p. 730).

One immediate problem the Bolsheviks faced was the Constituent Assembly, which had been initiated by the provisional government and was scheduled to meet in January 1918. Elections to the assembly by universal male suffrage had resulted in a defeat for the Bolsheviks, who had only 225 delegates compared to the 420 garnered by the Socialist Revolutionaries. But no matter. Lenin simply broke the Constituent Assembly by force. "To hand over power," he said, "to the Constituent Assembly would again be compromising with malignant bourgeoisie."

But the Bolsheviks (soon renamed the Communists) still had a long way to go. Lenin, ever the opportunist, realized the importance of winning mass support as quickly as possible by fulfilling Bolshevik promises. In his first law, Lenin declared the land nationalized and turned it over to local rural soviets. In effect, this action merely ratified the peasants' seizure of the land and assured the Bolsheviks of peasant support, especially against any attempt by the old landlords to restore their power. Lenin also met the demands of urban workers by turning over control of the factories to committees of workers. To Lenin, however, this was merely a temporary expedient.

The new government also introduced a number of social changes. Alexandra Kollontai (1872–1952), who had become a supporter of revolutionary socialism while in exile in Switzerland, took the lead in pushing a Bolshevik program for women's rights and social welfare reforms. As minister of social welfare, she tried to provide health care

Lenin and Trotsky. V. I. Lenin and Leon Trotsky were important figures in the success of the Bolsheviks in seizing power in Russia. On the left, Lenin is seen addressing a rally in Moscow in 1917. On the right, Trotsky, who became commissar of war in the new regime, is shown haranguing his troops.

Brown Brothers

© Underwood & Underwood/CORBIS

for women and children by establishing "palaces for the protection of maternity and children." Between 1918 and 1920, the new regime enacted a series of reforms that made marriage a civil act, legalized divorce, decreed the equality of men and women, and permitted abortions. Kollontai was also instrumental in establishing a women's bureau, known as Zhenotdel, within the Communist Party. This bureau sent men and women to all parts of the Russian Empire to explain the new social order. Members of Zhenotdel were especially eager to help women with matters of divorce and women's rights. In the eastern provinces, several Zhenotdel members were brutally murdered by angry males who objected to any kind of liberation for their wives and daughters. Much to Kollontai's disappointment, many of these Communist social reforms were later undone as the Communists came to face more pressing matters, including the survival of the new regime.

Lenin had also promised peace and that, he realized, was not an easy task because of the humiliating losses of Russian territory that it would entail. There was no real choice, however. On March 3, 1918, the new Communist government signed the Treaty of Brest-Litovsk with Germany and gave up eastern Poland, Ukraine, Finland, and the Baltic provinces. To his critics, Lenin argued that it made no difference since the spread of socialist revolution throughout Europe would make the treaty largely irrelevant. In any case, he had promised peace to the Russian people, but real peace did not come, for the country soon lapsed into civil war.

CIVIL WAR

There was great opposition to the new Bolshevik regime, not only from groups loyal to the tsar but also from bourgeois and aristocratic liberals and anti-Leninist socialists, including Mensheviks and Socialist Revolutionaries. In addition, thousands of Allied troops were eventually sent to different parts of Russia in the hope of bringing Russia back into the war.

Between 1918 and 1921, the Bolshevik (Red) Army was forced to fight on many fronts (see Map 25.4). The first serious threat to the Bolsheviks came from Siberia, where a White (anti-Bolshevik) force under Admiral Alexander Kolchak pushed westward and advanced almost to the Volga River before being stopped. Attacks also came from the Ukrainians in the southeast and from the Baltic regions. In mid-1919, White forces under General Anton Denikin, probably the most effective of the White generals, swept through the Ukraine and advanced almost to Moscow. At one point in late 1919, three separate White armies seemed to be closing in on the Bolsheviks but were eventually pushed back. By 1920, the major White forces had been defeated, and the Ukraine was retaken. The next year, the Communist regime regained control over the independent nationalist governments in the Caucasus: Georgia, Russian Armenia, and Azerbaijan.

The royal family was yet another victim of the civil war. After the tsar had abdicated, he, his wife, and their five children had been taken into custody. They were moved in

Ten Days That Shook the World: Lenin and the Bolshevik Seizure of Power

John Reed was an American journalist who helped found the American Communist Labor Party. Accused of sedition, he fled the United States and went to Russia. In *Ten Days That Shook the World,* Reed left an impassioned eyewitness account of the Russian Revolution. It is apparent from his comments that Reed considered Lenin the indispensable hero of the Bolshevik success.

John Reed, Ten Days That Shook the World

It was just 8:40 when a thundering wave of cheers announced the entrance of the presidium, with Lenin—great Lenin—among them. A short, stocky figure, with a big head set down in his shoulders, bald and bulging. Little eyes, a snubbish nose, wide, generous mouth, and heavy chin; clean-shaven now, but already beginning to bristle with the well-known beard of his past and future. Dressed in shabby clothes, his trousers much too long for him. Unimpressive, to be the idol of a mob, loved and revered as perhaps few leaders in history have been. A strange popular leader—a leader purely by virtue of intellect; colorless, humorless, uncompromising and detached; without picturesque idiosyncrasies—but with the power of explaining profound ideas in simple terms, of analyzing a concrete situation. And combined with shrewdness, the greatest intellectual audacity. . . .

Now Lenin, gripping the edge of the reading stand, letting his little winking eyes travel over the crowd as he stood there waiting, apparently oblivious to the long-rolling ovation, which lasted several minutes. When it finished, he said simply, "We shall now proceed to construct the Socialist order!" Again that overwhelming human roar.

"The first thing is the adoption of practical measures to realize peace. . . . We shall offer peace to the peoples of all the belligerent countries upon the basis of the Soviet terms—no annexations, no indemnities, and the right of self-determination of peoples. At the same time, according to our promise, we shall publish and repudiate the secret treaties. . . . The question of War and Peace is so clear that I think that I may, without preamble, read the project of a Proclamation to the Peoples of All the Belligerent Countries. . . ."

His great mouth, seeming to smile, opened wide as he spoke; his voice was hoarse—not unpleasantly so, but as if it had hardened that way after years and years of speaking—and went on monotonously, with the effect of being able to go forever. . . . For emphasis he bent forward slightly. No gestures. And before him, a thousand simple faces looking up in intent adoration.

[Reed then reproduces the full text of the Proclamation.]

When the grave thunder of applause had died away, Lenin spoke again: "We propose to the Congress to ratify this declaration. . . . This proposal of peace will meet with resistance on the part of the imperialist governments—we don't fool ourselves on that score. But we hope that revolution will soon break out in all the belligerent countries; that is why we address ourselves especially to the workers of France, England and Germany. . . ."

"The revolution of November 6th and 7th," he ended, "has opened the era of the Social Revolution. . . . The labor movement, in the name of peace and Socialism, shall win, and fulfill its destiny. . . ."

There was something quiet and powerful in all this, which stirred the souls of men. It was understandable why people believed when Lenin spoke.

August 1917 to Tobolsk in Siberia and in April 1918 to Ekaterinburg, a mining town in the Urals. On the night of July 16, members of the local soviet murdered the tsar and his family and burned their bodies in a nearby mine shaft.

How had Lenin and the Bolsheviks triumphed over what seemed at one time to be overwhelming forces? For one thing, the Red Army became a well-disciplined and formidable fighting force, largely due to the organizational genius of Leon Trotsky. As commissar of war, Trotsky reinstated the draft and even recruited and gave commands to former tsarist army officers. Trotsky insisted on rigid discipline; soldiers who deserted or refused to obey orders were summarily executed. The Red Army also had the advantage of interior lines of defense and was able to move its troops rapidly from one battlefront to the other.

The disunity of the anti-Communist forces seriously weakened the efforts of the Whites. Political differences created distrust among the Whites and prevented them from cooperating effectively with each other. Some Whites, such as Admiral Kolchak, insisted on restoring the tsarist regime, but others understood that only a more liberal and democratic program had any chance of success. Since the White forces were forced to operate on the exterior fringes of the Russian Empire, it was difficult enough to achieve military cooperation. Political differences made it virtually impossible.

The Whites' inability to agree on a common goal contrasted sharply with the Communists' single-minded sense of purpose. Inspired by their vision of a new socialist order, the Communists had the advantage of possessing the determination that comes from revolutionary fervor and revolutionary convictions.

The Communists also succeeded in translating their revolutionary faith into practical instruments of power. A policy of "war communism," for example, was used to ensure regular supplies for the Red Army. "War communism" included the nationalization of banks and most industries, the forcible requisition of grain from peasants, and the centralization of state administration under Bolshevik control. Another Bolshevik instrument was "revolutionary terror." Although the old tsarist secret police had been abolished, a new Red secret police—known as the Cheka—replaced it. The Red Terror instituted by the Cheka aimed at nothing less than the destruction of all those who opposed the new regime. "Class enemies"—the bourgeoisie—were especially singled out, at least according to a Cheka officer: "The first questions you should put to the accused person are: To what class does he belong, what is his origin, what was his education, and what is his profession? These should determine the fate of the accused." In practice, however, the Cheka promulgated terror against all classes, including the proletariat, if they opposed the new regime. Thousands were executed. The Red Terror added an element of fear to the Bolshevik regime.

Finally, the intervention of foreign armies enabled the Communists to appeal to the powerful force of Russian patriotism. Although the Allied Powers had initially intervened in Russia to encourage the Russians to remain in the war, the end of the war on November 11, 1918, had made that purpose inconsequential. Nevertheless, Allied troops remained, and more were even sent as Allied countries did not hide their anti-Bolshevik feelings. At one point, over

CHRONOLOGY

The Russian Revolution

	1917
March of women in Petrograd	March 8
General strike in Petrograd	March 10
Establishment of provisional government	March 15
Tsar abdicates	March 15
Formation of Petrograd soviet	March
Lenin arrives in Russia	April 3
Lenin's "April Theses"	April 20
Failed attempt to overthrow provisional government	July
Bolsheviks gain majority in Petrograd soviet	October
Bolsheviks overthrow provisional government	November 6–7
	1918
Lenin disbands Constituent Assembly	January
Treaty of Brest-Litovsk	March 3
Civil war	1918–1921

Map 25.4 The Russian Revolution and Civil War. The Russian Civil War lasted from 1918 to 1921. A variety of disparate groups, including victorious powers from World War I, sought to either overthrow the Bolsheviks or seize Russian territory. Lack of cohesion among enemies helped the Bolsheviks triumph, but at the cost of much hardship and bloodshed.
■ What was the most common method of Allied troop transport to Russia, and why?

100,000 foreign troops, mostly Japanese, British, American, and French, were stationed on Russian soil. These forces rarely engaged in pitched battles, however, nor did they pursue a common strategy, although they did give material assistance to anti-Bolshevik forces. This intervention by the Allies enabled the Communist government to appeal to patriotic Russians to fight the attempts of foreigners to control their country. Allied interference was never substantial enough to make a military difference in the civil war, but it did serve indirectly to help the Bolshevik cause.

By 1921, the Communists had succeeded in retaining control of Russia. In the course of the civil war, the Bolshevik regime had also transformed Russia into a bureaucratically centralized state dominated by a single party. It was also a state that was largely hostile to the Allied Powers that had sought to assist the Bolsheviks' enemies in the civil war. To most historians, the Russian Revolution is unthinkable without the total war of World War I, for only the collapse of Russia made it possible for a radical minority like the Bolsheviks to seize the reins of power. In turn, the Russian Revolution had an impact on the course of World War I.

CHRONOLOGY

World War I

	1914
Battle of Tannenberg	August 26–30
First Battle of the Marne	September 6–10
Battle of Masurian Lakes	September 15
Russia, Great Britain, and France declare war on Ottoman Empire	November
	1915
Battle of Gallipoli begins	April 25
Italy declares war on Austria-Hungary	May 23
Entry of Bulgaria into the war	September
	1916
Battle of Verdun	February 21–December 18
Battle of Jutland	May 31
Somme offensive	July 1–November 19
	1917
Germany returns to unrestricted submarine warfare	January
United States enters the war	April 6
The Champagne offensive	April 16–29
	1918
Last German offensive	March 21–July 18
Second Battle of the Marne	July 18
Allied counteroffensive	July 18–November 10
Armistice between Allies and Germany	November 11
	1919
Paris Peace Conference begins	January 18
Peace of Versailles	June 28

The Last Year of the War

For Germany, the withdrawal of the Russians from the war in March 1918 offered renewed hope for a favorable outcome. The victory over Russia persuaded Ludendorff and most German leaders to make one final military gamble—a grand offensive in the west to break the military stalemate. The German attack was launched in March and lasted into July. The German forces succeeded in advancing 40 miles to the Marne River, within 35 miles of Paris. But an Allied counterattack, led by the French General Ferdinand Foch and supported by the arrival of 140,000 fresh American troops, defeated the Germans at the Second Battle of the Marne on July 18. Ludendorff's gamble had failed. Having used up his reserves, Ludendorff knew that defeat was now inevitable. With the arrival of one million more American troops on the Continent, Allied forces began making a steady advance toward Germany.

On September 29, 1918, General Ludendorff informed German leaders that the war was lost. Unwilling to place the burden of defeat on the army, Ludendorff demanded that the government sue for peace at once. When German officials discovered that the Allies were unwilling to make peace with the autocratic imperial government, they instituted reforms to set up a liberal government. But these constitutional reforms came too late for the exhausted and angry German people. On November 3, naval units in Kiel mutinied, and within days, councils of workers and soldiers, German versions of the Russian soviets, were forming throughout northern Germany and taking over the supervision of civilian and military administrations. William II capitulated to public pressure and left the country on November 9, while the Socialists under Friedrich Ebert announced the establishment of a republic. Two days later, on November 11, 1918, an armistice agreed to by the new German government went into effect. The war was over, but the revolutionary forces set in motion by the war were not yet exhausted.

Revolutionary Upheavals in Germany and Austria-Hungary

Like Russia, Germany and Austria-Hungary experienced political revolution as a result of military defeat. In November 1918, when Germany began to disintegrate in a convulsion of mutinies and mass demonstrations (known as the November Revolution), only the Social Democrats were numerous and well organized enough to pick up the pieces. But the German socialists had divided into two groups during the war. A majority of the Social Democrats still favored parliamentary democracy as a gradual approach to social democracy and the elimination of the capitalist system. A minority of German socialists, however, disgusted with the Social Democrats' support of the war, had formed their own Independent Social Democratic Party in 1916. In 1918, the more radical members of the Independent Socialists favored an immediate social revolution carried out by the councils of soldiers, sailors, and workers. Led by Karl Liebknecht and Rosa Luxemburg, these radical, left-wing socialists formed the German Communist Party in December 1918. In effect, two parallel governments were established in Germany: the parliamentary republic proclaimed by the majority Social Democrats and the revolutionary socialist republic declared by the radicals.

Unlike Russia's Bolsheviks, Germany's radicals failed to achieve control of the government. By ending the war on November 11, the moderate socialists had removed a major source of dissatisfaction. When the radical socialists (now known as Communists) attempted to seize power in Berlin in January 1919, Friedrich Ebert and the moderate socialists called on the regular army and groups of antirevolutionary volunteers known as Free Corps to crush the rebels. The victorious forces brutally murdered Liebknecht and Luxemburg. A similar attempt at Communist revolution in the city of Munich in southern Germany was also crushed by the Free Corps and the regular army. The German republic had been saved, but only because the moderate socialists had relied on the traditional army—in effect, the same conservatives who had dominated the old imperial regime. Moreover, this "second revolution" of January 1919, bloodily crushed by the republican government, created a deep fear of communism among the German middle classes. All too soon, this fear would be cleverly manipulated by a politician named Adolf Hitler.

Austria-Hungary, too, experienced disintegration and revolution. In 1914, when it attacked Serbia, the imperial regime had tried to crush the nationalistic forces that it believed were destroying the empire. By 1918, those same nationalistic forces had brought the complete breakup of the Austro-Hungarian Empire. As war weariness took hold of the empire, ethnic minorities increasingly sought to achieve national independence. This desire was further encouraged by Allied war aims that included calls for the independence of the subject peoples. By the time the war ended, the Austro-Hungarian Empire had been replaced by the independent republics of Austria, Hungary, and Czechoslovakia and a new southern Slavic monarchical state called Yugoslavia. Other regions clamored to join Italy, Romania, and a reconstituted Poland. Rivalries among the nations that succeeded Austria-Hungary would weaken eastern Europe for the next eighty years. Ethnic pride and national statehood proved far more important to these states than class differences. Only in Hungary was there an attempt at social revolution when Béla Kun established a communist state. It was crushed after a brief five-month existence.

The Peace Settlement

In January 1919, the delegations of the victorious Allied nations gathered in Paris to conclude a final settlement of the Great War. Over the years, the reasons for fighting World War I had been transformed from selfish national interests to idealistic principles. At the end of 1917, after they had taken over the Russian government, Lenin and the Bolsheviks had publicly revealed the contents of secret wartime treaties found in the archives of the Russian foreign ministry. The documents made it clear that European nations had gone to war primarily to achieve territorial gains. But the American president, Woodrow Wilson, attempted at the beginning of 1918 to shift the discussion of war aims to a higher ground. Wilson outlined "Fourteen Points" to the American Congress that he believed justified the enormous military struggle then being waged. Later, Wilson spelled out additional steps for a truly just and lasting peace. Wilson's proposals included "open covenants of peace, openly arrived at" instead of secret diplomacy; the reduction of national armaments to a "point consistent with domestic safety"; and the self-determination of people so that "all well-defined national aspirations shall be accorded the utmost satisfaction." Wilson characterized World War I as a people's war waged against "absolutism and militarism," two scourges of liberty that could only be eliminated by creating democratic governments and a "general association of nations" that would guarantee the "political independence and territorial integrity to great and small states alike" (see the box on p. 734). As the spokesman for a new world order based on democracy and international cooperation, Wilson was enthusiastically cheered by many Europeans when he arrived in Europe for the peace conference.

Wilson soon found, however, that other states at the Paris Peace Conference were guided by considerably more pragmatic motives. The secret treaties and agreements, for example, that had been made before the war could not be totally ignored, even if they did conflict with the principle of self-determination enunciated by Wilson. National interests also complicated the deliberations of the Paris Peace Conference. David Lloyd George, prime minister of Great Britain, had won a decisive electoral victory in December of 1918 on a platform of making the Germans pay for this dreadful war.

France's approach to peace was primarily determined by considerations of national security. Georges Clemenceau, the feisty premier of France who had led his country to victory, believed the French people had borne the brunt of German aggression. They deserved revenge and security against future German aggression (see the box on p. 734). Clemenceau wanted a demilitarized Germany, vast German reparations to pay for the costs of the war, and a separate Rhineland as a buffer state between France and Germany—demands that Wilson viewed as vindictive and contrary to the principle of national self-determination.

Two Voices of Peacemaking: Woodrow Wilson and Georges Clemenceau

When the Allied Powers met at Paris in January 1919, it soon became apparent that the victors had different opinions on the kind of peace they expected. The first excerpt is from a speech of Woodrow Wilson in which the American president presented his idealistic goals for a peace based on justice and reconciliation. The French wanted revenge and security. In the second selection, from Georges Clemenceau's *Grandeur and Misery of Victory,* the French premier revealed his fundamental dislike and distrust of Germany.

Woodrow Wilson, May 26, 1917

We are fighting for the liberty, the self-government, and the undictated development of all peoples, and every feature of the settlement that concludes this war must be conceived and executed for that purpose. Wrongs must first be righted and then adequate safeguards must be created to prevent their being committed again. . . .

No people must be forced under sovereignty under which it does not wish to live. No territory must change hands except for the purpose of securing those who inhabit it a fair chance of life and liberty. No indemnities must be insisted on except those that constitute payment for manifest wrongs done. No readjustments of power must be made except such as will tend to secure the future peace of the world and the future welfare and happiness of its peoples.

And then the free peoples of the world must draw together in some common covenant, some genuine and practical cooperation that will in effect combine their force to secure peace and justice in the dealings of nations with one another.

Georges Clemenceau, **Grandeur and Misery of Victory**

War and peace, with their strong contrasts, alternate against a common background. For the catastrophe of 1914 the Germans are responsible. Only a professional liar would deny this. . . .

I have sometimes penetrated into the sacred cave of the Germanic cult, which is, as every one knows, the *Bierhaus* [beer hall]. A great aisle of massive humanity where there accumulate, amid the fumes of tobacco and beer, the popular rumblings of a nationalism upheld by the sonorous brasses blaring to the heavens the supreme voice of Germany, *Deutschland über alles! Germany above everything!* Men, women, and children, all petrified in reverence before the divine stoneware pot, brows furrowed with irrepressible power, eyes lost in a dream of infinity, mouths twisted by the intensity of willpower, drink in long draughts the celestial hope of vague expectations. These only remain to be realized presently when the chief marked out by Destiny shall have given the word. There you have the ultimate framework of an old but childish race.

Yet another consideration affected the negotiations at Paris: the fear that Bolshevik revolution would spread from Russia to other European countries. This concern led the Allies to enlarge and strengthen such eastern European states as Poland, Czechoslovakia, and Romania at the expense of both Germany and Bolshevik Russia.

Although twenty-seven nations were represented at the Paris Peace Conference, the most important decisions were made by Wilson, Clemenceau, and Lloyd George. Italy was considered one of the so-called Big Four powers but played a much less important role than the other three countries. Germany, of course, was not invited to attend, and Russia could not because of its civil war.

In view of the many conflicting demands at the conference table, it was inevitable that the Big Three would quarrel. Wilson was determined to create a "league of nations" to prevent future wars. Clemenceau and Lloyd George were equally determined to punish Germany. In the end, only compromise made it possible to achieve a peace settlement. On January 25, 1919, the conference adopted the principle of the League of Nations. The details of its structure were left for later sessions, and Wilson willingly agreed to make compromises on territorial arrangements to guarantee the establishment of the League, believing that a functioning League could later rectify bad arrangements. Clemenceau also compromised to obtain some guarantees for French security. He renounced France's desire for a separate Rhineland and instead accepted a defensive alliance with Great Britain and the United States. Both states pledged to help France if it were attacked by Germany.

The Treaty of Versailles

The final peace settlement of Paris consisted of five separate treaties with the defeated nations—Germany, Austria, Hungary, Bulgaria, and the Ottoman Empire. The Treaty of Versailles with Germany, signed on June 28, 1919, was by far the most important. The Germans considered it a harsh peace, conveniently overlooking that the Treaty of Brest-Litovsk, which they had imposed on Bolshevik Russia, was even more severe. The Germans were particularly unhappy with Article 231, the so-called War Guilt Clause, which declared Germany (and Austria) responsible for starting the war and ordered Germany to pay reparations for all the damage to which the Allied governments and their people were subjected as a result of the war "imposed upon them by the aggression of Germany and her allies." Reparations were a logical consequence of the wartime promises that Allied leaders had made to their people that the Germans would pay for the war effort. The treaty did

Hulton Archive/Getty Images

The Big Four at Paris. Shown here are the Big Four at the Paris Peace Conference: David Lloyd George of Britain, Vittorio Orlando of Italy, Georges Clemenceau of France, and Woodrow Wilson of the United States. Although Italy was considered one of the Big Four powers, Britain, France, and the United States (the Big Three) made the major decisions at the peace conference.

not establish the amount to be paid but left that to be determined later by a reparations commission (see Chapter 26).

The military and territorial provisions of the treaty also rankled the Germans, although they were by no means as harsh as the Germans claimed. Germany had to reduce its army to 100,000 men, cut back its navy, and eliminate its air force. German territorial losses included the cession of Alsace and Lorraine to France and sections of Prussia to the new Polish state. German land west and as far as 30 miles east of the Rhine was established as a demilitarized zone and stripped of all armaments or fortifications to serve as a barrier to any future German military moves westward against France. Outraged by the "dictated peace," the new German government vowed to resist rather than accept the treaty, but it had no real alternative. Rejection meant a renewal of the war, and as the army pointed out, that was no longer possible.

The Other Peace Treaties

The separate peace treaties made with the other Central Powers extensively redrew the map of eastern Europe. Many of these changes merely ratified what the war had already accomplished. The empires that had controlled eastern Europe for centuries had been destroyed or weakened, and a number of new states appeared on the map of Europe (see Map 25.5).

Both the German and Russian Empires lost considerable territory in eastern Europe, and the Austro-Hungarian Empire disappeared altogether. New nation-states emerged from the lands of these three empires: Finland, Latvia, Estonia, Lithuania, Poland, Czechoslovakia, Austria, and Hungary. Territorial rearrangements were also made in the Balkans. Romania acquired additional lands from Russia, Hungary, and Bulgaria. Serbia formed the nucleus of the new state of Yugoslavia (known until 1929 as the kingdom of the Serbs, Croats, and Slovenes).

Although the Paris Peace Conference was supposedly guided by the principle of self-determination, the mixtures of peoples in eastern Europe made it impossible to draw boundaries along neat ethnic lines. Compromises had to be made, sometimes to satisfy the national interest of the victors. France, for example, had lost Russia as its major ally on Germany's eastern border and wanted to strengthen and expand Poland, Czechoslovakia, Yugoslavia, and Romania as much as possible so that those states could serve as barriers against Germany and Communist Russia. As a result of compromises, virtually every eastern European state was left with a minorities problem that could lead to future conflicts. Germans in Poland, Hungarians, Poles, and Germans in Czechoslovakia, and the combination of Serbs, Croats, Slovenes, Macedonians, and Albanians in Yugoslavia all became sources of later conflict.

The centuries-old Ottoman Empire was dismembered by the peace settlement after the war. To gain Arab support against the Ottomans during the war, the Allies had promised to recognize the independence of Arab states in the Middle Eastern lands of the Ottoman Empire. But the imperialist habits of Europeans died hard. After the

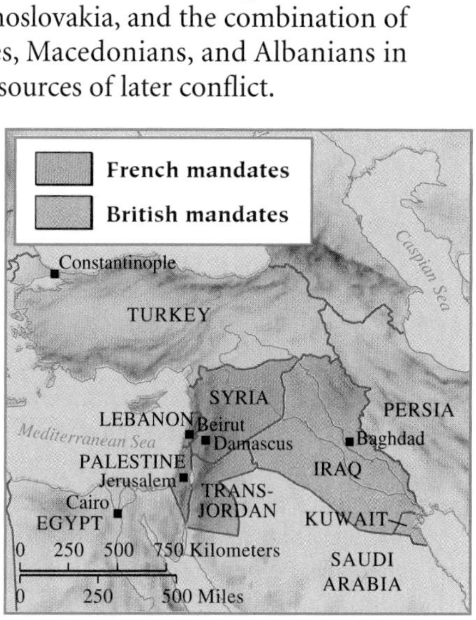

The Middle East in 1919

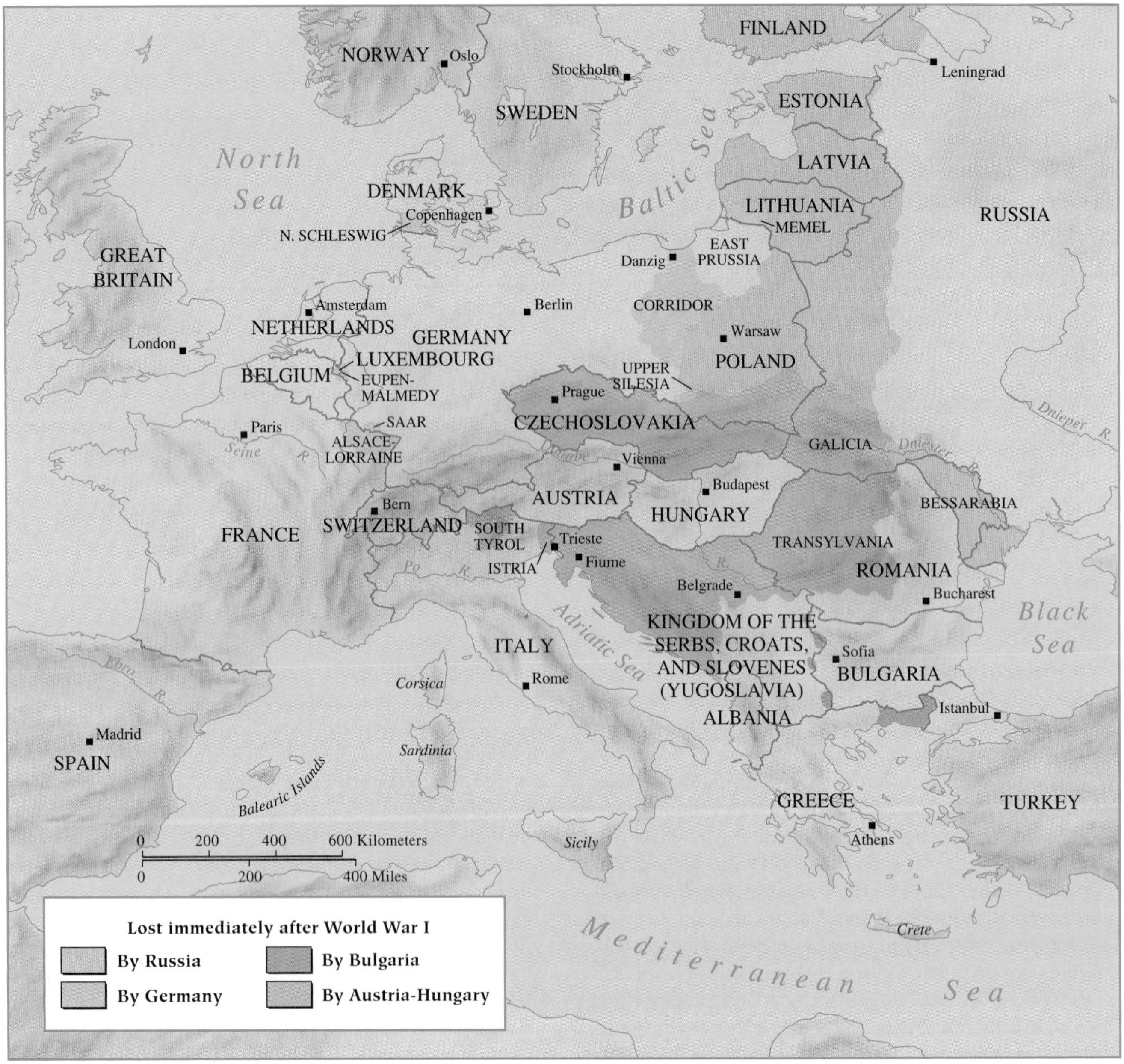

Map 25.5 Europe in 1919. The victorious allies met in Paris to determine the shape and nature of postwar Europe. At the urging of U.S. President Woodrow Wilson, many nationalist aspirations of former imperial subjects were realized with the creation of several new countries from the prewar territory of Austria-Hungary, Germany, and Russia. ■ What countries gained territory when Austria-Hungary was dismembered?

war, France took control of Lebanon and Syria, and Britain received Iraq and Palestine. Officially, both acquisitions were called mandates. Since Woodrow Wilson had opposed the outright annexation of colonial territories by the Allies, the peace settlement had created a system of mandates whereby a nation officially administered a territory on behalf of the League of Nations. The system of mandates could not hide the fact that the principle of national self-determination at the Paris Peace Conference was largely for Europeans.

The peace settlement negotiated at Paris soon came under attack, not only by the defeated Central Powers but also by others who felt that the peacemakers had been shortsighted. Some people agreed, however, that the settlement was the best that could be achieved under the circumstances. They believed that self-determination had served reasonably well as a central organizing principle, and the establishment of the League of Nations gave some hope that future conflicts could be resolved peacefully. Yet within twenty years, Europe would again be engaged in deadly conflict. As some historians have suggested, perhaps a lack of enforcement, rather than the structure of the settlement, may account for the failure of the peace of 1919.

Successful enforcement of the peace necessitated the active involvement of its principal architects, especially in helping the new German state develop a peaceful and democratic republic. The failure of the U.S. Senate to ratify the Treaty of Versailles, however, meant that the United States never joined the League of Nations. The Senate also rejected Wilson's defensive alliance with Great Britain and France. Already by the end of 1919, the United States was pursuing policies intended to limit its direct involvement in future European wars.

This retreat had dire consequences. American withdrawal from the defensive alliance with Britain and France led Britain to withdraw as well. By removing itself from European affairs, the United States forced France to stand alone facing its old enemy, leading the embittered nation to take strong actions against Germany that only intensified German resentment. By the end of 1919, it appeared that the peace of mere months earlier was already beginning to unravel.

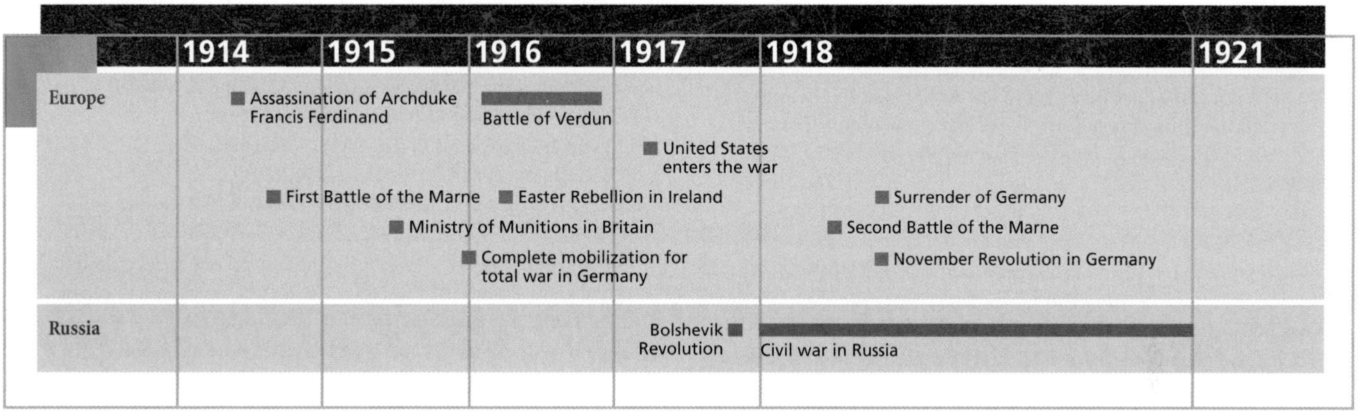

Conclusion

World War I shattered the liberal and rational assumptions of late-nineteenth- and early-twentieth-century European society. The incredible destruction and the deaths of almost ten million people undermined the whole idea of progress. New propaganda techniques had manipulated entire populations into sustaining their involvement in a meaningless slaughter.

World War I was a total war that involved a mobilization of resources and populations and increased government centralization of power over the lives of its citizens. Civil liberties, such as freedom of the press, speech, assembly, and movement, were circumscribed in the name of national security. Governments' need to plan the production and distribution of goods and to ration consumer goods restricted economic freedom. Although the late nineteenth and early twentieth centuries had witnessed the extension of government authority into such areas as mass education, social welfare legislation, and mass conscription, World War I made the practice of strong central authority a way of life.

Finally, World War I ended the age of European hegemony over world affairs. In 1917, the Russian Revolution laid the foundation for the creation of a new Eurasian power, the Soviet Union, and the United States had entered the war. The waning of the European age was not evident to all, however, for it was clouded by American isolationism and the withdrawal of the Soviets from world affairs while they nurtured the growth of their own socialist system. These developments, though temporary, created a political vacuum in Europe that all too soon was filled by the revival of German power.

Notes

1. Arnold Toynbee, *Surviving the Future* (New York, 1971), pp. 106–107.
2. Quoted in Joachim Remak, "1914—The Third Balkan War: Origins Reconsidered," *Journal of Modern History* 43 (1971): 364–365.
3. Quoted in Robert G. L. Waite, *Vanguard of Nazism* (New York, 1969), p. 22.
4. Quoted in J. M. Winter, *The Experience of World War I* (New York, 1989), p. 142.
5. Quoted in ibid., p. 137.
6. Quoted in Gail Braybon, *Women Workers in the First World War: The British Experience* (London, 1981), p. 79.
7. Quoted in Catherine W. Reilly, ed., *Scars upon My Heart: Women's Poetry and Verse of the First World War* (London, 1981), p. 90.
8. Quoted in Robert Paxton, *Europe in the Twentieth Century,* 2d ed. (New York, 1985), p. 110.
9. Quoted in William M. Mandel, *Soviet Women* (Garden City, N.Y., 1975), p. 43.

Suggestions for Further Reading

The historical literature on the causes of World War I is enormous. Good starting points are J. Joll, *The Origins of the First World War,* 2d ed. (London, 1992), and J. Remak, *The Origins of World War I, 1871–1914,* 2d ed. (Fort Worth, Tex., 1995). The belief that Germany was primarily responsible for the war was argued vigorously by the German scholar F. Fischer, *Germany's Aims in the First World War* (New York, 1967), *World Power or Decline: The Controversy over Germany's Aims in World War I* (New York, 1974), and *War of Illusions: German Policies from 1911 to 1914* (New York, 1975). The role of each great power has been reassessed in a series of books on the causes of World War I. They include V. R. Berghahn, *Germany and the Approach of War in 1914,* 2d ed. (London, 1993); Z. S. Steiner, *Britain and the Origins of the First World War* (New York, 1977); R. Bosworth, *Italy and the Approach of the First World War* (New York, 1983); J. F. Keiger, *France and the Origins of the First World* War (New York, 1984); and D. C. B. Lieven, *Russia and the Origins of the First World War* (New York, 1984). On the role of militarism, see D. Hermann, *The Arming of Europe and the Making of the First World War* (New York, 1997).

Two fine accounts of World War I are M. Gilbert, *The First World War* (New York, 1994), and the lavishly illustrated book by J. M. Winter, *The Experience of World War I* (New York, 1989). See also the brief work by N. Heyman, *World War I* (Westport, Conn., 1997). There is an excellent collection of articles in H. Strachan, *The Oxford Illustrated History of the First World War* (New York, 1998). The nature of trench warfare is examined in T. Ashworth, *Trench Warfare, 1914–1918: The Live-and-Let-Live System* (London, 1980). The use of poison gas is examined in L. F. Haber, *The Poisonous Cloud: Chemical Warfare in the First World War* (Oxford, 1985). The war at sea is examined in R. Hough, *The Great War at Sea, 1914–18* (Oxford, 1983). B. Tuchman, *The Guns of August* (New York, 1962), is a magnificently written account of the opening days of the war, although scholars do not always agree with the author's conclusions. For an interesting perspective on World War I and the beginnings of the modern world, see M. Eksteins, *Rites of Spring: The Great War and the Birth of the Modern Age* (Boston, 1989).

On the role of women in World War I, see G. Braybon, *Women Workers in the First World War: The British Experience* (London, 1981); J. M. Winter and R. M. Wall, eds., *The Upheaval of War: Family, Work and Welfare in Europe, 1914–1918* (Cambridge, 1988); G. Braybon and P. Summerfield, *Women's Experiences in Two World Wars* (London, 1987); and M. R. Higonnet, J. Jensen, S. Michel, and M. C. Weitz, *Behind the Lines: Gender and the Two World Wars* (New Haven, Conn., 1987).

A good introduction to the Russian Revolution can be found in R. A. Wade, *The Russian Revolution, 1917* (Cambridge, 2000), and S. Fitzpatrick, *The Russian Revolution, 1917–1932,* 2d ed. (New York, 1994). See also R. Pipes, *The Russian Revolution* (New York, 1990). On Lenin, see R. W. Clark, *Lenin* (New York, 1988), and the valuable work by A. B. Ulam, *The Bolsheviks* (New York, 1965). On social reforms, see W. Goldman, *Women, the State and Revolution* (Cambridge, 1993). A comprehensive study of the Russian civil war is W. B. Lincoln, *Red Victory: A History of the Russian Civil War* (New York, 1989). On the revolutions in Germany and Austria-Hungary, see F. L. Carsten, *Revolution in Central Europe* (Berkeley, Calif., 1972), and A. J. Ryder, *The German Revolution of 1918* (Cambridge, 1967).

The role of war aims in shaping the peace settlement is examined in V. H. Rothwell, *British War Aims and Peace Diplomacy, 1914–1918* (Oxford, 1971), and D. R. Stevenson, *French War Aims Against Germany, 1914–1919* (New York, 1982).

World War I and the Russian Revolution are also well covered in two good general surveys of European history in the twentieth century, R. Paxton, *Europe in the Twentieth Century,* 2d ed. (New York, 1985), and A. Rudhart, *Twentieth-Century Europe* (Englewood Cliffs, N.J., 1986).

For additional reading, go to InfoTrac College Edition, your online research library at http://web1.infotrac-college.com

Enter the search term *World War, 1914–1918* using the Subject Guide.

Enter the search term *Russia Revolution* using Key Terms.

Enter the search term *Bolshevik* using Key Terms.

Enter the search term *Versailles Treaty* using Key Terms.

CHAPTER

26

The Futile Search for Stability: Europe Between the Wars, 1919–1939

© Bildarchiv Preussischer Kulturbesitz, Berlin

CHAPTER OUTLINE

- An Uncertain Peace: The Search for Security
- The Democratic States
- Retreat from Democracy: The Authoritarian and Totalitarian States
- The Expansion of Mass Culture and Mass Leisure
- Cultural and Intellectual Trends in the Interwar Years
- Conclusion

FOCUS QUESTIONS

- How did France, Great Britain, and the United States respond to the various crises, including the Great Depression, that they faced in the interwar years?
- What conditions led to the emergence of Fascists in Italy and Nazis in Germany, and how did each group attain power?
- What are the characteristics of totalitarian states, and to what degree were these characteristics present in Fascist Italy, Nazi Germany, and Stalinist Russia?
- What new dimensions in mass culture and mass leisure emerged during the interwar years, and what role did these activities play in totalitarian states?
- What were the main cultural and intellectual trends in the interwar years?
- Why have some historians called the 1920s both an age of anxiety and a period of hope?

ONLY TWENTY YEARS after the Treaty of Versailles, Europeans were again at war. Yet in the 1920s, many people assumed that the world was about to enter a new era of international peace, economic growth, and political democracy. In all of these areas, the optimistic hopes of the 1920s failed to be realized. After 1919, most people wanted peace but were unsure how to maintain it. The League of Nations, conceived as a new instrument to provide for collective security, failed to work well. New treaties that renounced the use of war looked good on paper but had no means of enforcement. Then, too, virtually everyone favored disarmament, but few could agree on how to achieve it.

Europe faced serious economic hardships after World War I. The European economy did not begin to recover from the war until 1922, and even then it was beset by financial problems left over from the war and, most devastating of all, the severe depression that began at the end of 1929. The Great Depression brought misery to millions of people. Begging for food on the streets became widespread, especially when soup kitchens were unable to keep up with the demand. Larger and larger numbers of people were homeless and moved from place to place looking for work and shelter. In the United States, the homeless set up shantytowns they derisively named "Hoovervilles" after the U.S. president, Herbert Hoover. Some of the destitute saw but one solution; as one unemployed person expressed it: "Today, when I am experiencing this for the first time, I think that I should prefer to do away with myself, to take gas, to jump into the river, or leap from some high place. . . . Would I really come to such a decision? I do not know. Animals die, plants wither, but men always go on living." Social unrest spread rapidly, and some unemployed staged hunger marches to get attention. In democratic countries, more and more people began to listen to and vote for radical voices calling for extreme measures.

According to Woodrow Wilson, World War I had been fought to make the world safe for democracy, and for a while after 1919, political democracy seemed well on its way. But hope soon faded as authoritarian regimes spread into Italy and Germany and across eastern Europe.

An Uncertain Peace: The Search for Security

The peace treaties at the end of World War I had tried to fulfill the nineteenth-century dream of nationalism by redrawing boundaries and creating new states. However, this peace settlement had left nations unhappy. Conflicts over disputed border regions poisoned mutual relations in eastern Europe for years, and many Germans viewed the Peace of Versailles as a dictated peace and vowed to seek its revision.

U.S. President Woodrow Wilson had recognized that the peace treaties contained unwise provisions that could serve as new causes for conflicts and had placed many of his hopes for the future in the League of Nations. The League, however, was not particularly effective in maintaining the peace. The failure of the United States to join the League and the subsequent American determination to be less involved in European affairs undermined the effectiveness of the League from its beginning. Moreover, the League's sole weapon for halting aggression was economic sanctions.

The weakness of the League of Nations and the failure of both the United States and Great Britain to honor their promises to form defensive military alliances with France left France embittered and alone. Before World War I, France's alliance with Russia had served to threaten Germany with the possibility of a two-front war. But Communist Russia was now a hostile power. To compensate, France built a network of alliances in eastern Europe with Poland and the members of the so-called Little Entente (Czechoslovakia, Romania, Yugoslavia). Although these alliances looked good on paper as a way to contain Germany and maintain the new status quo, they overlooked the fundamental military weaknesses of those nations. Poland and the Little Entente states were no real substitutes for Russia.

The Little Entente

The French Policy of Coercion (1919–1924)

France's search for security between 1919 and 1924 was founded primarily on a strict enforcement of the Treaty of Versailles. This tough policy toward Germany began with the issue of reparations, the payments that the Germans were supposed to make to compensate for the "damage done to the civilian population of the Allied and Associated Powers and to their property," as the treaty asserted. In April 1921, the Allied Reparations Commission settled on a sum of 132 billion marks ($33 billion) for German reparations, payable in annual installments of 2.5 billion (gold) marks. Allied threats to occupy the Ruhr valley, Germany's chief industrial and mining center, led the new German republic to accept the reparations settlement and make its first payment in 1921. By the following year, however, facing financial problems, the German government announced that it was unable to pay any more. Outraged by what they considered Germany's violation of the peace settlement, the French government sent troops to occupy the Ruhr valley. Because the Germans would not pay reparations, the French would collect reparations in kind by operating and using the Ruhr mines and factories.

Both Germany and France suffered from the French occupation of the Ruhr. The German government adopted a policy of passive resistance that was largely financed by printing more paper money, but this only intensified the inflationary pressures that had already appeared in Germany by the end of the war. The German mark soon became worthless. In 1914, a dollar was worth 4.2 marks; by November 1, 1923, the rate had reached 130 billion to the dollar, and by the end of November, it had snowballed to an incredible 4.2 trillion marks to the dollar. Economic disaster fueled political upheavals as Communists staged

Hulton Archive/Getty Images

The Effects of Inflation. The inflationary pressures that had begun in Germany at the end of World War I intensified during the French occupation of the Ruhr. By the early 1920s, the value of the German mark had fallen precipitously. This photograph shows German children using bundles of worthless money as building blocks. The wads of money were cheaper than toys.

uprisings in October 1923, and Adolf Hitler's band of Nazis attempted to seize power in Munich in November (see "Hitler and Nazi Germany" later in this chapter). But the French were hardly victorious. The cost of the French occupation was not offset by the gains. Meanwhile, pressure from the United States and Great Britain against the French policy forced the French to agree to a new conference of experts to reassess the reparations problem. By the time the conference did its work in 1924, both France and Germany were opting to pursue a more conciliatory approach toward each other.

The Hopeful Years (1924–1929)

The formation of new governments in both Great Britain and France opened the door to conciliatory approaches to Germany and the reparations problem. At the same time, a new German government led by Gustav Stresemann (1878–1929) ended the policy of passive resistance and committed Germany to carry out most of the provisions of the Treaty of Versailles while seeking a new settlement of the reparations question.

In August 1924, an international commission produced a new plan for reparations. Named the Dawes Plan after the American banker who chaired the commission, it reduced reparations and stabilized Germany's payments on the basis of its ability to pay. The Dawes Plan also granted an initial $200 million loan for German recovery, which opened the door to heavy American investments in Europe that helped usher in a new era of European prosperity between 1924 and 1929.

With prosperity came new efforts at European diplomacy. A spirit of international cooperation was fostered by the foreign ministers of Germany and France, Gustav Stresemann and Aristide Briand (1862–1932), who concluded the Treaty of Locarno in 1925. This guaranteed Germany's new western borders with France and Belgium. Although Germany's new eastern borders with Poland were conspicuously absent from the agreement, a clear indication that Germany did not accept those borders as permanent, the Locarno pact was viewed by many as the beginning of a new era of European peace. On the day after the pact was concluded, the headline in the *New York Times* ran "France and Germany Ban War Forever," while the London *Times* declared, "Peace at Last."[1]

Germany's entry into the League of Nations in March 1926 soon reinforced the new spirit of conciliation engendered at Locarno. Two years later, similar optimistic attitudes prevailed in the Kellogg-Briand pact, drafted by the American secretary of state Frank B. Kellogg and the French foreign minister Aristide Briand. Sixty-three nations eventually agreed to the pact, in which they pledged "to renounce war as an instrument of national policy." Nothing was said, however, about what would be done if anyone violated the treaty.

The spirit of Locarno was based on little real substance. Germany lacked the military power to alter its western borders even if it wanted to. And the issue of disarmament soon proved that even the spirit of Locarno could not induce nations to cut back on their weapons. The League of Nations Covenant had suggested the "reduction of national armaments to the lowest point consistent with national safety." Germany, of course, had been disarmed with the expectation that other states would do likewise. Numerous disarmament conferences, however, failed to achieve anything substantial as states proved unwilling to trust their security to anyone but their own military forces. When a world disarmament conference finally met in Geneva in 1932, the issue was already dead.

One other hopeful sign in the years between 1924 and 1929 was the new coexistence of the West with Soviet Russia. By the beginning of 1924, Soviet hopes for communist revolutions in Western states had largely dissipated. In turn, these states had realized by then that the Bolshevik regime could not be ousted. By 1924, Germany, Britain, France, and Italy, as well as several smaller European countries, had established full diplomatic relations with Soviet Russia. Nevertheless, Western powers remained highly suspicious of Soviet intentions.

The Great Depression

After World War I, most European states hoped to return to the liberal ideal of a market economy based on private enterprise and largely free of state intervention. But the war had vastly strengthened business cartels and labor unions, making some government regulation of these powerful organizations appear necessary. Then, too, the economic integration of Europe before 1914 that had been based on free trade was soon undermined by a wave of protectionism and trade barriers, and reparations and war debts had further damaged the postwar international economy. Consequently, the prosperity that did occur between 1924 and 1929 was uncommonly fragile, and the dream of returning to a self-regulating market economy was mere illusion. Then, to dash the dream altogether, along came the Great Depression.

Two factors played an important role in bringing on the Great Depression: a downturn in domestic economies and an international financial crisis caused by the collapse of the American stock market in 1929. Already in the mid-1920s, prices for agricultural goods were beginning to decline rapidly due to overproduction of basic commodities, such as wheat. In 1925, states in central and eastern Europe began to impose tariffs to close their markets to other countries' goods. An increase in the use of oil and hydroelectricity led to a slump in the coal industry even before 1929.

Furthermore, much of Europe's prosperity between 1924 and 1929 had been built on American bank loans to Germany. Twenty-three billion marks had been invested in German municipal bonds and German industries since 1924. Already in 1928 and 1929, American investors had begun to pull money out of Germany in order to invest in the booming New York stock market. The crash of the American stock market in October 1929 led panicky American investors to withdraw even more of their funds from Germany and other European markets. The withdrawal of funds seriously weakened the banks of Germany and other central European states. The Credit-Anstalt, Vienna's most prestigious bank, collapsed on May 31, 1931. By that time, trade was slowing down, industrialists were cutting back production, and unemployment was increasing as the ripple effects of international bank failures had a devastating impact on domestic economies.

Economic depression was by no means a new phenomenon in European history. But the depth of the economic downturn after 1929 fully justifies the "Great Depression" label. During 1932, the worst year of the depression, one British worker in four was unemployed, and six million Germans—40 percent of the German labor force—were out of work. Between 1929 and 1932, industrial production plummeted almost 50 percent in the United States and nearly as much in Germany. The unemployed and homeless filled the streets of the cities throughout the advanced industrial countries (see the box on p. 743).

The economic crisis also had unexpected social repercussions. Women were often able to secure low-paying jobs as servants, housecleaners, or laundresses while many men

The Great Depression: Bread Lines in Paris. The Great Depression devastated the European economy and had serious political repercussions. Because of its more balanced economy, France did not feel the effects of the depression as quickly as other European countries. By 1931, however, even France was experiencing lines of unemployed people at free-food centers.

Roger-Viollet/Getty Images

The Great Depression: Unemployed and Homeless in Germany

In 1932, Germany had six million unemployed workers, many of them wandering aimlessly through the country, begging for food and seeking shelter in city lodging houses for the homeless. The Great Depression was an important factor in the rise to power of Adolf Hitler and the Nazis. This selection presents a description of unemployed homeless in 1932.

■ *Heinrich Hauser, "With Germany's Unemployed"*

An almost unbroken chain of homeless men extends the whole length of the great Hamburg-Berlin highway.... All the highways in Germany over which I have traveled this year presented the same aspect....

Most of the hikers paid no attention to me. They walked separately or in small groups, with their eyes on the ground. And they had the queer, stumbling gait of barefooted people, for their shoes were slung over their shoulders. Some of them were guild members—carpenters ... milkmen ... and bricklayers ... —but they were in a minority. Far more numerous were those whom one could assign to no special profession or craft—unskilled young people, for the most part, who had been unable to find a place for themselves in any city or town in Germany, and who had never had a job and never expected to have one. There was something else that had never been seen before—whole families that had piled all their goods into baby carriages and wheelbarrows that they were pushing along as they plodded forward in dumb despair. It was a whole nation on the march.

I saw them—and this was the strongest impression that the year 1932 left with me—I saw them, gathered into groups of fifty or a hundred men, attacking fields of potatoes. I saw them digging up the potatoes and throwing them into sacks while the farmer who owned the field watched them in despair and the local policeman looked on gloomily from the distance. I saw them staggering toward the lights of the city as night fell, with their sacks on their backs. What did it remind me of? Of the War, of the worst periods of starvation in 1917 and 1918, but even then people paid for the potatoes....

I saw that the individual can know what is happening only by personal experience. I know what it is to be a tramp. I know what cold and hunger are.... But there are two things that I have only recently experienced—begging and spending the night in a municipal lodging house.

I entered the huge Berlin municipal lodging house in a northern quarter of the city....

Distribution of spoons, distribution of enameled-ware bowls with the words "Property of the City of Berlin" written on their sides. Then the meal itself. A big kettle is carried. Men with yellow smocks have brought it in and men with yellow smocks ladle out the food. These men, too, are homeless and they have been expressly picked by the establishment and given free food and lodging and a little pocket money in exchange for their work about the house.

Where have I seen this kind of food distribution before? In a prison that I once helped to guard in the winter of 1919 during the German civil war. There was the same hunger then, the same trembling, anxious expectation of rations. Now the men are standing in a long row, dressed in their plain nightshirts that reach to the ground, and the noise of their shuffling feet is like the noise of big wild animals walking up and down the stone floor of their cages before feeding time. The men lean far over the kettle so that the warm steam from the food envelops them and they hold out their bowls as if begging and whisper to the attendant, "Give me a real helping. Give me a little more." A piece of bread is handed out with every bowl.

My next recollection is sitting at a table in another room on a crowded bench that is like a seat in a fourth-class railway carriage. Hundreds of hungry mouths make an enormous noise eating their food. The men sit bent over their food like animals who feel that someone is going to take it away from them. They hold their bowl with their left arm part way around it, so that nobody can take it away, and they also protect it with their other elbow and with their head and mouth, while they move the spoon as fast as they can between their mouth and the bowl.

remained unemployed, either begging on the streets or staying at home to do household tasks. Many unemployed men, resenting this reversal of traditional gender roles, were open to the shrill cries of demagogues with simple solutions to the economic crisis. High unemployment rates among young males often led them to join gangs that gathered in parks or other public places, arousing fear among local residents.

Governments seemed powerless to deal with the crisis. The classical liberal remedy for depression, a deflationary policy of balanced budgets, which involved cutting costs by lowering wages and raising tariffs to exclude other countries' goods from home markets, only served to worsen the economic crisis and create even greater mass discontent. This in turn led to serious political repercussions. Increased government activity in the economy was one reaction, even in countries like the United States that had a strong laissez-faire tradition. Another effect was a renewed interest in Marxist doctrines, since Marx had predicted that capitalism would destroy itself through overproduction. Communism took on new popularity, especially among workers and intellectuals. Finally, the

Great Depression increased the attractiveness of simplistic dictatorial solutions, especially from a new authoritarian movement known as fascism. Everywhere in Europe, democracy seemed on the defensive in the 1930s.

The Democratic States

Woodrow Wilson proclaimed that World War I had been fought to make the world safe for democracy, and in 1919, there seemed to be some justification for that claim. Four major European states and a host of minor ones had functioning political democracies. In a number of nations, universal male suffrage had even been replaced by universal suffrage as male politicians rewarded women for their contributions to World War I by granting them the right to vote (except in Italy, France, and Spain, where women had to wait until the end of World War II). Women also began to enter political life as deputies to parliamentary bodies. In the new German republic, for example, almost 10 percent of the deputies elected to the Reichstag in 1919 were women, although the number dropped to 6 percent by 1926.

Great Britain

After World War I, Great Britain went through a period of painful readjustment and serious economic difficulties. During the war, Britain had lost many of its markets for industrial products, especially to the United States and Japan. The postwar decline of such staple industries as coal, steel, and textiles led to a rise in unemployment, which reached the two million mark in 1921. The Liberal government of David Lloyd George proved unable to change this situation.

By 1923, British politics experienced a major transformation when the Labour Party surged ahead of the Liberals as the second most powerful party in Britain after the Conservatives. In fact, after the elections of November 1923, a Labour-Liberal coalition enabled Ramsay MacDonald (1866–1937) to become the first Labour prime minister of Britain. Dependent on Liberal support, MacDonald rejected any extreme social or economic experimentation. His government lasted only ten months, however, as the Conservative Party's charge that his administration was friendly toward communism proved to be a highly successful campaign tactic.

Under the direction of Stanley Baldwin (1867–1947) as prime minister, the Conservatives guided Britain during an era of renewed prosperity from 1925 to 1929. This prosperity, however, was relatively superficial. British exports in the 1920s never compensated for the overseas investments lost during the war, and even in these so-called prosperous years, unemployment remained at a startling 10 percent level. Coal miners were especially affected by the decline of the antiquated and inefficient British coal mines, which also suffered from a world glut of coal. Attempts by mine owners to lower coal miners' wages led to a national strike (the General Strike of 1926) by miners and sympathetic trade unions. A compromise settled the strike, but many miners refused to accept the settlement and were eventually forced back to work at lower wages for longer hours.

In 1929, just as the Great Depression was beginning, a second Labour government came into power, but its failure to solve the nation's economic problems caused it to fall in 1931. A National Government (a coalition of all three parties) claimed credit for bringing Britain out of the worst stages of the depression, primarily by using the traditional policies of balanced budgets and protective tariffs. By 1936, unemployment had dropped to 1.6 million after reaching a depression high of 3 million in 1932 (see the box on p. 745).

British politicians largely ignored the new ideas of a Cambridge economist, John Maynard Keynes (1883–1946), who published his *General Theory of Employment, Interest, and Money* in 1936. He condemned the traditional view that in a free economy, depressions should be left to work themselves out. Instead, Keynes argued that unemployment stemmed not from overproduction but from a decline in demand and that demand could be increased by public works, financed, if necessary, through deficit spending to stimulate production.

France

After the defeat of Germany, France had become the strongest power on the European continent. Its greatest need was to rebuild the devastated areas of northern and eastern France. The conservative National Bloc government, led by Raymond Poincaré (1860–1934), sought to use German reparations for this purpose, which resulted in Poincaré's hard-line policy toward Germany and the Ruhr invasion. When Poincaré's conservative government was forced to raise taxes in 1924 to pay for the cost of the Ruhr fiasco, his National Bloc was voted out of power and replaced by the so-called Cartel of the Left.

The Cartel of the Left was a coalition government formed by two French leftist parties, the Radicals and the Socialists. These parties shared a belief in antimilitarism, anticlericalism, and the importance of education. But despite their name, the Radicals were a democratic party of small property owners, whereas the Socialists were nominally committed to Marxist socialism. Although they cooperated to win elections, their differences on economic and financial issues made their efforts to solve France's financial problems between 1924 and 1926 largely futile. The failure of the Cartel of the Left led to the return of Raymond Poincaré, whose government from 1926 to 1929 stabilized the French economy during a period of relative prosperity.

France began to feel the full effects of the Great Depression in 1932, and that economic instability soon had political repercussions. During a nineteen-month period in 1932 and 1933, six different cabinets were formed as France faced political chaos. During the same time, French fascist groups, adhering to far-right policies similar to those

The Struggles of a Democracy: Unemployment and Slums in Great Britain

During the 1920s and 1930s, Britain struggled with the problems of economic depression. Unemployment was widespread, especially after the onset of the Great Depression. Even after Britain began to recover in the late 1930s, many Britons still lived in wretched conditions. These selections reflect Britain's economic and social problems.

Men Without Work: A Report Made to the Pilgrim Trust, 1938

A week's notice may end half a lifetime's service, with no prospects, if he is elderly, but the dole, followed by a still further reduction in his means of livelihood when the old age pension comes. We take as an example a shoe laster from Leicester, who had worked thirty-seven years with one firm. "When I heard the new manager going through and saying: 'The whole of this side of this room, this room, and this room is to be stopped,' I knew it would be uphill work to get something.'" He went on to describe to us how he had not been able to bring himself to tell his wife the bad news when he got home, how she had noticed that something was wrong, how confident she had been that he would get work elsewhere, but how he had known that the chances were heavily against him. For months and indeed often for years such men go on looking for work, and the same is true of many casual laborers. There were in the sample old men who have not a remote chance of working again but yet make it a practice to stand every morning at six o'clock at the works gates in the hope that perhaps they may catch the foreman's eye.

George Orwell, "A Woman in the Slums"

As we moved slowly through the outskirts of the town we passed row after row of little grey slum houses. . . . At the back of one of the houses a young woman was kneeling on the stones, poking a stick up the leaden wastepipe which ran from the sink inside, and which I suppose was blocked. . . . She had a round pale face, the usual exhausted face of the slum girl who is twenty-five and looks forty, thanks to miscarriages and drudgery; and it wore, for the second in which I saw it, the most desolate, hopeless expression I have ever seen. It struck me then that we are mistaken when we say that "It isn't the same for them as it would be for us," and that people bred in the slums can imagine nothing but the slums. For what I saw in her face was not the ignorant suffering of an animal. She knew well enough what was happening to her—understood as well as I did how dreadful a destiny it was to be kneeling there in the bitter cold, on the slimy stones of a slum backyard, poking a stick up a foul drain-pipe.

of the Fascists in Italy and the Nazis in Germany (see "Fascist Italy" and "Hitler and Nazi Germany" later in this chapter), marched through French streets in numerous demonstrations. The February riots of 1934, caused by a number of French fascist leagues, frightened many into believing that the fascists intended to seize power. These fears began to drive the leftist parties together despite their other differences and led in 1936 to the formation of the Popular Front.

The first Popular Front government was formed in June 1936 and was a coalition of the Communists, Socialists, and Radicals. The Socialist leader, Léon Blum (1872–1950), served as prime minister. The Popular Front succeeded in initiating a program for workers that some have called the French New Deal. It established the right of collective bargaining, a forty-hour workweek, two-week paid vacations, and minimum wages. The Popular Front's policies failed to solve the problems of the depression, however. By 1938, the French were experiencing a serious decline of confidence in their political system that left them unprepared to deal with their aggressive Nazi enemy to the east.

The Scandinavian Example

The Scandinavian states were particularly successful in coping with the Great Depression. Socialist parties had grown steadily in the late nineteenth and early twentieth centuries and between the wars came to head the governments of Sweden, Denmark, Norway, and Finland. These Social Democratic governments encouraged the development of rural and industrial cooperative enterprises. Ninety percent of the Danish milk industry, for example, was organized on a cooperative basis by 1933. Privately owned and managed, Scandinavian cooperatives seemed to avoid the pitfalls of either communist or purely capitalist economic systems.

Social Democratic governments also greatly expanded social services. Not only did Scandinavian governments increase old-age pensions and unemployment insurance, but they also provided such novel forms of assistance as subsidized housing, free prenatal care, maternity allowances, and annual paid vacations for workers. To achieve their social welfare states, the Scandinavian governments required high taxes and large bureaucracies, but these did not prevent both private and cooperative enterprises from prospering. Indeed, between 1900 and 1939, Sweden experienced a greater rise in real wages than any other European country.

The United States

After Germany, no Western nation was more affected by the Great Depression than the United States. By the end of 1932, industrial production was down almost 50 percent. By 1933, there were fifteen million unemployed. Under these circumstances, the Democrat Franklin Delano

CHRONOLOGY

The Democratic States

Great Britain	
First Labour Party government	1923
Conservative government	1925–1929
General strike	1926
Second Labour Party government	1929–1931
Beginnings of National Government coalition	1931
France	
Cartel of the Left	1924–1926
Poincaré's government	1926–1929
Formation of the Popular Front	1936
United States	
Election of Franklin D. Roosevelt	1932
Beginning of the New Deal	1933
Second New Deal	1935

Roosevelt (1882–1945) won the 1932 presidential election by an electoral landslide.

Roosevelt and his advisers pursued a policy of active government intervention in the economy that came to be known as the New Deal. The first New Deal created a variety of new agencies designed to bring relief, recovery, and reform. To support the nation's banks, the Federal Deposit Insurance Corporation was established; it insured the safety of bank deposits up to $5,000. The Federal Emergency Relief Administration provided funds to help states and local communities meet the needs of the destitute and the homeless. The Civilian Conservation Corps employed over two million people on reforestation projects.

By 1935, it was becoming apparent that the initial efforts of Roosevelt's administration had produced only a slow recovery at best. As his policies came under more and more criticism by people who advocated more radical change, Roosevelt inaugurated new efforts that collectively became known as the Second New Deal. These included a stepped-up program of public works, such as the Works Progress Administration (WPA), established in 1935. This government organization employed between two and three million people who worked at building bridges, roads, post offices, and airports. The Roosevelt administration was also responsible for social legislation that launched the American welfare state. In 1935, the Social Security Act created a system of old-age pensions and unemployment insurance. The National Labor Relations Act of 1935 encouraged the rapid growth of labor unions.

The New Deal provided some social reform measures that perhaps averted the possibility of social revolution in the United States. It did not, however, solve the unemployment problems of the Great Depression. After partial recovery between 1933 and 1937, the economy experienced another downturn during the winter of 1937–1938. In May 1937, American unemployment still stood at seven million; by the following year, it had increased to eleven million. Only World War II and the subsequent growth of armaments industries brought American workers back to full employment.

Retreat from Democracy: The Authoritarian and Totalitarian States

The apparent triumph of liberal democracy in 1919 proved extremely short-lived. By 1939, only two major states (France and Great Britain) and a host of minor ones (the Low Countries, the Scandinavian states, Switzerland, and Czechoslovakia) remained democratic. Italy and Germany had succumbed to fascism, while the Soviet Union, under Stalin, had moved toward a repressive totalitarian state. A host of other European states, especially in eastern Europe, adopted authoritarian structures of various kinds.

The dictatorial regimes between the wars assumed both old and new forms. Dictatorship was not a new phenomenon, but the modern totalitarian state was. The totalitarian regimes, whose best examples can be found in Stalinist Russia and Nazi Germany, extended the functions and power of the central state far beyond what they had been in the past. The immediate origins of totalitarianism can be found in the total warfare of World War I when governments, even in the democratic states, exercised controls over economic, political, and personal freedom in order to achieve victory.

The modern totalitarian state might have begun as an old-fashioned political dictatorship, but it soon moved beyond the ideal of passive obedience expected in a traditional dictatorship or authoritarian monarchy. The new "total states" expected the active loyalty and commitment of citizens to the regime's goals. They used modern mass propaganda techniques and high-speed modern communications to conquer the minds and hearts of their subjects. The total state aimed to control not only the economic, political, and social aspects of life but the intellectual and cultural aspects as well. But that control also had a purpose: the active involvement of the masses in the achievement of the regime's goals, whether they be war, a socialist state, or a thousand-year Reich.

The modern totalitarian state was to be led by a single leader and a single party. It ruthlessly rejected the liberal ideal of limited government power and constitutional guarantees of individual freedoms. Indeed, individual freedom was to be subordinated to the collective will of the masses, organized and determined for them by a leader or leaders. Modern technology also gave total states unprecedented police controls to enforce their wishes on their subjects.

Totalitarianism is an abstract term, and no state followed all its theoretical implications. The fascist states—

Italy and Nazi Germany—as well as Stalin's Soviet Union have all been labeled totalitarian, although their regimes exhibited significant differences and met with varying degrees of success. Totalitarianism transcended traditional political labels. Fascism in Italy and Nazism in Germany grew out of extreme rightist preoccupations with nationalism and, in the case of Germany, with racism. Communism in the Soviet Union emerged out of Marxist socialism, a radical leftist program. Thus totalitarianism could and did exist in what were perceived as extreme right-wing and left-wing regimes. This fact helped bring about a new concept of the political spectrum in which the extremes were no longer seen as opposites on a linear scale but came to be viewed as similar to each other in at least some respects.

Fascist Italy

In the early 1920s, in the wake of economic turmoil, political disorder, and the general insecurity and fear stemming from World War I, Benito Mussolini burst on the Italian scene with the first fascist movement in Europe.

THE BIRTH OF FASCISM

As a new European state after 1870, Italy faced a number of serious problems that were only magnified when it became a belligerent in World War I. An estimated 700,000 Italian soldiers died, and the treasury reckoned the cost of the war at 148 billion lire, twice the sum of all government expenditures between 1861 and 1913. Italy did gain some territory, namely, Trieste, and a new northern border that included the formerly Austrian South Tyrol area. Italy's demands for Fiume and Dalmatia on the Adriatic coast were rejected, however, which gave rise to the myth that Italy had been cheated of its just rewards by the other victors. The war created immense domestic confusion. Inflation undermined middle-class security. Demobilization of the troops created high unemployment and huge groups of dissatisfied veterans. The government proved unable to deal effectively with these problems.

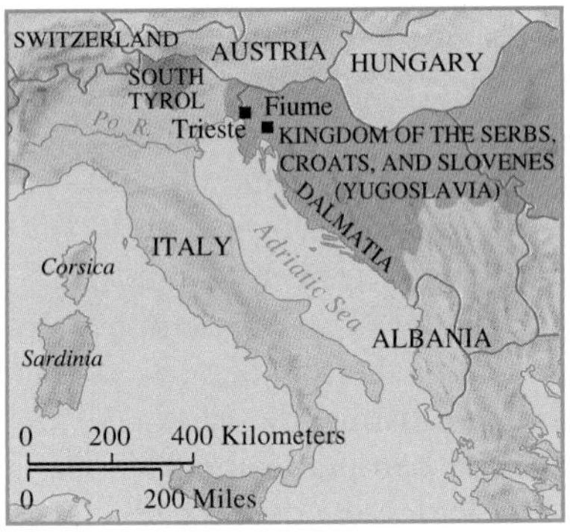

Gained Italian Territory

Benito Mussolini (1883–1945) was an unruly and rebellious child who ultimately received a diploma as an elementary school teacher. After an unsuccessful stint as a teacher, Mussolini became a socialist and gradually became well known in Italian socialist circles. In 1912, he obtained the important position of editor of *Avanti* (Forward), the official socialist daily newspaper. After editorially switching his position from ardent neutrality, the socialist position, to intervention in World War I, he was expelled from the Socialist Party.

In 1919, Mussolini laid the foundations for a new political movement that came to be called fascism after the name of his group, the *Fascio di Combattimento* (League of Combat). It received little attention in the elections of 1919, but political stalemate in Italy's parliamentary system and strong nationalist sentiment saved Mussolini and the Fascists.

The new parliament elected in November quickly proved incapable of governing Italy. Three major parties, the Socialists, Liberals, and Popolari (or Christian Democrats, a new Catholic party formed in January 1919), were unable to form an effective coalition. The Socialists, who had now become the largest party, spoke theoretically of the need for revolution, which alarmed conservatives, who quickly associated them with Bolsheviks or Communists. The success of the Communists in Russia had frightened the propertied classes, who were concerned about what a Communist takeover would mean. Thousands of industrial and agricultural strikes in 1919 and 1920 created a climate of class warfare and continual violence. Mussolini shifted quickly from leftist to rightist politics and began to gain support from middle-class industrialists fearful of working-class agitation and large landowners who objected to the agricultural strikes. Mussolini also perceived that Italians were angry over Italy's failure to receive more fruits of victory in the form of territorial acquisitions after World War I. He realized then that anticommunism, antistrike activity, and nationalist rhetoric combined with the use of brute force might help him obtain what he had been unable to achieve in free elections.

In 1920 and 1921, bands of armed Fascists called *squadristi* were formed and turned loose in attacks on Socialist offices and newspapers. Strikes by trade unionists and Socialist workers and peasant leagues were broken up by force. At the same time, Mussolini entered into a political alliance with the Liberals under then Prime Minister Giovanni Giolitti. No doubt, Giolitti and the Liberals believed that the Fascists could be used to crush socialism temporarily and then be dropped. In this game of mutual deceit, Mussolini soon proved to be the more skillful player. By allying with the government coalition, he gained respectability and a free hand for his violent *squadristi*. Mussolini's efforts were rewarded when the Fascists won thirty-five parliamentary seats, or 7 percent of the total, in the election of May 1921.

The use of violence was crucial to Mussolini's plans. By 1921, the black-shirted Fascist squads numbered 200,000 and had become a regular feature of Italian life. World War I veterans and students were especially attracted to the *squadristi* and relished the opportunity to use unrestrained violence. Administering large doses of castor oil to unwilling victims became one of their favorite tactics.

Mussolini and the Fascists believed that these terrorist tactics would eventually achieve political victory. They deliberately created conditions of disorder knowing that fascism would flourish in such an environment. The Fascists construed themselves as the party of order and drew the bulk of their support from the middle and upper classes; white-collar workers, professionals and civil servants, landowners, merchants and artisans, and students made up almost 60 percent of the membership of the

Fascist Party. The middle-class fear of socialism, communist revolution, and disorder made the Fascists attractive.

With the further deterioration of the Italian political situation, Mussolini and the Fascists were emboldened to plan a march on Rome in order to seize power. In a speech in Naples to Fascist blackshirts on October 24, 1922, Mussolini exclaimed: "Either we are allowed to govern, or we will seize power by marching on Rome" to "take by the throat the miserable political class that governs us."[2] Bold words, but in truth the planned march on Rome was really a calculated bluff to frighten the government into giving them power. The bluff worked, and the government capitulated even before the march occurred. On October 29, 1922, King Victor Emmanuel III (1900–1946) made Mussolini prime minister of Italy. Twenty-four hours later, the Fascist blackshirts were allowed to march into Rome in order to create the myth that they had gained power by an armed insurrection after a civil war.

MUSSOLINI AND THE ITALIAN FASCIST STATE

Since the Fascists constituted but a small minority in parliament, the new prime minister was forced to move slowly. In the summer of 1923, Mussolini began to prepare for a national election that would consolidate the power of his Fascist government and give him a more secure base from which to govern. In July 1923, parliament enacted the Acerbo Law, which stipulated that any party winning at least 25 percent of the votes in the next national election would automatically be allotted two-thirds of the seats in parliament. The national elections that were subsequently held on April 6, 1924, resulted in an enormous victory for the Fascists. They won 65 percent of the votes and garnered 374 seats out of a total of 535 in parliament. Although the elections were conducted in an atmosphere of Fascist fraud, force, and intimidation, the size of the victory indicated the growing popularity of Mussolini and his Fascists.

With this victory, Mussolini moved faster to consolidate his power. A campaign of intimidation of opposition deputies reached its high point with the assassination of the Socialist deputy Giacomo Matteotti in June 1924. Mussolini was severely challenged for his assumed complicity in the murder of Matteotti. The public outcry even caused numerous Italian political leaders to predict in December 1924 that Mussolini would have to resign. At the beginning of 1925, yielding to extremists within his own Fascist Party who demanded decisive action and a "second wave" of Fascist change, Mussolini counterattacked. To save himself, Mussolini now pushed to establish a full dictatorship. In a speech to parliament on January 3, Mussolini accepted responsibility for all Fascist violence and vowed to establish a new order: "Italy wants peace, tranquility, calm in which to work; we will give it to her, by means of love if possible, by force if necessary."

By 1926, Mussolini had established the institutional framework for his Fascist dictatorship. Press laws gave the government the right to suspend any publications that fostered disrespect for the Catholic church, the monarchy, or the state. The prime minister was made "head of government" with the power to legislate by decree. A police law empowered the police to arrest and confine anybody for nonpolitical or political crimes without due process of law. The government was given the power to dissolve political and cultural associations. In 1926, all anti-Fascist parties were outlawed. A secret police, known as the OVRA, was also established. By the end of 1926, Mussolini ruled Italy as *Il Duce,* the leader.

Mussolini conceived of the Fascist state as totalitarian: "Fascism is totalitarian, and the Fascist State, the synthesis and unity of all values, interprets, develops and gives strength to the whole life of the people"[3] (see the box on p. 750). Mussolini did try to create a totalitarian apparatus for police surveillance and for controlling mass communications, but this machinery was not all that effective. Police activities in Italy were never as repressive, efficient, or savage as those of Nazi Germany. Likewise, the Italian Fascists' attempt to exercise control over all forms of mass media, including newspapers, radio, and cinema, in order to use propaganda as an instrument to integrate the masses into the state failed to achieve its major goals. Most commonly, Fascist propaganda was disseminated through simple slogans, such as "Mussolini is always right," plastered on walls all over Italy.

Mussolini and the Fascists also attempted to mold Italians into a single-minded community by pursuing a Fascist educational policy and developing Fascist organizations. Because the secondary schools maintained considerable freedom from Fascist control, the regime relied more and more on the activities of youth organizations, known as the Young Fascists, to indoctrinate the young people of the nation in Fascist ideals. By 1939, about 6.8 million children, teenagers, and young adults of both sexes, or 66 percent of the population between eight and eighteen, were enrolled in some kind of Fascist youth group. Activities for these groups included unpopular Saturday afternoon marching drills and calisthenics, seaside and mountain summer camps, and competitions. An underlying motif for all of these activities was the Fascist insistence on militarization. Beginning in the 1930s, all male groups were given some kind of premilitary exercises to develop discipline and provide training for war. Results were mixed. Italian teenagers, who liked neither military training nor routine discipline of any kind, simply refused to attend Fascist youth meetings on a regular basis.

The Fascist organizations hoped to create a new Italian, hardworking, physically fit, disciplined, intellectually sharp, and martially inclined. In practice, the Fascists largely reinforced traditional social attitudes in Italy, as is evident in their policies regarding women. The Fascists portrayed the family as the pillar of the state and women as the basic foundation of the family. "Woman into the home" became the Fascist slogan. Women were to be homemakers and baby producers, "their natural and fundamental mission in life," according to Mussolini, who viewed population growth as an indicator of national strength. To Mussolini, female emancipation was "unfascist." Employment outside the home was an impediment distracting

AP/Wide World Photos

Mussolini, the Iron Duce. One of Mussolini's favorite images of himself was that of the Iron Duce—the strong leader who is always right. Consequently, he was often seen in military-style uniforms and military poses. This photograph shows Mussolini in one of his numerous uniforms with his Black Shirt bodyguards giving the Fascist salute.

women from conception. "It forms an independence and consequent physical and moral habits contrary to child bearing."[4] A practical consideration also underlay the Fascist attitude toward women: eliminating women from the job market reduced male unemployment figures in the depression economy of the 1930s.

In the 1930s, the Fascists translated their attitude toward women into law by a series of enactments that aimed at encouraging larger families by offering supplementary pay, loans, prizes, and subsidies for families with many offspring. Gold medals were given to mothers of many children. A national "Mother and Child" holiday was celebrated on December 24, with prizes awarded for fertility. Also in the 1930s, decrees were passed that set quotas on the employment of women, but they were not successful in accomplishing their goal.

Despite the instruments of repression, the use of propaganda, and the creation of numerous Fascist organizations, Mussolini failed to achieve the degree of totalitarian control accomplished in Hitler's Germany or Stalin's Soviet Union. Mussolini and the Fascist Party never really destroyed the old power structure. Some institutions, including the armed forces and the monarchy, were never absorbed into the Fascist state and managed to maintain their independence. Mussolini had boasted that he would help workers and peasants, but instead he generally allied himself with the interests of the industrialists and large landowners at the expense of the lower classes.

Even more indicative of Mussolini's compromise with the traditional institutions of Italy was his attempt to gain the support of the Catholic church. In the Lateran Accords of February 1929, Mussolini's regime recognized the sovereign independence of a small enclave of 109 acres within Rome, known as Vatican City, which had remained in the church's possession since the unification of Italy in 1870; in return, the papacy recognized the Italian state. The Lateran Accords also guaranteed the church a large grant of money and recognized Catholicism as the "sole religion of the state." In return, the Catholic church urged Italians to support the Fascist regime.

The Voice of Italian Fascism

In 1932, an article on fascism appeared in the *Italian Encyclopedia.* Supposedly authored by Mussolini, it was largely written by the philosopher Giovanni Gentile. Mussolini had always argued that fascism was based only on the need for action, not on doctrines, but after its success, he felt the need to summarize the basic political and social ideas of fascism. These excerpts are taken from Mussolini's article.

Benito Mussolini, "The Political and Social Doctrine of Fascism"

Above all, Fascism . . . believes neither in the possibility nor the utility of perpetual peace. It thus repudiates the doctrine of Pacifism—born of a renunciation of struggle and an act of cowardice in the face of sacrifice. War alone brings up to its highest tension all human energy and puts the stamp of nobility upon the peoples who have the courage to meet it. All other trials are substitutes, which never really put men into the position where they have to make the great decision—the alternative of life or death. Thus a doctrine which is founded upon this harmful postulate of peace is hostile to Fascism. . . . Thus the Fascist accepts life and loves it, knowing nothing of and despising suicide: he rather conceives of life as duty and struggle and conquest. . . .

Fascism is the complete opposite of Marxian socialism, the materialist conception of history; according to which the history of human civilization can be explained simply through the conflict of interests among the various social groups and by the change and development in the means and instruments of production. That the changes in the economic field have their importance no one can deny; but that these factors are sufficient to explain the history of humanity excluding all others is an absurd delusion. Fascism, now and always, believes in holiness and in heroism; that is to say, in actions influenced by no economic motive, direct or indirect. . . .

After Socialism, Fascism combats the whole complex system of democratic ideology, and repudiates it, whether in its theoretical premises or in its practical application. Fascism denies that the majority, by the simple fact that it is a majority, can direct human society; it denies that numbers alone can govern by means of a periodical consultation, and it affirms the immutable, beneficial, and fruitful inequality of mankind, which can never be permanently leveled through the mere operation of a mechanical process such as universal suffrage.

The foundation of Fascism is the conception of the State, its character, its duty and its aim. Fascism conceives of the State as an absolute, in comparison with which all individuals or groups are relative, only to be conceived of in their relation to the State. . . . The Fascist state organizes the nation, but leaves a sufficient margin of liberty to the individual; the latter is deprived of all useless and possibly harmful freedom, but retains what is essential; the deciding power in the question cannot be the individual, but the State alone. . . .

For Fascism, the growth of empire, that is to say the expansion of the nation, is an essential manifestation of vitality, and its opposite a sign of decadence. Peoples which are rising, or rising again after a period of decadence, are always imperialist; any renunciation is a sign of decay and of death. Fascism is the doctrine best adapted to represent the tendencies and the aspirations of a people, like the people of Italy, who are rising again after many centuries of abasement and foreign servitude. But Empire demands discipline, the coordination of all forces and a deeply felt sense of duty and sacrifice.

In all areas of Italian life under Mussolini and the Fascists, there was a noticeable dichotomy between Fascist ideals and practice. The Italian Fascists promised much but delivered considerably less, and they were soon overshadowed by a much more powerful fascist movement to the north.

Hitler and Nazi Germany

In 1923, a small, south German rightist party, known as the Nazis, led by an obscure Austrian rabble-rouser named Adolf Hitler, created a stir when it tried to seize power in southern Germany in conscious imitation of Mussolini's march on Rome in 1922. Although the attempt failed, Adolf Hitler and the Nazis achieved sudden national prominence. Within ten years, Hitler and his party had taken over complete power.

WEIMAR GERMANY

After Germany's defeat in World War I, a German democratic state known as the Weimar Republic had been established. From its beginnings, the Weimar Republic was plagued by problems. It had no outstanding political leaders. Its more able leaders, such as Friedrich Ebert, who served as president, and Gustav Stresemann, the foreign minister and chancellor, died in the 1920s. When Ebert died in 1925, Paul von Hindenburg, the World War I military hero, was elected president. Hindenburg was a traditional military man, monarchist in sentiment, who at heart was not in favor of the republic. The young republic also suffered politically from attempted uprisings and attacks from both the left and the right.

The Weimar Republic also faced serious economic difficulties. Germany experienced runaway inflation in 1922

CHRONOLOGY

Fascist Italy

Creation of *Fascio di Combattimento*	1919
Squadristi violence	1920–1921
Fascists win thirty-five seats in Parliament	1921
Mussolini is made prime minister	1922 (October 29)
Acerbo Law	1923
Electoral victory for Fascists	1924
Establishment of Fascist dictatorship	1925–1926
Lateran Accords with Catholic church	1929

and 1923 with serious social effects. Widows, orphans, the retired elderly, army officers, teachers, civil servants, and others who lived on fixed incomes all watched their monthly stipends become worthless or their lifetime savings disappear. Their economic losses increasingly pushed the middle class to the rightist parties that were hostile to the republic. To make matters worse, after a period of prosperity from 1924 to 1929, Germany faced the Great Depression. Unemployment increased to 4.38 million by December 1930. The depression paved the way for social discontent, fear, and extremist parties. The political, economic, and social problems of the Weimar Republic provided an environment in which Adolf Hitler and the Nazis were able to rise to power.

THE RISE OF THE NAZIS

Born on April 20, 1889, Adolf Hitler was the son of an Austrian customs official. He was a total failure in secondary school and eventually made his way to Vienna to become an artist. Rejected by the Vienna Academy of Fine Arts and supported by an inheritance and an orphan's pension, Hitler stayed on in Vienna to live the bohemian lifestyle of an artist. In his autobiography, *Mein Kampf* (My Struggle), Hitler characterized his years in Vienna from 1908 to 1913 as an important formative period in his life: "In this period there took shape within me a world picture and a philosophy which became the granite foundation of all my acts. In addition to what I then created, I have had to learn little, and I have had to alter nothing."[5]

Hitler experienced four major influences in Vienna. Georg von Schönerer, the leader of the Austrian Pan-German movement, was an extreme German nationalist who urged the union of all Germans in one national state. Karl Lueger was mayor of Vienna and leader of the anti-Semitic Christian Social Party. Hitler called him "the greatest German mayor of all time" and especially admired his demagogic methods and leadership of a mass party that was formed with the aid of emotional slogans. Much of Hitler's early anti-Semitism was imbibed from a former Catholic monk named Adolf Lanz who called himself Lanz von Liebenfels. Hitler was an avid reader of *Ostara,* a periodical published by Liebenfels in which he propagated his racial beliefs that the German Aryans were exalted beings destined to rule the earth. Liebenfels characterized the Jews and other allegedly inferior races as "animal-men" who must someday be eliminated by sterilization, deportation, forced labor, and even "direct liquidation." Finally, Hitler was also strongly influenced by Richard Wagner's operas, which he attended frequently in Vienna. Hitler absorbed Wagner's ideal of the true artist as a social outcast from the bourgeois world who is subject to his own rhythms. Wagner's music also spoke of a boundless will to power and a need to dominate.

In Vienna, then, Hitler established the basic ideas of an ideology from which he never deviated for the rest of his life. At the core of Hitler's ideas was racism, especially anti-Semitism (see the box on p. 752). His hatred of the Jews lasted to the very end of his life. Hitler had also become an extreme German nationalist who had learned from the mass politics of Vienna how political parties could effectively use propaganda and terror. Finally, in his Viennese years, Hitler also came to a firm belief in the need for struggle, which he saw as the "granite foundation of the world."

In 1913, Hitler moved to Munich, still without purpose and with no real future in sight. World War I saved him: "Overpowered by stormy enthusiasm, I fell down on my knees and thanked Heaven from an overflowing heart for granting me the good fortune of being permitted to live at this time."[6] As a dispatch runner on the Western Front, Hitler distinguished himself by his brave acts. At the end of the war, finding again that his life had no purpose or meaning, he returned to Munich and decided to enter politics and found, at last, his true profession.

Hitler joined the obscure German Workers' Party, one of a number of right-wing extreme nationalist parties in Munich. By the summer of 1921, Hitler had assumed total control of the party, which he renamed the National Socialist German Workers' Party (NSDAP), or Nazi for short (from the first two syllables of its name). His idea was that the party's name would distinguish the Nazis from the socialist parties while gaining support from both working-class and nationalist circles. Hitler worked assiduously to develop the party into a mass political movement with flags, badges, uniforms, its own newspaper, and its own police force or militia known as the SA, the *Sturmabteilung,* or Storm Troops. The SA was used to defend the party in meeting halls and to break up the meetings of other parties. Hitler's own oratorical skills were largely responsible for attracting an increasing number of followers. By 1923, the party had grown from its early hundreds into a membership of 55,000, plus another 15,000 in the SA.

In its early years, the Nazi Party had been only one of many radical right-wing political groups in southern Germany. By 1923, it had become the strongest. When it appeared that the Weimar Republic was on the verge of collapse in the fall of 1923, the Nazis and other right-wing

Adolf Hitler's Hatred of the Jews

A believer in Aryan racial supremacy, Adolf Hitler viewed the Jews as the archenemies of the Aryans. He believed that the first task of a true Aryan state would be the elimination of the Jewish threat. This is why Hitler's political career both began and ended with a warning against the Jews. In this excerpt from his autobiography, *Mein Kampf,* Hitler describes how he came to be an anti-Semite when he lived in Vienna in his early twenties.

■ *Adolf Hitler,* Mein Kampf

My views with regard to anti-Semitism thus succumbed to the passage of time, and this was my greatest transformation of all. . . .

Once, as I was strolling through the Inner City [of Vienna], I suddenly encountered an apparition in a black caftan and black hair locks. Is this a Jew? was my first thought.

For, to be sure, they had not looked like that in Linz. I observed the man furtively and cautiously, but the longer I stared at this foreign face, scrutinizing feature for feature, the more my first question assumed a new form: Is this a German?

As always in such cases, I now began to try to relieve my doubts by books. For a few pennies I bought the first anti-Semitic pamphlets of my life. . . .

Yet I could no longer very well doubt that the objects of my study were not Germans of a special religion, but a people in themselves; for since I had begun to concern myself with this question and to take cognizance of the Jews, Vienna appeared to me in a different light than before. Wherever I went, I began to see Jews, and the more I saw, the more sharply they became distinguished in my eyes from the rest of humanity. . . .

In a short time I was made more thoughtful than ever by my slowly rising insight into the type of activity carried on by the Jews in certain fields.

Was there any form of filth or profligacy, particularly in cultural life, without at least one Jew involved in it? . . .

Sometimes I stood there thunderstruck.

I didn't know what to be more amazed at: the agility of their tongues or their virtuosity at lying.

Gradually I began to hate them.

leaders in the south German state of Bavaria decided to march on Berlin to overthrow the Weimar government. When his fellow conspirators reneged, Hitler and the Nazis decided to act on their own by staging an armed uprising in Munich on November 8. The so-called Beer Hall Putsch was quickly crushed. Hitler was arrested, put on trial for treason, and sentenced to prison for five years, a lenient sentence indeed from sympathetic right-wing judges.

THE NAZI SEIZURE OF POWER

The Beer Hall Putsch proved to be a major turning point in Hitler's career. Rather than discouraging him, his trial and imprisonment reinforced his faith in himself and in his mission. He now saw clearly the need for a change in tactics. If the Nazis could not overthrow the Weimar Republic by force, they would have to use constitutional means to gain power. This implied the formation of a mass political movement that would actively compete for votes with the other political parties.

Hitler occupied himself in prison with the writing of *Mein Kampf,* an account of his movement and its underlying ideology. Extreme German nationalism, virulent anti-Semitism, and vicious anticommunism are linked together by a social Darwinian theory of struggle that stresses the right of superior nations to *Lebensraum* (living space) through expansion and the right of superior individuals to secure authoritarian leadership over the masses. What is perhaps most remarkable about *Mein Kampf* is its elaboration of a series of ideas that directed Hitler's actions once he took power. That others refused to take Hitler and his ideas seriously was one of his greatest advantages.

When Hitler was released, the Nazi Party was in shambles, and he set about to reestablish his sole control over the party and organize it for the lawful takeover of power. Hitler's position on leadership in the party was quite clear. There was to be no discussion of ideas in the party, and the party was to follow the *Führerprinzip,* the leadership principle, which entailed nothing less than a single-minded party under one leader. As Hitler expressed it: "A good National Socialist is one who would let himself be killed for his Führer at any time."[7]

In the late 1920s, Hitler worked to establish a highly structured party that could compete in elections and attract new recruits. He reorganized the Nazi Party on a regional basis and expanded it to all parts of Germany. By 1929, the Nazis had a national party organization. The party also grew from 27,000 members in 1925 to 178,000 by the end of 1929. Especially noticeable was the youthfulness of the regional, district, and branch leaders of the Nazi organization. Many were under thirty and were fiercely committed to Hitler because he gave them the kind of active politics they sought. Rather than democratic debate, they wanted brawls in beer halls, enthusiastic speeches, and comradeship in the building of a new Germany. One new young Nazi member expressed his excitement about the party:

> For me this was the start of a completely new life. There was only one thing in the world for me and that was service in the movement. All my thoughts were centered on the movement. I could talk only politics. I was no longer aware of anything else. At the time I was a promising athlete; I was very keen on sport, and it was going to be my career. But I had to give this up too. My only interest was agitation and propaganda.[8]

Hugo Jaeger, Life Magazine, © TimePix

Hitler and the Blood Flag Ritual. In developing his mass political movement, Adolf Hitler used ritualistic ceremonies as a means of binding party members to his own person. Hitler is shown here touching the "blood flag," which had supposedly been stained with the blood of Nazis killed during the Beer Hall Putsch, to an SS banner while the SS standard-bearer makes a "blood oath" of allegiance: "I vow to remain true to my Führer, Adolf Hitler. I bind myself to carry out all orders conscientiously and without reluctance. Standards and flags shall be sacred to me."

Such youthful enthusiasm gave Nazism the aura of a "young man's movement" and a sense of dynamism that the other parties could not match.

By 1929, the Nazi Party had also made a significant shift in strategy. Between 1925 and 1927, Hitler and the Nazis had pursued an urban strategy geared toward winning workers from the Socialists and Communists. But failure in the 1928 elections, when the Nazis gained only 2.6 percent of the vote and twelve seats in the Reichstag (parliament), convinced Hitler of the need for a change. By 1929, the party began to pursue middle-class and lower-middle-class votes in small towns and rural areas, especially in northern, central, and eastern Germany. By the end of 1929, the Nazis had successfully made their shift to the new strategy.

Germany's economic difficulties paved the way for the Nazis' rise to power. Unemployment rose dramatically, from 4.35 million in 1931 to 6 million by the winter of 1932. The economic and psychological impact of the Great Depression made extremist parties offering radical solutions more attractive. Already in the Reichstag elections of September 1930, the Nazis polled 18 percent of the vote and gained 107 seats in the Reichstag, making the Nazi Party one of the largest in Germany.

By 1930, Chancellor Heinrich Brüning (1885–1970) had found it impossible to form a working parliamentary majority in the Reichstag and relied on the use of emergency decrees by President Hindenburg to rule. In a real sense, then, parliamentary democracy was already dying in 1930, three years before Hitler destroyed it.

Hitler's quest for power from late 1930 to early 1933 depended on the political maneuvering around President Hindenburg. Nevertheless, the elections from 1930 through 1932 were indirectly responsible for the Nazis' rise to power since they showed the importance of the Nazi Party. The party itself grew dramatically during this period, from 289,000 members in September 1930 to 800,000 by 1932. The SA also rose to 500,000 members.

The Nazis proved very effective in developing modern electioneering techniques. They crossed Germany in whirlwind campaigns by car, train, and airplane. His "Hitler over Germany" campaign by airplane had Hitler speaking in fifty cities in fifteen days. In their election campaigns, party members pitched their themes to the needs and fears of different social groups. In working-class districts, for example, the Nazis attacked international high finance, but in middle-class neighborhoods, they exploited fears of a

Communist revolution and its threat to private property. At the same time that the Nazis made blatant appeals to class interests, they were denouncing conflicts of interest and maintaining that they stood above classes and parties. Hitler, in particular, claimed to stand above all differences and promised to create a new Germany free of class differences and party infighting. His appeal to national pride, national honor, and traditional militarism struck chords of emotion in his listeners.

Elections, however, proved to have their limits. In the elections of July 1932, the Nazis won 230 seats, making them the largest party in the Reichstag. But four months later, in November, they declined to 196 seats. It became apparent to many Nazis that they would not gain power simply by the ballot box. Hitler saw clearly, however, that the Reichstag after 1930 was not all that important, since the government ruled by decree with the support of President Hindenburg. Increasingly, the right-wing elites of Germany, the industrial magnates, landed aristocrats, military establishment, and higher bureaucrats, came to see Hitler as the man who had the mass support to establish a right-wing, authoritarian regime that would save Germany and their privileged positions from a Communist takeover. These people almost certainly thought that they could control Hitler and, like many others, may well have underestimated his abilities. Under pressure from these elites, President Hindenburg agreed to allow Hitler to become chancellor (on January 30, 1933) and to form a new government, but with supposed safeguards. There would be only three Nazis in the cabinet, and Franz von Papen (1878–1969), who had served as chancellor and done much to win over Hindenburg to the arrangements, would serve as vice-chancellor. When some reproached von Papen for giving power to Hitler, he responded: "What do you want? I have Hindenburg's trust. Within two months, we will have pushed Hitler so far into a corner that he will squeak."[9]

Within those two months, Hitler basically laid the foundations for the Nazis' complete control over Germany. One of Hitler's important cohorts, Hermann Göring (1893–1946), had been made minister of the interior and hence head of the police of the Prussian state, the largest of the federal states in Germany. He used his power to purge the police of non-Nazis and to establish an auxiliary police force composed of SA members. This action legitimized Nazi terror. On the day after a fire broke out in the Reichstag building (February 27), supposedly set by the Communists but possibly by the Nazis themselves, Hitler was also able to convince President Hindenburg to issue a decree that gave the government emergency powers. It suspended all basic rights of citizens for the full duration of the emergency, thus enabling the Nazis to arrest and imprison anyone without redress.

The crowning step of Hitler's legal seizure of power came after the Nazis had gained 288 Reichstag seats in the elections of March 5, 1933. Since they still did not possess an absolute majority, on March 23 the Nazis sought the passage of a bill that would empower the government to dispense with constitutional forms for four years while it issued laws that would deal with the country's problems. Since the Enabling Act was to be an amendment to the Weimar constitution, the Nazis needed and obtained a two-thirds vote to pass it. Only the Social Democrats had the courage to oppose Hitler. The Enabling Act provided the legal basis for Hitler's subsequent acts. He no longer needed either the Reichstag or President Hindenburg. In effect, Hitler became a dictator appointed by the parliamentary body itself.

With their new source of power, the Nazis acted quickly to enforce *Gleichschaltung,* the coordination of all institutions under Nazi control. The civil service was purged of Jews and democratic elements, concentration camps were established for opponents of the new regime, the autonomy of the federal states was eliminated, trade unions were dissolved and swallowed up by the gigantic Labor Front, and all political parties except the Nazis were abolished. By the end of the summer of 1933, within seven months of being appointed chancellor, Hitler and the Nazis had established the foundations for a totalitarian state.

Why had this seizure of power been so quick and easy? The Nazis were not only ruthless in their use of force but had also been ready to take control. The depression had weakened what little faith the Germans had in their democratic state. But negative factors alone cannot explain the Nazi success. To many Germans, the Nazis offered a national awakening. "Germany Awake," one of the many Nazi slogans, had a powerful appeal to a people psychologically crushed by their defeat in World War I. The Nazis presented a strong image of a dynamic new Germany that was above parties and above classes.

By the end of 1933, there were only two sources of potential danger to Hitler's authority: the armed forces and the SA within his own party. The SA, under the leadership of Ernst Röhm, openly criticized Hitler and spoke of the need for a "second revolution" and the replacement of the regular army by the SA. Neither the army nor Hitler favored such a possibility. Hitler solved both problems simultaneously on June 30, 1934, by having Ernst Röhm and a number of other SA leaders killed in return for the army's support in allowing Hitler to succeed Hindenburg when the president died. When Hindenburg died on August 2, 1934, the office of president was abolished, and Hitler became sole ruler of Germany. Public officials and soldiers were all required to take a personal oath of loyalty to Hitler as the "Führer of the German Reich and people." On August 19, 1934, Hitler held a plebiscite in which 85 percent of the German people indicated their approval of the new order. The Third Reich had begun.

THE NAZI STATE (1933–1939)

Having smashed the parliamentary state, Hitler now felt that the real task was at hand: to develop the "total state." Hitler's aims had not been simply power for power's sake or a tyranny based on personal power. He had larger ideological goals. The development of an Aryan racial state that would dominate Europe and possibly the world for generations to come required a massive movement in

Hugo Jaeger, Life Magazine, © TimePix

The Nazi Mass Spectacle. Hitler and the Nazis made clever use of mass spectacles to rally the German people behind the Nazi regime. These mass demonstrations evoked intense enthusiasm, as is evident in this photograph of Hitler arriving at the Bückeberg near Hamelin for the Harvest Festival in 1937. Almost one million people were present for the celebration.

which the German people would be actively involved, not passively cowed by force. Hitler stated:

> We must develop organizations in which an individual's entire life can take place. Then every activity and every need of every individual will be regulated by the collectivity represented by the party. There is no longer any arbitrary will, there are no longer any free realms in which the individual belongs to himself. . . . The time of personal happiness is over.[10]

The Nazis pursued the creation of this totalitarian state in a variety of ways. Mass demonstrations and spectacles were employed to integrate the German nation into a collective fellowship and to mobilize it as an instrument for Hitler's policies. These mass demonstrations, especially the Nuremberg party rallies that were held every September and the Harvest Festivals celebrated at the Bückeberg near Hamelin every fall, combined the symbolism of a religious service with the merriment of a popular amusement. They had great appeal and usually evoked mass enthusiasm and excitement (see the box on p. 756).

Some features of the state apparatus of Hitler's "total state" seem contradictory. One usually thinks of Nazi Germany as having an all-powerful government that maintained absolute control and order. In truth, Nazi Germany was the scene of almost constant personal and institutional conflict, which resulted in administrative chaos. In matters such as foreign policy, education, and economics, parallel government and party bureaucracies competed with each other over spheres of influence. Incessant struggle characterized relationships within the party, within the state, and between party and state. By fostering rivalry within the party and between party and state, Hitler became the ultimate decision maker.

In the economic sphere, Hitler and the Nazis also established control, but industry was not nationalized, as the left wing of the Nazi Party wanted. Hitler felt that it was irrelevant who owned the means of production so long as the owners recognized their master. Although the regime pursued the use of public works projects and "pump-priming" grants to private construction firms to foster employment and end the depression, there is little doubt that rearmament was a far more important contributor to solving the unemployment problem. Unemployment, which had stood at 6 million in 1932, dropped to 2.6 million in 1934 and less than 500,000 in 1937. The regime claimed full credit for solving Germany's economic woes, and this was an important factor in leading many Germans to accept the new regime, despite its excesses.

The German Labor Front under Robert Ley regulated the world of labor. The Labor Front was a state-controlled union. To control all laborers, it used the workbook. Every salaried worker had to have one in order to hold a job. Only by submitting to the policies of the Nazi-controlled Labor Front could a worker obtain and retain a workbook. The Labor Front also sponsored activities to keep the workers happy (see "Mass Leisure" later in this chapter).

Propaganda and Mass Meetings in Nazi Germany

Propaganda and mass rallies were two of the chief instruments that Hitler used to prepare the German people for the tasks he set before them. In the first selection, taken from a speech to a crowd at Nuremberg, Hitler describes the kind of mystical bond he hoped to create through his mass rallies. In the second excerpt, a Hamburg schoolteacher provides her impression of a Hitler rally.

Adolf Hitler, Speech at the Nuremberg Party Rally, *1936*

Do we not feel once again in this hour the miracle that brought us together? Once you heard the voice of a man, and it struck deep into your hearts; it awakened you, and you followed this voice. Year after year you went after it, though him who had spoken you never even saw. You heard only a voice, and you followed it. When we meet each other here, the wonder of our coming together fills us all. Not everyone of you sees me, and I do not see everyone of you. But I feel you, and you feel me. It is the belief in our people that has made us small men great, that has made us poor men rich, that has made brave and courageous men out of us wavering, spiritless, timid folk; this belief made us see our road when we were astray; it joined us together into one whole! . . . You come, that . . . you may, once in a while, gain the feeling that now we are together; we are with him and he with us, and we are now Germany!

A Teacher's Impression of a Hitler Rally

The April sun shone hot like in summer and turned everything into a picture of gay expectation. There was immaculate order and discipline, although the police left the whole square to the stewards and stood on the sidelines. Nobody spoke of "Hitler," always just "the Führer," "the Führer says," "the Führer wants," and what he said and wanted seemed right and good. The hours passed, the sun shone, expectations rose. In the background, at the edge of the track there were columns of carriers like ammunition carriers. . . . Aeroplanes above us. Testing of the loudspeakers, buzzing of the cine-cameras. It was nearly 3 P.M. "The Führer is coming!" A ripple went through the crowds. Around the speaker's platform one could see hands raised in the Hitler salute. A speaker opened the meeting, abused the "system," nobody listened to him. A second speaker welcomed Hitler and made way for the man who had drawn 120,000 people of all classes and ages. There stood Hitler in a simple black coat and looked over the crowd, waiting—a forest of swastika pennants swished up, the jubilation of this moment was given vent in a roaring salute. Main theme: Out of parties shall grow a nation, the German nation. He censured the "system" ("I want to know what there is left to be ruined in this state!"). "On the way here Socialists confronted me with a poster, 'Turn back, Adolf Hitler.' Thirteen years ago I was a simple unknown soldier. I went my way. I never turned back. Nor shall I turn back now." Otherwise he made no personal attacks, nor any promises, vague or definite. His voice was hoarse after all his speaking during the previous days. When the speech was over, there was roaring enthusiasm and applause. Hitler saluted, gave his thanks, the Horst Wessel song sounded out across the course. Hitler was helped into his coat. Then he went.—How many look up to him with touching faith! as their helper, their savior, their deliverer from unbearable distress—to him who rescues the Prussian prince, the scholar, the clergyman, the farmer, the worker, the unemployed, who rescues them from the parties back into the nation.

For those who needed coercion, the Nazi total state had its instruments of terror and repression. Especially important was the SS. Originally created as Hitler's personal bodyguard, the SS, under the direction of Heinrich Himmler (1900–1945), came to control all of the regular and secret police forces. Himmler and the SS functioned on the basis of two principles: terror and ideology. Terror included the instruments of repression and murder: the secret police, criminal police, concentration camps, and later the execution squads and death camps for the extermination of the Jews (see Chapter 27). For Himmler, the SS was a crusading order whose primary goal was to further the Aryan master race. SS members, who constituted a carefully chosen elite, were thoroughly indoctrinated in racial ideology.

Other institutions, such as the Catholic and Protestant churches, primary and secondary schools, and universities, were also brought under the control of the Nazi totalitarian state. Nazi professional organizations and leagues were formed for civil servants, teachers, women, farmers, doctors, and lawyers. Because the early indoctrination of the nation's youth would lay the foundation for a strong totalitarian state, youth organizations, the *Hitler Jugend* (Hitler Youth) and its female counterpart, the *Bund Deutscher Mädel* (German Girls Association), were given special attention. The oath required of Hitler Youth members demonstrates the degree of dedication expected of youth in the Nazi state: "In the presence of this blood banner, which represents our Führer, I swear to devote all my energies and my strength to the savior of our country, Adolf Hitler. I am willing and ready to give up my life for him, so help me God."

The Nazi total state was intended to be an Aryan racial state. From its beginning, the Nazi Party reflected the strong anti-Semitic beliefs of Adolf Hitler. Once in power, it did

© Bildarchiv Preussischer Kulturbesitz, Berlin

Anti-Semitism in Nazi Germany. At the core of Hitler's ideology was an intense anti-Semitism. Soon after seizing power, Hitler and the Nazis began to translate their anti-Semitic ideas into anti-Semitic policies. This photograph shows one example of Nazi action against the Jews. Two women clean up some of the debris on Potsdamer Strasse in Berlin the morning after *Kristallnacht,* the night of shattered glass.

not take long for the Nazis to translate anti-Semitic ideas into anti-Semitic policies. Already on April 1, 1933, the new Nazi government initiated a two-day boycott of Jewish businesses. A series of laws soon followed that excluded "non-Aryans" (defined as anyone "descended from non-Aryans, especially Jewish parents or grandparents") from the legal profession, civil service, judgeships, the medical profession, teaching positions, cultural and entertainment enterprises, and the press.

In 1935, the Nazis unleashed another stage of anti-Jewish activity when new racial laws were announced in September at the annual party rally in Nuremberg. These "Nuremberg laws" excluded German Jews from German citizenship and forbade marriages and extramarital relations between Jews and German citizens. The "Nuremberg laws" essentially separated Jews from the Germans politically, socially, and legally and were the natural extension of Hitler's stress on the preservation of a pure Aryan race.

Another considerably more violent phase of anti-Jewish activity took place in 1938 and 1939; it was initiated on November 9–10, 1938, the infamous *Kristallnacht,* or night of shattered glass. The assassination of a third secretary in the German embassy in Paris by a young Polish Jew became the occasion for a Nazi-led destructive rampage against the Jews in which synagogues were burned, seven thousand Jewish businesses were destroyed, and at least one hundred Jews were killed. Moreover, thirty thousand Jewish males were rounded up and sent to concentration camps. *Kristallnacht* also led to further drastic steps. Jews were barred from all public buildings and prohibited from owning, managing, or working in any retail store. Finally, under the direction of the SS, Jews were encouraged to "emigrate from Germany." After the outbreak of World War II, the policy of emigration was replaced by a more gruesome one.

The creation of the Nazi total state also had an impact on women. The Nazi attitude toward women was largely determined by ideological considerations. Women played a crucial role in the Aryan racial state as bearers of the children who would bring about the triumph of the Aryan race. To the Nazis, the differences between men and women were quite natural. Men were warriors and political leaders; women were destined to be wives and mothers. Motherhood was also exalted in an annual ceremony on August 12, Hitler's mother's birthday, when Hitler awarded the German Mother's Cross to a select group of German mothers. Those with four children received a bronze cross, those with six a silver cross, and those with eight or more a gold cross.

Nazi ideas determined employment opportunities for women. The Nazis hoped to drive women out of certain areas of the labor market. These included heavy industry

CHRONOLOGY

Nazi Germany

Hitler as Munich politician	1919–1923
Beer Hall Putsch	1923
Nazis win 107 seats in Reichstag	1930 (September)
Hitler is made chancellor	1933 (January 30)
Reichstag fire	1933 (February 27)
Enabling Act	1933 (March 23)
Purge of the SA	1934 (June 30)
Hindenburg dies; Hitler as sole ruler	1934 (August 2)
Nuremberg laws	1935
Kristallnacht	1938 (November 9–10)

or other jobs that might hinder women from bearing healthy children, as well as certain professions, including university teaching, medicine, and law, which were considered inappropriate for women, especially married women. The Nazis encouraged women to pursue professional occupations that had direct practical application, such as social work and nursing. In addition to restrictive legislation against females, the Nazi regime pursued its campaign against working women with such poster slogans as "Get hold of pots and pans and broom and you'll sooner find a groom!" Nazi policy toward female workers remained inconsistent, however. Especially after the rearmament boom and increased conscription of males for military service resulted in a labor shortage, the government encouraged women to work, even in areas previously dominated by males.

The Soviet Union

Yet another example of totalitarianism was to be found in the Soviet Union. The civil war in Russia had come to an end by the beginning of 1921. It had taken an enormous toll of life, but the Red Terror and the victories of the Red Army had guaranteed the survival of the Communist regime. During the civil war, Lenin had pursued a policy of "war communism." Under this policy of expedience, the government had nationalized transportation and communication facilities as well as banks, mines, factories, and businesses that employed more than ten workers. The government had also assumed the right to requisition the produce of peasants. War communism worked during the civil war, but once the war was over, peasants began to sabotage the program by hoarding food. Added to this problem was drought, which caused a great famine between 1920 and 1922 that claimed as many as five million lives. Industrial collapse paralleled the agricultural disaster. By 1921, industrial output was at only 20 percent of its 1913 levels. Russia was exhausted. As Leon Trotsky said: "The collapse of the productive forces surpassed anything of the kind that history had ever seen. The country, and the government with it, were at the very edge of the abyss."[11]

THE NEW ECONOMIC POLICY

In March 1921, Lenin pulled Russia back from the abyss by establishing his New Economic Policy (NEP). The NEP was a modified version of the old capitalist system. Peasants were now allowed to sell their produce openly, and retail stores as well as small industries that employed fewer than twenty employees could now operate under private ownership; heavy industry, banking, and mines remained in the hands of the government. In 1922, Lenin and the Communists formally created a new state called the Union of Soviet Socialist Republics, known by its initials as the USSR and commonly called the Soviet Union. Already in that year, a revived market and good harvest had brought the famine to an end; Soviet agriculture climbed to 75 percent of its prewar level. Industry, especially state-owned heavy industry, fared less well and continued to stagnate. Only coal production had reached prewar levels by 1926. Overall, the NEP had saved the Soviet Union from complete economic disaster even though Lenin and other leading Communists intended it to be only a temporary, tactical retreat from the goals of communism.

Between 1922 and 1924, Lenin suffered a series of strokes that finally led to his death on January 21, 1924. Although Communist Party rule theoretically rested on a principle of collective leadership, in fact, Lenin had provided an example of one-man rule. His death inaugurated a struggle for power among the members of the Politburo, the institution that had become the leading organ of the party.

In 1924, the Politburo of seven members was severely divided over the future direction of the nation. The Left, led by Leon Trotsky, wanted to end the NEP and launch the Soviet Union on the path of rapid industrialization, primarily at the expense of the peasantry. This same group wanted to carry the revolution on, believing that the survival of the Russian Revolution ultimately depended on the spread of communism abroad. Another group in the Politburo, called the Right, rejected the cause of world revolution and wanted instead to concentrate on constructing a socialist state. Believing that too rapid industrialization would worsen the living standards of the Soviet peasantry, this group also favored a continuation of Lenin's NEP.

These ideological divisions were underscored by an intense personal rivalry between Leon Trotsky and Joseph Stalin. Trotsky had been a key figure in the success of the Bolshevik Revolution and the Red Army. In 1924, he held the post of commissar of war and was the leading spokesman for the Left in the Politburo. Joseph Stalin (1879–1953) had joined the Bolsheviks in 1903 and had come to Lenin's attention after staging a daring bank robbery to obtain funds for the Bolshevik cause. Stalin, who was neither a dynamic speaker nor a forceful writer, was content to hold the dull bureaucratic job of party general secretary while other Politburo members held party positions that enabled them to display their brilliant oratorical abilities. He was a good organizer (his fellow Bolsheviks called him "Comrade Card-Index"), and the other members of the Politburo soon found that the position of party secretary was really the most important in the party hierarchy. The general secretary appointed the regional, district, city, and town party secretaries. In 1922, for example, Stalin had made some ten thousand appointments, many of them trusted followers whose holding of key positions proved valuable in the struggle for power. Although Stalin at first refused to support either the Left or the Right in the Politburo, he finally came to favor the goal of "socialism in one country" rather than world revolution.

Stalin used his post as party general secretary to gain complete control of the Communist Party. Trotsky was expelled from the party in 1927. Eventually, he made his way to Mexico, where he was murdered in 1940, no doubt on Stalin's orders. By 1929, Stalin had succeeded in eliminating the Old Bolsheviks of the revolutionary era from the Politburo and establishing a dictatorship so powerful that the Russian tsars of old would have been envious.

CHRONOLOGY

The Soviet Union

New Economic Policy begins	1921
Death of Lenin	1924
Trotsky is expelled from the Communist Party	1927
First five-year plan begins	1928
Stalin's dictatorship is established	1929
Stalin's purge	1936–1938

THE STALINIST ERA (1929–1939)

The Stalinist era marked the beginning of an economic, social, and political revolution that was more sweeping in its results than the revolutions of 1917. Stalin made a significant shift in economic policy in 1928 when he launched his first five-year plan. Its real goal was nothing less than the transformation of the Soviet Union from an agricultural country into an industrial state virtually overnight. Instead of consumer goods, the first five-year plan emphasized maximum production of capital goods and armaments and succeeded in quadrupling the production of heavy machinery and doubling oil production. Between 1928 and 1937, during the first two five-year plans, steel production increased from 4 to 18 million tons per year, and hard coal output went from 36 to 128 million tons.

The social and political costs of industrialization were enormous. Little provision was made for absorbing the expanded labor force into the cities. Though the industrial labor force increased by millions between 1932 and 1940, total investment in housing actually declined after 1929; as a result, millions of workers and their families lived in pitiful conditions. Real wages in industry also declined by 43 percent between 1928 and 1940, and strict laws limited workers' freedom of movement. To inspire and pacify the workers, government propaganda stressed the need for sacrifice to create the new socialist state. Soviet labor policy stressed high levels of achievement, typified by the Stakhanov cult. Alexei Stakhanov was a coal miner who mined 102 tons of coal in one shift, exceeding the norm by 1,300 percent. He was held up as an example to others.

Rapid industrialization was accompanied by an equally rapid collectivization of agriculture. Almost all of the Bolsheviks had been appalled by one result of Lenin's New Economic Policy, the growth of a class of well-to-do peasant proprietors known as kulaks who employed wage labor. Of the 26 million peasant households in 1929, 2 million were kulaks. It seemed an anomaly to have this capitalist group in the midst of a communist society. To rectify this, Stalin inaugurated a policy of collectivization of agriculture even before he initiated the first five-year plan. Its goal was to eliminate private farms and push people into collective farms (see the box on p. 761).

Initially, Stalin planned to collectivize only the wealthier kulaks, but strong resistance from peasants who hoarded crops and killed livestock led him to step up the program. By 1930, 10 million peasant households had been collectivized; by 1934, 26 million family farms had been collectivized into 250,000 units. This was done at tremendous cost, since the hoarding of food and the slaughter of livestock produced widespread famine. Stalin himself is supposed to have told Winston Churchill during World War II that 10 million peasants died in the artificially created famines of 1932 and 1933. The only concession Stalin made to the peasants was to allow each household to have one tiny, privately owned garden plot.

Stalin's program of rapid industrialization entailed additional costs as well. To achieve his goals, Stalin strengthened the party bureaucracy under his control. Those who resisted were sent into forced labor camps in Siberia. Stalin's desire for sole control of decision making also led to purges of the Old Bolsheviks. Between 1936 and 1938, the most prominent Old Bolsheviks were put on trial and condemned to death. During this same time, Stalin undertook a purge of army officers, diplomats, union officials, party members, intellectuals, and numerous ordinary citizens. Estimates are that eight million Russians were arrested; millions died in Siberian forced labor camps. This gave Stalin the distinction of being one of the greatest mass murderers in human history. The Stalinist bloodbath made what some Western intellectuals had hailed as the "new civilization" much less attractive by the late 1930s.

Disturbed by a rapidly declining birthrate, Stalin also reversed much of the permissive social legislation of the early 1920s. Advocating complete equality of rights for women, the Communists had made divorce and abortion

Stalin Signing a Death Warrant. Terror played an important role in the authoritarian system created by Joseph Stalin. Here Stalin is shown signing what is supposedly a death warrant in 1933. As the terror increased in the late 1930s, Stalin signed such lists every day.

David King Collection, London

easy to obtain while also encouraging women to work outside the home and liberate themselves sexually. After Stalin came to power, the family was praised as a miniature collective in which parents were responsible for inculcating values of duty, discipline, and hard work. Abortion was outlawed, and divorced fathers who did not support their children were fined heavily. The new divorce law of June 1936 imposed fines for repeated divorces, and homosexuality was declared a criminal activity. The regime now praised motherhood and urged women to have large families as a patriotic duty. But by this time, many Soviet women worked in factories and spent many additional hours waiting in line to purchase increasingly scarce consumer goods. There was no dramatic increase in the birthrate.

Authoritarianism in Eastern Europe

A number of other states in Europe were not totalitarian but did have conservative authoritarian governments. These states adopted some of the trappings of totalitarian states, especially wide police powers, but their greatest concern was not the creation of a mass movement aimed at the establishment of a new kind of society but rather the defense of the existing social order. Consequently, the authoritarian states tended to limit the participation of the masses and were content with passive obedience rather than active involvement in the goals of the regime. A number of states in eastern Europe adopted this kind of authoritarian government.

Nowhere had the map of Europe been more drastically altered by World War I than in eastern Europe. The new states of Austria, Poland, Czechoslovakia, and Yugoslavia adopted parliamentary systems, and the preexisting kingdoms of Romania and Bulgaria gained new parliamentary constitutions in 1920. Greece became a republic in 1924. Hungary's government was parliamentary in form but was controlled by its landed aristocrats. At the beginning of the 1920s, political democracy seemed well established, but almost everywhere in eastern Europe, parliamentary governments soon gave way to authoritarian regimes.

Eastern Europe After World War I

Several problems helped create this situation. Eastern European states had little tradition of liberalism or parliamentary politics and no substantial middle class to support them. Then, too, these states were largely rural and agrarian. Much of the land was still dominated by large landowners who feared the growth of agrarian peasant parties with their schemes for land redistribution. Ethnic conflicts also threatened to tear these countries apart. Fearful of land reform, communist agrarian upheaval, and ethnic conflict, powerful landowners, the churches, and even some members of the small middle class looked to authoritarian governments to maintain the old system.

Already in the 1920s, some eastern European states began to move away from political democracy toward authoritarian structures. Poland established an authoritarian regime in 1926 when Marshal Joseph Pilsudski created a military dictatorship. King Alexander I (1921–1934) abolished the constitution and imposed a royal dictatorship on Yugoslavia in 1929. King Boris III (1918–1943) established an authoritarian regime in Bulgaria in 1923. During the 1930s, all of the remaining parliamentary regimes except Czechoslovakia succumbed to authoritarianism. Eastern European states were increasingly attracted to the authoritarian examples of Fascist Italy and Nazi Germany.

The Formation of Collective Farms

Accompanying the rapid industrialization of the Soviet Union was the collectivization of agriculture, a feat that involved nothing less than transforming Russia's 26 million family farms into 250,000 collective farms (*kolkhozes*). This selection provides a firsthand account of how the process worked.

Max Belov, The History of a Collective Farm

General collectivization in our village was brought about in the following manner: Two representatives of the [Communist] Party arrived in the village. All the inhabitants were summoned by the ringing of the church bell to a meeting at which the policy of general collectivization was announced. . . . The upshot was that although the meeting lasted two days, from the viewpoint of the Party representatives nothing was accomplished.

After this setback the Party representatives divided the village into two sections and worked each one separately. Two more officials were sent to reinforce the first two. A meeting of our section of the village was held in a stable which had previously belonged to a kulak. The meeting dragged on until dark. Suddenly someone threw a brick at the lamp, and in the dark the peasants began to beat the Party representatives who jumped out the window and escaped from the village barely alive. The following day seven people were arrested. The militia was called in and stayed in the village until the peasants, realizing their helplessness, calmed down. . . .

By the end of 1930 there were two kolkhozes in our village. Though at first these collectives embraced at most only 70 percent of the peasant households, in the months that followed they gradually absorbed more and more of them.

In these kolkhozes the great bulk of the land was held and worked communally, but each peasant household owned a house of some sort, a small plot of ground and perhaps some livestock. All the members of the kolkhoz were required to work on the kolkhoz a certain number of days each month; the rest of the time they were allowed to work on their own holdings. They derived their income partly from what they grew on their garden strips and partly from their work in the kolkhoz.

When the harvest was over, and after the farm had met its obligations to the state and to various special funds (for instance, seed, etc.) and had sold on the market whatever undesignated produce was left, the remaining produce and the farm's monetary income were divided among the kolkhoz members according to the number of "labor days" each one had contributed to the farm's work. . . . It was in 1930 that the kolkhoz members first received their portions out of the "communal kettle." After they had received their earnings, at the rate of 1 kilogram of grain and 55 kopecks per labor day, one of them remarked, "You will live, but you will be very, very thin."

In the spring of 1931 a tractor worked the fields of the kolkhoz for the first time. The tractor was "capable of plowing every kind of hard soil and virgin soil," as Party representatives told us at the meeting in celebration of its arrival. The peasants did not then know that these "steel horses" would carry away a good part of the harvest in return for their work. . . .

By late 1932 more than 80 percent of the peasant households . . . had been collectivized. . . . That year the peasants harvested a good crop and had hopes that the calculations would work out to their advantage and would help strengthen them economically. These hopes were in vain. The kolkhoz workers received only 200 grams of flour per labor day for the first half of the year; the remaining grain, including the seed fund, was taken by the government. The peasants were told that industrialization of the country, then in full swing, demanded grain and sacrifices from them.

Although Admiral Miklós Horthy had ruled Hungary as "regent" since 1919, the appointment of Julius Gömbös as prime minister in 1932 brought Hungary even closer to Italy and Germany. In Austria, the Christian Socialist chancellor, Engelbert Dollfuss, used the armed forces to crush the Social Democrats and create his own brand of authoritarian state, a Christian corporate state. Romania witnessed the development of a strong fascist movement led by Corneliu Codreanu. Known as the Legion of the Archangel Michael, it possessed its own paramilitary squad called the Iron Guard. As Codreanu's fascist movement grew and became Romania's third largest political party, King Carol II (1930–1940) responded in 1938 by ending parliamentary rule, crushing the leadership of the legion, and imposing authoritarian rule. At the beginning of World War II, General Ian Antonescu seized power and established his own military dictatorship in Romania. In Greece, General John Metaxas imposed a dictatorship in 1936.

Only Czechoslovakia, with its substantial middle class, liberal tradition, and strong industrial base, maintained its political democracy. Thomas Masaryk, an able and fair leader who served as president from 1918 to 1935, was able to maintain an uneasy but stable alliance of reformist socialists, agrarians, and Catholics.

Dictatorship in the Iberian Peninsula

Parliamentary regimes also failed to survive in both Spain and Portugal. Both countries were largely agrarian, illiterate, and dominated by powerful landlords and Catholic clergy.

Spain's parliamentary monarchy was unable to deal with the social tensions generated by the industrial boom

CHRONOLOGY

The Authoritarian States

Eastern Europe	
Boris III establishes authoritarian regime in Bulgaria	1923
Pilsudski creates military dictatorship in Poland	1926
Alexander I creates royal dictatorship in Yugoslavia	1929
Gömbös is made prime minister in Hungary	1932
Dictatorship of General Metaxas in Greece	1936
Carol II crushes Iron Guard and imposes authoritarian rule in Romania	1938
Spain	
Dictatorship of Primo de Rivera	1923–1930
Creation of Spanish Republic	1931
Spanish Civil War	1936–1939
Dictatorship of Franco	1939–1975

and inflation that accompanied World War I. Supported by King Alfonso XIII (1886–1931), General Miguel Primo de Rivera led a successful military coup in September 1923 and created a personal dictatorship that lasted until 1930. But a faltering economy because of the Great Depression led to the collapse of Primo de Rivera's regime in January 1930 as well as to a widespread lack of support for the monarchy. King Alfonso XIII left Spain in 1931, and a new Spanish republic was instituted, governed by a coalition of democrats and reformist socialists. Political turmoil ensued as control of the government passed from leftists to rightists until the Popular Front, an antifascist coalition composed of democrats, socialists, and the revolutionary left, took over in 1936. The Popular Front was unacceptable, however, to senior army officers. Led by General Francisco Franco (1892–1975), Spanish military forces revolted against the government and inaugurated a brutal and bloody civil war that lasted three years.

Foreign intervention complicated the Spanish Civil War. The Popular Front was assisted by trucks, planes, tanks, and military advisers from the Soviet Union and forty thousand volunteers from other countries; Franco's forces were aided by arms, money, and men from the fascist regimes of Italy and Germany. Hitler used the Spanish Civil War as an opportunity to test the new weaponry of his revived air force. Gradually, Franco's forces wore down the Popular Front, and after they captured Madrid on March 28, 1939, the Spanish Civil War finally came to an end.

General Franco soon established a dictatorship that lasted until his death in 1975. It was not a fascist government, although it was unlikely to oppose the Fascists in Italy or the Nazis in Germany. The fascist movement in Spain, known as the Falange and led by José Antonio Primo de Rivera, son of the former dictator, contributed little to Franco's success and played a minor role in the new regime. Franco's government, which favored large landowners, business, and the Catholic clergy, was yet another example of a traditional, conservative, authoritarian regime.

In 1910, the Portuguese had overthrown their monarchy and established a republic. Severe inflation after World War I, however, undermined support for the republic and helped intensify political instability. In 1926, a group of army officers seized power, and by the early 1930s, the military junta's finance minister, Antonio Salazar (1889–1970), had become the strongman of the regime. Salazar controlled the Portuguese government for the next forty years.

The Expansion of Mass Culture and Mass Leisure

The Roaring Twenties was the name given to the decade of the 1920s, known for the exuberance of its popular culture. Berlin, the capital of Germany, became the entertainment center of Europe with its theaters, cabarets, cinemas, and jazz clubs. The Roaring Twenties was especially known for its dance crazes. People danced in clubs and dance halls, at home, and in the streets, doing the Charleston, the Bunny Hug, and a variety of other dances. An American singer and dancer, Josephine Baker (1906–1975), became especially well known in Europe, appearing at European clubs featuring American "Negro" jazz music. One critic said, "She dances for hours without the slightest trace of tiredness." She became a wonderful symbol of the popular "flapper," the unconventional and lively young woman of the 1920s.

So popular was jazz, a musical form that had originated with African American musicians in the United States, that the 1920s also became known as the Jazz Age. Known for its improvised qualities and forceful rhythms, jazz spread throughout the Western world as King Oliver, Bix Beiderbecke, Jelly Roll Morton, and others wrote and played some of the greatest jazz music of the time.

Radio and Movies

A series of technological inventions in the late nineteenth century had prepared the way for a revolution in mass communications. Especially important was Marconi's discovery of "wireless" radio waves. But it was not until June 16, 1920, that a radio broadcast (of a concert by soprano Nellie Melba from London) for a mass audience was attempted. Permanent broadcasting facilities were then constructed in the United States, Europe, and Japan during 1921 and 1922, while mass production of radios (receiving sets) also began. In 1926, when the British Broadcasting Corporation (BBC) was made into a public

The Charleston. Dancing became the rage during the Roaring Twenties, and the Charleston was the most popular and enduring dance of the decade. This photograph shows a couple dancing the Charleston in a scene from a London musical, *Just a Kiss,* performed in 1926.

corporation, there were 2.2 million radios in Great Britain. By the end of the 1930s, there were 9 million.

The technical foundation for motion pictures had already been developed in the 1890s when short moving pictures were produced as novelties for music halls. Shortly before World War I, full-length features, such as the Italian film *Quo Vadis* and the American film *Birth of a Nation,* became available and made it apparent that cinema was a new form of entertainment for the masses. By 1939, about 40 percent of adults in the more advanced industrial countries were attending the movies once a week. That figure increased to 60 percent by the end of World War II.

Mass forms of communication and entertainment were, of course, not new, but the increased size of audiences and the ability of radio and cinema, unlike the printed word, to provide an immediate shared experience added new dimensions to mass culture. Favorite film actors and actresses became stars who then became the focus of public adoration and scrutiny. Sensuous actresses such as Marlene Dietrich, whose appearance in the early sound film *The Blue Angel* catapulted her to fame, popularized new images of women's sexuality.

Of course, radio and movies could also be used for political purposes. Hitler had said that "without motor cars, sound films, and wireless, no victory of National Socialism." Radio seemed to offer great opportunities for reaching the masses, especially when it became apparent that the emotional harangues of a demagogue such as Hitler had just as much impact on people when heard on radio as in person. The Nazi regime encouraged radio listening by urging manufacturers to produce cheap radios that could be bought on the installment plan. The Nazis also erected loudspeaker pillars in the streets to encourage communal radio listening, especially to broadcasts of mass meetings.

Film, too, had propaganda potential, a possibility not lost on Joseph Goebbels (1897–1945), the propaganda minister of Nazi Germany. Believing that film constituted one of the "most modern and scientific means of influencing the masses," Goebbels created a special film section in his Propaganda Ministry and encouraged the production of both documentaries and popular feature films that carried the Nazi message. *The Triumph of the Will,* for example, was a documentary of the 1934 Nuremberg party rally that forcefully conveyed the power of National Socialism to viewers. Both Fascist Italy and Nazi Germany controlled and exploited the content of newsreels shown in movie theaters.

Mass Leisure

Mass leisure activities had developed at the turn of the century, but new work patterns after World War I dramatically expanded the amount of free time available to take advantage of them. By 1920, the eight-hour day had become the norm for many office and factory workers in northern and western Europe.

Professional sporting events for mass audiences became an especially important aspect of mass leisure. Attendance at association football (soccer) games increased dramatically, and the inauguration of the World Cup contest in 1930 added to the nationalistic rivalries that began to surround such mass sporting events. Increased attendance also made the 1920s and 1930s a great era of stadium building. For the 1936 Olympics, the Germans built a stadium in Berlin that seated 140,000 people.

Travel opportunities also added new dimensions to mass leisure activities. The military use of aircraft during World War I helped improve planes and make civilian air travel a reality. The first regular international airmail service began in 1919, and regular passenger service soon followed. Although air travel remained the preserve of the wealthy or the adventurous, trains, buses, and private cars made excursions to beaches or resorts more popular and more affordable. Beaches, such as the one at Brighton in England, were increasingly mobbed by crowds of people from all social classes.

Mass leisure provided totalitarian regimes with new ways to control their populations. Mussolini's Italy created the *Dopolavoro* (Afterwork) as a vast national recreation agency. The *Dopolavoro* was responsible for establishing clubhouses with libraries, radios, and athletic facilities in virtually every town and village. In some places, they included auditoriums for plays and films, as well as travel

Mass Leisure: Strength Through Joy

In November 1933, the German Labor Front established an organization called *Kraft durch Freude* (Strength Through Joy), whose purpose was to organize the leisure time of workers in the interests of the Nazi regime. These excerpts are taken from the reports of the Social Democratic Party's contact men in Germany and give a fairly accurate account of the attitudes of the German workers toward the *Kraft durch Freude* (KdF) program.

Reports of the SOPADE [Social Democratic Party in Exile]

■ *Central Germany, April 1939*

While Beauty of Labor [another Labor Front organization] makes no impressions whatsoever . . . Strength Through Joy is not without impact. However, workers' wages are only barely sufficient for essentials and nobody can afford a trip to Madeira, 150 Reichsmarks per person—300 RM with the wife. Even the shorter trips produce so many additional expenses that they often double the cost. But some people like them nonetheless. Anybody who has never made a trip in his life and sees the sea for the first time is much impressed. The effect is: "The Nazis have done some good things after all." The enthusiasm is, however, greater on the first trip. On the second, many are put off by the crowds.

■ *Berlin, February 1938*

Strength Through Joy is very popular. The events appeal to the yearning of the little man who wants an opportunity to get out and about himself and to take part in the pleasures of the "top people." It is a clever appeal to the petty bourgeois inclinations of the unpolitical workers. For such a man it really means something to have been on a trip to Scandinavia, or even if he only went to the Black Forest or the Harz Mountains, he imagines that he has thereby climbed up a rung on the social ladder.

■ *Bavaria, April 1939*

On the group tours there is a sharp social differentiation. The "top people" only go on big trips where there will be a more select clientele. The big mass trips are for the proletariat. People now look for places where there are no KdF visitors. "Not visited by KdF" is now a particular asset for summer vacations. A landlord in a mountain village in Upper Bavaria wrote in his prospects: "Not visited by KdF tourists." The Labor Front, which was sent the prospectus by someone, took the landlord to court. He had to withdraw the prospectus and was not allowed to receive summer guests. Nevertheless, information about summer Pensions [boardinghouses] which are not used by KdF is becoming more and more widespread.

agencies that arranged tours, cruises, and resort vacations on the Adriatic at reduced rates. *Dopolavoro* groups introduced many Italians to various facets of mass culture and mass leisure with activities such as band concerts, movies, choral groups, roller skating, and ballroom dancing. Essentially, the *Dopolavoro* enabled the Italian government to provide recreational activities and supervise them as well. By doing so, the state imposed new rules and regulations on previously spontaneous activities, thus breaking down old group solidarities and enabling these groups to be guided by the goals of the state.

The Nazi regime adopted a program similar to the *Dopolavoro* in its *Kraft durch Freude* (Strength Through Joy). The purpose of *Kraft durch Freude* was to coordinate the free time of the working class by offering a variety of leisure time activities, including concerts, operas, films, guided tours, and sporting events (see the box above). Especially popular were inexpensive vacations, much like modern package tours, such as cruises to Scandinavia or the Mediterranean or, more likely for workers, short trips to various sites in Germany. Some 130,000 workers took cruises in 1938; seven million took short trips.

More and more, mass culture and mass leisure had the effect of increasing the homogeneity of national populations, a process that had begun in the nineteenth century with the development of the national state. Local popular culture was increasingly replaced by national and even international culture as new forms of mass production and consumption brought similar styles of clothing and fashion to people throughout Europe.

Cultural and Intellectual Trends in the Interwar Years

The artistic and intellectual innovations of the pre–World War I period, which had shocked many Europeans, had been the preserve primarily of a small group of avant-garde artists and intellectuals. In the 1920s and 1930s, they became more widespread as artists and intellectuals continued to work out the implications of the ideas developed before 1914. But what made the prewar avant-garde culture acceptable in the 1920s and the 1930s? Perhaps the most important factor was the impact of World War I.

Four years of devastating war had left many Europeans with a profound sense of despair and disillusionment. The Great War indicated to many people that something was dreadfully wrong with Western values. In his *Decline of the West*, the German writer Oswald Spengler (1880–1936) reflected this disillusionment when he emphasized the decadence of Western civilization and posited its collapse. To many people, the experiences of the war seemed to confirm the prewar avant-garde belief that human beings were violent and irrational animals who were incapable of creating a sane and rational world. The Great Depression of the late 1920s and early 1930s, as well as the growth of fascist movements based on violence and the degradation of individual rights, only added to the uncertainties generated by the Great War. The crisis of confidence in Western civilization indeed ran deep and was well captured in the words of the French poet Paul Valéry in the early 1920s:

> The storm has died away, and still we are restless, uneasy, as if the storm were about to break. Almost all the affairs of men remain in a terrible uncertainty. We think of what has disappeared, and we are almost destroyed by what has been destroyed; we do not know what will be born, and we fear the future. . . . Doubt and disorder are in us and with us. There is no thinking man, however shrewd or learned he may be, who can hope to dominate this anxiety, to escape from this impression of darkness.[12]

Political and economic uncertainties were paralleled by social insecurities. The war had served to break down many traditional middle-class attitudes, especially toward sexuality. In the 1920s, women's physical appearance changed dramatically. Short skirts, short hair, the use of cosmetics that were once thought to be the preserve of prostitutes, and the new practice of suntanning gave women a new image. This change in physical appearance, which stressed more exposure of a woman's body, was also accompanied by frank discussions of sexual matters. In England in 1918, Marie Stopes published *Married Love,* which emphasized sexual pleasure in marriage and soon became a best-seller. In 1926, the Dutch physician Theodore van de Velde published *Ideal Marriage: Its Physiology and Technique.* Translated into a number of languages, it became an international best-seller. Van de Velde described female and male anatomy, discussed birth control techniques, and glorified sexual pleasure in marriage. New ideas on sexuality and birth control were also spread to the working classes by family planning clinics, such as those of Margaret Sanger in the United States and Marie Stopes in Britain.

Nightmares and New Visions: Art and Music

Uncertainty also pervaded the cultural and intellectual achievements of the interwar years. Postwar artistic trends were largely a working out of the implications of prewar developments. Abstract painting, for example, became ever more popular as many pioneering artists of the early twentieth century matured in the decades after the war. In addition, prewar fascination with the absurd and the unconscious contents of the mind seemed even more appropriate after the nightmare landscapes of World War I battlefronts. This gave rise to both the Dada movement and Surrealism.

Dadaism attempted to enshrine the purposelessness of life. Tristan Tzara (1896–1945), a Romanian-French poet and one of the founders of Dadaism, expressed the Dadaist contempt for the Western tradition in a lecture on Dada in 1922: "The acts of life have no beginning or end. Everything happens in a completely idiotic way. . . . Like everything in life, Dada is useless." Revolted by the insanity of life, the Dadaists tried to give it expression by creating anti-art. The 1918 Berlin Dada Manifesto maintained that "Dada is the international expression of our times, the great rebellion of artistic movements." In the hands of Hannah Höch (1889–1978), Dada became an instrument to comment on women's roles in the new mass culture. Höch was the only female member of the Berlin Dada Club, which featured the use of photomontage. Her work was part of the first Dada show in Berlin in 1920. In *Dada Dance,* she seemed to criticize the "new woman" by making fun of the way women were inclined to follow new fashion styles. In other works, however, she created positive images of the modern woman and expressed a keen interest in new freedoms for women.

Hannah Höch, *Cut with the Kitchen Knife Dada Through the Last Weimar Beer Belly Cultural Epoch of Germany.* Hannah Höch, a prominent figure in the postwar Dada movement, used photomontage to create images that reflected on women's issues. In *Cut with the Kitchen Knife* (1919), she combined pictures of German political leaders with sports stars, Dada artists, and scenes from urban life. One major theme emerged: the confrontation between the anti-Dada world of German political leaders and the Dada world of revolutionary ideals. Höch associated women with Dada and the new world.

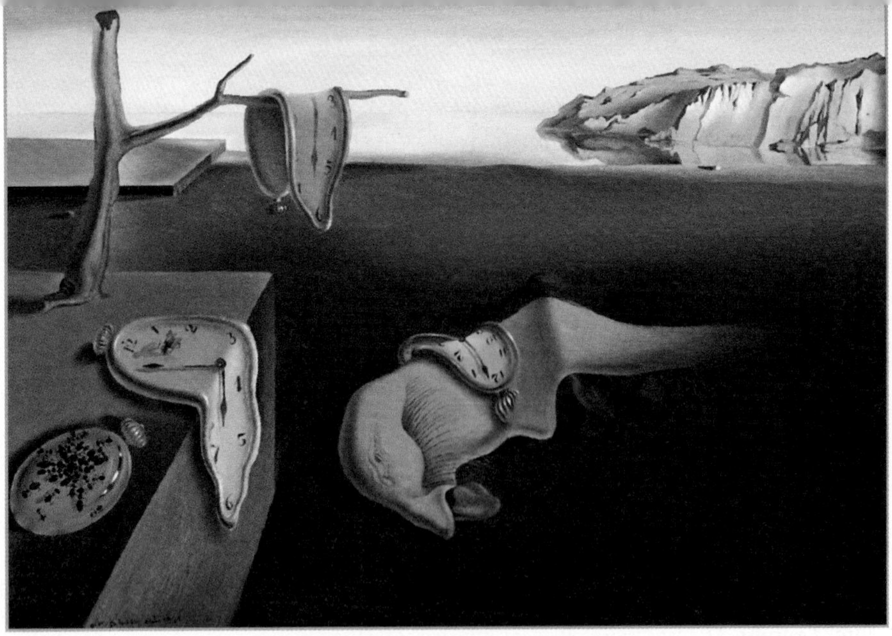

Museum of Modern Art, New York, © 2000 Artists Rights Society (ARS), New York

Salvador Dalí, *The Persistence of Memory.* Surrealism was another important artistic movement between the wars. Influenced by the theories of Freudian psychology, Surrealists sought to reveal the world of the unconscious, or the "greater reality" that they believed existed beyond the world of physical appearances. As is evident in this 1931 painting, Salvador Dalí sought to portray the world of dreams by painting recognizable objects in unrecognizable relationships.

Perhaps more important as an artistic movement was Surrealism, which sought a reality beyond the material, sensible world and found it in the world of the unconscious through the portrayal of fantasies, dreams, or nightmares. Employing logic to portray the illogical, the Surrealists created disturbing and evocative images. The Spaniard Salvador Dalí (1904–1989) became the high priest of Surrealism and in his mature phase became a master of representational Surrealism. In *The Persistence of Memory,* Dalí portrayed recognizable objects divorced from their normal context. By placing these objects into unrecognizable relationships, Dalí created a disturbing world in which the irrational had become tangible.

The move to functionalism in modern architecture also became more widespread in the 1920s and 1930s. First conceived near the end of the nineteenth century, functionalism meant that buildings, like the products of machines, should be "functional" or useful, fulfilling the purpose for which they were constructed. Art and engineering were to be unified, and all unnecessary ornamentation was to be stripped away.

The United States was a leader in these pioneering architectural designs. Unprecedented urban growth and the absence of restrictive architectural traditions allowed for new building methods, especially in the relatively "new city" of Chicago. The Chicago School of the 1890s, led by Louis H. Sullivan (1856–1924), used reinforced concrete, steel frames, and electric elevators to build skyscrapers virtually free of external ornamentation. One of Sullivan's most successful pupils was Frank Lloyd Wright (1869–1959), who became known for innovative designs in domestic architecture. Wright's private houses, built chiefly for wealthy patrons, featured geometric structures with long lines, overhanging roofs, and severe planes of brick and stone. The interiors were open spaces that included cathedral ceilings and built-in furniture and lighting fixtures. Wright pioneered the modern American house.

Especially important in the spread of functionalism was the Bauhaus School of art, architecture, and design, founded in 1919 at Weimar, Germany, by the Berlin architect Walter Gropius (1883–1969). The Bauhaus teaching staff consisted of architects, artists, and designers who worked together to blend the study of fine arts (painting and sculpture) with the applied arts (printing, weaving, and furnituremaking). Gropius urged his followers to foster a new union of arts and crafts to create the buildings and objects of the future. Gropius's own buildings were often unornamented steel boxes with walls of windows, reflecting his belief that the "sensibility of the artist must be combined with the knowledge of the technician to create new forms in architecture and design."

Important to the development of artistic expression between the wars was the search for a new popular audience. To attract a wider audience, artists and musicians began to involve themselves in the new mass culture. The German Kurt Weill, for example, had been a struggling composer of classical music before he turned to jazz rhythms and other popular musical idioms for the music for *The Threepenny Opera.* Some artists even regarded art as a means to transform society and located their studios in poor, working-class neighborhoods. Theater proved especially attractive as postwar artists sought to make an impact on popular audiences. The German director Erwin Piscator began his directing career by offering plays to workers on picket lines. Piscator hoped to reach workers by experimental drama with political messages. Like many other artists, however, he became frustrated by his failure to achieve a mass audience.

The postwar acceptance of modern art forms was by no means universal. Many traditionalists denounced what they considered degeneracy and decadence in the arts. Nowhere was this more evident than in the totalitarian states of Nazi Germany and the Soviet Union.

In the 1920s, Weimar Germany was one of the chief European centers for modern arts and sciences. Hitler and the Nazis rejected modern art as "degenerate" or "Jewish" art. In an address at the premiere of the Great German Art Exhibition in the newly opened House of German Art

Gian Berto Vanni/Art Resource, NY

Walter Gropius, The Bauhaus. Walter Gropius was one of Europe's pioneers in modern architecture. When the Bauhaus moved to Dessau in 1925, Gropius designed a building for its activities. His straightforward use of steel, reinforced concrete, and rows of windows reflects the move to functionalism in modern architecture.

in July 1937, Hitler proclaimed, "The people regarded this art [modern art] as the outcome of an impudent and unashamed arrogance or of a simply shocking lack of skill; . . . these achievements—which might have been produced by untalented children of from eight to ten years old—could never be valued as an expression of our own times or of the German future."[13] Hitler and the Nazis believed that they had laid the foundation for a new and genuine German art, which would glorify the strong, the healthy, and the heroic—all supposedly attributes of the Aryan race. The new German art was actually the old nineteenth-century genre art with its emphasis on realistic scenes of everyday life.

So, too, was the art produced by the school of "socialist realism" in the Soviet Union. After the bold experimentalism of the 1920s, the Stalinist era imposed a stifling uniformity on artistic creativity. Like German painting, Soviet painting was expected to focus on a nineteenth-century pictorial style aimed at realistic presentation. Both the new German art and "socialist realism" were intended to inculcate social values useful to the ruling regimes.

At the beginning of the twentieth century, a revolution in music parallel to the revolution in art had begun with the work of Igor Stravinsky (see Chapter 24). But Stravinsky still wrote music in a definite key. The Viennese composer Arnold Schönberg (1874–1951) began to experiment with a radically new style by creating musical pieces in which tonality is completely abandoned, a system that he called atonal music. Since the use of traditional forms was virtually impossible in atonal music, Schönberg created a new system of composition—twelve-tone composition—which used a scale of twelve notes independent of any tonal key. Resistance to modern music was even greater than to modern painting, and it did not begin to win favor until after World War II.

The Search for the Unconscious

The interest in the unconscious, evident in Surrealism, was also apparent in the new literary techniques that emerged in the 1920s. One of its most apparent manifestations was in the "stream of consciousness" technique in which the writer presented an interior monologue, or a report of the innermost thoughts of each character. One example of this genre was written by the Irish exile James Joyce (1882–1941). His *Ulysses,* published in 1922, told the story of one day in the life of ordinary people in Dublin by following the flow of their inner dialogue. Disconnected ramblings and veiled allusions pervade Joyce's work.

Another famous writer who used her own stream-of-consciousness technique was Virginia Woolf (1882–1942). Woolf belonged to a group of intellectuals and artists, known as the Bloomsbury Circle, who sought to create new artistic and literary forms. In her novels *Mrs. Dalloway* and *Jacob's Room,* Woolf used the inner monologues of her main characters to reveal their world of existence. Woolf came to believe that for a woman to be a writer, she would need to have her own income to free herself from the expected roles of wife and mother.

The German writer Hermann Hesse (1877–1962) dealt with the unconscious in a considerably different fashion. His novels reflected the influence of both Carl Jung's psychological theories and Eastern religions and focused among other things on the spiritual loneliness of modern human beings in a mechanized urban society. *Demian* was a psychoanalytic study of incest, and *Steppenwolf* mirrored the psychological confusion of modern existence. Hesse's novels made a large impact on German youth in the 1920s (see the box on p. 768). He won the Nobel Prize for literature in 1946.

The growing concern with the unconscious also led to greater popular interest in psychology. The full impact of Sigmund Freud's thought was not felt until after World War I. The 1920s witnessed a worldwide acceptance of his ideas. Freudian terms, such as *unconscious, repression, id, ego,* and *Oedipus complex,* entered the common vocabulary. Popularization of Freud's ideas led to the widespread misconception that an uninhibited sex life was necessary for a healthy mental life. Despite such misconceptions, psychoanalysis did develop into a major profession, especially in the United States. But Freud's ideas did not go unchallenged, even by his own pupils. One of the most prominent challenges came from Carl Jung.

A disciple of Freud, Carl Jung (1856–1961) came to believe that Freud's theories were too narrow and reflected Freud's own personal biases. Jung's study of dreams—his own and those of others—led him to diverge sharply from Freud. Whereas for Freud the unconscious was the seat of repressed desires or appetites, for Jung it was an opening to deep spiritual needs and ever-greater vistas for humans.

Hesse and the Unconscious

The novels of Hermann Hesse made a strong impact on young people, first in Germany in the 1920s and then in the United States in the 1960s after they had been translated into English. Many of these young people shared Hesse's fascination with the unconscious and his dislike of modern industrial civilization. This excerpt from *Demian* spoke directly to many of them.

Hermann Hesse, Demian

The following spring I was to leave the preparatory school and enter a university. I was still undecided, however, as to where and what I was to study. I had grown a thin mustache, I was a full-grown man, and yet I was completely helpless and without a goal in life. Only one thing was certain: the voice within me, the dream image. I felt the duty to follow this voice blindly wherever it might lead me. But it was difficult and each day I rebelled against it anew. Perhaps I was mad, as I thought at moments; perhaps I was not like other men? But I was able to do the same things the others did; with a little effort and industry I could read Plato, was able to solve problems in trigonometry or follow a chemical analysis. There was only one thing I could not do: wrest the dark secret goal from myself and keep it before me as others did who knew exactly what they wanted to be—professors, lawyers, doctors, artists, however long this would take them and whatever difficulties and advantages this decision would bear in its wake. This I could not do. Perhaps I would become something similar, but how was I to know? Perhaps I would have to continue my search for years on end and would not become anything, and would not reach a goal. Perhaps I would reach this goal but it would turn out to be an evil, dangerous, horrible one.

I wanted only to try to live in accord with the promptings which came from my true self. Why was that so very difficult?

Jung viewed the unconscious as twofold: a "personal unconscious" and, at a deeper level, a "collective unconscious." The collective unconscious was the repository of memories that all human beings share and consisted of archetypes, mental forms or images that appear in dreams. The archetypes are common to all people and have a special energy that creates myths, religions, and philosophies. To Jung, the archetypes proved that mind was only in part personal or individual because their origin was buried so far in the past that they seemed to have no human source. Their function was to bring the original mind of humans into a new, higher state of consciousness.

The "Heroic Age of Physics"

The prewar revolution in physics initiated by Max Planck and Albert Einstein continued in the interwar period. In fact, Ernest Rutherford (1871–1937), one of the physicists responsible for demonstrating that the atom could be split, dubbed the 1920s the "heroic age of physics." By the early 1940s, seven subatomic particles had been distinguished, and a sufficient understanding of the atom had been achieved to lay the foundations for the development of a sophisticated new explosive device, the atomic bomb.

The new picture of the universe that was unfolding continued to undermine the old scientific certainties of classical physics. Classical physics had rested on the fundamental belief that all phenomena could be predicted if they could be completely understood; thus the weather could be accurately predicted if we knew everything about the wind, sun, and water. In 1927, the German physicist Werner Heisenberg (1901–1976) upset this belief when he posited the "uncertainty principle." In essence, Heisenberg argued that no one could determine the path of an electron because the very act of observing the electron with light affected the electron's location. The "uncertainty principle" was more than an explanation for the path of an electron, however; it was a new worldview. Heisenberg shattered confidence in predictability and dared to propose that uncertainty was at the root of all physical laws.

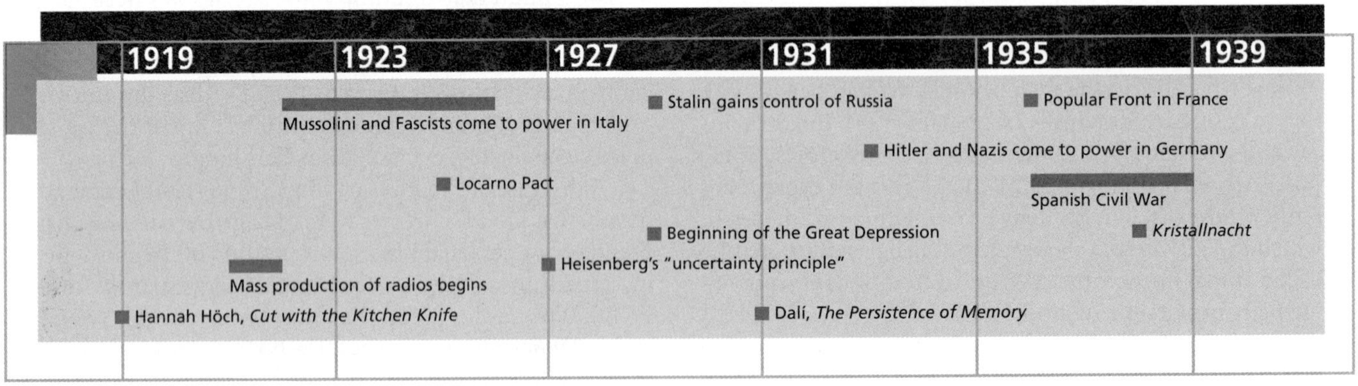

Conclusion

The devastation wrought by World War I destroyed the liberal optimism of the prewar era. Yet many in the 1920s still hoped that the progress of Western civilization, so seemingly evident before 1914, could somehow be restored. These hopes proved largely unfounded as plans for economic reconstruction gave way to inflation and to the even more devastating Great Depression at the end of the 1920s. Likewise, confidence in political democracy was soon shattered by the rise of authoritarian governments that not only restricted individual freedoms but, in the cases of Italy, Germany, and the Soviet Union, sought even greater control over the lives of their subjects in order to manipulate and guide them to achieve the goals of their totalitarian regimes. For many people, despite the loss of personal freedom, these mass movements at least offered some sense of security in a world that seemed fraught with uncertainty.

But the seeming security of these mass movements gave rise to even greater uncertainty as Europeans, after a brief twenty-year interlude of peace, once again plunged into war, this time on a scale even more horrendous than that of World War I. The twentieth-century crisis, begun in 1914, seemed only to be worsening in 1939.

Notes

1. Quoted in Robert Paxton, *Europe in the Twentieth Century,* 2d ed. (New York, 1985), p. 237.
2. Quoted in Denis Mack Smith, *Mussolini* (New York, 1982), p. 51.
3. Benito Mussolini, "The Doctrine of Fascism," in Adrian Lyttleton, ed., *Italian Fascisms from Pareto to Gentile* (London, 1973), p. 42.
4. Quoted in Alexander De Grand, "Women Under Italian Fascism," *Historical Journal* 19 (1976): 958–959.
5. Adolf Hitler, *Mein Kampf,* trans. Ralph Manheim (Boston, 1943), p. 22.
6. Ibid., p. 161.
7. Quoted in Joachim Fest, *Hitler,* trans. Richard Winston and Clara Winston (New York, 1974), p. 241.
8. Quoted in Jeremy Noakes and Geoffrey Pridham, eds., *Nazism, 1919–1945* (Exeter, England, 1983), vol. 1, pp. 50–51.
9. Quoted in Jackson J. Spielvogel, *Hitler and Nazi Germany: A History,* 3d ed. (Englewood Cliffs, N.J., 1996), p. 66.
10. Quoted in Fest, *Hitler,* p. 418.
11. Irving Howe, ed., *The Basic Writings of Trotsky* (London, 1963), p. 162.
12. Paul Valéry, *Variety,* trans. Malcolm Cowley (New York, 1927), pp. 27–28.
13. Norman H. Baynes, ed., *The Speeches of Adolf Hitler, 1922–1939* (Oxford, 1942), vol. 1, p. 591.

Suggestions for Further Reading

For a general introduction to the interwar period, see M. Kitchen, *Europe Between the Wars: A Political History* (London, 1988), and the general survey by R. Paxton, *Europe in the Twentieth Century,* 2d ed. (New York, 1985). On European security issues after the Peace of Paris, see S. Marks, *The Illusion of Peace: Europe's International Relations, 1918–1933* (New York, 1976). The best study on the problem of reparations is M. Trachtenberg, *Reparations in World Politics* (New York, 1980), which paints a positive view of French policies. On the Great Depression, see C. P. Kindleberger, *The World in Depression, 1929–39,* rev. ed. (Berkeley, Calif., 1986).

The best biography of Mussolini is D. Mack Smith, *Mussolini* (New York, 1982). Two brief but excellent surveys of Fascist Italy are A. Cassels, *Fascist Italy,* 2d ed. (Arlington Heights, Ill., 1985), and J. Whittam, *Fascist Italy* (New York, 1995).

On the Weimar Republic, see P. Bookbinder, *Weimar Germany* (New York, 1996), and R. Henig, *The Weimar Republic, 1919–1933* (New York, 1998). Two brief but sound surveys of Nazi Germany are J. J. Spielvogel, *Hitler and Nazi Germany: A History,* 4th ed. (Upper Saddle River, N.J., 2000), and J. Dülffer, *Nazi Germany, 1933–1945* (New York, 1996). A more detailed examination can be found in K. Bracher, *The German Dictatorship: The Origins, Structure, and Effects of National Socialism* (New York, 1970), and K. P. Fischer, *Nazi Germany: A New History* (New York, 1995). The best biographies of Hitler are A. Bullock, *Hitler: A Study in Tyranny* (New York, 1964); J. Fest, *Hitler,* trans. R. Winston and C. Winston (New York, 1974); and I. Kershaw, *Hitler, 1889–1936: Hubris* (New York, 1999), and *Hitler: Nemesis* (New York, 2000). Two recent works that examine the enormous literature on Hitler are J. Lukacs, *The Hitler of History* (New York, 1997), and R. Rosenbaum, *Explaining Hitler* (New York, 1998).A new perspective on Germany's economic recovery can be found in D. P. Silverman, *Hitler's Economy: Nazi Work Creation Programs, 1933–1936* (Cambridge, Mass., 1998). Basic studies of the SS include R. Koehl, *The Black Corps: The Structure and Power Struggles of the Nazi SS* (Madison, Wis., 1983), and H. Krausnick and M. Broszat, *Anatomy of the SS State* (London, 1970). On women, see J. Stephenson, *Women in Nazi Society* (London, 1975), and C. Koonz, *Mothers in the Fatherland: Women, the Family, and Nazi Politics* (New York, 1987). The Hitler Youth is examined in H. W. Koch, *The Hitler Youth* (New York, 1976). The books on the Holocaust cited in Chapter 27 contain background information on Nazi anti-Jewish policies between 1933 and 1939. The importance of racial ideology in Nazi Germany is evident in R. Proctor, *Racial Hygiene: Medicine Under the Nazis* (Cambridge, Mass., 1988).

For a general study of other fascist movements, see S. Payne, *A History of Fascism* (Madison, Wis., 1996). Starting points for the study of eastern Europe are J. Rothschild, *East Central Europe Between the Two World Wars* (New York, 1974), and B. Jelavich, *History of the Balkans,* vol. 2: *The Twentieth Century* (New York, 1983). On Franco, see J. W. D. Trythall, *El Caudillo: A Political Biography* (New York, 1970). On the Spanish Civil War, see S. G. Payne, *The Spanish Revolution* (New York, 1970), and H. Thomas, *The Spanish Civil War,* rev. ed. (New York, 1977).

The collectivization of agriculture in the Soviet Union is examined in S. Fitzpatrick, *Stalin's Peasants: Resistance and Survival in the Russian Village After Collectivization* (New York, 1995); industrialization is covered in H. Kuromiya, *Stalin's Industrial Revolution: Politics and Workers, 1928–1932* (New York, 1988). On Stalin, see R. H. McNeal, *Stalin: Man and Ruler* (New York, 1988); R. Tucker, *Stalin in Power: The Revolution from Above, 1928–1941* (New York, 1990); and R. W. Thurston, *Life and Terror in Stalin's Russia* (New Haven, Conn.,

1996). Stalin's purges are examined in R. Conquest, *The Great Terror: A Reassessment* (New York, 1990).

The use of cinema for propaganda purposes is well examined in D. Welch, *Propaganda and the German Cinema* (New York, 1985). Gender issues are discussed in S. K. Kent, *Making Peace: The Reconstruction of Gender in Interwar Britain* (Princeton, N.J., 1993); S. Pedersen, *Family, Dependence, and the Origins of the Welfare State: Britain and France, 1914–1945* (New York, 1994); and M. L. Roberts, *Civilization Without Sexes: Reconstructing Gender in Postwar France, 1917–1927* (Chicago, 1994). On the cultural and intellectual environment of Weimar Germany, see W. Laqueur, *Weimar: A Cultural History* (New York, 1974), and P. Gay, *Weimar Culture: The Outsider as Insider* (New York, 1968). For a study of Carl Jung, see G. Wehr, *Jung: A Biography* (New York, 1987).

For additional reading, go to InfoTrac College Edition, your online research library at http://web1.infotrac-college.com

Enter the search term *socialism history* using Key Terms.

Enter the search term *Great Depression* using Key Terms.

Enter the search term *Mussolini* using Key Terms.

Enter the search term *Hitler* using Key Terms.

C H A P T E R

27

The Deepening of the European Crisis: World War II

Bildarchiv Preussischer Kulturbesitz, Berlin

CHAPTER OUTLINE

- Prelude to War (1933–1939)
- The Course of World War II
- The Nazi New Order
- The Home Front
- The Aftermath of the War: The Emergence of the Cold War
- Conclusion

FOCUS QUESTIONS

- What were Hitler's foreign policy goals, and what steps did he take to achieve them between 1933 and 1939?
- What were the main events of World War II in Europe and in Asia, and why were the Allies ultimately victorious?
- What was the Holocaust, and what role did it play in Nazi policy?
- What were conditions like on the home front for the major Western nations involved in World War II?
- How did the Allies' visions of postwar Europe differ, and how did these differences contribute to the emergence of the Cold War?
- What was the relationship between World War I and World War II, and what were the differences in the way the wars were fought?

ON FEBRUARY 3, 1933, only four days after he had been appointed chancellor of Germany, Adolf Hitler met secretly with Germany's leading generals. He revealed to them his desire to remove the "cancer of democracy," create a new authoritarian leadership, and forge a new domestic unity. All Germans would need to realize that "only a struggle can save us and that everything else must be subordinated to this idea." Youth especially must be trained and their wills strengthened "to fight with all means." Since Germany's living space was too small for its people, above all, Hitler said, Germany must rearm and prepare for "the conquest of new living space in the east and its ruthless Germanization." Even before he had consolidated his power, Hitler had a clear vision of his goals, and their implementation meant another European war.

World War II was clearly Hitler's war. Although other countries may have helped make the war possible by not resisting Hitler's Germany earlier, it was Nazi Germany's actions that made World War II inevitable.

World War II was more than just Hitler's war, however. This chapter will focus on the European theater of war, but both European and American armies were also involved in fighting around the world. World War II consisted of two conflicts: one provoked by the ambitions of Germany in Europe, the other by the ambitions of Japan in Asia. By 1941, with the involvement of the United States in both wars, the two had merged into one global conflict.

Although World War I has been described as a total war, World War II was even more so and was fought on a scale unknown in history. Almost everyone in the warring countries was involved in one way or another: as soldiers; as workers in wartime industries; as ordinary citizens subject to invading armies, military occupation, or bombing raids; as refugees; or as victims of mass extermination. The world had never witnessed such widespread human-made death and destruction.

Prelude to War (1933–1939)

Only twenty years after the "war to end all war," Europe plunged back into the nightmare of total war. The efforts at collective security in the 1920s—the League of Nations, the attempts at disarmament, the pacts and treaties—all proved meaningless in view of the growth of Nazi Germany and its deliberate scrapping of the postwar settlement in the 1930s. Still weary from the last war, France and Britain refused to accept the possibility of another war. The Soviet Union, treated as an outcast by the Western powers, had turned in on itself, and the United States had withdrawn into its traditional isolationism. The small successor states to Austria-Hungary were too weak to oppose Germany. Thus the power vacuum in the heart of Europe encouraged a revived and militarized Germany to acquire the living space that Hitler claimed Germany needed for its rightful place in the world.

The Role of Hitler

World War II in Europe had its beginnings in the ideas of Adolf Hitler, who believed that only the Aryans were capable of building a great civilization. But to Hitler, the Germans, in his view the leading group of Aryans, were threatened from the east by a large mass of inferior peoples, the Slavs, who had learned to use German weapons and technology. Germany needed more land to support a larger population and be a great power. Hitler was a firm believer in the doctrine of *Lebensraum* (living space), espoused by Karl Haushofer, a professor of geography at the University of Munich. The doctrine of *Lebensraum* maintained that a nation's power depended on the amount and kind of land it occupied. Already in the 1920s, in the second volume of *Mein Kampf,* Hitler had indicated where a National Socialist regime would find this land: "And so we National Socialists . . . take up where we broke off six hundred years ago. We stop the endless German movement to the south and west, and turn our gaze toward the land in the east. . . . If we speak of soil in Europe today, we can primarily have in mind only Russia and her vassal border states."[1]

In Hitler's view, the Russian Revolution had created the conditions for Germany's acquisition of land to its east. Imperial Russia had been strong only because of its German leadership. The seizure of power by the Bolsheviks (who, in Hitler's mind, were Jewish) had left Russia weak and vulnerable. Once it had been conquered, the land of Russia could be resettled by German peasants, and the Slavic population could be used as slave labor to build the Aryan racial state that would dominate Europe for the next thousand years. Hitler's conclusion was clear: Germany must prepare for its inevitable war with the Soviet Union. Hitler's ideas were by no means secret. He had spelled them out in *Mein Kampf,* a book readily available to anyone who wished to read it (see the box on p. 773).

Hitler and the Nazis were neither the first Europeans nor the first Germans to undertake European conquest and world power. Certainly, a number of elite circles in Germany before World War I had argued that Germany needed to annex lands to its south, east, and west if it wished to compete with the large states and remain a great power. The defeat in World War I destroyed this dream of world power, but the traditional conservative elites in the German military and the Foreign Office supported Hitler's foreign policy until 1937, largely because it accorded with their own desires for German expansion. But, as they realized too late, Nazi policy went far beyond previous German goals. Hitler's desire to create an Aryan racial empire led to slave labor and even mass extermination on a scale that would have been incomprehensible to previous generations of Germans.

Although Hitler had defined his goals, he had no prearranged timetable for achieving them. During his rise to power, he had demonstrated the ability to be both ideologue and opportunist. After 1933, a combination of military and diplomatic situations, organizational chaos in the administration of Germany, and economic pressures, especially after 1936, caused Hitler periodically to take steps that seemed to contradict the foreign policy goals of *Mein Kampf.* But he always returned to his basic ideological plans for racial supremacy and empire. He was certain of one thing: only he had the ability to accomplish these goals, and his fears for his health pushed him to fulfill his mission as quickly as possible. His impatience would become a major cause of his own undoing.

Hitler's Foreign Policy Goals

Adolf Hitler was a firm believer in the geopolitical doctrine of *Lebensraum,* which advocated that nations must find sufficient living space to be strong. This idea was evident in *Mein Kampf,* but it was explained in even more detail in a treatise that Hitler wrote in 1928. It was not published in his lifetime.

Hitler's Secret Book, *1928*

1 have already dealt with Germany's various foreign policy possibilities in this book. Nevertheless I shall once more briefly present the possible foreign policy goals so that they may yield a basis for the critical examination of the relations of these individual foreign policy aims to those of other European states.

1. Germany can renounce setting a foreign policy goal altogether. This means that in reality she can decide for anything and need be committed to nothing at all. . . . [Hitler rejects this alternative.]
2. Germany desires to effect the sustenance of the German people by peaceful economic means, as up to now. Accordingly even in the future she will participate most decisively in world industry, export and trade. . . . From a folkish standpoint setting this foreign policy aim is calamitous, and it is madness from the point of view of power politics.
3. Germany establishes the restoration of the borders of the year 1914 as her foreign policy aim. This goal is insufficient from a national standpoint, unsatisfactory from a military point of view, impossible from a folkish standpoint with its eye on the future, and mad from the viewpoint of its consequences. . . .
4. Germany decides to go over to [her future aim] a clear, far-seeing territorial policy. Thereby she abandons all attempts at world-industry and world-trade and instead concentrates all her strength in order, through the allotment of sufficient living space for the next hundred years to our people, also to prescribe a path of life. Since this territory can be only in the East, the obligation to be a naval power also recedes into the background. Germany tries anew to champion her interests through the formation of a decisive power on land.

This aim is equally in keeping with the highest national as well as folkish requirements. It likewise presupposes great military power means for its execution, but does not necessarily bring Germany into conflict with all European great powers. As surely as France here will remain Germany's enemy, just as little does the nature of such a political aim contain a reason for England, and especially for Italy, to maintain the enmity of the World War.

The "Diplomatic Revolution" (1933–1936)

Between 1933 and 1936, Hitler and Nazi Germany achieved a "diplomatic revolution" in Europe. When Hitler became chancellor of Germany on January 30, 1933, Germany's position in Europe seemed weak. The Versailles treaty had created a demilitarized zone on Germany's western border that would allow the French to move into the heavily industrialized parts of Germany in the event of war. To Germany's east, the smaller states, such as Poland and Czechoslovakia, had defensive treaties with France. The Versailles treaty had also limited Germany's army to 100,000 troops with no air and limited naval forces.

The Germans were not without advantages, however. Germany was the second most populous European state after the Soviet Union and still possessed a great industrial capacity. Hitler was also well aware that Great Britain and France, dismayed by the costs and losses of World War I, wanted to avoid another war. Hitler knew that France posed a threat to an unarmed Germany, but he believed that if he could keep the French from acting against Germany in his first years, he could remove the restrictions imposed on Germany by Versailles and restore its strength.

Hitler's ability to rearm Germany and fulfill his expansionist policies depended initially on whether he could convince others that his intentions were peaceful. Posing as a man of peace in his public speeches, Hitler emphasized that Germany wished only to revise the unfair provisions of Versailles by peaceful means and achieve Germany's rightful place among the European states. During his first two years in office, Hitler pursued a prudent foreign policy without unnecessary risks. His dramatic action in October 1933, when he withdrew Germany from the Geneva Disarmament Conference and the League of Nations, was done primarily for domestic political reasons, to give the Germans the feeling that their country was no longer dominated by other European states.

By the beginning of 1935, Hitler had become convinced that Germany could break some of the provisions of the Treaty of Versailles without serious British and French opposition. Hitler had come to believe, based on their responses to his early actions, that both states wanted to maintain the international status quo, but without using force. Consequently, he decided to announce publicly what had been going on secretly for some time—Germany's military rearmament. On March 9, 1935, Hitler announced the creation of a new air force and, one week later, the introduction of a military draft that would expand Germany's army from 100,000 to 550,000 troops.

Hitler's unilateral repudiation of the disarmament clauses of the Versailles treaty brought a swift reaction as France, Great Britain, and Italy condemned Germany's action and warned against future aggressive steps. But nothing concrete was done. Even worse, Britain subsequently moved toward an open acceptance of Germany's right to rearm when it agreed to the Anglo-German Naval Pact on June 18, 1935. This treaty allowed Germany to build a navy that would be 35 percent of the size of the British navy, with equality in submarines. The British were starting a policy of appeasement, based on the belief that if European states satisfied the reasonable demands of dissatisfied powers, the latter would be content, and stability and peace would be achieved in Europe. British appeasement was grounded in large part on Britain's desire to avoid another war, but it was also fostered by British statesmen who believed that Nazi Germany offered a powerful bulwark against Soviet communism.

On March 7, 1936, buoyed by his conviction that the Western democracies had no intention of using force to maintain all aspects of the Treaty of Versailles, Hitler sent German troops into the demilitarized Rhineland. According to the Versailles treaty, the French had the right to use force against any violation of the demilitarized Rhineland. But France would not act without British support, and the British viewed the occupation of German territory by German troops as another reasonable action by a dissatisfied power. The London *Times* noted that the Germans were only "going into their own back garden." The French and British response only reinforced Hitler's growing conviction that they were weak nations unwilling to use force to defend the old order. At the same time, since the German generals had opposed his plan, Hitler became even more convinced of his own superior abilities. Many Germans expressed fresh enthusiasm for a leader who was restoring German honor.

Meanwhile, Hitler gained new allies. In October 1935, Benito Mussolini had committed Fascist Italy to imperial expansion by invading Ethiopia. Angered by French and British opposition to his invasion, Mussolini welcomed Hitler's support and began to draw closer to the German dictator he had once called a buffoon. The joint intervention of Germany and Italy on behalf of General Francisco Franco in the Spanish Civil War in 1936 also drew the two nations closer together. In October 1936, Mussolini and Hitler concluded an agreement that recognized their common political and economic interests, and one month later, Mussolini referred publicly to the new Rome-Berlin Axis. Also in November 1936, Germany and Japan (the rising military power in the East) concluded the Anti-Comintern Pact and agreed to maintain a common front against communism.

By the end of 1936, Hitler and Nazi Germany had achieved a "diplomatic revolution" in Europe. The Treaty of Versailles had been virtually scrapped, and Germany was once more a "world power," as Hitler proclaimed. Hitler had demonstrated a great deal of diplomatic skill in taking advantage of Europeans' burning desire for peace. He had used the tactic of peaceful revision as skillfully as he had used the tactic of legality in his pursuit of power in Germany. By the end of 1936, Nazi power had increased enough that Hitler could initiate an even more daring foreign policy. As Hitler perceived, if the Western states were so afraid of war that they resisted its use when they were strong and Germany was weak, then they would be even more reluctant to do so now that Germany was strong. Although many Europeans still wanted to believe that Hitler desired peace, his moves had actually made war more possible.

The Path to War (1937–1939)

On November 5, 1937, at a secret conference with his military leaders in Berlin, Adolf Hitler revealed his future aims. Germany's ultimate goal, he assured his audience, must be the conquest of living space in the east. Although this might mean war with France and Great Britain, Germany had no alternative if the basic needs of the German people were to be met. First, however, Germany must deal with Austria and Czechoslovakia and secure its eastern and southern flanks.

By the end of 1937, Hitler was convinced that neither the French nor the British would provide much opposition to his plans. Neville Chamberlain (1869–1940), who had become prime minister of Britain in May 1936, was a strong advocate of appeasement and believed that the survival of the British Empire depended on an accommodation with Germany. Chamberlain had made it known to Hitler in November 1937 that he would not oppose changes in central Europe, provided that they were executed peacefully.

AUSTRIA

Hitler decided to move first on Austria. By threatening Austria with invasion, Hitler coerced the Austrian chancellor, Kurt von Schuschnigg (1897–1977), into putting Austrian Nazis in charge of the government. The new government promptly invited German troops to enter Austria and assist in maintaining law and order. One day later, on March 13, 1938, after his triumphal return to his native land, Hitler formally annexed Austria to Germany. Great Britain's ready acknowledgment of Hitler's action and France's inability to respond due to a political crisis only increased the German dictator's contempt for Western weakness.

The annexation of Austria improved Germany's strategic position in central Europe and put Germany in position for Hitler's next objective, the destruction of Czechoslovakia (see Map 27.1). On May 30, 1938, Hitler had already told his generals that it was his "unalterable decision to smash Czechoslovakia by military action in the near future."[2] This goal might have seemed unrealistic since democratic Czechoslovakia was quite prepared to defend itself and was well supported by pacts with France and Soviet Russia. Nevertheless, Hitler believed that France and Britain would not use force to defend Czechoslovakia.

Hitler Arrives in Vienna. By threatening to invade Austria, Hitler forced the Austrian government to capitulate to his wishes. Austria was annexed to Germany. Shown here is the triumphal arrival of Hitler in Vienna on March 13, 1938. Seated in the car to Hitler's right is Arthur Seyss-Inquart, Hitler's new handpicked governor of Austria.

CZECHOSLOVAKIA

In the meantime, Hitler had stepped up his demands on the Czechs. Initially, the Germans had asked for autonomy for the Sudetenland, the mountainous northwestern border area of Czechoslovakia that was home to three million ethnic Germans. As Hitler knew, the Sudetenland also contained Czechoslovakia's most important frontier defenses and considerable industrial resources as well. But on September 15, 1938, Hitler demanded the cession of the Sudetenland to Germany and expressed his willingness to risk "world war" to achieve his objective. War was not necessary, however, as appeasement triumphed once again. On September 29, at the hastily arranged Munich Conference, the British, French, Germans, and Italians (neither the Czechs nor the Russians were invited) reached an agreement that essentially met all of Hitler's demands. German troops were allowed to occupy the Sudetenland as the Czechs, abandoned by their Western allies, stood by helplessly. The Munich Conference was the high point of Western appeasement of Hitler. When Chamberlain returned to England from Munich, he boasted that the Munich agreement meant "peace for our time." Hitler had promised Chamberlain that he had made his last demand; all other European problems could be settled by negotiation. Like many German politicians, Chamberlain had believed Hitler's assurances (see the box on p. 777).

In fact, Munich confirmed Hitler's perception that the Western democracies were weak and would not fight. Increasingly, Hitler was convinced of his own infallibility, and he had by no means been satisfied at Munich. Already at the end of October 1938, Hitler told his generals to prepare for the final liquidation of the Czechoslovakian state. Using the internal disorder that he had deliberately fostered as a pretext, Hitler occupied the Czech lands (Bohemia and Moravia) while the Slovaks, with Hitler's encouragement, declared their independence of the Czechs and became a puppet state (Slovakia) of Nazi Germany. On the evening of March 15, 1939, Hitler triumphantly declared in Prague that he would be known as the greatest German of them all.

POLAND

At last, the Western states reacted vigorously to Hitler's threat. After all, the Czechs were not Germans crying for reunion with Germany. Hitler's naked aggression made clear that his promises were utterly worthless. When Hitler began to demand the return to Germany of Danzig, which had been made a free city by the Treaty of Versailles to serve as a seaport for Poland, Britain recognized the danger and offered to protect Poland in the event of war. At the same time, both France and Britain realized that only the Soviet Union was powerful enough to help contain Nazi aggression and began political and military negotiations with Joseph Stalin and the Soviets. The West's distrust of Soviet communism, however, made an alliance unlikely.

Meanwhile, Hitler pressed on in the belief that the West would not really fight over Poland. He ordered his generals to prepare for the invasion of Poland on September 1, 1939. To preclude an alliance between the West and the Soviet Union, which would create the danger of a two-front war, Hitler, ever the opportunist, negotiated his own nonaggression pact with Stalin and shocked the world with its announcement on August 23, 1939. A secret protocol to the treaty created German and Soviet spheres of influence in eastern Europe: Finland, the Baltic states (Estonia, Latvia, and Lithuania), and eastern Poland would go

National Archives, (#306-NT-1222E)

Hitler Declares War. Adolf Hitler believed that it was necessary for Germany to gain living space through conquest in the east. This policy meant war. Hitler's nonaggression pact with the Soviet Union on August 23, 1939, paved the way for his invasion of Poland on September 1. On that day, Hitler spoke to the German Reichstag and announced the outbreak of war.

CHRONOLOGY

Prelude to War, 1933–1939

Hitler becomes chancellor	January 30, 1933
Germany withdraws from League of Nations and Geneva Disarmament Conference	October 1933
Hitler announces a German air force	March 9, 1935
Hitler announces military conscription	March 16, 1935
Anglo-German Naval Pact	June 18, 1935
Mussolini invades Ethiopia	October 1935
Hitler occupies demilitarized Rhineland	March 7, 1936
Mussolini and Hitler intervene in the Spanish Civil War	1936
Rome-Berlin Axis	October 1936
Anti-Comintern Pact (Japan and Germany)	November 1936
Japan invades China	1937
Germany annexes Austria	March 13, 1938
Munich Conference: Germany occupies Sudetenland	September 29, 1938
Germany occupies the rest of Czechoslovakia	March 1939
German-Soviet Nonaggression Pact	August 23, 1939
Germany invades Poland	September 1, 1939
Britain and France declare war on Germany	September 3, 1939
Soviet Union invades Poland	September 17, 1939

to the Soviet Union, while Germany would acquire western Poland. The treaty with the Soviet Union gave Hitler the freedom to attack Poland. He told his generals: "Now Poland is in the position in which I wanted her. . . . I am only afraid that at the last moment some swine or other will yet submit to me a plan for mediation."[3] He need not have worried. On September 1, German forces invaded Poland; two days later, Britain and France declared war on Germany. Two weeks later, on September 17, Germany's newfound ally, the Soviet Union, sent its troops into eastern Poland. Europe was again at war.

The Course of World War II

Nine days before he attacked Poland, Hitler made clear to his generals what was expected of them: "When starting and waging a war it is not right that matters, but victory. Close your hearts to pity. Act brutally. Eighty million people must obtain what is their right. . . . The wholesale destruction of Poland is the military objective. Speed is the main thing. Pursuit until complete annihilation."[4] Hitler's remarks set the tone for what became the most destructive war in human history.

Victory and Stalemate

Unleashing a *Blitzkrieg,* or "lightning war," Hitler stunned Europe with the speed and efficiency of the German attack. Armored columns or panzer divisions (a panzer division was a strike force of about three hundred tanks and accompanying forces and supplies) supported by airplanes broke quickly through Polish lines and encircled the overwhelmed Polish troops. Regular infantry units then moved in to hold the newly conquered territory. Within four weeks, Poland had surrendered. On September 28, 1939, Germany and the Soviet Union officially divided Poland between them.

Although Hitler's hopes of avoiding a war with the West were dashed when France and Britain declared war on September 3, he was confident that he could control the situation. Expecting another war of attrition and economic blockade, Britain and France refused to go on the offensive.

The Munich Conference

At the Munich Conference, the leaders of France and Great Britain capitulated to Hitler's demands on Czechoslovakia. While the British prime minister, Neville Chamberlain, defended his actions at Munich as necessary for peace, another British statesman, Winston Churchill, characterized the settlement at Munich as "a disaster of the first magnitude."

■ *Winston Churchill, Speech to the House of Commons, October 5, 1938*

I will begin by saying what everybody would like to ignore or forget but which must nevertheless be stated, namely, that we have sustained a total and unmitigated defeat, and that France has suffered even more than we have.... The utmost my right honorable Friend the Prime Minister ... has been able to gain for Czechoslovakia and in the matters which were in dispute has been that the German dictator, instead of snatching his victuals from the table, has been content to have them served to him course by course.... And I will say this, that I believe the Czechs, left to themselves and told they were going to get no help from the Western Powers, would have been able to make better terms than they have got....

We are in the presence of a disaster of the first magnitude which has befallen Great Britain and France. Do not let us blind ourselves to that....

And do not suppose that this is the end. This is only the beginning of the reckoning. This is only the first sip, the first foretaste of a bitter cup which will be proffered to us year by year unless by a supreme recovery of moral health and martial vigor, we arise again and take our stand for freedom as in the olden time.

■ *Neville Chamberlain, Speech to the House of Commons, October 6, 1938*

That is my answer to those who say that we should have told Germany weeks ago that, if her army crossed the border of Czechoslovakia, we should be at war with her. We had no treaty obligations and no legal obligations to Czechoslovakia.... When we were convinced, as we became convinced, that nothing any longer would keep the Sudetenland within the Czechoslovakian State, we urged the Czech Government as strongly as we could to agree to the cession of territory, and to agree promptly.... It was a hard decision for anyone who loved his country to take, but to accuse us of having by that advice betrayed the Czechoslovakian State is simply preposterous. What we did was to save her from annihilation and give her a chance of new life as a new State, which involves the loss of territory and fortifications, but may perhaps enable her to enjoy in the future and develop a national existence under a neutrality and security comparable to that which we see in Switzerland today. Therefore, I think the Government deserve the approval of this House for their conduct of affairs in this recent crisis which has saved Czechoslovakia from destruction and Europe from Armageddon.

Between 1930 and 1935, France had built a series of concrete and steel fortifications armed with heavy artillery—known as the Maginot Line—along its border with Germany. Now France was quite happy to remain in its defensive shell. After a winter of waiting (called the "phony war"), Hitler resumed the war on April 9, 1940, with another *Blitzkrieg*, this time against Denmark and Norway. One month later, on May 10, the Germans launched their attack on the Netherlands, Belgium, and France. The main assault through Luxembourg and the Ardennes forest was completely unexpected by the French and British forces. German panzer divisions broke through the weak French defensive positions there, outflanking the Maginot Line, and raced across northern France. The maneuver split the Allied armies and trapped French troops and the entire British army on the beaches of Dunkirk. A heroic rescue effort ensued with hundreds of ships and small boats ferrying troops from the French port to Britain. The British succeeded in evacuating an army of 330,000 Allied (mostly British) troops that would fight another day.

On June 5, the Germans launched another offensive into southern France. Five days later, Mussolini, believing that the war was over and eager to grab some of the spoils, declared war on France and invaded from the south. Dazed by the speed of the German offensive, the French were never able to mount an adequate resistance and surrendered on June 22. German armies occupied about three-fifths of France while the French hero of World War I, Marshal Henri Pétain (1856–1951), established an authoritarian regime (known as Vichy France) over the remainder. The Allies regarded the Pétain government as a Nazi puppet state, and a French government-in-exile took up residence in Britain. Germany was now in control of western and central Europe, but Britain still had not been defeated.

German victories in Denmark and Norway coincided with a change of government in Great Britain. On May 10, 1940, Winston Churchill (1874–1965), a longtime advocate for a hard-line policy toward Nazi Germany, replaced the apostle of appeasement, Neville Chamberlain. Churchill was confident that he could guide Britain to ultimate victory. "I thought I knew a great deal about it all," he later wrote, "and I was sure I should not fail." Churchill proved to be an inspiring leader who rallied the British people with stirring speeches. Hitler hoped that the British could be persuaded to make peace so that he could fulfill his long-awaited opportunity to gain living space in the east. Led by

Map 27.1 Changes in Central Europe, 1936–1939. Hitler's main objectives in the late 1930s were the incorporation into a greater Germany of lands that contained German people—the Rhineland, Austria, the Sudetenland—and the acquisition of *Lebensraum* (living space) in eastern Europe for the expansion of the German people. ■ What aspects of Czechoslovakia's location would have made it difficult for France and Britain to come directly to its aid in 1938?

the stubbornly determined Churchill, the British refused, and Hitler was forced to prepare for an invasion of Britain, a prospect that he faced with little confidence.

As Hitler realized, an amphibious invasion of Britain would be possible only if Germany gained control of the air. At the beginning of August 1940, the *Luftwaffe* (the German air force) launched a major offensive against British air and naval bases, harbors, communication centers, and war industries. The British fought back doggedly, supported by an effective radar system that gave them early warning of German attacks. Moreover, the Ultra intelligence operation, which had broken German military codes, gave the British air force information about the specific targets of German air attacks. Nevertheless, the British air force suffered critical losses by the end of August and was probably saved by Hitler's change of strategy. In September, in retaliation for a British attack on Berlin, Hitler ordered a shift from military targets to massive bombing

AKG London

German Troops in the Soviet Union. At first, the German attack on the Soviet Union was enormously successful, leading one German general to remark in his diary, "It is probably no overstatement to say that the Russian campaign has been won in the space of two weeks." Shown here is German artillery firing on Soviet positions.

of cities to break British morale. The British rebuilt their air strength quickly and were soon inflicting major losses on *Luftwaffe* bombers. By the end of September, Germany had lost the Battle of Britain, and the invasion of Britain had to be postponed.

At this point, Hitler pursued the possibility of a Mediterranean strategy, which would involve capturing Egypt and the Suez Canal and closing the Mediterranean to British ships, thereby shutting off Britain's supply of oil. Hitler's commitment to the Mediterranean was never wholehearted, however. His initial plan was to let the Italians, whose role was to secure the Balkan and Mediterranean flanks, defeat the British in North Africa, but this strategy failed when the British routed the Italian army. Although Hitler then sent German troops to the North African theater of war, his primary concern lay elsewhere: he had already reached the decision to fulfill his lifetime obsession with the acquisition of living space in the east.

Already at the end of July 1940, Hitler had told his army leaders to begin preparations for the invasion of the Soviet Union. Although he had no desire for a two-front war, Hitler became convinced that Britain was remaining in the war only because it expected Soviet support. If the Soviet Union were smashed, Britain's last hope would be eliminated. Moreover, Hitler had convinced himself that the Soviet Union, with its Jewish-Bolshevik leadership and a pitiful army, could be defeated quickly and decisively. Although the invasion of the Soviet Union was scheduled for spring 1941, the attack was delayed because of problems in the Balkans. Hitler had already obtained the political cooperation of Hungary, Bulgaria, and Romania. Mussolini's disastrous invasion of Greece in October 1940 exposed Hitler's southern flank to British air bases in Greece. To secure his Balkan flank, German troops seized both Yugoslavia and Greece in April. Now reassured, Hitler turned to the east and invaded the Soviet Union on June 22, 1941, in the belief that the Soviets could still be decisively defeated before winter set in.

The massive attack stretched out along an 1,800-mile front (see Map 27.2). German troops advanced rapidly, capturing two million Soviet soldiers. By November, one German army group had swept through the Ukraine while a second was besieging Leningrad; a third approached within 25 miles of Moscow, the Soviet capital. An early winter and unexpected Soviet resistance, however, brought the German advance to a halt. For the first time in the war, German armies had been stopped. Moreover, after the Japanese bombed Pearl Harbor, Hawaii, on December 7, 1941, Stalin concluded that the Japanese would not strike at the Soviet Union and transferred troops from eastern Siberia to the Moscow front. A counterattack in December 1941 by a Soviet army supposedly exhausted by Nazi victories brought an ominous ending to the year for the Germans. By that time, another of Hitler's decisions—the declaration of war on the United States—had probably made his defeat inevitable and turned another European conflict into a global war.

The War in Asia

The war in Asia arose from the ambitions of Japan, whose rise to the status of world power had been swift. Japan had defeated China in 1895 and Russia in 1905 and had taken over many of Germany's eastern and Pacific colonies in World War I. By 1933, the Japanese Empire included Korea, Formosa (Taiwan), Manchuria, and the Marshall, Caroline, and Mariana Islands in the Pacific.

By the early 1930s, Japan was experiencing severe internal tensions. Its population had exploded from thirty million in 1870 to eighty million by 1937. Much of Japan's ability to feed its population and to pay for industrial raw

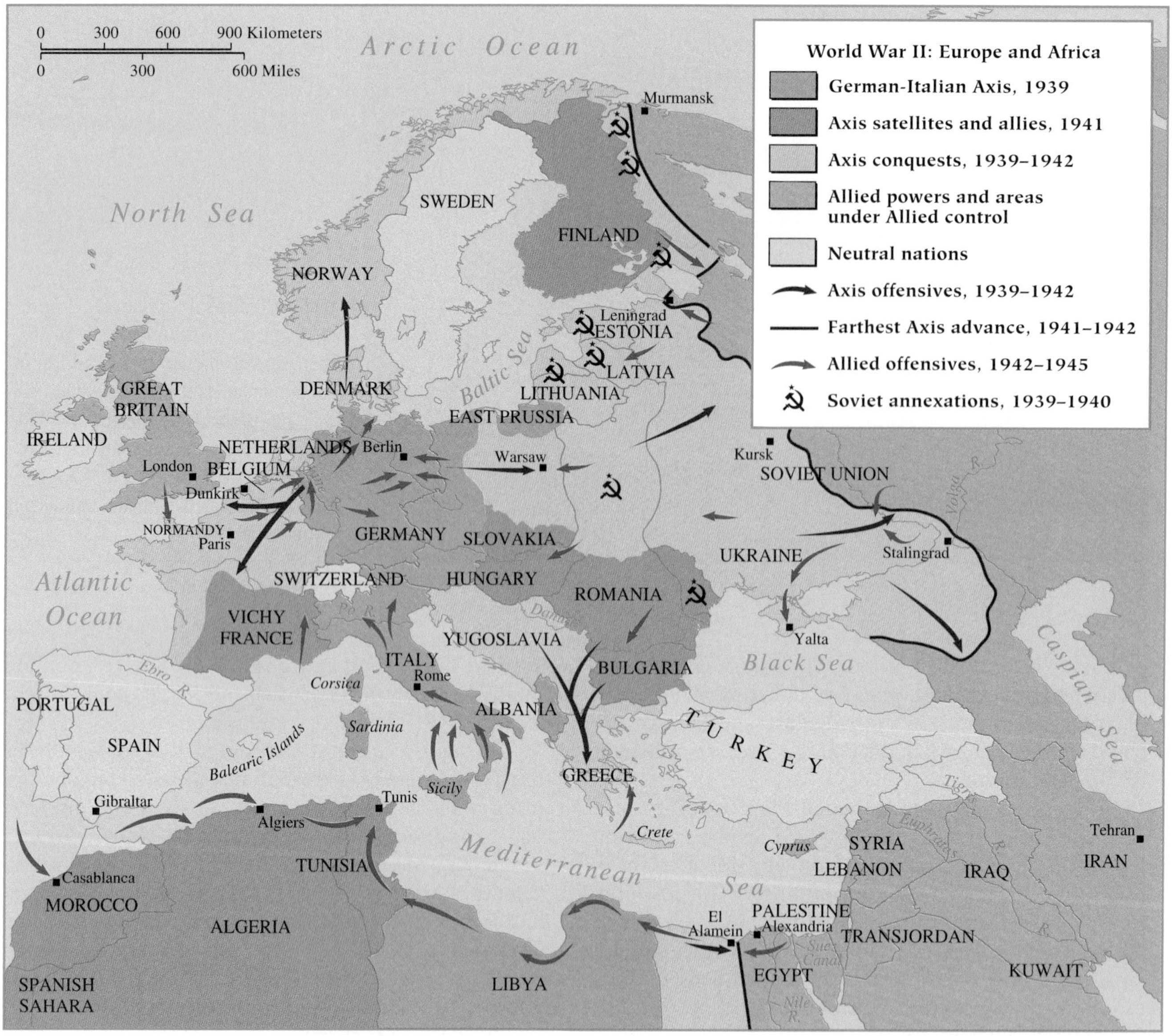

Map 27.2 World War II in Europe and North Africa. With its fast and effective military, Germany quickly overwhelmed much of western Europe. However, Hitler overestimated his country's capabilities and underestimated those of his foes. By late 1942, his invasion of the Soviet Union was failing, and the United States had become a major factor in the war. The Allies successfully invaded Italy in 1943 and France in 1944. ■ Which countries were neutral, and how did geography help make their neutrality an option?

materials depended on the manufacture of heavy industrial goods (especially ships) and textiles. But in the 1930s, Western nations established tariff barriers to protect their own economies from the effects of the depression. Japan was devastated, both economically and politically.

Although political power had been concentrated in the hands of the emperor and his cabinet, Japan had also experienced a slow growth of political democracy with universal male suffrage in 1924 and the emergence of mass political parties. The economic crises of the 1930s stifled this democratic growth. Right-wing patriotic societies allied themselves with the army and navy to push a program of expansion at the expense of China and the Soviet Union, while the navy hoped to make Japan self-sufficient in raw materials by conquering British Malaya and the Dutch East Indies. In 1935, Japan began to construct a modern naval fleet, and after 1936, the armed forces exercised much influence over the government.

The war in Asia began in July 1937 when Japanese troops invaded northern China. Moreover, Japanese naval expansion brought the Japanese into conflict with the European imperial powers—Britain (in India, Burma, Malaya),

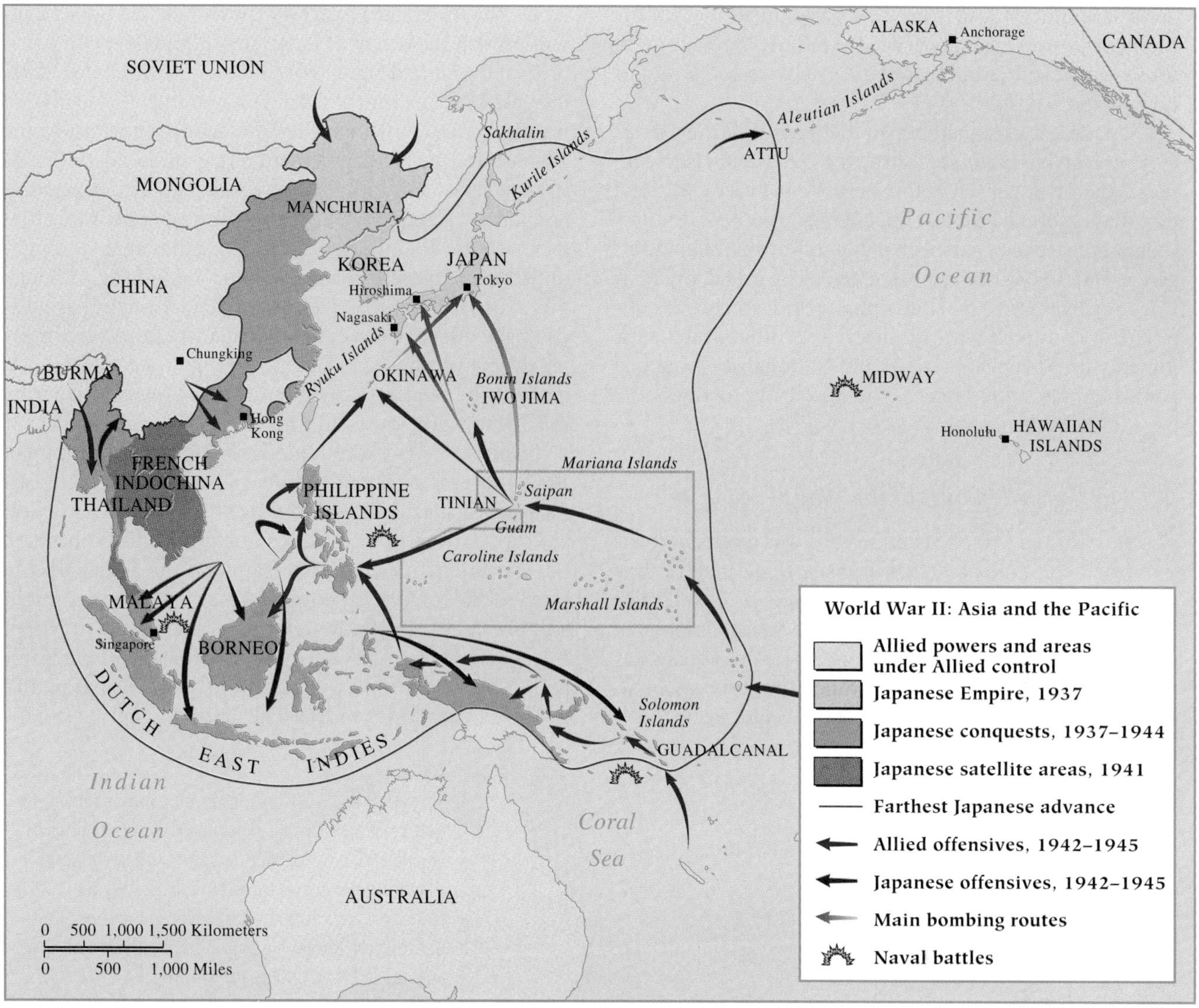

Map 27.3 World War II in Asia and the Pacific. In 1937, Japan invaded northern China, beginning its effort to create a "Great East Asia Co-Prosperity Sphere." Further expansion induced America to end iron and oil sales to Japan. Deciding that war with the United States was inevitable, Japan engineered a surprise attack on Pearl Harbor. ■ Why was control of the islands in the western Pacific of great importance both to the Japanese and to the Allies?

France (in Indochina), and the Netherlands (in the East Indies)—as well as with the other rising power in the Pacific, the United States. When the Japanese occupied Indochina in July 1941, the Americans responded by cutting off sales of vital scrap iron and oil to Japan. Japan's military leaders decided to preempt any further American response by attacking the American naval fleet in the Pacific.

On December 7, 1941, Japanese carrier-based aircraft attacked the United States naval base at Pearl Harbor in the Hawaiian Islands. The same day, other units launched additional assaults on the Philippines and began advancing toward the British colony of Malaya. The next day, the United States declared war on Japan. Three days later, Hitler declared war on the United States, although he was by no means required to do so by his loose alliance with Japan. This action enabled President Roosevelt to overcome strong American isolationist sentiment and to bring the United States into the European conflict.

Shortly after American entry into the war, Japanese forces invaded the Dutch East Indies and occupied a number of islands in the Pacific Ocean (see Map 27.3). In some cases, as on the Bataan peninsula and the island of Corregidor in the Philippines, resistance was fierce, but by the spring of 1942, almost all of Southeast Asia and much of the western Pacific had fallen into Japanese hands. Tokyo declared the creation of the Great East Asia Co-Prosperity Sphere, encompassing the entire region under Japanese tutelage, and announced its intention to liberate the colonial areas of Southeast Asia from Western colonial rule. For the moment, however, Japan needed the resources of the region for its war machine and placed the countries under its rule on a wartime basis.

Japanese leaders had hoped that their lightning strike at American bases would destroy the U.S. Pacific Fleet and persuade the Roosevelt administration to accept Japanese domination of the Pacific. The American people, in the eyes of Japanese leaders, had been made soft by material indulgence. But Tokyo had miscalculated. The attack on Pearl Harbor galvanized American opinion and won broad support for Roosevelt's war policy. The United States now joined with European nations and Nationalist China in a combined effort to defeat Japan and bring to an end its hegemony in the Pacific.

The Turning Point of the War (1942–1943)

The entry of the United States into the war created a coalition (the Grand Alliance) that ultimately defeated the Axis powers (Germany, Italy, Japan). Nevertheless, the three major Allies, Britain, the United States, and the Soviet Union, had to overcome mutual suspicions before they could operate as an effective alliance. Two factors aided that process. First, Hitler's declaration of war on the United States made it easier for the Americans to accept the British and Soviet contention that the defeat of Germany should be the first priority of the United States. For that reason, the United States increased the quantity of trucks, planes, and other arms that it sent to the British and Soviets. Also important to the alliance was the tacit agreement of the three chief Allies to stress military operations while ignoring political differences and larger strategic issues concerning any postwar settlement. At the beginning of 1943, the Allies agreed to fight until the Axis powers surrendered unconditionally. Although this principle of unconditional surrender might have discouraged dissident Germans and Japanese from overthrowing their governments in order to arrange a negotiated peace, it also had the effect of cementing the Grand Alliance by making it nearly impossible for Hitler to divide his foes.

Defeat was far from Hitler's mind at the beginning of 1942, however. As Japanese forces advanced into Southeast Asia and the Pacific after crippling the American naval fleet at Pearl Harbor, Hitler and his European allies continued the war in Europe against Britain and the Soviet Union. Until the fall of 1942, it appeared that the Germans might still prevail on the battlefield. Reinforcements in North Africa enabled the Afrika Korps under General Erwin Rommel to break through the British defenses in Egypt and advance toward Alexandria. The Germans were also con-

Topham/The Image Works

The Air War. Air power played a major role in the battles of World War II. Because his supply lines in North Africa were extended, the German general Erwin Rommel was forced to rely heavily on transport aircraft to keep his forces supplied. This photograph shows a group of German aircraft at an airfield in Libya during the summer of 1941. In the background are the three-engined Junkers Ju-52s used for transporting reinforcements and supplies. Two Messerschmidt fighter planes are in the foreground

A German Soldier at Stalingrad

The Soviet victory at Stalingrad was a major turning point in World War II. This excerpt comes from the diary of a German soldier who fought and died in the Battle of Stalingrad. His dreams of victory and a return home with medals were soon dashed by the realities of Soviet resistance.

Diary of a German Soldier

Today, after we'd had a bath, the company commander told us that if our future operations are as successful, we'll soon reach the Volga, take Stalingrad and then the war will inevitably soon be over. Perhaps we'll be home by Christmas.

July 29. The company commander says the Russian troops are completely broken, and cannot hold out any longer. To reach the Volga and take Stalingrad is not so difficult for us. The Führer knows where the Russians' weak point is. Victory is not far away. . . .

August 10. The Führer's orders were read out to us. He expects victory of us. We are all convinced that they can't stop us.

August 12. This morning outstanding soldiers were presented with decorations. . . . Will I really go back to Elsa without a decoration? I believe that for Stalingrad the Führer will decorate even me. . . .

September 4. We are being sent northward along the front toward Stalingrad. We marched all night and by dawn had reached Voroponovo Station. We can already see the smoking town. It's a happy thought that the end of the war is getting nearer. That's what everyone is saying. . . .

September 8. Two days of non-stop fighting. The Russians are defending themselves with insane stubbornness. Our regiment has lost many men. . . .

September 16. Our battalion, plus tanks, is attacking the [grain storage] elevator, from which smoke is pouring—the grain in it is burning, the Russians seem to have set light to it themselves. Barbarism. The battalion is suffering heavy losses. . . .

October 10. The Russians are so close to us that our planes cannot bomb them. We are preparing for a decisive attack. The Führer has ordered the whole of Stalingrad to be taken as rapidly as possible. . . .

October 22. Our regiment has failed to break into the factory. We have lost many men; every time you move you have to jump over bodies. . . .

November 10. A letter from Elsa today. Everyone expects us home for Christmas. In Germany everyone believes we already hold Stalingrad. How wrong they are. If they could only see what Stalingrad has done to our army. . . .

November 21. The Russians have gone over to the offensive along the whole front. Fierce fighting is going on. So, there it is—the Volga, victory and soon home to our families! We shall obviously be seeing them next in the other world.

November 29. We are encircled. It was announced this morning that the Führer has said: "The army can trust me to do everything necessary to ensure supplies and rapidly break the encirclement."

December 3. We are on hunger rations and waiting for the rescue that the Führer promised. . . .

December 14. Everybody is racked with hunger. Frozen potatoes are the best meal, but to get them out of the ice-covered ground under fire from Russian bullets is not so easy. . . .

December 26. The horses have already been eaten. I would eat a cat; they say its meat is also tasty. The soldiers look like corpses or lunatics, looking for something to put in their mouths. They no longer take cover from Russian shells; they haven't the strength to walk, run away and hide. A curse on this war!

tinuing their success in the Battle of the North Atlantic as their submarines continued to attack Allied ships carrying supplies to Great Britain. In the spring of 1942, a renewed German offensive in the Soviet Union led to the capture of the entire Crimea, causing Hitler to boast in August 1942:

> As the next step, we are going to advance south of the Caucasus and then help the rebels in Iran and Iraq against the English. Another thrust will be directed along the Caspian Sea toward Afghanistan and India. Then the English will run out of oil. In two years we'll be on the borders of India. Twenty to thirty elite German divisions will do. Then the British Empire will collapse.[5]

But this would be Hitler's last optimistic outburst. By the fall of 1942, the war had turned against the Germans.

In North Africa, British forces had stopped Rommel's troops at El Alamein in the summer of 1942 and then forced them back across the desert. In November 1942, British and American forces invaded French North Africa and forced the German and Italian troops to surrender in May 1943. By that time, new detection devices had enabled the Allies to destroy increasing numbers of German submarines in the shipping war in the Atlantic. On the Eastern Front, the turning point of the war occurred at Stalingrad. After the capture of the Crimea, Hitler's generals wanted him to concentrate on the Caucasus and its oil fields, but Hitler decided that Stalingrad, a major industrial center on the Volga, should be taken first. Between November 1942 and February 1943, German troops were stopped, then encircled, and finally forced to surrender on February 2, 1943 (see the box above). The entire German Sixth Army of 300,000 men was lost. By February 1943, German forces in the Soviet Union were back to their positions of

June 1942. By the spring of 1943, even Hitler knew that the Germans would not defeat the Soviet Union.

The tide of battle in Asia also turned dramatically in 1942. In the Battle of the Coral Sea on May 7–8, 1942, American naval forces stopped the Japanese advance and temporarily relieved Australia of the threat of invasion. On June 4, at the Battle of Midway Island, American planes destroyed all four of the attacking Japanese aircraft carriers and established American naval superiority in the Pacific. After a series of bitter engagements in the waters near the Solomon Islands from August to November, Japanese fortunes began to fade.

The Last Years of the War

By the beginning of 1943, the tide of battle had turned against Germany, Italy, and Japan, but it would take a long time to achieve the goal of unconditional surrender of the three Axis powers. After the Axis forces had surrendered in Tunisia on May 13, 1943, the Allies crossed the Mediterranean and carried the war to Italy, an area that Winston Churchill had called the "soft underbelly" of Europe. After taking Sicily, Allied troops began the invasion of mainland Italy in September. In the meantime, after the ouster and arrest of Benito Mussolini, a new Italian government offered to surrender to Allied forces. But Mussolini was liberated by the Germans in a daring raid and then set up as the head of a puppet German state in northern Italy while German troops moved in and occupied much of Italy. The new defensive lines established by the Germans in the hills south of Rome were so effective that the Allied advance up the Italian peninsula was a painstaking affair accompanied by heavy casualties. Rome did not fall to the Allies until June 4, 1944. By that time, the Italian war had assumed a secondary role anyway as the Allies opened their long-awaited "second front" in western Europe two days later.

Since the autumn of 1943, the Allies had been planning a cross-channel invasion of France from Britain. A series of Allied deceptions managed to trick the Germans into believing that the invasion would come on the flat plains of northern France. Instead, the Allies, under the direction of the American general, Dwight D. Eisenhower (1890–1969), landed five assault divisions on the Normandy beaches on June 6 in history's greatest naval invasion. An initially indecisive German response enabled the Allied forces to establish a beachhead. Within three months, they had landed two million men and a half-million vehicles that pushed inland and broke through the German defensive lines.

After the breakout, Allied troops moved south and east and liberated Paris by the end of August. Supply problems as well as a last-minute, desperate (and unsuccessful) offensive by German troops in the Battle of the Bulge slowed the Allied advance. Nevertheless, by March 1945, Allied armies had crossed the Rhine River and advanced further into Germany. At the end of April, Allied forces in northern Germany moved toward the Elbe River, where they finally linked up with the Soviets.

The Soviets had come a long way since the Battle of Stalingrad in 1943. In the summer of 1943, Hitler's generals had urged him to build an East Wall based on river barriers to halt the Soviets. Instead, Hitler gambled on taking the offensive by making use of newly developed heavy tanks. German forces were soundly defeated by the Soviets at the Battle of Kursk (July 5–12), the greatest tank battle of World War II. The Germans lost eighteen of their best panzer divisions. Soviet forces now began a relentless advance westward. The Soviets had reoccupied the Ukraine

National Archives, (#111-C-273)

Crossing the Rhine. After landing at Normandy, Allied forces liberated France and prepared to move into Germany. Makeshift bridges enabled the Allies to cross the Rhine in some areas and advance deeper into Germany. Units of the 7th U.S. Army of General Patch are shown here crossing the Rhine at Worms on a pontoon bridge constructed by battalions of engineers alongside the ruins of the old bridge.

CHRONOLOGY

The Course of World War II

Germany and the Soviet Union divide Poland	September 1939
Blitzkrieg against Denmark and Norway	April 1940
Blitzkrieg against Belgium, Netherlands, and France	May 1940
Churchill becomes British prime minister	May 10, 1940
France surrenders	June 22, 1940
Battle of Britain	Fall 1940
Nazi seizure of Yugoslavia and Greece	April 1941
Germany invades the Soviet Union	June 22, 1941
Japanese attack on Pearl Harbor	December 7, 1941
Battle of the Coral Sea	May 7–8, 1942
Battle of Midway Island	June 4, 1942
Allied invasion of North Africa	November 1942
German surrender at Stalingrad	February 2, 1943
Axis forces surrender in North Africa	May 13, 1943
Battle of Kursk	July 5–12, 1943
Invasion of mainland Italy	September 1943
Allied invasion of France	June 6, 1944
Hitler commits suicide	April 30, 1945
Surrender of Germany	May 7, 1945
Atomic bomb dropped on Hiroshima	August 6, 1945
Japan surrenders	August 14, 1945

by the end of 1943 and lifted the siege of Leningrad and moved into the Baltic states by the beginning of 1944. Advancing along a northern front, Soviet troops occupied Warsaw in January 1945 and entered Berlin in April. Meanwhile, Soviet troops swept along a southern front through Hungary, Romania, and Bulgaria.

In January 1945, Adolf Hitler had moved into a bunker 55 feet under Berlin to direct the final stages of the war. Hitler continued to arrange his armies on worn-out battle maps as if it still made a difference. In his final political testament, Hitler, consistent to the end in his rabid anti-Semitism, blamed the Jews for the war: "Above all I charge the leaders of the nation and those under them to scrupulous observance of the laws of race and to merciless opposition to the universal poisoner of all peoples, international Jewry."[6] Hitler committed suicide on April 30, two days after Mussolini had been shot by partisan Italian forces. On May 7, German commanders surrendered. The war in Europe was over.

The war in Asia continued. Beginning in 1943, American forces had gone on the offensive and advanced their way, slowly at times, across the Pacific. American forces took an increasing toll of enemy resources, especially at sea and in the air. When President Harry Truman (Roosevelt had died on April 12, 1945) and his advisers became convinced that American troops might suffer heavy casualties in the invasion of the Japanese homeland, they made the decision to drop the newly developed atomic bomb on Hiroshima and Nagasaki. The Japanese surrendered unconditionally on August 14. World War II, in which seventeen million died in battle and perhaps eighteen million civilians perished as well (some estimate total losses at fifty million), was finally over.

The Nazi New Order

After the German victories in Europe between 1939 and 1941, Nazi propagandists painted glowing images of a new European order based on "equal chances" for all nations and an integrated economic community. This was not Hitler's conception of the European New Order. He saw the Europe he had conquered simply as subject to German domination. Only the Germans, he once said, "can really organize Europe."

The Nazi Empire

The Nazi empire stretched across continental Europe from the English Channel in the west to the outskirts of Moscow in the east. In no way was this empire organized systematically or governed efficiently. Some states—Spain, Portugal, Switzerland, Sweden, and Turkey—remained neutral and outside the empire. Germany's allies—Italy, Romania, Bulgaria, Hungary, and Finland—kept their independence but found themselves increasingly restricted by the Germans as the war progressed. The remainder of Europe was largely organized in one of two ways. Some areas, such as western Poland, were directly annexed by Nazi Germany and made into German provinces. Most of occupied Europe was administered by German military or civilian officials, combined with varying degrees of indirect control from collaborationist regimes. Competing lines of authority by different offices in occupied Europe made German occupation inefficient.

Racial considerations played an important role in how conquered peoples were treated. German civil administrations were established in Norway, Denmark, and the Netherlands because the Nazis considered their peoples Aryan, racially akin to the Germans and hence worthy of more lenient treatment. "Inferior" Latin peoples, such as the occupied French, were given military administrations. By 1943, however, as Nazi losses continued to multiply, all the occupied territories of northern and western Europe were ruthlessly exploited for material goods and workers for Germany's war needs.

Because the conquered lands in the east contained the living space for German expansion and were populated

Hitler's Plans for a New Order in the East

Hitler's nightly monologues to his postdinner guests, which were recorded by the Führer's private secretary, Martin Bormann, reveal much about the New Order he wished to create. On the evening of October 17, 1941, he expressed his views on what the Germans would do with their newly conquered territories in the east.

Hitler's Secret Conversations, October 17, 1941

In comparison with the beauties accumulated in Central Germany, the new territories in the East seem to us like a desert. . . . This Russian desert, we shall populate it. . . . We'll take away its character of an Asiatic steppe, we'll Europeanize it. With this object, we have undertaken the construction of roads that will lead to the southernmost point of the Crimea and to the Caucasus. These roads will be studded along their whole length with German towns, and around these towns our colonists will settle.

As for the two or three million men whom we need to accomplish this task, we'll find them quicker than we think. They'll come from Germany, Scandinavia, the Western countries and America. I shall no longer be here to see all that, but in twenty years the Ukraine will already be a home for twenty million inhabitants besides the natives. In three hundred years, the country will be one of the loveliest gardens in the world.

As for the natives, we'll have to screen them carefully. The Jew, that destroyer, we shall drive out. . . . We shan't settle in the Russian towns, and we'll let them fall to pieces without intervening. And, above all, no remorse on this subject! We're not going to play at children's nurses; we're absolutely without obligations as far as these people are concerned. To struggle against the hovels, chase away the fleas, provide German teachers, bring out newspapers—very little of that for us! We'll confine ourselves, perhaps, to setting up a radio transmitter, under our control. For the rest, let them know just enough to understand our highway signs, so that they won't get themselves run over by our vehicles. . . . There's only one duty: to Germanize this country by the immigration of Germans, and to look upon the natives as Redskins. If these people had defeated us, Heaven have mercy! But we don't hate them. That sentiment is unknown to us. We are guided only by reason. . . .

All those who have the feeling for Europe can join in our work.

In this business I shall go straight ahead, cold-bloodedly. What they may think about me, at this juncture, is to me a matter of complete indifference. I don't see why a German who eats a piece of bread should torment himself with the idea that the soil that produces this bread has been won by the sword.

in Nazi eyes by racially inferior Slavic peoples, Nazi administration there was considerably more ruthless. Hitler's racial ideology and his plans for an Aryan racial empire were so important to him that he and the Nazis began to implement their racial program soon after the conquest of Poland. Heinrich Himmler, a strong believer in Nazi racial ideology and the leader of the SS, was put in charge of German resettlement plans in the east. Himmler's task was to evacuate the inferior Slavic peoples and replace them with Germans, a policy first applied to the new German provinces created from the lands of western Poland. One million Poles were uprooted and dumped in southern Poland. Hundreds of thousands of ethnic Germans (descendants of Germans who had migrated years earlier from Germany to various parts of southern and eastern Europe) were encouraged to colonize the designated areas in Poland. By 1942, two million ethnic Germans had been settled in Poland.

The invasion of the Soviet Union inflated Nazi visions of German colonization in the east. Hitler spoke to his intimate circle of a colossal project of social engineering after the war, in which Poles, Ukrainians, and Soviets would become slave labor and German peasants would settle on the abandoned lands and Germanize them (see the box above). Nazis involved in this kind of planning were well aware of the human costs. Himmler told a gathering of SS officers that although the destruction of thirty million Slavs was a prerequisite for German plans in the east: "Whether nations live in prosperity or starve to death interests me only insofar as we need them as slaves for our culture. Otherwise it is of no interest."[7]

Economically, the Nazi New Order meant the ruthless exploitation of conquered Europe's resources. In eastern Europe, economic exploitation was direct and severe. The Germans seized raw materials, machines, and food, leaving only enough to maintain local peoples at a bare subsistence level. Although the Germans adopted legal formalities in their economic exploitation of western Europe, military supplies and important raw materials were taken outright. As Nazi policies created drastic shortages of food, clothing, and shelter, many Europeans suffered severely.

Labor shortages in Germany led to a policy of ruthless mobilization of foreign labor for Germany. After the invasion of the Soviet Union, the four million Soviet prisoners of war captured by the Germans became a major source of heavy labor, but it was wasted by allowing three million of them to die from neglect. In 1942, a special office was created to recruit labor for German farms and industries. By the summer of 1944, seven million foreign workers were laboring in Germany and constituted 20 percent of Germany's labor force. At the same time, another seven million workers were supplying forced labor in their own countries on farms, in industries, and even in military camps. Forced labor often proved counterproductive, however, because it created economic chaos in occupied countries and disrupted industrial production that could have helped Germany. Even worse for the Germans, the brutal character of Germany's recruitment policies often led more and more people to resist the Nazi occupation forces.

Resistance Movements

German policies toward conquered peoples quickly led to the emergence of resistance movements throughout Europe, especially in the east, where brutality toward the native peoples produced a strong reaction. In the Ukraine and the Baltic states, for example, the Germans were initially hailed as liberators from Communist rule, but Hitler's policies of treating Slavic peoples as subhumans only drove those peoples to support and join guerrilla forces.

Resistance movements were formed throughout Europe. Active resisters committed acts of sabotage against German installations, assassinated German officials, spread anti-German newspapers, wrote anti-German sentiments on walls, and spied on German military positions for the Allies. Some anti-Nazi groups from occupied countries, such as the Free French movement under Charles de Gaulle, created governments-in-exile in London. In some countries, resistance groups even grew strong enough to take on the Germans in pitched battles. In Yugoslavia, for example, Josip Broz, known as Tito (1892–1980), led a band of guerrillas against German occupation forces. By 1944, his partisan army numbered 250,000, including 100,000 women.

After the invasion of the Soviet Union in 1941, Communists throughout Europe assumed leadership roles in underground resistance movements. This sometimes led to conflict with other local resistance groups who feared the postwar consequences of Communist power. Charles de Gaulle's Free French movement, for example, thwarted the attempt of French Communists to dominate the major French resistance groups.

Women, too, joined resistance movements in large numbers throughout Nazi-occupied Europe. Women served as message carriers, planted bombs in Nazi headquarters, assassinated Nazi officers, published and spread anti-German underground newspapers, spied on German military movements and positions, and used shopping baskets to carry weapons, medicines, and money to help their causes. In Norway, women smuggled Jews into neutral Sweden. In Greece, wives dressed their husbands as women to save them when the Nazis sought to stop acts of sabotage by vicious reprisals in which all the males of a village were executed.

Germany, too, had its resistance movements, although the increased control of the SS over everyday life made resistance both dangerous and ineffectual. The White Rose movement involved an attempt by a small group of students and one professor at the University of Munich to distribute pamphlets denouncing the Nazi regime as lawless, criminal, and godless. Its members were caught, arrested, and promptly executed. Likewise, Communist resistance groups were mostly crushed by the Gestapo.

Only one plot against Hitler and the Nazi regime came remotely close to success. It was the work primarily of a group of military officers and conservative politicians who were appalled at Hitler's warmongering and sickened by the wartime atrocities he had encouraged. One of their number, Colonel Count Claus von Stauffenberg (1907–1944), believed that only the elimination of Hitler would bring the overthrow of the Nazi regime. On July 20, 1944, a bomb planted by Stauffenberg in Hitler's East Prussian headquarters exploded, but it failed to kill the dictator. The plot was then quickly uncovered and crushed. Five thousand people were executed, and Hitler remained in control of Germany.

The Holocaust

There was no more terrifying aspect of the Nazi New Order than the deliberate attempt to exterminate the Jewish people of Europe. Racial struggle was a key element in Hitler's ideology and meant to him a clearly defined conflict of opposites: the Aryans, creators of human cultural development, against the Jews, parasites who were trying to destroy the Aryans. At a meeting of the Nazi Party in 1922, Hitler proclaimed: "There can be no compromise—there are only two possibilities: either victory of the Aryan or annihilation of the Aryan and the victory of the Jew."[8] Although Hitler later toned down his anti-Semitic message when his party sought mass electoral victories, anti-Semitism was a recurring theme in Nazism and resulted in a wave of legislative acts against the Jews between 1933 and 1939.

By the beginning of 1939, Nazi policy focused on promoting the "emigration" of German Jews from Germany. At the same time, Hitler had given ominous warnings about the future of European Jewry. When he addressed the German Reichstag on January 30, 1939, he stated:

> I have often been a prophet in life and was generally laughed at. During my struggle for power, the Jews primarily received with laughter my prophecies that I would someday assume the leadership of the state and thereby of the entire Volk and then, among many other things, achieve a solution of the Jewish problem. . . . Today I will be a prophet again: if international finance Jewry within Europe and abroad should succeed once more in plunging the peoples into a world war, then the consequence will be not the Bolshevization of the world and therewith a victory of Jewry, but on the contrary, the destruction of the Jewish race in Europe.[9]

At the time, emigration was still the favored policy. Once the war began in September 1939, the so-called Jewish problem took on new dimensions. For a while, there was discussion of the Madagascar Plan, which aspired to the mass shipment of Jews to the island of Madagascar, off the eastern coast of Africa. When war contingencies made this plan impracticable, an even more drastic policy was conceived.

Heinrich Himmler and the SS organization closely shared Adolf Hitler's racial ideology. The SS was given responsibility for what the Nazis called their Final Solution to the Jewish problem—the annihilation of the Jewish people. Reinhard Heydrich (1904–1942), head of the SS's Security Service, was given administrative responsibility for the Final Solution. After the defeat of Poland, Heydrich ordered the special strike forces (*Einsatzgruppen*) that he had created to round up all Polish Jews and concentrate them in ghettos established in a number of Polish cities.

In June 1941, the *Einsatzgruppen* were given new responsibilities as mobile killing units. These SS death squads followed the regular army's advance into the Soviet Union. Their job was to round up Jews in their villages and execute and bury them in mass graves, often giant pits dug by the victims themselves before they were shot. The leader of one of these death squads described the mode of operation:

> The unit selected for this task would enter a village or city and order the prominent Jewish citizens to call together all Jews for the purpose of resettlement. They were requested to hand over their valuables to the leaders of the unit, and shortly before the execution to surrender their outer clothing. The men, women, and children were led to a place of execution which in most cases was located next to a more deeply excavated anti-tank ditch. Then they were shot, kneeling or standing, and the corpses thrown into the ditch.[10]

Such regular killing created morale problems among the SS executioners. During a visit to Minsk in the Soviet Union, SS leader Himmler tried to build morale by pointing out that "he would not like it if Germans did such a thing gladly. But their conscience was in no way impaired, for they were soldiers who had to carry out every order unconditionally. He alone had responsibility before God and Hitler for everything that was happening, . . . and he was acting from a deep understanding of the necessity for this operation."[11]

Although it has been estimated that as many as one million Jews were killed by the *Einsatzgruppen,* this approach to solving the Jewish problem was soon perceived as inadequate. Instead, the Nazis opted for the systematic annihilation of the European Jewish population in specially built death camps. The plan was simple. Jews from countries occupied by Germany (or sympathetic to Germany) would be rounded up, packed like cattle into freight trains, and

The Holocaust: Activities of the *Einsatzgruppen.* The activities of the mobile killing units known as the *Einsatzgruppen* were the first stage in the mass killings of the Holocaust. This picture shows the execution of a Jew by a member of one of these SS killing squads. Onlookers include members of the German army, the German Labor Service, and even Hitler Youth. When it became apparent that this method of killing was inefficient, it was replaced by the death camps.

Library of Congress (2391, folder 401)

Map 27.4 The Holocaust. Hitler used the fiction of the Aryan race, to which Germans supposedly belonged, to help radicalize the German people and justify his hatred of Jews. Hitler's "Final Solution" to the "Jewish problem" was mass execution of Europe's Jews in extermination camps. ■ Which region lost the largest number of Jews in the camps, and what helps explain this?

shipped to Poland, where six extermination centers were built for this purpose (see Map 27.4). The largest and most infamous was Auschwitz-Birkenau. Technical assistance for the construction of the camps was provided by experts from the T-4 program, which had been responsible for the extermination of eighty thousand alleged racially unfit mental and physical defectives in Germany between 1938 and 1941. Based on their experiences, medical technicians chose Zyklon B (the commercial name for hydrogen cyanide) as the most effective gas for quickly killing large numbers of people in gas chambers designed to look like shower rooms to facilitate the cooperation of the victims. After gassing, the corpses would be burned in specially built crematoria.

To inform party and state officials of the general procedures for the Final Solution, a conference was held at Wannsee, outside Berlin, on January 20, 1942. Reinhard Heydrich outlined the steps that would now be taken to "solve the Jewish question." He explained how "in the course of the practical implementation of the final solution Europe is to be combed through from west to east" for Jews, who would then be brought "group by group, into so-called transit ghettos, to be transported from there farther to the east." The conference then worked out all of the bureaucratic details so that party and state officials would cooperate fully in the final elimination of the Jews.

By the spring of 1942, the death camps were in operation. Although initial priority was given to the elimination of the ghettos in Poland, by the summer of 1942, Jews were also being shipped from France, Belgium, and the Netherlands. In 1943, there were shipments of Jews from the capital cities of Berlin, Vienna, and Prague and from Greece, southern France, Italy, and Denmark. Even as the Allies were making important advances in 1944, Jews were being shipped from Greece and Hungary. These shipments depended on the cooperation of Germany's Transport Ministry, and despite desperate military needs, the Final Solution had priority in using railroad cars for the transportation of Jews to death camps. Even the military argument that Jews could be used to produce armaments was overridden by the demands of extermination.

A harrowing experience awaited the Jews when they arrived at one of the six death camps. Rudolf Höss, commandant at Auschwitz-Birkenau, described it:

> We had two SS doctors on duty at Auschwitz to examine the incoming transports of prisoners. The prisoners would be marched by one of the doctors who would make spot decisions as they walked by. Those who were fit for work were sent into the camp. Others were sent immediately to the extermination plants. Children of tender years were invariably exterminated since by reason of their youth they were unable to work. . . . At Auschwitz we endeavored to fool the victims into thinking that they were to go through a delousing process. Of course, frequently they realized our true intentions and we sometimes had riots and difficulties due to that fact.[12]

About 30 percent of the arrivals at Auschwitz were sent to a labor camp; the remainder went to the gas chambers (see the box on p. 791). After they had been gassed, the bodies were burned in the crematoria. The victims' goods and even their bodies were used for economic gain. Female hair was cut off, collected, and turned into mattresses or cloth. Some inmates were also subjected to cruel and painful "medical" experiments. The Germans killed between five and six million Jews, more than three million of them in the death camps. Virtually 90 percent of the Jewish populations of Poland, the Baltic countries, and Germany were exterminated. Overall, the Holocaust was responsible for the death of nearly two out of every three European Jews.

The Nazis were also responsible for the deliberate death by shooting, starvation, or overwork of at least another nine to ten million people. Because the Nazis also considered the Gypsies of Europe (like the Jews) a race containing alien blood, they were systematically rounded up for extermination. About 40 percent of Europe's one million Gypsies were killed in the death camps. The leading elements of the "subhuman" Slavic peoples—the clergy, intelligentsia, civil leaders, judges, and lawyers—were arrested and deliberately killed. Probably, an additional four million Poles, Ukrainians, and Belorussians lost their lives as slave laborers for Nazi Germany, and at least three to four million Soviet prisoners of war were killed in captivity. The Nazis also singled out homosexuals for persecution, and thousands lost their lives in concentration camps.

The Holocaust: The Extermination Camp at Auschwitz. After his initial successes in the east, Hitler set in motion the machinery for the physical annihilation of Europe's Jews. Shown here is a group of Hungarian Jews who have just arrived at Auschwitz. Hungarian Jews were not rounded up and shipped to the death camps until 1944, at a time when the Allies were making significant advances in the war.

Courtesy of the U.S. Holocaust Museum, Washington DC

The Holocaust: The Camp Commandant and the Camp Victims

The systematic annihilation of millions of men, women, and children in extermination camps makes the Holocaust one of the most horrifying events in history. The first document is taken from an account by Rudolf Höss, commandant of the extermination camp at Auschwitz-Birkenau. In the second document, a French doctor explains what happened to the victims at one of the crematoria described by Höss.

Commandant Höss Describes the Equipment

The two large crematoria, Nos. I and II, were built during the winter of 1942–43. . . . They each . . . could cremate c. 2,000 corpses within twenty-four hours. . . . Crematoria I and II both had underground undressing and gassing rooms which could be completely ventilated. The corpses were brought up to the ovens on the floor above by lift. The gas chambers could hold c. 3,000 people.

The firm of Topf had calculated that the two smaller crematoria, III and IV, would each be able to cremate 1,500 corpses within twenty-four hours. However, owing to the wartime shortage of materials, the builders were obliged to economize and so the undressing rooms and gassing rooms were built above ground and the ovens were of a less solid construction. But it soon became apparent that the flimsy construction of these two four-retort ovens was not up to the demands made on it. No. III ceased operating altogether after a short time and later was no longer used. No. IV had to be repeatedly shut down since after a short period in operation of 4–6 weeks, the ovens and chimneys had burnt out. The victims of the gassing were mainly burnt in pits behind crematorium IV.

The largest number of people gassed and cremated within twenty-four hours was somewhat over 9,000.

A French Doctor Describes the Victims

It is mid-day, when a long line of women, children, and old people enter the yard. The senior official in charge . . . climbs on a bench to tell them that they are going to have a bath and that afterward they will get a drink of hot coffee. They all undress in the yard. . . . The doors are opened and an indescribable jostling begins. The first people to enter the gas chamber begin to draw back. They sense the death which awaits them. The SS men put an end to this pushing and shoving with blows from their rifle butts beating the heads of the horrified women who are desperately hugging their children. The massive oak double doors are shut. For two endless minutes one can hear banging on the walls and screams which are no longer human. And then—not a sound. Five minutes later the doors are opened. The corpses, squashed together and distorted, fall out like a waterfall. . . . The bodies which are still warm pass through the hands of the hairdresser who cuts their hair and the dentist who pulls out their gold teeth. . . . One more transport has just been processed through No. IV crematorium.

The Home Front

World War II was even more of a total war than World War I. Fighting was much more widespread and covered most of the globe. Economic mobilization was more extensive; so too was the mobilization of women. The number of civilians killed was far higher; almost twenty million died as a result of bombing raids, mass extermination policies, and attacks by invading armies.

The Mobilization of Peoples: Four Examples

The home fronts of the major Western countries varied considerably, based on national circumstances.

GREAT BRITAIN

The British mobilized their resources more thoroughly than their allies or even Germany. By the summer of 1944, fully 55 percent of the British people were in the armed forces or civilian "war work." The British were especially determined to make use of women. Most women under forty years of age were called on to do war work of some kind. By 1944, women held almost 50 percent of the civil service positions, and the number of women in agriculture doubled as "land girls" performed agricultural labor usually undertaken by men.

The government encouraged the "Dig for Victory" campaign to increase food production. Fields normally reserved for athletic events were turned over to citizens to plant gardens in "Grow Your Own Food" campaigns. Even with 1.4 million new gardens in 1943, Britain still faced a shortage of food as German submarines continued to sink hundreds of British merchant vessels. Food rationing, with its weekly allotments of bacon, sugar, fats, and eggs, intensified during the war as the British became accustomed to a diet dominated by bread and potatoes. For many British people, hours after work were spent in such wartime activities as "Dig for Victory," the Civil Defence, or Home Guard. The Home Guard had been founded in 1940 to fight off German invaders. Even elderly people were expected to help manufacture airplane parts in their homes.

During the war, the British placed much emphasis on a planned economy. In 1942, the government created a ministry for fuel and power to control the coal industry and a ministry for production to oversee supplies for the

Imperial War Museum, London

Women in the Factories. Although only the Soviet Union used women in combat positions, the number of women working in industry increased dramatically in most belligerent countries. British women are shown here preparing artillery shells that will be filled with explosives.

armed forces. Although controls and bureaucratic "red tape" became unpopular, especially with businesspeople, most British citizens seemed to accept that total war required unusual governmental interference in people's lives. The British did make substantial gains in manufacturing war materials. Tank production quadrupled between 1940 and 1942, and the production of aircraft grew from 8,000 in 1939 to 26,000 in 1943 and 1944.

THE SOVIET UNION

World War II had an enormous impact on the Soviet Union. Known to the Soviets as the Great Patriotic War, the German-Soviet war witnessed the greatest land battles in history as well as incredible ruthlessness. To Nazi Germany, it was a war of oppression and annihilation that called for merciless measures. Two out of every five persons killed in World War II were Soviet citizens.

The shift to a war footing necessitated only limited administrative change in the Soviet Union. As the central authority, the dictator Joseph Stalin simply created a system of "supercentralization," by which he directed military and political affairs. All civil and military organizations were subjected to the control of the Communist Party and the Soviet police.

The initial defeats of the Soviet Union led to drastic emergency mobilization measures that affected the civilian population. Leningrad, for example, experienced nine hundred days of siege, during which its inhabitants became so desperate for food that they ate dogs, cats, and mice. As the German army made its rapid advance into Soviet territory, the factories in the western part of the Soviet Union were dismantled and shipped to the interior—to the Urals, western Siberia, and the Volga region. Machines were placed on the bare ground, and walls went up around them as workers began their work. The Kharkov Tank Factory produced its first 25 T-34 tanks only ten weeks after the plant had been rebuilt.

This widespread military, industrial, and economic mobilization created yet another Industrial Revolution for the Soviet Union. Stalin labeled it a "battle of machines," and the Soviets won, producing 78,000 tanks and 98,000 artillery pieces. Fifty-five percent of Soviet national income went for war matériel, compared to 15 percent in 1940. As a result of the emphasis on military goods, Soviet citizens experienced incredible shortages of both food and housing. Civilian food consumption fell by 40 percent during the war; in the Volga area, the Urals, and Siberia, workers lived in dugouts or dilapidated barracks.

Soviet women played a major role in the war effort. Women and girls worked in industries, mines, and railroads. Women constituted between 26 and 35 percent of the laborers in mines and 48 percent in the oil industry. Overall, the number of women working in industry increased almost 60 percent. Soviet women were also expected to dig antitank ditches and work as air-raid wardens. In addition, the Soviet Union was the only country in World War II to use women as combatants. Soviet women functioned as snipers and also as aircrews in bomber squadrons. The female pilots who helped defeat the Germans at Stalingrad were known as the "Night Witches."

Soviet peasants were asked to bear enormous burdens. Not only did the peasants furnish 60 percent of the military forces, but at the same time, they were expected to feed the Red Army and the Soviet people under very trying conditions. The German occupation in the early months of the war resulted in the loss of 47 percent of the country's grain-producing regions. Although new land was opened in the Urals, Siberia, and Soviet Asia, a shortage of labor and equipment hindered the effort to expand agricultural production. Because farm tractors and trucks were requisitioned to carry guns for the military, women and children were literally harnessed to do the plowing, and everywhere peasants worked long hours on collective farms for no pay. In 1943, the Soviet harvest was only 60 percent of its 1940 figure, a shortfall that meant extreme hardship for many people.

Total mobilization produced victory for the Soviet Union. Stalin and the Communist Party had quickly realized after the start of the German invasion that the Soviet people would not fight for communist ideology but would do battle to preserve "Mother Russia." Government propaganda played on patriotic feelings. In a speech on the anniversary of the Bolshevik Revolution in November 1941, Stalin rallied the Soviet people by speaking of the country's past heroes, including the famous tsars of Imperial Russia.

THE UNITED STATES

The home front in the United States was quite different from those of its two chief wartime allies, largely because the United States faced no threat of war in its own territory. Although the economy and labor force were slow to mobilize, eventually the United States became the arsenal of the Allied Powers, producing the military equipment they needed. The mobilization of the United States also had a great impact on American social and economic developments.

The American economy was never completely mobilized. In 1941, industries were hesitant to change over to full-time war operations because they feared that too much production would inundate postwar markets and cause another depression. Unemployment did not decrease significantly in the United States until mid-1943, a situation that affected the use of women in industrial jobs. Seventy-one percent of American women over eighteen years of age remained at home, in part due to male attitudes concerning women's traditional place in the home but also because the services of women were not really needed. During the high point of war production in the United States in November 1943, the nation was constructing six ships a day and $6 billion worth of other military equipment a month. Within a year, many small factories were being shut down because of overproduction.

Even this partial mobilization of the American economy caused social problems. The construction of new factories created boomtowns where thousands came to work but then faced a shortage of houses, health facilities, and schools. The dramatic expansion of small towns into large cities often brought a breakdown in traditional social mores, especially evident in the growth of teenage prostitution. Economic mobilization also led to a widespread movement of people, which in turn created new social tensions. Sixteen million men and women were enrolled in the military, and another sixteen million, mostly wives and sweethearts of the servicemen or workers looking for jobs, also relocated. Over one million African Americans migrated from the rural South to the industrial cities of the North and West, looking for jobs in industry. The presence of African Americans in areas where they had not lived before led to racial tensions and sometimes even racial riots. In Detroit in June 1943, white mobs roamed the streets attacking African Americans. Many of the one million African Americans who enlisted in the military, only to be segregated in their own battle units, were angered by the way they were treated. Some became militant and prepared to fight for their civil rights.

Japanese Americans were treated even more shabbily. On the West Coast, 110,000 Japanese Americans, 65 percent of whom had been born in the United States, were removed to camps encircled by barbed wire and required to take loyalty oaths. Although public officials claimed that this policy was necessary for security reasons, no similar treatment of German Americans or Italian Americans ever took place. The racism inherent in this treatment of Japanese Americans was evident when the California governor, Culbert Olson, said: "You know, when I look out at a group of Americans of German or Italian descent, I can tell whether they're loyal or not. I can tell how they think and even perhaps what they are thinking. But it is impossible for me to do this with inscrutable orientals, and particularly the Japanese."[13]

GERMANY

In August 1914, Germans had enthusiastically cheered their soldiers marching off to war. In September 1939, the streets were quiet. Many Germans were apathetic or, even worse for the Nazi regime, had a foreboding of disaster. Hitler was very aware of the importance of the home front. He believed that the collapse of the home front in World War I had caused Germany's defeat, and in his determination to avoid a repetition of that experience, he adopted economic policies that may indeed have cost Germany the war.

To maintain the morale of the home front during the first two years of the war, Hitler refused to convert production from consumer goods to armaments. *Blitzkrieg*

The Bombing of Civilians

The home front became a battle front when civilian populations became the targets of mass bombing raids. Many people believed that mass bombing could effectively weaken the morale of the people and shorten the war. Rarely did it achieve its goal. In these selections, British, German, and Japanese civilians relate their experiences during bombing raids.

London, 1940

Early last evening, the noise was terrible. My husband and Mr. P. were trying to play chess in the kitchen. I was playing draughts with Kenneth in the cupboard. . . . Presently I heard a stifled voice "Mummy! I don't know what's become of my glasses." "I should think they are tied up in my wool." My knitting had disappeared and wool seemed to be everywhere! We heard a whistle, a bang which shook the house, and an explosion. . . . Well, we straightened out, decided draughts and chess were no use under the circumstances, and waited for a lull so we could have a pot of tea.

Hamburg, 1943

As the many fires broke through the roofs of the burning buildings, a column of heated air rose more than two and a half miles high and one and a half miles in diameter. . . . This column was turbulent, and it was fed from its base by in-rushing cooler ground-surface air. One and one half miles from the fires this draught increased the wind velocity from eleven to thirty-three miles per hour. At the edge of the area the velocities must have been appreciably greater, as trees three feet in diameter were uprooted. In a short time the temperature reached ignition point for all combustibles, and the entire area was ablaze. In such fires complete burn-out occurred; that is, no trace of combustible material remained, and only after two days were the areas cool enough to approach.

Hiroshima, August 6, 1945

I heard the airplane; I looked up at the sky, it was a sunny day, the sky was blue. . . . Then I saw something drop—and pow!—a big explosion knocked me down. Then I was unconscious—I don't know for how long. Then I was conscious but I couldn't see anything. . . . Then I see people moving away and I just follow them. It is not light like it was before, it is more like evening. I look around; houses are all flat! . . . I follow the people to the river. I couldn't hear anything, my ears are blocked up. I am thinking a bomb has dropped! . . . I didn't know my hands were burned, nor my face. . . . My eyes were swollen and felt closed up.

allowed the Germans to win quick victories, after which they could plunder the food and raw materials of conquered countries in order to avoid diverting resources away from the civilian economy. After the German defeats on the Soviet front and the American entry into the war, the economic situation changed. Early in 1942, Hitler finally ordered a massive increase in armaments production and the size of the army. Hitler's personal architect, Albert Speer, was made minister for armaments and munitions in 1942. By eliminating waste and rationalizing procedures, Speer was able to triple the production of armaments between 1942 and 1943 despite the intense Allied air raids. Speer's urgent plea for a total mobilization of resources for the war effort went unheeded, however. Hitler, fearful of civilian morale problems that would undermine the home front, refused any dramatic cuts in the production of consumer goods. A total mobilization of the economy was not implemented until 1944, when schools, theaters, and cafés were closed and Speer was finally permitted to use all remaining resources for the production of a few basic military items. By that time, it was in vain. Total war mobilization was too little and too late in July 1944 to save Germany from defeat.

The war produced a reversal in Nazi attitudes toward women. Nazi resistance to female employment declined as the war progressed and more and more men were called up for military service. Nazi magazines now proclaimed: "We see the woman as the eternal mother of our people, but also as the working and fighting comrade of the man."[14] But the number of women working in industry, agriculture, commerce, and domestic service increased only slightly. The total number of employed women in September 1944 was 14.9 million, compared to 14.6 in May 1939. Many women, especially those of the middle class, resisted regular employment, particularly in factories. Even the introduction of labor conscription for women in January 1943 failed to achieve much as women found ingenious ways to avoid the regulations.

The Frontline Civilians: The Bombing of Cities

Bombing was used in World War II in a variety of ways: against nonhuman military targets, against enemy troops, and against civilian populations. The use of bombs made World War II as devastating for civilians as for frontline soldiers (see the box above). A small number of bombing raids in the last year of World War I had given rise to the argument, expressed in 1930 by the Italian general Giulio Douhet, that the public outcry generated by the bombing of civilian populations would be an effective way to coerce governments into making peace. Consequently, European air forces began to develop long-range bombers in the 1930s.

The first sustained use of civilian bombing contradicted Douhet's theory. Beginning in early September 1940, the German *Luftwaffe* subjected London and many other British cities and towns to nightly air raids, making the Blitz (as the British called the German air raids) a national experience. Londoners took the first heavy blows and set the standard for the rest of the British population by refusing to panic. One British woman expressed well what many others apparently felt:

> It was a beautiful summer night, so warm it was incredible, and made more beautiful than ever by the red glow from the East, where the docks were burning. We stood and stared for a minute, and I tried to fix the scene in my mind, because one day this will be history, and I shall be one of those who actually saw it. I wasn't frightened any more.[15]

But London morale was helped by the fact that German raids were widely scattered over a very large city. Smaller communities were more directly affected by the devastation. On November 14, 1940, for example, the *Luftwaffe* destroyed hundreds of shops and 100 acres of the city center of Coventry. The destruction of smaller cities did produce morale problems as wild rumors of heavy casualties spread quickly in these communities. Nevertheless, morale was soon restored. In any case, war production in these areas seems to have been little affected by the raids.

The British failed to learn from their own experience, however, and soon proceeded to bomb German cities. Churchill and his advisers believed that destroying German communities would break civilian morale and bring victory. Major bombing raids began in 1942 under the direction of Arthur Harris, the wartime leader of the British air force's Bomber Command, which was rearmed with four-engine heavy bombers capable of taking the war into the center of occupied Europe. On May 31, 1942, Cologne became the first German city to be subjected to an attack by one thousand bombers.

With the entry of the Americans into the war, the bombing strategy changed. American planes flew daytime missions aimed at the precision bombing of transportation facilities and war industries, while the British Bomber Command continued nighttime saturation bombing of all German cities with populations over 100,000. Bombing raids added an element of terror to circumstances already made difficult by growing shortages of food, clothing, and fuel. Germans especially feared the incendiary bombs, which created firestorms that swept destructive paths through the cities. Four raids on Hamburg in August 1943

The Destruction of Clydebank. The bombing of an enemy's cities brought the war home to civilian populations. This picture shows a street in Clydebank, near Glasgow in Scotland, the day after the city was bombed by the Germans in March 1941. Only 7 of the city's 12,000 houses were left undamaged; 35,000 of the 47,000 inhabitants became homeless overnight. Clydebank was Scotland's only severe bombing experience.

produced temperatures of 1,800 degrees Fahrenheit, obliterated half the city's buildings, and killed fifty thousand civilians. The ferocious bombing of Dresden from February 13 to 15, 1945, created a firestorm that may have killed as many as 100,000 inhabitants and refugees. Even some Allied leaders began to criticize what they saw as the unnecessary terror bombing of German cities. Urban dwellers became accustomed to living in air-raid shelters, usually cellars in businesses or houses. Occupants of shelters could be crushed to death if the shelters were hit directly or die by suffocation from the effects of high-explosive bombs. Not until 1943 did Nazi leaders begin to evacuate women and children to rural areas. This evacuation policy, however, created its own problems since people in country villages were often hostile to the urban newcomers.

Germany suffered enormously from the Allied bombing raids. Millions of buildings were destroyed, and possibly half a million civilians died in the raids. Nevertheless, it is highly unlikely that Allied bombing sapped the morale of the German people. Instead, Germans, whether pro-Nazi or anti-Nazi, fought on stubbornly, often driven simply by a desire to live. Nor did the bombing destroy Germany's industrial capacity. The Allied Strategic Bombing survey revealed that the production of war matériel actually increased between 1942 and 1944. Even in 1944 and 1945, Allied raids cut German production of armaments by only 7 percent. Nevertheless, the widespread destruction of transportation systems and fuel supplies made it extremely difficult for the new matériel to reach the German military. The destruction of German cities from the air did accomplish one major goal. There would be no stab-in-the-back myth after World War II as there had been after World War I. The loss of the war could not be blamed on the collapse of the home front. Many Germans understood that the home front had been a battlefront, and they had fought bravely on their front just as the soldiers had on theirs.

The bombing of civilians eventually reached a new level with the dropping of the first atomic bomb on Japan. Fearful of German attempts to create a superbomb through the use of uranium, the American government pursued a dual strategy. While sabotaging German efforts, the United States and Britain recruited scientists, including many who had fled from Germany, to develop an atomic bomb. Working under the direction of J. Robert Oppenheimer at a secret laboratory in Los Alamos, New Mexico, Allied scientists built and tested the first atomic bomb by the summer of 1945. A new era in warfare was about to begin.

Japan was especially vulnerable to air raids because its air force had been virtually destroyed in the course of the war, and its crowded cities were built of flimsy materials.

J. R. Eyerman, Life Magazine, © TimePix

Hiroshima. The most devastating destruction of civilians came near the end of World War II when the United States dropped atomic bombs on the Japanese cities of Hiroshima and Nagasaki. This panoramic view of Hiroshima after the bombing shows the incredible devastation produced by the atomic bomb.

Attacks on Japanese cities by the new American B-29 Superfortresses, the biggest bombers of the war, had begun on November 24, 1944. By the summer of 1945, many of Japan's factories had been destroyed, along with one-fourth of its dwellings. After the Japanese government decreed the mobilization of all people between the ages of thirteen and sixty into a "people's volunteer corps," President Truman and his advisers feared that Japanese fanaticism might mean a million American casualties. This concern led them to drop the atomic bomb on Hiroshima (August 6) and Nagasaki (August 9). The destruction was incredible. Of 76,000 buildings near the hypocenter of the explosion in Hiroshima, 70,000 were flattened; 140,000 of the city's 400,000 inhabitants died by the end of 1945. By the end of 1950, another 50,000 had perished from the effects of radiation.

The Aftermath of the War: The Emergence of the Cold War

The total victory of the Allies in World War II was succeeded not by true peace but by the beginnings of a new conflict known as the Cold War that dominated European and world politics until the end of the 1980s. The origins of the Cold War stemmed from the military, political, and ideological differences, especially between the Soviet Union and the United States, that became apparent at the Allied war conferences held in the last years of the war. Although Allied leaders were mostly preoccupied with how to end the war, they also were strongly motivated by differing and often conflicting visions of postwar Europe.

The Conferences at Tehran, Yalta, and Potsdam

Stalin, Roosevelt, and Churchill, the leaders of the Big Three of the Grand Alliance, met at Tehran (the capital of Iran) in November 1943 to decide the future course of the war. Their major tactical decision concerned the final assault on Germany. Churchill had wanted British and American forces to follow up their North African and Italian campaigns by an indirect attack on Germany through the Balkans. Although an extremely difficult route, this would give the Western Allies a better position in postwar central Europe. Stalin and Roosevelt, however, overruled Churchill and argued successfully for an American-British invasion of the Continent through France, which they scheduled for the spring of 1944. The acceptance of this plan had important consequences. It meant that Soviet and British-American forces would meet in defeated Germany along a north-south dividing line and that, most likely, eastern Europe would be liberated by Soviet forces. The Allies also agreed to a partition of postwar Germany, but differences over questions like the frontiers of Poland were carefully set aside. Roosevelt was pleased with the accord with Stalin. Harry Hopkins, one of Roosevelt's advisers at the conference, remarked:

> We really believed in our hearts that this was the dawn of the new day. . . . We were absolutely certain that we had won the first great victory of the peace—and by "we," I mean all of us, the whole civilized human race. The Russians had proved that they could be reasonable and far-seeing and there wasn't any doubt in the minds of the President or any of us that we could live with them and get along with them peacefully for as far into the future as any of us could imagine.[16]

Winston Churchill was more cautious about future relations with the Soviets. Although overruled at the Tehran Conference, Churchill met again with Stalin in Moscow in October 1944 and was able to pin him down to a more specific determination of postwar spheres of influence. The agreement between Churchill and Stalin, written on a scrap of paper, assigned the various Allies a certain percentage of political influence in a given area on the basis of past historical roles. The Soviet Union received 90 percent influence in Romania and 75 percent in Bulgaria, whereas Britain obtained 90 percent influence in Greece. Eastern European countries that had a strong tradition of Western ties, such as Yugoslavia and Hungary, were divided "fifty-fifty." Churchill perceived how callous this division of sovereign countries might seem from a distance. He remarked to Stalin, "Might it not be thought rather cynical if it seemed we had disposed of these issues, so fateful to millions of people, in such an offhand manner? Let us burn the paper." Stalin, not worried about what others might think, simply replied, "No, you keep it."[17]

By the time of the conference at Yalta in the Ukraine in February 1945, the defeat of Germany was a foregone conclusion. The Western powers, which had earlier believed that the Soviets were in a weak position, were now faced with the reality of eleven million Red Army soldiers taking possession of eastern and much of central Europe. Stalin was still operating under the notion of spheres of influence. He was deeply suspicious of the Western powers and desired a buffer to protect the Soviet Union from possible future Western aggression. At the same time, however, Stalin was eager to obtain economically important resources and strategic military positions. Roosevelt by this time was moving away from the notion of spheres of influence to the ideal of self-determination. He called for "the end of the system of unilateral action, exclusive alliances, and spheres of influence." The Grand Alliance approved the "Declaration on Liberated Europe." This was a pledge to assist liberated European nations in the creation of "democratic institutions of their own choice." Liberated countries were to hold free elections to determine their political systems.

At Yalta, Roosevelt sought Soviet military help against Japan. The atomic bomb was not yet assured, and American military planners feared the possible loss of as many as one million men in amphibious assaults on the Japanese home islands. Roosevelt therefore agreed to Stalin's price for military assistance against Japan: possession of Sakhalin and the Kurile Islands as well as two warm-water ports and railroad rights in Manchuria.

The Art Archive, London

The Victorious Allied Leaders at Yalta. Even before World War II ended, the leaders of the Big Three of the Grand Alliance, Churchill, Roosevelt, and Stalin (seated, left to right), met in wartime conferences to plan the final assault on Germany and negotiate the outlines of the postwar settlement. At the Yalta meeting (February 5–11, 1945), the three leaders concentrated on postwar issues. The American president, who died two months later, was already a worn-out man at Yalta.

The creation of the United Nations was a major American concern at Yalta. Roosevelt hoped to ensure the participation of the Big Three powers in a postwar international organization before difficult issues divided them into hostile camps. After a number of compromises, both Churchill and Stalin accepted Roosevelt's plans for a United Nations organization and set the first meeting for San Francisco in April 1945.

The issues of Germany and eastern Europe were treated less decisively. The Big Three reaffirmed that Germany must surrender unconditionally and created four occupation zones. Churchill, over the objections of the Soviets and Americans, insisted that the French be given one occupation zone, carved out of the British and American zones. German reparations were set at $20 billion. A compromise was also worked out in regard to Poland. It was agreed that a provisional government would be established with members of both the Lublin Poles, who were Polish Communists living in exile in the Soviet Union, and the London Poles, who were non-Communists exiled in Britain. Stalin also agreed to free elections in the future to determine a new government. But the issue of free elections in eastern Europe caused a serious rift between the Soviets and the Americans. The principle was that eastern European governments would be freely elected, but they were also supposed to be pro-Soviet. As Churchill expressed it: "The Poles will have their future in their own hands, with the single limitation that they must honestly follow in harmony with their allies, a policy friendly to Russia."[18] This attempt to reconcile two irreconcilable goals was doomed to failure, as soon became evident at the next conference of the Big Three powers.

Even before the conference at Potsdam took place in July 1945, Western relations with the Soviets were deteriorating rapidly. The Grand Alliance had been one of necessity in which disagreements had been subordinated to the pragmatic concerns of the war. The Allied Powers' only common aim was the defeat of Nazism. Once this aim had all but been accomplished, the many differences that troubled East-West relations came to the surface. Each side committed acts that the other viewed as unbecoming of "allies."

From the perspective of the Soviets, the United States' termination of Lend-Lease aid before the war was over and its failure to respond to the Soviet request for a $6 billion loan for reconstruction exposed the Western desire to keep the Soviet state weak. On the American side, the Soviet Union's failure to fulfill its Yalta pledge on the "Declaration on Liberated Europe" as applied to eastern Europe set a dangerous precedent. This was evident in Romania as early as February 1945, when the Soviets engineered a coup and installed a new government under the Communist Petra Groza, called the "Little Stalin." One month later, the Soviets sabotaged the Polish settlement by arresting the London Poles and their sympathizers and placing the Soviet-backed Lublin Poles in power. To the Americans, the Soviets seemed to be asserting control of eastern European countries under puppet Communist regimes (see Map 27.5).

The Potsdam Conference of July 1945 consequently began under a cloud of mistrust. Roosevelt had died on

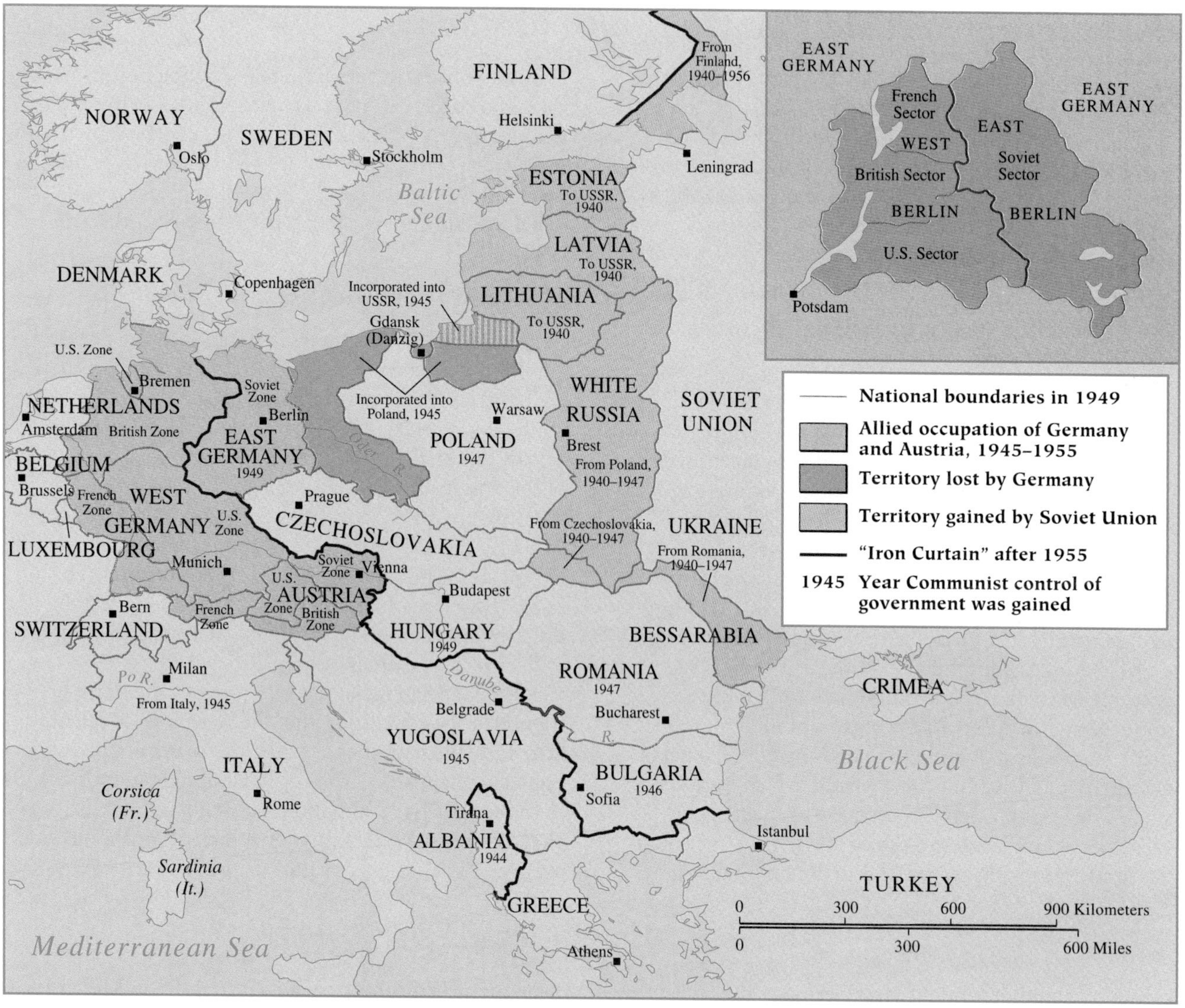

Map 27.5 Territorial Changes After World War II. In the last months of World War II, the Red Army occupied much of eastern Europe. Stalin sought pro-Soviet satellite states in the region as a buffer against future invasions from western Europe, whereas Britain and the United States wanted democratically elected governments. Soviet military control of the territory settled the question. ■ Which country gained the greatest territory at the expense of Germany?

April 12 and had been succeeded by Harry Truman. During the conference, Truman received word that the atomic bomb had been successfully tested. Some historians have argued that this knowledge resulted in Truman's stiffened resolve against the Soviets. Whatever the reasons, there was a new coldness in the relations between the Soviets and Americans. At Potsdam, Truman demanded free elections throughout eastern Europe. Stalin responded: "A freely elected government in any of these East European countries would be anti-Soviet, and that we cannot allow."[19] After a bitterly fought and devastating war, Stalin sought absolute military security. To him, it could only be gained by the presence of Communist states in eastern Europe. Free elections might result in governments hostile to the Soviets. By the middle of 1945, only an invasion by Western forces could undo developments in eastern Europe, and after the world's most destructive conflict had ended, few people favored such a policy.

The Soviets did not view their actions as dangerous expansionism but as legitimate security maneuvers. Was it not the West that had attacked the East? When Stalin sought help against the Nazis in the 1930s, had not the West turned a deaf ear? But there was little sympathy in the West for Soviet fears and even less trust in Stalin. When the American secretary of state, James Byrnes, proposed a twenty-five-year disarmament of Germany, the Soviet Union rejected it. In the West, many saw this as proof of Stalin's plans to expand in central Europe and create a Communist East German state. When Byrnes responded by announcing that American troops would be needed in Europe for an indefinite time and made moves that foreshadowed the

Emergence of the Cold War: Churchill and Stalin

Less than a year after the end of World War II, the major Allies that had fought together to destroy Hitler's Germany had divided into two hostile camps. These excerpts, taken from Winston Churchill's speech to an American audience on March 5, 1946, and Joseph Stalin's reply to Churchill only nine days later, reveal the divisions in the Western world that marked the beginning of the Cold War.

Churchill's Speech at Fulton, Missouri, March 5, 1946

From Stettin in the Baltic to Trieste in the Adriatic, an iron curtain has descended across the continent. Behind that line lie all the capitals of the ancient states of central and eastern Europe. Warsaw, Berlin, Prague, Vienna, Budapest, Belgrade, Bucharest, and Sofia, all these famous cities and the populations around them lie in the Soviet sphere and all are subject, in one form or another, not only to Soviet influence but to a very high and increasing measure of control from Moscow. . . .

The Russian-dominated Polish Government has been encouraged to make enormous and wrongful inroads upon Germany, and mass expulsions of millions of Germans on a scale grievous and undreamed of are now taking place. The Communist parties, which were very small in all these eastern states of Europe, have been raised to preeminence and power far beyond their numbers and are seeking everywhere to obtain totalitarian control. Police governments are prevailing in nearly every case, and so far, except in Czechoslovakia, there is no true democracy. . . . Whatever conclusions may be drawn from these facts—and facts they are—this is certainly not the liberated Europe we fought to build up. Nor is it one which contains the essentials of permanent peace.

Stalin's Reply to Churchill, March 14, 1946

In substance, Mr. Churchill now stands in the position of a firebrand of war. And Mr. Churchill is not alone here. He has friends not only in England but also in the United States of America.

In this respect, one is reminded remarkably of Hitler and his friends. Hitler began to set war loose by announcing his racial theory, declaring that only people speaking the German language represent a fully valuable nation. Mr. Churchill begins to set war loose, also by a racial theory, maintaining that only nations speaking the English language are fully valuable nations, called upon to decide the destinies of the entire world.

The German racial theory brought Hitler and his friends to the conclusion that the Germans, as the only fully valuable nation, must rule over other nations. The English racial theory brings Mr. Churchill and his friends to the conclusion that nations speaking the English language, being the only fully valuable nations, should rule over the remaining nations of the world.

creation of an independent West Germany, the Soviets saw this as a direct threat to Soviet security in Europe.

As the war slowly receded into the past, the reality of conflicting ideologies had reappeared. Many in the West interpreted Soviet policy as part of a worldwide Communist conspiracy. The Soviets, for their part, viewed Western, especially American, policy as nothing less than global capitalist expansionism or, in Leninist terms, economic imperialism. Vyacheslav Molotov, the Russian foreign minister, referred to the Americans as "insatiable imperialists" and "war-mongering groups of adventurers."[20] In March 1946, in a speech to an American audience, former British prime minister Winston Churchill declared that "an iron curtain" had "descended across the continent," dividing Germany and Europe into two hostile camps. Stalin branded Churchill's speech a "call to war with the Soviet Union" (see the box above). Only months after the world's most devastating conflict had ended, the world seemed once again bitterly divided. Would the twentieth-century crisis of Western civilization never end?

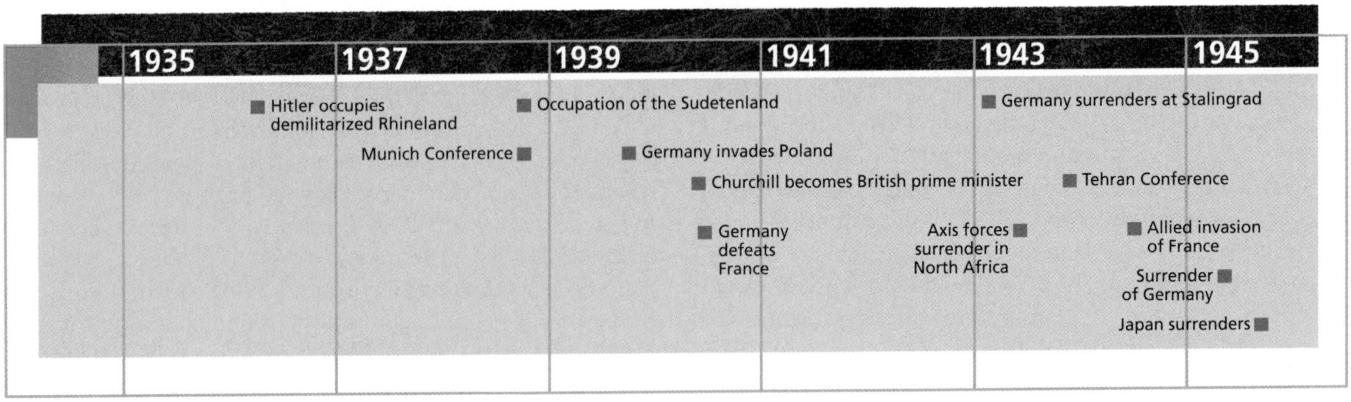

Conclusion

Between 1933 and 1939, Europeans watched as Adolf Hitler rebuilt Germany into a great military power. For Hitler, military power was an absolute prerequisite for the creation of a German racial empire that would dominate Europe and the world for generations to come. If Hitler had been successful, the Nazi New Order, built on authoritarianism, racial extermination, and the brutal oppression of peoples, would have meant a triumph of barbarism and the end of freedom and equality, which, however imperfectly realized, had become important ideals in Western civilization.

The Nazis lost, but only after tremendous sacrifices and costs. Much of European civilization lay in ruins, and the old Europe had disappeared forever. Europeans, who had been accustomed to dominating the world at the beginning of the twentieth century, now watched helplessly at mid-century as the two new superpowers created by the two world wars took control of their destinies. Even before the last battles had been fought, the United States and the Soviet Union had arrived at different visions of the postwar European world. No sooner had the war ended than their differences gave rise to a new and potentially even more devastating conflict known as the Cold War. Yet even though Europeans seemed merely pawns in the struggle between the two superpowers, they managed to stage a remarkable recovery of their own civilization.

Notes

1. Adolf Hitler, *Mein Kampf,* trans. Ralph Manheim (Boston, 1971), p. 654.
2. *Documents on German Foreign Policy* (London, 1956), ser. D, vol. 2, p. 358.
3. Ibid., vol. 7, p. 204.
4. Quoted in Norman Rich, *Hitler's War Aims* (New York, 1973), vol. 1, p. 129.
5. Albert Speer, *Spandau,* trans. Richard Winston and Clara Winston (New York, 1976), p. 50.
6. *Nazi Conspiracy and Aggression* (Washington, D.C., 1946), vol. 6, p. 262.
7. International Military Tribunal, *Trial of the Major War Criminals* (Nuremberg, 1947–1949), vol. 22, p. 480.
8. Adolf Hitler, *My New Order,* ed. Raoul de Roussy de Sales (New York, 1941), pp. 21–22.
9. Quoted in Lucy Dawidowicz, *The War Against the Jews* (New York, 1975), p. 106.
10. *Nazi Conspiracy and Aggression,* vol. 5, pp. 341–342.
11. Quoted in Raul Hilberg, *The Destruction of the European Jews,* rev. ed. (New York, 1985), vol. 1, pp. 332–333.
12. *Nazi Conspiracy and Aggression,* vol. 6, p. 789.
13. Quoted in John Campbell, *The Experience of World War II* (New York, 1989), p. 170.
14. Quoted in Claudia Koonz, "Mothers in the Fatherland: Women in Nazi Germany," in Renate Bridenthal and Claudia Koonz, eds., *Becoming Visible: Women in European History* (Boston, 1977), p. 466.
15. Quoted in Campbell, *The Experience of World War II,* p. 177.
16. Quoted in Robert E. Sherwood, *Roosevelt and Hopkins: An Intimate History* (New York, 1948), p. 870.
17. Quoted in Walter Laqueur, *Europe Since Hitler,* rev. ed. (New York, 1982), p. 102.
18. Quoted in Norman Graebner, *Cold War Diplomacy, 1945–1960* (Princeton, N.J., 1962), p. 117.
19. Quoted in ibid.
20. Quoted in Wilfried Loth, *The Division of the World, 1941–1955* (New York, 1988), p. 81.

Suggestions for Further Reading

The basic study of Germany's foreign policy from 1933 to 1939 can be found in G. Weinberg, *The Foreign Policy of Hitler's Germany: Diplomatic Revolution in Europe, 1933–36* (Chicago, 1970), and *The Foreign Policy of Hitler's Germany: Starting World War II, 1937–1939* (Chicago, 1980). For a detailed account of the immediate events leading to World War II, see D. C. Watt, *How War Came: The Immediate Origins of the Second World War, 1938–1939* (New York, 1989).

Hitler's war aims and the importance of ideology to those aims are examined in N. Rich, *Hitler's War Aims,* vol. 1, *Ideology, the Nazi State, and the Course of Expansion* (New York, 1973), and vol. 2, *The Establishment of the New Order* (New York, 1974). On the origins of the war in the Pacific, see A. Iriye, *The Origins of the Second World War in Asia and the Pacific* (London, 1987). General works on World War II include the comprehensive work by G. Weinberg, *A World at Arms: A Global History of World War II* (Cambridge, 1994); M. K. Dziewanowski, *War at Any Price: World War II in Europe, 1939–1945,* 2d ed. (Englewood Cliffs, N.J., 1991); J. Campbell, *The Experience of World War II* (New York, 1989); and G. Wright, *The Ordeal of Total War, 1939–1945* (New York, 1968). On Hitler as a military leader, see R. Lewin, *Hitler's Mistakes* (New York, 1986). The Eastern Front is covered in J. Erickson, *Stalin's War with Germany,* vol. 1, *The Road to Stalingrad;* vol. 2, *The Road to Berlin* (London, 1973, 1985), and O. Bartov, *The Eastern Front, 1941–45: German Troops and the Barbarisation of Warfare* (London, 1986). The second front in Europe is examined in C. D'Este, *Decision in Normandy* (London, 1983).

A standard work on the German New Order in Russia is A. Dallin, *German Rule in Russia, 1941–1945,* rev. ed. (London, 1981). On Poland, see J. T. Gross, *Polish Society Under German Occupation* (Princeton, N.J., 1981). On foreign labor, see E. Homze, *Foreign Labor in Nazi Germany* (Princeton, N.J., 1967). Resistance movements in Europe are covered in M. R. D. Foot, *Resistance: An Analysis of European Resistance to Nazism* (London, 1976). A fundamental study on resistance in Germany is P. Hoffmann, *The History of the German Resistance, 1933–1945,* trans. R. Barry (Cambridge, Mass., 1977). There is a good collection of articles in W. Benz and W. H. Pehle, eds., *Encyclopedia of German Resistance to the Nazi Movement* (New York, 1997). On women in resistance movements, see M. Rossiter, *Women in the Resistance* (New York, 1986).

The best studies of the Holocaust include R. Hilberg, *The Destruction of the European Jews,* rev. ed., 3 vols. (New York, 1985); L. Dawidowicz, *The War Against the Jews* (New York, 1975); L. Yahil, *The Holocaust* (Oxford, 1990); and M. Gilbert, *The Holocaust: The History of the Jews of Europe During the Second World War* (New York, 1985). For brief studies, see J. Fischel, *The Holocaust* (Westport, Conn., 1998), and R. S. Botwinick, *A History of the Holocaust* (Upper Saddle River,

N.J., 1996). On the extermination camps, see K. G. Feig, *Hitler's Death Camps: The Sanity of Madness* (New York, 1981). Other Nazi atrocities are examined in R. C. Lukas, F*orgotten Holocaust: The Poles Under German Occupation, 1939–44* (Lexington, Ky., 1986), and B. Wytwycky, *The Other Holocaust* (Washington, D.C., 1980).

General studies on the impact of total war include J. Costello, *Love, Sex and War: Changing Values, 1939–1945* (London, 1985); P. Summerfield, *Women Workers in the Second World War: Production and Patriarchy in Conflict* (London, 1984); and M. R. Marrus, *The Unwanted: European Refugees in the Twentieth Century* (New York, 1985). On the home front in Germany, see E. R. Beck, *Under the Bombs: The German Home Front, 1942–1945* (Lexington, Ky., 1986); M. Kitchen, *Nazi Germany at War* (New York, 1995); and J. Stephenson, *The Nazi Organisation of Women* (London, 1981). On the home front in Britain, see A. Marwick, *The Home Front* (London, 1976). The Soviet Union during the war is examined in M. Harrison, *Soviet Planning in Peace and War, 1938–1945* (Cambridge, 1985). On the American home front, see the collection of essays in K. P. O'Brien and L. H. Parsons, *The Home-Front War: World War II and American Society* (Westport, Conn., 1995).

On the destruction of Germany by bombing raids, see H. Rumpf, *The Bombing of Germany* (London, 1963). The German bombing of Britain is covered in T. Harrisson, *Living Through the Blitz* (London, 1985). On Hiroshima, see A. Chisholm, *Faces of Hiroshima* (London, 1985).

On the emergence of the Cold War, see W. Loth, *The Division of the World, 1941–1955* (New York, 1988), and the more extensive list of references at the end of Chapter 28. On the wartime summit conferences, see H. Feis, *Churchill, Roosevelt, Stalin: The War They Waged and the Peace They Sought,* 2d ed. (Princeton, N.J., 1967).

For additional reading, go to InfoTrac College Edition, your online research library at http://web1.infotrac-college.com

Enter the search term *World War, 1939–1945* using Key Terms.

Enter the search term *socialism history* using Key Terms.

Enter the search term *Holocaust* using the Subject Guide.

Enter the search term *Hitler* using Key Terms.

CHAPTER

28

Cold War and a New Western World, 1945–1970

© Bettmann/CORBIS

CHAPTER OUTLINE

- Development of the Cold War
- The End of European Colonies
- Recovery and Renewal in Europe
- The United States and Canada: A New Era
- The Emergence of a New Society
- Conclusion

FOCUS QUESTIONS

- Why were the United States and the Soviet Union suspicious of each other after World War II, and what events between 1945 and 1949 heightened the tensions between the two nations?
- What were the major changes in the European colonies in Africa, the Middle East, and Asia between 1945 and 1970?
- What were the main developments in the Soviet Union and Eastern Europe between 1945 and 1970?
- What were the main political developments in the nations of Western Europe and North America between 1945 and 1970?
- What major changes occurred in Western society between 1945 and 1970?
- What were the similarities and differences in the political, social, and economic history of Eastern Europe and Western Europe between 1945 and 1970?

THE END OF WORLD WAR II in Europe had been met with great joy. One visitor to Moscow reported: "I looked out of the window [at 2 A.M.], almost everywhere there were lights in the window—people were staying awake. Everyone embraced everyone else, someone sobbed aloud." But after the victory parades and celebrations, Europeans awoke to a devastating realization: their civilization was in ruins. Some wondered if Europe would ever regain its former prosperity and importance. Winston Churchill wrote: "What is Europe now? A rubble heap, a charnel house, a breeding ground of pestilence and hate." There was ample reason for his pessimism. Almost forty million people (both soldiers and civilians) had been killed during the preceding six years. Massive air raids and artillery bombardments had reduced many of the great cities of Europe to heaps of rubble. The Polish capital of Warsaw had been almost completely obliterated. An American general described Berlin: "Wherever we looked we saw desolation. It was like a city of the dead. Suffering and shock were visible in every face. Dead bodies still remained in canals and lakes and were being dug out from under bomb debris." Millions of Europeans faced starvation as grain harvests were only half of what they had been in 1939. Millions were also homeless. In the parts of the Soviet Union that had been occupied by the Germans, almost 25 million people were without homes. The destruction of bridges, roads, and railroads had left transportation systems paralyzed. Untold millions of people had been uprooted by the war; now they became "displaced persons," trying to find food and then their way home. Eleven million prisoners of war had to be returned to their native countries while fifteen million Germans and Eastern Europeans were driven out of countries where they were no longer wanted. Yet despite the chaos, Europe was soon on the road to a remarkable recovery. Already by 1950, Europe's industrial and agricultural output was 30 percent above prewar levels.

World War II had cost Europe more than physical destruction, however. European supremacy in world affairs had also been destroyed. After 1945, the colonial empires of the European nations disintegrated, and Europe's place in the world changed radically. As the Cold War conflict between the world's two superpowers—the United States and the Soviet Union—intensified, the European nations were divided into two armed camps dependent on one or the other of these two major powers. The United States and the Soviet Union, whose rivalry raised the specter of nuclear war, seemed to hold the survival of Europe and the world in their hands.

Development of the Cold War

Even before World War II had ended, the two major Allied Powers—the United States and the Soviet Union—had begun to disagree on the nature of the postwar European world. Unity had been maintained during the war because of the urgent need to defeat the Axis Powers, but once they were defeated, the differences between the Americans and Soviets again surged to the front.

Confrontation of the Superpowers

Considerable historical debate has been waged about who was responsible for starting the Cold War. Both the United States and the Soviet Union took steps at the end of World War II that were unwise or might have been avoided. Both nations, however, were working within a framework conditioned by the past. Ultimately, the rivalry between the two superpowers stemmed from their different historical perspectives and their irreconcilable political ambitions. Intense competition for political and military supremacy had long been a regular feature of Western civilization. The United States and the Soviet Union were the heirs of that European tradition of power politics, and it should not surprise us that two such different systems would seek to extend their way of life to the rest of the world. Because of its need to feel secure on its western border, the Soviet Union was not prepared to give up the advantages it had gained in Eastern Europe from Germany's defeat. But neither were American leaders willing to give up the power and prestige the United States had gained throughout the world. Suspicious of each other's motives, the United States and the Soviet Union soon raised their mutual fears to a level of intense competition. Between 1945 and 1949, a number of events embroiled the two countries in continual conflict.

Eastern Europe was the first area of disagreement. The United States and Great Britain had championed self-determination and democratic freedom for the liberated nations of Eastern Europe. Stalin, however, fearful that the Eastern European nations would return to traditional anti-Soviet attitudes if they were permitted free elections, opposed the West's plans. Having liberated Eastern Europe from the Nazis, the Red Army proceeded to install pro-Soviet governing regimes in Poland, Romania, Bulgaria, and Hungary. These pro-Soviet governments satisfied Stalin's desire for a buffer zone against the West, but the local populations and their sympathizers in the West saw the regimes as an expansion of Stalin's empire. Only another war could change this situation, and few people wanted another armed conflict.

A civil war in Greece provided another arena for confrontation between the superpowers. In 1946, the Communist People's Liberation Army and the anti-Communist forces supported by the British were fighting each other for control of Greece. President Harry S Truman of the United States, alarmed by British weakness and the possibility of Soviet expansion into the eastern Mediterranean, responded with the Truman Doctrine (see the box on p. 805). The Truman Doctrine said in essence that the United States would provide money to countries that claimed they were threatened by Communist expansion. If the Soviets were not stopped in Greece, the Truman argument ran, then the United States would have to face the spread of communism throughout the free world. As Dean Acheson, the American secretary of state explained: "Like apples in a barrel infected by disease, the corruption of Greece would infect Iran and all the East . . . likewise Africa . . . Italy . . . France. . . . Not since Rome and Carthage had there been such a polarization of power on this earth."[1] In March 1947, Truman requested $400 million in economic and military aid for Greece and Turkey from the U.S. Congress.

The proclamation of the Truman Doctrine was followed in June 1947 by the European Recovery Program,

The Truman Doctrine

By 1947, the battle lines had been clearly drawn in the Cold War. This selection is taken from a speech by President Harry S Truman to the U.S. Congress in which he justified his request for aid to Greece and Turkey. Truman expressed the urgent need to contain the expansion of communism.

President Harry S Truman, Address to Congress, March 12, 1947

The peoples of a number of countries of the world have recently had totalitarian regimes forced upon them against their will. The Government of the United States has made frequent protests against coercion and intimidation, in violation of the Yalta agreement, in Poland, Romania, and Bulgaria. I must also state that in a number of other countries there have been similar developments.

At the present moment in world history nearly every nation must choose between alternative ways of life. The choice is too often not a free one.

One way of life is based upon the will of the majority, and is distinguished by free institutions, representative government, free elections, guarantees of individual liberty, freedom of speech and religion, and freedom from political oppression.

The second way of life is based upon the will of a minority forcibly imposed upon the majority. It relies upon terror and oppression, a controlled press and radio, fixed elections, and the suppression of personal freedoms.

I believe that it must be the policy of the United States to support free peoples who are resisting attempted subjugation by armed minorities or by outside pressures.

I believe that we must assist free people to work out their own destinies in their own way.

I believe that our help should be primarily through economic and financial aid which is essential to economic stability and orderly political processes. . . . I therefore ask the Congress for assistance to Greece and Turkey in the amount of $400 million.

better known as the Marshall Plan. Intended to rebuild prosperity and stability, this program included $13 billion for the economic recovery of war-torn Europe. Underlying it was the belief that Communist aggression fed off economic turmoil. General George C. Marshall had noted in his commencement speech at Harvard: "Our policy is not directed against any country or doctrine but against hunger, poverty, desperation and chaos."[2] The Marshall Plan did not intend to shut out either the Soviet Union or its Eastern European satellite states, but they refused to participate. According to the Soviet view, the Marshall Plan aimed at the "construction of a bloc of states bound by obligations to the USA, and to guarantee the American loans in return for the relinquishing by the European states of their economic and later also their political independence."[3] The Soviets, however, were in no position to compete financially with the United States and could do little to counter the Marshall Plan.

By 1947, the split in Europe between East and West had become a fact of life. At the end of World War II, the United States had favored a quick end to its commitments in Europe. But American fears of Soviet aims caused the United States to play an increasingly important role in European affairs. In an article in *Foreign Affairs* in July 1947, George Kennan, a well-known American diplomat with much knowledge of Soviet affairs, advocated a policy of containment against further aggressive Soviet moves. Kennan favored the "adroit and vigilant application of counterforce at a series of constantly shifting geographical and political points, corresponding to the shifts and maneuvers of Soviet policy." After the Soviet blockade of Berlin in 1948, containment of the Soviet Union became formal American policy.

The fate of Germany also became a source of heated contention between East and West. Besides denazification and the partitioning of Germany (and Berlin) into four occupied zones, the Allied powers had agreed on little else with regard to the conquered nation. The Soviets, hardest hit by the war, took reparations from Germany in the form of booty. The technology-starved Soviets dismantled and removed to the Soviet Union 380 factories from the western zones of Berlin before transferring their control to the Western powers. By the summer of 1946, two hundred chemical, paper, and textile factories in the Soviets' East German zone had likewise been shipped to the Soviet Union. At the same time, the German Communist Party was reestablished under the control of Walter Ulbricht (1893–1973) and was soon in charge of the political reconstruction of the Soviet zone in eastern Germany.

At the same time, the British, French, and Americans gradually began to merge their zones economically and by February 1948 were making plans for the unification of these three western sections of Germany and the formal creation of a West German federal government. The Soviets responded with a blockade of West Berlin that allowed neither trucks nor trains to enter the three western zones of Berlin. The Soviets hoped to secure economic control of all Berlin and force the Western powers to halt the creation of a separate West German state.

The Western powers faced a dilemma. Direct military confrontation seemed dangerous, and no one wished to risk World War III. Therefore, an attempt to break through the blockade with tanks and trucks was ruled out. But how could the 2.5 million people in the three western zones of Berlin be kept alive when the whole city was inside the Soviet zone? The solution was the Berlin Air Lift. At its peak, 13,000 tons of supplies were flown to Berlin daily. The Soviets, also not wanting war, did not interfere and finally lifted the blockade in May 1949. The blockade of Berlin had severely increased tensions between the United States and the Soviet Union and brought the separation of Germany into two states. The West German Federal Republic was formally created in September 1949, and a month later, a separate German Democratic Republic was established in East Germany. Berlin remained a divided city and the source of much contention between East and West.

In that same year, the Cold War spread from Europe to the rest of the world. The victory of the Chinese Communists in 1949 in the Chinese civil war brought a new Communist regime and only intensified American fears about the spread of communism. The Soviet Union also detonated its first atomic bomb in 1949, and all too soon, both powers were involved in an escalating arms race that resulted in the construction of ever more destructive nuclear weapons. Soon the search for security took the form of mutual deterrence, the belief that an arsenal of nuclear weapons prevented war by assuring that even if one nation launched its nuclear weapons in a preemptive first strike, the other nation would still be able to respond and devastate the attacker. Therefore, the assumption was that neither side would risk using the massive arsenals that had been assembled.

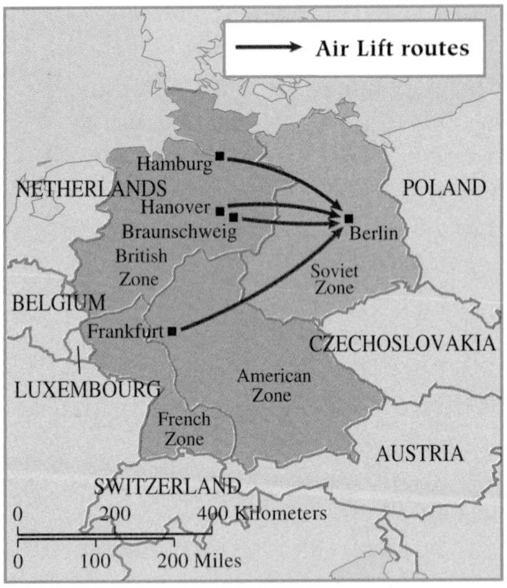

The Berlin Air Lift

The search for security in the new world of the Cold War also led to the formation of military alliances. The North Atlantic Treaty Organization (NATO) was formed in April 1949 when Belgium, Britain, Denmark, France, Iceland, Italy, Luxembourg, the Netherlands, Norway, and Portugal signed a treaty with the United States and Canada. All the powers agreed to provide mutual assistance if any one of them was attacked. A few years later West Germany, Greece, and Turkey joined NATO.

The Eastern European states soon followed suit. In 1949, they had already formed the Council for Mutual Economic Assistance (COMECON) for economic cooperation. Then in 1955, Albania, Bulgaria, Czechoslovakia, East Germany, Hungary, Poland, Romania, and the Soviet Union organized a formal military alliance in the Warsaw Pact. Once again, Europe was tragically divided into hostile alliance systems (see Map 28.1).

New Sources of Contention

A system of military alliances spread to the rest of the world after the United States became involved in the Korean War in 1950. Korea had been liberated from the Japanese in 1945 but was soon divided into two parts. The land north of the 38th parallel became the Democratic People's Republic of Korea (North Korea) and was supported by the Soviet

The Berlin Air Lift. The Berlin Air Lift enabled the United States to fly 13,000 tons of supplies daily to Berlin and thus break the Soviet land blockade of the city. In this photograph, residents of West Berlin are watching another American plane arrive with supplies for the city.

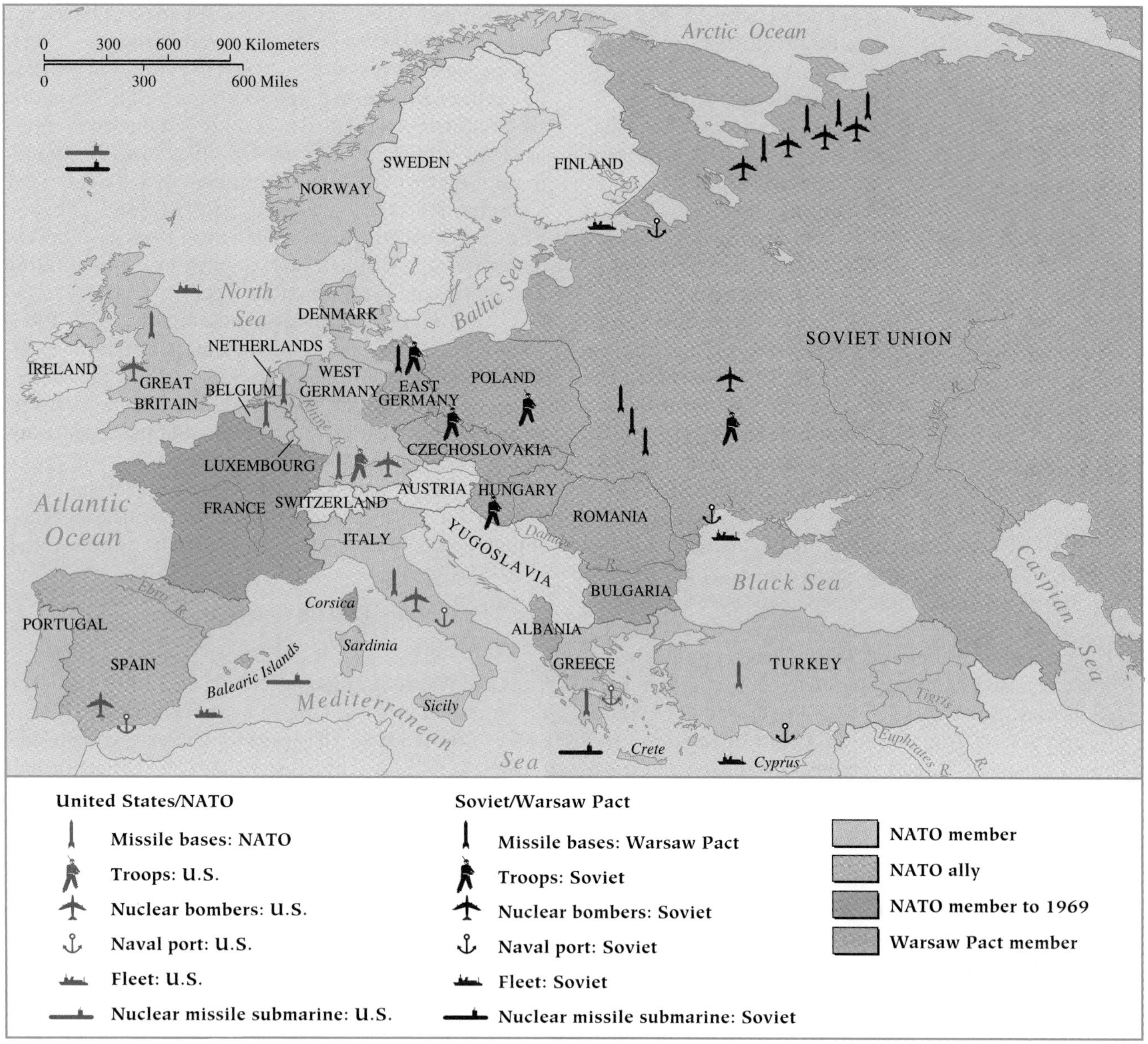

Map 28.1 The New European Alliance Systems in the 1950s and 1960s. With the United States as its leader, NATO formed in 1949 to counter the perceived military threat of the Soviet Union and its Eastern European satellites, which formally constituted the Warsaw Pact in 1955. Soviet and American troops, each backed by nuclear weapons, directly faced each other, heightening Cold War tensions. ■ Which NATO countries shared a border with one or more Warsaw Pact countries?

Union. The Republic of Korea (South Korea) received aid from the United States. On June 25, 1950, with the apparent approval of Joseph Stalin, North Korean troops invaded South Korea. The Americans, seeing this as yet another example of Communist aggression and expansion, gained the support of the United Nations and intervened by sending American troops to turn back the invasion. By September, United Nations forces (mostly Americans and South Koreans) under the command of General Douglas MacArthur marched northward across the 38th parallel with the aim of unifying Korea under a single non-Communist government. But Mao Zedong (1893–1976), the leader of Communist China, then sent Chinese forces into the fray and forced MacArthur's troops to retreat back to South Korea. Believing that the Chinese were simply the puppets of Moscow, American policymakers created an image of communism as a monolithic force directed by the Soviet Union. When two more years of fighting failed to produce a conclusive victory, an armistice was finally signed in 1953. The 38th parallel remained roughly the boundary

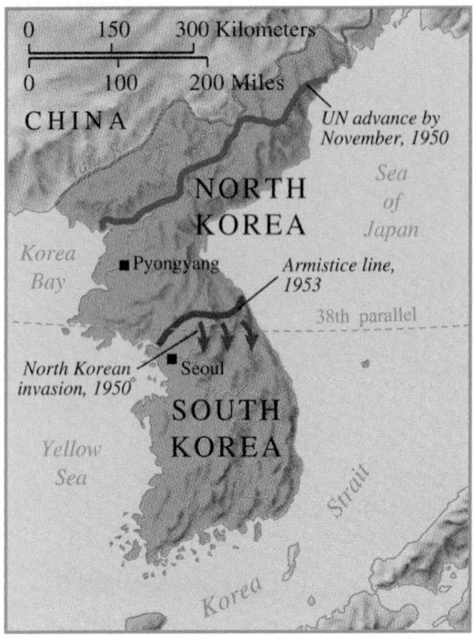

The Korean War

line between North and South Korea. To many Americans, the policy of containing communism had succeeded in Asia, just as it had earlier in Europe, despite the cost of losing more than fifty thousand men in the war.

The Korean experience seemed to confirm American fears of Communist expansion and reinforced American determination to contain Soviet power. In the mid-1950s, the administration of President Dwight D. Eisenhower (1890–1969) adopted a policy of massive retaliation, which advocated the full use of American nuclear bombs to counteract even a Soviet ground attack in Europe. Moreover, American military alliances were extended around the world. As President Eisenhower explained: "The freedom we cherish and defend in Europe and in the Americas is no different from the freedom that is imperiled in Asia." The Central Treaty Organization (CENTO) of Turkey, Iraq, Iran, Pakistan, Great Britain, and the United States was intended to prevent the Soviet Union from expanding at the expense of its southern neighbors. To stem Soviet aggression in the East, the United States, Britain, France, Pakistan, Thailand, the Philippines, Australia, and New Zealand formed the Southeast Asia Treaty Organization (SEATO). By the mid-1950s, the United States found itself allied militarily with forty-two states around the world.

Despite the continued escalation of the Cold War, hopes for a new era of peaceful coexistence also appeared. The death of Stalin in 1953 caused some people in the West to think that the new Soviet leadership might be more flexible in its policies. But this optimism proved premature. A summit conference at Geneva in 1955 between President Eisenhower and Nikolai Bulganin, then leader of the Soviet government, produced no real benefits. A year later, all talk of rapprochement between East and West temporarily ceased when the Soviet Union used its armed forces to crush Hungary's attempt to assert its independence from Soviet control.

A crisis over Berlin also added to the tension in the late 1950s. In August 1957, the Soviet Union had launched its first intercontinental ballistic missile (ICBM) and, shortly thereafter, *Sputnik I,* the first space satellite. Fueled by partisan political debate, fears of a "missile gap" between the United States and the Soviet Union seized the American public. Nikita Khrushchev (1894–1971), the new leader of the Soviet Union, attempted to take advantage of the American frenzy over missiles to solve the problem of West Berlin. West Berlin had remained a "Western island" of prosperity in the midst of the relatively poverty-stricken East Germany. Many East Germans also managed to escape East Germany by fleeing through West Berlin.

In November 1958, Khrushchev announced that, unless the West removed its forces from West Berlin within six months, he would turn over control of the access routes to Berlin to the East Germans. Unwilling to accept an ultimatum that would have abandoned West Berlin to the Communists, Eisenhower and the West stood firm, and Khrushchev eventually backed down. In 1961, the East German government built a wall separating West Berlin from East Berlin, and the Berlin issue faded.

It was revived when John F. Kennedy (1917–1963) became the American president. During a summit meeting in Vienna in June 1961, Khrushchev threatened Kennedy with another six-month ultimatum over West Berlin. Kennedy left Vienna convinced of the need to deal firmly with the Soviet Union, and Khrushchev was forced once again to lift his six-month ultimatum. Determined to achieve some foreign policy success, the Soviet leader soon embarked on an even more dangerous venture in Cuba.

The Cuban Missile Crisis and the Move Toward Détente

The Cold War confrontation between the United States and the Soviet Union reached frightening levels during the Cuban Missile Crisis. In 1959, a left-wing revolutionary named Fidel Castro (b. 1927) had overthrown the Cuban dictator Fulgencio Batista and established a Soviet-supported totalitarian regime. In 1961, an American-supported attempt to invade Cuba via the Bay of Pigs and overthrow Castro's regime ended in utter failure. The next year, in 1962, the Soviet Union decided to station nuclear missiles in Cuba. The United States was not prepared to allow nuclear weapons to be within such close striking distance of the American mainland, even though it had placed nuclear weapons in Turkey within easy range of the Soviet Union. Khrushchev was quick to point out that "your rockets are in Turkey. You are worried by Cuba . . . because it is 90 miles from the American coast. But Turkey is next to us."[4] When U.S. intelligence discovered that a Soviet fleet carrying missiles was heading to Cuba, President Kennedy decided to blockade Cuba and prevent the fleet from reaching its destination. This approach to the problem had the benefit of delaying confrontation and giving each side time to find a peaceful solution (see the box on p. 809). Khrushchev agreed to turn back the fleet if Kennedy pledged not to invade Cuba. In a conciliatory letter to Kennedy, Khrushchev wrote:

> We and you ought not to pull on the ends of the rope in which you have tied the knot of war, because the more the two of us pull, the tighter that knot will be tied. And a moment may come when that knot will be tied too tight that even he who tied it will not have the strength to untie it. . . . Let us not only relax the forces pulling on the ends of the rope, let us take measures to untie that knot. We are ready for this.[5]

The Cuban Missile Crisis brought the world frighteningly close to nuclear war. Indeed, in 1992, a high-ranking Soviet officer revealed that short-range rockets

The Cuban Missile Crisis from Khrushchev's Perspective

The Cuban Missile Crisis was one of the sobering experiences of the Cold War. It led the two superpowers to seek new ways to lessen the tensions between them. This version of the events is taken from the memoirs of Nikita Khrushchev.

Nikita Khrushchev, Khrushchev Remembers

I will explain what the Caribbean crisis of October 1962, was all about.... At the time that Fidel Castro led his revolution to victory and entered Havana with his troops, we had no idea what political course his regime would follow. ... All the while the Americans had been watching Castro closely. At first they thought that the capitalist underpinnings of the Cuban economy would remain intact. So by the time Castro announced that he was going to put Cuba on the road toward Socialism, the Americans had already missed their chance to do any thing about it by simply exerting their influence: there were no longer any forces left which could be organized to fight on America's behalf in Cuba. That left only one alternative—invasion!...

After Castro's crushing victory over the counterrevolutionaries we intensified our military aid to Cuba.... We were sure that the Americans would never reconcile themselves to the existence of Castro's Cuba. They feared, as much as we hoped, that a Socialist Cuba might become a magnet that would attract other Latin American countries to Socialism.... It was clear to me that we might very well lose Cuba if we didn't take some decisive steps in her defense.... We had to think up some way of confronting America with more than words. We had to establish a tangible and effective deterrent to American interference in the Caribbean. But what exactly? The logical answer was missiles. We knew that American missiles were aimed against us in Turkey and Italy, to say nothing of West Germany.... My thinking went like this: if we installed the missiles secretly and then if the United States discovered the missiles were there after they were already poised and ready to strike, the Americans would think twice before trying to liquidate our installations by military means.... I want to make one thing absolutely clear: when we put our ballistic missiles in Cuba we had no desire to start a war. On the contrary, our principal aim was only to deter America from starting a war....

President Kennedy issued an ultimatum, demanding that we remove our missiles and bombers from Cuba.... We sent the Americans a note saying that we agreed to remove our missiles and bombers on the condition that the President give us his assurance that there would be no invasion of Cuba by the forces of the United States or anybody else. Finally Kennedy gave in and agreed to make a statement giving us such an assurance.... It had been, to say the least, an interesting and challenging situation. The two most powerful nations of the world had been squared off against each other, each with its finger on the button. You'd have thought that war was inevitable. But both sides showed that if the desire to avoid war is strong enough, even the most pressing dispute can be solved by compromise. And a compromise over Cuba was indeed found. The episode ended in a triumph of common sense.... It was a great victory for us, though, that we had been able to extract from Kennedy a promise that neither America nor any of her allies would invade Cuba.... The Caribbean crisis was a triumph of Soviet foreign policy and a personal triumph in my own career as a statesman and as a member of the collective leadership. We achieved, I would say, a spectacular success without having to fire a single shot!

armed with nuclear devices would have been used against American troops if the United States had invaded Cuba, an option that President Kennedy fortunately had rejected. The intense feeling that the world might have been annihilated in a few days had a profound influence on both sides. A hotline communication system between Moscow and Washington was installed in 1963 to expedite rapid communication between the two superpowers in a time of crisis. In the same year, the two powers agreed to ban nuclear tests in the atmosphere, a step that at least served to lessen the tensions between the two nations.

The Vietnam War

By that time, the United States had also been drawn into a new confrontation that had an important impact on the Cold War—the Vietnam War. After Vietnamese forces had defeated their French colonial masters in 1954, Vietnam had been divided. A strongly nationalistic regime in the north under Ho Chi Minh (1890–1969) received Soviet aid, while American sponsors worked to establish a pro-Western regime in South Vietnam. President Kennedy maintained Eisenhower's policy of providing military and financial aid to the regime of Ngo Dinh Diem, the autocratic ruler of South Vietnam. But the Kennedy administration grew increasingly disenchanted with the Diem regime, which was corrupt and seemed incapable of gaining any strong support from the people. From the American point of view, this lack of support simply undermined the ability of the South Vietnamese government to deal with the Vietcong, the South Vietnamese Communist guerrillas who were being supported by the North Vietnamese. In November 1963, the American government supported a military coup that overthrew the Diem regime. However, the new military government seemed even less able to govern the country.

In 1964, under President Lyndon B. Johnson (1908–1973), increasing numbers of American troops were sent to

CHRONOLOGY

The Cold War

Truman Doctrine	1947
European Recovery Program (Marshall Plan)	1947
Berlin blockade	1948–1949
Communists win civil war in China	1949
Soviet Union explodes first atomic bomb	1949
Formation of North Atlantic Treaty Organization	1949
Formation of COMECON	1949
Korean War	1950–1953
Formation of Warsaw Pact	1955
Berlin Crisis	1958
Vienna summit	1961
Cuban Missile Crisis	1962
Vietnam War	1964–1973

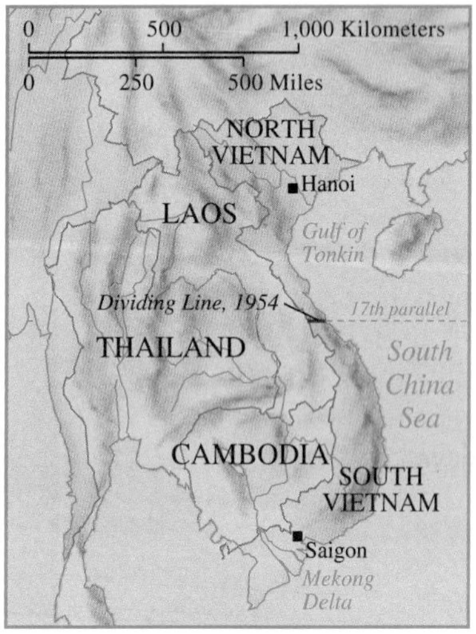

The Vietnam War

Vietnam to defeat the Vietcong and keep the Communist regime of the north from uniting the entire country under its control. Although nationalism played a powerful role in this conflict, American policymakers saw it in terms of a domino theory concerning the spread of communism. If the Communists succeeded in Vietnam, so the argument went, all the other countries in Asia freeing themselves from colonial domination would fall, like dominoes, to communism.

Despite their massive superiority in equipment and firepower, American forces failed to prevail over the persistence of the North Vietnamese and especially the Vietcong. These guerrilla forces were extremely effective against American troops. Natives of Vietnam, they were able to live off the land, disappear among the people, and attack when least expected. Many South Vietnamese villagers were so opposed to their own government that they sheltered and supported the Vietcong.

The growing number of American troops sent to Vietnam soon produced a persistent antiwar movement in the United States, especially among college students of draft age. The mounting destruction and increasing brutalization of the war, brought into American homes every evening on television, also turned American public opinion against the war. Finally, in 1973, President Richard Nixon (1913–1994) reached an agreement with North Vietnam that allowed the United

CORBIS

The Vietnam War. Between 1964 and 1973, U.S. troops fought against Vietcong guerrillas and North Vietnamese regular forces until they were finally withdrawn as a result of the Paris Agreement reached in January 1973. Shown here are U.S. troops after a Vietcong attack. The helicopter that is arriving would soon remove the American wounded from the battlefield.

States to withdraw its forces. Within two years, Vietnam had been forcibly reunited by Communist armies from the North.

Despite the success of the North Vietnamese Communists, the domino theory proved unfounded. A noisy rupture between Communist China and the Soviet Union put an end to the idea of a monolithic communism directed by Moscow. Under President Nixon, American relations with China were resumed. New nations in Southeast Asia also managed to avoid Communist governments. Above all, Vietnam helped show the limitations of American power. By the end of the Vietnam War, a new era in American-Soviet relations, known as détente, had begun to emerge.

The End of European Colonies

Not only did World War II leave Europe in ruins, but it also cost Europe its supremacy in world affairs. World War I had initiated nationalistic movements against colonial rule, and World War II greatly accelerated this process. The Japanese had already humiliated the Western states by overrunning their colonial empires during the war. In addition, colonial soldiers who had fought on behalf of the Allies were well aware that Allied war aims included the principle of self-determination for the peoples of the world. Equally important to the process of decolonization after the war, the power of the European states had been destroyed by the exhaustive struggles of World War II. The greatest colonial empire builder, Great Britain, no longer had the energy or the wealth to maintain its colonial empire after the war and quickly sought to let its colonies go. Given the combination of circumstances, a rush of decolonization swept through the world. Between 1947 and 1962, virtually every colony achieved independence and attained statehood. Although some colonial powers willingly relinquished their control, others had to be driven out by national wars of liberation. Decolonization was a difficult and even bitter process, but it created a new world as the non-Western states ended the long era of Western domination.

Africa: The Struggle for Independence

After World War II, Europeans reluctantly realized that colonial rule in Africa would have to come to an end, but little had been done to prepare Africans for self-rule. Political organizations that had been formed by Africans before the war to gain their rights became formal political parties with independence as their goal. In the Gold Coast, Kwame Nkrumah formed the Convention People's Party, the first African political party in black Africa. In the late 1940s, Jomo Kenyatta founded the Kenya African National Union, which focused on economic issues but also sought self-rule for Kenya.

For the most part, these political activities were nonviolent and were led by Western-educated African intellectuals. Their constituents were primarily merchants, urban professionals, and members of labor unions. But the demand for independence was not entirely restricted to the cities. In Kenya, for example, the widely publicized Mau Mau movement among the Kikuyu peoples used terrorism to demand *uhuru* (Swahili for "freedom") from the British. Mau Mau terrorism alarmed the European population and convinced the British in 1959 to promise eventual independence.

A similar process was occurring in Egypt, which had been a protectorate of Great Britain since the 1880s. In 1918, a formal political party called the Wafd was formed to promote Egyptian independence. Although Egypt gained its independence in 1922, it still remained under British control. Egyptian intellectuals, however, were opposed as much to the Egyptian monarchy as to the British, and in 1952, an army coup overthrew King Farouk and set up an independent republic.

In North Africa, the French, who were simply not strong enough to maintain control of their far-flung colonial empire, granted full independence to Morocco and Tunisia in 1956 (see Map 28.2). Since Algeria was home to two million French settlers, however, France chose to retain its dominion there. But a group of Algerian nationalists organized the National Liberation Front (FLN) and in 1954 initiated a guerrilla war to liberate their homeland (see the box on p. 812). The French people became so divided over this war that the French leader, Charles de Gaulle, accepted the inevitable and granted Algerian independence in 1962.

In areas such as South Africa, where the political system was dominated by European settlers, the transition to independence was more complicated. In South Africa, political activity by local blacks began with the formation of the African National Congress (ANC) in 1912. At first, it was a group of intellectuals whose goal was to gain economic and political reforms, including full equality for educated Africans, within the framework of the existing system. The ANC's efforts, however, met with little success. At the same time, by the 1950s, South African whites were strengthening the laws separating whites and blacks, creating a system of racial segregation in South Africa known as apartheid. When blacks demonstrated against the apartheid laws, the white government brutally repressed the demonstrators. After the arrest of Nelson Mandela, the ANC leader, in 1962, members of the ANC called for armed resistance to the white government.

When both the British and the French decided to let go of their colonial empires, most black African nations achieved their independence in the late 1950s and 1960s. The Gold Coast, now renamed Ghana and under the guidance of Kwame Nkrumah, was first in 1957. Nigeria, the Belgian Congo (renamed Zaire), Kenya, Tanganyika (later, when joined with Zanzibar, renamed Tanzania), and others soon followed. Seventeen new African nations emerged in 1960. Another eleven followed between 1961 and 1965. By the late 1960s, only parts of southern Africa and the Portuguese possessions of Mozambique and Angola remained under European rule. After a series of brutal guerrilla wars, the Portuguese finally gave up their colonies in the 1970s.

Conflict in the Middle East

For the countries of the Middle East, the period between the two world wars was a time of transition. With the fall of the Ottoman and the Persian Empires, new modernizing regimes emerged in Turkey and Iran. A fiercely independent government was established in Saudi Arabia in 1932. Iraq, too, gained its independence from Britain in the same year. Elsewhere in the Middle East, European influence remained strong; the British and the French had mandates in Syria, Lebanon, Jordan, and Palestine.

As in other areas of the world, the end of World War II led to the emergence of new independent states in the Middle East. Jordan, Syria, and Lebanon, all European mandates before the war, became independent (see Map 28.3). Sympathy for the idea of Arab unity led to the formation of the Arab League in 1945, but different points of view among its members prevented it from achieving anything of substance.

The one issue on which all Muslim states in the area could agree was the question of Palestine. As tensions between Jews and Arabs intensified in that mandate

Frantz Fanon and the Wretched of the Earth

Born on the island of Martinique, Frantz Fanon (1925–1961) studied psychiatry in France. His work as head of a psychiatric hospital in Algeria led him to favor violence as a necessary instrument to overthrow Western imperialism, which to Fanon was itself rooted in violence. *The Wretched of the Earth,* published in 1961, provided an argument for national liberation movements in the Third World. In the last part of the book, Fanon discussed the problem of mental disorders that arose from Algeria's war of national liberation.

■ The Wretched of the Earth: *Colonial War and Mental Disorders, Series B*

We have here brought together certain cases or groups of cases in which the event giving rise to the illness is in the first place the atmosphere of total war which reigns in Algeria.

Case No. 1: The murder by two young Algerians, thirteen and fourteen years old respectively, of their European playmate.

We had been asked to give expert medical advice in a legal matter. Two young Algerians thirteen and fourteen years old, pupils in a secondary school, were accused of having killed one of their European schoolmates. They admitted having done it. The crime was reconstructed, and photos were added to the record. Here one of the children could be seen holding the victim while the other struck at him with a knife. The little defendants did not go back on their declarations. We had long conversations with them. We here reproduce the most characteristic of their remarks:

The boy fourteen years old:

This young defendant was in marked contrast to his school fellow. He was already almost a man, and an adult in his muscular control, his appearance, and the content of his replies. He did not deny having killed either. Why had he killed? He did not reply to the question but asked me had I ever seen a European in prison. Had there ever been a European arrested and sent to prison after the murder of an Algerian? I replied that in fact I had never seen any Europeans in prison.

"And yet there are Algerians killed every day, aren't there?"

"Yes."

"So why are only Algerians found in the prisons? Can you explain that to me?"

"No. But tell me why you killed this boy who was your friend."

"I'll tell you why. You've heard tell of the Rivet business?" [Rivet was a village near Algiers where in 1956 the French militia dragged forty men from their own beds and afterward murdered them.]

"Yes."

"Two of my family were killed then. At home, they said that the French had sworn to kill us all, one after the other. And did they arrest a single Frenchman for all those Algerians who were killed?"

"I don't know."

"Well, nobody at all was arrested. I wanted to take to the mountains, but I was too young. So [my friend] and I said we'd kill a European."

"Why?"

"In your opinion, what should we have done?"

"I don't know. But you are a child and what is happening concerns grown-up people."

"But they kill children too."

"That is no reason for killing your friend."

"Well, kill him I did. Now you can do what you like."

"Had your friend done anything to harm you?"

"Not a thing."

"Well?"

"Well, there you are."

during the 1930s, the British reduced Jewish immigration into the area and firmly rejected Jewish proposals for an independent state in Palestine. The Zionists who wanted Palestine as a home for Jews were not to be denied, however. Many people had been shocked at the end of World War II when they learned about the Holocaust, and sympathy for the Jewish cause grew dramatically. As a result, the Zionists turned for support to the United States, and in March 1948, the Truman administration approved the concept of an independent Jewish state in Palestine, even though only about one-third of the local population were Jews. When a United Nations resolution divided Palestine into a Jewish state and an Arab state, the Jews in Palestine acted. On May 14, 1948, they proclaimed the state of Israel.

To its Arab neighbors, the new state was seen as a betrayal of the Palestinian people, 90 percent of whom were Muslim. Outraged at the lack of Western support for Muslim interests in the area, several Arab countries invaded the new Jewish state. The invasion failed, but both sides remained bitter. The Arab states refused to recognize the existence of Israel.

The growing Arab hostility was a constant threat to the security of Israel. At a meeting of Arab leaders held in Jerusalem in 1964, the Egyptians took the lead in forming the Palestine Liberation Organization (PLO) to represent the interests of the Palestinians. The PLO believed that only the Palestinian peoples (and not Jewish immigrants from abroad) had the right to form a state in Palestine. A guerrilla movement called al-Fatah, led by the PLO political leader Yasir Arafat (b. 1929), began to launch terrorist attacks on Israeli territory, prompting the Israeli government to raid PLO bases in Jordan in 1966.

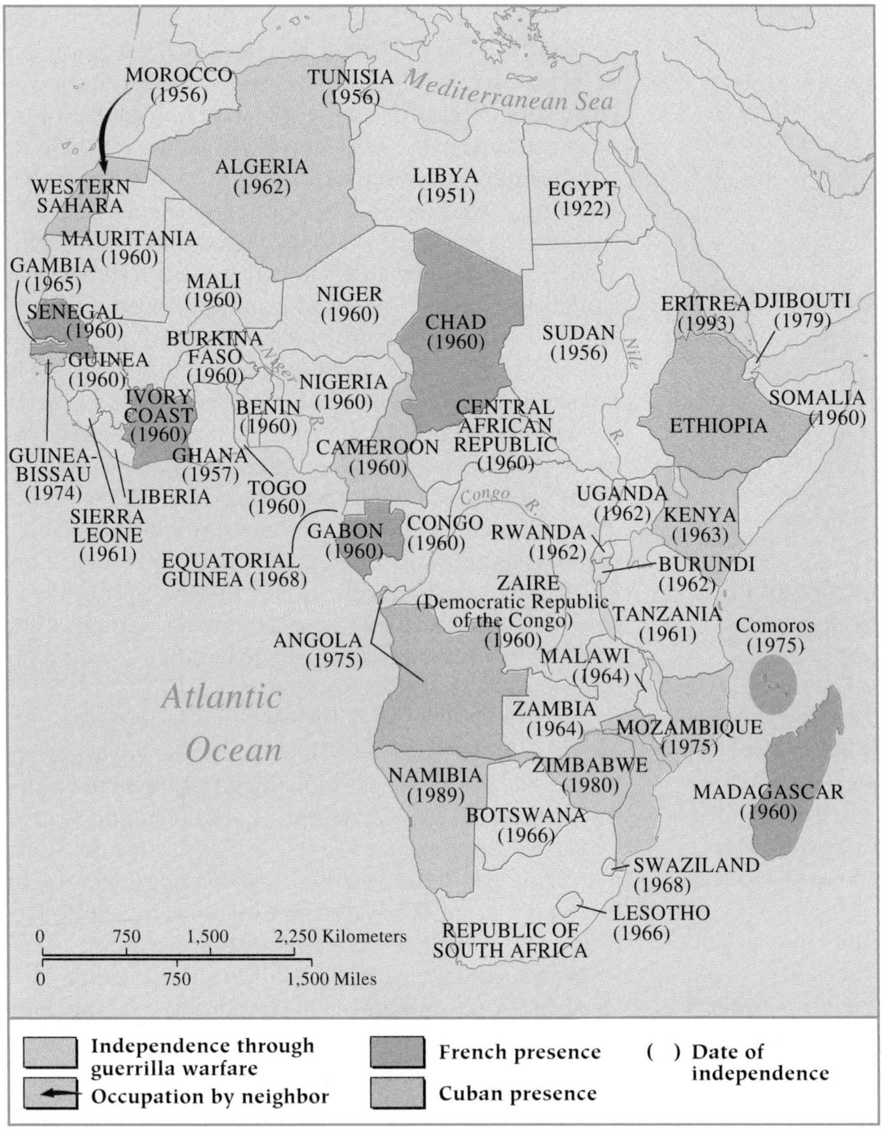

Map 28.2 Decolonization in Africa. By the late 1950s, Britain and France decided to allow independence for most of their African colonies, although France fought hard before relinquishing Algeria. Most of the new states had difficulty promoting economic growth and dealing with intertribal animosity. ■ Of the countries that gained independence from 1975 onward, what is a significant characteristic shared by a majority of them?

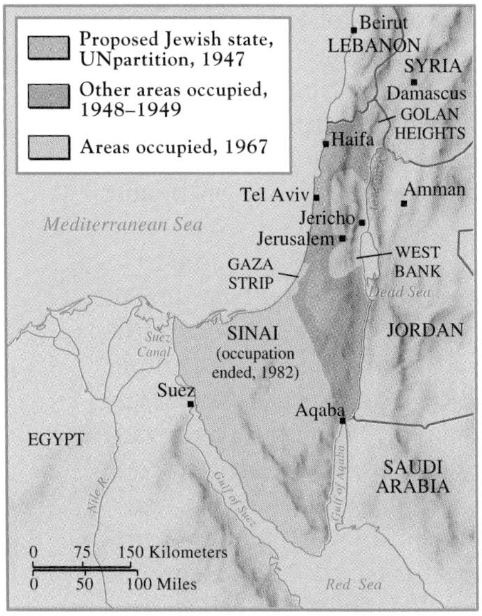

Israel and Its Neighbors

During the 1960s, the dispute between Israel and other states in the Middle East intensified. Essentially alone except for the sympathy of the United States and a few Western European countries, Israel adopted a policy of immediate retaliation against any hostile act by the PLO and its Arab neighbors. By the spring of 1967, Colonel Gamal Abdel Nasser (1918–1970), the ruler of Egypt, had stepped up his military activities and imposed a blockade against Israeli shipping through the Gulf of Aqaba. Learning that an attack was imminent, on June 5, 1967, Israel launched preemptive air strikes against Egypt and several of its Arab neighbors. Israeli warplanes bombed seventeen Egyptian airfields and wiped out most of the Egyptian air force. Israeli armies then broke the blockade at the head of the Gulf of Aqaba and occupied the Sinai peninsula. Other Israeli forces seized Jordanian territory on the West Bank of the Jordan River, occupied all of Jerusalem (formerly divided between Israel and Jordan), and attacked Syrian military positions in the Golan Heights area along the Israeli-Syrian border. In this brief Six-Day War, as it is called, Israel devastated Nasser's forces and tripled the size of its territory. The new Israel aroused even more bitter hatred among the Arabs. Besides, another million Palestinians now lived inside Israel's new borders, most of them on the West Bank. Israel's victories secured its existence, but the Arab-Israeli conflict continues to this day.

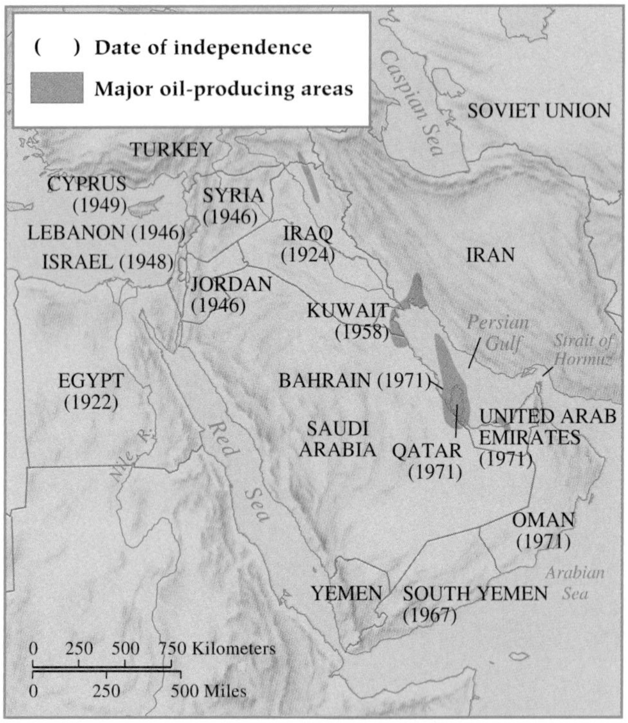

Map 28.3 Decolonization in the Middle East. Under the control of the Ottoman Empire prior to World War I, much of the Middle East was ruled directly or indirectly by the British and French after the war. Britain, the main colonial power, granted independence to most of its holdings in the first years after World War II, although it did maintain control of small states in the Persian Gulf and Arabian Sea region until 1971. ■ Which countries are major oil producers?

Asia: Nationalism and Communism

In Asia, the United States initiated the process of decolonization in 1946 when it granted independence to the Philippines (see Map 28.4). Britain soon followed suit with its oldest and largest nonwhite possession, India. But ethnic and religious differences made the process both difficult and violent.

At the end of World War II, the British negotiated with both the Indian National Congress, which was mostly Hindu, and the Muslim League. British India's Muslims and Hindus were bitterly divided and unwilling to accept a single Indian state. Britain soon realized that British India would have to be divided into two countries, one Hindu (India) and one Muslim (Pakistan). Pakistan would actually consist of two regions separated by more than 1,000 miles.

Among Congress leaders, only Mahatma Gandhi objected to the division of India. A Muslim woman criticized him for opposition to partition, asking him, "If two brothers were living together in the same house and wanted to separate and live in two different houses, would you object?" "Ah," Gandhi replied, "if only we could separate as two brothers. But we will not. It will be an orgy of blood. We shall tear ourselves asunder in the womb of the mother who bears us."[6]

On August 15, 1947, India and Pakistan became independent. But Gandhi had been right. The flight of millions of Hindus and Muslims across the new borders led to violence, and over a million people were killed. One of the dead was especially well known. On January 30, 1948, a Hindu militant assassinated Gandhi as he was going to morning prayer. India's new beginning had not been easy.

Other areas of Asia also achieved independence. In 1948, Britain granted independence to Ceylon (modern Sri Lanka) and Burma (modern Myanmar). When the Dutch failed to reestablish control over the Dutch East Indies, Indonesia emerged as an independent nation in 1949. The French effort to remain in Indochina led to a bloody struggle with the Vietminh, Vietnamese nationalist guerrillas, led by Ho Chi Minh, the Communist and nationalist leader of the Vietnamese. After their defeat in 1954, the French granted independence to Laos and Cambodia, and Vietnam was temporarily divided in anticipation of elections in 1956 that would decide its fate. But the elections were never held, and the division of Vietnam by Communist and pro-Western regimes eventually led to the Vietnam War.

CHINA UNDER COMMUNISM

At the end of World War II, two Chinese governments existed side by side. The Nationalist government of Chiang Kai-shek (1887–1975), based in southern and central China, was supported by the Americans, while the Communists, under the leadership of Mao Zedong (1893–1976), had built a strong base in North China. Their People's Liberation Army included nearly one million troops.

When efforts to form a coalition government in 1946 failed, full-scale war between the Nationalists and the Communists broke out. In the countryside, millions of peasants were attracted to the Communists by promises of land, and many joined Mao's People's Liberation Army. By 1948, the People's Liberation Army had surrounded Beijing. The following spring, the Communists crossed the Yangtze and occupied Shanghai. During the next few months, Chiang's government and two million of his followers fled to Taiwan, an island off the coast of mainland China. On October 1, 1949, Mao mounted the rostrum of the Gate of Heavenly Peace in Beijing and made a victory statement to the thousands gathered in the square before him. The Chinese people have stood up, he said, and no one will be able to humiliate us again.

The newly victorious Communist Party, under the leadership of its chairman, Mao, had a long-term goal of building a socialist society. In 1955, the Chinese government collectivized all private farmland and nationalized most industry and commerce. When the collective farms failed to increase food production, Mao began a more radical program known as the Great Leap Forward in 1958. Existing collective farms, normally the size of the traditional village, were combined into vast "people's communes," each containing more than thirty thousand people. Mao hoped this program would mobilize the people for a massive effort to speed up economic growth and reach the final stage of communism—the classless society—before

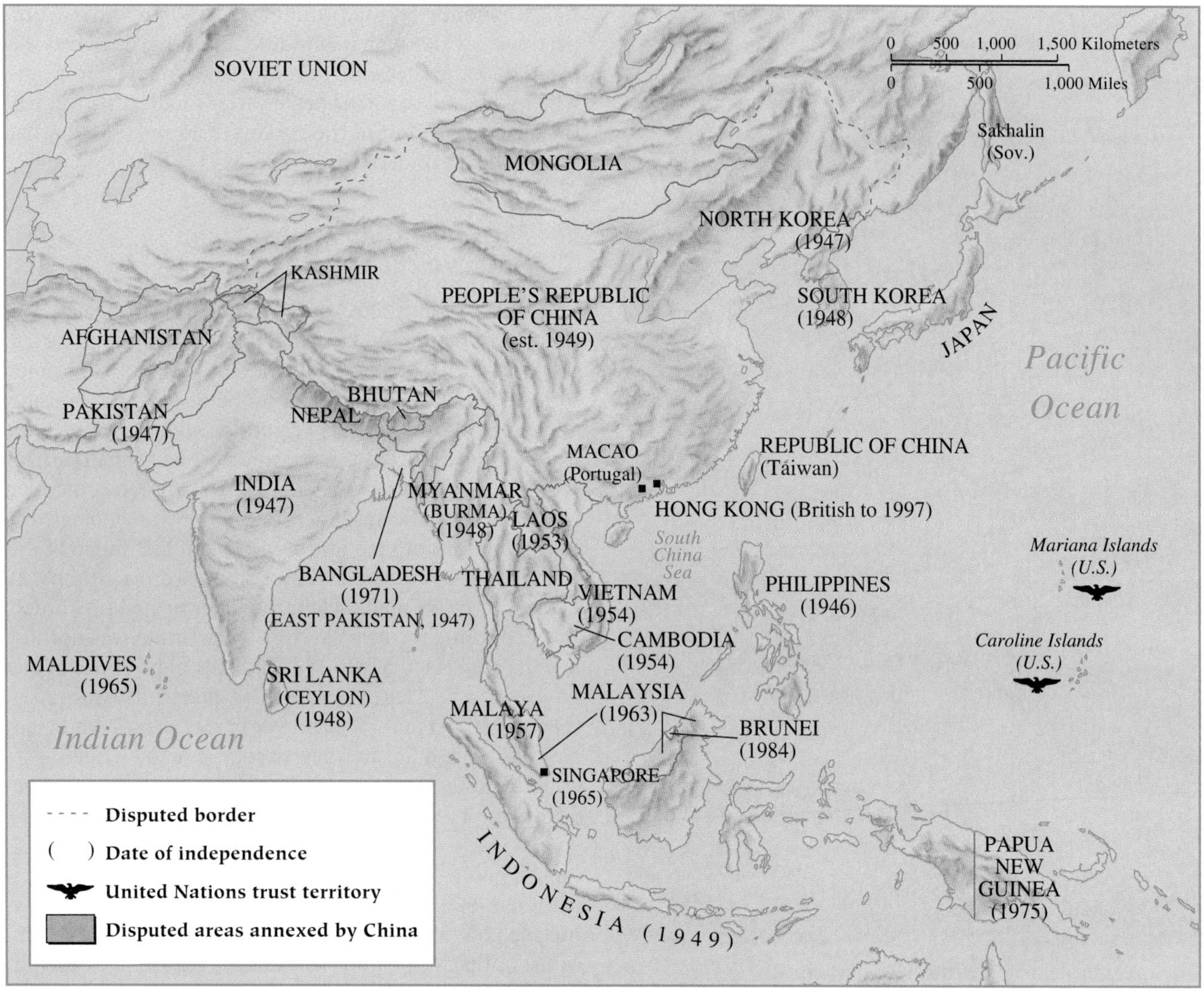

Map 28.4 Decolonization in Asia. Britain and the United States facilitated relatively peaceful transitions to independence for their possessions in Asia. France fought hard to hold Indochina but left after major military defeats. Cold War tensions in Asia led to both the Korean War and the Vietnam War. ■ The presence of what two neighboring countries helps explain why Korea has had difficulty maintaining complete independence throughout much of its history?

the end of the twentieth century. But the Great Leap Forward was a disaster. Bad weather and peasant hatred of the new system combined to drive food production downward.

Despite his failures, Mao was not yet ready to abandon his dream of a totally classless society. In 1966, he returned to the attack and unleashed the Red Guards, revolutionary units composed of unhappy Party members and discontented young people who were urged to take to the streets to cleanse Chinese society of impure elements guilty of taking the capitalist road. Schools, universities, factories, and even government ministries were all subject to the scrutiny of the Red Guards. Mao launched China on a new forced march toward communism, the so-called Great Proletarian Cultural Revolution (literally, the Chinese name translates as "great revolution to create a proletarian culture"). It lasted for ten years, from 1966 to 1976. Mao was convinced that only an atmosphere of constant revolutionary fervor could enable the Chinese to overcome the past and achieve the final stage of communism. Red Guards set out across the nation to eliminate the "four olds"—old ideas, old culture, old customs, and old habits. They destroyed temples, books written by foreigners, and jazz records. They tore down street signs and replaced them with ones carrying revolutionary names. Destruction of property was matched by vicious attacks on individuals who had supposedly deviated from Mao's thought. Those accused were humiliated at public meetings where they were forced to admit their "crimes." Many were brutally beaten, often to death.

Mao found, however, that it was not easy to maintain a constant mood of revolutionary enthusiasm. Key groups,

David King Collection

The Great Proletarian Cultural Revolution. The Cultural Revolution, which began in 1966, was a massive effort by Mao Zedong and his radical supporters to eliminate rival elements within the Chinese Communist Party and achieve the final stage of communism—a classless society. This enormous parade was held in Beijing in August 1968. The banner in the middle shows Mao waving to the people.

including Party members, urban professionals, and many military officers, did not share Mao's desire for "permanent revolution." People began to turn against the movement, and in September 1976, when Mao died, a group of practical-minded reformers seized power from the radicals and adopted a more practical approach to China's problems.

Recovery and Renewal in Europe

At the height of Nazi success in 1942, a new era of barbarism seemed to challenge the very existence of European civilization. But Europeans made a remarkable recovery, and within a few years after the defeat of Germany and Italy, economic revival brought renewed growth to European society, although major differences remained between Western and Eastern Europe. Moreover, many Europeans, who had feared that European states would suffer tremendously from the loss of their colonies, found that they had even adjusted to decolonization.

The Soviet Union: From Stalin to Khrushchev

World War II devastated the Soviet Union. To create a new industrial base, Stalin returned to the method that he had used in the 1930s—the acquisition of development capital from Soviet labor. Working hard for little pay, poor housing, and precious few consumer goods, Soviet laborers were expected to produce goods for export with little in return for themselves. The incoming capital from abroad could then be used to purchase machinery and Western technology. The loss of millions of men in the war meant that much of this tremendous workload fell upon Soviet women. Almost 40 percent of heavy manual labor was performed by women.

Economic recovery in the Soviet Union was nothing less than spectacular. By 1947, industrial production had attained prewar levels; three years later, it had surpassed them by 40 percent. New power plants, canals, and giant factories were built, and new industries and oil fields were established in Siberia and Soviet Central Asia. Stalin's five-year plan of 1946 reached its goals in less than five years.

STALIN'S POLICIES

Although Stalin's economic policy was successful in promoting growth in heavy industry, primarily for the benefit of the military, consumer goods were scarce. The development of thermonuclear weapons in 1953, MIG fighters from 1950 to 1953, and the first space satellite (*Sputnik*) in 1957 may have elevated the Soviet state's reputation as a world power abroad, but domestically, the Soviet people were shortchanged. Heavy industry grew at a rate three times that of personal consumption. Moreover, the housing shortage was acute. A British military attaché in Moscow reported that "all houses, practically without exception, show lights from every window after dark. This seems to indicate that every room is both a living room by day and a bedroom by night. There is no place in overcrowded Moscow for the luxury of eating and sleeping in separate rooms."[7]

When World War II ended in 1945, Stalin had been in power for more than fifteen years. During that time, he had removed all opposition to his rule and remained the undisputed master of the Soviet Union. Other leading members of the Communist Party were completely obedient to his will. Increasingly distrustful of competitors, Stalin exercised sole authority and pitted his subordinates against one another.

Stalin's morbid suspicions fueled the constantly increasing repression that was a characteristic of his regime. In 1946, the government decreed that all literary and scientific works must conform to the political needs of the state. Along with this anti-intellectual campaign came political terror. A new series of purges seemed imminent in 1953

Khrushchev Denounces Stalin

Three years after the death of Stalin, the new Soviet premier, Nikita Khrushchev, addressed the Twentieth Congress of the Communist Party and denounced the former Soviet dictator for his crimes. This denunciation was the beginning of a policy of destalinization.

Nikita Khrushchev, Address to the Twentieth Party Congress, February 1956

Comrades, . . . quite a lot has been said about the cult of the individual and about its harmful consequences. . . . The cult of the person of Stalin . . . became at a certain specific stage the source of a whole series of exceedingly serious and grave perversions of Party principles, of Party democracy, of revolutionary legality.

Stalin absolutely did not tolerate collegiality in leadership and in work and . . . practiced brutal violence, not only toward everything which opposed him, but also toward that which seemed to his capricious and despotic character, contrary to his concepts.

Stalin abandoned the method of ideological struggle for that of administrative violence, mass repressions and terror. . . . Arbitrary behavior by one person encouraged and permitted arbitrariness in others. Mass arrests and deportations of many thousands of people, execution without trial and without normal investigation created conditions of insecurity, fear and even desperation.

Stalin showed in a whole series of cases his intolerance, his brutality and his abuse of power. . . . He often chose the path of repression and annihilation, not only against actual enemies, but also against individuals who had not committed any crimes against the Party and the Soviet government. . . .

Many Party, Soviet and economic activists who were branded in 1937—8 as "enemies" were actually never enemies, spies, wreckers and so on, but were always honest communists; they were only so stigmatized, and often, no longer able to bear barbaric tortures, they charged themselves (at the order of the investigative judges-falsifiers) with all kinds of grave and unlikely crimes.

This was the result of the abuse of power by Stalin, who began to use mass terror against the Party cadres. . . . Stalin put the Party and the NKVD [the secret police] up to the use of mass terror when the exploiting classes had been liquidated in our country and when there were no serious reasons for the use of extraordinary mass terror. The terror was directed . . . against the honest workers of the Party and the Soviet state. . . .

Stalin was a very distrustful man, sickly suspicious. . . . Everywhere and in everything he saw "enemies," "two-facers" and "spies." Possessing unlimited power, he indulged in great willfulness and choked a person morally and physically. A situation was created where one could not express one's own will. When Stalin said that one or another would be arrested, it was necessary to accept on faith that he was an "enemy of the people." What proofs were offered? The confession of the arrested. . . . How is it possible that a person confesses to crimes that he had not committed? Only in one way—because of application of physical methods of pressuring him, tortures, bringing him to a state of unconsciousness, deprivation of his judgment, taking away of his human dignity.

when a number of Jewish doctors were implicated in a spurious plot to kill high-level party officials. Only Stalin's death on March 5, 1953, prevented more bloodletting.

KHRUSHCHEV'S RULE

A new collective leadership succeeded Stalin until Nikita Khrushchev emerged as the chief Soviet policymaker. Khrushchev had been responsible for ending the system of forced-labor camps, a regular feature of Soviet life under Stalin. At the Twentieth Congress of the Communist Party in 1956, Khrushchev condemned Stalin for his "administrative violence, mass repression, and terror" (see the box above).

Once in power, Khrushchev took steps to undo some of the worst features of Stalin's repressive regime. A certain degree of intellectual freedom was now permitted; Khrushchev said that "readers should be given the chance to make their own judgments" regarding the acceptability of controversial literature and that "police measures shouldn't be used."[8] In 1962, he allowed the publication of Alexander Solzhenitsyn's novel *A Day in the Life of Ivan Denisovich*, a grim portrayal of the horrors of the forced-labor camps. Most important, Khrushchev extended the process of destalinization by reducing the powers of the secret police and closing some of the Siberian prison camps. Nevertheless, Khrushchev's revelations about Stalin at the Twentieth Congress caused turmoil in Communist ranks everywhere and encouraged a spirit of rebellion in Soviet satellite countries in Eastern Europe. Soviet troops reacted by crushing an uprising in Hungary in 1956, and Khrushchev and the Soviet leaders, fearful of further undermining the basic foundations of the regime, downplayed their destalinization campaign.

Economically, Khrushchev tried to place more emphasis on light industry and consumer goods. Attempts to increase agricultural output by growing corn and cultivating vast lands east of the Ural Mountains proved less successful and damaged Khrushchev's reputation within the Party. These failures, combined with increased military spending, hurt the Soviet economy. The industrial growth rate, which had soared in the early 1950s, now declined dramatically from 13 percent in 1953 to 7.5 percent in 1964.

Khrushchev's personality also did not endear him to the higher Soviet officials, who frowned at his tendency to crack jokes and play the clown. Nor were the higher members of the Party bureaucracy pleased when Khrushchev tried to curb their privileges. Foreign policy failures caused additional damage to Khrushchev's reputation among his colleagues. His rash plan to place missiles in Cuba was the final straw. While he was on vacation in 1964, a special meeting of the Soviet Politburo voted him out of office (because of "deteriorating health") and forced him into retirement. Although a group of leaders succeeded him, real power came into the hands of Leonid Brezhnev (1906–1982), the "trusted" supporter of Khrushchev who had engineered his downfall.

Eastern Europe: Behind the Iron Curtain

At the end of World War II, Soviet military forces had occupied all of Eastern Europe and the Balkans (except Greece, Albania, and Yugoslavia). All of the occupied states came to be part of the Soviet sphere of influence and, after 1945, experienced similar political developments. Between 1945 and 1947, one-party Communist governments became firmly entrenched in East Germany, Bulgaria, Romania, Poland, and Hungary. In Czechoslovakia, which had a strong tradition of democratic institutions, the Communists did not achieve their goals until 1948. In the elections of 1946, the Communist Party of Czechoslovakia had become the largest party. But it was not all-powerful and shared control of the government with the non-Communist parties. When it appeared that the latter might win new elections early in 1948, the Communists seized control of the government on February 25. All other parties were dissolved, and Klement Gottwald, the leader of the Communists, became the new president of Czechoslovakia.

ALBANIA AND YUGOSLAVIA

Albania and Yugoslavia were exceptions to this progression of Soviet dominance in Eastern Europe. Both had had strong Communist resistance movements during the war, and in both countries, the Communist Party simply took over power when the war ended. In Albania, local Communists established a rigidly Stalinist regime, but one that grew increasingly independent of the Soviet Union.

In Yugoslavia, Josip Broz, known as Tito (1892–1980), leader of the Communist resistance movement, seemed to be a loyal Stalinist. After the war, however, he moved toward the establishment of an independent Communist state in Yugoslavia. Stalin hoped to take control of Yugoslavia, just as he had done in other Eastern European countries, but Tito refused to capitulate to Stalin's demands and gained the support of the people by portraying the struggle as one of Yugoslav national freedom. In 1958, the Yugoslav party congress asserted that Yugoslav Communists did not see themselves as deviating from communism, only Stalinism. They considered their way closer to the Marxist-Leninist ideal. This included a more decentralized economic and political system in which workers could manage themselves and local communes could exercise some political power.

Between 1948 and Stalin's death in 1953, the Eastern European satellite states followed a policy of Stalinization. They instituted Soviet-type five-year plans with emphasis on

Khrushchev's Visit to Yugoslavia. The leadership of Nikita Khrushchev appeared for a while to open the door to more flexible Soviet policies. In 1955, he visited Yugoslavia in an attempt to improve relations with a Communist state that had deviated from Soviet policies. Khrushchev is shown here making a conciliatory speech with Marshal Tito, the leader of Yugoslavia, looking on.

Camera Press, (Jugo) London

heavy industry rather than consumer goods. They began to collectivize agriculture. They eliminated all non-Communist parties and established the institutions of repression—secret police and military forces. But communism—a foreign import—had not developed deep roots among the peoples of Eastern Europe. Moreover, Soviet economic exploitation of Eastern Europe made living conditions harsh for most people. The Soviets demanded reparations from their defeated wartime enemies Bulgaria, Romania, and Hungary—often in the form of confiscated plants and factories removed to the Soviet Union—and forced all of the Eastern European states to trade with the Soviet Union to the latter's advantage.

CHRONOLOGY

The Soviet Union and Satellite States in Eastern Europe

Death of Stalin	1953
Khrushchev's denunciation of Stalin	1956
Attempt at reforms in Poland	1956
Hungarian revolt is crushed	1956
Berlin Wall is built	1961
Brezhnev replaces Khrushchev	1964
Soviets crush "Prague Spring" in Czechoslovakia	1968

UPHEAVAL IN EASTERN EUROPE

After Stalin's death, many Eastern European states began to pursue a new, more nationalistically oriented course as the new Soviet leaders, including Khrushchev, interfered less in the internal affairs of their satellites. But in the late 1950s and 1960s, the Soviet Union also made it clear, particularly in Poland, Hungary, and Czechoslovakia, that it would not allow its Eastern European satellites to become independent of Soviet control.

In 1956, after the circulation of Khrushchev's denunciation of Stalin, protests—especially by workers—erupted in Poland. In response, the Polish Communist Party adopted a series of reforms in October 1956 and elected Wladyslaw Gomulka (1905–1982) as first secretary. Gomulka declared that Poland had the right to follow its own socialist path. Fearful of Soviet armed response, however, the Poles compromised. Poland pledged to remain loyal to the Warsaw Pact, and the Soviets agreed to allow Poland to follow its own path to socialism.

The developments in Poland in 1956 inspired national Communists in Hungary to seek the same kinds of reforms and independence. Intense debates eventually resulted in the ouster of the ruling Stalinist and the selection of Imry Nagy (1896–1958) as the new Hungarian leader. Internal dissent, however, was not directed simply against the Soviets but against communism in general, which was viewed as a creation of the Soviets, not the Hungarians. The Stalinist secret police had also bred much terror and hatred. This dissatisfaction, combined with economic difficulties, created a situation ripe for revolt. To quell the rising rebellion, Nagy declared Hungary a free nation on November 1, 1956. He promised free elections, and the mood of the country made it clear that this could mean the end of Communist rule in Hungary. But Khrushchev was in no position at home to allow a member of the Communist flock to fly the coop. Just three days after Nagy's declaration, the Red Army invaded the capital city of Budapest (see the box on p. 820). The Soviets reestablished control over the country, and János Kádár (1912–1989), a reform-minded cabinet minister, replaced Nagy and worked with the Soviets to quash the revolt. By collaborating with the Soviet invaders, Kádár saved many of Nagy's economic reforms.

The developments in Poland and Hungary in 1956 did not generate similar revolts in Czechoslovakia. The "Little Stalin," Antonin Novotny (1904–1975), placed in power in 1952 by Stalin himself, remained firmly in control. By the late 1960s, however, Novotny had alienated many members of his own party and was particularly resented by Czechoslovakia's writers, such as the playwright Vaclav Havel (b. 1936). A writers' rebellion late in 1967, in fact, led to Novotny's resignation. In January 1968, Alexander Dubček (1921–1992) was elected first secretary of the Communist Party and soon introduced a number of reforms, including freedom of speech and the press, freedom to travel abroad, and a relaxation of secret police activities. Dubček hoped to create "communism with a human face." A period of euphoria erupted that came to be known as the "Prague Spring."

It proved short-lived. This euphoria had led many to call for more far-reaching reforms, including neutrality and withdrawal from the Soviet bloc. To forestall the spreading of this "spring" fever, the Red Army invaded Czechoslovakia in August 1968 and crushed the reform movement. Gustav Husák (1913–1991), a committed nonreformist, replaced Dubček, abolished his reforms, and reestablished the old order.

Soviet Invasion of Czechoslovakia, 1968. The attempt of Alexander Dubček, the new first secretary of the Communist Party, to liberalize Communist rule in Czechoslovakia failed when Soviet troops invaded and crushed the reform movement. This photograph shows a confrontation between Soviet tanks and Czechs in Prague. The tanks won.

Soviet Repression in Eastern Europe: Hungary, 1956

Developments in Poland in 1956 inspired the Communist leaders of Hungary to begin to remove their country from Soviet control. But there were limits to Khrushchev's tolerance, and he sent Soviet troops to crush Hungary's movement for independence. The first selection is a statement by the Soviet government justifying the use of Soviet troops; the second is a brief and tragic final statement from Imry Nagy, the Hungarian leader.

Statement of the Soviet Government, October 30, 1956

The Soviet Government regards it as indispensable to make a statement in connection with the events in Hungary.

The course of the events has shown that the working people of Hungary, who have achieved great progress on the basis of their people's democratic order, correctly raise the question of the necessity of eliminating serious shortcomings in the field of economic building, the further raising of the material well-being of the population, and the struggle against bureaucratic excesses in the state apparatus.

However, this just and progressive movement of the working people was soon joined by forces of black reaction and counterrevolution, which are trying to take advantage of the discontent of part of the working people to undermine the foundations of the people's democratic order in Hungary and to restore the old landlord and capitalist order.

The Soviet Government and all the Soviet people deeply regret that the development of events in Hungary has led to bloodshed. On the request of the Hungarian People's Government the Soviet Government consented to the entry into Budapest of the Soviet Army units to assist the Hungarian People's Army and the Hungarian authorities to establish order in the town.

The Last Message of Imry Nagy, November 4, 1956

This fight is the fight for freedom by the Hungarian people against the Russian intervention, and it is possible that I shall only be able to stay at my post for one or two hours. The whole world will see how the Russian armed forces, contrary to all treaties and conventions, are crushing the resistance of the Hungarian people. They will also see how they are kidnapping the Prime Minister of a country which is a Member of the United Nations, taking him from the capital, and therefore it cannot be doubted at all that this is the most brutal form of intervention. I should like in these last moments to ask the leaders of the revolution, if they can, to leave the country. I ask that all that I have said in my broadcast, and what we have agreed on with the revolutionary leaders during meetings in Parliament, should be put in a memorandum, and the leaders should turn to all the peoples of the world for help and explain that today it is Hungary and tomorrow, or the day after tomorrow, it will be the turn of other countries because the imperialism of Moscow does not know borders, and is only trying to play for time.

Western Europe: The Revival of Democracy and the Economy

All the countries of Western Europe faced similar kinds of problems at the end of World War II. They needed to rebuild their economies, re-create their democratic institutions, and contend with the growth of Communist parties.

The important role that Communists had played in the resistance movements against the Nazis gained them a new respectability and strength once the war was over. Communist parties did well in elections in Italy and France in 1946 and 1947 and even showed strength in some countries, such as Belgium and the Netherlands, where they had not been much of a political factor before the war. But Communist success was short-lived. After the hardening of the divisions in the Cold War, their advocacy of Soviet policies hurt the Communist parties at home, and support began to dwindle. Only in France and Italy, where social inequities remained their focus, did Communist parties retain significant support—about 25 percent of the vote.

As part of their electoral strategy, Communist parties had often joined forces with other left-wing parties, such as the Social Democrats. Socialist parties had also fared well immediately after the war as the desire to overthrow the old order led to the abandonment of conservative politics. But support for the Socialists soon waned. In France, for example, Socialists won 23 percent of the vote in 1945 but 18 percent in 1946 and only 12.6 percent in 1962. The Cold War also hurt the cause of socialism. Socialist parties had originally been formed in the late nineteenth century as Marxist parties, and their identification with Communist parties in postwar coalitions cost them dearly. In the late 1950s, many Socialist parties on the Continent perceived the need to eliminate their old doctrinal emphasis on class struggle and began to call for social justice and liberty. Although they advocated economic and social planning, they no longer demanded the elimination of the capitalist system.

By 1950, moderate political parties had made a remarkable comeback in Western Europe. Especially important was the rise of Christian Democratic parties. The new Christian Democrats were not connected to the prewar church-based parties that had been advocates of church interests and had crusaded against both liberal and socialist causes. The new Christian Democrats were sincerely interested in democracy and in significant economic reforms. They were especially strong in Italy and Germany and played a particularly important role in achieving Europe's economic restoration.

Western European countries recovered relatively rapidly from the devastation of World War II. The Marshall Plan played a significant role in this process. Between 1947 and 1950, European countries received $9.4 billion to be used for new equipment and raw materials. By 1950, industrial output in Europe was 30 percent above prewar levels. Between 1947 and 1950, steel production alone expanded by 70 percent. And this economic recovery continued well into the 1950s and 1960s. Those years were a time of dramatic economic growth and prosperity in Western Europe, which experienced virtually full employment.

FRANCE: THE DOMINATION OF DE GAULLE

The history of France for nearly a quarter century after the war was dominated by one man—Charles de Gaulle (1890–1970)—who possessed an unshakable faith that he had a historical mission to reestablish the greatness of the French nation. During the war, de Gaulle had assumed leadership of some resistance groups and played an important role in ensuring the establishment of a French provisional government after the war. The declaration of the Fourth Republic, with a return to a parliamentary system based on parties that de Gaulle considered weak, led him to withdraw from politics. Eventually, he formed the French Popular Movement, a decidedly rightist organization. It blamed the parties for France's political mess and called for an even stronger presidency, a goal that de Gaulle finally achieved in 1958.

The fragile political stability of the Fourth Republic had been badly shaken by the Algerian crisis. The French army had suffered defeat in Indochina in 1954 and was determined to resist Algerian demands for independence. But a strong antiwar movement among French intellectuals and church leaders led to bitter divisions that opened the door to the possibility of civil war in France. The panic-stricken leaders of the Fourth Republic offered to let de Gaulle take over the government and revise the constitution.

In 1958, de Gaulle immediately drafted a new constitution for the Fifth Republic that greatly enhanced the power of the president, who would now have the right to choose the prime minister, dissolve parliament, and supervise both defense and foreign policy. De Gaulle had always believed in strong leadership, and the new Fifth Republic was by no means a democratic system. As the new president, de Gaulle sought to return France to the position of a great power. He believed that playing a pivotal role in the Cold War might enhance France's stature. For that reason, he pulled France out of the NATO high command. He increased French prestige among Third World countries by consenting to Algerian independence despite strenuous opposition from the army. With an eye toward achieving the status of a world power, de Gaulle invested heavily in the nuclear arms race. France exploded its first nuclear bomb in 1960. Despite his successes, de Gaulle did not really achieve his ambitious goals of world power. Although his successors maintained that France was the "third nuclear power" after the United States and the Soviet Union, in truth France was too small for such global ambitions.

Although the cost of the nuclear program increased the defense budget, de Gaulle did not neglect the French economy. Economic decision making was centralized. Between 1958 and 1968, the French gross national product increased by 5.5 percent annually, faster than the U.S. economy was growing. By the end of de Gaulle's era, France was a major industrial producer and exporter, particularly in such areas as automobiles and armaments. Nevertheless, problems remained. The expansion of traditional industries, such as coal, steel, and railroads, which had all been nationalized (put under government ownership), led to large government deficits. The cost of living increased faster than in the rest of Europe. Consumer prices were 45 percent higher in 1968 than they had been ten years earlier.

Increased dissatisfaction with the inability of de Gaulle's government to deal with these problems soon led to more violent action. In May 1968, a series of student protests, followed by a general strike by the labor unions, shook the government. Although de Gaulle managed to restore order, the events of May 1968 seriously undermined the French people's respect for their aloof and imperious president. Tired and discouraged, de Gaulle resigned from office in April 1969 and died within a year.

Charles de Gaulle. As president, Charles de Gaulle sought to revive the greatness of the French nation. He is shown here dressed in his military uniform participating in a formal state ceremony.

WEST GERMANY: A NEW NATION?

Already by the end of 1945, the Western powers (the United States, Britain, and France) occupying Germany had allowed the reemergence of political parties in their zones. Three major parties came forth: the Social Democrats (SPD), the Christian Democrats (CDU), and the Free Democrats (FDP). Over the next three years, the occupation forces gradually allowed the political parties to play greater roles in their zones.

As a result of the pressures of the Cold War, the unification of the three Western zones into the Federal Republic of Germany became a reality in 1949. Konrad Adenauer (1876–1967), the leader of the CDU who served as chancellor from 1949 to 1963, became the "founding hero" of the Federal Republic. Adenauer sought respect for West Germany by cooperating with the United States and the other Western European nations. He was especially desirous of reconciliation with France, Germany's longtime enemy. The beginning of the Korean War in June 1950 had unexpected repercussions for West Germany. The fear that South Korea might fall to the Communist forces of the north led many Germans and Westerners to worry about the security of West Germany and led to calls for the rearmament of West Germany. Although many people, concerned about a revival of German militarism, condemned this proposal, Cold War tensions were decisive. West Germany rearmed in 1955 and became a member of NATO.

Adenauer's chancellorship is largely associated with the resurrection of the West German economy, often referred to as the "economic miracle." It was largely guided by the minister of finance, Ludwig Erhard. Although West Germany had only 75 percent of the population and 52 percent of the territory of prewar Germany, by 1955 the West German gross national product exceeded that of prewar Germany. Real wages doubled between 1950 and 1965 even though work hours were cut by 20 percent. Unemployment fell from 8 percent in 1950 to 0.4 percent in 1965. To maintain its economic expansion, West Germany even imported hundreds of thousands of "guest workers," primarily from Italy, Spain, Greece, Turkey, and Yugoslavia.

Throughout its postwar existence, West Germany was troubled by its Nazi past. The surviving major Nazi leaders had been tried and condemned as war criminals at war crimes trials held in Nuremberg in 1945 and 1946. As part of the denazification of Germany, the victorious Allies continued war crimes trials of lesser officials, but these diminished as the Cold War produced a shift in attitudes. By 1950, German courts had begun to take over the war crimes trials, and the German legal machine persisted in prosecuting cases. Beginning in 1953, the West German government also began to make payments to Israel and to Holocaust survivors and their relatives in order to make some restitution for the crimes of the Nazi era.

Adenauer resigned in 1963, after fourteen years of firmly guiding West Germany through its postwar recovery. Adenauer had wanted no grand experimentation at home or abroad; he was content to give Germany time to regain its equilibrium. Ludwig Erhard succeeded Adenauer and largely continued his policies. But an economic downturn in the mid-1960s opened the door to the rise of the Social Democrats, and in 1969, they became the leading party.

GREAT BRITAIN: THE WELFARE STATE

The end of World War II left Britain with massive economic problems. In elections held immediately after the war, the Labour Party overwhelmingly defeated Churchill's Conservative Party. The Labour Party had promised far-reaching reforms, particularly in the area of social welfare, and in a country with a tremendous shortage of consumer goods and housing, its platform was quite appealing. The new Labour government, with Clement Attlee (1883–1967) as prime minister, proceeded to enact the reforms that created a modern welfare state.

The establishment of the British welfare state began with the nationalization of the Bank of England, the coal and steel industries, public transportation, and public utilities, such as electricity and gas. In the area of social welfare, the new government enacted the National Insurance Act and the National Health Service Act in 1946. The insurance act established a comprehensive social security program and nationalized medical insurance, thereby enabling the state to subsidize the unemployed, the sick, and the aged. The health act created a system of socialized medicine that required doctors and dentists to work with state hospitals, although private practices could be maintained. This measure was especially costly for the state, but within a few years, 90 percent of medical practitioners were participating. The British welfare state became the model for most European states after the war.

The cost of building a welfare state at home forced the British to reduce expenses abroad. This meant the dismantling of the British Empire and the reduction of military aid to such countries as Greece and Turkey. It was not a belief in the morality of self-determination but economic necessity that brought an end to the British Empire.

Continuing economic problems, however, brought the Conservatives back into power from 1951 to 1964. Although they favored private enterprise, the Conservatives accepted the welfare state and even extended it when they undertook an ambitious construction program to improve British housing. Although the British economy had recovered from the war, it had done so at a slower rate than other European countries. Moreover, the slow rate of recovery masked a long-term economic decline caused by a variety of factors. The demands of British trade unions for wages that rose faster than productivity were certainly a problem in the late 1950s and 1960s. The unwillingness of the British to invest in modern industrial machinery and to adopt new methods also did not help. Underlying the immediate problems, however, was a deeper issue. As a result of World War II, Britain had lost much of its prewar revenues from abroad but was left with a burden of debt from its many international commitments.

At the same time, with the rise of the United States and the Soviet Union, Britain's ability to play the role of a world power declined substantially—as was evident in the Suez

Crisis. On July 26, 1956, Colonel Gamal Abdel Nasser, the leader of Egypt, nationalized the Suez Canal, an act strongly condemned by the British as a threat to their vital interests. On October 29, British, French, and Israeli forces attacked Egypt. Strong American opposition forced the British to accept a United Nations cease-fire resolution and withdraw their troops. The Suez debacle made it clear that Britain was no longer a world power.

ITALY: THE WEAKNESS OF COALITION GOVERNMENT

After the war, Italy faced a period of heavy reconstruction. No other Western country except Germany had sustained more physical destruction. The monarchy was abolished when 54 percent of Italian voters rejected the royal house, and in June 1946, Italy became a democratic republic.

In the first postwar parliamentary elections, held in April 1948, the Christian Democrats, still allied with the Catholic church, emerged as the leading political party. Alcide de Gasperi (1881–1954) served as prime minister from 1948 to 1953, an unusually long span of time for an Italian government. Like pre-Fascist governments, postwar Italian coalitions, largely dominated by the Christian Democrats, were famous for their instability and short lives. Although the Italian Communist Party was one of Italy's three largest parties, it was largely excluded from all of these government coalitions. It did, however, manage to gain power in a number of provinces and municipalities in the 1960s. The Christian Democrats were able to maintain control by keeping the support of the upper and middle classes and the southern peasantry.

Italy, too, experienced an "economic miracle" after the war, although it was far less publicized than Germany's. In 1945, Italy's industrial production was only 20 percent of prewar levels, and agricultural output was about 50 percent. The Marshall Plan helped stabilize the postwar Italian economy. Especially during the late 1950s and early 1960s, Italy made rapid strides in economic growth. The production of electrical appliances, cars, and office machinery made the most significant leap. As in other Western welfare states, the Italian economy combined private enterprise with government management, particularly of heavy industry. In 1965, for example, the government controlled 60 percent of Italy's steel production. The major economic problem continued to be the backwardness of southern Italy, a region that possessed 36 percent of the total population but generated only 25 percent of the national income. In the 1960s, millions of Italians from the south migrated to the more prosperous north.

Western Europe: The Move Toward Unity

As we have seen, the divisions created by the Cold War led the nations of Western Europe to form the North Atlantic Treaty Organization in 1949. But military unity was not the only kind of unity fostered in Europe after 1945. The destructiveness of two world wars caused many thoughtful Europeans to consider the need for some form of European unity. National feeling was still too powerful, however, for European nations to give up their political sovereignty. Consequently, the desire for a sense of solidarity was forced to focus primarily on the economic arena, not the political one.

In 1951, France, West Germany, the Benelux countries (Belgium, Netherlands, and Luxembourg), and Italy formed the European Coal and Steel Community (ECSC). Its purpose was to create a common market for coal and steel products among the six nations by eliminating tariffs and other trade barriers. The success of the ECSC encouraged its members to proceed further, and in 1957 they created the European Atomic Energy Community (EURATOM) to further European research on the peaceful uses of nuclear energy.

In the same year, these six nations signed the Rome Treaty, which created the European Economic Community (EEC), also known as the Common Market. The EEC eliminated customs barriers for the six member nations and created a large free-trade area protected from the rest of the world by a common external tariff. By promoting free trade, the EEC also encouraged cooperation and standardization in many aspects of the six nations' economies. All the member nations benefited economically. By the 1960s, the EEC nations had become an important trading bloc. With a total

The Common Market, 1957

CHRONOLOGY

Western Europe

Welfare state emerges in Great Britain	1946
Italy becomes a democratic republic	1946
Alcide de Gasperi becomes prime minister of Italy	1948
Konrad Adenauer becomes chancellor of West Germany	1949
Formation of European Coal and Steel Community	1951
West Germany joins NATO	1955
Suez Crisis	1956
Formation of EURATOM	1957
Formation of European Economic Community (Common Market)	1957
Charles de Gaulle assumes power in France	1958
Erhard becomes chancellor of Germany	1963
Student protests in France	1968

population of 165 million, the EEC became the world's largest exporter and purchaser of raw materials. Only the United States surpassed the EEC in steel production.

The United States and Canada: A New Era

At the end of World War II, the United States was undeniably one of the world's two superpowers. As the Cold War with the Soviet Union intensified, the United States worked hard to combat the spread of communism throughout the world. American domestic political life after 1945 was played out against a background of American military power abroad.

American Politics and Society in the 1950s

Between 1945 and 1970, the ideals of Franklin Roosevelt's New Deal largely determined the patterns of American domestic politics. The New Deal had brought basic changes to American society, including a dramatic increase in the role and power of the federal government, the rise of organized labor as a significant force in the economy and politics, the beginning of a welfare state, and a grudging realization of the need to deal fairly with the concerns of minorities.

The New Deal tradition was bolstered by the election of three Democratic presidents—Harry Truman in 1948, John Kennedy in 1960, and Lyndon Johnson in 1964. Even the election of a Republican president, Dwight Eisenhower, in 1952 and 1956 did not change the basic direction of American politics. As Eisenhower stated: "Should any political party attempt to abolish Social Security and eliminate labor laws and farm programs, you would not hear of that party again in our political history."

The economic boom after World War II fueled confidence in the American way of life. A shortage of consumer goods during the war had left Americans with both extra income and a pent-up desire to buy these goods after the war. Then, too, the growth of labor unions brought higher wages that enabled more and more workers to buy consumer goods. Between 1945 and 1973, real wages grew 3 percent a year on average, the most prolonged advance in American history.

Prosperity was not the only characteristic of the early 1950s. Cold War confrontations abroad had repercussions at home. The takeover of China by Mao Zedong's Communist forces in 1949 and Communist North Korea's invasion of South Korea in 1950 led to a fear that Communists had infiltrated the United States. President Truman's attorney general warned that Communists "are everywhere—in factories, offices, butcher stores, on street corners, in private businesses. And each carried in himself the germ of death for society." A demagogic senator from Wisconsin, Joseph R. McCarthy, helped intensify the "Red Scare" with his exposés of supposed Communists in high government positions. McCarthy went too far when he attacked alleged "Communist conspirators" in the U.S. Army and was censured by Congress in 1954. Very quickly, his anti-Communist crusade came to an end.

Decade of Upheaval: America in the 1960s

Between 1960 and 1970, the United States experienced a period of upheaval that brought to the fore problems that had been glossed over in the 1950s. The 1960s began on a youthful and optimistic note. At age forty-three, John F. Kennedy became the youngest elected president in the history of the United States. His own administration, cut short by an assassin's bullet on November 22, 1963, focused primarily on foreign affairs. Kennedy's successor, Lyndon B. Johnson, who won a new term as president in a landslide in 1964, used his stunning mandate to pursue what he called the Great Society, heir to the welfare state first begun in the New Deal. Johnson's programs included health care for the elderly, a "war on poverty" to be fought with food stamps and the new Job Corps, the new Department of Housing and Urban Development to deal with the problems of the cities, and federal assistance for education.

Johnson's other domestic passion was equal rights for African Americans. The civil rights movement had its beginnings in 1954 when the U.S. Supreme Court took the dramatic step of striking down the practice of racially segregating public schools. An eloquent Baptist minister named Martin Luther King Jr. (1929–1968) became the leader of a growing movement for racial equality, and by the early 1960s, a number of groups, including King's Southern Christian Leadership Conference (SCLC), were organizing sit-ins and demonstrations across the South to end racial segregation. In August 1963, King led the March on Washington for Jobs and Freedom to dramatize African Americans' desire for equal rights and opportunities. This march and King's impassioned plea for racial equality had an electrifying effect on the American people. By the end of 1963, 52 percent of Americans called civil rights the most significant national issue; eight months earlier, only 4 percent had done so.

President Johnson took up the cause of civil rights. As a result of his initiative, Congress passed the Civil Rights Act of 1964, which created the machinery to end segregation and discrimination in the workplace and all public places. A voting rights act the following year made it easier for blacks to vote in southern states. But laws alone could not guarantee the Great Society, and Johnson soon faced bitter social unrest, both from African Americans and from the burgeoning movement opposing the Vietnam War.

In the North and the West, African Americans had had voting rights for many years, but local patterns of segre-

© Bob Adelman/Magnum Photos

The Civil Rights Movement. In the early 1960s, Martin Luther King Jr. and his Southern Christian Leadership Conference organized a variety of activities to pursue the goal of racial equality. He is shown here with his wife Coretta (right) and Rosa Parks and Ralph Abernathy (far left) leading a march against racial discrimination in 1965.

gation led to higher unemployment rates for blacks than for whites and left African Americans segregated in huge urban ghettos. In these ghettos, the call for action by radical black leaders, such as Malcom X of the Black Muslims, attracted more attention than the nonviolent appeals of Martin Luther King. Malcom X's advice was straightforward: "If someone puts a hand on you, send him to the cemetery."

In the summer of 1965, race riots broke out in the Watts district of Los Angeles. Thirty-four people died and more than one thousand buildings were destroyed. Cleveland, San Francisco, Chicago, Newark, and Detroit likewise exploded in the summers of 1966 and 1967. After the assassination of Martin Luther King in 1968, more than one hundred cities experienced riots. The combination of riots and extremist comments by radical black leaders led to a "white backlash" and a severe division of the American population.

Antiwar protests also divided the American people after President Johnson sent American troops to war in Vietnam. As the war dragged on and a military draft ensued, protests escalated. Teach-ins, sit-ins, and the occupation of buildings at universities alternated with more radical demonstrations that led to violence. The killing of four student protesters at Kent State University in 1970 by the Ohio National Guard caused a reaction, and the antiwar movement began to decline. By that time, however, antiwar demonstrations had worn down the willingness of many Americans to continue the war. The combination of antiwar demonstrations and ghetto riots in the cities also heightened the appeal of a call for "law and order," used by Richard Nixon, the Republican presidential candidate in 1968. With Nixon's election in 1968, a shift to the right in American politics had begun.

The Development of Canada

Canada experienced many of the same developments as the United States in the postwar years. For twenty-five years after World War II, prosperous Canada set out on a new path of industrial development. Canada had always had a strong export economy based on its abundant natural resources. Now it also developed electronic, aircraft, nuclear, and chemical engineering industries on a large scale. Much of the Canadian growth, however, was financed by capital from the United States, which led to American ownership of Canadian businesses. Although many Canadians welcomed the economic growth, others feared American economic domination.

Canadians also worried about playing a secondary role politically and militarily to their neighboring superpower. Canada agreed to join NATO in 1949 and even sent military forces to fight in Korea the following year. At the same time, to avoid subordination to the United States, Canada actively supported the United Nations. Nevertheless, concerns about the United States did not keep Canada from maintaining a special relationship with its southern neighbor. The North American Air Defense Command (NORAD), formed in 1957, maintained close cooperation between the air forces of the two countries for the defense of North America against missile attack.

After 1945, the Liberal Party continued to dominate Canadian politics until 1957, when John Diefenbaker (1895–1979) achieved a Conservative Party victory. But major economic problems returned the Liberals to power, and under Lester Pearson (1897–1972), they created Canada's welfare state by enacting a national social security system (the Canada Pension Plan) and a national health insurance program.

The Emergence of a New Society

During the postwar era, Western society witnessed remarkably rapid change. Computers, television, jet planes, contraceptive devices, and new surgical techniques all dramatically and quickly altered the pace and nature of human life. The rapid changes in postwar society, fueled by scientific advances and rapid economic growth, led many to view it as a new society. In the 1960s, a wave of protests rocked this new society as blacks demanded civil rights, young people marched for an end to the war in Vietnam and a ban on nuclear weapons, and women argued for equal rights with men.

The Structure of European Society

The structure of European society was altered after 1945. Especially noticeable were the changes in the middle class. Such traditional middle-class groups as businesspeople and professionals in law, medicine, and the universities were greatly augmented by a new group of managers and technicians as large companies and government agencies employed increasing numbers of white-collar supervisory and administrative personnel. In both Eastern and Western Europe, the new managers and experts were very much alike. Everywhere their positions depended on specialized knowledge acquired from some form of higher education. Everywhere they focused on the effective administration of their organizations. Because their positions usually depended on their skills, they took steps to ensure that their own children would be educated.

Changes also occurred among the traditional lower classes. Especially noticeable was the dramatic shift of people from rural to urban areas. The number of people working in agriculture declined dramatically, yet the size of the industrial labor force remained the same. In West Germany, industrial workers made up 48 percent of the labor force throughout the 1950s and 1960s. Thereafter, the number of industrial workers began to dwindle as white-collar and service jobs increased. At the same time, a substantial increase in their real wages enabled the working classes to aspire to the consumption patterns of the middle class, leading to what some observers have called the "consumer society." Buying on the installment plan, which was introduced in the 1930s, became widespread in the 1950s and gave workers a chance to imitate the middle class by buying such products as televisions, washing machines, refrigerators, vacuum cleaners, and stereos. But the most visible symbol of mass consumerism was the automobile. Before World War II, cars were reserved mostly for the European upper classes. In 1948, there were 5 million cars in all of Europe, but by 1957, the number had tripled. By the 1960s, there were almost 45 million cars.

Rising incomes, combined with shorter working hours, created an even greater market for mass leisure activities. Between 1900 and 1960, the workweek was reduced from sixty hours to a little more than forty hours, and the number of paid holidays increased. In the 1960s, German and Italian workers received between thirty-two and thirty-five paid holidays a year. All aspects of popular culture—music, sports, media—became commercialized and offered opportunities for leisure activities, including concerts, sporting events, and television viewing.

Hulton Archive/Getty Images

Television in the Consumer Society. Buying on the installment plan made it possible for consumers to purchase a wide variety of new products. Television was one of the most popular. By 1956, fully 80 percent of all American families owned a television set. Many families considered television a necessity, not a luxury. Television advertising also encouraged even more consumption in the new consumer society.

Another visible symbol of mass leisure was the growth of mass tourism. Before World War II, mostly the upper and middle classes traveled for pleasure. After the war, the combination of more vacation time, increased prosperity, and the flexibility provided by package tours with their lower rates and less expensive lodgings enabled millions to expand their travel possibilities. By the mid-1960s, 100 million tourists were crossing European boundaries each year.

Creation of the Welfare State

One of the most noticeable social developments in postwar Europe was the creation of the welfare state. In one sense, the welfare state represents another extension of the power of the state over the lives of its citizens, a process that had increased dramatically as a result of two world wars. Yet the goal of the welfare state was to make it possible for people to live better and more meaningful lives. Advocates of the welfare state believed that eliminating poverty and homelessness, providing medical services for all, ensuring dignity for older people, and extending educational opportunities for all who wanted them would free people to achieve happiness by satisfying their material needs.

Social welfare schemes were not new to Europe. Beginning in the late nineteenth century, some states had provided for the welfare of the working class by instituting old-age pensions, medical insurance, and unemployment compensation. But these efforts were piecemeal and were by no means based on a general belief that society had a responsibility to care for all of its citizens.

The new postwar social legislation greatly extended earlier benefits and created new ones as well. Of course, social welfare benefits differed considerably from country to country in quantity and quality as well as in how they were paid for and managed. Nevertheless, there were some common trends.

In many countries, already existing benefits for sickness, accidents, unemployment, and old age were simply extended to cover more people and provide larger payments. Men were generally eligible for old-age pensions at age sixty-five and women at sixty. Old-age benefits were not always generous. In France and Britain, for example, a person was entitled to receive $40 per month after forty years of work.

Affordable health care for all people was another goal of the welfare state, although the methods of achieving this goal varied. In Britain, Italy, and Germany, for example, medical care was free to all people with some kind of insurance, but in France, the Scandinavian countries, Belgium, and Switzerland, people had to contribute toward the cost of their medical care. The amount ranged from 10 to 25 percent of the total cost.

Two other features of welfare states were family allowances and new educational policies. Family allowances were instituted in some countries to provide a minimum level of material care for children. Most family allowance programs provided a fixed amount per child. In 1964, for example, France granted $60 per month per child, Italy $24, and Britain only $10. Welfare states also sought to remove class barriers to opportunity by expanding the number of universities and providing scholarship aid to allow everyone to attend these institutions of higher learning. Overall, European states moved toward free tuition or modest fees for university attendance. These policies did not always achieve their goals, however. In the early 1960s, most students in Western European universities still came from privileged backgrounds. In Britain, 25 percent of university students came from working-class backgrounds; in France, the figure was only 17.6 percent.

The welfare state dramatically increased the amount of money states expended on social services. In 1967, such spending constituted 17 percent of the gross national product of the major European countries; by the 1980s, it absorbed 40 to 50 percent. To some critics, these figures proved that the welfare state had produced a new generation of citizens overly dependent on the state. But most people favored the benefits, and most leaders were well aware that it was political suicide to advocate curtailing or seriously lowering those benefits.

Gender issues also influenced the form that the welfare state took in different countries. One general question dominated the debate: Should women be recognized in a special category as mothers, or should they be regarded as individuals? William Beveridge, the economist who drafted the report that formed the basis for the British welfare state, said that women had "vital work to do in ensuring the adequate continuance of the British race." "During marriage," he said, "most women will not be gainfully employed. The small minority of women who undertake paid employment or other gainful employment or other gainful occupations after marriage require special treatment differing from that of single women."[9] Accordingly, the British welfare system was based on the belief that women should stay home with their children: women received subsidies for children, but married women who worked were given few or no benefits. Employers were also encouraged to pay women lower wages to discourage them from joining the workforce. Thus the British welfare system encouraged the dependence of wives on their husbands. So did the West German system. The West German government passed laws that discouraged women from working. In keeping its women at home, West Germany sought to differentiate itself from neighboring Communist countries in Eastern Europe and the Soviet Union, where women were encouraged to work outside the home. At the same time, to help working women raise families, Communist governments also provided day-care facilities, as well as family subsidies and maternity benefits.

France sought to maintain the individual rights of women in its welfare system. The French government recognized women as equal to men and thus as entitled to the same welfare benefits as men for working outside the home. At the same time, wanting to encourage population growth, the government provided incentives for women to stay home and bear children as well as day-care and afterschool programs for working mothers.

Women in the Postwar Western World

Despite their enormous contributions to the war effort, women were removed from the workforce at the end of World War II to provide jobs for the soldiers returning home. After the horrors of war, people seemed willing for a while to return to traditional family practices. Female participation in the workforce declined, and birthrates began to rise, creating a "baby boom." This increase in the birthrate did not last, however, and birthrates, and thus the size of families, began to decline by the end of the 1950s. Largely responsible for this decline was the widespread practice of birth control. Invented in the nineteenth century, the condom was already in wide use, but the development in the 1960s of oral contraceptives, known as birth control pills or simply "the pill," provided a reliable means of birth control that quickly spread to all Western countries.

The trend toward smaller families no doubt contributed to the change in the character of women's employment in both Europe and the United States as women experienced considerably more years when they were not involved in rearing children. The most important development was the increased number of married women in the workforce. At the beginning of the twentieth century, even working-class wives tended to stay at home if they could afford to do so. In the postwar period, this was no longer the case. In the United States, for example, in 1900, married women made up about 15 percent of the female labor force; by 1970, their number had increased to 62 percent. The percentage of married women in the female labor force in Sweden increased from 47 to 66 percent between 1963 and 1975. Figures for the Soviet Union and its satellites were even higher. In 1970, 92.5 percent of all women in the Soviet Union held jobs, compared to around 50 percent in France and West Germany. The industrial development of the Soviet Union relied on female labor.

But the increased number of women in the workforce did not change some old patterns. Working-class women in particular still earned salaries lower than those of men for equal work. In the 1960s, women earned only 60 percent of men's wages in Britain, 50 percent in France, and 63 percent in West Germany. In addition, women still tended to enter traditionally female jobs. As one Swedish female guidance counselor remarked in 1975: "Every girl now thinks in terms of a job. This is progress. They want children, but they don't pin their hopes on marriage. They don't intend to be housewives for some future husband. But there has been no change in their vocational choices."[10] Many European women also still faced the double burden of earning income on the one hand and raising a family and maintaining the household on the other. Such inequities led increasing numbers of women to rebel.

THE FEMINIST MOVEMENT: THE SEARCH FOR LIBERATION

The participation of women in World Wars I and II helped them achieve one of the major aims of the nineteenth-century women's movement—the right to vote. Already after World War I, many governments acknowledged the contributions of women to the war effort by granting them the right to vote. Sweden, Great Britain, Germany, Poland, Hungary, Austria, and Czechoslovakia did so in 1918, followed by the United States in 1920. Women in France and Italy did not obtain the right to vote until 1945. After World War II, European women tended to fall back into the traditional roles expected of them, and little was heard of fem-

Women's Liberation Movement. In the late 1960s, as women began once again to assert their rights, a revived women's liberation movement emerged. Feminists in the movement maintained that women themselves must alter the conditions of their lives. During this women's liberation rally, some women climbed the statue of Admiral Farragut in Washington, D.C., to exhibit their signs.

AP/Wide World Photos

The Voice of the Women's Liberation Movement

Simone de Beauvoir was an important figure in the emergence of the postwar women's liberation movement. This excerpt is taken from her influential book *The Second Sex,* in which she argued that women have been forced into a position subordinate to men.

Simone de Beauvoir, The Second Sex

Now, woman has always been man's dependent, if not his slave; the two sexes have never shared the world in equality. And even today woman is heavily handicapped, though her situation is beginning to change. Almost nowhere is her legal status the same as man's and frequently it is much to her disadvantage. Even when her rights are legally recognized in the abstract, long-standing custom prevents their full expression in the mores. In the economic sphere men and women can almost be said to make up two castes; other things being equal, the former hold the better jobs, get higher wages, and have more opportunity for success than their new competitors. In industry and politics men have a great many more positions and they monopolize the most important posts. In addition to all this they enjoy a traditional prestige that the education of children tends in every way to support, for the present enshrines the past—and in the past all history has been made by men. At the present time, when women are beginning to take part in the affairs of the world, it is still a world that belongs to men—they have no doubt of it at all and women have scarcely any. To decline to be the Other, to refuse to be a party to a deal—this would be for women to renounce all the advantages conferred upon them by their alliance with the superior caste. Man-the-sovereign will provide woman-the-liege with material protection and will undertake the moral justification of her existence; thus she can evade at once both economic risk and the metaphysical risk of a liberty in which ends and aims must be contrived without assistance. Indeed, along with the ethical urge of each individual to affirm his subjective existence, there is also the temptation to forgo liberty and become a thing. This is an inauspicious road, for he who takes it—passive, lost, ruined—becomes henceforth the creature of another's will, frustrated in his transcendence and deprived of every value. But it is an easy road; on it one avoids the strain involved in undertaking an authentic existence. When man makes of woman the *Other* he may, then, expect her to manifest deep-seated tendencies toward complicity. Thus woman may fail to lay claim to the status of subject because she lacks definite resources, because she feels the necessary bond that ties her to man regardless of reciprocity, and because she is often very well pleased with her role as the *Other.*

Now, what peculiarly signalizes the situation of woman is that she—a free and autonomous being like all human creatures—nevertheless finds herself living in a world where men compel her to assume the status of the Other.

inist concerns. But by the late 1960s, women began to assert their rights again and speak as feminists. Along with the student upheavals of the late 1960s came renewed interest in feminism, or the women's liberation movement, as it was now called. Increasingly, women protested that the acquisition of political and legal equality had not brought true equality with men:

> We are economically oppressed: in jobs we do full work for half pay, in the home we do unpaid work full time. We are commercially exploited by advertisement, television, and the press; legally, we often have only the status of children. We are brought up to feel inadequate, educated to narrower horizons than men. This is our specific oppression as women. It is as women that we are, therefore, organizing.[11]

These were the words of a British Women's Liberation Workshop in 1969.

Of great importance to the emergence of the postwar women's liberation movement was the work of Simone de Beauvoir (1908–1986). Born into a Catholic middle-class family and educated at the Sorbonne in Paris, she supported herself as a teacher and later as a novelist and writer. She maintained a lifelong relationship (but not marriage) with Jean-Paul Sartre. Her involvement in the existentialist movement—the leading intellectual movement of the time—led to her involvement in political causes. De Beauvoir believed that she lived a "liberated" life for a twentieth-century European woman, but for all her freedom, she still came to perceive that as a woman she faced limits that men did not. In 1949, she published her highly influential work, *The Second Sex,* in which she argued that as a result of male-dominated societies, women had been defined by their differences from men and consequently received second-class status: "What peculiarly signalizes the situation of woman is that she—a free and autonomous being like all human creatures—nevertheless finds herself living in a world where men compel her to assume the status of the Other."[12] De Beauvoir took an active role in the French women's movement of the 1970s, and her book was a major influence on both sides of the Atlantic (see the box above).

Another important contributor to the growth of a women's movement in the 1960s was Betty Friedan (b. 1921). A journalist and the mother of three children, Friedan grew increasingly uneasy with her attempt to fulfill the traditional role of the "ideal housewife and mother." In 1963, she published *The Feminine Mystique,* in which she analyzed the problems of middle-class American women in the 1950s and argued that women were being denied equality with men. She wrote: "The problem that has no name—which is simply the fact that American women are kept from growing to their full human capacities—is taking a far greater toll on the physical and mental health of our country than any known disease."[13]

The Feminine Mystique became a best-seller and propelled Friedan into a newfound celebrity. In 1966, she founded the National Organization for Women (NOW), whose stated goal was to take "action to bring women into full participation in the mainstream of American society *now,* exercising all the privileges and responsibilities thereof in truly equal partnership with men." Friedan's voice was also prominent in calling for the addition to the U.S. Constitution of an amendment guaranteeing equal rights for women.

The Permissive Society

The "permissive society" was yet another label used by critics to describe the new society of postwar Europe. World War I had seen the first significant crack in the rigid code of manners and morals of the nineteenth century. The 1920s had witnessed experimentation with drugs, the appearance of pornography, and a new sexual freedom (police in Berlin, for example, issued cards that permitted female and male homosexual prostitutes to practice their trade). But these indications of a new attitude appeared mostly in major cities and touched only small numbers of people. After World War II, changes in manners and morals were far more extensive and far more noticeable.

Sweden took the lead in the propagation of the so-called sexual revolution of the 1960s, and the rest of Europe and the United States soon followed. Sex education in the schools and the decriminalization of homosexuality were but two aspects of Sweden's liberal legislation. The introduction of the birth control pill, which became widely available by the mid-1960s, gave people more freedom in sexual behavior. Meanwhile, sexually explicit movies, plays, and books broke new ground in the treatment of once-hidden subjects. Cities like Amsterdam, which allowed open prostitution and the public sale of pornography, attracted thousands of curious tourists.

The new standards were evident in the breakdown of the traditional family. Divorce rates increased dramatically, especially in the 1960s, and premarital and extramarital sexual experiences also rose substantially. A survey in the Netherlands in 1968 revealed that 78 percent of men and 86 percent of women had engaged in extramarital sex. The appearance of *Playboy* magazine in the 1950s also added a new dimension to the sexual revolution for adult males. Along with photographs of nude women, *Playboy* offered well-written articles on various aspects of masculinity. *Playboy*'s message was clear: men were encouraged to seek sexual gratification outside marriage.

The decade of the 1960s also saw the emergence of a drug culture. Marijuana was widely used among college and university students as the recreational drug of choice.

The "Love-in." In the 1960s, a number of outdoor public festivals for young people combined music, drugs, and sex. Flamboyant dress, face painting, free-form dancing, and drugs were vital ingredients in creating an atmosphere dedicated to "love and peace." Shown here is a "love-in" that was held on the grounds of an English country estate during the Summer of Love, 1967.

Popperfoto/Archive/Getty Images

"The Times They Are a-Changin'": The Music of Youthful Protest

In the 1960s, the lyrics of rock and folk music reflected the rebellious mood of many young people. Bob Dylan (b. 1941) expressed the feelings of the younger generation. His song "The Times They Are a-Changin'," released in 1964, has been called an "anthem for the protest movement."

Bob Dylan, "The Times They Are a-Changin'"

Come gather round people
Wherever you roam
And admit that the waters
Around you have grown
And accept it that soon
You'll be drenched to the bone
If your time to you
Is worth savin'
Then you better start swimmin'
Or you'll sink like a stone
For the times they are a-changin'

Come writers and critics
Who prophesize with your pen
And keep your eyes wide
The chance won't come again
And don't speak too soon
For the wheel's still in spin
And there's no tellin' who
That it's namin'
For the loser now
Will be later to win
For the times they are a-changin'

Come senators, congressmen
please heed the call
Don't stand in the doorway
Don't block up the hall
For he that gets hurt
Will be he who has stalled
There's a battle outside
And it is ragin'
It'll soon shake your windows
And rattle your walls
For the times they are a-changin'

Come mothers and fathers
Throughout the land
And don't criticize
What you can't understand
Your sons and your daughters
Are beyond your command
Your old road
Is rapidly agin'
Please get out of the new one
If you can't lend your hand
For the times they are a-changin'

The line it is drawn
The curse it is cast
The slow one now
Will later be fast
As the present now
Will later be past
The order is
Rapidly fadin'
And the first one now
Will later be last
For the times they are a-changin'

For young people more interested in mind expansion into higher levels of consciousness, Timothy Leary, who had done psychedelic research at Harvard on the effects of LSD (lysergic acid diethylamide), became the high priest of hallucinogenic experiences.

New attitudes toward sex and the use of drugs were only two manifestations of a growing youth movement in the 1960s that questioned authority and fostered rebellion against the older generation. Spurred on by the Vietnam War and a growing political consciousness, the youth rebellion became a youth protest movement by the second half of the 1960s (see the box above).

Education and Student Revolt

Before World War II, higher education had largely remained the preserve of Europe's wealthier classes. After the war, European states began to foster greater equality of opportunity in higher education by reducing or eliminating fees, and universities experienced an influx of students from the middle and lower classes. Enrollments grew dramatically; in France, 4.5 percent of young people attended a university in 1950. By 1965, the figure had increased to 14.5 percent.

But there were problems. Classrooms with too many students, professors who paid little attention to their students, and administrators who acted in an authoritarian fashion led to student resentment. In addition, despite changes in the curriculum, students often felt that the universities were not providing an education relevant to the realities of the modern age. This discontent led to an outburst of student revolts in the late 1960s (see the box on p. 832). In part, these protests were an extension of the spontaneous disruptions in American universities in the mid-1960s, which were often sparked by student opposition to the Vietnam War. Perhaps the most famous student revolt occurred in France in 1968. It erupted at the

1968: The Year of Student Revolts

The outburst of student upheavals in the late 1960s reached its high point in 1968. These two very different selections illustrate some of the issues that prompted university students to occupy campus buildings and demand reforms.

A Student Manifesto in Search of a Real and Human Educational Alternative, University of British Columbia, June 1968

Today we as students are witnessing a deepening crisis within our society. We are intensely aware, in a way perhaps not possible for the older generation, that humanity stands on the edge of a new era. Because we are young, we have insights into the present and visions of the future that our parents do not have. Tasks of an immense gravity wait solution in our generation. We have inherited these tasks from our parents. We do not blame them so much for that . . . but we do blame them for being unwilling to admit that there are problems or for saying that it is we who have visited these problems on ourselves because of our perversity, ungratefulness and unwillingness to listen to "reason."

Much of the burden of solving the problems of the new era rests on the university. We have been taught to look to it for leadership. While we know that part of the reason for the university is to render direct services to the community, we are alarmed at its servility to industry and government as to what and how it teaches. We are scandalized that the university fails to realize its role in renewing and vivifying those intellectual and moral energies necessary to create a new society—one in which a sense of personal dignity and human community can be preserved.

Student Inscriptions on the Walls of Paris, May and June 1968

The dream is the reality.
May 1968. World revolution is the order of the day.
I decree a state of permanent happiness.
To be free in 1968 is to take part.
Take the trip every day of your life.
Make love, not war.
No exams.
The mind travels farther than the heart but it doesn't go as far.
Run, comrade, the old are behind you!
Don't make a revolution in the image of your confused and hide-bound university.
Exam = servility, social promotion, hierarchic society.
Love each other.
SEX. It's good, said Mao, but not too often.
Alcohol kills. Take LSD.
Are you consumers or participants?
Professors, you are as old as your culture; your modernism is only the modernization of the police.
Live in the present.
Revolution, I love you.
Long live direct democracy!

University of Nanterre outside Paris but soon spread to the Sorbonne, the main campus of the University of Paris. French students demanded a greater voice in the administration of the university, took over buildings, and then expanded the scale of their protests by inviting workers to support them. Half of France's workforce went on strike in May 1968. After the Gaullist government instituted a hefty wage hike, the workers returned to work and the police repressed the remaining student protesters.

The French revolt spurred student protests elsewhere in Europe, although none of them succeeded in becoming mass movements. In West Berlin, university students led a protest against Axel Springer, leader of Germany's largest newspaper establishment. Many German students were motivated by a desire to destroy what they considered to be the corrupt old order and were especially influenced by the ideas of the German-American social philosopher Herbert Marcuse. In *One-Dimensional Man,* published in 1964, Marcuse argued that capitalism had undermined the dissatisfaction of the oppressed masses by encouraging the consumption of material things. He proposed that a small cadre of unindoctrinated students could liberate the masses from the control of the capitalist ruling class. But the German students' attempt at revolutionary violence backfired as angry Berliners supported police repression of the students.

The student protest movement reached its high point in 1968, although scattered incidents lasted into the early 1970s. There were several reasons for the student radicalism. Some students were genuinely motivated by the desire to reform the university. Others were protesting the Vietnam War, which they viewed as a product of Western imperialism. They also attacked other aspects of Western society, such as its materialism, and expressed concern about becoming cogs in the large and impersonal bureaucratic jungles of the modern world. For many students, the calls for democratic decision making within the universities were a reflection of their deeper concerns about the direction of Western society. Although student revolts fizzled out in the 1970s, the larger issues they raised were increasingly revived in the 1990s.

Student Revolt in Paris, 1968. The discontent of university students exploded in the late 1960s in a series of student revolts. Perhaps best known was the movement in Paris in 1968. This photograph shows the barricades erected on a Parisian street on the morning of May 11 during the height of the revolt.

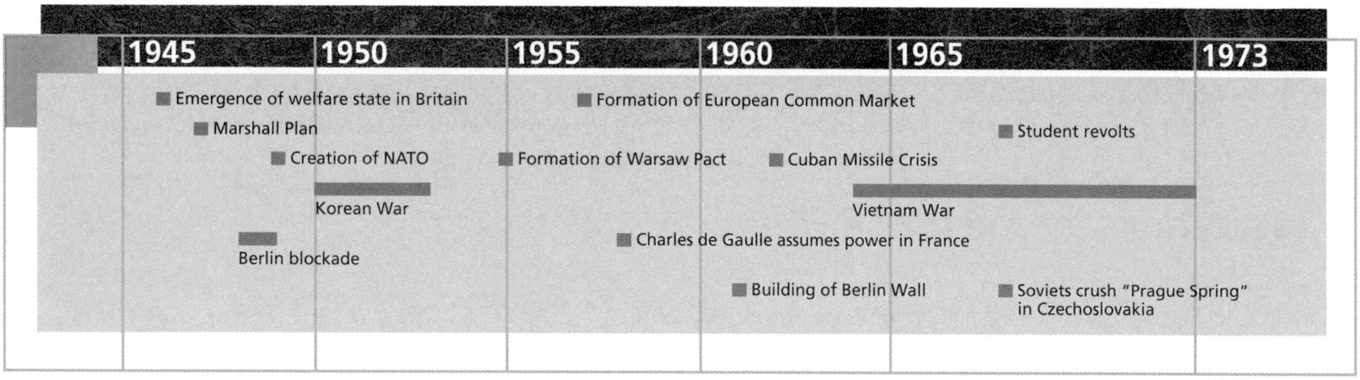

Conclusion

At the end of World War II, a new conflict erupted in the Western world as the two new superpowers, the United States and the Soviet Union, competed for political domination. Europeans, whether they wanted to or not, were forced to become supporters of one side or the other. But this ideological division also spread to the rest of the world as the United States fought in Korea and Vietnam to prevent the spread of communism and the Soviet Union used its armies to prop up pro-Soviet regimes in Eastern Europe.

In addition to the Cold War conflict, the postwar era was characterized by decolonization and the creation of a new Europe. After World War II, the colonial empires of the European states were largely dissolved, and the liberated territories of Africa, Asia, and the Middle East emerged as sovereign states. A global community was emerging.

Western Europe also emerged as a new community in the 1950s and the 1960s. Although Western Europeans staged a remarkable economic recovery, the Cuban Missile Crisis made it clear that their future still depended on the conflict between the two superpowers. At the same time, the student protests of the late 1960s caused many to rethink some of their basic assumptions. And yet, looking back, the student upheavals were not a "turning point in the history of postwar Europe," as some people thought at the time. In the 1970s and 1980s, student rebels would become middle-class professionals, and revolutionary politics would remain mostly a memory.

Notes

1. Quoted in Joseph M. Jones, *The Fifteen Weeks (February 21–June 5, 1947)*, 2d ed. (New York, 1964), pp. 140–141.
2. Quoted in Walter Laqueur, *Europe in Our Time* (New York, 1992), p. 111.
3. Quoted in Wilfried Loth, *The Division of the World, 1941–1955* (New York, 1988), pp. 160–161.
4. Quoted in Peter Lane, *Europe Since 1945: An Introduction* (Totowa, N.J., 1985), p. 248.
5. Quoted in Robert F. Kennedy, *Thirteen Days: A Memoir of the Cuban Missile Crisis* (New York, 1969), pp. 89–90.
6. Quoted in Larry Collins and Dominique Lapierre, *Freedom at Midnight* (New York, 1975), p. 252.
7. R. Hilton, *Military Attaché in Moscow* (London, 1949), p. 41.
8. Nikita Khrushchev, *Khrushchev Remembers*, trans. Strobe Talbott (Boston, 1970), p. 77.
9. Quoted in Bonnie G. Smith, *Changing Lives: Women in European History Since 1700* (Lexington, Mass., 1989), p. 513.
10. Quoted in Hilda Scott, *Sweden's "Right to Be Human"—Sex-Role Equality: The Goal and the Reality* (London, 1982), p. 125.
11. Quoted in Marsha Rowe et al., *Spare Rib Reader* (Harmondsworth, England, 1982), p. 574.
12. Simone de Beauvoir, *The Second Sex*, trans. H. M. Parshley (New York, 1961), p. xxviii.
13. Betty Friedan, *The Feminine Mystique* (New York, 1963), p. 10.

Suggestions for Further Reading

Three introductory surveys on postwar Europe are P. Lane, *Europe Since 1945: An Introduction* (Totowa, N.J., 1985); J. R. Wegs, *Europe Since 1945: A Concise History*, 2d ed. (New York, 1984); and W. Laqueur, *Europe in Our Time* (New York, 1992). There is a detailed literature on the Cold War. A general account is J. W. Langdon, *A Hard and Bitter Peace: A Global History of the Cold War* (Englewood Cliffs, N.J., 1995). Two brief works on the entire Cold War are J. H. Mason, *The Cold War* (New York, 1996), and J. Smith, *The Cold War, 1945–1991* (Oxford, 1998). For an illustrated history, see J. Isaacs and T. Downing, *Cold War: An Illustrated History, 1945–1991* (Boston, 1998). See also J. L. Gaddis, *We Now Know: Rethinking Cold War History* (New York, 1997). For a study of Soviet foreign policy, see J. L. Nogee, *Soviet Foreign Policy Since World War I*, 4th ed. (New York, 1992). The effects of the Cold War on Germany are examined in J. H. Backer, *The Decision to Divide Germany: American Foreign Policy in Transition* (Durham, N.C., 1978). For a good introduction to the arms race, see E. M. Bottome, *The Balance of Terror: A Guide to the Arms Race*, rev. ed. (Boston, 1986). On the Cuban Missile Crisis, see R. A. Chayes, *The Cuban Missile Crisis* (New York, 1974). On decolonization after World War II, see R. F. Betts, *Decolonization* (London, 1998).

For a general view of Soviet society, see D. K. Shipler, *Russia: Broken Idols, Solemn Dreams* (New York, 1983). On the Khrushchev years, see C. A. Linden, *Khrushchev and the Soviet Leadership* (Baltimore, 1990). For a general study of the Soviet satellites in Eastern Europe, see J. Rothschild, *Return to Diversity: A Political History of East Central Europe Since World War II*, 2d ed. (New York, 1992). On the Soviet Union's actions against Czechoslovakia in 1968, see J. Valenta, *Intervention in Czechoslovakia in 1968* (Baltimore, 1991). The unique path of Yugoslavia is examined in L. J. Cohen and P. Warwick, *Political Cohesion in a Fragile Mosaic: The Yugoslav Experience* (Boulder, Colo., 1983).

The rebuilding of postwar Europe is examined in D.W. Ellwood, *Rebuilding Europe: Western Europe, America, and Postwar Reconstruction* (London, 1992), and M. Hogan, *The Marshall Plan: America, Britain, and the Reconstruction of Western Europe, 1947–1952* (New York, 1987). On the building of common institutions in Western Europe, see S. Henig, *The Uniting of Europe: From Discord to Concord* (London, 1997). For surveys of West Germany, see H. A. Turner, *Germany from Partition to Reunification* (New Haven, Conn., 1992), and T. G. Ash, *In Europe's Name: Germany and the Enduring Balance* (New York, 1993). France under de Gaulle is examined in A. Shennen, *De Gaulle* (New York, 1993), and D. J. Mahoney, *De Gaulle: Statesmanship, Grandeur, and Modern Democracy* (Westport, Conn., 1996). On Britain, see K. O. Morgan, *The People's Peace: British History, 1945–1990* (Oxford, 1992). On Italy, see P. Ginsbourg, *A History of Contemporary Italy: Society and Politics, 1943–1988* (New York, 1990).

The student revolts of the late 1960s are put into a broader context in D. Caute, *The Year of the Barricades: A Journey Through 1968* (New York, 1988). On the welfare state, see A. de Swann, *In Care of the State: Health Care, Education, and Welfare in Europe and the United States in the Modern Era* (New York, 1988). On women and the welfare state, see E. Wilson, *Women and the Welfare State* (London, 1977), and D. Sainsbury, ed., *Gendering Welfare States* (London, 1994). On the women's liberation movement, see D. Bouchier, *The Feminist Challenge: The Movement for Women's Liberation in Britain and the United States* (New York, 1983); D. Meyer, *Sex and Power: The Rise of Women in America, Russia, Sweden, and Italy* (Middletown, Conn., 1987); T. Keefe, *Simone de Beauvoir* (New York, 1998); and C. Duchen, *Women's Rights and Women's Lives in France, 1944–1968* (New York, 1994). More general works that include much information on the contemporary period are B. G. Smith, *Changing Lives: Women in European History Since 1700* (Lexington, Mass., 1989), and F. Thebuad, ed., *A History of Women in the West*, vol. 5, *Toward a Cultural Identity in the Twentieth Century* (Cambridge, Mass., 1994).

For additional reading, go to InfoTrac College Edition, your online research library at http://web1.infotrac-college.com

Enter the search term *Cold War* using the Subject Guide.

Enter the search term *Soviet Union relations with the United States* using the Subject Guide.

Enter the search term *decolonization* using Key Terms.

Enter the search term *Khrushchev* using Key Terms.

C H A P T E R

29

The Western World (Since 1970)

Alexandra Avakian/Woodfin Camp & Associates

CHAPTER OUTLINE

- Moving Beyond the Cold War: A New World Order?
- Toward a New Western Order
- New Directions and New Problems in Western Society
- The World of Western Culture
- Toward a Global Civilization?

FOCUS QUESTIONS

- How and why did the Cold War end?
- What reforms did Gorbachev institute in the Soviet Union, and what role did he play in the Soviet Union's demise?
- What changes have occurred in Eastern Europe as a result of the revolutions of 1989?
- What are the major political and social developments in Western Europe and North America since 1970?
- What major cultural and intellectual trends have emerged since 1970?
- What are the similarities and differences between the feminist movement of the nineteenth century and the post–World War II feminist movement?

BETWEEN 1945 AND 1970, Europe not only overcame the devastating effects of World War II but actually experienced an economic recovery that seemed nothing less than miraculous to many people. Some historians have even labeled the years from 1950 to 1973 "the golden age of the European economy." Economic growth and virtually full employment continued so long that the first post–World War II recession in 1973 came as a shock to Western Europe.

By that time, too, after more than two decades of the Cold War, Europeans had become accustomed to a new division of Europe between West and East. A prosperous Western Europe allied to the United States stood opposed to a still-struggling Eastern Europe that remained largely subject to the Soviet Union. The division of Germany symbolized the new order, which seemed so well established. Yet within two decades, a revolutionary upheaval in the Soviet Union and Eastern Europe brought an end to the Cold War and ended the long-standing division of postwar Europe. Even the Soviet Union ceased to exist as a single nation. On August 19, 1991, a group of Soviet leaders opposed to reform arrested Mikhail Gorbachev, the president of the Soviet Union, and tried to seize control of the government. Hundreds of thousands of Russians, led by Boris Yeltsin, poured into the streets of Moscow and Leningrad to resist the attempted coup. Some army units, sent out to enforce the wishes of the rebels, defected to Yeltsin's side, and within days, the rebels were forced to surrender. This failed attempt to seize power had unexpected results as Russia and many of the other Soviet republics declared their independence. By the end of 1991, the Soviet Union—one of the largest empires in world history—had come to an end, and a new era of cooperation between the successor states in the old Soviet Union and the nations of the West had begun.

As the world adjusted to the transformation from Cold War to post–Cold War sensibilities, other changes shaped the Western outlook. New artistic and intellectual currents, the continued advance of science and technology, a religious revival, the coming to grips with environmental problems, the surge of the women's liberation movement—all spoke of a vibrant, ever-changing new world. At the same time, a devastating terrorist attack on the World Trade Center in New York City and the Pentagon outside Washington, D.C., in 2001 made the Western world vividly aware of its vulnerability to international terrorism.

Moving Beyond the Cold War: A New World Order?

By the 1970s, American-Soviet relations had entered a new phase known as détente, marked by a reduction of tensions between the two superpowers. An appropriate symbol of détente was the Antiballistic Missile Treaty, signed in 1972, in which the two nations agreed to limit their systems for launching antiballistic missiles (ABMs). The U.S. objective in pursuing the treaty was to make it unlikely that either superpower could win a nuclear exchange by launching a preemptive strike against the other. U.S. officials believed that a policy of "equivalence," in which there was a roughly equal power balance on each side, was the best way to avoid a nuclear confrontation.

In 1975, the Helsinki Agreements provided yet another example of reduced tensions between the superpowers. Signed by the United States, Canada, and all European nations, these accords recognized all borders that had been established in Europe since the end of World War II, thereby acknowledging the Soviet sphere of influence in Eastern Europe. The Helsinki Agreements also committed the signatory powers to recognize and protect the human rights of their citizens.

This protection of human rights became one of the major foreign policy goals of the next American president, Jimmy Carter (b. 1924). Although hopes ran high for the continuation of détente, the Soviet invasion of Afghanistan in 1979, undertaken to restore a pro-Soviet regime, hardened relations between the United States and the Soviet Union. President Carter canceled American participation in the 1980 Olympic Games in Moscow and placed an embargo on the shipment of American grain to the Soviet Union.

The early administration of President Ronald Reagan (b. 1911) witnessed a return to the harsh rhetoric, if not all of the harsh practices, of the Cold War. Calling the Soviet Union an "evil empire," Reagan began a military buildup that stimulated a renewed arms race. In 1982, the Reagan administration introduced the nuclear-tipped cruise missile, whose ability to fly at low altitudes made it difficult to detect. President Reagan also became an ardent proponent of the Strategic Defense Initiative (SDI), nicknamed "Star Wars." Its purpose was to create a space shield that could destroy incoming missiles. By providing military support to the Afghan insurgents, the Reagan administration helped maintain a Vietnam-like war in Afghanistan that the Soviet Union could not win. Like the Vietnam War, the war in Afghanistan demonstrated that the power of a superpower was actually limited in the face of strong nationalist, guerrilla-type opposition.

The End of the Cold War

The accession of Mikhail Gorbachev (b. 1931) to power in the Soviet Union (see "The Gorbachev Era" later in this chapter) in 1985 eventually brought a dramatic end to the Cold War. Gorbachev was willing to rethink many of the fundamental assumptions underlying Soviet foreign policy, and his "New Thinking," as it was called, opened the door to a series of stunning changes. For one, Gorbachev initiated a plan for arms limitation that led in 1987 to an agreement with the United States to eliminate intermediate-range nuclear weapons (the INF Treaty). Both sides had incentives to dampen the expensive arms race. Gorbachev hoped to make extensive economic and internal reforms, and the United States had serious deficit problems. During the Reagan years, the United States had moved from being a creditor nation to being the world's biggest debtor nation. By 1990, both countries were becoming aware that their large military budgets made it difficult for them to solve their serious social problems.

The years 1989 and 1990 were a crucial period in the ending of the Cold War. The postwar settlements came unstuck as a mostly peaceful revolutionary upheaval swept through Eastern Europe. Gorbachev's policy of allowing greater autonomy for the Communist regimes of Eastern Europe meant that the Soviet Union would no longer mil-

AP/Wide World Photos

Reagan and Gorbachev. The willingness of Mikhail Gorbachev and Ronald Reagan to dampen the arms race was a significant factor in ending the Cold War confrontation between the United States and the Soviet Union. Reagan and Gorbachev are shown here standing before Saint Basil's Cathedral during Reagan's visit to Moscow in 1988.

itarily support Communist governments that faced internal revolt. The unwillingness of the Soviet regime to use force to maintain the status quo, as it had in Hungary in 1956 and in Czechoslovakia in 1968, opened the door to the overthrow of the Communist regimes (see "Eastern Europe: The Collapse of the Communist Order" later in this chapter). The reunification of Germany on October 3, 1990, marked the end of one of the most prominent legacies of the Cold War.

The Persian Gulf War provided the first major opportunity for testing the new relationship between the United States and the Soviet Union in the post–Cold War era. In early August 1990, Iraqi military forces suddenly occupied the small neighboring country of Kuwait, in the northeastern corner of the Arabian peninsula at the head of the Persian Gulf. The Iraqi invasion of Kuwait sparked an international outcry, and an international force led by the United States liberated Kuwait and destroyed a substantial part of Iraq's armed forces in the early months of 1991.

The Gulf War was the first important military conflict in the post–Cold War period. Although Gorbachev tried to persuade Iraq to withdraw its forces from Kuwait before the war began, overall the Soviets played a minor role in the crisis and supported the American action. By the end of 1991, the Soviet Union had disintegrated, making any renewal of global rivalry between the superpowers impossible. Although this left the United States as the world's leading military power, its role in the creation of the "New World Order" that President George Bush envisioned was not clear. His successor, President Bill Clinton (b. 1946), began to reassert American power in the world. He sent American troops to Haiti in September 1994 to restore that country's fragile democratic system. In December 1995, the United States took the lead in bringing a negotiated end to the war in Bosnia. In 1999, the United States tried to arrange a settlement between Yugoslavia and the Kosovo Liberation Army. When Slobodan Milošević, the Yugoslav president, refused to accept a peace plan, the United States and its NATO allies began a bombing campaign against Yugoslavia that forced it to cooperate (see "The War in Kosovo" later in this chapter). After terrorists struck at the United States in September 2001, President George W. Bush declared war on terrorism and created an international coalition led by the United States to oppose it.

Toward a New Western Order

Between 1945 and 1970, economic recovery had brought renewed growth to Europe. Nevertheless, the political divisions between Western and Eastern Europe remained; so did disparities in prosperity. But in the late 1980s and early 1990s, the Soviet Union and its Eastern European satellite states underwent a revolutionary upheaval that dramatically altered the European landscape (see Map 29.1) and left many Europeans with both new hopes and new fears.

The Revolutionary Era in the Soviet Union

Between 1964 and 1982, significant change in the Soviet Union seemed highly unlikely. The man in charge, Leonid Brezhnev (1906–1982), lived by the slogan "No experimentation." Brezhnev had entered the ranks of the party leadership under Stalin and, after the overthrow of Khrushchev in 1964, had become head of both Party and state. He was always optimistic, yet reluctant to reform. Overall, the Brezhnev years were relatively calm, although the Brezhnev doctrine—the right of the Soviet Union to intervene if socialism was threatened in another socialist state—became an article of faith and led to the use of Soviet troops in Czechoslovakia in 1968.

Brezhnev benefited from the more relaxed atmosphere associated with détente. The Soviets had reached a rough parity with the United States in nuclear arms and enjoyed a sense of external security that seemed to allow for a relaxation of authoritarian rule. The regime permitted more access to Western styles of music, dress, and art, although dissenters were still punished. Andrei Sakharov, for example, who had played an important role in the development of the Soviet hydrogen bomb, was placed under house arrest for his defense of human rights.

In his economic policies, Brezhnev continued to emphasize heavy industry. Overall industrial growth declined, although the Soviet production of iron, steel, coal, and cement surpassed that of the United States. Two prob-

Map 29.1 The New Europe. The combination of an inefficient economy and high military spending had led to stagnation in the Soviet Union by the early 1980s. Mikhail Gorbachev came to power in 1985, unleashing political, economic, and nationalist forces that led to independence for the former Soviet republics and also for Eastern Europe.
■ Compare this map with Map 28.1: What new countries had emerged by the beginning of the twenty-first century?

lems bedeviled the Soviet economy. The government's insistence on vigorous central planning led to a huge, complex bureaucracy that discouraged efficiency and reduced productivity. Moreover, the Soviet system, based on guaranteed employment and a lack of incentives, bred apathy, complacency, absenteeism, and drunkenness. Agricultural problems added to Soviet economic woes. Bad harvests in the mid-1970s, caused by a series of droughts, heavy rains, and early frosts, forced the Soviet government to buy grain from the West, particularly the United States. To their chagrin, the Soviets were increasingly dependent on capitalist countries.

By the 1970s, the Soviet Union had developed a ruling system that depended on patronage as a major avenue of advancement. Those who aspired to rise in the party and the state bureaucracy needed the support of successful Communist Party leaders. At the same time, Party and state leaders—as well as leaders of the army and the secret police (KGB)—were granted awards and material privileges. Brezhnev was unwilling to tamper with the Party leadership and state bureaucracy despite the inefficiency and corruption that the system encouraged.

By 1980, the Soviet Union was ailing. A declining economy, a rise in infant mortality rates, a dramatic surge in alcoholism, and a deterioration in working conditions all gave impetus to a decline in morale and a growing perception that the system was foundering. Within the Party, a small group of reformers emerged who understood the real condition of the Soviet Union. One member of this group was Yuri Andropov (1914–1985), head of the KGB and successor to Brezhnev after the latter's death in November 1982. But Andropov was already old and in poor health when he came to power, and he was unable to make any substantive changes. His most significant move may have been his support for a young reformer, Mikhail Gorbachev, who was climbing the rungs of the Party ladder. When Party leaders chose Gorbachev as Party secretary in March 1985, a new era began.

THE GORBACHEV ERA

Born into a peasant family in 1931, Mikhail Gorbachev combined farm work with school and received the Order of the Red Banner for his agricultural efforts. This award and his good school record enabled him to study law at the University of Moscow. After receiving his law degree in 1955, he returned to his native southern Russia, where he eventually became first secretary of the Party in the city of Stavropol (he had joined the Party in 1952) and then first secretary of the regional Party committee. In 1978, Gorbachev was made a member of the Party's Central Committee in Moscow. Two years later, he became a full member of the ruling Politburo and secretary of the Central Committee. In March 1985, Party leaders elected him general secretary of the Party, and he became the new leader of the Soviet Union.

Educated during the years of reform under Khrushchev, Gorbachev seemed intent on taking earlier reforms to their logical conclusions. By the 1980s, Soviet economic problems were obvious. Rigid, centralized planning led to mismanagement and stifled innovation. Although the Soviets still excelled in space exploration, they fell behind the West in high technology, especially in the development and production of computers for private and public use. Most noticeable to the Soviet people was the actual decline in the standard of living. In February 1986, at the Twenty-Seventh Congress of the Communist Party, Gorbachev made clear the need for changes in Soviet society: "The practical actions of the Party and state agencies lag behind the demands of the times and of life itself. . . . Problems grow faster than they are solved. Sluggishness, ossification in the forms, and methods of management decrease the dynamism of work. . . . Stagnation begins to show up in the life of society."[1] Thus from the start, Gorbachev preached the need for radical reforms.

The cornerstone of Gorbachev's radical reforms was *perestroika,* or "restructuring" (see the box on p. 840). At first, this meant only a reordering of economic policy as Gorbachev called for the beginning of a market economy with limited free enterprise and some private property. However, Gorbachev soon perceived that in the Soviet system, the economic sphere was intimately tied to the social and political spheres. Attempting to reform the economy without political or social reform would be doomed to failure. One of the most important instruments of *perestroika* was *glasnost,* or "openness." Soviet citizens and officials were encouraged to discuss openly the strengths and weaknesses of the Soviet Union. *Pravda,* the official newspaper of the Communist Party, began to include reports of official corruption, sloppy factory work, and protests against government policy. The arts also benefited from the new policy. Previously banned works were now published, and music based on Western styles, such as jazz and rock, began to be performed openly.

Political reforms were equally revolutionary. At the Communist Party conference in 1988, Gorbachev called for the creation of a new Soviet parliament, the Congress of People's Deputies, whose members were to be chosen in competitive elections. It convened in 1989, the first such meeting in Russia since 1918. Early in 1990, Gorbachev legalized the formation of other political parties and struck Article 6, which had guaranteed the "leading role" of the Communist Party, from the Soviet constitution. At the same time, Gorbachev attempted to consolidate his power by creating a new state presidency. The new position was a consequence of the separation of the state from the Communist Party. Hitherto, the position of first secretary of the Party had been the most important post in the Soviet Union, but as the Communist Party became less closely associated with the state, the powers of this office diminished correspondingly. In March 1990, Gorbachev became the Soviet Union's first president.

One of Gorbachev's most serious problems stemmed from the nature of the nation he led. The Union of Soviet Socialist Republics was a truly multiethnic country, containing 92 nationalities and 112 recognized languages.

Gorbachev and Perestroika

After assuming the leadership of the Soviet Union in 1985, Mikhail Gorbachev worked to liberalize and restructure the country. His policies opened the door to rapid changes in Eastern Europe and in Soviet-American relations at the end of the 1980s. In his book *Perestroika,* Gorbachev explained some of his "New Thinking."

■ *Mikhail Gorbachev,* Perestroika

The fundamental principle of the new political outlook is very simple: *nuclear war cannot be a means of achieving political, economic, ideological or any other goals.* This conclusion is truly revolutionary, for it means discarding the traditional notions of war and peace. It is the political function of war that has always been a justification for war, a "rational" explanation. Nuclear war is senseless; it is irrational. There would be neither winners nor losers in a global nuclear conflict: world Civilization would inevitably perish. . . .

But military technology has developed to such an extent that even a non-nuclear war would now be comparable with a nuclear war in its destructive effect. That is why it is logical to include in our category of nuclear wars this "variant" of an armed clash between major powers as well.

Thereby, an altogether different situation has emerged. A way of thinking and a way of acting, based on the use of force in world politics, have formed over centuries, even millennia. It seems they have taken root as something unshakable. Today, they have lost all reasonable grounds. . . . For the first time in history, basing international politics on moral and ethical norms that are common to all humankind, as well as humanizing interstate relations, has become a vital requirement. . . .

There is a great thirst for mutual understanding and mutual communication in the world. It is felt among politicians, it is gaining momentum among the intelligentsia, representatives of culture, and the public at large. And if the Russian word "perestroika" has easily entered the international lexicon, this is due to more than just interest in what is going on in the Soviet Union. Now the whole world needs restructuring, i.e., progressive development, a fundamental change.

People feel this and understand this. They have to find their bearings, to understand the problems besetting mankind, to realize how they should live in the future. The restructuring is a must for a world overflowing with nuclear weapons; for a world ridden with serious economic and ecological problems; for a world laden with poverty, backwardness and disease; for a human race now facing the urgent need of ensuring its own survival.

We are all students, and our teacher is life and time. I believe that more and more people will come to realize that through RESTRUCTURING in the broad sense of the word, the integrity of the world will be enhanced. Having earned good marks from our main teacher—life—we shall enter the twenty-first century well prepared and sure that there will be further progress.

Previously, the iron hand of the Communist Party, centered in Moscow, had kept a lid on the centuries-old ethnic tensions that had periodically erupted. As Gorbachev released this iron grip, tensions resurfaced, a by-product of *glasnost* that Gorbachev had not anticipated. Ethnic groups took advantage of the new openness to protest what they perceived as ethnically motivated slights. When violence erupted, the Soviet army, in disrepair since Afghanistan, had difficulty controlling the situation.

The period 1988 to 1990 also witnessed the appearance of nationalist movements in the republics that made up the Soviet Union. Many were motivated by ethnic concerns, with calls for sovereignty and independence from the Russian-based rule centered in Moscow. These movements sprang up first in Georgia in late 1988 and then in Latvia, Estonia, Moldavia, Uzbekistan, Azerbaijan, and Lithuania. On March 11, 1990, the Lithuanian Supreme Council proclaimed Lithuania an independent state.

THE END OF THE SOVIET UNION

During 1990 and 1991, Gorbachev struggled to deal with Lithuania and the other problems unleashed by his reforms. On the one hand, he tried to appease conservatives who complained about the growing disorder within the Soviet Union. On the other hand, he tried to accommodate the liberal forces, especially those in the Soviet republics, who increasingly favored a new kind of decentralized Soviet federation. In particular, Gorbachev labored to cooperate more closely with Boris Yeltsin, who had been elected president of the Russian Republic in June 1991.

By 1991, the conservative leaders of the traditional Soviet institutions—the army, government, KGB, and military industries—had grown increasingly worried about the impending dissolution of the Soviet Union and its impact on their own fortunes. On August 19, 1991, a group of these discontented rightists arrested Gorbachev and attempted to seize power. Gorbachev's unwillingness to work with the conspirators and the brave resistance in Moscow of Yeltsin and thousands of Russians who had grown accustomed to their new liberties caused the coup to disintegrate rapidly. The actions of these right-wing plotters, however, served to accelerate the very process they had hoped to stop—the disintegration of the Soviet Union.

Despite desperate pleas by Gorbachev, the Soviet republics soon moved for complete independence. Ukraine voted for independence on December 1, 1991, and a week later, the leaders of Russia, Ukraine, and Belarus announced that the Soviet Union had "ceased to exist" and would be

AP/Wide World Photos

Yeltsin Resists a Right-Wing Coup. In August 1991, the attempt of right-wing plotters to overthrow Mikhail Gorbachev and seize power in the Soviet Union was thwarted by the efforts of Boris Yeltsin, president of the Russian Republic, and his supporters. Yeltsin (holding papers) is shown here atop a tank in front of the Russian parliament building in Moscow, urging the Russian people to resist the conspirators.

replaced by the new and voluntary Commonwealth of Independent States. Gorbachev resigned on December 25, 1991, and turned over his responsibilities as commander in chief to Boris Yeltsin, the president of Russia. By the end of 1991, one of the largest empires in world history had evaporated, and a new era had begun in its lands.

Within Russia, a new power struggle soon ensued. Yeltsin was committed to introducing a free market economy as quickly as possible, but the transition was not easy. Economic hardships and social disarray, made worse by a dramatic rise in the activities of organized crime mobs, led increasing numbers of Russians to support both former Communists and hard-line nationalists who criticized Russia's loss of prestige in world affairs. Yeltsin's brutal use of force against the Chechens, who wanted to secede from Russia and create their own independent republic, also undermined his support. Despite the odds against him, however, Yeltsin won reelection as Russia's president in 1996, although his precarious health raised serious questions about his ability to govern.

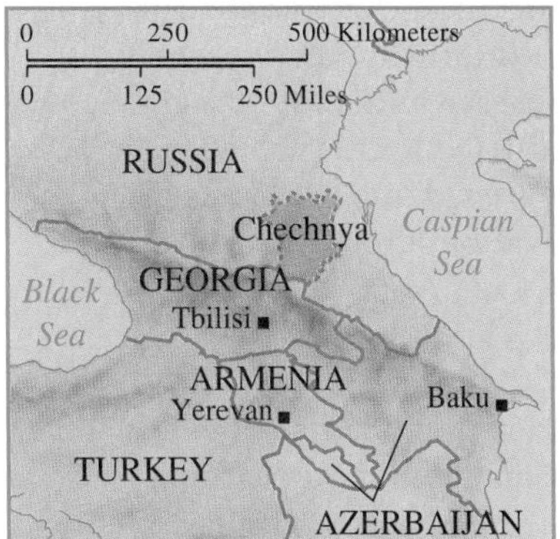

Chechnya

At the end of 1999, Yeltsin suddenly resigned and was replaced by Vladimir Putin, an ex-member of the KGB. Putin vowed to return the breakaway state of Chechnya to Russian authority and to adopt a more assertive role in international affairs. Fighting in Chechnya continued throughout 2000, nearly reducing the republic's capital city of Grozny to ruins. In July 2001, Putin launched reforms, which included the unrestricted sale and purchase of land and tax cuts aimed at boosting economic growth and budget revenues.

Eastern Europe: The Collapse of the Communist Order

Stalin's postwar order had imposed Communist regimes throughout Eastern Europe. The process of sovietization seemed so complete that few people believed that the new order could be undone. But discontent with their Soviet-style regimes always simmered beneath the surface of these satellite states, and after Mikhail Gorbachev made it clear that his government would not intervene militarily, the Communist regimes fell quickly in the revolutions of 1989.

POLAND

Under Wladyslaw Gomulka, Poland had achieved a certain stability in the 1960s, but economic problems led to his replacement in 1971 by Edward Gierek, who attempted to solve Poland's economic problems by borrowing heavily from the West. But in 1980, when he announced huge increases in food prices in an effort to pay off part of the Western debt, workers' protests erupted once again. Unlike the protests of 1956, however, this time the revolutionary demands of the workers led directly to the rise of the independent labor movement called Solidarity. Led by Lech Walesa (b. 1943), Solidarity represented 10 million of Poland's 35 million people. With the support of the workers, many intellectuals, and the Catholic church, Solidarity was able to win a series of concessions. The Polish government seemed powerless to stop the flow of concessions until December 1981, when it arrested Walesa and other Solidarity leaders, outlawed the union, and imposed military rule.

But martial rule did not solve Poland's serious economic problems, and in 1988, new demonstrations led the Polish regime to agree to free parliamentary elections—the first free elections in Eastern Europe in forty years. Bowing to the inevitable, the military regime allowed the newly elected Solidarity coalition to form a new government, thus ending forty-five years of Communist rule in Poland. In December 1990, Lech Walesa was chosen as the new Polish president. But Poland's new path was not an easy one. Rapid free market reforms led to severe unemployment and popular discontent, and in November 1995, Aleksander Kwasniewski, a former Communist, defeated Walesa and became president. However, he has continued Poland's move toward an increasingly prosperous free market economy.

HUNGARY

In Hungary, too, the process of liberation from Communist rule had begun before 1989. Remaining in power for over thirty years, the government of János Kádár enacted the most far-reaching economic reforms in Eastern Europe. In the early 1980s, Kádár legalized small private enterprises, such as retail stores, restaurants, and artisan shops. His economic reforms were termed "Communism with a capitalist facelift." Under his leadership, Hungary moved slowly away from its strict adherence to Soviet dominance and even established fairly friendly relations with the West.

As the 1980s progressed, however, the economy sagged, and Kádár fell from power in 1988. By 1989, the Hungarian Communist government was aware of the growing dissatisfaction and began to undertake reforms. But they came too late as new political parties called for Hungary to become a democratic republic. In elections in March 1990, the Communists came in fourth, winning only 8.5 percent of the vote, a clear repudiation. The Democratic Forum, a right-of-center, highly patriotic party, won the election and formed a new coalition government that committed Hungary to democratic government and the institution of a free market economy.

CZECHOSLOVAKIA

Communist regimes in Poland and Hungary had attempted to make some political and economic reforms in the 1970s and 1980s, but this was not the case in Czechoslovakia. After Soviet troops had crushed the reform movement in 1968, hard-line Czech Communists under Gustav Husák purged the Party and instituted a policy of massive repression to maintain their power. Only writers and other intellectuals provided any real opposition to the government, but they did not have any success until the late 1980s. Government attempts to suppress mass demonstrations in Prague and other cities in 1988 and 1989 only led to more and larger demonstrations. By November 1989, crowds as large as 500,000, which included many students, were forming in Prague. A new opposition group, the Civic Forum, emerged and was officially recognized on November 17. In December 1989, as demonstrations continued, the Communist government, lacking any real support, collapsed. President Husák resigned and at the end of December was replaced by Vaclav Havel (b. 1936), a dissident playwright who had played an important role in bringing the Communist government down. In January 1990, Havel declared amnesty for some thirty thousand political prisoners. He also set out on a goodwill tour to various Western countries in which he proved to be an eloquent spokesman for Czech democracy and a new order in Europe (see the box on p. 844).

Within Czechoslovakia, the shift to non-Communist rule was complicated by old problems, especially ethnic issues. Czechs and Slovaks disagreed over the makeup of the new state but were able to agree to a peaceful division of the country. On January 1, 1993, Czechoslovakia split into the Czech Republic and Slovakia. Vaclav Havel was elected the first president of the new Czech Republic.

ROMANIA

Czechoslovakia's revolutionary path was considerably less violent than Romania's. By 1948, with Soviet assistance, the Communist People's Democratic Front had assumed complete power in Romania. In 1965, leadership of the Communist government passed into the hands of Nicolae Ceaușescu (1918–1989), who with his wife, Elena, established a rigid and dictatorial regime. Ceaușescu ruled Romania with an iron grip, using a secret police force—the Securitate—as his personal weapon against dissent. Nevertheless, opposition to his regime grew as Ceaușescu rejected the reforms in Eastern Europe promoted by Gorbachev. Ceaușescu's regime had for years stood aloof from the Soviet Union, especially in foreign policy. In addition, Ceaușescu's extreme measures to reduce Romania's external debt led to economic difficulties. Although he was successful in reducing foreign debt, the sharp drop in living standards that resulted from those hardship measures angered many Romanians. Despite food shortages and the rationing of bread, flour, and sugar, Ceaușescu insisted that the country should continue exporting such goods. Ceaușescu's plan for rapid urbanization, especially a program that called for the bulldozing of entire villages, further angered the populace.

A small incident became the spark that ignited heretofore suppressed flames of discontent. The ruthless crushing of a demonstration in Timisoara in December 1989 led to other mass demonstrations. After the dictator was booed at a mass rally on December 21, the army refused to support any more repression. Ceaușescu and his wife were captured on December 22 and tried and executed on Christmas Day. Leadership now passed into the hands of the hastily formed National Salvation Front, which won elections in the spring of 1990.

BULGARIA

In Bulgaria, too, Soviet cooperation after the war enabled the local Communist Party to assume control of the country. In 1954, Todor Zhivkov (1911–1998) became the leader of the Bulgarian Communist Party and hence leader of the

Geroges Merillon/Getty Images

A Romanian Revolutionary. The revolt against Communist rule in Eastern Europe in 1989 came last to Romania. It was also more violent as the government at first tried to stem the revolt by massacring demonstrators. This picture shows a young Romanian rebel waving the national flag with the Communist emblem cut out of the center.

nation. Not until the late 1980s did a number of small opposition groups begin to emerge. In October 1989, antigovernment demonstrations were held in the capital city of Sofia, and a month later, Zhivkov was unexpectedly relieved of his post as general secretary of the Communist Party, a position he had held for thirty-five years. Elections in November 1991 brought about a new government coalition, led by the United Democratic Front. Nevertheless, the Socialist Party (the former Communists) remained a potent force in Bulgarian politics.

ALBANIA

Albania was Eastern Europe's smallest and poorest country. Isolated from its neighbors, Albania maintained its hard-line Stalinist political system well into the 1980s. The oppressive regime of Enver Hoxha (1908–1985) ruled the country from 1944 to 1985, when Hoxha's handpicked successor, Ramiz Alia (b. 1925), assumed power. Throughout this period, Albania remained a closed society; it had little contact with the rest of the world, which in turn knew little about it. Nevertheless, the revolutionary upheaval of 1989 also reached Albania. Antigovernment demonstrations broke out in the Albanian capital of Tirana in 1990, forcing Alia's government to promise reforms. New political parties were legalized, and Albania's first free election was held in March 1991. Political and social unrest and economic decline have continued to trouble the Republic of Albania.

The Reunification of Germany

Until 1989, the existence of two Germanies, West and East, remained the most powerful symbol of the division of postwar Europe. In the early 1950s, the ruling Communist government in East Germany, led by Walter Ulbricht, had consolidated its position and become a faithful Soviet satellite. Industry was nationalized and agriculture collectivized. After a workers' revolt in 1953 was crushed by Soviet tanks, a steady flight of East Germans to West Germany ensued, primarily through the divided city of Berlin. This exodus of mostly skilled laborers created economic problems and led the East German government in 1961 to build the infamous Berlin Wall separating West from East Berlin, as well as equally fearsome barriers along the entire border with West Germany.

Vaclav Havel: The Call for a New Politics

In attempting to deal with the world's problems, some European leaders have pointed to the need for a new perspective, especially a moral one, if people are to live in a sane world. These two excerpts are taken from speeches by Vaclav Havel, who was elected the new president of Czechoslovakia at the end of 1989. The first is from his inaugural address as president of Czechoslovakia on January 1, 1990; the second is from a speech given to the U.S. Congress.

Vaclav Havel, Address to the People of Czechoslovakia, January 1, 1990

But all this is still not the main problem [the environmental devastation of the country by its Communist leaders]. The worst thing is that we live in a contaminated moral environment. We fell morally ill because we became used to saying something different from what we thought. We learned not to believe in anything, to ignore each other, to care only about ourselves. Concepts such as love, friendship, compassion, humility, or forgiveness lost their depth and dimensions, and for many of us they represented only psychological peculiarities, or they resembled gone-astray greetings from ancients, a little ridiculous in the era of computers and spaceships. Only a few of us were able to cry out loud that the powers that be should not be all-powerful, and that special farms, which produce ecologically pure and top-quality food just for them should send their produce to schools, children's homes and hospitals if our agriculture was unable to offer them to all. The previous regime—armed with its arrogant and intolerant ideology—reduced man to a force of production and nature to a tool of production. In this it attacked both their very substance and their mutual relationship. It reduced gifted and autonomous people, skillfully working in their own country, to nuts and bolts of some monstrously huge, noisy, and stinking machine, whose real meaning is not clear to anyone.

Vaclav Havel, Speech to Congress, February 21, 1990

For this reason, the salvation of this human world lies nowhere else than in the human heart, in the human power to reflect, in human meekness and in human responsibility.

Without a global revolution in the sphere of human consciousness, nothing will change for the better in the sphere of our being as humans, and the catastrophe toward which this world is headed—be it ecological, social, demographic or a general breakdown of civilization—will be unavoidable. . . .

We are still a long way from that "family of man." In fact, we seem to be receding from the ideal rather than growing closer to it. Interests of all kinds—personal, selfish, state, nation, group, and if you like, company interests—still considerably outweigh genuinely common and global interests. We are still under the sway of the destructive and vain belief that man is the pinnacle of creation and not just a part of it and that therefore everything is permitted. . . .

In other words, we still don't know how to put morality ahead of politics, science and economics. We are still incapable of understanding that the only genuine backbone of all our actions, if they are to be moral, is responsibility.

Responsibility to something higher than my family, my country, my company, my success—responsibility to the order of being where all our actions are indelibly recorded and where and only where they will be properly judged.

The interpreter or mediator between us and this higher authority is what is traditionally referred to as human conscience.

After building the wall, East Germany succeeded in developing the strongest economy among the Soviet Union's Eastern European satellites. In 1971, Ulbricht was succeeded by Erich Honecker (1912–1992), a party hardliner who made use of the Stasi, the secret police, to rule with an iron fist for the next eighteen years.

In 1988, however, popular unrest, fueled in part by the economic slump of the 1980s (which affected most of Eastern Europe) as well as the ongoing oppressiveness of Honecker's regime, caused another mass exodus of East German refugees. Violent repression and Honecker's refusal to institute reforms only led to a larger exodus and mass demonstrations against the regime in the summer and fall of 1989. Capitulating to popular pressure on November 9, the Communist government opened the entire border with the West. Hundreds of thousands of Germans swarmed across the border, mostly to visit and return. The Berlin Wall, long the symbol of the Cold War, became the site of massive celebrations as thousands of people used sledgehammers to tear down the wall. By December, new political parties had emerged, and on March 18, 1990, in East Germany's first free elections ever, the Christian Democrats won almost 50 percent of the vote.

The Christian Democrats supported rapid monetary unification followed shortly by political unification with West Germany. On July 1, 1990, the economies of West and East Germany were united, with the West German deutsche mark becoming the official currency of the two countries. Political reunification was achieved on October 3, 1990. What had seemed almost impossible at the beginning of

Alexandra Avakian/Woodfin Camp & Associates

And the Wall Came Tumbling Down. The Berlin Wall, long a symbol of Europe's Cold War divisions, became the site of massive celebrations after the East German government opened its border with the West. The activities included spontaneous acts of demolition as Germans used sledgehammers and crowbars to tear down parts of the wall.

1989 had become a reality by the end of 1990—Germany was whole again, and the country of East Germany had ceased to exist.

The Disintegration of Yugoslavia

From its beginning in 1919, Yugoslavia had been an artificial creation. After World War II, the dictatorial Marshal Tito had managed to hold the six republics and two autonomous provinces that constituted Yugoslavia together. After his death in 1980, no strong leader emerged, and his responsibilities passed to a collective state presidency and the League of Communists of Yugoslavia. At the end of the 1980s, Yugoslavia was caught up in the reform movements sweeping through Eastern Europe. The League of Communists collapsed, and new parties quickly emerged.

The Yugoslav political scene was complicated by the development of separatist movements. In 1990, the republics of Slovenia, Croatia, Bosnia-Herzegovina, and Macedonia began to lobby for a new federal structure of Yugoslavia that would fulfill their separatist desires. Slobodan Milošević, who had become the leader of the Serbian Communist Party in 1987 and had managed to stay in power by emphasizing his Serbian nationalism, rejected these efforts. He asserted that these republics could be independent only if new border arrangements were made to accommodate the Serb minorities in those republics who did not want to live outside the boundaries of a Greater Serbian state. Serbs constituted 11.6 percent of Croatia's population and 32 percent of Bosnia-Herzegovina's in 1981.

After negotiations among the six republics failed, Slovenia and Croatia declared their independence in June 1991. Milošević's government sent the Yugoslavian army, which it controlled, into Slovenia, without much success. In September 1991, it began a full assault against Croatia. Increasingly, the Yugoslavian army was becoming the Serbian army, while Serbian irregular forces played a growing role in military operations. Before a cease-fire was arranged, the Serbian forces had captured one-third of Croatia's territory in brutal and destructive fighting.

THE WAR IN BOSNIA

The recognition of Bosnia-Herzegovina, Slovenia, and Croatia by many European states and the United States early in 1992 did not stop the Serbs from turning their guns on Bosnia. By mid-1993, Serbian forces had acquired 70 percent of Bosnian territory (see the box on p. 846). The Serbian policy of "ethnic cleansing"—killing or forcibly removing Bosnian Muslims from their lands—revived memories of Nazi atrocities in World War II. Nevertheless, despite worldwide outrage, European governments failed to take a decisive and forceful stand against these Serbian activities. By 1995, some 250,000 Bosnians (mostly civilians) had been killed, and two million others were left homeless.

Renewed offensives by mostly Muslim Bosnian government army forces and by the Croatian army regained considerable territory that had been lost to Serbian forces. Air strikes by NATO bombers, strongly advocated by U.S. President Bill Clinton, were launched in retaliation for Serb attacks on civilians and weakened the Serb military positions. All sides were now encouraged by the United States to end the war and met in Dayton, Ohio, in November 1995 for negotiations. A formal peace treaty was signed in Paris on December 14 that split Bosnia into a loose union of a Serb republic (with 49 percent of the land) and a Muslim-Croat federation (with 51 percent of the land). NATO agreed to send a force of 60,000 troops (20,000 American troops made up the largest single contingent) that would monitor the frontier between the new political entities (see Map 29.2).

THE WAR IN KOSOVO

Peace in Bosnia, however, did not bring peace to the remnants of Yugoslavia. A new war erupted in 1999 over Kosovo, which had been made an autonomous province within Yugoslavia in 1974. Kosovo's inhabitants were mainly ethnic Albanians who were allowed to keep their Albanian language. But Kosovo also contained a Serbian minority who considered Kosovo a sacred territory because it contained the site where Serbian forces had been defeated by the Ottoman Turks in the fourteenth century in a battle that became a defining moment in Serbian history.

Bosnia: Two Faces of War

In April 1993, Serbian forces surrounded the Muslim town of Srebrenica in eastern Bosnia. After ferocious shelling by the Serbs, the town appeared ready to surrender. On April 17, 1993, newspapers in Sarajevo (the capital of Bosnia-Herzegovina) and Belgrade (the capital of Serbia) gave their readers very different versions of what was happening in Srebrenica.

Olsobodjenje *(Sarajevo)*

Tomorrow, a Canadian battalion serving with the United Nations Protection Force should enter Srebrenica as a result of negotiations between Lieut. Gen. Lars-Eric Wahlgren, commander of the U.N. force, and the war criminal Karadzic [Radovan Karadzic, leader of the Bosnian Serbs]. A Golgotha continues for the citizens of Srebrenica.... Zlatko Lagumdzija, the Deputy Prime Minister of Bosnia and Herzegovina, has told the world that Mladic's army [General Ratko Mladic, commander of the Bosnian Serb forces], that is Milošević's army [President Slobodan Milošević of Serbia], has to be stopped, that the only thing that the aggressor army understands is force, and that the only way it can be stopped is by confronting it with a greater force.... The aggressor forces continued their offensive at Srebrenica throughout the day yesterday with undiminished intensity, and the people of the town continued to give a heroic account of themselves in resisting the attempt by the more numerous and better-armed attackers to penetrate the town's outskirts. Besides their push across the front lines, the Chetniks [Serbian forces] continued to use their heavy artillery to shell the center of Srebrenica, massacring civilians. During the morning hours alone, the Chetnik artillery killed six people and injured 15, including several children. In Tuzla ... local and foreign reporters were presented with a transcript of an intercepted radio-telephone conversation between war criminal Mladic and the Chetnik commanders in the area ... in which he ordered them to press the attacks so as to enter Srebrenica before he began his negotiations on a cease-fire.

Politika *(Belgrade)*

In spite of the fact that the Muslim armed forces are facing a total military defeat, they again launched attacks this morning from various directions from the territory of Srebrenica. According to Tanjug [Yugoslav news agency] reporting from this region, the Muslim units are using all their artillery and firing equipment. The Serbian sources say that Serbian defenders had tens of dead and wounded following attacks by Muslim forces which lasted for days. The army of the Republika Srpska [the name Serb nationalists gave to their self-proclaimed government in Bosnia] was forced to respond strongly in a counterattack and it has reached strategically important peaks around Srebrenica. The Serbian lines are only about one kilometer by air from Srebrenica. Using the fact that the Serbian side is not undertaking any action against Srebrenica itself, the Muslim extremists continued to attack. During the morning the most severe attacks of the Muslims were launched on Ratkovic, Zeleni Jadar, Podravanje and Milici. According to Tanjug, the Serbian sources are reporting that Muslim soldiers have started surrendering arms yesterday. There were such individual cases in the region of Skelani, Bratunac, Derventa and Podravanje. The Muslim extremists are in a hopeless situation from the military point of view. They are still reluctant to surrender because they were the ones to destroy 56 Serbian villages near Srebrenica, Bratunac and Skelani and on several occasions have killed in a most brutal way more than 1,300 Serbs, mostly women, children and aged people.

In 1989, Slobodan Milošević, the Yugoslav president, who had become an ardent Serbian nationalist to remain in power, stripped Kosovo of its autonomous status and outlawed any official use of the Albanian language. In 1993, some groups of ethnic Albanians founded the Kosovo Liberation Army (KLA) and began a campaign against Serbian rule in Kosovo. When Serb forces began to massacre ethnic Albanians in an effort to crush the KLA, the United States and its NATO allies sought to arrange a settlement. After months of negotiations, the Kosovo Albanians agreed to a peace plan that would have given the ethnic Albanians in Kosovo broad autonomy for a three-year interim period. When Milošević refused to sign the agreement, the United States and its NATO allies began a bombing campaign that forced the Yugoslavian government into compliance. In the fall elections of 2000, Milošević himself was ousted from power and later put on trial by an international tribunal for war crimes against humanity for his ethnic cleansing policies throughout Yugoslavia's disintegration.

Western Europe: The Winds of Change

After two decades of incredible economic growth, Europe experienced severe economic recessions in 1973–1974 and 1979–1983. Both inflation and unemployment rose dramatically. A substantial increase in the price of oil in 1973 was a major cause for the first downturn. But other factors were present as well. A worldwide recession had led to a decline in demand for European goods, and in Europe itself, the reconstruction of many European cities after their devastation in World War II had largely been completed. The economies of the Western European states recovered in the course of the 1980s, although problems remained. Unemployment was still high, even after almost a decade of

The War in Kosovo. In 1999, war erupted in Yugoslavia as Slobodan Milošević pursued a ruthless policy of ethnic cleansing in the province of Kosovo. Serbian troops forced hundreds of thousands of ethnic Albanians to flee their homeland in terror. This photograph shows ethnic Albanian refugees moving into a temporary relief camp after crossing the border into Macedonia on April 24, 1999.

growth. The unemployment rate in France reached 11.7 percent by the end of 1995. Yet despite their economic woes, Western Europeans were full participants in the technological growth of the age and seemed quite capable of standing up to American and Japanese economic competition.

Europeans also moved toward further integration of their economies after 1970. The European Economic Community expanded in 1973 when Great Britain, Ireland, and Denmark joined what its members now renamed the European Community (EC). By 1986, three additional members—Spain, Portugal, and Greece—had been added. The economic integration of the members of the European Community led to cooperative efforts in international and political affairs as well.

Nevertheless, the European Community was still primarily an economic union, not a political one. By 1992, the EC comprised 344 million people and constituted the world's largest single trading entity, transacting almost one-fourth of the world's commerce. In the 1990s, the EC moved toward even greater economic integration. The Treaty on European Union (also called the Maastricht Treaty after the city in the Netherlands where the agreement was reached) represented an attempt to create a true economic and monetary union of all EC members. On January 1, 1994, the EC became the European Union. One of its first goals was to introduce a common currency, called the euro, adopted by eleven EU nations early in 1999. The euro officially replaced eleven national currencies in 2001.

GERMANY RESTORED

After the Adenauer era, West German voters moved politically from the center-right politics of the Christian Democrats to center-left politics, and in 1969, the Social Democrats became the leading party. By forming a ruling coalition with the small Free Democratic Party (FPD), the Social Democrats remained in power until 1982. The first Social Democratic chancellor was Willy Brandt (1913–1992). Brandt was especially successful with his "opening toward the east" (known as *Ostpolitik*), for which he received the Nobel Peace Prize in 1972. In the same year, Brandt made a Basic Treaty with East Germany that called for "good neighborly" relations, which soon led to greater cultural, personal, and economic contacts between West and East Germany.

Brandt's successor, Helmut Schmidt (b. 1918), was more of a technocrat than a reform-minded socialist and concentrated primarily on the economic problems largely brought about by high oil prices between 1973 and 1975.

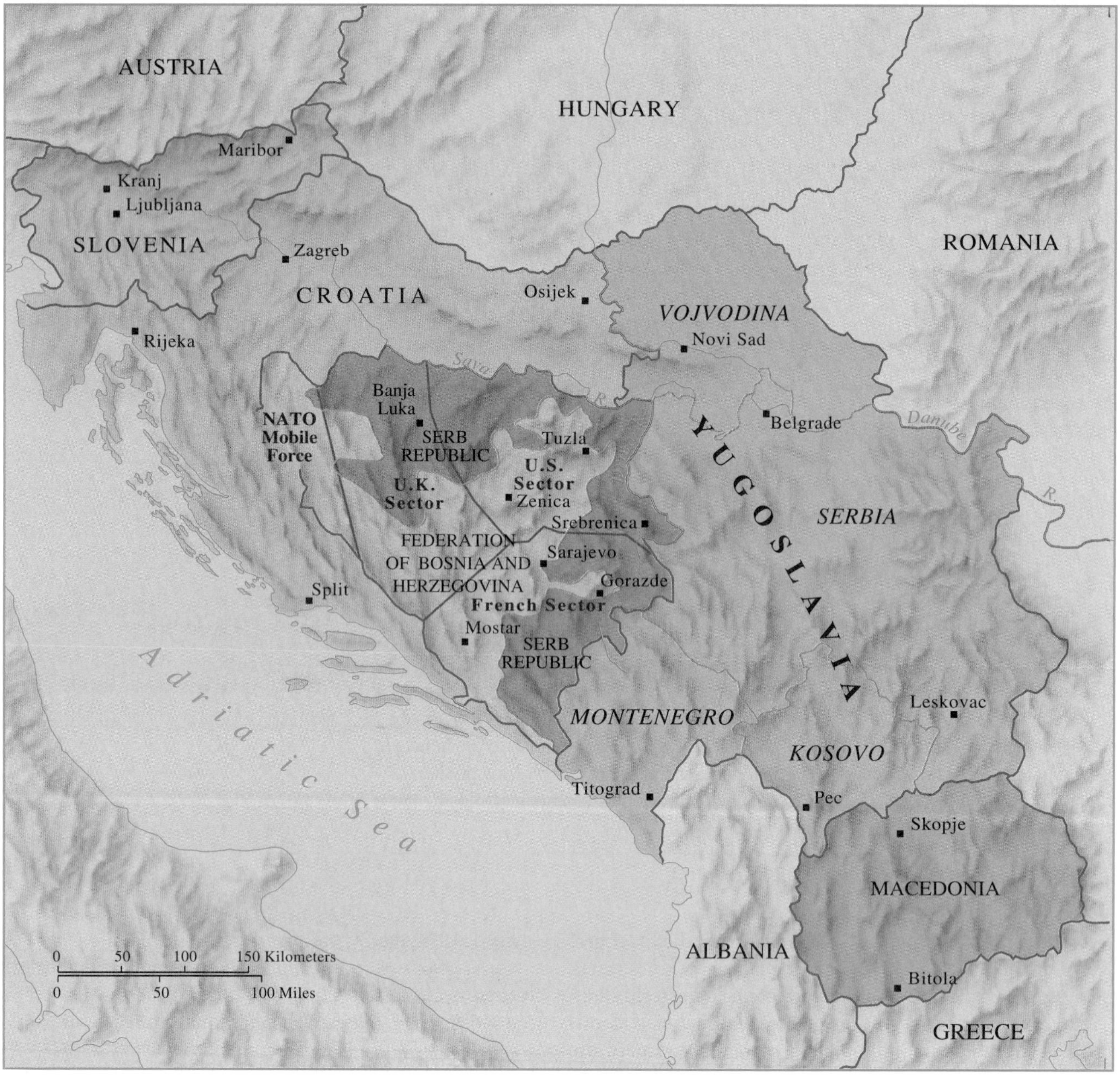

Map 29.2 The Lands of the Former Yugoslavia. By 1991, resurgent nationalism and the European independence wave overcame the forces that held Yugoslavia together. Independence declarations by Slovenia, Croatia, and Bosnia-Herzegovina brought war with the Serbian-dominated rump Yugoslavia of Slobodan Milošević. ■ What aspects of Slovenia's location help explain why its war of liberation was briefer and less bloody than others in the former Yugoslavia?

Schmidt was successful in eliminating a deficit of 10 billion marks in three years. In 1982, when the coalition of Schmidt's Social Democrats with the Free Democrats fell apart over the reduction of social welfare expenditures, the Free Democrats joined with the Christian Democratic Union of Helmut Kohl (b. 1930) to form a new government.

Kohl was a clever politician who benefited greatly from an economic boom in the mid-1980s. Gradually, however, discontent with the Christian Democrats increased, and by 1988, their political prospects seemed diminished. But unexpectedly, the 1989 revolution in East Germany led to the reunification of the two Germanies, leaving the new Germany, with its 79 million people, the leading power in Europe. Reunification, accomplished during Kohl's administration, brought rich political dividends to the Christian Democrats. In the first all-German federal election, Kohl's Christian Democrats won 44 percent of the vote, while their coalition partners, the Free Democrats, received 11 percent.

CHRONOLOGY

The Soviet Bloc and Its Demise

Rule of Enver Hoxha in Albania	1944–1985
Era of Brezhnev	1964–1982
Rule of Ceauşescu in Romania	1965–1989
Honecker succeeds Ulbricht in East Germany	1971
Emergence of Solidarity in Poland	1980
Gorbachev comes to power in the Soviet Union	1985
	1989
Zhivkov loses power in Bulgaria	November 10
Collapse of Communist government in Czechoslovakia	December
Collapse of East German government	December
Execution of Ceauşescu in Romania	December 25
	1990
Lithuania declares independence	March 11
East German elections—victory of Christian Democrats	March 18
Hungarian elections	March 25
Reunification of Germany	October 3
Walesa becomes president of Poland	December
	1991
Yeltsin becomes president of Russia	June
Slovenia and Croatia declare independence	June
Right-wing coup in the Soviet Union	August 19
Dissolution of the Soviet Union	December
	1992
Havel resigns as president of Czechoslovakia	July
	1993
Czechoslovakia splits into Czech Republic and Slovakia	January 1
Havel becomes president of Czech Republic	February 2
	1995
Aleksander Kwasniewski becomes Polish president	November
Dayton accords—end of war in Bosnia	December
War in Kosovo	1999
Putin as president of Russia	2000

But the excitement over reunification soon dissipated as new problems arose. All too soon, the realization set in that the revitalization of eastern Germany would take far more money than was originally thought, and Kohl's government was soon forced to face the politically undesirable task of raising taxes substantially. Moreover, the virtual collapse of the economy in eastern Germany led to extremely high levels of unemployment and severe discontent. One of the responses was a return to power for the Social Democrats as a result of elections in 1998.

GREAT BRITAIN: THATCHER AND THATCHERISM

Between 1964 and 1979, the Conservative and Labour Parties alternated in power. Neither could solve the problem of fighting between Catholics and Protestants in Northern Ireland. Violence increased as the Irish Republican Army (IRA) staged a series of dramatic terrorist acts in response to the suspension of Northern Ireland's parliament in 1972 and the establishment of direct rule by London. Nor was either party able to deal with Britain's ailing economy. Failure to modernize made British industry less and less competitive. Moreover, Britain was hampered by frequent labor strikes, many of them caused by conflicts between rival labor unions.

In 1979, after Britain's economic problems had seemed to worsen during five years under a Labour government, the Conservatives returned to power under Margaret Thatcher (b. 1925). She became the first woman to serve as prime minister in British history (see the box on p. 850). Thatcher pledged to lower taxes, reduce government bureaucracy, limit social welfare, restrict union power, and end inflation. The "Iron Lady," as she was called, did break the power of the labor unions. Although she did not eliminate the basic components of the social welfare system, she did use austerity measures to control inflation. "Thatcherism," as her economic policy was termed, improved the British

Margaret Thatcher. Great Britain's first female prime minister, Margaret Thatcher was a strong leader who dominated British politics in the 1980s. This picture of Thatcher was taken at the Chelsea Flower Show in May 1990. Six months later, a revolt within her own party caused her to resign as prime minister.

Mark Stewart/Camera Press, London

Margaret Thatcher: Entering a Man's World

In 1979, Margaret Thatcher became the first woman to serve as Britain's prime minster and went on to be its longest-serving prime minister as well. In this excerpt from her autobiography, Thatcher describes how she was interviewed by Conservative Party officials when they first considered her as a possible candidate for Parliament. Thatcher ran for Parliament for the first time in 1950; she lost but did increase the Conservative vote total in the district by 50 percent over the previous election.

■ *Margaret Thatcher,* The Path to Power

And, as always with me, there was politics. I immediately joined the Conservative Association and threw myself into the usual round of Party activities. In particular, I thoroughly enjoyed what was called the "'39–'45" discussion group, where Conservatives of the war generation met to exchange views and argue about the political topics of the day. . . . It was as a representative of the Oxford University Graduate Conservative Association (OUGCA) that I went to the Llandudno Conservative Party Conference in October 1948.

It had originally been intended that I should speak at the Conference, seconding an OUGCA motion deploring the abolition of university seats. At that time universities had separate representation in Parliament, and graduates had the right to vote in their universities as well as in the constituency where they lived. (I supported separate university representation, but not the principle that graduates should have more than one vote. . . .) It would have been my first Conference speech, but in the end the seconder chosen was a City man, because the City seats were also to be abolished.

My disappointment at this was, however, very quickly overcome and in a most unexpected way. After one of the debates, I found myself engaged in one of those speculative conversations which young people have about their future prospects. An Oxford friend, John Grant, said he supposed that one day I would like to be a Member of Parliament. "Well, yes," I replied, "but there's not much hope of that. The chances of my being selected are just nil at the moment." I might have added that with no private income of my own there was no way I could have afforded to be an MP on the salary then available. I had not even tried to get on the Party's list of approved candidates.

Later in the day, John Grant happened to be sitting next to the Chairman of the Dartford Conservative Association, John Miller. The Association was in search of a candidate. I learned afterwards that the conversation went something like this: "I understand that you're still looking for a candidate at Dartford?" . . .

"That's right. Any suggestions?"

"Well, there's a young woman, Margaret Roberts, that you might look at. She's very good."

"Oh, but Dartford is a real industrial stronghold. I don't think a woman would do at all."

"Well, you know best of course. But why not just look at her?"

And they did. I was invited to have lunch with John Miller and his wife, Phee, and the Dartford Woman's Chairman, Mrs. Fletcher, on the Saturday on Llandudno Pier. Presumably, and in spite of any reservations about the suitability of a woman candidate for their seat, they liked what they saw. I certainly got on well with them. . . .

I did not hear from Dartford until December, when I was asked to attend an interview at Palace Chambers, Bridge Street. . . . Very few outside the political arena know just how nerve-racking such occasions are. The interviewee who is not nervous and tense is very likely to perform badly: for, as any chemist will tell you, the adrenaline needs to flow if one is to perform at one's best. . . .

I found myself short-listed, and was asked to go to Dartford itself for a further interview. . . . As one of five would-be candidates, I had to give a fifteen-minute speech and answer questions for a further ten minutes.

It was the questions which were more likely to cause me trouble. There was a good deal of suspicion of woman candidates, particularly in what was regarded as a tough industrial seat like Dartford. This was quite definitely a man's world into which not just angels feared to tread. . . .

The most reliable sign that a political occasion has gone well is that you have enjoyed it. I enjoyed that evening at Dartford, and the outcome justified my confidence. I was selected.

economic situation, but at a price. The south of England, for example, prospered, but the old industrial areas of the Midlands and north declined and were beset by high unemployment, poverty, and sporadic violence. Cutbacks in education seriously undermined the quality of British education, long regarded as among the world's finest.

In the area of foreign policy, Thatcher, like Ronald Reagan in the United States, took a hard-line approach toward communism. She oversaw a large military buildup aimed at replacing older technology and reestablishing Britain as a world police officer. In 1982, when Argentina attempted to take control of the Falkland Islands (one of Britain's few remaining colonial outposts) 300 miles off its coast, the British successfully rebuked the Argentines. The Falklands War generated much popular patriotic support for Thatcher.

Margaret Thatcher dominated British politics in the 1980s. The Labour Party, beset by divisions between its moderate and radical wings, offered little effective opposition. Only in 1990 did Labour's fortunes seem to revive when Thatcher's government attempted to replace local property taxes with a flat-rate tax payable by every adult to his or her local authority. Though Thatcher maintained that this would make local government more responsive to its electors, many argued that this was nothing more than a poll tax that would enable the rich to pay the same rate as the poor. In 1990, after antitax riots broke out, Thatcher's once remarkable popularity fell to an all-time low. At the end of November, a revolt within her own party caused Thatcher to resign as prime minister. She was replaced by John Major, whose Conservative Party won a narrow victory in the general elections held in April 1992. His government, however, failed to capture the imagination of most Britons. In new elections on May 1, 1997, the Labour Party won a landslide victory. The new prime minister, Tony Blair (b. 1953), was a moderate whose youthful energy immediately instilled new vigor into the political scene. Blair was one of the major leaders in forming an international coalition against terrorism after the terrorist attack on the United States in 2001.

CHRONOLOGY

Western Europe

Willy Brandt as chancellor of West Germany	1969
Helmut Schmidt as chancellor of West Germany	1974
Margaret Thatcher as prime minister of Britain	1979
François Mitterrand as president of France	1981
Falklands War	1982
Helmut Kohl as chancellor of West Germany	1982
Reelection of Mitterrand	1988
First all-German federal election	1990
Treaty on European Union proposed	1991
Victory of Conservative Party under John Major	1992
Conservative victory in France	1993
Creation of European Union	1994
Jacques Chirac as president of France	1995
Victory of center-left coalition in Italy	1996
Election of Tony Blair in Britain	1997
Victory of Social Democrats in Germany	1998

UNCERTAINTIES IN FRANCE

The worsening of France's economic situation in the 1970s brought a shift to the left politically. By 1981, the Socialists had become the dominant party in the National Assembly, and the Socialist leader, François Mitterrand (1916–1995), was elected president. His first concern was with France's economic difficulties. In 1982, Mitterrand froze prices and wages in the hope of reducing the huge budget deficit and high inflation. He also passed a number of liberal measures to aid workers: an increased minimum wage, expanded social benefits, a mandatory fifth week of paid vacation for salaried workers, a thirty-nine-hour workweek, and higher taxes for the rich. Mitterrand's administrative reforms included both centralization (nationalization of banks and industry) and decentralization (granting local governments greater powers). Their victory had convinced the Socialists that they could enact some of their more radical reforms. Consequently, the government nationalized the steel industry, major banks, the space and electronics industries, and important insurance firms.

The Socialist policies largely failed to work, however, and within three years, a decline in support for the Socialists caused the Mitterrand government to turn portions of the economy back over to private enterprise. Some economic improvement in the late 1980s enabled Mitterrand to win a second seven-year term in the 1988 presidential elections. But France's economic decline continued. In 1993, French unemployment stood at 10.6 percent, and in the elections in March of that year, the Socialists won only 28 percent of the vote as a coalition of conservative parties gained 80 percent of the seats in the National Assembly. The move to the right in France was strengthened when the conservative mayor of Paris, Jacques Chirac, was elected president in May 1995.

CONFUSION IN ITALY

In the 1970s and 1980s, Italy continued to practice the politics of coalitions that had characterized much of its history. Italy witnessed the installation of its fiftieth postwar government in 1991, and its new prime minister, Giulio Andreotti, had already served six times in that office. Italian governments continued to consist of coalitions mostly led by the Christian Democrats.

In the 1980s, even the Communists had been included briefly in the government. The Italian Communists had become advocates of Eurocommunism, basically an attempt to broaden communism's support by dropping its Marxist ideology. Although its vote declined in the 1980s, even in 1987, the Communist Party still garnered 26 percent of the vote. The Communists also won a number of local elections and took charge of municipal governments in several cities, including Rome and Naples for a brief time.

In the 1970s, Italy suffered from a severe economic recession. The Italian economy, which depended on imported oil as its chief source of energy, was especially vulnerable to the steep increase in oil prices in 1973. Parallel to the economic problems was a host of political and social problems: student unrest, mass strikes, and terrorist attacks. In 1978, a former prime minister, Aldo Moro, was kidnapped and killed by the Red Brigades, a terrorist organization. Then, too, there was the all-pervasive and corrupting influence of the Mafia, which had always been an important factor in southern Italy but spread to northern Italy as well in the 1980s.

Italy survived the crises of the 1970s and in the 1980s began to experience remarkable economic growth. But severe problems remained. Corruption continued to trouble Italian politics. In 1993, hundreds of politicians and business leaders were under investigation for their involvement in a widespread scheme to use political bribes to secure public contracts. Public disgust with political corruption became so intense that in April 1996, Italian voters took the unusual step of giving control of the government to a center-left coalition that included the Communists.

The United States: Domestic Turmoil

With the election of Richard Nixon as president in 1968, American politics made a shift to the right. Nixon ended American involvement in Vietnam by gradually withdrawing American troops. Politically, he pursued a "southern strategy," carefully calculating that "law and order" issues and a slowdown in racial desegregation would appeal to southern whites. The South, which had once been a Democratic stronghold, began to form a new allegiance to the Republican Party. The Republican strategy also gained support among white Democrats in northern cities, where court-mandated busing to achieve racial integration had led to a white backlash.

As president, Nixon was paranoid about conspiracies and began to use illegal methods to gather political intelligence on his political opponents. One of the president's advisers explained that their intention was to "use the available Federal machinery to screw our political enemies." Nixon's zeal led to the Watergate scandal—the attempted bugging of Democratic National Headquarters, located in the Watergate apartment and hotel complex in Washington, D.C. Although Nixon repeatedly lied to the American public about his involvement in the affair, secret tapes of his own conversations in the White House revealed the truth. On August 9, 1974, Nixon resigned the presidency rather than face possible impeachment and then trial by the U.S. Congress.

After Watergate, American domestic politics focused on economic issues. Vice President Gerald Ford (b. 1913) became president when Nixon resigned, only to lose in the 1976 election to the former governor of Georgia, Jimmy Carter (b. 1924). Both Ford and Carter faced severe economic problems. The period from 1973 to the mid-1980s was one of economic stagnation, which came to be known as stagflation—a combination of high inflation and high unemployment. In part, the economic downturn stemmed from a dramatic change in oil prices. Oil was considered a cheap and abundant source of energy in the 1950s, and Americans had grown dependent on imported oil from the Middle East. But an oil embargo and price increases by the Organization of Petroleum Exporting Countries (OPEC) as a result of the Arab-Israeli War in 1973 quadrupled oil prices. Additional price hikes increased oil prices twentyfold by the end of the 1970s, encouraging inflationary tendencies throughout the entire economy.

By 1980, the Carter administration faced two devastating problems. High inflation and a noticeable decline in average weekly earnings were causing a drop in American living standards. At the same time, a crisis abroad had erupted when fifty-three Americans were taken hostage by the Iranian government of Ayatollah Khomeini. Carter's inability to gain the release of the hostages led to perceptions at home that he was a weak president. His overwhelming loss to Ronald Reagan (b. 1911) in the election of 1980 enabled the chief exponent of right-wing Republican policies to assume the presidency and initiate a new political order.

The Reagan Revolution, as it has been called, consisted of a number of new policies. Reversing decades of increased spending on social welfare, Reagan cut back on the welfare state by reducing spending on food stamps, school lunch programs, and job programs. At the same time, his administration fostered the largest peacetime military buildup in American history. Total federal spending rose from $631 billion in 1981 to over $1 trillion by 1986. But instead of raising taxes to pay for the new expenditures, which far outweighed the budget cuts in social areas, Reagan convinced Congress to rely on "supply-side economics." Massive tax cuts would supposedly stimulate rapid economic growth and produce new revenues. Much of the tax cut went to the wealthy. Reagan's policies seemed to work in the short run as the United States experienced an economic upturn that lasted until the end of the 1980s. The spending policies of the Reagan administration, however, also produced record government deficits, which loomed as an obstacle to long-term growth. In the 1970s, the total deficit was $420 billion. Between 1981 and 1987, Reagan's budget deficits were three times that amount.

The inability of George Bush (b. 1924), Reagan's successor, to deal with the deficit problem as well as an economic downturn, enabled a Democrat, Bill Clinton, to become president in November 1992. The new president was a southern Democrat who claimed to be a new Democrat—one who favored a number of the Republican policies of the 1980s. This was a clear indication that the Democratic victory had by no means halted the rightward drift in American politics. In fact, Clinton's reelection in 1996 was partially due to his adoption of Republican ideas and policies. Much of Clinton's second term, however, was overshadowed by charges of presidential misconduct stemming from the president's affair with Monica Lewinsky, a White House intern. After a bitter partisan struggle, the U.S. Senate acquitted the president on two articles of impeachment brought by the House of Representatives. But Clinton's problems helped the Republican candidate, George W. Bush, win the presidential election in 2000. Although Bush lost the popular vote to Al Gore, he narrowly won the electoral vote after a highly controversial victory in the state of Florida decided ultimately by the U.S. Supreme Court.

Contemporary Canada

In 1963, during a major economic recession, the Liberals had been returned to power in Canada. The most prominent Liberal government was that of Pierre Trudeau (1919–2000), who came to power in 1968. Although French in background, Trudeau was dedicated to Canada's federal union, and in 1968, his government passed the Official Languages Act that allowed both English and French to be used in the federal civil service. Although Trudeau's government vigorously pushed an industrialization program, high inflation and Trudeau's efforts to impose the will of the federal government on the powerful provincial governments alienated voters and weakened his government. Economic recession in the early 1980s brought Brian Mulroney (b. 1939), leader of the Progressive Conservative Party, to power in 1984. Mulroney's government sought greater privatization of Canada's state-run corporations and negotiated a free trade agreement with the United States. Bitterly resented by many Canadians, the agreement cost Mulroney's government much of its popularity. In 1993, the ruling Conservatives were overwhelmingly defeated, and the Liberal leader, Jean Chrétien (b. 1934), became prime minister.

Mulroney's government was also unable to settle the ongoing crisis over the French-speaking province of Quebec. In the late 1960s, the Parti Québécois, headed by René Lévesque, ran on a platform of Quebec's secession from the Canadian union. To pursue their dream of separation, some underground separatist groups even resorted to terrorist bombings. In 1976, the Parti Qué-bécois won Quebec's provincial elections and in 1980 called for a referendum that would enable the provincial government to negotiate Quebec's independence from the rest of Canada. Quebec voters narrowly rejected the plan in 1995, however, and debate over the province's status continues to divide Canada.

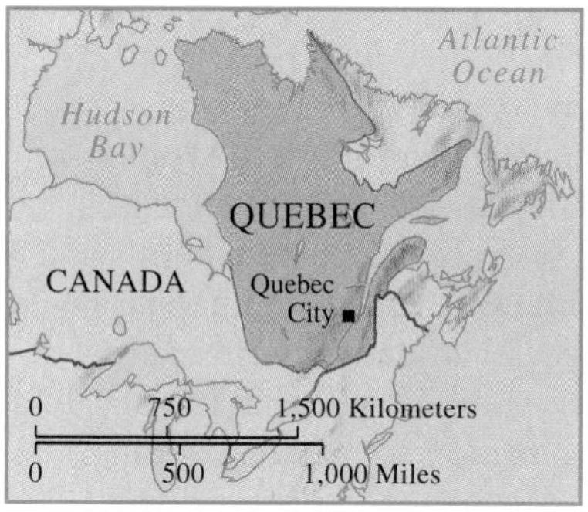

Quebec

New Directions and New Problems in Western Society

Dramatic social developments have accompanied political and economic changes since 1970. New opportunities for women emerged, and a reinvigorated women's movement sought to bring new meaning to the principle of equality with men. New problems for Western society also arose with the advent of terrorism, a reaction against foreign workers and immigrants, and a growing awareness of environmental dangers.

Transformation in Women's Lives

It is estimated that women need to average 2.1 children to ensure a natural replacement of a country's population. In many European countries, the population stopped growing in the 1960s, and the trend has continued since then. By the 1990s, birthrates had declined drastically; among the nations of the European Union, the average number of children per mother was 1.4. Italy's rate of 1.2 was the lowest in the world in 1997.

At the same time, the number of women in the workforce continued to rise. In Britain, for example, women made up 44 percent of the labor force in 1990, up from 32 percent in 1970. Moreover, women were entering new employment areas. Greater access to universities and professional schools enabled women to take jobs in law, medicine, government, business, and education. In the Soviet Union, for example, about 70 percent of doctors and teachers were women. Nevertheless, economic inequality still often prevailed; women received lower wages than men for comparable work and found fewer opportunities for advancement to management positions.

THE WOMEN'S MOVEMENT

Feminists in the women's liberation movement came to believe that women themselves must transform the fundamental conditions of their lives. They did so in a variety of ways after 1970. First, they formed numerous "consciousness-raising" groups to heighten awareness of women's issues. Women got together to share their personal experiences and become aware of the many ways that male dominance affected their lives. This consciousness-raising helped many women become activists.

Women sought and gained a measure of control over their own bodies by insisting that they had a right to both contraception and abortion. In the 1960s and 1970s, hundreds of thousands of European women worked, often successfully, to repeal the laws that outlawed contraception and abortion. In 1968, a French law permitted the sale of contraceptive devices, and in the 1970s, French feminists began to call for the legalization of abortion. One group of 343 prominent French women even signed a manifesto declaring that they had had abortions. In 1979, abortion became legal in France. Even in Catholic countries, where the church remained adamantly opposed to abortion, legislation allowing contraception and abortion was passed in the 1970s and 1980s.

As more women became activists, they also became involved in new issues. In the 1980s and 1990s, women faculty in universities concentrated on developing new cultural attitudes through the new academic field of women's studies. Courses in women's studies, which stressed the role and contributions of women in history, mushroomed in both American and European colleges and universities.

AP/Wide World Photos

An Antinuclear Protest. Women were active participants in the antinuclear movement of the 1980s. Shown here are some of the ten thousand antinuclear protesters who linked hands to form a human chain around the 9-mile perimeter of the U.S. Air Force base at Greenham Common, England, on December 13, 1982. They were protesting the planned siting of ninety-six U.S. cruise missiles at the base.

Other women began to try to affect the political environment by allying with the antinuclear movement. In 1982, a group of women protested American nuclear missiles in Britain by chaining themselves to the fence of an American military base. Thousands more joined in creating a peace camp around the military compound. Enthusiasm ran high; one participant said: "I'll never forget that feeling; it'll live with me forever. . . . We walked round, and we clasped hands. . . . It was for women; it was for peace; it was for the world."[2]

Some women joined the ecological movement. As one German writer who was concerned with environmental issues said, it is women "who must give birth to children, willingly or unwillingly, in this polluted world of ours." Especially prominent were the female members of the Green Party in Germany (see "The Environment and the Green Movements" later in this chapter), which supported environmental issues and elected forty-two delegates to the West German parliament in 1987. Among the delegates was Petra Kelly (b. 1947), one of the founders of the German Green Party and a tireless campaigner for the preservation of the environment as well as human rights and equality.

Women in the West have also reached out to work with women from the rest of the world in international conferences to change the conditions of their lives. Between 1975 and 1995, the United Nations held conferences in Mexico City, Copenhagen, Nairobi, and Beijing. These meetings made clear that women from Western and non-Western countries had different priorities. Whereas women from Western countries spoke about political, economic, cultural, and sexual rights, women from developing countries in Latin America, Africa, and Asia focused their attention on bringing an end to the violence, hunger, and disease that haunt their lives. Despite these differences, the meetings were an indication of how women in both developed and developing nations were organizing to make people aware of women's issues.

The Growth of Terrorism

Acts of terror by individuals and groups opposed to governments became a frightening aspect of modern Western society. During the late 1970s and early 1980s, concern about terrorism was often at the top of foreign policy agendas in the United States and many European countries. Small bands of terrorists used assassination; indiscriminate killing of civilians, especially by bombing; the taking of hostages; and the hijacking of airplanes to draw attention to their demands or to destabilize governments in the hope of achieving their political goals. Terrorist acts garnered considerable media attention. When Palestinian terrorists kidnapped and killed eleven Israeli athletes at the Munich Olympic Games in 1972, hundreds of millions of people watched the drama unfold on television. Indeed, some observers believe that media exposure has been an important catalyst for some terrorist groups.

Motivations for terrorist acts varied considerably. Left- and right-wing terrorist groups flourished in the late 1970s and early 1980s. Left-wing groups, such as the Baader-Meinhof gang (also known as the Red Army Faction) in Germany and the Red Brigades in Italy, consisted chiefly of affluent middle-class young people who denounced the injustices of capitalism and supported acts of revolutionary terrorism in an attempt to bring down the system. Right-wing terrorist groups, such as the New Order in Italy and the Charles Martel Club in France, used bombings to foment disorder and bring about authoritarian regimes. These groups received little or no public support, and authorities were able to crush them fairly quickly.

But terrorist acts also stemmed from militant nationalists who wished to create separatist states. Because they received considerable support from local populations sympathetic to their cause, these terrorist groups could maintain their activities over a long period of time. Most prominent was the Irish Republican Army (IRA), which resorted to vicious attacks against the ruling government and innocent civilians in Northern Ireland. Over a period of twenty years, IRA terrorists were responsible for the death of two thousand people in Northern Ireland; three-fourths of the victims were civilians.

Although left- and right-wing terrorist activities declined in Europe in the 1980s, international terrorism remained commonplace. Angered over the loss of their territory to Israel by 1967, some militant Palestinians responded with a policy of terrorist attacks against Israel's supporters. Palestinian terrorists operated throughout European countries, attacking both Europeans and American tourists; vacationers at airports in Rome and Vienna were massacred by Palestinian terrorists in 1985. State-sponsored terrorism was often an integral part of international terrorism. Militant governments, especially in Iran, Libya, and Syria, assisted terrorist organizations that made attacks on Europeans and Americans. On December 21, 1988, Pan American flight 103 from Frankfurt to New York exploded over Lockerbie, Scotland, killing all 259 passengers and crew members. A massive investigation finally revealed that the bomb responsible for the explosion had been planted by two Libyan terrorists who were connected to terrorist groups based in Iran and Syria.

TERRORIST ATTACK ON THE UNITED STATES

One of the most destructive acts of terrorism occurred on September 11, 2001, in the United States. Four groups of terrorists hijacked four commercial jet airplanes after takeoff from Boston, Newark, and Washington, D.C. The hijackers flew two of the airplanes directly into the towers of the World Trade Center in New York City, causing these buildings, as well as a number of surrounding buildings, to collapse. A third hijacked plane slammed into the Pentagon near Washington, D.C. The fourth plane, apparently headed for Washington, crashed instead in an isolated area of Pennsylvania, apparently as the result of an attempt by a group of heroic passengers to overcome the hijackers. In total, more than three thousand people were killed, including everyone aboard the four airliners.

These coordinated acts of terror were carried out by hijackers connected to an international terrorist organization known as al-Qaeda, run by Osama bin Laden. A native of Saudi Arabia, bin Laden used an inherited fortune to set up terrorist training camps in Afghanistan, under the protection of the nation's militant fundamentalist Islamic rulers known as the Taliban. Bin Laden was also suspected of directing earlier terrorist attacks against the United States, including the bombing of two U.S. embassies in Africa in 1998 and an attack on a naval ship, the U.S.S. *Cole,* in 2000.

Terrorist Attack on the World Trade Center in New York City On September 11, 2001, hijackers flew two commercial jetliners into the twin towers of the World Trade Center. Shown at left are the two towers in the New York skyline before the attack. The middle picture shows the second of the two jetliners about to hit one of the towers while smoke billows from the site of the first attack. In the scene below, firefighters are making their way through what was left of the 110-story towers after the collapse.

AP/Wide World Photos

AP/Wide World Photos

© Jeremy Walker/Stone/Getty Images

U.S. president George W. Bush vowed to wage a lengthy war on terrorism and worked to create a coalition of nations to assist in ridding the world of al-Qaeda and other terrorist groups. Within weeks of the attack on America, United States and NATO air forces began bombing Taliban-controlled command centers, airfields, and al-Qaeda hiding places in Afghanistan. On the ground, Afghan forces, assisted by U.S. special forces, pushed the Taliban out and gained control of the country by the end of November. A democratic multiethnic government was installed, and the focus of antiterrorism efforts shifted to other areas of the world.

Guest Workers and Immigrants

As the economies of the Western European countries revived in the 1950s and 1960s, a severe labor shortage forced them to rely on foreign workers. Scores of Turks and eastern and southern Europeans came to Germany, North Africans to France, and people from the Caribbean, India, and Pakistan to Great Britain. Overall, there were probably fifteen million "guest workers" in Europe in the 1980s. They constituted 17 percent of the labor force in Switzerland and 10 percent in Germany.

Although these workers were necessary for economic reasons, socially and politically their presence created problems for their host countries. Many foreign workers complained that they received lower wages and inferior social benefits. Moreover, their concentration in certain cities or certain sections of cities often created tensions with the local native populations. Foreign workers, many of them nonwhites, constituted almost one-fifth of the population in the German cities of Frankfurt, Munich, and Stuttgart. Having become settled in their new countries, many were unwilling to leave, even after the end of the postwar boom in the early 1970s led to mass unemployment. Moreover, as guest workers settled permanently in their host countries, additional family members migrated to join them. Although they had little success in getting guest workers already there to leave, some European countries passed legislation or took other measures to restrict new immigration. In 1991, thousands of Albanians fled their homeland after its Communist government began to fall apart, but when they arrived in Italy, the Italian authorities forcibly evicted them and sent them back to Albania.

In the 1980s, the problem of foreign workers was intensified by an influx of other refugees, especially to West Germany, which had liberal immigration laws that permitted people seeking asylum for political persecution to enter the country. During the 1970s and 1980s, West Germany absorbed over a million refugees from Eastern Europe and East Germany. In 1986 alone, 200,000 political refugees from Pakistan, Bangladesh, and Sri Lanka entered the country.

This great influx of foreigners, many of them nonwhite, strained not only the social services of European countries but also the patience of many native residents who opposed making their countries ethnically diverse. Antiforeign sentiment, especially in a time of growing unemployment, increased and was encouraged by new right-wing political parties that catered to people's complaints. Thus the National Front in France, organized by Jean-Marie Le Pen, and the Republican Party in Germany, led by Franz Schönhuber, a former SS officer, advocated restricting all new immigration and limiting the assimilation of settled immigrants. Although these parties have had only limited success in elections, even that modest accomplishment has encouraged traditional conservative and even moderately conservative parties to adopt more nationalistic policies. Even more frightening, however, have been the organized campaigns of violence, especially against African and Asian immigrants, by radical, right-wing groups (see the box on p. 857).

The Environment and the Green Movements

By the 1970s, serious ecological problems had become all too apparent. Air pollution, produced by nitrogen oxide and sulfur dioxide emissions from road vehicles, power plants, and industrial factories, was causing respiratory illnesses and having corrosive effects on buildings and monuments. Many rivers, lakes, and seas had become so polluted that they posed serious health risks. Dying forests and disappearing wildlife alarmed more and more people. A Soviet nuclear power disaster at Chernobyl in 1986 made Europeans even more aware of potential environmental hazards. The opening of Eastern Europe after the revolutions of 1989 brought to the world's attention the incredible environmental destruction of that region caused by unfettered industrial pollution. Environmental concerns forced the major political parties in Europe to advocate new regulations for the protection of the environment.

Growing ecological awareness also gave rise to the Green movements and Green parties that emerged throughout Europe in the 1970s. The origins of these movements were by no means uniform. Some came from the antinuclear movement; others arose out of such causes as women's liberation and concerns for foreign workers. Most started at the local level and then gradually expanded to include activities at the national level, where they became formally organized as political parties. Most visible was the Green Party in Germany, which was officially organized in 1979 and by 1987 had elected forty-two delegates to the West German parliament. Green parties also competed successfully in Sweden, Austria, and Switzerland.

Despite their repressive policies, Communist countries in Eastern Europe also witnessed the formation of ecologically conscious groups. In the 1980s, environmental groups emerged in East Germany and Czechoslovakia, two especially environmentally devastated countries, as well as in Poland and Hungary. The Czech dissident group, Charter 77, emphasized environmental damage as one of the chief crimes of its Communist government.

Violence Against Foreigners in Germany

As the number of foreign guest workers and immigrants increased in Europe, violent attacks against them also escalated. Especially in the former East Germany, where unemployment rose dramatically after reunification, gangs of neo-Nazi youth have perpetrated violent attacks on foreigners. This document is taken from a German press account of an attack on guest workers from Vietnam and Mozambique who had originally been recruited by the East German government.

Knud Pries, "East Germans Have Yet to Learn Tolerance"

The police headquarters in Dresden, the capital of Saxony, announced that "a political situation" had developed in the town of Hoyerswerda. Political leaders and the police needed to examine the problem and corresponding measures should be taken: "In the near future the residents of the asylum hostel will be moved."

The people of Hoyerswerda prefer to be more direct, referring to the problem of *Neger* (niggers) and *Fidschis* (a term for Asian foreigners). The loudmouths of the neo-fascist gangs make the message clear: "Niggers Go Home!"

It looks as if some Germans have had enough of bureaucratic officialese. What is more, they will soon make sure that no more foreign voices are heard in Hoyerswerda.

The municipality in northern Saxony has a population of just under 70,000, including 70 people from Mozambique and Vietnam who live in a hostel for foreigners and about 240 asylum-seekers in a hostel at the other end of town.

The "political situation" was triggered by an attack by a neo-Nazi gang on Vietnamese traders selling their goods on the market square on 17 September. After being dispersed by the police the Faschos carried out their first attack on the hostel for foreigners.

The attacks then turned into a regular evening "hunt" by a growing group of right-wing radicals, some of them minors, who presented their idea of a clean Germany by roaming the streets armed with truncheons, stones, steel balls, bottles and Molotov cocktails. Seventeen people were injured, some seriously.

After the police stepped in on a larger scale the extremists moved across the town to the asylum hostel. To begin with, only the gang itself and onlookers were outside the building, but on the evening of 22 September members of the "Human Rights League" and about 100 members of "autonomous" groups turned up to help the foreigners who had sought refuge in the already heavily damaged block of flats.

A large police contingent, reinforced by men from Dresden and the Border Guard, prevented the situation from becoming even more critical. Two people were seriously injured. The mob was disbanded with the help of dogs, tear gas and water-cannons.

Thirty-two people were arrested, and blank cartridge guns, knives, slings and clubs were seized. On 23 September, a police spokesman announced that the situation was under control. It seems doubtful whether things will stay this way, since the pogroms have become an evening ritual. Politicians and officials are racking their brains about how to grapple with the current crisis and the basic problem. One thing is clear: without a massive intervention by the police the problem cannot even be contained. But what then?

Saxony's Interior Minister, Rudolf Krause, initially recommended that the hostels concerned should be "fenced in," but then admitted that this was "not the final solution." Providing the Defense Ministry approves, the "provisional solution" will be to move the foreigners to a barracks in Kamenz.

Even if this operation is completed without violence it would represent a shameful success for the right-wing radicals. Although the Africans and Asians still living in Hoyerswerda will have to leave at the end of November anyway once the employment contracts drawn up in the former [East Germany] expire, they are unwilling to endure the terror that long. "Even if we're going anyway—they want all foreigners to go now," says the 29-year-old Martinho from Mozambique.

His impression is that the gangs of thugs are doing something for which others are grateful: "The neighbors are glad when the skinheads arrive."

Interior Minister Krause feels that the abuse of asylum laws, the social problems in East Germany and an historically rooted deficit explain this situation: "The problem is that we were unable in the past to practice the tolerance needed to accept alien cultures."

Although the Green movements and parties have played an important role in making people aware of ecological problems, they have by no means replaced the traditional political parties, as some political analysts in the mid-1980s forecast. For one thing, the coalitions that made up the Greens found it difficult to agree on all issues and tended to splinter into different cliques. Moreover, traditional political parties have co-opted the environmental issues of the Greens. By the 1990s, more and more European governments were beginning to sponsor projects to safeguard the environment and clean up the worst sources of pollution.

The World of Western Culture

Intellectually and culturally, the Western world during the second half of the twentieth century was notable for its diversity. Although many trends represented a continuation of prewar modern developments, new directions have led some observers to speak of a postmodern cultural world.

Recent Trends in Art, Music, and Literature

For the most part, the United States dominated the art world, much as it did the world of popular culture (see "Popular Culture and the Americanization of the World" later in this chapter). American art, often vibrantly colored and filled with activity, reflected the energy and exuberance of the postwar United States. After 1945, New York City became the artistic center of the Western world. The Guggenheim Museum, the Museum of Modern Art, and the Whitney Museum of American art, together with New York's numerous art galleries, promoted modern art and helped determine artistic tastes throughout much of the world.

Abstractionism, especially Abstract Expressionism, emerged as the artistic mainstream (see Chapters 24 and 26). American exuberance in Abstract Expressionism is evident in the enormous canvases of Jackson Pollock (1912–1956). In such works as *Lavender Mist* (1950), paint seems to explode, assaulting the viewer with emotion and movement. Pollock's swirling forms and seemingly chaotic patterns broke all conventions of form and structure. His drip paintings, with their total abstraction, were extremely influential with other artists, although the public was initially quite hostile to his work. Pollock also introduced the technique of painting with the canvas laid on the floor. He said: "On the floor I am more at ease. I feel nearer, more a part of the painting, since this way I can walk around in, work from four sides and be literally *in* the painting. When I am in the painting, I am not aware of what I am doing. There is pure harmony."

The early 1960s saw the emergence of pop art, which took images of popular culture and transformed them into works of fine art. Andy Warhol (1930–1987), who began as an advertising illustrator, was the most famous of the pop artists. Warhol adapted images from commercial art, such as the Campbell's soup cans, and photographs of such celebrities as Marilyn Monroe. Derived from mass culture, these works were mass-produced and deliberately "of the moment," expressing the fleeting whims of popular culture.

In the 1980s, styles emerged that some have referred to as "postmodern." Postmodernism tends to move away from the futurism or "cutting edge" qualities of Modernism. Instead it favors "tradition," whether that means using earlier styles of painting or elevating traditional crafts to the level of fine art. Weavers, potters, glassmakers, metalsmiths, and furniture makers have gained respect as artists.

Hans Namuth/Photo Researchers, Inc.

Jackson Pollock Painting. One of the best-known practitioners of Abstract Expressionism, which remained at the center of the artistic mainstream after World War II, was the American Jackson Pollock, who achieved his ideal of total abstraction in his drip paintings. He is shown here at work in his Long Island studio. Pollock found it easier to cover his large canvases with exploding patterns of color when he put them on the floor.

Another response to Modernism can be seen in a return to realism in the arts, a movement called Neorealism. Some Neorealists paint or sculpt with such minute attention to detail that their paintings appear to be photographs and their sculptures living human beings. Their subjects are often ordinary individuals, stuck in ordinary lives. These works are often pessimistic and cynical.

One of the best examples of a postmodern artist who makes use of Abstract Expressionism (thus creating a style called Neoexpressionism) is Anselm Kiefer. Born in Germany in 1945, Kiefer combines aspects of Abstract Expressionism, collage, and German Expressionism to create works that are stark and haunting. His *Departure from Egypt* (1984) is a meditation on Jewish history and its descent into the horrors of Nazism. Kiefer hoped that a portrayal of Germany's atrocities could free Germans from their past and bring some good out of evil. His international stature reflects a movement away from American

The Museum of Contemporary Art

Anselm Kiefer, *Departure for Egypt.* Although Western artists experimented with a variety of modern and even postmodern styles in the 1970s and 1980s, Abstract Expressionism continued to be popular. The German artist Anselm Kiefer used the tradition of Abstract Expressionism to create haunting images that reflect the horrors of Germany's Nazi past.

dominance in the fine arts, a trend that gained momentum in the 1980s.

MUSIC

Like modern art, modern music has focused on variety and radical experimentation. Also like modern art, modern classical music witnessed a continuation of prewar developments. Some composers, the neoclassicists, remained closely tied to nineteenth-century Romantic music, although they occasionally incorporated some twentieth-century developments, such as atonality and dissonance. Their style was strongly reminiscent of Stravinsky (see Chapter 24).

The major musical trend since the war, however, has been serialism. Inspired mostly by the twelve-tone music of Schönberg (see Chapter 26), serialism is a compositional procedure where an order of succession is set for specific values: pitch (for tones of the tempered scale), loudness (for dynamic levels), and units of time (for rhythm). By predetermining the order of succession, the composer restricts his or her intuitive freedom as the work to some extent creates itself. However, the mechanism the composer initially establishes could generate unanticipated musical events, thereby creating new and exciting compositions. Serialist composition diminishes the role of intuition and emotion in favor of intellect and mathematical precision. The first recognized serialist was the Frenchman Olivier Messiaen (1908–1992). Significantly, Messiaen was influenced in part by Indian and Greek music, plainchant, folk music, and birdsongs. Most critics have respected serialism, although the public has been largely indifferent, if not hostile, to it.

An offshoot of serialism that has won popular support, but not the same critical favor, is minimalism. Like serialism, this style uses repeated patterns and series and steady pulsation with gradual changes occurring over time. But whereas serialism is often atonal, minimalism is usually tonal and more harmonic. Perhaps the most successful minimalist composer is Philip Glass (b. 1937), who demonstrated in *Einstein on the Beach* that minimalist music could be adapted to full-scale opera. Like other modern American composers, Glass found no contradiction in moving between the worlds of classical music and popular music. His *Koyaanisqatsi* was used as background music to a documentary film on the disintegrative forces in Western society.

LITERATURE

The most significant new trend in postwar literature has been called the "Theater of the Absurd." This new convention in drama began in France in the 1950s, although its most famous proponent was the Irishman Samuel Beckett (1906–1990), who lived in France. In Beckett's *Waiting for Godot* (1952), it is readily apparent that the action on stage is not realistic. Two men wait incessantly for the appearance of someone, with whom they may or may not have an appointment. No background information on the two men is provided. During the course of the play, nothing seems to be happening. The audience is never told if the action in front of them is real or unreal. Unlike traditional theater, suspense is maintained not by having the audience wonder what is going to happen next but by having them ask simply, what is happening now?

The Theater of the Absurd reflected its time. The postwar period was a time of disillusionment with fixed ideological beliefs in politics or religion. A sense of the world's meaninglessness underscored the desolate worldview of absurdist drama and literature. This can be seen in Günter Grass's novel *The Tin Drum,* published in 1959, which reflected postwar Germany's preoccupation with the seemingly incomprehensibility of Nazi Germany.

Postmodernism was also evident in literature. In the Western world, the best examples were found in Latin America, in a literary style called "magic realism," and in central and Eastern Europe. Magic realism combined realistic events with dreamlike or fantastic backgrounds. One of the finest examples of magic realism can be found in the novel *One Hundred Years of Solitude,* by Gabriel García

The Voice of Existentialism

Jean-Paul Sartre, a famous French intellectual of the early postwar years, became identified with the existentialist movement. He himself had been a student of German philosophy and was especially affected by the ideas of Martin Heidegger, whose *Being and Time* is considered an influential existentialist work. This selection is taken from *Existentialism,* written by Sartre in 1946 to provide a general description of existentialism. In this passage, he discusses atheistic existentialism.

Jean-Paul Sartre, Existentialism

Dostoievsky said, "If God didn't exist, everything would be possible." That is the very starting point of existentialism. Indeed, everything is permissible if God does not exist, and as a result man is forlorn, because neither within him nor without does he find anything to cling to. He can't start making excuses for himself.

If existence really does precede essence, there is no explaining things away by reference to a fixed and given human nature. In other words, there is no determinism, man is free, man is freedom. On the other hand, if God does not exist, we find no values or commands to turn to which legitimize our conduct. So, in the bright realm of values, we have no excuse behind us, nor justification before us. We are alone with no excuses.

That is the idea I shall try to convey when I say that man is condemned to be free. Condemned, because he did not create himself, yet, in other respects is free; because, once thrown into the world, he is responsible for everything he does. The existentialist does not believe in the power of passion. He will never agree that a sweeping passion is a ravaging torrent which fatally leads a man to certain acts and is therefore an excuse. He thinks that man is responsible for his passion.

The existentialist does not think that man is going to help himself by finding in the world some omen by which to orient himself. Because he thinks that man will interpret the omen to suit himself. Therefore, he thinks that man, with no support and no aid, is condemned every moment to invent man. . . .

There can be no other truth to take off from than this: *I think; therefore, I exist.* There we have the absolute truth of consciousness becoming aware of itself. Every theory which takes man out of the moment in which he becomes aware of himself is, at its very beginning, a theory which confounds truth, for outside the Cartesian *cogito,* all views are only probable, and a doctrine of probability which is not bound to a truth dissolves into thin air. In order to describe the probable, you must have a firm hold on the true. Therefore, before there can be any truth whatsoever, there must be an absolute truth; and this one is simple and easily arrived at; it's on everyone's doorstep; it's a matter of grasping it directly.

Secondly, this theory is the only one which gives man dignity, the only one which does not reduce him to an object. The effect of all materialism is to treat all men, including the one philosophizing, as objects, that is, as an ensemble of determined reactions in no way distinguished from the ensemble of qualities and phenomena which constitute a table or a chair or a stone. We definitely wish to establish the human realm as an ensemble of values distinct from the material realm. . . .

Moreover, to say that we invent values means nothing else but this: life has no meaning a priori. Before you come alive, life is nothing; it's up to you to give it a meaning, and value is nothing else but the meaning that you choose. In that way, you see, there is a possibility of creating a human community.

Márquez, who won the Nobel Prize for literature in 1982. The novel is the story of the fictional town of Macondo as seen by several generations of the Buendias, its founding family. The author slips back and forth between fact and fantasy. Villagers are not surprised when a local priest rises into the air and floats. However, when wandering Gypsies introduce these villagers to magnets, telescopes, and magnifying glasses, the villagers are dumbfounded by what they see as magic. According to the author, fantasy and fact depend on one's point of view.

The European center of Postmodernism is well represented by the work of Milan Kundera (b. 1929) of Czechoslovakia. Like the magic realists of Latin America, Kundera also blended fantasy with realism. Unlike the magic realists, Kundera used fantasy to examine moral issues and remained optimistic about the human condition. Indeed, in his first novel, *The Unbearable Lightness of Being* (1984), Kundera does not despair because of the political repression that he so aptly describes in his native Czechoslovakia but allows his characters to use love as a way to a better life. The human spirit can be lessened but not destroyed.

The Philosophical Dilemma: Existentialism

The sense of meaninglessness that inspired the Theater of the Absurd also underscored the philosophy of existentialism. It was born largely of the desperation caused by two world wars and the breakdown of traditional values. Existentialism reflected the anxieties of the twentieth century and became especially well known after World War II through the works of two Frenchmen, Jean-Paul Sartre (1905–1980) and Albert Camus (1913–1960).

The beginning point of the existentialism of Sartre and Camus was the absence of God in the universe (see the box above). The death of God, though tragic, meant that humans had no preordained destiny and were utterly alone in the universe, with no future and no hope. As Camus expressed it:

> A world that can be explained even with bad reasons is a familiar world. But, on the other hand, in a universe suddenly divested of illusions and lights, man feels an alien, a stranger. His exile is without remedy since he is deprived of the memory of a lost home or the hope of a promised land. This divorce between man and his life, the actor and his setting, is properly the feeling of absurdity.[3]

According to Camus, then, the world was absurd and without meaning; humans, too, are without meaning and purpose. Reduced to despair and depression, humans have but one ground of hope—themselves.

Though the world might be absurd, Camus argued, it could not be absurd unless people judged it to be so. People are unique in the world, and their kind of being is quite different from that of all others. In the words of Sartre, human "existence precedes essence." Humans are beings who first exist and then define themselves. They determine what they will be. According to Sartre, "Man is nothing else but what he makes of himself. Such is the first principle of existentialism." People then must take full responsibility for what they are. They create their values and give their lives meaning. And this can only be done by their involvement in life. Only through a person's acts can one determine his or her values.

Existentialism, therefore, involved an ethics of action, of involvement in life. But people could not define themselves without their involvement with others. Thus existentialism's ethical message was just as important as its philosophy of being. Essentially, the message of existentialism was one of authenticity. Individuals true to themselves refused to be depersonalized by their society. As one author noted, "Existentialism is the struggle to discover the human person in a depersonalized age."

The Revival of Religion

Existentialism was one response to the despair generated by the apparent collapse of civilized values in the twentieth century. The revival of religion was another. Ever since the Enlightenment of the eighteenth century, Christianity and religion had been on the defensive. But a number of religious thinkers and leaders attempted to bring new life to Christianity in the twentieth century.

One expression of this religious revival was the attempt by such theologians as the Protestant Karl Barth (1886–1968) and the Catholic Karl Rahner (1904–1984) to infuse traditional Christian teachings with new life. In numerous writings, Barth attempted to reinterpret the religious insights of the Reformation era for the modern world. To Barth, the sinful and hence imperfect nature of human beings meant that humans could know religious truth not through reason but only through the grace of God. Rahner attempted to revitalize traditional Catholic theology by incorporating aspects of modern thought. He was careful, however, to emphasize the continuity between ancient and modern interpretations of Catholic doctrine.

In the Catholic church, attempts at religious renewal also came from two charismatic popes—John XXIII and John Paul II. Pope John XXIII (1881–1963) reigned as pope for only a short time (1958–1963) but sparked a dramatic revival of Catholicism when he summoned the twenty-first ecumenical council of the Catholic church. Known as Vatican II, the council liberalized a number of Catholic practices. New avenues of communication with other Christian faiths were also opened for the first time since the Reformation.

John Paul II (b. 1920), who had been the archbishop of Krakow in Poland before his elevation to the papacy in 1978, was the first non-Italian to be elected pope since the sixteenth century. Although he alienated a number of people by reasserting traditional Catholic teaching on such issues as birth control, women in the priesthood, and clerical celibacy, John Paul's numerous travels around the world helped strengthen the Catholic church throughout the non-Western world. A strong believer in social justice, John Paul II has been a powerful figure in reminding Europeans of their spiritual heritage and the need to temper the pursuit of materialism with spiritual concerns. He has also condemned nuclear weapons and constantly reminded leaders and laity of their obligations to prevent war (see the box on p. 862).

The New World of Science and Technology

Many of the scientific and technological achievements since World War II have revolutionized people's lives. Before World War II, theoretical science and technology were largely separated. Pure science was the domain of university professors who were far removed from the practical technological concerns of technicians and engineers. But during World War II, university scientists were recruited to work for their governments and develop new weapons and practical instruments of war. British physicists played a crucial role in the development of an improved radar system in 1940 that helped defeat the German air force in the Battle of Britain. German scientists created self-propelled rockets and jet airplanes to keep Hitler's hopes alive for a miraculous turnaround in the war. The computer, too, was a wartime creation. The British mathematician Alan Turing designed a primitive computer to assist British intelligence in breaking the secret codes of German ciphering machines. The most famous product of wartime scientific research was the atomic bomb, created by a team of American and European scientists under the guidance of the American physicist J. Robert Oppenheimer. Obviously, most wartime devices were created for destructive purposes, but merely to mention computers and jet airplanes demonstrates that they could easily be adapted for peacetime uses.

The sponsorship of research by governments and the military during World War II created a new scientific model. Science had become very complex, and only large

Pope John Paul II: An Appeal for Peace

Pope John Paul II became the spiritual leader of the Catholic church in 1978. He has made numerous trips to all parts of the globe, advocating a variety of spiritual and social issues. He has made a point of speaking directly to as many lay groups as possible, often focusing on one of his chief themes, the desire for peace.

Pope John Paul II, Speeches

Today peace has become, throughout the world, a preoccupation not only for those responsible for the destiny of nations but even more so for broad sections of the population and innumerable individuals who generously and tenaciously dedicate themselves to creating an outlook of peace and to establishing genuine peace between peoples and nations. This is comforting. But there is no hiding the fact that in spite of the efforts of all men and women of good will, there are still serious threats to peace in the world. Some of these threats take the form of divisions within various nations; others stem from deep-rooted and acute tensions between opposing nations and blocs within the world community. In reality, the confrontations that we witness today are distinguished from those of past history by certain new characteristics. In the first place they are worldwide: even a local conflict is often an expression of tensions originating elsewhere in the world. In the same way, it often happens that a conflict has profound effects far from where it broke out. Another characteristic is totality: present day tensions mobilize all the forces of the nations involved; moreover, selfish monopolization and even hostility are to be found today as much in the way economic life is run and in the technological application of science as in the way that the mass media or military resources are utilized. . . .

Elsewhere, fear of a precarious peace, military and political imperatives, and economic and commercial interests lead to the establishment of arms stockpiles or to the sale of weapons capable of appalling destruction. The arms race, then, prevails over the great tasks of peace, which ought to unite peoples in new solidarity; it fosters sporadic but murderous conflicts and builds up the gravest threats. It is true that at first sight the cause of peace seems to be handicapped to a crippling extent.

But we must reach peace. Peace, as I said earlier, is threatened when uncertainty, doubt, and suspicion reign, and violence makes good use of this. Do we really want peace? Then we must dig deep within ourselves, and going beyond the divisions we find within us and between us, we must find the areas in which we can strengthen our conviction that human beings' basic driving forces and the recognition of their real nature carry them toward openness to others, mutual respect, community, and peace. The course of this laborious search for the objective and universal truth about humanity, and the result of the search, will develop men and women of peace and dialogue, people who draw both strength and humility from a truth that they realize they must serve and not make use of for partisan interests.

organizations with teams of scientists, huge laboratories, and complex equipment could undertake such large-scale projects. Such facilities were so expensive that they could only be provided by governments and large corporations.

There was no more stunning example of how the new scientific establishment operated than the space race of the 1960s. The announcement by the Soviets in 1957 that they had sent the first space satellite, *Sputnik I,* into orbit around the earth caused the United States to launch a gigantic project to place a manned spacecraft on the moon within a decade. Massive government funds financed the scientific research and technological advances that attained this goal in 1969.

The postwar alliance of science and technology led to an accelerated rate of change that became a fact of life in Western society. One product of this alliance—the computer—may yet prove to be the most revolutionary of all the technological inventions of the twentieth century. Early computers, which required thousands of vacuum tubes to function, were large and took up considerable space. An important figure in the development of the early computer was Grace Hopper (1906–1992), a career Navy officer. Hopper was instrumental in inventing COBOL, a computer language that enabled computers to respond to words as well as numbers.

The development of the transistor and then the silicon chip produced a revolutionary new approach to computers. In 1971, the invention of the microprocessor, a machine that combines the equivalent of thousands of transistors on a single, tiny silicon chip, opened the road for the development of the personal computer.

The computer is a new kind of machine whose chief function is to store and produce information, now considered an essential element of our fast-paced civilization. By 2000, the personal computer had become a fixture in businesses, schools, and homes. It not only makes a whole host of tasks much easier, but it has also become an important tool in virtually every area of modern life. Indeed, other tools and machines now depend for their functioning on computers. Many of the second-by-second decisions involved in flying an airplane, for example, are made by a computer.

Despite the marvels that were produced by the alliance of science and technology, some people came to question the underlying assumption of this alliance—that scientific knowledge gave human beings the ability to manipulate the environment for their benefit. They maintained that some technological advances had far-reaching side effects damaging to the environment. The chemical fertilizers, for

On the Moon. The first landing on the moon in 1969 was one of the great technological achievements of the twentieth century. This picture shows astronaut James Irwin shortly after he erected the American flag during a moonwalk in 1971. The lunar module and lunar rover are also visible in the picture.

example, that were touted for producing larger crops wreaked havoc with the ecological balance of streams, rivers, and woodlands. *Small Is Beautiful,* written by the British economist E. F. Schumacher (1911–1977), was a fundamental critique of the dangers of the new science and technology (see the box on p. 864). The widespread proliferation of fouled beaches and dying forests and lakes made environmentalism one of the important issues of the late twentieth century.

After World War II, a number of physicists continued to explore the implications of Einstein's revolution in physics and raised fundamental questions about the nature of reality. To some physicists, quantum and relativity theory described the universe as a complicated web of relations in which there were no isolated building blocks. Thus the universe was not a "collection of physical objects" but a complicated web of relations between "various parts of a unified whole." Moreover, this web of relations that is the universe also included the human observer. Human beings could not be objective observers of objects detached from themselves because the very act of observation made them participants in the process. These speculations implied that the old Newtonian conception of the universe as a machine was an outdated tool for understanding the nature of the universe.

The Explosion of Popular Culture

Since World War II, popular culture has played an increasingly important role in helping Western people define themselves. At one level, popular culture is but the history of the ever-changing whims of mass taste, but on another level, "it is a history of how modern society has created images of itself and expressed its fantasies, its fears, its ambitions."[4]

The history of popular culture is also the history of the economic system that supports it, for this system manufactures, distributes, and sells the images that people consume as popular culture. As popular culture and its economic support system become increasingly intertwined, industries of leisure emerge. As one historian of popular culture has argued, "Industrial societies turn the provision of leisure into a commercial activity, in which their citizens are sold entertainment, recreation, pleasure, and appearance as commodities that differ from the goods at the drugstore only in the way they are used."[5] Modern popular culture is therefore inextricably tied to the mass consumer society in which it has emerged.

POPULAR CULTURE AND THE AMERICANIZATION OF THE WORLD

The United States has been the most influential force in shaping popular culture in the West and, to a lesser degree, the rest of the world. Through movies, music, advertising, and television, the United States has spread its particular form of consumerism and the American dream to millions around the world. Already in 1923, the New York *Morning Post* noted that "the film is to America what the flag was once to Britain. By its means Uncle Sam may hope some day . . . to Americanize the world."[6] In movies, television, and popular music, the impact of American popular culture on the Western world is apparent.

Motion pictures were the primary vehicle for the diffusion of American popular culture in the years immediately following the war, and they continued to dominate both European and American markets in the next decades (40 percent of Hollywood's income in the 1960s came from the European market). Nevertheless, the existence of a profitable art-house circuit in America and Europe enabled European filmmakers to make films whose themes and

Small Is Beautiful: The Limits of Modern Technology

Although science and technology have produced an amazing array of achievements in the postwar world, some voices have been raised in criticism of their sometimes destructive aspects. In 1975, in his book *Small Is Beautiful,* the British economist E. F. Schumacher examined the effects modern industrial technology has had on the earth's resources.

■ *E. F. Schumacher,* Small Is Beautiful

Is it not evident that our current methods of production are already eating into the very substance of industrial man? To many people this is not at all evident. Now that we have solved the problem of production, they say, have we ever had it so good? Are we not better fed, better clothed, and better housed than ever before—and better educated? Of course we are: most, but by no means all, of us: in the rich countries. But this is not what I mean by "substance." The substance of man cannot be measured by Gross National Product. Perhaps it cannot be measured at all, except for certain symptoms of loss. However, this is not the place to go into the statistics of these symptoms, such as crime, drug addiction, vandalism, mental breakdown, rebellion, and so forth. Statistics never prove anything.

I started by saying that one of the most fateful errors of our age is the belief that the problem of production has been solved. This illusion, I suggested, is mainly due to our inability to recognize that the modern industrial system, with all its intellectual sophistication, consumes the very basis on which it has been erected. To use the language of the economist, it lives on irreplaceable capital which it cheerfully treats as income. I specified three categories of such capital: fossil fuels, the tolerance margins of nature, and the human substance. Even if some readers should refuse to accept all three parts of my argument, I suggest that any one of them suffices to make my case.

And what is my case? Simply that our most important task is to get off our present collision course. And who is there to tackle such a task? I think every one of us. . . . To talk about the future is useful only if it leads to action *now.* And what can we do *now,* while we are still in the position of "never having had it so good"? To say the least . . . we must thoroughly understand the problem and begin to see the possibility of evolving a new life-style, with new methods of production and new patterns of consumption: a life-style designed for permanence. To give only three preliminary examples: in agriculture and horticulture, we can interest ourselves in the perfection of production methods which are biologically sound, build up soil fertility, and produce health, beauty and permanence. Productivity will then look after itself. In industry, we can interest ourselves in the evolution of small-scale technology, relatively nonviolent technology, "technology with a human face," so that people have a chance to enjoy themselves while they are working, instead of working solely for their pay packet and hoping, usually forlornly, for enjoyment solely during their leisure time.

avant-garde methods were quite different from those of Hollywood. Italy and Sweden, for example, developed a tradition of "national cinema" that reflected "specific cultural traits in a mode in which they could be successfully exported." The 1957 film *The Seventh Seal,* by the Swedish director Ingmar Bergman, was a good example of the successful European art film. Bergman's films caused him to be viewed as "an artist of comparable stature to a novelist or playwright." So too were François Truffaut in France and Federico Fellini in Italy; such directors gloried in experimenting with subject matter and technique and produced films dealing with more complex and daring themes than Hollywood would attempt.

Although developed in the 1930s, television did not become readily available until the late 1940s. By 1954, there were 32 million sets in the United States as television became the centerpiece of middle-class life. In the 1960s, as television spread around the world, American networks unloaded their products on Europe and the Third World at extraordinarily low prices. For instance, the British Broadcasting Corporation (BBC) could buy American programs for one-tenth the cost per viewer of producing its own. Only the establishment of quota systems prevented American television from completely inundating these countries. Nevertheless, American shows have remained popular in Europe.

The United States has dominated popular music since the end of World War II. Jazz, blues, rhythm and blues, rap, and rock-and-roll have been by far the most popular music forms in the Western world—and much of the non-Western world—during this time. All of them originated in the United States, and all are rooted in African American musical innovations. These forms later spread around the globe, inspiring local artists who then transformed the music in their own way. Often these transformed models then returned to the United States to inspire American artists. This was certainly the case with rock-and-roll. Through the 1950s, American figures such as Chuck Berry, Little Richard, and Elvis Presley inspired the Beatles and other British performers, who then led an "invasion" of the United States in the 1960s, creating a sensation and in part sparking new rockers in America. Rock music itself developed in the 1950s. In 1952, white disk jockeys began playing rhythm and blues and traditional blues music performed by African Americans to young white audiences. The music was popular with this audience, and record

AP/Wide World Photos

The Beatles. Although rock-and-roll originated in the United States, it inspired musical groups around the world. This was certainly true of Britain's Beatles, who created a sensation among young people when they came to the United States in the 1960s. Here the Beatles are shown during a performance on *The Ed Sullivan Show.*

companies began recording watered-down white "cover" versions of this music. It was not until performers such as Elvis Presley mixed white "folkabilly" with rhythm and blues that rock-and-roll became popular with the larger white audience.

The period from 1967 to 1973 was probably the true golden age of rock. During this brief period, much experimentation in rock music took place, as it did in society in general. Straightfoward rock-and-roll competed with a new hybrid blues rock, created in part by British performers such as the Rolling Stones, who were in turn inspired by African American blues artists. Many musicians also experimented with non-Western musical sounds, such as Indian sitars. Some of the popular music of the 1960s also focused on social issues. It was against the Vietnam War and materialism and promoted "peace and love" as alternatives to the prevailing "establishment" culture.

The same migration of a musical form from the United States to Britain and back to the United States occurred when the early punk movement in New York spread to Britain in the mid-1970s after failing to make an immediate impact in the United States. The more influential British punk movement of 1976–1979 was also fueled by an economic crisis that had resulted in large numbers of unemployed and undereducated young people. However, punk was not simply a proletarian movement. Many of its supporters, performers, and promoters were British art school graduates who applied avant-garde experimentation to the movement. Punk rockers rejected most social conventions and preached anarchy and rebellion. They often wore tattered clothes and pins in their cheeks, symbolizing their rejection of a materialistic and degenerate culture. Pure punk was short-lived, partly because its intense energy quickly burned out (as did many of its performers) and partly because, as ex-punk Mick Hucknall said, "the biggest mistake of the punks was that they rejected music." Offshoots of punk proliferated through the 1980s, however, and continue to influence rock-and-roll.

The introduction of the video music channel MTV in the early 1980s radically changed the music scene by making image as important as sound in the selling of records. In the mid-1990s, teen and preteen consumers made performers who made splashy videos into multimillion-dollar musical acts, regardless of their actual musical talent.

THE GROWTH OF MASS SPORTS

In the postwar years, sports have become a major product of both popular culture and the leisure industry. The development of satellite television and various electronic breakthroughs helped make sports a global phenomenon. Olympic Games could now be broadcast across the globe from anywhere in the world. Sports became a cheap form of entertainment since fans did not have to leave their homes to enjoy athletic competitions. In fact, some sports organizations initially resisted television fearing that it would hurt ticket sales. Soon, however, the tremendous revenues possible from television contracts overcame this hesitation. As sports television revenue escalated, many sports came to receive the bulk of their yearly revenue from television contracts. The Olympics, for example, are now funded primarily by American television. These contracts are paid for by advertising sponsors, mostly for products to be consumed along with the sport: beer, soda, and snack foods.

Sports have become big politics as well as big business. The politicization of sports has been one of the most significant trends in sports since World War II. Football (soccer) remains the dominant world sport and more than ever has become a vehicle for nationalist sentiment and expression. The World Cup is the most watched event on television. Although the sport can be a positive outlet for national and local pride, all too often it has been marred by violence as nationalistic energies have overcome rational behavior.

The most telling example of the potent mix of politics and sport continues to be the Olympic Games. When the Soviets entered Olympic competition in 1952, the Olympics began to take on Cold War implications and became known as the "war without weapons." The Soviets saw the Olympics as a way to stimulate nationalist spirit, as well as to promote the Communist system as the best path for social progress. The Soviets led the Olympics in terms of total medals won between 1956 and 1988. The nature of the Olympics, with their daily medal count by nation and elaborate ceremonies and rituals such as the playing of the national anthem of the winning athletes and the parade of nations, virtually ensured the politicization of the games originally intended to foster international cooperation through friendly competition.

The political nature of the games found expression in other ways as well. In 1956, six nations withdrew from the games to protest the Soviet crushing of the Hungarian uprising. In 1972, twenty-seven African nations threatened to pull out of the Munich Olympics because of apartheid in South Africa. Also at the Munich Games, the Palestinian terrorist group Black September seized eleven Israeli athletes as hostages, all of whom died in a confrontation at an airport. The United States led a boycott of the 1980 Moscow Games to protest the Soviet invasion of Afghanistan, and the Soviets responded by boycotting the Los Angeles Games in 1984.

POPULAR CULTURE: INCREASINGLY GLOBAL

Media critic and theorist Marshall McLuhan predicted in the 1960s that advances in mass communications technology, such as satellites and electronics, would eventually lead to a shrinking of the world, a lessening of cultural distinctions, and a breaking down of cultural barriers, all of which would in time transform the world into a single "global village." McLuhan was quite optimistic about these developments, and his ideas became quite popular at the time. Many critics have since argued that McLuhan was too utopian about the benefits of technological progress and maintain that the mass media that these technological breakthroughs created are still controlled by a small number of multinational corporations that "colonize the rest of the world, sometimes benignly, sometimes not." They argue that this has allowed Western popular culture to disrupt the traditional cultures of less developed countries and inculcate new patterns of behavior as well as new desires and new dissatisfactions.

Cultural contacts, however, often move in two directions. While the world has been "Americanized" to a great extent, formerly unfamiliar ways of life and styles of music have also come into the world of the West. This has expanded the horizons of Westerners and led to the creation of new cultural hybrids in music, philosophy, and religion. This emergence of a global culture has become part of the new globalism at the beginning of the twenty-first century.

Toward a Global Civilization?

More and more, people are becoming aware of the political and economic interdependence of the world's nations and the global nature of our contemporary problems. At the beginning of the twenty-first century, human beings are coming to understand that destructive forces generated in one part of the world soon affect the entire world. Nuclear proliferation makes nuclear war an ever-present possibility; nuclear war would mean radioactive fallout for the entire planet. Smokestack pollution in one nation can produce acid rain in another. Oil spills and dumping of wastes in the ocean have an impact on the shores of many nations. The consumption of drugs in the world's wealthy nations affects the stability of both wealthy and less developed nations. As crises of food, water, energy, and natural resources proliferate, one nation's solutions often become other nations' problems. The new globalism includes the recognition that the challenges that seem to threaten human existence at the beginning of the twenty-first century are global. In response to the recent terrorist crisis, Tony Blair, the British prime minister, said in October 2001, "We are realizing how fragile are our frontiers in the face of the world's new challenges. Today, conflicts rarely stay within national boundaries."

As the heirs of Western civilization have become aware that the problems humans face are not just national but global, they have responded to this challenge in different ways. One approach has been to develop grassroots social movements, including environmental, women's and men's liberation, human potential, appropriate-technology, and nonviolence movements. "Think globally, act locally" is frequently the slogan of these grassroots groups. Related to the emergence of these social movements is the growth of nongovernmental organizations (NGOs). According to one analyst, NGOs are an important instrument in the cultivation of global perspectives: "Since NGOs by definition are identified with interests that transcend national boundaries, we expect all NGOs to define problems in global terms, to take account of human interests and needs as they are found in all parts of the planet."[7] NGOs are often represented at the United Nations and include professional, business, and cooperative organizations; foundations; religious, peace, and disarmament groups; youth and women's organizations; environmental and human rights groups; and research institutes. The number of international NGOs increased from 176 in 1910 to 29,000 in 1995.

And yet hopes for global approaches to global problems have also been hindered by political, ethnic, and religious disputes. Pollution of the Rhine River by factories along its banks provokes angry disputes among European nations, and the United States and Canada have argued about the effects of acid rain on Canadian forests. The collapse of the Soviet Union and its satellite system seemed to provide an enormous boost to the potential for international cooperation on global issues. In fact, the collapse of the Soviet empire has had almost the opposite effect, as the disintegration of the Soviet Union has led to the emergence of squabbling new nations and an atmosphere of conflict and tension throughout much of Eastern Europe. The bloody conflict in Yugoslavia clearly indicates the dangers inherent in the rise of nationalist sentiment among various ethnic and religious groups in Eastern Europe. Many conflicts begin with regional issues and then develop into international concerns. Terrorism is an important example as international terrorist groups seek to wreak havoc around the world.

Thus even as the world becomes more global in culture and interdependent in its mutual relations, centrifugal forces are still at work attempting to redefine the political, cultural, and ethnic ways in which the world is divided. Such efforts are often disruptive and can sometimes work against measures to enhance our human destiny.

Many lessons can be learned from the history of Western civilization, but one of them is especially clear. Lack of involvement in the affairs of one's society can lead to a sense of powerlessness. In an age that is often crisis-laden and chaotic, an understanding of our Western heritage and its lessons can be instrumental in helping us create new models for the future. For we are all creators of history, and the future of Western and indeed world civilization depends on us.

Courtesy of NASA

The Earth. For many people in the West, as in the rest of the world, the view of earth from outer space fostered an important image of global unity. The American astronaut Russell Schweickart wrote: "From where you see it, the thing is a whole, and it is so beautiful." In a similar reaction, Yuri Gagarin, a Soviet cosmonaut, remarked: "What strikes me, is not only the beauty of the continents . . . but their closeness to one another . . . their essential unity."

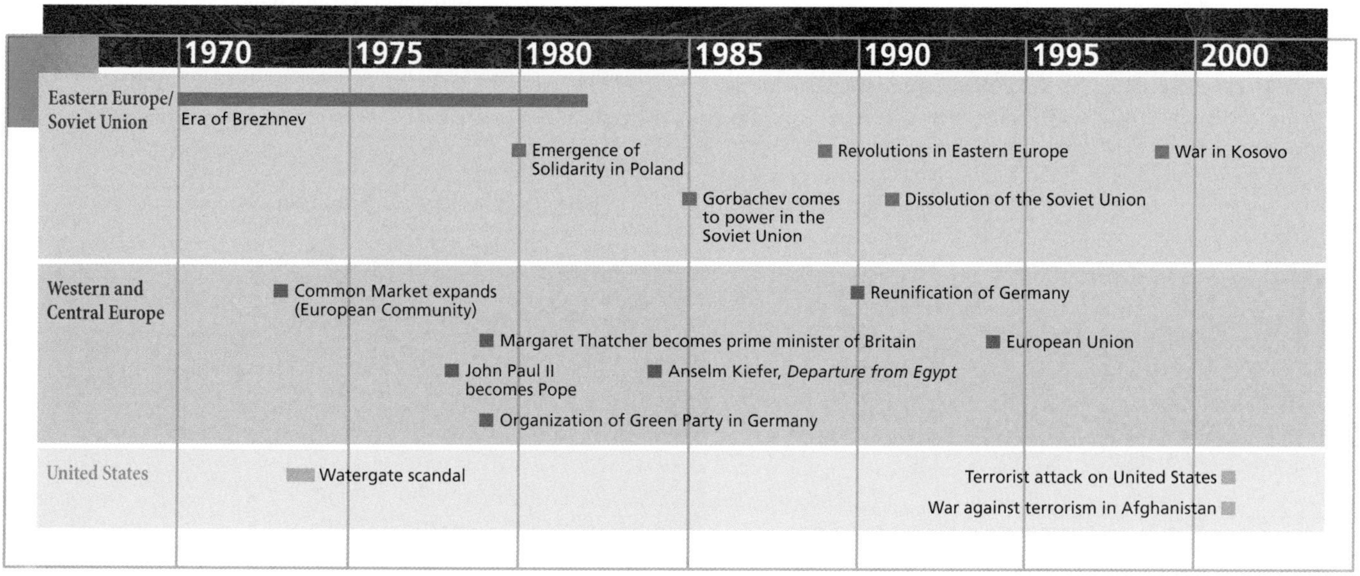

Notes

1. Mikhail Gorbachev, "Report to the 27th Party Congress," February 25, 1986, in *Current Soviet Policies* 9 (1986): 10.
2. Quoted in Renate Bridenthal, "Women in the New Europe," in Renate Bridenthal, Susan Mosher Stuard, and Merry E. Weisner, eds., *Becoming Visible: Women in European History,* 3d ed. (Boston, 1998), pp. 564–565.
3. Quoted in Henry Grosshans, *The Search for Modern Europe* (Boston, 1970), p. 421.
4. Richard Maltby, ed., *Passing Parade: A History of Popular Culture in the Twentieth Century* (Oxford, 1989), p. 8.
5. Ibid.
6. Quoted in ibid., p. 11.
7. Elise Boulding, *Women in the Twentieth-Century World* (New York, 1977), pp. 186–187.

Suggestions for Further Reading

For general surveys of contemporary European history, see the references in Chapter 28. General studies on the Cold War are also listed in Chapter 28. A detailed analysis of American-Soviet relations in the 1970s and 1980s is available in R. Garthoff, *Détente and Confrontation: American-Soviet Relations from Nixon to Reagan* (Washington, D.C., 1985). On the end of the Cold War, see B. Denitch, *The End of the Cold War* (Minneapolis, 1990); W. G. Hyland, *The Cold War Is Over* (New York, 1990); and W. Laqueur, *Soviet Union, 2000: Reform or Revolution?* (New York, 1990).

Recent problems in the Soviet Union are analyzed in A. Brown, *The Gorbachev Factor* (New York, 1996), G. Hosking, *The Awakening of the Soviet Union* (London, 1990); and S. White, *Gorbachev and After* (Cambridge, 1991). For a general study of the Soviet satellites in Eastern Europe, see G. Stokes, *The Walls Came Tumbling Down: The Collapse of Communism in Eastern Europe* (Oxford, 1993). Additional studies on the recent history of these countries include T. G. Ash, *The Polish Revolution: Solidarity* (New York, 1984); T. G. Ash, *The Magic Lantern: The Revolution of '89 Witnessed in Warsaw, Budapest, Berlin, and Prague* (New York, 1990); M. Shafir, *Romania: Politics, Economics and Society* (London, 1985); C. S. Maier, *Dissolution: The Crisis of Communism and the End of East Germany* (Princeton, N.J., 1997); and S. Ramet, *Nationalism and Federalism in Yugoslavia* (Bloomington, Ind., 1992).

For general works on Western Europe and individual countries, see the references in Chapter 28. On the recent history of these countries, see E. J. Evans, *Thatcher and Thatcherism* (New York, 1997); P. A. Hall, *Governing the Economy: The Politics of State Intervention in Britain and France* (New York, 1986); S. Baumann-Reynolds, *François Mitterrand* (Westport, Conn., 1995); R. J. Dalton, *Politics in West Germany* (Glenview, Ill., 1989); and K. Jarausch, *The Rush to German Unity* (New York, 1994).

The changing role of women is examined in C. Duchen, *Feminism in France* (London, 1986). On terrorism, see W. Laqueur, *Terrorism*, 2d ed. (New York, 1988), and R. Rubenstein, *Alchemists of Revolution: Terrorism in the Modern World* (London, 1987). The problems of guest workers and immigrants are examined in J. Miller, *Foreign Workers in Western Europe* (London, 1981), and S. Castles, *Here for Good: Western Europe's New Ethnic Minorities* (London, 1984). On the development of the Green parties, see M. O'Neill, *Green Parties and Political Change in Contemporary Europe* (Aldershot, England, 1997), and D. Richardson and C. Rootes, eds., *The Green Challenge: The Development of the Green Parties in Europe* (London, 1995).

For a general view of postwar thought, see R. N. Stromberg, *European Intellectual History Since 1789,* 5th ed. (Englewood Cliffs, N.J., 1990). On contemporary art, see R. Lambert, *Cambridge Introduction to the History of Art: The Twentieth Century* (Cambridge, 1981), and the general work by B. Cole and A. Gealt, *Art of the Western World* (New York, 1989). A physicist's view of science is contained in J. Ziman, *The Force of Knowledge: The Scientific Dimension of Society* (Cambridge, 1976). A physicist's view of a new conception of reality is D. Bohm, *Wholeness and the Implicate Order* (Boston, 1980). The space race is examined in W. A. McDougall, *The Heavens and the Earth: A Political History of the Space Age* (New York, 1984). A classic work on existentialism is W. Barrett, *Irrational Man* (Garden City, N.Y., 1962). An excellent survey of twentieth-century popular culture is R. Maltby, ed., *Passing Parade: A History of Popular Culture in the Twentieth Century* (Oxford, 1989). On film and the media, see L. May, *Screening Out the Past: The Birth of Mass Culture and the Motion Picture Industry* (New York, 1980), and F. Wheen, *Television* (London, 1985). On popular music, see P. Eberly, *Music in the Air* (New York, 1982). Sport is examined in A. Guttmann, *From Ritual to Record: The Nature of Modern Sports* (New York, 1978), and R. Mandell, *Sport: A Cultural History* (New York, 1984). On the "global village" idea, see M. McLuhan, *Understanding Media: The Extensions of Man* (New York, 1964).

For additional reading, go to InfoTrac College Edition, your online research library at http://web1.infotrac-college.com

Enter the search term *single European market* using the Subject Guide.

Enter the search term *Europe Communism* using Key Terms.

Enter the search term *perestroika* using the Subject Guide.

Enter the search term *Green parties* using Key Terms.

Glossary

absolutism a form of government where the sovereign power or ultimate authority rested in the hands of a monarch who claimed to rule by divine right and was therefore responsible only to God.

Agricultural (Neolithic) Revolution the shift from hunting animals and gathering plants for sustenance to producing food by systematic agriculture that occurred gradually between 10,000 and 4000 B.C. (the Neolithic or "New Stone" Age).

agricultural revolution the application of new agricultural techniques that allowed for a large increase in productivity in the eighteenth century.

anarchism a political theory that holds that all governments and existing social institutions are unnecessary and advocates a society based on voluntary cooperation.

anti-Semitism hostility toward or discrimination against Jews.

apartheid the system of racial segregation practiced in the Republic of South Africa until the 1990s, which involved political, legal, and economic discrimination against nonwhites.

appeasement the policy, followed by the European nations in the 1930s, of accepting Hitler's annexation of Austria and Czechoslovakia in the belief that meeting his demands would assure peace and stability.

Arianism a Christian heresy that taught that Jesus was inferior to God. Though condemned by the Council of Nicaea in 325, Arianism was adopted by many of the Germanic peoples who entered the Roman Empire over the next centuries.

aristocracy a class of hereditary nobility in medieval Europe; a warrior class who shared a distinctive lifestyle based on the institution of knighthood, although there were social divisions within the group based on extremes of wealth.

Ausgleich the "Compromise" of 1867 that created the dual monarchy of Austria-Hungary. Austria and Hungary each had its own capital, constitution, and legislative assembly, but were united under one monarch.

authoritarian state a state that has a dictatorial government and some other trappings of a totalitarian state, but does not demand that the masses be actively involved in the regime's goals as totalitarian states do.

auxiliaries troops enlisted from the subject peoples of the Roman Empire to supplement the regular legions composed of Roman citizens.

balance of power a distribution of power among several states such that no single nation can dominate or interfere with the interests of another.

benefice in the Christian church, a position, such as a bishopric, that consisted of both a sacred office and the right of the holder to the annual revenues from the position.

bicameral legislature a legislature with two houses.

Black Death the outbreak of plague (mostly bubonic) in the mid-fourteenth century that killed from 25 to 50 percent of Europe's population.

Blitzkrieg "lightning war." A war conducted with great speed and force, as in Germany's advance at the beginning of World War II.

Bolsheviks a small faction of the Russian Social Democratic Party who were led by Lenin and dedicated to violent revolution; seized power in Russia in 1917 and were subsequently renamed the Communists.

boyars the Russian nobility.

Brezhnev Doctrine the doctrine, enunciated by Leonid Brezhnev, that the Soviet Union had a right to intervene if socialism was threatened in another socialist state; used to justify the use of Soviet troops in Czechoslovakia in 1968.

caliph the secular leader of the Islamic community.

capital material wealth used or available for use in the production of more wealth.

cartel a combination of independent commercial enterprises that work together to control prices and limit competition.

Cartesian dualism Descartes's principle of the separation of mind and matter (and mind and body) that enabled scientists to view matter as something separate from themselves that could be investigated by reason.

chansons de geste a form of vernacular literature in the High Middle Ages that consisted of heroic epics focusing on the deeds of warriors.

chivalry the ideal of civilized behavior that emerged among the nobility in the eleventh and twelfth centuries under the influence of the church; a code of ethics knights were expected to uphold.

Christian (northern) humanism an intellectual movement in northern Europe in the late fifteenth and early sixteenth centuries that combined the interest in the classics of the Italian Renaissance with an interest in the sources of early Christianity, including the New Testament and the writings of the church fathers.

civic humanism an intellectual movement of the Italian Renaissance that saw Cicero, who was both an intellectual and a statesman, as the ideal and held that humanists should be involved in government and use their rhetorical training in the service of the state.

civil rights the basic rights of citizens including equality before the law, freedom of speech and press, and freedom from arbitrary arrest.

Cold War the ideological conflict between the Soviet Union and the United States after World War II.

collective farms large farms created in the Soviet Union by Stalin by combining many small holdings into one large farm worked by the peasants under government supervision.

collective security the use of an international army raised by an association of nations to deter aggression and keep the peace.

coloni free tenant farmers who worked as sharecroppers on the large estates of the Roman Empire (singular: *colonus*).

common law law common to the entire kingdom of England; imposed by the king's courts beginning in the twelfth century to replace the customary law used in county and feudal courts that varied from place to place.

commune in medieval Europe, an association of townspeople bound together by a sworn oath for the purpose of obtaining basic liberties from the lord of the territory in which the town was located; also, the self-governing town after receiving its liberties.

conciliarism a movement in fourteenth- and fifteenth-century Europe that held that final authority in spiritual matters resided with a general church council, not the pope; emerged in response to the Avignon papacy and the Great Schism and used to justify the summoning of the Council of Constance (1414–1418).

condottieri leaders of bands of mercenary soldiers in Renaissance Italy who sold their services to the highest bidder.

conquistadors "conquerors." Leaders in the Spanish conquests in the Americas, especially Mexico and Peru, in the sixteenth century.

conscription a military draft.

conservatism an ideology based on tradition and social stability that favored the maintenance of established institutions, organized religion, and obedience to authority and resisted change, especially abrupt change.

consuls the chief executive officers of the Roman Republic. Two were chosen annually to administer the government and lead the army in battle.

consumer society a term applied to Western society after World War II as the working classes adopted the consumption patterns of the middle class and installment plans, credit cards, and easy credit made consumer goods such as appliances and automobiles widely available.

Continental System Napoleon's effort to bar British goods from the Continent in the hope of weakening Britain's economy and destroying its capacity to wage war.

cosmopolitanism the quality of being sophisticated and having wide international experience.

cottage industry a system of textile manufacturing in which spinners and weavers worked at home in their cottages using raw materials supplied to them by capitalist entrepreneurs.

cultural relativism the belief that no culture is superior to another because culture is a matter of custom, not reason, and derives its meaning from the group holding it.

cuneiform "wedge-shaped." A system of writing developed by the Sumerians that consisted of wedge-shaped impressions made by a reed stylus on clay tablets.

decolonization the process of becoming free of colonial status and achieving statehood; occurred in most of the world's colonies between 1947 and 1962.

deism belief in God as the creator of the universe who, after setting it in motion, ceased to have any direct involvement in it and allowed it to run according to its own natural laws.

demesne the part of a manor retained under the direct control of the lord and worked by the serfs as part of their labor services.

depression a very severe, protracted economic downturn with high levels of unemployment.

destalinization the policy of denouncing and undoing the most repressive aspects of Stalin's regime; begun by Nikita Khrushchev in 1956.

détente the relaxation of tension between the Soviet Union and the United States that occurred in the 1970s.

dialectic logic, one of the seven liberal arts that made up the medieval curriculum. In Marxist thought, the process by which all change occurs through the clash of antagonistic elements.

Diaspora the scattering of Jews throughout the ancient world after the Babylonian captivity in the sixth century B.C.

dictator in the Roman Republic, an official granted unlimited power to run the state for a short period of time, usually six months, during an emergency.

diocese the area under the jurisdiction of a Christian bishop; based originally on Roman administrative districts.

direct representation a system of choosing delegates to a representative assembly in which citizens vote directly for the delegates who will represent them.

divination the practice of seeking to foretell future events by interpreting divine signs, which could appear in various forms, such as in entrails of animals, in patterns in smoke, or in dreams.

divine-right monarchy a monarchy based on the belief that monarchs receive their power directly from God and are responsible to no one except God.

domino theory the belief that if the Communists succeeded in Vietnam, other countries in Southeast and East Asia would also fall (like dominoes) to communism; a justification for the U.S. intervention in Vietnam.

dualism the belief that the universe is dominated by two opposing forces, one good and the other evil.

dynastic state a state where the maintenance and expansion of the interests of the ruling family is the primary consideration.

economic imperialism the process in which banks and corporations from developed nations invest in underdeveloped regions and establish a major presence there in the hope of making high profits; not necessarily the same as colonial expansion in that businesses invest where they can make a profit, which may not be in their own nation's colonies.

empiricism the practice of relying on observation and experiment.

enclosure movement in the eighteenth century, the fencing in of the old open fields, combining many small holdings into larger units that could be farmed more efficiently.

encyclical a letter from the pope to all the bishops of the Roman Catholic church.

enlightened absolutism an absolute monarchy where the ruler follows the principles of the Enlightenment by introducing reforms for the improvement of society, allowing freedom of speech and the press, permitting religious toleration, expanding education, and ruling in accordance with the laws.

Enlightenment an eighteenth-century intellectual movement, led by the philosophes, that stressed the application of reason and the scientific method to all aspects of life.

entrepreneur one who organizes, operates, and assumes the risk in a business venture in the expectation of making a profit.

Epicureanism a philosophy founded by Epicurus in the fourth century B.C. that taught that happiness (freedom from emotional turmoil) could be achieved through the pursuit of pleasure (intellectual rather than sensual pleasure).

equestrians a group of extremely wealthy men in the late Roman Republic who were effectively barred from high office, but sought political power commensurate with their wealth; called equestrians because many had gotten their start as cavalry officers (*equites*).

ethnic cleansing the policy of killing or forcibly removing people of another ethnic group; used by the Serbs against Bosnian Muslims in the 1990s.

eucharist a Christian sacrament in which consecrated bread and wine are consumed in celebration of Jesus' Last Supper; also called the Lord's Supper or communion.

evolutionary socialism a socialist doctrine espoused by Eduard Bernstein who argued that socialists should stress cooperation and evolution to attain power by democratic means rather than by conflict and revolution.

fascism an ideology or movement that exalts the nation above the individual and calls for a centralized government with a dictatorial leader, economic and social regimentation, and forcible suppression of opposition; in particular, the ideology of Mussolini's Fascist regime in Italy.

feminism the belief in the social, political, and economic equality of the sexes; also, organized activity to advance women's rights.

fief a landed estate granted to a vassal in exchange for military services.

Final Solution the physical extermination of the Jewish people by the Nazis during World War II.

folk culture the traditional arts and crafts, literature, music, and other customs of the people; something that people make, as opposed to modern popular culture, which is something people buy.

free trade the unrestricted international exchange of goods with low or no tariffs.

functionalism the idea that the function of an object should determine its design and materials.

general strike a strike by all or most workers in an economy; espoused by Georges Sorel as the heroic action that could be used to inspire the workers to destroy capitalist society.

gentry well-to-do English landowners below the level of the nobility; played an important role in the English Civil War of the seventeenth century.

geocentric theory the idea that the earth is at the center of the universe and that the sun and other celestial objects revolve around the earth.

glasnost "openness." Mikhail Gorbachev's policy of encouraging Soviet citizens to openly discuss the strengths and weaknesses of the Soviet Union.

good emperors the five emperors who ruled from 96 to 180 (Nerva, Trajan, Hadrian, Antoninus Pius, and Marcus Aurelius), a period of peace and prosperity for the Roman Empire.

Great Schism the crisis in the late medieval church when there were first two and then three popes; ended by the Council of Constance (1414–1418).

guest workers foreign workers working temporarily in European countries.

guild an association of people with common interests and concerns, especially people working in the same craft. In medieval Europe, guilds came to control much of the production process and to restrict entry into various trades.

gymnasium in classical Greece, a place for athletics; in the Hellenistic Age, a secondary school with a curriculum centered on music, physical exercise, and literature.

heliocentric theory the idea that the sun (not the earth) is at the center of the universe.

Hellenistic literally, "to imitate the Greeks"; the era after the death of Alexander the Great when Greek culture spread into the Near East and blended with the culture of that region.

helots serfs in ancient Sparta, who were permanently bound to the land that they worked for their Spartan masters.

heresy the holding of religious doctrines different from the official teachings of the church.

Hermeticism an intellectual movement beginning in the fifteenth century that taught that divinity is embodied in all aspects of nature; included works on alchemy and magic as well as theology and philosophy. The tradition continued into the seventeenth century and influenced many of the leading figures of the Scientific Revolution.

hetairai highly sophisticated courtesans in ancient Athens who offered intellectual and musical entertainment as well as sex.

hieroglyphics a highly pictorial system of writing used in ancient Egypt.

high culture the literary and artistic culture of the educated and wealthy ruling classes.

Holocaust the mass slaughter of European Jews by the Nazis during World War II.

hoplites heavily armed infantry soldiers used in ancient Greece in a phalanx formation.

Huguenots French Calvinists.

humanism an intellectual movement in Renaissance Italy based upon the study of the Greek and Roman classics

iconoclasm an eighth-century Byzantine movement against the use of icons (pictures of sacred figures), which was condemned as idolatry.

ideology a political philosophy such as conservatism or liberalism.

imperium "the right to command." In the Roman Republic, the chief executive officers (consuls and praetors) possessed the *imperium;* a military commander was an *imperator.* In the Roman Empire, the title *imperator,* or emperor, came to be used for the ruler.

indirect representation a system of choosing delegates to a representative assembly in which citizens do not choose the delegates directly but instead vote for electors who choose the delegates.

individualism emphasis on and interest in the unique traits of each person.

indulgence the remission of part or all of the temporal punishment in purgatory due to sin; granted for charitable contributions and other good deeds. Indulgences became a regular practice of the Christian church in the High Middle Ages, and their abuse was instrumental in sparking Luther's reform movement in the sixteenth century.

infanticide the practice of killing infants.

inflation a sustained rise in the price level.

intendants royal officials in seventeenth-century France who were sent into the provinces to execute the orders of the central government.

intervention, principle of the idea, after the Congress of Vienna, that the great powers of Europe had the right to send armies into countries experiencing revolution to restore legitimate monarchs to their thrones.

isolationism a foreign policy in which a nation refrains from making alliances or engaging actively in international affairs.

jihad "striving in the way of the Lord." In Islam, the practice of conducting raids against neighboring peoples, which was an expansion of the Arab tradition of tribal raids against their persecutors.

joint-stock company a company or association that raises capital by selling shares to individuals who receive dividends on their investment while a board of directors runs the company.

joint-stock investment bank a bank created by selling shares of stock to investors. Such banks potentially have access to much more capital than do private banks owned by one or a few individuals.

justification of faith the primary doctrine of the Protestant Reformation; taught that humans are saved not through good works, but by the grace of God, bestowed freely through the sacrifice of Jesus.

laissez-faire "to let alone." An economic doctrine that holds that an economy is best served when the government does not interfere but allows the economy to self-regulate according to the forces of supply and demand.

latifundia large landed estates in the Roman Empire (singular: *latifundium*).

lay investiture the practice in which a layperson chose a bishop and invested him with the symbols of both his temporal office and his spiritual office; led to the Investiture Controversy, which was ended by compromise in the Concordat of Worms in 1122.

Lebensraum "living space." The doctrine, adopted by Hitler, that a nation's power depends on the amount of land it occupies; thus, a nation must expand to be strong.

legitimacy, principle of the idea that after the Napoleonic wars peace could best be reestablished in Europe by restoring legitimate monarchs who would preserve traditional institutions; guided Metternich at the Congress of Vienna.

Leninism Lenin's revision of Marxism that held that Russia need not experience a bourgeois revolution before it could move toward socialism.

liberal arts the seven areas of study that formed the basis of education in medieval and early modern Europe. Following Boethius and other late Roman authors, they consisted of grammar, rhetoric, and dialectic or logic (the *trivium*) and arithmetic, geometry, astronomy, and music (the *quadrivium*).

liberalism an ideology based on the belief that people should be as free from restraint as possible. Economic liberalism is the idea that the government should not interfere in the workings of the economy. Political liberalism is the idea that there should be restraints on the exercise of power so that people can enjoy basic civil rights in a constitutional state with a representative assembly.

limited liability the principle that shareholders in a joint-stock corporation can be held responsible for the corporation's debts only up to the amount they have invested.

limited (constitutional) monarchy a system of government in which the monarch is limited by a representative assembly and by the duty to rule in accordance with the laws of the land.

mandates a system established after World War I whereby a nation officially administered a territory (mandate) on behalf of the League of Nations. Thus, France administered Lebanon and Syria as mandates, and Britain administered Iraq and Palestine.

manor an agricultural estate operated by a lord and worked by peasants who performed labor services and paid various rents and fees to the lord in exchange for protection and sustenance.

Marshall Plan the European Recovery Program, under which the United States provided financial aid to European countries to help them rebuild after World War II.

Marxism the political, economic, and social theories of Karl Marx, which included the idea that history is the story of class struggle and that ultimately the proletariat will overthrow the bourgeoisie and establish a dictatorship en route to a classless society.

mass education a state-run educational system, usually free and compulsory, that aims to ensure that all children in society have at least a basic education.

mass leisure forms of leisure that appeal to large numbers of people in a society including the working classes; emerged at the end of the nineteenth century to provide workers with amusements after work and on weekends; used during the twentieth century by totalitarian states to control their populations.

mass politics a political order characterized by mass political parties and universal male and (eventually) female suffrage.

mass society a society in which the concerns of the majority—the lower classes—play a prominent role; characterized by extension of voting rights, an improved standard of living for the lower classes, and mass education.

materialism the belief that everything mental, spiritual, or ideal is an outgrowth of physical forces and that truth is found in concrete material existence, not through feeling or intuition.

mercantilism an economic theory that held that a nation's prosperity depended on its supply of gold and silver and that the total volume of trade is unchangeable; therefore, advocated that the government play an active role in the economy by encouraging exports and discouraging imports, especially through the use of tariffs.

Mesolithic Age the period from 10,000 to 7000 B.C., characterized by a gradual transition from a food-gathering/hunting economy to a food-producing economy.

metics resident foreigners in ancient Athens; not permitted full rights of citizenship but did receive the protection of the laws.

militarism a policy of aggressive military preparedness; in particular, the large armies based on mass conscription and complex, inflexible plans for mobilization that most European nations had before World War I.

ministerial responsibility a tenet of nineteenth-century liberalism that held that ministers of the monarch should be responsible to the legislative assembly rather than to the monarch.

Modernism the new artistic and literary styles that emerged in the decades before 1914 as artists rebelled against traditional efforts to portray reality as accurately as possible (leading to Impressionism and Cubism) and writers explored new forms.

monotheistic/monotheism having only one god; the doctrine or belief that there is only one god.

mutual deterrence the belief that nuclear war could best be prevented if both the United States and the Soviet Union had sufficient nuclear weapons so that even if one nation launched a preemptive first strike, the other could respond and devastate the attacker.

mystery religions religions that involve initiation into secret rites that promise intense emotional involvement with spiritual forces and a greater chance of individual immortality.

nationalism a sense of national consciousness based on awareness of being part of a community—a "nation"—that has common institutions, traditions, language, and customs and that becomes the focus of the individual's primary political loyalty.

nationalities problem the dilemma faced by the Austro-Hungarian Empire in trying to unite a wide variety of ethnic groups including, among others, Austrians, Hungarians, Poles, Croats, Czechs, Serbs, Slovaks, and Slovenes in an era when nationalism and calls for self-determination were coming to the fore.

nationalization the process of converting a business or industry from private ownership to government control and ownership.

nation in arms the people's army raised by universal mobilization to repel the foreign enemies of the French Revolution.

nation-state a form of political organization in which a relatively homogeneous people inhabits a sovereign state, as opposed to a state containing people of several nationalities.

NATO the North Atlantic Treaty Organization; a military alliance formed in 1949 in which the signatories (Belgium, Canada, Denmark, France, Great Britain, Iceland, Italy, Luxembourg, the Netherlands, Norway, Portugal, and the United States) agreed to provide mutual assistance if any one of them was attacked; later expanded to include other nations.

natural laws a body of laws or specific principles held to be derived from nature and binding upon all human society even in the absence of positive laws.

natural rights certain inalienable rights to which all people are entitled; include the right to life, liberty, and property, freedom of speech and religion, and equality before the law.

natural selection Darwin's idea that organisms that are most adaptable to their environment survive and pass on the variations that enabled them to survive, while other, less adaptable organisms become extinct; "survival of the fittest."

Nazi New Order the Nazis' plan for their conquered territories; included the extermination of Jews and others considered inferior, ruthless exploitation of resources, German colonization in the east, and the use of Poles, Russians, and Ukrainians as slave labor.

Neoplatonism a revival of Platonic philosophy. In the third century A.D., a revival associated with Plotinus; in the Italian Renaissance, a revival associated with Marsilio Ficino who attempted to synthesize Christianity and Platonism.

New Economic Policy a modified version of the old capitalist system introduced in the Soviet Union by Lenin in 1921 to revive the economy after the ravages of the civil war and war communism.

new imperialism the revival of imperialism after 1880 in which European nations established colonies throughout much of Asia and Africa.

new monarchies the governments of France, England, and Spain at the end of the fifteenth century, where the rulers were successful in reestablishing or extending centralized royal authority, suppressing the nobility, controlling the church, and insisting upon the loyalty of all peoples living in their territories.

nobiles "nobles." The small group of families from both patrician and plebeian origins who produced most of the men who were elected to office in the late Roman Republic.

nominalism a school of thought in medieval Europe that, following Aristotle, held that only individual objects are real and that universals are only names created by humans.

nuclear family a family group consisting only of father, mother, and children.

old regime/old order the political and social system of France in the eighteenth century before the Revolution.

oligarchy rule by a few.

optimates "best men." Aristocratic leaders in the late Roman Republic who generally came from senatorial families and wished to retain their oligarchical privileges.

orders/estates the traditional tripartite division of European society based on heredity and quality rather than wealth or economic standing, first established in the Middle Ages and continuing into the eighteenth century; traditionally consisted of those who pray (the clergy), those who fight (the nobility), and those who work (all the rest).

organic evolution Darwin's principle that all plants and animals have evolved over a long period of time from earlier and simpler forms of life.

Paleolithic Age the period of human history when humans used simple stone tools (c. 2,500,000–10,000 B.C.).

pantheism a doctrine that equates God with the universe and all that is in it.

paterfamilias the dominant male in a Roman family whose powers over his wife and children were theoretically unlimited, though they were sometimes circumvented in practice.

patriarchal/patriarchy a society in which the father is supreme in the clan or family; more generally, a society dominated by men.

patriarchal family a family in which the husband/father dominates his wife and children.

patricians great landowners who became the ruling class in the Roman Republic.

patronage the practice of awarding titles and making appointments to government and other positions to gain political support.

Pax Romana "Roman peace." A term used to refer to the stability and prosperity that Roman rule brought to the Mediterranean world and much of western Europe during the first and second centuries A.D.

Pentateuch the first five books of the Hebrew Bible (Genesis, Exodus, Leviticus, Numbers, and Deuteronomy).

perestroika "restructuring." A term applied to Mikhail Gorbachev's economic, political, and social reforms in the Soviet Union.

permissive society a term applied to Western society after World War II to reflect the new sexual freedom and the emergence of a drug culture.

Petrine supremacy the doctrine that the bishop of Rome—the pope—as the successor of Saint Peter (traditionally considered the first bishop of Rome) should hold a preeminent position in the church.

phalanstery a self-sustaining cooperative community, as advocated by Charles Fourier in the early 19th century.

phalanx a rectangular formation of tightly massed infantry soldiers.

philosophes intellectuals of the eighteenth-century Enlightenment who believed in applying a spirit of rational criticism to all things, including religion and politics, and who focused on improving and enjoying this world, rather than on the afterlife.

plebeians the class of Roman citizens who included nonpatrician landowners, craftspeople, merchants, and small farmers in the Roman Republic. Their struggle for equal rights with the patricians dominated much of the Republic's history.

pluralism the practice in which one person holds several church offices simultaneously; a problem of the late medieval church.

pogroms organized massacres of Jews.

polis an ancient Greek city-state encompassing both an urban area and its surrounding countryside; a small but autonomous political unit where all major political and social activities were carried out in a central location.

political democracy a form of government characterized by universal suffrage and mass political parties.

politiques a group who emerged during the French Wars of Religion in the sixteenth century; placed politics above religion and believed that no religious truth was worth the ravages of civil war.

polytheistic/polytheism having many gods; belief in or the worship of more than one god.

popular culture as opposed to high culture, the unofficial, written and unwritten culture of the masses, much of which was passed down orally; centers on public and group activities such as festivals. In the twentieth century, refers to the entertainment, recreation, and pleasures that people purchase as part of mass consumer society.

populares "favoring the people." Aristocratic leaders in the late Roman Republic who tended to use the people's assemblies in an effort to break the stranglehold of the *nobiles* on political offices.

popular sovereignty the doctrine that government is created by and subject to the will of the people, who are the source of all political power.

populism a political philosophy or movement that supports the rights and power of ordinary people in their struggle against the privileged elite.

praetorian guard the military unit that served as the personal bodyguard of the Roman emperors.

predestination the belief, associated with Calvinism, that God, as a consequence of his foreknowledge of all events, has predetermined those who will be saved (the elect) and those who will be damned.

price revolution the dramatic rise in prices (inflation) that occurred throughout Europe in the sixteenth and early seventeenth centuries.

primogeniture an inheritance practice in which the eldest son receives all or the largest share of the parents' estate.

principate the form of government established by Augustus for the Roman Empire; continued the constitutional forms of the Republic and consisted of the *princeps* ("first citizen") and the senate, although the *princeps* was clearly the dominant partner.

proletariat the industrial working class. In Marxism, the class who will ultimately overthrow the bourgeoisie.

Puritans English Protestants inspired by Calvinist theology who wished to remove all traces of Catholicism from the Church of England.

querelles des femmes "arguments about women." A centuries-old debate about the nature of women that continued during the Scientific Revolution as those who argued for the inferiority of women found additional support in the new anatomy and medicine.

rationalism a system of thought based on the belief that human reason and experience are the chief sources of knowledge.

realism in medieval Europe, the school of thought that, following Plato, held that the individual objects we perceive are not real but merely manifestations of universal ideas existing in the mind of God. In the nineteenth century, a school of painting that emphasized the everyday life of ordinary people, depicted with photographic realism.

Realpolitik "politics of reality." Politics based on practical concerns rather than theory or ethics.

real wages/income/prices wages/income/prices that have been adjusted for inflation.

reason of state the principle that a nation should act on the basis of its long-term interests and not merely to further the dynastic interests of its ruling family.

relativity theory Einstein's theory that holds, among other things, that (1) space and time are not absolute but are relative to the observer and interwoven into a four-dimensional space-time continuum and (2) matter is a form of energy ($E = mc^2$).

relics the bones of Christian saints or objects intimately associated with saints that were considered worthy of veneration.

Renaissance the "rebirth" of classical culture that occurred in Italy between c. 1350 and c. 1550; also, the earlier revivals of classical culture that occurred under Charlemagne and in the twelfth century.

rentier a person who lives on income from property and is not personally involved in its operation.

reparations payments made by a defeated nation after a war to compensate another nation for damage sustained as a result of the war; required from Germany after World War I.

revisionism a socialist doctrine that rejected Marx's emphasis on class struggle and revolution and argued instead that workers should work through political parties to bring about gradual change.

revolution a fundamental change in the political and social organization of a state.

revolutionary socialism the socialist doctrine espoused by Georges Sorel who held that violent action was the only way to achieve the goals of socialism.

rhetoric the art of persuasive speaking; in the Middle Ages, one of the seven liberal arts.

sacraments rites considered imperative for a Christian's salvation. By the thirteenth century consisted of the eucharist or Lord's Supper, baptism, marriage, penance, extreme unction, holy orders, and confirmation of children; Protestant reformers of the sixteenth century generally recognized only two—baptism and communion (the Lord's Supper).

salons gatherings of philosophes and other notables to discuss the ideas of the Enlightenment; so-called from the elegant drawing rooms (salons) where they met.

sans-culottes the common people who did not wear the fine clothes of the upper classes (sans-culottes means "without breeches") and played an important role in the radical phase of the French Revolution.

satrap/satrapy a governor with both civil and military duties in the ancient Persian Empire, which was divided into satrapies, or provinces, each administered by a satrap.

scholasticism the philosophical and theological system of the medieval schools, which emphasized rigorous analysis of contradictory authorities; often used to try to reconcile faith and reason.

scientific method a method of seeking knowledge through inductive principles; uses experiments and observations to develop generalizations.

Scientific Revolution the transition from the medieval worldview to a largely secular, rational, and materialistic perspective; began in the seventeenth century and was popularized in the eighteenth.

secularization the process of becoming more concerned with material, worldly, temporal things and less with spiritual and religious things.

self-determination the doctrine that the people of a given territory or a particular nationality should have the right to determine their own government and political future.

senate/senators the leading council of the Roman Republic; composed of about 300 men (senators) who served for life and dominated much of the political life of the Republic.

serf a peasant who is bound to the land and obliged to provide labor services and pay various rents and fees to the lord; considered unfree but not a slave because serfs could not be bought and sold.

skepticism a doubtful or questioning attitude, especially about religion.

Social Darwinism the application of Darwin's principle of organic evolution to the social order; led to the belief that progress comes from the struggle for survival as the fittest advance and the weak decline.

socialism an ideology that calls for collective or government ownership of the means of production and the distribution of goods.

social security/social insurance government programs that provide social welfare measures such as old age pensions and sickness, accident, and disability insurance.

Socratic method a form of teaching that uses a question-and-answer format to enable students to reach conclusions by using their own reasoning.

Sophists wandering scholars and professional teachers in ancient Greece who stressed the importance of rhetoric and tended toward skepticism and relativism.

soviets councils of workers' and soldiers' deputies formed throughout Russia in 1917; played an important role in the Bolshevik Revolution.

sphere of influence a territory or region over which an outside nation exercises political or economic influence.

Stoicism a philosophy founded by Zeno in the fourth century B.C. that taught that happiness could be obtained by accepting one's lot and living in harmony with the will of God, thereby achieving inner peace.

subinfeudation the practice in which a lord's greatest vassals subdivided their fiefs and had vassals of their own, and those vassals, in turn, subdivided their fiefs and so on down to simple knights whose fiefs were too small to subdivide.

suffrage the right to vote.

suffragists those who advocate the extension of the right to vote (suffrage), especially to women.

surplus value in Marxism, the difference between a product's real value and the wages of the worker who produced the product.

syncretism the combining of different forms of belief or practice, as, for example, when two gods are regarded as different forms of the same underlying divine force and are fused together.

tariffs duties (taxes) imposed on imported goods; usually imposed both to raise revenue and to discourage imports and protect domestic industries.

tetrarchy rule by four; the system of government established by Diocletian (284–305) in which the Roman Empire was divided into two parts, each ruled by an "Augustus" assisted by a "Caesar."

theocracy a government ruled by a divine authority.

three-field system in medieval agriculture, the practice of dividing the arable land into three fields so that one could lie fallow while the others were planted in winter grains and spring crops.

tithe a tenth of one's harvest or income; paid by medieval peasants to the village church.

Torah the body of law in Hebrew Scripture, contained in the Pentateuch (the first five books of the Hebrew Bible).

totalitarian state a state characterized by government control over all aspects of economic, social, political, cultural, and intellectual life, the subordination of the individual to the state, and insistence that the masses be actively involved in the regime's goals.

total war warfare in which all of a nation's resources, including civilians at home as well as soldiers in the field, are mobilized for the war effort.

trade union an association of workers in the same trade, formed to help members secure better wages, benefits, and working conditions.

transformism a political system in Italy in the nineteenth and twentieth centuries in which old political groups were transformed into new government coalitions by political and economic bribery.

transubstantiation a doctrine of the Roman Catholic church that teaches that during the eucharist the substance of the bread and wine is miraculously transformed into the body and blood of Jesus.

trench warfare warfare in which the opposing forces attack and counterattack from a relatively permanent system of trenches protected by barbed wire; characteristic of World War I.

trivium* and *quadrivium together formed the seven liberal arts that were the basis of medieval and early modern education. Grammar, rhetoric, and dialectic or logic made up the *trivium;* arithmetic, geometry, astronomy, and music made up the *quadrivium.*

Truman Doctrine the doctrine, enunciated by Harry Truman in 1947, that the United States would provide economic aid to countries that said they were threatened by Communist expansion.

tyrant/tyranny in an ancient Greek *polis* (or an Italian city-state during the Renaissance), a ruler who came to power in an unconstitutional way and ruled without being subject to the law.

uncertainty principle a principle in quantum mechanics, posited by Heisenberg, that holds that one cannot determine the path of an electron because the very act of observing the electron would affect its location.

unconditional surrender complete, unqualified surrender of a belligerent nation.

utopian socialists intellectuals and theorists in the early nineteenth century who favored equality in social and economic conditions and wished to replace private property and competition with collective ownership and cooperation; deemed impractical and "utopian" by later socialists.

vassal a person granted a fief, or landed estate, in exchange for providing military services to the lord and fulfilling certain other obligations such as appearing at the lord's court when summoned and making a payment on the knighting of the lord's eldest son.

vernacular the everyday language of a region, as distinguished from a language used for special purposes. For example, in medieval Paris, French was the vernacular, but Latin was used for academic writing and for classes at the University of Paris.

volkish thought the belief that German culture is superior and that the German people have a universal mission to save Western civilization from inferior races.

war communism Lenin's policy of nationalizing industrial and other facilities and requisitioning the peasants' produce during the civil war in Russia.

War Guilt Clause the clause in the Treaty of Versailles that declared that Germany (and Austria) were responsible for starting World War I and ordered Germany to pay reparations for the damage the Allies had suffered as a result of the war.

Warsaw Pact a military alliance, formed in 1955, in which Albania, Bulgaria, Czechoslovakia, East Germany, Hungary, Poland, Romania, and the Soviet Union agreed to provide mutual assistance.

welfare state a social/political system in which the government assumes the primary responsibility for the social welfare of its citizens by providing such things as social security, unemployment benefits, and health care.

wergeld "money for a man." In early Germanic law, a person's value in monetary terms, which was paid by a wrongdoer to the family of the person who had been injured or killed.

world-machine Newton's conception of the universe as one huge, regulated, and uniform machine that operated according to natural laws in absolute time, space, and motion.

ziggurat a massive stepped tower upon which a temple dedicated to the chief god or goddess of a Sumerian city was built.

Zionism an international movement that called for the establishment of a Jewish state or a refuge for Jews in Palestine.

Zoroastrianism a religion founded by the Persian Zoroaster in the seventh century B.C.; characterized by worship of a supreme god Ahuramazda who represents the good against the evil spirit, identified as Ahriman.

Pronunciation Guide

Abbasid AB-uh-sid or a-BA-sid
Adenauer, Konrad AD-n'our-er
aediles EE-diles
Aeolians ee-OH-lee-uns
Aeschylus ESS-kuh-lus
Afrikaners a-fri-KAH-ners
Agincourt AJ-in-kor
Ahlwardt, Hermann ARL-vart
Ahuramazda ah-HOOR-ah-MAHZ-duh
Akhenaten ah-kuh-NAH-tun
Akkadians a-KAY-dee-uns
al-Abbas, Abu al-AH-bus, AH-boo
Albigensians al-bi-GEN-see-uns
Albuquerque, Afonso de AL-buh-kur-kee, ah-FON-soh d'
Alcibiades al-suh-BY-uh-deez
Alcuin AL-kwin
Aliz, Ramiz AL-ee-uh, ra-MEEZ
Allah AH-luh or AL-uh
al-Ma'mun al-MAH-moon
al-Rahman, Abd al-RAH-mun, abd
Amenhotep ah-mun-HOE-tep
Andreotti, Giulio ahn-dray-AH-tee, JOOL-yoh
Andropov, Yuri an-DROP-ov, YOOR-ee
Anjou AN-joo
Antigonid an-TIG-oh-nid
Antigonus Gonatus an-TIG-oh-nus goh-NAH-tus
Antiochus an-TIE-uh-kus
Antonescu, Ion An-tuh-NES-koo, YON
Antoninus Pius an-toh-NIGH-nus PIE-us
apella a-PELL-uh
Apollonius ap-uh-LOH-nee-us
Aquinas, Thomas uh-KWIGH-nus
aratrum a-RA-trum
Archimedes are-kuh-MEE-deez
Argonautica ARE-guh-NOT-i-kuh
Aristarchus ar-is-TAR-kus
Aristotle ar-i-STAH-tul
Arsinoë ar-SIN-oh-ee
artium baccalarius are-TEE-um back-uh-LAR-ee-us
artium magister are-TEE-um ma-GIS-ter
Ashkenazic ash-kuh-NAH-zic
Ashurnasirpal ah-shoor-NAH-suh-pul
asiento a-SEE-en-toh
assignat as-seen-YAH or AS-sig-nat
Assyrians uh-SEER-ee-uns
Astell, Mary AST-uhl
Atahualpa ah-tuh-WALL-puh
Attalid AT-a-lid
audiencias ah-DEE-en-CEE-ahs
Augustine AW-gus-STEEN
Auschwitz-Birkenau OUSH-vitz-BUR-kuh-now
Ausgleich OUS-glike
Avicenna av-i-SEN-uh
Avignon ah-veen-YONE
Babeuf, Gracchus bah-BUHF, GRAK-us
Bach, Johann Sebastian BAHK, yoh-HAHN suh-BASS-chen
Bakunin, Michael ba-KOO-nin
Balboa, Vasco Nuñez de bal-BOH-uh, VASH-koh NOON-yez duh
Ballin, Albert BAHLL-een
Banque de Belgique BAWNK duh bel-JEEK
Barbarossa bar-buh-ROH-suh
Barth, Karl BAHRT
Bastille ba-STEEL
Bauhaus BOW-hows
Bayle, Pierre BAYL, PYER
Beauvoir, Simone de boh-VWAH, see-MOAN duh
Bebel, August BAY-bul
Beccaria, Cesare bek-KAH-ree-uh, CHAY-zahr-ay
Beguines bi-GEENS
Belgioioso, Cristina bayl-joh-YOH-soh
Belisarius bell-i-SAR-ee-us
benefice BEN-uh-fiss
Bergson, Henri BERG-son, AWN-ree
Berlioz, Hector BER-lee-ohz
Bernini, Gian Lorenzo bur-NEE-nee, JAHN loh-RENT-soh
Bernstein, Eduard BURN-stine, AY-doo-art
Bethman-Hollweg, Theobald von BET-mun-HOL-veg, THAY-oh-bald von
Blitzkrieg BLITZ-kreeg
Blum, Léon BLOOM, LAY-OHN
Boccaccio, Giovanni boh-KAH-chee-oh, joe-VAHN-nee
Bodichon, Barbara BOH-duh-chon
Boer BOHR
Boethius boh-EETH-ee-us
Boleyn, Anne BUH-lin

Bólívar, Simón BOH-luh-VAR, see-MOAN
Bologna buh-LOHN-yuh
Bossuet, Jacques baw-SWAY, ZHAHK
Bottai, Giuseppe BOT-tah, joo-ZEP-pay
Botticelli, Sandro BOT-i-CHELL-ee, SAHN-droh
Boulanger, Georges boo-lahn-ZHAY, ZHORZH
Bracciolini, Poggio braht-choh-LEE-nee, POD-joh
Brahe, Tycho BRAH, TIE-koh
Bramante, Donato brah-MAHN-tee, doe-NAY-toe
Brandt, Willy BRAHNT, VIL-ee
Brétigny bray-tee-NYEE
Brezhnev, Leonid BREZH-nef, lyi-on-YEET
Briand, Aristide bree-AHN, a-ree-STEED
Brunelleschi, Filippo BROO-nuh-LES-kee, fee-LEEP-poe
Brüning, Heinrich BROO-ning, HINE-rik
Bulganin, Nicolai bul-GAN-in, nyik-uh-LYE
Bund deutscher Mädel BUNT DOICHer MAIR-del
Bundesrat BUN-duhs-raht
Burckhardt, Jacob BORK-hart, YAK-ob
Burschenschaften BOOR-shen-shaft-un
cahiers de doléances ca-HEAR duh DOL-ay-AHNZ
Calais ka-LAY
Calas, Jean ka-LAH, ZHAHN
Caligula ka-LIG-yuh-luh
caliph/caliphate KAY-lif/KAY-li-FATE
Calonne, Charles de kah-LAWN, SHARL duh
Cambyses kam-BY-seez
Camus, Albert kuh-MOO, al-BEAR
Canaanites KAY-nuh-nites
Capet/Capetian ka-PAY or KAY-put/kuh-PEE-shun
Caraffa, Gian Pietro kah-RAH-fuh, JAHN PYEE-troh
carbonari kar-buh-NAH-ree
Carolingian kar-oh-LIN-jun
carruca ca-ruh-kuh
Carthage/Carthaginian KAR-thij/KAR-thuh-JIN-ee-un
Cartier, Jacques kahr-TYAY, ZHAK
Cassiodorus kass-ee-oh-DOR-us
Castiglione, Baldassare kas-tel-YOH-neh, bal-daz-AH-reh
Catharism KA-tha-ri-zem
Catullus ka-TULL-us
Cavendish, Margaret KAV-un-dish
Cavour, Camillo di ka-VOOR, kah-MIL-oh
Ceausescu, Nicolai chow-SHES-koo, nee-koh-LYE
cenobitic sen-oh-BIT-ik
Cereta, Laura Seh-REE-tuh, LOW-ruh
Cèzanne, Paul say-ZAN
Chaeronea ker-oh-NEE-uh
Chaldean kal-DEE-un
Chandragupta Maurya chun-druh-GUP-tuh MOWR-yuh
chanson de geste shahn-SAWN duh ZHEST
Charlemagne SHAR-luh-mane
Chateaubriand, François-René de shah-TOH-bree-AHN, FRAN-swah-ruh-NAY duh
Cheka CHEK-uh
Chiang Kai-Shek CHANG KIGH-shek
Chirac, Jacques CHI-rak, ZHAK
Chrétien de Troyes KRAY-tee-ahn duh TRWAH
Chrétien, Jean kray-TYEN, ZHAHN
Cicero SIS-uh-roh
ciompi CHOM-pee
Cistercians si-STIR-shuns
Claudius KLAW-dee-us
Cleisthenes KLISE-thuh-neez
Clemenceau, Georges klem-un-SOH, ZHORZH
Clovis KLOH-vis
Codreanu, Corneliu kaw-dree-AH-noo, kor-NELL-yoo
Colbert, Jean-Baptiste KOL-ber, ZHAHN bap-TEEST
colonus kuh-LOH-nus
Columbanus kol-um-BAHN-us
comitia centuriata kuh-MISH-ee-uh sen-TYOO-ree-ah-tuh
Commodus KOM-uh-dus
Comnenus kom-NEE-nus
Comte, Auguste KOHNT
concilium plebis con-CIL-ee-um PLE-bis
Concordat of Worms kon-KOR-dat of WURMZ or VAWRMZ
Condorcet, Marie-Jean de kawn-dar-SAY, mur-REE-ZHAHN duh
condottieri kon-dah-TEE-AIR-ee
consul KON-sul
Contarini, Gasparo kahn-tuh-REE-nee, GAHS-pah-roh
conversos kon-VAIR-sohs
Copernicus, Nicolaus koh-PURR-nuh-kus, nee-koh-LAH-us
Corinth KOR-inth
Corpus Hermeticum KOR-pus her-MET-i-koom
Corpus Iuris Civilis KOR-pus YOR-is SIV-i-lis
corregidores kor-REG-uh-DOR-ays
Cortés, Hernán kor-TEZ, er-NAHN
Corvinus, Matthias kor-VIE-nus, muh-THIGH-us
Courbet, Gustave koor-BAY, guh-STAWV
Crassus KRASS-us
Crécy kray-SEE
Crédit Mobilier kred-EE mohb-eel-YAY
Croesus KREE-sus
cum manu koom MAH-nu
Curie, Marie kyu-REE
Cypselus SIP-suh-luhs
d'Albret, Jeanne dahl-BRAy, ZHAHN
d'Este, Isabella ES-tay
d'Holbach, Paul awl-BAHK
Daimler, Gottlieb DYM-luhr, GOT-leeb
Danton, Georges dahn-TAWN, ZHORZH
Darius duh-RYE-us
dauphin DAW-fin
David, Jacques-Louis dah-VEED, ZHAHK-LWEE
de Gaulle, Charles duh GOLL, SHARL
De Rerum Novarum day RARE-um no-VAR-um

Debelleyme, Louis-Maurice de-bel-AME, LOO-ee-mo-REES
Debussy, Claude de-BYOO-see, KLODE
Decameron di-KAM-uh-run
decemviri de-kem-VI-ree
Deffand, marquise du di-FAHN, mar-KEEZ doo
Delacroix, Eugène del-uh-KWAW, yoo-ZHAHN
Démar, Claire DAY-mar
Demosthenes di-MOSS-thuh-neez
Denikin, Anton dyi-NYEE-kin, an-TAWN
Descartes, René day-KART, ruh-NAY
Diaghilev, Sergei dee-AHG-uh-lef, syir-GYAY
Dias, Bartholomeu DEE-us, bar-too-loo-MAY
Diaspora die-AS-pur-uh
Diderot, Denis DEE-duh-roh, duh-NEE
Diocletian die-uh-KLEE-shun
Disraeli, Benjamin diz-RAY-lee
Djoser ZHO-suh
Dollfuss, Engelbert DOLL-foos
Domesday Book DOOMZ-day
Domitian doh-MISH-un
Donatus/Donatist doh-NAY-tus/DOH-nuh-tist
Dopolavoro duh-puh-LAHR-vuh-roh
Dorians DOR-ee-uns
Dostoevsky, Fyodor DOS-tuh-YEF-skee, FYOD-ur
Douhet, Giulio doo-EE, JOOL-yoh
Dreyfus, Alfred DRY-fus
Dubček, Alexander DOOB-chek
Dufay, Guillaume doo-FAY, gwee-YOHM
Duma DOO-muh
Dürer, Albrecht DOO-er, AWL-brekt
Ebert, Friedrich AY-bert, FREE-drik
ecclesia eh-KLEE-zee-uh
Eckhart, Meister EK-hart, MY-ster
Einsatzgruppen INE-satz-grup-uhn
Einstein, Albert INE-stine
encomienda en-koh-mee-EN-dah
Engels, Friedrich ENG-ulz, FREE-drik
Enki EN-ki
Enlil EN-lil
Entente Cordiale ahn-TAHNT kor-DYALL
Epaminondas i-PAM-uh-NAHN-dus
ephor EF-or
Epicurus/Epicureanism EP-i-KYOOR-us/EP-i-kyoo-REE-uh-ni-zem
equestrians i-KWES-tree-uns
equites EK-wuh-tays
Erasistratus er-uh-SIS-truh-tus
Erasmus, Desiderius i-RAZZ-mus, des-i-DIR-ee-us
Eratosthenes er-uh-TOSS-thuh-neez
eremitical air-uh-MITT-i-cul
Erhard, Ludwig AIR-hart
Etruscans i-TRUSS-kuhns
Euclid YOO-klid
Euripides yoo-RIP-i-deez
exchequer EX-chek-ur
fasces FASS-eez
Fascio di Combattimento FASH-ee-oh di com-BATT-ee-men-toh
Fatimid FAT-i-mid
Fedele, Cassandra FAY-del-ee
Feltre, Vittorino da FELL-tree, vee-tor-EE-noh dah
Ficino, Marsilio fee-CHEE-noh, mar-SIL-ee-oh
Flaubert, Gustave floh-BEAR, guh-STAWV
Fleury, Cardinal floe-REE
Foch, Ferdinand FAWSH, FER-di-nawn
Fontainebleau FAWN-tin-BLOW
Fontenelle, Bernard de fawnt-NELL, BER-nar duh
Fouquet, Nicolas foo-KAY, nee-KOH-lah
Frequens FREE-kwens
Friedan, Betty fri-DAN
Friedrich, Caspar David FREE-drik, KAS-puh dah-VEED
Frimaire free-MARE
Fronde FROND
Führerprinzip FYOOR-ur-PRIN-tseep
gabelle gah-BELL
Gama, Vasco da GAM-uh, VASH-koh duh
Gamond, Zoé Gatti de gah-MAHN, zaw-ay GAHT-tee duh
Garibaldi, Giuseppe gar-uh-BAWL-dee, joo-ZEP-pay
Gasperi, Alcide de GAHS-pe-ree, awl-CHEE-day de
Gaugamela gaw-guh-MEE-luh
Gentileschi, Artemisia jen-tul-ESS-kee, are-tee-MISS-ee-uh
Geoffrin, Marie-Thérèse de JOF-ran, ma-REE-tuh-RAYZ duh
gerousia juh-ROO-see-uh
Gesamtkunstwerk guh-SAMT-kuns-vuhk
Gierek, Edward GYER-ek
Gilgamesh GILL-guh-mesh
Giolitti, Giovanni joh-LEET-tee, joe-VAHN-nee
Giotto JAW-toh
Girondins juh-RAHN-dins
glasnost GLAZ-nohst
Gleichschaltung GLIKE-shalt-ung
Goebbels, Joseph GUHR-bulz
Gömbös, Julius GERM-berz, JOO-li-uhs
Gomulka, Wladyslaw goh-MOOL-kuh, vla-DIS-lawf
gonfaloniere gon-fa-loh-NEE-ree
Gorbachev, Mikhail GOR-buh-chof, meek-HALE
Gottwald, Clement GORT-vald, CLE-ment
Gracchus, Tiberius and Gaius GRAK-us, tie-BIR-ee-us and GAY-us or GUY-us
grandi GRAHN-dee
Grieg, Edvard GREEG, ED-vart
Groote, Gerard GROH-tuh
Gropius, Walter GROH-pee-us, VAHL-ter
Grossdeutsch gross-DOICH
Groza, Petra GRO-zhuh, PET-ruh
Guicciardini, Francesco gwee-char-DEE-nee, frahn-CHASE-koh

Guindorf, Reine GWIN-dorf, RY-nuh
Guizot, François gee-ZOH, FRAN-swah
Gustavus Adolphus gus-STAY-vus a-DOLF-us
Guzman, Gaspar de goos-MAHN, gahs-PAR day
Habsburg HAPS-burg
Hadrian HAY-dree-un
Hagia Sophia HAG-ee-uh soh-FEE-uh
hajj HAJ
Hammurabi ham-uh-RAH-bee
Handel, George Friedrich HAN-dul
Hannibal HAN-uh-bul
Hanukkah HAH-nuh-kuh
Harappa huh-RAP-uh
Hardenberg, Karl von HAR-d'n-burg
Harun al-Rashid huh-ROON al-ra-SHEED
Hatshepsut hat-SHEP-soot
Haushofer, Karl HOUS-ho-fuh
Haussmann, Baron HOUS-mun
Havel, Vaclav HAH-vuhl, VAHT-slaf
Haydn, Franz Joseph HIDE-n, FRAHNTS
hegemon HEJ-uh-mon
Heisenberg, Werner HIGH-zun-burg, VUR-nur
Hellenistic hell-uh-NIS-tik
helots HELL-uts
Herodotus hi-ROD-oh-tus
Herophilus hi-ROF-uh-lus
Herzen, Alexander HER-tsun
Herzl, Theodor HERT-sul, TAY-oh-dor
Hesiod HEE-see-ud
Hesse, Hermann HES-uh
hetairai het-EYE-ree
Heydrich, Reinhard HIGH-drik, RINE-hart
hieroglyph HIGH-ur-oh-glif
Hildegard of Bingen HILL-duh-gard of BING-en
Hindenburg, Paul von HIN-duhn-berg, POWL vuhn
Hiroshima hi-ruh-SHEE-muh
Hitler Jugend JOO-gunt
Ho Chi Minh HOE CHEE MIN
Höch, Hannah HOKH
Hohenstaufen HOE-un-SHTAU-fun
Hohenzollern HOE-un-ZAHL-lurn
Honecker, Erich HOE-nuh-ker
hoplites HOP-lites
Horace HOR-us
Horthy, Miklós HOR-tee, MIK-lohsh
Höss, Rudolf HERS
Hoxha, Enver HAW-jah
Huguenots HYOO-guh-nots
Husák, Gustav HOO-sahk, guh-STAHV
Ibn Sina ib-en SEE-nuh
Ignatius of Loyola ig-NAY-shus of loi-OH-luh
Il Duce eel DOO-chay
imperator im-puh-RAH-tor
imperium im-PIER-ee-um
intendant in-TEN-duhnt
Isis EYE-sis
Issus ISS-us
ius gentium YOOS GEN-tee-um
Jacobin JAK-uh-bin
Jacquerie zhah-KREE
Jahn, Friedrich Ludwig YAHN, FREE-drik
Jaurés, Jean zhaw-RESS, ZHAHN
jihad ji-HAHD
Joffre, Joseph ZHOR-fruh
Judaea joo-DEE-uh
Judas Maccabaeus JOO-dus mak-uh-BEE-us
Jung, Carl YOONG
Junkers YOONG-kers
Jupiter Optimus Maximus JOO-pi-ter OPP-tuh-mus MAK-suh-mus
Justinian juh-STIN-ee-un
Juvenal JOO-vuh-nul
Kádár, János KAY-dahr, YAHN-us
Kadinsky, Wassily kan-DIN-skee, vus-YEEL-yee
Kangxi GANG-zhee
Kant, Immanuel KAHNT, i-MAN-yoo-el
Karlowitz KARL-oh-vitz
Kaunitz, Wenzel von KOU-nits, VENT-sul
Kenyatta, Jomo ken-YAHT-uh, JO-mo
Kerensky, Alexander kuh-REN-skee
Keynes, John Maynard KAYNZ
Khrushchev, Nikita KROOSH-chef, nuh-KEE-tuh
Khubilai Khan KOO-bluh KAHN
Kleindeutsch kline-DOICH
Kohl, Helmut KOLE, HELL-mut
koiné koi-NAY
Kolchak, Alexander KAWL-chok
Kollantai, Alexandra kawl-un-TIE
Kornikov, Lavr KAW-ni-kuhf, LAH-vuh
Kosciuszko, Thaddeus kos-ee-US-koh, tah-DE-us
Kossuth, Louis KOSS-ooth
kouros KOO-raws
Kraft durch Freude CRAFT durch FROI-duh
Kreditanstalt kre-deet-AHN-shtalt
Kristallnacht KRIS-tal-NAHCHT
Krupp, Alfred KROOP
Kuchuk-Kainarji koo-CHOOK-kigh-NAR-jee
kulaks koo-LAKS
kulturkampf kool-TOOR-kahmf
Kun, Béla KOON, BAY-luh
Kundera, Milan kun-DER-uh, MEE-lahn
Kwasniewski, Aleksander kwah-shnee-EF-skee, a-lek-ZAHN-duh
L'Ouverture, Toussaint loo-vuh-TYOR, TOO-sane
Lafayette, marquis de lah-fee-ETTE, mar-KEE duh
laissez-faire les-ay-FAIR

Lamarck, Jean-Baptiste luh-MAHRK, ZHAHN-buh-TEEST
Lancaster LAN-kas-ter
latifundia lat-uh-FUN-dee-uh
Latium LAY-shee-um
Laurier, Wilfred LAWR-ee-ay
Le Tellier, François Michel luh tel-YAY, FRAN-swah-mee-SHELL
Lebensraum LAY-benz-roum
Lespinasse, Julie de les-peen-AHS
Lévesque, René luh-VEK, ruh-NAY
Leyster, Judith LE-ster
Liebenfels, Lanz von LEE-bun-felz, LAHNZ
Liebknecht, Karl LEEP-knekt
Liebknecht, Wilhelm LEEP-knekt, VIL-helm
Lionne, Hugues de LYAWN, UGH
List, Friedrich LIST, FREE-drik
Liszt, Franz LIST, FRAHNZ
Livy LIV-ee
Lucretius loo-KREE-shus
Luddites LUD-ites
Ludendorff, Erich LOOD-un-dorf
Lueger, Karl LOO-ger
Luftwaffe LUFT-vaf-uh
Luxemburg, Rosa LUK-sum-burg
Machiavelli, Niccolò mak-ee-uh-VELL-ee, nee-koh-LOH
Maginot Line mah-zhee-NO
Magna Graecia MAG-nuh GREE-shuh
Magyars MAG-yars
Maistre, Joseph de MES-truh
Mallarmé, Stéphane mah-lahr-MAY, STE-fahn
Malleus Maleficarum mall-EE-us mal-uh-FIK-ar-um
Manetho MAN-uh-THOH
Mao Zedong mau zee-DONG
Marcus Aurelius MAR-kus au-REE-lee-us
Marcuse, Herbert mar-KOO-zuh
Marie Antoinette muh-REE an-twuh-NET
Marius MAR-ee-us
Marsiglio of Padua mar-SIL-ee-oh of PA-juh-wuh
Masaryk, Thomas MAS-uh-rik
Matteotti, Giacomo mat-ee-OH-tee, JAHK-oh-moh
Mazarin maz-uh-RAN
Mazzini, Giuseppe maht-SEE-nee, joo-ZEP-pay
Meiji MAY-jee
Mein Kampf mine KAHMF
Melanchthon, Philip muh-LANGK-thun
Menander me-NAN-der
Mendeleyev, Dmitri men-duh-LAY-ef, di-MEE-tri
Mercator, Gerardus muh-KAY-tuh, je-RAR-duhs
Merian, Maria Sibylla MARE-ee-un
Mesopotamia mess-oh-poh-TAME-ee-uh
Messiaen, Olivier me-SYAHN, 0-LEEV-yay
Metaxas, John me-TAK-sus
Metternich, Klemens von MET-er-nik, KLAY-mens
Michel, Louise mee-SHELL
Michelangelo my-kell-AN-juh-loh
Mieszko MYESH-koh
Millet, Jean-François mi-LAY, ZHAHN-FRAN-swah
Milošević, Slobodan mi-LOH-suh-vik, SLOW-buh-dan
Miltiades mil-TIE-uh-deez
Mirandola, Pico della muh-RAN-duh-luh, PEE-koh DELL-uh
missi dominici MISS-ee doe-MIN-ee-chee
Mitterrand, François MEE-tuh-rawn
Moctezuma mahk-tuh-ZOO-muh
Mohács MOH-hach
Mohenjo-Daro mo-HEN-jo-DAH-ro
Moldavia mahl-DAY-vee-uh
Molière, Jean-Baptiste mole-YAIR, ZHAHN-buh-TEEST
Monet, Claude moh-NAY, KLODE
Montaigne, Michel de mahn-TANE, mee-SHELL duh
Montefeltro, Federigo da mahn-tuh-FELL-troh, fay-day-REE-goh dah
Montesquieu MONT-ess-skyoo
Montessori, Maria mon-ti-SOR-ee
Morisot, Berthe mor-ee-ZOH, BERT
Mozart, Wolfgang Amadeus MO-tzart, VOLF-gang a-mah-DAY-us
Muawiya moo-AH-wee-yah
Mughal MOO-gool
Muhammad moe-HA-mud
Mühlberg mool-BERK
Müntzer, Thomas MOON-tsur
Muslim MUZ-lum
Mutsuhito moo-tsoo-HEE-toe
Mycenaean my-suh-NEE-un
Nabonidas na-bun-EYE-dus
Nagasaki na-ga-SAH-ki
Nagy, Imry NAHJD, IM-re
Navarre nuh-VARR
Nebuchadnezzar neb-uh-kad-NWZZ-ar
Nero NEE-roh
Nerva NUR-vuh
Neumann, Balthasar NOI-mahn, BAHL-tah-zar
Neumann, Solomon NOI-mahn
Nevsky, Alexander NEW-skee
Newcomen, Thomas new-KUH-mun
Ngo Dinh Diem NGOH din dee-EM
Nietzsche, Friedrich NEE-chuh, FREE-drik
Nimwegen NIM-vay-gun
Ninhursaga nin-HUR-sah-guh
Nkrumah, Kwame en-KROO-muh, KWA-may
nobiles no-BEE-lez
Nogarola, Isotta NOH-guh-roll-uh, eye-SOT-tuh
Novalis, Friedrich noh-VAH-lis, FREE-drik
Novotny, Antonin noh-VOT-nee, AN-ton-yeen
Nystadt nee-STAHD
Octavian ok-TAY-vee-un
Odoacer oh-doh-AY-ser

optimates opp-tuh-MAH-tays
Oresteia uh-res-TY-uh
Osiris oh-SIGH-ris
Ostpolitik ost-POL-i-tik
Ovid OV-id
Pachakuti PAR-char-koo-tee
Paleologus pay-lee-OHL-uh-gus
papal curia PAY-pul KOOR-ee-uh
Papen, Franz von PAH-pun, FRAHNTZ fahn
Paracelsus par-uh-SELL-sus
Parlement par-luh-MAHN
Pascal, Blaise pass-KAL, BLEZ
Pasteur, Louis pas-TUHR, LOO-ee
paterfamilias pay-ter-fuh-MILL-ee-us
Pentateuch PEN-tuh-tuke
Pepin PEP-in
perestroika pair-ess-TROY-kuh
Pergamum PURR-guh-mum
Pericles PER-i-kleez
perioeci per-ee-EE-sie
Pétain, Henri pay-TAN, AHN-ree
Petrarch PE-trark
Petronius pi-TROH-nee-us
phalansteries fa-LUHN-stuh-rees
philosophe fee-luh-ZAWF
Phoenicians fi-NISH-uns
Photius FOH-shus
Picasso, Pablo pi-KAW-soh
Pilsudski, Joseph peel-SOOT-skee
Piscator, Erwin pis-KAR-tor, ER-vin
Pisistratus pi-SIS-truh-tus
Pissarro, Camille pi-SARR-oh, kah-MEEYL
Pizan, Christine de PEE-zhan, kris-TEEN duh
Pizarro, Francesco pi-ZARR-oh, frahn-CHASE-koh
Planck, Max PLAHNK
Plantagenet plan-TA-juh-net
Plato PLAY-toe
Plautus PLAW-tus
plebiscita ple-bi-SEE-tuh
Poincaré, Raymond pwan-kah-RAY, re-MOAN
polis POE-lis
politiques puh-lee-TEEKS
Pollaiuolo, Antonio pohl-ly-WAHR-loh
Polybius poe-LIB-ee-us
Pombal, marquis de pom-BAHL, mar-KEE duh
Pompadour, madame de POM-puh-door, muh-DAM duh
Pompey POM-pee
populares POP-yoo-lar-ays
populo grasso POP-uh-loh GRAH-soh
Poussin, Nicholas poo-SAN, NEE-kaw-lah
Praecepter Germaniae PREE-sep-ter ger-MAN-ee-eye
praetor PREE-ter
princeps PRIN-seps
Procopius proh-KOH-pee-us
procurator PROK-yuh-ray-ter
Ptolemy/Ptolemaic TOL-uh-mee/TOL-uh-MAY-ik
Pugachev, Emelyan POO-guh-choff, yim-yil-YAHN
Punic PYOO-nik
Putin, Vladimir POO-tin
Pyrrhus/Pyrrhic PIR-us/PIR-ik
Qianlong CHAN-lung
quadrivium kwa-DRI-vi-um
quaestors KWES-ters
Quesnay, François kay-NAY, FRAHN-swuh
Quetzelcoatl ket-SAHL-koh-ATE-ul
Quran kuh-RAN
Racine, Jean-Baptiste ra-SEEN, ZHAHN-buh-TEEST
Rahner, Karl RAH-nuh
Ramesses RAM-i-seez
Raphael RAFF-ee-ul
Rasputin rass-PYOO-tin
Rathenau, Walter RAH-tuh-now, VAL-tuh
Realpolitik ray-AHL-poe-li-teek
Reichsrat RIKES-raht
Reichstag RYK-zhtahg
Rembrandt van Rijn REM-brant vahn RINE
Renan, Ernst re-NAHN
Ricci, Matteo REECH-ee, mah-TAY-oh
Richelieu RISH-uh-loo
Rilke, Rainer Maria RILL-kuh, RYE-ner
Rimbaud, Arthur ram-BO
risorgimento ree-SOR-jee-men-toe
Robespierre, Maximilien ROHBZ-pee-air, mak-SEE-meel-yahn
Rococo ro-KOH-koh
Röhm, Ernst RURM
Rousseau, Jean-Jacques roo-SOH ZHAHN-ZHAHK
Rurik ROOR-ik
Ryswick RIZ-wik
Sacrosancta sak-roh-SANK-tuh
Saint-Just san-ZHOOST
Saint-Simon, Henri de san-see-MOAN, AHN-ree duh
Sakharov, Andrei SAH-kuh-rof, ahn-DRAY
Saladin SAL-uh-din
Salazar, Antonio SAL-uh-zahr
Sallust SALL-ust
Samnites SAM-nites
San Martín, José de san mar-TEEN, hoe-SAY day
Sartre, Jean-Paul SAR-truh, ZHAHN-PAUL
satrap/satrapy SAY-trap/SAY-truh-pee
Satyricon SAY-tir-ee-kon
Schaumburg-Lippe SHAHM-berkh-LI-puh
Schleswig-Holstein SCHLES-vig-HOLE-stine
Schlieffen, Alfred von SHLEE-fun
Schliemann, Heinrich SCHLEE-mahn, HINE-rik
Schmidt, Helmut SHMIT, HELL-mut
Schönberg, Arnold SHURN-burg, ARR-nawlt

Schönerer, George von SHURN-er-er, ZHORSH
Schuschnigg, Kurt von SHOOSH-nik
Schutzmannschaft SHOOTS-mun-shaft
Scipio Aemilianus SI-pee-oh i-mill-ee-AY-nus
Scipio Africanus SI-pee-oh af-ri-KAY-nus
scriptoria skrip-TOR-ee-uh
Sejm SAME
Seleucus/Seleucid si-LOO-kus/si-LOO-sid
Seljuk Turks SELL-juke
Seneca SEN-i-kuh
Sephardic suh-FAR-dik
Septimius Severus sep-TIM-ee-us se-VIR-us
Sforza, Ludovico SFORT-zuh, loo-doe-VEE-koh
Shang SHAHNG
Sieveking, Amalie SEEVE-king
Sieyès, Abbé sye-YES, a-BAY
signoria seen YOOR-ee-uh
sine manu si-ne MAH-noo
Société Générale so-si-YAY-tay jeh-neh-RAHL
Socrates SOK-ruh-teez
Solon SOH-lun
Solzhenitsyn, Alexander SOLE-zhuh-NEET-sin
Sophocles SOF-uh-kleez
Sor Juana Inés de la Cruz saw WAH-na ee-NAHS duh lah KROOZ
Sorel, Georges sah-RELL, ZHORZH
Spartacus SPAR-tuh-kus
Spartiates spah-ti-AH-tees
Speer, Albert SHPIER
Speransky, Michael spyuh-RAHN-skee
Spinoza, Benedict de spi-NOH-zuh
squadristi sqah-DREES-tee
Staël, Germaine de STAWL, ZHER-men duh
Stakhanov, Alexei stuh-KAHN-uhv, a-LEX-ay
Stauffenberg, Claus von ZHTOW-fen-berg
Stein, Heinrich von STINE, HINE-rik
Stoicism STOH-i-siz-um
Stolypin, Peter stuh-LEE-pyin
Stravinsky, Igor struh-VIN-skee, EE-gor
Stresemann, Gustav SHTRAY-zuh-mahn, GUS-tahf
Struensee, John Frederick SHTROO-un-zay
Sturmabteilung shtorm-AP-ty-lung
Sudetenland soo-DAY-tun-land
Sulla SULL-uh
Sumerians soo-MER-ee-uns
Suppiluliumas suh-pil-oo-LEE-uh-mus
Suttner, Bertha von ZOOT-ner
Taafe, Edward von TAH-fuh
Tacitus TASS-i-tus
taille TAH-yuh or TIE
Talleyrand, Prince TAL-ee-ran
Tenochtitlán tay-NAWCH-teet-LAWN
Tertullian tur-TULL-yun
Theocritus thee-OCK-ri-tus
Theodora thee-uh-DOR-uh
Theognis thee-OGG-nus
Thermidor ter-mee-DOR
Thermopylae thur-MOP-uh-lee
Thiers, Adolphe tee-ER, a-DOLF
Thucydides thoo-SID-uh-deez
Thutmosis thoot-MOH-sus
Tiberius tie-BIR-ee-us
Tiglath-pileser TIG-lath-puh-LEE-zur
Tirpitz, Admiral von TUR-puts
Tito TEE-toh
Tlaxcala tlah-SKAHL-uh
Togugawa Ieyasu to-koo-GAH-wah ee-yeh-YAH-soo
Torah TOR-uh
Tordesillas tor-duh-SEE-yus
Trajan TRAY-jun
Trevithick, Richard TREV-uh-thik
Tristan, Flora TRIS-tun
trivium TRIV-i-um
Trudeau, Pierre troo-DOH, pee-AIR
Tsara, Tristan ZAR-rah
Tyche TIE-kee
Uccello, Paolo oo-CHEL-oh, POW-loh
Ulbricht, Walter UL-brikt, VAHL-ter
Umayyads oo-MY-ads
Unam Sanctam OON-ahm SANK-tahm
universitas yoo-ni-VER-si-tahs
Valéry, Paul vah-lar-REE, POWL
Valois VAL-wah
Van de Velde, Theodore vahn duh VEL-duh, THAY-oh-dor
van Eyck, Jan van IKE
van Gogh, Vincent van GOE
Vasa, Gustavus VAH-suh, gus-STAY-vus
Vega, Lope de VAY-guh, LOH-pay day
Vendée vahn-DAY
Venetia vuh-NEE-shee-uh
Vergerio, Pietro Paolo ver-JER-i-oh, pee-AY-tro POW-lo
Vesalius, Andreas vi-SAY-lee-us, ahn-DRAY-us
Vespasian ves-PAY-zhun
Vespucci, Amerigo ves-POO-chee, ahm-ay-REE-goe
Vichy VISH-ee
Vierzenheiligen feer-tsun-HILE-i-gun
Virchow, Rudolf FEER-koh, roo-DOLF
Virgil VUR-jul
Visconti, Giangaleazzo vis-KAHN-tee, jee-AHN-jah-li-AH-zoh
Voilquin, Suzanne VWA-kan
Volkschulen FOLK-shool-un
Voltaire vole-TAIR
von Bora, Katherina BOR-uh
Wafd WAHFT
Wagner, Richard VAHG-ner, RIK-art
Walesa, Lech va-WENZ-uh, LEK

Wallachia wah-lay-KEE-uh
Wallenstein, Albrecht von WOLL-un-stine, AWL-brekt
Wannsee VAHN-say
Watteau, Antoine wah-TOE, AHN-twahn
Weill, Kurt VYL
Weizsäcker, Richard von VITS-zek-er, RIK-art
wergeld wur-GELD
Windischgrätz, Alfred vin-dish-GRETS
Winkelmann, Maria VING-kul-mun
Witte, Sergei VIT-uh, syir-GYAY
Worms, Edict of WURMZ or VAWRMZ
Wyclif, John WIK-lif
Xavier, Francis ZAY-vee-ur
Xerxes ZURK-seez
Xhosa KOH-suh
Ximenes hee-MAY-nus
Yahweh YAH-wah
Yeats, William Butler YATES
Yeltsin, Boris YELT-sun
yishuv YISH-uv
Zemsky Sobor ZEM-skee SOH-bur
zemstvos ZEMPST-voh
Zeno ZEE-noh
Zeus ZOOS
Zhenotdel zhe-NOT-del
Zhivkov, Todor ZHEV-kof, toh-DOR
ziggurat ZIG-guh-rat
Zimmermann, Domenikus TSIM-ur-mahn, doe-MEE-nee-kus
Zinzendorf, Nikolaus von ZIN-zun-dorf, nee-koh-LAH-us
Zola, Emile ZOH-luh, ay-MEEL
zollverein TSOL-fuh-rine
Zoroaster ZOR-oh-as-ter

Photo Credits

CHAPTER 1

Erich Lessing/ Art Resource, NY; **4** © Francois Ducasse/Photo Researchers, Inc.; **5** Courtesy of the Hashemite Kingdom of Jordan, Dept. of Antiquities; **8** © The British Museum; **10** Réunion des Musées Nationaux/Art Resource, NY; **12** Robert Harding Picture Library; **14 top** from *Cultural Atlas of Mesopotamia & the Ancient Near East* by Michael Roaf/ Andromeda Oxford Limited, Oxford, England; **14 bottom** Réunion des Musées Nationaux/ Art Resource, NY; **18** Pair Statue of King Mycerinus and His Queen; From Giza, Dynasty IV, 2599-1571 B.C., Slate Schist, 54 1/2 in. Harvard MFA Expedition. Courtesy Museum of Fine Arts, Boston.; **20** © The British Museum; **21** © Will and Deni McIntyre/Photo Researchers, Inc.; **24** Scala/Art Resource, NY; **25** © Brian Blake/ Photo Researchers, Inc.; **26** Erich Lessing/Art Resource, NY; **27** © Adam Woolfit/Robert Harding Picture Library

CHAPTER 2

30 © The British Museum; **32** Ronald Sheridan/The Ancient Art & Architecture Collection; **33** © The British Museum; **35** Art Resource, NY; **37** © The British Museum; **40** Erich Lessing/ Art Resource, NY; **42** © The British Museum; **43** Bildarchiv Preussischer Kulturbesitz, Berlin; **45** © G. Dagli Orti ; **47** Réunion des Musées Nationaux/Art Resource, NY

CHAPTER 3

50 Scala/Art Resource, NY; **51** © Robert Harding Picture Library; **53** Erich Lessing/Art Resource, NY; **54** © Michael Holford, London; **56** Scala/Art Resource, NY; **61** The Metropolitan Museum of Art, New York, Fletcher Fund, 1932 (32.11.1) Photograph © 1997 The Metropolitan Museum of Art; **64 left** © G. Dagli Orti; **64 right** Courtesy of William M. Murray; **66** © The British Museum; **71** © The British Museum; **73** Art Resource, NY; **74** left © Michael Holford, London; **74** right Scala/Art Resource, NY; **77** © Archaeological Receipts Fund, Athens, Greece; **78** Metropolitan Museum of Art, New York, Fletcher Fund, 1931 (31.11.10) Photograph © 1999 The Metropolitan Museum of Art

CHAPTER 4

82 Scala/Art Resource, NY; **83** Thessalonike Museum, © Archaeological Receipts Fund, Athens, Greece ; **84** Réunion des Musées Nationaux/Art Resource, NY; **85** Scala/Art Resource, NY; **88** Giraudon/Art Resource, NY; **90** Scala/Art Resource, NY; **92** Metropolitan Museum of Art, New York, Rogers Fund, 1920, (20.2.21) Photograph © 1986 The Metropolitan Museum of Art; **97 left** Scala/Art Resource, NY; **97 right** Metropolitan Museum of Art, New York, Rogers Fund, 1909, (09.39) Photograph © 1997 The Metropolitan Museum of Art; **98** Metropolitan Museum of Art, New York, Rogers Fund, 1911, (11.90) All rights reserved, The Metropolitan Museum of Art; **100** © Leonard von Matt/Photo Researchers, Inc.

CHAPTER 5

103 © Leonard von Matt/Photo Researchers, Inc.; **105** Photo: AKG, London; **106** Alinari/Art Resource, NY; **111 top** SEF/Art Resource, NY; **111 bottom** The Art Archive, London/Museo di Villa Giulia/ G. Dagli Orti (A) ; **115** Scala/Art Resource, NY; **117 top** © Leslye and Roy Adkins Picture Library; **117 bottom** Erich Lessing/Art Resource, NY; **118** Metropolitan Museum of Art, New York, Rogers Fund, 1903 (3.14.5) Photograph © 1986 The Metropolitan Museum of Art; **120** © Leonard von Matt/Photo Researchers, Inc.; **124 left** The Ny Carlsberg Glyptotek, Copenhagen; **124 right** Scala/Art Resource, NY; **127** Scala/Art Resource, NY

CHAPTER 6

133 Réunion des Musées Nationaux/Art Resource, NY; **134** Photo, Vatican Museums; **136** Réunion des Musées Nationaux/Art Resource, NY; **142** © Vanni Archive/CORBIS; **143** Photo © Eberhard Theim, Lotos-Film, Kaufbeuren, Germany; **146 top** SEF/Art Resource, NY; **146 bottom left** © Michael S. Yamashita/CORBIS; **146 bottom right** © Fred Mayer/Magnum Photos; **148** © Thomas S. England/Photo Researchers, Inc.; **149** Scala/Art Resource, NY; **153** Scala/Art Resource, NY; **157** Scala/Art Resource, NY

CHAPTER 7

162 Sonia Halliday Photographs; **165** Kunsthistorisches Museum, Vienna; **167** Bibliotheque Nationale, Paris, France; **171** Sonia Halliday Photographs; **172** Vat. lat 1202F.80r, Foto Biblioteca Apostolica Vaticana; **174** The Board of Trinity College Dublin; **180** Scala/Art Resource, NY; **182** Erich Lessing/Art Resource, NY; **184** Byzantine Museum, Athens © Archaeological Receipts Fund, Athens, Greece; **185** Edinburgh University Library (Or. Ms.161, f. 10v); **186** Bibliotheque Nationale, Paris, France

CHAPTER 8

190 Bibliotheque Nationale, Paris, France/Bridgeman Art Library; **193** Réunion des Musées Nationaux/Art Resource, NY; **195 top** The Granger Collection; **195 bottom** Bibliotheque Mazarine, Paris, France/Archives Charmet/Bridgeman Art Library; **198** MS Hunter 252, f.70, Courtesy of the Librarian, Glasgow University Library; **201 left** Bibliotheque Nationale, Paris, France/Bridgeman Art Library; **201 right** Bibliotheque Nationale, Paris, France; **202 left** The Pierpont Library/Art Resource, NY; **202 right** © University Museum of Cultural Heritage–University of Oslo, Norway, Photograph by Eirik Irgens Johnsen; **204** Leiden, University Library, BPL 20, f.60r; **207** Art Archive, London, from the British Library, Psalter, Calendar, c1250 1260; **210** Byzantine Visual Resources, Dumbarton Oaks, Washington, D.C., © 1996; **214** Scala/Art Resource, NY

CHAPTER 9

217 Staatliche Museen, Berlin, Photo © Bildarchiv Preussischer Kulturbesitz, Berlin; **219** Victoria & Albert Museum, London, UK/Bridgeman Art Library; **220** Giraudon/Art Resource, NY; **222** Giraudon/Art Resource, NY; **224 top** Visual Arts Library/Art Resource, NY; **224 bottom** Bibliotheque Nationale, Paris, France; **227** © Wysocki/Explorer/Photo Researchers, Inc.; **228** British Library, London, Harley 4379, f. 64; **230** Bibliotheque Nationale, Paris, France; **233** Staatliche Museen, Berlin, Photo © Bildarchiv Preussischer Kulturbesitz, Berlin; **238** G. Dagli Orti; **239 left** © Russell Thompson/OmniPhoto Communications; **239 right** G. Dagli Orti; **240** Sonia Halliday Photographs

CHAPTER 10

243 The Granger Collection; **244** Michael Holford; **248** The Granger Collection; **252** Giraudon/Art Resource, NY; **258** Scala/Art Resource, NY; **259 left** Giraudon/Art Resource, NY; **259 right** © Bibliotheque royale Albert ler (Ms IV 119, fol.72 verso); **261** Bibliotheque Nationale, Paris, France; **263** British Library, London, UK/Bridgeman Art Library; **268** Bibliotheque Nationale, Paris, France; **269** Bibliotheque Nationale, Paris, France

CHAPTER 11

273 Bibliotheque Nationale, Paris, France; **276** © Bibliotheque royale Albert ler, Bruxelles (Ms. 13076-77, f. 12v); **278** Metropolitan Museum of Art , New York, The Cloisters Collection, 1954 (54.1.1) Photograph © 1987 The Metropolitan Museum of Art; **279** Bibliotheque Nationale, Paris, France; **282** Bibliotheque Nationale, Paris, France/Bridgeman Art Library; **284** Giraudon/Art Resource, NY; **288** British Library, London; **290** British Library, London, Ms. Add.23923,f.2; **295** British Library, London, folio 290, Harley ms. 4431; **296** Scala/Art Resource, NY; **298** Meister des Marienlebens, "Geburt Mariae," Alte Pinakothek, Munich, Photo © Artothek; **299** British Library, London, Ms. Sloane 1977, f.7

CHAPTER 12

302 Staatliche Landesbildstelle Hamburg; **305** Staatliche Landesbildstelle Hamburg; **308** Private Collection/Bridgeman Art Library; **311 left** Scala/Art Resource, NY; **311 right** Scala/Art Resource, NY; **313** © ARCHIV/Photo Researchers, Inc.; **320** Scala/Art Resource, NY; **321 top** Erich Lessing/Art Resource, NY; **321 bottom** Scala/Art Resource, NY; **322 top** Scala/Art Resource, NY; **322 bottom** Scala/Art Resource, NY; **323** Erich Lessing/Art Resource, NY; **324 top** Photo, Vatican Museums; **324 bottom** Scala/Art Resource, NY; **325** Art Resource, NY; **326** Jan van Eyck, *Giovanni Arnolfini and His Bride*, reproduced by Courtesy of the Trustees, The National Gallery, London; **327** Alinari/Art Resource, NY ; **333** Scala/Art Resource, NY;

CHAPTER 13

336 The Royal Collection © Her Majesty Queen Elizabeth II; **338** Oeffentliche Kunstsammlung Basel, Kunstmuseum: Colorphoto Hans Hinz; **340** Scala/Art Resource, NY ; **342** Staatliche Museen Preussischer Kulturbesitz, Kupferstich-kabinett, Berlin, Photo: Jorg P. Anders; **345** Alte Pinakothek, Munich; **348** National Gallery of Scotland, Edinburgh, Scotland/ Bridgeman Art Library; **351** The Royal Collection © Her Majesty Queen Elizabeth II; **352** © Bibliotheque Publique et Universitaire, Geneva; **355** Oeffentliche Kunstsammlung Basel, Kunstmuseum: Colorphoto Hans Hinz; **357** Scala/Art Resource, NY; **360** François Dubois, La Saint Barthelémy, 1572/84, Huile sur bois, 94 x 154 cm, Musée cantonal des Beaux-Arts de Lausanne, Photo: J.-C. Ducret, Musée cantonal des Beaux-Arts de Lausanne; **361** Scala/Art Resource, NY; **364** Courtesy of J. K. Wingfield Digby, Sherborne Castle

CHAPTER 14

368 © Michael Holford, London; **370** The Huntington Library, San Marino CA Claudius Ptolemy, Cosmographia, Ulm, 1482; **371** Hulton Archive/Getty Images; **374** The Metropolitan Museum of Art, Gift of J. Pierpont Morgan, 1900 (00.18.2) Photograph © 1979 The Metropolitan Museum of Art; **377** William Clements Library, University of Michigan, USA/ Bridgeman Art Library; **382** Bibliotheque des Arts Decoratifs, Paris, France/Archives Charmet/Bridgeman Art Library; **384** The Art Archive/London; **388** © Michael Holford, London; **389** The Art Archive/London; **392** Herzog Anton Ulrich Museum, Braunschweig; **397** The Huntington Library, San Marino, CA

CHAPTER 15

400 © Archivo Iconografico SA/CORBIS; **406** Giraudon/Art Resource, NY; **408** Reproduced by Courtesy of the Trustees, The National Gallery, London; **411** Réunion des Musées Nationaux/Art Resource, NY; **412** © Archivo Iconografico SA/CORBIS; **413** Giraudon/Art Resource, NY; **419** Russian School, *Czar Peter the Great,* Rijksmuseum, Amsterdam; **425** Giraudon/Art Resource, NY; **427** Robert Walker, Oliver Cromwell, 1649, By Courtesy of the National Portrait Gallery; **431** *Laocoön,* El Greco, National Gallery of Art, Washington: Samuel H. Kress Collection; **432 left** Scala/Art Resource, NY; **432 right** Giraudon/Art Resource, NY; **433** Réunion des Musées Nationaux/Art Resource, NY; **434** Rembrandt Van Rijn, *Syndics of the Cloth Guild,* Rijksmuseum, Amsterdam

CHAPTER 16

438 Réunion des Musées Nationaux/Art Resource, NY; **442** Courtesy of the Lilly Library, Indiana University, Bloomington, Indiana; **443 top** Courtesy of the Lilly Library, Indiana University, Bloomington, Indiana; **443 bottom** Deutsches Museum, Munich; **447** Erich Lessing/Art Resource, NY; **449** National Portrait Gallery, London; **451** © CORBIS; **454** Réunion des Musées Nationaux/Art Resource, NY; **457** Réunion des Musées Nationaux/Art Resource, NY; **459 top** Giraudon/Art Resource, NY; **459 bottom** Reproduced by Courtesy of the Science Museum, (neg. 4534)

CHAPTER 17

463 Réunion des Musées Nationaux/Art Resource, NY; **465** By permission of the Houghton Library, Harvard University; **470 top** Mary Evans Picture Library; **470 bottom** Réunion des Musées Nationaux/Art Resource, NY; **473** Allan Ramsay, *Jean-Jacques Rousseau,* National Gallery of Scotland; **475** Giraudon/Art Resource, NY; **476** Réunion des Musées Nationaux/Art Resource, NY; **477 top** Courtesy of James R. Spencer; **477 bottom** Scala/Art Resource, NY; **478** Réunion des Musées Nationaux/Art Resource, NY; **479** Musee Conde, Chantilly, Photo Giraudon/Art Resource, NY;

481 Photo © Michael Holford; **487** Nathaniel Hone, John Wesley, ca.1766, By courtesy of the National Portrait Gallery, London

CHAPTER 18

491 By courtesy of the National Portrait Gallery, London; **495** National Portrait Gallery; **497** Giraudon/Art Resource, NY; **499** Kunsthistorisches Museum, Vienna; **500** Scala/Art Resource, NY; **505** By courtesy of the National Portrait Gallery, London; **508** Arthur Devis, *The John Bacon Family,* c. 1742 3, Yale Center for British Art, Paul Mellon Collection; **509** Germanisches Nationalmuseum; **513** Hulton Archive/Getty Images; **516 left** Collection of the Earl of Pembroke, WIlton House, Wilts., UK/Bridgeman Art Library; **516 right** Erich Lessing/Art Resource, NY; **519** Giovanni Michele Graneri, *Market in Piazza San Carlo,* 1752, Museo Civico di Torino

CHAPTER 19

522 Giraudon/Art Resource, NY; **527** © Bettmann/CORBIS; **529** Giraudon/Art Resource, NY; **530** Réunion des Musées Nationaux/Art Resource, NY; **534** Réunion des Musées Nationaux/Art Resource, NY; **536** The Art Archive; **537** Giraudon/Art Resource, NY; **541** Giraudon/Art Resource, NY; **542** Giraudon/Art Resource, NY; **544** Réunion des Musées Nationaux/Art Resource, NY; **545** Réunion des Musées Nationaux/Art Resource, NY

CHAPTER 20

552 © CORBIS; **556** Reproduced by Permission of the Trustees of the Science Museum (neg. 607.56); **557 top** Mansell/TimePix; **557 bottom** Thomas V. Robins, *Opening of the Royal Albert Bridge, Saltash, 2 May 1859,* Elton Collection/Ironbridge Gorge; **558** © CORBIS; **560** Guildhall Library, Corporation of London, UK/Bridgeman Art Library; **564** North Wind Picture Archives; **567** © Ann Ronan/Image Select; **568** Gustave Dore, *Over London by Rail,* from London, A Pilgramage, Billy Rose Theatre Collection, The New York Public Library, Astor Lenox and Tilden Foundations; **572** © CORBIS; **575** Trades Union Congress, London, UK/Bridgeman Art Library

CHAPTER 21

579 Giraudon/Art Resource, NY; **580** Austrian Information Service; **583** © G. Dagli Orti; **588** © British Museum; **592** The Art Archive, London; **593** Giraudon/Art Resource, NY; **598** Historisches Museum der Stadt Wien; **601** Mansell/TimePix; **604** © Ed Pritchard/Stone/Getty Images; **606 top** Caspar David Friedrich, *Man and Woman Gazing at the Moon,* Nationalgalerie SMPK Berlin, Photo Jorg P. Anders, © Bildarchiv Preussischer Kulturbesitz, Berlin; **606 bottom** J.M.W. Turner, *Rain, Steam, Speed—The Great Western Railway,* Reproduced by Courtesy of the Trustees, The National Gallery, London; **607** Erich Lessing/Art Resource, NY

CHAPTER 22

611 Proclamation of the German Empire at Versailles, 1871, Anton von Werner, Photo © Bildarchiv Preussischer Kulturbesitz, Berlin; **612** Réunion des Musées Nationaux/Art Resource, NY; **615** Wellcome Institute Library, London; **617** Stock Montage; **621** Proclamation of the German Empire at Versailles, 1871, Anton von Werner, Photo © Bildarchiv Preussischer Kulturbesitz, Berlin; **626** Novosti Agency; **627** Hulton Archive/Getty Images ; **630** Opening of the Suez Canal, Photo © Bildarchiv Preussischer Kulturbesitz, Berlin; **631** The Granger Collection, New York; **635** Thomas Eakins, *The Gross Clinic,* Jefferson Medical College of Thomas Jefferson University, Philadelphia, PA; **638 top** Gustave Courbet, *The Stonebreakers,* Gemaldegalerie Neue Meister, Staatliche Kunstsammlungen Dresden, Photo by Reinhold, Leipzig-Molkau; **638 bottom** Erich Lessing/Art Resource, NY

CHAPTER 23

642 Verein fur Geschichte der Arbeiterbewegung, Vienna; **644** The Fotomas Index; **648** Private Collection/Archives Charmet/ Bridgeman Art Library; **649** Verein fur Geschichte der Arbeiterbewegung, Vienna; **652** Bradford Art Galleries & Museums, West Yorkshire, UK/Bridgeman Art Library; **656** Hulton Archive/Getty Images; **660** Harrogate Museums and Art Gallery, North Yorkshire, UK/Bridgeman Art Library; **662** Courtesy, Vassar College Library; **664** Hulton Archive/Getty Images; **665** Mansell/TimePix; **668** © CORBIS

CHAPTER 24

672 Metropolitan Museum of Art, New York, Gift of Lincoln Kirstein, 1959 (JP 3276), Photograph by Otto E. Nelson Photograph © 1986 The Metropolitan Museum of Art; **674** AP/Wide World Photos; **676** Bild-Archiv der Osterreichischen Nationalbibliothek, Vienna; **679 top** Scala/Art Resource, NY; **679 bottom** Erich Lessing/Art Resource, NY; **680** Réunion des Musées Nationaux/Art Resource, NY; **681** Vincent van Gogh, *The Starry Night,* (1889) Oil on canvas 29 x 36 1/4″, Collection, The Museum of Modern Art, New York, Acquired through the Lillie P. Bliss Bequest; **682 top** Pablo Picasso, *Les Demoiselles d'Avignon,* Paris (Begun May reworked July 1907), Oil on canvas, 8′ x 7′ 8″, Collection, The Museum of Modern Art, New York, Acquired through the Lillie P. Bliss Bequest, © 2000 Estate of Pablo Picasso/Artist Right's Society (ARS), New York; **682 bottom** Vasily Kandinsky, *Painting with White Border,* May 1913, The Solomon R. Guggenheim Museum, New York, © Artists Rights Society, ARS, NY/ADAGP, Paris; **684** © Popperfoto; **690** David King Collection, London; **691** North Wind Picture Archives; **699** Metropolitan Museum of Art, New York, Gift of Lincoln Kirstein, 1959 (JP 3276), Photograph by Otto E. Nelson Photograph © 1986 The Metropolitan Museum of Art; **703** The Art Archive, London

CHAPTER 25

707 Libraire Larousse, Paris; **710** © CORBIS; **712** Libraire Larousse, Paris ; **714 top** © Roger-Viollet/Getty Images; **714 bottom** Libraire Larousse, Paris; **716** Hulton Archive/Getty Images; **717** Bilderdienst Suddeutscher Verlag, Munich; **720** © CORBIS; **722** The Art Archive, London; **723** © Ullstein Bilderdienst; **727** Sovfoto; **729 left** Brown Brothers; **729 right** © Underwood & Underwood/CORBIS; **735** Hulton Archive/Getty Images

CHAPTER 26

739 Paulman, 10 November, 1938, Photo © Bildarchiv Preussischer Kulturbesitz, Berlin; **741** Hulton Archive/Getty Images; **742** © Roger-Viollet/Getty Images; **749** AP/Wide World

Photos; **753** Hugo Jaeger/TimePix; **755** Hugo Jaeger/TimePix; **757** Paulman, 10 November, 1938, Photo © Bildarchiv Preussischer Kulturbesitz, Berlin; **760** David King Collection, London; **763** Hulton Archive/Getty Images; **765** Erich Lessing/ Art Resource, NY Hoech, Hannah. *The Kitchen knife cuts through Germany's first Weimar beer-belly culture.* Photomontage. 1919. © 2000 Copyright Artist's Rights Society, (ARS), NY, VG Bild-Kunst, Bonn; **766** Salvador Dali, *The Persistence of Memory,* 1931, Oil on canvas, 9 1/2 x 13″, Collection the Museum of Modern Art, New York, Given Anonymously, © 2000 Artist Right's Society, (ARS), New York; **767** Gian Berto Vanni/Art Resource, NY

CHAPTER 27

775 Bildarchiv Preussischer Kulturbesitz, Berlin; **775** Bildarchiv Preussischer Kulturbesitz, Berlin; **776** National Archives, (#306-NT-1222E); **779** AKG London; **782** © Topham/ The Image Works; **784** National Archives, (#111-C-273); **788** Library of Congress (2391, folder 401); **790** Courtesy of the U.S. Holocaust Museum, Washington DC; **792** Imperial War Museum, London; **795** The Herald and Evening Times Picture Library, © Caledonian Newspapers, LTD.; **796** J.R. Eyerman, Life Magazine, © TimePix; **798** The Art Archive, London

CHAPTER 28

803 © Bettmann/CORBIS; **806** © Bettmann/CORBIS; **810** © CORBIS; **816** David King Collection, London; **818** Camera Press, (Jugo) London; **819** © Prache-Lewin/CORBIS Sygma; **821** © Pierre Boulat-Cosmos/Woodfin Camp & Associates; **825** © Bob Adelman/Magnum Photos; **826** Hulton Archive/Getty Images; **828** AP/Wide World Photos; **830** © Popperfoto/Hulton Archive/Getty Images; **833** © C. Raimond-Dityvon/Woodfin Camp & Associates

CHAPTER 29

835 © Alexandra Avakian/Woodfin Camp & Associates; **837** AP/Wide World Photos; **841** AP/Wide World Photos; **843** © Georges Merillon/Getty Images; **845** © Alexandra Avakian/Woodfin Camp & Associates; **847** AP/Wide World Photos; **849** Mark Stewart/Camera Press, London; **854** AP/Wide World Photos; **855 left** © Jeremy Walker/Stone/Getty Images; **855 middle and right** AP/Wide World Photos; **858** © Hans Namuth/Photo Researchers, Inc.; **859** The Museum of Contemporary Art, Los Angeles. Purchased with funds provided by Douglas S. Cramer, Beatrice and Philip Gersh, Lenore S. and Bernard A. Greenberg, Joan and Fred Nicholas, Robert A. Rowan, Pippa Scott and an anonymous donor; **863** Courtesy of NASA; **865** AP/Wide World Photos; **867** Courtesy of NASA

Documents

Continued from page xx

William Shakespeare: In Praise of England 435
Excerpt from *Richard II* in *Shakespeare, The Complete Works* by G. B. Harrison, copyright ©1968 by Harcourt Brace & Company.

CHAPTER 16

Magic & Science: The Case of Girolamo Cardano 440
From *The Book of My Life* by Jerome Cardan, translated by Jean Stoner, copyright 1930 by E. P. Dutton. Used by permission of Dutton, a division of Penguin Putnam, Inc.

On the Revolutions of the Heavenly Spheres 444
From *On the Revolutions* by Nicolaus Copernicus, pp. 4–5, 20. Copyright ©1978 by The Johns Hopkins University Press. Reprinted with permission of the publisher.

Kepler and the Emerging Scietific Community 445
From *Johannes Kepler, Life and Letters* by Carola Baumgardt, copyright 1951 by the Philosophical Library. Used by permission.

The Starry Messenger 446
From *Discoveries and Opinions of Galileo* by Galileo Galilei, translated by Stillman Drake, copyright ©1957 by Stillman Drake. Used by permission of Doubleday, a division of Random House, Inc.

Newton's Rules of Reasoning 448
From Isaac Newton, *The Mathematical Principles of Natural Philosophy,* 2 volumes (London, 1803), vol. 2: pp. 160–162

The "Natural" Inferiority of Women 453
From *A Political Treaties,* Benedict de Spinoza, copyright 1895 by George Routledge & Sons.

Father of Modern Rationalism 455
From *Descartes, Philosophical Writings,* translated by Norman Kemp Smith, copyright ©1958 by Macmillan Education. Reprinted with permission of the publisher, Macmillan, London, & Basingstoke.

Pascal: "What Is a Man in the Infinite?" 458
From *The Pensees* by Pascal, translated by J. M. Cohen ©1961 by J. M. Cohen. Reprinted with permission of the Estate of J. M. Cohen.

CHAPTER 17

The Separation of Powers 468
From *Les Philosophes* by Norman L. Torrey, copyright ©1961 by Norman L. Torrey. Used by permission of G. P. Putnam's Sons, a division of Penguin Putnam, Inc.

The Attack on Religious Intolerance 469
The Ignorant Philosopher
Reprinted with permission of Macmillan Publishing Company. *From Absolutism to Revolution 1648–1848* by Herbert H. Rowen. Copyright ©1963 by Macmillan Publishing Company.
Candide
From *Candide* by Voltaire, translated by John Butt (Penguin Classics, 1947) copyright ©John Butt, 1947, pp. 26–27. Reproduced by permission of Penguin Books, Ltd.

Diderot Questions Christian Sexual Standards 471
From *Rameau's Nephew and Other Works* by Denis Diderot. Copyright ©1956 by Jacques Barzun and Ralph Bowen. Used by permission of Jacques Barzun.

A Social Contract 473
From *The Social Contact,* Jean Jacques Rousseau, translated by Maurice Cranston. Copyright ©1968 by Penguin Books. Reprinted by permission of the Peters Fraser & Dunlop Group Ltd.

The Rights of Women 475
From *First Feminists: British Women Writers, 1578–1799* by Moira Ferguson. Copyright ©1985. Reprinted with permission of Indiana University Press.

Gibbon and the Idea of Progress 480
From Edward Gibbons, *The History of the Decline and Fall of the Roman Empire, Vol. 4,* J. B. Bury, ed., 1901. Used with permission of the publishers, Methuen & Co.

The Punishment of Crime 483
From *European Society in the Eighteenth Century* by Robert Forster and Elborg Forster. Copyright ©1969 by Robert and Elborg Forster. Reprinted by permission of HarperCollins Publishers, Inc.

The Conversion Experience in Wesley's Methodism 488
From *European Society in the Eighteenth Century* by Robert Forster and Elborg Forster. Copyright ©1969 by Robert and Elborg Forster. Reprinted by permission of HarperCollins Publishers, Inc.

CHAPTER 18

The French King's Bedtime 494
From *European Society in the Eighteenth Century* by Robert Forster and Elborg Forster. Copyright ©1969 by Robert and Elborg Forster. Reprinted by permission of HarperCollins Publishers, Inc.

Frederick the Great and His Father 498
From *Readings in European History,* James Harvey Robinson (Lexington, Mass: Ginn and Co., 1934).

The Proposals of Catherine II for a New Law Code 500
From *Documents of Catherine the Great,* W. F. Reddaway. Copyright ©1931 by Cambridge University Press. Reprinted with permission of Cambridge University Press.

British Victory in India 506
From James Harvey Robinson, *Readings in European History,* 1934.

Marital Arrangements 510
From *The Rivals* by Richard Sheridan (London,1775).

Propaganda for the New Agriculture 511
Arthur Young, *Travels during the Years, 1787, 1788, and 1789 . . . in the Kingdom of France* (London: W. Richardson, 1794).

The Beginnings of Mechanized Industry: The Attack on New Machines 514
Excerpt from *Society and Politics in England 1780–1960* by J. F. C. Harrison. Copyright by J. F. C. Harrison. Reprinted by permission of Harper & Row, Publishers, Inc.

Poverty in France 518
From *European Society in the Eighteenth Century* by Robert Forster and Elborg Forster. Copyright ©1969 by Robert and Elborg Forster. Reprinted by permission of HarperCollins Publishers, Inc.

President Abraham Lincoln, Emancipation Proclamation, January 1, 1863
From *U. S. Statutes at Large* (Washinton, D.C., Government Printing Office, 1875), vol. 12, pp. 1268–1269.

The Classless Society 632
From *The Communist Manifesto* by Karl Marx and Frederick Engels.

Darwin and the Descent of Man 634
From *The Descent of Man* by Charles Darwin (New York: Appleton, 1876), pp. 606–607, 619.

Anesthesia and Modern Surgery 636
From *Source Books of Medical History,* Logan Clendening, ed. Copyright ©1960 by Dover Publications. Reprinted by permission of the publisher.

Realism: Charles Dickens and an Image of Hell on Earth 639
Mary Ann Frese Witt, Charlotte Vestal Brown, Roberta Ann Dunbar, Frank Tirro, and Ronald G. Witt, *The Humanities* (Lexington, Mass.: D. C. Heath & Co., 1980), vol. 2, pp. 200–201.

CHAPTER 23

The Department Store and the Beginnings of Mass Consumerism 645
From *Documents of European Economic History, Vol. I* by Sidney Pollard & Colin Holmes. Copyright ©Sidney Pollard and Colin Holmes. Reprinted with permission of Palgrave and Edward Arnold.

The Voice of Evolutionary Socialism: Eduard Bernstein 650
Eduard Bernstein, *Evolutionary Socialism,* Edith C. Harney, trans. (New York: B. W. Huebsch, 1911), pp. x–xii, xiv.

The Housing Venture of Octavia Hill 655
Extract taken from *Human Documents of the Victorian Age* by E. Royston Pike, copyright ©1967 by Frederick A. Praeger.

Advice to Women: Be Dependent 659
Elizabeth Poole Sanford, *Women in Her Social and Domestic Character* (Boston: Otis Boraders & Co., 1842), pp. 5–7, 15–16.

The Fight Song: Sports in the English Public School 663
From *Athleticism and the Victorian in Edwardian Public School* by J. A. Mangan. Copyright ©1981 by Cambridge University Press. Reprinted with permission of Cambridge University Press.

A Leader of the Paris Commune 666
From *The Red Virgin: Memoirs of Louise Michel* edited by Bullitt Lowry and Elizabeth Ellington Gunter (University, Alabama: University of Alabama Press, 19810, pp. 64, 66.

Bismarck and the Welfare of the Workers 669
From *Bismarck,* by Frederick B. M. Hollyday (Englewood Cliffs, NJ: Prentice-Hall, Inc. 1970), pp. 60, 63, 65.

CHAPTER 24

Freud and the Concept of Repression 675
From *The Standard Edition of the Complete Psychological Works of Sigmund Freud,* edited and translated by James Strachey, London, 1957, ©1961 by James Strachey. Vol. XI, pp. 23–24. Used by permission of W. W. Norton & Company, Inc. Canadian rights arranged with Mark Paterson & Associates.

Symbolist Poetry: Art for Art's Sake 683
"The Drunken Boat" by Arthur Rimbaud from *Realism, Naturalism, Symbolism: Mode of Thought and Expression in Europe* by Roland Stromberg. English Translation Copyright ©1968 by Roland Stromberg. Reprinted by permission of HarperCollins Publishers, Inc.

Advice to Women: Be Independent 685
From *Roots of Western Civilization* by Wesley D. Camp. Copyright ©1983 by John Wiley & Sons.

The Voice fo Zionism: Theodor Herzl and the Jewish State 687
From Theodor Herzl, *The Jewish State, 3rd ed.,* Sylvie d'Anigdor, trans., copyright 1936. Reprinted by permission of the Central Zionist Organization.

Bloody Sunday 689
From *Eyewitness to History,* ed. John Carey (originally published under The Faber Book of Reportage), ©1987.

The White Man's Burden 694
From *Verse* by Rudyard Kipling. Copyright 1920 by Doubleday, a division of Bantam, Doubleday, Dell Publishing Group, Inc.

The Black Man's Burden 695
From Louis L. Snyder (ed.), *The Imperial Reader* (Princeton: Van Nostrand, 1962). By permission of Louis L. Snyder.

The Emperor's Big Mouth 701
From *The Daily Telegraph,* London, October 28, 1908.

CHAPTER 25

"You Have to Bear the Responsibility for War or Peace" 711
From *The Western World: From 1700, Vol. II,* by W. E. Adams, R. B. Barlow, G. R. Kleinfeld, and R. D. Smith (Dodd, Mead, and Co., 1968), pp. 421–422.

The Excitement of War 713
From *The World of Yesterday* by Stefan Zweig, translated by Helmut Ripperger. Translation copyright 1943 by the Viking Press, renewed.

The Reality of War: Trench Warfare 718
All Quiet on the Western Front by Erich Maria Remarque. "Im Westen Nichts Neues," copyright 1928 by Ullstein A. G.; copyright renewed ©1956 by Erich Maria Remarque. "All Quiet on the Western Front," copyright 1929, 1930 by Little, Brown and Company; Copyright renewed ©1957, 1958 by Erich Maria Remarque. All Rights Reserved.

The Songs of World War I 719
Copyright 1917 (renewed 1945) Leo Feist, Inc. All rights of Leo Feist, Inc., assigned to EMI Catalogue Partnership. All rights controlled and administered by EMI Feist Catalgoue, Inc. International copyright secured. Made in U.S.A. All rights reserved.

Women in Factories 724
From "Munition Work" by Naomi Loughnan in *Women War Workers,* edited by Gilbert Stone (London: George Harrap and Company, 1917), pp. 25, 35–38.

The Reality of War: War and the Family 725
Personal Letters of Reginald B. Mott family.

Vaclav Havel: The Call for a New Politics 844
From *The Washington Post,* February 22, 1990, p. 28d. Copyright ©The Washington Post.

Bosnia: Two Faces of War 846
Copyright ©1993 by the New York Times Co. Reprinted by permission.

Margaret Thatcher: Entering a Man's World 850
Excerpt on "Entering a Man's World" from *The Path to Power* by Margaret Thatcher. Copyright ©1995 by Margaret Thatcher. Reprinted by permission of HarperCollins Publishers, Inc.

Violence Against Foreigners in Germany 857
Published in English in *The German Tribune,* October 6, 1991, pp. 3–5; reprinted in Merry Wiesner, Julius R. H. William Wheeler, eds. *Discovering the Western Past: A Look at the Evidence, 2nd ed.* (Boston: Houghton Mifflin Company, 1993), pp. 446–447.

The Voice of Existentialism 860
©1946 Philosophical Library, New York. Reprinted by permission.

Pope John Paul II: An Appeal for Peace 862
From *John Paul II and the Laity,* Leonard Doohan (The Jesuit Educational Center for Human Development; published by Le Jacq Publishing, Inc., 1984), pp. 48–50.

Small Is Beautiful: The Limits of Modern Technology 864
Excerpt from *Small Is Beautiful: Economics as if People Mattered* by E. F. Schumacher. Copryight ©1973 by E. F. Schumacher. Reprinted by permission of HarperCollins Publishers, Inc. and the Random House Group, Ltd.

Index

Note: Page references in *italics* indicate map or figure.

B

D

E

H

I

N

O

P

X

Y

Z